BUSINESS STATISTICS OF THE UNITED STATES

BUSINESS STATISTICS OF THE UNITED STATES

PATTERNS OF ECONOMIC CHANGE

18TH EDITION
2013

Edited by Cornelia J. Strawser

Associate Editor
Mary Meghan Ryan

Lanham • Boulder • New York • Toronto • Plymouth, UK

Published by Bernan Press
A wholly owned subsidiary of Rowman & Littlefield
4501 Forbes Boulevard, Suite 200, Lanham, Maryland 20706
www.rowman.com
800-865-3457; info@bernan.com

ISBN: 978-1-59888-635-1

eISBN: 978-1-59888-636-8

ISSN: 1086-8488

∞™ The paper used in this publication meets the minimum requirements of American
National Standard for Information Sciences Permanence of Paper for Printed Library
Materials, ANSI/NISO Z39.48-1992.

Printed in the United States of America

CONTENTS

PREFACE

Business Statistics of the United States: Patterns of Economic Change, 18th Edition, 2013 is a basic desk reference for anyone requiring statistics on the U.S. economy. It contains over 3,000 economic time series portraying the period from World War II to December 2012 in comprehensive industry, product, and demographic detail. In the case of about 200 key series, the period from 1929 through 1948 is depicted as well.

For three important statistical series that have been compiled monthly on a continuous basis, monthly and annual data are included going back to 1919 for industrial production and 1913 for consumer and producer prices. In this edition, annual data for money and credit have also been taken back before 1929, including money supply figures back to 1892 and some interest rates back to 1919. Annual estimates of the unemployment rate from 1890 to 1929, not official but using a method similar to that used by BLS for its 1929-48 unemployment estimates, are also included for the first time.

The National Income and Product Accounts (NIPAs) were comprehensively revised in July 2013, changing some measurement concepts, changing base periods for price indexes and real output, and as a result altering all the data back to 1929. This edition of *Business Statistics* incorporates fully revised data for over 700 series from this data set, and also includes the comprehensive August 2013 revision of the productivity and costs series that are based on the revised NIPAs. The important new concepts introduced in the NIPA revision are explained in the Notes and Definitions to Chapters 1, 4, 5, and 6. In all, this edition provides, in one volume, unparalleled, up-to-date background information on the course of the U.S. economy.

The data are predominantly from federal government sources. Of equal importance are the extensive background notes for each chapter, which help users to understand the data, use them appropriately, and, if desired, seek additional information from the source agencies.

Chapters are organized according to subject matter. For most time series, users will find an initial page displaying the latest two years of monthly data, or three years of quarterly data, for the most recent completed years, along with annual averages for the last completed 40, 50, or even 60 years.

For the most important series for which we have long-term historical data, this initial page will be labeled with "A" after the table number, and identified in the title by the additional words "Recent Data". It will be immediately followed by pages labeled with "B" after the table number and identified by the words "Historical Data", which will show all available historical data annually back as far as possible, and monthly or quarterly back to the earliest available postwar year. In some cases, additional tables of historical data will be included.

The monthly index of industrial production is shown all the way back to 1919, and monthly indexes of consumer and producer prices back to 1913. In both cases, these are the earliest dates for which the originating agencies (respectively, the Federal Reserve Board and the Bureau of Labor Statistics [BLS]) have compiled a continuous series.

The leading article "Cycle and Growth Perspectives" discusses the impact of the NIPA revision and provides other information and techniques to assist in using and interpreting the data.

The plan of the book

The history of the U.S. economy is told in major U.S. government sets of statistical data: the national income and product accounts compiled by the Bureau of Economic Analysis (BEA); the data on labor force, employment, hours, earnings, and productivity compiled by the Bureau of Labor Statistics (BLS); the price indexes collected by BLS; and the financial market and industrial production data compiled primarily by the Board of Governors of the Federal Reserve System (FRB). All of these sets exist in annual and either monthly or quarterly form beginning in 1946, 1947, or 1948; many are available, at least annually, as far back as 1929, and a few even farther back; and three are available monthly back to the teens of the 20th century.

In Part A, *Business Statistics* presents the aggregate United States economy in a number of important dimensions. The presentations begin with the national income and product accounts, or NIPAs. The NIPAs comprise a comprehensive, thorough, and internally consistent body of data. They measure the value of the total output of the U.S. economy (the gross domestic product, or GDP) and they allocate that value between its quantity, or "real," and price components. They show how the value of aggregate demand is generated by consumers, business investors, government, and foreign customers; how much of aggregate demand is supplied by imports and how much by domestic production; and how the income generated in domestic production is distributed between labor and capital.

Production estimates covering only the sectors of the economy that used to be labeled "industrial"—manufacturing, mining, and utilities—are shown in Chapter 2, after the presentation of the overall NIPAs in Chapter 1.

The distribution of personal income, median income—the best measure of the economic well-being of the "typical" American—and poverty statistics from a Census household survey are presented in Chapter 3.

Then, more detail from the NIPAs is presented for the demand components of economic activity. GDP, by its product-side definition, consists of the sum of consumption expenditures, business investment, government purchases of goods and services, and exports minus imports—the elementary economics blackboard identity "GDP = C + I + G + X – M." Chapters on each of these components—consumption, investment, government, and foreign trade—are presented in Part A.

Following these chapters, there are a chapter on prices, two chapters on the compensation of labor and capital inputs and the amount and productivity of labor input, one chapter on energy inputs into production and consumption, and one chapter on money and financial markets.

At the end of Part A, comparisons of output, prices, and labor markets among major industrial countries are presented, along with statistics on the value of the dollar against other currencies.

While GDP is initially defined and measured by adding up its demand categories and subtracting imports, this output is produced in industries—some in the old-line heavy industries such as manufacturing, mining, and utilities, but an increasing share in the huge and heterogeneous group known as "service-providing" industries. Part A gives a number of summary measures of activity classified by industry or industrial sector: industrial production, profits, and employment-related data. Further industry information is provided in Part B.

Industry data collection is important because demands for goods and services are channeled into demands for labor and capital through the industries responsible for producing the requested goods and services. These data are reported using the North American Industry Classification System (NAICS). This system, introduced in 1997 to replace the older Standard Industrial Classification System (SIC), delineates industries that are better defined in relation to today's demands and more closely related to each other by technology. Notable examples include more detailed data available on service industries, a more rational grouping of the Computer and electronic product manufacturing subsector, and the creation of the Information sector. See the References at the end of this Preface.

NAICS industries are groupings of producing units—not of products as such—and are grouped according to similarity of production processes. This is done in order to collect consistent data on inputs and outputs, which are then used to measure important concepts, such as productivity and input-output parameters. Emphasis on the production process helps to explain a number of ways in which the NAICS differs from the SIC.

- Manufacturing activities at retail locations, such as bakeries, have been classified separately from retail activity and put into the Food manufacturing industry.

- Central administrative offices of companies have a new sector of their own, Management of companies and enterprises (sector 55). For example, the headquarters office of a food-producing corporation is considered part of the new sector instead of part of the Food manufacturing industry.

- Reproduction of packaged software, which was classified as a business service in the SIC, is now classified in sector 334, Computer and electronic product manufacturing, as a manufacturing process.

- Electronic markets and agents and brokers, formerly undifferentiated components of wholesale trade industries, have a sector of their own (425).

- Retail trade in NAICS (sectors 44 and 45) now includes establishments such as office supply stores, computer and software stores, building materials dealers, plumbing supply stores, and electrical supply stores, that display merchandise and use mass-media advertising to sell to individuals as well as to businesses, which were formerly classified in wholesale trade.

In Part B, *Business Statistics* shows GDP, income, employment, hours, and earnings by industry, followed by statistics for key sectors such as petroleum, housing, manufacturing, retail trade, and services.

Regional and state data formerly included in *Business Statistics* will be incorporated in a new and broader, more comprehensive compendium of time series for sub-national groupings.

Notes and definitions. Productive use of economic data requires accurate knowledge about the sources and meaning of the data. The notes and definitions for each chapter, shown immediately after that chapter's tables, contain definitions, descriptions of recent data revisions, and references to sources of additional technical information. They also include information about data availability and revision and release schedules, which helps users to readily access the latest current values if they need to keep up with the data month by month or quarter by quarter.

A note on the importance of economic statistics

To retrieve money and credit data for earlier years, the editor of *Business Statistics* had to consult old printed volumes, where she encountered some inspiring prefatory words in the Federal Reserve Board volume *Banking and Monetary Statistics* (1943). These words were written by the Fed's longtime statistics chief E. A. Goldenweiser, in the stately cadences of an earlier era, just to apply to the financial statistics collected in that volume. But they well express the hope and expectation of statisticians and economists that their work can lead to better economic decisions:

"These serried ranks of organized statistics on banking and finance, even though they may inspire awe, should also inspire confidence. They are an augury that credit policy can be based in the future, as in the past, on fact rather than on fancy."

The history of *Business Statistics*

The history of *Business Statistics* began with the publication, many years ago, of the first edition of a volume with the same name by the U.S. Department of Commerce's Bureau of Economic Analysis (BEA). After 27 periodic editions, the last of which appeared in 1992, BEA found it necessary, for budgetary and other reasons, to discontinue both the publication and the maintenance of the database from which the publication was derived.

The individual statistical series gathered together here are publicly available. However, the task of gathering them from the numerous different sources within the government and assembling them into one coherent database is impractical for most data users. Even when current data are readily available, obtaining the full historical time series is often time-consuming and difficult. Definitions and other documentation can also be inconvenient to find. Believing that a *Business Statistics* compilation was too valuable to be lost to the public, Bernan Press published the first edition of the present publication, edited by Dr. Courtenay M. Slater, in 1995. The first edition received a warm welcome from users of economic data. Dr. Slater, formerly chief economist of the Department of Commerce, continued to develop *Business Statistics* through four subsequent annual editions. The current editor worked with Dr. Slater on the fourth and fifth editions. In

subsequent editions, she has continued in the tradition established by Dr. Slater of ensuring high-quality data, while revising and expanding the book's scope to include significant new aspects of the U.S. economy and longer historical background.

Nearly all of the statistical data in this book are from federal government sources and all are available in the public domain. Sources are given in the applicable notes and definitions.

The data in this volume meet the publication standards of the federal statistical agencies from which they were obtained. Every effort has been made to select data that are accurate, meaningful, and useful. All statistical data are subject to error arising from sampling variability, reporting errors, incomplete coverage, imputation, and other causes. The responsibility of the editor and publisher of this volume is limited to reasonable care in the reproduction and presentation of data obtained from established sources.

The 2013 edition has been edited by Cornelia J. Strawser, in association with Mary Meghan Ryan, who prepared all the tables and graphs and whose ability and experience have been essential in producing a timely and accurate reference work.

Dr. Strawser is the senior economic consultant to Bernan Press. She edited the seventh through seventeenth editions and was the co-editor of two previous editions of *Business Statistics*. She was co-editor of *Foreign Trade of the United States, 2001,* and also worked on the *Handbook of U.S. Labor Statistics*. She was formerly a senior economist for the U.S. House of Representatives Budget Committee and has also served at the Senate Budget Committee, at the Congressional Budget Office, and on the Federal Reserve Board staff.

The editor assumes full responsibility for the interpretations presented in this volume.

References

The NAICS is explained and laid out in *North American Industry Classification System: United States, 2007,* from the Executive Office of the President, Office of Management and Budget. This presents the second five-year updating of the system, which was first introduced in 1997. Changes introduced in these updatings have been minor and have not affected the definitions of the industry divisions presented in *Business Statistics.*

Information on differences between NAICS and SIC can be found in *North American Industry Classification System: United States, 1997,* from the Executive Office of the President, Office of Management and Budget (which contains matches between the 1997 NAICS and the 1987 SIC); and

North American Industry Classification System: United States, 2002 (which contains matches that show the relatively few changes from the 1997 NAICS to the 2002 NAICS).

All three of these volumes are available from Bernan Press. These volumes fully describe the development and application of the new classification system and are the sources for the material presented in this volume. Information is also available on the NAICS Web site at http://www.census.gov/naics. Additional background information can also be found in Bernan Press's *Business Statistics of the United States: 2002* (8th edition), pp. xxiv–xxviii.

CYCLE AND GROWTH PERSPECTIVES

This 18th edition of *Business Statistics of the United States* presents comprehensive and detailed data on U.S. economic performance through December 2012. These tables incorporate a comprehensive revision of the National Income and Product Accounts (NIPAs). In addition to the usual incorporation of new and better data for recent years, the Bureau of Economic Analysis (BEA) expanded the category of fixed investment to include research and development and the creation of certain entertainment, literary, and other artistic originals.

The revision raised the level of current-dollar GDP for all years, but did not significantly change the basic historical picture of change in the real U.S. economy. For the entire period from 1929 to 2011, the average annual growth rate is now indicated to have been 3.3 instead of 3.2 percent—barely noticeable in the graph of annual real GDP growth shown below in Figure A-1. Revisions to productivity growth are similar.

For the most recent years of cyclical recovery, from 2009 to 2012, the real GDP growth rate is now shown as 2.4 percent per year, 0.3 percentage point higher than in previous estimates, with the greatest revision in 2012 reflecting new data. Even with the new data, the recovery still appears subpar compared with recoveries from previous severe recessions in the 1970s and 1980s.

There has not yet been time to assess the full importance of the expanded measurement of fixed investment. Revised and expanded estimates of the stock of capital using the new data have not yet been issued. It can be hoped that such new measures will provide new resources for understanding, modeling, and forecasting the sources of productivity growth.

In order to provide further perspective on the data presented in *Business Statistics,* this article begins with a general discussion of business cycles in the United States economy, including a chronology of the cycles occurring in the years covered by this volume.

- Following this is an example of the use of monthly data, such as those provided in this book, to track recession and recovery.

- Then, other examples are provided of important analytical techniques for extracting key information from statistical records, particularly for focusing on growth issues.

- The last section of this article concerns measuring the standard of living.

Figure A-1. Percent Changes in Real GDP, Before and After Comprehensive Revision

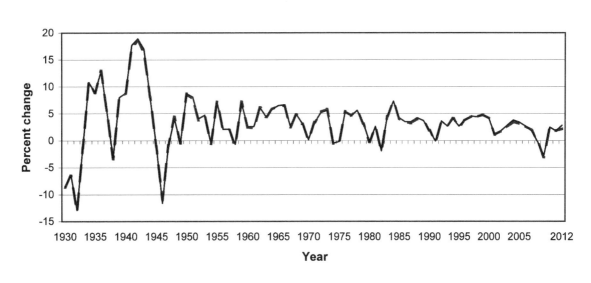

Business cycles in the U.S. economy

The study of economic fluctuations in the United States was pioneered by Wesley C. Mitchell and Arthur F. Burns early in the twentieth century, and was carried on subsequently by other researchers affiliated with the National Bureau of Economic Research (NBER), an independent, nonpartisan research organization. These analysts observed that indicators of the general state of business activity tended to move up and down over periods that were longer than a year and were therefore not accounted for by seasonal variation. Although these periods of expansion and contraction were not uniform in length, and thus not "cycles" in any strict mathematical sense, their recurrent nature caused them to be called "business cycles." NBER has identified 32 complete peak-to-peak business cycles over the period beginning with December 1854.

The first NBER-established business cycle dates, identifying the monthly peaks and troughs in general economic activity, were published in 1929. Currently, the dates are established by the NBER Business Cycle Dating Committee, first formed in 1978. It consists of eight economists who are university professors, associated with research organizations, or both.

Business cycle dates are based on monthly data, and have been identified for periods long before the availability of quarterly data on real gross national product (GDP). It is important to understand that even in the recent period for which such data are available, the NBER identification of a recession does not always coincide with the frequently cited definition of recession as two consecutive quarters of decline in real GDP.

The NBER monthly and quarterly dates of the cycles from 1891 to the latest announced turning point—the June 2009 trough ending the recession that began in December 2007—are shown in Table A-1 below. The quarterly turning points are identified by Roman numerals. NBER considers that the trough month is both the end of the decline and the beginning of the recovery, based on the concept that the actual turning point was some particular day within that month. Thus, the latest recession ended in June 2009, and the recovery also began in June 2009.

For additional information on NBER and its business cycle studies, see the NBER Web site at http://www.nber.org/cycles.

Table A-1. Business Cycle Reference Dates, 1891–2009

TROUGH	PEAK
May 1891 (II)	January 1893 (I)
June 1894 (II)	December 1895 (IV)
June 1897 (II)	June 1899 (III)
December 1900 (IV)	September 1902 (IV)
August 1904 (III)	May 1907 (II)
June 1908 (II)	January 1910 (I)
January 1912 (IV)	January 1913 (I)
December 1914 (IV)	August 1918 (III)
March 1919 (I)	January 1920 (I)
July 1921 (III)	May 1923 (II)
July 1924 (III)	October 1926 (III)
November 1927 (IV)	August 1929 (III)
March 1933 (I)	May 1937 (II)
June 1938 (II)	February 1945 (I)
October 1945 (IV)	November 1948 (IV)
October 1949 (IV)	July 1953 (II)
May 1954 (II)	August 1957 (III)
April 1958 (II)	April 1960 (II)
February 1961 (I)	December 1969 (IV)
November 1970 (IV)	November 1973 (IV)
March 1975 (I)	January 1980 (I)
July 1980 (III)	July 1981 (III)
November 1982 (IV)	July 1990 (III)
March 1991 (I)	March 2001 (I)
November 2001 (IV)	December 2007 (IV)
June 2009 (II)	

Source: National Bureau of Economic Research, http://www.nber.org/cycles.

What was the Great Depression?

Most of the 1930s, after the March 1933 trough, is identified as a period of expansion by NBER, in apparent conflict with the fact that the entire decade is often considered to be in the "Great Depression." The NBER does not identify "depressions;" the popular usage denotes a prolonged period of idle resources. People interested in the economics and politics of the 1930s may wish to distinguish, as NBER does, between that part of the period when output and employment declined precipitously—the 43-month collapse from August 1929 through March 1933, sometimes called The Great Contraction—and the subsequent period when output and employment, though still far below a likely trend line, were rising most of the time, before accepting at face value statements like "the New Deal failed to end the Depression."

The article that follows this one, "The U.S. Economy 1929-1948," includes five graphs depicting the economic course of the Depression and World War II periods, accompanied by some explanatory narration. The Notes and Definitions to Chapter 10 discuss the important issue of the statistical treatment of work relief employment during the Depression.

Tracking recession and recovery: Total payroll employment

Figure A-2 shows how current data can be tracked month by month in comparison with earlier business cycles. The figure depicts proportional movements in total payroll employment (see Tables 10-8 and 10-9 and the associated Notes and Definitions), beginning with the cycle peak and continuing over the following 5 years—through December 2012 in the case of the latest cycle.

Many economists would prefer to track cycles using a comprehensive measure of aggregate output, not employment. However, we do not have a satisfactory monthly measure of gross domestic product (GDP); attempts to estimate it have proved to be volatile, "noisy," and subject to excessive revision.

The reliable and long-established monthly index of industrial production is a narrower measure of output, limited to manufacturing, mining, and utilities. It is presented in Chapter 2 of this volume. Mining and utilities are of little significance in the business cycle process; in fact, short-term variation in the utility sector is mostly influenced not by cycles in demand but by unusual weather conditions. As a result, the cyclical movements of the industrial production index are dominated by the manufacturing sector. Because manufacturing now accounts for only about 10 percent of total nonfarm employment, the industrial production index is an imperfect general business cycle gauge, but it is still one of the major indicators monitored by the Business Cycle Dating Committee. Furthermore, it is the only such indicator that extends monthly all the way back to 1919; these historical data are now shown in *Business Statistics*.

The employment count—covering the entire nonfarm economy, based on a large and long-established sample of large and small businesses, and available shortly after the end of each month—is a widely accepted indicator, more reliable and less subject either to substantial revision or to excessive random variation than any available broad monthly production measure. It is viewed as "the most reliable comprehensive estimate of employment" by the Business Cycle Dating Committee.

For ease of comparing proportional effects in this graph, the employment totals for each recession period are converted to indexes with the cycle's peak month set at 100. For example, the line labeled "From July 1981" represents employment at the peak and in each of the 60 successive months, July 1981 through July 1986, divided by the July 1981 value and multiplied by 100. The line labeled "From December 2007" represents employment in each month, December 2007 through December 2012, divided by the December 2007 value and multiplied by 100.

Looked at in this way, the similarities among the four recessions in the first 10 months of decline were striking: nearly a year after the peak, employment was down about 1½ percent in each case. Two months later, the four declines no longer looked similar. Employment had leveled off in 1991 and 2002, but lurched further downward in winter 2008–2009 as it did in mid-1982.

**Figure A-2. Four Recession-Recoveries Compared:
Total Payroll Employment Relative to NBER Cycle Peak**

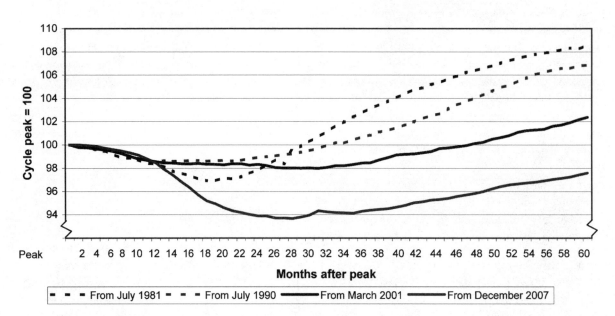

Figure A-2 shows that the slide in employment from the July 1981 peak continued for a year and a half and then began a brisk recovery. However, the downward turn in the latest period was deeper and much longer. The low point was not reached until February 2010, more than two years after the employment peak and eight months past the NBER cycle trough.

In comparing the end-of-recession and beginning-of-recovery periods 1982–1984 and 2009–2011, it should be noted that both periods saw fiscal stimulus enacted, but the monetary conditions are strikingly different. A look at Table 12-9B shows that the federal funds rate (the rate banks charge on overnight loans, set by Federal Reserve open market operations) was 19 percent in July 1981, fell to 13 percent in July 1982, and was 9 percent by July 1983. The Fed had maintained a very tight policy in early 1981 to break the back of inflation, but then had plenty of room to reduce rates once the recession was under way. The housing industry was not burdened then with a huge overhang of household debt and excess housing inventory, and was able to play its usual role in sparking the recovery.

In contrast, the federal funds rate was already close to zero at the cycle peak in December 2007, and the initial obstacles to renewed credit flows and construction activity were not high interest rates but deflation, an overbuilt housing inventory, and deteriorating financial balance sheets. Later, as some of these conditions improved, other obstacles including new problems overseas and policy debates at home have been said to be impeding recovery. Furthermore, as will be seen in Chapters 1 and 9, a declining share of the value of private-

sector output has been paid to workers and a rising share to profits, especially financial sector profits. This change in the flows of economic circulation may be hindering recovery as well: lower payments to workers lead to lower growth in consumption, and consumption markets do not grow enough to provide incentive to invest the profits, contributing to a vicious circle of stagnation instead of a more vigorous, virtuous circle of recovery.

Analytical techniques for growth issues

In assessing the performance of an economy over longer periods of time, it is important to use analytical techniques that highlight the most important aspects of the series. In this article and in the graphs and text that accompany nearly every *Business Statistics* data chapter, the editor will frequently make use of three powerful tools: the ratio-scale graph, the calculation of compound annual growth rates, and the use of cyclically comparable years to estimate trends and to separate trend from cyclical behavior. Econometricians use more elaborate methods of statistical analysis to estimate relationships and construct models, but much can be discerned just by using these relatively simple techniques.

Ratio-scale graphs. At the beginning of Chapter 1 (Figure 1-1) is a time series graph of output per capita from 1946 through 2012, drawn on a ratio scale. Output per capita is the constant-dollar value of each year's U.S. gross domestic product (GDP), divided by the size of that year's U.S. population.

The reader will quickly see that equal distances on the vertical scale of this graph do not represent equal differences in 2009-dollar values. However, equal vertical distances do represent equal *percent changes*. Any upward-sloping straight line plotted on this scale represents a constant percentage rate of growth over the period, and any downward-sloping straight line represents a constant percentage rate of decline. (The same method of ratio-scale charting is used regularly in graphs of individual stock prices in *The Wall Street Journal*.)

This ratio-scale graph was produced by the following three steps: (1) The values to be graphed were converted into natural (base e) logarithms. (2) The natural logarithms were graphed. (3) For ease of interpretation, the vertical scale on this graph of the logarithms was re-labeled, replacing the numerical value of the logarithm that was plotted with the numerical value of its antilog—that is, the original value of per capita output.

This technique is only valid for data series that do not include zeroes or negative numbers, for which logarithms do not exist. Because percentage values such as the unemployment rate and percent changes such as the inflation rate are already in percentage terms, and because percent changes may include zero and/or negative values, they are not and should not be graphed in this fashion.

Compound annual growth rates. In the text of this article and in the highlights pages that precede and accompany each chapter, the editor often uses compound annual growth rates to summarize the history of important economic processes such as economic and demographic growth and inflation.

The compound annual growth rate is the percentage rate which, when compounded annually, would cause a quantity or price "X(t)" observed in a base period "t" to grow (or decline) to the observed quantity or price "X(t+i)" over a period of "i" years. Using this procedure, growth percentages for different periods spanning different numbers of years can be reduced to a common scale—the annual rate—for comparison. The formula for calculating such a growth rate, "r," is as follows:

$$r = \left(\sqrt[i]{X(t+i) \big/ X(t)} - 1 \right) x 100$$

When growth rates are functionally related to each other, such as the growth rates for output, hours worked, and output per hour worked (productivity), those rates will be arithmetically consistent as in the following formula, where "o" is the percentage growth rate for output, "h" the rate for hours worked, and "p" the growth rate for output per hour worked:

$$p = \left[\left[(100 + o) / (100 + h) \right] - 1 \right] x 100$$

When the percentage growth rates are not very far from zero, relationships of this kind can be approximated or verified by simple addition or subtraction of the relevant percentage rates. For example, the productivity growth rate of 2.2 percent in output per hour at nonfarm business from 1948 to 2000 is approximately the difference between the output growth rate of 3.7 percent and the hours growth rate of 1.5 percent in that period.

Using cyclically comparable end points. For economic processes that have significant business-cycle components, such as output and employment, it is important to use comparable points in the business cycle for estimating underlying—that is, long-term sustainable—growth rates. One commonly used method is to calculate growth rates between years with similar, high rates of resource utilization. The broadest readily available measure of resource utilization is the unemployment rate—actually, of course, a measure of "un-utilization"—which was 3.8 percent in 1948, 5.8 in 1979, 5.6 percent in 1990, 4.0 percent in 2000, and 4.6 percent in 2007. These years were all at or near the cycle low points for unemployment, that is, the high points of labor utilization. (See Tables 10-1A and B and Figure 10.2.) A narrower measure that focuses on capital rather than labor, namely capacity utilization in manufacturing, was 82.5 percent in 1948, 84.0 percent in 1979, 81.7 percent in 1990, 79.8 percent in 2000, and 78.5 percent in 2007. These rates were near their cycle highs. (See Tables 2-3 and 2-4A and Figure 2-1.)

End points that are not comparable: What difference does it make?

An interesting example of non-cyclically comparable end points appeared in a commentary by Richard W. Rahn in the *Washington Times* (January 27, 2010). He wrote that "In the nine quarter-century periods since the American republic was founded in 1789, the one with highest economic growth and job creation was the period from 1983 through 2007." He showed an annual average growth rate of 3.33 percent during that period, which he measured from the year 1982 as a base. (All the growth rates in this discussion are based on the GDP statistics available at the time the article was written.)

However, November 1982 was the trough of a deep recession, and December 2007 a cycle peak. If GDP growth is measured between the years of the two full cycle peaks nearest to this general time span, 1979 and 2007, it averages 2.95 percent; if it is measured between the two nearest troughs, 1982 and 2009, it averages 2.90 percent. This suggests that long-term growth in potential output during that period was more like 3.0 percent than like 3 1/3 percent, although of course higher growth rates can—and should—be attained temporarily when starting from an underutilization low.

Similarly, growth in payroll employment 1982–2007 averaged 1.73 percent; but between 1979 and 2007, it was 1.53 percent and between 1982 and 2009, 1.41 percent.

Furthermore, the period between 1979 and 2007 includes three full cycles with somewhat different growth rates and other characteristics, including possible differences in potential labor input, capital input, and productivity—the determinants of long-term sustainable growth—as well as different economic policy settings.

All of these facts suggest that long-term growth rates using non-comparable end points will not provide a solid basis for policy analysis. Comparisons based on other artificial demarcation points, such as decades, may be subject to similar distortions.

Whose standard of living?

Many widely used economic indicators are averages, such as GDP and personal income per capita and output per hour worked. Averages are calculated by dividing some aggregate measure (income or production, for example) by another aggregate measure (population or total hours worked, for example). It is important to note that such an average, known technically to statisticians as a "mean," is only one way of describing the central tendency of any set of statistical data, and for many purposes, is not necessarily the method that produces the most representative number.

To give an important example, most researchers who are interested in the economic well-being of a typical American family or household find that the best single number to characterize that well-being is the standard of living of the family or household situated at the middle of the income distribution. Half of all families or households have higher

incomes and half have lower incomes. This is the measure known as the "median." Medians are not the same as averages or means, and in the case of income distributions, they are invariably lower.

This reason behind this difference is sometimes illustrated by calling up the image of a billionaire walking into a working-class bar. The "average income" (mean income) of each person in the bar would jump, as a billion dollars was added to the numerator of the average and just one unit was added to the denominator. However, the median would be little if at all changed—at most, the addition of one person to the group might mean that the median income moved up from one worker to the next best-paid worker—and this would accord with an accurate perception that the *typical* person in that bar had not experienced any significant increase in his or her income. Thus, when a few individuals or households have very high incomes (and there is, as well, a zero lower bound on measured incomes), means are higher than medians and not representative of the typical individual or household.

Furthermore, if over time the incomes of people at the upper end of the distribution increase *faster* than the incomes of those at the middle and bottom of the distribution (which happens when the income distribution becomes more unequal), then the means will also *increase* more than the medians.

Once a year, as a supplement to the Current Population Survey, the Census Bureau collects data on the incomes of its sample of households. These data are used to produce a report on median incomes, the distribution of incomes, and the poverty rate, providing extensive data on the economic well-being of households and individuals throughout the income distribution. This survey is the source for all of the data in Chapter 3 of *Business Statistics,* including median earnings and median household income. These median indicators grow less than per capita income and other averages, consistent with the continued trend toward income inequality displayed in Tables 3-4 and 3-5.

THE U.S. ECONOMY 1929–1948

While there has been much discussion in recent years of the "Great Depression," there is surprisingly little familiarity with the basic statistical record of the period between 1929 and the end of World War II. Reproducing material from Chapter 18 of the 15th edition of Business Statistics, we present here an explanation of that period from the NBER business cycle perspective, followed by a graphic overview and narration of its economic developments as recorded in the statistics now presented in Part A of this volume.

The NBER chronology, presented in Table A-1 in the preceding article "Cycle and Growth Perspectives," may surprise readers who are looking for "The Great Depression" and are not familiar with the NBER approach to business cycles. As NBER perceives it, a downtrend in economic activity began in August 1929 (*before* the stock market crash) and lasted until March 1933. This 43-month period has been called the "Great Contraction": it was the longest period of economic decline since the 1870s, and more than double the length of the longest recession identified and completed since that time (the latest one, which lasted 18 months). For the rest of the 1930s—except a 13-month recession in 1937–1938—the economy is viewed by the NBER as being in an expansion phase. The NBER chronology does not use the term "depression."

However, the term "Great Depression" is often colloquially used for the entire 1929–1939 period, even though the economy was expanding for most of the period following March 1933. This is because economic activity during that time, though increasing, remained below the likely capacity of the economy, as is indicated in Figures A-3 and A-4 below.

It should also be noted that NBER construes the entire period from June 1938 through February 1945 as a business cycle expansion. The recovery from the 1937–1938 recession merged into a further, continued rise in activity that reflected the outbreak of war in Europe in September 1939, a consequent preparedness effort in the United States, and an increase in demand from abroad for U.S. output. The United States entered the war after being attacked by Japan in December 1941, launching an all-out war production effort at that time.

The February 1945 end of the "wartime expansion" (as NBER terms the period June 1938–February 1945) preceded the end of the war, as the European war ended in May 1945 and the Pacific war concluded in August 1945. A brief demobilization recession occurred from February to October 1945, followed by the first postwar expansion, which lasted from October 1945 to November 1948.

Figure A-3. Employment, 1929–1948
(ratio scale)

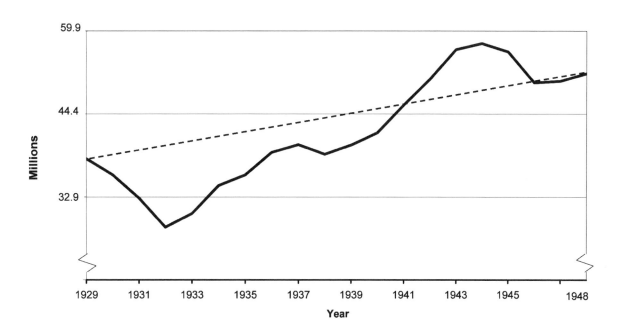

In Figures A-3 through A-7, summary annual statistics for the years 1929 through 1948 are presented, depicting the economy during two of its most tumultuous decades. This period encompasses the "great contraction," the economic collapse that began in August 1929 and lasted until March 1933; a subsequent period of recovery, which failed to return many important economic indicators to their expected trend levels and was interrupted by a new, though less severe, recession; apprehension of coming war, then the outbreak of war in Europe in September 1939, leading to increased war-related production; United States participation in all-out war, beginning with the Japanese attack on Pearl Harbor on December 7, 1941, and ending in 1945, with supercharged production and employment rates; then, rapid demobilization, and return to a high peacetime rate of economic activity by 1948.

For a first overall view of the economy during these decades, Figure A-3 shows total U.S. employment as calculated by the Bureau of Economic Analysis, including all private and government jobs, both civilian and military. In this graph a "trend" line is shown connecting the two peacetime high employment levels of 1929 and 1948.

• More than one-fifth of all the jobs held in the U.S. economy in 1929 were gone by 1932. In the subsequent recovery, total employment was back at the 1929 level by 1936, but only because of government employment, including over 3 ½ million work relief jobs; private industry employment would not recover to its 1929 level until 1941. (Table 10-21)

• Because the recovery was incomplete and economic activity did not recover to a trend level until after the decade's end, the entire decade of the 1930s is often described as "The Great Depression."

• During the war, men were drafted into the armed forces, practically all of the unemployed were put back to work, and women were drawn into the labor force, resulting in a period of what might be called "super-employment." After the war, employment fell back to a more normal trend level. (Tables 10-1C and 10-21)

• The unemployment rates for the prewar period calculated by the Bureau of Labor Statistics, unlike the employment data used in Figure A-3, count people on government work relief programs as unemployed. By this reckoning, unemployment rose from 3.2 percent of the civilian labor force in 1929 to a peak of 24.9 percent in 1933, and got no lower than 14.3 percent for the rest of the 1930s, as shown in Figure A-4. (Table 10-1C)

Figure A-4. Unemployment Rates, 1929–1948

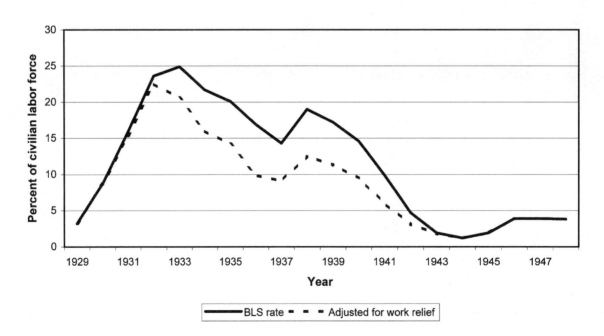

Figure A-5. Per Capita Real Output and Consumption, 1929–1948
(ratio scale)

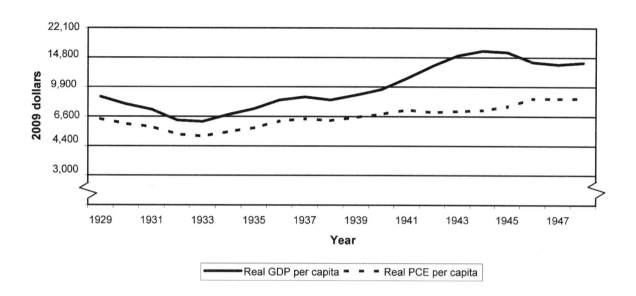

Figure A-6. Inflation and Nominal and Real Interest Rates, 1929–1948

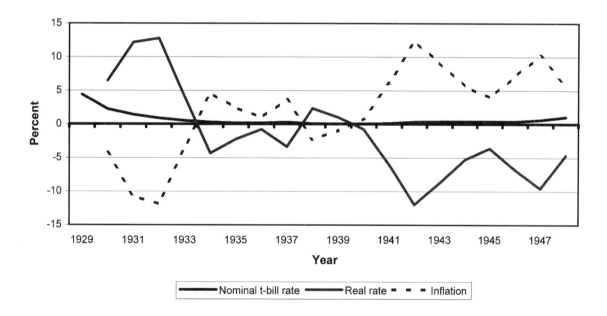

• State and local governments started hiring people for work relief in 1930. The Federal government's programs began in 1933, and in 1936 and 1938 agencies such as the WPA and the CCC employed over 3 ½ million people. When workers in these programs are counted as employed rather than unemployed, the high point for unemployment was 22.5 percent in 1932, and it was reduced to 9.1 percent in 1937, as shown by the dashed line in Figure A-4. (Tables 10-1C and 10-21; see Notes and Definitions to Chapter 10 for further explanation.)

• By 1943, the economy reached a state of over-full employment, which would have been associated with runaway inflation if not for comprehensive price, wage, and production controls; the years of full wartime production, 1943 through 1945, all saw unemployment rates below 2 percent. After demobilization, the unemployment rate returned to just under 4 percent. (Table 10-1C)

• Real GDP declined 26.7 percent from 1929 to 1933—28.9 percent on a per capita basis. Per capita output recovered almost to the 1929 level in 1937 but fell back 4.1 percent in the 1938 recession. Output then nearly doubled from 1939 to the peak war production year, 1944; the per capita annual growth rate was 12.4 percent. Output fell back during the demobilization, but in 1948 was still at a per capita level representing a 4.9 percent growth rate since 1939. (Table 1-3B)

• Per capita personal consumption expenditures fell 20.9 percent from 1929 to 1933. The decline would have been greater if consumers had not dipped into their assets to keep their living standards from declining as steeply as their incomes; the personal saving rate was negative in 1932 and 1933. Real per capita consumption recovered to the 1929 level by 1937. Despite rationing and shortages, real per capita consumption spending declined little during the war years. In 1948, it was 29.3 percent above the 1939 level. (Table 1-3B)

• Why was the 1929-1933 contraction so deep and long-lasting? By some, blame is placed on U.S. government tax increases and imposition of new trade barriers (the Smoot-Hawley Tariff), which undoubtedly made their contribution. A substantial number of well-regarded economists, however, point primarily to deflation and its interaction with debt. The price index for personal consumption expenditures, whose rate of change is shown in Figure A-6, declined 27.2 percent from 1929 to 1933, for an annual average *deflation* rate of 7.6 percent. Current and prospective price declines make debt more burdensome and debtors more likely to default, as interest payments remain fixed while incomes and asset values decline. (Table 1-6B)

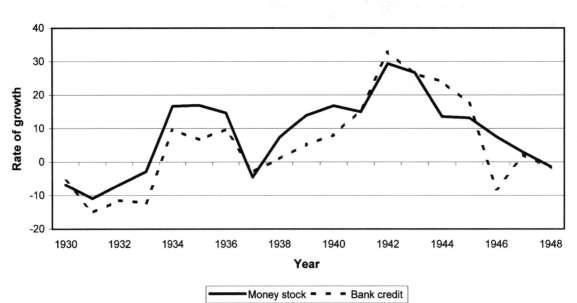

Figure A-7. Money and Credit Growth, 1930–1948
(percent)

THE U.S. ECONOMY 1929–1948

• Current and prospective price declines also make borrowing prohibitively expensive; a low nominal interest rate becomes high in real terms (since the real rate is the nominal rate *minus* the inflation rate, and subtraction means changing the sign and adding). A dollar in the hands of a prospective lender will be worth more in terms of purchasing power if he simply holds on to it than if he invests it in some real economic asset or activity whose price will be lower at the end of the year. There is no feasible way for a central bank to lower interest rates below zero in order to reduce real rates in the presence of deflation. As Figure A-6 shows, real rates were high from 1930 through 1933 despite near-zero market nominal rates on Treasury bills. (Tables 12-9B and 1-6B)

• Deflation was rooted in deep and sustained declines in the dollar volumes of money and credit, as shown in Tables 12-1B and 12-4B and illustrated in Figure A-7. The money stock (currency and demand deposits) declined 27 percent from June 30, 1929, to June 30, 1933. Loans and investments at all commercial banks declined 29 percent over the same period. Commercial paper outstanding plunged 76 percent between December 1929 and December 1932, and bankers' acceptances were down 59 percent.

• Positive money and credit growth after 1933 was reflected in moderate rates of price increase and moderately negative—which means stimulative—real interest rates. As can be seen in Figures A-6 and A-7, there was a monetary component to the 1937-38 recession. There was also a premature federal budget retrenchment at that time (Table 6-14B).

• During the war, monetary policy was pre-empted by wartime needs. Interest rates were held low to facilitate the financing of huge federal deficits (Tables 6-14B and 12-9B).

• Worker incomes increased during the wartime boom as employment, average hours, and hourly wages all rose. But inflation and consumer spending were held down by price and production controls and rationing. Personal saving rates soared when there was little to buy and the government emphasized the sale of "war bonds"; the saving rate reached 26 percent in 1943 and 1944, then fell back to 4.2 percent in 1947, almost equal to its 1929 level. (Tables 1-6B, 4-1B, 8-1C, and 10-9)

GENERAL NOTES

These notes provide general information about the data in Tables 1-1 through 16-15. Specific notes with information about data sources, definitions, methodology, revisions, and sources of additional information follow the tables in each chapter.

Main divisions of the book

The tables are presented in two parts:

Part A (Tables 1-1 through 13-8) pertains to the U.S. economy as a whole. Generally, each table presents, on its initial page, annual averages as far back as data availability and space permit, and quarterly or monthly values for the most recent year or years. For many important series, this initial page is followed by full annual and quarterly or monthly histories as far back as they are available on a continuous, consistent basis. Some chapters present data for the United States only in aggregate, while others—such as the chapters concerning industrial production and capacity utilization (chapter 2), capital expenditures (chapter 5), profits (chapter 9), and employment, hours, and earnings (chapter 10)—also have detail for major industry groups.

Data by industry are classified using the new North American Industry Classification System (NAICS), as far back as such data are made available by the source agencies.

Part B focuses on the individual industries that together produce the gross domestic product (GDP).

• Chapter 14 contains data on the value of GDP, quantity production trends, and factor income by NAICS industry group.

• Chapter 15 provides further detail on payroll employment, hours, and earnings classified according to NAICS.

• Chapter 16 presents various data sets for key economic sectors. Some of the tables are based on definitions of products, rather than of producing establishments, and are valid for either classification system. This is the case for Tables 16-1, Petroleum and Petroleum Products; 16-2, New Construction; 16-3, Housing Starts and Building Permits, New House Sales, and Prices; and 16-8, Motor Vehicle Sales and Inventories. Tables 16-4 through 16-7 and 16-9, 16-11, and 16-12, which cover manufacturing and retail and wholesale trade, show data classified according to NAICS. Table 16-15 presents data for services industries classified according to NAICS.

Characteristics of the tables and the data

The subtitles or column headings for the data tables normally indicate whether the data are *seasonally adjusted*, *not seasonally adjusted*, or *at a seasonally adjusted annual rate*. These descriptions refer to the monthly or quarterly data, rather than the annual data. Annual data by definition require no seasonal adjustment. Annual values are normally calculated as totals or averages, as appropriate, of unadjusted data. Such annual values are shown in either or both adjusted or unadjusted data columns.

Seasonal adjustment removes from the time series the average impact of variations that normally occur at about the same time each year, due to occurrences such as weather, holidays, and tax payment dates.

A simplified example of the process of seasonal adjustment, or deseasonalizing, can indicate its importance in the interpretation of economic time series. Statisticians compare actual monthly data for a number of years with "moving average" trends of the monthly data for the 12 months centered on each month's data. For example, they may find that in November, sales values are usually about 95 percent of the moving average, while in December, usual sales values are 110 percent of the average. Suppose that actual November sales in the current year are $100 and December sales are $105. The seasonally adjusted value for November will be $105 ($100/0.95) while the value for December will be $95 ($105/1.10). Thus, an apparent increase in the unadjusted data turns out to be a decrease when adjusted for the usual seasonal pattern.

The statistical method used to achieve the seasonal adjustment may vary from one data set to another. Many of the data are adjusted by a computer method known as X-12-ARIMA, developed by the Census Bureau. A description of the method is found in "New Capabilities and Methods of the X-12-ARIMA Seasonal Adjustment Program," by David F. Findley, Brian C. Monsell, William R. Bell, Mark C. Otto and Bor-Chung Chen (*Journal of Business and Economic Statistics*, April 1998). This article can be downloaded from the Bureau of the Census Web site at http://www.census.gov.

Production and sales data presented at *annual rates*—such as NIPA data in dollars, or motor vehicle data in number of units—show values at their annual equivalents: the values that would be registered if the seasonally adjusted rate of activity measured during a particular month or quarter were maintained for a full year. Specifically, seasonally adjusted monthly values are multiplied by 12 and quarterly values by 4 to yield seasonally adjusted annual rates.

Percent changes at seasonally adjusted annual rates for quarterly time periods are calculated using a compound interest formula, by raising the quarter-to-quarter percent change in a seasonally adjusted series to the fourth power. See the article "Cycle and Growth Perspectives" for an explanation of compound annual growth rates.

Indexes. In many of the most important data sets presented in this volume, aggregate measures of prices and quantities are expressed in the form of indexes. The most basic and familiar form of index, the original Consumer Price Index, begins with a "market basket" of goods and services purchased in a base period, with each product category valued at its dollar prices—the amount spent on that category by the average consumer. The value weight ascribed to each component of the market basket is moved forward by the observed change in the price of the item selected to represent that component. These weighted component prices—which constitute the quantities in the base period repriced in the prices of subsequent periods—are aggregated, divided by the base period aggregate, and multiplied by 100 to provide an index number. An index calculated in this way is known as a *Laspeyres index.* In general, economists believe that Laspeyres price indexes have an upward bias, showing more price increase than they would if account were taken of consumers' ability to change spending patterns *and maintain the same level of satisfaction* in response to changing relative prices.

A *Paasche index* is one that uses the weights of the current period. Since the weights in the Paasche index change in each period, Paasche indexes only provide acceptable indications of change relative to the base period. Paasche indexes for two periods neither of which is the base period cannot be correctly compared: for example, a Paasche price index for a recent period might increase from the period just preceding even if no prices changed between those two periods, if there was a change in the composition of output toward prices that had previously increased more from the base period. When the national income and product account (NIPA) measures of real output were Laspeyres measures, using the weights of a single base year, the implicit deflators (current-dollar values divided by constant-dollar values) were Paasche indexes. Just as Laspeyres price indexes are upward-biased, Paasche price indexes are downward-biased because they overestimate consumers' ability to maintain the same level of satisfaction by changing spending patterns.

In recent years, government statisticians—with the aid of complex computer programs—have developed measures of real output and prices that minimize bias by using the weights of both periods and updating the weights for each period-to-period comparison. Such measures are described as chained indexes and are used in the NIPAs, the index of industrial production, and an experimental consumer price index. Chained measures are discussed more fully in the notes and definitions for Chapter 1, Chapter 2, and Chapter 8. The "Fisher Ideal" index, the "superlative" index, and the "Tornqvist formula" are all types of chained indexes that use weights for both periods under comparison.

Detail may not sum to totals due to rounding. Since annual data are typically calculated by source agencies as the annual totals or averages of not-seasonally-adjusted data, they therefore will not be precisely equal to the annual totals or averages of monthly seasonally-adjusted data. Also, seasonal adjustment procedures are typically multiplicative rather than additive, which may also prevent seasonally adjusted data from adding or averaging to the annual figure. Percent changes and growth rates may have been calculated using unrounded data and therefore differ from those using the published figures.

The data in this volume are from federal government sources and may be reproduced freely. A list of data sources is shown below.

The tables in this volume incorporate data revisions and corrections released by the source agencies through mid-2013, including the July comprehensive revision of the NIPAs and the resulting August revision of productivity and costs.

Data sources

The source agencies for the data in this volume are listed below. The specific source or sources for each particular data set are identified at the beginning of the notes and definitions for the relevant data pages.

Board of Governors of the Federal Reserve System
20th Street & Constitution Avenue NW
Washington, DC 20551

Data Inquiries and Publication Sales: Publications Services
Mail Stop 127
Board of Governors of the Federal Reserve System
Washington, DC 20551
Phone: (202) 452-3245

Quarterly Publication:
As of 2006, the *Federal Reserve Bulletin* is available free of charge and only on the Federal Reserve Web site.

URL:
http://www.federalreserve.gov

Census Bureau
U.S. Department of Commerce
4700 Silver Hill Road
Washington, DC 20233

URL:
http://www.census.gov

Ordering Data Products:
Call Center: (301) 763-INFO (4636)

E-mail Questions:
webmaster@census.gov

E-sales:
http://www.census.gov/mp/www/censtore.html

Bureau of Economic Analysis
U.S. Department of Commerce
Washington, DC 20230

Data Inquiries:
Public Information Office
Phone: (202) 606-9900

Monthly Publication:
Survey of Current Business
Available online.

URL:
http://www.bea.gov

Bureau of Labor Statistics
U.S. Department of Labor
2 Massachusetts Avenue NE
Washington, DC 20212-0001
(202) 691-5200

URL:
http://www.bls.gov

Data Inquiries:
Blsdata_staff@bls.gov

Monthly Publications available online:
Monthly Labor Review
Employment and Earnings
Compensation and Working Conditions
Producer Price Indexes
CPI Detailed Report

Employment and Training Administration
U.S. Department of Labor
200 Constitution Avenue NW
Washington, DC 20210
(877) US2-JOBS

URL:
http://www.doleta.gov
http://www.itsc.state.md.us

Energy Information Administration
U.S. Department of Energy
1000 Independence Avenue SW
Washington, DC 20585

Data Inquiries and Publications:
National Energy Information Center
Phone: (202) 586-8800
E-mail: infoctr@eia.doe.gov

Monthly Publication:
Monthly Energy Review, as of 2007 available only on the EIA
Web site, free of charge.

URL:
http://www.eia.doe.gov

Federal Housing Finance Agency
FHFAinfo@FHFA.gov
(202) 414-6921,6922
(202) 414-6376

URL:
http://www.fhfa.gov/hpi

U.S. Department of the Treasury
Office of International Affairs
Treasury International Capital System

URL:
http://www.treas.gov/tic

To order government publications
Superintendent of Documents
Government Printing Office
Washington, DC 20402
(202) 512-1800

URL:
http://bookstore.gpo.gov

PART A

THE U.S. ECONOMY

CHAPTER 1: NATIONAL INCOME AND PRODUCT

Section 1a: Gross Domestic Product: Values, Quantities, and Prices

Figure 1-1. Output Per Capita, 1950–2012

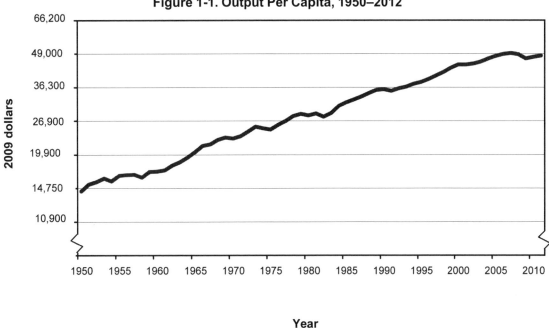

Year

- Total output of goods and services in the United States (real gross domestic product, or GDP), expressed in constant 2009-value dollars to remove the effect of inflation, rose from $2.18 trillion in 1950 to $15.47 trillion in 2012. This was a seven-fold increase in real value over the 62-year period, with an annual average growth rate of 3.2 percent per year. (Table 1-2A)

- Real GDP per capita—the constant-dollar average value of production for each man, woman, and child in the population—rose from $14,384 (2009 dollars) in 1950 to a peak value of $49,311 in 2007, a growth rate of 2.2 percent per year. Reflecting the recession that began in December 2007, it declined 4.8 percent from 2007 to 2009. In the three years since then, per capita GDP recovered to its 2007 peak. The history of per capita GDP is charted in Figure 1-1. It is graphed on a "ratio scale," with equal vertical distances signifying equal percent changes. (Table 1-3A)

- Measured in current dollars, the value of GDP has increased even faster, reflecting increases in the average price level. Current-dollar GDP rose from $300 billion in 1950 to over $16 trillion currently. (Table 1-1A) The price level in 2012 was 7.7 times that in 1950, reflecting an average inflation rate of 3.3 percent per year. (Table 1-6A) Annual changes in the chain-type price index for GDP ranged from inflation of 9 percent or more in 1947, 1974–1975, and 1980–1981 to changes of no more than 1.2 percent in 1949–1950, 1954, 1959, 1961, 1963, 1998, 2009, and 2010. Over the last 12 years, inflation averaged 2.1 percent per year; it was 1.7 percent in 2012. (Tables 1-6A and B)

Table 1-1A. Gross Domestic Product: Recent Data

(Billions of dollars, quarterly data are at seasonally adjusted annual rates.)   **NIPA Tables 1.1.5, 1.2.5**

Year and quarter	Gross domestic product	Personal consumption expenditures	Gross private domestic investment — Total	Fixed investment — Nonresidential	Fixed investment — Residential	Change in private inventories	Net exports	Exports	Imports	Government — Total	Government — Federal	Government — State and local	Addendum: final sales of domestic product
1950	300.2	192.2	56.5	30.0	20.7	5.8	0.7	12.4	11.6	50.7	29.5	21.3	294.4
1951	347.3	208.5	62.8	34.2	18.7	9.9	2.5	17.1	14.6	73.5	50.0	23.6	337.4
1952	367.7	219.5	57.3	34.9	18.9	3.5	1.2	16.5	15.3	89.8	64.8	25.0	364.2
1953	389.7	233.0	60.4	38.8	19.7	1.9	-0.7	15.3	16.0	97.0	70.3	26.7	387.8
1954	391.1	239.9	58.1	38.6	21.4	-1.9	0.4	15.8	15.4	92.8	63.3	29.5	393.1
1955	426.2	258.7	73.8	43.4	25.4	5.0	0.5	17.7	17.2	93.3	61.0	32.2	421.2
1956	450.1	271.6	77.7	49.7	24.0	4.0	2.4	21.3	18.9	98.5	63.1	35.4	446.2
1957	474.9	286.7	76.5	53.1	22.6	0.8	4.1	24.0	19.9	107.5	68.4	39.1	474.1
1958	482.0	296.0	70.9	48.5	22.8	-0.4	0.5	20.6	20.0	114.5	71.5	43.0	482.4
1959	522.5	317.5	85.7	53.1	28.6	3.9	0.4	22.7	22.3	118.9	73.5	45.3	518.5
1960	543.3	331.6	86.5	56.4	26.9	3.2	4.2	27.0	22.8	121.0	72.8	48.2	540.1
1961	563.3	342.0	86.6	56.6	27.0	3.0	4.9	27.6	22.7	129.8	77.4	52.5	560.3
1962	605.1	363.1	97.0	61.2	29.6	6.1	4.1	29.1	25.0	140.9	85.5	55.4	599.0
1963	638.6	382.5	103.3	64.8	32.9	5.6	4.9	31.1	26.1	147.9	87.8	60.0	633.0
1964	685.8	411.2	112.2	72.2	35.1	4.8	6.9	35.0	28.1	155.5	90.2	65.3	681.0
1965	743.7	443.6	129.6	85.2	35.2	9.2	5.6	37.1	31.5	164.9	93.1	71.7	734.5
1966	815.0	480.6	144.2	97.2	33.4	13.6	3.9	40.9	37.1	186.4	106.5	79.8	801.4
1967	861.7	507.4	142.7	99.2	33.6	9.9	3.6	43.5	39.9	208.1	120.0	88.1	851.9
1968	942.5	557.4	156.9	107.7	40.2	9.1	1.4	47.9	46.6	226.8	127.9	98.8	933.4
1969	1 019.9	604.5	173.6	120.0	44.4	9.2	1.4	51.9	50.5	240.4	131.1	109.3	1 010.7
1970	1 075.9	647.7	170.1	124.6	43.4	2.0	4.0	59.7	55.8	254.2	132.7	121.4	1 073.9
1971	1 167.8	701.0	196.8	130.4	58.2	8.3	0.6	63.0	62.3	269.3	134.4	134.9	1 159.5
1972	1 282.4	769.4	228.1	146.6	72.4	9.1	-3.4	70.8	74.2	288.2	141.5	146.7	1 273.3
1973	1 428.5	851.1	266.9	172.7	78.3	15.9	4.1	95.3	91.2	306.4	145.6	160.8	1 412.7
1974	1 548.8	932.0	274.5	191.1	69.5	14.0	-0.8	126.7	127.5	343.1	158.1	185.0	1 534.8
1975	1 688.9	1 032.8	257.3	196.8	66.7	-6.3	16.0	138.7	122.7	382.9	172.8	210.2	1 695.2
1976	1 877.6	1 150.2	323.2	219.3	86.8	17.1	-1.6	149.5	151.1	405.8	183.8	222.1	1 860.5
1977	2 086.0	1 276.7	396.6	259.1	115.2	22.3	-23.1	159.4	182.4	435.8	198.8	237.0	2 063.6
1978	2 356.6	1 426.2	478.4	314.6	138.0	25.8	-25.4	186.9	212.3	477.4	216.7	260.7	2 330.8
1979	2 632.1	1 589.5	539.7	373.8	147.8	18.0	-22.5	230.1	252.7	525.5	237.7	287.8	2 614.2
1980	2 862.5	1 754.6	530.1	406.9	129.5	-6.3	-13.1	280.8	293.8	590.8	272.4	318.5	2 868.8
1981	3 210.9	1 937.5	631.2	472.9	128.5	29.8	-12.5	305.2	317.8	654.7	311.7	343.0	3 181.1
1982	3 345.0	2 073.9	581.0	485.1	110.8	-14.9	-20.0	283.2	303.2	710.0	345.6	364.4	3 359.9
1983	3 638.1	2 286.5	637.5	482.2	161.1	-5.8	-51.7	277.0	328.6	765.7	380.2	385.6	3 643.9
1984	4 040.7	2 498.2	820.1	564.3	190.4	65.4	-102.7	302.4	405.1	825.2	407.6	417.5	3 975.3
1985	4 346.7	2 722.7	829.6	607.7	200.1	21.8	-114.0	303.2	417.2	908.4	449.3	459.2	4 324.9
1986	4 590.1	2 898.4	849.1	607.8	234.8	6.6	-131.9	321.0	452.9	974.5	478.4	496.1	4 583.6
1987	4 870.2	3 092.1	892.2	615.2	249.8	27.1	-144.8	363.9	508.7	1 030.8	500.2	530.5	4 843.1
1988	5 252.6	3 346.9	937.0	662.3	256.2	18.5	-109.4	444.6	554.0	1 078.2	508.8	569.3	5 234.1
1989	5 657.7	3 592.8	999.7	716.0	256.0	27.7	-86.8	504.3	591.0	1 151.9	531.4	620.5	5 630.0
1990	5 979.6	3 825.6	993.5	739.2	239.7	14.5	-77.9	551.9	629.7	1 238.4	560.0	678.3	5 965.0
1991	6 174.0	3 960.2	944.3	723.6	221.2	-0.4	-28.6	594.9	623.5	1 298.2	580.7	717.4	6 174.4
1992	6 539.3	4 215.7	1 013.0	741.9	254.7	16.3	-34.8	633.0	667.8	1 345.4	586.6	758.8	6 522.9
1993	6 878.7	4 471.0	1 106.8	799.2	286.8	20.8	-65.2	654.8	720.0	1 366.1	578.4	787.7	6 857.9
1994	7 308.7	4 741.0	1 256.5	868.9	323.8	63.8	-92.5	720.9	813.4	1 403.7	572.7	831.1	7 244.9
1995	7 664.0	4 984.2	1 317.5	962.2	324.1	31.2	-89.8	812.8	902.6	1 452.2	575.4	876.8	7 632.9
1996	8 100.2	5 268.1	1 432.1	1 043.2	358.1	30.8	-96.4	867.6	964.0	1 496.4	578.2	918.2	8 069.4
1997	8 608.5	5 560.7	1 595.6	1 149.1	375.6	70.9	-102.0	953.8	1 055.8	1 554.2	582.4	971.8	8 537.5
1998	9 089.1	5 903.0	1 735.3	1 252.8	418.8	63.7	-162.7	952.9	1 115.7	1 613.5	584.1	1 029.4	9 025.4
1999	9 665.7	6 316.9	1 884.2	1 361.6	461.8	60.8	-261.4	989.2	1 250.6	1 726.0	610.4	1 115.6	9 604.9
2000	10 289.7	6 801.6	2 033.8	1 493.8	485.4	54.5	-380.1	1 094.3	1 474.4	1 834.4	632.4	1 202.0	10 235.2
2001	10 625.3	7 106.9	1 928.6	1 453.9	513.0	-38.3	-369.0	1 028.8	1 397.8	1 958.8	669.2	1 289.5	10 663.5
2002	10 980.2	7 385.3	1 925.0	1 348.9	557.6	18.5	-425.0	1 004.7	1 429.7	2 094.9	740.6	1 354.3	10 961.7
2003	11 512.2	7 764.4	2 027.9	1 371.7	636.9	19.3	-500.9	1 043.4	1 544.3	2 220.8	824.8	1 396.0	11 493.0
2004	12 277.0	8 257.8	2 276.7	1 463.1	749.7	63.9	-614.8	1 183.1	1 797.9	2 357.4	892.4	1 465.0	12 213.2
2005	13 095.4	8 790.3	2 527.1	1 611.5	856.1	59.6	-715.7	1 310.4	2 026.1	2 493.7	946.3	1 547.4	13 035.8
2006	13 857.9	9 297.5	2 680.6	1 776.3	837.4	67.0	-762.4	1 478.5	2 240.9	2 642.2	1 002.0	1 640.2	13 790.9
2007	14 480.3	9 744.4	2 643.7	1 920.6	688.7	34.5	-709.8	1 665.7	2 375.5	2 801.9	1 049.8	1 752.2	14 445.9
2008	14 720.3	10 005.5	2 424.8	1 941.0	515.9	-32.0	-713.2	1 843.1	2 556.4	3 003.2	1 155.6	1 847.6	14 752.3
2009	14 417.9	9 842.9	1 878.1	1 633.4	392.2	-147.6	-392.2	1 583.8	1 976.0	3 089.1	1 217.7	1 871.4	14 565.5
2010	14 958.3	10 201.9	2 100.8	1 658.2	381.1	61.5	-518.5	1 843.5	2 362.0	3 174.0	1 303.9	1 870.2	14 896.7
2011	15 533.8	10 711.8	2 232.1	1 809.9	385.8	36.4	-568.7	2 101.2	2 669.9	3 158.7	1 304.1	1 854.7	15 497.4
2012	16 244.6	11 149.6	2 475.2	1 970.0	439.2	66.1	-547.2	2 195.9	2 743.1	3 167.0	1 295.7	1 871.3	16 178.5
2010													
1st quarter	14 672.5	10 042.3	1 989.5	1 594.4	383.1	12.1	-495.1	1 746.4	2 241.4	3 135.7	1 269.2	1 866.5	14 660.4
2nd quarter	14 879.2	10 134.7	2 092.7	1 641.8	400.8	50.1	-529.7	1 807.0	2 336.7	3 181.5	1 304.6	1 876.9	14 829.0
3rd quarter	15 049.8	10 234.3	2 164.6	1 677.4	365.6	121.5	-543.8	1 860.3	2 404.0	3 194.7	1 321.6	1 873.1	14 928.2
4th quarter	15 231.7	10 396.3	2 156.5	1 719.3	374.7	62.4	-505.3	1 960.4	2 465.7	3 184.2	1 320.1	1 864.2	15 169.3
2011													
1st quarter	15 242.9	10 527.1	2 120.4	1 721.8	377.1	21.5	-554.7	2 029.5	2 584.1	3 150.0	1 297.4	1 852.6	15 221.4
2nd quarter	15 461.9	10 662.6	2 199.9	1 773.1	381.0	45.8	-572.2	2 095.5	2 667.7	3 171.7	1 315.4	1 856.3	15 416.2
3rd quarter	15 611.8	10 778.6	2 222.2	1 848.9	386.8	-13.5	-553.7	2 143.4	2 697.1	3 164.6	1 308.5	1 856.1	15 625.3
4th quarter	15 818.7	10 878.9	2 385.7	1 895.7	398.1	91.9	-594.4	2 136.2	2 730.7	3 148.5	1 294.9	1 853.6	15 726.8
2012													
1st quarter	16 041.6	11 019.1	2 453.6	1 932.3	418.4	102.9	-590.8	2 173.4	2 764.2	3 159.7	1 291.8	1 867.9	15 938.7
2nd quarter	16 160.4	11 100.2	2 449.3	1 961.4	425.7	66.8	-557.9	2 197.4	2 755.3	3 164.1	1 293.8	1 870.3	16 093.6
3rd quarter	16 356.0	11 193.6	2 493.3	1 968.0	443.7	81.6	-524.4	2 199.2	2 723.5	3 193.5	1 322.1	1 871.4	16 274.4
4th quarter	16 420.3	11 285.5	2 499.9	2 018.2	468.8	13.0	-515.8	2 213.7	2 729.5	3 150.7	1 275.2	1 875.4	16 407.3

Table 1-1B. Gross Domestic Product: Historical

(Billions of dollars, quarterly data are at seasonally adjusted annual rates.)   **NIPA Tables 1.1.5, 1.2.5**

Year and quarter	Gross domestic product	Personal consumption expenditures	Gross private domestic investment				Exports and imports of goods and services			Government consumption expenditures and gross investment			Addendum: Final sales of domestic product
			Total	Fixed investment		Change in private inventories	Net exports	Exports	Imports	Total	Federal	State and local	
				Nonresidential	Residential								
1929	104.6	77.4	17.2	11.6	4.1	1.5	0.4	5.9	5.6	9.6	1.9	7.7	103.0
1930	92.2	70.1	11.4	9.2	2.5	-0.2	0.3	4.4	4.1	10.3	2.0	8.3	92.4
1931	77.4	60.7	6.5	5.8	1.9	-1.1	0.0	2.9	2.9	10.2	2.0	8.1	78.5
1932	59.5	48.7	1.8	3.3	0.9	-2.4	0.0	2.0	1.9	9.0	2.0	7.0	61.9
1933	57.2	45.9	2.3	3.0	0.7	-1.4	0.1	2.0	1.9	8.9	2.4	6.5	58.6
1934	66.8	51.5	4.3	3.8	1.0	-0.6	0.3	2.6	2.2	10.7	3.4	7.3	67.4
1935	74.3	55.9	7.4	4.8	1.4	1.1	-0.2	2.8	3.0	11.2	3.6	7.6	73.1
1936	84.9	62.2	9.4	6.4	1.8	1.2	-0.1	3.0	3.2	13.4	5.8	7.7	83.7
1937	93.0	66.8	13.0	8.2	2.2	2.6	0.1	4.0	4.0	13.1	5.3	7.9	90.4
1938	87.4	64.3	7.9	6.3	2.2	-0.6	1.0	3.8	2.8	14.2	5.9	8.3	88.0
1939	93.5	67.2	10.2	6.9	3.2	0.2	0.8	4.0	3.1	15.2	6.2	9.0	93.3
1940	102.9	71.3	14.6	8.5	3.6	2.4	1.5	4.9	3.4	15.6	6.8	8.8	100.6
1941	129.4	81.1	19.4	10.8	4.2	4.3	1.0	5.5	4.4	27.9	19.1	8.8	125.0
1942	166.0	89.0	11.8	7.5	2.4	1.9	-0.3	4.4	4.6	65.5	56.7	8.8	164.1
1943	203.1	99.9	7.4	6.6	1.6	-0.7	-2.2	4.0	6.3	98.1	89.5	8.6	203.9
1944	224.6	108.6	9.2	8.6	1.5	-0.9	-2.0	4.9	6.9	108.7	100.1	8.6	225.5
1945	228.2	120.0	12.4	12.1	1.8	-1.5	-0.8	6.8	7.5	96.6	87.3	9.3	229.6
1946	227.8	144.3	33.1	19.2	8.0	6.0	7.2	14.2	7.0	43.2	32.1	11.1	221.8
1947	249.9	162.0	37.1	25.5	12.2	-0.6	10.8	18.7	7.9	40.0	25.8	14.2	250.5
1948	274.8	175.0	50.3	28.9	15.8	5.7	5.5	15.5	10.1	44.0	27.1	16.9	269.1
1949	272.8	178.5	39.1	26.9	14.8	-2.7	5.2	14.5	9.2	50.0	30.5	19.6	275.5
1947													
1st quarter	243.1	156.3	35.9	24.8	10.5	0.5	10.9	18.4	7.5	40.1	26.6	13.4	242.6
2nd quarter	246.3	160.2	34.5	25.2	10.6	-1.2	11.3	19.5	8.2	40.3	26.5	13.8	247.5
3rd quarter	250.1	163.7	34.9	25.4	12.5	-2.9	11.8	19.4	7.7	39.8	25.3	14.5	253.0
4th quarter	260.3	167.8	43.2	26.5	15.3	1.5	9.3	17.6	8.3	40.0	24.8	15.2	258.9
1948													
1st quarter	266.2	170.5	47.2	28.2	15.3	3.6	7.3	16.9	9.6	41.2	25.5	15.7	262.5
2nd quarter	272.9	174.3	50.3	28.0	16.4	5.9	5.2	15.2	10.0	43.1	26.7	16.4	267.0
3rd quarter	279.5	177.2	52.5	29.1	16.3	7.2	4.9	15.4	10.5	44.8	27.5	17.3	272.3
4th quarter	280.7	178.1	51.3	30.2	15.2	6.0	4.5	14.6	10.1	46.8	28.7	18.0	274.7
1949													
1st quarter	275.4	177.0	43.1	28.6	14.2	0.4	6.5	16.1	9.6	48.8	30.2	18.6	275.0
2nd quarter	271.7	178.6	36.2	27.5	13.9	-5.1	6.3	15.6	9.4	50.6	31.3	19.3	276.8
3rd quarter	273.3	177.9	39.5	26.1	14.7	-1.3	5.2	14.1	8.9	50.6	30.5	20.1	274.6
4th quarter	271.0	180.4	37.5	25.6	16.5	-4.7	3.0	12.1	9.1	50.1	29.8	20.3	275.7
1950													
1st quarter	281.2	183.1	46.7	26.4	18.3	2.0	2.2	11.7	9.5	49.2	28.6	20.6	279.2
2nd quarter	290.7	187.0	52.3	28.9	20.6	2.8	1.6	11.9	10.2	49.9	29.0	20.9	287.9
3rd quarter	308.5	200.7	58.6	31.9	22.6	4.2	-0.7	12.3	13.0	50.0	28.4	21.5	304.3
4th quarter	320.3	198.1	68.4	32.9	21.5	14.0	-0.2	13.5	13.7	53.9	31.8	22.1	306.3
1951													
1st quarter	336.4	209.4	64.6	33.1	21.1	10.4	0.2	15.0	14.9	62.3	39.6	22.7	326.0
2nd quarter	344.5	205.1	67.4	34.1	18.5	14.8	1.9	17.1	15.2	70.0	46.6	23.4	329.7
3rd quarter	351.8	207.8	62.0	34.8	17.4	9.7	3.7	18.1	14.3	78.3	54.3	24.0	342.0
4th quarter	356.6	211.7	57.1	34.6	17.7	4.7	4.2	18.2	14.0	83.6	59.3	24.2	351.9
1952													
1st quarter	360.2	213.1	58.1	35.1	18.3	4.7	3.7	18.7	15.0	85.3	60.9	24.3	355.5
2nd quarter	361.4	217.2	53.0	35.8	18.8	-1.5	2.0	16.6	14.6	89.2	64.1	25.1	362.9
3rd quarter	368.1	219.7	57.2	32.9	18.8	5.6	0.0	15.2	15.3	91.2	66.2	25.0	362.5
4th quarter	381.2	227.9	60.7	35.8	19.6	5.3	-1.0	15.3	16.3	93.7	68.1	25.6	376.0
1953													
1st quarter	388.5	231.5	61.7	37.8	20.0	3.9	-0.7	15.1	15.8	96.0	69.7	26.4	384.6
2nd quarter	392.3	233.2	62.1	38.5	20.1	3.6	-1.3	15.2	16.4	98.2	71.9	26.2	388.7
3rd quarter	391.7	233.9	61.4	39.6	19.5	2.3	-0.6	15.8	16.3	96.9	70.0	26.9	389.4
4th quarter	386.5	233.4	56.4	39.2	19.3	-2.0	-0.3	15.2	15.5	97.0	69.5	27.5	388.5
1954													
1st quarter	385.9	235.4	55.7	38.3	19.4	-2.0	-0.4	14.4	14.8	95.1	66.8	28.4	387.9
2nd quarter	386.7	238.2	55.4	38.2	20.7	-3.4	0.3	16.4	16.2	92.8	63.7	29.1	390.1
3rd quarter	391.6	240.6	59.0	38.9	22.2	-2.1	0.6	15.9	15.3	91.4	61.3	30.1	393.7
4th quarter	400.3	245.4	62.1	38.9	23.6	-0.3	1.1	16.6	15.5	91.6	61.2	30.4	400.7
1955													
1st quarter	413.8	251.8	68.7	39.5	25.4	3.8	1.1	17.3	16.2	92.2	60.7	31.5	409.9
2nd quarter	422.2	256.8	72.7	42.1	26.0	4.6	-0.2	16.9	17.1	92.8	60.9	32.0	417.6
3rd quarter	430.9	261.0	74.7	44.8	25.6	4.3	0.7	18.1	17.4	94.4	61.9	32.5	426.6
4th quarter	437.8	265.1	78.9	47.1	24.6	7.2	0.2	18.3	18.1	93.6	60.5	33.1	430.6
1956													
1st quarter	440.5	266.6	78.3	47.8	24.1	6.4	0.4	19.4	18.9	95.2	61.0	34.2	434.1
2nd quarter	446.8	269.3	77.0	49.1	24.4	3.6	1.9	20.9	19.0	98.6	63.5	35.1	443.2
3rd quarter	452.0	272.5	78.3	50.7	24.0	3.6	2.6	21.8	19.3	98.6	62.8	35.8	448.4
4th quarter	461.3	277.9	77.1	51.4	23.5	2.2	4.5	23.1	18.5	101.7	65.2	36.5	459.0
1957													
1st quarter	470.6	282.3	77.7	52.5	23.1	2.2	4.8	24.9	20.1	105.7	67.9	37.8	468.4
2nd quarter	472.8	284.6	77.9	52.6	22.6	2.7	4.1	24.4	20.3	106.2	67.5	38.7	470.2
3rd quarter	480.3	289.2	79.3	54.1	22.5	2.8	4.0	23.8	19.8	107.8	68.4	39.4	477.5
4th quarter	475.7	290.8	71.0	53.2	22.3	-4.5	3.4	23.0	19.6	110.4	70.0	40.4	480.2
1958													
1st quarter	468.4	290.3	66.7	49.4	21.4	-4.0	1.1	20.5	19.5	110.2	68.7	41.5	472.4
2nd quarter	472.8	293.2	65.1	47.8	21.5	-4.2	0.5	20.5	20.1	114.0	71.5	42.5	477.0
3rd quarter	486.7	298.3	72.0	47.4	23.0	1.5	0.9	20.6	19.7	115.5	71.9	43.6	485.1
4th quarter	500.4	302.2	80.0	49.3	25.4	5.2	-0.3	20.6	20.8	118.4	73.9	44.5	495.1

Table 1-1B. Gross Domestic Product: Historical—*Continued*

(Billions of dollars, quarterly data are at seasonally adjusted annual rates.)   **NIPA Tables 1.1.5, 1.2.5**

Year and quarter	Gross domestic product	Personal consumption expenditures	Gross private domestic investment				Exports and imports of goods and services			Government consumption expenditures and gross investment			Addendum: Final sales of domestic product
			Total	Fixed investment		Change in private inventories	Net exports	Exports	Imports	Total	Federal	State and local	
				Nonresidential	Residential								
1959													
1st quarter	511.1	309.9	83.2	50.9	28.3	3.9	0.4	21.8	21.4	117.6	72.3	45.3	507.2
2nd quarter	524.2	315.9	89.4	52.7	29.4	7.3	0.0	22.6	22.5	119.0	73.6	45.4	517.0
3rd quarter	525.2	321.1	83.6	54.4	28.8	0.4	0.6	23.5	22.9	119.9	74.5	45.4	524.8
4th quarter	529.3	323.2	86.5	54.4	28.0	4.1	0.6	23.1	22.5	119.0	73.8	45.2	525.2
1960													
1st quarter	543.3	326.7	96.5	56.3	29.0	11.2	2.7	26.0	23.3	117.4	70.9	46.5	532.1
2nd quarter	542.7	332.6	87.1	57.2	26.7	3.2	4.2	27.6	23.5	118.9	71.0	47.8	539.5
3rd quarter	546.0	332.5	86.4	56.2	25.9	4.3	4.2	27.0	22.9	122.9	74.1	48.8	541.7
4th quarter	541.1	334.5	76.0	55.9	25.9	-5.8	5.8	27.5	21.7	124.9	75.3	49.6	546.9
1961													
1st quarter	545.9	335.0	78.4	55.0	25.9	-2.5	5.8	27.5	21.7	126.8	75.3	51.5	548.5
2nd quarter	557.4	339.9	84.1	56.2	26.1	1.8	5.5	27.4	21.9	127.9	76.2	51.7	555.6
3rd quarter	568.2	342.8	90.9	56.7	27.6	6.7	3.9	27.2	23.3	130.6	78.1	52.5	561.6
4th quarter	581.6	350.1	92.9	58.5	28.5	6.0	4.4	28.3	23.9	134.2	79.9	54.3	575.6
1962													
1st quarter	595.2	355.4	98.1	59.7	29.0	9.4	4.0	28.3	24.3	137.8	83.3	54.5	585.8
2nd quarter	602.6	361.0	96.7	61.4	29.9	5.4	5.8	30.7	24.9	139.1	84.1	55.0	597.1
3rd quarter	609.6	364.9	98.2	62.1	29.9	6.2	3.8	29.0	25.1	142.7	87.0	55.7	603.4
4th quarter	613.1	371.1	95.0	61.8	29.8	3.4	2.8	28.4	25.6	144.2	87.6	56.6	609.8
1963													
1st quarter	622.7	374.7	99.7	62.0	30.8	6.9	3.9	29.1	25.2	144.4	86.2	58.2	615.8
2nd quarter	631.8	378.9	101.6	63.9	32.9	4.8	6.5	32.4	25.9	144.8	85.7	59.1	627.0
3rd quarter	645.0	385.8	104.6	65.7	33.2	5.7	3.9	30.6	26.7	150.6	89.8	60.8	639.2
4th quarter	654.8	390.5	107.2	67.7	34.5	5.1	5.4	32.2	26.8	151.7	89.6	62.1	649.8
1964													
1st quarter	671.2	400.1	110.5	69.1	36.2	5.1	7.3	34.2	27.0	153.3	90.0	63.2	666.0
2nd quarter	680.8	408.1	110.5	71.1	35.0	4.5	7.1	34.8	27.7	155.1	90.1	65.0	676.3
3rd quarter	692.8	417.0	112.6	73.4	34.5	4.7	6.4	34.8	28.4	156.8	90.8	66.0	688.1
4th quarter	698.4	419.6	115.0	75.3	34.6	5.0	6.9	36.2	29.3	156.9	89.9	67.0	693.4
1965													
1st quarter	719.2	430.3	126.5	80.2	34.8	11.5	4.6	33.1	28.5	157.8	89.4	68.4	707.7
2nd quarter	732.4	437.2	127.0	83.4	35.1	8.6	7.5	39.1	31.7	160.6	90.1	70.6	723.8
3rd quarter	750.2	446.4	131.2	86.7	35.3	9.3	4.9	36.9	32.0	167.6	94.4	73.2	740.9
4th quarter	773.1	460.4	133.8	90.6	35.5	7.6	5.5	39.5	33.9	173.5	98.7	74.8	765.5
1966													
1st quarter	797.3	470.8	144.2	94.4	35.9	13.9	4.4	39.4	35.0	177.9	101.2	76.8	783.5
2nd quarter	807.2	475.9	143.5	96.8	34.4	12.3	5.2	41.5	36.2	182.6	104.0	78.6	794.8
3rd quarter	820.8	485.0	143.2	98.3	33.0	11.9	2.2	40.4	38.2	190.4	109.9	80.5	808.9
4th quarter	834.9	490.8	145.9	99.2	30.2	16.5	3.6	42.4	38.8	194.7	111.1	83.5	818.4
1967													
1st quarter	846.0	495.1	142.8	98.0	29.4	15.4	4.6	44.0	39.4	203.6	117.9	85.7	830.6
2nd quarter	851.1	504.2	137.5	98.3	32.9	6.3	4.5	43.5	39.0	204.8	117.9	87.0	844.7
3rd quarter	866.6	511.4	142.8	98.8	34.8	9.3	2.9	42.4	39.5	209.4	120.9	88.5	857.4
4th quarter	883.2	518.9	147.7	101.7	37.5	8.4	2.2	43.9	41.7	214.4	123.1	91.2	874.8
1968													
1st quarter	911.1	536.9	152.3	105.6	38.3	8.4	1.1	45.5	44.4	220.9	126.3	94.5	902.7
2nd quarter	936.3	550.6	158.9	105.3	39.6	14.1	1.9	47.4	45.4	224.8	127.1	97.7	922.2
3rd quarter	952.3	566.7	155.7	107.6	40.4	7.7	1.3	49.5	48.2	228.6	128.5	100.1	944.7
4th quarter	970.1	575.6	160.8	112.2	42.6	6.0	1.1	49.2	48.2	232.7	129.7	103.0	964.1
1969													
1st quarter	995.4	587.8	172.4	116.0	44.9	11.5	0.2	44.0	43.8	235.0	129.6	105.5	983.9
2nd quarter	1 011.4	599.2	172.7	118.4	45.1	9.2	1.2	53.9	52.7	238.2	129.7	108.5	1 002.1
3rd quarter	1 032.0	609.5	177.6	122.4	45.0	10.2	1.0	53.3	52.4	240.0	133.3	110.6	1 021.8
4th quarter	1 040.7	621.5	171.6	123.3	42.5	5.8	3.3	56.5	53.1	244.3	131.9	112.4	1 035.0
1970													
1st quarter	1 053.5	632.6	168.1	123.8	42.5	1.8	3.4	56.9	53.5	249.4	133.5	115.9	1 051.7
2nd quarter	1 070.1	642.5	171.5	125.0	41.4	5.1	5.4	60.6	55.2	250.7	131.7	119.0	1 065.0
3rd quarter	1 088.5	654.5	173.9	126.3	42.6	5.1	3.8	60.3	56.4	256.2	132.3	123.9	1 083.4
4th quarter	1 091.5	661.2	166.8	123.5	47.2	-4.0	3.2	61.1	57.9	260.4	133.5	126.9	1 095.4
1971													
1st quarter	1 137.8	680.2	189.5	126.3	51.0	12.3	4.4	63.1	58.7	263.7	133.3	130.4	1 125.6
2nd quarter	1 159.4	694.3	197.3	129.5	57.0	10.9	-0.2	63.1	63.3	268.0	134.2	133.8	1 148.5
3rd quarter	1 180.3	706.7	202.1	131.2	60.7	10.2	-0.1	65.4	65.5	271.7	135.5	136.2	1 170.1
4th quarter	1 193.6	722.9	198.4	134.7	64.0	-0.3	-1.7	60.3	61.9	274.0	134.7	139.3	1 193.9
1972													
1st quarter	1 233.8	740.1	213.0	140.6	69.2	3.2	-3.5	68.6	72.2	284.3	141.4	142.9	1 230.6
2nd quarter	1 270.1	758.6	226.8	144.0	70.8	12.0	-4.3	67.2	71.4	289.0	144.6	144.4	1 258.1
3rd quarter	1 293.8	777.1	233.1	147.0	72.4	13.7	-2.6	71.5	74.1	286.3	138.5	147.8	1 280.1
4th quarter	1 332.0	801.9	239.7	155.0	77.3	7.5	-3.1	76.1	79.2	293.5	141.7	151.8	1 324.5
1973													
1st quarter	1 380.7	826.5	254.3	162.8	80.9	10.6	-1.4	84.0	85.4	301.3	145.9	155.4	1 370.1
2nd quarter	1 417.6	842.0	268.2	171.3	78.7	18.2	2.5	91.9	89.5	304.9	146.5	158.4	1 399.4
3rd quarter	1 436.8	860.5	264.3	176.6	77.9	9.8	6.4	97.6	91.1	305.6	143.4	162.2	1 427.1
4th quarter	1 479.1	875.6	280.9	180.1	75.7	25.0	9.0	107.6	98.7	313.7	146.5	167.2	1 454.1
1974													
1st quarter	1 494.7	893.8	268.4	183.4	72.4	12.5	6.4	116.7	110.3	326.1	151.9	174.3	1 482.1
2nd quarter	1 534.2	922.3	277.4	188.8	71.2	17.4	-2.7	126.7	129.4	337.3	154.7	182.5	1 516.8
3rd quarter	1 563.4	951.1	271.0	194.5	70.9	5.6	-7.0	126.6	133.6	348.3	159.5	188.8	1 557.8
4th quarter	1 603.0	960.9	281.3	197.6	63.3	20.4	0.0	136.6	136.6	360.8	166.4	194.4	1 582.6

Table 1-1B. Gross Domestic Product: Historical—*Continued*

(Billions of dollars, quarterly data are at seasonally adjusted annual rates.)

NIPA Tables 1.1.5, 1.2.5

Year and quarter	Gross domestic product	Personal consumption expenditures	Gross private domestic investment				Exports and imports of goods and services			Government consumption expenditures and gross investment			Addendum: Final sales of domestic product
			Total	Fixed investment		Change in private inventories	Net exports	Exports	Imports	Total	Federal	State and local	
				Nonresidential	Residential								
1975													
1st quarter	1 619.6	987.1	244.3	193.1	61.2	-10.0	16.5	141.4	124.9	371.7	167.6	204.1	1 629.6
2nd quarter	1 656.4	1 015.8	243.3	193.3	64.0	-14.0	21.6	136.8	115.2	375.8	169.0	206.8	1 670.4
3rd quarter	1 713.8	1 049.6	265.2	197.8	68.8	-1.4	12.0	134.1	122.1	387.0	174.9	212.1	1 715.2
4th quarter	1 765.9	1 078.5	276.2	202.9	73.0	0.3	13.8	142.5	128.7	397.3	179.7	217.6	1 765.5
1976													
1st quarter	1 824.5	1 112.3	304.6	209.5	80.4	14.7	4.7	143.6	138.9	402.9	180.5	222.4	1 809.8
2nd quarter	1 856.9	1 132.0	322.3	215.0	84.8	22.4	-0.5	146.6	147.1	403.2	182.0	221.2	1 834.5
3rd quarter	1 890.5	1 161.3	328.3	222.6	84.9	20.8	-4.1	151.8	155.8	404.9	183.6	221.3	1 869.7
4th quarter	1 938.4	1 195.1	337.6	230.2	96.9	10.5	-6.6	156.1	162.7	412.3	189.0	223.3	1 927.9
1977													
1st quarter	1 992.5	1 230.6	360.3	243.3	102.2	14.8	-21.1	155.4	176.4	422.7	192.9	229.8	1 977.7
2nd quarter	2 060.2	1 258.5	389.7	253.7	116.5	19.5	-21.1	161.9	183.0	433.1	197.7	235.3	2 040.7
3rd quarter	2 122.4	1 289.7	414.1	263.3	120.0	30.9	-20.6	162.3	182.9	439.1	200.0	239.1	2 091.5
4th quarter	2 168.7	1 327.9	422.3	275.9	122.2	24.1	-29.6	157.8	187.4	448.1	204.5	243.6	2 144.6
1978													
1st quarter	2 208.7	1 357.8	434.8	282.4	126.9	25.5	-38.7	164.6	203.3	454.8	207.7	247.1	2 183.2
2nd quarter	2 336.6	1 415.3	470.6	309.3	137.0	24.3	-22.6	186.2	208.8	473.3	214.8	258.5	2 312.3
3rd quarter	2 398.9	1 446.2	492.4	325.1	142.3	25.0	-23.8	191.3	215.1	484.0	218.6	265.4	2 373.9
4th quarter	2 482.2	1 485.4	515.8	341.4	145.8	28.5	-16.4	205.4	221.8	497.4	225.8	271.7	2 453.7
1979													
1st quarter	2 531.6	1 521.0	525.8	356.7	145.3	23.9	-18.2	211.7	229.8	502.9	229.1	273.8	2 507.7
2nd quarter	2 595.9	1 561.5	539.3	364.3	147.6	27.4	-22.2	220.9	243.1	517.3	234.9	282.4	2 568.5
3rd quarter	2 670.4	1 616.0	545.6	383.0	150.5	12.1	-23.0	234.3	257.3	531.8	238.8	293.0	2 658.3
4th quarter	2 730.7	1 659.5	547.9	391.3	148.0	8.6	-26.8	253.7	280.5	550.2	248.1	302.1	2 722.2
1980													
1st quarter	2 796.5	1 706.5	554.6	404.5	140.2	9.9	-35.8	268.5	304.3	571.2	259.7	311.6	2 786.6
2nd quarter	2 799.9	1 708.9	519.3	394.7	116.9	7.8	-15.2	277.4	292.6	586.9	271.0	315.9	2 792.2
3rd quarter	2 860.0	1 767.7	495.1	405.7	123.2	-33.9	5.5	284.7	279.2	591.8	272.0	319.8	2 893.9
4th quarter	2 993.5	1 835.4	551.5	422.8	137.8	-9.1	-6.7	292.5	299.2	613.4	286.8	326.6	3 002.6
1981													
1st quarter	3 131.8	1 890.7	619.4	443.0	137.6	38.8	-14.3	305.5	319.7	636.0	296.5	339.4	3 093.0
2nd quarter	3 167.2	1 921.9	609.8	462.9	135.3	11.7	-13.5	308.4	322.0	649.0	309.4	339.6	3 155.5
3rd quarter	3 261.2	1 961.2	652.3	482.1	126.2	44.0	-7.6	302.3	309.9	655.2	312.5	342.7	3 217.2
4th quarter	3 283.5	1 976.1	643.4	503.8	114.8	24.8	-14.8	304.7	319.4	678.8	328.5	350.3	3 258.7
1982													
1st quarter	3 273.8	2 014.4	588.3	500.1	109.7	-21.5	-16.3	293.2	309.5	687.4	332.5	354.9	3 295.3
2nd quarter	3 331.3	2 041.1	593.6	490.1	107.7	-4.2	-4.4	294.7	299.1	701.0	339.5	361.5	3 335.4
3rd quarter	3 367.1	2 089.2	593.0	478.7	108.4	5.8	-29.7	279.6	309.3	714.5	347.6	366.9	3 361.3
4th quarter	3 407.8	2 150.9	549.2	471.5	117.5	-39.8	-29.6	265.3	294.9	737.2	362.9	374.4	3 447.6
1983													
1st quarter	3 480.3	2 190.6	565.5	462.1	138.5	-35.1	-24.6	270.7	295.3	748.8	370.1	378.7	3 515.4
2nd quarter	3 583.8	2 254.5	613.8	466.4	155.0	-7.7	-45.4	272.5	318.0	761.0	378.8	382.2	3 591.5
3rd quarter	3 692.3	2 324.3	652.3	485.4	171.1	-4.2	-65.2	278.2	343.4	780.9	391.7	389.2	3 696.5
4th quarter	3 796.1	2 376.7	718.5	514.7	179.9	23.9	-71.4	286.6	358.0	772.3	380.1	392.2	3 772.2
1984													
1st quarter	3 912.8	2 422.8	790.9	531.5	186.4	73.0	-95.0	293.0	388.0	794.2	391.1	403.0	3 839.8
2nd quarter	4 015.0	2 481.2	818.9	558.3	191.3	69.3	-104.3	302.2	406.5	819.2	406.9	412.2	3 945.7
3rd quarter	4 087.4	2 519.7	838.9	576.6	190.9	71.3	-103.9	305.7	409.6	832.7	409.5	423.2	4 016.0
4th quarter	4 147.6	2 568.9	831.7	590.9	192.9	48.0	-107.8	308.6	416.4	854.7	423.0	431.7	4 099.6
1985													
1st quarter	4 237.0	2 643.9	809.9	599.4	194.2	16.2	-91.3	306.0	397.3	874.5	432.2	442.3	4 220.8
2nd quarter	4 302.3	2 691.2	827.0	609.1	196.3	21.6	-114.5	304.1	418.6	898.5	443.8	454.7	4 280.6
3rd quarter	4 394.6	2 764.7	822.2	604.4	201.4	16.3	-116.9	297.3	414.2	924.6	458.7	465.9	4 378.3
4th quarter	4 453.1	2 790.9	859.5	618.1	208.4	33.1	-133.4	305.4	438.9	936.1	462.4	473.7	4 420.0
1986													
1st quarter	4 516.3	2 834.7	863.5	613.5	219.5	30.4	-126.0	313.4	439.4	944.2	459.7	484.4	4 485.9
2nd quarter	4 555.2	2 863.0	855.2	605.0	234.6	15.7	-128.9	315.1	444.0	965.8	474.5	491.3	4 539.6
3rd quarter	4 619.6	2 929.7	835.8	602.0	240.9	-7.0	-139.0	320.5	459.4	993.0	492.9	500.2	4 626.6
4th quarter	4 669.4	2 966.1	842.1	610.6	244.3	-12.8	-133.6	335.0	468.6	994.8	486.4	508.4	4 682.1
1987													
1st quarter	4 736.2	2 998.3	871.2	596.6	246.7	28.0	-141.2	336.4	477.7	1 008.0	489.6	518.4	4 708.2
2nd quarter	4 821.4	3 068.8	874.6	608.4	249.7	16.5	-147.0	355.4	502.3	1 025.0	499.2	525.9	4 804.9
3rd quarter	4 900.5	3 133.5	876.5	625.5	250.0	1.0	-145.5	371.8	517.3	1 036.0	502.2	533.7	4 899.5
4th quarter	5 022.7	3 167.6	946.5	630.5	252.8	63.1	-145.4	392.1	537.5	1 054.0	509.8	544.2	4 959.6
1988													
1st quarter	5 090.6	3 249.0	908.6	641.5	250.1	17.0	-124.0	418.7	542.7	1 057.0	504.0	553.0	5 073.6
2nd quarter	5 207.7	3 309.0	934.5	659.4	255.5	19.6	-106.6	439.5	546.1	1 070.8	505.4	565.4	5 188.0
3rd quarter	5 299.5	3 378.3	942.0	666.3	257.5	18.2	-99.3	453.6	552.8	1 078.4	505.8	572.6	5 281.3
4th quarter	5 412.7	3 451.3	962.8	681.9	261.7	19.1	-107.7	466.6	574.3	1 106.4	520.0	586.4	5 393.6
1989													
1st quarter	5 527.3	3 506.1	1 005.4	696.3	260.9	48.1	-101.0	485.2	586.2	1 116.9	517.5	599.3	5 479.2
2nd quarter	5 628.4	3 569.5	1 001.0	708.9	255.8	36.3	-88.2	507.2	595.4	1 146.1	531.8	614.3	5 592.2
3rd quarter	5 711.5	3 625.6	996.5	731.2	255.5	9.8	-75.1	509.3	584.4	1 164.6	538.5	626.1	5 701.7
4th quarter	5 763.4	3 670.1	995.9	727.5	251.9	16.6	-82.8	515.4	598.2	1 180.2	537.7	642.5	5 746.9
1990													
1st quarter	5 890.8	3 754.5	1 010.8	740.9	256.0	14.0	-88.6	538.2	626.8	1 214.0	552.6	661.4	5 876.9
2nd quarter	5 974.6	3 800.2	1 014.8	734.2	246.9	33.7	-68.9	545.9	614.8	1 228.6	559.5	669.1	5 940.9
3rd quarter	6 029.5	3 863.4	1 000.7	744.3	234.5	21.9	-75.0	555.1	630.1	1 240.4	558.0	682.4	6 007.6
4th quarter	6 023.3	3 884.4	947.6	737.6	221.3	-11.3	-79.1	568.2	647.3	1 270.4	570.0	700.5	6 034.6

Table 1-1B. Gross Domestic Product: Historical—*Continued*

(Billions of dollars, quarterly data are at seasonally adjusted annual rates.)

NIPA Tables 1.1.5, 1.2.5

Year and quarter	Gross domestic product	Personal consumption expenditures	Gross private domestic investment Total	Fixed investment Nonresidential	Fixed investment Residential	Change in private inventories	Net exports	Exports	Imports	Government consumption expenditures and gross investment Total	Federal	State and local	Addendum: Final sales of domestic product
1991													
1st quarter	6 054.8	3 890.2	924.6	729.8	210.3	-15.5	-47.2	573.2	620.3	1 287.2	582.9	704.3	6 070.4
2nd quarter	6 143.6	3 943.7	926.6	726.8	217.8	-18.0	-23.2	590.7	613.9	1 296.6	585.5	711.1	6 161.6
3rd quarter	6 218.4	3 989.6	947.5	720.1	226.5	0.8	-21.1	600.6	621.7	1 302.4	580.9	721.5	6 217.6
4th quarter	6 279.3	4 017.1	978.8	717.6	230.1	31.1	-23.1	615.2	638.3	1 306.5	573.7	732.9	6 248.1
1992													
1st quarter	6 380.8	4 117.7	956.8	714.2	242.4	0.2	-20.6	625.3	645.8	1 326.9	578.6	748.3	6 380.5
2nd quarter	6 492.3	4 173.4	1 013.1	736.7	253.2	23.2	-32.8	626.1	659.0	1 338.7	582.2	756.5	6 469.1
3rd quarter	6 586.5	4 245.4	1 024.2	748.6	255.1	20.5	-38.5	639.3	677.9	1 355.4	592.7	762.8	6 566.0
4th quarter	6 697.5	4 326.2	1 058.0	768.3	268.3	21.3	-47.2	641.4	688.5	1 360.5	593.0	767.5	6 676.2
1993													
1st quarter	6 748.2	4 368.5	1 083.9	776.6	271.4	35.9	-55.7	643.6	699.3	1 351.5	577.0	774.5	6 712.2
2nd quarter	6 829.6	4 437.5	1 094.5	792.4	278.0	24.1	-63.2	653.1	716.3	1 360.9	575.6	785.3	6 805.5
3rd quarter	6 904.2	4 506.0	1 095.9	798.4	290.9	6.6	-68.4	650.9	719.3	1 370.6	578.9	791.7	6 897.6
4th quarter	7 032.8	4 572.0	1 153.0	829.5	306.9	16.6	-73.5	671.6	745.0	1 381.3	582.0	799.3	7 016.2
1994													
1st quarter	7 136.2	4 640.9	1 202.1	841.1	315.6	45.4	-80.6	681.2	761.8	1 373.9	564.4	809.5	7 090.9
2nd quarter	7 269.8	4 702.9	1 265.1	855.7	327.9	81.4	-90.6	707.0	797.6	1 392.4	569.0	823.4	7 188.4
3rd quarter	7 352.2	4 773.1	1 251.6	871.9	326.4	53.2	-96.9	736.9	833.8	1 424.4	584.0	840.5	7 299.0
4th quarter	7 476.6	4 847.2	1 307.2	906.6	325.4	75.1	-101.9	758.6	860.6	1 424.2	573.4	850.8	7 401.5
1995													
1st quarter	7 545.3	4 883.3	1 327.3	944.3	321.8	61.2	-105.4	781.5	886.9	1 440.0	577.6	862.4	7 484.1
2nd quarter	7 604.9	4 955.0	1 303.8	956.6	313.5	33.8	-109.5	798.8	908.3	1 455.6	579.7	875.9	7 571.1
3rd quarter	7 706.5	5 020.5	1 303.2	965.5	326.4	11.3	-74.5	831.4	905.8	1 457.3	576.9	880.4	7 695.2
4th quarter	7 799.5	5 077.9	1 335.6	982.5	334.6	18.4	-69.8	839.4	909.2	1 455.7	567.3	888.5	7 781.0
1996													
1st quarter	7 893.1	5 153.8	1 355.2	1 003.6	344.7	6.9	-88.8	847.9	936.7	1 472.9	577.2	895.8	7 886.2
2nd quarter	8 061.5	5 244.1	1 418.6	1 026.6	361.4	30.5	-93.7	859.0	952.8	1 492.5	582.5	910.0	8 031.0
3rd quarter	8 159.0	5 298.3	1 474.4	1 059.1	364.3	51.1	-114.2	859.5	973.8	1 500.5	576.9	923.6	8 107.9
4th quarter	8 287.0	5 376.1	1 480.0	1 083.5	361.8	34.7	-88.9	903.8	992.6	1 519.8	576.3	943.6	8 252.3
1997													
1st quarter	8 402.0	5 456.7	1 522.0	1 106.8	365.4	49.8	-108.9	918.3	1 027.2	1 532.2	572.1	960.1	8 352.3
2nd quarter	8 551.9	5 495.1	1 589.9	1 129.2	372.3	88.4	-85.2	954.4	1 039.7	1 552.2	585.7	966.5	8 463.5
3rd quarter	8 691.7	5 603.5	1 625.3	1 178.4	379.0	67.9	-96.9	974.0	1 070.9	1 559.8	585.4	974.4	8 623.8
4th quarter	8 788.3	5 687.6	1 645.3	1 181.9	385.8	77.7	-117.0	968.3	1 085.3	1 572.4	586.5	985.9	8 710.6
1998													
1st quarter	8 889.7	5 745.9	1 712.3	1 212.4	394.8	105.1	-135.3	963.0	1 098.2	1 566.7	571.5	995.3	8 784.6
2nd quarter	8 994.7	5 857.8	1 694.8	1 246.1	411.3	37.3	-162.4	947.3	1 109.6	1 604.4	586.6	1 017.8	8 957.4
3rd quarter	9 146.5	5 952.8	1 739.8	1 259.8	427.6	52.4	-174.7	935.2	1 109.9	1 628.6	584.7	1 043.8	9 094.1
4th quarter	9 325.6	6 055.5	1 794.4	1 292.9	441.5	60.0	-178.7	966.3	1 145.0	1 654.3	593.6	1 060.8	9 265.6
1999													
1st quarter	9 450.3	6 134.7	1 850.6	1 319.9	447.4	83.4	-210.9	959.2	1 170.2	1 676.0	594.5	1 081.5	9 367.0
2nd quarter	9 561.5	6 263.1	1 845.8	1 351.4	459.3	35.1	-251.1	970.9	1 221.9	1 703.7	601.1	1 102.6	9 526.4
3rd quarter	9 718.7	6 371.4	1 890.9	1 383.8	466.6	40.5	-283.8	997.2	1 281.0	1 740.2	614.6	1 125.6	9 678.2
4th quarter	9 932.3	6 498.5	1 949.4	1 391.4	473.8	84.2	-299.9	1 029.3	1 329.2	1 784.2	631.6	1 152.7	9 848.0
2000													
1st quarter	10 036.1	6 652.8	1 945.9	1 445.5	484.2	16.2	-357.7	1 053.0	1 410.7	1 795.1	618.1	1 177.0	10 020.0
2nd quarter	10 283.7	6 745.3	2 071.8	1 494.7	486.6	90.4	-362.2	1 090.2	1 452.4	1 828.9	639.3	1 189.6	10 193.3
3rd quarter	10 363.8	6 854.7	2 055.8	1 515.5	483.1	57.2	-391.6	1 120.8	1 512.5	1 845.0	636.2	1 208.9	10 306.6
4th quarter	10 475.3	6 953.8	2 061.6	1 519.4	487.8	54.3	-408.7	1 113.3	1 522.0	1 868.7	636.1	1 232.6	10 421.0
2001													
1st quarter	10 512.5	7 025.3	1 967.5	1 501.5	496.7	-30.6	-392.2	1 097.9	1 490.1	1 911.9	652.5	1 259.4	10 543.1
2nd quarter	10 641.6	7 078.0	1 967.0	1 467.6	511.0	-11.6	-362.1	1 057.4	1 419.5	1 958.6	666.4	1 292.3	10 653.1
3rd quarter	10 644.3	7 107.3	1 937.3	1 445.0	522.4	-30.1	-365.8	998.5	1 364.3	1 965.5	674.9	1 290.6	10 674.4
4th quarter	10 702.7	7 216.9	1 842.7	1 401.5	522.1	-80.8	-356.0	961.4	1 317.3	1 999.1	683.3	1 315.8	10 783.5
2002													
1st quarter	10 837.3	7 253.2	1 910.0	1 371.9	538.3	-0.2	-374.3	973.7	1 348.0	2 048.3	714.4	1 333.9	10 837.5
2nd quarter	10 938.0	7 347.9	1 925.6	1 351.6	554.8	19.1	-416.1	1 007.0	1 423.1	2 080.6	733.1	1 347.6	10 918.9
3rd quarter	11 039.8	7 437.5	1 927.9	1 343.7	558.9	25.3	-433.2	1 022.8	1 456.1	2 107.7	746.2	1 361.6	11 014.5
4th quarter	11 105.7	7 502.6	1 936.5	1 328.4	578.3	29.8	-476.5	1 015.3	1 491.8	2 143.1	768.8	1 374.2	11 075.9
2003													
1st quarter	11 230.8	7 593.1	1 960.2	1 327.8	601.4	31.0	-500.5	1 015.4	1 515.9	2 178.0	789.3	1 388.7	11 199.8
2nd quarter	11 371.4	7 685.2	1 970.5	1 359.1	611.9	-0.4	-501.3	1 013.8	1 515.1	2 216.9	831.4	1 385.5	11 371.8
3rd quarter	11 628.4	7 844.6	2 048.3	1 388.5	651.6	8.1	-495.7	1 044.1	1 539.9	2 231.2	830.5	1 400.8	11 620.2
4th quarter	11 818.5	7 934.5	2 132.8	1 411.5	682.9	38.4	-506.1	1 100.2	1 606.4	2 257.3	848.1	1 409.3	11 780.1
2004													
1st quarter	11 991.4	8 076.8	2 155.2	1 400.3	706.0	48.9	-543.6	1 141.1	1 684.7	2 303.1	872.5	1 430.6	11 942.6
2nd quarter	12 183.5	8 183.6	2 259.5	1 440.2	743.1	76.2	-603.2	1 173.6	1 776.8	2 343.6	886.7	1 456.8	12 107.3
3rd quarter	12 369.4	8 309.4	2 311.3	1 485.6	763.4	62.3	-633.0	1 188.4	1 821.4	2 381.8	906.9	1 474.9	12 307.1
4th quarter	12 563.8	8 461.3	2 380.8	1 526.5	786.2	68.0	-679.4	1 229.4	1 908.8	2 401.2	903.3	1 497.9	12 495.8
2005													
1st quarter	12 816.2	8 573.5	2 475.2	1 560.5	815.1	99.5	-674.7	1 266.4	1 941.1	2 442.2	931.2	1 511.0	12 716.6
2nd quarter	12 975.7	8 720.6	2 469.5	1 595.2	843.7	30.6	-684.1	1 302.9	1 987.1	2 469.7	938.2	1 531.5	12 945.0
3rd quarter	13 206.5	8 882.0	2 527.2	1 633.8	875.5	17.9	-724.3	1 313.9	2 038.2	2 521.6	963.1	1 558.4	13 188.6
4th quarter	13 383.3	8 985.3	2 636.5	1 656.4	889.9	90.2	-779.7	1 358.2	2 138.0	2 541.3	952.8	1 588.5	13 293.1
2006													
1st quarter	13 649.8	9 128.1	2 699.7	1 729.4	895.9	74.4	-770.1	1 420.4	2 190.6	2 592.2	995.3	1 596.9	13 575.4
2nd quarter	13 802.9	9 247.2	2 697.0	1 761.0	858.7	77.3	-771.9	1 466.9	2 238.8	2 630.7	998.7	1 631.9	13 725.6
3rd quarter	13 910.5	9 369.6	2 684.4	1 793.6	813.7	77.1	-798.9	1 482.9	2 281.8	2 655.4	1 000.4	1 655.0	13 833.4
4th quarter	14 068.4	9 444.9	2 641.6	1 821.2	781.3	39.1	-708.6	1 543.9	2 252.6	2 690.6	1 013.5	1 677.0	14 029.3

Table 1-1B. Gross Domestic Product: Historical—*Continued*

(Billions of dollars, quarterly data are at seasonally adjusted annual rates.)   **NIPA Tables 1.1.5, 1.2.5**

| Year and quarter | Gross domestic product | Personal consumption expenditures | Gross private domestic investment | | | | Exports and imports of goods and services | | | Government consumption expenditures and gross investment | | | Addendum: Final sales of domestic product |
| | | | Total | Fixed investment | | Change in private inventories | Net exports | Exports | Imports | Total | Federal | State and local | |
				Nonresidential	Residential								
2007													
1st quarter	14 235.0	9 588.5	2 634.2	1 864.7	749.3	20.2	-723.4	1 578.8	2 302.2	2 735.6	1 018.3	1 717.3	14 214.8
2nd quarter	14 424.5	9 696.7	2 671.9	1 907.5	717.3	47.1	-726.5	1 624.4	2 351.0	2 782.5	1 040.8	1 741.7	14 377.4
3rd quarter	14 571.9	9 790.2	2 658.2	1 937.9	671.7	48.6	-700.9	1 693.1	2 394.0	2 824.3	1 063.9	1 760.5	14 523.2
4th quarter	14 690.0	9 902.5	2 610.6	1 972.3	616.4	21.9	-688.4	1 766.6	2 455.0	2 865.3	1 076.1	1 789.1	14 668.0
2008													
1st quarter	14 672.9	9 967.1	2 527.0	1 981.6	565.5	-20.1	-745.0	1 816.1	2 561.2	2 923.8	1 110.7	1 813.1	14 693.0
2nd quarter	14 817.1	10 090.4	2 493.3	1 978.7	538.4	-23.9	-749.9	1 918.9	2 668.8	2 983.4	1 140.5	1 842.9	14 841.0
3rd quarter	14 844.3	10 113.2	2 435.9	1 947.3	507.4	-18.8	-760.6	1 930.1	2 690.7	3 055.9	1 180.0	1 875.9	14 863.1
4th quarter	14 546.7	9 851.3	2 243.1	1 856.2	452.1	-65.1	-597.4	1 707.5	2 304.9	3 049.7	1 191.2	1 858.5	14 611.9
2009													
1st quarter	14 381.2	9 763.3	1 972.1	1 712.3	405.5	-145.6	-389.6	1 519.3	1 908.9	3 035.4	1 182.2	1 853.1	14 526.8
2nd quarter	14 342.1	9 764.9	1 825.9	1 637.5	376.3	-187.9	-335.2	1 521.5	1 856.7	3 086.5	1 214.6	1 871.9	14 530.0
3rd quarter	14 384.4	9 887.4	1 786.4	1 600.3	392.0	-205.9	-402.0	1 591.0	1 993.1	3 112.5	1 233.2	1 879.3	14 590.3
4th quarter	14 564.1	9 956.2	1 928.0	1 583.6	395.2	-50.8	-442.1	1 703.2	2 145.3	3 122.0	1 240.7	1 881.3	14 614.9
2010													
1st quarter	14 672.5	10 042.3	1 989.5	1 594.4	383.1	12.1	-495.1	1 746.4	2 241.4	3 135.7	1 269.2	1 866.5	14 660.4
2nd quarter	14 879.2	10 134.7	2 092.7	1 641.8	400.8	50.1	-529.7	1 807.0	2 336.7	3 181.5	1 304.6	1 876.9	14 829.0
3rd quarter	15 049.8	10 234.3	2 164.6	1 677.4	365.6	121.5	-543.8	1 860.3	2 404.0	3 194.7	1 321.6	1 873.1	14 928.2
4th quarter	15 231.7	10 396.3	2 156.5	1 719.3	374.7	62.4	-505.3	1 960.4	2 465.7	3 184.2	1 320.1	1 864.2	15 169.3
2011													
1st quarter	15 242.9	10 527.1	2 120.4	1 721.8	377.1	21.5	-554.7	2 029.5	2 584.1	3 150.0	1 297.4	1 852.6	15 221.4
2nd quarter	15 461.9	10 662.6	2 199.9	1 773.1	381.0	45.8	-572.2	2 095.5	2 667.7	3 171.7	1 315.4	1 856.3	15 416.2
3rd quarter	15 611.8	10 778.6	2 222.2	1 848.9	386.8	-13.5	-553.7	2 143.4	2 697.1	3 164.6	1 308.5	1 856.1	15 625.3
4th quarter	15 818.7	10 878.9	2 385.7	1 895.7	398.1	91.9	-594.4	2 136.2	2 730.7	3 148.5	1 294.9	1 853.6	15 726.8
2012													
1st quarter	16 041.6	11 019.1	2 453.6	1 932.3	418.4	102.9	-590.8	2 173.4	2 764.2	3 159.7	1 291.8	1 867.9	15 938.7
2nd quarter	16 160.4	11 100.2	2 454.0	1 961.4	425.7	66.8	-557.9	2 197.4	2 755.3	3 164.1	1 293.8	1 870.3	16 093.6
3rd quarter	16 356.0	11 193.6	2 493.3	1 968.0	443.7	81.6	-524.4	2 199.2	2 723.5	3 193.5	1 322.1	1 871.4	16 274.4
4th quarter	16 420.3	11 285.5	2 499.9	2 018.2	468.8	13.0	-515.8	2 213.7	2 729.5	3 150.7	1 275.2	1 875.4	16 407.3

Table 1-2A. Real Gross Domestic Product: Recent Data

(Billions of chained [2009] dollars, quarterly data are at seasonally adjusted annual rates.)   **NIPA Tables 1.1.6, 1.2.6**

| Year and quarter | Gross domestic product | Personal consumption expenditures | Gross private domestic investment | | | | Exports and imports of goods and services | | | Government consumption expenditures and gross investment | | | Residual | Addendum: final sales of domestic product |
| | | | Total | Fixed investment | | Change in private inventories | Net exports | Exports | Imports | Total | Federal | State and local | | |
				Nonresidential	Residential									
1950	2 181.9	1 360.5	293.7	...	...	...	...	58.2	70.7	569.6	...	...	-29.4	2 165.0
1951	2 357.7	1 381.7	294.5	...	...	...	...	71.3	73.4	778.9	...	...	-95.3	2 326.3
1952	2 453.7	1 425.3	270.4	...	...	...	...	68.2	79.9	931.7	...	...	-162.0	2 455.1
1953	2 568.9	1 493.4	285.6	...	...	...	...	63.6	87.4	994.8	...	...	-181.1	2 578.0
1954	2 554.4	1 524.7	274.4	...	...	...	...	66.7	83.1	931.1	...	...	-159.4	2 586.4
1955	2 736.4	1 637.3	337.7	...	...	...	...	73.8	93.1	901.0	...	...	-120.3	2 731.3
1956	2 794.7	1 685.1	336.8	...	...	...	...	86.0	100.7	903.2	...	...	-115.7	2 797.8
1957	2 853.5	1 726.8	324.2	...	...	...	...	93.5	104.9	944.8	...	...	-130.9	2 871.9
1958	2 832.6	1 741.7	300.6	...	...	...	...	80.9	109.9	976.7	...	...	-157.4	2 855.8
1959	3 028.1	1 840.5	358.4	...	...	...	...	89.2	121.4	1 000.9	...	...	-139.5	3 029.0
1960	3 105.8	1 891.0	359.7	...	...	...	...	104.7	123.0	1 007.0	...	...	-133.6	3 111.1
1961	3 185.1	1 930.0	360.9	...	...	...	...	105.2	122.2	1 060.6	...	...	-149.4	3 192.7
1962	3 379.9	2 025.4	403.8	...	...	...	...	110.6	136.1	1 129.5	...	...	-153.3	3 371.2
1963	3 527.1	2 108.9	431.2	...	...	...	...	118.5	139.8	1 157.1	...	...	-148.8	3 522.0
1964	3 730.5	2 234.4	465.2	...	...	...	...	132.4	147.2	1 185.9	...	...	-140.2	3 731.2
1965	3 972.9	2 376.1	529.6	...	...	...	...	136.1	162.8	1 224.2	...	...	-130.3	3 951.4
1966	4 234.9	2 510.6	577.1	...	...	...	...	145.5	187.1	1 331.0	...	...	-142.2	4 192.9
1967	4 351.2	2 585.6	556.9	...	...	...	...	148.9	200.7	1 436.4	...	...	-175.9	4 330.0
1968	4 564.7	2 734.1	590.2	...	...	...	...	160.6	230.6	1 485.7	...	...	-175.3	4 549.0
1969	4 707.9	2 836.3	623.1	...	...	...	...	168.4	243.7	1 488.0	...	...	-164.2	4 693.1
1970	4 717.7	2 903.1	585.2	...	...	...	...	186.5	254.1	1 457.7	...	...	-160.7	4 736.1
1971	4 873.0	3 013.9	645.5	...	...	...	...	189.6	267.7	1 431.0	...	...	-139.3	4 866.0
1972	5 128.8	3 198.7	718.2	...	...	...	...	203.9	297.8	1 424.2	...	...	-118.4	5 120.4
1973	5 418.2	3 357.3	796.8	...	...	...	...	242.3	311.6	1 419.6	...	...	-86.2	5 386.5
1974	5 390.2	3 329.6	744.0	...	...	...	...	261.5	304.6	1 451.8	...	...	-92.1	5 372.5
1975	5 379.5	3 405.2	623.5	...	...	...	...	259.8	270.7	1 483.8	...	...	-122.1	5 428.6
1976	5 669.3	3 595.1	742.5	...	...	...	...	271.1	323.6	1 491.6	...	...	-107.4	5 645.7
1977	5 930.6	3 746.6	848.4	...	...	...	...	277.7	359.0	1 509.2	...	...	-92.3	5 894.4
1978	6 260.4	3 911.3	946.6	...	...	...	...	306.9	390.1	1 553.7	...	...	-68.0	6 218.7
1979	6 459.2	4 004.2	979.8	...	...	...	...	337.4	396.6	1 582.6	...	...	-48.2	6 443.3
1980	6 443.4	3 991.6	881.2	...	...	...	...	373.7	370.3	1 612.5	...	...	-45.3	6 485.0
1981	6 610.6	4 050.8	958.7	...	...	...	...	378.3	380.0	1 628.0	...	...	-25.2	6 579.8
1982	6 484.3	4 108.4	833.7	...	...	...	...	349.4	375.2	1 658.0	...	...	-90.0	6 539.6
1983	6 784.7	4 342.6	911.5	...	...	...	...	340.4	422.6	1 721.6	...	...	-108.8	6 823.2
1984	7 277.2	4 571.6	1 160.3	...	...	...	...	368.2	525.4	1 783.2	...	...	-80.7	7 188.5
1985	7 585.7	4 812.0	1 159.5	...	...	...	...	380.5	559.5	1 904.0	...	...	-110.8	7 573.5
1986	7 852.1	5 014.1	1 161.3	...	...	...	...	409.7	607.3	2 007.7	...	...	-133.4	7 864.1
1987	8 123.9	5 183.7	1 194.4	...	...	...	...	454.4	643.3	2 066.9	...	...	-132.2	8 104.4
1988	8 465.4	5 400.5	1 223.8	...	...	...	...	528.0	668.6	2 094.8	...	...	-113.1	8 457.8
1989	8 777.0	5 558.2	1 273.4	...	...	...	...	589.1	698.0	2 155.1	...	...	-100.8	8 756.0
1990	8 945.4	5 672.7	1 240.6	...	...	...	...	641.1	723.0	2 224.3	...	...	-110.3	8 943.0
1991	8 938.9	5 685.7	1 158.8	...	...	...	...	683.6	721.9	2 250.9	...	...	-118.2	8 959.0
1992	9 256.7	5 896.6	1 243.7	...	...	...	...	730.9	772.5	2 262.1	...	...	-104.1	9 252.5
1993	9 510.8	6 101.5	1 343.1	...	...	...	...	754.8	839.3	2 243.3	...	...	-92.6	9 500.7
1994	9 894.7	6 338.1	1 502.3	...	...	...	...	821.5	939.5	2 245.5	...	...	-73.2	9 827.0
1995	10 163.7	6 527.7	1 550.8	...	...	...	...	905.9	1 014.6	2 257.5	...	...	-63.6	10 140.2
1996	10 549.5	6 755.7	1 686.7	...	...	...	...	980.0	1 102.9	2 279.2	...	...	-49.2	10 525.0
1997	11 022.9	7 010.0	1 879.0	...	...	...	...	1 096.8	1 251.4	2 322.0	...	...	-33.5	10 944.0
1998	11 513.4	7 384.8	2 058.3	...	...	...	...	1 122.4	1 397.7	2 370.5	...	...	-24.9	11 439.8
1999	12 071.4	7 788.1	2 231.4	1 510.1	633.8	75.5	-382.3	1 174.1	1 556.4	2 451.7	815.3	1 643.6	-114.0	12 000.3
2000	12 565.2	8 182.1	2 375.5	1 647.7	637.9	66.2	-482.7	1 272.4	1 755.1	2 498.2	817.7	1 689.1	-84.3	12 500.4
2001	12 684.4	8 387.5	2 231.4	1 608.4	643.7	-46.2	-504.2	1 200.5	1 704.7	2 592.4	849.8	1 751.5	-90.5	12 731.7
2002	12 909.7	8 600.4	2 218.2	1 498.0	682.7	22.5	-584.9	1 178.1	1 763.0	2 705.8	910.8	1 802.4	-70.3	12 889.9
2003	13 270.0	8 866.2	2 308.7	1 526.1	744.5	22.6	-641.6	1 197.2	1 838.8	2 764.3	973.0	1 795.3	-45.4	13 247.9
2004	13 774.0	9 205.6	2 511.3	1 605.4	818.9	71.4	-731.9	1 309.3	2 041.2	2 808.2	1 017.1	1 792.8	-19.2	13 702.7
2005	14 235.6	9 527.8	2 672.6	1 717.4	872.6	64.3	-777.1	1 388.4	2 165.5	2 826.2	1 034.8	1 792.3	-1.7	14 170.1
2006	14 615.2	9 814.9	2 730.0	1 839.6	806.6	71.6	-786.2	1 512.4	2 298.6	2 869.3	1 060.9	1 808.8	-3.5	14 543.6
2007	14 876.8	10 035.5	2 644.1	1 948.4	654.8	35.5	-703.6	1 647.3	2 350.9	2 914.4	1 078.7	1 836.1	-9.5	14 839.2
2008	14 833.6	9 999.2	2 396.0	1 934.4	497.7	-33.7	-546.9	1 741.8	2 288.7	2 994.8	1 152.3	1 842.4	-13.4	14 868.9
2009	14 417.9	9 842.9	1 878.1	1 633.4	392.2	-147.6	-392.2	1 583.8	1 976.0	3 089.1	1 217.7	1 871.4	0.1	14 565.5
2010	14 779.4	10 035.9	2 120.4	1 673.8	382.4	58.2	-462.6	1 765.6	2 228.1	3 091.4	1 270.7	1 820.8	-1.2	14 717.7
2011	15 052.4	10 291.3	2 224.6	1 800.5	384.3	33.6	-445.9	1 890.5	2 336.4	2 992.3	1 237.9	1 754.5	-9.0	15 014.4
2012	15 470.7	10 517.6	2 436.0	1 931.8	433.7	57.6	-430.8	1 957.4	2 388.2	2 963.1	1 220.3	1 742.8	-13.0	15 403.2
2010														
1st quarter	14 597.7	9 915.4	2 012.9	1 615.0	383.0	9.8	-413.6	1 700.4	2 113.9	3 084.3	1 247.8	1 836.5	3.9	14 584.3
2nd quarter	14 738.0	9 995.3	2 116.9	1 659.3	403.5	48.8	-474.3	1 739.3	2 213.6	3 106.2	1 273.4	1 832.8	-1.9	14 686.3
3rd quarter	14 839.3	10 063.7	2 185.7	1 692.8	368.1	116.2	-504.9	1 784.9	2 289.8	3 103.5	1 285.0	1 818.5	-2.3	14 718.3
4th quarter	14 942.4	10 169.0	2 166.1	1 728.1	375.1	58.1	-457.5	1 837.7	2 295.2	3 071.5	1 276.4	1 795.2	-5.0	14 881.8
2011														
1st quarter	14 894.0	10 221.3	2 124.3	1 724.1	376.7	22.0	-456.5	1 854.7	2 311.3	3 012.0	1 241.6	1 770.5	-10.1	14 871.9
2nd quarter	15 011.3	10 258.9	2 196.1	1 765.3	379.2	42.9	-438.3	1 876.9	2 315.2	3 002.4	1 247.0	1 755.5	-3.1	14 961.8
3rd quarter	15 062.1	10 311.9	2 209.9	1 835.0	384.9	-11.0	-433.9	1 908.9	2 342.8	2 983.2	1 236.4	1 746.9	-13.3	15 072.7
4th quarter	15 242.1	10 373.1	2 368.2	1 877.3	396.2	80.6	-454.7	1 921.7	2 376.4	2 971.7	1 226.7	1 745.0	-9.1	15 151.3
2012														
1st quarter	15 381.6	10 447.8	2 427.8	1 903.8	417.2	89.2	-439.2	1 941.4	2 380.6	2 961.3	1 219.1	1 742.2	-7.5	15 278.9
2nd quarter	15 427.7	10 496.8	2 418.0	1 925.0	423.0	56.8	-435.3	1 959.8	2 395.1	2 963.5	1 218.5	1 745.0	-11.6	15 360.8
3rd quarter	15 534.0	10 541.0	2 456.5	1 926.4	437.3	77.2	-436.5	1 961.6	2 398.0	2 988.8	1 244.6	1 744.3	-11.0	15 444.9
4th quarter	15 539.6	10 584.8	2 441.8	1 971.9	457.5	7.3	-412.1	1 967.0	2 379.1	2 938.8	1 198.9	1 739.8	-22.2	15 528.3

Note: Chained (2009) dollar series are calculated as the product of the chain-type quantity index and the 2009 current-dollar value of the corresponding series, divided by 100. Because the formula for the chain-type quantity indexes uses weights from more than one period, the corresponding chained-dollar estimates are usually not additive. The residual column is the difference between the total and the sum of the most detailed components shown in the Bureau of Economic Analysis (BEA) published data.

. . . = Not available.

Table 1-2B. Real Gross Domestic Product: Historical

(Billions of chained [2009] dollars, quarterly data are at seasonally adjusted annual rates.)   **NIPA Tables 1.1.6, 1.2.6**

Year and quarter	Gross domestic product	Personal consump-tion expen-ditures	Gross private domestic investment				Exports and imports of goods and services			Government consumption expenditures and gross investment			Residual	Adden-dum: Final sales of domestic product
			Total	Nonresi-dential	Residential	Change in private inventories	Net exports	Exports	Imports	Total	Federal	State and local		
1929	1 055.6	781.0	123.6	...	...	...	...	40.3	52.8	165.7	...	...	-2.2	1 066.6
1930	965.8	739.2	84.2	...	...	...	...	33.3	45.9	182.5	...	...	-27.5	994.6
1931	904.1	716.1	54.7	...	...	...	...	27.7	40.0	190.1	...	...	-44.5	936.9
1932	787.5	652.0	20.2	...	...	...	...	21.7	33.2	184.2	...	...	-57.4	831.6
1933	777.6	637.6	27.3	...	...	...	...	21.8	34.6	178.0	...	...	-52.5	806.7
1934	861.4	683.1	45.2	...	...	...	...	24.3	35.4	199.7	...	...	-55.5	882.9
1935	938.2	724.6	78.6	...	...	...	...	25.6	46.3	206.0	...	...	-50.3	938.2
1936	1 059.6	798.3	99.3	...	...	...	...	26.9	45.8	239.1	...	...	-58.2	1 061.1
1937	1 113.6	827.8	122.3	...	...	...	...	33.9	51.5	229.4	...	...	-48.3	1 105.3
1938	1 076.7	814.6	84.2	...	...	...	...	33.5	40.1	246.8	...	...	-62.3	1 090.7
1939	1 162.6	860.2	105.6	...	...	...	...	35.4	42.1	268.3	...	...	-64.8	1 170.3
1940	1 265.0	904.7	143.8	...	...	...	...	40.2	43.1	277.9	...	...	-58.5	1 250.5
1941	1 488.9	968.7	176.0	...	...	...	...	41.3	53.0	467.1	...	...	-111.2	1 459.5
1942	1 770.3	945.7	98.0	...	...	...	...	27.3	48.1	1 084.2	...	...	-336.8	1 769.6
1943	2 072.0	972.0	61.1	...	...	...	...	23.0	60.6	1 626.0	...	...	-549.5	2 098.8
1944	2 237.5	999.7	73.0	...	...	...	...	24.7	63.5	1 826.3	...	...	-622.7	2 267.0
1945	2 215.9	1 061.5	93.9	...	...	...	...	34.6	67.5	1 604.5	...	...	-511.1	2 251.8
1946	1 959.0	1 193.6	225.0	...	...	...	...	74.7	55.9	566.8	...	...	-45.2	1 930.8
1947	1 937.6	1 216.4	216.5	...	...	...	...	85.1	53.1	482.5	...	...	-9.8	1 965.8
1948	2 018.0	1 243.9	272.9	...	...	...	...	67.0	62.0	510.6	...	...	-14.4	1 999.2
1949	2 007.0	1 278.5	210.9	...	...	...	...	66.4	59.8	566.1	...	...	-55.1	2 044.9
1947														
1st quarter	1 932.6	1 199.4	222.7	...	...	...	...	90.7	54.8	478.7	...	...	-4.1	1 947.9
2nd quarter	1 930.4	1 219.3	205.6	...	...	...	...	89.5	55.9	482.8	...	...	-10.9	1 960.9
3rd quarter	1 928.4	1 223.3	199.6	...	...	...	...	85.0	49.5	485.9	...	...	-15.9	1 976.0
4th quarter	1 958.8	1 223.7	238.2	...	...	...	...	75.3	52.2	482.5	...	...	-8.7	1 978.4
1948														
1st quarter	1 987.6	1 229.8	262.6	...	...	...	...	71.9	58.9	488.6	...	...	-6.4	1 985.2
2nd quarter	2 019.9	1 244.1	278.9	...	...	...	...	65.2	61.2	505.0	...	...	-12.1	1 995.9
3rd quarter	2 031.2	1 245.9	281.7	...	...	...	...	66.7	64.4	515.0	...	...	-13.7	1 999.9
4th quarter	2 033.3	1 255.9	268.3	...	...	...	...	64.4	63.4	533.8	...	...	-25.7	2 015.8
1949														
1st quarter	2 005.6	1 257.9	228.0	...	...	...	...	72.1	61.5	548.6	...	...	-39.5	2 023.8
2nd quarter	1 998.8	1 277.2	197.7	...	...	...	...	71.5	60.6	572.5	...	...	-59.5	2 049.9
3rd quarter	2 020.8	1 280.1	214.1	...	...	...	...	65.5	58.1	577.6	...	...	-58.4	2 049.0
4th quarter	2 002.7	1 298.8	203.6	...	...	...	...	56.7	59.0	565.8	...	...	-63.2	2 056.8
1950														
1st quarter	2 082.5	1 320.4	251.9	...	...	...	...	55.8	60.6	557.1	...	...	-42.1	2 089.7
2nd quarter	2 145.5	1 342.1	278.9	...	...	...	...	56.4	64.0	566.6	...	...	-34.5	2 145.7
3rd quarter	2 228.2	1 411.0	302.9	...	...	...	...	57.9	78.9	557.3	...	...	-22.0	2 221.8
4th quarter	2 271.2	1 368.4	341.3	...	...	...	...	62.6	79.1	597.2	...	...	-19.2	2 202.7
1951														
1st quarter	2 302.3	1 401.5	306.5	...	...	...	...	65.7	79.1	660.9	...	...	-53.2	2 269.4
2nd quarter	2 342.3	1 361.9	313.6	...	...	...	...	72.2	76.5	748.8	...	...	-77.7	2 282.5
3rd quarter	2 390.5	1 377.7	290.5	...	...	...	...	73.9	70.0	830.9	...	...	-112.5	2 358.9
4th quarter	2 395.8	1 385.8	267.3	...	...	...	...	73.3	68.2	874.8	...	...	-137.2	2 394.3
1952														
1st quarter	2 421.1	1 388.9	274.3	...	...	...	...	77.2	76.1	900.5	...	...	-143.7	2 415.4
2nd quarter	2 426.2	1 416.1	253.6	...	...	...	...	68.7	75.7	930.7	...	...	-167.2	2 456.0
3rd quarter	2 443.7	1 423.0	267.2	...	...	...	...	63.2	80.3	940.0	...	...	-169.4	2 434.4
4th quarter	2 523.9	1 473.3	286.5	...	...	...	...	63.7	87.5	955.6	...	...	-167.7	2 514.5
1953														
1st quarter	2 570.9	1 490.8	292.6	...	...	...	...	62.6	85.4	985.5	...	...	-175.2	2 568.4
2nd quarter	2 591.0	1 499.9	294.3	...	...	...	...	63.0	89.8	1 005.9	...	...	-182.3	2 589.3
3rd quarter	2 576.4	1 496.3	288.1	...	...	...	...	65.5	89.4	995.2	...	...	-179.3	2 584.0
4th quarter	2 537.3	1 486.4	267.3	...	...	...	...	63.4	85.0	992.4	...	...	-187.2	2 570.4
1954														
1st quarter	2 525.6	1 491.9	265.4	...	...	...	...	60.5	80.1	967.3	...	...	-179.4	2 555.8
2nd quarter	2 528.3	1 511.3	264.8	...	...	...	...	69.2	87.3	934.3	...	...	-164.0	2 565.4
3rd quarter	2 556.9	1 531.8	277.6	...	...	...	...	67.0	82.1	914.3	...	...	-151.7	2 591.2
4th quarter	2 606.8	1 564.0	289.7	...	...	...	...	70.1	82.8	908.6	...	...	-142.8	2 633.2
1955														
1st quarter	2 681.2	1 599.1	318.7	...	...	...	...	72.7	87.7	909.2	...	...	-130.8	2 683.5
2nd quarter	2 724.8	1 629.7	337.9	...	...	...	...	71.0	92.7	900.5	...	...	-121.6	2 718.3
3rd quarter	2 761.5	1 649.8	343.1	...	...	...	...	75.6	94.3	906.1	...	...	-118.8	2 758.0
4th quarter	2 778.1	1 670.5	351.1	...	...	...	...	76.0	97.7	888.3	...	...	-110.1	2 765.4
1956														
1st quarter	2 767.4	1 673.3	341.1	...	...	...	...	79.6	101.8	888.1	...	...	-112.9	2 761.0
2nd quarter	2 790.2	1 678.8	338.4	...	...	...	...	85.0	101.3	905.9	...	...	-116.6	2 792.5
3rd quarter	2 787.9	1 682.6	335.4	...	...	...	...	87.8	102.1	898.3	...	...	-114.1	2 794.7
4th quarter	2 833.5	1 705.8	332.2	...	...	...	...	91.7	97.5	920.7	...	...	-119.4	2 843.0
1957														
1st quarter	2 851.8	1 717.6	327.1	...	...	...	...	97.7	105.2	940.7	...	...	-126.1	2 868.5
2nd quarter	2 845.5	1 720.6	326.8	...	...	...	...	94.8	106.0	935.7	...	...	-126.4	2 858.6
3rd quarter	2 873.2	1 734.1	334.2	...	...	...	...	92.1	104.0	943.5	...	...	-126.7	2 880.6
4th quarter	2 843.7	1 734.9	308.5	...	...	...	...	89.4	104.3	959.3	...	...	-144.1	2 879.8
1958														
1st quarter	2 770.0	1 711.1	287.7	...	...	...	...	80.5	105.9	950.8	...	...	-154.2	2 809.3
2nd quarter	2 788.3	1 725.1	281.9	...	...	...	...	80.9	110.4	974.7	...	...	-163.9	2 825.3

Note: Chained (2009) dollar series are calculated as the product of the chain-type quantity index and the 2009 current-dollar value of the corresponding series, divided by 100. Because the formula for the chain-type quantity indexes uses weights from more than one period, the corresponding chained-dollar estimates are usually not additive. The residual column is the difference between the total and the sum of the most detailed components shown in the Bureau of Economic Analysis (BEA) published data.

. . . = Not available.

Table 1-2B. Real Gross Domestic Product: Historical—*Continued*

(Billions of chained [2009] dollars, quarterly data are at seasonally adjusted annual rates.)   NIPA Tables 1.1.6, 1.2.6

| Year and quarter | Gross domestic product | Personal consumption expenditures | Gross private domestic investment | | | | Exports and imports of goods and services | | | Government consumption expenditures and gross investment | | | Residual | Addendum: Final sales of domestic product |
| | | | Total | Fixed investment | | Change in private inventories | Net exports | Exports | Imports | Total | Federal | State and local | | |
				Nonresidential	Residential									
3rd quarter	2 852.7	1 753.6	303.5	...	...	...	...	81.2	108.7	980.6	...	...	-157.5	2 866.3
4th quarter	2 919.5	1 777.1	329.4	...	...	...	...	80.9	114.4	1 000.7	...	...	-154.2	2 922.3
1959														
1st quarter	2 973.8	1 809.5	347.4	...	...	...	...	86.3	117.4	989.4	...	...	-141.4	2 977.8
2nd quarter	3 046.1	1 837.4	374.4	...	...	...	...	89.1	123.1	1 001.7	...	...	-133.4	3 027.0
3rd quarter	3 040.2	1 856.5	350.2	...	...	...	...	91.9	124.2	1 010.3	...	...	-144.5	3 060.3
4th quarter	3 052.2	1 858.6	361.6	...	...	...	...	89.5	121.1	1 002.1	...	...	-138.5	3 050.8
1960														
1st quarter	3 120.2	1 876.4	398.0	...	...	...	...	100.7	125.6	985.2	...	...	-114.5	3 084.8
2nd quarter	3 108.4	1 900.1	360.9	...	...	...	...	107.1	126.6	995.8	...	...	-128.9	3 115.6
3rd quarter	3 116.1	1 892.5	360.0	...	...	...	...	104.4	122.9	1 020.0	...	...	-137.9	3 114.2
4th quarter	3 078.4	1 895.0	320.1	...	...	...	...	106.6	117.1	1 026.8	...	...	-153.0	3 129.9
1961														
1st quarter	3 099.3	1 894.4	328.4	...	...	...	...	105.8	116.5	1 042.0	...	...	-154.8	3 135.6
2nd quarter	3 156.9	1 922.7	351.4	...	...	...	...	104.4	117.9	1 044.4	...	...	-148.1	3 169.7
3rd quarter	3 209.6	1 932.0	378.7	...	...	...	...	103.8	125.7	1 066.4	...	...	-145.6	3 196.6
4th quarter	3 274.6	1 970.8	385.0	...	...	...	...	107.0	128.7	1 089.7	...	...	-149.2	3 268.8
1962														
1st quarter	3 333.6	1 991.7	405.7	...	...	...	...	106.7	132.6	1 110.7	...	...	-148.6	3 309.5
2nd quarter	3 369.5	2 016.2	402.5	...	...	...	...	117.0	135.5	1 116.0	...	...	-146.7	3 364.3
3rd quarter	3 401.6	2 032.5	409.4	...	...	...	...	110.4	137.3	1 141.7	...	...	-155.1	3 391.6
4th quarter	3 414.8	2 061.3	397.4	...	...	...	...	108.1	138.9	1 149.6	...	...	-162.7	3 419.5
1963														
1st quarter	3 452.8	2 075.3	418.3	...	...	...	...	110.6	135.7	1 134.1	...	...	-149.8	3 436.3
2nd quarter	3 497.8	2 095.1	425.0	...	...	...	...	123.5	138.9	1 135.1	...	...	-142.0	3 495.8
3rd quarter	3 566.1	2 123.7	438.0	...	...	...	...	116.9	142.4	1 185.4	...	...	-155.5	3 560.4
4th quarter	3 591.5	2 141.4	443.4	...	...	...	...	122.8	142.0	1 173.7	...	...	-147.8	3 595.4
1964														
1st quarter	3 669.2	2 183.6	460.0	...	...	...	...	130.3	141.8	1 177.3	...	...	-140.2	3 671.2
2nd quarter	3 712.9	2 222.0	458.3	...	...	...	...	132.5	145.0	1 187.9	...	...	-142.8	3 716.3
3rd quarter	3 763.3	2 262.9	469.0	...	...	...	...	131.5	148.9	1 189.4	...	...	-140.6	3 762.4
4th quarter	3 776.6	2 269.2	473.5	...	...	...	...	135.4	152.9	1 189.0	...	...	-137.6	3 775.1
1965														
1st quarter	3 869.8	2 319.8	518.6	...	...	...	...	120.8	147.4	1 187.7	...	...	-129.7	3 836.3
2nd quarter	3 922.7	2 345.5	520.0	...	...	...	...	143.4	164.8	1 202.0	...	...	-123.4	3 905.4
3rd quarter	4 002.4	2 385.9	538.1	...	...	...	...	135.2	165.5	1 241.7	...	...	-133.0	3 979.2
4th quarter	4 096.7	2 453.0	541.6	...	...	...	...	145.0	173.6	1 265.4	...	...	-134.7	4 084.7
1966														
1st quarter	4 197.9	2 489.1	584.9	...	...	...	...	142.5	178.1	1 289.0	...	...	-129.5	4 154.7
2nd quarter	4 215.1	2 495.4	576.2	...	...	...	...	148.7	182.5	1 313.4	...	...	-136.1	4 176.6
3rd quarter	4 245.2	2 523.8	572.0	...	...	...	...	143.1	192.7	1 349.1	...	...	-150.1	4 213.2
4th quarter	4 281.6	2 534.2	575.3	...	...	...	...	147.9	194.9	1 372.4	...	...	-153.3	4 227.3
1967														
1st quarter	4 320.9	2 549.0	561.2	...	...	...	...	150.7	197.9	1 429.8	...	...	-171.9	4 272.7
2nd quarter	4 324.7	2 583.8	540.9	...	...	...	...	149.3	196.4	1 424.2	...	...	-177.1	4 319.1
3rd quarter	4 362.0	2 596.9	556.8	...	...	...	...	145.7	199.0	1 440.2	...	...	-178.6	4 344.1
4th quarter	4 397.1	2 612.7	568.8	...	...	...	...	149.9	209.4	1 451.4	...	...	-176.3	4 384.1
1968														
1st quarter	4 486.4	2 674.8	580.2	...	...	...	...	154.2	221.8	1 477.2	...	...	-178.2	4 474.7
2nd quarter	4 562.2	2 715.7	602.4	...	...	...	...	157.3	225.2	1 485.0	...	...	-173.0	4 520.5
3rd quarter	4 595.0	2 766.6	586.0	...	...	...	...	166.5	238.7	1 489.7	...	...	-175.1	4 585.8
4th quarter	4 615.4	2 779.2	592.3	...	...	...	...	164.4	236.7	1 491.0	...	...	-174.8	4 615.1
1969														
1st quarter	4 687.1	2 810.3	627.2	...	...	...	...	144.7	214.4	1 494.7	...	...	-175.4	4 662.6
2nd quarter	4 702.1	2 828.2	623.5	...	...	...	...	177.1	256.7	1 490.0	...	...	-160.0	4 686.6
3rd quarter	4 731.5	2 842.0	636.2	...	...	...	...	172.9	253.3	1 493.5	...	...	-159.8	4 710.7
4th quarter	4 711.0	2 864.7	605.5	...	...	...	...	178.9	250.5	1 473.9	...	...	-161.5	4 712.5
1970														
1st quarter	4 702.8	2 882.4	587.4	...	...	...	...	180.4	249.7	1 466.9	...	...	-164.6	4 723.8
2nd quarter	4 711.1	2 895.7	588.7	...	...	...	...	188.3	254.7	1 450.2	...	...	-157.1	4 715.1
3rd quarter	4 752.8	2 921.1	598.3	...	...	...	...	187.7	254.1	1 456.5	...	...	-156.7	4 757.1
4th quarter	4 703.9	2 913.2	566.5	...	...	...	...	189.4	258.0	1 457.2	...	...	-164.4	4 748.4
1971														
1st quarter	4 829.9	2 968.9	632.5	...	...	...	...	190.2	255.0	1 436.1	...	...	-142.8	4 805.9
2nd quarter	4 857.4	2 996.2	650.5	...	...	...	...	189.8	274.2	1 432.8	...	...	-137.7	4 839.0
3rd quarter	4 895.3	3 020.1	658.4	...	...	...	...	197.6	280.3	1 432.4	...	...	-132.9	4 880.5
4th quarter	4 909.5	3 070.3	640.6	...	...	...	...	181.0	261.3	1 422.6	...	...	-143.7	4 938.5
1972														
1st quarter	4 997.0	3 110.8	682.9	...	...	...	...	200.2	299.5	1 429.3	...	...	-126.7	5 007.4
2nd quarter	5 112.7	3 170.2	721.6	...	...	...	...	194.4	288.8	1 438.0	...	...	-122.7	5 089.0
3rd quarter	5 159.8	3 219.1	731.9	...	...	...	...	206.1	294.8	1 409.3	...	...	-111.8	5 133.1
4th quarter	5 245.5	3 294.7	736.5	...	...	...	...	214.8	308.1	1 420.1	...	...	-112.5	5 252.0

Note: Chained (2009) dollar series are calculated as the product of the chain-type quantity index and the 2009 current-dollar value of the corresponding series, divided by 100. Because the formula for the chain-type quantity indexes uses weights from more than one period, the corresponding chained-dollar estimates are usually not additive. The residual column is the difference between the total and the sum of the most detailed components shown in the Bureau of Economic Analysis (BEA) published data.

. . . = Not available.

Table 1-2B. Real Gross Domestic Product: Historical—*Continued*

(Billions of chained [2009] dollars, quarterly data are at seasonally adjusted annual rates.) **NIPA Tables 1.1.6, 1.2.6**

Year and quarter	Gross domestic product	Personal consumption expenditures	Gross private domestic investment — Total	Fixed investment — Nonresidential	Fixed investment — Residential	Change in private inventories	Net exports	Exports	Imports	Government consumption expenditures and gross investment — Total	Federal	State and local	Residual	Addendum: Final sales of domestic product
1973														
1st quarter	5 374.7	3 354.8	779.6	. . .	. . .	. . .	. . .	230.6	322.3	1 431.6	. . .	. . .	-99.6	5 362.8
2nd quarter ...	5 435.6	3 353.4	812.9	. . .	. . .	. . .	. . .	241.7	313.1	1 424.5	. . .	. . .	-83.8	5 388.9
3rd quarter	5 406.1	3 365.4	783.4	. . .	. . .	. . .	. . .	242.5	304.4	1 406.4	. . .	. . .	-87.2	5 394.0
4th quarter	5 456.5	3 355.5	811.3	. . .	. . .	. . .	. . .	254.4	306.7	1 415.8	. . .	. . .	-73.8	5 400.5
1974														
1st quarter	5 411.2	3 326.3	765.0	. . .	. . .	. . .	. . .	257.7	296.3	1 442.4	. . .	. . .	-83.9	5 395.1
2nd quarter ...	5 425.4	3 337.9	761.9	. . .	. . .	. . .	. . .	270.2	312.0	1 451.6	. . .	. . .	-84.2	5 401.6
3rd quarter	5 372.8	3 351.7	722.4	. . .	. . .	. . .	. . .	255.6	306.5	1 453.5	. . .	. . .	-103.9	5 384.9
4th quarter	5 351.4	3 302.5	726.8	. . .	. . .	. . .	. . .	262.3	303.5	1 459.9	. . .	. . .	-96.6	5 308.3
1975														
1st quarter	5 286.7	3 330.2	609.7	. . .	. . .	. . .	. . .	264.2	273.0	1 476.1	. . .	. . .	-120.5	5 346.7
2nd quarter ...	5 327.4	3 385.8	591.6	. . .	. . .	. . .	. . .	256.5	251.2	1 466.2	. . .	. . .	-121.5	5 401.5
3rd quarter	5 415.5	3 434.1	637.5	. . .	. . .	. . .	. . .	252.2	272.1	1 489.5	. . .	. . .	-125.7	5 449.7
4th quarter	5 488.5	3 470.5	655.2	. . .	. . .	. . .	. . .	266.4	286.6	1 503.4	. . .	. . .	-120.4	5 516.5
1976														
1st quarter	5 612.4	3 539.9	718.5	. . .	. . .	. . .	. . .	264.6	304.5	1 506.5	. . .	. . .	-112.6	5 593.4
2nd quarter ...	5 654.8	3 572.5	746.9	. . .	. . .	. . .	. . .	267.2	317.7	1 491.4	. . .	. . .	-105.5	5 613.1
3rd quarter	5 683.6	3 610.4	749.5	. . .	. . .	. . .	. . .	275.0	330.7	1 483.9	. . .	. . .	-104.5	5 648.6
4th quarter	5 726.2	3 657.5	755.1	. . .	. . .	. . .	. . .	277.8	341.6	1 484.4	. . .	. . .	-107.0	5 727.9
1977														
1st quarter	5 792.9	3 699.4	790.1	. . .	. . .	. . .	. . .	273.3	357.8	1 497.3	. . .	. . .	-109.4	5 782.2
2nd quarter ...	5 906.6	3 719.8	846.8	. . .	. . .	. . .	. . .	280.7	361.1	1 512.0	. . .	. . .	-91.6	5 874.3
3rd quarter	6 011.1	3 755.2	889.6	. . .	. . .	. . .	. . .	282.9	356.1	1 515.4	. . .	. . .	-75.9	5 936.1
4th quarter	6 011.7	3 811.8	867.3	. . .	. . .	. . .	. . .	273.8	361.1	1 512.1	. . .	. . .	-92.2	5 985.2
1978														
1st quarter	6 032.6	3 833.9	884.2	. . .	. . .	. . .	. . .	280.2	385.4	1 513.9	. . .	. . .	-94.2	5 993.4
2nd quarter ...	6 267.2	3 915.7	941.6	. . .	. . .	. . .	. . .	309.4	386.6	1 554.1	. . .	. . .	-67.0	6 228.4
3rd quarter	6 328.5	3 932.1	969.1	. . .	. . .	. . .	. . .	312.8	391.6	1 566.4	. . .	. . .	-60.3	6 285.5
4th quarter	6 413.3	3 963.6	991.5	. . .	. . .	. . .	. . .	325.3	397.0	1 580.6	. . .	. . .	-50.7	6 367.5
1979														
1st quarter	6 426.1	3 983.7	993.1	. . .	. . .	. . .	. . .	325.5	395.9	1 566.9	. . .	. . .	-47.2	6 389.4
2nd quarter ...	6 433.9	3 981.3	992.2	. . .	. . .	. . .	. . .	326.4	398.0	1 583.0	. . .	. . .	-51.0	6 391.0
3rd quarter	6 480.1	4 020.5	975.5	. . .	. . .	. . .	. . .	338.1	392.0	1 585.1	. . .	. . .	-47.1	6 482.3
4th quarter	6 496.8	4 031.3	958.2	. . .	. . .	. . .	. . .	359.4	400.5	1 595.4	. . .	. . .	-47.0	6 510.6
1980														
1st quarter	6 517.9	4 025.1	951.6	. . .	. . .	. . .	. . .	369.4	400.8	1 620.2	. . .	. . .	-47.6	6 523.5
2nd quarter ...	6 385.7	3 934.5	870.7	. . .	. . .	. . .	. . .	376.4	371.7	1 625.9	. . .	. . .	-50.1	6 396.9
3rd quarter	6 376.0	3 976.9	813.3	. . .	. . .	. . .	. . .	375.6	345.0	1 601.9	. . .	. . .	-46.7	6 480.0
4th quarter	6 494.1	4 029.7	889.2	. . .	. . .	. . .	. . .	373.3	363.5	1 601.8	. . .	. . .	-36.4	6 539.7
1981														
1st quarter	6 628.6	4 050.9	971.7	. . .	. . .	. . .	. . .	380.4	379.1	1 622.8	. . .	. . .	-18.1	6 574.1
2nd quarter ...	6 580.2	4 050.1	931.3	. . .	. . .	. . .	. . .	382.4	379.6	1 627.9	. . .	. . .	-31.9	6 590.0
3rd quarter	6 655.7	4 066.4	983.5	. . .	. . .	. . .	. . .	374.3	375.3	1 621.6	. . .	. . .	-14.8	6 595.0
4th quarter	6 578.0	4 035.9	948.4	. . .	. . .	. . .	. . .	376.0	386.1	1 639.9	. . .	. . .	-36.1	6 560.3
1982														
1st quarter	6 468.0	4 062.7	854.9	. . .	. . .	. . .	. . .	359.7	375.1	1 638.2	. . .	. . .	-72.4	6 537.4
2nd quarter ...	6 503.3	4 077.7	853.8	. . .	. . .	. . .	. . .	361.9	368.9	1 648.9	. . .	. . .	-70.1	6 535.8
3rd quarter	6 479.8	4 109.2	845.7	. . .	. . .	. . .	. . .	345.9	386.0	1 659.3	. . .	. . .	-94.3	6 495.1
4th quarter	6 486.2	4 184.2	780.3	. . .	. . .	. . .	. . .	330.0	370.9	1 685.8	. . .	. . .	-123.2	6 590.0
1983														
1st quarter	6 571.1	4 224.8	807.5	. . .	. . .	. . .	. . .	335.4	379.4	1 701.9	. . .	. . .	-119.1	6 664.3
2nd quarter ...	6 721.1	4 308.5	879.1	. . .	. . .	. . .	. . .	336.4	408.6	1 719.1	. . .	. . .	-113.4	6 762.4
3rd quarter	6 852.7	4 384.1	934.2	. . .	. . .	. . .	. . .	341.4	440.4	1 747.3	. . .	. . .	-113.9	6 887.3
4th quarter	6 994.0	4 453.2	1 025.1	. . .	. . .	. . .	. . .	348.3	462.0	1 718.0	. . .	. . .	-88.6	6 978.8
1984														
1st quarter	7 132.9	4 490.9	1 124.2	. . .	. . .	. . .	. . .	355.6	499.1	1 738.1	. . .	. . .	-76.8	7 031.2
2nd quarter ...	7 258.2	4 555.0	1 160.7	. . .	. . .	. . .	. . .	364.5	520.0	1 777.1	. . .	. . .	-79.1	7 162.0
3rd quarter	7 329.6	4 590.0	1 185.8	. . .	. . .	. . .	. . .	372.5	533.5	1 791.8	. . .	. . .	-77.0	7 229.0
4th quarter	7 388.1	4 650.7	1 170.4	. . .	. . .	. . .	. . .	380.1	549.1	1 826.0	. . .	. . .	-90.0	7 331.9
1985														
1st quarter	7 461.5	4 729.7	1 138.3	. . .	. . .	. . .	. . .	381.0	537.0	1 848.0	. . .	. . .	-98.5	7 458.3
2nd quarter ...	7 529.9	4 774.1	1 157.7	. . .	. . .	. . .	. . .	380.2	563.4	1 891.0	. . .	. . .	-109.7	7 520.5
3rd quarter	7 647.0	4 865.8	1 149.8	. . .	. . .	. . .	. . .	374.7	557.9	1 935.4	. . .	. . .	-120.8	7 642.0
4th quarter	7 704.4	4 878.3	1 192.2	. . .	. . .	. . .	. . .	385.9	579.8	1 941.8	. . .	. . .	-114.0	7 673.4
1986														
1st quarter	7 775.8	4 919.7	1 191.9	. . .	. . .	. . .	. . .	398.0	579.3	1 958.0	. . .	. . .	-112.5	7 749.5
2nd quarter ...	7 811.5	4 974.7	1 171.0	. . .	. . .	. . .	. . .	402.4	604.0	1 997.8	. . .	. . .	-130.4	7 811.7
3rd quarter	7 890.1	5 064.8	1 139.5	. . .	. . .	. . .	. . .	411.6	620.7	2 043.4	. . .	. . .	-148.5	7 923.7
4th quarter	7 931.0	5 097.2	1 143.0	. . .	. . .	. . .	. . .	426.9	625.5	2 031.5	. . .	. . .	-142.1	7 971.7
1987														
1st quarter	7 986.4	5 098.0	1 173.8	. . .	. . .	. . .	. . .	427.2	621.7	2 044.3	. . .	. . .	-135.2	7 963.4
2nd quarter ...	8 076.1	5 168.7	1 174.4	. . .	. . .	. . .	. . .	444.8	637.2	2 062.9	. . .	. . .	-137.5	8 074.4
3rd quarter	8 149.4	5 228.6	1 174.6	. . .	. . .	. . .	. . .	464.1	649.6	2 067.7	. . .	. . .	-136.0	8 172.6
4th quarter	8 283.8	5 239.6	1 254.6	. . .	. . .	. . .	. . .	481.4	664.6	2 092.8	. . .	. . .	-120.0	8 207.1

Note: Chained (2009) dollar series are calculated as the product of the chain-type quantity index and the 2009 current-dollar value of the corresponding series, divided by 100. Because the formula for the chain-type quantity indexes uses weights from more than one period, the corresponding chained-dollar estimates are usually not additive. The residual column is the difference between the total and the sum of the most detailed components shown in the Bureau of Economic Analysis (BEA) published data.

. . . = Not available.

Table 1-2B. Real Gross Domestic Product: Historical—*Continued*

(Billions of chained [2009] dollars, quarterly data are at seasonally adjusted annual rates.)   **NIPA Tables 1.1.6, 1.2.6**

Year and quarter	Gross domestic product	Personal consumption expenditures	Gross private domestic investment				Exports and imports of goods and services			Government consumption expenditures and gross investment			Residual	Adden-dum: Final sales of domestic product
			Total	Fixed investment		Change in private inventories	Net exports	Exports	Imports	Total	Federal	State and local		
				Nonresi-dential	Residential									
1988														
1st quarter	8 330.4	5 332.7	1 194.4	...	...	...	...	508.1	661.5	2 078.6	...	...	-121.9	8 329.7
2nd quarter	8 440.5	5 371.9	1 222.9	...	...	...	...	522.4	653.8	2 086.1	...	...	-109.0	8 433.2
3rd quarter	8 489.2	5 417.7	1 229.7	...	...	...	...	532.7	669.3	2 087.5	...	...	-109.1	8 480.5
4th quarter	8 601.6	5 479.8	1 248.4	...	...	...	...	548.9	689.7	2 126.8	...	...	-112.6	8 587.8
1989														
1st quarter	8 688.4	5 505.1	1 290.7	...	...	...	...	565.3	692.9	2 117.2	...	...	-97.0	8 636.1
2nd quarter	8 756.7	5 531.0	1 278.3	...	...	...	...	590.0	696.2	2 151.8	...	...	-98.2	8 721.9
3rd quarter	8 822.1	5 585.9	1 266.9	...	...	...	...	596.0	695.2	2 169.8	...	...	-101.3	8 827.8
4th quarter	8 840.7	5 610.6	1 257.7	...	...	...	...	605.1	707.8	2 181.5	...	...	-106.4	8 838.2
1990														
1st quarter	8 937.5	5 658.8	1 270.0	...	...	...	...	631.3	730.2	2 215.8	...	...	-108.2	8 937.9
2nd quarter	8 972.1	5 676.5	1 270.4	...	...	...	...	639.2	729.0	2 221.2	...	...	-106.2	8 942.0
3rd quarter	8 974.3	5 699.4	1 245.6	...	...	...	...	644.1	726.1	2 219.9	...	...	-108.6	8 961.5
4th quarter	8 897.8	5 656.3	1 176.3	...	...	...	...	649.7	706.6	2 240.2	...	...	-118.1	8 930.5
1991														
1st quarter	8 856.1	5 636.8	1 137.1	...	...	...	...	653.8	698.6	2 251.2	...	...	-124.2	8 896.2
2nd quarter	8 924.9	5 684.1	1 137.2	...	...	...	...	677.6	711.0	2 259.2	...	...	-122.2	8 969.1
3rd quarter	8 967.7	5 711.7	1 159.8	...	...	...	...	693.6	731.0	2 250.8	...	...	-117.2	8 987.0
4th quarter	9 006.8	5 710.1	1 201.0	...	...	...	...	709.2	747.1	2 242.3	...	...	-108.7	8 983.8
1992														
1st quarter	9 113.2	5 817.4	1 178.9	...	...	...	...	722.1	752.6	2 259.7	...	...	-112.3	9 131.3
2nd quarter	9 213.7	5 857.3	1 245.7	...	...	...	...	722.4	764.9	2 256.8	...	...	-103.6	9 199.6
3rd quarter	9 303.3	5 920.7	1 255.8	...	...	...	...	737.7	777.0	2 268.4	...	...	-102.3	9 294.2
4th quarter	9 396.5	5 991.1	1 294.2	...	...	...	...	741.4	795.6	2 263.5	...	...	-98.1	9 385.0
1993														
1st quarter	9 414.0	6 013.9	1 324.6	...	...	...	...	743.1	812.8	2 237.8	...	...	-92.6	9 378.4
2nd quarter	9 469.9	6 067.9	1 332.1	...	...	...	...	752.0	829.6	2 240.3	...	...	-92.8	9 452.0
3rd quarter	9 516.1	6 134.8	1 323.1	...	...	...	...	750.0	840.5	2 245.1	...	...	-96.4	9 532.0
4th quarter	9 643.1	6 189.2	1 392.5	...	...	...	...	774.2	874.3	2 250.0	...	...	-88.5	9 640.5
1994														
1st quarter	9 737.6	6 260.1	1 446.2	...	...	...	...	781.7	894.7	2 222.1	...	...	-77.8	9 693.4
2nd quarter	9 870.7	6 308.7	1 517.1	...	...	...	...	808.1	928.0	2 235.1	...	...	-70.3	9 777.6
3rd quarter	9 928.9	6 357.6	1 492.2	...	...	...	...	838.3	954.1	2 272.7	...	...	-77.8	9 877.3
4th quarter	10 041.6	6 426.0	1 553.5	...	...	...	...	857.7	981.0	2 252.2	...	...	-66.8	9 959.7
1995														
1st quarter	10 075.9	6 443.0	1 570.3	...	...	...	...	874.2	1 002.5	2 256.8	...	...	-65.9	10 010.6
2nd quarter	10 111.1	6 500.8	1 537.7	...	...	...	...	886.5	1 012.0	2 268.6	...	...	-70.5	10 081.7
3rd quarter	10 197.7	6 560.4	1 528.6	...	...	...	...	924.8	1 015.5	2 262.4	...	...	-63.0	10 202.6
4th quarter	10 270.1	6 606.5	1 566.7	...	...	...	...	938.0	1 028.5	2 242.1	...	...	-54.7	10 266.0
1996														
1st quarter	10 337.4	6 667.8	1 590.6	...	...	...	...	949.3	1 061.9	2 246.8	...	...	-55.2	10 350.2
2nd quarter	10 517.9	6 740.2	1 667.7	...	...	...	...	964.8	1 085.7	2 282.8	...	...	-51.9	10 500.4
3rd quarter	10 615.2	6 780.8	1 744.5	...	...	...	...	972.6	1 120.9	2 285.2	...	...	-47.0	10 553.7
4th quarter	10 727.4	6 834.1	1 743.9	...	...	...	...	1 033.2	1 143.0	2 301.9	...	...	-42.7	10 695.7
1997														
1st quarter	10 809.1	6 906.2	1 781.6	...	...	...	...	1 052.9	1 191.8	2 301.3	...	...	-41.1	10 770.6
2nd quarter	10 972.2	6 937.5	1 880.0	...	...	...	...	1 095.0	1 231.8	2 325.3	...	...	-33.8	10 862.9
3rd quarter	11 112.0	7 056.2	1 913.6	...	...	...	...	1 120.4	1 277.2	2 329.0	...	...	-30.0	11 035.2
4th quarter	11 198.2	7 140.0	1 940.7	...	...	...	...	1 118.8	1 304.7	2 332.5	...	...	-29.1	11 107.5
1998														
1st quarter	11 309.0	7 213.7	2 027.1	...	...	...	...	1 123.9	1 353.6	2 319.0	...	...	-21.1	11 183.1
2nd quarter	11 418.7	7 341.1	2 013.4	...	...	...	...	1 111.5	1 384.7	2 366.0	...	...	-28.6	11 375.9
3rd quarter	11 568.1	7 437.7	2 067.2	...	...	...	...	1 106.5	1 403.4	2 387.6	...	...	-27.5	11 507.0
4th quarter	11 757.9	7 546.9	2 125.5	...	...	...	...	1 147.7	1 448.9	2 409.4	...	...	-22.7	11 693.3
1999														
1st quarter	11 867.8	7 625.8	2 186.1	1 459.0	623.0	97.5	-342.7	1 142.7	1 485.4	2 418.1	801.2	1 624.5	-138.9	11 776.7
2nd quarter	11 967.7	7 744.1	2 188.0	1 497.3	632.7	45.3	-377.1	1 154.9	1 532.0	2 431.7	805.2	1 634.0	-113.6	11 926.9
3rd quarter	12 120.1	7 836.8	2 242.8	1 539.3	637.4	51.5	-402.8	1 183.3	1 586.1	2 460.3	819.4	1 648.0	-101.3	12 073.3
4th quarter	12 329.8	7 945.9	2 308.6	1 544.9	642.1	107.5	-406.6	1 215.5	1 622.1	2 496.7	835.6	1 668.1	-102.8	12 224.4
2000														
1st quarter	12 365.2	8 067.1	2 287.8	1 599.9	645.3	23.6	-454.1	1 234.8	1 688.9	2 476.2	804.6	1 680.8	-80.9	12 346.0
2nd quarter	12 598.7	8 142.1	2 424.5	1 650.5	641.9	108.7	-467.5	1 268.4	1 735.9	2 506.4	832.8	1 681.2	-84.0	12 489.6
3rd quarter	12 614.8	8 223.1	2 394.1	1 667.9	632.0	68.7	-497.2	1 298.3	1 795.5	2 501.2	818.9	1 691.0	-85.2	12 547.4
4th quarter	12 682.0	8 296.1	2 395.6	1 672.3	632.6	63.9	-512.0	1 288.0	1 799.9	2 509.0	814.6	1 703.6	-87.1	12 618.4
2001														
1st quarter	12 645.7	8 325.7	2 285.3	1 658.8	635.3	-37.9	-497.1	1 271.4	1 768.5	2 546.3	832.3	1 722.9	-83.3	12 684.2
2nd quarter	12 712.8	8 348.3	2 277.1	1 621.2	645.2	-12.8	-488.1	1 229.8	1 717.9	2 596.4	848.7	1 756.8	-100.5	12 728.2
3rd quarter	12 674.1	8 376.3	2 236.6	1 600.0	649.2	-36.9	-509.2	1 166.5	1 675.7	2 594.6	855.9	1 747.3	-104.5	12 712.1
4th quarter	12 705.2	8 499.8	2 126.9	1 553.6	645.0	-97.4	-522.3	1 134.3	1 656.6	2 632.4	862.6	1 778.9	-72.8	12 802.4
2002														
1st quarter	12 824.6	8 527.0	2 202.8	1 522.1	666.2	-3.8	-545.7	1 152.3	1 698.0	2 671.3	884.0	1 795.9	-79.8	12 830.4
2nd quarter	12 894.7	8 572.2	2 224.9	1 501.9	682.7	26.5	-570.0	1 184.4	1 754.3	2 696.9	904.7	1 799.8	-74.6	12 872.1
3rd quarter	12 956.7	8 633.0	2 224.6	1 493.0	684.7	32.4	-589.2	1 193.3	1 782.5	2 717.8	919.0	1 805.9	-60.5	12 926.8
4th quarter	12 962.9	8 669.1	2 220.7	1 475.1	697.1	35.1	-634.5	1 182.5	1 817.0	2 737.1	935.7	1 807.9	-66.7	12 930.1

Note: Chained (2009) dollar series are calculated as the product of the chain-type quantity index and the 2009 current-dollar value of the corresponding series, divided by 100. Because the formula for the chain-type quantity indexes uses weights from more than one period, the corresponding chained-dollar estimates are usually not additive. The residual column is the difference between the total and the sum of the most detailed components shown in the Bureau of Economic Analysis (BEA) published data.

. . . = Not available.

Table 1-2B. Real Gross Domestic Product: Historical—*Continued*

(Billions of chained [2009] dollars, quarterly data are at seasonally adjusted annual rates.)   **NIPA Tables 1.1.6, 1.2.6**

Year and quarter	Gross domestic product	Personal consump-tion expen-ditures	Gross private domestic investment				Exports and imports of goods and services			Government consumption expenditures and gross investment			Residual	Adden-dum: Final sales of domestic product
			Total	Fixed investment		Change in private inventories	Net exports	Exports	Imports	Total	Federal	State and local		
				Nonresi-dential	Residential									
2003														
1st quarter	13 028.6	8 712.2	2 239.5	1 478.6	709.8	36.3	-622.7	1 170.8	1 793.5	2 728.3	935.9	1 798.5	-62.4	12 992.8
2nd quarter ...	13 151.8	8 810.1	2 251.3	1 514.3	721.0	-0.2	-650.7	1 166.6	1 817.3	2 771.2	982.8	1 791.7	-50.7	13 152.3
3rd quarter	13 374.0	8 938.2	2 330.9	1 544.7	762.3	7.6	-639.1	1 198.1	1 837.2	2 771.2	977.1	1 798.0	-37.3	13 366.3
4th quarter	13 525.7	9 004.3	2 413.1	1 566.8	785.0	46.6	-653.9	1 253.3	1 907.2	2 786.3	996.0	1 793.0	-31.9	13 480.2
2004														
1st quarter	13 606.6	9 096.3	2 414.5	1 549.4	794.2	56.4	-676.0	1 283.7	1 959.7	2 793.9	1 003.0	1 793.3	-28.0	13 551.2
2nd quarter ...	13 710.7	9 152.4	2 500.9	1 583.8	819.5	81.9	-732.6	1 301.5	2 034.0	2 809.9	1 013.0	1 799.0	-21.8	13 628.7
3rd quarter	13 831.0	9 239.3	2 539.4	1 626.9	825.3	71.1	-749.3	1 310.5	2 059.8	2 820.7	1 030.7	1 791.0	-16.1	13 759.8
4th quarter	13 947.7	9 334.5	2 590.6	1 661.4	836.7	76.2	-769.6	1 341.5	2 111.0	2 808.2	1 021.8	1 787.7	-10.9	13 871.2
2005														
1st quarter	14 100.2	9 409.5	2 664.4	1 681.9	856.4	111.3	-773.4	1 357.0	2 130.4	2 814.1	1 027.6	1 787.6	-10.0	13 989.9
2nd quarter ...	14 177.2	9 507.8	2 630.5	1 706.1	872.3	33.0	-765.6	1 386.0	2 151.6	2 818.9	1 029.8	1 790.2	-0.1	14 142.9
3rd quarter	14 292.9	9 578.9	2 657.9	1 737.4	881.9	18.2	-770.4	1 386.8	2 157.2	2 841.0	1 048.6	1 792.9	4.1	14 272.8
4th quarter	14 372.0	9 614.9	2 737.6	1 744.3	879.9	94.8	-799.0	1 423.8	2 222.9	2 830.7	1 033.2	1 798.6	-1.9	14 274.9
2006														
1st quarter	14 546.4	9 722.7	2 773.8	1 808.7	871.7	78.6	-792.3	1 478.4	2 270.7	2 853.5	1 058.9	1 794.9	1.7	14 469.0
2nd quarter ...	14 591.6	9 774.2	2 755.7	1 831.3	827.8	84.4	-790.5	1 505.4	2 295.9	2 864.1	1 057.7	1 806.9	-4.2	14 508.3
3rd quarter	14 604.4	9 833.4	2 727.6	1 853.1	781.6	81.9	-813.4	1 502.2	2 315.6	2 870.4	1 058.0	1 813.0	-6.4	14 522.0
4th quarter	14 718.4	9 929.2	2 663.0	1 865.2	745.2	41.4	-748.6	1 563.7	2 312.3	2 889.1	1 069.0	1 820.6	-5.4	14 675.2
2007														
1st quarter	14 728.1	9 987.1	2 638.5	1 897.2	711.2	19.6	-765.3	1 586.5	2 351.8	2 882.7	1 054.5	1 829.0	-6.6	14 705.3
2nd quarter ...	14 841.5	10 020.4	2 674.7	1 934.4	682.7	49.4	-746.5	1 614.4	2 360.9	2 907.0	1 071.2	1 836.4	-7.1	14 788.4
3rd quarter	14 941.5	10 060.1	2 658.1	1 964.4	639.2	50.2	-691.2	1 671.2	2 362.4	2 928.0	1 091.6	1 836.7	-10.3	14 888.9
4th quarter	14 996.1	10 074.5	2 605.2	1 997.6	586.1	23.0	-611.2	1 717.1	2 328.3	2 939.8	1 097.5	1 842.5	-15.2	14 974.4
2008														
1st quarter	14 895.4	10 054.1	2 517.5	1 998.1	540.0	-20.2	-611.2	1 738.7	2 349.9	2 952.0	1 115.2	1 836.9	-20.0	14 915.3
2nd quarter ...	14 969.2	10 073.0	2 472.6	1 986.6	516.3	-26.4	-539.9	1 788.4	2 328.3	2 975.0	1 135.7	1 839.3	-17.7	14 998.7
3rd quarter	14 895.1	9 993.7	2 403.8	1 933.0	490.9	-20.7	-512.4	1 772.8	2 285.2	3 016.2	1 169.1	1 847.1	-6.8	14 914.1
4th quarter	14 574.6	9 876.2	2 190.0	1 820.1	443.6	-67.4	-524.0	1 667.4	2 191.5	3 035.9	1 189.3	1 846.6	-10.1	14 647.6
2009														
1st quarter	14 372.1	9 843.6	1 937.7	1 688.3	401.0	-144.5	-447.1	1 534.8	1 981.9	3 040.5	1 180.1	1 860.4	-9.8	14 524.4
2nd quarter ...	14 356.9	9 801.5	1 820.5	1 634.0	377.0	-190.1	-360.1	1 537.5	1 897.6	3 096.0	1 218.9	1 877.1	-2.0	14 547.2
3rd quarter	14 402.5	9 862.7	1 804.7	1 613.1	395.4	-206.1	-380.4	1 588.7	1 969.1	3 113.0	1 235.6	1 877.4	4.7	14 605.2
4th quarter	14 540.2	9 863.9	1 949.6	1 598.4	395.7	-49.6	-381.2	1 674.2	2 055.5	3 106.8	1 236.2	1 870.6	6.8	14 585.2
2010														
1st quarter	14 597.7	9 915.4	2 012.9	1 615.0	383.0	9.8	-413.6	1 700.4	2 113.9	3 084.3	1 247.8	1 836.5	3.9	14 584.3
2nd quarter ...	14 738.0	9 995.3	2 116.9	1 659.3	403.5	48.8	-474.3	1 739.3	2 213.6	3 106.2	1 273.4	1 832.8	-1.9	14 686.3
3rd quarter	14 839.3	10 063.7	2 185.7	1 692.8	368.1	116.2	-504.9	1 784.9	2 289.8	3 103.5	1 285.0	1 818.5	-2.3	14 718.3
4th quarter	14 942.4	10 169.0	2 166.1	1 728.1	375.1	58.1	-457.5	1 837.7	2 295.2	3 071.5	1 276.4	1 795.2	-5.0	14 881.8
2011														
1st quarter	14 894.0	10 221.3	2 124.3	1 724.1	376.7	22.0	-456.5	1 854.7	2 311.3	3 012.0	1 241.6	1 770.5	-10.1	14 871.9
2nd quarter ...	15 011.3	10 258.9	2 196.1	1 765.3	379.2	42.9	-438.3	1 876.9	2 315.2	3 002.4	1 247.0	1 755.5	-3.1	14 961.8
3rd quarter	15 062.1	10 311.9	2 209.9	1 835.0	384.9	-11.0	-433.9	1 908.9	2 342.8	2 983.2	1 236.4	1 746.9	-13.3	15 072.7
4th quarter	15 242.1	10 373.1	2 368.2	1 877.3	396.2	80.6	-454.7	1 921.7	2 376.4	2 971.7	1 226.7	1 745.0	-9.1	15 151.3
2012														
1st quarter	15 381.6	10 447.8	2 427.8	1 903.8	417.2	89.2	-439.2	1 941.4	2 380.6	2 961.3	1 219.1	1 742.2	-7.5	15 278.9
2nd quarter ...	15 427.7	10 496.8	2 418.0	1 925.0	423.0	56.8	-435.3	1 959.8	2 395.1	2 963.5	1 218.5	1 745.0	-11.6	15 360.8
3rd quarter	15 534.0	10 541.0	2 456.5	1 926.4	437.3	77.2	-436.5	1 961.6	2 398.0	2 988.8	1 244.6	1 744.3	-11.0	15 444.9
4th quarter	15 539.6	10 584.8	2 441.8	1 971.9	457.5	7.3	-412.1	1 967.0	2 379.1	2 938.8	1 198.9	1 739.8	-22.2	15 528.3

Note: Chained (2009) dollar series are calculated as the product of the chain-type quantity index and the 2009 current-dollar value of the corresponding series, divided by 100. Because the formula for the chain-type quantity indexes uses weights from more than one period, the corresponding chained-dollar estimates are usually not additive. The residual column is the difference between the total and the sum of the most detailed components shown in the Bureau of Economic Analysis (BEA) published data.

Table 1-3A. U.S. Population and Per Capita Product and Income: Recent Data

(Dollars, except as noted; quarterly data are at seasonally adjusted annual rates.)   **NIPA Table 7.1**

Year and quarter	Population (mid-period, thousands)	Current dollars							Chained (2009) dollars					
		Gross domestic product	Personal income	Dispos-able personal income	Personal consumption expenditures				Gross domestic product	Dispos-able personal income	Personal consumption expenditures			
					Total	Durable goods	Nondur-able goods	Services			Total	Durable goods	Nondur-able goods	Services
1950	151 684	1 979	1 542	1 417	1 267	214	556	497	14 384	10 033	8 969	446	3 254	5 281
1951	154 287	2 251	1 714	1 539	1 351	206	603	543	15 281	10 197	8 956	402	3 248	5 498
1952	156 954	2 343	1 801	1 597	1 398	199	621	578	15 633	10 371	9 081	387	3 313	5 647
1953	159 565	2 443	1 877	1 669	1 460	217	628	615	16 099	10 697	9 359	425	3 360	5 788
1954	162 391	2 409	1 863	1 678	1 477	208	628	641	15 730	10 662	9 389	416	3 354	5 886
1955	165 275	2 579	1 964	1 765	1 565	247	645	673	16 557	11 172	9 906	496	3 466	6 074
1956	168 221	2 676	2 071	1 854	1 614	239	666	710	16 614	11 502	10 017	469	3 525	6 253
1957	171 274	2 772	2 151	1 924	1 674	245	686	742	16 661	11 589	10 082	465	3 532	6 353
1958	174 141	2 768	2 179	1 958	1 700	227	701	772	16 266	11 519	10 002	422	3 520	6 451
1959	177 130	2 950	2 276	2 038	1 793	253	721	818	17 095	11 811	10 391	464	3 616	6 655
1960	180 760	3 006	2 338	2 083	1 834	252	727	855	17 182	11 877	10 461	464	3 602	6 776
1961	183 742	3 066	2 401	2 143	1 861	241	733	888	17 335	12 097	10 504	441	3 615	6 912
1962	186 590	3 243	2 514	2 238	1 946	265	748	933	18 114	12 482	10 855	484	3 670	7 128
1963	189 300	3 373	2 603	2 315	2 021	286	760	974	18 632	12 766	11 140	521	3 695	7 325
1964	191 927	3 573	2 753	2 482	2 142	310	796	1 037	19 437	13 485	11 642	562	3 816	7 655
1965	194 347	3 827	2 937	2 641	2 282	342	840	1 101	20 442	14 144	12 226	624	3 958	7 978
1966	196 599	4 146	3 157	2 819	2 445	365	905	1 175	21 541	14 726	12 770	668	4 130	8 276
1967	198 752	4 336	3 350	2 983	2 553	372	931	1 250	21 893	15 198	13 009	670	4 173	8 522
1968	200 745	4 695	3 640	3 207	2 777	423	995	1 359	22 739	15 728	13 620	737	4 307	8 882
1969	202 736	5 031	3 947	3 432	2 982	446	1 057	1 479	23 222	16 102	13 990	757	4 382	9 186
1970	205 089	5 246	4 216	3 713	3 158	439	1 116	1 604	23 003	16 643	14 155	729	4 428	9 438
1971	207 692	5 623	4 488	3 998	3 375	493	1 154	1 728	23 463	17 191	14 511	792	4 455	9 642
1972	209 924	6 109	4 876	4 287	3 665	555	1 226	1 885	24 432	17 822	15 237	881	4 586	10 088
1973	211 939	6 740	5 372	4 747	4 016	616	1 350	2 050	25 565	18 725	15 841	964	4 673	10 466
1974	213 898	7 241	5 841	5 135	4 357	609	1 502	2 246	25 200	18 344	15 566	894	4 517	10 571
1975	215 981	7 820	6 329	5 645	4 782	658	1 617	2 507	24 907	18 614	15 766	887	4 512	10 863
1976	218 086	8 609	6 869	6 079	5 274	773	1 732	2 769	25 996	19 002	16 485	988	4 681	11 221
1977	220 289	9 469	7 509	6 613	5 795	871	1 854	3 070	26 922	19 406	17 007	1 065	4 740	11 569
1978	222 629	10 585	8 352	7 322	6 406	958	2 022	3 425	28 120	20 080	17 569	1 109	4 859	11 977
1979	225 106	11 693	9 231	8 037	7 061	1 005	2 273	3 783	28 694	20 248	17 788	1 091	4 930	12 207
1980	227 726	12 570	10 174	8 861	7 705	994	2 518	4 193	28 295	20 159	17 528	993	4 865	12 262
1981	230 008	13 960	11 286	9 785	8 424	1 061	2 719	4 644	28 741	20 459	17 612	993	4 877	12 351
1982	232 218	14 405	11 966	10 442	8 931	1 090	2 783	5 058	27 923	20 685	17 692	982	4 881	12 477
1983	234 333	15 525	12 673	11 170	9 758	1 259	2 897	5 602	28 953	21 214	18 532	1 112	4 994	13 009
1984	236 394	17 093	13 880	12 284	10 568	1 447	3 052	6 068	30 784	22 480	19 339	1 259	5 155	13 393
1985	238 506	18 225	14 741	12 991	11 416	1 595	3 175	6 646	31 805	22 961	20 176	1 373	5 264	13 972
1986	240 683	19 071	15 477	13 661	12 042	1 751	3 217	7 075	32 624	23 632	20 833	1 491	5 402	14 292
1987	242 843	20 055	16 288	14 274	12 733	1 820	3 353	7 559	33 453	23 930	21 346	1 507	5 446	14 802
1988	245 061	21 434	17 446	15 386	13 657	1 939	3 519	8 200	34 544	24 826	22 038	1 578	5 539	15 328
1989	247 387	22 870	18 668	16 380	14 523	1 998	3 757	8 768	35 479	25 340	22 467	1 598	5 635	15 666
1990	250 181	23 901	19 604	17 235	15 291	1 987	3 974	9 331	35 756	25 556	22 675	1 573	5 637	15 957
1991	253 530	24 352	20 002	17 688	15 620	1 882	4 024	9 714	35 258	25 395	22 426	1 469	5 546	16 004
1992	256 922	25 452	21 060	18 684	16 408	1 978	4 107	10 324	36 029	26 134	22 951	1 533	5 579	16 431
1993	260 282	26 428	21 695	19 211	17 178	2 119	4 191	10 868	36 540	26 216	23 442	1 626	5 647	16 718
1994	263 455	27 742	22 526	19 906	17 996	2 305	4 325	11 366	37 557	26 611	24 058	1 735	5 797	17 025
1995	266 588	28 749	23 544	20 753	18 696	2 385	4 426	11 886	38 125	27 180	24 486	1 782	5 870	17 328
1996	269 714	30 032	24 700	21 615	19 532	2 507	4 603	12 422	39 114	27 719	25 048	1 893	5 970	17 630
1997	272 958	31 538	25 920	22 527	20 372	2 621	4 731	13 020	40 383	28 398	25 682	2 023	6 073	17 977
1998	276 154	32 913	27 476	23 759	21 376	2 822	4 814	13 740	41 692	29 724	26 742	2 241	6 226	18 587
1999	279 328	34 603	28 582	24 617	22 615	3 063	5 124	14 428	43 216	30 351	27 882	2 500	6 465	19 134
2000	282 398	36 437	30 569	26 206	24 085	3 232	5 454	15 399	44 495	31 525	28 974	2 685	6 599	19 871
2001	285 225	37 252	31 509	27 179	24 917	3 301	5 553	16 063	44 472	32 077	29 407	2 798	6 647	20 111
2002	287 955	38 132	31 774	28 127	25 647	3 422	5 602	16 623	44 832	32 754	29 867	2 975	6 706	20 281
2003	290 626	39 612	32 645	29 201	26 716	3 501	5 863	17 352	45 660	33 345	30 507	3 157	6 877	20 527
2004	293 262	41 864	34 267	30 700	28 158	3 682	6 208	18 269	46 968	34 224	31 391	3 386	7 037	20 985
2005	295 993	44 242	35 846	31 763	29 698	3 808	6 598	19 291	48 094	34 428	32 189	3 537	7 204	21 451
2006	298 818	46 376	38 116	33 591	31 114	3 869	6 960	20 285	48 910	35 461	32 846	3 653	7 370	21 819
2007	301 696	47 996	39 761	34 829	32 299	3 927	7 216	21 157	49 311	35 870	33 264	3 784	7 422	22 043
2008	304 543	48 336	40 817	36 104	32 854	3 619	7 465	21 770	48 708	36 082	32 834	3 557	7 272	22 002
2009	307 240	46 927	39 325	35 598	32 037	3 331	7 080	21 626	46 927	35 598	32 037	3 331	7 080	21 626
2010	309 776	48 287	40 143	36 296	32 933	3 456	7 399	22 077	47 710	35 706	32 397	3 505	7 178	21 716
2011	312 036	49 782	42 275	37 776	34 329	3 621	7 925	22 783	48 239	36 293	32 981	3 708	7 262	22 020
2012	314 278	51 689	43 731	38 965	35 477	3 827	8 168	23 482	49 226	36 756	33 466	3 967	7 308	22 218
2010														
1st quarter	308 900	47 499	39 477	35 768	32 510	3 367	7 331	21 811	47 257	35 316	32 099	3 383	7 127	21 587
2nd quarter	309 457	48 082	39 987	36 213	32 750	3 441	7 306	22 003	47 625	35 715	32 299	3 478	7 148	21 674
3rd quarter	310 067	48 537	40 321	36 420	33 007	3 467	7 377	22 162	47 858	35 813	32 457	3 527	7 179	21 752
4th quarter	310 679	49 027	40 782	36 781	33 463	3 550	7 582	22 332	48 096	35 977	32 731	3 629	7 257	21 851
2011														
1st quarter	311 192	48 982	41 871	37 449	33 828	3 583	7 767	22 478	47 861	36 361	32 846	3 671	7 271	21 910
2nd quarter	311 718	49 602	42 181	37 690	34 206	3 582	7 929	22 695	48 157	36 263	32 911	3 657	7 271	21 988
3rd quarter	312 319	49 987	42 532	37 981	34 512	3 615	7 983	22 913	48 227	36 336	33 017	3 696	7 248	22 082
4th quarter	312 917	50 552	42 514	37 981	34 766	3 704	8 019	23 043	48 710	36 215	33 150	3 808	7 258	22 100
2012														
1st quarter	313 425	51 182	43 227	38 560	35 157	3 779	8 120	23 258	49 076	36 561	33 334	3 892	7 286	22 178
2nd quarter	313 960	51 473	43 483	38 769	35 355	3 788	8 119	23 448	49 139	36 661	33 434	3 913	7 307	22 236
3rd quarter	314 564	51 996	43 557	38 800	35 585	3 835	8 197	23 552	49 383	36 538	33 510	3 985	7 321	22 232
4th quarter	315 162	52 101	44 654	39 727	35 809	3 905	8 235	23 668	49 307	37 260	33 585	4 078	7 319	22 226

Table 1-3B. U.S. Population and Per Capita Product and Income: Historical

(Dollars, except as noted; quarterly data are at seasonally adjusted annual rates.)   **NIPA Table 7.1**

Year and quarter	Population (mid-period, thousands)	Current dollars							Chained (2009) dollars					
		Gross domestic product	Personal income	Disposable personal income	Personal consumption expenditures				Gross domestic product	Disposable personal income	Personal consumption expenditures			
					Total	Durable goods	Nondurable goods	Services			Total	Durable goods	Nondurable goods	Services
1929	121 878	858	700	685	635	81	278	276	8 661	6 917	6 408	263	2 479	3 812
1930	123 188	748	621	608	569	62	248	260	7 840	6 411	6 000	215	2 325	3 693
1931	124 149	623	529	521	489	48	208	233	7 282	6 145	5 768	185	2 282	3 571
1932	124 949	476	402	396	390	32	161	197	6 303	5 306	5 218	140	2 068	3 334
1933	125 690	455	376	369	366	30	159	177	6 187	5 122	5 073	135	2 048	3 191
1934	126 485	528	427	420	407	36	189	182	6 811	5 579	5 401	154	2 201	3 327
1935	127 362	583	478	469	439	43	205	191	7 366	6 080	5 689	185	2 311	3 419
1936	128 181	662	540	530	485	53	228	205	8 266	6 802	6 228	224	2 559	3 607
1937	128 961	721	579	564	518	57	240	221	8 635	6 990	6 419	234	2 606	3 753
1938	129 969	672	532	517	494	47	230	217	8 284	6 556	6 268	193	2 623	3 694
1939	131 028	713	562	551	513	55	235	224	8 873	7 046	6 565	227	2 721	3 807
1940	132 122	779	601	588	540	63	245	232	9 574	7 464	6 848	257	2 813	3 921
1941	133 402	970	734	716	608	77	279	252	11 161	8 559	7 261	294	2 954	4 113
1942	134 860	1 231	940	903	660	57	322	282	13 127	9 598	7 012	185	2 929	4 293
1943	136 739	1 485	1 142	1 020	731	55	357	319	15 153	9 923	7 109	163	2 907	4 572
1944	138 397	1 623	1 226	1 099	785	56	381	348	16 167	10 109	7 223	149	2 933	4 769
1945	139 928	1 631	1 256	1 117	857	65	418	374	15 836	9 885	7 586	164	3 080	4 970
1946	141 389	1 611	1 292	1 170	1 021	121	489	411	13 856	9 679	8 442	292	3 324	5 142
1947	144 126	1 734	1 350	1 213	1 124	151	538	434	13 444	9 109	8 440	336	3 241	5 066
1948	146 631	1 874	1 457	1 326	1 194	167	566	461	13 762	9 426	8 483	352	3 210	5 111
1949	149 188	1 829	1 416	1 304	1 196	178	546	472	13 453	9 340	8 570	374	3 202	5 144
1947														
1st quarter	143 156	1 698	1 328	1 194	1 092	145	523	424	13 500	9 167	8 378	326	3 225	5 057
2nd quarter	143 803	1 713	1 320	1 185	1 114	148	535	431	13 424	9 022	8 479	331	3 266	5 107
3rd quarter	144 462	1 731	1 369	1 232	1 133	151	544	438	13 349	9 212	8 468	334	3 266	5 073
4th quarter	145 135	1 794	1 382	1 239	1 156	162	551	443	13 496	9 036	8 431	354	3 208	5 023
1948														
1st quarter	145 761	1 826	1 418	1 272	1 170	162	559	449	13 636	9 176	8 437	351	3 205	5 055
2nd quarter	146 341	1 865	1 450	1 320	1 191	164	568	458	13 803	9 424	8 501	352	3 223	5 114
3rd quarter	146 973	1 902	1 481	1 356	1 206	172	568	466	13 820	9 537	8 477	356	3 190	5 119
4th quarter	147 659	1 901	1 478	1 353	1 206	169	567	470	13 771	9 546	8 505	350	3 217	5 147
1949														
1st quarter	148 298	1 857	1 431	1 311	1 193	165	558	471	13 524	9 319	8 482	342	3 215	5 157
2nd quarter	148 891	1 825	1 418	1 304	1 199	177	550	472	13 425	9 326	8 578	370	3 211	5 162
3rd quarter	149 529	1 827	1 408	1 299	1 190	183	537	471	13 515	9 346	8 561	386	3 170	5 129
4th quarter	150 211	1 804	1 405	1 299	1 201	189	539	473	13 333	9 356	8 646	399	3 207	5 121
1950														
1st quarter	150 852	1 864	1 501	1 391	1 214	194	540	479	13 805	10 035	8 753	413	3 234	5 162
2nd quarter	151 385	1 921	1 505	1 389	1 235	197	547	491	14 173	9 969	8 866	415	3 260	5 275
3rd quarter	152 039	2 029	1 554	1 429	1 320	246	570	504	14 656	10 051	9 280	511	3 302	5 333
4th quarter	152 724	2 097	1 605	1 457	1 297	218	567	512	14 872	10 067	8 960	446	3 214	5 342
1951														
1st quarter	153 336	2 194	1 659	1 500	1 365	232	600	533	15 015	10 038	9 140	458	3 260	5 466
2nd quarter	153 947	2 237	1 711	1 539	1 332	200	594	539	15 215	10 221	8 847	391	3 200	5 482
3rd quarter	154 655	2 275	1 731	1 552	1 343	195	602	546	15 457	10 290	8 909	382	3 252	5 525
4th quarter	155 389	2 295	1 753	1 562	1 363	196	614	553	15 418	10 223	8 918	379	3 275	5 512
1952														
1st quarter	156 033	2 308	1 759	1 561	1 366	197	607	561	15 517	10 176	8 901	380	3 234	5 557
2nd quarter	156 644	2 307	1 778	1 574	1 387	198	617	572	15 488	10 265	9 041	385	3 297	5 622
3rd quarter	157 324	2 340	1 815	1 610	1 397	187	626	583	15 533	10 425	9 045	361	3 340	5 672
4th quarter	158 043	2 412	1 849	1 640	1 442	213	635	594	15 970	10 601	9 322	421	3 374	5 727
1953														
1st quarter	158 648	2 449	1 870	1 660	1 459	222	634	604	16 205	10 689	9 397	434	3 382	5 763
2nd quarter	159 234	2 463	1 888	1 678	1 465	220	631	613	16 271	10 788	9 419	430	3 385	5 810
3rd quarter	159 963	2 449	1 879	1 671	1 463	216	624	622	16 106	10 688	9 354	425	3 338	5 819
4th quarter	160 713	2 405	1 870	1 665	1 452	210	622	621	15 788	10 602	9 249	411	3 328	5 749
1954														
1st quarter	161 389	2 391	1 862	1 675	1 459	204	627	628	15 649	10 612	9 244	397	3 346	5 778
2nd quarter	162 044	2 386	1 852	1 667	1 470	208	625	637	15 602	10 579	9 327	414	3 323	5 854
3rd quarter	162 792	2 405	1 856	1 672	1 478	204	628	646	15 707	10 642	9 410	414	3 350	5 929
4th quarter	163 585	2 447	1 880	1 694	1 500	214	632	654	15 935	10 794	9 561	438	3 390	5 971
1955														
1st quarter	164 266	2 519	1 911	1 720	1 533	234	636	662	16 322	10 924	9 735	475	3 411	6 017
2nd quarter	164 926	2 560	1 949	1 753	1 557	247	643	667	16 522	11 121	9 881	499	3 460	6 036
3rd quarter	165 674	2 601	1 985	1 784	1 576	256	645	674	16 668	11 273	9 958	512	3 467	6 071
4th quarter	166 481	2 630	2 006	1 801	1 592	249	655	688	16 687	11 350	10 034	497	3 521	6 161
1956														
1st quarter	167 190	2 635	2 031	1 819	1 594	237	661	696	16 552	11 418	10 008	472	3 545	6 194
2nd quarter	167 869	2 661	2 057	1 841	1 604	237	663	704	16 621	11 480	10 001	471	3 522	6 228
3rd quarter	168 654	2 680	2 079	1 860	1 616	235	667	714	16 530	11 484	9 977	460	3 508	6 264
4th quarter	169 497	2 721	2 113	1 890	1 640	245	671	724	16 717	11 601	10 064	473	3 519	6 314
1957														
1st quarter	170 218	2 765	2 131	1 904	1 659	250	678	730	16 754	11 586	10 090	479	3 525	6 312
2nd quarter	170 915	2 766	2 150	1 922	1 665	247	682	737	16 648	11 620	10 067	466	3 524	6 340
3rd quarter	171 684	2 798	2 168	1 940	1 684	244	695	745	16 735	11 631	10 101	461	3 557	6 357
4th quarter	172 463	2 758	2 154	1 929	1 686	240	690	755	16 489	11 509	10 059	453	3 517	6 397

Table 1-3B. U.S. Population and Per Capita Product and Income: Historical—*Continued*

(Dollars, except as noted; quarterly data are at seasonally adjusted annual rates.)   NIPA Table 7.1

Year and quarter	Population (mid-period, thou-sands)	Current dollars							Chained (2009) dollars					
		Gross domestic product	Personal income	Dispos-able personal income	Personal consumption expenditures				Gross domestic product	Dispos-able personal income	Personal consumption expenditures			
					Total	Durable goods	Nondur-able goods	Services			Total	Durable goods	Nondur-able goods	Services
1958														
1st quarter	173 116	2 705	2 151	1 931	1 677	228	692	757	16 001	11 379	9 884	421	3 473	6 365
2nd quarter	173 781	2 721	2 157	1 940	1 687	222	697	768	16 045	11 412	9 927	413	3 491	6 433
3rd quarter	174 535	2 788	2 195	1 972	1 709	226	705	779	16 345	11 590	10 047	420	3 539	6 492
4th quarter	175 340	2 854	2 211	1 986	1 724	232	708	784	16 650	11 678	10 135	434	3 571	6 504
1959														
1st quarter	176 045	2 903	2 240	2 009	1 760	248	716	796	16 892	11 730	10 278	455	3 603	6 557
2nd quarter	176 727	2 966	2 279	2 041	1 787	257	719	811	17 236	11 872	10 397	471	3 619	6 629
3rd quarter	177 481	2 959	2 282	2 042	1 809	261	722	826	17 130	11 805	10 460	478	3 618	6 690
4th quarter	178 268	2 969	2 304	2 058	1 813	247	726	839	17 121	11 837	10 426	453	3 624	6 741
1960														
1st quarter	179 694	3 024	2 321	2 069	1 818	253	721	844	17 364	11 883	10 442	464	3 604	6 748
2nd quarter	180 335	3 009	2 341	2 086	1 844	257	732	855	17 237	11 915	10 536	473	3 631	6 798
3rd quarter	181 094	3 015	2 345	2 088	1 836	254	727	856	17 207	11 886	10 450	467	3 594	6 761
4th quarter	181 915	2 974	2 343	2 087	1 839	246	728	865	16 922	11 827	10 417	453	3 580	6 796
1961														
1st quarter	182 634	2 989	2 358	2 103	1 834	231	730	872	16 970	11 895	10 373	426	3 587	6 837
2nd quarter	183 337	3 040	2 383	2 127	1 854	236	732	886	17 219	12 030	10 487	434	3 622	6 911
3rd quarter	184 103	3 086	2 412	2 154	1 862	242	731	889	17 434	12 139	10 494	442	3 609	6 903
4th quarter	184 894	3 146	2 449	2 189	1 894	252	736	905	17 711	12 320	10 659	462	3 643	6 995
1962														
1st quarter	185 553	3 208	2 478	2 211	1 915	257	743	915	17 966	12 394	10 734	470	3 660	7 036
2nd quarter	186 203	3 236	2 508	2 235	1 939	263	745	930	18 096	12 480	10 828	481	3 662	7 116
3rd quarter	186 926	3 261	2 523	2 243	1 952	265	749	938	18 198	12 497	10 873	483	3 676	7 149
4th quarter	187 680	3 267	2 546	2 261	1 978	275	754	949	18 195	12 557	10 983	502	3 682	7 211
1963														
1st quarter	188 299	3 307	2 567	2 279	1 990	279	757	954	18 337	12 623	11 021	510	3 690	7 215
2nd quarter	188 906	3 345	2 584	2 296	2 006	285	756	964	18 516	12 700	11 091	520	3 690	7 271
3rd quarter	189 631	3 401	2 612	2 324	2 035	288	766	981	18 805	12 791	11 199	524	3 710	7 370
4th quarter	190 362	3 440	2 651	2 361	2 051	293	763	995	18 867	12 949	11 249	530	3 691	7 442
1964														
1st quarter	190 954	3 515	2 693	2 412	2 095	304	778	1 013	19 215	13 162	11 435	549	3 742	7 538
2nd quarter	191 560	3 554	2 734	2 474	2 130	310	791	1 029	19 382	13 474	11 600	562	3 802	7 619
3rd quarter	192 256	3 604	2 774	2 506	2 169	319	806	1 044	19 574	13 598	11 770	578	3 862	7 691
4th quarter	192 938	3 620	2 810	2 534	2 175	308	808	1 059	19 574	13 703	11 761	558	3 856	7 769
1965														
1st quarter	193 467	3 718	2 859	2 565	2 224	336	815	1 073	20 002	13 827	11 991	609	3 882	7 836
2nd quarter	193 994	3 775	2 901	2 600	2 254	334	829	1 091	20 221	13 946	12 091	608	3 908	7 934
3rd quarter	194 647	3 854	2 965	2 672	2 293	343	843	1 108	20 562	14 279	12 258	627	3 954	8 016
4th quarter	195 279	3 959	3 024	2 725	2 358	354	873	1 130	20 979	14 520	12 561	651	4 087	8 126
1966														
1st quarter	195 763	4 073	3 081	2 767	2 405	369	889	1 146	21 444	14 628	12 715	680	4 107	8 189
2nd quarter	196 277	4 112	3 123	2 789	2 424	355	903	1 166	21 475	14 628	12 714	651	4 135	8 256
3rd quarter	196 877	4 169	3 181	2 836	2 463	367	913	1 183	21 563	14 760	12 819	671	4 152	8 298
4th quarter	197 481	4 228	3 240	2 883	2 485	368	913	1 204	21 681	14 886	12 833	668	4 127	8 362
1967														
1st quarter	197 967	4 274	3 287	2 927	2 501	359	921	1 220	21 827	15 071	12 876	654	4 164	8 419
2nd quarter	198 455	4 288	3 314	2 957	2 541	375	927	1 238	21 792	15 151	13 019	681	4 184	8 479
3rd quarter	199 012	4 355	3 374	3 003	2 570	375	933	1 261	21 918	15 251	13 049	673	4 169	8 570
4th quarter	199 572	4 425	3 423	3 042	2 600	379	941	1 280	22 033	15 318	13 092	673	4 176	8 617
1968														
1st quarter	199 995	4 556	3 513	3 120	2 684	404	968	1 312	22 432	15 547	13 375	713	4 249	8 732
2nd quarter	200 452	4 671	3 605	3 197	2 747	414	987	1 346	22 759	15 770	13 548	727	4 291	8 848
3rd quarter	200 997	4 738	3 687	3 230	2 820	436	1 009	1 375	22 861	15 767	13 764	758	4 348	8 937
4th quarter	201 538	4 814	3 755	3 279	2 856	436	1 017	1 403	22 901	15 831	13 790	751	4 337	9 011
1969														
1st quarter	201 955	4 929	3 819	3 311	2 911	446	1 034	1 431	23 209	15 830	13 915	764	4 376	9 073
2nd quarter	202 419	4 996	3 905	3 383	2 960	447	1 048	1 465	23 230	15 968	13 972	760	4 376	9 163
3rd quarter	202 986	5 084	4 000	3 487	3 003	446	1 064	1 492	23 310	16 260	14 001	756	4 380	9 210
4th quarter	203 584	5 112	4 064	3 545	3 053	446	1 079	1 527	23 140	16 339	14 071	750	4 396	9 297
1970														
1st quarter	204 086	5 162	4 125	3 612	3 100	439	1 100	1 561	23 043	16 459	14 123	737	4 423	9 374
2nd quarter	204 721	5 227	4 199	3 684	3 139	445	1 107	1 587	23 013	16 601	14 144	743	4 407	9 404
3rd quarter	205 419	5 299	4 255	3 765	3 186	448	1 118	1 620	23 137	16 804	14 220	744	4 423	9 479
4th quarter	206 130	5 295	4 283	3 791	3 208	424	1 138	1 646	22 820	16 703	14 133	692	4 460	9 494
1971														
1st quarter	206 763	5 503	4 367	3 892	3 290	474	1 141	1 675	23 359	16 986	14 359	764	4 464	9 530
2nd quarter	207 362	5 591	4 467	3 982	3 348	487	1 152	1 709	23 425	17 184	14 449	779	4 461	9 598
3rd quarter	208 000	5 675	4 522	4 030	3 397	497	1 156	1 744	23 535	17 222	14 520	797	4 439	9 659
4th quarter	208 642	5 721	4 595	4 089	3 465	514	1 168	1 783	23 531	17 369	14 716	828	4 455	9 781
1972														
1st quarter	209 142	5 899	4 714	4 142	3 539	529	1 181	1 828	23 893	17 407	14 874	845	4 459	9 922
2nd quarter	209 637	6 059	4 787	4 198	3 619	544	1 213	1 862	24 388	17 543	15 122	865	4 569	10 019
3rd quarter	210 181	6 156	4 897	4 305	3 697	559	1 237	1 900	24 549	17 835	15 316	885	4 620	10 128
4th quarter	210 737	6 321	5 104	4 501	3 805	586	1 272	1 947	24 891	18 493	15 634	929	4 695	10 283

Table 1-3B. U.S. Population and Per Capita Product and Income: Historical—*Continued*

(Dollars, except as noted; quarterly data are at seasonally adjusted annual rates.)   **NIPA Table 7.1**

Year and quarter	Population (mid-period, thousands)	Current dollars							Chained (2009) dollars					
		Gross domestic product	Personal income	Disposable personal income	Personal consumption expenditures				Gross domestic product	Disposable personal income	Personal consumption expenditures			
					Total	Durable goods	Nondurable goods	Services			Total	Durable goods	Nondurable goods	Services
1973														
1st quarter	211 192	6 538	5 177	4 578	3 913	624	1 304	1 985	25 449	18 585	15 885	986	4 713	10 392
2nd quarter	211 663	6 697	5 304	4 693	3 978	620	1 329	2 029	25 680	18 691	15 843	972	4 662	10 457
3rd quarter	212 191	6 771	5 420	4 788	4 055	616	1 366	2 072	25 477	18 726	15 860	961	4 673	10 501
4th quarter	212 708	6 954	5 586	4 928	4 116	603	1 399	2 114	25 652	18 885	15 775	936	4 643	10 515
1974														
1st quarter	213 144	7 012	5 651	4 981	4 193	594	1 449	2 150	25 387	18 536	15 606	913	4 571	10 478
2nd quarter	213 602	7 183	5 760	5 063	4 318	611	1 489	2 218	25 399	18 324	15 627	915	4 531	10 559
3rd quarter	214 147	7 301	5 915	5 191	4 441	637	1 530	2 274	25 090	18 295	15 651	918	4 529	10 584
4th quarter	214 700	7 466	6 037	5 303	4 475	592	1 541	2 342	24 925	18 225	15 382	829	4 437	10 663
1975														
1st quarter	215 135	7 528	6 117	5 382	4 588	613	1 563	2 413	24 574	18 159	15 479	845	4 437	10 740
2nd quarter	215 652	7 681	6 249	5 687	4 710	634	1 599	2 478	24 704	18 956	15 700	859	4 524	10 848
3rd quarter	216 289	7 924	6 399	5 693	4 853	679	1 646	2 528	25 038	18 626	15 878	910	4 555	10 869
4th quarter	216 848	8 143	6 548	5 817	4 974	707	1 659	2 608	25 310	18 719	16 005	934	4 532	10 994
1976														
1st quarter	217 314	8 396	6 684	5 938	5 118	751	1 691	2 676	25 826	18 898	16 289	979	4 614	11 098
2nd quarter	217 776	8 527	6 782	6 006	5 198	762	1 713	2 723	25 966	18 956	16 404	981	4 675	11 148
3rd quarter	218 338	8 659	6 932	6 127	5 319	778	1 743	2 798	26 031	19 047	16 536	990	4 699	11 256
4th quarter	218 917	8 855	7 077	6 244	5 459	801	1 780	2 878	26 157	19 109	16 707	1 003	4 735	11 382
1977														
1st quarter	219 427	9 081	7 199	6 340	5 608	838	1 807	2 963	26 400	19 060	16 859	1 037	4 721	11 491
2nd quarter	219 956	9 366	7 401	6 513	5 722	860	1 835	3 026	26 853	19 250	16 912	1 059	4 710	11 507
3rd quarter	220 573	9 622	7 592	6 694	5 847	879	1 858	3 109	27 252	19 491	17 025	1 072	4 720	11 600
4th quarter	221 201	9 804	7 842	6 901	6 003	907	1 915	3 181	27 178	19 810	17 232	1 091	4 807	11 677
1978														
1st quarter	221 719	9 962	8 004	7 049	6 124	894	1 944	3 286	27 208	19 904	17 292	1 060	4 817	11 835
2nd quarter	222 281	10 512	8 249	7 247	6 367	973	2 001	3 393	28 195	20 050	17 616	1 136	4 842	11 982
3rd quarter	222 933	10 760	8 465	7 406	6 487	972	2 044	3 471	28 387	20 135	17 638	1 117	4 865	12 032
4th quarter	223 583	11 102	8 688	7 583	6 644	994	2 099	3 550	28 684	20 235	17 728	1 123	4 913	12 059
1979														
1st quarter	224 152	11 294	8 919	7 788	6 785	996	2 162	3 628	28 668	20 398	17 772	1 107	4 922	12 151
2nd quarter	224 737	11 551	9 076	7 911	6 948	988	2 225	3 735	28 628	20 169	17 715	1 079	4 900	12 195
3rd quarter	225 418	11 846	9 339	8 121	7 169	1 024	2 317	3 827	28 747	20 204	17 836	1 105	4 942	12 207
4th quarter	226 117	12 077	9 588	8 328	7 339	1 013	2 385	3 941	28 732	20 230	17 828	1 074	4 953	12 275
1980														
1st quarter	226 754	12 333	9 835	8 582	7 526	1 023	2 469	4 033	28 744	20 242	17 751	1 054	4 937	12 259
2nd quarter	227 389	12 313	9 922	8 640	7 515	932	2 489	4 095	28 083	19 892	17 303	938	4 856	12 147
3rd quarter	228 070	12 540	10 245	8 923	7 751	988	2 528	4 235	27 956	20 075	17 437	976	4 830	12 246
4th quarter	228 689	13 090	10 689	9 297	8 026	1 033	2 585	4 407	28 397	20 413	17 621	1 003	4 836	12 394
1981														
1st quarter	229 155	13 667	10 924	9 483	8 251	1 074	2 680	4 497	28 926	20 317	17 677	1 030	4 869	12 341
2nd quarter	229 674	13 790	11 106	9 617	8 368	1 049	2 712	4 607	28 650	20 266	17 634	987	4 879	12 391
3rd quarter	230 301	14 161	11 494	9 947	8 516	1 094	2 732	4 690	28 900	20 625	17 657	1 015	4 877	12 346
4th quarter	230 903	14 220	11 617	10 092	8 558	1 026	2 753	4 779	28 488	20 611	17 479	939	4 883	12 325
1982														
1st quarter	231 395	14 148	11 731	10 210	8 705	1 065	2 765	4 875	27 952	20 592	17 557	967	4 881	12 348
2nd quarter	231 906	14 365	11 892	10 344	8 801	1 075	2 754	4 972	28 043	20 665	17 583	969	4 862	12 403
3rd quarter	232 498	14 482	12 039	10 536	8 986	1 084	2 795	5 107	27 871	20 723	17 674	974	4 870	12 490
4th quarter	233 074	14 621	12 202	10 674	9 229	1 134	2 818	5 277	27 829	20 765	17 952	1 016	4 908	12 668
1983														
1st quarter	233 546	14 902	12 337	10 837	9 380	1 151	2 813	5 415	28 136	20 901	18 090	1 024	4 914	12 806
2nd quarter	234 028	15 314	12 526	10 992	9 634	1 237	2 876	5 520	28 719	21 006	18 410	1 096	4 962	12 942
3rd quarter	234 603	15 738	12 747	11 277	9 907	1 289	2 934	5 684	29 210	21 271	18 687	1 136	5 025	13 092
4th quarter	235 153	16 143	13 080	11 570	10 107	1 358	2 962	5 787	29 742	21 678	18 938	1 189	5 074	13 193
1984														
1st quarter	235 605	16 607	13 442	11 911	10 283	1 407	2 998	5 878	30 275	22 078	19 061	1 232	5 077	13 230
2nd quarter	236 082	17 007	13 769	12 202	10 510	1 446	3 060	6 005	30 745	22 400	19 294	1 258	5 178	13 313
3rd quarter	236 657	17 271	14 056	12 435	10 647	1 445	3 062	6 140	30 972	22 653	19 395	1 255	5 169	13 454
4th quarter	237 232	17 483	14 252	12 585	10 829	1 492	3 089	6 248	31 143	22 784	19 604	1 293	5 196	13 575
1985														
1st quarter	237 673	17 827	14 499	12 682	11 124	1 548	3 124	6 452	31 394	22 687	19 900	1 335	5 218	13 796
2nd quarter	238 176	18 063	14 637	13 007	11 299	1 567	3 161	6 572	31 615	23 075	20 045	1 348	5 248	13 898
3rd quarter	238 789	18 404	14 797	13 033	11 578	1 660	3 185	6 733	32 024	22 938	20 377	1 431	5 278	14 054
4th quarter	239 387	18 602	15 031	13 241	11 658	1 603	3 231	6 825	32 184	23 144	20 378	1 378	5 311	14 141
1986														
1st quarter	239 861	18 829	15 250	13 475	11 818	1 633	3 249	6 937	32 418	23 386	20 511	1 403	5 368	14 165
2nd quarter	240 368	18 951	15 393	13 609	11 911	1 694	3 193	7 024	32 498	23 647	20 696	1 450	5 404	14 228
3rd quarter	240 962	19 172	15 563	13 741	12 158	1 850	3 200	7 109	32 744	23 756	21 019	1 570	5 402	14 323
4th quarter	241 539	19 332	15 701	13 815	12 280	1 826	3 225	7 229	32 835	23 741	21 103	1 541	5 433	14 451
1987														
1st quarter	242 009	19 570	15 911	14 051	12 389	1 729	3 295	7 365	33 001	23 891	21 065	1 447	5 430	14 635
2nd quarter	242 520	19 881	16 125	14 017	12 654	1 811	3 349	7 494	33 301	23 609	21 312	1 503	5 460	14 755
3rd quarter	243 120	20 157	16 379	14 370	12 889	1 894	3 376	7 619	33 520	23 978	21 506	1 561	5 451	14 854
4th quarter	243 721	20 608	16 732	14 654	12 997	1 846	3 392	7 758	33 989	24 239	21 498	1 515	5 444	14 961

Table 1-3B. U.S. Population and Per Capita Product and Income: Historical—*Continued*

(Dollars, except as noted; quarterly data are at seasonally adjusted annual rates.)   **NIPA Table 7.1**

Year and quarter	Population (mid-period, thou-sands)	Current dollars							Chained (2009) dollars					
		Gross domestic product	Personal income	Dispos-able personal income	Personal consumption expenditures				Gross domestic product	Dispos-able personal income	Personal consumption expenditures			
					Total	Durable goods	Nondur-able goods	Services			Total	Durable goods	Nondur-able goods	Services
1988														
1st quarter	244 208	20 845	17 005	14 953	13 304	1 926	3 433	7 945	34 112	24 544	21 837	1 584	5 492	15 139
2nd quarter	244 716	21 281	17 272	15 242	13 522	1 934	3 488	8 100	34 491	24 744	21 951	1 581	5 524	15 240
3rd quarter	245 354	21 599	17 599	15 538	13 769	1 917	3 549	8 303	34 600	24 918	22 081	1 556	5 547	15 419
4th quarter	245 966	22 006	17 904	15 806	14 031	1 977	3 603	8 452	34 971	25 096	22 279	1 593	5 591	15 512
1989														
1st quarter	246 460	22 427	18 385	16 148	14 226	1 974	3 662	8 590	35 253	25 355	22 337	1 582	5 605	15 585
2nd quarter	247 017	22 786	18 565	16 278	14 450	1 997	3 756	8 697	35 450	25 223	22 391	1 600	5 601	15 614
3rd quarter	247 698	23 058	18 738	16 437	14 637	2 041	3 780	8 816	35 616	25 325	22 551	1 632	5 642	15 680
4th quarter	248 374	23 205	18 981	16 654	14 777	1 980	3 830	8 966	35 594	25 459	22 589	1 578	5 690	15 786
1990														
1st quarter	248 936	23 664	19 327	16 995	15 082	2 070	3 913	9 098	35 903	25 615	22 732	1 641	5 670	15 837
2nd quarter	249 711	23 926	19 571	17 197	15 218	1 996	3 928	9 294	35 930	25 689	22 732	1 581	5 659	15 980
3rd quarter	250 595	24 061	19 748	17 358	15 417	1 970	4 003	9 444	35 812	25 608	22 743	1 560	5 648	16 053
4th quarter	251 482	23 951	19 767	17 385	15 446	1 912	4 051	9 483	35 382	25 315	22 492	1 512	5 571	15 958
1991														
1st quarter	252 258	24 003	19 748	17 454	15 422	1 870	4 020	9 531	35 107	25 291	22 345	1 465	5 557	15 905
2nd quarter	253 063	24 277	19 919	17 612	15 584	1 878	4 038	9 668	35 267	25 385	22 461	1 468	5 572	16 015
3rd quarter	253 965	24 485	20 048	17 733	15 709	1 907	4 034	9 769	35 311	25 387	22 490	1 485	5 561	16 024
4th quarter	254 835	24 641	20 291	17 951	15 763	1 874	4 005	9 884	35 344	25 516	22 407	1 456	5 495	16 069
1992														
1st quarter	255 585	24 965	20 689	18 394	16 111	1 941	4 060	10 109	35 656	25 988	22 761	1 509	5 560	16 286
2nd quarter	256 439	25 317	21 006	18 648	16 274	1 954	4 084	10 237	35 929	26 172	22 841	1 514	5 565	16 360
3rd quarter	257 386	25 590	21 164	18 779	16 494	1 990	4 122	10 382	36 145	26 189	23 003	1 541	5 577	16 475
4th quarter	258 277	25 932	21 377	18 911	16 750	2 025	4 161	10 564	36 381	26 189	23 197	1 566	5 614	16 601
1993														
1st quarter	259 039	26 051	21 446	19 074	16 864	2 038	4 166	10 661	36 342	26 258	23 216	1 577	5 603	16 614
2nd quarter	259 826	26 285	21 646	19 178	17 079	2 109	4 181	10 789	36 447	26 224	23 354	1 623	5 630	16 645
3rd quarter	260 714	26 482	21 727	19 208	17 283	2 135	4 191	10 958	36 500	26 150	23 531	1 635	5 667	16 778
4th quarter	261 547	26 889	21 957	19 383	17 481	2 194	4 226	11 061	36 870	26 239	23 664	1 669	5 688	16 835
1994														
1st quarter	262 250	27 212	22 094	19 535	17 696	2 245	4 259	11 192	37 131	26 352	23 871	1 705	5 749	16 929
2nd quarter	263 020	27 640	22 437	19 794	17 880	2 276	4 289	11 315	37 528	26 553	23 986	1 718	5 777	16 999
3rd quarter	263 870	27 863	22 615	19 989	18 089	2 309	4 357	11 423	37 628	26 625	24 094	1 730	5 808	17 061
4th quarter	264 678	28 248	22 956	20 300	18 314	2 387	4 394	11 532	37 939	26 912	24 279	1 786	5 852	17 109
1995														
1st quarter	265 388	28 431	23 250	20 537	18 401	2 341	4 397	11 663	37 967	27 096	24 278	1 744	5 857	17 185
2nd quarter	266 142	28 575	23 430	20 641	18 618	2 356	4 422	11 840	37 991	27 081	24 426	1 757	5 869	17 312
3rd quarter	267 000	28 863	23 642	20 842	18 803	2 407	4 433	11 963	38 194	27 235	24 571	1 801	5 871	17 385
4th quarter	267 820	29 122	23 849	20 990	18 960	2 435	4 449	12 075	38 347	27 309	24 668	1 826	5 884	17 430
1996														
1st quarter	268 487	29 398	24 224	21 257	19 196	2 458	4 511	12 227	38 503	27 502	24 835	1 842	5 907	17 560
2nd quarter	269 251	29 940	24 640	21 541	19 477	2 512	4 604	12 361	39 064	27 686	25 033	1 895	5 966	17 614
3rd quarter	270 128	30 204	24 838	21 734	19 614	2 515	4 614	12 484	39 297	27 816	25 102	1 902	5 989	17 652
4th quarter	270 991	30 581	25 093	21 926	19 839	2 545	4 680	12 613	39 586	27 872	25 219	1 933	6 018	17 691
1997														
1st quarter	271 709	30 923	25 484	22 185	20 083	2 597	4 715	12 771	39 782	28 077	25 418	1 980	6 039	17 801
2nd quarter	272 487	31 385	25 707	22 365	20 166	2 556	4 690	12 920	40 267	28 236	25 460	1 968	6 025	17 885
3rd quarter	273 391	31 792	26 036	22 615	20 496	2 644	4 747	13 106	40 645	28 478	25 810	2 049	6 101	18 040
4th quarter	274 246	32 045	26 447	22 938	20 739	2 688	4 770	13 281	40 833	28 796	26 035	2 095	6 125	18 179
1998														
1st quarter	274 950	32 332	26 967	23 366	20 898	2 683	4 754	13 461	41 131	29 335	26 236	2 106	6 153	18 347
2nd quarter	275 703	32 625	27 356	23 669	21 247	2 790	4 789	13 668	41 417	29 663	26 627	2 207	6 211	18 537
3rd quarter	276 564	33 072	27 659	23 908	21 524	2 839	4 827	13 858	41 828	29 872	26 893	2 262	6 236	18 703
4th quarter	277 400	33 618	27 919	24 091	21 830	2 975	4 886	13 969	42 386	30 024	27 206	2 389	6 301	18 760
1999														
1st quarter	278 103	33 981	28 168	24 308	22 059	2 948	4 980	14 131	42 674	30 216	27 421	2 388	6 401	18 889
2nd quarter	278 864	34 287	28 342	24 431	22 459	3 065	5 085	14 309	42 916	30 208	27 770	2 495	6 443	19 045
3rd quarter	279 751	34 741	28 636	24 646	22 775	3 114	5 146	14 514	43 325	30 314	28 013	2 547	6 452	19 214
4th quarter	280 592	35 397	29 178	25 081	23 160	3 123	5 283	14 754	43 942	30 668	28 318	2 570	6 564	19 388
2000														
1st quarter	281 304	35 677	30 007	25 724	23 650	3 274	5 303	15 073	43 957	31 193	28 678	2 706	6 490	19 637
2nd quarter	282 002	36 467	30 393	26 046	23 919	3 198	5 443	15 278	44 676	31 439	28 873	2 649	6 603	19 815
3rd quarter	282 769	36 651	30 840	26 442	24 241	3 224	5 507	15 510	44 612	31 721	29 081	2 687	6 628	19 952
4th quarter	283 518	36 948	31 033	26 608	24 527	3 230	5 563	15 733	44 731	31 744	29 261	2 699	6 674	20 078
2001														
1st quarter	284 169	36 994	31 519	26 953	24 722	3 261	5 532	15 929	44 500	31 941	29 298	2 737	6 619	20 116
2nd quarter	284 838	37 360	31 574	26 994	24 849	3 228	5 583	16 038	44 632	31 839	29 309	2 728	6 635	20 123
3rd quarter	285 584	37 272	31 466	27 581	24 887	3 235	5 571	16 081	44 380	32 506	29 331	2 752	6 648	20 096
4th quarter	286 311	37 381	31 476	27 188	25 206	3 478	5 524	16 204	44 375	32 021	29 687	2 974	6 687	20 110
2002														
1st quarter	286 935	37 769	31 552	27 840	25 278	3 398	5 523	16 358	44 695	32 729	29 718	2 931	6 697	20 195
2nd quarter	287 574	38 035	31 768	28 134	25 551	3 407	5 592	16 553	44 840	32 822	29 809	2 953	6 686	20 272
3rd quarter	288 303	38 292	31 805	28 168	25 797	3 481	5 607	16 709	44 941	32 696	29 944	3 032	6 685	20 303
4th quarter	289 007	38 427	31 970	28 363	25 960	3 402	5 687	16 871	44 853	32 773	29 996	2 983	6 756	20 353

Table 1-3B. U.S. Population and Per Capita Product and Income: Historical—*Continued*

(Dollars, except as noted; quarterly data are at seasonally adjusted annual rates.) **NIPA Table 7.1**

Year and quarter	Population (mid-period, thousands)	Current dollars							Chained (2009) dollars					
		Gross domestic product	Personal income	Disposable personal income	Personal consumption expenditures				Gross domestic product	Disposable personal income	Personal consumption expenditures			
					Total	Durable goods	Nondurable goods	Services			Total	Durable goods	Nondurable goods	Services
2003														
1st quarter	289 609	38 779	32 102	28 587	26 219	3 363	5 810	17 046	44 987	32 800	30 083	2 986	6 788	20 404
2nd quarter	290 253	39 177	32 457	28 961	26 478	3 472	5 748	17 257	45 312	33 200	30 353	3 116	6 823	20 475
3rd quarter	290 974	39 964	32 810	29 542	26 960	3 582	5 921	17 457	45 963	33 661	30 718	3 247	6 932	20 571
4th quarter	291 669	40 520	33 208	29 711	27 204	3 586	5 973	17 644	46 374	33 716	30 872	3 280	6 963	20 655
2004														
1st quarter	292 237	41 033	33 547	30 097	27 638	3 635	6 088	17 915	46 560	33 896	31 127	3 328	7 002	20 819
2nd quarter	292 875	41 600	34 034	30 540	27 942	3 659	6 151	18 132	46 814	34 156	31 250	3 354	7 009	20 909
3rd quarter	293 603	42 130	34 423	30 803	28 301	3 693	6 219	18 389	47 108	34 250	31 469	3 411	7 045	21 026
4th quarter	294 334	42 686	35 057	31 356	28 747	3 741	6 370	18 636	47 387	34 592	31 714	3 450	7 091	21 184
2005														
1st quarter	294 957	43 451	35 108	31 149	29 067	3 765	6 428	18 874	47 804	34 186	31 901	3 479	7 167	21 264
2nd quarter	295 588	43 898	35 573	31 537	29 502	3 859	6 485	19 159	47 963	34 383	32 166	3 570	7 183	21 409
3rd quarter	296 340	44 566	36 088	31 965	29 972	3 865	6 682	19 426	48 231	34 473	32 324	3 602	7 181	21 537
4th quarter	297 086	45 049	36 611	32 399	30 245	3 744	6 798	19 703	48 376	34 669	32 364	3 497	7 285	21 594
2006														
1st quarter	297 736	45 845	37 639	33 220	30 658	3 874	6 847	19 938	48 857	35 383	32 655	3 632	7 329	21 690
2nd quarter	298 408	46 255	37 955	33 451	30 988	3 844	6 955	20 190	48 898	35 357	32 755	3 620	7 337	21 797
3rd quarter	299 180	46 495	38 224	33 699	31 318	3 870	7 051	20 396	48 815	35 367	32 868	3 660	7 354	21 848
4th quarter	299 946	46 903	38 643	33 994	31 489	3 888	6 986	20 615	49 070	35 737	33 103	3 699	7 458	21 938
2007														
1st quarter	300 609	47 354	39 307	34 460	31 897	3 903	7 081	20 912	48 994	35 892	33 223	3 733	7 457	22 023
2nd quarter	301 284	47 877	39 645	34 723	32 184	3 933	7 190	21 062	49 261	35 883	33 259	3 778	7 425	22 041
3rd quarter	302 062	48 241	39 869	34 920	32 411	3 940	7 231	21 240	49 465	35 883	33 305	3 810	7 416	22 063
4th quarter	302 829	48 509	40 220	35 211	32 700	3 930	7 359	21 411	49 520	35 823	33 268	3 816	7 392	22 046
2008														
1st quarter	303 494	48 347	40 731	35 692	32 841	3 797	7 427	21 618	49 080	36 004	33 128	3 699	7 335	22 088
2nd quarter	304 160	48 715	41 138	36 742	33 175	3 748	7 624	21 803	49 215	36 679	33 117	3 679	7 370	22 063
3rd quarter	304 902	48 686	40 912	36 181	33 169	3 614	7 702	21 853	48 852	35 754	32 777	3 558	7 255	21 963
4th quarter	305 616	47 598	40 488	35 803	32 234	3 322	7 108	21 805	47 689	35 893	32 316	3 294	7 128	21 896
2009														
1st quarter	306 237	46 961	39 311	35 407	31 881	3 305	6 939	21 638	46 931	35 699	32 144	3 294	7 119	21 733
2nd quarter	306 866	46 737	39 427	35 760	31 821	3 274	6 986	21 562	46 786	35 894	31 941	3 267	7 053	21 621
3rd quarter	307 573	46 767	39 199	35 537	32 147	3 400	7 150	21 597	46 826	35 448	32 066	3 416	7 063	21 587
4th quarter	308 285	47 242	39 361	35 687	32 295	3 343	7 243	21 709	47 165	35 356	31 996	3 346	7 083	21 566
2010														
1st quarter	308 900	47 499	39 477	35 768	32 510	3 367	7 331	21 811	47 257	35 316	32 099	3 383	7 127	21 587
2nd quarter	309 457	48 082	39 987	36 213	32 750	3 441	7 306	22 003	47 625	35 715	32 299	3 478	7 148	21 674
3rd quarter	310 067	48 537	40 321	36 420	33 007	3 467	7 377	22 162	47 858	35 813	32 457	3 527	7 179	21 752
4th quarter	310 679	49 027	40 782	36 781	33 463	3 550	7 582	22 332	48 096	35 977	32 731	3 629	7 257	21 851
2011														
1st quarter	311 192	48 982	41 871	37 449	33 828	3 583	7 767	22 478	47 861	36 361	32 846	3 671	7 271	21 910
2nd quarter	311 718	49 602	42 181	37 690	34 206	3 582	7 929	22 695	48 157	36 263	32 911	3 657	7 271	21 988
3rd quarter	312 319	49 987	42 532	37 981	34 512	3 615	7 983	22 913	48 227	36 336	33 017	3 696	7 248	22 082
4th quarter	312 917	50 552	42 514	37 981	34 766	3 704	8 019	23 043	48 710	36 215	33 150	3 808	7 258	22 100
2012														
1st quarter	313 425	51 182	43 227	38 560	35 157	3 779	8 120	23 258	49 076	36 561	33 334	3 892	7 286	22 178
2nd quarter	313 960	51 473	43 483	38 769	35 355	3 788	8 119	23 448	49 139	36 661	33 434	3 913	7 307	22 236
3rd quarter	314 564	51 996	43 557	38 800	35 585	3 835	8 197	23 552	49 383	36 538	33 510	3 985	7 321	22 232
4th quarter	315 162	52 101	44 654	39 727	35 809	3 905	8 235	23 668	49 307	37 260	33 585	4 078	7 319	22 226

Table 1-4A. Contributions to Percent Change in Real Gross Domestic Product: Recent Data

(Percent, percentage points.)   NIPA Table 1.1.2

| Year and quarter | Percent change at seasonally adjusted annual rate, real GDP | Personal consump-tion expen-ditures | Gross private domestic investment | | | | Exports and imports of goods and services | | | Government consumption expenditures and gross investment | | |
| | | | Total | Fixed investment | | Change in private inventories | Net exports | Exports | Imports | Total | Federal | State and local |
				Nonresi-dential	Residential							
1950	8.7	4.20	5.68	0.91	1.99	2.78	-1.28	-0.65	-0.63	0.11	-0.47	0.58
1951	8.1	1.00	0.05	0.42	-1.11	0.74	0.80	0.96	-0.16	6.22	6.16	0.06
1952	4.1	1.90	-1.44	-0.01	-0.09	-1.34	-0.57	-0.21	-0.36	4.18	4.07	0.11
1953	4.7	2.85	0.87	0.95	0.19	-0.27	-0.68	-0.30	-0.38	1.65	1.32	0.33
1954	-0.6	1.25	-0.61	-0.14	0.42	-0.89	0.39	0.19	0.20	-1.60	-2.20	0.59
1955	7.1	4.50	3.44	1.06	0.88	1.50	-0.04	0.43	-0.47	-0.78	-1.31	0.54
1956	2.1	1.76	-0.05	0.70	-0.47	-0.28	0.36	0.69	-0.33	0.05	-0.20	0.25
1957	2.1	1.49	-0.64	0.20	-0.31	-0.53	0.24	0.41	-0.17	1.01	0.55	0.47
1958	-0.7	0.52	-1.16	-1.04	0.05	-0.17	-0.87	-0.67	-0.19	0.77	0.07	0.69
1959	6.9	3.49	2.82	0.81	1.18	0.83	0.00	0.44	-0.44	0.59	0.29	0.30
1960	2.6	1.67	0.06	0.56	-0.37	-0.13	0.70	0.76	-0.06	0.14	-0.24	0.38
1961	2.6	1.26	0.05	0.08	0.02	-0.05	0.05	0.03	0.03	1.19	0.65	0.54
1962	6.1	3.00	1.82	0.81	0.46	0.55	-0.21	0.25	-0.45	1.50	1.23	0.28
1963	4.4	2.47	1.08	0.59	0.57	-0.07	0.23	0.34	-0.11	0.57	0.03	0.54
1964	5.8	3.56	1.27	1.08	0.31	-0.12	0.35	0.57	-0.22	0.58	-0.05	0.63
1965	6.5	3.79	2.26	1.75	-0.13	0.64	-0.29	0.14	-0.44	0.74	0.10	0.63
1966	6.6	3.37	1.56	1.40	-0.40	0.56	-0.28	0.35	-0.63	1.94	1.34	0.61
1967	2.7	1.76	-0.62	-0.04	-0.11	-0.47	-0.21	0.12	-0.33	1.82	1.32	0.50
1968	4.9	3.38	0.99	0.55	0.53	-0.09	-0.29	0.39	-0.68	0.83	0.22	0.62
1969	3.1	2.21	0.93	0.79	0.14	0.00	-0.03	0.24	-0.28	0.04	-0.33	0.37
1970	0.2	1.39	-1.03	-0.10	-0.22	-0.70	0.33	0.54	-0.21	-0.49	-0.80	0.31
1971	3.3	2.29	1.63	-0.01	1.08	0.56	-0.18	0.09	-0.28	-0.44	-0.80	0.36
1972	5.2	3.66	1.90	0.97	0.87	0.06	-0.20	0.41	-0.61	-0.11	-0.37	0.26
1973	5.6	2.97	1.95	1.50	-0.04	0.48	0.80	1.08	-0.28	-0.07	-0.40	0.32
1974	-0.5	-0.50	-1.24	0.10	-1.08	-0.26	0.73	0.56	0.17	0.49	0.07	0.42
1975	-0.2	1.36	-2.90	-1.13	-0.54	-1.23	0.86	-0.05	0.91	0.49	0.05	0.43
1976	5.4	3.41	2.91	0.66	0.88	1.37	-1.05	0.36	-1.40	0.12	0.02	0.10
1977	4.6	2.59	2.47	1.26	0.97	0.24	-0.70	0.19	-0.89	0.26	0.21	0.04
1978	5.6	2.69	2.21	1.72	0.38	0.12	0.04	0.80	-0.76	0.61	0.24	0.37
1979	3.2	1.44	0.71	1.33	-0.22	-0.40	0.64	0.80	-0.16	0.38	0.21	0.16
1980	-0.2	-0.19	-2.07	0.00	-1.18	-0.89	1.64	0.95	0.69	0.38	0.40	-0.02
1981	2.6	0.91	1.63	0.87	-0.37	1.13	-0.15	0.12	-0.27	0.20	0.43	-0.23
1982	-1.9	0.86	-2.55	-0.53	-0.72	-1.30	-0.59	-0.71	0.12	0.38	0.36	0.01
1983	4.6	3.54	1.60	-0.06	1.38	0.28	-1.32	-0.21	-1.10	0.81	0.67	0.14
1984	7.3	3.32	4.73	2.18	0.65	1.90	-1.54	0.61	-2.15	0.76	0.35	0.41
1985	4.2	3.25	-0.01	0.91	0.11	-1.03	-0.39	0.24	-0.63	1.38	0.80	0.59
1986	3.5	2.63	0.03	-0.24	0.58	-0.31	-0.29	0.53	-0.82	1.14	0.61	0.53
1987	3.5	2.14	0.53	0.01	0.10	0.41	0.17	0.76	-0.59	0.63	0.39	0.24
1988	4.2	2.66	0.45	0.63	-0.05	-0.13	0.81	1.22	-0.41	0.28	-0.13	0.42
1989	3.7	1.86	0.72	0.71	-0.16	0.17	0.51	0.97	-0.46	0.59	0.16	0.43
1990	1.9	1.31	-0.45	0.14	-0.38	-0.21	0.40	0.78	-0.37	0.66	0.20	0.46
1991	-0.1	0.15	-1.09	-0.48	-0.35	-0.25	0.62	0.61	0.01	0.25	0.00	0.25
1992	3.6	2.38	1.11	0.34	0.49	0.28	-0.04	0.66	-0.70	0.11	-0.14	0.24
1993	2.7	2.24	1.23	0.84	0.32	0.07	-0.56	0.31	-0.87	-0.17	-0.31	0.14
1994	4.0	2.52	1.90	0.91	0.38	0.61	-0.40	0.84	-1.24	0.02	-0.30	0.32
1995	2.7	1.94	0.55	1.15	-0.15	-0.44	0.12	1.02	-0.89	0.10	-0.21	0.31
1996	3.8	2.28	1.49	1.13	0.35	0.02	-0.15	0.86	-1.01	0.18	-0.09	0.27
1997	4.5	2.45	2.00	1.37	0.11	0.52	-0.31	1.26	-1.57	0.35	-0.06	0.40
1998	4.4	3.45	1.76	1.42	0.38	-0.04	-1.13	0.25	-1.39	0.38	-0.06	0.44
1999	4.8	3.55	1.60	1.32	0.29	-0.02	-0.91	0.48	-1.39	0.61	0.13	0.49
2000	4.1	3.31	1.25	1.27	0.03	-0.05	-0.81	0.86	-1.67	0.34	0.02	0.32
2001	1.0	1.66	-1.19	-0.34	0.04	-0.89	-0.19	-0.59	0.40	0.67	0.24	0.43
2002	1.8	1.70	-0.11	-0.93	0.29	0.53	-0.62	-0.18	-0.44	0.81	0.46	0.35
2003	2.8	2.08	0.71	0.23	0.47	0.02	-0.42	0.15	-0.56	0.42	0.46	-0.05
2004	3.8	2.58	1.55	0.62	0.56	0.37	-0.64	0.85	-1.49	0.31	0.33	-0.02
2005	3.4	2.35	1.20	0.83	0.41	-0.04	-0.32	0.59	-0.91	0.12	0.13	0.00
2006	2.7	2.02	0.42	0.87	-0.50	0.04	-0.06	0.90	-0.96	0.29	0.18	0.11
2007	1.8	1.51	-0.61	0.76	-1.13	-0.23	0.59	0.96	-0.37	0.30	0.12	0.18
2008	-0.3	-0.24	-1.71	-0.09	-1.12	-0.49	1.12	0.67	0.45	0.54	0.50	0.04
2009	-2.8	-1.06	-3.52	-2.04	-0.73	-0.76	1.14	-1.10	2.24	0.64	0.44	0.20
2010	2.5	1.34	1.66	0.28	-0.07	1.45	-0.51	1.28	-1.79	0.02	0.37	-0.35
2011	1.8	1.74	0.69	0.84	0.01	-0.16	0.10	0.89	-0.79	-0.68	-0.23	-0.46
2012	2.8	1.52	1.36	0.85	0.32	0.20	0.10	0.48	-0.38	-0.20	-0.12	-0.08
2010												
1st quarter	1.6	1.42	1.77	0.46	-0.35	1.66	-0.96	0.73	-1.70	-0.63	0.32	-0.95
2nd quarter	3.9	2.21	2.86	1.21	0.56	1.09	-1.77	1.10	-2.87	0.61	0.71	-0.10
3rd quarter	2.8	1.87	1.86	0.90	-0.94	1.90	-0.88	1.27	-2.15	-0.07	0.32	-0.39
4th quarter	2.8	2.86	-0.51	0.94	0.19	-1.64	1.32	1.47	-0.15	-0.87	-0.23	-0.63
2011												
1st quarter	-1.3	1.42	-1.11	-0.09	0.04	-1.06	0.01	0.48	-0.46	-1.61	-0.94	-0.67
2nd quarter	3.2	1.03	1.88	1.09	0.07	0.72	0.53	0.64	-0.11	-0.25	0.16	-0.41
3rd quarter	1.4	1.42	0.36	1.81	0.15	-1.60	0.10	0.92	-0.82	-0.52	-0.29	-0.23
4th quarter	4.9	1.65	4.13	1.10	0.29	2.73	-0.60	0.38	-0.98	-0.31	-0.25	-0.05
2012												
1st quarter	3.7	1.98	1.57	0.68	0.53	0.36	0.44	0.56	-0.12	-0.28	-0.20	-0.08
2nd quarter	1.2	1.28	-0.23	0.53	0.15	-0.91	0.10	0.51	-0.41	0.05	-0.02	0.07
3rd quarter	2.8	1.15	0.99	0.04	0.35	0.60	-0.03	0.05	-0.08	0.67	0.69	-0.02
4th quarter	0.1	1.13	-0.36	1.13	0.50	-2.00	0.68	0.15	0.53	-1.31	-1.19	-0.12

Table 1-4B. Contributions to Percent Change in Real Gross Domestic Product: Historical

(Percent; percentage points.)   **NIPA Table 1.1.2**

Year and quarter	Percent change at seasonally adjusted annual rate, real GDP	Personal consumption expenditures	Gross private domestic investment				Exports and imports of goods and services			Government consumption expenditures and gross investment		
			Total	Fixed investment		Change in private inventories	Net exports	Exports	Imports	Total	Federal	State and local
				Nonresidential	Residential							
1929	. . .	. . .	. . .	. . .	. . .	. . .	. . .	. . .	. . .	. . .	. . .	. . .
1930	-8.5	-3.96	-5.18	-1.84	-1.50	-1.84	-0.31	-0.96	0.65	0.94	0.19	0.74
1931	-6.4	-2.37	-4.28	-3.32	-0.40	-0.56	-0.22	-0.77	0.54	0.48	0.08	0.40
1932	-12.9	-7.00	-5.28	-2.78	-1.02	-1.48	-0.20	-0.80	0.61	-0.42	0.05	-0.47
1933	-1.3	-1.79	1.16	-0.44	-0.24	1.84	-0.11	0.02	-0.13	-0.52	0.76	-1.28
1934	10.8	5.71	2.83	1.31	0.38	1.14	0.33	0.41	-0.08	1.91	1.37	0.54
1935	8.9	4.69	4.54	1.41	0.56	2.58	-0.83	0.21	-1.04	0.50	0.14	0.36
1936	12.9	7.68	2.58	2.10	0.47	0.01	0.24	0.19	0.05	2.44	2.43	0.01
1937	5.1	2.72	2.57	1.42	0.17	0.98	0.45	0.93	-0.48	-0.64	-0.65	0.02
1938	-3.3	-1.15	-4.13	-2.13	0.01	-2.01	0.88	-0.05	0.93	1.09	0.60	0.49
1939	8.0	4.11	2.39	0.71	1.03	0.65	0.07	0.24	-0.17	1.41	0.49	0.92
1940	8.8	3.72	3.99	1.60	0.42	1.97	0.52	0.61	-0.08	0.57	0.87	-0.30
1941	17.7	4.90	3.13	1.58	0.21	1.34	-0.64	0.12	-0.76	10.31	10.83	-0.52
1942	18.9	-1.50	-6.45	-3.16	-1.55	-1.74	-1.19	-1.51	0.32	28.04	28.65	-0.61
1943	17.0	1.52	-2.63	-0.72	-0.55	-1.36	-1.16	-0.42	-0.73	19.31	19.76	-0.44
1944	8.0	1.42	0.72	0.88	-0.10	-0.05	0.01	0.15	-0.15	5.84	5.98	-0.14
1945	-1.0	3.01	1.20	1.40	0.10	-0.30	0.66	0.86	-0.19	-5.84	-5.97	0.14
1946	-11.6	6.29	7.36	2.30	2.30	2.76	3.71	3.15	0.56	-28.95	-29.34	0.39
1947	-1.1	1.21	-0.56	1.28	1.02	-2.86	1.05	0.89	0.16	-2.80	-3.46	0.66
1948	4.1	1.47	3.89	0.48	0.96	2.45	-2.13	-1.59	-0.54	0.93	0.57	0.35
1949	-0.5	1.77	-4.15	-0.94	-0.43	-2.79	0.08	-0.05	0.13	1.77	0.85	0.92
1947												
1st quarter	. . .	. . .	. . .	. . .	. . .	. . .	. . .	. . .	. . .	. . .	. . .	. . .
2nd quarter	-0.4	4.30	-4.71	-0.59	-0.88	-3.25	-0.68	-0.42	-0.26	0.65	0.34	0.31
3rd quarter	-0.4	0.93	-1.83	-0.66	2.67	-3.84	-0.16	-1.68	1.52	0.65	0.12	0.52
4th quarter	6.5	0.24	10.67	1.33	3.97	5.37	-4.22	-3.52	-0.70	-0.24	-0.62	0.38
1948												
1st quarter	6.0	1.50	6.26	2.62	-0.31	3.95	-2.98	-1.31	-1.67	1.23	1.23	0.00
2nd quarter	6.7	3.11	4.31	-1.26	1.38	4.18	-3.00	-2.37	-0.63	2.24	1.57	0.67
3rd quarter	2.2	0.37	0.91	0.21	-0.75	1.46	-0.32	0.49	-0.81	1.30	0.88	0.42
4th quarter	0.4	1.83	-3.04	1.00	-1.74	-2.30	-0.60	-0.79	0.20	2.24	1.66	0.57
1949												
1st quarter	-5.4	0.17	-9.95	-2.06	-1.63	-6.26	2.84	2.44	0.40	1.58	0.59	0.99
2nd quarter	-1.3	3.56	-7.86	-1.55	-0.33	-5.98	0.02	-0.16	0.18	2.94	1.48	1.45
3rd quarter	4.5	0.15	4.98	-1.76	1.74	5.00	-1.31	-1.87	0.55	0.66	-0.50	1.16
4th quarter	-3.5	3.27	-2.51	-0.36	2.67	-4.82	-2.86	-2.66	-0.19	-1.44	-2.01	0.57
1950												
1st quarter	16.9	4.04	14.11	1.36	2.88	9.87	-0.56	-0.21	-0.36	-0.66	-1.46	0.80
2nd quarter	12.7	4.01	7.60	3.32	2.62	1.66	-0.49	0.23	-0.72	1.53	1.26	0.27
3rd quarter	16.3	13.39	6.42	3.45	1.60	1.37	-2.77	0.44	-3.21	-0.71	-0.75	0.04
4th quarter	8.0	-7.71	9.62	-0.07	-1.35	11.04	1.25	1.29	-0.04	4.79	4.78	0.02
1951												
1st quarter	5.6	6.32	-8.87	-1.16	-1.40	-6.32	0.80	0.82	-0.02	7.34	7.61	-0.27
2nd quarter	7.1	-6.88	1.66	0.47	-3.37	4.56	2.33	1.78	0.55	10.01	9.55	0.46
3rd quarter	8.5	2.88	-5.57	0.52	-1.36	-4.73	1.96	0.50	1.46	9.23	9.09	0.14
4th quarter	0.9	1.31	-5.40	-0.54	0.18	-5.03	0.15	-0.17	0.32	4.83	4.86	-0.03
1952												
1st quarter	4.3	0.32	1.72	0.54	0.51	0.66	-0.76	1.14	-1.90	3.02	2.91	0.10
2nd quarter	0.8	4.48	-4.71	0.75	0.37	-5.82	-2.22	-2.19	-0.03	3.29	2.71	0.58
3rd quarter	2.9	1.07	3.26	-2.95	-0.21	6.42	-2.41	-1.36	-1.05	1.00	1.72	-0.72
4th quarter	13.8	8.60	4.66	3.34	1.13	0.19	-1.28	0.20	-1.48	1.81	1.15	0.65
1953												
1st quarter	7.7	2.86	1.35	2.06	0.34	-1.05	0.24	-0.18	0.42	3.20	2.62	0.58
2nd quarter	3.2	1.33	0.40	0.41	0.07	-0.08	-0.70	0.15	-0.85	2.13	2.16	-0.03
3rd quarter	-2.2	-0.71	-1.20	0.92	-0.76	-1.36	0.67	0.65	0.03	-0.99	-1.70	0.71
4th quarter	-5.9	-1.76	-4.24	-0.28	-0.16	-3.80	0.24	-0.53	0.77	-0.17	-0.85	0.67
1954												
1st quarter	-1.9	0.65	-0.16	-0.97	0.22	0.58	0.13	-0.73	0.86	-2.45	-3.47	1.01
2nd quarter	0.4	2.97	0.07	-0.27	1.32	-0.98	0.67	2.11	-1.44	-3.28	-3.41	0.12
3rd quarter	4.6	3.19	3.02	1.09	1.32	0.61	0.36	-0.58	0.94	-1.94	-2.79	0.84
4th quarter	8.0	5.10	2.89	0.04	1.43	1.42	0.48	0.70	-0.22	-0.44	-0.60	0.16
1955												
1st quarter	11.9	5.56	6.40	0.77	1.76	3.87	-0.39	0.57	-0.95	0.34	-0.95	1.29
2nd quarter	6.7	4.64	4.05	2.31	0.33	1.41	-1.37	-0.43	-0.94	-0.64	-1.05	0.41
3rd quarter	5.5	2.96	1.06	2.00	-0.55	-0.39	0.70	1.03	-0.33	0.77	0.79	-0.02
4th quarter	2.4	3.07	1.54	1.22	-1.01	1.33	-0.56	0.05	-0.61	-1.62	-1.82	0.20
1956												
1st quarter	-1.5	0.38	-2.11	-0.61	-0.60	-0.90	0.07	0.80	-0.73	0.13	-0.21	0.34
2nd quarter	3.3	0.79	-0.58	0.73	-0.15	-1.17	1.25	1.20	0.05	1.88	1.47	0.41
3rd quarter	-0.3	0.51	-0.61	0.39	-0.43	-0.57	0.42	0.62	-0.20	-0.66	-0.82	0.17
4th quarter	6.7	3.34	-0.54	0.00	-0.33	-0.21	1.63	0.88	0.75	2.27	1.93	0.34
1957												
1st quarter	2.6	1.64	-0.95	0.23	-0.29	-0.90	-0.01	1.31	-1.32	1.93	1.15	0.79
2nd quarter	-0.9	0.41	-0.06	-0.08	-0.47	0.49	-0.80	-0.62	-0.18	-0.43	-0.71	0.28
3rd quarter	4.0	1.93	1.43	0.93	-0.25	0.75	-0.26	-0.55	0.30	0.85	0.38	0.47
4th quarter	-4.1	0.12	-5.17	-0.99	-0.02	-4.16	-0.61	-0.55	-0.06	1.63	0.81	0.82

. . . = Not available.

Table 1-4B. Contributions to Percent Change in Real Gross Domestic Product: Historical—*Continued*

(Percent; percentage points.)   NIPA Table 1.1.2

Year and quarter	Percent change at seasonally adjusted annual rate, real GDP	Personal consumption expenditures	Gross private domestic investment				Exports and imports of goods and services			Government consumption expenditures and gross investment		
			Total	Fixed investment		Change in private inventories	Net exports	Exports	Imports	Total	Federal	State and local
				Nonresidential	Residential							
1958												
1st quarter	-10.0	-3.24	-4.12	-2.69	-0.71	-0.71	-2.05	-1.83	-0.22	-0.57	-1.54	0.97
2nd quarter	2.7	2.11	-1.23	-1.53	0.07	0.23	-0.63	0.12	-0.74	2.41	1.89	0.52
3rd quarter	9.6	4.25	4.41	-0.41	1.31	3.50	0.28	0.10	0.18	0.63	-0.16	0.79
4th quarter	9.7	3.49	5.26	1.45	1.96	1.84	-0.97	-0.01	-0.96	1.91	1.25	0.66
1959												
1st quarter	7.7	4.59	3.82	1.18	2.27	0.36	0.52	1.12	-0.59	-1.27	-1.40	0.13
2nd quarter	10.1	3.95	5.37	1.14	0.77	3.46	-0.31	0.61	-0.92	1.08	0.97	0.11
3rd quarter	-0.8	2.61	-4.41	1.07	-0.42	-5.06	0.34	0.56	-0.22	0.69	0.66	0.04
4th quarter	1.6	0.32	2.05	-0.11	-0.62	2.77	-0.03	-0.47	0.44	-0.77	-0.59	-0.17
1960												
1st quarter	9.2	2.37	6.61	1.48	0.67	4.47	1.65	2.23	-0.58	-1.42	-2.02	0.59
2nd quarter	-1.5	3.05	-6.62	0.63	-1.73	-5.52	1.13	1.22	-0.09	0.93	0.09	0.84
3rd quarter	1.0	-0.97	-0.19	-0.72	-0.58	1.11	0.02	-0.51	0.53	2.14	1.61	0.52
4th quarter	-4.8	0.34	-6.92	-0.07	-0.02	-6.83	1.21	0.41	0.80	0.61	0.21	0.40
1961												
1st quarter	2.7	-0.05	1.52	-0.57	0.08	2.02	-0.07	-0.14	0.07	1.35	0.17	1.18
2nd quarter	7.7	3.70	4.17	0.92	0.08	3.18	-0.47	-0.27	-0.19	0.24	0.48	-0.25
3rd quarter	6.8	1.22	4.81	0.40	1.02	3.39	-1.13	-0.10	-1.04	1.94	1.62	0.32
4th quarter	8.4	4.89	1.22	1.22	0.67	-0.67	0.22	0.60	-0.39	2.03	1.02	1.01
1962												
1st quarter	7.4	2.58	3.55	0.79	0.35	2.42	-0.54	-0.05	-0.49	1.80	2.07	-0.27
2nd quarter	4.4	2.95	-0.46	1.07	0.61	-2.14	1.46	1.81	-0.36	0.44	0.19	0.25
3rd quarter	3.9	1.95	1.12	0.50	-0.01	0.64	-1.34	-1.13	-0.21	2.13	1.68	0.45
4th quarter	1.6	3.40	-1.89	-0.16	-0.03	-1.71	-0.61	-0.41	-0.20	0.66	0.28	0.38
1963												
1st quarter	4.5	1.65	3.28	0.10	0.69	2.48	0.83	0.44	0.39	-1.23	-1.92	0.69
2nd quarter	5.3	2.33	1.07	1.24	1.42	-1.60	1.82	2.19	-0.37	0.11	-0.23	0.33
3rd quarter	8.0	3.32	2.10	1.12	0.40	0.58	-1.48	-1.07	-0.41	4.10	3.10	1.00
4th quarter	2.9	1.99	0.83	1.18	0.65	-0.99	1.01	0.95	0.06	-0.95	-1.46	0.51
1964												
1st quarter	8.9	4.77	2.60	0.88	1.30	0.43	1.25	1.22	0.03	0.31	-0.26	0.58
2nd quarter	4.8	4.21	-0.18	0.97	-1.08	-0.07	-0.01	0.34	-0.35	0.82	-0.04	0.85
3rd quarter	5.5	4.44	1.56	1.35	-0.33	0.53	-0.58	-0.15	-0.43	0.13	-0.29	0.41
4th quarter	1.4	0.69	0.59	0.92	-0.35	0.03	0.16	0.60	-0.44	-0.02	-0.43	0.41
1965												
1st quarter	10.2	5.47	6.38	2.81	0.10	3.46	-1.59	-2.22	0.63	-0.02	-0.38	0.36
2nd quarter	5.6	2.70	0.17	1.66	0.17	-1.66	1.62	3.46	-1.85	1.10	0.12	0.98
3rd quarter	8.4	4.19	2.49	1.68	0.10	0.72	-1.27	-1.20	-0.06	2.97	1.87	1.10
4th quarter	9.8	6.79	0.61	1.89	-0.37	-0.91	0.62	1.44	-0.82	1.76	1.17	0.59
1966												
1st quarter	10.3	3.58	5.71	1.96	0.46	3.29	-0.79	-0.35	-0.44	1.75	1.27	0.48
2nd quarter	1.6	0.60	-1.05	0.75	-1.42	-0.38	0.43	0.86	-0.43	1.67	1.38	0.30
3rd quarter	2.9	2.69	-0.51	0.62	-0.56	-0.57	-1.76	-0.77	-0.99	2.47	2.01	0.46
4th quarter	3.5	0.98	0.42	0.01	-1.69	2.11	0.47	0.65	-0.19	1.61	0.60	1.00
1967												
1st quarter	3.7	1.38	-1.72	-0.75	-0.40	-0.58	0.14	0.40	-0.26	3.93	3.44	0.49
2nd quarter	0.3	3.20	-2.45	-0.10	1.60	-3.95	-0.02	-0.19	0.17	-0.38	-0.60	0.23
3rd quarter	3.5	1.22	1.90	-0.08	0.83	1.15	-0.72	-0.49	-0.23	1.09	0.93	0.16
4th quarter	3.3	1.46	1.42	0.92	0.93	-0.43	-0.40	0.56	-0.95	0.78	0.06	0.72
1968												
1st quarter	8.4	5.66	1.43	1.37	0.06	0.00	-0.52	0.58	-1.10	1.80	1.03	0.77
2nd quarter	6.9	3.64	2.62	-0.57	0.42	2.77	0.11	0.41	-0.30	0.56	-0.26	0.82
3rd quarter	2.9	4.42	-1.84	0.60	0.34	-2.79	0.01	1.18	-1.16	0.32	-0.28	0.60
4th quarter	1.8	1.07	0.71	1.21	0.24	-0.74	-0.10	-0.26	0.17	0.10	-0.25	0.35
1969												
1st quarter	6.4	2.67	3.97	1.17	0.60	2.20	-0.55	-2.43	1.88	0.28	-0.12	0.40
2nd quarter	1.3	1.50	-0.40	0.49	-0.17	-0.72	0.48	3.94	-3.46	-0.30	-0.66	0.36
3rd quarter	2.5	1.14	1.41	1.06	-0.14	0.49	-0.24	-0.51	0.27	0.21	0.10	0.11
4th quarter	-1.7	1.88	-3.30	-0.24	-1.20	-1.86	0.94	0.72	0.23	-1.25	-1.17	-0.08
1970												
1st quarter	-0.7	1.46	-1.93	-0.32	0.01	-1.62	0.25	0.18	0.07	-0.47	-0.88	0.41
2nd quarter	0.7	1.11	0.14	-0.31	-1.00	1.45	0.55	0.95	-0.40	-1.10	-1.34	0.24
3rd quarter	3.6	2.15	1.04	0.15	0.88	0.01	-0.02	-0.07	0.05	0.42	-0.60	1.01
4th quarter	-4.1	-0.59	-3.41	-1.62	1.58	-3.37	-0.11	0.21	-0.32	0.06	-0.18	0.24
1971												
1st quarter	11.2	4.79	7.28	0.36	0.92	6.00	0.38	0.11	0.26	-1.30	-1.52	0.22
2nd quarter	2.3	2.24	1.85	0.58	1.73	-0.46	-1.59	-0.04	-1.54	-0.21	-0.55	0.34
3rd quarter	3.2	1.94	0.83	0.21	0.91	-0.29	0.41	0.89	-0.48	-0.03	-0.19	0.16
4th quarter	1.2	3.98	-1.81	0.96	0.79	-3.57	-0.35	-1.86	1.52	-0.65	-1.23	0.59
1972												
1st quarter	7.3	3.21	4.52	1.54	1.40	1.57	-0.85	2.16	-3.01	0.44	0.31	0.13
2nd quarter	9.6	4.62	4.14	0.83	0.43	2.88	0.22	-0.64	0.87	0.60	0.67	-0.07
3rd quarter	3.7	3.67	1.09	0.70	0.10	0.29	0.79	1.26	-0.46	-1.82	-2.18	0.36
4th quarter	6.8	5.63	0.57	2.19	0.80	-2.43	-0.10	0.92	-1.03	0.71	0.08	0.63
1973												
1st quarter	10.2	4.46	4.38	1.96	0.79	1.63	0.58	1.68	-1.10	0.79	0.57	0.22
2nd quarter	4.6	-0.10	3.23	1.74	-1.22	2.72	1.89	1.16	0.73	-0.41	-0.48	0.07
3rd quarter	-2.2	0.84	-2.67	0.73	-0.96	-2.43	0.75	0.06	0.69	-1.09	-1.56	0.47
4th quarter	3.8	-0.69	2.78	0.36	-0.98	3.41	1.12	1.34	-0.21	0.57	0.01	0.56

Table 1-4B. Contributions to Percent Change in Real Gross Domestic Product: Historical—*Continued*

(Percent; percentage points.)   **NIPA Table 1.1.2**

Year and quarter	Percent change at seasonally adjusted annual rate, real GDP	Personal consump-tion expen-ditures	Gross private domestic investment				Exports and imports of goods and services			Government consumption expenditures and gross investment		
			Total	Fixed investment		Change in private inventories	Net exports	Exports	Imports	Total	Federal	State and local
				Nonresi-dential	Residential							
1974												
1st quarter	-3.3	-2.06	-4.15	-0.06	-1.34	-2.76	1.34	0.36	0.98	1.59	1.01	0.58
2nd quarter	1.0	0.87	-0.24	-0.09	-0.78	0.63	-0.14	1.51	-1.65	0.57	-0.02	0.58
3rd quarter	-3.8	1.04	-3.79	-0.48	-0.61	-2.69	-1.21	-1.81	0.59	0.15	0.21	-0.06
4th quarter	-1.6	-3.49	0.29	-1.28	-2.34	3.91	1.19	0.85	0.35	0.42	0.39	0.03
1975												
1st quarter	-4.7	2.06	-11.55	-2.77	-0.88	-7.90	3.69	0.24	3.45	1.06	-0.38	1.44
2nd quarter	3.1	4.11	-1.89	-1.14	0.44	-1.19	1.47	-1.01	2.48	-0.57	-0.21	-0.36
3rd quarter	6.8	3.56	4.52	0.50	1.02	2.99	-2.80	-0.54	-2.25	1.50	0.86	0.63
4th quarter	5.5	2.61	1.78	0.53	0.69	0.56	0.25	1.76	-1.51	0.87	0.21	0.65
1976												
1st quarter	9.3	4.91	6.25	0.96	1.57	3.72	-2.05	-0.22	-1.83	0.23	-0.33	0.56
2nd quarter	3.1	2.23	2.73	0.58	0.44	1.72	-1.02	0.31	-1.33	-0.88	-0.04	-0.84
3rd quarter	2.0	2.59	0.26	1.00	-0.29	-0.45	-0.38	0.91	-1.29	-0.42	-0.10	-0.31
4th quarter	3.0	3.23	0.49	0.91	2.18	-2.61	-0.74	0.33	-1.08	0.06	0.19	-0.14
1977												
1st quarter	4.7	2.90	3.14	1.77	0.61	0.75	-2.08	-0.50	-1.57	0.77	0.34	0.44
2nd quarter	8.1	1.44	5.22	1.40	2.29	1.53	0.56	0.85	-0.30	0.87	0.59	0.28
3rd quarter	7.3	2.37	3.94	1.05	-0.07	2.96	0.75	0.25	0.51	0.20	0.25	-0.05
4th quarter	0.0	3.62	-1.88	1.56	-0.28	-3.17	-1.49	-1.00	-0.49	-0.21	-0.27	0.06
1978												
1st quarter	1.4	1.36	1.69	0.52	0.20	0.97	-1.70	0.65	-2.35	0.05	0.06	-0.01
2nd quarter	16.5	5.44	5.67	4.12	1.13	0.41	3.12	3.19	-0.07	2.26	0.90	1.36
3rd quarter	4.0	1.00	2.48	1.81	0.27	0.40	-0.14	0.34	-0.47	0.63	0.12	0.51
4th quarter	5.5	1.93	2.02	1.74	-0.04	0.32	0.79	1.28	-0.49	0.73	0.31	0.42
1979												
1st quarter	0.8	1.21	0.15	1.21	-0.57	-0.49	0.13	0.03	0.10	-0.69	0.04	-0.73
2nd quarter	0.5	-0.16	-0.07	-0.10	-0.41	0.44	-0.10	0.09	-0.18	0.81	0.41	0.40
3rd quarter	2.9	2.35	-1.39	1.61	-0.28	-2.72	1.84	1.22	0.62	0.11	-0.04	0.14
4th quarter	1.0	0.61	-1.46	0.11	-0.91	-0.66	1.37	2.18	-0.81	0.51	0.03	0.48
1980												
1st quarter	1.3	-0.42	-0.56	0.59	-1.69	0.54	1.04	1.00	0.04	1.24	1.05	0.20
2nd quarter	-7.9	-5.48	-6.68	-2.67	-3.71	-0.30	3.98	0.73	3.25	0.31	0.89	-0.58
3rd quarter	-0.6	2.62	-4.94	0.35	0.51	-5.81	2.96	-0.07	3.03	-1.24	-0.55	-0.70
4th quarter	7.6	3.32	6.53	1.19	1.62	3.73	-2.25	-0.19	-2.07	0.02	0.23	-0.21
1981												
1st quarter	8.5	1.36	6.97	1.18	-0.43	6.22	-0.88	0.82	-1.70	1.09	0.74	0.36
2nd quarter	-2.9	-0.02	-3.31	1.17	-0.55	-3.93	0.18	0.25	-0.07	0.26	1.08	-0.82
3rd quarter	4.7	0.99	4.32	1.39	-1.32	4.24	-0.34	-0.80	0.45	-0.30	-0.18	-0.12
4th quarter	-4.6	-1.80	-2.82	1.44	-1.61	-2.65	-0.90	0.17	-1.08	0.93	0.60	0.33
1982												
1st quarter	-6.5	1.61	-7.60	-1.45	-0.81	-5.34	-0.49	-1.61	1.12	-0.05	0.07	-0.11
2nd quarter	2.2	0.89	-0.06	-1.89	-0.44	2.26	0.81	0.19	0.61	0.56	0.41	0.15
3rd quarter	-1.4	1.88	-0.62	-1.71	-0.02	1.11	-3.22	-1.57	-1.65	0.53	0.53	-0.01
4th quarter	0.4	4.51	-5.37	-1.05	1.01	-5.33	-0.10	-1.53	1.43	1.35	1.03	0.32
1983												
1st quarter	5.3	2.45	2.36	-0.92	2.36	0.92	-0.29	0.50	-0.78	0.82	0.67	0.15
2nd quarter	9.4	5.06	5.96	0.67	1.86	3.43	-2.46	0.11	-2.57	0.89	0.98	-0.08
3rd quarter	8.1	4.50	4.40	2.13	1.70	0.57	-2.25	0.47	-2.72	1.42	1.05	0.37
4th quarter	8.5	4.06	6.94	3.14	0.79	3.01	-1.13	0.63	-1.76	-1.36	-1.39	0.03
1984												
1st quarter	8.2	2.26	7.23	1.71	0.58	4.94	-2.31	0.65	-2.96	1.01	0.47	0.54
2nd quarter	7.2	3.64	2.57	2.52	0.34	-0.29	-0.87	0.76	-1.63	1.87	1.31	0.56
3rd quarter	4.0	1.95	1.69	1.70	-0.22	0.21	-0.35	0.66	-1.02	0.70	0.00	0.71
4th quarter	3.2	3.29	-1.08	1.34	0.02	-2.44	-0.56	0.60	-1.16	1.58	1.16	0.42
1985												
1st quarter	4.0	4.23	-2.14	0.67	0.05	-2.86	0.94	0.07	0.87	1.01	0.48	0.52
2nd quarter	3.7	2.35	1.34	0.83	0.16	0.35	-1.90	-0.08	-1.83	1.93	1.18	0.76
3rd quarter	6.4	4.82	-0.43	-0.62	0.34	-0.15	-0.01	-0.42	0.41	1.98	1.31	0.68
4th quarter	3.0	0.62	2.80	1.00	0.40	1.40	-0.66	0.78	-1.44	0.27	-0.05	0.32
1986												
1st quarter	3.8	2.10	0.04	-0.55	0.76	-0.17	0.92	0.82	0.10	0.70	-0.09	0.78
2nd quarter	1.9	2.77	-1.30	-1.12	1.12	-1.30	-1.33	0.27	-1.60	1.70	1.28	0.42
3rd quarter	4.1	4.55	-1.97	-0.63	0.28	-1.62	-0.45	0.62	-1.07	1.95	1.55	0.40
4th quarter	2.1	1.62	0.24	0.48	0.05	-0.29	0.71	1.03	-0.32	-0.48	-0.63	0.15
1987												
1st quarter	2.8	0.05	1.98	-1.26	-0.04	3.28	0.23	0.03	0.20	0.57	0.35	0.23
2nd quarter	4.6	3.54	0.08	1.00	0.07	-0.99	0.14	1.18	-1.05	0.81	0.71	0.10
3rd quarter	3.7	2.97	0.03	1.39	-0.17	-1.19	0.45	1.28	-0.83	0.23	0.08	0.15
4th quarter	6.8	0.57	4.94	-0.05	0.04	4.95	0.18	1.16	-0.97	1.08	0.49	0.59
1988												
1st quarter	2.3	4.49	-3.62	0.41	-0.36	-3.68	1.94	1.74	0.20	-0.54	-1.00	0.47
2nd quarter	5.4	1.89	1.72	1.14	0.25	0.33	1.44	0.94	0.50	0.34	-0.21	0.55
3rd quarter	2.3	2.17	0.38	0.32	0.01	0.05	-0.31	0.66	-0.97	0.08	-0.12	0.20
4th quarter	5.4	2.93	1.11	0.71	0.13	0.27	-0.21	1.04	-1.25	1.56	1.04	0.53
1989												
1st quarter	4.1	1.18	2.41	0.80	-0.19	1.80	0.85	1.03	-0.17	-0.35	-0.70	0.35
2nd quarter	3.2	1.20	-0.70	0.68	-0.59	-0.79	1.35	1.53	-0.18	1.34	0.86	0.48
3rd quarter	3.0	2.52	-0.64	1.29	-0.08	-1.84	0.44	0.37	0.07	0.70	0.28	0.42
4th quarter	0.9	1.13	-0.53	-0.52	-0.38	0.37	-0.20	0.54	-0.73	0.45	-0.15	0.59

Table 1-4B. Contributions to Percent Change in Real Gross Domestic Product: Historical—*Continued*

(Percent; percentage points.)   NIPA Table 1.1.2

Year and quarter	Percent change at seasonally adjusted annual rate, real GDP	Personal consumption expenditures	Gross private domestic investment				Exports and imports of goods and services			Government consumption expenditures and gross investment		
			Total	Fixed investment		Change in private inventories	Net exports	Exports	Imports	Total	Federal	State and local
				Nonresidential	Residential							
1990												
1st quarter	4.4	2.21	0.69	0.63	0.16	-0.10	0.25	1.56	-1.31	1.30	0.61	0.69
2nd quarter	1.6	0.80	0.03	-0.66	-0.68	1.38	0.52	0.46	0.07	0.20	0.11	0.09
3rd quarter	0.1	1.02	-1.30	0.32	-0.89	-0.73	0.44	0.28	0.16	-0.05	-0.36	0.31
4th quarter	-3.4	-1.96	-3.64	-0.78	-0.90	-1.96	1.47	0.33	1.13	0.76	0.24	0.52
1991												
1st quarter	-1.9	-0.92	-2.04	-1.00	-0.78	-0.26	0.69	0.24	0.45	0.41	0.34	0.07
2nd quarter	3.1	2.14	0.05	-0.26	0.42	-0.12	0.65	1.38	-0.73	0.30	0.11	0.19
3rd quarter	1.9	1.24	1.21	-0.42	0.48	1.16	-0.21	0.91	-1.12	-0.30	-0.58	0.28
4th quarter	1.8	-0.07	2.15	-0.05	0.29	1.91	-0.02	0.87	-0.89	-0.31	-0.63	0.33
1992												
1st quarter	4.8	4.85	-1.15	-0.19	0.84	-1.80	0.44	0.72	-0.28	0.67	0.07	0.60
2nd quarter	4.5	1.79	3.40	1.44	0.52	1.43	-0.63	0.03	-0.66	-0.08	-0.02	-0.07
3rd quarter	4.0	2.80	0.51	0.69	0.01	-0.19	0.19	0.82	-0.64	0.45	0.43	0.02
4th quarter	4.1	3.08	1.92	1.19	0.60	0.13	-0.77	0.20	-0.97	-0.16	-0.13	-0.03
1993												
1st quarter	0.7	0.97	1.48	0.44	0.01	1.03	-0.79	0.09	-0.88	-0.92	-1.06	0.14
2nd quarter	2.4	2.32	0.38	0.88	0.22	-0.72	-0.40	0.46	-0.86	0.09	-0.28	0.37
3rd quarter	2.0	2.86	-0.41	0.36	0.61	-1.38	-0.66	-0.10	-0.55	0.17	-0.07	0.24
4th quarter	5.4	2.33	3.38	1.65	0.87	0.87	-0.45	1.22	-1.67	0.18	-0.04	0.22
1994												
1st quarter	4.0	2.99	2.58	0.50	0.26	1.82	-0.62	0.37	-1.00	-0.97	-1.15	0.18
2nd quarter	5.6	2.04	3.37	0.70	0.57	2.09	-0.30	1.29	-1.59	0.46	-0.06	0.52
3rd quarter	2.4	2.02	-1.15	0.77	-0.27	-1.65	0.22	1.45	-1.23	1.29	0.76	0.53
4th quarter	4.6	2.83	2.79	1.83	-0.27	1.24	-0.32	0.93	-1.25	-0.68	-0.86	0.18
1995												
1st quarter	1.4	0.71	0.70	1.80	-0.39	-0.70	-0.20	0.78	-0.98	0.16	-0.19	0.36
2nd quarter	1.4	2.33	-1.49	0.47	-0.52	-1.43	0.15	0.58	-0.43	0.41	0.05	0.36
3rd quarter	3.5	2.40	-0.41	0.31	0.61	-1.33	1.66	1.82	-0.15	-0.19	-0.24	0.05
4th quarter	2.9	1.83	1.69	0.97	0.33	0.40	0.01	0.62	-0.61	-0.66	-0.90	0.24
1996												
1st quarter	2.6	2.41	1.07	1.22	0.45	-0.59	-1.01	0.53	-1.54	0.17	0.25	-0.08
2nd quarter	7.2	2.88	3.39	1.36	0.77	1.26	-0.33	0.73	-1.05	1.22	0.56	0.66
3rd quarter	3.8	1.59	3.23	1.59	-0.04	1.68	-1.15	0.36	-1.51	0.08	-0.32	0.39
4th quarter	4.3	2.08	-0.05	1.30	-0.20	-1.14	1.73	2.64	-0.91	0.53	-0.12	0.65
1997												
1st quarter	3.1	2.78	1.47	1.20	0.09	0.18	-1.13	0.85	-1.98	-0.04	-0.46	0.42
2nd quarter	6.2	1.23	3.98	1.11	0.25	2.62	0.20	1.78	-1.57	0.76	0.59	0.17
3rd quarter	5.2	4.44	1.33	2.33	0.17	-1.17	-0.70	1.05	-1.75	0.12	-0.05	0.17
4th quarter	3.1	3.07	1.06	0.33	0.19	0.55	-1.10	-0.05	-1.05	0.11	-0.07	0.18
1998												
1st quarter	4.0	2.67	3.36	1.65	0.37	1.35	-1.62	0.21	-1.83	-0.40	-0.75	0.35
2nd quarter	3.9	4.58	-0.50	1.74	0.62	-2.86	-1.59	-0.47	-1.12	1.45	0.63	0.81
3rd quarter	5.3	3.45	2.04	0.79	0.54	0.71	-0.83	-0.18	-0.65	0.67	-0.15	0.82
4th quarter	6.7	3.88	2.18	1.55	0.44	0.18	-0.01	1.53	-1.54	0.68	0.32	0.37
1999												
1st quarter	3.8	2.74	2.16	1.17	0.07	0.91	-1.38	-0.18	-1.20	0.27	-0.23	0.50
2nd quarter	3.4	4.06	0.05	1.44	0.30	-1.68	-1.11	0.43	-1.54	0.41	0.13	0.27
3rd quarter	5.2	3.19	1.94	1.57	0.15	0.22	-0.80	1.00	-1.80	0.86	0.45	0.40
4th quarter	7.1	3.74	2.33	0.22	0.15	1.97	-0.06	1.13	-1.19	1.09	0.52	0.57
2000												
1st quarter	1.2	4.03	-0.71	2.00	0.10	-2.81	-1.57	0.66	-2.24	-0.59	-0.95	0.36
2nd quarter	7.8	2.54	4.72	1.85	-0.10	2.97	-0.39	1.17	-1.55	0.90	0.88	0.02
3rd quarter	0.5	2.61	-1.01	0.60	-0.29	-1.31	-0.95	1.01	-1.95	-0.15	-0.42	0.27
4th quarter	2.1	2.34	0.06	0.13	0.02	-0.08	-0.48	-0.33	-0.15	0.23	-0.13	0.35
2001												
1st quarter	-1.1	0.92	-3.60	-0.51	0.08	-3.17	0.47	-0.54	1.01	1.07	0.53	0.54
2nd quarter	2.1	0.71	-0.24	-1.31	0.29	0.77	0.24	-1.35	1.59	1.43	0.49	0.95
3rd quarter	-1.2	0.88	-1.29	-0.72	0.12	-0.69	-0.75	-2.04	1.29	-0.05	0.21	-0.26
4th quarter	1.0	3.92	-3.54	-1.55	-0.13	-1.86	-0.47	-1.04	0.57	1.07	0.20	0.88
2002												
1st quarter	3.8	0.88	2.51	-1.02	0.64	2.89	-0.68	0.56	-1.24	1.11	0.64	0.47
2nd quarter	2.2	1.42	0.73	-0.66	0.49	0.90	-0.68	1.00	-1.67	0.72	0.62	0.11
3rd quarter	1.9	1.91	0.00	-0.31	0.06	0.25	-0.56	0.28	-0.83	0.59	0.42	0.17
4th quarter	0.2	1.12	-0.14	-0.64	0.37	0.13	-1.34	-0.33	-1.01	0.55	0.50	0.05
2003												
1st quarter	2.0	1.34	0.57	0.04	0.39	0.15	0.37	-0.36	0.73	-0.24	0.02	-0.26
2nd quarter	3.8	3.05	0.37	1.09	0.34	-1.06	-0.82	-0.12	-0.69	1.23	1.42	-0.19
3rd quarter	6.9	3.98	2.51	0.95	1.25	0.31	0.41	0.98	-0.56	0.02	-0.16	0.18
4th quarter	4.6	2.02	2.53	0.69	0.67	1.16	-0.35	1.66	-2.02	0.42	0.56	-0.13
2004												
1st quarter	2.4	2.76	0.07	-0.50	0.27	0.30	-0.63	0.90	-1.52	0.21	0.20	0.01
2nd quarter	3.1	1.68	2.60	1.06	0.75	0.79	-1.62	0.52	-2.15	0.44	0.29	0.15
3rd quarter	3.6	2.57	1.16	1.30	0.17	-0.31	-0.48	0.27	-0.75	0.30	0.51	-0.21
4th quarter	3.4	2.79	1.52	1.02	0.34	0.15	-0.56	0.91	-1.47	-0.33	-0.25	-0.08
2005												
1st quarter	4.5	2.19	2.17	0.60	0.60	0.97	-0.09	0.46	-0.55	0.18	0.17	0.00
2nd quarter	2.2	2.80	-0.99	0.69	0.47	-2.16	0.25	0.84	-0.60	0.14	0.06	0.07
3rd quarter	3.3	2.02	0.81	0.90	0.29	-0.38	-0.11	0.03	-0.14	0.60	0.53	0.07
4th quarter	2.2	1.00	2.32	0.20	-0.06	2.18	-0.80	1.06	-1.86	-0.29	-0.43	0.15

Table 1-4B. Contributions to Percent Change in Real Gross Domestic Product: Historical—*Continued*

(Percent; percentage points.)

NIPA Table 1.1.2

Year and quarter	Percent change at seasonally adjusted annual rate, real GDP	Personal consump-tion expen-ditures	Gross private domestic investment				Exports and imports of goods and services			Government consumption expenditures and gross investment		
			Total	Fixed investment		Change in private inventories	Net exports	Exports	Imports	Total	Federal	State and local
				Nonresi-dential	Residential							
2006												
1st quarter	4.9	3.01	1.10	1.84	-0.25	-0.49	0.23	1.56	-1.33	0.61	0.71	-0.11
2nd quarter	1.3	1.41	-0.50	0.63	-1.33	0.19	0.07	0.76	-0.69	0.27	-0.04	0.31
3rd quarter	0.3	1.62	-0.80	0.61	-1.39	-0.02	-0.63	-0.09	-0.54	0.16	0.01	0.16
4th quarter	3.2	2.63	-1.83	0.34	-1.09	-1.07	1.85	1.75	0.10	0.51	0.30	0.20
2007												
1st quarter	0.3	1.58	-0.71	0.89	-1.01	-0.58	-0.45	0.64	-1.09	-0.16	-0.39	0.23
2nd quarter	3.1	0.91	1.02	1.03	-0.84	0.83	0.53	0.78	-0.26	0.66	0.46	0.20
3rd quarter	2.7	1.08	-0.44	0.81	-1.26	0.01	1.53	1.58	-0.05	0.56	0.55	0.01
4th quarter	1.5	0.39	-1.43	0.88	-1.53	-0.79	2.21	1.26	0.95	0.31	0.16	0.15
2008												
1st quarter	-2.7	-0.55	-2.36	0.00	-1.31	-1.05	-0.07	0.58	-0.65	0.32	0.47	-0.15
2nd quarter	2.0	0.53	-1.21	-0.31	-0.67	-0.24	2.05	1.42	0.63	0.62	0.56	0.07
3rd quarter	-2.0	-2.11	-1.86	-1.42	-0.71	0.26	0.88	-0.45	1.33	1.13	0.91	0.22
4th quarter	-8.3	-3.08	-5.74	-3.00	-1.29	-1.45	-0.08	-2.92	2.85	0.56	0.56	0.00
2009												
1st quarter	-5.4	-0.83	-7.02	-3.58	-1.17	-2.26	2.25	-3.59	5.84	0.15	-0.24	0.39
2nd quarter	-0.4	-1.13	-3.25	-1.46	-0.66	-1.12	2.40	0.10	2.29	1.56	1.09	0.47
3rd quarter	1.3	1.73	-0.40	-0.54	0.52	-0.38	-0.53	1.45	-1.98	0.48	0.47	0.01
4th quarter	3.9	0.05	4.05	-0.37	0.01	4.40	-0.05	2.42	-2.47	-0.17	0.02	-0.19
2010												
1st quarter	1.6	1.42	1.77	0.46	-0.35	1.66	-0.96	0.73	-1.70	-0.63	0.32	-0.95
2nd quarter	3.9	2.21	2.86	1.21	0.56	1.09	-1.77	1.10	-2.87	0.61	0.71	-0.10
3rd quarter	2.8	1.87	1.86	0.90	-0.94	1.90	-0.88	1.27	-2.15	-0.07	0.32	-0.39
4th quarter	2.8	2.86	-0.51	0.94	0.19	-1.64	1.32	1.47	-0.15	-0.87	-0.23	-0.63
2011												
1st quarter	-1.3	1.42	-1.11	-0.09	0.04	-1.06	0.01	0.48	-0.46	-1.61	-0.94	-0.67
2nd quarter	3.2	1.03	1.88	1.09	0.07	0.72	0.53	0.64	-0.11	-0.25	0.16	-0.41
3rd quarter	1.4	1.42	0.36	1.81	0.15	-1.60	0.10	0.92	-0.82	-0.52	-0.29	-0.23
4th quarter	4.9	1.65	4.13	1.10	0.29	2.73	-0.60	0.38	-0.98	-0.31	-0.25	-0.05
2012												
1st quarter	3.7	1.98	1.57	0.68	0.53	0.36	0.44	0.56	-0.12	-0.28	-0.20	-0.08
2nd quarter	1.2	1.28	-0.23	0.53	0.15	-0.91	0.10	0.51	-0.41	0.05	-0.02	0.07
3rd quarter	2.8	1.15	0.99	0.04	0.35	0.60	-0.03	0.05	-0.08	0.67	0.69	-0.02
4th quarter	0.1	1.13	-0.36	1.13	0.50	-2.00	0.68	0.15	0.53	-1.31	-1.19	-0.12

Table 1-5A. Chain-Type Quantity Indexes for Gross Domestic Product and Domestic Purchases: Recent Data

(Index numbers, 2009 = 100.)   NIPA Tables 1.1.3, 1.4.3, 2.3.3

Year and quarter	Gross domestic product												Gross domestic purchases
	Gross domestic product, total	Personal consumption expenditures		Private fixed investment			Exports and imports of goods and services		Government consumption expenditures and gross investment			
		Total	Excluding food and energy	Total	Nonresidential	Residential	Exports	Imports	Total	Federal	State and local	
1950	15.1	13.8	11.3	13.9	8.3	49.3	3.7	3.6	18.4	21.5	16.0	15.0
1951	16.4	14.0	11.5	13.3	8.7	41.4	4.5	3.7	25.2	35.1	16.1	16.1
1952	17.0	14.5	11.8	13.2	8.7	40.7	4.3	4.0	30.2	45.0	16.4	16.8
1953	17.8	15.2	12.4	14.3	9.5	42.2	4.0	4.4	32.2	48.4	17.2	17.7
1954	17.7	15.5	12.6	14.5	9.4	45.7	4.2	4.2	30.1	42.5	18.7	17.6
1955	19.0	16.6	13.7	16.4	10.4	53.1	4.7	4.7	29.2	39.1	20.0	18.8
1956	19.4	17.1	14.0	16.6	11.1	48.9	5.4	5.1	29.2	38.6	20.7	19.2
1957	19.8	17.5	14.3	16.5	11.3	46.0	5.9	5.3	30.6	40.1	21.9	19.5
1958	19.6	17.7	14.4	15.5	10.3	46.5	5.1	5.6	31.6	40.3	23.7	19.5
1959	21.0	18.7	15.3	17.6	11.1	58.1	5.6	6.1	32.4	41.1	24.5	20.9
1960	21.5	19.2	15.8	17.8	11.7	54.2	6.6	6.2	32.6	40.4	25.6	21.3
1961	22.1	19.6	16.2	17.9	11.8	54.4	6.6	6.2	34.3	42.3	27.1	21.8
1962	23.4	20.6	17.2	19.4	12.7	59.6	7.0	6.9	36.6	46.1	27.9	23.2
1963	24.5	21.4	18.0	20.9	13.5	66.6	7.5	7.1	37.5	46.2	29.6	24.2
1964	25.9	22.7	19.2	22.8	14.9	70.6	8.4	7.4	38.4	46.1	31.6	25.5
1965	27.6	24.1	20.5	25.2	17.4	68.8	8.6	8.2	39.6	46.4	33.7	27.2
1966	29.4	25.5	21.7	26.8	19.6	63.0	9.2	9.5	43.1	51.4	35.8	29.1
1967	30.2	26.3	22.4	26.5	19.5	61.4	9.4	10.2	46.5	56.6	37.5	30.0
1968	31.7	27.8	23.8	28.4	20.4	69.7	10.1	11.7	48.1	57.4	39.8	31.6
1969	32.7	28.8	24.7	30.0	21.8	71.9	10.6	12.3	48.2	56.0	41.2	32.6
1970	32.7	29.5	25.2	29.4	21.7	68.1	11.8	12.9	47.2	52.6	42.4	32.5
1971	33.8	30.6	26.3	31.4	21.6	86.2	12.0	13.5	46.3	49.2	43.7	33.7
1972	35.6	32.5	28.2	35.0	23.5	101.2	12.9	15.1	46.1	47.7	44.7	35.5
1973	37.6	34.1	29.9	38.0	26.6	100.6	15.3	15.8	46.0	46.0	45.9	37.2
1974	37.4	33.8	29.9	35.9	26.9	80.8	16.5	15.4	47.0	46.3	47.6	36.7
1975	37.3	34.6	30.5	32.4	24.4	71.1	16.4	13.7	48.0	46.6	49.3	36.3
1976	39.3	36.5	32.3	35.6	25.8	86.8	17.1	16.4	48.3	46.6	49.7	38.7
1977	41.1	38.1	33.9	40.4	28.6	104.6	17.5	18.2	48.9	47.7	49.9	40.8
1978	43.4	39.7	35.7	45.1	32.6	111.6	19.4	19.7	50.3	48.9	51.6	43.0
1979	44.8	40.7	36.8	47.7	35.8	107.4	21.3	20.1	51.2	50.0	52.3	44.1
1980	44.7	40.6	36.7	44.9	35.8	84.9	23.6	18.7	52.2	52.2	52.2	43.2
1981	45.9	41.2	37.5	46.1	38.0	77.9	23.9	19.2	52.7	54.5	51.2	44.4
1982	45.0	41.7	38.1	43.0	36.6	63.8	22.1	19.0	53.7	56.6	51.2	43.8
1983	47.1	44.1	40.6	46.2	36.5	90.6	21.5	21.4	55.7	60.2	51.9	46.4
1984	50.5	46.4	43.1	53.7	42.6	104.0	23.2	26.6	57.7	62.2	53.9	50.5
1985	52.6	48.9	45.6	56.6	45.4	106.4	24.0	28.3	61.6	67.2	56.9	52.7
1986	54.5	50.9	47.7	57.7	44.6	119.6	25.9	30.7	65.0	71.1	59.8	54.7
1987	56.3	52.7	49.6	58.0	44.6	121.9	28.7	32.6	66.9	73.8	61.1	56.4
1988	58.7	54.9	51.8	59.9	46.9	120.8	33.3	33.8	67.8	72.8	63.4	58.3
1989	60.9	56.5	53.4	61.8	49.5	116.9	37.2	35.3	69.8	74.1	66.0	60.1
1990	62.0	57.6	54.7	61.0	50.1	107.0	40.5	36.6	72.0	75.6	68.7	61.0
1991	62.0	57.8	54.8	57.8	48.1	97.5	43.2	36.5	72.9	75.6	70.2	60.6
1992	64.2	59.9	57.2	61.0	49.5	110.9	46.1	39.1	73.2	74.5	71.6	62.8
1993	66.0	62.0	59.3	65.7	53.2	120.0	47.7	42.5	72.6	71.9	72.5	64.8
1994	68.6	64.4	61.8	71.0	57.4	130.7	51.9	47.5	72.7	69.4	74.5	67.7
1995	70.5	66.3	63.9	75.4	63.0	126.3	57.2	51.3	73.1	67.6	76.5	69.4
1996	73.2	68.6	66.3	82.1	68.7	136.6	61.9	55.8	73.8	66.8	78.3	72.1
1997	76.5	71.2	69.1	89.1	76.1	139.9	69.2	63.3	75.2	66.2	81.1	75.5
1998	79.9	75.0	73.2	98.2	84.3	152.0	70.9	70.7	76.7	65.7	84.3	79.7
1999	83.7	79.1	77.4	106.9	92.4	161.6	74.1	78.8	79.4	67.0	87.8	84.2
2000	87.1	83.1	81.7	114.3	100.9	162.6	80.3	88.8	80.9	67.2	90.3	88.2
2001	88.0	85.2	84.0	112.6	98.5	164.1	75.8	86.3	83.9	69.8	93.6	89.2
2002	89.5	87.4	86.4	108.7	91.7	174.0	74.4	89.2	87.6	74.8	96.3	91.3
2003	92.0	90.1	89.2	113.0	93.4	189.8	75.6	93.1	89.5	79.9	95.9	94.1
2004	95.5	93.5	92.9	120.6	98.3	208.8	82.7	103.3	90.9	83.5	95.8	98.1
2005	98.7	96.8	96.2	128.9	105.1	222.5	87.7	109.6	91.5	85.0	95.8	101.5
2006	101.4	99.7	99.4	131.4	112.6	205.6	95.5	116.3	92.9	87.1	96.7	104.2
2007	103.2	102.0	101.8	128.8	119.3	166.9	104.0	119.0	94.3	88.6	98.1	105.3
2008	102.9	101.6	101.7	120.1	118.4	126.9	110.0	115.8	96.9	94.6	98.5	103.9
2009	100.0	100.0	100.0	100.0	100.0	100.0	100.0	100.0	100.0	100.0	100.0	100.0
2010	102.5	102.0	102.0	101.5	102.5	97.5	111.5	112.8	100.1	104.4	97.3	102.9
2011	104.4	104.6	105.0	107.8	110.2	98.0	119.4	118.2	96.9	101.7	93.8	104.7
2012	107.3	106.9	107.7	116.8	118.3	110.6	123.6	120.9	95.9	100.2	93.1	107.4
2010												
1st quarter	101.2	100.7	100.7	98.6	98.9	97.6	107.4	107.0	99.8	102.5	98.1	101.4
2nd quarter	102.2	101.5	101.6	101.8	101.6	102.9	109.8	112.0	100.6	104.6	97.9	102.7
3rd quarter	102.9	102.2	102.3	101.7	103.6	93.8	112.7	115.9	100.5	105.5	97.2	103.6
4th quarter	103.6	103.3	103.4	103.8	105.8	95.6	116.0	116.2	99.4	104.8	95.9	104.0
2011												
1st quarter	103.3	103.8	104.1	103.7	105.6	96.0	117.1	117.0	97.5	102.0	94.6	103.7
2nd quarter	104.1	104.2	104.6	105.9	108.1	96.7	118.5	117.2	97.2	102.4	93.8	104.3
3rd quarter	104.5	104.8	105.2	109.6	112.3	98.1	120.5	118.6	96.6	101.5	93.3	104.6
4th quarter	105.7	105.4	106.1	112.2	114.9	101.0	121.3	120.3	96.2	100.7	93.2	106.0
2012												
1st quarter	106.7	106.1	107.1	114.6	116.6	106.4	122.6	120.5	95.9	100.1	93.1	106.8
2nd quarter	107.0	106.6	107.3	115.9	117.8	107.9	123.7	121.2	95.9	100.1	93.2	107.1
3rd quarter	107.7	107.1	107.8	116.7	117.9	111.5	123.9	121.4	96.8	102.2	93.2	107.8
4th quarter	107.8	107.5	108.5	119.9	120.7	116.6	124.2	120.4	95.1	98.5	93.0	107.7

Table 1-5B. Chain-Type Quantity Indexes for Gross Domestic Product and Domestic Purchases: Historical

(Index numbers, 2009 = 100.)   **NIPA Tables 1.1.3, 1.4.3, 2.3.3**

Year and quarter	Gross domestic product, total	Personal consumption expenditures		Private fixed investment			Exports and imports of goods and services		Government consumption expenditures and gross investment			Gross domestic purchases
		Total	Excluding food and energy	Total	Nonresidential	Residential	Exports	Imports	Total	Federal	State and local	
1929	7.3	7.9	6.5	7.6	5.5	20.4	2.5	2.7	5.4	2.1	10.4	7.3
1930	6.7	7.5	6.1	5.9	4.5	12.6	2.1	2.3	5.9	2.4	11.5	6.7
1931	6.3	7.3	5.9	4.2	3.1	10.7	1.7	2.0	6.2	2.4	12.0	6.3
1932	5.5	6.6	5.3	2.6	1.9	6.1	1.4	1.7	6.0	2.5	11.4	5.5
1933	5.4	6.5	5.1	2.3	1.8	5.1	1.4	1.8	5.8	3.0	10.2	5.4
1934	6.0	6.9	5.4	3.0	2.2	6.6	1.5	1.8	6.5	4.0	10.7	6.0
1935	6.5	7.4	5.7	3.7	2.8	9.0	1.6	2.3	6.7	4.1	11.1	6.5
1936	7.3	8.1	6.3	4.9	3.7	11.2	1.7	2.3	7.7	6.2	11.1	7.4
1937	7.7	8.4	6.5	5.7	4.4	12.1	2.1	2.6	7.4	5.6	11.1	7.7
1938	7.5	8.3	6.3	4.6	3.3	12.1	2.1	2.0	8.0	6.1	11.7	7.4
1939	8.1	8.7	6.8	5.4	3.7	17.0	2.2	2.1	8.7	6.6	12.9	8.0
1940	8.8	9.2	7.1	6.5	4.4	19.0	2.5	2.2	9.0	7.5	12.5	8.7
1941	10.3	9.8	7.7	7.4	5.3	20.2	2.6	2.7	15.1	19.8	11.7	10.3
1942	12.3	9.6	7.5	4.4	3.3	10.5	1.7	2.4	35.1	59.1	10.7	12.3
1943	14.4	9.9	8.0	3.5	2.8	6.5	1.5	3.1	52.6	94.1	9.8	14.6
1944	15.5	10.2	8.2	4.2	3.5	5.6	1.6	3.2	59.1	107.2	9.4	15.7
1945	15.4	10.8	8.7	5.5	4.8	6.4	2.2	3.4	51.9	92.7	9.8	15.5
1946	13.6	12.1	9.6	9.8	7.0	25.5	4.7	2.8	18.3	26.0	10.7	13.1
1947	13.4	12.4	9.9	11.6	8.0	32.6	5.4	2.7	15.6	19.5	12.2	12.8
1948	14.0	12.6	10.2	12.7	8.4	39.0	4.2	3.1	16.5	20.7	12.9	13.7
1949	13.9	13.0	10.5	11.7	7.6	36.1	4.2	3.0	18.3	22.4	14.8	13.6
1947												
1st quarter	13.4	12.2	. . .	11.5	8.1	30.0	5.7	2.8	15.5	19.6	11.9	12.8
2nd quarter	13.4	12.4	. . .	11.2	8.0	28.5	5.7	2.8	15.6	19.7	12.0	12.8
3rd quarter	13.4	12.4	. . .	11.5	7.8	32.9	5.4	2.5	15.7	19.7	12.3	12.7
4th quarter	13.6	12.4	. . .	12.5	8.1	39.2	4.8	2.6	15.6	19.3	12.5	13.1
1948												
1st quarter	13.8	12.5	. . .	12.9	8.5	38.7	4.5	3.0	15.8	19.7	12.5	13.4
2nd quarter	14.0	12.6	. . .	12.8	8.2	40.9	4.1	3.1	16.3	20.4	12.8	13.7
3rd quarter	14.1	12.7	. . .	12.7	8.3	39.6	4.2	3.3	16.7	20.8	13.0	13.8
4th quarter	14.1	12.8	. . .	12.6	8.5	36.7	4.1	3.2	17.3	21.8	13.3	13.8
1949												
1st quarter	13.9	12.8	. . .	11.9	8.1	34.0	4.6	3.1	17.8	22.2	13.9	13.5
2nd quarter	13.9	13.0	. . .	11.5	7.8	33.4	4.5	3.1	18.5	23.0	14.6	13.5
3rd quarter	14.0	13.0	. . .	11.5	7.4	36.3	4.1	2.9	18.7	22.7	15.2	13.7
4th quarter	13.9	13.2	. . .	11.9	7.3	40.7	3.6	3.0	18.3	21.7	15.5	13.7
1950												
1st quarter	14.4	13.4	. . .	12.6	7.5	45.3	3.5	3.1	18.0	20.8	15.9	14.2
2nd quarter	14.9	13.6	. . .	13.7	8.2	49.6	3.6	3.2	18.3	21.3	16.0	14.7
3rd quarter	15.5	14.3	. . .	14.7	8.8	52.3	3.7	4.0	18.0	20.6	16.0	15.4
4th quarter	15.8	13.9	. . .	14.4	8.8	49.9	4.0	4.0	19.3	23.2	16.1	15.6
1951												
1st quarter	16.0	14.2	. . .	13.9	8.6	47.3	4.1	4.0	21.4	27.6	15.9	15.8
2nd quarter	16.2	13.8	. . .	13.3	8.7	41.0	4.6	3.9	24.2	33.1	16.2	16.0
3rd quarter	16.6	14.0	. . .	13.1	8.8	38.4	4.7	3.5	26.9	38.4	16.2	16.2
4th quarter	16.6	14.1	. . .	13.0	8.6	38.8	4.6	3.4	28.3	41.4	16.2	16.3
1952												
1st quarter	16.8	14.1	. . .	13.2	8.7	39.8	4.9	3.9	29.2	43.0	16.3	16.5
2nd quarter	16.8	14.4	. . .	13.4	8.9	40.5	4.3	3.8	30.1	44.7	16.6	16.6
3rd quarter	16.9	14.5	. . .	12.7	8.2	40.1	4.0	4.1	30.4	45.8	16.2	16.8
4th quarter	17.5	15.0	. . .	13.7	8.9	42.3	4.0	4.4	30.9	46.5	16.5	17.4
1953												
1st quarter	17.8	15.1	. . .	14.2	9.4	43.0	4.0	4.3	31.9	48.1	16.9	17.7
2nd quarter	18.0	15.2	. . .	14.3	9.5	43.1	4.0	4.5	32.6	49.5	16.9	17.9
3rd quarter	17.9	15.2	. . .	14.3	9.7	41.5	4.1	4.5	32.2	48.3	17.3	17.8
4th quarter	17.6	15.1	. . .	14.2	9.6	41.2	4.0	4.3	32.1	47.7	17.7	17.5
1954												
1st quarter	17.5	15.2	. . .	14.0	9.4	41.6	3.8	4.1	31.3	45.3	18.4	17.4
2nd quarter	17.5	15.4	. . .	14.2	9.3	44.3	4.4	4.4	30.2	43.0	18.4	17.4
3rd quarter	17.7	15.6	. . .	14.8	9.5	47.0	4.2	4.2	29.6	41.1	18.9	17.6
4th quarter	18.1	15.9	. . .	15.1	9.5	50.0	4.4	4.2	29.4	40.7	19.0	17.9
1955												
1st quarter	18.6	16.2	. . .	15.7	9.7	53.6	4.6	4.4	29.4	39.9	19.8	18.4
2nd quarter	18.9	16.6	. . .	16.3	10.2	54.4	4.5	4.7	29.2	39.1	20.1	18.8
3rd quarter	19.2	16.8	. . .	16.7	10.7	53.2	4.8	4.8	29.3	39.5	20.0	19.0
4th quarter	19.3	17.0	. . .	16.8	11.0	51.0	4.8	4.9	28.8	38.1	20.2	19.1

. . . = Not available.

Table 1-5B. Chain-Type Quantity Indexes for Gross Domestic Product and Domestic Purchases: Historical—*Continued*

(Index numbers, 2009 = 100.)

NIPA Tables 1.1.3, 1.4.3, 2.3.3

Year and quarter	Gross domestic product											Gross domestic purchases
	Gross domestic product, total	Personal consumption expenditures		Private fixed investment			Exports and imports of goods and services		Government consumption expenditures and gross investment			
		Total	Excluding food and energy	Total	Nonresidential	Residential	Exports	Imports	Total	Federal	State and local	
1956												
1st quarter	19.2	17.0	. . .	16.5	10.9	49.7	5.0	5.2	28.7	37.9	20.4	19.0
2nd quarter	19.4	17.1	. . .	16.7	11.1	49.5	5.4	5.1	29.3	38.8	20.6	19.1
3rd quarter	19.3	17.1	. . .	16.7	11.2	48.5	5.5	5.2	29.1	38.2	20.7	19.1
4th quarter	19.7	17.3	. . .	16.6	11.2	47.8	5.8	4.9	29.8	39.5	20.9	19.3
1957												
1st quarter	19.8	17.5	. . .	16.6	11.3	47.1	6.2	5.3	30.5	40.3	21.5	19.5
2nd quarter	19.7	17.5	. . .	16.4	11.3	46.0	6.0	5.4	30.3	39.8	21.6	19.5
3rd quarter	19.9	17.6	. . .	16.6	11.5	45.4	5.8	5.3	30.5	39.9	21.9	19.7
4th quarter	19.7	17.6	. . .	16.3	11.2	45.4	5.6	5.3	31.1	40.4	22.5	19.5
1958												
1st quarter	19.2	17.4	. . .	15.4	10.5	43.6	5.1	5.4	30.8	39.2	23.1	19.1
2nd quarter	19.3	17.5	. . .	15.0	10.1	43.7	5.1	5.6	31.6	40.5	23.5	19.2
3rd quarter	19.8	17.8	. . .	15.3	10.0	46.9	5.1	5.5	31.7	40.3	24.0	19.7
4th quarter	20.2	18.1	. . .	16.2	10.4	51.8	5.1	5.8	32.4	41.2	24.4	20.2
1959												
1st quarter	20.6	18.4	15.0	17.1	10.7	57.6	5.4	5.9	32.0	40.4	24.5	20.5
2nd quarter	21.1	18.7	15.3	17.6	11.0	59.6	5.6	6.2	32.4	41.1	24.6	21.0
3rd quarter	21.1	18.9	15.5	17.8	11.3	58.5	5.8	6.3	32.7	41.7	24.6	21.0
4th quarter	21.2	18.9	15.5	17.6	11.3	56.8	5.7	6.1	32.4	41.2	24.5	21.0
1960												
1st quarter	21.6	19.1	15.7	18.2	11.7	58.6	6.4	6.4	31.9	39.7	24.9	21.4
2nd quarter	21.6	19.3	15.9	17.9	11.8	53.8	6.8	6.4	32.2	39.8	25.5	21.3
3rd quarter	21.6	19.2	15.8	17.5	11.6	52.2	6.6	6.2	33.0	41.0	25.9	21.4
4th quarter	21.4	19.3	15.9	17.5	11.6	52.1	6.7	5.9	33.2	41.1	26.2	21.0
1961												
1st quarter	21.5	19.2	15.8	17.3	11.4	52.3	6.7	5.9	33.7	41.3	27.0	21.2
2nd quarter	21.9	19.5	16.1	17.6	11.7	52.6	6.6	6.0	33.8	41.6	26.8	21.6
3rd quarter	22.3	19.6	16.2	18.0	11.8	55.4	6.6	6.4	34.5	42.8	27.0	22.0
4th quarter	22.7	20.0	16.6	18.6	12.2	57.3	6.8	6.5	35.3	43.6	27.8	22.5
1962												
1st quarter	23.1	20.2	16.8	18.9	12.4	58.3	6.7	6.7	36.0	45.3	27.6	22.9
2nd quarter	23.4	20.5	17.1	19.5	12.8	60.1	7.4	6.9	36.1	45.4	27.7	23.1
3rd quarter	23.6	20.6	17.2	19.6	12.9	60.1	7.0	6.9	37.0	46.8	28.1	23.4
4th quarter	23.7	20.9	17.5	19.6	12.9	60.0	6.8	7.0	37.2	47.0	28.4	23.5
1963												
1st quarter	23.9	21.1	17.6	19.8	12.9	62.1	7.0	6.9	36.7	45.4	28.9	23.7
2nd quarter	24.3	21.3	17.9	20.7	13.3	66.5	7.8	7.0	36.7	45.2	29.2	23.9
3rd quarter	24.7	21.6	18.1	21.2	13.7	67.8	7.4	7.2	38.4	47.8	29.9	24.5
4th quarter	24.9	21.8	18.3	21.9	14.1	69.9	7.8	7.2	38.0	46.5	30.3	24.6
1964												
1st quarter	25.4	22.2	18.7	22.6	14.4	74.2	8.2	7.2	38.1	46.3	30.8	25.0
2nd quarter	25.8	22.6	19.1	22.6	14.7	70.5	8.4	7.3	38.5	46.3	31.5	25.4
3rd quarter	26.1	23.0	19.4	22.9	15.2	69.4	8.3	7.5	38.5	46.0	31.8	25.7
4th quarter	26.2	23.1	19.5	23.1	15.5	68.2	8.5	7.7	38.5	45.6	32.2	25.8
1965												
1st quarter	26.8	23.6	20.0	24.2	16.5	68.5	7.6	7.5	38.4	45.2	32.4	26.6
2nd quarter	27.2	23.8	20.2	24.9	17.1	69.1	9.1	8.3	38.9	45.3	33.3	26.8
3rd quarter	27.8	24.2	20.6	25.5	17.7	69.4	8.5	8.4	40.2	47.0	34.2	27.5
4th quarter	28.4	24.9	21.1	26.1	18.4	68.1	9.2	8.8	41.0	48.1	34.7	28.1
1966												
1st quarter	29.1	25.3	21.5	27.1	19.2	69.8	9.0	9.0	41.7	49.2	35.1	28.8
2nd quarter	29.2	25.4	21.6	26.9	19.5	64.4	9.4	9.2	42.5	50.6	35.4	28.9
3rd quarter	29.4	25.6	21.8	26.9	19.8	62.2	9.0	9.8	43.7	52.5	35.8	29.3
4th quarter	29.7	25.7	22.0	26.2	19.8	55.7	9.3	9.9	44.4	53.1	36.7	29.5
1967												
1st quarter	30.0	25.9	22.0	25.7	19.4	54.2	9.5	10.0	46.3	56.5	37.1	29.7
2nd quarter	30.0	26.3	22.4	26.3	19.4	60.4	9.4	9.9	46.1	55.9	37.4	29.8
3rd quarter	30.3	26.4	22.5	26.6	19.4	63.6	9.2	10.1	46.6	56.9	37.5	30.1
4th quarter	30.5	26.5	22.6	27.4	19.8	67.3	9.5	10.6	47.0	56.9	38.2	30.4
1968												
1st quarter	31.1	27.2	23.2	28.0	20.3	67.5	9.7	11.2	47.8	57.9	38.9	31.0
2nd quarter	31.6	27.6	23.6	28.0	20.1	69.1	9.9	11.4	48.1	57.6	39.6	31.5
3rd quarter	31.9	28.1	24.1	28.4	20.4	70.5	10.5	12.1	48.2	57.3	40.2	31.8
4th quarter	32.0	28.2	24.2	29.1	20.9	71.5	10.4	12.0	48.3	57.0	40.5	31.9

. . . = Not available.

Table 1-5B. Chain-Type Quantity Indexes for Gross Domestic Product and Domestic Purchases: Historical—*Continued*

(Index numbers, 2009 = 100.)   NIPA Tables 1.1.3, 1.4.3, 2.3.3

Year and quarter	Gross domestic product, total	Personal consumption expenditures		Private fixed investment			Exports and imports of goods and services		Government consumption expenditures and gross investment			Gross domestic purchases
		Total	Excluding food and energy	Total	Nonresidential	Residential	Exports	Imports	Total	Federal	State and local	
1969												
1st quarter	32.5	28.6	24.4	29.9	21.5	73.9	9.1	10.8	48.4	56.8	40.9	32.5
2nd quarter	32.6	28.7	24.6	30.0	21.7	73.2	11.2	13.0	48.2	56.1	41.2	32.5
3rd quarter	32.8	28.9	24.8	30.5	22.2	72.6	10.9	12.8	48.3	56.2	41.3	32.7
4th quarter	32.7	29.1	24.9	29.8	22.1	67.7	11.3	12.7	47.7	55.0	41.3	32.5
1970												
1st quarter	32.6	29.3	25.0	29.6	21.9	67.7	11.4	12.6	47.5	54.0	41.7	32.4
2nd quarter	32.7	29.4	25.2	29.0	21.8	63.5	11.9	12.9	46.9	52.6	41.9	32.5
3rd quarter	33.0	29.7	25.4	29.5	21.8	67.2	11.9	12.9	47.1	52.0	42.8	32.7
4th quarter	32.6	29.6	25.2	29.5	21.1	74.0	12.0	13.1	47.2	51.8	43.1	32.4
1971												
1st quarter	33.5	30.2	25.8	30.1	21.3	77.8	12.0	12.9	46.5	50.1	43.2	33.3
2nd quarter	33.7	30.4	26.1	31.3	21.6	85.3	12.0	13.9	46.4	49.5	43.6	33.6
3rd quarter	34.0	30.7	26.4	31.8	21.7	89.2	12.5	14.2	46.4	49.3	43.7	33.8
4th quarter	34.1	31.2	26.9	32.6	22.1	92.7	11.4	13.2	46.1	48.0	44.3	33.9
1972												
1st quarter	34.7	31.6	27.4	34.0	22.8	98.7	12.6	15.2	46.3	48.4	44.4	34.6
2nd quarter	35.5	32.2	27.9	34.6	23.2	100.6	12.3	14.6	46.5	49.0	44.3	35.4
3rd quarter	35.8	32.7	28.3	35.0	23.5	101.0	13.0	14.9	45.6	46.7	44.7	35.7
4th quarter	36.4	33.5	29.0	36.5	24.6	104.6	13.6	15.6	46.0	46.7	45.3	36.3
1973												
1st quarter	37.3	34.1	29.8	38.0	25.7	108.1	14.6	16.3	46.3	47.3	45.5	37.1
2nd quarter	37.7	34.1	29.9	38.2	26.6	102.5	15.3	15.8	46.1	46.7	45.6	37.3
3rd quarter	37.5	34.2	30.0	38.1	27.0	98.1	15.3	15.4	45.5	45.0	46.0	37.1
4th quarter	37.8	34.1	30.0	37.8	27.2	93.6	16.1	15.5	45.8	45.0	46.6	37.3
1974												
1st quarter	37.5	33.8	30.0	37.1	27.2	87.5	16.3	15.0	46.7	46.1	47.2	36.8
2nd quarter	37.6	33.9	30.0	36.6	27.2	84.0	17.1	15.8	47.0	46.1	47.8	36.9
3rd quarter	37.3	34.1	30.0	36.0	26.9	81.2	16.1	15.5	47.1	46.3	47.7	36.7
4th quarter	37.1	33.6	29.5	34.1	26.2	70.6	16.6	15.4	47.3	46.7	47.7	36.5
1975												
1st quarter	36.7	33.8	29.8	32.1	24.7	66.6	16.7	13.8	47.8	46.2	49.1	35.7
2nd quarter	37.0	34.4	30.2	31.8	24.1	68.5	16.2	12.7	47.5	46.0	48.8	35.8
3rd quarter	37.6	34.9	30.8	32.5	24.3	73.0	15.9	13.8	48.2	46.9	49.4	36.7
4th quarter	38.1	35.3	31.3	33.2	24.6	76.2	16.8	14.5	48.7	47.1	50.0	37.2
1976												
1st quarter	38.9	36.0	31.9	34.5	25.2	83.4	16.7	15.4	48.8	46.7	50.6	38.2
2nd quarter	39.2	36.3	32.1	35.1	25.5	85.4	16.9	16.1	48.3	46.7	49.7	38.6
3rd quarter	39.4	36.7	32.4	35.5	26.1	84.1	17.4	16.7	48.0	46.5	49.4	38.8
4th quarter	39.7	37.2	32.8	37.2	26.6	94.3	17.5	17.3	48.1	46.7	49.2	39.2
1977												
1st quarter	40.2	37.6	33.3	38.5	27.5	97.1	17.3	18.1	48.5	47.1	49.7	39.9
2nd quarter	41.0	37.8	33.7	40.5	28.3	107.7	17.7	18.3	48.9	47.8	50.0	40.6
3rd quarter	41.7	38.2	34.0	41.0	28.9	107.4	17.9	18.0	49.1	48.1	49.9	41.2
4th quarter	41.7	38.7	34.5	41.7	29.7	106.2	17.3	18.3	49.0	47.7	50.0	41.4
1978												
1st quarter	41.8	39.0	34.8	42.1	30.0	107.1	17.7	19.5	49.0	47.8	50.0	41.7
2nd quarter	43.5	39.8	35.8	44.9	32.3	112.3	19.5	19.6	50.3	48.9	51.5	43.0
3rd quarter	43.9	39.9	36.0	46.2	33.4	113.6	19.8	19.8	50.7	49.1	52.1	43.4
4th quarter	44.5	40.3	36.3	47.2	34.5	113.4	20.5	20.1	51.2	49.5	52.6	43.9
1979												
1st quarter	44.6	40.5	36.4	47.6	35.3	110.6	20.6	20.0	50.7	49.6	51.7	44.0
2nd quarter	44.6	40.4	36.5	47.3	35.3	108.6	20.6	20.1	51.2	50.2	52.2	44.0
3rd quarter	44.9	40.8	37.0	48.1	36.3	107.3	21.4	19.8	51.3	50.1	52.4	44.1
4th quarter	45.1	41.0	37.1	47.7	36.4	103.0	22.7	20.3	51.6	50.1	53.0	44.1
1980												
1st quarter	45.2	40.9	37.0	47.1	36.8	95.1	23.3	20.3	52.4	51.6	53.2	44.1
2nd quarter	44.3	40.0	36.0	43.2	35.1	77.5	23.8	18.8	52.6	52.8	52.5	42.8
3rd quarter	44.2	40.4	36.7	43.7	35.3	79.8	23.7	17.5	51.9	52.0	51.7	42.5
4th quarter	45.0	40.9	37.3	45.4	36.1	87.3	23.6	18.4	51.9	52.3	51.5	43.5
1981												
1st quarter	46.0	41.2	37.7	45.8	36.8	85.2	24.0	19.2	52.5	53.3	51.9	44.5
2nd quarter	45.6	41.1	37.5	46.2	37.6	82.4	24.1	19.2	52.7	54.8	50.9	44.2
3rd quarter	46.2	41.3	37.7	46.2	38.4	76.0	23.6	19.0	52.5	54.6	50.7	44.7
4th quarter	45.6	41.0	37.3	46.0	39.3	68.1	23.7	19.5	53.1	55.4	51.1	44.3

Table 1-5B. Chain-Type Quantity Indexes for Gross Domestic Product and Domestic Purchases: Historical—*Continued*

(Index numbers, 2009 = 100.)   NIPA Tables 1.1.3, 1.4.3, 2.3.3

| Year and quarter | Gross domestic product | | | | | | | | | | | Gross domestic purchases |
| | Gross domestic product, total | Personal consumption expenditures | | Private fixed investment | | | Exports and imports of goods and services | | Government consumption expenditures and gross investment | | | |
		Total	Excluding food and energy	Total	Nonresi-dential	Residential	Exports	Imports	Total	Federal	State and local	
1982												
1st quarter	44.9	41.3	37.5	44.6	38.3	64.2	22.7	19.0	53.0	55.4	51.0	43.6
2nd quarter	45.1	41.4	37.7	43.1	37.0	62.1	22.9	18.7	53.4	56.0	51.2	43.8
3rd quarter	44.9	41.7	38.1	42.1	36.0	62.0	21.8	19.5	53.7	56.7	51.2	44.0
4th quarter	45.0	42.5	38.9	42.1	35.3	67.0	20.8	18.8	54.6	58.1	51.6	44.0
1983												
1st quarter	45.6	42.9	39.4	43.1	34.8	78.5	21.2	19.2	55.1	59.0	51.7	44.6
2nd quarter	46.6	43.8	40.3	44.7	35.3	87.6	21.2	20.7	55.7	60.4	51.6	45.9
3rd quarter	47.5	44.5	41.0	47.2	36.8	96.2	21.6	22.3	56.6	61.8	52.1	47.1
4th quarter	48.5	45.2	41.7	49.9	39.0	100.2	22.0	23.4	55.6	59.7	52.1	48.1
1984												
1st quarter	49.5	45.6	42.3	51.4	40.3	103.2	22.5	25.3	56.3	60.4	52.8	49.4
2nd quarter	50.3	46.3	42.8	53.4	42.1	105.0	23.0	26.3	57.5	62.3	53.5	50.3
3rd quarter	50.8	46.6	43.2	54.5	43.4	103.8	23.5	27.0	58.0	62.3	54.4	50.9
4th quarter	51.2	47.2	43.9	55.5	44.4	103.9	24.0	27.8	59.1	64.0	54.9	51.3
1985												
1st quarter	51.8	48.1	44.7	56.0	44.9	104.1	24.1	27.2	59.8	64.8	55.6	51.7
2nd quarter	52.2	48.5	45.3	56.7	45.6	105.0	24.0	28.5	61.2	66.6	56.6	52.4
3rd quarter	53.0	49.4	46.2	56.4	45.1	107.0	23.7	28.2	62.7	68.7	57.5	53.2
4th quarter	53.4	49.6	46.2	57.5	45.9	109.3	24.4	29.3	62.9	68.6	58.0	53.7
1986												
1st quarter	53.9	50.0	46.7	57.7	45.4	113.8	25.1	29.3	63.4	68.5	59.0	54.0
2nd quarter	54.2	50.5	47.3	57.7	44.5	120.3	25.4	30.6	64.7	70.7	59.6	54.5
3rd quarter	54.7	51.5	48.3	57.4	44.0	121.9	26.0	31.4	66.1	73.3	60.2	55.1
4th quarter	55.0	51.8	48.6	57.9	44.4	122.3	27.0	31.7	65.8	72.1	60.4	55.2
1987												
1st quarter	55.4	51.8	48.7	56.9	43.4	122.1	27.0	31.5	66.2	72.7	60.7	55.6
2nd quarter	56.0	52.5	49.4	57.8	44.3	122.5	28.1	32.2	66.8	73.9	60.8	56.2
3rd quarter	56.5	53.1	50.1	58.8	45.5	121.5	29.3	32.9	66.9	74.0	61.0	56.6
4th quarter	57.5	53.2	50.2	58.7	45.4	121.7	30.4	33.6	67.7	74.7	61.8	57.5
1988												
1st quarter	57.8	54.2	51.1	58.8	45.8	119.5	32.1	33.5	67.3	72.9	62.5	57.5
2nd quarter	58.5	54.6	51.5	59.9	46.8	121.0	33.0	33.1	67.5	72.4	63.3	58.1
3rd quarter	58.9	55.0	51.9	60.2	47.1	121.1	33.6	33.9	67.6	72.1	63.6	58.4
4th quarter	59.7	55.7	52.6	60.9	47.8	121.8	34.7	34.9	68.8	74.0	64.4	59.2
1989												
1st quarter	60.3	55.9	52.9	61.4	48.5	120.7	35.7	35.1	68.5	72.6	64.9	59.7
2nd quarter	60.7	56.2	53.2	61.5	49.2	116.9	37.3	35.2	69.7	74.3	65.6	60.0
3rd quarter	61.2	56.8	53.8	62.6	50.4	116.3	37.6	35.2	70.2	74.8	66.2	60.3
4th quarter	61.3	57.0	53.9	61.8	49.9	113.9	38.2	35.8	70.6	74.5	67.1	60.5
1990												
1st quarter	62.0	57.5	54.7	62.5	50.6	114.9	39.9	37.0	71.7	75.7	68.1	61.1
2nd quarter	62.2	57.7	54.7	61.3	49.9	110.3	40.4	36.9	71.9	75.9	68.3	61.3
3rd quarter	62.2	57.9	54.9	60.8	50.3	104.4	40.7	36.7	71.9	75.2	68.7	61.2
4th quarter	61.7	57.5	54.5	59.2	49.5	98.4	41.0	35.8	72.5	75.7	69.5	60.5
1991												
1st quarter	61.4	57.3	54.4	57.6	48.5	93.2	41.3	35.4	72.9	76.4	69.6	60.1
2nd quarter	61.9	57.7	54.7	57.8	48.2	96.1	42.8	36.0	73.1	76.6	69.9	60.5
3rd quarter	62.2	58.0	55.0	57.8	47.8	99.3	43.8	37.0	72.9	75.4	70.3	60.8
4th quarter	62.5	58.0	55.2	58.1	47.8	101.3	44.8	37.8	72.6	74.1	70.8	61.0
1992												
1st quarter	63.2	59.1	56.4	58.7	47.6	107.1	45.6	38.1	73.2	74.2	71.7	61.7
2nd quarter	63.9	59.5	56.7	60.7	49.2	110.7	45.6	38.7	73.1	74.2	71.6	62.5
3rd quarter	64.5	60.2	57.5	61.4	49.9	110.8	46.6	39.3	73.4	75.0	71.6	63.1
4th quarter	65.2	60.9	58.2	63.2	51.2	115.0	46.8	40.3	73.3	74.7	71.6	63.8
1993												
1st quarter	65.3	61.1	58.4	63.6	51.8	115.1	46.9	41.1	72.4	72.5	71.8	64.1
2nd quarter	65.7	61.6	59.0	64.8	52.8	116.6	47.5	42.0	72.5	71.9	72.4	64.5
3rd quarter	66.0	62.3	59.6	65.8	53.2	121.0	47.4	42.5	72.7	71.7	72.8	64.9
4th quarter	66.9	62.9	60.2	68.4	55.1	127.2	48.9	44.2	72.8	71.6	73.1	65.8
1994												
1st quarter	67.5	63.6	61.0	69.3	55.7	129.1	49.4	45.3	71.9	69.1	73.4	66.6
2nd quarter	68.5	64.1	61.4	70.7	56.6	133.3	51.0	47.0	72.4	69.0	74.2	67.5
3rd quarter	68.9	64.6	62.0	71.2	57.5	131.3	52.9	48.3	73.6	70.7	75.1	67.9
4th quarter	69.6	65.3	62.8	73.0	59.8	129.3	54.2	49.6	72.9	68.7	75.4	68.7
1995												
1st quarter	69.9	65.5	63.0	74.5	62.0	126.4	55.2	50.7	73.1	68.3	76.0	69.0
2nd quarter	70.1	66.0	63.6	74.5	62.6	122.5	56.0	51.2	73.4	68.4	76.6	69.2
3rd quarter	70.7	66.7	64.2	75.5	63.0	127.0	58.4	51.4	73.2	67.8	76.6	69.5
4th quarter	71.2	67.1	64.7	77.0	64.3	129.5	59.2	52.0	72.6	65.8	77.0	70.0
1996												
1st quarter	71.7	67.7	65.3	79.0	65.9	132.8	59.9	53.7	72.7	66.3	76.9	70.6
2nd quarter	73.0	68.5	66.1	81.4	67.6	138.6	60.9	54.9	73.9	67.5	78.0	71.9
3rd quarter	73.6	68.9	66.7	83.3	69.8	138.3	61.4	56.7	74.0	66.8	78.7	72.8
4th quarter	74.4	69.4	67.2	84.6	71.5	136.8	65.2	57.8	74.5	66.4	79.9	73.2

Table 1-5B. Chain-Type Quantity Indexes for Gross Domestic Product and Domestic Purchases: Historical—*Continued*

(Index numbers, 2009 = 100.)   **NIPA Tables 1.1.3, 1.4.3, 2.3.3**

Year and quarter	Gross domestic product, total	Personal consumption expenditures		Private fixed investment			Exports and imports of goods and services		Government consumption expenditures and gross investment			Gross domestic purchases
		Total	Excluding food and energy	Total	Nonresi-dential	Residential	Exports	Imports	Total	Federal	State and local	
1997												
1st quarter	75.0	70.2	68.0	86.1	73.1	137.5	66.5	60.3	74.5	65.3	80.7	74.0
2nd quarter	76.1	70.5	68.3	87.8	74.7	139.4	69.1	62.3	75.3	66.7	81.0	75.1
3rd quarter	77.1	71.7	69.7	90.9	78.0	140.7	70.7	64.6	75.4	66.5	81.3	76.2
4th quarter	77.7	72.5	70.5	91.6	78.5	142.2	70.6	66.0	75.5	66.4	81.6	77.0
1998												
1st quarter	78.4	73.3	71.4	94.3	81.0	145.2	71.0	68.5	75.1	64.5	82.2	78.0
2nd quarter	79.2	74.6	72.7	97.4	83.7	150.2	70.2	70.1	76.6	66.1	83.7	79.1
3rd quarter	80.2	75.6	73.7	99.3	85.0	154.6	69.9	71.0	77.3	65.7	85.2	80.3
4th quarter	81.6	76.7	75.0	102.0	87.4	158.2	72.5	73.3	78.0	66.4	85.9	81.6
1999												
1st quarter	82.3	77.5	75.8	103.7	89.3	158.8	72.1	75.2	78.3	65.8	86.8	82.6
2nd quarter	83.0	78.7	76.9	106.2	91.7	161.3	72.9	77.5	78.7	66.1	87.3	83.5
3rd quarter	84.1	79.6	77.9	108.6	94.2	162.5	74.7	80.3	79.6	67.3	88.1	84.7
4th quarter	85.5	80.7	79.1	109.1	94.6	163.7	76.7	82.1	80.8	68.6	89.1	86.1
2000												
1st quarter	85.8	82.0	80.7	112.2	97.9	164.5	78.0	85.5	80.2	66.1	89.8	86.7
2nd quarter	87.4	82.7	81.3	114.7	101.0	163.7	80.1	87.8	81.1	68.4	89.8	88.4
3rd quarter	87.5	83.5	82.2	115.1	102.1	161.1	82.0	90.9	81.0	67.3	90.4	88.7
4th quarter	88.0	84.3	82.8	115.4	102.4	161.3	81.3	91.1	81.2	66.9	91.0	89.2
2001												
1st quarter	87.7	84.6	83.2	114.8	101.6	162.0	80.3	89.5	82.4	68.4	92.1	88.9
2nd quarter	88.2	84.8	83.6	113.3	99.2	164.5	77.6	86.9	84.1	69.7	93.9	89.3
3rd quarter	87.9	85.1	83.9	112.4	98.0	165.5	73.7	84.8	84.0	70.3	93.4	89.2
4th quarter	88.1	86.4	85.3	109.8	95.1	164.4	71.6	83.8	85.2	70.8	95.1	89.5
2002												
1st quarter	88.9	86.6	85.7	109.1	93.2	169.8	72.8	85.9	86.5	72.6	96.0	90.5
2nd quarter	89.4	87.1	86.1	108.9	91.9	174.1	74.8	88.8	87.3	74.3	96.2	91.1
3rd quarter	89.9	87.7	86.7	108.5	91.4	174.6	75.3	90.2	88.0	75.5	96.5	91.6
4th quarter	89.9	88.1	87.0	108.2	90.3	177.7	74.7	92.0	88.6	76.8	96.6	92.0
2003												
1st quarter	90.4	88.5	87.5	108.9	90.5	181.0	73.9	90.8	88.3	76.9	96.1	92.3
2nd quarter	91.2	89.5	88.6	111.3	92.7	183.8	73.7	92.0	89.7	80.7	95.7	93.4
3rd quarter	92.8	90.8	90.0	114.8	94.6	194.4	75.6	93.0	89.7	80.2	96.1	94.8
4th quarter	93.8	91.5	90.7	117.0	95.9	200.1	79.1	96.5	90.2	81.8	95.8	95.9
2004												
1st quarter	94.4	92.4	91.6	116.6	94.9	202.5	81.1	99.2	90.4	82.4	95.8	96.6
2nd quarter	95.1	93.0	92.3	119.6	97.0	208.9	82.2	102.9	91.0	83.2	96.1	97.7
3rd quarter	95.9	93.9	93.3	122.0	99.6	210.4	82.7	104.2	91.3	84.6	95.7	98.6
4th quarter	96.7	94.8	94.2	124.3	101.7	213.3	84.7	106.8	90.9	83.9	95.5	99.5
2005												
1st quarter	97.8	95.6	94.9	126.3	103.0	218.3	85.7	107.8	91.1	84.4	95.5	100.6
2nd quarter	98.3	96.6	96.1	128.3	104.4	222.4	87.5	108.9	91.3	84.6	95.7	101.1
3rd quarter	99.1	97.3	96.8	130.3	106.4	224.8	87.6	109.2	92.0	86.1	95.8	101.9
4th quarter	99.7	97.7	97.1	130.6	106.8	224.3	89.9	112.5	91.6	84.8	96.1	102.6
2006												
1st quarter	100.9	98.8	98.5	133.3	110.7	222.2	93.3	114.9	92.4	87.0	95.9	103.7
2nd quarter	101.2	99.3	98.9	132.1	112.1	211.1	95.1	116.2	92.7	86.9	96.6	104.0
3rd quarter	101.3	99.9	99.5	130.8	113.4	199.3	94.8	117.2	92.9	86.9	96.9	104.3
4th quarter	102.1	100.9	100.6	129.5	114.2	190.0	98.7	117.0	93.5	87.8	97.3	104.6
2007												
1st quarter	102.2	101.5	101.1	129.3	116.1	181.3	100.2	119.0	93.3	86.6	97.7	104.8
2nd quarter	102.9	101.8	101.6	129.6	118.4	174.0	101.9	119.5	94.1	88.0	98.1	105.4
3rd quarter	103.6	102.2	102.1	128.8	120.3	163.0	105.5	119.6	94.8	89.6	98.1	105.7
4th quarter	104.0	102.4	102.4	127.7	122.3	149.4	108.4	117.8	95.2	90.1	98.5	105.5
2008												
1st quarter	103.3	102.1	102.1	125.3	122.3	137.7	109.8	118.9	95.6	91.6	98.2	104.8
2nd quarter	103.8	102.3	102.4	123.6	121.6	131.6	112.9	117.8	96.3	93.3	98.3	104.8
3rd quarter	103.3	101.5	101.9	119.7	118.3	125.2	111.9	115.6	97.6	96.0	98.7	104.1
4th quarter	101.1	100.3	100.5	111.8	111.4	113.1	105.3	110.9	98.3	97.7	98.7	102.0
2009												
1st quarter	99.7	100.0	100.0	103.1	103.4	102.2	96.9	100.3	98.4	96.9	99.4	100.1
2nd quarter	99.6	99.6	99.5	99.3	100.0	96.1	97.1	96.0	100.2	100.1	100.3	99.4
3rd quarter	99.9	100.2	100.2	99.1	98.8	100.8	100.3	99.6	100.8	101.5	100.3	99.8
4th quarter	100.8	100.2	100.2	98.4	97.9	100.9	105.7	104.0	100.6	101.5	100.0	100.7
2010												
1st quarter	101.2	100.7	100.7	98.6	98.9	97.6	107.4	107.0	99.8	102.5	98.1	101.4
2nd quarter	102.2	101.5	101.6	101.8	101.6	102.9	109.8	112.0	100.6	104.6	97.9	102.7
3rd quarter	102.9	102.2	102.3	101.7	103.6	93.8	112.7	115.9	100.5	105.5	97.2	103.6
4th quarter	103.6	103.3	103.4	103.8	105.8	95.6	116.0	116.2	99.4	104.8	95.9	104.0
2011												
1st quarter	103.3	103.8	104.1	103.7	105.6	96.0	117.1	117.0	97.5	102.0	94.6	103.7
2nd quarter	104.1	104.2	104.6	105.9	108.1	96.7	118.5	117.2	97.2	102.4	93.8	104.3
3rd quarter	104.5	104.8	105.2	109.6	112.3	98.1	120.5	118.6	96.6	101.5	93.3	104.6
4th quarter	105.7	105.4	106.1	112.2	114.9	101.0	121.3	120.3	96.2	100.7	93.2	106.0

Table 1-5B. Chain-Type Quantity Indexes for Gross Domestic Product and Domestic Purchases: Historical—*Continued*

(Index numbers, 2009 = 100.)   **NIPA Tables 1.1.3, 1.4.3, 2.3.3**

Year and quarter	Gross domestic product, total	Personal consumption expenditures		Private fixed investment			Exports and imports of goods and services		Government consumption expenditures and gross investment			Gross domestic purchases
		Total	Excluding food and energy	Total	Nonresi-dential	Residential	Exports	Imports	Total	Federal	State and local	
2012												
1st quarter	106.7	106.1	107.1	114.6	116.6	106.4	122.6	120.5	95.9	100.1	93.1	106.8
2nd quarter	107.0	106.6	107.3	115.9	117.8	107.9	123.7	121.2	95.9	100.1	93.2	107.1
3rd quarter	107.7	107.1	107.8	116.7	117.9	111.5	123.9	121.4	96.8	102.2	93.2	107.8
4th quarter	107.8	107.5	108.5	119.9	120.7	116.6	124.2	120.4	95.1	98.5	93.0	107.7

Table 1-6A. Chain-Type Price Indexes for Gross Domestic Product and Domestic Purchases: Recent Data

(Index numbers, 2009 = 100.)   **NIPA Tables 1.1.4, 1.6.4, 2.3.4**

Year and quarter	Gross domestic product, total	Personal consumption expenditures		Private fixed investment			Exports and imports of goods and services		Government consumption expenditures and gross investment			Gross domestic purchases
		Total	Excluding food and energy	Total	Nonresi-dential	Residential	Exports	Imports	Total	Federal	State and local	
1950	13.7	14.1	14.3	18.2	22.2	10.7	21.2	16.4	8.9	11.3	7.1	13.5
1951	14.7	15.1	15.2	19.7	24.3	11.5	24.0	19.9	9.4	11.7	7.8	14.4
1952	15.0	15.4	15.5	20.2	24.8	11.8	24.1	19.1	9.6	11.8	8.1	14.7
1953	15.2	15.6	15.8	20.3	25.1	11.9	24.1	18.3	9.8	11.9	8.3	14.9
1954	15.3	15.7	16.0	20.5	25.3	12.0	23.7	18.6	10.0	12.2	8.4	15.1
1955	15.6	15.8	16.1	20.8	25.7	12.2	23.9	18.5	10.4	12.8	8.6	15.3
1956	16.1	16.1	16.5	22.0	27.6	12.5	24.7	18.8	10.9	13.4	9.2	15.8
1957	16.7	16.6	17.0	22.8	28.9	12.5	25.7	19.0	11.4	14.0	9.5	16.3
1958	17.1	17.0	17.4	22.9	29.1	12.5	25.4	18.2	11.7	14.6	9.7	16.7
1959	17.3	17.3	17.8	23.1	29.5	12.6	25.5	18.4	11.9	14.7	9.9	16.9
1960	17.5	17.5	18.1	23.3	29.7	12.6	25.8	18.6	12.0	14.8	10.1	17.1
1961	17.7	17.7	18.3	23.2	29.6	12.7	26.2	18.6	12.2	15.0	10.3	17.3
1962	17.9	17.9	18.6	23.2	29.6	12.7	26.3	18.3	12.5	15.2	10.6	17.5
1963	18.1	18.1	18.8	23.2	29.6	12.6	26.2	18.7	12.8	15.6	10.8	17.7
1964	18.4	18.4	19.1	23.3	29.8	12.7	26.4	19.1	13.1	16.1	11.1	18.0
1965	18.7	18.7	19.3	23.7	30.2	13.0	27.3	19.4	13.5	16.5	11.4	18.3
1966	19.3	19.2	19.8	24.2	30.6	13.5	28.1	19.8	14.0	17.0	11.9	18.8
1967	19.8	19.6	20.4	24.9	31.4	14.0	29.2	19.9	14.5	17.4	12.5	19.3
1968	20.7	20.4	21.2	25.9	32.5	14.7	29.8	20.2	15.3	18.3	13.3	20.2
1969	21.7	21.3	22.2	27.2	33.9	15.7	30.8	20.7	16.2	19.2	14.2	21.1
1970	22.8	22.3	23.3	28.3	35.5	16.2	32.0	21.9	17.4	20.7	15.3	22.3
1971	24.0	23.3	24.4	29.8	37.1	17.2	33.2	23.3	18.8	22.4	16.5	23.4
1972	25.0	24.1	25.2	31.0	38.4	18.2	34.7	24.9	20.2	24.4	17.6	24.5
1973	26.4	25.4	26.1	32.8	40.0	19.9	39.3	29.3	21.6	26.0	18.7	25.9
1974	28.8	28.0	28.2	36.0	43.8	21.9	48.4	41.9	23.6	28.0	20.8	28.5
1975	31.4	30.3	30.6	40.4	49.6	23.9	53.4	45.3	25.8	30.5	22.8	31.1
1976	33.2	32.0	32.4	42.7	52.3	25.5	55.1	46.7	27.2	32.4	23.9	32.8
1977	35.2	34.1	34.5	46.0	55.8	28.1	57.4	50.8	28.9	34.3	25.4	35.0
1978	37.7	36.5	36.8	49.8	59.5	31.5	60.9	54.4	30.7	36.4	27.0	37.5
1979	40.8	39.7	39.5	54.3	64.3	35.1	68.2	63.7	33.2	39.0	29.4	40.7
1980	44.5	44.0	43.1	59.4	70.0	38.9	75.1	79.4	36.6	42.9	32.6	45.0
1981	48.7	47.9	46.9	64.8	76.7	42.0	80.7	83.6	40.2	46.9	35.8	49.1
1982	51.6	50.6	49.9	68.5	81.0	44.3	81.1	80.8	42.8	50.2	38.0	51.9
1983	53.7	52.7	52.5	68.7	80.9	45.3	81.4	77.8	44.5	51.8	39.7	53.7
1984	55.6	54.7	54.6	69.4	81.2	46.7	82.1	77.1	46.3	53.8	41.4	55.5
1985	57.3	56.7	56.9	70.4	82.0	48.0	79.7	74.6	47.7	54.9	43.1	57.2
1986	58.5	57.9	58.8	72.1	83.4	50.1	78.3	74.6	48.5	55.2	44.3	58.3
1987	59.9	59.6	60.7	73.6	84.4	52.2	80.1	79.1	49.9	55.7	46.4	60.0
1988	62.0	62.0	63.3	75.6	86.5	54.1	84.2	82.9	51.5	57.4	48.0	62.1
1989	64.5	64.6	65.9	77.6	88.5	55.8	85.6	84.7	53.5	58.9	50.3	64.5
1990	66.8	67.4	68.5	79.3	90.4	57.1	86.1	87.1	55.7	60.8	52.8	67.0
1991	69.1	69.7	70.9	80.7	92.1	57.8	87.0	86.4	57.7	63.1	54.6	69.1
1992	70.6	71.5	73.0	80.7	91.8	58.6	86.6	86.4	59.5	64.6	56.6	70.7
1993	72.3	73.3	75.0	81.6	92.0	60.9	86.7	85.8	60.9	66.0	58.0	72.3
1994	73.9	74.8	76.7	82.9	92.7	63.2	87.8	86.6	62.5	67.8	59.6	73.8
1995	75.4	76.4	78.3	84.2	93.6	65.4	89.7	89.0	64.3	69.9	61.2	75.4
1996	76.8	78.0	79.8	84.3	93.0	66.8	88.5	87.4	65.7	71.1	62.6	76.7
1997	78.1	79.3	81.2	84.4	92.5	68.4	87.0	84.4	66.9	72.2	64.0	77.9
1998	78.9	79.9	82.2	84.0	91.0	70.2	84.9	79.8	68.1	73.1	65.3	78.4
1999	80.1	81.1	83.3	84.2	90.2	72.9	84.2	80.4	70.4	74.9	67.9	79.6
2000	81.9	83.1	84.7	85.5	90.7	76.1	86.0	84.0	73.4	77.3	71.2	81.6
2001	83.8	84.7	86.3	86.3	90.4	79.7	85.7	82.0	75.6	78.7	73.6	83.2
2002	85.1	85.9	87.7	86.6	90.0	81.7	85.3	81.1	77.4	81.3	75.1	84.4
2003	86.8	87.6	89.0	87.7	89.9	85.5	87.2	84.0	80.3	84.8	77.8	86.2
2004	89.1	89.7	90.8	90.5	91.1	91.5	90.4	88.1	83.9	87.7	81.7	88.7
2005	92.0	92.3	92.7	94.5	93.8	98.1	94.4	93.6	88.2	91.4	86.3	91.9
2006	94.8	94.7	94.8	98.2	96.6	103.8	97.8	97.5	92.1	94.4	90.7	94.8
2007	97.3	97.1	96.8	100.0	98.6	105.2	101.1	101.1	96.1	97.3	95.4	97.4
2008	99.2	100.1	98.8	101.0	100.3	103.6	105.8	111.7	100.3	100.3	100.3	100.2
2009	100.0	100.0	100.0	100.0	100.0	100.0	100.0	100.0	100.0	100.0	100.0	100.0
2010	101.2	101.7	101.3	99.2	99.1	99.6	104.4	106.0	102.7	102.6	102.7	101.5
2011	103.2	104.1	102.7	100.5	100.5	100.4	111.1	114.3	105.6	105.3	105.7	103.9
2012	105.0	106.0	104.6	101.9	102.0	101.2	112.2	114.9	106.9	106.2	107.4	105.6
2010												
1st quarter	100.5	101.3	100.9	99.0	98.7	100.0	102.7	106.1	101.7	101.7	101.6	101.0
2nd quarter	101.0	101.4	101.2	99.0	99.0	99.3	103.9	105.6	102.4	102.5	102.4	101.3
3rd quarter	101.4	101.7	101.4	99.1	99.1	99.3	104.3	105.0	102.9	102.9	103.0	101.6
4th quarter	101.9	102.2	101.6	99.6	99.5	99.9	106.7	107.4	103.7	103.4	103.8	102.2
2011												
1st quarter	102.4	103.0	102.0	99.9	99.9	100.1	109.4	111.8	104.6	104.5	104.6	102.9
2nd quarter	103.0	103.9	102.5	100.5	100.5	100.5	111.7	115.2	105.6	105.5	105.7	103.8
3rd quarter	103.7	104.5	103.0	100.7	100.8	100.5	112.3	115.1	106.1	105.8	106.2	104.3
4th quarter	103.8	104.9	103.5	100.9	101.0	100.5	111.2	114.9	105.9	105.6	106.2	104.5
2012												
1st quarter	104.3	105.5	104.0	101.3	101.5	100.3	112.0	116.1	106.7	106.0	107.2	105.1
2nd quarter	104.8	105.8	104.5	101.7	101.9	100.7	112.1	115.0	106.8	106.2	107.2	105.4
3rd quarter	105.3	106.2	104.8	102.0	102.2	101.5	112.1	113.6	106.9	106.2	107.3	105.7
4th quarter	105.6	106.6	105.2	102.4	102.4	102.5	112.5	114.7	107.2	106.4	107.8	106.2

Table 1-6B. Chain-Type Price Indexes for Gross Domestic Product and Domestic Purchases: Historical

(Index numbers, 2009 = 100.)   NIPA Tables 1.1.4, 1.6.4, 2.3.4

Year and quarter	Gross domestic product, total	Personal consumption expenditures		Private fixed investment			Exports and imports of goods and services		Government consumption expenditures and gross investment			Gross domestic purchases
		Total	Excluding food and energy	Total	Nonresidential	Residential	Exports	Imports	Total	Federal	State and local	
1929	9.9	9.9	10.1	10.3	13.2	5.1	14.7	10.5	5.8	7.3	4.0	9.7
1930	9.5	9.5	9.7	9.9	12.5	5.0	13.3	9.0	5.6	6.9	3.9	9.3
1931	8.6	8.5	8.9	9.1	11.7	4.6	10.5	7.3	5.4	6.9	3.6	8.4
1932	7.6	7.5	7.9	8.1	10.6	3.7	9.1	5.8	4.9	6.6	3.3	7.4
1933	7.4	7.2	7.5	7.9	10.3	3.7	9.1	5.6	5.0	6.6	3.4	7.2
1934	7.8	7.5	7.7	8.3	10.7	4.1	10.5	6.3	5.4	7.0	3.6	7.5
1935	7.9	7.7	7.8	8.3	10.8	4.0	10.8	6.4	5.4	7.1	3.7	7.7
1936	8.0	7.8	7.9	8.4	10.8	4.2	11.2	6.9	5.6	7.7	3.7	7.8
1937	8.3	8.1	8.2	9.1	11.6	4.6	11.9	7.7	5.7	7.8	3.8	8.1
1938	8.2	7.9	8.2	9.2	11.7	4.8	11.4	7.1	5.8	7.9	3.8	7.9
1939	8.0	7.8	8.1	9.2	11.6	4.8	11.2	7.5	5.7	7.8	3.7	7.8
1940	8.1	7.9	8.2	9.4	11.9	4.9	12.2	8.0	5.6	7.5	3.8	7.9
1941	8.7	8.4	8.6	10.1	12.6	5.4	13.3	8.4	6.0	7.9	4.0	8.4
1942	9.4	9.4	9.6	11.1	14.0	5.8	16.1	9.6	6.0	7.9	4.4	9.1
1943	9.8	10.3	10.3	11.7	14.6	6.3	17.6	10.4	6.0	7.8	4.7	9.5
1944	10.1	10.9	11.1	12.1	15.0	6.9	19.8	10.9	6.0	7.7	4.9	9.7
1945	10.3	11.3	11.6	12.5	15.4	7.3	19.6	11.2	6.0	7.7	5.1	10.0
1946	11.6	12.1	12.3	13.7	17.0	8.0	19.0	12.5	7.6	10.1	5.6	11.3
1947	12.9	13.3	13.3	16.1	19.7	9.5	22.0	14.9	8.3	10.9	6.2	12.6
1948	13.6	14.1	14.1	17.4	21.3	10.3	23.2	16.2	8.6	10.8	7.0	13.3
1949	13.6	14.0	14.1	17.8	21.8	10.5	21.8	15.5	8.8	11.2	7.1	13.3
1947												
1st quarter	12.6	13.0	...	15.4	18.9	9.0	20.2	13.7	8.4	11.2	6.1	12.3
2nd quarter	12.8	13.1	...	15.9	19.4	9.5	21.7	14.7	8.4	11.0	6.2	12.5
3rd quarter	13.0	13.4	...	16.3	20.0	9.7	22.8	15.4	8.2	10.6	6.3	12.6
4th quarter	13.2	13.7	...	16.7	20.3	9.9	23.4	16.0	8.3	10.6	6.5	12.9
1948												
1st quarter	13.4	13.9	...	16.8	20.4	10.1	23.5	16.3	8.4	10.7	6.7	13.1
2nd quarter	13.6	14.0	...	17.2	21.0	10.2	23.4	16.4	8.5	10.7	6.9	13.2
3rd quarter	13.8	14.2	...	17.7	21.7	10.5	23.1	16.2	8.7	10.8	7.1	13.5
4th quarter	13.8	14.2	...	17.9	22.0	10.5	22.8	16.0	8.8	10.9	7.2	13.5
1949												
1st quarter	13.7	14.1	...	17.9	21.9	10.6	22.3	15.6	8.9	11.2	7.2	13.4
2nd quarter	13.7	14.0	...	17.9	21.8	10.6	21.9	15.5	8.8	11.2	7.0	13.3
3rd quarter	13.5	13.9	...	17.7	21.7	10.3	21.6	15.4	8.8	11.0	7.0	13.2
4th quarter	13.6	13.9	...	17.6	21.6	10.4	21.4	15.4	8.9	11.3	7.0	13.3
1950												
1st quarter	13.5	13.9	...	17.6	21.6	10.3	21.0	15.7	8.8	11.3	6.9	13.2
2nd quarter	13.6	13.9	...	17.9	21.9	10.6	21.1	16.1	8.8	11.2	7.0	13.3
3rd quarter	13.8	14.2	...	18.4	22.3	11.0	21.2	16.6	9.0	11.3	7.2	13.6
4th quarter	14.1	14.5	...	18.7	23.1	11.0	21.6	17.4	9.0	11.3	7.4	13.8
1951												
1st quarter	14.5	14.9	...	19.4	23.8	11.3	22.9	18.8	9.4	11.8	7.6	14.3
2nd quarter	14.6	15.1	...	19.6	24.2	11.5	23.8	19.8	9.4	11.6	7.7	14.4
3rd quarter	14.7	15.1	...	19.8	24.4	11.5	24.4	20.4	9.4	11.6	7.9	14.4
4th quarter	14.9	15.3	...	20.0	24.7	11.6	24.8	20.5	9.6	11.8	8.0	14.6
1952												
1st quarter	14.9	15.4	...	20.1	24.8	11.7	24.2	19.6	9.5	11.6	8.0	14.6
2nd quarter	14.9	15.4	...	20.2	24.9	11.8	24.2	19.3	9.6	11.8	8.1	14.7
3rd quarter	15.1	15.5	...	20.2	24.8	11.9	24.1	19.0	9.7	11.9	8.3	14.8
4th quarter	15.1	15.5	...	20.2	24.8	11.8	24.1	18.7	9.8	12.1	8.3	14.8
1953												
1st quarter	15.1	15.5	...	20.2	24.8	11.9	24.2	18.5	9.7	11.9	8.3	14.8
2nd quarter	15.2	15.6	...	20.3	25.0	11.9	24.1	18.3	9.8	11.9	8.3	14.9
3rd quarter	15.2	15.6	...	20.5	25.2	12.0	24.0	18.2	9.7	11.9	8.3	14.9
4th quarter	15.3	15.7	...	20.4	25.2	11.9	23.9	18.2	9.8	12.0	8.3	15.0
1954												
1st quarter	15.3	15.8	...	20.4	25.3	11.9	23.8	18.4	9.8	12.1	8.3	15.0
2nd quarter	15.4	15.8	...	20.5	25.4	11.9	23.7	18.5	9.9	12.2	8.4	15.1
3rd quarter	15.3	15.7	...	20.5	25.2	12.0	23.7	18.6	10.0	12.2	8.5	15.1
4th quarter	15.4	15.7	...	20.5	25.3	12.0	23.7	18.7	10.1	12.4	8.5	15.1
1955												
1st quarter	15.4	15.8	...	20.6	25.2	12.1	23.8	18.4	10.1	12.5	8.5	15.1
2nd quarter	15.5	15.8	...	20.7	25.4	12.2	23.9	18.4	10.3	12.8	8.5	15.2
3rd quarter	15.6	15.8	...	20.9	25.8	12.3	24.0	18.5	10.4	12.9	8.7	15.3
4th quarter	15.7	15.9	...	21.2	26.3	12.3	24.2	18.5	10.5	13.0	8.8	15.4
1956												
1st quarter	15.9	15.9	...	21.6	27.0	12.4	24.3	18.6	10.7	13.2	9.0	15.6
2nd quarter	16.0	16.1	...	21.9	27.2	12.6	24.6	18.7	10.9	13.4	9.1	15.7
3rd quarter	16.2	16.2	...	22.2	27.9	12.6	24.9	18.8	11.0	13.5	9.2	15.9
4th quarter	16.3	16.3	...	22.4	28.2	12.5	25.2	19.0	11.1	13.6	9.3	16.0
1957												
1st quarter	16.5	16.4	...	22.6	28.7	12.5	25.5	19.1	11.2	13.9	9.4	16.1
2nd quarter	16.6	16.6	...	22.7	28.8	12.5	25.7	19.1	11.4	14.0	9.6	16.3
3rd quarter	16.7	16.7	...	22.9	29.0	12.6	25.8	19.0	11.4	14.1	9.6	16.4
4th quarter	16.8	16.8	...	23.0	29.2	12.6	25.7	18.8	11.5	14.2	9.6	16.5
1958												
1st quarter	17.0	17.0	...	22.8	29.0	12.5	25.5	18.4	11.6	14.4	9.6	16.6
2nd quarter	17.0	17.0	...	22.9	29.1	12.5	25.4	18.2	11.7	14.5	9.7	16.7
3rd quarter	17.1	17.0	...	22.9	29.2	12.5	25.4	18.2	11.8	14.6	9.7	16.7
4th quarter	17.1	17.0	...	23.0	29.3	12.5	25.4	18.2	11.8	14.7	9.8	16.7

. . . = Not available.

Table 1-6B. Chain-Type Price Indexes for Gross Domestic Product and Domestic Purchases: Historical—*Continued*

(Index numbers, 2009 = 100.) **NIPA Tables 1.1.4, 1.6.4, 2.3.4**

Year and quarter	Gross domestic product, total	Gross domestic product Personal consumption expenditures Total	Excluding food and energy	Private fixed investment Total	Nonresidential	Residential	Exports and imports of goods and services Exports	Imports	Government consumption expenditures and gross investment Total	Federal	State and local	Gross domestic purchases
1959												
1st quarter	17.2	17.1	17.6	23.0	29.3	12.5	25.3	18.2	11.9	14.7	9.9	16.8
2nd quarter	17.2	17.2	17.7	23.1	29.5	12.6	25.3	18.3	11.9	14.7	9.9	16.9
3rd quarter	17.3	17.3	17.8	23.2	29.6	12.6	25.5	18.4	11.9	14.7	9.9	16.9
4th quarter	17.4	17.4	17.9	23.2	29.7	12.6	25.8	18.6	11.9	14.7	9.9	17.0
1960												
1st quarter	17.4	17.4	18.0	23.2	29.7	12.6	25.8	18.5	11.9	14.7	10.0	17.0
2nd quarter	17.5	17.5	18.0	23.3	29.7	12.6	25.8	18.5	11.9	14.7	10.0	17.1
3rd quarter	17.6	17.6	18.1	23.3	29.7	12.6	25.9	18.6	12.1	14.9	10.1	17.2
4th quarter	17.6	17.7	18.2	23.2	29.7	12.7	25.8	18.6	12.2	15.0	10.1	17.2
1961												
1st quarter	17.7	17.7	18.2	23.2	29.6	12.6	25.9	18.6	12.2	15.0	10.2	17.3
2nd quarter	17.7	17.7	18.3	23.2	29.6	12.7	26.3	18.6	12.2	15.0	10.3	17.3
3rd quarter	17.7	17.8	18.4	23.2	29.6	12.7	26.2	18.6	12.2	15.0	10.4	17.3
4th quarter	17.8	17.8	18.4	23.2	29.6	12.7	26.4	18.5	12.3	15.0	10.4	17.4
1962												
1st quarter	17.9	17.9	18.5	23.2	29.6	12.7	26.5	18.3	12.4	15.1	10.6	17.4
2nd quarter	17.9	17.9	18.5	23.2	29.6	12.7	26.2	18.4	12.5	15.2	10.6	17.5
3rd quarter	18.0	18.0	18.6	23.2	29.6	12.7	26.2	18.3	12.5	15.3	10.6	17.5
4th quarter	18.0	18.0	18.6	23.2	29.6	12.7	26.2	18.4	12.5	15.3	10.7	17.6
1963												
1st quarter	18.1	18.1	18.7	23.2	29.6	12.7	26.3	18.6	12.7	15.6	10.8	17.7
2nd quarter	18.1	18.1	18.8	23.2	29.6	12.6	26.2	18.6	12.8	15.6	10.8	17.7
3rd quarter	18.1	18.2	18.8	23.1	29.6	12.5	26.2	18.8	12.7	15.4	10.9	17.7
4th quarter	18.2	18.2	18.9	23.2	29.7	12.6	26.2	18.9	12.9	15.8	10.9	17.8
1964												
1st quarter	18.3	18.3	19.0	23.1	29.7	12.4	26.3	19.0	13.0	16.0	11.0	17.9
2nd quarter	18.4	18.4	19.1	23.3	29.8	12.6	26.3	19.1	13.1	16.0	11.0	18.0
3rd quarter	18.4	18.4	19.1	23.3	29.8	12.7	26.5	19.1	13.2	16.2	11.1	18.0
4th quarter	18.5	18.5	19.2	23.6	30.0	13.0	26.8	19.2	13.2	16.2	11.1	18.1
1965												
1st quarter	18.6	18.6	19.2	23.6	30.0	12.9	27.4	19.3	13.3	16.2	11.3	18.2
2nd quarter	18.7	18.7	19.3	23.6	30.1	13.0	27.3	19.2	13.4	16.3	11.3	18.3
3rd quarter	18.8	18.7	19.4	23.7	30.2	12.9	27.3	19.4	13.5	16.5	11.4	18.4
4th quarter	18.9	18.8	19.4	24.0	30.3	13.3	27.2	19.6	13.7	16.9	11.5	18.5
1966												
1st quarter	19.0	18.9	19.5	23.9	30.3	13.1	27.7	19.7	13.8	16.9	11.7	18.6
2nd quarter	19.2	19.1	19.7	24.2	30.6	13.6	27.9	19.9	13.9	16.9	11.9	18.8
3rd quarter	19.4	19.2	19.8	24.2	30.7	13.5	28.2	19.8	14.1	17.2	12.0	18.9
4th quarter	19.5	19.4	20.0	24.5	30.9	13.8	28.7	19.9	14.2	17.2	12.2	19.1
1967												
1st quarter	19.6	19.4	20.1	24.6	31.1	13.8	29.2	19.9	14.2	17.1	12.3	19.1
2nd quarter	19.7	19.5	20.3	24.7	31.2	13.9	29.2	19.9	14.4	17.3	12.4	19.2
3rd quarter	19.9	19.7	20.4	24.9	31.4	14.0	29.1	19.9	14.5	17.5	12.6	19.4
4th quarter	20.1	19.9	20.6	25.2	31.7	14.2	29.3	19.9	14.8	17.8	12.8	19.6
1968												
1st quarter	20.3	20.1	20.9	25.5	32.0	14.5	29.5	20.0	15.0	17.9	13.0	19.8
2nd quarter	20.6	20.3	21.1	25.7	32.3	14.6	30.1	20.2	15.1	18.1	13.2	20.0
3rd quarter	20.8	20.5	21.4	25.9	32.6	14.6	29.7	20.2	15.4	18.4	13.3	20.2
4th quarter	21.0	20.7	21.6	26.4	33.1	15.2	30.0	20.4	15.6	18.7	13.6	20.5
1969												
1st quarter	21.3	20.9	21.8	26.7	33.3	15.5	30.4	20.4	15.7	18.7	13.8	20.7
2nd quarter	21.5	21.2	22.1	27.0	33.6	15.7	30.5	20.5	16.0	19.0	14.1	21.0
3rd quarter	21.8	21.5	22.4	27.3	34.0	15.8	30.9	20.7	16.3	19.5	14.3	21.3
4th quarter	22.1	21.7	22.6	27.6	34.4	16.0	31.6	21.2	16.6	19.7	14.6	21.6
1970												
1st quarter	22.4	22.0	22.9	27.8	34.8	16.0	31.6	21.4	17.0	20.3	14.9	21.9
2nd quarter	22.7	22.2	23.1	28.4	35.4	16.6	32.2	21.7	17.3	20.6	15.2	22.2
3rd quarter	22.9	22.4	23.4	28.4	35.6	16.1	32.1	22.2	17.6	20.9	15.5	22.4
4th quarter	23.2	22.7	23.7	28.7	36.1	16.3	32.2	22.4	17.9	21.2	15.8	22.7
1971												
1st quarter	23.6	22.9	24.0	29.2	36.6	16.7	33.2	23.0	18.4	21.8	16.1	23.0
2nd quarter	23.9	23.2	24.3	29.6	37.0	17.1	33.2	23.1	18.7	22.2	16.4	23.3
3rd quarter	24.1	23.4	24.5	30.0	37.3	17.4	33.1	23.4	19.0	22.6	16.7	23.6
4th quarter	24.3	23.6	24.7	30.2	37.6	17.6	33.3	23.7	19.3	23.0	16.8	23.8
1972												
1st quarter	24.7	23.8	24.9	30.6	38.0	17.9	34.3	24.1	19.9	24.0	17.2	24.2
2nd quarter	24.9	23.9	25.1	30.8	38.3	18.0	34.6	24.7	20.1	24.2	17.4	24.4
3rd quarter	25.1	24.2	25.3	31.1	38.5	18.3	34.7	25.1	20.3	24.4	17.7	24.6
4th quarter	25.4	24.4	25.4	31.6	38.8	18.8	35.5	25.7	20.7	24.9	17.9	24.9

Table 1-6B. Chain-Type Price Indexes for Gross Domestic Product and Domestic Purchases: Historical—*Continued*

(Index numbers, 2009 = 100.)   **NIPA Tables 1.1.4, 1.6.4, 2.3.4**

Year and quarter	Gross domestic product, total	Personal consumption expenditures		Private fixed investment			Exports and imports of goods and services		Government consumption expenditures and gross investment			Gross domestic purchases
		Total	Excluding food and energy	Total	Nonresidential	Residential	Exports	Imports	Total	Federal	State and local	
1973												
1st quarter	25.7	24.7	25.6	31.9	39.1	19.1	36.5	26.5	21.0	25.3	18.3	25.2
2nd quarter	26.1	25.1	25.9	32.4	39.7	19.6	38.1	28.5	21.4	25.7	18.6	25.7
3rd quarter	26.6	25.6	26.3	33.1	40.3	20.2	40.3	29.9	21.7	26.2	18.8	26.1
4th quarter	27.1	26.1	26.7	33.6	40.8	20.6	42.4	32.1	22.2	26.7	19.2	26.6
1974												
1st quarter	27.6	26.9	27.1	34.2	41.5	21.0	45.3	37.2	22.6	27.0	19.7	27.3
2nd quarter	28.3	27.6	27.8	35.2	42.8	21.5	46.9	41.5	23.2	27.6	20.4	28.1
3rd quarter	29.1	28.4	28.6	36.6	44.5	22.2	49.5	43.6	24.0	28.3	21.1	28.9
4th quarter	30.0	29.1	29.3	38.0	46.5	22.8	52.0	45.0	24.7	29.3	21.8	29.8
1975												
1st quarter	30.7	29.7	29.9	39.3	48.2	23.4	53.5	45.7	25.2	29.8	22.2	30.4
2nd quarter	31.1	30.0	30.3	40.2	49.4	23.8	53.4	45.9	25.6	30.2	22.7	30.8
3rd quarter	31.7	30.6	30.8	40.7	50.1	24.0	53.2	44.8	26.0	30.6	23.0	31.4
4th quarter	32.2	31.1	31.3	41.3	50.8	24.5	53.5	44.9	26.4	31.3	23.2	31.9
1976												
1st quarter	32.6	31.4	31.8	41.7	51.3	24.6	54.3	45.6	26.7	31.7	23.5	32.2
2nd quarter	32.9	31.7	32.1	42.4	52.0	25.3	54.9	46.3	27.0	32.0	23.8	32.5
3rd quarter	33.3	32.2	32.6	43.0	52.7	25.7	55.2	47.2	27.3	32.4	24.0	33.0
4th quarter	33.9	32.7	33.1	43.7	53.4	26.2	56.2	47.7	27.8	33.2	24.2	33.5
1977												
1st quarter	34.4	33.3	33.7	44.6	54.5	26.9	56.8	49.3	28.2	33.7	24.7	34.1
2nd quarter	35.0	33.9	34.2	45.4	55.3	27.6	57.7	50.7	28.6	34.0	25.2	34.7
3rd quarter	35.4	34.4	34.8	46.4	56.3	28.5	57.4	51.4	29.0	34.2	25.6	35.2
4th quarter	36.0	34.9	35.3	47.4	57.2	29.4	57.7	51.9	29.6	35.2	26.0	35.8
1978												
1st quarter	36.6	35.4	35.9	48.3	58.1	30.2	58.8	52.8	30.0	35.7	26.4	36.4
2nd quarter	37.3	36.2	36.5	49.3	59.0	31.1	60.3	54.0	30.5	36.0	26.8	37.1
3rd quarter	38.0	36.8	37.1	50.3	60.0	32.0	61.2	54.9	30.9	36.6	27.2	37.8
4th quarter	38.8	37.5	37.8	51.3	61.0	32.8	63.3	55.9	31.5	37.4	27.6	38.5
1979												
1st quarter	39.5	38.2	38.3	52.4	62.3	33.5	65.1	58.1	32.1	37.9	28.3	39.2
2nd quarter	40.4	39.2	39.1	53.7	63.7	34.6	67.8	61.1	32.7	38.5	28.9	40.2
3rd quarter	41.2	40.2	39.8	55.0	65.0	35.7	69.4	65.7	33.6	39.1	29.9	41.2
4th quarter	42.0	41.2	40.7	56.1	66.3	36.6	70.6	70.0	34.5	40.6	30.5	42.2
1980												
1st quarter	43.0	42.4	41.7	57.4	67.7	37.6	72.7	75.8	35.3	41.3	31.3	43.4
2nd quarter	43.9	43.5	42.6	58.7	69.3	38.4	73.7	78.6	36.1	42.2	32.1	44.4
3rd quarter	44.9	44.5	43.5	60.0	70.8	39.3	75.8	80.8	36.9	42.9	33.0	45.4
4th quarter	46.2	45.6	44.6	61.3	72.2	40.2	78.3	82.2	38.3	45.0	33.9	46.6
1981												
1st quarter	47.4	46.7	45.6	62.9	74.2	41.1	80.3	84.3	39.2	45.7	35.0	47.8
2nd quarter	48.2	47.5	46.4	64.3	76.0	41.8	80.6	84.8	39.9	46.3	35.7	48.7
3rd quarter	49.1	48.3	47.3	65.4	77.4	42.3	80.8	82.6	40.4	47.1	36.1	49.5
4th quarter	50.0	49.0	48.1	66.7	79.1	42.9	81.0	82.8	41.4	48.7	36.6	50.3
1982												
1st quarter	50.7	49.7	48.8	67.5	80.0	43.6	81.5	82.5	42.0	49.3	37.2	51.0
2nd quarter	51.3	50.1	49.5	68.4	81.0	44.2	81.5	81.1	42.5	49.8	37.7	51.5
3rd quarter	52.0	50.9	50.3	68.8	81.5	44.6	80.9	80.1	43.1	50.4	38.3	52.2
4th quarter	52.6	51.5	51.0	69.0	81.7	44.8	80.4	79.5	43.7	51.3	38.8	52.8
1983												
1st quarter	53.0	51.9	51.7	68.8	81.2	45.0	80.7	77.8	44.0	51.5	39.1	53.1
2nd quarter	53.4	52.4	52.1	68.6	80.9	45.1	81.0	77.8	44.3	51.5	39.5	53.4
3rd quarter	53.9	53.1	52.9	68.6	80.8	45.4	81.5	78.0	44.7	52.0	39.9	54.0
4th quarter	54.3	53.5	53.3	68.8	80.7	45.8	82.3	77.5	45.0	52.3	40.2	54.3
1984												
1st quarter	54.9	54.0	53.8	68.9	80.8	46.1	82.4	77.7	45.7	53.2	40.8	54.9
2nd quarter	55.4	54.6	54.4	69.3	81.1	46.4	82.9	78.1	46.1	53.6	41.2	55.3
3rd quarter	55.8	55.0	55.0	69.6	81.3	46.9	82.1	76.8	46.5	54.0	41.6	55.7
4th quarter	56.2	55.3	55.4	69.8	81.4	47.3	81.2	75.8	46.8	54.3	42.0	56.0
1985												
1st quarter	56.8	56.0	56.1	70.0	81.6	47.5	80.3	74.0	47.3	54.8	42.5	56.6
2nd quarter	57.2	56.5	56.6	70.2	81.8	47.7	80.0	74.3	47.5	54.7	42.9	56.9
3rd quarter	57.5	56.9	57.2	70.5	82.1	48.0	79.3	74.3	47.8	54.8	43.3	57.3
4th quarter	57.8	57.3	57.6	70.9	82.5	48.6	79.1	75.7	48.2	55.3	43.7	57.7
1986												
1st quarter	58.1	57.7	58.2	71.3	82.7	49.2	78.7	75.8	48.2	55.1	43.9	58.0
2nd quarter	58.3	57.6	58.6	71.8	83.2	49.7	78.3	73.5	48.3	55.2	44.1	58.1
3rd quarter	58.6	57.9	59.0	72.4	83.7	50.4	77.9	74.0	48.6	55.3	44.4	58.4
4th quarter	59.0	58.3	59.5	72.9	84.1	50.9	78.5	74.9	49.0	55.4	45.0	58.8
1987												
1st quarter	59.3	58.8	59.9	73.2	84.2	51.5	78.8	76.9	49.3	55.3	45.7	59.3
2nd quarter	59.7	59.4	60.4	73.3	84.2	52.0	79.9	78.9	49.7	55.5	46.2	59.7
3rd quarter	60.1	59.9	61.0	73.6	84.2	52.5	80.2	79.7	50.1	55.8	46.7	60.2
4th quarter	60.6	60.5	61.6	74.3	85.0	53.0	81.5	80.9	50.4	56.0	47.0	60.7

Table 1-6B. Chain-Type Price Indexes for Gross Domestic Product and Domestic Purchases: Historical—*Continued*

(Index numbers, 2009 = 100.)   **NIPA Tables 1.1.4, 1.6.4, 2.3.4**

Year and quarter	Gross domestic product, total	Personal consumption expenditures		Private fixed investment			Exports and imports of goods and services		Government consumption expenditures and gross investment			Gross domestic purchases
		Total	Excluding food and energy	Total	Nonresi-dential	Residential	Exports	Imports	Total	Federal	State and local	
1988												
1st quarter	61.1	60.9	62.2	74.9	85.8	53.4	82.4	82.1	50.9	56.8	47.3	61.2
2nd quarter	61.7	61.6	62.9	75.4	86.2	53.9	84.2	83.5	51.3	57.3	47.7	61.8
3rd quarter	62.4	62.4	63.7	75.8	86.6	54.2	85.2	82.6	51.7	57.6	48.1	62.4
4th quarter	63.0	63.0	64.4	76.5	87.4	54.8	85.0	83.3	52.0	57.7	48.7	63.0
1989												
1st quarter	63.6	63.7	65.0	76.9	87.9	55.1	85.8	84.6	52.8	58.5	49.4	63.7
2nd quarter	64.3	64.5	65.6	77.4	88.3	55.8	86.0	85.5	53.3	58.8	50.0	64.4
3rd quarter	64.8	64.9	66.1	77.8	88.8	56.0	85.4	84.1	53.7	59.1	50.5	64.8
4th quarter	65.2	65.4	66.7	78.2	89.2	56.4	85.2	84.5	54.1	59.3	51.2	65.2
1990												
1st quarter	65.9	66.3	67.5	78.7	89.7	56.8	85.3	85.8	54.8	60.0	51.9	66.1
2nd quarter	66.6	66.9	68.2	79.0	90.0	57.0	85.4	84.3	55.3	60.5	52.4	66.6
3rd quarter	67.2	67.8	68.9	79.5	90.7	57.3	86.2	86.7	55.9	60.9	53.0	67.3
4th quarter	67.7	68.7	69.4	79.9	91.3	57.3	87.5	91.6	56.7	61.8	53.8	68.1
1991												
1st quarter	68.4	69.0	70.0	80.6	92.2	57.5	87.7	88.8	57.2	62.7	54.0	68.6
2nd quarter	68.8	69.4	70.6	80.7	92.2	57.8	87.2	86.3	57.4	62.8	54.3	68.9
3rd quarter	69.3	69.9	71.2	80.8	92.2	58.1	86.6	85.0	57.9	63.3	54.8	69.3
4th quarter	69.7	70.4	71.7	80.5	91.9	57.9	86.7	85.4	58.3	63.6	55.3	69.7
1992												
1st quarter	70.0	70.8	72.3	80.4	91.8	57.7	86.6	85.8	58.7	64.0	55.8	70.1
2nd quarter	70.5	71.3	72.8	80.6	91.7	58.3	86.7	86.2	59.3	64.5	56.4	70.5
3rd quarter	70.8	71.7	73.2	80.7	91.8	58.7	86.7	87.3	59.8	64.9	56.9	70.9
4th quarter	71.3	72.2	73.8	81.0	91.8	59.5	86.5	86.6	60.1	65.2	57.3	71.4
1993												
1st quarter	71.7	72.6	74.3	81.3	91.9	60.1	86.6	86.0	60.4	65.4	57.6	71.8
2nd quarter	72.1	73.1	74.8	81.6	91.9	60.8	86.8	86.3	60.7	65.8	58.0	72.2
3rd quarter	72.5	73.5	75.3	81.7	91.9	61.3	86.8	85.6	61.0	66.3	58.1	72.5
4th quarter	72.9	73.9	75.6	82.0	92.2	61.5	86.8	85.2	61.4	66.7	58.4	72.9
1994												
1st quarter	73.3	74.1	76.0	82.4	92.4	62.3	87.2	85.2	61.8	67.0	58.9	73.2
2nd quarter	73.7	74.6	76.5	82.7	92.6	62.7	87.5	86.0	62.3	67.7	59.3	73.6
3rd quarter	74.0	75.1	76.9	83.0	92.8	63.4	87.9	87.4	62.7	67.9	59.8	74.1
4th quarter	74.4	75.4	77.3	83.4	92.9	64.2	88.5	87.8	63.2	68.5	60.3	74.5
1995												
1st quarter	74.9	75.8	77.7	83.9	93.3	64.9	89.4	88.5	63.8	69.5	60.7	74.9
2nd quarter	75.2	76.2	78.2	84.2	93.6	65.3	90.1	89.8	64.2	69.6	61.1	75.3
3rd quarter	75.6	76.5	78.5	84.5	93.8	65.5	89.9	89.2	64.4	69.9	61.4	75.6
4th quarter	75.9	76.9	78.9	84.4	93.6	65.9	89.5	88.4	64.9	70.8	61.6	75.9
1996												
1st quarter	76.3	77.3	79.2	84.3	93.3	66.2	89.3	88.2	65.5	71.5	62.2	76.3
2nd quarter	76.6	77.8	79.6	84.2	92.9	66.5	89.0	87.7	65.4	70.8	62.3	76.5
3rd quarter	76.9	78.1	80.0	84.4	92.9	67.2	88.4	86.9	65.7	71.0	62.7	76.8
4th quarter	77.3	78.7	80.4	84.3	92.7	67.5	87.4	86.8	66.1	71.2	63.2	77.3
1997												
1st quarter	77.6	79.0	80.7	84.4	92.6	67.8	87.2	86.2	66.6	71.9	63.6	77.6
2nd quarter	78.0	79.2	81.1	84.4	92.6	68.1	87.2	84.4	66.8	72.1	63.8	77.7
3rd quarter	78.2	79.4	81.3	84.5	92.5	68.7	86.9	83.8	67.0	72.2	64.1	77.9
4th quarter	78.5	79.7	81.6	84.5	92.1	69.2	86.5	83.1	67.4	72.6	64.6	78.2
1998												
1st quarter	78.6	79.7	81.8	84.1	91.6	69.4	85.7	81.1	67.6	72.8	64.7	78.1
2nd quarter	78.8	79.8	82.1	84.0	91.1	69.8	85.2	80.1	67.8	72.9	65.0	78.2
3rd quarter	79.1	80.0	82.3	83.9	90.8	70.5	84.5	79.1	68.2	73.1	65.5	78.4
4th quarter	79.3	80.2	82.6	84.0	90.5	71.2	84.2	79.0	68.7	73.4	66.0	78.7
1999												
1st quarter	79.6	80.5	82.9	84.1	90.5	71.8	83.9	78.8	69.3	74.2	66.6	78.9
2nd quarter	79.9	80.9	83.1	84.2	90.3	72.6	84.1	79.8	70.1	74.7	67.5	79.4
3rd quarter	80.2	81.3	83.4	84.1	89.9	73.2	84.3	80.8	70.7	75.0	68.3	79.8
4th quarter	80.6	81.8	83.8	84.4	90.1	73.8	84.7	82.0	71.5	75.6	69.1	80.2
2000												
1st quarter	81.2	82.5	84.2	84.9	90.4	75.0	85.3	83.5	72.5	76.8	70.0	81.0
2nd quarter	81.6	82.9	84.5	85.3	90.6	75.8	86.0	83.7	73.0	76.8	70.8	81.4
3rd quarter	82.2	83.4	84.9	85.7	90.9	76.4	86.3	84.2	73.8	77.7	71.5	81.9
4th quarter	82.6	83.8	85.3	85.9	90.9	77.1	86.5	84.6	74.5	78.1	72.4	82.4
2001												
1st quarter	83.1	84.4	85.8	85.9	90.5	78.2	86.4	84.3	75.1	78.4	73.1	82.8
2nd quarter	83.7	84.8	86.1	86.2	90.5	79.2	86.0	82.7	75.4	78.5	73.6	83.2
3rd quarter	84.0	84.9	86.4	86.4	90.3	80.5	85.6	81.5	75.8	78.9	73.9	83.3
4th quarter	84.2	84.9	86.8	86.5	90.2	80.9	84.8	79.6	75.9	79.2	74.0	83.4
2002												
1st quarter	84.5	85.1	87.1	86.4	90.1	80.8	84.5	79.4	76.7	80.8	74.3	83.7
2nd quarter	84.8	85.7	87.6	86.5	90.0	81.3	85.0	81.2	77.2	81.0	74.9	84.2
3rd quarter	85.2	86.2	88.0	86.6	90.0	81.6	85.7	81.7	77.6	81.2	75.4	84.6
4th quarter	85.7	86.5	88.3	87.0	90.1	83.0	85.9	82.1	78.3	82.2	76.0	85.0

Table 1-6B. Chain-Type Price Indexes for Gross Domestic Product and Domestic Purchases: Historical—*Continued*

(Index numbers, 2009 = 100.)   NIPA Tables 1.1.4, 1.6.4, 2.3.4

Year and quarter	Gross domestic product, total	Personal consumption expenditures		Private fixed investment			Exports and imports of goods and services		Government consumption expenditures and gross investment			Gross domestic purchases
		Total	Excluding food and energy	Total	Nonresi-dential	Residential	Exports	Imports	Total	Federal	State and local	
2003												
1st quarter	86.2	87.2	88.5	87.4	89.8	84.8	86.7	84.5	79.8	84.3	77.2	85.8
2nd quarter	86.5	87.2	88.9	87.4	89.7	84.9	86.9	83.4	80.0	84.6	77.3	85.9
3rd quarter	86.9	87.8	89.2	87.7	89.9	85.5	87.2	83.8	80.5	85.0	77.9	86.4
4th quarter	87.4	88.1	89.5	88.4	90.1	87.0	87.8	84.2	81.0	85.1	78.6	86.8
2004												
1st quarter	88.1	88.8	90.0	89.2	90.4	88.9	88.9	86.0	82.4	87.0	79.8	87.6
2nd quarter	88.8	89.4	90.6	90.1	90.9	90.7	90.2	87.4	83.4	87.5	81.0	88.4
3rd quarter	89.4	89.9	91.0	91.0	91.3	92.5	90.7	88.5	84.4	88.0	82.3	89.1
4th quarter	90.1	90.7	91.4	91.9	91.9	94.0	91.7	90.5	85.5	88.4	83.8	89.9
2005												
1st quarter	90.9	91.1	92.0	92.9	92.8	95.2	93.3	91.2	86.8	90.6	84.5	90.6
2nd quarter	91.5	91.7	92.5	93.9	93.5	96.8	94.0	92.4	87.6	91.1	85.6	91.3
3rd quarter	92.4	92.7	92.9	95.1	94.0	99.3	94.8	94.5	88.8	91.8	86.9	92.3
4th quarter	93.1	93.5	93.5	96.3	95.0	101.1	95.4	96.2	89.8	92.2	88.3	93.2
2006												
1st quarter	93.8	93.9	94.0	97.2	95.6	102.7	96.1	96.5	90.8	94.0	89.0	93.9
2nd quarter	94.6	94.6	94.6	97.9	96.2	103.7	97.5	97.5	91.9	94.4	90.3	94.6
3rd quarter	95.3	95.3	95.1	98.4	96.8	104.1	98.7	98.5	92.5	94.6	91.3	95.3
4th quarter	95.6	95.1	95.5	99.2	97.7	104.8	98.8	97.4	93.1	94.8	92.1	95.4
2007												
1st quarter	96.7	96.0	96.2	99.8	98.3	105.3	99.5	97.9	94.9	96.6	93.9	96.4
2nd quarter	97.2	96.8	96.5	100.0	98.6	105.1	100.7	99.6	95.7	97.2	94.8	97.1
3rd quarter	97.5	97.3	97.0	100.0	98.6	105.1	101.3	101.3	96.5	97.5	95.9	97.6
4th quarter	97.9	98.3	97.6	100.1	98.7	105.2	102.9	105.4	97.5	98.1	97.1	98.4
2008												
1st quarter	98.5	99.1	98.2	100.3	99.1	104.8	104.5	109.0	99.1	99.6	98.7	99.3
2nd quarter	98.9	100.2	98.7	100.5	99.6	104.4	107.4	114.7	100.3	100.4	100.2	100.2
3rd quarter	99.6	101.2	99.1	101.2	100.7	103.4	108.9	117.8	101.3	100.9	101.6	101.2
4th quarter	99.8	99.7	99.3	101.9	102.0	102.0	102.5	105.3	100.5	100.2	100.6	100.3
2009												
1st quarter	100.0	99.2	99.4	101.4	101.4	101.2	99.0	96.4	99.8	100.2	99.6	99.7
2nd quarter	99.9	99.6	99.9	100.2	100.2	99.8	99.0	97.9	99.7	99.7	99.7	99.7
3rd quarter	99.9	100.3	100.1	99.2	99.2	99.1	100.2	101.3	100.0	99.8	100.1	100.0
4th quarter	100.2	100.9	100.7	99.3	99.1	99.9	101.8	104.4	100.5	100.4	100.6	100.6
2010												
1st quarter	100.5	101.3	100.9	99.0	98.7	100.0	102.7	106.1	101.7	101.7	101.6	101.0
2nd quarter	101.0	101.4	101.2	99.0	99.0	99.3	103.9	105.6	102.4	102.5	102.4	101.3
3rd quarter	101.4	101.7	101.4	99.1	99.1	99.3	104.3	105.0	102.9	102.9	103.0	101.6
4th quarter	101.9	102.2	101.6	99.6	99.5	99.9	106.7	107.4	103.7	103.4	103.8	102.2
2011												
1st quarter	102.4	103.0	102.0	99.9	99.9	100.1	109.4	111.8	104.6	104.5	104.6	102.9
2nd quarter	103.0	103.9	102.5	100.5	100.5	100.5	111.7	115.2	105.6	105.5	105.7	103.8
3rd quarter	103.7	104.5	103.0	100.7	100.8	100.5	112.3	115.1	106.1	105.8	106.2	104.3
4th quarter	103.8	104.9	103.5	100.9	101.0	100.5	111.2	114.9	105.9	105.6	106.2	104.5
2012												
1st quarter	104.3	105.5	104.0	101.3	101.5	100.3	112.0	116.1	106.7	106.0	107.2	105.1
2nd quarter	104.8	105.8	104.5	101.7	101.9	100.7	112.1	115.0	106.8	106.2	107.2	105.4
3rd quarter	105.3	106.2	104.8	102.0	102.2	101.5	112.1	113.6	106.8	106.2	107.3	105.7
4th quarter	105.6	106.6	105.2	102.4	102.4	102.5	112.5	114.7	107.2	106.4	107.8	106.2

Table 1-7. Final Sales

(Quarterly dollar data are at seasonally adjusted annual rates.)

NIPA Tables 1.4.4, 1.4.5, 1.4.6

Year and quarter	Final sales of domestic product			Final sales to domestic purchasers		
	Billions of dollars	Billions of chained (2009) dollars	Chain-type price index, 2009 = 100	Billions of dollars	Billions of chained (2009) dollars	Chain-type price index, 2009 = 100
1950	294.4	2 165.0	13.6	293.7	2 201.7	13.4
1951	337.4	2 326.3	14.5	334.9	2 348.0	14.3
1952	364.2	2 455.1	14.9	363.1	2 493.0	14.6
1953	387.8	2 578.0	15.1	388.5	2 635.5	14.8
1954	393.1	2 586.4	15.2	392.7	2 633.7	14.9
1955	421.2	2 731.3	15.4	420.7	2 782.5	15.1
1956	446.2	2 797.8	16.0	443.8	2 840.2	15.7
1957	474.1	2 871.9	16.5	470.0	2 908.9	16.2
1958	482.4	2 855.8	16.9	481.9	2 917.9	16.5
1959	518.5	3 029.0	17.1	518.1	3 095.0	16.8
1960	540.1	3 111.1	17.4	535.8	3 157.2	17.0
1961	560.3	3 192.7	17.6	555.4	3 238.9	17.2
1962	599.0	3 371.2	17.8	594.9	3 428.4	17.4
1963	633.0	3 522.0	18.0	628.0	3 574.8	17.6
1964	681.0	3 731.2	18.3	674.1	3 775.9	17.9
1965	734.5	3 951.4	18.6	728.9	4 012.3	18.2
1966	801.4	4 192.9	19.1	797.5	4 271.0	18.7
1967	851.9	4 330.0	19.7	848.3	4 420.7	19.2
1968	933.4	4 549.0	20.5	932.1	4 658.2	20.0
1969	1 010.7	4 693.1	21.6	1 009.3	4 807.6	21.0
1970	1 073.9	4 736.1	22.7	1 069.9	4 835.6	22.2
1971	1 159.5	4 866.0	23.9	1 158.9	4 977.5	23.3
1972	1 273.3	5 120.4	24.9	1 276.7	5 247.9	24.4
1973	1 412.7	5 386.5	26.3	1 408.6	5 477.8	25.7
1974	1 534.8	5 372.5	28.6	1 535.6	5 423.2	28.4
1975	1 695.2	5 428.6	31.3	1 679.2	5 432.9	30.9
1976	1 860.5	5 645.7	33.0	1 862.1	5 709.5	32.7
1977	2 063.6	5 894.4	35.1	2 086.7	6 000.7	34.8
1978	2 330.8	6 218.7	37.5	2 356.1	6 324.4	37.3
1979	2 614.2	6 443.3	40.6	2 636.7	6 509.1	40.6
1980	2 868.8	6 485.0	44.3	2 881.9	6 445.0	44.8
1981	3 181.1	6 579.8	48.4	3 193.7	6 548.2	48.9
1982	3 359.9	6 539.6	51.4	3 379.9	6 547.0	51.7
1983	3 643.9	6 823.2	53.5	3 695.5	6 915.3	53.5
1984	3 975.3	7 188.5	55.4	4 078.0	7 385.7	55.3
1985	4 324.9	7 573.5	57.2	4 438.9	7 800.0	57.0
1986	4 583.6	7 864.1	58.3	4 715.5	8 113.4	58.2
1987	4 843.1	8 104.4	59.8	4 987.8	8 340.7	59.8
1988	5 234.1	8 457.8	61.9	5 343.5	8 628.1	61.9
1989	5 630.0	8 756.0	64.3	5 716.7	8 882.9	64.4
1990	5 965.0	8 943.0	66.7	6 042.9	9 034.2	66.9
1991	6 174.4	8 959.0	68.9	6 203.1	8 994.7	69.0
1992	6 522.9	9 252.5	70.5	6 557.7	9 291.6	70.6
1993	6 857.9	9 500.7	72.2	6 923.1	9 591.3	72.2
1994	7 244.9	9 827.0	73.7	7 337.5	9 956.2	73.7
1995	7 632.9	10 140.2	75.3	7 722.6	10 257.4	75.3
1996	8 069.4	10 525.0	76.7	8 165.8	10 657.9	76.6
1997	8 537.5	10 944.0	78.0	8 639.5	11 110.4	77.8
1998	9 025.4	11 439.8	78.9	9 188.2	11 734.4	78.3
1999	9 604.9	12 000.3	80.0	9 866.3	12 404.5	79.5
2000	10 235.2	12 500.4	81.9	10 615.3	13 005.7	81.6
2001	10 663.5	12 731.7	83.8	11 032.6	13 262.4	83.2
2002	10 961.7	12 889.9	85.0	11 386.7	13 501.3	84.3
2003	11 493.0	13 247.9	86.8	11 993.9	13 916.1	86.2
2004	12 213.2	13 702.7	89.1	12 828.0	14 458.7	88.7
2005	13 035.8	14 170.1	92.0	13 751.6	14 971.7	91.9
2006	13 790.9	14 543.6	94.8	14 553.3	15 354.2	94.8
2007	14 445.9	14 839.2	97.3	15 155.7	15 564.2	97.4
2008	14 752.3	14 868.9	99.2	15 465.5	15 427.8	100.2
2009	14 565.5	14 565.5	100.0	14 957.7	14 957.7	100.0
2010	14 896.7	14 717.7	101.2	15 415.2	15 183.2	101.5
2011	15 497.4	15 014.4	103.2	16 066.2	15 463.4	103.9
2012	16 178.5	15 403.2	105.0	16 725.7	15 835.2	105.6
2010						
1st quarter	14 660.4	14 584.3	100.5	15 155.5	14 998.4	101.1
2nd quarter	14 829.0	14 686.3	101.0	15 358.8	15 164.0	101.3
3rd quarter	14 928.2	14 718.3	101.4	15 472.0	15 228.0	101.6
4th quarter	15 169.3	14 881.8	101.9	15 674.6	15 342.3	102.2
2011						
1st quarter	15 221.4	14 871.9	102.4	15 776.1	15 332.1	102.9
2nd quarter	15 416.2	14 961.8	103.0	15 988.4	15 402.4	103.8
3rd quarter	15 625.3	15 072.7	103.7	16 179.0	15 508.9	104.3
4th quarter	15 726.8	15 151.3	103.8	16 321.2	15 610.2	104.6
2012						
1st quarter	15 938.7	15 278.9	104.3	16 529.5	15 720.4	105.2
2nd quarter	16 093.6	15 360.8	104.8	16 651.4	15 797.9	105.4
3rd quarter	16 274.4	15 444.9	105.4	16 798.8	15 882.8	105.8
4th quarter	16 407.3	15 528.3	105.7	16 923.1	15 939.7	106.2

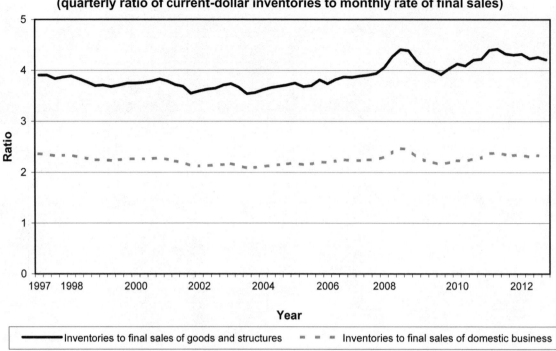

Figure 1-2. Private Nonfarm Inventory-Sales Ratios, 1997–2012
(quarterly ratio of current-dollar inventories to monthly rate of final sales)

- Inventories play an important role in the business cycle. The change in inventories is a GDP component that, although small, can be volatile and even negative. When inventory change is positive, the economy is producing more than is sold; when it is negative, production is below the rate of sales—which could be because sales rose faster than anticipated, causing involuntary inventory reduction, or on the other hand because production was deliberately cut back in order to get rid of unwanted stocks.

- In 2009, following a rapid and unwanted rise in inventory/sales ratios, stocks were reduced at a record rate of $148 billion, contributing 0.76 percentage points to the 2.8 percent decline in GDP. In 2010, the return to inventory-building contributed 1.45 percentage points, more than half of the 2.5 percent GDP increase. This was the largest positive contribution from inventories since 1984. (Tables 1-2A, 1-8A and 1-4A).

- Current-dollar inventory-sales ratios, such as those shown in Figure 1-2, show stocks in recent periods to be still relatively high, while estimated constant-dollar ratios are more ambiguous. Inventory investment has been moderate and variable during the recovery. (Tables 1-8A and B)

Table 1-8A. Inventory Change and Inventory-Sales Ratios: Recent Data

(Quarterly dollar data are at seasonally adjusted annual rates.)   **NIPA Tables 5.7.5B, 5.7.6B, 5.8.5B, 5.8.6B**

Year and quarter	Change in private inventories				Ratio, inventories at end of quarter to monthly rate of sales during the quarter					
	Billions of current dollars		Billions of chained dollars [1]		Total private inventories to final sales of domestic business		Nonfarm inventories to final sales of domestic business		Nonfarm inventories to final sales of goods and structures	
	Farm	Nonfarm	Farm	Nonfarm	Current dollars	Chained dollars[1]	Current dollars	Chained dollars[1]	Current dollars	Chained dollars[1]
OLD BASIS										
1950	-0.1	5.9	-0.3	22.8	5.81	3.67	3.04	2.30	3.94	3.97
1951	1.0	8.9	2.1	28.4	5.85	3.76	3.15	2.46	4.07	4.24
1952	1.4	2.1	3.1	7.4	5.24	3.74	3.06	2.45	3.98	4.23
1953	0.7	1.2	2.0	4.5	5.04	3.74	3.08	2.45	4.04	4.22
1954	0.2	-2.1	0.5	-7.5	4.74	3.52	2.88	2.28	3.81	3.94
1955	-0.6	5.6	-1.9	18.7	4.43	3.44	2.95	2.29	3.87	3.94
1956	-1.0	4.9	-3.2	15.6	4.47	3.45	3.03	2.35	4.00	4.07
1957	0.1	0.7	0.4	2.4	4.46	3.48	3.01	2.37	4.01	4.14
1958	2.0	-2.3	5.8	-7.7	4.50	3.44	2.90	2.30	3.88	4.00
1959	-1.6	5.5	-4.7	19.9	4.26	3.37	2.90	2.32	3.94	4.08
1960	0.6	2.7	1.7	9.9	4.22	3.37	2.89	2.34	3.93	4.10
1961	0.9	2.1	2.5	7.8	4.12	3.30	2.81	2.29	3.84	4.03
1962	0.6	5.5	1.7	20.4	4.14	3.32	2.82	2.34	3.87	4.11
1963	0.5	5.1	1.4	19.0	3.95	3.25	2.78	2.32	3.81	4.07
1964	-1.2	6.0	-3.8	21.8	3.79	3.17	2.75	2.31	3.79	4.07
1965	0.8	8.4	2.5	30.5	3.77	3.09	2.72	2.29	3.71	3.99
1966	-0.5	14.1	-1.4	50.2	3.92	3.26	2.92	2.50	4.01	4.38
1967	0.9	9.0	2.5	31.5	3.90	3.35	2.99	2.59	4.14	4.57
1968	1.4	7.7	4.1	26.5	3.79	3.33	2.90	2.58	4.03	4.56
1969	0.0	9.2	0.0	30.9	3.88	3.40	2.98	2.68	4.18	4.76
1970	-0.8	2.8	-2.4	8.6	3.81	3.39	2.96	2.68	4.23	4.83
1971	1.7	6.6	4.1	20.6	3.76	3.33	2.88	2.64	4.12	4.75
1972	0.3	8.8	0.4	26.7	3.74	3.18	2.77	2.55	3.94	4.53
1973	1.5	14.4	1.8	40.5	4.20	3.22	2.98	2.62	4.22	4.67
1974	-2.8	16.8	-4.4	39.0	4.52	3.46	3.54	2.88	5.11	5.26
1975	3.4	-9.6	5.8	-21.4	4.04	3.26	3.16	2.66	4.59	4.88
1976	-0.8	18.0	-1.6	37.6	3.95	3.23	3.19	2.68	4.68	4.92
1977	4.5	17.8	7.2	35.7	3.89	3.22	3.16	2.67	4.63	4.87
1978	1.4	24.4	2.1	44.9	3.98	3.14	3.15	2.63	4.54	4.73
1979	3.6	14.4	4.2	23.8	4.19	3.16	3.34	2.64	4.85	4.75
1980	-6.1	-0.2	-7.2	-0.4	4.24	3.13	3.44	2.65	5.08	4.82
1981	8.8	21.0	10.1	28.2	4.17	3.28	3.49	2.75	5.20	5.03
1982	5.8	-20.7	7.5	-27.4	3.97	3.23	3.30	2.68	5.10	4.99
1983	-15.4	9.6	-17.4	10.7	3.69	2.98	3.08	2.52	4.77	4.64
1984	5.7	59.7	6.3	72.3	3.72	3.05	3.16	2.60	4.89	4.72
1985	5.8	16.1	7.0	18.4	3.51	2.98	3.01	2.53	4.74	4.65
1986	-1.5	8.0	-2.3	10.4	3.25	2.90	2.82	2.47	4.49	4.53
1987	-6.4	33.6	-9.1	41.1	3.33	2.90	2.90	2.50	4.65	4.62
1988	-11.9	30.4	-13.1	35.4	3.29	2.81	2.86	2.47	4.63	4.55
1989	0.0	27.7	0.0	30.8	3.23	2.80	2.83	2.47	4.63	4.56
1990	2.4	12.2	2.5	14.0	3.22	2.83	2.82	2.49	4.71	4.66
1991	-1.3	0.9	-1.8	0.4	3.06	2.83	2.70	2.50	4.62	4.74
1992	6.3	10.1	7.1	11.0	2.92	2.73	2.56	2.39	4.41	4.53
1993	-6.2	27.0	-7.5	29.8	2.85	2.68	2.51	2.38	4.33	4.47
1994	12.0	51.8	13.7	55.9	2.89	2.72	2.56	2.40	4.39	4.47
1995	-11.1	42.2	-13.0	44.3	2.88	2.69	2.58	2.40	4.45	4.46
1996	8.6	22.1	8.3	23.2	2.76	2.62	2.47	2.33	4.24	4.28
1997	3.3	67.7	3.7	73.6	2.70	2.65	2.42	2.37	4.17	4.32
NEW BASIS										
1997	3.3	67.7	4.1	80.5	2.60	2.66	2.33	2.37	3.87	4.17
1998	1.3	62.5	1.9	76.4	2.46	2.62	2.24	2.35	3.70	4.09
1999	-2.7	63.5	-4.2	77.7	2.48	2.60	2.26	2.34	3.75	4.08
2000	-1.4	55.9	-2.0	67.1	2.50	2.61	2.28	2.36	3.83	4.12
2001	0.0	-38.3	0.1	-45.8	2.32	2.53	2.12	2.28	3.55	3.97
2002	-2.5	21.0	-3.5	25.5	2.37	2.55	2.15	2.31	3.71	4.09
2003	0.1	19.2	0.1	22.4	2.31	2.42	2.09	2.19	3.56	3.86
2004	8.8	55.1	9.0	62.4	2.38	2.44	2.16	2.20	3.71	3.89
2005	0.2	59.4	0.3	63.9	2.42	2.44	2.20	2.21	3.81	3.89
2006	-3.6	70.5	-4.2	75.4	2.43	2.45	2.23	2.23	3.86	3.93
2007	-0.7	35.2	-0.9	36.5	2.53	2.43	2.30	2.22	4.06	3.93
2008	1.6	-33.6	1.1	-35.0	2.52	2.49	2.30	2.27	4.18	4.13
2009	-1.6	-146.0	-1.6	-146.0	2.41	2.35	2.19	2.13	4.03	3.89
2010	-7.3	68.9	-7.0	65.9	2.53	2.35	2.28	2.14	4.22	3.91
2011	-6.4	42.8	-4.5	39.7	2.60	2.32	2.33	2.13	4.30	3.85
2012	-11.7	77.8	-7.2	68.7	2.57	2.30	2.31	2.13	4.21	3.81
2010										
1st quarter	-1.3	13.3	-3.0	12.9	2.46	2.35	2.23	2.13	4.13	3.90
2nd quarter	-5.9	56.1	-5.8	54.6	2.43	2.34	2.21	2.13	4.09	3.89
3rd quarter	-11.6	133.2	-9.9	126.8	2.49	2.37	2.26	2.16	4.20	3.97
4th quarter	-10.5	72.8	-9.5	69.1	2.53	2.35	2.28	2.14	4.22	3.91
2011										
1st quarter	-7.9	29.4	-5.5	28.7	2.64	2.35	2.37	2.15	4.40	3.94
2nd quarter	-9.6	55.4	-6.1	51.1	2.65	2.34	2.38	2.14	4.42	3.93
3rd quarter	-4.6	-8.8	-3.9	-6.6	2.61	2.31	2.34	2.12	4.33	3.87
4th quarter	-3.3	95.2	-2.5	85.5	2.60	2.32	2.33	2.13	4.30	3.85
2012										
1st quarter	-0.1	103.0	-0.8	92.5	2.61	2.32	2.34	2.13	4.32	3.85
2nd quarter	-7.4	74.3	-4.9	64.7	2.57	2.31	2.30	2.13	4.23	3.85
3rd quarter	-23.9	105.5	-13.6	97.3	2.59	2.33	2.33	2.15	4.26	3.87
4th quarter	-15.6	28.6	-9.6	20.3	2.57	2.30	2.31	2.13	4.21	3.81

[1]Before 1997, 2005 dollars; 1997 forward, 2009 dollars.

Table 1-8B. Inventory Change and Inventory-Sales Ratios: Historical

(Quarterly dollar data are at seasonally adjusted annual rates.)   **NIPA Tables 5.7.5B, 5.7.6B, 5.8.5B, 5.8.6B**

Year and quarter	Change in private inventories				Ratio, inventories at end of quarter to monthly rate of sales during the quarter					
	Billions of current dollars		Billions of chained dollars[1]		Total private inventories to final sales of domestic business		Nonfarm inventories to final sales of domestic business		Nonfarm inventories to final sales of goods and structures	
	Farm	Nonfarm	Farm	Nonfarm	Current dollars	Chained dollars[1]	Current dollars	Chained dollars[1]	Current dollars	Chained dollars[1]
OLD BASIS										
1929	-0.10	1.70	-0.60	10.60	...	...	...	...	...	...
1930	-0.30	0.00	-1.70	-2.40	...	...	...	...	...	...
1931	0.50	-1.60	3.10	-13.40	...	...	...	...	...	...
1932	0.10	-2.50	0.80	-21.20	...	...	...	...	...	...
1933	-0.10	-1.30	-1.10	-9.40	...	...	...	...	...	...
1934	-0.80	0.20	-5.70	1.00	...	...	...	...	...	...
1935	0.70	0.40	4.00	2.50	...	...	...	...	...	...
1936	-0.90	2.00	-5.40	15.50	...	...	...	...	...	...
1937	0.90	1.70	4.10	7.90	...	...	...	...	...	...
1938	0.40	-1.00	2.80	-6.00	...	...	...	...	...	...
1939	-0.10	0.30	-1.10	2.70	...	...	...	...	...	...
1940	0.50	1.90	2.80	12.40	...	...	...	...	...	...
1941	0.40	3.90	1.90	24.30	...	...	...	...	...	...
1942	1.30	0.60	5.60	3.00	...	...	...	...	...	...
1943	-0.20	-0.50	-1.10	-2.30	...	...	...	...	...	...
1944	-0.30	-0.60	-1.50	-2.50	...	...	...	...	...	...
1945	-0.90	-0.60	-3.30	-3.80	...	...	...	...	...	...
1946	-0.20	6.20	-1.00	31.80	...	...	...	...	...	...
1947	-1.80	1.20	-4.50	4.40	...	...	...	...	...	...
1948	2.70	3.00	6.10	12.40	...	...	...	...	...	...
1949	-0.60	-2.10	-1.90	-8.60	...	...	...	...	...	...
1947										
1st quarter	-1.10	1.60	-0.40	6.60	5.93	3.88	2.82	2.27	3.71	3.99
2nd quarter	-2.70	1.50	-4.50	4.20	5.89	3.84	2.82	2.27	3.69	4.00
3rd quarter	-2.50	-0.40	-6.80	-3.70	6.02	3.76	2.76	2.23	3.61	3.93
4th quarter	-0.80	2.30	-6.30	10.50	6.30	3.74	2.81	2.25	3.65	3.93
1948										
1st quarter	1.30	2.40	1.60	11.70	6.00	3.76	2.87	2.27	3.71	3.96
2nd quarter	2.80	3.00	7.70	11.90	6.02	3.81	2.89	2.30	3.76	4.03
3rd quarter	3.40	3.70	8.30	15.00	5.88	3.88	2.97	2.34	3.85	4.10
4th quarter	3.10	2.90	6.60	11.10	5.74	3.91	3.00	2.36	3.90	4.13
1949										
1st quarter	-0.20	0.60	-1.20	-0.40	5.66	3.90	2.97	2.36	3.88	4.14
2nd quarter	-1.20	-4.00	-3.00	-15.10	5.38	3.82	2.83	2.30	3.70	4.02
3rd quarter	-0.90	-0.40	-2.30	-0.60	5.39	3.81	2.82	2.29	3.69	4.00
4th quarter	-0.20	-4.50	-0.90	-18.40	5.23	3.73	2.77	2.23	3.61	3.87
1950										
1st quarter	-0.10	2.20	-1.00	9.70	5.26	3.69	2.76	2.22	3.61	3.84
2nd quarter	-1.30	4.20	-2.50	16.20	5.27	3.62	2.75	2.20	3.57	3.79
3rd quarter	0.50	3.70	0.60	15.20	5.21	3.47	2.72	2.12	3.50	3.63
4th quarter	0.70	13.40	1.50	50.20	5.81	3.67	3.04	2.30	3.94	3.97
1951										
1st quarter	1.20	9.20	2.60	29.00	5.94	3.68	3.12	2.33	4.01	4.01
2nd quarter	0.90	13.80	2.50	44.30	5.99	3.81	3.25	2.45	4.23	4.28
3rd quarter	0.80	9.00	1.60	29.30	5.89	3.79	3.20	2.47	4.16	4.29
4th quarter	1.10	3.60	1.70	11.00	5.85	3.76	3.15	2.46	4.07	4.24
1952										
1st quarter	1.00	3.80	2.70	12.80	5.77	3.79	3.16	2.49	4.11	4.31
2nd quarter	1.90	-3.40	3.60	-10.50	5.63	3.75	3.08	2.44	4.01	4.24
3rd quarter	2.20	3.40	4.50	11.20	5.63	3.85	3.15	2.51	4.13	4.38
4th quarter	0.50	4.80	1.50	16.20	5.24	3.74	3.06	2.45	3.98	4.23
1953										
1st quarter	0.80	3.10	2.50	10.60	5.06	3.69	3.02	2.42	3.93	4.17
2nd quarter	-0.70	4.30	-0.20	14.10	5.00	3.69	3.06	2.43	3.99	4.20
3rd quarter	0.70	1.60	1.80	5.80	4.99	3.72	3.09	2.45	4.05	4.23
4th quarter	2.10	-4.10	3.80	-12.30	5.04	3.74	3.08	2.45	4.04	4.22
1954										
1st quarter	0.80	-2.80	2.10	-9.20	5.02	3.72	3.04	2.42	4.01	4.20
2nd quarter	-0.20	-3.20	0.50	-10.80	4.91	3.66	2.98	2.38	3.93	4.11
3rd quarter	0.70	-2.80	0.80	-9.10	4.85	3.59	2.93	2.32	3.89	4.04
4th quarter	-0.50	0.20	-1.50	-0.90	4.74	3.52	2.88	2.28	3.81	3.94
1955										
1st quarter	-0.10	3.90	-1.70	14.00	4.68	3.46	2.86	2.25	3.77	3.88
2nd quarter	-1.10	5.70	-2.10	20.00	4.57	3.44	2.87	2.26	3.73	3.83
3rd quarter	-1.30	5.60	-2.00	17.90	4.47	3.42	2.89	2.26	3.77	3.85
4th quarter	0.30	6.90	-1.60	22.70	4.43	3.44	2.95	2.29	3.87	3.94
1956										
1st quarter	0.00	6.40	-2.90	20.80	4.50	3.48	3.00	2.33	3.96	4.02
2nd quarter	-1.50	5.00	-3.40	16.20	4.57	3.48	3.03	2.35	3.99	4.04
3rd quarter	-0.80	4.30	-3.20	13.20	4.50	3.48	3.02	2.36	3.98	4.07
4th quarter	-1.60	3.90	-3.30	12.10	4.47	3.45	3.03	2.35	4.00	4.07
1957										
1st quarter	0.30	1.90	-0.90	5.70	4.44	3.44	3.02	2.35	3.97	4.05
2nd quarter	0.70	2.00	-0.20	6.80	4.48	3.48	3.04	2.38	4.00	4.11
3rd quarter	0.50	2.30	1.80	7.50	4.46	3.47	3.03	2.38	3.99	4.10
4th quarter	-1.00	-3.50	1.10	-10.20	4.46	3.48	3.01	2.37	4.01	4.14

[1]Before 1997, 2005 dollars; 1997 forward, 2009 dollars.
. . . = Not available.

Table 1-8B. Inventory Change and Inventory-Sales Ratios: Historical—*Continued*

(Quarterly dollar data are at seasonally adjusted annual rates.)   **NIPA Tables 5.7.5B, 5.7.6B, 5.8.5B, 5.8.6B**

Year and quarter	Change in private inventories				Ratio, inventories at end of quarter to monthly rate of sales during the quarter					
	Billions of current dollars		Billions of chained dollars [1]		Total private inventories to final sales of domestic business		Nonfarm inventories to final sales of domestic business		Nonfarm inventories to final sales of goods and structures	
	Farm	Nonfarm	Farm	Nonfarm	Current dollars	Chained dollars[1]	Current dollars	Chained dollars[1]	Current dollars	Chained dollars[1]
1958										
1st quarter	2.20	-6.30	7.60	-20.40	4.67	3.56	3.04	2.41	4.06	4.20
2nd quarter	1.60	-5.80	6.90	-18.60	4.65	3.56	3.00	2.38	4.00	4.17
3rd quarter	2.20	-0.70	6.20	-2.50	4.58	3.48	2.92	2.32	3.92	4.07
4th quarter	1.80	3.40	2.50	10.60	4.50	3.44	2.90	2.30	3.88	4.00
1959										
1st quarter	-0.30	4.20	-3.50	14.90	4.37	3.35	2.83	2.25	3.79	3.93
2nd quarter	-1.90	9.20	-5.30	33.80	4.33	3.34	2.86	2.27	3.85	3.98
3rd quarter	-2.30	2.60	-5.40	9.60	4.25	3.31	2.84	2.27	3.82	3.96
4th quarter	-1.80	5.90	-4.60	21.10	4.26	3.37	2.90	2.32	3.94	4.08
1960										
1st quarter	0.60	10.60	0.40	39.00	4.29	3.37	2.93	2.35	3.96	4.10
2nd quarter	0.90	2.40	1.90	9.00	4.21	3.36	2.91	2.34	3.95	4.11
3rd quarter	1.00	3.30	3.10	12.10	4.27	3.41	2.95	2.38	3.99	4.15
4th quarter	-0.20	-5.60	1.50	-20.20	4.22	3.37	2.89	2.34	3.93	4.10
1961										
1st quarter	0.60	-3.10	2.50	-11.30	4.19	3.35	2.86	2.32	3.90	4.07
2nd quarter	0.60	1.20	2.20	4.70	4.12	3.33	2.83	2.30	3.89	4.07
3rd quarter	0.90	5.70	2.60	21.00	4.17	3.35	2.85	2.32	3.89	4.08
4th quarter	1.40	4.60	2.80	16.80	4.12	3.30	2.81	2.29	3.84	4.03
1962										
1st quarter	1.50	7.90	2.50	29.00	4.15	3.32	2.82	2.32	3.85	4.07
2nd quarter	0.20	5.20	0.80	19.20	4.09	3.29	2.80	2.31	3.84	4.06
3rd quarter	0.20	5.90	1.40	22.00	4.17	3.32	2.83	2.33	3.87	4.09
4th quarter	0.40	3.00	2.20	11.30	4.14	3.32	2.82	2.34	3.87	4.11
1963										
1st quarter	1.90	4.90	7.50	18.20	4.12	3.34	2.83	2.35	3.87	4.12
2nd quarter	0.10	4.80	0.70	17.40	4.04	3.29	2.79	2.32	3.83	4.08
3rd quarter	-0.60	6.40	-1.70	23.60	4.00	3.27	2.79	2.33	3.81	4.07
4th quarter	0.60	4.50	-0.80	16.70	3.95	3.25	2.78	2.32	3.81	4.07
1964										
1st quarter	-0.60	5.80	-3.90	21.10	3.85	3.19	2.74	2.29	3.75	4.01
2nd quarter	-1.20	5.70	-4.30	20.70	3.79	3.17	2.73	2.29	3.75	4.02
3rd quarter	-1.80	6.50	-4.20	23.80	3.78	3.15	2.73	2.29	3.74	4.00
4th quarter	-1.10	6.10	-3.10	21.70	3.79	3.17	2.75	2.31	3.79	4.07
1965										
1st quarter	0.30	11.20	0.90	40.80	3.81	3.17	2.76	2.33	3.79	4.08
2nd quarter	1.10	7.40	2.90	26.90	3.82	3.15	2.75	2.32	3.79	4.08
3rd quarter	0.80	8.50	3.10	30.50	3.78	3.14	2.76	2.32	3.78	4.06
4th quarter	1.00	6.60	3.20	23.70	3.77	3.09	2.72	2.29	3.71	3.99
1966										
1st quarter	0.60	13.20	1.10	46.80	3.80	3.09	2.73	2.31	3.71	4.00
2nd quarter	-1.70	14.00	-2.70	50.20	3.86	3.16	2.80	2.38	3.83	4.16
3rd quarter	-0.60	12.40	-1.70	43.70	3.91	3.19	2.84	2.42	3.88	4.22
4th quarter	-0.40	16.90	-2.30	59.90	3.92	3.26	2.92	2.50	4.01	4.38
1967										
1st quarter	1.70	13.70	3.40	48.60	3.94	3.32	2.98	2.55	4.11	4.50
2nd quarter	2.10	4.20	7.60	14.70	3.92	3.31	2.95	2.54	4.07	4.46
3rd quarter	0.50	8.70	1.40	29.70	3.92	3.34	2.97	2.57	4.10	4.52
4th quarter	-0.90	9.30	-2.20	33.10	3.90	3.35	2.99	2.59	4.14	4.57
1968										
1st quarter	3.00	5.40	7.30	19.10	3.87	3.32	2.94	2.57	4.08	4.51
2nd quarter	4.30	9.80	13.40	33.90	3.87	3.34	2.93	2.58	4.07	4.55
3rd quarter	0.20	7.50	1.20	25.10	3.81	3.32	2.90	2.56	4.03	4.51
4th quarter	-2.00	8.00	-5.50	27.80	3.79	3.33	2.90	2.58	4.03	4.56
1969										
1st quarter	1.80	9.70	3.90	33.00	3.79	3.32	2.90	2.59	4.02	4.54
2nd quarter	1.40	7.80	4.40	26.60	3.83	3.35	2.91	2.61	4.06	4.61
3rd quarter	-1.20	11.40	-2.50	38.60	3.83	3.38	2.94	2.64	4.10	4.67
4th quarter	-1.90	7.70	-5.80	25.50	3.88	3.40	2.98	2.68	4.18	4.76
1970										
1st quarter	1.60	0.20	3.40	0.00	3.86	3.38	2.96	2.66	4.18	4.74
2nd quarter	0.40	4.70	1.90	14.90	3.85	3.40	2.96	2.68	4.20	4.80
3rd quarter	-1.80	6.90	-4.40	21.90	3.84	3.39	2.97	2.67	4.22	4.79
4th quarter	-3.50	-0.50	-10.30	-2.20	3.81	3.39	2.96	2.68	4.23	4.83
1971										
1st quarter	2.50	9.70	6.60	31.30	3.83	3.38	2.95	2.68	4.21	4.81
2nd quarter	4.20	6.70	10.70	20.60	3.81	3.39	2.94	2.68	4.20	4.81
3rd quarter	2.30	7.90	5.80	25.20	3.80	3.38	2.93	2.68	4.18	4.80
4th quarter	-2.30	2.00	-6.80	5.40	3.76	3.33	2.88	2.64	4.12	4.75
1972										
1st quarter	-0.50	3.70	0.10	11.10	3.72	3.30	2.84	2.62	4.06	4.69
2nd quarter	2.00	10.00	6.80	30.60	3.75	3.27	2.83	2.60	4.03	4.64
3rd quarter	1.00	12.70	1.90	38.50	3.77	3.26	2.83	2.60	4.05	4.66
4th quarter	-1.40	8.90	-7.10	26.50	3.74	3.18	2.77	2.55	3.94	4.53

[1]Before 1997, 2005 dollars; 1997 forward, 2009 dollars.

Table 1-8B. Inventory Change and Inventory-Sales Ratios: Historical—*Continued*

(Quarterly dollar data are at seasonally adjusted annual rates.)   **NIPA Tables 5.7.5B, 5.7.6B, 5.8.5B, 5.8.6B**

Year and quarter	Change in private inventories				Ratio, inventories at end of quarter to monthly rate of sales during the quarter					
	Billions of current dollars		Billions of chained dollars [1]		Total private inventories to final sales of domestic business		Nonfarm inventories to final sales of domestic business		Nonfarm inventories to final sales of goods and structures	
	Farm	Nonfarm	Farm	Nonfarm	Current dollars	Chained dollars[1]	Current dollars	Chained dollars[1]	Current dollars	Chained dollars[1]
1973										
1st quarter	-4.20	14.80	-10.70	42.90	3.86	3.11	2.79	2.52	3.92	4.45
2nd quarter	5.00	13.20	12.00	38.30	4.03	3.15	2.86	2.54	4.02	4.51
3rd quarter	2.60	7.20	3.50	20.00	4.11	3.16	2.87	2.56	4.05	4.55
4th quarter	2.80	22.20	2.30	60.90	4.20	3.22	2.98	2.62	4.22	4.67
1974										
1st quarter	-3.30	15.90	-5.20	39.70	4.26	3.27	3.13	2.68	4.42	4.76
2nd quarter	1.00	16.40	0.90	39.60	4.29	3.31	3.28	2.72	4.67	4.86
3rd quarter	-0.10	5.70	1.70	11.70	4.45	3.34	3.40	2.75	4.84	4.93
4th quarter	-8.70	29.20	-15.00	64.90	4.52	3.46	3.54	2.88	5.11	5.26
1975										
1st quarter	7.10	-17.10	16.40	-38.30	4.32	3.42	3.41	2.82	4.94	5.16
2nd quarter	3.10	-17.10	5.40	-38.60	4.26	3.35	3.30	2.75	4.81	5.06
3rd quarter	0.80	-2.20	-1.00	-5.00	4.18	3.31	3.24	2.71	4.69	4.95
4th quarter	2.50	-2.10	2.30	-3.70	4.04	3.26	3.16	2.66	4.59	4.88
1976										
1st quarter	-0.50	15.20	0.10	33.20	4.00	3.22	3.14	2.64	4.56	4.83
2nd quarter	-1.80	24.30	-1.90	51.80	4.07	3.26	3.21	2.69	4.67	4.91
3rd quarter	2.00	18.80	5.40	38.90	4.04	3.28	3.23	2.70	4.74	4.96
4th quarter	-3.00	13.60	-9.80	26.50	3.95	3.23	3.19	2.68	4.68	4.92
1977										
1st quarter	-1.30	16.10	-7.00	33.00	3.96	3.22	3.21	2.68	4.72	4.92
2nd quarter	5.30	14.20	11.30	27.80	3.88	3.19	3.16	2.65	4.62	4.84
3rd quarter	4.40	26.50	16.30	53.80	3.86	3.22	3.16	2.67	4.63	4.88
4th quarter	9.80	14.40	8.40	28.10	3.89	3.22	3.16	2.67	4.63	4.87
1978										
1st quarter	-0.60	26.10	-3.60	48.90	4.02	3.26	3.21	2.72	4.78	5.00
2nd quarter	0.40	23.90	0.20	44.20	3.92	3.14	3.12	2.62	4.55	4.75
3rd quarter	7.20	17.80	11.10	32.30	3.95	3.15	3.13	2.62	4.54	4.74
4th quarter	-1.50	30.00	0.50	54.10	3.98	3.14	3.15	2.63	4.54	4.73
1979										
1st quarter	4.20	19.60	6.60	33.00	4.15	3.17	3.22	2.65	4.66	4.78
2nd quarter	3.10	24.30	5.30	40.40	4.19	3.21	3.29	2.69	4.78	4.87
3rd quarter	6.60	5.50	7.00	8.20	4.16	3.16	3.28	2.64	4.74	4.73
4th quarter	0.30	8.30	-1.90	13.40	4.19	3.16	3.34	2.64	4.85	4.75
1980										
1st quarter	-0.60	10.50	-2.60	17.40	4.25	3.17	3.45	2.66	5.02	4.78
2nd quarter	-5.20	13.00	-5.90	19.30	4.40	3.28	3.57	2.76	5.26	5.02
3rd quarter	-12.50	-21.40	-14.20	-32.60	4.34	3.18	3.50	2.68	5.15	4.88
4th quarter	-6.10	-3.00	-6.00	-5.80	4.24	3.13	3.44	2.65	5.08	4.82
1981										
1st quarter	6.80	31.90	10.30	44.60	4.26	3.17	3.48	2.67	5.13	4.84
2nd quarter	9.90	1.80	10.90	1.70	4.24	3.18	3.47	2.67	5.15	4.87
3rd quarter	11.80	32.10	14.50	42.60	4.20	3.22	3.48	2.71	5.16	4.93
4th quarter	6.50	18.30	4.50	23.80	4.17	3.28	3.49	2.75	5.20	5.03
1982										
1st quarter	5.10	-26.50	6.70	-34.30	4.19	3.28	3.46	2.74	5.20	5.03
2nd quarter	4.30	-8.50	6.40	-12.20	4.15	3.28	3.42	2.74	5.17	5.04
3rd quarter	9.00	-3.20	12.00	-5.50	4.12	3.33	3.43	2.77	5.26	5.15
4th quarter	4.60	-44.40	4.90	-57.50	3.97	3.23	3.30	2.68	5.10	4.99
1983										
1st quarter	-7.30	-27.80	-10.40	-37.30	3.89	3.15	3.19	2.62	4.98	4.89
2nd quarter	-13.00	5.30	-12.60	6.50	3.81	3.09	3.14	2.58	4.89	4.80
3rd quarter	-32.40	28.20	-37.70	34.30	3.73	3.03	3.12	2.55	4.86	4.73
4th quarter	-8.80	32.70	-9.00	39.40	3.69	2.98	3.08	2.52	4.77	4.64
1984										
1st quarter	5.50	67.50	7.40	81.90	3.78	3.02	3.15	2.56	4.87	4.71
2nd quarter	5.60	63.70	6.40	77.20	3.76	3.03	3.16	2.57	4.88	4.69
3rd quarter	6.80	64.50	8.10	78.90	3.75	3.06	3.18	2.60	4.93	4.75
4th quarter	5.00	43.00	3.30	51.00	3.72	3.05	3.16	2.60	4.89	4.72
1985										
1st quarter	7.90	8.30	8.40	8.80	3.60	3.00	3.06	2.55	4.77	4.65
2nd quarter	4.20	17.40	4.80	20.30	3.55	2.99	3.04	2.55	4.76	4.66
3rd quarter	6.60	9.70	9.10	12.00	3.47	2.96	2.98	2.51	4.67	4.60
4th quarter	4.30	28.80	5.90	32.70	3.51	2.98	3.01	2.53	4.74	4.65
1986										
1st quarter	2.50	27.80	1.70	33.30	3.42	2.97	2.94	2.52	4.65	4.63
2nd quarter	-3.50	19.10	-5.90	22.30	3.37	2.97	2.92	2.53	4.63	4.65
3rd quarter	-3.10	-3.90	-4.30	-5.50	3.29	2.92	2.85	2.49	4.52	4.55
4th quarter	-1.80	-11.00	-0.60	-8.50	3.25	2.90	2.82	2.47	4.49	4.53
1987										
1st quarter	-7.70	35.60	-9.70	44.50	3.31	2.94	2.86	2.51	4.62	4.66
2nd quarter	-10.70	27.20	-14.50	33.10	3.30	2.90	2.86	2.49	4.60	4.60
3rd quarter	-4.00	5.00	-5.20	4.10	3.25	2.85	2.82	2.45	4.52	4.51
4th quarter	-3.30	66.40	-7.00	82.50	3.33	2.90	2.90	2.50	4.65	4.62

[1]Before 1997, 2005 dollars; 1997 forward, 2009 dollars.

Table 1-8B. Inventory Change and Inventory-Sales Ratios: Historical—*Continued*

(Quarterly dollar data are at seasonally adjusted annual rates.)   **NIPA Tables 5.7.5B, 5.7.6B, 5.8.5B, 5.8.6B**

| Year and quarter | Change in private inventories | | | | Ratio, inventories at end of quarter to monthly rate of sales during the quarter | | | | | |
| | Billions of current dollars | | Billions of chained dollars [1] | | Total private inventories to final sales of domestic business | | Nonfarm inventories to final sales of domestic business | | Nonfarm inventories to final sales of goods and structures | |
	Farm	Nonfarm	Farm	Nonfarm	Current dollars	Chained dollars[1]	Current dollars	Chained dollars[1]	Current dollars	Chained dollars[1]
1988										
1st quarter	-4.40	21.40	-7.60	25.10	3.30	2.86	2.86	2.47	4.61	4.56
2nd quarter	-12.20	31.90	-15.20	38.00	3.29	2.83	2.85	2.46	4.60	4.52
3rd quarter	-11.20	29.40	-11.40	32.60	3.30	2.83	2.85	2.47	4.63	4.57
4th quarter	-19.70	38.80	-18.30	45.90	3.29	2.81	2.86	2.47	4.63	4.55
1989										
1st quarter	7.20	41.00	7.80	46.60	3.32	2.83	2.89	2.48	4.70	4.58
2nd quarter	2.90	33.20	3.60	37.60	3.28	2.83	2.87	2.48	4.65	4.56
3rd quarter	-5.50	15.50	-5.80	16.90	3.21	2.79	2.82	2.45	4.55	4.49
4th quarter	-4.60	21.20	-5.60	22.30	3.23	2.80	2.83	2.47	4.63	4.56
1990										
1st quarter	1.80	12.10	1.70	13.30	3.18	2.78	2.78	2.45	4.53	4.50
2nd quarter	-1.50	35.30	-2.60	39.90	3.17	2.81	2.78	2.47	4.58	4.60
3rd quarter	4.00	17.90	4.40	20.30	3.20	2.82	2.82	2.48	4.67	4.63
4th quarter	5.20	-16.60	6.70	-17.70	3.22	2.83	2.82	2.49	4.71	4.66
1991										
1st quarter	0.00	-15.60	0.70	-18.10	3.18	2.85	2.78	2.51	4.65	4.71
2nd quarter	-0.70	-17.30	-0.50	-20.60	3.08	2.81	2.70	2.47	4.55	4.66
3rd quarter	-10.90	11.70	-13.80	13.10	3.04	2.81	2.69	2.48	4.54	4.67
4th quarter	6.40	24.70	6.10	27.10	3.06	2.83	2.70	2.50	4.62	4.74
1992										
1st quarter	8.00	-7.80	10.50	-7.50	3.00	2.78	2.63	2.44	4.52	4.64
2nd quarter	9.40	13.80	10.90	13.20	2.99	2.77	2.62	2.43	4.50	4.61
3rd quarter	5.10	15.40	4.70	16.60	2.96	2.75	2.60	2.41	4.47	4.57
4th quarter	2.50	18.90	2.40	21.60	2.92	2.73	2.56	2.39	4.41	4.53
1993										
1st quarter	-5.60	41.60	-6.20	46.50	2.95	2.75	2.58	2.42	4.47	4.60
2nd quarter	-4.90	29.00	-5.30	32.30	2.92	2.74	2.57	2.41	4.44	4.56
3rd quarter	-12.50	19.10	-14.20	20.60	2.89	2.72	2.54	2.40	4.42	4.55
4th quarter	-1.70	18.30	-4.10	19.90	2.85	2.68	2.51	2.38	4.33	4.47
1994										
1st quarter	16.50	28.80	19.40	31.10	2.87	2.69	2.51	2.38	4.33	4.48
2nd quarter	17.10	64.30	21.00	70.00	2.86	2.71	2.53	2.39	4.37	4.49
3rd quarter	10.70	42.50	10.60	46.10	2.86	2.71	2.53	2.39	4.36	4.48
4th quarter	3.70	71.50	3.70	76.30	2.89	2.72	2.56	2.40	4.39	4.47
1995										
1st quarter	-5.80	67.00	-5.90	71.20	2.93	2.75	2.62	2.43	4.49	4.52
2nd quarter	-13.70	47.40	-13.60	50.10	2.94	2.75	2.64	2.44	4.55	4.55
3rd quarter	-20.40	31.70	-26.40	32.80	2.90	2.71	2.60	2.41	4.49	4.50
4th quarter	-4.40	22.80	-6.20	22.90	2.88	2.69	2.58	2.40	4.45	4.46
1996										
1st quarter	1.10	5.80	-2.90	6.20	2.84	2.66	2.55	2.38	4.39	4.42
2nd quarter	11.80	18.60	7.40	19.80	2.81	2.63	2.51	2.35	4.30	4.35
3rd quarter	17.10	34.00	27.40	35.00	2.81	2.65	2.50	2.35	4.29	4.34
4th quarter	4.50	30.20	1.30	31.70	2.76	2.62	2.47	2.33	4.24	4.28
1997										
1st quarter	-0.50	50.30	-10.80	53.30	2.74	2.62	2.45	2.33	4.21	4.28
2nd quarter	0.80	87.60	8.20	95.70	2.73	2.65	2.44	2.36	4.21	4.33
3rd quarter	8.30	59.60	10.10	65.50	2.69	2.63	2.41	2.34	4.14	4.27
4th quarter	4.70	73.10	7.20	79.80	2.70	2.65	2.42	2.37	4.17	4.32
NEW BASIS										
1997										
1st quarter	-0.60	50.30	-9.00	59.30	2.64	2.62	2.36	2.33	3.91	4.13
2nd quarter	0.80	87.60	8.70	104.20	2.63	2.65	2.35	2.36	3.91	4.18
3rd quarter	8.30	59.60	10.00	71.10	2.59	2.63	2.32	2.34	3.84	4.12
4th quarter	4.60	73.10	6.60	87.30	2.60	2.66	2.33	2.37	3.87	4.17
1998										
1st quarter	5.60	99.50	6.20	121.10	2.59	2.69	2.33	2.40	3.89	4.23
2nd quarter	-4.90	42.20	-2.60	51.40	2.54	2.66	2.30	2.37	3.83	4.17
3rd quarter	0.50	51.90	3.00	63.90	2.50	2.65	2.27	2.37	3.77	4.15
4th quarter	3.80	56.20	0.90	69.10	2.46	2.62	2.24	2.35	3.70	4.09
1999										
1st quarter	4.10	79.30	-1.90	97.50	2.47	2.64	2.24	2.36	3.71	4.12
2nd quarter	-0.20	35.30	1.10	43.60	2.45	2.62	2.23	2.34	3.68	4.07
3rd quarter	-9.10	49.60	-12.00	60.60	2.46	2.60	2.24	2.33	3.71	4.06
4th quarter	-5.70	90.00	-3.90	109.10	2.48	2.60	2.26	2.34	3.75	4.08
2000										
1st quarter	-17.70	33.90	-20.50	41.00	2.47	2.58	2.26	2.33	3.75	4.05
2nd quarter	5.90	84.50	6.90	101.40	2.47	2.59	2.26	2.34	3.76	4.08
3rd quarter	-1.10	58.40	-2.30	69.70	2.47	2.60	2.27	2.35	3.79	4.10
4th quarter	7.30	47.00	7.90	56.30	2.50	2.61	2.28	2.36	3.83	4.12
2001										
1st quarter	5.60	-36.20	6.70	-43.50	2.47	2.59	2.25	2.34	3.79	4.09
2nd quarter	-3.00	-8.60	-3.30	-9.70	2.43	2.58	2.22	2.33	3.72	4.07
3rd quarter	1.80	-31.90	1.70	-38.00	2.40	2.58	2.19	2.33	3.69	4.07
4th quarter	-4.30	-76.60	-4.60	-92.20	2.32	2.53	2.12	2.28	3.55	3.97

[1]Before 1997, 2005 dollars; 1997 forward, 2009 dollars.

Table 1-8B. Inventory Change and Inventory-Sales Ratios: Historical—*Continued*

(Quarterly dollar data are at seasonally adjusted annual rates.)   **NIPA Tables 5.7.5B, 5.7.6B, 5.8.5B, 5.8.6B**

| Year and quarter | Change in private inventories | | | | Ratio, inventories at end of quarter to monthly rate of sales during the quarter | | | | | |
| | Billions of current dollars | | Billions of chained dollars [1] | | Total private inventories to final sales of domestic business | | Nonfarm inventories to final sales of domestic business | | Nonfarm inventories to final sales of goods and structures | |
	Farm	Nonfarm	Farm	Nonfarm	Current dollars	Chained dollars[1]	Current dollars	Chained dollars[1]	Current dollars	Chained dollars[1]
2002										
1st quarter	4.10	-4.30	2.70	-6.10	2.32	2.52	2.12	2.28	3.59	3.99
2nd quarter	-10.30	29.50	-10.90	35.80	2.33	2.53	2.13	2.28	3.63	4.03
3rd quarter	-2.90	28.20	-3.70	35.50	2.34	2.53	2.14	2.29	3.65	4.04
4th quarter	-0.80	30.60	-2.00	36.80	2.37	2.55	2.15	2.31	3.71	4.09
2003										
1st quarter	2.80	28.20	3.30	33.00	2.39	2.53	2.17	2.29	3.74	4.06
2nd quarter	-1.40	1.00	-1.00	0.70	2.34	2.49	2.13	2.25	3.67	4.00
3rd quarter	0.90	7.30	0.20	7.40	2.30	2.43	2.08	2.19	3.54	3.87
4th quarter	-2.10	40.50	-1.90	48.60	2.31	2.42	2.09	2.19	3.56	3.86
2004										
1st quarter	4.40	44.40	5.70	50.70	2.34	2.43	2.11	2.20	3.62	3.89
2nd quarter	18.40	57.80	15.70	65.90	2.37	2.44	2.13	2.21	3.66	3.90
3rd quarter	7.70	54.60	8.40	62.80	2.37	2.44	2.15	2.20	3.69	3.89
4th quarter	4.70	63.40	6.00	70.30	2.38	2.44	2.16	2.20	3.71	3.89
2005										
1st quarter	-6.70	106.20	-5.00	115.80	2.40	2.45	2.18	2.22	3.75	3.90
2nd quarter	0.90	29.70	0.80	32.10	2.36	2.42	2.15	2.20	3.68	3.85
3rd quarter	4.30	13.60	3.30	14.90	2.37	2.41	2.16	2.18	3.70	3.82
4th quarter	2.30	87.90	1.90	92.60	2.42	2.44	2.20	2.21	3.81	3.89
2006										
1st quarter	3.70	70.70	1.70	76.90	2.39	2.42	2.19	2.20	3.74	3.83
2nd quarter	-8.10	85.40	-7.30	90.80	2.42	2.44	2.22	2.22	3.82	3.89
3rd quarter	-6.30	83.40	-6.30	87.70	2.45	2.47	2.24	2.25	3.87	3.96
4th quarter	-3.60	42.70	-4.70	46.20	2.43	2.45	2.23	2.23	3.86	3.93
2007										
1st quarter	5.30	14.90	3.20	16.40	2.45	2.45	2.23	2.23	3.89	3.94
2nd quarter	-5.00	52.00	-3.80	53.20	2.46	2.45	2.24	2.23	3.91	3.94
3rd quarter	-2.30	51.00	-2.00	52.30	2.47	2.44	2.25	2.23	3.94	3.94
4th quarter	-0.80	22.80	-1.10	24.10	2.53	2.43	2.30	2.22	4.06	3.93
2008										
1st quarter	-6.90	-13.30	-4.90	-15.00	2.63	2.44	2.39	2.23	4.27	3.97
2nd quarter	3.90	-27.80	2.20	-28.80	2.72	2.42	2.46	2.21	4.41	3.92
3rd quarter	6.60	-25.40	4.60	-25.70	2.70	2.44	2.45	2.23	4.39	3.97
4th quarter	2.80	-67.90	2.70	-70.40	2.52	2.49	2.30	2.27	4.18	4.13
2009										
1st quarter	-0.30	-145.30	-0.70	-144.20	2.45	2.48	2.23	2.26	4.05	4.13
2nd quarter	-1.00	-186.90	-1.00	-189.30	2.42	2.43	2.20	2.21	4.00	4.03
3rd quarter	-5.00	-200.90	-4.20	-201.60	2.37	2.36	2.15	2.14	3.92	3.89
4th quarter	0.00	-50.80	-0.50	-48.80	2.41	2.35	2.19	2.13	4.03	3.89
2010										
1st quarter	-1.30	13.30	-3.00	12.90	2.46	2.35	2.23	2.13	4.13	3.90
2nd quarter	-5.90	56.10	-5.80	54.60	2.43	2.34	2.21	2.13	4.09	3.89
3rd quarter	-11.60	133.20	-9.90	126.80	2.49	2.37	2.26	2.16	4.20	3.97
4th quarter	-10.50	72.80	-9.50	69.10	2.53	2.35	2.28	2.14	4.22	3.91
2011										
1st quarter	-7.90	29.40	-5.50	28.70	2.64	2.35	2.37	2.15	4.40	3.94
2nd quarter	-9.60	55.40	-6.10	51.10	2.65	2.34	2.38	2.14	4.42	3.93
3rd quarter	-4.60	-8.80	-3.90	-6.60	2.61	2.31	2.34	2.12	4.33	3.87
4th quarter	-3.30	95.20	-2.50	85.50	2.60	2.32	2.33	2.13	4.30	3.85
2012										
1st quarter	-0.10	103.00	-0.80	92.50	2.61	2.32	2.34	2.13	4.32	3.85
2nd quarter	-7.40	74.30	-4.90	64.70	2.57	2.31	2.30	2.13	4.23	3.85
3rd quarter	-23.90	105.50	-13.60	97.30	2.59	2.33	2.33	2.15	4.26	3.87
4th quarter	-15.60	28.60	-9.60	20.30	2.57	2.30	2.31	2.13	4.21	3.81

[1]Before 1997, 2005 dollars; 1997 forward, 2009 dollars.

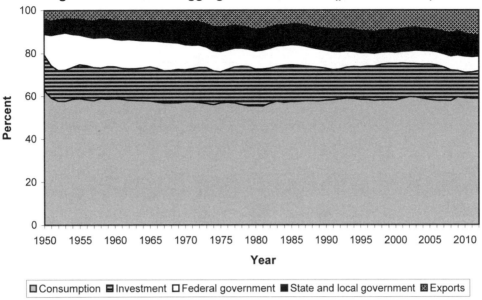

Figure 1-3. Shares of Aggregate Final Demand (percent of total)

□ Consumption ▣ Investment □ Federal government ■ State and local government ▨ Exports

- People often want to know how various sources of demand, especially consumption spending, affect GDP. Often, it is said that consumption "accounts for" about 70 percent of GDP. That is based on a NIPA table showing the components of GDP as a percent of total GDP. In such a calculation, personal consumption expenditures (PCE) amounted to 68.6 percent of total GDP in 2012, up from a range of 60 to 65 percent earlier in the postwar period. (These ratios are slightly lower than before the revision, which added new investment categories to GDP. All such calculations must be made in current dollars, since for reasons stated in the notes and definitions, the 2009-dollar values do not sum to the total GDP.) (Table 1-1A)

- Does this mean that consumption "accounts for" 69 percent of GDP? No, because the value of PCE includes imported goods and services—coffee, cocoa, and bananas; crude oil from the Middle East, transformed into gasoline; clothing, cars, and toys manufactured overseas—even the money that U.S. consumers spend when they travel. The imports included in PCE don't contribute to demand for U.S. GDP, which excludes imports; instead, they contribute to demand for GDP in China and other countries that export to us.

- It is not possible with NIPA data to precisely estimate and subtract out the import content of PCE, and so there is no way to precisely estimate PCE's contribution to GDP. What we can do is calculate PCE and the other sources of aggregate final demand for U.S. output as shares of *total final demand*; this is shown in Table 1-10 and Figure 1-3. These shares approximate their contributions to GDP if each demand source has about the same percentage import content as total GDP.

- Consumption spending has remained under 60 percent of final demand ever since 1951. (It was greater in 1946 through 1950, as consumers made up for wartime deprivations.) The shares of exports and state and local government spending have increased to more than 10 percent each, while the federal government direct spending share remains at less than half of its Korean War highs. (This measure of government spending does not include government financing of medical care and other consumption spending through transfer payment programs such as Social Security and Medicare.) Nonresidential and residential investment display the most cyclical variation in their shares. (Table 1-10)

- The share of imports in the total supply of goods and services in the U.S. market rose from around 4 percent in the 1950s to 15 percent in 2008. The recession and associated inventory liquidation reduced the import share to 12 percent in 2009, but it has recovered to around 14 1/2 percent. (Table 1-9)

Table 1-9. Shares of Aggregate Supply

(Billions of dollars, quarterly dollar data are at seasonally adjusted rates, percents.)   **NIPA Table 1.1.5**

Year and quarter	Aggregate supply (billions of dollars)			Shares of aggregate supply (percent)	
	Total	GDP	Imports	Domestic production (GDP)	Imports
1950	311.8	300.2	11.6	96.3	3.7
1951	361.9	347.3	14.6	96.0	4.0
1952	383.0	367.7	15.3	96.0	4.0
1953	405.7	389.7	16.0	96.1	3.9
1954	406.5	391.1	15.4	96.2	3.8
1955	443.4	426.2	17.2	96.1	3.9
1956	469.0	450.1	18.9	96.0	4.0
1957	494.8	474.9	19.9	96.0	4.0
1958	502.0	482.0	20.0	96.0	4.0
1959	544.8	522.5	22.3	95.9	4.1
1960	566.1	543.3	22.8	96.0	4.0
1961	586.0	563.3	22.7	96.1	3.9
1962	630.1	605.1	25.0	96.0	4.0
1963	664.7	638.6	26.1	96.1	3.9
1964	713.9	685.8	28.1	96.1	3.9
1965	775.2	743.7	31.5	95.9	4.1
1966	852.1	815.0	37.1	95.6	4.4
1967	901.6	861.7	39.9	95.6	4.4
1968	989.1	942.5	46.6	95.3	4.7
1969	1 070.4	1 019.9	50.5	95.3	4.7
1970	1 131.7	1 075.9	55.8	95.1	4.9
1971	1 230.1	1 167.8	62.3	94.9	5.1
1972	1 356.6	1 282.4	74.2	94.5	5.5
1973	1 519.7	1 428.5	91.2	94.0	6.0
1974	1 676.3	1 548.8	127.5	92.4	7.6
1975	1 811.6	1 688.9	122.7	93.2	6.8
1976	2 028.7	1 877.6	151.1	92.6	7.4
1977	2 268.4	2 086.0	182.4	92.0	8.0
1978	2 568.9	2 356.6	212.3	91.7	8.3
1979	2 884.8	2 632.1	252.7	91.2	8.8
1980	3 156.3	2 862.5	293.8	90.7	9.3
1981	3 528.7	3 210.9	317.8	91.0	9.0
1982	3 648.2	3 345.0	303.2	91.7	8.3
1983	3 966.7	3 638.1	328.6	91.7	8.3
1984	4 445.8	4 040.7	405.1	90.9	9.1
1985	4 763.9	4 346.7	417.2	91.2	8.8
1986	5 043.0	4 590.1	452.9	91.0	9.0
1987	5 378.9	4 870.2	508.7	90.5	9.5
1988	5 806.6	5 252.6	554.0	90.5	9.5
1989	6 248.7	5 657.7	591.0	90.5	9.5
1990	6 609.3	5 979.6	629.7	90.5	9.5
1991	6 797.5	6 174.0	623.5	90.8	9.2
1992	7 207.1	6 539.3	667.8	90.7	9.3
1993	7 598.7	6 878.7	720.0	90.5	9.5
1994	8 122.1	7 308.7	813.4	90.0	10.0
1995	8 566.6	7 664.0	902.6	89.5	10.5
1996	9 064.2	8 100.2	964.0	89.4	10.6
1997	9 664.3	8 608.5	1 055.8	89.1	10.9
1998	10 204.8	9 089.1	1 115.7	89.1	10.9
1999	10 916.3	9 665.7	1 250.6	88.5	11.5
2000	11 764.1	10 289.7	1 474.4	87.5	12.5
2001	12 023.1	10 625.3	1 397.8	88.4	11.6
2002	12 409.9	10 980.2	1 429.7	88.5	11.5
2003	13 056.5	11 512.2	1 544.3	88.2	11.8
2004	14 074.9	12 277.0	1 797.9	87.2	12.8
2005	15 121.5	13 095.4	2 026.1	86.6	13.4
2006	16 098.8	13 857.9	2 240.9	86.1	13.9
2007	16 855.8	14 480.3	2 375.5	85.9	14.1
2008	17 276.7	14 720.3	2 556.4	85.2	14.8
2009	16 393.9	14 417.9	1 976.0	87.9	12.1
2010	17 320.3	14 958.3	2 362.0	86.4	13.6
2011	18 203.7	15 533.8	2 669.9	85.3	14.7
2012	18 987.7	16 244.6	2 743.1	85.6	14.4
2010					
1st quarter	16 913.9	14 672.5	2 241.4	86.7	13.3
2nd quarter	17 215.9	14 879.2	2 336.7	86.4	13.6
3rd quarter	17 453.8	15 049.8	2 404.0	86.2	13.8
4th quarter	17 697.4	15 231.7	2 465.7	86.1	13.9
2011					
1st quarter	17 827.0	15 242.9	2 584.1	85.5	14.5
2nd quarter	18 129.6	15 461.9	2 667.7	85.3	14.7
3rd quarter	18 308.9	15 611.8	2 697.1	85.3	14.7
4th quarter	18 549.4	15 818.7	2 730.7	85.3	14.7
2012					
1st quarter	18 805.8	16 041.6	2 764.2	85.3	14.7
2nd quarter	18 915.7	16 160.4	2 755.3	85.4	14.6
3rd quarter	19 079.5	16 356.0	2 723.5	85.7	14.3
4th quarter	19 149.8	16 420.3	2 729.5	85.7	14.3

Table 1-10. Shares of Aggregate Final Demand

(Billions of dollars, quarterly dollar data are at seasonally adjusted rates, percents.)   **NIPA Table 1.1.5**

Year and quarter	Aggregate final demand (billions of dollars)							Shares of aggregate final demand (percent)					
	Total	Consumption (PCE)	Nonresidential fixed investment	Residential investment	Exports	Government consumption and gross investment		PCE	Nonresidential investment	Residential investment	Exports	Federal government	State and local government
						Federal	State and local						
1950	306.1	192.2	30.0	20.7	12.4	29.5	21.3	62.8	9.8	6.8	4.1	9.6	7.0
1951	352.1	208.5	34.2	18.7	17.1	50.0	23.6	59.2	9.7	5.3	4.9	14.2	6.7
1952	379.6	219.5	34.9	18.9	16.5	64.8	25.0	57.8	9.2	5.0	4.3	17.1	6.6
1953	403.8	233.0	38.8	19.7	15.3	70.3	26.7	57.7	9.6	4.9	3.8	17.4	6.6
1954	408.5	239.9	38.6	21.4	15.8	63.3	29.5	58.7	9.4	5.2	3.9	15.5	7.2
1955	438.4	258.7	43.4	25.4	17.7	61.0	32.2	59.0	9.9	5.8	4.0	13.9	7.3
1956	465.1	271.6	49.7	24.0	21.3	63.1	35.4	58.4	10.7	5.2	4.6	13.6	7.6
1957	493.9	286.7	53.1	22.6	24.0	68.4	39.1	58.0	10.8	4.6	4.9	13.8	7.9
1958	502.4	296.0	48.5	22.8	20.6	71.5	43.0	58.9	9.7	4.5	4.1	14.2	8.6
1959	540.7	317.5	53.1	28.6	22.7	73.5	45.3	58.7	9.8	5.3	4.2	13.6	8.4
1960	562.9	331.6	56.4	26.9	27.0	72.8	48.2	58.9	10.0	4.8	4.8	12.9	8.6
1961	583.1	342.0	56.6	27.0	27.6	77.4	52.5	58.7	9.7	4.6	4.7	13.3	9.0
1962	623.9	363.1	61.2	29.6	29.1	85.5	55.4	58.2	9.8	4.7	4.7	13.7	8.9
1963	659.1	382.5	64.8	32.9	31.1	87.8	60.0	58.0	9.8	5.0	4.7	13.3	9.1
1964	709.0	411.2	72.2	35.1	35.0	90.2	65.3	58.0	10.2	5.0	4.9	12.7	9.2
1965	765.9	443.6	85.2	35.2	37.1	93.1	71.7	57.9	11.1	4.6	4.8	12.2	9.4
1966	838.4	480.6	97.2	33.4	40.9	106.5	79.8	57.3	11.6	4.0	4.9	12.7	9.5
1967	891.8	507.4	99.2	33.6	43.5	120.0	88.1	56.9	11.1	3.8	4.9	13.5	9.9
1968	979.9	557.4	107.7	40.2	47.9	127.9	98.8	56.9	11.0	4.1	4.9	13.1	10.1
1969	1 061.2	604.5	120.0	44.4	51.9	131.1	109.3	57.0	11.3	4.2	4.9	12.4	10.3
1970	1 129.5	647.7	124.6	43.4	59.7	132.7	121.4	57.3	11.0	3.8	5.3	11.7	10.7
1971	1 221.9	701.0	130.4	58.2	63.0	134.4	134.9	57.4	10.7	4.8	5.2	11.0	11.0
1972	1 347.4	769.4	146.6	72.4	70.8	141.5	146.7	57.1	10.9	5.4	5.3	10.5	10.9
1973	1 503.8	851.1	172.7	78.3	95.3	145.6	160.8	56.6	11.5	5.2	6.3	9.7	10.7
1974	1 662.4	932.0	191.1	69.5	126.7	158.1	185.0	56.1	11.5	4.2	7.6	9.5	11.1
1975	1 818.0	1 032.8	196.8	66.7	138.7	172.8	210.2	56.8	10.8	3.7	7.6	9.5	11.6
1976	2 011.7	1 150.2	219.3	86.8	149.5	183.8	222.1	57.2	10.9	4.3	7.4	9.1	11.0
1977	2 246.2	1 276.7	259.1	115.2	159.4	198.8	237.0	56.8	11.5	5.1	7.1	8.9	10.6
1978	2 543.1	1 426.2	314.6	138.0	186.9	216.7	260.7	56.1	12.4	5.4	7.3	8.5	10.3
1979	2 866.7	1 589.5	373.8	147.8	230.1	237.7	287.8	55.4	13.0	5.2	8.0	8.3	10.0
1980	3 162.7	1 754.6	406.9	129.5	280.8	272.4	318.5	55.5	12.9	4.1	8.9	8.6	10.1
1981	3 498.8	1 937.5	472.9	128.5	305.2	311.7	343.0	55.4	13.5	3.7	8.7	8.9	9.8
1982	3 663.0	2 073.9	485.1	110.8	283.2	345.6	364.4	56.6	13.2	3.0	7.7	9.4	9.9
1983	3 972.6	2 286.5	482.2	161.1	277.0	380.2	385.6	57.6	12.1	4.1	7.0	9.6	9.7
1984	4 380.4	2 498.2	564.3	190.4	302.4	407.6	417.5	57.0	12.9	4.3	6.9	9.3	9.5
1985	4 742.2	2 722.7	607.7	200.1	303.2	449.3	459.2	57.4	12.8	4.2	6.4	9.5	9.7
1986	5 036.5	2 898.4	607.8	234.8	321.0	478.4	496.1	57.5	12.1	4.7	6.4	9.5	9.9
1987	5 351.7	3 092.1	615.2	249.8	363.9	500.2	530.5	57.8	11.5	4.7	6.8	9.3	9.9
1988	5 788.1	3 346.9	662.3	256.2	444.6	508.8	569.3	57.8	11.4	4.4	7.7	8.8	9.8
1989	6 221.0	3 592.8	716.0	256.0	504.3	531.4	620.5	57.8	11.5	4.1	8.1	8.5	10.0
1990	6 594.7	3 825.6	739.2	239.7	551.9	560.0	678.3	58.0	11.2	3.6	8.4	8.5	10.3
1991	6 798.0	3 960.2	723.6	221.2	594.9	580.7	717.4	58.3	10.6	3.3	8.8	8.5	10.6
1992	7 190.7	4 215.7	741.9	254.7	633.0	586.6	758.8	58.6	10.3	3.5	8.8	8.2	10.6
1993	7 577.9	4 471.0	799.2	286.8	654.8	578.4	787.7	59.0	10.5	3.8	8.6	7.6	10.4
1994	8 058.4	4 741.0	868.9	323.8	720.9	572.7	831.1	58.8	10.8	4.0	8.9	7.1	10.3
1995	8 535.5	4 984.2	962.2	324.1	812.8	575.4	876.8	58.4	11.3	3.8	9.5	6.7	10.3
1996	9 033.4	5 268.1	1 043.2	358.1	867.6	578.2	918.2	58.3	11.5	4.0	9.6	6.4	10.2
1997	9 593.4	5 560.7	1 149.1	375.6	953.8	582.4	971.8	58.0	12.0	3.9	9.9	6.1	10.1
1998	10 141.0	5 903.0	1 252.8	418.8	952.9	584.1	1 029.4	58.2	12.4	4.1	9.4	5.8	10.2
1999	10 855.5	6 316.9	1 361.6	461.8	989.2	610.4	1 115.6	58.2	12.5	4.3	9.1	5.6	10.3
2000	11 709.5	6 801.6	1 493.8	485.4	1 094.3	632.4	1 202.0	58.1	12.8	4.1	9.3	5.4	10.3
2001	12 061.3	7 106.9	1 453.9	513.0	1 028.8	669.2	1 289.5	58.9	12.1	4.3	8.5	5.5	10.7
2002	12 391.4	7 385.3	1 348.9	557.6	1 004.7	740.6	1 354.3	59.6	10.9	4.5	8.1	6.0	10.9
2003	13 037.2	7 764.4	1 371.7	636.9	1 043.4	824.8	1 396.0	59.6	10.5	4.9	8.0	6.3	10.7
2004	14 011.1	8 257.8	1 463.1	749.7	1 183.1	892.4	1 465.0	58.9	10.4	5.4	8.4	6.4	10.5
2005	15 062.0	8 790.3	1 611.5	856.1	1 310.4	946.3	1 547.4	58.4	10.7	5.7	8.7	6.3	10.3
2006	16 031.9	9 297.5	1 776.3	837.4	1 478.5	1 002.0	1 640.2	58.0	11.1	5.2	9.2	6.3	10.2
2007	16 821.4	9 744.4	1 920.6	688.7	1 665.7	1 049.8	1 752.2	57.9	11.4	4.1	9.9	6.2	10.4
2008	17 308.7	10 005.5	1 941.0	515.9	1 843.1	1 155.6	1 847.6	57.8	11.2	3.0	10.6	6.7	10.7
2009	16 541.4	9 842.9	1 633.4	392.2	1 583.8	1 217.7	1 871.4	59.5	9.9	2.4	9.6	7.4	11.3
2010	17 258.8	10 201.9	1 658.2	381.1	1 843.5	1 303.9	1 870.2	59.1	9.6	2.2	10.7	7.6	10.8
2011	18 167.5	10 711.8	1 809.9	385.8	2 101.2	1 304.1	1 854.7	59.0	10.0	2.1	11.6	7.2	10.2
2012	18 921.7	11 149.6	1 970.0	439.2	2 195.9	1 295.7	1 871.3	58.9	10.4	2.3	11.6	6.8	9.9
2010													
1st quarter	16 901.9	10 042.3	1 594.4	383.1	1 746.4	1 269.2	1 866.5	59.4	9.4	2.3	10.3	7.5	11.0
2nd quarter	17 165.8	10 134.7	1 641.8	400.8	1 807.0	1 304.6	1 876.9	59.0	9.6	2.3	10.5	7.6	10.9
3rd quarter	17 332.3	10 234.3	1 677.4	365.6	1 860.3	1 321.6	1 873.1	59.0	9.7	2.1	10.7	7.6	10.8
4th quarter	17 635.0	10 396.3	1 719.3	374.7	1 960.4	1 320.1	1 864.2	59.0	9.7	2.1	11.1	7.5	10.6
2011													
1st quarter	17 805.5	10 527.1	1 721.8	377.1	2 029.5	1 297.4	1 852.6	59.1	9.7	2.1	11.4	7.3	10.4
2nd quarter	18 083.9	10 662.6	1 773.1	381.0	2 095.5	1 315.4	1 856.3	59.0	9.8	2.1	11.6	7.3	10.3
3rd quarter	18 322.3	10 778.6	1 848.9	386.8	2 143.4	1 308.5	1 856.1	58.8	10.1	2.1	11.7	7.1	10.1
4th quarter	18 457.4	10 878.9	1 895.7	398.1	2 136.2	1 294.9	1 853.6	58.9	10.3	2.2	11.6	7.0	10.0
2012													
1st quarter	18 702.9	11 019.1	1 932.3	418.4	2 173.4	1 291.8	1 867.9	58.9	10.3	2.2	11.6	6.9	10.0
2nd quarter	18 848.8	11 100.2	1 961.4	425.7	2 197.4	1 293.8	1 870.3	58.9	10.4	2.3	11.7	6.9	9.9
3rd quarter	18 998.0	11 193.6	1 968.0	443.7	2 199.2	1 322.1	1 871.4	58.9	10.4	2.3	11.6	7.0	9.9
4th quarter	19 136.8	11 285.5	2 018.2	468.8	2 213.7	1 275.2	1 875.4	59.0	10.5	2.4	11.6	6.7	9.8

Section 1b: Income and Value Added

Figure 1-4. Shares of Income

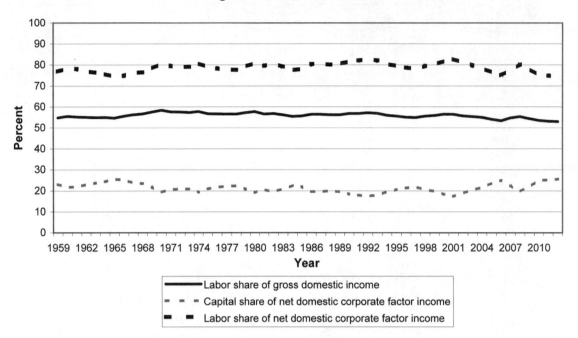

- Recent years have seen a decline in the share of national income paid to workers—not just in worker wages, but in total compensation, including all health and other benefits and executive compensation including exercised stock options. One indicator of this can be seen in a later chapter, in Tables 9-3A and B, where Bureau of Labor Statistics calculations (based on BEA data) document a declining labor share in the value of output of private nonfarm business. In the tables in Section 1b immediately following this page, BEA compilations show the composition of domestic income, national income, and corporate value added; Table 1-16 shows income share percentages calculated by the editors based on these data.

- One broad calculation is based on gross domestic income (GDI), the income-side counterpart of total gross domestic product. Total GDI includes the contribution of government to GDP and income, which is defined as employee compensation and consumption of fixed capital (CFC), and has no capital-type net surplus income. Employee compensation was around 55 percent of gross domestic income in the 1960s and edged even higher between then and the early 2000s, but since then has fallen to 53 percent in 2012, as shown in Figure 1-4. One factor has been a rise in the share of output value required for CFC, to replace used-up capital, reflecting increased use of capital per unit of production. The "net operating surplus" includes profits and interest—clearly capital-type income—but also proprietor's income, in which it is difficult to separate the returns to labor and to capital. (BLS does make such an estimate in its compensation and share calculations.) This surplus is variable over the cycle, but was higher in 2011 and 2012 than in most years since 1968. (Tables 1-12 and 1-16)

- If we narrow the focus to the corporate business sector, the demarcation lines are clearer. Total net factor income (that is, net of capital consumption) can be completely attributed to either labor or capital, since the net operating surplus is composed almost entirely of profits and interest. These shares are charted in Figure 1-4. Between 1959 and 2004, the shares vary cyclically but seem remarkably stable over time, averaging 79 percent for labor and 21 percent for capital. Since then, they have broken out of that range, with the capital share trending up and averaging 23.5 percent between 2005 and 2012, even including the recession low in 2008. (Tables 1-14 and 1-16)

Table 1-11. Relation of Gross Domestic Product, Gross and Net National Product, National Income, and Personal Income

(Billions of dollars, quarterly data are at seasonally adjusted annual rates.)   **NIPA Table 1.7.5**

Year and quarter	Gross domestic product	Plus: Income receipts from the rest of the world	Less: Income payments to the rest of the world	Equals: Gross national product	Less: Consumption of fixed capital										Equals: Net national product
					Total	Private						Government			
						Total	Domestic business				House-holds and institutions	Total	General government	Government enter-prises	
							Total	Capital consumption allowances	Less: Capital consumption adjustment						
1955	426.2	3.5	1.1	428.6	48.9	35.0	28.9	28.3	-0.6	6.1	13.9	13.1	0.8	379.7
1956	450.1	3.9	1.1	452.9	54.1	38.8	32.2	30.8	-1.3	6.6	15.3	14.5	0.9	398.8
1957	474.9	4.3	1.2	477.9	58.9	42.3	35.2	33.5	-1.7	7.1	16.7	15.7	0.9	419.0
1958	482.0	3.9	1.2	484.7	62.4	44.9	37.5	35.3	-2.3	7.4	17.5	16.5	1.0	422.2
1959	522.5	4.3	1.5	525.2	65.4	46.8	39.0	37.5	-1.5	7.8	18.6	17.6	1.0	459.8
1960	543.3	4.9	1.8	546.4	67.9	48.2	40.0	39.7	-0.3	8.2	19.7	18.6	1.1	478.5
1961	563.3	5.3	1.8	566.8	70.6	49.8	41.3	41.7	0.4	8.5	20.8	19.7	1.2	496.2
1962	605.1	5.9	1.8	609.2	74.1	51.8	42.9	46.6	3.6	8.8	22.3	21.1	1.2	535.1
1963	638.6	6.5	2.1	643.1	78.0	54.2	44.9	49.9	5.0	9.3	23.8	22.5	1.3	565.1
1964	685.8	7.2	2.3	690.7	82.4	57.3	47.4	53.2	5.8	9.9	25.1	23.7	1.4	608.3
1965	743.7	7.9	2.6	749.0	88.0	61.6	50.9	57.0	6.1	10.7	26.4	24.9	1.5	661.0
1966	815.0	8.1	3.0	820.1	95.3	67.2	55.6	61.9	6.2	11.5	28.1	26.5	1.6	724.8
1967	861.7	8.7	3.3	867.1	103.5	73.3	60.9	66.9	6.0	12.4	30.2	28.4	1.8	763.6
1968	942.5	10.1	4.0	948.6	113.3	80.6	67.0	72.5	5.6	13.6	32.7	30.8	2.0	835.2
1969	1 019.9	11.8	5.7	1 026.0	124.9	89.4	74.2	79.7	5.5	15.2	35.4	33.2	2.2	901.1
1970	1 075.9	12.8	6.4	1 082.3	136.8	98.3	81.8	85.9	4.1	16.5	38.5	36.1	2.5	945.5
1971	1 167.8	14.0	6.4	1 175.4	148.9	107.6	89.4	92.3	2.9	18.2	41.2	38.4	2.8	1 026.5
1972	1 282.4	16.3	7.7	1 291.0	160.9	117.5	97.2	102.3	5.2	20.3	43.4	40.3	3.1	1 130.1
1973	1 428.5	23.5	10.9	1 441.2	178.1	131.5	108.2	111.9	3.7	23.3	46.6	43.1	3.5	1 263.1
1974	1 548.8	29.8	14.3	1 564.3	206.2	153.2	126.1	123.9	-2.2	27.0	53.0	48.7	4.3	1 358.2
1975	1 688.9	28.0	15.0	1 701.9	237.5	178.8	147.9	135.9	-12.0	30.9	58.7	53.7	5.1	1 464.4
1976	1 877.6	32.4	15.5	1 894.4	259.2	196.5	162.2	147.4	-14.8	34.3	62.7	57.2	5.5	1 635.2
1977	2 086.0	37.2	16.9	2 106.2	288.3	221.1	181.5	167.0	-14.5	39.6	67.2	61.2	6.0	1 817.9
1978	2 356.6	46.3	24.7	2 378.2	325.1	252.1	205.5	189.4	-16.2	46.6	72.9	66.3	6.7	2 053.1
1979	2 632.1	68.3	36.4	2 664.1	371.1	290.7	236.4	216.1	-20.2	54.4	80.4	72.8	7.6	2 292.9
1980	2 862.5	79.1	44.9	2 896.7	426.0	335.0	272.8	245.8	-26.9	62.2	91.0	82.3	8.8	2 470.7
1981	3 210.9	92.0	59.1	3 243.9	485.0	381.9	313.5	301.2	-12.3	68.5	103.1	93.1	10.0	2 758.8
1982	3 345.0	101.0	64.5	3 381.5	534.3	420.4	347.5	343.1	-4.4	72.9	113.9	103.1	10.9	2 847.2
1983	3 638.1	101.9	64.8	3 675.2	560.5	438.8	362.8	385.6	22.8	76.0	121.8	110.3	11.5	3 114.7
1984	4 040.7	121.9	85.6	4 077.0	594.3	463.5	382.7	435.6	52.9	80.9	130.8	118.7	12.2	3 482.6
1985	4 346.7	112.7	87.3	4 372.1	636.7	496.4	410.3	493.5	83.2	86.2	140.2	127.3	12.9	3 735.4
1986	4 590.1	111.3	94.4	4 607.1	682.2	531.6	438.1	512.0	73.9	93.4	150.6	136.8	13.8	3 924.9
1987	4 870.2	123.3	105.8	4 887.7	728.0	566.3	464.5	533.1	68.6	101.8	161.6	147.0	14.6	4 159.7
1988	5 252.6	152.1	129.5	5 275.3	782.4	608.3	498.4	563.7	65.3	109.9	174.1	158.5	15.6	4 492.9
1989	5 657.7	177.7	152.9	5 682.5	836.1	650.1	531.8	589.5	57.7	118.2	186.0	169.3	16.7	4 846.4
1990	5 979.6	188.8	154.2	6 014.3	886.8	689.0	563.9	596.0	32.1	125.1	197.8	180.0	17.9	5 127.4
1991	6 174.0	168.4	136.8	6 205.6	931.1	722.4	591.8	611.6	19.8	130.6	208.8	189.9	18.8	5 274.5
1992	6 539.3	152.1	121.0	6 570.4	959.7	744.2	607.9	628.4	20.5	136.3	215.6	195.8	19.8	5 610.6
1993	6 878.7	155.6	123.6	6 910.7	1 003.6	780.0	634.2	658.9	24.7	145.7	223.6	202.5	21.1	5 907.1
1994	7 308.7	184.5	160.7	7 332.6	1 055.6	824.3	669.0	701.6	32.6	155.3	231.2	208.9	22.4	6 277.0
1995	7 664.0	229.8	201.1	7 692.8	1 122.8	882.6	717.8	753.9	36.2	164.8	240.2	216.6	23.6	6 570.0
1996	8 100.2	246.4	214.6	8 131.9	1 176.0	931.0	758.4	808.3	50.0	172.7	245.0	220.4	24.6	6 955.9
1997	8 608.5	280.1	256.0	8 632.6	1 240.0	990.1	807.9	877.0	69.1	182.1	249.9	224.6	25.3	7 392.6
1998	9 089.1	286.8	268.5	9 107.4	1 310.3	1 054.9	860.4	941.4	81.0	194.5	255.3	228.9	26.4	7 797.1
1999	9 665.7	321.4	294.3	9 692.8	1 400.9	1 135.9	925.0	1 023.8	98.9	210.9	264.9	236.9	28.0	8 292.0
2000	10 289.7	382.7	345.7	10 326.8	1 514.2	1 236.6	1 006.5	1 096.1	89.5	230.1	277.7	247.7	30.0	8 812.5
2001	10 625.3	325.3	273.5	10 677.1	1 604.0	1 317.7	1 067.5	1 180.1	112.6	250.2	286.3	254.9	31.4	9 073.1
2002	10 980.2	315.8	267.2	11 028.8	1 662.1	1 368.0	1 101.4	1 284.9	183.5	266.6	294.1	261.2	32.9	9 366.7
2003	11 512.2	356.1	288.1	11 580.3	1 727.2	1 422.4	1 131.6	1 305.4	173.9	290.8	304.9	270.3	34.6	9 853.1
2004	12 277.0	451.4	361.4	12 367.1	1 831.7	1 509.3	1 185.9	1 335.4	149.4	323.4	322.4	284.9	37.5	10 535.4
2005	13 095.4	575.8	482.3	13 189.0	1 982.0	1 635.3	1 273.2	1 174.2	-99.0	362.1	346.7	305.6	41.0	11 207.0
2006	13 857.9	724.2	655.7	13 926.3	2 136.0	1 765.0	1 368.8	1 250.0	-118.8	396.2	371.0	326.6	44.4	11 790.3
2007	14 480.3	875.5	749.1	14 606.8	2 264.4	1 865.0	1 451.2	1 330.0	-121.2	413.7	399.4	351.4	48.0	12 342.4
2008	14 720.3	856.8	683.8	14 893.2	2 363.4	1 936.9	1 522.3	1 584.7	62.4	414.6	426.5	375.5	51.0	12 529.8
2009	14 417.9	643.7	496.5	14 565.1	2 368.4	1 925.7	1 522.4	1 558.6	36.2	403.3	442.7	390.3	52.5	12 196.7
2010	14 958.3	720.0	514.1	15 164.2	2 381.6	1 923.5	1 523.0	1 599.9	76.9	400.5	458.1	403.8	54.3	12 782.6
2011	15 533.8	802.8	542.1	15 794.6	2 452.6	1 974.4	1 571.6	1 837.2	265.7	402.9	478.1	421.2	57.0	13 342.0
2012	16 244.6	818.6	565.7	16 497.4	2 542.9	2 049.3	1 639.4	1 595.0	-44.4	409.9	493.6	434.2	59.4	13 954.6
2010														
1st quarter	14 672.5	696.5	493.0	14 875.9	2 369.8	1 919.7	1 517.4	1 533.8	16.4	402.3	450.2	396.9	53.3	12 506.1
2nd quarter	14 879.2	711.9	506.7	15 084.3	2 374.9	1 918.9	1 519.4	1 531.8	12.4	399.5	456.0	402.1	53.9	12 709.4
3rd quarter	15 049.8	720.5	520.8	15 249.5	2 382.5	1 921.9	1 522.7	1 598.9	76.2	399.3	460.5	405.8	54.7	12 867.0
4th quarter	15 231.7	751.2	535.7	15 447.2	2 399.1	1 933.6	1 532.7	1 735.3	202.6	400.9	465.5	410.2	55.3	13 048.1
2011														
1st quarter	15 242.9	772.5	524.2	15 491.2	2 417.9	1 947.3	1 545.8	1 801.5	255.7	401.5	470.6	414.7	55.8	13 073.4
2nd quarter	15 461.9	804.5	554.2	15 712.1	2 443.4	1 967.1	1 564.7	1 829.3	264.6	402.5	476.2	419.7	56.6	13 268.8
3rd quarter	15 611.8	822.3	550.1	15 884.0	2 465.1	1 984.1	1 580.9	1 851.2	270.4	403.2	481.0	423.7	57.4	13 419.0
4th quarter	15 818.7	812.0	539.7	16 091.0	2 483.9	1 999.3	1 594.9	1 867.0	272.1	404.4	484.7	426.6	58.1	13 607.1
2012														
1st quarter	16 041.6	818.0	570.0	16 289.6	2 507.6	2 018.7	1 613.9	1 577.3	-36.6	404.8	488.9	430.3	58.7	13 782.0
2nd quarter	16 160.4	814.4	555.7	16 419.2	2 533.7	2 041.0	1 633.7	1 588.3	-45.5	407.2	492.7	433.5	59.2	13 885.5
3rd quarter	16 356.0	812.0	564.4	16 603.7	2 555.1	2 059.8	1 648.4	1 600.2	-48.2	411.4	495.3	435.6	59.7	14 048.5
4th quarter	16 420.3	829.8	572.8	16 677.3	2 575.0	2 077.6	1 661.4	1 614.1	-47.3	416.2	497.4	437.3	60.2	14 102.3

Table 1-11. Relation of Gross Domestic Product, Gross and Net National Product, National Income, and Personal Income—*Continued*

(Billions of dollars, quarterly data are at seasonally adjusted annual rates.)

NIPA Table 1.7.5

Year and quarter	Net national product	Less: Statistical discrepancy	Equals: National income	Corporate profits with IVA and CCAdj	Taxes on production and imports less subsidies	Contributions for government social insurance, domestic	Net interest and miscellaneous payments on assets	Business current transfer payments, net	Current surplus of government enterprises	Personal income receipts on assets	Personal current transfer receipts	Equals: Personal income	Addendum: Gross national income
						Less:				**Plus:**			
1955	379.7	2.1	377.6	50.2	31.3	9.1	6.3	1.3	. . .	29.4	15.7	324.6	426.5
1956	398.8	-2.1	400.9	49.6	33.5	10.0	6.9	1.7	. . .	32.4	16.8	348.4	455.0
1957	419.0	-0.4	419.4	49.1	35.5	11.4	8.1	1.8	. . .	35.6	19.5	368.5	478.3
1958	422.2	0.6	421.6	43.9	36.4	11.4	9.6	1.7	. . .	37.3	23.5	379.5	484.1
1959	459.8	0.1	459.6	55.5	40.0	13.8	9.7	1.7	0.5	40.6	24.2	403.2	525.1
1960	478.5	-1.4	479.9	54.7	43.4	16.4	10.7	1.7	0.5	44.3	25.7	422.5	547.8
1961	496.2	-1.0	497.2	55.9	45.0	17.0	12.6	1.9	0.3	47.2	29.5	441.1	567.8
1962	535.1	-0.1	535.2	64.0	48.1	19.1	14.3	2.1	0.4	51.6	30.4	469.1	609.3
1963	565.1	-1.5	566.6	70.5	51.2	21.7	15.3	2.5	0.8	56.0	32.2	492.8	644.6
1964	608.3	0.0	608.3	77.7	54.5	22.4	17.5	3.0	0.8	62.5	33.5	528.4	690.7
1965	661.0	0.8	660.3	89.3	57.7	23.4	19.8	3.5	0.7	68.7	36.2	570.8	748.2
1966	724.8	5.1	719.7	96.1	59.3	31.3	22.5	3.4	0.3	74.2	39.6	620.6	815.0
1967	763.6	3.4	760.2	93.9	64.1	34.9	25.7	3.6	0.2	79.8	48.0	665.7	863.7
1968	835.2	3.2	832.1	101.7	72.2	38.7	27.6	4.2	0.3	87.3	56.1	730.7	945.4
1969	901.1	1.6	899.5	98.4	79.3	44.1	33.6	4.8	0.0	98.7	62.3	800.3	1 024.4
1970	945.5	5.3	940.1	86.2	86.6	46.4	40.5	4.4	-1.2	112.7	74.7	864.6	1 076.9
1971	1 026.5	9.5	1 017.0	100.6	95.8	51.2	45.2	4.2	-1.7	122.3	88.1	932.1	1 165.9
1972	1 130.1	7.1	1 123.0	117.2	101.3	59.2	49.3	4.8	-1.2	133.3	97.9	1 023.6	1 283.9
1973	1 263.1	6.1	1 257.0	133.4	112.0	75.5	57.2	5.7	-2.2	150.6	112.6	1 138.5	1 435.1
1974	1 358.2	7.4	1 350.8	125.7	121.6	85.2	73.5	6.8	-2.7	175.4	133.3	1 249.3	1 556.9
1975	1 464.4	13.2	1 451.1	138.9	130.8	89.3	85.9	9.0	-4.4	195.3	170.0	1 366.9	1 688.7
1976	1 635.2	20.5	1 614.8	174.3	141.3	101.3	89.9	9.1	-2.7	212.6	184.0	1 498.1	1 874.0
1977	1 817.9	19.3	1 798.7	205.8	152.6	113.1	105.9	8.1	-3.3	243.4	194.2	1 654.2	2 087.0
1978	2 053.1	23.2	2 029.9	238.6	162.0	131.3	118.8	10.4	-2.8	278.0	209.6	1 859.5	2 355.0
1979	2 292.9	44.8	2 248.2	249.0	171.6	152.7	141.0	12.8	-3.2	318.3	235.3	2 077.9	2 619.3
1980	2 470.7	43.9	2 426.8	223.6	190.5	166.2	186.2	14.0	-5.1	386.0	279.5	2 316.8	2 852.8
1981	2 758.8	36.7	2 722.1	247.5	224.2	195.7	238.4	16.9	-5.2	472.9	318.4	2 595.9	3 207.2
1982	2 847.2	6.8	2 840.4	229.9	225.9	208.9	277.5	19.3	-3.8	541.3	354.8	2 778.8	3 374.7
1983	3 114.7	54.2	3 060.5	279.8	242.0	226.0	291.8	21.7	-2.3	584.3	383.7	2 969.7	3 621.1
1984	3 482.6	38.7	3 444.0	337.9	268.7	257.5	336.1	29.2	-1.4	665.1	400.1	3 281.3	4 038.3
1985	3 735.4	51.2	3 684.2	354.5	286.8	281.4	348.0	34.1	1.3	712.8	424.9	3 515.9	4 320.8
1986	3 924.9	76.7	3 848.2	324.4	298.5	303.4	365.2	36.0	2.0	755.3	451.0	3 725.1	4 530.4
1987	4 159.7	40.5	4 119.2	366.0	317.3	323.1	369.5	33.3	2.2	779.9	467.6	3 955.3	4 847.2
1988	4 492.9	-0.5	4 493.4	414.9	345.0	361.5	394.7	32.8	5.0	839.4	496.5	4 275.3	5 275.8
1989	4 846.4	64.2	4 782.2	414.2	371.4	385.2	442.7	38.3	6.7	951.9	542.6	4 618.2	5 618.3
1990	5 127.4	91.3	5 036.1	417.2	398.0	410.1	450.1	39.2	3.2	991.2	594.9	4 904.5	5 922.9
1991	5 274.5	88.4	5 186.1	451.3	429.6	430.2	408.5	38.9	7.8	985.5	665.9	5 071.1	6 117.3
1992	5 610.6	110.9	5 499.7	475.3	453.3	455.0	383.7	39.7	9.9	982.1	745.8	5 410.8	6 459.5
1993	5 907.1	152.3	5 754.8	522.0	466.4	477.4	371.4	39.4	10.8	988.6	790.8	5 646.8	6 758.4
1994	6 277.0	136.8	6 140.2	621.9	512.7	508.2	365.9	40.7	11.8	1 029.4	826.4	5 934.7	7 195.8
1995	6 570.0	90.5	6 479.5	703.0	523.1	532.8	376.5	45.0	15.6	1 114.0	878.9	6 276.5	7 602.3
1996	6 955.9	56.5	6 899.4	786.1	545.5	555.1	381.9	52.6	16.9	1 176.5	924.1	6 661.9	8 075.4
1997	7 392.6	12.3	7 380.4	865.8	577.8	587.2	414.7	50.1	17.5	1 258.5	949.2	7 075.0	8 620.3
1998	7 797.1	-60.2	7 857.3	804.1	603.1	624.7	477.8	64.1	16.3	1 342.5	977.9	7 587.7	9 167.6
1999	8 292.0	-32.4	8 324.4	830.2	628.4	661.3	488.0	67.8	16.2	1 329.7	1 021.6	7 983.8	9 725.3
2000	8 812.5	-94.5	8 907.0	781.2	662.7	705.8	565.0	85.3	10.7	1 453.5	1 083.0	8 632.8	10 421.3
2001	9 073.1	-111.6	9 184.6	754.0	669.0	733.2	566.4	99.1	5.2	1 441.3	1 188.1	8 987.1	10 788.6
2002	9 366.7	-70.1	9 436.8	907.2	721.2	751.5	490.5	80.7	7.0	1 390.4	1 280.3	9 149.5	11 098.9
2003	9 853.1	-12.1	9 865.1	1 056.4	758.9	779.3	466.2	76.3	3.9	1 420.5	1 342.9	9 487.6	11 592.3
2004	10 535.4	-6.5	10 541.9	1 283.3	817.6	829.2	403.5	81.4	-1.8	1 503.7	1 416.7	10 049.2	12 373.6
2005	11 207.0	-33.8	11 240.8	1 477.7	873.6	873.3	496.8	93.9	-6.4	1 666.5	1 512.0	10 610.3	13 222.7
2006	11 790.3	-215.3	12 005.6	1 646.5	940.5	922.6	580.9	82.6	-9.3	1 938.4	1 609.6	11 389.8	14 141.6
2007	12 342.4	20.2	12 322.3	1 529.0	980.0	961.4	663.4	98.6	-16.4	2 166.6	1 722.8	11 995.7	14 586.6
2008	12 529.8	99.0	12 430.8	1 285.1	989.4	988.2	693.4	116.4	-21.2	2 167.1	1 884.0	12 430.6	14 794.2
2009	12 196.7	72.2	12 124.5	1 392.6	967.8	964.4	563.1	127.2	-20.6	1 811.8	2 140.2	12 082.1	14 492.9
2010	12 782.6	43.1	12 739.5	1 740.6	1 001.2	984.1	489.4	128.5	-22.9	1 739.6	2 276.9	12 435.2	15 121.1
2011	13 342.0	-53.7	13 395.7	1 877.7	1 037.2	918.2	456.9	129.6	-23.8	1 884.6	2 306.9	13 191.3	15 848.3
2012	13 954.6	-17.0	13 971.6	2 009.5	1 065.6	950.7	439.6	106.9	-27.7	1 958.5	2 358.3	13 743.8	16 514.5
2010													
1st quarter	12 506.1	45.1	12 461.0	1 655.2	987.3	972.0	508.0	129.3	-21.2	1 710.7	2 253.3	12 194.3	14 830.9
2nd quarter	12 709.4	85.4	12 624.0	1 660.8	998.7	984.0	485.8	126.5	-22.6	1 722.8	2 260.9	12 374.3	14 998.9
3rd quarter	12 867.0	-0.7	12 867.8	1 807.0	1 006.9	988.4	482.2	131.1	-23.5	1 738.0	2 288.4	12 502.1	15 250.2
4th quarter	13 048.1	42.7	13 005.4	1 839.2	1 012.1	992.0	481.6	127.0	-24.3	1 787.0	2 305.1	12 670.0	15 404.5
2011													
1st quarter	13 073.4	-83.3	13 156.7	1 755.0	1 026.5	912.6	473.8	142.6	-23.8	1 850.4	2 309.6	13 029.9	15 574.6
2nd quarter	13 268.8	-51.7	13 320.4	1 868.7	1 040.0	916.4	436.7	125.6	-23.1	1 883.4	2 309.0	13 148.5	15 763.8
3rd quarter	13 419.0	-83.0	13 502.0	1 893.8	1 035.4	924.7	459.7	128.3	-23.7	1 899.3	2 300.5	13 283.6	15 967.1
4th quarter	13 607.1	3.4	13 603.6	1 993.4	1 046.9	919.1	457.5	121.8	-24.4	1 905.4	2 308.5	13 303.2	16 087.6
2012													
1st quarter	13 782.0	-63.0	13 845.0	1 979.9	1 066.6	942.5	453.9	115.7	-24.5	1 909.1	2 328.5	13 548.6	16 352.6
2nd quarter	13 885.5	10.1	13 875.3	1 998.4	1 064.6	945.1	419.0	110.0	-26.1	1 935.3	2 352.2	13 651.8	16 409.0
3rd quarter	14 048.5	86.4	13 962.1	2 012.3	1 062.8	947.4	455.3	102.6	-28.5	1 926.9	2 364.4	13 701.6	16 517.2
4th quarter	14 102.3	-101.7	14 204.0	2 047.2	1 068.6	967.9	430.3	99.5	-31.8	2 062.8	2 388.0	14 073.1	16 779.1

. . . = Not available.

Table 1-12. Gross Domestic Income by Type of Income

(Billions of dollars, quarterly data are at seasonally adjusted annual rates.)   **NIPA Tables 1.1.5, 1.10**

Year and quarter	Gross domestic income	Compensation of employees			Taxes on production and imports	Less: Subsidies	Net operating surplus					
							Total	Private enterprises				
		Total	Wages and salaries	Supplements to wages and salaries				Total	Net interest and miscellaneous payments, domestic industries	Business current transfer payments, net	Proprietors' income with IVA and CCAdj	Rental income of persons with CCAdj
1955	424.1	231.0	212.2	18.7	31.5	0.2	. . .	112.9	6.1	1.3	44.3	13.4
1956	452.2	249.7	229.1	20.6	34.2	0.7	. . .	114.9	6.9	1.7	45.8	13.7
1957	475.2	263.1	240.0	23.0	36.6	1.1	. . .	117.8	8.1	1.8	47.8	14.1
1958	481.4	265.2	241.4	23.8	37.7	1.4	. . .	117.5	9.5	1.7	50.2	14.8
1959	522.3	286.4	259.9	26.5	41.1	1.1	130.5	129.9	9.6	1.7	50.3	15.6
1960	544.6	302.0	273.0	29.0	44.5	1.1	131.3	130.9	10.5	1.7	50.6	16.5
1961	564.3	311.2	280.7	30.6	47.0	2.0	137.5	137.2	12.2	1.9	53.2	17.2
1962	605.2	333.0	299.5	33.6	50.4	2.3	150.0	149.6	13.9	2.1	55.2	18.0
1963	640.1	351.2	314.9	36.3	53.4	2.2	159.7	158.9	14.8	2.5	56.4	18.7
1964	685.8	376.9	337.8	39.0	57.3	2.7	172.0	171.2	17.0	3.0	59.1	18.8
1965	743.0	406.3	363.8	42.6	60.7	3.0	190.9	190.2	19.2	3.5	63.7	19.3
1966	809.9	450.3	400.3	50.0	63.2	3.9	205.1	204.8	22.0	3.4	67.9	19.9
1967	858.3	482.9	429.0	53.9	67.9	3.8	207.8	207.6	25.1	3.6	69.5	20.3
1968	939.3	532.1	472.0	60.1	76.4	4.2	221.7	221.4	27.1	4.2	73.8	20.1
1969	1 018.3	586.0	518.3	67.7	83.9	4.5	228.1	228.1	34.1	4.8	77.0	20.4
1970	1 070.5	625.1	551.5	73.6	91.4	4.8	222.0	223.2	41.2	4.4	77.8	20.7
1971	1 158.3	667.0	584.5	82.5	100.5	4.7	246.6	248.3	45.5	4.2	83.9	21.9
1972	1 275.3	733.6	638.8	94.9	107.9	6.6	279.5	280.6	50.3	4.8	95.1	22.8
1973	1 422.4	815.1	708.8	106.3	117.2	5.2	317.3	319.5	59.5	5.7	112.5	23.3
1974	1 541.4	890.3	772.3	118.0	124.9	3.3	323.3	326.0	75.4	6.8	112.2	23.3
1975	1 675.7	950.2	814.9	135.3	135.3	4.5	357.1	361.5	87.5	9.0	118.2	22.5
1976	1 857.1	1 051.3	899.8	151.5	146.4	5.1	405.4	408.1	89.6	9.1	131.0	20.6
1977	2 066.7	1 169.0	994.2	174.8	159.7	7.1	456.8	460.1	104.6	8.1	144.5	16.2
1978	2 333.4	1 320.3	1 120.7	199.7	170.9	8.9	526.1	528.9	120.0	10.4	166.0	16.9
1979	2 587.4	1 481.1	1 253.4	227.7	180.1	8.5	563.6	566.8	143.6	12.8	179.4	16.6
1980	2 818.6	1 626.3	1 373.5	252.8	200.3	9.8	575.7	580.8	187.4	14.0	171.6	19.7
1981	3 174.2	1 795.4	1 511.5	283.9	235.6	11.5	669.6	674.8	235.0	16.9	179.7	25.4
1982	3 338.2	1 894.5	1 587.7	306.8	240.9	15.0	683.5	687.3	273.4	19.3	171.2	26.1
1983	3 584.0	2 014.1	1 677.7	336.4	263.3	21.3	767.4	769.7	289.6	21.7	186.3	27.5
1984	4 002.0	2 217.6	1 845.1	372.5	289.8	21.1	921.4	922.8	336.2	29.2	228.2	27.9
1985	4 295.5	2 389.2	1 982.8	406.4	308.1	21.4	982.9	981.6	360.6	34.1	241.1	29.5
1986	4 513.4	2 545.6	2 104.1	441.5	323.4	24.9	987.1	985.2	385.9	36.0	256.5	21.9
1987	4 829.7	2 725.7	2 257.6	468.0	347.5	30.3	1 058.8	1 056.6	398.7	33.3	286.5	20.2
1988	5 253.1	2 950.9	2 440.6	510.3	374.5	29.5	1 174.8	1 169.8	428.2	32.8	325.8	25.1
1989	5 593.5	3 143.9	2 584.3	559.5	398.9	27.4	1 242.1	1 235.4	483.7	38.3	341.9	24.4
1990	5 888.2	3 345.0	2 743.5	601.5	425.0	27.0	1 258.4	1 255.2	489.1	39.2	354.4	31.4
1991	6 085.7	3 454.7	2 817.2	637.5	457.1	27.5	1 270.2	1 262.3	450.6	38.9	356.0	42.0
1992	6 428.4	3 674.1	2 968.5	705.6	483.4	30.1	1 341.3	1 331.4	422.8	39.7	402.4	64.3
1993	6 726.4	3 824.0	3 082.7	741.3	503.1	36.7	1 432.4	1 421.6	413.0	39.4	430.5	93.6
1994	7 171.9	4 014.1	3 240.6	773.5	545.2	32.5	1 589.5	1 577.7	416.0	40.7	459.5	117.5
1995	7 573.5	4 206.7	3 422.1	784.6	557.9	34.8	1 720.9	1 705.3	436.6	45.0	484.5	129.2
1996	8 043.6	4 426.2	3 620.6	805.6	580.8	35.2	1 895.9	1 879.0	447.9	52.6	547.4	147.0
1997	8 596.2	4 719.1	3 881.2	837.8	611.6	33.8	2 059.4	2 041.9	493.7	50.1	587.9	152.0
1998	9 149.3	5 082.4	4 186.2	896.2	639.5	36.4	2 153.6	2 137.3	557.8	64.1	644.2	169.9
1999	9 698.1	5 417.5	4 465.2	952.3	673.6	45.2	2 251.4	2 235.2	575.7	67.8	700.4	183.1
2000	10 384.1	5 863.1	4 832.4	1 030.7	708.6	45.8	2 344.2	2 333.4	667.6	85.3	757.8	187.7
2001	10 736.8	6 053.8	4 961.6	1 092.1	727.7	58.7	2 410.1	2 404.9	677.8	99.1	836.8	207.5
2002	11 050.3	6 149.7	5 004.2	1 145.5	762.6	41.4	2 517.3	2 510.3	592.9	80.7	871.0	217.3
2003	11 524.3	6 372.7	5 146.1	1 226.6	808.0	49.1	2 665.4	2 661.5	557.4	76.3	900.1	238.0
2004	12 283.5	6 748.8	5 431.2	1 317.6	863.9	46.4	2 885.5	2 887.3	510.1	81.4	962.1	255.4
2005	13 129.2	7 097.9	5 703.1	1 394.8	934.5	60.9	3 175.7	3 182.1	632.2	93.9	979.0	238.4
2006	14 073.2	7 513.7	6 068.8	1 444.9	991.9	51.5	3 483.0	3 492.3	758.1	82.6	1 053.7	207.5
2007	14 460.1	7 908.8	6 405.7	1 503.1	1 034.6	54.6	3 307.0	3 323.5	880.7	98.6	979.2	189.4
2008	14 621.2	8 090.0	6 543.6	1 546.4	1 041.9	52.6	3 178.6	3 199.8	916.4	116.4	1 026.5	262.1
2009	14 345.7	7 795.7	6 260.1	1 535.6	1 026.1	58.3	3 213.9	3 234.5	760.9	127.2	973.0	333.7
2010	14 915.2	7 975.3	6 385.6	1 589.8	1 057.1	55.9	3 557.0	3 579.9	670.6	128.5	1 032.7	402.8
2011	15 587.5	8 286.6	6 646.8	1 639.8	1 097.1	60.0	3 811.2	3 834.9	624.6	129.6	1 155.1	484.4
2012	16 261.6	8 620.0	6 935.1	1 684.9	1 122.9	57.3	4 033.2	4 060.9	597.4	106.9	1 224.9	541.2
2010												
1st quarter	14 627.4	7 811.8	6 247.0	1 564.7	1 042.2	54.9	3 458.5	3 479.7	694.6	129.3	1 017.6	380.5
2nd quarter	14 793.7	7 960.8	6 373.6	1 587.2	1 054.2	55.5	3 459.3	3 481.9	667.1	126.5	1 024.7	397.3
3rd quarter	15 050.5	8 035.0	6 434.8	1 600.1	1 063.1	56.2	3 626.2	3 649.7	658.7	131.1	1 029.2	408.3
4th quarter	15 189.0	8 093.9	6 486.8	1 607.1	1 069.0	56.9	3 683.9	3 708.3	661.9	127.0	1 059.3	425.0
2011												
1st quarter	15 326.2	8 215.0	6 585.2	1 629.9	1 085.2	58.7	3 666.8	3 690.7	645.7	142.6	1 116.5	458.5
2nd quarter	15 513.6	8 264.3	6 629.0	1 635.4	1 099.9	59.9	3 765.9	3 789.0	605.9	125.6	1 140.7	475.5
3rd quarter	15 694.9	8 351.6	6 706.3	1 645.3	1 095.9	60.5	3 842.8	3 866.5	629.9	128.3	1 175.3	489.9
4th quarter	15 815.3	8 315.3	6 666.7	1 648.7	1 107.5	60.6	3 969.1	3 993.5	617.0	121.8	1 188.0	513.5
2012												
1st quarter	16 104.6	8 522.3	6 850.3	1 672.1	1 124.4	57.8	4 008.1	4 032.5	613.6	115.7	1 214.4	524.8
2nd quarter	16 150.3	8 562.6	6 882.3	1 680.3	1 122.2	57.6	3 989.4	4 015.5	580.8	110.0	1 217.8	537.8
3rd quarter	16 269.6	8 599.5	6 913.2	1 686.2	1 118.8	56.0	4 052.2	4 080.7	611.7	102.6	1 220.0	546.7
4th quarter	16 522.0	8 795.5	7 094.6	1 700.9	1 126.3	57.7	4 083.0	4 114.8	583.3	99.5	1 247.5	555.4

. . . = Not available.

Table 1-12. Gross Domestic Income by Type of Income—*Continued*

(Billions of dollars, quarterly data are at seasonally adjusted annual rates.)   **NIPA Tables 1.1.5, 1.10**

| Year and quarter | Net operating surplus—*Continued* Private enterprises—*Continued* Corporate profits with IVA and CCAdj, domestic industries | | | | | Current surplus of government enterprises | Consumption of fixed capital | | | Statistical discrepancy | Gross domestic product |
	Total	Taxes on corporate income	Profits after tax Total	Profits after tax Net dividends	Profits after tax Undistributed corporate profits		Total	Private	Government		
1955	47.8	22.0	25.8	8.9	16.9	...	48.9	35.0	13.9	2.1	426.2
1956	46.8	22.0	24.8	9.5	15.4	...	54.1	38.8	15.3	-2.1	450.1
1957	46.0	21.4	24.6	9.9	14.8	...	58.9	42.3	16.7	-0.4	474.9
1958	41.3	19.0	22.4	9.8	12.5	...	62.4	44.9	17.5	0.6	482.0
1959	52.8	23.7	29.1	10.7	18.4	0.5	65.4	46.8	18.6	0.1	522.5
1960	51.5	22.8	28.8	11.4	17.4	0.5	67.9	48.2	19.7	-1.4	543.3
1961	52.6	22.9	29.7	11.5	18.2	0.3	70.6	49.8	20.8	-1.0	563.3
1962	60.3	24.1	36.2	12.4	23.8	0.4	74.1	51.8	22.3	-0.1	605.1
1963	66.4	26.4	40.1	13.6	26.5	0.8	78.0	54.2	23.8	-1.5	638.6
1964	73.2	28.2	45.1	15.0	30.1	0.8	82.4	57.3	25.1	0.0	685.8
1965	84.6	31.1	53.5	16.9	36.6	0.7	88.0	61.6	26.4	0.8	743.7
1966	91.6	33.9	57.7	17.8	39.9	0.3	95.3	67.2	28.1	5.1	815.0
1967	89.1	32.9	56.2	18.3	37.9	0.2	103.5	73.3	30.2	3.4	861.7
1968	96.1	39.6	56.5	20.2	36.3	0.3	113.3	80.6	32.7	3.2	942.5
1969	91.8	40.0	51.8	20.4	31.4	0.0	124.9	89.4	35.4	1.6	1 019.9
1970	79.1	34.8	44.4	20.4	24.0	-1.2	136.8	98.3	38.5	5.3	1 075.9
1971	92.8	38.2	54.6	20.3	34.3	-1.7	148.9	107.6	41.2	9.5	1 167.8
1972	107.7	42.3	65.3	21.9	43.4	-1.2	160.9	117.5	43.4	7.1	1 282.4
1973	118.5	50.0	68.5	23.1	45.4	-2.2	178.1	131.5	46.6	6.1	1 428.5
1974	108.2	52.8	55.5	23.5	32.0	-2.7	206.2	153.2	53.0	7.4	1 548.8
1975	124.2	51.6	72.6	26.4	46.2	-4.4	237.5	178.8	58.7	13.2	1 688.9
1976	157.8	65.3	92.5	30.1	62.4	-2.7	259.2	196.5	62.7	20.5	1 877.6
1977	186.7	74.4	112.2	33.7	78.5	-3.3	288.3	221.1	67.2	19.3	2 086.0
1978	215.7	84.9	130.8	39.6	91.2	-2.8	325.1	252.1	72.9	23.2	2 356.6
1979	214.4	90.0	124.4	41.5	82.9	-3.2	371.1	290.7	80.4	44.8	2 632.1
1980	188.1	87.2	100.9	47.3	53.6	-5.1	426.0	335.0	91.0	43.9	2 862.5
1981	217.8	84.3	133.5	58.3	75.2	-5.2	485.0	381.9	103.1	36.7	3 210.9
1982	197.3	66.5	130.8	61.3	69.4	-3.8	534.3	420.4	113.9	6.8	3 345.0
1983	244.7	80.6	164.1	71.3	92.7	-2.3	560.5	438.8	121.8	54.2	3 638.1
1984	301.3	97.5	203.8	78.5	125.3	-1.4	594.3	463.5	130.8	38.7	4 040.7
1985	316.4	99.4	217.0	85.7	131.3	1.3	636.7	496.4	140.2	51.2	4 346.7
1986	284.9	109.7	175.2	88.3	86.9	2.0	682.2	531.6	150.6	76.7	4 590.1
1987	318.0	130.4	187.5	95.6	91.9	2.2	728.0	566.3	161.6	40.5	4 870.2
1988	357.9	141.6	216.3	98.0	118.2	5.0	782.4	608.3	174.1	-0.5	5 252.6
1989	347.1	146.1	201.0	126.4	74.7	6.7	836.1	650.1	186.0	64.2	5 657.7
1990	341.1	145.4	195.6	144.1	51.6	3.2	886.8	689.0	197.8	91.3	5 979.6
1991	374.9	138.6	236.3	156.2	80.1	7.8	931.1	722.4	208.8	88.4	6 174.0
1992	402.2	148.7	253.5	161.5	92.0	9.9	959.7	744.2	215.6	110.9	6 539.3
1993	445.1	171.0	274.0	184.7	89.3	10.8	1 003.6	780.0	223.6	152.3	6 878.7
1994	543.9	193.1	350.8	197.8	153.0	11.8	1 055.6	824.3	231.2	136.8	7 308.7
1995	610.1	217.8	392.2	226.2	166.1	15.6	1 122.8	882.6	240.2	90.5	7 664.0
1996	684.1	231.5	452.6	263.1	189.5	16.9	1 176.0	931.0	245.0	56.5	8 100.2
1997	758.2	245.4	512.8	292.2	220.6	17.5	1 240.0	990.1	249.9	12.3	8 608.5
1998	701.3	248.4	453.0	314.8	138.2	16.3	1 310.3	1 054.9	255.3	-60.2	9 089.1
1999	708.2	258.8	449.4	306.4	143.1	16.2	1 400.9	1 135.9	264.9	-32.4	9 665.7
2000	635.0	265.1	369.9	355.4	14.5	10.7	1 514.2	1 236.6	277.7	-94.5	10 289.7
2001	583.6	203.3	380.3	329.9	50.4	5.2	1 604.0	1 317.7	286.3	-111.6	10 625.3
2002	748.4	192.3	556.1	352.3	203.8	7.0	1 662.1	1 368.0	294.1	-70.1	10 980.2
2003	889.7	243.8	646.0	401.9	244.1	3.9	1 727.2	1 422.4	304.9	-12.1	11 512.2
2004	1 078.3	306.1	772.2	501.8	270.4	-1.8	1 831.7	1 509.3	322.4	-6.5	12 277.0
2005	1 238.7	412.4	826.3	319.7	506.6	-6.4	1 982.0	1 635.3	346.7	-33.8	13 095.4
2006	1 390.3	473.4	917.0	648.1	268.9	-9.3	2 136.0	1 765.0	371.0	-215.3	13 857.9
2007	1 175.6	445.5	730.1	678.5	51.6	-16.4	2 264.4	1 865.0	399.4	20.2	14 480.3
2008	878.4	309.1	569.3	628.1	-58.8	-21.2	2 363.4	1 936.9	426.5	99.0	14 720.3
2009	1 039.8	269.4	770.3	456.9	313.5	-20.6	2 368.4	1 925.7	442.7	72.2	14 417.9
2010	1 345.4	370.6	974.8	442.5	532.3	-22.9	2 381.6	1 923.5	458.1	43.1	14 958.3
2011	1 441.2	374.2	1 067.0	545.1	521.8	-23.8	2 452.6	1 974.4	478.1	-53.7	15 533.8
2012	1 590.5	434.8	1 155.7	613.6	542.2	-27.7	2 542.9	2 049.3	493.6	-17.0	16 244.6
2010											
1st quarter	1 257.7	344.8	912.9	418.9	494.0	-21.2	2 369.8	1 919.7	450.2	45.1	14 672.5
2nd quarter	1 266.4	351.7	914.7	410.9	503.8	-22.6	2 374.9	1 918.9	456.0	85.4	14 879.2
3rd quarter	1 422.4	387.5	1 034.9	462.8	572.1	-23.5	2 382.5	1 921.9	460.5	-0.7	15 049.8
4th quarter	1 435.1	398.3	1 036.8	477.6	559.2	-24.3	2 399.1	1 933.6	465.5	42.7	15 231.7
2011											
1st quarter	1 327.2	393.0	934.2	510.9	423.3	-23.8	2 417.9	1 947.3	470.6	-83.3	15 242.9
2nd quarter	1 441.3	384.3	1 057.0	543.1	514.0	-23.1	2 443.4	1 967.1	476.2	-51.7	15 461.9
3rd quarter	1 443.0	351.0	1 092.0	573.7	518.3	-23.7	2 465.1	1 984.1	481.0	-83.0	15 611.8
4th quarter	1 553.2	368.6	1 184.6	553.0	631.6	-24.4	2 483.9	1 999.3	484.7	3.4	15 818.7
2012											
1st quarter	1 564.0	437.2	1 126.8	569.1	557.8	-24.5	2 507.6	2 018.7	488.9	-63.0	16 041.6
2nd quarter	1 569.1	429.7	1 139.4	572.5	566.9	-26.1	2 533.7	2 041.0	492.7	10.1	16 160.4
3rd quarter	1 599.8	439.1	1 160.7	577.3	583.4	-28.5	2 555.1	2 059.8	495.3	86.4	16 356.0
4th quarter	1 629.1	433.2	1 196.0	735.3	460.7	-31.8	2 575.0	2 077.6	497.4	-101.7	16 420.3

. . . = Not available.

Table 1-13A. National Income by Type of Income: Recent Data

(Billions of dollars, quarterly data are at seasonally adjusted annual rates.)   **NIPA Tables 1.7.5, 1.12**

Year and quarter	National income, total	Compensation of employees Total	Wages and salaries Total	Government	Other	Supplements to wages and salaries Total	Employer contributions for: Employee pension and insurance funds	Government social insurance	Proprietors' income with IVA and CCAdj Total	Farm	Nonfarm	Rental income of persons with CCAdj
1950	267.0	158.5	147.3	22.6	124.6	11.2	7.8	3.4	37.5	12.9	24.6	8.8
1951	308.0	185.9	171.6	29.2	142.4	14.3	10.2	4.1	42.6	15.3	27.3	9.7
1952	326.5	201.3	185.6	33.4	152.3	15.7	11.6	4.1	43.0	14.3	28.7	10.8
1953	344.4	215.5	199.0	34.3	164.7	16.5	12.3	4.2	42.0	12.2	29.8	12.0
1954	344.4	214.4	197.3	34.9	162.4	17.2	12.6	4.6	42.3	11.7	30.5	13.1
1955	377.6	230.9	212.2	36.6	175.6	18.7	13.6	5.2	44.3	10.7	33.6	13.4
1956	400.9	249.6	229.0	38.8	190.2	20.6	14.9	5.7	45.8	10.6	35.2	13.7
1957	419.4	263.0	240.0	41.0	198.9	23.0	16.7	6.4	47.8	10.6	37.2	14.1
1958	421.6	265.1	241.3	44.1	197.2	23.8	17.5	6.3	50.2	12.4	37.7	14.8
1959	459.6	286.3	259.8	46.1	213.8	26.5	18.6	7.9	50.3	10.0	40.3	15.6
1960	479.9	301.9	272.9	49.2	223.7	29.0	19.7	9.3	50.6	10.6	39.9	16.5
1961	497.2	311.1	280.5	52.5	228.0	30.6	21.0	9.6	53.2	11.2	42.0	17.2
1962	535.2	332.9	299.4	56.3	243.0	33.6	22.4	11.2	55.2	11.2	44.0	18.0
1963	566.6	351.2	314.9	60.0	254.8	36.3	23.9	12.4	56.4	11.0	45.4	18.7
1964	608.3	376.8	337.8	64.9	272.9	39.0	26.4	12.6	59.1	9.8	49.4	18.8
1965	660.3	406.3	363.8	69.9	293.8	42.6	29.5	13.1	63.7	12.0	51.6	19.3
1966	719.7	450.3	400.3	78.4	321.9	50.0	33.1	16.8	67.9	13.0	54.9	19.9
1967	760.2	482.9	429.0	86.5	342.5	53.9	35.9	18.0	69.5	11.6	57.8	20.3
1968	832.1	532.1	472.0	96.7	375.3	60.1	40.2	20.0	73.8	11.7	62.2	20.1
1969	899.5	586.0	518.3	105.6	412.7	67.7	44.9	22.8	77.0	12.8	64.2	20.4
1970	940.1	625.1	551.6	117.2	434.3	73.6	49.7	23.8	77.8	12.9	64.9	20.7
1971	1 017.0	667.0	584.5	126.8	457.8	82.5	56.0	26.4	83.9	13.4	70.5	21.9
1972	1 123.0	733.6	638.8	137.9	500.9	94.9	63.7	31.2	95.1	17.0	78.1	22.8
1973	1 257.0	815.0	708.8	148.8	560.0	106.3	66.5	39.8	112.5	29.1	83.4	23.3
1974	1 350.8	890.3	772.3	160.5	611.8	118.0	73.3	44.7	112.2	23.5	88.7	23.3
1975	1 451.1	950.2	814.8	176.2	638.6	135.3	88.6	46.7	118.2	22.0	96.2	22.5
1976	1 614.8	1 051.2	899.7	188.9	710.8	151.5	97.1	54.4	131.0	17.2	113.8	20.6
1977	1 798.7	1 169.0	994.2	202.6	791.6	174.8	113.7	61.1	144.5	16.0	128.5	16.2
1978	2 029.9	1 320.2	1 120.6	220.0	900.6	199.7	128.1	71.5	166.0	19.9	146.1	16.9
1979	2 248.2	1 481.0	1 253.3	237.1	1 016.2	227.7	145.1	82.6	179.4	22.2	157.3	16.6
1980	2 426.8	1 626.2	1 373.4	261.5	1 112.0	252.8	163.9	88.9	171.6	11.7	159.9	19.7
1981	2 722.1	1 795.3	1 511.4	285.8	1 225.5	283.9	180.3	103.6	179.7	19.0	160.7	25.4
1982	2 840.4	1 894.3	1 587.5	307.5	1 280.0	306.8	197.0	109.8	171.2	13.3	157.9	26.1
1983	3 060.5	2 013.9	1 677.5	324.8	1 352.7	336.4	216.5	119.9	186.3	6.2	180.1	27.5
1984	3 444.0	2 217.4	1 844.9	348.1	1 496.8	372.5	233.5	139.0	228.2	20.9	207.3	27.9
1985	3 684.2	2 389.0	1 982.6	373.9	1 608.7	406.4	258.7	147.7	241.1	21.0	220.1	29.5
1986	3 848.2	2 543.8	2 102.3	397.2	1 705.1	441.5	283.6	157.9	256.5	22.8	233.7	21.9
1987	4 119.2	2 724.3	2 256.3	423.1	1 833.2	468.0	301.8	166.3	286.5	28.9	257.6	20.2
1988	4 493.4	2 950.0	2 439.8	452.0	1 987.7	510.3	325.6	184.6	325.8	26.8	299.1	25.1
1989	4 782.2	3 142.6	2 583.1	481.1	2 101.9	559.5	365.8	193.7	341.9	33.0	308.9	24.4
1990	5 036.1	3 342.7	2 741.2	519.0	2 222.2	601.5	395.0	206.5	354.4	32.2	322.3	31.4
1991	5 186.1	3 452.0	2 814.5	548.8	2 265.7	637.5	422.4	215.1	356.0	26.8	329.2	42.0
1992	5 499.7	3 671.1	2 965.5	572.0	2 393.5	705.6	477.2	228.4	402.4	34.8	367.6	64.3
1993	5 754.8	3 820.7	3 079.3	589.0	2 490.3	741.3	501.7	239.7	430.5	31.4	399.2	93.6
1994	6 140.2	4 010.1	3 236.6	609.5	2 627.1	773.5	519.4	254.1	459.5	34.7	424.8	117.5
1995	6 479.5	4 202.6	3 418.0	629.0	2 789.0	784.6	520.5	264.1	484.5	22.0	462.4	129.2
1996	6 899.4	4 422.1	3 616.5	648.1	2 968.4	805.6	530.8	274.8	547.4	37.3	510.1	147.0
1997	7 380.4	4 714.7	3 876.8	671.9	3 205.0	837.8	548.3	289.6	587.9	32.4	555.5	152.0
1998	7 857.8	5 077.8	4 181.6	701.3	3 480.3	896.2	589.0	307.2	644.2	28.4	615.7	169.9
1999	8 324.4	5 410.3	4 458.0	733.8	3 724.2	952.3	629.0	323.3	700.4	28.1	672.3	183.1
2000	8 907.0	5 856.6	4 825.9	779.8	4 046.1	1 030.7	685.5	345.2	757.8	31.5	726.3	187.7
2001	9 184.6	6 046.5	4 954.4	822.0	4 132.4	1 092.1	734.1	358.0	836.8	32.1	804.7	207.5
2002	9 436.8	6 141.9	4 996.4	873.2	4 123.3	1 145.5	779.5	366.0	871.0	19.9	851.1	217.3
2003	9 865.1	6 365.4	5 138.8	913.3	4 225.5	1 226.6	844.1	382.5	900.1	38.0	862.0	238.0
2004	10 541.9	6 740.5	5 422.9	952.7	4 470.2	1 317.6	908.9	408.7	962.1	50.4	911.6	255.4
2005	11 240.8	7 087.8	5 692.9	991.5	4 701.4	1 394.8	966.8	428.1	979.0	46.4	932.6	238.4
2006	12 005.6	7 503.2	6 058.2	1 035.0	5 023.3	1 444.9	997.6	447.4	1 053.7	36.0	1 017.7	207.5
2007	12 322.3	7 899.1	6 396.0	1 088.8	5 307.2	1 503.1	1 041.4	461.7	979.2	38.1	941.1	189.4
2008	12 430.8	8 079.2	6 532.8	1 144.1	5 388.7	1 546.4	1 075.1	471.3	1 026.5	47.0	979.5	262.1
2009	12 124.5	7 787.8	6 252.2	1 175.1	5 077.1	1 535.6	1 077.5	458.1	973.0	35.5	937.5	333.7
2010	12 739.5	7 967.3	6 377.5	1 191.1	5 186.4	1 589.8	1 120.4	469.4	1 032.7	46.0	986.7	402.8
2011	13 395.7	8 278.5	6 638.7	1 194.4	5 444.3	1 639.8	1 145.4	494.4	1 155.1	72.6	1 082.6	484.4
2012	13 971.6	8 611.6	6 926.8	1 197.3	5 729.4	1 684.9	1 170.6	514.3	1 224.9	75.4	1 149.6	541.2
2010												
1st quarter	12 461.0	7 804.3	6 239.6	1 187.4	5 052.1	1 564.7	1 100.3	464.4	1 017.6	39.2	978.5	380.5
2nd quarter	12 624.0	7 952.7	6 365.5	1 196.8	5 168.7	1 587.2	1 117.4	469.8	1 024.7	43.2	981.5	397.3
3rd quarter	12 867.8	8 026.5	6 426.4	1 190.3	5 236.1	1 600.1	1 128.9	471.2	1 029.2	48.4	980.8	408.3
4th quarter	13 005.4	8 085.7	6 478.6	1 189.8	5 288.8	1 607.1	1 135.1	472.0	1 059.3	53.2	1 006.0	425.0
2011												
1st quarter	13 156.7	8 207.4	6 577.6	1 190.6	5 387.0	1 629.9	1 138.2	491.7	1 116.5	71.7	1 044.9	458.5
2nd quarter	13 320.4	8 256.3	6 621.0	1 197.9	5 423.0	1 635.4	1 141.9	493.5	1 140.7	67.5	1 073.2	475.5
3rd quarter	13 502.0	8 343.3	6 698.0	1 198.2	5 499.7	1 645.3	1 147.2	498.1	1 175.3	74.1	1 101.2	489.9
4th quarter	13 603.6	8 306.9	6 658.2	1 191.0	5 467.2	1 648.7	1 154.4	494.3	1 188.0	76.9	1 111.1	513.5
2012												
1st quarter	13 845.0	8 514.3	6 842.2	1 199.4	5 642.8	1 672.1	1 162.2	509.9	1 214.4	74.6	1 139.7	524.8
2nd quarter	13 875.3	8 553.8	6 873.5	1 195.5	5 678.0	1 680.3	1 169.1	511.2	1 217.8	77.0	1 140.8	537.8
3rd quarter	13 962.1	8 591.0	6 904.7	1 195.1	5 709.7	1 686.2	1 174.1	512.2	1 220.0	75.3	1 144.7	546.7
4th quarter	14 204.0	8 787.4	7 086.6	1 199.3	5 887.2	1 700.9	1 176.8	524.0	1 247.5	74.5	1 173.0	555.4

Table 1-13A. National Income by Type of Income: Recent Data—*Continued*

(Billions of dollars, quarterly data are at seasonally adjusted annual rates.)   **NIPA Tables 1.7.5, 1.12**

| Year and quarter | Corporate profits with IVA and CCAdj | | | | | Net interest and miscel-laneous payments | Taxes on production and imports | Less: Subsidies | Business current transfer payments, net | | | Current surplus of govern-ment enterprises | Addendum: Net national factor income |
| | Total | Taxes on corporate income | Profits after tax | | | | | | | | | | |
			Total	Net dividends	Undis-tributed corporate profits				Total 1	To persons	To govern-ment		
1950	36.1	17.9	18.1	8.8	9.3	3.2	23.0	0.8	0.8	0.6	0.3	. . .	244.0
1951	41.2	22.6	18.6	8.6	10.1	3.7	24.7	1.0	1.2	0.9	0.3	. . .	283.1
1952	39.7	19.4	20.3	8.6	11.7	4.1	27.1	0.8	1.2	0.9	0.3	. . .	299.0
1953	40.3	20.3	20.0	8.9	11.1	4.8	29.1	0.5	1.2	0.8	0.3	. . .	314.6
1954	39.5	17.6	21.8	9.3	12.6	5.7	28.9	0.3	0.9	0.6	0.3	. . .	314.9
1955	50.2	22.0	28.1	10.5	17.6	6.3	31.5	0.2	1.3	0.9	0.4	. . .	345.1
1956	49.6	22.0	27.7	11.3	16.4	6.9	34.2	0.7	1.7	1.2	0.4	. . .	365.7
1957	49.1	21.4	27.7	11.7	16.0	8.1	36.6	1.1	1.8	1.4	0.4	. . .	382.1
1958	43.9	19.0	24.9	11.6	13.3	9.6	37.7	1.4	1.7	1.2	0.5	. . .	383.6
1959	55.5	23.7	31.8	12.6	19.2	9.7	41.1	1.1	1.7	1.3	0.3	0.5	417.4
1960	54.7	22.8	31.9	13.4	18.5	10.7	44.5	1.1	1.7	1.3	0.4	0.5	434.3
1961	55.9	22.9	33.1	13.9	19.2	12.6	47.0	2.0	1.9	1.4	0.5	0.3	450.0
1962	64.0	24.1	39.9	15.0	24.9	14.3	50.4	2.3	2.1	1.5	0.6	0.4	484.6
1963	70.5	26.4	44.1	16.2	27.9	15.3	53.4	2.2	2.5	1.9	0.7	0.8	512.1
1964	77.7	28.2	49.6	18.2	31.4	17.5	57.3	2.7	3.0	2.2	0.8	0.8	550.0
1965	89.3	31.1	58.2	20.2	38.0	19.8	60.7	3.0	3.5	2.3	1.2	0.7	598.4
1966	96.1	33.9	62.2	20.7	41.6	22.5	63.2	3.9	3.4	2.1	1.3	0.3	656.8
1967	93.9	32.9	61.0	21.5	39.5	25.7	67.9	3.8	3.6	2.3	1.4	0.2	692.3
1968	101.7	39.6	62.1	23.5	38.6	27.6	76.4	4.2	4.2	2.8	1.4	0.3	755.3
1969	98.4	40.0	58.4	24.2	34.2	33.6	83.9	4.5	4.8	3.3	1.5	0.0	815.4
1970	86.2	34.8	51.5	24.3	27.2	40.5	91.4	4.8	4.4	2.9	1.4	-1.2	850.4
1971	100.6	38.2	62.5	25.0	37.5	45.2	100.5	4.7	4.2	2.7	1.5	-1.7	918.7
1972	117.2	42.3	74.9	26.8	48.0	49.3	107.9	6.6	4.8	3.1	1.7	-1.2	1 018.1
1973	133.4	50.0	83.4	29.9	53.5	57.2	117.2	5.2	5.7	3.9	1.8	-2.2	1 141.5
1974	125.7	52.8	72.9	33.2	39.7	73.5	124.9	3.3	6.8	4.7	2.1	-2.7	1 225.1
1975	138.9	51.6	87.2	33.0	54.3	85.9	135.3	4.5	9.0	6.8	2.2	-4.4	1 315.7
1976	174.3	65.3	109.1	39.0	70.0	89.9	146.4	5.1	9.1	6.7	2.4	-2.7	1 467.1
1977	205.8	74.4	131.3	44.8	86.6	105.9	159.7	7.1	8.1	5.1	3.0	-3.3	1 641.3
1978	238.6	84.9	153.7	50.8	102.9	118.8	170.9	8.9	10.4	6.5	3.9	-2.8	1 860.5
1979	249.0	90.0	159.0	57.5	101.4	141.0	180.1	8.5	12.8	8.2	4.5	-3.2	2 067.0
1980	223.6	87.2	136.4	64.1	72.3	186.2	200.3	9.8	14.0	8.6	5.4	-5.1	2 227.3
1981	247.5	84.3	163.2	73.8	89.4	238.4	235.6	11.5	16.9	11.2	5.7	-5.2	2 486.2
1982	229.9	66.5	163.4	77.7	85.6	277.5	240.9	15.0	19.3	12.4	6.9	-3.8	2 599.0
1983	279.8	80.6	199.1	83.5	115.7	291.8	263.3	21.3	21.7	13.8	7.9	-2.3	2 799.2
1984	337.9	97.5	240.4	90.8	149.5	336.1	289.8	21.1	29.2	19.7	9.4	-1.4	3 147.5
1985	354.5	99.4	255.1	97.5	157.5	348.0	308.1	21.4	34.1	22.3	11.8	1.3	3 362.0
1986	324.4	109.7	214.7	106.2	108.5	365.2	323.4	24.9	36.0	22.9	13.0	2.0	3 511.8
1987	366.0	130.4	235.5	112.3	123.2	369.5	347.5	30.3	33.3	20.2	13.1	2.2	3 766.5
1988	414.9	141.6	273.2	129.9	143.3	394.7	374.5	29.5	32.8	20.6	12.2	5.0	4 110.6
1989	414.2	146.1	268.2	158.0	110.2	442.7	398.9	27.4	38.3	23.2	15.1	6.7	4 365.8
1990	417.2	145.4	271.7	169.1	102.7	450.1	425.0	27.0	39.2	22.2	17.0	3.2	4 595.7
1991	451.3	138.6	312.7	180.5	132.2	408.5	457.1	27.5	38.9	17.6	21.3	7.8	4 709.8
1992	475.3	148.7	326.6	189.5	137.1	383.7	483.4	30.1	39.7	16.3	23.6	9.9	4 996.8
1993	522.0	171.0	351.0	205.3	145.6	371.4	503.1	36.7	39.4	14.1	25.6	10.8	5 238.2
1994	621.9	193.1	428.8	236.0	192.8	365.9	545.2	32.5	40.7	13.3	27.9	11.8	5 575.0
1995	703.0	217.8	485.2	259.0	226.2	376.5	557.9	34.8	45.0	18.7	24.9	15.6	5 895.8
1996	786.1	231.5	554.6	303.5	251.1	381.9	580.8	35.2	52.6	22.9	30.7	16.9	6 284.3
1997	865.8	245.4	620.3	339.5	280.9	414.7	611.6	33.8	50.1	19.4	29.8	17.5	6 735.1
1998	804.1	248.4	555.7	357.1	198.7	477.8	639.5	36.4	64.1	26.0	34.3	16.3	7 173.8
1999	830.2	258.8	571.4	347.9	223.5	488.0	673.6	45.2	67.8	34.0	36.5	16.2	7 612.0
2000	781.2	265.1	516.1	384.7	131.4	565.0	708.6	45.8	85.3	42.4	41.9	10.7	8 148.3
2001	754.0	203.3	550.7	370.6	180.2	566.4	727.7	58.7	99.1	46.8	43.9	5.2	8 411.4
2002	907.2	192.3	714.8	400.2	314.7	490.5	762.6	41.4	80.7	34.2	46.2	7.0	8 628.0
2003	1 056.4	243.8	812.6	434.0	378.6	466.2	808.0	49.1	76.3	26.3	48.3	3.9	9 026.0
2004	1 283.3	306.1	977.3	564.1	413.2	403.5	863.9	46.4	81.4	16.8	52.4	-1.8	9 644.8
2005	1 477.7	412.4	1 065.3	580.5	484.8	496.8	934.5	60.9	93.9	25.7	53.4	-6.4	10 279.6
2006	1 646.5	473.4	1 173.1	726.0	447.1	580.9	991.9	51.5	82.6	21.5	58.3	-9.3	10 991.8
2007	1 529.0	445.5	1 083.5	818.9	264.6	663.4	1 034.6	54.6	98.6	30.6	62.0	-16.4	11 260.2
2008	1 285.1	309.1	976.0	808.6	167.3	693.4	1 041.9	52.6	116.4	36.6	72.6	-21.2	11 346.2
2009	1 392.6	269.4	1 123.1	568.7	554.4	563.1	1 026.1	58.3	127.2	38.7	90.7	-20.6	11 050.2
2010	1 740.6	370.6	1 370.0	563.9	806.0	489.4	1 057.1	55.9	128.5	43.0	87.2	-22.9	11 632.7
2011	1 877.7	374.2	1 503.5	701.6	801.9	456.9	1 097.1	60.0	129.6	46.7	90.1	-23.8	12 252.7
2012	2 009.5	434.8	1 574.7	770.3	804.3	439.6	1 122.9	57.3	106.9	41.4	70.6	-27.7	12 826.8
2010													
1st quarter	1 655.2	344.8	1 310.4	521.8	788.6	508.0	1 042.2	54.9	129.3	40.6	85.4	-21.2	11 365.5
2nd quarter	1 660.8	351.7	1 309.2	542.8	766.4	485.8	1 054.2	55.5	126.5	41.9	84.5	-22.6	11 521.3
3rd quarter	1 807.0	387.5	1 419.6	576.0	843.5	482.2	1 063.1	56.2	131.1	43.3	89.2	-23.5	11 753.3
4th quarter	1 839.2	398.3	1 440.9	615.2	825.7	481.6	1 069.0	56.9	127.0	46.1	89.7	-24.3	11 890.7
2011													
1st quarter	1 755.0	393.0	1 362.0	668.3	693.7	473.8	1 085.2	58.7	142.6	46.8	92.3	-23.8	12 011.4
2nd quarter	1 868.7	384.3	1 484.4	692.9	791.4	436.7	1 099.9	59.9	125.6	47.3	90.2	-23.1	12 178.0
3rd quarter	1 893.8	351.0	1 542.8	717.5	825.3	459.7	1 095.9	60.5	128.3	46.9	91.0	-23.7	12 362.0
4th quarter	1 993.4	368.6	1 624.8	727.6	897.3	457.5	1 107.5	60.6	121.8	45.7	86.9	-24.4	12 459.3
2012													
1st quarter	1 979.9	437.2	1 542.7	727.4	815.3	453.9	1 124.4	57.8	115.7	43.3	81.4	-24.5	12 687.1
2nd quarter	1 998.4	429.7	1 568.7	739.6	829.1	419.0	1 122.2	57.6	110.0	41.7	75.1	-26.1	12 726.9
3rd quarter	2 012.3	439.1	1 573.2	746.7	826.5	455.3	1 118.8	56.0	102.6	40.6	66.2	-28.5	12 825.3
4th quarter	2 047.2	433.2	1 614.0	867.6	746.4	430.3	1 126.3	57.7	99.5	40.1	59.7	-31.8	13 067.8

1Includes net transfer payments to the rest of the world, not shown separately.
. . . = Not available.

Table 1-13B. National Income by Type of Income: Historical

(Billions of dollars, quarterly data are at seasonally adjusted annual rates.)   **NIPA Tables 1.7.5, 1.12**

Year and quarter	National income, total	Compensation of employees							Proprietors' income with IVA and CCAdj			Rental income of persons with CCAdj
		Total	Wages and salaries			Supplements to wages and salaries			Total	Farm	Nonfarm	
			Total	Government	Other	Total	Employer contributions for:					
							Employee pension and insurance funds	Government social insurance				
1929	94.2	51.4	50.5	5.0	45.5	1.0	1.0	0.0	14.0	5.7	8.4	6.1
1930	83.1	47.2	46.2	5.2	41.0	1.0	1.0	0.0	10.9	3.9	7.0	5.4
1931	67.7	40.1	39.2	5.3	33.9	1.0	1.0	0.0	8.3	3.0	5.3	4.4
1932	51.3	31.4	30.5	5.0	25.5	0.9	0.9	0.0	5.0	1.8	3.3	3.6
1933	49.0	29.8	29.0	5.2	23.9	0.8	0.8	0.0	5.3	2.2	3.0	2.9
1934	58.3	34.6	33.7	6.1	27.6	0.9	0.8	0.0	7.0	2.6	4.4	2.5
1935	66.4	37.7	36.7	6.5	30.2	1.0	1.0	0.0	10.1	4.9	5.2	2.6
1936	75.2	43.3	42.0	7.9	34.1	1.4	1.1	0.2	10.4	3.9	6.4	2.7
1937	83.7	48.4	46.1	7.5	38.6	2.2	1.2	1.0	12.5	5.6	6.9	3.0
1938	77.1	45.5	43.0	8.3	34.8	2.5	1.3	1.2	10.6	4.0	6.6	3.5
1939	82.5	48.6	46.0	8.2	37.7	2.6	1.3	1.3	11.1	4.0	7.1	3.7
1940	91.6	52.8	49.9	8.5	41.4	2.9	1.6	1.4	12.2	4.1	8.2	3.8
1941	117.4	66.2	62.1	10.2	51.9	4.2	2.4	1.7	16.7	6.0	10.6	4.4
1942	152.4	88.1	82.1	16.0	66.1	6.0	4.0	2.0	23.3	9.7	13.7	5.5
1943	187.3	112.8	105.8	26.6	79.2	7.0	4.7	2.3	28.2	11.5	16.7	6.0
1944	201.0	124.4	116.7	33.0	83.8	7.7	5.1	2.5	29.3	11.4	17.9	6.3
1945	201.4	126.4	117.5	34.9	82.6	8.9	5.4	3.5	30.8	11.8	19.0	6.6
1946	201.5	122.6	112.0	20.7	91.3	10.6	5.5	5.1	35.7	14.2	21.5	6.9
1947	219.0	132.5	123.1	17.5	105.6	9.4	5.5	3.9	34.6	14.3	20.2	6.9
1948	245.1	144.5	135.6	19.0	116.5	8.9	5.9	3.0	39.3	16.7	22.6	7.5
1949	240.0	144.5	134.7	20.8	113.9	9.8	6.4	3.3	34.7	12.0	22.7	7.8
1947												
1st quarter	213.6	129.1	118.9	17.1	101.7	10.3	5.6	4.7	36.2	16.0	20.2	6.7
2nd quarter	215.9	130.9	121.3	17.3	103.9	9.7	5.4	4.3	33.3	12.4	20.9	6.8
3rd quarter	219.3	132.9	124.0	17.6	106.4	8.9	5.4	3.5	33.9	14.1	19.8	7.0
4th quarter	227.2	137.0	128.3	18.0	110.3	8.7	5.5	3.2	35.0	14.9	20.0	7.2
1948												
1st quarter	236.1	140.6	131.7	18.3	113.4	8.9	5.7	3.2	36.4	14.5	21.9	7.3
2nd quarter	244.3	142.2	133.4	18.6	114.7	8.9	5.9	3.0	40.2	18.0	22.3	7.5
3rd quarter	249.1	147.0	138.1	19.3	118.8	8.9	6.0	2.9	40.6	17.9	22.7	7.5
4th quarter	251.0	148.1	139.1	19.9	119.2	9.0	6.1	2.9	39.9	16.4	23.5	7.6
1949												
1st quarter	243.6	146.4	136.7	20.4	116.4	9.7	6.2	3.5	35.4	12.7	22.7	7.5
2nd quarter	240.1	144.9	135.0	20.7	114.3	9.9	6.3	3.5	34.9	12.1	22.8	7.7
3rd quarter	240.2	143.8	134.0	21.1	112.9	9.8	6.5	3.3	34.2	11.6	22.6	7.9
4th quarter	236.3	143.0	133.2	21.2	112.0	9.8	6.7	3.0	34.2	11.5	22.7	8.1
1950												
1st quarter	246.7	147.2	136.9	21.2	115.6	10.3	7.1	3.3	36.2	12.2	24.0	8.5
2nd quarter	258.8	153.8	143.0	21.8	121.2	10.8	7.5	3.3	36.8	12.2	24.6	8.7
3rd quarter	275.5	162.5	151.0	23.0	128.1	11.5	8.1	3.4	38.5	13.1	25.4	8.8
4th quarter	286.4	170.3	158.1	24.5	133.5	12.3	8.7	3.6	38.5	13.9	24.6	9.1
1951												
1st quarter	298.2	178.8	165.3	26.7	138.6	13.5	9.4	4.0	40.9	15.0	25.9	9.3
2nd quarter	305.6	185.1	171.0	28.5	142.5	14.1	10.0	4.1	42.5	15.4	27.1	9.6
3rd quarter	310.9	188.1	173.5	30.2	143.3	14.6	10.5	4.1	43.2	15.1	28.1	9.9
4th quarter	317.4	191.7	176.6	31.5	145.1	15.1	11.0	4.1	43.7	15.7	28.0	10.1
1952												
1st quarter	318.9	196.4	181.0	32.4	148.6	15.3	11.2	4.1	41.7	13.7	28.0	10.4
2nd quarter	320.9	197.7	182.1	33.1	149.0	15.6	11.5	4.1	43.0	14.5	28.4	10.7
3rd quarter	327.4	201.8	186.0	33.8	152.2	15.8	11.7	4.1	44.7	16.0	28.8	10.9
4th quarter	338.9	209.6	193.5	34.2	159.3	16.1	11.9	4.2	42.8	13.0	29.7	11.3
1953												
1st quarter	345.0	213.4	197.1	34.3	162.7	16.3	12.1	4.2	43.0	13.0	29.9	11.6
2nd quarter	347.8	216.5	200.0	34.4	165.7	16.5	12.3	4.2	42.3	12.4	29.9	11.9
3rd quarter	346.2	216.8	200.1	34.3	165.9	16.7	12.4	4.3	41.2	11.7	29.5	12.2
4th quarter	338.6	215.4	198.7	34.4	164.3	16.7	12.5	4.2	41.6	11.5	30.0	12.5
1954												
1st quarter	340.2	213.4	196.4	34.4	162.0	17.0	12.4	4.6	42.7	12.9	29.8	12.8
2nd quarter	340.5	213.0	196.0	34.7	161.2	17.0	12.4	4.6	42.1	11.7	30.4	13.0
3rd quarter	343.9	213.5	196.3	35.1	161.2	17.2	12.6	4.6	42.2	11.8	30.5	13.1
4th quarter	352.9	217.8	200.4	35.4	165.0	17.5	12.8	4.6	42.0	10.7	31.3	13.3
1955												
1st quarter	365.3	222.2	204.1	35.5	168.6	18.2	13.1	5.0	43.7	10.9	32.7	13.3
2nd quarter	374.7	228.4	209.9	36.2	173.6	18.6	13.4	5.1	44.3	11.3	33.0	13.4
3rd quarter	382.1	234.2	215.2	37.4	177.8	19.0	13.7	5.2	44.6	10.7	33.9	13.4
4th quarter	388.4	238.7	219.5	37.3	182.2	19.3	14.0	5.3	44.5	10.0	34.5	13.5
1956												
1st quarter	392.1	243.2	223.3	37.8	185.4	19.9	14.3	5.6	44.9	10.2	34.7	13.6
2nd quarter	397.9	247.9	227.5	38.5	189.0	20.4	14.7	5.7	45.3	10.4	34.9	13.6
3rd quarter	402.7	250.8	230.0	39.2	190.8	20.8	15.2	5.7	46.4	10.9	35.5	13.7
4th quarter	410.9	256.7	235.4	39.7	195.7	21.4	15.6	5.8	46.8	10.9	35.8	13.8
1957												
1st quarter	417.6	260.6	238.3	40.2	198.0	22.4	16.0	6.4	46.9	9.9	37.0	13.9
2nd quarter	419.7	262.5	239.6	40.7	198.9	22.8	16.4	6.4	47.7	10.5	37.2	14.0
3rd quarter	423.4	265.1	241.8	41.5	200.3	23.3	16.9	6.4	48.8	11.0	37.8	14.1
4th quarter	416.9	263.7	240.1	41.6	198.5	23.6	17.3	6.3	47.7	10.7	37.0	14.3

Table 1-13B. National Income by Type of Income: Historical—*Continued*

(Billions of dollars, quarterly data are at seasonally adjusted annual rates.)   **NIPA Tables 1.7.5, 1.12**

Year and quarter	Corporate profits with IVA and CCAdj — Total	Taxes on corporate income	Profits after tax — Total	Net dividends	Undistributed corporate profits	Net interest and miscellaneous payments	Taxes on production and imports	Less: Subsidies	Business current transfer payments, net — Total ¹	To persons	To government	Current surplus of government enterprises	Addendum: Net national factor income
1929	10.8	1.4	9.5	5.8	3.7	4.6	6.8	0.0	0.5	0.4	0.1	. . .	86.9
1930	7.5	0.8	6.7	5.5	1.2	4.8	7.0	0.1	0.5	0.4	0.1	. . .	75.8
1931	3.0	0.5	2.5	4.1	-1.6	4.8	6.7	0.1	0.5	0.4	0.1	. . .	60.6
1932	-0.2	0.4	-0.6	2.5	-3.1	4.5	6.6	0.1	0.6	0.5	0.1	. . .	44.3
1933	-0.2	0.5	-0.7	2.0	-2.7	4.0	6.9	0.2	0.5	0.4	0.1	. . .	41.7
1934	2.5	0.7	1.8	2.6	-0.8	4.0	7.6	0.5	0.5	0.4	0.1	. . .	50.7
1935	4.0	1.0	3.1	2.8	0.2	4.1	8.0	0.6	0.5	0.4	0.1	. . .	58.5
1936	6.2	1.4	4.8	4.5	0.3	3.8	8.5	0.3	0.5	0.4	0.1	. . .	66.4
1937	7.1	1.5	5.6	4.7	0.9	3.7	8.9	0.3	0.5	0.4	0.1	. . .	74.6
1938	5.0	1.0	4.0	3.2	0.8	3.6	8.9	0.5	0.4	0.3	0.2	. . .	68.2
1939	6.6	1.4	5.2	3.8	1.4	3.6	9.1	0.8	0.4	0.3	0.2	. . .	73.7
1940	9.9	2.8	7.0	4.0	3.0	3.3	9.8	0.8	0.5	0.3	0.2	. . .	82.1
1941	15.7	7.6	8.1	4.4	3.7	3.3	11.1	0.5	0.5	0.4	0.2	. . .	106.3
1942	20.8	11.4	9.4	4.3	5.1	3.2	11.5	0.5	0.5	0.3	0.2	. . .	140.9
1943	24.9	14.1	10.8	4.4	6.4	2.9	12.4	0.6	0.6	0.4	0.3	. . .	174.8
1944	25.0	12.9	12.0	4.6	7.4	2.4	13.7	1.0	0.8	0.4	0.4	. . .	187.5
1945	20.5	10.7	9.8	4.6	5.2	2.3	15.1	1.1	0.9	0.5	0.4	. . .	186.6
1946	18.2	9.1	9.1	5.6	3.6	1.9	16.8	1.4	0.7	0.4	0.3	. . .	185.3
1947	24.2	11.3	12.9	6.3	6.6	2.5	18.1	0.4	0.7	0.4	0.3	. . .	200.6
1948	31.4	12.4	19.0	7.0	11.9	2.6	19.7	0.5	0.7	0.4	0.3	. . .	225.2
1949	29.1	10.2	18.9	7.2	11.6	2.9	20.9	0.5	0.7	0.4	0.3	. . .	219.0
1947													
1st quarter	21.5	11.6	9.9	6.0	3.9	2.3	17.7	0.5	0.7	0.4	0.3	. . .	195.7
2nd quarter	24.5	10.9	13.5	6.3	7.2	2.4	17.7	0.4	0.7	0.4	0.3	. . .	197.9
3rd quarter	24.6	10.8	13.8	6.5	7.3	2.6	18.0	0.4	0.7	0.4	0.3	. . .	200.9
4th quarter	26.1	11.8	14.3	6.4	7.9	2.6	19.0	0.3	0.7	0.4	0.3	. . .	207.8
1948													
1st quarter	30.0	12.1	17.8	7.0	10.8	2.5	19.0	0.4	0.7	0.4	0.4	. . .	216.8
2nd quarter	31.8	12.8	19.0	6.7	12.3	2.6	19.7	0.3	0.7	0.4	0.3	. . .	224.3
3rd quarter	31.2	12.6	18.6	7.1	11.5	2.7	20.0	0.6	0.7	0.4	0.3	. . .	229.0
4th quarter	32.7	12.2	20.5	7.4	13.2	2.7	20.3	0.9	0.7	0.4	0.3	. . .	230.9
1949													
1st quarter	31.0	11.0	20.0	7.2	12.7	2.8	20.4	0.6	0.7	0.3	0.3	. . .	223.2
2nd quarter	28.7	9.7	18.9	7.2	11.7	2.9	20.8	0.4	0.7	0.3	0.3	. . .	219.0
3rd quarter	29.9	10.1	19.8	7.1	12.7	2.9	21.3	0.5	0.7	0.4	0.3	. . .	218.8
4th quarter	26.6	9.9	16.7	7.4	9.3	3.0	21.2	0.5	0.7	0.4	0.3	. . .	214.9
1950													
1st quarter	30.1	13.6	16.4	8.3	8.1	3.1	21.6	0.7	0.7	0.4	0.3	. . .	225.1
2nd quarter	33.9	16.3	17.6	8.4	9.2	3.2	22.5	0.8	0.8	0.5	0.3	. . .	236.4
3rd quarter	38.4	19.9	18.5	9.2	9.4	3.2	24.4	0.8	0.9	0.6	0.3	. . .	251.4
4th quarter	41.8	21.8	20.0	9.5	10.5	3.3	23.4	1.1	0.9	0.7	0.3	. . .	263.2
1951													
1st quarter	40.7	26.3	14.4	8.4	6.1	3.4	25.1	1.2	1.1	0.8	0.3	. . .	273.2
2nd quarter	40.6	22.3	18.3	8.6	9.7	3.7	24.1	1.1	1.2	0.9	0.3	. . .	281.5
3rd quarter	41.1	20.1	21.0	8.6	12.4	3.8	24.5	0.9	1.2	0.9	0.3	. . .	286.1
4th quarter	42.4	21.5	20.8	8.7	12.2	3.9	25.3	1.0	1.2	0.9	0.3	. . .	291.8
1952													
1st quarter	40.0	19.8	20.2	8.2	12.1	3.9	26.1	0.8	1.2	0.9	0.3	. . .	292.4
2nd quarter	38.1	18.7	19.5	8.7	10.8	4.1	26.9	0.8	1.2	0.9	0.3	. . .	293.5
3rd quarter	38.1	18.6	19.5	8.6	10.9	4.2	27.3	0.8	1.2	0.9	0.3	. . .	299.7
4th quarter	42.4	20.5	21.9	8.8	13.1	4.3	28.1	0.7	1.2	0.9	0.3	. . .	310.3
1953													
1st quarter	43.3	21.6	21.7	8.4	13.3	4.5	28.7	0.7	1.2	0.9	0.3	. . .	315.8
2nd quarter	42.5	21.7	20.8	9.2	11.6	4.7	29.2	0.4	1.2	0.9	0.3	. . .	317.9
3rd quarter	41.3	21.2	20.1	9.0	11.0	4.9	29.3	0.7	1.2	0.8	0.3	. . .	316.4
4th quarter	34.0	16.6	17.4	8.9	8.5	5.1	29.2	0.2	1.1	0.8	0.3	. . .	308.5
1954													
1st quarter	36.5	16.4	20.1	9.4	10.7	5.3	28.7	0.1	1.0	0.6	0.3	. . .	310.7
2nd quarter	37.8	16.9	20.9	8.9	12.1	5.6	28.8	0.7	0.9	0.5	0.3	. . .	311.5
3rd quarter	39.9	17.9	22.0	9.3	12.7	5.8	28.7	0.3	0.9	0.5	0.4	. . .	314.6
4th quarter	43.6	19.3	24.3	9.5	14.8	6.0	29.3	0.2	0.9	0.6	0.3	. . .	322.7
1955													
1st quarter	48.8	21.3	27.5	10.0	17.4	6.2	30.2	0.3	1.1	0.7	0.4	. . .	334.2
2nd quarter	50.1	21.6	28.5	10.2	18.3	6.3	31.2	0.3	1.2	0.9	0.4	. . .	342.5
3rd quarter	50.2	22.2	28.0	10.8	17.2	6.3	31.9	0.0	1.4	1.0	0.4	. . .	348.8
4th quarter	51.6	23.1	28.5	10.9	17.6	6.4	32.5	0.2	1.5	1.1	0.4	. . .	354.7
1956													
1st quarter	49.4	22.0	27.4	11.2	16.2	6.7	33.0	0.3	1.6	1.2	0.4	. . .	357.7
2nd quarter	49.6	22.5	27.2	11.2	16.0	6.8	33.6	0.5	1.6	1.2	0.4	. . .	363.2
3rd quarter	49.3	21.1	28.2	11.2	17.0	7.1	34.6	0.9	1.7	1.3	0.4	. . .	367.3
4th quarter	50.2	22.3	27.9	11.6	16.3	7.1	35.7	1.2	1.7	1.3	0.4	. . .	374.6
1957													
1st quarter	51.7	22.8	28.8	11.6	17.2	7.8	36.1	1.3	1.8	1.4	0.4	. . .	380.9
2nd quarter	50.3	21.9	28.4	11.8	16.6	8.0	36.6	1.2	1.8	1.4	0.4	. . .	382.5
3rd quarter	49.3	21.4	27.9	11.9	16.0	8.3	37.0	1.1	1.8	1.4	0.4	. . .	385.6
4th quarter	45.3	19.6	25.7	11.7	14.0	8.3	36.7	1.0	1.8	1.4	0.4	. . .	379.3

¹Includes net transfer payments to the rest of the world, not shown separately.
. . . = Not available.

Table 1-13B. National Income by Type of Income: Historical—*Continued*

(Billions of dollars, quarterly data are at seasonally adjusted annual rates.)   **NIPA Tables 1.7.5, 1.12**

Year and quarter	National income, total	Compensation of employees								Proprietors' income with IVA and CCAdj			Rental income of persons with CCAdj
		Total	Wages and salaries			Supplements to wages and salaries							
			Total	Government	Other	Total	Employer contributions for:		Total	Farm	Nonfarm	
							Employee pension and insurance funds	Government social insurance				
1958												
1st quarter	411.1	260.2	236.7	42.0	194.7	23.5	17.2	6.3	50.3	13.3	36.9	14.6
2nd quarter	413.0	259.9	236.3	43.1	193.2	23.6	17.3	6.3	50.3	13.0	37.3	14.8
3rd quarter	425.3	267.7	243.8	46.1	197.7	23.8	17.5	6.4	50.1	12.1	38.0	14.9
4th quarter	437.1	272.7	248.4	45.3	203.2	24.3	17.8	6.4	49.9	11.2	38.7	15.0
1959												
1st quarter	449.2	280.2	254.0	45.5	208.6	26.2	18.5	7.8	50.1	10.9	39.2	15.0
2nd quarter	463.2	286.9	260.6	45.8	214.7	26.4	18.5	7.9	50.3	9.9	40.5	15.4
3rd quarter	460.5	287.4	260.9	46.2	214.7	26.5	18.6	7.9	50.4	9.4	41.0	15.8
4th quarter	465.7	290.7	263.9	46.7	217.2	26.8	18.9	7.9	50.6	10.1	40.5	16.0
1960												
1st quarter	479.1	299.3	270.7	47.7	223.0	28.5	19.3	9.3	49.7	9.6	40.1	16.2
2nd quarter	479.8	302.3	273.4	48.6	224.8	28.9	19.6	9.3	50.7	10.6	40.1	16.4
3rd quarter	481.2	303.2	274.0	49.9	224.1	29.2	19.9	9.3	50.9	11.0	39.9	16.5
4th quarter	479.4	302.7	273.3	50.5	222.8	29.4	20.2	9.2	51.0	11.3	39.7	16.7
1961												
1st quarter	481.4	303.7	273.8	51.1	222.7	30.0	20.5	9.5	52.3	11.5	40.8	16.9
2nd quarter	491.1	308.0	277.6	51.8	225.8	30.3	20.8	9.6	52.6	10.9	41.8	17.1
3rd quarter	500.9	313.0	282.3	52.8	229.5	30.8	21.1	9.6	53.3	11.0	42.3	17.3
4th quarter	515.5	319.7	288.4	54.2	234.2	31.2	21.5	9.8	54.5	11.5	43.0	17.5
1962												
1st quarter	524.6	326.2	293.3	55.3	238.0	32.9	21.9	11.0	55.3	11.9	43.5	17.7
2nd quarter	531.8	332.1	298.7	56.0	242.8	33.4	22.2	11.2	55.0	11.1	43.9	18.0
3rd quarter	538.2	334.9	301.2	56.5	244.7	33.8	22.5	11.2	54.9	10.7	44.2	18.2
4th quarter	546.2	338.4	304.2	57.6	246.6	34.1	22.9	11.3	55.8	11.3	44.5	18.3
1963												
1st quarter	553.0	343.4	308.0	58.6	249.3	35.4	23.2	12.2	56.0	11.4	44.6	18.5
2nd quarter	562.1	348.3	312.4	59.4	253.0	36.0	23.6	12.3	55.8	10.8	45.0	18.7
3rd quarter	570.6	353.4	316.8	60.2	256.7	36.6	24.1	12.5	56.2	10.7	45.5	18.8
4th quarter	580.6	359.6	322.2	61.9	260.3	37.3	24.7	12.6	57.6	11.1	46.5	18.8
1964												
1st quarter	593.0	366.0	328.2	63.1	265.1	37.8	25.3	12.4	57.9	9.9	48.0	18.8
2nd quarter	603.1	373.5	334.8	64.2	270.7	38.6	26.1	12.6	58.8	9.5	49.3	18.8
3rd quarter	614.5	380.9	341.4	65.7	275.7	39.5	26.7	12.7	59.3	9.3	50.0	18.9
4th quarter	622.7	387.0	346.7	66.8	279.9	40.3	27.5	12.8	60.5	10.4	50.1	18.8
1965												
1st quarter	641.3	393.8	352.8	67.5	285.4	41.0	28.2	12.8	61.9	11.4	50.5	19.1
2nd quarter	652.6	400.8	358.9	68.5	290.3	42.0	29.0	13.0	63.2	12.0	51.2	19.3
3rd quarter	663.8	409.3	366.2	70.5	295.7	43.1	29.9	13.2	64.0	12.2	51.8	19.5
4th quarter	683.2	421.4	377.1	73.2	304.0	44.3	30.9	13.4	65.6	12.5	53.0	19.5
1966												
1st quarter	703.5	434.1	385.8	74.9	310.8	48.3	31.9	16.5	69.2	14.9	54.4	19.8
2nd quarter	713.4	445.4	395.9	76.9	319.0	49.5	32.8	16.7	67.2	12.7	54.5	19.8
3rd quarter	724.7	456.7	406.1	79.8	326.3	50.6	33.6	17.0	67.2	12.3	54.9	20.0
4th quarter	737.2	464.9	413.5	82.0	331.5	51.4	34.3	17.2	68.1	12.2	55.9	20.0
1967												
1st quarter	743.5	471.1	418.8	83.5	335.4	52.3	34.7	17.6	68.9	11.9	57.0	20.3
2nd quarter	750.2	476.8	423.6	85.0	338.6	53.2	35.4	17.8	68.5	11.1	57.4	20.4
3rd quarter	765.6	486.4	432.0	87.1	344.9	54.4	36.3	18.2	70.5	12.0	58.6	20.4
4th quarter	781.5	497.4	441.6	90.4	351.2	55.8	37.3	18.6	70.0	11.5	58.4	20.3
1968												
1st quarter	802.5	512.2	454.2	92.8	361.5	57.9	38.5	19.4	71.7	11.6	60.1	20.1
2nd quarter	823.7	525.3	465.9	95.2	370.7	59.4	39.6	19.8	73.2	11.2	61.9	20.1
3rd quarter	842.8	539.2	478.3	98.7	379.6	60.9	40.7	20.1	75.0	11.8	63.2	20.2
4th quarter	859.3	551.7	489.4	100.1	389.4	62.3	41.9	20.5	75.5	12.0	63.5	20.0
1969												
1st quarter	875.7	564.2	499.1	101.3	397.8	65.2	43.1	22.1	75.6	11.6	64.1	20.2
2nd quarter	892.1	578.2	511.4	103.1	408.3	66.9	44.3	22.5	77.1	12.5	64.6	20.3
3rd quarter	910.8	595.0	526.4	108.2	418.3	68.6	45.6	23.0	78.0	13.1	64.8	20.5
4th quarter	919.4	606.6	536.5	109.8	426.6	70.1	46.7	23.4	77.3	14.1	63.2	20.5
1970												
1st quarter	923.9	616.7	545.1	114.4	430.7	71.6	47.9	23.7	77.1	13.5	63.5	20.5
2nd quarter	935.8	622.0	549.1	116.5	432.6	72.9	49.1	23.9	76.7	12.4	64.3	20.3
3rd quarter	950.3	630.0	555.7	118.3	437.4	74.3	50.3	23.9	78.5	13.2	65.3	20.9
4th quarter	950.6	631.8	556.4	119.7	436.6	75.5	51.6	23.9	78.9	12.5	66.4	21.2
1971												
1st quarter	987.4	649.9	570.5	123.9	446.6	79.4	53.3	26.1	80.3	13.1	67.2	21.2
2nd quarter	1 007.3	661.8	580.4	125.6	454.8	81.4	55.0	26.4	82.8	13.3	69.6	21.8
3rd quarter	1 025.5	672.2	588.8	128.0	460.8	83.4	56.9	26.5	84.6	13.0	71.6	22.2
4th quarter	1 047.9	684.2	598.4	129.6	468.8	85.8	59.0	26.8	87.9	14.2	73.6	22.6
1972												
1st quarter	1 081.2	710.6	618.5	134.2	484.3	92.1	61.5	30.6	87.9	13.1	74.8	23.2
2nd quarter	1 101.7	724.7	630.4	135.7	494.7	94.4	63.3	31.0	91.3	15.4	75.9	20.3
3rd quarter	1 131.4	738.1	642.3	138.4	503.9	95.8	64.6	31.2	95.5	17.2	78.4	24.0
4th quarter	1 177.6	761.2	664.0	143.3	520.7	97.2	65.4	31.8	105.6	22.4	83.3	23.9

Table 1-13B. National Income by Type of Income: Historical—*Continued*

(Billions of dollars, quarterly data are at seasonally adjusted annual rates.)

NIPA Tables 1.7.5, 1.12

Year and quarter	Corporate profits with IVA and CCAdj					Net interest and miscellaneous payments	Taxes on production and imports	Less: Subsidies	Business current transfer payments, net			Current surplus of government enterprises	Addendum: Net national factor income
	Total	Taxes on corporate income	Profits after tax						Total [1]	To persons	To government		
			Total	Net dividends	Undistributed corporate profits								
1958													
1st quarter	39.5	16.9	22.5	11.6	11.0	9.1	36.8	1.1	1.8	1.3	0.5	. . .	373.6
2nd quarter	40.6	17.2	23.4	11.7	11.7	9.6	37.3	1.3	1.7	1.3	0.5	. . .	375.2
3rd quarter	44.8	19.4	25.4	11.7	13.7	9.9	37.8	1.5	1.7	1.2	0.5	. . .	387.3
4th quarter	50.6	22.3	28.3	11.4	16.9	10.0	38.9	1.6	1.6	1.2	0.4	. . .	398.2
1959													
1st quarter	54.3	23.5	30.8	12.1	18.7	8.9	39.8	1.1	1.6	1.3	0.3	0.5	408.4
2nd quarter	59.1	25.7	33.3	12.5	20.9	9.9	40.3	0.9	1.7	1.3	0.3	0.5	421.6
3rd quarter	54.2	23.1	31.1	12.8	18.3	9.9	41.7	1.1	1.7	1.3	0.3	0.5	417.6
4th quarter	54.5	22.6	32.0	13.0	19.0	10.2	42.4	1.1	1.7	1.4	0.3	0.6	422.1
1960													
1st quarter	58.6	25.1	33.5	13.2	20.3	10.3	43.7	1.0	1.7	1.3	0.4	0.5	434.1
2nd quarter	54.8	23.1	31.7	13.2	18.5	10.3	44.3	1.3	1.7	1.3	0.4	0.6	434.4
3rd quarter	53.8	22.0	31.8	13.5	18.2	10.9	44.9	1.0	1.7	1.3	0.4	0.4	435.2
4th quarter	51.5	20.9	30.6	13.5	17.1	11.3	45.3	1.2	1.8	1.3	0.5	0.4	433.2
1961													
1st quarter	50.2	20.7	29.6	13.6	16.0	11.8	45.8	1.6	1.9	1.3	0.5	0.3	435.0
2nd quarter	54.5	22.1	32.4	13.6	18.7	12.3	46.5	2.0	1.9	1.3	0.5	0.3	444.5
3rd quarter	57.2	23.4	33.9	13.9	19.9	12.7	47.3	2.2	1.9	1.4	0.5	0.3	453.6
4th quarter	61.8	25.4	36.4	14.5	21.9	13.5	48.4	2.3	2.0	1.4	0.6	0.5	466.9
1962													
1st quarter	62.6	23.9	38.6	14.6	24.1	13.3	49.4	2.3	2.0	1.5	0.6	0.4	475.1
2nd quarter	62.5	23.7	38.9	15.0	23.9	14.3	49.9	2.4	2.1	1.5	0.6	0.3	481.8
3rd quarter	64.2	24.4	39.9	15.2	24.7	14.7	50.9	2.2	2.1	1.6	0.6	0.4	486.9
4th quarter	66.9	24.5	42.4	15.4	27.0	15.1	51.3	2.2	2.2	1.6	0.6	0.4	494.5
1963													
1st quarter	67.2	24.6	42.6	15.8	26.9	14.8	52.0	2.0	2.4	1.8	0.6	0.7	499.9
2nd quarter	70.2	26.3	44.0	16.1	27.9	15.0	52.9	2.2	2.5	1.8	0.7	0.8	508.0
3rd quarter	71.7	27.0	44.7	16.3	28.3	15.5	53.9	2.3	2.5	1.9	0.7	0.8	515.6
4th quarter	73.0	27.7	45.3	16.8	28.5	15.9	54.7	2.4	2.6	2.0	0.7	0.9	524.9
1964													
1st quarter	77.1	27.9	49.1	17.5	31.7	16.7	55.7	2.7	2.7	2.1	0.6	0.9	536.5
2nd quarter	77.3	28.0	49.4	18.0	31.3	17.3	56.7	2.9	2.8	2.2	0.6	0.8	545.6
3rd quarter	78.4	28.6	49.9	18.4	31.4	18.0	57.9	2.6	3.2	2.2	1.0	0.6	555.5
4th quarter	78.0	28.2	49.9	18.9	31.0	18.2	58.8	2.7	3.3	2.3	1.0	0.8	562.5
1965													
1st quarter	85.8	29.6	56.3	19.2	37.1	19.1	60.2	2.9	3.5	2.3	1.2	0.7	579.8
2nd quarter	88.0	30.5	57.5	19.9	37.7	19.6	60.3	3.0	3.5	2.3	1.2	0.8	590.9
3rd quarter	89.3	31.1	58.2	20.5	37.6	20.1	60.5	3.0	3.5	2.2	1.2	0.7	602.2
4th quarter	94.0	33.1	60.9	21.2	39.7	20.1	61.8	3.1	3.4	2.2	1.3	0.5	620.6
1966													
1st quarter	97.4	34.2	63.2	21.3	41.9	21.3	61.4	3.6	3.4	2.2	1.3	0.5	641.8
2nd quarter	96.4	34.2	62.2	20.9	41.3	22.0	62.8	3.9	3.4	2.1	1.3	0.3	650.7
3rd quarter	94.8	33.9	61.0	20.5	40.4	22.8	63.7	4.1	3.4	2.1	1.3	0.1	661.6
4th quarter	95.9	33.3	62.6	20.0	42.6	23.9	64.9	4.2	3.4	2.1	1.3	0.2	672.9
1967													
1st quarter	93.3	32.5	60.8	21.1	39.8	24.7	65.6	4.0	3.5	2.2	1.3	0.1	678.3
2nd quarter	92.2	32.2	60.0	21.7	38.3	25.6	66.8	3.9	3.6	2.2	1.4	0.2	683.4
3rd quarter	93.2	32.5	60.7	22.1	38.7	26.0	68.7	3.7	3.7	2.3	1.4	0.3	696.6
4th quarter	96.7	34.4	62.3	21.2	41.1	26.4	70.6	3.7	3.8	2.4	1.4	0.0	710.8
1968													
1st quarter	98.1	38.7	59.4	22.6	36.8	26.8	73.4	4.0	3.9	2.5	1.4	0.3	728.9
2nd quarter	102.1	39.5	62.6	23.4	39.2	27.3	75.4	4.2	4.1	2.7	1.4	0.3	748.0
3rd quarter	102.6	39.7	63.0	24.0	39.0	27.7	77.7	4.2	4.3	2.9	1.4	0.3	764.7
4th quarter	104.1	40.6	63.5	24.2	39.3	28.4	79.1	4.2	4.4	3.0	1.4	0.2	779.8
1969													
1st quarter	103.5	41.5	62.0	24.0	38.1	31.2	80.6	4.3	4.7	3.3	1.5	0.0	794.7
2nd quarter	100.3	40.4	59.9	24.1	35.8	32.9	82.9	4.5	4.8	3.4	1.5	0.0	808.9
3rd quarter	97.4	39.1	58.3	24.3	34.0	34.6	85.2	4.7	4.8	3.4	1.5	0.0	825.5
4th quarter	92.4	38.9	53.6	24.6	29.0	35.7	86.7	4.7	4.8	3.3	1.5	0.0	832.5
1970													
1st quarter	84.7	34.5	50.2	24.5	25.7	37.4	88.5	4.7	4.6	3.1	1.5	-0.7	836.3
2nd quarter	88.5	34.7	53.8	24.3	29.6	39.5	90.5	4.8	4.5	3.0	1.5	-1.3	846.9
3rd quarter	88.4	35.7	52.7	24.2	28.4	41.8	92.5	4.7	4.2	2.8	1.4	-1.3	859.5
4th quarter	83.5	34.2	49.3	24.2	25.1	43.2	94.1	4.8	4.1	2.8	1.4	-1.5	858.7
1971													
1st quarter	96.6	37.8	58.8	25.0	33.8	44.3	97.7	4.8	4.1	2.7	1.5	-1.9	892.3
2nd quarter	98.7	38.6	60.2	25.0	35.2	45.3	98.9	4.8	4.1	2.7	1.4	-1.4	910.5
3rd quarter	101.4	37.9	63.5	25.2	38.4	45.5	101.7	4.5	4.2	2.7	1.5	-1.8	925.9
4th quarter	105.8	38.4	67.4	24.9	42.5	45.8	103.7	4.6	4.2	2.8	1.5	-1.7	946.3
1972													
1st quarter	111.5	40.4	71.2	26.1	45.0	46.6	104.6	6.1	4.5	2.9	1.6	-1.6	979.8
2nd quarter	113.4	40.7	72.8	26.4	46.3	47.9	106.8	6.2	4.7	3.0	1.7	-1.3	997.6
3rd quarter	118.2	42.0	76.2	27.1	49.1	50.2	108.9	7.2	4.9	3.2	1.7	-1.1	1 026.0
4th quarter	125.7	46.4	79.4	27.7	51.7	52.4	111.5	7.1	5.0	3.3	1.7	-0.7	1 068.8

[1] Includes net transfer payments to the rest of the world, not shown separately.
. . . = Not available.

Table 1-13B. National Income by Type of Income: Historical—*Continued*

(Billions of dollars, quarterly data are at seasonally adjusted annual rates.)

NIPA Tables 1.7.5, 1.12

Year and quarter	National income, total	Compensation of employees Total	Wages and salaries Total	Government	Other	Supplements Total	Employee pension and insurance funds	Government social insurance	Proprietors' income with IVA and CCAdj Total	Farm	Nonfarm	Rental income of persons with CCAdj
1973												
1st quarter	1 214.7	787.8	683.4	145.0	538.3	104.4	65.7	38.7	104.1	21.8	82.4	23.6
2nd quarter	1 239.4	805.6	700.2	147.2	553.0	105.4	66.0	39.3	109.9	27.6	82.4	23.5
3rd quarter	1 267.8	822.8	716.2	149.6	566.6	106.6	66.6	39.9	113.8	29.5	84.3	22.5
4th quarter	1 306.0	844.1	735.3	153.4	582.0	108.7	67.6	41.1	122.2	37.5	84.7	23.4
1974												
1st quarter	1 318.2	860.9	748.2	155.6	592.5	112.7	69.1	43.6	115.7	28.6	87.1	23.7
2nd quarter	1 338.9	881.1	765.3	158.2	607.1	115.8	71.3	44.5	108.6	20.1	88.5	23.1
3rd quarter	1 364.9	902.8	783.1	161.3	621.8	119.7	74.4	45.3	111.0	21.5	89.5	23.4
4th quarter	1 381.1	916.5	792.5	166.9	625.6	124.0	78.6	45.4	113.5	23.7	89.8	23.2
1975												
1st quarter	1 388.0	921.2	791.9	170.5	621.4	129.3	83.5	45.7	112.7	19.7	93.0	22.9
2nd quarter	1 418.8	934.1	800.4	174.5	625.9	133.8	87.8	46.0	114.3	20.1	94.2	22.6
3rd quarter	1 477.0	959.0	821.3	177.8	643.5	137.7	90.7	47.0	120.7	23.8	96.9	22.5
4th quarter	1 520.8	986.4	845.8	182.2	663.6	140.6	92.4	48.2	125.2	24.3	100.8	22.1
1976												
1st quarter	1 571.3	1 017.6	871.2	184.8	686.4	146.4	93.3	53.1	126.4	19.4	107.0	21.9
2nd quarter	1 596.9	1 038.4	889.4	187.3	702.1	149.0	95.1	53.9	128.6	17.0	111.6	20.8
3rd quarter	1 628.9	1 061.2	908.5	189.5	719.0	152.8	97.9	54.9	132.7	16.1	116.6	20.3
4th quarter	1 661.9	1 087.7	929.9	194.1	735.8	157.7	102.1	55.7	136.2	16.3	119.9	19.4
1977												
1st quarter	1 705.6	1 116.3	950.0	196.7	753.3	166.2	107.2	59.1	138.6	16.0	122.6	17.1
2nd quarter	1 776.0	1 153.4	980.9	199.7	781.2	172.5	111.9	60.6	140.5	14.1	126.4	16.6
3rd quarter	1 832.8	1 185.3	1 007.5	203.7	803.8	177.8	116.1	61.7	142.4	11.8	130.6	15.8
4th quarter	1 880.3	1 221.0	1 038.2	210.3	827.9	182.8	119.8	63.0	156.5	22.0	134.5	15.3
1978												
1st quarter	1 920.3	1 255.8	1 064.2	214.0	850.3	191.6	122.8	68.8	158.5	18.5	140.0	16.5
2nd quarter	2 014.3	1 302.9	1 106.0	217.2	888.8	197.0	126.0	71.0	166.1	20.9	145.2	16.2
3rd quarter	2 060.3	1 339.2	1 137.1	221.5	915.6	202.0	129.8	72.3	168.3	20.8	147.6	17.4
4th quarter	2 124.8	1 383.0	1 175.0	227.4	947.6	208.0	133.9	74.1	170.9	19.5	151.4	17.6
1979												
1st quarter	2 181.1	1 427.3	1 208.4	231.1	977.2	219.0	138.5	80.5	180.1	23.8	156.3	17.8
2nd quarter	2 219.6	1 458.3	1 234.0	233.1	1 000.9	224.2	142.6	81.6	179.2	21.8	157.3	15.6
3rd quarter	2 270.7	1 498.8	1 268.2	238.2	1 030.0	230.6	147.3	83.3	180.7	22.3	158.5	15.4
4th quarter	2 321.2	1 539.7	1 302.7	246.1	1 056.6	237.0	152.1	84.9	177.8	20.8	157.0	17.6
1980												
1st quarter	2 366.6	1 579.2	1 334.9	251.3	1 083.6	244.4	157.0	87.3	167.6	13.3	154.3	20.0
2nd quarter	2 358.0	1 600.5	1 351.0	257.7	1 093.3	249.5	161.7	87.7	160.3	3.1	157.2	14.1
3rd quarter	2 425.7	1 631.2	1 376.1	263.0	1 113.1	255.1	166.2	89.0	173.4	11.7	161.7	17.0
4th quarter	2 556.8	1 694.0	1 431.7	273.8	1 157.9	262.3	170.5	91.7	185.0	18.7	166.3	27.8
1981												
1st quarter	2 642.6	1 745.2	1 469.1	278.7	1 190.3	276.2	174.5	101.7	188.2	17.6	170.6	26.2
2nd quarter	2 684.2	1 777.5	1 496.2	282.1	1 214.1	281.3	178.3	102.9	176.4	18.2	158.2	24.4
3rd quarter	2 773.6	1 815.4	1 528.7	286.8	1 241.9	286.7	182.1	104.5	182.3	23.3	158.9	24.1
4th quarter	2 788.1	1 843.0	1 551.5	295.7	1 255.8	291.5	186.2	105.3	171.8	17.0	154.9	27.0
1982												
1st quarter	2 791.9	1 866.4	1 567.2	300.4	1 266.8	299.2	190.2	109.0	165.2	14.4	150.8	27.6
2nd quarter	2 838.1	1 885.1	1 580.9	304.6	1 276.3	304.1	194.5	109.6	169.4	12.8	156.6	24.0
3rd quarter	2 858.0	1 905.3	1 596.1	309.2	1 286.9	309.3	199.1	110.1	170.7	11.9	158.8	25.9
4th quarter	2 873.7	1 920.4	1 605.9	316.0	1 289.9	314.6	204.3	110.3	179.5	14.2	165.3	27.0
1983												
1st quarter	2 934.4	1 949.9	1 623.1	319.3	1 303.7	326.9	209.8	117.1	183.3	12.9	170.4	27.4
2nd quarter	3 014.3	1 988.6	1 655.1	323.0	1 332.1	333.5	214.7	118.7	182.6	7.9	174.8	27.4
3rd quarter	3 094.5	2 031.2	1 691.8	327.1	1 364.7	339.5	219.0	120.5	183.8	0.2	183.6	27.4
4th quarter	3 198.8	2 085.9	1 740.1	329.7	1 410.4	345.8	222.6	123.2	195.3	3.8	191.5	27.7
1984												
1st quarter	3 331.3	2 147.1	1 785.2	339.0	1 446.2	361.9	226.3	135.6	221.9	19.5	202.4	26.9
2nd quarter	3 418.3	2 196.8	1 828.2	344.8	1 483.4	368.6	230.4	138.2	231.8	21.3	210.5	25.2
3rd quarter	3 484.7	2 242.6	1 866.7	351.6	1 515.2	375.9	235.6	140.3	232.4	20.4	211.9	27.6
4th quarter	3 541.8	2 283.1	1 899.5	357.2	1 542.4	383.5	241.5	142.0	226.9	22.5	204.4	31.9
1985												
1st quarter	3 607.4	2 327.0	1 933.8	365.6	1 568.2	393.3	248.6	144.7	240.7	22.8	217.8	30.2
2nd quarter	3 655.4	2 365.0	1 963.2	370.0	1 593.2	401.8	255.3	146.4	238.5	20.4	218.0	29.2
3rd quarter	3 716.2	2 406.7	1 996.1	376.8	1 619.3	410.6	262.1	148.5	240.7	19.3	221.5	30.3
4th quarter	3 757.7	2 457.1	2 037.1	383.0	1 654.0	420.0	268.7	151.4	244.3	21.4	223.0	28.4
1986												
1st quarter	3 809.1	2 493.3	2 063.5	387.9	1 675.6	429.8	274.7	155.0	245.6	18.3	227.4	24.8
2nd quarter	3 820.4	2 519.1	2 081.8	393.6	1 688.3	437.2	280.8	156.4	251.6	19.6	232.0	24.2
3rd quarter	3 859.9	2 557.1	2 111.7	399.7	1 712.0	445.3	286.6	158.7	264.4	26.6	237.8	20.5
4th quarter	3 903.4	2 605.9	2 152.2	407.6	1 744.6	453.7	292.4	161.3	264.2	26.6	237.6	18.1
1987												
1st quarter	3 975.2	2 651.0	2 193.7	414.6	1 779.1	457.3	294.4	162.9	275.4	27.3	248.2	18.8
2nd quarter	4 073.4	2 694.2	2 230.1	420.1	1 810.0	464.2	299.4	164.7	282.3	29.0	253.3	17.4
3rd quarter	4 167.3	2 741.8	2 270.6	424.9	1 845.7	471.2	304.2	167.0	289.5	28.8	260.7	21.0
4th quarter	4 260.9	2 810.3	2 330.7	432.8	1 897.8	479.6	309.2	170.4	298.6	30.4	268.2	23.7

Table 1-13B. National Income by Type of Income: Historical—*Continued*

(Billions of dollars, quarterly data are at seasonally adjusted annual rates.)

NIPA Tables 1.7.5, 1.12

| Year and quarter | Corporate profits with IVA and CCAdj | | | | | Net interest and miscellaneous payments | Taxes on production and imports | Less: Subsidies | Business current transfer payments, net | | | Current surplus of government enterprises | Addendum: Net national factor income |
| | Total | Taxes on corporate income | Profits after tax | | | | | | | | | | |
			Total	Net dividends	Undistributed corporate profits				Total [1]	To persons	To government		
1973													
1st quarter	133.5	49.7	83.8	28.4	55.4	53.0	114.6	5.9	5.6	3.6	1.9	-1.6	1 102.1
2nd quarter	131.3	50.2	81.0	29.3	51.7	54.8	116.2	5.7	5.9	3.9	2.0	-2.0	1 125.0
3rd quarter	133.0	48.6	84.4	30.4	54.0	58.9	118.4	4.7	5.6	4.1	1.6	-2.4	1 150.9
4th quarter	135.8	51.4	84.4	31.5	52.9	62.3	119.7	4.6	5.8	4.2	1.6	-2.8	1 187.8
1974													
1st quarter	130.3	49.7	80.6	32.5	48.0	66.8	120.8	3.6	6.3	4.3	2.0	-2.7	1 197.3
2nd quarter	128.9	52.2	76.8	33.3	43.5	71.6	124.1	2.9	6.6	4.5	2.1	-2.1	1 213.3
3rd quarter	124.3	57.3	67.0	33.6	33.4	75.2	127.1	3.2	7.0	4.9	2.1	-2.7	1 236.8
4th quarter	119.3	51.9	67.4	33.5	33.9	80.4	127.7	3.6	7.3	5.2	2.1	-3.2	1 252.9
1975													
1st quarter	117.8	43.8	74.0	32.9	41.0	84.4	128.8	4.2	8.4	6.1	2.2	-4.0	1 259.0
2nd quarter	128.9	46.8	82.2	32.7	49.5	85.1	133.0	4.3	9.1	6.9	2.2	-4.2	1 285.1
3rd quarter	149.8	57.2	92.6	32.9	59.7	86.7	138.2	4.6	9.3	7.1	2.2	-4.6	1 338.7
4th quarter	159.0	58.8	100.2	33.4	66.8	87.3	141.1	4.9	9.4	7.2	2.2	-4.7	1 380.0
1976													
1st quarter	175.1	66.6	108.5	36.2	72.3	86.8	141.7	5.1	9.5	7.0	2.5	-2.7	1 427.9
2nd quarter	173.2	65.2	108.0	38.1	69.9	89.3	144.9	4.8	9.4	7.0	2.4	-2.7	1 450.3
3rd quarter	174.7	64.9	109.9	39.9	69.9	90.9	147.7	5.1	9.1	6.7	2.4	-2.6	1 479.9
4th quarter	174.3	64.5	109.9	41.9	68.0	92.6	151.3	5.5	8.6	6.1	2.5	-2.7	1 510.2
1977													
1st quarter	184.1	68.8	115.3	42.7	72.6	95.2	154.8	5.8	8.2	5.5	2.7	-3.0	1 551.4
2nd quarter	204.9	74.4	130.5	43.9	86.6	103.6	158.0	5.9	7.8	5.0	2.8	-3.1	1 619.0
3rd quarter	219.6	76.7	142.9	45.6	97.3	110.1	161.5	6.4	8.0	4.9	3.2	-3.6	1 673.3
4th quarter	214.5	77.8	136.6	46.8	89.8	114.5	164.3	10.3	8.3	5.0	3.3	-3.7	1 721.7
1978													
1st quarter	209.9	72.5	137.4	48.3	89.2	115.7	166.9	8.7	9.4	5.6	3.7	-3.6	1 756.4
2nd quarter	239.7	86.6	153.1	49.5	103.7	117.8	173.1	8.4	10.0	6.2	3.9	-3.2	1 842.8
3rd quarter	246.2	87.4	158.8	51.8	107.0	118.9	169.7	8.3	10.7	6.7	4.0	-1.9	1 890.0
4th quarter	258.4	92.9	165.5	53.7	111.8	122.7	173.9	10.4	11.4	7.3	4.1	-2.7	1 952.6
1979													
1st quarter	249.7	90.1	159.6	55.4	104.2	128.7	176.4	8.4	12.3	7.9	4.4	-2.8	2 003.6
2nd quarter	252.1	90.9	161.2	56.9	104.3	134.9	178.5	8.8	12.7	8.2	4.5	-2.9	2 040.1
3rd quarter	250.1	90.6	159.5	58.0	101.4	143.2	180.9	8.1	13.0	8.4	4.6	-3.1	2 088.1
4th quarter	244.0	88.4	155.6	59.7	95.9	157.3	184.6	8.9	13.1	8.5	4.6	-4.0	2 136.4
1980													
1st quarter	237.5	97.0	140.5	61.8	78.7	173.0	189.5	9.2	13.2	8.2	5.0	-4.1	2 177.2
2nd quarter	207.0	77.2	129.8	64.3	65.5	180.1	196.9	9.6	13.4	8.3	5.1	-4.8	2 162.1
3rd quarter	214.6	83.2	131.5	64.7	66.8	186.6	204.3	10.1	13.7	8.7	5.0	-5.1	2 222.8
4th quarter	235.1	91.4	143.8	65.6	78.2	205.0	210.6	10.3	15.7	9.3	6.4	-6.2	2 347.0
1981													
1st quarter	244.4	91.1	153.2	68.7	84.5	208.6	230.8	10.6	16.4	10.4	6.1	-6.6	2 412.5
2nd quarter	240.8	82.6	158.2	72.7	85.5	228.4	235.5	10.7	16.6	11.0	5.6	-4.6	2 447.5
3rd quarter	257.8	86.2	171.7	75.9	95.8	255.6	237.5	11.1	17.1	11.5	5.6	-5.1	2 535.2
4th quarter	246.9	77.4	169.5	77.7	91.8	260.9	238.8	13.5	17.5	11.9	5.7	-4.4	2 549.6
1982													
1st quarter	221.8	65.7	156.1	77.7	78.4	272.7	237.4	14.0	18.6	12.0	6.6	-3.8	2 553.7
2nd quarter	236.2	68.4	167.8	76.5	91.2	283.2	238.3	13.6	19.2	12.3	6.9	-3.7	2 598.0
3rd quarter	233.7	68.6	165.1	77.1	87.9	278.0	241.8	13.0	19.5	12.5	7.0	-3.9	2 613.6
4th quarter	227.7	63.2	164.5	79.5	85.0	276.1	246.3	19.4	20.0	12.7	7.2	-3.8	2 630.6
1983													
1st quarter	244.6	64.2	180.4	81.0	99.4	281.1	250.7	19.9	20.3	12.8	7.5	-3.0	2 686.3
2nd quarter	274.7	79.2	195.5	82.1	113.4	282.9	261.2	21.6	20.9	13.2	7.7	-2.5	2 756.2
3rd quarter	291.2	88.3	203.0	84.3	118.6	295.8	267.5	22.2	21.9	14.0	7.9	-2.1	2 829.5
4th quarter	308.6	90.9	217.6	86.4	131.3	307.2	273.7	21.5	23.6	15.3	8.4	-1.6	2 924.6
1984													
1st quarter	336.6	103.9	232.7	88.6	144.1	313.8	281.6	21.2	26.7	17.6	9.1	-2.1	3 046.4
2nd quarter	338.2	102.9	235.3	90.9	144.5	332.6	287.7	21.0	28.6	19.2	9.4	-1.6	3 124.5
3rd quarter	333.6	91.1	242.5	91.1	151.5	348.3	292.2	20.9	30.1	20.6	9.6	-1.3	3 184.5
4th quarter	343.1	92.3	250.8	92.7	158.1	349.7	297.5	21.2	31.2	21.5	9.7	-0.5	3 234.7
1985													
1st quarter	347.9	98.7	249.2	95.4	153.8	349.3	301.0	21.1	32.2	21.9	10.3	0.2	3 295.1
2nd quarter	351.5	97.0	254.6	97.0	157.6	346.9	305.7	21.0	38.1	22.1	16.0	1.5	3 331.0
3rd quarter	368.9	102.3	266.6	98.3	168.3	344.5	311.9	21.3	32.8	22.3	10.5	1.8	3 391.1
4th quarter	349.7	99.7	250.0	99.5	150.5	351.5	313.9	22.0	33.1	22.6	10.5	1.6	3 431.0
1986													
1st quarter	340.7	106.6	234.1	103.2	130.9	366.4	317.5	23.1	42.1	23.3	18.7	1.9	3 470.8
2nd quarter	326.6	106.3	220.2	106.4	113.9	367.2	319.5	24.2	34.5	23.5	11.1	2.0	3 488.7
3rd quarter	315.6	107.3	208.2	107.5	100.8	366.4	326.2	25.5	33.2	23.0	10.2	2.0	3 524.0
4th quarter	314.7	118.5	196.2	107.6	88.6	360.8	330.4	26.8	34.0	22.0	12.0	2.1	3 563.8
1987													
1st quarter	325.9	118.7	207.1	108.8	98.3	359.9	336.0	28.3	34.0	21.3	12.7	2.5	3 630.9
2nd quarter	362.9	132.8	230.1	109.8	120.2	366.1	344.4	30.4	34.4	20.6	13.8	2.2	3 722.9
3rd quarter	386.4	137.9	248.5	113.3	135.2	373.1	352.4	31.3	32.5	19.7	12.8	2.0	3 811.7
4th quarter	388.8	132.4	256.4	117.2	139.2	378.9	357.4	31.1	32.3	19.3	13.0	2.0	3 900.3

[1] Includes net transfer payments to the rest of the world, not shown separately.

Table 1-13B. National Income by Type of Income: Historical—*Continued*

(Billions of dollars, quarterly data are at seasonally adjusted annual rates.)

NIPA Tables 1.7.5, 1.12

Year and quarter	National income, total	Compensation of employees							Proprietors' income with IVA and CCAdj			Rental income of persons with CCAdj
		Total	Wages and salaries			Supplements to wages and salaries			Total	Farm	Nonfarm	
			Total	Government	Other	Total	Employer contributions for:					
							Employee pension and insurance funds	Government social insurance				
1988												
1st quarter	4 351.7	2 861.0	2 367.3	442.8	1 924.4	493.8	314.1	179.6	319.3	33.3	286.0	23.0
2nd quarter	4 444.5	2 926.1	2 422.1	449.0	1 973.0	504.0	320.6	183.4	322.8	27.4	295.3	22.6
3rd quarter	4 536.1	2 978.0	2 463.0	454.7	2 008.3	514.9	328.7	186.2	334.0	28.8	305.2	23.9
4th quarter	4 641.2	3 035.1	2 506.8	461.6	2 045.2	528.3	339.0	189.3	327.3	17.7	309.7	30.9
1989												
1st quarter	4 723.2	3 084.0	2 542.2	470.8	2 071.3	541.8	351.0	190.9	348.7	36.7	312.0	26.8
2nd quarter	4 755.2	3 117.5	2 563.4	476.8	2 086.6	554.1	361.7	192.4	340.3	32.6	307.7	24.7
3rd quarter	4 806.5	3 157.6	2 592.0	484.9	2 107.1	565.6	371.3	194.3	338.0	30.3	307.7	22.7
4th quarter	4 843.8	3 211.2	2 634.6	491.9	2 142.7	576.6	379.4	197.2	340.7	32.5	308.2	23.4
1990												
1st quarter	4 952.2	3 278.8	2 686.8	505.9	2 180.9	592.0	389.0	203.0	346.7	34.5	312.2	25.9
2nd quarter	5 034.8	3 334.8	2 735.9	515.8	2 220.1	598.9	392.6	206.2	352.3	32.7	319.6	30.2
3rd quarter	5 064.7	3 373.9	2 768.7	523.2	2 245.5	605.2	396.9	208.3	360.3	31.8	328.5	34.8
4th quarter	5 092.6	3 383.2	2 773.4	531.3	2 242.1	609.8	401.6	208.2	358.4	29.7	328.8	34.6
1991												
1st quarter	5 120.9	3 395.1	2 776.0	543.9	2 232.1	619.1	407.1	212.0	349.1	26.2	322.9	36.2
2nd quarter	5 156.4	3 430.2	2 801.2	547.1	2 254.1	629.0	415.2	213.8	354.8	27.8	326.9	38.6
3rd quarter	5 204.7	3 469.2	2 826.5	550.0	2 276.5	642.7	426.3	216.4	355.5	24.5	331.0	43.0
4th quarter	5 262.5	3 513.5	2 854.2	554.0	2 300.2	659.3	441.0	218.3	364.5	28.6	335.9	50.2
1992												
1st quarter	5 392.4	3 597.6	2 913.5	564.8	2 348.7	684.2	459.1	225.1	380.8	32.9	347.9	53.9
2nd quarter	5 476.6	3 654.4	2 952.8	570.6	2 382.2	701.6	473.8	227.8	397.4	35.4	362.0	61.1
3rd quarter	5 516.2	3 690.7	2 976.1	574.7	2 401.4	714.6	484.6	230.0	410.1	36.7	373.4	68.0
4th quarter	5 613.8	3 741.9	3 019.9	577.9	2 442.0	722.0	491.3	230.7	421.2	34.0	387.1	74.3
1993												
1st quarter	5 619.9	3 747.9	3 018.5	585.4	2 433.1	729.4	494.7	234.7	421.3	28.6	392.8	83.2
2nd quarter	5 722.7	3 803.3	3 065.5	585.7	2 479.8	737.8	498.9	238.9	432.0	34.9	397.1	91.9
3rd quarter	5 768.5	3 838.0	3 093.3	591.5	2 501.9	744.7	503.7	241.0	426.0	26.1	399.9	96.3
4th quarter	5 908.1	3 893.5	3 140.1	593.5	2 546.5	753.4	509.3	244.1	442.6	35.8	406.8	103.2
1994												
1st quarter	5 974.2	3 917.2	3 152.8	601.2	2 551.6	764.4	515.0	249.4	452.9	41.8	411.2	112.7
2nd quarter	6 101.4	3 997.2	3 224.6	608.4	2 616.2	772.6	519.2	253.3	456.9	36.7	420.3	117.4
3rd quarter	6 190.2	4 035.1	3 258.0	611.8	2 646.2	777.0	521.8	255.3	459.7	32.1	427.5	120.7
4th quarter	6 295.2	4 091.0	3 310.9	616.5	2 694.4	780.1	521.6	258.6	468.5	28.0	440.4	119.0
1995												
1st quarter	6 362.0	4 141.3	3 360.6	624.9	2 735.7	780.8	519.9	260.8	470.5	20.3	450.2	122.2
2nd quarter	6 424.1	4 177.6	3 395.2	627.6	2 767.7	782.3	519.5	262.9	475.2	18.4	456.8	126.1
3rd quarter	6 523.3	4 223.7	3 438.2	630.2	2 808.0	785.4	520.1	265.3	487.8	21.4	466.4	130.2
4th quarter	6 608.4	4 268.0	3 478.0	633.4	2 844.6	790.0	522.5	267.5	504.4	28.0	476.3	138.3
1996												
1st quarter	6 729.8	4 321.4	3 525.9	641.5	2 884.4	795.5	525.9	269.6	526.8	36.9	489.9	143.9
2nd quarter	6 857.6	4 393.5	3 590.6	646.3	2 944.3	802.8	529.4	273.4	551.0	44.2	506.9	146.0
3rd quarter	6 938.5	4 455.7	3 646.7	650.1	2 996.5	809.0	532.5	276.5	551.1	33.5	517.6	148.0
4th quarter	7 071.6	4 517.9	3 702.7	654.5	3 048.2	815.2	535.5	279.7	560.6	34.7	525.8	149.9
1997												
1st quarter	7 192.4	4 599.5	3 777.3	663.2	3 114.1	822.2	538.4	283.8	579.4	37.8	541.6	149.0
2nd quarter	7 304.3	4 665.8	3 835.5	667.8	3 167.7	830.2	543.2	287.1	579.0	28.1	550.9	149.9
3rd quarter	7 453.0	4 745.4	3 903.7	674.8	3 228.9	841.7	550.7	291.0	592.5	32.4	560.0	152.6
4th quarter	7 571.8	4 848.1	3 990.9	681.6	3 309.2	857.2	560.8	296.5	600.6	31.2	569.4	156.8
1998												
1st quarter	7 673.1	4 950.4	4 076.3	691.2	3 385.1	874.1	573.0	301.1	621.4	27.9	593.5	161.5
2nd quarter	7 799.0	5 035.9	4 146.2	698.1	3 448.1	889.7	584.5	305.2	633.7	26.4	607.2	167.2
3rd quarter	7 930.2	5 120.9	4 216.8	705.0	3 511.8	904.1	594.7	309.3	649.0	26.6	622.5	172.6
4th quarter	8 026.8	5 204.2	4 287.1	710.9	3 576.2	917.0	603.7	313.3	672.7	32.9	639.7	178.1
1999												
1st quarter	8 178.6	5 298.8	4 368.9	721.3	3 647.6	929.9	610.7	319.3	686.0	33.6	652.3	180.8
2nd quarter	8 250.1	5 352.5	4 410.7	728.1	3 682.7	941.7	620.7	321.0	694.1	28.1	665.9	184.1
3rd quarter	8 343.6	5 429.7	4 472.0	737.6	3 734.5	957.7	634.0	323.6	703.8	26.2	677.6	183.9
4th quarter	8 525.4	5 560.2	4 580.3	748.1	3 832.3	979.9	650.4	329.4	717.9	24.5	693.4	183.6
2000												
1st quarter	8 766.2	5 759.9	4 752.9	765.9	3 987.1	1 006.9	665.8	341.2	724.9	27.0	697.8	184.2
2nd quarter	8 856.3	5 800.8	4 780.1	778.6	4 001.4	1 020.7	679.1	341.6	755.2	33.4	721.9	184.3
3rd quarter	8 976.8	5 914.0	4 872.6	784.2	4 088.4	1 041.4	693.5	347.9	764.7	31.8	732.8	186.9
4th quarter	9 028.7	5 951.7	4 897.8	790.4	4 107.4	1 053.8	703.7	350.2	786.3	33.7	752.6	195.4
2001												
1st quarter	9 171.5	6 059.4	4 982.8	804.5	4 178.2	1 076.7	717.4	359.3	816.2	34.0	782.1	201.7
2nd quarter	9 208.8	6 050.2	4 963.8	815.5	4 148.3	1 086.3	727.9	358.4	835.0	32.5	802.5	207.5
3rd quarter	9 165.5	6 033.7	4 936.6	828.6	4 108.0	1 097.1	740.1	357.0	851.5	32.6	819.0	210.1
4th quarter	9 192.7	6 042.9	4 934.6	839.4	4 095.2	1 108.3	751.1	357.2	844.4	29.2	815.2	210.8
2002												
1st quarter	9 317.6	6 074.8	4 952.5	861.6	4 090.9	1 122.3	759.7	362.6	861.1	17.9	843.3	215.2
2nd quarter	9 394.5	6 137.7	5 000.7	870.4	4 130.3	1 137.0	770.7	366.3	864.8	12.8	852.0	217.4
3rd quarter	9 455.5	6 161.4	5 010.9	877.8	4 133.1	1 150.6	783.4	367.1	873.9	21.3	852.6	216.8
4th quarter	9 579.7	6 193.7	5 021.5	882.7	4 138.8	1 172.1	804.0	368.1	884.3	27.7	856.6	219.8

Table 1-13B. National Income by Type of Income: Historical—*Continued*

(Billions of dollars, quarterly data are at seasonally adjusted annual rates.)   **NIPA Tables 1.7.5, 1.12**

Year and quarter	Corporate profits with IVA and CCAdj					Net interest and miscellaneous payments	Taxes on production and imports	Less: Subsidies	Business current transfer payments, net			Current surplus of government enterprises	Addendum: Net national factor income
	Total	Taxes on corporate income	Profits after tax						Total [1]	To persons	To government		
			Total	Net dividends	Undistributed corporate profits								
1988													
1st quarter	394.5	129.3	265.2	121.7	143.4	386.3	365.1	30.4	31.1	19.6	11.5	1.7	3 984.1
2nd quarter	409.1	136.6	272.4	126.4	146.0	383.6	372.6	29.8	31.7	20.1	11.6	5.9	4 064.2
3rd quarter	415.7	146.7	269.1	132.8	136.3	396.9	377.6	29.2	33.2	20.8	12.4	6.0	4 148.5
4th quarter	440.2	153.9	286.3	138.7	147.6	412.1	382.5	28.6	35.1	21.9	13.2	6.5	4 245.7
1989													
1st quarter	423.9	158.4	265.5	148.0	117.5	432.9	391.1	28.0	37.2	23.3	14.0	6.5	4 316.3
2nd quarter	415.9	145.0	270.8	155.7	115.1	442.5	397.4	27.4	37.7	23.1	14.5	6.7	4 340.9
3rd quarter	416.5	140.4	276.1	161.1	115.0	449.2	403.8	27.1	39.1	23.2	15.9	6.6	4 384.0
4th quarter	400.7	140.5	260.3	167.1	93.1	446.0	403.2	27.3	39.0	23.1	16.0	6.8	4 422.1
1990													
1st quarter	413.5	139.3	274.2	170.2	104.0	451.0	419.4	27.1	39.4	23.3	16.1	4.6	4 516.0
2nd quarter	433.4	144.9	288.5	169.9	118.6	449.3	419.5	26.9	39.0	22.9	16.0	3.3	4 600.0
3rd quarter	407.1	149.8	257.3	170.0	87.3	447.0	426.9	26.9	38.9	21.9	17.0	2.8	4 623.1
4th quarter	414.6	147.7	266.9	166.2	100.8	452.9	434.2	27.0	39.5	20.7	18.8	2.2	4 643.7
1991													
1st quarter	454.0	141.6	312.3	175.2	137.1	424.2	444.3	27.1	39.8	19.2	20.6	5.5	4 658.5
2nd quarter	451.5	136.8	314.7	180.2	134.6	410.3	451.6	27.2	38.7	17.9	20.7	8.0	4 685.3
3rd quarter	449.4	137.4	311.9	183.1	128.8	407.3	461.2	27.5	38.5	17.0	21.5	8.2	4 724.3
4th quarter	450.5	138.5	312.0	183.6	128.4	392.3	471.3	28.1	38.7	16.4	22.2	9.6	4 771.0
1992													
1st quarter	476.5	148.2	328.3	185.2	143.2	387.8	476.2	28.6	38.6	16.5	22.4	9.4	4 896.7
2nd quarter	477.8	149.8	328.1	188.2	139.9	385.6	481.1	29.2	38.4	16.5	22.0	10.2	4 976.2
3rd quarter	463.2	144.0	319.2	191.0	128.2	379.1	485.9	30.4	38.9	16.3	22.7	10.7	5 011.1
4th quarter	483.5	152.8	330.7	193.7	137.0	382.4	490.3	32.2	43.0	15.9	27.1	9.4	5 103.3
1993													
1st quarter	481.3	158.1	323.1	196.6	126.6	382.5	489.8	35.5	40.2	15.1	25.1	9.1	5 116.2
2nd quarter	509.4	170.1	339.3	201.1	138.2	375.1	497.9	37.6	39.3	14.4	25.1	11.3	5 211.7
3rd quarter	523.6	162.1	361.5	207.6	153.9	367.5	505.0	37.7	38.7	13.7	25.4	11.1	5 251.4
4th quarter	573.7	193.8	379.9	216.0	163.9	360.4	519.8	36.0	39.3	13.1	26.9	11.6	5 373.4
1994													
1st quarter	581.6	174.5	407.0	225.6	181.4	358.5	531.9	33.6	40.7	12.8	28.7	12.2	5 422.9
2nd quarter	604.5	183.6	420.9	233.8	187.1	361.8	544.2	32.4	39.7	12.8	27.7	12.1	5 537.8
3rd quarter	638.5	201.1	437.4	240.0	197.4	364.9	550.2	31.9	41.3	13.2	28.4	11.7	5 619.0
4th quarter	663.1	213.3	449.8	244.5	205.3	378.6	554.7	32.2	41.2	14.2	26.8	11.3	5 720.2
1995													
1st quarter	664.7	217.6	447.1	247.8	199.3	383.1	554.9	34.0	43.6	16.0	25.9	15.7	5 781.8
2nd quarter	689.2	214.8	474.5	253.2	221.2	376.6	553.7	34.6	44.9	17.8	25.1	15.4	5 844.7
3rd quarter	723.2	221.7	501.5	261.8	239.7	373.1	559.2	35.1	45.8	19.6	24.6	15.6	5 937.9
4th quarter	735.0	217.3	517.7	273.0	244.6	373.1	563.9	35.5	45.5	21.4	23.9	15.8	6 018.8
1996													
1st quarter	768.9	221.6	547.4	286.3	261.1	370.3	570.8	35.5	46.8	22.8	24.7	16.5	6 131.3
2nd quarter	781.4	233.4	548.0	298.8	249.3	378.5	577.7	35.4	48.2	23.5	25.8	16.7	6 250.4
3rd quarter	786.6	233.8	552.8	309.8	243.0	384.7	581.6	35.2	48.9	23.2	26.8	17.2	6 326.0
4th quarter	807.3	237.1	570.2	319.3	250.9	394.0	592.9	34.8	66.7	21.9	45.5	17.3	6 429.6
1997													
1st quarter	835.3	238.2	597.0	327.7	269.4	403.8	595.6	34.4	46.9	19.7	27.8	17.4	6 566.9
2nd quarter	857.7	242.9	614.8	335.7	279.0	409.9	610.3	33.6	47.4	18.7	28.5	18.1	6 662.2
3rd quarter	892.6	255.1	637.5	343.5	294.0	416.0	616.6	33.4	53.5	19.0	33.4	17.3	6 799.0
4th quarter	877.5	245.5	632.0	350.9	281.1	429.1	624.0	33.8	52.5	20.4	29.6	17.1	6 912.0
1998													
1st quarter	808.5	248.5	560.0	357.1	202.8	460.7	629.1	33.8	58.9	22.8	31.1	16.4	7 002.5
2nd quarter	805.2	245.5	559.7	359.9	199.8	479.6	635.5	35.0	60.4	25.1	30.4	16.7	7 121.4
3rd quarter	813.2	252.2	561.0	358.5	202.6	489.0	643.0	36.8	62.6	27.1	31.8	16.6	7 244.8
4th quarter	789.6	247.2	542.3	352.8	189.5	482.1	650.3	39.9	74.3	28.9	43.9	15.4	7 326.6
1999													
1st quarter	842.2	256.2	586.0	344.5	241.4	473.2	657.5	42.4	65.2	31.2	35.6	17.3	7 481.0
2nd quarter	835.6	254.1	581.5	341.8	239.7	478.7	667.1	45.0	66.4	32.8	36.2	16.7	7 545.0
3rd quarter	819.2	259.2	560.0	346.6	213.5	490.3	679.0	46.4	67.9	34.8	36.2	16.2	7 627.0
4th quarter	823.9	265.7	558.3	358.7	199.6	509.6	690.8	46.9	71.8	37.1	37.8	14.5	7 795.2
2000													
1st quarter	803.3	274.3	529.0	375.7	153.2	547.1	698.6	45.1	79.1	39.8	41.0	14.2	8 019.4
2nd quarter	792.8	273.1	519.6	386.9	132.8	565.3	707.3	45.5	83.3	41.5	41.8	12.8	8 098.4
3rd quarter	775.8	254.7	521.1	390.2	130.9	573.3	711.3	45.8	87.2	43.3	42.0	9.4	8 214.8
4th quarter	753.0	258.3	494.7	386.0	108.8	574.1	717.1	47.0	91.7	45.2	42.8	6.5	8 260.4
2001													
1st quarter	743.6	224.5	519.1	374.2	144.9	577.4	724.1	55.2	98.5	47.9	42.8	5.8	8 398.4
2nd quarter	774.0	216.6	557.4	368.3	189.1	575.5	724.1	62.0	100.5	48.3	43.2	4.0	8 442.3
3rd quarter	742.3	195.0	547.3	367.1	180.2	564.8	725.4	71.2	100.1	47.0	44.2	8.8	8 402.4
4th quarter	756.2	177.0	579.2	372.7	206.5	548.0	737.2	46.4	97.5	43.9	45.2	2.2	8 402.4
2002													
1st quarter	850.7	179.3	671.5	386.8	284.6	521.3	745.0	42.6	87.8	39.1	46.6	4.3	8 523.2
2nd quarter	881.0	186.0	695.1	398.8	296.2	490.5	756.6	39.8	81.4	35.2	45.9	4.8	8 591.5
3rd quarter	910.1	193.7	716.4	403.7	312.7	475.5	771.8	41.4	77.5	32.3	45.9	9.8	8 637.7
4th quarter	986.8	210.4	776.4	411.4	365.0	474.8	777.0	41.7	76.0	30.2	46.6	9.1	8 759.4

[1] Includes net transfer payments to the rest of the world, not shown separately.

Table 1-13B. National Income by Type of Income: Historical—*Continued*

(Billions of dollars, quarterly data are at seasonally adjusted annual rates.)   **NIPA Tables 1.7.5, 1.12**

Year and quarter	National income, total	Compensation of employees								Proprietors' income with IVA and CCAdj			Rental income of persons with CCAdj
		Total	Wages and salaries			Supplements to wages and salaries				Total	Farm	Nonfarm	
			Total	Government	Other	Total	Employer contributions for:						
							Employee pension and insurance funds	Government social insurance					
2003													
1st quarter	9 638.1	6 227.5	5 031.9	904.8	4 127.1	1 195.6	821.2	374.4		880.2	31.1	849.1	226.8
2nd quarter	9 779.0	6 319.6	5 102.9	912.4	4 190.5	1 216.7	836.8	379.9		894.1	38.9	855.3	234.0
3rd quarter	9 933.9	6 404.8	5 167.8	915.6	4 252.2	1 237.0	852.1	384.9		907.2	39.8	867.4	239.9
4th quarter	10 109.4	6 509.6	5 252.5	920.4	4 332.1	1 257.1	866.2	390.9		918.7	42.4	876.3	251.3
2004													
1st quarter	10 293.3	6 566.6	5 282.3	941.8	4 340.5	1 284.4	885.0	399.4		947.2	55.3	891.9	254.6
2nd quarter	10 467.5	6 691.2	5 384.6	950.6	4 434.0	1 306.6	900.4	406.2		961.9	53.0	908.9	258.7
3rd quarter	10 660.3	6 824.3	5 493.1	955.7	4 537.4	1 331.2	917.6	413.6		962.1	44.9	917.2	254.6
4th quarter	10 746.6	6 879.8	5 531.6	962.6	4 569.0	1 348.2	932.6	415.6		977.1	48.7	928.4	253.8
2005													
1st quarter	10 982.6	6 953.5	5 580.9	982.5	4 598.4	1 372.7	950.8	421.9		953.3	45.4	907.9	246.1
2nd quarter	11 119.5	7 028.3	5 640.7	987.6	4 653.0	1 387.7	962.6	425.0		960.5	49.0	911.6	242.9
3rd quarter	11 325.4	7 143.2	5 738.2	994.5	4 743.8	1 405.0	974.2	430.8		991.7	48.4	943.3	231.6
4th quarter	11 535.6	7 225.9	5 811.9	1 001.4	4 810.4	1 414.1	979.5	434.5		1 010.3	42.7	967.7	233.1
2006													
1st quarter	11 865.1	7 407.8	5 977.0	1 018.9	4 958.2	1 430.7	986.2	444.6		1 058.7	36.9	1 021.8	223.2
2nd quarter	11 955.9	7 453.9	6 016.1	1 028.1	4 988.0	1 437.7	992.1	445.6		1 062.2	35.9	1 026.3	211.9
3rd quarter	12 062.4	7 509.4	6 061.7	1 040.8	5 021.0	1 447.7	1 000.9	446.7		1 051.1	35.0	1 016.1	204.3
4th quarter	12 139.0	7 641.7	6 178.1	1 052.1	5 126.0	1 463.6	1 011.1	452.5		1 042.7	36.1	1 006.7	190.7
2007													
1st quarter	12 226.7	7 833.0	6 348.8	1 076.2	5 272.6	1 484.2	1 023.5	460.7		992.3	39.2	953.2	177.9
2nd quarter	12 323.9	7 867.9	6 372.0	1 082.5	5 289.6	1 495.9	1 035.8	460.1		972.8	34.3	938.5	189.6
3rd quarter	12 328.8	7 902.8	6 394.6	1 092.4	5 302.2	1 508.2	1 047.7	460.5		966.0	35.2	930.9	192.9
4th quarter	12 409.6	7 992.8	6 468.7	1 104.4	5 364.4	1 524.1	1 058.7	465.4		985.5	43.8	941.8	197.2
2008													
1st quarter	12 475.9	8 079.4	6 540.5	1 127.6	5 412.9	1 538.9	1 068.0	470.9		1 017.7	55.6	962.2	225.3
2nd quarter	12 515.5	8 078.1	6 532.4	1 137.9	5 394.5	1 545.7	1 074.9	470.8		1 045.9	50.0	995.9	250.0
3rd quarter	12 545.3	8 095.7	6 544.7	1 151.0	5 393.7	1 551.0	1 078.6	472.4		1 040.9	42.8	998.1	273.4
4th quarter	12 186.6	8 063.6	6 513.7	1 160.0	5 353.7	1 549.9	1 078.8	471.1		1 001.3	39.6	961.7	299.8
2009													
1st quarter	12 006.6	7 763.0	6 231.3	1 166.9	5 064.4	1 531.8	1 075.3	456.5		944.2	30.2	914.0	310.8
2nd quarter	11 996.4	7 791.2	6 257.0	1 176.0	5 081.0	1 534.2	1 074.9	459.3		944.6	31.9	912.8	325.0
3rd quarter	12 121.5	7 774.9	6 239.8	1 177.7	5 062.1	1 535.0	1 077.4	457.7		976.9	35.7	941.2	344.4
4th quarter	12 373.6	7 822.1	6 280.8	1 180.0	5 100.8	1 541.3	1 082.3	458.9		1 026.3	44.1	982.2	354.6
2010													
1st quarter	12 461.0	7 804.3	6 239.6	1 187.4	5 052.1	1 564.7	1 100.3	464.4		1 017.6	39.2	978.5	380.5
2nd quarter	12 624.0	7 952.7	6 365.5	1 196.8	5 168.7	1 587.2	1 117.4	469.8		1 024.7	43.2	981.5	397.3
3rd quarter	12 867.8	8 026.5	6 426.4	1 190.3	5 236.1	1 600.1	1 128.9	471.2		1 029.2	48.4	980.8	408.3
4th quarter	13 005.4	8 085.7	6 478.6	1 189.8	5 288.8	1 607.1	1 135.1	472.0		1 059.3	53.2	1 006.0	425.0
2011													
1st quarter	13 156.7	8 207.4	6 577.6	1 190.6	5 387.0	1 629.9	1 138.2	491.7		1 116.5	71.7	1 044.9	458.5
2nd quarter	13 320.4	8 256.3	6 621.0	1 197.9	5 423.0	1 635.4	1 141.9	493.5		1 140.7	67.5	1 073.2	475.5
3rd quarter	13 502.0	8 343.3	6 698.0	1 198.2	5 499.7	1 645.3	1 147.2	498.1		1 175.3	74.1	1 101.2	489.9
4th quarter	13 603.6	8 306.9	6 658.2	1 191.0	5 467.2	1 648.7	1 154.4	494.3		1 188.0	76.9	1 111.1	513.5
2012													
1st quarter	13 845.0	8 514.3	6 842.2	1 199.4	5 642.8	1 672.1	1 162.2	509.9		1 214.4	74.6	1 139.7	524.8
2nd quarter	13 875.3	8 553.8	6 873.5	1 195.5	5 678.0	1 680.3	1 169.1	511.2		1 217.8	77.0	1 140.8	537.8
3rd quarter	13 962.1	8 591.0	6 904.7	1 195.1	5 709.7	1 686.2	1 174.1	512.2		1 220.0	75.3	1 144.7	546.7
4th quarter	14 204.0	8 787.4	7 086.6	1 199.3	5 887.2	1 700.9	1 176.8	524.0		1 247.5	74.5	1 173.0	555.4

Table 1-13B. National Income by Type of Income: Historical—*Continued*

(Billions of dollars, quarterly data are at seasonally adjusted annual rates.)   **NIPA Tables 1.7.5, 1.12**

| Year and quarter | Corporate profits with IVA and CCAdj | | | | | Net interest and miscellaneous payments | Taxes on production and imports | Less: Subsidies | Business current transfer payments, net | | | Current surplus of government enterprises | Addendum: Net national factor income |
| | Total | Taxes on corporate income | Profits after tax | | | | | | Total [1] | To persons | To government | | |
			Total	Net dividends	Undistributed corporate profits								
2003													
1st quarter	988.2	231.5	756.6	411.5	345.2	488.0	788.6	45.0	77.7	29.6	47.2	6.1	8 810.7
2nd quarter	1 028.9	227.0	801.9	412.8	389.1	477.9	800.7	57.1	76.4	28.0	47.6	4.5	8 954.5
3rd quarter	1 076.4	247.2	829.1	436.4	392.8	458.9	814.8	47.0	75.9	25.5	48.6	3.0	9 087.2
4th quarter	1 132.1	269.3	862.8	475.3	387.5	439.9	828.0	47.2	75.0	22.0	49.7	2.0	9 251.7
2004													
1st quarter	1 238.7	277.6	961.1	515.5	445.6	409.6	843.4	44.7	77.8	17.5	51.5	0.1	9 416.7
2nd quarter	1 266.8	298.2	968.6	543.1	425.5	398.5	855.5	43.7	79.5	15.4	52.5	-0.9	9 577.1
3rd quarter	1 325.7	320.4	1 005.3	549.0	456.2	394.4	868.6	45.1	78.5	15.7	53.0	-2.7	9 761.0
4th quarter	1 302.2	328.1	974.1	648.7	325.4	411.5	888.4	52.0	89.6	18.4	52.5	-3.7	9 824.4
2005													
1st quarter	1 427.8	405.1	1 022.7	556.6	466.0	460.4	908.4	56.5	94.5	23.5	52.2	-4.9	10 041.1
2nd quarter	1 446.0	395.6	1 050.4	571.4	478.9	481.3	929.5	60.7	97.4	26.4	53.1	-5.7	10 159.1
3rd quarter	1 474.3	403.1	1 071.2	576.8	494.4	516.5	944.7	62.1	93.0	27.2	53.4	-7.3	10 357.2
4th quarter	1 562.9	445.7	1 117.2	617.3	499.9	528.9	955.6	64.3	90.7	25.8	54.9	-7.6	10 561.2
2006													
1st quarter	1 627.4	460.7	1 166.7	687.4	479.3	553.1	975.7	55.7	80.8	22.2	56.7	-5.9	10 870.3
2nd quarter	1 649.2	475.2	1 174.0	718.3	455.7	571.1	988.3	51.5	79.1	20.5	57.7	-8.1	10 948.2
3rd quarter	1 693.5	496.7	1 196.8	734.9	461.9	583.5	996.9	49.9	84.0	20.6	58.8	-10.4	11 041.8
4th quarter	1 615.9	460.8	1 155.0	763.4	391.6	616.1	1 007.0	48.7	86.4	22.6	59.9	-12.8	11 107.1
2007													
1st quarter	1 530.9	474.2	1 056.8	781.9	274.8	634.2	1 022.0	49.5	101.5	26.5	60.9	-15.7	11 168.4
2nd quarter	1 596.9	468.1	1 128.8	822.6	306.2	639.9	1 032.0	58.2	98.8	29.7	60.9	-15.7	11 267.0
3rd quarter	1 518.1	431.1	1 087.1	833.6	253.5	682.1	1 038.8	55.9	99.6	32.2	61.6	-15.6	11 262.0
4th quarter	1 470.0	408.8	1 061.2	837.6	223.7	697.6	1 045.5	54.7	94.3	34.1	64.5	-18.8	11 343.2
2008													
1st quarter	1 383.4	355.3	1 028.1	867.8	160.3	691.4	1 038.1	51.9	112.6	35.3	67.5	-20.2	11 397.3
2nd quarter	1 367.6	344.1	1 023.5	829.8	193.7	688.5	1 047.9	51.6	110.4	36.3	67.7	-21.2	11 430.1
3rd quarter	1 371.3	312.6	1 058.7	800.2	258.6	678.1	1 049.2	52.1	110.1	37.1	68.0	-21.5	11 459.5
4th quarter	1 017.9	224.4	793.5	736.7	56.8	715.6	1 032.4	54.7	132.6	37.8	87.3	-21.9	11 098.2
2009													
1st quarter	1 252.7	215.0	1 037.7	667.8	369.9	668.0	1 014.1	55.2	130.9	37.9	91.7	-21.8	10 938.6
2nd quarter	1 295.5	240.4	1 055.1	574.6	480.5	560.2	1 019.4	55.4	136.3	38.3	101.3	-20.4	10 916.6
3rd quarter	1 449.6	285.0	1 164.6	523.0	641.7	514.4	1 030.1	67.1	117.7	38.9	82.9	-19.5	11 060.2
4th quarter	1 572.5	337.4	1 235.1	509.6	725.5	509.8	1 041.0	55.7	123.8	39.7	87.2	-20.7	11 285.2
2010													
1st quarter	1 655.2	344.8	1 310.4	521.8	788.6	508.0	1 042.2	54.9	129.3	40.6	85.4	-21.2	11 365.5
2nd quarter	1 660.8	351.7	1 309.2	542.8	766.4	485.8	1 054.2	55.5	126.5	41.9	84.5	-22.6	11 521.3
3rd quarter	1 807.0	387.5	1 419.6	576.0	843.5	482.2	1 063.1	56.2	131.1	43.3	89.2	-23.5	11 753.3
4th quarter	1 839.2	398.3	1 440.9	615.2	825.7	481.6	1 069.0	56.9	127.0	46.1	89.7	-24.3	11 890.7
2011													
1st quarter	1 755.0	393.0	1 362.0	668.3	693.7	473.8	1 085.2	58.7	142.6	46.8	92.3	-23.8	12 011.4
2nd quarter	1 868.7	384.3	1 484.4	692.9	791.4	436.7	1 099.9	59.9	125.6	47.3	90.2	-23.1	12 178.0
3rd quarter	1 893.8	351.0	1 542.8	717.5	825.3	459.7	1 095.9	60.5	128.3	46.9	91.0	-23.7	12 362.0
4th quarter	1 993.4	368.6	1 624.8	727.6	897.3	457.5	1 107.5	60.6	121.8	45.7	86.9	-24.4	12 459.3
2012													
1st quarter	1 979.9	437.2	1 542.7	727.4	815.3	453.9	1 124.4	57.8	115.7	43.3	81.4	-24.5	12 687.1
2nd quarter	1 998.4	429.7	1 568.7	739.6	829.1	419.0	1 122.2	57.6	110.0	41.7	75.1	-26.1	12 726.9
3rd quarter	2 012.3	439.1	1 573.2	746.7	826.5	455.3	1 118.8	56.0	102.6	40.6	66.2	-28.5	12 825.3
4th quarter	2 047.2	433.2	1 614.0	867.6	746.4	430.3	1 126.3	57.7	99.5	40.1	59.7	-31.8	13 067.8

[1] Includes net transfer payments to the rest of the world, not shown separately.

Table 1-14. Gross and Net Value Added of Domestic Corporate Business

(Billions of dollars, quarterly data are at seasonally adjusted annual rates.)   **NIPA Table 1.14**

Year and quarter	Gross value added of corporate business, total	Consumption of fixed capital	Net value added											Gross value added of financial corporate business
						Net operating surplus								
									Corporate profits with IVA and CCAdj					
											Profits after tax			
			Total	Compensation of employees	Taxes on production and imports less subsidies	Total	Net interest and miscellaneous payments	Business current transfer payments	Total	Taxes on corporate income	Total	Net dividends	Undistributed	
1950	162.2	13.3	148.9	98.7	14.8	35.4	-0.1	0.7	34.8	17.9	16.9	7.9	9.0	7.3
1951	185.8	15.1	170.7	114.6	15.9	40.3	-0.2	1.0	39.5	22.6	16.9	7.4	9.5	8.2
1952	195.1	16.1	179.0	123.0	17.3	38.6	-0.2	1.0	37.8	19.4	18.4	7.5	10.9	9.2
1953	209.3	17.3	192.0	134.0	18.5	39.5	0.0	1.0	38.5	20.3	18.2	7.8	10.5	10.2
1954	206.9	18.3	188.6	132.2	17.9	38.5	0.2	0.7	37.5	17.6	19.9	7.9	12.0	10.8
1955	233.1	19.6	213.6	144.6	19.8	49.1	0.2	1.1	47.8	22.0	25.8	8.9	16.9	11.8
1956	250.2	22.1	228.1	158.2	21.5	48.4	0.1	1.4	46.8	22.0	24.8	9.5	15.4	12.9
1957	261.8	24.6	237.2	166.5	22.8	47.9	0.3	1.6	46.0	21.4	24.6	9.9	14.8	13.8
1958	256.9	26.4	230.5	164.0	23.1	43.4	0.7	1.4	41.3	19.0	22.4	9.8	12.5	14.7
1959	287.5	27.6	259.9	180.3	25.6	54.1	-0.1	1.4	52.8	23.7	29.1	10.7	18.4	15.9
1960	300.0	28.5	271.5	190.7	27.8	52.9	-0.1	1.5	51.5	22.8	28.8	11.4	17.4	17.5
1961	308.8	29.5	279.3	195.6	28.9	54.8	0.5	1.7	52.6	22.9	29.7	11.5	18.2	18.4
1962	336.0	30.8	305.2	211.0	31.2	63.0	0.9	1.9	60.3	24.1	36.2	12.4	23.8	19.3
1963	357.5	32.4	325.0	222.7	33.2	69.2	0.5	2.3	66.4	26.4	40.1	13.6	26.5	19.6
1964	386.1	34.4	351.7	239.2	35.6	76.9	0.9	2.7	73.2	28.2	45.1	15.0	30.1	21.6
1965	423.9	37.1	386.7	259.9	37.8	89.1	1.3	3.1	84.6	31.1	53.5	16.9	36.6	23.2
1966	465.2	40.9	424.3	288.5	38.9	96.9	2.4	2.9	91.6	33.9	57.7	17.8	39.9	25.1
1967	491.3	45.1	446.2	308.4	41.4	96.4	4.2	3.1	89.1	32.9	56.2	18.3	37.9	28.1
1968	542.2	50.0	492.2	340.2	47.8	104.2	4.4	3.7	96.1	39.6	56.5	20.2	36.3	31.3
1969	590.8	55.7	535.1	377.5	52.9	104.7	8.6	4.3	91.8	40.0	51.8	20.4	31.4	36.2
1970	612.3	61.8	550.5	398.0	57.0	95.5	12.6	3.7	79.1	34.8	44.4	20.4	24.0	39.4
1971	661.1	67.6	593.5	421.7	62.8	109.0	12.8	3.4	92.8	38.2	54.6	20.3	34.3	43.1
1972	733.2	73.4	659.7	468.2	67.3	124.3	12.7	3.9	107.7	42.3	65.3	21.9	43.4	47.2
1973	820.5	82.0	738.5	526.1	74.1	138.4	15.1	4.8	118.5	50.0	68.5	23.1	45.4	51.7
1974	889.9	96.0	793.9	577.3	78.6	138.0	23.4	6.3	108.2	52.8	55.5	23.5	32.0	59.9
1975	966.0	113.5	852.4	607.8	84.5	160.1	27.7	8.2	124.2	51.6	72.6	26.4	46.2	67.6
1976	1 087.8	125.0	962.7	682.8	91.4	188.5	23.2	7.6	157.8	65.3	92.5	30.1	62.4	73.0
1977	1 233.0	140.5	1 092.5	771.7	100.0	220.8	28.1	6.0	186.7	74.4	112.2	33.7	78.5	85.5
1978	1 407.5	159.3	1 248.3	884.7	108.7	254.9	31.3	7.9	215.7	84.9	130.8	39.6	91.2	103.4
1979	1 565.0	183.4	1 381.7	1 004.4	115.0	262.2	37.0	10.8	214.4	90.0	124.4	41.5	82.9	114.6
1980	1 702.7	212.1	1 490.7	1 102.0	128.6	260.1	59.9	12.0	188.1	87.2	100.9	47.3	53.6	128.5
1981	1 935.2	244.9	1 690.3	1 220.6	154.4	315.3	83.3	14.3	217.8	84.3	133.5	58.3	75.2	146.8
1982	2 018.8	272.5	1 746.2	1 275.1	161.3	309.8	95.9	16.6	197.3	66.5	130.8	61.3	69.4	164.5
1983	2 172.9	285.9	1 887.1	1 353.0	177.4	356.6	92.4	19.5	244.7	80.6	164.1	71.3	92.7	187.4
1984	2 435.3	303.2	2 132.1	1 501.1	195.6	435.4	107.2	26.9	301.3	97.5	203.8	78.5	125.3	209.7
1985	2 605.8	326.9	2 279.0	1 615.9	209.0	454.0	106.7	30.9	316.4	99.4	217.0	85.7	131.3	236.3
1986	2 712.5	349.9	2 362.6	1 723.4	219.6	419.6	105.4	29.3	284.9	109.7	175.2	88.3	86.9	247.1
1987	2 902.9	371.3	2 531.6	1 847.6	233.4	450.6	107.7	24.9	318.0	130.4	187.5	95.6	91.9	260.4
1988	3 151.3	399.4	2 751.9	2 002.3	252.0	497.6	113.3	26.4	357.9	141.6	216.3	98.0	118.2	276.8
1989	3 329.0	427.2	2 901.8	2 119.3	267.5	514.9	134.2	33.6	347.1	146.1	201.0	126.4	74.7	308.2
1990	3 477.3	455.3	3 022.0	2 234.9	284.5	502.6	127.6	34.0	341.1	145.4	195.6	144.1	51.6	316.0
1991	3 564.1	480.9	3 083.2	2 277.8	307.9	497.5	89.0	33.7	374.9	138.6	236.3	156.2	80.1	332.3
1992	3 750.6	496.2	3 254.3	2 420.5	325.9	507.9	71.8	34.0	402.2	148.7	253.5	161.5	92.0	373.4
1993	3 926.9	519.8	3 407.1	2 515.7	343.8	547.6	70.8	31.8	445.1	171.0	274.0	184.7	89.3	391.6
1994	4 219.3	550.4	3 668.9	2 649.0	376.1	643.8	67.6	32.2	543.9	193.1	350.8	197.8	153.0	402.8
1995	4 483.9	593.6	3 890.3	2 787.9	384.8	717.6	70.7	36.9	610.1	217.8	392.2	226.2	166.1	442.5
1996	4 780.2	629.8	4 150.4	2 953.7	398.4	798.3	70.4	43.7	684.1	231.5	452.6	263.1	189.5	484.0
1997	5 153.6	674.0	4 479.6	3 176.6	416.9	886.1	93.5	34.4	758.2	245.4	512.8	292.2	220.6	545.2
1998	5 485.8	719.3	4 766.5	3 447.5	430.8	888.3	134.1	52.8	701.3	248.4	453.0	314.8	138.2	612.1
1999	5 815.5	774.6	5 040.9	3 684.3	454.0	902.6	140.5	53.9	708.2	258.8	449.4	306.4	143.1	645.6
2000	6 227.3	844.5	5 382.8	4 008.9	479.8	894.1	186.6	72.4	635.0	265.1	369.9	355.4	14.5	714.3
2001	6 226.0	894.9	5 331.1	4 015.6	476.3	839.2	170.4	85.1	583.6	203.3	380.3	329.9	50.4	754.8
2002	6 318.8	920.5	5 398.3	3 973.9	506.3	918.1	107.7	61.9	748.4	192.3	556.1	352.3	203.8	779.9
2003	6 544.3	941.5	5 602.8	4 042.0	532.6	1 028.1	87.3	51.0	889.7	243.8	646.0	401.9	244.1	819.8
2004	6 967.7	982.7	5 985.0	4 241.5	571.5	1 172.0	39.2	54.5	1 078.3	306.1	772.2	501.8	270.4	859.8
2005	7 484.0	1 051.6	6 432.4	4 444.5	616.5	1 371.4	72.9	59.8	1 238.7	412.4	826.3	319.7	506.6	951.9
2006	8 026.3	1 128.6	6 897.7	4 683.2	655.8	1 558.7	120.1	48.2	1 390.3	473.4	917.0	648.1	268.9	1 038.3
2007	8 189.1	1 197.5	6 991.6	4 893.0	681.2	1 417.4	172.9	68.9	1 175.6	445.5	730.1	678.5	51.6	985.2
2008	8 094.2	1 259.2	6 835.0	4 939.7	685.0	1 210.3	234.5	97.4	878.4	309.1	569.3	628.1	-58.8	836.0
2009	7 825.9	1 260.6	6 565.3	4 610.0	659.3	1 296.0	157.5	98.7	1 039.8	269.4	770.3	456.9	313.5	964.4
2010	8 237.3	1 262.5	6 974.9	4 714.7	685.9	1 574.3	129.1	99.8	1 345.4	370.6	974.8	442.5	532.3	994.2
2011	8 636.2	1 306.0	7 330.2	4 952.7	718.4	1 659.2	109.9	108.1	1 441.2	374.2	1 067.0	545.1	521.8	999.8
2012	9 089.7	1 365.7	7 724.0	5 202.9	740.5	1 780.6	110.7	79.4	1 590.5	434.8	1 155.7	613.6	542.2	1 067.5
2010														
1st quarter	8 017.4	1 256.8	6 760.6	4 592.3	676.9	1 491.4	134.3	99.4	1 257.7	344.8	912.9	418.9	494.0	941.3
2nd quarter	8 137.7	1 259.5	6 878.2	4 698.7	683.8	1 495.7	132.1	97.1	1 266.4	351.7	914.7	410.9	503.8	943.9
3rd quarter	8 364.8	1 262.4	7 102.4	4 760.2	689.4	1 652.8	127.8	102.7	1 422.4	387.5	1 034.9	462.8	572.1	1 018.0
4th quarter	8 429.5	1 271.1	7 158.3	4 807.8	693.3	1 657.2	122.2	99.9	1 435.1	398.3	1 036.8	477.6	559.2	1 073.6
2011														
1st quarter	8 455.4	1 283.1	7 172.3	4 900.3	710.5	1 561.6	114.9	119.4	1 327.2	393.0	934.2	510.9	423.3	991.0
2nd quarter	8 609.6	1 299.9	7 309.8	4 933.3	720.1	1 656.4	110.1	104.9	1 441.3	384.3	1 057.0	543.1	514.0	971.7
3rd quarter	8 693.8	1 314.2	7 379.6	5 003.3	717.6	1 658.7	108.0	107.7	1 443.0	351.0	1 092.0	573.7	518.3	978.2
4th quarter	8 785.8	1 326.6	7 459.2	4 973.9	725.2	1 760.1	106.8	100.2	1 553.2	368.6	1 184.6	553.0	631.6	1 058.3
2012														
1st quarter	8 970.6	1 343.7	7 626.9	5 124.1	741.4	1 761.4	108.5	88.9	1 564.0	437.2	1 126.8	569.1	557.8	1 025.5
2nd quarter	9 018.3	1 361.2	7 657.1	5 156.6	739.3	1 761.2	110.2	81.9	1 569.1	429.7	1 139.4	572.5	566.9	1 019.4
3rd quarter	9 082.8	1 373.6	7 709.2	5 185.1	738.3	1 785.8	111.3	74.6	1 599.8	439.1	1 160.7	577.3	583.4	1 090.3
4th quarter	9 287.1	1 384.4	7 902.7	5 345.7	743.0	1 814.1	112.8	72.1	1 629.1	433.2	1 196.0	735.3	460.7	1 135.0

Table 1-15. Gross Value Added of Nonfinancial Domestic Corporate Business in Current and Chained Dollars

(Billions of dollars, quarterly data are at seasonally adjusted annual rates.)   NIPA Table 1.14

Year and quarter	Current-dollar gross value added													Gross value added in billions of chained (2009) dollars
	Total	Consumption of fixed capital	Net value added											
			Total	Compensation of employees	Taxes on production and imports less subsidies	Net operating surplus								
						Total	Net interest and miscellaneous payments	Business current transfer payments	Corporate profits with IVA and CCAdj					
									Total	Taxes on corporate income	Profits after tax			
											Total	Net dividends	Undistributed	
1955	221.4	18.9	202.5	137.9	19.2	45.4	1.7	1.0	42.7	20.1	22.6	8.4	14.2	1 044.8
1956	237.2	21.4	215.9	150.8	20.8	44.3	1.8	1.0	41.4	19.9	21.5	9.0	12.5	1 080.9
1957	247.9	23.8	224.2	158.4	22.0	43.7	2.3	1.1	40.3	19.0	21.4	9.2	12.1	1 095.4
1958	242.2	25.5	216.8	155.2	22.3	39.2	2.8	1.2	35.2	16.1	19.2	9.1	10.0	1 054.0
1959	271.6	26.7	245.0	170.8	24.4	49.8	3.0	1.3	45.5	20.7	24.8	9.8	15.0	1 172.5
1960	282.5	27.6	254.9	180.4	26.6	47.9	3.3	1.3	43.3	19.1	24.2	10.5	13.7	1 212.1
1961	290.4	28.6	261.9	184.5	27.6	49.7	3.8	1.4	44.5	19.4	25.1	10.6	14.5	1 241.0
1962	316.8	29.8	287.0	199.3	29.9	57.8	4.5	1.6	51.8	20.6	31.2	11.6	19.6	1 346.1
1963	337.8	31.3	306.5	210.1	31.7	64.7	4.8	1.6	58.3	22.8	35.5	12.4	23.1	1 429.1
1964	364.5	33.3	331.3	225.7	33.9	71.7	5.3	1.9	64.6	23.9	40.7	14.0	26.7	1 529.4
1965	400.7	35.8	364.9	245.4	36.0	83.5	6.0	2.1	75.4	27.1	48.3	16.2	32.1	1 658.0
1966	440.1	39.4	400.7	272.9	37.0	90.9	7.2	2.6	81.1	29.5	51.6	16.8	34.8	1 780.6
1967	463.2	43.5	419.7	291.1	39.3	89.3	8.6	2.7	78.1	27.8	50.2	17.3	33.0	1 831.6
1968	510.9	48.1	462.8	320.9	45.5	96.4	10.1	2.9	83.4	33.5	49.8	19.0	30.8	1 950.4
1969	554.6	53.5	501.1	356.1	50.2	94.9	13.5	3.0	78.3	33.3	45.0	19.0	25.9	2 028.4
1970	572.8	59.3	513.6	374.5	54.2	84.8	17.8	3.2	63.9	27.3	36.6	18.3	18.3	2 010.8
1971	618.0	64.7	553.3	396.2	59.5	97.6	18.8	3.6	75.2	30.0	45.2	18.1	27.0	2 090.0
1972	685.9	70.2	615.8	439.9	63.7	112.2	20.0	3.9	88.3	33.8	54.5	19.7	34.8	2 248.4
1973	768.8	78.2	690.7	495.1	70.1	125.5	23.7	4.5	97.2	40.4	56.8	20.8	36.1	2 385.0
1974	830.1	91.4	738.7	542.9	74.4	121.3	30.2	3.7	87.4	42.8	44.6	21.5	23.0	2 348.8
1975	898.3	107.7	790.6	569.0	80.2	141.4	32.4	4.7	104.3	41.9	62.4	24.6	37.8	2 315.5
1976	1 014.8	118.3	896.5	640.0	86.7	169.8	30.1	6.7	133.0	53.5	79.6	27.8	51.8	2 505.0
1977	1 147.5	132.6	1 015.0	723.3	94.6	197.0	33.2	8.7	155.1	60.6	94.6	30.9	63.6	2 689.5
1978	1 304.1	150.2	1 154.0	829.5	102.7	221.7	36.8	9.2	175.8	67.6	108.2	35.9	72.3	2 864.2
1979	1 450.4	172.4	1 278.0	942.4	108.8	226.8	43.8	9.0	174.0	70.6	103.4	37.6	65.8	2 956.0
1980	1 574.2	198.9	1 375.4	1 030.7	121.5	223.1	57.8	9.6	155.7	68.2	87.5	44.7	42.8	2 927.1
1981	1 788.4	229.1	1 559.3	1 139.9	146.7	272.8	72.2	10.7	189.9	66.0	123.9	52.5	71.4	3 045.9
1982	1 854.3	253.9	1 600.4	1 183.3	152.9	264.2	82.8	8.1	173.3	48.8	124.5	54.1	70.5	2 979.4
1983	1 985.5	264.6	1 720.9	1 250.1	168.0	302.8	82.3	10.0	210.5	61.7	148.8	63.2	85.6	3 125.2
1984	2 225.5	279.0	1 946.6	1 388.2	185.0	373.4	93.5	10.9	268.9	75.9	193.0	67.2	125.8	3 403.6
1985	2 369.5	299.0	2 070.6	1 490.1	196.6	383.9	97.5	15.4	271.1	71.1	200.0	72.0	128.0	3 561.3
1986	2 465.3	317.9	2 147.5	1 578.2	204.6	364.7	107.6	26.9	230.2	76.2	154.0	72.9	81.1	3 654.2
1987	2 642.5	334.7	2 307.8	1 685.5	216.8	405.5	116.5	29.7	259.4	94.2	165.1	76.3	88.9	3 848.0
1988	2 874.5	357.7	2 516.8	1 825.3	233.8	457.7	136.2	27.0	294.5	104.0	190.5	82.2	108.4	4 084.4
1989	3 020.8	380.1	2 640.7	1 934.8	248.2	457.8	160.1	23.5	274.1	101.2	172.9	105.4	67.6	4 162.0
1990	3 161.2	403.0	2 758.3	2 037.5	263.5	457.2	170.2	24.9	262.1	98.5	163.7	118.3	45.4	4 222.2
1991	3 231.8	424.5	2 807.3	2 071.1	285.7	450.5	157.2	26.1	267.2	88.6	178.6	125.5	53.1	4 200.4
1992	3 377.1	437.8	2 939.4	2 188.7	302.5	448.2	132.0	30.7	285.6	94.4	191.1	134.3	56.9	4 328.5
1993	3 535.3	457.9	3 077.3	2 271.0	319.3	487.0	117.9	29.5	339.6	108.0	231.6	149.2	82.4	4 435.2
1994	3 816.5	484.8	3 331.8	2 398.7	350.7	582.3	116.9	34.7	430.8	132.4	298.4	158.0	140.4	4 708.1
1995	4 041.4	523.7	3 517.7	2 524.6	358.7	634.4	126.3	30.2	477.9	140.3	337.6	178.0	159.6	4 935.4
1996	4 296.1	557.4	3 738.8	2 667.7	371.7	699.4	119.7	37.3	542.3	152.9	389.4	197.6	191.8	5 224.7
1997	4 608.4	598.4	4 010.0	2 862.6	388.9	758.6	127.0	38.5	593.1	161.4	431.7	215.9	215.8	5 573.4
1998	4 873.7	638.2	4 235.5	3 093.8	402.9	738.7	146.8	34.1	557.8	158.7	399.2	241.0	158.1	5 889.8
1999	5 169.9	683.4	4 486.5	3 310.0	424.6	751.9	159.9	45.6	546.4	171.4	375.0	224.7	150.4	6 210.3
2000	5 513.0	741.9	4 771.1	3 597.3	449.9	723.9	198.4	45.5	480.1	170.2	309.9	251.3	58.6	6 550.6
2001	5 471.2	785.3	4 685.9	3 584.6	445.0	656.3	219.1	55.3	382.0	111.2	270.7	245.4	25.3	6 411.5
2002	5 538.9	804.7	4 734.2	3 542.0	472.9	719.3	198.6	52.3	468.4	97.1	371.3	254.8	116.5	6 466.3
2003	5 724.4	818.0	4 906.5	3 595.7	495.8	815.0	169.8	61.8	583.4	132.9	450.5	293.4	157.2	6 606.8
2004	6 107.9	850.2	5 257.7	3 762.8	530.9	964.1	159.9	62.0	742.2	187.0	555.2	364.5	190.7	6 904.1
2005	6 532.1	909.9	5 622.2	3 930.3	573.2	1 118.7	173.6	74.2	870.9	271.9	599.1	170.8	428.3	7 131.7
2006	6 988.0	979.4	6 008.7	4 129.3	610.1	1 269.3	183.9	70.4	1 015.0	307.7	707.3	471.1	236.2	7 406.3
2007	7 203.9	1 040.3	6 163.6	4 305.3	632.5	1 225.8	249.0	62.2	914.6	293.8	620.8	484.6	136.2	7 480.5
2008	7 258.1	1 093.9	6 164.2	4 353.0	632.7	1 173.5	307.5	51.7	814.3	227.4	586.9	474.2	112.7	7 385.3
2009	6 861.4	1 092.0	5 769.4	4 088.4	605.9	1 075.1	283.7	73.4	718.1	177.8	540.2	351.7	188.5	6 861.4
2010	7 243.1	1 094.6	6 148.6	4 168.0	633.0	1 347.5	286.2	83.2	978.2	220.6	757.6	375.5	382.1	7 244.4
2011	7 636.4	1 135.8	6 500.6	4 374.3	664.2	1 462.1	287.2	89.3	1 085.6	222.3	863.3	440.3	423.0	7 464.6
2012	8 022.1	1 188.2	6 833.9	4 600.8	685.3	1 547.8	286.8	92.5	1 168.5	256.9	911.6	478.8	432.8	7 734.8
2010														
1st quarter	7 076.1	1 087.8	5 988.3	4 086.7	624.6	1 277.1	282.7	80.5	913.9	208.8	705.0	356.8	348.2	7 178.5
2nd quarter	7 193.8	1 091.6	6 102.2	4 157.3	631.1	1 313.7	286.1	81.2	946.5	220.2	726.2	346.3	379.9	7 227.4
3rd quarter	7 346.8	1 095.1	6 251.8	4 198.2	636.3	1 417.3	287.6	85.0	1 044.6	229.3	815.3	394.3	421.0	7 314.7
4th quarter	7 355.8	1 103.9	6 252.0	4 229.8	640.1	1 382.1	288.3	86.0	1 007.8	223.9	783.9	404.4	379.4	7 257.2
2011														
1st quarter	7 464.4	1 115.3	6 349.1	4 339.7	656.9	1 352.4	287.6	88.3	976.5	216.1	760.4	411.0	349.4	7 365.1
2nd quarter	7 638.0	1 130.4	6 507.5	4 361.5	665.7	1 480.3	287.3	88.1	1 104.9	226.0	878.9	439.5	439.4	7 479.5
3rd quarter	7 715.6	1 143.2	6 572.4	4 407.7	663.5	1 501.2	287.5	90.5	1 123.2	229.8	893.5	466.5	427.0	7 465.6
4th quarter	7 727.5	1 154.1	6 573.4	4 388.3	670.5	1 514.6	286.5	90.3	1 137.8	217.3	920.5	444.2	476.3	7 548.1
2012														
1st quarter	7 945.1	1 168.8	6 776.3	4 549.1	685.8	1 541.4	286.3	99.5	1 155.6	252.5	903.1	456.0	447.2	7 681.1
2nd quarter	7 998.9	1 184.1	6 814.7	4 570.5	684.8	1 559.5	286.5	96.3	1 176.7	257.8	918.9	457.5	461.4	7 728.7
3rd quarter	7 992.4	1 195.2	6 797.2	4 589.1	683.2	1 524.9	286.7	89.7	1 148.4	249.1	899.4	461.2	438.1	7 701.9
4th quarter	8 152.2	1 204.7	6 947.5	4 694.5	687.6	1 565.4	287.7	84.3	1 193.4	268.4	925.0	540.4	384.6	7 827.4

Table 1-16. Shares of Income

(Billions of dollars, percent, quarterly data are at seasonally adjusted annual rates.)   **NIPA Table 1.10, 1.14**

Year and quarter	Gross domestic income, total economy									Net factor income, domestic corporate business				
	Billions of dollars					Percent of total				Billions of dollars			Percent of total	
	Total	Compensation of employees	Taxes on production and imports less subsidies	Net operating surplus	Consumption of fixed capital	Compensation of employees	Taxes on production and imports less subsidies	Net operating surplus	Consumption of fixed capital	Total	Compensation of employees	Net operating surplus	Compensation	Net operating surplus
1959	522.3	286.4	40.0	130.5	65.4	54.8	7.7	25.0	12.5	234.4	180.3	54.1	76.9	23.1
1960	544.6	302.0	43.4	131.3	67.9	55.5	8.0	24.1	12.5	243.6	190.7	52.9	78.3	21.7
1961	564.3	311.2	45.0	137.5	70.6	55.1	8.0	24.4	12.5	250.4	195.6	54.8	78.1	21.9
1962	605.2	333.0	48.1	150.0	74.1	55.0	7.9	24.8	12.2	274.0	211.0	63.0	77.0	23.0
1963	640.1	351.2	51.2	159.7	78.0	54.9	8.0	24.9	12.2	291.9	222.7	69.2	76.3	23.7
1964	685.8	376.9	54.6	172.0	82.4	55.0	8.0	25.1	12.0	316.1	239.2	76.9	75.7	24.3
1965	743.0	406.3	57.7	190.9	88.0	54.7	7.8	25.7	11.8	349.0	259.9	89.1	74.5	25.5
1966	809.9	450.3	59.3	205.1	95.3	55.6	7.3	25.3	11.8	385.4	288.5	96.9	74.9	25.1
1967	858.3	482.9	64.1	207.8	103.5	56.3	7.5	24.2	12.1	404.8	308.4	96.4	76.2	23.8
1968	939.3	532.1	72.2	221.7	113.3	56.6	7.7	23.6	12.1	444.4	340.2	104.2	76.6	23.4
1969	1 018.3	586.0	79.4	228.1	124.9	57.5	7.8	22.4	12.3	482.2	377.5	104.7	78.3	21.7
1970	1 070.5	625.1	86.6	222.0	136.8	58.4	8.1	20.7	12.8	493.5	398.0	95.5	80.6	19.4
1971	1 158.3	667.0	95.8	246.6	148.9	57.6	8.3	21.3	12.9	530.7	421.7	109.0	79.5	20.5
1972	1 275.3	733.6	101.3	279.5	160.9	57.5	7.9	21.9	12.6	592.5	468.2	124.3	79.0	21.0
1973	1 422.4	815.1	112.0	317.3	178.1	57.3	7.9	22.3	12.5	664.5	526.1	138.4	79.2	20.8
1974	1 541.4	890.3	121.6	323.3	206.2	57.8	7.9	21.0	13.4	715.3	577.3	138.0	80.7	19.3
1975	1 675.7	950.2	130.8	357.1	237.5	56.7	7.8	21.3	14.2	767.9	607.8	160.1	79.2	20.8
1976	1 857.1	1 051.3	141.3	405.4	259.2	56.6	7.6	21.8	14.0	871.3	682.8	188.5	78.4	21.6
1977	2 066.7	1 169.0	152.6	456.8	288.3	56.6	7.4	22.1	13.9	992.5	771.7	220.8	77.8	22.2
1978	2 333.4	1 320.3	162.0	526.1	325.1	56.6	6.9	22.5	13.9	1 139.6	884.7	254.9	77.6	22.4
1979	2 587.4	1 481.1	171.6	563.6	371.1	57.2	6.6	21.8	14.3	1 266.6	1 004.4	262.2	79.3	20.7
1980	2 818.6	1 626.3	190.5	575.7	426.0	57.7	6.8	20.4	15.1	1 362.1	1 102.0	260.1	80.9	19.1
1981	3 174.2	1 795.4	224.1	669.6	485.0	56.6	7.1	21.1	15.3	1 535.9	1 220.6	315.3	79.5	20.5
1982	3 338.2	1 894.5	225.9	683.5	534.3	56.8	6.8	20.5	16.0	1 584.9	1 275.1	309.8	80.5	19.5
1983	3 584.0	2 014.1	242.0	767.4	560.5	56.2	6.8	21.4	15.6	1 709.6	1 353.0	356.6	79.1	20.9
1984	4 002.0	2 217.6	268.7	921.4	594.3	55.4	6.7	23.0	14.9	1 936.5	1 501.1	435.4	77.5	22.5
1985	4 295.5	2 389.2	286.7	982.9	636.7	55.6	6.7	22.9	14.8	2 069.9	1 615.9	454.0	78.1	21.9
1986	4 513.4	2 545.6	298.5	987.1	682.2	56.4	6.6	21.9	15.1	2 143.0	1 723.4	419.6	80.4	19.6
1987	4 829.7	2 725.7	317.2	1 058.8	728.0	56.4	6.6	21.9	15.1	2 298.2	1 847.6	450.6	80.4	19.6
1988	5 253.1	2 950.9	345.0	1 174.8	782.4	56.2	6.6	22.4	14.9	2 499.9	2 002.3	497.6	80.1	19.9
1989	5 593.5	3 143.9	371.5	1 242.1	836.1	56.2	6.6	22.2	14.9	2 634.2	2 119.3	514.9	80.5	19.5
1990	5 888.2	3 345.0	398.0	1 258.4	886.8	56.8	6.8	21.4	15.1	2 737.5	2 234.9	502.6	81.6	18.4
1991	6 085.7	3 454.7	429.6	1 270.2	931.1	56.8	7.1	20.9	15.3	2 775.3	2 277.8	497.5	82.1	17.9
1992	6 428.4	3 674.1	453.3	1 341.3	959.7	57.2	7.1	20.9	14.9	2 928.4	2 420.5	507.9	82.7	17.3
1993	6 726.4	3 824.0	466.4	1 432.4	1 003.6	56.9	6.9	21.3	14.9	3 063.3	2 515.7	547.6	82.1	17.9
1994	7 171.9	4 014.1	512.7	1 589.5	1 055.6	56.0	7.1	22.2	14.7	3 292.8	2 649.0	643.8	80.4	19.6
1995	7 573.5	4 206.7	523.1	1 720.9	1 122.8	55.5	6.9	22.7	14.8	3 505.5	2 787.9	717.6	79.5	20.5
1996	8 043.6	4 426.2	545.6	1 895.9	1 176.0	55.0	6.8	23.6	14.6	3 752.0	2 953.7	798.3	78.7	21.3
1997	8 596.2	4 719.1	577.8	2 059.4	1 240.0	54.9	6.7	24.0	14.4	4 062.7	3 176.6	886.1	78.2	21.8
1998	9 149.3	5 082.4	603.1	2 155.6	1 310.3	55.5	6.6	23.5	14.3	4 335.8	3 447.5	888.3	79.5	20.5
1999	9 698.1	5 417.5	628.4	2 251.4	1 400.9	55.9	6.5	23.2	14.4	4 586.9	3 684.3	902.6	80.3	19.7
2000	10 384.3	5 863.1	662.8	2 344.2	1 514.2	56.5	6.4	22.6	14.6	4 903.0	4 008.9	894.1	81.8	18.2
2001	10 736.8	6 053.8	669.0	2 410.1	1 604.0	56.4	6.2	22.4	14.9	4 854.8	4 015.6	839.2	82.7	17.3
2002	11 050.3	6 149.7	721.2	2 517.3	1 662.1	55.7	6.5	22.8	15.0	4 892.0	3 973.9	918.1	81.2	18.8
2003	11 524.3	6 372.7	758.9	2 665.4	1 727.2	55.3	6.6	23.1	15.0	5 070.1	4 042.0	1 028.1	79.7	20.3
2004	12 283.5	6 748.8	817.5	2 885.5	1 831.7	54.9	6.7	23.5	14.9	5 413.5	4 241.5	1 172.0	78.4	21.6
2005	13 129.2	7 097.9	873.6	3 175.7	1 982.0	54.1	6.7	24.2	15.1	5 815.9	4 444.5	1 371.4	76.4	23.6
2006	14 073.2	7 513.7	940.4	3 483.0	2 136.0	53.4	6.7	24.7	15.2	6 241.9	4 683.2	1 558.7	75.0	25.0
2007	14 460.1	7 908.8	980.0	3 307.0	2 264.4	54.7	6.8	22.9	15.7	6 310.4	4 893.0	1 417.4	77.5	22.5
2008	14 621.2	8 090.0	989.3	3 178.6	2 363.4	55.3	6.8	21.7	16.2	6 150.0	4 939.7	1 210.3	80.3	19.7
2009	14 345.7	7 795.7	967.8	3 213.9	2 368.4	54.3	6.7	22.4	16.5	5 906.0	4 610.0	1 296.0	78.1	21.9
2010	14 915.2	7 975.3	1 001.2	3 557.0	2 381.6	53.5	6.7	23.8	16.0	6 289.0	4 714.7	1 574.3	75.0	25.0
2011	15 587.5	8 286.6	1 037.1	3 811.2	2 452.6	53.2	6.7	24.5	15.7	6 611.9	4 952.7	1 659.2	74.9	25.1
2012	16 261.6	8 620.0	1 065.6	4 033.2	2 542.9	53.0	6.6	24.8	15.6	6 983.5	5 202.9	1 780.6	74.5	25.5
2010														
1st quarter	14 627.4	7 811.8	987.3	3 458.5	2 369.8	53.4	6.7	23.6	16.2	6 083.7	4 592.3	1 491.4	75.5	24.5
2nd quarter	14 793.7	7 960.8	998.7	3 459.3	2 374.9	53.8	6.8	23.4	16.1	6 194.4	4 698.7	1 495.7	75.9	24.1
3rd quarter	15 050.5	8 035.0	1 006.9	3 626.2	2 382.5	53.4	6.7	24.1	15.8	6 413.0	4 760.2	1 652.8	74.2	25.8
4th quarter	15 189.0	8 093.9	1 012.1	3 683.9	2 399.1	53.3	6.7	24.3	15.8	6 465.0	4 807.8	1 657.2	74.4	25.6
2011														
1st quarter	15 326.2	8 215.0	1 026.5	3 666.8	2 417.9	53.6	6.7	23.9	15.8	6 461.9	4 900.3	1 561.6	75.8	24.2
2nd quarter	15 513.6	8 264.3	1 040.0	3 765.9	2 443.4	53.3	6.7	24.3	15.8	6 589.7	4 933.3	1 656.4	74.9	25.1
3rd quarter	15 694.9	8 351.6	1 035.4	3 842.8	2 465.1	53.2	6.6	24.5	15.7	6 662.0	5 003.3	1 658.7	75.1	24.9
4th quarter	15 815.3	8 315.3	1 046.9	3 969.1	2 483.9	52.6	6.6	25.1	15.7	6 734.0	4 973.9	1 760.1	73.9	26.1
2012														
1st quarter	16 104.6	8 522.3	1 066.6	4 008.1	2 507.6	52.9	6.6	24.9	15.6	6 885.5	5 124.1	1 761.4	74.4	25.6
2nd quarter	16 150.3	8 562.6	1 064.6	3 989.4	2 533.7	53.0	6.6	24.7	15.7	6 917.8	5 156.6	1 761.2	74.5	25.5
3rd quarter	16 269.6	8 599.5	1 062.8	4 052.2	2 555.1	52.9	6.5	24.9	15.7	6 970.9	5 185.1	1 785.8	74.4	25.6
4th quarter	16 522.0	8 795.5	1 068.6	4 083.0	2 575.0	53.2	6.5	24.7	15.6	7 159.8	5 345.7	1 814.1	74.7	25.3

Table 1-17. Rates of Return and Related Data for Domestic Nonfinancial Corporations

Year	Rates of return (percent)					Shares of net value added (percent)					Value of produced assets (billions of dollars)	Tax liability as a percent of produced assets	Q3 ratio
	Net operating surplus		Corporate profits		Net interest	Net operating surplus		Corporate profits		Net interest			
	Before tax	After tax	Before tax	After tax		Before tax	After tax	Before tax	After tax				
1960	9.6	5.7	8.7	4.7	0.7	18.4	10.9	16.6	9.1	1.3	487.5	3.9	0.75
1961	9.7	5.8	8.7	4.8	0.7	18.6	11.1	16.6	9.1	1.4	498.3	3.9	0.89
1962	11.1	7.1	9.9	5.9	0.9	19.9	12.7	17.8	10.6	1.5	512.9	4.0	0.85
1963	11.9	7.6	10.6	6.4	0.9	20.7	13.2	18.6	11.1	1.5	530.9	4.3	0.92
1964	12.7	8.3	11.4	7.1	0.9	21.3	14.0	19.1	11.9	1.6	554.8	4.3	1.05
1965	13.8	9.2	12.4	7.8	1.0	22.4	15.0	20.2	12.7	1.6	590.3	4.6	1.12
1966	13.7	9.1	12.2	7.6	1.1	22.0	14.6	19.6	12.2	1.8	640.6	4.6	0.94
1967	12.4	8.4	10.8	6.8	1.2	20.7	14.1	18.0	11.4	2.0	697.6	4.0	1.10
1968	12.2	7.8	10.6	6.1	1.3	20.2	12.9	17.4	10.1	2.1	758.6	4.4	1.20
1969	10.9	6.9	9.0	5.0	1.5	18.2	11.5	15.0	8.4	2.6	831.7	4.0	0.95
1970	8.9	5.9	6.7	3.7	1.8	15.8	10.5	11.9	6.6	3.2	910.1	3.0	0.86
1971	9.4	6.4	7.3	4.3	1.8	16.9	11.5	13.1	7.6	3.2	991.1	3.0	0.92
1972	9.8	6.7	7.7	4.6	1.7	17.2	11.7	13.5	8.0	3.0	1 076.5	3.1	1.03
1973	9.7	6.3	7.5	4.1	1.8	16.8	11.0	13.0	7.1	3.2	1 198.5	3.4	0.74
1974	7.7	4.7	5.4	2.4	1.9	14.8	9.0	10.5	4.7	3.7	1 426.6	3.0	0.41
1975	8.1	5.5	6.1	3.5	1.7	16.9	11.6	12.6	7.3	3.6	1 645.7	2.6	0.57
1976	8.6	5.6	6.8	3.8	1.4	17.3	11.3	13.6	7.6	2.9	1 801.0	3.0	0.62
1977	9.0	5.9	7.1	4.1	1.4	17.7	11.7	14.0	8.0	2.8	1 991.8	3.0	0.53
1978	8.8	5.8	6.9	3.9	1.5	17.2	11.3	13.5	7.6	2.9	2 243.8	3.0	0.50
1979	7.8	5.0	5.8	3.0	1.6	15.8	10.2	11.7	6.2	3.3	2 577.1	2.7	0.52
1980	6.7	4.4	4.5	2.2	1.8	14.4	9.5	9.7	4.8	4.0	2 961.1	2.3	0.57
1981	7.4	5.4	5.0	3.0	2.0	15.9	11.6	10.8	6.5	4.3	3 350.5	2.0	0.48
1982	6.6	5.2	4.2	2.9	2.1	14.9	11.9	9.5	6.5	4.9	3 619.9	1.4	0.51
1983	7.5	5.8	5.2	3.5	2.1	16.4	12.8	11.3	7.7	4.5	3 744.6	1.7	0.55
1984	8.8	6.9	6.3	4.4	2.2	17.9	13.9	12.8	8.9	4.4	3 911.5	1.9	0.51
1985	8.6	6.9	6.0	4.3	2.2	17.2	13.8	12.0	8.5	4.5	4 119.3	1.7	0.60
1986	8.1	6.3	5.2	3.4	2.2	16.2	12.6	10.4	6.8	4.5	4 267.9	1.8	0.67
1987	8.7	6.6	5.9	3.7	2.2	16.9	12.7	11.3	7.2	4.2	4 440.9	2.1	0.65
1988	9.4	7.2	6.5	4.3	2.3	17.8	13.6	12.3	8.1	4.4	4 695.5	2.2	0.67
1989	9.0	7.0	5.7	3.7	2.9	17.2	13.3	10.8	7.0	5.4	4 967.2	2.0	0.78
1990	8.5	6.7	5.3	3.4	2.8	16.4	12.8	10.1	6.5	5.4	5 225.4	1.9	0.72
1991	7.9	6.2	4.9	3.2	2.5	15.4	12.2	9.5	6.3	4.9	5 391.8	1.6	0.89
1992	7.7	6.0	5.3	3.5	2.0	14.8	11.5	10.0	6.8	3.9	5 508.9	1.7	0.97
1993	8.2	6.4	5.9	4.0	1.8	15.5	12.0	11.2	7.6	3.4	5 716.9	1.9	1.01
1994	9.1	6.9	6.9	4.7	1.7	16.7	12.6	12.7	8.6	3.1	6 015.6	2.2	0.94
1995	9.4	7.2	7.1	4.9	1.8	17.3	13.2	13.1	9.0	3.3	6 371.1	2.2	1.12
1996	10.0	7.8	7.8	5.5	1.7	18.3	14.2	14.2	10.1	3.1	6 712.3	2.3	1.10
1997	10.4	8.1	8.1	5.8	1.8	18.7	14.6	14.6	10.5	3.2	7 056.0	2.3	1.29
1998	9.9	7.7	. . .	. . .	. . .	17.4	13.6	. . .	. . .	. . .	7 341.1	. . .	1.51
1999	9.6	7.4	. . .	. . .	. . .	16.9	13.0	. . .	. . .	. . .	7 729.9	. . .	1.83
2000	8.6	6.5	. . .	. . .	. . .	15.1	11.5	. . .	. . .	. . .	8 219.5	. . .	1.41
2001	7.2	5.9	. . .	. . .	. . .	13.6	11.2	. . .	. . .	. . .	8 648.3	. . .	1.17
2002	7.2	6.1	. . .	. . .	. . .	13.9	11.8	. . .	. . .	. . .	8 952.1	. . .	0.85
2003	7.6	6.1	. . .	. . .	. . .	14.5	11.7	. . .	. . .	. . .	9 238.2	. . .	1.09
2004	9.0	7.1	. . .	. . .	. . .	16.9	13.3	. . .	. . .	. . .	9 746.6	. . .	1.13
2005	9.7	7.1	. . .	. . .	. . .	18.4	13.5	. . .	. . .	. . .	10 550.8	. . .	1.01
2006	10.2	7.5	. . .	. . .	. . .	19.6	14.4	. . .	. . .	. . .	11 405.9	. . .	1.06
2007	9.4	6.9	. . .	. . .	. . .	18.6	13.8	. . .	. . .	. . .	12 155.1	. . .	1.09
2008	8.3	6.6	. . .	. . .	. . .	17.5	13.8	. . .	. . .	. . .	12 838.6	. . .	0.70
2009	7.5	6.1	. . .	. . .	. . .	16.8	13.8	. . .	. . .	. . .	12 906.1	. . .	0.82
2010	9.1	7.3	. . .	. . .	. . .	19.3	15.5	. . .	. . .	. . .	12 807.2	. . .	0.85
2011	9.3	7.5	. . .	. . .	. . .	19.8	15.9	. . .	. . .	. . .	13 507.5	. . .	0.74

Note: See notes and definitions for explanation.
. . . = Not available.

NOTES AND DEFINITIONS, CHAPTER 1

Tables 1-1 through 1-17:
National Income and Product

SOURCE: U.S. DEPARTMENT OF COMMERCE, BUREAU OF ECONOMIC ANALYSIS (BEA)

These tables, and others in the chapters that follow, incorporate the results of the 14th comprehensive benchmark revision of the National Income and Product Accounts (NIPAs) of the United States. The 2013 revision has altered the numbers all the way back to 1929. In this revision, BEA adopted an expansion of the basic concept of production embodied in the accounts and changed the method of accounting for an important category of pension plans. Also, the constant-dollar or "real" estimates have all been restated to 2009 dollars, so that the levels shown are different even if the indicated rates of change are the same. And, as is done every year, new, revised, and updated source data have been introduced to improve accuracy.

Fixed investment, one of the basic building blocks of the estimation of gross domestic product, is expanded in this revision by recognizing expenditures for research and development by business, government, and nonprofit institutions serving households (NPISHs) as investment.

The workers and capital that produce this R&D have always been reported in the labor and capital tabulations, but were treated as if they were costs of producing this year's output only. In the national income accounting as in conventional business accounting, the full costs of the R&D were subtracted from current-year business receipts in calculating business profit.

Now, in the NIPAs, the estimated value of the research over the whole life of the product—for example, from the estimated future sales of a new drug—is added to the value produced this year. However, this R&D will lose value over time and, as with a piece of machinery, its use and obsolescence, called consumption of fixed capital (CFC), is estimated and charged against GDP in each year that this capital is in use. For that reason, this change adds more to gross national product than to net national product and income.

The basic concept of the NIPAs requires equivalence (except for measurement error) between the value of output and the income and other charges against that value. The higher values of production are balanced on the income side of the accounts by the higher capital consumption allowances and by addition, to profits and other operating surplus (nonlabor income) components, of the net R&D investment—the difference between gross investment value and current year's CFC. (This does not change the tax accounting treatment. The firm still gets to charge off the entire expenditure in the year it is made, which is the most favorable treatment possible.)

Similarly, BEA is now capitalizing private spending for certain entertainment, literary, and other artistic originals as fixed investment. This includes movies, books, music, and long-lived TV programs such as situation comedies and drama (but not news, sports, games, or reality shows).

In a third expansion of the GDP investment definition, all ownership transfer costs for residential and nonresidential structures are capitalized (instead of only broker's commissions as in the previous treatment).

The other important conceptual change introduced in this revision is the adoption of accrual instead of cash accounting for defined benefit pension plans. This does not increase income and saving (or dis-saving) overall, but relocates it. Pension benefits will be credited to the labor income and saving of employees when earned instead of when paid—matched by an equal and opposite change in the surplus or deficit of the employing government or business.

All the quarterly NIPA data published here, including indexes of quantity and price, are seasonally adjusted; this is not specifically noted on each table. All of the quarterly level values in current and constant dollars are also expressed at annual rates, which means that seasonally adjusted quarterly levels have been multiplied by four so that their scale will be comparable with the annual values shown, and this is noted on the pertinent *Business Statistics* tables. Where quarterly percent changes are shown, they are expressed as seasonally adjusted annual rates, which means that the quarter-to-quarter change in the level of GDP is calculated and then raised to the 4th power in order to express what that rate of change would be if continued over an entire year; this is noted in the column headings. For further information on these concepts see "General Notes" at the front of this volume.

Each table is notated, just above the table at the right-hand side, with the numbers of the NIPA tables from which the data are drawn.

All data and references are available on the BEA website, http://www.bea.gov.pdf.

Definitions and notes on the data: Basic concepts of total output and income (Tables 1-1, 1-11, 1-12, and 1-13)

The NIPAs depict the U.S. economy in several different dimensions. The basic concept, and the measure that is now most frequently cited, is gross domestic product (GDP), which is the market value of all goods and services produced by labor and property located in the United States.

In principle, GDP can be measured by summing the values created by each industry in the economy. However, it can also, and more readily, be measured by summing all the final demands for the economy's output. This final-demand approach also has the advantage of depicting the origins of demand for economic production, whether from consumers, businesses, or government.

Since production for the market necessarily generates incomes equal to its value, there is also an income total that corresponds to the production value total. This income can be measured and its distribution among labor, capital, and other income recipients can be depicted.

The relationships of several of these major concepts are illustrated in Table 1-11. The definitions of these concepts are as follows:

Gross domestic product (GDP), the featured measure of the value of U.S. output, is the market value of the goods and services produced by labor and property located in the United States. Market values represent output valued at the prices paid by the final customer, and therefore include taxes on production and imports, such as sales taxes, customs duties, and taxes on property.

The term "gross" in gross domestic product and gross national product is used to indicate that capital consumption allowances (economic depreciation) have not been deducted.

GDP is primarily measured by summing the values of all of the final demands in the economy, net of the demands met by imports; this is shown in Table 1-1. Specifically, GDP is the sum of personal consumption expenditures (PCE), gross private domestic investment (including change in private inventories and before deduction of charges for consumption of fixed capital), net exports of goods and services, and government consumption expenditures and gross investment. GDP measured in this way excludes duplication involving "intermediate" purchases of goods and services (goods and services purchased by industries and used in production), the value of which is already included in the value of the final products. Production of any intermediate goods that are not used in further production in the current period is captured in the measurement of inventory change.

In concept, GDP is equal to the sum of the economic value added by (also referred to as "gross product originating in") all industries in the United States. This, in turn, also makes it the conceptual equivalent of *gross domestic income (GDI),* a

new concept introduced in the 2003 revision. GDI is the sum of the incomes earned in each domestic industry, plus the taxes on production and imports and less the subsidies that account for the difference between output value and factor input value. This derivation is shown in Table 1-12. Since the incomes and taxes can be measured directly, they can be summed to a total that is equivalent to GDP in concept but differs due to imperfections in measurement. The difference between the two is known as the *statistical discrepancy*. It is defined as GDP minus GDI, and is shown in Tables 1-11 and 1-12.

Gross national product (GNP) refers to all goods and services produced by labor and property supplied by U.S. residents—whether located in the United States or abroad—expressed at market prices. It is equal to GDP, plus *income receipts from the rest of the world*, less *income payments to the rest of the world*. *Domestic* production and income refer to the location of the factors of production, with only factors located in the United States included; *national* production and income refer to the ownership of the factors of production, with only factors owned by United States residents included.

Before the comprehensive NIPA revisions that were made in 1991, GNP was the commonly used measure of U.S. production. However, GDP is clearly preferable to GNP when used in conjunction with indicators such as employment, hours worked, and capital utilized—for example, in the calculation of labor and capital productivity—because it is confined to production taking place within the borders of the United States. It is also the measure used by almost all other countries, thus facilitating international comparisons such as those shown in Chapter 13.

The income-side aggregate corresponding to GNP is *gross national income (GNI),* shown as an addendum to Table 1-11. It consists of gross domestic income plus income receipts from the rest of the world, less income payments to the rest of the world. It is used as the denominator for a national saving-income ratio, presented in Chapter 5. National income is the preferred measure for calculating and comparing saving, since it is the income aggregate from which that saving arises. As with GDP and gross domestic income, the statistical discrepancy indicates the difference between the product-side and income-side measurement of the same concept.

Net national product is the market value, net of depreciation, of goods and services attributable to the labor and property supplied by U.S. residents. It is equal to GNP minus the *consumption of fixed capital (CFC)*. CFC relates only to fixed capital located in the United States. (Investment in that capital is measured by private fixed investment and government gross investment.) As of the 2009 comprehensive revision, CFC represents only the normal using-up of capital in the process of production, and no longer includes extraordinary disaster losses such as those caused by Hurricane Katrina and the 9/11 attacks. These losses are still estimated and used to write down the estimates of the capital stock, but they no longer have negative effects on our calculation of current income from production.

National income has been redefined and now includes all net incomes (net of the consumption of fixed capital) earned by U.S. residents, and also includes not only "factor incomes"—net incomes received by labor and capital as a result of their participation in the production process, but also "nonfactor charges"—taxes on production and imports, business transfer payments, and the current surplus of government enterprises, less subsidies. This change has been made to conform with the international guidelines for national accounts, *System of National Accounts (SNA) 1993.* According to *SNA 1993,* these charges cannot be eliminated from the input and output prices.

Since national income now includes the nonfactor charges, it is conceptually equivalent to *net national product* and differs only by the amount of the statistical discrepancy.

The concept formerly known as "national income," which excludes the nonfactor charges, is still included in the accounts as an addendum item, now called "net national factor income." It is shown in Table 1-13. *Net national factor income* consists of compensation of employees, proprietors' income with inventory valuation and capital consumption adjustments (IVA and CCadj, respectively), rental income of persons with capital consumption adjustment, corporate profits with inventory valuation and capital consumption adjustments, and net interest.

By definition, national income and its components exclude all income from capital gains (increases in the value of owned assets). Such increases have no counterpart on the production side of the accounts. This exclusion is partly accomplished by means of the inventory valuation and capital consumption adjustments, which will be described in the definitions of the components of product and income.

Definitions and notes on the data: Imputation

The term *imputation* will appear from time to time in the definitions of product and income components. Imputed values are values estimated by BEA statisticians for certain important product and income components that are not explicitly valued in the source data, usually because a market transaction in money terms is not involved. Imputed values

appear on both the product and income side of the accounts; they add equal amounts to income and spending, so that no imputed saving is created.

One important example is the imputed rent on owner-occupied housing. The building of such housing is counted as investment, yet in the monetary accounts of the household sector, there is no income from that investment nor any rental paid for it. In the NIPAs, the rent that each such dwelling would earn if rented is estimated and added to both national and personal income (as part of rental income receipts) and to personal consumption expenditures (as part of expenditures on housing services).

Another important example is imputed interest. For example, many individuals keep monetary balances in a bank or other financial institution, receiving either no interest or below-market interest, but receiving the institution's services, such as clearing checks and otherwise facilitating payments, with little or no charge. In this case, where is the product generated by the institution's workers and capital? In the NIPAs, the depositor is imputed a market-rate-based interest return on his or her balance, which is then imputed as a service charge received by the institution, and therefore included in the value of the institution's output.

Definitions and notes on the data: Components of product (Tables 1-1 through 1-6)

Personal consumption expenditures (PCE) is goods and services purchased by persons residing in the United States. PCE consists mainly of purchases of new goods and services by individuals from businesses. It includes purchases that are financed by insurance, such as government-provided and private medical insurance. In addition, PCE includes purchases of new goods and services by nonprofit institutions, net purchases of used goods ("net" here indicates purchases of used goods from business less sales of used goods to business) by individuals and nonprofit institutions, and purchases abroad of goods and services by U.S. residents traveling or working in foreign countries. PCE also includes purchases for certain goods and services provided by government agencies. (See the notes and definitions for Chapter 4 for additional information.) In the 2009 revision, new detail was provided on the allocation of PCE between the household and nonprofit sectors.

Gross private domestic investment consists of gross private fixed investment and change in private inventories.

Private fixed investment consists of both nonresidential and residential fixed investment. The term "residential" refers to the construction and equipping of living quarters for permanent occupancy. Hotels and motels are included in *nonresidential fixed investment*, as described subsequently in this section.

Private fixed investment consists of purchases of fixed assets, which are commodities that will be used in a production process for more than one year, including replacements and additions to the capital stock, and now also including research and development and other intellectual property. It is measured "gross," before a deduction for consumption of existing fixed capital. It covers all investment by private businesses and nonprofit institutions in the United States, regardless of whether the investment is owned by U.S. residents. The residential component includes investment in owner-occupied housing; the homeowner is treated equivalently to a business in these investment accounts. (However, when GDP by sector is calculated, owner-occupied housing is no longer included in the business sector. It is allocated to the households and institutions sector.) Private fixed investment does not include purchases of the same types of equipment and structures by government agencies, which are included in government gross investment, nor does it include investment by U.S. residents in other countries.

Nonresidential fixed investment is the total of nonresidential structures, nonresidential equipment, and intellectual property.

Nonresidential structures consists of new construction, brokers' commissions and other ownership transfer costs on sales of structures, and net purchases of used structures by private business and by nonprofit institutions from government agencies (that is, purchases of used structures from government minus sales of used structures to government). New construction also includes hotels and motels and mining exploration, shafts, and wells.

Nonresidential equipment consists of private business purchases on capital account of new machinery, equipment, and vehicles; dealers' margins on sales of used equipment; and net purchases of used equipment from government agencies, persons, and the rest of the world (that is, purchases of such equipment minus sales of such equipment). It does not include the estimated personal-use portion of equipment purchased for both business and personal use, which is allocated to PCE.

Intellectual property consists of purchases and in-house production of software; research and development; and private expenditures for specified entertainment, literary, and artistic originals. (See above for further description.)

Residential private fixed investment consists of both residential structures and residential producers' durable equipment (including such equipment as appliances owned by

landlords and rented to tenants). Investment in structures consists of new units, improvements to existing units, purchases of manufactured homes, brokers' commissions and other ownership transfer costs on the sale of residential property, and net purchases of used residential structures from government agencies (that is, purchases of such structures from government minus sales of such structures to government). As noted above, it includes investment in owner-occupied housing.

Change in private inventories is the change in the physical volume of inventories held by businesses, with that change being valued at the average price of the period. It differs from the change in the book value of inventories reported by most businesses; an *inventory valuation adjustment (IVA)* converts book value change using historical cost valuations to the change in physical volume, valued at average replacement cost.

Net exports of goods and services is *exports of goods and services* less *imports of goods and services*. It does not include income payments or receipts or transfer payments to and from the rest of the world.

Government consumption expenditures is the estimated value of the services produced by governments (federal, state, and local) for current consumption. Since these are generally not sold, there is no market valuation and they are priced at the cost of inputs. The input costs consist of the compensation of general government employees; the estimated consumption of general government fixed capital including software and R&D (CFC, or economic depreciation); and the cost of goods and services purchased by government less the value of sales to other sectors. The value of investment in equipment and structures produced by government workers and capital is also subtracted, and is instead included in government investment. Government sales to other sectors consist primarily of receipts of tuition payments for higher education and receipts of charges for medical care.

This definition of government consumption expenditures differs in concept—but not in the amount contributed to GDP—from the treatment in existence before the 2003 revision of the NIPAs. In the current definition, goods and services purchased by government are considered to be intermediate output. In the previous definition, they were considered to be final sales. Since their value is added to the other components to yield total government consumption expenditures, the dollar total contributed to GDP is the same. The only practical difference is that the goods purchased disappear from the goods account and appear in the services account instead. In the industry sector accounts, the value added by government is also unchanged. It continues to be measured as the sum of compensation and CFC, or equivalently as gross government output less the value of goods and services purchased.

Gross government investment consists of general government and government enterprise expenditures for fixed assets (structures, equipment, software, and R&D). Government inventory investment is included in government consumption expenditures.

Definitions and notes on the data: Real values, quantity and price indexes (Tables 1-2 through 1-7)

Real, or chained (2009) dollar, estimates are estimates from which the effect of price change has been removed. Prior to the 1996 comprehensive revision, constant-dollar measures were obtained by combining real output measures for different goods and services using the relative prices of a single year as weights for the entire time span of the series. In the recent environment of rapid technological change, which has caused the prices of computers and electronic components to decline rapidly relative to other prices, this method distorts the measurement of economic growth and causes excessive revisions of growth rates at each benchmark revision. The current, chained-dollar measure changes the relative price weights each year, as relative prices shift over time. As a result, recent changes in relative prices do not change historical growth rates.

Chained-dollar estimates, although expressed for continuity's sake as if they had occurred according to the prices of a single year (currently 2009), are usually not additive. This means that because of the changes in price weights each year, the chained (2009) dollar components in any given table for any year other than 2009 usually do not add to the chained (2009) dollar total. The amount of the difference for the major components of GDP is called the *residual* and is shown in Table 1-2. In time periods close to the base year, the residual is usually quite small; over longer periods, the differences become much larger. For this reason, BEA no longer publishes chained-dollar estimates prior to 1999, except for selected aggregate series. For the more detailed components of GDP, historical trends and fluctuations in real volumes are represented by *chain-type quantity indexes,* which are presented in Tables 1-5, 4-3, 5-4, 5-6, 6-6, 6-7, 6-11, 6-16, 7-2, 7-5, and 14-2.

Chain-weighting leads to complexity in estimating the contribution of economic sectors to an overall change in output: it becomes difficult, for someone without access to the complicated statistical methods that BEA uses, to find the correct answers to questions such as "How much is the rise in

defense spending contributing to GDP growth?" Because of this, BEA is now calculating and publishing estimates of the arithmetic contribution of each major component to the total change in real GDP. *Business Statistics* reproduces these calculations in Table 1-4. As will be explained later, these calculations are of limited analytical value because imports are treated as a negative contribution to GDP instead of being subtracted from the demand components that give rise to them. For further information, see J. Steven Landefeld, Brent R. Moulton, and Cindy M. Vojtech, "Chained-Dollar Indexes: Issues, Tips on Their Use, and Upcoming Changes," *Survey of Current Business* (November 2003); and J. Steven Landefeld and Robert P. Parker, "BEA's Chain Indexes, Time Series, and Measures of Long-Term Economic Growth," *Survey of Current Business* (May 1997).

GDP price indexes measure price changes between any two adjacent years (or quarters) for a fixed "market basket" of goods and services consisting of the average quantities purchased in those two years (or quarters). The annual measures are chained together to form an index with prices in 2009 set to equal 100. Using average quantities as weights while changing weights each period eliminates the substitution bias that arises in more conventional indexes, in which weights are taken from a single base period that usually takes place early in the period under measurement. Generally, using a single, early base period leads to an overstatement of price increase. The CPI-U and the CPI-W are examples of such conventional indexes, technically known as "Laspeyres" indexes. See the "General Notes" at the beginning of this volume and the notes and definitions for Chapter 8 for further explanation.

The chain-type formula guarantees that a GDP price index change will differ only trivially from the change in the implicit deflator (ratio of current-dollar to real value, expressed as a percent). Therefore, *Business Statistics* is no longer publishing a separate table of implicit deflators.

Definitions and notes on the data: Aggregates of sales and purchases (Tables 1-1 and 1-5 through 1-7)

Final sales of domestic product is GDP minus change in private inventories. It is the sum of personal consumption expenditures, gross private domestic fixed investment, government consumption expenditures and gross investment, and net exports of goods and services.

Gross domestic purchases is the market value of goods and services purchased by U.S. residents, regardless of where those goods and services were produced. It is GDP minus net exports (that is, minus exports plus imports) of goods and services; equivalently, it is the sum of personal consumption expenditures, gross private domestic investment, and government consumption expenditures and gross investment. The price index for gross domestic purchases is therefore a measure of price change for goods and services purchased by (rather than produced by) U.S. residents.

Final sales to domestic purchasers is gross domestic purchases minus change in private inventories.

Definitions and notes on the data: U.S. population and per capita product and income estimates (Table 1-3)

In Table 1-3, annual and quarterly measures of product, income, and consumption spending are expressed in per capita terms—the aggregate dollar amount divided by the U.S. population. Population data from 1991 forward reflect the results of Census 2000.

Definitions and notes on the data: Inventory-sales ratios (Table 1-8)

Inventories to sales ratios. The ratios shown in Table 1-8 are based on the inventory estimates underlying the measurement of inventory change in the NIPAs. They include data and estimates for not only the inventories held in manufacturing and trade (which are shown in Chapter 16), but also stocks held by all other businesses in the U.S. economy.

For the current-dollar ratios, inventories at the end of each quarter are valued in the prices that prevailed at the end of that quarter. For the constant-dollar ratios, they are valued in chained (2009) dollars. In both cases, the inventory-sales ratio is the value of the inventories at the end of the quarter divided by quarterly total sales at monthly rates (quarterly totals divided by 3). In other words, they represent how many months' supply businesses had on hand at the end of the period. This makes them comparable in concept and order of magnitude to the ratios shown in Chapter 16. Annual ratios are those for the fourth quarter.

At the time this volume went to press, inventory data consistent with the 2013 revision were only available from 1997 to date. Tables 1-8A and B show the old estimates for earlier years with an overlap period.

Definitions and notes on the data: Shares of aggregate supply and demand (Tables 1-9 and 1-10)

These tables, developed by the editor of *Business Statistics*, are not official NIPA calculations. They are components of

current-dollar GDP rearranged in order to highlight relationships that are not always apparent in the official presentation of the NIPAs.

Aggregate supply combines domestic production (GDP) and imports, the two sources that, between them, supply the goods and services demanded by consumers, businesses, and governments in the U.S. economy. In this table the user can observe the growing share of imports that satisfy demands in the U.S. marketplace.

Aggregate final demand is the sum of all final (that is, excluding inventory change) demands for goods and services in the U.S. market—consumption spending, fixed investment, exports, and government consumption and investment. It is different from *final sales of domestic product* (Tables 1-1 and 1-7) because imports are not subtracted; in this table, imports are considered a source of supply, not a negative element of demand. It is different from *gross domestic purchases* (Tables 1-5 and 1-6) because it includes exports, since they are a source of demand for U.S. output, but excludes inventory change. It is like *final sales to domestic purchasers* (Table 1-7) in excluding inventory change, but different because it also includes exports.

Table 1-10 provides alternative data on the question of the relative importance of consumption spending and other final demands to the U.S. economy. NIPA statistics on PCE as a percent of GDP are frequently cited, but there is a problem with this, since PCE includes the value of imports while GDP does not.

Definitions and notes on the data: Components of income (Tables 1-11, 1-12 and 1-13)

There are now two different presentations of aggregate income for the United States: *gross domestic income* (Table 1-12) and *national income* (Table 1-13). As noted above, domestic income refers to income generated from production within the United States, while national income refers to income received by residents of the United States. This means that some of the income components differ between the two tables. Domestic income payments include payments to the rest of the world from domestic industries. National income payments exclude payments to the rest of the world but include payments received by U.S. residents from the rest of the world. These differences are seen in employee compensation, interest, and corporate profits. Taxes on production and imports, taxes on corporate income, business transfer payments, subsidies, proprietors' income, rental income, and the current surplus of government enterprises are the same in both accounts.

All income entries are now calculated on an accrual basis, associating the income with the period in which it was earned rather than when it was paid.

A third important income aggregate is *personal income.* The derivation of this well-known statistic from national income is shown in Table 1-11. See Chapter 4 and its notes and definitions for more information.

Compensation of employees is the income accruing to employees as remuneration for their work. It is the sum of wage and salary accruals and supplements to wages and salaries. In the domestic income account, it refers to all payments generated by domestic production, including those to workers residing in the "rest of the world." In the national and personal income accounts, there is a slightly different "compensation of employees," including that received by U.S. residents from the rest of the world but excluding that paid from the domestic production account to workers residing elsewhere.

Wages and salaries consists of the monetary remuneration of employees, including the compensation of corporate officers; corporate directors' fees paid to directors who are also employees of the corporation; commissions, tips, and bonuses; voluntary employee contributions to certain deferred compensation plans, such as 401(k) plans; and receipts-in-kind that represent income. As of the 2003 revision, it also includes judicial fees to jurors and witnesses, compensation of prison inmates, and marriage fees to justices of the peace, all of which were formerly included in "other labor income."

In concept, wages and salaries include the value of the exercise by employees of "nonqualified stock options," in which an employee is allowed to buy stock for less than its current market price. (Actual measurement of these values involves a number of problems, particularly in the short run. Such stock options are not included in the monthly wage data from the Bureau of Labor Statistics, which are the main source for current extrapolations of wages and salaries, and are not consistently reported in corporate financial statements. They are, however, generally included in the unemployment insurance wage data that are used to correct the preliminary wage and salary estimates.) Another form of stock option, the "incentive stock option," leads to a capital gain only and is thus not included in the definition of wages and salaries.

Supplements to wages and salaries consists of *employer contributions for employee pension and insurance funds* and *employer contributions for government social insurance.*

Employer contributions for employee pension and insurance funds consists of employer payments (including payments-in-kind) to private pension and profit-sharing plans, private

group health and life insurance plans, privately administered workers' compensation plans, government employee retirement plans, and supplemental unemployment benefit plans. They are now measured in the period in which the employee earns the obligation rather than when the employer makes the cash payment into the fund. This includes the major part of what was once called "other labor income." The remainder of "other labor income" has been reclassified as wages and salaries, as noted above.

Employer contributions for government social insurance consists of employer payments under the following federal, state, and local government programs: old-age, survivors, and disability insurance (Social Security); hospital insurance (Medicare); unemployment insurance; railroad retirement; pension benefit guaranty; veterans' life insurance; publicly administered workers' compensation; military medical insurance; and temporary disability insurance.

Taxes on production and imports is included in the gross domestic income account to make it comparable in concept to gross domestic product. It consists of federal excise taxes and customs duties and of state and local sales taxes, property taxes (including residential real estate taxes), motor vehicle license taxes, severance taxes, special assessments, and other taxes. It is equal to the former "indirect business taxes and nontax liabilities" less most of the nontax liabilities, which have now been reclassified as "business transfer payments."

Subsidies (payments by government to business other than purchases of goods and services) are now presented separately from the current surplus of government enterprises, which is presented as a component of net operating surplus. However, for years before 1959, subsidies continue to be presented as net of the current surplus of government enterprises, since detailed data to separate the series for this period are not available.

Net operating surplus is a new aggregate introduced in the 2003 NIPA revision—a grouping of the business income components of the gross domestic income account. It represents the net income accruing to business capital. It is equal to gross domestic income minus compensation of employees, taxes on production and imports less subsidies (that is, the taxes are taken out of income and the subsidies are put in), and consumption of fixed capital (CFC). Net operating surplus consists of the surplus for private enterprises and the current surplus of government enterprises. The net operating surplus of private enterprises comprises net interest and miscellaneous payments, business current transfer payments, proprietors' income, rental income of persons, and corporate profits.

Net interest and miscellaneous payments, domestic industries consists of interest paid by domestic private enterprises and of rents and royalties paid by private enterprises to government, less interest received by domestic private enterprises. Interest received does not include interest received by noninsured pension plans, which are recorded as being directly received by persons in personal income. Both interest categories include monetary and imputed interest. In the *national* account, interest paid to the rest of the world is subtracted from the interest paid by domestic industries and interest received from the rest of the world is added. Interest payments on mortgage and home improvement loans and on home equity loans are included as net interest in the private enterprises account.

It should be noted that net interest does not include interest paid by federal, state, or local governments. In fact, government interest does not enter into the national and domestic income accounts, though it does appear as a component of personal income. The NIPAs draw a distinction between interest paid by government and that paid by business.

The reasoning behind this distinction is that interest paid by business is one of the income counterparts of the production side of the account. The value of business production (as measured by its output of goods and services) includes the value added by business capital, and interest paid by business to its lenders is part of the total return to business capital.

However, there is no product flow in the accounts that is a counterpart to the payment of interest by government. The output of government does not have a market value. For purposes of GDP measurement, BEA estimates the government contribution to GDP as the sum of government's compensation of employees, purchases of goods and services, and consumption of government fixed capital. (See above, and also the notes and definitions to Chapter 6.) This implies an estimate (described as "conservative" by BEA) that the net return to government capital is zero—that is, that the gross return is just sufficient to pay down the depreciation. Consequently, this assumption generates no income, imputed or actual, that might correspond to the government's interest payment.

Supporting the distinction between business and government interest payments, it may be noted that most federal government debt was not incurred to finance investment, but rather to finance wars, to avoid tax increases and spending cuts during recessions, or to stimulate the economy. Furthermore, some of the largest and most productive government investments—highways—are typically financed by taxes on a pay-as-you-go basis and not by borrowing.

Business current transfer payments, net consists of payments to persons, government, and the rest of the world by private business for which no current services are performed. Net insurance settlements—actual insured losses (or claims payable) less a normal level of losses—are treated as transfer payments. Payments to government consist of federal deposit insurance premiums, fines, regulatory and inspection fees, tobacco settlements, and other miscellaneous payments previously classified as "nontaxes." Taxes paid by domestic corporations to foreign governments, formerly classified as transfer payments, are now counted as taxes on corporate income.

In the NIPAs, capital income other than interest—corporate profits, proprietors' income, and rental income—is converted from the basis usually shown in the books of business, and reported to the Internal Revenue Service, to a basis that more closely represents income from current production. In the business accounts that provide the source data, depreciation of structures and equipment typically reflects a historical cost basis and a possibly arbitrary service life allowed by law to be used for tax purposes. BEA adjusts these values to reflect the average actual life of the capital goods and the cost of replacing them in the current period's prices. This conversion is done for all three forms of capital income. In addition, corporate and proprietors' incomes also require an adjustment for inventory valuation to exclude any profits or losses that might appear in the books, should the cost of inventory acquisition not be valued in the current period's prices. These two adjustments are called the *capital consumption adjustment (CCAdj)* and the *inventory valuation adjustment (IVA)*. They are described in more detail below.

Proprietors' income with inventory valuation and capital consumption adjustments is the current-production income (including income-in-kind) of sole proprietorships and partnerships and of tax-exempt cooperatives. The imputed net rental income of owner-occupants of farm dwellings is included, but the imputed net rental income of owner-occupants of nonfarm dwellings is included in rental income of persons. Fees paid to outside directors of corporations are included. Proprietors' income excludes dividends and monetary interest received by nonfinancial business and rental incomes received by persons not primarily engaged in the real estate business; these incomes are included in dividends, net interest, and rental income of persons, respectively.

Rental income of persons with capital consumption adjustment is the net current-production income of persons from the rental of real property (except for the income of persons primarily engaged in the real estate business), the imputed net rental income of owner-occupants of nonfarm dwellings, and the royalties received by persons from patents, copyrights, and rights to natural resources. Consistent with the classification of investment in owner-occupied housing as business investment, the homeowner is considered to be paying himself or herself the rental value of the house (classified as PCE for services) and receiving as net income the amount of the rental that remains after paying interest and other costs.

Corporate profits with inventory valuation and capital consumption adjustments, often referred to as "economic profits," is the current-production income, net of economic depreciation, of organizations treated as corporations in the NIPAs. These organizations consist of all entities required to file federal corporate tax returns, including mutual financial institutions and cooperatives subject to federal income tax; private noninsured pension funds; nonprofit institutions that primarily serve business; Federal Reserve Banks, which accrue income stemming from the conduct of monetary policy; and federally sponsored credit agencies. This income is measured as receipts less expenses as defined in federal tax law, except for the following differences: receipts exclude capital gains and dividends received; expenses exclude depletion and capital losses and losses resulting from bad debts; inventory withdrawals are valued at replacement cost; and depreciation is on a consistent accounting basis and is valued at replacement cost.

Since *national* income is defined as the income of U.S. residents, its profits component includes income earned abroad by U.S. corporations and excludes income earned by the rest of the world within the United States.

Taxes on corporate income consists of taxes on corporate income paid to government and to the rest of the world.

Taxes on corporate income paid to government is the sum of federal, state, and local income taxes on all income subject to taxes. This income includes capital gains and other income excluded from profits before tax. These taxes are measured on an accrual basis, net of applicable tax credits.

Taxes on corporate income paid to the rest of the world consists of nonresident taxes, which are those paid by domestic corporations to foreign governments. These taxes were formerly classified as "business transfer payments to the rest of the world."

Profits after tax is total corporate profits with IVA and CCAdj less taxes on corporate income. It consists of dividends and undistributed corporate profits.

Dividends is payments in cash or other assets, excluding those made using corporations' own stock, that are made by corporations to stockholders. In the domestic account, these are payments by domestic industries to stockholders in the United States and abroad; in the national account, these are dividends received by U.S. residents from domestic and foreign industries. The payments are measured net of dividends received by U.S. corporations. Dividends paid to state and local government social insurance funds and general government are included.

Undistributed profits is corporate profits after tax with IVA and CCAdj less dividends.

The *inventory valuation adjustment (IVA)* is the difference between the cost of inventory withdrawals valued at replacement cost and the cost as valued in the source data used to determine profits before tax, which in many cases charge inventories at acquisition cost. It is calculated separately for corporate profits and for nonfarm proprietors' income. Its behavior is determined by price changes, especially for materials. When prices are rising, which has been typical of much of the postwar period, the business-reported value of inventory change will include a capital gains component, which needs to be removed from reported inventory change on the product side in order to correctly measure the change in the volume of inventories, and from reported profits on the income side of the accounts in order to remove the capital gains element. At such times, the IVA will be a negative figure, which is added to reported profits to yield economic profits. Occasionally, falling prices—especially for petroleum and products—will result in a positive IVA. No adjustment is needed for farm proprietors' income, as farm inventories are measured on a current-market-cost basis.

Consumption of fixed capital (CFC) is a charge for the using-up of private and government fixed capital located in the United States. It is not based on the depreciation schedules allowed in tax law, but instead on studies of prices of used equipment and structures in resale markets and other service life information.

For general government and for nonprofit institutions that primarily serve individuals, CFC on their capital assets is recorded in government consumption expenditures and in personal consumption expenditures, respectively. It is considered to be the value of the current services of the fixed capital assets owned and used by these entities.

Private capital consumption allowances consists of tax-return-based depreciation charges for corporations and nonfarm proprietorships; BEA estimates for R&D and other intellectual property; and historical cost depreciation (calculated by BEA using a geometric pattern of price declines) for farm proprietorships, rental income of persons, and nonprofit institutions.

The *private capital consumption adjustment (CCAdj)* is the difference between private capital consumption allowances and private consumption of fixed capital. The CCAdj has two parts:

• The first component of CCAdj converts tax-return-based depreciation to consistent historical cost accounting based on actual service lives of capital. In the postwar period, this has usually been a large positive number, that is, a net addition to profits and subtraction from reported depreciation. This is the case because U.S. tax law typically allows depreciation periods shorter than actual service lives. Tax depreciation was accelerated even further for 2001 through 2004. This component is a reallocation of gross business saving from depreciation to profits; gross saving is unchanged, with exactly offsetting changes in capital consumption and net saving.

• The second component is analogous to the IVA: it converts reported business capital consumption allowances from the historical cost basis to a replacement cost basis. It is determined by the price behavior of capital goods. These prices have had an upward drift in the postwar period, which has been much more stable than the changes in materials prices. Hence, this component is consistently negative (serving to reduce economic profits relative to the reported data) but less volatile than the IVA.

In 1982 through 2004, positive values for the first component outweighed negative values for the second, resulting in a net positive CCAdj, an addition to profits. However, when the accelerated depreciation expired in 2005, there was a sharp decline in the consistent-accounting adjustment and it was outweighed by the price adjustment. This led to negative CCAdjs in 2005 through 2007, reducing profits from the reported numbers.

Definitions and notes on the data: Gross value added of domestic corporate business (Tables 1-14 and 1-15)

Gross value added is the term now used for what was formerly called "gross domestic product originating." It represents the share of the GDP that is produced in the specified sector or industry. Tables 1-14 and 1-15 show the current-dollar value of gross value added for all domestic corporate business and its financial and nonfinancial components. For the total and for nonfinancial corporations, consumption of fixed capital and net value added are shown, as is the allocation of net value added among employee compensation, taxes and transfer payments, and capital income. Constant-dollar values are also shown for nonfinancial corporations.

The data for nonfinancial corporations are often considered to be somewhat sturdier than data for the other sectors of the economy, since they exclude sectors whose outputs are difficult to evaluate—households, institutions, general government, and financial business—as well as excluding all noncorporate business, in which the separate contributions of labor and capital are not readily measured.

Data availability and revisions

Annual data are available beginning with 1929. Quarterly data begin with 1946 for current-dollar values and 1947 for quantity and price measures such as real GDP and the GDP price index. Not all data are available for all time periods.

New data are normally released toward the end of each month. The "advance" estimate of GDP for each calendar quarter is released at the end of the month after the quarter's end. The "second" estimate, including more complete product data and the first estimates of corporate profits, is released at the end of the second month after the quarter's end, and a "third" estimate including still more complete data at the end of the third month. Wage and salary and related income-side components may be revised for previous quarters as well.

At the end of each July, there is an "annual" revision, incorporating more complete data and other improvements, affecting at least the previous 3 years. Every five years, there is a "comprehensive" revision, such as the 2013 revision incorporated in this volume, corresponding with updated statistics from the quinquennial benchmark input-output accounts and incorporating a revision of the base year for constant-price and index numbers.

The most recent data are published each month in the Survey of Current Business. Current and historical data may be obtained from the BEA Web site at http://www.bea.gov.pdf and the STAT-USA subscription Web site at http://www.stat-usa.gov.pdf.

References

The revised data shown in this edition of *Business Statistics* were made available on the BEA website on July 31, 2013, and briefly described in a release on that date titled "National Income and Product Accounts." The changes in definitions and presentations are described in "Preview of the 2013 Comprehensive Revision of the National Income and Product Accounts," *Survey of Current Business (SCB),* March 2013. The results will be more fully presented and described in an article in the September 2013 *SCB.* Earlier revisions are described in annual *SCB* articles in September or August issues.

Selected documentation available on the BEA Web site at http://www.bea.gov.pdf includes the following: "NIPA Handbook: Concepts and Methods of the U.S. National Income and Product Accounts, October 2009"; separate chapters from the Handbook on Personal Consumption Expenditures, Private Fixed Investment, and Change in Private Inventories; "Measuring the Economy: A Primer on GDP and the National Income and Product Accounts"; "An Introduction to the National Income and Product Accounts"; and "Taking the Pulse of the Economy: Measuring GDP," *Journal of Economic Perspectives*, Spring 2008.

The treatment of employee stock options is discussed in Carol Moylan, "Treatment of Employee Stock Options in the U.S. National Economic Accounts," available on the BEA Web site at http://www.bea.gov.pdf.

The data for 1929 through 1946 published here have been calculated after the fact and differ from the national income data that were currently available during the 1930s and 1940s. For an article on what was available at that time and the history of the NIPAs during that period, see Rosemary D. Marcuss and Richard E. Kane, "U.S. National Income and Product Statistics: Born of the Great Depression and World War II," *Survey of Current Business,* February 2007, pp. 32–46.

Definitions and notes on the data: Rates of return and related data for domestic nonfinancial corporations (Table 1-17)

Table 1-17 shows various measures of the return to capital in domestic nonfinancial corporate business. The measure of capital is the *value of produced assets,* which is the current-cost value of the net stock of equipment and software and structures and the replacement-cost value of inventories. The basic measure of the total return to capital is the *net operating surplus,* which is the sum of corporate profits, net interest paid, and net business transfer payments. Table 1-15 displays the same concept, but the numbers may not be exactly the same as those shown in Table 1-17, since the latter data set was compiled before the latest data revisions. (See below for the date of the Table 1-17 data.) In both cases, corporate profits are adjusted to an economic profits basis by including the inventory valuation and capital consumption adjustments.

Rates of return are total net operating surplus and its major components, before and after corporate taxes, as a percent of the value of produced assets. *Tax liability* is also shown as a percent of produced assets.

Shares of net value added are total net operating surplus and its major components, before and after corporate taxes, as a percent of net value added in nonfinancial domestic corporate business. Net value added, shown in Table 1-15, is the value of the industry's output after deducting the consumption of fixed capital, and is the sum of compensation of employees, the net operating surplus, and taxes on production and imports less subsidies.

A *Q ratio* (often known as "Tobin's Q" for the economist James Tobin, who originally proposed it) is the ratio of the valuation of assets in financial markets to the current-cost value of produced assets. A value of Q above 1 indicates that ownership claims to existing assets are more expensive than the cost of purchasing new assets. A high value of Q is therefore more conducive to new investment. Table 1-17 shows the BEA calculation of a ratio termed *Q3*. The numerator is the sum of the market value of outstanding equity and an estimate of the market value of outstanding corporate bonds, minus net liquid assets. The denominator is the estimated current-dollar value of the net stock of produced assets.

The rate of return data do not follow the general NIPA publication and revision schedule. They were presented and described in "Note on the Returns for Domestic Nonfinancial Corporations in 1960–2005," *Survey of Current Business* (May 2006), pp. 6–10. The rates of return for the net operating surplus, the shares of net value added, the values of produced assets, and the Q3 ratio were revised and updated most recently in "Returns for Domestic Nonfinancial Business," *Survey of Current Business* (June 2012), pp. 14–17. They do not, therefore, reflect the 2013 comprehensive revision.

CHAPTER 2: INDUSTRIAL PRODUCTION AND CAPACITY UTILIZATION

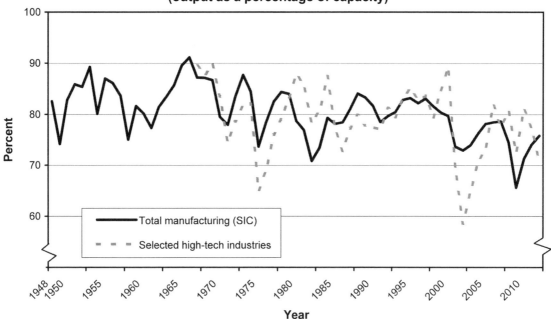

Figure 2-1. Capacity Utilization: Total Manufacturing and High-Tech Industries (output as a percentage of capacity)

- Manufacturing capacity utilization is a key statistic for the U.S. economy, despite being limited to a sector that by some measures has diminished in importance. The Federal Reserve also provides measures of capacity utilization for "total industry"—manufacturing, mining, and utilities. However, mining and utilities are less significant in the context of business cycle analysis, and much of the variation in capacity use by utilities is a result of transitory weather variations, not economic factors. Manufacturing utilization is an important indicator of inflationary pressure and also measures an important element in the demand for new capital goods. (Tables 2-3 and 2-4A)

- Industrial production peaked at 100.8 percent of its 2007 average in November and December 2007 and then fell to a low of 83.8 percent in June 2009, a decline of 17 percent. The preliminary index for April 2013, at 98.7 percent, was up 17 percent from its low point—though still 2 percent below the previous high, as the increase is calculated from a lower base. (Table 2-4A and recent data)

- Manufacturing capacity utilization reached a high point of 79.1 percent in April 2007—lower than in previous periods of high activity—and then drifted down slightly for the rest of 2007, as capacity growth exceeded the increase in output. Then output plunged in 2008 and early 2009, and utilization collapsed to 64.0 percent in May and June 2009, by far the lowest in the entire postwar period. The preliminary April 2013 reading was 75.9 percent. (Table 2-4A and recent data)

- Capacity utilization in the high-tech industries (computers and office equipment, communications equipment, and semiconductors and related electronic components) has been somewhat more volatile than in the rest of industry, as seen in Figure 2-1. (Table 2-4A)

Table 2-1. Industrial Production Indexes by Market Groups

(Seasonally adjusted, 2007 = 100.)

Year and month	Total industrial production	Final products and nonindustrial supplies							
		Total	Consumer goods						
			Total	Durable consumer goods					Nondurable consumer goods
				Total	Automotive products	Home electronics	Appliances, furniture, and carpeting	Miscellaneous durable goods	Total
1967	35.0	34.6	42.7	29.6	28.4	0.8	45.6	45.1	49.1
1968	37.0	36.3	45.2	33.0	33.8	0.9	49.0	48.1	51.0
1969	38.7	37.6	46.9	34.4	34.0	0.9	51.7	52.0	52.8
1970	37.4	36.4	46.4	31.7	28.6	0.9	51.1	50.2	53.7
1971	37.9	37.0	49.1	35.9	36.4	0.9	54.0	52.9	55.2
1972	41.6	40.4	53.0	40.2	39.3	1.1	63.4	59.5	58.7
1973	45.0	43.4	55.4	43.3	42.6	1.3	68.5	62.2	60.5
1974	44.8	43.3	53.8	39.4	36.9	1.2	62.4	59.9	60.6
1975	40.9	40.3	51.7	35.7	35.5	1.0	53.5	53.1	59.5
1976	44.1	43.1	55.9	40.3	40.4	1.2	60.4	59.2	63.2
1977	47.4	46.7	59.4	45.3	45.7	1.4	67.7	65.5	65.6
1978	50.0	49.5	61.3	46.4	45.4	1.5	71.3	67.8	67.9
1979	51.5	51.1	60.3	44.7	40.8	1.5	71.5	68.4	67.5
1980	50.2	50.4	58.1	38.9	31.5	1.6	66.6	62.7	67.6
1981	50.9	51.5	58.5	39.5	32.4	1.7	65.7	63.6	67.9
1982	48.3	50.2	58.3	37.2	31.5	1.5	59.5	60.2	69.1
1983	49.6	51.6	60.5	41.4	36.6	2.1	65.6	62.0	69.9
1984	54.0	55.9	63.3	46.2	40.9	2.6	73.1	68.5	71.3
1985	54.7	57.3	63.9	46.2	40.8	2.7	72.7	68.6	72.2
1986	55.2	58.5	66.1	49.3	43.9	3.5	76.2	70.8	73.9
1987	58.1	61.4	68.9	52.2	47.0	3.5	80.3	75.3	76.6
1988	61.1	64.4	71.5	54.9	49.2	4.6	81.7	78.6	79.1
1989	61.6	65.0	71.8	56.0	50.8	4.8	82.5	79.1	78.9
1990	62.2	65.8	72.1	54.5	47.8	5.6	80.4	78.4	80.2
1991	61.3	64.8	72.1	52.2	44.9	6.7	74.9	75.6	81.4
1992	63.0	66.4	74.2	57.1	52.1	7.3	79.3	78.0	82.0
1993	65.1	68.5	76.5	61.7	57.2	9.3	83.7	81.5	83.2
1994	68.5	71.5	79.7	67.2	62.8	12.1	89.6	86.0	85.2
1995	71.8	74.4	82.0	70.0	64.7	17.5	89.2	88.5	87.3
1996	74.9	77.3	83.5	72.2	65.8	21.1	90.2	91.5	88.5
1997	80.4	82.4	86.5	77.1	70.9	29.3	94.1	93.6	90.5
1998	85.0	87.0	89.5	82.6	76.2	38.1	100.3	96.8	92.5
1999	88.7	89.7	91.5	89.1	84.6	48.3	103.6	99.0	92.5
2000	92.2	92.5	93.2	91.6	86.1	55.0	106.6	101.8	93.9
2001	89.1	90.1	92.2	87.3	82.8	55.5	101.9	94.4	94.1
2002	89.3	89.7	94.0	92.5	90.9	56.1	104.4	96.8	94.6
2003	90.3	90.8	95.3	95.3	95.7	61.3	104.4	96.8	95.2
2004	92.5	92.5	96.4	97.0	95.7	70.3	107.6	98.7	96.1
2005	95.5	96.2	99.0	98.0	94.2	79.0	109.7	101.7	99.3
2006	97.6	98.4	99.5	98.3	93.0	94.6	106.5	103.3	99.9
2007	100.0	100.0	100.0	100.0	100.0	100.0	100.0	100.0	100.0
2008	96.6	95.8	95.1	88.8	84.8	109.4	87.4	92.5	97.2
2009	85.7	85.0	88.6	74.0	73.1	93.8	66.2	76.3	93.4
2010	90.6	87.7	89.6	79.4	83.3	60.8	65.6	81.5	92.9
2011	93.6	89.7	90.9	83.3	90.0	61.7	65.3	83.7	93.5
2012	97.0	92.5	92.4	90.3	101.2	60.8	67.7	87.8	93.3
2011									
January	92.6	88.9	90.3	80.1	84.0	59.2	63.5	83.8	93.7
February	92.2	88.8	90.1	81.8	86.7	60.0	64.9	84.0	92.8
March	93.1	89.2	90.6	83.4	89.3	61.3	67.6	83.6	93.0
April	92.6	88.7	90.2	80.7	84.8	61.5	64.9	83.0	93.4
May	92.9	89.2	90.6	81.9	86.6	63.5	65.3	83.7	93.5
June	93.1	89.1	90.5	81.6	86.6	62.2	64.8	83.1	93.4
July	93.6	89.8	91.2	83.1	89.7	62.4	64.1	83.8	93.9
August	94.1	90.3	91.7	84.1	91.8	63.0	65.2	83.5	94.2
September	94.2	90.4	91.6	84.7	92.5	62.6	65.2	84.3	93.9
October	94.7	90.6	91.7	86.2	96.0	62.5	65.4	83.9	93.7
November	95.0	90.4	91.2	85.3	94.2	61.0	65.1	83.9	93.3
December	95.5	90.9	91.4	87.1	97.6	61.2	67.1	83.4	93.0
2012									
January	96.2	91.4	91.7	89.0	100.4	61.8	67.9	84.7	92.8
February	96.7	92.1	92.1	89.3	100.4	62.1	67.9	85.5	93.3
March	96.1	91.6	91.3	89.2	100.6	60.9	67.0	85.8	92.2
April	96.9	92.4	92.1	90.2	101.9	61.5	67.2	86.8	92.9
May	97.1	92.8	92.8	89.9	100.5	61.1	67.7	87.5	94.0
June	97.1	92.8	92.6	90.6	102.0	61.9	67.4	87.7	93.5
July	97.6	93.1	92.9	90.9	101.5	60.3	68.1	89.2	93.8
August	96.8	92.5	92.0	89.3	98.5	60.4	67.7	88.6	93.2
September	97.0	92.7	92.4	89.3	99.2	58.9	67.3	87.9	93.7
October	96.8	92.1	91.9	89.6	99.6	58.4	67.7	88.1	92.9
November	98.1	93.5	93.2	91.8	102.4	61.4	68.7	89.9	94.0
December	98.2	93.5	93.2	94.1	106.7	61.2	67.8	91.5	93.3

Table 2-1. Industrial Production Indexes by Market Groups—*Continued*

(Seasonally adjusted, 2007 = 100.)

Year and month	Final products and nonindustrial supplies—*Continued*												
	Consumer goods—*Continued*						Business equipment				Defense and space equipment	Construction supplies	Business supplies
	Nondurable consumer goods—*Continued*					Consumer energy products	Total	Transit	Information processing	Industrial and other			
	Nondurable non-energy consumer goods												
	Total	Foods and tobacco	Clothing	Chemical products	Paper products								
1967	51.3	54.5	318.0	21.0	58.5	39.3	15.9	55.3	1.0	46.2	66.2	45.7	30.8
1968	53.1	55.9	329.5	22.9	57.9	42.1	16.6	61.7	1.1	46.1	66.4	48.1	32.7
1969	54.6	57.4	334.4	24.0	60.0	45.0	17.6	60.8	1.2	49.1	63.2	50.2	34.8
1970	55.2	58.2	324.7	26.1	57.8	47.6	17.0	53.3	1.3	47.4	53.5	48.4	34.9
1971	56.6	60.0	322.8	27.6	59.0	49.9	16.2	51.6	1.2	45.3	48.1	49.9	36.0
1972	60.3	63.4	351.3	30.2	59.5	52.6	18.4	56.3	1.4	51.5	46.8	56.7	39.6
1973	62.3	65.1	358.1	32.4	61.5	53.6	21.3	67.2	1.6	58.6	51.2	61.5	42.1
1974	62.0	65.4	335.7	34.2	60.6	55.0	22.6	65.5	2.0	61.1	52.9	60.0	41.9
1975	60.4	64.3	326.1	33.0	57.1	56.2	20.1	57.6	1.9	53.5	53.4	50.8	38.7
1976	64.3	68.5	343.5	35.9	59.4	59.1	21.5	59.6	2.2	55.7	51.8	54.7	41.2
1977	66.6	69.9	360.4	37.4	64.9	61.4	24.8	70.8	2.9	60.7	46.4	59.6	44.7
1978	69.2	72.5	369.0	39.7	68.1	62.6	28.0	82.1	3.7	65.0	47.3	63.0	47.1
1979	68.3	72.0	348.7	39.8	68.9	64.2	31.5	95.8	4.7	69.0	50.6	64.6	48.7
1980	69.1	73.1	355.0	39.6	69.7	61.8	32.3	90.3	5.9	66.7	60.1	59.8	47.6
1981	69.7	73.5	354.8	40.2	71.5	61.4	33.2	84.5	6.9	66.6	65.1	58.8	48.8
1982	71.0	75.8	353.8	40.3	73.3	61.8	30.4	64.8	7.9	57.6	77.8	53.4	48.2
1983	71.9	76.0	363.9	40.8	76.4	62.3	30.6	63.8	9.1	53.4	78.4	57.2	50.5
1984	73.2	76.9	365.5	41.7	80.3	64.2	35.1	65.8	11.2	60.9	89.8	62.2	54.9
1985	74.3	79.2	350.1	42.2	84.4	64.2	36.4	68.1	12.0	61.6	100.5	63.7	56.3
1986	76.2	80.5	349.9	45.4	85.6	65.5	35.9	62.3	12.1	61.3	106.7	65.9	58.1
1987	78.9	82.4	353.1	49.0	90.5	67.9	38.3	63.2	13.9	63.5	109.0	70.1	61.6
1988	81.2	84.7	347.9	51.9	93.0	71.4	42.3	70.6	15.6	69.0	110.0	71.7	63.9
1989	80.8	84.1	332.1	53.0	93.3	71.9	43.7	74.2	16.0	71.3	110.1	71.4	64.8
1990	82.6	86.5	325.7	54.9	95.1	71.4	45.3	79.4	17.3	70.8	106.2	70.9	66.3
1991	83.5	86.9	324.8	56.9	95.6	73.6	44.5	82.5	17.3	67.1	98.3	67.0	65.4
1992	84.5	88.1	332.1	56.7	96.8	72.6	46.3	80.6	19.6	68.2	91.1	69.8	66.9
1993	85.2	87.4	338.7	58.3	99.0	75.8	48.6	75.5	21.4	72.8	86.0	72.8	69.0
1994	87.5	90.9	344.9	59.5	98.0	76.7	51.8	73.1	24.1	77.7	80.7	78.1	71.8
1995	89.6	93.3	343.5	62.1	98.6	78.8	56.5	71.2	29.0	82.6	77.9	79.8	74.7
1996	90.2	93.0	334.5	65.1	98.3	82.3	62.0	75.4	35.5	85.5	75.8	83.4	77.6
1997	93.0	94.4	333.4	68.8	107.0	81.6	71.2	88.7	44.8	90.8	74.6	87.4	83.2
1998	95.4	96.8	313.5	72.2	112.0	81.7	79.1	104.2	53.2	93.5	77.8	92.1	87.9
1999	94.7	94.9	301.8	73.5	114.2	84.5	83.4	102.0	64.7	91.4	75.4	94.4	91.6
2000	96.0	96.4	289.4	76.2	113.8	86.3	89.6	90.3	78.2	96.8	67.0	96.5	95.3
2001	96.1	96.3	250.5	80.5	110.6	87.3	84.0	87.0	75.9	87.5	73.6	92.1	91.7
2002	95.8	94.6	192.9	87.1	109.0	91.1	78.5	80.0	66.1	86.1	74.5	92.2	91.9
2003	96.5	95.8	181.5	89.2	105.0	91.6	78.3	75.4	68.7	85.7	79.2	92.0	93.4
2004	97.2	97.1	150.8	91.4	105.6	92.9	82.1	79.6	74.3	88.0	77.2	94.2	95.1
2005	100.5	100.4	141.9	96.3	104.6	96.1	87.7	87.1	80.0	92.8	84.9	98.7	98.2
2006	101.4	100.5	132.1	99.6	104.5	95.8	95.8	101.2	91.0	96.4	84.0	101.1	99.2
2007	100.0	100.0	100.0	100.0	100.0	100.0	100.0	100.0	100.0	100.0	100.0	100.0	100.0
2008	96.4	96.5	88.4	96.4	95.4	99.7	97.7	92.6	101.2	98.0	107.0	90.7	96.0
2009	91.5	95.0	60.7	88.6	86.2	99.8	80.1	71.6	89.9	78.5	102.4	69.9	86.0
2010	90.2	95.4	62.3	84.7	83.3	102.0	86.7	84.7	91.0	84.9	110.1	72.5	88.1
2011	90.8	95.8	60.4	86.5	81.7	102.5	91.6	86.7	90.9	93.2	106.1	74.6	89.0
2012	91.4	98.4	58.5	85.1	76.9	99.9	99.2	99.4	97.4	99.1	111.8	78.5	90.3
2011													
January	90.4	95.6	63.2	84.9	82.4	104.7	90.6	83.1	91.0	92.8	107.0	73.1	88.7
February	90.0	95.1	63.0	84.9	81.8	102.5	90.9	84.4	91.0	92.6	106.2	72.9	88.5
March	90.3	95.3	61.0	85.4	81.9	102.3	90.5	85.9	90.8	91.5	105.5	73.7	89.1
April	91.0	96.0	61.5	86.4	82.1	101.6	89.7	83.8	89.9	91.3	104.8	73.4	88.5
May	90.7	95.5	61.4	86.6	81.4	103.1	90.5	84.9	89.9	92.3	104.7	74.4	88.9
June	90.7	95.3	60.9	87.0	80.7	102.5	90.4	85.3	88.8	92.4	104.1	74.5	88.6
July	91.2	96.0	60.9	87.5	81.0	103.1	91.1	85.1	90.3	93.1	104.6	75.4	89.1
August	91.3	95.8	59.2	87.9	81.6	104.1	91.9	87.6	90.8	93.3	105.7	75.0	89.5
September	91.1	95.7	58.3	87.3	82.2	103.6	92.3	87.5	91.4	93.8	105.8	75.2	89.9
October	91.5	96.5	59.0	87.2	82.2	101.2	93.1	90.3	91.7	94.1	107.2	75.5	89.3
November	90.8	96.1	58.7	86.2	81.5	101.5	93.7	91.1	92.0	94.8	109.3	75.6	88.7
December	91.3	96.5	58.2	87.0	81.4	99.1	94.7	91.1	93.3	96.0	108.9	76.9	89.3
2012													
January	91.8	97.2	60.9	87.1	80.9	96.8	96.1	92.2	95.4	97.2	109.5	77.6	89.6
February	92.0	98.0	60.6	86.8	80.8	97.9	97.0	94.2	96.0	97.8	111.6	79.2	90.2
March	91.3	97.1	59.4	86.3	79.3	95.9	97.4	95.3	95.5	98.2	111.9	78.7	89.6
April	91.7	98.0	59.4	86.4	78.4	97.3	98.3	96.9	96.7	98.8	111.1	79.5	90.4
May	91.6	98.1	59.2	85.8	77.8	102.4	99.0	98.9	96.1	99.4	109.8	78.6	90.9
June	91.3	98.4	58.4	85.0	76.4	100.9	100.3	99.9	97.2	100.9	109.7	77.9	90.7
July	91.5	99.3	57.9	84.5	75.2	102.0	100.4	102.8	98.0	99.5	112.1	77.8	90.8
August	90.9	99.0	56.7	83.5	74.7	101.0	100.3	101.8	97.7	99.9	112.4	77.7	90.2
September	91.7	100.4	57.5	83.5	74.1	100.8	100.1	100.6	98.1	99.9	113.1	78.0	90.1
October	90.0	97.4	56.1	83.3	74.5	103.0	98.9	100.6	97.5	98.1	112.8	77.8	89.9
November	91.2	99.0	57.6	83.9	75.4	103.5	101.3	105.1	99.8	99.5	114.0	79.6	90.7
December	92.0	99.5	57.9	85.4	75.1	97.7	101.7	104.1	101.3	100.1	113.3	80.1	90.5

Table 2-1. Industrial Production Indexes by Market Groups—*Continued*

(Seasonally adjusted, 2007 = 100.)

Year and month		Materials										
	Total	Non-energy materials										Energy materials
		Total	Durable				Nondurable					
			Total	Consumer parts	Equipment parts	Other	Total	Textile	Paper	Chemicals		
1967	34.6	27.3	20.6	49.8	4.4	54.1	44.9	103.7	50.5	28.5		67.4
1968	36.9	29.3	21.8	56.1	4.5	56.9	49.3	114.5	52.8	33.1		70.6
1969	39.1	31.2	22.9	56.4	4.8	60.6	53.4	117.6	57.3	36.8		74.2
1970	37.8	29.3	20.8	47.3	4.4	56.6	53.7	113.3	56.8	37.6		77.8
1971	38.3	29.9	20.9	52.4	4.4	54.5	56.0	118.6	59.4	39.9		78.5
1972	42.2	33.5	23.6	58.3	5.1	61.6	61.7	124.9	63.3	46.4		81.5
1973	46.0	37.1	27.0	67.7	6.0	68.3	64.8	121.6	68.3	51.2		83.5
1974	45.9	37.0	26.7	59.9	6.3	68.1	65.7	113.7	71.7	52.6		83.1
1975	40.8	31.7	22.3	48.3	5.4	56.9	58.8	111.3	62.4	44.1		82.4
1976	44.4	35.3	24.9	61.7	5.8	61.1	65.2	123.9	68.6	50.5		84.2
1977	47.5	38.3	27.1	67.6	6.6	64.7	69.9	132.0	71.7	56.1		86.9
1978	49.9	40.7	29.3	71.5	7.4	69.0	72.5	130.6	75.2	59.6		87.9
1979	51.2	41.8	30.2	67.5	8.2	70.7	73.9	129.4	78.2	62.0		90.3
1980	49.3	39.4	28.0	52.1	8.4	65.5	71.5	126.5	78.8	57.4		91.0
1981	49.6	39.5	28.1	49.5	8.6	65.6	72.1	123.7	80.3	57.9		91.9
1982	45.8	35.6	24.5	42.1	7.9	55.4	68.3	113.1	81.0	51.9		88.0
1983	47.0	38.0	26.1	51.2	8.0	57.9	73.1	126.7	86.1	57.4		85.2
1984	51.4	42.4	30.3	60.8	9.6	64.1	76.3	126.3	91.5	61.0		90.6
1985	51.4	42.4	30.5	63.3	9.6	63.7	75.7	119.4	91.0	59.9		90.0
1986	51.3	43.2	30.9	62.7	9.8	64.9	78.1	124.3	94.9	62.8		86.5
1987	54.0	46.1	33.0	64.4	10.7	69.4	82.7	139.2	99.5	68.3		88.6
1988	57.0	49.0	35.7	69.7	11.7	74.4	85.8	137.8	102.8	72.4		91.6
1989	57.4	49.3	35.8	66.1	12.1	74.7	86.6	140.7	102.8	73.4		92.5
1990	57.8	49.4	35.9	61.6	12.5	75.0	86.8	133.6	103.1	74.2		94.4
1991	57.0	48.4	34.9	58.2	12.5	71.8	85.8	133.5	100.9	73.1		94.5
1992	58.8	50.7	37.2	65.4	13.2	75.6	87.9	141.2	103.4	74.9		93.6
1993	60.8	53.0	39.6	74.0	14.0	78.5	88.9	146.9	103.4	75.4		93.8
1994	64.7	57.2	44.0	85.4	15.9	84.4	91.6	155.8	107.3	77.7		95.3
1995	68.4	61.2	48.7	88.8	19.5	87.5	92.5	153.2	110.1	78.3		96.8
1996	71.9	65.0	53.8	91.1	23.9	90.1	91.6	148.9	106.6	78.7		98.3
1997	77.7	71.8	61.3	98.0	30.3	94.7	95.9	155.5	107.7	84.4		98.2
1998	82.4	77.2	68.0	101.3	37.4	97.2	97.2	154.1	108.8	84.6		98.4
1999	87.3	83.2	75.7	111.6	45.9	98.8	98.4	151.0	110.4	87.0		97.9
2000	91.8	88.3	83.1	111.6	57.2	99.7	97.8	144.6	108.6	87.2		99.6
2001	87.7	83.4	78.8	98.6	57.0	92.9	91.4	127.8	103.0	80.8		98.2
2002	88.6	84.7	80.0	103.5	57.7	92.9	93.1	129.6	103.3	83.6		97.9
2003	89.8	86.2	82.7	102.4	64.3	92.1	92.3	122.9	99.9	84.1		97.9
2004	92.4	89.8	87.2	102.5	71.1	95.8	94.1	117.5	101.1	88.5		97.9
2005	94.6	93.4	92.2	103.6	80.3	97.9	95.2	120.4	100.7	89.3		96.9
2006	96.5	95.7	95.7	100.8	87.9	100.1	95.6	109.3	99.9	91.2		98.0
2007	100.0	100.0	100.0	100.0	100.0	100.0	100.0	100.0	100.0	100.0		100.0
2008	97.6	95.6	97.5	84.3	106.6	95.3	92.7	86.9	95.5	89.1		100.9
2009	86.6	79.7	76.8	56.4	89.7	74.6	84.0	71.4	83.8	79.4		98.4
2010	94.2	89.1	89.5	74.5	106.1	82.9	88.4	79.4	85.3	87.3		102.5
2011	98.7	93.8	98.1	81.3	122.7	87.3	87.7	78.1	85.2	86.2		106.4
2012	102.8	97.6	104.1	93.1	130.7	90.3	88.6	80.2	83.3	87.7		110.9
2011												
January	97.3	93.0	95.9	79.1	118.2	86.4	88.8	77.6	86.6	87.6		104.0
February	96.5	92.7	96.1	80.7	118.5	86.0	87.9	78.8	85.8	86.5		102.3
March	98.2	93.6	97.1	82.5	119.6	86.8	88.8	76.4	86.0	88.1		105.2
April	97.5	92.7	96.2	78.8	119.0	86.7	87.7	78.5	85.8	86.0		105.1
May	97.6	93.0	97.2	78.5	120.7	87.5	87.1	78.5	85.0	85.3		104.9
June	98.2	93.1	97.5	79.8	122.3	86.8	87.0	78.5	85.3	85.0		106.2
July	98.5	93.6	97.9	80.4	122.4	87.2	87.6	78.7	85.7	85.8		106.3
August	99.0	93.6	98.3	81.0	124.4	86.9	86.9	76.5	84.6	85.1		107.8
September	99.1	94.1	98.9	82.0	124.5	87.5	87.5	77.4	85.0	86.1		106.9
October	100.0	94.7	99.6	82.8	125.8	87.9	87.9	77.5	84.1	86.5		108.4
November	100.7	95.0	100.6	83.1	127.5	88.7	87.3	78.9	84.3	85.7		109.8
December	101.4	96.3	102.1	87.0	129.2	89.2	88.4	80.2	84.9	87.0		109.4
2012												
January	102.2	97.5	103.5	90.1	130.4	90.2	89.2	82.3	84.8	88.0		109.7
February	102.4	97.9	104.5	90.3	131.8	91.3	88.8	82.3	85.4	87.0		109.4
March	101.9	97.0	103.5	89.3	131.9	89.7	88.2	80.9	84.0	86.7		109.4
April	102.6	97.8	104.6	92.4	132.5	90.4	88.6	81.6	84.1	87.1		109.9
May	102.6	97.1	103.9	91.8	131.9	89.6	87.9	79.2	84.2	86.2		111.3
June	102.6	97.5	104.5	93.1	133.3	89.7	87.7	81.5	82.9	86.3		110.8
July	103.3	97.8	104.9	97.1	130.7	90.4	88.1	80.2	82.2	86.8		112.0
August	102.3	97.0	103.2	93.6	127.8	90.1	88.3	79.9	82.4	87.2		110.7
September	102.4	96.9	103.0	92.7	129.0	89.3	88.6	80.1	81.8	88.1		111.2
October	102.8	97.1	103.3	92.5	129.5	89.6	88.5	80.2	82.0	88.2		112.1
November	103.9	98.4	105.1	95.4	130.0	91.8	89.3	77.7	82.3	89.4		112.7
December	104.1	99.2	105.6	98.5	130.1	91.8	90.4	76.0	83.5	91.3		111.7

Table 2-1. Industrial Production Indexes by Market Groups—*Continued*

(Seasonally adjusted, 2007 = 100.)

Year and month	Special aggregates											Total non-energy, excluding high-tech
	Energy						Non-energy					
									Selected high-tech			
	Total	Consumer energy products	Commercial energy products	Oil and gas well drilling	Converted fuels	Primary energy	Total	Total	Computers and peripheral equipment	Communications equipment	Semiconductors and related components	
1967	54.4	39.3	26.7	. . .	52.0	80.4	31.6	0.1	. . .	. . .	. . .	48.6
1968	57.3	42.1	29.0	. . .	55.7	82.7	33.3	0.1	. . .	. . .	. . .	51.3
1969	60.4	45.0	30.5	. . .	59.6	85.6	34.8	0.1	. . .	. . .	. . .	53.4
1970	63.3	47.6	32.8	. . .	62.7	89.7	33.3	0.1	. . .	. . .	. . .	50.9
1971	64.5	49.9	34.5	. . .	64.4	89.0	33.7	0.1	. . .	. . .	. . .	51.8
1972	67.4	52.6	36.4	57.1	68.4	90.4	37.3	0.1	0.0	3.3	0.1	57.0
1973	69.2	53.6	38.4	53.7	71.1	91.5	40.7	0.2	0.1	3.6	0.1	61.9
1974	69.5	55.0	38.4	62.4	70.1	91.9	40.5	0.2	0.1	3.9	0.1	61.2
1975	69.7	56.2	39.8	70.4	67.6	92.7	36.2	0.2	0.1	3.8	0.1	54.6
1976	72.0	59.1	41.9	79.3	71.3	92.7	39.4	0.3	0.1	4.0	0.1	59.1
1977	74.8	61.4	43.3	100.7	74.0	95.4	42.7	0.3	0.2	4.8	0.2	63.6
1978	76.1	62.6	44.6	103.9	73.4	97.7	45.4	0.4	0.3	5.3	0.2	67.1
1979	78.3	64.2	46.7	111.3	76.1	99.9	46.8	0.5	0.4	6.3	0.2	68.4
1980	78.6	61.8	45.9	133.2	74.6	102.0	45.3	0.7	0.6	7.6	0.3	65.2
1981	79.8	61.4	47.1	161.6	73.6	104.0	45.8	0.8	0.8	8.1	0.3	65.3
1982	76.9	61.8	47.7	141.2	67.7	101.0	43.2	0.9	1.0	8.6	0.3	60.9
1983	74.7	62.3	48.7	107.6	67.6	96.6	45.3	1.1	1.4	9.1	0.4	63.1
1984	79.0	64.2	51.3	117.9	71.8	102.7	49.8	1.5	2.0	9.7	0.5	68.6
1985	78.8	64.2	53.2	107.3	71.5	102.1	50.7	1.5	2.4	9.4	0.5	69.6
1986	76.1	65.5	54.7	56.3	68.9	97.9	51.8	1.6	2.5	8.9	0.6	71.2
1987	78.3	67.9	57.6	54.3	72.4	98.6	54.8	1.9	3.3	9.9	0.7	74.5
1988	81.4	71.4	59.5	65.2	75.8	101.4	57.8	2.3	4.0	11.9	0.8	77.8
1989	82.2	71.9	61.7	56.8	78.6	100.7	58.3	2.4	4.2	12.3	0.9	78.2
1990	83.6	71.4	63.5	60.1	79.2	103.4	58.7	2.7	4.5	14.6	1.0	78.2
1991	84.0	73.6	64.4	46.8	79.3	103.5	57.6	2.9	4.7	15.2	1.1	76.2
1992	82.9	72.6	64.0	32.7	80.8	100.9	59.7	3.5	5.9	17.4	1.3	78.2
1993	84.4	75.8	65.9	45.5	82.3	100.1	61.9	4.1	7.3	20.0	1.5	80.3
1994	86.1	76.7	68.5	54.0	83.6	101.8	65.5	5.3	9.1	24.0	2.0	83.8
1995	87.8	78.8	70.9	52.6	84.8	103.4	69.0	7.4	12.6	29.4	3.0	86.0
1996	90.0	82.3	73.2	56.4	86.3	104.8	72.3	10.6	17.9	36.9	4.6	87.3
1997	90.5	81.6	76.2	64.7	87.6	103.8	78.5	15.6	25.4	50.4	7.2	91.6
1998	90.7	81.7	77.5	60.5	88.7	103.4	83.8	21.8	34.9	59.8	10.8	94.9
1999	91.3	84.5	80.5	47.4	90.3	101.4	87.9	31.3	45.9	76.3	17.3	96.1
2000	93.6	86.3	83.7	67.2	92.4	102.7	91.6	43.8	53.5	102.9	26.6	96.8
2001	93.6	87.3	85.1	81.4	89.2	102.4	87.9	44.8	54.1	95.5	28.9	92.1
2002	94.0	91.1	86.9	58.7	91.2	100.7	88.0	44.5	53.3	71.4	33.5	92.3
2003	95.0	91.6	91.2	68.2	91.8	100.4	89.1	53.3	57.8	73.8	44.9	92.3
2004	95.7	92.9	94.1	74.5	94.0	99.3	91.6	60.6	58.4	81.9	54.0	94.2
2005	96.3	96.1	96.7	83.7	95.3	97.4	95.2	71.1	69.6	80.8	67.5	97.1
2006	97.4	95.8	97.3	96.6	95.2	98.9	97.6	84.9	86.5	98.0	78.7	98.5
2007	100.0	100.0	100.0	100.0	100.0	100.0	100.0	100.0	100.0	100.0	100.0	100.0
2008	100.7	99.7	100.2	104.4	98.2	101.7	95.2	115.6	118.9	96.0	123.6	94.1
2009	97.7	99.8	98.5	61.4	93.0	100.1	81.8	103.1	104.0	81.2	113.6	80.6
2010	101.6	102.0	99.9	82.3	98.9	103.6	87.0	128.2	84.9	81.5	173.4	84.9
2011	104.7	102.5	100.8	99.2	98.2	109.0	90.0	147.4	68.8	88.7	215.8	87.4
2012	107.2	99.9	100.7	103.9	98.6	114.9	93.7	153.1	65.5	91.2	227.6	91.0
2011												
January	103.4	104.7	100.7	90.1	99.4	105.4	89.0	145.5	74.7	85.3	211.1	86.4
February	101.7	102.5	99.4	90.8	96.9	104.0	89.0	145.3	73.1	86.4	210.8	86.4
March	103.8	102.3	101.9	91.7	98.0	107.5	89.5	143.9	71.9	86.5	208.5	87.0
April	103.5	101.6	100.0	94.9	98.1	107.3	89.0	143.8	71.1	86.1	208.9	86.4
May	103.9	103.1	101.3	97.0	98.1	107.0	89.3	145.1	70.5	86.2	211.9	86.7
June	104.6	102.5	101.0	98.0	98.9	108.5	89.3	146.5	69.8	87.4	214.3	86.7
July	104.9	103.1	101.1	100.5	100.2	108.2	89.9	146.9	69.0	89.1	214.5	87.3
August	106.2	104.1	102.2	103.3	99.5	110.4	90.1	149.5	67.6	90.7	219.5	87.4
September	105.7	103.6	102.7	104.8	97.5	109.9	90.4	148.9	65.7	91.3	218.9	87.8
October	106.0	101.2	101.2	106.7	96.9	112.2	91.0	148.6	64.7	91.5	218.7	88.4
November	106.8	101.5	99.6	106.5	97.8	113.7	91.0	151.2	63.8	91.7	224.3	88.3
December	105.9	99.1	99.0	106.9	97.0	113.4	92.1	153.3	63.5	92.2	228.4	89.3
2012												
January	105.5	96.8	98.3	107.2	95.8	114.2	93.1	152.9	64.0	92.9	227.0	90.4
February	105.8	97.9	99.8	106.7	98.2	113.0	93.6	152.6	64.3	93.1	225.9	90.9
March	105.1	95.9	98.1	107.1	98.7	112.9	93.1	152.6	65.0	92.7	226.0	90.4
April	106.0	97.3	100.4	106.2	99.3	113.3	93.8	153.6	65.8	91.7	228.2	91.1
May	108.2	102.4	102.6	106.1	103.1	113.8	93.4	153.7	66.1	90.6	228.8	90.7
June	107.5	100.9	101.5	106.5	100.0	114.3	93.7	154.5	65.8	89.9	231.1	90.9
July	108.5	102.0	102.2	105.3	100.4	115.7	93.9	153.1	65.4	89.6	228.6	91.2
August	107.4	101.0	101.6	103.6	97.8	114.9	93.3	149.1	65.3	89.7	220.4	90.7
September	107.5	100.8	100.7	102.0	97.5	115.7	93.4	150.7	65.6	90.2	223.2	90.8
October	108.7	103.0	102.2	99.9	98.6	116.6	92.9	155.1	66.1	90.3	231.9	90.1
November	109.2	103.5	102.4	98.8	99.0	117.2	94.4	155.2	66.5	92.2	230.9	91.7
December	106.8	97.7	99.2	97.3	94.6	117.4	95.3	154.2	66.2	91.8	229.2	92.5

. . . = Not available.

Table 2-2. Industrial Production Indexes by NAICS Industry Groups

(Seasonally adjusted, 2007 = 100.)

Year and month	Total industrial production	Manufacturing (SIC)	Manufacturing (NAICS) Total	Durable goods manufacturing Total	Wood products	Nonmetallic mineral products	Primary metals	Fabricated metal products	Machinery	Computer and electronic products	Electrical equipment, appliances, and components	Motor vehicles and parts	Aerospace and miscellaneous transport equipment
1967	35.0	31.7	...	...	...	...	...	...	...	...	...	...	...
1968	37.0	33.4	...	...	...	...	...	...	...	...	...	...	...
1969	38.7	34.9	...	...	...	...	...	...	...	...	...	...	...
1970	37.4	33.4	...	...	...	...	...	...	...	...	...	...	...
1971	37.9	33.9	...	...	...	...	...	...	...	...	...	...	...
1972	41.6	37.4	36.0	25.5	70.7	67.7	110.2	60.3	56.4	0.7	67.9	43.3	55.5
1973	45.0	40.8	39.3	28.6	68.4	72.6	128.2	66.6	65.2	0.9	76.4	49.5	63.3
1974	44.8	40.7	39.2	28.4	62.2	71.8	131.4	65.4	68.3	1.0	74.6	42.6	64.3
1975	40.9	36.4	35.0	24.7	57.7	64.3	101.9	56.5	59.5	0.9	59.9	37.1	61.1
1976	44.1	39.7	38.3	27.0	64.9	67.9	108.2	60.6	62.1	1.1	67.6	47.3	57.2
1977	47.4	43.1	41.6	29.7	70.0	72.3	109.3	65.7	67.8	1.3	74.5	53.8	57.6
1978	50.0	45.7	44.1	32.0	70.9	77.0	116.2	68.9	73.1	1.7	79.1	56.1	63.6
1979	51.5	47.1	45.5	33.6	68.6	76.9	118.9	72.0	77.1	2.0	82.3	51.4	74.0
1980	50.2	45.5	43.8	32.1	63.5	69.4	104.4	67.9	73.4	2.5	77.4	37.9	79.6
1981	50.9	46.0	44.2	32.5	62.1	66.4	104.5	67.4	72.7	2.9	76.4	36.9	75.8
1982	48.3	43.5	41.7	29.7	55.7	58.8	73.9	60.4	60.8	3.2	68.9	33.3	71.0
1983	49.6	45.6	43.7	31.2	64.6	63.3	75.7	60.8	54.9	3.7	71.2	42.5	67.8
1984	54.0	50.0	48.1	35.6	69.1	68.3	83.1	66.2	64.0	4.6	80.2	50.9	72.3
1985	54.7	50.8	48.9	36.4	70.0	69.6	76.7	67.2	64.2	4.9	78.9	52.9	77.3
1986	55.2	52.0	50.0	37.0	76.1	72.5	74.9	66.7	63.2	5.1	80.4	52.8	81.3
1987	58.1	54.9	52.8	39.2	82.9	76.5	80.7	68.0	64.5	5.8	81.5	54.7	84.3
1988	61.1	57.8	55.8	42.1	82.8	78.0	90.3	71.4	71.0	6.4	85.5	58.5	88.7
1989	61.6	58.3	56.3	42.6	81.6	77.4	88.2	70.9	73.7	6.6	84.2	57.9	94.0
1990	62.2	58.7	56.8	42.7	80.7	76.2	87.1	70.0	71.9	7.2	82.0	54.4	94.4
1991	61.3	57.6	55.7	41.4	75.5	70.2	81.8	66.8	67.5	7.5	77.8	52.0	91.1
1992	63.0	59.7	57.9	43.5	79.6	73.2	83.8	68.9	67.3	8.4	82.4	59.2	84.2
1993	65.1	61.8	60.0	45.9	80.5	74.8	87.9	71.5	72.3	9.3	87.6	65.4	78.5
1994	68.5	65.4	63.8	49.8	85.3	79.0	94.6	77.7	79.2	10.9	94.0	75.1	70.5
1995	71.8	68.8	67.3	54.0	87.3	81.3	95.6	82.5	84.8	14.0	96.2	77.3	67.0
1996	74.9	72.2	70.7	58.9	90.2	86.6	97.9	85.5	87.8	18.2	99.1	77.9	69.6
1997	80.4	78.2	76.7	65.9	92.9	89.4	102.0	89.4	92.6	24.4	102.8	84.0	77.7
1998	85.0	83.4	81.8	72.9	97.0	94.0	103.8	92.3	94.9	31.3	106.6	88.4	90.0
1999	88.7	87.6	86.0	79.0	100.6	94.9	103.7	92.9	93.0	41.0	108.4	98.1	86.6
2000	92.2	91.3	89.8	84.8	99.3	94.9	100.3	96.6	97.7	53.6	113.9	97.4	76.0
2001	89.1	87.5	86.3	80.9	93.1	91.4	91.3	89.6	86.4	54.4	102.5	88.8	80.8
2002	89.3	87.8	86.7	80.8	96.6	91.6	91.3	87.6	83.3	53.0	94.5	97.6	76.5
2003	90.3	88.9	88.0	82.9	96.6	92.4	89.8	86.6	82.8	60.3	92.1	101.1	73.1
2004	92.5	91.4	90.6	86.2	99.2	95.3	97.7	86.9	86.3	68.3	93.7	101.7	72.0
2005	95.5	95.0	94.4	91.2	105.9	99.4	95.2	90.9	91.6	76.9	95.3	102.3	80.2
2006	97.6	97.4	97.0	95.4	106.9	101.1	98.0	95.9	95.9	87.4	96.0	100.8	85.2
2007	100.0	100.0	100.0	100.0	100.0	100.0	100.0	100.0	100.0	100.0	100.0	100.0	100.0
2008	96.6	95.3	95.4	96.6	85.4	88.4	100.0	96.4	97.3	108.1	96.3	80.0	101.9
2009	85.7	82.4	82.4	78.6	65.3	66.6	74.0	74.2	75.7	97.0	75.6	58.6	92.8
2010	90.6	87.4	87.9	87.3	67.6	68.6	91.1	79.0	84.6	111.6	78.6	77.8	94.0
2011	93.6	90.3	91.1	93.2	68.4	70.2	97.4	85.3	95.6	122.5	83.4	84.8	94.3
2012	97.0	93.9	95.0	99.9	71.3	71.0	99.4	91.4	102.2	130.3	86.3	99.6	102.0
2011													
January	92.6	89.3	90.1	91.2	68.4	67.3	95.4	82.7	94.5	121.0	83.0	80.3	91.1
February	92.2	89.3	90.1	91.7	68.1	69.1	94.8	82.5	94.7	121.1	83.7	83.3	90.8
March	93.1	89.9	90.7	92.3	69.7	69.5	96.8	83.3	94.2	120.6	84.3	86.4	90.9
April	92.6	89.3	90.0	91.2	68.2	70.1	96.0	83.9	93.1	120.1	82.8	80.1	91.7
May	92.9	89.5	90.3	92.0	68.8	70.9	95.8	84.7	94.1	121.0	82.9	81.4	92.3
June	93.1	89.6	90.4	92.2	67.6	70.7	95.9	85.8	95.0	120.5	83.3	81.1	93.2
July	93.6	90.2	91.0	92.9	67.6	71.2	96.4	86.3	95.6	121.7	81.9	83.4	93.7
August	94.1	90.6	91.4	93.7	66.9	71.5	96.9	86.3	95.6	123.4	82.6	85.7	95.1
September	94.2	90.9	91.7	94.1	68.7	71.4	98.3	86.1	96.1	123.7	83.3	86.3	95.8
October	94.7	91.4	92.2	95.1	68.8	70.5	99.6	86.5	96.7	123.9	85.4	89.4	97.7
November	95.0	91.4	92.2	95.5	68.7	70.0	100.8	87.4	97.4	125.3	83.7	88.1	99.7
December	95.5	92.3	93.2	96.7	69.5	70.1	101.8	88.1	99.6	127.3	83.6	92.0	99.0
2012													
January	96.2	93.3	94.2	98.2	71.0	70.8	102.2	89.0	101.4	128.7	84.8	96.0	98.6
February	96.7	93.9	94.8	99.1	70.6	72.3	102.9	90.1	102.3	128.9	86.3	96.0	101.5
March	96.1	93.4	94.3	98.9	70.4	71.4	99.6	90.3	103.1	128.4	85.8	96.9	101.3
April	96.9	93.9	94.9	99.8	70.6	71.5	101.6	90.9	103.4	129.8	86.0	99.5	100.8
May	97.1	93.7	94.7	99.7	70.6	70.8	99.6	91.4	103.0	129.3	86.3	99.2	101.1
June	97.1	94.0	95.1	100.3	70.0	71.0	97.7	91.8	105.3	130.9	85.7	100.9	101.4
July	97.6	94.2	95.4	100.7	70.4	70.1	100.2	92.3	102.3	130.8	86.2	102.6	102.6
August	96.8	93.5	94.7	99.7	70.2	70.0	99.7	92.0	101.5	128.8	85.4	99.2	102.7
September	97.0	93.6	94.8	99.5	70.4	70.2	95.1	92.2	102.1	129.7	86.9	97.8	103.2
October	96.8	93.2	94.4	99.3	72.3	70.0	96.1	91.6	99.8	131.0	85.7	98.1	103.7
November	98.1	94.5	95.8	101.3	73.9	71.2	98.9	92.6	100.9	132.9	88.2	103.2	103.6
December	98.2	95.3	96.6	102.0	75.5	72.3	99.1	92.9	101.5	133.9	87.9	105.9	102.8

. . . = Not available.

Table 2-2. Industrial Production Indexes by NAICS Industry Groups—*Continued*

(Seasonally adjusted, 2007 = 100.)

Year and month	Manufacturing (NAICS)—*Continued*											Other manu-facturing (non-NAICS)
	Durable goods manufacturing—*Continued*		Nondurable goods manufacturing									
	Furniture and related products	Miscel-laneous manu-facturing	Total	Food, beverage, and tobacco products	Textile and product mills	Apparel and leather	Paper	Printing and support	Petroleum and coal products	Chemicals	Plastics and rubber products	
1967	. . .	. . .	. . .	. . .	. . .	. . .	. . .	. . .	. . .	. . .	. . .	. . .
1968	. . .	. . .	. . .	. . .	. . .	. . .	. . .	. . .	. . .	. . .	. . .	. . .
1969	. . .	. . .	. . .	. . .	. . .	. . .	. . .	. . .	. . .	. . .	. . .	. . .
1970	. . .	. . .	. . .	. . .	. . .	. . .	. . .	. . .	. . .	. . .	. . .	. . .
1971	. . .	. . .	. . .	. . .	. . .	. . .	. . .	. . .	. . .	. . .	. . .	. . .
1972	55.7	37.6	57.2	62.0	112.9	292.8	68.1	49.4	65.5	41.1	34.7	75.3
1973	58.4	38.8	59.9	62.8	111.9	297.7	73.7	52.0	64.4	45.0	39.2	77.7
1974	53.8	37.9	60.1	63.6	103.0	280.0	76.9	50.4	69.5	46.8	37.8	78.2
1975	46.0	35.4	55.7	62.5	99.6	272.7	66.5	47.1	68.5	41.1	31.9	74.4
1976	51.2	38.5	60.8	66.8	110.8	286.9	73.4	50.5	75.9	46.0	35.2	76.7
1977	58.6	41.9	64.9	68.3	120.9	300.8	76.6	54.7	81.2	50.1	41.6	84.1
1978	63.1	42.8	67.3	70.7	120.6	307.5	80.1	57.9	82.1	52.6	43.5	87.0
1979	62.7	43.1	67.7	70.4	120.2	288.8	81.3	59.6	87.7	53.8	42.9	88.8
1980	60.5	40.8	65.7	71.5	115.4	294.5	81.1	60.1	77.7	50.9	38.4	91.9
1981	60.0	42.3	66.3	72.3	113.0	294.2	82.2	61.6	74.1	51.7	40.6	94.2
1982	56.6	42.8	65.3	74.4	105.0	292.5	80.8	66.2	70.8	48.4	40.0	95.2
1983	62.0	42.8	68.4	74.5	118.0	300.7	86.0	71.2	72.0	51.7	43.5	97.8
1984	69.5	46.3	71.5	75.5	120.9	300.7	90.4	77.5	73.5	54.8	50.2	102.3
1985	70.1	46.9	71.9	78.0	116.5	287.7	88.6	80.6	72.5	54.4	52.2	106.3
1986	73.3	48.0	74.0	79.0	121.1	286.6	92.3	84.7	72.1	56.8	54.4	108.5
1987	78.4	51.7	78.0	80.6	133.2	289.8	95.3	91.0	75.5	61.2	60.2	114.7
1988	77.6	56.5	80.6	82.8	131.9	284.9	99.1	93.9	77.8	64.8	62.9	114.2
1989	77.2	57.3	81.1	82.4	134.0	272.5	100.2	94.2	77.0	66.0	65.0	112.6
1990	75.6	60.1	82.4	84.7	128.5	266.5	100.1	97.8	77.1	67.5	66.8	111.2
1991	69.9	61.3	82.1	85.3	126.6	265.0	100.3	94.7	76.0	67.3	66.1	106.7
1992	75.5	63.9	84.2	86.4	133.4	272.4	102.8	99.9	75.7	68.3	71.1	104.5
1993	78.6	67.5	85.4	86.2	138.5	278.1	104.0	100.2	76.2	69.1	76.2	105.3
1994	81.3	68.0	88.4	89.1	145.9	281.5	108.5	101.3	78.3	70.9	82.5	104.4
1995	82.7	70.6	89.9	91.6	144.4	279.7	110.1	102.8	79.7	72.1	84.6	104.4
1996	83.4	74.1	90.2	90.9	141.0	273.3	106.6	103.5	81.6	73.6	87.4	103.4
1997	92.1	76.1	93.5	92.8	148.5	272.9	108.9	105.6	84.3	78.0	92.8	112.1
1998	98.6	80.5	94.9	95.6	147.3	257.1	109.8	106.8	82.7	79.2	96.1	118.8
1999	101.9	82.2	95.5	93.9	147.3	245.8	110.6	106.8	86.0	80.8	101.2	122.2
2000	103.6	86.8	95.9	95.3	144.2	235.2	107.7	107.8	85.2	81.9	102.3	121.9
2001	97.1	85.8	93.1	95.0	129.0	201.0	101.6	104.2	84.7	80.5	96.4	114.0
2002	100.8	90.6	94.2	94.1	129.3	158.8	102.9	102.1	89.3	85.1	99.8	110.1
2003	99.1	93.4	94.4	95.9	124.2	147.5	100.4	98.1	87.9	86.5	99.9	106.9
2004	101.8	93.4	95.9	96.3	122.7	129.3	101.2	98.5	93.1	90.0	101.1	107.7
2005	105.5	99.5	98.3	99.8	124.5	126.1	100.7	98.6	95.6	92.9	102.2	107.3
2006	103.9	102.6	98.8	99.9	113.0	123.1	99.6	97.8	97.3	95.2	102.8	106.1
2007	100.0	100.0	100.0	100.0	100.0	100.0	100.0	100.0	100.0	100.0	100.0	100.0
2008	90.3	101.6	94.1	97.2	87.9	80.6	95.8	93.8	95.6	92.5	90.6	93.5
2009	65.5	94.2	86.9	96.5	69.7	59.4	85.4	78.8	94.3	83.5	75.8	80.7
2010	64.7	97.5	88.7	96.7	74.4	60.0	87.2	78.8	93.5	86.3	82.6	76.4
2011	66.5	98.4	88.9	96.8	74.0	58.9	87.3	78.0	94.7	86.3	84.0	74.8
2012	69.6	103.8	90.0	99.6	75.3	57.4	85.2	76.9	95.6	86.4	86.7	72.1
2011												
January	65.3	99.0	88.9	96.6	73.2	61.0	88.8	77.8	92.6	86.5	84.2	74.9
February	65.2	99.1	88.4	96.1	74.3	60.7	87.5	78.9	91.4	86.1	83.9	74.7
March	66.9	98.3	89.1	96.5	73.2	59.0	88.0	78.9	93.7	87.0	83.9	74.5
April	66.1	97.7	88.8	97.0	74.2	59.5	87.5	79.0	92.0	86.2	84.1	74.5
May	67.6	97.9	88.5	96.4	74.2	59.7	87.0	78.8	93.5	85.7	84.1	74.3
June	65.4	98.0	88.5	96.3	74.1	59.2	87.4	78.0	94.0	85.8	83.6	73.8
July	66.0	98.0	89.1	96.9	74.0	59.3	87.3	78.5	95.9	86.3	84.1	74.4
August	67.4	98.0	89.0	96.6	72.8	57.9	86.5	78.1	96.5	86.3	83.8	75.2
September	67.0	98.9	89.2	96.6	73.5	57.3	87.1	77.9	97.0	86.6	83.9	75.5
October	66.7	98.7	89.3	97.5	73.8	58.2	86.5	77.0	96.5	86.6	84.3	75.3
November	66.8	98.4	88.9	97.1	74.6	57.9	86.8	76.1	96.7	85.7	83.7	74.9
December	67.5	98.2	89.6	97.5	75.7	57.3	87.2	77.1	97.0	86.8	84.4	75.5
2012												
January	69.1	100.5	90.1	98.4	76.6	59.6	87.0	78.0	96.4	87.4	84.9	75.2
February	70.2	100.4	90.4	99.1	76.7	59.0	87.1	78.2	98.3	86.7	85.9	75.7
March	69.5	100.8	89.6	98.1	75.8	58.3	85.6	77.2	97.0	86.4	85.6	74.9
April	70.1	102.4	89.9	99.1	76.0	58.3	86.0	77.5	95.4	86.6	86.2	74.1
May	69.8	103.3	89.7	99.3	74.4	58.1	85.7	77.6	96.0	85.9	85.6	73.3
June	69.3	103.8	89.8	99.5	76.4	57.5	84.3	77.9	95.7	86.0	86.4	72.1
July	70.5	105.3	89.9	100.6	75.2	56.9	84.0	77.5	94.3	85.8	88.0	70.7
August	69.9	104.7	89.6	100.2	74.9	55.6	84.3	77.1	94.4	85.5	86.9	70.5
September	69.4	104.1	90.0	101.4	75.1	56.5	84.0	75.8	93.9	86.0	86.9	69.8
October	68.9	103.5	89.3	98.7	75.3	55.0	84.5	74.9	96.0	85.8	86.7	69.3
November	69.3	107.4	90.1	100.1	74.2	56.7	84.7	74.8	94.8	86.7	88.1	69.7
December	69.4	109.2	91.1	100.7	73.5	57.1	85.4	76.4	95.8	88.3	89.3	69.4

. . . = Not available.

Table 2-2. Industrial Production Indexes by NAICS Industry Groups—*Continued*

(Seasonally adjusted, 2007 = 100.)

Year and month	Mining	Utilities			Selected high-tech industries	Excluding selected high-tech industries	Stage-of-process groups		
		Total	Electric	Natural gas			Crude	Primary and semi-finished	Finished
1967	. . .	. . .	. . .	. . .	0.1	50.0	. . .	. . .	. . .
1968	. . .	. . .	. . .	. . .	0.1	52.7	. . .	. . .	. . .
1969	. . .	. . .	. . .	. . .	0.1	55.0	. . .	. . .	. . .
1970	. . .	. . .	. . .	. . .	0.1	53.1	. . .	. . .	. . .
1971	. . .	. . .	. . .	. . .	0.1	54.1	. . .	. . .	. . .
1972	106.2	46.4	37.0	112.2	0.1	59.1	82.5	. . .	34.7
1973	106.8	49.1	40.3	107.7	0.2	63.6	86.9	. . .	37.2
1974	105.3	48.9	40.5	104.1	0.2	63.0	88.0	. . .	36.7
1975	102.7	49.8	42.3	97.4	0.2	57.4	79.9	. . .	34.7
1976	103.5	52.1	45.0	96.3	0.3	61.6	84.5	. . .	38.1
1977	105.9	54.2	47.9	93.0	0.3	65.9	89.0	. . .	41.3
1978	109.2	55.6	49.4	93.8	0.4	69.0	90.7	. . .	43.9
1979	112.5	56.8	50.5	96.3	0.5	70.5	93.1	. . .	44.7
1980	114.5	57.3	51.3	94.2	0.7	67.9	92.5	. . .	43.8
1981	117.5	58.1	52.7	92.1	0.8	68.3	93.6	. . .	44.8
1982	111.7	56.2	51.4	86.5	0.9	64.3	87.3	. . .	44.0
1983	105.8	56.7	52.9	81.0	1.1	65.5	87.5	. . .	46.0
1984	112.6	60.0	55.9	86.0	1.5	70.6	93.3	. . .	50.2
1985	110.4	61.3	58.0	82.5	1.5	71.3	90.8	. . .	51.5
1986	102.4	61.8	59.2	78.4	1.6	72.0	88.3	50.5	53.5
1987	103.4	64.7	62.0	82.0	1.9	75.1	92.3	53.4	56.1
1988	106.0	68.4	65.5	87.0	2.3	78.4	95.9	56.2	59.3
1989	104.8	70.6	67.5	90.2	2.4	78.9	96.4	56.6	60.1
1990	106.3	71.9	69.4	87.1	2.7	79.1	98.3	56.7	61.2
1991	104.0	73.7	71.1	89.5	2.9	77.5	96.6	55.7	60.6
1992	101.7	73.6	70.7	92.0	3.5	79.0	97.5	58.0	62.1
1993	101.7	76.2	73.2	95.5	4.1	81.0	96.0	60.7	63.8
1994	104.0	77.7	74.8	96.1	5.3	84.2	97.9	64.9	66.4
1995	103.9	80.5	77.5	98.6	7.4	86.3	98.8	68.5	69.6
1996	105.6	82.8	79.5	103.3	10.6	87.7	98.0	72.4	72.4
1997	107.6	82.8	79.8	101.3	15.6	91.4	100.8	78.0	78.1
1998	105.6	84.9	83.1	94.7	21.8	94.2	99.3	83.0	83.5
1999	100.1	87.4	85.5	97.4	31.3	95.3	99.1	88.5	85.9
2000	102.8	89.9	87.9	100.3	43.8	96.3	97.8	92.9	88.9
2001	103.2	89.5	87.7	98.9	44.8	92.5	92.6	88.8	86.9
2002	98.4	92.3	90.5	101.8	44.5	92.7	93.2	90.2	86.0
2003	98.5	94.1	92.4	102.7	53.3	92.9	92.7	91.2	87.5
2004	98.2	95.3	94.2	100.5	60.6	94.5	95.8	93.5	89.6
2005	97.0	97.3	97.0	98.9	71.1	96.9	94.5	96.6	94.0
2006	99.3	96.7	97.5	93.0	84.9	98.2	96.4	97.8	97.2
2007	100.0	100.0	100.0	100.0	100.0	100.0	100.0	100.0	100.0
2008	101.2	99.9	99.4	102.3	115.6	95.8	96.1	96.0	96.3
2009	95.7	97.5	96.9	100.4	103.1	85.0	89.1	82.3	86.6
2010	100.7	101.0	100.7	102.2	128.2	89.2	96.6	88.8	88.9
2011	106.8	100.8	100.4	102.3	147.4	91.8	98.7	92.0	91.2
2012	113.6	98.7	98.7	97.4	153.1	95.1	100.8	94.2	95.7
2011									
January	103.2	102.9	102.2	106.7	145.5	90.8	98.3	91.5	89.6
February	101.0	101.4	101.1	102.4	145.3	90.4	96.7	91.1	90.0
March	104.3	101.8	101.2	104.9	143.9	91.4	98.8	91.9	90.6
April	105.1	100.5	100.3	101.5	143.8	90.8	97.7	91.1	89.6
May	106.3	100.4	99.5	105.4	145.1	91.1	97.8	91.3	90.2
June	106.8	100.9	100.6	101.7	146.5	91.3	98.0	91.6	90.2
July	106.2	102.1	102.1	101.8	146.9	91.8	98.1	92.3	90.9
August	108.2	101.9	101.6	102.7	149.5	92.3	98.6	92.5	91.8
September	107.7	101.0	100.6	103.3	148.9	92.4	99.0	92.6	92.0
October	109.9	99.4	98.9	102.2	148.6	92.9	100.0	92.4	93.2
November	111.3	99.9	99.9	99.1	151.2	93.1	100.3	92.8	92.7
December	112.2	97.1	97.2	95.4	153.3	93.6	101.2	93.1	93.9
2012									
January	113.0	95.5	95.9	91.6	152.9	94.3	101.8	93.3	95.2
February	112.4	96.3	96.5	93.5	152.6	94.8	100.7	94.2	95.6
March	111.6	95.8	97.6	81.1	152.6	94.2	99.6	93.6	95.5
April	112.2	98.0	98.7	91.9	153.6	95.0	100.0	94.4	96.4
May	112.2	102.4	103.2	95.3	153.7	95.2	99.6	95.0	96.5
June	112.8	99.5	99.3	99.7	154.5	95.2	99.9	94.4	96.9
July	113.8	101.2	101.0	101.6	153.1	95.7	100.3	94.7	97.3
August	113.0	99.5	99.1	101.8	149.1	95.0	100.1	93.8	96.6
September	114.3	99.0	98.3	103.3	150.7	95.1	101.0	93.5	96.7
October	115.1	100.2	99.2	106.7	155.1	94.9	101.3	94.1	95.6
November	116.5	101.0	100.0	107.7	155.2	96.2	102.6	95.0	97.7
December	116.0	95.6	95.7	93.3	154.2	96.3	103.0	94.3	98.8

. . . = Not available.

Table 2-3. Capacity Utilization by NAICS Industry Groups

(Output as a percentage of capacity, seasonally adjusted.)

Year and month	Total industry	Total manufac-turing (SIC)	Manufacturing (NAICS) Total	Durable goods manufacturing Total	Wood products	Nonmetallic mineral products	Primary metals	Fabricated metal products	Machinery	Computer and electronic products	Electrical equipment, appliances, and components	Motor vehicles and parts	Aerospace and miscellaneous transportation equipment
1967	87.0	87.2	...	87.5	...	75.7	85.0	86.4	90.4	...	...	78.9	94.1
1968	87.3	87.1	...	87.4	...	78.4	84.8	87.2	85.1	...	...	90.1	90.2
1969	87.4	86.6	...	87.1	...	79.7	88.4	86.1	86.7	...	...	86.7	86.2
1970	81.3	79.4	...	77.8	...	73.9	79.5	78.4	79.7	...	...	66.4	75.2
1971	79.6	77.9	...	75.5	...	75.5	73.1	78.3	73.8	...	...	79.1	66.8
1972	84.7	83.4	83.3	82.1	92.2	79.5	82.9	85.0	83.1	80.7	89.8	84.3	65.6
1973	88.3	87.7	87.8	88.6	87.8	84.1	94.6	90.9	92.4	85.2	97.7	91.8	73.5
1974	85.1	84.4	84.5	84.7	77.9	81.7	96.5	86.1	91.9	83.1	91.6	76.7	74.4
1975	75.8	73.7	73.5	71.8	70.2	73.0	75.2	72.3	77.7	68.7	70.7	66.0	70.8
1976	79.8	78.3	78.4	76.4	79.5	77.6	78.6	75.9	79.9	72.1	78.7	81.8	66.2
1977	83.4	82.5	82.4	81.2	86.2	82.6	79.2	80.1	85.5	77.9	85.5	90.0	66.2
1978	85.1	84.4	84.3	83.8	84.8	86.5	84.2	80.8	88.6	80.4	87.8	90.7	72.4
1979	85.0	84.0	84.0	84.1	80.0	84.4	86.1	81.6	90.1	83.6	88.9	80.9	81.9
1980	80.7	78.6	78.4	77.5	72.4	75.0	75.9	75.0	83.5	86.8	81.8	59.8	84.5
1981	79.6	76.9	76.5	75.1	70.7	72.4	77.8	72.5	80.5	84.5	79.0	57.2	76.8
1982	73.6	70.9	70.3	66.4	63.7	65.0	56.9	64.5	66.6	81.0	69.8	50.7	69.7
1983	74.9	73.4	72.9	68.7	75.2	70.6	59.5	66.5	60.5	81.9	73.0	67.2	66.3
1984	80.4	79.3	78.9	76.9	81.0	75.8	69.0	73.5	70.9	87.5	82.5	81.6	69.7
1985	79.2	78.1	77.6	75.7	79.6	76.0	67.3	73.9	70.6	80.3	79.1	83.4	72.2
1986	78.7	78.4	78.0	75.4	83.6	78.5	69.5	73.7	70.2	77.5	80.2	79.3	73.8
1987	81.2	81.0	80.5	77.6	85.6	80.7	78.3	75.4	72.0	79.8	82.4	78.2	75.3
1988	84.3	84.0	83.8	82.1	84.1	81.8	88.9	80.3	80.4	81.4	87.2	82.9	79.8
1989	83.8	83.3	83.2	81.9	82.2	80.9	86.5	80.0	84.1	78.7	86.2	81.3	85.4
1990	82.5	81.7	81.6	79.5	80.4	79.2	85.3	78.0	81.7	78.7	83.9	72.3	85.0
1991	79.8	78.5	78.4	75.3	76.3	73.2	79.7	74.4	76.6	77.6	79.0	64.3	82.9
1992	80.6	79.6	79.6	77.2	78.8	77.0	81.2	76.6	75.4	79.4	82.1	72.6	77.5
1993	81.4	80.4	80.3	78.5	79.0	78.8	85.3	77.5	78.9	77.5	86.5	79.0	72.7
1994	83.6	82.8	82.9	81.6	82.9	81.6	90.8	81.9	83.5	80.1	91.7	86.4	66.7
1995	84.0	83.2	83.2	82.2	80.8	81.8	88.9	83.7	85.6	83.1	91.2	83.5	64.7
1996	83.4	82.2	82.3	81.5	81.1	85.2	88.7	83.1	84.7	81.3	90.0	80.5	67.2
1997	84.1	83.1	82.9	82.2	81.1	84.3	89.8	81.9	84.9	81.6	88.5	81.6	73.3
1998	82.8	81.5	81.3	80.5	81.1	84.4	86.3	79.8	81.7	77.8	86.2	78.7	81.4
1999	81.6	80.4	80.0	79.8	81.5	81.9	84.2	77.5	76.2	80.7	83.9	83.2	75.5
2000	81.4	79.7	79.3	79.4	78.4	78.6	82.0	78.4	77.4	84.4	86.6	81.5	65.3
2001	76.0	73.6	73.2	71.2	72.7	73.7	73.7	72.3	68.2	69.7	77.4	72.6	69.5
2002	74.8	72.9	72.5	69.9	75.1	73.7	75.5	71.3	67.2	60.7	73.7	78.6	66.1
2003	76.0	73.9	73.5	71.1	76.2	73.7	73.8	72.7	68.8	65.0	74.8	78.3	63.3
2004	77.9	76.2	75.9	73.8	79.2	74.1	81.5	74.9	72.6	71.2	77.4	77.0	62.8
2005	79.8	78.1	77.9	76.0	81.0	74.9	79.2	78.5	76.2	72.5	81.0	77.4	69.3
2006	80.2	78.4	78.3	77.3	77.9	73.4	78.9	83.3	79.3	77.3	83.0	72.3	72.5
2007	80.5	78.6	78.7	78.2	72.3	68.5	80.4	85.7	82.2	76.3	87.7	72.0	84.1
2008	77.5	74.5	74.3	74.4	64.4	59.2	77.3	80.8	79.7	77.3	85.3	58.6	83.1
2009	68.7	65.7	65.4	61.2	51.8	45.8	55.1	64.0	62.7	70.6	68.1	44.0	72.8
2010	74.0	71.3	71.4	68.6	57.0	49.8	69.3	71.2	70.6	77.5	73.3	59.3	72.0
2011	76.5	74.0	74.4	72.3	60.3	53.1	73.8	77.6	79.2	76.2	79.2	64.4	69.6
2012	77.6	75.8	76.3	75.4	64.3	55.6	74.8	82.4	82.4	74.1	81.6	73.3	73.1
2011													
January	76.1	73.4	73.8	71.6	59.3	50.0	72.8	75.3	78.8	80.8	78.3	61.0	68.5
February	75.7	73.4	73.8	71.9	59.3	51.5	72.3	75.3	79.0	79.9	79.1	63.3	68.1
March	76.5	73.9	74.3	72.2	60.9	52.0	73.7	75.9	78.5	78.6	79.8	65.7	67.9
April	76.0	73.4	73.7	71.2	59.7	52.6	73.0	76.5	77.4	77.2	78.5	60.9	68.3
May	76.1	73.5	73.9	71.7	60.5	53.4	72.7	77.2	78.2	76.7	78.7	61.9	68.4
June	76.2	73.5	73.9	71.6	59.6	53.4	72.7	78.2	78.8	75.3	79.2	61.7	68.9
July	76.5	74.0	74.4	72.0	59.7	54.0	73.0	78.6	79.3	75.0	77.9	63.5	69.0
August	76.8	74.2	74.5	72.4	59.2	54.4	73.2	78.6	79.1	75.1	78.6	65.2	69.8
September	76.7	74.3	74.7	72.6	60.9	54.5	74.1	78.3	79.4	74.3	79.4	65.5	70.1
October	77.0	74.7	75.1	73.1	61.1	54.0	75.1	78.6	79.7	73.6	81.4	67.7	71.3
November	77.0	74.5	74.9	73.2	61.2	53.7	75.9	79.3	80.1	73.7	79.7	66.6	72.6
December	77.3	75.2	75.6	74.0	62.0	54.0	76.6	79.9	81.7	74.2	79.7	69.4	71.9
2012													
January	77.7	75.8	76.3	74.9	63.5	54.7	76.8	80.7	83.0	74.5	80.8	72.2	71.5
February	77.9	76.2	76.7	75.4	63.3	56.0	77.4	81.6	83.6	74.2	82.1	71.9	73.4
March	77.3	75.7	76.2	75.2	63.2	55.5	74.8	81.6	84.0	73.6	81.6	72.4	73.1
April	77.7	76.1	76.6	75.7	63.4	55.7	76.3	82.1	83.9	74.1	81.7	74.0	72.6
May	77.8	75.8	76.3	75.4	63.6	55.2	74.9	82.5	83.3	73.7	81.8	73.4	72.7
June	77.7	75.9	76.5	75.8	63.1	55.6	73.5	82.8	85.0	74.4	81.2	74.4	72.7
July	77.9	76.0	76.6	75.9	63.6	55.0	75.4	83.1	82.3	74.3	81.6	75.3	73.5
August	77.2	75.4	76.0	75.0	63.4	55.0	75.1	82.8	81.4	73.0	80.7	72.5	73.4
September	77.2	75.3	75.9	74.7	63.7	55.3	71.7	82.9	81.6	73.4	81.9	71.2	73.6
October	77.0	74.9	75.5	74.5	65.5	55.3	72.5	82.3	79.6	74.0	80.7	71.1	73.8
November	77.9	75.8	76.5	75.8	67.0	56.4	74.7	83.2	80.2	74.9	82.9	74.5	73.6
December	77.8	76.4	77.1	76.2	68.5	57.3	74.9	83.4	80.5	75.2	82.4	76.3	72.8

. . . = Not available.

Table 2-3. Capacity Utilization by NAICS Industry Groups—*Continued*

(Output as a percentage of capacity, seasonally adjusted.)

Year and month	Durable goods manufacturing—Continued		Manufacturing (NAICS)—Continued — Nondurable goods manufacturing									Other manufacturing (non-NAICS)
	Furniture and related products	Miscellaneous manufacturing	Total	Food, beverage, and tobacco products	Textile and product mills	Apparel and leather	Paper	Printing and support	Petroleum and coal products	Chemicals	Plastics and rubber products	
1967	91.9	. . .	86.3	85.0	. . .	. . .	89.7	. . .	94.9	78.9	88.3	. . .
1968	91.4	. . .	86.5	84.8	. . .	. . .	89.3	. . .	95.7	80.1	91.1	. . .
1969	92.8	. . .	86.1	85.1	. . .	. . .	91.1	. . .	96.0	79.1	90.3	. . .
1970	84.1	. . .	82.1	84.0	. . .	. . .	86.2	. . .	96.0	76.1	79.2	. . .
1971	85.0	. . .	81.7	84.0	. . .	. . .	86.9	. . .	94.7	75.4	79.8	. . .
1972	94.0	80.4	85.2	85.1	88.9	81.6	91.4	92.3	93.1	80.1	88.5	85.7
1973	95.4	79.5	86.6	84.8	86.3	82.2	94.9	94.0	90.4	83.7	92.5	84.7
1974	82.3	74.6	84.2	83.8	76.3	76.3	94.9	88.0	92.6	84.1	84.2	82.7
1975	68.2	67.7	76.1	80.1	72.5	74.5	80.5	79.6	83.7	71.8	70.1	77.3
1976	75.7	72.3	81.1	83.2	81.4	78.2	87.6	82.3	86.0	77.8	77.3	77.6
1977	83.8	77.6	84.3	82.8	88.5	81.6	90.1	86.0	87.7	81.4	88.4	83.2
1978	85.5	78.7	85.1	83.4	87.7	83.9	92.1	87.4	86.4	82.5	88.7	85.1
1979	80.2	78.4	83.8	81.0	87.2	78.9	90.7	86.0	88.6	82.9	83.8	85.6
1980	74.6	73.2	79.6	80.8	83.3	79.8	88.2	83.7	76.2	76.6	74.2	86.8
1981	71.6	75.7	78.8	80.4	80.6	78.7	86.8	81.2	72.8	76.0	77.6	87.5
1982	66.4	73.7	76.4	81.4	74.4	77.8	83.8	82.4	71.2	69.2	74.5	87.3
1983	72.2	70.8	79.4	80.9	84.1	81.1	88.8	84.4	74.4	72.9	81.5	87.9
1984	79.2	76.0	82.1	81.4	85.8	81.3	91.2	87.2	78.5	76.0	91.1	89.5
1985	77.3	74.1	80.5	82.6	81.6	77.9	87.9	84.9	80.1	73.4	86.9	90.4
1986	79.2	74.0	81.8	82.8	84.3	79.8	90.2	85.6	81.9	75.9	85.2	88.8
1987	82.9	77.2	84.7	83.8	91.5	82.1	90.2	89.2	82.4	80.9	89.4	90.6
1988	80.5	81.8	86.1	85.3	88.9	82.2	91.3	90.3	83.2	84.3	88.9	88.6
1989	79.0	79.8	85.0	83.7	88.6	80.4	90.4	88.9	84.2	83.3	86.9	85.4
1990	76.1	79.7	84.2	84.0	83.6	79.1	89.3	88.9	84.7	82.9	83.7	83.7
1991	70.7	78.3	82.3	82.8	81.7	80.5	87.7	84.1	82.7	81.1	78.6	80.8
1992	76.8	77.0	82.7	82.4	85.5	82.9	88.4	86.1	85.3	79.9	81.9	80.0
1993	79.4	77.1	82.7	81.0	87.9	84.0	89.0	84.5	89.1	79.2	86.6	81.3
1994	80.9	76.9	84.6	83.4	90.1	85.3	90.7	83.7	89.0	80.5	91.4	81.4
1995	80.3	79.2	84.5	84.5	86.2	85.1	89.4	83.0	89.5	80.7	89.7	82.2
1996	79.0	80.5	83.3	82.6	82.3	83.8	85.4	82.8	91.7	80.6	88.6	80.6
1997	83.3	78.6	83.9	82.5	84.5	83.7	87.3	81.2	95.2	81.6	89.3	85.5
1998	82.8	78.8	82.4	83.0	82.3	77.5	87.2	79.7	92.7	78.9	88.0	86.7
1999	80.5	76.2	80.3	78.7	81.8	76.7	86.6	78.0	90.4	77.4	86.7	87.1
2000	77.3	75.7	79.1	77.7	79.7	79.6	84.4	77.3	89.0	76.4	82.7	87.4
2001	70.5	71.9	75.7	76.5	71.9	74.4	80.0	74.9	88.1	72.1	76.8	82.8
2002	72.4	73.2	76.0	75.7	73.7	67.0	82.1	75.3	88.6	73.6	78.8	81.5
2003	71.2	74.4	76.7	77.6	72.8	69.9	81.8	74.3	89.7	73.5	79.1	81.4
2004	76.6	74.6	78.5	77.7	74.8	70.6	83.2	75.4	92.8	76.0	83.0	82.6
2005	80.0	77.3	80.0	79.5	78.0	75.8	83.6	76.1	92.1	76.4	83.8	82.0
2006	79.2	76.7	79.6	79.0	74.8	75.4	83.5	75.1	89.6	77.0	82.0	79.9
2007	75.8	73.1	79.3	78.5	71.6	76.4	83.6	76.6	87.8	77.8	79.1	76.5
2008	71.8	74.0	74.2	76.3	67.3	75.7	81.8	71.2	82.0	71.1	71.1	77.3
2009	58.6	69.9	70.5	75.8	56.7	60.6	76.7	62.0	78.6	67.7	61.8	70.7
2010	61.7	74.2	74.9	76.4	63.9	66.1	81.6	65.7	80.8	74.1	71.2	67.3
2011	65.5	75.6	76.8	78.0	65.8	67.8	82.1	66.6	84.0	76.1	72.8	65.6
2012	70.5	77.3	77.4	80.5	69.8	67.8	81.0	66.8	83.6	75.3	73.6	63.5
2011												
January	63.3	76.1	76.4	77.2	64.2	69.2	83.7	66.0	82.3	75.9	73.3	65.8
February	63.4	76.3	76.1	76.9	65.3	69.0	82.5	67.0	81.4	75.6	73.0	65.6
March	65.2	75.7	76.8	77.3	64.5	67.3	82.9	67.1	83.5	76.6	73.0	65.4
April	64.6	75.3	76.6	77.9	65.5	68.1	82.4	67.2	82.0	76.0	73.2	65.4
May	66.3	75.4	76.5	77.6	65.7	68.4	81.8	67.1	83.3	75.6	73.1	65.2
June	64.3	75.5	76.5	77.6	65.7	68.1	82.1	66.5	83.6	75.8	72.6	64.7
July	65.0	75.5	77.1	78.2	65.8	68.4	82.1	67.0	85.2	76.2	73.0	65.2
August	66.6	75.5	77.0	78.1	65.0	66.9	81.3	66.8	85.5	76.3	72.6	66.0
September	66.4	76.1	77.2	78.1	65.7	66.4	81.8	66.6	85.8	76.5	72.6	66.2
October	66.3	75.8	77.3	79.0	66.2	67.5	81.3	66.0	85.2	76.4	72.8	66.0
November	66.5	75.4	76.9	78.7	67.1	67.3	81.6	65.3	85.2	75.6	72.2	65.7
December	67.4	75.1	77.5	79.1	68.4	66.7	82.0	66.2	85.2	76.5	72.6	66.2
2012												
January	69.2	76.6	77.9	79.8	69.4	69.6	81.9	67.1	84.6	77.0	72.9	66.0
February	70.5	76.3	78.1	80.4	69.7	69.1	82.1	67.4	86.1	76.2	73.7	66.5
March	70.0	76.3	77.4	79.6	69.2	68.3	80.8	66.7	84.8	75.8	73.3	65.9
April	70.7	77.2	77.6	80.3	69.7	68.5	81.4	67.1	83.4	75.9	73.6	65.2
May	70.6	77.6	77.3	80.4	68.5	68.4	81.2	67.3	83.8	75.1	73.0	64.5
June	70.1	77.6	77.3	80.5	70.6	67.9	80.0	67.6	83.5	75.0	73.5	63.5
July	71.5	78.3	77.4	81.3	69.8	67.4	79.9	67.4	82.3	74.7	74.6	62.3
August	71.0	77.5	77.0	80.9	69.9	65.9	80.4	67.2	82.3	74.3	73.5	62.2
September	70.6	76.7	77.3	81.8	70.4	67.2	80.2	66.2	81.9	74.6	73.3	61.7
October	70.2	75.9	76.7	79.6	70.9	65.5	80.8	65.5	83.7	74.2	72.9	61.3
November	70.8	78.4	77.2	80.6	70.1	67.7	81.1	65.5	82.7	74.9	73.9	61.7
December	70.9	79.2	78.0	81.0	69.6	68.4	82.0	67.0	83.6	76.0	74.7	61.5

. . . = Not available.

Table 2-3. Capacity Utilization by NAICS Industry Groups—*Continued*

(Output as a percentage of capacity, seasonally adjusted.)

Year and month	Mining	Utilities	Selected high-tech industries				Measures excluding selected high-tech industries		Stage-of-process groups		
			Total	Computers and peripheral equipment	Communications equipment	Semiconductors and related electronic components	Total industry	Manufacturing	Crude	Primary and semi-finished	Finished
1967	81.2	94.5	89.4	. . .	. . .	. . .	86.9	86.8	81.1	85.0	88.2
1968	83.6	95.1	87.6	. . .	. . .	. . .	87.2	87.0	83.4	86.8	87.1
1969	86.7	96.8	89.8	. . .	. . .	. . .	87.1	86.4	85.6	88.1	85.6
1970	89.2	96.3	83.5	. . .	. . .	. . .	81.0	79.2	85.1	81.5	78.2
1971	87.8	94.7	74.4	. . .	. . .	. . .	80.0	78.3	84.3	81.6	75.7
1972	90.7	95.3	78.6	81.5	73.2	84.6	84.9	83.6	88.4	88.2	79.6
1973	91.5	93.3	81.6	82.0	75.1	91.1	88.5	87.9	90.0	92.1	83.3
1974	91.0	86.9	82.0	88.3	73.3	87.5	85.2	84.5	90.9	87.3	80.3
1975	89.3	85.1	65.0	69.0	62.1	64.7	76.2	74.0	83.9	75.3	73.7
1976	89.4	85.5	68.8	76.8	62.0	69.7	80.2	78.8	86.9	80.1	76.8
1977	89.5	86.6	75.9	77.8	72.4	78.2	83.7	82.8	89.1	84.5	79.9
1978	89.7	86.9	79.0	77.7	77.4	82.1	85.3	84.6	88.7	86.2	82.1
1979	91.3	87.0	83.2	78.2	85.6	87.2	85.1	84.0	89.9	85.9	81.7
1980	91.4	85.5	87.8	86.9	91.7	85.1	80.5	78.2	89.4	78.8	79.3
1981	90.9	84.4	85.7	85.3	89.2	83.3	79.3	76.4	89.3	77.2	77.4
1982	84.2	80.2	78.2	70.3	87.2	81.4	73.4	70.4	82.3	70.5	73.0
1983	79.8	79.6	80.5	75.8	85.9	81.6	74.6	73.0	79.9	74.5	73.0
1984	85.9	82.2	87.4	85.4	85.4	90.9	80.1	78.8	85.7	81.2	77.2
1985	84.4	81.9	77.2	76.4	78.7	76.9	79.3	78.2	83.8	79.9	76.6
1986	77.6	81.1	72.8	72.9	75.3	71.0	79.0	78.8	78.4	79.8	77.1
1987	80.3	83.6	77.2	73.8	79.4	79.4	81.4	81.2	81.6	82.8	78.7
1988	84.3	86.7	79.8	76.2	84.0	80.9	84.6	84.3	83.8	85.9	81.8
1989	85.0	86.9	77.9	74.8	79.9	79.3	84.2	83.7	82.6	84.7	81.7
1990	86.6	86.5	77.4	71.4	82.1	80.2	82.8	82.0	82.0	82.7	80.7
1991	85.0	87.9	77.0	73.7	78.4	78.7	80.0	78.6	80.2	79.9	78.2
1992	84.7	86.3	81.2	78.3	79.5	83.7	80.6	79.5	81.7	81.6	78.1
1993	85.5	88.3	79.5	79.8	81.5	78.1	81.6	80.4	82.6	83.3	78.2
1994	87.0	88.4	82.9	75.7	83.1	86.4	83.6	82.8	84.3	86.4	79.1
1995	87.6	89.4	85.1	80.4	79.3	89.8	83.9	83.0	85.0	86.4	79.8
1996	90.3	90.9	82.8	86.0	76.7	84.3	83.5	82.1	84.8	85.6	79.3
1997	91.5	90.4	83.6	81.7	80.1	86.2	84.2	83.0	86.0	86.1	80.3
1998	89.0	92.7	79.3	78.0	84.6	77.3	83.1	81.8	84.3	84.2	80.1
1999	85.8	94.2	84.7	83.2	88.6	83.3	81.4	79.9	85.2	84.1	77.8
2000	90.6	93.9	89.2	80.6	90.9	92.0	80.8	78.7	86.0	84.0	76.7
2001	90.2	89.6	69.6	71.0	69.6	69.1	76.5	74.1	77.4	77.3	72.3
2002	86.1	87.6	58.6	69.0	45.5	62.3	76.1	74.2	73.5	77.1	70.6
2003	88.0	85.7	64.7	73.6	46.1	73.3	76.7	74.6	75.5	78.1	71.5
2004	88.3	84.5	70.8	77.9	52.9	78.9	78.4	76.6	78.6	79.9	73.2
2005	88.6	84.8	73.2	75.8	55.3	82.3	80.2	78.4	79.4	81.5	75.3
2006	90.2	83.0	81.9	78.0	74.8	88.1	80.1	78.2	81.9	81.0	76.1
2007	89.4	85.5	77.5	75.9	76.3	78.0	80.6	78.7	80.2	80.7	77.0
2008	89.7	84.1	80.6	76.3	85.6	81.0	77.4	74.1	79.2	76.8	74.0
2009	80.2	80.7	72.5	88.3	80.4	64.6	68.5	65.3	73.3	66.2	68.4
2010	84.3	83.0	81.0	86.5	80.4	78.4	73.7	70.8	77.6	72.2	72.1
2011	87.1	81.4	77.4	77.9	79.1	76.9	76.5	73.8	77.4	74.5	74.5
2012	88.2	78.1	70.7	68.5	76.2	69.8	77.8	76.0	75.1	75.4	76.3
2011											
January	86.0	83.9	85.5	86.4	82.4	86.3	75.8	72.9	85.5	74.6	73.6
February	83.9	82.5	83.8	84.3	82.5	84.1	75.5	73.0	83.9	74.2	73.8
March	86.4	82.7	81.3	82.8	81.4	81.1	76.3	73.6	85.8	74.8	74.2
April	86.7	81.6	79.4	81.6	79.8	79.1	75.8	73.1	85.4	74.1	73.8
May	87.4	81.3	78.4	80.6	78.5	78.1	76.1	73.3	85.6	74.2	74.1
June	87.4	81.6	77.3	79.5	78.3	76.8	76.1	73.3	85.7	74.3	74.0
July	86.5	82.5	75.8	78.1	78.6	74.8	76.5	73.9	85.1	74.7	74.5
August	87.8	82.1	75.5	76.2	78.7	74.7	76.8	74.1	86.0	74.7	74.9
September	87.0	81.3	73.8	73.6	78.2	72.8	76.8	74.4	85.7	74.7	74.9
October	88.3	79.9	72.4	71.9	77.4	71.3	77.2	74.8	86.7	74.5	75.5
November	89.0	80.1	72.5	70.4	76.8	71.8	77.2	74.6	87.0	74.7	75.2
December	89.4	77.7	72.6	69.6	76.6	72.1	77.5	75.3	87.3	74.8	75.7
2012											
January	89.6	76.3	71.7	69.6	76.8	70.7	77.9	76.1	87.8	74.9	76.5
February	88.8	76.8	70.9	69.3	76.7	69.8	78.2	76.5	86.8	75.5	76.7
March	87.8	76.2	70.6	69.5	76.3	69.4	77.6	76.0	86.1	75.0	76.2
April	87.9	77.8	70.8	69.7	75.6	69.8	78.0	76.3	86.1	75.6	76.7
May	87.6	81.2	70.7	69.6	74.9	69.9	78.1	76.0	85.8	76.0	76.4
June	87.7	78.8	71.1	68.7	74.6	70.6	77.9	76.2	86.0	75.5	76.6
July	88.2	80.0	70.5	67.8	74.7	69.9	78.2	76.2	86.4	75.8	76.7
August	87.2	78.5	68.7	67.4	75.2	67.4	77.5	75.7	85.7	75.0	76.0
September	88.0	78.1	69.5	67.4	76.0	68.4	77.5	75.6	86.4	74.8	76.0
October	88.3	78.9	71.5	67.7	76.5	71.0	77.2	75.0	86.5	75.2	74.9
November	89.0	79.4	71.6	67.9	78.4	70.7	78.1	76.0	87.4	75.9	76.0
December	88.4	75.1	71.1	67.5	78.3	70.0	78.1	76.7	87.3	75.3	76.6

. . . = Not available.

Table 2-4A. Industrial Production and Capacity Utilization: Historical Data, 1947–2012

(Seasonally adjusted.)

Year and month	Production indexes, 2007 = 100										Capacity utilization (output as percentage of capacity)	
	Total industry	Manufac-turing (SIC)	Market groups								Total industry	Manufac-turing (SIC)
			Consumer goods			Business equipment	Defense and space equipment	Construction supplies	Business supplies	Materials		
			Total	Durable	Nondurable							
1947	13.8	12.5	18.1	12.0	21.3	6.0	6.8	21.3	11.7	13.7	. . .	. . .
1948	14.4	13.0	18.7	12.5	21.9	6.3	8.0	22.8	12.1	14.3	. . .	82.5
1949	13.6	12.3	18.6	11.8	22.1	5.5	8.3	20.9	12.0	13.1	. . .	74.2
1950	15.7	14.3	21.2	15.8	23.9	5.9	9.8	25.2	13.4	15.6	. . .	82.8
1951	17.1	15.4	21.0	13.7	24.8	7.2	24.1	26.2	14.2	17.3	. . .	85.8
1952	17.7	16.1	21.5	13.3	25.8	8.1	33.9	26.0	14.1	17.6	. . .	85.4
1953	19.2	17.5	22.8	15.6	26.5	8.5	40.6	27.9	15.0	19.5	. . .	89.3
1954	18.2	16.4	22.6	14.5	26.8	7.4	35.8	27.5	15.2	18.0	. . .	80.1
1955	20.5	18.5	25.3	17.8	28.9	8.1	32.7	31.6	17.0	21.3	. . .	87.0
1956	21.4	19.2	26.2	17.2	30.8	9.4	32.0	32.5	18.1	21.8	. . .	86.1
1957	21.7	19.4	26.8	17.2	31.7	9.7	33.4	32.1	18.3	21.8	. . .	83.6
1958	20.3	18.1	26.6	15.3	32.7	8.2	33.6	31.0	18.1	19.7	. . .	75.0
1959	22.7	20.4	29.2	18.1	34.9	9.2	35.4	34.7	19.7	22.7	. . .	81.6
1960	23.2	20.8	30.3	19.1	36.0	9.5	36.4	33.9	20.4	23.0	. . .	80.1
1961	23.4	20.8	30.9	18.8	37.2	9.2	36.9	34.2	21.0	23.0	. . .	77.3
1962	25.3	22.7	33.0	21.3	39.0	10.0	42.8	36.3	22.4	25.0	. . .	81.4
1963	26.8	24.1	34.8	23.1	40.7	10.5	46.1	38.0	23.8	26.7	. . .	83.5
1964	28.6	25.7	36.7	24.8	42.7	11.7	44.7	40.3	25.5	28.8	. . .	85.6
1965	31.5	28.5	39.6	29.1	44.6	13.4	49.4	42.7	27.2	32.1	. . .	89.5
1966	34.3	31.1	41.6	30.8	46.7	15.6	58.1	44.5	29.3	35.0	. . .	91.1
1967	35.0	31.7	42.7	29.6	49.1	15.9	66.2	45.7	30.8	34.6	87.0	87.2
1968	37.0	33.4	45.2	33.0	51.0	16.6	66.4	48.1	32.7	36.9	87.3	87.1
1969	38.7	34.9	46.9	34.4	52.8	17.6	63.2	50.2	34.8	39.1	87.4	86.6
1970	37.4	33.4	46.4	31.7	53.7	17.0	53.5	48.4	34.9	37.8	81.3	79.4
1971	37.9	33.9	49.1	35.9	55.2	16.2	48.1	49.9	36.0	38.3	79.6	77.9
1972	41.6	37.4	53.0	40.2	58.7	18.4	46.8	56.7	39.6	42.2	84.7	83.4
1973	45.0	40.8	55.4	43.3	60.5	21.3	51.2	61.5	42.1	46.0	88.3	87.7
1974	44.8	40.7	53.8	39.4	60.6	22.6	52.9	60.0	41.9	45.9	85.1	84.4
1975	40.9	36.4	51.7	35.7	59.5	20.1	53.4	50.8	38.7	40.8	75.8	73.7
1976	44.1	39.7	55.9	40.3	63.2	21.5	51.8	54.7	41.2	44.4	79.8	78.3
1977	47.4	43.1	59.4	45.3	65.6	24.8	46.4	59.6	44.7	47.5	83.4	82.5
1978	50.0	45.7	61.3	46.4	67.9	28.0	47.3	63.0	47.1	49.9	85.1	84.4
1979	51.5	47.1	60.3	44.7	67.5	31.5	50.6	64.6	48.7	51.2	85.0	84.0
1980	50.2	45.5	58.1	38.9	67.6	32.3	60.1	59.8	47.6	49.3	80.7	78.6
1981	50.9	46.0	58.5	39.5	67.9	33.2	65.1	58.8	48.8	49.6	79.6	76.9
1982	48.3	43.5	58.3	37.2	69.1	30.4	77.8	53.4	48.2	45.8	73.6	70.9
1983	49.6	45.6	60.5	41.4	69.9	30.6	78.4	57.2	50.5	47.0	74.9	73.4
1984	54.0	50.0	63.3	46.2	71.3	35.1	89.8	62.2	54.9	51.4	80.4	79.3
1985	54.7	50.8	63.9	46.2	72.2	36.4	100.5	63.7	56.3	51.4	79.2	78.1
1986	55.2	52.0	66.1	49.3	73.9	35.9	106.7	65.9	58.1	51.3	78.7	78.4
1987	58.1	54.9	68.9	52.2	76.6	38.3	109.0	70.1	61.6	54.0	81.2	81.0
1988	61.1	57.8	71.5	54.9	79.1	42.3	110.0	71.7	63.9	57.0	84.3	84.0
1989	61.6	58.3	71.8	56.0	78.9	43.7	110.1	71.4	64.8	57.4	83.8	83.3
1990	62.2	58.7	72.1	54.5	80.2	45.3	106.2	70.9	66.3	57.8	82.5	81.7
1991	61.3	57.6	72.1	52.2	81.4	44.5	98.3	67.0	65.4	57.0	79.8	78.5
1992	63.0	59.7	74.2	57.1	82.0	46.3	91.1	69.8	66.9	58.8	80.6	79.6
1993	65.1	61.8	76.5	61.7	83.2	48.6	86.0	72.8	69.0	60.8	81.4	80.4
1994	68.5	65.4	79.7	67.2	85.2	51.8	80.7	78.1	71.8	64.7	83.6	82.8
1995	71.8	68.8	82.0	70.0	87.3	56.5	77.9	79.8	74.7	68.4	84.0	83.2
1996	74.9	72.2	83.5	72.2	88.5	62.0	75.8	83.4	77.6	71.9	83.4	82.2
1997	80.4	78.2	86.5	77.1	90.5	71.2	74.6	87.4	83.2	77.7	84.1	83.1
1998	85.0	83.4	89.5	82.6	92.5	79.1	77.8	92.1	87.9	82.4	82.8	81.5
1999	88.7	87.6	91.5	89.1	92.5	83.4	75.4	94.4	91.6	87.3	81.6	80.4
2000	92.2	91.3	93.2	91.6	93.9	89.6	67.0	96.5	95.3	91.8	81.4	79.7
2001	89.1	87.5	92.2	87.3	94.1	84.0	73.6	92.1	91.7	87.7	76.0	73.6
2002	89.3	87.8	94.0	92.5	94.6	78.5	74.5	92.2	91.9	88.6	74.8	72.9
2003	90.3	88.9	95.3	95.3	95.2	78.3	79.2	92.0	93.4	89.8	76.0	73.9
2004	92.5	91.4	96.4	97.0	96.1	82.1	77.2	94.2	95.1	92.4	77.9	76.2
2005	95.5	95.0	99.0	98.0	99.3	87.7	84.9	98.7	98.2	94.6	79.8	78.1
2006	97.6	97.4	99.5	98.3	99.9	95.8	84.0	101.1	99.2	96.5	80.2	78.4
2007	100.0	100.0	100.0	100.0	100.0	100.0	100.0	100.0	100.0	100.0	80.5	78.6
2008	96.6	95.3	95.1	88.8	97.2	97.7	107.0	90.7	96.0	97.6	77.5	74.5
2009	85.7	82.4	88.6	74.0	93.4	80.1	102.4	69.9	86.0	86.6	68.7	65.7
2010	90.6	87.4	89.6	79.4	92.9	86.7	110.1	72.5	88.1	94.2	74.0	71.3
2011	93.6	90.3	90.9	83.3	93.5	91.6	106.1	74.6	89.0	98.7	76.5	74.0
2012	97.0	93.9	92.4	90.3	93.3	99.2	111.8	78.5	90.3	102.8	77.6	75.8
1947												
January	13.6	12.4	18.0	11.3	21.6	5.8	7.0	20.2	11.5	13.5	. . .	. . .
February	13.7	12.4	17.9	11.6	21.2	5.9	6.9	20.9	11.6	13.6	. . .	. . .
March	13.8	12.5	18.0	11.9	21.2	5.9	6.8	21.1	11.6	14.1	. . .	. . .
April	13.7	12.5	17.9	12.0	21.0	6.0	6.8	21.3	11.7	13.7	. . .	. . .
May	13.7	12.4	17.8	11.9	20.9	6.0	6.7	21.5	11.7	13.8	. . .	. . .
June	13.7	12.4	17.8	12.0	20.9	6.1	6.7	21.6	11.6	13.6	. . .	. . .
July	13.7	12.3	17.9	11.7	21.1	6.0	6.6	21.0	11.6	13.5	. . .	. . .
August	13.7	12.4	18.0	11.6	21.3	6.1	6.6	21.3	11.5	13.5	. . .	. . .
September	13.8	12.5	18.2	12.0	21.4	6.2	6.6	21.5	11.6	13.7	. . .	. . .
October	14.0	12.6	18.5	12.2	21.7	6.2	6.8	21.5	11.6	13.8	. . .	. . .
November	14.2	12.8	18.8	12.5	22.0	6.2	6.9	21.9	11.8	14.1	. . .	. . .
December	14.2	12.9	18.8	12.7	21.9	6.3	7.1	22.0	12.0	13.9	. . .	. . .

. . . = Not available.

Table 2-4A. Industrial Production and Capacity Utilization: Historical Data, 1947–2012—*Continued*

(Seasonally adjusted.)

Year and month	Production indexes, 2007 = 100										Capacity utilization (output as percentage of capacity)	
	Total industry	Manufac-turing (SIC)	Market groups								Total industry	Manufac-turing (SIC)
			Consumer goods			Business equipment	Defense and space equipment	Construction supplies	Business supplies	Materials		
			Total	Durable	Nondurable							
1948												
January	14.3	12.9	18.7	12.6	21.8	6.3	7.1	22.9	12.0	14.0	. . .	84.4
February	14.3	12.9	18.8	12.4	22.0	6.3	7.4	22.7	12.1	14.1	. . .	84.0
March	14.2	12.9	18.5	12.5	21.7	6.3	7.6	22.8	12.1	13.9	. . .	83.4
April	14.2	12.9	18.7	12.4	22.0	6.3	7.7	22.6	12.0	13.8	. . .	82.8
May	14.4	13.0	18.6	12.1	22.0	6.3	7.6	22.8	12.1	14.5	. . .	83.3
June	14.6	13.1	18.9	12.7	22.2	6.3	7.8	22.6	12.2	14.6	. . .	83.6
July	14.6	13.2	18.9	13.0	21.9	6.4	8.0	23.2	12.1	14.7	. . .	83.4
August	14.6	13.1	18.7	12.8	21.8	6.4	8.2	23.1	12.3	14.5	. . .	82.7
September	14.5	13.0	18.6	12.4	21.8	6.3	8.4	22.8	12.1	14.5	. . .	81.5
October	14.6	13.1	18.8	12.8	21.9	6.2	8.5	23.3	12.2	14.5	. . .	81.7
November	14.4	12.9	18.6	12.3	22.0	6.2	8.7	22.6	12.2	14.4	. . .	80.2
December	14.3	12.8	18.4	11.8	21.8	6.2	8.7	22.4	12.2	14.3	. . .	79.3
1949												
January	14.1	12.7	18.2	11.5	21.7	6.0	8.6	21.8	12.0	14.1	. . .	77.9
February	14.0	12.5	18.1	11.3	21.8	6.0	8.6	21.3	11.8	14.0	. . .	76.9
March	13.7	12.4	18.3	11.3	22.0	5.8	8.5	21.1	11.9	13.4	. . .	75.9
April	13.6	12.2	18.2	11.3	21.9	5.8	8.4	20.7	11.8	13.2	. . .	74.2
May	13.4	12.1	18.2	11.2	22.0	5.6	8.5	20.5	11.9	12.9	. . .	73.2
June	13.4	12.1	18.4	11.5	22.0	5.5	8.6	20.5	11.9	12.7	. . .	73.1
July	13.4	12.1	18.6	11.9	22.1	5.4	8.5	20.2	11.9	12.6	. . .	73.1
August	13.5	12.3	18.8	12.1	22.3	5.4	8.4	20.4	12.0	12.8	. . .	73.6
September	13.7	12.5	19.1	12.5	22.4	5.3	8.3	21.1	12.1	13.1	. . .	74.8
October	13.2	12.0	19.1	12.7	22.5	5.1	8.0	20.4	12.3	11.7	. . .	71.7
November	13.5	12.1	18.9	12.0	22.4	5.0	8.0	21.1	12.2	12.8	. . .	72.0
December	13.7	12.4	18.7	11.9	22.2	5.0	7.9	22.0	12.3	13.4	. . .	73.6
1950												
January	14.0	12.7	19.4	13.3	22.7	5.1	7.8	21.7	12.4	13.5	. . .	74.9
February	14.0	12.8	19.5	13.2	22.7	5.2	7.8	22.6	12.7	13.3	. . .	75.4
March	14.5	13.0	19.9	13.8	23.0	5.3	7.9	23.1	12.8	14.2	. . .	76.4
April	15.0	13.6	20.4	14.8	23.3	5.4	8.1	24.3	13.0	14.8	. . .	79.2
May	15.3	13.9	20.9	15.5	23.5	5.7	8.4	24.5	13.1	15.2	. . .	81.0
June	15.8	14.3	21.4	16.8	23.7	5.9	8.7	25.4	13.2	15.8	. . .	83.1
July	16.3	14.8	22.1	17.5	24.2	6.1	9.1	26.1	13.5	16.2	. . .	85.5
August	16.8	15.3	22.8	18.1	25.1	6.4	10.1	26.6	13.9	16.7	. . .	88.4
September	16.7	15.2	22.2	17.2	24.7	6.3	11.1	26.6	13.8	16.9	. . .	87.2
October	16.8	15.3	22.1	16.9	24.6	6.4	11.9	26.9	14.0	17.1	. . .	87.5
November	16.8	15.3	22.0	16.5	24.6	6.4	12.8	26.9	14.0	16.9	. . .	87.0
December	17.1	15.5	22.3	16.4	25.3	6.5	13.8	26.9	14.2	17.2	. . .	88.1
1951												
January	17.1	15.6	22.4	16.1	25.7	6.6	15.4	27.2	14.4	17.0	. . .	88.3
February	17.2	15.6	22.4	16.1	25.6	6.7	17.8	26.9	14.2	17.1	. . .	88.3
March	17.3	15.7	22.1	16.0	25.1	6.8	20.2	27.0	14.5	17.5	. . .	88.4
April	17.3	15.7	21.7	15.3	25.0	7.0	22.1	26.9	14.8	17.6	. . .	88.2
May	17.3	15.6	21.3	14.5	24.8	7.1	22.8	26.7	14.6	17.7	. . .	87.4
June	17.2	15.6	21.0	13.8	24.7	7.1	24.0	26.5	14.4	17.8	. . .	86.6
July	16.9	15.3	20.3	12.4	24.5	7.2	25.4	25.9	14.2	17.5	. . .	84.9
August	16.8	15.1	19.9	11.5	24.3	7.3	26.2	25.8	14.1	17.2	. . .	83.6
September	16.9	15.2	20.1	12.0	24.3	7.5	27.1	25.7	14.0	17.3	. . .	83.7
October	16.9	15.1	19.9	11.9	24.2	7.6	28.2	25.5	13.6	17.1	. . .	83.1
November	17.0	15.3	20.3	12.2	24.6	7.7	29.8	25.3	13.7	17.1	. . .	83.6
December	17.1	15.4	20.4	12.3	24.7	7.8	30.5	25.3	13.8	17.1	. . .	83.9
1952												
January	17.3	15.5	20.6	12.3	25.0	8.0	31.0	25.7	13.8	17.5	. . .	84.4
February	17.4	15.6	20.7	12.2	25.3	8.1	31.3	25.9	13.8	17.4	. . .	84.6
March	17.4	15.7	20.8	12.5	25.3	8.2	31.4	25.7	13.9	17.4	. . .	84.7
April	17.3	15.6	20.8	12.4	25.3	8.1	31.8	25.3	13.8	17.1	. . .	83.6
May	17.1	15.5	20.8	12.7	25.1	8.2	32.8	24.9	13.7	16.8	. . .	83.1
June	17.0	15.4	21.4	12.9	26.0	8.2	33.8	24.8	14.0	15.9	. . .	81.9
July	16.7	15.0	21.0	11.6	26.0	7.8	34.0	24.7	14.1	15.5	. . .	79.8
August	17.8	16.1	21.4	12.8	26.1	8.0	34.5	26.4	14.2	17.5	. . .	85.1
September	18.4	16.7	22.0	14.1	26.1	8.2	35.1	26.7	14.4	18.6	. . .	87.7
October	18.6	16.9	22.3	14.6	26.3	8.2	36.3	27.0	14.6	18.5	. . .	88.8
November	19.0	17.3	22.8	15.5	26.6	8.4	37.0	27.5	14.7	19.1	. . .	90.2
December	19.1	17.4	22.8	15.6	26.6	8.4	38.1	27.6	14.7	19.1	. . .	90.5
1953												
January	19.1	17.4	23.0	16.2	26.5	8.5	38.7	28.1	14.5	19.0	. . .	90.5
February	19.2	17.6	23.2	16.3	26.7	8.5	39.5	28.5	14.8	19.5	. . .	91.1
March	19.4	17.7	23.2	16.5	26.6	8.6	40.3	28.6	15.1	19.7	. . .	91.4
April	19.5	17.8	23.1	16.3	26.7	8.6	40.8	28.7	15.1	19.9	. . .	91.5
May	19.6	17.9	23.2	16.4	26.8	8.6	41.5	28.1	15.2	20.3	. . .	91.7
June	19.5	17.8	22.9	15.8	26.7	8.5	41.8	27.9	15.2	20.3	. . .	90.7
July	19.8	17.9	22.9	15.7	26.6	8.6	42.1	28.3	15.3	20.5	. . .	91.0
August	19.6	17.9	22.8	15.6	26.5	8.6	41.8	28.1	15.3	20.0	. . .	90.6
September	19.2	17.5	22.5	14.9	26.4	8.5	41.8	27.6	15.2	19.5	. . .	88.3
October	19.1	17.3	22.5	14.8	26.5	8.5	41.4	27.7	15.0	18.9	. . .	87.2
November	18.6	16.9	22.1	14.3	26.3	8.2	38.7	27.2	15.0	18.4	. . .	84.7
December	18.2	16.4	21.8	13.8	26.0	8.1	39.0	26.6	14.8	18.0	. . .	82.3

. . . = Not available.

Table 2-4A. Industrial Production and Capacity Utilization: Historical Data, 1947–2012—*Continued*

(Seasonally adjusted.)

Year and month	Production indexes, 2007 = 100										Capacity utilization (output as percentage of capacity)	
	Total industry	Manufac-turing (SIC)	Market groups								Total industry	Manufac-turing (SIC)
			Consumer goods			Business equipment	Defense and space equipment	Construction supplies	Business supplies	Materials		
			Total	Durable	Nondurable							
1954												
January	18.0	16.3	21.9	13.6	26.3	7.8	38.2	27.1	14.8	17.8	. . .	81.3
February	18.1	16.2	22.1	13.9	26.5	7.7	38.0	27.2	14.9	17.7	. . .	80.8
March	18.0	16.2	22.2	13.9	26.5	7.6	37.5	27.0	14.9	17.6	. . .	80.2
April	17.9	16.1	22.2	14.0	26.4	7.5	36.8	27.0	15.0	17.5	. . .	79.4
May	18.0	16.2	22.3	14.3	26.4	7.5	36.3	27.3	15.0	17.8	. . .	79.8
June	18.0	16.2	22.4	14.4	26.5	7.4	35.7	26.7	15.1	18.0	. . .	79.9
July	18.1	16.2	22.5	14.2	26.8	7.4	35.6	26.6	14.9	18.1	. . .	79.4
August	18.0	16.1	22.5	14.4	26.8	7.3	34.8	26.5	15.0	18.0	. . .	78.8
September	18.1	16.2	22.8	14.5	27.0	7.2	34.5	27.8	15.5	17.8	. . .	79.2
October	18.3	16.4	22.8	14.7	27.1	7.2	34.1	28.7	15.6	18.2	. . .	79.7
November	18.6	16.7	23.3	15.1	27.6	7.3	33.9	29.0	15.8	18.5	. . .	80.9
December	18.8	16.9	23.7	15.7	27.8	7.4	33.4	29.2	16.0	18.9	. . .	81.8
1955												
January	19.2	17.4	24.3	16.8	27.9	7.4	33.2	29.7	16.2	19.5	. . .	83.5
February	19.5	17.5	24.4	16.9	27.9	7.5	33.2	30.1	16.4	20.0	. . .	84.1
March	19.9	18.0	24.8	17.4	28.4	7.6	33.0	31.1	16.8	20.5	. . .	85.8
April	20.2	18.2	25.0	17.7	28.6	7.9	33.0	31.3	16.7	20.9	. . .	86.7
May	20.5	18.5	25.3	18.1	28.8	8.0	33.0	31.4	17.0	21.3	. . .	87.9
June	20.5	18.6	25.1	17.8	28.7	8.1	32.7	32.0	17.1	21.4	. . .	87.6
July	20.7	18.6	25.2	18.0	28.7	8.1	32.6	32.0	17.1	21.7	. . .	87.7
August	20.7	18.6	25.3	18.0	28.7	8.2	32.4	32.0	17.0	21.6	. . .	87.3
September	20.8	18.7	25.4	18.1	29.0	8.2	32.5	32.2	17.4	21.9	. . .	87.5
October	21.1	19.0	25.9	18.2	29.7	8.6	32.3	32.2	17.5	22.1	. . .	88.4
November	21.2	19.0	26.0	18.0	29.9	8.6	32.3	32.6	17.8	22.0	. . .	88.3
December	21.3	19.3	26.1	17.9	30.2	8.8	32.4	32.8	17.6	22.2	. . .	89.0
1956												
January	21.4	19.2	26.1	17.8	30.3	8.8	32.0	33.3	17.8	22.3	. . .	88.2
February	21.2	19.1	26.1	17.4	30.4	9.0	31.7	33.2	17.8	21.9	. . .	87.4
March	21.2	19.1	26.0	17.5	30.4	9.1	31.0	33.1	18.0	21.8	. . .	87.0
April	21.4	19.3	26.1	17.7	30.4	9.3	31.2	33.0	18.2	21.9	. . .	87.8
May	21.2	19.1	26.0	17.3	30.5	9.3	31.3	32.5	18.0	21.5	. . .	86.3
June	21.0	18.9	25.9	16.9	30.6	9.3	31.3	32.1	18.0	21.2	. . .	85.3
July	20.4	18.2	26.0	16.9	30.7	9.3	31.3	30.5	18.0	19.5	. . .	81.5
August	21.2	19.0	26.1	16.9	30.9	9.4	31.7	32.0	18.1	21.3	. . .	84.9
September	21.7	19.3	26.1	16.7	31.0	9.5	32.0	32.9	18.1	22.5	. . .	86.0
October	21.9	19.5	26.3	16.9	31.2	9.6	32.8	32.6	18.2	22.8	. . .	86.5
November	21.7	19.4	26.2	16.6	31.1	9.7	33.3	32.4	18.2	22.3	. . .	85.8
December	22.0	19.7	26.4	17.3	31.0	9.8	34.1	33.0	18.3	22.7	. . .	86.8
1957												
January	21.9	19.7	26.5	17.4	31.2	10.0	34.2	32.5	18.4	22.3	. . .	86.2
February	22.1	19.9	26.9	17.7	31.5	10.2	34.4	33.5	18.4	22.4	. . .	87.0
March	22.1	19.9	26.9	17.6	31.7	10.1	34.4	32.9	18.3	22.3	. . .	86.4
April	21.8	19.6	26.7	17.1	31.6	9.9	34.5	32.2	18.4	22.0	. . .	85.0
May	21.7	19.5	26.7	17.0	31.7	9.8	33.9	32.1	18.5	21.9	. . .	84.2
June	21.8	19.6	26.8	17.3	31.7	9.8	34.1	32.3	18.3	22.0	. . .	84.6
July	21.9	19.6	26.9	17.1	32.0	9.8	33.8	32.4	18.4	22.2	. . .	84.3
August	21.9	19.6	27.1	17.6	31.9	9.8	33.8	32.1	18.4	22.2	. . .	84.2
September	21.7	19.5	27.1	17.5	32.0	9.7	33.1	31.9	18.4	21.9	. . .	83.2
October	21.4	19.1	26.7	16.9	31.7	9.4	32.3	31.5	18.2	21.6	. . .	81.4
November	20.9	18.7	26.6	16.9	31.6	9.2	31.2	31.1	18.0	20.8	. . .	79.4
December	20.5	18.3	26.4	16.1	31.9	8.9	31.0	30.7	18.0	20.1	. . .	77.5
1958												
January	20.1	17.9	26.1	15.5	31.8	8.7	31.4	30.3	17.9	19.5	. . .	75.7
February	19.7	17.5	25.9	14.9	31.8	8.4	31.6	29.3	17.8	18.9	. . .	73.8
March	19.5	17.3	25.7	14.4	31.8	8.2	32.2	29.1	17.9	18.4	. . .	72.7
April	19.1	17.0	25.4	13.9	31.8	8.1	32.7	28.8	17.7	18.0	. . .	71.3
May	19.3	17.2	25.8	14.4	32.1	7.9	33.1	29.7	17.7	18.2	. . .	71.9
June	19.8	17.8	26.3	14.8	32.6	7.9	34.0	30.9	17.9	18.9	. . .	73.9
July	20.1	17.9	26.7	15.0	33.0	7.9	34.1	30.7	17.9	19.4	. . .	74.3
August	20.5	18.3	26.8	15.3	33.0	8.1	34.4	32.1	18.2	20.0	. . .	75.7
September	20.7	18.5	26.5	14.2	33.2	8.1	34.6	32.2	18.4	20.5	. . .	76.2
October	21.0	18.6	26.7	14.9	33.2	8.2	34.6	32.1	18.7	20.9	. . .	76.4
November	21.6	19.3	28.0	17.5	33.6	8.4	34.9	33.4	18.8	21.5	. . .	79.1
December	21.6	19.3	28.1	17.5	33.6	8.4	34.9	33.0	18.7	21.5	. . .	79.0
1959												
January	21.9	19.6	28.5	17.6	34.1	8.6	35.1	33.6	19.2	21.9	. . .	80.2
February	22.4	20.0	28.7	17.7	34.4	8.7	34.7	34.5	19.4	22.6	. . .	81.4
March	22.7	20.3	28.7	18.0	34.3	8.8	34.9	35.4	19.5	23.2	. . .	82.5
April	23.2	20.7	29.1	18.1	34.8	9.1	35.1	36.4	19.5	23.8	. . .	84.0
May	23.5	21.0	29.3	18.5	34.8	9.3	35.4	36.7	19.5	24.4	. . .	84.9
June	23.5	21.1	29.1	18.7	34.6	9.6	35.5	36.6	19.7	24.2	. . .	84.8
July	23.0	20.7	29.5	19.0	34.9	9.6	35.6	35.1	20.0	22.8	. . .	83.0
August	22.2	19.9	29.5	18.5	35.3	9.5	35.4	32.9	19.9	21.1	. . .	79.5
September	22.2	19.8	29.4	17.9	35.5	9.4	35.6	32.6	20.0	21.1	. . .	79.0
October	22.0	19.6	29.3	18.4	35.0	9.4	35.6	32.7	20.0	20.8	. . .	78.2
November	22.1	19.8	28.7	16.1	35.5	9.2	35.5	33.8	20.0	21.7	. . .	78.5
December	23.5	21.1	29.6	18.1	35.6	9.3	35.8	36.4	20.1	24.0	. . .	83.6

. . . = Not available.

Table 2-4A. Industrial Production and Capacity Utilization: Historical Data, 1947–2012—*Continued*

(Seasonally adjusted.)

Year and month	Total industry	Manufac-turing (SIC)	Consumer goods Total	Durable	Nondurable	Business equipment	Defense and space equipment	Construction supplies	Business supplies	Materials	Capacity utilization Total industry	Manufac-turing (SIC)
1960												
January	24.1	21.7	30.6	20.1	35.8	9.7	36.1	36.2	20.4	24.7	. . .	85.6
February	23.9	21.5	30.2	19.9	35.4	9.8	36.3	35.8	20.4	24.4	. . .	84.6
March	23.7	21.3	30.2	19.5	35.8	9.8	36.4	34.7	20.4	24.0	. . .	83.2
April	23.5	21.1	30.4	19.4	36.1	9.7	36.2	34.7	20.6	23.4	. . .	82.3
May	23.5	21.0	30.6	19.6	36.3	9.7	36.6	34.3	20.8	23.2	. . .	81.5
June	23.2	20.7	30.4	19.4	36.1	9.6	35.7	33.7	20.5	22.8	. . .	80.2
July	23.1	20.7	30.1	18.7	36.1	9.5	36.6	34.0	20.6	22.8	. . .	79.7
August	23.1	20.6	30.2	18.9	36.1	9.3	36.8	33.2	20.4	22.7	. . .	79.1
September	22.8	20.4	30.1	18.7	36.0	9.3	36.7	32.9	20.3	22.4	. . .	77.9
October	22.8	20.4	30.4	18.9	36.4	9.2	36.3	33.0	20.4	22.3	. . .	77.5
November	22.5	20.0	29.8	18.2	36.0	9.2	36.4	32.6	20.4	21.7	. . .	75.8
December	22.1	19.6	29.6	17.6	36.0	8.9	35.9	32.2	20.0	21.1	. . .	74.3
1961												
January	22.1	19.7	29.4	17.0	36.1	9.0	36.3	31.9	20.3	21.3	. . .	74.1
February	22.1	19.6	29.5	16.9	36.3	8.9	36.0	31.8	20.4	21.1	. . .	73.5
March	22.2	19.7	29.5	16.9	36.3	8.9	35.9	32.6	20.6	21.3	. . .	73.9
April	22.7	20.2	30.2	18.1	36.7	9.0	36.0	33.4	20.7	22.0	. . .	75.4
May	23.0	20.5	30.6	18.7	36.9	9.0	36.0	33.5	20.8	22.6	. . .	76.4
June	23.3	20.8	30.9	19.3	37.1	9.1	36.0	34.2	20.9	23.0	. . .	77.3
July	23.6	21.1	31.2	19.6	37.2	9.1	36.3	34.8	21.2	23.3	. . .	78.1
August	23.8	21.3	31.4	19.7	37.6	9.2	36.4	35.2	21.3	23.7	. . .	79.0
September	23.8	21.2	30.9	18.6	37.4	9.3	37.2	35.5	21.2	23.8	. . .	78.2
October	24.2	21.6	31.7	19.6	38.0	9.3	38.1	35.7	21.5	24.2	. . .	79.6
November	24.6	22.0	32.3	20.5	38.4	9.6	39.0	35.5	21.7	24.5	. . .	80.8
December	24.8	22.3	32.4	20.9	38.4	9.6	39.7	35.7	21.9	24.9	. . .	81.6
1962												
January	24.6	22.0	32.1	20.4	38.2	9.6	40.1	34.1	21.9	24.7	. . .	80.2
February	25.0	22.4	32.3	20.5	38.5	9.7	40.8	36.0	22.1	25.1	. . .	81.4
March	25.1	22.6	32.6	20.8	38.7	9.8	41.4	36.5	22.0	25.1	. . .	81.9
April	25.2	22.6	32.8	21.3	38.7	9.9	41.7	36.0	22.0	25.1	. . .	81.7
May	25.2	22.5	33.0	21.5	39.0	9.9	42.0	36.0	22.4	24.8	. . .	81.3
June	25.1	22.5	32.8	21.1	38.9	10.0	42.4	36.2	22.4	24.7	. . .	80.9
July	25.4	22.7	33.4	21.6	39.4	10.1	43.3	36.1	22.3	24.9	. . .	81.5
August	25.4	22.7	33.0	21.3	39.0	10.2	43.9	36.7	22.5	24.9	. . .	81.4
September	25.5	22.9	33.2	21.5	39.2	10.2	44.0	37.2	22.7	25.2	. . .	81.8
October	25.6	22.9	33.1	21.6	39.1	10.2	44.1	36.5	22.6	25.2	. . .	81.4
November	25.7	23.1	33.3	21.7	39.2	10.2	44.6	36.7	22.8	25.4	. . .	81.8
December	25.7	23.1	33.5	21.8	39.4	10.1	44.7	37.0	22.6	25.2	. . .	81.7
1963												
January	25.9	23.2	33.9	22.0	40.0	10.1	46.8	36.1	22.8	25.3	. . .	81.9
February	26.2	23.4	34.3	22.3	40.4	10.2	46.5	36.2	23.0	25.7	. . .	82.4
March	26.3	23.6	34.4	22.3	40.6	10.2	46.2	36.6	22.8	26.1	. . .	82.6
April	26.6	23.9	34.6	22.5	40.7	10.3	46.2	37.8	23.6	26.3	. . .	83.5
May	26.9	24.1	34.6	22.9	40.6	10.2	46.2	38.7	23.8	26.9	. . .	84.0
June	27.0	24.2	34.8	23.3	40.7	10.3	46.1	38.5	23.7	27.0	. . .	83.9
July	26.9	24.1	34.7	23.2	40.5	10.4	45.7	38.4	23.9	26.8	. . .	83.3
August	26.9	24.2	35.0	23.3	40.9	10.7	45.8	38.5	24.0	26.5	. . .	83.5
September	27.2	24.4	35.1	23.7	40.8	10.7	46.0	38.2	24.2	27.1	. . .	83.8
October	27.4	24.6	35.4	23.7	41.1	10.8	46.0	38.8	24.4	27.2	. . .	84.3
November	27.5	24.6	35.4	24.0	41.1	10.9	45.8	39.2	24.7	27.4	. . .	84.3
December	27.5	24.6	35.6	24.0	41.5	10.9	46.0	38.7	24.5	27.2	. . .	84.0
1964												
January	27.7	24.9	35.9	24.1	41.9	11.2	45.5	38.9	24.8	27.4	. . .	84.5
February	27.9	25.0	35.9	24.2	41.7	11.1	45.1	39.9	24.9	27.9	. . .	84.7
March	27.9	25.0	35.7	24.0	41.6	11.3	45.0	40.0	25.1	27.9	. . .	84.4
April	28.3	25.5	36.6	24.7	42.6	11.5	44.9	40.2	25.4	28.2	. . .	85.6
May	28.5	25.6	36.9	24.8	43.0	11.7	44.1	40.4	25.6	28.4	. . .	85.6
June	28.6	25.6	36.8	25.1	42.7	11.7	43.9	40.1	25.7	28.6	. . .	85.4
July	28.8	25.8	37.3	25.5	43.3	11.9	43.8	40.9	25.7	28.7	. . .	85.9
August	29.0	26.0	37.3	25.7	43.0	11.9	44.0	40.5	25.6	29.3	. . .	86.1
September	29.1	26.1	36.8	25.1	42.7	12.0	44.3	40.2	25.6	29.7	. . .	86.2
October	28.7	25.7	36.1	22.5	43.3	11.9	44.6	40.3	25.6	29.2	. . .	84.6
November	29.5	26.5	37.5	25.5	43.4	12.3	45.1	41.3	25.8	30.1	. . .	86.8
December	29.9	27.0	38.2	27.0	43.7	12.5	45.4	40.7	26.1	30.4	. . .	88.0
1965												
January	30.2	27.3	38.8	27.5	44.3	12.5	45.9	41.0	26.3	30.8	. . .	88.6
February	30.4	27.5	38.9	27.9	44.2	12.7	46.4	42.1	26.4	30.9	. . .	88.7
March	30.8	27.8	39.2	28.6	44.2	12.8	47.2	42.4	26.7	31.4	. . .	89.3
April	30.9	28.0	39.1	28.6	44.1	13.0	47.8	41.8	26.7	31.7	. . .	89.3
May	31.2	28.2	39.4	28.8	44.4	13.1	48.8	42.2	27.0	31.8	. . .	89.4
June	31.4	28.4	39.5	29.0	44.4	13.3	49.4	42.3	27.1	32.2	. . .	89.5
July	31.7	28.8	39.5	29.2	44.3	13.6	50.2	43.5	27.1	32.5	. . .	90.3
August	31.9	28.8	39.5	28.9	44.4	13.6	50.6	43.0	27.4	32.8	. . .	89.9
September	31.9	28.9	40.0	29.5	45.0	13.8	50.7	42.7	27.4	32.5	. . .	89.6
October	32.3	29.1	40.3	29.8	45.1	14.0	51.4	43.3	27.7	32.9	. . .	89.8
November	32.4	29.2	40.5	30.0	45.4	14.3	51.8	43.9	27.9	32.8	. . .	89.6
December	32.8	29.7	40.7	30.6	45.3	14.6	52.4	44.9	28.3	33.1	. . .	90.5

. . . = Not available.

Table 2-4A. Industrial Production and Capacity Utilization: Historical Data, 1947–2012—*Continued*

(Seasonally adjusted.)

Year and month	Production indexes, 2007 = 100										Capacity utilization (output as percentage of capacity)	
			Market groups									
	Total industry	Manufac-turing (SIC)	Consumer goods			Business equipment	Defense and space equipment	Construction supplies	Business supplies	Materials	Total industry	Manufac-turing (SIC)
			Total	Durable	Nondurable							
1966												
January	33.1	30.0	40.9	30.7	45.6	14.9	53.5	44.8	28.3	33.6	. . .	90.9
February	33.3	30.2	41.0	30.6	45.8	14.8	54.3	44.4	28.6	33.9	. . .	90.9
March	33.8	30.6	41.3	30.9	46.2	15.1	54.7	45.2	28.9	34.6	. . .	91.6
April	33.8	30.8	41.5	31.4	46.1	15.2	55.9	45.2	28.6	34.5	. . .	91.5
May	34.2	31.0	41.5	30.9	46.4	15.4	56.9	45.5	29.0	34.9	. . .	91.6
June	34.3	31.1	41.6	30.9	46.6	15.6	57.7	44.8	29.4	35.1	. . .	91.5
July	34.5	31.3	41.6	30.4	46.9	15.8	58.5	45.2	29.7	35.2	. . .	91.4
August	34.5	31.3	41.4	29.9	47.0	15.9	59.3	43.9	29.6	35.5	. . .	91.1
September	34.9	31.6	41.6	30.1	47.1	16.1	60.1	43.9	29.8	35.8	. . .	91.2
October	35.1	31.9	42.4	31.6	47.5	16.0	61.0	44.0	29.8	36.0	. . .	91.6
November	34.9	31.6	42.2	30.7	47.7	15.8	62.1	44.0	29.9	35.4	. . .	90.1
December	34.9	31.7	42.1	30.3	47.8	16.0	62.8	43.9	29.9	35.4	. . .	90.0
1967												
January	35.1	31.8	42.5	29.6	48.9	15.9	63.8	45.1	30.5	35.3	89.4	89.8
February	34.7	31.4	41.9	28.8	48.5	15.9	64.6	44.7	30.3	34.6	88.0	88.4
March	34.5	31.3	42.1	29.0	48.5	15.9	65.3	44.8	30.4	34.0	87.1	87.5
April	34.8	31.5	42.8	29.2	49.5	15.9	65.9	44.6	30.6	34.3	87.5	87.7
May	34.5	31.3	42.0	28.8	48.5	15.9	66.4	45.3	30.1	33.9	86.4	86.6
June	34.5	31.2	42.1	28.5	48.9	15.9	66.2	45.6	30.3	33.9	86.0	86.1
July	34.5	31.1	42.0	28.9	48.5	15.5	66.6	45.8	30.4	33.8	85.4	85.3
August	35.1	31.7	42.4	29.2	49.0	15.8	66.7	46.3	31.2	34.9	86.6	86.5
September	35.1	31.7	42.5	29.1	49.2	15.8	66.9	46.7	31.3	34.6	86.1	86.1
October	35.3	31.9	43.1	29.7	49.7	15.6	67.4	46.4	31.5	35.1	86.4	86.4
November	35.8	32.5	44.0	31.3	50.1	16.0	67.6	46.7	31.6	35.5	87.3	87.5
December	36.2	32.8	44.7	32.6	50.5	16.2	67.5	46.7	31.6	35.9	87.8	88.0
1968												
January	36.2	32.8	44.1	31.6	50.1	16.3	67.3	47.0	31.7	36.1	87.4	87.4
February	36.3	32.9	44.4	32.1	50.2	16.3	68.0	47.5	31.9	36.1	87.4	87.4
March	36.4	33.0	44.6	32.1	50.7	16.4	66.7	47.6	31.9	36.2	87.3	87.2
April	36.5	33.0	44.6	32.1	50.6	16.3	65.4	47.8	32.2	36.5	87.1	86.9
May	36.9	33.4	44.8	32.5	50.7	16.6	66.3	48.0	32.5	37.0	87.7	87.6
June	37.0	33.5	45.1	32.8	50.9	16.5	66.6	48.1	32.7	37.2	87.7	87.4
July	37.0	33.4	45.0	32.5	50.9	16.4	66.7	48.1	32.6	37.2	87.2	86.7
August	37.1	33.5	45.5	33.0	51.5	16.5	66.8	48.3	33.0	37.0	87.1	86.8
September	37.2	33.6	45.7	33.3	51.6	16.7	66.8	47.9	33.1	37.1	87.1	86.5
October	37.3	33.8	46.0	33.7	51.7	16.9	65.0	47.9	33.3	37.2	86.9	86.6
November	37.8	34.3	46.6	34.5	52.2	16.9	65.7	49.0	33.7	37.7	87.7	87.5
December	37.9	34.3	46.3	34.8	51.5	17.0	65.3	49.9	33.9	37.9	87.7	87.1
1969												
January	38.1	34.5	46.6	34.7	52.0	17.3	65.4	50.3	34.0	38.1	87.9	87.3
February	38.4	34.7	46.9	34.7	52.6	17.3	65.0	50.7	33.9	38.5	88.1	87.7
March	38.7	35.0	47.3	34.9	53.0	17.4	65.2	50.9	35.0	38.7	88.5	88.0
April	38.5	34.9	46.6	34.0	52.5	17.6	64.7	50.5	34.5	38.8	87.8	87.3
May	38.4	34.7	46.2	33.5	52.2	17.5	64.6	50.1	34.8	38.7	87.2	86.6
June	38.8	34.9	46.8	34.7	52.3	17.7	63.7	50.4	35.1	39.3	87.7	86.8
July	39.0	35.2	47.6	34.7	53.6	17.9	63.4	49.9	34.9	39.3	87.9	87.1
August	39.1	35.2	47.5	35.0	53.2	17.8	62.5	49.9	35.0	39.7	87.8	86.9
September	39.0	35.2	47.1	34.7	52.9	18.0	62.1	49.9	35.0	39.8	87.4	86.5
October	39.1	35.2	47.1	34.9	52.8	18.0	61.5	50.1	35.1	39.8	87.2	86.2
November	38.7	34.9	46.7	33.4	53.1	17.6	60.4	49.8	34.9	39.6	86.0	85.0
December	38.6	34.7	46.8	33.3	53.3	17.5	59.7	49.5	35.3	39.3	85.5	84.2
1970												
January	37.9	33.9	46.0	31.5	53.2	17.3	58.9	47.9	35.2	38.4	83.7	82.1
February	37.8	33.9	46.5	32.0	53.6	17.4	57.9	47.8	35.0	38.2	83.3	81.9
March	37.8	33.8	46.4	32.3	53.3	17.4	56.6	48.2	35.2	38.1	83.0	81.4
April	37.7	33.7	46.6	32.3	53.6	17.4	55.3	48.7	35.0	37.9	82.5	80.9
May	37.7	33.6	46.9	32.3	54.0	17.4	54.1	48.7	34.9	37.7	82.1	80.5
June	37.5	33.5	47.0	32.9	53.8	17.3	53.2	48.5	34.9	37.6	81.6	80.0
July	37.6	33.6	47.1	33.0	53.9	17.2	52.3	49.1	35.0	37.8	81.6	80.0
August	37.6	33.4	46.3	32.0	53.3	17.2	51.9	48.9	34.7	38.2	81.2	79.2
September	37.3	33.1	46.1	31.1	53.6	16.8	51.4	48.8	34.9	37.9	80.4	78.3
October	36.6	32.4	45.5	29.3	53.9	16.3	50.7	48.3	34.8	36.9	78.5	76.3
November	36.3	32.2	45.2	29.4	53.4	16.2	50.3	47.7	34.9	36.7	77.8	75.6
December	37.2	33.0	47.2	32.8	54.3	16.4	49.7	48.2	34.9	37.6	79.4	77.3
1971												
January	37.4	33.3	47.9	34.1	54.5	16.0	50.1	48.2	35.1	38.1	79.7	77.8
February	37.4	33.3	47.9	34.8	54.0	16.1	48.9	48.6	35.4	37.9	79.4	77.6
March	37.3	33.3	48.0	34.9	54.2	15.9	48.5	48.4	35.1	37.9	79.1	77.2
April	37.5	33.4	48.4	35.1	54.7	15.9	48.5	48.8	35.5	38.2	79.3	77.4
May	37.7	33.7	48.4	35.7	54.4	15.7	49.1	49.1	35.6	38.6	79.5	77.8
June	37.9	33.8	48.8	35.9	54.8	15.8	48.4	49.6	35.4	38.8	79.7	77.8
July	37.8	33.8	49.5	36.6	55.5	15.8	48.0	50.0	36.3	37.9	79.2	77.7
August	37.6	33.4	49.0	36.2	54.9	16.1	48.0	49.2	35.9	37.6	78.6	76.6
September	38.2	34.1	49.4	36.2	55.6	16.5	47.5	51.0	36.5	38.4	79.7	77.9
October	38.5	34.6	50.1	36.8	56.3	16.6	47.2	51.7	36.7	38.5	80.1	78.9
November	38.6	34.7	50.5	37.2	56.7	16.7	46.8	51.9	37.1	38.5	80.2	79.0
December	39.1	35.0	50.8	37.4	57.1	16.8	46.1	52.8	37.3	39.3	80.9	79.5

. . . = Not available.

Table 2-4A. Industrial Production and Capacity Utilization: Historical Data, 1947–2012—*Continued*

(Seasonally adjusted.)

Year and month	Production indexes, 2007 = 100										Capacity utilization (output as percentage of capacity)	
	Total industry	Manufac-turing (SIC)	Market groups								Total industry	Manufac-turing (SIC)
			Consumer goods			Business equipment	Defense and space equipment	Construction supplies	Business supplies	Materials		
			Total	Durable	Nondurable							
1972												
January	40.0	35.9	47.9	38.5	57.6	17.3	46.1	54.2	37.9	40.6	82.7	81.4
February	40.4	36.2	47.9	38.6	57.9	17.6	46.2	54.4	38.6	41.0	83.2	81.8
March	40.7	36.5	48.0	38.4	58.2	17.8	46.6	54.8	39.0	41.4	83.7	82.2
April	41.1	36.9	48.4	39.5	58.4	18.1	46.8	55.4	39.0	41.8	84.3	82.9
May	41.1	36.9	48.4	39.2	58.2	18.1	46.4	55.7	39.2	41.9	84.1	82.7
June	41.2	37.1	48.8	39.2	58.2	18.2	46.4	56.2	39.5	42.0	84.1	82.8
July	41.2	37.1	49.5	40.0	58.3	18.2	46.3	57.0	39.5	41.7	83.8	82.6
August	41.7	37.6	49.0	40.4	59.0	18.5	46.3	57.4	40.0	42.3	84.7	83.5
September	42.0	37.9	49.4	40.8	59.2	18.7	46.7	57.9	40.0	42.7	85.1	83.9
October	42.6	38.4	50.1	41.7	59.9	19.1	46.7	58.7	40.7	43.1	86.0	84.9
November	43.1	38.9	50.5	42.7	59.8	19.5	48.0	59.2	40.8	43.8	86.8	85.7
December	43.6	39.4	50.8	43.6	60.0	19.7	48.8	59.0	40.9	44.5	87.5	86.6
1973												
January	43.9	39.7	55.1	43.4	59.9	20.0	49.4	59.7	41.2	44.8	87.8	86.9
February	44.6	40.4	55.8	44.2	60.5	20.5	50.4	60.8	41.7	45.5	88.8	88.1
March	44.6	40.4	55.9	44.3	60.7	20.6	50.2	61.2	41.7	45.4	88.6	88.0
April	44.5	40.4	55.4	43.6	60.2	20.8	50.0	61.0	41.7	45.5	88.1	87.5
May	44.8	40.6	55.7	43.5	60.8	21.0	50.3	61.3	41.9	45.8	88.4	87.8
June	44.8	40.6	55.3	43.4	60.3	21.2	50.8	61.4	42.0	45.8	88.1	87.4
July	45.0	40.8	55.2	43.3	60.1	21.4	51.9	61.9	42.2	46.0	88.2	87.5
August	44.9	40.7	54.7	42.0	60.2	21.5	51.9	62.0	42.2	46.1	87.8	87.0
September	45.3	41.0	55.6	43.4	60.7	21.9	51.9	61.9	42.3	46.3	88.3	87.5
October	45.6	41.4	55.8	43.1	61.2	22.1	53.1	61.8	42.7	46.6	88.6	87.9
November	45.9	41.7	55.9	43.1	61.5	22.3	52.6	62.3	42.7	47.0	88.8	88.3
December	45.8	41.7	54.9	42.2	60.4	22.4	52.3	62.7	42.3	47.2	88.3	88.1
1974												
January	45.4	41.4	54.2	40.1	60.7	22.4	52.1	62.8	42.4	46.8	87.4	87.1
February	45.3	41.2	54.0	39.9	60.5	22.3	52.5	62.1	42.2	46.7	86.9	86.5
March	45.3	41.2	54.1	40.0	60.6	22.5	52.5	62.2	42.2	46.5	86.7	86.2
April	45.2	41.0	53.9	39.7	60.5	22.3	52.4	61.7	42.3	46.5	86.2	85.6
May	45.5	41.3	54.4	39.8	61.2	22.6	52.6	61.9	42.5	46.8	86.6	85.9
June	45.5	41.3	54.6	40.4	61.3	22.7	51.8	61.6	42.7	46.6	86.4	85.8
July	45.5	41.2	54.5	40.2	61.1	22.6	52.4	60.4	42.3	46.8	86.2	85.4
August	45.0	40.9	54.5	40.2	61.1	22.6	53.5	59.7	42.2	45.9	85.2	84.5
September	45.1	41.0	54.0	40.1	60.4	23.1	53.6	59.3	41.9	46.1	85.1	84.4
October	44.9	40.6	54.1	39.6	60.8	23.1	54.4	58.2	41.7	45.8	84.6	83.6
November	43.4	39.4	52.5	37.7	59.5	22.8	54.1	56.3	40.8	43.8	81.6	80.9
December	41.9	37.7	50.9	34.6	59.0	21.8	53.5	53.7	40.0	42.1	78.6	77.1
1975												
January	41.3	36.9	49.7	33.2	58.0	21.4	53.8	53.5	39.4	41.8	77.4	75.5
February	40.4	35.9	49.0	32.2	57.6	20.6	51.1	51.9	38.6	40.8	75.5	73.2
March	39.9	35.4	49.2	32.6	57.5	20.3	51.6	49.9	38.0	40.2	74.6	72.1
April	40.0	35.3	50.2	33.9	58.4	20.1	51.3	49.4	38.2	39.9	74.5	71.9
May	39.9	35.3	50.5	34.7	58.2	19.9	53.7	49.5	38.0	39.7	74.2	71.7
June	40.2	35.7	51.2	35.1	59.2	19.7	54.5	49.2	38.1	40.0	74.6	72.2
July	40.6	36.2	52.5	36.9	60.1	19.8	53.9	50.0	38.5	40.2	75.3	73.2
August	40.9	36.5	52.8	37.4	60.2	19.7	53.5	50.5	38.8	40.8	75.8	73.7
September	41.5	37.1	53.5	38.1	60.9	20.0	55.1	51.0	38.9	41.3	76.6	74.7
October	41.6	37.3	53.6	38.0	61.1	20.0	55.0	51.3	39.1	41.5	76.7	74.9
November	41.7	37.4	53.8	38.0	61.4	20.0	52.8	51.5	39.2	41.7	76.8	75.0
December	42.3	37.9	54.2	38.7	61.7	20.3	54.4	51.6	39.6	42.3	77.6	75.8
1976												
January	42.9	38.4	55.0	39.4	62.5	20.6	54.3	52.9	40.0	43.0	78.6	76.7
February	43.3	38.9	55.2	39.8	62.4	20.7	54.3	53.7	40.2	43.6	79.1	77.6
March	43.3	39.0	55.0	39.8	62.3	20.8	54.3	52.9	40.3	43.8	79.0	77.6
April	43.6	39.3	55.2	39.8	62.5	21.0	53.1	53.6	40.5	44.1	79.4	78.0
May	43.8	39.5	55.7	39.8	63.2	21.2	52.7	54.2	40.7	44.2	79.5	78.2
June	43.8	39.5	55.4	39.6	63.0	21.2	52.0	54.6	40.4	44.3	79.4	78.0
July	44.0	39.8	55.8	39.8	63.4	21.4	50.6	55.8	41.1	44.4	79.7	78.4
August	44.3	40.0	55.9	40.4	63.2	21.8	50.7	55.2	41.2	44.9	80.0	78.7
September	44.5	40.1	55.9	40.2	63.4	21.7	50.3	55.6	42.1	45.0	80.1	78.8
October	44.5	40.1	56.4	40.7	63.8	21.8	50.2	55.6	42.3	44.7	80.0	78.6
November	45.2	40.6	57.3	42.0	64.5	22.5	49.9	55.9	42.5	45.3	80.9	79.4
December	45.6	41.1	57.9	43.0	64.8	22.9	48.9	56.2	42.9	45.8	81.6	80.0
1977												
January	45.4	40.9	57.8	42.8	64.7	22.9	48.3	55.3	42.8	45.4	80.9	79.6
February	46.0	41.7	58.5	43.3	65.5	23.4	48.2	56.5	43.3	46.0	81.9	80.7
March	46.6	42.3	58.5	44.5	64.8	23.8	47.2	57.7	43.6	46.9	82.8	81.7
April	47.0	42.7	58.9	44.9	65.2	24.2	47.5	59.1	44.1	47.3	83.4	82.4
May	47.4	43.1	59.0	45.1	65.1	24.7	47.4	60.0	44.5	47.7	83.8	82.9
June	47.8	43.5	59.4	46.0	65.2	25.2	47.3	60.5	44.9	47.9	84.2	83.3
July	47.9	43.5	59.6	46.0	65.4	25.4	47.2	60.5	45.1	47.9	84.1	83.1
August	47.9	43.7	59.6	46.0	65.5	25.4	46.9	61.0	45.3	47.8	83.9	83.3
September	48.1	43.8	59.8	46.2	65.6	25.6	47.0	60.7	45.5	48.2	84.1	83.2
October	48.2	43.9	60.3	46.2	66.4	25.5	42.8	60.8	45.5	48.4	84.1	83.1
November	48.3	43.9	60.2	46.2	66.4	25.5	42.4	61.0	45.5	48.4	83.9	83.0
December	48.3	44.4	60.8	46.4	67.1	25.8	45.2	61.7	45.9	48.0	83.8	83.6

Table 2-4A. Industrial Production and Capacity Utilization: Historical Data, 1947–2012—*Continued*

(Seasonally adjusted.)

Year and month	Production indexes, 2007 = 100										Capacity utilization (output as percentage of capacity)	
	Total industry	Manufac-turing (SIC)	Market groups								Total industry	Manufac-turing (SIC)
			Consumer goods			Business equipment	Defense and space equipment	Construction supplies	Business supplies	Materials		
			Total	Durable	Nondurable							
1978												
January	47.7	43.8	59.3	44.0	66.3	25.3	45.8	60.5	45.8	47.5	82.4	82.1
February	47.9	43.9	60.3	45.1	67.1	25.9	43.4	60.3	45.9	47.4	82.5	82.2
March	48.8	44.7	61.4	46.5	68.1	26.7	47.3	61.5	46.6	48.1	83.9	83.4
April	49.8	45.4	61.8	47.4	68.2	27.3	47.1	62.8	46.7	49.6	85.3	84.4
May	50.0	45.5	61.4	46.6	68.0	27.3	47.3	62.8	46.9	50.1	85.4	84.4
June	50.3	45.9	61.8	46.9	68.4	27.8	47.9	63.3	47.4	50.3	85.7	84.8
July	50.3	45.9	61.5	46.9	67.8	28.0	47.8	63.2	47.3	50.3	85.4	84.5
August	50.5	46.1	61.4	46.7	67.8	28.6	48.3	63.3	47.3	50.4	85.5	84.7
September	50.7	46.3	61.5	46.4	68.2	28.9	48.4	63.6	47.5	50.5	85.6	84.8
October	51.1	46.7	61.4	46.6	68.0	29.5	47.9	64.2	47.7	51.1	86.0	85.2
November	51.4	47.1	61.6	46.7	68.2	30.0	47.6	64.6	47.9	51.5	86.4	85.7
December	51.7	47.5	61.8	46.9	68.4	30.3	48.3	65.7	48.3	51.7	86.7	86.1
1979												
January	51.4	47.1	61.6	47.2	67.9	30.6	48.6	64.0	48.3	51.0	85.9	85.1
February	51.7	47.3	61.2	46.7	67.7	31.0	49.6	64.5	48.8	51.4	86.1	85.2
March	51.8	47.5	61.5	46.6	68.1	31.2	49.2	65.3	49.0	51.5	86.2	85.4
April	51.3	46.7	60.4	44.3	67.8	30.6	48.0	64.2	48.7	51.2	85.0	83.8
May	51.7	47.3	60.7	45.6	67.6	31.4	48.8	64.6	48.9	51.5	85.5	84.6
June	51.7	47.4	60.5	45.0	67.5	31.6	49.2	64.9	48.6	51.5	85.3	84.5
July	51.6	47.4	60.0	44.5	67.1	31.9	50.1	64.9	48.7	51.3	85.0	84.4
August	51.3	46.8	59.3	42.6	67.3	31.5	50.8	64.2	48.9	51.1	84.2	83.1
September	51.3	47.0	59.7	44.1	66.9	32.4	51.2	64.4	48.3	50.8	84.1	83.1
October	51.6	47.1	59.8	43.8	67.3	31.9	52.8	64.8	48.8	51.3	84.4	83.2
November	51.5	47.0	59.7	43.1	67.5	31.9	54.0	64.7	49.0	51.1	84.2	82.8
December	51.6	47.1	59.7	42.9	67.7	32.1	55.1	64.9	49.0	51.1	84.0	82.8
1980												
January	51.8	47.3	59.4	42.1	67.7	32.7	55.8	64.7	48.6	51.4	84.2	82.9
February	51.8	47.3	59.7	41.9	68.3	32.8	58.0	63.7	48.7	51.3	84.1	82.7
March	51.7	46.9	59.3	41.1	68.1	32.6	58.6	63.0	48.6	51.3	83.7	81.9
April	50.6	46.0	58.3	39.4	67.7	32.3	59.2	60.0	47.8	50.0	81.8	80.0
May	49.4	44.6	57.1	36.9	67.3	31.7	59.5	57.6	46.8	48.6	79.7	77.4
June	48.8	43.9	56.8	36.3	67.3	31.4	60.2	56.4	46.3	47.7	78.5	76.1
July	48.5	43.5	56.9	36.2	67.4	31.4	60.7	56.1	46.5	47.0	77.9	75.2
August	48.6	43.8	57.1	36.5	67.5	31.4	60.9	56.8	46.7	47.1	77.9	75.5
September	49.4	44.5	57.6	38.2	67.2	31.9	61.0	58.2	47.3	48.1	79.0	76.5
October	50.0	45.3	58.0	38.9	67.5	32.6	61.9	59.5	47.4	48.7	79.8	77.6
November	50.9	46.2	58.3	39.9	67.3	33.1	62.7	60.7	48.0	49.9	81.0	78.9
December	51.2	46.3	58.3	39.3	67.6	33.2	62.9	60.7	48.5	50.3	81.3	78.9
1981												
January	50.9	46.2	58.3	39.2	67.8	33.3	62.6	60.5	48.6	49.8	80.6	78.4
February	50.7	45.9	58.2	39.0	67.7	32.9	62.5	60.0	48.1	49.6	80.1	77.7
March	50.9	46.0	58.2	39.6	67.3	33.2	62.6	60.2	48.1	49.9	80.3	77.8
April	50.7	46.3	58.3	40.1	67.2	33.6	62.6	60.2	48.4	49.2	79.7	77.9
May	51.0	46.5	58.9	40.7	67.8	33.6	63.1	60.2	49.0	49.5	80.0	78.1
June	51.3	46.3	58.5	40.3	67.4	33.4	63.5	59.2	49.2	50.2	80.2	77.5
July	51.6	46.4	58.9	40.5	67.9	33.4	64.3	59.3	49.4	50.5	80.5	77.4
August	51.6	46.4	58.9	40.3	68.0	33.5	65.2	59.2	49.1	50.5	80.3	77.3
September	51.2	46.2	58.4	39.3	67.7	33.4	66.4	58.7	49.2	50.1	79.6	76.7
October	50.9	45.7	58.7	39.2	68.5	33.3	67.9	57.0	48.8	49.4	78.8	75.8
November	50.3	45.2	58.7	38.5	68.8	32.8	69.6	56.1	48.6	48.5	77.8	74.7
December	49.8	44.4	58.1	36.9	68.9	32.3	71.4	55.1	48.5	47.9	76.7	73.3
1982												
January	48.8	43.4	57.1	35.9	68.0	31.1	70.7	53.3	47.8	47.1	75.1	71.4
February	49.7	44.6	58.6	37.2	69.5	32.1	74.6	55.1	48.8	47.6	76.4	73.2
March	49.4	44.2	58.2	37.0	69.0	31.7	75.8	53.9	48.6	47.3	75.7	72.4
April	48.9	43.9	58.2	37.8	68.6	31.3	76.7	53.6	48.4	46.7	74.9	71.8
May	48.6	43.8	58.3	37.8	68.6	31.1	78.2	53.9	48.1	46.2	74.3	71.6
June	48.5	43.8	58.6	38.0	69.0	30.5	78.5	53.4	48.1	46.0	73.9	71.3
July	48.3	43.7	58.8	38.2	69.1	30.5	79.6	53.3	48.1	45.7	73.5	71.2
August	47.9	43.4	58.6	37.7	69.2	29.8	79.5	53.3	48.1	45.2	72.8	70.5
September	47.8	43.3	58.6	37.2	69.5	29.6	80.5	53.5	48.2	45.0	72.5	70.2
October	47.4	42.8	58.7	36.7	69.9	29.0	80.0	52.7	48.0	44.4	71.8	69.3
November	47.2	42.5	58.5	36.7	69.7	28.8	80.3	52.4	48.0	44.2	71.5	68.8
December	46.8	42.4	57.8	36.6	68.5	29.1	79.7	52.0	47.8	43.9	70.9	68.5
1983												
January	47.7	43.4	59.0	38.2	69.5	29.2	79.3	53.9	48.4	44.9	72.2	70.1
February	47.4	43.3	58.3	38.1	68.4	29.1	77.9	53.6	48.3	44.7	71.7	70.0
March	47.8	43.8	58.5	38.6	68.4	29.4	78.0	54.3	49.1	45.1	72.3	70.7
April	48.4	44.3	59.7	39.5	69.8	29.4	77.3	55.0	49.6	45.7	73.2	71.4
May	48.7	44.8	59.9	40.3	69.7	29.8	77.1	56.0	49.7	46.0	73.7	72.3
June	49.0	45.1	60.1	41.0	69.5	30.0	76.5	57.0	49.9	46.3	74.0	72.8
July	49.8	45.8	60.9	41.9	70.2	30.6	77.4	58.2	50.6	47.1	75.1	73.8
August	50.3	46.1	61.5	42.7	70.6	30.8	77.9	58.4	51.1	47.7	75.9	74.3
September	51.1	47.0	62.3	43.5	71.4	31.7	78.8	59.2	52.0	48.4	77.0	75.7
October	51.5	47.5	61.9	44.0	70.5	32.1	79.7	60.1	52.2	49.1	77.6	76.5
November	51.6	47.7	61.9	44.0	70.5	32.3	80.1	59.9	52.4	49.3	77.8	76.7
December	51.9	47.8	62.0	45.0	70.0	32.7	80.9	60.1	52.5	49.5	78.1	76.8

Table 2-4A. Industrial Production and Capacity Utilization: Historical Data, 1947–2012—*Continued*

(Seasonally adjusted.)

Year and month	Production indexes, 2007 = 100										Capacity utilization (output as percentage of capacity)	
	Total industry	Manufac-turing (SIC)	Market groups								Total industry	Manufac-turing (SIC)
			Consumer goods			Business equipment	Defense and space equipment	Construction supplies	Business supplies	Materials		
			Total	Durable	Nondurable							
1984												
January	52.9	48.7	63.3	46.1	71.4	33.4	83.2	60.5	53.5	50.5	79.6	78.1
February	53.2	49.3	63.2	46.2	71.1	33.7	84.9	61.9	53.6	50.8	79.9	78.9
March	53.5	49.5	63.4	46.3	71.4	34.0	85.5	61.5	54.1	51.0	80.1	79.1
April	53.8	49.7	63.6	46.3	71.7	34.3	87.6	61.9	54.1	51.4	80.5	79.4
May	54.1	49.9	63.3	45.8	71.6	34.5	88.5	62.1	54.8	51.8	80.8	79.4
June	54.2	50.1	63.3	45.9	71.4	35.0	89.6	62.5	55.1	51.9	80.9	79.6
July	54.4	50.3	63.3	46.4	71.1	35.4	88.7	62.3	55.3	52.1	81.0	79.8
August	54.5	50.4	62.9	46.7	70.4	35.8	91.7	62.5	55.4	52.0	80.9	79.7
September	54.4	50.3	62.8	46.1	70.6	36.0	93.8	62.8	55.3	51.8	80.6	79.4
October	54.3	50.5	63.3	45.7	71.6	36.2	94.5	62.5	55.6	51.3	80.3	79.4
November	54.5	50.7	63.5	46.4	71.5	36.5	93.8	62.4	55.9	51.5	80.4	79.5
December	54.6	50.9	63.8	46.9	71.7	36.8	95.6	63.1	55.5	51.3	80.3	79.5
1985												
January	54.4	50.7	63.4	46.4	71.3	36.6	96.0	61.9	55.6	51.4	79.9	79.0
February	54.7	50.5	63.9	46.0	72.3	36.4	96.9	62.1	56.1	51.6	80.0	78.5
March	54.7	50.9	63.8	46.5	71.9	36.7	98.4	63.7	56.0	51.5	79.9	78.9
April	54.6	50.7	63.4	45.8	71.7	36.4	98.7	63.7	56.3	51.5	79.5	78.3
May	54.7	50.8	63.5	45.8	71.8	36.5	99.2	63.9	56.5	51.5	79.4	78.2
June	54.7	50.9	63.7	45.7	72.3	36.6	100.6	64.4	56.1	51.4	79.3	78.2
July	54.3	50.6	63.4	45.8	71.8	36.3	99.7	64.0	55.7	51.0	78.6	77.5
August	54.6	50.9	63.8	46.3	72.0	36.4	101.4	64.2	56.3	51.1	78.8	77.8
September	54.8	50.9	64.2	46.3	72.6	36.3	102.0	64.2	56.7	51.4	78.9	77.7
October	54.6	50.8	64.1	46.0	72.6	36.2	103.1	64.3	56.2	51.1	78.5	77.4
November	54.8	51.1	64.4	47.1	72.5	36.6	104.4	64.3	56.4	51.1	78.6	77.8
December	55.3	51.3	65.1	47.3	73.5	36.5	105.5	64.0	57.2	51.8	79.3	78.0
1986												
January	55.6	51.9	65.8	48.5	73.9	36.5	106.1	65.5	57.6	51.9	79.6	78.8
February	55.2	51.6	65.2	48.1	73.2	36.1	104.6	64.8	57.1	51.7	79.0	78.2
March	54.9	51.4	65.0	48.2	72.9	36.1	105.6	65.0	56.9	51.2	78.4	78.0
April	54.9	51.6	65.4	48.1	73.5	35.9	105.8	65.6	57.4	51.1	78.4	78.2
May	55.0	51.7	65.8	48.2	74.0	35.8	106.2	66.0	57.8	51.0	78.4	78.3
June	54.8	51.5	65.9	48.8	73.8	35.4	106.6	65.3	58.3	50.8	78.1	77.9
July	55.2	51.9	66.3	49.4	74.2	35.6	107.6	65.8	58.3	51.2	78.5	78.3
August	55.0	52.0	66.2	49.6	73.9	35.7	107.5	66.4	58.3	50.9	78.3	78.4
September	55.1	52.1	66.3	50.0	73.8	35.7	107.2	66.4	58.4	51.0	78.3	78.4
October	55.4	52.3	66.6	50.0	74.2	35.7	107.5	66.4	58.8	51.3	78.6	78.6
November	55.6	52.5	67.0	50.7	74.6	35.7	108.1	66.6	58.9	51.6	78.8	78.8
December	56.1	53.0	67.6	51.6	75.0	36.1	108.2	67.0	59.7	52.0	79.4	79.4
1987												
January	56.0	52.8	67.0	51.3	74.1	36.2	108.6	67.7	59.2	51.9	79.6	78.9
February	56.7	53.6	67.8	52.2	74.9	37.0	109.2	69.0	59.7	52.5	79.0	79.9
March	56.8	53.6	68.0	51.9	75.4	36.9	108.9	68.6	60.1	52.6	78.4	79.8
April	57.1	53.9	67.9	51.6	75.4	37.2	109.0	69.0	60.7	53.1	78.4	80.0
May	57.5	54.3	68.5	51.9	76.1	37.5	108.7	69.5	61.4	53.4	78.4	80.4
June	57.8	54.5	68.6	51.4	76.6	37.9	108.3	69.8	61.7	53.7	78.1	80.5
July	58.2	54.9	69.0	51.3	77.3	38.0	108.0	70.0	62.1	54.1	78.5	80.9
August	58.6	55.2	69.5	51.8	77.7	38.5	109.0	70.5	62.3	54.5	78.3	81.1
September	58.7	55.5	69.1	52.2	76.9	39.1	109.3	70.8	62.5	54.7	78.3	81.4
October	59.6	56.4	70.4	53.9	77.9	40.0	109.0	71.9	63.0	55.5	78.6	82.6
November	60.0	56.8	70.4	53.9	78.0	40.4	109.5	71.9	63.0	56.0	78.8	82.9
December	60.2	57.1	70.5	53.5	78.4	40.8	110.4	72.5	63.1	56.3	79.4	83.3
1988												
January	60.3	57.0	70.9	53.2	79.0	40.9	112.7	71.3	63.4	56.1	83.4	83.1
February	60.5	57.1	71.2	53.2	79.5	41.1	111.1	71.9	63.8	56.3	83.7	83.2
March	60.6	57.3	71.2	53.7	79.2	41.5	110.3	72.2	63.8	56.5	83.8	83.4
April	61.0	57.8	71.6	54.9	79.2	42.0	109.3	71.9	63.8	56.9	84.2	84.0
May	60.9	57.7	71.3	54.9	78.8	42.2	109.2	72.1	63.3	56.9	84.1	83.9
June	61.1	57.8	71.3	55.2	78.7	42.6	108.4	71.6	63.5	57.1	84.3	84.0
July	61.1	57.8	71.3	53.9	79.3	42.3	109.7	71.6	63.8	57.3	84.4	84.0
August	61.4	57.8	71.9	54.4	79.9	42.4	109.4	71.1	64.4	57.5	84.7	84.0
September	61.2	58.0	71.4	55.4	78.6	42.7	109.8	71.4	63.9	57.2	84.4	84.2
October	61.5	58.3	71.9	55.9	79.2	43.1	109.9	71.6	64.2	57.4	84.7	84.6
November	61.6	58.5	72.0	56.5	78.9	43.2	109.7	71.9	64.1	57.6	84.8	84.8
December	61.9	58.7	72.3	57.2	79.1	43.3	110.2	72.1	64.4	57.9	85.1	85.0
1989												
January	62.0	59.2	72.3	58.4	78.4	43.7	110.3	73.3	64.4	58.0	85.2	85.6
February	61.8	58.6	72.4	57.8	78.8	43.6	110.2	71.5	64.6	57.6	84.7	84.6
March	62.0	58.6	72.5	56.9	79.6	43.4	109.4	71.7	65.3	57.8	84.8	84.4
April	62.0	58.7	72.4	57.4	79.1	44.0	111.0	71.7	64.8	57.7	84.7	84.4
May	61.6	58.2	71.6	56.1	78.6	43.4	111.5	71.1	64.5	57.5	84.0	83.5
June	61.6	58.3	71.7	55.4	79.1	44.0	111.2	71.2	64.8	57.3	83.9	83.5
July	61.0	57.7	70.2	53.7	77.7	43.5	111.7	71.2	64.2	57.0	82.9	82.4
August	61.5	58.1	71.3	55.6	78.4	44.1	112.2	71.2	64.5	57.3	83.4	82.8
September	61.4	58.0	71.0	55.6	78.0	44.0	111.6	71.1	64.7	57.1	83.0	82.5
October	61.3	57.9	71.3	54.6	78.9	43.3	107.5	71.3	64.8	57.3	82.8	82.1
November	61.5	58.0	71.5	55.0	79.1	43.6	105.9	71.3	65.1	57.4	82.8	82.1
December	61.9	58.1	72.8	55.6	80.7	44.2	108.3	70.5	65.5	57.3	83.1	81.9

Table 2-4A. Industrial Production and Capacity Utilization: Historical Data, 1947–2012—*Continued*

(Seasonally adjusted.)

Year and month	Production indexes, 2007 = 100										Capacity utilization (output as percentage of capacity)	
	Total industry	Manufac-turing (SIC)	Market groups								Total industry	Manufac-turing (SIC)
			Consumer goods			Business equipment	Defense and space equipment	Construction supplies	Business supplies	Materials		
			Total	Durable	Nondurable							
1990												
January	61.5	57.9	71.1	52.5	79.8	43.9	108.8	72.0	66.0	57.1	82.4	81.5
February	62.1	58.8	72.0	55.8	79.4	44.6	108.5	72.4	65.8	57.7	83.0	82.5
March	62.4	59.1	72.5	56.8	79.6	45.3	108.0	72.2	66.2	57.9	83.3	82.7
April	62.3	58.9	72.3	55.6	79.9	45.2	107.2	71.5	66.2	57.9	83.0	82.3
May	62.4	59.0	72.2	56.1	79.5	45.6	106.3	71.1	66.6	58.0	83.0	82.3
June	62.6	59.2	73.0	56.9	80.3	45.7	106.0	71.3	66.4	58.1	83.1	82.3
July	62.6	59.1	72.4	55.3	80.2	45.9	106.7	70.7	66.7	58.1	82.8	82.0
August	62.7	59.2	72.6	55.2	80.5	46.0	105.0	70.7	66.6	58.4	82.9	82.1
September	62.9	59.2	73.3	55.5	81.4	46.1	104.7	70.4	66.7	58.4	82.9	81.9
October	62.4	58.8	72.2	53.7	80.7	45.8	105.0	69.5	66.6	58.1	82.2	81.1
November	61.6	58.1	71.4	50.9	80.9	44.7	103.3	69.6	66.2	57.4	81.1	80.0
December	61.2	57.6	70.9	50.1	80.6	44.4	104.4	69.1	65.8	56.9	80.4	79.3
1991												
January	60.9	57.2	71.2	50.1	81.1	44.1	103.2	66.5	65.6	56.5	79.9	78.5
February	60.5	56.9	70.6	49.0	80.7	43.9	102.2	66.3	65.1	56.3	79.3	77.9
March	60.2	56.5	70.6	49.3	80.6	43.9	101.6	65.5	64.3	55.8	78.8	77.3
April	60.3	56.6	70.6	50.3	80.1	43.8	98.8	66.0	64.7	56.1	78.8	77.4
May	60.9	57.0	71.8	51.2	81.5	44.1	96.9	66.1	65.3	56.5	79.5	77.8
June	61.5	57.7	72.9	52.6	82.3	44.8	97.4	67.3	65.7	56.9	80.2	78.6
July	61.5	57.8	72.5	53.4	81.3	44.7	96.5	67.0	65.2	57.3	80.1	78.7
August	61.6	58.0	72.5	52.6	81.7	44.7	97.2	67.8	65.6	57.4	80.1	78.8
September	62.1	58.6	73.6	54.8	82.2	45.3	96.9	68.0	66.0	57.7	80.7	79.5
October	62.0	58.4	73.3	54.5	82.0	44.9	97.1	67.3	65.8	57.8	80.5	79.3
November	61.9	58.3	73.4	54.6	82.1	44.9	96.4	67.9	65.9	57.6	80.3	79.0
December	61.7	58.2	72.5	54.2	80.9	45.0	95.6	67.9	65.8	57.6	79.9	78.8
1992												
January	61.3	57.9	71.7	51.8	81.0	44.0	94.3	68.0	65.7	57.5	79.3	78.2
February	61.8	58.4	72.5	53.9	81.0	45.1	93.7	68.5	65.7	57.8	79.8	78.8
March	62.3	59.0	73.2	55.1	81.5	45.4	93.3	68.9	66.2	58.3	80.3	79.4
April	62.7	59.3	73.8	56.1	82.0	45.9	91.5	69.5	66.7	58.6	80.7	79.6
May	63.0	59.6	74.3	57.8	81.8	46.4	91.2	70.2	66.8	58.7	80.8	79.9
June	63.0	59.8	73.8	57.0	81.5	46.5	91.0	69.8	66.7	58.9	80.6	79.9
July	63.5	60.3	74.8	58.5	82.2	46.9	90.1	70.2	67.2	59.4	81.2	80.4
August	63.2	60.1	74.9	58.0	82.5	46.7	89.9	70.4	67.1	58.7	80.6	79.8
September	63.3	60.1	74.5	57.8	82.0	46.9	89.7	70.3	67.3	59.1	80.6	79.7
October	63.8	60.5	75.5	59.1	83.0	47.2	89.5	70.5	67.6	59.4	81.0	80.0
November	64.1	60.7	75.7	59.6	83.0	47.5	89.5	70.3	67.8	59.8	81.2	80.1
December	64.1	60.6	75.8	60.3	82.8	47.7	89.4	70.5	68.1	59.6	81.0	79.8
1993												
January	64.4	61.3	76.1	61.1	82.9	48.1	88.7	70.8	68.2	60.0	81.3	80.4
February	64.6	61.4	76.2	60.9	83.1	48.0	88.2	71.9	68.5	60.4	81.5	80.4
March	64.6	61.2	76.3	61.2	83.0	48.1	87.1	71.3	69.0	60.2	81.3	80.1
April	64.8	61.6	76.4	61.6	83.0	48.4	87.2	71.6	69.0	60.5	81.4	80.4
May	64.6	61.5	75.8	61.6	82.1	48.5	86.2	72.5	68.7	60.3	81.0	80.2
June	64.7	61.4	75.9	61.0	82.6	48.1	85.6	72.4	68.8	60.6	81.1	80.0
July	64.9	61.6	76.6	60.9	83.7	48.1	86.5	72.8	68.9	60.6	81.2	80.1
August	64.9	61.5	76.5	60.3	83.9	47.8	84.9	73.0	69.1	60.7	81.1	79.8
September	65.2	61.9	76.7	61.5	83.6	48.5	85.3	73.4	69.2	60.9	81.4	80.2
October	65.7	62.4	77.1	63.0	83.4	49.4	84.5	74.1	69.4	61.4	81.8	80.8
November	65.9	62.7	77.2	63.6	83.3	49.7	84.4	74.7	69.4	61.8	82.0	81.0
December	66.3	63.0	77.3	63.8	83.4	50.0	83.6	75.6	69.9	62.2	82.3	81.2
1994												
January	66.5	63.1	77.9	64.8	83.8	50.3	82.8	75.3	70.4	62.3	82.4	81.2
February	66.6	63.2	78.1	64.7	84.0	49.9	81.4	74.7	70.4	62.5	82.3	81.1
March	67.3	64.0	78.7	65.3	84.7	50.4	82.3	76.1	70.9	63.2	82.9	82.0
April	67.6	64.6	78.8	66.1	84.5	50.8	82.5	77.3	71.2	63.7	83.2	82.4
May	68.0	65.0	79.4	66.4	85.1	50.9	81.4	77.9	71.3	64.1	83.4	82.7
June	68.4	65.2	80.0	66.9	85.8	51.2	80.3	78.0	72.0	64.6	83.7	82.7
July	68.6	65.4	79.6	67.1	85.2	51.8	79.8	78.7	71.7	64.9	83.6	82.7
August	68.9	66.0	80.5	68.2	85.9	51.9	78.7	78.7	71.8	65.3	83.8	83.1
September	69.2	66.2	80.1	68.5	85.2	52.4	79.5	79.4	72.2	65.6	83.7	83.2
October	69.8	66.9	80.9	69.4	86.0	53.3	79.3	79.8	72.7	66.1	84.2	83.7
November	70.2	67.4	80.9	69.3	86.1	53.9	80.2	79.9	73.0	66.7	84.4	84.0
December	70.9	68.2	81.5	69.9	86.6	54.4	80.0	80.7	73.5	67.7	85.0	84.6
1995												
January	71.1	68.3	81.4	70.3	86.3	54.7	80.3	80.8	73.7	67.8	84.9	84.5
February	71.0	68.2	81.7	70.0	86.8	54.7	78.9	79.8	73.7	67.7	84.5	84.0
March	71.2	68.4	81.6	69.9	86.8	55.1	79.1	79.7	74.0	67.8	84.4	83.8
April	71.1	68.3	81.3	69.8	86.4	55.2	78.5	79.2	73.9	68.0	84.0	83.4
May	71.3	68.3	81.5	69.2	87.0	55.7	78.5	78.7	74.2	68.1	83.9	83.1
June	71.6	68.7	81.9	69.6	87.4	56.4	79.0	78.9	74.6	68.1	83.9	83.2
July	71.3	68.3	81.5	68.2	87.4	56.3	78.2	78.7	74.6	67.8	83.3	82.3
August	72.2	69.0	82.8	70.4	88.3	57.4	78.0	79.4	75.4	68.6	84.1	82.9
September	72.5	69.6	82.9	71.1	88.0	57.9	77.6	80.7	75.4	68.9	84.1	83.2
October	72.4	69.6	82.2	70.3	87.4	57.7	76.5	80.6	75.6	69.0	83.6	82.8
November	72.6	69.6	82.4	70.3	87.8	57.9	74.8	80.6	75.9	69.2	83.5	82.4
December	72.8	69.9	82.7	70.8	87.9	58.4	75.0	81.1	75.9	69.5	83.4	82.3

Table 2-4A. Industrial Production and Capacity Utilization: Historical Data, 1947–2012—*Continued*

(Seasonally adjusted.)

Year and month	Production indexes, 2007 = 100										Capacity utilization (output as percentage of capacity)	
	Total industry	Manufacturing (SIC)	Market groups								Total industry	Manufacturing (SIC)
			Consumer goods			Business equipment	Defense and space equipment	Construction supplies	Business supplies	Materials		
			Total	Durable	Nondurable							
1996												
January	72.4	69.3	81.7	68.9	87.4	57.6	74.1	79.8	75.6	69.4	82.5	81.3
February	73.5	70.4	83.1	70.9	88.5	59.2	76.2	80.8	76.5	70.3	83.5	82.2
March	73.4	70.3	82.6	68.6	88.8	59.0	76.4	81.7	76.5	70.3	83.0	81.6
April	74.0	71.0	83.3	71.8	88.4	60.4	76.2	82.0	76.4	70.9	83.3	82.0
May	74.5	71.5	83.4	72.1	88.4	61.2	76.3	82.9	77.2	71.4	83.5	82.2
June	75.2	72.3	84.1	73.6	88.7	62.2	75.8	84.3	77.4	72.0	83.9	82.6
July	75.1	72.5	83.4	74.0	87.5	62.9	76.2	83.7	77.4	72.0	83.4	82.4
August	75.6	73.0	83.3	73.3	87.7	63.5	76.1	84.6	78.2	72.7	83.6	82.5
September	76.0	73.4	84.0	73.4	88.6	63.9	76.1	84.9	78.6	73.0	83.6	82.6
October	76.0	73.4	83.6	72.2	88.6	63.8	75.7	85.0	78.8	73.2	83.2	82.1
November	76.6	74.0	84.5	73.1	89.6	64.7	75.1	85.6	79.4	73.6	83.5	82.3
December	77.1	74.6	84.8	74.3	89.4	66.0	75.2	85.2	79.8	74.1	83.6	82.5
1997												
January	77.2	74.7	84.5	73.7	89.2	66.2	74.1	84.4	80.4	74.3	83.3	82.1
February	78.1	75.7	85.0	75.0	89.3	67.3	74.6	86.0	81.2	75.4	83.9	82.8
March	78.7	76.6	85.6	76.0	89.8	68.5	74.4	87.0	81.5	75.9	84.1	83.3
April	78.8	76.4	84.7	74.0	89.5	68.8	74.4	86.6	81.8	76.3	83.7	82.6
May	79.3	77.1	85.3	74.8	89.9	69.7	74.3	87.2	82.3	76.7	83.9	82.8
June	79.7	77.6	85.4	76.3	89.3	70.7	74.2	87.0	82.6	77.1	83.8	82.8
July	80.1	78.0	85.7	74.9	90.4	70.8	74.7	87.2	83.3	77.8	83.8	82.7
August	81.2	79.3	87.0	78.3	90.7	72.9	74.8	87.7	83.5	78.7	84.4	83.4
September	81.9	79.9	87.7	79.3	91.3	73.3	74.8	88.2	84.5	79.5	84.6	83.6
October	82.5	80.4	88.9	79.6	92.9	74.2	75.0	88.7	85.4	79.5	84.6	83.5
November	83.2	81.3	89.2	81.6	92.4	75.7	74.6	89.0	85.7	80.5	84.8	83.8
December	83.5	81.7	88.7	81.4	91.8	76.1	75.6	90.1	85.9	81.1	84.6	83.5
1998												
January	83.9	82.3	89.1	81.7	92.1	77.1	76.2	90.7	85.9	81.4	84.4	83.6
February	84.0	82.4	88.9	81.6	92.0	77.3	76.6	91.1	86.1	81.4	84.0	83.0
March	84.1	82.3	89.1	81.8	92.2	77.6	76.2	90.5	86.6	81.3	83.5	82.3
April	84.4	82.7	89.6	82.1	92.8	77.8	76.1	90.9	86.9	81.6	83.3	82.1
May	84.9	83.2	90.0	82.7	93.1	78.3	77.0	92.0	87.7	82.2	83.3	82.0
June	84.4	82.6	89.0	78.7	93.4	78.3	77.3	91.8	87.8	81.7	82.3	80.8
July	84.1	82.2	88.1	75.3	93.6	77.7	78.4	92.1	88.3	81.4	81.5	80.0
August	85.9	84.3	90.8	84.8	93.4	80.4	78.7	92.5	88.9	82.8	82.8	81.5
September	85.6	84.0	89.9	84.3	92.3	80.3	78.2	92.2	88.8	82.8	82.1	80.7
October	86.3	84.8	90.4	86.0	92.2	81.3	79.9	93.3	89.1	83.6	82.3	81.1
November	86.2	84.9	89.8	85.8	91.5	81.2	79.7	93.4	89.4	83.7	81.9	80.7
December	86.5	85.4	89.8	86.5	91.1	81.4	79.1	94.5	89.3	84.3	81.8	80.7
1999												
January	86.9	85.6	90.7	86.5	92.5	81.6	78.9	94.0	90.0	84.5	81.8	80.6
February	87.3	86.2	91.0	87.2	92.6	82.2	79.6	94.0	90.1	85.0	81.8	80.8
March	87.5	86.2	90.9	87.0	92.5	82.0	79.3	93.1	90.5	85.5	81.6	80.3
April	87.7	86.5	90.8	88.0	91.9	82.2	78.4	93.3	90.7	86.0	81.5	80.3
May	88.3	87.3	91.7	88.8	92.9	83.4	77.5	93.7	91.2	86.5	81.8	80.6
June	88.1	87.0	90.8	88.3	91.8	83.0	76.3	93.6	91.1	86.8	81.3	80.0
July	88.7	87.4	90.4	88.3	91.3	83.8	75.8	94.3	91.8	88.0	81.5	80.1
August	89.1	88.0	91.6	90.4	92.1	84.2	75.2	94.2	91.8	88.0	81.6	80.2
September	88.9	87.7	91.0	89.4	91.7	84.0	72.8	94.4	91.9	87.9	81.0	79.6
October	90.0	89.0	92.7	92.1	93.0	84.6	72.0	95.5	92.7	89.0	81.8	80.5
November	90.4	89.6	92.6	91.4	93.1	84.6	70.3	96.1	93.2	90.0	81.9	80.6
December	91.2	90.3	93.6	91.4	94.4	85.2	69.2	97.0	93.9	90.7	82.2	80.9
2000												
January	91.2	90.4	92.4	93.2	92.1	86.7	69.2	97.4	94.2	91.0	82.0	80.7
February	91.6	90.7	93.0	92.8	93.1	87.4	67.7	97.7	94.3	91.3	82.0	80.6
March	91.9	91.3	92.7	92.7	92.8	88.2	67.3	97.8	95.0	91.9	82.1	80.8
April	92.5	91.8	93.6	93.8	93.5	89.3	66.1	98.1	96.0	92.2	82.3	80.9
May	92.7	91.7	93.7	93.4	93.8	89.8	65.6	96.6	96.0	92.4	82.2	80.4
June	92.7	91.8	93.7	93.0	94.0	89.9	66.4	96.3	95.8	92.5	81.9	80.3
July	92.5	91.8	93.1	90.6	94.1	90.7	67.9	96.7	95.9	92.1	81.5	79.9
August	92.3	91.2	92.8	91.1	93.5	90.3	66.3	96.0	95.6	92.0	81.0	79.1
September	92.7	91.7	93.8	91.8	94.6	91.4	63.4	96.2	95.5	92.2	81.2	79.3
October	92.3	91.3	92.9	90.8	93.7	91.0	66.5	95.7	95.1	92.0	80.6	78.6
November	92.3	91.0	93.2	88.7	95.0	90.8	68.5	95.5	95.4	91.7	80.3	78.1
December	92.0	90.4	93.7	87.4	96.2	89.9	69.1	94.2	95.0	91.1	79.8	77.4
2001												
January	91.3	89.8	93.0	85.8	95.8	89.7	70.9	94.5	94.8	90.0	79.0	76.6
February	90.8	89.3	92.3	85.7	94.9	89.3	70.6	93.5	93.6	89.7	78.3	75.9
March	90.5	89.0	92.1	87.4	94.0	89.0	72.5	93.7	93.0	89.3	77.9	75.5
April	90.3	88.8	92.6	88.0	94.4	86.8	73.2	93.4	92.4	89.1	77.5	75.1
May	89.6	88.1	92.4	88.6	93.9	85.3	73.5	92.9	91.8	88.3	76.7	74.3
June	89.0	87.5	92.2	87.7	93.9	84.5	74.6	92.3	91.3	87.4	76.0	73.6
July	88.6	87.2	92.0	88.7	93.3	83.7	75.5	92.2	91.3	86.8	75.5	73.2
August	88.4	86.7	91.9	87.2	93.8	82.2	74.5	91.2	91.0	87.0	75.1	72.6
September	88.1	86.5	91.5	86.5	93.5	81.0	75.1	91.2	91.1	86.9	74.7	72.3
October	87.7	86.0	92.0	85.9	94.3	79.4	74.8	90.0	90.5	86.4	74.2	71.8
November	87.2	85.7	91.8	87.2	93.6	79.0	74.1	89.9	89.8	85.7	73.6	71.4
December	87.2	85.9	92.3	89.2	93.6	78.5	73.8	90.7	90.0	85.5	73.5	71.6

Table 2-4A. Industrial Production and Capacity Utilization: Historical Data, 1947–2012—*Continued*

(Seasonally adjusted.)

Year and month	Production indexes, 2007 = 100										Capacity utilization (output as percentage of capacity)	
			Market groups									
	Total industry	Manufac-turing (SIC)	Consumer goods			Business equipment	Defense and space equipment	Construction supplies	Business supplies	Materials	Total industry	Manufac-turing (SIC)
			Total	Durable	Nondurable							
2002												
January	87.8	86.4	93.3	89.2	94.9	78.4	73.4	90.5	89.8	86.3	73.9	71.9
February	87.7	86.3	92.7	89.8	93.9	78.1	72.9	90.8	89.8	86.7	73.7	71.8
March	88.4	86.9	93.5	90.4	94.7	78.4	72.9	92.1	90.7	87.3	74.2	72.2
April	88.7	87.1	93.4	91.7	94.1	77.9	72.9	92.0	91.4	88.2	74.4	72.3
May	89.2	87.6	93.7	92.1	94.3	78.5	73.0	92.6	91.9	88.7	74.8	72.8
June	90.1	88.7	94.8	93.3	95.5	79.0	73.9	93.2	92.5	89.6	75.5	73.6
July	89.8	88.2	94.6	94.0	94.9	78.2	73.9	91.9	92.5	89.4	75.2	73.2
August	89.9	88.6	94.2	93.8	94.4	79.1	74.3	92.4	92.4	89.7	75.3	73.5
September	89.9	88.6	94.4	93.8	94.6	78.8	75.7	93.1	92.7	89.6	75.3	73.6
October	89.6	88.3	94.2	92.8	94.7	78.5	76.2	92.7	93.1	89.0	75.1	73.3
November	90.1	88.7	94.9	95.2	94.8	78.6	75.7	92.7	92.8	89.7	75.5	73.6
December	89.7	88.3	94.0	93.5	94.3	78.0	78.7	92.0	92.8	89.5	75.2	73.3
2003												
January	90.4	88.8	94.6	94.8	94.5	78.3	78.6	92.3	94.3	90.1	75.8	73.7
February	90.7	89.0	95.7	93.8	96.5	78.3	79.7	91.7	94.1	90.2	76.1	73.9
March	90.5	89.1	95.7	94.0	96.4	78.5	79.7	91.5	94.1	89.7	76.0	74.0
April	89.8	88.3	94.8	93.1	95.5	77.6	79.1	90.3	92.9	89.2	75.4	73.3
May	89.8	88.3	94.7	93.2	95.2	77.5	79.7	91.5	93.2	89.1	75.4	73.4
June	89.8	88.6	94.7	94.4	94.8	77.6	79.9	91.8	92.5	89.2	75.5	73.7
July	90.1	88.7	95.6	96.2	95.3	77.2	79.4	91.5	93.2	89.3	75.8	73.8
August	90.0	88.4	95.0	94.9	95.0	77.9	79.4	92.0	93.0	89.3	75.7	73.5
September	90.5	89.1	95.9	98.2	95.1	78.6	79.6	91.8	93.0	89.7	76.2	74.1
October	90.5	89.0	95.0	96.4	94.4	78.5	79.4	92.3	93.3	90.2	76.2	74.1
November	91.2	89.9	95.7	97.5	95.0	80.1	78.7	93.4	93.8	90.7	76.8	74.8
December	91.1	89.7	95.8	97.6	95.1	79.6	76.7	93.2	93.6	90.8	76.7	74.7
2004												
January	91.4	89.7	96.3	98.8	95.4	79.9	74.4	93.4	94.0	90.9	77.0	74.8
February	91.9	90.3	96.8	98.7	96.0	81.0	76.1	93.3	94.6	91.3	77.4	75.3
March	91.4	90.2	95.6	97.6	94.8	80.8	76.2	93.3	93.8	91.2	77.0	75.2
April	91.8	90.5	96.2	97.9	95.6	80.8	76.1	93.1	94.4	91.5	77.4	75.6
May	92.4	91.2	96.7	96.9	96.6	81.6	76.8	94.2	95.1	92.2	77.9	76.1
June	91.7	90.5	95.4	94.9	95.6	81.4	75.8	93.6	94.8	91.6	77.3	75.6
July	92.4	91.3	95.5	95.0	95.7	83.0	77.0	94.8	95.4	92.5	77.9	76.3
August	92.6	91.9	96.1	96.5	96.0	82.9	77.6	94.8	95.3	92.5	78.1	76.7
September	92.6	91.8	96.1	95.6	96.3	83.0	78.5	94.0	95.3	92.6	78.1	76.6
October	93.5	92.8	97.0	97.7	96.8	83.8	78.7	95.6	95.7	93.5	78.8	77.4
November	93.7	92.7	96.9	96.5	97.1	83.3	79.5	95.3	96.1	94.0	78.9	77.2
December	94.3	93.3	97.6	97.6	97.6	83.9	80.2	95.2	96.9	94.7	79.4	77.6
2005												
January	94.7	93.9	98.0	97.0	98.4	85.1	80.1	96.2	97.5	94.7	79.7	78.0
February	95.3	94.7	98.4	99.1	98.2	86.1	83.3	96.9	97.4	95.4	80.1	78.5
March	95.2	94.3	98.2	97.6	98.4	85.8	84.9	96.0	97.6	95.5	80.0	78.0
April	95.3	94.5	98.0	96.4	98.5	86.8	86.4	97.7	97.9	95.3	80.0	78.1
May	95.5	94.9	98.7	96.6	99.3	87.6	86.1	97.9	97.9	95.0	80.0	78.2
June	95.9	95.1	99.5	97.2	100.2	87.5	86.9	97.1	98.4	95.4	80.2	78.2
July	95.8	94.9	99.3	96.0	100.3	87.5	86.2	97.9	98.1	95.2	80.0	78.0
August	95.9	95.2	99.5	98.1	99.9	88.1	87.3	98.2	98.2	95.1	80.0	78.0
September	94.0	94.2	99.6	99.6	99.6	85.7	83.8	99.6	98.3	91.3	78.3	77.0
October	95.2	95.6	99.5	100.7	99.2	90.1	84.7	101.5	98.6	92.5	79.2	78.0
November	96.1	96.3	99.3	99.3	99.3	91.4	84.7	102.1	98.9	94.3	79.8	78.5
December	96.7	96.4	100.1	97.8	100.8	90.8	84.6	102.9	99.3	95.1	80.2	78.4
2006												
January	96.8	97.2	99.0	99.3	98.9	92.1	82.9	103.6	99.1	95.7	80.2	78.9
February	96.8	97.0	98.8	98.5	98.9	92.7	83.6	102.8	99.2	95.9	80.1	78.6
March	97.1	96.9	99.6	99.3	99.7	93.5	81.5	102.5	99.5	95.8	80.2	78.5
April	97.4	97.5	99.7	99.3	99.8	95.3	81.9	102.0	99.5	96.2	80.4	78.8
May	97.3	97.1	99.5	98.8	99.8	95.0	81.4	101.2	99.3	96.2	80.2	78.4
June	97.7	97.4	100.0	99.7	100.2	95.7	82.0	100.7	99.4	96.6	80.4	78.5
July	97.8	97.2	99.2	96.3	100.2	96.9	83.5	101.1	99.4	96.8	80.3	78.2
August	98.0	97.6	99.9	98.5	100.4	97.3	83.5	100.3	99.1	96.9	80.3	78.4
September	97.8	97.7	99.5	97.4	100.2	97.4	84.5	100.0	98.8	96.9	80.1	78.4
October	97.7	97.2	99.5	95.8	100.7	97.5	86.2	98.8	99.0	96.7	79.9	77.9
November	97.6	97.3	99.7	97.1	100.5	97.2	87.8	98.5	98.5	96.5	79.6	77.8
December	98.6	98.8	100.1	99.9	100.1	98.4	89.7	101.5	99.2	97.7	80.2	78.8
2007												
January	98.2	98.3	99.6	97.9	100.2	96.2	91.8	99.6	99.2	97.5	79.7	78.2
February	99.3	98.7	101.2	99.2	101.8	97.2	92.7	100.1	100.2	98.4	80.4	78.3
March	99.3	99.4	100.1	99.3	100.3	99.3	91.7	101.1	100.0	98.8	80.3	78.7
April	100.1	100.1	100.8	101.6	100.5	100.4	94.5	100.7	100.6	99.5	80.7	79.1
May	100.1	100.0	100.4	100.9	100.2	100.2	96.7	100.5	100.3	99.9	80.6	78.8
June	100.1	100.3	100.4	102.0	99.9	99.8	100.1	100.9	100.0	99.9	80.5	78.9
July	100.1	100.5	100.4	101.2	100.1	99.6	101.3	100.5	99.5	100.2	80.4	78.8
August	100.3	100.1	100.2	100.7	100.1	99.5	103.3	99.9	99.9	100.5	80.4	78.3
September	100.7	100.6	100.3	99.6	100.5	101.4	106.0	99.9	100.5	100.8	80.7	78.6
October	100.2	100.3	99.0	99.2	98.9	101.0	105.8	98.9	99.9	100.9	80.3	78.2
November	100.8	100.8	99.0	99.3	98.9	102.2	107.8	98.8	100.2	101.8	80.7	78.5
December	100.8	100.9	98.7	99.2	98.6	103.2	108.3	99.3	99.7	101.8	80.8	78.5

Table 2-4A. Industrial Production and Capacity Utilization: Historical Data, 1947–2012—*Continued*

(Seasonally adjusted.)

Year and month	Total industry	Manufac-turing (SIC)	Consumer goods Total	Durable	Nondurable	Business equipment	Defense and space equipment	Construction supplies	Business supplies	Materials	Total industry	Manufac-turing (SIC)
2008												
January	100.5	100.5	98.4	96.6	99.0	103.5	108.7	99.0	99.7	101.2	80.5	78.1
February	100.3	99.9	98.2	95.3	99.2	104.2	107.8	97.2	99.7	101.0	80.4	77.7
March	100.0	99.6	97.3	94.3	98.3	104.0	108.3	95.8	99.1	101.1	80.2	77.5
April	99.2	98.5	96.7	92.1	98.1	102.0	108.0	94.2	98.2	100.6	79.6	76.6
May	98.8	98.0	96.3	91.6	97.8	102.3	107.3	93.4	97.6	100.0	79.3	76.3
June	98.6	97.5	96.0	91.9	97.4	102.1	109.4	92.3	96.9	99.9	79.2	76.0
July	98.1	96.4	95.0	88.4	97.1	101.5	107.3	92.3	96.3	99.8	78.8	75.3
August	96.5	95.1	93.6	86.0	96.1	98.1	107.7	90.1	95.4	98.3	77.5	74.4
September	92.5	91.9	93.1	85.9	95.5	90.0	105.2	87.8	94.2	92.0	74.2	72.0
October	93.2	91.3	93.3	83.7	96.4	87.4	105.5	86.4	93.7	94.5	74.8	71.6
November	92.2	89.3	92.7	81.4	96.4	88.6	104.9	82.1	92.0	93.1	73.9	70.2
December	89.6	86.3	91.0	78.3	95.2	89.3	103.8	77.6	89.4	89.4	71.7	67.9
2009												
January	87.5	83.8	88.9	70.3	95.1	84.5	103.1	74.7	88.4	88.0	70.0	66.1
February	87.0	83.6	89.0	71.6	94.8	84.2	102.4	73.4	87.1	87.4	69.6	66.1
March	85.7	82.0	88.8	71.8	94.4	82.0	100.8	70.9	86.1	85.8	68.5	65.0
April	84.9	81.4	88.4	72.2	93.8	80.1	100.1	69.3	85.6	85.2	67.9	64.6
May	84.1	80.5	87.2	69.0	93.2	78.1	99.9	69.1	85.1	84.7	67.2	64.0
June	83.8	80.3	86.8	68.7	92.8	77.2	100.8	69.0	85.1	84.4	66.9	64.0
July	84.5	81.2	87.8	74.6	92.1	77.7	102.3	69.1	84.9	85.3	67.6	64.8
August	85.4	82.1	88.7	76.4	92.7	78.7	103.3	69.4	85.2	86.4	68.3	65.7
September	86.0	82.8	89.4	79.1	92.8	78.8	104.4	69.0	85.3	87.1	68.9	66.3
October	86.2	82.9	89.7	77.3	93.8	79.3	103.8	68.1	86.1	87.4	69.2	66.5
November	86.6	83.8	89.3	79.0	92.6	79.2	103.9	69.4	86.0	88.5	69.7	67.4
December	87.0	83.8	89.2	78.0	92.9	80.9	104.2	67.8	87.5	88.8	70.1	67.6
2010												
January	88.0	84.6	89.8	78.3	93.5	82.0	106.4	68.9	87.4	90.1	71.0	68.4
February	88.3	84.6	89.1	77.0	93.0	81.7	107.1	69.2	87.2	91.3	71.5	68.5
March	89.0	85.7	89.3	77.9	93.0	83.3	110.2	70.5	87.0	92.0	72.2	69.5
April	89.3	86.4	88.3	78.0	91.6	84.7	111.4	72.6	87.4	92.6	72.6	70.2
May	90.7	87.7	90.1	80.6	93.2	86.6	111.5	73.0	88.2	94.0	73.9	71.4
June	90.9	87.7	89.8	79.6	93.1	87.2	111.4	73.2	88.3	94.5	74.2	71.5
July	91.4	88.3	90.2	82.2	92.9	88.8	112.9	73.1	88.5	94.9	74.8	72.1
August	91.6	88.4	89.9	79.6	93.3	88.9	113.4	73.6	88.5	95.6	75.1	72.3
September	91.9	88.5	89.6	79.7	92.8	89.5	111.1	73.6	88.5	96.2	75.4	72.5
October	91.6	88.5	89.6	80.9	92.5	88.8	109.5	74.0	87.7	95.8	75.2	72.6
November	91.8	88.7	89.2	79.6	92.4	89.4	108.8	74.5	88.6	96.3	75.5	72.8
December	92.7	89.2	90.3	79.3	93.9	89.9	107.9	73.4	89.2	97.6	76.2	73.3
2011												
January	92.6	89.3	90.3	80.1	93.7	90.6	107.0	73.1	88.7	97.3	76.1	73.4
February	92.2	89.3	90.1	81.8	92.8	90.9	106.2	72.9	88.5	96.5	75.7	73.4
March	93.1	89.9	90.6	83.4	93.0	90.5	105.5	73.7	89.1	98.2	76.5	73.9
April	92.6	89.3	90.2	80.7	93.4	89.7	104.8	73.4	88.5	97.5	76.0	73.4
May	92.9	89.5	90.6	81.9	93.5	90.5	104.7	74.4	88.9	97.6	76.1	73.5
June	93.1	89.6	90.5	81.6	93.4	90.4	104.1	74.5	88.6	98.2	76.2	73.5
July	93.6	90.2	91.2	83.1	93.9	91.1	104.6	75.4	89.1	98.5	76.5	74.0
August	94.1	90.6	91.7	84.1	94.2	91.9	105.7	75.0	89.5	99.0	76.8	74.2
September	94.2	90.9	91.6	84.7	93.9	92.3	105.8	75.2	89.9	99.1	76.7	74.3
October	94.7	91.4	91.7	86.2	93.7	93.1	107.2	75.5	89.3	100.0	77.0	74.7
November	95.0	91.4	91.2	85.3	93.3	93.7	109.3	75.6	88.7	100.7	77.0	74.5
December	95.5	92.3	91.4	87.1	93.0	94.7	108.9	76.9	89.3	101.4	77.3	75.2
2012												
January	96.2	93.3	91.7	89.0	92.8	96.1	109.5	77.6	89.6	102.2	77.7	75.8
February	96.7	93.9	92.1	89.3	93.3	97.0	111.6	79.2	90.2	102.4	77.9	76.2
March	96.1	93.4	91.3	89.2	92.2	97.4	111.9	78.7	89.6	101.9	77.3	75.7
April	96.9	93.9	92.1	90.2	92.9	98.3	111.1	79.5	90.4	102.6	77.7	76.1
May	97.1	93.7	92.8	89.9	94.0	99.0	109.8	78.6	90.9	102.6	77.8	75.8
June	97.1	94.0	92.6	90.6	93.5	100.3	109.7	77.9	90.7	102.6	77.7	75.9
July	97.6	94.2	92.9	90.9	93.8	100.4	112.1	77.8	90.8	103.3	77.9	76.0
August	96.8	93.5	92.0	89.3	93.2	100.3	112.4	77.7	90.2	102.3	77.2	75.4
September	97.0	93.6	92.4	89.3	93.7	100.1	113.1	78.0	90.1	102.4	77.2	75.3
October	96.8	93.2	91.9	89.6	92.9	98.9	112.8	77.8	89.9	102.8	77.0	74.9
November	98.1	94.5	93.2	91.8	94.0	101.3	114.0	79.6	90.7	103.9	77.9	75.8
December	98.2	95.3	93.2	94.1	93.3	101.7	113.3	80.1	90.5	104.1	77.8	76.4

Production indexes, 2007 = 100 — Market groups; Capacity utilization (output as percentage of capacity)

Table 2-4B. Industrial Production: Historical Data, 1919–1947

(Seasonally adjusted, 2007 = 100.)

Year and month	January	February	March	April	May	June	July	August	September	October	November	December	Annual averages
1919													
Industrial production, total ...	4.86	4.64	4.51	4.59	4.62	4.91	5.21	5.29	5.18	5.13	5.05	5.13	4.92
Manufacturing	4.60	4.50	4.33	4.43	4.40	4.72	4.98	5.10	4.91	4.81	4.98	4.89	4.72
1920													
Industrial production, total ..	5.61	5.61	5.50	5.21	5.34	5.39	5.26	5.29	5.10	4.88	4.48	4.21	5.16
Manufacturing	5.39	5.39	5.27	4.96	5.13	5.13	4.93	4.96	4.84	4.57	4.09	3.80	4.87
1921													
Industrial production, total ..	3.97	3.89	3.78	3.78	3.89	3.86	3.84	3.97	4.00	4.24	4.19	4.16	3.97
Manufacturing	3.61	3.61	3.51	3.51	3.63	3.61	3.61	3.75	3.80	3.97	4.02	3.97	3.72
1922													
Industrial production, total ..	4.32	4.51	4.75	4.59	4.83	5.07	5.07	4.96	5.23	5.53	5.77	5.93	5.05
Manufacturing	4.07	4.16	4.36	4.55	4.79	5.01	5.05	4.86	5.01	5.22	5.42	5.58	4.84
1923													
Industrial production, total ..	5.80	5.88	6.07	6.20	6.28	6.23	6.17	6.07	5.93	5.90	5.90	5.77	6.02
Manufacturing	5.49	5.54	5.78	5.85	5.97	5.90	5.80	5.66	5.63	5.54	5.54	5.46	5.68
1924													
Industrial production, total ...	5.90	6.01	5.90	5.72	5.47	5.23	5.15	5.34	5.53	5.66	5.77	5.93	5.64
Manufacturing	5.56	5.68	5.58	5.44	5.17	4.91	4.84	5.01	5.20	5.34	5.46	5.66	5.32
1925													
Industrial production, total ..	6.12	6.12	6.12	6.17	6.15	6.09	6.25	6.15	6.07	6.31	6.44	6.52	6.21
Manufacturing	5.82	5.85	5.87	5.87	5.82	5.80	5.92	5.82	5.85	6.09	6.26	6.40	5.95
1926													
Industrial production, total ..	6.41	6.41	6.49	6.49	6.44	6.52	6.55	6.63	6.74	6.74	6.71	6.68	6.57
Manufacturing	6.26	6.21	6.19	6.19	6.14	6.21	6.21	6.28	6.40	6.35	6.31	6.28	6.25
1927													
Industrial production, total ..	6.66	6.71	6.79	6.63	6.68	6.66	6.58	6.58	6.47	6.33	6.33	6.36	6.56
Manufacturing	6.23	6.28	6.33	6.31	6.33	6.33	6.28	6.23	6.14	6.04	6.02	6.09	6.22
1928													
Industrial production, total ..	6.49	6.55	6.60	6.58	6.66	6.71	6.79	6.92	6.98	7.11	7.25	7.38	6.83
Manufacturing	6.21	6.28	6.31	6.28	6.38	6.45	6.55	6.69	6.72	6.84	6.98	7.10	6.56
1929													
Industrial production, total ..	7.49	7.46	7.49	7.62	7.76	7.81	7.92	7.84	7.78	7.65	7.27	6.95	7.59
Manufacturing	7.15	7.12	7.20	7.29	7.44	7.53	7.61	7.56	7.41	7.34	6.93	6.52	7.26
1930													
Industrial production, total ..	6.95	6.92	6.82	6.76	6.66	6.47	6.17	6.04	5.93	5.77	5.64	5.50	6.30
Manufacturing	6.59	6.55	6.33	6.43	6.31	6.14	5.85	5.63	5.58	5.39	5.25	5.13	5.93
1931													
Industrial production, total ..	5.47	5.50	5.61	5.64	5.56	5.42	5.34	5.15	4.91	4.72	4.67	4.64	5.22
Manufacturing	5.13	5.17	5.27	5.27	5.22	5.03	4.96	4.79	4.57	4.36	4.28	4.26	4.86
1932													
Industrial production, total ..	4.51	4.40	4.35	4.05	3.92	3.78	3.68	3.78	4.03	4.16	4.16	4.08	4.07
Manufacturing	4.21	4.09	3.95	3.71	3.61	3.49	3.37	3.47	3.71	3.80	3.83	3.75	3.75
1933													
Industrial production, total ..	4.00	4.03	3.78	4.05	4.72	5.45	5.96	5.72	5.39	5.13	4.83	4.86	4.83
Manufacturing	3.71	3.61	3.39	3.75	4.40	5.13	5.66	5.32	5.05	4.77	4.45	4.50	4.48
1934													
Industrial production, total ..	5.02	5.26	5.50	5.50	5.61	5.50	5.13	5.07	4.78	4.99	5.05	5.37	5.23
Manufacturing	4.65	4.91	5.10	5.20	5.27	5.15	4.74	4.72	4.45	4.62	4.69	5.03	4.88
1935													
Industrial production, total ..	5.80	5.90	5.88	5.77	5.77	5.85	5.85	6.07	6.23	6.41	6.55	6.63	6.06
Manufacturing	5.49	5.58	5.51	5.46	5.44	5.42	5.58	5.80	5.94	6.11	6.26	6.33	5.74
1936													
Industrial production, total ..	6.52	6.36	6.44	6.84	6.98	7.11	7.25	7.35	7.49	7.59	7.81	8.05	7.15
Manufacturing	6.21	6.02	6.14	6.52	6.69	6.84	6.96	7.08	7.20	7.32	7.51	7.75	6.85
1937													
Industrial production, total ..	8.02	8.13	8.32	8.32	8.35	8.24	8.29	8.24	7.97	7.38	6.66	6.07	7.83
Manufacturing	7.75	7.87	7.92	8.04	8.09	7.94	7.99	7.89	7.61	6.98	6.16	5.51	7.48
1938													
Industrial production, total ..	5.93	5.88	5.88	5.77	5.64	5.69	6.01	6.33	6.52	6.68	6.95	7.03	6.19
Manufacturing	5.42	5.39	5.42	5.25	5.22	5.22	5.54	5.90	6.09	6.28	6.57	6.62	5.74

Table 2-4B. Industrial Production: Historical Data, 1919–1947—*Continued*

(Seasonally adjusted, 2007 = 100.)

Year and month	January	February	March	April	May	June	July	August	September	October	November	December	Annual averages
1939													
Industrial production, total	7.03	7.08	7.11	7.08	7.06	7.22	7.43	7.54	8.00	8.40	8.61	8.61	7.60
Products	7.09	7.11	7.19	7.19	7.24	7.32	7.46	7.54	7.77	7.98	8.14	8.20	7.52
Consumer goods	10.61	10.61	10.79	10.79	10.82	10.93	11.06	11.10	11.27	11.38	11.48	11.52	11.03
Materials	6.72	6.82	6.82	6.61	6.58	6.90	7.19	7.27	8.10	8.87	9.03	9.03	7.50
Manufacturing	6.31	6.35	6.35	6.28	6.28	6.43	6.62	6.81	7.20	7.61	7.75	7.85	6.82
1940													
Industrial production, total	8.51	8.24	8.05	8.21	8.45	8.72	8.83	8.88	9.07	9.21	9.42	9.74	8.78
Products	8.12	8.04	7.96	8.04	8.14	8.33	8.33	8.43	8.67	8.83	8.99	9.31	8.43
Consumer goods	11.48	11.45	11.31	11.38	11.45	11.55	11.52	11.52	11.83	12.04	12.28	12.67	11.71
Materials	8.79	8.31	7.99	8.23	8.61	9.06	9.30	9.38	9.49	9.59	9.78	10.13	9.06
Manufacturing	7.73	7.49	7.32	7.39	7.70	8.04	8.14	8.26	8.42	8.54	8.69	9.00	8.06
1941													
Industrial production, total	9.98	10.28	10.60	10.63	11.11	11.19	11.33	11.46	11.46	11.57	11.62	11.81	11.09
Products	9.60	9.89	10.15	10.36	10.71	10.81	10.89	11.02	11.05	11.16	11.21	11.37	10.69
Consumer goods	12.91	13.29	13.64	13.88	14.30	14.34	14.34	14.37	14.30	14.30	14.34	14.34	14.03
Materials	10.26	10.55	10.93	10.69	11.35	11.51	11.67	11.75	11.75	11.80	11.88	12.12	11.36
Manufacturing	9.17	9.51	9.75	10.01	10.35	10.47	10.59	10.66	10.64	10.73	10.76	10.90	10.30
1942													
Industrial production, total	12.05	12.26	12.40	12.05	12.08	12.10	12.40	12.77	13.07	13.50	13.82	14.14	12.72
Products	11.71	12.00	12.14	11.37	11.40	11.45	11.77	12.11	12.53	12.98	13.40	13.83	12.22
Consumer goods	14.61	14.44	14.44	12.46	12.32	12.11	12.28	12.39	12.42	12.63	12.70	12.98	12.98
Materials	12.15	12.34	12.44	12.76	12.74	12.76	13.00	13.38	13.54	13.91	14.12	14.28	13.12
Manufacturing	11.14	11.41	11.58	11.24	11.29	11.36	11.72	12.11	12.47	12.92	13.29	13.65	12.01
1943													
Industrial production, total	14.28	14.65	14.76	14.95	15.06	14.98	15.43	15.75	16.16	16.40	16.61	16.40	15.45
Products	13.88	14.20	14.36	14.54	14.67	14.83	15.23	15.49	15.92	16.15	16.39	16.05	15.14
Consumer goods	12.60	12.70	12.74	12.87	13.08	13.29	13.50	13.57	13.67	13.57	13.54	13.26	13.20
Materials	14.50	14.87	15.03	15.16	15.14	14.76	15.32	15.62	16.02	16.28	16.42	16.41	15.46
Manufacturing	13.84	14.13	14.25	14.42	14.51	14.56	14.90	15.21	15.62	15.96	16.17	15.91	14.96
1944													
Industrial production, total	16.59	16.72	16.69	16.69	16.59	16.53	16.50	16.72	16.61	16.67	16.53	16.48	16.61
Products	16.26	16.42	16.42	16.47	16.44	16.50	16.63	16.82	16.68	16.71	16.50	16.37	16.52
Consumer goods	13.40	13.47	13.64	13.71	13.81	13.88	13.95	14.27	13.95	13.99	13.95	13.95	13.83
Materials	16.57	16.71	16.63	16.57	16.34	16.10	15.86	16.04	16.02	16.07	16.10	16.18	16.26
Manufacturing	16.15	16.27	16.25	16.22	16.10	16.08	16.08	16.29	16.20	16.25	16.10	16.10	16.17
1945													
Industrial production, total	16.32	16.26	16.16	15.86	15.43	15.08	14.73	13.20	12.02	11.54	11.97	12.02	14.22
Products	16.23	16.05	15.81	15.52	15.10	14.81	14.57	12.98	11.63	11.34	11.50	11.53	13.92
Consumer goods	14.16	14.06	14.02	14.13	14.16	14.27	14.23	13.60	14.27	14.47	14.89	15.07	14.28
Materials	15.99	16.15	16.18	15.94	15.51	15.11	14.55	13.19	12.20	11.54	12.34	12.47	14.26
Manufacturing	15.89	15.81	15.64	15.31	14.83	14.42	14.08	12.37	11.00	10.57	10.85	10.98	13.48
1946													
Industrial production, total	11.35	10.79	11.92	11.70	11.27	11.97	12.37	12.83	13.07	13.31	13.39	13.47	12.29
Products	11.40	11.29	11.55	11.74	11.61	11.74	12.00	12.40	12.74	12.95	13.09	13.22	12.14
Consumer goods	15.73	16.35	16.25	16.42	16.49	16.53	16.91	17.47	17.82	18.02	18.27	18.37	17.05
Materials	10.93	9.62	12.10	11.30	10.45	11.91	12.60	13.08	13.16	13.46	13.43	13.51	12.13
Manufacturing	10.23	9.58	10.78	10.81	10.30	10.88	11.24	11.75	11.99	12.25	12.40	12.44	11.22
1947													
Industrial production, total	13.63	13.71	13.79	13.69	13.74	13.74	13.66	13.74	13.85	13.98	14.17	14.22	13.83
Products	13.35	13.40	13.46	13.46	13.48	13.46	13.43	13.51	13.64	13.83	14.01	14.09	13.59
Consumer goods	17.99	17.92	17.99	17.92	17.78	17.82	17.88	18.02	18.20	18.48	18.75	18.79	18.13
Materials	13.51	13.62	14.07	13.72	13.78	13.64	13.51	13.48	13.67	13.78	14.10	13.94	13.73
Manufacturing	12.40	12.44	12.49	12.52	12.42	12.42	12.35	12.42	12.47	12.64	12.83	12.85	12.52

NOTES AND DEFINITIONS, CHAPTER 2

Tables 2-1 through 2-4: Industrial Production and Capacity Utilization

SOURCE: BOARD OF GOVERNORS OF THE FEDERAL RESERVE SYSTEM

The *industrial production index* measures changes in the physical volume or quantity of output of manufacturing, mining, and electric and gas utilities. *Capacity utilization* is calculated by dividing a seasonally adjusted industrial production index for an industry or group of industries by a related index of productive capacity.

The index of industrial production is one of the oldest continuous statistical series maintained by the Federal government, and one of the few economic indicators for which monthly data are available before the post-World-War-II period. This edition of *Business Statistics* reprints monthly and annual values for total industrial production and its manufacturing component beginning with January 1919.

On March 25, 2011, a revision of the entire industrial production data system included rebasing all of the indexes from the previous comparison base, 2002 = 100, to 2007 = 100. This affected the levels of all current and historical production indexes, though not necessarily the changes that they record over time.

Around the 15th day of each month, the Federal Reserve issues estimates of industrial production and capacity utilization for the previous month. The production estimates are in the form of index numbers (2007 = 100) that reflect the monthly levels of total output of the nation's factories, mines, and gas and electric utilities expressed as a percent of the monthly average in the 2007 base year. Capacity estimates are expressed as index numbers, 2007 output = 100 (not 2007 capacity), and capacity utilization is measured by the production index as a percent of the capacity index. Since the bases of those two indexes are the same for each industry, this procedure yields production as a percent of capacity. Monthly estimates are subject to revision in subsequent months, as well as to annual and comprehensive revisions in subsequent years.

Definitions and notes on the data

The index of industrial production measures a large portion of the goods output of the national economy on a monthly basis. That portion, together with construction, has also accounted for the bulk of the variation in output over the course of many historical business cycles. The substantial industrial detail included in the index illuminates structural developments in the economy.

The total industrial production index and the indexes for its major components are constructed from individual industry series (312 series for data from 1997 forward) based on the 2007 North American Industry Classification System (NAICS). See the Preface to this volume for information on NAICS.

The Federal Reserve has been able to provide a longer continuous historical series on the NAICS basis than some other government agencies. In a major research effort, the Fed and the Census Bureau's Center for Economic Studies re-coded data from seven Censuses of Manufactures, beginning in 1963, to establish benchmark NAICS data for output, value added, and capacity utilization. The resulting indexes are shown annually for the last 41 years (46 years for aggregate levels) in Tables 2-1 through 2-3.

The Fed's featured indexes for total industry and total manufacturing on the Standard Industrial Classification (SIC) basis do not observe the reclassifications under NAICS of the logging industry to the Agriculture sector and the publishing industry to the Information sector. (The reason cited by the Fed was to avoid "changing the scope or historical continuity of these statistics.") One advantage of the SIC index for capacity utilization is that it is a continuous series back to 1948 (shown in Table 2-4A). On the new NAICS basis, production and capacity utilization are shown back to 1972 in Tables 2-2 and 2-3.

The individual series components of the indexes are grouped in two ways: market groups and industry groups.

Market groups. For analyzing market trends and product flows, the individual series are grouped into two major divisions: *final products and nonindustrial supplies* and *materials. Final products* consists of products purchased by consumers, businesses, or government for final use. *Nonindustrial supplies* are expected to become inputs in nonindustrial sectors: the two major subgroups are *construction supplies* and *business supplies. Materials* comprises industrial output that requires further processing within the industrial sector. This twofold division distinguishes between products that are ready to ship outside the industrial sector and those that will stay within the sector for further processing.

Final products are divided into *consumer goods* and *equipment*, and *equipment* is divided into *business equipment* and *defense and space equipment*. Further subdivisions of each market group are based on type of product and the market destination for the product.

Industry groups are typically groupings by 3-digit NAICS industries and major aggregates of these industries—for example, *durable goods* and *nondurable goods manufacturing*, *mining*, and *utilities*. Indexes are also calculated for *stage-of-process* industry groups—*crude, primary and semifinished*, and *finished* processing. The stage-of-process grouping was a new feature in the 2002 revision, replacing the two narrower and less well-defined "primary processing manufacturing" and "advanced processing manufacturing" groups that were previously published. *Crude processing* consists of logging, much of mining, and certain basic manufacturing activities in the chemical, paper, and metals industries. *Primary and semifinished processing* represents industries that produce materials and parts used as inputs by other industries. *Finished processing* includes industries that produce goods in their finished form for use by consumers, business investment, or government.

The indexes of industrial production are constructed with data from a variety of sources. Current monthly estimates of production are based on measures of physical output where possible and appropriate. For a few high-tech industries, the estimated value of nominal output is deflated by a corresponding price index. For industries in which such direct measurement is not possible on a monthly basis, output is inferred from production-worker hours, adjusted for trends in worker productivity derived from annual and benchmark revisions. (Between the 1960s and 1997, electric power consumption was used as a monthly output indicator for some industries instead of hours. However, the coverage of the electric power consumption survey deteriorated, and in the 2005 revision, the decision was made to resume the use of hours in those industries, beginning with the data for 1997.)

In annual and benchmark revisions, the individual indexes are revised using data from the quinquennial Censuses of Manufactures and Mineral Industries, the Annual Survey of Manufactures, and the quarterly Survey of Plant Capacity, prepared by the Census Bureau; deflators from the Producer Price Indexes and other sources; the *Minerals Yearbook*, prepared by the Department of the Interior; publications from the Department of Energy; and other sources.

The weights used in computing the indexes are based on Census value added—the difference between the value of production and the cost of materials and supplies consumed. Census value added differs in some respects from the economic concept of industry value added used in the national income and product accounts (NIPAs). Industry value added as defined in the NIPAs is not available in sufficient detail for the industrial production indexes. See Chapter 14 for data and a description of NIPA value added (equivalently, gross domestic product) by major industry group.

Before 1972, a linked-Laspeyres formula (base period prices) is used to compute the weighted individual indexes. Beginning with 1972, the index uses a version of the Fisher-ideal index formula—a chain-weighting (updated average price) system similar to that in the NIPAs. See the "General Notes" article at the front of this book and the notes and definitions for Chapter 1 for more information. Chain-weighting keeps the index from being distorted by the use of obsolete relative prices.

For the purpose of these value-added weights, value added per unit of output is based on data from the Censuses of Manufacturing and Mineral Industries, the Census Bureau's Annual Survey of Manufactures, and revenue and expense data reported by the Department of Energy and the American Gas Association, which are projected into recent years by using changes in relevant Producer Price Indexes.

To separate seasonal movements from cyclical patterns and underlying trends, each component of the index is seasonally adjusted by the Census X-12-ARIMA method.

The index does not cover production on farms, in the construction industry, in transportation, or in various trade and service industries. A number of groups and subgroups include data for individual series not published separately.

Capacity utilization is calculated for the manufacturing, mining, and electric and gas utilities industries. Output is measured by seasonally adjusted indexes of industrial production. The capacity indexes attempt to capture the concept of sustainable maximum output, which is defined as the greatest level of output that a plant can maintain within the framework of a realistic work schedule, taking account of normal downtime and assuming sufficient availability of inputs to operate the machinery and equipment in place. The 89 individual industry capacity indexes are based on a variety of data, including capacity data measured in physical units compiled by government agencies and trade associations, Census Bureau surveys of utilization rates and investment, and estimates of growth of the capital stock.

In its monthly release, the Federal Reserve includes the following "Perspective. Over the 1972–2012 period, the average total industry utilization rate is 80.2 percent; for manufacturing, the average factory operating rate has been 78.7 percent. Industrial plants usually operate at capacity utilization rates that are well below 100 percent: none of the broad aggregates has ever reached 100 percent. For total industry and total manufacturing, utilization rates have exceeded 90 percent only in wartime."

Revisions

Revisions normally occur annually. The data shown in this volume are as revised in the annual revision released March 22, 2013, and subsequent updates through May 2013. New data incorporated in this revision include information from the 2011 Annual Survey of Manufactures, new minerals data through 2012, and new capacity data including the Census Quarterly Survey of Plant Capacity through the fourth quarter of 2012.

Data availability

Data are available monthly in Federal Reserve release G.17. Current and historical data and background information are available on the Federal Reserve Web site at http://www.federalreserve.gov.

Chain-weighting makes it difficult for the user to analyze in detail the sources of aggregate output change. An "Explanatory Note," included in each month's index release, provides some assistance for the user, including a reference to an Internet location with the exact contribution of a monthly change in a component index to the monthly change in the total index.

References

The G.17 release each month contains extensive explanatory material, as well as references for further detail.

An earlier detailed description of the industrial production index, together with a history of the index, a glossary of terms, and a bibliography is presented in *Industrial Production—1986 Edition*, available from Publication Services, Mail Stop 127, Board of Governors of the Federal Reserve System, Washington, DC 20551.

CHAPTER 3: INCOME DISTRIBUTION AND POVERTY

Section 3a: Household and Family Income

Figure 3-1. Median and Mean Household Income, 1967–2011
(2011 dollars)

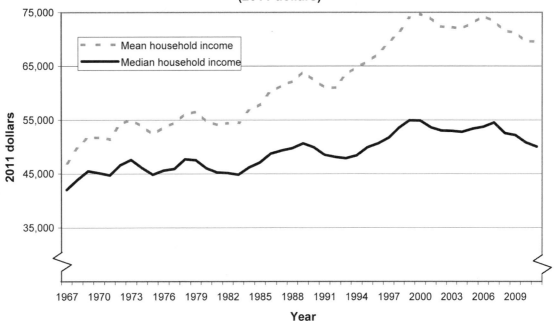

- Measured as cash income before taxes, median household income in 2011 was $50,054—down 1.5 percent from the previous year, in constant (2011) dollars. It was the fourth straight year of decline, for a total of 8.1 percent since 2007. Income was 8.8 percent below the all-time peak in 1999, and the lowest since 1995. Over the latest completed business cycle, from 1999 to 2007, real median household income declined 0.8 percent. In contrast, between the 1969 business cycle peak and 1999, income rose an average 0.6 percent per year. Median income is the income of the household at the middle of the income distribution. (Table 3-1)

- The Census Bureau also tabulates "mean income," which is the sum of all the reported household incomes divided by the number of households; this is also shown in Figure 3-1 above. Mean income is higher than median income when the distribution of income is skewed upward by very large incomes at the top of the distribution. (Table 3-1)

- Household income inequality, as measured by the "Gini coefficient," rose to a new postwar record in 2011. A new measure of inequality based on "equivalence-adjusted income," which takes account of the size and composition of the household, also rose to a new record; it is slightly lower in level than the raw "Gini" but has increased 28 percent since 1967, compared with 20 percent for the unadjusted measure. (Table 3-4)

- The ratio of women's to men's earnings for year-round, full-time workers increased from about 0.6 through 1981 to 0.778 in 2007, fell back somewhat over the next three years, and rose back to 0.774 in 2011. Men's median earnings at the cycle high in 2007 were 3.3 percent below their all-time high in 1973, in real terms. The men's median was actually higher in 2009 and 2010 than in 2007, as the number of full-time workers dropped sharply—apparently leaving proportionately more of the better-paid workers in their jobs. Women's real earnings in 2007 were up 32.8 percent since 1973, but in 2011 were down 2.5 percent from 2007. (Table 3-1)

Table 3-1. Median and Mean Household Income and Median Earnings

(2011 dollars, except as noted.)

Year	Number of households (thousands)	Average size of household (number of people)	Median household income — All races	Median household income — White Total	Median household income — White Not Hispanic	Median household income — Black	Median household income — Asian [1]	Median household income — Hispanic (any race)	Mean household income, all races	Median earnings — Male workers	Median earnings — Female workers	Median earnings — Ratio, female to male
1960	...	...	...	...	...	...	...	...	...	35 675	21 646	0.607
1961	...	...	...	...	...	...	...	...	...	36 813	21 812	0.592
1962	...	...	...	...	...	...	...	...	...	37 486	22 228	0.593
1963	...	...	...	...	...	...	...	...	...	38 428	22 652	0.589
1964	...	...	...	...	...	...	...	...	...	39 325	23 260	0.591
1965	...	...	...	...	...	...	...	...	...	39 886	23 901	0.599
1966	...	...	...	...	...	...	...	...	...	41 628	23 959	0.576
1967	60 813	...	42 056	43 857	...	25 464	...	...	47 037	42 285	24 434	0.578
1968	62 214	...	43 868	45 675	...	26 934	...	...	49 630	43 421	25 251	0.582
1969	63 401	...	45 499	47 484	...	28 702	...	...	51 763	45 857	26 993	0.589
1970	64 778	...	45 146	47 023	...	28 621	...	...	51 695	46 345	27 515	0.594
1971	66 676	...	44 707	46 762	...	27 622	...	...	51 417	46 544	27 697	0.595
1972	68 251	...	46 622	48 910	49 608	28 549	...	36 910	54 262	49 050	28 381	0.579
1973	69 859	...	47 563	49 848	50 287	29 342	...	36 849	55 006	50 613	28 664	0.566
1974	71 163	...	46 057	48 167	48 578	28 645	...	36 633	53 860	48 796	28 670	0.588
1975	72 867	2.89	44 851	46 903	47 257	28 157	...	33 695	52 373	48 492	28 522	0.588
1976	74 142	2.86	45 595	47 762	48 736	28 401	...	34 392	53 632	48 359	29 109	0.602
1977	76 030	2.81	45 884	48 250	49 207	28 473	...	35 995	54 430	49 447	29 135	0.589
1978	77 330	2.78	47 659	49 545	50 478	29 774	...	37 342	56 094	49 766	29 581	0.594
1979	80 776	2.76	47 527	49 831	50 532	29 256	...	37 655	56 457	49 123	29 308	0.597
1980	82 368	2.73	46 024	48 555	49 415	27 973	...	35 475	54 737	48 368	29 098	0.602
1981	83 527	2.72	45 260	47 820	48 510	26 835	...	36 305	54 070	48 074	28 477	0.592
1982	83 918	2.73	45 139	47 256	48 048	26 782	...	33 965	54 399	47 166	29 123	0.617
1983	85 407	2.71	44 823	47 006	...	26 675	...	34 137	54 516	46 961	29 864	0.636
1984	86 789	2.69	46 215	48 755	49 768	27 774	...	35 034	56 625	47 871	30 473	0.637
1985	88 458	2.67	47 079	49 651	50 767	29 540	...	34 814	57 939	48 229	31 144	0.646
1986	89 479	2.66	48 746	51 248	52 413	29 525	...	35 932	60 223	49 449	31 781	0.643
1987	91 124	2.64	49 358	52 003	53 433	29 682	61 034	36 621	61 382	49 140	32 028	0.652
1988	92 830	2.62	49 737	52 579	54 028	29 974	58 948	37 193	62 145	48 697	32 164	0.660
1989	93 347	2.63	50 624	53 251	54 396	31 669	63 226	38 391	63 958	47 865	32 871	0.687
1990	94 312	2.63	49 950	52 099	53 290	31 155	64 142	37 251	62 395	46 172	33 067	0.716
1991	95 669	2.62	48 516	50 840	52 054	30 287	58 699	36 542	61 071	47 381	33 099	0.699
1992	96 426	2.66	48 117	50 588	52 286	29 457	59 371	35 491	61 003	47 428	33 572	0.708
1993	97 107	2.67	47 884	50 518	52 377	29 939	58 775	35 078	63 497	46 605	33 332	0.715
1994	98 990	2.65	48 418	51 065	52 713	31 555	60 751	35 147	64 729	46 302	33 323	0.720
1995	99 627	2.65	49 935	52 411	54 480	32 815	59 516	33 499	65 852	46 154	32 967	0.714
1996	101 018	2.64	50 661	53 044	55 365	33 518	61 772	35 551	67 263	45 882	33 844	0.738
1997	102 528	2.62	51 704	54 452	56 695	35 000	63 222	37 205	69 430	47 050	34 892	0.742
1998	103 874	2.61	53 582	56 376	58 480	34 933	64 265	39 038	71 455	48 704	35 637	0.732
1999	106 434	2.60	54 932	57 131	59 604	37 673	68 787	41 501	73 885	49 121	35 522	0.723
2000	108 209	2.58	54 841	57 356	59 586	38 747	72 821	43 319	74 621	48 653	35 867	0.737
2001	109 297	2.58	53 646	56 554	58 825	37 438	68 137	42 640	73 947	48 624	37 114	0.763
2002	111 278	2.57	53 019	...	...	...	...	41 385	72 326	49 294	37 759	0.766
2003	112 000	2.57	52 973	...	...	...	...	40 351	72 232	49 732	37 572	0.755
2004	113 343	2.57	52 788	...	...	...	...	40 806	71 997	48 576	37 197	0.766
2005	114 384	2.57	53 371	...	...	...	...	41 437	72 977	47 680	36 703	0.770
2006	116 011	2.56	53 768	...	...	...	...	42 145	74 259	47 142	36 271	0.769
2007	116 783	2.56	54 489	...	...	...	...	41 956	73 337	48 935	38 076	0.778
2008	117 181	2.57	52 546	...	...	...	...	39 604	71 455	48 435	37 339	0.771
2009	117 538	2.59	52 195	...	...	...	...	39 887	71 278	49 416	38 040	0.770
2010	119 927	2.56	50 831	...	...	...	...	38 818	69 518	49 464	38 052	0.769
2011	121 084	2.55	50 054	...	...	...	...	38 624	69 677	48 202	37 118	0.770
By race												
Race alone												
2002	...	...	...	56 366	58 634	36 288	65 792	...	...	...	...	...
2003	...	...	...	55 801	58 426	36 252	68 113	...	...	...	...	...
2004	...	...	...	55 556	58 237	35 834	68 470	...	...	...	...	...
2005	...	...	...	55 938	58 507	35 551	70 385	...	...	...	...	...
2006	...	...	...	56 526	58 478	35 661	71 658	...	...	...	...	...
2007	...	...	...	56 531	59 573	36 790	71 704	...	...	...	...	...
2008	...	...	...	54 645	58 006	35 744	68 564	...	...	...	...	...
2009	...	...	...	54 380	57 106	34 167	68 649	...	...	...	...	...
2010	...	...	...	53 340	56 178	33 137	66 286	...	...	...	...	...
2011	...	...	...	52 214	55 412	32 229	65 129	...	...	...	...	...
Race alone or in combination												
2002	...	...	...	...	...	36 477	65 366	...	...	...	...	...
2003	...	...	...	...	...	36 306	67 579	...	...	...	...	...
2004	...	...	...	...	...	36 001	68 404	...	...	...	...	...
2005	...	...	...	...	...	35 661	70 332	...	...	...	...	...
2006	...	...	...	...	...	35 843	71 281	...	...	...	...	...
2007	...	...	...	...	...	36 979	71 458	...	...	...	...	...
2008	...	...	...	...	...	35 877	68 491	...	...	...	...	...
2009	...	...	...	...	...	34 341	68 234	...	...	...	...	...
2010	...	...	...	...	...	33 170	65 531	...	...	...	...	...
2011	...	...	...	...	...	32 366	64 995	...	...	...	...	...

[1]For 1987 through 2001, Asian and Pacific Islander.
. . . = Not available.

Table 3-2. Median Income and Poverty Rates by Race and Hispanic Origin Using 3-Year Moving Averages

(Income in 2011 dollars; percent of population.)

Race and Hispanic origin	Median household income, 2011 dollars									
	2000–2002	2001–2003	2002–2004	2003–2005	2004–2006	2005–2007	2006–2008	2007–2009	2008–2010	2009–2011
All Races	53 835	53 213	52 927	53 044	53 309	53 876	53 601	53 077	51 857	51 026
White alone or in combination	56 708	56 165	55 804	55 669	55 913	56 238	55 826	55 097	54 009	53 184
White alone	56 759	56 240	55 908	55 765	56 007	56 332	55 901	55 185	54 122	53 311
Not Hispanic	59 015	58 628	58 432	58 390	58 407	58 853	58 686	58 228	57 097	56 232
Black alone or in combination	37 554	36 740	36 261	35 989	35 835	36 161	36 233	35 732	34 463	33 292
Black alone	37 491	36 659	36 125	35 879	35 682	36 001	36 065	35 567	34 349	33 178
American Indian and Alaskan Native alone or in combination	41 404	42 471	43 154	42 882	41 683	41 251	41 154	40 621	39 561	37 987
American Indian and Alaskan Native alone	40 863	40 372	39 361	38 745	37 586	37 901	37 156	37 225	35 343	33 939
Asian alone or in combination	68 775	67 027	67 116	68 772	70 006	71 024	70 410	69 394	67 419	66 253
Asian alone	68 917	67 347	67 458	68 989	70 171	71 249	70 642	69 639	67 833	66 688
Native Hawaiian and Other Pacific Islander alone or in combination	. . .	. . .	62 085	61 765	61 212	62 479	62 402	60 582	59 485	57 283
Native Hawaiian and Other Pacific Islander alone	. . .	. . .	61 492	62 585	61 342	61 046	60 735	59 992	59 558	57 341
Hispanic (any race)	42 448	41 459	40 847	40 865	41 463	41 846	41 235	40 482	39 436	39 110

Race and Hispanic origin	Poverty rates									
	2000–2002	2001–2003	2002–2004	2003–2005	2004–2006	2005–2007	2006–2008	2007–2009	2008–2010	2009–2011
All Races	11.7	12.1	12.4	12.6	12.5	12.5	12.7	13.4	14.2	14.8
White alone or in combination	9.9	10.3	10.6	10.7	10.7	10.5	10.8	11.5	12.3	12.9
White alone	9.9	10.2	10.5	10.6	10.6	10.4	10.7	11.3	12.2	12.7
Not Hispanic	7.7	8.0	8.3	8.4	8.4	8.2	8.3	8.7	9.3	9.7
Black alone or in combination	23.0	23.6	24.3	24.6	24.5	24.4	24.4	25.0	26.0	26.9
Black alone	23.1	23.7	24.4	24.7	24.6	24.6	24.5	25.0	26.0	26.9
American Indian and Alaskan Native alone or in combination	21.6	20.0	19.2	19.7	20.9	21.2	21.6	21.9	23.7	24.4
American Indian and Alaskan Native alone	23.1	23.3	24.3	25.3	27.2	26.6	26.7	26.1	27.8	28.3
Asian alone or in combination	10.0	10.7	10.5	10.8	10.3	10.4	10.6	11.4	12.0	12.2
Asian alone	10.1	10.7	10.6	10.9	10.4	10.5	10.8	11.5	12.1	12.3
Native Hawaiian and Other Pacific Islander alone or in combination	. . .	. . .	. . .	. . .	. . .	. . .	. . .	. . .	. . .	. . .
Native Hawaiian and Other Pacific Islander alone	. . .	. . .	. . .	. . .	. . .	. . .	. . .	. . .	. . .	. . .
Hispanic (any race)	21.6	21.9	22.1	22.0	21.4	21.3	21.8	23.3	25.0	25.7

. . . = Not available.

Table 3-3. Median Family Income by Type of Family

(2011 dollars, except as noted.)

Year	All families	Married couples			Male householder [1]	Female householder [1]	4-person families	Average size of family (number of people)
		Total	Wife in paid labor force	Wife not in paid labor force				
1947	26 697	27 384	. . .	. . .	25 860	19 131	28 996	3.64
1948	25 992	26 685	. . .	. . .	26 873	16 833	28 283	3.58
1949	25 656	26 383	31 849	25 251	23 294	17 366	27 894	3.54
1950	27 068	28 104	32 647	27 036	25 405	15 675	29 972	3.54
1951	28 034	29 001	35 003	27 467	26 091	16 780	31 156	3.54
1952	28 873	30 143	36 370	28 294	26 832	16 589	32 458	3.53
1953	31 275	32 226	39 850	30 354	30 324	18 100	. . .	3.59
1954	30 450	31 663	38 993	29 603	29 332	16 763	. . .	3.59
1955	32 428	33 757	41 265	31 753	30 755	18 137	36 105	3.58
1956	34 548	35 943	43 055	33 572	30 117	19 905	38 443	3.60
1957	34 751	36 088	42 974	33 821	32 057	19 335	38 404	3.64
1958	34 644	36 197	42 319	33 936	29 012	18 667	38 717	3.65
1959	36 590	38 245	45 290	35 914	31 159	18 670	41 000	3.67
1960	37 350	39 031	45 857	36 685	32 299	19 725	41 836	3.70
1961	37 734	39 722	47 295	36 794	33 352	19 693	42 353	3.67
1962	38 802	40 802	48 607	37 551	37 206	20 398	44 014	3.68
1963	40 157	42 367	50 053	38 807	36 693	20 634	45 869	3.70
1964	41 646	43 947	51 796	40 181	36 720	21 923	47 472	3.70
1965	43 439	45 362	53 678	41 160	38 387	22 053	48 702	3.69
1966	45 732	47 590	56 139	43 279	39 053	24 347	50 644	3.67
1967	46 707	49 698	58 618	44 811	40 119	25 282	52 954	3.63
1968	48 905	51 806	60 542	46 542	41 477	25 365	55 715	3.60
1969	51 161	54 242	63 072	48 157	45 233	26 153	57 615	3.58
1970	51 003	54 357	63 455	48 093	46 583	26 326	57 722	3.57
1971	50 932	54 423	63 648	48 253	43 192	25 325	57 572	3.53
1972	53 444	57 228	66 815	50 752	49 545	25 684	61 579	3.48
1973	54 527	58 947	68 942	51 663	48 604	26 229	62 033	3.44
1974	53 070	57 270	66 722	50 310	47 953	26 687	61 572	3.42
1975	52 145	56 508	65 516	48 469	49 393	26 014	60 237	3.39
1976	53 761	58 236	67 322	50 070	46 220	25 917	62 232	3.37
1977	54 123	59 555	68 521	50 924	49 082	26 252	63 298	3.33
1978	55 809	61 188	69 948	51 114	50 513	27 009	64 630	3.31
1979	56 552	61 871	71 780	51 121	48 529	28 526	64 997	3.29
1980	54 633	60 137	69 852	49 303	45 527	27 048	63 233	3.27
1981	53 123	59 475	69 399	48 228	47 194	26 006	62 344	3.25
1982	52 438	58 225	67 899	47 663	45 069	25 699	61 806	3.26
1983	52 754	58 561	68 908	46 980	46 884	25 302	62 635	3.24
1984	54 499	61 054	71 478	48 621	48 091	26 397	64 116	3.23
1985	55 286	61 994	72 620	48 949	45 094	27 229	65 336	3.21
1986	57 676	64 229	75 078	50 520	48 873	26 720	67 971	3.19
1987	58 655	66 058	77 179	50 454	47 742	27 808	70 238	3.17
1988	58 809	66 478	78 024	49 728	49 010	28 035	71 342	3.16
1989	59 918	67 508	79 276	50 345	48 769	28 795	71 389	3.17
1990	58 975	66 552	78 033	50 488	48 454	28 246	69 148	3.18
1991	57 877	66 020	77 573	48 434	45 657	26 881	69 339	3.17
1992	57 442	65 793	78 177	47 392	43 311	26 740	69 501	3.19
1993	56 648	65 914	78 481	46 316	40 566	26 735	69 219	3.20
1994	58 199	67 469	80 000	46 785	41 645	27 366	70 550	3.19
1995	59 511	68 964	81 803	47 442	44 486	28 855	72 811	3.20
1996	60 379	70 952	83 333	48 172	45 106	28 421	73 537	3.19
1997	62 271	72 083	84 767	50 337	46 052	29 374	74 541	3.18
1998	64 402	74 659	87 847	51 207	49 167	30 540	77 251	3.18
1999	65 913	76 266	89 733	51 941	50 401	32 074	80 658	3.15
2000	66 259	77 186	90 424	52 218	49 273	33 586	81 850	3.14
2001	65 307	76 649	89 986	51 809	46 483	32 706	80 387	3.15
2002	64 610	76 424	91 021	50 135	47 181	33 034	78 427	3.13
2003	64 421	76 162	91 924	50 287	46 509	32 467	79 601	3.13
2004	64 370	75 759	91 510	50 265	48 058	32 112	78 614	3.13
2005	64 740	75 929	90 732	51 218	47 363	31 387	81 005	3.13
2006	65 153	77 420	92 350	51 042	46 677	32 159	81 895	3.13
2007	66 554	78 739	93 759	51 339	48 116	32 863	82 087	3.15
2008	64 264	75 987	90 484	50 665	45 514	31 473	79 880	3.15
2009	63 007	75 106	90 123	49 963	43 517	31 216	78 020	3.16
2010	62 136	74 520	90 154	50 270	44 569	30 075	77 108	3.14
2011	60 974	73 790	89 017	50 414	43 069	30 259	75 570	3.13

[1]No spouse present.
. . . = Not available.

Table 3-4. Shares of Aggregate Income Received by Each Fifth and Top 5 Percent of Households

Year	Money income							Equivalence-adjusted income						
	Share of aggregate income (percent)						Gini coefficient	Share of aggregate income (percent)						Gini coefficient
	Lowest fifth	Second fifth	Third fifth	Fourth fifth	Highest fifth	Top 5 percent		Lowest fifth	Second fifth	Third fifth	Fourth fifth	Highest fifth	Top 5 percent	
1967	4.0	10.8	17.3	24.2	43.6	17.2	0.397	5.6	12.0	17.1	23.2	42.1	. . .	0.362
1968	4.2	11.1	17.6	24.5	42.6	16.3	0.386	5.8	12.3	17.4	23.4	41.1	. . .	0.351
1969	4.1	10.9	17.5	24.5	43.0	16.6	0.391	5.8	12.2	17.3	23.4	41.3	. . .	0.353
1970	4.1	10.8	17.4	24.5	43.3	16.6	0.394	5.7	12.1	17.3	23.4	41.5	. . .	0.357
1971	4.1	10.6	17.3	24.5	43.5	16.7	0.396	5.7	12.0	17.2	23.4	41.7	. . .	0.359
1972	4.1	10.4	17.0	24.5	43.9	17.0	0.401	5.6	11.9	17.2	23.4	41.9	. . .	0.362
1973	4.2	10.4	17.0	24.5	43.9	16.9	0.400	5.6	12.0	17.2	23.5	41.7	. . .	0.360
1974	4.3	10.6	17.0	24.6	43.5	16.5	0.395	5.8	12.1	17.3	23.6	41.2	. . .	0.354
1975	4.3	10.4	17.0	24.7	43.6	16.5	0.397	5.6	11.9	17.3	23.6	41.6	. . .	0.359
1976	4.3	10.3	17.0	24.7	43.7	16.6	0.398	5.6	11.8	17.4	23.8	41.5	. . .	0.359
1977	4.2	10.2	16.9	24.7	44.0	16.8	0.402	5.5	11.7	17.3	23.7	41.7	. . .	0.362
1978	4.2	10.2	16.8	24.7	44.1	16.8	0.402	5.4	11.8	17.3	23.7	41.8	. . .	0.363
1979	4.1	10.2	16.8	24.6	44.2	16.9	0.404	5.3	11.7	17.2	23.8	41.9	. . .	0.366
1980	4.2	10.2	16.8	24.7	44.1	16.5	0.403	5.2	11.6	17.3	24.0	41.9	. . .	0.367
1981	4.1	10.1	16.7	24.8	44.3	16.5	0.406	5.0	11.4	17.2	24.0	42.4	. . .	0.373
1982	4.0	10.0	16.5	24.5	45.0	17.0	0.412	4.7	11.1	17.0	23.9	43.2	. . .	0.384
1983	4.0	9.9	16.4	24.6	45.1	17.0	0.414	4.6	11.0	16.9	24.0	43.5	. . .	0.389
1984	4.0	9.9	16.3	24.6	45.2	17.1	0.415	4.6	11.0	16.8	24.0	43.6	. . .	0.389
1985	3.9	9.8	16.2	24.4	45.6	17.6	0.419	4.6	10.9	16.7	23.7	44.1	. . .	0.394
1986	3.8	9.7	16.2	24.3	46.1	18.0	0.425	4.5	10.8	16.6	23.8	44.3	. . .	0.397
1987	3.8	9.6	16.1	24.3	46.2	18.2	0.426	4.4	10.8	16.7	23.8	44.4	. . .	0.399
1988	3.8	9.6	16.0	24.2	46.3	18.3	0.426	4.4	10.7	16.5	23.7	44.7	. . .	0.402
1989	3.8	9.5	15.8	24.0	46.8	18.9	0.431	4.4	10.5	16.3	23.4	45.4	. . .	0.408
1990	3.8	9.6	15.9	24.0	46.6	18.5	0.428	4.4	10.6	16.3	23.5	45.1	. . .	0.406
1991	3.8	9.6	15.9	24.2	46.5	18.1	0.428	4.3	10.6	16.5	23.7	45.0	. . .	0.406
1992	3.8	9.4	15.8	24.2	46.9	18.6	0.433	4.1	10.3	16.3	23.7	45.5	. . .	0.413
1993	3.6	9.0	15.1	23.5	48.9	21.0	0.454	3.9	9.8	15.6	23.0	47.7	. . .	0.436
1994	3.6	8.9	15.0	23.4	49.1	21.2	0.456	4.0	9.8	15.6	22.8	47.8	. . .	0.436
1995	3.7	9.1	15.2	23.3	48.7	21.0	0.450	4.1	9.9	15.6	22.8	47.6	. . .	0.433
1996	3.6	9.0	15.1	23.3	49.0	21.4	0.455	4.0	9.8	15.5	22.7	47.9	. . .	0.437
1997	3.6	8.9	15.0	23.2	49.4	21.7	0.459	4.0	9.8	15.4	22.6	48.3	. . .	0.440
1998	3.6	9.0	15.0	23.2	49.2	21.4	0.456	4.0	9.8	15.4	22.7	48.1	. . .	0.439
1999	3.6	8.9	14.9	23.2	49.4	21.5	0.458	4.0	9.7	15.3	22.6	48.4	. . .	0.441
2000	3.6	8.9	14.8	23.0	49.8	22.1	0.462	4.1	9.8	15.2	22.3	48.6	. . .	0.442
2001	3.5	8.7	14.6	23.0	50.1	22.4	0.466	4.0	9.6	15.2	22.4	48.8	. . .	0.446
2002	3.5	8.8	14.8	23.3	49.7	21.7	0.462	4.0	9.6	15.2	22.7	48.4	. . .	0.443
2003	3.4	8.7	14.8	23.4	49.8	21.4	0.464	3.9	9.5	15.2	22.8	48.6	. . .	0.445
2004	3.4	8.7	14.7	23.2	50.1	21.8	0.466	3.8	9.6	15.2	22.7	48.7	. . .	0.447
2005	3.4	8.6	14.6	23.0	50.4	22.2	0.469	3.8	9.5	15.1	22.6	49.1	. . .	0.450
2006	3.4	8.6	14.5	22.9	50.5	22.3	0.470	3.8	9.4	14.9	22.5	49.3	. . .	0.452
2007	3.4	8.7	14.8	23.4	49.7	21.2	0.463	3.8	9.5	15.3	22.9	48.5	. . .	0.444
2008	3.4	8.6	14.7	23.3	50.0	21.5	0.466	3.7	9.4	15.1	22.8	48.9	21.4	0.450
2009	3.4	8.6	14.6	23.2	50.3	21.7	0.468	3.6	9.3	15.0	22.9	49.4	21.7	0.456
2010	3.3	8.5	14.6	23.4	50.3	21.3	0.470	3.4	9.2	15.0	23.1	49.2	21.0	0.456
2011	3.2	8.4	14.3	23.0	51.1	22.3	0.477	3.4	9.0	14.8	22.8	50.0	22.1	0.463

. . . = Not available.

Table 3-5. Shares of Aggregate Income Received by Each Fifth and Top 5 Percent of Families

Year	Number of families (thousands)	Share of aggregate income (percent)						Mean family income (2011 dollars)						Gini coefficient
		Lowest fifth	Second fifth	Third fifth	Fourth fifth	Highest fifth	Top 5 percent	Lowest fifth	Second fifth	Third fifth	Fourth fifth	Highest fifth	Top 5 percent	
1947	37 237	5.0	11.9	17.0	23.1	43.0	17.5	...	...	...	...	...	...	0.376
1948	38 624	4.9	12.1	17.3	23.2	42.4	17.1	...	...	...	...	...	...	0.371
1949	39 303	4.5	11.9	17.3	23.5	42.7	16.9	...	...	...	...	...	...	0.378
1950	39 929	4.5	12.0	17.4	23.4	42.7	17.3	...	...	...	...	...	...	0.379
1951	40 578	5.0	12.4	17.6	23.4	41.6	16.8	...	...	...	...	...	...	0.363
1952	40 832	4.9	12.3	17.4	23.4	41.9	17.4	...	...	...	...	...	...	0.368
1953	41 202	4.7	12.5	18.0	23.9	40.9	15.7	...	...	...	...	...	...	0.359
1954	41 951	4.5	12.1	17.7	23.9	41.8	16.3	...	...	...	...	...	...	0.371
1955	42 889	4.8	12.3	17.8	23.7	41.3	16.4	...	...	...	...	...	...	0.363
1956	43 497	5.0	12.5	17.9	23.7	41.0	16.1	...	...	...	...	...	...	0.358
1957	43 696	5.1	12.7	18.1	23.8	40.4	15.6	...	...	...	...	...	...	0.351
1958	44 232	5.0	12.5	18.0	23.9	40.6	15.4	...	...	...	...	...	...	0.354
1959	45 111	4.9	12.3	17.9	23.8	41.1	15.9	...	...	...	...	...	...	0.361
1960	45 539	4.8	12.2	17.8	24.0	41.3	15.9	...	...	...	...	...	...	0.364
1961	46 418	4.7	11.9	17.5	23.8	42.2	16.6	...	...	...	...	...	...	0.374
1962	47 059	5.0	12.1	17.6	24.0	41.3	15.7	...	...	...	...	...	...	0.362
1963	47 540	5.0	12.1	17.7	24.0	41.2	15.8	...	...	...	...	...	...	0.362
1964	47 956	5.1	12.0	17.7	24.0	41.2	15.9	...	...	...	...	...	...	0.361
1965	48 509	5.2	12.2	17.8	23.9	40.9	15.5	...	...	...	...	...	...	0.356
1966	49 214	5.6	12.4	17.8	23.8	40.5	15.6	14 238	31 609	45 228	60 547	103 334	158 672	0.349
1967	50 111	5.4	12.2	17.5	23.5	41.4	16.4	14 460	32 335	46 478	62 333	110 065	174 141	0.358
1968	50 823	5.6	12.4	17.7	23.7	40.5	15.6	15 586	33 993	48 565	64 950	110 982	171 082	0.348
1969	51 586	5.6	12.4	17.7	23.7	40.6	15.6	16 081	35 514	50 820	68 078	116 592	179 078	0.349
1970	52 227	5.4	12.2	17.6	23.8	40.9	15.6	15 838	35 020	50 636	68 303	117 456	178 853	0.353
1971	53 296	5.5	12.0	17.6	23.8	41.1	15.7	15 851	34 506	50 486	68 373	117 764	179 560	0.355
1972	54 373	5.5	11.9	17.5	23.9	41.4	15.9	16 544	36 097	53 021	72 406	125 577	192 516	0.359
1973	55 053	5.5	11.9	17.5	24.0	41.1	15.5	16 977	36 772	54 029	73 838	126 686	191 189	0.356
1974	55 698	5.7	12.0	17.6	24.1	40.6	14.8	17 276	36 469	53 243	72 946	122 914	179 283	0.355
1975	56 245	5.6	11.9	17.7	24.2	40.7	14.9	16 599	35 090	52 175	71 438	120 387	176 598	0.357
1976	56 710	5.6	11.9	17.7	24.2	40.7	14.9	17 000	35 977	53 667	73 327	123 415	180 630	0.358
1977	57 215	5.5	11.7	17.6	24.3	40.9	14.9	16 927	36 184	54 420	75 070	126 467	184 370	0.363
1978	57 804	5.4	11.7	17.6	24.2	41.1	15.1	17 167	37 228	55 901	77 019	130 693	191 517	0.363
1979	59 550	5.4	11.6	17.5	24.1	41.4	15.3	17 318	37 442	56 466	77 739	133 338	197 372	0.365
1980	60 309	5.3	11.6	17.6	24.4	41.1	14.6	16 661	36 268	54 789	76 013	127 983	181 938	0.365
1981	61 019	5.3	11.4	17.5	24.6	41.2	14.4	16 142	35 104	53 690	75 381	126 480	176 734	0.369
1982	61 393	5.0	11.3	17.2	24.4	42.2	15.3	15 228	34 552	52 758	74 843	129 325	185 031	0.380
1983	62 015	4.9	11.2	17.2	24.5	42.4	15.3	14 995	34 502	53 084	75 656	131 180	189 136	0.382
1984	62 706	4.8	11.1	17.1	24.5	42.5	15.4	15 507	35 504	54 778	78 332	136 138	196 832	0.383
1985	63 558	4.8	11.0	16.9	24.3	43.1	16.1	15 686	35 994	55 573	79 659	141 567	211 557	0.389
1986	64 491	4.7	10.9	16.9	24.1	43.4	16.5	16 129	37 241	57 696	82 438	148 484	225 483	0.392
1987	65 204	4.6	10.7	16.8	24.0	43.8	17.2	16 112	37 710	58 556	83 806	153 158	239 759	0.393
1988	65 837	4.6	10.7	16.7	24.0	44.0	17.2	16 250	37 842	58 888	84 572	155 175	242 456	0.395
1989	66 090	4.6	10.6	16.5	23.7	44.6	17.9	16 575	38 561	59 906	86 188	162 283	259 963	0.401
1990	66 322	4.6	10.8	16.6	23.8	44.3	17.4	16 403	38 260	58 924	84 739	157 483	247 098	0.396
1991	67 173	4.5	10.7	16.6	24.1	44.2	17.1	15 676	37 209	57 736	83 738	153 845	238 050	0.397
1992	68 216	4.3	10.5	16.5	24.0	44.7	17.6	15 056	36 314	57 370	83 390	155 180	244 320	0.404
1993	68 506	4.1	9.9	15.7	23.3	47.0	20.3	14 927	35 850	56 812	84 217	170 157	293 687	0.429
1994	69 313	4.2	10.0	15.7	23.3	46.9	20.1	15 588	36 879	58 238	86 088	173 491	297 639	0.426
1995	69 597	4.4	10.1	15.8	23.2	46.5	20.0	16 508	38 034	59 549	87 128	175 046	300 205	0.421
1996	70 241	4.2	10.0	15.8	23.1	46.8	20.3	16 255	38 321	60 617	88 573	179 320	310 252	0.425
1997	70 884	4.2	9.9	15.7	23.0	47.2	20.7	16 846	39 474	62 281	91 326	187 624	328 373	0.429
1998	71 551	4.2	9.9	15.7	23.0	47.3	20.7	17 260	40 625	64 299	94 295	194 082	339 698	0.430
1999	73 206	4.3	9.9	15.6	23.0	47.2	20.3	17 963	41 755	65 907	97 277	199 371	343 751	0.429
2000	73 778	4.3	9.8	15.4	22.7	47.7	21.1	18 444	42 171	66 278	97 681	204 944	363 164	0.433
2001	74 340	4.2	9.7	15.4	22.9	47.7	21.0	17 812	41 244	65 473	97 370	202 809	356 104	0.435
2002	75 616	4.2	9.7	15.5	23.0	47.6	20.8	17 524	40 657	64 846	96 446	199 153	348 540	0.434
2003	76 232	4.1	9.6	15.5	23.2	47.6	20.5	16 963	40 228	64 832	97 479	199 723	344 200	0.436
2004	76 866	4.0	9.6	15.4	23.0	47.9	20.9	16 907	40 242	64 587	96 495	200 827	349 872	0.438
2005	77 418	4.0	9.6	15.3	22.9	48.1	21.1	17 013	40 480	64 778	96 884	203 102	355 572	0.440
2006	78 454	4.0	9.5	15.1	22.9	48.5	21.5	17 334	41 016	65 240	98 604	209 033	370 014	0.444
2007	77 908	4.1	9.7	15.6	23.3	47.3	20.1	17 429	41 549	66 650	99 666	202 333	343 445	0.432
2008	78 874	4.0	9.6	15.5	23.1	47.8	20.5	16 615	39 825	64 328	96 270	198 890	341 506	0.438
2009	78 867	3.9	9.4	15.3	23.2	48.2	20.7	16 032	38 844	62 817	95 380	198 690	340 810	0.443
2010	79 559	3.8	9.5	15.4	23.5	47.8	20.0	15 394	38 075	62 059	94 681	193 022	322 745	0.440
2011	80 529	3.8	9.3	15.1	23.0	48.9	21.3	15 282	37 556	61 032	93 232	197 932	344 531	0.450

. . . = Not available.

Section 3b: Poverty

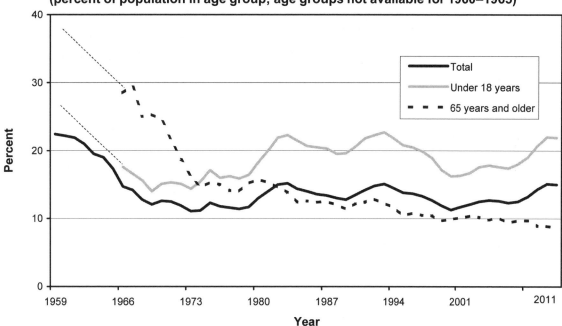

Figure 3-2: Poverty Rates, Total, Children, and Seniors, 1959–2011 (percent of population in age group; age groups not available for 1960–1965)

- The number of Americans with family money incomes below the official poverty line was 15.0 percent of the population in 2011, little changed from 2010, which was the highest rate since 1993. (Table 3-7)

- Poverty affecting children changed little in 2011, with 21.9 percent living below the poverty threshold, while poverty for those 65 and older edged down to 8.7 percent, an all-time low. In 1959, the first poverty rate calculations showed more than one-third of all seniors living in poverty, compared with 17 percent of working-age adults. Between 1959 and 1974, ad hoc legislative changes raised Social Security benefits by a cumulative 104 percent—exceeding the 69 percent increase in consumer prices—and since then, each year's benefits have been indexed to the rate of change in the Consumer Price Index, Urban Wage Earners and Clerical Workers (CPI-W). As a result, since the early 1980s, officially-measured senior poverty has been consistently lower than the population average. (Table 3-9)

- However, the official thresholds do not specifically include medical expenses or account for the disproportionate effect of medical price inflation on senior budgets. The new Supplemental Poverty Measure (SPM) estimates that the poverty rate for persons 65 and older was 15.1 percent in 2011, little different from the 16.1 percent SPM for all ages. (Table 3-13)

- The poverty rate for children, on the other hand, has always been higher than the average, and remains so even in the SPM (18.1 percent, compared with the official 21.9 percent), which takes account of government programs benefitting families with children. (Tables 3-9 and 3-13)

- The official poverty rate among Hispanics (who may be of any race) was 25.3 percent in 2011, compared with 9.8 percent for non-Hispanic Whites. Poverty among Blacks was 27.6 percent and poverty among Asians was 12.3 percent. (Table 3-7)

Table 3-6. Weighted Average Poverty Thresholds by Family Size

(Dollars.)

Year	Unrelated individuals			Families of 2 people			Families, all ages								CPI-U, all items (1982–1984 = 100)
	All ages	Under 65 years	65 years and older	All ages	House-holder under 65 years	House-holder 65 years and older	3 people	4 people	5 people	6 people	7 people or more (before 1980)	7 people	8 people	9 people or more	
1959	1 467	1 503	1 397	1 894	1 952	1 761	2 324	2 973	3 506	3 944	4 849	. . .	. . .	. . .	29.2
1960	1 490	1 526	1 418	1 924	1 982	1 788	2 359	3 022	3 560	4 002	4 921	. . .	. . .	. . .	29.6
1961	1 506	1 545	1 433	1 942	2 005	1 808	2 383	3 054	3 597	4 041	4 967	. . .	. . .	. . .	29.9
1962	1 519	1 562	1 451	1 962	2 027	1 828	2 412	3 089	3 639	4 088	5 032	. . .	. . .	. . .	30.3
1963	1 539	1 581	1 470	1 988	2 052	1 850	2 442	3 128	3 685	4 135	5 092	. . .	. . .	. . .	30.6
1964	1 558	1 601	1 488	2 015	2 079	1 875	2 473	3 169	3 732	4 193	5 156	. . .	. . .	. . .	31.0
1965	1 582	1 626	1 512	2 048	2 114	1 906	2 514	3 223	3 797	4 264	5 248	. . .	. . .	. . .	31.5
1966	1 628	1 674	1 556	2 107	2 175	1 961	2 588	3 317	3 908	4 388	5 395	. . .	. . .	. . .	32.5
1967	1 675	1 722	1 600	2 168	2 238	2 017	2 661	3 410	4 019	4 516	5 550	. . .	. . .	. . .	33.4
1968	1 748	1 797	1 667	2 262	2 333	2 102	2 774	3 553	4 188	4 706	5 789	. . .	. . .	. . .	34.8
1969	1 840	1 893	1 757	2 383	2 458	2 215	2 924	3 743	4 415	4 958	6 101	. . .	. . .	. . .	36.7
1970	1 954	2 010	1 861	2 525	2 604	2 348	3 099	3 968	4 680	5 260	6 468	. . .	. . .	. . .	38.8
1971	2 040	2 098	1 940	2 633	2 716	2 448	3 229	4 137	4 880	5 489	6 751	. . .	. . .	. . .	40.5
1972	2 109	2 168	2 005	2 724	2 808	2 530	3 339	4 275	5 044	5 673	6 983	. . .	. . .	. . .	41.8
1973	2 247	2 307	2 130	2 895	2 984	2 688	3 548	4 540	5 358	6 028	7 435	. . .	. . .	. . .	44.4
1974	2 495	2 562	2 364	3 211	3 312	2 982	3 936	5 038	5 950	6 699	8 253	. . .	. . .	. . .	49.3
1975	2 724	2 797	2 581	3 506	3 617	3 257	4 293	5 500	6 499	7 316	9 022	. . .	. . .	. . .	53.8
1976	2 884	2 959	2 730	3 711	3 826	3 445	4 540	5 815	6 876	7 760	9 588	. . .	. . .	. . .	56.9
1977	3 075	3 152	2 906	3 951	4 072	3 666	4 833	6 191	7 320	8 261	10 216	. . .	. . .	. . .	60.6
1978	3 311	3 392	3 127	4 249	4 383	3 944	5 201	6 662	7 880	8 891	11 002	. . .	. . .	. . .	65.2
1979	3 689	3 778	3 479	4 725	4 878	4 390	5 784	7 412	8 775	9 914	12 280	. . .	. . .	. . .	72.6
1980	4 190	4 290	3 949	5 363	5 537	4 983	6 565	8 414	9 966	11 269	13 955	12 761	14 199	16 896	82.4
1981	4 620	4 729	4 359	5 917	6 111	5 498	7 250	9 287	11 007	12 449	. . .	14 110	15 655	18 572	90.9
1982	4 901	5 019	4 626	6 281	6 487	5 836	7 693	9 862	11 684	13 207	. . .	15 036	16 719	19 698	96.5
1983	5 061	5 180	4 775	6 483	6 697	6 023	7 938	10 178	12 049	13 630	. . .	15 500	17 170	20 310	99.6
1984	5 278	5 400	4 979	6 762	6 983	6 282	8 277	10 609	12 566	14 207	. . .	16 096	17 961	21 247	103.9
1985	5 469	5 593	5 156	6 998	7 231	6 503	8 573	10 989	13 007	14 696	. . .	16 656	18 512	22 083	107.6
1986	5 572	5 701	5 255	7 138	7 372	6 630	8 737	11 203	13 259	14 986	. . .	17 049	18 791	22 497	109.6
1987	5 778	5 909	5 447	7 397	7 641	6 872	9 056	11 611	13 737	15 509	. . .	17 649	19 515	23 105	113.6
1988	6 022	6 155	5 674	7 704	7 958	7 157	9 435	12 092	14 304	16 146	. . .	18 232	20 253	24 129	118.3
1989	6 310	6 451	5 947	8 076	8 343	7 501	9 885	12 674	14 990	16 921	. . .	19 162	21 328	25 480	124.0
1990	6 652	6 800	6 268	8 509	8 794	7 905	10 419	13 359	15 792	17 839	. . .	20 241	22 582	26 848	130.7
1991	6 932	7 086	6 532	8 865	9 165	8 241	10 860	13 924	16 456	18 587	. . .	21 058	23 582	27 942	136.2
1992	7 143	7 299	6 729	9 137	9 443	8 487	11 186	14 335	16 952	19 137	. . .	21 594	24 053	28 745	140.3
1993	7 363	7 518	6 930	9 414	9 728	8 740	11 522	14 763	17 449	19 718	. . .	22 383	24 838	29 529	144.5
1994	7 547	7 710	7 108	9 661	9 976	8 967	11 821	15 141	17 900	20 235	. . .	22 923	25 427	30 300	148.2
1995	7 763	7 929	7 309	9 933	10 259	9 219	12 158	15 569	18 408	20 804	. . .	23 552	26 237	31 280	152.4
1996	7 995	8 163	7 525	10 233	10 564	9 491	12 516	16 036	18 952	21 389	. . .	24 268	27 091	31 971	156.9
1997	8 183	8 350	7 698	10 473	10 805	9 712	12 802	16 400	19 380	21 886	. . .	24 802	27 593	32 566	160.5
1998	8 316	8 480	7 818	10 634	10 972	9 862	13 003	16 660	19 680	22 228	. . .	25 257	28 166	33 339	163.0
1999	8 499	8 667	7 990	10 864	11 213	10 075	13 289	17 030	20 128	22 730	. . .	25 918	28 970	34 436	166.6
2000	8 791	8 959	8 259	11 235	11 589	10 418	13 740	17 604	20 815	23 533	. . .	26 750	29 701	35 150	172.2
2001	9 039	9 214	8 494	11 569	11 920	10 715	14 128	18 104	21 405	24 195	. . .	27 517	30 627	36 286	177.1
2002	9 183	9 359	8 628	11 756	12 110	10 885	14 348	18 392	21 744	24 576	. . .	28 001	30 907	37 062	179.9
2003	9 393	9 573	8 825	12 015	12 384	11 133	14 680	18 810	22 245	25 122	. . .	28 544	31 589	37 656	184.0
2004	9 646	9 827	9 060	12 335	12 714	11 430	15 066	19 307	22 830	25 787	. . .	29 233	32 641	39 062	188.9
2005	9 973	10 160	9 367	12 755	13 145	11 815	15 577	19 971	23 613	26 683	. . .	30 249	33 610	40 288	195.3
2006	10 294	10 488	9 669	13 167	13 569	12 201	16 079	20 614	24 382	27 560	. . .	31 205	34 774	41 499	201.6
2007	10 590	10 787	9 944	13 540	13 954	12 550	16 530	21 203	25 080	28 323	. . .	32 233	35 816	42 739	207.3
2008	10 991	11 201	10 326	14 051	14 417	13 014	17 163	22 025	26 049	29 456	. . .	33 529	37 220	44 346	215.3
2009	10 956	11 161	10 289	13 991	14 439	12 982	17 098	21 954	25 991	29 405	. . .	33 372	37 252	44 366	214.5
2010	11 137	11 344	10 458	14 216	14 676	13 194	17 373	22 315	26 442	29 904	. . .	34 019	37 953	45 224	218.1
2011	11 484	11 702	10 788	14 657	15 139	13 609	17 916	23 021	27 251	30 847	. . .	35 085	39 064	46 572	224.9

. . . = Not available.

Table 3-7. Poverty Status of People by Race and Hispanic Origin

(Thousands of people, percent of population.)

Year	Number of people, all races	Below poverty level											
		All races		White		White, not Hispanic		Black		Asian [1]		Hispanic (any race)	
		Number	Poverty rate (percent)	Number	Poverty rate (percent)	Number	Poverty rate (percent)	Number	Poverty rate (percent)	Number	Poverty rate (percent)	Number	Poverty rate (percent)
1959	176 557	39 490	22.4	28 484	18.1	. . .	. . .	9 927	55.1	. . .	. . .	. . .	. . .
1960	179 503	39 851	22.2	28 309	17.8	. . .	. . .	. . .	. . .	. . .	. . .	. . .	. . .
1961	181 277	39 628	21.9	27 890	17.4	. . .	. . .	. . .	. . .	. . .	. . .	. . .	. . .
1962	184 276	38 625	21.0	26 672	16.4	. . .	. . .	. . .	. . .	. . .	. . .	. . .	. . .
1963	187 258	36 436	19.5	25 238	15.3	. . .	. . .	. . .	. . .	. . .	. . .	. . .	. . .
1964	189 710	36 055	19.0	24 957	14.9	. . .	. . .	. . .	. . .	. . .	. . .	. . .	. . .
1965	191 413	33 185	17.3	22 496	13.3	. . .	. . .	. . .	. . .	. . .	. . .	. . .	. . .
1966	193 388	28 510	14.7	19 290	11.3	. . .	. . .	8 867	41.8	. . .	. . .	. . .	. . .
1967	195 672	27 769	14.2	18 983	11.0	. . .	. . .	8 486	39.3	. . .	. . .	. . .	. . .
1968	197 628	25 389	12.8	17 395	10.0	. . .	. . .	7 616	34.7	. . .	. . .	. . .	. . .
1969	199 517	24 147	12.1	16 659	9.5	. . .	. . .	7 095	32.2	. . .	. . .	. . .	. . .
1970	202 183	25 420	12.6	17 484	9.9	. . .	. . .	7 548	33.5	. . .	. . .	. . .	. . .
1971	204 554	25 559	12.5	17 780	9.9	. . .	. . .	7 396	32.5	. . .	. . .	. . .	. . .
1972	206 004	24 460	11.9	16 203	9.0	. . .	. . .	7 710	33.3	. . .	. . .	2 414	22.8
1973	207 621	22 973	11.1	15 142	8.4	12 864	7.5	7 388	31.4	. . .	. . .	2 366	21.9
1974	209 362	23 370	11.2	15 736	8.6	13 217	7.7	7 182	30.3	. . .	. . .	2 575	23.0
1975	210 864	25 877	12.3	17 770	9.7	14 883	8.6	7 545	31.3	. . .	. . .	2 991	26.9
1976	212 303	24 975	11.8	16 713	9.1	14 025	8.1	7 595	31.1	. . .	. . .	2 783	24.7
1977	213 867	24 720	11.6	16 416	8.9	13 802	8.0	7 726	31.3	. . .	. . .	2 700	22.4
1978	215 656	24 497	11.4	16 259	8.7	13 755	7.9	7 625	30.6	. . .	. . .	2 607	21.6
1979	222 903	26 072	11.7	17 214	9.0	14 419	8.1	8 050	31.0	. . .	. . .	2 921	21.8
1980	225 027	29 272	13.0	19 699	10.2	16 365	9.1	8 579	32.5	. . .	. . .	3 491	25.7
1981	227 157	31 822	14.0	21 553	11.1	17 987	9.9	9 173	34.2	. . .	. . .	3 713	26.5
1982	229 412	34 398	15.0	23 517	12.0	19 362	10.6	9 697	35.6	. . .	. . .	4 301	29.9
1983	231 700	35 303	15.2	23 984	12.1	19 538	10.8	9 882	35.7	. . .	. . .	4 633	28.0
1984	233 816	33 700	14.4	22 955	11.5	18 300	10.0	9 490	33.8	. . .	. . .	4 806	28.4
1985	236 594	33 064	14.0	22 860	11.4	17 839	9.7	8 926	31.3	. . .	. . .	5 236	29.0
1986	238 554	32 370	13.6	22 183	11.0	17 244	9.4	8 983	31.1	. . .	. . .	5 117	27.3
1987	240 982	32 221	13.4	21 195	10.4	16 029	8.7	9 520	32.4	1 021	16.1	5 422	28.0
1988	243 530	31 745	13.0	20 715	10.1	15 565	8.4	9 356	31.3	1 117	17.3	5 357	26.7
1989	245 992	31 528	12.8	20 785	10.0	15 599	8.3	9 302	30.7	939	14.1	5 430	26.2
1990	248 644	33 585	13.5	22 326	10.7	16 622	8.8	9 837	31.9	858	12.2	6 006	28.1
1991	251 192	35 708	14.2	23 747	11.3	17 741	9.4	10 242	32.7	996	13.8	6 339	28.7
1992	256 549	38 014	14.8	25 259	11.9	18 202	9.6	10 827	33.4	985	12.7	7 592	29.6
1993	259 278	39 265	15.1	26 226	12.2	18 882	9.9	10 877	33.1	1 134	15.3	8 126	30.6
1994	261 616	38 059	14.5	25 379	11.7	18 110	9.4	10 196	30.6	974	14.6	8 416	30.7
1995	263 733	36 425	13.8	24 423	11.2	16 267	8.5	9 872	29.3	1 411	14.6	8 574	30.3
1996	266 218	36 529	13.7	24 650	11.2	16 462	8.6	9 694	28.4	1 454	14.5	8 697	29.4
1997	268 480	35 574	13.3	24 396	11.0	16 491	8.6	9 116	26.5	1 468	14.0	8 308	27.1
1998	271 059	34 476	12.7	23 454	10.5	15 799	8.2	9 091	26.1	1 360	12.5	8 070	25.6
1999	276 208	32 791	11.9	22 169	9.8	14 735	7.7	8 441	23.6	1 285	10.7	7 876	22.7
2000	278 944	31 581	11.3	21 645	9.5	14 366	7.4	7 982	22.5	1 258	9.9	7 747	21.5
2001	281 475	32 907	11.7	22 739	9.9	15 271	7.8	8 136	22.7	1 275	10.2	7 997	21.4
2002	285 317	34 570	12.1	. . .	. . .	. . .	. . .	. . .	. . .	. . .	. . .	8 555	21.8
2003	287 699	35 861	12.5	. . .	. . .	. . .	. . .	. . .	. . .	. . .	. . .	9 051	22.5
2004	290 617	37 040	12.7	. . .	. . .	. . .	. . .	. . .	. . .	. . .	. . .	9 122	21.9
2005	293 135	36 950	12.6	. . .	. . .	. . .	. . .	. . .	. . .	. . .	. . .	9 368	21.8
2006	296 450	36 460	12.3	. . .	. . .	. . .	. . .	. . .	. . .	. . .	. . .	9 243	20.6
2007	298 699	37 276	12.5	. . .	. . .	. . .	. . .	. . .	. . .	. . .	. . .	9 890	21.5
2008	301 041	39 829	13.2	. . .	. . .	. . .	. . .	. . .	. . .	. . .	. . .	10 987	23.2
2009	303 820	43 569	14.3	. . .	. . .	. . .	. . .	. . .	. . .	. . .	. . .	12 350	25.3
2010	306 130	46 343	15.1	. . .	. . .	. . .	. . .	. . .	. . .	. . .	. . .	13 522	26.5
2011	308 456	46 247	15.0	. . .	. . .	. . .	. . .	. . .	. . .	. . .	. . .	13 244	25.3
By race													
Race alone													
2002	. . .	. . .	. . .	23 466	10.2	15 567	8.0	8 602	24.1	1 161	10.1	. . .	. . .
2003	. . .	. . .	. . .	24 272	10.5	15 902	8.2	8 781	24.4	1 401	11.8	. . .	. . .
2004	. . .	. . .	. . .	25 327	10.8	16 908	8.7	9 014	24.7	1 201	9.8	. . .	. . .
2005	. . .	. . .	. . .	24 872	10.6	16 227	8.3	9 168	24.9	1 402	11.1	. . .	. . .
2006	. . .	. . .	. . .	24 416	10.3	16 013	8.2	9 048	24.3	1 353	10.3	. . .	. . .
2007	. . .	. . .	. . .	25 120	10.5	16 032	8.2	9 237	24.5	1 349	10.2	. . .	. . .
2008	. . .	. . .	. . .	26 990	11.2	17 024	8.6	9 379	24.7	1 576	11.8	. . .	. . .
2009	. . .	. . .	. . .	29 830	12.3	18 530	9.4	9 944	25.8	1 746	12.5	. . .	. . .
2010	. . .	. . .	. . .	31 083	13.0	19 251	9.9	10 746	27.4	1 899	12.2	. . .	. . .
2011	. . .	. . .	. . .	30 849	12.8	19 171	9.8	10 929	27.6	1 973	12.3	. . .	. . .
Race alone or in combination													
2002	. . .	. . .	. . .	. . .	. . .	. . .	. . .	8 884	23.9	1 243	10.0	. . .	. . .
2003	. . .	. . .	. . .	. . .	. . .	. . .	. . .	9 108	24.3	1 527	11.8	. . .	. . .
2004	. . .	. . .	. . .	. . .	. . .	. . .	. . .	9 411	24.7	1 295	9.7	. . .	. . .
2005	. . .	. . .	. . .	. . .	. . .	. . .	. . .	9 517	24.7	1 501	10.9	. . .	. . .
2006	. . .	. . .	. . .	. . .	. . .	. . .	. . .	9 447	24.2	1 447	10.1	. . .	. . .
2007	. . .	. . .	. . .	. . .	. . .	. . .	. . .	9 668	24.4	1 467	10.2	. . .	. . .
2008	. . .	. . .	. . .	. . .	. . .	. . .	. . .	9 882	24.6	1 686	11.6	. . .	. . .
2009	. . .	. . .	. . .	. . .	. . .	. . .	. . .	10 575	25.9	1 901	12.4	. . .	. . .
2010	. . .	. . .	. . .	. . .	. . .	. . .	. . .	11 597	27.4	2 064	12.0	. . .	. . .
2011	. . .	. . .	. . .	. . .	. . .	. . .	. . .	11 730	27.5	2 189	12.3	. . .	. . .

[1] For 1987 through 2001, Asian and Pacific Islander.
. . . = Not available.

Table 3-8. Poverty Status of Families by Type of Family

(Thousands of families, percent.)

Year	Married couple families — Number of families — Total	Total below poverty level	Poverty rate (percent) Total	With children under 18 years	Families with no spouse present — Male householder — Familes below poverty level	Poverty rate Total	With children under 18 years	Female householder — Familes below poverty level	Poverty rate Total	With children under 18 years	Unrelated individuals — Below poverty level	Poverty rate
1959	39 335	...	...	...	...	...	...	1 916	42.6	59.9	4 928	46.1
1960	39 624	...	...	...	...	...	...	1 955	42.4	56.3	4 926	45.2
1961	40 405	...	...	...	...	...	...	1 954	42.1	56.0	5 119	45.9
1962	40 923	...	...	...	...	...	...	2 034	42.9	59.7	5 002	45.4
1963	41 311	...	...	...	...	...	...	1 972	40.4	55.7	4 938	44.2
1964	41 648	...	...	...	...	...	...	1 822	36.4	49.7	5 143	42.7
1965	42 107	...	...	...	...	...	...	1 916	38.4	52.2	4 827	39.8
1966	42 553	...	...	...	...	...	...	1 721	33.1	47.1	4 701	38.3
1967	43 292	...	...	...	...	...	...	1 774	33.3	44.5	4 998	38.1
1968	43 842	...	...	...	...	...	...	1 755	32.3	44.6	4 694	34.0
1969	44 436	...	...	...	...	...	...	1 827	32.7	44.9	4 972	34.0
1970	44 739	...	...	...	...	...	...	1 952	32.5	43.8	5 090	32.9
1971	45 752	...	...	...	...	...	...	2 100	33.9	44.9	5 154	31.6
1972	46 314	...	...	...	...	...	...	2 158	32.7	44.5	4 883	29.0
1973	46 812	2 482	5.3	...	154	10.7	...	2 193	32.2	43.2	4 674	25.6
1974	47 069	2 474	5.3	6.0	125	8.9	15.4	2 324	32.1	43.7	4 553	24.1
1975	47 318	2 904	6.1	7.2	116	8.0	11.7	2 430	32.5	44.0	5 088	25.1
1976	47 497	2 606	5.5	6.4	162	10.8	15.4	2 543	33.0	44.1	5 344	24.9
1977	47 385	2 524	5.3	6.3	177	11.1	14.8	2 610	31.7	41.8	5 216	22.6
1978	47 692	2 474	5.2	5.9	152	9.2	14.7	2 654	31.4	42.2	5 435	22.1
1979	49 112	2 640	5.4	6.1	176	10.2	15.5	2 645	30.4	39.6	5 743	21.9
1980	49 294	3 032	6.2	7.7	213	11.0	18.0	2 972	32.7	42.9	6 227	22.9
1981	49 630	3 394	6.8	8.7	205	10.3	14.0	3 252	34.6	44.3	6 490	23.4
1982	49 908	3 789	7.6	9.8	290	14.4	20.6	3 434	36.3	47.8	6 458	23.1
1983	50 081	3 815	7.6	10.1	268	13.2	20.2	3 564	36.0	47.1	6 740	23.1
1984	50 350	3 488	6.9	9.4	292	13.1	18.1	3 498	34.5	45.7	6 609	21.8
1985	50 933	3 438	6.7	8.9	311	12.9	17.1	3 474	34.0	45.4	6 725	21.5
1986	51 537	3 123	6.1	8.0	287	11.4	17.8	3 613	34.6	46.0	6 846	21.6
1987	51 675	3 011	5.8	7.7	340	12.0	16.8	3 654	34.2	45.5	6 857	20.8
1988	52 100	2 897	5.6	7.2	336	11.8	18.0	3 642	33.4	44.7	7 070	20.6
1989	52 317	2 931	5.6	7.3	348	12.1	18.1	3 504	32.2	42.8	6 760	19.2
1990	52 147	2 981	5.7	7.8	349	12.0	18.8	3 768	33.4	44.5	7 446	20.7
1991	52 457	3 158	6.0	8.3	392	13.0	19.6	4 161	35.6	47.1	7 773	21.1
1992	53 090	3 385	6.4	8.6	484	15.8	22.5	4 275	35.4	46.2	8 075	21.9
1993	53 181	3 481	6.5	9.0	488	16.8	22.5	4 424	35.6	46.1	8 388	22.1
1994	53 865	3 272	6.1	8.3	549	17.0	22.6	4 232	34.6	44.0	8 287	21.5
1995	53 570	2 982	5.6	7.5	493	14.0	19.7	4 057	32.4	41.5	8 247	20.9
1996	53 604	3 010	5.6	7.5	531	13.8	20.0	4 167	32.6	41.9	8 452	20.8
1997	54 321	2 821	5.2	7.1	507	13.0	18.7	3 995	31.6	41.0	8 687	20.8
1998	54 778	2 879	5.3	6.9	476	12.0	16.6	3 831	29.9	38.7	8 478	19.9
1999	56 290	2 748	4.9	6.4	485	11.8	16.3	3 559	27.8	35.7	8 400	19.1
2000	56 598	2 637	4.7	6.0	485	11.3	15.3	3 278	25.4	33.0	8 653	19.0
2001	56 755	2 760	4.9	6.1	583	13.1	17.7	3 470	26.4	33.6	9 226	19.9
2002	57 327	3 052	5.3	6.8	564	12.1	16.6	3 613	26.5	33.7	9 618	20.4
2003	57 725	3 115	5.4	7.0	636	13.5	19.1	3 856	28.0	35.5	9 713	20.4
2004	57 983	3 216	5.5	7.0	657	13.4	17.1	3 962	28.3	35.9	9 926	20.4
2005	58 189	2 944	5.1	6.5	669	13.0	17.6	4 044	28.7	36.2	10 425	21.1
2006	58 964	2 910	4.9	6.4	671	13.2	17.9	4 087	28.3	36.5	9 977	20.0
2007	58 395	2 849	4.9	6.7	696	13.6	17.5	4 078	28.3	37.0	10 189	19.7
2008	59 137	3 261	5.5	7.5	723	13.8	17.6	4 163	28.7	37.2	10 710	20.8
2009	58 428	3 409	5.8	8.3	942	16.9	23.7	4 441	29.9	38.5	11 678	22.0
2010	58 667	3 681	6.3	9.0	892	15.8	24.1	4 827	31.7	40.9	12 449	22.9
2011	58 963	3 652	6.2	8.8	950	16.1	22.0	4 894	31.2	40.9	12 416	22.8

. . . = Not available.

Table 3-9. Poverty Status of People by Sex and Age

(Thousands of people, percent of population.)

Year	Poverty status of people by sex				Poverty status of people by age					
	Males below poverty level		Females below poverty level		Children under 18 years below poverty level		People 18 to 64 years below poverty level		People 65 years and older below poverty level	
	Number (thousands)	Poverty rate (percent)	Number (thousands)	Poverty rate (percent)	Number (thousands)	Poverty rate (percent)	Number (thousands)	Poverty rate (percent)	Number (thousands)	Poverty rate (percent)
1959	...	...	...	...	17 552	27.3	16 457	17.0	5 481	35.2
1966	12 225	13.0	16 265	16.3	12 389	17.6	11 007	10.5	5 114	28.5
1967	11 813	12.5	15 951	15.8	11 656	16.6	10 725	10.0	5 388	29.5
1968	10 793	11.3	14 578	14.3	10 954	15.6	9 803	9.0	4 632	25.0
1969	10 292	10.6	13 978	13.6	9 691	14.0	9 669	8.7	4 787	25.3
1970	10 879	11.1	14 632	14.0	10 440	15.1	10 187	9.0	4 793	24.6
1971	10 708	10.8	14 841	14.1	10 551	15.3	10 735	9.3	4 273	21.6
1972	10 190	10.2	14 258	13.4	10 284	15.1	10 438	8.8	3 738	18.6
1973	9 642	9.6	13 316	12.5	9 642	14.4	9 977	8.3	3 354	16.3
1974	10 313	10.2	13 881	12.9	10 156	15.4	10 132	8.3	3 085	14.6
1975	10 908	10.7	14 970	13.8	11 104	17.1	11 456	9.2	3 317	15.3
1976	10 373	10.1	14 603	13.4	10 273	16.0	11 389	9.0	3 313	15.0
1977	10 340	10.0	14 381	13.0	10 288	16.2	11 316	8.8	3 177	14.1
1978	10 017	9.6	14 480	13.0	9 931	15.9	11 332	8.7	3 233	14.0
1979	10 535	10.0	14 810	13.2	10 377	16.4	12 014	8.9	3 682	15.2
1980	12 207	11.2	17 065	14.7	11 543	18.3	13 858	10.1	3 871	15.7
1981	13 360	12.1	18 462	15.8	12 505	20.0	15 464	11.1	3 853	15.3
1982	14 842	13.4	19 556	16.5	13 647	21.9	17 000	12.0	3 751	14.6
1983	15 182	13.5	20 084	16.8	13 911	22.3	17 767	12.4	3 625	13.8
1984	14 537	12.8	19 163	15.9	13 420	21.5	16 952	11.7	3 330	12.4
1985	14 140	12.3	18 923	15.6	13 010	20.7	16 598	11.3	3 456	12.6
1986	13 721	11.8	18 649	15.2	12 876	20.5	16 017	10.8	3 477	12.4
1987	14 029	12.0	18 518	15.0	12 843	20.3	15 815	10.6	3 563	12.5
1988	13 599	11.5	18 146	14.5	12 455	19.5	15 809	10.5	3 481	12.0
1989	13 366	11.2	18 162	14.4	12 590	19.6	15 575	10.2	3 363	11.4
1990	14 211	11.7	19 373	15.2	13 431	20.6	16 496	10.7	3 658	12.2
1991	15 082	12.3	20 626	16.0	14 341	21.8	17 586	11.4	3 781	12.4
1992	16 222	12.9	21 792	16.6	15 294	22.3	18 793	11.9	3 928	12.9
1993	16 900	13.3	22 365	16.9	15 727	22.7	19 781	12.4	3 755	12.2
1994	16 316	12.8	21 744	16.3	15 289	21.8	19 107	11.9	3 663	11.7
1995	15 683	12.2	20 742	15.4	14 665	20.8	18 442	11.4	3 318	10.5
1996	15 611	12.0	20 918	15.4	14 463	20.5	18 638	11.4	3 428	10.8
1997	15 187	11.6	20 387	14.9	14 113	19.9	18 085	10.9	3 376	10.5
1998	14 712	11.1	19 764	14.3	13 467	18.9	17 623	10.5	3 386	10.5
1999	14 079	10.4	18 712	13.2	12 280	17.1	17 289	10.1	3 222	9.7
2000	13 536	9.9	18 045	12.6	11 587	16.2	16 671	9.6	3 323	9.9
2001	14 327	10.4	18 580	12.9	11 733	16.3	17 760	10.1	3 414	10.1
2002	15 162	10.9	19 408	13.3	12 133	16.7	18 861	10.6	3 576	10.4
2003	15 783	11.2	20 078	13.7	12 866	17.6	19 443	10.8	3 552	10.2
2004	16 399	11.5	20 641	13.9	13 041	17.8	20 545	11.3	3 453	9.8
2005	15 950	11.1	21 000	14.1	12 896	17.6	20 450	11.1	3 603	10.1
2006	16 000	11.0	20 460	13.6	12 827	17.4	20 239	10.8	3 394	9.4
2007	16 302	11.1	20 973	13.8	13 324	18.0	20 396	10.9	3 556	9.7
2008	17 698	12.0	22 131	14.4	14 068	19.0	22 105	11.7	3 656	9.7
2009	19 475	13.0	24 094	15.6	15 451	20.7	24 684	12.9	3 433	8.9
2010	20 893	14.0	25 451	16.3	16 286	22.0	26 499	13.8	3 558	8.9
2011	20 501	13.6	25 746	16.3	16 134	21.9	26 492	13.7	3 620	8.7

... = Not available.

Table 3-10. Poor People Age 16 Years and Older by Work Experience

(Thousands of people, percent of population [poverty rate], percent of total poor people.)

Year	Total number of poor people, 16 years and older	Worked		Worked year-round, full-time			Worked less than year-round or full-time			Did not work		
		Number	Percent of total poor	Number	Poverty rate (percent)	Percent of total poor	Number	Poverty rate (percent)	Percent of total poor	Number	Poverty rate (percent)	Percent of total poor
1978	16 914	6 599	39.0	1 309	...	7.7	5 290	...	31.3	10 315	...	61.0
1979	16 803	6 601	39.3	1 394	...	8.3	5 207	...	31.0	10 202	...	60.7
1980	18 892	7 674	40.6	1 644	...	8.7	6 030	...	31.9	11 218	...	59.4
1981	20 571	8 524	41.4	1 881	...	9.1	6 643	...	32.3	12 047	...	58.6
1982	22 100	9 013	40.8	1 999	...	9.0	7 014	...	31.7	13 087	...	59.2
1983	22 741	9 329	41.0	2 064	...	9.1	7 265	...	31.9	13 412	...	59.0
1984	21 541	8 999	41.8	2 076	...	9.6	6 923	...	32.1	12 542	...	58.2
1985	21 243	9 008	42.4	1 972	...	9.3	7 036	...	33.1	12 235	...	57.6
1986	20 688	8 743	42.3	2 007	...	9.7	6 736	...	32.6	11 945	...	57.7
1987	20 546	8 258	40.2	1 821	2.4	8.9	6 436	12.5	31.3	12 288	21.6	59.8
1988	20 323	8 363	41.2	1 929	2.4	9.5	6 434	12.7	31.7	11 960	21.2	58.8
1989	19 952	8 376	42.0	1 908	2.4	9.6	6 468	12.5	32.4	11 576	20.8	58.0
1990	21 242	8 716	41.0	2 076	2.6	9.8	6 639	12.6	31.3	12 526	22.1	59.0
1991	22 530	9 208	40.9	2 103	2.6	9.3	7 105	13.4	31.5	13 322	22.8	59.1
1992	23 951	9 739	40.6	2 211	2.7	9.2	7 529	14.1	31.4	14 212	23.7	59.3
1993	24 832	10 144	40.8	2 408	2.9	9.7	7 737	14.6	31.2	14 688	24.2	59.1
1994	24 108	9 829	40.8	2 520	2.9	10.5	7 309	13.9	30.3	14 279	23.6	59.2
1995	23 077	9 484	41.1	2 418	2.7	10.5	7 066	13.7	30.6	13 593	22.3	58.9
1996	23 472	9 586	40.8	2 263	2.5	9.6	7 322	14.1	31.2	13 886	22.7	59.2
1997	22 753	9 444	41.5	2 345	2.5	10.3	7 098	13.8	31.2	13 309	21.7	58.5
1998	22 256	9 133	41.0	2 804	2.9	12.6	6 330	12.7	28.4	13 123	21.1	59.0
1999	21 762	9 251	42.5	2 559	2.6	11.8	6 692	13.2	30.8	12 511	19.9	57.5
2000	21 080	8 511	40.4	2 439	2.4	11.6	6 072	12.1	28.8	12 569	19.8	59.6
2001	22 245	8 530	38.3	2 567	2.6	11.5	5 964	11.8	26.8	13 715	20.6	61.7
2002	23 601	8 954	37.9	2 635	2.6	11.2	6 318	12.4	26.8	14 647	21.0	62.1
2003	24 266	8 820	36.3	2 636	2.6	10.9	6 183	12.2	25.5	15 446	21.5	63.7
2004	25 256	9 384	37.2	2 891	2.8	11.4	6 493	12.8	25.7	15 872	21.7	62.8
2005	25 381	9 340	36.8	2 894	2.8	11.4	6 446	12.8	25.4	16 041	21.8	63.2
2006	24 896	9 181	36.9	2 906	2.7	11.7	6 275	12.6	25.2	15 715	21.1	63.1
2007	25 297	9 089	35.9	2 768	2.5	10.9	6 320	12.7	25.0	16 208	21.5	64.1
2008	27 216	10 085	37.1	2 754	2.6	10.1	7 331	13.5	26.9	17 131	22.0	62.9
2009	29 625	10 680	36.1	2 641	2.7	8.9	8 039	14.5	27.1	18 945	22.7	63.9
2010	31 731	10 742	33.9	2 640	2.7	8.3	8 102	15.0	25.5	20 989	23.9	66.1
2011	31 630	10 588	33.5	2 770	2.7	8.8	7 818	14.9	24.7	21 042	23.6	66.5

. . . = Not available.

Section 3c: Alternative Measures of Income and Poverty

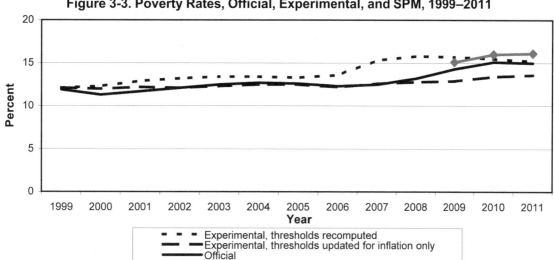

Figure 3-3. Poverty Rates, Official, Experimental, and SPM, 1999–2011

- A special panel of the National Academy of Sciences (NAS) has recommended a complete redesign of poverty calculations, redefining both needs and resources. For the years 1999 forward, the Census Bureau has calculated experimental poverty measures according to several versions of the NAS recommendations. For 2009 through 2011 the Bureau has released a "Supplemental Poverty Measure" (SPM), based on further refinement of the NAS recommendations. In Figure 3-3, two of the experimental measures are shown along with the official rate and the SPM. The SPM and all of the experimental measures use more comprehensive and realistic definitions of both needs and resources than the official rate. The SPM and the two experimental measures shown in the graph both include adjustment for geographic differences in the cost of living, and adjust for differing health care needs by excluding medical out-of-pocket expenses from the resources of the measurement unit. (Table 3-12)

- The thresholds for the experimental measures were initially based on needs estimated for the year 1999; in that year, the two experimental measures shown in Figure 3-3 indicated a poverty rate of 12.1 percent, compared with 11.9 percent in the official rate. (Table 3-12)

- One of those experimental measures updates the thresholds for inflation only, using the CPI-U, as is the case with the official series. This measure tracks the official series fairly closely through 2007. In the recession years 2008 through 2010, it increases much less than the official measure, probably because resources are on an after-tax basis and include food aid and the Employment Tax Credit. (Table 3-12)

- The other experimental measure recomputes the thresholds each year using the percent increase in a 3-year average of median expenditures on necessities instead of the percent increase in the CPI. The poverty rate with this method of recomputing thresholds rises even in a year of economic expansion such as 2000, diverges even more sharply upward in 2007 and 2008, and then declines in the next three recession years. (Table 3-12)

- The SPM indicates a poverty rate similar to the higher of the experimental rates in 2009, but it increases in 2010 and remains high in 2011, like both the official and the CPI-based experimental rates. It also changes poverty incidence among demographic groups. Reflecting the inclusion of need-based benefits for families, child poverty is somewhat lower than in the official measure, though still above adult poverty rates. But reflecting the adjustment for out-of-pocket medical care spending, poverty for those 65 and older is considerably higher in the SPM. (Tables 3-12 and 3-13)

Table 3-11. Poverty Rates and Income Distribution Coefficients for People, Based on Alternative Definitions of Income

Year	Definition 1, MI: Money income excluding capital gains (current official measure)			Definition 4: Money income before taxes and cash transfers, plus realized capital gains (losses) and health insurance supplements		
	Poverty rate (percent)		Gini coefficient [2]	Poverty rate (percent)		Gini coefficient
	Official threshold	CPI-U-RS threshold [1]		Official threshold	CPI-U-RS threshold [1]	
1979	11.7	10.6	0.403	18.8	17.8	0.460
1980	13.0	11.5	0.401	20.1	19.0	0.462
1981	14.0	12.2	0.404	21.1	19.8	0.466
1982	15.0	13.2	0.409	22.0	20.6	0.475
1983	15.2	13.7	0.412	21.8	20.6	0.478
1984	14.4	12.8	0.413	20.8	19.5	0.477
1985	14.0	12.5	0.418	20.4	19.1	0.486
1986	13.6	12.2	0.423	19.9	18.7	0.505
1987	13.4	12.1	0.424	19.7	18.7	0.488
1988	13.0	11.7	0.425	19.7	18.5	0.489
1989	12.8	11.3	0.429	19.4	18.1	0.492
1990	13.5	11.9	0.426	19.9	18.7	0.487
1991	14.2	12.4	0.425	21.1	19.7	0.490
1992	14.8	13.1	0.430	22.1	20.6	0.497
1993	15.1	13.4	0.448	22.6	21.1	0.514
1994	14.5	12.6	0.450	22.0	20.3	0.515
1995	13.8	11.7	0.444	21.1	19.5	0.509
1996	13.7	11.6	0.447	20.8	19.1	0.511
1997	13.3	11.3	0.448	20.3	18.7	0.513
1998	12.7	10.6	0.446	19.3	17.4	0.509
1999	11.9	9.9	0.445	18.7	16.9	0.508
2000	11.3	9.7	0.447	18.0	16.5	0.506
2001	11.7	9.9	0.450	18.5	16.9	0.510
2002	12.1	10.1	0.448	19.0	17.4	. . .
2003	12.5	10.5	0.450	19.5	17.8	. . .
2004	12.7	10.8	0.450	20.0	18.3	0.503
2005	12.6	10.8	0.450	19.7	18.1	0.501
2006	12.3	10.5	0.447	18.9	17.3	0.495
2007	12.5	11.0	0.443	19.3	18.0	0.492
2008 [4]	13.2	11.7	0.446	20.8	19.6	0.497
2009 [4]	14.3	12.8	0.447	23.0	21.6	0.505

Year	Definition 14, MI - Tx + NC: Income after all taxes and transfers			Definition 15, MI - Tx + NC + HE: Income after all taxes and transfers, plus net imputed return on equity in own home		
	Poverty rate (percent)		Gini coefficient [3]	Poverty rate (percent)		Gini coefficient [3]
	Official threshold	CPI-U-RS threshold [1]		Official threshold	CPI-U-RS threshold [1]	
1979	8.9	7.9	0.359	7.5	6.7	0.352
1980	10.1	8.6	0.354	8.2	7.0	0.347
1981	11.5	9.8	0.358	8.7	7.3	0.350
1982	12.3	10.6	0.366	9.9	8.5	0.359
1983	12.7	11.0	0.374	10.4	9.0	0.368
1984	12.0	10.4	0.378	9.9	8.6	0.372
1985	11.7	10.1	0.385	9.9	8.6	0.381
1986	11.3	9.8	0.409	10.1	8.6	0.404
1987	11.0	9.5	0.382	9.7	8.2	0.380
1988	10.8	9.4	0.385	9.4	8.2	0.384
1989	10.4	8.8	0.389	9.1	7.6	0.387
1990	10.9	9.3	0.382	9.8	8.3	0.381
1991	11.4	9.7	0.380	10.3	8.6	0.379
1992	11.9	10.2	0.385	10.7	9.1	0.381
1993	12.1	10.3	0.398	11.2	9.4	0.395
1994	11.1	9.2	0.400	10.0	8.3	0.395
1995	10.3	8.5	0.394	9.4	7.6	0.388
1996	10.2	8.4	0.398	9.3	7.6	0.392
1997	10.0	8.2	0.403	9.2	7.5	0.397
1998	9.5	7.7	0.405	8.8	7.1	0.399
1999	8.9	7.2	0.408	8.2	6.5	0.402
2000	8.8	7.2	0.410	8.0	6.5	0.402
2001	9.0	7.3	0.412	8.3	6.7	0.407
2002	9.3	7.7	0.394	8.6	7.1	0.388
2003	9.7	7.9	0.394	9.0	7.4	0.390
2004	9.6	7.9	0.404	8.8	7.2	0.398
2005	9.6	8.1	0.402	8.9	7.4	0.398
2006	9.3	7.9	0.405	8.7	7.4	0.400
2007	9.5	8.3	0.403	9.1	7.9	0.399
2008 [4]	9.8	8.4	0.392	9.2	7.9	0.389
2009 [4]	10.1	8.7	0.392	9.7	8.4	0.388

[1]Before 1987, threshold based on CPI-U-X1.
[2]Calculated for comparability by same method as the other coefficients in this table; differs from official calculation in Table 3-4.
[3]Earlier years not comparable with 2002 and subsequent years because of a change in tax estimating model.
[4]2008 and 2009 data do not include estimates of capital gains (losses).
. . . = Not available.

Table 3-12. Official and Experimental Poverty Rates and Supplemental Poverty Measure

(Percent of population.)

Measurement method	Capital gains included in income								
	1999	2000	2001	2002 (new tax model)	2003	2004 (revised)	2005	2006	2007
Official measure	11.9	11.3	11.7	12.1	12.5	12.7	12.6	12.3	12.5
Experimental									
MSI-GA-CPI	12.1	12.0	12.2	12.1	12.3	12.5	12.5	12.2	12.6
MIT-GA-CPI	12.7	12.5	12.5	12.6	12.7	13.0	13.0	12.6	13.0
MSI-NGA-CPI	12.2	12.1	12.3	12.3	12.4	12.7	12.6	12.4	12.6
MIT-NGA-CPI	12.8	12.7	12.7	12.8	12.7	13.1	13.0	12.8	12.9
MSI-GA-CE	12.1	12.3	12.9	13.2	13.4	13.4	13.3	13.6	15.3
MIT-GA-CE	12.7	12.8	13.2	13.7	13.9	14.0	14.1	14.1	15.9
MSI-NGA-CE	12.2	12.5	13.0	13.4	13.5	13.4	13.5	13.7	15.1
MIT-NGA-CE	12.8	13.0	13.4	13.9	14.1	14.1	14.2	14.2	16.0
Supplemental poverty measure	...	...	...	...	...	...	...	...	...

Measurement method	Capital gains excluded from income				
	2007	2008	2009	2010	2011
Official measure	12.5	13.2	14.3	15.1	15.0
Experimental					
MSI-GA-CPI	12.6	12.8	12.9	13.4	13.6
MIT-GA-CPI	13.0	13.2	13.2	13.8	13.9
MSI-NGA-CPI	12.6	12.8	12.8	13.5	13.5
MIT-NGA-CPI	13.0	13.1	13.3	14.0	13.8
MSI-GA-CE	15.3	15.8	15.7	15.5	15.2
MIT-GA-CE	15.9	16.9	17.3	17.2	16.9
MSI-NGA-CE	15.2	15.7	15.7	15.6	15.0
MIT-NGA-CE	16.1	17.1	17.3	17.3	16.9
Supplemental poverty measure	...	...	15.3	16.0	16.1

Note: The Census Bureau changed the way it modeled taxes, effective with the revised 2002 estimates. Consequently, comparisons of 2002 and later data with earlier years may be affected.

MSI means "Medical out-of-pocket expenses subtracted from income."
MIT means "Medical out-of-pocket expenses in the thresholds."
GA means "Geographic adjustment (of poverty thresholds)."
NGA means "No geographic adjustment (of poverty thresholds)."
CPI means "Thresholds were adjusted since 1999 using the Consumer Price Index for All Urban Consumers."
CE means "Thresholds were recomputed since 1999 using data from the Consumer Expenditure Survey."

See notes and definitions for further explanation.
... = Not available.

Table 3-13. Number and Percent of People in Poverty using SPM and Comparison with Official Measure

(Numbers in thousands; percent of population.)

Characteristic	SPM 2010		SPM 2011		Official, 2011[1]	
	Number	Percent	Number	Percent	Number	Percent
All People	49 094	16.0	49 695	16.1	46 618	15.1
Sex						
Male	...	...	23 112	15.3	20 686	13.7
Female	...	...	26 583	16.9	25 932	16.4
Age						
Under 18 years	13 622	18.2	13 429	18.1	16 506	22.3
18 to 64 years	29 235	15.2	30 020	15.5	26 492	13.7
65 years and older	6 237	15.9	6 247	15.1	3 620	8.7
Type of Unit						
In married-couple unit	18 295	9.9	18 576	10.0	13 849	7.4
In female householder unit	17 991	29.0	18 996	30.0	18 773	29.6
In male household unit	7 317	22.7	7 071	21.9	5 582	17.3
In new SPM unit	5 490	21.0	5 052	18.8	8 414	31.2
Race and Hispanic Origin						
White	34 747	14.3	34 427	14.3	31 101	12.9
White, not Hispanic	21 876	11.1	21 427	11.0	19 358	9.9
Black	9 932	25.4	10 214	25.7	11 016	27.8
Asian	2 397	16.7	2 719	16.9	1 981	12.3
Hispanic, any race	14 088	28.2	14 670	28.0	13 323	25.4
Nativity						
Native born	39 329	14.7	39 368	14.6	39 022	14.5
Foreign born	9 765	25.5	10 327	25.8	7 596	19.0
Naturalized citizen	2 829	16.8	3 286	18.3	2 233	12.5
Not a citizen	6 936	32.4	7 041	31.9	5 363	24.3
Tenure						
Owner	20 205	9.7	19 978	9.7	16 217	7.8
Owner/ mortgage	11 419	8.3	11 138	8.1	7 932	5.8
Owner/no-mortgage/rent-free	9 581	13.3	9 592	13.1	9 232	12.6
Renter	28 093	29.4	28 966	29.3	29 454	29.8
Residence						
Inside MSAa	42 979	16.6	43 322	16.6	38 502	14.7
Inside principal cities	20 748	21.0	21 748	21.7	20 127	20.1
outside principal cities	22 231	13.9	21 574	13.4	18 375	11.4
Outside MSAs	6 114	12.8	6 373	13.5	8 116	17.1
Region						
Northeast	7 969	14.5	8 262	15.0	7 266	13.2
Midwest	8 678	13.1	8 454	12.8	9 313	14.1
South	18 503	16.3	18 432	16.0	18 512	16.1
West	13 944	19.4	14 547	20.0	11 527	15.9
Health Insurance Coverage						
With private insurance	14 631	7.5	15 010	7.6	9 806	5.0
With public, no private insurance	19 126	31.7	19 677	31.3	23 077	36.7
Not insured	15 337	30.7	15 008	30.9	13 736	28.3
Work Experience						
Total, 18 to 64 years	...	...	30 020	15.5	26 492	13.7
All workers	...	...	13 611	9.4	10 345	7.2
Full-time, year-round	...	...	4 983	5.1	2 732	2.8
Less than full-time, year-round	...	...	8 628	18.5	7 614	16.3
Did not work at least 1 week	...	...	16 409	33.5	16 147	32.9
Disability Status						
Total, 18 to 64 years	...	...	30 020	15.5	26 492	13.7
With a disability	...	...	4 133	27.6	4 313	28.8
With no disability	...	...	25 795	14.5	22 105	12.5

[1]Differs from published official rates because these figures include unrelated individuals under 15 years of age as does the SPM.
. . . = Not available.

NOTES AND DEFINITIONS, CHAPTER 3

Tables 3-1 through 3-13: Income Distribution and Poverty

SOURCE: U.S. DEPARTMENT OF COMMERCE, BUREAU OF THE CENSUS

All data in this chapter are derived from the Current Population Survey (CPS), which is also the source of the data on labor force, employment, and unemployment used in Chapter 10. (See the notes and definitions for Tables 10-1 through 10-5.) In March of each year (with some data also collected in February and April), the households in this monthly survey are asked additional questions concerning earnings and other income in the previous year. This additional information, informally known as the "March Supplement," is now formally known as the Current Population Survey Annual Social and Economic Supplement (CPS-ASEC). It was previously called the Annual Demographic Supplement.

The population represented by the income and poverty survey is the civilian noninstitutional population of the United States and members of the armed forces in the United States living off post or with their families on post, but excluding all other members of the armed forces. This is slightly different from the population base for the civilian employment and unemployment data, which excludes those armed forces households. As it is a survey of households, homeless persons are not included.

Definitions: Racial classification and Hispanic Origin

In 2002 and all earlier years, the CPS required respondents to report identification with only one race group. Since 2003, the CPS has allowed respondents to choose more than one race group. Income data for 2002 were collected in early 2003; thus, in the data for 2002 and all subsequent years, an individual could report identification with more than one race group. In the 2000 census, about 2.6 percent of people reported identification with more than one race.

Therefore, data from 2002 onward that are classified by race are not strictly comparable with race-classified data for 2001 and earlier years. As alternative approaches to dealing with this problem, the Census Bureau has tabulated two different race concepts for each racial category in a number of cases. In the case of Blacks, for example, this means there is one income measure for "Black alone," consisting of persons who report Black and no other race, and one for "Black alone or in combination," which includes all the "Black alone" reporters plus those who report Black in combination with any other

race. The tables in this volume show both the "alone" and the "alone or in combination" values where available.

The race classifications now used in the CPS are *White, Black, Asian, American Indian and Alaska Native,* and *Native Hawaiian and Other Pacific Islander.* (Native Hawaiians and other Pacific Islanders were included in the "Asian" category in the data for 1987 through 2001.) The last two of these five racial groups are too small to provide reliable data for a single year, but in new Census Bureau tables available on the website, household income and poverty data for all five groups are presented in 2- and 3-year averages. Table 3-2 displays some of these data.

Hispanic origin is a separate question in the survey—not a racial classification—and Hispanics may be of any race. A subgroup of *White non-Hispanic* is shown in some tables. According to the Census Bureau, "Being Hispanic was reported by 13.8 percent of White householders who reported only one race, 4.5 percent of Black householders who reported only one race, and 3.5 percent of Asian householders who reported only one race . . . Data users should exercise caution when interpreting aggregate results for the Hispanic population or for race groups because these populations consist of many distinct groups that differ in socioeconomic characteristics, culture, and recent immigration status." ("Income, Poverty, and Health Insurance Coverage in the United States: 2011," footnote 2, p. 2)

Definitions: General

A *household* consists of all persons who occupy a housing unit. A household includes the related family members and all the unrelated persons, if any (such as lodgers, foster children, wards, or employees), who share the housing unit. A person living alone in a housing unit or a group of unrelated persons sharing a housing unit as partners is also counted as a household. The count of households excludes group quarters.

Earnings includes all income from work, including wages, salaries, armed forces pay, commissions, tips, piece-rate payments, and cash bonuses, before deductions such as taxes, bonds, pensions, and union dues. This category also includes net income from nonfarm self-employment and farm self-employment. Wage and salary supplements that are paid directly by the employer, such as the employer share of Social Security taxes and the cost of employer-provided health insurance, are not included.

Income, in the official definition used in the survey, is money income, including *earnings* from work as defined above; unemployment compensation; workers' compensation; Social Security; Supplemental Security Income; cash public assistance (welfare payments); veterans' payments; survivor benefits; disability benefits; pension or retirement income; interest income; dividends (but not capital gains); rents, royalties, and payments from estates or trusts; educational assistance, such as scholarships or grants; child support; alimony; financial assistance from outside of the household; and other cash income regularly received, such as foster child payments, military family allotments, and foreign government pensions. Receipts not counted as income include capital gains or losses, withdrawals of bank deposits, money borrowed, tax refunds, gifts, and lump-sum inheritances or insurance payments.

A *year-round, full-time worker* is a person who worked 35 or more hours per week and 50 or more weeks during the previous calendar year.

A *family* is a group of two or more persons related by birth, marriage, or adoption who reside together.

Unrelated individuals are persons 15 years old and over who are not living with any relatives. In the official poverty measure, the poverty status of unrelated individuals is determined independently of and is not affected by the incomes of other persons with whom they may share a household.

Median income is the amount of income that divides a ranked income distribution into two equal groups, with half having incomes above the median, and half having incomes below the median. The median income for persons is based on persons 15 years old and over with income.

Mean income is the amount obtained by dividing the total aggregate income of a group by the number of units in that group. In this survey, as in most surveys of incomes, means are higher than medians because of the skewed nature of the income distribution; see the section "Whose standard of living?" in the article at the beginning of this book.

Historical income figures are shown in constant *2011 dollars*. All constant-dollar figures are converted from current-dollar values using the *CPI-U-RS* (the Consumer Price Index, All Urban, Research Series), which measures changes in prices for past periods using the methodologies of the current CPI, and is similar in concept and behavior to the deflators used in the NIPAs for consumer income and spending. See Chapter 8 for CPI-U-RS data and the corresponding notes and definitions.

Definitions: Income distribution

Income distribution is portrayed by dividing the total ranked distribution of families or households into *fifths*, also known as *quintiles,* and also by separately tabulating the top 5 percent (which is included in the highest fifth). The households or families are arrayed from those with the lowest income to those with the highest income, then divided into five groups, with each group containing one-fifth of the total number of households. Within each quintile, incomes are summed and calculated as a share of total income for all quintiles, and are averaged to show the average (mean) income within that quintile.

A statistical measure that summarizes the dispersion of income across the entire income distribution is the *Gini coefficient* (also known as Gini ratio, Gini index, or index of income concentration), which can take values ranging from 0 to 1. A Gini value of 1 indicates "perfect" inequality; that is, one household has all the income and the rest have none. A value of 0 indicates "perfect" equality, a situation in which each household has the same income.

There are differences between the Gini coefficients for the official income measure presented in the report's main tables and those presented in Table 3-11. In the latter, the coefficients were recalculated, using a slightly different method, for comparability with the other income definitions.

A new "equivalence-adjusted" measure of household income inequality was introduced recently and is displayed in Table 3-4. For a Census-defined household, a given level of money income can have different implications for that household's well-being, depending on the size of the household and how many children, if any, are in the household. Since there have been substantial changes over past decades in the average size and composition of households, some have questioned the pertinence of standard income distribution tables. In response, the Census Bureau now also reports measures of income inequality for households using "equivalence-adjusted" income.

The equivalence adjustment is based on a three-parameter scale reflecting the size of the household and the facts that children consume less than adults; that as family size increases, expenses do not increase at the same rate; and that the increase in expenses is larger for the first child of a single-parent family than the first child of a two-adult family. The same equivalence concept is used in the poverty thresholds for the NAS-based alternative poverty estimates shown in Tables 3-12 and 3-13 and described later in these Notes.

As can be seen in Table 3-4, the equivalence-adjusted measures generally show somewhat less inequality than the raw money income measures, but they show a greater rise in inequality over the period 1967–2011.

Definitions: Poverty

The *number of people below poverty level,* or the number of poor people, is the number of people with family or individual incomes below a specified level that is intended to measure the cost of a minimum standard of living. These minimum levels vary by size and composition of family and are known as *poverty thresholds.*

The official poverty thresholds are based on a definition developed in 1964 by Mollie Orshansky of the Social Security Administration. She calculated food budgets for families of various sizes and compositions, using an "economy food plan" developed by the U.S. Department of Agriculture (the cheapest of four plans developed). Reflecting a 1955 Department of Agriculture survey that found that families of three or more persons spent about one-third of their after-tax incomes on food, Orshansky multiplied the costs of the food plan by 3 to arrive at a set of thresholds for poverty income for families of three or larger. For 2-person families, the multiplier was 3.7; for 1-person families, the threshold was 80 percent of the two-person threshold.

These poverty thresholds have been adjusted each year for price increases, using the percent change in the Consumer Price Index for All Urban Consumers (CPI-U).

For more information on the Orshansky thresholds (the description of which has been simplified here), see Gordon Fisher, "The Development of the Orshansky Thresholds and Their Subsequent History as the Official U.S. Poverty Measure" (May 1992), available on the Census Bureau Web site at http://www.census.gov/hhes/poverty/povmeas/papers/orshansky.html.

The *poverty rate* for a demographic group is the number of poor people or poor families in that group expressed as a percentage of the total number of people or families in the group.

Average poverty thresholds. The thresholds used to calculate the official poverty rates vary not only with the size of the family but with the number of children in the family. For example, the threshold for a three-person family in 2011 was $17,595 if there were no children in the family but $18,123 if the family consisted of 1 adult and 2 children. There are 48 different threshold values depending on size of household, number of children, and whether the householder is 65 years old or over (with lower thresholds for the older householders). The full matrix of thresholds is shown in the report referenced below. To give a general sense of the "poverty line," the Census Bureau also publishes the average threshold for each size family, based on the actual mix of family types in that year. These are the values shown in *Business Statistics* in

Table 3-6 to represent the history of poverty thresholds. The average value for 3-person families in 2011, as shown in Table 3-6, was $17,916, a weighted average of the values actually used for the 3 different possible family compositions.

A person with *work experience* (Table 3-10) is one who, during the preceding calendar year and on a part-time or full-time basis, did any work for pay or profit or worked without pay on a family-operated farm or business at any time during the year. A *year-round* worker is one who worked for 50 weeks or more during the preceding calendar year. A person is classified as having worked *full time* if he or she worked 35 hours or more per week during a majority of the weeks worked. A *year-round, full-time worker* is a person who worked 35 or more hours per week and 50 or more weeks during the previous calendar year.

Toward better measures of income and poverty

The definition of the official poverty rate is established by the Office of Management of Budget in the Executive Office of the President and has not been substantially changed since 1969. Criticisms of the current definition are legion. In response to these criticisms, the Census Bureau has published extensive research work illustrating the effects of various ways of modifying income definitions and poverty thresholds. Some of the results of this work are published here in Tables 3-11 through 3-13 and explained in the notes and definitions below.

Improving the income concept

One type of criticism accepted the general concept of the Orshansky threshold but recommended making the income definition more realistic by including some or all of the following: capital gains; taxes and tax credits; noncash food, housing, and health benefits provided by government and employers; and the value of homeownership. There is debate about whether it is appropriate to use income data augmented in this way in conjunction with the official thresholds. The original 1964 thresholds made no allowance for health insurance or other health expenses—in effect, they assumed that the poor would get free medical care, or at least that the poverty calculation was not required to allow for medical needs—and because of the imprecision of Orshansky's multiplier it is not clear to what extent they include housing expenses in a way that is comparable with the inclusion of a homeownership component in income. Nevertheless, the Census Bureau has calculated and published income and poverty figures based on broadened income definitions and either the official thresholds or thresholds that are closely related to the official ones. Some of these calculations are presented in Table 3-11 and described below.

Still accepting the validity of the basic Orshansky threshold concept, some critics have also argued that use of the CPI-U in the official measure to update the thresholds each year has overstated the price increase, and that an inflator such as the CPI-U-RS should be used instead. (See the notes and definitions for Chapter 8.) Use of the CPI-U-RS leads to lower poverty thresholds beginning in the late 1970s, when the CPI began to be distorted by housing and other biases subsequently corrected by new methods; these newer methods were not carried backward to revise the official CPI-U. Table 3-11 also shows poverty rates using the lower CPI-U-RS thresholds. Use of the CPI-U-RS, which does carry current methods back and thereby revises the CPI time series, eliminates a presumed upward bias in the poverty rate relative to the poverty rates estimated before the bias emerged. This is a bias in the behavior of the time series given the concept of the Orshansky threshold, not necessarily a bias in the current level of poverty, since all the other criticisms of the Orshansky thresholds need to be considered when assessing the general adequacy of today's poverty measurements.

Alternative definitions of income with Orshansky-type poverty thresholds—Table 3-11

The Census Bureau has calculated "alternative" income and poverty measures based on a number of different definitions of income. In many cases, these measures require simulation—use of data from sources other than the CPS to estimate elements of family and individual income and expenses. One system of income definition alternatives, shown in Table 3-11, was used for data through 2003 and has been selectively updated through 2009. The updated data for 2009 are shown on the website under the category "Effect of Benefits and Taxes on Income and Poverty: 2009." This system provides poverty rates including and excluding the effects of government tax and transfer programs, demonstrating the effects of these programs in alleviating poverty.

Table 3-11 shows household income distribution and poverty data through 2009 according to this system of alternative income definitions, which was last used in published reports for 2003 data, issued in June 2005.

Definition 1, also known as "MI," is the official Census Bureau definition of money income described above.

Definition 4 is Definition 1 income minus government cash transfers (Social Security, unemployment compensation, workers' compensation, veterans' payments, railroad retirement, Black Lung payments, government education assistance, Supplemental Security Income, and welfare payments), plus realized capital gains and employers' payments for health insurance coverage. Capital gains and health insurance were not collected in the CPS but were simulated using statistical data from the Internal Revenue Service and the National Medical Care Expenditure Survey. Definition 4 is the closest approach in this set of calculations to a measure of the income generated by the workings of the economy before government interventions in the form of taxes and transfer payments.

Definition 14, also known as "MI – Tx + NC," is income after all government income and earnings tax and transfer interventions. It consists of Definition 4 income minus payroll taxes and federal and state income taxes, plus the Earned Income Credit; plus all of the cash transfers listed above as being subtracted from money income to yield Definition 4; plus the "fungible" value of Medicare and Medicaid (see below for definition); plus the value of regular-price school lunches provided by government; and plus the value of noncash transfers, including food stamps (now called the Supplemental Nutrition Assistance Program, or SNAP), rent subsidies, and free and reduced-price school lunches. The tax information is not collected in the CPS but was simulated using statistical data from the Internal Revenue Service, Social Security payroll tax formulas, and a model of each state's income tax regulations.

The "fungible" value approach to medical benefits counts such benefits as income only to the extent that they free up resources that would have been spent on medical care. Therefore, if family income is not sufficient to cover the family's basic food and housing requirements, Medicare and Medicaid are treated as having no income value. Data on average Medicare and Medicaid outlays per enrollee are used in the valuation process. It appears that the inclusion of these estimates of fungible values makes little difference in the overall poverty rate, reducing it by just 0.2 percentage points in 2009.

Food stamp or SNAP values are reported in the March CPS. Estimates of other government subsidy payments use data from the Department of Agriculture (for school lunches) and the 1985 American Housing Survey.

Definition 15 ("MI – Tx + NC + HE") is Definition 14 income plus the net imputed return on equity in owner-occupied housing—the calculated annual benefit of converting one's home equity into an annuity, net of property taxes. This concept can be thought of as measuring the extent to which equity in the home relieves the owner of the need for rental or mortgage payments. Information from the 1987 American

Housing Survey is used to assign values of home equity and amounts of property taxes. Since disposable personal income in the national income and product accounts (NIPAs) includes the imputed rent on owner-occupied housing plus most of the cash and in-kind transfers included in Definitions 14 and 15, Definition 15 is the Census Bureau income definition closest to the NIPA concept.

Improving the concepts of income and poverty together

Another type of criticism argues that the official thresholds are also no longer relevant to today's needs, and that the concepts of income (or "resources") and of the threshold level that depicts a minimum adequate standard of living need to be rethought together. These critics cite the availability of more up-to-date and detailed information about consumer spending at various income levels. The Consumer Expenditure Survey (CEX), originally designed to provide the weights for the Consumer Price Index, is now conducted quarterly and provides extensive data on consumer spending patterns. To give just one example of the information available now that was not available to Mollie Orshansky, the CEX indicates that food now accounts for one-sixth, not one-third, of total family expenditures, even among low-income families. (For data from, and notes on, the Consumer Expenditure Survey, see Bernan Press, *Handbook of U.S. Labor Statistics.)*

A special panel of the National Academy of Sciences (NAS) undertook a study that reconsidered both resources and thresholds. The Census Bureau has calculated and published experimental poverty rates for 1999 through 2011, developed following NAS recommendations, which are presented in Table 3-12. Beginning in November 2011 the Bureau has issued "The Research Supplemental Poverty Measure" or SPM for the most recent two years, a further refinement of the NAS recommendations; SPM measures are presented in Tables 3-12 and 3-13.

Experimental measures based on NAS recommendations—Table 3-12

Several alternative poverty rates that redefined both resources and needs were presented in "Alternative Poverty Estimates in the United States: 2003" (see below for complete reference) and have been updated through 2011 on the Census Bureau Web site at http://www.census.gov, under the general heading "NAS-based Experimental Poverty Estimates."

To derive these estimates, a baseline set of poverty thresholds for the year 1999, based on data from the CEX for the years 1997–1999, was developed as follows:

• A reference family type was selected: a 2-adult, 2-child family.

• The definition of necessities for the purpose of the poverty threshold was expenditures on food, clothing, shelter, and utilities (FCSU), augmented by a multiplier of between 1.15 and 1.25 to include other needs such as household and personal supplies. The definition of food includes food away from home. Expenses on shelter include interest (but not principal repayment) for homeowners and rent for renters.

• The numerical estimates were derived as follows: FCSU expenditures for reference families falling between the 30th and 35th percentile of the distribution of expenditures in the CEX, based on 1997–1999 data but expressed in 1999 dollars, were calculated and expanded by the multiplier percentages. The midpoint of these estimates was then selected as the poverty threshold; it turned out to be 96.725 percent of FCSU expenditures by the median household.

• For health care, three different treatments were developed; these treatments are described below.

• Three-parameter equivalence scale adjustments were used to convert the threshold for the reference family to thresholds for other family sizes and compositions, accounting for the differing needs of adults and children and the economies of scale of living in larger families.

• For some of the experimental measures, thresholds were adjusted geographically to reflect differences in the cost of living (in practice, difference in housing costs) in different areas.

The family incomes to be compared with these poverty thresholds were defined and measured to include the effects of all taxes, tax credits, and in-kind benefits such as food stamps, but not the value of homeownership, and to allow for expenses such as child care that are necessary to hold a job.

The eight experimental measures shown in Table 3-12 are as originally presented in Table B-3 in "Alternative Poverty Estimates in the United States: 2003," and most recently updated in the table "Official and National Academy of Sciences (NAS) Based Poverty Rates: 1999 to 2011" on the Census Bureau Web site. The following abbreviations are used to define the alternative definitions of poverty that are presented in this table.

• *MSI* indicates that in calculating the poverty rate, medical out-of-pocket expenses are subtracted from family income before comparing that income to the family's threshold.

• *MIT* indicates that poverty thresholds were increased to take the family's potential medical out-of-pocket expenses into account, using the CEX and the 1996 Medical Expenditures Panel Survey, with the amounts depending on family size, age, and health insurance coverage.

• *GA* indicates that the thresholds were adjusted for geographic differences in the cost of living. Measures labeled *NGA* were not.

• *CPI* indicates that the thresholds established for 1999 were updated to succeeding years using the percent change in the CPI-U. In effect, the thresholds for these measures have been held constant in real (inflation-adjusted) terms since 1999, just as the official thresholds have been held constant in real terms—in intention, and in fact except for bias in the price indexes—since 1964.

• *CE* indicates that the thresholds were updated using the percent change in median FCSU expenditures from the latest available 12 quarters of CEX data. This means that if the actual real FCSU spending of middle-income families rises (or falls), the real standard of living represented by the poverty thresholds will rise (or fall) commensurately.

Supplemental Poverty Measure—Tables 3-12 and 3-13

In March of 2010, an Interagency Technical Working Group produced suggestions for a Supplemental Poverty Measure (SPM), which were first implemented in the "Research Supplemental Poverty Measure: 2010" issued by the Census Bureau in November 2011. The SPM goes beyond the experimental measures just described, and takes advantage of new data from questions introduced in the CPS-ASEC in recent years. In the new SPM:

• The measurement unit now covers not just the family but "all related individuals who live at the same address, including any coresident unrelated children who are cared for by the family (such as foster children) and any cohabitors and their children." This redefinition adds unrelated individuals under the age of 15 to the universe measured by the official rate. The "official" measures shown in Table 3-13 have been adjusted to include these individuals, and are therefore slightly higher than the regular published official rates shown in Tables 3-7 through 3-12.

• The SPM thresholds are calculated separately for three housing status groups: owners with mortgages, owners without mortgages, and renters. For each of these three groups the basic threshold represents the 33rd percentile of expenditures on food, clothing, shelter, and utilities (FCSU), averaged over a five-year period, by consumer units with two children, multiplied by 1.2 to allow for other needs. (Before averaging, the expenditures are converted to their dollar

values in the prices of the threshold year using the CPI-U.) The consumer units selected for calculating the threshold include not only two-adult two-child families but also other types with two children, such as single-parent families. But they are adjusted to a four-person basis, using the equivalence scales, before averaging them to determine the basic threshold appropriate to a two-adult two-child household. Then that threshold is used as the basis for calculating thresholds for other size measurement units, again using the three-parameter equivalence scales for family size and composition, and for geographic differences.

• The thresholds are updated each year, using an updated five-year moving average of FCSU at the 33rd percentile, expressed in the prices of the new threshold year. Thus the thresholds are adjusted for inflation, but in addition, the "real" (constant-dollar) purchasing power of the poverty threshold will change (gradually) over time as the real standard of FCSU spending in the 33rd percentile changes. The real value of the threshold will likely change more slowly and gradually than in the "experimental" measures described above, because of using five instead of three years in the average.

• Family resources include cash income, plus in-kind benefits that families can use to meet their FCSU needs (for example, the Supplemental Nutrition Assistance Program [SNAP] formerly known as food stamps), minus income and payroll taxes, plus tax credits, minus childcare and other work-related expenses, minus child support payments to another household, and minus out-of-pocket medical expenses.

The SPM is not intended to replace the official poverty measure and is not to be used in calculations affecting program eligibility and funding distribution. According to the report referenced above, it is "designed to provide information on aggregate levels of economic need at a national level or within large subpopulations or areas…providing further understanding of economic conditions and trends." Census Bureau presentation of the SPM has focused on the different distribution of the poverty population indicated by the new measures, as shown in Table 3-13.

Notes on the data

The following are the principal changes that may affect year-to-year comparability of all income and poverty data from the CPS.

• Beginning in 1952, the estimates are based on 1950 census population controls. Earlier figures were based on 1940 census population controls.

• Beginning in 1962, 1960 census–based sample design and population controls are fully implemented.

• With 1971 and 1972 data, 1970 census–based sample design and population controls were introduced.

• With 1983–1985 data, 1980 census–based sample design was introduced; 1980 population controls were introduced; and these were extended back to 1979 data.

• With 1993 data, there was a major redesign of the CPS, including the introduction of computer-assisted interviewing. The limits used to "code" reported income amounts were changed, resulting in reporting of higher income values for the highest-income families and, consequently, an exaggerated year-to-year increase in income inequality. (It is possible that this jump actually reflects in one year an increase that had emerged more gradually, so that the distribution measures for 1993 and later years may be properly comparable with data for decades earlier even if they should not be directly compared with 1992.) In addition, 1990 census–based population controls were introduced, and these were extended back to the 1992 data.

• With 1995 data, the 1990 census–based sample design was implemented and the sample was reduced by 7,000 households.

• Data for 2001 implemented population controls based on the 2000 census, which were carried back to 2000 and 1999 data as well. Data from 2000 forward also incorporate results from a 28,000-household sample expansion.

• Beginning with the data for 2010 presented here, population controls based on the 2010 census were implemented. (This resulted in some revision of CPS data initially published for 2010.)

For more information on these and other changes that could affect comparability, see "Current Population Survey Technical Paper 63RV: Design and Methodology" (March 2002) and footnotes to CPS historical income tables, both available on the Census Bureau Web site at http://www.census.gov/hhes/income.

Data availability

Data embodying the official definitions of income and poverty are published annually in late summer or early fall by the Census Bureau, as part of a series with the general title *Current Population Reports: Consumer Income, P60*. Most of the data in this chapter were derived from report P60-243, "Income, Poverty, and Health Insurance Coverage in the United States: 2011" (September 2012), and from the "Historical Income Tables" and "Historical Poverty Tables" on the Census Web site (see below).

The data in Table 3-11 were first published in two reports, both issued in June 2005: P60-228, "Alternative Income Estimates in the United States: 2003," and P60-227, "Alternative Poverty Estimates in the United States: 2003." Updates available on the website are cited in the table description above. Corrections to the 2006 data on the website were obtained from Census Bureau staff.

The NAS-based experimental data used in Table 3-12 are from the Census Bureau Web site, as specified in the description above.

The SPM data in Tables 3-12 and 3-13 are from the reports "The Research Supplemental Poverty Measure: 2011" (P60-244) and "The Research Supplemental Poverty Measure: 2010" (P60-241), available on the Census Web site.

All these reports and related data, including historical tabulations, used in *Business Statistics* are available on the Census Bureau Web site at http://www.census.gov, under the general headings of "Income" and "Poverty."

References

Definitions and descriptions of the concepts and data of all series are provided in the source documents listed above and in the references contained therein.

CHAPTER 4: CONSUMER INCOME AND SPENDING

Figure 4-1. Personal Saving Rate, 1955–2012
(saving as a percent of disposable personal income)

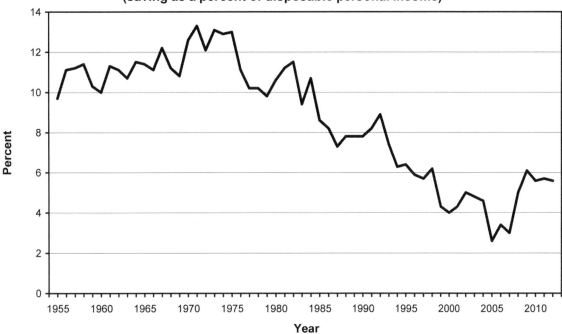

- In the 2013 revision of the National Income and Product Accounts, the personal saving rate is generally higher than was shown before the revision. This does not mean that more money has been discovered in the savings accounts of individuals. It is the result of a change from cash accounting to accrual accounting for the defined benefit pension plans of private and government employers. This accounting change does not create new saving out of thin air, but rather attributes the accrual of the earned benefit to the employee instead of to the employer. What it adds to personal saving is subtracted from government saving, or added to government deficits.

- The newly-defined personal saving rate is markedly higher in the 1950s through early 1970s than the previous series, but it starts to trend down sooner. From rates as high as 13 percent in the early 1970s, it falls to an average of 6.7 percent in the 1990s and 4.3 percent in the 2000s. Between 2010 and 2012, the rate averaged 5.6 percent. (Table 4-1A)

- It should be noted that personal income does not, by definition, include any capital gains. Despite that, taxes on realized capital gains are deducted (along with all other income taxes) from personal income to get after-tax income. Capital gains, both realized and unrealized, can be a source of spending power in addition to current disposable income; during the housing price bubble they were converted into cash by asset sales, refinancing, and home equity loans, all of which were reflected in low saving rates. (Table 12-11)

- Government social benefits were 4.5 percent of personal income in 1955, rising to 14.1 percent in the high-employment year 2007. In the recession they rose further, to 18.0 percent in 2010, falling back somewhat to 16.9 percent in 2010. It should be understood that this income category includes all spending financed by government health insurance programs such as Medicare and Medicaid, and this spending is counted as personal consumption expenditures rather than direct government spending in the NIPAs. (Table 4-1)

Table 4-1A. Personal Income and Its Disposition: Recent Data

(Billions of current dollars, except as noted; quarterly data are at seasonally adjusted annual rates.)   **NIPA Table 2.1**

Year and quarter	Total	Compensation of employees	Proprietors' income with IVA and CCAdj	Rental income of persons with CCAdj	Personal income receipts on assets		Personal current transfer receipts — Government social benefits to persons					
					Personal interest income	Personal dividend income	Total	Social Security and Medicare	Government unemployment insurance	Veterans	Medicaid	Other government benefits to persons
1955	324.6	230.9	44.3	13.4	18.9	10.5	14.8	4.9	1.6	4.4	. . .	3.9
1956	348.4	249.6	45.8	13.7	21.2	11.3	15.6	5.7	1.6	4.3	. . .	4.0
1957	368.5	263.0	47.8	14.1	23.8	11.7	18.1	7.3	1.9	4.5	. . .	4.4
1958	379.5	265.1	50.2	14.8	25.8	11.6	22.2	8.5	4.2	4.6	. . .	4.9
1959	403.2	286.3	50.3	15.6	28.0	12.6	22.9	10.2	2.9	4.5	. . .	5.4
1960	422.5	301.9	50.6	16.5	31.0	13.4	24.4	11.1	3.1	4.5	. . .	5.7
1961	441.1	311.1	53.2	17.2	33.2	13.9	28.1	12.6	4.4	4.9	. . .	6.2
1962	469.1	332.9	55.2	18.0	36.6	15.0	28.8	14.3	3.2	4.6	. . .	6.8
1963	492.8	351.2	56.4	18.7	39.8	16.2	30.3	15.2	3.1	4.8	. . .	7.3
1964	528.4	376.8	59.1	18.8	44.3	18.2	31.3	16.0	2.8	4.6	. . .	7.9
1965	570.8	406.3	63.7	19.3	48.5	20.2	33.9	18.1	2.4	4.8	. . .	8.6
1966	620.6	450.3	67.9	19.9	53.5	20.7	37.5	20.8	1.9	4.8	1.9	8.1
1967	665.7	482.9	69.5	20.3	58.3	21.5	45.8	25.8	2.2	5.5	2.7	9.4
1968	730.7	532.1	73.8	20.1	63.8	23.5	53.3	30.5	2.2	5.9	4.0	10.8
1969	800.3	586.0	77.0	20.4	74.4	24.2	59.0	33.1	2.3	6.6	4.6	12.4
1970	864.6	625.1	77.8	20.7	88.3	24.3	71.7	38.7	4.2	7.5	5.5	16.0
1971	932.1	667.0	83.9	21.9	97.3	25.0	85.4	44.6	6.2	8.4	6.7	19.4
1972	1 023.6	733.6	95.1	22.8	106.5	26.8	94.8	49.7	6.0	9.4	8.2	21.4
1973	1 138.5	815.0	112.5	23.3	120.8	29.9	108.6	60.9	4.6	10.2	9.6	23.3
1974	1 249.3	890.3	112.2	23.3	142.2	33.2	128.6	70.3	7.0	11.6	11.2	28.4
1975	1 366.9	950.2	118.2	22.5	162.4	32.9	163.1	81.5	18.1	14.0	13.9	35.7
1976	1 498.1	1 051.2	131.0	20.6	173.6	39.0	177.3	93.3	16.4	13.8	15.5	38.4
1977	1 654.2	1 169.0	144.5	16.2	198.7	44.7	189.1	105.3	13.1	13.3	16.7	40.6
1978	1 859.5	1 320.2	166.0	16.9	227.3	50.7	203.2	116.9	9.4	13.6	18.6	44.6
1979	2 077.9	1 481.0	179.4	16.6	260.9	57.4	227.1	132.5	9.7	14.2	21.1	49.7
1980	2 316.8	1 626.2	171.6	19.7	322.0	64.0	270.8	154.8	16.1	14.7	23.9	61.4
1981	2 595.9	1 795.3	179.7	25.4	399.2	73.6	307.2	182.1	15.9	15.8	27.7	65.6
1982	2 778.8	1 894.3	171.2	26.1	463.7	77.6	342.4	204.6	25.2	16.3	30.2	66.1
1983	2 969.7	2 013.9	186.3	27.5	501.0	83.3	369.9	222.2	26.4	16.4	33.9	71.0
1984	3 281.3	2 217.4	228.2	27.9	574.4	90.6	380.4	237.7	16.0	16.3	36.6	73.8
1985	3 515.9	2 389.0	241.1	29.5	615.4	97.4	402.6	253.0	15.9	16.6	39.7	77.6
1986	3 725.1	2 543.8	256.5	21.9	649.3	106.0	428.0	268.9	16.5	16.6	43.6	82.4
1987	3 955.3	2 724.3	286.5	20.2	667.7	112.2	447.4	282.6	14.6	16.5	47.8	85.9
1988	4 275.3	2 950.0	325.8	25.1	709.6	129.7	475.9	300.2	13.3	16.7	53.0	92.6
1989	4 618.2	3 142.6	341.9	24.4	794.2	157.8	519.4	325.6	14.4	17.2	60.8	101.4
1990	4 904.5	3 342.7	354.4	31.4	822.4	168.8	572.7	351.7	18.2	17.7	73.1	111.9
1991	5 071.1	3 452.0	356.0	42.0	805.3	180.2	648.2	381.7	26.8	18.1	96.9	124.7
1992	5 410.8	3 671.1	402.4	64.3	793.1	189.1	729.5	414.4	39.6	18.6	116.2	140.6
1993	5 646.8	3 820.7	430.5	93.6	783.9	204.7	776.7	444.7	34.8	19.3	130.1	147.7
1994	5 934.7	4 010.1	459.5	117.5	794.2	235.2	813.1	476.6	23.9	19.7	139.4	153.5
1995	6 276.5	4 202.6	484.5	129.2	856.0	258.0	860.2	508.9	21.7	20.5	149.6	159.5
1996	6 661.9	4 422.1	547.4	147.0	874.3	302.2	901.2	536.9	22.3	21.4	158.2	162.4
1997	7 075.0	4 714.7	587.9	152.0	920.5	337.9	929.8	563.5	20.1	22.3	163.1	160.7
1998	7 587.7	5 077.8	644.2	169.9	987.1	355.4	951.9	574.8	19.7	23.3	170.2	164.0
1999	7 983.8	5 410.3	700.4	183.1	983.3	346.4	987.6	588.6	20.5	24.1	184.6	169.8
2000	8 632.8	5 856.6	757.8	187.7	1 070.2	383.3	1 040.6	620.5	20.7	25.0	199.5	174.8
2001	8 987.1	6 046.5	836.8	207.5	1 072.2	369.2	1 141.3	667.7	31.9	26.6	227.3	187.9
2002	9 149.5	6 141.9	871.0	217.3	991.8	398.6	1 246.2	706.1	53.5	29.5	250.0	207.0
2003	9 487.6	6 365.4	900.1	238.0	988.2	432.3	1 316.6	740.2	53.2	31.8	264.5	226.8
2004	10 049.2	6 740.5	962.1	255.4	941.7	562.1	1 399.9	789.9	36.4	34.0	289.8	249.7
2005	10 610.3	7 087.8	979.0	238.4	1 088.1	578.3	1 486.3	844.9	31.8	36.4	304.4	268.8
2006	11 389.8	7 503.2	1 053.7	207.5	1 214.7	723.7	1 588.2	943.3	30.4	38.9	299.1	276.5
2007	11 995.7	7 899.1	979.2	189.4	1 350.1	816.5	1 692.2	1 004.7	32.7	41.7	324.2	288.9
2008	12 430.6	8 079.2	1 026.5	262.1	1 361.6	805.4	1 847.3	1 068.4	51.1	45.0	338.3	344.4
2009	12 082.1	7 787.8	973.0	333.7	1 263.9	547.9	2 101.5	1 159.1	131.2	51.5	369.2	390.4
2010	12 435.2	7 967.3	1 032.7	402.8	1 195.0	544.6	2 234.0	1 204.0	138.9	58.0	396.6	436.5
2011	13 191.3	8 278.5	1 155.1	484.4	1 204.1	680.5	2 260.3	1 250.3	107.6	63.3	405.5	433.7
2012	13 743.8	8 611.6	1 224.9	541.2	1 211.6	746.9	2 316.8	1 323.0	84.2	70.2	417.1	422.5
2010												
1st quarter	12 194.3	7 804.3	1 017.6	380.5	1 206.1	504.6	2 212.7	1 184.0	159.8	55.9	381.7	431.4
2nd quarter	12 374.3	7 952.7	1 024.7	397.3	1 198.7	524.1	2 219.0	1 199.9	140.5	57.1	385.3	436.1
3rd quarter	12 502.1	8 026.5	1 029.2	408.3	1 182.8	555.2	2 245.1	1 210.2	130.7	58.9	405.4	439.9
4th quarter	12 670.0	8 085.7	1 059.3	425.0	1 192.5	594.6	2 259.0	1 221.9	124.4	59.9	414.1	438.7
2011												
1st quarter	13 029.9	8 207.4	1 116.5	458.5	1 202.9	647.5	2 262.8	1 232.5	118.1	61.5	418.8	431.9
2nd quarter	13 148.5	8 256.3	1 140.7	475.5	1 210.8	672.6	2 261.8	1 247.9	109.1	62.5	408.7	433.5
3rd quarter	13 283.6	8 343.3	1 175.3	489.9	1 203.0	696.3	2 253.6	1 255.5	102.9	64.7	396.1	434.4
4th quarter	13 303.2	8 306.9	1 188.0	513.5	1 199.6	705.7	2 262.8	1 265.0	100.2	64.4	398.3	435.0
2012												
1st quarter	13 548.6	8 514.3	1 214.4	524.8	1 204.9	704.2	2 285.2	1 301.0	96.8	67.1	400.8	419.5
2nd quarter	13 651.8	8 553.8	1 217.8	537.8	1 219.4	715.9	2 310.5	1 314.6	85.9	68.9	420.9	420.3
3rd quarter	13 701.6	8 591.0	1 220.0	546.7	1 203.7	723.2	2 323.8	1 328.8	78.7	71.3	421.5	423.5
4th quarter	14 073.1	8 787.4	1 247.5	555.4	1 218.4	844.3	2 347.9	1 347.4	75.3	73.3	425.1	426.8

. . . = Not available.

Table 4-1A. Personal Income and Its Disposition: Recent Data—*Continued*

(Billions of current dollars, except as noted; quarterly data are at seasonally adjusted annual rates.)   **NIPA Table 2.1**

Year and quarter	Personal income—Continued: Personal current transfer receipts—Continued: From business, net	Less: Contributions for government social insurance, domestic	Less: Personal current taxes	Equals: Disposable personal income	Less: Personal outlays: Total	Personal consumption expenditures	Personal interest payments	Personal current transfer payments: Total	To government	To the rest of the world, net	Equals: Personal saving: Billions of dollars	Percent of disposable personal income	Billions of chained (2009) dollars: Percent income excluding current transfers	Disposable personal income
1955	0.9	9.1	32.9	291.7	263.5	258.7	4.0	0.9	0.4	0.4	28.2	9.7	1 955.2	1 846.5
1956	1.2	10.0	36.6	311.8	277.1	271.6	4.6	1.0	0.5	0.5	34.7	11.1	2 057.5	1 934.8
1957	1.4	11.4	38.9	329.6	292.7	286.7	4.9	1.1	0.6	0.5	36.9	11.2	2 101.5	1 984.9
1958	1.2	11.4	38.5	340.9	302.0	296.0	5.0	1.0	0.6	0.4	38.9	11.4	2 094.7	2 005.9
1959	1.3	13.8	42.3	360.9	323.8	317.5	5.5	0.8	0.3	0.5	37.1	10.3	2 196.7	2 092.1
1960	1.3	16.4	46.1	376.5	338.6	331.6	6.2	0.8	0.3	0.5	37.8	10.0	2 262.9	2 146.9
1961	1.4	17.0	47.3	393.8	349.5	342.0	6.5	1.0	0.5	0.5	44.4	11.3	2 323.1	2 222.7
1962	1.5	19.1	51.6	417.5	371.2	363.1	7.0	1.1	0.5	0.6	46.4	11.1	2 447.1	2 329.1
1963	1.9	21.7	54.6	438.3	391.6	382.5	7.9	1.2	0.5	0.7	46.7	10.7	2 539.7	2 416.5
1964	2.2	22.4	52.1	476.3	421.4	411.2	8.9	1.3	0.6	0.7	54.8	11.5	2 689.0	2 588.1
1965	2.3	23.4	57.7	513.2	454.9	443.6	9.9	1.4	0.6	0.8	58.3	11.4	2 863.9	2 748.9
1966	2.1	31.3	66.4	554.2	492.8	480.6	10.7	1.6	0.8	0.8	61.4	11.1	3 034.8	2 895.0
1967	2.3	34.9	73.0	592.8	520.6	507.4	11.1	2.0	1.0	1.0	72.2	12.2	3 147.7	3 020.6
1968	2.8	38.7	87.0	643.8	571.7	557.4	12.2	2.0	1.0	1.0	72.1	11.2	3 308.9	3 157.4
1969	3.3	44.1	104.5	695.8	620.7	604.5	14.0	2.2	1.1	1.1	75.0	10.8	3 462.5	3 264.4
1970	2.9	46.4	103.1	761.5	665.5	647.7	15.2	2.6	1.3	1.3	96.1	12.6	3 540.7	3 413.4
1971	2.7	51.2	101.7	830.4	720.3	701.0	16.6	2.8	1.5	1.4	110.1	13.3	3 628.8	3 570.4
1972	3.1	59.2	123.6	899.9	790.7	769.4	18.1	3.2	1.8	1.4	109.2	12.1	3 848.2	3 741.3
1973	3.9	75.5	132.4	1 006.1	874.3	851.1	19.8	3.4	1.8	1.6	131.8	13.1	4 046.8	3 968.6
1974	4.7	85.2	151.0	1 098.3	956.6	932.0	21.2	3.4	2.1	1.4	141.7	12.9	3 987.2	3 923.7
1975	6.8	89.3	147.6	1 219.3	1 060.3	1 032.8	23.7	3.8	2.5	1.3	159.0	13.0	3 946.4	4 020.2
1976	6.7	101.3	172.3	1 325.8	1 178.5	1 150.2	23.9	4.4	3.0	1.4	147.3	11.1	4 107.5	4 144.0
1977	5.1	113.1	197.5	1 456.7	1 308.5	1 276.7	27.0	4.8	3.5	1.4	148.2	10.2	4 284.5	4 274.8
1978	6.5	131.3	229.4	1 630.1	1 463.5	1 426.2	31.9	5.4	3.9	1.6	166.6	10.2	4 524.7	4 470.5
1979	8.2	152.7	268.7	1 809.3	1 631.7	1 589.5	36.2	6.0	4.3	1.7	177.5	9.8	4 641.9	4 557.8
1980	8.6	166.2	298.9	2 018.0	1 804.8	1 754.6	43.2	6.9	5.0	2.0	213.2	10.6	4 634.7	4 590.6
1981	11.2	195.7	345.2	2 250.7	1 998.3	1 937.5	49.2	11.5	6.0	5.6	252.5	11.2	4 761.7	4 705.7
1982	12.4	208.9	354.1	2 424.7	2 147.0	2 073.9	59.3	13.8	7.1	6.7	277.7	11.5	4 802.0	4 803.4
1983	13.8	226.0	352.3	2 617.4	2 370.4	2 286.5	68.8	15.1	8.1	7.0	247.0	9.4	4 911.4	4 971.0
1984	19.7	257.5	377.4	2 903.9	2 591.8	2 498.2	76.6	17.1	9.2	7.9	312.1	10.7	5 272.5	5 314.0
1985	22.3	281.4	417.3	3 098.5	2 833.4	2 722.7	92.0	18.8	10.4	8.3	265.1	8.6	5 462.9	5 476.3
1986	22.9	303.4	437.2	3 287.9	3 018.5	2 898.4	99.0	21.1	12.0	9.1	269.4	8.2	5 664.1	5 687.9
1987	20.2	323.1	489.1	3 466.3	3 214.2	3 092.1	98.9	23.2	13.2	10.0	252.1	7.3	5 847.1	5 811.1
1988	20.6	361.5	504.9	3 770.4	3 475.7	3 346.9	103.1	25.6	14.8	10.8	294.7	7.8	6 097.6	6 083.9
1989	23.2	385.2	566.1	4 052.1	3 735.6	3 592.8	114.8	28.0	16.5	11.6	316.5	7.8	6 305.1	6 268.8
1990	22.2	410.1	592.7	4 311.8	3 976.3	3 825.6	120.1	30.6	18.4	12.2	335.4	7.8	6 390.3	6 393.6
1991	17.6	430.2	586.6	4 484.5	4 118.6	3 960.2	121.8	36.7	22.6	14.1	365.9	8.2	6 324.7	6 438.5
1992	16.3	455.0	610.5	4 800.3	4 374.2	4 215.7	118.1	40.5	26.0	14.5	426.0	8.9	6 525.1	6 714.3
1993	14.1	477.4	646.5	5 000.2	4 632.6	4 471.0	116.0	45.6	28.6	17.1	367.6	7.4	6 626.8	6 823.6
1994	13.3	508.2	690.5	5 244.2	4 912.8	4 741.0	122.0	49.8	30.9	18.9	331.4	6.3	6 829.1	7 010.8
1995	18.7	532.8	743.9	5 532.6	5 179.6	4 984.2	142.6	52.9	32.6	20.3	352.9	6.4	7 069.1	7 245.9
1996	22.9	555.1	832.0	5 829.9	5 484.7	5 268.1	159.1	57.6	34.9	22.6	345.2	5.9	7 358.1	7 476.2
1997	19.4	587.2	926.2	6 148.9	5 796.7	5 560.7	172.1	63.9	38.2	25.7	352.2	5.7	7 722.3	7 751.4
1998	26.0	624.7	1 026.4	6 561.3	6 156.0	5 903.0	183.4	69.5	39.9	29.7	405.3	6.2	8 269.0	8 208.3
1999	34.0	661.3	1 107.5	6 876.3	6 583.3	6 316.9	190.2	76.2	44.1	32.2	293.0	4.3	8 583.8	8 477.8
2000	42.4	705.8	1 232.3	7 400.5	7 102.6	6 801.6	217.5	83.4	48.8	34.6	297.9	4.0	9 082.1	8 902.5
2001	46.8	733.2	1 234.8	7 752.3	7 421.1	7 106.9	223.2	91.0	52.9	38.1	331.2	4.3	9 204.4	9 149.3
2002	34.2	751.5	1 050.3	8 099.2	7 695.3	7 385.3	213.0	97.0	56.4	40.6	403.9	5.0	9 163.8	9 431.7
2003	26.3	779.3	1 000.9	8 486.7	8 075.9	7 764.4	209.8	101.7	60.5	41.2	410.8	4.8	9 300.5	9 691.0
2004	16.8	829.2	1 046.0	9 003.2	8 590.0	8 257.8	221.8	110.5	66.9	43.6	413.2	4.6	9 623.4	10 036.7
2005	25.7	873.3	1 208.5	9 401.8	9 159.1	8 790.3	248.8	120.0	71.6	48.4	242.7	2.6	9 861.5	10 190.5
2006	21.5	922.6	1 352.1	10 037.7	9 700.8	9 297.5	275.1	128.2	76.6	51.6	336.9	3.4	10 324.5	10 596.4
2007	30.6	961.4	1 487.9	10 507.9	10 190.6	9 744.4	305.9	140.3	81.0	59.3	317.2	3.0	10 579.9	10 821.8
2008	36.6	988.2	1 435.2	10 995.4	10 444.0	10 005.5	289.6	148.9	82.8	66.2	551.3	5.0	10 540.0	10 988.4
2009	38.7	964.4	1 144.9	10 937.2	10 266.5	9 842.9	273.9	149.6	83.5	66.1	670.7	6.1	9 941.9	10 937.2
2010	43.0	984.1	1 191.5	11 243.7	10 609.5	10 201.9	250.8	156.9	83.9	73.0	634.2	5.6	9 993.0	11 060.8
2011	46.7	918.2	1 404.0	11 787.4	11 119.1	10 711.8	248.0	159.4	85.3	74.1	668.2	5.7	10 457.1	11 324.6
2012	41.4	950.7	1 498.0	12 245.8	11 558.4	11 149.6	248.4	160.4	88.5	71.9	687.4	5.6	10 740.1	11 551.6
2010														
1st quarter	40.6	972.0	1 145.6	11 048.7	10 459.9	10 042.3	259.2	158.4	84.0	74.4	588.9	5.3	9 815.4	10 909.1
2nd quarter	41.9	984.0	1 167.9	11 206.4	10 542.4	10 134.7	252.4	155.2	83.9	71.4	664.0	5.9	9 974.3	11 052.2
3rd quarter	43.3	988.4	1 209.4	11 292.6	10 637.5	10 234.3	246.8	156.5	83.8	72.7	655.2	5.8	10 043.5	11 104.4
4th quarter	46.1	992.0	1 242.9	11 427.1	10 798.4	10 396.3	244.7	157.4	83.7	73.6	628.7	5.5	10 138.3	11 177.3
2011														
1st quarter	46.8	912.6	1 376.0	11 653.9	10 936.0	10 527.1	251.0	157.9	84.1	73.8	717.9	6.2	10 408.9	11 315.4
2nd quarter	47.3	916.4	1 399.9	11 748.6	11 069.5	10 662.6	247.7	159.2	84.7	74.5	679.1	5.8	10 429.2	11 303.9
3rd quarter	46.9	924.7	1 421.6	11 862.1	11 185.8	10 778.6	248.7	158.5	85.6	72.9	676.2	5.7	10 507.5	11 348.4
4th quarter	45.7	919.1	1 418.4	11 884.8	11 285.2	10 878.9	244.5	161.8	86.8	75.0	599.6	5.0	10 483.5	11 332.3
2012														
1st quarter	43.3	942.5	1 462.8	12 085.7	11 428.4	11 019.1	248.6	160.7	87.7	73.0	657.3	5.4	10 638.4	11 459.2
2nd quarter	41.7	945.1	1 480.0	12 171.9	11 507.9	11 100.2	247.0	160.8	88.4	72.4	663.9	5.5	10 685.5	11 510.2
3rd quarter	40.6	947.4	1 496.4	12 205.1	11 601.0	11 193.6	250.7	156.7	88.8	67.9	604.1	4.9	10 676.2	11 493.6
4th quarter	40.1	967.9	1 552.8	12 520.4	11 696.2	11 285.5	247.3	163.4	89.0	74.4	824.1	6.6	10 959.6	11 743.0

Table 4-1B. Personal Income and Its Disposition: Historical

(Billions of current dollars, except as noted; quarterly data are at seasonally adjusted annual rates.)   **NIPA Table 2.1**

| Year and quarter | Personal income | | | | | | | Less: Personal current taxes | Equals: Disposable personal income | Less: Personal outlays | Equals: Personal saving | | Billions of chained (2009) dollars | |
	Total	Compen-sation of employees	Pro-prietors' income with IVA and CCAdj	Rental income of persons with CCAdj	Personal income receipts on assets	Personal current transfer receipts	Less: Contribu-tions for govern-ment social insurance, domestic				Billions of dollars	Percent of disposable personal income	Personal income excluding current transfers	Disposable personal income
1929	85.3	51.4	14.0	6.1	12.6	1.2	0.1	1.7	83.5	79.6	3.9	4.7	848.5	843.1
1930	76.5	47.2	10.9	5.4	11.9	1.2	0.1	1.6	74.9	71.6	3.3	4.4	793.4	789.7
1931	65.6	40.1	8.3	4.4	10.5	2.3	0.1	1.0	64.6	61.8	2.8	4.3	747.0	762.9
1932	50.3	31.4	5.0	3.6	8.6	1.7	0.1	0.7	49.5	49.7	-0.1	-0.2	649.3	663.0
1933	47.2	29.8	5.3	2.9	7.6	1.7	0.1	0.8	46.4	46.8	-0.4	-0.8	631.6	643.8
1934	54.1	34.6	7.0	2.5	8.3	1.8	0.1	0.9	53.2	52.3	0.9	1.7	694.4	705.7
1935	60.8	37.7	10.1	2.6	8.5	2.0	0.1	1.1	59.8	56.8	3.0	5.1	762.5	774.3
1936	69.2	43.3	10.4	2.7	10.0	3.1	0.3	1.3	67.9	63.1	4.8	7.0	848.9	871.9
1937	74.7	48.4	12.5	3.0	10.4	2.0	1.5	1.9	72.8	67.9	4.9	6.7	900.7	901.4
1938	69.1	45.5	10.6	3.5	8.8	2.4	1.6	1.9	67.2	65.3	2.0	2.9	845.2	852.0
1939	73.6	48.6	11.1	3.7	9.4	2.5	1.8	1.5	72.1	68.2	3.9	5.4	910.0	923.2
1940	79.4	52.8	12.2	3.8	9.7	2.7	1.9	1.7	77.7	72.4	5.3	6.8	973.6	986.2
1941	97.9	66.2	16.7	4.4	10.2	2.7	2.3	2.3	95.6	82.3	13.3	13.9	1 137.7	1 141.8
1942	126.7	88.1	23.3	5.5	10.0	2.7	2.9	4.9	121.8	90.0	31.9	26.2	1 318.0	1 294.4
1943	156.2	112.8	28.2	6.0	10.4	2.5	3.8	16.7	139.4	100.8	38.6	27.7	1 495.5	1 356.8
1944	169.7	124.4	29.3	6.3	10.9	3.1	4.3	17.7	152.0	109.7	42.4	27.9	1 533.0	1 399.0
1945	175.8	126.4	30.8	6.6	11.7	5.6	5.3	19.4	156.3	121.2	35.2	22.5	1 505.2	1 383.1
1946	182.7	122.6	35.7	6.9	13.6	10.6	6.6	17.2	165.5	145.9	19.6	11.8	1 423.6	1 368.6
1947	194.6	132.5	34.6	6.9	15.4	10.8	5.6	19.8	174.8	163.8	11.0	6.3	1 380.3	1 312.9
1948	213.7	144.5	39.3	7.5	16.8	10.3	4.6	19.2	194.5	177.2	17.2	8.9	1 445.8	1 382.2
1949	211.2	144.5	34.7	7.8	17.9	11.2	4.9	16.7	194.5	180.9	13.6	7.0	1 432.9	1 393.3
1950	233.9	158.5	37.5	8.8	20.7	14.0	5.5	18.9	215.0	195.0	20.0	9.3	1 556.8	1 521.9
1951	264.5	185.9	42.6	9.7	21.4	11.4	6.6	27.1	237.4	211.5	25.9	10.9	1 677.0	1 573.3
1952	282.7	201.3	43.0	10.8	22.5	11.9	6.9	32.0	250.7	222.8	27.8	11.1	1 758.5	1 627.8
1953	299.6	215.5	42.0	12.0	24.6	12.5	7.1	33.2	266.3	237.1	29.2	11.0	1 839.7	1 706.9
1954	302.6	214.4	42.3	13.1	26.6	14.3	8.1	30.2	272.4	244.2	28.2	10.3	1 832.1	1 731.4
1947														
1st quarter	190.2	129.1	36.2	6.7	14.8	9.7	6.3	19.2	171.0	158.1	12.9	7.5	1 384.8	1 312.3
2nd quarter ...	189.9	130.9	33.3	6.8	15.3	9.6	6.0	19.5	170.4	161.9	8.5	5.0	1 372.7	1 297.4
3rd quarter	197.8	132.9	33.9	7.0	15.7	13.5	5.2	19.7	178.0	165.5	12.5	7.0	1 377.6	1 330.8
4th quarter	200.6	137.0	35.0	7.2	15.8	10.5	4.8	20.8	179.8	169.7	10.2	5.7	1 386.5	1 311.5
1948														
1st quarter	206.6	140.6	36.4	7.3	16.5	10.7	4.8	21.2	185.4	172.7	12.8	6.9	1 413.2	1 337.4
2nd quarter ...	212.1	142.2	40.2	7.5	16.3	10.4	4.6	18.9	193.2	176.5	16.7	8.6	1 439.9	1 379.1
3rd quarter	217.6	147.0	40.6	7.5	16.9	10.1	4.6	18.2	199.4	179.4	19.9	10.0	1 458.9	1 401.7
4th quarter	218.3	148.1	39.9	7.6	17.4	9.8	4.5	18.4	199.9	180.4	19.5	9.8	1 470.7	1 409.6
1949														
1st quarter	212.2	146.4	35.4	7.5	17.5	10.5	5.2	17.8	194.4	179.2	15.2	7.8	1 434.0	1 381.9
2nd quarter ...	211.2	144.9	34.9	7.7	17.7	11.0	5.1	17.0	194.2	180.9	13.2	6.8	1 431.2	1 388.6
3rd quarter	210.6	143.8	34.2	7.9	17.9	11.5	4.8	16.3	194.3	180.4	13.9	7.2	1 431.8	1 397.6
4th quarter	211.0	143.0	34.2	8.1	18.5	11.8	4.5	15.8	195.2	182.9	12.3	6.3	1 434.4	1 405.4
1950														
1st quarter	226.5	147.2	36.2	8.5	19.7	20.2	5.3	16.6	209.9	185.7	24.2	11.5	1 487.9	1 513.7
2nd quarter ...	227.8	153.8	36.8	8.7	20.1	13.8	5.3	17.6	210.2	189.7	20.6	9.8	1 536.5	1 509.2
3rd quarter	236.2	162.5	38.5	8.8	21.1	10.8	5.5	18.9	217.3	203.5	13.8	6.3	1 585.1	1 528.1
4th quarter	245.1	170.3	38.5	9.1	21.8	11.1	5.8	22.5	222.6	201.0	21.5	9.7	1 616.5	1 537.5
1951														
1st quarter	254.4	178.8	40.9	9.3	20.9	11.1	6.6	24.4	229.9	212.3	17.6	7.7	1 628.5	1 539.3
2nd quarter ...	263.3	185.1	42.5	9.6	21.4	11.4	6.7	26.4	237.0	208.0	28.9	12.2	1 672.9	1 573.5
3rd quarter	267.8	188.1	43.2	9.9	21.6	11.6	6.6	27.8	240.0	210.7	29.3	12.2	1 698.9	1 591.4
4th quarter	272.3	191.7	43.7	10.1	21.9	11.6	6.7	29.6	242.7	214.7	28.0	11.5	1 706.9	1 588.5
1952														
1st quarter	274.5	196.4	41.7	10.4	21.6	11.4	6.9	30.9	243.6	216.2	27.4	11.3	1 714.7	1 587.7
2nd quarter ...	278.4	197.7	43.0	10.7	22.4	11.5	6.8	31.8	246.6	220.4	26.2	10.6	1 740.2	1 607.9
3rd quarter	285.5	201.8	44.7	10.9	22.7	12.3	6.9	32.3	253.2	223.1	30.1	11.9	1 769.7	1 640.2
4th quarter	292.2	209.6	42.8	11.3	23.3	12.3	7.1	33.1	259.1	231.5	27.6	10.7	1 809.3	1 675.4
1953														
1st quarter	296.7	213.4	43.0	11.6	23.5	12.4	7.1	33.4	263.3	235.3	28.0	10.6	1 831.4	1 695.8
2nd quarter ...	300.6	216.5	42.3	11.9	24.7	12.3	7.1	33.4	267.1	237.3	29.9	11.2	1 853.7	1 717.9
3rd quarter	300.5	216.8	41.2	12.2	25.0	12.5	7.2	33.2	267.3	238.1	29.2	10.9	1 841.9	1 709.7
4th quarter	300.5	215.4	41.6	12.5	25.2	12.9	7.1	32.9	267.6	237.7	29.9	11.2	1 831.6	1 704.0
1954														
1st quarter	300.5	213.4	42.7	12.8	26.2	13.5	8.1	30.2	270.3	239.7	30.6	11.3	1 818.5	1 712.7
2nd quarter ...	300.2	213.0	42.1	13.0	26.0	14.1	8.0	30.0	270.2	242.4	27.8	10.3	1 815.0	1 714.3
3rd quarter	302.2	213.5	42.2	13.1	26.8	14.5	8.1	30.0	272.2	245.1	27.0	9.9	1 831.3	1 732.5
4th quarter	307.6	217.8	42.0	13.3	27.4	15.2	8.1	30.5	277.1	249.8	27.3	9.9	1 863.1	1 765.7
1955														
1st quarter	313.9	222.2	43.7	13.3	28.3	15.3	8.9	31.4	282.5	256.3	26.3	9.3	1 896.9	1 794.5
2nd quarter ...	321.5	228.4	44.3	13.4	28.8	15.6	9.0	32.4	289.1	261.6	27.5	9.5	1 940.8	1 834.1
3rd quarter	328.9	234.2	44.6	13.4	29.9	15.9	9.2	33.4	295.5	266.0	29.5	10.0	1 978.3	1 867.7
4th quarter	334.0	238.7	44.5	13.5	30.6	16.0	9.3	34.2	299.8	270.2	29.6	9.9	2 004.7	1 889.6

Table 4-1B. Personal Income and Its Disposition: Historical—*Continued*

(Billions of current dollars, except as noted; quarterly data are at seasonally adjusted annual rates.) **NIPA Table 2.1**

Year and quarter	Total	Compensation of employees	Proprietors' income with IVA and CCAdj	Rental income of persons with CCAdj	Personal income receipts on assets	Personal current transfer receipts	Less: Contributions for government social insurance, domestic	Less: Personal current taxes	Equals: Disposable personal income	Less: Personal outlays	Billions of dollars	Percent of disposable personal income	Personal income excluding current transfers	Disposable personal income
1956														
1st quarter	339.5	243.2	44.9	13.6	31.4	16.3	9.9	35.4	304.1	272.0	32.1	10.6	2 028.4	1 909.0
2nd quarter ...	345.3	247.9	45.3	13.6	32.0	16.6	10.0	36.2	309.1	274.8	34.3	11.1	2 049.8	1 927.2
3rd quarter	350.6	250.8	46.4	13.7	32.7	17.1	10.0	36.9	313.7	278.1	35.6	11.3	2 059.4	1 936.9
4th quarter	358.2	256.7	46.8	13.8	33.7	17.3	10.1	37.9	320.3	283.6	36.8	11.5	2 092.4	1 966.4
1957														
1st quarter	362.8	260.6	46.9	13.9	34.5	18.2	11.4	38.6	324.2	288.2	36.0	11.1	2 096.0	1 972.1
2nd quarter ...	367.5	262.5	47.7	14.0	35.4	19.4	11.4	39.0	328.5	290.5	38.0	11.6	2 104.2	1 986.1
3rd quarter	372.2	265.1	48.8	14.1	36.0	19.6	11.5	39.2	333.0	295.2	37.8	11.4	2 114.1	1 996.8
4th quarter	371.5	263.7	47.7	14.3	36.3	20.8	11.3	38.8	332.7	296.8	35.9	10.8	2 092.1	1 984.9
1958														
1st quarter	372.4	260.2	50.3	14.6	36.6	22.1	11.3	38.2	334.2	296.4	37.8	11.3	2 064.5	1 969.8
2nd quarter ...	374.8	259.9	50.3	14.8	37.2	23.9	11.3	37.7	337.1	299.2	37.8	11.2	2 064.2	1 983.1
3rd quarter	383.1	267.7	50.1	14.9	37.6	24.2	11.4	38.9	344.1	304.2	39.9	11.6	2 109.7	2 022.9
4th quarter	387.6	272.7	49.9	15.0	37.9	23.7	11.5	39.4	348.2	308.2	40.0	11.5	2 140.2	2 047.7
1959														
1st quarter	394.4	280.2	50.1	15.0	38.8	24.0	13.7	40.8	353.6	315.8	37.8	10.7	2 162.8	2 065.0
2nd quarter ...	402.7	286.9	50.3	15.4	40.0	23.9	13.9	42.0	360.7	322.0	38.7	10.7	2 203.1	2 098.1
3rd quarter	405.0	287.4	50.4	15.8	41.2	24.2	13.9	42.7	362.4	327.4	34.9	9.6	2 202.1	2 095.1
4th quarter	410.7	290.7	50.6	16.0	42.4	24.8	13.9	43.7	366.9	329.8	37.1	10.1	2 218.8	2 110.1
1960														
1st quarter	417.1	299.3	49.7	16.2	43.6	24.6	16.4	45.3	371.8	333.5	38.3	10.3	2 253.9	2 135.2
2nd quarter ...	422.1	302.3	50.7	16.4	43.9	25.3	16.5	46.0	376.1	339.6	36.5	9.7	2 267.2	2 148.6
3rd quarter	424.7	303.2	50.9	16.5	44.6	26.0	16.5	46.5	378.2	339.7	38.5	10.2	2 269.1	2 152.5
4th quarter	426.2	302.7	51.0	16.7	45.1	27.0	16.4	46.4	379.7	341.8	38.0	10.0	2 261.5	2 151.5
1961														
1st quarter	430.7	303.7	52.3	16.9	45.6	28.8	16.7	46.5	384.1	342.4	41.7	10.9	2 272.5	2 172.5
2nd quarter ...	436.9	308.0	52.6	17.1	46.4	29.7	16.9	46.9	390.0	347.4	42.6	10.9	2 303.1	2 205.5
3rd quarter	444.0	313.0	53.3	17.3	47.5	29.9	17.1	47.4	396.6	350.3	46.2	11.7	2 333.6	2 234.8
4th quarter	452.8	319.7	54.5	17.5	49.1	29.4	17.3	48.1	404.7	357.8	46.9	11.6	2 383.4	2 277.9
1962														
1st quarter	459.7	326.2	55.3	17.7	49.4	30.0	18.9	49.4	410.3	363.1	47.2	11.5	2 408.4	2 299.7
2nd quarter ...	467.0	332.1	55.0	18.0	51.1	30.0	19.1	50.9	416.1	369.0	47.2	11.3	2 440.8	2 323.9
3rd quarter	471.7	334.9	54.9	18.2	52.5	30.4	19.2	52.3	419.4	373.1	46.3	11.0	2 458.0	2 336.0
4th quarter	477.9	338.4	55.8	18.3	53.6	31.2	19.3	53.6	424.3	379.5	44.8	10.6	2 481.3	2 356.7
1963														
1st quarter	483.3	343.4	56.0	18.5	54.0	32.6	21.3	54.1	429.2	383.4	45.8	10.7	2 495.7	2 376.9
2nd quarter ...	488.1	348.3	55.8	18.7	55.2	31.7	21.5	54.3	433.8	387.8	46.0	10.6	2 524.2	2 399.0
3rd quarter	495.3	353.4	56.2	18.8	56.6	32.0	21.8	54.6	440.7	395.1	45.5	10.3	2 550.1	2 425.5
4th quarter	504.7	359.6	57.6	18.8	58.2	32.5	22.0	55.2	449.5	400.1	49.4	11.0	2 589.3	2 465.0
1964														
1st quarter	514.3	366.0	57.9	18.8	60.0	33.6	22.0	53.8	460.6	409.9	50.7	11.0	2 623.5	2 513.4
2nd quarter ...	523.7	373.5	58.8	18.8	61.7	33.2	22.3	49.7	474.0	418.2	55.8	11.8	2 670.9	2 581.0
3rd quarter	533.3	380.9	59.3	18.9	63.3	33.5	22.5	51.6	481.7	427.5	54.3	11.3	2 712.4	2 614.4
4th quarter	542.1	387.0	60.5	18.8	64.8	33.7	22.7	53.2	488.8	430.3	58.6	12.0	2 749.2	2 643.9
1965														
1st quarter	553.1	393.8	61.9	19.1	66.1	35.0	22.9	57.0	496.2	441.1	55.1	11.1	2 793.4	2 675.1
2nd quarter ...	562.7	400.8	63.2	19.3	68.0	34.6	23.2	58.4	504.3	448.5	55.8	11.1	2 833.0	2 705.5
3rd quarter	577.1	409.3	64.0	19.5	69.7	38.1	23.6	57.0	520.1	457.9	62.1	11.9	2 880.3	2 779.5
4th quarter	590.4	421.4	65.6	19.5	71.1	36.9	24.0	58.3	532.2	472.0	60.1	11.3	2 949.3	2 835.4
1966														
1st quarter	603.1	434.1	69.2	19.8	72.5	37.8	30.4	61.5	541.6	482.6	59.0	10.9	2 988.7	2 863.5
2nd quarter ...	613.0	445.4	67.2	19.8	73.6	37.9	30.8	65.6	547.5	488.0	59.5	10.9	3 016.3	2 871.1
3rd quarter	626.3	456.7	67.2	20.0	74.7	39.6	31.9	67.9	558.4	497.3	61.1	10.9	3 053.0	2 905.9
4th quarter	639.8	464.9	68.1	20.0	75.8	43.1	32.2	70.6	569.3	503.3	65.9	11.6	3 081.3	2 939.7
1967														
1st quarter	650.6	471.1	68.9	20.3	77.9	46.1	33.6	71.2	579.5	507.9	71.6	12.3	3 112.8	2 983.6
2nd quarter ...	657.7	476.8	68.5	20.4	79.4	47.2	34.6	70.9	586.7	517.6	69.1	11.8	3 128.3	3 006.8
3rd quarter	671.6	486.4	70.5	20.4	80.7	48.7	35.2	73.8	597.7	524.6	73.2	12.2	3 162.7	3 035.1
4th quarter	683.1	497.4	70.0	20.3	81.3	50.0	36.0	75.9	607.2	532.2	75.0	12.4	3 187.2	3 057.1
1968														
1st quarter	702.6	512.2	71.7	20.1	83.9	52.4	37.6	78.6	624.1	550.4	73.7	11.8	3 239.6	3 109.3
2nd quarter ...	722.6	525.3	73.2	20.1	86.5	55.9	38.4	81.7	640.9	564.6	76.4	11.9	3 288.2	3 161.2
3rd quarter	741.0	539.2	75.0	20.2	88.4	57.3	39.1	91.9	649.1	581.2	67.9	10.5	3 337.6	3 169.0
4th quarter	756.7	551.7	75.5	20.0	90.4	58.7	39.7	95.9	660.8	590.5	70.3	10.6	3 370.1	3 190.6
1969														
1st quarter	771.3	564.2	75.6	20.2	93.7	60.4	42.9	102.6	668.7	603.2	65.5	9.8	3 398.6	3 197.0
2nd quarter ...	790.4	578.2	77.1	20.3	96.9	61.5	43.7	105.7	684.8	615.3	69.5	10.1	3 440.6	3 232.3
3rd quarter	812.0	595.0	78.0	20.5	100.2	62.9	44.6	104.1	707.9	626.0	81.9	11.6	3 492.9	3 300.6
4th quarter	827.3	606.6	77.3	20.5	103.9	64.3	45.3	105.6	721.7	638.4	83.2	11.5	3 516.7	3 326.5

Table 4-1B. Personal Income and Its Disposition: Historical—*Continued*

(Billions of current dollars, except as noted; quarterly data are at seasonally adjusted annual rates.)   **NIPA Table 2.1**

Year and quarter	Personal income							Less: Personal current taxes	Equals: Disposable personal income	Less: Personal outlays	Equals: Personal saving		Billions of chained (2009) dollars	
	Total	Compensation of employees	Proprietors' income with IVA and CCAdj	Rental income of persons with CCAdj	Personal income receipts on assets	Personal current transfer receipts	Less: Contributions for government social insurance, domestic				Billions of dollars	Percent of disposable personal income	Personal income excluding current transfers	Disposable personal income
1970														
1st quarter	841.8	616.7	77.1	20.5	107.4	66.1	46.0	104.6	737.2	649.9	87.3	11.8	3 534.4	3 359.1
2nd quarter ...	859.6	622.0	76.7	20.3	110.8	76.1	46.3	105.5	754.1	660.2	93.9	12.5	3 531.2	3 398.5
3rd quarter ...	874.0	630.0	78.5	20.9	115.0	76.3	46.7	100.7	773.4	672.4	101.0	13.1	3 560.3	3 451.8
4th quarter ...	882.9	631.8	78.9	21.2	117.3	80.1	46.5	101.5	781.4	679.4	102.0	13.1	3 537.3	3 442.9
1971														
1st quarter	903.0	649.9	80.3	21.2	120.0	82.0	50.5	98.3	804.6	698.8	105.8	13.2	3 583.2	3 512.0
2nd quarter ...	926.4	661.8	82.8	21.8	121.4	89.6	51.0	100.7	825.7	713.3	112.4	13.6	3 611.4	3 563.4
3rd quarter ...	940.5	672.2	84.6	22.2	123.3	89.6	51.3	102.3	838.2	726.3	111.9	13.4	3 636.6	3 582.2
4th quarter ...	958.7	684.2	87.9	22.6	124.6	91.3	51.9	105.5	853.2	743.0	110.2	12.9	3 684.3	3 624.0
1972														
1st quarter	986.0	710.6	87.9	23.2	128.1	94.3	58.1	119.8	866.2	760.7	105.5	12.2	3 747.5	3 640.6
2nd quarter ...	1 003.5	724.7	91.3	20.3	131.0	94.9	58.8	123.4	880.1	779.8	100.3	11.4	3 796.8	3 677.8
3rd quarter ...	1 029.2	738.1	95.5	24.0	135.0	96.0	59.5	124.3	904.9	798.7	106.3	11.7	3 865.5	3 748.5
4th quarter ...	1 075.7	761.2	105.6	23.9	139.0	106.4	60.4	127.1	948.6	823.8	124.8	13.2	3 982.4	3 897.2
1973														
1st quarter	1 093.3	787.8	104.1	23.6	142.3	109.1	73.6	126.4	966.9	848.6	118.3	12.2	3 995.3	3 924.9
2nd quarter ...	1 122.6	805.6	109.9	23.5	146.9	111.5	74.7	129.2	993.4	864.8	128.7	13.0	4 026.8	3 956.2
3rd quarter ...	1 150.0	822.8	113.8	22.5	153.8	113.3	76.1	134.1	1 016.0	883.6	132.3	13.0	4 054.9	3 973.6
4th quarter ...	1 188.2	844.1	122.2	23.4	159.6	116.5	77.6	140.0	1 048.2	900.3	147.9	14.1	4 107.1	4 017.1
1974														
1st quarter	1 204.4	860.9	115.7	23.7	165.4	121.9	83.1	142.8	1 061.6	917.4	144.2	13.6	4 028.7	3 950.9
2nd quarter ...	1 230.4	881.1	108.6	23.1	172.4	129.9	84.7	148.9	1 081.5	946.4	135.0	12.5	3 982.8	3 914.0
3rd quarter ...	1 266.6	902.8	111.0	23.4	178.6	137.1	86.4	154.9	1 111.7	976.0	135.7	12.2	3 980.4	3 917.7
4th quarter ...	1 296.0	916.5	113.5	23.2	185.2	144.3	86.6	157.6	1 138.5	986.5	152.0	13.3	3 958.6	3 912.9
1975														
1st quarter	1 315.9	921.2	112.7	22.9	190.8	155.9	87.6	158.0	1 157.9	1 014.0	143.9	12.4	3 913.7	3 906.7
2nd quarter ...	1 347.5	934.1	114.3	22.6	192.9	171.5	88.0	121.1	1 226.5	1 043.0	183.5	15.0	3 919.7	4 088.0
3rd quarter ...	1 384.1	959.0	120.7	22.5	196.8	174.8	89.8	152.8	1 231.3	1 077.5	153.8	12.5	3 956.6	4 028.6
4th quarter ...	1 420.0	986.4	125.2	22.1	200.5	177.6	91.8	158.5	1 261.5	1 106.7	154.8	12.3	3 997.8	4 059.2
1976														
1st quarter	1 452.6	1 017.6	126.4	21.9	204.2	181.4	98.9	162.1	1 290.5	1 140.1	150.3	11.7	4 045.5	4 106.9
2nd quarter ...	1 477.0	1 038.4	128.6	20.8	210.0	179.7	100.4	169.0	1 308.1	1 159.9	148.1	11.3	4 094.4	4 128.2
3rd quarter ...	1 513.5	1 061.2	132.7	20.3	215.0	186.4	102.2	175.8	1 337.7	1 189.7	148.0	11.1	4 125.6	4 158.6
4th quarter ...	1 549.3	1 087.7	136.2	19.4	221.3	188.5	103.8	182.4	1 366.9	1 224.1	142.8	10.4	4 164.7	4 183.4
1977														
1st quarter	1 579.6	1 116.3	138.6	17.1	226.3	190.6	109.3	188.4	1 391.2	1 260.9	130.3	9.4	4 175.7	4 182.2
2nd quarter ...	1 627.9	1 153.4	140.5	16.6	238.5	191.1	112.1	195.3	1 432.6	1 289.9	142.7	10.0	4 246.8	4 234.2
3rd quarter ...	1 674.7	1 185.3	142.4	15.8	249.3	196.2	114.3	198.2	1 476.5	1 322.0	154.5	10.5	4 304.9	4 299.1
4th quarter ...	1 734.7	1 221.0	156.5	15.3	259.6	199.0	116.7	208.1	1 526.5	1 361.3	165.2	10.8	4 408.3	4 382.1
1978														
1st quarter	1 774.6	1 255.8	158.5	16.5	266.9	203.1	126.2	211.7	1 562.9	1 392.8	170.1	10.9	4 437.5	4 413.0
2nd quarter ...	1 833.7	1 302.9	166.1	16.2	273.7	204.9	130.1	222.8	1 610.9	1 452.0	158.9	9.9	4 506.4	4 456.8
3rd quarter ...	1 887.1	1 339.2	168.3	17.4	281.3	213.6	132.8	236.0	1 651.0	1 484.4	166.6	10.1	4 549.7	4 488.8
4th quarter ...	1 942.5	1 383.0	170.9	17.6	290.1	216.9	136.0	247.0	1 695.5	1 524.9	170.7	10.1	4 604.4	4 524.3
1979														
1st quarter	1 999.1	1 427.3	180.1	17.8	300.2	222.5	148.8	253.4	1 745.7	1 561.2	184.5	10.6	4 653.2	4 572.3
2nd quarter ...	2 039.6	1 458.3	179.2	15.6	310.3	227.1	150.9	261.8	1 777.9	1 602.9	175.0	9.8	4 621.0	4 532.8
3rd quarter ...	2 105.1	1 498.8	180.7	15.4	321.7	242.7	154.2	274.6	1 830.5	1 658.8	171.8	9.4	4 633.5	4 554.2
4th quarter ...	2 168.0	1 539.7	177.8	17.6	341.2	248.9	157.1	285.0	1 883.0	1 704.1	178.9	9.5	4 661.9	4 574.3
1980														
1st quarter	2 230.1	1 579.2	167.6	20.0	367.7	258.7	163.1	284.2	1 946.0	1 756.3	189.7	9.7	4 649.8	4 589.9
2nd quarter ...	2 256.1	1 600.5	160.3	14.1	380.5	263.9	163.2	291.5	1 964.6	1 758.6	206.0	10.5	4 586.8	4 523.2
3rd quarter ...	2 336.6	1 631.2	173.4	17.0	385.6	295.9	166.6	301.5	2 035.0	1 816.9	218.1	10.7	4 591.1	4 578.4
4th quarter ...	2 444.4	1 694.0	185.0	27.8	410.1	299.3	171.8	318.2	2 126.2	1 887.3	239.0	11.2	4 709.7	4 668.3
1981														
1st quarter	2 503.3	1 745.2	188.2	26.2	429.4	305.9	191.6	330.3	2 173.0	1 947.3	225.8	10.4	4 708.0	4 655.7
2nd quarter ...	2 550.8	1 777.5	176.4	24.4	457.4	309.3	194.1	342.1	2 208.8	1 981.0	227.8	10.3	4 723.6	4 654.6
3rd quarter ...	2 647.1	1 815.4	182.3	24.1	495.2	327.9	197.7	356.3	2 290.9	2 023.5	267.3	11.7	4 808.8	4 749.9
4th quarter ...	2 682.3	1 843.0	171.8	27.0	509.5	330.4	199.4	352.0	2 330.3	2 041.2	289.0	12.4	4 803.3	4 759.1
1982														
1st quarter	2 714.5	1 866.4	165.2	27.6	526.8	335.7	207.2	351.9	2 362.6	2 083.1	279.5	11.8	4 797.6	4 764.9
2nd quarter ...	2 757.9	1 885.1	169.4	24.0	542.9	344.9	208.4	359.1	2 398.8	2 113.1	285.7	11.9	4 820.8	4 792.4
3rd quarter ...	2 799.1	1 905.3	170.7	25.9	545.5	361.5	209.8	349.5	2 449.6	2 163.8	285.8	11.7	4 794.4	4 818.0
4th quarter ...	2 843.9	1 920.4	179.5	27.0	549.9	377.3	210.2	355.9	2 487.9	2 228.2	259.7	10.4	4 798.3	4 839.8
1983														
1st quarter	2 881.3	1 949.9	183.3	27.4	560.8	380.2	220.4	350.3	2 530.9	2 270.4	260.6	10.3	4 823.7	4 881.3
2nd quarter ...	2 931.4	1 988.6	182.6	27.4	570.0	386.4	223.6	359.0	2 572.4	2 337.0	235.4	9.2	4 863.7	4 916.0
3rd quarter ...	2 990.5	2 031.2	183.8	27.4	593.3	381.9	227.2	344.9	2 645.6	2 409.7	235.9	8.9	4 920.2	4 990.1
4th quarter ...	3 075.8	2 085.9	195.3	27.7	613.0	386.5	232.6	355.1	2 720.6	2 464.5	256.1	9.4	5 038.9	5 097.7

Table 4-1B. Personal Income and Its Disposition: Historical—*Continued*

(Billions of current dollars, except as noted; quarterly data are at seasonally adjusted annual rates.)   **NIPA Table 2.1**

Year and quarter	Personal income							Less: Personal current taxes	Equals: Disposable personal income	Less: Personal outlays	Equals: Personal saving		Billions of chained (2009) dollars	
	Total	Compensation of employees	Proprietors' income with IVA and CCAdj	Rental income of persons with CCAdj	Personal income receipts on assets	Personal current transfer receipts	Less: Contributions for government social insurance, domestic				Billions of dollars	Percent of disposable personal income	Personal income excluding current transfers	Disposable personal income
1984														
1st quarter	3 166.9	2 147.1	221.9	26.9	628.6	393.4	251.0	360.7	2 806.3	2 512.1	294.2	10.5	5 141.1	5 201.8
2nd quarter ...	3 250.7	2 196.8	231.8	25.2	655.0	397.8	255.8	369.9	2 880.7	2 573.4	307.4	10.7	5 237.3	5 288.3
3rd quarter	3 326.5	2 242.6	232.4	27.6	683.3	400.5	259.9	383.6	2 942.9	2 614.9	328.0	11.1	5 330.1	5 360.9
4th quarter	3 381.1	2 283.1	226.9	31.9	693.4	408.9	263.1	395.4	2 985.6	2 666.8	318.8	10.7	5 380.7	5 405.0
1985														
1st quarter	3 445.9	2 327.0	240.7	30.2	703.9	419.6	275.4	431.8	3 014.1	2 749.7	264.4	8.8	5 413.9	5 392.0
2nd quarter	3 486.1	2 365.0	238.5	29.2	710.1	422.1	278.8	388.1	3 098.0	2 800.5	297.6	9.6	5 435.4	5 495.9
3rd quarter	3 533.3	2 406.7	240.7	30.3	710.9	427.5	282.8	421.1	3 112.2	2 877.2	235.1	7.6	5 466.1	5 477.4
4th quarter	3 598.1	2 457.1	244.3	28.4	726.3	430.4	288.4	428.4	3 169.7	2 906.3	263.4	8.3	5 537.0	5 540.4
1986														
1st quarter	3 657.9	2 493.3	245.6	24.8	749.5	442.6	297.9	425.7	3 232.2	2 952.9	279.3	8.6	5 580.1	5 609.5
2nd quarter	3 700.1	2 519.1	251.6	24.2	757.4	448.5	300.7	428.8	3 271.2	2 982.6	288.6	8.8	5 649.8	5 684.0
3rd quarter	3 750.0	2 557.1	264.4	20.5	757.6	455.5	305.0	438.9	3 311.2	3 050.2	260.9	7.9	5 695.5	5 724.2
4th quarter	3 792.4	2 605.9	264.2	18.1	756.9	457.2	310.1	455.4	3 336.9	3 088.4	248.6	7.4	5 731.4	5 734.5
1987														
1st quarter	3 850.6	2 651.0	275.4	18.8	759.2	462.6	316.5	450.2	3 400.4	3 118.8	281.6	8.3	5 760.6	5 781.7
2nd quarter ...	3 910.6	2 694.2	282.3	17.4	769.4	467.6	320.2	511.1	3 399.5	3 189.9	209.6	6.2	5 799.0	5 725.6
3rd quarter	3 982.2	2 741.8	289.5	21.0	785.8	468.6	324.5	488.4	3 493.7	3 256.6	237.1	6.8	5 862.6	5 829.6
4th quarter	4 077.9	2 810.3	298.6	23.7	805.0	471.6	331.2	506.4	3 571.5	3 291.5	280.0	7.8	5 965.2	5 907.6
1988														
1st quarter	4 152.8	2 861.0	319.3	23.0	812.6	488.9	352.1	501.1	3 651.7	3 374.4	277.3	7.6	6 013.7	5 993.8
2nd quarter	4 226.8	2 926.1	322.8	22.6	821.9	492.5	359.1	496.8	3 730.0	3 436.5	293.5	7.9	6 062.3	6 055.3
3rd quarter	4 317.9	2 978.0	334.0	23.9	847.9	498.6	364.4	505.7	3 812.3	3 507.9	304.4	8.0	6 124.9	6 113.6
4th quarter	4 403.9	3 035.1	327.3	30.9	875.1	505.8	370.3	516.2	3 887.7	3 583.8	303.8	7.8	6 189.3	6 172.7
1989														
1st quarter	4 531.1	3 084.0	348.7	26.8	921.6	529.8	379.8	551.3	3 979.8	3 644.0	335.8	8.4	6 282.6	6 248.9
2nd quarter	4 586.0	3 117.5	340.3	24.7	949.2	537.2	382.8	565.0	4 021.0	3 711.4	309.5	7.7	6 273.7	6 230.5
3rd quarter	4 641.4	3 157.6	338.0	22.7	963.2	546.2	386.4	569.9	4 071.5	3 769.6	301.9	7.4	6 309.5	6 272.9
4th quarter	4 714.5	3 211.2	340.7	23.4	973.9	557.2	391.9	578.2	4 136.3	3 817.5	318.8	7.7	6 355.4	6 323.3
1990														
1st quarter	4 811.3	3 278.8	346.7	25.9	986.4	577.5	404.1	580.5	4 230.7	3 902.7	328.1	7.8	6 381.1	6 376.6
2nd quarter	4 887.0	3 334.8	352.3	30.2	989.5	588.5	408.3	592.6	4 294.4	3 949.0	345.3	8.0	6 420.9	6 414.7
3rd quarter	4 948.7	3 373.9	360.3	34.8	995.7	598.0	414.1	598.8	4 349.9	4 015.5	334.5	7.7	6 418.2	6 417.1
4th quarter	4 970.9	3 383.2	358.4	34.6	993.1	615.5	413.9	598.9	4 372.0	4 038.1	333.9	7.6	6 342.0	6 366.3
1991														
1st quarter	4 981.5	3 395.1	349.1	36.2	986.3	639.4	424.5	578.5	4 403.0	4 046.7	356.3	8.1	6 291.6	6 379.8
2nd quarter ...	5 040.7	3 430.2	354.8	38.6	985.7	659.1	427.7	583.7	4 457.0	4 101.8	355.2	8.0	6 315.2	6 424.0
3rd quarter	5 091.4	3 469.2	355.5	43.0	987.8	668.5	432.6	588.0	4 503.4	4 148.7	354.7	7.9	6 332.0	6 447.3
4th quarter	5 170.8	3 513.5	364.5	50.2	982.0	696.5	435.9	596.4	4 574.5	4 177.2	397.3	8.7	6 360.1	6 502.4
1992														
1st quarter	5 287.9	3 597.6	380.8	53.9	979.5	724.7	448.7	586.5	4 701.4	4 274.3	427.1	9.1	6 446.8	6 642.0
2nd quarter	5 386.8	3 654.4	397.4	61.1	984.4	743.3	453.7	604.9	4 782.0	4 330.8	451.1	9.4	6 517.1	6 711.5
3rd quarter	5 447.3	3 690.7	410.1	68.0	981.0	755.3	457.8	613.9	4 833.5	4 408.3	425.1	8.8	6 543.5	6 740.8
4th quarter	5 521.1	3 741.9	421.2	74.3	983.7	759.7	459.6	636.9	4 884.2	4 483.5	400.8	8.2	6 593.8	6 763.9
1993														
1st quarter	5 555.4	3 747.9	421.3	83.2	991.0	779.4	467.5	614.6	4 940.8	4 529.3	411.5	8.3	6 575.0	6 801.9
2nd quarter	5 624.3	3 803.3	432.0	91.9	988.8	783.8	475.6	641.3	4 982.9	4 598.9	384.0	7.7	6 619.0	6 813.8
3rd quarter	5 664.6	3 838.0	426.0	96.3	986.7	797.7	480.1	657.0	5 007.7	4 667.0	340.6	6.8	6 626.2	6 817.8
4th quarter	5 742.7	3 893.5	442.6	103.2	987.9	802.1	486.6	673.3	5 069.5	4 735.1	334.4	6.6	6 688.2	6 862.6
1994														
1st quarter	5 794.2	3 917.2	452.9	112.7	994.1	815.6	498.4	671.1	5 123.1	4 805.6	317.5	6.2	6 715.8	6 910.7
2nd quarter	5 901.5	3 997.2	456.9	117.4	1 016.1	820.3	506.4	695.3	5 206.2	4 872.0	334.3	6.4	6 816.2	6 983.9
3rd quarter	5 967.3	4 035.1	459.7	120.7	1 038.1	824.3	510.6	692.8	5 274.5	4 948.2	326.3	6.2	6 850.3	7 025.4
4th quarter	6 075.9	4 091.0	468.5	119.0	1 069.3	845.4	517.4	702.9	5 373.0	5 025.4	347.5	6.5	6 934.1	7 123.0
1995														
1st quarter	6 170.3	4 141.3	470.5	122.2	1 092.6	869.4	525.7	720.0	5 450.3	5 065.6	384.6	7.1	6 993.8	7 191.0
2nd quarter	6 235.7	4 177.6	475.2	126.1	1 108.1	879.0	530.1	742.2	5 493.5	5 147.6	345.9	6.3	7 028.0	7 207.3
3rd quarter	6 312.5	4 223.7	487.8	130.2	1 120.4	885.9	535.3	747.7	5 564.8	5 219.4	345.5	6.2	7 091.3	7 271.8
4th quarter	6 387.3	4 268.0	504.4	138.3	1 135.1	881.5	540.0	765.7	5 621.6	5 286.0	335.7	6.0	7 163.2	7 313.9
1996														
1st quarter	6 503.8	4 321.4	526.8	143.9	1 145.0	910.9	544.2	796.5	5 707.2	5 363.0	344.3	6.0	7 235.9	7 383.8
2nd quarter	6 634.2	4 393.5	551.0	146.0	1 164.5	931.3	552.1	834.4	5 799.8	5 458.2	341.7	5.9	7 329.9	7 454.4
3rd quarter	6 709.5	4 455.7	551.1	148.0	1 186.7	926.7	558.7	838.4	5 871.1	5 517.8	353.3	6.0	7 400.9	7 513.8
4th quarter	6 800.1	4 517.9	560.6	149.9	1 209.6	927.5	565.4	858.4	5 941.6	5 600.0	341.7	5.8	7 465.2	7 553.0
1997														
1st quarter	6 924.2	4 599.5	579.4	149.0	1 227.3	944.6	575.5	896.4	6 027.7	5 684.0	343.8	5.7	7 568.0	7 628.9
2nd quarter	7 004.8	4 665.8	579.0	149.9	1 248.0	944.3	582.2	910.5	6 094.3	5 728.6	365.7	6.0	7 651.3	7 694.0
3rd quarter	7 118.1	4 745.4	592.5	152.6	1 267.4	950.5	590.2	935.4	6 182.7	5 842.5	340.2	5.5	7 766.7	7 785.7
4th quarter	7 252.9	4 848.1	600.6	156.8	1 291.1	957.4	601.0	962.2	6 290.7	5 931.6	359.2	5.7	7 903.2	7 897.2

Table 4-1B. Personal Income and Its Disposition: Historical—*Continued*

(Billions of current dollars, except as noted; quarterly data are at seasonally adjusted annual rates.)   **NIPA Table 2.1**

| Year and quarter | Personal income | | | | | | | Less: Personal current taxes | Equals: Disposable personal income | Less: Personal outlays | Equals: Personal saving | | Billions of chained (2009) dollars | |
	Total	Compensation of employees	Proprietors' income with IVA and CCAdj	Rental income of persons with CCAdj	Personal income receipts on assets	Personal current transfer receipts	Less: Contributions for government social insurance, domestic				Billions of dollars	Percent of disposable personal income	Personal income excluding current transfers	Disposable personal income
1998														
1st quarter	7 414.6	4 950.4	621.4	161.5	1 324.4	968.7	611.8	990.1	6 424.4	5 988.5	435.9	6.8	8 092.4	8 065.5
2nd quarter ...	7 542.1	5 035.9	633.7	167.2	1 350.7	975.1	620.4	1 016.4	6 525.7	6 110.3	415.4	6.4	8 229.8	8 178.1
3rd quarter ...	7 649.4	5 120.9	649.0	172.6	1 357.3	978.5	629.0	1 037.2	6 612.1	6 209.6	402.6	6.1	8 334.8	8 261.5
4th quarter ...	7 744.8	5 204.2	672.7	178.1	1 337.8	989.4	637.4	1 062.0	6 682.8	6 315.4	367.4	5.5	8 419.1	8 328.6
1999														
1st quarter	7 833.5	5 298.8	686.0	180.8	1 310.4	1 010.0	652.5	1 073.5	6 760.0	6 391.4	368.6	5.5	8 482.2	8 403.2
2nd quarter ...	7 903.7	5 352.5	694.1	184.1	1 316.2	1 013.2	656.4	1 090.8	6 812.9	6 527.8	285.2	4.2	8 519.9	8 424.0
3rd quarter ...	8 010.9	5 429.7	703.8	183.9	1 329.3	1 026.3	662.2	1 116.2	6 894.7	6 640.6	254.1	3.7	8 591.0	8 480.4
4th quarter ...	8 187.2	5 560.2	717.9	183.6	1 362.8	1 036.8	674.1	1 149.6	7 037.6	6 773.5	264.1	3.8	8 743.0	8 605.1
2000														
1st quarter	8 441.0	5 759.9	724.9	184.2	1 417.0	1 052.4	697.5	1 204.7	7 236.3	6 938.5	297.8	4.1	8 959.3	8 774.7
2nd quarter ...	8 571.0	5 800.8	755.2	184.3	1 450.1	1 079.4	698.9	1 226.1	7 344.9	7 039.0	306.0	4.2	9 043.0	8 865.9
3rd quarter ...	8 720.6	5 914.0	764.7	186.9	1 472.4	1 093.7	711.2	1 243.6	7 477.0	7 163.4	313.5	4.2	9 149.4	8 969.6
4th quarter ...	8 798.5	5 951.7	786.3	195.4	1 474.5	1 106.5	715.8	1 254.6	7 543.8	7 269.4	274.5	3.6	9 176.8	9 000.0
2001														
1st quarter	8 956.7	6 059.4	816.2	201.7	1 463.7	1 151.2	735.5	1 297.6	7 659.1	7 341.1	318.0	4.2	9 250.3	9 076.8
2nd quarter ...	8 993.4	6 050.2	835.0	207.5	1 451.9	1 182.9	734.0	1 304.5	7 689.0	7 394.3	294.7	3.8	9 212.3	9 068.9
3rd quarter ...	8 986.2	6 033.7	851.5	210.1	1 434.7	1 187.7	731.5	1 109.5	7 876.7	7 423.3	453.4	5.8	9 190.9	9 283.1
4th quarter ...	9 012.0	6 042.9	844.4	210.8	1 415.0	1 230.7	731.7	1 227.7	7 784.4	7 525.7	258.7	3.3	9 164.6	9 168.1
2002														
1st quarter	9 053.4	6 074.8	861.1	215.2	1 392.0	1 255.6	745.4	1 065.2	7 988.2	7 559.5	428.7	5.4	9 167.3	9 391.1
2nd quarter ...	9 135.5	6 137.7	864.8	217.4	1 390.4	1 277.3	752.1	1 045.0	8 090.5	7 659.6	431.0	5.3	9 167.6	9 438.7
3rd quarter ...	9 169.6	6 161.4	873.9	216.8	1 383.7	1 287.2	753.5	1 048.8	8 120.8	7 750.4	370.5	4.6	9 149.5	9 426.3
4th quarter ...	9 239.6	6 193.7	884.3	219.8	1 395.5	1 301.3	755.0	1 042.4	8 197.2	7 811.9	385.3	4.7	9 172.6	9 471.7
2003														
1st quarter	9 296.9	6 227.5	880.2	226.8	1 407.5	1 319.2	764.4	1 017.9	8 279.0	7 894.8	384.3	4.6	9 153.5	9 499.2
2nd quarter ...	9 420.8	6 319.6	894.1	234.0	1 411.3	1 336.0	774.2	1 014.7	8 406.1	7 997.3	408.8	4.9	9 268.1	9 636.4
3rd quarter ...	9 546.8	6 404.8	907.2	239.9	1 421.1	1 357.2	783.4	950.7	8 596.0	8 157.9	438.1	5.1	9 331.3	9 794.4
4th quarter ...	9 685.8	6 509.6	918.7	251.3	1 442.1	1 359.1	795.0	1 020.1	8 665.7	8 253.5	412.1	4.8	9 449.4	9 834.0
2004														
1st quarter	9 803.7	6 566.6	947.2	254.6	1 451.7	1 394.0	810.4	1 008.3	8 795.4	8 396.3	399.1	4.5	9 471.2	9 905.6
2nd quarter ...	9 967.7	6 691.2	961.9	258.7	1 468.2	1 411.7	823.9	1 023.3	8 944.5	8 510.6	433.9	4.9	9 569.0	10 003.3
3rd quarter ...	10 106.8	6 824.3	962.1	254.6	1 484.6	1 419.9	838.7	1 062.9	9 043.9	8 646.4	397.5	4.4	9 659.1	10 056.0
4th quarter ...	10 318.6	6 879.8	977.1	253.8	1 610.5	1 441.1	843.7	1 089.4	9 229.2	8 806.8	422.4	4.6	9 793.6	10 181.7
2005														
1st quarter	10 355.3	6 953.5	953.3	246.1	1 577.6	1 484.5	859.8	1 167.8	9 187.5	8 932.3	255.2	2.8	9 735.8	10 083.5
2nd quarter ...	10 514.8	7 028.3	960.5	242.9	1 641.9	1 508.3	867.1	1 193.0	9 321.8	9 089.9	231.9	2.5	9 819.6	10 163.3
3rd quarter ...	10 694.3	7 143.2	991.7	231.6	1 684.2	1 522.7	879.1	1 221.9	9 472.4	9 254.8	217.6	2.3	9 891.1	10 215.6
4th quarter ...	10 876.6	7 225.9	1 010.3	233.1	1 762.1	1 532.5	887.3	1 251.4	9 625.3	9 359.4	265.9	2.8	9 998.9	10 299.7
2006														
1st quarter	11 206.4	7 407.8	1 058.7	223.2	1 847.6	1 584.4	915.4	1 315.7	9 890.7	9 513.1	377.6	3.8	10 248.7	10 534.9
2nd quarter ...	11 326.2	7 453.9	1 062.2	211.9	1 917.5	1 599.5	918.8	1 344.2	9 981.9	9 643.2	338.7	3.4	10 281.0	10 550.8
3rd quarter ...	11 436.0	7 509.4	1 051.1	204.3	1 969.0	1 624.2	921.9	1 354.0	10 082.0	9 776.6	305.4	3.0	10 297.5	10 581.0
4th quarter ...	11 590.8	7 641.7	1 042.7	190.7	2 019.5	1 630.5	934.3	1 394.5	10 196.2	9 870.3	325.9	3.2	10 471.1	10 719.1
2007														
1st quarter	11 816.2	7 833.0	992.3	177.9	2 069.2	1 701.4	957.7	1 457.3	10 358.9	10 014.0	344.8	3.3	10 535.3	10 789.6
2nd quarter ...	11 944.3	7 867.9	972.8	189.6	2 128.9	1 703.1	958.0	1 482.7	10 461.6	10 140.6	321.0	3.1	10 583.1	10 810.9
3rd quarter ...	12 042.9	7 902.8	966.0	192.9	2 213.4	1 727.6	959.8	1 494.8	10 548.1	10 249.7	298.4	2.8	10 599.7	10 838.9
4th quarter ...	12 179.7	7 992.8	985.5	197.2	2 215.1	1 759.1	970.1	1 516.7	10 662.9	10 358.1	304.8	2.9	10 601.7	10 848.2
2008														
1st quarter	12 361.7	8 079.4	1 017.7	225.3	2 228.0	1 797.7	986.5	1 529.4	10 832.3	10 415.1	417.2	3.9	10 656.2	10 926.9
2nd quarter ...	12 512.5	8 078.1	1 045.9	250.0	2 185.7	1 940.0	987.2	1 337.0	11 175.5	10 532.5	643.0	5.8	10 554.2	11 156.2
3rd quarter ...	12 474.2	8 095.7	1 040.9	273.4	2 174.9	1 879.9	990.7	1 442.4	11 031.8	10 558.1	473.6	4.3	10 469.2	10 901.5
4th quarter ...	12 373.9	8 063.6	1 001.3	299.8	2 079.6	1 918.2	988.6	1 432.0	10 941.8	10 270.4	671.5	6.1	10 482.0	10 969.5
2009														
1st quarter	12 038.5	7 763.0	944.2	310.8	1 949.3	2 032.5	961.3	1 195.5	10 843.0	10 182.2	660.9	6.1	10 088.3	10 932.3
2nd quarter ...	12 098.7	7 791.2	944.6	325.0	1 833.8	2 170.3	966.3	1 125.2	10 973.5	10 191.2	782.3	7.1	9 965.7	11 014.7
3rd quarter ...	12 056.7	7 774.9	976.9	344.4	1 753.0	2 171.0	963.4	1 126.4	10 930.2	10 316.2	614.1	5.6	9 861.0	10 902.9
4th quarter ...	12 134.4	7 822.1	1 026.3	354.6	1 711.0	2 187.1	966.6	1 132.6	11 001.9	10 376.4	625.4	5.7	9 855.1	10 899.8
2010														
1st quarter	12 194.3	7 804.3	1 017.6	380.5	1 710.7	2 253.3	972.0	1 145.6	11 048.7	10 459.9	588.9	5.3	9 815.4	10 909.1
2nd quarter ...	12 374.3	7 952.7	1 024.7	397.3	1 722.8	2 260.9	984.0	1 167.9	11 206.4	10 542.4	664.0	5.9	9 974.3	11 052.2
3rd quarter ...	12 502.1	8 026.5	1 029.2	408.3	1 738.0	2 288.4	988.4	1 209.4	11 292.6	10 637.5	655.2	5.8	10 043.5	11 104.4
4th quarter ...	12 670.0	8 085.7	1 059.3	425.0	1 787.0	2 305.1	992.0	1 242.9	11 427.1	10 798.4	628.7	5.5	10 138.3	11 177.3

Table 4-2. Personal Consumption Expenditures by Major Type of Product

(Billions of dollars, quarterly data are at seasonally adjusted rates.)   **NIPA Table 2.3.5**

| | | Goods | | | | | | | | | | | |
| | | | Durable goods | | | | | Nondurable goods | | | | | |
Year and quarter	Personal consumption expend- itures, total	Total goods	Durable goods, total	Motor vehicles and parts	Furnishings and household equipment	Recreational goods and vehicles	Other durable goods	Nondurable goods, total	Food and beverages off-premises	Clothing and footwear	Gasoline and other energy goods	Other nondurable goods
1950	192.2	116.8	32.4	13.7	11.8	4.1	2.9	84.4	41.4	18.9	8.9	15.2
1951	208.5	124.8	31.7	12.1	12.4	4.1	3.2	93.0	46.0	20.5	9.6	16.9
1952	219.5	128.8	31.2	11.4	12.2	4.3	3.4	97.5	48.4	21.2	10.2	17.8
1953	233.0	134.8	34.6	13.8	12.6	4.7	3.5	100.2	49.3	21.3	10.8	18.8
1954	239.9	135.8	33.7	12.7	12.5	4.9	3.6	102.1	50.6	21.4	11.3	18.8
1955	258.7	147.4	40.7	17.7	14.0	5.3	3.7	106.7	52.0	22.4	12.4	19.9
1956	271.6	152.2	40.2	15.7	14.8	5.7	4.0	112.0	54.2	23.4	13.3	21.1
1957	286.7	159.6	42.0	17.5	14.8	5.8	4.0	117.6	57.1	23.6	14.2	22.6
1958	296.0	161.6	39.5	15.0	14.6	5.9	4.1	122.0	59.8	23.9	14.7	23.6
1959	317.5	172.6	44.9	18.8	15.5	6.4	4.2	127.7	61.6	25.4	15.3	25.5
1960	331.6	177.0	45.6	19.6	15.4	6.4	4.3	131.4	62.6	25.9	15.8	27.1
1961	342.0	178.8	44.2	17.7	15.6	6.6	4.3	134.6	63.7	26.6	15.7	28.6
1962	363.1	189.0	49.5	21.4	16.4	6.9	4.7	139.5	64.7	27.9	16.3	30.7
1963	382.5	198.2	54.2	24.2	17.5	7.6	4.9	143.9	65.9	28.6	16.9	32.5
1964	411.2	212.3	59.6	25.8	19.5	8.8	5.5	152.7	69.5	31.1	17.7	34.5
1965	443.6	229.7	66.4	29.6	20.7	10.1	6.0	163.3	74.4	32.7	19.1	37.1
1966	480.6	249.6	71.7	29.9	22.6	12.3	6.9	177.9	80.6	35.8	20.7	40.8
1967	507.4	259.0	74.0	29.6	23.7	13.6	7.1	185.0	82.6	37.5	21.9	43.0
1968	557.4	284.6	84.8	35.4	26.1	15.3	8.0	199.8	88.8	41.3	23.2	46.5
1969	604.5	304.7	90.5	37.4	27.6	16.7	8.7	214.2	95.4	44.3	25.0	49.5
1970	647.7	318.8	90.0	34.5	28.2	17.9	9.4	228.8	103.5	45.5	26.3	53.6
1971	701.0	342.1	102.4	43.2	29.9	19.2	10.1	239.7	107.1	49.0	27.6	55.9
1972	769.4	373.8	116.4	49.4	33.5	22.6	11.0	257.4	114.5	53.5	29.4	60.0
1973	851.1	416.6	130.5	54.4	38.0	25.3	12.9	286.1	126.7	59.2	34.3	65.8
1974	932.0	451.5	130.2	48.2	40.9	26.6	14.5	321.4	143.0	62.4	43.8	72.1
1975	1 032.8	491.3	142.2	52.6	42.6	30.4	16.5	349.2	156.6	66.9	48.0	77.7
1976	1 150.2	546.3	168.6	68.2	47.2	34.2	19.1	377.7	167.3	72.2	53.0	85.2
1977	1 276.7	600.4	192.0	79.8	53.4	37.7	21.1	408.4	179.8	79.3	57.8	91.5
1978	1 426.2	663.6	213.3	89.2	59.0	41.7	23.5	450.2	196.1	89.3	61.5	103.3
1979	1 589.5	737.9	226.3	90.2	65.3	45.8	25.1	511.6	218.4	96.4	80.4	116.5
1980	1 754.6	799.8	226.4	84.4	67.8	46.5	27.6	573.4	239.2	103.0	101.9	129.3
1981	1 937.5	869.4	243.9	93.0	71.5	49.9	29.6	625.4	255.3	113.2	113.4	143.5
1982	2 073.9	899.3	253.0	100.0	71.8	51.3	29.9	646.3	267.1	116.7	108.4	154.0
1983	2 286.5	973.8	295.0	122.9	79.8	58.7	33.7	678.8	277.0	126.4	106.5	168.8
1984	2 498.2	1 063.7	342.2	147.2	88.8	67.8	38.3	721.5	291.1	137.6	108.2	184.6
1985	2 722.7	1 137.6	380.4	170.1	94.6	74.1	41.6	757.2	303.0	146.8	110.5	196.9
1986	2 898.4	1 195.6	421.4	187.5	103.5	83.0	47.5	774.2	316.4	157.2	91.2	209.4
1987	3 092.1	1 256.3	442.0	188.2	109.5	91.8	52.5	814.3	324.3	167.7	96.4	225.9
1988	3 346.9	1 337.3	475.1	202.2	115.2	99.9	57.8	862.3	342.8	178.2	99.9	241.4
1989	3 592.8	1 423.8	494.3	207.8	121.4	103.9	61.3	929.5	365.4	190.4	110.4	263.3
1990	3 825.6	1 491.3	497.1	205.1	120.9	105.6	65.5	994.2	391.2	195.2	124.2	283.6
1991	3 960.2	1 497.4	477.2	185.7	118.8	107.7	64.9	1 020.3	403.0	199.1	121.1	297.1
1992	4 215.7	1 563.3	508.1	204.8	124.3	111.0	68.0	1 055.2	404.5	211.2	125.0	314.5
1993	4 471.0	1 642.3	551.5	224.7	131.4	123.5	72.0	1 090.8	413.5	219.1	126.9	331.4
1994	4 741.0	1 746.6	607.2	249.8	140.5	140.3	76.5	1 139.4	432.1	227.4	129.2	350.6
1995	4 984.2	1 815.5	635.7	255.7	146.7	153.7	79.6	1 179.8	443.7	231.2	133.4	371.4
1996	5 268.1	1 917.7	676.3	273.5	153.5	164.9	84.3	1 241.4	461.9	239.5	144.7	395.2
1997	5 560.7	2 006.8	715.5	293.1	160.5	174.6	87.3	1 291.2	474.8	247.5	147.7	421.3
1998	5 903.0	2 108.7	779.3	320.2	173.6	191.4	94.2	1 329.4	487.4	257.8	132.4	451.8
1999	6 316.9	2 286.8	855.6	350.7	191.2	210.9	102.7	1 431.2	515.5	271.1	146.5	498.0
2000	6 801.6	2 452.9	912.6	363.2	208.1	230.9	110.4	1 540.3	540.6	280.8	184.5	534.4
2001	7 106.9	2 525.2	941.5	383.3	214.9	234.9	108.4	1 583.7	564.0	277.9	178.0	563.9
2002	7 385.3	2 598.6	985.4	401.3	225.9	244.8	113.4	1 613.2	575.1	278.8	167.9	591.4
2003	7 764.4	2 721.6	1 017.5	401.5	235.2	259.2	121.7	1 704.0	599.6	285.3	196.4	622.7
2004	8 257.8	2 900.3	1 079.8	409.3	254.3	284.1	132.1	1 820.4	632.6	297.5	232.7	657.6
2005	8 790.3	3 080.3	1 127.2	410.0	271.3	305.0	141.0	1 953.1	668.2	310.7	283.8	690.4
2006	9 297.5	3 235.8	1 156.1	395.0	283.6	324.1	153.5	2 079.7	700.3	320.2	319.7	739.6
2007	9 744.4	3 361.6	1 184.6	400.6	283.5	335.8	164.8	2 176.9	737.3	323.7	345.5	770.4
2008	10 005.5	3 375.7	1 102.3	339.6	268.7	329.3	164.6	2 273.4	772.9	319.5	389.1	791.9
2009	9 842.9	3 198.4	1 023.3	317.1	244.3	303.8	158.2	2 175.1	770.0	306.5	284.5	814.2
2010	10 201.9	3 362.8	1 070.7	342.0	250.4	312.7	165.6	2 292.1	788.9	320.6	333.4	849.2
2011	10 711.8	3 602.7	1 129.9	368.7	260.1	321.1	179.9	2 472.8	833.0	338.3	408.9	892.6
2012	11 149.6	3 769.7	1 202.7	401.7	275.1	334.5	191.3	2 567.0	863.3	354.6	417.0	932.1
2010												
1st quarter	10 042.3	3 304.9	1 040.2	321.3	247.8	309.1	161.9	2 264.7	785.4	316.1	328.5	834.7
2nd quarter	10 134.7	3 325.6	1 064.7	337.4	251.9	312.6	162.9	2 260.9	782.0	318.9	317.6	842.4
3rd quarter	10 234.3	3 362.4	1 075.1	345.8	249.7	313.6	165.9	2 287.3	786.6	319.5	326.9	854.3
4th quarter	10 396.3	3 458.4	1 102.8	363.4	252.3	315.6	171.6	2 355.6	801.6	327.7	360.7	865.5
2011												
1st quarter	10 527.1	3 532.2	1 115.1	368.7	253.7	317.8	174.9	2 417.1	815.6	331.1	393.1	877.3
2nd quarter	10 662.6	3 588.2	1 116.6	358.6	258.2	319.6	180.3	2 471.5	831.2	337.3	414.3	888.7
3rd quarter	10 778.6	3 622.3	1 129.0	363.4	261.7	321.5	182.4	2 493.3	839.9	339.5	417.2	896.7
4th quarter	10 878.9	3 668.2	1 158.9	384.4	266.7	325.7	182.1	2 509.3	845.2	345.3	411.2	907.6
2012												
1st quarter	11 019.1	3 729.3	1 184.3	395.4	273.0	329.9	186.0	2 545.0	854.3	352.0	416.9	921.8
2nd quarter	11 100.2	3 738.4	1 189.3	394.6	273.3	332.2	189.1	2 549.2	861.0	352.1	410.1	926.0
3rd quarter	11 193.6	3 784.9	1 206.5	401.8	276.2	336.1	192.4	2 578.4	866.0	357.1	419.5	935.9
4th quarter	11 285.5	3 826.1	1 230.7	415.1	277.9	339.9	197.8	2 595.4	871.8	357.4	421.6	944.7

Table 4-2. Personal Consumption Expenditures by Major Type of Product—*Continued*

(Billions of dollars, quarterly data are at seasonally adjusted rates.)   **NIPA Table 2.3.5**

Year and quarter	Services	Household consumption expenditures for services								Nonprofit institutions serving households (NPISHs)		
		Household services, total	Housing and utilities	Health care	Transportation services	Recreation services	Food services and accommodations	Financial services and insurance	Other services	Final consumption expenditures	Gross output	Less: receipts from sales of goods and services
1950	75.4	72.9	25.1	6.4	5.4	3.6	12.7	5.6	14.1	2.4	. . .	. . .
1951	83.7	81.1	28.1	6.9	6.0	3.8	15.0	6.3	15.1	2.6	. . .	. . .
1952	90.7	87.8	31.2	7.6	6.3	4.0	16.0	6.7	16.0	2.9	. . .	. . .
1953	98.2	95.2	34.5	8.4	6.8	4.2	16.5	7.8	17.1	3.0	. . .	. . .
1954	104.2	100.9	37.4	9.3	6.8	4.5	16.6	8.6	17.8	3.2	. . .	. . .
1955	111.3	107.9	40.0	9.9	7.1	4.8	17.0	9.6	19.4	3.4	. . .	. . .
1956	119.4	115.6	42.9	10.9	7.6	5.2	17.7	10.4	20.9	3.8	. . .	. . .
1957	127.1	123.1	45.9	12.0	8.0	5.2	18.5	11.1	22.4	4.0	. . .	. . .
1958	134.5	130.1	49.2	13.4	8.1	5.4	18.7	11.6	23.8	4.3	. . .	. . .
1959	144.9	140.0	52.8	14.8	8.7	5.9	19.7	12.5	25.5	4.9	13.9	9.0
1960	154.6	149.5	56.7	16.0	9.2	6.5	20.5	13.6	27.1	5.1	14.8	9.8
1961	163.2	157.9	60.3	17.1	9.6	6.9	21.0	14.8	28.3	5.2	15.8	10.5
1962	174.1	168.7	64.5	19.1	10.1	7.5	22.3	15.4	29.9	5.5	16.9	11.5
1963	184.3	178.6	68.2	21.0	10.6	7.9	23.3	15.9	31.6	5.8	18.3	12.6
1964	198.9	192.5	72.1	24.2	11.4	8.5	24.9	17.7	33.8	6.4	20.3	13.8
1965	213.9	206.9	76.6	26.0	12.1	9.0	27.2	19.4	36.6	7.0	22.1	15.1
1966	231.0	223.5	81.2	28.7	13.1	9.8	29.6	21.3	39.9	7.5	24.3	16.9
1967	248.4	240.4	86.3	31.9	14.3	10.5	31.0	22.8	43.6	8.0	27.0	18.9
1968	272.8	264.0	92.7	36.6	15.9	11.7	34.6	25.8	46.8	8.8	30.3	21.6
1969	299.8	290.4	101.0	42.1	18.0	12.9	37.5	28.5	50.5	9.4	34.0	24.6
1970	328.9	318.4	109.4	47.7	20.0	14.0	41.6	31.1	54.6	10.5	38.1	27.6
1971	358.9	347.2	120.0	53.7	22.4	15.1	43.8	34.1	58.1	11.7	42.8	31.1
1972	395.6	382.8	131.2	59.8	24.5	16.3	48.9	38.3	63.7	12.8	47.4	34.5
1973	434.5	420.8	143.5	67.2	26.1	18.3	54.8	41.5	69.3	13.8	51.8	38.1
1974	480.5	465.0	158.6	76.1	28.5	20.9	60.6	45.9	74.4	15.5	58.8	43.3
1975	541.4	524.4	176.5	89.0	32.0	23.7	68.8	54.0	80.3	17.0	67.2	50.2
1976	603.9	584.9	194.7	101.8	36.2	26.5	77.8	59.3	88.6	19.0	76.3	57.3
1977	676.3	655.7	217.8	115.7	41.4	29.6	85.7	67.8	97.7	20.6	85.2	64.5
1978	762.6	739.6	244.3	131.2	45.2	32.9	97.1	80.6	108.3	23.0	96.7	73.6
1979	851.6	825.4	273.4	148.8	50.7	36.7	110.9	87.6	117.2	26.1	109.4	83.2
1980	954.8	924.8	312.5	171.7	55.4	40.8	121.7	95.6	127.1	30.0	126.1	96.1
1981	1 068.1	1 034.0	352.1	201.9	59.8	47.1	133.9	102.0	137.2	34.1	145.7	111.5
1982	1 174.6	1 136.7	387.5	225.2	61.7	52.5	142.5	116.3	150.9	38.0	163.8	125.8
1983	1 312.7	1 272.0	421.2	253.1	68.9	59.4	153.6	145.9	169.9	40.8	179.2	138.5
1984	1 434.5	1 389.1	457.5	276.5	80.0	66.1	164.9	156.6	187.5	45.4	194.4	149.0
1985	1 585.1	1 537.2	500.6	302.2	90.1	74.0	174.3	188.1	207.9	47.9	209.3	161.4
1986	1 702.8	1 650.2	537.0	330.2	95.0	80.4	186.7	199.8	221.2	52.6	227.3	174.7
1987	1 835.8	1 780.1	571.6	366.0	103.1	87.3	204.4	205.3	242.4	55.7	246.9	191.2
1988	2 009.6	1 946.3	614.4	410.1	114.2	99.2	225.8	219.8	262.8	63.3	275.5	212.2
1989	2 169.0	2 101.0	655.2	451.2	121.8	110.7	242.6	238.4	281.1	68.0	301.2	233.2
1990	2 334.3	2 258.5	696.5	506.2	126.4	121.8	262.7	247.4	297.5	75.9	334.4	258.6
1991	2 462.7	2 382.6	735.2	555.8	123.7	127.2	273.4	266.8	300.5	80.1	362.9	282.8
1992	2 652.4	2 564.5	771.1	612.8	133.6	139.8	286.3	295.1	325.7	87.9	396.4	308.5
1993	2 828.7	2 738.6	814.9	648.8	146.1	153.4	298.4	332.6	344.4	90.1	418.7	328.7
1994	2 994.5	2 896.7	863.3	680.5	161.9	164.7	308.3	346.9	371.2	97.8	440.1	342.3
1995	3 168.6	3 066.3	913.7	719.9	177.9	181.1	316.1	366.4	391.2	102.3	458.5	356.2
1996	3 350.4	3 240.4	962.4	752.1	195.0	195.6	326.6	392.3	416.4	110.0	483.1	373.1
1997	3 554.0	3 448.4	1 009.8	790.9	214.3	208.3	343.4	429.2	452.3	105.6	502.6	397.0
1998	3 794.3	3 670.5	1 065.5	832.0	227.6	220.2	361.8	467.3	496.0	123.8	542.5	418.7
1999	4 030.1	3 891.9	1 123.1	863.6	244.1	238.1	380.3	509.1	533.6	138.2	576.3	438.1
2000	4 348.8	4 190.7	1 198.6	918.4	263.5	254.4	408.8	566.3	580.7	158.0	621.6	463.6
2001	4 581.6	4 402.5	1 287.5	996.6	264.7	262.3	419.7	552.8	619.0	179.1	676.4	497.4
2002	4 786.7	4 588.4	1 333.6	1 082.9	258.2	271.4	436.3	562.6	643.5	198.3	737.1	538.7
2003	5 042.8	4 837.3	1 394.1	1 154.6	265.5	289.2	461.9	588.5	683.5	205.5	774.6	569.1
2004	5 357.5	5 151.1	1 469.1	1 240.1	276.6	312.1	496.4	635.3	721.5	206.4	819.0	612.6
2005	5 710.1	5 499.8	1 583.6	1 322.3	289.4	328.9	530.6	689.6	755.3	210.3	868.5	658.2
2006	6 061.7	5 822.5	1 682.4	1 394.2	302.1	351.9	566.3	724.2	801.4	239.2	932.2	693.0
2007	6 382.9	6 134.1	1 758.2	1 481.8	312.2	375.8	595.6	768.5	841.9	248.8	983.1	734.4
2008	6 629.8	6 347.7	1 839.1	1 556.5	311.7	384.5	612.5	771.5	871.9	282.1	1 040.9	758.8
2009	6 644.5	6 368.5	1 881.0	1 627.4	289.7	376.0	600.3	719.0	875.1	276.0	1 072.6	796.5
2010	6 839.1	6 563.7	1 909.0	1 690.7	292.9	385.1	617.7	763.2	905.1	275.4	1 105.9	830.5
2011	7 109.1	6 831.2	1 960.9	1 767.8	308.2	399.7	658.7	801.1	934.8	277.9	1 141.6	863.7
2012	7 379.9	7 089.4	2 013.9	1 847.6	318.1	416.6	701.7	821.0	970.4	290.5	1 194.1	903.6
2010												
1st quarter	6 737.4	6 461.6	1 898.4	1 654.5	289.0	380.5	607.1	740.5	891.5	275.9	1 085.4	809.6
2nd quarter	6 809.1	6 531.7	1 899.8	1 678.8	291.7	380.9	614.7	764.7	901.2	277.3	1 101.0	823.7
3rd quarter	6 871.9	6 597.1	1 912.4	1 703.1	294.0	387.9	620.6	768.1	911.1	274.7	1 113.1	838.3
4th quarter	6 937.9	6 664.4	1 925.3	1 726.4	297.1	391.0	628.4	779.6	916.6	273.5	1 124.0	850.6
2011												
1st quarter	6 995.0	6 722.7	1 935.9	1 742.0	301.2	390.7	639.9	788.2	924.7	272.2	1 127.3	855.0
2nd quarter	7 074.4	6 798.8	1 952.2	1 763.9	306.8	399.1	654.1	792.1	930.7	275.6	1 139.6	864.0
3rd quarter	7 156.3	6 871.6	1 975.9	1 768.3	310.9	403.1	665.8	810.8	936.9	284.7	1 142.1	857.4
4th quarter	7 210.7	6 931.6	1 979.5	1 796.9	314.0	405.9	674.9	813.3	947.0	279.1	1 157.4	878.3
2012												
1st quarter	7 289.7	7 009.5	1 982.7	1 826.2	315.5	412.8	688.1	820.9	963.4	280.2	1 175.9	895.7
2nd quarter	7 361.8	7 071.3	2 013.9	1 835.9	318.1	415.2	698.2	821.3	968.6	290.5	1 185.4	894.9
3rd quarter	7 408.7	7 117.2	2 029.5	1 855.9	318.9	419.2	703.4	817.9	972.4	291.5	1 202.7	911.2
4th quarter	7 459.4	7 159.6	2 029.4	1 872.5	319.8	419.0	717.2	824.2	977.5	299.8	1 212.5	912.7

. . . = Not available.

Table 4-3. Chain-Type Quantity Indexes for Personal Consumption Expenditures by Major Type of Product

(Index numbers, 2009 = 100.)   **NIPA Table 2.3.3**

Year and quarter	Personal consumption expend-itures, total	Total goods	Goods										
			Durable goods					Nondurable goods				
			Durable goods, total	Motor vehicles and parts	Furnishings and household equipment	Recreational goods and vehicles	Other durable goods	Nondurable goods, total	Food and beverages off-premises	Clothing and footwear	Gasoline and other energy goods	Other nondurable goods
1955	16.6	17.7	8.0	20.6	12.6	0.8	8.4	26.3	41.3	14.3	44.2	15.6
1956	17.1	18.0	7.7	17.5	13.2	0.9	8.8	27.3	42.7	14.7	46.1	16.3
1957	17.5	18.3	7.8	18.3	12.9	0.9	8.9	27.8	43.7	14.6	47.3	16.9
1958	17.7	18.1	7.2	15.2	12.8	0.9	9.0	28.2	43.9	14.7	49.4	17.2
1959	18.7	19.2	8.0	18.1	13.6	1.0	9.2	29.4	45.7	15.5	50.6	18.2
1960	19.2	19.5	8.2	19.2	13.4	1.0	9.3	29.9	46.0	15.6	51.4	19.1
1961	19.6	19.7	7.9	17.3	13.5	1.0	9.5	30.5	46.7	15.9	51.1	20.1
1962	20.6	20.7	8.8	20.5	14.2	1.1	10.4	31.5	47.0	16.6	52.7	21.5
1963	21.4	21.5	9.6	23.1	15.2	1.2	10.8	32.2	47.4	16.9	54.5	22.5
1964	22.7	22.8	10.5	24.4	16.9	1.4	11.7	33.7	49.0	18.2	57.5	23.5
1965	24.1	24.4	11.8	28.2	18.0	1.6	12.9	35.4	51.4	19.0	60.2	24.9
1966	25.5	26.0	12.8	28.7	19.6	2.0	14.8	37.3	53.4	20.3	63.5	26.9
1967	26.3	26.5	13.0	28.0	20.0	2.2	14.9	38.1	54.7	20.4	65.1	27.7
1968	27.8	28.1	14.5	32.4	21.2	2.4	16.4	39.7	57.1	21.2	67.9	28.8
1969	28.8	29.0	15.0	33.5	21.7	2.5	17.0	40.8	58.6	21.6	70.8	29.6
1970	29.5	29.2	14.6	30.0	21.6	2.7	17.9	41.8	60.3	21.4	73.5	30.6
1971	30.6	30.4	16.1	35.9	22.6	2.8	18.7	42.5	61.0	22.3	76.1	30.7
1972	32.5	32.4	18.1	40.8	24.9	3.3	19.7	44.3	62.2	23.9	79.9	32.2
1973	34.1	34.1	20.0	44.8	27.6	3.6	22.4	45.5	61.1	25.6	84.5	34.4
1974	33.8	32.8	18.7	37.4	27.5	3.6	23.5	44.4	59.9	25.1	77.6	34.3
1975	34.6	33.1	18.7	37.2	26.0	3.9	24.9	44.8	61.0	25.7	79.5	33.2
1976	36.5	35.4	21.1	44.7	27.6	4.2	27.4	46.9	64.0	26.9	83.7	34.5
1977	38.1	36.9	22.9	49.4	30.2	4.5	28.9	48.0	64.9	28.4	85.2	35.1
1978	39.7	38.4	24.1	51.7	31.7	4.8	30.5	49.7	64.6	31.4	86.6	37.6
1979	40.7	39.0	24.0	48.6	33.0	5.1	30.1	51.0	65.5	33.2	84.1	39.8
1980	40.6	38.0	22.1	42.4	31.8	4.9	27.5	50.9	66.2	34.2	76.6	40.4
1981	41.2	38.5	22.3	43.3	31.2	5.0	28.0	51.6	66.0	36.4	75.7	41.4
1982	41.7	38.8	22.3	44.5	29.8	5.0	28.0	52.1	67.3	37.0	75.8	41.2
1983	44.1	41.2	25.5	53.0	32.3	5.8	30.5	53.8	69.0	39.5	77.4	42.3
1984	46.4	44.2	29.1	61.7	35.6	6.8	34.0	56.0	70.4	42.8	79.5	44.6
1985	48.9	46.5	32.0	69.7	37.5	7.6	36.5	57.7	72.4	44.7	81.1	45.8
1986	50.9	49.1	35.1	74.7	40.5	8.8	40.7	59.8	73.9	48.1	85.2	46.8
1987	52.7	50.0	35.8	71.7	42.3	9.8	42.2	60.8	73.4	49.8	86.8	48.5
1988	54.9	51.9	37.8	75.9	43.8	10.7	43.6	62.4	75.4	51.3	89.3	49.6
1989	56.5	53.2	38.6	75.7	46.0	11.2	44.1	64.1	76.3	54.0	90.7	51.3
1990	57.6	53.5	38.5	74.5	45.4	11.5	44.4	64.8	77.9	53.6	89.1	52.6
1991	57.8	52.4	36.4	65.6	44.3	11.9	42.4	64.6	77.8	53.7	88.4	52.3
1992	59.9	54.1	38.5	71.0	45.9	12.6	43.3	65.9	77.5	56.5	91.9	53.4
1993	62.0	56.3	41.4	75.0	48.2	14.5	45.5	67.6	78.1	58.9	94.2	55.3
1994	64.4	59.3	44.7	79.7	50.8	16.9	47.6	70.2	80.3	62.2	95.7	58.1
1995	66.3	61.1	46.4	78.4	53.1	19.3	48.7	71.9	80.7	64.8	97.5	60.5
1996	68.6	63.8	49.9	82.2	55.4	22.3	51.9	74.0	81.5	67.9	99.0	63.2
1997	71.2	66.9	54.0	87.8	58.0	25.8	54.5	76.2	82.2	70.2	101.0	66.6
1998	75.0	71.3	60.5	97.0	62.8	30.8	59.9	79.0	83.4	74.5	103.9	70.2
1999	79.1	76.9	68.2	105.9	70.1	37.2	67.0	83.0	86.8	79.3	106.3	74.4
2000	83.1	80.9	74.1	109.3	76.8	43.5	73.0	85.7	88.9	83.2	103.5	78.1
2001	85.2	83.4	78.0	114.9	80.8	47.5	71.4	87.2	90.1	84.0	103.4	80.6
2002	87.4	86.6	83.7	120.9	86.7	52.9	75.8	88.8	90.5	86.5	104.2	83.0
2003	90.1	90.8	89.7	124.4	92.8	59.8	82.9	91.9	92.6	90.8	104.3	87.2
2004	93.5	95.4	97.0	127.9	101.6	68.9	90.3	94.9	94.8	95.0	105.2	91.0
2005	96.8	99.3	102.3	126.2	108.4	78.2	96.9	98.0	98.4	100.1	104.7	94.1
2006	99.7	102.9	106.7	121.5	113.9	88.5	104.0	101.2	101.4	103.6	104.5	98.7
2007	102.0	105.7	111.6	123.9	114.8	98.4	108.9	103.0	102.8	105.7	104.3	101.3
2008	101.6	103.1	105.9	107.5	109.6	101.6	105.3	101.8	101.5	105.2	99.6	101.7
2009	100.0	100.0	100.0	100.0	100.0	100.0	100.0	100.0	100.0	100.0	100.0	100.0
2010	102.0	103.4	106.1	102.0	107.0	110.9	104.2	102.2	102.1	105.3	99.2	102.3
2011	104.6	106.9	113.1	107.0	113.0	122.0	109.8	104.2	103.8	109.3	96.7	105.8
2012	106.9	110.5	121.8	114.8	119.8	135.2	116.1	105.6	105.1	110.6	95.4	108.7
2010												
1st quarter	100.7	101.5	102.1	96.6	104.0	106.7	102.5	101.2	102.1	103.1	98.2	100.8
2nd quarter	101.5	102.8	105.2	100.8	107.0	109.9	102.7	101.7	101.4	104.7	99.3	101.8
3rd quarter	102.2	103.8	106.9	102.7	107.5	112.2	104.6	102.3	101.8	105.0	99.9	102.8
4th quarter	103.3	105.7	110.2	107.9	109.7	114.7	107.1	103.6	103.3	108.3	99.4	103.9
2011												
1st quarter	103.8	106.4	111.6	108.9	110.3	117.6	108.0	104.0	103.6	109.0	98.6	104.7
2nd quarter	104.2	106.4	111.4	104.1	111.9	120.2	110.1	104.2	104.0	110.3	96.3	105.5
3rd quarter	104.8	106.8	112.8	104.5	113.4	123.2	111.0	104.1	103.7	108.4	96.2	106.2
4th quarter	105.4	108.1	116.5	110.7	116.2	126.9	110.1	104.4	103.7	109.5	96.0	106.9
2012												
1st quarter	106.1	109.3	119.2	113.6	118.5	130.2	112.2	105.0	104.4	110.8	94.9	107.9
2nd quarter	106.6	109.9	120.1	112.4	118.8	133.3	115.0	105.5	105.0	109.7	96.6	108.2
3rd quarter	107.1	110.9	122.5	114.6	120.4	137.0	117.0	105.9	105.4	111.1	95.8	108.8
4th quarter	107.5	111.9	125.6	118.5	121.7	140.5	120.2	106.0	105.7	110.6	94.5	109.9

Table 4-3. Chain-Type Quantity Indexes for Personal Consumption Expenditures by Major Type of Product—*Continued*

(Index numbers, 2009 = 100.)

NIPA Table 2.3.3

Year and quarter	Services	Household consumption expenditures for services								Nonprofit institutions serving households (NPISHs)		
		Household services, total	Housing and utilities	Health care	Transportation services	Recreation services	Food services and accommodations	Financial services and insurance	Other services	Final consumption expenditures	Gross output	Less: receipts from sales of goods and services
1955	15.1	16.1	16.6	11.2	20.9	9.9	27.4	10.3	20.0	2.5	. . .	. . .
1956	15.8	16.8	17.5	11.9	21.4	10.4	28.2	10.9	20.8	2.7	. . .	. . .
1957	16.4	17.4	18.4	12.6	21.8	10.0	28.6	11.2	21.6	2.8	. . .	. . .
1958	16.9	18.0	19.3	13.6	21.5	10.0	28.1	11.5	22.3	2.9	. . .	. . .
1959	17.7	18.8	20.4	14.6	22.4	10.7	28.7	11.8	23.2	3.2	13.2	20.1
1960	18.4	19.5	21.5	14.8	23.1	11.3	29.0	12.2	24.0	3.6	13.7	20.1
1961	19.1	20.2	22.6	15.4	23.4	11.7	29.1	12.9	24.8	3.7	14.3	21.2
1962	20.0	21.2	23.9	16.8	24.2	12.3	30.2	12.9	25.7	3.8	15.1	22.6
1963	20.9	22.1	25.0	17.9	25.3	12.8	30.9	13.3	26.7	3.9	15.9	24.1
1964	22.1	23.4	26.2	20.0	26.7	13.3	32.5	14.3	27.9	4.3	17.2	25.6
1965	23.3	24.7	27.6	20.9	28.0	13.8	34.8	15.2	29.5	4.6	18.2	27.2
1966	24.5	25.9	28.9	22.0	29.7	14.7	36.5	15.7	31.2	4.7	19.4	29.4
1967	25.5	27.0	30.2	23.1	31.2	15.2	36.2	16.5	33.0	4.9	20.6	31.4
1968	26.8	28.4	31.7	24.8	33.2	16.1	38.4	17.4	33.9	5.2	22.0	33.7
1969	28.0	29.7	33.4	26.7	35.5	17.1	39.2	17.6	34.9	5.2	23.1	36.0
1970	29.1	30.9	34.7	28.1	36.7	17.7	40.6	18.3	36.1	5.6	24.3	37.7
1971	30.1	31.9	36.2	30.1	38.3	18.3	40.6	18.9	36.2	5.9	26.0	40.6
1972	31.9	33.7	38.1	32.2	40.4	19.3	43.7	20.0	37.8	6.2	27.5	43.0
1973	33.4	35.4	39.9	34.5	41.1	20.9	45.8	21.2	38.9	6.2	28.3	44.5
1974	34.0	36.1	41.8	35.7	41.4	22.3	45.4	21.7	37.6	6.1	28.6	45.6
1975	35.3	37.5	43.1	37.5	41.9	23.5	47.3	23.8	37.9	6.2	29.7	47.9
1976	36.8	39.1	44.4	39.2	44.0	25.1	50.2	25.1	39.4	6.6	31.3	50.3
1977	38.4	40.7	45.6	41.1	47.1	26.7	51.5	26.6	41.3	6.7	32.5	52.6
1978	40.1	42.6	47.8	43.0	48.2	28.0	53.7	28.0	43.5	7.0	34.3	55.6
1979	41.4	43.9	49.5	44.4	49.7	29.3	55.4	28.8	43.9	7.2	35.3	57.1
1980	42.0	44.6	51.2	45.7	46.8	30.3	55.4	29.2	43.6	7.6	36.4	58.4
1981	42.8	45.3	51.9	47.9	45.0	32.9	55.9	29.0	43.4	8.2	37.9	60.1
1982	43.6	46.0	52.3	48.0	44.0	34.5	56.3	31.2	44.3	9.7	39.5	60.5
1983	45.9	48.2	53.4	49.5	47.4	37.4	58.1	35.7	47.2	11.2	41.0	60.8
1984	47.7	49.9	55.2	50.3	52.9	39.9	59.8	36.1	49.6	13.0	42.4	60.7
1985	50.2	52.5	57.4	51.8	58.5	42.8	60.6	40.0	53.0	14.1	43.9	62.1
1986	51.8	54.0	58.8	53.4	61.0	44.8	62.3	41.8	53.6	16.0	46.1	63.6
1987	54.1	56.4	60.4	55.6	63.5	46.8	65.6	44.2	57.3	17.3	47.9	65.5
1988	56.5	58.7	62.5	57.8	67.2	51.3	69.5	45.1	59.6	19.8	50.5	67.3
1989	58.3	60.4	64.0	58.5	68.7	54.5	71.4	47.6	61.5	22.8	52.3	67.6
1990	60.1	61.8	65.2	60.4	68.6	56.8	73.9	48.7	62.6	27.8	55.5	68.8
1991	61.1	62.6	66.6	61.6	65.3	56.4	74.0	52.8	60.3	31.7	57.5	69.4
1992	63.5	64.8	68.0	63.5	68.7	60.1	75.9	56.5	62.7	38.3	60.6	70.4
1993	65.5	66.7	69.8	63.8	72.5	63.9	77.5	60.5	64.1	41.4	62.1	71.1
1994	67.5	68.6	72.1	64.3	79.4	67.2	78.7	61.9	66.6	45.1	63.5	71.4
1995	69.5	70.6	74.3	65.6	85.4	72.3	78.9	64.0	67.9	47.2	64.3	71.6
1996	71.6	72.7	76.0	67.0	92.4	75.6	79.3	66.3	70.3	49.9	66.0	72.8
1997	73.9	75.3	77.7	69.0	99.4	78.0	81.0	69.7	74.3	46.0	66.9	75.9
1998	77.3	78.6	80.1	71.3	103.7	80.4	83.1	75.9	79.8	50.5	70.1	78.5
1999	80.4	81.7	82.4	72.4	109.6	84.3	85.2	83.3	83.8	54.4	72.5	80.2
2000	84.5	85.7	85.1	74.9	114.9	86.7	89.1	91.7	89.5	58.9	75.3	82.0
2001	86.3	87.4	87.4	78.6	114.1	86.5	88.9	89.8	92.6	63.8	78.9	85.0
2002	87.9	88.7	87.9	83.3	110.7	87.0	90.2	89.3	92.6	70.3	83.5	88.7
2003	89.8	90.5	89.1	85.6	111.5	90.0	93.5	89.4	94.9	74.7	85.3	89.2
2004	92.6	93.4	91.3	88.6	114.4	94.6	97.3	93.0	97.0	76.2	87.5	91.8
2005	95.6	96.5	95.1	91.6	115.5	97.0	100.8	97.9	97.9	76.1	89.7	94.9
2006	98.1	98.7	96.9	93.7	115.8	100.4	104.1	100.2	100.5	85.7	93.1	95.9
2007	100.1	100.6	97.9	96.1	117.0	104.3	105.4	103.3	102.7	88.0	95.3	98.0
2008	100.8	100.9	98.9	98.2	110.9	103.5	104.3	102.6	102.2	99.1	98.4	98.1
2009	100.0	100.0	100.0	100.0	100.0	100.0	100.0	100.0	100.0	100.0	100.0	100.0
2010	101.2	101.3	101.2	101.3	99.1	101.3	101.5	102.1	101.0	100.8	101.3	101.4
2011	103.4	103.5	102.5	104.1	101.6	103.4	105.6	105.1	102.5	101.0	102.6	103.1
2012	105.1	105.0	103.3	106.8	102.9	104.9	109.4	103.8	104.2	106.4	105.6	105.3
2010												
1st quarter	100.4	100.3	100.9	99.9	98.2	100.8	100.5	100.3	100.3	101.2	100.0	99.6
2nd quarter	100.9	100.9	100.8	100.8	98.8	100.3	101.2	102.4	100.7	102.1	101.1	100.7
3rd quarter	101.5	101.5	101.4	101.8	99.4	101.7	101.8	102.3	101.3	100.5	101.7	102.1
4th quarter	102.2	102.3	101.9	102.8	100.0	102.5	102.7	103.3	101.7	99.5	102.3	103.2
2011												
1st quarter	102.6	102.8	102.0	103.3	100.3	101.9	104.0	104.4	102.3	99.1	102.1	103.1
2nd quarter	103.2	103.3	102.3	104.0	101.4	103.4	105.2	104.5	102.3	99.7	102.4	103.4
3rd quarter	103.8	103.8	103.0	103.8	102.2	104.1	106.1	106.1	102.4	103.8	102.4	102.0
4th quarter	104.1	104.2	102.7	105.1	102.5	104.3	107.2	105.6	102.9	101.6	103.3	103.8
2012												
1st quarter	104.6	104.7	102.5	106.3	102.4	104.8	108.3	105.3	104.1	102.5	104.7	105.4
2nd quarter	105.1	105.0	103.6	106.4	102.9	104.9	109.0	104.5	104.0	106.3	105.0	104.6
3rd quarter	105.3	105.2	104.0	107.0	103.1	105.2	109.3	102.7	104.4	107.2	106.1	105.8
4th quarter	105.4	105.3	103.2	107.6	103.1	104.7	111.0	102.6	104.4	109.5	106.4	105.4

. . . = Not available.

Table 4-4. Chain-Type Price Indexes for Personal Consumption Expenditures by Major Type of Product

(Index numbers, 2009 =1000.)   NIPA Table 2.3.4

Year and quarter	Personal consumption expend-itures, total	Total goods	Goods									
			Durable goods					Nondurable goods				
			Durable goods, total	Motor vehicles and parts	Furnishings and household equipment	Recreational goods and vehicles	Other durable goods	Nondurable goods, total	Food and beverages off-premises	Clothing and footwear	Gasoline and other energy goods	Other nondurable goods
1955	15.8	26.1	49.8	27.1	45.6	208.8	28.2	18.6	16.4	51.0	9.8	15.7
1956	16.1	26.5	51.0	28.3	46.0	211.1	28.5	18.9	16.5	52.0	10.1	16.0
1957	16.6	27.3	52.9	30.1	46.8	218.6	28.6	19.4	17.0	52.7	10.6	16.5
1958	17.0	28.0	53.8	31.2	46.7	224.6	28.7	19.9	17.7	53.0	10.5	16.9
1959	17.3	28.1	54.7	32.8	46.7	218.1	28.8	19.9	17.5	53.4	10.6	17.1
1960	17.5	28.3	54.5	32.2	47.1	219.6	28.9	20.2	17.7	54.1	10.8	17.4
1961	17.7	28.4	54.6	32.4	47.3	218.4	28.8	20.3	17.7	54.5	10.8	17.5
1962	17.9	28.6	54.8	32.9	47.2	216.0	28.7	20.4	17.9	54.6	10.9	17.5
1963	18.1	28.8	55.0	33.2	47.3	215.6	28.9	20.6	18.1	55.1	10.9	17.8
1964	18.4	29.1	55.3	33.4	47.3	213.0	29.6	20.9	18.4	55.6	10.8	18.0
1965	18.7	29.4	54.8	33.1	47.0	210.0	29.4	21.2	18.8	56.1	11.2	18.3
1966	19.2	30.1	54.7	32.9	47.4	207.7	29.4	21.9	19.6	57.6	11.4	18.6
1967	19.6	30.6	55.6	33.4	48.5	209.0	30.1	22.3	19.6	60.0	11.8	19.1
1968	20.4	31.7	57.4	34.5	50.4	213.1	30.8	23.1	20.2	63.4	12.0	19.8
1969	21.3	32.9	59.0	35.2	52.2	218.0	32.3	24.1	21.1	66.8	12.4	20.6
1970	22.3	34.2	60.3	36.3	53.3	218.3	33.2	25.2	22.3	69.3	12.6	21.5
1971	23.3	35.2	62.4	38.0	54.3	226.0	34.1	25.9	22.8	71.8	12.8	22.3
1972	24.1	36.1	63.0	38.1	55.0	229.3	35.2	26.7	23.9	73.1	12.9	22.9
1973	25.4	38.2	64.0	38.3	56.3	232.8	36.3	28.9	26.9	75.5	14.3	23.5
1974	28.0	43.0	68.2	40.7	60.9	243.1	39.1	33.3	31.0	81.1	19.9	25.8
1975	30.3	46.5	74.3	44.7	67.0	259.2	42.1	35.8	33.3	84.8	21.2	28.8
1976	32.0	48.3	78.3	48.1	69.9	268.1	44.1	37.0	34.0	87.5	22.3	30.3
1977	34.1	50.9	81.8	50.9	72.4	275.8	46.1	39.1	36.0	91.2	23.9	32.0
1978	36.5	54.0	86.4	54.4	76.1	285.7	48.6	41.6	39.4	92.9	24.9	33.8
1979	39.7	59.1	92.2	58.5	80.8	298.5	52.7	46.1	43.3	94.8	33.6	36.0
1980	44.0	65.7	100.2	62.9	87.4	315.0	63.4	51.8	46.9	98.2	46.7	39.3
1981	47.9	70.6	106.8	67.7	93.9	329.2	66.9	55.8	50.3	101.5	52.7	42.6
1982	50.6	72.6	111.0	71.0	98.7	336.8	67.6	57.0	51.6	103.0	50.3	45.9
1983	52.7	73.9	113.3	73.2	101.0	332.7	69.7	58.0	52.2	104.4	48.3	49.1
1984	54.7	75.3	114.9	75.3	102.2	328.0	71.2	59.2	53.7	104.9	47.8	50.9
1985	56.7	76.5	116.2	77.0	103.3	322.3	72.0	60.3	54.3	107.2	47.9	52.9
1986	57.9	76.1	117.4	79.1	104.4	312.0	73.7	59.5	55.6	106.7	37.6	55.0
1987	59.6	78.6	120.8	82.8	106.1	308.1	78.7	61.6	57.4	109.8	39.0	57.2
1988	62.0	80.6	122.8	84.1	107.6	306.1	83.9	63.5	59.1	113.3	39.3	59.7
1989	64.6	83.7	125.0	86.5	107.9	305.3	87.8	66.7	62.2	115.0	42.8	63.0
1990	67.4	87.2	126.3	86.8	109.0	302.8	93.3	70.5	65.2	118.7	49.0	66.2
1991	69.7	89.3	128.1	89.3	109.6	299.0	96.7	72.6	67.3	121.0	48.2	69.7
1992	71.5	90.4	129.0	90.9	110.9	289.8	99.3	73.6	67.8	121.9	47.8	72.4
1993	73.3	91.2	130.3	94.5	111.5	279.4	100.1	74.2	68.7	121.3	47.3	73.6
1994	74.8	92.1	132.8	98.9	113.2	273.6	101.7	74.6	69.9	119.2	47.5	74.1
1995	76.4	92.9	133.8	102.8	113.1	262.1	103.3	75.4	71.4	116.4	48.1	75.4
1996	78.0	94.0	132.5	104.9	113.4	243.5	102.7	77.1	73.6	115.0	51.4	76.8
1997	79.3	93.9	129.6	105.3	113.2	223.1	101.3	77.9	75.0	115.1	51.4	77.6
1998	79.9	92.4	125.9	104.1	113.1	204.3	99.4	77.3	75.9	113.0	44.8	79.1
1999	81.1	92.9	122.5	104.5	111.7	186.5	96.9	79.2	77.2	111.5	48.5	82.2
2000	83.1	94.8	120.3	104.8	110.8	174.8	95.7	82.7	79.0	110.1	62.7	84.0
2001	84.7	94.7	118.0	105.3	108.9	162.9	96.0	83.5	81.3	108.0	60.5	85.9
2002	85.9	93.8	115.0	104.7	106.7	152.4	94.6	83.5	82.5	105.1	56.6	87.5
2003	87.6	93.7	110.9	101.8	103.7	142.7	92.8	85.3	84.1	102.5	66.2	87.8
2004	89.7	95.0	108.8	100.9	102.4	135.7	92.5	88.2	86.7	102.2	77.8	88.8
2005	92.3	97.0	107.7	102.5	102.4	128.4	91.9	91.6	88.2	101.3	95.2	90.1
2006	94.7	98.3	105.9	102.5	101.9	120.6	93.3	94.4	89.7	100.9	107.5	92.1
2007	97.1	99.4	103.8	102.0	101.1	112.3	95.7	97.2	93.2	99.9	116.4	93.4
2008	100.1	102.4	101.8	99.7	100.4	106.7	98.9	102.7	98.9	99.1	137.3	95.6
2009	100.0	100.0	100.0	100.0	100.0	100.0	100.0	100.0	100.0	100.0	100.0	100.0
2010	101.7	101.6	98.6	105.7	95.8	92.9	100.4	103.1	100.3	99.3	118.1	102.0
2011	104.1	105.3	97.6	108.6	94.2	86.7	103.6	109.1	104.3	101.0	148.6	103.6
2012	106.0	106.7	96.5	110.4	94.0	81.4	104.2	111.8	106.7	104.7	153.6	105.3
2010												
1st quarter	101.3	101.8	99.5	104.9	97.6	95.3	99.8	102.9	99.9	100.1	117.5	101.7
2nd quarter	101.4	101.1	98.9	105.5	96.3	93.6	100.2	102.2	100.2	99.3	112.4	101.7
3rd quarter	101.7	101.3	98.3	106.2	95.0	91.9	100.3	102.8	100.4	99.3	115.1	102.1
4th quarter	102.2	102.3	97.8	106.3	94.1	90.6	101.3	104.5	100.8	98.7	127.6	102.3
2011												
1st quarter	103.0	103.8	97.6	106.8	94.1	88.9	102.4	106.8	102.2	99.1	140.2	102.9
2nd quarter	103.9	105.4	97.9	108.6	94.5	87.4	103.5	109.1	103.8	99.8	151.2	103.4
3rd quarter	104.5	106.1	97.8	109.7	94.5	85.9	103.9	110.1	105.1	102.2	152.4	103.8
4th quarter	104.9	106.1	97.2	109.5	93.9	84.5	104.6	110.5	105.9	102.9	150.5	104.3
2012												
1st quarter	105.5	106.7	97.1	109.7	94.3	83.4	104.8	111.4	106.3	103.6	154.4	105.0
2nd quarter	105.8	106.4	96.8	110.8	94.2	82.0	103.9	111.1	106.5	104.7	149.3	105.1
3rd quarter	106.2	106.7	96.2	110.6	93.9	80.7	104.0	112.0	106.7	104.9	154.0	105.6
4th quarter	106.6	106.9	95.7	110.5	93.5	79.6	104.0	112.5	107.2	105.4	156.9	105.5

Table 4-4. Chain-Type Price Indexes for Personal Consumption Expenditures by Major Type of Product—*Continued*

(Index numbers, 2009 =1000.)

NIPA Table 2.3.4

| Year and quarter | Services | Household consumption expenditures for services | | | | | | | | Nonprofit institutions serving households (NPISHs) | | |
		Household services, total	Housing and utilities	Health care	Transportation services	Recreation services	Food services and accommodations	Financial services and insurance	Other services	Final consumption expenditures	Gross output	Less: receipts from sales of goods and services
1955	11.1	10.6	12.8	5.4	11.8	13.1	10.3	13.2	10.9	48.3	. . .	. . .
1956	11.4	10.8	13.0	5.6	12.2	13.5	10.4	13.6	11.3	50.5	. . .	. . .
1957	11.7	11.1	13.3	5.8	12.7	14.0	10.8	14.0	11.7	52.8	. . .	. . .
1958	12.0	11.4	13.5	6.1	13.1	14.5	11.1	14.3	12.0	54.2	. . .	. . .
1959	12.3	11.7	13.7	6.2	13.4	14.9	11.5	15.1	12.3	55.2	9.8	5.7
1960	12.6	12.0	14.0	6.7	13.7	15.4	11.8	15.7	12.7	51.4	10.1	6.1
1961	12.9	12.3	14.2	6.8	14.1	15.8	12.0	16.3	12.8	52.0	10.3	6.2
1962	13.1	12.5	14.3	7.0	14.4	16.2	12.3	16.9	13.0	52.7	10.5	6.4
1963	13.3	12.7	14.5	7.2	14.5	16.6	12.6	17.0	13.3	53.6	10.7	6.5
1964	13.6	12.9	14.6	7.4	14.7	17.0	12.8	17.7	13.6	53.8	11.0	6.8
1965	13.8	13.2	14.8	7.7	14.9	17.4	13.0	18.1	14.0	55.3	11.3	7.0
1966	14.2	13.5	15.0	8.0	15.2	17.8	13.5	19.2	14.4	57.3	11.7	7.2
1967	14.7	14.0	15.2	8.5	15.8	18.5	14.3	19.7	14.8	59.2	12.2	7.6
1968	15.3	14.6	15.6	9.0	16.5	19.4	15.0	21.1	15.5	61.4	12.9	8.0
1969	16.1	15.4	16.1	9.7	17.5	20.3	15.9	23.0	16.2	65.3	13.7	8.6
1970	17.0	16.2	16.8	10.4	18.9	21.2	17.1	24.2	17.0	68.1	14.6	9.2
1971	17.9	17.1	17.6	11.0	20.2	22.1	18.0	25.6	18.0	72.0	15.3	9.6
1972	18.7	17.8	18.3	11.4	21.0	22.7	18.7	27.2	19.0	74.9	16.1	10.1
1973	19.6	18.7	19.1	12.0	21.9	23.5	19.9	27.8	20.1	79.8	17.1	10.7
1974	21.3	20.2	20.2	13.1	23.8	25.1	22.2	30.1	22.2	91.3	19.1	11.9
1975	23.1	22.0	21.8	14.6	26.4	27.0	24.2	32.3	23.8	99.7	21.1	13.2
1976	24.7	23.5	23.3	16.0	28.4	28.3	25.8	33.6	25.3	104.9	22.7	14.3
1977	26.6	25.3	25.4	17.3	30.3	29.7	27.7	36.2	26.6	112.0	24.4	15.4
1978	28.6	27.3	27.2	18.8	32.3	31.5	30.1	41.0	28.0	119.4	26.3	16.6
1979	31.0	29.5	29.4	20.6	35.2	33.5	33.4	43.2	30.1	131.1	28.9	18.3
1980	34.2	32.6	32.5	23.1	40.9	36.1	36.6	46.5	32.8	143.3	32.3	20.6
1981	37.7	36.0	36.0	25.9	45.8	38.4	39.9	50.0	36.1	150.4	35.9	23.3
1982	40.6	38.9	39.4	28.8	48.4	40.5	42.2	52.9	39.0	142.5	38.7	26.1
1983	43.2	41.5	41.9	31.5	50.2	42.2	44.0	58.0	41.1	131.8	40.8	28.6
1984	45.4	43.8	44.0	33.8	52.2	44.1	46.0	61.7	43.2	126.1	42.7	30.8
1985	47.7	46.1	46.4	35.9	53.2	46.0	47.9	66.9	44.8	123.3	44.5	32.6
1986	49.6	48.1	48.6	38.0	53.8	47.7	49.9	67.9	47.2	119.3	46.0	34.5
1987	51.1	49.6	50.3	40.4	56.0	49.6	51.9	64.7	48.3	117.0	48.0	36.7
1988	53.5	52.1	52.3	43.6	58.7	51.5	54.2	67.7	50.3	115.6	50.9	39.6
1989	56.0	54.6	54.4	47.4	61.2	54.0	56.6	69.7	52.2	108.1	53.7	43.3
1990	58.5	57.3	56.8	51.5	63.6	57.0	59.2	70.7	54.3	99.0	56.2	47.2
1991	60.7	59.8	58.7	55.4	65.3	60.0	61.6	70.3	56.9	91.5	58.8	51.1
1992	62.8	62.1	60.3	59.3	67.2	61.8	62.9	72.6	59.4	83.2	61.0	55.0
1993	65.0	64.5	62.0	62.5	69.5	63.8	64.1	76.5	61.4	78.7	62.8	58.0
1994	66.8	66.3	63.6	65.0	70.4	65.2	65.2	77.9	63.7	78.6	64.6	60.2
1995	68.6	68.2	65.4	67.4	71.9	66.6	66.8	79.6	65.8	78.5	66.5	62.4
1996	70.5	70.0	67.3	69.0	72.8	68.8	68.6	82.4	67.7	79.9	68.3	64.3
1997	72.4	72.0	69.1	70.4	74.4	71.0	70.6	85.6	69.6	83.3	70.0	65.7
1998	73.9	73.3	70.8	71.7	75.8	72.8	72.5	85.7	71.0	88.9	72.1	67.0
1999	75.4	74.8	72.4	73.3	76.9	75.1	74.4	85.0	72.7	92.1	74.1	68.6
2000	77.5	76.8	74.9	75.4	79.2	78.0	76.5	85.9	74.1	97.2	77.0	70.9
2001	79.9	79.1	78.4	77.9	80.1	80.6	78.6	85.6	76.4	101.7	80.0	73.5
2002	82.0	81.2	80.6	79.9	80.5	82.9	80.5	87.7	79.4	102.2	82.3	76.2
2003	84.5	84.0	83.2	82.9	82.2	85.5	82.2	91.5	82.3	99.6	84.7	80.1
2004	87.1	86.6	85.5	86.0	83.4	87.7	85.0	95.0	85.0	98.1	87.3	83.8
2005	89.9	89.5	88.6	88.7	86.5	90.2	87.7	97.9	88.2	100.2	90.3	87.1
2006	93.0	92.6	92.3	91.4	90.0	93.2	90.6	100.6	91.1	101.1	93.3	90.7
2007	96.0	95.7	95.5	94.8	92.1	95.9	94.2	103.5	93.7	102.4	96.2	94.0
2008	98.9	98.8	98.9	97.4	97.0	98.8	97.8	104.6	97.5	103.1	98.6	97.1
2009	100.0	100.0	100.0	100.0	100.0	100.0	100.0	100.0	100.0	100.0	100.0	100.0
2010	101.7	101.8	100.2	102.5	102.0	101.1	101.3	104.0	102.4	98.9	101.8	102.8
2011	103.5	103.6	101.7	104.4	104.7	102.8	103.9	106.0	104.3	99.6	103.8	105.2
2012	105.7	106.0	103.6	106.3	106.8	105.6	106.8	110.1	106.4	98.9	105.5	107.7
2010												
1st quarter	101.0	101.1	100.1	101.8	101.5	100.4	100.7	102.6	101.5	98.8	101.2	102.0
2nd quarter	101.5	101.7	100.2	102.3	101.9	101.0	101.2	103.9	102.3	98.4	101.6	102.7
3rd quarter	101.9	102.0	100.3	102.8	102.1	101.4	101.5	104.5	102.8	99.0	102.1	103.1
4th quarter	102.2	102.3	100.4	103.2	102.6	101.5	102.0	105.0	103.0	99.5	102.5	103.5
2011												
1st quarter	102.6	102.7	100.9	103.6	103.7	102.0	102.5	105.0	103.3	99.5	103.0	104.1
2nd quarter	103.2	103.3	101.4	104.2	104.4	102.7	103.6	105.4	104.0	100.2	103.7	104.9
3rd quarter	103.8	104.0	102.0	104.7	105.0	103.0	104.5	106.3	104.6	99.4	104.0	105.6
4th quarter	104.3	104.5	102.4	105.1	105.8	103.5	104.9	107.1	105.2	99.5	104.5	106.2
2012												
1st quarter	104.9	105.1	102.8	105.6	106.4	104.8	105.8	108.4	105.7	99.0	104.7	106.7
2nd quarter	105.5	105.7	103.3	106.0	106.7	105.3	106.7	109.3	106.5	99.0	105.3	107.4
3rd quarter	105.9	106.3	103.8	106.6	106.7	106.0	107.2	110.8	106.5	98.5	105.7	108.2
4th quarter	106.5	106.8	104.5	106.9	107.1	106.4	107.6	111.7	107.0	99.2	106.2	108.7

. . . = Not available.

Figure 4-2. Household Consumption Expenditures by Function, 1948 and 2011
1948   2011

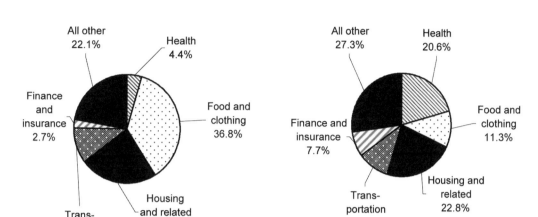

- Figure 4-2 compares the composition of household consumer spending (excluding the net spending of nonprofit institutions) in 1948 and 2011, the latest available data at the time *Business Statistics* went to press.

- Household spending on health in 2011 made up 20.6 percent of all household consumption spending—four and one/half times the percentage in 1948. It is important to recognize that household consumption spending, as presented in these data, includes (in health spending and in the total) medical care payments made by government and private insurance on behalf of individuals as well as out-of-pocket consumer payments. (Table 4-5)

- In 2011, a much smaller share was required for food and clothing than in 1948, as seen in Figure 4-2. The shares of housing-related spending and transportation were similar in the two years. The share of finance and insurance spending nearly tripled, and households also spent a larger share on the remaining category, here labeled "all other," which includes communication, recreation, education, food services, accommodations, and other miscellaneous goods and services. (Table 4-5)

Table 4-5. Household Consumption Expenditures by Function

(Billions of dollars.)   NIPA Table 2.5.5

Year	Household consumption expenditures, total	Food and beverages off-premises	Clothing, footwear, and related services	Housing, utilities, and fuels	Furnishings, household equipment, and maintenance	Health	Transportation	Communication	Recreation	Education	Food services and accommodations	Financial services and insurance	Other goods and services	Foreign travel and expenditures, net
1939	66.2	15.2	7.7	12.3	5.5	2.8	6.3	0.7	3.6	0.6	4.1	2.3	5.0	0.2
1940	70.2	15.9	8.1	12.8	6.0	3.0	7.0	0.7	3.9	0.6	4.4	2.4	5.3	0.1
1941	80.0	18.2	9.5	13.7	7.1	3.2	8.3	0.8	4.5	0.6	5.3	2.5	6.0	0.1
1942	87.7	21.6	11.8	14.8	7.4	3.6	5.4	1.0	4.9	0.7	6.9	2.6	6.8	0.2
1943	98.4	24.3	14.4	15.5	7.4	4.0	5.4	1.2	5.3	0.8	9.1	2.8	8.0	0.3
1944	107.0	26.0	15.7	16.2	8.0	4.5	5.7	1.3	5.8	0.9	10.9	3.0	8.5	0.6
1945	118.2	28.2	17.6	16.9	8.9	4.8	6.6	1.4	6.5	0.9	12.7	3.2	9.3	1.2
1946	142.3	34.9	19.7	18.8	12.7	5.9	12.1	1.6	9.0	1.0	12.7	3.8	10.3	-0.1
1947	159.9	40.2	20.4	21.2	15.5	6.6	15.4	1.7	9.8	1.2	12.5	4.2	11.1	0.0
1948	172.7	41.8	21.8	23.9	16.8	7.6	18.0	1.9	10.3	1.3	12.6	4.7	11.7	0.3
1949	176.1	40.4	21.1	25.6	16.3	7.9	21.2	2.1	10.6	1.4	12.4	4.9	11.8	0.6
1950	189.8	41.4	21.4	28.4	18.7	8.5	24.6	2.3	11.7	1.5	12.7	5.6	12.2	0.7
1951	205.9	46.0	23.1	31.6	19.7	9.3	24.2	2.6	12.3	1.6	15.0	6.3	13.3	0.9
1952	216.6	48.4	23.9	34.6	19.3	10.1	24.4	2.9	13.0	1.7	16.0	6.7	14.3	1.1
1953	230.0	49.3	24.2	37.9	20.0	11.0	28.0	3.2	13.8	1.8	16.5	7.8	15.0	1.5
1954	236.7	50.6	24.3	40.9	19.9	11.9	27.4	3.3	14.3	1.9	16.6	8.6	15.4	1.5
1955	255.3	52.0	25.4	43.8	22.3	12.8	33.4	3.6	15.4	2.1	17.0	9.6	16.3	1.6
1956	267.8	54.2	26.5	46.8	23.6	14.1	32.7	3.9	16.4	2.4	17.7	10.4	17.5	1.7
1957	282.7	57.1	26.8	50.0	23.9	15.5	35.7	4.3	16.8	2.6	18.5	11.1	18.8	1.7
1958	291.7	59.8	27.1	53.3	24.1	17.1	33.7	4.5	17.3	2.9	18.7	11.6	19.9	1.9
1959	312.6	61.6	28.6	56.9	25.6	18.8	38.8	4.8	18.8	3.1	19.7	12.5	21.4	2.0
1960	326.5	62.6	29.3	60.5	26.2	20.4	40.8	5.2	19.7	3.4	20.5	13.6	22.4	2.1
1961	336.7	63.7	29.9	64.0	26.8	21.8	39.3	5.6	20.5	3.6	21.0	14.8	23.7	2.0
1962	357.6	64.7	31.3	68.2	28.3	24.3	44.1	5.9	22.1	4.0	22.3	15.4	24.9	2.3
1963	376.7	65.9	32.1	72.2	29.8	26.4	47.8	6.4	23.9	4.3	23.3	15.9	26.2	2.5
1964	404.8	69.5	34.7	76.2	32.7	29.8	50.7	6.9	26.3	4.8	24.9	17.7	27.8	2.6
1965	436.6	74.4	36.5	81.0	34.7	32.0	56.5	7.5	28.9	5.5	27.2	19.4	30.2	2.9
1966	473.1	80.6	39.8	85.9	37.8	35.0	59.0	8.1	33.4	6.2	29.6	21.3	33.3	3.1
1967	499.4	82.6	41.7	91.1	39.7	38.4	61.0	8.9	35.8	6.9	31.0	22.8	35.8	3.8
1968	548.7	88.8	45.6	97.4	43.2	43.8	69.8	9.7	39.9	7.7	34.6	25.8	38.6	3.7
1969	595.0	95.4	48.8	105.5	45.4	50.0	75.9	10.7	43.7	8.7	37.5	28.5	41.0	4.0
1970	637.2	103.5	49.9	113.8	46.6	56.8	76.5	11.6	47.0	9.9	41.6	31.1	44.3	4.5
1971	689.3	107.1	53.4	124.5	48.8	63.4	88.7	12.8	50.1	10.9	43.8	34.1	47.0	4.8
1972	756.6	114.5	58.0	136.2	53.5	70.4	98.3	14.4	56.2	11.7	48.9	38.3	51.0	5.2
1973	837.4	126.7	63.7	149.7	59.9	78.7	108.6	16.1	63.0	13.0	54.8	41.5	56.9	4.7
1974	916.5	143.0	66.9	166.3	64.6	88.7	112.8	17.7	68.9	14.2	60.6	45.9	62.2	4.7
1975	1 015.7	156.6	71.4	184.8	67.8	102.7	124.4	20.0	77.1	15.9	68.8	54.0	67.8	4.4
1976	1 131.2	167.3	76.9	204.6	75.0	116.8	147.4	22.4	86.2	17.4	77.8	59.3	76.3	3.8
1977	1 256.0	179.8	84.3	228.7	84.0	131.6	168.1	24.3	94.9	18.8	85.7	67.8	83.8	4.3
1978	1 403.2	196.1	94.6	255.6	93.6	149.4	184.5	27.0	106.3	20.9	97.1	80.6	93.2	4.3
1979	1 563.4	218.4	101.9	287.5	104.3	169.9	207.1	29.4	118.9	22.9	110.9	87.6	100.4	4.1
1980	1 723.9	239.2	108.8	327.0	110.7	195.5	226.5	31.8	127.4	25.4	121.7	95.6	110.7	3.5
1981	1 903.2	255.3	119.1	367.5	118.3	228.9	250.7	36.0	141.6	28.3	133.9	102.0	121.2	0.4
1982	2 035.4	267.1	122.7	401.2	121.0	254.9	255.9	41.1	151.4	31.0	142.5	116.3	127.8	2.5
1983	2 245.7	277.0	132.9	434.5	132.3	287.1	284.9	44.8	169.3	34.3	153.6	145.9	143.4	5.4
1984	2 453.5	291.1	144.7	471.9	147.1	315.2	321.8	48.4	190.0	37.7	164.9	156.6	157.7	6.6
1985	2 667.3	303.0	154.3	514.0	156.0	345.3	357.4	53.1	207.2	41.2	174.3	180.5	173.3	7.7
1986	2 841.4	316.4	165.1	546.8	168.7	378.4	362.6	56.9	225.4	44.5	186.7	196.7	190.0	3.3
1987	3 038.4	324.3	176.4	582.8	176.9	419.9	376.6	60.0	247.0	48.8	204.4	207.1	208.2	6.1
1988	3 283.3	342.8	188.2	625.9	186.6	470.7	404.8	63.1	273.4	54.4	225.8	219.4	225.4	2.8
1989	3 522.8	365.4	201.4	667.3	197.5	519.0	428.3	67.3	295.7	60.6	242.6	235.7	245.7	-3.7
1990	3 755.8	391.2	207.0	709.1	200.6	583.7	442.9	70.1	314.7	66.0	262.7	253.2	262.3	-7.7
1991	3 895.8	403.0	210.4	747.8	199.1	638.4	418.3	73.9	326.3	70.6	273.4	282.0	268.0	-15.2
1992	4 144.5	404.5	223.0	783.3	209.4	700.4	451.3	81.1	346.8	76.4	286.3	311.8	290.1	-20.0
1993	4 389.0	413.5	231.0	826.9	221.9	741.7	485.3	85.8	378.4	81.1	298.6	341.0	304.5	-20.7
1994	4 648.4	432.1	239.7	879.2	238.6	779.9	528.2	93.3	414.0	86.4	308.7	349.0	316.9	-17.5
1995	4 880.1	443.7	244.1	926.8	251.7	826.0	554.1	98.9	449.8	92.3	316.7	364.7	332.7	-21.5
1996	5 157.9	461.9	252.7	975.5	263.7	868.3	598.9	108.3	481.5	99.6	327.4	393.6	350.8	-24.5
1997	5 458.4	474.8	262.0	1 023.1	277.3	919.9	641.8	120.1	509.5	107.1	344.6	431.3	368.4	-21.5
1998	5 787.5	486.5	273.0	1 076.8	296.8	979.7	669.2	130.6	546.0	115.2	363.0	469.6	394.8	-13.7
1999	6 197.4	513.6	287.1	1 137.4	319.7	1 033.3	730.5	144.7	593.6	123.9	381.6	514.2	431.6	-13.8
2000	6 665.0	537.5	297.3	1 214.5	342.5	1 109.6	798.4	162.1	639.9	134.3	410.1	570.0	462.3	-13.3
2001	6 962.6	559.7	294.3	1 303.2	351.1	1 209.4	814.1	171.3	655.7	143.6	421.2	562.8	483.5	-7.4
2002	7 234.2	569.6	295.2	1 349.1	363.5	1 317.1	818.4	177.5	680.9	149.5	438.2	576.2	504.3	-5.1
2003	7 592.9	587.5	301.7	1 410.6	374.7	1 405.7	857.0	182.9	715.5	159.9	464.2	602.5	531.2	-0.5
2004	8 061.2	613.0	314.6	1 480.2	397.0	1 507.5	909.1	189.1	770.6	169.8	499.1	651.7	558.9	0.6
2005	8 591.8	644.5	330.2	1 602.6	418.7	1 605.1	978.0	193.8	817.7	181.9	533.9	698.4	587.0	0.0
2006	9 061.0	674.2	344.2	1 706.8	436.5	1 694.5	1 007.0	206.8	872.0	194.6	570.2	732.6	617.9	3.8
2007	9 518.4	711.2	352.7	1 777.9	442.5	1 798.4	1 049.9	220.9	918.7	208.6	600.5	790.3	649.9	-3.2
2008	9 750.9	746.4	348.0	1 857.0	432.9	1 884.9	1 029.7	230.7	923.5	222.2	618.3	807.0	666.6	-16.3
2009	9 566.4	742.3	333.2	1 892.2	402.7	1 966.7	879.2	229.0	881.0	233.8	607.2	741.8	668.9	-11.6
2010	9 936.1	760.6	347.9	1 914.2	410.2	2 044.1	960.5	237.0	907.0	249.9	631.0	796.3	693.7	-16.3
2011	10 437.1	810.2	366.1	1 954.5	429.6	2 155.0	1 079.4	246.7	952.0	265.9	670.9	807.1	723.6	-23.8

Table 4-6. Personal Saving: Households and Nonprofit Institutions Serving Households

(Billions of dollars, except as noted.)   **NIPA Table 2.9**

Year	Personal saving as a percentage of disposable personal income (percent)	Households				Nonprofit Institutions Serving Households (NPISHs)					
		Disposable income	Less: outlays	Equals: household saving		Income	Less: gross output	Plus: receipts from sales	Less: transfer payments	Saving	
				Billions of dollars	Percent of income					Billions of dollars	Percent of income and receipts from sales
1992	7.3	4 710.6	4 378.8	331.8	7.0	131.7	400.8	308.5	23.2	16.3	3.7
1993	5.8	4 896.4	4 625.5	270.9	5.5	135.3	423.3	328.7	26.2	14.5	3.1
1994	5.2	5 157.1	4 898.3	258.8	5.0	142.9	444.7	342.3	28.6	11.9	2.5
1995	5.2	5 423.1	5 152.3	270.8	5.0	151.3	463.4	356.2	28.7	15.5	3.0
1996	4.9	5 726.3	5 466.8	259.5	4.5	170.9	488.8	373.1	33.5	21.6	4.0
1997	4.6	6 039.8	5 799.2	240.6	4.0	188.8	509.3	397.0	36.7	39.9	6.8
1998	5.3	6 473.4	6 154.0	319.4	4.9	196.7	550.5	419.6	43.7	22.1	3.6
1999	3.1	6 776.2	6 596.0	180.1	2.7	221.8	585.3	439.9	48.8	27.6	4.2
2000	2.9	7 298.6	7 117.2	181.4	2.5	248.7	632.0	466.6	51.7	31.7	4.4
2001	2.7	7 630.3	7 421.5	208.9	2.7	241.0	688.0	501.8	58.7	-4.0	-0.5
2002	3.5	7 999.9	7 691.6	308.3	3.9	240.8	749.7	544.7	61.9	-26.1	-3.3
2003	3.5	8 370.9	8 047.3	323.5	3.9	243.0	785.9	574.7	65.6	-33.9	-4.1
2004	3.6	8 882.0	8 555.3	326.7	3.7	270.6	827.6	618.2	69.8	-8.5	-1.0
2005	1.5	9 262.2	9 125.4	136.9	1.5	294.7	874.3	662.6	76.7	6.3	0.7
2006	2.6	9 896.5	9 630.1	266.5	2.7	310.2	935.2	695.2	80.1	-9.8	-1.0
2007	2.4	10 404.5	10 130.3	274.2	2.6	315.0	989.4	735.5	86.5	-25.5	-2.4
2008	5.4	11 013.1	10 359.4	653.8	5.9	316.2	1 046.5	761.9	93.0	-61.4	-5.7
2009	4.7	10 711.2	10 129.3	581.9	5.4	302.1	1 078.7	799.2	96.4	-73.8	-6.7
2010	5.1	11 114.6	10 488.7	625.9	5.6	326.2	1 113.4	833.7	105.7	-59.2	-5.1
2011	4.2	11 532.7	10 984.5	548.2	4.8	342.4	1 164.5	872.5	109.3	-58.9	-4.8

NOTES AND DEFINITIONS, CHAPTER 4

SOURCE: U.S. DEPARTMENT OF COMMERCE, BUREAU OF ECONOMIC ANALYSIS (BEA)

All personal income and personal consumption expenditure series are from the national income and product accounts (NIPAs). All quarterly series are shown at seasonally adjusted annual rates. Current and constant dollar values are in billions of dollars. Indexes of price and quantity are based on the average for the year 2009, which equals 100.

The 2013 NIPA revision introduced in this volume includes a major definitional revision: accrual accounting for defined benefit pension programs. This caused upward revisions to personal income receipts on assets for 1929–2012 and upward revisions to the supplements component of employee compensation for 1929–1975, 1989–2002, and 2004–2011.

Tables 4-1 through 4-4 cover all income and spending by the personal sector, which includes nonprofit institutions serving households (NPISHs). In a new feature introduced in the 2009 comprehensive revision of the NIPAs, Tables 4-2, 4-3, and 4-4 show the services component of personal consumption expenditures broken down into separate aggregates for "household consumption expenditures for services" and "final consumption expenditures" by NPISHs. The last two tables give further details of the separate accounts for households and NPISHs that are only available annually, and do not reflect the 2013 revision. Table 4-5 shows a more detailed functional breakdown of household consumption expenditures, not including NPISHs. Table 4-6 shows income, spending, and saving data estimated separately for households and NPISHs.

In several cases, the notes and definitions below will refer to *imputations* or *imputed values*. See the notes and definitions to Chapter 1 for an explanation of imputation and the role it plays in national and personal income measurement.

Tables 4-1 through 4-4: Sources and Disposition of Personal Income; Personal Consumption Expenditures by Major Type of Product

Definitions

Personal income is the income received by persons residing in the United States from participation in production, from government and business transfer payments, and from government interest, which is treated similarly to a transfer payment rather than as income from participation in production. *Persons* denotes the total for individuals, *nonprofit institutions that primarily serve households (NPISHs)*, private noninsured welfare funds, and private trust funds. Personal income, outlays, and saving excluding NPISHs are referred to as *household* income, outlays, and saving. All proprietors' income is treated as received by individuals. Life insurance carriers and private noninsured pension funds are not counted as persons, but their saving is credited to persons.

Income from the sale of illegal goods and services is excluded by definition from national and personal income, and the value of purchases of illegal goods and services is not included in personal consumption expenditures.

Personal income is the sum of compensation received by employees, proprietors' income with inventory valuation and capital consumption adjustments (IVA and CCAdj), rental income of persons with capital consumption adjustment, personal receipts on assets, and personal current transfer receipts, less contributions for social insurance.

Personal income differs from national income in that it includes current transfer payments and interest received by persons, regardless of source, while it excludes the following national income components: employee and employer contributions for social insurance; business transfer payments, interest payments, and other payments on assets other than to persons; taxes on production and imports less subsidies; the current surplus of government enterprises; and undistributed corporate profits with IVA and CCAdj. The relationships of GDP, gross and net national product, national income, and personal income are displayed in Table 1-11.

Compensation of employees is the sum of wages and salaries and supplements to wages and salaries, as defined in the *national* income account (see Table 1-13 and the notes and definitions to Chapter 1).

As in *national* income, the *compensation of employees* component of personal income refers to compensation received by residents of the United States, including compensation from the rest of the world, but excludes compensation from domestic industries to workers residing in the rest of the world.

Wages and salaries consists of the monetary remuneration of employees, including wages and salaries as conventionally defined; the compensation of corporate officers; corporate directors' fees paid to directors who are also employees of the corporation; the value of employee exercise of "nonqualified stock options"; commissions, tips, and bonuses; voluntary employee contributions to certain deferred-compensation plans, such as 401(k) plans; and receipts in kind that represent income. This category also now includes judicial fees to jurors and witnesses, compensation of prison inmates, and marriage fees to justices of the peace, which before the latest comprehensive revision were classified as "other labor income". As of the 2013 revision, wages and salaries are now measured on an accrual basis, that is to say when earned rather than when paid, consistent with the treatment in the gross domestic income and national income tables.

Supplements to wages and salaries consists of employer contributions to employee pension and insurance funds and to government social insurance funds. In a substantial change introduced in the 2013 revision, defined benefit pension plan transactions are now recorded on an accrual basis instead of a cash transactions basis: employees are now credited with defined pension benefits, based on actuarial estimates of pension costs, at the time they earn them. (This was already the case with defined contribution plans.)

The following two categories, *proprietors' income* and *rental income,* are both measured net of depreciation of the capital (structures and equipment) involved. BEA calculates normal depreciation, based on the estimated life of the capital, and subtracts it from the estimated value of receipts to yield net income.

Proprietors' income with inventory valuation and capital consumption adjustments is the current-production income (including income-in-kind) of sole proprietors and partnerships and of tax-exempt cooperatives. The imputed net rental income of owner-occupants of farm dwellings is included. Dividends and monetary interest received by proprietors of nonfinancial business and rental incomes received by persons not primarily engaged in the real estate business are excluded. These incomes are included in personal income receipts on assets and rental income of persons, respectively. Fees paid to outside directors of corporations are included. The two valuation adjustments are designed to obtain income measures that exclude any element of capital gains: inventory withdrawals are valued at replacement cost, rather than historical cost, and charges for depreciation are on an economically consistent accounting basis and are valued at replacement cost.

Rental income of persons with capital consumption adjustment consists of the net current-production income of persons from the rental of real property (other than the incomes of persons primarily engaged in the real estate business), the imputed net rental income of owner-occupants of nonfarm dwellings, and the royalties received by persons from patents, copyrights, and rights to natural resources. The capital consumption adjustment converts charges for depreciation to an economically consistent accounting basis valued at replacement cost. Rental income is net of interest and other expenses, and hence is affected by changing

indebtedness and interest payments on owner-occupied and other housing.

Personal income receipts on assets consists of personal interest income and personal dividend income.

Personal interest income is the interest income (monetary and imputed) of persons from all sources, including interest paid by government to government employee retirement plans as well as government interest paid directly to persons.

Personal dividend income is the dividend income of persons from all sources, excluding capital gains distributions. It equals net dividends paid by corporations (dividends paid by corporations minus dividends received by corporations) less a small amount of corporate dividends received by general government. Dividends received by government employee retirement systems are included in personal dividend income.

Personal current transfer receipts is income payments to persons for which no current services are performed. It consists of government social benefits to persons and net receipts from business.

Government social benefits to persons consists of benefits from the following categories of programs:

• *Social Security and Medicare*, consisting of federal old-age, survivors, disability, and health insurance;

• *Medicaid,* the federal-state means-tested program covering medical expenses for lower-income children and adults as well as nursing care expenses;

• *Unemployment insurance*;

• *Veterans' benefits;*

• *Other government benefits to persons*, which includes pension benefit guaranty; workers' compensation; military medical insurance; temporary disability insurance; food stamps; Black Lung benefits; supplemental security income; family assistance, which consists of aid to families with dependent children and (beginning in 1996) assistance programs operating under the Personal Responsibility and Work Opportunity Reconciliation Act of 1996; educational assistance; and the earned income credit. Government payments to nonprofit institutions, other than for work under research and development contracts, also are included. Payments from government employee retirement plans are not included.

Note that the value of Medicare and Medicaid spending, though in practice it is usually paid directly from the government to the health care provider, is treated as if it were cash income to the consumer which is then expended in personal consumption expenditures; this value is not treated in the national accounts as a government purchase of medical services but as a government benefit paid to persons, which then finances personal consumption spending.

Contributions for government social insurance, domestic, which is subtracted to arrive at personal income, includes payments by U.S. employers, employees, self-employed, and other individuals who participate in the following programs: old-age, survivors, and disability insurance (Social Security); hospital insurance and supplementary medical insurance (Medicare); unemployment insurance; railroad retirement; veterans' life insurance; and temporary disability insurance. Contributions to government employee retirement plans are not included in this item.

In the 2009 comprehensive revision, most transactions between the U.S. government and economic agents in Guam, the U.S. Virgin Islands, American Samoa, Puerto Rico, and the Northern Mariana Islands are treated as government transactions with the rest of the world. Since the NIPAs only cover the 50 states and the District of Columbia, the *domestic* contributions to government social insurance funds are the only ones that need to be subtracted from NIPA payroll data to calculate personal income. The social insurance receipts of governments, shown in Chapter 6, will be somewhat larger than this personal income entry because they will include contributions from residents of those territories and commonwealths.

Personal current taxes is tax payments (net of refunds) by persons residing in the United States that are not chargeable to business expenses, including taxes on income, on realized net capital gains, and on personal property. As of the 1999 revisions, estate and gift taxes are classified as capital transfers and are not included in personal current taxes.

Disposable personal income is personal income minus personal current taxes. It is the income from current production that is available to persons for spending or saving. However, it is not the cash flow available, since it excludes realized capital gains. Disposable personal income in chained (2009) dollars represents the inflation-adjusted value of disposable personal income, using the implicit price deflator for personal consumption expenditures.

Personal income excluding current transfer receipts, also shown in chained (2009) dollars using the implicit price deflator for personal consumption expenditures, is an important business cycle indicator, to which particular attention is paid because it is calculated monthly as well as quarterly and annually, and thus can help establish monthly cycle turning point dates. As a pre-income-tax measure which excludes transfer payments, it is more directly related to the workings of the economy than alternative monthly income indicators such as total or disposable personal income.

Personal outlays is the sum of *personal consumption expenditures* (defined below), *personal interest payments,* and *personal current transfer payments.*

Personal interest payments is nonmortgage interest paid by households. As noted above in the definition of rental income, mortgage interest has been subtracted from gross rental or imputed rental receipts of persons to yield a net rental income estimate; hence, it is not included as an interest outlay in this category.

Personal current transfer payments to government includes donations, fees, and fines paid to federal, state, and local governments.

Personal current transfer payments to the rest of the world (net) is personal remittances in cash and in kind to the rest of the world less such remittances from the rest of the world.

Personal saving is derived by subtracting personal outlays from disposable personal income. It is the current net saving of individuals (including proprietors), nonprofit institutions that primarily serve individuals, life insurance carriers, retirement funds (including those of government employees), private noninsured welfare funds, and private trust funds. Conceptually, personal saving may also be viewed as the sum of the net acquisition of financial assets and the change in physical assets less the sum of net borrowing and consumption of fixed capital. In either case, it is defined to exclude both realized and unrealized capital gains.

Note that in the context of national income accounting, the term just defined is *saving,* not "savings." *Saving* refers to a flow of income during a particular time span (such as a year or a quarter) that is not consumed. It is therefore available to finance a commensurate flow of investment during that time span. Strictly defined, "savings" denotes an accumulated stock of monetary funds—possibly the cumulative effects of successive periods of *saving*—available to the owner in asset form, such as in a bank savings account.

Personal consumption expenditures (PCE) is goods and services purchased by persons residing in the United States. Persons are defined as individuals and nonprofit institutions that primarily serve individuals. PCE mostly consists of purchases of new goods and services by individuals from business, including purchases financed by insurance (such as both private and government medical insurance). In addition, PCE includes purchases of new goods and services by nonprofit institutions, net purchases of used goods by individuals and nonprofit institutions, and purchases abroad of goods and services by U.S. residents traveling or working in foreign countries. PCE also includes purchases for certain goods and services provided by the government, primarily tuition payments for higher education, charges for medical care, and charges for water and sanitary services. Finally, PCE includes imputed purchases that keep PCE invariant to changes in the way that certain activities are carried out. For example, to take account of the value of the services provided by owner-occupied housing, PCE includes an imputation equal to what (estimated) rent homeowners would pay if they rented their houses from themselves. (See the discussion of imputation in the notes and definitions to Chapter 1.) Actual purchases of residential structures by individuals are classified as gross private domestic investment.

In the 2009 comprehensive revision, the classification system used for breakdowns of PCE was revised, and new calculations were introduced separating the consumption spending of the household sector proper from that of nonprofit institutions serving households.

Goods is the sum of *Durable* and *Nondurable goods.*

The PCE category *Durable goods* is subdivided into *Motor vehicles and parts, Furnishings and household equipment* (which includes appliances), *Recreational goods and vehicles* (which includes video, audio, photographic, and information processing equipment and media), and *Other durable goods.*

Nondurable goods encompasses *Food and beverages off-premises, Clothing and footwear, Gasoline and other energy goods,* and *Other nondurable goods.* This food and beverages category no longer includes meals and beverages purchased for consumption on the premises, which are now included in services, since they have a high service component and since their prices are much more stable than those of off-premises food and beverages.

Services, total is subdivided into *Household services* and *Final consumption expenditures of nonprofit institutions serving households (NPISHs).* The latter is the difference between the *Gross output* of NPISHs and the amounts that they receive from sales of goods and services to households—for example, payments for services of a nonprofit hospital. Such sales of goods and services appear in the appropriate category of household expenditures—for example, *Health* in the case of the hospital services.

The components of *Household services* are *Housing and utilities, Health care, Transportation services, Recreation services, Food services and accommodations* (which includes meals and beverages purchased for consumption on premises, as well as payments for hotels and similar accommodations), *Financial services and insurance,* and *Other services.*

These are the categories used in the quarterly data presented in Tables 4-2, 4-3, and 4-4. This classification system is not particularly helpful with respect to the objective of spending. For example, the *Health care* component of services does not include drugs and medicines, which are included instead in nondurable goods. For a more precise classification of consumption spending by objective, see Table 4-5, Household Consumption Expenditures by Function, described in more detail below. This classification by type of expenditure is only available on an annual basis, and later than the principal quarterly NIPA data.

Data availability

Monthly data on personal income and spending are made available in a BEA press release, usually distributed the first business day following the monthly release of the latest quarterly national income and product account (NIPA) estimates. Monthly and quarterly data are subsequently published each month in the BEA's Survey of Current Business. Current and historical data are available on the BEA Web site at http://www.bea.gov, and may also be obtained from the STAT-USA subscription Web site at http://www.stat-usa.gov.

References

References can be found in the notes and definitions to Chapter 1. A discussion of monthly estimates of personal income and its disposition appears in the November 1979 edition of the *Survey of Current Business.* Additional and more recent information can be found in the articles listed in the notes and definitions for Chapter 1.

Table 4-5: Household Consumption Expenditures by Function

SOURCE: BUREAU OF ECONOMIC ANALYSIS (BEA)

In this table, also derived from the NIPAs, annual estimates of the current-dollar value of PCE by households—excluding the "final" consumption expenditures of nonprofit institutions serving households (NPISHs); see definition above—are presented by function.

Definitions

Food and beverages includes food and beverages (including alcoholic beverages) purchased for home consumption and food produced and consumed on farms.

Clothing, footwear, and related services includes purchases, rental, cleaning, and repair of clothing and footwear.

Housing, utilities, and fuels includes rents paid for rental housing, imputed rent of owner-occupied dwellings, and purchase of fuels and utility services.

Furnishings, household equipment, and routine household maintenance includes furniture, floor coverings, household textiles, appliances, tableware etc., tools, and other supplies and services.

Health includes drugs, other medical products and equipment, and outpatient, hospital, and nursing home services.

Transportation includes the purchase and operation of motor vehicles and public transportation services.

Communication includes telephone equipment, postal and delivery services, telecommunication services, and Internet access.

Recreation includes video and audio equipment, computers, and related services; sports vehicles and other sports goods and services; memberships and admissions; magazines, newspapers, books, and stationery; pets and related goods and services; photo goods and services; tour services; and legal gambling. (As noted earlier, purchases of goods and services that are illegal and the incomes from such purchases are outside the scope of the national income and product accounts.)

Education includes educational services and books.

Food services and accommodations includes meals and beverages purchased for consumption on the premises, food furnished to employees, and hotel and other accommodations including housing at schools.

Financial services and insurance consists of financial services and life, household, medical care, motor vehicle, and other insurance.

Other goods and services includes personal goods (such as cosmetics, jewelry, and luggage) and services, social services and religious activities, professional and other services, and tobacco.

Foreign travel and expenditures, net consists of foreign travel spending and other expenditures abroad by U.S. residents minus expenditures in the United States by nonresidents. A negative figure indicates that foreigners spent more here than U.S. residents spent abroad. Positive values for this foreign travel category, indicating that U.S. residents spent more abroad than foreigners spent here, appear in the 1980s when the dollar was strong against other major currencies. (The

international value of the dollar is shown in Table 13-8.) Negative values in subsequent years have resulted in part from the weakening of the dollar, which discouraged U.S. residents' travel abroad and encouraged tourism by foreigners in the United States. The negative sign does not indicate a drain on GDP—these effects of a weaker dollar are in fact positive for GDP—but rather reflects the fact that the goods and services purchased by foreigners in the United States must be subtracted from the total consumer purchases recorded elsewhere in this table in order to be added to other exports and classified in the category of exports rather than in the consumption spending of U.S. residents.

Data availability and revisions

Data are updated once a year, after the general midyear revision of the NIPAs, and are available on the BEA Web site at http://www.bea.gov.

Table 4-6: Personal Saving: Households and Nonprofit Institutions Serving Households

SOURCE: BUREAU OF ECONOMIC ANALYSIS (BEA)

As noted above, the "personal" sector includes not only households but also "nonprofit institutions serving households" (NPISHs). This category comprises all nonprofit institutions except those that are considered to be serving government and business, such as chambers of commerce and trade associations. Those institutions are included in the business sector instead.

For annual (not quarterly) data beginning with 1992, BEA now compiles and makes available tables showing personal income and its disposition for households and NPISHs separately. Each major type of income and expenditure is estimated separately for the two groups. Household receipts from NPISHs, purchases from NPISHs, and contributions to NPISHs are identified separately instead of being netted out as they are in the quarterly accounts. Selected aggregates for households and NPISHs are shown in Table 4-6.

Data availability and references

These data and the data on income and outlays for the household and nonprofit sectors on which they are based become available about two months after the release of the midyear revision of the NIPAs. They are published in Table 2.9 in the NIPA tables on the BEA Web site at http://www.bea.gov. An article from the April 2003 *Survey*, "Income and Outlays of Households and of Nonprofit

Institutions Serving Households," can also be found on the BEA Web site.

CHAPTER 5: SAVING AND INVESTMENT

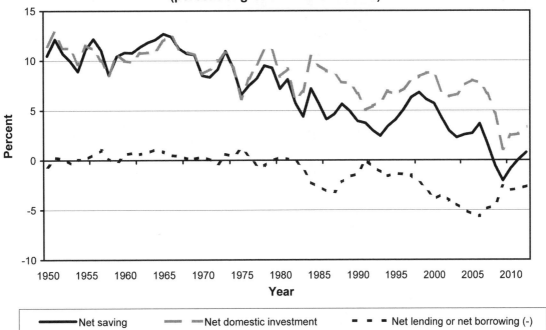

Figure 5-1. National Saving, Investment, and Borrowing, 1950–2012
(percent of gross national income)

- In the 2013 revision of the National Income and Product Accounts, the inclusion of new categories of investment tended to increase measured gross saving and investment. However, they also increased estimated capital consumption allowances, which are subtracted in arriving at net saving and investment. The revised paths of national net saving, net investment, and borrowing were little different from those previously depicted.

- Net national saving—the middle line in Figure 5-1—averaged 4.9 percent of gross national income (GNI) in the years 1984 through 2000, which was already lower than the rates seen in the 1950s and 1960s. Net saving is gross saving by U.S. persons, businesses, and governments, less the consumption of fixed capital—that is, saving available for investment over and above the replacement of the existing capital stock.

- In the years 2001–2007 the national saving rate fell even more, averaging 2.9 percent. Record net borrowing from the rest of the world was required to finance net investment that far exceeded domestic net saving.

- In the recession that began at the end of 2007, national saving fell into negative territory for the first time since the depression years 1931 through 1934. Government deficits soared as the Great Recession cut deeply into tax revenues and called forth both automatic and discretionary anti-recession spending.

Table 5-1A. Saving and Investment: Recent Data

(Billions of dollars, except as noted; quarterly data are at seasonally adjusted annual rates.)

NIPA Tables 1.7.5, 5.1

Year and quarter	Gross saving Total	Net saving Total	Net saving Private Total	Net saving Private Personal saving	Net saving Private Domestic corporate business	Net saving Government Federal	Net saving Government State and local	Consumption of fixed capital Total	Consumption of fixed capital Private Total	Consumption of fixed capital Private Domestic business	Consumption of fixed capital Private Households and institutions	Consumption of fixed capital Government Federal	Consumption of fixed capital Government State and local
1955	96.4	47.5	45.9	28.2	17.6	-0.6	2.2	48.9	35.0	28.9	6.1	10.7	3.2
1956	109.6	55.4	51.1	34.7	16.4	1.4	3.0	54.1	38.8	32.2	6.6	11.7	3.6
1957	111.8	52.9	52.9	36.9	16.0	-2.6	2.6	58.9	42.3	35.2	7.1	12.7	3.9
1958	103.8	41.3	52.2	38.9	13.3	-12.0	1.1	62.4	44.9	37.5	7.4	13.4	4.1
1959	120.1	54.7	56.4	37.1	19.2	-3.9	2.2	65.4	46.8	39.0	7.8	14.3	4.4
1960	127.0	59.1	56.4	37.8	18.5	0.2	2.6	67.9	48.2	40.0	8.2	15.1	4.5
1961	131.7	61.1	63.5	44.4	19.2	-4.7	2.2	70.6	49.8	41.3	8.5	16.0	4.8
1962	143.5	69.4	71.3	46.4	24.9	-5.3	3.4	74.1	51.8	42.9	8.8	17.1	5.2
1963	154.2	76.2	74.6	46.7	27.9	-2.1	3.7	78.0	54.2	44.9	9.3	18.3	5.5
1964	166.0	83.6	86.2	54.8	31.4	-6.9	4.3	82.4	57.3	47.4	9.9	19.2	5.9
1965	182.9	94.9	96.3	58.3	38.0	-5.5	4.1	88.0	61.6	50.9	10.7	20.0	6.4
1966	196.4	101.1	102.9	61.4	41.6	-7.0	5.2	95.3	67.2	55.6	11.5	21.0	7.1
1967	200.4	96.9	111.7	72.2	39.5	-19.5	4.7	103.5	73.3	60.9	12.4	22.4	7.8
1968	214.5	101.2	110.7	72.1	38.6	-13.7	4.3	113.3	80.6	67.0	13.6	24.1	8.6
1969	233.1	108.2	109.2	75.0	34.2	-5.1	4.1	124.9	89.4	74.2	15.2	25.8	9.7
1970	228.2	91.4	123.2	96.1	27.2	-34.8	3.0	136.8	98.3	81.8	16.5	27.6	10.9
1971	246.2	97.3	147.5	110.1	37.5	-50.8	0.6	148.9	107.6	89.4	18.2	29.0	12.2
1972	277.7	116.8	157.2	109.2	48.0	-48.9	8.4	160.9	117.5	97.2	20.3	30.1	13.3
1973	335.3	157.2	185.3	131.8	53.5	-37.7	9.6	178.1	131.5	108.2	23.3	31.7	14.9
1974	349.3	143.1	181.4	141.7	39.7	-40.6	2.3	206.2	153.2	126.1	27.0	34.7	18.3
1975	348.2	110.7	213.3	159.0	54.3	-97.0	-5.6	237.5	178.8	147.9	30.9	37.8	21.0
1976	399.5	140.3	217.3	147.3	70.0	-79.9	2.8	259.2	196.5	162.2	34.3	40.6	22.1
1977	459.6	171.3	234.7	148.2	86.6	-71.9	8.4	288.3	221.1	181.5	39.6	43.7	23.5
1978	548.2	223.1	269.5	166.6	102.9	-59.8	13.4	325.1	252.1	205.5	46.6	47.5	25.5
1979	613.8	242.7	279.0	177.5	101.4	-44.5	8.2	371.1	290.7	236.4	54.4	51.8	28.6
1980	630.6	204.6	285.5	213.2	72.3	-86.3	5.4	426.0	335.0	272.8	62.2	57.9	33.1
1981	745.2	260.2	341.9	252.5	89.4	-85.8	4.1	485.0	381.9	313.5	68.5	65.3	37.8
1982	727.9	193.6	363.3	277.7	85.6	-164.6	-5.1	534.3	420.4	347.5	72.9	72.7	41.3
1983	719.5	158.9	362.7	247.0	115.7	-205.0	1.3	560.5	438.8	362.8	76.0	79.0	42.8
1984	884.5	290.2	461.6	312.1	149.5	-192.3	20.9	594.3	463.5	382.7	80.9	86.4	44.4
1985	884.0	247.3	422.7	265.1	157.5	-195.6	20.3	636.7	496.4	410.3	86.2	93.3	46.9
1986	867.8	185.6	377.9	269.4	108.5	-212.7	20.4	682.2	531.6	438.1	93.4	100.3	50.3
1987	952.2	224.2	375.3	252.1	123.2	-163.2	12.1	728.0	566.3	464.5	101.8	107.5	54.1
1988	1 080.1	297.7	438.1	294.7	143.3	-157.3	17.0	782.4	608.3	498.4	109.9	116.3	57.8
1989	1 113.6	277.5	426.7	316.5	110.2	-156.6	7.4	836.1	650.1	531.8	118.2	124.2	61.9
1990	1 117.6	230.7	438.1	335.4	102.7	-200.9	-6.5	886.8	689.0	563.9	125.1	131.1	66.7
1991	1 157.9	226.8	498.1	365.9	132.2	-246.2	-25.1	931.1	722.4	591.8	130.6	137.9	70.9
1992	1 152.7	192.9	563.1	426.0	137.1	-332.7	-37.5	959.7	744.2	607.9	136.3	141.4	74.1
1993	1 167.8	164.3	513.3	367.6	145.6	-311.8	-37.2	1 003.6	780.0	634.2	145.7	145.3	78.3
1994	1 299.1	243.6	524.2	331.4	192.8	-253.7	-27.0	1 055.6	824.3	669.0	155.3	148.3	82.9
1995	1 429.5	306.8	579.2	352.9	226.2	-240.8	-31.5	1 122.8	882.6	717.8	164.8	151.9	88.3
1996	1 581.3	405.3	596.3	345.2	251.1	-178.5	-12.5	1 176.0	931.0	758.4	172.7	152.4	92.6
1997	1 783.6	543.6	633.1	352.2	280.9	-91.2	1.7	1 240.0	990.1	807.9	182.1	153.0	96.9
1998	1 932.4	622.1	604.0	405.3	198.7	2.7	15.4	1 310.3	1 054.9	860.4	194.5	153.6	101.8
1999	1 993.2	592.3	516.5	293.0	223.5	66.5	9.2	1 400.9	1 135.9	925.0	210.9	156.8	108.1
2000	2 109.4	595.2	429.4	297.9	131.4	155.9	9.9	1 514.2	1 236.6	1 006.5	230.1	161.5	116.2
2001	2 064.1	460.1	511.4	331.2	180.2	14.0	-65.3	1 604.0	1 317.7	1 067.5	250.2	163.3	123.0
2002	1 988.7	326.7	718.5	403.9	314.7	-270.9	-120.9	1 662.1	1 368.0	1 101.4	266.6	165.0	129.0
2003	1 991.7	264.5	789.4	410.8	378.6	-403.5	-121.4	1 727.2	1 422.4	1 131.6	290.8	170.3	134.5
2004	2 149.9	318.2	826.4	413.2	413.2	-399.8	-108.4	1 831.7	1 509.3	1 185.9	323.4	178.6	143.8
2005	2 337.4	355.5	727.5	242.7	484.8	-305.4	-66.6	1 982.0	1 635.3	1 273.2	362.1	189.4	157.3
2006	2 652.6	516.5	784.0	336.9	447.1	-228.1	-39.4	2 136.0	1 765.0	1 368.8	396.2	200.7	170.3
2007	2 506.7	242.4	581.8	317.2	264.6	-266.7	-72.7	2 264.4	1 865.0	1 451.2	413.7	212.8	186.6
2008	2 281.9	-81.5	718.7	551.3	167.3	-635.1	-165.1	2 363.4	1 936.9	1 522.3	414.6	226.3	200.2
2009	2 071.7	-296.6	1 225.1	670.7	554.4	-1 249.8	-271.9	2 368.4	1 925.7	1 522.4	403.3	234.5	208.2
2010	2 255.0	-126.6	1 440.3	634.2	806.0	-1 329.5	-237.3	2 381.6	1 923.5	1 523.0	400.5	245.3	212.7
2011	2 461.4	8.8	1 470.2	668.2	801.9	-1 248.3	-213.1	2 452.6	1 974.4	1 571.6	402.9	256.5	221.7
2012	2 672.2	129.4	1 491.7	687.4	804.3	-1 109.7	-252.7	2 542.9	2 049.3	1 639.4	409.9	262.3	231.4
2010													
1st quarter	2 134.6	-235.2	1 377.4	588.9	788.6	-1 352.3	-260.3	2 369.8	1 919.7	1 517.4	402.3	240.2	210.0
2nd quarter	2 202.4	-172.5	1 430.4	664.0	766.4	-1 340.0	-262.9	2 374.9	1 918.9	1 519.4	399.5	244.1	211.9
3rd quarter	2 339.5	-43.0	1 498.7	655.2	843.5	-1 320.1	-221.6	2 382.5	1 921.9	1 522.7	399.3	246.9	213.6
4th quarter	2 343.5	-55.6	1 454.4	628.7	825.7	-1 305.7	-204.4	2 399.1	1 933.6	1 532.7	400.9	250.1	215.4
2011													
1st quarter	2 374.3	-43.6	1 411.7	717.9	693.7	-1 244.9	-210.3	2 417.9	1 947.3	1 545.8	401.5	253.2	217.4
2nd quarter	2 411.9	-31.5	1 470.5	679.1	791.4	-1 313.4	-188.6	2 443.4	1 967.1	1 564.7	402.5	256.1	220.2
3rd quarter	2 511.8	46.7	1 501.5	676.2	825.3	-1 231.7	-223.1	2 465.1	1 984.1	1 580.9	403.2	257.9	223.1
4th quarter	2 547.5	63.6	1 496.9	599.6	897.3	-1 203.0	-230.3	2 483.9	1 999.3	1 594.9	404.4	258.6	226.1
2012													
1st quarter	2 645.0	137.4	1 472.6	657.3	815.3	-1 094.0	-241.1	2 507.6	2 018.7	1 613.9	404.8	260.4	228.5
2nd quarter	2 624.6	90.9	1 493.0	663.9	829.1	-1 146.9	-255.2	2 533.7	2 041.0	1 633.7	407.2	261.9	230.8
3rd quarter	2 606.4	51.2	1 430.6	604.1	826.5	-1 119.3	-260.1	2 555.1	2 059.8	1 648.4	411.4	262.9	232.4
4th quarter	2 812.8	237.8	1 570.5	824.1	746.4	-1 078.5	-254.2	2 575.0	2 077.6	1 661.4	416.2	263.7	233.7

Table 5-1A. Saving and Investment: Recent Data—*Continued*

(Billions of dollars, except as noted; quarterly data are at seasonally adjusted annual rates.)

Year and quarter	Gross domestic investment, capital account transactions, and net lending, NIPAs				Capital account transactions, net	Net lending or net borrowing (-), NIPAs	Statistical discrepancy	Net domestic investment	Gross national income	Gross saving as a percent of gross national income	Net saving as a percent of gross national income
	Total	Gross domestic investment									
		Total	Private	Government							
1955	98.5	98.1	73.8	24.4	. . .	0.4	2.1	49.2	426.5	22.6	11.1
1956	107.5	104.8	77.7	27.1	. . .	2.7	-2.1	50.7	455.0	24.1	12.2
1957	111.5	106.7	76.5	30.2	. . .	4.7	-0.4	47.8	478.3	23.4	11.1
1958	104.4	103.6	70.9	32.6	. . .	0.8	0.6	41.1	484.1	21.4	8.5
1959	120.2	121.5	85.7	35.9	. . .	-1.3	0.1	56.1	525.1	22.9	10.4
1960	125.6	122.5	86.5	36.0	. . .	3.2	-1.4	54.6	547.8	23.2	10.8
1961	130.7	126.5	86.6	39.9	. . .	4.2	-1.0	55.9	567.8	23.2	10.8
1962	143.4	139.6	97.0	42.6	. . .	3.8	-0.1	65.5	609.3	23.5	11.4
1963	152.7	147.7	103.3	44.4	. . .	4.9	-1.5	69.7	644.6	23.9	11.8
1964	166.0	158.5	112.2	46.4	. . .	7.5	0.0	76.2	690.7	24.0	12.1
1965	183.7	177.5	129.6	47.9	. . .	6.2	0.8	89.5	748.2	24.4	12.7
1966	201.6	197.8	144.2	53.6	. . .	3.8	5.1	102.5	815.0	24.1	12.4
1967	203.8	200.4	142.7	57.7	. . .	3.5	3.4	96.8	863.7	23.2	11.2
1968	217.7	216.2	156.9	59.2	. . .	1.5	3.2	102.8	945.4	22.7	10.7
1969	234.7	233.1	173.6	59.5	0.0	1.6	1.6	108.2	1 024.4	22.8	10.6
1970	233.6	229.8	170.1	59.8	0.0	3.7	5.3	93.1	1 076.9	21.2	8.5
1971	255.6	255.3	196.8	58.5	0.0	0.3	9.5	106.5	1 165.9	21.1	8.3
1972	284.8	288.8	228.1	60.7	0.0	-4.1	7.1	127.9	1 283.9	21.6	9.1
1973	341.4	332.6	266.9	65.6	0.0	8.8	6.1	154.5	1 435.1	23.4	11.0
1974	356.7	350.7	274.5	76.2	0.0	5.9	7.4	144.5	1 556.9	22.4	9.2
1975	361.5	341.7	257.3	84.4	0.1	19.8	13.2	104.1	1 688.7	20.6	6.6
1976	420.0	412.9	323.2	89.6	0.1	7.0	20.5	153.7	1 874.0	21.3	7.5
1977	478.9	489.8	396.6	93.2	0.1	-11.0	19.3	201.4	2 087.0	22.0	8.2
1978	571.3	583.9	478.4	105.6	0.1	-12.7	23.2	258.9	2 355.0	23.3	9.5
1979	658.6	659.8	539.7	120.1	0.1	-1.3	44.8	288.6	2 619.3	23.4	9.3
1980	674.6	666.1	530.1	136.0	0.1	8.4	43.9	240.0	2 852.8	22.1	7.2
1981	781.9	778.6	631.2	147.3	0.1	3.2	36.7	293.5	3 207.2	23.2	8.1
1982	734.7	738.0	581.0	156.9	0.1	-3.4	6.8	203.7	3 374.7	21.6	5.7
1983	773.6	808.7	637.5	171.2	0.1	-35.2	54.2	248.1	3 621.1	19.9	4.4
1984	923.2	1 013.3	820.1	193.2	0.1	-90.2	38.7	418.9	4 038.3	21.9	7.2
1985	935.2	1 049.5	829.6	219.9	0.1	-114.5	51.2	412.9	4 320.8	20.5	5.7
1986	944.5	1 087.2	849.1	238.1	0.1	-142.8	76.7	405.1	4 530.4	19.2	4.1
1987	992.7	1 146.8	892.2	254.6	0.1	-154.2	40.5	418.9	4 847.2	19.6	4.6
1988	1 079.6	1 195.4	937.0	258.4	0.1	-115.9	-0.5	413.0	5 275.8	20.5	5.6
1989	1 177.8	1 270.1	999.7	270.4	0.3	-92.7	64.2	434.0	5 618.3	19.8	4.9
1990	1 208.9	1 283.8	993.5	290.4	7.4	-82.3	91.3	397.0	5 922.9	18.9	3.9
1991	1 246.3	1 238.4	944.3	294.1	5.3	2.6	88.4	307.3	6 117.3	18.9	3.7
1992	1 263.5	1 309.1	1 013.0	296.1	-1.3	-44.3	110.9	349.4	6 459.5	17.8	3.0
1993	1 320.2	1 398.7	1 106.8	291.9	0.9	-79.4	152.3	395.1	6 758.4	17.3	2.4
1994	1 435.9	1 550.7	1 256.5	294.2	1.3	-116.0	136.8	495.1	7 195.8	18.1	3.4
1995	1 520.1	1 625.2	1 317.5	307.7	0.4	-105.5	90.5	502.4	7 602.3	18.8	4.0
1996	1 637.9	1 752.0	1 432.1	320.0	0.2	-114.4	56.5	576.0	8 075.4	19.6	5.0
1997	1 795.8	1 925.1	1 595.6	329.5	0.5	-129.8	12.3	685.2	8 620.3	20.7	6.3
1998	1 872.2	2 076.7	1 735.3	341.4	0.2	-204.8	-60.2	766.5	9 167.6	21.1	6.8
1999	1 960.7	2 252.7	1 884.2	368.5	4.5	-296.4	-32.4	851.8	9 725.3	20.5	6.1
2000	2 014.9	2 424.0	2 033.8	390.3	0.3	-409.5	-94.5	909.8	10 421.3	20.2	5.7
2001	1 952.5	2 342.3	1 928.6	413.6	-12.9	-376.8	-111.6	738.3	10 788.6	19.1	4.3
2002	1 918.6	2 368.6	1 925.0	443.6	0.5	-450.4	-70.1	706.5	11 098.9	17.9	2.9
2003	1 979.7	2 493.2	2 027.9	465.3	2.1	-515.7	-12.1	766.0	11 592.3	17.2	2.3
2004	2 143.5	2 765.1	2 276.7	488.5	-2.8	-618.9	-6.5	933.4	12 373.6	17.4	2.6
2005	2 303.6	3 040.8	2 527.1	513.6	-12.9	-724.3	-33.8	1 058.8	13 222.7	17.7	2.7
2006	2 437.3	3 233.0	2 680.6	552.3	2.1	-797.8	-215.3	1 097.0	14 141.6	18.8	3.7
2007	2 526.9	3 236.0	2 643.7	592.2	-0.1	-709.0	20.2	971.6	14 586.6	17.2	1.7
2008	2 380.9	3 059.4	2 424.8	634.6	-5.4	-673.1	99.0	696.1	14 794.2	15.4	-0.6
2009	2 144.0	2 525.1	1 878.1	647.0	0.6	-381.7	72.2	156.8	14 492.9	14.3	-2.0
2010	2 298.1	2 752.6	2 100.8	651.8	0.7	-455.2	43.1	371.0	15 121.1	14.9	-0.8
2011	2 407.7	2 864.7	2 232.1	632.6	1.7	-458.6	-53.7	412.1	15 848.3	15.5	0.1
2012	2 655.2	3 094.2	2 475.2	619.0	-6.6	-432.4	-17.0	551.3	16 514.5	16.2	0.8
2010											
1st quarter	2 179.7	2 624.9	1 989.5	635.4	0.5	-445.8	45.1	255.1	14 830.9	14.4	-1.6
2nd quarter	2 287.8	2 748.0	2 092.7	655.3	0.6	-460.7	85.4	373.1	14 998.9	14.7	-1.2
3rd quarter	2 338.7	2 825.1	2 164.6	660.5	1.1	-487.5	-0.7	442.6	15 250.2	15.3	-0.3
4th quarter	2 386.2	2 812.5	2 156.5	656.0	0.5	-426.8	42.7	413.4	15 404.5	15.2	-0.4
2011											
1st quarter	2 290.9	2 754.4	2 120.4	633.9	0.6	-464.0	-83.3	336.5	15 574.6	15.2	-0.3
2nd quarter	2 360.3	2 833.1	2 199.9	633.2	3.8	-476.6	-51.7	389.7	15 763.8	15.3	-0.2
3rd quarter	2 428.7	2 853.8	2 222.2	631.6	1.6	-426.7	-83.0	388.7	15 967.1	15.7	0.3
4th quarter	2 551.0	3 017.5	2 385.7	631.8	0.6	-467.2	3.4	533.6	16 087.6	15.8	0.4
2012											
1st quarter	2 582.1	3 071.0	2 453.6	617.3	0.4	-489.3	-63.0	563.4	16 352.6	16.2	0.8
2nd quarter	2 634.7	3 079.3	2 454.0	625.3	1.4	-445.9	10.1	545.6	16 409.0	16.0	0.6
3rd quarter	2 692.8	3 113.9	2 493.3	620.6	2.3	-423.4	86.4	558.8	16 517.2	15.8	0.3
4th quarter	2 711.1	3 112.5	2 499.9	612.5	-30.3	-371.1	-101.7	537.4	16 779.1	16.8	1.4

. . . = Not available.

Table 5-1B. Saving and Investment: Historical

(Billions of dollars, except as noted; quarterly data are at seasonally adjusted annual rates.)   **NIPA Tables 1.7.5, 5.1**

Year and quarter	Gross saving									Gross domestic investment and net lending, NIPAs				Net domestic invest-ment	Gross national income	Net saving as a percent-age of gross national income
	Total	Net saving			Consumption of fixed capital					Gross domestic investment			Net lending or net borrow-ing (-), NIPAs			
		Private	Government		Total	Private	Government			Total	Private	Govern-ment				
			Federal	State and local			Federal	State and local								
1929	20.1	7.6	0.8	1.3	10.4	9.4	0.2	0.8		20.1	17.2	2.9	0.8	9.7	104.6	9.3
1930	15.8	4.5	0.0	1.1	10.2	9.2	0.2	0.8		14.7	11.4	3.3	0.7	4.5	93.3	6.0
1931	9.1	1.2	-2.3	0.8	9.5	8.6	0.2	0.7		9.6	6.5	3.1	0.2	0.1	77.2	-0.5
1932	4.0	-3.2	-1.6	0.5	8.3	7.5	0.2	0.7		4.1	1.8	2.3	0.2	-4.2	59.6	-7.3
1933	3.9	-3.1	-1.2	0.2	8.0	7.0	0.2	0.7		4.3	2.3	2.0	0.2	-3.7	57.0	-7.1
1934	7.0	0.1	-2.6	1.1	8.4	7.3	0.3	0.9		7.0	4.3	2.7	0.4	-1.4	66.7	-2.1
1935	10.4	3.2	-2.3	1.0	8.5	7.3	0.3	0.8		10.2	7.4	2.9	-0.1	1.8	74.8	2.6
1936	12.3	5.1	-3.6	2.1	8.8	7.5	0.3	0.9		13.6	9.4	4.2	-0.1	4.8	83.9	4.2
1937	17.1	5.8	-0.2	1.8	9.7	8.4	0.4	1.0		16.9	13.0	3.9	0.2	7.1	93.4	7.9
1938	12.7	2.8	-1.8	1.7	10.0	8.6	0.4	1.0		12.2	7.9	4.3	1.2	2.2	87.1	3.1
1939	14.6	5.3	-2.5	1.7	10.1	8.6	0.4	1.1		14.8	10.2	4.6	1.0	4.7	92.6	4.8
1940	19.5	8.3	-1.0	1.6	10.6	9.0	0.5	1.1		19.0	14.6	4.4	1.5	8.4	102.2	8.7
1941	31.1	16.9	0.6	1.6	12.1	10.0	0.9	1.2		30.2	19.4	10.8	1.3	18.1	129.5	14.7
1942	41.6	37.0	-11.4	1.1	14.9	11.2	2.2	1.4		40.7	11.8	29.0	-0.1	25.9	167.3	16.0
1943	47.0	45.0	-17.1	1.1	18.0	11.5	5.0	1.5		47.3	7.4	39.9	-2.1	29.3	205.3	14.1
1944	42.8	49.8	-29.5	1.1	21.4	12.0	7.9	1.5		47.3	9.2	38.1	-2.0	25.9	222.4	9.7
1945	32.6	40.3	-32.1	1.1	23.2	12.5	9.3	1.4		37.7	12.4	25.3	-1.3	14.5	224.6	4.2
1946	41.5	23.1	-8.2	0.8	25.8	14.2	10.0	1.6		37.8	33.1	4.7	4.9	12.1	227.2	6.9
1947	49.3	17.6	2.4	0.1	29.2	17.7	9.6	1.9		42.8	37.1	5.7	9.3	13.6	248.2	8.1
1948	61.5	29.2	0.9	0.1	31.4	20.8	8.4	2.1		58.8	50.3	8.5	2.4	27.4	276.5	10.9
1949	49.6	25.3	-8.5	0.5	32.3	22.6	7.6	2.2		50.4	39.1	11.3	0.9	18.1	272.4	6.3
1950	64.9	29.3	1.8	0.3	33.4	24.3	6.9	2.2		68.0	56.5	11.5	-1.8	34.6	300.4	10.5
1951	79.8	36.0	4.5	1.5	37.8	27.7	7.4	2.6		82.3	62.8	19.6	0.9	44.6	345.8	12.2
1952	79.9	39.5	-2.1	1.9	40.6	29.5	8.3	2.8		81.9	57.3	24.6	0.6	41.3	367.1	10.7
1953	82.0	40.4	-4.2	2.3	43.5	31.3	9.2	2.9		87.1	60.4	26.7	-1.3	43.6	387.9	9.9
1954	80.8	40.7	-8.0	2.0	46.0	33.0	10.1	3.0		83.5	58.1	25.4	0.2	37.5	390.4	8.9
1947																
1st quarter	47.5	16.8	2.8	0.1	27.7	16.3	9.7	1.8		40.8	35.9	5.0	9.4	13.1	241.3	8.2
2nd quarter	46.8	15.7	2.1	0.2	28.8	17.3	9.6	1.8		39.6	34.5	5.1	9.9	10.9	244.6	7.4
3rd quarter	48.9	19.8	-0.7	0.0	29.8	18.2	9.7	1.9		41.0	34.9	6.1	10.1	11.2	249.1	7.7
4th quarter	53.8	18.1	5.3	-0.1	30.5	19.1	9.4	2.0		49.8	43.2	6.6	7.8	19.3	257.7	9.0
1948																
1st quarter	59.0	23.6	5.0	-0.3	30.8	19.9	8.9	2.0		54.7	47.2	7.5	4.9	24.0	266.9	10.6
2nd quarter	62.7	29.0	2.5	0.1	31.2	20.6	8.5	2.1		58.6	50.3	8.3	3.0	27.4	275.5	11.5
3rd quarter	62.0	31.4	-1.1	0.0	31.7	21.2	8.3	2.2		61.3	52.5	8.8	0.9	29.6	280.8	10.8
4th quarter	62.4	32.7	-2.7	0.4	32.0	21.7	8.1	2.2		60.7	51.3	9.4	0.8	28.7	283.0	10.7
1949																
1st quarter	54.7	27.9	-6.0	0.6	32.3	22.1	8.0	2.2		53.4	43.1	10.2	2.2	21.1	275.9	8.1
2nd quarter	48.6	25.0	-9.2	0.4	32.3	22.4	7.7	2.2		47.5	36.2	11.3	1.7	15.2	272.4	6.0
3rd quarter	50.1	26.6	-9.5	0.6	32.3	22.8	7.4	2.2		51.5	39.5	11.9	0.6	19.1	272.5	6.5
4th quarter	44.8	21.6	-9.5	0.3	32.4	23.1	7.2	2.2		49.2	37.5	11.8	-1.0	16.8	268.7	4.6
1950																
1st quarter	53.2	32.3	-11.6	0.0	32.5	23.4	7.0	2.1		57.4	46.7	10.7	-1.0	25.0	279.1	7.4
2nd quarter	61.7	29.8	-0.6	-0.3	32.8	23.9	6.8	2.1		63.4	52.3	11.1	-1.2	30.6	291.6	9.9
3rd quarter	67.1	23.1	9.6	0.8	33.6	24.6	6.8	2.2		70.4	58.6	11.7	-2.7	36.8	309.5	10.8
4th quarter	77.6	32.0	10.0	0.8	34.9	25.5	7.0	2.3		80.8	68.4	12.3	-2.5	45.9	321.3	13.3
1951																
1st quarter	74.3	23.7	12.7	1.7	36.3	26.6	7.2	2.5		79.5	64.6	14.9	-1.7	43.2	334.5	11.4
2nd quarter	82.5	38.6	5.0	1.5	37.4	27.5	7.3	2.6		85.6	67.4	18.2	0.4	48.2	342.9	13.2
3rd quarter	80.8	41.7	-0.6	1.3	38.3	28.2	7.4	2.7		83.1	62.0	21.1	2.2	44.8	349.2	12.2
4th quarter	81.6	40.1	0.7	1.6	39.1	28.7	7.7	2.7		81.2	57.1	24.1	2.7	42.1	356.4	11.9
1952																
1st quarter	82.0	39.5	1.2	1.8	39.6	29.0	7.9	2.7		82.2	58.1	24.1	3.5	42.7	358.5	11.8
2nd quarter	76.0	37.0	-2.4	1.3	40.2	29.3	8.1	2.8		77.3	53.0	24.3	1.1	37.1	361.1	9.9
3rd quarter	79.3	41.0	-4.8	2.1	41.0	29.7	8.4	2.9		82.1	57.2	24.8	-1.1	41.1	368.4	10.4
4th quarter	82.3	40.8	-2.5	2.3	41.7	30.2	8.7	2.8		86.0	60.7	25.3	-1.2	44.3	380.6	10.7
1953																
1st quarter	84.0	41.3	-1.5	1.7	42.5	30.7	8.9	2.9		88.2	61.7	26.5	-1.3	45.7	387.5	10.7
2nd quarter	84.2	41.5	-3.3	2.8	43.2	31.1	9.2	2.9		89.3	62.1	27.1	-1.8	46.0	391.1	10.5
3rd quarter	83.7	40.2	-2.6	2.3	43.8	31.6	9.3	2.9		88.4	61.4	27.0	-1.2	44.6	390.0	10.2
4th quarter	76.0	38.5	-9.3	2.4	44.4	32.0	9.5	2.9		82.4	56.4	25.9	-0.9	38.0	382.9	8.3
1954																
1st quarter	78.9	41.3	-9.8	2.4	45.0	32.4	9.8	2.8		82.1	55.7	26.4	-0.5	37.2	385.2	8.8
2nd quarter	79.3	39.8	-8.4	2.1	45.7	32.8	10.0	3.0		81.4	55.4	25.9	0.3	35.7	386.2	8.7
3rd quarter	80.2	39.7	-7.6	1.8	46.3	33.2	10.2	3.0		83.7	59.0	24.7	-0.1	37.4	390.2	8.7
4th quarter	84.7	42.1	-6.3	1.9	47.0	33.5	10.4	3.0		86.6	62.1	24.5	0.9	39.7	399.8	9.4
1955																
1st quarter	89.9	43.7	-2.9	1.7	47.5	33.9	10.5	3.0		92.9	68.7	24.1	0.5	45.4	412.8	10.3
2nd quarter	95.4	45.8	-0.6	2.0	48.2	34.5	10.6	3.1		97.4	72.7	24.8	-0.2	49.2	422.9	11.2
3rd quarter	97.9	46.8	-0.7	2.5	49.3	35.3	10.8	3.2		99.0	74.7	24.3	0.8	49.7	431.4	11.2
4th quarter	102.3	47.2	1.9	2.6	50.6	36.2	11.0	3.3		103.2	78.9	24.3	0.4	52.6	439.0	11.8
1956																
1st quarter	105.7	48.3	2.3	2.9	52.1	37.3	11.4	3.5		103.9	78.3	25.6	0.9	51.7	444.2	12.1
2nd quarter	107.6	50.3	0.7	3.1	53.5	38.4	11.6	3.6		103.6	77.0	26.6	2.2	50.1	451.4	12.0
3rd quarter	111.6	52.6	1.2	3.1	54.8	39.3	11.8	3.7		106.0	78.3	27.7	3.0	51.2	457.5	12.4
4th quarter	113.4	53.1	1.4	2.9	56.0	40.2	12.0	3.8		105.8	77.1	28.6	4.5	49.8	466.9	12.3

Table 5-1B. Saving and Investment: Historical—*Continued*

(Billions of dollars, except as noted; quarterly data are at seasonally adjusted annual rates.)   **NIPA Tables 1.7.5, 5.1**

Year and quarter	Gross saving											Gross domestic investment and net lending, NIPAs					Net domestic invest-ment	Gross national income	Net saving as a percent-age of gross national income
	Total	Net saving				Consumption of fixed capital						Gross domestic investment			Net lending or net borrow-ing (-), NIPAs			
		Private	Government			Total	Private	Government				Total	Private	Govern-ment				
			Federal	State and local				Federal	State and local									
1957																		
1st quarter	114.3	53.2	0.4	3.4		57.3	41.1	12.4	3.8			107.5	77.7	29.8	5.6	50.2	474.9	12.0
2nd quarter	114.3	54.6	-1.5	2.8		58.4	41.9	12.6	3.9			107.6	77.9	29.7	4.8	49.2	478.1	11.7
3rd quarter	114.2	53.8	-1.6	2.5		59.5	42.7	12.8	4.0			109.9	79.3	30.6	4.9	50.4	482.9	11.3
4th quarter	104.6	49.9	-7.7	1.9		60.4	43.4	13.1	4.0			101.9	71.0	30.8	3.6	41.4	477.3	9.2
1958																		
1st quarter	100.7	48.8	-10.2	1.0		61.1	44.0	13.1	4.0			98.0	66.7	31.3	1.5	36.9	472.2	8.4
2nd quarter	97.3	49.5	-15.0	0.8		62.0	44.7	13.2	4.1			97.0	65.1	32.0	0.8	35.1	475.0	7.4
3rd quarter	104.9	53.6	-12.5	0.9		62.9	45.2	13.5	4.2			104.9	72.0	32.9	1.0	42.0	488.2	8.6
4th quarter	112.1	56.9	-10.6	1.9		63.8	45.7	13.8	4.2			114.3	80.0	34.3	-0.1	50.6	500.9	9.6
1959																		
1st quarter	117.8	56.5	-4.5	1.4		64.5	46.2	14.0	4.3			119.4	83.2	36.2	-1.5	54.9	513.6	10.4
2nd quarter	124.9	59.6	-1.8	2.0		65.1	46.6	14.2	4.3			125.5	89.4	36.1	-2.1	60.4	528.3	11.3
3rd quarter	117.3	53.2	-4.2	2.6		65.8	47.0	14.4	4.4			119.7	83.6	36.1	-0.6	54.0	526.2	9.8
4th quarter	120.4	56.1	-4.9	2.8		66.4	47.4	14.6	4.4			121.5	86.5	34.9	-0.9	55.1	532.1	10.1
1960																		
1st quarter	133.1	58.7	4.7	2.7		67.0	47.7	14.8	4.5			131.6	96.5	35.1	1.7	64.6	546.0	12.1
2nd quarter	126.4	55.0	1.3	2.5		67.6	48.0	15.0	4.5			122.3	87.1	35.2	2.5	54.7	547.3	10.8
3rd quarter	127.1	56.7	-0.4	2.5		68.2	48.4	15.2	4.6			123.2	86.4	36.8	3.7	55.0	549.4	10.7
4th quarter	121.5	55.0	-4.9	2.5		68.8	48.7	15.5	4.6			112.8	76.0	36.9	4.8	44.0	548.3	9.6
1961																		
1st quarter	124.7	57.8	-4.7	2.1		69.5	49.1	15.7	4.7			118.0	78.4	39.6	5.3	48.5	550.9	10.0
2nd quarter	127.1	61.4	-6.4	1.9		70.2	49.5	15.9	4.8			122.6	84.1	38.5	4.0	52.4	561.3	10.1
3rd quarter	134.6	66.1	-4.9	2.4		70.9	50.0	16.1	4.8			130.8	90.9	39.9	3.8	59.8	571.8	11.1
4th quarter	140.3	68.8	-2.9	2.6		71.8	50.5	16.4	4.9			134.5	92.9	41.6	3.7	62.8	587.2	11.7
1962																		
1st quarter	141.6	71.3	-5.4	3.0		72.7	51.0	16.7	5.0			140.0	98.1	42.0	3.1	67.3	597.3	11.5
2nd quarter	142.1	71.0	-5.6	3.2		73.5	51.5	16.9	5.1			138.6	96.7	41.9	4.8	65.0	605.3	11.3
3rd quarter	144.5	71.0	-4.9	3.8		74.6	52.1	17.3	5.2			141.3	98.2	43.1	4.1	66.7	612.7	11.4
4th quarter	145.6	71.8	-5.5	3.7		75.6	52.6	17.7	5.3			138.4	95.0	43.5	3.2	62.8	621.8	11.3
1963																		
1st quarter	149.2	72.7	-3.4	3.4		76.5	53.2	17.9	5.4			142.9	99.7	43.3	3.9	66.4	629.5	11.5
2nd quarter	153.9	73.9	-1.1	3.6		77.5	53.8	18.2	5.5			145.2	101.6	43.6	5.3	67.7	639.6	11.9
3rd quarter	154.7	73.8	-1.6	4.0		78.5	54.5	18.4	5.6			150.4	104.6	45.8	4.6	72.0	649.0	11.7
4th quarter	159.0	78.0	-2.3	3.8		79.5	55.2	18.7	5.7			152.3	107.2	45.1	6.0	72.8	660.2	12.0
1964																		
1st quarter	161.9	82.4	-5.5	4.5		80.6	55.9	18.9	5.8			156.2	110.5	45.8	8.2	75.6	673.6	12.1
2nd quarter	163.0	87.2	-10.2	4.3		81.8	56.8	19.1	5.9			157.0	110.5	46.5	6.7	75.3	684.9	11.9
3rd quarter	166.4	85.7	-6.7	4.4		83.0	57.7	19.3	6.0			159.2	112.6	46.6	7.6	76.2	697.5	12.0
4th quarter	172.8	89.5	-5.1	4.1		84.2	58.7	19.5	6.1			161.7	115.0	46.7	7.3	77.5	706.9	12.5
1965																		
1st quarter	180.7	92.2	-0.9	3.9		85.6	59.7	19.6	6.2			172.7	126.5	46.2	5.7	87.2	726.9	13.1
2nd quarter	182.7	93.5	-2.0	4.1		87.1	60.9	19.8	6.4			173.9	127.0	46.9	7.0	86.8	739.7	12.9
3rd quarter	183.2	99.8	-9.4	4.1		88.8	62.1	20.1	6.5			180.1	131.2	48.9	6.0	91.3	752.6	12.6
4th quarter	184.9	99.8	-9.6	4.2		90.5	63.5	20.3	6.7			183.2	133.8	49.5	5.9	92.8	773.7	12.2
1966																		
1st quarter	194.3	100.9	-4.1	5.2		92.3	65.0	20.5	6.8			196.1	144.2	51.9	4.7	103.8	795.8	12.8
2nd quarter	194.8	100.7	-5.6	5.4		94.3	66.4	20.9	7.0			195.4	143.5	51.9	3.9	101.1	807.7	12.4
3rd quarter	195.3	101.5	-7.8	5.4		96.3	67.9	21.2	7.2			197.4	143.2	54.2	2.7	101.1	821.0	12.1
4th quarter	201.3	108.6	-10.3	4.8		98.3	69.4	21.5	7.4			202.1	145.9	56.2	3.9	103.8	835.5	12.3
1967																		
1st quarter	197.6	111.3	-19.3	5.2		100.2	70.9	21.8	7.5			200.7	142.8	57.9	4.4	100.5	843.8	11.5
2nd quarter	194.0	107.4	-20.5	4.7		102.3	72.5	22.2	7.7			194.0	137.5	56.6	3.6	91.7	852.5	10.7
3rd quarter	201.8	111.8	-18.8	4.2		104.6	74.1	22.6	7.9			200.8	142.8	57.9	3.2	96.2	870.2	11.2
4th quarter	208.4	116.1	-19.4	4.8		106.9	75.8	23.1	8.1			205.9	147.7	58.3	2.8	99.0	888.4	11.4
1968																		
1st quarter	207.2	110.5	-16.9	4.3		109.4	77.6	23.5	8.3			210.6	152.3	58.4	1.7	101.2	911.9	10.7
2nd quarter	214.0	115.6	-18.6	5.1		111.9	79.5	23.9	8.5			218.5	158.9	59.5	2.2	106.5	935.6	10.9
3rd quarter	215.4	106.9	-10.1	4.0		114.5	81.6	24.3	8.6			215.2	155.7	59.5	1.5	100.7	957.3	10.5
4th quarter	221.4	109.6	-9.3	3.6		117.4	83.7	24.7	8.9			220.3	160.8	59.5	0.8	102.9	976.7	10.6
1969																		
1st quarter	229.9	103.6	2.2	3.7		120.5	86.1	25.2	9.2			233.9	172.4	61.5	1.6	113.4	996.2	11.0
2nd quarter	231.1	105.3	-1.5	3.9		123.5	88.3	25.6	9.5			232.4	172.7	59.7	0.6	109.0	1 015.6	10.6
3rd quarter	238.1	115.9	-8.6	4.6		126.3	90.6	26.0	9.8			237.5	177.6	59.9	1.4	111.2	1 037.1	10.8
4th quarter	233.2	112.2	-12.5	4.3		129.2	92.8	26.4	10.1			228.6	171.6	57.0	2.7	99.4	1 048.6	9.9
1970																		
1st quarter	227.2	113.0	-22.2	4.3		132.2	94.9	26.9	10.4			227.1	168.1	59.0	3.8	94.9	1 056.1	9.0
2nd quarter	229.8	123.5	-32.6	3.7		135.2	97.1	27.4	10.8			230.3	171.5	58.8	5.2	95.1	1 071.0	8.8
3rd quarter	231.1	129.4	-39.5	3.0		138.3	99.4	27.8	11.1			234.1	173.9	60.2	3.5	95.8	1 088.6	8.5
4th quarter	224.7	127.1	-44.7	0.9		141.4	101.7	28.2	11.5			227.8	166.8	61.1	2.4	86.4	1 092.0	7.6
1971																		
1st quarter	238.6	139.6	-45.5	0.0		144.6	104.1	28.6	11.8			247.5	189.5	58.0	4.3	103.0	1 132.0	8.3
2nd quarter	243.2	147.6	-52.4	0.5		147.5	106.5	28.9	12.1			255.7	197.3	58.3	0.1	108.1	1 154.8	8.3
3rd quarter	249.1	150.3	-51.7	0.2		150.3	108.8	29.1	12.3			261.2	202.1	59.2	-0.4	110.9	1 175.8	8.4
4th quarter	253.7	152.7	-53.7	1.7		153.1	111.1	29.3	12.7			256.9	198.4	58.5	-2.8	103.8	1 201.0	8.4

Table 5-1B. Saving and Investment: Historical—*Continued*

(Billions of dollars, except as noted; quarterly data are at seasonally adjusted annual rates.)   **NIPA Tables 1.7.5, 5.1**

Year and quarter	Gross saving Total	Net saving Private	Net saving Government Federal	Net saving Government State and local	Consumption of fixed capital Total	Consumption of fixed capital Private	Consumption of fixed capital Government Federal	Consumption of fixed capital Government State and local	Gross domestic investment Total	Gross domestic investment Private	Gross domestic investment Government	Net lending or net borrowing (-), NIPAs	Net domestic investment	Gross national income	Net saving as a percentage of gross national income
1972															
1st quarter	263.3	150.5	-45.7	2.4	156.1	113.4	29.8	12.9	273.0	213.0	60.0	-5.1	116.9	1 237.4	8.7
2nd quarter	265.5	146.6	-51.4	11.2	159.0	116.0	29.9	13.1	287.8	226.8	61.0	-4.8	128.7	1 260.7	8.4
3rd quarter	279.7	155.4	-40.7	2.6	162.4	118.8	30.2	13.4	292.2	233.1	59.1	-3.6	129.8	1 293.8	9.1
4th quarter	302.2	176.4	-57.8	17.5	166.0	121.8	30.4	13.8	302.3	239.7	62.6	-2.8	136.3	1 343.7	10.1
1973															
1st quarter	316.3	173.6	-40.0	12.4	170.2	125.2	30.9	14.2	320.5	254.3	66.2	2.2	150.3	1 384.9	10.5
2nd quarter	324.5	180.4	-40.8	9.7	175.1	129.0	31.4	14.6	333.8	268.2	65.6	5.4	158.7	1 414.5	10.6
3rd quarter	338.9	186.4	-36.6	8.7	180.4	133.4	32.0	15.0	328.9	264.3	64.6	12.4	148.5	1 448.3	10.9
4th quarter	361.7	200.8	-33.4	7.7	186.6	138.3	32.6	15.6	347.1	280.9	66.2	15.3	160.5	1 492.6	11.7
1974															
1st quarter	355.9	192.2	-35.3	5.4	193.6	143.8	33.3	16.5	339.3	268.4	71.0	16.5	145.7	1 511.8	10.7
2nd quarter	346.1	178.5	-37.9	3.8	201.6	149.7	34.1	17.8	353.5	277.4	76.1	2.6	151.9	1 540.5	9.4
3rd quarter	346.1	169.1	-36.2	2.8	210.3	156.1	35.2	19.1	349.1	271.0	78.1	0.3	138.8	1 575.3	8.6
4th quarter	349.0	185.9	-53.3	-2.7	219.1	163.0	36.1	20.0	360.8	281.3	79.5	4.4	141.7	1 600.2	8.1
1975															
1st quarter	330.0	185.0	-75.1	-7.5	227.7	170.3	36.8	20.6	327.4	244.3	83.1	17.8	99.7	1 615.7	6.3
2nd quarter	329.6	233.0	-132.4	-5.9	235.0	176.6	37.5	20.8	322.5	243.3	79.2	21.4	87.5	1 653.8	5.7
3rd quarter	360.3	213.5	-89.7	-4.6	241.1	182.0	38.1	21.1	350.6	265.2	85.4	18.3	109.5	1 718.1	6.9
4th quarter	373.1	221.6	-90.7	-4.3	246.4	186.3	38.8	21.4	366.1	276.2	89.9	21.6	119.7	1 767.3	7.2
1976															
1st quarter	392.5	222.7	-80.8	-0.1	250.8	189.6	39.5	21.7	397.6	304.6	92.9	13.1	146.8	1 822.1	7.8
2nd quarter	399.4	218.0	-76.2	1.8	255.8	193.7	40.1	22.0	411.3	322.3	89.0	8.9	155.5	1 852.7	7.8
3rd quarter	402.5	217.9	-79.5	2.3	261.7	198.6	41.0	22.2	417.0	328.3	88.7	2.4	155.3	1 890.7	7.4
4th quarter	403.5	210.8	-83.0	7.2	268.5	204.2	41.9	22.4	425.6	337.6	87.9	3.8	157.0	1 930.4	7.0
1977															
1st quarter	412.2	202.9	-72.2	5.3	276.2	210.7	42.6	22.9	451.8	360.3	91.5	-8.1	175.6	1 981.7	6.9
2nd quarter	454.2	229.3	-66.3	7.2	284.1	217.5	43.4	23.3	483.9	389.7	94.2	-8.9	199.8	2 060.1	8.3
3rd quarter	481.6	251.7	-73.1	10.8	292.2	224.5	44.0	23.7	507.8	414.1	93.6	-7.9	215.6	2 125.0	8.9
4th quarter	490.3	255.0	-76.0	10.4	300.9	231.8	45.0	24.1	515.6	422.3	93.3	-19.0	214.7	2 181.2	8.7
1978															
1st quarter	502.9	259.2	-78.2	11.9	309.9	239.4	46.0	24.6	528.4	434.8	93.6	-25.1	218.5	2 230.3	8.7
2nd quarter	541.4	262.5	-58.9	18.1	319.7	247.5	47.0	25.2	575.6	470.6	105.0	-12.9	255.9	2 334.0	9.5
3rd quarter	561.2	273.7	-53.1	10.7	330.0	256.2	48.0	25.8	602.1	492.4	109.7	-11.5	272.1	2 390.3	9.7
4th quarter	587.1	282.5	-49.2	13.1	340.7	265.4	48.8	26.4	629.7	515.8	113.9	-1.4	289.0	2 465.4	10.0
1979															
1st quarter	609.9	288.7	-39.6	8.7	352.2	275.2	49.8	27.2	635.6	525.8	109.8	-1.9	283.4	2 533.3	10.2
2nd quarter	612.3	279.3	-39.2	7.8	364.5	285.3	51.0	28.1	656.3	539.3	117.0	-2.8	291.8	2 584.0	9.6
3rd quarter	615.0	273.2	-44.8	9.3	377.3	295.8	52.4	29.1	671.0	545.6	125.4	2.3	293.6	2 648.1	9.0
4th quarter	618.0	274.8	-54.4	7.1	390.5	306.6	53.8	30.2	676.1	547.9	128.2	-2.7	285.6	2 711.7	8.4
1980															
1st quarter	615.9	268.4	-63.5	6.9	404.2	317.7	55.3	31.3	690.3	554.6	135.8	-10.8	286.1	2 770.8	7.6
2nd quarter	604.6	271.6	-87.4	2.0	418.5	329.0	57.0	32.5	654.0	519.3	134.7	9.7	235.6	2 776.5	6.7
3rd quarter	622.0	284.9	-100.3	4.3	433.2	340.7	58.7	33.8	629.4	495.1	134.4	28.0	196.2	2 858.8	6.6
4th quarter	680.0	317.1	-93.7	8.4	448.2	352.5	60.6	35.0	690.4	551.5	138.9	6.6	242.2	3 004.9	7.7
1981															
1st quarter	710.2	310.3	-71.8	8.4	463.3	364.7	62.4	36.3	765.8	619.4	146.4	1.5	302.5	3 105.9	7.9
2nd quarter	720.6	313.3	-75.6	4.6	478.3	376.4	64.4	37.4	755.2	609.8	145.4	0.0	276.9	3 162.5	7.7
3rd quarter	777.2	363.1	-82.6	4.3	492.4	387.8	66.2	38.4	798.0	652.3	145.7	6.9	305.6	3 266.0	8.7
4th quarter	773.0	380.8	-113.3	-0.7	506.2	398.8	68.1	39.3	795.3	643.4	151.9	4.5	289.0	3 294.3	8.1
1982															
1st quarter	740.8	358.0	-133.2	-3.5	519.6	409.4	70.0	40.2	738.5	588.3	150.2	0.5	219.0	3 311.5	6.7
2nd quarter	764.6	377.0	-139.3	-4.1	531.1	418.0	72.0	41.0	750.2	593.6	156.6	17.3	219.1	3 369.1	6.9
3rd quarter	732.3	373.7	-175.8	-5.6	540.0	424.7	73.6	41.7	750.5	593.0	157.5	-14.2	210.5	3 398.0	5.7
4th quarter	674.0	344.7	-210.2	-7.2	546.7	429.5	75.1	42.1	712.8	549.2	163.6	-17.4	166.1	3 420.4	3.7
1983															
1st quarter	693.5	359.9	-207.0	-10.8	551.3	432.3	76.6	42.4	730.1	565.5	164.5	-8.0	178.8	3 485.7	4.1
2nd quarter	703.8	348.8	-200.8	-0.8	556.6	436.0	78.0	42.6	781.1	613.8	167.3	-27.7	224.5	3 570.9	4.1
3rd quarter	706.8	354.6	-217.3	6.2	563.4	440.6	79.8	42.9	826.9	652.3	174.7	-48.0	263.5	3 657.9	3.9
4th quarter	773.8	387.4	-194.9	10.4	570.9	446.2	81.5	43.2	896.7	718.5	178.2	-56.9	325.8	3 769.7	5.4
1984															
1st quarter	857.7	438.3	-179.8	19.1	580.0	452.6	83.8	43.6	974.7	790.9	183.8	-78.6	394.7	3 911.4	7.1
2nd quarter	875.8	451.8	-189.0	23.7	589.3	459.5	85.6	44.2	1 008.7	818.9	189.8	-88.0	419.4	4 007.6	7.1
3rd quarter	901.4	479.5	-195.4	18.3	599.0	467.0	87.3	44.7	1 032.9	838.9	194.1	-90.5	433.9	4 083.6	7.4
4th quarter	903.4	476.9	-205.2	22.7	609.1	474.9	89.0	45.2	1 036.8	831.7	205.1	-103.5	427.7	4 150.9	7.1
1985															
1st quarter	893.1	418.2	-167.8	22.6	620.1	483.4	90.8	45.9	1 017.7	809.9	207.9	-89.6	397.6	4 227.5	6.5
2nd quarter	890.7	455.1	-217.1	21.8	630.9	492.0	92.4	46.5	1 045.7	827.0	218.7	-111.5	414.8	4 286.3	6.1
3rd quarter	868.9	403.3	-196.1	19.5	642.1	500.7	94.2	47.2	1 048.9	822.2	226.7	-121.4	406.8	4 358.3	5.2
4th quarter	883.1	413.9	-201.5	17.1	653.5	509.6	95.9	48.0	1 085.8	859.5	226.2	-135.3	432.3	4 411.2	5.2
1986															
1st quarter	899.3	410.2	-201.5	25.6	665.0	518.6	97.6	48.8	1 092.0	863.5	228.6	-128.5	427.1	4 474.0	5.2
2nd quarter	874.3	402.5	-224.2	19.4	676.6	527.4	99.4	49.8	1 089.9	855.2	234.7	-142.0	413.3	4 497.0	4.4
3rd quarter	841.8	361.7	-229.9	22.3	687.8	536.0	101.1	50.7	1 082.1	835.8	246.3	-150.3	394.3	4 547.7	3.4
4th quarter	855.8	337.2	-195.1	14.5	699.3	544.3	103.2	51.8	1 084.8	842.1	242.8	-150.4	385.5	4 602.7	3.4

Table 5-1B. Saving and Investment: Historical—*Continued*

(Billions of dollars, except as noted; quarterly data are at seasonally adjusted annual rates.)   **NIPA Tables 1.7.5, 5.1**

Year and quarter	Gross saving								Gross domestic investment and net lending, NIPAs				Net domestic invest-ment	Gross national income	Net saving as a percent-age of gross national income
	Total	Net saving			Consumption of fixed capital				Gross domestic investment			Net lending or net borrow-ing (-), NIPAs			
		Private	Government		Total	Private	Government		Total	Private	Govern-ment				
			Federal	State and local			Federal	State and local							
1987															
1st quarter	902.1	379.9	-194.7	7.1	709.8	552.3	104.8	52.7	1 118.6	871.2	247.4	-151.1	408.8	4 685.0	4.1
2nd quarter	929.0	329.8	-141.6	19.5	721.2	561.2	106.4	53.7	1 128.3	874.6	253.7	-154.5	407.1	4 794.7	4.3
3rd quarter	964.1	372.3	-153.3	11.5	733.7	570.7	108.4	54.6	1 135.5	876.5	259.0	-154.2	401.8	4 901.0	4.7
4th quarter	1 013.5	419.2	-163.1	10.2	747.1	581.0	110.6	55.4	1 204.9	946.5	258.4	-157.2	457.8	5 008.0	5.3
1988															
1st quarter	1 032.9	420.7	-163.8	14.4	761.6	592.1	113.1	56.4	1 162.1	908.6	253.5	-127.0	400.5	5 113.2	5.3
2nd quarter	1 072.7	439.5	-155.8	13.3	775.6	603.0	115.4	57.3	1 193.0	934.5	258.5	-110.1	417.4	5 220.1	5.7
3rd quarter	1 100.1	440.7	-151.2	21.2	789.4	613.8	117.4	58.3	1 200.7	942.0	258.7	-106.6	411.4	5 325.4	5.8
4th quarter	1 114.8	451.4	-158.6	19.0	803.0	624.4	119.4	59.2	1 225.6	962.8	262.8	-119.8	422.6	5 444.2	5.7
1989															
1st quarter	1 152.0	453.3	-136.3	18.5	816.4	634.9	121.4	60.2	1 268.8	1 005.4	263.4	-106.8	452.4	5 539.6	6.1
2nd quarter	1 109.8	424.7	-158.2	13.6	829.7	645.1	123.3	61.3	1 268.5	1 001.0	267.5	-93.7	438.8	5 585.0	5.0
3rd quarter	1 103.3	416.9	-163.5	7.2	842.8	655.2	125.1	62.4	1 271.5	996.5	275.0	-81.8	428.7	5 649.3	4.6
4th quarter	1 089.3	411.9	-168.5	-9.7	855.5	665.1	126.8	63.6	1 271.7	995.9	275.8	-88.5	416.2	5 699.3	4.1
1990															
1st quarter	1 107.5	432.1	-195.3	2.5	868.2	674.8	128.7	64.8	1 297.5	1 010.8	286.6	-90.9	429.2	5 820.5	4.1
2nd quarter	1 139.6	463.9	-201.7	-3.4	880.8	684.4	130.3	66.1	1 303.2	1 014.8	288.4	-73.0	422.4	5 915.5	4.4
3rd quarter	1 110.4	421.7	-196.7	-7.9	893.3	693.8	132.0	67.5	1 291.4	1 000.7	290.7	-82.6	398.1	5 958.0	3.6
4th quarter	1 112.8	434.7	-209.9	-17.0	905.0	703.0	133.6	68.5	1 243.2	947.6	295.7	-82.7	338.2	5 997.7	3.5
1991															
1st quarter	1 205.7	493.5	-184.1	-20.9	917.2	712.1	135.7	69.4	1 215.4	924.6	290.7	42.1	298.1	6 038.1	4.8
2nd quarter	1 148.4	489.7	-244.1	-25.0	927.8	719.9	137.4	70.5	1 221.7	926.6	295.1	14.2	293.9	6 084.1	3.6
3rd quarter	1 127.8	483.5	-269.3	-23.0	936.6	726.2	139.0	71.4	1 243.0	947.5	295.6	-29.1	306.4	6 141.3	3.1
4th quarter	1 149.8	525.7	-287.4	-31.4	942.9	731.2	139.6	72.1	1 273.7	978.8	294.9	-17.0	330.8	6 205.4	3.3
1992															
1st quarter	1 161.6	570.3	-324.7	-31.4	947.4	734.8	139.9	72.7	1 257.1	956.8	300.3	-22.0	309.7	6 339.8	3.4
2nd quarter	1 178.2	591.1	-331.4	-36.0	954.6	740.0	140.9	73.7	1 310.8	1 013.1	297.7	-39.8	356.2	6 431.2	3.5
3rd quarter	1 129.3	553.3	-343.9	-43.1	963.0	746.7	141.7	74.6	1 318.5	1 024.2	294.3	-46.8	355.5	6 479.2	2.6
4th quarter	1 141.6	537.8	-330.6	-39.5	973.9	755.1	143.2	75.6	1 350.2	1 058.0	292.2	-68.6	376.3	6 587.7	2.5
1993															
1st quarter	1 135.3	538.1	-340.6	-48.0	985.8	765.0	144.0	76.8	1 372.3	1 083.9	288.4	-59.2	386.6	6 605.7	2.3
2nd quarter	1 173.5	522.2	-306.0	-40.5	997.7	774.9	144.9	78.0	1 387.8	1 094.5	293.3	-73.9	390.1	6 720.4	2.6
3rd quarter	1 147.4	494.5	-317.2	-39.2	1 009.3	784.9	145.6	78.8	1 387.4	1 095.9	291.4	-77.0	378.1	6 777.8	2.0
4th quarter	1 215.3	498.3	-283.5	-21.2	1 021.6	795.0	146.7	79.8	1 447.3	1 153.0	294.3	-107.6	425.8	6 929.6	2.8
1994															
1st quarter	1 236.1	498.9	-266.5	-29.5	1 033.2	805.1	146.9	81.1	1 485.3	1 202.1	283.3	-92.3	452.2	7 007.3	2.9
2nd quarter	1 301.7	521.4	-236.8	-29.6	1 046.8	816.9	147.7	82.2	1 555.4	1 265.1	290.3	-111.9	508.7	7 148.2	3.6
3rd quarter	1 311.3	523.7	-254.6	-20.3	1 062.4	830.2	148.7	83.6	1 553.9	1 251.6	302.4	-121.9	491.5	7 252.6	3.4
4th quarter	1 347.5	552.8	-256.8	-28.4	1 079.9	845.1	150.0	84.9	1 607.9	1 307.2	300.7	-137.9	528.0	7 375.1	3.6
1995															
1st quarter	1 400.0	584.0	-254.1	-29.4	1 099.5	861.7	151.5	86.4	1 632.8	1 327.3	305.5	-118.7	533.3	7 461.6	4.0
2nd quarter	1 397.1	567.1	-241.8	-44.3	1 116.1	876.6	151.7	87.7	1 613.9	1 303.8	310.1	-118.3	497.8	7 540.2	3.7
3rd quarter	1 439.3	585.2	-245.2	-31.9	1 131.3	890.1	152.3	88.9	1 609.9	1 303.2	306.7	-101.0	478.6	7 654.6	4.0
4th quarter	1 481.7	580.3	-222.3	-20.5	1 144.3	902.0	152.2	90.1	1 644.1	1 335.6	308.4	-84.0	499.8	7 752.7	4.4
1996															
1st quarter	1 522.5	605.4	-223.1	-15.8	1 156.0	912.3	152.5	91.2	1 670.0	1 355.2	314.7	-102.3	514.0	7 885.8	4.6
2nd quarter	1 562.5	590.9	-179.9	-16.9	1 168.3	923.9	152.4	92.0	1 736.5	1 418.6	317.9	-108.7	568.1	8 025.9	4.9
3rd quarter	1 598.6	596.2	-169.6	-10.3	1 182.3	936.9	152.4	93.1	1 796.1	1 474.4	321.7	-132.8	613.8	8 120.9	5.1
4th quarter	1 641.7	592.6	-141.4	-6.8	1 197.4	951.1	152.2	94.1	1 805.5	1 480.0	325.5	-113.6	608.1	8 269.0	5.4
1997															
1st quarter	1 701.9	613.1	-120.7	-4.8	1 214.2	966.6	152.5	95.2	1 852.3	1 522.0	330.4	-131.5	638.1	8 406.7	5.8
2nd quarter	1 771.3	644.7	-102.5	-2.6	1 231.7	982.2	153.1	96.3	1 919.9	1 589.9	330.0	-101.7	688.2	8 535.9	6.3
3rd quarter	1 820.4	634.2	-68.7	6.5	1 248.5	997.9	153.3	97.3	1 956.6	1 625.3	331.3	-122.7	708.2	8 701.4	6.6
4th quarter	1 840.6	640.3	-72.8	7.7	1 265.5	1 013.6	153.1	98.7	1 971.8	1 645.3	326.5	-163.3	706.3	8 837.3	6.5
1998															
1st quarter	1 912.0	638.8	-22.6	13.9	1 281.9	1 029.5	152.7	99.7	2 036.9	1 712.3	324.6	-164.3	754.9	8 955.1	7.0
2nd quarter	1 917.5	615.2	-8.8	11.0	1 300.1	1 046.0	153.3	100.8	2 031.7	1 694.8	336.9	-195.5	731.5	9 099.2	6.8
3rd quarter	1 960.4	605.2	21.7	14.2	1 319.3	1 063.2	153.7	102.5	2 091.5	1 739.8	351.8	-224.1	772.2	9 249.5	6.9
4th quarter	1 939.6	556.9	20.6	22.5	1 339.7	1 081.0	154.6	104.0	2 146.8	1 794.4	352.4	-235.2	807.1	9 366.4	6.4
1999															
1st quarter	2 029.9	610.0	47.5	12.2	1 360.2	1 099.5	155.2	105.5	2 206.9	1 850.6	356.3	-243.7	846.7	9 538.8	7.0
2nd quarter	1 976.6	524.9	62.8	3.9	1 385.1	1 121.5	156.3	107.3	2 210.0	1 845.8	364.2	-280.0	824.9	9 635.2	6.1
3rd quarter	1 960.2	467.5	71.1	8.7	1 412.8	1 146.9	157.0	108.9	2 261.5	1 890.9	370.6	-314.7	848.7	9 756.3	5.6
4th quarter	2 006.0	463.7	84.8	12.1	1 445.4	1 175.8	158.6	111.0	2 332.2	1 949.4	382.8	-347.2	886.8	9 970.8	5.6
2000															
1st quarter	2 128.4	451.0	174.2	22.0	1 481.2	1 208.2	160.0	112.9	2 333.6	1 945.9	387.7	-386.0	852.5	10 247.4	6.3
2nd quarter	2 116.1	438.7	146.2	22.2	1 508.9	1 232.5	161.0	115.4	2 457.7	2 071.8	386.0	-389.7	948.8	10 365.2	5.9
3rd quarter	2 132.7	444.4	153.6	6.5	1 528.1	1 248.7	162.1	117.3	2 447.4	2 055.8	391.6	-427.0	919.2	10 505.0	5.8
4th quarter	2 060.4	383.2	149.5	-11.2	1 538.7	1 256.8	162.8	119.1	2 457.3	2 061.6	395.7	-435.1	918.6	10 567.4	4.9
2001															
1st quarter	2 138.2	462.9	129.2	-24.7	1 570.8	1 287.0	162.9	120.9	2 369.2	1 967.5	401.7	-420.5	798.4	10 742.3	5.3
2nd quarter	2 121.3	483.8	92.3	-53.5	1 598.7	1 313.2	163.3	122.3	2 388.7	1 967.0	421.7	-383.8	790.0	10 807.5	4.8
3rd quarter	2 042.7	633.6	-130.3	-76.5	1 616.0	1 328.9	163.4	123.6	2 344.0	1 937.3	406.7	-359.1	728.1	10 781.5	4.0
4th quarter	1 953.9	465.2	-35.2	-106.5	1 630.4	1 341.6	163.6	125.2	2 267.1	1 842.7	424.4	-343.8	636.7	10 823.2	3.0

Table 5-1B. Saving and Investment: Historical—*Continued*

(Billions of dollars, except as noted; quarterly data are at seasonally adjusted annual rates.)   **NIPA Tables 1.7.5, 5.1**

Year and quarter	Gross saving									Gross domestic investment and net lending, NIPAs				Net domestic invest-ment	Gross national income	Net saving as a percent-age of gross national income
	Total	Net saving			Consumption of fixed capital				Gross domestic investment			Net lending or net borrow-ing (-), NIPAs			
		Private	Government		Total	Private	Government		Total	Private	Govern-ment				
			Federal	State and local			Federal	State and local							
2002															
1st quarter	2 008.0	713.4	-228.2	-117.3	1 640.2	1 349.3	164.1	126.8	2 344.4	1 910.0	434.4	-406.1	704.2	10 957.8	3.4
2nd quarter	1 989.3	727.2	-267.2	-123.3	1 652.5	1 359.6	164.5	128.4	2 365.0	1 925.6	439.4	-452.6	712.5	11 047.0	3.0
3rd quarter	1 958.8	683.1	-277.5	-116.1	1 669.3	1 374.1	165.4	129.8	2 375.8	1 927.9	448.0	-455.8	706.6	11 124.7	2.6
4th quarter	1 998.9	750.4	-310.9	-126.9	1 686.3	1 389.0	166.2	131.1	2 389.0	1 936.5	452.5	-487.3	702.7	11 266.1	2.8
2003															
1st quarter	1 942.5	729.4	-334.0	-154.9	1 702.0	1 401.6	167.7	132.7	2 415.5	1 960.2	455.3	-531.9	713.6	11 340.1	2.1
2nd quarter	1 974.8	797.9	-402.9	-136.7	1 716.5	1 413.2	169.4	133.9	2 431.6	1 970.5	461.0	-521.5	715.1	11 495.5	2.2
3rd quarter	1 985.8	830.9	-473.0	-107.0	1 735.0	1 428.6	171.3	135.1	2 520.5	2 048.3	472.2	-512.6	785.5	11 668.9	2.1
4th quarter	2 063.7	799.6	-404.3	-87.0	1 755.4	1 446.0	173.0	136.4	2 605.2	2 132.8	472.4	-496.7	849.8	11 864.9	2.6
2004															
1st quarter	2 071.4	844.7	-441.5	-115.2	1 783.3	1 470.1	175.0	138.1	2 630.4	2 155.2	475.3	-534.8	847.2	12 076.5	2.4
2nd quarter	2 147.0	859.3	-402.9	-122.6	1 813.2	1 494.4	177.4	141.3	2 747.1	2 259.5	487.6	-612.6	933.9	12 280.7	2.7
3rd quarter	2 216.6	853.7	-374.1	-109.1	1 846.1	1 520.7	179.7	145.8	2 805.7	2 311.3	494.4	-618.1	959.6	12 506.3	3.0
4th quarter	2 164.9	747.7	-380.6	-86.6	1 884.3	1 552.0	182.4	149.9	2 877.4	2 380.8	496.6	-710.1	993.1	12 630.9	2.2
2005															
1st quarter	2 262.9	721.3	-313.8	-66.6	1 922.0	1 584.9	185.2	151.9	2 973.3	2 475.2	498.2	-703.9	1 051.3	12 904.6	2.6
2nd quarter	2 288.4	710.8	-311.1	-70.7	1 959.3	1 616.0	187.9	155.4	2 979.1	2 469.5	509.6	-701.8	1 019.8	13 078.9	2.5
3rd quarter	2 334.4	712.0	-308.7	-69.9	2 000.9	1 650.8	190.6	159.5	3 046.6	2 527.2	519.4	-667.4	1 045.7	13 326.3	2.5
4th quarter	2 463.9	765.8	-288.2	-59.3	2 045.5	1 689.5	193.7	162.4	3 163.9	2 636.5	527.4	-823.9	1 118.4	13 581.1	3.1
2006															
1st quarter	2 669.0	856.9	-243.6	-26.5	2 082.2	1 721.4	196.6	164.2	3 233.9	2 699.7	534.3	-791.2	1 151.7	13 947.3	4.2
2nd quarter	2 646.2	794.4	-246.0	-21.3	2 119.1	1 751.1	199.4	168.6	3 250.7	2 697.0	553.7	-807.6	1 131.6	14 075.0	3.7
3rd quarter	2 635.0	767.4	-235.4	-49.7	2 152.8	1 779.0	202.0	171.8	3 240.2	2 684.4	555.8	-852.1	1 087.4	14 215.1	3.4
4th quarter	2 660.0	717.5	-187.5	-60.1	2 190.0	1 808.6	204.8	176.6	3 207.2	2 641.6	565.7	-740.2	1 017.2	14 329.0	3.3
2007															
1st quarter	2 566.1	619.7	-215.0	-66.0	2 227.4	1 837.5	208.2	181.7	3 209.8	2 634.2	575.6	-793.6	982.3	14 454.1	2.3
2nd quarter	2 572.5	627.2	-253.0	-55.4	2 253.7	1 857.5	211.3	185.0	3 262.6	2 671.9	590.7	-750.0	1 009.0	14 577.6	2.2
3rd quarter	2 464.9	551.8	-288.6	-74.9	2 276.5	1 874.0	214.4	188.1	3 255.5	2 658.2	597.2	-675.7	979.0	14 605.3	1.3
4th quarter	2 423.4	528.5	-310.3	-94.6	2 299.8	1 891.0	217.3	191.6	3 215.9	2 610.6	605.3	-616.6	916.1	14 709.4	0.8
2008															
1st quarter	2 378.5	577.5	-409.5	-117.3	2 327.7	1 911.7	221.2	194.9	3 138.4	2 527.0	611.4	-709.3	810.6	14 803.7	0.3
2nd quarter	2 285.8	836.6	-782.9	-120.9	2 353.0	1 930.3	224.8	197.9	3 126.0	2 493.3	632.8	-706.8	773.0	14 868.5	-0.5
3rd quarter	2 263.9	732.2	-664.8	-183.2	2 379.7	1 949.6	228.4	201.6	3 081.6	2 435.9	645.8	-671.7	701.9	14 925.0	-0.8
4th quarter	2 199.3	728.3	-683.3	-238.9	2 393.0	1 955.9	231.0	206.2	2 891.7	2 243.1	648.6	-604.9	498.7	14 579.6	-1.3
2009															
1st quarter	2 108.6	1 030.8	-1 040.7	-267.1	2 385.6	1 944.4	232.7	208.5	2 614.9	1 972.1	642.7	-395.2	229.3	14 392.2	-1.9
2nd quarter	2 026.5	1 262.8	-1 336.6	-266.7	2 367.0	1 924.8	234.0	208.1	2 477.8	1 825.9	651.9	-353.5	110.8	14 363.3	-2.4
3rd quarter	1 983.6	1 255.7	-1 341.7	-285.6	2 355.2	1 912.6	234.8	207.7	2 437.8	1 786.4	651.4	-380.5	82.6	14 476.7	-2.6
4th quarter	2 168.3	1 351.0	-1 280.2	-268.3	2 365.8	1 920.7	236.6	208.4	2 570.1	1 928.0	642.1	-397.7	204.3	14 739.3	-1.3
2010															
1st quarter	2 134.6	1 377.4	-1 352.3	-260.3	2 369.8	1 919.7	240.2	210.0	2 624.9	1 989.5	635.4	-445.8	255.1	14 830.9	-1.6
2nd quarter	2 202.4	1 430.4	-1 340.0	-262.9	2 374.9	1 918.9	244.1	211.9	2 748.0	2 092.7	655.3	-460.7	373.1	14 998.9	-1.2
3rd quarter	2 339.5	1 498.7	-1 320.1	-221.6	2 382.5	1 921.9	246.9	213.6	2 825.1	2 164.6	660.5	-487.5	442.6	15 250.2	-0.3
4th quarter	2 343.5	1 454.4	-1 305.7	-204.4	2 399.1	1 933.6	250.1	215.4	2 812.5	2 156.5	656.0	-426.8	413.4	15 404.5	-0.4
2011															
1st quarter	2 374.3	1 411.7	-1 244.9	-210.3	2 417.9	1 947.3	253.2	217.4	2 754.4	2 120.4	633.9	-464.0	336.5	15 574.6	-0.3
2nd quarter	2 411.9	1 470.5	-1 313.4	-188.6	2 443.4	1 967.1	256.1	220.2	2 833.1	2 199.9	633.2	-476.6	389.7	15 763.8	-0.2
3rd quarter	2 511.8	1 501.5	-1 231.7	-223.1	2 465.1	1 984.1	257.9	223.1	2 853.8	2 222.2	631.6	-426.7	388.7	15 967.1	0.3
4th quarter	2 547.5	1 496.9	-1 203.0	-230.3	2 483.9	1 999.3	258.6	226.1	3 017.5	2 385.7	631.8	-467.2	533.6	16 087.6	0.4
2012															
1st quarter	2 645.0	1 472.6	-1 094.0	-241.1	2 507.6	2 018.7	260.4	228.5	3 071.0	2 453.6	617.3	-489.3	563.4	16 352.6	0.8
2nd quarter	2 624.6	1 493.0	-1 146.9	-255.2	2 533.7	2 041.0	261.9	230.8	3 079.3	2 454.0	625.3	-445.9	545.6	16 409.0	0.6
3rd quarter	2 606.4	1 430.6	-1 119.3	-260.1	2 555.1	2 059.8	262.9	232.4	3 113.9	2 493.3	620.6	-423.4	558.8	16 517.2	0.3
4th quarter	2 812.8	1 570.5	-1 078.5	-254.2	2 575.0	2 077.6	263.7	233.7	3 112.5	2 499.9	612.5	-371.1	537.4	16 779.1	1.4

Table 5-2. Gross Private Fixed Investment by Type

(Billions of dollars, quarterly data are at seasonally adjusted annual rates.)   **NIPA Table 5.3.5**

Year and quarter	Total gross private fixed investment	Nonresidential											
			Structures						Equipment				
										Information processing equipment			
		Total	Total	Comm-ercial and health care	Manufac-turing	Power and communi-cation	Mining explor-ation, shafts, and wells	Other non-residential structures	Total	Total	Computers and peripheral equipment	Other information processing	Industrial equipment
1955	68.8	43.4	15.2	3.4	2.3	3.3	2.5	3.7	23.9	2.8	. . .	2.8	7.3
1956	73.7	49.7	18.2	4.2	3.2	4.1	2.7	4.0	26.3	3.4	. . .	3.4	8.8
1957	75.7	53.1	19.0	4.1	3.6	4.5	2.6	4.1	28.6	4.0	. . .	4.0	9.6
1958	71.3	48.5	17.6	4.2	2.4	4.4	2.4	4.2	24.9	3.6	. . .	3.6	8.2
1959	81.7	53.1	18.1	4.6	2.1	4.3	2.5	4.7	28.3	4.0	0.0	4.0	8.5
1960	83.2	56.4	19.6	4.8	2.9	4.4	2.3	5.2	29.7	4.7	0.2	4.6	9.4
1961	83.6	56.6	19.7	5.5	2.8	4.1	2.3	5.0	28.9	5.1	0.3	4.8	8.8
1962	90.9	61.2	20.8	6.2	2.8	4.1	2.5	5.2	32.1	5.5	0.3	5.1	9.3
1963	97.7	64.8	21.2	6.1	2.9	4.4	2.3	5.6	34.4	6.1	0.7	5.4	10.0
1964	107.3	72.2	23.7	6.8	3.6	4.8	2.4	6.2	38.7	6.8	0.9	5.9	11.4
1965	120.4	85.2	28.3	8.2	5.1	5.4	2.4	7.2	45.8	7.8	1.2	6.7	13.7
1966	130.6	97.2	31.3	8.3	6.6	6.3	2.5	7.8	53.0	9.7	1.7	8.0	16.2
1967	132.8	99.2	31.5	8.2	6.0	7.1	2.4	7.8	53.7	10.1	1.9	8.2	16.9
1968	147.9	107.7	33.6	9.4	6.0	8.3	2.6	7.3	58.5	10.6	1.9	8.7	17.3
1969	164.4	120.0	37.7	11.7	6.8	8.7	2.8	7.8	65.2	12.8	2.4	10.4	19.1
1970	168.0	124.6	40.3	12.5	7.0	10.2	2.8	7.8	66.4	14.3	2.7	11.6	20.3
1971	188.6	130.4	42.7	14.9	6.3	11.0	2.7	7.9	69.1	14.9	2.8	12.2	19.5
1972	219.0	146.6	47.2	17.6	5.9	12.1	3.1	8.6	78.9	16.7	3.5	13.2	21.4
1973	251.1	172.7	55.0	19.8	7.9	13.8	3.5	9.9	95.1	19.9	3.5	16.3	26.0
1974	260.5	191.1	61.2	20.6	10.0	15.1	5.2	10.3	104.3	23.1	3.9	19.2	30.7
1975	263.5	196.8	61.4	17.7	10.6	15.7	7.4	10.1	107.6	23.8	3.6	20.2	31.3
1976	306.1	219.3	65.9	18.1	10.1	18.2	8.6	11.0	121.2	27.5	4.4	23.1	34.1
1977	374.3	259.1	74.6	20.3	11.1	19.3	11.5	12.5	148.7	33.7	5.7	28.0	39.4
1978	452.6	314.6	93.6	25.3	16.2	21.4	15.4	15.2	180.6	42.3	7.6	34.8	47.7
1979	521.7	373.8	117.7	33.5	22.0	24.6	19.0	18.5	208.1	50.4	10.2	40.2	56.2
1980	536.4	406.9	136.2	41.0	20.5	27.3	27.4	20.0	216.4	58.9	12.5	46.4	60.7
1981	601.4	472.9	167.3	48.3	25.4	30.0	42.5	21.2	240.9	69.6	17.1	52.5	65.5
1982	595.9	485.1	177.6	55.8	26.1	29.6	44.8	21.3	234.9	74.2	18.9	55.3	62.7
1983	643.3	482.2	154.3	55.8	19.5	25.8	30.0	23.3	246.5	83.7	23.9	59.8	58.9
1984	754.7	564.3	177.4	70.6	20.9	26.5	31.3	28.1	291.9	101.2	31.6	69.6	68.1
1985	807.8	607.7	194.5	84.1	24.1	26.5	27.9	31.8	307.9	106.6	33.7	72.9	72.5
1986	842.6	607.8	176.5	80.9	21.0	28.3	15.7	30.7	317.7	111.1	33.4	77.7	75.4
1987	865.0	615.2	174.2	80.8	21.2	25.4	13.1	33.7	320.9	112.2	35.8	76.4	76.7
1988	918.5	662.3	182.8	86.3	23.2	25.0	15.7	32.5	346.8	120.8	38.0	82.8	84.2
1989	972.0	716.0	193.7	88.3	28.8	27.5	14.9	34.3	372.2	130.7	43.1	87.6	93.3
1990	978.9	739.2	202.9	87.5	33.6	26.3	17.9	37.6	371.9	129.6	38.6	90.9	92.1
1991	944.7	723.6	183.6	68.9	31.4	31.6	18.5	33.2	360.8	129.2	37.7	91.5	89.3
1992	996.7	741.9	172.6	64.5	29.0	33.9	14.2	31.0	381.7	142.1	44.0	98.1	93.0
1993	1 086.0	799.2	177.2	69.4	23.6	33.2	16.6	34.5	425.1	153.3	47.9	105.4	102.2
1994	1 192.7	868.9	186.8	75.4	28.9	31.2	16.4	34.9	476.4	167.0	52.4	114.6	113.6
1995	1 286.3	962.2	207.3	83.1	35.5	33.1	15.0	40.6	528.1	188.4	66.1	122.3	129.0
1996	1 401.3	1 043.2	224.6	91.5	38.2	29.2	16.8	48.9	565.3	204.7	72.8	131.9	136.5
1997	1 524.7	1 149.1	250.3	104.3	37.6	28.8	22.4	57.2	610.9	222.8	81.4	141.4	140.4
1998	1 671.6	1 252.8	275.1	116.0	40.5	34.2	22.3	62.2	660.0	240.1	87.9	152.2	147.4
1999	1 823.4	1 361.6	283.9	125.4	35.1	40.4	18.3	64.7	713.6	259.8	97.2	162.5	149.1
2000	1 979.2	1 493.8	318.1	139.3	37.6	48.1	23.7	69.4	766.1	293.8	103.2	190.6	162.9
2001	1 966.9	1 453.9	329.7	137.3	37.8	51.1	34.6	68.9	711.5	265.9	87.6	178.4	151.9
2002	1 906.5	1 348.9	282.9	119.4	22.7	51.0	30.2	59.5	659.6	236.7	79.7	157.0	141.7
2003	2 008.7	1 371.7	281.8	115.0	21.4	48.1	38.5	58.8	669.0	241.0	78.3	162.8	143.4
2004	2 212.8	1 463.1	301.8	125.3	23.2	43.1	47.3	62.9	719.2	253.1	81.5	171.6	144.2
2005	2 467.5	1 611.5	345.6	135.9	28.4	48.1	69.4	63.9	790.7	262.8	80.0	182.8	162.4
2006	2 613.7	1 776.3	415.6	156.3	32.3	55.8	96.0	75.1	856.1	282.3	86.4	195.9	181.6
2007	2 609.3	1 920.6	496.9	181.8	40.2	81.6	102.2	91.1	885.8	303.2	87.7	215.5	194.1
2008	2 456.8	1 941.0	552.4	181.8	52.8	95.6	117.0	105.2	825.1	291.2	83.8	207.5	192.9
2009	2 025.7	1 633.4	438.2	126.7	56.3	95.8	75.0	84.5	644.3	256.1	76.8	179.3	152.1
2010	2 039.3	1 658.2	362.0	92.0	39.8	83.8	86.2	60.3	731.8	276.7	81.3	195.4	152.9
2011	2 195.6	1 809.9	380.6	93.2	38.9	81.8	110.2	56.5	832.7	280.4	76.8	203.6	182.0
2012	2 409.1	1 970.0	437.3	103.2	45.8	100.5	125.5	62.3	907.6	284.5	79.2	205.4	195.3
2010													
1st quarter	1 977.5	1 594.4	352.4	96.6	45.0	73.4	74.1	63.4	682.7	271.9	84.8	187.1	143.7
2nd quarter	2 042.6	1 641.8	364.5	92.1	43.0	83.2	85.2	61.1	719.0	273.3	83.2	190.1	152.5
3rd quarter	2 043.0	1 677.4	361.1	89.8	37.9	82.5	91.7	59.1	751.2	277.1	79.5	197.6	154.6
4th quarter	2 094.1	1 719.3	370.1	89.5	33.3	96.1	93.8	57.4	774.4	284.7	77.6	207.0	160.9
2011													
1st quarter	2 098.9	1 721.8	340.8	87.0	31.6	71.7	97.7	52.8	798.0	278.7	73.1	205.6	171.3
2nd quarter	2 154.1	1 773.1	370.1	91.9	36.8	79.3	105.6	56.5	809.9	282.1	77.5	204.6	173.1
3rd quarter	2 235.7	1 848.9	397.5	96.0	42.2	86.8	114.8	57.7	849.8	280.1	77.5	202.6	187.1
4th quarter	2 293.8	1 895.7	413.9	97.9	44.8	89.4	122.7	59.1	873.0	280.6	79.1	201.5	196.5
2012													
1st quarter	2 350.7	1 932.3	422.0	100.1	43.9	93.6	125.1	59.3	895.4	290.1	83.5	206.6	190.1
2nd quarter	2 387.1	1 961.4	431.3	102.2	45.4	93.8	127.4	62.5	907.9	281.2	79.2	202.0	195.5
3rd quarter	2 411.7	1 968.0	438.3	105.5	46.0	97.9	125.0	63.8	902.2	277.5	71.5	206.0	195.9
4th quarter	2 486.9	2 018.2	457.8	105.1	48.0	116.5	124.5	63.7	925.0	289.4	82.5	206.9	199.6

. . . = Not available.

Table 5-2. Gross Private Fixed Investment by Type—*Continued*

(Billions of dollars, quarterly data are at seasonally adjusted annual rates.)   **NIPA Table 5.3.5**

Year and quarter	Equipment—*Continued*		Intellectual property				Total	Residential						Residential equipment
	Transportation equipment	Other nonresidential equipment	Total	Software [1]	Research and development [2]	Entertainment, literary, and artistic originals		Residential structures		Permanent site			Other residential structures	
								Total	Total	Total	Single family	Multifamily		
1955	7.5	6.3	4.3	...	2.7	1.6	25.4	25.0	18.6	...	...	6.4	0.4
1956	7.4	6.7	5.2	...	3.6	1.7	24.0	23.5	16.5	...	...	7.0	0.5
1957	8.3	6.7	5.6	...	3.7	1.9	22.6	22.2	15.1	...	...	7.1	0.5
1958	6.1	6.9	6.0	...	4.0	2.0	22.8	22.3	15.4	13.1	2.3	6.9	0.5
1959	8.3	7.6	6.6	0.0	4.4	2.2	28.6	28.1	19.7	16.7	3.0	8.4	0.6
1960	8.5	7.1	7.1	0.1	4.9	2.2	26.9	26.3	17.5	14.9	2.6	8.8	0.5
1961	8.0	7.0	8.0	0.2	5.2	2.7	27.0	26.5	17.4	14.1	3.3	9.1	0.5
1962	9.8	7.5	8.4	0.2	5.6	2.6	29.6	29.1	19.9	15.1	4.8	9.2	0.5
1963	9.4	8.8	9.2	0.4	6.0	2.8	32.9	32.3	22.4	16.0	6.4	9.8	0.6
1964	10.6	9.9	9.8	0.5	6.5	2.8	35.1	34.5	24.1	17.6	6.4	10.4	0.6
1965	13.2	11.0	11.1	0.7	7.2	3.2	35.2	34.5	23.8	17.8	6.0	10.6	0.7
1966	14.5	12.7	12.8	1.0	8.1	3.7	33.4	32.7	21.8	16.6	5.2	10.9	0.7
1967	14.3	12.4	14.0	1.2	9.0	3.8	33.6	32.9	21.5	16.8	4.7	11.4	0.7
1968	17.6	13.0	15.6	1.3	9.9	4.3	40.2	39.3	26.7	19.5	7.2	12.6	0.9
1969	18.9	14.4	17.2	1.8	11.0	4.4	44.4	43.4	29.2	19.7	9.5	14.1	1.0
1970	16.2	15.6	17.9	2.3	11.5	4.1	43.4	42.3	27.1	17.5	9.5	15.2	1.1
1971	18.4	16.3	18.7	2.4	11.9	4.4	58.2	56.9	38.7	25.8	12.9	18.2	1.3
1972	21.8	19.0	20.6	2.8	12.9	4.9	72.4	70.9	50.1	32.8	17.2	20.8	1.5
1973	26.6	22.6	22.7	3.2	14.6	4.9	78.3	76.6	54.6	35.2	19.4	22.0	1.7
1974	26.3	24.3	25.5	3.9	16.4	5.2	69.5	67.6	43.4	29.7	13.7	24.2	1.9
1975	25.2	27.4	27.8	4.8	17.5	5.5	66.7	64.8	36.3	29.6	6.7	28.5	1.9
1976	30.0	29.6	32.2	5.2	19.6	7.4	86.8	84.6	50.8	43.9	6.9	33.9	2.1
1977	39.3	36.3	35.8	5.5	21.8	8.6	115.2	112.8	72.2	62.2	10.0	40.6	2.4
1978	47.3	43.2	40.4	6.3	24.9	9.1	138.0	135.3	85.6	72.8	12.8	49.7	2.7
1979	53.6	47.9	48.1	8.1	29.1	10.9	147.8	144.7	89.3	72.3	17.0	55.4	3.2
1980	48.4	48.3	54.4	9.8	34.2	10.3	129.5	126.1	69.6	52.9	16.7	56.5	3.4
1981	50.6	55.2	64.8	11.8	39.7	13.2	128.5	124.9	69.4	52.0	17.5	55.4	3.6
1982	46.8	51.2	72.7	14.0	44.8	13.9	110.8	107.2	57.0	41.5	15.5	50.2	3.7
1983	53.5	50.4	81.3	16.4	49.6	15.3	161.1	156.9	95.0	72.5	22.4	61.9	4.2
1984	64.4	58.1	95.1	20.4	56.9	17.8	190.4	185.6	114.6	86.4	28.2	71.0	4.7
1985	69.0	59.9	105.3	23.8	63.0	18.6	200.1	195.0	115.9	87.4	28.5	79.1	5.1
1986	70.5	60.7	113.5	25.6	66.5	21.4	234.8	229.3	135.2	104.1	31.0	94.1	5.5
1987	68.1	63.9	120.1	29.0	69.2	21.9	249.8	244.0	142.7	117.2	25.5	101.3	5.8
1988	72.9	69.0	132.7	34.2	75.5	23.0	256.2	250.1	142.4	120.1	22.3	107.7	6.1
1989	67.9	80.2	150.1	41.9	82.8	25.4	256.0	249.9	143.2	120.9	22.3	106.6	6.1
1990	70.0	80.2	164.4	47.6	89.3	27.5	239.7	233.7	132.1	112.9	19.3	101.5	6.0
1991	71.5	70.8	179.1	53.7	96.0	29.4	221.2	215.4	114.6	99.4	15.1	100.8	5.7
1992	74.7	72.0	187.7	57.9	98.6	31.2	254.7	248.8	135.1	122.0	13.1	113.8	5.9
1993	89.4	80.2	196.9	64.3	99.2	33.4	286.8	280.7	150.9	140.1	10.8	129.8	6.1
1994	107.7	88.1	205.7	68.3	101.3	36.1	323.8	317.6	176.4	162.3	14.1	141.2	6.2
1995	116.1	94.7	226.8	74.6	112.0	40.2	324.1	317.7	171.4	153.5	17.9	146.3	6.3
1996	123.2	101.0	253.3	85.5	123.6	44.3	358.1	351.7	191.1	170.8	20.3	160.6	6.3
1997	135.5	112.1	288.0	107.5	134.4	46.1	375.6	369.3	198.1	175.2	22.9	171.3	6.3
1998	147.1	125.4	317.7	126.0	143.3	48.3	418.8	412.1	224.0	199.4	24.6	188.2	6.7
1999	174.4	130.4	364.0	157.3	155.7	51.0	461.8	454.5	251.3	223.8	27.4	203.2	7.3
2000	170.8	138.6	409.5	184.5	169.5	55.6	485.4	477.7	265.0	236.8	28.3	212.7	7.7
2001	154.2	139.5	412.6	186.6	171.3	54.7	513.0	505.2	279.4	249.1	30.3	225.8	7.8
2002	141.6	139.6	406.4	183.0	165.7	57.6	557.6	549.6	298.8	265.9	33.0	250.7	8.0
2003	134.1	150.5	420.9	191.0	167.2	62.7	636.9	628.7	345.7	310.6	35.1	283.0	8.3
2004	159.2	162.7	442.1	205.1	173.0	64.1	749.7	740.7	417.5	377.6	39.9	323.2	9.0
2005	179.6	186.0	475.1	217.2	188.1	69.8	856.1	846.4	480.8	433.5	47.3	365.6	9.6
2006	194.3	198.0	504.6	228.9	204.5	71.2	837.4	827.4	468.8	416.0	52.8	358.6	10.0
2007	188.8	199.6	537.9	244.2	223.3	70.4	688.7	678.8	354.1	305.2	49.0	324.7	9.9
2008	146.2	194.9	563.4	258.5	237.7	67.2	515.9	506.5	230.1	185.8	44.3	276.4	9.3
2009	70.6	165.6	550.9	256.8	229.0	65.1	392.2	383.9	133.9	105.3	28.5	250.1	8.3
2010	127.5	174.7	564.3	252.0	240.2	72.2	381.1	372.7	127.3	112.6	14.7	245.5	8.3
2011	171.8	198.6	596.6	267.6	255.2	73.8	385.8	377.2	123.2	108.2	15.0	254.0	8.6
2012	214.4	213.4	625.0	281.6	269.1	74.3	439.2	430.2	154.2	132.0	22.2	275.9	9.0
2010													
1st quarter	101.5	165.7	559.2	254.4	236.6	68.3	383.1	374.8	130.8	114.7	16.1	244.0	8.3
2nd quarter	121.4	171.9	558.3	248.9	237.5	71.9	400.8	392.3	133.3	118.8	14.5	259.0	8.5
3rd quarter	141.6	177.9	565.1	250.7	240.6	73.9	365.6	357.3	124.5	110.4	14.1	232.8	8.3
4th quarter	145.5	183.3	574.8	253.9	246.1	74.9	374.7	366.4	120.4	106.4	14.1	246.0	8.3
2011													
1st quarter	156.2	191.9	582.9	259.7	249.3	73.9	377.1	368.9	120.7	106.9	13.8	248.2	8.3
2nd quarter	159.2	195.5	593.1	264.6	254.9	73.6	381.0	372.6	120.2	106.0	14.2	252.4	8.4
3rd quarter	176.2	206.5	601.6	270.0	257.9	73.7	386.8	378.1	124.1	108.5	15.6	253.9	8.7
4th quarter	195.4	200.6	608.8	275.9	259.0	73.9	398.1	389.3	127.8	111.3	16.5	261.5	8.8
2012													
1st quarter	209.0	206.3	614.9	276.8	264.1	74.0	418.4	409.5	137.4	119.4	17.9	272.1	8.9
2nd quarter	220.6	210.6	622.2	280.6	267.5	74.1	425.7	416.8	146.7	125.6	21.1	270.2	8.9
3rd quarter	212.3	216.5	627.5	281.9	271.3	74.4	443.7	434.7	158.6	135.1	23.5	276.1	9.0
4th quarter	215.7	220.3	635.4	287.3	273.4	74.7	468.8	459.7	174.3	148.0	26.4	285.3	9.1

[1]Excludes software "embedded," or bundled, in computers and other equipment. Includes software development expenditures.
[2]Excludes software development.
. . . = Not available.

Table 5-3. Real Gross Private Fixed Investment by Type

(Billions of chained [2009] dollars, quarterly data are at seasonally adjusted annual rates.)   **NIPA Table 5.3.6**

Year and quarter	Total gross private fixed investment	Nonresidential											
		Total	Structures						Equipment				
			Total	Commer-cial and health care	Manufac-turing	Power and communi-cation	Mining explor-ation, shafts, and wells	Other non-residential structures	Total	Information processing equipment			Industrial equipment
										Total	Computers and peripheral equipment¹	Other information processing	
1999	2 165.9	1 510.1	494.9	199.0	53.9	62.8	64.5	94.7	662.4	149.5	...	127.3	182.8
2000	2 316.2	1 647.7	533.5	212.3	55.6	72.5	80.5	97.5	726.9	180.4	...	153.2	198.5
2001	2 280.0	1 608.4	525.4	202.0	54.1	74.7	94.9	93.0	695.7	178.2	...	148.5	183.9
2002	2 201.1	1 498.0	432.5	171.1	31.6	72.9	69.4	78.6	658.0	169.9	...	135.0	171.6
2003	2 289.5	1 526.1	415.8	160.3	29.2	67.2	79.3	75.6	679.0	185.8	...	147.3	172.2
2004	2 443.9	1 605.4	414.1	164.2	30.1	56.1	84.2	76.7	731.2	204.5	...	160.7	169.1
2005	2 611.0	1 717.4	421.2	162.8	34.2	58.1	92.1	72.7	801.6	222.2	...	172.6	183.6
2006	2 662.5	1 839.6	451.5	172.6	36.5	61.7	99.5	79.7	870.8	250.9	...	187.5	199.1
2007	2 609.6	1 948.4	509.0	189.9	43.1	85.9	97.9	91.8	898.3	279.9	...	207.9	205.3
2008	2 432.6	1 934.4	540.2	182.8	53.8	94.5	105.0	103.4	836.1	281.0	...	204.2	195.5
2009	2 025.7	1 633.4	438.2	126.7	56.3	95.8	75.0	84.5	644.3	256.1	...	179.3	152.1
2010	2 056.2	1 673.8	366.3	95.2	40.8	80.4	87.8	62.0	746.7	281.4	...	196.8	151.3
2011	2 184.6	1 800.5	374.1	94.8	39.1	74.1	109.0	57.3	841.7	287.9	...	204.3	175.0
2012	2 365.3	1 931.8	421.6	102.3	45.0	88.0	124.1	61.9	905.9	295.7	...	207.8	184.6
2003													
1st quarter	2 206.8	1 478.6	408.5	156.7	27.2	71.7	74.3	73.4	649.5	175.4	...	138.7	170.1
2nd quarter	2 254.4	1 514.3	419.3	158.5	29.7	69.0	79.9	77.8	671.3	178.9	...	142.4	177.0
3rd quarter	2 325.9	1 544.7	417.5	162.4	29.9	64.4	80.5	76.3	691.0	189.1	...	150.3	172.8
4th quarter	2 370.9	1 566.8	418.0	163.6	30.1	63.5	82.5	75.0	704.3	199.7	...	157.8	169.0
2004													
1st quarter	2 362.5	1 549.4	409.3	161.2	29.1	60.0	82.0	74.1	692.8	198.7	...	158.1	162.5
2nd quarter	2 422.8	1 583.8	411.6	167.5	28.1	52.7	83.2	77.2	719.9	204.2	...	162.3	166.5
3rd quarter	2 472.0	1 626.9	417.9	167.1	29.1	55.6	85.4	78.0	744.6	206.1	...	161.5	171.9
4th quarter	2 518.2	1 661.4	417.7	161.2	34.1	56.2	86.1	77.5	767.4	209.2	...	161.1	175.4
2005													
1st quarter	2 558.8	1 681.9	423.1	164.0	34.8	57.2	90.9	74.5	774.2	214.3	...	168.6	179.4
2nd quarter	2 599.2	1 706.1	420.9	163.3	33.4	58.3	93.1	71.6	791.0	218.0	...	170.5	177.4
3rd quarter	2 640.4	1 737.4	418.6	161.1	34.0	57.9	92.9	71.6	817.9	226.2	...	176.2	185.0
4th quarter	2 645.5	1 744.3	422.3	162.8	34.6	59.1	91.5	73.0	823.4	230.3	...	175.2	192.6
2006													
1st quarter	2 700.7	1 808.7	437.8	166.5	34.4	60.7	99.5	75.2	866.5	246.3	...	187.8	190.8
2nd quarter	2 676.8	1 831.3	450.9	171.9	36.8	59.6	100.8	80.1	869.6	247.6	...	185.9	202.6
3rd quarter	2 649.6	1 853.1	458.9	176.7	38.5	61.8	99.6	80.9	871.9	255.1	...	188.4	201.2
4th quarter	2 622.8	1 865.2	458.4	175.4	36.1	64.7	98.1	82.6	875.2	254.7	...	187.9	201.7
2007													
1st quarter	2 618.2	1 897.2	474.8	183.8	37.3	72.6	97.7	82.4	886.1	270.6	...	200.0	197.7
2nd quarter	2 624.9	1 934.4	500.6	189.7	39.4	82.3	98.3	90.2	896.2	272.7	...	203.8	210.6
3rd quarter	2 609.0	1 964.4	524.0	192.8	46.2	90.6	98.6	95.5	900.9	279.5	...	207.7	211.7
4th quarter	2 586.3	1 997.6	536.8	193.2	49.7	98.2	96.9	98.9	910.0	296.7	...	220.0	201.2
2008													
1st quarter	2 539.1	1 998.1	539.0	191.3	50.0	100.2	96.5	101.0	899.4	294.6	...	213.8	201.0
2nd quarter	2 503.4	1 986.6	547.7	188.9	53.8	95.4	103.4	105.6	876.6	294.1	...	212.4	199.4
3rd quarter	2 424.1	1 933.0	543.7	183.3	55.1	90.0	108.7	105.7	831.6	281.2	...	205.2	195.6
4th quarter	2 263.8	1 820.1	530.3	167.8	56.3	92.2	111.4	101.4	736.8	254.1	...	185.4	186.0
2009													
1st quarter	2 089.3	1 688.3	490.5	146.2	61.5	93.8	96.7	92.0	653.9	245.6	...	175.8	161.0
2nd quarter	2 011.0	1 634.0	453.3	133.1	60.1	96.3	73.6	90.3	631.6	246.4	...	173.1	152.5
3rd quarter	2 008.4	1 613.1	422.6	120.1	55.1	100.9	63.9	82.6	639.9	261.4	...	183.9	148.5
4th quarter	1 994.1	1 598.4	386.5	107.4	48.5	92.0	65.7	73.1	651.9	270.9	...	184.5	146.3
2010													
1st quarter	1 997.9	1 615.0	359.7	99.7	46.2	72.7	76.5	65.0	697.7	276.0	...	188.5	143.0
2nd quarter	2 062.8	1 659.3	369.8	95.6	44.2	80.4	86.8	62.9	735.2	277.8	...	191.5	151.1
3rd quarter	2 060.8	1 692.8	364.4	93.1	38.8	78.3	93.1	60.9	766.2	282.5	...	199.5	152.8
4th quarter	2 103.1	1 728.1	371.2	92.4	34.1	90.0	94.7	59.0	787.8	289.5	...	207.7	158.3
2011													
1st quarter	2 100.7	1 724.1	339.8	89.5	32.4	66.3	97.9	54.1	810.6	283.6	...	205.2	166.7
2nd quarter	2 144.4	1 765.3	365.3	94.1	37.4	72.3	104.5	57.5	819.2	289.0	...	205.1	166.8
3rd quarter	2 219.8	1 835.0	388.9	97.4	42.3	78.1	112.8	58.4	858.0	288.6	...	203.8	179.0
4th quarter	2 273.4	1 877.3	402.2	98.2	44.4	79.6	121.0	59.2	879.1	290.4	...	203.2	187.7
2012													
1st quarter	2 320.8	1 903.8	409.0	100.0	43.3	82.6	123.7	59.4	896.9	300.0	...	208.0	180.5
2nd quarter	2 347.9	1 925.0	416.0	101.4	44.6	82.2	125.8	62.2	908.5	292.0	...	204.1	184.9
3rd quarter	2 363.5	1 926.4	422.0	104.4	45.2	85.6	123.7	63.1	899.5	288.6	...	208.7	185.0
4th quarter	2 429.1	1 971.9	439.4	103.5	47.0	101.6	123.1	62.7	918.8	302.1	...	210.3	187.8

¹See notes and definitions.
. . . = Not available.

Table 5-3. Real Gross Private Fixed Investment by Type—*Continued*

(Billions of chained [2009] dollars, quarterly data are at seasonally adjusted annual rates.)   **NIPA Table 5.3.6**

Year and quarter	Nonresidential—*Continued*						Residential						
	Equipment—*Continued*		Intellectual property					Residential structures					Residential equipment
	Transportation equipment	Other nonresidential equipment	Total	Software [2]	Research and development [3]	Entertainment, literary, and artistic originals	Total	Total	Permanent site			Other residential structures	
									Total	Single family	Multifamily		
1999	208.4	161.4	391.1	154.5	183.9	55.9	633.8	626.5	357.7	311.2	43.6	269.4	7.2
2000	204.1	170.5	426.1	175.9	193.0	59.3	637.9	630.1	360.6	314.6	42.8	270.1	7.6
2001	184.9	169.2	428.0	177.1	195.6	57.5	643.7	635.7	362.7	315.1	44.7	273.5	7.8
2002	167.2	167.9	425.9	176.9	190.5	60.3	682.7	674.5	377.3	327.3	47.1	297.2	8.0
2003	154.8	179.3	442.2	189.0	189.1	64.8	744.5	735.9	414.2	362.2	48.3	321.9	8.5
2004	176.5	192.4	464.9	207.9	191.0	65.8	818.9	809.2	462.2	405.7	52.0	347.6	9.5
2005	197.9	210.9	495.0	221.2	202.3	71.3	872.6	862.5	494.8	433.0	57.2	368.3	9.9
2006	212.6	219.6	517.5	230.3	215.0	72.1	806.6	796.3	451.6	390.7	57.6	345.2	10.1
2007	203.6	217.0	542.4	244.2	227.9	70.3	654.8	644.9	336.1	283.7	51.0	309.3	9.8
2008	156.9	206.5	558.8	256.2	235.5	67.1	497.7	488.4	223.1	178.2	44.9	265.6	9.3
2009	70.6	165.6	550.9	256.8	229.0	65.1	392.2	383.9	133.9	105.3	28.5	250.1	8.3
2010	136.9	179.8	561.3	254.2	234.4	72.7	382.4	373.6	128.5	114.4	14.3	245.1	8.8
2011	181.0	201.8	586.1	269.8	241.8	74.6	384.3	375.1	123.9	109.2	15.0	251.1	9.2
2012	221.0	209.7	605.8	285.9	245.7	74.8	433.7	424.2	154.0	132.1	22.1	270.4	9.5
2003													
1st quarter	144.7	173.1	433.0	180.7	190.5	63.3	709.8	701.6	393.5	342.6	47.6	308.3	8.0
2nd quarter	155.9	174.9	436.6	182.5	190.0	65.2	721.0	712.5	398.8	347.8	47.6	313.8	8.3
3rd quarter	159.0	183.2	446.2	192.7	188.3	65.5	762.3	753.4	420.1	367.2	49.1	333.4	8.7
4th quarter	159.6	186.1	452.9	199.9	187.5	65.4	785.0	775.9	444.5	391.2	48.9	332.0	8.9
2004													
1st quarter	156.1	184.6	454.7	202.4	187.4	64.7	794.2	784.8	447.2	393.4	49.3	338.1	9.2
2nd quarter	170.2	189.1	457.8	203.7	189.5	64.7	819.5	809.9	461.9	406.0	51.3	348.5	9.4
3rd quarter	183.2	195.9	468.6	209.8	192.8	65.9	825.3	815.5	469.6	411.6	53.6	346.6	9.5
4th quarter	196.4	200.2	478.4	215.7	194.5	68.0	836.7	826.7	470.0	411.6	54.0	357.2	9.7
2005													
1st quarter	189.7	203.7	487.0	216.6	200.6	69.7	856.4	846.4	483.4	423.4	55.4	363.6	9.7
2nd quarter	196.7	212.2	495.0	221.8	202.1	70.9	872.3	862.2	491.5	429.8	57.3	371.3	9.8
3rd quarter	206.9	213.0	499.9	223.1	204.9	71.8	881.9	871.8	498.0	435.4	58.2	374.4	9.8
4th quarter	198.4	214.9	498.0	223.3	201.6	72.9	879.9	869.6	506.2	443.5	58.1	364.0	10.1
2006													
1st quarter	219.6	221.9	503.8	225.7	205.2	72.6	871.7	861.1	504.4	441.8	58.0	357.4	10.3
2nd quarter	209.9	221.5	511.0	228.1	210.6	72.2	827.8	817.5	470.2	408.9	57.5	347.9	10.1
3rd quarter	209.0	217.2	522.9	231.7	219.6	71.7	781.6	771.4	433.7	374.2	56.6	338.1	10.0
4th quarter	211.8	217.7	532.1	235.9	224.7	71.7	745.2	735.2	398.0	337.8	58.3	337.6	9.8
2007													
1st quarter	212.8	213.2	537.0	241.5	224.7	70.8	711.2	701.1	371.9	313.7	56.6	329.7	9.9
2nd quarter	201.8	219.5	538.9	242.2	226.2	70.5	682.7	672.8	355.2	301.4	52.0	318.1	9.8
3rd quarter	199.2	217.9	541.1	244.7	225.9	70.5	639.2	629.4	328.0	277.7	48.8	301.8	9.7
4th quarter	200.5	217.4	552.4	248.3	234.7	69.4	586.1	576.4	289.4	241.8	46.7	287.5	9.7
2008													
1st quarter	198.5	211.1	561.2	256.0	236.6	68.6	540.0	530.5	255.7	209.4	46.0	275.2	9.5
2nd quarter	175.8	211.8	563.3	257.0	238.6	67.7	516.3	506.7	239.5	193.0	46.4	267.6	9.6
3rd quarter	147.7	210.6	558.2	257.7	234.2	66.3	490.9	481.7	213.5	168.2	45.3	268.4	9.2
4th quarter	105.5	192.7	552.5	254.2	232.7	65.6	443.6	434.9	183.9	142.2	41.8	251.0	8.6
2009													
1st quarter	68.6	178.8	543.6	252.8	226.2	64.6	401.0	392.6	147.0	109.5	37.6	245.6	8.4
2nd quarter	67.2	165.5	549.4	255.2	229.1	65.1	377.0	368.8	124.5	93.1	31.4	244.4	8.1
3rd quarter	70.0	159.9	550.9	257.7	228.4	64.7	395.4	387.1	132.1	106.8	25.3	255.0	8.3
4th quarter	76.5	158.2	559.8	261.4	232.3	66.1	395.7	387.2	131.9	112.0	20.0	255.3	8.4
2010													
1st quarter	109.7	170.7	557.6	256.0	232.7	68.9	383.0	374.4	131.3	115.7	15.8	243.1	8.6
2nd quarter	130.9	177.8	554.7	250.9	231.5	72.3	403.5	394.6	135.5	121.7	14.1	259.1	8.9
3rd quarter	152.0	182.2	563.0	253.3	235.6	74.0	368.1	359.3	126.0	112.6	13.7	233.3	8.8
4th quarter	155.1	188.3	570.0	256.7	237.8	75.4	375.1	366.2	121.2	107.7	13.8	245.0	8.9
2011													
1st quarter	166.0	197.9	575.2	261.8	239.0	74.4	376.7	367.7	121.6	108.2	13.6	246.1	9.0
2nd quarter	167.7	199.6	582.0	266.7	241.2	74.1	379.2	370.1	121.1	107.2	14.1	248.9	9.1
3rd quarter	185.5	208.9	589.6	272.2	242.9	74.6	384.9	375.7	124.9	109.5	15.6	250.7	9.3
4th quarter	204.6	200.7	597.6	278.6	244.1	75.2	396.2	386.8	128.1	111.7	16.5	258.7	9.4
2012													
1st quarter	217.0	204.8	599.6	279.7	245.3	74.8	417.2	407.8	138.4	120.8	17.9	269.4	9.4
2nd quarter	229.1	207.7	602.3	284.0	244.1	74.7	423.0	413.7	147.3	126.6	21.0	266.5	9.3
3rd quarter	218.8	211.6	606.4	286.6	245.7	74.6	437.3	427.7	157.8	134.6	23.4	270.1	9.5
4th quarter	219.4	214.5	614.9	293.1	247.6	74.9	457.5	447.8	172.3	146.4	26.2	275.8	9.7

[2]Excludes software "embedded," or bundled, in computers and other equipment.
[3]Excludes software development.

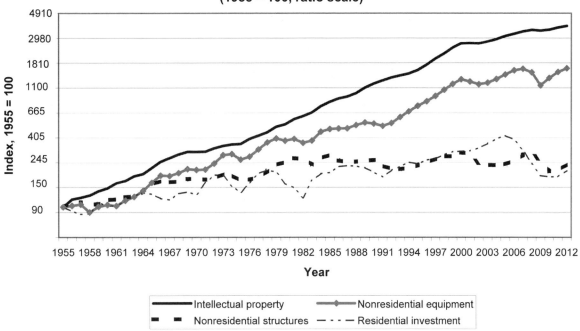

Figure 5-2. Real Private Fixed Investment by Major Type
(1955 = 100, ratio scale)

- Between 1955 and 2006, which was the recent high point for total real (constant-dollar) investment, the quantity of real gross private fixed investment increased eightfold, with an average annual growth rate of 4.2 percent. Every major type of investment grew in real terms between those two years, but as Figure 5-2 indicates, by far the fastest-growing major category has been "intellectual property products." Computer software is the main driver of growth in this category, but it also includes research and development and "entertainment, literary, and artistic originals." (Table 5-4)

- Between 2006 and 2009, gross investment fell 24 percent in real terms—a collapse unprecedented in the postwar period. (Table 5-4)

- By 2012, real equipment purchases had recovered to their pre-recession high, and all three categories of intellectual property spending had surpassed their previous peaks. But spending on both nonresidential and especially residential structures remained far below earlier levels. (Table 5-4)

Table 5-4. Chain-Type Quantity Indexes for Private Fixed Investment by Type

(Index numbers, 2009 = 100, quarterly data are seasonally adjusted.)   **NIPA Table 5.3.3**

Year and quarter	Total gross private fixed investment	Nonresidential											
		Total	Structures						Equipment				
			Total	Commercial and health care	Manufacturing	Power and communication	Mining exploration, shafts, and wells	Other nonresidential structures	Total	Information processing equipment			Industrial equipment
										Total	Computers and peripheral equipment[1]	Other information processing	
1955	16.4	10.4	40.7	29.5	42.7	29.9	84.6	43.9	8.7	0.2	...	2.8	37.0
1956	16.6	11.1	45.0	33.3	56.1	35.0	81.8	43.4	8.9	0.3	...	3.2	40.8
1957	16.5	11.3	45.0	31.6	59.5	36.3	77.2	43.4	9.1	0.3	...	3.7	41.3
1958	15.5	10.3	42.5	33.3	41.0	34.9	72.2	45.4	7.8	0.3	...	3.3	34.4
1959	17.6	11.1	43.5	36.1	36.6	33.5	74.1	50.2	8.7	0.3	0.0	3.6	35.0
1960	17.8	11.7	47.0	38.4	49.6	33.8	69.6	55.7	9.1	0.4	0.0	4.1	37.7
1961	17.9	11.8	47.6	43.8	48.5	31.6	70.9	54.4	8.9	0.4	0.0	4.4	35.7
1962	19.4	12.7	49.8	48.9	49.0	31.8	74.3	55.6	9.9	0.5	0.0	4.6	37.5
1963	20.9	13.5	50.4	47.3	49.2	34.0	69.8	58.8	10.7	0.5	0.0	4.8	40.5
1964	22.8	14.9	55.6	51.4	59.1	37.0	74.8	64.4	12.0	0.6	0.0	5.3	45.8
1965	25.2	17.4	64.5	60.3	81.7	40.9	73.8	72.5	14.2	0.7	0.0	6.0	54.0
1966	26.8	19.6	68.9	58.9	101.6	46.7	70.0	75.2	16.4	0.9	0.0	7.0	62.1
1967	26.5	19.5	67.2	56.6	89.4	51.1	66.9	73.6	16.2	1.0	0.0	7.0	62.4
1968	28.4	20.4	68.1	61.9	86.0	56.7	67.3	65.0	17.2	1.0	0.0	7.2	61.1
1969	30.0	21.8	71.8	71.5	90.5	56.7	70.1	64.5	18.6	1.2	0.0	8.4	65.2
1970	29.4	21.7	72.0	72.4	87.4	62.1	66.0	60.6	18.3	1.4	0.0	9.0	66.1
1971	31.4	21.6	70.8	79.1	72.1	62.6	61.1	56.8	18.4	1.4	0.0	9.1	60.7
1972	35.0	23.5	73.0	86.4	63.0	65.3	65.5	57.5	20.8	1.6	0.0	9.7	65.5
1973	38.0	26.6	79.0	90.3	78.1	69.4	69.9	61.9	24.6	2.0	0.0	11.7	77.4
1974	35.9	26.9	77.3	84.7	89.0	65.0	83.1	56.6	25.2	2.2	0.0	13.0	83.3
1975	32.4	24.4	69.2	66.0	85.3	59.9	97.1	49.9	22.5	2.2	0.0	12.5	70.7
1976	35.6	25.8	70.8	65.1	78.8	65.3	104.8	52.4	23.9	2.5	0.0	13.7	71.0
1977	40.4	28.6	73.7	68.5	80.9	64.3	118.3	55.3	27.6	3.1	0.1	16.4	75.3
1978	45.1	32.6	84.4	78.1	107.9	67.4	134.9	62.8	31.8	4.0	0.1	19.6	83.7
1979	47.7	35.8	95.1	93.1	132.6	70.0	143.7	69.0	34.4	4.9	0.2	22.0	89.7
1980	44.9	35.8	100.7	102.4	110.9	70.6	201.9	67.0	32.9	5.7	0.3	23.7	85.9
1981	46.1	38.0	108.7	110.8	125.9	72.4	234.7	64.9	34.1	6.6	0.4	25.0	84.5
1982	43.0	36.6	106.9	120.7	121.6	68.4	217.0	61.2	31.5	6.6	0.4	25.2	77.2
1983	46.2	36.5	95.4	117.1	87.9	58.8	179.6	64.6	33.0	7.7	0.6	26.5	71.1
1984	53.7	42.6	108.7	142.6	91.0	60.1	204.2	75.7	39.4	9.8	1.0	30.1	81.3
1985	56.6	45.4	116.4	164.6	101.8	59.4	182.0	83.3	41.5	10.7	1.2	31.1	85.1
1986	57.7	44.6	103.7	152.9	85.5	63.4	106.6	78.3	42.0	11.5	1.4	32.4	84.7
1987	58.0	44.6	100.7	147.4	83.3	56.4	104.2	82.9	42.1	12.0	1.8	31.1	82.6
1988	59.9	46.9	101.3	151.8	87.9	53.2	114.3	77.3	44.9	13.1	2.0	33.2	86.7
1989	61.8	49.5	103.3	149.8	105.4	55.3	103.4	78.9	47.3	14.4	2.5	34.7	92.8
1990	61.0	50.1	104.9	143.9	119.3	51.4	119.5	83.8	46.3	14.6	2.5	35.6	87.4
1991	57.8	48.1	93.2	111.8	109.9	61.1	116.8	72.7	44.2	14.9	2.7	35.4	81.8
1992	61.0	49.5	87.6	103.9	100.9	64.7	96.7	67.4	46.8	17.0	3.7	37.5	83.3
1993	65.7	53.2	87.3	108.1	79.3	61.7	112.4	72.7	52.8	19.4	4.7	40.4	90.4
1994	71.0	57.4	88.9	113.1	93.8	56.0	109.2	71.1	59.2	22.0	5.8	44.2	98.4
1995	75.4	63.0	94.6	119.8	110.6	57.1	92.7	79.6	66.4	26.5	8.8	47.5	108.0
1996	82.1	68.7	100.0	129.1	116.3	49.1	98.8	93.6	72.7	32.1	12.7	52.1	112.0
1997	89.1	76.1	107.3	142.6	111.1	47.4	116.2	106.2	80.8	38.7	18.4	56.6	114.5
1998	98.2	84.3	112.8	151.5	114.8	55.6	101.6	112.0	91.4	47.8	26.7	63.7	119.4
1999	106.9	92.4	112.9	157.0	95.8	65.6	86.0	112.1	102.8	58.4	38.0	71.0	120.2
2000	114.3	100.9	121.7	167.6	98.8	75.7	107.4	115.4	112.8	70.4	46.1	85.4	130.6
2001	112.6	98.5	119.9	159.4	96.0	78.0	126.6	110.1	108.0	69.6	47.2	82.8	120.9
2002	108.7	91.7	98.7	135.0	56.1	76.1	92.6	93.0	102.1	66.3	49.5	75.3	112.8
2003	113.0	93.4	94.9	126.5	51.9	70.1	105.8	89.5	105.4	72.5	54.4	82.2	113.3
2004	120.6	98.3	94.5	129.6	53.5	58.6	112.3	90.8	113.5	79.9	61.0	89.7	111.2
2005	128.9	105.1	96.1	128.5	60.8	60.7	122.9	86.0	124.4	86.8	67.9	96.3	120.7
2006	131.4	112.6	103.0	136.3	64.8	64.4	132.7	94.3	135.2	98.0	83.8	104.6	130.9
2007	128.8	119.3	116.2	149.9	76.6	89.7	130.6	108.6	139.4	109.3	94.7	115.9	135.0
2008	120.1	118.4	123.3	144.3	95.6	98.6	140.1	122.4	129.8	109.7	100.4	113.9	128.5
2009	100.0	100.0	100.0	100.0	100.0	100.0	100.0	100.0	100.0	100.0	100.0	100.0	100.0
2010	101.5	102.5	83.6	75.1	72.5	83.9	117.1	73.3	115.9	109.9	110.3	109.8	99.5
2011	107.8	110.2	85.4	74.8	69.5	77.3	145.5	67.8	130.6	112.4	108.6	113.9	115.1
2012	116.8	118.3	96.2	80.8	80.0	91.9	165.5	73.2	140.6	115.5	114.5	115.9	121.4
2010													
1st quarter	98.6	98.9	82.1	78.7	82.1	75.9	102.1	77.0	108.3	107.8	114.1	105.1	94.0
2nd quarter	101.8	101.6	84.4	75.4	78.4	83.9	115.8	74.5	114.1	108.5	112.6	106.8	99.4
3rd quarter	101.7	103.6	83.1	73.5	69.0	81.8	124.1	72.1	118.9	110.3	108.1	111.2	100.5
4th quarter	103.8	105.8	84.7	73.0	60.5	94.0	126.3	69.8	122.3	113.0	106.3	115.8	104.1
2011													
1st quarter	103.7	105.6	77.5	70.7	57.5	69.2	130.6	64.0	125.8	110.7	101.6	114.4	109.6
2nd quarter	105.9	108.1	83.4	74.3	66.4	75.5	139.3	68.0	127.1	112.8	109.0	114.4	109.7
3rd quarter	109.6	112.3	88.8	76.9	75.2	81.6	150.5	69.1	133.2	112.7	110.3	113.6	117.7
4th quarter	112.2	114.9	91.8	77.5	78.9	83.1	161.4	70.1	136.4	113.4	113.7	113.3	123.4
2012													
1st quarter	114.6	116.6	93.3	79.0	76.8	86.3	165.0	70.4	139.2	117.2	120.2	116.0	118.7
2nd quarter	115.9	117.8	94.9	80.1	79.2	85.8	167.8	73.7	141.0	114.0	114.5	113.8	121.6
3rd quarter	116.7	117.9	96.3	82.4	80.3	89.4	165.1	74.7	139.6	112.7	103.5	116.4	121.7
4th quarter	119.9	120.7	100.3	81.7	83.5	106.1	164.2	74.2	142.6	118.0	119.9	117.3	123.5

[1]See notes and definitions.
. . . = Not available.

Table 5-4. Chain-Type Quantity Indexes for Private Fixed Investment by Type—*Continued*

(Index numbers, 2009 = 100, quarterly data are seasonally adjusted.)   **NIPA Table 5.3.3**

Year and quarter	Nonresidential—*Continued*						Residential						
	Equipment—*Continued*		Intellectual property					Residential structures					
							Total	Total	Permanent site			Other residential structures	Residential equipment
	Transportation equipment	Other nonresidential equipment	Total	Software [2]	Research and development [3]	Entertainment, literary, and artistic originals			Total	Single family	Multifamily		
1955	54.1	26.3	2.9	. . .	6.2	17.1	53.1	55.0	123.1	. . .	. . .	20.2	8.9
1956	48.6	27.1	3.4	. . .	7.9	16.8	48.9	50.5	106.6	. . .	. . .	21.6	9.9
1957	52.0	25.7	3.5	. . .	8.0	18.0	46.0	47.4	96.9	. . .	. . .	21.9	9.9
1958	37.9	26.0	3.6	. . .	8.5	18.4	46.5	47.9	99.4	103.2	77.8	21.4	10.5
1959	50.2	28.0	4.0	0.0	9.2	20.3	58.1	60.0	126.6	131.3	100.0	25.8	12.1
1960	51.8	25.7	4.2	0.0	10.1	18.9	54.2	55.9	111.8	116.1	88.0	26.9	11.3
1961	48.9	25.4	4.7	0.0	10.7	22.8	54.4	56.1	111.2	110.0	110.9	27.5	11.4
1962	60.3	27.1	4.9	0.1	11.6	21.9	59.6	61.5	126.8	117.3	161.3	27.9	12.0
1963	58.4	31.5	5.4	0.1	12.5	23.5	66.6	68.8	143.9	125.3	216.5	30.1	13.4
1964	66.1	34.9	5.6	0.2	13.4	22.3	70.6	72.9	153.6	137.4	215.0	31.4	14.4
1965	82.8	38.8	6.3	0.2	15.0	24.8	68.8	70.8	146.9	134.3	193.3	31.6	16.1
1966	91.0	43.6	7.2	0.3	16.8	27.0	63.0	64.7	128.9	119.6	162.0	31.5	16.5
1967	88.0	41.2	7.7	0.4	18.5	26.8	61.4	63.0	122.8	117.2	140.7	31.9	16.9
1968	105.8	41.7	8.3	0.4	20.0	28.1	69.7	71.4	144.3	128.9	203.3	33.7	20.1
1969	110.0	44.5	8.8	0.6	21.3	26.5	71.9	73.5	148.5	122.3	252.9	34.7	22.9
1970	90.3	46.5	8.8	0.7	21.4	23.2	68.1	69.4	134.3	106.3	247.6	35.6	25.0
1971	97.5	46.3	8.8	0.7	21.4	22.9	86.2	88.2	181.0	147.6	315.1	40.3	28.0
1972	113.3	52.5	9.4	0.9	22.4	24.6	101.2	103.4	219.0	175.4	394.5	44.1	33.6
1973	136.2	61.3	9.9	1.0	23.9	23.6	100.6	102.5	218.0	171.6	405.6	43.2	37.8
1974	123.3	60.6	10.2	1.2	24.0	23.9	80.8	81.9	157.7	131.7	261.1	42.6	38.5
1975	106.2	56.1	10.2	1.4	23.6	23.1	71.1	71.9	120.7	120.2	116.5	46.0	35.8
1976	118.1	56.5	11.4	1.5	25.1	29.4	86.8	88.1	158.7	167.4	112.8	51.2	37.7
1977	143.6	63.6	12.1	1.5	26.4	32.8	104.6	106.4	204.8	215.1	149.6	55.5	41.3
1978	158.7	70.1	13.0	1.8	28.5	32.2	111.6	113.5	214.2	222.2	168.5	61.3	44.9
1979	165.6	71.4	14.5	2.3	30.6	37.0	107.4	108.9	200.4	196.9	205.8	61.4	49.2
1980	135.2	64.2	15.2	2.7	32.7	33.5	84.9	85.7	140.8	129.4	184.3	56.5	49.2
1981	131.5	65.9	16.9	3.1	34.8	40.5	77.9	78.4	129.9	117.8	177.2	51.3	49.2
1982	116.5	57.0	17.9	3.6	36.6	40.8	63.8	63.9	101.2	90.3	144.5	44.1	47.2
1983	131.2	55.0	19.3	4.3	38.6	43.0	90.6	91.4	165.4	156.8	197.8	52.8	52.7
1984	156.3	62.3	22.0	5.4	42.6	47.9	104.0	105.0	194.3	181.9	241.7	58.6	58.5
1985	162.4	62.8	23.9	6.4	46.3	47.7	106.4	107.2	191.8	180.4	235.5	63.1	63.1
1986	156.2	61.7	25.6	7.2	48.2	52.7	119.6	120.6	214.1	206.5	242.5	71.8	68.2
1987	148.5	63.4	26.6	8.2	49.1	51.8	121.9	123.0	217.0	223.1	191.3	73.7	71.0
1988	157.2	66.5	28.5	9.7	51.1	52.3	120.8	121.7	209.2	220.4	163.2	75.7	73.4
1989	141.8	74.2	31.8	12.5	54.4	54.7	116.9	117.7	204.0	214.0	162.8	72.4	73.8
1990	139.9	71.4	34.5	14.8	57.3	56.6	107.0	107.5	184.3	194.5	142.0	67.1	71.6
1991	136.0	61.0	36.7	16.7	59.9	57.2	97.5	97.8	158.6	170.5	109.5	65.3	68.8
1992	139.1	60.7	38.9	19.7	60.0	60.0	110.9	111.6	185.0	207.0	93.0	72.6	70.9
1993	165.8	66.5	40.6	22.0	59.7	63.3	120.0	120.9	197.5	226.7	75.0	80.0	72.3
1994	194.3	71.8	42.2	24.2	59.7	66.6	130.7	131.9	221.1	250.9	96.9	84.7	72.8
1995	209.0	75.7	45.3	26.6	62.7	72.1	126.3	127.3	206.5	227.8	120.1	85.1	73.8
1996	215.9	78.6	50.4	31.2	68.2	77.3	136.6	138.0	225.9	248.8	132.8	91.1	73.4
1997	231.5	86.2	57.0	40.4	72.1	79.6	139.9	141.4	227.1	248.0	143.1	95.5	72.8
1998	250.3	95.0	63.1	48.8	75.7	83.4	152.0	153.6	248.7	275.1	141.5	102.8	77.9
1999	295.3	97.5	71.0	60.2	80.3	85.9	161.6	163.2	267.2	295.4	152.7	107.7	86.1
2000	289.3	102.9	77.3	68.5	84.3	91.0	162.6	164.1	269.3	298.7	150.1	108.0	91.6
2001	262.1	102.2	77.7	69.0	85.4	88.2	164.1	165.6	270.9	299.1	156.6	109.4	93.3
2002	237.0	101.4	77.3	68.9	83.2	92.6	174.0	175.7	281.8	310.7	164.9	118.9	96.1
2003	219.4	108.3	80.3	73.6	82.6	99.6	189.8	191.7	309.4	343.8	169.2	128.7	102.0
2004	250.1	116.2	84.4	81.0	83.4	101.1	208.8	210.8	345.2	385.1	182.4	139.0	113.7
2005	280.5	127.4	89.8	86.1	88.3	109.5	222.5	224.7	369.6	411.1	200.6	147.3	118.7
2006	301.3	132.6	93.9	89.7	93.9	110.7	205.6	207.4	337.3	370.9	201.9	138.1	121.0
2007	288.5	131.0	98.4	95.1	99.5	108.0	166.9	168.0	251.1	269.3	178.8	123.7	117.5
2008	222.3	124.7	101.4	99.8	102.8	103.0	126.9	127.2	166.7	169.2	157.2	106.2	111.3
2009	100.0	100.0	100.0	100.0	100.0	100.0	100.0	100.0	100.0	100.0	100.0	100.0	100.0
2010	194.0	108.6	101.9	99.0	102.4	111.6	97.5	97.3	96.0	108.6	50.2	98.0	106.0
2011	256.4	121.9	106.4	105.1	105.6	114.5	98.0	97.7	92.6	103.6	52.4	100.4	110.7
2012	313.3	126.6	110.0	111.3	107.3	114.8	110.6	110.5	115.0	125.4	77.4	108.2	114.0
2010													
1st quarter	155.4	103.1	101.2	99.7	101.6	105.8	97.6	97.5	98.1	109.8	55.2	97.2	103.6
2nd quarter	185.5	107.4	100.7	97.7	101.1	111.0	102.9	102.8	101.2	115.5	49.6	103.6	107.0
3rd quarter	215.4	110.1	102.2	98.6	102.9	113.6	93.8	93.6	94.1	106.9	47.9	93.3	105.8
4th quarter	219.8	113.7	103.5	100.0	103.9	115.8	95.6	95.4	90.5	102.2	48.2	98.0	107.6
2011													
1st quarter	235.3	119.5	104.4	102.0	104.4	114.2	96.0	95.8	90.8	102.8	47.7	98.4	108.6
2nd quarter	237.6	120.6	105.6	103.9	105.3	113.8	96.7	96.4	90.5	101.8	49.5	99.5	109.9
3rd quarter	262.9	126.2	107.0	106.0	106.1	114.5	98.1	97.9	93.3	103.9	54.8	100.3	111.3
4th quarter	290.0	121.2	108.5	108.5	106.6	115.5	101.0	100.7	95.7	106.1	57.9	103.4	113.2
2012													
1st quarter	307.5	123.7	108.8	108.9	107.1	114.9	106.4	106.2	103.4	114.6	62.6	107.7	112.9
2nd quarter	324.7	125.4	109.3	110.6	106.6	114.8	107.9	107.8	110.1	120.2	73.4	106.6	112.4
3rd quarter	310.0	127.8	110.1	111.6	107.3	114.5	111.5	111.4	117.8	127.8	81.9	108.0	114.5
4th quarter	310.9	129.6	111.6	114.2	108.1	115.1	116.6	116.6	128.7	139.0	91.7	110.3	116.3

[2] Excludes software "embedded," or bundled, in computers and other equipment.
[3] Excludes software development.
. . . = Not available.

Table 5-5A. Current-Cost Net Stock of Fixed Assets: Recent Data

(Billions of dollars, year-end estimates.)

Year	Total	Private					Government				Private and government fixed assets			Government, by level	
		Total	Nonresidential			Resi-dential	Total	Nonresidential		Resi-dential	Nonresidential		Resi-dential	Federal	State and local
			Total	Equip-ment and software	Struc-tures			Equip-ment and software	Struc-tures		Equip-ment and software	Struc-tures			
1950	871.7	661.5	321.6	99.6	222.1	339.9	210.2	40.3	163.6	6.4	139.8	385.6	346.3	101.0	109.2
1951	955.8	719.7	350.7	109.7	241.0	369.0	236.1	44.1	184.1	7.9	153.8	425.1	376.9	113.2	122.8
1952	1 010.2	757.4	369.6	115.5	254.1	387.8	252.9	50.5	194.9	7.4	166.0	449.0	395.1	122.7	130.1
1953	1 046.3	787.6	385.4	125.0	260.4	402.2	258.7	57.3	193.5	7.8	182.3	454.0	410.0	130.0	128.8
1954	1 093.1	819.0	395.2	128.7	266.5	423.8	274.1	63.9	199.7	10.5	192.6	466.2	434.3	139.7	134.5
1955	1 187.7	891.9	435.4	141.7	293.7	456.5	295.8	69.4	218.8	7.6	211.2	512.5	464.1	146.5	149.3
1956	1 288.5	959.8	481.2	159.1	322.1	478.6	328.7	74.0	245.8	8.9	233.1	567.9	487.5	159.4	169.3
1957	1 351.1	1 008.4	513.8	173.4	340.4	494.6	342.7	76.1	257.2	9.4	249.5	597.6	504.0	165.3	177.4
1958	1 393.3	1 032.5	523.0	178.8	344.2	509.6	360.8	77.8	272.8	10.2	256.6	616.9	519.8	171.3	189.5
1959	1 447.4	1 076.3	544.6	187.3	357.3	531.7	371.1	82.4	277.6	11.1	269.7	634.9	542.8	175.3	195.7
1960	1 492.9	1 108.3	555.7	193.4	362.3	552.6	384.6	85.2	287.7	11.7	278.6	650.0	564.3	179.5	205.1
1961	1 547.5	1 143.5	570.8	196.9	373.9	572.7	404.0	89.1	302.3	12.5	286.0	676.2	585.3	186.5	217.4
1962	1 615.1	1 185.0	591.2	204.6	386.6	593.8	430.1	96.4	320.3	13.4	301.0	706.9	607.2	197.4	232.7
1963	1 671.7	1 220.8	612.4	213.4	399.0	608.4	450.9	99.1	338.1	13.7	312.5	737.1	622.1	202.9	248.1
1964	1 779.1	1 305.9	648.5	226.5	422.1	657.4	473.2	102.0	356.7	14.6	328.4	778.7	671.9	208.5	264.7
1965	1 895.6	1 392.2	694.2	244.3	449.9	698.0	503.4	104.6	383.6	15.3	348.8	833.4	713.3	215.4	288.0
1966	2 054.1	1 510.2	755.4	272.3	483.1	754.9	543.9	109.3	418.1	16.4	381.6	901.2	771.3	225.7	318.2
1967	2 210.2	1 622.5	816.3	298.5	517.8	806.2	587.7	116.1	454.4	17.3	414.6	972.2	823.4	240.0	347.7
1968	2 426.1	1 788.0	897.3	329.5	567.8	890.7	638.1	120.7	498.0	19.4	450.2	1 065.9	910.1	252.2	385.9
1969	2 643.2	1 940.9	988.0	363.8	624.1	952.9	702.4	124.9	555.9	21.6	488.8	1 180.0	974.5	266.6	435.8
1970	2 877.7	2 096.1	1 087.4	399.6	687.8	1 008.7	781.6	131.0	627.5	23.0	530.7	1 315.3	1 031.8	284.5	497.1
1971	3 177.5	2 331.0	1 197.2	428.3	768.9	1 133.8	846.4	131.9	688.7	25.8	560.2	1 457.6	1 159.7	298.5	547.9
1972	3 493.6	2 570.9	1 303.2	462.0	841.2	1 267.8	922.7	134.1	759.7	28.9	596.0	1 600.9	1 296.7	321.8	600.8
1973	3 959.3	2 921.4	1 468.8	515.2	953.6	1 452.6	1 037.9	136.2	869.0	32.7	651.3	1 822.7	1 485.3	348.6	689.3
1974	4 716.7	3 441.4	1 788.4	635.3	1 153.2	1 653.0	1 275.3	149.5	1 089.2	36.6	784.8	2 242.4	1 689.6	402.1	873.2
1975	5 102.5	3 762.5	1 970.4	727.4	1 243.0	1 792.1	1 340.0	164.5	1 135.4	40.1	891.8	2 378.4	1 832.2	425.5	914.4
1976	5 562.7	4 146.2	2 157.0	805.3	1 351.7	1 989.1	1 416.5	178.5	1 193.3	44.7	983.8	2 545.0	2 033.9	461.3	955.2
1977	6 225.1	4 719.6	2 398.1	904.1	1 494.0	2 321.5	1 505.5	194.9	1 259.1	51.5	1 099.0	2 753.1	2 372.9	484.2	1 021.3
1978	7 047.6	5 401.0	2 723.7	1 033.1	1 690.6	2 677.3	1 646.6	207.9	1 379.2	59.5	1 240.9	3 069.8	2 736.8	522.6	1 124.0
1979	8 126.3	6 251.6	3 143.2	1 199.7	1 943.5	3 108.4	1 874.7	225.0	1 579.0	70.8	1 424.6	3 522.5	3 179.2	581.7	1 293.0
1980	9 259.6	7 113.1	3 608.4	1 392.6	2 215.8	3 504.7	2 146.5	251.4	1 817.4	77.7	1 644.0	4 033.2	3 582.3	645.6	1 500.8
1981	10 209.7	7 851.6	4 081.8	1 553.6	2 528.1	3 769.8	2 358.1	282.7	1 990.3	85.1	1 836.4	4 518.5	3 854.9	694.7	1 663.5
1982	10 770.9	8 281.7	4 341.2	1 646.8	2 694.5	3 940.5	2 489.2	307.6	2 091.4	90.2	1 954.4	4 785.8	4 030.7	733.5	1 755.6
1983	11 121.6	8 573.3	4 474.1	1 702.6	2 771.5	4 099.2	2 548.3	337.3	2 110.3	100.7	2 039.9	4 881.8	4 200.0	769.9	1 778.4
1984	11 721.2	9 072.5	4 741.8	1 796.8	2 945.0	4 330.6	2 648.7	361.3	2 182.9	104.5	2 158.1	5 127.9	4 435.1	809.0	1 839.7
1985	12 334.2	9 570.4	5 007.4	1 903.8	3 103.6	4 563.0	2 763.8	383.6	2 274.5	105.6	2 287.5	5 378.1	4 668.6	840.4	1 923.4
1986	13 106.8	10 172.9	5 244.8	2 010.7	3 234.2	4 928.1	2 933.9	411.7	2 412.6	109.5	2 422.4	5 646.8	5 037.6	883.6	2 050.3
1987	13 864.0	10 774.8	5 528.1	2 112.2	3 415.9	5 246.7	3 089.2	436.4	2 533.4	119.4	2 548.5	5 949.3	5 366.1	918.8	2 170.4
1988	14 703.8	11 455.3	5 882.3	2 238.6	3 643.7	5 573.0	3 248.4	470.7	2 642.7	135.0	2 709.4	6 286.4	5 708.0	975.1	2 273.3
1989	15 539.4	12 113.9	6 234.3	2 374.7	3 859.5	5 879.6	3 425.5	507.9	2 773.4	144.2	2 882.7	6 633.0	6 023.8	1 028.9	2 396.6
1990	16 268.3	12 670.5	6 563.5	2 506.7	4 056.7	6 107.0	3 597.8	550.8	2 898.1	148.9	3 057.5	6 954.9	6 255.9	1 076.8	2 521.0
1991	16 656.7	12 937.2	6 694.0	2 577.7	4 116.2	6 243.2	3 719.6	583.7	2 985.8	150.0	3 161.5	7 102.1	6 393.2	1 120.6	2 599.0
1992	17 370.2	13 487.9	6 902.2	2 650.3	4 251.9	6 585.7	3 882.3	612.9	3 110.6	158.8	3 263.2	7 362.5	6 744.5	1 167.3	2 715.1
1993	18 267.0	14 204.1	7 214.1	2 761.4	4 452.8	6 990.0	4 062.9	637.2	3 255.7	170.0	3 398.5	7 708.5	7 160.0	1 208.7	2 854.2
1994	19 374.3	15 080.9	7 594.8	2 911.5	4 683.4	7 486.0	4 293.4	665.5	3 446.4	181.5	3 577.0	8 129.8	7 667.5	1 259.7	3 033.7
1995	20 314.7	15 810.6	7 989.8	3 099.5	4 890.3	7 820.8	4 504.1	675.2	3 640.8	188.1	3 774.7	8 531.1	8 008.9	1 291.5	3 212.6
1996	21 305.4	16 624.9	8 371.9	3 261.8	5 110.1	8 253.0	4 680.5	675.0	3 809.1	196.4	3 936.8	8 919.2	8 449.4	1 315.0	3 365.5
1997	22 429.2	17 542.6	8 828.2	3 418.1	5 410.2	8 714.4	4 886.6	670.6	4 021.5	194.5	4 088.7	9 431.7	8 908.8	1 335.8	3 550.8
1998	23 705.1	18 618.1	9 332.6	3 607.9	5 724.7	9 285.5	5 087.0	677.8	4 204.8	204.4	4 285.7	9 929.5	9 489.9	1 357.7	3 729.3
1999	25 244.6	19 857.6	9 883.1	3 853.2	6 029.9	9 974.6	5 386.9	699.3	4 470.2	217.3	4 552.5	10 500.2	10 191.9	1 403.7	3 983.2
2000	26 932.4	21 230.4	10 562.7	4 134.1	6 428.6	10 667.7	5 702.0	703.7	4 769.3	229.0	4 837.8	11 197.9	10 896.7	1 431.5	4 270.5
2001	28 535.4	22 575.0	11 114.1	4 283.0	6 831.1	11 460.9	5 960.5	703.8	5 012.8	243.8	4 986.9	11 843.9	11 704.7	1 449.3	4 511.2
2002	29 973.8	23 739.4	11 541.6	4 378.9	7 162.7	12 197.7	6 234.4	716.5	5 260.6	257.4	5 095.4	12 423.3	12 455.1	1 478.7	4 755.7
2003	31 665.4	25 170.6	11 932.8	4 495.6	7 437.3	13 237.7	6 494.8	731.6	5 487.6	275.7	5 227.1	12 924.9	13 513.4	1 513.6	4 981.3
2004	34 978.0	27 735.5	12 910.7	4 702.4	8 208.4	14 824.8	7 242.5	767.4	6 172.1	303.0	5 469.7	14 380.5	15 127.8	1 636.5	5 606.0
2005	38 511.9	30 593.2	14 063.3	4 936.7	9 126.6	16 529.9	7 918.7	802.3	6 784.5	331.8	5 739.0	15 911.2	16 861.7	1 743.8	6 174.9
2006	41 713.1	32 956.6	15 274.6	5 277.1	9 997.6	17 682.0	8 756.5	850.1	7 560.8	345.6	6 127.2	17 558.4	18 027.6	1 861.9	6 894.6
2007	43 563.5	34 080.8	16 124.7	5 513.4	10 611.3	17 956.2	9 482.7	895.4	8 244.5	342.8	6 408.8	18 855.8	18 299.0	1 947.5	7 535.2
2008	45 058.6	34 869.3	17 184.8	5 765.9	11 419.0	17 684.5	10 189.3	956.3	8 900.1	332.9	6 722.2	20 319.0	18 017.4	2 036.4	8 152.9
2009	44 177.3	33 982.7	16 608.1	5 687.5	10 920.7	17 374.5	10 194.6	991.0	8 877.9	325.7	6 678.5	19 798.5	17 700.3	2 024.3	8 170.3
2010	44 977.7	34 388.3	16 946.0	5 757.2	11 188.8	17 442.3	10 589.4	1 044.0	9 215.8	329.6	6 801.2	20 404.6	17 771.9	2 095.3	8 494.1
2011	46 385.2	35 193.2	17 632.0	5 943.6	11 688.4	17 561.2	11 192.0	1 088.8	9 769.9	333.3	7 032.4	21 458.3	17 894.5	2 176.1	9 016.0

Table 5-5B. Current-Cost Net Stock of Fixed Assets: Historical

(Billions of dollars, year-end estimates.)

Year	Total	Private					Government				Private and government fixed assets			Government, by level	
		Total	Nonresidential			Resi-dential	Total	Nonresidential		Resi-dential	Nonresidential		Resi-dential	Federal	State and local
			Total	Equip-ment and software	Struc-tures			Equip-ment and software	Struc-tures		Equip-ment and software	Struc-tures			
1925	263.3	225.0	124.3	31.3	93.0	100.7	38.3	2.9	35.4	0.0	34.2	128.4	100.7	9.2	29.1
1926	272.3	233.2	128.8	33.1	95.6	104.5	39.1	2.8	36.3	0.0	35.9	132.0	104.5	9.0	30.1
1927	278.5	238.6	131.4	33.8	97.5	107.2	40.0	2.8	37.2	0.0	36.6	134.7	107.2	8.7	31.3
1928	291.1	250.5	134.8	34.5	100.3	115.7	40.6	2.6	38.0	0.0	37.1	138.3	115.7	8.3	32.3
1929	294.5	253.7	133.9	34.7	99.2	119.8	40.8	2.4	38.4	0.0	37.1	137.6	119.8	7.9	32.9
1930	280.9	241.2	126.9	33.0	93.9	114.3	39.6	2.3	37.3	0.0	35.3	131.2	114.3	7.4	32.2
1931	242.7	206.6	113.1	30.0	83.1	93.5	36.1	2.3	33.7	0.0	32.3	116.8	93.6	6.8	29.2
1932	224.2	188.5	104.6	27.0	77.6	84.0	35.6	2.3	33.3	0.0	29.2	111.0	84.0	6.7	29.0
1933	239.7	197.9	106.1	26.7	79.5	91.8	41.8	2.3	39.4	0.0	29.0	118.9	91.8	7.6	34.2
1934	245.8	200.0	107.3	26.7	80.6	92.7	45.8	2.6	43.2	0.0	29.4	123.8	92.7	8.7	37.2
1935	249.7	201.0	106.8	26.2	80.6	94.2	48.7	2.8	45.8	0.0	29.0	126.4	94.2	9.9	38.8
1936	276.3	222.2	117.5	28.2	89.3	104.7	54.1	2.9	51.1	0.1	31.1	140.4	104.8	11.4	42.7
1937	290.8	233.6	122.2	30.3	91.9	111.4	57.2	3.2	53.8	0.2	33.5	145.7	111.6	12.6	44.6
1938	293.0	233.9	120.7	30.3	90.4	113.2	59.2	3.3	55.6	0.2	33.6	146.0	113.4	13.3	45.9
1939	299.2	237.6	120.8	30.9	89.9	116.8	61.5	3.6	57.7	0.3	34.5	147.6	117.1	13.9	47.6
1940	324.1	256.5	128.3	33.2	95.1	128.2	67.5	4.0	63.0	0.5	37.2	158.1	128.7	15.7	51.8
1941	369.1	284.7	144.8	38.3	106.5	139.9	84.5	7.7	75.8	1.0	45.9	182.2	141.0	24.3	60.1
1942	421.2	304.2	153.6	39.2	114.4	150.7	117.0	20.9	94.4	1.7	60.1	208.8	152.4	49.6	67.4
1943	468.4	319.2	155.6	39.6	116.0	163.6	149.2	45.3	101.3	2.6	84.9	217.3	166.2	80.7	68.4
1944	501.2	331.6	156.7	39.5	117.2	174.9	169.6	65.2	101.5	2.8	104.7	218.8	177.7	102.7	66.9
1945	543.4	355.5	171.0	44.7	126.2	184.5	187.9	75.4	109.5	3.0	120.1	235.8	187.5	118.5	69.4
1946	637.8	438.4	211.1	54.5	156.7	227.3	199.3	70.2	125.2	4.0	124.7	281.8	231.3	121.6	77.8
1947	734.7	521.6	254.0	66.6	187.4	267.6	213.1	61.7	145.8	5.6	128.3	333.2	273.2	119.8	93.3
1948	780.3	567.0	278.8	81.3	197.5	288.3	213.3	51.9	156.5	5.0	133.1	353.9	293.2	111.8	101.5
1949	785.5	586.5	283.7	85.4	198.3	302.8	199.0	44.1	149.8	5.2	129.5	348.1	307.9	102.1	96.9

Table 5-6A. Chain-Type Quantity Indexes for Net Stock of Fixed Assets: Recent Data

(Index numbers, 2005 = 100.)

Year	Total	Private					Government				Private and government fixed assets			Government, by level	
		Total	Nonresidential			Resi-dential	Total	Nonresidential		Resi-dential	Nonresidential		Resi-dential	Federal	State and local
			Total	Equip-ment and software	Struc-tures			Equip-ment and software	Struc-tures		Equip-ment and software	Struc-tures			
1950	19.76	18.40	17.51	9.35	25.20	19.44	24.87	26.11	24.74	16.67	11.62	25.04	19.41	51.61	16.57
1951	20.50	19.08	18.12	9.88	25.84	20.20	25.86	27.93	25.51	17.92	12.32	25.74	20.18	53.76	17.20
1952	21.28	19.71	18.66	10.32	26.44	20.92	27.23	31.23	26.43	19.33	13.13	26.48	20.92	57.55	17.83
1953	22.12	20.39	19.29	10.84	27.13	21.67	28.68	34.72	27.42	20.60	14.03	27.30	21.68	61.43	18.54
1954	22.90	21.07	19.83	11.18	27.84	22.50	29.92	36.54	28.54	21.18	14.57	28.19	22.50	63.75	19.44
1955	23.78	21.89	20.51	11.70	28.63	23.48	30.96	37.30	29.68	21.64	15.13	29.12	23.48	64.94	20.43
1956	24.63	22.70	21.26	12.23	29.56	24.34	31.98	38.01	30.80	22.22	15.68	30.14	24.33	66.02	21.44
1957	25.44	23.45	22.00	12.76	30.46	25.12	33.01	38.47	31.96	23.28	16.20	31.15	25.11	66.88	22.52
1958	26.16	24.05	22.46	12.92	31.22	25.88	34.22	39.11	33.27	25.16	16.43	32.14	25.91	68.11	23.73
1959	27.06	24.82	23.00	13.21	32.00	26.93	35.63	40.78	34.57	27.28	16.89	33.14	26.97	70.16	24.95
1960	27.93	25.59	23.64	13.59	32.89	27.85	36.90	41.86	35.87	28.84	17.37	34.21	27.91	71.65	26.16
1961	28.83	26.33	24.24	13.89	33.78	28.76	38.40	43.58	37.29	30.74	17.86	35.32	28.84	73.78	27.48
1962	29.84	27.20	24.98	14.37	34.74	29.77	39.98	45.63	38.71	32.87	18.55	36.48	29.88	76.08	28.84
1963	30.91	28.17	25.77	14.95	35.68	30.95	41.47	46.89	40.28	33.97	19.22	37.69	31.05	77.63	30.33
1964	32.11	29.28	26.77	15.74	36.79	32.19	42.99	47.95	41.92	35.16	20.05	39.03	32.29	78.90	31.95
1965	33.43	30.54	28.11	16.89	38.19	33.37	44.49	48.44	43.67	36.43	21.11	40.58	33.47	79.69	33.68
1966	34.81	31.85	29.68	18.34	39.69	34.37	46.17	49.45	45.52	37.80	22.52	42.23	34.48	80.88	35.53
1967	36.10	33.02	31.06	19.55	41.09	35.30	47.94	50.81	47.39	39.34	23.76	43.84	35.42	82.04	37.49
1968	37.44	34.29	32.46	20.82	42.49	36.41	49.52	51.03	49.28	40.85	24.90	45.45	36.54	82.18	39.53
1969	38.79	35.63	33.99	22.23	44.00	37.55	50.86	50.74	50.96	42.76	26.09	47.03	37.70	81.84	41.41
1970	39.97	36.84	35.35	23.38	45.46	38.57	51.98	50.20	52.41	44.72	27.02	48.49	38.74	81.23	43.06
1971	41.19	38.16	36.59	24.38	46.85	40.01	52.80	48.18	53.78	46.61	27.62	49.87	40.18	79.69	44.59
1972	42.59	39.72	38.00	25.68	48.27	41.74	53.58	46.57	55.04	48.19	28.53	51.21	41.91	78.45	46.00
1973	44.13	41.45	39.76	27.56	49.83	43.44	54.42	45.34	56.26	49.70	29.97	52.62	43.60	77.54	47.39
1974	45.44	42.87	41.38	29.29	51.26	44.62	55.37	45.07	57.42	51.12	31.43	53.93	44.80	77.17	48.74
1975	46.44	43.88	42.47	30.30	52.39	45.55	56.33	45.06	58.53	52.82	32.31	55.04	45.74	77.02	50.02
1976	47.59	45.09	43.61	31.41	53.49	46.84	57.29	45.38	59.59	54.15	33.32	56.13	47.03	77.11	51.25
1977	48.99	46.65	45.04	33.00	54.66	48.55	58.12	45.63	60.51	55.41	34.73	57.19	48.73	77.23	52.31
1978	50.66	48.49	46.91	35.13	56.18	50.37	59.09	45.92	61.62	56.47	36.61	58.53	50.54	77.43	53.55
1979	52.42	50.41	49.04	37.45	58.03	52.07	60.20	46.86	62.76	57.48	38.76	60.08	52.23	77.87	54.86
1980	53.87	51.95	50.93	39.13	60.05	53.22	61.32	47.98	63.87	58.77	40.36	61.71	53.38	78.49	56.15
1981	55.28	53.45	52.94	40.76	62.33	54.19	62.32	49.27	64.79	60.30	41.96	63.40	54.36	79.39	57.18
1982	56.34	54.56	54.49	41.64	64.45	54.81	63.22	50.92	65.53	61.71	42.93	64.92	55.00	80.46	58.02
1983	57.55	55.82	55.78	42.56	66.04	56.04	64.24	53.46	66.22	63.41	44.08	66.12	56.25	82.07	58.87
1984	59.23	57.60	57.79	44.38	68.14	57.58	65.53	56.80	67.10	64.85	46.11	67.69	57.78	84.08	59.94
1985	61.03	59.45	59.94	46.16	70.57	59.11	67.13	61.17	68.15	66.62	48.23	69.53	59.32	86.69	61.23
1986	62.80	61.22	61.65	47.61	72.45	60.95	68.87	65.94	69.33	68.51	50.13	71.11	61.16	89.56	62.63
1987	64.52	62.93	63.19	48.79	74.27	62.82	70.65	70.76	70.56	70.49	51.77	72.67	63.03	92.57	64.04
1988	66.20	64.63	64.81	50.23	76.00	64.63	72.26	74.47	71.80	72.24	53.50	74.19	64.84	94.55	65.54
1989	67.86	66.30	66.49	51.83	77.69	66.28	73.89	78.51	73.01	73.78	55.41	75.67	66.49	96.36	67.11
1990	69.42	67.80	68.07	53.07	79.52	67.71	75.68	82.64	74.41	75.49	57.02	77.31	67.93	98.21	68.87
1991	70.64	68.90	69.11	53.86	80.77	68.87	77.35	85.68	75.85	76.97	58.09	78.65	69.10	99.57	70.65
1992	71.88	70.05	70.09	54.88	81.67	70.20	78.94	88.19	77.29	78.58	59.31	79.78	70.43	100.69	72.39
1993	73.35	71.56	71.48	56.66	82.66	71.84	80.28	89.30	78.65	79.98	61.00	80.93	72.07	101.07	74.02
1994	74.96	73.27	73.12	59.06	83.56	73.64	81.44	89.58	79.96	81.13	63.14	82.01	73.86	100.83	75.62
1995	76.75	75.20	75.21	62.05	84.82	75.40	82.72	89.70	81.44	82.54	65.75	83.37	75.62	100.68	77.35
1996	78.80	77.40	77.62	65.45	86.33	77.39	84.21	89.93	83.14	83.94	68.75	84.96	77.59	101.09	79.17
1997	80.98	79.79	80.41	69.49	88.06	79.38	85.56	89.74	84.73	85.93	72.23	86.63	79.58	100.37	81.17
1998	83.42	82.49	83.60	74.29	89.94	81.60	87.03	90.17	86.36	91.35	76.45	88.40	81.78	99.92	83.22
1999	86.06	85.37	87.02	79.80	91.78	83.97	88.72	91.26	88.15	92.73	81.36	90.22	84.13	99.68	85.49
2000	88.82	88.40	90.75	85.70	93.91	86.35	90.45	92.14	90.04	93.80	86.58	92.25	86.49	99.17	87.90
2001	91.19	90.91	93.43	89.50	95.81	88.70	92.26	92.81	92.03	95.10	89.96	94.18	88.82	98.63	90.40
2002	93.27	93.01	95.05	91.82	96.97	91.23	94.29	94.15	94.19	96.48	92.14	95.78	91.32	98.68	93.02
2003	95.41	95.17	96.49	93.91	97.99	94.03	96.34	95.65	96.35	97.80	94.15	97.29	94.10	98.94	95.59
2004	97.70	97.56	98.14	96.61	99.00	97.06	98.26	97.01	98.38	99.02	96.67	98.73	97.10	99.47	97.91
2005	100.00	100.00	100.00	100.00	100.00	100.00	100.00	100.00	100.00	100.00	100.00	100.00	100.00	100.00	100.00
2006	102.57	102.74	102.47	104.19	101.56	102.98	101.93	103.51	101.81	100.48	104.10	101.67	102.93	100.77	102.25
2007	104.87	105.15	105.15	108.20	103.71	105.06	103.83	107.17	103.59	101.13	108.06	103.65	104.98	101.67	104.43
2008	106.63	106.85	107.59	110.56	106.05	106.15	105.82	111.92	105.34	101.86	110.75	105.74	106.07	103.12	106.56
2009	107.43	107.31	108.00	109.43	107.22	106.67	107.74	116.13	107.07	102.78	110.37	107.15	106.60	104.74	108.56
2010	108.17	107.73	108.41	109.73	107.69	107.10	109.54	120.23	108.63	104.42	111.21	108.12	107.05	106.64	110.33
2011	109.01	108.42	109.40	111.61	108.24	107.50	110.86	123.09	109.80	105.52	113.23	108.95	107.46	107.78	111.69

Table 5-6B. Chain-Type Quantity Indexes for Net Stock of Fixed Assets: Historical

(Index numbers, 2005 = 100.)

Year	Total	Private					Government				Private and government fixed assets			Government, by level	
		Total	Nonresidential			Resi-dential	Total	Nonresidential		Resi-dential	Nonresidential		Resi-dential	Federal	State and local
			Total	Equip-ment and software	Struc-tures			Equip-ment and software	Struc-tures		Equip-ment and software	Struc-tures			
1925	11.82	13.28	13.23	5.52	20.86	13.30	7.44	2.20	9.61	0.00	4.65	15.80	13.04	7.15	7.65
1926	12.26	13.78	13.67	5.73	21.52	13.88	7.72	2.17	10.02	0.00	4.80	16.34	13.61	7.04	8.07
1927	12.67	14.22	14.04	5.84	22.16	14.41	8.06	2.19	10.49	0.00	4.89	16.91	14.13	6.94	8.57
1928	13.07	14.64	14.40	5.96	22.77	14.88	8.44	2.20	11.01	0.00	4.99	17.47	14.59	6.88	9.10
1929	13.45	15.01	14.84	6.15	23.44	15.18	8.83	2.22	11.54	0.03	5.14	18.08	14.89	6.85	9.64
1930	13.69	15.19	15.09	6.17	23.95	15.29	9.32	2.23	12.23	0.05	5.16	18.66	14.99	6.90	10.29
1931	13.78	15.17	15.00	5.97	24.05	15.34	9.84	2.26	12.94	0.08	5.00	19.03	15.04	7.04	10.95
1932	13.71	14.97	14.69	5.62	23.88	15.27	10.25	2.25	13.52	0.10	4.73	19.18	14.98	7.27	11.43
1933	13.60	14.74	14.36	5.32	23.61	15.18	10.53	2.24	13.92	0.13	4.50	19.20	14.89	7.72	11.65
1934	13.57	14.60	14.14	5.14	23.38	15.13	10.90	2.38	14.38	0.15	4.38	19.30	14.84	8.35	11.94
1935	13.62	14.54	14.02	5.09	23.21	15.14	11.30	2.55	14.88	0.22	4.37	19.44	14.86	9.21	12.20
1936	13.82	14.61	14.08	5.21	23.16	15.21	11.95	2.65	15.73	0.63	4.48	19.80	14.93	10.03	12.80
1937	14.05	14.74	14.26	5.43	23.24	15.30	12.49	2.76	16.41	1.19	4.67	20.16	15.03	10.77	13.27
1938	14.20	14.76	14.22	5.41	23.19	15.39	13.10	2.93	17.19	1.41	4.68	20.49	15.12	11.49	13.86
1939	14.43	14.87	14.24	5.45	23.17	15.59	13.79	3.12	18.07	1.83	4.74	20.88	15.34	12.14	14.58
1940	14.72	15.08	14.40	5.66	23.22	15.85	14.43	3.30	18.83	3.06	4.93	21.25	15.61	13.13	15.10
1941	15.30	15.34	14.65	5.95	23.34	16.13	16.15	6.14	20.12	5.56	5.61	21.89	15.94	19.20	15.38
1942	16.24	15.29	14.52	5.86	23.19	16.18	20.65	17.96	22.56	8.30	7.27	22.92	16.04	38.15	15.41
1943	17.31	15.16	14.31	5.73	22.92	16.13	26.08	40.88	23.53	11.80	10.30	23.22	16.07	62.38	15.28
1944	18.18	15.11	14.26	5.76	22.76	16.07	30.50	62.85	23.82	12.64	13.25	23.27	16.03	82.62	15.11
1945	18.56	15.19	14.48	6.10	22.77	16.02	32.03	70.52	23.95	12.84	14.55	23.33	16.02	89.91	14.98
1946	18.49	15.69	15.07	6.70	23.26	16.45	29.62	57.86	23.73	14.24	13.43	23.51	16.43	79.20	14.99
1947	18.60	16.33	15.74	7.54	23.67	17.06	27.57	46.06	23.76	14.68	12.61	23.75	17.04	69.52	15.17
1948	18.89	17.05	16.43	8.33	24.18	17.80	26.07	36.24	24.00	14.95	12.02	24.14	17.78	61.67	15.47
1949	19.26	17.62	16.93	8.80	24.65	18.46	25.57	31.13	24.48	15.86	11.78	24.62	18.44	57.69	15.97

Table 5-7. Capital Expenditures

(Millions of dollars, except as noted.)

Capital expenditures	All companies											
	2000	2001	2002	2003	2004	2005	2006	2007	2008	2009	2010	2011
TOTAL (billions)	1 161.0	1 109.0	997.9	975.0	1 042.1	1 144.8	1 309.9	1 354.7	1 374.2	1 090.1	1 105.7	1 225.6
Structures	364 407	363 748	358 484	344 641	368 707	401 653	488 701	525 273	562 381	448 132	428 713	454 658
New	329 525	335 538	321 191	305 291	324 680	365 938	448 861	480 839	522 999	421 044	394 517	425 101
Used	34 882	28 210	37 293	39 350	44 028	35 715	39 840	44 434	39 382	27 088	34 196	29 557
Equipment	796 622	745 256	639 410	630 373	673 353	743 130	821 238	829 455	811 779	641 938	676 989	770 900
New	750 626	706 617	598 668	579 414	628 591	701 247	777 059	790 407	765 279	606 935	639 214	729 934
Used	45 996	38 639	40 741	50 960	44 762	41 884	44 179	39 048	46 501	35 003	37 775	40 966
Not distributed as structures or equipment	0	0	0	0	0	0	0	0	0	0	0	0
CAPITALIZED COMPUTER SOFTWARE [1]	...	...	...	...	...	...	...	...	...	...	...	...
Prepackaged	...	...	...	...	...	...	...	...	...	...	...	...
Vendor-customized	...	...	...	...	...	...	...	...	...	...	...	...
Internally-developed	...	...	...	...	...	...	...	...	...	...	...	...
CAPITAL LEASE AND CAPITALIZED INTEREST EXPENSES [1]												
Capital leases	19 545	15 529	15 334	15 641	17 996	18 103	24 442	20 210	20 169	17 410	15 780	20 498
Capitalized interest	...	...	...	...	...	...	...	...	...	...	...	...

Capital expenditures	Companies with employees											
	2000	2001	2002	2003	2004	2005	2006	2007	2008	2009	2000	2011
TOTAL (billions)	1 089.9	1 052.3	917.5	886.8	953.2	1 062.5	1 217.1	1 270.5	1 294.5	1 014.7	1 089.9	1 152.2
Structures	338 120	346 221	325 168	314 021	335 405	368 791	453 893	490 779	529 393	412 638	338 120	423 772
New	309 541	323 871	299 941	281 892	300 371	341 223	420 090	457 233	500 474	393 286	309 541	397 314
Used	28 579	22 349	25 227	32 128	35 034	27 568	33 802	33 546	28 919	19 352	28 579	26 458
Equipment	751 742	706 123	592 321	572 825	617 766	693 745	763 215	779 744	765 098	602 060	751 742	728 434
New	718 227	679 090	564 218	540 611	588 110	664 648	734 160	750 353	728 322	577 410	718 227	697 668
Used	33 515	27 033	28 103	32 214	29 656	29 096	29 055	29 391	36 776	24 650	33 515	30 766
Not distributed as structures or equipment	0	0	0	0	0	0	0	0	0	0	0	0
CAPITALIZED COMPUTER SOFTWARE [1]	...	...	...	49 869	49 868	49 149	58 522	63 116	72 241	66 704	...	71 130
Prepackaged	...	...	...	17 307	17 306	17 630	21 181	21 777	26 260	21 407	...	23 238
Vendor-customized	...	...	...	15 554	15 553	13 876	16 912	17 990	19 259	18 610	...	20 329
Internally-developed	...	...	...	17 008	17 008	17 643	20 433	23 350	26 723	26 687	...	27 563
CAPITAL LEASE AND CAPITALIZED INTEREST EXPENSES [1]												
Capital leases	19 184	15 500	15 092	15 137	17 526	17 640	23 923	19 432	19 422	16 832	19 184	20 133
Capitalized interest	11 423	11 969	...	...	...	...	...	...	...	...	11 423	...

Capital expenditures	Companies without employees											
	2000	2001	2002	2003	2004	2005	2006	2007	2008	2009	2010	2011
TOTAL (billions)	71.2	56.7	80.4	88.2	88.9	82.2	92.8	84.2	79.7	75.4	69.5	73.4
Structures	26 287	17 527	33 316	30 621	33 302	32 862	34 809	34 494	32 988	35 493	33 182	30 886
New	19 984	11 667	21 250	23 399	24 309	24 715	28 771	23 606	22 525	27 758	27 664	27 787
Used	6 303	5 860	12 066	7 222	8 993	8 146	6 038	10 888	10 463	7 735	5 518	3 099
Equipment	44 880	39 133	47 088	57 549	55 587	49 386	58 023	49 711	46 681	39 878	36 357	42 467
New	32 399	27 528	34 450	38 803	40 481	36 598	42 899	40 054	36 957	29 525	26 773	32 267
Used	12 481	11 605	12 638	18 746	15 106	12 787	15 124	9 657	9 724	10 353	9 585	10 200
Not distributed as structures or equipment	0	0	0	0	0	0	0	0	0	0	0	0
CAPITALIZED COMPUTER SOFTWARE [1]	...	...	...	...	...	...	...	...	...	...	...	...
Prepackaged	...	...	...	...	...	...	...	...	...	...	...	...
Vendor-customized	...	...	...	...	...	...	...	...	...	...	...	...
Internally-developed	...	...	...	...	...	...	...	...	...	...	...	...
CAPITAL LEASE AND CAPITALIZED INTEREST EXPENSES [1]												
Capital leases	361	29	242	504	469	463	519	778	747	577	568	365
Capitalized interest	...	...	...	...	...	...	...	...	...	...	...	...

[1]Included in structures and equipment data shown above.
. . . = Not available.

Table 5-8. Capital Expenditures for Structures and Equipment for Companies with Employees by Major NAICS Industry Sector

(Millions of dollars.)

Year and type of expenditure	Total	Forestry, fishing, and agricultural services (113–115)	Mining (21)	Utilities (22)	Construction (23)	Manufacturing (31–33) Total	Durable goods industries (321, 327, 33)	Nondurable goods industries (31, 322–326)	Wholesale trade (42)	Retail trade (44–45)	Transportation and warehousing (48–49)	Information (51)
1998												
Total expenditures	896 452	854	40 424	36 010	26 867	203 587	117 901	85 685	29 169	57 276	51 287	96 487
Structures, total	300 283	206	26 503	18 574	7 062	39 028	19 406	19 622	7 480	25 105	13 036	24 721
New	260 008	158	24 714	17 771	4 749	37 122	18 449	18 673	6 738	23 104	12 365	24 218
Used	40 275	49	1 789	804	2 313	1 906	957	949	742	2 001	671	503
Equipment, total	596 169	648	13 921	17 436	19 805	164 559	98 496	66 063	21 690	32 171	38 251	71 766
New	570 397	603	12 625	17 266	15 346	159 363	95 571	63 792	20 470	30 359	33 409	70 827
Used	25 773	46	1 296	170	4 458	5 196	2 925	2 271	1 220	1 812	4 842	939
1999												
Total expenditures	974 631	1 716	30 586	42 802	23 110	196 399	117 005	79 394	32 442	64 063	57 299	122 827
Structures, total	293 787	344	17 626	21 241	1 753	33 985	17 320	16 665	7 264	29 494	14 122	34 924
New	276 094	331	17 039	20 784	1 505	32 814	16 581	16 233	6 508	28 670	13 859	33 733
Used	17 693	13	587	457	248	1 171	739	432	756	824	263	1 191
Equipment, total	680 843	1 371	12 960	21 561	21 356	162 414	99 685	62 729	25 179	34 569	43 178	87 903
New	656 344	1 190	12 167	20 545	18 600	157 715	96 434	61 281	23 714	33 567	40 425	85 310
Used	24 499	182	793	1 016	2 756	4 699	3 251	1 448	1 465	1 002	2 752	2 593
2000												
Total expenditures	1 089 862	1 488	42 522	61 302	25 049	214 827	133 786	81 041	33 579	69 791	59 851	160 177
Structures, total	338 120	139	28 620	29 472	2 803	39 434	21 228	18 207	8 923	32 037	13 457	41 502
New	309 541	134	25 500	29 258	2 583	36 643	19 748	16 895	8 364	30 413	13 190	40 062
Used	28 579	5	3 120	214	220	2 791	1 480	1 312	559	1 624	267	1 440
Equipment, total	751 742	1 350	13 902	31 830	22 245	175 393	112 558	62 835	24 656	37 754	46 394	118 675
New	718 227	1 086	12 854	27 937	17 788	169 454	108 703	60 751	23 610	36 428	43 455	117 835
Used	33 515	264	1 048	3 893	4 458	5 939	3 856	2 083	1 046	1 326	2 938	841
2001												
Total expenditures	1 052 344	1 532	51 278	82 823	24 802	192 835	118 875	73 959	29 981	66 917	57 756	144 793
Structures, total	346 221	226	32 678	38 093	3 859	39 815	22 032	17 784	6 932	30 010	16 594	41 742
New	323 871	149	31 825	36 504	3 389	38 001	20 701	17 301	5 357	29 118	14 479	41 384
Used	22 349	77	853	1 588	470	1 814	1 331	483	1 575	892	2 116	358
Equipment, total	706 123	1 306	18 600	44 731	20 943	153 019	96 844	56 176	23 049	36 906	41 161	103 051
New	679 090	1 091	17 567	42 939	17 432	148 397	94 251	54 145	20 757	35 074	38 521	102 410
Used	27 033	215	1 033	1 792	3 511	4 623	2 592	2 030	2 292	1 833	2 640	641
2002												
Total expenditures	917 490	1 910	42 467	65 502	24 773	157 243	84 062	73 181	26 789	59 316	47 124	88 156
Structures, total	325 168	184	30 685	29 893	1 890	32 643	15 133	17 510	5 885	26 286	14 498	33 607
New	299 941	118	29 775	29 008	1 254	31 022	14 396	16 626	5 447	25 051	13 870	33 472
Used	25 227	66	910	886	456	1 622	737	885	438	1 234	628	135
Equipment, total	592 321	1 726	11 783	35 609	23 063	124 600	68 929	55 671	20 904	33 030	32 626	54 550
New	564 218	1 319	10 262	34 816	19 257	118 621	66 112	52 510	18 562	31 157	29 178	54 247
Used	28 103	407	1 520	793	3 806	5 978	2 817	3 161	2 342	1 873	3 447	303
2003												
Total expenditures	886 846	1 894	50 548	54 569	23 159	149 065	80 226	68 839	26 014	65 868	44 460	80 524
Structures, total	314 021	202	36 617	24 841	1 676	31 108	13 330	17 778	5 615	29 675	13 005	30 765
New	281 892	177	35 897	24 580	1 424	29 315	12 631	16 685	4 921	27 393	11 779	30 406
Used	32 128	25	720	261	251	1 793	700	1 093	694	2 282	1 226	358
Equipment, total	572 825	1 692	13 931	29 729	21 484	117 956	66 895	51 061	20 399	36 193	31 454	49 759
New	540 611	1 267	12 135	29 044	16 170	112 102	62 810	49 292	19 457	32 162	26 786	47 857
Used	32 214	425	1 796	685	5 313	5 855	4 086	1 769	942	4 031	4 668	1 902
2004												
Total expenditures	953 171	2 081	51 253	50 409	28 627	156 651	85 119	71 532	32 314	72 170	46 054	83 488
Structures, total	335 405	324	34 564	24 398	4 511	31 823	13 606	18 217	7 133	33 308	13 992	28 636
New	300 371	309	33 583	23 626	4 167	30 016	12 818	17 198	6 555	31 486	13 018	26 253
Used	35 034	15	982	772	345	1 807	788	1 019	578	1 822	975	2 384
Equipment, total	617 766	1 757	16 689	26 011	24 115	124 828	71 513	53 315	25 181	38 862	32 062	54 852
New	588 110	1 507	15 415	25 724	18 939	120 481	68 904	51 576	21 888	36 965	28 472	53 120
Used	29 656	250	1 274	286	5 176	4 347	2 609	1 738	3 293	1 897	3 590	1 732
2005												
Total expenditures	1 062 536	2 702	66 746	58 032	30 072	165 634	92 180	73 455	40 578	73 531	56 926	91 373
Structures, total	368 791	344	46 433	24 186	2 544	34 132	14 735	19 397	9 184	34 119	17 855	31 977
New	341 223	283	45 655	23 485	2 247	32 564	14 033	18 531	8 830	33 360	16 954	31 716
Used	27 568	61	777	701	297	1 569	703	866	355	759	901	262
Equipment, total	693 745	2 358	20 313	33 847	27 528	131 502	77 444	54 058	31 394	39 412	39 072	59 396
New	664 648	2 016	18 495	33 083	22 082	126 387	73 889	52 498	28 224	38 301	34 953	59 071
Used	29 096	341	1 818	764	5 446	5 115	3 555	1 560	3 169	1 111	4 119	325
2006												
Total expenditures	1 217 107	2 672	99 309	69 757	30 257	192 364	106 843	85 521	36 600	86 735	68 021	104 373
Structures, total	453 893	391	68 662	30 587	2 556	41 617	17 515	24 103	10 375	43 188	20 852	31 947
New	420 090	316	67 322	29 294	2 217	39 419	16 243	23 176	9 956	41 985	19 765	31 621
Used	33 802	75	1 340	1 293	338	2 198	1 272	926	419	1 203	1 087	326
Equipment, total	763 215	2 281	30 647	39 170	27 701	150 747	89 328	61 419	26 226	43 547	47 168	72 425
New	734 160	1 846	28 813	37 617	23 276	146 551	86 637	59 914	24 366	41 943	41 258	71 830
Used	29 055	435	1 833	1 553	4 425	4 196	2 692	1 504	1 860	1 604	5 911	595

Note: Detail may not sum to total because of rounding.

182   BUSINESS STATISTICS OF THE UNITED STATES (BERNAN PRESS)

Table 5-8. Capital Expenditures for Structures and Equipment for Companies with Employees by Major NAICS Industry Sector—*Continued*

(Millions of dollars.)

Year and type of expenditure	Finance and insurance (52)	Real estate and rental and leasing (53)	Professional, scientific, and technical services (54)	Management of companies and enterprises (55)	Administrative and support and waste management (56)	Educational services (61)	Health care and social assistance (62)	Arts, entertainment, and recreation (71)	Accommodation and food services (72)	Other services, except public administration (81)	Structure and equipment expenditures serving multiple industries
1998											
Total expenditures	118 173	85 184	22 277	1 821	13 110	12 983	47 109	8 994	20 822	20 627	3 392
Structures, total	27 221	36 775	4 886	753	4 288	9 109	23 971	5 045	12 045	13 737	738
New	16 858	24 109	4 572	502	3 745	8 734	21 328	4 838	10 402	13 280	699
Used	10 362	12 666	314	251	543	374	2 643	206	1 643	457	39
Equipment, total	90 952	48 409	17 390	1 068	8 822	3 874	23 138	3 949	8 777	6 890	2 654
New	90 058	46 877	16 868	1 030	8 346	3 825	22 465	3 752	8 005	6 296	2 609
Used	894	1 532	522	38	476	49	672	197	772	594	46
1999											
Total expenditures	130 101	100 629	29 546	6 065	16 227	13 532	51 342	13 355	23 328	16 902	2 359
Structures, total	20 080	33 903	6 780	1 668	2 875	9 767	25 922	8 119	13 431	9 975	516
New	17 918	30 295	6 168	1 509	2 773	9 140	24 159	7 971	11 391	9 033	495
Used	2 162	3 608	613	159	102	627	1 763	148	2 040	941	21
Equipment, total	110 021	66 726	22 766	4 397	13 353	3 766	25 420	5 236	9 897	6 928	1 843
New	109 577	63 555	22 153	4 319	12 323	3 668	24 945	5 125	9 324	6 370	1 752
Used	444	3 171	613	78	1 029	97	475	111	573	558	91
2000											
Total expenditures	133 684	92 456	34 055	5 054	17 506	18 223	52 166	19 125	26 307	21 125	1 572
Structures, total	23 010	24 815	8 141	1 570	4 032	13 699	26 868	12 245	13 873	13 274	206
New	20 298	17 793	7 470	955	3 504	12 965	23 999	11 627	12 879	11 705	200
Used	2 712	7 022	671	615	528	735	2 869	618	993	1 569	6
Equipment, total	110 675	67 641	25 914	3 484	13 475	4 523	25 299	6 880	12 434	7 852	1 366
New	109 678	62 175	24 847	3 403	12 723	4 338	24 407	6 161	11 501	7 192	1 357
Used	997	5 466	1 067	81	752	186	892	719	933	659	10
2001											
Total expenditures	131 105	82 674	30 464	3 035	15 785	17 377	52 932	14 974	21 365	29 006	911
Structures, total	22 744	20 489	7 258	933	3 527	12 852	27 030	8 998	12 248	20 031	163
New	19 571	17 325	6 793	869	3 367	11 860	25 241	8 157	11 402	18 918	162
Used	3 173	3 164	465	64	160	991	1 789	841	846	1 112	0
Equipment, total	108 361	62 185	23 206	2 102	12 258	4 525	25 902	5 976	9 117	8 976	749
New	107 268	60 295	22 330	2 019	11 644	4 238	24 573	5 590	7 921	8 300	725
Used	1 093	1 891	876	83	613	287	1 329	386	1 196	676	24
2002											
Total expenditures	128 444	94 529	25 864	3 430	14 719	19 532	59 311	13 169	22 409	21 269	1 532
Structures, total	24 308	35 579	7 129	933	3 276	14 655	30 291	7 758	12 157	13 261	250
New	19 748	30 227	6 424	913	2 948	13 601	27 273	7 332	10 848	11 363	248
Used	4 739	5 352	706	21	328	1 055	3 018	425	1 309	1 899	2
Equipment, total	103 956	58 949	18 735	2 497	11 443	4 876	29 021	5 412	10 252	8 007	1 282
New	103 421	56 847	18 021	2 481	10 585	4 690	28 196	5 132	9 290	6 858	1 276
Used	535	2 102	714	16	857	186	825	280	962	1 149	6
2003											
Total expenditures	120 787	87 952	24 703	3 298	16 612	16 667	61 151	11 029	21 036	26 035	1 476
Structures, total	26 200	25 028	5 314	925	3 976	11 984	30 996	6 800	10 568	18 518	209
New	17 908	16 446	4 671	869	3 213	11 569	28 885	6 532	9 417	16 288	202
Used	8 292	8 583	643	56	763	415	2 111	268	1 151	2 230	7
Equipment, total	94 587	62 923	19 389	2 373	12 636	4 683	30 155	4 229	10 468	7 517	1 267
New	94 205	61 253	18 675	2 368	11 374	4 569	29 497	4 038	9 684	6 706	1 263
Used	383	1 671	714	5	1 262	114	658	192	783	811	4
2004											
Total expenditures	153 629	91 606	26 688	2 825	17 455	18 919	64 561	12 165	20 641	19 701	1 572
Structures, total	43 919	27 277	6 007	860	2 567	13 728	32 608	7 360	9 860	12 278	321
New	30 216	21 610	5 714	798	2 309	12 781	30 668	7 196	9 126	10 867	307
Used	13 703	5 667	293	62	259	947	1 939	164	734	1 411	13
Equipment, total	109 710	64 329	20 681	1 965	14 888	5 190	31 953	4 804	10 781	7 423	1 252
New	109 244	61 947	20 081	1 931	12 692	4 965	31 280	4 677	10 373	6 788	1 248
Used	466	2 382	600	34	2 196	225	673	128	408	635	3
2005											
Total expenditures	161 389	103 022	33 066	2 809	18 194	17 484	73 825	14 165	30 718	20 105	2 163
Structures, total	39 383	24 791	8 717	857	3 051	12 711	39 089	9 242	17 679	12 036	460
New	31 023	17 341	7 633	795	2 759	11 913	37 493	8 805	16 567	11 350	452
Used	8 360	7 450	1 084	62	292	798	1 597	436	1 112	686	8
Equipment, total	122 005	78 231	24 350	1 951	15 143	4 773	34 736	4 924	13 039	8 069	1 703
New	121 511	76 894	23 887	1 917	13 523	4 597	34 110	4 757	11 950	7 209	1 681
Used	494	1 337	463	34	1 620	176	626	166	1 089	861	22
2006											
Total expenditures	163 069	132 073	30 284	3 306	19 231	22 615	75 296	17 156	36 217	25 959	1 813
Structures, total	41 326	40 794	6 971	875	3 613	17 537	41 197	11 733	22 585	16 621	467
New	34 028	30 240	6 375	799	3 485	16 203	37 765	11 326	21 774	15 754	446
Used	7 298	10 554	596	76	128	1 334	3 433	406	811	866	21
Equipment, total	121 743	91 280	23 313	2 432	15 618	5 078	34 099	5 424	13 632	9 339	1 346
New	121 157	88 957	22 867	2 188	14 932	4 983	33 508	5 121	13 161	8 463	1 322
Used	586	2 323	446	244	686	95	591	303	472	875	24

Note: Detail may not sum to total because of rounding.

Table 5-8. Capital Expenditures for Structures and Equipment for Companies with Employees by Major NAICS Industry Sector—*Continued*

(Millions of dollars.)

Year and type of expenditure	Total	Forestry, fishing, and agricultural services (113–115)	Mining (21)	Utilities (22)	Construction (23)	Manufacturing (31–33)			Wholesale trade (42)	Retail trade (44–45)	Transportation and warehousing (48–49)	Information (51)
						Total	Durable goods industries (321, 327, 33)	Nondurable goods industries (31, 322–326)				
2007												
Total expenditures	1 270 522	2 149	120 681	85 354	36 692	197 298	107 664	89 633	30 776	82 511	67 351	106 084
Structures, total	490 779	469	85 242	40 178	3 529	42 458	17 879	24 579	7 526	41 527	23 712	29 081
New	457 233	320	83 206	37 647	2 704	41 247	17 431	23 816	7 091	40 471	22 808	28 304
Used	33 546	149	2 036	2 531	824	1 211	447	763	436	1 056	904	777
Equipment, total	779 744	1 681	35 440	45 176	33 164	154 840	89 786	65 054	23 250	40 983	43 639	77 003
New	750 353	1 368	33 095	44 107	27 325	150 333	87 020	63 313	21 690	39 668	39 238	76 143
Used	29 391	313	2 344	1 069	5 838	4 507	2 766	1 741	1 560	1 316	4 400	861
2008												
Total expenditures	1 294 491	2 337	149 272	98 668	40 838	213 117	103 022	110 095	32 370	73 234	79 617	103 327
Structures, total	529 393	421	109 683	43 515	11 129	49 346	18 896	30 450	8 387	36 147	30 078	27 376
New	500 474	417	105 064	41 746	10 525	48 184	18 168	30 015	7 958	35 342	29 214	27 080
Used	28 919	4	4 618	1 769	603	1 162	728	434	430	805	863	296
Equipment, total	765 098	1 917	39 590	55 154	29 709	163 771	84 125	79 645	23 982	37 087	49 539	75 951
New	728 322	1 610	35 928	53 486	22 404	158 104	80 690	77 414	22 554	36 328	41 877	75 342
Used	36 776	307	3 662	1 668	7 305	5 667	3 435	2 232	1 429	759	7 662	609
2009												
Total expenditures	1 015 322	2 168	100 564	103 024	19 751	155 153	76 039	79 114	25 252	58 428	55 702	88 373
Structures, total	414 051	460	72 255	45 973	4 556	35 735	13 054	22 680	5 485	28 205	22 088	21 764
New	395 022	453	69 942	45 168	4 215	34 537	12 273	22 264	5 131	27 220	21 128	21 410
Used	19 030	7	2 313	805	341	1 198	782	416	354	985	961	354
Equipment, total	601 270	1 708	28 308	57 051	15 195	119 418	62 985	56 434	19 767	30 223	33 614	66 609
New	577 051	1 428	26 790	54 848	11 815	115 470	60 699	54 772	18 512	29 063	30 182	65 879
Used	24 219	279	1 518	2 204	3 380	3 948	2 286	1 662	1 255	1 160	3 432	731
2010												
Total expenditures	1 036 153	3 255	115 749	94 462	17 856	160 798	86 570	74 227	31 075	65 252	58 952	97 150
Structures, total	396 398	679	85 221	43 896	2 633	31 166	14 099	17 068	6 879	29 169	23 401	21 771
New	367 759	671	82 147	42 853	2 361	30 069	13 492	16 576	5 709	27 608	22 622	20 696
Used	28 639	8	3 074	1 044	272	1 098	606	491	1 170	1 561	778	1 074
Equipment, total	639 755	2 576	30 528	50 566	15 223	129 631	72 472	57 160	24 196	36 084	35 551	75 379
New	611 573	1 979	28 820	48 675	11 377	125 911	70 692	55 219	21 756	34 457	29 912	74 657
Used	28 182	597	1 708	1 891	3 846	3 720	1 780	1 940	2 440	1 626	5 639	723
2011												
Total expenditures	1 152 206	3 063	149 504	98 047	21 778	193 365	110 846	82 519	35 471	67 449	72 258	99 654
Structures, total	423 772	529	108 292	46 729	2 867	36 605	17 654	18 951	7 907	27 048	28 205	20 297
New	397 314	516	104 217	45 882	2 590	35 032	16 944	18 088	7 430	26 136	27 327	19 877
Used	26 458	13	4 075	847	277	1 573	710	863	477	912	878	421
Equipment, total	728 434	2 534	41 213	51 319	18 910	156 760	93 192	63 568	27 564	40 401	44 053	79 357
New	697 668	2 050	39 356	48 843	13 895	152 037	90 098	61 939	26 496	39 177	37 965	79 110
Used	30 766	485	1 857	2 476	5 015	4 723	3 094	1 629	1 069	1 224	6 088	247

Note: Detail may not sum to total because of rounding.

Table 5-8. Capital Expenditures for Structures and Equipment for Companies with Employees by Major NAICS Industry Sector—Continued

(Millions of dollars.)

Year and type of expenditure	Finance and insurance (52)	Real estate and rental and leasing (53)	Professional, scientific, and technical services (54)	Management of companies and enterprises (55)	Administrative and support and waste management (56)	Educational services (61)	Health care and social assistance (62)	Arts, entertainment, and recreation (71)	Accommodation and food services (72)	Other services, except public administration (81)	Structure and equipment expenditures serving multiple industries
2007											
Total expenditures	172 894	117 969	31 804	4 542	18 167	23 238	84 160	18 769	38 021	29 680	2 380
Structures, total	45 159	41 222	7 453	1 472	3 859	17 910	45 361	12 589	22 211	19 165	656
New	36 507	34 026	6 944	1 404	3 677	17 322	43 522	11 894	21 226	16 264	650
Used	8 652	7 196	509	69	182	588	1 839	695	984	2 901	6
Equipment, total	127 735	76 747	24 351	3 070	14 308	5 328	38 799	6 180	15 810	10 515	1 725
New	126 763	74 735	23 931	2 943	13 599	5 253	38 258	5 916	14 671	9 593	1 724
Used	972	2 012	420	127	709	75	541	264	1 139	922	1
2008											
Total expenditures	132 913	106 910	32 980	4 567	16 552	27 426	90 248	17 109	40 519	28 312	4 175
Structures, total	25 058	45 929	8 836	1 304	4 133	21 698	50 105	11 594	24 947	18 673	1 035
New	22 640	36 532	8 481	1 241	3 789	20 632	47 205	11 224	24 271	17 899	1 030
Used	2 418	9 397	355	63	344	1 065	2 900	370	675	775	6
Equipment, total	107 855	60 981	24 144	3 264	12 420	5 728	40 143	5 515	15 572	9 638	3 139
New	107 108	59 117	23 349	3 146	11 687	5 672	39 161	5 340	14 012	8 974	3 124
Used	747	1 864	794	117	733	56	981	175	1 560	664	15
2009											
Total expenditures	99 466	72 902	28 163	4 719	19 234	28 018	79 370	16 265	26 439	29 296	3 034
Structures, total	21 825	26 564	6 669	1 371	5 876	22 388	44 375	11 035	14 735	22 054	641
New	20 419	22 350	5 975	1 334	5 361	21 577	42 188	10 804	13 607	21 564	639
Used	1 406	4 214	694	36	515	810	2 187	231	1 128	490	2
Equipment, total	77 641	46 339	21 494	3 349	13 359	5 630	34 994	5 230	11 704	7 243	2 393
New	77 169	44 594	20 980	3 311	12 471	5 403	34 271	5 073	10 858	6 545	2 389
Used	473	1 745	514	38	888	227	723	157	846	698	4
2010											
Total expenditures	103 093	81 282	28 203	4 946	16 873	23 368	78 381	12 121	19 915	20 951	2 471
Structures, total	16 209	32 375	5 706	1 567	3 552	17 673	42 861	7 709	9 765	13 605	562
New	13 653	23 085	5 365	1 517	3 466	16 678	40 113	7 551	9 051	11 987	558
Used	2 556	9 290	341	50	86	995	2 748	158	714	1 618	4
Equipment, total	86 884	48 908	22 497	3 379	13 321	5 695	35 520	4 412	10 151	7 346	1 909
New	86 401	47 593	21 889	3 359	12 626	5 553	34 808	4 164	8 856	6 879	1 902
Used	483	1 315	608	20	695	142	713	248	1 294	467	7
2011											
Total expenditures	109 580	91 096	28 177	5 187	18 425	21 018	83 162	11 275	24 844	16 060	2 794
Structures, total	14 490	33 539	6 553	1 367	3 537	15 037	42 946	6 514	12 029	8 673	608
New	11 857	24 762	6 161	1 307	3 423	14 404	40 570	. . .	11 354	7 865	. . .
Used	2 633	8 776	392	60	114	633	2 376	675	807	. . .	. . .
Equipment, total	95 090	57 557	21 624	3 820	14 888	5 981	40 216	4 760	12 814	7 387	2 186
New	94 802	55 153	21 067	3 759	14 342	5 909	39 354	. . .	10 893	7 029	. . .
Used	287	2 404	557	61	546	72	862	. . .	1 922	358	. . .

. . . = Not available.
Note: Detail may not sum to total because of rounding.

NOTES AND DEFINITIONS, CHAPTER 5

Tables 5-1 through 5-4: Gross Saving and Investment Accounts

SOURCE: U.S. DEPARTMENT OF COMMERCE, BUREAU OF ECONOMIC ANALYSIS (BEA)

All of the data in these tables are from the National Income and Product Accounts, which are described in the Notes and Definitions to Chapter 1. All quarterly series are shown at seasonally adjusted annual rates. Current and constant dollar values are in billions of dollars. Constant dollar values are in 2009 dollars. Indexes of quantity are based on the average for the year 2009, set to equal 100.

The 2013 revision includes a major expansion of the investment accounts. Expenditures for research and development are now recognized as fixed investment. Previously, they were treated as if they were costs of producing this year's output. R&D spending by business, government, and nonprofit institutions serving households (NPISHs) is now counted as fixed investment. It is depreciated (with the estimated depreciation added to capital consumption allowances), so that there can be either positive or negative net investment in R&D. A similar treatment is now given to expenditures by private enterprises for the creation of entertainment, literary, and artistic originals. Finally, an expanded set of ownership transfer costs for residential fixed assets is recognized as fixed investment.

Definitions: Table 5-1

Gross saving is saving before the deduction of allowances for the consumption of fixed capital. It represents the amount of saving available to finance gross investment. *Net saving* is gross saving less allowances for fixed capital consumption. It represents the amount of saving available for financing expansion of the capital stock, and comprises net private saving (the sum of personal saving, undistributed corporate profits, and wage accruals less disbursements) and the net saving of federal, state, and local governments.

Personal saving is derived by subtracting personal outlays from disposable personal income. (See Chapter 4 for more information.) It is the current net saving of individuals (including proprietors of unincorporated businesses), nonprofit institutions that primarily serve individuals, life insurance carriers, retirement funds, private noninsured welfare funds, and private trust funds. Conceptually, personal saving may also be viewed as the sum for all persons (including institutions as previously defined) of the net acquisition of financial assets and the change in physical

assets, less the sum of net borrowing and consumption of fixed capital. In either case, it is defined to exclude capital gains. That is, it excludes profits on the increase in the value of homes, securities, and other property—whether realized or unrealized—and therefore includes the noncorporate inventory valuation adjustment and the capital consumption adjustment (IVA and CCAdj, respectively). (See notes and definitions to Chapter 1.)

The net saving of *Domestic corporate business* is corporate profits after tax less dividends plus the corporate IVA and corporate CCAdj. (See notes and definitions for Chapter 1.)

Government net saving was formerly called "current surplus or deficit (-) of general government." (See Chapter 6 for further detail from the government accounts.) Where current receipts of government exceed current expenditures, government has a current surplus (indicated by a positive value) and saving is made available to finance investment by government or other sectors—for example, by the repayment of debt, which can free up funds for private investment. Where current expenditures exceed current receipts, there is a government deficit (indicated by a negative value) and government must borrow, drawing on funds that would otherwise be available for private investment. In these accounts, current expenditures are defined to include a charge for the consumption of fixed capital.

Consumption of fixed capital is an accounting charge for the using-up of private and government fixed capital, including software, located in the United States. It is based on studies of prices of used equipment and structures in resale markets. As of the 2013 revision, it also includes estimated charges for the using-up of the research and development and other intellectual property capital now defined as investment spending.

For general government and nonprofit institutions that primarily serve individuals, consumption of fixed capital is recorded in government consumption expenditures and in personal consumption expenditures (PCE), respectively, and taken to be the value of the current services of the fixed capital assets owned and used by these entities and the estimated using-up of R&D and other intellectual property.

Private consumption of fixed capital consists of tax-return-based depreciation charges for corporations and nonfarm proprietorships and historical-cost depreciation (calculated by the Bureau of Economic Analysis [BEA] using a geometric pattern of price declines) for farm proprietorships, rental income of persons, and nonprofit institutions, minus the capital consumption adjustments. (In other words, in the NIPA treatment of saving, the amount of the CCAdj is taken out of book depreciation and added to income and profits—a reallocation from one form of gross saving to another.) It also includes the charges for the using-up of private R&D and other intellectual property, as described above.

Gross private domestic investment consists of gross private fixed investment and change in private inventories. (See the notes and definitions for Chapter 1.)

Gross government investment consists of federal, state, and local general government and government enterprise expenditures for fixed assets (structures, equipment, and intellectual property). Government inventory investment is included in government consumption expenditures. For further detail, see Chapter 6.

Capital account transactions, net are the net cash or in-kind transfers between the United States and the rest of the world that are linked to the acquisition or disposition of assets rather than the purchase or sale of currently-produced goods and services. When positive, it represents a net transfer from the United States to the rest of the world; when negative, it represents a net transfer to the United States from the rest of the world. This is a definitional category that was introduced in the 1999 revision of the NIPAs. Estimates are available only from 1982 forward. With the new treatment of disaster losses and disaster insurance introduced in the 2009 revision, this line will include disaster-related insurance payouts to the rest of the world less what is received from the rest of the world.

Net lending or net borrowing (-), NIPAs is equal to the international balance on current account as measured in the NIPAs (see Chapter 7) less capital account transactions, net. When positive, this represents net investment by the United States in the rest of the world; when negative, it represents net borrowing by the United States from the rest of the world. For data before 1982, net lending or net borrowing equals the NIPA balance on current account, because estimates of capital account transactions are not available.

By definition, gross national saving must equal the sum of gross domestic investment, capital account transactions, and net international lending (where net international borrowing appears as negative lending). In practice, due to differences in measurement, these two aggregates differ by the *statistical discrepancy* calculated in the product and income accounts. (See Chapter 1.) Gross saving is therefore equal to the sum of gross domestic investment, capital account transactions, and net international lending minus the statistical discrepancy. Where the statistical discrepancy is negative, it means that the sum of measured investment, capital transactions, and net international lending has fallen short of measured saving.

Net domestic investment is gross domestic investment minus consumption of fixed capital, calculated by the editors from the data shown in the table.

Gross national income is national income plus the consumption of fixed capital. (See Chapter 1 for further information.) This is a new concept introduced in the 2003 revision. It is conceptually equal to gross national product, but differs by the statistical discrepancy. Gross national income is an appropriate denominator for the national saving ratios. Saving was previously shown as a percentage of gross national product; in the revision, it is instead shown as a percentage of the income-side equivalent of gross national product. Since saving is measured as a residual from income, it is appropriate to involve consistent measurements—and consistent imperfections in those measurements—in both the numerator and the denominator of the fraction.

Definitions: Tables 5-2 through 5-4

Gross private fixed investment comprises both nonresidential and residential fixed investment. It consists of purchases of fixed assets, which are commodities that will be used in a production process for more than one year, including replacements and additions to the capital stock, and intellectual property, including software, research and development, and entertainment, literary, and artistic originals. It is "gross" in the sense that it is measured before a deduction for consumption of fixed capital. It covers investment by private businesses and nonprofit institutions in the United States, regardless of whether the investment is owned by U.S. residents. It does not include purchases of the same types of equipment, structures, or intellectual property by government agencies, which are included in government gross investment. It also does not include investment by U.S. residents in other countries.

Gross nonresidential fixed investment consists of structures, equipment, and intellectual property that are not related to personal residences.

Nonresidential structures consists of new construction, brokers' commissions on sales of structures, and net purchases (purchases less sales) of used structures by private business and by nonprofit institutions from government agencies. New construction includes hotels, motels, and mining exploration, shafts, and wells.

Other nonresidential structures consists primarily of religious, educational, vocational, lodging, railroads, farm, and amusement and recreational structures, net purchases of used structures, and brokers' commissions on the sale of structures.

Nonresidential equipment consists of private business purchases—on capital account—of new machinery, equipment, and vehicles; dealers' margins on sales of used equipment; and net purchases (purchases less sales) of used equipment from government agencies, persons, and the rest of the world. (However, it does not include the personal-use portion of equipment purchased for both business and personal use. This is included in PCE.)

Computers have displayed phenomenal growth in numbers and power not easily represented by index numbers or constant-dollar estimates at the scale shown in these tables. Zero entries shown in the quantity indexes for early years actually represent very small quantities. Because of rapid growth in computing power and declines in its price, constant-dollar measures are deemed not meaningful and are not calculated by BEA.

Other information processing includes communication equipment, nonmedical instruments, medical equipment and instruments, photocopy and related equipment, and office and accounting equipment.

Other nonresidential equipment consists primarily of furniture and fixtures, agricultural machinery, construction machinery, mining and oilfield machinery, service industry machinery, and electrical equipment not elsewhere classified.

Intellectual property comprises information processing software, research and development, and entertainment, literary, and artistic originals.

Software excludes the value of software "embedded," or bundled, in computers and other equipment, which is instead included in the value of that equipment.

Research and development consists of expenditures for both purchased and own-account R&D by businesses, NPISHs, and general governments. Government R&D expenditures are treated as investment regardless of whether the R&D is protected or made freely available to the public. Investment is measured as the sum of production costs.

Entertainment, literary, and other artistic originals include theatrical movies, long-lived television programs, books, music, and other miscellaneous entertainment.

Residential private fixed investment consists of both *structures* and residential producers' durable *equipment*—that is, equipment owned by landlords and rented to tenants. Investment in *structures* consists of new units, improvements to existing units, manufactured homes, brokers' commissions and other ownership transfer costs on the sale of residential property, and net purchases (purchases less sales) of used structures from government agencies.

Other residential structures consists primarily of manufactured homes, improvements, dormitories, net purchases of used structures, and brokers' commissions on the sale of residential structures.

Real gross private investment (Table 5-3) and *chain-type quantity indexes for private fixed investment* (Table 5-4) are defined and explained in the notes and definitions to Chapter 1. The chained-dollar (2009) estimates in Table 5-3 are constructed by applying the changes in the chain-type quantity indexes, as shown in Table 5-4, to the 2009 current-dollar values. Thus, they do not contain any information about time trends that is not already present in the quantity indexes.

In Table 5-4, the user may wish to distinguish between the use of the "not available" symbol (. . .) and the publication of zero values (0.0). The "not available" values shown for computers and software mean that BEA has no separate estimates of their values; they are included in total "information processing equipment and software." The zeroes indicate quantities so small relative to the 2009 base that they round to zero, but they do exist and are included in the higher-level aggregates.

As the quantity indexes are chain-weighted at the basic level of aggregation, chained constant-dollar components generally do not add to the chained constant-dollar totals. For this reason, BEA only makes available year-2009-dollar estimates back to 1999 (except for the very highest levels of aggregation of gross domestic product [GDP]), since the addition problem is less severe for years close to the base year. However, the addition problem is so severe for computers that BEA does not even publish recent year-2009-dollar values for this component. BEA notes that "The quantity index for computers can be used to accurately measure the real growth rate of this component. However, because computers exhibit rapid changes in prices relative to other prices in the economy, the chained-dollar estimates should not be used to measure the component's relative importance or its contribution to the growth rate of more aggregate series." (Footnote to BEA Table 5.3.6, *Survey of Current Business*, available on the BEA Web site at http://www.bea.gov.) Accurate estimates of these contributions are shown in BEA Table 5.3.2, which is published in the *Survey of Current Business* and can be found on the BEA Web site.

Data availability, revisions, and references

See the information on the NIPAs at the end of the notes and definitions to Chapter 1. All current and historical data are available on the BEA Web site at http://www.bea.gov or the STAT-USA subscription Web site at http://www.stat-usa.gov.

Tables 5-5 and 5-6: Current-Cost Net Stock of Fixed Assets; Chain-Type Quantity Indexes for Net Stock of Fixed Assets

SOURCE: U.S. DEPARTMENT OF COMMERCE, BUREAU OF ECONOMIC ANALYSIS (BEA)

The Bureau of Economic Analysis (BEA) calculates measurements, integrated with the national income and product accounts (NIPAs), of the level of the stock of fixed assets in the U.S. economy, or what is commonly called the "capital stock." (The fixed investment component of the GDP is a flow, or the increment of new capital goods into the capital stock.) Data on consumer stocks of durable goods are also included in the accounts, but are not shown here. Historical data are available back to 1901, with detailed annual estimates of net stocks, depreciation, and investment by type and by NAICS (North American Industry Classification System) industry. This volume of *Business Statistics* presents time series data on the net stock of fixed assets valued in current dollars and also as constant-dollar quantity indexes.

At the time of compiling *Business Statistics*, the 2013 revision of the NIPAs with its new investment categories had not been incorporated in this data set, which was only available on the old basis through 2011.

Definitions and methods

The definitions of capital stock categories are the same as used in pre-revision GDP investment categories. Equipment includes software, and R&D and entertainment, literary, and artistic originals are not included.

The values of fixed capital and depreciation typically reported by businesses are inadequate for economic analysis and are not typically used in these measures. In business reports, capital is generally valued at historical costs—each year's capital acquisition in the prices of the year acquired—and the totals thus represent a mixture of pricing bases. Reported depreciation is generally based on historical cost and on depreciation rates allowable by federal income tax law, rather than on a realistic rate of economic depreciation.

In these data, the *net stock of fixed assets* is measured by a perpetual inventory method. In other words, net stock at any given time is the cumulative value of past gross investment less the cumulative value of past depreciation (measured by "consumption of fixed capital," the component of the NIPAs that is subtracted from GDP in order to yield net domestic product) and also less damages from disasters and war losses that exceed normal depreciation (such as Hurricane Katrina and the terrorist attacks of September 11, 2001).

The initial calculations using this perpetual inventory method are performed in real terms for each type of asset. They are then aggregated to higher levels using an annual-weighted Fisher-type index. (See the definition of *real or chained-dollar estimates* in the notes and definitions for Chapter 1.) This provides the *chain-type quantity indexes* shown in Table 5-6. Growth rates in these indexes measure real growth in the capital stock.

The real values are then converted to a *current-cost* basis to yield the values shown in Table 5-5. They are converted by multiplying the real values by the appropriate price index for the period under consideration. A major use of the current-cost net stock figures is comparison with the value of output in that year; for example, the current-cost net stock of fixed assets for the total economy divided by the current-dollar value of GDP yields a capital-output ratio for the entire economy. Growth rates in current-cost values will reflect both the real growth measured by the quantity indexes and the increase in the value at current prices of the existing stock.

Data availability and references

The latest comprehensive revision was presented and described in "Fixed Assets and Consumer Durable Goods for 1999–2008," *Survey of Current Business* (November 2009). Annual data are available on the BEA Web site at http://www.bea.gov/national/FA2004/Index.asp.

Tables 5-7 and 5-8: Annual Capital Expenditures

SOURCE: U.S. DEPARTMENT OF COMMERCE, CENSUS BUREAU

These data are from the Census Bureau's Annual Capital Expenditures Survey (ACES). The survey provides detailed information on capital investment in new and used structures and equipment by nonfarm businesses.

The survey is based on a stratified random sample of approximately 47,000 companies with employees and 30,000 non-employer businesses (businesses with an owner but no employees). For companies with employees, the Census Bureau reports data for 132 separate industry categories from the North American Industry Classification System (NAICS); Table 5-8 shows these data for the major NAICS sectors. Total capital expenditures, with no industry detail, are reported for the nonemployer businesses and are shown in Table 5-7, where they can be compared with the totals for companies with employees. The 1999 ACES was the first to use NAICS, providing data for the years 1998 forward on that basis.

Definitions

Capital expenditures include all capitalized costs during the year for both new and used structures and equipment, including software, that were chargeable to fixed asset accounts for which depreciation or amortization accounts are ordinarily maintained. For projects lasting longer than one year, this definition includes gross additions to construction-in-progress accounts, even if the asset was not in use and not yet depreciated. For *capital leases*, the company using the asset (lessee) is asked to include the cost or present value of the leased assets in the year in which the lease was entered. Also included in capital expenditures are capitalized leasehold improvements and capitalized interest charges on loans used to finance capital projects.

Structures consist of the capitalized costs of buildings and other structures and all necessary expenditures to acquire, construct, and prepare the structures. The costs of any machinery and equipment that is integral to or built-in features of the structures are classified as structures. Also included are major additions and alterations to existing structures and capitalized repairs and improvements to buildings.

New structures include new buildings and other structures not previously owned, as well as buildings and other structures that have been previously owned but not used or occupied.

Used structures are buildings and other structures that have been previously owned and occupied.

Equipment includes machinery, furniture and fixtures, computers, and vehicles used in the production and distribution of goods and services. Expenditures for machinery and equipment that is housed in structures and can be removed or replaced without significantly altering the structure are classified as equipment.

New equipment consists of machinery and equipment purchased new, as well as equipment produced in the company for the company's own use.

Used equipment is secondhand machinery and equipment.

Capital leases consist of new assets acquired under capital lease arrangements entered into during the year. Capital leases are defined by the criteria in the Financial Accounting Standards (FASB) Number 13.

Capitalized computer software consists of costs of materials and services directly related to the development or acquisition of software; payroll and payroll-related costs for employees directly associated with software development; and interest cost incurred while developing the software. Capitalized computer software is defined by the criteria in Statement of Position 98-1, Accounting for the Costs of Computer Software Developed or Obtained for Internal Use.

Prepackaged software is purchased off-the-shelf through retailers or other mass-market outlets for internal use by the company and includes the cost of licensing fees and service/maintenance agreements.

Vendor-customized software is externally developed by vendors and customized for the company's use.

Internally-developed software is developed by the company's employees for internal use and includes loaded payroll (salaries, wages, benefits, and bonuses related to all software development activities).

Data availability and references

Current and historical data and references are available on the Census Bureau Web site at http://www.census.gov/econ/aces.

CHAPTER 6: GOVERNMENT

Section 6a: Federal Government in the National Income and Product Accounts

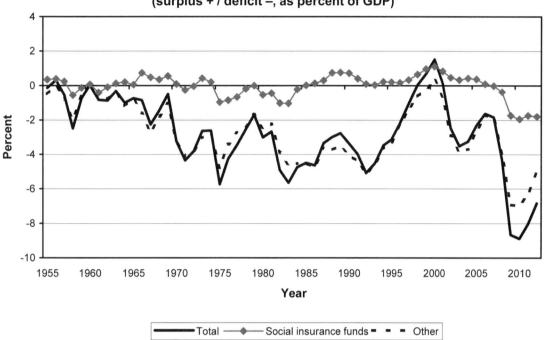

Figure 6-1. Federal Government Saving and Dis-saving, 1955–2012
(surplus + / deficit –, as percent of GDP)

- In the recovery and economic expansion of the 2000s, the federal budget never got back to a surplus such as those achieved in 1999 and 2000. With the onset of the most severe recession of the postwar period beginning in December 2007, deficits grew rapidly as receipts fell while expenditures continued to rise. In calendar 2010, the NIPA budget deficit peaked at 8.9 percent of GDP, including a 1.9 percent deficit in social insurance funds. This was not as great as World War II deficits but exceeded in scale the deficits of the 1930s. The NIPA deficit fell back to 6.8 percent of GDP in 2012 and appears to be falling further in 2013. (Tables 6-1, 1-1, and 6-14B)

- The main contributors to the rise in the deficit from 2007 to 2010 were increasing social benefits to persons, such as Social Security and unemployment insurance, and a drop in tax receipts. (Tables 6-1, 6-2, 6-3, and 1-1)

- Total federal government current expenditures increased from 16.8 percent of gross domestic product (GDP) in 1955 to 24.9 percent in 2010, falling back a bit to 23.2 percent in 2012. The composition of current expenditures changed significantly over that period. "Consumption" spending on defense and nondefense programs fell from 65 percent of total spending to 27 percent, while social benefits to persons, such as Social Security and Medicare, rose from 16 percent to 47 percent. Grants to state and local governments increased from 3 percent to 12 percent. Interest payments were 11 percent in both years. (Tables 6-1 and 1-1)

Table 6-1. Federal Government Current Receipts and Expenditures

(National income and product accounts, calendar years, billions of dollars, quarterly data are at seasonally adjusted annual rates.)

NIPA Table 3.2

Year and quarter	Total current receipts	Current receipts													
		Current tax receipts						Taxes from the rest of the world	Contributions for government social insurance	Income receipts on assets			Current transfer receipts	Current surplus of government enterprises
		Total tax receipts	Personal current taxes	Taxes on production and imports		Taxes on corporate income				Interest receipts	Dividends	Rents and royalties		
				Excise taxes	Customs duties	Federal Reserve banks	Other corporate taxes							
1955	71.1	62.0	30.5	9.8	0.7	0.3	20.8	. . .	8.8	. . .	. . .	0.1	0.2	. . .
1956	75.8	65.8	33.9	10.2	0.7	0.4	20.5	. . .	9.6	. . .	. . .	0.1	0.3	. . .
1957	79.3	67.9	36.0	10.7	0.8	0.5	19.9	. . .	11.0	. . .	. . .	0.1	0.3	. . .
1958	76.1	64.6	35.5	10.4	0.8	0.5	17.4	. . .	11.0	. . .	. . .	0.1	0.3	. . .
1959	86.6	73.2	38.5	11.2	1.0	0.9	21.6	0.1	13.5	. . .	. . .	0.1	0.3	-0.5
1960	93.6	76.5	41.8	12.0	1.1	0.9	20.6	0.1	16.0	1.3	. . .	0.2	0.3	-0.7
1961	95.1	77.5	42.7	12.1	1.0	0.7	20.8	0.1	16.6	1.4	. . .	0.2	0.4	-0.9
1962	103.2	83.3	46.5	12.9	1.2	0.8	21.7	0.1	18.6	1.6	. . .	0.2	0.4	-0.9
1963	111.3	88.6	49.1	13.5	1.2	0.9	23.7	0.2	21.1	1.7	. . .	0.2	0.5	-0.7
1964	111.3	87.7	46.0	14.1	1.3	1.6	24.6	0.2	21.8	1.7	. . .	0.2	0.6	-0.8
1965	120.4	95.6	51.1	13.8	1.6	1.3	27.6	0.2	22.7	1.8	. . .	0.2	0.9	-0.9
1966	137.4	104.7	58.6	12.6	1.9	1.6	29.8	0.2	30.6	2.0	. . .	0.2	1.0	-1.2
1967	146.3	109.8	64.4	13.3	1.9	1.9	28.1	0.2	34.1	2.3	. . .	0.3	1.0	-1.3
1968	170.6	129.7	76.4	14.6	2.3	2.5	33.6	0.3	37.9	2.7	. . .	0.3	1.0	-1.0
1969	191.8	146.0	91.7	15.4	2.4	3.0	33.0	0.4	43.3	2.5	. . .	0.3	1.0	-1.3
1970	185.1	137.9	88.9	15.6	2.5	3.5	27.1	0.4	45.5	2.8	. . .	0.4	1.0	-2.5
1971	190.7	138.6	85.8	15.9	3.1	3.4	30.1	0.4	50.3	3.1	. . .	0.5	0.9	-2.8
1972	219.0	158.2	102.8	15.5	3.0	3.2	33.4	0.4	58.3	3.3	. . .	0.5	1.1	-2.4
1973	249.2	173.0	109.6	16.5	3.3	4.3	38.9	0.4	74.5	3.4	. . .	0.7	1.0	-3.4
1974	278.5	192.1	126.5	16.4	3.7	5.6	39.6	0.4	84.1	3.6	. . .	0.9	1.1	-3.3
1975	276.8	186.8	120.7	16.2	5.9	5.4	38.2	0.5	88.1	4.3	. . .	1.0	1.1	-4.4
1976	322.2	217.9	141.2	16.8	4.6	5.9	48.7	0.7	99.8	5.2	. . .	1.1	1.2	-2.9
1977	363.5	247.2	162.2	17.3	5.4	5.9	55.7	0.7	111.1	5.8	. . .	1.3	1.6	-3.4
1978	423.6	286.6	188.9	18.2	7.1	7.0	64.4	1.0	128.7	7.4	. . .	1.5	2.2	-2.9
1979	486.8	325.9	224.6	18.2	7.5	9.3	65.1	1.1	149.8	9.2	. . .	2.1	2.5	-2.7
1980	533.0	355.5	250.0	26.5	7.2	11.7	58.6	1.6	163.6	11.3	. . .	3.0	3.1	-3.6
1981	620.4	407.7	290.6	41.3	8.6	14.0	51.7	1.5	193.0	14.8	. . .	4.4	3.1	-2.6
1982	618.0	386.3	295.0	32.3	8.6	15.2	33.8	1.4	206.0	18.3	. . .	5.1	4.4	-2.1
1983	644.2	393.2	286.2	35.3	9.1	14.2	47.1	1.2	223.1	20.4	. . .	4.3	5.2	-1.9
1984	710.7	425.2	301.4	35.4	11.9	16.1	59.2	1.3	254.1	22.8	. . .	4.9	6.3	-2.7
1985	775.3	460.2	336.0	33.9	12.2	17.8	58.5	1.9	277.9	25.6	. . .	4.6	8.6	-1.6
1986	817.3	479.2	350.0	30.0	13.7	17.8	66.0	1.7	298.9	28.8	. . .	3.3	7.6	-0.6
1987	899.0	543.6	392.5	30.4	15.5	17.7	85.4	2.0	317.4	25.1	. . .	3.1	10.2	-0.5
1988	961.4	566.2	402.8	33.4	16.4	17.4	93.8	2.4	354.8	27.4	. . .	2.8	9.6	0.7
1989	1 040.8	621.2	451.5	32.3	17.5	21.6	95.6	2.7	378.0	25.9	. . .	3.0	11.8	1.1
1990	1 085.7	642.2	470.1	33.4	17.5	23.6	94.5	3.0	402.0	26.9	. . .	3.5	13.3	-2.3
1991	1 105.6	635.6	461.3	44.9	16.8	20.8	89.2	2.6	420.6	26.2	. . .	3.8	17.2	2.1
1992	1 152.1	659.9	475.2	45.0	18.3	16.8	102.0	2.6	444.0	22.2	. . .	3.5	18.4	4.1
1993	1 228.8	713.0	505.5	46.5	19.8	16.0	122.5	2.7	465.5	22.8	. . .	3.8	20.2	3.5
1994	1 326.7	781.4	542.5	57.5	21.4	20.5	136.3	3.1	496.2	20.0	. . .	3.6	21.6	4.0
1995	1 412.9	844.6	585.8	55.7	19.8	23.4	155.9	3.9	521.9	20.8	. . .	3.0	17.5	5.0
1996	1 531.2	931.9	663.3	53.6	19.2	20.1	170.5	5.2	545.4	22.5	. . .	4.1	22.7	4.5
1997	1 661.6	1 030.1	744.2	58.2	19.6	20.7	182.3	5.1	579.4	21.0	. . .	4.5	20.1	6.6
1998	1 783.8	1 115.8	825.2	61.1	19.6	26.6	177.7	5.7	617.4	17.3	. . .	4.2	21.5	7.6
1999	1 900.7	1 195.4	893.0	64.3	19.2	25.4	187.6	5.9	654.8	17.1	. . .	4.0	22.3	7.2
2000	2 063.2	1 309.6	995.6	66.1	21.1	25.3	194.1	7.3	698.6	19.3	. . .	6.3	24.1	5.3
2001	2 026.8	1 249.4	991.8	64.6	20.6	27.1	137.6	7.7	723.3	18.0	. . .	8.4	24.9	2.8
2002	1 865.8	1 073.3	828.5	66.9	19.9	24.5	126.0	7.6	739.4	15.3	. . .	6.5	24.4	6.9
2003	1 889.7	1 071.0	774.1	68.7	21.4	22.0	175.8	9.0	763.2	16.5	. . .	7.0	25.5	6.7
2004	2 022.2	1 154.0	798.5	72.0	23.3	18.1	232.2	10.0	808.9	16.6	0.1	8.7	29.0	4.9
2005	2 298.1	1 384.5	932.1	74.1	25.3	21.5	319.5	12.1	853.4	17.3	0.2	9.7	32.0	0.9
2006	2 531.7	1 558.5	1 049.6	72.6	26.7	29.1	366.0	14.6	905.7	18.8	0.3	9.9	36.8	1.8
2007	2 660.8	1 637.1	1 164.4	65.8	28.8	34.6	328.2	15.3	947.2	22.1	0.2	11.1	41.0	2.0
2008	2 505.7	1 448.1	1 101.7	64.7	29.2	31.7	202.0	18.8	974.4	19.5	0.6	13.8	48.6	0.8
2009	2 230.1	1 163.7	857.2	68.3	23.1	47.4	153.0	14.8	950.8	22.8	18.7	7.0	66.2	0.8
2010	2 391.7	1 305.0	893.8	68.2	28.6	79.3	219.4	15.7	970.9	29.5	17.0	8.0	64.4	-3.1
2011	2 516.7	1 496.1	1 077.0	76.7	31.9	75.4	218.8	16.3	904.3	28.5	18.8	10.1	66.1	-7.3
2012	2 663.0	1 636.0	1 149.2	84.5	33.5	88.4	262.6	17.8	937.8	22.2	21.1	9.6	49.7	-13.4
2010														
1st quarter	2 309.0	1 238.1	854.2	66.8	26.2	72.1	204.7	14.1	958.7	27.2	14.9	6.7	63.8	-0.4
2nd quarter	2 363.1	1 279.8	885.8	68.5	27.8	70.2	212.2	15.3	970.9	28.9	16.3	7.8	61.7	-2.4
3rd quarter	2 429.9	1 334.9	908.7	68.9	30.0	85.7	227.1	14.5	975.2	30.8	18.6	8.4	66.0	-3.9
4th quarter	2 465.0	1 367.1	926.7	68.4	30.3	89.1	233.6	18.9	978.8	31.3	18.3	9.1	66.1	-5.6
2011														
1st quarter	2 506.3	1 486.7	1 055.5	72.0	30.9	87.3	226.5	14.5	898.7	30.9	18.7	9.7	68.0	-6.2
2nd quarter	2 523.1	1 503.1	1 072.2	76.4	32.0	80.2	227.0	15.2	902.5	29.9	18.1	10.1	65.6	-6.4
3rd quarter	2 515.7	1 488.2	1 091.5	76.7	32.5	69.4	200.9	17.3	910.8	27.8	18.9	10.8	66.8	-7.6
4th quarter	2 521.6	1 506.6	1 088.7	81.9	32.0	64.7	220.9	18.4	905.4	25.4	19.5	9.9	63.8	-8.9
2012														
1st quarter	2 645.4	1 611.7	1 122.4	84.9	32.3	96.5	258.9	16.8	929.2	23.5	21.0	9.4	60.3	-9.7
2nd quarter	2 641.1	1 614.0	1 133.1	84.9	33.7	93.9	251.0	17.4	932.1	21.6	21.2	9.4	54.6	-11.8
3rd quarter	2 656.6	1 638.6	1 147.2	84.4	33.7	85.5	270.6	17.1	934.6	21.7	21.2	9.4	45.6	-14.4
4th quarter	2 709.0	1 679.8	1 194.0	83.8	34.2	77.8	270.0	19.9	955.3	22.2	20.9	10.2	38.4	-17.8

. . . = Not available.

Table 6-1. Federal Government Current Receipts and Expenditures—*Continued*

(National income and product accounts, calendar years, billions of dollars, quarterly data are at seasonally adjusted annual rates.)

NIPA Table 3.2

Year and quarter	Total current expenditures	Consumption expenditures	Government social benefits — Benefits to persons	Benefits to the rest of the world	Other current transfer payments — Grants-in-aid to state and local governments	Payments to the rest of the world	Interest payments — Total	To persons and business	To the rest of the world	Subsidies	Net federal government saving, NIPA (surplus + / deficit -) — Total	Social insurance funds	Other
1955	71.6	46.8	11.5	...	2.3	2.2	7.9	...	0.1	0.9	-0.6	1.5	-2.1
1956	74.4	47.4	12.3	...	2.4	2.0	8.8	...	0.2	1.5	1.4	1.7	-0.3
1957	81.9	50.9	14.5	...	2.8	1.9	9.9	...	0.2	1.9	-2.6	1.1	-3.7
1958	88.1	52.6	18.2	...	3.2	2.0	10.0	...	0.1	2.1	-12.0	-2.7	-9.4
1959	90.5	51.8	18.6	...	3.6	4.0	11.4	...	0.3	1.1	-3.9	-0.7	-3.2
1960	93.4	50.9	19.9	0.2	3.8	3.5	13.9	13.5	0.3	1.1	0.2	0.4	-0.2
1961	99.8	52.7	23.1	0.3	4.3	3.5	13.9	13.6	0.3	2.0	-4.7	-2.3	-2.4
1962	108.5	59.0	23.5	0.3	4.7	3.6	15.1	14.8	0.3	2.3	-5.3	-0.6	-4.8
1963	113.5	61.2	24.6	0.3	5.2	3.6	16.3	15.9	0.4	2.2	-2.1	0.8	-3.0
1964	118.2	63.1	25.2	0.3	6.0	3.4	17.5	17.0	0.5	2.7	-6.9	1.3	-8.1
1965	125.9	66.5	27.3	0.5	6.6	3.6	18.6	18.1	0.5	3.0	-5.5	0.4	-5.9
1966	144.3	76.5	29.9	0.5	9.4	4.0	20.3	19.7	0.5	3.9	-7.0	6.0	-13.0
1967	165.7	88.0	36.5	0.6	10.9	4.0	21.9	21.3	0.6	3.8	-19.5	4.1	-23.6
1968	184.3	96.8	41.9	0.6	11.8	4.5	24.6	23.9	0.7	4.1	-13.7	3.2	-16.9
1969	196.9	100.4	45.8	0.6	13.7	4.5	27.5	26.7	0.8	4.5	-5.1	5.7	-10.8
1970	219.9	102.3	55.6	0.7	18.3	4.8	33.3	32.4	0.9	4.8	-34.8	1.0	-35.7
1971	241.5	106.6	66.1	0.8	22.1	6.0	35.2	33.5	1.8	4.6	-50.8	-3.0	-47.8
1972	267.9	112.2	72.9	1.0	30.5	7.2	37.6	35.1	2.6	6.6	-48.9	-0.6	-48.2
1973	286.9	113.9	84.5	1.2	33.5	5.4	43.3	39.6	3.7	5.1	-37.7	5.9	-43.6
1974	319.1	122.5	103.3	1.3	34.9	6.0	48.0	43.9	4.0	3.2	-40.6	3.2	-43.9
1975	373.8	132.9	132.3	2.0	43.6	6.1	52.5	48.1	4.3	4.3	-97.0	-16.3	-80.7
1976	402.1	139.0	143.1	2.5	49.1	4.5	58.9	54.6	4.3	4.9	-79.9	-16.0	-63.8
1977	435.4	149.6	152.1	2.6	54.8	4.2	65.3	60.0	5.2	6.9	-71.9	-14.1	-57.8
1978	483.4	162.0	162.4	2.7	63.5	5.0	79.1	70.9	8.2	8.7	-59.8	-4.7	-55.1
1979	531.3	176.0	182.8	3.0	64.0	5.8	91.5	80.9	10.6	8.2	-44.5	0.0	-44.5
1980	619.3	202.1	219.6	3.5	69.7	7.3	107.5	95.7	11.9	9.4	-86.3	-15.8	-70.5
1981	706.3	231.3	250.1	4.3	69.4	6.7	133.4	117.2	16.3	11.1	-85.8	-14.3	-71.5
1982	782.7	255.7	281.2	4.1	66.3	8.1	152.7	134.7	18.0	14.6	-164.6	-34.4	-130.3
1983	849.2	277.9	303.0	3.6	67.9	8.9	167.0	148.9	18.1	20.9	-205.0	-37.9	-167.2
1984	903.0	292.0	309.2	3.7	72.3	11.2	193.8	173.7	20.2	20.7	-192.3	-9.4	-183.0
1985	970.9	316.8	325.4	4.0	76.2	13.8	213.7	191.6	22.2	21.0	-195.6	0.9	-196.5
1986	1 030.0	336.5	343.7	4.4	82.4	14.2	224.2	200.9	23.3	24.6	-212.7	5.7	-218.3
1987	1 062.1	347.8	356.7	4.3	78.4	12.7	232.3	208.2	24.1	30.0	-163.2	14.5	-177.6
1988	1 118.8	360.8	377.4	4.6	85.7	13.2	247.9	219.2	28.8	29.2	-157.3	39.1	-196.4
1989	1 197.5	380.2	410.1	5.1	91.8	13.5	269.7	235.1	34.5	27.1	-156.6	42.6	-199.3
1990	1 286.6	401.8	445.1	6.2	104.4	13.5	289.0	253.0	36.1	26.6	-200.9	42.4	-243.3
1991	1 351.8	423.9	491.7	6.3	124.0	-25.6	304.4	268.3	36.1	27.1	-246.2	24.7	-270.9
1992	1 484.7	430.2	549.5	6.2	141.7	20.6	306.9	272.6	34.3	29.7	-332.7	5.4	-338.0
1993	1 540.6	427.7	581.5	6.2	155.7	21.7	311.4	277.3	34.2	36.3	-311.8	2.8	-314.6
1994	1 580.4	427.3	606.4	6.8	166.8	19.9	320.8	284.5	36.4	32.2	-253.7	15.4	-269.0
1995	1 653.7	427.7	642.6	6.8	174.5	15.4	352.3	305.2	47.1	34.5	-240.8	15.6	-256.5
1996	1 709.7	428.4	676.9	7.6	181.5	20.4	360.0	303.2	56.8	34.9	-178.5	12.9	-191.4
1997	1 752.8	438.7	702.2	7.9	188.1	17.0	365.6	295.9	69.7	33.4	-91.2	28.9	-120.1
1998	1 781.0	436.4	716.1	8.2	200.8	18.0	365.6	293.5	72.1	35.9	2.7	58.3	-55.6
1999	1 834.2	455.6	735.3	8.5	219.2	18.7	352.2	285.4	66.7	44.8	66.5	92.5	-26.0
2000	1 907.3	475.1	769.1	8.7	233.1	22.3	353.7	289.3	64.4	45.3	155.9	114.3	41.6
2001	2 012.8	505.4	836.3	9.4	261.3	18.2	331.2	274.1	57.1	51.1	14.0	88.1	-74.2
2002	2 136.7	560.3	913.1	9.7	287.2	23.3	302.7	253.4	49.3	40.5	-270.9	49.7	-320.7
2003	2 293.5	628.5	963.0	10.1	321.7	28.6	292.6	245.2	47.4	49.0	-403.5	37.8	-441.4
2004	2 422.0	681.4	1 014.9	10.7	332.2	30.8	306.1	251.3	54.8	46.0	-399.8	51.2	-451.0
2005	2 603.5	723.4	1 079.7	11.2	343.4	40.9	344.4	276.4	68.0	60.5	-305.4	48.4	-353.9
2006	2 759.8	763.9	1 184.2	12.4	340.8	35.0	372.3	286.5	85.9	51.1	-228.1	11.8	-239.9
2007	2 927.5	798.4	1 258.9	13.3	359.0	42.3	408.2	309.2	99.0	47.5	-266.7	-4.1	-262.7
2008	3 140.8	879.8	1 391.9	15.5	371.0	45.0	388.0	290.9	97.1	49.6	-635.1	-54.9	-580.2
2009	3 479.9	933.7	1 608.9	16.0	458.1	52.7	353.6	264.8	88.8	56.3	-1 249.8	-253.1	-996.7
2010	3 721.3	1 003.9	1 710.1	16.5	505.3	50.6	380.6	288.0	92.6	54.3	-1 329.5	-290.9	-1 038.6
2011	3 764.9	1 008.7	1 728.2	17.1	472.5	56.5	422.6	325.1	97.5	59.4	-1 248.3	-271.8	-976.4
2012	3 772.7	1 011.7	1 772.5	18.0	443.2	49.9	420.6	327.6	93.0	56.8	-1 109.7	-293.9	-815.8
2010													
1st quarter	3 661.3	979.1	1 704.7	16.3	492.2	55.1	360.8	272.7	88.1	53.2	-1 352.3	-301.8	-1 050.6
2nd quarter	3 703.1	1 005.1	1 706.4	16.5	492.3	44.3	385.2	295.0	90.2	53.4	-1 340.0	-288.0	-1 052.0
3rd quarter	3 750.0	1 018.8	1 711.8	16.6	517.2	49.7	381.2	286.4	94.8	54.6	-1 320.1	-285.4	-1 034.6
4th quarter	3 770.6	1 012.7	1 717.6	16.7	519.5	53.2	395.1	297.8	97.3	55.9	-1 305.7	-288.5	-1 017.1
2011													
1st quarter	3 751.3	1 001.1	1 717.4	16.9	495.4	54.9	407.6	310.6	97.0	57.9	-1 244.9	-267.4	-977.5
2nd quarter	3 836.4	1 017.4	1 726.4	17.0	500.5	62.0	453.5	356.0	97.5	59.5	-1 313.4	-271.6	-1 041.8
3rd quarter	3 747.4	1 013.4	1 731.0	17.2	453.8	54.9	417.2	318.7	98.4	60.1	-1 231.7	-266.1	-965.6
4th quarter	3 724.6	1 002.7	1 738.1	17.3	440.3	54.1	411.9	315.0	96.9	60.2	-1 203.0	-282.2	-920.8
2012													
1st quarter	3 739.4	1 009.3	1 757.9	17.7	436.1	54.7	406.4	312.2	94.2	57.3	-1 094.0	-289.1	-804.9
2nd quarter	3 787.9	1 007.4	1 762.9	17.9	440.7	51.6	450.1	357.4	92.7	57.2	-1 146.9	-292.2	-854.7
3rd quarter	3 775.8	1 036.1	1 775.0	18.1	447.7	52.3	391.1	298.4	92.7	55.6	-1 119.3	-299.7	-819.6
4th quarter	3 787.5	993.9	1 794.2	18.1	448.4	40.9	434.7	342.3	92.4	57.3	-1 078.5	-294.6	-784.0

. . . = Not available.

Table 6-2. Federal Government Consumption Expenditures and Gross Investment

(National income and product accounts, calendar years, billions of dollars, quarterly data are at seasonally adjusted annual rates.)

NIPA Tables 3.9.5, 3.10.5

Year and quarter	Federal government consumption expenditures and gross investment												
	Total	Consumption expenditures					Gross investment						
		Total	Compensation of general government employees	Consumption of general government fixed capital	Intermediate goods and services purchased [1]	Less: Own-account investment and sales to other sectors	Total	National defense			Nondefense		
								Structures	Equipment	Intellectual property	Structures	Equipment	Intellectual property
1955	61.0	46.8	22.9	10.7	15.5	2.2	14.2	2.1	7.8	3.0	0.6	0.2	0.4
1956	63.1	47.4	23.5	11.6	14.1	1.8	15.8	2.1	7.8	4.1	0.9	0.2	0.6
1957	68.4	50.9	24.3	12.6	16.4	2.4	17.6	2.3	8.2	4.9	1.1	0.2	0.9
1958	71.5	52.6	25.3	13.3	16.5	2.6	18.9	2.6	8.5	5.2	1.4	0.2	1.1
1959	73.5	51.8	25.8	14.2	14.5	2.7	21.8	2.5	10.7	5.7	1.5	0.2	1.1
1960	72.8	50.9	26.6	15.0	12.0	2.7	21.9	2.2	10.1	5.9	1.7	0.3	1.7
1961	77.4	52.7	27.7	15.9	11.9	2.8	24.6	2.4	11.5	6.5	1.9	0.3	2.1
1962	85.5	59.0	29.5	17.0	15.6	3.1	26.5	2.0	12.5	6.7	2.1	0.3	2.9
1963	87.8	61.2	30.8	18.1	15.6	3.4	26.7	1.6	10.9	6.9	2.3	0.4	4.5
1964	90.2	63.1	33.0	19.0	14.9	3.8	27.1	1.3	10.1	6.9	2.5	0.6	5.7
1965	93.1	66.5	34.8	19.8	16.0	4.2	26.7	1.1	8.9	6.7	2.8	0.5	6.8
1966	106.5	76.5	39.8	20.8	20.6	4.7	30.1	1.3	10.4	7.0	2.8	0.6	7.9
1967	120.0	88.0	43.8	22.2	26.5	4.5	31.9	1.2	12.2	7.9	2.2	0.6	7.8
1968	127.9	96.8	48.3	23.8	29.3	4.6	31.1	1.2	10.8	7.9	2.1	0.5	8.6
1969	131.1	100.4	51.4	25.5	28.7	5.1	30.7	1.5	9.7	8.2	1.9	0.6	8.8
1970	132.7	102.3	55.2	27.2	25.3	5.4	30.5	1.3	9.5	8.1	2.1	0.7	8.8
1971	134.4	106.6	58.8	28.6	25.0	5.8	27.8	1.8	5.5	8.4	2.5	0.8	8.9
1972	141.5	112.2	62.6	29.6	26.9	6.9	29.3	1.8	5.3	9.2	2.7	1.1	9.2
1973	145.6	113.9	64.6	31.2	25.8	7.7	31.7	2.1	6.0	9.7	3.1	1.1	9.6
1974	158.1	122.5	67.8	34.0	29.2	8.6	35.7	2.2	8.2	10.0	3.4	1.5	10.4
1975	172.8	132.9	72.5	37.0	31.8	8.4	39.8	2.3	9.9	10.5	4.1	1.6	11.5
1976	183.8	139.0	76.5	39.8	31.3	8.5	44.7	2.1	12.1	11.3	4.6	1.8	12.7
1977	198.8	149.6	80.9	42.8	35.6	9.7	49.2	2.4	13.3	12.3	5.0	2.3	14.0
1978	216.7	162.0	87.1	46.4	39.3	10.8	54.7	2.5	14.3	13.3	6.1	2.7	15.9
1979	237.7	176.0	92.0	50.6	45.8	12.4	61.7	2.5	17.4	14.9	6.3	2.7	17.9
1980	272.4	202.1	100.8	56.6	58.4	13.6	70.3	3.2	19.8	17.2	7.1	3.2	19.8
1981	311.7	231.3	112.2	63.8	69.6	14.3	80.4	3.2	24.1	20.9	7.7	3.3	21.2
1982	345.6	255.7	122.0	71.0	77.6	14.9	90.0	4.0	29.1	25.2	6.8	3.9	21.1
1983	380.2	277.9	127.7	77.2	88.8	15.9	102.3	4.8	35.2	29.8	6.7	4.3	21.6
1984	407.6	292.0	136.5	84.6	88.3	17.4	115.6	4.9	41.1	35.0	7.0	4.7	22.8
1985	449.3	316.8	145.0	91.4	99.1	18.7	132.5	6.2	47.9	41.3	7.3	5.1	24.6
1986	478.4	336.5	149.1	98.2	108.8	19.6	141.9	6.8	52.7	43.9	8.0	4.8	25.7
1987	500.2	347.8	153.1	105.4	110.2	20.9	152.4	7.7	55.0	48.1	9.0	5.2	27.4
1988	508.8	360.8	161.9	114.0	107.4	22.5	148.0	7.4	49.6	48.5	6.8	6.1	29.6
1989	531.4	380.2	168.5	121.6	114.0	23.9	151.2	6.4	51.5	47.3	6.9	7.2	31.9
1990	560.0	401.8	176.0	128.3	123.1	25.6	158.2	6.1	54.6	46.6	8.0	8.1	34.8
1991	580.7	423.9	186.5	134.8	129.4	26.8	156.8	4.6	53.4	43.3	9.2	8.9	37.4
1992	586.6	430.2	189.6	138.1	129.4	26.9	156.4	5.2	50.7	41.3	10.3	10.0	38.9
1993	578.4	427.7	188.1	141.7	125.1	27.2	150.7	5.3	44.7	39.2	11.2	9.9	40.4
1994	572.7	427.3	186.1	144.5	126.1	29.3	145.4	5.8	41.9	38.1	10.2	7.5	41.9
1995	575.4	427.7	183.3	148.0	123.5	27.3	147.7	6.7	39.8	38.4	10.8	8.6	43.4
1996	578.2	428.4	182.2	148.3	125.5	27.6	149.8	6.3	39.9	38.9	11.3	9.7	43.8
1997	582.4	438.7	183.5	148.9	131.9	25.6	143.7	6.1	33.6	39.2	9.9	10.0	44.9
1998	584.1	436.4	185.8	149.2	128.1	26.6	147.7	5.8	34.0	39.4	10.8	10.2	47.5
1999	610.4	455.6	191.7	152.0	137.4	25.6	154.9	5.4	36.8	39.3	10.7	11.9	50.7
2000	632.4	475.1	202.4	156.3	144.6	28.2	157.4	5.4	37.8	40.2	8.4	10.8	54.8
2001	669.2	505.4	211.2	158.0	165.8	29.6	163.8	5.3	39.9	42.5	8.1	10.0	58.1
2002	740.6	560.3	236.4	159.8	195.6	31.5	180.3	6.1	45.6	47.0	10.0	12.0	59.6
2003	824.8	628.5	266.9	165.1	229.9	33.5	196.4	7.1	50.2	53.7	10.3	12.4	62.7
2004	892.4	681.4	284.2	173.3	258.5	34.6	211.0	6.9	56.7	59.8	9.6	13.4	64.6
2005	946.3	723.4	303.7	183.8	275.2	39.2	222.9	7.2	60.7	64.5	8.1	15.2	67.3
2006	1 002.0	763.9	314.8	194.8	294.4	40.0	238.0	7.8	66.8	67.5	9.4	17.4	69.2
2007	1 049.8	798.4	329.6	206.7	302.3	40.2	251.4	10.0	70.8	71.9	11.4	16.1	71.3
2008	1 155.6	879.8	350.2	220.1	352.3	42.8	275.8	13.7	83.8	73.8	11.4	17.6	75.5
2009	1 217.7	933.7	375.5	228.1	374.4	44.3	284.0	17.1	86.0	71.8	12.0	17.7	79.3
2010	1 303.9	1 003.9	404.8	238.8	406.6	46.3	300.0	16.7	90.3	72.6	16.0	19.1	85.3
2011	1 304.1	1 008.7	413.2	249.7	395.5	49.8	295.4	13.4	87.0	72.7	16.7	18.5	87.2
2012	1 295.7	1 011.7	411.1	255.3	389.6	44.3	284.0	8.4	86.2	70.5	14.2	19.5	85.3
2010													
1st quarter	1 269.2	979.1	397.5	233.7	393.3	45.5	290.1	16.0	85.9	72.3	14.3	18.9	82.7
2nd quarter	1 304.6	1 005.1	408.2	237.6	406.0	46.7	299.5	16.7	90.0	72.4	17.0	19.2	84.2
3rd quarter	1 321.6	1 018.8	406.4	240.4	419.6	47.7	302.9	17.2	90.7	72.8	16.4	19.3	86.4
4th quarter	1 320.1	1 012.7	406.9	243.6	407.5	45.3	307.4	16.7	94.6	73.0	16.1	19.2	87.9
2011													
1st quarter	1 297.4	1 001.1	410.8	246.6	388.8	45.0	296.3	15.4	83.6	73.0	18.0	18.7	87.6
2nd quarter	1 315.4	1 017.4	413.1	249.4	401.7	46.8	297.9	14.4	87.5	72.9	17.4	18.4	87.4
3rd quarter	1 308.5	1 013.4	414.5	251.2	407.9	60.2	295.1	12.7	87.7	72.6	16.4	18.3	87.4
4th quarter	1 294.9	1 002.7	414.6	251.8	383.5	47.1	292.2	10.9	89.1	72.2	14.9	18.6	86.4
2012													
1st quarter	1 291.8	1 009.3	413.3	253.6	387.4	45.0	282.4	9.5	82.7	71.2	14.8	19.2	85.1
2nd quarter	1 293.8	1 007.4	411.6	255.0	386.6	45.7	286.4	8.4	88.1	70.6	14.4	19.4	85.5
3rd quarter	1 322.1	1 036.1	410.2	256.0	413.6	43.7	286.0	7.2	89.5	70.2	13.7	19.6	85.8
4th quarter	1 275.2	993.9	409.3	256.7	370.9	43.0	281.4	8.7	84.4	70.0	13.9	19.7	84.7

[1]Includes general government intermediate inputs for goods and services sold to other sectors and for own-account investment.

Table 6-3. Federal Government Defense and Nondefense Consumption Expenditures by Type

(National income and product accounts, calendar years, billions of dollars, quarterly data are at seasonally adjusted annual rates.)

NIPA Table 3.10.5

Year and quarter	Defense consumption expenditures [1]						Nondefense consumption expenditures [1]					
	Total	Compensation of general government employees	Consumption of general government fixed capital	Intermediate goods and services purchased [2]			Total	Compensation of general government employees	Consumption of general government fixed capital	Intermediate goods and services purchased [2]		
				Durable goods	Nondurable goods	Services				Durable goods	Nondurable goods	Services
1950	19.0	10.0	6.3	1.7	0.9	0.6	4.9	3.3	0.6	0.0	0.5	0.9
1951	33.1	16.7	6.6	4.4	2.3	4.0	4.3	3.4	0.7	0.0	-0.2	0.8
1952	42.2	19.8	7.5	8.0	2.8	4.9	5.4	3.6	0.8	0.1	0.5	1.1
1953	44.2	19.7	8.4	9.1	4.2	3.8	7.4	3.5	0.8	0.1	2.4	1.2
1954	39.9	19.0	9.2	6.8	3.0	2.8	7.3	3.4	0.8	0.1	2.2	1.4
1955	39.4	19.3	9.8	6.0	1.7	3.9	7.4	3.7	0.8	0.0	2.4	1.5
1956	40.9	19.6	10.7	5.9	1.7	4.2	6.4	3.9	0.9	0.1	0.5	1.7
1957	44.6	20.1	11.7	6.7	2.0	5.6	6.3	4.2	0.9	0.1	0.3	1.8
1958	46.0	20.6	12.3	7.0	2.0	5.8	6.6	4.8	1.0	0.0	0.5	1.2
1959	42.0	20.7	13.0	5.0	1.8	3.2	9.8	5.1	1.1	0.1	2.4	2.1
1960	42.6	21.1	13.8	4.4	1.7	3.5	8.3	5.6	1.2	0.0	0.5	1.9
1961	44.2	21.7	14.5	3.6	2.2	4.0	8.5	6.1	1.4	0.1	-0.3	2.3
1962	48.6	22.9	15.4	4.6	2.8	4.7	10.4	6.5	1.6	0.1	1.1	2.4
1963	50.5	23.6	16.3	4.7	2.5	5.2	10.7	7.2	1.9	0.1	0.6	2.6
1964	51.4	25.2	16.7	4.0	2.8	4.7	11.7	7.8	2.3	0.1	0.3	3.0
1965	53.9	26.4	17.1	4.2	3.2	5.1	12.5	8.3	2.7	0.1	0.4	3.1
1966	63.8	30.8	17.5	6.2	4.7	7.0	12.7	9.0	3.3	0.1	-0.7	3.3
1967	73.7	34.2	18.4	6.2	7.3	9.7	14.3	9.7	3.8	0.1	0.1	3.1
1968	81.4	37.6	19.4	7.5	8.4	10.5	15.4	10.7	4.4	0.1	0.8	2.0
1969	82.6	40.0	20.3	6.5	7.6	10.5	17.8	11.5	5.1	0.1	1.4	2.6
1970	81.8	41.9	21.3	6.1	5.4	9.6	20.5	13.3	5.9	0.1	0.5	3.6
1971	82.3	43.4	21.9	4.6	4.4	10.6	24.3	15.5	6.7	0.1	0.9	4.4
1972	84.4	45.6	22.3	5.5	4.7	9.5	27.8	17.0	7.3	0.2	1.2	5.8
1973	84.3	46.1	23.0	5.3	4.3	9.3	29.6	18.4	8.2	0.2	1.0	5.8
1974	88.8	47.7	24.6	5.0	5.2	10.7	33.6	20.1	9.4	0.2	1.4	6.7
1975	94.3	50.2	26.3	5.8	5.1	10.9	38.6	22.3	10.7	0.3	2.1	7.6
1976	98.2	51.8	28.1	5.7	4.4	11.7	40.8	24.7	11.7	0.3	2.1	7.1
1977	104.9	53.9	30.0	7.6	4.5	12.7	44.7	27.0	12.8	0.4	2.5	7.8
1978	113.0	57.6	32.2	9.0	4.9	13.3	49.0	29.5	14.2	0.5	3.2	8.4
1979	122.9	60.9	34.5	10.8	6.2	14.9	53.0	31.1	16.1	0.6	3.3	10.0
1980	140.8	66.7	38.1	12.3	10.0	18.7	61.3	34.0	18.4	0.8	5.5	11.2
1981	162.9	76.3	42.8	15.7	11.8	22.0	68.4	35.9	21.0	0.8	8.7	10.5
1982	184.6	84.8	47.8	19.1	11.5	28.1	71.1	37.2	23.2	0.8	7.5	10.7
1983	199.6	89.3	52.5	24.6	11.3	28.9	78.3	38.4	24.7	0.8	10.1	13.1
1984	213.6	95.9	58.2	26.6	10.4	30.7	78.4	40.7	26.3	0.9	5.8	13.9
1985	230.5	102.4	63.7	29.0	9.9	34.7	86.2	42.6	27.7	0.9	8.9	15.7
1986	245.8	106.2	69.4	31.7	10.2	38.3	90.7	42.9	28.8	0.9	11.7	16.1
1987	259.2	109.5	75.3	33.6	10.2	40.9	88.6	43.6	30.1	1.0	6.2	18.3
1988	274.2	113.8	81.9	33.4	10.6	45.4	86.7	48.1	32.1	1.1	-0.8	17.7
1989	283.5	117.9	87.5	32.0	10.8	46.5	96.7	50.6	34.1	1.2	5.1	18.2
1990	295.4	121.2	92.2	31.6	11.0	51.8	106.4	54.8	36.1	1.4	5.0	22.2
1991	310.6	126.8	96.4	31.0	10.7	58.1	113.3	59.7	38.4	1.5	5.9	22.3
1992	307.5	126.8	98.1	28.4	9.4	57.6	122.7	62.8	40.1	1.6	6.5	25.9
1993	300.8	121.0	99.7	26.4	8.5	58.1	126.9	67.1	42.0	1.6	7.6	22.9
1994	294.5	117.4	100.8	22.9	7.6	60.3	132.8	68.7	43.7	1.5	6.1	27.7
1995	291.1	114.1	101.8	20.9	6.3	60.1	136.6	69.2	46.2	1.4	7.5	27.3
1996	291.5	112.0	100.6	20.8	7.6	62.9	136.9	70.2	47.7	1.5	6.6	26.0
1997	292.5	111.4	99.5	20.9	7.6	65.0	146.2	72.0	49.4	1.6	8.5	28.4
1998	288.5	110.8	98.2	20.9	7.0	63.0	148.0	75.1	51.0	1.5	9.4	26.2
1999	301.2	112.7	98.4	22.2	8.2	71.3	154.3	79.0	53.6	1.7	7.2	26.9
2000	308.3	116.9	99.4	22.1	10.4	71.8	166.8	85.5	56.9	1.8	9.3	29.0
2001	325.1	123.2	99.0	22.3	10.3	84.6	180.3	88.0	59.0	1.9	12.2	34.6
2002	358.1	139.4	99.0	23.2	11.5	101.1	202.2	97.0	60.8	2.2	12.7	44.8
2003	408.9	160.5	101.9	25.7	13.4	124.4	219.5	106.4	63.2	2.3	15.6	48.5
2004	446.8	172.2	107.3	28.8	17.1	138.8	234.6	112.1	66.0	2.5	17.2	54.0
2005	475.9	186.1	114.4	29.6	20.9	144.1	247.5	117.6	69.4	2.7	19.1	58.8
2006	500.3	192.9	121.8	33.0	22.3	151.6	263.6	121.9	73.0	3.0	20.2	64.3
2007	526.1	201.5	129.9	36.3	23.8	156.5	272.3	128.1	76.9	3.0	20.0	62.7
2008	582.8	214.4	139.1	42.9	30.5	179.1	297.0	135.9	81.0	3.3	23.7	72.9
2009	613.3	228.8	144.6	45.8	24.4	192.8	320.4	146.7	83.5	3.5	26.4	81.4
2010	653.2	245.0	151.1	47.0	26.8	206.8	350.7	159.7	87.7	3.9	28.4	93.7
2011	662.8	251.2	157.9	44.8	33.3	200.4	345.8	162.0	91.8	3.7	26.6	86.7
2012	652.0	248.6	161.1	44.2	31.2	190.9	359.7	162.5	94.3	3.8	28.4	91.0
2010												
1st quarter	637.8	242.7	148.2	43.6	26.5	200.0	341.3	154.8	85.5	3.8	27.7	91.7
2nd quarter	650.2	244.5	150.5	46.0	27.4	205.2	354.9	163.7	87.1	3.9	28.6	95.0
3rd quarter	665.6	245.9	151.9	48.2	26.0	217.3	353.2	160.5	88.6	3.9	29.0	95.3
4th quarter	659.2	247.0	153.9	50.3	27.4	204.7	353.4	160.0	89.7	3.9	28.4	92.8
2011												
1st quarter	650.0	249.3	155.9	41.8	31.1	196.4	351.1	161.4	90.7	3.7	27.3	88.4
2nd quarter	669.4	250.8	157.9	44.3	33.5	207.8	348.0	162.3	91.5	3.7	26.3	86.1
3rd quarter	678.7	252.3	158.9	45.7	34.6	212.2	334.7	162.2	92.3	3.7	26.1	85.7
4th quarter	653.3	252.5	158.9	47.4	34.0	185.3	349.4	162.0	92.9	3.7	26.5	86.5
2012												
1st quarter	652.9	250.1	160.1	43.2	33.3	190.5	356.4	163.2	93.5	3.8	27.7	89.0
2nd quarter	649.6	248.9	161.0	43.6	30.5	189.6	357.9	162.7	94.1	3.8	28.3	90.7
3rd quarter	675.0	248.3	161.4	45.5	29.6	214.1	361.1	161.9	94.6	3.9	28.6	92.0
4th quarter	630.6	247.0	161.7	44.4	31.5	169.5	363.3	162.2	95.0	3.9	29.1	92.4

[1]Excludes government sales to other sectors and government own-account investment (construction and software).
[2]Includes general government intermediate inputs for goods and services sold to other sectors and for own-account investment.

Table 6-4. National Defense Consumption Expenditures and Gross Investment: Selected Detail

(National income and product accounts, calendar years, billions of dollars, quarterly data are at seasonally adjusted annual rates.)

NIPA Table 3.11.5

Year and quarter	Compensation of general government employees		Intermediate goods and services purchased [1]						Gross investment				
			Durable goods	Nondurable goods		Services							Research and develop-ment
	Military	Civilian	Aircraft	Petroleum products	Ammu-nition	Installation support	Weapons support	Personnel support	Aircraft	Missiles	Ships	Software	
1972	30.2	15.4	2.7	1.8	2.0	3.8	1.6	1.3	2.6	1.5	1.8	0.3	8.9
1973	30.3	15.8	2.4	1.7	1.7	3.8	1.5	1.4	2.3	1.5	1.6	0.3	9.4
1974	30.9	16.7	2.0	2.8	1.4	4.6	1.8	1.5	2.3	1.7	2.2	0.4	9.6
1975	32.0	18.2	2.1	2.9	1.1	4.8	1.7	1.6	3.6	1.3	2.2	0.5	10.0
1976	32.6	19.2	2.0	2.5	0.6	5.3	1.9	1.7	3.4	1.4	2.4	0.5	10.8
1977	33.7	20.2	3.3	2.4	0.8	5.8	1.9	1.9	3.7	1.2	3.1	0.6	11.7
1978	35.4	22.2	3.5	2.5	1.0	5.9	2.1	2.1	3.7	1.1	3.9	0.7	12.6
1979	37.4	23.5	4.8	3.6	1.2	6.6	2.7	2.1	4.8	1.8	4.3	0.8	14.0
1980	41.5	25.2	5.6	6.8	1.4	8.3	3.9	2.3	6.1	2.3	4.1	1.0	16.2
1981	48.8	27.6	7.8	7.7	1.6	9.6	4.8	2.9	7.5	2.8	5.1	1.3	19.6
1982	54.9	29.9	10.2	6.8	2.1	12.6	6.3	3.6	8.4	3.4	6.2	1.4	23.7
1983	57.8	31.5	13.6	6.4	2.5	12.4	7.0	3.9	10.1	4.6	7.1	1.7	28.1
1984	62.0	33.9	14.0	5.9	2.2	13.8	7.2	3.7	10.9	5.7	8.0	2.2	32.8
1985	66.2	36.1	15.4	5.8	1.3	15.1	8.4	5.0	13.4	6.6	9.0	2.7	38.6
1986	69.4	36.8	17.2	3.6	3.6	16.0	9.4	6.2	17.9	7.9	8.9	3.2	40.7
1987	72.2	37.3	18.2	3.9	2.8	17.7	9.2	6.8	17.6	8.7	8.8	3.6	44.5
1988	74.8	39.0	17.9	3.5	3.5	18.3	10.3	9.5	13.5	7.8	8.6	4.3	44.3
1989	76.5	41.4	16.4	4.2	3.1	18.0	10.5	10.2	12.2	8.8	10.0	4.8	42.5
1990	78.5	42.7	14.8	5.3	2.8	21.4	11.6	10.1	12.0	11.2	10.8	5.2	41.4
1991	82.4	44.4	13.6	4.7	2.7	22.9	10.0	9.5	9.2	10.8	10.2	5.4	37.9
1992	80.9	45.9	12.2	3.5	2.6	23.1	9.4	13.7	8.3	10.6	10.1	5.6	35.6
1993	75.1	45.9	10.7	3.2	2.5	25.2	8.8	14.7	9.3	7.9	8.7	5.4	33.7
1994	71.7	45.7	9.2	3.0	1.8	26.2	9.4	16.3	10.5	5.7	8.1	5.3	32.8
1995	69.5	44.6	8.9	2.8	1.2	25.2	9.5	17.0	9.0	4.7	8.0	5.3	33.1
1996	67.7	44.3	8.8	3.4	1.4	26.0	9.0	19.3	9.2	4.1	6.8	5.5	33.4
1997	67.8	43.6	9.4	2.9	1.7	25.1	10.5	21.3	5.8	2.9	6.1	5.6	33.6
1998	68.0	42.8	9.9	2.1	1.9	23.9	10.0	20.6	5.8	3.3	6.4	5.9	33.5
1999	69.8	42.9	10.5	2.6	1.9	25.0	11.3	26.0	7.0	2.9	6.8	5.9	33.3
2000	72.9	44.1	9.8	4.1	1.8	25.1	11.7	26.1	7.8	2.7	6.6	6.0	34.2
2001	78.4	44.8	9.8	4.2	2.1	27.4	14.8	32.4	8.5	3.3	7.2	5.8	36.7
2002	89.7	49.7	9.8	4.6	2.5	30.7	18.2	42.1	9.4	3.3	8.7	5.6	41.4
2003	107.4	53.1	11.3	5.3	2.6	35.7	22.5	49.5	9.4	3.5	9.5	5.4	48.2
2004	113.9	58.3	12.0	7.0	3.6	36.6	23.5	61.9	11.1	4.0	10.0	5.7	54.1
2005	123.3	62.7	10.7	10.1	4.0	35.8	26.1	66.3	13.5	4.0	9.8	5.9	58.5
2006	127.8	65.1	11.1	11.4	4.2	38.2	27.5	71.0	13.6	4.5	10.5	6.2	61.3
2007	133.2	68.3	11.5	12.2	4.1	38.2	28.6	70.0	12.9	4.3	10.3	6.5	65.4
2008	142.8	71.6	12.8	17.6	4.5	41.4	30.9	86.1	13.7	4.3	11.0	6.9	67.0
2009	152.0	76.8	14.7	10.5	4.2	44.1	32.6	93.6	13.5	5.1	11.1	6.8	65.0
2010	159.6	85.5	16.1	13.7	4.2	46.2	36.8	99.1	16.9	5.6	11.8	7.3	65.3
2011	160.7	90.6	17.9	19.4	4.3	45.1	35.7	96.4	20.2	5.1	11.7	7.6	65.0
2012	158.8	89.7	19.4	17.8	4.3	43.3	34.1	95.9	21.0	6.9	11.9	7.7	62.9
2006													
1st quarter	128.7	64.7	10.6	10.5	4.1	37.6	26.1	71.1	13.0	4.8	9.7	6.0	60.1
2nd quarter	127.5	64.9	10.4	11.2	4.1	38.9	28.5	74.1	15.2	4.8	11.1	6.1	60.7
3rd quarter	127.5	65.0	10.8	12.9	4.2	36.8	24.9	67.0	11.9	3.4	10.6	6.2	61.6
4th quarter	127.7	65.7	12.7	11.0	4.4	39.5	30.5	71.7	14.4	5.0	10.7	6.4	62.7
2007													
1st quarter	132.0	67.9	10.3	11.1	4.2	37.1	26.7	65.6	12.1	5.5	9.8	6.5	64.0
2nd quarter	132.6	68.2	11.0	11.6	3.7	37.7	28.3	68.2	13.9	4.5	10.2	6.5	65.0
3rd quarter	133.9	68.3	11.9	11.7	4.4	38.9	30.1	71.9	13.1	3.7	10.2	6.5	65.9
4th quarter	134.2	68.9	12.8	14.3	3.9	39.1	29.4	74.1	12.5	3.7	11.1	6.5	66.6
2008													
1st quarter	138.7	70.8	11.5	16.9	4.5	39.7	29.8	78.9	8.9	4.4	9.7	6.9	67.1
2nd quarter	141.5	71.5	12.4	20.1	4.1	39.2	27.5	80.6	14.6	4.7	11.0	6.9	67.2
3rd quarter	144.5	72.2	13.4	20.3	4.6	43.4	33.9	90.7	14.5	4.5	11.7	7.0	67.0
4th quarter	146.4	72.0	14.0	13.2	4.7	43.2	32.5	94.4	16.8	3.8	11.7	6.8	66.5
2009													
1st quarter	150.6	74.8	13.5	8.6	3.8	42.4	29.5	87.7	12.5	4.2	10.5	6.7	65.6
2nd quarter	152.0	74.6	14.3	9.0	4.3	43.8	32.1	94.4	15.2	4.7	10.9	6.8	65.0
3rd quarter	153.0	77.5	14.9	11.6	4.1	44.7	33.9	96.1	12.8	6.5	10.9	6.8	64.7
4th quarter	152.4	80.4	16.0	12.7	4.5	45.3	35.0	96.3	13.5	4.9	12.3	7.0	64.6
2010													
1st quarter	160.1	82.6	13.8	13.1	4.2	44.9	33.6	97.4	15.0	5.6	10.7	7.2	65.1
2nd quarter	160.1	84.4	15.4	14.0	4.5	46.0	36.2	98.6	17.0	5.7	11.3	7.2	65.2
3rd quarter	159.3	86.6	16.3	13.4	3.9	48.3	40.6	103.4	16.0	5.4	11.9	7.4	65.4
4th quarter	158.8	88.2	19.0	14.2	4.2	45.7	36.8	97.2	19.6	5.5	13.2	7.5	65.5
2011													
1st quarter	160.5	88.8	15.6	17.6	4.1	43.4	32.2	95.9	18.4	5.2	10.6	7.6	65.5
2nd quarter	160.9	89.9	17.5	19.8	4.1	46.3	37.7	99.6	20.1	5.7	11.5	7.6	65.3
3rd quarter	161.0	91.3	18.8	20.4	4.3	47.5	39.8	101.9	21.3	5.1	11.4	7.6	64.9
4th quarter	160.3	92.2	19.8	19.7	4.6	43.0	33.0	88.3	21.0	4.6	13.1	7.7	64.5
2012													
1st quarter	159.7	90.4	18.4	20.1	3.9	43.4	34.0	93.3	19.4	6.9	10.7	7.6	63.5
2nd quarter	159.0	89.8	18.6	17.1	4.1	42.9	33.6	94.8	21.2	7.0	12.6	7.7	62.9
3rd quarter	158.6	89.6	19.9	15.7	4.8	48.5	43.1	105.5	23.8	6.7	11.6	7.6	62.6
4th quarter	157.9	89.1	20.7	18.5	4.3	38.2	25.6	90.0	19.6	7.0	12.9	7.7	62.3

[1] Includes general government intermediate inputs for goods and services sold to other sectors and for own-account investment.

Table 6-5. Federal Government Output, Lending and Borrowing, and Net Investment

(National income and product accounts, calendar years, billions of dollars, quarterly data are at seasonally adjusted annual rates.)

NIPA Tables 3.2, 3.10.5

Year and quarter	Output						Net lending (net borrowing -)							Net investment
	Gross		Value added		Intermediate goods and services purchased[1]		Net saving, current (surplus +, deficit -)	Plus: capital transfer receipts	Minus			Plus: Consumption of fixed capital	Equals: Net lending (borrowing -)	
	Defense	Non-defense	Defense	Non-defense	Defense	Non-defense			Gross investment	Capital transfer payments	Net purchases of non-produced assets			
1960	44.4	9.2	34.8	6.8	9.6	2.4	0.2	1.8	21.9	2.6	0.5	15.1	-7.9	6.8
1961	46.0	9.6	36.2	7.4	9.8	2.1	-4.7	2.0	24.6	2.9	0.5	16.0	-14.7	8.6
1962	50.4	11.6	38.4	8.1	12.1	3.5	-5.3	2.1	26.5	3.1	0.6	17.1	-16.3	9.4
1963	52.3	12.3	39.9	9.1	12.4	3.2	-2.1	2.2	26.7	3.6	0.5	18.3	-12.3	8.4
1964	53.3	13.6	41.9	10.1	11.4	3.5	-6.9	2.6	27.1	4.1	0.6	19.2	-16.9	7.9
1965	55.9	14.7	43.5	11.1	12.4	3.6	-5.5	2.8	26.7	4.0	0.5	20.0	-13.9	6.7
1966	66.1	15.0	48.3	12.3	17.9	2.7	-7.0	3.0	30.1	4.4	0.6	21.0	-18.0	9.1
1967	75.7	16.8	52.5	13.5	23.2	3.3	-19.5	3.1	31.9	4.3	-0.2	22.4	-30.0	9.5
1968	83.4	18.0	57.0	15.1	26.4	2.9	-13.7	3.1	31.1	6.0	-0.9	24.1	-22.7	7.0
1969	84.9	20.7	60.3	16.6	24.6	4.1	-5.1	3.6	30.7	5.9	0.1	25.8	-12.5	4.9
1970	84.2	23.5	63.2	19.2	21.0	4.3	-34.8	3.7	30.5	5.3	-0.3	27.6	-38.9	2.9
1971	84.9	27.5	65.3	22.1	19.6	5.4	-50.8	4.6	27.8	5.9	-0.4	29.0	-50.5	-1.2
1972	87.6	31.5	67.9	24.4	19.7	7.2	-48.9	5.4	29.3	6.1	-0.7	30.1	-48.1	-0.8
1973	88.0	33.6	69.2	26.6	18.9	6.9	-37.7	5.1	31.7	6.0	-3.2	31.7	-35.3	0.0
1974	93.2	37.8	72.3	29.5	20.9	8.3	-40.6	4.8	35.7	7.9	-5.7	34.7	-39.1	1.0
1975	98.4	43.0	76.6	33.0	21.8	10.0	-97.0	4.9	39.8	9.7	-0.4	37.8	-103.4	2.0
1976	101.7	45.9	79.9	36.3	21.8	9.5	-79.9	5.6	44.7	10.6	-2.4	40.6	-86.6	4.1
1977	108.7	50.5	83.9	39.8	24.9	10.8	-71.9	7.2	49.2	11.2	-1.4	43.7	-80.0	5.5
1978	117.0	55.8	89.8	43.7	27.2	12.1	-59.8	5.2	54.7	12.0	-0.6	47.5	-73.2	7.2
1979	127.3	61.1	95.4	47.1	31.9	13.9	-44.5	5.5	61.7	14.5	-2.8	51.8	-60.7	9.9
1980	145.8	69.9	104.9	52.5	40.9	17.4	-86.3	6.5	70.3	16.7	-4.1	57.9	-104.8	12.4
1981	168.7	76.9	119.1	56.9	49.6	20.1	-85.8	6.9	80.4	15.7	-5.5	65.3	-104.3	15.1
1982	191.3	79.4	132.6	60.4	58.7	19.0	-164.6	7.5	90.0	14.7	-3.7	72.7	-185.4	17.3
1983	206.5	87.2	141.7	63.2	64.8	24.0	-205.0	5.8	102.3	15.6	-4.9	79.0	-233.2	23.3
1984	221.8	87.6	154.1	67.0	67.7	20.5	-192.3	6.0	115.6	17.8	-4.0	86.4	-229.4	29.2
1985	239.7	95.7	166.1	70.3	73.7	25.4	-195.6	6.4	132.5	19.6	-1.2	93.3	-246.8	39.2
1986	255.7	100.3	175.6	71.7	80.1	28.6	-212.7	7.0	141.9	20.1	-3.0	100.3	-264.3	41.6
1987	269.5	99.2	184.8	73.7	84.8	25.5	-163.2	7.2	152.4	19.1	-0.4	107.5	-219.5	44.9
1988	285.1	98.2	195.7	80.2	89.4	18.0	-157.3	7.6	148.0	19.8	-0.2	116.3	-201.0	31.7
1989	294.8	109.2	205.4	84.7	89.4	24.5	-156.6	8.9	151.2	20.2	-0.7	124.2	-194.3	27.0
1990	307.9	119.5	213.4	90.9	94.5	28.6	-200.9	11.6	158.2	28.2	-0.8	131.1	-243.8	27.1
1991	322.9	127.9	223.1	98.2	99.7	29.7	-246.2	11.0	156.8	26.5	0.1	137.9	-280.8	18.9
1992	320.2	136.9	224.8	102.9	95.4	34.0	-332.7	11.3	156.4	22.6	0.2	141.4	-359.1	15.0
1993	313.7	141.1	220.7	109.0	93.0	32.1	-311.8	12.9	150.7	24.3	0.2	145.3	-328.8	5.4
1994	309.0	147.7	218.2	112.5	90.8	35.3	-253.7	15.1	145.4	26.0	0.1	148.3	-261.7	-2.9
1995	303.3	151.6	215.9	115.4	87.4	36.2	-240.8	14.9	147.7	27.9	-7.9	151.9	-241.6	-4.2
1996	304.0	152.0	212.6	117.9	91.4	34.1	-178.5	17.5	149.8	28.4	-4.8	152.4	-182.0	-2.6
1997	304.3	159.9	210.9	121.4	93.5	38.5	-91.2	20.6	143.7	29.2	-8.8	153.0	-81.7	-9.3
1998	299.9	163.2	208.9	126.1	91.0	37.1	2.7	25.2	147.7	28.9	-6.0	153.6	10.9	-5.9
1999	312.7	168.4	211.0	132.7	101.7	35.7	66.5	28.8	154.9	36.6	-1.2	156.8	61.9	-1.9
2000	320.7	182.6	216.3	142.4	104.4	40.2	155.9	28.1	157.4	37.0	-0.6	161.5	151.7	-4.1
2001	339.4	195.6	222.2	147.0	117.2	48.7	14.0	28.0	163.8	42.5	-1.5	163.3	0.3	0.5
2002	374.2	217.6	238.3	157.8	135.8	59.8	-270.9	25.3	180.3	49.7	-0.3	165.0	-310.3	15.3
2003	426.0	235.9	262.5	169.6	163.6	66.3	-403.5	22.0	196.4	63.1	-0.9	170.3	-469.8	26.1
2004	464.2	251.8	279.5	178.1	184.7	73.8	-399.8	24.6	211.0	64.0	-0.8	178.6	-470.7	32.4
2005	495.1	267.5	300.5	187.0	194.6	80.5	-305.4	25.0	222.9	85.3	-2.0	189.4	-397.3	33.5
2006	521.6	282.4	314.7	194.9	206.9	87.5	-228.1	27.8	238.0	71.0	-14.4	200.7	-294.2	37.3
2007	548.0	290.6	331.4	204.9	216.6	85.7	-266.7	26.5	251.4	79.4	-3.3	212.8	-354.9	38.6
2008	605.9	316.7	353.4	216.9	252.4	99.9	-635.1	28.3	275.8	145.9	-20.4	226.3	-781.8	49.5
2009	636.5	341.5	373.5	230.2	263.1	111.3	-1 249.8	20.6	284.0	206.9	-8.9	234.5	-1 476.7	49.5
2010	676.8	373.4	396.1	247.5	280.6	126.0	-1 329.5	15.1	300.0	141.4	-1.0	245.3	-1 509.5	54.7
2011	687.7	370.8	409.2	253.8	278.5	116.9	-1 248.3	9.6	295.4	123.4	-0.9	256.5	-1 400.1	38.9
2012	675.9	380.1	409.6	256.8	266.3	123.3	-1 109.7	14.1	284.0	98.7	-1.4	262.3	-1 214.8	21.7
2010														
1st quarter	661.1	363.5	391.0	240.3	270.2	123.2	-1 352.3	17.5	290.1	151.0	-0.8	240.2	-1 535.0	49.9
2nd quarter	673.5	378.3	395.0	250.8	278.5	127.5	-1 340.0	15.8	299.5	181.1	-1.7	244.1	-1 559.0	55.4
3rd quarter	689.2	377.3	397.7	249.1	291.4	128.2	-1 320.1	14.3	302.9	121.8	-1.1	246.9	-1 482.4	56.0
4th quarter	683.3	374.7	400.9	249.7	282.4	125.1	-1 305.7	12.6	307.4	111.7	-0.2	250.1	-1 461.7	57.3
2011														
1st quarter	674.6	371.6	405.3	252.1	269.3	119.5	-1 244.9	9.8	296.3	100.1	-0.2	253.2	-1 378.1	43.1
2nd quarter	694.3	370.0	408.7	253.8	285.6	116.1	-1 313.4	9.5	297.9	126.1	-0.7	256.1	-1 471.1	41.8
3rd quarter	703.7	370.0	411.2	254.5	292.5	115.5	-1 231.7	9.4	295.1	122.2	-1.6	257.9	-1 380.0	37.2
4th quarter	678.2	371.6	411.5	254.9	266.8	116.7	-1 203.0	9.8	292.2	145.3	-1.0	258.6	-1 371.1	33.6
2012														
1st quarter	677.2	377.1	410.2	256.7	267.0	120.4	-1 094.0	12.2	282.4	100.9	-1.4	260.4	-1 203.3	22.0
2nd quarter	673.5	379.6	409.8	256.8	263.7	122.8	-1 146.9	13.3	286.4	85.7	-1.3	261.9	-1 242.5	24.5
3rd quarter	698.8	381.0	409.7	256.5	289.1	124.5	-1 119.3	14.7	286.0	88.7	-1.4	262.9	-1 215.0	23.1
4th quarter	654.2	382.6	408.7	257.2	245.5	125.4	-1 078.5	16.1	281.4	119.6	-1.4	263.7	-1 198.3	17.7

[1]Includes general government intermediate inputs for goods and services sold to other sectors and for own-account investment.

Table 6-6. Chain-Type Quantity Indexes for Federal Government Defense and Nondefense Consumption Expenditures and Gross Investment

(Seasonally adjusted, 2009 = 100.)

NIPA Tables 3.9.3, 3.10.3

| | Defense consumption expenditures [1] | | | | | | | Nondefense consumption expenditures [1] | | | | | | |
| | | | | Intermediate goods and services purchased [2] | | | | | | | Intermediate goods and services purchased [2] | | | |
Year and quarter	Total	Compensation of general government employees	Consumption of general government fixed capital	Durable goods	Non-durable goods	Services	Defense gross investment	Total	Compensation of general government employees	Consumption of general government fixed capital	Durable goods	Non-durable goods excluding CCC inventory change	Services	Non-defense gross investment
1960	57.5	121.2	45.2	36.9	61.5	17.5	41.2	21.3	50.1	6.9	2.0	5.5	15.6	13.9
1961	59.0	123.8	47.2	30.3	78.3	19.4	45.5	21.0	51.4	7.7	2.7	8.5	18.6	16.3
1962	64.0	129.1	49.5	37.4	102.6	22.2	46.7	24.9	54.1	8.6	3.3	12.7	18.5	20.1
1963	64.3	126.8	51.5	37.7	91.6	23.2	42.8	24.8	57.2	10.2	3.7	12.7	19.4	26.8
1964	63.0	126.8	52.8	31.9	104.3	19.1	40.1	25.8	58.6	12.1	4.7	12.9	22.0	32.2
1965	63.9	127.0	53.5	33.1	117.8	19.6	36.4	26.7	59.7	14.3	4.9	13.6	21.6	36.8
1966	72.6	139.9	54.1	48.2	168.0	25.1	40.4	25.9	62.1	17.0	5.2	13.7	22.3	41.2
1967	81.7	152.3	55.7	47.5	257.7	32.0	45.4	28.6	65.1	19.5	5.1	15.4	20.3	37.9
1968	85.4	154.3	57.1	55.1	295.9	33.2	41.4	28.9	66.6	22.0	3.4	10.2	12.5	38.6
1969	82.5	154.5	57.6	46.0	262.6	31.0	38.6	31.6	67.2	24.3	3.5	10.6	15.2	37.2
1970	75.8	143.3	57.3	41.2	182.8	28.7	35.3	32.9	68.1	26.3	4.0	13.4	20.8	35.8
1971	70.1	132.4	55.8	29.6	149.5	29.2	27.6	35.8	70.4	28.0	5.1	16.5	24.2	35.7
1972	65.7	122.4	54.0	36.8	152.3	24.6	24.8	39.0	72.4	29.5	8.1	20.1	31.8	36.9
1973	61.2	116.1	52.6	33.6	113.2	22.7	25.9	39.0	72.6	31.0	7.4	19.2	30.1	37.0
1974	59.5	114.4	51.5	29.1	97.8	23.8	27.8	41.6	76.2	32.3	8.0	20.3	31.2	37.2
1975	58.3	112.8	50.8	30.7	81.0	21.9	28.9	43.4	77.6	33.7	8.6	18.4	31.6	38.2
1976	57.0	110.6	50.6	27.8	65.0	21.9	30.7	43.3	81.4	35.1	9.0	18.3	26.5	40.5
1977	57.4	109.6	50.6	34.8	61.4	21.9	31.4	45.0	83.2	36.7	11.7	18.0	28.8	43.0
1978	57.8	110.4	50.7	38.3	62.2	21.0	31.7	46.7	85.4	38.7	13.3	26.6	29.6	47.5
1979	58.3	109.5	51.1	41.7	64.1	21.6	34.7	47.6	85.3	40.8	15.6	26.1	32.3	48.1
1980	60.0	110.1	51.9	44.0	70.1	24.0	37.3	50.8	87.6	42.9	17.5	25.4	33.0	49.3
1981	63.0	113.5	53.3	51.6	74.1	26.0	41.2	52.1	85.0	44.8	16.5	47.5	28.0	48.4
1982	66.5	116.1	55.4	56.8	73.8	31.3	46.5	51.1	83.4	46.3	15.1	35.5	26.5	44.8
1983	69.5	117.9	58.5	67.9	77.3	31.4	53.9	54.6	84.6	47.7	16.3	44.3	32.0	44.7
1984	71.3	119.6	62.6	69.0	73.1	32.7	61.0	52.9	84.7	49.0	17.6	46.2	32.9	46.1
1985	75.1	121.8	67.9	74.7	71.3	36.3	72.0	55.9	84.8	50.4	18.2	40.1	35.7	48.6
1986	79.1	122.3	73.9	80.2	90.4	38.8	79.8	57.8	83.6	51.9	17.9	34.2	35.5	49.9
1987	81.9	123.4	79.8	85.3	88.5	39.7	86.7	56.3	85.1	53.3	20.3	39.7	39.9	53.3
1988	83.8	121.9	84.7	87.9	85.8	42.0	81.2	53.1	87.2	54.9	21.5	39.5	37.6	52.6
1989	84.3	121.9	88.1	84.5	83.0	42.0	79.2	57.5	87.7	56.5	24.2	35.3	37.3	55.2
1990	84.7	121.1	90.6	81.5	74.1	44.3	79.1	61.6	92.1	58.3	27.7	37.5	44.2	59.4
1991	86.0	120.7	91.8	77.7	75.5	47.8	72.8	62.0	91.8	60.3	29.2	32.9	43.8	63.2
1992	82.4	113.7	91.9	69.9	69.8	46.5	68.9	65.6	93.5	62.1	31.8	40.9	49.4	67.0
1993	79.6	108.9	90.9	63.6	64.0	45.8	61.7	65.0	93.4	63.8	31.0	44.5	41.8	68.3
1994	76.1	103.3	89.1	54.5	58.3	46.3	57.8	65.6	90.8	65.3	29.2	37.4	49.2	65.1
1995	73.1	97.6	87.1	49.7	47.7	44.7	55.4	65.0	87.2	66.8	28.6	42.2	47.4	66.6
1996	71.8	93.5	85.2	49.3	52.7	45.8	55.0	63.7	84.8	68.6	32.5	36.4	44.7	68.5
1997	70.8	90.1	83.4	49.5	53.1	46.5	51.1	66.4	84.3	70.1	35.1	44.4	47.5	68.2
1998	68.9	87.2	81.6	49.9	54.8	44.2	51.2	66.0	85.3	72.1	35.1	48.3	43.5	72.0
1999	70.0	85.1	80.2	53.0	61.3	49.2	51.7	66.8	85.4	74.6	39.4	36.0	44.1	76.4
2000	69.0	84.4	79.0	52.5	64.3	48.1	52.3	69.5	88.1	77.2	43.5	40.9	46.2	75.4
2001	71.0	85.0	78.3	52.9	66.1	54.7	55.3	73.5	88.0	79.4	46.6	54.3	53.0	77.2
2002	74.8	87.2	78.1	55.0	75.5	63.6	62.5	79.0	89.7	81.6	57.2	59.5	67.0	82.6
2003	80.7	90.2	79.5	60.5	81.8	75.5	69.5	82.4	91.9	83.8	59.0	73.3	70.7	85.6
2004	84.8	91.9	81.9	66.9	93.0	81.6	76.1	84.4	91.1	85.9	65.2	81.9	76.3	86.4
2005	85.7	92.2	85.1	67.4	93.6	82.4	80.0	85.5	90.9	88.4	71.3	82.3	80.3	87.5
2006	86.6	90.8	88.5	73.4	91.5	83.8	84.5	88.2	90.9	91.3	79.9	80.1	85.0	91.4
2007	88.0	90.5	92.1	80.6	92.6	84.1	89.2	88.1	91.5	94.2	81.6	78.0	80.1	92.5
2008	94.0	93.9	96.1	94.2	95.6	93.1	97.9	93.6	94.9	97.1	92.6	88.1	90.0	95.8
2009	100.0	100.0	100.0	100.0	100.0	100.0	100.0	100.0	100.0	100.0	100.0	100.0	100.0	100.0
2010	103.7	103.2	103.1	102.5	96.4	105.4	101.4	105.9	104.3	102.8	110.6	105.6	111.9	108.2
2011	102.3	104.3	105.3	97.1	99.4	99.0	95.6	101.6	103.1	105.8	104.6	93.3	99.9	108.0
2012	99.5	102.2	106.2	94.8	92.3	93.1	90.6	105.1	103.6	108.6	109.1	96.3	103.4	104.8
2010														
1st quarter	102.0	102.7	101.9	95.1	98.3	102.9	99.0	104.3	102.5	101.5	107.9	104.3	110.7	105.5
2nd quarter	103.3	103.1	102.8	100.1	98.7	104.7	101.3	107.4	107.2	102.4	111.3	107.3	113.4	108.5
3rd quarter	105.5	103.4	103.6	104.9	93.9	110.4	102.2	106.1	104.1	103.3	112.5	107.7	113.5	109.2
4th quarter	104.0	103.8	104.3	109.8	94.8	103.5	103.3	105.6	103.4	104.0	110.8	103.3	109.9	109.5
2011														
1st quarter	101.2	103.9	104.7	90.9	98.2	98.0	95.4	104.2	104.0	104.8	106.8	97.0	103.1	110.1
2nd quarter	103.0	104.1	105.2	96.1	96.2	102.4	96.6	102.3	103.6	105.5	103.9	92.1	99.0	108.7
3rd quarter	104.2	104.3	105.5	98.8	100.6	104.2	95.2	97.9	102.6	106.2	103.4	91.4	98.2	107.7
4th quarter	100.7	104.7	105.8	102.4	102.4	91.3	95.2	102.2	102.3	106.9	104.3	92.7	99.2	105.7
2012														
1st quarter	100.0	103.2	106.0	92.8	97.6	93.4	89.8	104.2	103.9	107.6	106.8	93.8	101.5	104.9
2nd quarter	99.2	102.5	106.2	93.7	91.0	92.4	91.5	104.6	103.8	108.3	108.4	97.1	102.9	105.0
3rd quarter	103.0	102.0	106.3	97.6	88.7	104.2	91.3	105.6	103.3	108.9	110.1	96.7	104.5	105.0
4th quarter	95.9	101.2	106.4	95.3	91.9	82.3	89.6	106.2	103.4	109.5	111.1	97.8	104.8	104.3

[1] Excludes government sales to other sectors and government own-account investment (construction and software).
[2] Includes general government intermediate inputs for goods and services sold to other sectors and for own-account investment.

Table 6-7. Chain-Type Quantity Indexes for National Defense Consumption Expenditures and Gross Investment: Selected Detail

(Seasonally adjusted, 2009 = 100.)   **NIPA Table 3.11.3**

Year and quarter	Consumption expenditures								Gross investment				
	Compensation of general government employees		Intermediate goods and services purchased [1]										Research and development
			Durable goods	Nondurable goods		Services			Aircraft	Missiles	Ships	Software	
	Military	Civilian	Aircraft	Petroleum products	Ammu-nition	Installation support	Weapons support	Personnel support					
1972	120.6	124.4	61.0	309.3	189.9	40.3	22.0	11.6	25.7	30.4	73.8	6.0	51.7
1973	113.8	119.3	51.0	195.8	148.1	37.3	20.3	10.9	22.6	31.8	62.2	7.2	51.4
1974	109.8	122.4	39.6	177.9	101.3	40.6	21.9	10.7	22.7	35.2	76.8	8.3	47.8
1975	107.4	122.4	36.5	149.7	70.5	39.7	18.6	9.9	34.3	25.7	68.7	9.7	46.0
1976	104.8	120.9	30.6	124.1	35.4	40.8	19.8	9.5	32.1	21.9	70.4	10.2	47.4
1977	103.9	119.8	46.7	105.6	48.4	40.5	18.8	9.7	33.5	17.1	82.2	10.5	48.8
1978	102.9	124.0	47.7	105.0	55.9	37.9	18.5	9.5	31.7	14.1	92.5	12.3	49.4
1979	101.3	124.6	59.4	106.8	62.1	39.8	22.4	8.4	39.7	28.4	95.2	14.7	51.3
1980	102.3	124.4	64.5	118.2	62.3	45.1	29.0	8.3	47.5	41.0	83.7	16.8	54.0
1981	105.6	127.9	83.1	116.1	70.4	48.9	31.9	9.3	54.9	47.6	95.4	20.0	60.0
1982	107.5	132.1	97.2	109.3	86.7	59.8	39.6	11.1	55.2	61.4	111.2	22.0	67.6
1983	109.4	133.7	118.3	117.0	101.7	56.6	41.6	12.2	62.7	77.8	123.6	25.5	76.7
1984	110.7	135.9	111.8	116.7	86.1	61.2	41.7	11.3	67.4	93.5	130.9	33.7	85.8
1985	112.3	139.6	120.1	118.7	51.3	65.3	47.4	14.7	92.0	106.6	143.9	41.1	98.8
1986	113.3	138.8	132.9	118.6	138.2	65.7	52.4	17.3	140.3	135.1	138.9	48.9	102.6
1987	114.7	139.2	142.3	121.8	104.9	69.9	50.6	17.6	161.0	153.7	135.1	54.6	110.4
1988	113.9	136.2	147.3	102.6	121.0	69.6	55.0	20.9	132.3	139.9	128.0	63.3	105.1
1989	113.3	137.5	138.9	112.6	101.2	67.8	53.9	21.3	121.0	160.2	142.1	72.5	97.8
1990	113.6	134.3	122.0	111.7	91.3	76.2	57.5	19.6	111.6	208.1	149.9	78.6	93.1
1991	115.0	130.1	109.2	110.3	86.1	80.7	47.2	17.4	80.3	209.2	134.5	80.8	82.6
1992	105.2	129.4	95.2	92.3	81.8	80.0	42.5	24.0	70.3	206.9	130.0	87.2	75.9
1993	99.8	125.8	82.5	88.7	81.2	86.3	38.3	25.0	75.7	150.2	109.7	83.2	70.5
1994	95.0	118.6	70.1	91.3	55.9	87.4	39.9	26.8	75.6	110.3	98.7	81.9	67.0
1995	90.1	111.6	66.8	82.9	35.8	81.1	39.5	26.9	61.1	92.9	92.9	80.4	64.8
1996	86.8	105.8	66.2	83.8	41.9	82.6	36.6	29.6	59.3	82.7	78.5	84.5	64.4
1997	84.5	100.3	70.8	75.2	51.5	79.4	41.6	32.0	41.2	61.2	69.6	86.9	63.3
1998	82.6	95.7	75.1	73.4	58.3	74.7	39.2	30.2	41.5	68.9	73.6	92.7	62.2
1999	81.1	92.3	79.3	81.2	59.3	76.9	43.7	36.9	43.2	62.4	78.0	92.4	60.7
2000	81.8	89.2	73.8	74.9	56.4	76.3	43.8	35.5	50.4	58.8	74.2	91.2	60.4
2001	83.5	87.7	72.8	87.6	64.4	81.0	54.4	42.5	58.9	73.8	81.3	86.4	64.6
2002	86.6	88.4	73.1	100.9	78.3	88.3	65.8	53.4	67.9	73.8	97.3	84.5	72.7
2003	91.3	88.2	82.4	97.9	81.1	98.2	79.7	60.9	68.3	76.0	104.7	82.6	83.2
2004	92.3	91.0	85.9	103.2	106.3	96.3	81.1	74.3	82.0	86.3	106.2	86.4	91.4
2005	91.8	93.1	75.8	100.5	110.6	90.1	87.6	77.8	102.8	83.7	101.2	89.5	96.6
2006	89.6	93.3	76.3	99.4	108.7	92.5	90.0	81.0	104.7	93.0	105.2	92.4	99.2
2007	88.9	93.8	79.2	98.4	101.8	89.0	91.7	77.2	99.8	88.6	98.3	96.4	103.1
2008	92.9	96.1	88.0	99.3	104.2	93.1	96.6	93.4	102.2	86.0	101.2	100.6	102.7
2009	100.0	100.0	100.0	100.0	100.0	100.0	100.0	100.0	100.0	100.0	100.0	100.0	100.0
2010	101.6	106.5	109.9	101.4	99.2	101.8	111.3	104.7	124.2	108.1	103.4	107.4	98.1
2011	101.2	110.3	121.6	105.8	95.6	94.9	105.2	100.1	144.7	95.1	97.7	111.7	94.9
2012	98.5	109.5	130.7	96.8	95.0	90.6	98.5	98.1	154.2	124.9	98.7	112.5	90.6
2006													
1st quarter	89.6	92.8	74.2	91.6	111.5	92.6	86.2	82.2	100.2	99.4	98.4	90.4	97.4
2nd quarter	89.1	92.7	71.4	93.8	107.4	94.4	93.3	85.0	117.1	99.0	112.0	91.2	98.5
3rd quarter	90.1	93.3	73.7	109.5	105.6	88.4	81.4	76.0	90.2	70.4	105.7	92.7	99.8
4th quarter	89.8	94.3	86.0	102.9	110.3	94.5	98.9	80.9	111.3	102.9	104.6	95.5	101.0
2007													
1st quarter	88.8	93.4	70.1	98.6	107.0	87.8	86.0	73.0	94.4	112.5	94.3	96.7	102.1
2nd quarter	88.2	93.3	75.7	100.8	93.6	88.2	91.2	75.4	108.8	92.1	97.6	96.3	102.9
3rd quarter	89.5	93.7	82.3	98.7	110.8	90.0	96.1	79.0	101.1	75.5	96.6	96.4	103.4
4th quarter	89.3	94.7	88.6	95.5	95.8	90.0	93.5	81.2	94.7	74.3	104.8	96.1	104.0
2008													
1st quarter	90.5	94.3	79.6	96.0	108.8	90.5	94.2	86.2	66.9	87.5	91.2	100.7	103.6
2nd quarter	91.2	95.7	85.4	101.1	95.2	87.9	86.4	87.6	108.9	92.8	101.2	101.3	103.1
3rd quarter	93.8	97.1	92.0	98.7	104.5	96.5	105.6	98.0	108.9	89.0	106.0	101.2	102.2
4th quarter	96.0	97.3	95.0	101.6	108.3	97.7	99.9	101.8	123.8	74.8	106.3	99.4	101.7
2009													
1st quarter	97.3	97.1	91.5	92.7	91.4	97.6	90.2	93.9	92.2	83.7	94.4	98.2	101.1
2nd quarter	99.7	98.5	97.3	97.5	102.6	100.2	98.5	100.9	112.4	93.0	97.5	98.9	100.4
3rd quarter	101.5	100.6	102.0	107.9	98.8	100.8	104.0	102.5	94.8	127.7	97.8	100.5	99.9
4th quarter	101.4	103.8	109.1	102.0	107.2	101.4	107.3	102.6	100.7	95.6	110.3	102.4	98.6
2010													
1st quarter	101.9	104.3	94.1	102.1	100.3	99.6	102.3	103.4	111.8	110.2	94.9	105.8	98.8
2nd quarter	101.9	105.3	104.7	104.1	105.2	101.3	109.8	104.3	126.4	111.9	98.8	105.5	98.1
3rd quarter	101.5	107.2	111.1	100.0	93.1	106.6	122.7	108.9	117.9	105.8	104.3	108.4	98.3
4th quarter	101.1	109.0	129.6	99.3	98.0	99.7	110.4	102.0	140.7	104.5	115.6	109.8	97.2
2011													
1st quarter	101.1	109.4	106.2	104.8	92.5	93.0	96.0	100.1	128.4	98.5	89.9	110.7	96.3
2nd quarter	101.3	109.7	118.8	101.4	91.6	96.8	111.6	103.5	145.0	104.3	96.9	111.4	95.0
3rd quarter	101.3	110.4	127.4	107.4	96.2	99.1	117.0	105.5	151.9	93.5	94.8	111.8	94.3
4th quarter	101.2	111.7	134.1	109.4	102.1	90.7	96.4	91.2	153.6	84.0	109.1	112.9	94.0
2012													
1st quarter	99.7	110.2	124.5	106.8	86.6	91.2	98.9	95.9	141.6	122.3	88.6	111.6	92.3
2nd quarter	98.8	109.6	125.2	94.4	90.5	89.7	97.1	97.1	153.7	128.6	103.5	112.5	90.7
3rd quarter	98.3	109.4	133.7	87.4	107.4	101.6	124.0	107.7	174.8	121.5	95.5	112.3	90.0
4th quarter	97.4	108.7	139.6	98.7	95.7	79.8	73.8	91.6	146.9	127.2	107.2	113.9	89.7

[1] Includes general government intermediate inputs for goods and services sold to other sectors and for own-account investment.

Section 6b: State and Local Government in the National Income and Product Accounts

Figure 6-2. State and Local Government Current Receipts and Expenditures, 1946–2012 (percent of GDP)

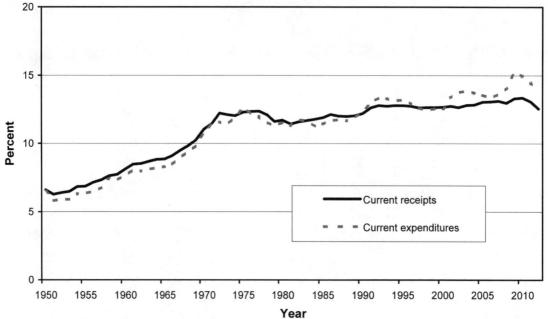

- New definitions introduced to the National Income and Product Accounts (NIPAs) in their 2013 comprehensive revision have caused a noticeable change in the entire time series recording the aggregate surplus+/deficit- of U.S. state and local governments. Compared with the balances shown in this table last year in *Business Statistics,* which were based on cash accounting for defined benefit pension plans, surpluses are now smaller and have morphed into deficits even in some years of prosperity such as 2007, and deficits are larger—with the onset of recession, rising to 1.9 percent of GDP in 2009. The reason for this change is that defined pension benefits for employees are now recorded as government spending when the employees earn them instead of when the benefits are paid. (Table 6-8)

- Both current receipts and current spending of state and local governments have increased as a share of gross domestic product (GDP) over the postwar period, but the growth slowed markedly after the early 1970s. (Tables 6-8 and 1-1)

- State and local gross investment in structures, equipment, R&D, and software rose at an annual rate of 2.1 percent in real terms from 1960 to 2012, compared with 4.0 percent for federal nondefense investment. (Tables 6-6 and 6-11)

Table 6-8. State and Local Government Current Receipts and Expenditures

(National income and product accounts, calendar years, billions of dollars, quarterly data are at seasonally adjusted annual rates.)

NIPA Table 3.3

Year and quarter	Total current receipts	Current tax receipts								Contributions for government social insurance	Income receipts on assets		
		Total tax receipts	Personal current taxes		Taxes on production and imports			Taxes on corporate income			Interest receipts	Dividends	Rents and royalties
			Income taxes	Other personal taxes	Sales taxes	Property taxes	Other taxes on prod. and imports						
1950	19.8	16.5	0.8	0.7	4.8	7.1	2.3	0.8	0.2	0.3	. . .	0.2
1951	21.8	18.1	0.9	0.8	5.4	7.7	2.5	0.9	0.2	0.4	. . .	0.2
1952	23.5	19.7	1.0	0.8	5.8	8.4	2.8	0.8	0.3	0.4	. . .	0.2
1953	25.3	21.1	1.0	0.9	6.3	9.1	3.0	0.8	0.3	0.5	. . .	0.3
1954	26.7	22.2	1.1	1.0	6.5	9.7	3.2	0.8	0.3	0.5	. . .	0.3
1955	29.2	24.4	1.3	1.0	7.1	10.4	3.5	1.0	0.3	0.6	. . .	0.3
1956	32.2	27.0	1.6	1.1	8.0	11.5	3.8	1.0	0.4	0.7	. . .	0.3
1957	34.8	29.0	1.7	1.2	8.6	12.6	3.9	1.0	0.4	0.7	. . .	0.3
1958	36.8	30.6	1.8	1.2	10.0	13.8	2.8	1.0	0.4	0.8	. . .	0.4
1959	40.4	33.8	2.2	1.6	11.1	14.8	2.9	1.2	0.4	0.9	. . .	0.3
1960	44.2	37.0	2.5	1.7	12.2	16.2	3.1	1.2	0.5	1.0	. . .	0.3
1961	47.7	39.7	2.8	1.8	13.0	17.6	3.2	1.3	0.5	1.1	. . .	0.4
1962	51.6	42.8	3.2	1.8	14.0	19.0	3.3	1.5	0.5	1.1	. . .	0.4
1963	55.5	45.8	3.4	2.0	15.0	20.2	3.5	1.7	0.6	1.2	. . .	0.4
1964	60.6	49.8	4.0	2.1	16.5	21.7	3.7	1.8	0.7	1.5	. . .	0.4
1965	65.8	53.9	4.4	2.2	18.2	23.2	3.9	2.0	0.8	1.8	. . .	0.4
1966	74.1	58.8	5.4	2.4	20.0	24.5	4.3	2.2	0.8	2.1	. . .	0.5
1967	81.6	64.0	6.1	2.5	21.4	27.0	4.4	2.6	0.9	2.4	. . .	0.6
1968	92.5	73.4	7.8	2.7	25.1	29.9	4.6	3.3	0.9	2.8	. . .	0.7
1969	104.3	82.5	9.8	3.0	28.6	32.8	4.7	3.6	1.0	3.6	. . .	0.8
1970	118.9	91.3	10.9	3.3	31.6	36.7	5.0	3.7	1.1	4.3	. . .	0.8
1971	133.6	101.7	12.4	3.5	35.4	40.4	5.7	4.3	1.2	4.6	. . .	0.9
1972	156.9	115.6	17.2	3.7	39.8	43.2	6.4	5.3	1.3	4.9	. . .	1.0
1973	172.8	126.3	18.9	4.0	44.1	46.4	7.0	6.0	1.5	6.6	0.0	1.1
1974	186.4	136.0	20.4	4.2	48.2	49.0	7.7	6.7	1.7	8.9	0.0	1.3
1975	207.7	147.4	22.5	4.4	51.7	53.4	8.1	7.3	1.8	9.8	0.0	1.3
1976	231.9	165.7	26.3	4.8	57.8	58.2	9.0	9.6	2.2	9.0	0.0	1.3
1977	257.9	183.7	30.4	5.0	64.0	63.2	9.7	11.4	2.8	10.4	0.0	1.3
1978	285.3	198.2	35.0	5.5	71.0	63.7	10.9	12.1	3.4	13.3	0.1	1.3
1979	305.8	212.0	38.2	5.8	77.3	64.4	12.7	13.6	3.9	18.1	0.1	1.9
1980	335.3	230.0	42.6	6.3	82.9	68.8	15.0	14.5	3.6	23.1	0.1	3.1
1981	367.0	255.8	47.9	6.7	90.7	77.1	17.9	15.4	3.9	28.5	0.1	3.3
1982	388.1	273.2	51.9	7.3	96.2	85.3	18.5	14.0	4.0	33.1	0.2	3.5
1983	424.8	300.9	58.3	7.8	107.7	91.9	19.4	15.9	4.1	37.0	0.2	4.3
1984	475.6	337.3	67.5	8.6	121.0	99.7	21.8	18.8	4.7	42.6	0.2	4.9
1985	516.9	363.7	72.1	9.2	131.1	107.5	23.5	20.2	4.9	50.1	0.2	5.4
1986	556.8	389.5	77.4	9.8	139.9	116.2	23.7	22.7	6.0	52.6	0.2	6.2
1987	585.0	422.1	86.0	10.6	150.3	126.4	24.9	23.9	7.2	53.0	0.2	5.3
1988	629.9	452.8	90.6	11.5	162.4	136.5	25.7	26.0	8.4	56.6	0.2	4.4
1989	680.8	488.0	102.3	12.4	172.3	149.9	26.9	24.2	9.0	62.3	0.2	4.1
1990	729.6	519.1	109.6	13.0	184.3	161.5	28.3	22.5	10.0	64.1	0.2	4.2
1991	779.5	544.3	111.7	13.6	190.7	176.1	28.6	23.6	11.6	62.4	0.3	4.5
1992	835.6	579.8	120.4	14.9	204.3	184.7	31.1	24.4	13.1	58.8	0.5	4.8
1993	877.1	604.7	126.2	14.8	216.4	187.3	33.1	26.9	14.1	56.0	0.6	4.5
1994	934.1	644.2	132.2	15.7	231.4	199.4	35.5	30.0	14.5	58.2	0.8	4.5
1995	979.8	672.1	141.7	16.4	242.7	202.6	37.0	31.7	13.6	63.6	1.0	4.5
1996	1 032.6	709.6	152.3	16.3	256.2	212.4	39.4	33.0	12.5	67.7	1.4	4.6
1997	1 085.8	749.9	164.7	17.3	268.7	223.5	41.6	34.1	10.8	71.8	1.5	4.8
1998	1 148.7	794.9	183.0	18.2	283.9	231.0	43.9	34.9	10.4	75.0	1.6	4.6
1999	1 221.8	840.4	195.5	19.0	301.6	242.8	45.8	35.8	9.8	78.6	1.5	5.1
2000	1 303.1	893.2	217.4	19.4	316.8	254.7	49.8	35.2	10.8	86.3	1.4	6.3
2001	1 352.6	914.3	223.3	19.7	321.8	268.0	52.6	28.9	13.7	81.3	1.4	6.5
2002	1 388.4	928.5	201.3	20.5	331.1	289.3	55.4	30.9	15.8	70.5	1.6	6.6
2003	1 474.6	978.6	204.7	22.1	348.9	307.0	62.0	34.0	19.9	64.5	1.7	7.6
2004	1 575.1	1 057.8	223.6	23.8	371.1	326.2	71.5	41.7	24.7	66.4	2.0	8.5
2005	1 708.8	1 166.5	251.5	24.9	402.5	351.3	81.4	54.9	24.6	76.8	2.0	9.8
2006	1 810.9	1 254.5	276.2	26.3	431.8	375.0	85.9	59.2	21.5	94.7	2.1	10.4
2007	1 900.6	1 321.3	296.4	27.1	448.9	403.8	87.2	57.9	18.9	104.2	2.2	11.5
2008	1 909.1	1 328.9	307.0	26.5	444.8	413.8	89.4	47.4	18.7	91.0	2.6	12.1
2009	1 919.2	1 268.1	259.5	28.3	423.9	435.1	75.8	45.6	18.6	74.4	2.1	11.2
2010	1 998.5	1 305.6	267.1	30.5	446.0	435.0	79.4	47.7	18.1	69.1	2.3	11.2
2011	2 029.9	1 366.3	296.1	30.9	463.7	436.9	87.9	50.7	18.3	66.3	2.3	11.4
2012	2 039.4	1 405.2	317.3	31.6	474.9	440.0	90.0	51.4	17.5	64.2	2.4	11.9
2010												
1st quarter	1 963.7	1 285.1	261.6	29.9	431.8	436.7	80.7	44.5	18.2	69.9	2.3	11.1
2nd quarter	1 965.4	1 285.6	251.7	30.5	443.4	434.9	79.5	45.6	18.1	69.5	2.4	11.2
3rd quarter	2 020.5	1 315.5	269.9	30.9	452.2	434.2	77.8	50.6	18.1	68.8	2.2	11.2
4th quarter	2 044.5	1 336.4	285.5	30.7	456.5	434.4	79.4	49.9	18.2	68.2	2.3	11.3
2011												
1st quarter	2 040.7	1 355.4	289.8	30.7	460.4	435.5	86.5	52.5	18.3	67.5	2.1	11.3
2nd quarter	2 059.0	1 367.6	296.9	30.8	467.7	436.5	87.2	48.4	18.4	66.6	2.2	11.4
3rd quarter	2 013.1	1 367.5	299.1	31.0	460.6	437.4	88.8	50.7	18.3	66.0	2.4	11.5
4th quarter	2 006.7	1 374.7	298.7	31.1	466.2	438.1	89.3	51.4	18.1	65.1	2.4	11.6
2012												
1st quarter	2 024.4	1 398.3	309.1	31.4	476.0	438.7	92.5	50.7	17.8	64.1	2.2	11.7
2nd quarter	2 034.1	1 403.1	315.3	31.6	473.2	439.5	91.0	52.5	17.6	63.8	2.5	11.9
3rd quarter	2 039.6	1 400.9	317.7	31.5	473.0	440.4	87.2	51.1	17.4	64.0	2.4	12.0
4th quarter	2 059.7	1 418.4	326.9	31.8	477.3	441.4	89.6	51.3	17.3	64.9	2.3	12.1

. . . = Not available.

Table 6-8. State and Local Government Current Receipts and Expenditures—*Continued*

(National income and product accounts, calendar years, billions of dollars, quarterly data are at seasonally adjusted annual rates.)

NIPA Table 3.3

Year and quarter	Current receipts—*Continued*				Current surplus of government enterprises	Current expenditures					Net state and local government saving, NIPA (surplus + / deficit -)		
	Current transfer receipts					Total	Consumption expenditures	Government social benefits to persons	Interest payments	Subsidies	Total	Social insurance funds	Other
	Total	Federal grants-in-aid	From business, net	From persons									
1950	2.2	1.8	0.1	0.3	0.4	19.5	15.4	3.2	1.0	...	0.3	0.1	0.2
1951	2.4	2.0	0.1	0.3	0.4	20.2	16.5	2.6	1.1	...	1.5	0.1	1.5
1952	2.5	2.1	0.1	0.3	0.4	21.7	17.6	2.9	1.2	...	1.9	0.1	1.8
1953	2.7	2.2	0.1	0.3	0.5	23.0	18.8	3.0	1.3	...	2.3	0.1	2.2
1954	2.8	2.2	0.2	0.4	0.6	24.7	20.2	3.1	1.4	...	2.0	0.1	1.9
1955	2.9	2.3	0.2	0.4	0.7	27.0	22.1	3.3	1.6	...	2.2	0.1	2.1
1956	3.0	2.4	0.2	0.4	0.8	29.2	24.0	3.3	1.9	...	3.0	0.1	2.9
1957	3.5	2.8	0.2	0.5	0.8	32.1	26.4	3.6	2.1	...	2.6	0.1	2.5
1958	4.0	3.2	0.2	0.5	0.8	35.7	29.4	4.0	2.3	...	1.1	0.0	1.1
1959	4.0	3.6	0.1	0.3	1.0	38.2	31.2	4.3	2.7	0.0	2.2	0.0	2.2
1960	4.3	3.8	0.2	0.3	1.2	41.6	34.1	4.6	3.0	0.0	2.6	0.0	2.5
1961	4.9	4.3	0.2	0.4	1.2	45.5	37.2	5.0	3.3	0.0	2.2	0.0	2.2
1962	5.5	4.7	0.2	0.5	1.3	48.2	39.3	5.3	3.5	0.0	3.4	0.0	3.4
1963	6.0	5.2	0.3	0.5	1.5	51.8	42.3	5.7	3.8	0.0	3.7	0.0	3.7
1964	6.8	6.0	0.3	0.5	1.5	56.3	46.0	6.2	4.1	0.0	4.3	0.0	4.3
1965	7.4	6.6	0.3	0.5	1.6	61.7	50.6	6.7	4.5	0.0	4.1	0.1	4.0
1966	10.4	9.4	0.3	0.7	1.5	68.9	56.4	7.6	4.9	0.0	5.2	0.1	5.1
1967	12.3	10.9	0.5	0.9	1.4	76.9	62.4	9.2	5.2	0.0	4.7	0.1	4.6
1968	13.3	11.8	0.5	1.0	1.3	88.2	70.7	11.4	6.0	0.0	4.3	0.1	4.1
1969	15.3	13.7	0.5	1.1	1.3	100.2	80.4	13.2	6.6	0.0	4.1	0.2	3.9
1970	20.1	18.3	0.6	1.2	1.3	115.9	92.1	16.1	7.7	0.0	3.0	0.2	2.8
1971	24.1	22.1	0.6	1.4	1.1	133.0	104.2	19.3	9.4	0.0	0.6	0.2	0.4
1972	32.8	30.5	0.7	1.7	1.2	148.5	115.4	22.0	11.1	0.1	8.4	0.3	8.2
1973	36.1	33.5	0.9	1.7	1.2	163.1	126.8	24.1	12.2	0.1	9.6	0.3	9.3
1974	37.9	34.9	1.1	2.0	0.6	184.1	144.5	25.3	14.2	0.1	2.3	0.4	1.9
1975	47.2	43.6	1.2	2.4	0.1	213.3	165.6	30.8	16.7	0.2	-5.6	0.5	-6.0
1976	53.3	49.1	1.4	2.9	0.2	229.1	177.2	34.1	17.6	0.2	2.8	0.6	2.2
1977	59.6	54.8	1.6	3.3	0.1	249.5	193.0	37.0	19.2	0.2	8.4	1.0	7.5
1978	69.0	63.5	1.9	3.7	0.0	271.9	209.9	40.8	21.0	0.2	13.4	1.5	12.0
1979	70.3	64.0	2.2	4.1	-0.5	297.6	229.4	44.3	23.5	0.3	8.2	1.8	6.4
1980	76.9	69.7	2.5	4.7	-1.4	329.9	252.8	51.2	25.6	0.4	5.4	1.3	4.1
1981	78.0	69.4	2.9	5.7	-2.6	362.9	276.1	57.1	29.3	0.4	4.1	1.3	2.8
1982	75.9	66.3	3.2	6.4	-1.7	393.2	297.4	61.2	34.2	0.5	-5.1	1.2	-6.3
1983	78.7	67.9	3.6	7.2	-0.4	423.6	316.7	66.9	39.5	0.4	1.3	1.2	0.1
1984	84.7	72.3	4.2	8.1	1.3	454.7	340.0	71.2	43.2	0.4	20.9	1.4	19.5
1985	89.8	76.2	4.4	9.2	2.9	496.7	371.8	77.3	47.3	0.3	20.3	1.3	18.9
1986	99.8	82.4	6.7	10.6	2.6	536.4	399.9	84.3	51.8	0.3	20.4	1.9	18.6
1987	94.4	78.4	4.9	11.2	2.7	572.9	428.3	90.7	53.5	0.3	12.1	2.2	9.9
1988	103.1	85.7	5.4	12.0	4.4	612.9	458.9	98.5	55.1	0.4	17.0	2.5	14.5
1989	111.6	91.8	6.4	13.4	5.6	673.4	501.3	109.3	62.3	0.4	7.4	2.3	5.1
1990	126.4	104.4	7.1	14.9	5.6	736.0	546.2	127.7	61.8	0.4	-6.5	2.0	-8.4
1991	150.7	124.0	7.9	18.7	5.7	804.6	580.1	156.5	67.6	0.4	-25.1	2.4	-27.5
1992	172.8	141.7	9.2	21.9	5.8	873.1	619.0	180.0	73.6	0.4	-37.5	3.1	-40.7
1993	189.8	155.7	10.5	23.5	7.3	914.3	646.5	195.2	72.2	0.4	-37.2	4.2	-41.4
1994	204.1	166.8	12.0	25.2	7.8	961.0	682.2	206.7	71.8	0.3	-27.0	4.6	-31.6
1995	214.4	174.5	13.5	26.5	10.6	1 011.4	716.8	217.6	76.6	0.3	-31.5	4.0	-35.6
1996	224.4	181.5	15.2	27.8	12.4	1 045.0	748.1	224.3	72.4	0.3	-12.5	2.8	-15.3
1997	236.1	188.1	17.7	30.3	10.9	1 084.1	785.9	227.6	70.2	0.4	1.7	1.2	0.5
1998	253.5	200.8	21.6	31.1	8.7	1 133.3	835.7	235.8	61.4	0.4	15.4	1.7	13.7
1999	277.4	219.2	24.0	34.2	9.0	1 212.6	902.0	252.3	57.8	0.4	9.2	1.7	7.5
2000	299.7	233.1	28.6	38.0	5.4	1 293.2	969.1	271.4	52.1	0.5	9.9	2.0	7.9
2001	333.1	261.3	29.8	42.0	2.4	1 417.9	1 039.7	305.1	65.4	7.7	-65.3	2.6	-67.9
2002	365.4	287.2	32.6	45.6	0.1	1 509.4	1 091.0	333.0	84.4	0.9	-120.9	1.4	-122.3
2003	405.0	321.7	33.8	49.5	-2.8	1 596.0	1 127.1	353.6	115.2	0.1	-121.4	3.2	-124.7
2004	422.4	332.2	36.5	53.7	-6.7	1 683.4	1 187.6	385.0	110.5	0.4	-108.4	7.3	-115.7
2005	436.4	343.4	36.5	56.5	-7.3	1 775.4	1 256.6	406.6	111.8	0.4	-66.6	7.2	-73.8
2006	438.9	340.8	38.8	59.3	-11.1	1 850.3	1 325.9	403.9	120.1	0.4	-39.4	4.6	-44.0
2007	460.9	359.0	40.5	61.4	-18.5	1 973.3	1 411.4	433.3	121.5	7.1	-72.7	2.7	-75.4
2008	477.8	371.0	43.6	63.3	-22.0	2 074.1	1 488.7	455.4	127.0	3.0	-165.1	1.7	-166.8
2009	566.1	458.1	44.0	64.0	-21.4	2 191.2	1 508.4	492.6	188.8	1.4	-271.9	2.2	-274.1
2010	612.0	505.3	43.4	63.2	-19.8	2 235.8	1 518.3	523.8	192.1	1.6	-237.3	3.2	-240.5
2011	581.8	472.5	44.2	65.2	-16.5	2 243.0	1 517.4	532.0	192.9	0.5	-213.1	4.2	-217.3
2012	552.6	443.2	41.9	67.5	-14.3	2 292.1	1 536.4	544.3	211.0	0.5	-252.7	3.9	-256.6
2010													
1st quarter	597.8	492.2	42.4	63.2	-20.7	2 224.0	1 521.2	508.0	193.1	1.6	-260.3	2.7	-263.1
2nd quarter	598.9	492.3	43.6	63.0	-20.2	2 228.4	1 521.0	512.5	192.6	2.1	-262.9	3.0	-266.0
3rd quarter	624.2	517.2	43.9	63.1	-19.6	2 242.1	1 515.4	533.3	191.8	1.6	-221.6	3.3	-224.9
4th quarter	626.9	519.5	43.9	63.5	-18.7	2 248.9	1 515.6	541.4	191.0	1.0	-204.4	3.7	-208.0
2011													
1st quarter	603.8	495.4	44.2	64.2	-17.6	2 251.1	1 515.0	545.4	189.8	0.9	-210.3	4.0	-214.3
2nd quarter	609.7	500.5	44.4	64.9	-16.8	2 247.6	1 521.1	535.3	190.8	0.4	-188.6	4.2	-192.9
3rd quarter	563.6	453.8	44.3	65.5	-16.1	2 236.3	1 519.7	522.7	193.5	0.4	-223.1	4.3	-227.5
4th quarter	550.2	440.3	43.8	66.1	-15.5	2 236.9	1 514.0	524.7	197.7	0.4	-230.3	4.2	-234.5
2012													
1st quarter	544.8	436.1	42.2	66.6	-14.8	2 265.5	1 533.0	527.3	204.8	0.5	-241.1	4.0	-245.2
2nd quarter	549.6	440.7	41.7	67.2	-14.3	2 289.3	1 531.3	547.5	209.9	0.5	-255.2	3.9	-259.1
3rd quarter	557.0	447.7	41.6	67.8	-14.1	2 299.7	1 536.8	548.8	213.7	0.5	-260.1	3.9	-264.0
4th quarter	558.7	448.4	42.0	68.3	-14.0	2 313.9	1 544.3	553.7	215.5	0.5	-254.2	3.9	-258.2

. . . = Not available.

Table 6-9. State and Local Government Consumption Expenditures and Gross Investment

(National income and product accounts, calendar years, billions of dollars, quarterly data are at seasonally adjusted annual rates.)

NIPA Tables 3.9.5, 3.10.5

Year and quarter	Total	Consumption expenditures [1] Total	Compensation of general government employees	Consumption of general government fixed capital	Intermediate goods and services purchased [2]	Less: Own-account investment	Less: Sales to other sectors Total [3]	Less: Tuition and related educational charges	Less: Health and hospital charges	Gross investment Total	Structures	Equipment	Intellectual property
1960	48.2	34.1	26.4	3.6	8.9	0.9	3.9	0.4	1.0	14.1	12.7	1.2	0.2
1961	52.5	37.2	29.1	3.8	9.6	1.0	4.3	0.5	1.0	15.3	13.8	1.2	0.2
1962	55.4	39.3	31.2	4.1	10.1	1.1	4.9	0.6	1.3	16.1	14.5	1.3	0.2
1963	60.0	42.3	33.9	4.4	10.8	1.3	5.6	0.7	1.3	17.8	16.0	1.5	0.3
1964	65.3	46.0	37.0	4.7	11.9	1.3	6.3	0.8	1.5	19.3	17.2	1.7	0.3
1965	71.7	50.6	40.7	5.1	13.4	1.4	7.2	1.0	1.8	21.2	19.0	1.8	0.4
1966	79.8	56.4	45.5	5.7	14.9	1.5	8.2	1.2	2.1	23.5	21.0	2.0	0.4
1967	88.1	62.4	50.6	6.2	16.4	1.6	9.3	1.4	2.5	25.7	23.0	2.2	0.5
1968	98.8	70.7	57.6	6.9	18.6	1.8	10.7	1.6	3.1	28.1	25.2	2.3	0.6
1969	109.3	80.4	64.6	7.8	21.8	1.9	11.8	1.9	3.5	28.8	25.6	2.6	0.7
1970	121.4	92.1	73.2	8.8	25.3	2.1	13.1	2.4	3.8	29.3	25.8	2.8	0.8
1971	134.9	104.2	82.4	9.9	29.1	2.2	14.9	2.9	4.6	30.7	27.0	2.9	0.8
1972	146.7	115.4	91.7	10.7	32.0	2.3	16.7	3.2	5.6	31.3	27.1	3.3	0.9
1973	160.8	126.8	100.7	11.9	35.3	2.4	18.7	3.7	6.6	34.0	29.1	3.8	1.0
1974	185.0	144.5	110.5	14.7	42.6	2.8	20.5	4.0	7.4	40.5	34.7	4.6	1.2
1975	210.2	165.6	124.0	16.7	50.5	3.0	22.6	4.3	8.5	44.6	38.1	5.1	1.3
1976	222.1	177.2	133.3	17.4	55.0	3.0	25.6	4.7	9.9	44.9	38.1	5.3	1.5
1977	237.0	193.0	145.1	18.4	60.8	3.1	28.3	5.2	10.9	44.0	36.9	5.4	1.6
1978	260.7	209.9	158.9	19.9	66.6	3.5	32.0	5.8	12.7	50.8	42.8	6.1	1.9
1979	287.8	229.4	174.2	22.2	73.9	4.3	36.6	6.4	15.2	58.4	49.0	7.1	2.2
1980	318.5	252.8	191.6	25.7	81.6	4.9	41.2	7.2	17.3	65.7	55.1	8.1	2.6
1981	343.0	276.1	208.5	29.4	91.1	5.3	47.6	8.3	21.0	66.9	55.4	8.5	3.0
1982	364.4	297.4	224.8	32.1	100.0	5.7	53.8	9.4	24.5	67.0	54.2	9.4	3.4
1983	385.6	316.7	240.9	33.1	109.0	6.1	60.1	10.6	27.8	68.8	54.2	10.8	3.8
1984	417.5	340.0	259.2	34.1	118.4	7.0	64.7	11.7	29.4	77.6	60.5	12.7	4.4
1985	459.2	371.8	283.2	35.9	131.4	7.9	70.8	12.7	32.0	87.3	67.6	14.8	5.0
1986	496.1	399.9	305.8	38.6	141.7	8.8	77.4	13.8	34.8	96.2	74.2	16.4	5.6
1987	530.5	428.3	329.6	41.6	150.0	9.5	83.4	15.0	37.0	102.2	78.8	17.2	6.2
1988	569.3	458.9	356.3	44.5	159.8	10.4	91.2	16.6	40.3	110.4	84.8	18.6	7.0
1989	620.5	501.3	391.1	47.7	175.8	11.9	101.4	18.4	45.0	119.2	88.7	21.9	8.6
1990	678.3	546.2	428.7	51.6	190.5	13.1	111.6	20.3	50.0	132.2	98.5	23.9	9.7
1991	717.4	580.1	458.5	55.1	204.7	14.1	124.1	22.6	57.0	137.3	103.2	23.5	10.6
1992	758.8	619.0	495.3	57.6	218.9	14.4	138.4	25.4	65.3	139.7	104.2	24.0	11.4
1993	787.7	646.5	519.2	60.8	233.8	14.8	152.5	27.4	73.1	141.2	104.5	24.9	11.9
1994	831.1	682.2	545.5	64.3	251.3	15.4	163.5	29.3	78.8	148.8	108.7	28.1	12.0
1995	876.8	716.8	569.6	68.6	270.3	16.1	175.6	31.1	85.0	160.0	117.3	30.5	12.3
1996	918.2	748.1	591.4	72.0	285.5	16.8	184.0	32.9	86.6	170.2	126.8	30.5	12.8
1997	971.8	785.9	619.0	75.7	304.1	18.5	194.3	35.4	89.9	185.8	139.5	32.0	14.3
1998	1 029.4	835.7	652.5	79.8	326.4	19.3	203.7	37.9	93.4	193.7	143.6	34.7	15.5
1999	1 115.6	902.0	695.1	84.9	357.1	20.7	214.4	40.5	96.7	213.6	159.7	37.4	16.5
2000	1 202.0	969.1	740.4	91.4	391.9	22.8	231.8	43.6	104.0	232.9	176.0	38.8	18.1
2001	1 289.5	1 039.7	794.4	96.9	425.0	25.2	251.4	46.1	116.2	249.8	192.3	38.4	19.1
2002	1 354.3	1 091.0	836.4	101.4	444.0	26.1	264.6	49.3	120.7	263.3	205.8	38.0	19.4
2003	1 396.0	1 127.1	876.5	105.2	450.8	26.6	278.8	53.4	124.8	268.9	211.1	37.6	20.2
2004	1 465.0	1 187.6	926.3	111.6	472.2	27.8	294.7	56.7	130.9	277.5	219.1	37.2	21.2
2005	1 547.4	1 256.6	965.0	121.8	507.3	29.6	308.0	60.9	132.3	290.8	231.5	37.1	22.1
2006	1 640.2	1 325.9	1 011.1	131.7	542.2	31.6	327.5	65.7	141.3	314.3	251.2	39.1	24.0
2007	1 752.2	1 411.4	1 065.5	144.7	577.8	33.6	343.0	69.6	149.8	340.8	271.2	43.9	25.8
2008	1 847.6	1 488.7	1 117.7	155.5	606.6	35.8	355.2	73.8	157.6	358.8	285.3	45.7	27.8
2009	1 871.4	1 508.4	1 141.9	162.1	609.9	36.2	369.4	79.2	167.0	363.0	289.8	44.5	28.7
2010	1 870.2	1 518.3	1 167.4	164.9	610.0	35.2	388.8	85.2	175.3	351.9	280.5	41.8	29.5
2011	1 854.7	1 517.4	1 168.0	171.4	623.7	34.8	410.9	92.2	184.5	337.2	265.8	40.9	30.6
2012	1 871.3	1 536.4	1 178.5	178.8	642.4	35.2	428.2	98.7	192.0	334.9	262.7	41.1	31.2
2010													
1st quarter	1 866.5	1 521.2	1 157.9	163.2	616.9	34.8	381.9	83.0	172.5	345.3	272.4	43.6	29.3
2nd quarter	1 876.9	1 521.0	1 169.3	164.4	609.6	35.4	386.8	84.5	174.5	355.8	284.6	41.9	29.3
3rd quarter	1 873.1	1 515.4	1 171.3	165.4	605.2	35.6	390.9	85.9	176.2	357.6	287.3	40.7	29.6
4th quarter	1 864.2	1 515.6	1 171.3	166.6	608.3	35.1	395.5	87.4	177.9	348.6	277.8	40.9	29.9
2011													
1st quarter	1 852.6	1 515.0	1 166.9	168.1	616.9	34.5	402.4	89.4	180.9	337.7	266.8	40.6	30.2
2nd quarter	1 856.3	1 521.1	1 170.6	170.3	622.9	34.6	408.2	91.3	183.4	335.2	263.6	41.2	30.5
3rd quarter	1 856.1	1 519.7	1 169.9	172.5	626.5	34.8	414.3	93.2	185.8	336.4	264.3	41.4	30.7
4th quarter	1 853.6	1 514.0	1 164.5	174.8	628.4	35.2	418.5	95.0	187.8	339.6	268.3	40.3	31.0
2012													
1st quarter	1 867.9	1 533.0	1 176.7	176.7	637.1	35.1	422.5	96.7	189.5	334.9	263.4	40.5	31.0
2nd quarter	1 870.3	1 531.3	1 176.6	178.5	638.2	35.4	426.6	98.2	191.2	339.0	266.5	41.3	31.1
3rd quarter	1 871.4	1 536.8	1 178.4	179.6	644.6	35.3	430.5	99.5	192.9	334.6	262.5	40.9	31.2
4th quarter	1 875.4	1 544.3	1 182.2	180.6	649.7	35.0	433.2	100.3	194.2	331.2	258.3	41.4	31.4

[1] Excludes government sales to other sectors and government own-account investment (construction and software).
[2] Includes general government intermediate inputs for goods and services sold to other sectors and for own-account investment.
[3] Includes components not shown separately.

Table 6-10. State and Local Government Output, Lending and Borrowing, and Net Investment

(National income and product accounts, calendar years, billions of dollars, quarterly data are at seasonally adjusted annual rates.)

NIPA Tables 3.3, 3.10.5

Year and quarter	Output			Net lending (net borrowing -)								Net investment
	Gross	Value added	Intermediate goods and services purchased [1]	Net saving, current (surplus +, deficit -)	Plus: Capital transfer receipts	Minus			Plus: consumption of fixed capital	Equals: Net lending (borrowing -)	
						Gross investment	Capital transfer payments	Net purchases of nonproduced assets			
1955	25.1	19.1	6.0	2.2	1.0	10.1	. . .	0.6	3.2	-4.4	6.9
1956	27.2	21.3	5.9	3.0	1.1	11.4	. . .	0.7	3.6	-4.3	7.8
1957	30.0	23.6	6.4	2.6	1.6	12.7	. . .	0.7	3.9	-5.1	8.8
1958	33.4	25.9	7.5	1.1	2.7	13.7	. . .	0.8	4.1	-6.5	9.6
1959	35.8	27.4	8.3	2.2	3.5	14.1	. . .	0.8	4.4	-4.9	9.7
1960	38.9	30.0	8.9	2.6	3.0	14.1	. . .	0.9	4.5	-4.8	9.6
1961	42.6	32.9	9.6	2.2	3.3	15.3	. . .	1.0	4.8	-5.9	10.5
1962	45.4	35.3	10.1	3.4	3.5	16.1	. . .	1.1	5.2	-5.1	10.9
1963	49.1	38.3	10.8	3.7	4.1	17.8	. . .	1.2	5.5	-5.5	12.3
1964	53.6	41.7	11.9	4.3	4.7	19.3	. . .	1.3	5.9	-5.6	13.4
1965	59.2	45.8	13.4	4.1	4.7	21.2	. . .	1.3	6.4	-7.2	14.8
1966	66.1	51.2	14.9	5.2	5.1	23.5	. . .	1.4	7.1	-7.4	16.4
1967	73.3	56.9	16.4	4.7	5.1	25.7	. . .	1.4	7.8	-9.5	17.9
1968	83.2	64.5	18.6	4.3	6.8	28.1	. . .	1.4	8.6	-9.8	19.5
1969	94.2	72.4	21.8	4.1	6.8	28.8	. . .	1.0	9.7	-9.2	19.1
1970	107.3	82.0	25.3	3.0	6.2	29.3	. . .	1.1	10.9	-10.3	18.4
1971	121.4	92.2	29.1	0.6	7.0	30.7	. . .	1.6	12.2	-12.5	18.5
1972	134.4	102.4	32.0	8.4	7.3	31.3	. . .	1.7	13.3	-4.0	18.0
1973	147.9	112.6	35.3	9.6	7.3	34.0	. . .	1.7	14.9	-3.9	19.1
1974	167.8	125.2	42.6	2.3	9.2	40.5	. . .	1.9	18.3	-12.6	22.2
1975	191.2	140.7	50.5	-5.6	11.0	44.6	. . .	1.9	21.0	-20.1	23.6
1976	205.7	150.8	55.0	2.8	12.0	44.9	. . .	1.7	22.1	-9.7	22.8
1977	224.4	163.5	60.8	8.4	13.1	44.0	. . .	1.6	23.5	-0.5	20.5
1978	245.4	178.8	66.6	13.4	13.7	50.8	. . .	1.8	25.5	0.0	25.3
1979	270.3	196.4	73.9	8.2	16.2	58.4	. . .	2.0	28.6	-7.3	29.8
1980	298.9	217.3	81.6	5.4	18.6	65.7	. . .	2.2	33.1	-10.8	32.6
1981	329.0	237.8	91.1	4.1	17.8	66.9	. . .	2.2	37.8	-9.4	29.1
1982	356.9	256.9	100.0	-5.1	16.9	67.0	. . .	2.2	41.3	-16.1	25.7
1983	382.9	273.9	109.0	1.3	18.0	68.8	. . .	2.2	42.8	-9.0	26.0
1984	411.7	293.3	118.4	20.9	20.1	77.6	. . .	2.6	44.4	5.3	33.2
1985	450.5	319.1	131.4	20.3	22.0	87.3	. . .	3.1	46.9	-1.3	40.4
1986	486.1	344.4	141.7	20.4	23.0	96.2	. . .	3.7	50.3	-6.1	45.9
1987	521.3	371.2	150.0	12.1	22.3	102.2	. . .	4.2	54.1	-17.9	48.1
1988	560.5	400.8	159.8	17.0	23.1	110.4	. . .	4.3	57.8	-16.9	52.6
1989	614.6	438.8	175.8	7.4	23.4	119.2	0.0	4.9	61.9	-31.4	57.3
1990	670.8	480.3	190.5	-6.5	25.0	132.2	0.0	5.7	66.7	-52.7	65.5
1991	718.3	513.7	204.7	-25.1	25.8	137.3	0.0	5.8	70.9	-71.6	66.4
1992	771.9	553.0	218.9	-37.5	26.9	139.7	0.0	5.9	74.1	-82.0	65.6
1993	813.8	580.0	233.8	-37.2	28.2	141.2	0.0	5.9	78.3	-77.8	62.9
1994	861.1	609.9	251.3	-27.0	29.9	148.8	0.0	6.2	82.9	-69.1	65.9
1995	908.6	638.2	270.3	-31.5	32.4	160.0	0.0	6.6	88.3	-77.5	71.7
1996	948.9	663.4	285.5	-12.5	33.8	170.2	0.0	6.0	92.6	-62.2	77.6
1997	998.7	694.7	304.1	1.7	35.2	185.8	0.0	5.8	96.9	-57.9	88.9
1998	1 058.7	732.3	326.4	15.4	35.9	193.7	0.0	7.6	101.8	-48.3	91.9
1999	1 137.1	780.0	357.1	9.2	40.0	213.6	0.0	8.6	108.1	-64.8	105.5
2000	1 223.7	831.8	391.9	9.9	44.2	232.9	0.0	8.6	116.2	-71.2	116.7
2001	1 316.3	891.3	425.0	-65.3	51.7	249.8	0.0	10.1	123.0	-150.5	126.8
2002	1 381.8	937.8	444.0	-120.9	52.9	263.3	0.0	11.2	129.0	-213.5	134.3
2003	1 432.5	981.7	450.8	-121.4	52.0	268.9	0.0	11.4	134.5	-215.2	134.4
2004	1 510.1	1 037.9	472.2	-108.4	52.4	277.5	4.5	11.3	143.8	-205.4	133.7
2005	1 594.1	1 086.8	507.3	-66.6	56.8	290.8	6.4	10.0	157.3	-159.7	133.5
2006	1 685.0	1 142.8	542.2	-39.4	57.8	314.3	0.0	11.0	170.3	-136.6	144.0
2007	1 788.0	1 210.2	577.8	-72.7	59.3	340.8	0.0	13.6	186.6	-181.2	154.2
2008	1 879.7	1 273.2	606.6	-165.1	63.2	358.8	0.0	13.8	200.2	-274.3	158.6
2009	1 913.9	1 304.0	609.9	-271.9	67.7	363.0	0.0	12.3	208.2	-371.4	154.8
2010	1 942.3	1 332.3	610.0	-237.3	76.7	351.9	0.0	10.6	212.7	-310.3	139.2
2011	1 963.1	1 339.4	623.7	-213.1	73.9	337.2	0.0	10.1	221.7	-264.8	115.5
2012	1 999.7	1 357.3	642.4	-252.7	74.1	334.9	0.0	10.2	231.4	-292.4	103.5
2010											
1st quarter	1 937.9	1 321.0	616.9	-260.3	65.0	345.3	0.0	11.1	210.0	-341.7	135.3
2nd quarter	1 943.3	1 333.7	609.6	-262.9	76.3	355.8	0.0	10.7	211.9	-341.2	143.9
3rd quarter	1 941.9	1 336.7	605.2	-221.6	83.5	357.6	0.0	10.3	213.6	-292.5	144.0
4th quarter	1 946.1	1 337.9	608.3	-204.4	82.1	348.6	0.0	10.2	215.4	-265.7	133.2
2011											
1st quarter	1 951.9	1 335.0	616.9	-210.3	72.7	337.7	0.0	10.1	217.4	-268.0	120.3
2nd quarter	1 963.9	1 340.9	622.9	-188.6	72.7	335.2	0.0	10.1	220.2	-241.1	115.0
3rd quarter	1 968.8	1 342.4	626.5	-223.1	73.8	336.4	0.0	10.1	223.1	-272.8	113.3
4th quarter	1 967.7	1 339.3	628.4	-230.3	76.5	339.6	0.0	10.2	226.1	-277.5	113.5
2012											
1st quarter	1 990.6	1 353.4	637.1	-241.1	70.6	334.9	0.0	10.3	228.5	-287.2	106.4
2nd quarter	1 993.3	1 355.1	638.2	-255.2	72.0	339.0	0.0	10.3	230.8	-301.7	108.2
3rd quarter	2 002.6	1 358.0	644.6	-260.1	73.2	334.6	0.0	10.2	232.4	-299.3	102.2
4th quarter	2 012.5	1 362.8	649.7	-254.2	80.5	331.2	0.0	10.1	233.7	-281.2	97.5

[1]Includes general government intermediate inputs for goods and services sold to other sectors and for own-account investment.
. . . = Not available.

Table 6-11. Chain-Type Quantity Indexes for State and Local Government Consumption Expenditures and Gross Investment

(Seasonally adjusted, 2009 = 100.)   **NIPA Tables 3.9.3, 3.10.3**

Year and quarter	Total	State and local government consumption expenditures and gross investment											
		Consumption expenditures [1]								Gross investment			
		Total	Compensation of general government employees	Consumption of general government fixed capital	Intermediate goods and services purchased [2]	Less				Total	Structures	Equipment	Intellectual property
						Own-account investment	Sales to other sectors						
							Total [3]	Tuition and related educational charges	Health and hospital charges				
1955	20.0	18.9	25.1	10.9	8.1	13.1	9.9	7.3	6.7	23.2	35.8	3.3	1.6
1956	20.7	19.6	26.7	11.5	7.8	14.6	10.4	8.4	7.7	23.7	36.4	3.7	1.7
1957	21.9	20.6	28.1	12.2	8.2	14.8	11.1	9.7	8.7	25.5	38.6	4.5	1.8
1958	23.7	22.2	29.8	12.9	9.4	15.9	12.3	11.0	11.0	28.0	42.7	4.5	2.0
1959	24.5	23.0	31.0	13.7	10.0	21.2	13.1	12.6	11.5	28.8	43.9	4.8	2.1
1960	25.6	24.3	32.6	14.5	10.5	20.3	13.8	14.0	10.6	29.2	44.0	5.4	2.4
1961	27.1	25.6	34.3	15.3	11.2	21.4	14.9	15.3	10.9	31.5	47.7	5.5	2.7
1962	27.9	26.3	35.5	16.1	11.7	23.0	16.6	17.3	12.7	32.7	49.2	5.9	3.0
1963	29.6	27.5	37.3	17.1	12.4	25.8	18.5	19.7	13.2	35.6	53.3	6.7	3.6
1964	31.6	29.3	39.5	18.2	13.6	26.1	20.4	23.1	14.2	38.2	56.8	7.6	4.0
1965	33.7	31.1	41.9	19.4	15.0	27.2	22.8	26.8	16.3	40.9	60.8	8.1	4.5
1966	35.8	33.0	44.3	20.6	16.2	29.0	24.9	30.4	18.6	43.6	64.7	8.8	5.2
1967	37.5	34.5	46.1	22.0	17.5	29.3	27.4	33.9	21.1	46.4	68.8	9.2	5.9
1968	39.8	36.8	48.8	23.3	19.3	30.9	29.9	38.1	24.6	48.5	71.9	9.6	6.3
1969	41.2	39.1	51.0	24.7	21.4	31.4	31.0	41.9	25.5	46.5	68.1	10.2	7.0
1970	42.4	41.5	53.3	25.9	23.6	32.2	32.3	48.8	25.9	43.7	63.1	10.6	7.7
1971	43.7	43.6	55.4	27.0	25.8	32.6	35.1	55.0	30.2	42.6	61.0	10.7	8.0
1972	44.7	45.2	57.3	28.0	27.4	32.3	37.6	58.4	34.6	41.2	58.0	12.0	8.4
1973	45.9	46.8	59.3	29.1	28.2	32.2	39.1	63.0	38.4	41.5	57.5	13.4	8.9
1974	47.6	48.9	61.5	30.1	29.5	33.8	39.0	62.8	39.6	41.9	57.4	14.6	9.2
1975	49.3	51.3	63.3	31.1	31.9	32.7	39.5	62.8	40.7	41.5	56.9	14.1	9.9
1976	49.7	52.0	64.1	32.1	32.9	30.6	41.8	64.9	43.2	40.9	55.9	13.8	10.5
1977	49.9	53.0	65.0	32.8	34.0	29.3	43.2	67.5	44.0	38.5	52.2	13.4	11.0
1978	51.6	54.1	66.5	33.6	35.0	31.6	45.4	71.2	47.1	41.9	57.1	14.0	12.2
1979	52.3	54.4	67.6	34.5	35.0	35.3	47.6	73.2	51.1	44.0	59.6	15.2	13.4
1980	52.2	54.2	68.5	35.4	33.7	36.8	48.4	75.7	51.5	44.3	59.3	16.1	14.2
1981	51.2	54.0	68.2	36.2	33.9	36.2	50.2	77.3	54.8	40.6	53.5	15.8	15.1
1982	51.2	54.8	68.6	36.9	35.4	36.8	51.5	77.2	56.4	38.2	49.1	16.6	16.2
1983	51.9	55.5	68.1	37.7	37.8	37.2	53.3	79.5	57.9	38.8	48.6	18.9	17.5
1984	53.9	56.7	68.3	38.7	39.8	40.5	53.4	79.3	56.5	43.4	53.9	22.1	19.4
1985	56.9	59.2	70.2	40.1	43.1	43.9	55.3	79.3	57.8	48.1	59.1	25.5	21.8
1986	59.8	61.9	72.2	41.8	46.7	48.0	57.3	79.9	59.3	51.5	62.8	28.0	24.2
1987	61.1	63.2	73.4	43.5	47.7	49.9	58.5	80.5	59.3	52.9	64.2	29.2	25.9
1988	63.4	65.4	75.8	45.3	49.2	52.3	59.7	82.9	59.4	55.7	67.0	31.1	28.8
1989	66.0	67.8	78.0	47.6	51.6	56.9	61.4	85.5	59.8	58.7	68.4	35.9	34.2
1990	68.7	70.0	80.1	50.2	53.3	59.7	62.6	87.4	60.5	63.3	73.5	38.6	38.0
1991	70.2	71.5	80.8	52.7	56.0	62.1	64.7	88.8	63.0	64.8	76.0	37.2	40.9
1992	71.6	73.1	82.0	55.0	58.7	61.5	67.6	90.4	66.7	65.6	76.3	38.0	44.4
1993	72.5	74.4	82.8	57.1	61.3	61.4	70.7	89.3	70.6	65.0	74.5	39.3	45.4
1994	74.5	76.4	84.1	59.2	64.7	62.2	73.1	89.4	73.4	66.9	75.1	44.2	45.9
1995	76.5	78.2	85.6	61.3	67.3	63.0	75.7	89.7	76.7	69.7	77.7	48.4	45.7
1996	78.3	79.7	86.7	63.6	69.1	64.7	77.1	90.0	76.4	72.9	81.6	49.7	48.0
1997	81.1	81.8	88.2	66.2	72.6	70.2	79.7	92.1	78.2	78.4	87.1	54.3	53.8
1998	84.3	85.1	89.8	69.3	78.3	72.1	82.1	94.6	80.5	80.7	86.9	61.8	58.9
1999	87.8	88.0	90.9	72.7	83.7	75.4	84.3	97.4	81.9	87.1	93.1	69.3	62.4
2000	90.3	89.9	92.6	76.1	87.0	79.8	88.5	100.8	85.9	92.0	98.2	73.2	66.7
2001	93.6	92.9	94.5	79.5	93.2	86.1	93.3	101.4	93.1	96.6	103.8	74.8	69.7
2002	96.3	95.4	96.2	82.5	96.8	88.0	95.2	101.4	93.5	100.1	108.1	76.3	71.2
2003	95.9	94.8	96.5	84.9	94.3	87.5	95.7	101.4	91.9	100.8	108.3	77.0	74.5
2004	95.8	94.9	96.6	87.4	94.3	88.4	96.6	98.2	92.2	99.6	106.3	76.9	78.0
2005	95.8	95.5	97.0	89.7	94.7	90.9	97.0	98.2	90.1	97.0	102.2	78.1	81.1
2006	96.7	96.2	97.6	92.1	96.2	94.6	99.1	99.2	92.6	98.7	102.3	84.9	87.0
2007	98.1	97.7	98.8	94.8	97.6	97.5	99.7	99.1	95.0	99.7	101.0	97.2	91.9
2008	98.5	97.9	99.9	97.6	95.2	99.9	98.9	98.9	97.1	100.6	100.7	102.1	96.9
2009	100.0	100.0	100.0	100.0	100.0	100.0	100.0	100.0	100.0	100.0	100.0	100.0	100.0
2010	97.3	97.4	99.0	101.9	96.2	95.7	102.2	102.3	102.2	96.7	96.4	94.7	102.1
2011	93.8	94.6	97.6	103.4	92.9	92.5	105.0	105.4	105.4	90.2	88.3	93.1	104.5
2012	93.1	94.6	97.4	104.7	93.8	91.8	106.5	107.6	107.3	86.8	84.1	92.8	105.3
2010													
1st quarter	98.1	98.8	99.5	101.2	98.1	95.2	101.3	101.3	101.2	95.5	94.4	98.6	101.6
2nd quarter	97.9	97.9	99.3	101.7	96.7	96.4	101.8	101.7	101.8	98.0	98.1	94.9	101.5
3rd quarter	97.2	97.0	98.7	102.1	95.5	96.5	102.4	102.5	102.4	98.1	98.6	92.4	102.4
4th quarter	95.9	96.1	98.4	102.5	94.3	94.5	103.1	103.6	103.2	95.2	94.7	93.0	103.0
2011													
1st quarter	94.6	95.3	98.0	102.9	93.3	92.6	104.0	104.4	104.4	91.6	90.3	92.7	103.7
2nd quarter	93.8	94.7	97.7	103.2	92.8	92.1	104.7	105.3	105.1	90.1	88.2	93.9	104.1
3rd quarter	93.3	94.3	97.4	103.6	92.7	92.3	105.4	105.7	105.9	89.5	87.3	94.2	104.7
4th quarter	93.2	94.2	97.3	103.9	92.8	92.9	105.8	106.4	106.4	89.4	87.5	91.4	105.4
2012													
1st quarter	93.1	94.4	97.4	104.2	93.3	91.9	106.1	107.0	107.0	87.5	85.2	91.7	104.9
2nd quarter	93.2	94.5	97.3	104.6	93.8	92.5	106.4	107.5	107.2	87.9	85.4	93.4	105.1
3rd quarter	93.2	94.8	97.6	104.9	94.0	91.9	106.7	107.9	107.4	86.4	83.7	92.4	105.2
4th quarter	93.0	94.8	97.4	105.2	94.1	91.0	106.7	107.9	107.6	85.3	82.0	93.7	106.1

[1] Excludes government sales to other sectors and government own-account investment (construction and software).
[2] Includes general government intermediate inputs for goods and services sold to other sectors and for own-account investment.
[3] Includes components not shown separately.

Table 6-12. State Government Current Receipts and Expenditures

(National income and product accounts, calendar years, billions of dollars.)   **NIPA Table 3.20**

Year	Current receipts Total [1]	Current tax receipts Total	Personal current taxes Total [1]	Personal current taxes Income taxes	Taxes on production and imports Total	Taxes on production and imports Sales taxes	Taxes on production and imports Property taxes	Taxes on production and imports Other	Taxes on corporate income	Contributions for government social insurance	Income receipts on assets Total [1]	Income receipts on assets Interest receipts	Income receipts on assets Rents and royalties
1959	21.8	16.7	3.1	2.0	12.5	10.0	0.5	2.0	1.1	0.4	0.5	0.3	0.2
1960	23.5	18.1	3.4	2.3	13.5	10.8	0.5	2.2	1.2	0.5	0.5	0.4	0.2
1961	25.2	19.3	3.7	2.5	14.4	11.6	0.5	2.3	1.3	0.5	0.6	0.4	0.2
1962	27.5	21.0	4.0	2.8	15.4	12.6	0.6	2.3	1.5	0.5	0.6	0.4	0.2
1963	29.6	22.4	4.3	3.1	16.4	13.4	0.6	2.4	1.6	0.6	0.6	0.4	0.2
1964	32.3	24.5	4.9	3.6	17.7	14.5	0.6	2.6	1.8	0.7	0.7	0.4	0.2
1965	35.8	26.9	5.4	3.9	19.6	16.1	0.7	2.8	1.9	0.8	0.8	0.5	0.3
1966	42.3	30.2	6.4	4.8	21.7	18.0	0.7	3.0	2.2	0.8	0.9	0.6	0.3
1967	46.5	32.7	7.0	5.3	23.3	19.4	0.7	3.1	2.5	0.9	1.1	0.8	0.3
1968	54.7	38.6	8.8	6.9	26.7	22.8	0.8	3.2	3.1	0.9	1.7	1.4	0.3
1969	62.6	44.0	10.8	8.6	29.9	25.7	0.9	3.3	3.4	1.0	2.1	1.8	0.3
1970	70.1	48.1	12.0	9.6	32.7	28.2	0.9	3.6	3.5	1.1	2.5	2.2	0.3
1971	79.4	53.8	13.4	11.0	36.3	31.4	1.0	3.9	4.0	1.2	2.7	2.3	0.4
1972	96.3	63.5	17.9	15.2	40.7	35.2	1.1	4.4	5.0	1.3	2.9	2.5	0.4
1973	104.5	70.2	19.8	16.8	44.7	38.8	1.2	4.7	5.7	1.5	3.9	3.3	0.5
1974	113.5	75.9	21.1	18.0	48.4	42.0	1.1	5.3	6.3	1.7	5.0	4.4	0.6
1975	127.4	81.9	23.2	19.9	51.8	44.7	1.4	5.6	6.9	1.8	5.6	5.0	0.6
1976	143.4	93.8	27.0	23.4	57.7	49.9	1.5	6.3	9.1	2.2	5.3	4.7	0.6
1977	160.0	105.1	30.9	27.2	63.4	55.0	1.5	6.9	10.8	2.8	6.1	5.4	0.6
1978	179.3	117.4	35.6	31.6	70.3	60.8	1.9	7.6	11.5	3.4	7.4	6.7	0.6
1979	197.3	128.9	38.9	34.6	77.1	65.7	2.3	9.0	12.9	3.9	10.3	9.2	1.1
1980	218.7	140.9	43.7	39.1	83.4	70.0	2.6	10.8	13.7	3.6	13.4	11.2	2.0
1981	239.5	155.6	48.5	43.6	92.7	76.5	2.7	13.6	14.5	3.9	15.6	13.2	2.2
1982	247.9	162.3	52.3	47.0	97.0	80.3	2.8	13.9	13.1	4.0	17.5	15.3	2.1
1983	272.9	180.5	58.9	53.2	106.8	90.0	3.0	13.8	14.9	4.1	19.5	17.2	2.2
1984	308.2	205.4	68.2	61.9	119.7	100.9	3.4	15.5	17.4	4.7	22.4	19.8	2.5
1985	333.1	220.9	73.2	66.1	129.0	109.0	3.5	16.5	18.7	4.9	25.9	23.1	2.6
1986	359.1	234.0	78.3	70.7	134.9	115.8	3.6	15.6	20.7	6.0	27.3	24.5	2.7
1987	380.5	253.7	87.5	79.1	144.3	124.6	3.7	16.0	21.8	7.2	28.3	25.5	2.6
1988	408.8	269.4	90.4	81.5	155.2	135.1	3.8	16.3	23.8	8.4	30.5	27.7	2.7
1989	441.7	288.4	102.4	92.9	163.5	142.3	4.3	17.0	22.4	9.0	32.4	29.8	2.4
1990	476.7	305.6	109.6	99.6	175.4	152.5	4.6	18.3	20.5	10.0	33.9	31.4	2.3
1991	512.4	314.2	111.8	101.4	180.8	157.5	4.9	18.3	21.6	11.6	34.4	31.5	2.6
1992	559.9	338.8	120.6	109.0	195.9	169.7	6.1	20.1	22.2	13.1	33.9	30.8	2.7
1993	594.0	357.1	126.3	114.9	206.3	179.4	5.9	21.0	24.5	14.1	32.5	29.4	2.5
1994	630.6	380.4	132.1	120.2	220.8	191.7	7.0	22.1	27.5	14.5	33.8	30.5	2.5
1995	663.5	401.5	140.9	128.4	231.3	200.5	7.2	23.6	29.2	13.6	36.6	33.1	2.6
1996	696.8	425.9	150.9	138.6	245.0	211.8	8.2	25.0	29.9	12.5	39.3	35.2	2.7
1997	731.2	449.1	162.7	149.7	255.4	221.3	8.1	26.0	31.0	10.8	41.8	37.5	2.7
1998	777.3	480.7	180.4	166.8	268.8	233.3	8.5	27.0	31.6	10.4	43.4	39.3	2.4
1999	828.2	507.9	192.6	178.4	283.0	245.9	9.1	27.9	32.3	9.8	47.1	42.9	2.6
2000	884.1	540.1	213.5	199.2	294.8	255.5	7.8	31.6	31.7	10.8	49.5	44.5	3.6
2001	922.5	546.8	220.1	205.7	300.8	259.9	8.1	32.8	25.9	13.7	47.0	41.9	3.7
2002	940.6	536.4	199.1	184.2	309.6	267.9	7.7	34.0	27.7	15.9	43.0	37.7	3.7
2003	991.8	561.2	201.8	185.8	328.9	282.0	9.1	37.8	30.5	20.1	42.0	35.9	4.4
2004	1 072.2	610.8	221.4	204.4	352.3	300.5	8.3	43.5	37.1	24.1	44.6	37.5	5.1
2005	1 161.8	681.2	246.7	229.2	385.4	325.7	9.0	50.6	49.1	24.8	50.5	42.5	6.0
2006	1 220.0	732.1	271.2	252.9	408.9	346.3	9.7	52.9	52.0	21.8	59.5	50.7	6.4
2007	1 277.5	765.0	289.5	270.6	424.8	358.5	9.8	56.4	50.8	18.9	63.3	53.5	7.4
2008	1 299.0	769.6	301.1	282.3	427.1	355.1	9.7	62.4	41.5	19.0	59.9	49.2	7.8
2009	1 301.4	690.1	257.4	237.2	393.9	335.4	10.3	48.2	38.7	19.0	56.1	47.0	6.9
2010	1 372.4	722.8	267.4	245.3	417.2	354.5	10.9	51.7	38.2	18.4	53.9	45.1	6.5
2011	1 386.0	769.0	290.5	267.6	437.9	370.8	10.9	56.2	40.6	18.3	52.6	43.7	6.6

[1] Includes components not shown separately.

Table 6-12. State Government Current Receipts and Expenditures—*Continued*

(National income and product accounts, calendar years, billions of dollars.)   **NIPA Table 3.20**

| Year | Current receipts—*Continued* | | | | | Current expenditures | | | | | Net state government saving, NIPA (surplus + / deficit -) | | |
| | Current transfer receipts | | | | | Total [1] | Consumption expenditures | Government social benefits to persons | Grants-in-aid to local governments | Interest payments | Total | Social insurance funds | Other |
	Total	Federal grants-in-aid	Local grants-in-aid	From business, net	From persons								
1959	3.8	3.4	0.2	0.0	0.1	20.8	8.6	3.6	7.7	0.8	1.0	0.0	1.0
1960	3.9	3.5	0.2	0.0	0.1	22.6	9.3	3.8	8.6	0.9	0.9	0.0	0.9
1961	4.4	4.0	0.3	0.0	0.1	24.5	9.9	4.1	9.4	0.9	0.8	0.0	0.8
1962	4.9	4.4	0.3	0.1	0.2	26.6	10.7	4.4	10.3	1.0	0.9	0.0	0.9
1963	5.4	4.9	0.3	0.1	0.2	28.9	11.6	4.7	11.3	1.1	0.7	0.0	0.6
1964	5.9	5.4	0.3	0.1	0.2	31.4	12.5	5.1	12.4	1.2	0.9	0.0	0.9
1965	6.7	6.1	0.3	0.1	0.3	35.1	13.9	5.5	14.3	1.3	0.6	0.1	0.5
1966	9.6	8.9	0.4	0.1	0.3	40.2	15.6	6.4	16.7	1.4	2.1	0.1	2.0
1967	11.1	10.3	0.5	0.1	0.3	46.4	17.9	7.7	19.1	1.6	0.0	0.1	-0.1
1968	12.6	11.6	0.6	0.1	0.3	53.6	20.2	9.5	22.0	1.8	1.0	0.1	0.9
1969	14.6	13.3	0.8	0.1	0.4	61.4	23.2	10.8	25.4	1.8	1.1	0.2	1.0
1970	17.6	16.2	0.9	0.1	0.4	71.3	26.7	12.9	29.2	2.2	-1.2	0.2	-1.3
1971	21.0	19.4	1.0	0.1	0.4	81.1	29.8	15.3	33.0	2.8	-1.7	0.2	-2.0
1972	27.6	25.8	1.1	0.2	0.5	90.6	32.6	17.5	36.9	3.2	5.8	0.3	5.5
1973	27.9	25.8	1.2	0.2	0.7	101.2	36.5	19.4	41.1	3.6	3.3	0.3	3.0
1974	30.0	27.6	1.3	0.2	0.8	114.3	43.6	19.9	45.9	4.1	-0.8	0.4	-1.1
1975	36.9	33.9	1.7	0.2	1.0	132.4	51.0	24.2	51.4	4.7	-5.0	0.5	-5.4
1976	40.8	37.1	2.3	0.3	1.2	145.1	55.6	26.9	56.2	5.3	-1.8	0.6	-2.4
1977	44.6	40.6	2.4	0.3	1.4	157.5	60.6	29.1	60.7	5.8	2.5	1.0	1.5
1978	49.5	45.2	2.5	0.3	1.5	171.8	64.7	32.0	67.3	6.3	7.5	1.5	6.0
1979	52.4	48.3	2.2	0.4	1.6	191.9	72.0	35.4	75.4	7.3	5.3	1.8	3.6
1980	59.2	54.7	2.3	0.4	1.7	216.5	81.2	41.3	83.8	8.2	2.2	1.3	0.9
1981	62.8	57.7	2.7	0.5	2.0	238.7	89.8	46.7	90.4	9.4	0.8	1.3	-0.5
1982	61.9	56.0	3.1	0.6	2.3	255.9	96.6	51.0	94.5	11.3	-8.0	1.2	-9.2
1983	66.0	58.6	4.2	0.6	2.6	273.7	102.6	55.9	99.0	13.5	-0.8	1.2	-2.0
1984	72.1	63.3	5.0	0.8	3.0	297.3	110.2	59.8	108.7	15.5	10.9	1.4	9.5
1985	76.9	67.3	5.2	0.9	3.6	323.6	118.8	65.2	120.0	16.3	9.5	1.3	8.2
1986	86.7	74.5	5.3	2.8	4.1	343.3	124.4	71.4	128.9	15.0	15.8	1.9	13.9
1987	85.8	74.9	5.5	0.9	4.5	372.6	135.6	77.4	137.8	17.6	7.9	2.2	5.7
1988	93.9	82.1	5.6	1.1	5.2	402.7	146.9	84.4	148.1	18.4	6.1	2.5	3.6
1989	104.6	91.5	5.8	1.3	5.9	436.1	157.9	94.4	159.5	19.2	5.5	2.3	3.2
1990	119.5	104.7	6.2	1.6	6.9	478.6	171.5	111.0	169.4	21.2	-1.9	2.0	-3.9
1991	144.2	124.6	7.6	2.0	10.0	528.1	179.6	137.6	181.9	23.1	-15.7	2.4	-18.0
1992	165.4	141.8	9.0	2.6	12.1	569.8	186.4	159.5	194.8	23.1	-9.9	3.1	-13.0
1993	181.0	155.9	10.1	2.9	12.1	603.8	195.7	173.6	206.0	22.6	-9.8	4.2	-14.0
1994	191.9	165.1	11.0	3.4	12.4	640.5	207.8	184.4	218.9	23.2	-9.9	4.6	-14.5
1995	201.0	173.6	11.1	4.1	12.2	674.2	217.1	194.8	231.6	24.0	-10.7	4.0	-14.8
1996	207.5	178.4	12.0	5.0	12.0	701.5	223.6	202.5	242.4	25.3	-4.7	2.8	-7.5
1997	217.3	184.3	13.5	6.6	13.0	731.9	235.3	206.8	255.1	26.2	-0.7	1.2	-1.9
1998	230.9	194.6	13.3	9.8	13.2	775.6	252.0	214.6	273.3	26.7	1.7	1.7	0.0
1999	251.8	212.7	12.9	11.4	14.9	844.3	280.5	230.3	296.4	27.8	-16.1	1.7	-17.8
2000	272.9	226.7	14.0	15.0	17.2	903.8	297.9	248.4	318.7	29.1	-19.7	2.0	-21.7
2001	304.4	253.6	14.9	16.1	19.8	985.3	319.0	281.0	336.7	31.1	-62.7	2.6	-65.3
2002	334.6	280.3	15.5	17.2	21.5	1 033.8	332.0	307.2	351.9	31.3	-93.2	1.5	-94.7
2003	356.9	301.5	16.4	16.6	22.3	1 068.1	333.5	326.1	366.7	31.3	-76.4	3.4	-79.8
2004	380.4	320.5	17.6	17.7	24.6	1 117.1	339.5	355.2	379.5	32.7	-44.9	6.9	-51.8
2005	392.1	330.2	16.6	18.4	26.9	1 177.7	360.7	373.9	397.8	34.9	-15.9	7.4	-23.3
2006	393.8	332.4	15.0	18.4	28.0	1 218.9	374.4	371.2	423.0	38.3	1.2	4.7	-3.5
2007	420.2	353.8	17.1	19.5	29.8	1 303.2	395.6	400.1	445.9	41.4	-25.7	1.9	-27.5
2008	441.3	370.8	17.1	21.7	31.6	1 358.3	417.0	421.2	459.6	43.7	-59.3	1.2	-60.5
2009	527.0	457.0	16.0	22.3	31.7	1 398.6	424.2	456.8	460.6	41.4	-97.2	1.7	-98.9
2010	568.7	498.9	16.4	21.4	32.1	1 440.9	438.2	487.0	458.0	41.4	-68.5	2.2	-70.7
2011	537.4	466.1	16.8	21.1	33.3	1 480.2	459.9	496.9	465.2	42.5	-94.2	2.8	-96.9

[1] Includes components not shown separately.

Table 6-13. Local Government Current Receipts and Expenditures

(National income and product accounts, calendar years, billions of dollars.)   **NIPA Table 3.21**

Year	Current receipts Total [1]	Current tax receipts Total	Personal current taxes Total [1]	Personal current taxes Income taxes	Taxes on production and imports Total	Taxes on production and imports Sales taxes	Taxes on production and imports Property taxes	Taxes on production and imports Other	Taxes on corporate income	Contributions for government social insurance	Income receipts on assets Total [1]	Income receipts on assets Interest receipts	Income receipts on assets Rents and royalties
1959	26.9	17.1	0.8	0.2	16.4	1.2	14.3	0.9	0.0	. . .	0.7	0.5	0.1
1960	29.9	18.8	0.8	0.3	18.0	1.3	15.7	0.9	0.0	. . .	0.8	0.7	0.1
1961	32.6	20.3	0.9	0.3	19.4	1.4	17.0	1.0	0.0	. . .	0.9	0.7	0.2
1962	35.2	21.8	1.0	0.3	20.8	1.5	18.4	1.0	0.0	. . .	1.0	0.8	0.2
1963	38.2	23.4	1.1	0.4	22.3	1.6	19.7	1.0	0.0	. . .	1.0	0.9	0.2
1964	41.8	25.3	1.2	0.5	24.1	1.9	21.1	1.1	0.0	. . .	1.3	1.1	0.2
1965	45.5	27.0	1.2	0.5	25.7	2.1	22.5	1.1	0.0	. . .	1.4	1.2	0.2
1966	49.9	28.5	1.4	0.6	27.1	2.0	23.8	1.3	0.0	. . .	1.7	1.4	0.3
1967	55.8	31.3	1.6	0.8	29.5	1.9	26.2	1.3	0.2	. . .	2.0	1.6	0.3
1968	61.7	34.8	1.7	0.9	32.8	2.3	29.1	1.4	0.3	. . .	1.7	1.4	0.4
1969	69.2	38.4	2.0	1.1	36.1	2.9	31.9	1.4	0.3	. . .	2.2	1.8	0.4
1970	80.3	43.2	2.3	1.3	40.6	3.5	35.7	1.5	0.2	. . .	2.6	2.2	0.5
1971	89.8	47.9	2.5	1.5	45.2	4.0	39.5	1.8	0.3	. . .	2.8	2.3	0.5
1972	100.5	52.0	3.0	2.0	48.8	4.6	42.2	2.0	0.3	. . .	3.0	2.4	0.6
1973	112.8	56.1	3.0	2.0	52.7	5.2	45.2	2.3	0.3	. . .	3.9	3.3	0.6
1974	122.6	60.2	3.4	2.3	56.4	6.1	47.9	2.4	0.3	. . .	5.2	4.5	0.7
1975	136.5	65.5	3.7	2.5	61.4	7.0	51.9	2.5	0.4	. . .	5.6	4.9	0.7
1976	150.1	71.9	4.1	2.8	67.3	7.9	56.7	2.7	0.5	. . .	5.1	4.4	0.7
1977	164.5	78.6	4.5	3.2	73.6	9.0	61.7	2.9	0.6	. . .	5.6	4.9	0.7
1978	179.6	80.8	4.9	3.4	75.3	10.2	61.8	3.3	0.6	. . .	7.2	6.5	0.7
1979	190.4	83.1	5.1	3.6	77.3	11.5	62.1	3.7	0.6	. . .	9.8	8.9	0.9
1980	207.6	89.1	5.1	3.5	83.3	12.8	66.2	4.2	0.7	. . .	12.9	11.8	1.1
1981	226.1	100.2	6.2	4.3	93.0	14.3	74.4	4.3	1.0	. . .	16.4	15.3	1.1
1982	243.7	110.8	6.9	4.9	103.0	15.9	82.5	4.6	1.0	. . .	19.2	17.8	1.4
1983	261.7	120.4	7.2	5.1	112.1	17.7	88.9	5.5	1.0	. . .	21.9	19.8	2.1
1984	288.9	131.9	7.8	5.6	122.7	20.1	96.3	6.3	1.4	. . .	25.2	22.8	2.4
1985	316.8	142.8	8.2	6.0	133.1	22.1	104.0	7.0	1.5	. . .	28.9	26.2	2.7
1986	341.0	155.6	8.9	6.8	144.7	24.1	112.6	8.1	2.0	. . .	31.1	27.5	3.5
1987	358.5	168.5	9.1	6.8	157.3	25.7	122.7	8.9	2.1	. . .	29.9	27.2	2.7
1988	386.1	183.3	11.7	9.1	169.4	27.2	132.7	9.4	2.3	. . .	30.0	28.3	1.7
1989	417.1	199.6	12.3	9.4	185.6	30.1	145.6	10.0	1.8	. . .	33.3	31.6	1.7
1990	443.3	213.6	12.9	10.0	198.7	31.8	157.0	9.9	2.0	. . .	34.5	32.7	1.8
1991	473.3	230.1	13.5	10.3	214.5	33.2	171.1	10.2	2.1	. . .	33.6	31.6	1.9
1992	497.1	241.0	14.7	11.4	224.2	34.6	178.6	11.0	2.1	. . .	30.9	28.8	2.0
1993	517.1	247.7	14.8	11.3	230.5	37.0	181.3	12.1	2.4	. . .	28.8	26.7	2.1
1994	551.4	263.8	15.9	12.0	245.4	39.7	192.4	13.3	2.5	. . .	29.5	27.5	2.0
1995	578.9	270.7	17.2	13.3	251.0	42.2	195.3	13.4	2.5	. . .	31.9	29.9	2.0
1996	611.5	283.7	17.8	13.7	262.9	44.4	204.2	14.4	3.1	. . .	34.2	32.2	2.0
1997	646.5	300.8	19.3	14.9	278.4	47.4	215.5	15.6	3.1	. . .	36.4	34.3	2.1
1998	683.8	314.2	20.9	16.2	290.0	50.6	222.5	16.9	3.4	. . .	38.1	35.9	2.2
1999	731.8	332.5	21.9	17.1	307.1	55.6	233.7	17.8	3.5	. . .	38.7	36.2	2.5
2000	782.0	353.1	23.2	18.1	326.5	61.3	246.9	18.3	3.5	. . .	44.8	42.1	2.7
2001	814.6	367.5	22.9	17.6	341.6	61.9	260.0	19.8	3.0	. . .	43.1	40.3	2.8
2002	851.7	392.3	22.7	17.1	366.4	63.2	281.7	21.5	3.1	. . .	36.7	33.8	2.9
2003	899.6	416.5	24.4	18.2	388.6	66.8	297.7	24.2	3.5	. . .	31.9	28.7	3.2
2004	937.2	448.6	27.2	20.3	416.8	70.2	318.4	28.2	4.6	. . .	32.6	29.2	3.4
2005	995.0	481.9	30.0	22.5	446.0	76.5	337.8	31.7	5.8	. . .	37.7	33.9	3.8
2006	1 061.5	517.0	31.3	23.1	478.6	84.2	360.3	34.1	7.2	. . .	44.0	40.1	3.9
2007	1 123.9	548.5	33.6	25.3	507.9	88.5	386.2	33.2	7.0	. . .	51.2	47.1	4.0
2008	1 138.4	556.7	33.3	25.4	517.5	88.9	398.7	29.9	5.9	. . .	46.9	42.7	4.2
2009	1 152.4	574.8	30.2	22.0	537.9	86.9	420.9	30.1	6.8	. . .	39.0	34.8	4.2
2010	1 160.6	581.7	33.2	24.8	542.3	88.1	422.5	31.6	6.3	. . .	34.9	30.6	4.4
2011	1 177.0	591.8	32.2	23.7	552.5	90.6	428.9	33.0	7.0	. . .	33.8	29.3	4.5

[1]Includes components not shown separately.
. . . = Not available.

Table 6-13. Local Government Current Receipts and Expenditures—*Continued*

(National income and product accounts, calendar years, billions of dollars.)   **NIPA Table 3.21**

Year	Current receipts—*Continued*					Current expenditures					Net local government saving, NIPA (surplus + / deficit -)		
	Current transfer receipts					Total [1]	Consumption expenditures	Government social benefits to persons	Grants-in-aid to state governments	Interest payments	Total	Social insurance funds	Other
	Total	Federal grants-in-aid	State grants-in-aid	From business, net	From persons								
1959	8.3	0.4	7.7	0.1	0.1	24.1	22.1	0.7	0.2	1.0	2.8	. . .	2.8
1960	9.4	0.5	8.6	0.1	0.2	26.4	24.2	0.8	0.2	1.2	3.4	. . .	3.4
1961	10.4	0.6	9.4	0.2	0.3	29.1	26.6	0.9	0.3	1.3	3.5	. . .	3.5
1962	11.5	0.6	10.3	0.2	0.3	30.9	28.3	0.9	0.3	1.4	4.3	. . .	4.3
1963	12.6	0.8	11.3	0.2	0.3	33.2	30.4	1.0	0.3	1.5	5.0	. . .	5.0
1964	14.0	1.1	12.4	0.2	0.3	36.3	33.3	1.0	0.3	1.7	5.5	. . .	5.5
1965	15.9	1.1	14.3	0.3	0.3	39.6	36.3	1.1	0.3	1.8	5.9	. . .	5.9
1966	18.6	1.2	16.7	0.2	0.4	44.2	40.5	1.3	0.4	2.0	5.7	. . .	5.7
1967	21.6	1.5	19.1	0.4	0.6	48.9	44.7	1.6	0.5	2.1	7.0	. . .	7.0
1968	24.2	1.1	22.0	0.4	0.7	55.2	50.2	2.0	0.6	2.4	6.5	. . .	6.5
1969	27.7	1.3	25.4	0.4	0.7	62.4	56.6	2.4	0.8	2.5	6.9	. . .	6.9
1970	33.6	3.2	29.2	0.4	0.8	72.0	64.9	3.2	0.9	3.1	8.3	. . .	8.3
1971	38.2	3.8	33.0	0.5	0.9	81.6	72.9	4.0	1.0	3.8	8.2	. . .	8.2
1972	44.4	5.9	36.9	0.5	1.1	90.6	80.6	4.5	1.1	4.3	9.9	. . .	9.9
1973	51.8	9.0	41.1	0.7	1.0	100.4	89.5	4.7	1.2	4.9	12.4	. . .	12.4
1974	56.6	8.7	45.9	0.9	1.1	112.5	100.1	5.4	1.3	5.6	10.1	. . .	10.1
1975	65.0	11.2	51.4	1.0	1.4	129.1	114.1	6.6	1.7	6.4	7.4	. . .	7.4
1976	72.6	13.6	56.2	1.1	1.7	140.9	123.9	7.3	2.3	7.2	9.1	. . .	9.1
1977	79.9	16.0	60.7	1.3	1.9	153.9	135.3	8.0	2.4	7.9	10.6	. . .	10.6
1978	91.4	20.4	67.3	1.5	2.2	168.5	148.5	8.7	2.5	8.6	11.2	. . .	11.2
1979	97.8	18.1	75.4	1.8	2.6	182.8	161.3	8.9	2.2	9.9	7.7	. . .	7.7
1980	106.4	17.6	83.8	2.0	3.0	201.0	177.2	9.9	2.3	11.2	6.6	. . .	6.6
1981	111.3	14.8	90.4	2.4	3.7	219.4	192.5	10.4	2.7	13.4	6.8	. . .	6.8
1982	114.8	13.5	94.5	2.7	4.1	237.9	208.2	10.2	3.1	15.8	5.8	. . .	5.8
1983	119.5	13.0	99.0	3.0	4.5	256.0	221.5	11.0	4.2	18.8	5.7	. . .	5.7
1984	130.6	13.3	108.7	3.4	5.2	275.9	237.4	11.4	5.0	21.5	13.1	. . .	13.1
1985	142.7	13.6	120.0	3.5	5.7	304.0	263.0	12.1	5.2	23.0	12.8	. . .	12.8
1986	152.4	13.2	128.9	3.9	6.5	336.1	293.7	12.9	5.3	23.1	4.9	. . .	4.9
1987	157.4	9.0	137.8	4.0	6.7	354.4	305.8	13.4	5.5	28.6	4.1	. . .	4.1
1988	168.8	9.5	148.1	4.3	6.9	375.0	324.1	14.1	5.6	30.0	11.1	. . .	11.1
1989	178.8	6.8	159.5	5.1	7.5	402.5	346.5	15.0	5.8	34.0	14.6	. . .	14.6
1990	189.6	6.7	169.4	5.5	8.0	435.3	375.5	16.6	6.2	35.6	8.1	. . .	8.1
1991	203.5	7.0	181.9	5.9	8.7	463.4	397.9	18.9	7.6	37.7	9.9	. . .	9.9
1992	218.6	7.4	194.8	6.7	9.8	488.6	419.9	20.5	9.0	37.9	8.5	. . .	8.5
1993	233.1	8.1	206.0	7.7	11.4	508.3	438.4	21.6	10.1	36.8	8.8	. . .	8.8
1994	250.3	9.9	218.9	8.6	12.9	533.3	460.4	22.4	11.0	38.2	18.1	. . .	18.1
1995	265.9	10.6	231.6	9.4	14.3	559.0	484.2	22.9	11.1	39.4	19.9	. . .	19.9
1996	280.9	12.7	242.4	10.2	15.7	583.8	506.6	21.8	12.0	42.0	27.7	. . .	27.7
1997	297.6	14.1	255.1	11.1	17.3	609.5	529.3	20.8	13.5	44.5	37.0	. . .	37.0
1998	321.0	18.0	273.3	11.8	17.9	638.7	556.6	21.1	13.3	46.0	45.2	. . .	45.2
1999	348.6	20.2	296.4	12.7	19.3	674.0	590.1	22.1	12.9	47.4	57.9	. . .	57.9
2000	373.7	20.6	318.7	13.5	20.8	721.1	632.8	23.0	14.0	49.7	61.0	. . .	61.0
2001	395.2	22.5	336.7	13.7	22.3	767.8	675.3	24.0	14.9	51.9	46.8	. . .	46.8
2002	415.2	23.8	351.9	15.4	24.1	812.6	717.4	25.8	15.5	52.2	39.1	. . .	39.1
2003	447.5	36.5	366.7	17.2	27.1	862.0	763.0	27.3	16.4	53.8	37.6	. . .	37.6
2004	456.1	28.7	379.5	18.8	29.1	900.7	799.5	29.1	17.6	52.9	36.6	. . .	36.6
2005	476.6	31.1	397.8	18.1	29.6	953.2	851.4	30.9	16.6	52.4	41.9	. . .	41.9
2006	500.9	26.6	423.0	20.0	31.3	1 011.6	907.9	31.7	15.0	54.7	49.9	. . .	49.9
2007	528.0	27.0	445.9	21.7	33.4	1 086.0	973.3	33.6	17.1	59.7	37.9	. . .	37.9
2008	540.4	24.7	459.6	22.6	33.6	1 151.3	1 032.2	35.5	17.1	64.4	-12.9	. . .	-12.9
2009	543.1	25.5	460.6	22.7	34.3	1 168.4	1 049.1	38.3	16.0	63.3	-16.0	. . .	-16.0
2010	548.9	32.2	458.0	23.4	35.3	1 181.7	1 058.0	41.3	16.4	64.6	-21.1	. . .	-21.1
2011	557.3	31.7	465.2	24.3	36.1	1 184.8	1 058.1	41.7	16.8	66.7	-7.8	. . .	-7.8

[1] Includes components not shown separately.
. . . = Not available.

Section 6c: Federal Government Budget Accounts

Figure 6-3. Federal Debt as a Percent of GDP, 1940–2012

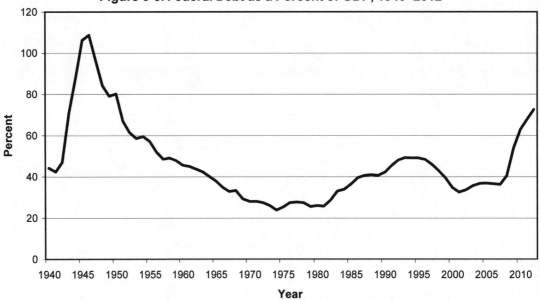

- The "debt held by the public" is generally thought to be a more significant measure of the burden of the federal debt on credit markets than the gross debt, because it nets out the intragovernmental debt of the Social Security and other U.S. government trust funds. The ratio of this debt to GDP was reduced in the late 1990s, began to creep back upward after 2001, and then rose rapidly beginning in 2008, as the recession reduced revenues and increased spending, and taxes were reduced further. The spending increases were a result of both automatic stabilizer programs, such as unemployment insurance, and an unprecedented level of spending for stimulus and financial rescue programs. At the end of fiscal year 2012, the debt held by the public was 72.6 percent of GDP, the highest since 1950. (Tables 6-14 and 6-15)

- From the end of fiscal year 2001 through the end of fiscal year 2012, foreign investors bought 56 percent of the Treasury debt sold to the public to finance the deficits of 2002 through 2012. At the end of 2012, foreign residents—including central banks—held $5.5 trillion of Treasury debt, 49 percent of the $11.3 trillion total debt held by the public. (Table 6-15)

Table 6-14A. Federal Government Receipts and Outlays by Fiscal Year

(Budget accounts, millions of dollars.)

Year	Total receipts, net	Total outlays, net	Budget surplus or deficit (-) Total	On-budget	Off-budget	Borrowing from the public	Other financing	Individual income taxes	Corporate income taxes	Employment taxes and contributions	Unemployment insurance	Other retirement contributions
1940	6 548	9 468	-2 920	-3 484	564	. . .	. . .	892	1 197	725	1 015	45
1941	8 712	13 653	-4 941	-5 594	653	5 451	-510	1 314	2 124	827	1 056	57
1942	14 634	35 137	-20 503	-21 333	830	19 530	973	3 263	4 719	1 064	1 299	89
1943	24 001	78 555	-54 554	-55 595	1 041	60 013	-5 459	6 505	9 557	1 338	1 477	229
1944	43 747	91 304	-47 557	-48 735	1 178	57 030	-9 473	19 705	14 838	1 557	1 644	272
1945	45 159	92 712	-47 553	-48 720	1 167	50 386	-2 833	18 372	15 988	1 592	1 568	291
1946	39 296	55 232	-15 936	-16 964	1 028	6 679	9 257	16 098	11 883	1 517	1 316	282
1947	38 514	34 496	4 018	2 861	1 157	-17 522	13 504	17 935	8 615	1 835	1 329	259
1948	41 560	29 764	11 796	10 548	1 248	-8 069	-3 727	19 315	9 678	2 168	1 343	239
1949	39 415	38 835	580	-684	1 263	-1 948	1 368	15 552	11 192	2 246	1 205	330
1950	39 443	42 562	-3 119	-4 702	1 583	4 701	-1 582	15 755	10 449	2 648	1 332	358
1951	51 616	45 514	6 102	4 259	1 843	-4 697	-1 405	21 616	14 101	3 688	1 609	377
1952	66 167	67 686	-1 519	-3 383	1 864	432	1 087	27 934	21 226	4 315	1 712	418
1953	69 608	76 101	-6 493	-8 259	1 766	3 625	2 868	29 816	21 238	4 722	1 675	423
1954	69 701	70 855	-1 154	-2 831	1 677	6 116	-4 962	29 542	21 101	5 192	1 561	455
1955	65 451	68 444	-2 993	-4 091	1 098	2 117	876	28 747	17 861	5 981	1 449	431
1956	74 587	70 640	3 947	2 494	1 452	-4 460	513	32 188	20 880	7 059	1 690	571
1957	79 990	76 578	3 412	2 639	773	-2 836	-576	35 620	21 167	7 405	1 950	642
1958	79 636	82 405	-2 769	-3 315	546	7 016	-4 247	34 724	20 074	8 624	1 933	682
1959	79 249	92 098	-12 849	-12 149	-700	8 365	4 484	36 719	17 309	8 821	2 131	770
1960	92 492	92 191	301	510	-209	2 139	-2 440	40 715	21 494	11 248	2 667	768
1961	94 388	97 723	-3 335	-3 766	431	1 517	1 818	41 338	20 954	12 679	2 903	857
1962	99 676	106 821	-7 146	-5 881	-1 265	9 653	-2 507	45 571	20 523	12 835	3 337	875
1963	106 560	111 316	-4 756	-3 966	-789	5 968	-1 212	47 588	21 579	14 746	4 112	946
1964	112 613	118 528	-5 915	-6 546	632	2 871	3 044	48 697	23 493	16 959	3 997	1 007
1965	116 817	118 228	-1 411	-1 605	194	3 929	-2 518	48 792	25 461	17 358	3 803	1 081
1966	130 835	134 532	-3 698	-3 068	-630	2 936	762	55 446	30 073	20 662	3 755	1 129
1967	148 822	157 464	-8 643	-12 620	3 978	2 912	5 731	61 526	33 971	27 823	3 575	1 221
1968	152 973	178 134	-25 161	-27 742	2 581	22 919	2 242	68 726	28 665	29 224	3 346	1 354
1969	186 882	183 640	3 242	-507	3 749	-11 437	8 195	87 249	36 678	34 236	3 328	1 451
1970	192 807	195 649	-2 842	-8 694	5 852	5 090	-2 248	90 412	32 829	39 133	3 464	1 765
1971	187 139	210 172	-23 033	-26 052	3 019	19 839	3 194	86 230	26 785	41 699	3 674	1 952
1972	207 309	230 681	-23 373	-26 068	2 695	19 340	4 033	94 737	32 166	46 120	4 357	2 097
1973	230 799	245 707	-14 908	-15 246	338	18 533	-3 625	103 246	36 153	54 876	6 051	2 187
1974	263 224	269 359	-6 135	-7 198	1 063	2 789	3 346	118 952	38 620	65 888	6 837	2 347
1975	279 090	332 332	-53 242	-54 148	906	51 001	2 241	122 386	40 621	75 199	6 771	2 565
1976	298 060	371 792	-73 732	-69 427	-4 306	82 704	-8 972	131 603	41 409	79 901	8 054	2 814
TQ	81 232	95 975	-14 744	-14 065	-679	18 105	-3 361	38 801	8 460	21 801	2 698	720
1977	355 559	409 218	-53 659	-49 933	-3 726	53 595	64	157 626	54 892	92 199	11 312	2 974
1978	399 561	458 746	-59 185	-55 416	-3 770	58 022	1 163	180 988	59 952	103 881	13 850	3 237
1979	463 302	504 028	-40 726	-39 633	-1 093	33 180	7 546	217 841	65 677	120 058	15 387	3 494
1980	517 112	590 941	-73 830	-73 141	-689	71 617	2 213	244 069	64 600	138 748	15 336	3 719
1981	599 272	678 241	-78 968	-73 859	-5 109	77 487	1 481	285 917	61 137	162 973	15 763	3 984
1982	617 766	745 743	-127 977	-120 593	-7 384	135 165	-7 188	297 744	49 207	180 686	16 600	4 212
1983	600 562	808 364	-207 802	-207 692	-110	212 693	-4 891	288 938	37 022	185 766	18 799	4 429
1984	666 438	851 805	-185 367	-185 269	-98	169 707	15 660	298 415	56 893	209 658	25 138	4 580
1985	734 037	946 344	-212 308	-221 529	9 222	200 285	12 023	334 531	61 331	234 646	25 758	4 759
1986	769 155	990 382	-221 227	-237 915	16 688	233 363	-12 136	348 959	63 143	255 062	24 098	4 742
1987	854 288	1 004 017	-149 730	-168 357	18 627	149 130	600	392 557	83 926	273 028	25 575	4 715
1988	909 238	1 064 416	-155 178	-192 265	37 087	161 863	-6 685	401 181	94 508	305 093	24 584	4 658
1989	991 105	1 143 744	-152 639	-205 393	52 754	139 100	13 539	445 690	103 291	332 859	22 011	4 546
1990	1 031 958	1 252 994	-221 036	-277 626	56 590	220 842	194	466 884	93 507	353 891	21 635	4 522
1991	1 054 988	1 324 226	-269 238	-321 435	52 198	277 441	-8 203	467 827	98 086	370 526	20 922	4 568
1992	1 091 208	1 381 529	-290 321	-340 408	50 087	310 738	-20 417	475 964	100 270	385 491	23 410	4 788
1993	1 154 335	1 409 386	-255 051	-300 398	45 347	248 659	6 392	509 680	117 520	396 939	26 556	4 805
1994	1 258 566	1 461 753	-203 186	-258 840	55 654	184 669	18 517	543 055	140 385	428 810	28 004	4 661
1995	1 351 790	1 515 742	-163 952	-226 367	62 415	171 313	-7 361	590 244	157 004	451 045	28 878	4 550
1996	1 453 053	1 560 484	-107 431	-174 019	66 588	129 695	-22 264	656 417	171 824	476 361	28 584	4 469
1997	1 579 232	1 601 116	-21 884	-103 248	81 364	38 271	-16 387	737 466	182 293	506 751	28 202	4 418
1998	1 721 728	1 652 458	69 270	-29 925	99 195	-51 245	-18 025	828 586	188 677	540 014	27 484	4 333
1999	1 827 452	1 701 842	125 610	1 920	123 690	-88 736	-36 874	879 480	184 680	580 880	26 480	4 473
2000	2 025 191	1 788 950	236 241	86 422	149 819	-222 559	-13 682	1 004 462	207 289	620 451	27 640	4 761
2001	1 991 082	1 862 846	128 236	-32 445	160 681	-90 189	-38 047	994 339	151 075	661 442	27 812	4 713
2002	1 853 136	2 010 894	-157 758	-317 417	159 659	220 812	-63 054	858 345	148 044	668 547	27 619	4 594
2003	1 782 314	2 159 899	-377 585	-538 418	160 833	373 016	4 569	793 699	131 778	674 981	33 366	4 631
2004	1 880 114	2 292 841	-412 727	-567 961	155 234	382 101	30 626	808 959	189 371	689 360	39 453	4 594
2005	2 153 611	2 471 957	-318 346	-493 611	175 265	296 668	21 678	927 222	278 282	747 664	42 002	4 459
2006	2 406 869	2 655 050	-248 181	-434 494	186 313	236 760	11 421	1 043 908	353 915	790 043	43 420	4 358
2007	2 567 985	2 728 686	-160 701	-342 153	181 452	206 157	-45 456	1 163 472	370 243	824 258	41 091	4 258
2008	2 523 991	2 982 544	-458 553	-641 848	183 295	767 921	-309 368	1 145 747	304 346	856 459	39 527	4 169
2009	2 104 989	3 517 677	-1 412 688	-1 549 681	136 993	1 741 657	-328 969	915 308	138 229	848 885	37 889	4 143
2010	2 162 706	3 457 079	-1 294 373	-1 371 378	77 005	1 474 175	-179 802	898 549	191 437	815 894	44 823	4 097
2011	2 303 466	3 603 059	-1 299 593	-1 366 775	67 182	1 109 305	190 288	1 091 473	181 085	758 516	56 241	4 035
2012	2 450 164	3 537 127	-1 086 963	-1 148 876	61 913	1 152 937	-65 974	1 132 206	242 289	774 927	66 647	3 740

. . . = Not available.

Table 6-14A. Federal Government Receipts and Outlays by Fiscal Year—*Continued*

(Budget accounts, millions of dollars.)

Year	Excise taxes	Estate and gift taxes	Customs duties and fees	Federal reserve deposits	All other	National defense	International affairs	General science, space, and technology	Energy	Natural resources and environment	Agriculture	Commerce and housing credit
1940	1 977	353	331	...	14	1 660	51	0	88	997	369	550
1941	2 552	403	365	...	14	6 435	145	0	91	817	339	398
1942	3 399	420	369	...	11	25 658	968	4	156	819	344	1 521
1943	4 096	441	308	...	50	66 699	1 286	1	116	726	343	2 151
1944	4 759	507	417	...	48	79 143	1 449	48	65	642	1 275	624
1945	6 265	637	341	...	105	82 965	1 913	111	25	455	1 635	-2 630
1946	6 998	668	424	...	109	42 681	1 935	34	41	482	610	-1 857
1947	7 211	771	477	15	69	12 808	5 791	5	18	700	814	-923
1948	7 356	890	403	100	68	9 105	4 566	1	292	780	69	306
1949	7 502	780	367	187	54	13 150	6 052	48	341	1 080	1 924	800
1950	7 550	698	407	192	55	13 724	4 673	55	327	1 308	2 049	1 035
1951	8 648	708	609	189	72	23 566	3 647	51	383	1 310	-323	1 228
1952	8 852	818	533	278	81	46 089	2 691	49	474	1 233	176	1 278
1953	9 877	881	596	298	81	52 802	2 119	49	425	1 289	2 253	910
1954	9 945	934	542	341	88	49 266	1 596	46	432	1 007	1 817	-184
1955	9 131	924	585	251	90	42 729	2 223	74	325	940	3 514	92
1956	9 929	1 161	682	287	140	42 523	2 414	79	174	870	3 486	506
1957	10 534	1 365	735	434	139	45 430	3 147	122	240	1 098	2 288	1 424
1958	10 638	1 393	782	664	123	46 815	3 364	141	348	1 407	2 411	930
1959	10 578	1 333	925	491	171	49 015	3 144	294	382	1 632	4 509	1 933
1960	11 676	1 606	1 105	1 093	119	48 130	2 988	599	464	1 559	2 623	1 618
1961	11 860	1 896	982	788	130	49 601	3 184	1 042	510	1 779	2 641	1 203
1962	12 534	2 016	1 142	718	125	52 345	5 639	1 723	604	2 044	3 562	1 424
1963	13 194	2 167	1 205	828	194	53 400	5 308	3 051	530	2 251	4 384	62
1964	13 731	2 394	1 252	947	139	54 757	4 945	4 897	572	2 364	4 609	418
1965	14 570	2 716	1 442	1 372	222	50 620	5 273	5 823	699	2 531	3 954	1 157
1966	13 062	3 066	1 767	1 713	163	58 111	5 580	6 717	612	2 719	2 447	3 245
1967	13 719	2 978	1 901	1 805	302	71 417	5 566	6 233	782	2 869	2 990	3 979
1968	14 079	3 051	2 038	2 091	400	81 926	5 301	5 524	1 037	2 988	4 544	4 280
1969	15 222	3 491	2 319	2 662	247	82 497	4 600	5 020	1 010	2 900	5 826	-119
1970	15 705	3 644	2 430	3 266	158	81 692	4 330	4 511	997	3 065	5 166	2 112
1971	16 614	3 735	2 591	3 533	325	78 872	4 159	4 182	1 035	3 915	4 290	2 366
1972	15 477	5 436	3 287	3 252	380	79 174	4 781	4 175	1 296	4 241	5 227	2 222
1973	16 260	4 917	3 188	3 495	425	76 681	4 149	4 032	1 237	4 775	4 821	931
1974	16 844	5 035	3 334	4 845	523	79 347	5 710	3 980	1 303	5 697	2 194	4 705
1975	16 551	4 611	3 676	5 777	935	86 509	7 097	3 991	2 916	7 346	2 997	9 947
1976	16 963	5 216	4 074	5 451	2 576	89 619	6 433	4 373	4 204	8 184	3 109	7 619
TQ	4 473	1 455	1 212	1 500	111	22 269	2 458	1 162	1 129	2 524	972	931
1977	17 548	7 327	5 150	5 908	623	97 241	6 353	4 736	5 770	10 032	6 734	3 093
1978	18 376	5 285	6 573	6 641	778	10 449	7 482	4 926	7 991	10 983	11 301	6 254
1979	18 745	5 411	7 439	8 327	925	11 634	7 459	5 234	9 179	12 135	11 176	4 686
1980	24 329	6 389	7 174	11 767	981	13 399	12 714	5 831	10 156	13 858	8 774	9 390
1981	40 839	6 787	8 083	12 834	956	15 751	13 104	6 468	15 166	13 568	11 241	8 206
1982	36 311	7 991	8 854	15 186	975	18 530	12 300	7 199	13 527	12 998	15 866	6 256
1983	35 300	6 053	8 655	14 492	1 108	20 990	11 848	7 934	9 353	12 672	22 814	6 681
1984	37 361	6 010	11 370	15 684	1 328	22 741	15 869	8 311	7 073	12 586	13 526	6 959
1985	35 992	6 422	12 079	17 059	1 460	25 274	16 169	8 622	5 608	13 345	25 477	4 337
1986	32 919	6 958	13 327	18 374	1 574	27 337	14 146	8 962	4 690	13 628	31 368	5 058
1987	32 457	7 493	15 085	16 817	2 635	28 199	11 645	9 200	4 072	13 355	26 513	6 434
1988	35 227	7 594	16 198	17 163	3 031	29 036	10 466	10 820	2 296	14 601	17 137	19 163
1989	34 386	8 745	16 334	19 604	3 639	30 355	9 583	12 821	2 705	16 169	16 859	29 709
1990	35 345	11 500	16 707	24 319	3 647	29 932	13 758	14 426	3 341	17 055	11 804	67 599
1991	42 402	11 138	15 949	19 158	4 412	27 328	15 846	16 092	2 436	18 544	15 054	76 270
1992	45 569	11 143	17 359	22 920	4 293	29 834	16 090	16 389	4 499	20 001	15 087	10 918
1993	48 057	12 577	18 802	14 908	4 491	29 108	17 218	17 006	4 319	20 224	20 245	-21 853
1994	55 225	15 225	20 099	18 023	5 081	28 164	17 067	16 189	5 218	21 000	14 914	-4 228
1995	57 484	14 763	19 301	23 378	5 143	27 206	16 429	16 692	4 936	21 889	9 671	-17 808
1996	54 014	17 189	18 670	20 477	5 048	26 574	13 487	16 684	2 839	21 503	9 035	-10 478
1997	56 924	19 845	17 928	19 636	5 769	27 050	15 173	17 136	1 475	21 201	8 889	-14 640
1998	57 673	24 076	18 297	24 540	8 048	26 819	13 054	18 172	1 270	22 278	12 077	1 007
1999	70 414	27 782	18 336	25 917	9 010	27 476	15 239	18 084	911	23 943	22 879	2 641
2000	68 865	29 010	19 914	32 293	10 506	29 436	17 213	18 594	-761	25 003	36 458	3 207
2001	66 232	28 400	19 369	26 124	11 576	30 473	16 485	19 753	9	25 532	26 252	5 731
2002	66 989	26 507	18 602	23 683	10 206	34 845	22 315	20 734	475	29 426	21 965	-407
2003	67 524	21 959	19 862	21 878	12 636	404 744	21 199	20 831	-736	29 667	22 496	727
2004	69 855	24 831	21 083	19 652	12 956	455 833	26 870	23 029	-167	30 694	15 439	5 265
2005	73 094	24 764	23 379	19 297	13 448	495 308	34 565	23 597	429	27 980	26 565	7 566
2006	73 961	27 877	24 810	29 945	14 632	521 827	29 499	23 584	782	33 021	25 969	6 187
2007	65 069	26 044	26 010	32 043	15 497	551 271	28 482	24 407	-860	31 716	17 662	487
2008	67 334	28 844	27 568	33 598	16 399	616 072	28 857	26 773	628	31 817	18 387	27 870
2009	62 483	23 482	22 453	34 318	17 799	661 023	37 529	28 417	4 749	35 568	22 237	291 535
2010	66 909	18 885	25 298	75 845	20 969	693 498	45 195	30 100	11 611	43 661	21 356	-82 316
2011	72 381	7 399	29 519	82 546	20 271	705 557	45 685	29 466	12 174	45 470	20 662	-12 573
2012	79 061	13 973	30 307	81 957	25 057	677 856	47 189	29 060	14 857	41 628	17 791	40 823

. . . = Not available.

Table 6-14A. Federal Government Receipts and Outlays by Fiscal Year—*Continued*

(Budget accounts, millions of dollars.)

Year	Transportation	Community and regional development	Education, employment, and social services	Health	Medicare	Income security	Social Security	Veterans benefits and services	Administration of justice	General government	Net interest
					Outlays by function—*Continued*						
1940	392	285	1 972	55	0	1 514	28	570	81	274	899
1941	353	123	1 592	60	0	1 855	91	560	92	306	943
1942	1 283	113	1 062	71	0	1 828	137	501	117	397	1 052
1943	3 220	219	375	92	0	1 739	177	276	154	673	1 529
1944	3 901	238	160	174	0	1 503	217	-126	192	900	2 219
1945	3 654	243	134	211	0	1 137	267	110	178	581	3 112
1946	1 970	200	85	201	0	2 384	358	2 465	176	825	4 111
1947	1 130	302	102	177	0	2 820	466	6 344	176	1 114	4 204
1948	787	78	191	162	0	2 499	558	6 457	170	1 045	4 341
1949	916	-33	178	197	0	3 174	657	6 599	184	824	4 523
1950	967	30	241	268	0	4 097	781	8 834	193	986	4 812
1951	956	47	235	323	0	3 352	1 565	5 526	218	1 097	4 665
1952	1 124	73	339	347	0	3 655	2 063	5 341	267	1 163	4 701
1953	1 264	117	441	336	0	3 823	2 717	4 519	243	1 209	5 156
1954	1 229	100	370	307	0	4 434	3 352	4 613	257	799	4 811
1955	1 246	129	445	291	0	5 071	4 427	4 675	256	651	4 850
1956	1 450	92	591	359	0	4 734	5 478	4 891	302	1 201	5 079
1957	1 662	135	590	479	0	5 427	6 661	5 005	303	1 360	5 354
1958	2 334	169	643	541	0	7 535	8 219	5 350	325	655	5 604
1959	3 655	211	789	685	0	8 239	9 737	5 443	356	926	5 762
1960	4 126	224	968	795	0	7 378	11 602	5 441	366	1 184	6 947
1961	3 987	275	1 063	913	0	9 683	12 474	5 705	400	1 354	6 716
1962	4 290	469	1 241	1 198	0	9 207	14 365	5 619	429	1 049	6 889
1963	4 596	574	1 458	1 451	0	9 311	15 788	5 514	465	1 230	7 740
1964	5 242	933	1 555	1 788	0	9 657	16 620	5 675	489	1 518	8 199
1965	5 763	1 114	2 140	1 791	0	9 469	17 460	5 716	536	1 499	8 591
1966	5 730	1 105	4 363	2 543	64	9 678	20 694	5 916	564	1 603	9 386
1967	5 936	1 108	6 453	3 351	2 748	10 261	21 725	6 735	618	1 719	10 268
1968	6 316	1 382	7 634	4 390	4 649	11 816	23 854	7 032	659	1 757	11 090
1969	6 526	1 552	7 548	5 162	5 695	13 076	27 298	7 631	766	1 939	12 699
1970	7 008	2 392	8 634	5 907	6 213	15 655	30 270	8 669	959	2 320	14 380
1971	8 052	2 917	9 849	6 843	6 622	22 946	35 872	9 768	1 307	2 442	14 841
1972	8 392	3 423	12 529	8 674	7 479	27 650	40 157	10 720	1 684	2 960	15 478
1973	9 066	4 605	12 745	9 356	8 052	28 276	49 090	12 003	2 174	9 774	17 349
1974	9 172	4 229	12 457	10 733	9 639	33 713	55 867	13 374	2 505	10 032	21 449
1975	10 918	4 322	16 022	12 930	12 875	50 176	64 658	16 584	3 028	10 374	23 244
1976	13 739	5 442	18 910	15 734	15 834	60 799	73 899	18 419	3 430	9 706	26 727
TQ	3 358	1 569	5 169	3 924	4 264	14 985	19 763	3 960	918	3 878	6 949
1977	14 829	7 021	21 104	17 302	19 345	61 060	85 061	18 022	3 701	12 791	29 901
1978	15 521	11 841	26 710	18 524	22 768	61 505	93 861	18 961	3 923	11 961	35 458
1979	18 079	10 480	30 223	20 494	26 495	66 376	104 073	19 914	4 286	12 241	42 633
1980	21 329	11 252	31 843	23 169	32 090	86 557	118 547	21 169	4 702	12 975	52 533
1981	23 379	10 568	33 152	26 866	39 149	100 299	139 584	22 973	4 908	11 373	68 766
1982	20 625	8 347	26 612	27 445	46 567	108 155	155 964	23 938	4 842	10 861	85 032
1983	21 334	7 564	26 197	28 641	52 588	123 031	170 724	24 824	5 246	11 181	89 808
1984	23 669	7 673	26 920	30 417	57 540	113 352	178 223	25 575	5 811	11 746	111 102
1985	25 838	7 676	28 592	33 541	65 822	128 979	188 623	26 251	6 426	11 515	129 478
1986	28 113	7 233	29 776	35 933	70 164	120 633	198 757	26 314	6 735	12 491	136 017
1987	26 222	5 049	28 921	39 964	75 120	124 088	207 352	26 729	7 715	7 487	138 611
1988	27 272	5 293	30 931	44 483	78 878	130 377	219 341	29 367	9 397	9 399	151 803
1989	27 608	5 362	35 328	48 380	84 964	137 426	232 542	30 003	9 644	9 316	168 981
1990	29 485	8 531	37 171	57 699	98 102	148 668	248 623	29 034	10 185	10 460	184 347
1991	31 099	6 810	41 235	71 168	104 489	172 462	269 015	31 275	12 486	11 566	194 448
1992	33 332	6 836	42 741	89 486	119 024	199 562	287 584	34 037	14 650	12 881	199 344
1993	35 004	9 146	47 380	99 401	130 552	209 969	304 585	35 642	15 193	12 943	198 713
1994	38 066	10 620	43 286	107 107	144 747	217 166	319 565	37 559	15 516	11 159	202 932
1995	39 350	10 746	51 027	115 399	159 855	223 799	335 846	37 862	16 508	13 799	232 134
1996	39 565	10 741	48 321	119 365	174 225	229 736	349 671	36 956	17 898	11 755	241 053
1997	40 767	11 049	48 975	123 832	190 016	235 032	365 251	39 283	20 617	12 547	243 984
1998	40 343	9 771	50 512	131 425	192 822	237 750	379 215	41 741	23 359	15 544	241 118
1999	42 532	11 865	50 605	141 048	190 447	242 478	390 037	43 155	26 536	15 363	229 755
2000	46 853	10 623	53 764	154 504	197 113	253 724	409 423	46 989	28 499	13 013	222 949
2001	54 447	11 773	57 094	172 233	217 384	269 774	432 958	44 974	30 201	14 358	206 167
2002	61 833	12 981	70 566	196 497	230 855	312 720	455 980	50 929	35 061	16 951	170 949
2003	67 069	18 850	82 587	219 541	249 433	334 632	474 680	56 984	35 340	23 164	153 073
2004	64 627	15 820	87 974	240 122	269 360	333 059	495 548	59 746	45 576	22 338	160 245
2005	67 894	26 262	97 555	250 548	298 638	345 847	523 305	70 120	40 019	16 997	183 986
2006	70 244	54 465	118 482	252 739	329 868	352 477	548 549	69 811	41 016	18 177	226 603
2007	72 905	29 567	91 656	266 382	375 407	365 975	586 153	72 818	42 362	17 425	237 109
2008	77 616	23 952	91 287	280 599	390 758	431 313	617 027	84 653	48 097	20 323	252 757
2009	84 289	27 676	79 749	334 335	430 093	533 224	682 963	95 429	52 581	22 017	186 902
2010	91 972	23 894	128 598	369 068	451 636	622 210	706 737	108 384	54 383	23 014	196 194
2011	92 966	23 883	101 233	372 504	485 653	597 352	730 811	127 189	56 056	27 476	229 962
2012	93 019	25 132	90 823	346 742	471 793	541 344	773 290	124 595	56 277	28 036	220 408

Table 6-14B. The Federal Budget and GDP

(Billions of dollars; percent.)

Year	Fiscal year GDP	Billions of dollars — Receipts — Total	Individual income taxes	Corporate income taxes	Outlays — Total	National defense	Budget surplus or deficit	Percent of GDP — Receipts — Total	Individual income taxes	Corporate income taxes	Outlays — Total	National defense	Budget surplus or deficit
1929	...	3.9	...	...	3.1	...	0.7	...	...	...	...	...	...
1930	97.4	4.1	...	...	3.3	...	0.7	4.2	...	...	3.4	...	0.8
1931	83.9	3.1	...	...	3.6	...	-0.5	3.7	...	...	4.3	...	-0.6
1932	67.6	1.9	...	...	4.7	...	-2.7	2.8	...	...	6.9	...	-4.0
1933	57.6	2.0	...	...	4.6	...	-2.6	3.5	...	...	8.0	...	-4.5
1934	61.2	3.0	0.4	0.4	6.5	...	-3.6	4.8	0.7	0.6	10.7	...	-5.9
1935	69.6	3.6	0.5	0.5	6.4	...	-2.8	5.2	0.8	0.8	9.2	...	-4.0
1936	78.5	3.9	0.7	0.7	8.2	...	-4.3	5.0	0.9	0.9	10.5	...	-5.5
1937	87.8	5.4	1.1	1.0	7.6	...	-2.2	6.1	1.2	1.2	8.6	...	-2.5
1938	89.0	6.8	1.3	1.3	6.8	...	-0.1	7.6	1.4	1.4	7.7	...	-0.1
1939	89.1	6.3	1.0	1.1	9.1	...	-2.8	7.1	1.2	1.3	10.3	...	-3.2
1940	96.8	6.5	0.9	1.2	9.5	1.7	-2.9	6.8	0.9	1.2	9.8	1.7	-3.0
1941	114.1	8.7	1.3	2.1	13.7	6.4	-4.9	7.6	1.2	1.9	12.0	5.6	-4.3
1942	144.3	14.6	3.3	4.7	35.1	25.7	-20.5	10.1	2.3	3.3	24.3	17.8	-14.2
1943	180.3	24.0	6.5	9.6	78.6	66.7	-54.6	13.3	3.6	5.3	43.6	37.0	-30.3
1944	209.2	43.7	19.7	14.8	91.3	79.1	-47.6	20.9	9.4	7.1	43.6	37.8	-22.7
1945	221.4	45.2	18.4	16.0	92.7	83.0	-47.6	20.4	8.3	7.2	41.9	37.5	-21.5
1946	222.6	39.3	16.1	11.9	55.2	42.7	-15.9	17.7	7.2	5.3	24.8	19.2	-7.2
1947	233.2	38.5	17.9	8.6	34.5	12.8	4.0	16.5	7.7	3.7	14.8	5.5	1.7
1948	256.6	41.6	19.3	9.7	29.8	9.1	11.8	16.2	7.5	3.8	11.6	3.5	4.6
1949	271.3	39.4	15.6	11.2	38.8	13.2	0.6	14.5	5.7	4.1	14.3	4.8	0.2
1950	273.1	39.4	15.8	10.4	42.6	13.7	-3.1	14.4	5.8	3.8	15.6	5.0	-1.1
1951	320.2	51.6	21.6	14.1	45.5	23.6	6.1	16.1	6.8	4.4	14.2	7.4	1.9
1952	348.7	66.2	27.9	21.2	67.7	46.1	-1.5	19.0	8.0	6.1	19.4	13.2	-0.4
1953	372.5	69.6	29.8	21.2	76.1	52.8	-6.5	18.7	8.0	5.7	20.4	14.2	-1.7
1954	377.0	69.7	29.5	21.1	70.9	49.3	-1.2	18.5	7.8	5.6	18.8	13.1	-0.3
1955	395.9	65.5	28.7	17.9	68.4	42.7	-3.0	16.5	7.3	4.5	17.3	10.8	-0.8
1956	427.0	74.6	32.2	20.9	70.6	42.5	3.9	17.5	7.5	4.9	16.5	10.0	0.9
1957	450.9	80.0	35.6	21.2	76.6	45.4	3.4	17.7	7.9	4.7	17.0	10.1	0.8
1958	460.0	79.6	34.7	20.1	82.4	46.8	-2.8	17.3	7.5	4.4	17.9	10.2	-0.6
1959	490.2	79.2	36.7	17.3	92.1	49.0	-12.8	16.2	7.5	3.5	18.8	10.0	-2.6
1960	518.9	92.5	40.7	21.5	92.2	48.1	0.3	17.8	7.8	4.1	17.8	9.3	0.1
1961	529.9	94.4	41.3	21.0	97.7	49.6	-3.3	17.8	7.8	4.0	18.4	9.4	-0.6
1962	567.8	99.7	45.6	20.5	106.8	52.3	-7.1	17.6	8.0	3.6	18.8	9.2	-1.3
1963	599.2	106.6	47.6	21.6	111.3	53.4	-4.8	17.8	7.9	3.6	18.6	8.9	-0.8
1964	641.5	112.6	48.7	23.5	118.5	54.8	-5.9	17.6	7.6	3.7	18.5	8.5	-0.9
1965	687.5	116.8	48.8	25.5	118.2	50.6	-1.4	17.0	7.1	3.7	17.2	7.4	-0.2
1966	755.8	130.8	55.4	30.1	134.5	58.1	-3.7	17.3	7.3	4.0	17.8	7.7	-0.5
1967	810.0	148.8	61.5	34.0	157.5	71.4	-8.6	18.4	7.6	4.2	19.4	8.8	-1.1
1968	868.4	153.0	68.7	28.7	178.1	81.9	-25.2	17.6	7.9	3.3	20.5	9.4	-2.9
1969	948.1	186.9	87.2	36.7	183.6	82.5	3.2	19.7	9.2	3.9	19.4	8.7	0.3
1970	1 012.7	192.8	90.4	32.8	195.6	81.7	-2.8	19.0	8.9	3.2	19.3	8.1	-0.3
1971	1 080.0	187.1	86.2	26.8	210.2	78.9	-23.0	17.3	8.0	2.5	19.5	7.3	-2.1
1972	1 176.5	207.3	94.7	32.2	230.7	79.2	-23.4	17.6	8.1	2.7	19.6	6.7	-2.0
1973	1 310.6	230.8	103.2	36.2	245.7	76.7	-14.9	17.6	7.9	2.8	18.7	5.9	-1.1
1974	1 438.5	263.2	119.0	38.6	269.4	79.3	-6.1	18.3	8.3	2.7	18.7	5.5	-0.4
1975	1 560.2	279.1	122.4	40.6	332.3	86.5	-53.2	17.9	7.8	2.6	21.3	5.5	-3.4
1976	1 738.1	298.1	131.6	41.4	371.8	89.6	-73.7	17.1	7.6	2.4	21.4	5.2	-4.2
1977	1 973.5	355.6	157.6	54.9	409.2	97.2	-53.7	18.0	8.0	2.8	20.7	4.9	-2.7
1978	2 217.5	399.6	181.0	60.0	458.7	104.5	-59.2	18.0	8.2	2.7	20.7	4.7	-2.7
1979	2 501.4	463.3	217.8	65.7	504.0	116.3	-40.7	18.5	8.7	2.6	20.1	4.7	-1.6
1980	2 724.2	517.1	244.1	64.6	590.9	134.0	-73.8	19.0	9.0	2.4	21.7	4.9	-2.7
1981	3 057.0	599.3	285.9	61.1	678.2	157.5	-79.0	19.6	9.4	2.0	22.2	5.2	-2.6
1982	3 223.7	617.8	297.7	49.2	745.7	185.3	-128.0	19.2	9.2	1.5	23.1	5.7	-4.0
1983	3 440.7	600.6	288.9	37.0	808.4	209.9	-207.8	17.5	8.4	1.1	23.5	6.1	-6.0
1984	3 844.4	666.4	298.4	56.9	851.8	227.4	-185.4	17.3	7.8	1.5	22.2	5.9	-4.8
1985	4 146.3	734.0	334.5	61.3	946.3	252.7	-212.3	17.7	8.1	1.5	22.8	6.1	-5.1
1986	4 403.9	769.2	349.0	63.1	990.4	273.4	-221.2	17.5	7.9	1.4	22.5	6.2	-5.0
1987	4 651.4	854.3	392.6	83.9	1 004.0	282.0	-149.7	18.4	8.4	1.8	21.6	6.1	-3.2
1988	5 008.5	909.2	401.2	94.5	1 064.4	290.4	-155.2	18.2	8.0	1.9	21.3	5.8	-3.1
1989	5 399.5	991.1	445.7	103.3	1 143.7	303.6	-152.6	18.4	8.3	1.9	21.2	5.6	-2.8
1990	5 734.5	1 032.0	466.9	93.5	1 253.0	299.3	-221.0	18.0	8.1	1.6	21.9	5.2	-3.9
1991	5 930.5	1 055.0	467.8	98.1	1 324.2	273.3	-269.2	17.8	7.9	1.7	22.3	4.6	-4.5
1992	6 242.0	1 091.2	476.0	100.3	1 381.5	298.3	-290.3	17.5	7.6	1.6	22.1	4.8	-4.7
1993	6 587.3	1 154.3	509.7	117.5	1 409.4	291.1	-255.1	17.5	7.7	1.8	21.4	4.4	-3.9
1994	6 976.6	1 258.6	543.1	140.4	1 461.8	281.6	-203.2	18.0	7.8	2.0	21.0	4.0	-2.9

. . . = Not available.

Table 6-14B. The Federal Budget and GDP—*Continued*

(Billions of dollars; percent.)

Year		Billions of dollars							Percent of GDP					
	Fiscal year GDP	Receipts			Outlays		Budget surplus or deficit		Receipts			Outlays		Budget surplus or deficit
		Total	Individual income taxes	Corporate income taxes	Total	National defense			Total	Individual income taxes	Corporate income taxes	Total	National defense	
1995	7 341.1	1 351.8	590.2	157.0	1 515.7	272.1	-164.0		18.4	8.0	2.1	20.6	3.7	-2.2
1996	7 718.3	1 453.1	656.4	171.8	1 560.5	265.7	-107.4		18.8	8.5	2.2	20.2	3.4	-1.4
1997	8 211.7	1 579.2	737.5	182.3	1 601.1	270.5	-21.9		19.2	9.0	2.2	19.5	3.3	-0.3
1998	8 663.0	1 721.7	828.6	188.7	1 652.5	268.2	69.3		19.9	9.6	2.2	19.1	3.1	0.8
1999	9 208.4	1 827.5	879.5	184.7	1 701.8	274.8	125.6		19.8	9.6	2.0	18.5	3.0	1.4
2000	9 821.0	2 025.2	1 004.5	207.3	1 789.0	294.4	236.2		20.6	10.2	2.1	18.2	3.0	2.4
2001	10 225.3	1 991.1	994.3	151.1	1 862.8	304.7	128.2		19.5	9.7	1.5	18.2	3.0	1.3
2002	10 543.9	1 853.1	858.3	148.0	2 010.9	348.5	-157.8		17.6	8.1	1.4	19.1	3.3	-1.5
2003	10 980.2	1 782.3	793.7	131.8	2 159.9	404.7	-377.6		16.2	7.2	1.2	19.7	3.7	-3.4
2004	11 676.0	1 880.1	809.0	189.4	2 292.8	455.8	-412.7		16.1	6.9	1.6	19.6	3.9	-3.5
2005	12 428.6	2 153.6	927.2	278.3	2 472.0	495.3	-318.3		17.3	7.5	2.2	19.9	4.0	-2.6
2006	13 206.5	2 406.9	1 043.9	353.9	2 655.1	521.8	-248.2		18.2	7.9	2.7	20.1	4.0	-1.9
2007	13 861.4	2 568.0	1 163.5	370.2	2 728.7	551.3	-160.7		18.5	8.4	2.7	19.7	4.0	-1.2
2008	14 334.4	2 524.0	1 145.7	304.3	2 982.5	616.1	-458.6		17.6	8.0	2.1	20.8	4.3	-3.2
2009	13 960.7	2 105.0	915.3	138.2	3 517.7	661.0	-1 412.7		15.1	6.6	1.0	25.2	4.7	-10.1
2010	14 348.4	2 162.7	898.5	191.4	3 457.1	693.5	-1 294.4		15.1	6.3	1.3	24.1	4.8	-9.0
2011	14 929.4	2 303.5	1 091.5	181.1	3 603.1	705.6	-1 299.6		15.4	7.3	1.2	24.1	4.7	-8.7
2012	15 547.4	2 450.2	1 132.2	242.3	3 537.1	677.9	-1 087.0		15.8	7.3	1.6	22.8	4.4	-7.0

Table 6-15. Federal Government Debt by Fiscal Year

(Billions of dollars, except as noted.)

Year	Federal government debt held by the public at end of fiscal year		Gross federal debt at end of fiscal year held by:						
	Debt held by the public	Debt/GDP ratio (percent)	Total	Social Security funds	Other U.S. government accounts	Federal Reserve System	Private investors		
							Total	Foreign residents	Domestic investors
1940	43	44.2	51	2	6	2	40	. . .	. . .
1941	48	42.3	58	2	7	2	46	. . .	. . .
1942	68	47.0	79	3	8	3	65	. . .	. . .
1943	128	70.9	143	4	11	7	121	. . .	. . .
1944	185	88.3	204	5	14	15	170	. . .	. . .
1945	235	106.2	260	7	18	22	213	. . .	. . .
1946	242	108.7	271	8	21	24	218	. . .	. . .
1947	224	96.2	257	9	24	22	202	. . .	. . .
1948	216	84.3	252	10	26	21	195	. . .	. . .
1949	214	79.0	253	11	27	19	195	. . .	. . .
1950	219	80.2	257	13	25	18	201	. . .	. . .
1951	214	66.9	255	15	26	23	191	. . .	. . .
1952	215	61.6	259	17	28	23	192	. . .	. . .
1953	218	58.6	266	18	29	25	194	. . .	. . .
1954	224	59.5	271	20	26	25	199	. . .	. . .
1955	227	57.2	274	21	27	24	203	. . .	. . .
1956	222	52.0	273	23	28	24	198	. . .	. . .
1957	219	48.6	272	23	30	23	196	. . .	. . .
1958	226	49.2	280	24	29	25	201	. . .	. . .
1959	235	47.9	287	23	30	26	209	. . .	. . .
1960	237	45.6	291	23	31	27	210	. . .	. . .
1961	238	45.0	293	23	31	27	211	. . .	. . .
1962	248	43.7	303	22	33	30	218	. . .	. . .
1963	254	42.4	310	21	35	32	222	. . .	. . .
1964	257	40.0	316	22	37	35	222	. . .	. . .
1965	261	37.9	322	22	39	39	222	12	210
1966	264	34.9	328	22	43	42	222	12	210
1967	267	32.9	340	26	48	47	220	11	209
1968	290	33.3	369	28	51	52	237	11	226
1969	278	29.3	366	32	56	54	224	10	214
1970	283	28.0	381	38	60	58	225	14	211
1971	303	28.1	408	41	64	66	238	32	206
1972	322	27.4	436	44	70	71	251	49	202
1973	341	26.0	466	44	81	75	266	59	207
1974	344	23.9	484	46	94	81	263	57	206
1975	395	25.3	542	48	99	85	310	66	244
1976	477	27.5	629	45	107	95	383	70	313
1977	549	27.8	706	40	118	105	444	96	348
1978	607	27.4	777	35	134	115	492	121	371
1979	640	25.6	829	33	156	116	525	120	405
1980	712	26.1	909	32	165	121	591	122	469
1981	789	25.8	995	27	178	124	665	131	534
1982	925	28.7	1 137	19	193	134	790	141	649
1983	1 137	33.1	1 372	32	202	156	982	160	822
1984	1 307	34.0	1 565	32	225	155	1 152	176	976
1985	1 507	36.4	1 817	40	270	170	1 337	223	1 114
1986	1 741	39.5	2 121	46	334	191	1 550	266	1 284
1987	1 890	40.6	2 346	65	391	212	1 678	280	1 398
1988	2 052	41.0	2 601	104	445	229	1 822	346	1 476
1989	2 191	40.6	2 868	157	520	220	1 971	395	1 576
1990	2 412	42.1	3 206	215	580	234	2 177	464	1 713
1991	2 689	45.3	3 598	268	641	259	2 430	506	1 924
1992	3 000	48.1	4 002	319	683	296	2 703	563	2 140
1993	3 248	49.3	4 351	366	737	326	2 923	619	2 304
1994	3 433	49.2	4 643	423	788	355	3 078	682	2 396
1995	3 604	49.1	4 921	483	833	374	3 230	820	2 410
1996	3 734	48.4	5 181	550	898	391	3 343	993	2 350
1997	3 772	45.9	5 369	631	966	425	3 348	1 231	2 117
1998	3 721	43.0	5 478	730	1 027	458	3 263	1 224	2 039
1999	3 632	39.4	5 606	855	1 118	497	3 136	1 281	1 855
2000	3 410	34.7	5 629	1 007	1 212	511	2 898	1 039	1 859
2001	3 320	32.5	5 770	1 170	1 280	534	2 785	1 006	1 779
2002	3 540	33.6	6 198	1 329	1 329	604	2 936	1 201	1 735
2003	3 913	35.6	6 760	1 485	1 362	656	3 257	1 454	1 803
2004	4 296	36.8	7 355	1 635	1 424	700	3 595	1 799	1 796
2005	4 592	36.9	7 905	1 809	1 504	736	3 856	1 930	1 926
2006	4 829	36.6	8 451	1 994	1 628	769	4 060	2 025	2 035
2007	5 035	36.3	8 951	2 181	1 735	780	4 255	2 235	2 020
2008	5 803	40.5	9 986	2 366	1 817	491	5 312	2 802	2 510
2009	7 545	54.0	11 876	2 504	1 827	769	6 776	3 571	3 205
2010	9 019	62.9	13 529	2 585	1 925	812	8 207	4 324	3 883
2011	10 128	67.8	14 764	2 654	1 982	1 665	8 464	4 912	3 551
2012	11 281	72.6	16 051	2 718	2 052	1 645	9 636	5 475	4 160

. . . = Not available.

Section 6d: Government Output and Employment

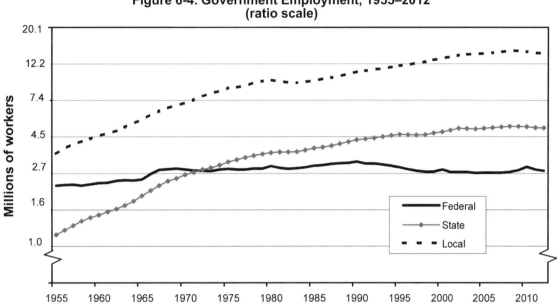

Figure 6-4. Government Employment, 1955–2012
(ratio scale)

- Since 1955, total reported employment of civilians by all levels of government has increased 212 percent—an annual rate of 2.0 percent per year—and government's proportion of total nonfarm payroll employment has risen from 13.8 percent to 16.4 percent. Federal employment rose 23 percent; state government employment rose 333 percent, with 53 percent of this increase due to education; and local government rose 295 percent, with 57 percent of this increase due to education. (Tables 6-17 and 10-8B)

- Contracting and outsourcing of federal government spending can be seen in comparisons between government purchases and government value added. From 1955 to 2012, the volume (measured by the quantity index) of "intermediate" goods and services purchased for nondefense purposes rose 1- 1/2 times as fast as real nondefense value added by government itself. (Real value added comprises the input of government employees and government-owned capital, valued in constant dollars). For defense, government value added rose 25 percent over that period, while purchases of goods and services rose 180 percent in real terms. (Table 6-16)

- A similar process has occurred at state and local governments, where real value added increased 331 percent while goods and services purchased rose 1,058 percent. (Table 6-16)

Table 6-16. Chain-Type Quantity Indexes for Government Output

(Seasonally adjusted, 2009 = 100.)　　　　　　　　　　　　　　　　　　　　　　　　**NIPA Table 3.10.3**

| Year and quarter | Federal government | | | | | | | | | State and local government | | |
| | Gross output of general government | | | Value added | | | Intermediate goods and services purchased [1] | | | Gross output of general government | Value added | Intermediate goods and services purchased [1] |
	Total	Defense	Nondefense	Total	Defense	Nondefense	Total	Defense	Nondefense			
1955	46.5	60.3	22.5	59.9	83.0	22.8	27.4	33.4	16.1	17.3	22.8	8.1
1956	44.8	59.7	18.8	59.7	82.4	23.3	24.4	32.9	9.7	18.0	24.3	7.8
1957	46.5	62.4	18.6	60.2	82.7	24.1	27.1	37.9	8.8	18.9	25.6	8.2
1958	46.0	61.8	18.0	59.2	80.7	25.0	27.0	38.8	7.0	20.5	27.2	9.4
1959	45.1	56.4	25.3	59.3	80.6	25.4	25.1	27.5	19.2	21.4	28.3	10.0
1960	44.0	56.8	21.6	61.0	82.1	27.4	21.0	26.7	10.4	22.5	29.8	10.5
1961	44.9	58.2	21.5	62.9	84.6	28.5	20.5	26.9	9.0	23.8	31.3	11.2
1962	49.4	63.0	25.5	66.0	88.4	30.4	26.4	32.6	14.5	24.6	32.5	11.7
1963	49.8	63.1	26.3	67.2	88.9	32.8	25.8	32.5	13.2	26.0	34.2	12.4
1964	49.6	62.1	27.5	68.5	89.8	34.7	23.7	29.0	13.5	27.8	36.2	13.6
1965	50.7	63.1	28.8	69.6	90.3	36.7	24.8	30.6	13.7	29.7	38.4	15.0
1966	56.0	71.7	28.4	74.4	96.4	39.4	30.5	42.1	9.8	31.6	40.7	16.2
1967	62.3	79.9	31.2	79.4	102.8	42.4	37.7	52.4	11.8	33.2	42.4	17.5
1968	64.6	83.4	31.5	81.4	104.6	44.6	40.3	57.9	9.8	35.5	45.0	19.3
1969	63.9	80.8	34.2	82.3	105.0	46.3	37.8	51.6	13.1	37.6	47.0	21.4
1970	60.2	74.4	35.2	79.7	99.8	47.8	32.9	43.7	13.4	39.8	49.1	23.6
1971	57.7	68.9	37.9	76.8	93.8	49.9	31.0	38.6	16.5	41.9	51.1	25.8
1972	56.7	65.2	41.4	73.9	88.0	51.7	32.4	37.5	21.8	43.7	52.9	27.4
1973	54.0	61.1	41.2	71.9	84.2	52.6	28.8	32.7	20.3	45.2	54.8	28.2
1974	54.0	59.7	43.7	72.0	82.8	55.1	28.6	31.2	22.5	46.9	56.8	29.5
1975	53.6	58.1	45.4	71.9	81.7	56.5	27.8	29.0	24.3	48.9	58.5	31.9
1976	52.6	56.5	45.5	72.1	80.5	59.2	25.3	27.0	21.0	49.8	59.3	32.9
1977	53.6	56.9	47.5	72.5	80.1	60.9	26.9	28.4	23.0	50.8	60.2	34.0
1978	54.6	57.3	49.6	73.6	80.5	63.1	27.8	28.8	24.7	52.1	61.6	35.0
1979	55.4	57.9	50.9	73.9	80.3	64.1	29.2	30.2	26.2	52.8	62.8	35.0
1980	57.5	59.6	53.6	75.2	81.0	66.4	32.0	32.9	29.1	52.8	63.6	33.7
1981	59.6	62.6	54.3	76.6	83.4	66.1	34.9	36.2	30.9	52.8	63.6	33.9
1982	61.5	66.1	53.0	78.1	85.8	66.2	37.1	40.7	28.0	53.8	64.0	35.4
1983	64.6	69.0	56.5	80.2	88.4	67.5	41.1	43.8	34.0	54.6	63.8	37.8
1984	65.4	71.0	54.9	82.4	91.5	68.3	40.1	44.5	29.3	55.7	64.2	39.8
1985	69.0	74.9	57.9	85.3	95.5	69.2	44.3	47.9	35.0	58.1	66.0	43.1
1986	72.3	78.9	59.9	87.5	98.9	69.3	48.9	52.5	39.4	60.7	68.0	46.7
1987	73.8	81.7	58.9	90.3	102.5	70.8	48.6	54.2	34.9	62.0	69.3	47.7
1988	74.1	83.6	56.2	92.1	104.3	72.7	47.0	56.2	25.6	64.0	71.7	49.2
1989	75.9	84.1	60.6	93.6	106.1	73.8	49.2	55.2	35.0	66.3	73.9	51.6
1990	77.6	84.7	64.4	95.4	107.0	77.0	50.7	55.3	39.7	68.4	76.1	53.3
1991	78.6	85.7	65.3	96.0	107.4	77.9	52.1	57.0	40.6	70.0	77.1	56.0
1992	77.4	82.3	68.3	94.4	103.9	79.6	51.4	53.8	45.6	71.8	78.4	58.7
1993	75.2	79.5	67.3	92.9	100.9	80.4	48.5	51.4	41.5	73.4	79.5	61.3
1994	73.5	76.5	68.0	90.3	97.2	79.8	48.0	49.4	44.7	75.5	80.9	64.7
1995	71.0	73.0	67.3	87.5	93.3	78.5	45.9	46.4	44.8	77.4	82.5	67.3
1996	69.7	71.8	65.9	85.4	90.2	78.1	45.7	47.4	41.8	78.9	83.8	69.1
1997	69.5	70.6	67.7	84.0	87.6	78.5	47.4	48.0	46.0	81.2	85.4	72.6
1998	68.4	68.6	68.0	83.1	85.2	79.9	45.9	46.5	44.2	84.3	87.2	78.3
1999	69.1	69.7	68.1	82.5	83.4	81.1	48.5	51.2	42.0	87.0	88.7	83.7
2000	69.6	68.9	71.0	83.0	82.5	83.8	49.1	50.6	45.7	89.4	90.5	87.0
2001	72.3	71.1	74.5	83.3	82.5	84.7	55.1	55.6	53.9	92.8	92.7	93.2
2002	76.6	75.0	79.5	84.8	83.6	86.6	63.8	63.3	65.0	95.3	94.5	96.8
2003	81.5	80.8	82.9	87.0	85.9	88.8	72.8	73.6	70.7	94.9	95.1	94.3
2004	84.7	84.7	84.8	88.4	87.9	89.1	79.0	80.2	76.1	95.1	95.5	94.3
2005	86.1	85.8	86.6	89.6	89.4	89.9	80.6	80.9	79.8	95.7	96.1	94.7
2006	87.5	87.0	88.5	90.3	89.9	91.1	83.0	82.8	83.4	96.7	96.9	96.2
2007	88.3	88.3	88.2	91.6	91.1	92.5	82.9	84.4	79.5	98.1	98.3	97.6
2008	94.0	94.3	93.6	95.1	94.8	95.7	92.3	93.6	89.4	98.2	99.6	95.2
2009	100.0	100.0	100.0	100.0	100.0	100.0	100.0	100.0	100.0	100.0	100.0	100.0
2010	104.3	103.5	105.8	103.4	103.2	103.8	105.8	104.0	110.1	98.3	99.3	96.2
2011	102.2	102.2	102.2	104.4	104.7	104.1	98.7	98.8	98.3	96.6	98.3	92.9
2012	101.1	99.4	104.2	104.4	103.8	105.4	95.9	93.4	101.8	96.9	98.3	93.8
2010												
1st quarter	102.7	101.9	104.3	102.3	102.4	102.1	103.4	101.1	108.6	99.2	99.7	98.1
2nd quarter	104.6	103.1	107.5	103.9	103.0	105.5	105.8	103.3	111.5	98.7	99.6	96.7
3rd quarter	105.7	105.3	106.5	103.6	103.5	103.8	109.0	107.8	112.0	98.0	99.2	95.5
4th quarter	104.3	103.9	105.1	103.8	104.0	103.6	105.1	103.7	108.2	97.4	98.9	94.3
2011												
1st quarter	102.0	101.2	103.4	104.3	104.2	104.3	98.4	97.0	101.7	96.9	98.6	93.3
2nd quarter	102.6	103.0	102.0	104.4	104.5	104.2	99.7	100.7	97.4	96.6	98.4	92.8
3rd quarter	103.1	104.1	101.5	104.4	104.8	103.8	101.1	103.0	96.5	96.4	98.1	92.7
4th quarter	101.1	100.7	101.9	104.7	105.1	104.0	95.5	94.5	97.7	96.4	98.1	92.8
2012												
1st quarter	101.2	99.9	103.4	104.6	104.3	105.2	95.6	93.9	99.8	96.6	98.2	93.3
2nd quarter	100.9	99.1	104.1	104.4	103.9	105.4	95.2	92.5	101.4	96.8	98.2	93.8
3rd quarter	103.4	102.7	104.5	104.3	103.7	105.3	101.8	101.4	102.7	97.0	98.5	94.0
4th quarter	99.0	95.9	104.9	104.1	103.2	105.6	90.9	85.6	103.3	97.0	98.4	94.1

[1]Includes general government intermediate inputs for goods and services sold to other sectors and for own-account investment.

Table 6-17. Government Employment

(Calendar years, payroll employment in thousands.)

Year and month	Total government employment	Federal			State			Local		
		Total	Department of Defense	Postal Service	Total	Education	State government hospitals	Total	Education	Local government hospitals
1950	6 120	2 023	533	516	. . .	. . .	. . .	. . .	. . .	. . .
1951	6 502	2 415	797	521	. . .	. . .	. . .	. . .	. . .	. . .
1952	6 727	2 539	868	542	. . .	. . .	. . .	. . .	. . .	. . .
1953	6 758	2 418	818	530	. . .	. . .	. . .	. . .	. . .	. . .
1954	6 858	2 295	744	533	. . .	. . .	. . .	. . .	. . .	. . .
1955	7 021	2 295	744	534	1 168	308	. . .	3 558	1 751	. . .
1956	7 386	2 318	749	539	1 249	334	. . .	3 819	1 884	. . .
1957	7 724	2 326	729	555	1 328	363	. . .	4 071	2 026	. . .
1958	7 946	2 298	695	567	1 415	389	. . .	4 232	2 115	. . .
1959	8 192	2 342	699	578	1 484	420	. . .	4 366	2 198	. . .
1960	8 464	2 381	681	591	1 536	448	. . .	4 547	2 314	. . .
1961	8 706	2 391	683	601	1 607	474	. . .	4 708	2 411	. . .
1962	9 004	2 455	697	601	1 669	511	. . .	4 881	2 522	. . .
1963	9 341	2 473	687	603	1 747	557	. . .	5 121	2 674	. . .
1964	9 711	2 463	676	604	1 856	609	. . .	5 392	2 839	. . .
1965	10 191	2 495	679	619	1 996	679	. . .	5 700	3 031	. . .
1966	10 910	2 690	741	686	2 141	775	. . .	6 080	3 297	. . .
1967	11 525	2 852	802	719	2 302	873	. . .	6 371	3 490	. . .
1968	11 972	2 871	801	729	2 442	958	. . .	6 660	3 649	. . .
1969	12 330	2 893	815	737	2 533	1 042	. . .	6 904	3 785	. . .
1970	12 687	2 865	756	741	2 664	1 104	. . .	7 158	3 912	. . .
1971	13 012	2 828	731	731	2 747	1 149	. . .	7 437	4 091	. . .
1972	13 465	2 815	720	703	2 859	1 188	459	7 790	4 262	467
1973	13 862	2 794	696	698	2 923	1 205	472	8 146	4 433	477
1974	14 303	2 858	698	710	3 039	1 267	483	8 407	4 584	483
1975	14 820	2 882	704	699	3 179	1 323	503	8 758	4 722	489
1976	15 001	2 863	693	676	3 273	1 371	518	8 865	4 786	492
1977	15 258	2 859	676	657	3 377	1 385	538	9 023	4 859	494
1978	15 812	2 893	661	660	3 474	1 367	541	9 446	4 958	535
1979	16 068	2 894	649	673	3 541	1 378	538	9 633	4 989	571
1980	16 375	3 000	645	673	3 610	1 398	530	9 765	5 090	604
1981	16 180	2 922	655	675	3 640	1 420	515	9 619	5 095	622
1982	15 982	2 884	690	684	3 640	1 433	494	9 458	5 049	635
1983	16 011	2 915	699	685	3 662	1 450	471	9 434	5 020	644
1984	16 159	2 943	716	706	3 734	1 488	459	9 482	5 076	623
1985	16 533	3 014	738	750	3 832	1 540	449	9 687	5 221	608
1986	16 838	3 044	736	792	3 893	1 561	438	9 901	5 358	601
1987	17 156	3 089	736	815	3 967	1 586	439	10 100	5 469	606
1988	17 540	3 124	719	835	4 076	1 621	446	10 339	5 590	619
1989	17 927	3 136	735	838	4 182	1 668	442	10 609	5 740	632
1990	18 415	3 196	722	825	4 305	1 730	426	10 914	5 902	646
1991	18 545	3 110	702	813	4 355	1 768	417	11 081	5 994	653
1992	18 787	3 111	702	800	4 408	1 799	419	11 267	6 076	665
1993	18 989	3 063	670	793	4 488	1 834	414	11 438	6 206	673
1994	19 275	3 018	657	821	4 576	1 882	407	11 682	6 329	673
1995	19 432	2 949	627	850	4 635	1 919	395	11 849	6 453	669
1996	19 539	2 877	597	867	4 606	1 911	376	12 056	6 592	648
1997	19 664	2 806	588	866	4 582	1 904	360	12 276	6 759	632
1998	19 909	2 772	550	881	4 612	1 922	346	12 525	6 921	630
1999	20 307	2 769	525	890	4 709	1 983	344	12 829	7 120	626
2000	20 790	2 865	510	880	4 786	2 031	343	13 139	7 294	622
2001	21 118	2 764	504	873	4 905	2 113	345	13 449	7 479	628
2002	21 513	2 766	499	842	5 029	2 243	349	13 718	7 654	642
2003	21 583	2 761	486	809	5 002	2 255	348	13 820	7 709	651
2004	21 621	2 730	473	782	4 982	2 238	348	13 909	7 765	656
2005	21 804	2 732	488	774	5 032	2 260	350	14 041	7 856	655
2006	21 974	2 732	493	770	5 075	2 293	357	14 167	7 913	647
2007	22 218	2 734	491	769	5 122	2 318	360	14 362	7 987	654
2008	22 509	2 762	496	747	5 177	2 354	361	14 571	8 084	659
2009	22 555	2 832	519	703	5 169	2 360	359	14 554	8 079	661
2010	22 490	2 977	545	659	5 137	2 373	354	14 376	8 013	650
2011	22 086	2 859	559	631	5 078	2 374	348	14 150	7 873	648
2012	21 917	2 814	550	611	5 052	2 385	347	14 051	7 779	654

. . . = Not available.

NOTES AND DEFINITIONS, CHAPTER 6

Tables 6-1 through 6-13 and 6-16: Federal, State, and Local Government in the National Income and Product Accounts

SOURCE: U.S. DEPARTMENT OF COMMERCE, BUREAU OF ECONOMIC ANALYSIS (BEA)

These data are from the national income and product accounts (NIPAs), as published in the 2013 comprehensive NIPA revision. For general information about the NIPAs and the 2013 revision, see the notes and definitions for Chapter 1.

Changes in definitions made in this latest revision had significant effects on some components of the government accounts. Recognition of research and development spending as fixed, depreciable capital investment increased the amount of investment and capital consumption charges. The change to accrual accounting for defined benefit plans, which increased personal income and saving by recognizing benefits of such plans when earned instead of when paid, generally increased employee compensation spending and government deficits. (An exception occurs in the Federal accounts in some years when the Federal government has made large cash contributions to its pension funds as "catch up" payments, which under the previous cash accounting was registered as personal income and compensation at the time instead of when accrued. In those years, the redefinition makes employee compensation smaller.)

The framework for the government accounts

In the 2003 revision, a new framework was introduced for government consumption expenditures—federal, state, and local—that explicitly recognizes the services produced by general government. Governments serve several functions in the economy. Three of these functions are recognized in the NIPAs: the production of nonmarket services; the consumption of these services, as the value of services provided to the general public is treated as government consumption expenditures; and the provision of transfer payments. These functions are financed through taxation, through contributions to social insurance funds, and in the world's capital markets.

In this framework, the value of the government services produced and consumed (most of which are not sold in the market) is measured as the sum of the costs of the three major inputs: compensation of government employees, consumption of fixed capital (CFC), and intermediate goods and services purchased. The purchase from the private sector of goods and services by government, classified as final sales to

government before the 2003 revision, was reclassified as intermediate purchases.

The value of government final purchases of consumption expenditures and gross investment, which constitutes the contribution of government demand to the gross domestic product (GDP), was not changed by this reclassification, since the previous definition of that contribution was the sum of compensation, CFC, and goods and services purchased. However, the distribution of GDP by type of product was changed—final sales of goods were reduced by the amount of goods purchased by government, and services were increased by the same amount.

In addition to this change in the conceptual framework, a number of the categories of government receipts and expenditures were redefined to make more precise distinctions. For example, items that used to be called "nontax payments" and included with taxes are now classified as transfer or fee payments and not included in taxes.

Finally, the concept previously known as "current surplus or deficit (-), national income and product accounts" was renamed "net government saving." This recognizes, in part, the role of government in the capital markets. When government runs a current surplus, net government saving is positive and funds are made available (for example, by repayment of outstanding debt) to finance investment—both private-sector capital spending and government investment. When government runs a current deficit, or "dis-saves," it must borrow funds that would otherwise be available to finance investment.

However, this definition of net government saving does not give a complete picture of governments' role in capital markets, because it is based on current receipts and expenditures alone and does not include government investment activity.

In the NIPAs, the capital spending of all levels of government is treated the same way as the accounts treat private investment spending. A depreciation, or more precisely "consumption of fixed capital" (CFC), entry for existing capital is calculated, using estimated replacement costs and realistic depreciation rates. In the government accounts this CFC value is entered as one element of current expenditures and output. Capital spending is excluded from government current expenditures but appears in the account for "net lending or borrowing (-)."

The basic concept expressed in the net lending section of the NIPAs is that when CFC exceeds actual investment expenditures, governments have a positive net cash flow and can lend (or repay debt); if gross investment exceeds CFC, government must borrow to finance the difference, indicating negative net cash flow and requiring borrowing. (As will be seen below in the definitions, capital transfer and purchase accounts also enter into the calculation of net lending.)

The federal *budget* accounts (see Tables 6-14 and 6-15) do not draw a distinction between current and capital spending. The budget accounts of individual state and local governments typically separate capital from current spending and allow capital spending to be financed by borrowing—even when deficit financing of current spending is constitutionally forbidden. However, neither federal nor state and local government budget accounts typically show depreciation as a current expense in the way that is standard to private-sector accounting or in the way adopted in the NIPAs.

Notes on the data

Government receipts and expenditures data are derived from the U.S. government accounts and from Census Bureau censuses and surveys of the finances of state and local governments. However, BEA makes a number of adjustments to the data to convert them from fiscal year to calendar year and quarter bases and to agree with the concepts of national income accounting. Data are converted from the cash basis usually found in financial statements to the timing bases required for the NIPAs. In the NIPAs, receipts from businesses are generally on an accrual basis, purchases of goods and services are recorded when delivered, and receipts from and transfer payments to persons are on a cash basis. The federal receipts and expenditure data from the NIPAs in Table 6-1 therefore differ from the federal receipts and outlay data in Table 6-14. Among other differences, the latter are by fiscal year and are on a modified cash basis.

The NIPA data on government receipts and expenditures record transactions of governments (federal, state, and local) with other U.S. residents and foreigners. Each entry in the government receipts and expenditures account has a corresponding entry elsewhere in the NIPAs. Thus, for example, the sum of personal current taxes received by federal and state and local governments (Tables 6-1 and 6-8) is equal to personal current taxes paid, as shown in personal income (Table 4-1).

Definitions: General

In the 2003 revision of the NIPAs, several items appear separately that were previously treated as "negative expenditures" and netted against other items on the expenditures side. This grossing-up of the accounts raises both receipts and outlays and has no effect on net saving. Grossing-

up has been applied to taxes from the rest of the world, interest receipts (back to 1960 for the federal government and back to 1946 for state and local governments), dividends, and subsidies and the current surplus of government enterprises (back to 1959).

Definitions: Current receipts

Current tax receipts includes personal current taxes, taxes on production and imports, taxes on corporate income and (for the federal government only) taxes from the rest of the world. The category *total tax receipts* does not include *contributions for government social insurance,* which are the taxes levied to finance Social Security, unemployment insurance, and Medicare, and are included in *receipts* in the budget accounts (Table 6-14). Analysts using NIPA data to analyze tax burdens as they are usually understood should add *contributions for government social insurance* to *tax receipts* for this purpose.

Personal current taxes is personal tax payments from residents of the United States that are not chargeable to business expense. Personal taxes consist of taxes on income, including on realized net capital gains, and on personal property. Personal contributions for social insurance are not included in this category. As of the 1999 revisions, estate and gift taxes are classified as capital transfers and are no longer included in personal current taxes. However, estate and gift taxes continue to be included in federal government receipts in Table 6-14.

Taxes on production and imports in the case of the federal government consists of *excise taxes* and *customs duties*. In the case of state and local governments, these taxes include *sales taxes*, *property taxes* (including residential real estate taxes), and *Other* taxes such as motor vehicle licenses, severance taxes, and special assessments. Before the 2003 revision, these taxes were a component of "indirect business tax and nontax liabilities."

Taxes on corporate income covers federal, state, and local government taxes on all corporate income subject to taxes. This taxable income includes capital gains and other income excluded from NIPA profits. The taxes are measured on an accrual basis, net of applicable tax credits. Federal corporate income tax receipts in the NIPAs include receipts from *Federal Reserve Banks* that represent the return of their surplus earnings. (In the budget accounts in Table 6-14, these are included under "Miscellaneous receipts.")

Contributions for social insurance includes employer and personal contributions for Social Security, Medicare, unemployment insurance, and other government social insurance programs. As of the 1999 revisions, contributions to government employee retirement plans are no longer included in this category; these plans are now treated the same as private pension plans.

Income receipts on assets consists of *interest*, *dividends* and *rents and royalties*.

Interest receipts (1960 to the present for federal government; 1946 to the present for state and local governments) consists of monetary and imputed interest received on loans and investments. In the NIPAs, this no longer includes interest received by government employee retirement plans, which is now credited to personal income. However, such interest received is still deducted from interest paid in the budget accounts that are shown in Table 6-14. Before the indicated years, receipts are deducted from aggregate interest payments in the NIPAs. Hence, they are not shown as receipts, and net interest is presented on the expenditure side. In the federal budget accounts in Table 6-14, net interest (total interest expenditures minus interest receipts) is the interest "expenditure" concept used throughout the period covered.

Current transfer receipts includes receipts in categories other than those specified above from persons and business. In the case of state and local government accounts (Table 6-8), it also includes *federal grants-in-aid,* a component of federal expenditures. Receipts from *business* and *persons* were previously included with income taxes in "tax and nontax payments." They consist of federal deposit insurance premiums and other nontaxes (largely fines and regulatory and inspection fees), state and local fines and other nontaxes (largely donations and tobacco settlements), and net insurance settlements paid to governments as policyholders.

The *current surplus of government enterprises* is the current operating revenue and subsidies received from other levels of government by such enterprises less their current expenses. No deduction is made for depreciation charges or net interest paid. Before 1959, this category of receipts is treated as a deduction from subsidies. In the federal NIPA accounts before 1959, there is no entry shown for the current surplus on the receipts side, and on the expenditure side, there is an entry for subsidies, which is net of the current surplus. (Subsidies are usually a larger amount than the enterprise surplus in the federal accounts.) In the state and local NIPA accounts before 1959, there is an entry for the surplus on the receipts side, which is net of subsidies. (Subsidies are typically smaller than the enterprise surplus in state and local finance.)

Definitions: Consumption expenditures, saving, and gross investment

Government consumption expenditures is expenditures by governments (federal or state and local) on services for current consumption. It includes *compensation of general government employees* (including employer contributions to government employee retirement plans, as of the 1999 revision); an allowance for *consumption of general government fixed capital (CFC),* including R&D and software (depreciation); and *intermediate goods and services purchased.* (See the general discussion above for an explanation.) The estimated value of *own-account investment*—investment goods, including R&D and software, produced by government resources and purchased inputs—is subtracted here, and added to *government gross investment. Sales to other sectors*—primarily tuition payments received from individuals for higher education and charges for medical care to individuals—are also deducted.

Government social benefits consists of payments to individuals for which the individuals do not render current services. Examples are Social Security benefits, Medicare, Medicaid, unemployment benefits, and public assistance. Retirement payments to retired government employees from their pension plans are no longer included in this category.

Government social benefits to persons consists of payments to persons residing in the United States (with a corresponding entry of an equal amount in the personal income receipts accounts). Government social benefits to the *rest of the world* appear only in the federal government account, and are transfers, mainly retirement benefits, to former residents of the United States.

Other current transfer payments (federal account only) includes *grants-in-aid to state and local governments* and *grants to the rest of the world*—military and nonmilitary grants to foreign governments.

Federal grants-in-aid comprises net payments from federal to state and local governments that are made to help finance programs such as health (Medicaid), public assistance (the old Aid to Families with Dependent Children and the new Temporary Assistance for Needy Families), and education. Investment grants to state and local governments for highways, transit, air transportation, and water treatment plants are now classified as capital transfers and are no longer included in this category. However, such investment grants continue to be included as federal government outlays in Table 6-14.

Interest payments is monetary interest paid to U.S. and foreign persons and businesses and to foreign governments for public debt and other financial obligations. As noted above, from 1960 forward for the federal government and from 1946 forward for state and local governments, this represents gross total (not net) interest payments. Before those dates in the NIPAs, and throughout the federal budget accounts presented in Table 6-14, net instead of aggregate interest is shown; that is, gross total interest paid less interest received.

Subsidies are monetary grants paid by government to business, including to government enterprises at another level of government. Subsidies no longer include federal maritime construction subsidies, which are now classified as a capital transfer. For years prior to 1959, subsidies continue to be presented net of the *current surplus of government enterprises*, because detailed data to separate the series are not available for this period. See the entry for *current surplus of government enterprises*, described above, for explanation of the pre-1959 treatment of this item in the federal accounts in *Business Statistics*, which differs from the treatment in the state and local accounts.

Net saving, NIPA (surplus+/deficit-), is the sum of current receipts less the sum of current expenditures. This is shown separately for *social insurance funds* (which, in the case of the federal government, include Social Security and other trust funds) and *other* (all other government).

Gross government investment consists of general government and government enterprise expenditures for fixed assets—*structures*, *equipment*, and *intellectual property* (R&D and software). The expenditures include the compensation of government employees producing the assets and the purchase of goods and services as intermediate inputs to be incorporated in the assets. Government inventory investment is included in government consumption expenditures.

Capital consumption. Consumption of fixed capital (CFC; economic depreciation) is included in government consumption expenditures as a partial measure of the value of the services of general government fixed assets, including structures, equipment, R&D, and software.

Definitions: Output, lending and borrowing, and net investment

In Tables 6-5 and 6-10, current-dollar values of gross output and value added of government are presented, as described in the general discussion above. *Gross output* of government is the sum of the *intermediate goods and services purchased* by government and the value added by government as a producing industry. *Value added* consists of compensation of general government employees and consumption of general

government fixed capital. Since this depreciation allowance is the only entry on the product side of the accounts measuring the output associated with such capital, a zero net return on these assets is implicitly assumed.

Gross output minus own-account investment and sales to other sectors (see the previous description) yields *government consumption expenditures*, which represents the contribution of government consumption spending to final demands in GDP.

Net lending (net borrowing -) consists of current *net saving* as defined above, plus the *consumption of fixed capital* (CFC, from the current expenditure account), minus *gross investment*, plus *capital transfer receipts*, and minus *capital transfer payments* and *net purchases of non-produced assets*.

Capital transfer receipts and *payments* include grants between levels of government, or between government and the private sector, associated with acquisition or disposal of assets rather than with current consumption expenditures. Examples are federal grants to state and local government for highways, transit, air transportation, and water treatment plants; federal shipbuilding subsidies and other subsidies to businesses; and lump-sum payments to amortize the unfunded liability of the Uniformed Services Retiree Health Care Fund. Government capital transfer receipts include estate and gift taxes, which are no longer included in personal tax receipts. (Federal estate and gift taxes are shown in Table 6-14 and, although they are reported on a fiscal year basis, are almost identical to the calendar year values for federal capital transfer receipts in Table 6-5.)

Non-produced assets are land and radio spectrum. Unusually large negative entries for net purchases of non-produced assets in recent years result from the negative purchase–that is, the sale–of spectrum.

The values of *net investment* shown in these tables are calculated by the editor, as gross investment minus the consumption of fixed capital.

Definitions: Chain-type quantity indexes

Chain-type quantity indexes represent changes over time in real values, removing the effects of inflation. Indexes for key categories in the government expenditure accounts, as well as for government gross output, value added, and intermediate goods and services purchased, use the chain formula described in the notes and definitions for Chapter 1 and are expressed as index numbers, with the average for the year 2009 equal to 100.

Data availability

The most recent data are published each month in the Survey of Current Business. Current and historical data may be obtained from the BEA Web site at http://www.bea.gov and the STAT-USA subscription Web site at http://www.stat-usa.gov.

References

See the references regarding the 2013 comprehensive revision of the NIPAs in the notes and definitions for Chapter 1. NIPA concepts and their differences from the budget estimates are discussed in "NIPA Estimates of the Federal Sector and the Federal Budget Estimates," *Survey of Current Business,* March 2007, p. 11.

For information about the classification of government expenditures into current consumption and gross investment, first undertaken in the 1996 comprehensive revisions, see the Survey of Current Business article, "Preview of the Comprehensive Revision of the National Income and Product Accounts: Recognition of Government Investment and Incorporation of a New Methodology for Calculating Depreciation" September 1995. Other sources of information about the NIPAs are listed in the notes and definitions for Chapter 1.

Tables 6-12 and 6-13: State Government Current Receipts and Expenditures; Local Government Current Receipts and Expenditures

SOURCE: BUREAU OF ECONOMIC ANALYSIS (BEA)

In the standard presentation of the state and local sector of the national income and product accounts (NIPAs) such as in Tables 6-8 through 6-11 above, state and local governments are combined. Annual measures for aggregate state governments and aggregate local governments are also available on the BEA Web site. These measures are shown in Tables 6-12 and 6-13. The definitions are the same as in the other NIPA tables described above.

These data, like other BEA annual-only tables, are available later than the quarterly NIPA series. The data shown here were issued in 2012 and therefore do not reflect the 2013 comprehensive revision that is incorporated in the quarterly and annual data elsewhere in this chapter and this volume.

Two new categories appear in each table, detailing inter-governmental flows that are consolidated in Table 6-8. State government receipts include not only *federal grants-in-aid* but also *local grants-in-aid*, and state government expenditures

include *grants-in-aid to local governments*. Local government receipts include not only *federal grants-in-aid* but also *state grants-in-aid*, and local government expenditures include *grants-in-aid to state governments*. To make room for these columns, the components *current surplus of government enterprises* and *subsidies* are not shown, though they are included in total current receipts and total current expenditures respectively.

These measures are described in "Receipts and Expenditures of State Governments and of Local Governments," *Survey of Current Business*, October 2005. Data back to 1959 are available on the BEA Web site at http://www.bea.gov.

Tables 6-14A and 6-14B: Federal Government Receipts and Outlays by Fiscal Year; The Federal Budget and GDP

SOURCE: U.S. OFFICE OF MANAGEMENT AND BUDGET

These data on federal government receipts and outlays are on a modified cash basis and are from the *Budget of the United States Government: Historical Tables*. The data are by federal fiscal years, which are defined as July 1 through June 30 through 1976 and October 1 through September 30 for 1977 and subsequent years. They are identified by the year of the final fiscal quarter—i.e., the year from July 1, 1975, through June 30, 1976, is identified as Fiscal 1976, and the year from October 1, 1976, through June 30, 1977, is identified as Fiscal Year 1977. The period July 1 through September 30, 1976, is a separate fiscal period known as the transition quarter (TQ) and is not included in any fiscal year.

There are numerous differences in both timing and definition between these estimates and the NIPA estimates in Tables 6-1 through 6-7. See the notes and definitions for those tables for the definitional differences that were introduced with the 1999 comprehensive revision of the NIPAs.

Definitions

The definitions for these tables are not affected by the 2013, 2003, or 1999 changes in the government sectors of the NIPAs.

Table references will be given indicating the source of each item in the *Historical Tables*; for example, "HT Table 1.1."

Receipts consist of gifts and of taxes or other compulsory payments to the government. Other types of payments to the government are netted against outlays. (HT Table 1.1)

Outlays occur when the federal government liquidates an obligation through a cash payment or when interest accrues on public debt issues. Beginning with the data for 1992, outlays include the subsidy cost of direct and guaranteed loans made. Before 1992, the costs and repayments associated with such loans are recorded on a cash basis. As noted previously, various types of nontax receipts are netted against cash outlays. These accounts do not distinguish between investment outlays and current consumption and do not include allowances for depreciation. (HT Table 1.1)

The *total surplus (deficit-)* is receipts minus outlays. (HT Table 1.1)

On-budget and off-budget. By law, two government programs that are included in the federal receipts and outlays totals are "off-budget"—old-age, survivors, and disability insurance (Social Security) and the Postal Service. The former accounts for nearly all of the off-budget activity. The *surplus (deficit-)* not accounted for by these two programs is the on-budget surplus or deficit. (HT Table 1.1)

Sources of financing is the means by which the total deficit is financed or the surplus is distributed. By definition, sources of financing sum to the total deficit or surplus with the sign reversed. The principal source is *borrowing from the public*, shown as a positive number, that is, the increase in the debt held by the public. (This entry is calculated by the editors as the change in the debt held by the public as shown in HT Table 7.1.) When there is a budget surplus, as in fiscal years 1998 to 2001, this provides resources for debt reduction, which is indicated by a minus sign in this column. *Other financing* includes drawdown (or buildup, shown here with a minus sign) in Treasury cash balances, seigniorage on coins, direct and guaranteed loan account cash transactions, and miscellaneous other transactions. Large negative "other financing" in 2008 through 2010 resulted from direct loans and asset purchases under TARP and other emergency financial procedures; in other words, the government borrowed from the public to undertake these loans and asset purchases, but they are not included in budget expenditures or the budget deficit. *Other financing* is calculated by the editors, by reversing the sign of the surplus/deficit—so that the deficit becomes a positive number—and subtracting the value of borrowing from the public.

Some of the categories of *receipts by source* are self-explanatory. *Employment taxes and contributions* includes taxes for old-age, survivors, and disability insurance (Social Security), hospital insurance (Medicare), and railroad retirement funds. *Other retirement contributions* includes the employee share of payments for retirement pensions, mainly those for federal employees. *Excise taxes* includes federal taxes on alcohol, tobacco, telephone service, and transportation fuels, as well as taxes funding smaller programs

such as black lung disability and vaccine injury compensation. *Miscellaneous receipts* includes deposits of earnings by the Federal Reserve system and all other receipts. (HT Tables 2.1, 2.4, and 2.5)

Outlays by function presents outlays according to the major purpose of the spending. Functional classifications cut across departmental and agency lines. Most categories of offsetting receipts are netted against cash outlays in the appropriate function, which explains how recorded outlays in *energy* and *commerce and housing credit* (which, as its name suggests, includes loan programs) can be negative. There is also a category of "undistributed offsetting receipts" (not shown), always with a negative sign, that includes proceeds from the sale or lease of assets and payments from federal agencies to federal retirement funds and the Social Security and Medicare trust funds. Note that *Social Security* is recorded separately from other *income security* outlays, and *Medicare* separately from other *health* outlays. (HT Table 3.1) For further explanation, consult the *Budget of the United States Government.*

In order to provide authoritative comparisons of these budget values with the overall size of the economy, a special calculation of gross domestic product by fiscal year is supplied to the Office of Management and Budget by the BEA, and is shown in Table 6-14B. These are the values that were available when the Budget was prepared, at the beginning of the year, and do not reflect the comprehensive revison made in mid-2013. That table also displays selected budget aggregates in dollar values and as a percent of GDP. (HT Tables 1.2, 1.3, 2.3, and 3.1)

Data availability and references

Definitions, budget concepts, and historical data are from *Budget of the United States Government for Fiscal Year 2014: Historical Tables*, available on the Office of Management and Budget Web site at http://www.whitehouse.gov/omb/Budget/historicals.

Similarly defined data for the latest month, the year-ago month, and the current and year-ago fiscal year to date are published in the *Monthly Treasury Statement* prepared by the Financial Management Service, U.S. Department of the Treasury. For those who need up-to-date budget information, this publication is available on the Financial Management Service Web site at http://www.fms.treas.gov. As these monthly figures are never revised to agree with the final annual data, they are not published in this volume.

Table 6-15: Federal Government Debt by Fiscal Year

SOURCE: U.S. OFFICE OF MANAGEMENT AND BUDGET

Debt outstanding at the end of each fiscal year is from the *Budget of the United States Government.* Most securities are recorded at sales price plus amortized discount or less amortized premium.

Definitions

Federal government debt held by the public consists of all federal debt held outside the federal government accounts—by individuals, financial institutions (including the Federal Reserve Banks), and foreign individuals, businesses, and central banks. It does not include federal debt held by federal government trust funds such as the Social Security trust fund. The level and change of the ratio of this debt to the value of gross domestic product (GDP) provide proportional measures of the impact of federal borrowing on credit markets. (HT Table 7.1) This measure of debt held by the public is very similar in concept and scope to the total federal government credit market debt outstanding in the flow-of-funds accounts, shown in Business Statistics in Table 12-5; however, it is not identical, being priced somewhat differently, and is shown here in Chapter 6 on a fiscal year rather than calendar year basis.

Gross federal debt—total. This is the total debt owed by the U.S. Treasury. It includes a small amount of matured debt. (HT Table 7.1)

Debt held by Social Security funds is the sum of the end-year trust fund balances for old age and survivors insurance and disability insurance. The separate disability trust fund begins in 1957. (HT Table 13.1)

Debt held by other U.S. government accounts is calculated by the editors by subtracting the Social Security debt holdings from the total debt held by federal government accounts, which is shown in HT Table 7.1. It includes the balances in all the other trust funds, including the Medicare funds, federal employee retirement funds, and the highway trust fund.

Debt held by the Federal Reserve System is the total value of Treasury securities held by the 12 Federal Reserve Banks, which are acquired in open market operations that carry out monetary policy. (HT Table 7.1)

Debt held by private investors is calculated by subtracting the Federal Reserve debt from the total debt held by the public, and is shown as "Debt Held by the Public: Other" in HT Table 7.1.

Debt held by foreign residents is based on surveys by the Treasury Department. (Table 5-7, *Budget of the United States for Fiscal Year 2014: Analytical Perspectives,* p. 76.)

Debt held by domestic investors is calculated by the editors by subtracting the foreign-held debt from the total debt held by private investors.

The "debt subject to statutory limitation," not shown here, is close to the gross federal debt in concept and size, but there are some relatively minor definitional differences specified by law. The debt limit can only be changed by an Act of Congress. For information about the debt subject to limit and other debt subjects, see the latest *Budget of the United States Government: Historical Statistics* and *Analytical Perspectives.*

Data availability and references

For the end-of-fiscal-year data, see *Historical Tables* and *Analytical Perspectives* in the *Budget of the United States Government,* which is available on the OMB Web site at http://www.whitehouse.gov/omb/Budget. In the *Analytical Perspectives,* debt analysis and data are included in the "Economic and Budget Analysis" section.

Recent quarterly data, measured on a somewhat different basis, are found in the *Treasury Bulletin* in the chapter on "Ownership of Federal Securities (OFS)," in Tables OFS-1 and OFS-2. The *Treasury Bulletin* can be accessed on the Internet at http://www.fms.treas.gov/bulletin. Holdings by Social Security funds are also available in the *Bulletin* in the chapter on "Federal Debt," Table FD-3. The Disability Fund is listed separately from the Old-Age and Survivors Fund.

Table 6-17: Government Employment

SOURCE: U.S. DEPARTMENT OF LABOR, BUREAU OF LABOR STATISTICS (SEE NOTES AND DEFINITIONS FOR TABLE 10-8)

Government payroll employment includes federal, state, and local activities such as legislative, executive, and judicial functions, as well as all government-owned and government-operated business enterprises, establishments, and institutions (arsenals, navy yards, hospitals, etc.), and government force account construction. The figures relate to civilian employment only. The Bureau of Labor Statistics (BLS) considers regular full-time teachers (private and governmental) to be employed during the summer vacation period, regardless of whether they are specifically paid in those months.

Employment in federal government establishments reflects employee counts as of the pay period containing the 12th of the month. Federal government employment excludes employees of the Central Intelligence Agency and the National Security Agency.

CHAPTER 7: U.S. FOREIGN TRADE AND FINANCE

Section 7a: Foreign Transactions in the National Income and Product Accounts

Figure 7-1. Receipts, Payments, and Balance on Current Account, 1950–2012

- Beginning in 1983, chronic current-account deficits in U.S. transactions with the rest of the world have emerged and increased, requiring increasing net capital inflows from abroad to finance them. The only current-account surplus since then occurred in 1991, when payments from other countries financed most of the cost of the first Gulf War. In 2006 the NIPA deficit reached a record $796 billion, 5.7 percent of GDP. (Tables 7-1 and 1-1A)

- U.S. current-account deficits typically diminish somewhat during recessions, as receipts hold up somewhat better than payments. The deficit diminished to $381 billion, 2.6 percent of GDP, in 2009, the recession's low point. The gap was $439 billion in 2012, 2.7 percent of GDP. (Tables 7-1 and 1-1A)

- The NIPA current-account deficit of $439 billion in 2012 comprised a deficit of $759 billion on goods, a surplus of $212 billion on services, net income receipts of $253 billion, and net payments of $145 billion in taxes and transfer payments. (Table 7-1)

- Looking at quarterly data on the real volume of flows of goods and services in U.S. trade, the quantity index for exports of goods and services reached a high point in the second quarter of 2008 and fell 14 percent over the next year. By the end of 2010, the volume of exports recovered fully to the level in 2008:II, and by the end of 2012 it was 10 percent past the 2008 peak. Imports of goods and services, also in real terms, peaked earlier, in mid-2007, and plunged 20 percent between then and the second quarter of 2009. In 2012, the volume of U.S. imports was only slightly above its 2007 peak. (Table 7-2)

Table 7-1. Foreign Transactions in the National Income and Product Accounts

(Billions of dollars, quarterly data are at seasonally adjusted annual rates.)   **NIPA Table 4.1**

Year and quarter	Current receipts from the rest of the world					Current payments to the rest of the world						Balance on current account, NIPAs	Net lending or net borrowing (-), NIPAs
	Total	Exports of goods and services			Income receipts	Total	Imports of goods and services			Income payments	Current taxes and transfer payments, net		
		Goods [1]		Services [1]			Goods [1]		Services [1]				
		Durable	Nondurable				Durable	Nondurable					
1950	14.5	5.1	5.1	2.1	2.2	16.4	3.0	6.1	2.5	0.7	4.0	-1.8	-1.8
1951	19.9	6.6	7.6	2.9	2.8	19.0	3.8	7.4	3.4	0.9	3.5	0.9	0.9
1952	19.3	6.9	6.5	3.0	2.9	18.7	4.1	6.7	4.5	0.9	2.6	0.6	0.6
1953	18.2	6.9	5.5	2.9	2.8	19.5	4.1	6.9	5.0	0.9	2.5	-1.3	-1.3
1954	18.9	7.1	5.8	2.9	3.0	18.7	3.6	6.7	5.1	0.9	2.3	0.2	0.2
1955	21.2	8.2	6.2	3.3	3.5	20.8	4.5	7.1	5.7	1.1	2.6	0.4	0.4
1956	25.2	9.8	7.8	3.7	3.9	22.5	5.2	7.6	6.1	1.1	2.5	2.7	2.7
1957	28.3	10.9	8.6	4.5	4.3	23.6	5.3	8.0	6.7	1.2	2.4	4.7	4.7
1958	24.4	9.0	7.4	4.1	3.9	23.6	5.0	8.0	7.1	1.2	2.4	0.8	0.8
1959	27.0	8.9	7.5	6.3	4.3	28.3	6.6	8.7	7.0	1.5	4.4	-1.3	-1.3
1960	31.9	11.3	9.2	6.6	4.9	28.8	6.4	8.9	7.6	1.8	4.1	3.2	3.2
1961	32.9	11.5	9.4	6.7	5.3	28.7	6.0	9.0	7.6	1.8	4.2	4.2	4.2
1962	35.0	12.0	9.7	7.4	5.9	31.2	6.9	9.9	8.1	1.8	4.4	3.8	3.8
1963	37.6	12.7	10.7	7.7	6.5	32.7	7.4	10.3	8.4	2.1	4.5	4.9	4.9
1964	42.3	14.7	12.0	8.3	7.2	34.8	8.4	11.0	8.7	2.3	4.4	7.5	7.5
1965	45.0	15.8	12.0	9.4	7.9	38.9	10.4	11.8	9.3	2.6	4.7	6.2	6.2
1966	49.0	17.5	13.2	10.2	8.1	45.2	13.3	13.1	10.7	3.0	5.1	3.8	3.8
1967	52.1	18.4	13.7	11.3	8.7	48.7	14.5	13.2	12.2	3.3	5.5	3.5	3.5
1968	58.0	21.0	14.3	12.6	10.1	56.5	18.8	15.1	12.6	4.0	5.9	1.5	1.5
1969	63.7	23.7	14.6	13.7	11.8	62.1	20.8	16.1	13.7	5.7	5.9	1.6	1.6
1970	72.5	27.1	17.4	15.2	12.8	68.8	22.8	18.1	14.9	6.4	6.6	3.7	3.7
1971	77.0	27.5	18.0	17.4	14.0	76.7	26.6	19.9	15.8	6.4	7.9	0.3	0.3
1972	87.1	31.0	20.8	19.0	16.3	91.2	33.3	23.6	17.3	7.7	9.2	-4.0	-4.1
1973	118.8	41.4	32.6	21.3	23.5	109.9	40.8	31.0	19.3	10.9	7.9	8.9	8.8
1974	156.5	56.5	44.5	25.7	29.8	150.5	50.3	54.2	22.9	14.3	8.7	6.0	5.9
1975	166.7	63.8	45.8	29.1	28.0	146.9	45.6	53.4	23.7	15.0	9.1	19.8	19.8
1976	181.9	69.0	48.7	31.7	32.4	174.8	56.8	67.8	26.5	15.5	8.1	7.1	7.0
1977	196.6	72.0	51.6	35.7	37.2	207.5	69.2	83.4	29.8	16.9	8.1	-10.9	-11.0
1978	233.1	85.3	60.1	41.5	46.3	245.8	89.0	88.4	34.8	24.7	8.8	-12.6	-12.7
1979	298.5	108.0	76.0	46.1	68.3	299.6	100.4	112.3	39.9	36.4	10.6	-1.2	-1.3
1980	359.9	133.3	92.5	55.0	79.1	351.4	111.9	136.6	45.3	44.9	12.6	8.5	8.4
1981	397.3	140.1	99.0	66.1	92.0	393.9	126.0	141.8	49.9	59.1	17.0	3.4	3.2
1982	384.2	124.7	90.3	68.2	101.0	387.5	125.1	125.4	52.6	64.5	19.8	-3.3	-3.4
1983	378.9	120.4	86.9	69.7	101.9	413.9	147.3	125.4	56.0	64.8	20.5	-35.1	-35.2
1984	424.2	132.4	93.2	76.7	121.9	514.3	192.4	143.9	68.8	85.6	23.6	-90.1	-90.2
1985	415.9	137.2	85.0	81.0	112.7	530.2	204.2	139.1	73.9	87.3	25.7	-114.3	-114.5
1986	432.3	142.6	83.4	95.0	111.3	575.0	238.8	131.2	82.9	94.4	27.8	-142.7	-142.8
1987	487.2	162.9	94.6	106.4	123.3	641.3	264.2	150.6	93.9	105.8	26.8	-154.1	-154.2
1988	596.7	208.8	117.0	118.8	152.1	712.4	294.8	157.3	101.9	129.5	29.0	-115.7	-115.9
1989	682.0	239.8	129.5	134.9	177.7	774.3	310.3	174.5	106.2	152.9	30.4	-92.4	-92.7
1990	740.7	262.0	134.7	155.2	188.8	815.6	314.5	193.5	121.7	154.2	31.7	-74.9	-82.3
1991	763.3	282.3	141.3	171.3	168.4	755.4	315.5	185.2	122.8	136.8	-4.9	7.9	2.6
1992	785.1	300.5	147.4	185.1	152.1	830.7	346.7	198.2	122.9	121.0	41.9	-45.6	-44.3
1993	810.4	314.0	146.0	194.8	155.6	888.9	386.4	206.4	127.2	123.6	45.4	-78.6	-79.4
1994	905.5	349.6	160.4	210.8	184.5	1 020.2	454.0	222.8	136.6	160.7	46.1	-114.7	-116.0
1995	1 042.6	394.0	189.3	229.5	229.8	1 147.7	510.8	246.7	145.1	201.1	44.1	-105.1	-105.5
1996	1 114.0	421.1	197.2	249.2	246.4	1 228.1	533.4	274.1	156.5	214.6	49.5	-114.1	-114.4
1997	1 233.8	482.3	205.4	266.1	280.1	1 363.2	588.5	297.1	170.1	256.0	51.4	-129.3	-129.8
1998	1 239.7	486.6	194.3	272.1	286.8	1 444.3	637.7	293.0	184.9	268.5	60.0	-204.5	-204.8
1999	1 310.6	508.7	202.7	277.7	321.4	1 602.5	715.5	334.8	200.3	294.3	57.6	-291.9	-296.4
2000	1 477.0	573.4	223.7	297.2	382.7	1 886.1	822.4	428.0	224.0	345.7	66.1	-409.1	-409.5
2001	1 354.1	525.3	218.4	285.1	325.3	1 743.9	757.1	418.4	222.3	273.5	72.6	-389.8	-376.8
2002	1 320.5	492.8	219.8	292.1	315.8	1 770.4	773.7	424.4	231.6	267.2	73.5	-449.9	-450.4
2003	1 399.5	501.8	239.0	302.6	356.1	1 913.0	805.6	488.9	249.6	288.1	80.7	-513.5	-515.7
2004	1 634.6	565.7	267.1	350.3	451.4	2 256.2	935.3	573.6	289.0	361.4	96.9	-621.7	-618.9
2005	1 886.1	629.8	295.5	385.1	575.8	2 623.3	1 024.2	692.0	309.9	482.3	114.9	-737.1	-724.3
2006	2 202.7	715.0	333.1	430.4	724.2	2 998.4	1 129.7	766.8	344.5	655.7	101.7	-795.7	-797.8
2007	2 541.3	783.2	382.1	500.4	875.5	3 250.3	1 174.6	825.7	375.3	749.1	125.7	-709.1	-709.0
2008	2 699.9	829.4	468.2	545.5	856.8	3 378.4	1 162.0	984.4	410.0	683.8	138.3	-678.5	-673.1
2009	2 227.5	671.9	392.8	519.1	643.7	2 608.7	893.1	694.2	388.7	496.5	136.1	-381.2	-381.7
2010	2 563.5	801.2	477.2	565.1	720.0	3 018.1	1 108.3	842.9	410.8	514.1	142.0	-454.5	-455.2
2011	2 904.0	897.4	576.2	627.6	802.8	3 360.9	1 234.5	1 000.1	435.3	542.1	149.0	-457.0	-458.6
2012	3 014.5	946.1	589.9	659.9	818.6	3 453.5	1 324.9	970.5	447.7	565.7	144.6	-439.0	-432.4
2010													
1st quarter	2 442.8	754.1	451.4	540.9	696.5	2 888.1	1 018.2	824.1	399.1	493.0	153.6	-445.2	-445.8
2nd quarter	2 518.9	796.5	459.1	551.4	711.9	2 979.1	1 097.6	835.5	403.5	506.7	135.7	-460.2	-460.7
3rd quarter	2 580.8	810.6	475.8	574.0	720.5	3 067.2	1 142.7	842.9	418.5	520.8	142.3	-486.4	-487.5
4th quarter	2 711.6	843.8	522.6	594.0	751.2	3 137.9	1 174.8	869.1	421.9	535.7	136.5	-426.3	-426.8
2011													
1st quarter	2 802.0	865.7	557.5	606.3	772.5	3 265.5	1 201.6	962.2	420.3	524.2	157.1	-463.4	-464.0
2nd quarter	2 899.9	892.3	576.9	626.2	804.5	3 372.7	1 212.1	1 022.5	433.0	554.2	150.8	-472.8	-476.6
3rd quarter	2 965.7	912.6	584.3	646.4	822.3	3 390.8	1 249.6	1 002.8	444.6	550.1	143.6	-425.0	-426.7
4th quarter	2 948.2	919.1	585.9	631.2	812.0	3 414.7	1 274.8	1 012.8	443.1	539.7	144.4	-466.5	-467.2
2012													
1st quarter	2 991.4	946.8	573.8	652.7	818.0	3 480.4	1 315.0	1 004.5	444.6	570.0	146.1	-488.9	-489.3
2nd quarter	3 011.8	949.1	590.3	657.9	814.4	3 456.4	1 329.6	977.8	447.8	555.7	145.4	-444.6	-445.9
3rd quarter	3 011.2	945.8	599.8	653.6	812.0	3 432.3	1 322.9	952.1	448.6	564.4	144.3	-421.1	-423.4
4th quarter	3 043.5	942.6	595.7	675.5	829.8	3 444.9	1 332.2	947.5	449.9	572.8	142.6	-401.4	-371.1

[1]Exports and imports of certain goods, primarily military equipment purchased and sold by the federal government, are included in services. Beginning with 1986, repairs and alterations of equipment are reclassified from goods to services.

Table 7-2. Chain-Type Quantity Indexes for Exports and Imports of Goods and Services

(Index numbers, 2009 = 100; quarterly indexes are seasonally adjusted.)   NIPA Table 4.2.3

| Year and quarter | Exports of goods and services | | | | | Imports of goods and services | | | | |
| | Total | Goods [1] | | | Services [1] | Total | Goods [1] | | | Services [1] |
		Total	Durable	Nondurable			Total	Durable	Nondurable	
1967	9.40	8.92	6.63	15.59	10.70	10.16	8.56	4.78	18.29	18.31
1968	10.14	9.63	7.26	16.50	11.52	11.67	10.32	6.09	20.72	18.64
1969	10.63	10.14	7.85	16.66	11.95	12.33	10.89	6.51	21.49	19.81
1970	11.77	11.29	8.58	19.10	13.01	12.86	11.32	6.69	22.66	20.85
1971	11.97	11.25	8.52	19.13	14.02	13.55	12.26	7.36	24.06	20.25
1972	12.87	12.46	9.41	21.27	13.93	15.07	13.93	8.47	26.87	21.11
1973	15.30	15.32	11.73	25.67	14.91	15.77	14.92	9.02	28.99	20.40
1974	16.51	16.53	13.54	25.44	16.08	15.41	14.50	9.05	27.18	20.38
1975	16.40	16.15	13.26	24.76	17.06	13.70	12.67	7.40	25.21	19.49
1976	17.12	16.92	13.44	27.14	17.57	16.38	15.54	9.06	30.94	20.84
1977	17.53	17.14	13.41	28.09	18.70	18.17	17.43	10.26	34.46	21.88
1978	19.38	19.05	14.95	31.11	20.27	19.74	19.00	11.85	35.58	23.44
1979	21.30	21.30	17.02	33.91	20.89	20.07	19.32	12.12	35.99	23.76
1980	23.60	23.84	18.98	38.14	22.19	18.74	17.89	12.22	30.99	23.23
1981	23.89	23.58	18.30	39.14	24.56	19.23	18.26	13.24	30.06	24.57
1982	22.06	21.45	15.91	37.96	23.88	18.99	17.80	13.39	28.31	25.88
1983	21.49	20.84	15.58	36.44	23.48	21.39	20.22	16.14	30.15	27.96
1984	23.25	22.48	17.26	37.87	25.57	26.59	25.11	21.47	34.33	34.98
1985	24.02	23.31	18.65	36.89	26.18	28.32	26.68	23.62	34.75	37.64
1986	25.87	24.51	19.74	38.36	29.97	30.74	29.41	25.81	38.85	38.06
1987	28.69	27.23	22.54	40.65	33.10	32.56	30.78	26.95	40.80	42.55
1988	33.34	32.36	27.96	44.81	36.31	33.83	32.02	28.07	42.36	43.99
1989	37.20	36.21	31.90	48.43	40.17	35.32	33.40	29.32	44.08	46.12
1990	40.48	39.26	35.31	50.47	44.14	36.59	34.37	30.09	45.57	49.14
1991	43.16	41.97	37.94	53.41	46.76	36.53	34.53	30.26	45.71	47.86
1992	46.15	45.11	40.96	56.89	49.37	39.10	37.78	33.43	49.20	46.57
1993	47.66	46.58	43.09	56.49	51.00	42.48	41.57	37.39	52.51	47.82
1994	51.87	51.11	48.31	59.16	54.42	47.54	47.12	43.57	56.41	50.37
1995	57.20	57.09	55.19	62.97	58.12	51.35	51.36	48.56	58.72	51.88
1996	61.88	62.12	61.55	65.07	61.95	55.81	56.17	53.76	62.66	54.60
1997	69.25	71.06	72.67	69.30	65.62	63.33	64.27	62.63	69.17	59.34
1998	70.87	72.64	75.02	69.19	67.33	70.73	71.89	70.89	75.49	65.80
1999	74.13	76.93	79.45	73.26	68.27	78.77	81.02	81.08	82.43	68.88
2000	80.34	84.72	89.19	76.86	70.92	88.82	91.63	93.37	89.87	76.48
2001	75.80	79.51	81.79	76.40	67.87	86.27	88.66	87.52	92.26	75.82
2002	74.39	76.74	77.20	77.67	69.44	89.22	91.97	91.23	94.87	77.17
2003	75.59	78.18	78.58	79.27	70.14	93.06	96.47	95.14	100.52	78.17
2004	82.67	84.79	87.22	81.87	78.27	103.30	107.19	108.40	107.17	86.36
2005	87.66	91.03	95.41	84.46	80.59	109.59	114.32	117.60	111.34	89.04
2006	95.49	99.61	105.69	90.04	86.84	116.33	121.10	128.08	113.20	95.60
2007	104.01	107.11	114.76	94.86	97.52	118.97	123.32	131.34	114.12	100.07
2008	109.98	113.69	120.62	102.59	102.19	115.83	118.76	126.33	110.07	103.18
2009	100.00	100.00	100.00	100.00	100.00	100.00	100.00	100.00	100.00	100.00
2010	111.48	114.32	116.77	110.28	105.59	112.76	115.16	122.79	105.97	102.75
2011	119.37	122.47	127.33	114.80	112.94	118.24	121.18	133.76	106.69	105.93
2012	123.59	127.10	133.41	117.35	116.30	120.86	123.75	143.39	102.31	108.78
2006										
1st quarter	93.34	97.72	103.68	88.31	84.14	114.91	119.52	126.61	111.50	94.92
2nd quarter	95.05	99.12	105.02	89.87	86.49	116.19	121.03	127.56	113.72	95.17
3rd quarter	94.85	99.26	105.18	90.00	85.55	117.18	122.35	128.33	115.74	94.75
4th quarter	98.73	102.33	108.88	91.96	91.18	117.02	121.50	129.81	111.83	97.55
2007										
1st quarter	100.17	103.73	110.59	92.81	92.71	119.02	123.59	131.12	114.97	99.18
2nd quarter	101.93	105.36	112.99	93.10	94.75	119.48	123.93	131.27	115.57	100.18
3rd quarter	105.52	108.46	116.40	95.72	99.37	119.56	123.80	132.59	113.63	101.12
4th quarter	108.42	110.90	119.06	97.82	103.23	117.83	121.97	130.37	112.30	99.81
2008										
1st quarter	109.78	113.70	120.74	102.42	101.55	118.92	122.65	131.90	112.12	102.69
2nd quarter	112.92	117.20	125.04	104.73	103.93	117.83	121.56	131.52	110.38	101.54
3rd quarter	111.93	116.49	124.45	103.83	102.35	115.65	118.48	127.27	108.51	103.53
4th quarter	105.28	107.38	112.23	99.38	100.95	110.90	112.34	114.61	109.27	104.98
2009										
1st quarter	96.91	96.52	97.57	94.79	97.69	100.30	100.26	97.12	104.26	100.46
2nd quarter	97.08	95.84	94.83	97.59	99.62	96.03	95.24	93.30	97.65	99.26
3rd quarter	100.31	100.53	99.98	101.41	99.87	99.65	99.60	100.47	98.42	99.86
4th quarter	105.71	107.12	107.62	106.22	102.82	104.02	104.90	109.11	99.67	100.41
2010										
1st quarter	107.36	109.95	110.66	108.74	102.02	106.98	108.54	112.92	103.08	100.52
2nd quarter	109.82	113.02	116.31	107.63	103.18	112.02	114.56	121.42	106.22	101.47
3rd quarter	112.70	115.37	118.31	110.55	107.16	115.88	118.53	127.04	108.29	104.85
4th quarter	116.03	118.94	121.82	114.19	109.99	116.15	119.02	129.76	106.29	104.17
2011										
1st quarter	117.11	120.22	123.82	114.35	110.64	116.97	120.31	131.24	107.44	102.85
2nd quarter	118.50	121.32	126.69	112.92	112.70	117.17	120.11	131.03	107.28	104.81
3rd quarter	120.52	123.02	128.73	114.14	115.42	118.56	121.15	134.70	105.75	107.79
4th quarter	121.34	125.33	130.06	117.80	113.00	120.26	123.12	138.06	106.30	108.28
2012										
1st quarter	122.58	125.88	133.58	114.17	115.72	120.48	123.39	141.99	103.02	108.25
2nd quarter	123.74	127.48	133.69	117.87	115.95	121.21	124.15	143.84	102.68	108.87
3rd quarter	123.85	128.00	133.61	119.24	115.20	121.36	124.28	143.56	103.18	109.14
4th quarter	124.20	127.04	132.76	118.13	118.32	120.40	123.17	144.17	100.37	108.86

[1]Exports and imports of certain goods, primarily military equipment purchased and sold by the federal government, are included in services. Beginning with 1986, repairs and alterations of equipment are reclassified from goods to services.

Table 7-3. Chain-Type Price Indexes for Exports and Imports of Goods and Services

(Index numbers, 2009 = 100; quarterly indexes are seasonally adjusted.)   NIPA Table 4.2.4

Year and quarter	Exports of goods and services					Imports of goods and services				
	Total	Goods [1]			Services [1]	Total	Goods [1]			Services [1]
		Total	Durable	Nondurable			Total	Durable	Nondurable	
1967	29.19	33.86	41.38	22.43	20.33	19.89	20.44	34.06	10.41	17.08
1968	29.83	34.39	43.05	22.01	21.14	20.19	20.72	34.61	10.51	17.41
1969	30.84	35.46	44.93	22.28	22.02	20.72	21.30	35.71	10.76	17.76
1970	32.02	37.06	47.03	23.23	22.45	21.94	22.75	38.14	11.49	18.40
1971	33.20	38.05	48.12	23.97	23.92	23.29	23.91	40.46	11.94	20.06
1972	34.75	39.06	49.09	24.85	26.35	24.92	25.75	44.02	12.67	21.06
1973	39.32	45.33	52.49	32.29	27.57	29.25	30.35	50.67	15.43	24.36
1974	48.44	57.37	62.08	44.56	30.76	41.85	45.41	62.26	28.73	28.97
1975	53.39	63.76	71.64	47.12	32.83	45.34	49.21	69.09	30.49	31.32
1976	55.14	65.39	76.44	45.71	34.81	46.70	50.53	70.21	31.58	32.74
1977	57.39	67.77	79.94	46.78	36.77	50.82	55.16	75.56	34.88	35.06
1978	60.89	71.68	84.86	49.22	39.43	54.41	58.84	84.12	35.78	38.25
1979	68.21	81.14	94.45	57.08	42.50	63.71	69.38	92.77	44.96	43.19
1980	75.13	88.95	104.52	61.71	47.73	79.36	87.55	102.58	63.51	50.13
1981	80.69	95.23	113.94	64.38	51.88	83.62	92.42	106.64	67.93	52.31
1982	81.06	94.14	116.65	60.59	55.03	80.80	88.69	104.67	63.82	52.34
1983	81.38	93.45	115.00	60.73	57.18	77.77	84.98	102.25	59.90	51.49
1984	82.13	94.26	114.13	62.69	57.81	77.10	84.39	100.38	60.36	50.60
1985	79.69	89.55	109.51	58.67	59.58	74.57	81.07	96.80	57.68	50.54
1986	78.34	86.61	107.53	55.34	61.05	74.57	79.26	103.61	48.65	56.01
1987	80.10	88.85	107.59	59.26	61.91	79.08	84.91	109.78	53.16	56.81
1988	84.20	94.57	111.12	66.49	63.03	82.87	88.95	117.59	53.50	59.58
1989	85.60	95.80	111.89	68.10	64.71	84.68	91.44	118.51	57.02	59.26
1990	86.08	94.89	110.43	67.94	67.73	87.10	93.12	117.05	61.18	63.70
1991	87.03	94.80	110.74	67.35	70.59	86.38	91.36	116.78	58.37	66.02
1992	86.61	93.27	109.20	65.98	72.22	86.45	90.86	116.15	58.04	67.87
1993	86.75	92.75	108.44	65.78	73.60	85.78	89.85	115.72	56.61	68.45
1994	87.76	93.74	107.71	69.05	74.63	86.59	90.50	116.71	56.89	69.78
1995	89.72	95.96	106.25	76.52	76.06	88.96	92.91	117.78	60.51	71.96
1996	88.53	93.48	101.84	77.15	77.50	87.41	90.56	111.10	63.00	73.76
1997	86.96	90.90	98.78	75.46	78.11	84.37	86.82	105.23	61.87	73.75
1998	84.90	88.03	96.53	71.50	77.85	79.83	81.57	100.74	55.91	72.32
1999	84.25	86.87	95.30	70.45	78.36	80.35	81.67	98.82	58.50	74.81
2000	86.01	88.37	95.68	74.11	80.73	84.01	85.97	98.62	68.60	75.36
2001	85.70	87.86	95.59	72.78	80.92	82.00	83.53	96.86	65.32	75.43
2002	85.28	87.21	95.00	72.05	81.03	81.10	82.07	94.96	64.44	77.22
2003	87.15	89.00	95.04	76.76	83.10	83.98	84.54	94.81	70.06	82.21
2004	90.36	92.25	96.54	83.06	86.22	88.08	88.69	96.61	77.09	86.11
2005	94.38	95.47	98.25	89.06	92.04	93.56	94.57	97.52	89.52	89.55
2006	97.76	98.83	100.69	94.18	95.48	97.49	98.66	98.77	97.57	92.70
2007	101.12	102.19	101.57	102.56	98.85	101.05	102.19	100.14	104.22	96.48
2008	105.82	107.20	102.35	116.19	102.83	111.70	113.86	103.00	128.82	102.23
2009	100.00	100.00	100.00	100.00	100.00	100.00	100.00	100.00	100.00	100.00
2010	104.42	105.03	102.12	110.18	103.10	106.01	106.74	101.07	114.57	102.85
2011	111.14	113.01	104.90	127.78	107.04	114.27	116.18	103.35	135.02	105.71
2012	112.19	113.51	105.54	127.98	109.31	114.86	116.86	103.46	136.63	105.90
2006										
1st quarter	96.09	96.96	99.29	91.40	94.29	96.49	97.69	97.69	96.72	91.52
2nd quarter	97.45	98.48	100.42	93.69	95.27	97.52	98.74	98.39	98.31	92.49
3rd quarter	98.73	99.89	101.29	96.14	96.26	98.55	99.83	99.27	99.72	93.20
4th quarter	98.76	99.99	101.77	95.50	96.09	97.41	98.38	99.71	95.54	93.62
2007										
1st quarter	99.54	100.56	101.63	97.49	97.39	97.87	98.82	99.56	96.82	94.21
2nd quarter	100.65	101.75	101.74	100.90	98.31	99.56	100.53	99.79	100.67	95.75
3rd quarter	101.35	102.37	101.37	103.55	99.17	101.32	102.35	100.32	104.33	97.28
4th quarter	102.93	104.07	101.56	108.30	100.54	105.45	107.05	100.90	115.04	98.67
2008										
1st quarter	104.51	105.76	101.82	112.82	101.89	109.03	111.10	101.25	124.47	100.04
2nd quarter	107.36	109.41	103.00	121.40	102.90	114.68	117.32	103.73	136.15	103.09
3rd quarter	108.93	110.96	103.65	124.82	104.52	117.82	120.83	104.52	143.62	104.49
4th quarter	102.46	102.69	100.92	105.74	102.01	105.25	106.19	102.48	111.06	101.29
2009										
1st quarter	99.04	98.56	99.41	96.98	100.02	96.39	95.71	99.79	90.61	99.18
2nd quarter	99.00	99.09	99.08	99.12	98.81	97.91	97.66	99.19	95.60	98.95
3rd quarter	100.19	100.36	100.10	100.88	99.84	101.28	101.59	100.06	103.43	100.02
4th quarter	101.77	101.98	101.41	103.02	101.33	104.42	105.03	100.96	110.37	101.84
2010										
1st quarter	102.75	103.03	101.45	105.79	102.16	106.05	106.96	100.99	115.11	102.16
2nd quarter	103.94	104.40	101.94	108.70	102.97	105.57	106.32	101.23	113.29	102.33
3rd quarter	104.26	104.77	101.98	109.65	103.20	104.99	105.52	100.71	112.12	102.71
4th quarter	106.71	107.94	103.10	116.58	104.05	107.43	108.17	101.37	117.77	104.20
2011										
1st quarter	109.44	111.21	104.06	124.14	105.59	111.81	113.30	102.52	128.99	105.15
2nd quarter	111.66	113.76	104.84	130.06	107.05	115.23	117.22	103.59	137.28	106.30
3rd quarter	112.29	114.29	105.52	130.31	107.90	115.13	117.14	103.89	136.58	106.13
4th quarter	111.16	112.79	105.18	126.61	107.62	114.92	117.06	103.40	137.21	105.27
2012										
1st quarter	111.96	113.46	105.50	127.95	108.67	116.12	118.43	103.70	140.45	105.68
2nd quarter	112.13	113.42	105.66	127.51	109.31	115.04	117.08	103.51	137.17	105.82
3rd quarter	112.11	113.41	105.35	128.08	109.29	113.57	115.32	103.18	132.92	105.74
4th quarter	112.54	113.73	105.67	128.39	109.97	114.72	116.59	103.46	135.98	106.34

[1] Exports and imports of certain goods, primarily military equipment purchased and sold by the federal government, are included in services. Beginning with 1986, repairs and alterations of equipment are reclassified from goods to services.

Table 7-4. Exports and Imports of Selected NIPA Types of Product

(Billions of dollars, quarterly data are at seasonally adjusted annual rates.)   **NIPA Table 4.2.5**

Year and quarter	Exports Goods — Foods, feeds, and beverages	Industrial supplies and materials	Capital goods, except auto-motive	Auto-motive vehicles, engines, and parts	Consumer goods, except auto-motive	Services Travel	Other private services (financial, profes-sional, etc.)	Imports Goods — Foods, feeds, and beverages	Industrial supplies and materials, except petroleum and products	Petroleum and products	Capital goods, except auto-motive	Auto-motive vehicles, engines, and parts	Consumer goods, except auto-motive	Services Travel	Other private services (financial, profes-sional, etc.)
1967	5.0	10.0	9.9	2.8	2.1	1.6	0.7	4.6	9.9	2.1	2.5	2.4	4.2	3.2	0.4
1968	4.8	11.0	11.1	3.5	2.3	1.8	0.8	5.3	12.0	2.4	2.8	4.0	5.4	3.0	0.5
1969	4.7	11.7	12.4	3.9	2.6	2.0	0.9	5.2	11.7	2.6	3.4	5.1	6.5	3.4	0.6
1970	5.9	13.8	14.7	3.9	2.8	2.3	1.0	6.1	12.2	2.9	4.0	5.7	7.4	4.0	0.6
1971	6.1	12.6	15.4	4.7	2.9	2.5	1.3	6.4	13.6	3.7	4.3	7.6	8.4	4.4	0.7
1972	7.5	13.9	16.9	5.5	3.6	2.8	1.5	7.3	16.0	4.7	5.9	9.0	11.1	5.0	0.8
1973	15.2	19.7	22.0	7.0	4.8	3.4	1.7	9.1	19.2	8.4	8.3	10.7	12.9	5.5	0.9
1974	18.6	29.9	30.9	8.8	6.4	4.0	3.0	10.6	27.0	26.6	9.8	12.4	14.4	6.0	1.9
1975	19.2	29.3	36.6	10.8	6.6	4.7	3.7	9.6	23.6	27.0	10.2	12.1	13.2	6.4	2.3
1976	19.8	31.6	39.1	12.2	8.0	5.7	4.5	11.5	28.5	34.6	12.3	16.8	17.2	6.9	2.9
1977	19.7	33.2	39.8	13.5	8.9	6.2	4.9	14.0	33.4	45.0	14.0	19.4	21.8	7.5	3.2
1978	25.7	38.4	47.5	15.2	11.4	7.2	6.2	15.8	39.3	42.6	19.3	25.0	29.4	8.5	3.9
1979	30.5	53.3	60.2	17.9	14.0	8.4	7.3	18.0	45.0	60.4	24.6	26.6	31.3	9.4	4.6
1980	36.3	68.0	76.3	17.4	17.8	10.6	8.6	18.6	47.3	79.5	31.6	28.3	34.3	10.4	5.1
1981	38.8	65.7	84.2	19.7	17.7	12.9	13.2	18.6	52.0	78.4	37.1	31.0	38.4	11.5	6.3
1982	32.2	61.8	76.5	17.2	16.1	12.4	16.9	17.5	45.4	62.0	38.4	34.3	39.7	12.4	7.4
1983	32.1	57.1	71.7	18.5	14.9	10.9	17.6	18.8	51.1	55.1	43.7	43.0	47.3	13.2	7.3
1984	32.2	61.9	77.0	22.4	15.1	17.2	18.6	21.9	62.6	58.1	60.4	56.5	61.1	22.9	8.2
1985	24.6	59.4	79.3	24.9	14.6	17.8	19.4	21.8	59.2	51.4	61.3	64.9	66.3	24.6	9.4
1986	23.5	59.0	82.8	25.1	16.7	20.4	28.3	24.4	62.5	34.3	72.0	78.1	79.4	25.9	13.8
1987	25.2	67.4	92.7	27.6	20.3	23.6	29.6	24.8	66.1	42.9	85.1	85.2	88.8	29.3	17.3
1988	33.8	84.2	119.1	33.4	27.0	29.4	31.4	24.9	76.6	39.6	102.2	87.9	96.4	32.1	18.4
1989	36.3	95.4	136.9	35.1	35.9	36.2	37.0	24.9	78.8	50.9	112.3	87.4	103.6	33.4	19.9
1990	35.1	101.9	153.0	36.2	43.5	43.0	40.6	26.4	78.2	62.3	116.4	88.2	105.0	37.4	23.3
1991	35.7	106.2	166.6	39.9	46.6	48.4	48.1	26.2	75.7	51.7	121.1	85.5	107.7	35.3	26.8
1992	40.3	105.2	176.4	46.9	51.2	54.7	50.3	27.6	82.4	51.6	134.8	91.5	122.4	38.6	25.4
1993	40.5	102.9	182.7	51.6	54.5	57.9	53.5	27.9	88.7	51.5	153.2	102.1	133.7	40.7	27.8
1994	42.4	115.4	205.7	57.5	59.7	58.4	60.8	31.0	105.0	51.3	185.0	118.1	145.9	43.8	31.6
1995	50.8	141.0	234.4	61.4	64.2	63.4	65.0	33.2	119.6	56.0	222.1	123.7	159.7	44.9	35.2
1996	56.0	141.3	254.0	64.4	69.3	69.8	73.3	35.7	124.6	72.7	228.4	128.7	172.5	48.1	39.7
1997	52.0	153.0	295.8	73.4	77.0	73.4	83.9	39.7	134.7	71.8	253.6	139.4	195.2	52.1	43.2
1998	46.8	143.3	299.8	72.5	79.4	71.3	91.8	41.3	142.2	50.9	269.8	148.6	218.5	56.5	47.6
1999	46.0	145.7	311.2	75.3	80.9	75.2	96.8	44.1	149.8	72.1	296.1	178.2	243.9	59.3	55.9
2000	47.9	171.1	357.0	80.4	89.3	82.9	100.8	46.5	175.1	126.1	347.7	195.0	284.7	65.4	61.1
2001	49.4	159.5	321.7	75.4	88.3	72.6	106.9	47.2	167.4	109.4	299.2	188.7	287.1	60.9	66.6
2002	49.6	157.3	290.4	78.9	84.3	67.4	115.1	50.3	161.4	109.3	284.9	202.8	311.4	59.5	73.2
2003	55.0	173.3	293.7	80.6	89.9	65.2	123.8	56.5	177.3	140.4	297.6	209.2	338.6	58.3	80.3
2004	56.6	206.3	327.5	89.2	103.2	75.5	141.5	63.0	228.2	189.9	346.1	227.3	378.3	66.7	90.6
2005	59.0	236.8	358.4	98.4	115.3	82.2	153.7	69.1	268.0	263.2	382.8	238.7	412.9	69.9	97.7
2006	66.0	279.1	404.0	107.3	129.1	86.2	176.8	76.1	293.5	316.7	422.6	256.0	447.9	73.0	127.3
2007	84.3	316.3	433.0	121.3	146.0	97.4	211.6	83.0	297.9	346.7	449.1	258.5	480.0	77.1	149.8
2008	108.3	386.9	457.7	121.5	161.3	110.4	232.0	90.4	318.7	476.1	458.7	233.2	486.7	80.5	172.5
2009	93.9	293.5	391.5	81.7	149.5	94.2	237.3	82.9	196.6	267.7	374.1	159.2	431.4	74.1	174.6
2010	107.7	388.6	447.8	112.0	165.2	103.5	256.0	92.5	249.4	353.6	450.4	225.6	486.5	75.5	186.4
2011	126.2	484.7	493.3	132.8	175.0	115.6	279.6	108.3	293.0	462.1	513.5	255.2	517.5	78.2	199.7
2012	132.8	482.3	527.7	146.1	181.7	126.2	294.5	111.1	290.0	433.9	551.7	298.5	519.6	83.5	201.2
2007															
1st quarter	74.5	294.1	420.4	114.9	141.3	88.2	200.2	81.7	289.2	296.8	442.0	254.9	484.9	75.5	142.2
2nd quarter	77.1	310.4	424.3	122.3	144.1	92.8	209.0	81.6	305.0	326.5	446.3	257.7	476.5	75.8	146.6
3rd quarter	87.9	319.8	439.5	124.1	147.9	101.5	216.9	83.9	302.9	345.0	453.5	265.8	474.2	77.4	154.1
4th quarter	97.6	340.8	447.8	123.8	150.6	106.9	220.4	84.7	294.6	418.5	454.6	255.6	484.3	79.8	156.5
2008															
1st quarter	108.9	371.1	454.4	122.2	157.6	109.3	226.7	87.8	309.3	469.0	465.0	257.9	490.9	82.6	163.8
2nd quarter	116.5	418.1	470.8	126.4	164.7	112.6	235.9	91.2	334.5	520.2	476.6	252.5	499.7	80.9	170.1
3rd quarter	115.3	430.8	473.3	130.3	167.8	115.5	232.6	92.8	347.5	554.2	466.5	229.2	498.3	79.8	176.7
4th quarter	92.6	327.7	432.2	106.9	155.0	104.4	232.9	89.9	283.6	361.1	426.7	193.2	457.9	78.7	179.5
2009															
1st quarter	86.0	262.8	394.3	68.3	145.2	94.8	235.6	83.0	209.2	222.6	372.2	129.8	426.8	76.4	169.5
2nd quarter	95.6	272.4	377.3	68.0	144.4	92.6	234.9	82.1	174.9	239.8	352.0	129.2	420.7	71.3	173.3
3rd quarter	93.5	308.2	383.7	88.3	149.8	93.9	234.6	82.3	187.5	289.0	371.1	174.4	426.9	74.2	175.3
4th quarter	100.6	330.7	410.7	102.3	158.3	95.4	244.2	84.1	214.9	319.4	400.9	203.4	451.2	74.6	180.2
2010															
1st quarter	104.0	355.1	423.8	106.5	162.5	100.5	240.6	88.1	237.1	353.8	410.4	203.1	456.8	74.7	180.5
2nd quarter	96.8	385.5	443.1	111.0	160.5	101.4	246.2	91.6	251.2	355.1	442.0	225.5	481.4	73.0	184.2
3rd quarter	106.4	388.6	455.5	112.5	164.0	104.2	262.2	94.2	252.2	346.4	466.3	234.2	504.5	76.5	187.9
4th quarter	123.6	425.1	469.0	118.0	174.0	107.7	275.0	96.0	257.2	359.3	483.0	239.8	503.3	77.8	193.1
2011															
1st quarter	128.0	462.0	473.2	127.5	169.5	109.5	274.0	103.0	282.2	444.2	491.9	250.1	511.4	75.7	191.3
2nd quarter	126.8	487.6	490.7	128.5	175.2	115.7	278.2	108.9	298.6	476.4	507.2	232.2	521.1	78.4	199.7
3rd quarter	125.2	495.8	500.1	136.7	176.7	119.4	286.2	108.3	301.5	460.2	519.2	264.7	516.7	79.0	204.6
4th quarter	124.8	493.5	509.0	138.7	178.3	117.6	280.2	112.8	289.6	467.8	535.6	274.0	520.7	79.8	203.1
2012															
1st quarter	120.4	487.7	525.6	145.6	177.7	121.0	292.2	111.7	289.6	472.9	550.4	292.7	511.1	83.8	199.1
2nd quarter	131.1	489.3	526.6	148.3	183.0	125.5	293.8	110.3	290.4	440.3	557.1	297.3	519.7	84.6	199.3
3rd quarter	146.7	474.8	532.0	145.9	182.2	128.3	287.9	111.0	291.6	408.1	548.5	303.0	521.0	82.8	201.0
4th quarter	133.1	477.5	526.4	144.8	184.1	130.1	304.2	111.4	288.2	414.1	550.7	301.2	526.8	82.6	205.5

Table 7-5. Chain-Type Quantity Indexes for Exports and Imports of Selected NIPA Types of Product

(Index numbers, 2009 = 100; quarterly indexes are seasonally adjusted.) NIPA Table 4.2.3

Year and quarter	Exports Goods — Foods, feeds, and beverages	Industrial supplies and materials	Capital goods, except automotive	Automotive vehicles, engines, and parts	Consumer goods, except automotive	Services — Travel	Other private services (financial, professional, etc.)	Imports Goods — Foods, feeds, and beverages	Industrial supplies and materials, except petroleum and products	Petroleum and products	Capital goods, except automotive	Automotive vehicles, engines, and parts	Consumer goods, except automotive	Services — Travel	Other private services (financial, professional, etc.)
1967	22.01	18.04	3.59	18.39	5.03	11.54	1.35	26.91	27.62	18.59	0.63	11.28	4.00	21.55	0.79
1968	21.66	20.52	3.70	22.66	5.47	11.92	1.40	30.53	32.87	21.41	0.73	17.54	5.05	19.53	0.89
1969	21.21	21.46	3.92	24.50	5.85	13.02	1.54	28.93	31.11	23.89	0.85	21.42	5.96	21.19	0.99
1970	25.60	24.03	4.38	23.93	6.20	14.04	1.65	30.90	31.43	25.80	0.88	21.91	6.41	24.45	1.04
1971	24.92	21.72	4.58	27.13	6.22	14.66	1.91	31.90	34.26	29.51	0.87	26.72	6.74	24.42	1.15
1972	29.42	23.14	5.01	30.44	7.28	15.74	2.13	33.96	37.59	36.04	1.12	28.95	8.22	26.41	1.19
1973	38.08	28.47	6.36	35.75	8.87	18.09	2.32	34.83	37.84	51.20	1.38	29.88	8.43	24.92	1.33
1974	34.13	29.29	7.95	39.87	11.04	19.68	3.79	32.22	36.86	49.29	1.47	31.73	7.59	22.37	2.67
1975	36.10	25.63	8.07	41.98	10.17	21.28	4.40	28.50	31.05	48.47	1.40	25.18	5.89	21.58	3.02
1976	40.97	27.68	7.96	43.89	11.47	24.24	5.09	32.44	37.81	58.45	1.69	33.37	7.59	22.95	3.62
1977	40.93	27.91	7.83	44.21	12.41	24.29	5.24	32.11	40.68	70.32	1.81	35.35	9.17	23.65	3.79
1978	50.57	30.84	8.94	45.39	14.33	26.10	6.21	36.05	44.55	66.48	2.33	38.25	11.26	24.43	4.44
1979	53.65	35.32	10.73	45.68	15.06	27.98	6.92	37.01	42.80	67.25	2.85	36.99	11.35	23.83	5.02
1980	60.48	40.09	12.53	38.47	18.25	31.25	7.40	32.21	37.35	54.31	3.36	36.64	11.43	23.80	5.13
1981	61.74	37.39	12.58	38.03	17.50	34.50	10.57	33.51	40.55	47.59	3.96	35.46	12.52	25.18	6.04
1982	58.01	36.26	11.12	31.16	15.75	30.75	12.75	34.16	36.76	40.93	4.31	37.96	13.09	29.85	6.85
1983	55.45	34.50	10.72	32.24	14.40	25.97	12.60	37.08	43.65	40.50	5.21	46.46	15.75	33.81	6.42
1984	53.96	36.26	11.88	38.04	14.33	38.73	12.78	42.00	54.14	42.78	7.79	59.69	19.88	61.81	7.19
1985	46.69	36.47	13.05	41.40	13.91	38.34	12.75	43.82	54.44	40.18	8.78	66.89	21.70	68.22	8.01
1986	48.17	38.10	14.24	40.71	15.38	42.78	18.06	44.85	57.34	49.67	9.96	72.41	24.05	63.42	11.46
1987	51.56	39.05	16.44	43.89	18.10	47.21	18.10	45.97	56.77	51.88	11.38	74.30	24.82	75.20	13.10
1988	56.66	44.02	20.91	52.09	23.12	56.95	18.95	44.15	57.39	57.38	13.11	72.43	25.19	77.27	13.99
1989	58.94	48.95	24.25	53.55	29.64	68.07	21.90	45.14	56.09	62.05	14.83	70.59	26.36	79.62	16.32
1990	60.80	51.84	28.05	53.62	34.77	76.78	23.02	46.87	56.97	62.71	16.02	70.69	25.89	85.06	17.70
1991	61.96	55.36	30.70	57.51	36.03	81.35	26.20	44.75	55.91	62.49	17.23	65.91	26.34	77.03	19.70
1992	70.23	56.40	33.63	66.29	38.81	90.25	26.66	47.24	61.46	65.31	19.96	69.30	29.08	79.31	18.47
1993	69.88	54.90	35.83	72.27	40.77	94.67	27.79	47.80	66.69	71.54	23.28	76.15	31.50	83.19	19.59
1994	70.61	57.75	41.35	79.89	44.55	95.14	31.17	48.89	76.61	76.38	28.55	85.39	34.12	86.15	22.09
1995	78.00	62.30	49.27	84.20	47.22	102.00	32.64	50.12	80.21	75.00	35.15	86.87	36.81	86.82	24.32
1996	76.75	65.46	57.10	87.31	50.36	109.70	36.08	55.13	84.78	81.32	41.30	89.81	39.64	90.23	26.63
1997	77.23	71.17	69.99	98.83	55.55	112.84	40.79	60.71	91.77	84.69	51.83	97.07	45.40	98.01	28.57
1998	76.45	70.38	72.97	97.49	57.23	108.37	44.66	65.16	101.92	90.53	59.61	103.35	51.52	110.80	31.92
1999	78.68	72.60	77.01	100.56	58.54	111.21	48.00	71.99	107.93	97.29	68.42	123.08	57.93	113.65	37.55
2000	82.62	79.02	88.59	106.20	64.38	117.14	49.82	76.69	114.96	100.84	82.20	133.14	68.14	127.03	41.87
2001	84.84	75.82	79.80	99.25	63.86	102.10	53.18	80.13	110.83	103.81	72.86	128.78	69.25	121.18	45.93
2002	83.09	76.19	72.87	103.34	61.31	95.45	57.29	84.40	114.21	101.38	71.74	137.92	75.92	113.90	48.80
2003	84.53	78.33	74.59	104.81	64.97	90.49	60.65	90.90	115.87	108.15	75.94	141.51	82.72	104.00	52.61
2004	79.37	83.58	83.51	115.18	73.91	101.25	67.58	96.41	133.78	115.31	89.47	151.45	91.96	110.98	59.27
2005	83.67	85.65	91.13	125.49	81.63	94.47	70.91	99.77	142.44	117.63	99.63	157.13	99.46	108.97	63.60
2006	90.30	91.99	102.00	135.12	90.25	94.86	78.62	105.93	148.63	115.42	110.93	167.81	107.45	109.30	78.50
2007	98.17	96.91	110.29	151.02	99.96	103.52	90.99	107.24	142.84	112.68	118.39	167.81	113.64	106.90	89.78
2008	104.78	107.53	116.90	149.67	108.15	112.37	96.93	106.02	132.28	108.81	120.33	147.91	112.44	104.20	100.02
2009	100.00	100.00	100.00	100.00	100.00	100.00	100.00	100.00	100.00	100.00	100.00	100.00	100.00	100.00	100.00
2010	110.34	115.61	113.70	136.42	109.37	106.60	105.54	102.28	114.57	100.47	121.33	140.87	112.82	99.89	105.04
2011	109.95	123.07	124.27	159.12	114.26	113.27	112.09	104.32	122.11	98.55	138.01	154.58	117.91	100.89	111.17
2012	108.91	125.24	131.84	171.98	116.96	120.32	116.10	108.15	125.40	90.48	147.98	177.39	116.69	107.93	112.16
2007															
1st quarter	92.72	94.43	106.07	143.56	97.61	96.13	86.98	110.01	143.20	112.58	116.15	166.26	115.22	109.74	86.60
2nd quarter	93.39	95.77	107.86	152.67	98.79	99.28	90.59	107.73	147.11	114.15	117.79	168.01	113.27	106.11	88.46
3rd quarter	101.62	97.42	112.32	154.28	101.10	107.27	92.92	106.87	145.09	111.80	119.53	172.65	112.08	105.90	91.73
4th quarter	104.97	100.03	114.93	153.58	102.35	111.40	93.46	104.36	135.96	112.20	120.11	164.30	113.98	105.84	92.34
2008															
1st quarter	108.71	105.53	116.88	152.17	106.41	112.03	95.03	107.82	137.06	110.10	122.93	165.17	114.53	107.42	96.18
2nd quarter	107.28	110.90	120.36	155.92	110.25	113.82	98.65	106.48	135.03	106.74	124.53	160.05	115.08	101.36	98.52
3rd quarter	104.26	110.69	120.51	159.92	111.99	114.67	96.24	104.66	134.53	105.08	121.67	144.64	114.45	101.78	101.06
4th quarter	98.86	102.99	109.86	130.67	103.95	108.96	97.79	105.13	122.52	113.33	112.21	121.77	105.67	106.22	104.30
2009															
1st quarter	94.80	93.43	100.78	83.52	97.32	101.53	99.82	101.73	105.57	109.85	99.02	81.85	98.76	105.07	98.54
2nd quarter	99.25	95.69	96.90	83.34	97.29	99.64	100.21	100.18	92.92	98.57	94.26	81.62	97.58	96.55	99.95
3rd quarter	98.57	104.10	98.15	108.18	99.95	99.42	98.62	99.42	97.41	96.88	99.32	109.47	99.10	99.29	99.80
4th quarter	107.39	106.79	104.17	124.97	105.44	99.41	101.36	98.67	104.10	94.70	107.41	127.06	104.57	99.10	101.72
2010															
1st quarter	110.87	110.76	107.72	129.83	108.22	104.19	99.74	101.93	109.82	97.93	110.41	127.19	105.73	99.11	101.58
2nd quarter	103.51	115.45	112.59	135.45	106.57	105.03	101.52	103.06	115.38	102.67	119.19	141.29	111.25	97.19	103.99
3rd quarter	109.97	116.28	115.75	137.04	108.70	107.48	108.32	103.79	117.14	103.77	125.77	146.18	117.11	101.55	106.32
4th quarter	117.01	119.95	118.73	143.37	113.99	109.72	112.57	100.36	115.93	97.51	129.93	148.81	117.18	101.72	108.26
2011															
1st quarter	113.14	121.50	119.69	154.38	111.25	109.32	110.68	102.09	119.85	101.91	132.11	154.23	118.15	98.12	106.39
2nd quarter	109.56	121.44	123.72	154.69	114.56	113.50	111.21	102.88	123.26	98.23	136.11	140.27	119.27	100.22	110.96
3rd quarter	107.19	122.96	125.72	163.04	114.91	116.03	114.08	103.38	123.28	96.84	139.49	159.25	117.15	101.41	113.96
4th quarter	109.91	126.38	127.94	164.37	116.33	114.26	112.41	108.92	122.04	97.23	144.33	164.56	117.06	103.82	113.35
2012															
1st quarter	105.18	124.03	131.55	171.93	114.92	115.99	116.06	107.49	124.98	92.62	147.29	174.94	114.69	108.56	110.94
2nd quarter	110.84	126.42	131.51	174.22	117.73	119.75	115.95	106.60	125.09	91.47	149.37	176.81	116.60	109.68	111.01
3rd quarter	115.45	125.14	133.03	171.42	117.11	122.19	113.50	108.75	127.64	90.19	147.19	179.93	117.27	107.46	112.06
4th quarter	104.16	125.38	131.28	170.36	118.06	123.36	118.90	109.75	123.90	87.66	148.07	177.89	118.18	106.02	114.62

Section 7b: U.S. International Transactions Accounts

Figure 7-2. Balance on Current Account and Financial Inflows and Outflows, 1960–2012

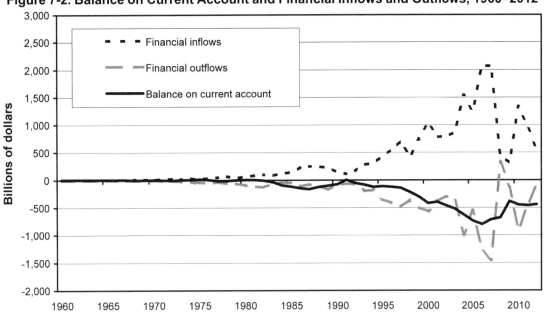

- The U.S. current-account international balance is also recorded in the International Transactions Accounts (ITAs). The definitional differences between this balance and the balance in the NIPAs are minor, and the trends in the two measures are similar. The ITAs measure the current account surplus or deficit (commonly known as the "balance of payments") and directly measure the financial flows required to finance it. (Table 7-6A and B)

- Figure 7-2 above shows the current-account balance since 1960, culminating in a $440 billion deficit in 2012, and the corresponding estimated financial flows. U.S. net investment in assets abroad contributed a further outflow, amounting to $97 billion, in 2012. Financing the sum of these was a financial inflow, that is a net increase in foreign-owned assets in the United States, estimated at $544 billion. The net of the estimated financial flows does not exactly equal the current-account balance because of small capital transactions, a negative net derivatives balance of $7 billion, and an unusually small ITA statistical discrepancy. (Table 7-6A)

- Large quarterly and annual variations during the last several years in many types of financial flows, including those involving official assets, are evidence of an extreme amount of international financial turbulence and official intervention. (Table 7-6A and B)

- Through the early 1980s, the United States was still a net creditor with respect to the rest of the world, meaning that the value of the stock of U.S.-owned assets abroad exceeded the value of foreign-owned assets in the United States. Since then, the persistent net financial inflows associated with current-account deficits have cumulated, resulting in a growing net debtor status, with the value of foreign-owned assets in the United States exceeding the value of U.S.-owned assets abroad by $3.9 trillion as of the end of 2012. (Table 7-8)

Table 7-6A. U.S. International Transactions: Recent Data

(Millions of dollars, seasonally adjusted.)

Year and quarter	Current account									
	Exports of goods and services and income receipts									
	Total	Exports of goods and services	Exports of goods	Exports of services	Income receipts					Compensation of employees
					Total	Income receipts on U.S.-owned assets abroad				
						Total	Direct investment receipts	Other private receipts	U.S. government receipts	
1960	30 556	25 940	19 650	6 290	4 616	4 616	3 621	646	349	. . .
1961	31 402	26 403	20 108	6 295	4 999	4 999	3 823	793	383	. . .
1962	33 340	27 722	20 781	6 941	5 618	5 618	4 241	904	473	. . .
1963	35 776	29 620	22 272	7 348	6 157	6 157	4 636	1 022	499	. . .
1964	40 165	33 341	25 501	7 840	6 824	6 824	5 106	1 256	462	. . .
1965	42 722	35 285	26 461	8 824	7 437	7 437	5 506	1 421	510	. . .
1966	46 454	38 926	29 310	9 616	7 528	7 528	5 260	1 669	599	. . .
1967	49 353	41 333	30 666	10 667	8 021	8 021	5 603	1 781	636	. . .
1968	54 911	45 543	33 626	11 917	9 367	9 367	6 591	2 021	756	. . .
1969	60 132	49 220	36 414	12 806	10 913	10 913	7 649	2 338	925	. . .
1970	68 387	56 640	42 469	14 171	11 748	11 748	8 169	2 671	907	. . .
1971	72 384	59 677	43 319	16 358	12 707	12 707	9 160	2 641	906	. . .
1972	81 986	67 222	49 381	17 841	14 765	14 765	10 949	2 949	866	. . .
1973	113 050	91 242	71 410	19 832	21 808	21 808	16 542	4 330	936	. . .
1974	148 484	120 897	98 306	22 591	27 587	27 587	19 157	7 356	1 074	. . .
1975	157 936	132 585	107 088	25 497	25 351	25 351	16 595	7 644	1 112	. . .
1976	172 090	142 716	114 745	27 971	29 375	29 375	18 999	9 043	1 332	. . .
1977	184 655	152 301	120 816	31 485	32 354	32 354	19 673	11 057	1 625	. . .
1978	220 516	178 428	142 075	36 353	42 088	42 088	25 458	14 788	1 843	. . .
1979	287 965	224 131	184 439	39 692	63 834	63 834	38 183	23 356	2 295	. . .
1980	344 440	271 834	224 250	47 584	72 606	72 606	37 146	32 898	2 562	. . .
1981	380 928	294 398	237 044	57 354	86 529	86 529	32 549	50 300	3 680	. . .
1982	366 983	275 236	211 157	64 079	91 747	91 747	. . .	58 160	4 118	. . .
1983	356 106	266 106	201 799	64 307	90 000	90 000	31 750	53 418	4 832	. . .
1984	399 913	291 094	219 926	71 168	108 819	108 819	35 325	68 267	5 227	. . .
1985	387 612	289 070	215 915	73 155	98 542	98 542	35 410	57 633	5 499	. . .
1986	407 098	310 033	223 344	86 689	97 064	96 156	36 938	52 806	6 413	908
1987	457 053	348 869	250 208	98 661	108 184	107 190	46 288	55 592	5 311	994
1988	567 862	431 149	320 230	110 919	136 713	135 718	58 445	70 571	6 703	995
1989	648 290	487 003	359 916	127 087	161 287	160 270	61 981	92 638	5 651	1 017
1990	706 975	535 233	387 401	147 832	171 742	170 570	65 973	94 072	10 525	1 172
1991	727 557	578 344	414 083	164 261	149 214	147 924	58 718	81 186	8 019	1 290
1992	750 648	616 883	439 631	177 252	133 766	131 970	57 538	67 316	7 115	1 796
1993	778 920	642 863	456 943	185 920	136 057	134 237	67 246	61 865	5 126	1 820
1994	869 775	703 254	502 859	200 395	166 521	164 578	77 344	83 106	4 128	1 943
1995	1 004 631	794 387	575 204	219 183	210 244	208 065	95 260	108 092	4 713	2 179
1996	1 077 731	851 602	612 113	239 489	226 129	223 948	102 505	116 852	4 591	2 181
1997	1 191 257	934 453	678 366	256 087	256 804	254 534	115 323	135 652	3 559	2 270
1998	1 194 993	933 174	670 416	262 758	261 819	259 382	103 963	151 818	3 601	2 437
1999	1 262 431	967 008	698 218	268 790	295 423	291 177	131 626	156 354	3 197	4 246
2000	1 425 260	1 072 782	784 781	288 002	352 478	348 083	151 839	192 398	3 846	4 395
2001	1 300 156	1 007 725	731 189	276 537	292 430	287 918	128 665	155 692	3 561	4 512
2002	1 263 580	980 879	697 439	283 440	282 701	278 131	145 590	129 238	3 303	4 570
2003	1 346 348	1 023 937	729 816	294 121	322 411	317 740	186 417	126 529	4 794	4 671
2004	1 579 517	1 163 724	821 986	341 739	415 793	411 059	250 606	157 313	3 140	4 734
2005	1 825 596	1 288 257	911 686	376 571	537 339	532 542	294 538	235 120	2 884	4 796
2006	2 145 469	1 460 792	1 039 406	421 386	684 677	679 608	324 816	352 122	2 670	5 069
2007	2 486 810	1 652 859	1 163 605	489 255	833 951	828 732	370 758	455 436	2 538	5 219
2008	2 654 418	1 840 332	1 307 329	533 003	814 086	808 721	413 739	389 881	5 101	5 364
2009	2 184 786	1 578 187	1 069 475	508 712	606 599	600 859	362 520	233 547	4 792	5 740
2010	2 522 520	1 844 468	1 288 795	555 674	678 051	672 120	440 906	229 720	1 494	5 931
2011	2 873 654	2 112 825	1 495 853	616 973	760 829	754 724	478 803	273 999	1 923	6 105
2012	2 986 949	2 210 585	1 561 239	649 346	776 364	770 079	470 233	297 891	1 954	6 286
2009										
1st quarter	527 063	378 600	254 016	124 584	148 463	147 042	79 660	64 906	2 476	1 421
2nd quarter	523 402	378 626	253 796	124 829	144 776	143 344	84 586	57 641	1 117	1 432
3rd quarter	550 164	396 852	270 087	126 765	153 313	151 870	95 398	55 733	739	1 443
4th quarter	584 157	424 111	291 577	132 534	160 046	158 603	102 876	55 267	460	1 444
2010										
1st quarter	600 890	436 943	303 979	132 964	163 947	162 471	107 022	55 013	435	1 476
2nd quarter	618 315	450 707	315 122	135 585	167 609	166 124	109 149	56 636	339	1 484
3rd quarter	635 337	465 899	324 746	141 153	169 438	167 952	110 025	57 574	353	1 486
4th quarter	667 977	490 919	344 947	145 972	177 058	175 573	114 710	60 497	367	1 484
2011										
1st quarter	692 037	509 057	360 094	148 963	182 980	181 456	118 228	62 802	426	1 523
2nd quarter	715 865	525 282	371 315	153 967	190 583	189 056	120 758	67 787	511	1 527
3rd quarter	735 595	540 553	381 584	158 970	195 041	193 510	121 767	71 217	525	1 531
4th quarter	730 158	537 933	382 860	155 073	192 225	190 703	118 049	72 193	461	1 523
2012										
1st quarter	742 117	548 046	387 559	160 487	194 071	192 550	119 118	72 752	680	1 521
2nd quarter	746 799	553 702	391 867	161 835	193 097	191 551	115 731	75 384	436	1 546
3rd quarter	744 602	552 275	391 474	160 802	192 327	190 748	115 735	74 554	459	1 579
4th quarter	753 430	556 561	390 339	166 222	196 869	195 230	119 649	75 201	380	1 639

. . . = Not available.

Table 7-6A. U.S. International Transactions: Recent Data—*Continued*

(Millions of dollars, seasonally adjusted.)

Year and quarter	Current account—*Continued*									
	Imports of goods and services and income payments [1]									
						Income payments				
							Income payments on foreign-owned assets in the U.S.			
	Total	Imports of goods and services	Imports of goods	Imports of services	Total	Total	Direct investment payments	Other private payments	U.S. government payments	Compensation of employees
1960	-23 670	-22 432	-14 758	-7 674	-1 238	-1 238	-394	-511	-332	. . .
1961	-23 453	-22 208	-14 537	-7 671	-1 245	-1 245	-432	-535	-278	. . .
1962	-25 676	-24 352	-16 260	-8 092	-1 324	-1 324	-399	-586	-339	. . .
1963	-26 970	-25 410	-17 048	-8 362	-1 560	-1 560	-459	-701	-401	. . .
1964	-29 102	-27 319	-18 700	-8 619	-1 783	-1 783	-529	-802	-453	. . .
1965	-32 708	-30 621	-21 510	-9 111	-2 088	-2 088	-657	-942	-489	. . .
1966	-38 468	-35 987	-25 493	-10 494	-2 481	-2 481	-711	-1 221	-549	. . .
1967	-41 476	-38 729	-26 866	-11 863	-2 747	-2 747	-821	-1 328	-598	. . .
1968	-48 671	-45 293	-32 991	-12 302	-3 378	-3 378	-876	-1 800	-702	. . .
1969	-53 998	-49 129	-35 807	-13 322	-4 869	-4 869	-848	-3 244	-777	. . .
1970	-59 901	-54 386	-39 866	-14 520	-5 515	-5 515	-875	-3 617	-1 024	. . .
1971	-66 414	-60 979	-45 579	-15 400	-5 435	-5 435	-1 164	-2 428	-1 844	. . .
1972	-79 237	-72 665	-55 797	-16 868	-6 572	-6 572	-1 284	-2 604	-2 684	. . .
1973	-98 997	-89 342	-70 499	-18 843	-9 655	-9 655	-1 610	-4 209	-3 836	. . .
1974	-137 274	-125 190	-103 811	-21 379	-12 084	-12 084	-1 331	-6 491	-4 262	. . .
1975	-132 745	-120 181	-98 185	-21 996	-12 564	-12 564	-2 234	-5 788	-4 542	. . .
1976	-162 109	-148 798	-124 228	-24 570	-13 311	-13 311	-3 110	-5 681	-4 520	. . .
1977	-193 764	-179 547	-151 907	-27 640	-14 217	-14 217	-2 834	-5 841	-5 542	. . .
1978	-229 870	-208 191	-176 002	-32 189	-21 680	-21 680	-4 211	-8 795	-8 674	. . .
1979	-281 657	-248 696	-212 007	-36 689	-32 961	-32 961	-6 357	-15 481	-11 122	. . .
1980	-333 774	-291 241	-249 750	-41 491	-42 532	-42 532	-8 635	-21 214	-12 684	. . .
1981	-364 196	-310 570	-265 067	-45 503	-53 626	-53 626	-6 898	-29 415	-17 313	. . .
1982	-355 975	-299 391	-247 642	-51 749	-56 583	-56 583	-2 114	-35 187	-19 282	. . .
1983	-377 488	-323 874	-268 901	-54 973	-53 614	-53 614	-4 120	-30 501	-18 993	. . .
1984	-473 923	-400 166	-332 418	-67 748	-73 756	-73 756	-8 443	-44 158	-21 155	. . .
1985	-483 769	-410 950	-338 088	-72 862	-72 819	-72 819	-6 945	-42 745	-23 129	. . .
1986	-530 142	-448 572	-368 425	-80 147	-81 571	-78 893	-6 856	-47 412	-24 625	-2 678
1987	-594 443	-500 552	-409 765	-90 787	-93 891	-91 553	-7 676	-57 659	-26 218	-2 338
1988	-663 741	-545 715	-447 189	-98 526	-118 026	-116 179	-12 150	-72 314	-31 715	-1 847
1989	-721 607	-580 144	-477 665	-102 479	-141 463	-139 177	-7 045	-93 768	-38 364	-2 286
1990	-759 290	-616 097	-498 438	-117 659	-143 192	-139 728	-3 450	-95 508	-40 770	-3 464
1991	-734 563	-609 479	-491 020	-118 459	-125 084	-121 058	2 266	-82 452	-40 872	-4 026
1992	-765 626	-656 094	-536 528	-119 566	-109 531	-104 779	-2 189	-63 509	-39 081	-4 752
1993	-823 914	-713 173	-589 394	-123 779	-110 741	-105 609	-7 943	-58 290	-39 376	-5 132
1994	-951 122	-801 747	-668 690	-133 057	-149 375	-143 423	-22 150	-77 081	-44 192	-5 952
1995	-1 080 124	-890 771	-749 374	-141 397	-189 353	-183 090	-30 318	-97 149	-55 623	-6 263
1996	-1 159 478	-955 667	-803 113	-152 554	-203 811	-197 511	-33 093	-97 800	-66 618	-6 300
1997	-1 286 921	-1 042 726	-876 794	-165 932	-244 195	-237 529	-42 950	-112 878	-81 701	-6 666
1998	-1 356 868	-1 099 314	-918 637	-180 677	-257 554	-250 560	-38 418	-127 988	-84 154	-6 994
1999	-1 514 255	-1 230 764	-1 035 592	-195 172	-283 492	-272 082	-53 437	-138 120	-80 525	-11 410
2000	-1 783 419	-1 450 119	-1 231 722	-218 397	-333 300	-322 345	-56 910	-180 918	-84 517	-10 955
2001	-1 632 766	-1 370 065	-1 153 701	-216 364	-262 702	-250 989	-12 783	-159 825	-78 381	-11 713
2002	-1 656 570	-1 399 044	-1 173 281	-225 762	-257 526	-245 164	-43 244	-127 012	-74 908	-12 362
2003	-1 794 133	-1 514 482	-1 272 089	-242 393	-279 651	-266 743	-73 750	-119 051	-73 942	-12 908
2004	-2 120 285	-1 768 622	-1 488 349	-280 272	-351 664	-337 691	-99 754	-155 266	-82 671	-13 973
2005	-2 465 880	-1 996 171	-1 695 820	-300 352	-469 709	-453 800	-121 333	-228 408	-104 059	-15 909
2006	-2 854 530	-2 213 191	-1 878 194	-334 998	-641 338	-624 912	-150 770	-338 897	-135 245	-16 426
2007	-3 085 270	-2 351 925	-1 986 347	-365 577	-733 345	-717 623	-126 174	-426 796	-164 653	-15 722
2008	-3 210 575	-2 542 634	-2 141 287	-401 348	-667 941	-650 880	-129 447	-354 609	-166 824	-17 061
2009	-2 444 863	-1 961 844	-1 580 025	-381 819	-483 019	-468 600	-104 828	-219 417	-144 355	-14 418
2010	-2 844 240	-2 343 847	-1 938 950	-404 897	-500 392	-486 430	-152 890	-196 390	-137 150	-13 962
2011	-3 197 844	-2 669 663	-2 239 991	-429 672	-528 181	-513 997	-168 243	-213 350	-132 404	-14 184
2012	-3 297 677	-2 745 240	-2 302 714	-442 527	-552 437	-537 815	-176 747	-233 336	-127 732	-14 622
2009										
1st quarter	-595 820	-472 674	-377 709	-94 964	-123 146	-119 332	-16 363	-64 045	-38 924	-3 814
2nd quarter	-580 164	-459 751	-366 041	-93 710	-120 413	-116 755	-26 094	-54 283	-36 378	-3 658
3rd quarter	-610 977	-495 587	-400 231	-95 356	-115 391	-111 877	-26 230	-50 739	-34 908	-3 514
4th quarter	-657 902	-533 833	-436 044	-97 788	-124 069	-120 637	-36 142	-50 350	-34 145	-3 433
2010										
1st quarter	-675 379	-555 217	-456 924	-98 294	-120 161	-116 823	-33 905	-48 958	-33 960	-3 339
2nd quarter	-703 234	-579 856	-480 442	-99 414	-123 378	-119 884	-36 699	-49 002	-34 183	-3 494
3rd quarter	-723 784	-597 173	-494 007	-103 166	-126 611	-123 011	-40 189	-48 166	-34 656	-3 600
4th quarter	-741 842	-611 601	-507 578	-104 023	-130 241	-126 712	-42 097	-50 264	-34 351	-3 529
2011										
1st quarter	-773 337	-645 442	-541 789	-103 653	-127 895	-124 474	-39 567	-51 485	-33 422	-3 421
2nd quarter	-800 980	-665 833	-558 987	-106 846	-135 148	-131 630	-45 705	-53 166	-32 759	-3 518
3rd quarter	-809 215	-675 242	-565 472	-109 771	-133 973	-130 361	-42 881	-54 301	-33 179	-3 612
4th quarter	-814 311	-683 147	-573 745	-109 402	-131 165	-127 532	-40 090	-54 398	-33 044	-3 633
2012										
1st quarter	-830 188	-690 993	-581 163	-109 830	-139 195	-135 665	-46 476	-56 638	-32 551	-3 530
2nd quarter	-824 644	-689 004	-578 355	-110 649	-135 639	-131 898	-41 436	-58 311	-32 151	-3 742
3rd quarter	-819 001	-681 304	-570 454	-110 850	-137 697	-133 996	-44 874	-57 394	-31 728	-3 701
4th quarter	-823 844	-683 939	-572 742	-111 197	-139 905	-136 256	-43 961	-60 993	-31 302	-3 649

[1] A minus sign indicates imports of goods and services or payments of incomes.
. . . = Not available.

Table 7-6A. U.S. International Transactions: Recent Data—*Continued*

(Millions of dollars, seasonally adjusted.)

Year and quarter	Current account—*Continued*				Capital account transactions, net [2]	Financial account					
	Unilateral current transfers, net [2]					U.S.-owned assets abroad, net, excluding financial derivatives [2]					
		U.S. government		Private remittances and other transfers				U.S. official reserve assets, net			
	Total	Grants	Pensions and other transfers			Total	Total	Gold	Special drawing rights	Reserve position in the IMF	Foreign currencies
1960	-4 062	-3 367	-273	-423	. . .	-4 099	2 145	1 703	0	442	0
1961	-4 127	-3 320	-373	-434	. . .	-5 538	607	857	0	-135	-115
1962	-4 277	-3 453	-347	-477	. . .	-4 174	1 535	890	0	626	19
1963	-4 392	-3 479	-339	-575	. . .	-7 270	378	461	0	29	-112
1964	-4 240	-3 227	-399	-614	. . .	-9 560	171	125	0	266	-220
1965	-4 583	-3 444	-463	-677	. . .	-5 716	1 225	1 665	0	-94	-346
1966	-4 955	-3 802	-499	-655	. . .	-7 321	570	571	0	537	-538
1967	-5 294	-3 844	-571	-879	. . .	-9 757	53	1 170	0	-94	-1 023
1968	-5 629	-4 256	-537	-836	. . .	-10 977	-870	1 173	0	-870	-1 173
1969	-5 735	-4 259	-537	-939	. . .	-11 585	-1 179	-967	0	-1 034	822
1970	-6 156	-4 449	-611	-1 096	. . .	-9 337	2 481	787	-851	389	2 156
1971	-7 402	-5 589	-696	-1 117	. . .	-12 475	2 349	866	-249	1 350	382
1972	-8 544	-6 665	-770	-1 109	. . .	-14 497	-4	547	-703	153	-1
1973	-6 913	-4 748	-915	-1 250	. . .	-22 874	158	0	9	-33	182
1974	-9 249	-7 293	-939	-1 017	. . .	-34 745	-1 467	0	-172	-1 265	-30
1975	-7 075	-5 101	-1 068	-906	. . .	-39 703	-849	0	-66	-466	-317
1976	-5 686	-3 519	-1 250	-917	. . .	-51 269	-2 558	0	-78	-2 212	-268
1977	-5 226	-2 990	-1 378	-859	. . .	-34 785	-375	-118	-121	-294	158
1978	-5 788	-3 412	-1 532	-844	. . .	-61 130	732	-65	1 249	4 231	-4 683
1979	-6 593	-4 015	-1 658	-920	. . .	-66 054	-1 133	-65	-1 136	-189	257
1980	-8 349	-5 486	-1 818	-1 044	. . .	-86 967	-8 155	0	-16	-1 667	-6 472
1981	-11 702	-5 145	-2 041	-4 516	. . .	-114 147	-5 175	*	-1 823	-2 491	-861
1982	-16 544	-6 087	-2 251	-8 207	. . .	-127 882	-4 965	0	-1 371	-2 552	-1 041
1983	-17 310	-6 469	-2 207	-8 635	. . .	-66 373	-1 196	0	-66	-4 434	3 304
1984	-20 335	-8 696	-2 159	-9 479	. . .	-40 376	-3 131	0	-979	-995	-1 156
1985	-21 998	-11 268	-2 138	-8 593	. . .	-44 752	-3 858	0	-897	908	-3 869
1986	-24 132	-11 883	-2 372	-9 877	. . .	-111 723	312	0	-246	1 501	-942
1987	-23 265	-10 309	-2 409	-10 548	. . .	-79 296	9 149	0	-509	2 070	7 588
1988	-25 274	-10 537	-2 709	-12 028	. . .	-106 573	-3 912	0	127	1 025	-5 064
1989	-26 169	-10 860	-2 775	-12 534	-207	-175 383	-25 293	0	-535	471	-25 229
1990	-26 654	-10 359	-3 224	-13 070	-7 220	-81 234	-2 158	0	-192	731	-2 697
1991	9 904	29 193	-3 775	-15 514	-5 130	-64 388	5 763	0	-177	-367	6 307
1992	-36 636	-16 320	-4 043	-16 273	1 449	-74 410	3 901	0	2 316	-2 692	4 277
1993	-39 812	-17 036	-4 104	-18 672	-714	-200 552	-1 379	0	-537	-44	-797
1994	-40 265	-14 978	-4 556	-20 731	-1 111	-178 937	5 346	0	-441	494	5 293
1995	-38 074	-11 190	-3 451	-23 433	-222	-352 264	-9 742	0	-808	-2 466	-6 468
1996	-43 017	-15 401	-4 466	-23 150	-7	-413 409	6 668	0	370	-1 280	7 578
1997	-45 062	-12 472	-4 191	-28 399	-256	-485 475	-1 010	0	-350	-3 575	2 915
1998	-53 187	-13 270	-4 305	-35 612	-8	-353 829	-6 783	0	-147	-5 119	-1 517
1999	-48 954	-13 774	-3 352	-31 828	-4 176	-504 062	8 747	0	10	5 484	3 253
2000	-58 159	-16 836	-4 595	-36 728	-1	-560 523	-290	0	-722	2 308	-1 876
2001	-64 086	-11 591	-5 534	-46 962	13 198	-382 616	-4 911	0	-630	-3 600	-681
2002	-64 810	-17 139	-5 085	-42 586	-141	-294 646	-3 681	0	-475	-2 632	-574
2003	-70 873	-22 175	-5 278	-43 420	-1 821	-325 424	1 523	0	601	1 494	-572
2004	-88 559	-23 704	-5 997	-58 857	3 049	-100 087	2 805	0	-398	3 826	-623
2005	-99 512	-33 615	-5 249	-60 647	13 116	-546 631	14 096	0	4 511	10 200	-615
2006	-89 417	-27 767	-6 273	-55 377	-1 788	-128 572	2 374	0	-223	3 331	-734
2007	-114 929	-34 567	-6 694	-73 668	384	-145 360	-122	0	-154	1 021	-989
2008	-125 185	-36 461	-6 325	-82 398	6 010	332 109	-4 848	0	-106	-3 473	-1 269
2009	-121 559	-42 699	-6 589	-72 271	-140	-128 860	-52 256	0	-48 230	-3 357	-669
2010	-127 751	-42 736	-6 645	-78 371	-157	-909 953	-1 834	0	-31	-1 293	-510
2011	-133 535	-47 350	-7 837	-78 349	-1 212	-452 304	-15 877	0	1 752	-18 079	450
2012	-129 688	-46 090	-3 685	-79 913	6 956	-97 469	-4 460	0	-37	-4 032	-391
2009											
1st quarter	-27 476	-8 932	-711	-17 832	-20	125 090	-982	0	-15	-754	-213
2nd quarter	-31 439	-11 184	-1 968	-18 287	-29	48 192	-3 632	0	-8	-3 485	-139
3rd quarter	-32 943	-13 315	-2 233	-17 395	-36	-309 132	-49 021	0	-47 720	-1 098	-203
4th quarter	-29 704	-9 267	-1 679	-18 757	-56	6 990	1 379	0	-487	1 980	-114
2010											
1st quarter	-34 906	-11 772	-1 715	-21 419	-3	-251 291	-773	0	-7	-581	-185
2nd quarter	-30 438	-9 479	-1 371	-19 588	-2	-158 216	-165	0	-6	-77	-82
3rd quarter	-32 045	-10 560	-1 630	-19 855	-146	-285 382	-1 096	0	-8	-956	-132
4th quarter	-30 362	-10 925	-1 929	-17 509	-7	-215 064	200	0	-10	321	-111
2011											
1st quarter	-35 343	-11 136	-2 154	-22 053	-29	-355 433	-3 619	0	1 961	-6 428	848
2nd quarter	-33 788	-13 486	-1 624	-18 678	-829	20 385	-6 267	0	-159	-5 974	-134
3rd quarter	-32 005	-11 176	-2 196	-18 633	-300	-84 425	-4 079	0	-27	-3 909	-143
4th quarter	-32 401	-11 551	-1 865	-18 985	-55	-32 831	-1 912	0	-23	-1 768	-121
2012											
1st quarter	-32 771	-11 912	-1 649	-19 210	-1	93 519	-1 233	0	-11	-1 078	-144
2nd quarter	-32 668	-11 473	-1 435	-19 761	-241	192 062	-3 289	0	-10	-3 179	-100
3rd quarter	-32 343	-11 823	-1 270	-19 250	-470	-267 054	-833	0	-10	-744	-79
4th quarter	-31 906	-10 882	668	-21 692	7 668	-115 996	895	0	-6	969	-68

[2]A minus sign indicates increases in U.S. official assets or financial outflows.
. . . = Not available.
* = Less than $500,000 (+/-).

Table 7-6A. U.S. International Transactions: Recent Data—*Continued*

(Millions of dollars, seasonally adjusted.)

Year and quarter	U.S. government assets other than official reserve assets, net				U.S. private assets, net				
	Total	U.S. credits and other long-term assets	Repayments on U.S. credits and other long-term assets	U.S. foreign currency holdings and short-term assets, net	Total	Direct investment	Foreign securities	U.S. claims	
								On unaffiliated foreigners reported by U.S. nonbanking concerns	Reported by U.S. banks, and securities brokers
1960	-1 100	-1 214	642	-528	-5 144	-2 940	-663	-394	-1 148
1961	-910	-1 928	1 279	-261	-5 235	-2 653	-762	-558	-1 261
1962	-1 085	-2 128	1 288	-245	-4 623	-2 851	-969	-354	-450
1963	-1 662	-2 204	988	-447	-5 986	-3 483	-1 105	157	-1 556
1964	-1 680	-2 382	720	-19	-8 050	-3 760	-677	-1 108	-2 505
1965	-1 605	-2 463	874	-16	-5 336	-5 011	-759	341	93
1966	-1 543	-2 513	1 235	-265	-6 347	-5 418	-720	-442	233
1967	-2 423	-3 638	1 005	209	-7 386	-4 805	-1 308	-779	-495
1968	-2 274	-3 722	1 386	62	-7 833	-5 295	-1 569	-1 203	233
1969	-2 200	-3 489	1 200	89	-8 206	-5 960	-1 549	-126	-570
1970	-1 589	-3 293	1 721	-16	-10 229	-7 590	-1 076	-596	-967
1971	-1 884	-4 181	2 115	182	-12 940	-7 618	-1 113	-1 229	-2 980
1972	-1 568	-3 819	2 086	165	-12 925	-7 747	-618	-1 054	-3 506
1973	-2 644	-4 638	2 596	-602	-20 388	-11 353	-671	-2 383	-5 980
1974	366	-5 001	4 826	541	-33 643	-9 052	-1 854	-3 221	-19 516
1975	-3 474	-5 941	2 475	-9	-35 380	-14 244	-6 247	-1 357	-13 532
1976	-4 214	-6 943	2 596	133	-44 498	-11 949	-8 885	-2 296	-21 368
1977	-3 693	-6 445	2 719	33	-30 717	-11 890	-5 460	-1 940	-11 427
1978	-4 660	-7 470	2 941	-131	-57 202	-16 056	-3 626	-3 853	-33 667
1979	-3 746	-7 697	3 926	25	-61 176	-25 222	-4 726	-5 014	-26 213
1980	-5 162	-9 860	4 456	242	-73 651	-19 222	-3 568	-4 023	-46 838
1981	-5 097	-9 674	4 413	164	-103 875	-9 624	-5 699	-4 377	-84 175
1982	-6 131	-10 063	4 292	-360	-116 786	-4 556	-7 983	6 823	-111 070
1983	-5 006	-9 967	5 012	-51	-60 172	-12 528	-6 762	-10 954	-29 928
1984	-5 489	-9 599	4 490	-379	-31 757	-16 407	-4 756	533	-11 127
1985	-2 821	-7 657	4 719	117	-38 074	-18 927	-7 481	-10 342	-1 323
1986	-2 022	-9 084	6 089	973	-110 014	-23 995	-4 271	-21 773	-59 975
1987	1 006	-6 506	7 625	-113	-89 450	-35 034	-5 251	-7 046	-42 119
1988	2 967	-7 680	10 370	277	-105 628	-22 528	-7 980	-21 193	-53 927
1989	1 233	-5 608	6 725	115	-151 323	-43 447	-22 070	-27 646	-58 160
1990	2 317	-8 410	10 856	-130	-81 393	-37 183	-28 765	-27 824	12 379
1991	2 924	-12 879	16 776	-974	-73 075	-37 889	-45 673	11 097	-610
1992	-1 667	-7 408	5 807	-66	-76 644	-48 266	-49 166	-387	21 175
1993	-351	-6 311	6 270	-310	-198 822	-83 950	-146 253	766	30 615
1994	-390	-5 383	5 088	-95	-183 893	-80 167	-63 190	-36 336	-4 200
1995	-984	-4 859	4 125	-250	-341 538	-98 750	-122 394	-45 286	-75 108
1996	-989	-5 025	3 930	106	-419 088	-91 885	-149 315	-86 333	-91 555
1997	68	-5 417	5 438	47	-484 533	-104 803	-116 852	-121 760	-141 118
1998	-422	-4 678	4 111	145	-346 624	-142 644	-130 204	-38 204	-35 572
1999	2 750	-6 175	9 559	-634	-515 559	-224 934	-122 236	-97 704	-70 685
2000	-941	-5 182	4 265	-24	-559 292	-159 212	-127 908	-138 790	-133 382
2001	-486	-4 431	3 873	72	-377 219	-142 349	-90 644	-8 520	-135 706
2002	345	-5 251	5 701	-105	-291 310	-154 460	-48 568	-50 022	-38 260
2003	537	-7 279	7 981	-165	-327 484	-149 564	-146 722	-18 184	-13 014
2004	1 710	-3 044	4 716	38	-1 005 385	-316 223	-170 549	-152 566	-366 047
2005	5 539	-2 255	5 603	2 191	-566 266	-36 235	-251 199	-71 207	-207 625
2006	5 346	-2 992	8 329	9	-1 293 449	-244 922	-365 129	-181 299	-502 099
2007	-22 273	-2 475	4 104	-23 902	-1 431 209	-414 039	-366 512	-928	-649 730
2008	-529 615	-2 202	2 354	-529 766	866 571	-329 081	197 347	456 177	542 128
2009	541 342	-4 069	2 133	543 278	-617 946	-310 382	-227 024	154 139	-234 679
2010	7 540	-4 976	2 408	10 108	-915 659	-301 080	-139 084	31 326	-506 821
2011	-103 666	-7 307	3 333	-99 692	-332 761	-409 004	-143 770	4 147	215 866
2012	85 331	-8 202	2 546	90 987	-178 341	-388 293	-144 823	-25 723	380 498
2009									
1st quarter	244 102	-240	484	243 858	-118 030	-72 892	-36 497	18 261	-26 902
2nd quarter	193 750	-1 947	432	195 265	-141 926	-65 916	-94 166	36 999	-18 843
3rd quarter	57 736	-616	534	57 818	-317 848	-86 451	-54 256	84 790	-261 931
4th quarter	45 754	-1 266	683	46 337	-40 143	-85 124	-42 105	14 089	72 997
2010									
1st quarter	9 433	-1 247	399	10 281	-259 950	-95 076	-42 160	43 586	-166 300
2nd quarter	-2 441	-1 835	783	-1 389	-155 610	-66 131	-15 759	6 381	-80 101
3rd quarter	788	-1 027	679	1 136	-285 074	-83 354	-39 342	2 639	-165 017
4th quarter	-240	-867	547	80	-215 024	-56 518	-41 823	-21 280	-95 403
2011									
1st quarter	-547	-1 307	610	150	-351 267	-98 181	-84 722	-80 578	-87 786
2nd quarter	-1 358	-2 337	1 259	-279	28 009	-126 287	-56 444	9 444	201 296
3rd quarter	-1 137	-1 396	812	-553	-79 209	-73 760	-39 360	9 766	24 145
4th quarter	-100 624	-2 267	653	-99 010	69 705	-110 777	36 756	65 515	78 211
2012									
1st quarter	51 087	-2 655	386	53 356	43 665	-113 038	2 276	-67 175	221 602
2nd quarter	16 650	-2 538	680	18 508	178 701	-86 202	-22 920	16 793	271 030
3rd quarter	15 206	-1 038	847	15 397	-281 428	-93 635	-51 183	6 325	-142 935
4th quarter	2 388	-1 971	633	3 726	-119 279	-95 418	-72 996	18 334	30 801

[3]A minus sign indicates increases in U.S. official assets or financial outflows.

Table 7-6A. U.S. International Transactions: Recent Data—*Continued*

(Millions of dollars, seasonally adjusted.)

Year and quarter	Financial account—Continued												
	Foreign-owned assets in the United States, net, excluding financial derivatives [4]												
	Foreign official assets in the United States, net							Other foreign assets in the United States, net				
	Total	Total	U.S. government securities			Other U.S. government liabilities	U.S. liabilities reported by U.S. banks and securities brokers	Other foreign official assets	Total	Direct investment	U.S. Treasury securities	U.S. securities other than Treasury securities	U.S. currency
			Total	U.S. Treasury securities	Other								
1960	2 294	1 473	655	655	0	215	603	0	821	315	-364	282	. . .
1961	2 705	765	233	233	0	25	508	0	1 939	311	151	324	. . .
1962	1 911	1 270	1 409	1 410	-1	152	-291	0	641	346	-66	134	. . .
1963	3 217	1 986	816	803	12	429	742	0	1 231	231	-149	287	. . .
1964	3 643	1 660	432	434	-2	298	930	0	1 983	322	-146	-85	. . .
1965	742	134	-141	-134	-7	65	210	0	607	415	-131	-358	. . .
1966	3 661	-672	-1 527	-1 548	21	113	742	0	4 333	425	-356	906	. . .
1967	7 379	3 451	2 261	2 222	39	83	1 106	0	3 928	698	-135	1 016	. . .
1968	9 928	-774	-769	-798	29	-15	10	0	10 703	807	136	4 414	. . .
1969	12 702	-1 301	-2 343	-2 269	-74	251	792	0	14 002	1 263	-68	3 130	. . .
1970	7 226	7 775	9 439	9 411	28	411	-2 075	0	-550	1 464	81	2 189	. . .
1971	23 687	27 596	26 570	26 578	-8	207	819	0	-3 909	367	-24	2 289	. . .
1972	22 171	11 185	8 470	8 213	257	892	1 638	185	10 986	949	-39	4 507	. . .
1973	18 388	6 026	641	59	582	936	4 126	323	12 362	2 800	-216	4 041	. . .
1974	35 227	10 546	4 172	3 270	902	301	5 818	254	24 682	4 760	697	378	986
1975	16 870	7 027	5 563	4 658	905	1 517	-2 158	2 104	9 843	2 603	2 590	2 503	1 200
1976	37 839	17 693	9 892	9 319	573	4 627	969	2 205	20 147	4 347	2 783	1 284	1 321
1977	52 770	36 816	32 538	30 230	2 308	1 400	773	2 105	15 954	3 728	534	2 437	1 451
1978	66 275	33 678	24 221	23 555	666	2 476	5 551	1 430	32 597	7 897	2 178	2 254	2 239
1979	40 693	-12 526	-21 972	-22 435	463	1 099	7 213	1 135	53 218	11 877	4 060	1 351	1 702
1980	62 037	16 649	11 895	9 708	2 187	1 767	-159	3 145	45 388	16 918	2 645	5 457	2 773
1981	85 684	6 053	6 322	5 019	1 303	755	-3 670	2 646	79 631	25 195	2 927	6 905	1 559
1982	95 056	3 593	5 085	5 779	-694	605	-1 747	-350	91 464	12 635	7 027	6 085	2 467
1983	87 399	5 845	6 496	6 972	-476	602	545	-1 798	81 554	10 372	8 689	8 164	4 105
1984	116 048	3 140	4 703	4 690	13	739	555	-2 857	112 908	24 468	23 001	12 568	2 396
1985	144 231	-1 119	-1 139	-838	-301	844	645	-1 469	145 349	19 742	20 433	50 962	3 316
1986	228 330	35 648	33 150	34 364	-1 214	2 195	1 187	-884	192 681	35 420	3 809	70 969	2 421
1987	247 100	45 387	44 802	43 238	1 564	-2 326	3 918	-1 007	201 713	58 470	-7 643	42 120	3 866
1988	244 833	39 758	43 050	41 741	1 309	-467	-319	-2 506	205 075	57 735	20 239	26 353	4 111
1989	222 777	8 503	1 532	149	1 383	160	4 976	1 835	214 274	68 274	29 618	38 767	3 749
1990	139 357	33 910	30 243	29 576	667	1 868	3 385	-1 586	105 447	48 494	-2 534	1 592	16 586
1991	108 221	17 389	16 147	14 846	1 301	1 367	-1 484	1 359	90 833	23 171	18 826	35 144	12 813
1992	168 349	40 477	22 403	18 454	3 949	2 191	16 571	-688	127 872	19 823	37 131	30 043	11 086
1993	279 758	71 753	53 014	48 952	4 062	1 313	14 841	2 585	208 005	51 362	24 381	80 092	16 618
1994	303 174	39 583	36 827	30 750	6 077	1 564	3 665	-2 473	263 591	46 121	34 274	56 971	20 585
1995	435 102	109 880	72 712	68 977	3 735	-105	34 008	3 265	325 222	57 776	91 544	77 249	8 840
1996	547 885	126 724	120 679	115 671	5 008	-982	5 704	1 323	421 161	86 502	147 022	103 272	14 151
1997	704 452	19 036	-2 161	-6 690	4 529	-881	22 286	-208	685 416	105 603	130 435	161 409	22 425
1998	420 794	-19 903	-3 589	-9 921	6 332	-3 326	-9 501	-3 487	440 697	179 045	28 581	156 315	13 847
1999	742 210	43 543	32 527	12 177	20 350	-2 863	12 964	915	698 667	289 444	-44 497	298 834	24 407
2000	1 038 224	42 758	35 710	-5 199	40 909	-1 825	5 746	3 127	995 466	321 274	-69 983	459 889	-3 357
2001	782 870	28 059	54 620	33 700	20 920	-2 309	-29 978	5 726	754 811	167 021	-14 378	393 885	23 794
2002	795 161	115 945	90 971	60 466	30 505	137	21 221	3 616	679 216	84 372	100 403	283 299	18 861
2003	858 303	278 069	224 874	184 931	39 943	-723	48 643	5 275	580 234	63 750	91 455	220 705	10 591
2004	1 533 201	397 755	314 941	273 279	41 662	-134	69 245	13 703	1 135 446	145 966	93 608	381 493	13 301
2005	1 247 347	259 268	213 334	112 841	100 493	-421	26 260	20 095	988 079	112 638	132 300	450 386	8 447
2006	2 065 169	487 939	428 401	208 564	219 837	2 816	22 365	34 357	1 577 230	243 151	-58 229	683 245	2 227
2007	2 064 642	481 043	269 897	98 432	171 465	5 436	109 019	96 691	1 583 599	221 166	66 845	605 414	-10 675
2008	431 406	554 634	591 381	548 653	42 728	9 029	-149 676	103 900	-123 228	310 092	162 944	-165 639	29 187
2009	315 063	480 286	437 324	569 893	-132 569	58 206	-68 848	53 604	-165 223	150 442	-15 451	1 855	12 632
2010	1 333 921	398 309	353 294	442 012	-88 718	12 442	-7 967	40 540	935 612	205 851	298 341	140 939	28 319
2011	969 006	253 816	149 101	169 813	-20 712	9 563	27 474	67 678	715 190	230 224	188 045	-54 462	54 996
2012	543 884	393 922	314 660	433 155	-118 495	8 241	-1 572	72 593	149 962	166 411	156 385	196 908	57 141
2009													
1st quarter	-118 782	109 442	145 512	163 809	-18 297	2 455	-43 319	4 794	-228 224	-2 335	45 873	-67 748	11 816
2nd quarter	-37 806	129 253	120 776	149 213	-28 437	926	-4 555	12 106	-167 059	30 243	-30 093	-279	-1 935
3rd quarter	335 518	109 204	69 961	126 593	-56 632	53 415	-33 650	19 478	226 314	54 849	-28 060	48 758	4 179
4th quarter	136 134	132 387	101 075	130 278	-29 203	1 410	12 676	17 226	3 747	67 686	-3 171	21 124	-1 428
2010													
1st quarter	312 270	89 967	84 837	97 364	-12 527	4 069	-15 851	16 912	222 303	36 712	84 213	5 098	2 265
2nd quarter	180 695	65 882	43 553	30 077	13 476	2 561	4 545	15 223	114 813	30 636	83 621	-15 923	2 100
3rd quarter	533 623	168 673	151 633	220 891	-69 258	1 851	9 981	5 208	364 950	82 515	74 766	93 331	10 514
4th quarter	307 333	73 787	73 271	93 680	-20 409	3 961	-6 642	3 197	233 546	55 988	55 741	58 433	13 440
2011													
1st quarter	560 627	72 443	67 719	56 274	11 445	2 827	-3 734	5 631	488 184	32 922	58 940	4 490	12 576
2nd quarter	112 919	121 361	97 184	104 363	-7 179	2 228	15 311	6 638	-8 442	60 576	-2 386	-4 962	13 989
3rd quarter	256 164	53 851	15 428	30 461	-15 033	2 420	7 948	28 055	202 313	61 038	84 134	-24 908	9 614
4th quarter	39 296	6 161	-31 230	-21 285	-9 945	2 088	7 949	27 354	33 135	75 688	47 357	-29 082	18 817
2012													
1st quarter	177 381	144 468	124 225	143 100	-18 875	2 939	-14 458	31 762	32 913	35 756	64 974	28 297	18 057
2nd quarter	-176 468	57 374	42 927	96 213	-53 286	2 773	406	11 268	-233 842	49 524	-4 652	-39 577	7 116
3rd quarter	300 570	107 684	87 309	100 571	-13 262	1 722	7 066	11 587	192 886	38 839	62 548	64 694	16 156
4th quarter	242 401	84 396	60 199	93 271	-33 072	807	5 414	17 976	158 005	42 292	33 515	143 494	15 812

[4]A minus sign indicates financial outflows or a decrease in foreign official assets in the United States.
. . . = Not available.

Table 7-6A. U.S. International Transactions: Recent Data—*Continued*

(Millions of dollars, seasonally adjusted.)

Year and quarter	Financial account—Continued			Statistical discrepancy 5		Balance on goods	Balance on services	Balance on goods and services	Balance on income	Balance on goods, services, and income	Unilateral current transfers, net	Balance on current account
	Foreign-owned assets in the United States, net 4—Cont.		Financial derivatives, net	Total	Seasonal adjustment discrepancy							
	Other foreign assets in the United States, net—Cont.											
	U.S. liabilities											
	To unaffiliated foreigners reported by U.S. nonbanking concerns	Reported by U.S. banks and securities brokers										
1960	-90	678	...	-1 019	0	4 892	-1 385	3 508	3 379	6 887	-4 062	2 824
1961	226	928	...	-989	0	5 571	-1 376	4 195	3 755	7 950	-4 127	3 822
1962	-110	336	...	-1 124	0	4 521	-1 151	3 370	4 294	7 664	-4 277	3 387
1963	-37	898	...	-360	0	5 224	-1 014	4 210	4 596	8 806	-4 392	4 414
1964	75	1 818	...	-907	0	6 801	-779	6 022	5 041	11 063	-4 240	6 823
1965	178	503	...	-457	0	4 951	-287	4 664	5 350	10 014	-4 583	5 431
1966	476	2 882	...	629	0	3 817	-877	2 940	5 047	7 987	-4 955	3 031
1967	584	1 765	...	-205	0	3 800	-1 196	2 604	5 274	7 878	-5 294	2 583
1968	1 475	3 871	...	438	0	635	-385	250	5 990	6 240	-5 629	611
1969	792	8 886	...	-1 516	0	607	-516	91	6 044	6 135	-5 735	399
1970	2 014	-6 298	...	-219	0	2 603	-349	2 254	6 233	8 487	-6 156	2 331
1971	369	-6 911	...	-9 779	0	-2 260	957	-1 303	7 272	5 969	-7 402	-1 433
1972	815	4 754	...	-1 879	0	-6 416	973	-5 443	8 192	2 749	-8 544	-5 795
1973	1 035	4 702	...	-2 654	0	911	989	1 900	12 153	14 053	-6 913	7 140
1974	1 844	16 017	...	-2 444	0	-5 505	1 213	-4 292	15 503	11 211	-9 249	1 962
1975	319	628	...	4 717	0	8 903	3 501	12 404	12 787	25 191	-7 075	18 116
1976	-578	10 990	...	9 134	0	-9 483	3 401	-6 082	16 063	9 981	-5 686	4 295
1977	1 086	6 719	...	-3 650	0	-31 091	3 845	-27 246	18 137	-9 109	-5 226	-14 335
1978	1 889	16 141	...	9 997	0	-33 927	4 164	-29 763	20 408	-9 355	-5 788	-15 143
1979	1 621	32 607	...	25 647	0	-27 568	3 003	-24 565	30 873	6 308	-6 593	-285
1980	6 852	10 743	...	22 613	0	-25 500	6 093	-19 407	30 073	10 666	-8 349	2 317
1981	917	42 128	...	23 433	0	-28 023	11 852	-16 172	32 903	16 731	-11 702	5 030
1982	-2 383	65 633	...	38 362	0	-36 485	12 329	-24 156	35 164	11 008	-16 544	-5 536
1983	-118	50 342	...	17 666	0	-67 102	9 335	-57 767	36 386	-21 381	-17 310	-38 691
1984	16 626	33 849	...	18 672	0	-112 492	3 419	-109 073	35 063	-74 010	-20 335	-94 344
1985	9 851	41 045	...	18 677	0	-122 173	294	-121 880	25 723	-96 157	-21 998	-118 155
1986	3 325	76 737	...	30 570	0	-145 081	6 543	-138 538	15 494	-123 044	-24 132	-147 177
1987	18 363	86 537	...	-7 149	0	-159 557	7 874	-151 684	14 293	-137 391	-23 265	-160 655
1988	32 893	63 744	...	-17 107	0	-126 959	12 393	-114 566	18 687	-95 879	-25 274	-121 153
1989	22 086	51 780	...	52 299	0	-117 749	24 607	-93 142	19 824	-73 318	-26 169	-99 486
1990	45 133	-3 824	...	28 066	0	-111 037	30 173	-80 864	28 550	-52 314	-26 654	-78 968
1991	-3 115	3 994	...	-41 601	0	-76 937	45 802	-31 135	24 130	-7 005	9 904	2 898
1992	13 573	16 216	...	-43 775	0	-96 897	57 685	-39 212	24 234	-14 978	-36 636	-51 613
1993	10 489	25 063	...	6 314	0	-132 451	62 141	-70 310	25 316	-44 994	-39 812	-84 806
1994	1 302	104 338	...	-1 514	0	-165 831	67 338	-98 493	17 146	-81 347	-40 265	-121 612
1995	59 637	30 176	...	30 951	0	-174 170	77 786	-96 384	20 891	-75 493	-38 074	-113 567
1996	53 736	16 478	...	-9 705	0	-191 000	86 935	-104 065	22 318	-81 747	-43 017	-124 764
1997	116 518	149 026	...	-77 995	0	-198 428	90 155	-108 273	12 609	-95 664	-45 062	-140 726
1998	23 140	39 769	...	148 105	0	-248 221	82 081	-166 140	4 265	-161 875	-53 187	-215 062
1999	76 247	54 232	...	66 806	0	-337 374	73 618	-263 755	11 931	-251 824	-48 954	-300 778
2000	170 672	116 971	...	-61 382	0	-446 942	69 605	-377 337	19 118	-358 159	-58 159	-416 317
2001	66 110	118 379	...	-16 755	0	-422 512	60 173	-362 339	29 728	-332 611	-64 086	-396 697
2002	95 871	96 410	...	-42 574	0	-475 842	57 678	-418 165	25 175	-392 990	-64 810	-457 800
2003	96 526	97 207	...	-12 401	0	-542 273	51 728	-490 545	42 760	-447 785	-70 873	-518 657
2004	165 872	335 206	...	93 947	0	-666 364	61 466	-604 897	64 129	-540 768	-88 559	-629 327
2005	69 572	214 736	...	25 964	0	-784 133	76 219	-707 914	67 630	-640 284	-99 512	-739 796
2006	244 793	462 043	29 710	-8 884	0	-838 788	86 389	-752 399	43 338	-709 061	-89 417	-798 478
2007	183 221	517 628	6 222	95 745	0	-822 743	123 677	-699 065	100 606	-598 459	-114 929	-713 389
2008	-31 475	-428 337	-32 947	-55 235	0	-833 957	131 655	-702 302	146 144	-556 158	-125 185	-681 343
2009	9 536	-324 237	44 816	150 757	0	-510 550	126 893	-383 657	123 580	-260 077	-121 559	-381 636
2010	67 985	194 177	14 076	11 585	0	-650 156	150 777	-499 379	177 659	-321 720	-127 751	-449 471
2011	6 053	290 334	35 006	-92 771	0	-744 139	187 301	-556 838	232 648	-324 190	-133 535	-457 725
2012	-39 505	-387 378	-7 064	-5 891	0	-741 475	206 819	-534 656	223 928	-310 728	-129 688	-440 416
2009												
1st quarter	-7 532	-208 298	7 146	82 799	11 065	-123 693	29 619	-94 074	25 317	-68 757	-27 476	-96 233
2nd quarter	15 848	-180 843	7 561	70 282	-7 588	-112 245	31 119	-81 126	24 364	-56 762	-31 439	-88 201
3rd quarter	20 775	125 813	10 645	56 761	-21 970	-130 144	31 409	-98 735	37 922	-60 813	-32 943	-93 756
4th quarter	-19 555	-60 909	19 464	-59 083	18 494	-144 468	34 745	-109 722	35 977	-73 745	-29 704	-103 449
2010												
1st quarter	22 388	71 627	16 152	32 267	12 982	-152 945	34 670	-118 275	43 786	-74 489	-34 906	-109 395
2nd quarter	12 778	1 601	9 980	82 900	-11 560	-165 320	36 170	-129 150	44 230	-84 920	-30 438	-115 357
3rd quarter	10 944	92 880	-11 893	-115 711	-21 473	-169 260	37 987	-131 274	42 827	-88 447	-32 045	-120 492
4th quarter	21 875	28 069	-163	12 130	20 051	-162 631	41 949	-120 682	46 817	-73 865	-30 362	-104 228
2011												
1st quarter	40 692	338 564	2 952	-91 475	13 068	-181 694	45 310	-136 385	55 085	-81 300	-35 343	-116 643
2nd quarter	24 774	-100 433	9 806	-23 377	-15 466	-187 672	47 121	-140 551	55 435	-85 116	-33 788	-118 903
3rd quarter	-17 898	90 333	-1 617	-64 196	-24 180	-183 888	49 199	-134 689	61 068	-73 621	-32 005	-105 626
4th quarter	-41 515	-38 130	23 865	86 279	26 580	-190 885	45 671	-145 214	61 061	-84 153	-32 401	-116 554
2012												
1st quarter	13 279	-127 450	-7 339	-142 718	13 576	-193 604	50 657	-142 947	54 876	-88 071	-32 771	-120 842
2nd quarter	-25 581	-220 672	2 419	92 741	-16 117	-186 487	51 186	-135 302	57 457	-77 845	-32 668	-110 513
3rd quarter	-4 763	15 412	-5 129	78 825	-21 229	-178 980	49 952	-129 029	54 630	-74 399	-32 343	-106 742
4th quarter	-22 440	-54 668	2 985	-34 738	23 771	-182 403	55 025	-127 378	56 965	-70 413	-31 906	-102 320

4A minus sign indicates financial outflows or a decrease in foreign official assets in the United States.
5Sum of credits and debits with the sign reversed.
. . . = Not available.

Table 7-6B. U.S. International Transactions: Historical

(Millions of dollars, seasonally adjusted.)

| Year and quarter | Exports of goods, services, and income | | | | Imports of goods, services, and income [1] | | | | Unilateral current transfers, net [2] | U.S.-owned assets abroad, net, excluding financial derivatives [3] | | | U.S. private assets, net | | |
	Total	Goods	Services	Income receipts	Total	Goods	Services	Income payments		Total	U.S. official reserve assets, net	U.S. government assets other than official reserve assets, net	Total	Direct investment	Foreign securities
1960															
1st quarter	7 355	4 685	1 543	1 127	-6 050	-3 812	-1 907	-331	-955	-1 066	159	-237	-988	-664	-266
2nd quarter	7 762	4 916	1 715	1 131	-6 078	-3 858	-1 906	-314	-1 154	-1 156	175	-339	-992	-586	-166
3rd quarter	7 650	5 031	1 453	1 166	-5 925	-3 648	-1 970	-307	-889	-956	740	-160	-1 536	-754	-111
4th quarter	7 791	5 018	1 580	1 193	-5 619	-3 440	-1 892	-287	-1 064	-923	1 071	-365	-1 629	-936	-120
1961															
1st quarter	7 827	5 095	1 481	1 251	-5 599	-3 394	-1 912	-293	-989	-1 320	371	-381	-1 310	-774	-135
2nd quarter	7 773	4 806	1 758	1 209	-5 659	-3 438	-1 922	-299	-1 208	-1 029	-320	471	-1 180	-551	-246
3rd quarter	7 757	5 038	1 468	1 251	-6 026	-3 809	-1 900	-317	-887	-1 928	-212	-486	-1 230	-737	-124
4th quarter	8 047	5 169	1 590	1 288	-6 171	-3 896	-1 939	-336	-1 043	-1 260	768	-513	-1 515	-592	-257
1962															
1st quarter	8 015	5 077	1 666	1 272	-6 256	-3 966	-1 971	-319	-1 113	-1 301	427	-406	-1 322	-545	-196
2nd quarter	8 719	5 336	2 004	1 379	-6 402	-4 080	-1 992	-330	-1 272	-1 461	-163	-381	-917	-716	-308
3rd quarter	8 295	5 331	1 567	1 397	-6 455	-4 116	-2 005	-334	-879	-279	881	8	-1 168	-811	-87
4th quarter	8 315	5 037	1 709	1 569	-6 567	-4 098	-2 126	-343	-1 016	-1 134	390	-306	-1 218	-779	-378
1963															
1st quarter	8 428	5 063	1 849	1 516	-6 478	-4 064	-2 057	-357	-1 107	-1 922	32	-482	-1 472	-980	-522
2nd quarter	9 244	5 599	2 150	1 495	-6 674	-4 226	-2 066	-382	-1 371	-2 631	124	-654	-2 101	-874	-536
3rd quarter	8 832	5 671	1 620	1 541	-6 893	-4 372	-2 122	-399	-918	-887	227	-86	-1 028	-721	-100
4th quarter	9 275	5 939	1 731	1 605	-6 926	-4 386	-2 118	-422	-999	-1 831	-5	-440	-1 386	-908	53
1964															
1st quarter	9 885	6 242	1 922	1 721	-6 982	-4 416	-2 140	-426	-993	-2 086	-51	-288	-1 747	-822	20
2nd quarter	9 975	6 199	2 088	1 688	-7 179	-4 598	-2 142	-439	-1 269	-2 018	303	-386	-1 935	-970	-206
3rd quarter	10 009	6 423	1 851	1 735	-7 349	-4 756	-2 153	-440	-935	-2 255	70	-414	-1 911	-1 018	2
4th quarter	10 299	6 637	1 982	1 680	-7 594	-4 930	-2 186	-478	-1 043	-3 200	-151	-592	-2 457	-949	-494
1965															
1st quarter	9 689	5 768	2 047	1 874	-7 395	-4 711	-2 187	-497	-1 037	-1 576	843	-374	-2 045	-1 606	-198
2nd quarter	11 263	6 876	2 448	1 939	-8 208	-5 428	-2 269	-511	-1 478	-1 270	69	-536	-803	-1 250	-147
3rd quarter	10 625	6 643	2 120	1 862	-8 307	-5 516	-2 263	-528	-1 013	-1 454	42	-254	-1 242	-1 030	-209
4th quarter	11 149	7 174	2 212	1 763	-8 802	-5 855	-2 393	-554	-1 058	-1 416	271	-441	-1 246	-1 125	-205
1966															
1st quarter	11 190	7 242	2 124	1 824	-9 068	-6 012	-2 483	-573	-1 140	-1 465	424	-321	-1 568	-1 115	-437
2nd quarter	11 726	7 169	2 705	1 852	-9 390	-6 195	-2 601	-594	-1 547	-1 967	68	-504	-1 531	-1 373	-115
3rd quarter	11 470	7 290	2 301	1 879	-9 912	-6 576	-2 693	-643	-1 073	-1 681	83	-339	-1 425	-1 314	-115
4th quarter	12 068	7 609	2 487	1 972	-10 098	-6 710	-2 717	-671	-1 194	-2 208	-5	-380	-1 823	-1 616	-53
1967															
1st quarter	12 439	7 751	2 731	1 957	-10 248	-6 708	-2 866	-674	-1 315	-1 203	1 027	-643	-1 587	-1 186	-265
2nd quarter	12 275	7 693	2 666	1 916	-10 136	-6 475	-2 986	-675	-1 472	-2 339	-419	-543	-1 377	-964	-261
3rd quarter	12 134	7 530	2 540	2 064	-10 262	-6 526	-3 059	-677	-1 309	-3 155	-375	-551	-2 229	-1 359	-419
4th quarter	12 506	7 692	2 731	2 083	-10 833	-7 157	-2 955	-721	-1 199	-3 060	-180	-685	-2 195	-1 297	-363
1968															
1st quarter	13 016	7 998	2 816	2 202	-11 571	-7 796	-2 997	-778	-1 249	-1 299	912	-706	-1 505	-981	-449
2nd quarter	13 577	8 324	2 936	2 317	-11 885	-8 051	-2 990	-844	-1 363	-2 427	-135	-632	-1 660	-1 172	-283
3rd quarter	14 195	8 745	3 039	2 411	-12 611	-8 612	-3 129	-870	-1 445	-3 447	-572	-568	-2 307	-1 573	-318
4th quarter	14 126	8 559	3 129	2 438	-12 604	-8 532	-3 185	-887	-1 573	-3 803	-1 075	-368	-2 360	-1 568	-519
1969															
1st quarter	12 921	7 468	2 884	2 569	-11 622	-7 444	-3 174	-1 004	-1 177	-2 595	-45	-406	-2 144	-1 556	-366
2nd quarter	15 492	9 536	3 283	2 673	-13 978	-9 527	-3 303	-1 148	-1 645	-3 428	-298	-632	-2 498	-1 663	-498
3rd quarter	15 439	9 400	3 245	2 794	-14 072	-9 380	-3 368	-1 324	-1 319	-3 361	-685	-703	-1 973	-1 548	-546
4th quarter	16 279	10 010	3 394	2 875	-14 329	-9 456	-3 481	-1 392	-1 593	-2 199	-151	-459	-1 589	-1 192	-139
1970															
1st quarter	16 461	10 258	3 235	2 968	-14 458	-9 587	-3 449	-1 422	-1 383	-3 478	-386	-399	-2 693	-1 958	-306
2nd quarter	17 419	10 744	3 645	3 030	-14 861	-9 766	-3 690	-1 405	-1 586	-1 725	1 025	-348	-2 402	-2 144	80
3rd quarter	17 267	10 665	3 625	2 977	-15 141	-10 049	-3 715	-1 377	-1 611	-2 146	802	-423	-2 525	-1 718	-517
4th quarter	17 241	10 802	3 666	2 773	-15 443	-10 464	-3 668	-1 311	-1 576	-1 989	1 040	-419	-2 610	-1 771	-333
1971															
1st quarter	17 980	10 920	4 048	3 012	-15 551	-10 600	-3 724	-1 227	-1 746	-3 464	151	-573	-3 042	-2 033	-408
2nd quarter	18 163	10 878	4 087	3 198	-16 764	-11 614	-3 867	-1 283	-1 808	-2 534	839	-567	-2 806	-1 949	-368
3rd quarter	18 676	11 548	3 972	3 156	-17 460	-12 171	-3 861	-1 428	-1 752	-3 390	1 377	-387	-4 380	-2 308	-346
4th quarter	17 564	9 973	4 251	3 340	-16 639	-11 194	-3 948	-1 497	-2 098	-3 084	-18	-355	-2 711	-1 327	9
1972															
1st quarter	19 757	11 833	4 473	3 451	-19 153	-13 501	-4 173	-1 479	-2 297	-4 295	-90	-212	-3 993	-2 187	-476
2nd quarter	19 427	11 618	4 233	3 576	-19 105	-13 254	-4 228	-1 623	-2 011	-2 125	-60	-271	-1 794	-1 481	-318
3rd quarter	20 788	12 351	4 634	3 803	-19 767	-14 022	-4 095	-1 650	-2 306	-3 952	96	-518	-3 530	-2 435	203
4th quarter	22 015	13 579	4 503	3 933	-21 212	-15 020	-4 371	-1 821	-1 933	-4 125	50	-566	-3 609	-1 644	-28
1973															
1st quarter	24 681	15 474	4 579	4 628	-23 000	-16 285	-4 613	-2 102	-1 536	-7 886	213	-572	-7 527	-3 785	55
2nd quarter	27 127	17 112	4 828	5 187	-24 301	-17 168	-4 741	-2 392	-1 953	-4 154	11	-423	-3 742	-2 691	-86
3rd quarter	29 329	18 271	5 145	5 913	-24 841	-17 683	-4 640	-2 518	-1 751	-3 189	-23	-608	-2 558	-2 159	-196
4th quarter	31 912	20 553	5 279	6 080	-26 855	-19 363	-4 849	-2 643	-1 674	-7 646	-43	-1 042	-6 561	-2 718	-445

[1] A minus sign indicates imports of goods or services or income payments.
[2] A minus sign indicates net unilateral transfers to foreigners.
[3] A minus sign indicates financial outflows or increases in U.S. official assets.

Table 7-6B. U.S. International Transactions: Historical—*Continued*

(Millions of dollars, seasonally adjusted.)

Year and quarter	U.S.-owned assets abroad, net [3] —Continued / U.S. private assets, net—Continued / U.S. claims / On unaffiliated foreigners reported by U.S. nonbanking concerns	Reported by U.S. banks and securities brokers	Foreign-owned assets in the United States, net, excluding financial derivatives [4] — Total	Foreign official assets in the United States, net	Other foreign assets in the United States, net — Total	Direct invest-ment	U.S. Treasury securities and U.S. currency flows	U.S. securities other than U.S. Treasury securities	U.S. liabilities — To unaffiliated foreigners reported by U.S. nonbanking concerns	Reported by U.S. banks and securities brokers	Statistical discrep-ancy [5]	Balance on goods and services	Balance on current account
1960													
1st quarter	38	-96	926	380	546	89	-100	170	-1	388	-210	509	350
2nd quarter	-100	-140	912	435	477	102	-143	118	-50	450	-286	867	530
3rd quarter	-51	-620	381	283	98	93	-99	5	-11	110	-261	866	836
4th quarter	-281	-292	77	377	-300	31	-22	-11	-28	-270	-262	1 266	1 108
1961													
1st quarter	-117	-284	435	438	-3	68	-82	104	73	-166	-354	1 270	1 239
2nd quarter	-164	-219	620	-307	927	86	-38	152	72	655	-497	1 204	906
3rd quarter	-149	-220	934	673	261	58	83	3	14	103	150	797	844
4th quarter	-128	-538	715	-41	756	99	188	66	67	336	-288	924	833
1962													
1st quarter	-186	-395	737	. . .	737	89	193	145	-14	324	-82	806	646
2nd quarter	-5	112	675	503	172	130	-51	7	-64	150	-259	1 268	1 045
3rd quarter	-181	-89	-277	178	-455	59	-109	-23	16	-398	-405	777	961
4th quarter	17	-78	779	591	188	68	-99	6	-47	260	-377	522	732
1963													
1st quarter	-27	57	1 191	946	245	40	25	14	-36	202	-112	791	843
2nd quarter	-108	-583	1 527	910	617	108	-109	119	69	430	-95	1 457	1 199
3rd quarter	47	-254	205	56	149	105	1	52	11	-20	-339	797	1 021
4th quarter	245	-776	295	75	220	-22	-66	102	-80	286	186	1 166	1 350
1964													
1st quarter	-206	-739	462	393	69	87	32	-42	0	-8	-286	1 608	1 910
2nd quarter	-166	-593	630	227	403	109	-108	14	19	369	-139	1 547	1 527
3rd quarter	-532	-363	769	275	494	56	-65	-30	37	496	-239	1 365	1 725
4th quarter	-204	-810	1 781	763	1 018	70	-5	-27	19	961	-243	1 503	1 662
1965													
1st quarter	286	-527	208	-202	410	184	60	57	3	106	111	917	1 257
2nd quarter	165	429	-330	-194	-136	-21	64	-243	63	1	23	1 627	1 577
3rd quarter	-19	16	587	115	472	147	-149	-227	49	652	-438	984	1 305
4th quarter	-91	175	280	421	-141	104	-106	54	63	-256	-153	1 138	1 289
1966													
1st quarter	-159	143	458	-164	622	143	-102	173	68	340	25	871	982
2nd quarter	-68	25	961	-57	1 018	133	-316	518	78	605	217	1 078	789
3rd quarter	-105	109	909	-342	1 251	-37	66	107	195	920	287	322	485
4th quarter	-110	-44	1 332	-111	1 443	187	-4	108	135	1 017	100	669	776
1967													
1st quarter	-107	-29	401	708	-307	169	-6	133	219	-822	-74	908	876
2nd quarter	-69	-83	1 884	1 100	784	174	-61	329	66	276	-212	898	667
3rd quarter	-40	-411	2 513	548	1 965	127	-36	520	164	1 190	79	485	563
4th quarter	-563	28	2 584	1 098	1 486	228	-32	34	135	1 121	2	311	474
1968													
1st quarter	-231	156	1 374	-533	1 907	367	22	855	207	456	-271	21	196
2nd quarter	-567	362	2 192	-2 007	4 199	133	86	1 122	478	2 380	-94	219	329
3rd quarter	-213	-203	2 809	442	2 367	148	-8	1 124	315	788	499	43	139
4th quarter	-191	-82	3 550	1 321	2 229	160	36	1 312	474	247	304	-29	-51
1969													
1st quarter	-132	-90	3 664	-1 117	4 781	359	-125	1 388	90	3 069	-1 191	-266	122
2nd quarter	-21	-316	3 896	-766	4 662	267	-35	365	181	3 884	-337	-11	-131
3rd quarter	141	-20	3 833	1 256	2 577	261	79	396	345	1 496	-520	-103	48
4th quarter	-114	-144	1 311	-672	1 983	376	13	981	176	437	531	467	357
1970													
1st quarter	-366	-63	3 027	3 697	-670	592	16	304	222	-1 804	-169	457	620
2nd quarter	-73	-265	848	694	154	212	-35	374	534	-931	-95	933	972
3rd quarter	-157	-133	1 940	1 411	529	357	1	720	510	-1 059	-309	526	515
4th quarter	0	-506	1 413	1 975	-562	303	99	792	748	-2 504	354	336	222
1971													
1st quarter	-355	-246	3 809	5 895	-2 086	196	179	559	-62	-2 958	-1 028	644	683
2nd quarter	-131	-358	5 154	5 630	-476	140	1 862	196	-34	-2 640	-2 211	-516	-409
3rd quarter	-337	-1 389	8 726	10 367	-1 641	-293	-795	626	79	-1 258	-4 800	-512	-536
4th quarter	-406	-987	5 997	5 704	293	324	-1 270	908	386	-55	-1 740	-918	-1 173
1972													
1st quarter	-248	-1 082	5 077	3 472	1 605	-136	-3	1 059	-14	699	911	-1 368	-1 693
2nd quarter	-185	190	4 277	1 103	3 174	373	-83	961	250	1 673	-463	-1 631	-1 689
3rd quarter	-241	-1 057	6 382	4 740	1 642	310	-12	718	216	410	-1 145	-1 132	-1 285
4th quarter	-380	-1 557	6 437	1 871	4 566	403	59	1 769	363	1 972	-1 182	-1 309	-1 130
1973													
1st quarter	-809	-2 988	10 743	9 937	806	631	-119	1 718	246	-1 670	-3 002	-845	145
2nd quarter	-202	-763	3 056	-403	3 458	835	-185	489	54	2 265	225	31	873
3rd quarter	-502	299	2 168	-772	2 940	539	-205	1 173	454	979	-1 716	1 093	2 737
4th quarter	-870	-2 528	2 423	-2 736	5 159	795	293	662	281	3 128	1 840	1 620	3 383

[3]A minus sign indicates financial outflows or increases in U.S. official assets.
[4]A minus sign indicates financial outflows or decreases in foreign official assets in the United States.
[5]Sum of credits and debits with the sign reversed.
. . . = Not available.

Table 7-6B. U.S. International Transactions: Historical—*Continued*

(Millions of dollars, seasonally adjusted.)

Year and quarter	Exports of goods, services, and income				Imports of goods, services, and income [1]				Unilateral current transfers, net [2]	U.S.-owned assets abroad, net, excluding financial derivatives [3]			U.S. private assets, net		
	Total	Goods	Services	Income receipts	Total	Goods	Services	Income payments		Total	U.S. official reserve assets, net	U.S. government assets other than official reserve assets, net	Total	Direct investment	Foreign securities
1974															
1st quarter	34 698	22 614	5 189	6 895	-29 643	-21 952	-4 985	-2 706	-3 443	-5 914	-246	1 389	-7 057	900	-600
2nd quarter	37 295	24 500	5 691	7 104	-34 710	-26 346	-5 359	-3 005	-2 475	-10 318	-358	267	-10 227	-1 790	-272
3rd quarter	37 385	24 629	5 633	7 123	-36 004	-27 368	-5 360	-3 276	-1 676	-7 694	-1 002	-354	-6 338	-4 385	-282
4th quarter	39 105	26 563	6 078	6 464	-36 918	-28 145	-5 675	-3 098	-1 656	-10 818	139	-938	-10 019	-3 776	-699
1975															
1st quarter	40 047	27 480	6 454	6 113	-33 797	-24 980	-5 580	-3 237	-2 043	-10 576	-327	-877	-9 372	-4 022	-1 931
2nd quarter	38 675	25 866	6 807	6 002	-31 284	-22 832	-5 309	-3 143	-2 377	-9 591	-28	-875	-8 688	-3 990	-985
3rd quarter	38 347	26 109	5 886	6 352	-33 078	-24 487	-5 379	-3 212	-1 189	-5 099	-333	-745	-4 021	-1 495	-938
4th quarter	40 868	27 633	6 351	6 884	-34 588	-25 886	-5 729	-2 973	-1 467	-14 436	-161	-977	-13 298	-4 736	-2 393
1976															
1st quarter	41 183	27 575	6 556	7 052	-37 464	-28 176	-5 883	-3 405	-1 153	-12 364	-777	-749	-10 838	-3 923	-2 467
2nd quarter	42 309	28 256	6 660	7 393	-39 494	-30 182	-5 980	-3 332	-1 167	-11 701	-1 580	-914	-9 207	-2 017	-1 405
3rd quarter	43 818	29 056	7 311	7 451	-41 737	-32 213	-6 231	-3 293	-2 165	-10 618	-408	-1 428	-8 782	-3 327	-2 751
4th quarter	44 780	29 858	7 444	7 478	-43 416	-33 657	-6 478	-3 281	-1 201	-16 588	207	-1 124	-15 671	-2 682	-2 262
1977															
1st quarter	44 916	29 668	7 494	7 754	-46 360	-36 585	-6 676	-3 099	-1 243	-1 198	-420	-1 062	284	-1 880	-749
2nd quarter	46 796	30 852	7 901	8 043	-48 401	-38 063	-6 940	-3 398	-1 426	-12 182	-24	-885	-11 273	-3 783	-1 784
3rd quarter	47 125	30 752	7 991	8 382	-48 511	-38 005	-6 894	-3 612	-1 371	-6 297	112	-1 001	-5 408	-2 762	-2 177
4th quarter	45 818	29 544	8 098	8 176	-50 495	-39 254	-7 133	-4 108	-1 185	-15 109	-43	-746	-14 320	-3 466	-749
1978															
1st quarter	48 847	30 470	8 704	9 673	-54 471	-42 487	-7 612	-4 372	-1 396	-15 219	187	-1 009	-14 397	-4 771	-1 115
2nd quarter	54 213	35 674	8 772	9 767	-56 513	-43 419	-7 768	-5 326	-1 477	-5 606	248	-1 257	-4 597	-3 720	-1 094
3rd quarter	56 058	36 523	9 203	10 332	-58 300	-44 422	-8 248	-5 630	-1 425	-9 703	115	-1 394	-8 424	-2 753	-510
4th quarter	61 399	39 408	9 673	12 318	-60 587	-45 674	-8 561	-6 352	-1 491	-30 601	182	-999	-29 784	-4 812	-907
1979															
1st quarter	64 530	41 475	9 664	13 391	-63 492	-47 582	-8 649	-7 261	-1 462	-8 980	-3 585	-1 094	-4 301	-5 465	-908
2nd quarter	68 445	43 885	9 713	14 847	-67 584	-50 778	-8 960	-7 846	-1 552	-15 565	322	-970	-14 917	-7 220	-492
3rd quarter	74 411	47 104	9 936	17 371	-71 856	-54 002	-9 329	-8 525	-1 632	-27 156	2 779	-779	-29 156	-7 166	-2 331
4th quarter	80 577	51 975	10 378	18 224	-78 726	-59 645	-9 751	-9 330	-1 949	-14 353	-649	-904	-12 800	-5 370	-995
1980															
1st quarter	85 274	54 237	10 997	20 040	-86 559	-65 815	-10 335	-10 409	-2 174	-13 814	-3 268	-1 441	-9 105	-5 188	-787
2nd quarter	83 441	55 967	11 491	15 983	-82 734	-62 274	-10 106	-10 354	-2 340	-24 724	502	-1 159	-24 067	-2 659	-1 387
3rd quarter	86 148	55 830	12 543	17 775	-79 906	-59 010	-10 292	-10 604	-1 909	-19 666	-1 109	-1 382	-17 175	-4 156	-944
4th quarter	89 578	58 216	12 554	18 808	-84 577	-62 651	-10 760	-11 166	-2 618	-28 761	-4 279	-1 178	-23 304	-7 219	-450
1981															
1st quarter	94 665	60 317	13 684	20 664	-91 024	-67 004	-11 360	-12 660	-2 678	-23 015	-4 529	-1 361	-17 125	-2 044	-473
2nd quarter	96 294	60 141	14 392	21 761	-92 303	-67 181	-11 447	-13 675	-2 763	-24 158	-905	-1 491	-21 762	-5 709	-1 564
3rd quarter	95 013	58 031	14 835	22 147	-89 787	-64 407	-11 236	-14 144	-3 145	-17 945	-4	-1 268	-16 673	-1 124	-697
4th quarter	94 958	58 555	14 446	21 957	-91 082	-66 475	-11 460	-13 147	-3 117	-49 028	262	-976	-48 314	-745	-2 966
1982															
1st quarter	94 006	55 163	16 032	22 811	-90 336	-63 502	-12 749	-14 085	-3 955	-36 335	-1 089	-800	-34 446	. . .	-628
2nd quarter	96 060	55 344	16 187	24 529	-88 318	-60 580	-13 096	-14 642	-3 953	-42 754	-1 132	-1 727	-39 895	1 074	-471
3rd quarter	90 925	52 089	16 003	22 833	-90 938	-63 696	-12 794	-14 448	-4 027	-23 547	-794	-2 524	-20 229	903	-3 397
4th quarter	85 993	48 561	15 857	21 575	-86 379	-59 864	-13 109	-13 406	-4 611	-25 246	-1 949	-1 080	-22 217	-3 838	-3 488
1983															
1st quarter	86 146	49 198	16 239	20 709	-85 097	-59 757	-12 951	-12 389	-3 566	-28 890	-787	-1 136	-26 967	-862	-1 549
2nd quarter	87 214	49 340	16 093	21 781	-91 096	-64 783	-13 557	-12 756	-3 951	-2 974	16	-1 263	-1 727	-1 842	-2 813
3rd quarter	89 919	50 324	16 308	23 287	-98 481	-70 370	-14 113	-13 978	-4 339	-12 191	529	-1 171	-11 549	-4 861	-1 308
4th quarter	92 831	52 937	15 671	24 223	-102 822	-73 991	-14 337	-14 494	-5 453	-22 318	-953	-1 436	-19 929	-4 962	-1 093
1984															
1st quarter	96 000	52 991	17 353	25 656	-112 576	-79 740	-16 131	-16 705	-4 354	-8 338	-657	-2 033	-5 648	-1 837	758
2nd quarter	100 257	54 626	18 045	27 586	-119 220	-83 798	-16 885	-18 537	-4 476	-25 718	-565	-1 342	-23 811	-1 967	-764
3rd quarter	102 296	55 893	17 936	28 467	-120 533	-83 918	-17 168	-19 447	-5 147	15 298	-799	-1 392	17 489	-3 209	-1 106
4th quarter	101 361	56 416	17 834	27 111	-121 591	-84 962	-17 564	-19 065	-6 359	-21 618	-1 109	-720	-19 789	-9 396	-3 644
1985															
1st quarter	97 794	54 866	18 227	24 701	-116 249	-80 319	-17 707	-18 223	-5 064	-5 491	-233	-760	-4 498	-2 783	-2 474
2nd quarter	97 437	54 154	18 214	25 069	-120 891	-84 565	-18 276	-18 050	-5 235	-2 340	-356	-1 053	-931	-4 374	-2 219
3rd quarter	94 771	52 836	17 961	23 974	-120 285	-83 909	-18 151	-18 225	-5 789	-5 776	-121	-453	-5 202	-4 698	-1 572
4th quarter	97 612	54 059	18 756	24 797	-126 349	-89 295	-18 732	-18 322	-5 911	-31 146	-3 147	-555	-27 444	-7 073	-1 217
1986															
1st quarter	100 332	53 536	21 052	25 744	-129 342	-89 220	-19 855	-20 267	-5 199	-17 406	-115	-266	-17 025	-9 781	-5 930
2nd quarter	102 206	56 828	20 912	24 466	-131 690	-91 743	-19 066	-20 881	-6 208	-24 945	16	-230	-24 731	-7 298	-1 051
3rd quarter	101 288	55 645	21 969	23 674	-132 879	-92 801	-20 448	-19 630	-6 458	-32 615	280	-1 554	-31 341	-4 975	181
4th quarter	103 275	57 335	22 761	23 179	-136 232	-94 661	-20 778	-20 793	-6 269	-36 753	132	29	-36 914	-1 938	2 529
1987															
1st quarter	104 750	56 696	23 602	24 452	-138 887	-96 023	-21 273	-21 591	-5 128	8 177	1 956	-5	6 226	-6 547	-1 749
2nd quarter	111 642	60 202	24 740	26 700	-146 125	-100 648	-22 537	-22 940	-5 502	-26 738	3 419	-168	-29 989	-7 541	-287
3rd quarter	116 688	64 217	24 986	27 485	-151 111	-104 412	-22 833	-23 866	-5 706	-27 791	32	310	-28 133	-8 795	-1 159
4th quarter	123 968	69 093	25 329	29 546	-158 324	-108 682	-24 146	-25 496	-6 926	-32 943	3 742	868	-37 553	-12 150	-2 056

[1] A minus sign indicates imports of goods or services or income payments.
[2] A minus sign indicates net unilateral transfers to foreigners.
[3] A minus sign indicates financial outflows or increases in U.S. official assets.
. . . = Not available.

Table 7-6B. U.S. International Transactions: Historical—*Continued*

(Millions of dollars, seasonally adjusted.)

Year and quarter	U.S.-owned assets abroad, net [3] —Continued / U.S. private assets, net—Continued / U.S. claims: On unaffiliated foreigners reported by U.S. nonbanking concerns	Reported by U.S. banks and securities brokers	Foreign-owned assets in the United States, net, excluding financial derivatives [4] / Total	Foreign official assets in the United States, net	Other foreign assets in the United States, net / Total	Direct invest-ment	U.S. Treasury securities and U.S. currency flows	U.S. securities other than U.S. Treasury securities	U.S. liabilities / To unaffiliated foreigners reported by U.S. nonbanking concerns	Reported by U.S. banks and securities brokers	Statistical discrep-ancy [5]	Balance on goods and services	Balance on current account
1974													
1st quarter	-2 113	-5 244	6 444	-1 138	7 582	1 784	266	712	354	4 466	-2 142	866	1 612
2nd quarter	-588	-7 577	9 897	4 434	5 463	539	-5	363	390	4 176	311	-1 514	110
3rd quarter	273	-1 944	9 310	3 062	6 248	1 610	407	227	239	3 765	-1 321	-2 466	-295
4th quarter	-793	-4 751	9 577	4 188	5 389	828	1 015	-925	861	3 610	710	-1 179	531
1975													
1st quarter	353	-3 772	2 701	3 419	-718	278	805	344	359	-2 504	3 668	3 374	4 207
2nd quarter	112	-3 825	4 307	2 244	2 063	870	-54	385	55	807	270	4 532	5 014
3rd quarter	-939	-649	2 934	-1 731	4 665	86	2 367	737	-163	1 638	-1 915	2 129	4 080
4th quarter	-883	-5 286	6 929	3 095	3 834	1 369	672	1 038	68	687	2 694	2 369	4 813
1976													
1st quarter	-747	-3 701	7 709	3 699	4 010	1 471	677	1 036	154	672	2 089	72	2 566
2nd quarter	-999	-4 786	8 425	4 039	4 386	1 086	-119	134	-231	3 516	1 628	-1 246	1 648
3rd quarter	616	-3 320	9 062	2 958	6 104	999	3 267	64	-184	1 958	1 640	-2 077	-84
4th quarter	-1 166	-9 561	12 644	6 997	5 647	790	279	51	-317	4 844	3 781	-2 833	163
1977													
1st quarter	-771	3 684	2 968	5 554	-2 586	980	1 087	749	-98	-5 304	917	-6 099	-2 687
2nd quarter	-1 124	-4 582	14 673	7 888	6 785	965	-907	589	-102	6 240	540	-6 250	-3 031
3rd quarter	1 310	-1 779	14 585	8 257	6 328	1 023	1 560	337	768	2 640	-5 531	-6 156	-2 757
4th quarter	-1 355	-8 750	20 547	15 117	5 430	761	245	763	518	3 143	424	-8 745	-5 862
1978													
1st quarter	-2 241	-6 270	18 461	15 448	3 013	1 356	1 158	396	507	-404	3 778	-10 925	-7 020
2nd quarter	315	-98	1 412	-5 113	6 525	2 313	1 354	1 082	304	1 472	7 971	-6 741	-3 777
3rd quarter	-29	-5 132	17 390	4 903	12 487	2 620	-560	296	912	9 219	-4 020	-6 944	-3 667
4th quarter	-1 898	-22 167	29 013	18 440	10 573	1 608	2 465	480	166	5 854	2 267	-5 154	-679
1979													
1st quarter	-3 854	5 926	3 472	-7 558	11 030	1 554	2 590	409	-296	6 773	5 932	-5 092	-424
2nd quarter	716	-7 921	7 379	-9 775	17 154	3 354	459	524	799	12 018	8 877	-6 140	-691
3rd quarter	-1 826	-17 833	25 063	6 036	19 027	3 382	2 116	166	210	13 153	1 170	-6 291	923
4th quarter	-50	-6 385	4 780	-1 228	6 008	3 588	597	252	908	663	9 671	-7 043	-98
1980													
1st quarter	-1 927	-1 203	10 180	-6 261	16 441	3 321	3 746	2 435	340	6 599	7 093	-10 916	-3 459
2nd quarter	144	-20 165	10 994	7 731	3 264	5 756	-150	496	1 671	-4 509	14 671	-4 922	-941
3rd quarter	365	-12 440	14 599	7 564	7 035	4 713	-109	263	1 252	916	734	-929	4 333
4th quarter	-2 605	-13 030	26 263	7 614	18 649	3 128	1 931	2 263	3 590	7 737	115	-2 641	2 383
1981													
1st quarter	-2 944	-11 664	10 303	6 595	3 708	3 146	1 877	2 357	121	-3 793	11 749	-4 363	963
2nd quarter	513	-15 002	14 906	-3 159	18 065	5 294	1 183	3 512	13	8 063	8 024	-4 095	1 228
3rd quarter	458	-15 310	17 212	-5 992	23 204	5 505	-567	704	1 084	16 478	-1 348	-2 777	2 081
4th quarter	-2 404	-42 199	43 264	8 609	34 655	11 251	1 993	332	-301	21 380	5 005	-4 934	759
1982													
1st quarter	2 220	-33 343	26 797	-3 265	30 062	. . .	854	1 263	-65	25 856	9 823	-5 056	-285
2nd quarter	-1 095	-39 403	34 995	1 534	33 461	2 945	3 928	2 486	-2 023	26 125	3 970	-2 145	3 789
3rd quarter	3 670	-21 405	18 267	2 694	15 573	2 849	1 695	555	-282	10 756	9 320	-8 398	-4 040
4th quarter	2 028	-16 919	14 995	2 629	12 366	4 685	3 017	1 781	-13	2 896	15 248	-8 555	-4 997
1983													
1st quarter	-4 253	-20 303	15 870	-38	15 908	1 254	3 317	2 873	-2 763	11 227	15 537	-7 271	-2 517
2nd quarter	-590	3 518	16 049	1 612	14 437	3 287	4 340	2 470	-64	4 404	-5 242	-12 907	-7 833
3rd quarter	-1 764	-3 616	20 106	-2 689	22 795	4 059	1 994	1 777	1 311	13 654	4 986	-17 871	-12 901
4th quarter	-4 347	-9 527	35 373	6 960	28 413	1 771	3 143	1 044	1 398	21 057	2 389	-19 720	-15 444
1984													
1st quarter	-3 012	-1 557	22 780	-2 956	25 736	4 858	1 928	1 333	6 092	11 525	6 488	-25 527	-20 930
2nd quarter	-934	-20 146	42 415	-156	42 571	8 625	7 762	362	4 232	21 590	6 742	-28 012	-23 439
3rd quarter	3 987	17 817	7 158	-884	8 042	4 432	5 693	1 447	1 662	-5 192	928	-27 257	-23 384
4th quarter	492	-7 241	43 694	7 136	36 558	6 552	10 014	9 426	4 640	5 926	4 513	-28 276	-26 589
1985													
1st quarter	475	284	17 783	-10 962	28 745	4 913	2 831	9 615	-720	12 106	11 227	-24 933	-23 519
2nd quarter	2 337	3 325	28 903	8 502	20 401	4 376	6 457	7 194	1 724	650	2 126	-30 473	-28 689
3rd quarter	-2 779	3 847	37 802	2 506	35 296	4 839	8 675	11 669	2 801	7 312	-723	-31 263	-31 303
4th quarter	-10 375	-8 779	59 746	-1 165	60 911	5 618	5 786	22 484	6 046	20 977	6 048	-35 212	-34 648
1986													
1st quarter	-6 230	4 916	40 898	2 712	38 186	3 431	5 829	18 730	696	9 500	10 717	-34 487	-34 209
2nd quarter	-2 722	-13 660	53 279	15 918	37 361	5 520	4 189	22 752	1 635	3 265	7 358	-33 069	-35 692
3rd quarter	-7 638	-18 909	70 490	15 789	54 701	8 746	-1 240	17 107	1 947	28 141	174	-35 635	-38 049
4th quarter	-5 183	-32 322	63 662	1 229	62 433	17 723	-2 548	12 380	-953	35 831	12 317	-35 343	-39 226
1987													
1st quarter	-5 715	20 237	41 667	14 199	27 468	12 883	-2 906	18 372	6 151	-7 032	-10 579	-36 998	-39 265
2nd quarter	712	-22 873	57 020	10 444	46 576	8 593	-1 042	15 960	5 595	17 470	9 703	-38 243	-39 985
3rd quarter	-1 319	-16 860	82 791	764	82 027	20 763	-2 189	12 676	6 656	44 121	-14 871	-38 042	-40 129
4th quarter	-724	-22 623	65 621	19 980	45 641	16 230	2 360	-4 888	-39	31 978	8 604	-38 406	-41 282

[3]A minus sign indicates financial outflows or increases in U.S. official assets.
[4]A minus sign indicates financial outflows or decreases in foreign official assets in the United States.
[5]Sum of credits and debits with the sign reversed.
. . . = Not available.

Table 7-6B. U.S. International Transactions: Historical—*Continued*

(Millions of dollars, seasonally adjusted.)

Year and quarter	Exports of goods, services, and income				Imports of goods, services, and income [1]				Unilateral current transfers, net [2]	U.S.-owned assets abroad, net, excluding financial derivatives [3]			U.S. private assets, net		
	Total	Goods	Services	Income receipts	Total	Goods	Services	Income payments		Total	U.S. official reserve assets, net	U.S. government assets other than official reserve assets, net	Total	Direct investment	Foreign securities
1988															
1st quarter	134 932	75 655	26 598	32 679	-161 810	-109 963	-24 503	-27 344	-6 074	2 892	1 502	-1 597	2 987	-5 037	-4 504
2nd quarter	139 984	79 542	27 567	32 875	-163 265	-110 836	-24 282	-28 147	-5 615	-23 428	39	-854	-22 613	-2 594	1 318
3rd quarter	143 879	80 941	28 453	34 485	-165 901	-110 901	-24 588	-30 412	-5 902	-49 965	-7 380	1 960	-44 545	-7 791	-1 500
4th quarter	149 068	84 092	28 302	36 674	-172 770	-115 489	-25 157	-32 124	-7 685	-36 074	1 925	3 457	-41 456	-7 105	-3 294
1989															
1st quarter	155 853	86 322	30 576	38 955	-178 297	-118 709	-25 140	-34 448	-6 048	-53 703	-4 000	961	-50 664	-12 136	-2 225
2nd quarter	163 435	91 482	31 110	40 843	-182 850	-121 012	-25 241	-36 597	-5 753	-8 202	-12 095	-306	4 199	-7 686	-6 192
3rd quarter	163 560	90 743	32 316	40 501	-178 980	-117 459	-25 792	-35 729	-6 630	-51 678	-5 996	489	-46 171	-8 704	-9 149
4th quarter	165 444	91 369	33 087	40 988	-181 480	-120 485	-26 306	-34 689	-7 739	-61 803	-3 202	87	-58 688	-14 922	-4 504
1990															
1st quarter	171 856	95 070	35 016	41 770	-188 962	-124 947	-28 173	-35 842	-6 540	37 828	-3 177	-756	41 761	-10 391	-8 580
2nd quarter	174 266	96 273	35 988	42 005	-186 146	-121 782	-28 764	-35 600	-7 644	-37 204	371	-796	-36 779	-4 651	-11 037
3rd quarter	176 466	97 227	37 402	41 837	-190 664	-124 132	-29 923	-36 609	-7 339	-43 716	1 739	-338	-45 117	-17 898	-1 037
4th quarter	184 389	98 831	39 428	46 130	-193 514	-127 577	-30 795	-35 142	-5 133	-38 142	-1 092	4 205	-41 255	-4 240	-8 111
1991															
1st quarter	181 296	101 258	37 891	42 147	-186 167	-122 326	-29 801	-34 040	14 828	-10 570	-353	549	-10 766	-14 318	-9 960
2nd quarter	180 627	102 674	40 745	37 208	-181 695	-120 103	-29 660	-31 932	3 593	745	1 014	-423	154	-1 230	-12 021
3rd quarter	181 647	104 238	41 860	35 549	-182 800	-122 448	-29 200	-31 152	-3 033	-15 900	3 878	3 256	-23 034	-9 356	-12 550
4th quarter	183 993	105 913	43 766	34 314	-183 906	-126 143	-29 799	-27 964	-5 488	-38 664	1 226	-459	-39 431	-12 987	-11 142
1992															
1st quarter	186 444	108 062	44 164	34 218	-185 468	-127 962	-29 762	-27 744	-7 210	-11 428	-1 057	-259	-10 112	-20 695	-8 668
2nd quarter	186 873	107 941	44 133	34 799	-190 414	-132 484	-29 443	-28 487	-8 349	-16 235	1 464	-302	-17 397	-10 268	-8 196
3rd quarter	188 127	110 847	44 609	32 671	-193 313	-136 048	-30 175	-27 090	-9 517	-13 570	1 952	-392	-15 130	-5 157	-13 059
4th quarter	189 201	112 781	44 343	32 077	-196 427	-140 034	-30 182	-26 211	-11 561	-33 177	1 542	-715	-34 004	-12 145	-19 243
1993															
1st quarter	191 422	112 099	45 984	33 339	-197 860	-142 331	-29 996	-25 533	-8 339	-21 491	-983	487	-20 995	-14 982	-28 208
2nd quarter	193 169	113 257	46 457	33 455	-204 737	-146 800	-30 661	-27 276	-9 111	-45 843	822	-304	-46 361	-23 264	-29 833
3rd quarter	194 153	112 982	46 707	34 464	-205 549	-147 763	-30 922	-26 864	-9 906	-52 975	-544	-194	-52 237	-13 155	-51 940
4th quarter	200 170	118 605	46 766	34 799	-215 772	-152 500	-32 202	-31 070	-12 456	-80 243	-673	-340	-79 230	-32 550	-36 272
1994															
1st quarter	204 240	118 833	48 362	37 045	-220 726	-156 303	-32 809	-31 614	-8 495	-39 740	-59	399	-40 080	-28 554	-19 540
2nd quarter	211 812	122 251	49 978	39 583	-231 476	-163 200	-33 023	-35 253	-8 914	-45 677	3 537	477	-49 691	-14 932	-11 834
3rd quarter	222 795	128 947	50 667	43 181	-244 319	-171 342	-33 624	-39 353	-10 084	-31 948	-165	-323	-31 460	-17 316	-13 368
4th quarter	230 930	132 828	51 391	46 711	-254 602	-177 845	-33 603	-43 154	-12 773	-61 574	2 033	-943	-62 664	-19 367	-18 448
1995															
1st quarter	241 117	138 370	52 173	50 574	-263 108	-183 966	-34 426	-44 716	-9 443	-64 771	-5 318	-553	-58 900	-19 325	-8 596
2nd quarter	248 705	142 520	53 163	53 022	-271 587	-189 910	-35 097	-46 580	-9 131	-118 089	-2 722	-225	-115 142	-15 078	-27 964
3rd quarter	255 495	146 536	56 436	52 523	-272 929	-187 685	-35 604	-49 640	-9 543	-47 311	-1 893	252	-45 670	-21 772	-42 116
4th quarter	259 310	147 778	57 408	54 124	-272 501	-187 813	-36 272	-48 416	-9 956	-122 091	191	-458	-121 824	-42 573	-43 718
1996															
1st quarter	263 221	150 552	57 442	55 227	-279 419	-194 445	-37 090	-47 884	-11 242	-80 431	17	-210	-80 238	-23 759	-43 538
2nd quarter	266 995	152 861	59 350	54 784	-287 312	-200 070	-37 606	-49 636	-9 523	-68 123	-523	-568	-67 032	-15 096	-30 579
3rd quarter	266 854	151 856	58 664	56 334	-293 261	-202 367	-38 836	-52 058	-9 651	-91 580	7 489	105	-99 174	-23 129	-33 178
4th quarter	280 655	156 844	64 029	59 782	-299 487	-206 231	-39 023	-54 233	-12 603	-173 272	-315	-316	-172 641	-29 898	-42 020
1997															
1st quarter	287 279	162 670	62 515	62 094	-313 391	-214 209	-40 405	-58 777	-9 967	-152 729	4 480	-76	-157 133	-29 544	-24 352
2nd quarter	299 679	170 249	64 292	65 138	-318 210	-217 296	-40 879	-60 035	-10 267	-93 152	-236	-298	-92 618	-24 883	-31 275
3rd quarter	303 542	173 155	64 855	65 532	-325 593	-220 974	-42 078	-62 541	-10 666	-119 387	-730	377	-119 034	-21 217	-51 401
4th quarter	300 762	172 292	64 429	64 041	-329 728	-224 315	-42 571	-62 842	-14 160	-120 209	-4 524	65	-115 750	-29 161	-9 824
1998															
1st quarter	302 195	171 060	64 690	66 445	-334 146	-227 667	-43 304	-63 175	-12 053	-74 438	-444	-80	-73 914	-41 844	-19 451
2nd quarter	298 846	165 559	66 174	67 113	-337 834	-228 497	-44 627	-64 710	-12 361	-138 628	-1 945	-483	-136 200	-44 689	-42 961
3rd quarter	293 115	164 054	64 786	64 275	-338 864	-227 854	-45 784	-65 226	-13 140	-58 520	-2 025	188	-56 683	-20 479	7 783
4th quarter	300 835	169 743	67 106	63 986	-346 026	-234 619	-46 965	-64 442	-15 633	-82 245	-2 369	-47	-79 829	-35 634	-75 575
1999															
1st quarter	301 005	167 904	65 610	67 491	-352 454	-239 941	-46 880	-65 632	-11 892	-84 623	4 068	118	-88 809	-68 498	2 696
2nd quarter	307 938	170 270	66 299	71 370	-367 959	-251 343	-48 322	-68 295	-11 352	-182 426	1 159	-392	-183 193	-50 190	-69 682
3rd quarter	320 396	176 349	67 896	76 150	-389 381	-265 946	-49 585	-73 850	-11 813	-123 490	1 951	-686	-124 755	-64 062	-39 790
4th quarter	333 095	183 695	68 984	80 416	-404 462	-278 362	-50 386	-75 714	-13 895	-113 524	1 569	3 710	-118 803	-42 185	-15 460
2000															
1st quarter	342 570	188 447	70 444	83 680	-428 500	-295 400	-53 020	-80 080	-12 711	-207 606	-554	-127	-206 925	-34 934	-32 542
2nd quarter	356 151	194 625	72 372	89 154	-442 363	-303 489	-53 889	-84 985	-13 367	-107 301	2 020	-570	-108 751	-52 029	-38 171
3rd quarter	361 296	201 770	72 323	87 202	-454 936	-314 558	-55 928	-84 450	-14 194	-84 847	-346	114	-84 615	-39 618	-32 363
4th quarter	365 246	199 939	72 864	92 443	-457 623	-318 276	-55 563	-83 784	-17 889	-160 771	-1 410	-358	-159 003	-32 633	-24 832
2001															
1st quarter	351 600	196 761	72 512	82 327	-443 855	-311 376	-55 064	-77 415	-15 075	-216 194	190	77	-216 461	-35 381	-25 355
2nd quarter	335 986	188 487	71 249	76 250	-417 632	-292 071	-56 276	-69 285	-15 392	-86 702	-1 343	-783	-84 576	-26 783	-50 200
3rd quarter	313 257	175 917	68 065	69 275	-401 463	-279 859	-53 405	-68 199	-16 316	32 858	-3 559	77	36 340	-44 327	11 639
4th quarter	299 313	170 023	64 711	64 580	-369 816	-270 395	-51 617	-47 804	-17 298	-112 577	-199	143	-112 521	-35 857	-26 728

[1] A minus sign indicates imports of goods or services or income payments.
[2] A minus sign indicates net unilateral transfers to foreigners.
[3] A minus sign indicates financial outflows or increases in U.S. official assets.

Table 7-6B. U.S. International Transactions: Historical—*Continued*

(Millions of dollars, seasonally adjusted.)

Year and quarter	U.S.-owned assets abroad, net³ —Continued / U.S. private assets, net—Continued / U.S. claims — On unaffiliated foreigners reported by U.S. nonbanking concerns	Reported by U.S. banks and securities brokers	Foreign-owned assets in the United States, net, excluding financial derivatives⁴ — Total	Foreign official assets in the United States, net	Other foreign assets in the United States, net — Total	Direct investment	U.S. Treasury securities and U.S. currency flows	U.S. securities other than U.S. Treasury securities	U.S. liabilities — To unaffiliated foreigners reported by U.S. nonbanking concerns	Reported by U.S. banks and securities brokers	Statistical discrepancy⁵	Balance on goods and services	Balance on current account
1988													
1st quarter	-3 454	15 982	31 524	24 925	6 599	8 425	6 007	2 423	12 593	-22 849	-1 464	-32 213	-32 952
2nd quarter	-9 954	-11 383	74 187	6 006	68 181	13 717	7 329	9 702	6 742	30 691	-21 863	-28 009	-28 896
3rd quarter	-5 217	-30 037	52 329	-1 974	54 303	13 778	4 275	7 464	6 399	22 387	25 560	-26 095	-27 924
4th quarter	-2 568	-28 489	86 793	10 801	75 992	21 815	6 739	6 764	7 159	33 515	-19 332	-28 252	-31 387
1989													
1st quarter	-9 293	-27 010	66 021	7 700	58 321	18 584	10 316	8 544	6 637	14 240	16 174	-26 951	-28 492
2nd quarter	-5 767	23 844	10 571	-5 114	15 685	15 325	4 380	9 365	12 000	-25 385	22 799	-23 661	-25 168
3rd quarter	-5 924	-22 394	73 526	13 060	60 466	11 519	12 202	10 270	-1 121	27 596	202	-20 192	-22 050
4th quarter	-6 662	-32 600	72 660	-7 142	79 802	22 846	6 469	10 588	4 570	35 329	13 125	-22 335	-23 775
1990													
1st quarter	3 019	57 713	-23 477	-6 421	-17 056	15 774	1 056	1 311	12 904	-48 101	9 467	-23 034	-23 646
2nd quarter	-5 069	-16 022	40 868	6 207	34 661	13 773	5 910	2 114	6 713	6 151	15 860	-18 285	-19 524
3rd quarter	-15 514	-10 668	62 621	13 937	48 684	8 313	5 434	-2 874	16 838	20 973	2 632	-19 426	-21 537
4th quarter	-10 260	-18 644	59 345	20 186	39 159	10 635	1 652	1 041	8 678	17 153	104	-20 113	-14 258
1991													
1st quarter	-40	13 552	7 590	5 569	2 021	4 076	8 782	5 023	-586	-15 274	-5 909	-12 978	9 957
2nd quarter	7 902	5 503	12 016	-4 913	16 929	13 378	14 999	14 872	-2 549	-23 771	-15 187	-6 344	2 525
3rd quarter	3 341	-4 469	32 574	3 854	28 720	-1 354	2 342	10 310	4 761	12 661	-8 528	-5 550	-4 186
4th quarter	-106	-15 196	56 043	12 879	43 164	7 072	5 516	4 939	-4 741	30 378	-11 976	-6 263	-5 401
1992													
1st quarter	7 562	11 689	30 212	20 988	9 224	2 086	1 119	4 569	5 689	-4 239	-12 537	-5 498	-6 234
2nd quarter	-6 620	7 687	49 732	20 879	28 853	5 916	10 759	10 467	3 954	-2 243	-21 545	-9 853	-11 890
3rd quarter	-3 737	6 823	34 931	-7 524	42 455	2 898	10 470	2 531	4 854	21 702	-8 187	-10 767	-14 703
4th quarter	2 408	-5 024	53 472	6 133	47 339	8 922	25 869	12 476	-924	996	-1 503	-13 092	-18 787
1993													
1st quarter	-6 130	28 325	24 531	10 937	13 594	8 060	15 795	9 694	-215	-19 740	12 359	-14 244	-14 777
2nd quarter	-725	7 461	58 599	17 466	41 133	11 386	5 169	15 205	6 531	2 842	7 936	-17 747	-20 679
3rd quarter	5 896	6 962	84 967	19 073	65 894	11 688	8 931	17 782	288	27 205	-10 622	-18 996	-21 302
4th quarter	1 725	-12 133	111 662	24 277	87 385	20 229	11 104	37 411	3 885	14 756	-3 350	-19 331	-28 058
1994													
1st quarter	-2 215	10 229	89 488	10 568	78 920	5 883	14 620	21 070	5 856	31 491	-24 759	-21 917	-24 981
2nd quarter	-20 966	-1 959	56 279	9 455	46 824	5 767	-1 361	12 352	4 269	25 797	18 842	-23 994	-28 578
3rd quarter	-960	184	81 239	19 358	61 881	13 709	9 666	13 389	-1 620	26 737	-17 455	-25 352	-31 608
4th quarter	-12 195	-12 654	76 168	202	75 966	20 762	31 934	10 160	-7 203	20 313	21 861	-27 229	-36 445
1995													
1st quarter	-2 631	-28 348	96 842	21 956	74 886	9 924	33 337	12 400	17 764	1 461	-629	-27 849	-31 434
2nd quarter	-24 580	-47 520	121 385	37 072	84 313	11 888	29 574	15 851	11 864	15 136	28 598	-29 324	-32 013
3rd quarter	13 729	4 489	115 499	39 302	76 197	16 764	36 327	26 218	13 493	-16 605	-40 767	-20 317	-26 977
4th quarter	-31 804	-3 729	101 376	11 550	89 826	19 200	1 146	22 780	16 516	30 184	43 751	-18 899	-23 147
1996													
1st quarter	-15 210	2 269	84 335	51 771	32 564	28 518	12 726	20 356	4 350	-33 386	23 538	-23 541	-27 440
2nd quarter	-22 000	643	100 610	13 503	87 107	16 184	28 719	24 686	15 259	2 259	-2 645	-25 465	-29 840
3rd quarter	-9 090	-33 777	143 269	23 020	120 249	15 257	43 276	29 719	28 925	3 072	-15 630	-30 683	-36 058
4th quarter	-40 033	-60 690	219 670	38 430	181 240	26 542	76 452	28 511	5 202	44 533	-14 962	-24 381	-31 435
1997													
1st quarter	-38 112	-65 125	172 247	27 763	144 484	28 626	31 779	38 490	25 055	20 534	16 577	-29 429	-36 079
2nd quarter	-9 885	-26 575	140 222	-6 019	146 241	23 150	38 253	45 651	6 461	32 726	-18 184	-23 634	-28 798
3rd quarter	-22 173	-24 243	166 609	23 474	143 135	17 865	42 095	52 544	25 550	5 081	-14 392	-25 042	-32 717
4th quarter	-51 590	-25 175	225 372	-26 182	251 554	35 960	40 733	24 724	59 452	90 685	-61 998	-30 165	-43 126
1998													
1st quarter	-7 822	-4 797	78 365	11 072	67 293	19 759	-6 594	63 237	39 833	-48 942	40 079	-35 221	-44 004
2nd quarter	-20 363	-28 187	154 539	-10 235	164 774	20 391	23 647	56 146	30 722	33 868	35 435	-41 391	-51 349
3rd quarter	-15 658	-28 329	75 193	-46 640	121 833	23 490	1 425	6 628	14 976	75 314	42 229	-44 798	-58 889
4th quarter	5 639	25 741	112 697	25 900	86 797	115 405	23 950	30 304	-62 391	-20 471	30 369	-44 735	-60 824
1999													
1st quarter	-47 211	24 204	108 317	4 381	103 936	28 759	-11 853	49 157	51 307	-13 434	39 654	-53 308	-63 341
2nd quarter	-27 021	-36 300	247 211	-757	247 968	140 759	-9 004	70 205	16 928	29 080	6 589	-63 096	-71 373
3rd quarter	-13 663	-7 240	156 060	12 625	143 435	50 758	7 584	86 202	-8 777	7 668	48 232	-71 286	-80 799
4th quarter	-9 809	-51 349	230 623	27 294	203 329	69 169	-6 817	93 270	16 789	30 918	-27 673	-76 069	-85 261
2000													
1st quarter	-79 800	-59 649	242 782	22 542	220 240	52 094	-23 776	129 306	72 433	-9 817	63 465	-89 530	-98 641
2nd quarter	-25 287	6 736	246 564	6 952	239 612	91 669	-22 889	88 189	28 796	53 847	-39 687	-90 380	-99 578
3rd quarter	-14 121	1 487	245 064	11 354	233 710	79 979	-13 777	122 138	16 914	28 456	-52 372	-96 393	-107 835
4th quarter	-19 582	-81 956	303 816	1 910	301 906	97 534	-12 898	120 256	52 529	44 485	-32 785	-101 036	-110 266
2001													
1st quarter	-46 769	-108 956	330 767	21 333	309 434	59 145	-16 736	129 474	112 097	25 454	-7 243	-97 167	-107 331
2nd quarter	-7 507	-86	206 867	-19 965	226 832	59 338	-10 143	108 537	-173	69 273	-23 131	-88 610	-97 038
3rd quarter	1 824	67 204	24 226	15 653	8 573	13 783	1 495	60 748	-23 171	-44 282	34 249	-89 282	-104 521
4th quarter	43 932	-93 868	221 010	11 038	209 972	34 755	34 800	95 126	-22 643	67 934	-20 639	-87 279	-87 801

³A minus sign indicates financial outflows or increases in U.S. official assets.
⁴A minus sign indicates financial outflows or decreases in foreign official assets in the United States.
⁵Sum of credits and debits with the sign reversed.

Table 7-6B. U.S. International Transactions: Historical—*Continued*

(Millions of dollars, seasonally adjusted.)

| Year and quarter | Exports of goods, services, and income | | | | Imports of goods, services, and income [1] | | | | Unilateral current transfers, net [2] | U.S.-owned assets abroad, net, excluding financial derivatives [3] | | | U.S. private assets, net | | |
	Total	Goods	Services	Income receipts	Total	Goods	Services	Income payments		Total	U.S. official reserve assets, net	U.S. government assets other than official reserve assets, net	Total	Direct investment	Foreign securities
2002															
1st quarter	304 361	168 672	68 817	66 873	-389 740	-274 921	-54 899	-59 920	-18 538	-84 841	390	133	-85 364	-48 155	-9 012
2nd quarter	316 088	175 682	70 205	70 201	-416 463	-293 371	-55 196	-67 896	-14 988	-139 712	-1 843	42	-137 911	-36 163	-20 735
3rd quarter	323 800	178 288	71 214	74 298	-424 466	-299 455	-56 553	-68 457	-15 040	892	-1 416	-27	2 335	-33 165	4 884
4th quarter	319 332	174 798	73 201	71 333	-425 899	-305 534	-59 114	-61 252	-16 244	-70 987	-812	197	-70 372	-36 979	-23 705
2003															
1st quarter	323 916	177 427	71 206	75 283	-440 291	-312 769	-58 808	-68 714	-18 245	-82 315	83	53	-82 451	-22 656	-31 947
2nd quarter	326 683	178 414	70 232	78 038	-439 044	-313 208	-57 724	-68 112	-17 080	-157 427	-170	310	-157 567	-46 512	-32 734
3rd quarter	337 199	182 186	74 142	80 871	-449 031	-316 504	-61 514	-71 013	-17 500	-755	-611	483	-627	-40 597	-27 677
4th quarter	358 545	191 790	78 540	88 215	-465 768	-329 607	-64 347	-71 814	-18 049	-84 924	2 221	-309	-86 836	-39 796	-54 364
2004															
1st quarter	377 320	197 823	82 809	96 687	-490 501	-347 597	-67 198	-75 706	-23 514	-353 976	557	727	-355 260	-77 283	-36 045
2nd quarter	388 822	203 914	84 354	100 554	-523 205	-367 997	-69 355	-85 853	-21 351	-170 502	1 122	-2	-171 622	-75 377	-44 702
3rd quarter	398 252	207 198	85 186	105 868	-535 559	-376 563	-70 542	-88 454	-21 106	-169 462	429	484	-170 375	-51 998	-53 988
4th quarter	415 122	213 050	89 389	112 684	-571 021	-396 192	-73 179	-101 651	-22 588	-306 929	697	501	-308 127	-111 564	-35 814
2005															
1st quarter	436 728	219 215	92 329	125 184	-582 103	-403 172	-73 202	-105 728	-23 842	-129 175	5 331	2 591	-137 097	-58 799	-59 599
2nd quarter	449 234	227 630	92 605	129 000	-602 838	-415 859	-74 645	-112 334	-24 774	-222 397	-797	989	-222 589	-41 548	-57 317
3rd quarter	459 154	228 111	94 393	136 650	-619 166	-426 218	-75 652	-117 296	-24 505	-204 361	4 766	1 501	-210 628	12 163	-66 383
4th quarter	480 478	236 730	97 245	146 503	-661 773	-450 570	-76 853	-134 350	-26 390	9 302	4 796	459	4 047	51 948	-67 900
2006															
1st quarter	505 910	249 307	100 796	155 807	-683 087	-458 054	-82 038	-142 995	-19 023	-387 689	513	1 049	-389 251	-58 801	-75 689
2nd quarter	532 406	257 793	104 550	170 063	-709 547	-467 891	-83 159	-158 497	-23 192	-223 953	-560	1 765	-225 158	-35 160	-80 203
3rd quarter	542 826	261 991	104 636	176 199	-732 007	-480 544	-83 461	-168 002	-25 320	-295 389	1 006	1 570	-297 965	-72 149	-72 552
4th quarter	564 327	270 314	111 405	182 608	-729 889	-471 705	-86 340	-171 845	-21 882	-378 698	1 415	962	-381 075	-78 812	-136 685
2007															
1st quarter	581 768	276 438	114 425	190 905	-747 883	-479 603	-88 389	-179 891	-32 456	-487 524	-72	445	-487 897	-101 224	-122 024
2nd quarter	610 537	285 540	118 228	206 769	-772 397	-491 220	-90 794	-190 384	-26 448	-563 522	26	-596	-562 951	-88 737	-107 067
3rd quarter	637 850	295 248	125 119	217 484	-779 400	-499 623	-93 125	-186 652	-27 496	-189 912	-54	623	-189 880	-77 349	-113 821
4th quarter	656 655	306 378	131 484	218 793	-785 588	-515 902	-93 268	-176 418	-28 532	-212 647	-22	-22 744	-189 880	-146 729	-23 600
2008															
1st quarter	670 403	323 291	131 285	215 827	-815 067	-540 391	-97 519	-177 157	-34 868	-238 333	-276	3 268	-241 325	-92 199	-11 990
2nd quarter	692 207	342 602	135 430	214 176	-837 586	-563 433	-99 711	-174 442	-31 204	177 984	-1 267	-41 592	220 844	-95 140	-4 820
3rd quarter	690 696	346 831	135 464	208 401	-834 277	-566 834	-103 083	-164 360	-31 207	113 445	-179	-225 997	339 621	-66 710	115 406
4th quarter	601 113	294 606	130 825	175 682	-723 645	-470 629	-101 034	-151 982	-27 908	279 012	-3 126	-265 293	547 432	-75 031	98 751
2009															
1st quarter	527 063	254 016	124 584	148 463	-595 820	-377 709	-94 964	-123 146	-27 476	125 090	-982	244 102	-118 030	-72 892	-36 497
2nd quarter	523 402	253 796	124 829	144 776	-580 164	-366 041	-93 710	-120 413	-31 439	48 192	-3 632	193 750	-141 926	-65 916	-94 166
3rd quarter	550 164	270 087	126 765	153 313	-610 977	-400 231	-95 356	-115 391	-32 943	-309 132	-49 021	57 736	-317 848	-86 451	-54 256
4th quarter	584 157	291 577	132 534	160 046	-657 902	-436 044	-97 788	-124 069	-29 704	6 990	1 379	45 754	-40 143	-85 124	-42 105
2010															
1st quarter	600 890	303 979	132 964	163 947	-675 379	-456 924	-98 294	-120 161	-34 906	-251 291	-773	9 433	-259 950	-95 076	-42 160
2nd quarter	618 315	315 122	135 585	167 609	-703 234	-480 442	-99 414	-123 378	-30 438	-158 216	-165	-2 441	-155 610	-66 131	-15 759
3rd quarter	635 337	324 746	141 153	169 438	-723 784	-494 007	-103 166	-126 611	-32 045	-285 382	-1 096	788	-285 074	-83 354	-39 342
4th quarter	667 977	344 947	145 972	177 058	-741 842	-507 578	-104 023	-130 241	-30 362	-215 064	200	-240	-215 024	-56 518	-41 823
2011															
1st quarter	692 037	360 094	148 963	182 980	-773 337	-541 789	-103 653	-127 895	-35 343	-355 433	-3 619	-547	-351 267	-98 181	-84 722
2nd quarter	715 865	371 315	153 967	190 583	-800 980	-558 987	-106 846	-135 148	-33 788	20 385	-6 267	-1 358	28 009	-126 287	-56 444
3rd quarter	735 595	381 584	158 970	195 041	-809 215	-565 472	-109 771	-133 973	-32 005	-84 425	-4 079	-1 137	-79 209	-73 760	-39 360
4th quarter	730 158	382 860	155 073	192 225	-814 311	-573 745	-109 402	-131 165	-32 401	-32 831	-1 912	-100 624	69 705	-110 777	36 756
2012															
1st quarter	742 117	387 559	160 487	194 071	-830 188	-581 163	-109 830	-139 195	-32 771	93 519	-1 233	51 087	43 665	-113 038	2 276
2nd quarter	746 799	391 867	161 835	193 097	-824 644	-578 355	-110 649	-135 639	-32 668	192 062	-3 289	16 650	178 701	-86 202	-22 920
3rd quarter	744 602	391 474	160 802	192 327	-819 001	-570 454	-110 850	-137 697	-32 343	-267 054	-833	15 206	-281 428	-93 635	-51 183
4th quarter	753 430	390 339	166 222	196 869	-823 844	-572 742	-111 197	-139 905	-31 906	-115 996	895	2 388	-119 279	-95 418	-72 996

[1] A minus sign indicates imports of goods or services or income payments.
[2] A minus sign indicates net unilateral transfers to foreigners.
[3] A minus sign indicates financial outflows or increases in U.S. official assets.

Table 7-6B. U.S. International Transactions: Historical—*Continued*

(Millions of dollars, seasonally adjusted.)

| Year and quarter | U.S.-owned assets abroad, net [3] —Continued / U.S. private assets, net—Continued / U.S. claims | | Foreign-owned assets in the United States, net, excluding financial derivatives [4] | | | | | | | | Statistical discrepancy [5] | Balance on goods and services | Balance on current account |
	On unaffiliated foreigners reported by U.S. nonbanking concerns	Reported by U.S. banks and securities brokers	Total	Foreign official assets in the United States, net	Other foreign assets in the United States, net: Total	Direct investment	U.S. Treasury securities and U.S. currency flows	U.S. securities other than U.S. Treasury securities	U.S. liabilities: To unaffiliated foreigners reported by U.S. nonbanking concerns	U.S. liabilities: Reported by U.S. banks and securities brokers			
2002													
1st quarter	-27 798	-399	173 225	12 801	160 424	24 485	13 964	73 750	57 788	-9 563	15 526	-92 332	-103 916
2nd quarter	-13 680	-67 333	231 325	53 312	178 013	7 194	26 042	99 689	17 805	27 283	23 752	-102 681	-115 363
3rd quarter	-7 443	38 059	160 335	18 328	142 007	13 929	55 166	43 282	7 515	22 115	-45 452	-106 506	-115 706
4th quarter	-1 101	-8 587	230 275	31 504	198 771	38 763	24 092	66 578	12 763	56 575	-36 399	-116 649	-122 812
2003													
1st quarter	1 757	-29 605	240 908	50 531	190 377	37 169	10 894	52 209	68 460	21 645	-23 892	-122 944	-134 619
2nd quarter	-15 089	-63 232	217 732	66 877	150 855	-5 460	48 179	81 187	15 129	11 820	70 387	-122 286	-129 440
3rd quarter	21 261	46 386	129 177	64 397	64 780	-1 574	36 749	15 354	9 137	5 114	1 403	-121 691	-129 332
4th quarter	-26 113	33 437	270 487	96 264	174 223	33 616	6 224	71 955	3 800	58 628	-60 296	-123 624	-125 272
2004													
1st quarter	-67 088	-174 844	459 483	147 636	311 847	26 000	29 034	47 862	61 265	147 686	31 245	-134 162	-136 695
2nd quarter	-11 754	-39 789	331 630	79 949	251 681	32 658	73 376	87 270	21 013	37 364	-5 394	-149 083	-155 734
3rd quarter	-9 235	-55 154	274 147	76 120	198 027	34 113	-3 198	86 577	29 957	50 578	50 554	-154 720	-158 413
4th quarter	-64 489	-96 260	467 941	94 050	373 891	53 195	7 697	159 784	53 637	99 578	17 543	-166 932	-178 487
2005													
1st quarter	-64 051	45 352	234 182	25 052	209 130	38 871	76 819	75 631	86 298	-68 489	66 369	-164 831	-169 216
2nd quarter	59 260	-182 984	304 880	81 292	223 588	-9 004	-13 197	107 694	-26 159	164 254	95 977	-170 269	-178 377
3rd quarter	-69 527	-86 881	425 404	54 736	370 668	38 016	26 597	141 900	51 727	112 428	-51 887	-179 366	-184 517
4th quarter	3 111	16 888	282 881	98 188	184 693	44 755	50 528	125 161	-42 294	6 543	-84 496	-193 448	-207 685
2006													
1st quarter	-41 792	-212 969	545 648	130 427	415 221	44 357	-25 884	167 589	66 064	163 095	37 828	-189 989	-196 200
2nd quarter	-48 226	-61 569	407 652	127 303	280 349	65 611	-26 369	139 681	59 820	41 606	3 031	-188 706	-200 333
3rd quarter	-57 478	-95 786	525 441	121 843	403 598	55 495	-23 914	197 877	69 975	104 165	-30 683	-197 378	-214 501
4th quarter	-33 803	-131 775	586 428	108 366	478 062	77 688	20 165	178 098	48 934	153 177	-19 060	-176 325	-187 444
2007													
1st quarter	-36 540	-228 109	726 910	165 888	561 022	49 999	35 962	183 458	83 177	208 426	-55 611	-177 129	-198 571
2nd quarter	-156 215	-210 932	717 694	88 383	629 311	65 513	-15 072	310 289	124 643	143 938	34 700	-178 245	-188 308
3rd quarter	88 737	-88 048	269 827	47 707	171 146	19 421	17 528	121 493	78 299	49 886	83 246	-172 382	-169 046
4th quarter	103 090	-122 641	350 211	179 065	171 146	19 421	17 752	121 493	-102 898	115 378	33 410	-171 308	-157 465
2008													
1st quarter	120 047	-257 183	456 245	216 229	240 016	88 544	7 665	-15 059	72 442	86 424	-30 406	-183 334	-179 532
2nd quarter	75 492	245 312	-19 863	181 419	-201 282	66 637	19 031	20 240	-61 088	-246 102	20 834	-185 113	-176 583
3rd quarter	121 264	169 661	72 116	142 224	-70 108	62 738	71 998	-123 022	85 846	-167 668	-11 930	-187 622	-174 788
4th quarter	139 374	384 338	-77 093	14 762	-91 855	92 172	93 437	-47 798	-128 675	-100 991	-33 732	-146 233	-150 440
2009													
1st quarter	18 261	-26 902	-118 782	109 442	-228 224	-2 335	57 689	-67 748	-7 532	-208 298	82 799	-94 074	-96 233
2nd quarter	36 999	-18 843	-37 806	129 253	-167 059	30 243	-32 028	-279	15 848	-180 843	70 282	-81 126	-88 201
3rd quarter	84 790	-261 931	335 518	109 204	226 314	54 849	-23 881	48 758	20 775	125 813	56 761	-98 735	-93 756
4th quarter	14 089	72 997	136 134	132 387	3 747	67 686	-4 599	21 124	-19 555	-60 909	-59 083	-109 722	-103 449
2010													
1st quarter	43 586	-166 300	312 270	89 967	222 303	36 712	86 478	5 098	22 388	71 627	32 267	-118 275	-109 395
2nd quarter	6 381	-80 101	180 695	65 882	114 813	30 636	85 721	-15 923	12 778	1 601	82 900	-129 150	-115 357
3rd quarter	2 639	-165 017	533 623	168 673	364 950	82 515	85 280	93 331	10 944	92 880	-115 711	-131 274	-120 492
4th quarter	-21 280	-95 403	307 333	73 787	233 546	55 988	69 181	58 433	21 875	28 069	12 130	-120 682	-104 228
2011													
1st quarter	-80 578	-87 786	560 627	72 443	488 184	32 922	71 516	4 490	40 692	338 564	-91 475	-136 385	-116 643
2nd quarter	9 444	201 296	112 919	121 361	-8 442	60 576	11 603	-4 962	24 774	-100 433	-23 377	-140 551	-118 903
3rd quarter	9 766	24 145	256 164	53 851	202 313	61 038	93 748	-24 908	-17 898	90 333	-64 196	-134 689	-105 626
4th quarter	65 515	78 211	39 296	6 161	33 135	75 688	66 174	-29 082	-41 515	-38 130	86 279	-145 214	-116 554
2012													
1st quarter	-67 175	221 602	177 381	144 468	32 913	35 756	83 031	28 297	13 279	-127 450	-142 718	-142 947	-120 842
2nd quarter	16 793	271 030	-176 468	57 374	-233 842	49 524	2 464	-39 577	-25 581	-220 672	92 741	-135 302	-110 513
3rd quarter	6 325	-142 935	300 570	107 684	192 886	38 839	78 704	64 694	-4 763	15 412	78 825	-129 029	-106 742
4th quarter	18 334	30 801	242 401	84 396	158 005	42 292	49 327	143 494	-22 440	-54 668	-34 738	-127 378	-102 320

[3] A minus sign indicates financial outflows or increases in U.S. official assets.
[4] A minus sign indicates financial outflows or decreases in foreign official assets in the United States.
[5] Sum of credits and debits with the sign reversed.

Table 7-7. Foreigners' Transactions in Long-Term Securities with U.S. Residents

(Billions of dollars, not seasonally adjusted.)

Year and month	Gross purchases from U.S. residents	Gross sales to U.S. residents	Transactions in U.S. domestic securities between foreigners and U.S. residents — Net purchases — Total	Private Total	Private Treasury bonds and notes	Private Government agency bonds	Private Corporate bonds	Private Equities	Official Total	Official Treasury bonds and notes
1977	60.7	30.1	30.6	. . .	. . .	. . .	. . .	. . .	. . .	. . .
1978	60.5	51.1	9.4	3.6	1.0	0.6	0.3	1.7	5.8	3.7
1979	72.9	67.2	5.7	2.5	1.2	0.1	0.2	1.1	3.2	1.7
1980	106.9	91.1	15.8	6.6	1.0	0.4	0.9	4.3	9.2	3.9
1981	126.5	100.5	26.0	10.2	3.3	0.3	1.9	4.8	15.6	11.7
1982	159.5	136.8	22.7	9.2	2.8	0.3	2.5	3.6	13.5	14.6
1983	223.4	211.7	11.7	13.2	4.6	0.5	1.7	6.4	-1.5	0.8
1984	335.5	304.0	31.5	33.8	21.0	1.2	12.5	-0.9	-2.4	0.5
1985	667.2	588.9	78.3	71.9	21.1	4.6	41.4	4.8	6.3	8.1
1986	1 355.4	1 266.9	88.5	76.4	5.2	8.2	45.1	18.0	12.1	14.2
1987	1 692.1	1 623.0	69.1	37.5	-5.5	3.5	22.7	16.8	31.7	31.1
1988	1 827.9	1 753.1	74.8	49.4	22.2	5.4	21.3	0.4	25.4	26.6
1989	2 431.7	2 335.2	96.5	66.5	27.4	13.7	17.5	7.9	30.0	26.8
1990	2 111.2	2 092.4	18.8	-3.6	-5.3	5.6	9.8	-13.7	22.5	23.3
1991	2 382.1	2 324.0	58.1	54.3	18.7	8.9	16.5	10.1	3.8	1.2
1992	2 677.8	2 604.6	73.2	63.1	32.4	14.3	20.0	-3.7	10.1	6.9
1993	3 212.5	3 101.4	111.1	103.2	22.2	31.4	29.9	19.6	7.9	1.3
1994	3 351.1	3 210.7	140.4	94.9	37.0	15.6	38.0	4.3	45.4	41.8
1995	3 737.6	3 505.7	231.9	185.3	94.5	25.0	57.6	8.2	46.5	39.6
1996	4 667.6	4 297.4	370.2	278.1	146.4	36.7	82.2	12.7	92.1	85.8
1997	6 573.3	6 185.3	388.0	339.7	140.2	45.3	82.8	71.3	48.3	44.0
1998	7 633.5	7 355.7	277.8	270.8	44.9	50.5	121.7	53.7	6.9	4.1
1999	7 483.5	7 133.3	350.2	338.8	-0.1	71.9	158.8	108.2	11.4	-9.9
2000	8 684.1	8 226.3	457.8	420.1	-47.7	111.9	182.1	173.8	37.7	-6.3
2001	10 261.8	9 740.9	520.8	494.2	15.0	146.6	218.2	114.4	26.7	3.5
2002	13 022.9	12 475.4	547.6	508.3	112.8	166.6	176.7	52.2	39.3	7.1
2003	13 526.0	12 806.1	719.9	585.0	159.7	129.9	260.3	35.0	134.9	103.8
2004	15 178.9	14 262.4	916.5	680.9	150.9	205.7	298.0	26.2	235.6	201.1
2005	17 157.5	16 145.9	1 011.6	891.1	269.4	187.6	353.1	81.0	120.4	68.7
2006	21 077.1	19 933.9	1 143.2	946.6	125.9	193.8	482.2	144.6	196.6	69.6
2007	29 730.6	28 724.8	1 005.8	818.1	195.0	99.9	342.8	180.4	187.8	3.0
2008	30 724.9	30 310.0	414.9	311.9	238.7	-7.4	59.2	21.4	103.0	76.2
2009	20 479.7	19 840.9	638.9	511.0	377.0	31.4	-38.4	141.1	127.9	161.4
2010	25 017.0	24 108.7	908.3	776.1	531.6	146.2	-14.0	112.3	132.2	172.1
2011	27 818.8	27 325.5	493.4	322.6	288.4	57.6	-44.0	20.6	170.7	144.2
2012	24 583.6	23 949.6	634.0	408.1	207.4	134.2	-30.9	97.4	225.9	209.9
2010										
January	1 709.0	1 672.6	36.4	40.6	61.0	-1.3	-24.9	5.8	-4.2	0.6
February	1 899.6	1 848.4	51.3	52.4	47.1	5.0	-12.2	12.6	-1.2	1.1
March	2 308.4	2 152.8	155.6	122.8	79.4	18.0	13.7	11.8	32.7	28.3
April	1 998.0	1 890.8	107.2	89.4	62.5	9.7	8.1	9.1	17.7	14.7
May	2 321.5	2 293.8	27.7	19.6	8.8	22.9	-13.2	1.0	8.1	6.1
June	2 085.0	2 055.5	29.5	12.9	20.3	14.6	-17.5	-4.7	16.6	11.4
July	1 694.4	1 621.6	72.7	68.5	21.9	28.7	5.5	12.4	4.3	8.2
August	2 125.0	1 989.5	135.5	112.9	87.4	13.3	7.7	4.5	22.6	30.6
September	2 154.2	2 075.3	79.0	69.4	35.8	7.8	4.4	21.4	9.6	41.4
October	2 043.4	1 995.1	48.4	55.5	24.0	7.0	7.4	17.2	-7.2	-0.7
November	2 537.2	2 444.8	92.4	72.1	44.0	10.0	3.5	14.5	20.3	16.6
December	2 141.2	2 068.5	72.8	60.0	39.3	10.5	3.6	6.7	12.7	13.7
2011										
January	2 197.1	2 121.1	76.0	46.3	30.6	2.1	-0.2	13.9	29.6	18.2
February	2 281.1	2 247.6	33.4	13.6	17.0	-6.8	-3.3	6.6	19.9	15.7
March	2 663.5	2 606.2	57.2	46.8	21.9	9.2	1.2	14.6	10.4	7.4
April	2 030.8	1 985.5	45.3	13.8	-4.4	5.1	-3.6	16.6	31.5	29.6
May	2 481.4	2 427.8	53.6	30.3	27.1	-9.2	4.5	7.9	23.3	21.6
June	2 574.2	2 581.2	-7.0	-16.1	-9.4	2.1	-11.8	2.9	9.1	11.3
July	2 099.4	2 075.5	23.9	9.4	1.2	6.4	2.3	-0.5	14.5	14.2
August	3 201.9	3 132.9	69.0	77.6	76.7	8.6	-1.2	-6.5	-8.6	-9.7
September	2 343.7	2 267.2	76.5	39.6	55.9	8.2	-5.2	-19.4	36.9	38.4
October	2 172.2	2 153.8	18.4	22.5	27.5	4.1	-10.9	1.8	-4.0	-6.0
November	2 121.7	2 057.1	64.6	47.0	37.1	11.5	3.5	-5.2	17.7	23.7
December	1 652.0	1 669.5	-17.6	-8.1	7.2	16.4	-19.3	-12.3	-9.5	-20.3
2012										
January	2 055.7	1 953.5	102.2	68.3	54.5	11.3	-0.8	3.3	34.0	33.1
February	2 194.6	2 172.1	22.5	2.1	-0.2	1.7	-7.8	8.4	20.4	13.3
March	2 222.9	2 200.3	22.6	-5.7	-16.5	9.2	-3.3	5.0	28.3	34.0
April	2 136.5	2 095.4	41.1	25.4	27.5	2.0	-4.1	-0.1	15.7	19.2
May	2 332.6	2 248.9	83.7	51.2	52.8	4.4	-7.1	1.1	32.5	22.2
June	1 998.1	1 988.4	9.7	0.4	10.6	16.6	-20.8	-6.0	9.3	22.9
July	1 922.9	1 850.7	72.3	47.0	24.7	16.5	-1.1	6.9	25.3	31.9
August	2 048.1	1 967.3	80.8	50.7	19.7	16.3	9.5	5.3	30.1	19.0
September	1 988.5	1 964.0	24.5	9.4	-22.5	14.2	-6.5	24.1	15.1	2.2
October	2 094.3	2 060.4	33.9	27.7	6.9	15.0	3.4	2.5	6.2	7.1
November	1 817.2	1 752.5	64.7	64.7	28.2	8.0	6.0	22.4	0.1	-3.5
December	1 772.1	1 696.1	76.0	66.9	21.8	18.9	1.7	24.6	9.2	8.4

. . . = Not available.

Table 7-7. Foreigners' Transactions in Long-Term Securities with U.S. Residents—*Continued*

(Billions of dollars, not seasonally adjusted.)

Year and month	Transactions in U.S. domestic securities between foreigners and U.S. residents—*Continued* Net purchases—*Continued* Official—*Continued* Government agency bonds	Corporate bonds	Equities	Transactions in foreign securities between foreigners and U.S. residents Gross purchases from U.S. residents	Gross sales to U.S. residents	Net purchases [1] Total	Bonds	Equities	Net long-term securities transactions	Other acquisitions of long-term securities, net	Net foreign acquisition of long-term securities
1977	. . .	. . .	. . .	10.3	15.8	-5.5	-5.1	-0.4	25.1	. . .	. . .
1978	0.7	0.7	0.7	14.8	18.5	-3.7	-4.2	0.5	5.7	. . .	. . .
1979	0.5	0.4	0.6	17.3	22.1	-4.8	-4.0	-0.8	0.9	0.1	1.0
1980	2.2	2.0	1.1	25.0	28.1	-3.1	-1.0	-2.1	12.7	-1.6	11.0
1981	1.3	1.6	1.0	26.9	32.6	-5.7	-5.5	-0.2	20.3	-5.2	15.0
1982	-0.7	-0.7	0.3	34.3	42.3	-8.0	-6.6	-1.3	14.7	-5.4	9.3
1983	-0.5	-0.8	-1.0	49.6	56.6	-7.0	-3.2	-3.8	4.7	-3.2	1.5
1984	0.0	-0.8	-2.1	70.8	75.9	-5.1	-3.9	-1.1	26.4	-1.5	24.9
1985	-0.3	-1.6	0.1	102.1	110.0	-7.9	-4.0	-3.9	70.4	-2.3	68.1
1986	-1.2	-1.6	0.7	216.1	221.7	-5.6	-3.7	-1.9	82.9	-2.3	80.8
1987	1.6	-0.4	-0.6	294.5	301.4	-6.9	-8.0	1.1	62.2	-1.0	61.3
1988	1.3	-0.1	-2.4	293.9	303.3	-9.4	-7.4	-2.0	65.4	0.2	65.6
1989	1.4	-0.2	2.0	344.6	363.2	-18.6	-5.5	-13.1	77.9	0.0	78.0
1990	0.7	-0.1	-1.4	437.7	468.9	-31.2	-21.9	-9.2	-12.4	3.9	-8.5
1991	1.3	0.4	0.9	450.9	497.7	-46.8	-14.8	-32.0	11.3	0.4	11.7
1992	3.9	0.8	-1.5	663.6	711.5	-47.9	-15.6	-32.3	25.3	-0.3	25.0
1993	4.0	0.6	2.0	991.4	1 134.5	-143.1	-80.4	-62.7	-32.0	1.1	-30.8
1994	6.1	0.0	-2.5	1 234.5	1 291.8	-57.3	-9.2	-48.1	83.1	0.5	83.5
1995	3.7	0.2	3.0	1 235.1	1 333.8	-98.7	-48.4	-50.3	133.2	0.4	133.6
1996	5.0	1.5	-0.2	1 564.4	1 675.0	-110.6	-51.4	-59.3	259.6	-0.5	259.1
1997	4.5	1.5	-1.7	2 207.7	2 296.8	-89.1	-48.1	-40.9	298.9	0.0	298.9
1998	6.3	0.2	-3.7	2 257.8	2 269.0	-11.2	-17.3	6.2	266.6	0.1	266.7
1999	20.4	1.5	-0.6	1 975.6	1 965.6	10.0	-5.7	15.6	360.2	0.0	360.2
2000	40.9	2.0	1.1	2 761.1	2 778.3	-17.1	-4.1	-13.1	440.7	-59.8	380.8
2001	17.4	3.8	2.0	2 557.8	2 577.4	-19.6	30.5	-50.1	501.2	-41.5	459.8
2002	28.6	5.6	-2.0	2 640.0	2 613.0	27.0	28.5	-1.5	574.6	-39.3	535.2
2003	25.9	5.4	-0.3	2 761.8	2 818.4	-56.5	32.0	-88.6	663.3	-138.9	524.5
2004	20.8	11.5	2.2	3 123.1	3 276.0	-152.8	-67.9	-85.0	763.6	-38.8	724.8
2005	31.6	19.1	1.0	3 700.0	3 872.4	-172.4	-45.1	-127.3	839.2	-143.0	696.2
2006	92.6	28.6	5.8	5 515.9	5 766.8	-250.9	-144.5	-106.5	892.3	-174.6	717.7
2007	119.1	50.6	15.1	8 189.1	8 418.3	-229.2	-133.9	-95.3	776.6	-235.2	541.4
2008	-31.3	34.7	23.4	7 714.9	7 640.7	74.2	53.9	20.2	489.1	-197.9	291.2
2009	-42.9	-2.3	11.7	5 121.4	5 308.3	-186.8	-127.5	-59.4	452.0	-205.1	246.9
2010	-38.2	0.8	-2.5	7 323.8	7 439.1	-115.3	-54.6	-60.6	793.0	-234.7	558.3
2011	23.3	-1.2	4.5	7 499.3	7 623.6	-124.3	-52.6	-71.7	369.0	-172.2	196.8
2012	-1.3	7.0	10.3	7 379.8	7 402.5	-22.6	17.0	-39.7	611.4	-237.2	374.1
2010											
January	-3.8	0.3	-1.2	589.9	611.3	-21.4	-16.0	-5.4	15.0	-16.1	-1.1
February	-2.4	-0.3	0.4	619.0	621.0	-1.9	-0.5	-1.4	49.4	-6.1	43.3
March	2.6	1.6	0.3	770.8	786.6	-15.9	-13.0	-2.8	139.7	-20.2	119.5
April	2.8	-0.4	0.7	713.1	742.6	-29.5	-16.2	-13.3	77.6	-20.9	56.7
May	3.3	-0.4	-1.0	675.1	670.9	4.2	14.2	-10.0	31.9	-21.6	10.3
June	4.9	0.0	0.4	583.0	569.6	13.5	9.4	4.1	43.0	-21.4	21.6
July	-4.2	-0.1	0.3	513.5	526.8	-13.3	-7.1	-6.2	59.4	-17.7	41.7
August	-8.2	-0.2	0.4	487.7	496.7	-9.0	-16.0	6.9	126.5	-28.1	98.4
September	-31.3	0.3	-0.8	607.0	610.5	-3.5	2.0	-5.5	75.4	-21.0	54.4
October	-5.3	-0.2	-1.0	611.7	630.6	-19.0	-9.0	-10.0	29.4	-20.8	8.6
November	4.0	0.9	-1.2	602.3	610.3	-8.0	0.6	-8.6	84.4	-20.0	64.3
December	-0.4	-0.7	0.1	550.8	562.2	-11.5	-3.0	-8.5	61.3	-20.8	40.5
2011											
January	9.9	-0.5	2.1	592.3	619.7	-27.4	-8.5	-18.9	48.6	-20.7	27.8
February	5.8	-1.1	-0.5	636.3	648.1	-11.8	1.6	-13.4	21.7	-14.9	6.8
March	2.7	0.4	-0.1	781.8	825.2	-43.3	-29.4	-13.9	13.9	-12.0	1.9
April	1.8	-1.0	1.2	639.1	662.7	-23.5	-10.4	-13.1	21.7	-11.0	10.8
May	0.6	-0.4	1.4	649.0	681.2	-32.2	-25.8	-6.4	21.4	-15.3	6.1
June	-2.4	-0.7	0.8	698.2	688.9	9.3	7.6	1.6	2.3	-11.5	-9.3
July	1.4	-0.4	-0.6	590.7	612.6	-21.9	-6.0	-15.9	2.0	-16.8	-14.8
August	-0.9	2.0	0.0	631.1	642.1	-11.1	-7.9	-3.2	57.9	-10.6	47.4
September	-1.8	0.3	0.0	575.2	575.3	0.0	-2.0	2.0	76.4	-12.5	63.9
October	0.7	0.4	0.9	574.2	578.3	-4.1	-1.9	-2.2	14.3	-14.2	0.1
November	-5.3	1.3	-2.0	588.1	584.8	3.3	2.0	1.4	68.0	-16.1	51.9
December	10.8	-1.4	1.3	543.4	504.9	38.5	28.2	10.3	20.9	-16.7	4.2
2012											
January	-0.1	-0.2	1.1	592.3	582.3	9.9	14.4	-4.5	112.1	-17.1	95.0
February	7.4	0.7	-1.1	644.5	659.4	-14.9	-8.6	-6.3	7.6	-13.5	-6.0
March	-5.4	-0.8	0.4	719.3	704.6	14.7	18.0	-3.3	37.3	-18.0	19.3
April	-6.2	0.5	2.2	614.3	615.0	-0.7	2.7	-3.4	40.3	-19.1	21.2
May	8.5	0.7	1.1	639.1	632.7	6.4	16.0	-9.6	90.1	-17.4	72.7
June	-14.3	-2.8	3.5	601.3	595.6	5.7	11.7	-6.0	15.4	-17.8	-2.4
July	-8.0	0.6	0.8	557.6	549.1	8.5	8.8	-0.3	80.7	-19.1	61.7
August	9.4	1.6	0.1	520.5	509.6	10.9	13.3	-2.4	91.7	-17.9	73.8
September	9.8	2.7	0.4	620.9	635.6	-14.7	-21.7	6.9	9.8	-21.8	-12.0
October	-3.0	0.9	1.2	665.5	691.6	-26.1	-26.2	0.1	7.8	-14.8	-6.9
November	1.4	2.2	-0.1	626.9	637.0	-10.1	-4.0	-6.2	54.6	-39.4	15.2
December	-0.7	0.9	0.6	577.7	589.9	-12.2	-7.3	-4.8	63.8	-21.3	42.5

[1](-) indicates net U.S. acquisitions of foreign securities.
. . . = Not available.

Table 7-8. International Investment Position of the United States at Year-End

(Millions of dollars.)

Year	U.S. net international investment position	U.S.-owned assets abroad									
		Total	Financial derivatives	Official reserve assets	Other U.S. government assets	Direct investment		Foreign bonds	Foreign corporate stocks	U.S. nonbank claims	U.S. bank claims
						Current cost	Market value				
1980	360 347	929 806	...	171 412	65 573	388 072	...	43 524	18 930	38 429	203 866
1981	340 385	1 001 667	...	124 568	70 893	407 804	...	45 675	16 467	42 752	293 508
1982	331 373	1 108 436	...	143 445	76 903	374 059	226 638	56 604	17 442	35 405	404 578
1983	302 404	1 210 974	...	123 110	81 664	355 643	274 342	58 569	26 154	131 329	434 505
1984	166 747	1 204 900	...	105 040	86 945	348 342	270 574	62 810	25 994	130 138	445 631
1985	61 739	1 287 396	...	117 930	89 792	371 036	386 352	75 020	44 383	141 872	447 363
1986	-27 759	1 469 396	...	139 875	91 850	404 818	530 074	85 724	72 399	167 392	507 338
1987	-70 919	1 646 527	...	162 370	90 681	478 062	590 246	93 889	94 700	177 368	549 457
1988	-167 458	1 829 665	...	144 179	87 892	513 761	692 461	104 187	128 662	197 757	653 227
1989	-246 232	2 070 868	...	168 714	86 643	553 093	832 460	116 949	197 345	234 307	713 817
1990	-230 375	2 178 978	...	174 664	84 344	616 655	731 762	144 717	197 596	265 315	695 687
1991	-291 754	2 286 456	...	159 223	81 422	643 364	827 537	176 774	278 976	256 295	690 402
1992	-411 021	2 331 696	...	147 435	83 022	663 830	798 630	200 817	314 266	254 303	668 023
1993	-284 460	2 753 648	...	164 945	83 382	723 526	1 061 299	309 666	543 862	242 022	686 245
1994	-298 458	2 987 118	...	163 394	83 908	786 565	1 114 582	310 391	626 762	322 980	693 118
1995	-430 194	3 486 272	...	176 061	85 064	885 506	1 363 792	413 310	790 615	367 567	768 149
1996	-463 338	4 032 307	...	160 739	86 123	989 810	1 608 340	481 411	1 006 135	450 578	857 511
1997	-786 174	4 567 906	...	134 836	86 198	1 068 063	1 879 285	543 396	1 207 787	545 524	982 102
1998	-858 363	5 095 546	...	146 006	86 768	1 196 021	2 279 601	594 400	1 474 983	588 322	1 009 046
1999	-731 068	5 974 394	...	136 418	84 227	1 414 355	2 839 639	548 233	2 003 716	704 517	1 082 928
2000	-1 337 014	6 238 785	...	128 400	85 168	1 531 607	2 694 014	572 692	1 852 842	836 559	1 231 517
2001	-1 875 032	6 308 681	...	129 961	85 654	1 693 131	2 314 934	557 062	1 612 673	839 303	1 390 897
2002	-2 044 631	6 649 079	...	158 602	85 309	1 867 043	2 022 588	702 742	1 373 980	901 946	1 559 457
2003	-2 093 794	7 638 086	...	183 577	84 772	2 054 464	2 729 126	868 948	2 079 422	594 004	1 772 899
2004	-2 253 026	9 340 634	...	189 591	83 062	2 498 494	3 362 796	984 978	2 560 418	793 556	2 230 535
2005	-1 932 149	11 961 552	1 190 029	188 043	77 523	2 651 721	3 637 996	1 011 554	3 317 705	1 018 462	2 506 515
2006	-2 191 653	14 428 137	1 238 995	219 853	72 189	2 948 172	4 470 343	1 275 515	4 328 960	1 184 073	3 160 380
2007	-1 796 005	18 399 676	2 559 332	277 211	94 471	3 553 095	5 274 991	1 587 089	5 247 990	1 233 341	3 847 147
2008	-3 260 158	19 464 717	6 127 450	293 732	624 099	3 748 512	3 102 418	1 237 284	2 748 428	930 909	3 754 303
2009	-2 275 186	18 558 536	3 489 779	403 804	82 774	4 077 369	4 322 122	1 570 341	3 995 295	930 033	4 009 141
2010	-2 250 297	20 554 995	3 652 313	488 673	75 235	4 273 559	4 809 587	1 731 316	4 900 246	879 575	4 554 078
2011	-3 730 590	21 636 152	4 716 578	537 037	178 901	4 663 142	4 513 863	1 939 912	4 501 438	792 953	4 306 191
2012	-3 863 892	21 637 618	3 619 761	572 368	93 570	5 077 750	5 249 539	2 140 685	5 390 538	844 752	3 898 194

Year	Foreign-owned assets in the United States										
	Total	Financial derivatives	Foreign official assets	Direct investment in the United States		U.S. Treasury securities	Corporate and other bonds	Corporate stocks	U.S. currency	U.S. nonbank liabilities	U.S. bank liabilities
				Current cost	Market value						
1980	569 459	...	181 217	127 105	...	16 113	9 545	64 569	19 415	30 426	121 069
1981	661 282	...	186 128	164 623	...	18 505	10 694	64 391	20 974	30 606	165 361
1982	777 063	...	194 514	184 842	130 428	25 758	16 709	76 279	23 441	27 532	227 988
1983	908 570	...	199 598	193 708	153 318	33 846	17 454	96 357	27 546	61 731	278 330
1984	1 038 153	...	204 481	223 538	172 377	62 121	32 421	96 056	29 942	77 415	312 179
1985	1 225 657	...	207 864	247 223	219 996	87 954	82 290	125 578	33 258	86 993	354 497
1986	1 497 155	...	247 219	284 701	272 966	96 078	140 863	168 940	35 679	90 703	432 972
1987	1 717 446	...	290 009	334 552	316 200	82 588	166 089	175 643	39 545	110 187	518 833
1988	1 997 123	...	328 629	401 766	391 530	100 877	191 314	200 978	43 656	144 548	585 355
1989	2 317 100	...	348 185	467 886	534 734	166 541	231 673	251 191	47 405	167 093	637 126
1990	2 409 353	...	380 263	505 346	539 601	152 452	238 903	221 741	63 991	213 406	633 251
1991	2 578 210	...	405 546	533 404	669 137	170 295	274 136	271 872	76 804	208 908	637 245
1992	2 742 717	...	444 000	540 270	696 177	197 739	299 287	300 160	87 890	220 666	652 705
1993	3 038 108	...	516 152	593 313	768 398	221 501	355 822	340 627	104 508	229 038	677 147
1994	3 285 576	...	542 380	617 982	757 853	235 684	368 077	371 618	125 093	239 817	784 925
1995	3 916 466	...	690 156	680 066	1 005 726	326 995	459 080	510 769	133 933	300 424	815 043
1996	4 495 645	...	827 868	745 619	1 229 118	433 903	539 308	625 805	148 084	346 810	828 248
1997	5 354 080	...	880 327	824 136	1 637 408	538 137	618 837	893 888	170 509	459 407	968 839
1998	5 953 909	...	903 073	920 044	2 179 035	543 323	724 619	1 178 824	184 356	485 675	1 013 995
1999	6 705 462	...	957 813	1 101 709	2 798 193	440 685	825 175	1 526 116	208 763	578 046	1 067 155
2000	7 575 799	...	1 037 092	1 421 017	2 783 235	381 630	1 068 566	1 554 448	205 406	738 904	1 168 736
2001	8 183 713	...	1 115 229	1 518 473	2 560 294	375 059	1 343 071	1 478 301	229 200	798 314	1 326 066
2002	8 693 710	...	1 257 638	1 499 952	2 021 817	473 503	1 530 982	1 248 085	248 061	897 335	1 538 154
2003	9 731 880	...	1 569 845	1 580 994	2 454 877	527 223	1 710 787	1 712 069	258 652	450 884	1 921 426
2004	11 593 660	...	2 019 508	1 742 716	2 717 383	561 610	2 035 149	1 960 357	271 953	600 161	2 402 206
2005	13 893 701	1 132 114	2 313 295	1 905 979	2 817 970	643 793	2 243 135	2 109 863	280 400	658 177	2 606 945
2006	16 619 790	1 179 159	2 832 999	2 154 062	3 293 053	567 861	2 824 871	2 547 468	282 627	799 471	3 431 272
2007	20 195 681	2 487 860	3 411 831	2 345 923	3 551 307	639 755	3 289 070	2 900 948	271 952	863 140	3 985 202
2008	22 724 875	5 967 815	3 943 862	2 397 396	2 486 446	852 458	2 770 606	1 850 055	301 139	740 553	3 900 991
2009	20 833 722	3 363 444	4 402 809	2 398 208	2 995 459	790 985	2 825 638	2 494 310	313 771	706 655	3 537 902
2010	22 805 292	3 541 931	4 912 848	2 623 646	3 422 293	1 094 066	2 916 409	3 018 454	342 090	648 796	3 707 052
2011	25 366 742	4 630 539	5 256 358	2 879 531	3 510 395	1 386 274	2 894 604	3 256 948	397 086	630 925	4 034 477
2012	25 501 510	3 561 985	5 692 448	3 057 326	3 923 969	1 541 569	3 061 963	3 842 087	454 227	656 522	3 633 383

. . . = Not available.

Section 7c: Exports and Imports

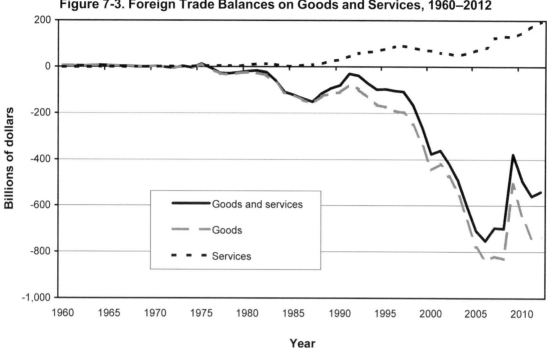

Figure 7-3. Foreign Trade Balances on Goods and Services, 1960–2012

- U.S. imports of goods and services exceeded exports by a record $752 billion in 2006. This negative "trade balance" (to differentiate it from the more comprehensive "current account deficit" shown in earlier pages) diminished to $384 billion in 2009 but was back at $535 billion in 2012. (Table 7-9)

- By 2012, all major U.S. goods export categories had recovered to above pre-recession values. The value of imports of food, capital goods, autos and other consumer goods, and advanced technology (which is also included in other categories, especially in capital goods) also had recovered to above pre-recession levels in 2012. (Tables 7-10 and 7-11)

- Canada and Mexico are the principal trading partners of the United States, with relations governed by the North American Free Trade Agreement (NAFTA). In 2012, U.S. goods exports to those two countries brought in $508 billion, compared with $265 billion in exports to the European Union and $315 billion in exports to China, Japan, and the newly industrialized countries of Asia (the NICS—Hong Kong, South Korea, Singapore, and Taiwan). (Table 7-13)

- U.S. goods imports from Canada and Mexico in 2012 amounted to $602 billion, more than the $381 billion imported from the European Union but less than the $695 billion from China, Japan, and the Asian NICS. (Table 7-14)

- The value of imports from China, which grew by an average 23 percent per year from 2001 to 2006, slowed to a 7 percent annual rate of increase between 2006 and 2012. (Table 7-14)

- For U.S. services trade, "other private services" is the largest single category among both exports and imports. This includes such activities as education, financial services, and many other types of business and professional services. The United States had a surplus of $93 billion on "other private services" in 2012, nearly half of the total $207 billion surplus on services. (Tables 7-9, 7-15 and 7-16)

Table 7-9. U.S. Exports and Imports of Goods and Services

(Balance of payments basis; millions of dollars, seasonally adjusted.)

Year and month	Goods and services			Goods			Services		
	Exports	Imports	Balance	Exports	Imports	Balance	Exports	Imports	Balance
1970	56 640	54 386	2 254	42 469	39 866	2 603	14 171	14 520	-349
1971	59 677	60 979	-1 302	43 319	45 579	-2 260	16 358	15 400	958
1972	67 222	72 665	-5 443	49 381	55 797	-6 416	17 841	16 868	973
1973	91 242	89 342	1 900	71 410	70 499	911	19 832	18 843	989
1974	120 897	125 190	-4 293	98 306	103 811	-5 505	22 591	21 379	1 212
1975	132 585	120 181	12 404	107 088	98 185	8 903	25 497	21 996	3 501
1976	142 716	148 798	-6 082	114 745	124 228	-9 483	27 971	24 570	3 401
1977	152 301	179 547	-27 246	120 816	151 907	-31 091	31 485	27 640	3 845
1978	178 428	208 191	-29 763	142 075	176 002	-33 927	36 353	32 189	4 164
1979	224 131	248 696	-24 565	184 439	212 007	-27 568	39 692	36 689	3 003
1980	271 834	291 241	-19 407	224 250	249 750	-25 500	47 584	41 491	6 093
1981	294 398	310 570	-16 172	237 044	265 067	-28 023	57 354	45 503	11 851
1982	275 236	299 391	-24 156	211 157	247 642	-36 485	64 079	51 749	12 329
1983	266 106	323 874	-57 767	201 799	268 901	-67 102	64 307	54 973	9 335
1984	291 094	400 166	-109 072	219 926	332 418	-112 492	71 168	67 748	3 420
1985	289 070	410 950	-121 880	215 915	338 088	-122 173	73 155	72 862	294
1986	310 033	448 572	-138 538	223 344	368 425	-145 081	86 689	80 147	6 543
1987	348 869	500 552	-151 684	250 208	409 765	-159 557	98 661	90 787	7 874
1988	431 149	545 715	-114 566	320 230	447 189	-126 959	110 919	98 526	12 393
1989	487 003	580 144	-93 141	359 916	477 665	-117 749	127 087	102 479	24 607
1990	535 233	616 097	-80 864	387 401	498 438	-111 037	147 832	117 659	30 173
1991	578 344	609 479	-31 135	414 083	491 020	-76 937	164 261	118 459	45 802
1992	616 882	656 094	-39 212	439 631	536 528	-96 897	177 251	119 566	57 685
1993	642 863	713 174	-70 311	456 943	589 394	-132 451	185 920	123 780	62 141
1994	703 254	801 747	-98 493	502 859	668 690	-165 831	200 395	133 057	67 338
1995	794 387	890 771	-96 384	575 204	749 374	-174 170	219 183	141 397	77 786
1996	851 602	955 667	-104 065	612 113	803 113	-191 000	239 489	152 554	86 935
1997	934 453	1 042 726	-108 273	678 366	876 794	-198 428	256 087	165 932	90 155
1998	933 174	1 099 314	-166 140	670 416	918 637	-248 221	262 758	180 677	82 081
1999	967 008	1 230 168	-263 160	698 218	1 034 389	-336 171	268 790	195 779	73 011
2000	1 072 783	1 449 532	-376 749	784 781	1 230 568	-445 787	288 002	218 964	69 038
2001	1 007 726	1 369 496	-361 771	731 189	1 152 464	-421 276	276 537	217 032	59 505
2002	980 879	1 398 311	-417 432	697 439	1 171 930	-474 491	283 440	226 381	57 059
2003	1 023 519	1 514 503	-490 984	729 816	1 270 225	-540 409	293 703	244 278	49 425
2004	1 163 146	1 768 502	-605 357	821 986	1 485 492	-663 507	341 160	283 010	58 150
2005	1 287 441	1 996 065	-708 624	911 686	1 692 416	-780 730	375 755	303 649	72 106
2006	1 459 823	2 213 111	-753 288	1 039 406	1 875 095	-835 689	420 417	338 016	82 401
2007	1 654 561	2 351 289	-696 728	1 163 957	1 982 843	-818 886	490 604	368 446	122 158
2008	1 842 682	2 541 020	-698 338	1 307 499	2 137 608	-830 109	535 183	403 413	131 770
2009	1 578 945	1 958 099	-379 154	1 069 733	1 575 491	-505 758	509 212	382 608	126 603
2010	1 842 485	2 337 222	-494 737	1 288 882	1 934 006	-645 124	553 603	403 216	150 387
2011	2 103 367	2 663 247	-559 880	1 497 406	2 235 819	-738 413	605 961	427 428	178 533
2012	2 195 925	2 736 286	-540 362	1 563 578	2 299 281	-735 702	632 346	437 005	195 341
2010									
January	143 622	180 850	-37 228	99 281	148 319	-49 037	44 341	32 532	11 809
February	144 675	185 644	-40 969	100 501	152 565	-52 065	44 174	33 078	11 096
March	148 646	188 723	-40 077	104 197	156 040	-51 842	44 449	32 684	11 765
April	147 331	188 265	-40 935	103 259	155 845	-52 586	44 071	32 420	11 651
May	151 958	193 313	-41 355	106 469	160 141	-53 672	45 489	33 172	12 317
June	151 418	198 278	-46 860	105 394	164 456	-59 062	46 024	33 822	12 202
July	154 530	195 753	-41 223	108 061	161 613	-53 552	46 469	34 140	12 329
August	155 320	200 800	-45 480	108 346	166 459	-58 113	46 974	34 341	12 633
September	156 049	200 620	-44 571	108 339	165 935	-57 596	47 709	34 685	13 025
October	161 577	202 241	-40 665	113 288	167 399	-54 111	48 288	34 842	13 446
November	163 165	201 680	-38 514	114 572	167 024	-52 452	48 593	34 655	13 937
December	166 177	207 680	-41 503	117 086	173 155	-56 068	49 091	34 525	14 565
2011									
January	168 079	215 874	-47 795	118 776	181 242	-62 466	49 303	34 632	14 671
February	166 635	211 849	-45 213	117 388	177 575	-60 187	49 247	34 274	14 974
March	174 342	217 719	-43 377	123 930	182 971	-59 042	50 412	34 748	15 665
April	175 948	218 074	-42 125	125 314	182 895	-57 581	50 635	35 179	15 456
May	176 153	223 595	-47 442	124 796	187 890	-63 093	51 357	35 705	15 652
June	173 180	224 164	-50 984	121 205	188 202	-66 997	51 975	35 962	16 013
July	179 465	224 926	-45 461	126 455	188 457	-62 002	53 010	36 469	16 541
August	179 917	224 591	-44 674	126 626	188 048	-61 422	53 291	36 543	16 748
September	181 172	225 725	-44 553	128 503	188 966	-60 464	52 669	36 759	15 910
October	180 547	226 630	-46 083	128 563	190 073	-61 510	51 984	36 557	15 427
November	178 267	226 050	-47 783	126 685	189 688	-63 003	51 582	36 362	15 220
December	179 118	230 467	-51 349	127 611	193 984	-66 372	51 507	36 483	15 024
2012									
January	179 477	230 871	-51 393	127 311	194 445	-67 134	52 167	36 426	15 740
February	182 064	225 827	-43 763	128 383	189 349	-60 966	53 680	36 478	17 202
March	186 505	234 295	-47 790	131 865	197 369	-65 504	54 640	36 926	17 714
April	184 267	230 892	-46 625	130 246	193 935	-63 689	54 021	36 957	17 064
May	184 217	230 464	-46 247	130 175	193 562	-63 386	54 042	36 902	17 139
June	185 218	227 648	-42 430	131 446	190 858	-59 412	53 773	36 790	16 982
July	183 375	226 826	-43 451	130 276	189 741	-59 464	53 099	37 085	16 013
August	182 071	226 078	-44 007	128 446	189 064	-60 619	53 625	37 014	16 611
September	186 829	228 400	-41 570	132 752	191 649	-58 897	54 078	36 751	17 327
October	182 655	225 304	-42 650	127 987	188 346	-60 360	54 668	36 958	17 710
November	185 220	231 641	-46 422	129 667	194 529	-64 862	55 552	37 112	18 440
December	188 686	226 994	-38 307	132 685	189 866	-57 182	56 002	37 127	18 874

Table 7-10. U.S. Exports of Goods by End-Use and Advanced Technology Categories

(Census basis, except as noted; billions of dollars; seasonally adjusted, except as noted.)

Year and month	Total exports of goods — Total, balance of payments basis	Net adjustments	Total, Census basis	Foods, feeds, and beverages	Industrial supplies and materials — Total	Industrial supplies and materials — Petroleum and products	Capital goods, except automotive	Automotive vehicles, engines, and parts	Consumer goods, except automotive	Other goods	Advanced technology products [1]
1980	224.25	3.55	220.70	36.28	72.09	3.57	76.28	17.44	17.75	. . .	. . .
1981	237.04	3.31	233.74	38.84	70.19	4.56	84.17	19.69	17.70	. . .	. . .
1982	211.16	-1.12	212.28	32.20	64.05	6.87	76.50	17.23	16.13	. . .	. . .
1983	201.80	0.09	201.71	32.09	58.94	5.59	71.66	18.46	14.93	. . .	. . .
1984	219.93	1.18	218.74	32.20	64.12	5.43	77.01	22.42	15.09	. . .	. . .
1985	215.92	3.29	212.62	24.57	61.16	5.71	79.32	24.95	14.59	. . .	. . .
1986	223.34	-3.13	226.47	23.52	64.72	4.43	82.82	25.10	16.73	. . .	. . .
1987	250.21	-3.70	253.90	25.23	70.05	4.63	92.71	27.58	20.31	. . .	. . .
1988	320.23	-3.11	323.34	33.77	90.02	4.48	119.10	33.40	26.98	. . .	. . .
1989	359.92	-3.08	363.00	36.34	98.36	6.46	136.94	35.05	36.01	. . .	. . .
1990	387.40	-5.57	392.97	35.18	105.55	8.36	153.07	36.07	43.60	20.73	. . .
1991	414.08	-7.77	421.85	35.79	109.69	8.40	166.72	39.72	46.65	23.66	. . .
1992	439.63	-8.54	448.17	40.34	109.59	7.62	176.50	46.71	51.31	24.39	. . .
1993	456.94	-7.92	464.86	40.59	111.89	7.49	182.85	51.35	54.56	23.89	. . .
1994	502.86	-9.77	512.63	41.96	121.55	6.97	205.82	57.31	59.86	26.50	. . .
1995	575.20	-9.54	584.74	50.47	146.37	8.10	234.46	61.26	64.31	28.72	. . .
1996	612.11	-12.96	625.08	55.53	147.98	9.63	253.99	64.24	70.11	33.85	. . .
1997	678.37	-10.82	689.18	51.51	158.32	10.42	295.87	73.30	77.96	33.51	. . .
1998	670.42	-11.72	682.14	46.40	148.31	8.08	299.87	72.39	80.29	35.44	. . .
1999	683.97	-11.83	695.80	45.98	147.52	8.62	310.79	75.26	80.92	35.32	. . .
2000	771.99	-9.92	781.92	47.87	172.62	12.01	356.93	80.36	89.38	34.77	227.39
2001	718.71	-10.39	729.10	49.41	160.10	10.64	321.71	75.44	88.33	34.11	199.63
2002	682.42	-10.68	693.10	49.62	156.81	10.34	290.44	78.94	84.36	32.94	178.57
2003	713.42	-11.36	724.77	55.03	173.04	12.69	293.67	80.63	89.91	32.49	180.21
2004	807.52	-11.26	818.78	56.57	203.96	17.08	331.56	89.21	103.08	34.40	201.42
2005	894.63	-11.35	905.98	58.96	233.05	22.66	363.32	98.41	115.29	36.96	216.06
2006	1 015.81	-10.16	1 025.97	66.00	276.00	31.57	404.00	107.30	129.10	43.60	252.71
2007	1 138.38	-9.82	1 148.20	84.30	316.40	37.76	433.00	121.30	146.00	47.30	264.88
2008	1 307.50	20.06	1 287.44	108.35	388.03	67.18	457.66	121.45	161.28	50.67	270.13
2009	1 069.73	13.69	1 056.04	93.91	296.51	49.18	391.24	81.72	149.46	43.22	244.71
2010	1 288.80	10.30	1 278.50	107.72	391.66	70.83	447.54	112.01	165.23	54.34	273.31
2011	1 495.85	15.56	1 480.29	126.21	500.46	113.58	493.01	132.85	174.96	52.81	286.83
2012	1 561.24	15.53	1 545.71	132.81	501.07	123.52	527.38	146.13	181.75	56.58	305.15
2010											
January	99.28	0.98	98.30	8.81	29.02	4.59	34.45	8.71	13.59	3.73	21.31
February	100.50	0.95	99.56	8.60	29.57	4.87	35.22	9.03	13.21	3.93	19.86
March	104.20	0.67	103.53	8.58	31.21	5.46	36.19	8.89	13.82	4.84	23.95
April	103.26	0.86	102.40	8.12	31.77	5.98	36.06	9.16	13.02	4.28	21.20
May	106.47	0.95	105.52	8.11	32.57	6.02	37.60	9.31	13.62	4.31	21.76
June	105.39	0.90	104.49	7.98	32.08	5.62	37.05	9.29	13.48	4.62	23.36
July	108.06	0.82	107.25	8.31	32.64	6.07	38.49	9.17	13.61	5.02	23.93
August	108.35	0.92	107.43	8.98	33.41	5.81	37.40	9.45	13.75	4.45	21.94
September	108.34	0.61	107.73	9.32	32.60	6.02	37.91	9.50	13.63	4.77	22.87
October	113.29	0.56	112.73	10.15	34.81	6.71	38.69	9.98	14.02	5.08	23.74
November	114.57	1.05	113.52	10.39	35.48	7.04	38.62	9.64	14.87	4.53	23.23
December	117.09	1.05	116.04	10.38	36.52	6.64	39.85	9.88	14.62	4.80	26.16
2011											
January	118.78	1.28	117.50	10.36	39.23	8.22	38.97	10.60	14.04	4.31	21.11
February	117.39	1.56	115.82	10.50	38.50	7.68	39.08	10.08	13.90	3.76	20.99
March	123.93	1.49	122.45	11.13	40.94	7.88	40.19	11.19	14.44	4.55	25.37
April	125.31	1.28	124.04	10.78	42.66	9.64	41.08	10.62	14.63	4.27	23.03
May	124.80	1.27	123.53	10.73	41.58	9.44	41.35	10.84	14.40	4.63	23.38
June	121.21	1.30	119.91	10.18	39.90	8.80	40.18	10.68	14.78	4.18	24.71
July	126.46	1.37	125.09	10.50	42.40	10.07	41.73	11.74	14.39	4.33	23.56
August	126.63	1.27	125.36	10.48	43.18	10.39	41.52	11.09	14.73	4.37	23.83
September	128.50	1.48	127.02	10.33	44.20	10.03	41.72	11.34	15.07	4.36	24.23
October	128.56	1.12	127.44	10.35	43.09	10.31	42.69	11.59	14.87	4.85	25.68
November	126.69	1.09	125.59	10.41	42.30	10.43	42.23	11.29	14.92	4.44	24.74
December	127.61	1.06	126.55	10.46	42.48	10.70	42.27	11.79	14.79	4.77	26.21
2012											
January	127.31	1.36	125.95	10.17	41.73	9.32	43.07	12.24	14.63	4.12	22.56
February	128.38	1.45	126.94	9.80	42.12	9.78	43.46	12.10	14.82	4.63	23.42
March	131.87	1.24	130.63	10.13	43.65	10.39	44.80	12.05	14.97	5.03	28.06
April	130.25	1.48	128.76	10.60	42.87	10.43	43.46	12.21	15.12	4.50	23.76
May	130.18	1.08	129.10	11.45	41.82	10.07	44.22	12.20	14.99	4.41	25.03
June	131.45	1.23	130.22	10.73	42.39	10.39	43.91	12.66	15.63	4.91	26.55
July	130.28	1.44	128.84	12.65	40.33	9.95	43.98	12.40	15.20	4.28	24.58
August	128.45	1.34	127.11	11.59	39.48	9.25	44.25	12.18	15.05	4.55	25.61
September	132.75	1.34	131.42	12.43	42.30	11.09	44.71	11.89	15.31	4.78	25.81
October	127.99	1.28	126.70	11.27	39.78	10.49	43.49	11.79	15.46	4.92	26.11
November	129.67	1.14	128.53	11.01	40.68	10.79	44.19	12.31	15.41	4.93	26.10
December	132.68	1.16	131.52	10.98	43.92	11.57	43.84	12.09	15.16	5.53	27.56

[1] Not seasonally adjusted.
. . . = Not available.

Table 7-11. U.S. Imports of Goods by End-Use and Advanced Technology Categories

(Census basis, except as noted; billions of dollars; seasonally adjusted, except as noted.)

Year and month	Total imports of goods			Principal end-use category							Advanced technology products [1]
	Total, balance of payments basis	Net adjustments	Total, Census basis	Foods, feeds, and beverages	Industrial supplies and materials		Capital goods, except automotive	Automotive vehicles, engines, and parts	Consumer goods, except automotive	Other goods	
					Total	Petroleum and products					
1980	249.75	4.23	245.52	18.55	124.96	. . .	30.72	28.13	34.22	. . .	. . .
1981	265.07	3.76	261.31	18.53	131.10	. . .	36.86	30.80	38.30	. . .	. . .
1982	247.64	3.70	243.94	17.47	107.82	. . .	38.22	34.26	39.66	. . .	. . .
1983	268.90	7.18	261.72	18.56	105.63	. . .	42.61	42.04	46.59	. . .	. . .
1984	332.42	1.91	330.51	21.92	122.72	. . .	60.15	56.77	61.19	. . .	. . .
1985	338.09	1.71	336.38	21.89	112.48	. . .	60.81	65.21	66.43	. . .	. . .
1986	368.43	2.75	365.67	24.40	101.37	. . .	71.86	78.25	79.43	. . .	. . .
1987	409.77	3.48	406.28	24.81	110.67	. . .	84.77	85.17	88.82	. . .	. . .
1988	447.19	5.26	441.93	24.93	118.06	. . .	101.79	87.95	96.42	. . .	. . .
1989	477.37	3.72	473.65	25.08	132.40	. . .	112.45	87.38	102.26	. . .	. . .
1990	498.34	2.36	495.98	26.65	143.41	62.16	116.04	87.69	105.29	16.09	. . .
1991	490.98	2.53	488.45	26.21	131.38	51.78	120.80	84.94	107.78	15.94	. . .
1992	536.46	3.80	532.66	27.61	138.64	51.60	134.25	91.79	122.66	17.71	. . .
1993	589.44	8.78	580.66	27.87	145.61	51.50	152.37	102.42	134.02	18.39	. . .
1994	668.59	5.33	663.26	27.87	145.61	51.28	152.37	102.42	134.02	18.39	. . .
1995	749.57	6.03	743.54	33.18	181.85	56.16	221.43	123.80	159.91	23.39	. . .
1996	803.33	8.04	796.77	35.74	204.43	72.75	228.07	128.95	172.00	26.11	. . .
1997	876.37	6.66	869.70	39.69	213.77	71.77	253.28	139.81	193.81	29.34	. . .
1998	917.18	5.28	911.90	41.24	200.14	50.90	269.56	149.05	216.52	35.39	. . .
1999	1 029.99	5.37	1 024.62	43.60	221.39	67.81	295.72	178.96	241.91	43.04	. . .
2000	1 224.42	6.40	1 218.02	45.98	298.98	120.28	347.03	195.88	281.83	48.33	222.08
2001	1 145.90	4.90	1 141.00	46.64	273.87	103.59	297.99	189.78	284.29	48.42	195.18
2002	1 164.72	3.35	1 161.37	49.69	267.69	103.51	283.32	203.74	307.84	49.08	195.15
2003	1 260.72	3.60	1 257.12	55.83	313.82	133.10	295.87	210.14	333.88	47.59	207.03
2004	1 477.09	7.39	1 469.70	62.14	412.83	180.46	343.49	228.20	372.94	50.11	238.28
2005	1 681.78	8.33	1 673.46	68.09	523.77	251.86	379.33	239.45	407.24	55.57	290.76
2006	1 861.38	7.44	1 853.94	74.94	601.99	302.43	418.26	256.63	442.64	59.49	290.76
2007	1 969.38	12.41	1 956.96	81.68	634.75	330.98	444.49	258.92	474.89	62.23	326.81
2008	2 137.61	33.97	2 103.64	89.00	779.48	453.28	453.74	231.24	481.64	68.54	331.18
2009	1 575.49	15.87	1 559.63	81.62	462.38	253.69	370.48	157.65	427.33	60.17	300.89
2010	1 938.95	25.09	1 913.86	91.75	603.10	336.11	449.39	225.10	483.23	61.30	354.25
2011	2 239.99	31.94	2 208.06	107.48	755.82	439.34	510.85	254.62	514.12	65.17	386.48
2012	2 302.71	27.39	2 275.32	110.26	730.37	414.78	548.61	297.81	516.34	71.92	396.12
2010											
January	148.32	1.51	146.81	7.15	48.08	27.47	33.69	16.58	36.26	5.05	24.38
February	152.57	2.05	150.52	7.21	48.91	28.04	34.18	16.62	38.35	5.26	23.62
March	156.04	2.06	153.98	7.47	50.54	28.93	34.56	17.48	38.84	5.11	28.65
April	155.85	2.14	153.71	7.39	50.96	29.38	35.86	17.49	37.38	4.63	26.98
May	160.14	2.01	158.13	7.59	50.55	28.49	36.78	18.83	39.70	4.68	27.50
June	164.46	2.25	162.20	7.71	49.26	26.50	37.65	19.91	42.52	5.15	31.64
July	161.61	1.95	159.66	7.69	49.46	26.93	37.50	19.04	40.97	5.00	30.67
August	166.46	1.93	164.53	7.83	50.35	28.24	38.62	19.82	42.60	5.31	30.70
September	165.94	2.10	163.84	7.90	49.50	27.00	40.18	19.53	41.72	5.01	32.32
October	167.40	2.10	165.30	7.78	50.17	27.21	39.55	20.04	42.42	5.35	32.38
November	167.02	2.13	164.89	7.96	50.57	27.17	40.42	19.69	40.97	5.30	33.78
December	173.16	2.87	170.29	8.09	54.76	30.75	40.41	20.07	41.49	5.46	31.64
2011											
January	181.24	2.48	178.77	8.35	61.09	36.14	41.85	21.08	41.48	4.92	28.32
February	177.58	2.50	175.07	8.58	57.48	32.85	39.91	20.21	43.90	4.98	27.01
March	182.97	2.54	180.43	8.61	62.97	36.79	40.82	21.07	41.63	5.34	32.12
April	182.90	2.60	180.29	8.87	62.04	35.65	41.57	19.07	43.29	5.47	30.15
May	187.89	2.80	185.09	9.00	66.23	39.13	42.28	19.33	42.83	5.42	31.41
June	188.20	2.84	185.37	9.15	65.21	38.39	42.33	19.51	43.33	5.84	33.47
July	188.46	2.71	185.75	8.88	63.76	36.84	42.98	22.05	43.01	5.06	32.50
August	188.05	2.66	185.39	8.93	63.24	36.20	42.95	21.36	43.03	5.89	33.02
September	188.97	2.86	186.11	9.12	63.67	36.09	43.13	22.60	42.30	5.29	32.69
October	190.07	2.90	187.17	9.49	62.44	35.79	44.18	22.12	43.60	5.35	36.15
November	189.69	2.54	187.15	9.29	63.01	37.18	43.67	22.68	42.70	5.81	35.63
December	193.98	2.50	191.48	9.23	64.70	38.30	45.17	23.54	43.04	5.81	34.02
2012											
January	194.45	2.52	191.92	9.48	65.05	39.21	44.87	24.06	42.71	5.76	29.36
February	189.35	2.28	187.07	9.00	62.05	35.89	44.82	24.49	40.79	5.92	29.23
March	197.37	2.41	194.96	9.21	64.46	38.05	47.16	24.45	43.38	6.31	35.07
April	193.94	2.26	191.68	9.21	63.76	37.41	45.63	24.14	43.03	5.91	30.48
May	193.56	2.26	191.30	9.11	61.13	34.85	46.78	24.63	43.44	6.21	33.72
June	190.86	2.29	188.57	9.03	59.32	33.12	46.02	25.37	42.64	6.19	33.51
July	189.74	2.23	187.51	9.15	57.91	31.56	45.58	25.97	43.00	5.91	33.01
August	189.06	2.26	186.81	9.18	58.95	32.77	45.11	25.20	42.35	6.03	32.26
September	191.65	2.29	189.36	9.25	59.89	33.02	45.66	24.40	44.12	6.05	32.91
October	188.35	2.28	186.07	8.94	59.88	34.71	45.59	24.58	41.09	5.98	36.04
November	194.53	2.17	192.36	9.38	60.66	33.56	45.61	25.61	45.07	6.03	37.80
December	189.87	2.16	187.71	9.33	57.33	30.63	45.79	24.92	44.72	5.63	32.75

[1] Not seasonally adjusted.
. . . = Not available.

Table 7-12. U.S. Exports and Imports of Goods by Principal End-Use Category in Constant Dollars

(Census basis; billions of 2009 chain-weighted dollars, except as noted; seasonally adjusted.)

Year and month	Exports							Imports						
	Total	Foods, feeds, and beverages	Industrial supplies and materials	Capital goods, except auto-motive	Auto-motive vehicles, engines, and parts	Consumer goods, except automotive	Other goods	Total	Foods, feeds, and beverages	Industrial supplies and materials	Capital goods, except auto-motive	Auto-motive vehicles, engines, and parts	Consumer goods, except automotive	Other goods
1986 I	227.20	22.30	57.30	75.80	21.70	. . .	. . .	365.40	24.40	101.30	71.80	78.20	79.40	. . .
1987 I	254.10	24.30	66.70	86.20	24.60	. . .	. . .	406.20	24.80	111.00	84.50	85.00	88.70	. . .
1988 I	322.40	32.30	85.10	109.20	29.30	. . .	. . .	441.00	24.80	118.30	101.40	87.70	95.90	. . .
1989 I	363.80	37.20	99.30	138.80	34.80	. . .	. . .	473.20	25.10	132.30	113.30	86.10	102.90	. . .
1990 I	393.60	35.10	104.40	152.70	37.40	39.22	18.70	495.30	26.60	146.20	116.40	87.30	105.70	14.46
1991 I	421.70	35.70	109.70	166.70	40.00	40.42	21.11	488.50	26.50	131.60	120.70	85.70	108.00	14.15
1992 I	448.20	40.30	109.10	175.90	47.00	43.60	21.71	532.70	27.60	138.60	134.30	91.80	122.70	15.46
1993 I	471.17	40.19	111.08	190.02	51.93	54.03	23.91	591.45	28.03	151.26	160.16	100.73	132.92	18.35
1994 I	522.29	40.43	114.17	225.76	56.54	58.97	26.41	675.05	29.52	168.80	199.56	112.13	144.22	20.82
1994	550.74	70.21	177.34	158.53	64.72	68.86	34.59	718.78	40.30	351.05	104.93	134.94	149.71	24.36
1995	607.14	77.48	189.34	184.12	68.50	72.85	35.52	780.92	41.33	361.34	126.52	137.25	161.15	25.72
1996	671.49	75.01	200.96	218.55	71.29	78.19	41.47	862.39	45.76	383.36	152.61	141.93	172.59	28.71
1997	761.13	74.80	217.46	267.75	80.44	85.87	41.19	982.15	50.15	409.79	191.10	153.44	196.50	32.48
1998	779.10	74.33	216.64	279.58	78.51	89.22	44.60	1 097.87	53.96	449.16	219.20	163.03	222.76	40.02
1999	804.15	76.88	218.21	294.71	81.30	89.85	44.57	1 230.04	58.93	456.33	251.42	194.72	250.12	48.84
2000	892.79	81.16	240.09	341.04	85.97	98.62	42.90	1 393.19	62.76	484.79	301.69	211.69	294.21	54.02
2001	837.60	83.31	229.28	307.59	80.38	97.52	42.14	1 347.00	65.19	482.40	266.29	205.19	299.06	54.53
2002	799.01	81.43	225.53	280.73	83.78	93.44	40.58	1 395.87	69.49	484.45	261.65	219.65	326.76	56.27
2003	822.70	82.79	235.44	288.75	85.14	98.54	39.09	1 472.99	75.91	503.93	279.49	225.32	354.90	53.72
2004	894.61	76.45	251.33	324.20	93.52	112.18	39.64	1 646.37	80.59	566.27	329.08	240.95	393.62	54.98
2005	957.75	79.97	258.79	353.83	102.09	123.61	40.79	1 762.48	83.57	595.14	365.98	250.33	425.74	58.94
2006	1 054.35	85.72	278.59	398.12	110.10	135.92	46.00	1 867.72	88.43	597.42	408.89	267.07	459.94	61.62
2007	1 138.01	91.11	297.50	428.78	123.19	149.94	47.50	1 904.34	89.18	579.33	435.52	264.43	485.82	65.33
2008	1 219.45	96.38	333.48	455.75	122.03	162.16	48.10	1 848.83	87.20	552.02	445.24	232.70	480.18	65.65
2009	1 056.04	93.91	296.51	391.24	81.72	149.46	43.22	1 559.63	81.62	462.38	370.48	157.65	427.33	60.17
2010	1 213.96	103.02	339.99	447.21	111.51	161.64	51.24	1 790.74	84.71	488.95	453.76	223.75	482.77	59.53
2011	1 305.45	100.89	369.77	493.82	130.25	167.89	45.75	1 900.87	87.26	497.23	514.63	246.10	505.47	60.39
2012	1 359.30	100.62	374.84	529.04	141.08	172.56	48.74	1 947.63	90.09	479.28	554.95	282.53	500.30	66.46
2009														
January	83.24	7.04	22.95	32.76	5.40	11.37	3.66	133.94	6.81	44.09	31.43	11.23	35.77	4.99
February	86.01	7.29	23.10	33.25	5.86	12.63	3.79	127.29	6.83	40.26	29.99	10.51	34.43	5.38
March	85.75	7.66	24.04	32.42	5.79	12.32	3.50	127.69	6.87	40.17	30.05	10.43	35.43	4.84
April	82.80	7.75	22.42	31.30	5.82	12.02	3.44	125.07	6.77	37.69	29.13	10.68	35.86	4.83
May	84.45	7.86	24.11	31.24	5.57	12.24	3.43	122.18	6.74	36.36	28.91	10.25	34.79	4.98
June	85.56	7.82	24.50	32.05	5.61	12.14	3.45	122.41	6.77	36.79	29.18	11.16	33.61	4.78
July	88.11	7.91	25.12	32.11	6.85	12.47	3.66	129.72	6.92	38.00	30.47	13.34	35.49	5.38
August	87.05	7.68	25.26	31.02	7.48	12.30	3.33	127.08	6.74	36.37	30.18	14.13	34.83	4.74
September	91.10	7.63	26.60	32.94	7.77	12.59	3.57	133.00	6.72	38.22	31.45	15.73	35.49	5.27
October	94.01	8.15	26.73	33.69	8.03	13.51	3.93	134.80	6.84	37.75	32.32	16.17	36.66	5.05
November	92.49	8.59	25.39	33.61	8.63	12.79	3.58	136.82	6.74	38.24	32.93	16.44	37.64	4.85
December	95.48	8.54	26.29	34.88	8.91	13.08	3.87	139.63	6.88	38.44	34.45	17.58	37.32	5.08
2010														
January	95.03	8.59	26.39	34.39	8.70	13.45	3.59	137.27	6.99	38.64	33.91	16.53	36.18	4.95
February	96.82	8.75	27.17	35.14	9.00	13.01	3.81	141.04	6.96	39.60	34.43	16.56	38.30	5.14
March	100.05	8.64	28.23	36.06	8.87	13.61	4.65	143.63	7.06	40.43	34.94	17.45	38.70	4.98
April	98.06	8.24	27.94	35.91	9.13	12.77	4.08	143.26	6.96	40.79	36.24	17.43	37.18	4.50
May	100.64	8.13	28.36	37.44	9.28	13.38	4.09	147.97	7.02	41.12	37.14	18.78	39.47	4.54
June	100.39	8.03	28.38	37.03	9.25	13.30	4.41	153.86	7.21	41.66	38.07	19.86	42.35	5.01
July	103.05	8.24	29.04	38.47	9.14	13.37	4.80	151.57	7.18	41.84	37.96	18.95	40.92	4.87
August	102.15	8.56	29.06	37.42	9.41	13.50	4.20	155.45	7.16	42.07	39.06	19.69	42.64	5.17
September	101.81	8.76	28.04	37.93	9.45	13.26	4.47	154.49	7.19	41.23	40.59	19.37	41.72	4.87
October	105.37	9.31	29.18	38.75	9.93	13.57	4.70	154.66	6.98	40.68	39.90	19.83	42.69	5.18
November	104.54	8.96	28.97	38.72	9.57	14.32	4.12	152.29	7.01	39.61	40.78	19.45	41.05	5.09
December	106.06	8.82	29.25	39.95	9.80	14.12	4.33	155.26	7.01	41.29	40.75	19.87	41.57	5.23
2011														
January	106.74	8.59	30.92	39.16	10.51	13.64	3.86	159.61	7.14	43.51	42.21	20.81	41.40	4.67
February	103.76	8.43	29.48	39.23	9.99	13.45	3.32	154.96	7.20	40.27	40.10	19.91	43.65	4.69
March	108.50	8.87	30.56	40.30	11.04	13.91	3.96	157.17	6.89	42.42	40.98	20.65	41.49	5.00
April	109.25	8.56	31.36	41.17	10.47	14.07	3.70	154.83	6.96	40.52	41.77	18.49	42.88	5.07
May	108.42	8.55	30.34	41.33	10.66	13.85	3.99	157.59	7.13	42.32	42.48	18.62	42.34	5.01
June	105.01	8.00	29.15	40.08	10.50	14.16	3.60	157.89	7.41	41.73	42.55	18.71	42.68	5.40
July	109.53	8.41	30.85	41.66	11.51	13.73	3.72	159.04	7.10	41.54	43.27	21.19	42.21	4.66
August	109.18	8.21	31.14	41.46	10.84	14.03	3.73	157.73	7.21	40.49	43.24	20.51	42.11	5.41
September	110.07	7.93	31.55	41.77	11.05	14.35	3.70	158.71	7.37	41.11	43.47	21.67	41.29	4.84
October	112.56	8.47	31.91	42.75	11.27	14.24	4.20	160.57	7.74	40.94	44.74	21.22	42.35	4.93
November	110.40	8.35	30.98	42.40	10.97	14.30	3.83	159.96	7.55	40.94	44.22	21.72	41.43	5.35
December	112.03	8.53	31.55	42.52	11.46	14.17	4.13	162.82	7.55	41.45	45.62	22.61	41.66	5.37
2012														
January	111.29	8.26	30.90	43.34	11.88	13.95	3.57	162.26	7.58	41.18	45.22	23.03	41.40	5.33
February	111.52	7.98	30.77	43.64	11.72	14.11	3.99	158.50	7.41	39.39	45.20	23.41	39.52	5.48
March	114.42	8.09	31.86	44.89	11.64	14.23	4.32	164.17	7.40	40.41	47.49	23.32	41.99	5.81
April	112.64	8.32	31.27	43.59	11.77	14.39	3.86	162.25	7.44	40.57	46.15	22.90	41.61	5.45
May	113.65	8.92	31.25	44.29	11.76	14.21	3.81	163.12	7.42	39.66	47.35	23.37	42.05	5.73
June	116.38	8.59	32.84	43.98	12.21	14.83	4.30	162.92	7.34	40.14	46.55	24.07	41.29	5.72
July	114.57	9.44	31.31	44.16	11.93	14.46	3.73	163.48	7.51	40.18	46.18	24.61	41.70	5.49
August	111.99	8.34	30.07	44.45	11.77	14.31	3.92	162.19	7.62	40.20	45.74	23.88	41.16	5.60
September	114.53	8.81	31.39	44.89	11.46	14.50	4.07	163.20	7.52	40.17	46.17	23.08	42.87	5.60
October	110.36	8.13	29.37	43.62	11.38	14.62	4.19	158.84	7.31	39.09	46.18	23.19	39.74	5.51
November	112.61	7.87	30.66	44.28	11.89	14.59	4.23	165.26	7.78	40.24	46.26	24.16	43.63	5.56
December	115.33	7.87	33.16	43.93	11.67	14.37	4.75	161.43	7.76	38.08	46.48	23.51	43.33	5.18

IData on the 2009 chain-weighted dollar basis are only available from 1994 forward. To provide more historical range, values in 1992 dollars are shown for the years 1986–1994.
. . . = Not available.

Table 7-13. U.S. Exports of Goods by Selected Regions and Countries

(Census f.a.s. basis; millions of dollars, not seasonally adjusted.)

Year and month	Total, all countries	Selected regions [1]					Selected countries				
		European Union, 15 countries	European Union	Euro area	Asian NICS	OPEC	Brazil	Canada	China	Japan	Mexico
1978	...	32 051	...	...	...	16 655	2 981	30 540	824	12 885	6 680
1979	...	42 582	...	...	...	15 051	3 442	37 599	1 724	17 581	9 847
1980	...	53 679	...	...	...	17 759	4 344	40 331	3 755	20 790	15 145
1981	...	52 363	...	...	...	21 533	3 798	44 602	3 603	21 823	17 789
1982	...	47 932	...	...	...	22 863	3 423	37 887	2 912	20 966	11 817
1983	201 708	44 311		...	...	16 905	2 557	43 345	2 173	21 894	9 082
1984	218 743	46 976		...	...	14 387	2 640	51 777	3 004	23 575	11 992
1985	212 621	48 994		...	16 918	12 478	3 140	47 251	3 856	22 631	13 635
1986	226 471	53 154		...	18 290	10 844	3 885	45 333	3 106	26 882	12 392
1987	254 122	60 575		...	23 547	11 057	4 040	59 814	3 497	28 249	14 582
1988	322 426	75 755		...	34 816	13 994	4 266	71 622	5 022	37 725	20 629
1989	363 812	86 331		...	38 429	13 196	4 804	78 809	5 755	44 494	24 982
1990	393 592	98 027		...	40 734	13 703	5 048	83 674	4 806	48 580	28 279
1991	421 730	103 123		...	45 628	19 054	6 148	85 150	6 278	48 125	33 277
1992	448 165	102 958		...	48 592	21 960	5 751	90 594	7 419	47 813	40 592
1993	465 090	96 973		...	52 501	19 500	6 058	100 444	8 763	47 892	41 581
1994	512 625	102 818		...	59 595	17 868	8 102	114 439	9 282	53 488	50 844
1995	584 740	123 671		...	74 234	19 533	11 439	127 226	11 754	64 343	46 292
1996	625 073	127 710		...	75 768	22 275	12 718	134 210	11 993	67 607	56 792
1997	689 180	140 773		...	78 225	25 525	15 915	151 767	12 862	65 549	71 389
1998	682 139	149 035		...	63 269	25 154	15 142	156 604	14 241	57 831	78 773
1999	695 797	151 814		...	70 989	20 166	13 203	166 600	13 111	57 466	86 909
2000	781 918	165 065	...	116 212	84 624	19 078	15 321	178 941	16 185	64 924	111 349
2001	729 101	158 768	...	112 903	71 981	20 052	15 879	163 424	19 182	57 452	101 297
2002	693 101	143 691	...	105 838	69 770	18 812	12 376	160 923	22 128	51 449	97 470
2003	724 771	151 731	...	113 132	71 601	17 279	11 211	169 924	28 368	52 004	97 412
2004	814 875	168 572	171 230	127 158	82 997	22 256	13 886	189 880	34 428	53 569	110 731
2005	901 082	...	185 166	137 497	86 003	31 641	15 372	211 899	41 192	54 681	120 248
2006	1 025 967	...	211 887	155 735	96 496	38 658	18 887	230 656	53 673	58 459	133 722
2007	1 148 199	...	244 166	180 232	105 751	48 485	24 172	248 888	62 937	61 160	135 918
2008	1 287 442	...	271 810	199 986	108 947	64 880	32 299	261 150	69 733	65 142	151 220
2009	1 056 043	...	220 599	162 002	90 380	49 857	26 095	204 658	69 497	51 134	128 892
2010	1 278 495	...	239 591	176 587	120 450	54 226	35 418	249 256	91 911	60 472	163 665
2011	1 480 290	...	268 455	195 904	136 851	64 625	42 938	281 292	103 986	65 686	198 069
2012	1 545 709	...	265 360	193 946	134 619	81 722	43 806	292 540	110 484	69 955	215 931
2010											
January	92 601	...	18 550	13 768	8 724	3 758	2 265	17 239	6 898	4 840	11 522
February	93 858	...	17 852	12 791	8 877	4 349	2 360	18 545	6 840	4 625	11 715
March	110 510	...	20 956	14 880	10 737	4 627	3 086	22 189	7 401	5 073	14 201
April	102 477	...	18 950	14 031	9 568	4 505	2 758	20 970	6 601	4 494	13 249
May	105 463	...	19 431	14 400	9 760	4 660	2 917	21 371	6 755	5 193	13 279
June	107 153	...	20 335	15 045	10 039	4 583	3 025	22 275	6 734	5 010	13 892
July	104 051	...	18 785	13 627	10 425	4 367	3 365	19 644	7 339	5 130	13 210
August	106 871	...	19 356	14 307	9 941	4 571	3 427	21 214	7 210	4 922	14 178
September	107 683	...	20 308	15 140	10 459	4 325	2 979	21 835	7 114	4 959	13 953
October	117 262	...	21 831	16 212	10 277	4 883	3 201	22 205	9 417	5 552	14 905
November	113 117	...	20 993	15 816	10 273	4 621	3 023	21 101	9 476	5 175	14 916
December	117 447	...	22 243	16 720	11 369	4 979	3 010	20 668	10 126	5 499	14 643
2011											
January	110 186	...	20 219	14 841	10 346	4 321	3 225	20 651	8 018	4 996	14 850
February	109 539	...	19 907	15 060	10 129	4 234	2 866	20 508	8 383	5 274	13 908
March	131 724	...	24 398	17 595	12 017	5 281	3 606	25 698	9 564	5 920	17 338
April	124 047	...	23 439	17 141	11 886	5 341	3 436	23 869	8 001	5 188	16 032
May	124 066	...	22 712	16 317	11 164	5 467	3 619	24 480	7 845	5 630	16 779
June	123 047	...	22 729	16 416	11 056	5 221	3 540	24 298	7 728	5 370	16 602
July	120 245	...	21 405	15 519	11 352	5 278	3 714	22 250	8 160	5 314	16 046
August	126 734	...	22 365	16 437	11 407	5 254	3 967	24 983	8 422	5 414	17 765
September	127 031	...	23 190	16 526	12 789	5 895	4 070	23 959	8 371	5 459	17 097
October	131 088	...	23 339	17 415	11 340	6 344	3 931	24 579	9 746	6 142	17 634
November	125 693	...	22 005	16 217	11 645	5 484	3 578	23 299	9 999	5 561	17 664
December	126 891	...	22 748	16 498	11 720	6 507	3 387	22 718	9 749	5 418	16 353
2012											
January	117 839	...	21 098	15 177	9 568	5 857	3 053	22 067	8 360	5 599	17 017
February	123 609	...	22 542	15 919	11 746	5 713	3 150	23 499	8 786	5 468	16 940
March	140 233	...	25 201	18 114	12 789	7 294	3 971	26 410	9 812	6 123	19 018
April	127 405	...	22 344	16 336	11 817	6 310	3 641	24 486	8 465	5 809	17 224
May	131 342	...	22 853	17 023	11 247	6 438	3 478	25 903	8 959	5 684	18 434
June	132 547	...	23 214	17 449	11 979	7 212	3 590	25 845	8 481	5 985	17 471
July	121 412	...	20 606	14 920	10 166	6 373	3 473	22 766	8 516	5 571	17 540
August	128 587	...	21 480	15 809	10 155	6 637	3 958	24 826	8 618	6 260	19 220
September	128 198	...	21 339	15 513	10 827	6 978	3 922	24 138	8 764	6 077	17 454
October	133 600	...	21 682	15 879	10 417	6 717	4 143	25 673	10 825	5 674	20 467
November	130 182	...	21 380	15 581	11 166	7 347	3 837	24 672	10 587	5 684	18 762
December	130 756	...	21 622	16 033	12 740	8 847	3 590	22 255	10 311	6 021	16 382

[1]See notes and definitions for definitions of regions.
. . . = Not available.

Table 7-14. U.S. Imports of Goods by Selected Regions and Countries

(Census Customs basis; millions of dollars, not seasonally adjusted.)

Year and month	Total, all countries	Selected regions [1]					Selected countries				
		European Union, 15 countries	European Union	Euro area	Asian NICS	OPEC	Brazil	Canada	China	Japan	Mexico
1978	...	29 009	...	...	...	...	2 826	33 525	...	24 458	6 094
1979	...	33 295	...	...	...	...	3 118	38 046	...	26 248	8 800
1980	...	35 958	...	...	...	...	3 715	41 455	...	30 701	12 520
1981	...	41 624	...	...	...	...	4 475	46 414	...	37 612	13 765
1982	...	42 509	...	...	...	...	4 285	46 477	...	37 744	15 566
1983	261 723	43 892	...	...	...	...	4 946	52 130	...	41 183	16 776
1984	330 510	57 360	...	...	...	...	7 621	66 478	...	57 135	18 020
1985	336 383	67 822	...	...	39 066	22 801	7 526	69 006	3 862	68 783	19 132
1986	365 672	75 736	...	...	46 136	19 751	6 813	68 253	4 771	81 911	17 302
1987	406 241	81 188	...	...	57 663	23 952	7 865	71 085	6 294	84 575	20 271
1988	440 952	84 939	...	...	63 030	22 962	9 294	81 398	8 511	89 519	23 260
1989	473 211	85 153	...	...	62 774	30 611	8 410	87 953	11 990	93 553	27 162
1990	495 311	91 868	...	...	60 573	38 052	7 898	91 380	15 237	89 684	30 157
1991	488 453	86 481	...	...	59 276	32 644	6 717	91 064	18 969	91 511	31 130
1992	532 662	93 993	...	...	62 384	33 200	7 609	98 630	25 728	97 414	35 211
1993	580 656	97 941	...	...	64 572	31 739	7 479	111 216	31 540	107 246	39 918
1994	663 252	110 875	...	...	71 388	31 685	8 683	128 406	38 787	119 156	49 494
1995	743 545	131 871	...	...	82 008	35 606	8 833	144 370	45 543	123 479	62 100
1996	795 287	142 947	...	...	82 770	44 285	8 773	155 893	51 513	115 187	74 297
1997	869 703	157 528	...	...	86 164	44 025	9 625	167 234	62 558	121 663	85 938
1998	911 897	176 380	...	...	85 960	33 925	10 102	173 256	71 169	121 845	94 629
1999	1 024 616	195 227	...	...	95 103	41 977	11 314	198 711	81 788	130 864	109 721
2000	1 218 023	220 019	...	163 520	111 438	67 090	13 853	230 838	100 018	146 479	135 926
2001	1 140 998	220 057	...	166 373	93 202	59 754	14 466	216 268	102 278	126 473	131 338
2002	1 161 366	225 771	...	172 573	91 850	53 245	15 781	209 088	125 193	121 429	134 616
2003	1 257 121	244 826	...	187 204	92 818	68 344	17 910	221 595	152 436	118 037	138 060
2004	1 469 705	272 439	281 959	209 606	105 476	92 099	21 160	256 360	196 682	129 805	155 902
2005	1 673 454	298 879	309 628	228 881	102 609	127 169	24 436	290 384	243 470	138 004	170 109
2006	1 853 938	319 590	330 482	246 667	109 730	150 758	26 367	302 438	287 774	148 181	198 253
2007	1 956 961	...	354 409	266 074	111 260	165 651	25 644	317 057	321 443	145 463	210 714
2008	2 103 641	...	367 617	277 658	106 763	242 579	30 453	339 491	337 773	139 262	215 942
2009	1 559 625	...	281 801	212 557	86 854	111 602	20 070	226 248	296 374	95 804	176 654
2010	1 913 857	...	319 264	242 215	106 446	149 893	23 958	277 637	364 953	120 552	229 986
2011	2 208 055	...	368 475	284 943	121 592	191 504	31 737	315 367	399 379	128 928	262 874
2012	2 275 320	...	381 208	293 950	123 441	180 770	32 123	323 936	425 579	146 392	277 570
2010											
January	136 725	...	21 293	16 711	7 293	10 966	1 942	21 654	25 216	8 341	16 089
February	133 899	...	23 125	17 068	6 601	10 781	1 432	21 233	23 343	8 776	16 459
March	157 729	...	28 264	21 709	7 970	13 657	1 958	24 316	24 292	10 485	20 089
April	153 165	...	24 771	18 856	8 412	13 838	2 002	23 657	25 920	9 442	18 594
May	156 153	...	25 739	19 596	8 904	12 495	1 884	23 658	29 052	8 641	19 419
June	168 324	...	27 710	21 140	9 452	13 518	2 217	24 694	32 843	10 218	20 049
July	163 910	...	28 485	21 784	9 415	12 405	2 400	21 300	33 267	10 091	18 214
August	171 004	...	27 553	20 772	9 440	13 549	2 082	23 457	35 375	10 729	20 252
September	167 120	...	26 630	19 912	9 768	13 312	1 707	23 041	35 197	10 057	19 908
October	170 320	...	28 698	22 169	9 880	10 495	2 088	23 444	35 083	11 282	21 024
November	168 989	...	28 213	21 317	10 212	11 579	1 875	22 909	34 564	11 092	20 530
December	166 518	...	28 784	21 620	9 100	13 297	2 370	24 273	30 800	11 399	19 357
2011											
January	167 048	...	26 134	19 709	9 401	14 358	2 206	24 793	31 377	9 885	19 606
February	156 315	...	26 833	21 289	8 613	13 499	1 984	23 215	27 245	10 567	19 054
March	185 978	...	33 505	25 742	9 646	16 045	2 055	28 306	27 600	11 807	23 270
April	178 294	...	31 134	24 106	10 408	14 848	2 495	25 936	29 580	8 829	21 360
May	188 954	...	31 677	23 910	11 211	16 916	2 909	26 965	32 788	8 317	22 970
June	191 582	...	32 345	25 324	10 982	18 833	2 820	26 858	34 375	9 421	22 715
July	187 265	...	30 175	23 236	10 943	17 190	2 922	25 446	35 153	10 859	21 091
August	196 347	...	31 372	24 245	10 365	18 515	2 349	27 147	37 379	11 829	23 153
September	189 570	...	29 529	22 983	10 282	16 420	2 892	27 235	36 419	10 858	22 304
October	191 861	...	31 528	24 332	10 386	14 423	2 584	26 729	37 824	12 388	22 854
November	190 323	...	31 746	24 574	10 023	14 734	3 095	26 177	36 765	12 124	23 147
December	184 519	...	32 498	25 014	9 333	15 723	3 427	26 558	32 874	12 044	21 352
2012											
January	183 522	...	29 591	22 782	9 331	15 767	3 003	26 779	34 419	11 756	21 504
February	171 866	...	28 530	21 726	9 236	12 163	2 635	26 276	28 105	12 433	22 617
March	197 310	...	34 908	26 919	10 216	16 584	3 303	29 151	31 433	13 308	25 115
April	189 417	...	31 281	23 900	10 850	17 769	2 908	27 766	33 011	12 086	22 757
May	198 370	...	33 450	25 576	10 963	17 677	2 484	27 579	34 938	12 111	24 814
June	191 851	...	31 537	24 457	10 557	15 731	2 908	27 308	35 953	11 996	23 514
July	192 707	...	33 252	25 113	10 909	14 738	2 660	24 941	37 929	12 488	22 526
August	194 769	...	32 885	25 524	10 205	14 755	3 060	26 997	37 276	12 953	23 763
September	185 488	...	29 381	23 142	10 445	14 172	2 396	26 015	37 884	10 974	22 151
October	198 614	...	32 395	24 747	11 020	15 227	2 300	27 622	40 252	12 681	24 818
November	194 431	...	33 593	26 210	10 135	13 965	2 302	27 724	39 537	11 790	23 711
December	176 975	...	30 404	23 547	9 573	12 222	2 164	25 780	34 843	11 816	20 279

[1]See notes and definitions for definitions of regions.
. . . = Not available.

Table 7-15. U.S. Exports of Services

(Balance of payments basis, millions of dollars, seasonally adjusted.)

Year and month	Total	Travel	Passenger fares	Other transportation	Royalties and license fees	Other private services (financial, professional, etc.)	Transfers under U.S. military sales contracts [1]	U.S. government miscellaneous services
1960	6 290	919	175	1 607	837	570	2 030	153
1961	6 295	947	183	1 620	906	607	1 867	164
1962	6 941	957	191	1 764	1 056	585	2 193	195
1963	7 348	1 015	205	1 898	1 162	613	2 219	236
1964	7 840	1 207	241	2 076	1 314	651	2 086	265
1965	8 824	1 380	271	2 175	1 534	714	2 465	285
1966	9 616	1 590	317	2 333	1 516	814	2 721	326
1967	10 667	1 646	371	2 426	1 747	951	3 191	336
1968	11 917	1 775	411	2 548	1 867	1 024	3 939	353
1969	12 806	2 043	450	2 652	2 019	1 160	4 138	343
1970	14 171	2 331	544	3 125	2 331	1 294	4 214	332
1971	16 358	2 534	615	3 299	2 545	1 546	5 472	347
1972	17 841	2 817	699	3 579	2 770	1 764	5 856	357
1973	19 832	3 412	975	4 465	3 225	1 985	5 369	401
1974	22 591	4 032	1 104	5 697	3 821	2 321	5 197	419
1975	25 497	4 697	1 039	5 840	4 300	2 920	6 256	446
1976	27 971	5 742	1 229	6 747	4 353	3 584	5 826	489
1977	31 485	6 150	1 366	7 090	4 920	3 848	7 554	557
1978	36 353	7 183	1 603	8 136	5 885	4 717	8 209	620
1979	39 692	8 441	2 156	9 971	6 184	5 439	6 981	520
1980	47 584	10 588	2 591	11 618	7 085	6 276	9 029	398
1981	57 354	12 913	3 111	12 560	7 284	10 250	10 720	517
1982	64 079	12 393	3 174	12 317	5 603	17 444	12 572	576
1983	64 307	10 947	3 610	12 590	5 778	18 192	12 524	666
1984	71 168	17 177	4 067	13 809	6 177	19 255	9 969	714
1985	73 155	17 762	4 411	14 674	6 678	20 035	8 718	878
1986	86 689	20 385	5 582	15 438	8 113	28 027	8 549	595
1987	98 661	23 563	7 003	17 027	10 174	29 263	11 106	526
1988	110 919	29 434	8 976	19 311	12 139	31 111	9 284	664
1989	127 087	36 205	10 657	20 526	13 818	36 729	8 564	587
1990	147 832	43 007	15 298	22 042	16 634	40 251	9 932	668
1991	164 261	48 385	15 854	22 631	17 819	47 748	11 135	690
1992	177 252	54 742	16 618	21 531	20 841	50 292	12 387	841
1993	185 920	57 875	16 528	21 958	21 695	53 510	13 471	883
1994	200 395	58 417	16 997	23 754	26 712	60 841	12 787	887
1995	219 183	63 395	18 909	26 081	30 289	65 048	14 643	818
1996	239 489	69 809	20 422	26 074	32 470	73 340	16 446	928
1997	256 087	73 426	20 868	27 006	33 228	83 929	16 675	955
1998	262 758	71 325	20 098	25 604	35 626	91 774	17 405	926
1999	268 790	75 161	19 425	23 792	47 731	96 812	5 211	657
2000	288 002	82 891	20 197	25 562	51 808	100 792	6 210	542
2001	276 537	72 638	17 181	24 534	49 489	106 909	5 213	573
2002	283 440	67 360	16 291	25 620	53 859	115 051	4 698	560
2003	294 121	65 159	15 091	26 354	56 813	124 154	5 918	631
2004	341 739	75 465	17 932	29 791	67 094	141 857	8 751	849
2005	376 571	82 160	20 609	32 013	74 448	154 133	12 082	1 125
2006	421 386	86 187	21 638	35 824	83 549	177 276	15 587	1 324
2007	489 255	97 355	25 187	40 638	97 803	209 307	17 444	1 522
2008	533 003	110 423	30 957	44 016	102 125	228 770	14 899	1 814
2009	508 712	94 187	26 103	36 087	98 406	235 744	16 277	1 908
2010	555 674	103 463	30 987	40 669	107 521	255 989	14 958	2 087
2011	616 973	115 552	36 763	43 067	120 717	279 645	18 821	2 408
2012	649 346	126 214	39 360	43 855	124 182	294 527	18 520	2 688
2011								
January	49 303	9 112	2 777	3 509	9 598	22 697	1 416	193
February	49 247	8 990	2 710	3 444	9 750	22 702	1 456	196
March	50 412	9 281	2 853	3 569	9 842	23 112	1 557	198
April	50 635	9 548	2 939	3 579	9 919	22 819	1 634	197
May	51 357	9 574	3 013	3 658	10 044	23 205	1 665	198
June	51 975	9 799	3 009	3 526	10 246	23 516	1 680	200
July	53 010	9 970	3 306	3 671	10 434	23 766	1 660	203
August	53 291	9 943	3 321	3 575	10 477	24 127	1 643	205
September	52 669	9 928	3 266	3 681	10 312	23 660	1 618	205
October	51 984	9 919	3 219	3 643	10 072	23 411	1 517	203
November	51 582	9 830	3 189	3 641	9 952	23 278	1 488	204
December	51 507	9 658	3 161	3 571	10 072	23 353	1 487	205
2012								
January	52 167	9 590	3 082	3 580	10 317	23 861	1 528	208
February	53 680	10 153	3 232	3 675	10 494	24 386	1 529	211
March	54 640	10 500	3 335	3 776	10 482	24 811	1 520	215
April	54 021	10 433	3 306	3 678	10 347	24 553	1 482	222
May	54 042	10 370	3 390	3 697	10 211	24 680	1 468	225
June	53 773	10 566	3 373	3 733	10 168	24 225	1 479	228
July	53 099	10 440	3 283	3 631	10 206	23 825	1 482	231
August	53 625	10 801	3 321	3 630	10 278	23 859	1 504	232
September	54 078	10 838	3 242	3 595	10 343	24 285	1 543	232
October	54 668	10 597	3 202	3 555	10 397	25 052	1 637	228
November	55 552	10 972	3 314	3 552	10 446	25 374	1 667	227
December	56 002	10 954	3 280	3 753	10 493	25 614	1 680	228

[1]Contains goods that cannot be separately identified.

Table 7-16. U.S. Imports of Services

(Balance of payments basis, millions of dollars, seasonally adjusted.)

Year and month	Total	Travel	Passenger fares	Other transportation	Royalties and license fees	Other private services (financial, professional, etc.)	Direct defense expenditures [1]	U.S. government miscellaneous services
1960	7 674	1 750	513	1 402	74	593	3 087	254
1961	7 671	1 785	506	1 437	89	588	2 998	268
1962	8 092	1 939	567	1 558	100	528	3 105	296
1963	8 362	2 114	612	1 701	112	493	2 961	370
1964	8 619	2 211	642	1 817	127	527	2 880	415
1965	9 111	2 438	717	1 951	135	461	2 952	457
1966	10 494	2 657	753	2 161	140	506	3 764	513
1967	11 863	3 207	829	2 157	166	565	4 378	561
1968	12 302	3 030	885	2 367	186	668	4 535	631
1969	13 322	3 373	1 080	2 455	221	751	4 856	586
1970	14 520	3 980	1 215	2 843	224	827	4 855	576
1971	15 400	4 373	1 290	3 130	241	956	4 819	592
1972	16 868	5 042	1 596	3 520	294	1 043	4 784	589
1973	18 843	5 526	1 790	4 694	385	1 180	4 629	640
1974	21 379	5 980	2 095	5 942	346	1 262	5 032	722
1975	21 996	6 417	2 263	5 708	472	1 551	4 795	789
1976	24 570	6 856	2 568	6 852	482	2 006	4 895	911
1977	27 640	7 451	2 748	7 972	504	2 190	5 823	951
1978	32 189	8 475	2 896	9 124	671	2 573	7 352	1 099
1979	36 689	9 413	3 184	10 906	831	2 822	8 294	1 239
1980	41 491	10 397	3 607	11 790	724	2 909	10 851	1 214
1981	45 503	11 479	4 487	12 474	650	3 562	11 564	1 287
1982	51 749	12 394	4 772	11 710	795	8 159	12 460	1 460
1983	54 973	13 149	6 003	12 222	943	8 001	13 087	1 568
1984	67 748	22 913	5 735	14 843	1 168	9 040	12 516	1 534
1985	72 862	24 558	6 444	15 643	1 170	10 203	13 108	1 735
1986	80 147	25 913	6 505	17 766	1 401	13 146	13 730	1 686
1987	90 787	29 310	7 283	19 010	1 857	16 485	14 950	1 893
1988	98 526	32 114	7 729	20 891	2 601	17 667	15 604	1 921
1989	102 479	33 416	8 249	22 172	2 528	18 930	15 313	1 871
1990	117 659	37 349	10 531	24 966	3 135	22 229	17 531	1 919
1991	118 459	35 322	10 012	24 975	4 035	25 590	16 409	2 116
1992	119 566	38 552	10 603	23 767	5 161	25 386	13 835	2 263
1993	123 779	40 713	11 410	24 524	5 032	27 760	12 086	2 255
1994	133 057	43 782	13 062	26 019	5 852	31 565	10 217	2 560
1995	141 397	44 916	14 663	27 034	6 919	35 199	10 043	2 623
1996	152 554	48 078	15 809	27 403	7 837	39 679	11 061	2 687
1997	165 932	52 051	18 138	28 959	9 161	43 154	11 707	2 762
1998	180 677	56 483	19 971	30 363	11 235	47 591	12 185	2 849
1999	195 172	59 332	20 946	31 494	13 302	55 885	11 849	2 364
2000	218 397	65 366	23 613	37 209	16 606	61 085	12 131	2 386
2001	216 364	60 912	21 921	34 909	16 661	66 639	12 869	2 452
2002	225 762	59 495	19 189	35 052	19 493	73 181	16 798	2 554
2003	242 393	58 311	20 125	40 619	19 259	80 460	21 882	1 737
2004	280 272	66 738	23 730	48 945	23 691	90 872	24 125	2 172
2005	300 352	69 930	25 189	54 212	25 577	97 989	25 200	2 255
2006	334 998	72 959	26 646	55 320	25 038	127 681	25 122	2 231
2007	365 577	77 127	27 681	55 773	26 479	150 257	25 850	2 410
2008	401 348	80 494	31 841	56 696	29 623	173 814	26 193	2 687
2009	381 819	74 132	25 117	42 601	31 297	177 212	28 331	3 130
2010	404 897	75 505	27 256	51 202	32 551	186 423	28 478	3 483
2011	429 672	78 229	31 079	54 630	34 786	199 654	27 752	3 541
2012	442 527	83 451	34 654	55 445	39 889	201 227	24 734	3 127
2011								
January	34 632	6 322	2 510	4 570	2 737	15 850	2 346	297
February	34 274	6 233	2 423	4 377	2 727	15 875	2 353	287
March	34 748	6 378	2 485	4 475	2 674	16 098	2 358	280
April	35 179	6 484	2 489	4 555	2 619	16 386	2 374	272
May	35 705	6 542	2 607	4 629	2 628	16 656	2 371	273
June	35 962	6 567	2 555	4 589	2 738	16 875	2 359	279
July	36 469	6 592	2 664	4 689	2 905	16 987	2 328	304
August	36 543	6 523	2 668	4 577	3 061	17 097	2 306	311
September	36 759	6 635	2 738	4 574	3 149	17 067	2 281	315
October	36 557	6 646	2 630	4 523	3 181	17 013	2 250	315
November	36 362	6 577	2 650	4 489	3 184	16 927	2 225	310
December	36 483	6 730	2 660	4 583	3 184	16 825	2 201	300
2012								
January	36 426	6 777	2 715	4 646	3 198	16 633	2 183	275
February	36 478	7 005	2 848	4 394	3 238	16 568	2 160	265
March	36 926	7 178	2 903	4 574	3 306	16 568	2 136	261
April	36 957	7 055	2 947	4 645	3 364	16 573	2 105	269
May	36 902	7 057	2 910	4 611	3 356	16 618	2 083	267
June	36 790	7 027	2 927	4 608	3 259	16 641	2 065	263
July	37 085	6 988	2 946	4 740	3 432	16 669	2 060	250
August	37 014	6 772	2 857	4 576	3 783	16 737	2 041	247
September	36 751	6 949	2 932	4 662	3 098	16 843	2 019	248
October	36 958	6 935	2 877	4 642	3 206	17 052	1 984	262
November	37 112	6 909	2 882	4 674	3 305	17 120	1 960	262
December	37 127	6 799	2 910	4 673	3 343	17 206	1 938	259

[1]Contains goods that cannot be separately identified.

Table 7-17. U.S. Export and Import Price Indexes by End-Use Category

(2000 = 100, not seasonally adjusted.)

Year and month	Exports			Imports		
	All commodities	Agricultural	Nonagricultural	All commodities	Petroleum [1]	Nonpetroleum
1990	95.5	105.1	94.4	94.0	75.5	97.1
1991	96.3	103.4	95.4	94.2	67.3	98.7
1992	96.3	102.5	95.7	94.9	62.9	100.0
1993	96.9	104.4	96.2	94.6	57.7	100.6
1994	98.9	109.4	98.0	96.2	54.3	103.2
1995	103.9	119.0	102.5	100.6	59.8	107.2
1996	104.5	132.6	101.6	101.6	71.1	106.4
1997	103.1	120.6	101.3	99.1	66.0	104.1
1998	99.7	108.8	98.8	93.1	44.8	100.4
1999	98.4	101.1	98.2	93.9	60.1	99.0
2000	100.0	100.0	100.0	100.0	100.0	100.0
2001	99.2	101.2	99.0	96.5	82.8	98.5
2002	98.2	103.2	97.8	94.1	85.3	96.2
2003	99.7	112.3	98.8	96.9	103.2	97.3
2004	103.6	123.4	102.1	102.3	134.6	99.8
2005	106.9	121.0	105.9	110.0	185.1	102.5
2006	110.7	125.8	109.6	115.4	223.3	104.2
2007	116.1	150.9	113.6	120.2	249.1	107.0
2008	123.1	183.5	118.8	134.1	343.2	112.7
2009	117.4	160.0	114.3	118.6	219.9	108.0
2010	123.1	172.6	119.6	126.8	282.2	111.0
2011	133.0	211.0	127.5	140.6	385.1	115.9
2012	133.5	216.1	127.6	141.0	384.0	116.3
2009						
January	116.6	159.7	113.5	113.0	143.8	109.0
February	116.3	157.0	113.3	113.0	151.6	108.2
March	115.5	151.6	112.9	113.6	168.5	107.3
April	116.1	157.2	113.1	114.8	185.5	107.1
May	116.6	162.8	113.4	116.8	206.1	107.3
June	117.8	169.7	114.1	120.0	241.5	107.4
July	117.4	161.3	114.2	119.3	235.8	107.2
August	118.1	161.6	115.0	121.1	253.7	107.6
September	117.9	156.9	115.1	121.3	252.2	107.9
October	117.9	155.8	115.2	122.3	258.3	108.4
November	118.9	161.8	115.8	124.1	272.2	109.1
December	119.7	164.7	116.5	124.4	269.3	109.7
2010						
January	120.7	166.8	117.3	125.9	279.6	110.3
February	120.3	160.2	117.4	125.8	277.4	110.4
March	121.2	163.3	118.1	126.3	284.2	110.3
April	122.5	162.7	119.6	127.7	294.5	110.8
May	123.1	165.3	120.0	126.7	278.9	111.2
June	122.2	165.3	119.1	125.2	267.4	110.7
July	122.0	165.0	118.9	125.2	269.6	110.5
August	123.0	172.0	119.5	125.7	273.4	110.7
September	123.7	176.1	120.0	125.7	269.8	111.0
October	124.7	181.0	120.7	127.1	282.4	111.3
November	126.6	194.7	121.7	129.2	296.6	112.2
December	127.5	198.5	122.4	131.0	313.0	112.6
2011						
January	129.1	204.7	123.6	133.0	324.7	113.6
February	130.8	214.1	124.8	135.3	342.5	114.4
March	132.7	218.8	126.5	139.3	380.2	115.0
April	133.8	217.8	127.7	142.9	410.7	115.9
May	134.3	215.5	128.4	143.1	407.6	116.4
June	134.5	217.2	128.6	142.2	397.8	116.4
July	134.0	208.5	128.7	142.4	399.2	116.5
August	134.6	211.9	129.1	141.9	390.0	116.8
September	135.3	216.0	129.5	141.7	386.5	117.0
October	132.6	201.9	127.7	141.2	385.5	116.6
November	132.7	205.3	127.5	142.2	398.8	116.3
December	132.1	200.5	127.3	142.2	397.8	116.4
2012						
January	132.5	202.8	127.5	142.2	397.9	116.4
February	133.1	202.0	128.3	142.2	399.0	116.3
March	134.1	206.9	128.9	144.2	418.5	116.7
April	134.7	211.0	129.2	144.1	416.0	116.7
May	134.0	212.0	128.4	142.0	392.3	116.6
June	131.7	204.5	126.5	138.7	357.2	116.3
July	132.2	216.7	126.2	137.7	348.8	115.9
August	133.4	227.0	126.7	139.4	370.5	115.8
September	134.5	229.9	127.6	140.8	385.5	116.0
October	134.6	226.0	128.0	141.2	385.3	116.4
November	133.8	227.1	127.1	140.2	374.0	116.4
December	133.6	227.4	126.9	139.4	363.1	116.5

[1] Petroleum and petroleum products.

NOTES AND DEFINITIONS, CHAPTER 7

This chapter presents data from two different data systems on international flows of goods, services, income payments, and financial transactions as they affect the U.S. economy. Tables 7-1 through 7-5 present data on the value, quantities, and prices of foreign transactions in the national income and product accounts (NIPAs). Tables 7-6 through 7-8 show foreign transactions and investment positions in current-dollar values as depicted in the U.S. international transactions accounts (ITAs). Both sets of accounts are prepared by the Bureau of Economic Analysis (BEA) and draw on the same original source data. The Census Bureau source data for exports and imports of goods and services are presented in greater detail in Tables 7-9 through 7-16. Table 7-17 shows selected summary values for export and import price indexes compiled by the Bureau of Labor Statistics (BLS).

Due to a few differences in concept, scope, and definitions, the aggregate values of international transactions in the NIPAs (shown in Tables 7-1 and 7-4) are not exactly equal to the values for similar concepts in the ITAs or the Census values that serve as their sources, shown in Tables 7-6 through 7-16. The principal sources of differences are as follows:

• The NIPAs cover only the 50 states and the District of Columbia. The ITAs include the U.S. territories and Puerto Rico as part of the U.S. economy.

• Gold is treated differently.

• Services without payment by financial intermediaries except life insurance carriers (imputed interest) is treated differently.

A reconciliation of the two sets of international accounts is published from time to time in the *Survey of Current Business*.

In addition, certain conventions of presentation differ between the two sets of international accounts. In the NIPAs (Tables 7-1 through 7-5) and in Census tables of exports and imports of goods and services (Tables 7-9 through 7-16), values of imports are shown as positive values, even though they are in fact subtracted in the calculation of gross domestic product (GDP). In the ITA balance of payments (Table 7-6), however, values of imports of goods and services and of all other transactions that result in a payment to the rest of the world—income payments to foreigners, net transfers to foreigners, and net acquisition of assets from abroad—are presented with a minus sign.

Tables 7-1 and 7-4: Foreign Transactions in the National Income and Product Accounts

SOURCE: U.S. DEPARTMENT OF COMMERCE, BUREAU OF ECONOMIC ANALYSIS

See the notes and definitions to Chapter 1 for an overview of the national income and product accounts (NIPAs).

In the 2003 comprehensive revision, the NIPA foreign transactions account was split into two accounts—the current account and the capital account. (This change had already been made in the ITAs.) Most international transactions fall into the current account, but occasionally there are substantial flows in the capital account when major already-existing assets are transferred. An example of this is the U.S. government's transfer of the Panama Canal to the Republic of Panama in 1999.

Definitions

In accordance with the split between current and capital account, there are now two NIPA measures of the balance of international transactions.

The *balance on current account, national income and product accounts* is *current receipts from the rest of the world* minus *current payments to the rest of the world*. A negative value indicates that current payments exceed current receipts.

Net lending or net borrowing (-), national income and product accounts is equal to the balance on current account less capital account transactions with the rest of the world (net). Capital account transactions with the rest of the world (net) is not shown separately in Table 7-1 (for space reasons) but can be calculated from that table as the difference between net lending/borrowing and the current account balance. (A similar measure, a component of the ITAs, is shown explicitly in Table 7-6.) Capital account transactions with the rest of the world are cash or in-kind transfers linked to the acquisition or disposition of an existing, nonproduced, nonfinancial asset. In contrast, the current account is limited to flows associated with current production of goods and services.

Net lending or net borrowing provides an indirect measure of the net acquisition of foreign assets by U.S. residents less the net acquisition of U.S. assets by foreign residents. These asset flows are measured directly in the ITAs. See Table 7-6 and its notes and definitions for a more extensive discussion of the relationship between the balances on current and capital account and international asset flows.

Current receipts from the rest of the world is *exports of goods and services* plus *income receipts*.

Current payments to the rest of the world is *imports of goods and services* plus *income payments* plus *current taxes and transfer payments (net)*.

Exports and imports of goods and services. Goods, in general, are products that can be stored or inventoried. *Services*, in general, are products that cannot be stored and are consumed at the place and time of their purchase. Goods imports include expenditures abroad by U.S. residents, except for travel. Services include foreign travel by U.S. residents, expenditures in the United States by foreign travelers, and exports and imports of certain goods—primarily military equipment purchased and sold by the federal government. See the following paragraph for the definition of *travel*.

Table 7-4 shows values for selected components of total goods and services; the components shown will not add to the total because of omitted items. In the case of goods, a miscellaneous "other" category is not shown. In the case of services, only two components are shown in this table. One is *travel*, which does not include passenger fares but includes as exports spending by foreign tourists in the United States, and includes as imports all other spending abroad by tourists from the United States. The other component shown here is a category called *other private services*, which includes the professional and financial services (for example, computer services) that have accounted for a large part of the long-term growth in the service category. The remaining components of total services are transfers under U.S. military agency sales contracts; passenger fares; other transportation; royalties and license fees; and a miscellaneous, smaller *other* category. They are shown separately in Tables 7-15 and 7-16.

Income receipts and payments. Income receipts—receipts from abroad of factor (labor or capital) income by U.S. residents—are analogous to exports and are combined with them to yield total *current receipts from the rest of the world. Income payments* by U.S. entities of factor income to entities abroad are analogous to imports.

Current taxes and transfer payments (net) consists of net payments between the United States and abroad that do not involve payment for the services of the labor or capital factors of production, purchase of currently-produced goods and services, or transfer of an existing asset. It includes net flows from persons, government, and business. The types of payments included are personal remittances from U.S. residents to the rest of the world, net of remittances from foreigners to U.S. residents; government grants; and transfer payments from businesses. Only the net payment to the rest of the world is shown. It usually appears in these accounts as a positive value, with transfers from the United States to abroad exceeding the reverse flow. An exception came in 1991, when

U.S. allies in the Gulf War reimbursed the United States for the cost of the war. This resulted in net payments to the United States from the rest of the world and appears as a negative entry in the net transfer payments column of the NIPA accounts. (Note that these signs are reversed in the ITAs, because of the differing measurement conventions described above.)

Tables 7-2, 7-3 and 7-5: Chain-Type Quantity and Price Indexes for NIPA Foreign Transactions

These indexes represent the separation of the current-dollar values in Tables 7-1 and 7-4 into their real quantity and price trends components. (See the notes and definitions to Chapter 1 for a general explanation of chained-dollar estimates of real output and prices.) As those notes explain, quantity indexes are shown instead of constant-dollar estimates, because BEA no longer publishes its real output estimates before 1995 in any detail in the constant-dollar form. Therefore, quantity indexes are the only comprehensive source of information about longer-term trends in real volumes.

Table 7-6A: U.S. International Transactions: Recent Data

SOURCE: U.S. DEPARTMENT OF COMMERCE, BUREAU OF ECONOMIC ANALYSIS

The U.S. international transactions accounts (ITAs), or "balance of payments accounts," provide a comprehensive view of economic and financial transactions between the United States and foreign countries, measured in current dollars only—unlike the NIPAs, in which price and quantity trends are also estimated. Direct measurement of financial asset flows further distinguishes this set of accounts from the NIPAs.

The ITAs are subdivided into three sets of accounts, with each comprising credit and debit items. In concept, all of these items together provide a complete accounting for U.S. international transactions and should therefore sum to zero. In practice, there are substantial discrepancies due to measurement problems. See the definitions below for an explanation of the *statistical discrepancy* in these accounts, which is different from the measure of the same name in the NIPAs.

The *balance on current account* is the most frequently quoted statistic from these accounts, and is often, but imprecisely, called the "trade balance." (See the definitions below for the correct definitions of "trade balance" and "merchandise trade balance," both of which differ from the current account balance.) The *current account* includes exports and imports of goods and of travel, transportation, and other services; receipts and payments of income between U.S. and foreign residents; and foreign aid and other current transfers. The *financial account* covers most international flows of private and official capital, including direct investment. The *capital account*, which is small relative to the other two accounts, includes certain transactions in existing assets.

More detailed data on exports and imports of goods and services as measured in these accounts are shown in Tables 7-9 through 7-16.

Definitions

Unlike the practice in the NIPA accounts, each category of transaction in the ITAs is presented either as a *credit,* with an implicit plus sign, or as a *debit*, with a clearly marked minus sign. The signs indicate the direction of the ultimate impact on the overall balance.

Credits (+): The following items are treated as credits in the international transactions accounts: exports of goods and services and income receipts; unilateral current transfers to the United States; capital account transactions receipts; and financial inflows, which are increases in foreign-owned assets (U.S. liabilities) and decreases in U.S.-owned assets (U.S. claims). Credits represent payments of funds to U.S. entities, whether earned (as with exports), received as gifts, received in payment for assets, or received in exchange for a claim, such as a stock, bond, or loan agreement, on a U.S. entity.

Debits (-): The following items are treated as debits in the international transactions accounts, indicated by minus signs in the data cells: imports of goods and services and income payments; unilateral current transfers to foreigners; capital accounts transactions payments; financial outflows, which are decreases in foreign-owned assets (U.S. liabilities) and increases in U.S.-owned assets (U.S. claims). Debits represent requirements for U.S. entities to make payments to foreigners, whether for imports, as gifts, or as payments for the acquisition of real or financial assets.

This convention of credits and debits is used only in the ITAs in Table 7-6. In Table 7-6, import values all have a negative sign. Import values are shown without negative signs both in the NIPA tables (Tables 7-1 and 7-4) and in the detailed tables from the Census Bureau on exports and imports of goods and services (Tables 7-9 through 7-16).

The *balance on goods* is the excess of exports of goods over imports of goods—the algebraic sum of the two, in ITA transactions accounting. A minus sign indicates an excess of imports over exports. A similar concept, which appears in

monthly trade reports, is called the "merchandise trade balance."

The *balance on services* is the excess of service exports over service imports. A minus sign indicates an excess of imports over exports.

The *balance on goods and services* is the sum of the balance on goods and the balance on services. This concept is accurately described as the "balance of trade."

The *balance on income* is the excess of income receipts from abroad over income payments to foreigners. A minus sign indicates an excess of payments over receipts.

The *balance on goods, services, and income* is the excess of exports of goods and services and income receipts over imports of goods and services and income payments. It is equal to the sum of the balance on goods and services and the balance on income. A minus sign indicates an excess of imports and payments over exports and receipts.

Unilateral current transfers, net is equal to unilateral transfers to the United States minus transfers from the United States. This category includes U.S. government grants, pensions, and other transfers, and private remittances and other transfers. In the July 2009 revision, insurance payments for extraordinary disaster losses were shifted from this account to the *capital account*.

The *balance on current account* is equal to the sum of the balance on goods, services, and income and the net balance on unilateral transfers. It is the featured measure of the U.S. balance of payments.

The *capital account* covers net capital transfers and the acquisition and disposal of nonproduced nonfinancial assets.

The major type of *capital transfers* is debt forgiveness. As of the 2010 comprehensive revision, and beginning with the data for 1982, migrants' transfers—the net worth of individuals who immigrate or emigrate during a period—are excluded from the capital account, as they do not generate transactions between a resident and a nonresident. This change is in accordance with international guidelines. Migrants' investments in their country of origin will continue to be recorded in the international investment position accounts (shown in Table 7-8) when migration changes the status of these investments from domestic to international, but they will enter the position as "other changes in value."

Nonproduced nonfinancial assets include rights to natural resources, patents, copyrights, trademarks, franchises, and leases. In the July 2009 revision, insurance payments for extraordinary disaster losses such as those caused by major hurricanes and the 2001 terror attack were shifted to the capital account from the current unilateral transfers account.

The *financial account* includes all other inflows and outflows of capital, or changes in U.S.-owned assets abroad and foreign-owned assets in the United States, including official reserve assets, direct investment, securities, currency, and bank deposits. Most of the categories are self-explanatory.

U.S. government assets other than official reserve assets, net and its component *U.S. foreign currency holdings and short-term assets, net* include the initiation and reversal of large swap positions under temporary reciprocal currency arrangements between the U.S. Federal Reserve System and foreign central banks, undertaken in order to deal with the international financial crisis in late 2008. The accounts indicate creation of a half-trillion dollars' worth of swaps in 2008 (because a minus sign in these accounts indicates increases in U.S. official assets) and the reversal of about the same amount in 2009.

Direct investment financial flows are those associated with the acquisition of a significant interest (10 percent or more) in a business enterprise in one country by a resident of another country.

U.S. claims reported by U.S. banks and securities brokers, a component of *U.S. private assets, net*. Beginning with 2003, these entries include securities brokers' claims on their foreign affiliates. Prior to 2003, such claims are included in the claims of nonbanking concerns.

U.S. liabilities reported by U.S. banks and securities brokers, components of *Foreign official assets in the United States, net* and *Other foreign assets in the United States, net*. Beginning with 2003, these entries include securities brokers' liabilities to their foreign affiliates. Prior to 2003, such liabilities are included in the liabilities of nonbanking concerns.

Foreign official assets in the United States. U.S. Treasury securities includes bills, certificates, marketable bonds and notes, and nonmarketable convertible and nonconvertible bonds and notes. *Other U.S. government securities* consists of U.S. Treasury and Export-Import Bank obligations, not included elsewhere, and of debt securities of U.S. government corporations and agencies. *Other U.S. government liabilities* primarily includes U.S. government liabilities to foreign official authorities associated with military agency sales contracts and other transactions arranged with or through foreign official agencies. *Other foreign official assets* consists of official investments in U.S. corporate stocks and in debt securities of private corporations and state and local governments.

In concept, the balance on current account is exactly offset by the net financial and capital inflow or outflow. For example, a U.S. current account deficit results in more dollars held by foreigners, which must be reflected in additional claims on the United States held by foreigners, whether in the form of U.S. currency, dollar bank accounts, securities, loans, or other forms of ownership or obligation. However, because of different and incomplete data sources, the measured financial and capital accounts do not exactly offset the measured current account. The *statistical discrepancy* in the U.S. international accounts—the sum of all credits and debits, with the sign reversed—measures the amount by which the measured net financial and capital flow would have to be augmented (or diminished, in the case of a negative discrepancy) to exactly offset the current account balance. In the quarterly accounts, a part of this discrepancy, the *seasonal adjustment discrepancy*, results from separate seasonal adjustments of the components of the accounts. The statistical discrepancy in the international accounts is not the same as the statistical discrepancy in the national income and product accounts, which arises from measurement differences between domestic output and domestic income.

Notes on the data

There are "breaks" (discontinuities) in the historical series for several of the components of the balance of payments accounts. See Technical Notes in the June 1989–1990, 1992–1995, and July 1996–2007 issues of the *Survey of Current Business.*

Exports and imports of goods. In the 2010 comprehensive revision, and beginning with the statistics for 1999, new adjustments were introduced to reclassify goods transactions by the U.S. military and by air and ocean carriers from services, where they had previously been included due to data deficiencies, to the goods categories. The goods data also reflect various other adjustments (for valuation, coverage, and timing) of Census Bureau statistics to a balance-of-payments basis. See the notes and definitions to Tables 7-9 through 7-16 for further information.

U.S. government grants includes transfers of goods and services under U.S. military grant programs. The positive value in 1991 reflects net grants to the United States from other countries.

Beginning in 1982, *private remittances and other transfers* includes taxes paid by U.S. private residents to foreign governments and taxes paid by private nonresidents to the U.S. government.

At the present time, all U.S. Treasury-owned *gold* is held in the United States.

Repayments on U.S. credits and other long-term assets includes sales of foreign obligations to foreigners.

Beginning with the data for 1982, *direct investment income payments* and the reinvested earnings component of *direct investment* financial flows are measured on a current-cost (replacement-cost) basis after adjustment to reported depreciation, depletion, and expensed exploration and development costs. For prior years, depreciation is valued in terms of the historical cost of assets and reflects a mix of prices for the various years in which capital investments were made. See *Survey of Current Business,* July 1999, pages 65–67, and *Survey of Current Business*, June 1992, pages 72ff.

The U.S. Treasury securities component of other foreign assets in the United States includes foreign-currency denominated notes sold to private residents abroad for 1978 through 1983.

Estimates of *U.S. currency flows abroad* were introduced for the first time as part of the July 1997 revisions. Data for 1974 and subsequent years were affected (see *Survey of Current Business*, July 1997). Beginning with the 1998 revisions, currency flows are published separately from U.S. Treasury securities.

Financial derivatives, net are estimated for the first time for 2006. (Previously, they were partly measured in other financial flow components and in part contributed to the statistical discrepancy.) They are reported on a net basis only. See "References," below, for more explanation.

Data availability

Quarterly estimates are reported in a press release around the middle of the third month of each quarter, available on the BEA Web site at http://www.bea.gov. The data published here were released on June 14, 2013. Complete historical data are available on the BEA Web site at http://www.bea.gov/.

References

An article in the May 2013 *Survey of Current Business* entitled "Modernizing and Enhancing BEA's International Economic Accounts" outlines changes in these accounts scheduled for June 2013 and June 2014. Previous discussions of the impact of changes in methodology and incorporation of new data sources when they occur are found in July issues (the June issues for 1995 and earlier years) of the *Survey of*

Current Business. An article in the July 2007 *Survey* includes an extensive discussion of the new data on financial derivatives and their role in the ITA financial account and investment position data. The *SCB* is available on the BEA Web site.

The Balance of Payments of the United States: Concepts, Data Sources, and Estimating Procedures (May 1990), available on the BEA Web site or from the National Technical Information Service (Accession No. PB 90-268715), describes the methodology in detail and provides a list of data sources.

Table 7-6B: U.S. International Transactions: Historical

The definitions and data descriptions for this historical table are the same as those for Table 7-6A, with the following exceptions.

For space reasons, the amounts for *U.S. Treasury securities and U.S. currency flows* under the heading *Other foreign assets in the United States, net*, which are separate columns in Table 7-6A, are combined in Table 7-6B.

The *Balance on current account* as shown in the final column of Table 7-6B includes some items not shown separately, which are displayed in Table 7-6A. They are *Capital account transactions, net* and *Financial derivatives, net.*

Table 7-7: Foreigners' Transactions in Long-Term Securities with U.S. Residents

SOURCE: U.S. DEPARTMENT OF THE TREASURY

Some of the transactions that go into the ITA financial account are collected monthly. Since December 2003, these transactions have been reported by the Treasury Department in a monthly press release. They are presented in Table 7-7.

These data cover transactions in long-term securities, measured at market value plus or minus commissions and fees, between foreigners and U.S. residents. They have more reporting gaps than the more comprehensive quarterly current account data in Table 7-6. These monthly data do not include direct investment, currency flows, changes in bank accounts, or transactions in short-term securities. They may be distorted by inappropriate reporting of repurchases and securities lending transactions. The data are more timely but less detailed than other information sources and are not reliable for country-by-country detail. They are based on a reporting panel of some 250 banks, securities dealers, and other enterprises with cross-border transactions of at least $50 million. This survey was designed to provide timely information for the balance of payments accounts, and its use for other applications—particularly those involving country detail—is less appropriate.

Definitions and notes on the data

U.S. residents includes any individual, corporation, or organization located in the United States (including branches, subsidiaries, and affiliates of foreign entities located in the United States) and any corporation incorporated in the United States, even if it has no physical presence in the country.

Gross purchases minus *gross sales* equals *net purchases.* Positive values for net purchases of U.S. securities by foreigners indicate capital inflows from foreigners to U.S. residents (and increased liabilities to foreigners on the part of the U.S. residents). Negative values for net purchases of foreign securities from U.S. residents indicate a capital outflow from U.S. residents to foreigners (and increased liabilities to U.S. residents on the part of foreigners). The algebraic sum of the two net purchases components gives *net long-term securities transactions.* When positive, this indicates that the net capital inflows on U.S. securities exceed the net U.S. acquisitions of foreign securities.

Other acquisitions of long-term securities, net consists of estimated foreign acquisitions of U.S. equity through stock swaps, plus the increase in nonmarketable treasury bonds and notes issued to official institutions and other residents of foreign countries, minus estimated unrecorded principal payments to foreigners on domestic corporate and agency asset-backed securities, minus estimated U.S. acquisitions of foreign equity through stock swaps.

Net foreign acquisition of long-term securities is the sum of *net long-term securities transactions* and *other acquisitions of long-term securities.*

Revisions

The monthly and annual data are revised frequently, when quarterly and annual benchmark data become available. The June release usually includes the final results from an annual survey of foreign holding of U.S. securities.

Data availability and references

Data for the latest month and recent historical data are published in a press release available around the middle of the second following month. The press release, supporting descriptions, references, and other relevant information concerning the Treasury International Capital System (TIC) can be found online at http://www.treas.gov/tic.

Table 7-8: International Investment Position of the United States

SOURCE: U.S. DEPARTMENT OF COMMERCE, BUREAU OF ECONOMIC ANALYSIS

The data presented in Tables 7-1 through 7-7 all represent flows of goods, services, and money over the designated time periods. Table 7-8, in contrast, is a measure of stocks, or total holdings of money and other claims. The data on the international investment position of the United States measure the extent to which the United States and its residents hold claims of ownership on foreigners or are creditors of foreigners; the extent to which foreigners, including foreign governments, hold claims of ownership on assets located in the United States or are creditors of U.S. residents and entities; and the net difference between the two amounts. This difference measures the amount by which the United States is a net creditor of the rest of the world or a net debtor to the rest of the world. A position of net U.S. indebtedness is represented by a minus sign in the net international investment position.

Changes in the net investment position can arise in two principal ways:

• The first way is through inflows or outflows of capital. A net inflow of capital increases U.S. indebtedness to foreigners, while a net outflow increases foreigners' indebtedness to the United States. A deficit in the U.S. international current account requires an equivalent inflow of foreign capital, while a surplus would require an equivalent outflow of U.S. capital; see the notes for Table 7-6 for further explanation.

• The second way is through valuation adjustments, which are of several kinds: changes in market prices of assets; changes in exchange rates, which can cause revaluation of foreign-currency-denominated assets; and miscellaneous other adjustments due to changes in coverage, statistical discrepancies, and the like. Valuation adjustments are shown separately from financial flows in the *Survey of Current Business* articles accompanying each annual update (see below for reference). They were particularly sharp in 2008 and 2009, far exceeding the actual net volume of financial flows in both years.

Two new features were introduced into the investment position accounts with the 2007 revision.

• First, only one version of the net position is now published, the one in which direct investment is measured at current cost. (See definitions below.) However, alternative measures of direct investment measured at market prices are also published, so that the user can calculate the position with market valuation of direct investment.

• Second, for the years 2005 forward, assets and the net position include financial derivatives, which introduces a break in the series. The values for financial derivatives are shown separately so that the user can eliminate them from the calculation if desired. The net U.S. balance on derivatives was reported to be $58 billion at the end of 2012. Without including derivatives, the U.S. international investment position would have been net indebtedness of $3.92 trillion instead of the net indebtedness of $3.86 trillion shown in Table 7-8.

Definitions: Direct investment, current cost, and market value

Direct investment occurs when an individual or business in one country (the parent) obtains a lasting interest in, and a degree of influence over the management of, a business enterprise in another country (the affiliate). The U.S. data define this degree of interest to be ownership of at least 10 percent of the voting securities of an incorporated business enterprise or the equivalent interest in an unincorporated business enterprise.

When direct investment positions are valued at the historical costs carried on the books of the affiliated companies, much of the investment will reflect the price levels of earlier time periods. Therefore, before calculating the overall U.S. position, BEA re-estimates the aggregate direct investment totals using two alternative valuation bases. Detailed direct investment data by country and industry are available only on a historical cost basis.

At *current cost*, the portion of the direct investment position representing the parents' shares of their affiliates' tangible assets (property, plant, equipment, and inventories) is revalued to replacement cost in today's money, using a perpetual inventory model, appropriate price indexes, and appropriate depreciation allowances. (The same methodology is used for the U.S. stock of fixed assets; see the notes and definitions to Tables 5-5 and 5-6 for further information.) This is an adjustment made to the asset side of the balance sheet and reflects prices of tangible assets only.

The *market value* method revalues the owners' equity portion of the direct investment positions using general country indexes of stock market prices. This adjustment is made on the liability and owner's equity side of the balance sheet. Stock price changes reflect changes not only in the value of tangible assets, but also in the value of intangible assets and in the outlook for a country or industry.

Market values are more volatile than current cost, reflecting the nature of stock markets and the additional uncertainties

concerning the intangibles included in the valuation. Typically, the total market value of U.S.-owned direct investment abroad is greater than the current replacement cost, though by varying proportions. However, in 1982 through 1984 and in 2008 and 2011, aggregate market values fell below the estimated replacement costs. For foreign-owned investments in the United States, the pattern has been different. Market values were below replacement cost through 1988, but have been higher every year since then.

Definitions: Net international investment position

U.S. net international investment position is defined as the value of *U.S.-owned assets abroad* minus the value of *foreign-owned assets in the United States.*

U.S.-owned assets abroad is the sum of *financial derivatives, official reserve assets, other U.S. government assets, direct investment at current cost, foreign bonds, foreign corporate stocks, U.S. nonbank claims,* and *U.S. bank claims.*

As a component of U.S.-owned assets, the *financial derivatives* category is the sum of derivatives positions with a positive "fair value" to U.S. residents. The fair value of a derivatives contract is the amount for which the contract could be exchanged between willing parties. A derivatives contract between a U.S. and a foreign resident with a positive fair value represents the amount that the foreign resident would have to pay to the U.S. resident if the contract was terminated.

U.S. official reserve assets includes gold, valued at the current market price; special drawing rights; the U.S. reserve position in the International Monetary Fund; and official holdings of foreign currencies.

Other U.S. government assets includes other U.S. government claims on foreigners and holdings of foreign currency and short-term assets.

U.S. nonbank claims includes U.S. claims on affiliated foreigners reported by U.S. nonbanking concerns.

U.S. bank claims consists of claims on foreigners, such as loans and commercial paper, held by U.S. banks and not reported elsewhere in the accounts.

Foreign-owned assets in the United States includes *financial derivatives, foreign official assets, direct investment in the United States at current cost, U.S. Treasury securities, U.S. currency, corporate and other bonds, corporate stocks, U.S. nonbank liabilities,* and *U.S. bank liabilities.*

As a component of foreign-owned assets in the United States, *financial derivatives* consists of derivatives positions with a negative "fair value" to U.S. residents. A contract with a negative fair value represents the amount that the U.S. resident would have to pay to the foreign resident if the contract was terminated.

Foreign official assets includes foreign government holdings of claims on the United States, including U.S. government securities and other liabilities and deposits held by such governments in U.S. banks.

Foreign-owned assets in the United States, other than official assets, also include *U.S. Treasury securities, U.S. currency, corporate and other bonds, corporate stocks, U.S. liabilities (to foreigners) reported by U.S. nonbanking concerns,* and *U.S. bank liabilities to foreigners* (such as deposits).

Data availability

The annual (year-end) data, along with revisions for earlier years, are released around the middle of the following year; the data shown in this edition of *Business Statistics* were released June 25, 2013. On March 26, 2013, BEA released quarterly estimates for the first time. The quarterly data are available from December 2005. All the data are available on the BEA Web site at http://www.bea.gov.

References

Articles entitled "The International Investment Position of the United States at Yearend" are published each July in the *Survey of Current Business* describing and analyzing the estimates. The article in the July 2007 *Survey* includes extensive data and discussion of the new coverage of financial derivatives. For background on the valuation of direct investment and other components, see "Valuation of the U.S. Net International Investment Position," *Survey of Current Business*, May 1991. Also see the references for Table 7-6.

Tables 7-9 through 7-16: Exports and Imports of Goods and Services

SOURCES: U.S. DEPARTMENT OF COMMERCE, CENSUS BUREAU AND BUREAU OF ECONOMIC ANALYSIS

These tables present the source data used to build up the aggregate measures of goods and services flows shown in Tables 7-1 through 7-6. These data are compiled and published monthly, making trends evident before the publication of the quarterly aggregate estimates. They also provide more detail than the quarterly aggregates.

Monthly and annual data on exports and imports of *goods* are compiled by the Census Bureau from documents collected by the U.S. Customs Service. The Bureau of Economic Analysis

(BEA) makes certain adjustments to these data (as described below) to place the estimates on a *balance of payments* basis—a basis consistent with the national and international accounts.

Data on exports and imports of *services* are prepared by BEA from a variety of sources. Monthly data on services are available from January 1992. Annual and quarterly data for earlier years are available as part of the international transactions accounts. Current data on goods and services are available each month in a joint Census Bureau-BEA press release.

In the case of some of the detailed breakdowns of exports and imports, such as by end-use categories, monthly data may not sum exactly to annual totals. This is due to later revisions, which are made only to annual data and are not allocated to monthly data. Also, the constant-dollar figures expressed in 2009 dollars are now calculated using chain weights. Therefore, the 2009-dollar detail will not add to the 2009-dollar totals.

In addition, monthly and annual data on exports and imports of goods for individual countries and various country groupings do not reflect subsequent revisions of annual total data. These country data are compiled by the Census Bureau for all countries, although this volume includes only a selection of the most significant countries and areas. The full set of data can be accessed on the Census Web site at http://www.census.gov.

Definitions: Goods

Goods: Census basis. The Census basis goods data are compiled from documents collected by the U.S. Customs Service. They reflect the movement of goods between foreign countries and the 50 states, the District of Columbia, Puerto Rico, the U.S. Virgin Islands, and U.S. Foreign Trade Zones. They include government and nongovernment shipments of goods, and exclude shipments between the United States and its territories and possessions; transactions with U.S. military, diplomatic, and consular installations abroad; U.S. goods returned to the United States by its armed forces; personal and household effects of travelers; and in-transit shipments. The general import values reflect the total arrival of merchandise from foreign countries that immediately enters consumption channels, warehouses, or Foreign Trade Zones.

For *imports,* the value reported is the U.S. Customs Service appraised value of merchandise (generally, the price paid for merchandise for export to the United States). Import duties, freight, insurance, and other charges incurred in bringing merchandise to the United States are excluded.

Exports are valued at the f.a.s. (free alongside ship) value of merchandise at the U.S. port of export, based on the transaction price including inland freight, insurance, and other charges incurred in placing the merchandise alongside the carrier at the U.S. port of exportation.

Goods: balance of payments (BOP) basis. Goods on a Census basis are adjusted by BEA to goods on a BOP basis to bring the data in line with the concepts and definitions used to prepare the international and national accounts. In general, the adjustments include changes in ownership that occur without goods passing into or out of the customs territory of the United States. These adjustments are necessary to supplement coverage of the Census basis data, to eliminate duplication of transactions recorded elsewhere in the international accounts, and to value transactions according to a standard definition. With the June 4, 2013 release, improved BOP adjustments involving U.S. military transactions were introduced for data beginning with 1999.

The *export* adjustments include the following: (1) The deduction of *U.S. military sales contracts*. The Census Bureau has included these contracts in the goods data, but BEA includes them in the service category "Transfers Under U.S. Military Sales Contracts." BEA's source material for these contracts is more comprehensive but does not distinguish between goods and services. (2) The addition of *private gift parcels* mailed to foreigners by individuals through the U.S. Postal Service. Only commercial shipments are covered in Census goods exports. (3) The addition to *nonmonetary gold exports* of gold purchased by foreign official agencies from private dealers in the United States and held at the Federal Reserve Bank of New York. The Census data include only gold that leaves the customs territory. (4) *Smaller adjustments* includes deductions for repairs of goods, exposed motion picture film, and military grant aid, and additions for sales of fish in U.S. territorial waters, exports of electricity to Mexico, and vessels and oil rigs that change ownership without export documents being filed.

The *import* adjustments include the following: (1) On *inland freight in Canada*, the customs value for imports for certain Canadian goods is the point of origin in Canada. BEA makes an addition for the inland freight charges of transporting these Canadian goods to the U.S. border. (2) An addition is made to *nonmonetary gold imports* for gold sold by foreign official agencies to private purchasers out of stock held at the Federal Reserve Bank of New York. The Census Bureau data include only gold that enters the customs territory. (3) A deduction is made for *imports by U.S. military agencies*. The Census Bureau has included these contracts in the goods data, but BEA includes them in the service category "Direct Defense Expenditures." BEA's source material is more comprehensive

but does not distinguish between goods and services. (4) *Smaller adjustments* includes deductions for repairs of goods and for exposed motion picture film and additions for imported electricity from Mexico, conversion of vessels for commercial use, and repairs to U.S. vessels abroad.

Definitions: Services

The statistics are estimates of service transactions between foreign countries and the 50 states, the District of Columbia, Puerto Rico, the U.S. Virgin Islands, and other U.S. territories and possessions. Transactions with U.S. military, diplomatic, and consular installations abroad are excluded because they are considered to be part of the U.S. economy. Services are shown in the broad categories described below. For six of these categories, the definitions are the same for imports and exports. For the seventh, the export category is "Transfers under U.S. Military Sales Contracts," while for imports, the category is "Direct Defense Expenditures."

Travel includes purchases of services and goods by U.S. travelers abroad and by foreign visitors to the United States. A traveler is defined as a person who stays for a period of less than one year in a country where the person is not a resident. Included are expenditures for food, lodging, recreation, gifts, and other items incidental to a foreign visit. Not included are the international costs of the travel itself, which are covered in *passenger fares* (see below).

Passenger fares consists of fares paid by residents of one country to residents in other countries. Receipts consist of fares received by U.S. carriers from foreign residents for travel between the United States and foreign countries and between two foreign points. Payments consist of fares paid by U.S. residents to foreign carriers for travel between the United States and foreign countries.

Break in series: travel and passenger fares. Beginning with data for 1984, these items incorporate results from a survey administered by the U.S. Travel and Tourism Administration. See *Survey of Current Business,* June 1989, pages 57ff.

Other transportation includes charges for the transportation of goods by ocean, air, waterway, pipeline, and rail carriers to and from the United States. Included are freight charges, operating expenses that transportation companies incur in foreign ports, and payments for vessel charter and aircraft and freight car rentals. (*Break in series*: Estimates of freight charges for the transportation of goods by truck between the United States and Canada are included in the data beginning with 1986. Reliable estimates for earlier years are not available. See *Survey of Current Business*, June 1994, pages 70ff.)

Royalties and license fees consists of transactions with foreign residents involving intangible assets and proprietary rights, such as the use of patents, techniques, processes, formulas, designs, know-how, trademarks, copyrights, franchises, and manufacturing rights. The term *royalties* generally refers to payments for the utilization of copyrights or trademarks, and the term *license fees* generally refers to payments for the use of patents or industrial processes.

Other private services includes transactions with "affiliated" foreigners for which no identification by type is available and transactions with unaffiliated foreigners.

The term "affiliated" refers to a direct investment relationship, which exists when a U.S. person has ownership or control (directly or indirectly) of 10 percent or more of a foreign business enterprise, or when a foreign person has a similar interest in a U.S. enterprise.

Transactions with "unaffiliated" foreigners in this "other private services" category consist of education services, financial services, insurance services, telecommunications services, and business, professional, and technical services. Included in the last group are advertising services; computer and data processing services; database and other information services; research, development, and testing services; management, consulting, and public relations services; legal services; construction, engineering, architectural, and mining services; industrial engineering services; installation, maintenance, and repair of equipment; and other services, including medical services and film and tape rental.

The insurance component of "other private services" was measured before the July 2003 revision as premiums less actual losses paid or recovered. Furthermore, catastrophic losses were entered immediately when the loss occurred, rather than when the insurance claim was actually paid out. This led to sharp swings for any month in which catastrophic losses occurred, such as Hurricane Katrina in August 2005 or the September 11, 2001, terror attacks. In the accounts as revised in July 2003 and presented here, insurance services are now measured as premiums less "normal" losses. Normal losses consist of a measure of expected regularly occurring losses based on six years of past experience plus an additional allowance for catastrophic loss. Catastrophic losses, when they occur, are added in equal increments to the estimate of regularly occurring losses over the 20 years following the occurrence. As adoption of this methodology introduces a difference between actual and normal losses, an amount equal to the difference is entered in the international accounts as a capital account transaction.

BEA conducts surveys of international transactions in financial services and "selected services" (largely business, professional, and technical services). Beginning with data for 1986, *other private services* includes estimates of business, professional, and technical services from the BEA surveys of selected services. (See *Survey of Current Business*, June 1989, pages 57ff.)

Breaks in series: royalties and license fees and other private services. These items are presented on a gross basis beginning in 1982. The definition of exports is revised to exclude U.S. parents' payments to foreign affiliates and to include U.S. affiliates' receipts from foreign parents. The definition of imports is revised to include U.S. parents' payments to foreign affiliates and to exclude U.S. affiliates' receipts from foreign parents.

Transfers under U.S. military sales contracts (exports only) includes exports in which U.S. government military agencies participate. This category has included both goods, such as equipment, and services, such as repair services and training, that could not be separately identified. In the 2010 and 2013 annual revisions, more precise breakdowns between goods and services in this category were introduced and incorporated as revised estimates of services and of the BOP goods adjustment, beginning with the data for 2007. Transfers of goods and services under U.S. military grant programs are included.

Direct defense expenditures (imports only) consists of expenditures incurred by U.S. military agencies abroad, including expenditures by U.S. personnel, payments of wages to foreign residents, construction expenditures, payments for foreign contractual services, and procurement of foreign goods. Improved breakdowns between goods and services are now incorporated beginning with statistics for 1999.

U.S. government miscellaneous services includes transactions of U.S. government nonmilitary agencies with foreign residents. Most of these transactions involve the provision of services to, or purchases of services from, foreigners. Transfers of some goods are also included.

Services estimates are based on quarterly, annual, and benchmark surveys and partial information generated from monthly reports. Service transactions are estimated at market prices. Estimates are seasonally adjusted when statistically significant seasonal patterns are present.

Definitions: Area groupings

The Census trade statistics for groups of countries present "groups as they were at the time of reporting", which means that as multinational organizations such as the European Union expand, the statistics for trade with that group include the added country only beginning with the year it entered the group. The European Union was expanded from 15 to 25 nations on May 1, 2004, and data for that year are available for both the new and the old group; to provide historical perspective, they are both shown here, along with the historical data back to 1974 for the original group.

The *European Union* now includes Austria, Belgium, Bulgaria, Cyprus, Czech Republic, Denmark, Estonia, Finland, France, Germany, Greece, Hungary, Ireland, Italy, Latvia, Lithuania, Luxembourg, Malta, Netherlands, Poland, Portugal, Romania, Slovakia, Slovenia, Spain, Sweden, and the United Kingdom.

The *Euro area* now includes Austria, Belgium, Cyprus, Estonia, Finland, France, Germany, Greece, Ireland, Italy, Luxembourg, Malta, the Netherlands, Portugal, Slovakia, Slovenia, and Spain. See the notes and definitions to Table 13-8 for further information about the euro.

The *Asian Newly Industrialized Countries (NICS)* includes Hong Kong SAR, South Korea, Singapore, and Taiwan.

The *Organization of Petroleum Exporting Countries (OPEC)* currently consists of Algeria, Angola, Ecuador, Iran, Iraq, Kuwait, Libya, Nigeria, Qatar, Saudi Arabia, the United Arab Emirates, and Venezuela. Indonesia is no longer a member as of January 2009.

Notes on the data

U.S./Canada data exchange and substitution. The data for U.S. exports to Canada are derived from import data compiled by Canada. The use of Canada's import data to produce U.S. export data requires several alignments in order to compare the two series.

• *Coverage*: Canadian imports are based on country of origin. U.S. goods shipped from a third country are included, but U.S. exports exclude these foreign shipments. U.S. export coverage also excludes certain Canadian postal shipments.

• *Valuation*: Canadian imports are valued at their point of origin in the United States. However, U.S. exports are valued at the port of exit in the United States and include inland freight charges, making the U.S. export value slightly larger. Canada requires inland freight to be reported.

• *Reexports*: U.S. exports include re-exports of foreign goods. Again, the aggregate U.S. export figure is slightly larger.

• *Exchange Rate*: Average monthly exchange rates are applied to convert the published data to U.S. currency.

End-use categories and seasonal adjustment of trade in goods. Goods are initially classified under the Harmonized

System, which describes and measures the characteristics of goods traded. Combining trade into approximately 140 export and 140 import end-use categories makes it possible to examine goods according to their principal uses. These categories are used as the basis for computing the seasonal and working-day adjusted data. Adjusted data are then summed to the six end-use aggregates for publication.

The seasonal adjustment procedure is based on a model that estimates the monthly movements as percentages above or below the general level of each end-use commodity series (unlike other methods that redistribute the actual series values over the calendar year). Imports of petroleum and petroleum products are adjusted for the length of the month.

Data availability

Data are released monthly in a joint Census Bureau-BEA press release (FT-900), which is published about six weeks after the end of the month to which the data pertain. The release and historical data are available on the Census Bureau Web site at http://www.census.gov/foreign-trade/www/.

Revisions

Data for recent years are normally revised annually. In some cases, revisions to annual totals are not distributed to monthly data; therefore, monthly data may not sum to the revised total shown. Data on trade in services may be subject to extensive revision as part of BEA's annual revision of the international transactions accounts (ITAs), usually released in July.

References

Discussion of the impact of changes in methodology and incorporation of new data sources are found in the discussions of annual revisions of the ITAs in the July issues of BEA's *Survey of Current Business*. The most recent pertinent article is "Annual Revision of the U.S. International Accounts" (July 2012).

Table 7-17: Export and Import Price Indexes

SOURCE: U.S. DEPARTMENT OF LABOR, BUREAU OF LABOR STATISTICS

The International Price Program of the Bureau of Labor Statistics (BLS) collects price data for nonmilitary goods traded between the United States and the rest of the world and for selected transportation services in international markets. BLS aggregates the goods price data into export and import price indexes. Summary values of these price indexes for goods are presented in *Business Statistics*. For product and locality detail on international prices for both goods and services, see the *Handbook of U.S. Labor Statistics,* also published by Bernan Press.

Definitions

The *export* price index provides a measure of price change for all goods sold by U.S. residents (businesses and individuals located within the geographic boundaries of the United States, whether or not owned by U.S. citizens) to foreign buyers.

The *import* price index provides a measure of price change for goods purchased from other countries by U.S. residents.

Notes on the data

Published index series use a base year of 2000 = 100 whenever possible.

The product universe for both the import and export indexes includes raw materials, agricultural products, and manufactures. Price data are primarily collected by mail questionnaire, and directly from the exporter or importer in all but a few cases.

To the greatest extent possible, the data refer to prices at the U.S. border for exports and at either the foreign border or the U.S. border for imports. For nearly all products, the prices refer to transactions completed during the first week of the month and represent the actual price for which the product was bought or sold, including discounts, allowances, and rebates.

For the export price indexes, the preferred pricing basis is f.a.s. (free alongside ship) U.S. port of exportation. Where necessary, adjustments are made to reported prices to place them on this basis. An attempt is made to collect two prices for imports: f.o.b. (free on board) at the port of exportation and c.i.f. (cost, insurance, and freight) at the U.S. port of importation. Adjustments are made to account for changes in product characteristics in order to obtain a pure measure of price change.

The indexes are weighted indexes of the Laspeyres type. (See "General Notes" at the beginning of this volume for further explanation.) The values assigned to each weight category are based on trade value figures compiled by the Census Bureau. They are reweighted annually, with a two-year lag (as concurrent value data are not available) in revisions.

The merchandise price indexes are published using three different classification systems: the Harmonized System, the Bureau of Economic Analysis End-Use System, and the Standard International Trade Classification (SITC) system. The aggregate indexes shown here are from the End-Use System.

Data availability

Indexes are published monthly in a press release and a more detailed report. Indexes are published for detailed product categories, as well as for all commodities. Aggregate import indexes by country or region of origin also are available, as are indexes for selected categories of internationally traded services. Additional information is available from the Division of International Prices in the Bureau of Labor Statistics. Complete historical data are available on the BLS Web site at http://www.bls.gov.

References

The indexes are described in "BLS to Produce Monthly Indexes of Export and Import Prices," *Monthly Labor Review* (December 1988), and Chapter 15, "International Price Indexes," *BLS Handbook of Methods* Bulletin 2490 (April 1997).

CHAPTER 8: PRICES

Figure 8-1. Inflation Indicators, 1946–2012
(year-to-year percent change in price index)

- Figure 8-1 shows annual rates of change in the Consumer Price Index for All Urban Consumers (CPI-U), the most widely used measure of the general price level. It also shows changes in the chain-type price index for personal consumption expenditures (PCE) excluding food and energy, which provides one widely used measure of the "core" or underlying rate of inflation. (Tables 8-1, 8-4, and 1-6)

- Sharp swings in energy prices caused the all-items CPI to drop 0.4 percent in 2009—the first year-to-year deflation registered since 1955—and swing back to 3.2 percent inflation in 2011; it rose 2.1 percent in 2012. (Table 8-4)

- The core PCE inflation rate strips out volatile food and energy prices, in order to try to isolate the "underlying" rate of inflation, and is based on a concept slightly different from the CPI (see Notes and definitions for details). It shows a deceleration of inflation from 2.2 percent in 2005-2007 to about 1.3 percent in 2009 through 2011; it rose 1.9 percent in 2012. (Table 8-4)

- From 1965 to 2012, commodity prices in the CPI-U rose at an average rate of 3.5 percent per year, but services prices increased at an average annual rate of 5.0 percent. (Table 8-1A)

- The Producer Price Index (PPI) measures prices at the point of production, rather than at the consumer level. The most widely used product of the PPI system—the PPI for Finished Goods—only covers commodities, whereas the CPI covers both commodities and services. The Finished Goods PPI rose at a 3.7 percent annual rate from 1965 to 2012, very similar to the rate for commodities alone in the CPI. (Table 8-1A)

- The PPI data set also includes prices for intermediate materials, supplies, and components and crude materials for further processing. Indexes for all three stage-of-processing groups that exclude the more volatile and supply-dominated food and energy components are also available, and are followed more closely by analysts of general inflationary pressures. The price index for crude nonfood materials less energy is a sensitive leading indicator, not of aggregate prices, but of general business conditions. (Table 8-1A)

Table 8-1A. Summary Consumer and Producer Price Indexes: Recent Data

(Seasonally adjusted.)

| Year and month | Consumer Price Index, 1982–1984 = 100 | | | | | | | Producer Price Index, 1982 = 100 | | | | | |
| | Urban wage earners and clerical workers (CPI-W), all items | All urban consumers (CPI-U) | | | | | | Finished goods | | Intermediate materials, supplies, and components | | Crude materials for further processing | |
		All items	Food	Energy	All items less food and energy	Commod-ities	Services	Total	Less food and energy	Total	Less food and energy	Total	Crude nonfood less energy
1965	31.7	31.5	32.2	22.9	32.7	35.2	26.6	34.1	. . .	31.2	. . .	31.1	. . .
1966	32.6	32.4	33.8	23.3	33.5	36.1	27.6	35.2	. . .	32.0	. . .	33.1	. . .
1967	33.6	33.4	34.1	23.8	34.7	36.8	28.8	35.6	. . .	32.2	. . .	31.3	. . .
1968	35.0	34.8	35.3	24.2	36.3	38.1	30.3	36.6	. . .	33.0	. . .	31.8	. . .
1969	36.9	36.7	37.1	24.8	38.4	39.9	32.4	38.0	. . .	34.1	. . .	33.9	. . .
1970	39.0	38.8	39.2	25.5	40.8	41.7	35.0	39.3	. . .	35.4	. . .	35.2	. . .
1971	40.7	40.5	40.4	26.5	42.7	43.2	37.0	40.5	. . .	36.8	. . .	36.0	. . .
1972	42.1	41.8	42.1	27.2	44.0	44.5	38.4	41.8	. . .	38.2	. . .	39.9	. . .
1973	44.7	44.4	48.2	29.4	45.6	47.8	40.1	45.6	48.1	42.4	44.3	54.5	70.8
1974	49.6	49.3	55.1	38.1	49.4	53.5	43.8	52.6	53.6	52.5	54.0	61.4	83.3
1975	54.1	53.8	59.8	42.1	53.9	58.2	48.0	58.2	59.7	58.0	60.2	61.6	69.3
1976	57.2	56.9	61.6	45.1	57.4	60.7	52.0	60.8	63.1	60.9	63.8	63.4	80.2
1977	60.9	60.6	65.5	49.4	61.0	64.2	56.0	64.7	66.9	64.9	67.6	65.5	79.8
1978	65.6	65.2	72.0	52.5	65.5	68.8	60.8	69.8	71.9	69.5	72.5	73.4	87.8
1979	73.1	72.6	79.9	65.7	71.9	76.6	67.5	77.6	78.3	78.4	80.7	85.9	106.2
1980	82.9	82.4	86.8	86.0	80.8	86.0	77.9	88.0	87.1	90.3	90.3	95.3	113.1
1981	91.4	90.9	93.6	97.7	89.2	93.2	88.1	96.1	94.6	98.6	97.7	103.0	111.7
1982	96.9	96.5	97.4	99.2	95.8	97.0	96.0	100.0	100.0	100.0	100.0	100.0	100.0
1983	99.8	99.6	99.4	99.9	99.6	99.8	99.4	101.6	103.0	100.6	101.6	101.3	105.3
1984	103.3	103.9	103.2	100.9	104.6	103.2	104.6	103.7	105.5	103.1	104.7	103.5	111.7
1985	106.9	107.6	105.6	101.6	109.1	105.4	109.9	104.7	108.1	102.7	105.2	95.8	104.9
1986	108.6	109.6	109.0	88.2	113.5	104.4	115.4	103.2	110.6	99.1	104.9	87.7	103.1
1987	112.5	113.6	113.5	88.6	118.2	107.7	120.2	105.4	113.3	101.5	107.8	93.7	115.7
1988	117.0	118.3	118.2	89.3	123.4	111.5	125.7	108.0	117.0	107.1	115.2	96.0	133.0
1989	122.6	124.0	125.1	94.3	129.0	116.7	131.9	113.6	122.1	112.0	120.2	103.1	137.9
1990	129.0	130.7	132.4	102.1	135.5	122.8	139.2	119.2	126.6	114.5	120.9	108.9	136.3
1991	134.3	136.2	136.3	102.5	142.1	126.6	146.3	121.7	131.1	114.4	121.4	101.2	128.2
1992	138.2	140.3	137.9	103.0	147.3	129.1	152.0	123.2	134.2	114.7	122.0	100.4	128.4
1993	142.1	144.5	140.9	104.2	152.2	131.5	157.9	124.7	135.8	116.2	123.8	102.4	140.2
1994	145.6	148.2	144.3	104.6	156.5	133.8	163.1	125.5	137.1	118.5	127.1	101.8	156.2
1995	149.8	152.4	148.4	105.2	161.2	136.4	168.7	127.9	140.0	124.9	135.2	102.7	173.6
1996	154.1	156.9	153.3	110.1	165.6	139.9	174.1	131.3	142.0	125.7	134.0	113.8	155.8
1997	157.6	160.5	157.3	111.5	169.5	141.8	179.4	131.8	142.4	125.6	134.2	111.1	156.5
1998	159.7	163.0	160.7	102.9	173.4	141.9	184.2	130.7	143.7	123.0	133.5	96.8	142.1
1999	163.2	166.6	164.1	106.6	177.0	144.4	188.8	133.0	146.1	123.2	133.1	98.2	135.2
2000	168.9	172.2	167.8	124.6	181.3	149.2	195.3	138.0	148.0	129.2	136.6	120.6	145.2
2001	173.5	177.1	173.1	129.3	186.1	150.7	203.4	140.7	150.0	129.7	136.4	121.0	130.7
2002	175.9	179.9	176.2	121.7	190.5	149.7	209.8	138.9	150.2	127.8	135.8	108.1	135.7
2003	179.8	184.0	180.0	136.5	193.2	151.2	216.5	143.3	150.5	133.7	138.5	135.3	152.5
2004	184.5	188.9	186.2	151.4	196.6	154.7	222.8	148.5	152.7	142.6	146.5	159.0	193.0
2005	191.0	195.3	190.7	177.1	200.9	160.2	230.1	155.7	156.4	154.0	154.6	182.2	202.4
2006	197.1	201.6	195.2	196.9	205.9	164.0	238.9	160.4	158.7	164.0	163.8	184.8	244.5
2007	202.8	207.3	202.9	207.7	210.7	167.5	246.8	166.6	161.7	170.7	168.4	207.1	282.6
2008	211.1	215.3	214.1	236.7	215.6	174.8	255.5	177.1	167.2	188.3	180.9	251.8	324.4
2009	209.6	214.5	218.0	193.1	219.2	169.7	259.2	172.5	171.5	172.5	173.4	175.2	248.4
2010	214.0	218.1	219.6	211.4	221.3	174.6	261.3	179.8	173.6	183.4	180.8	212.2	329.1
2011	221.6	224.9	227.8	243.9	225.0	183.9	265.8	190.5	177.8	199.8	192.0	249.4	390.4
2012	226.2	229.6	233.8	246.1	229.8	187.6	271.4	194.2	182.4	200.7	192.6	241.3	369.6
2011													
January	217.3	221.1	222.5	229.2	222.7	178.8	263.1	185.6	175.5	191.6	186.6	239.8	382.0
February	218.2	221.9	223.6	233.0	223.1	179.8	263.7	187.6	176.0	194.7	188.8	247.9	390.4
March	219.6	223.1	225.2	241.1	223.4	181.9	264.2	188.9	176.5	197.3	190.2	246.8	384.5
April	220.5	223.9	226.0	245.3	223.8	183.0	264.6	190.2	177.0	200.0	192.5	256.8	394.4
May	221.5	224.7	226.9	248.7	224.4	184.2	265.1	191.0	177.2	201.7	193.6	252.1	390.5
June	221.7	225.1	227.4	247.0	224.9	184.4	265.4	190.9	177.7	202.3	193.8	254.0	397.5
July	222.3	225.6	228.5	247.3	225.4	185.0	266.0	192.0	178.5	203.2	194.4	254.4	401.2
August	222.9	226.2	229.6	247.4	225.9	185.6	266.5	191.4	178.7	201.8	194.2	250.5	403.7
September	223.6	226.8	230.6	250.6	226.1	186.2	267.0	193.1	179.2	202.8	194.3	252.8	402.5
October	223.5	226.7	231.0	246.7	226.5	185.8	267.4	192.5	179.5	200.5	193.1	246.9	384.6
November	223.8	227.0	231.2	246.5	226.9	186.0	267.8	193.3	179.7	200.8	192.3	252.6	377.7
December	223.8	227.1	231.7	243.7	227.2	185.7	268.3	193.1	180.2	200.0	191.2	247.8	376.3
2012													
January	224.3	227.6	232.2	243.5	227.7	186.1	268.9	193.3	181.0	199.9	191.9	249.3	384.2
February	225.0	228.3	232.3	248.6	227.9	187.2	269.1	193.9	181.4	200.9	193.2	250.2	382.6
March	225.8	229.0	232.7	251.4	228.4	188.1	269.6	194.0	181.7	202.9	194.6	246.1	385.2
April	225.6	229.0	233.1	246.8	228.9	187.5	270.2	193.6	181.9	201.8	194.8	236.7	379.2
May	225.2	228.6	233.2	239.6	229.4	186.4	270.7	192.4	182.1	200.2	194.2	232.1	372.1
June	225.4	228.9	233.6	238.2	229.9	186.3	271.3	192.5	182.4	198.8	192.2	225.3	356.6
July	225.3	228.8	233.8	235.2	230.1	186.0	271.4	193.2	183.3	198.1	191.5	231.7	354.7
August	226.7	230.0	234.2	246.1	230.2	188.0	271.8	195.2	183.3	200.0	191.3	242.7	363.3
September	228.1	231.2	234.4	255.9	230.6	189.7	272.5	197.2	183.4	202.3	192.1	246.4	366.5
October	228.4	231.6	234.8	256.1	231.0	189.9	273.1	196.9	183.4	202.2	192.2	246.5	359.8
November	227.6	231.1	235.4	247.3	231.3	188.2	273.7	196.0	183.6	200.5	192.1	247.3	365.6
December	227.6	231.1	235.7	245.3	231.5	187.7	274.3	195.8	183.9	200.6	192.4	250.4	370.4

. . . = Not available.

Table 8-1B. Summary Consumer and Producer Price Indexes: Historical, 1946–2010

(Seasonally adjusted.)

Year and month	Consumer Price Index, 1982–1984 = 100							Producer Price Index, 1982 = 100					
	Urban wage earners and clerical workers (CPI-W), all items	All urban consumers (CPI-U)						Finished goods		Intermediate materials, supplies, and components		Crude materials for further processing	
		All items	Food	Energy	All items less food and energy	Commodities	Services	Total	Less food and energy	Total	Less food and energy	Total	Crude nonfood less energy
1946	19.6	19.5	19.8	...	...	22.9	14.1	...	...	...	...	...	...
1947	22.5	22.3	24.1	...	...	27.6	14.7	26.4	...	23.3	...	31.7	...
1948	24.2	24.1	26.1	...	...	29.6	15.6	28.5	...	25.2	...	34.7	...
1949	24.0	23.8	25.0	...	...	28.8	16.4	27.7	...	24.2	...	30.1	...
1950	24.2	24.1	25.4	...	...	29.0	16.9	28.2	...	25.3	...	32.7	...
1951	26.1	26.0	28.2	...	...	31.6	17.8	30.8	...	28.4	...	37.6	...
1952	26.7	26.5	28.7	...	...	32.0	18.6	30.6	...	27.5	...	34.5	...
1953	26.9	26.7	28.3	...	...	31.9	19.4	30.3	...	27.7	...	31.9	...
1954	27.0	26.9	28.2	...	...	31.6	20.0	30.4	...	27.9	...	31.6	...
1955	26.9	26.8	27.8	...	...	31.3	20.4	30.5	...	28.4	...	30.4	...
1956	27.3	27.2	28.0	...	...	31.6	20.9	31.3	...	29.6	...	30.6	...
1957	28.3	28.1	28.9	21.5	28.9	32.6	21.8	32.5	...	30.3	...	31.2	...
1958	29.1	28.9	30.2	21.5	29.6	33.3	22.6	33.2	...	30.4	...	31.9	...
1959	29.3	29.1	29.7	21.9	30.2	33.3	23.3	33.1	...	30.8	...	31.1	...
1960	29.8	29.6	30.0	22.4	30.6	33.6	24.1	33.4	...	30.8	...	30.4	...
1961	30.1	29.9	30.4	22.5	31.0	33.8	24.5	33.4	...	30.6	...	30.2	...
1962	30.4	30.2	30.6	22.6	31.4	34.1	25.0	33.5	...	30.6	...	30.5	...
1963	30.8	30.6	31.1	22.6	31.8	34.4	25.5	33.4	...	30.7	...	29.9	...
1964	31.2	31.0	31.5	22.5	32.3	34.8	26.0	33.5	...	30.8	...	29.6	...
1947													
January	21.6	21.5	22.8	...	...	...	...	...	...	...	...	...	...
February	21.7	21.6	23.1	...	...	...	...	...	...	...	...	...	...
March	22.1	22.0	23.8	...	...	...	...	...	...	...	...	...	...
April	22.1	22.0	23.5	...	...	...	...	26.0	...	23.1	...	30.7	...
May	22.1	22.0	23.4	...	...	...	...	26.1	...	23.0	...	30.4	...
June	22.2	22.1	23.5	...	...	...	...	26.2	...	23.2	...	30.6	...
July	22.4	22.2	23.8	...	...	...	...	26.2	...	23.2	...	31.0	...
August	22.5	22.4	24.1	...	...	...	...	26.3	...	23.3	...	31.6	...
September	23.0	22.8	24.8	...	...	...	...	26.7	...	23.7	...	32.4	...
October	23.0	22.9	24.9	...	...	...	...	26.8	...	24.0	...	33.7	...
November	23.2	23.1	25.2	...	...	...	...	27.1	...	24.3	...	33.9	...
December	23.5	23.4	25.7	...	...	...	...	27.7	...	24.5	...	35.3	...
1948													
January	23.8	23.7	26.1	...	...	...	...	28.1	...	25.0	...	36.2	...
February	23.8	23.7	25.9	...	...	...	...	27.9	...	24.7	...	34.4	...
March	23.6	23.5	25.3	...	...	...	...	28.0	...	24.8	...	33.5	...
April	24.0	23.8	26.0	...	...	...	...	28.1	...	25.1	...	34.2	...
May	24.1	24.0	26.3	...	...	...	...	28.4	...	25.1	...	35.3	...
June	24.3	24.2	26.5	...	...	...	...	28.6	...	25.4	...	36.2	...
July	24.5	24.4	26.7	...	...	...	...	28.8	...	25.4	...	36.1	...
August	24.6	24.4	26.5	...	...	...	...	28.9	...	25.5	...	35.5	...
September	24.5	24.4	26.3	...	...	...	...	28.8	...	25.5	...	34.9	...
October	24.4	24.3	26.1	...	...	...	...	28.7	...	25.5	...	33.8	...
November	24.3	24.2	25.7	...	...	...	...	28.5	...	25.4	...	33.5	...
December	24.2	24.1	25.5	...	...	...	...	28.5	...	25.2	...	33.0	...
1949													
January	24.2	24.0	25.4	...	...	...	...	28.3	...	25.2	...	32.0	...
February	24.1	23.9	25.3	...	...	...	...	28.0	...	24.8	...	30.9	...
March	24.0	23.9	25.3	...	...	...	...	28.0	...	24.7	...	30.8	...
April	24.1	23.9	25.3	...	...	...	...	27.9	...	24.5	...	30.2	...
May	24.0	23.9	25.2	...	...	...	...	27.8	...	24.3	...	30.1	...
June	24.1	23.9	25.3	...	...	...	...	27.7	...	24.1	...	29.7	...
July	23.8	23.7	24.8	...	...	...	...	27.5	...	24.1	...	29.2	...
August	23.8	23.7	24.8	...	...	...	...	27.4	...	23.9	...	29.2	...
September	23.9	23.8	25.0	...	...	...	...	27.4	...	23.9	...	29.5	...
October	23.8	23.7	24.8	...	...	...	...	27.3	...	23.8	...	29.5	...
November	23.8	23.7	24.8	...	...	...	...	27.2	...	23.7	...	29.6	...
December	23.8	23.6	24.5	...	...	...	...	27.2	...	23.8	...	29.6	...
1950													
January	23.6	23.5	24.3	...	...	...	...	27.2	...	23.8	...	29.6	...
February	23.7	23.6	24.7	...	...	...	...	27.2	...	23.9	...	30.5	...
March	23.8	23.6	24.6	...	...	...	...	27.3	...	24.1	...	30.3	...
April	23.8	23.7	24.6	...	...	...	...	27.3	...	24.2	...	30.5	...
May	23.9	23.8	24.8	...	...	...	...	27.5	...	24.6	...	31.6	...
June	24.0	23.9	25.1	...	...	...	...	27.6	...	24.7	...	32.1	...
July	24.2	24.1	25.6	...	...	...	...	28.0	...	25.3	...	33.3	...
August	24.3	24.2	25.8	...	...	...	...	28.6	...	25.6	...	34.0	...
September	24.5	24.3	25.8	...	...	...	...	28.9	...	26.2	...	34.5	...
October	24.6	24.5	26.0	...	...	...	...	29.0	...	26.7	...	34.5	...
November	24.7	24.6	26.1	...	...	...	...	29.4	...	26.9	...	35.4	...
December	25.1	25.0	26.9	...	...	...	...	30.0	...	27.8	...	36.7	...

. . . = Not available.

Table 8-1B. Summary Consumer and Producer Price Indexes: Historical, 1946–2010—*Continued*

(Seasonally adjusted.)

Year and month	Urban wage earners and clerical workers (CPI-W), all items	All items	Food	Energy	All items less food and energy	Commodit-ies	Services	Total	Less food and energy	Total	Less food and energy	Total	Crude nonfood less energy
1951													
January	25.5	25.4	27.6	...	...	...	...	30.5	...	28.5	...	38.2	...
February	26.0	25.8	28.5	...	...	...	...	30.8	...	28.7	...	39.6	...
March	26.0	25.9	28.4	...	...	...	...	30.9	...	28.8	...	39.1	...
April	26.1	25.9	28.2	...	...	...	...	30.9	...	28.8	...	39.1	...
May	26.1	26.0	28.3	...	...	...	...	31.1	...	28.8	...	38.4	...
June	26.1	25.9	28.0	...	...	...	...	31.0	...	28.7	...	38.1	...
July	26.1	25.9	27.9	...	...	...	...	30.8	...	28.4	...	36.8	...
August	26.0	25.9	27.8	...	...	...	...	30.7	...	28.0	...	36.2	...
September	26.2	26.0	27.9	...	...	...	...	30.6	...	28.0	...	35.9	...
October	26.3	26.2	28.4	...	...	...	...	30.8	...	27.9	...	36.7	...
November	26.5	26.3	28.6	...	...	...	...	30.9	...	27.9	...	36.4	...
December	26.6	26.5	28.9	...	...	...	...	30.9	...	27.8	...	36.6	...
1952													
January	26.6	26.5	28.9	...	...	...	...	30.8	...	27.8	...	35.8	...
February	26.6	26.4	28.6	...	...	...	...	30.7	...	27.7	...	35.5	...
March	26.5	26.4	28.5	...	...	...	...	30.9	...	27.6	...	35.0	...
April	26.6	26.5	28.7	...	...	...	...	30.7	...	27.5	...	34.9	...
May	26.6	26.5	28.7	...	...	...	...	30.7	...	27.5	...	34.8	...
June	26.7	26.5	28.6	...	...	...	...	30.7	...	27.6	...	34.6	...
July	26.8	26.7	28.9	...	...	...	...	30.8	...	27.5	...	34.6	...
August	26.8	26.7	28.9	...	...	...	...	30.7	...	27.6	...	34.7	...
September	26.8	26.6	28.7	...	...	...	...	30.6	...	27.6	...	33.8	...
October	26.8	26.7	28.8	...	...	...	...	30.5	...	27.5	...	33.8	...
November	26.8	26.7	28.8	...	...	...	...	30.4	...	27.4	...	33.7	...
December	26.9	26.7	28.6	...	...	...	...	30.2	...	27.3	...	32.9	...
1953													
January	26.8	26.6	28.4	...	...	...	...	30.3	...	27.4	...	32.5	...
February	26.7	26.6	28.3	...	...	...	...	30.2	...	27.4	...	32.4	...
March	26.8	26.6	28.3	...	...	...	...	30.3	...	27.5	...	32.4	...
April	26.8	26.7	28.1	...	...	...	...	30.2	...	27.5	...	31.6	...
May	26.9	26.7	28.2	...	...	...	...	30.3	...	27.6	...	31.8	...
June	26.9	26.8	28.4	...	...	...	...	30.4	...	27.7	...	31.4	...
July	26.9	26.8	28.2	...	...	...	...	30.5	...	28.0	...	32.3	...
August	27.0	26.9	28.3	...	...	...	...	30.4	...	27.9	...	31.8	...
September	27.0	26.9	28.4	...	...	...	...	30.4	...	27.9	...	32.0	...
October	27.1	27.0	28.4	...	...	...	...	30.4	...	27.9	...	31.4	...
November	27.0	26.9	28.1	...	...	...	...	30.3	...	27.8	...	31.2	...
December	27.0	26.9	28.3	...	...	...	...	30.4	...	27.8	...	31.7	...
1954													
January	27.1	26.9	28.5	...	...	...	...	30.5	...	27.9	...	32.0	...
February	27.1	27.0	28.5	...	...	...	...	30.4	...	27.9	...	32.0	...
March	27.1	26.9	28.4	...	...	...	...	30.4	...	27.9	...	32.1	...
April	27.0	26.9	28.4	...	...	...	...	30.6	...	27.9	...	32.2	...
May	27.1	26.9	28.4	...	...	...	...	30.6	...	27.9	...	32.1	...
June	27.1	26.9	28.4	...	...	...	...	30.4	...	27.8	...	31.5	...
July	27.0	26.9	28.4	...	...	...	...	30.5	...	27.9	...	31.4	...
August	27.0	26.9	28.3	...	...	...	...	30.4	...	27.9	...	31.3	...
September	27.0	26.8	28.0	...	...	...	...	30.3	...	27.8	...	31.5	...
October	26.9	26.7	27.9	...	...	...	...	30.2	...	27.8	...	31.2	...
November	26.9	26.8	27.9	...	...	...	...	30.3	...	27.9	...	31.4	...
December	26.9	26.8	27.8	...	...	...	...	30.3	...	27.9	...	30.8	...
1955													
January	26.9	26.8	27.8	...	...	...	...	30.4	...	27.9	...	31.1	...
February	27.0	26.8	28.0	...	...	...	...	30.5	...	28.0	...	31.0	...
March	26.9	26.8	28.0	...	...	...	...	30.3	...	28.0	...	30.7	...
April	26.9	26.8	28.0	...	...	...	...	30.4	...	28.1	...	31.0	...
May	26.9	26.8	27.9	...	...	...	...	30.4	...	28.1	...	30.2	...
June	26.9	26.7	27.7	...	...	...	...	30.5	...	28.2	...	30.7	...
July	26.9	26.8	27.7	...	...	...	...	30.4	...	28.4	...	30.4	...
August	26.9	26.7	27.6	...	...	...	...	30.4	...	28.5	...	30.1	...
September	27.0	26.9	27.8	...	...	...	...	30.5	...	28.8	...	30.4	...
October	27.0	26.8	27.7	...	...	...	...	30.6	...	28.9	...	30.4	...
November	27.0	26.9	27.6	...	...	...	...	30.6	...	28.9	...	29.4	...
December	27.0	26.9	27.6	...	...	...	...	30.7	...	29.0	...	29.5	...
1956													
January	27.0	26.8	27.5	...	...	31.2	20.7	30.7	...	29.1	...	29.4	...
February	27.0	26.9	27.5	...	...	31.1	20.7	30.8	...	29.2	...	29.9	...
March	27.1	26.9	27.5	...	...	31.2	20.7	30.9	...	29.4	...	29.8	...
April	27.1	26.9	27.6	...	...	31.3	20.8	31.0	...	29.5	...	30.3	...
May	27.2	27.0	27.8	...	...	31.4	20.8	31.2	...	29.6	...	30.7	...
June	27.3	27.2	28.1	...	...	31.5	20.9	31.4	...	29.6	...	30.5	...
July	27.4	27.3	28.4	...	...	31.8	20.9	31.3	...	29.4	...	30.5	...
August	27.5	27.3	28.2	...	...	31.7	21.0	31.4	...	29.7	...	31.0	...
September	27.5	27.4	28.2	...	...	31.8	21.1	31.6	...	29.8	...	31.0	...
October	27.7	27.5	28.3	...	...	32.0	21.1	31.8	...	30.0	...	31.0	...
November	27.7	27.5	28.4	...	...	32.0	21.2	31.9	...	30.0	...	31.1	...
December	27.8	27.6	28.5	...	...	32.1	21.3	31.9	...	30.1	...	31.7	...

. . . = Not available.

Table 8-1B. Summary Consumer and Producer Price Indexes: Historical, 1946–2010—*Continued*

(Seasonally adjusted.)

Year and month	Urban wage earners and clerical workers (CPI-W), all items	Consumer Price Index, 1982–1984 = 100						Producer Price Index, 1982 = 100					
		All urban consumers (CPI-U)						Finished goods		Intermediate materials, supplies, and components		Crude materials for further processing	
		All items	Food	Energy	All items less food and energy	Commodities	Services	Total	Less food and energy	Total	Less food and energy	Total	Crude nonfood less energy
1957													
January	27.8	27.7	28.4	21.3	28.5	32.1	21.4	32.1	. . .	30.3	. . .	31.3	. . .
February	28.0	27.8	28.7	21.4	28.6	32.3	21.4	32.2	. . .	30.3	. . .	31.0	. . .
March	28.0	27.9	28.6	21.5	28.7	32.3	21.6	32.1	. . .	30.3	. . .	30.9	. . .
April	28.1	27.9	28.6	21.6	28.8	32.4	21.6	32.3	. . .	30.2	. . .	30.8	. . .
May	28.2	28.0	28.7	21.6	28.8	32.4	21.7	32.3	. . .	30.2	. . .	30.7	. . .
June	28.3	28.1	28.9	21.6	28.9	32.5	21.8	32.5	. . .	30.3	. . .	31.5	. . .
July	28.4	28.2	29.1	21.5	29.0	32.6	21.8	32.6	. . .	30.3	. . .	32.0	. . .
August	28.4	28.3	29.4	21.4	29.0	32.8	21.9	32.6	. . .	30.4	. . .	32.0	. . .
September	28.5	28.3	29.2	21.4	29.1	32.8	22.0	32.6	. . .	30.4	. . .	31.2	. . .
October	28.5	28.3	29.2	21.4	29.2	32.7	22.1	32.7	. . .	30.3	. . .	31.0	. . .
November	28.6	28.4	29.2	21.5	29.3	32.8	22.2	32.9	. . .	30.4	. . .	31.1	. . .
December	28.6	28.5	29.2	21.5	29.3	32.9	22.2	33.0	. . .	30.4	. . .	31.5	. . .
1958													
January	28.8	28.6	29.8	21.6	29.3	33.1	22.3	33.2	. . .	30.4	. . .	31.4	. . .
February	28.9	28.7	29.9	21.3	29.4	33.2	22.4	33.2	. . .	30.3	. . .	31.9	. . .
March	29.0	28.9	30.5	21.4	29.5	33.4	22.4	33.4	. . .	30.3	. . .	32.3	. . .
April	29.1	28.9	30.6	21.4	29.5	33.5	22.5	33.2	. . .	30.2	. . .	31.8	. . .
May	29.1	28.9	30.5	21.5	29.5	33.5	22.6	33.2	. . .	30.3	. . .	32.4	. . .
June	29.1	28.9	30.3	21.5	29.6	33.4	22.6	33.3	. . .	30.3	. . .	32.0	. . .
July	29.1	28.9	30.2	21.6	29.6	33.3	22.7	33.2	. . .	30.3	. . .	32.1	. . .
August	29.1	28.9	30.1	21.7	29.6	33.3	22.7	33.2	. . .	30.4	. . .	31.9	. . .
September	29.1	28.9	30.0	21.7	29.7	33.3	22.8	33.2	. . .	30.4	. . .	31.6	. . .
October	29.1	28.9	30.0	21.7	29.7	33.2	22.8	33.2	. . .	30.4	. . .	31.9	. . .
November	29.1	29.0	30.0	21.4	29.8	33.3	22.8	33.2	. . .	30.5	. . .	32.1	. . .
December	29.1	29.0	29.9	21.4	29.9	33.3	22.8	33.1	. . .	30.6	. . .	31.6	. . .
1959													
January	29.2	29.0	30.0	21.4	29.9	33.3	22.9	33.1	. . .	30.6	. . .	31.6	. . .
February	29.2	29.0	29.8	21.6	29.9	33.3	23.0	33.2	. . .	30.7	. . .	31.4	. . .
March	29.1	29.0	29.7	21.7	30.0	33.2	23.0	33.2	. . .	30.7	. . .	31.5	. . .
April	29.1	29.0	29.5	21.8	30.0	33.2	23.1	33.2	. . .	30.7	. . .	31.7	. . .
May	29.2	29.0	29.5	21.8	30.1	33.3	23.2	33.3	. . .	30.9	. . .	31.5	. . .
June	29.3	29.1	29.7	21.9	30.2	33.3	23.2	33.2	. . .	30.9	. . .	31.3	. . .
July	29.3	29.2	29.6	21.8	30.2	33.3	23.3	33.1	. . .	30.8	. . .	31.0	. . .
August	29.3	29.2	29.6	21.9	30.2	33.3	23.4	33.0	. . .	30.8	. . .	30.7	. . .
September	29.4	29.3	29.7	21.9	30.3	33.5	23.5	33.4	. . .	30.8	. . .	30.9	. . .
October	29.5	29.4	29.7	22.2	30.4	33.5	23.6	33.1	. . .	30.8	. . .	30.7	. . .
November	29.5	29.4	29.7	22.2	30.4	33.5	23.6	33.0	. . .	30.9	. . .	30.5	. . .
December	29.6	29.4	29.6	22.3	30.5	33.5	23.7	33.0	. . .	30.9	. . .	30.3	. . .
1960													
January	29.5	29.4	29.6	22.3	30.5	33.5	23.7	33.1	. . .	30.8	. . .	30.4	. . .
February	29.6	29.4	29.5	22.2	30.6	33.4	23.8	33.1	. . .	30.9	. . .	30.4	. . .
March	29.6	29.4	29.6	22.3	30.6	33.5	23.9	33.4	. . .	30.9	. . .	30.7	. . .
April	29.7	29.5	30.0	22.4	30.6	33.6	23.9	33.4	. . .	30.8	. . .	30.8	. . .
May	29.7	29.6	30.0	22.3	30.6	33.6	24.0	33.4	. . .	30.8	. . .	30.8	. . .
June	29.8	29.6	30.0	22.4	30.7	33.6	24.0	33.4	. . .	30.9	. . .	30.4	. . .
July	29.7	29.6	29.9	22.5	30.6	33.5	24.1	33.5	. . .	30.8	. . .	30.4	. . .
August	29.8	29.6	30.0	22.5	30.6	33.6	24.1	33.4	. . .	30.8	. . .	29.8	. . .
September	29.8	29.6	30.1	22.6	30.6	33.6	24.2	33.4	. . .	30.8	. . .	30.0	. . .
October	29.9	29.8	30.3	22.5	30.8	33.7	24.2	33.7	. . .	30.8	. . .	30.2	. . .
November	30.0	29.8	30.5	22.7	30.8	33.8	24.3	33.7	. . .	30.7	. . .	30.2	. . .
December	30.0	29.8	30.5	22.6	30.7	33.9	24.3	33.6	. . .	30.7	. . .	30.3	. . .
1961													
January	30.0	29.8	30.5	22.7	30.8	33.8	24.4	33.6	. . .	30.6	. . .	30.4	. . .
February	30.0	29.8	30.5	22.6	30.8	33.8	24.4	33.7	. . .	30.7	. . .	30.5	. . .
March	30.0	29.8	30.5	22.6	30.9	33.8	24.4	33.6	. . .	30.8	. . .	30.3	. . .
April	30.0	29.8	30.4	22.2	30.9	33.8	24.5	33.4	. . .	30.7	. . .	30.2	. . .
May	30.0	29.8	30.3	22.4	30.9	33.8	24.5	33.3	. . .	30.6	. . .	29.9	. . .
June	30.0	29.8	30.2	22.5	31.0	33.8	24.5	33.3	. . .	30.5	. . .	29.5	. . .
July	30.1	29.9	30.3	22.5	31.0	33.9	24.5	33.3	. . .	30.5	. . .	29.7	. . .
August	30.1	29.9	30.3	22.5	31.1	33.9	24.6	33.4	. . .	30.5	. . .	30.5	. . .
September	30.2	30.0	30.3	22.6	31.1	33.9	24.6	33.3	. . .	30.5	. . .	30.3	. . .
October	30.2	30.0	30.3	22.4	31.1	33.9	24.7	33.3	. . .	30.4	. . .	30.3	. . .
November	30.2	30.0	30.3	22.5	31.2	33.8	24.7	33.4	. . .	30.5	. . .	30.2	. . .
December	30.2	30.0	30.3	22.4	31.2	33.9	24.8	33.4	. . .	30.6	. . .	30.6	. . .
1962													
January	30.2	30.0	30.4	22.4	31.2	33.9	24.8	33.5	. . .	30.5	. . .	30.6	. . .
February	30.3	30.1	30.5	22.6	31.2	34.0	24.8	33.6	. . .	30.6	. . .	30.5	. . .
March	30.4	30.2	30.6	22.4	31.3	34.0	24.9	33.5	. . .	30.6	. . .	30.5	. . .
April	30.4	30.2	30.7	22.7	31.3	34.1	24.9	33.5	. . .	30.6	. . .	30.1	. . .
May	30.4	30.2	30.6	22.7	31.4	34.1	25.0	33.4	. . .	30.6	. . .	30.1	. . .
June	30.4	30.2	30.5	22.5	31.4	34.1	25.0	33.4	. . .	30.6	. . .	29.9	. . .
July	30.4	30.2	30.4	22.3	31.4	34.0	25.1	33.4	. . .	30.6	. . .	30.2	. . .
August	30.5	30.3	30.6	22.4	31.5	34.1	25.1	33.5	. . .	30.6	. . .	30.5	. . .
September	30.6	30.4	30.9	22.8	31.5	34.3	25.1	33.8	. . .	30.6	. . .	31.2	. . .
October	30.6	30.4	30.8	22.7	31.5	34.2	25.1	33.6	. . .	30.5	. . .	30.8	. . .
November	30.6	30.4	30.9	22.7	31.5	34.3	25.2	33.6	. . .	30.5	. . .	31.0	. . .
December	30.6	30.4	30.7	22.8	31.6	34.2	25.2	33.5	. . .	30.5	. . .	30.6	. . .

. . . = Not available.

Table 8-1B. Summary Consumer and Producer Price Indexes: Historical, 1946–2010—*Continued*

(Seasonally adjusted.)

Year and month	Urban wage earners and clerical workers (CPI-W), all items	Consumer Price Index, 1982–1984 = 100						Producer Price Index, 1982 = 100					
		All urban consumers (CPI-U)						Finished goods		Intermediate materials, supplies, and components		Crude materials for further processing	
		All items	Food	Energy	All items less food and energy	Commodities	Services	Total	Less food and energy	Total	Less food and energy	Total	Crude nonfood less energy
1963													
January	30.6	30.4	31.0	22.8	31.5	34.3	25.3	33.4	...	30.5	...	30.3	...
February	30.7	30.5	31.1	22.7	31.6	34.3	25.3	33.4	...	30.5	...	30.0	...
March	30.7	30.5	31.0	22.7	31.7	34.3	25.3	33.3	...	30.5	...	29.6	...
April	30.7	30.5	30.9	22.6	31.7	34.3	25.4	33.3	...	30.5	...	29.8	...
May	30.7	30.5	30.9	22.6	31.7	34.3	25.4	33.4	...	30.7	...	29.6	...
June	30.8	30.6	31.0	22.5	31.8	34.4	25.5	33.5	...	30.7	...	29.9	...
July	30.9	30.7	31.2	22.7	31.8	34.5	25.5	33.4	...	30.7	...	30.0	...
August	30.9	30.8	31.2	22.6	31.9	34.6	25.6	33.4	...	30.7	...	29.9	...
September	30.9	30.7	31.1	22.5	31.9	34.5	25.6	33.4	...	30.7	...	29.8	...
October	30.9	30.8	31.0	22.7	32.0	34.5	25.6	33.5	...	30.8	...	29.9	...
November	31.0	30.8	31.2	22.6	32.0	34.6	25.7	33.5	...	30.8	...	30.2	...
December	31.1	30.9	31.3	22.6	32.1	34.7	25.8	33.4	...	30.8	...	29.4	...
1964													
January	31.1	30.9	31.4	22.8	32.2	34.7	25.8	33.5	...	30.8	...	29.8	...
February	31.1	30.9	31.4	22.2	32.2	34.7	25.8	33.5	...	30.8	...	29.4	...
March	31.1	30.9	31.4	22.6	32.2	34.7	25.8	33.4	...	30.8	...	29.5	...
April	31.1	31.0	31.4	22.5	32.2	34.7	25.9	33.5	...	30.8	...	29.5	...
May	31.2	31.0	31.4	22.5	32.2	34.7	25.9	33.5	...	30.7	...	29.4	...
June	31.2	31.0	31.4	22.6	32.3	34.7	26.0	33.5	...	30.6	...	29.0	...
July	31.2	31.0	31.5	22.5	32.3	34.7	26.0	33.5	...	30.7	...	29.2	...
August	31.2	31.1	31.4	22.6	32.3	34.7	26.0	33.6	...	30.6	...	29.4	...
September	31.3	31.1	31.6	22.5	32.3	34.8	26.0	33.6	...	30.7	...	30.1	...
October	31.3	31.1	31.6	22.5	32.4	34.8	26.1	33.6	...	30.8	...	29.8	...
November	31.4	31.2	31.7	22.5	32.5	34.9	26.2	33.6	...	30.8	...	29.9	...
December	31.4	31.3	31.7	22.6	32.5	35.0	26.2	33.6	...	30.9	...	29.8	...
1965													
January	31.5	31.3	31.6	22.8	32.6	35.0	26.3	33.6	...	30.9	...	29.5	...
February	31.5	31.3	31.5	22.7	32.6	34.9	26.4	33.7	...	30.9	...	29.9	...
March	31.5	31.3	31.7	22.6	32.6	35.0	26.4	33.7	...	31.0	...	30.0	...
April	31.6	31.4	31.8	22.9	32.7	35.0	26.5	34.0	...	31.1	...	30.4	...
May	31.7	31.5	32.1	23.0	32.7	35.1	26.5	34.1	...	31.1	...	30.8	...
June	31.8	31.6	32.6	23.1	32.7	35.3	26.5	34.2	...	31.2	...	31.6	...
July	31.8	31.6	32.5	23.0	32.7	35.3	26.6	34.1	...	31.2	...	31.2	...
August	31.7	31.6	32.4	23.0	32.7	35.2	26.6	34.2	...	31.3	...	31.5	...
September	31.8	31.6	32.3	23.1	32.8	35.2	26.7	34.3	...	31.3	...	31.4	...
October	31.8	31.7	32.5	23.0	32.8	35.3	26.8	34.4	...	31.3	...	31.8	...
November	31.9	31.8	32.6	23.1	32.9	35.4	26.9	34.5	...	31.4	...	32.1	...
December	32.0	31.9	32.8	23.1	33.0	35.5	26.9	34.7	...	31.4	...	32.7	...
1966													
January	32.1	31.9	33.0	23.1	33.0	35.6	27.0	34.7	...	31.4	...	33.1	...
February	32.3	32.1	33.5	23.2	33.1	35.8	27.0	35.0	...	31.6	...	33.7	...
March	32.4	32.2	33.8	23.2	33.1	35.9	27.1	35.0	...	31.7	...	33.5	...
April	32.5	32.3	33.8	23.2	33.3	36.0	27.3	35.1	...	31.8	...	33.3	...
May	32.5	32.4	33.7	23.2	33.4	36.0	27.4	35.1	...	32.0	...	33.0	...
June	32.6	32.4	33.7	23.3	33.5	36.0	27.5	34.9	...	32.0	...	33.0	...
July	32.6	32.5	33.5	23.4	33.6	36.1	27.7	35.1	...	32.2	...	33.4	...
August	32.8	32.7	34.0	23.3	33.7	36.2	27.7	35.4	...	32.3	...	33.5	...
September	32.9	32.8	34.1	23.4	33.8	36.4	27.9	35.6	...	32.2	...	33.4	...
October	33.0	32.9	34.2	23.4	34.0	36.4	28.0	35.5	...	32.1	...	32.9	...
November	33.1	32.9	34.1	23.5	34.0	36.4	28.2	35.5	...	32.2	...	32.3	...
December	33.1	32.9	34.0	23.5	34.1	36.4	28.2	35.4	...	32.2	...	32.1	...
1967													
January	33.1	32.9	33.9	23.6	34.2	36.4	28.3	35.4	...	32.2	...	32.2	...
February	33.2	33.0	33.8	23.7	34.2	36.4	28.4	35.3	...	32.1	...	31.5	...
March	33.2	33.0	33.8	23.6	34.3	36.4	28.5	35.3	...	32.1	...	31.1	...
April	33.3	33.1	33.7	23.9	34.4	36.4	28.6	35.3	...	32.1	...	30.7	...
May	33.3	33.1	33.7	23.9	34.5	36.5	28.6	35.4	...	32.1	...	31.1	...
June	33.5	33.3	34.0	23.8	34.6	36.6	28.8	35.7	...	32.2	...	31.4	...
July	33.6	33.4	34.1	23.8	34.7	36.8	28.8	35.7	...	32.2	...	31.3	...
August	33.7	33.5	34.3	23.9	34.9	37.0	28.9	35.8	...	32.2	...	31.3	...
September	33.8	33.6	34.3	24.0	35.0	37.0	29.0	35.8	...	32.3	...	31.2	...
October	33.9	33.7	34.4	23.9	35.1	37.1	29.2	35.9	...	32.3	...	31.3	...
November	34.0	33.9	34.5	24.0	35.2	37.2	29.2	35.9	...	32.4	...	31.1	...
December	34.1	34.0	34.6	23.9	35.4	37.4	29.4	36.0	...	32.6	...	31.5	...
1968													
January	34.3	34.1	34.6	24.0	35.5	37.5	29.5	36.1	...	32.6	...	31.4	...
February	34.4	34.2	34.8	24.1	35.7	37.6	29.6	36.2	...	32.7	...	31.5	...
March	34.5	34.3	34.9	24.1	35.8	37.7	29.8	36.3	...	32.8	...	31.6	...
April	34.6	34.4	35.0	24.0	35.9	37.8	29.9	36.5	...	32.8	...	31.7	...
May	34.7	34.5	35.1	24.1	36.0	37.8	30.0	36.5	...	32.8	...	31.5	...
June	34.9	34.7	35.2	24.2	36.2	38.0	30.2	36.6	...	32.9	...	31.3	...
July	35.0	34.9	35.3	24.2	36.4	38.1	30.4	36.7	...	33.0	...	31.6	...
August	35.2	35.0	35.4	24.3	36.5	38.3	30.6	36.8	...	33.0	...	31.7	...
September	35.3	35.1	35.6	24.3	36.7	38.4	30.7	37.0	...	33.1	...	31.9	...
October	35.5	35.3	35.9	24.3	36.9	38.6	30.9	37.0	...	33.2	...	32.1	...
November	35.6	35.4	35.9	24.4	37.1	38.7	31.0	37.1	...	33.2	...	32.8	...
December	35.8	35.6	36.0	24.3	37.2	38.8	31.2	37.1	...	33.4	...	32.4	...

. . . = Not available.

Table 8-1B. Summary Consumer and Producer Price Indexes: Historical, 1946–2010—*Continued*

(Seasonally adjusted.)

Year and month	Urban wage earners and clerical workers (CPI-W), all items	Consumer Price Index, 1982–1984 = 100						Producer Price Index, 1982 = 100					
		All urban consumers (CPI-U)						Finished goods		Intermediate materials, supplies, and components		Crude materials for further processing	
		All items	Food	Energy	All items less food and energy	Commodities	Services	Total	Less food and energy	Total	Less food and energy	Total	Crude nonfood less energy
1969													
January	35.9	35.7	36.1	24.4	37.3	38.9	31.4	37.2	. . .	33.6	. . .	32.6	. . .
February	36.0	35.8	36.1	24.4	37.6	39.0	31.5	37.2	. . .	33.7	. . .	32.3	. . .
March	36.3	36.1	36.2	24.7	37.8	39.3	31.8	37.4	. . .	33.9	. . .	32.7	. . .
April	36.5	36.3	36.4	24.9	38.1	39.4	32.0	37.6	. . .	33.8	. . .	33.1	. . .
May	36.6	36.4	36.6	24.8	38.1	39.5	32.2	37.8	. . .	33.9	. . .	34.0	. . .
June	36.8	36.6	37.0	25.0	38.3	39.8	32.3	38.0	. . .	34.0	. . .	34.5	. . .
July	37.0	36.8	37.3	24.9	38.5	39.9	32.5	38.1	. . .	34.0	. . .	34.1	. . .
August	37.1	36.9	37.5	24.9	38.7	40.1	32.7	38.2	. . .	34.2	. . .	34.4	. . .
September	37.3	37.1	37.7	25.0	38.9	40.2	33.0	38.3	. . .	34.2	. . .	34.4	. . .
October	37.5	37.3	37.8	25.0	39.1	40.4	33.1	38.5	. . .	34.4	. . .	34.8	. . .
November	37.7	37.5	38.2	25.0	39.2	40.6	33.3	38.8	. . .	34.6	. . .	35.2	. . .
December	37.9	37.7	38.6	25.1	39.4	40.8	33.5	38.9	. . .	34.7	. . .	35.1	. . .
1970													
January	38.1	37.9	38.7	25.1	39.6	41.0	33.8	39.1	. . .	35.0	. . .	35.1	. . .
February	38.3	38.1	38.9	25.1	39.8	41.2	34.0	39.0	. . .	35.0	. . .	35.2	. . .
March	38.5	38.3	38.9	25.0	40.1	41.2	34.4	39.1	. . .	34.9	. . .	35.6	. . .
April	38.7	38.5	39.0	25.5	40.4	41.4	34.6	39.1	. . .	35.1	. . .	35.5	. . .
May	38.8	38.6	39.2	25.4	40.5	41.5	34.8	39.1	. . .	35.2	. . .	35.0	. . .
June	39.0	38.8	39.2	25.3	40.8	41.6	35.0	39.2	. . .	35.3	. . .	35.0	. . .
July	39.1	38.9	39.2	25.5	40.9	41.7	35.2	39.2	. . .	35.5	. . .	35.1	. . .
August	39.2	39.0	39.2	25.4	41.1	41.8	35.4	39.2	. . .	35.5	. . .	34.7	. . .
September	39.4	39.2	39.4	25.6	41.3	42.0	35.6	39.6	. . .	35.6	. . .	35.5	. . .
October	39.6	39.4	39.5	25.9	41.5	42.2	35.8	39.6	. . .	35.8	. . .	35.5	. . .
November	39.8	39.6	39.5	26.0	41.8	42.3	36.0	39.8	. . .	35.9	. . .	35.1	. . .
December	40.0	39.8	39.5	26.2	42.0	42.5	36.2	39.8	. . .	35.9	. . .	34.5	. . .
1971													
January	40.1	39.9	39.4	26.3	42.1	42.5	36.4	39.9	. . .	36.0	. . .	34.8	. . .
February	40.2	39.9	39.5	26.2	42.2	42.6	36.5	40.1	. . .	36.1	. . .	35.9	. . .
March	40.2	40.0	39.8	26.2	42.2	42.7	36.5	40.2	. . .	36.3	. . .	35.4	. . .
April	40.4	40.1	40.1	26.1	42.4	42.9	36.6	40.3	. . .	36.3	. . .	36.0	. . .
May	40.5	40.3	40.3	26.2	42.6	43.1	36.7	40.5	. . .	36.5	. . .	36.0	. . .
June	40.7	40.5	40.5	26.3	42.8	43.2	37.0	40.6	. . .	36.7	. . .	36.2	. . .
July	40.9	40.6	40.6	26.3	42.9	43.3	37.1	40.4	. . .	36.9	. . .	35.9	. . .
August	41.0	40.7	40.6	26.8	43.0	43.4	37.3	40.7	. . .	37.2	. . .	35.8	. . .
September	41.0	40.8	40.6	26.9	43.0	43.4	37.4	40.7	. . .	37.2	. . .	35.7	. . .
October	41.1	40.9	40.7	27.0	43.1	43.5	37.5	40.7	. . .	37.1	. . .	36.4	. . .
November	41.2	41.0	40.9	26.9	43.2	43.5	37.6	40.8	. . .	37.2	. . .	37.0	. . .
December	41.4	41.1	41.3	27.0	43.3	43.8	37.7	41.1	. . .	37.4	. . .	37.2	. . .
1972													
January	41.5	41.2	41.1	27.0	43.5	43.8	37.9	41.0	. . .	37.5	. . .	37.8	. . .
February	41.6	41.4	41.7	26.8	43.6	44.0	38.0	41.3	. . .	37.7	. . .	38.1	. . .
March	41.7	41.4	41.6	26.9	43.6	44.0	38.1	41.3	. . .	37.8	. . .	38.1	. . .
April	41.7	41.5	41.6	26.9	43.8	44.1	38.2	41.3	. . .	37.9	. . .	38.7	. . .
May	41.8	41.6	41.7	27.0	43.9	44.2	38.3	41.5	. . .	38.0	. . .	39.3	. . .
June	41.9	41.7	41.9	27.0	44.0	44.3	38.4	41.7	. . .	38.0	. . .	39.4	. . .
July	42.1	41.8	42.1	27.1	44.1	44.5	38.5	41.8	. . .	38.1	. . .	40.0	. . .
August	42.2	41.9	42.2	27.3	44.3	44.5	38.6	42.0	. . .	38.2	. . .	40.3	. . .
September	42.3	42.1	42.5	27.6	44.3	44.8	38.7	42.2	. . .	38.5	. . .	40.5	. . .
October	42.5	42.2	42.8	27.7	44.4	44.9	38.8	42.0	. . .	38.7	. . .	40.9	. . .
November	42.6	42.4	43.0	27.9	44.4	45.1	38.9	42.3	. . .	39.0	. . .	42.0	. . .
December	42.8	42.5	43.2	27.8	44.6	45.2	39.0	42.7	. . .	39.6	. . .	43.8	. . .
1973													
January	43.0	42.7	44.0	27.9	44.6	45.5	39.1	43.0	. . .	39.8	. . .	45.0	. . .
February	43.2	43.0	44.6	28.2	44.8	45.9	39.2	43.5	. . .	40.4	. . .	47.1	. . .
March	43.6	43.4	45.8	28.3	45.0	46.4	39.4	44.4	. . .	41.1	. . .	49.3	. . .
April	43.9	43.7	46.5	28.6	45.1	46.8	39.5	44.7	. . .	41.3	. . .	50.1	. . .
May	44.2	43.9	47.1	28.8	45.3	47.2	39.6	45.0	. . .	42.2	. . .	52.5	. . .
June	44.4	44.2	47.6	29.2	45.4	47.5	39.8	45.5	. . .	43.0	. . .	55.0	. . .
July	44.5	44.2	47.7	29.2	45.5	47.5	39.9	45.4	. . .	42.3	. . .	52.5	. . .
August	45.3	45.0	50.5	29.4	45.7	48.7	40.2	47.0	. . .	43.5	. . .	64.1	. . .
September	45.4	45.2	50.4	29.4	46.0	48.7	40.5	46.9	. . .	43.0	. . .	60.9	. . .
October	45.8	45.6	50.7	30.3	46.3	49.0	41.0	46.8	. . .	43.4	. . .	58.5	. . .
November	46.2	45.9	51.4	31.5	46.5	49.5	41.3	47.2	. . .	43.8	. . .	59.0	. . .
December	46.5	46.3	51.9	32.5	46.7	49.9	41.5	47.6	. . .	44.8	. . .	59.1	. . .
1974													
January	47.0	46.8	52.5	34.1	46.9	50.5	41.8	48.8	49.7	45.9	47.5	63.3	86.3
February	47.6	47.3	53.6	35.4	47.2	51.3	42.0	49.7	50.0	46.8	48.1	64.3	86.5
March	48.1	47.8	54.2	36.9	47.6	51.9	42.4	50.2	50.5	48.1	49.5	62.3	88.3
April	48.3	48.1	54.1	37.6	47.9	52.1	42.6	50.7	51.1	49.0	50.9	60.6	89.7
May	48.8	48.6	54.5	38.3	48.5	52.7	43.1	51.3	52.2	50.6	52.5	58.3	83.8
June	49.2	49.0	54.5	38.6	49.0	53.1	43.5	51.3	53.1	51.5	53.7	55.4	82.9
July	49.6	49.3	54.3	38.9	49.5	53.3	44.0	52.7	54.0	53.4	55.2	59.8	84.2
August	50.2	49.9	55.1	39.2	50.2	54.1	44.5	53.7	55.0	55.8	57.0	62.9	85.5
September	50.9	50.6	56.2	39.3	50.7	54.8	45.0	54.3	55.7	55.9	57.6	60.9	82.5
October	51.3	51.0	56.8	39.2	51.2	55.3	45.4	55.3	56.7	57.2	58.2	63.2	80.6
November	51.8	51.5	57.5	39.4	51.6	55.8	45.8	56.4	57.4	57.8	58.8	64.2	77.6
December	52.2	51.9	58.2	39.6	52.0	56.3	46.2	56.4	57.9	57.8	59.1	61.5	71.6

. . . = Not available.

Table 8-1B. Summary Consumer and Producer Price Indexes: Historical, 1946–2010—*Continued*

(Seasonally adjusted.)

Year and month	Consumer Price Index, 1982–1984 = 100							Producer Price Index, 1982 = 100					
	Urban wage earners and clerical workers (CPI-W), all items	All urban consumers (CPI-U)						Finished goods		Intermediate materials, supplies, and components		Crude materials for further processing	
		All items	Food	Energy	All items less food and energy	Commodities	Services	Total	Less food and energy	Total	Less food and energy	Total	Crude nonfood less energy
1975													
January	52.6	52.3	58.4	40.0	52.3	56.7	46.5	56.7	58.3	58.0	59.6	59.6	69.8
February	52.9	52.6	58.5	40.3	52.8	56.9	46.9	56.6	58.7	57.8	59.8	57.9	69.2
March	53.1	52.8	58.4	40.6	53.0	57.1	47.0	56.6	59.0	57.4	59.7	57.1	68.2
April	53.3	53.0	58.3	41.0	53.3	57.2	47.3	57.1	59.2	57.5	59.7	59.5	67.7
May	53.4	53.1	58.6	41.3	53.5	57.5	47.5	57.4	59.3	57.3	59.7	61.2	68.8
June	53.8	53.5	59.2	41.7	53.8	57.9	47.8	57.9	59.5	57.3	59.8	61.5	66.5
July	54.3	54.0	60.3	42.5	54.0	58.6	48.0	58.4	59.8	57.5	59.9	62.4	66.5
August	54.5	54.2	60.3	42.8	54.2	58.7	48.3	58.9	59.9	58.0	60.1	63.0	67.7
September	54.9	54.6	60.7	43.2	54.5	59.0	48.7	59.3	60.2	58.2	60.3	64.5	71.2
October	55.2	54.9	61.3	43.5	54.8	59.4	49.0	59.8	60.6	58.8	61.0	65.1	71.5
November	55.6	55.3	61.7	43.9	55.2	59.7	49.6	60.0	61.0	59.0	61.4	64.4	71.9
December	55.9	55.6	62.1	44.1	55.5	59.9	49.9	60.1	61.4	59.2	61.8	64.0	73.1
1976													
January	56.2	55.8	61.9	44.5	55.9	60.0	50.5	60.0	61.7	59.4	62.1	63.0	72.4
February	56.2	55.9	61.3	44.4	56.2	59.9	50.8	59.9	61.9	59.6	62.3	62.1	73.8
March	56.3	56.0	60.9	44.1	56.5	59.8	51.1	60.0	62.2	59.8	62.6	61.5	74.5
April	56.5	56.1	60.9	43.9	56.7	59.9	51.3	60.3	62.3	60.0	62.8	63.9	78.1
May	56.7	56.4	61.1	44.1	57.0	60.2	51.4	60.4	62.4	60.3	63.2	63.6	80.6
June	57.0	56.7	61.3	44.4	57.2	60.4	51.7	60.5	62.8	60.8	63.6	65.2	82.8
July	57.3	57.0	61.6	44.8	57.6	60.7	52.1	60.7	63.1	61.1	63.9	64.8	87.3
August	57.6	57.3	61.8	45.2	57.9	61.0	52.4	60.9	63.5	61.3	64.3	63.6	84.1
September	57.9	57.6	62.1	45.7	58.2	61.3	52.8	61.1	63.9	61.9	64.7	63.4	84.4
October	58.2	57.9	62.4	46.1	58.5	61.6	53.1	61.4	64.1	62.0	65.0	63.0	82.2
November	58.4	58.1	62.3	46.8	58.7	61.7	53.4	61.9	64.6	62.4	65.3	63.4	81.8
December	58.7	58.4	62.5	47.5	58.9	62.0	53.7	62.4	64.9	62.8	65.6	64.5	81.1
1977													
January	59.1	58.7	62.7	48.1	59.3	62.3	54.1	62.5	65.1	63.0	65.8	64.3	78.7
February	59.6	59.3	63.9	48.1	59.7	63.0	54.4	63.2	65.4	63.3	65.9	65.7	79.7
March	59.9	59.6	64.2	48.4	60.0	63.2	54.8	63.7	65.7	63.9	66.4	66.6	81.5
April	60.3	60.0	65.0	48.6	60.3	63.7	55.2	64.0	65.9	64.4	66.7	68.3	82.1
May	60.6	60.2	65.3	48.9	60.6	63.9	55.4	64.4	66.1	64.9	67.1	67.6	82.5
June	60.9	60.5	65.7	48.9	61.0	64.2	55.8	64.6	66.5	64.9	67.4	65.5	79.7
July	61.2	60.8	65.9	49.1	61.2	64.4	56.3	64.8	66.8	65.1	67.9	64.7	78.8
August	61.4	61.1	66.2	49.5	61.5	64.6	56.6	65.2	67.3	65.4	68.2	63.9	79.2
September	61.7	61.3	66.4	49.8	61.8	64.8	56.9	65.5	67.8	65.7	68.7	63.7	79.2
October	61.9	61.6	66.6	50.5	62.0	65.0	57.2	65.9	68.2	65.8	68.8	64.0	78.5
November	62.3	62.0	67.1	51.3	62.3	65.5	57.6	66.4	68.8	66.3	69.1	65.4	78.4
December	62.6	62.3	67.4	51.6	62.7	65.7	57.9	66.7	69.0	66.6	69.4	66.4	80.1
1978													
January	63.0	62.7	67.9	51.1	63.1	66.1	58.3	67.0	69.2	66.9	69.8	67.3	80.3
February	63.3	63.0	68.6	50.6	63.4	66.4	58.7	67.5	69.5	67.4	70.3	68.4	80.6
March	63.8	63.4	69.5	51.0	63.8	66.8	59.1	67.8	69.9	67.8	70.6	69.8	80.3
April	64.2	63.9	70.6	51.4	64.3	67.4	59.6	68.6	70.6	68.1	71.1	72.1	82.2
May	64.8	64.5	71.6	51.7	64.7	68.0	60.0	69.1	71.1	68.7	71.6	72.8	84.6
June	65.3	65.0	72.7	51.9	65.2	68.6	60.5	69.7	71.7	69.2	72.2	74.6	87.4
July	65.8	65.5	73.0	52.1	65.6	69.1	61.0	70.3	72.3	69.4	72.5	74.2	89.6
August	66.2	65.9	73.3	52.6	66.1	69.4	61.5	70.4	72.8	69.9	73.2	73.7	90.4
September	66.7	66.5	73.6	53.2	66.7	70.0	62.1	71.1	73.5	70.5	73.7	75.1	92.3
October	67.4	67.1	74.2	54.1	67.2	70.6	62.6	71.4	73.4	71.3	74.5	77.0	94.7
November	67.8	67.5	74.7	54.9	67.6	71.1	63.1	72.0	74.1	71.9	75.2	77.4	96.3
December	68.3	67.9	75.1	55.9	68.0	71.6	63.3	72.8	74.7	72.4	75.6	78.0	96.8
1979													
January	68.8	68.5	76.4	55.8	68.5	72.2	63.8	73.7	75.3	73.1	76.3	80.1	96.4
February	69.6	69.2	77.7	55.9	69.2	72.9	64.4	74.4	75.9	73.7	77.0	82.1	99.6
March	70.3	69.9	78.4	57.4	69.8	73.8	64.9	75.0	76.4	74.6	77.8	83.8	104.2
April	71.1	70.6	79.0	59.5	70.3	74.7	65.5	75.8	77.0	75.7	78.9	84.4	105.1
May	71.9	71.4	79.7	62.0	70.8	75.6	66.2	76.2	77.4	76.6	79.6	84.7	106.7
June	72.7	72.2	80.0	64.7	71.3	76.4	66.8	76.6	78.0	77.5	80.1	85.6	111.6
July	73.5	73.0	80.5	67.3	71.9	77.2	67.6	77.4	78.5	78.7	81.1	86.5	109.4
August	74.2	73.7	80.4	69.7	72.7	77.9	68.5	78.2	78.8	79.8	81.8	85.5	106.4
September	75.0	74.4	80.9	71.9	73.3	78.6	69.2	79.5	79.7	81.1	82.7	87.9	106.5
October	75.7	75.2	81.5	73.5	74.0	79.3	70.1	80.4	80.4	82.4	83.9	88.8	108.9
November	76.5	76.0	82.0	74.8	74.8	80.0	71.1	81.4	81.0	83.2	84.5	90.0	111.3
December	77.3	76.9	82.8	76.8	75.7	80.8	72.0	82.2	81.7	84.0	85.2	91.2	111.3
1980													
January	78.5	78.0	83.3	79.1	76.7	82.0	73.1	83.4	83.3	86.0	87.2	90.9	112.6
February	79.4	79.0	83.4	81.9	77.5	82.8	74.1	84.6	84.2	87.6	88.2	92.6	115.3
March	80.6	80.1	84.1	84.5	78.6	83.9	75.4	85.5	84.7	88.2	88.6	90.8	111.7
April	81.4	80.9	84.7	85.4	79.5	84.4	76.6	86.2	85.5	88.5	88.8	88.3	109.9
May	82.2	81.7	85.2	86.4	80.1	84.9	77.6	86.6	85.7	89.0	89.1	89.5	107.2
June	83.0	82.5	85.7	86.5	81.0	85.3	79.0	87.3	86.6	89.8	89.8	90.1	106.1
July	83.1	82.6	86.6	86.7	80.8	85.9	78.5	88.7	87.7	90.5	90.3	94.6	109.6
August	83.7	83.2	88.0	87.2	81.3	86.9	78.5	89.7	88.4	91.5	91.1	99.0	112.4
September	84.4	83.9	89.1	87.5	82.1	87.8	79.0	90.1	88.8	91.9	91.4	100.4	116.2
October	85.3	84.7	89.8	88.0	83.0	88.5	80.0	90.8	89.6	92.8	92.1	102.2	118.2
November	86.2	85.6	90.8	88.8	83.9	89.2	81.1	91.4	90.1	93.5	92.6	103.5	119.8
December	87.0	86.4	91.3	90.7	84.9	89.7	82.2	91.8	90.4	94.4	93.7	102.7	119.3

Table 8-1B. Summary Consumer and Producer Price Indexes: Historical, 1946–2010—*Continued*

(Seasonally adjusted.)

Year and month	Urban wage earners and clerical workers (CPI-W), all items	Consumer Price Index, 1982–1984 = 100						Producer Price Index, 1982 = 100					
		All urban consumers (CPI-U)						Finished goods		Intermediate materials, supplies, and components		Crude materials for further processing	
		All items	Food	Energy	All items less food and energy	Commodit-ies	Services	Total	Less food and energy	Total	Less food and energy	Total	Crude nonfood less energy
1981													
January	87.7	87.2	91.6	92.1	85.4	90.4	83.0	92.8	91.4	95.6	94.7	103.4	113.3
February	88.6	88.0	92.1	95.2	85.9	91.4	83.7	93.6	92.0	96.1	94.9	104.2	106.2
March	89.1	88.6	92.6	97.4	86.4	91.9	84.4	94.7	92.6	97.1	95.6	103.8	108.9
April	89.6	89.1	92.8	97.6	87.0	92.0	85.3	95.7	93.5	98.3	96.6	104.2	111.9
May	90.2	89.7	92.8	97.9	87.8	92.4	86.4	96.0	94.0	98.7	97.1	103.8	113.7
June	90.9	90.5	93.2	97.3	88.6	92.9	87.5	96.5	94.6	99.0	97.7	104.9	115.5
July	92.0	91.5	93.9	97.3	89.8	93.6	88.9	96.7	94.8	99.2	98.4	105.0	116.4
August	92.7	92.2	94.4	97.8	90.7	94.0	89.9	96.8	95.3	99.7	98.9	104.0	115.5
September	93.5	93.1	94.8	98.6	91.8	94.6	91.2	97.2	95.9	99.7	99.3	102.7	112.6
October	93.8	93.4	95.0	99.2	92.1	94.7	91.7	97.6	96.5	99.8	99.5	101.2	110.8
November	94.2	93.8	95.1	100.5	92.5	94.9	92.5	97.9	97.0	99.9	99.7	99.7	107.5
December	94.5	94.1	95.3	101.5	93.0	95.1	93.0	98.3	97.6	100.0	99.8	98.8	106.0
1982													
January	94.8	94.4	95.6	100.6	93.3	95.2	93.5	98.9	98.1	100.4	99.9	99.7	101.2
February	95.1	94.7	96.3	98.0	93.8	95.4	93.9	98.8	98.1	100.3	100.0	100.0	100.7
March	95.0	94.7	96.2	96.6	93.9	95.3	94.0	98.8	98.7	99.9	99.9	99.7	100.0
April	95.3	95.0	96.4	94.2	94.7	95.1	94.9	99.0	99.0	99.7	99.8	100.2	101.1
May	96.1	95.9	97.2	95.7	95.4	96.0	95.7	99.0	99.4	99.7	100.1	101.9	102.2
June	97.3	97.0	98.1	98.4	96.1	97.4	96.5	99.8	99.9	99.8	100.0	101.8	101.0
July	97.8	97.5	98.2	99.3	96.7	97.9	97.0	100.2	100.1	100.0	99.8	100.7	101.4
August	98.1	97.7	98.0	99.8	97.1	97.9	97.6	100.6	100.6	99.9	99.7	99.8	100.0
September	98.1	97.7	98.2	100.3	97.2	97.8	97.6	100.7	100.8	100.0	100.2	99.2	98.9
October	98.5	98.1	98.2	101.7	97.5	98.2	97.9	101.0	101.3	99.9	100.2	98.7	97.7
November	98.4	98.0	98.2	102.5	97.3	98.3	97.7	101.4	101.6	100.1	100.2	99.2	96.3
December	98.1	97.7	98.2	102.8	97.2	98.3	96.9	101.8	102.2	100.1	100.3	98.8	95.9
1983													
January	98.2	97.9	98.1	99.6	97.6	98.3	97.5	101.0	101.8	99.8	100.3	98.8	97.3
February	98.2	98.0	98.2	97.7	98.0	98.1	97.9	101.1	102.2	100.0	100.8	100.0	99.8
March	98.5	98.1	98.8	96.8	98.2	98.2	98.1	101.0	102.5	99.7	100.8	100.5	102.2
April	99.1	98.8	99.2	98.9	98.6	98.9	98.7	101.1	102.4	99.5	100.9	101.2	102.1
May	99.5	99.2	99.5	100.4	98.9	99.5	98.9	101.4	102.6	99.8	101.0	100.9	103.4
June	99.7	99.4	99.6	100.6	99.2	99.8	99.2	101.6	102.8	100.2	101.3	100.5	104.8
July	100.0	99.8	99.6	100.9	99.8	100.2	99.6	101.6	103.1	100.5	101.8	99.5	106.2
August	100.5	100.1	99.7	101.2	100.1	100.5	99.8	101.9	103.5	100.9	102.0	102.2	108.4
September	100.7	100.4	100.0	101.0	100.5	100.7	100.2	102.2	103.5	101.6	102.3	103.3	109.0
October	101.0	100.8	100.3	100.8	101.0	101.0	100.7	102.2	103.6	101.7	102.5	103.2	109.1
November	101.2	101.1	100.3	100.5	101.5	101.1	101.3	102.0	103.8	101.8	102.8	102.3	109.9
December	101.3	101.4	100.6	100.0	101.8	101.2	101.6	102.3	104.1	101.9	103.1	103.5	111.2
1984													
January	101.8	102.1	102.0	100.2	102.5	101.9	102.1	103.0	104.5	102.1	103.4	104.6	111.5
February	102.0	102.6	102.7	101.4	102.8	102.4	102.6	103.4	104.7	102.5	103.8	103.8	113.8
March	102.0	102.9	102.9	101.4	103.2	102.6	103.0	103.8	105.2	103.0	104.4	105.7	114.8
April	102.2	103.3	102.9	101.7	103.7	102.9	103.5	103.9	105.3	103.2	104.5	105.2	115.1
May	102.5	103.5	102.7	101.6	104.1	103.0	103.9	103.8	105.3	103.4	104.6	104.5	115.7
June	102.7	103.7	103.1	100.8	104.5	103.1	104.2	103.8	105.5	103.6	104.8	103.3	114.1
July	103.2	104.1	103.3	100.5	105.0	103.2	104.9	104.0	105.7	103.4	104.9	104.0	112.0
August	104.1	104.4	103.9	100.1	105.4	103.4	105.4	103.8	105.9	103.2	105.1	103.3	109.6
September	104.5	104.7	103.8	100.6	105.8	103.6	105.9	103.8	106.2	103.1	105.0	102.8	110.5
October	104.7	105.1	104.0	101.1	106.2	103.9	106.3	103.6	105.9	103.2	105.1	101.5	108.5
November	104.8	105.3	104.1	100.8	106.4	103.9	106.7	104.0	106.2	103.3	105.3	101.9	107.7
December	104.9	105.5	104.5	100.1	106.8	103.9	107.1	104.0	106.3	103.2	105.3	101.4	107.3
1985													
January	105.2	105.7	104.7	100.3	107.1	104.1	107.4	104.0	106.9	103.1	105.3	99.9	107.4
February	105.7	106.3	105.2	100.3	107.7	104.7	107.9	104.1	107.3	102.8	105.3	99.4	107.2
March	106.1	106.8	105.5	101.3	108.1	105.1	108.4	104.1	107.6	102.7	105.2	97.6	107.0
April	106.4	107.0	105.4	102.3	108.4	105.4	108.7	104.6	107.6	102.9	105.2	96.7	107.4
May	106.6	107.2	105.2	102.2	108.8	105.2	109.4	104.9	107.8	103.2	105.3	95.8	105.3
June	106.9	107.5	105.5	102.2	109.1	105.3	109.8	104.6	108.2	102.6	105.5	95.2	103.6
July	107.0	107.7	105.5	102.2	109.4	105.3	110.3	104.7	108.4	102.3	105.3	94.9	104.3
August	107.1	107.9	105.6	101.2	109.8	105.2	110.7	104.5	108.5	102.3	105.3	92.9	103.6
September	107.3	108.1	105.8	101.2	110.0	105.4	111.0	103.8	107.9	102.2	105.2	91.8	103.3
October	107.7	108.5	105.8	101.2	110.5	105.6	111.5	104.9	108.9	102.3	105.1	94.1	103.7
November	108.2	109.0	106.5	101.8	111.1	106.1	112.1	105.5	109.1	102.5	105.1	95.7	103.0
December	108.7	109.5	107.3	102.4	111.4	106.6	112.5	106.0	109.1	102.9	105.1	95.5	102.4
1986													
January	109.1	109.9	107.5	102.6	111.9	106.9	113.1	105.5	109.3	102.4	105.0	94.2	103.6
February	108.8	109.7	107.3	99.5	112.2	106.0	113.5	104.1	109.5	101.2	104.9	90.5	103.5
March	108.1	109.1	107.5	92.6	112.5	104.5	114.1	102.8	109.6	99.9	105.0	88.2	103.8
April	107.7	108.7	107.7	87.2	112.9	103.3	114.6	102.3	110.1	98.9	104.7	85.6	103.9
May	107.8	109.0	108.2	87.2	113.1	103.5	114.8	102.8	110.2	98.7	104.6	86.5	104.1
June	108.3	109.4	108.3	88.8	113.4	103.8	115.5	103.1	110.5	98.6	104.7	86.2	104.7
July	108.3	109.5	109.1	85.6	113.8	103.7	115.7	102.3	110.7	98.0	104.8	86.4	105.3
August	108.4	109.6	110.1	83.6	114.2	103.6	116.1	102.7	110.8	98.0	104.9	86.7	99.7
September	108.8	110.0	110.2	84.4	114.6	104.0	116.5	102.9	110.7	98.5	105.1	86.6	100.3
October	108.9	110.2	110.5	82.8	115.0	104.0	116.9	103.5	111.8	98.3	105.1	87.4	102.0
November	109.2	110.4	111.1	82.1	115.3	104.2	117.2	103.4	112.0	98.3	105.2	87.6	102.8
December	109.5	110.8	111.4	82.5	115.6	104.5	117.5	103.6	112.1	98.5	105.3	86.9	104.1

Table 8-1B. Summary Consumer and Producer Price Indexes: Historical, 1946–2010—*Continued*

(Seasonally adjusted.)

Year and month	Urban wage earners and clerical workers (CPI-W), all items	Consumer Price Index, 1982–1984 = 100						Producer Price Index, 1982 = 100					
		All urban consumers (CPI-U)						Finished goods		Intermediate materials, supplies, and components		Crude materials for further processing	
		All items	Food	Energy	All items less food and energy	Commodities	Services	Total	Less food and energy	Total	Less food and energy	Total	Crude nonfood less energy
1987													
January	110.2	111.4	111.8	85.4	115.9	105.5	117.9	104.1	112.5	99.0	105.6	89.3	105.4
February	110.7	111.8	112.2	87.4	116.2	106.1	118.3	104.4	112.3	99.8	105.9	90.2	106.2
March	111.1	112.2	112.4	87.6	116.6	106.5	118.6	104.5	112.4	99.9	106.2	90.5	106.5
April	111.6	112.7	112.6	87.6	117.3	106.9	119.2	105.1	112.9	100.3	106.5	92.5	107.5
May	111.9	113.0	113.2	87.1	117.7	107.2	119.6	105.2	113.0	100.8	107.0	93.8	110.0
June	112.4	113.5	113.9	88.5	117.9	107.7	120.0	105.5	113.1	101.4	107.5	94.5	113.2
July	112.7	113.8	113.7	89.2	118.3	108.0	120.3	105.7	113.3	101.9	107.9	95.6	115.9
August	113.2	114.3	113.9	90.5	118.7	108.5	120.9	105.9	113.6	102.4	108.3	96.5	119.1
September	113.6	114.7	114.3	90.3	119.2	108.8	121.4	106.2	113.9	102.6	108.9	96.0	122.8
October	113.9	115.0	114.5	89.6	119.8	109.0	121.8	106.0	114.0	103.1	109.6	95.8	126.6
November	114.2	115.4	114.5	90.0	120.1	109.3	122.2	106.0	114.2	103.5	110.1	95.1	127.5
December	114.4	115.6	115.1	89.5	120.4	109.3	122.6	105.8	114.3	103.8	110.7	94.9	127.9
1988													
January	114.7	116.0	115.6	88.8	120.9	109.5	123.0	106.4	115.0	104.1	111.8	94.2	129.4
February	114.9	116.2	115.6	88.7	121.2	109.5	123.5	106.3	115.3	104.4	112.2	95.2	131.7
March	115.2	116.5	115.8	88.4	121.7	109.8	123.9	106.6	115.6	104.8	112.8	94.1	133.0
April	115.8	117.2	116.4	88.8	122.3	110.5	124.4	107.0	115.9	105.5	113.6	95.4	132.1
May	116.2	117.5	116.9	88.5	122.7	110.7	124.8	107.2	116.2	106.2	114.3	95.8	130.7
June	116.6	118.0	117.6	88.9	123.2	111.2	125.4	107.5	116.6	107.4	114.9	97.0	131.1
July	117.3	118.5	118.8	89.4	123.6	111.9	125.8	108.4	117.2	108.3	115.8	96.7	133.2
August	117.7	119.0	119.4	90.1	124.0	112.2	126.4	108.8	117.7	108.5	116.3	97.0	134.3
September	118.2	119.5	120.1	89.8	124.7	112.8	126.9	109.0	118.1	108.7	116.8	97.0	133.3
October	118.6	119.9	120.3	89.8	125.2	113.0	127.5	109.2	118.4	108.6	117.3	96.6	133.6
November	118.9	120.3	120.5	89.8	125.6	113.3	127.9	109.6	118.7	108.8	118.0	95.2	136.0
December	119.3	120.7	121.1	89.6	126.0	113.5	128.4	110.0	119.2	109.4	118.6	98.1	137.6
1989													
January	119.9	121.2	121.6	90.3	126.5	114.1	128.9	111.1	119.9	110.8	119.5	102.0	140.6
February	120.3	121.6	122.5	90.8	126.9	114.5	129.4	111.9	120.5	111.3	119.9	101.7	140.3
March	120.9	122.2	123.2	91.8	127.4	115.1	130.0	112.3	120.7	111.9	120.2	102.9	140.6
April	121.9	123.1	123.9	96.6	127.8	116.5	130.5	113.1	120.8	112.5	120.5	104.1	140.3
May	122.5	123.7	124.7	97.4	128.3	117.1	131.1	114.0	121.6	112.6	120.6	104.5	139.8
June	122.8	124.1	125.1	96.9	128.8	117.2	131.6	114.0	122.2	112.5	120.6	103.2	137.9
July	123.2	124.5	125.6	96.7	129.2	117.3	132.3	113.8	122.1	112.2	120.3	103.5	135.9
August	123.2	124.5	125.9	94.9	129.5	117.0	132.8	113.4	122.7	111.8	120.2	101.2	136.8
September	123.4	124.8	126.3	93.8	129.9	117.2	133.1	114.0	123.1	112.1	120.2	102.5	137.5
October	123.9	125.4	126.8	94.4	130.6	117.8	133.7	114.6	123.5	112.2	120.3	102.7	137.9
November	124.4	125.9	127.4	93.9	131.1	118.1	134.3	114.8	123.9	112.0	120.0	103.5	134.9
December	124.9	126.3	127.8	94.2	131.6	118.4	134.9	115.5	124.2	112.2	119.8	105.1	132.8
1990													
January	126.1	127.5	129.7	98.9	132.1	120.2	135.4	117.7	124.5	113.7	120.0	106.7	132.7
February	126.6	128.0	130.8	98.2	132.7	120.7	136.0	117.6	124.9	112.8	119.9	106.8	131.6
March	127.0	128.6	131.0	97.6	133.5	120.9	136.8	117.5	125.3	112.9	120.2	105.1	133.9
April	127.3	128.9	130.8	97.5	134.0	121.0	137.4	117.4	125.5	113.1	120.5	102.7	137.0
May	127.5	129.1	131.1	96.7	134.4	121.0	137.9	117.5	126.0	113.1	120.6	103.1	138.0
June	128.2	129.9	132.1	97.3	135.1	121.6	138.8	117.6	126.4	112.9	120.4	100.6	137.3
July	128.8	130.5	132.8	97.1	135.8	122.0	139.6	117.9	126.6	112.8	120.6	101.0	138.0
August	129.9	131.6	133.2	101.6	136.6	123.2	140.6	119.2	127.1	114.0	120.8	110.5	140.1
September	130.9	132.5	133.6	106.5	137.1	124.5	141.1	120.7	127.7	115.8	121.5	115.8	139.9
October	131.7	133.4	134.1	110.8	137.6	125.8	141.6	121.9	128.0	117.4	122.1	125.8	138.4
November	132.1	133.7	134.5	111.2	138.0	126.0	142.2	122.6	128.4	117.7	122.3	117.8	135.7
December	132.5	134.2	134.6	111.0	138.6	126.3	142.7	122.0	128.6	116.9	122.1	110.8	133.8
1991													
January	132.9	134.7	135.0	108.5	139.5	126.3	143.7	122.6	129.5	116.9	122.4	113.3	134.2
February	132.9	134.8	135.1	104.5	140.2	125.9	144.4	121.8	129.8	115.9	122.1	104.1	133.7
March	133.0	134.8	135.3	101.9	140.5	125.5	144.7	121.3	130.1	114.7	121.7	100.5	131.8
April	133.3	135.1	136.1	101.2	140.9	126.0	144.9	121.3	130.4	114.2	121.5	100.2	131.7
May	133.8	135.6	136.6	102.1	141.3	126.4	145.4	121.6	130.6	114.1	121.3	100.9	130.4
June	134.1	136.0	137.4	101.1	141.8	126.7	145.9	121.4	130.7	113.9	121.3	99.2	126.1
July	134.3	136.2	136.7	100.7	142.3	126.6	146.5	121.1	131.0	113.6	121.1	99.4	125.4
August	134.6	136.6	136.2	101.1	142.9	126.8	146.9	121.3	131.3	113.8	121.0	99.1	125.8
September	135.0	137.0	136.4	101.5	143.4	127.0	147.6	121.5	131.8	114.0	121.0	98.4	125.7
October	135.2	137.2	136.2	101.6	143.7	127.0	148.0	121.9	132.3	114.0	121.1	100.8	125.4
November	135.8	137.8	136.7	102.4	144.2	127.6	148.5	122.4	132.5	114.1	121.1	100.7	124.4
December	136.2	138.2	137.0	103.1	144.7	127.9	149.2	122.3	132.6	114.0	121.1	98.2	123.4
1992													
January	136.2	138.3	136.6	101.5	145.1	127.6	149.6	122.0	133.0	113.4	121.0	97.2	123.4
February	136.5	138.6	137.1	101.2	145.4	127.8	149.9	122.3	133.1	113.8	121.3	98.6	125.2
March	136.9	139.1	137.6	101.2	145.9	128.2	150.4	122.4	133.4	113.9	121.5	97.1	127.7
April	137.2	139.4	137.5	101.4	146.3	128.3	150.9	122.5	133.8	114.1	121.7	98.1	128.4
May	137.5	139.7	137.2	102.0	146.8	128.6	151.3	122.9	134.3	114.5	121.8	100.3	129.1
June	138.0	140.1	137.6	103.3	147.1	129.1	151.7	123.4	134.1	115.1	122.0	101.6	128.8
July	138.4	140.5	137.4	103.7	147.6	129.3	152.2	123.3	134.3	115.2	122.1	101.6	129.6
August	138.7	140.8	138.4	103.5	147.9	129.6	152.6	123.4	134.3	115.1	122.3	100.7	130.4
September	139.0	141.1	138.9	103.6	148.1	129.9	152.9	123.7	134.6	115.3	122.4	102.8	130.4
October	139.5	141.7	138.9	104.3	148.8	130.2	153.7	124.2	134.9	115.3	122.4	102.8	128.9
November	139.8	142.1	138.7	105.1	149.2	130.3	154.3	124.1	135.1	115.1	122.4	102.5	128.2
December	140.1	142.3	138.8	105.3	149.6	130.5	154.7	124.2	135.2	115.1	122.5	101.3	130.5

Table 8-1B. Summary Consumer and Producer Price Indexes: Historical, 1946–2010—*Continued*

(Seasonally adjusted.)

Year and month	Urban wage earners and clerical workers (CPI-W), all items	Consumer Price Index, 1982–1984 = 100 — All urban consumers (CPI-U)						Producer Price Index, 1982 = 100 — Finished goods		Intermediate materials, supplies, and components		Crude materials for further processing	
		All items	Food	Energy	All items less food and energy	Commodities	Services	Total	Less food and energy	Total	Less food and energy	Total	Crude nonfood less energy
1993													
January	140.5	142.8	139.1	105.0	150.1	130.7	155.3	124.4	135.6	115.4	122.9	101.7	135.0
February	140.8	143.1	139.6	104.3	150.6	131.1	155.6	124.7	135.9	115.9	123.5	101.2	136.8
March	141.0	143.3	139.6	104.9	150.8	131.1	156.0	125.0	136.1	116.3	123.8	101.7	137.0
April	141.4	143.8	140.0	104.9	151.4	131.4	156.7	125.7	136.5	116.6	124.0	103.2	138.4
May	141.8	144.2	141.0	104.3	151.8	131.6	157.3	125.7	136.6	116.3	123.7	105.6	140.3
June	142.0	144.3	140.6	103.9	152.1	131.3	157.8	125.2	136.4	116.3	123.7	103.8	140.3
July	142.1	144.5	140.6	103.4	152.3	131.3	158.1	125.1	136.6	116.3	123.7	101.6	142.1
August	142.4	144.8	141.1	103.4	152.8	131.6	158.6	123.9	134.9	116.2	123.9	100.8	140.4
September	142.5	145.0	141.4	103.0	152.9	131.3	159.0	124.1	134.9	116.3	124.0	101.2	140.7
October	143.2	145.6	142.0	105.3	153.4	132.2	159.4	124.2	135.0	116.4	124.0	103.7	142.6
November	143.4	146.0	142.3	104.4	153.9	132.4	159.9	124.4	135.3	116.5	124.3	103.0	144.1
December	143.7	146.3	142.8	103.7	154.3	132.4	160.5	124.4	135.7	116.2	124.5	101.7	145.3
1994													
January	143.8	146.3	142.9	102.8	154.5	132.3	160.8	124.8	136.3	116.5	124.7	103.8	148.3
February	144.0	146.7	142.7	104.1	154.8	132.4	161.4	125.0	136.3	116.9	124.9	102.1	151.0
March	144.3	147.1	142.7	104.3	155.3	132.5	162.0	125.1	136.4	117.1	125.1	103.8	151.5
April	144.5	147.2	143.0	103.7	155.5	132.6	162.2	125.1	136.6	117.1	125.3	103.8	150.7
May	144.8	147.5	143.3	102.8	155.9	132.9	162.4	125.1	137.0	117.2	125.6	102.2	149.7
June	145.3	147.9	143.8	103.1	156.4	133.5	162.8	125.2	137.2	117.8	126.3	102.7	151.2
July	145.9	148.4	144.6	104.5	156.7	134.1	163.1	125.7	137.3	118.3	126.7	101.7	155.5
August	146.5	149.0	145.1	106.7	157.1	134.7	163.8	126.2	137.6	119.1	127.4	101.6	158.8
September	146.8	149.3	145.3	106.1	157.5	134.8	164.1	125.9	137.7	119.6	128.4	99.7	160.5
October	146.9	149.4	145.3	105.7	157.8	134.8	164.5	125.5	137.4	120.1	129.3	98.6	161.3
November	147.3	149.8	145.6	106.1	158.2	135.0	165.0	126.1	137.6	121.0	130.3	99.8	166.6
December	147.6	150.1	146.8	105.9	158.3	135.4	165.2	126.6	137.9	121.5	131.0	101.1	169.9
1995													
January	148.0	150.5	146.7	105.7	159.0	135.4	166.0	126.9	138.4	122.8	132.6	102.1	174.5
February	148.4	150.9	147.3	105.8	159.4	135.6	166.5	127.2	138.7	123.7	133.7	102.9	176.5
March	148.6	151.2	147.1	105.5	159.9	135.6	167.1	127.4	139.0	124.3	134.3	102.3	177.8
April	149.2	151.8	148.1	105.6	160.4	136.2	167.7	127.7	139.3	125.0	135.2	103.7	180.2
May	149.5	152.1	148.2	105.8	160.7	136.4	168.1	127.8	139.7	125.2	135.5	102.4	179.6
June	149.8	152.4	148.3	106.7	161.1	136.6	168.5	127.8	139.8	125.5	135.7	103.0	179.5
July	149.9	152.6	148.5	105.8	161.4	136.6	168.9	128.0	140.2	125.6	136.1	101.6	176.4
August	150.2	152.9	148.6	105.6	161.8	136.8	169.3	127.9	140.2	125.6	136.1	99.7	173.4
September	150.4	153.1	149.1	104.1	162.2	136.8	169.7	128.1	140.2	125.5	136.2	102.0	170.9
October	150.8	153.5	149.5	104.4	162.7	137.1	170.3	128.4	141.0	125.4	135.8	101.9	166.6
November	150.9	153.7	149.6	103.4	163.0	137.0	170.7	128.7	141.3	125.2	135.5	104.1	163.6
December	151.3	153.9	149.9	104.4	163.1	137.3	170.9	129.3	141.5	125.4	135.2	106.5	162.3
1996													
January	152.0	154.7	150.4	106.9	163.7	138.2	171.5	129.7	141.5	125.5	134.8	109.8	162.6
February	152.3	155.0	150.8	107.1	164.0	138.3	172.0	129.7	141.6	125.0	134.4	111.6	162.1
March	152.9	155.5	151.4	108.3	164.4	139.0	172.4	130.5	141.6	125.3	134.1	109.8	158.2
April	153.4	156.1	152.0	111.2	164.6	139.6	172.8	130.9	141.6	125.7	133.8	114.2	156.7
May	153.8	156.4	151.9	112.0	165.0	139.7	173.4	130.9	142.0	126.2	134.0	114.6	157.6
June	154.0	156.7	152.9	110.3	165.4	139.8	173.8	131.3	142.2	125.8	133.9	112.2	154.6
July	154.3	157.0	153.4	110.1	165.7	139.8	174.4	131.2	142.2	125.5	133.6	114.6	152.2
August	154.5	157.2	153.9	109.7	166.0	139.8	174.9	131.6	142.3	125.6	133.6	115.3	152.5
September	154.9	157.7	154.6	109.8	166.5	140.3	175.4	131.7	142.2	126.1	134.0	112.7	153.5
October	155.4	158.2	155.5	110.5	166.8	140.8	175.8	132.4	142.3	126.0	133.7	111.9	153.3
November	155.9	158.7	156.1	111.8	167.2	141.4	176.3	132.5	142.1	125.8	133.7	115.7	153.0
December	156.3	159.1	156.3	113.9	167.4	141.7	176.7	132.9	142.3	126.4	133.9	122.5	153.6
1997													
January	156.6	159.4	155.9	115.2	167.8	141.8	177.3	133.0	142.5	126.6	134.1	127.5	156.2
February	156.9	159.7	156.5	115.0	168.1	142.1	177.6	132.7	142.4	126.5	134.1	116.6	157.6
March	156.9	159.8	156.6	113.0	168.4	141.8	178.0	132.6	142.6	126.1	134.2	107.5	158.7
April	157.0	159.9	156.5	111.0	168.9	141.6	178.4	131.8	142.6	125.6	134.1	107.8	155.8
May	157.0	159.9	156.6	108.8	169.2	141.4	178.7	131.5	142.4	125.4	134.2	109.1	157.0
June	157.3	160.2	156.9	110.0	169.4	141.5	179.2	131.3	142.4	125.4	134.2	106.2	156.9
July	157.4	160.4	157.2	109.1	169.7	141.4	179.7	130.9	142.2	125.1	134.2	106.2	155.7
August	157.8	160.8	157.7	110.9	169.8	141.9	179.9	131.4	142.3	125.3	134.3	106.8	156.8
September	158.2	161.2	158.0	112.4	170.2	142.2	180.4	131.6	142.6	125.5	134.3	108.4	155.8
October	158.4	161.5	158.3	111.8	170.6	142.2	180.9	131.9	142.6	125.4	134.3	113.4	156.7
November	158.6	161.7	158.6	111.4	170.8	142.1	181.4	131.6	142.4	125.6	134.4	115.8	156.5
December	158.6	161.8	158.7	109.8	171.2	142.1	181.7	131.4	142.3	125.4	134.4	108.8	154.2
1998													
January	158.8	162.0	159.5	107.5	171.6	142.0	182.1	130.7	142.4	124.6	134.3	102.8	150.4
February	158.7	162.0	159.4	105.1	171.9	141.8	182.3	130.6	142.6	124.2	134.2	100.8	150.1
March	158.7	162.0	159.7	103.3	172.2	141.4	182.8	130.5	143.3	123.7	134.1	99.5	148.7
April	158.8	162.2	159.7	102.4	172.5	141.3	183.3	130.7	143.4	123.6	134.0	100.6	147.3
May	159.3	162.6	160.3	103.2	172.9	141.7	183.7	130.5	143.5	123.5	133.9	99.6	146.2
June	159.5	162.8	160.2	103.6	173.2	141.8	184.0	130.4	143.5	123.1	133.6	97.1	145.9
July	159.8	163.2	160.6	103.3	173.5	142.1	184.3	130.7	143.8	123.0	133.5	97.4	143.4
August	160.0	163.4	161.0	102.1	174.0	142.2	184.7	130.4	143.8	122.7	133.4	93.6	139.4
September	160.1	163.5	161.1	101.3	174.2	142.0	185.1	130.4	144.0	122.3	133.1	91.4	137.6
October	160.5	163.9	162.0	101.5	174.4	142.3	185.5	130.9	144.2	122.2	132.7	93.9	134.0
November	160.7	164.1	162.2	101.1	174.8	142.2	186.0	130.8	144.3	122.0	132.5	93.6	131.6
December	161.1	164.4	162.4	100.1	175.4	142.5	186.4	131.3	145.8	121.3	132.2	90.2	129.4

Table 8-1B. Summary Consumer and Producer Price Indexes: Historical, 1946–2010—*Continued*

(Seasonally adjusted.)

Year and month	Urban wage earners and clerical workers (CPI-W), all items	Consumer Price Index, 1982–1984 = 100						Producer Price Index, 1982 = 100					
		All urban consumers (CPI-U)						Finished goods		Intermediate materials, supplies, and components		Crude materials for further processing	
		All items	Food	Energy	All items less food and energy	Commodities	Services	Total	Less food and energy	Total	Less food and energy	Total	Crude nonfood less energy
1999													
January	161.4	164.7	163.0	99.7	175.6	142.8	186.6	131.7	145.6	121.2	132.0	91.0	128.7
February	161.3	164.7	163.3	99.2	175.6	142.4	186.9	131.2	145.7	120.8	131.8	89.0	130.5
March	161.4	164.8	163.3	100.4	175.7	142.4	187.4	131.5	145.7	121.1	131.9	89.6	129.6
April	162.4	165.9	163.5	105.5	176.3	144.0	187.9	132.1	145.7	121.9	132.0	91.3	128.7
May	162.6	166.0	163.8	104.9	176.5	143.9	188.1	132.3	145.7	122.2	132.4	96.8	130.5
June	162.6	166.0	163.7	104.5	176.6	143.8	188.3	132.4	145.8	122.6	132.8	97.0	131.6
July	163.3	166.7	163.9	106.7	177.1	144.5	188.9	132.7	145.8	123.4	133.3	97.3	133.6
August	163.8	167.1	164.2	109.5	177.3	145.0	189.3	133.5	145.7	124.1	133.6	102.4	136.3
September	164.6	167.8	164.6	111.8	177.8	145.9	189.8	134.5	146.5	124.6	133.9	106.4	138.8
October	164.9	168.1	165.0	112.0	178.1	146.1	190.2	134.4	146.9	124.9	134.3	103.8	142.5
November	165.1	168.4	165.3	111.5	178.4	145.9	190.9	134.9	146.9	125.4	134.5	109.7	144.4
December	165.6	168.8	165.5	113.8	178.7	146.5	191.2	135.2	147.0	125.8	134.7	104.4	147.6
2000													
January	166.0	169.3	165.6	115.0	179.3	146.7	192.0	135.2	146.8	126.4	135.1	106.8	150.5
February	166.7	170.0	166.2	118.8	179.4	147.6	192.5	136.6	147.3	127.5	135.5	111.0	151.3
March	167.8	171.0	166.5	124.3	180.0	149.1	193.1	137.3	147.4	128.4	136.0	113.2	150.5
April	167.6	170.9	166.7	120.9	180.3	148.5	193.5	136.9	147.4	128.3	136.5	111.3	148.8
May	167.9	171.2	167.3	120.0	180.7	148.5	194.0	137.0	147.8	128.2	136.6	115.1	147.8
June	169.0	172.2	167.4	126.8	181.1	149.6	194.9	138.1	147.8	129.3	136.9	124.8	145.1
July	169.5	172.7	168.3	127.3	181.5	149.8	195.7	138.2	148.1	129.6	137.1	122.1	142.8
August	169.3	172.7	168.7	123.8	181.9	149.2	196.3	137.9	148.2	129.3	136.9	117.6	141.2
September	170.3	173.6	168.9	129.2	182.3	150.4	196.9	139.0	148.6	130.3	137.0	125.6	142.9
October	170.5	173.9	169.0	129.6	182.6	150.1	197.7	139.5	148.5	130.7	137.1	130.2	142.1
November	170.8	174.2	169.2	129.2	183.1	150.3	198.1	140.2	148.7	130.7	136.9	129.1	139.6
December	171.2	174.6	170.0	130.1	183.3	150.4	198.8	140.5	148.9	131.3	136.9	141.1	139.5
2001													
January	172.2	175.6	170.3	135.0	183.9	150.6	200.6	141.7	149.5	132.1	137.1	165.6	138.7
February	172.5	176.0	171.2	134.1	184.4	150.8	201.2	141.9	149.2	131.8	137.3	141.7	136.5
March	172.6	176.1	171.7	131.7	184.7	150.5	201.6	141.2	149.5	131.0	137.4	132.4	135.0
April	173.0	176.4	172.1	132.3	185.1	150.9	202.0	142.0	149.8	130.9	137.3	133.0	131.3
May	174.0	177.3	172.4	138.4	185.3	151.9	202.7	142.3	150.1	131.1	137.3	130.5	130.9
June	174.2	177.7	173.1	136.9	186.0	151.9	203.5	141.8	150.2	130.9	137.1	119.9	129.7
July	173.8	177.4	173.6	129.6	186.4	150.9	203.8	140.1	150.5	129.4	136.4	113.3	130.6
August	173.8	177.4	174.0	127.3	186.7	150.4	204.4	140.7	150.5	129.1	135.9	112.3	128.4
September	174.7	178.1	174.2	130.9	187.1	151.6	204.5	141.3	150.7	129.3	135.9	107.2	128.8
October	173.9	177.6	174.8	122.9	187.4	150.3	204.8	139.0	149.8	127.6	135.4	97.4	126.5
November	173.7	177.5	174.9	116.9	188.1	149.2	205.6	138.5	150.2	127.0	135.1	102.7	126.2
December	173.4	177.4	174.7	113.9	188.4	148.3	206.1	138.0	150.4	126.1	134.8	95.5	125.7
2002													
January	173.7	177.7	175.3	114.2	188.7	148.3	206.8	137.7	150.0	125.7	134.7	99.8	126.2
February	173.9	178.0	175.7	113.5	189.1	148.3	207.5	138.0	150.1	125.5	134.6	98.4	127.5
March	174.5	178.5	176.1	117.6	189.2	149.0	207.9	138.8	150.0	126.4	135.0	103.8	128.1
April	175.4	179.3	176.4	121.5	189.7	150.0	208.5	138.7	150.3	127.2	135.3	108.1	130.8
May	175.5	179.5	175.8	121.9	190.0	149.7	209.0	138.4	150.2	127.1	135.3	109.0	134.2
June	175.7	179.6	175.9	121.6	190.2	149.7	209.3	138.8	150.5	127.3	135.6	105.1	138.2
July	176.1	180.0	176.1	122.4	190.5	149.9	209.9	138.6	150.0	127.7	136.0	106.5	140.8
August	176.6	180.5	176.1	123.1	191.1	150.2	210.6	138.7	149.9	128.0	136.2	108.3	140.0
September	176.8	180.8	176.5	123.7	191.3	150.2	211.1	139.2	150.3	128.9	136.5	110.8	140.2
October	177.2	181.2	176.4	126.9	191.5	150.5	211.7	140.0	150.5	129.8	136.7	112.6	140.0
November	177.5	181.5	176.9	126.7	191.9	150.5	212.4	140.0	150.3	129.9	136.8	116.6	141.0
December	177.7	181.8	177.1	127.1	192.1	150.3	213.0	139.7	149.5	130.0	136.7	118.9	141.3
2003													
January	178.6	182.6	177.1	133.5	192.4	151.3	213.7	141.1	149.8	131.4	137.2	128.0	143.3
February	179.7	183.6	178.1	140.8	192.5	152.7	214.2	142.7	149.9	133.8	138.1	134.3	148.1
March	180.1	183.9	178.4	143.9	192.5	152.6	215.0	144.0	150.7	136.3	138.6	152.2	147.5
April	179.2	183.2	178.5	136.5	192.5	151.1	215.1	142.2	149.9	133.1	138.3	128.2	145.9
May	178.7	182.9	178.8	129.4	192.9	149.4	216.0	141.9	150.1	132.4	138.4	129.9	146.0
June	178.9	183.1	179.7	129.8	193.0	149.7	216.2	142.7	150.1	133.1	138.4	135.5	145.7
July	179.4	183.7	179.8	132.2	193.4	150.3	216.8	142.8	150.3	133.3	138.2	131.9	148.5
August	180.3	184.5	180.5	137.8	193.6	151.4	217.2	143.7	150.5	133.9	138.4	130.8	152.1
September	180.9	185.1	180.9	142.9	193.7	152.1	217.8	144.0	150.4	133.8	138.8	134.4	156.2
October	180.6	184.9	181.6	137.8	194.0	151.1	218.4	144.8	151.1	134.2	139.1	138.2	160.2
November	180.6	185.0	182.6	136.9	194.0	151.1	218.6	144.6	151.0	134.2	139.3	137.9	165.6
December	181.0	185.5	183.5	138.8	194.2	151.6	219.0	145.1	151.0	135.0	139.6	142.4	171.0
2004													
January	181.9	186.3	183.4	143.9	194.6	152.5	219.7	145.9	151.4	136.6	140.5	148.7	179.7
February	182.4	186.7	183.9	145.8	194.9	153.1	220.1	145.8	151.3	137.8	141.8	150.8	190.0
March	182.7	187.1	184.2	145.1	195.5	153.3	220.8	146.2	151.8	138.4	142.9	153.2	195.0
April	182.8	187.4	184.6	143.4	195.9	153.0	221.4	147.2	151.9	140.1	144.6	156.2	187.1
May	183.8	188.2	186.1	147.6	196.2	154.2	221.9	148.4	152.3	141.7	145.7	160.6	177.6
June	184.4	188.9	186.4	151.5	196.6	154.9	222.7	148.4	152.8	142.2	146.2	161.5	176.3
July	184.6	189.1	186.8	151.1	196.8	154.6	223.2	148.2	152.5	142.9	146.9	161.3	195.7
August	184.7	189.2	187.0	151.5	196.9	154.4	223.7	148.6	152.9	144.4	148.4	161.7	201.6
September	185.3	189.8	186.9	152.9	197.5	154.9	224.2	148.8	153.2	144.8	149.6	154.0	198.3
October	186.4	190.8	187.8	158.6	197.9	156.7	224.6	151.2	153.7	146.6	150.2	161.0	204.6
November	187.4	191.7	188.4	163.8	198.3	157.8	225.4	152.1	154.1	147.9	150.7	172.7	208.9
December	187.4	191.7	188.4	162.3	198.6	157.4	225.8	151.4	154.5	147.7	151.3	167.2	206.0

Table 8-1B. Summary Consumer and Producer Price Indexes: Historical, 1946–2010—*Continued*

(Seasonally adjusted.)

Year and month	Urban wage earners and clerical workers (CPI-W), all items	Consumer Price Index, 1982–1984 = 100						Producer Price Index, 1982 = 100					
		All urban consumers (CPI-U)						Finished goods		Intermediate materials, supplies, and components		Crude materials for further processing	
		All items	Food	Energy	All items less food and energy	Commodit-ies	Services	Total	Less food and energy	Total	Less food and energy	Total	Crude nonfood less energy
2005													
January	187.2	191.6	188.7	157.2	199.0	156.8	226.2	151.9	155.4	148.5	152.4	164.2	203.7
February	188.0	192.4	188.6	161.8	199.4	157.5	226.9	152.7	155.3	149.5	153.2	162.9	200.2
March	188.6	193.1	189.1	163.5	200.1	157.9	228.0	153.7	155.6	150.7	153.8	170.5	199.6
April	189.3	193.7	190.4	166.7	200.2	158.6	228.5	154.2	156.0	151.3	153.9	175.0	203.5
May	189.1	193.6	190.6	163.3	200.5	158.1	228.9	153.9	156.4	150.6	153.5	169.1	196.6
June	189.3	193.7	190.5	163.7	200.6	158.0	229.1	153.9	156.2	151.1	153.3	165.5	188.9
July	190.6	194.9	190.9	172.8	200.9	159.6	229.9	155.0	156.8	152.3	153.5	174.4	190.5
August	192.0	196.1	191.1	183.5	201.1	161.5	230.4	156.3	156.9	153.2	153.4	181.5	200.9
September	195.1	198.8	191.5	208.2	201.3	166.0	231.4	158.8	157.1	157.2	155.0	200.3	211.3
October	195.2	199.1	192.0	205.9	202.0	164.8	233.1	160.5	156.8	162.3	157.2	212.7	207.7
November	193.7	198.1	192.6	191.0	202.5	161.8	234.2	158.7	156.8	160.3	157.9	209.9	214.0
December	193.7	198.1	192.9	187.6	202.8	161.5	234.4	159.6	156.8	160.2	158.5	202.0	216.7
2006													
January	195.1	199.3	193.6	196.6	203.2	162.9	235.5	160.5	157.5	162.4	159.9	203.2	216.7
February	195.0	199.4	193.7	194.1	203.6	162.5	235.9	158.7	158.0	161.6	160.4	186.6	224.0
March	195.3	199.7	194.0	192.0	204.3	162.6	236.5	159.3	158.4	161.5	161.1	179.6	227.1
April	196.4	200.7	193.8	198.5	204.8	164.1	237.1	160.6	158.5	163.0	162.0	182.9	238.2
May	197.0	201.3	194.1	199.8	205.4	164.6	237.8	160.6	158.9	164.4	163.7	184.4	259.1
June	197.4	201.8	194.7	199.8	205.9	164.8	238.5	161.4	159.0	165.2	164.7	178.5	255.3
July	198.6	202.9	195.2	207.9	206.3	166.4	239.2	161.0	158.1	165.5	165.6	180.5	259.5
August	199.5	203.8	195.7	211.9	206.8	167.2	239.9	162.1	158.7	166.5	166.3	187.0	251.7
September	198.3	202.8	196.3	198.1	207.2	164.6	240.7	160.2	159.2	164.7	166.2	182.7	255.2
October	197.1	201.9	196.9	184.1	207.6	162.5	241.0	158.7	158.5	163.0	166.2	168.6	249.7
November	197.2	202.0	197.0	184.1	207.8	162.0	241.7	160.0	159.9	163.8	165.5	189.4	249.8
December	198.4	203.1	197.1	192.7	208.1	163.4	242.4	161.1	160.0	164.7	165.6	195.4	253.7
2007													
January	198.6	203.4	198.4	190.3	208.6	163.3	243.2	160.9	160.2	164.1	165.6	184.9	257.2
February	199.4	204.2	199.7	192.3	209.1	164.1	244.1	162.7	160.9	165.3	165.6	201.6	265.9
March	200.7	205.3	200.4	200.2	209.4	165.6	244.7	164.1	160.9	166.7	166.3	203.6	282.7
April	201.3	205.9	201.0	203.3	209.7	166.2	245.3	165.3	161.0	168.3	167.7	204.0	285.1
May	202.3	206.8	201.7	208.6	210.1	167.3	245.9	166.0	161.4	169.7	168.6	204.8	280.3
June	202.7	207.2	202.6	209.8	210.4	167.5	246.6	166.1	161.7	170.4	169.0	205.9	280.7
July	203.0	207.6	203.2	209.6	210.8	167.8	247.1	167.2	162.1	171.8	169.6	203.7	283.0
August	203.0	207.7	204.0	206.4	211.1	167.5	247.5	166.0	162.3	170.1	168.9	198.6	284.2
September	204.0	208.5	205.0	210.7	211.6	168.5	248.2	167.6	162.3	171.4	169.0	203.2	290.8
October	204.7	209.2	205.7	212.4	212.1	169.0	249.1	169.3	162.9	172.7	169.7	214.4	295.0
November	206.5	210.8	206.5	223.8	212.7	171.5	249.8	172.4	163.4	176.7	171.0	229.5	293.4
December	207.1	211.4	206.9	225.6	213.2	172.0	250.5	171.7	163.4	176.9	171.2	235.6	294.7
2008													
January	207.9	212.2	208.1	226.8	213.8	172.7	251.3	173.3	164.1	179.2	172.7	243.3	309.4
February	208.4	212.6	208.9	229.7	213.9	173.0	251.8	173.9	164.8	180.8	173.8	253.3	319.5
March	209.2	213.4	209.3	233.3	214.4	173.7	252.9	175.4	165.1	184.6	175.9	264.2	329.6
April	209.8	214.0	211.1	234.8	214.6	174.1	253.6	175.9	165.8	186.4	178.3	272.8	362.2
May	211.1	215.2	212.0	243.9	214.9	175.5	254.7	178.4	166.3	191.1	181.1	287.3	368.9
June	213.7	217.5	213.3	262.1	215.4	178.8	255.8	181.2	166.6	195.3	183.7	294.2	372.2
July	215.5	219.1	215.4	271.1	216.0	180.7	257.1	183.4	167.4	200.6	187.4	303.4	384.8
August	215.0	218.7	216.5	262.6	216.4	179.6	257.6	182.0	168.1	198.1	188.6	270.3	373.5
September	215.1	218.9	217.8	260.1	216.7	179.8	257.6	182.7	168.9	198.0	188.8	255.2	338.4
October	212.7	217.0	218.7	238.1	216.8	175.8	257.7	178.3	170.5	189.4	184.9	215.9	278.6
November	207.9	213.1	219.1	195.2	216.9	168.0	257.8	172.9	170.4	179.7	180.4	187.3	226.9
December	205.9	211.4	219.1	176.6	216.9	164.5	258.0	169.7	170.8	172.3	176.2	176.7	223.0
2009													
January	206.5	212.0	219.2	178.8	217.3	165.3	258.4	171.1	171.0	172.2	174.8	173.4	225.5
February	207.4	212.8	219.0	184.9	217.8	166.8	258.7	170.7	171.1	170.5	173.5	163.7	224.2
March	207.1	212.6	218.5	178.8	218.3	166.2	258.7	169.2	171.4	168.0	172.7	160.6	221.2
April	207.4	212.7	218.2	177.1	218.7	166.5	258.7	170.1	171.5	168.2	171.8	162.8	221.9
May	207.8	213.0	217.8	179.7	218.9	167.2	258.6	170.4	171.4	169.2	171.5	168.2	232.5
June	209.9	214.7	217.8	196.9	219.2	170.7	258.7	173.6	172.0	171.3	171.9	175.8	240.8
July	210.0	214.7	217.4	195.6	219.3	170.5	258.7	171.6	171.6	170.7	172.3	169.0	247.0
August	210.9	215.5	217.4	201.5	219.5	171.3	259.3	174.1	171.9	173.7	173.3	176.7	264.2
September	211.3	215.9	217.3	202.8	219.9	171.9	259.6	173.7	171.8	174.0	174.2	174.6	269.1
October	211.9	216.5	217.5	204.6	220.5	172.7	260.0	174.5	171.7	174.7	174.5	187.6	274.0
November	212.7	217.1	217.6	210.3	220.6	173.8	260.2	176.9	172.3	176.6	175.0	196.1	274.4
December	213.0	217.3	217.9	210.3	220.8	174.2	260.3	177.4	172.3	177.6	176.0	201.1	288.1
2010													
January	213.4	217.5	218.4	213.5	220.5	174.9	259.8	179.2	172.8	180.4	177.0	217.4	305.0
February	213.3	217.4	218.6	210.9	220.6	174.4	260.0	178.0	172.8	180.2	178.4	213.8	305.2
March	213.3	217.4	218.9	210.0	220.8	174.2	260.4	179.2	173.1	181.1	179.6	212.2	321.6
April	213.2	217.4	219.1	208.1	220.9	173.6	260.7	178.9	173.1	182.5	181.4	208.3	331.3
May	212.9	217.2	219.3	205.5	221.0	173.2	261.0	178.9	173.6	183.0	181.8	204.9	327.1
June	212.9	217.2	219.3	204.4	221.3	173.1	261.3	178.4	173.8	182.0	181.0	200.7	315.8
July	213.5	217.6	219.2	206.9	221.5	173.5	261.5	178.9	174.0	181.6	180.3	205.4	313.2
August	213.9	218.1	219.5	209.0	221.6	174.1	261.7	179.7	174.1	182.6	180.6	210.5	324.9
September	214.3	218.4	220.3	210.1	221.7	174.5	261.8	180.4	174.5	183.3	181.0	210.7	335.8
October	215.1	219.0	220.6	216.5	221.8	175.7	262.0	181.7	174.4	185.4	182.1	219.4	347.5
November	215.5	219.4	221.0	218.8	222.1	176.3	262.3	182.8	174.4	187.1	183.2	221.3	357.2
December	216.6	220.4	221.3	227.7	222.2	178.0	262.7	184.4	174.8	189.1	184.2	233.3	368.0

Table 8-1C. Consumer and Producer Price Indexes: Historical, 1913–1949

(Not seasonally adjusted.)

Year and month	Consumer price indexes, 1982–1984 =100				Producer Price Index, 1982 = 100			
	All urban consumers (CPI-U)		Urban wage earners and clerical workers (CPI-W)		All commodities		Farm products	Industrial commodities
	Index	Percent change	Index	Percent change	Index	Percent change		
1913	9.9	. . .	10.0	. . .	12.0	. . .	18.0	11.9
1914	10.0	1.0	10.1	1.0	11.8	-1.7	17.9	11.3
1915	10.1	1.0	10.2	1.0	12.0	1.7	18.0	11.6
1916	10.9	7.9	11.0	7.8	14.7	22.5	21.3	15.0
1917	12.8	17.4	12.9	17.3	20.2	37.4	32.6	19.5
1918	15.1	18.0	15.1	17.1	22.6	11.9	37.4	21.1
1919	17.3	14.6	17.4	15.2	23.9	5.8	39.8	22.0
1920	20.0	15.6	20.1	15.5	26.6	11.3	38.0	27.4
1921	17.9	-10.5	18.0	-10.4	16.8	-36.8	22.3	17.8
1922	16.8	-6.1	16.9	-6.1	16.7	-0.6	23.7	17.4
1923	17.1	1.8	17.2	1.8	17.3	3.6	24.9	17.8
1924	17.1	0.0	17.2	0.0	16.9	-2.3	25.2	17.0
1925	17.5	2.3	17.6	2.3	17.8	5.3	27.7	17.5
1926	17.7	1.1	17.8	1.1	17.2	-3.4	25.3	17.0
1927	17.4	-1.7	17.5	-1.7	16.5	-4.1	25.1	16.0
1928	17.1	-1.7	17.2	-1.7	16.7	1.2	26.7	15.8
1929	17.1	0.0	17.2	0.0	16.4	-1.8	26.4	15.6
1930	16.7	-2.3	16.8	-2.3	14.9	-9.1	22.4	14.5
1931	15.2	-9.0	15.3	-8.9	12.6	-15.4	16.4	12.8
1932	13.7	-9.9	13.7	-10.5	11.2	-11.1	12.2	11.9
1933	13.0	-5.1	13.0	-5.1	11.4	1.8	13.0	12.1
1934	13.4	3.1	13.5	3.8	12.9	13.2	16.5	13.3
1935	13.7	2.2	13.8	2.2	13.8	7.0	19.8	13.3
1936	13.9	1.5	13.9	0.7	13.9	0.7	20.4	13.5
1937	14.4	3.6	14.4	3.6	14.9	7.2	21.8	14.5
1938	14.1	-2.1	14.2	-1.4	13.5	-9.4	17.3	13.9
1939	13.9	-1.4	14.0	-1.4	13.3	-1.5	16.5	13.9
1940	14.0	0.7	14.1	0.7	13.5	1.5	17.1	14.1
1941	14.7	5.0	14.8	5.0	15.1	11.9	20.8	15.1
1942	16.3	10.9	16.4	10.8	17.0	12.6	26.7	16.2
1943	17.3	6.1	17.4	6.1	17.8	4.7	30.9	16.5
1944	17.6	1.7	17.7	1.7	17.9	0.6	31.2	16.7
1945	18.0	2.3	18.1	2.3	18.2	1.7	32.4	17.0
1946	19.5	8.3	19.6	8.3	20.8	14.3	37.5	18.6
1947	22.3	14.4	22.5	14.8	25.6	23.1	45.1	22.7
1948	24.1	8.1	24.2	7.6	27.7	8.2	48.5	24.6
1949	23.8	-1.2	24.0	-0.8	26.3	-5.1	41.9	24.1
1913								
January	9.8	. . .	9.9	. . .	12.1	. . .	17.6	12.3
February	9.8	0.0	9.8	-1.0	12.0	-0.8	17.5	12.2
March	9.8	0.0	9.8	0.0	12.0	0.0	17.6	12.1
April	9.8	0.0	9.9	1.0	12.0	0.0	17.5	12.0
May	9.7	-1.0	9.8	-1.0	11.9	-0.8	17.4	11.9
June	9.8	1.0	9.8	0.0	11.9	0.0	17.6	11.8
July	9.9	1.0	9.9	1.0	12.0	0.8	18.1	11.8
August	9.9	0.0	10.0	1.0	12.0	0.0	18.2	11.7
September	10.0	1.0	10.0	0.0	12.2	1.7	18.8	11.8
October	10.0	0.0	10.1	1.0	12.2	0.0	18.8	11.8
November	10.1	1.0	10.1	0.0	12.1	-0.8	18.9	11.7
December	10.0	-1.0	10.1	0.0	11.9	-1.7	18.5	11.6
1914								
January	10.0	0.0	10.1	0.0	11.8	-0.8	18.4	11.5
February	9.9	-1.0	10.0	-1.0	11.8	0.0	18.3	11.5
March	9.9	0.0	10.0	0.0	11.7	-0.8	18.2	11.5
April	9.8	-1.0	9.9	-1.0	11.7	0.0	18.0	11.5
May	9.9	1.0	9.9	0.0	11.6	-0.9	18.0	11.4
June	9.9	0.0	10.0	1.0	11.6	0.0	18.1	11.3
July	10.0	1.0	10.1	1.0	11.6	0.0	18.0	11.2
August	10.2	2.0	10.2	1.0	12.0	3.4	18.3	11.2
September	10.2	0.0	10.3	1.0	12.1	0.8	17.9	11.3
October	10.1	-1.0	10.2	-1.0	11.7	-3.3	17.2	11.0
November	10.2	1.0	10.2	0.0	11.7	0.0	17.6	11.0
December	10.1	-1.0	10.2	0.0	11.6	-0.9	17.4	11.0
1915								
January	10.1	0.0	10.2	0.0	11.8	1.7	18.1	11.1
February	10.0	-1.0	10.1	-1.0	11.8	0.0	18.4	11.0
March	9.9	-1.0	10.0	-1.0	11.8	0.0	17.9	11.0
April	10.0	1.0	10.1	1.0	11.8	0.0	18.2	11.1
May	10.1	1.0	10.1	0.0	11.9	0.8	18.2	11.2
June	10.1	0.0	10.2	1.0	11.8	-0.8	17.7	11.4
July	10.1	0.0	10.2	0.0	11.9	0.8	18.1	11.5
August	10.1	0.0	10.2	0.0	11.8	-0.8	17.9	11.5
September	10.1	0.0	10.2	0.0	11.8	0.0	17.5	11.7
October	10.2	1.0	10.3	1.0	12.1	2.5	18.1	11.9
November	10.3	1.0	10.4	1.0	12.3	1.7	18.0	12.3
December	10.3	0.0	10.4	0.0	12.8	4.1	18.4	12.9

. . . = Not available.

Table 8-1C. Consumer and Producer Price Indexes: Historical, 1913–1949—*Continued*

(Not seasonally adjusted.)

Year and month	Consumer price indexes, 1982–1984 =100				Producer Price Index, 1982 = 100			
	All urban consumers (CPI-U)		Urban wage earners and clerical workers (CPI-W)		All commodities		Farm products	Industrial commodities
	Index	Percent change	Index	Percent change	Index	Percent change		
1916								
January	10.4	1.0	10.5	1.0	13.3	3.9	19.4	13.6
February	10.4	0.0	10.5	0.0	13.5	1.5	19.4	14.0
March	10.5	1.0	10.6	1.0	13.9	3.0	19.4	14.4
April	10.6	1.0	10.7	0.9	14.1	1.4	19.6	14.6
May	10.7	0.9	10.7	0.0	14.2	0.7	19.8	14.7
June	10.8	0.9	10.9	1.9	14.3	0.7	19.7	14.8
July	10.8	0.0	10.9	0.0	14.4	0.7	20.3	14.6
August	10.9	0.9	11.0	0.9	14.7	2.1	21.7	14.6
September	11.1	1.8	11.2	1.8	15.0	2.0	22.6	14.8
October	11.3	1.8	11.3	0.9	15.7	4.7	23.7	15.5
November	11.5	1.8	11.5	1.8	16.8	7.0	25.3	16.8
December	11.6	0.9	11.6	0.9	17.1	1.8	25.0	17.7
1917								
January	11.7	0.9	11.8	1.7	17.6	2.9	26.2	18.3
February	12.0	2.6	12.0	1.7	18.0	2.3	27.2	18.6
March	12.0	0.0	12.1	0.8	18.5	2.8	28.6	18.8
April	12.6	5.0	12.6	4.1	19.7	6.5	31.6	19.0
May	12.8	1.6	12.9	2.4	20.8	5.6	33.6	19.8
June	13.0	1.6	13.0	0.8	21.0	1.0	33.8	20.4
July	12.8	-1.5	12.9	-0.8	21.2	1.0	34.0	20.7
August	13.0	1.6	13.1	1.6	21.5	1.4	34.6	20.7
September	13.3	2.3	13.3	1.5	21.3	-0.9	34.3	20.1
October	13.5	1.5	13.6	2.3	21.1	-0.9	35.2	19.1
November	13.5	0.0	13.6	0.0	21.2	0.5	36.0	19.2
December	13.7	1.5	13.8	1.5	21.2	0.0	35.6	19.5
1918								
January	14.0	2.2	14.0	1.4	21.6	1.9	37.0	19.9
February	14.1	0.7	14.2	1.4	21.1	-2.3	37.1	19.0
March	14.0	-0.7	14.1	-0.7	21.8	3.3	37.3	20.2
April	14.2	1.4	14.3	1.4	22.1	1.4	36.6	20.7
May	14.5	2.1	14.5	1.4	22.1	0.0	35.4	21.0
June	14.7	1.4	14.8	2.1	22.2	0.5	35.4	21.3
July	15.1	2.7	15.2	2.7	22.7	2.3	37.0	21.5
August	15.4	2.0	15.4	1.3	23.2	2.2	38.6	21.7
September	15.7	1.9	15.8	2.6	23.7	2.2	39.6	22.1
October	16.0	1.9	16.1	1.9	23.5	-0.8	38.2	22.1
November	16.3	1.9	16.3	1.2	23.5	0.0	38.0	22.1
December	16.5	1.2	16.6	1.8	23.5	0.0	38.1	21.8
1919								
January	16.5	0.0	16.6	0.0	23.2	-1.3	38.9	21.1
February	16.2	-1.8	16.2	-2.4	22.4	-3.4	37.5	20.6
March	16.4	1.2	16.5	1.9	22.6	0.9	38.5	20.1
April	16.7	1.8	16.8	1.8	22.9	1.3	40.0	20.0
May	16.9	1.2	17.0	1.2	23.3	1.7	40.9	20.2
June	16.9	0.0	17.0	0.0	23.4	0.4	39.6	21.1
July	17.4	3.0	17.5	2.9	24.3	3.8	41.5	22.1
August	17.7	1.7	17.8	1.7	24.9	2.5	41.3	23.1
September	17.8	0.6	17.9	0.6	24.3	-2.4	38.7	23.2
October	18.1	1.7	18.2	1.7	24.4	0.4	38.5	23.5
November	18.5	2.2	18.6	2.2	24.9	2.0	40.3	23.8
December	18.9	2.2	19.0	2.2	26.0	4.4	41.8	24.7
1920								
January	19.3	2.1	19.4	2.1	27.2	4.6	43.0	26.1
February	19.5	1.0	19.6	1.0	27.1	-0.4	41.2	27.1
March	19.7	1.0	19.8	1.0	27.3	0.7	41.5	27.7
April	20.3	3.0	20.4	3.0	28.5	4.4	42.5	28.7
May	20.6	1.5	20.7	1.5	28.8	1.1	42.8	29.0
June	20.9	1.5	21.0	1.4	28.7	-0.3	42.3	29.0
July	20.8	-0.5	20.9	-0.5	28.6	-0.3	40.5	29.5
August	20.3	-2.4	20.4	-2.4	27.8	-2.8	37.8	29.7
September	20.0	-1.5	20.1	-1.5	26.8	-3.6	36.4	28.5
October	19.9	-0.5	20.0	-0.5	24.9	-7.1	32.2	26.9
November	19.8	-0.5	19.9	-0.5	23.0	-7.6	30.0	24.5
December	19.4	-2.0	19.5	-2.0	20.8	-9.6	26.4	22.7
1921								
January	19.0	-2.1	19.1	-2.1	19.6	-5.8	25.6	21.1
February	18.4	-3.2	18.5	-3.1	18.1	-7.7	23.4	19.4
March	18.3	-0.5	18.4	-0.5	17.7	-2.2	22.7	18.7
April	18.1	-1.1	18.2	-1.1	17.0	-4.0	20.9	18.4
May	17.7	-2.2	17.8	-2.2	16.6	-2.4	21.0	17.9
June	17.6	-0.6	17.7	-0.6	16.1	-3.0	20.3	17.4
July	17.7	0.6	17.8	0.6	16.1	0.0	21.8	16.9
August	17.7	0.0	17.8	0.0	16.1	0.0	22.5	16.5
September	17.5	-1.1	17.6	-1.1	16.1	0.0	22.7	16.5
October	17.5	0.0	17.6	0.0	16.2	0.6	22.7	17.0
November	17.4	-0.6	17.5	-0.6	16.2	0.0	22.1	17.3
December	17.3	-0.6	17.4	-0.6	16.0	-1.2	22.2	17.0

Table 8-1C. Consumer and Producer Price Indexes: Historical, 1913–1949—*Continued*

(Not seasonally adjusted.)

Year and month	Consumer price indexes, 1982–1984 =100				Producer Price Index, 1982 = 100			
	All urban consumers (CPI-U)		Urban wage earners and clerical workers (CPI-W)		All commodities		Farm products	Industrial commodities
	Index	Percent change	Index	Percent change	Index	Percent change		
1922								
January	16.9	-2.3	17.0	-2.3	15.7	-1.9	22.2	16.7
February	16.9	0.0	17.0	0.0	16.0	1.9	24.0	16.6
March	16.7	-1.2	16.8	-1.2	16.0	0.0	23.6	16.5
April	16.7	0.0	16.8	0.0	16.1	0.6	23.4	16.6
May	16.7	0.0	16.8	0.0	16.6	3.1	23.8	17.4
June	16.7	0.0	16.8	0.0	16.6	0.0	23.4	17.4
July	16.8	0.6	16.9	0.6	17.1	3.0	24.1	18.1
August	16.6	-1.2	16.7	-1.2	17.0	-0.6	23.0	18.2
September	16.6	0.0	16.7	0.0	17.1	0.6	23.3	18.2
October	16.7	0.6	16.8	0.6	17.2	0.6	23.8	17.9
November	16.8	0.6	16.9	0.6	17.3	0.6	24.7	17.7
December	16.9	0.6	17.0	0.6	17.3	0.0	25.0	17.7
1923								
January	16.8	-0.6	16.9	-0.6	17.6	1.7	25.1	18.2
February	16.8	0.0	16.9	0.0	17.8	1.1	25.3	18.6
March	16.8	0.0	16.9	0.0	18.0	1.1	25.3	18.8
April	16.9	0.6	17.0	0.6	17.9	-0.6	24.8	18.7
May	16.9	0.0	17.0	0.0	17.5	-2.2	24.4	18.3
June	17.0	0.6	17.1	0.6	17.3	-1.1	24.2	17.9
July	17.2	1.2	17.3	1.2	17.0	-1.7	23.7	17.6
August	17.1	-0.6	17.2	-0.6	16.9	-0.6	24.2	17.4
September	17.2	0.6	17.3	0.6	17.2	1.8	25.3	17.3
October	17.3	0.6	17.4	0.6	17.1	-0.6	25.4	17.1
November	17.3	0.0	17.4	0.0	17.0	-0.6	25.7	16.9
December	17.3	0.0	17.4	0.0	16.9	-0.6	25.5	16.9
1924								
January	17.3	0.0	17.4	0.0	17.2	1.8	25.6	17.4
February	17.2	-0.6	17.3	-0.6	17.2	0.0	25.0	17.6
March	17.1	-0.6	17.2	-0.6	17.0	-1.2	24.2	17.5
April	17.0	-0.6	17.1	-0.6	16.7	-1.8	24.6	17.3
May	17.0	0.0	17.1	0.0	16.5	-1.2	24.0	17.0
June	17.0	0.0	17.1	0.0	16.4	-0.6	23.8	16.7
July	17.1	0.6	17.2	0.6	16.5	0.6	24.9	16.6
August	17.0	-0.6	17.1	-0.6	16.7	1.2	25.7	16.6
September	17.1	0.6	17.2	0.6	16.7	0.0	25.3	16.6
October	17.2	0.6	17.3	0.6	16.9	1.2	26.0	16.6
November	17.2	0.0	17.3	0.0	17.1	1.2	26.2	16.8
December	17.3	0.6	17.4	0.6	17.5	2.3	27.3	17.1
1925								
January	17.3	0.0	17.4	0.0	17.7	1.1	28.7	17.3
February	17.2	-0.6	17.3	-0.6	17.9	1.1	28.4	17.7
March	17.3	0.6	17.4	0.6	17.9	0.0	28.5	17.5
April	17.2	-0.6	17.3	-0.6	17.5	-2.2	27.1	17.2
May	17.3	0.6	17.4	0.6	17.5	0.0	27.1	17.3
June	17.5	1.2	17.6	1.1	17.7	1.1	27.6	17.5
July	17.7	1.1	17.8	1.1	18.0	1.7	28.3	17.6
August	17.7	0.0	17.8	0.0	17.9	-0.6	28.1	17.4
September	17.7	0.0	17.8	0.0	17.8	-0.6	27.7	17.4
October	17.7	0.0	17.8	0.0	17.8	0.0	27.0	17.5
November	18.0	1.7	18.1	1.7	18.0	1.1	27.3	17.6
December	17.9	-0.6	18.0	-0.6	17.8	-1.1	26.6	17.6
1926								
January	17.9	0.0	18.0	0.0	17.8	0.0	27.1	17.5
February	17.9	0.0	18.0	0.0	17.6	-1.1	26.5	17.3
March	17.8	-0.6	17.9	-0.6	17.3	-1.7	25.7	17.1
April	17.9	0.6	18.0	0.6	17.3	0.0	26.0	17.0
May	17.8	-0.6	17.9	-0.6	17.3	0.0	25.8	17.0
June	17.7	-0.6	17.8	-0.6	17.3	0.0	25.5	17.0
July	17.5	-1.1	17.6	-1.1	17.1	-1.2	24.9	16.9
August	17.4	-0.6	17.5	-0.6	17.1	0.0	24.6	16.9
September	17.5	0.6	17.6	0.6	17.2	0.6	25.1	16.9
October	17.6	0.6	17.7	0.6	17.1	-0.6	24.7	16.9
November	17.7	0.6	17.8	0.6	17.0	-0.6	23.9	16.9
December	17.7	0.0	17.8	0.0	16.9	-0.6	24.0	16.7
1927								
January	17.5	-1.1	17.6	-1.1	16.4	-3.0	24.3	16.4
February	17.4	-0.6	17.5	-0.6	16.6	1.2	24.1	16.3
March	17.3	-0.6	17.4	-0.6	16.5	-0.6	23.8	16.1
April	17.3	0.0	17.4	0.0	16.3	-1.2	23.8	15.9
May	17.4	0.6	17.5	0.6	16.2	-0.6	24.3	15.9
June	17.6	1.1	17.7	1.1	16.2	0.0	24.3	15.9
July	17.3	-1.7	17.4	-1.7	16.2	0.0	24.6	15.9
August	17.2	-0.6	17.3	-0.6	16.4	1.2	25.8	15.9
September	17.3	0.6	17.4	0.6	16.6	1.2	26.7	16.0
October	17.4	0.6	17.5	0.6	16.7	0.6	26.5	15.9
November	17.3	-0.6	17.4	-0.6	16.6	-0.6	26.3	15.8
December	17.3	0.0	17.4	0.0	16.6	0.0	26.3	15.9

Table 8-1C. Consumer and Producer Price Indexes: Historical, 1913–1949—*Continued*

(Not seasonally adjusted.)

| Year and month | Consumer price indexes, 1982–1984 =100 | | | | Producer Price Index, 1982 = 100 | | | |
| | All urban consumers (CPI-U) | | Urban wage earners and clerical workers (CPI-W) | | All commodities | | Farm products | Industrial commodities |
	Index	Percent change	Index	Percent change	Index	Percent change		
1928								
January	17.3	0.0	17.4	0.0	16.6	0.0	26.8	15.8
February	17.1	-1.2	17.2	-1.1	16.5	-0.6	26.4	15.8
March	17.1	0.0	17.2	0.0	16.5	0.0	26.1	15.8
April	17.1	0.0	17.2	0.0	16.7	1.2	27.1	15.8
May	17.2	0.6	17.3	0.6	16.8	0.6	27.7	15.8
June	17.1	-0.6	17.2	-0.6	16.7	-0.6	26.9	15.8
July	17.1	0.0	17.2	0.0	16.8	0.6	27.4	15.8
August	17.1	0.0	17.2	0.0	16.8	0.0	27.0	15.8
September	17.3	1.2	17.4	1.2	17.0	1.2	27.5	15.8
October	17.2	-0.6	17.3	-0.6	16.7	-1.8	26.1	15.8
November	17.2	0.0	17.3	0.0	16.5	-1.2	25.7	15.8
December	17.1	-0.6	17.2	-0.6	16.5	0.0	26.2	15.8
1929								
January	17.1	0.0	17.2	0.0	16.5	0.0	26.7	15.7
February	17.1	0.0	17.2	0.0	16.4	-0.6	26.6	15.6
March	17.0	-0.6	17.1	-0.6	16.6	1.2	27.1	15.7
April	16.9	-0.6	17.0	-0.6	16.5	-0.6	26.5	15.6
May	17.0	0.6	17.1	0.6	16.3	-1.2	25.8	15.6
June	17.1	0.6	17.2	0.6	16.4	0.6	26.1	15.6
July	17.3	1.2	17.4	1.2	16.6	1.2	27.1	15.6
August	17.3	0.0	17.4	0.0	16.6	0.0	27.1	15.5
September	17.3	0.0	17.4	0.0	16.6	0.0	26.9	15.6
October	17.3	0.0	17.4	0.0	16.4	-1.2	26.2	15.6
November	17.3	0.0	17.4	0.0	16.1	-1.8	25.5	15.5
December	17.2	-0.6	17.3	-0.6	16.1	0.0	25.7	15.4
1930								
January	17.1	-0.6	17.2	-0.6	15.9	-1.2	25.5	15.2
February	17.0	-0.6	17.1	-0.6	15.7	-1.3	24.7	15.1
March	16.9	-0.6	17.0	-0.6	15.5	-1.3	23.9	15.0
April	17.0	0.6	17.1	0.6	15.5	0.0	24.2	15.0
May	16.9	-0.6	17.0	-0.6	15.3	-1.3	23.5	14.9
June	16.8	-0.6	16.9	-0.6	15.0	-2.0	22.5	14.6
July	16.6	-1.2	16.7	-1.2	14.5	-3.3	21.0	14.4
August	16.5	-0.6	16.6	-0.6	14.5	0.0	21.4	14.2
September	16.6	0.6	16.7	0.6	14.5	0.0	21.5	14.2
October	16.5	-0.6	16.6	-0.6	14.3	-1.4	20.8	14.0
November	16.4	-0.6	16.5	-0.6	14.0	-2.1	20.0	13.8
December	16.1	-1.8	16.2	-1.8	13.7	-2.1	19.0	13.6
1931								
January	15.9	-1.2	16.0	-1.2	13.5	-1.5	18.4	13.4
February	15.7	-1.3	15.7	-1.9	13.2	-2.2	17.7	13.3
March	15.6	-0.6	15.6	-0.6	13.1	-0.8	17.8	13.1
April	15.5	-0.6	15.5	-0.6	12.9	-1.5	17.7	12.9
May	15.3	-1.3	15.4	-0.6	12.6	-2.3	16.9	12.8
June	15.1	-1.3	15.2	-1.3	12.4	-1.6	16.5	12.6
July	15.1	0.0	15.2	0.0	12.4	0.0	16.4	12.6
August	15.1	0.0	15.1	-0.7	12.4	0.0	16.1	12.6
September	15.0	-0.7	15.1	0.0	12.3	-0.8	15.3	12.6
October	14.9	-0.7	15.0	-0.7	12.1	-1.6	14.8	12.4
November	14.7	-1.3	14.8	-1.3	12.1	0.0	14.8	12.5
December	14.6	-0.7	14.7	-0.7	11.8	-2.5	14.1	12.3
1932								
January	14.3	-2.1	14.4	-2.0	11.6	-1.7	13.3	12.2
February	14.1	-1.4	14.2	-1.4	11.4	-1.7	12.8	12.1
March	14.0	-0.7	14.1	-0.7	11.4	0.0	12.7	12.0
April	13.9	-0.7	14.0	-0.7	11.3	-0.9	12.4	12.0
May	13.7	-1.4	13.8	-1.4	11.1	-1.8	11.8	11.9
June	13.6	-0.7	13.7	-0.7	11.0	-0.9	11.6	11.9
July	13.6	0.0	13.7	0.0	11.1	0.9	12.1	11.8
August	13.5	-0.7	13.5	-1.5	11.2	0.9	12.4	11.9
September	13.4	-0.7	13.5	0.0	11.3	0.9	12.4	11.9
October	13.3	-0.7	13.4	-0.7	11.1	-1.8	11.8	11.9
November	13.2	-0.8	13.3	-0.7	11.0	-0.9	11.8	11.9
December	13.1	-0.8	13.2	-0.8	10.8	-1.8	11.1	11.7
1933								
January	12.9	-1.5	13.0	-1.5	10.5	-2.8	10.8	11.4
February	12.7	-1.6	12.8	-1.5	10.3	-1.9	10.3	11.2
March	12.6	-0.8	12.7	-0.8	10.4	1.0	10.8	11.2
April	12.6	0.0	12.6	-0.8	10.4	0.0	11.2	11.1
May	12.6	0.0	12.7	0.8	10.8	3.8	12.7	11.3
June	12.7	0.8	12.8	0.8	11.2	3.7	13.4	11.7
July	13.1	3.1	13.2	3.1	11.9	6.3	15.2	12.3
August	13.2	0.8	13.3	0.8	12.0	0.8	14.6	12.6
September	13.2	0.0	13.3	0.0	12.2	1.7	14.4	13.0
October	13.2	0.0	13.3	0.0	12.3	0.8	14.1	13.1
November	13.2	0.0	13.3	0.0	12.3	0.0	14.3	13.1
December	13.2	0.0	13.2	-0.8	12.2	-0.8	14.0	13.2

Table 8-1C. Consumer and Producer Price Indexes: Historical, 1913–1949—*Continued*

(Not seasonally adjusted.)

Year and month	Consumer price indexes, 1982–1984 =100				Producer Price Index, 1982 = 100			
	All urban consumers (CPI-U)		Urban wage earners and clerical workers (CPI-W)		All commodities		Farm products	Industrial commodities
	Index	Percent change	Index	Percent change	Index	Percent change		
1934								
January	13.2	0.0	13.3	0.8	12.4	1.6	14.8	13.3
February	13.3	0.8	13.4	0.8	12.7	2.4	15.5	13.4
March	13.3	0.0	13.4	0.0	12.7	0.0	15.5	13.4
April	13.3	0.0	13.4	0.0	12.7	0.0	15.1	13.4
May	13.3	0.0	13.4	0.0	12.7	0.0	15.1	13.4
June	13.4	0.8	13.4	0.0	12.9	1.6	16.0	13.3
July	13.4	0.0	13.4	0.0	12.9	0.0	16.3	13.3
August	13.4	0.0	13.5	0.7	13.2	2.3	17.6	13.3
September	13.6	1.5	13.7	1.5	13.4	1.5	18.5	13.3
October	13.5	-0.7	13.6	-0.7	13.2	-1.5	17.8	13.3
November	13.5	0.0	13.5	-0.7	13.2	0.0	17.8	13.3
December	13.4	-0.7	13.5	0.0	13.3	0.8	18.2	13.3
1935								
January	13.6	1.5	13.7	1.5	13.6	2.3	19.6	13.2
February	13.7	0.7	13.8	0.7	13.7	0.7	20.0	13.2
March	13.7	0.0	13.8	0.0	13.7	0.0	19.7	13.2
April	13.8	0.7	13.9	0.7	13.8	0.7	20.3	13.1
May	13.8	0.0	13.8	-0.7	13.8	0.0	20.3	13.2
June	13.7	-0.7	13.8	0.0	13.8	0.0	19.8	13.3
July	13.7	0.0	13.7	-0.7	13.7	-0.7	19.5	13.3
August	13.7	0.0	13.7	0.0	13.9	1.5	20.0	13.3
September	13.7	0.0	13.8	0.7	13.9	0.0	20.1	13.2
October	13.7	0.0	13.8	0.0	13.9	0.0	19.7	13.3
November	13.8	0.7	13.9	0.7	13.9	0.0	19.6	13.4
December	13.8	0.0	13.9	0.0	14.0	0.7	19.8	13.4
1936								
January	13.8	0.0	13.9	0.0	13.9	-0.7	19.7	13.4
February	13.8	0.0	13.8	-0.7	13.9	0.0	20.1	13.4
March	13.7	-0.7	13.8	0.0	13.7	-1.4	19.3	13.4
April	13.7	0.0	13.8	0.0	13.7	0.0	19.4	13.4
May	13.7	0.0	13.8	0.0	13.5	-1.5	19.0	13.4
June	13.8	0.7	13.9	0.7	13.7	1.5	19.7	13.4
July	13.9	0.7	14.0	0.7	13.9	1.5	20.5	13.5
August	14.0	0.7	14.1	0.7	14.0	0.7	21.2	13.5
September	14.0	0.0	14.1	0.0	14.0	0.0	21.2	13.5
October	14.0	0.0	14.1	0.0	14.0	0.0	21.2	13.6
November	14.0	0.0	14.1	0.0	14.2	1.4	21.5	13.8
December	14.0	0.0	14.1	0.0	14.5	2.1	22.4	14.0
1937								
January	14.1	0.7	14.2	0.7	14.8	2.1	23.1	14.2
February	14.1	0.0	14.2	0.0	14.9	0.7	23.1	14.3
March	14.2	0.7	14.3	0.7	15.1	1.3	23.8	14.5
April	14.3	0.7	14.4	0.7	15.2	0.7	23.3	14.7
May	14.4	0.7	14.4	0.0	15.1	-0.7	22.7	14.7
June	14.4	0.0	14.5	0.7	15.0	-0.7	22.3	14.6
July	14.5	0.7	14.5	0.0	15.2	1.3	22.6	14.7
August	14.5	0.0	14.6	0.7	15.1	-0.7	21.8	14.6
September	14.6	0.7	14.7	0.7	15.1	0.0	21.7	14.6
October	14.6	0.0	14.6	-0.7	14.7	-2.6	20.3	14.5
November	14.5	-0.7	14.5	-0.7	14.4	-2.0	19.1	14.3
December	14.4	-0.7	14.5	0.0	14.1	-2.1	18.4	14.2
1938								
January	14.2	-1.4	14.3	-1.4	14.0	-0.7	18.1	14.2
February	14.1	-0.7	14.2	-0.7	13.8	-1.4	17.6	14.1
March	14.1	0.0	14.2	0.0	13.7	-0.7	17.7	14.1
April	14.2	0.7	14.2	0.0	13.5	-1.5	17.2	14.0
May	14.1	-0.7	14.2	0.0	13.5	0.0	17.0	13.9
June	14.1	0.0	14.2	0.0	13.5	0.0	17.3	13.8
July	14.1	0.0	14.2	0.0	13.6	0.7	17.5	13.9
August	14.1	0.0	14.2	0.0	13.4	-1.5	17.0	13.9
September	14.1	0.0	14.2	0.0	13.5	0.7	17.2	13.9
October	14.0	-0.7	14.1	-0.7	13.4	-0.7	16.8	13.8
November	14.0	0.0	14.1	0.0	13.4	0.0	17.1	13.7
December	14.0	0.0	14.1	0.0	13.3	-0.7	17.0	13.6
1939								
January	14.0	0.0	14.0	-0.7	13.3	0.0	17.0	13.6
February	13.9	-0.7	14.0	0.0	13.3	0.0	16.9	13.6
March	13.9	0.0	13.9	-0.7	13.2	-0.8	16.6	13.7
April	13.8	-0.7	13.9	0.0	13.1	-0.8	16.1	13.7
May	13.8	0.0	13.9	0.0	13.1	0.0	16.1	13.7
June	13.8	0.0	13.9	0.0	13.0	-0.8	15.7	13.6
July	13.8	0.0	13.9	0.0	13.0	0.0	15.8	13.6
August	13.8	0.0	13.9	0.0	12.9	-0.8	15.4	13.6
September	14.1	2.2	14.2	2.2	13.6	5.4	17.3	14.0
October	14.0	-0.7	14.1	-0.7	13.7	0.7	16.9	14.2
November	14.0	0.0	14.1	0.0	13.6	-0.7	17.0	14.3
December	14.0	0.0	14.0	-0.7	13.7	0.7	17.1	14.3

Table 8-1C. Consumer and Producer Price Indexes: Historical, 1913–1949—*Continued*

(Not seasonally adjusted.)

Year and month	Consumer price indexes, 1982–1984 =100				Producer Price Index, 1982 = 100			
	All urban consumers (CPI-U)		Urban wage earners and clerical workers (CPI-W)		All commodities		Farm products	Industrial commodities
	Index	Percent change	Index	Percent change	Index	Percent change		
1940								
January	13.9	-0.7	14.0	0.0	13.7	0.0	17.4	14.3
February	14.0	0.7	14.1	0.7	13.6	-0.7	17.3	14.2
March	14.0	0.0	14.1	0.0	13.5	-0.7	17.1	14.1
April	14.0	0.0	14.1	0.0	13.5	0.0	17.5	14.0
May	14.0	0.0	14.1	0.0	13.5	0.0	17.1	14.0
June	14.1	0.7	14.1	0.0	13.4	-0.7	16.7	14.0
July	14.0	-0.7	14.1	0.0	13.4	0.0	16.8	14.0
August	14.0	0.0	14.1	0.0	13.4	0.0	16.5	14.0
September	14.0	0.0	14.1	0.0	13.4	0.0	16.7	14.0
October	14.0	0.0	14.1	0.0	13.6	1.5	16.8	14.2
November	14.0	0.0	14.1	0.0	13.7	0.7	17.2	14.3
December	14.1	0.7	14.2	0.7	13.8	0.7	17.6	14.3
1941								
January	14.1	0.0	14.2	0.0	13.9	0.7	18.1	14.3
February	14.1	0.0	14.2	0.0	13.9	0.0	17.7	14.3
March	14.2	0.7	14.2	0.0	14.0	0.7	18.1	14.4
April	14.3	0.7	14.4	1.4	14.4	2.9	18.8	14.6
May	14.4	0.7	14.5	0.7	14.6	1.4	19.3	14.9
June	14.7	2.1	14.7	1.4	15.0	2.7	20.7	15.1
July	14.7	0.0	14.8	0.7	15.3	2.0	21.7	15.2
August	14.9	1.4	14.9	0.7	15.6	2.0	22.1	15.5
September	15.1	1.3	15.2	2.0	15.8	1.3	23.0	15.6
October	15.3	1.3	15.4	1.3	15.9	0.6	22.7	15.9
November	15.4	0.7	15.5	0.6	15.9	0.0	22.9	15.9
December	15.5	0.6	15.5	0.0	16.2	1.9	23.9	15.9
1942								
January	15.7	1.3	15.7	1.3	16.5	1.9	25.5	16.1
February	15.8	0.6	15.9	1.3	16.7	1.2	25.6	16.1
March	16.0	1.3	16.1	1.3	16.8	0.6	26.0	16.2
April	16.1	0.6	16.2	0.6	17.0	1.2	26.4	16.2
May	16.3	1.2	16.3	0.6	17.0	0.0	26.3	16.3
June	16.3	0.0	16.4	0.6	17.0	0.0	26.3	16.3
July	16.4	0.6	16.5	0.6	17.0	0.0	26.6	16.3
August	16.5	0.6	16.6	0.6	17.1	0.6	26.8	16.2
September	16.5	0.0	16.6	0.0	17.2	0.6	27.2	16.2
October	16.7	1.2	16.8	1.2	17.2	0.0	27.5	16.2
November	16.8	0.6	16.9	0.6	17.3	0.6	27.9	16.3
December	16.9	0.6	17.0	0.6	17.4	0.6	28.7	16.3
1943								
January	16.9	0.0	17.0	0.0	17.5	0.6	29.5	16.4
February	16.9	0.0	17.0	0.0	17.7	1.1	30.0	16.4
March	17.2	1.8	17.3	1.8	17.8	0.6	31.0	16.4
April	17.4	1.2	17.5	1.2	17.9	0.6	31.2	16.5
May	17.5	0.6	17.6	0.6	17.9	0.0	31.7	16.5
June	17.5	0.0	17.6	0.0	17.9	0.0	31.9	16.5
July	17.4	-0.6	17.5	-0.6	17.8	-0.6	31.5	16.5
August	17.3	-0.6	17.4	-0.6	17.8	0.0	31.2	16.5
September	17.4	0.6	17.5	0.6	17.8	0.0	31.0	16.5
October	17.4	0.0	17.5	0.0	17.8	0.0	30.9	16.5
November	17.4	0.0	17.5	0.0	17.7	-0.6	30.6	16.6
December	17.4	0.0	17.5	0.0	17.8	0.6	30.7	16.6
1944								
January	17.4	0.0	17.5	0.0	17.8	0.0	30.7	16.6
February	17.4	0.0	17.5	0.0	17.8	0.0	30.9	16.7
March	17.4	0.0	17.5	0.0	17.9	0.6	31.2	16.7
April	17.5	0.6	17.6	0.6	17.9	0.0	31.1	16.7
May	17.5	0.0	17.6	0.0	17.9	0.0	31.0	16.7
June	17.6	0.6	17.7	0.6	18.0	0.6	31.5	16.7
July	17.7	0.6	17.8	0.6	17.9	-0.6	31.3	16.7
August	17.7	0.0	17.8	0.0	17.9	0.0	30.9	16.8
September	17.7	0.0	17.8	0.0	17.9	0.0	31.0	16.8
October	17.7	0.0	17.8	0.0	17.9	0.0	31.2	16.8
November	17.7	0.0	17.8	0.0	18.0	0.6	31.4	16.8
December	17.8	0.6	17.9	0.6	18.0	0.0	31.6	16.8
1945								
January	17.8	0.0	17.9	0.0	18.1	0.6	31.9	16.8
February	17.8	0.0	17.9	0.0	18.1	0.0	32.1	16.9
March	17.8	0.0	17.9	0.0	18.1	0.0	32.1	16.9
April	17.8	0.0	17.9	0.0	18.2	0.6	32.5	16.9
May	17.9	0.6	18.0	0.6	18.3	0.5	32.8	16.9
June	18.1	1.1	18.2	1.1	18.3	0.0	32.9	16.9
July	18.1	0.0	18.2	0.0	18.3	0.0	32.5	17.0
August	18.1	0.0	18.2	0.0	18.2	-0.5	32.0	17.0
September	18.1	0.0	18.2	0.0	18.1	-0.5	31.4	17.0
October	18.1	0.0	18.2	0.0	18.2	0.6	32.1	17.0
November	18.1	0.0	18.2	0.0	18.4	1.1	33.1	17.0
December	18.2	0.6	18.3	0.5	18.4	0.0	33.2	17.1

Table 8-1C. Consumer and Producer Price Indexes: Historical, 1913–1949—*Continued*

(Not seasonally adjusted.)

| Year and month | Consumer price indexes, 1982–1984 =100 | | | | Producer Price Index, 1982 = 100 | | | |
| | All urban consumers (CPI-U) | | Urban wage earners and clerical workers (CPI-W) | | All commodities | | Farm products | Industrial commodities |
	Index	Percent change	Index	Percent change	Index	Percent change		
1946								
January	18.2	0.0	18.3	0.0	18.4	0.0	32.7	17.1
February	18.1	-0.5	18.2	-0.5	18.5	0.5	33.0	17.2
March	18.3	1.1	18.4	1.1	18.8	1.6	33.6	17.4
April	18.4	0.5	18.5	0.5	19.0	1.1	34.1	17.5
May	18.5	0.5	18.6	0.5	19.1	0.5	34.7	17.7
June	18.7	1.1	18.8	1.1	19.4	1.6	35.4	18.0
July	19.8	5.9	19.9	5.9	21.5	10.8	39.6	18.6
August	20.2	2.0	20.3	2.0	22.2	3.3	40.6	19.0
September	20.4	1.0	20.5	1.0	21.4	-3.6	39.0	19.1
October	20.8	2.0	20.9	2.0	23.1	7.9	41.7	19.7
November	21.3	2.4	21.5	2.9	24.1	4.3	42.8	20.6
December	21.5	0.9	21.6	0.5	24.3	0.8	42.4	21.2
1947								
January	21.5	0.0	21.6	0.0	24.5	0.8	41.6	21.8
February	21.5	0.0	21.6	0.0	24.7	0.8	42.6	22.0
March	21.9	1.9	22.1	2.3	25.3	2.4	45.5	22.3
April	21.9	0.0	22.1	0.0	25.1	-0.8	44.0	22.4
May	21.9	0.0	22.0	-0.5	25.0	-0.4	43.6	22.3
June	22.0	0.5	22.2	0.9	25.0	0.0	43.8	22.4
July	22.2	0.9	22.4	0.9	25.3	1.2	44.3	22.5
August	22.5	1.4	22.6	0.9	25.6	1.2	44.8	22.8
September	23.0	2.2	23.1	2.2	26.1	2.0	46.6	23.1
October	23.0	0.0	23.1	0.0	26.4	1.1	47.4	23.3
November	23.1	0.4	23.3	0.9	26.7	1.1	47.7	23.6
December	23.4	1.3	23.6	1.3	27.2	1.9	50.1	23.9
1948								
January	23.7	1.3	23.8	0.8	27.7	1.8	51.2	24.3
February	23.5	-0.8	23.6	-0.8	27.2	-1.8	47.7	24.1
March	23.4	-0.4	23.6	0.0	27.2	0.0	47.6	24.1
April	23.8	1.7	23.9	1.3	27.4	0.7	48.3	24.3
May	23.9	0.4	24.1	0.8	27.5	0.4	49.4	24.3
June	24.1	0.8	24.2	0.4	27.7	0.7	50.4	24.4
July	24.4	1.2	24.5	1.2	28.0	1.1	50.2	24.6
August	24.5	0.4	24.6	0.4	28.2	0.7	49.6	24.9
September	24.5	0.0	24.6	0.0	28.1	-0.4	48.8	25.0
October	24.4	-0.4	24.5	-0.4	27.8	-1.1	46.9	25.0
November	24.2	-0.8	24.4	-0.4	27.8	0.0	46.3	25.1
December	24.1	-0.4	24.2	-0.8	27.6	-0.7	45.2	25.1
1949								
January	24.0	-0.4	24.2	0.0	27.3	-1.1	43.8	24.9
February	23.8	-0.8	23.9	-1.2	26.8	-1.8	42.0	24.7
March	23.8	0.0	24.0	0.4	26.8	0.0	42.7	24.6
April	23.9	0.4	24.0	0.0	26.5	-1.1	42.7	24.3
May	23.8	-0.4	24.0	0.0	26.3	-0.8	42.7	24.0
June	23.9	0.4	24.0	0.0	26.0	-1.1	41.8	23.8
July	23.7	-0.8	23.8	-0.8	26.0	0.0	41.7	23.7
August	23.8	0.4	23.9	0.4	26.0	0.0	41.7	23.8
September	23.9	0.4	24.0	0.4	26.1	0.4	41.8	23.8
October	23.7	-0.8	23.9	-0.4	26.0	-0.4	41.0	23.8
November	23.8	0.4	23.9	0.0	26.0	0.0	40.9	23.8
December	23.6	-0.8	23.8	-0.4	25.9	-0.4	40.3	23.8

Figure 8-2. Consumer Prices: All Items, Medical Care, and Apparel, 1970–2012 (ratio scale)

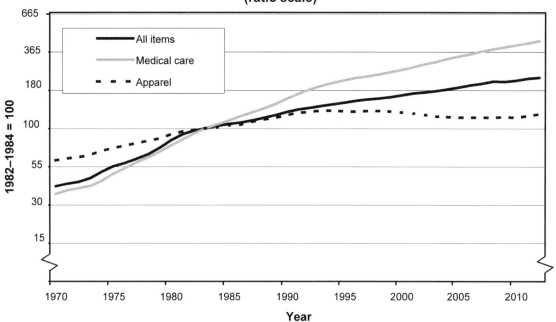

- Figure 8-2 charts two components of the Consumer Price Index for All Urban Consumers (CPI-U) along with the all-items total. Since all three indexes have the base years 1982–1984, they converge around 100 in those years. However, over the entire postwar period, the trends of the two components are very different. (Table 8-2)

- Apparel has been one of the areas most subject to international competition, and the apparel index shows far less growth than the overall average of prices.

- Medical care, on the other hand, has little price competition from producers in other countries. It is often paid for by third-party insurers, both government and private, rather than directly by consumers. Furthermore, it is characterized by trend growth in demand, due to rising income and expectations and to technological progress. All of these economic factors cause medical care prices to rise faster than the general price level.

- Medical care has arguably been overstated in the CPI due to the difficulties of making quality adjustments. Quality adjustments in the indexes have been much improved in recent years, although such improvements are not retroactively introduced into the official CPIs. But even since 1997, when a major improvement was introduced into the hospital cost component of the CPI, measured medical care prices have increased at a 3.9 percent annual rate, while the total CPI rose at a 2.4 percent average annual rate. (Table 8-2)

Table 8-2. Consumer Price Indexes and Purchasing Power of the Dollar

(1982–1984 = 100, seasonally adjusted, except as noted.)

Year and month	CPI-U, All items					CPI-U, Food and beverages									
	Not seasonally adjusted	Seasonally adjusted		Total	Total food	Food at home							Food away from home [1]	Alcoholic beverages
		Index	Percent change from previous period			Total	Cereals and bakery products	Meats, poultry, fish, and eggs	Dairy and related products[1]	Fruits and vegetables	Non-alcoholic beverages	Other food at home		
1970	38.8	38.8	5.7	40.1	39.2	39.9	37.1	44.6	44.7	37.8	27.1	32.9	37.5	52.1
1971	40.5	40.5	4.4	41.4	40.4	40.9	38.8	44.1	46.1	39.7	28.1	34.3	39.4	54.2
1972	41.8	41.8	3.2	43.1	42.1	42.7	39.0	48.0	46.8	41.6	28.0	34.6	41.0	55.4
1973	44.4	44.4	6.2	48.8	48.2	49.7	43.5	60.9	51.2	47.4	30.1	36.7	44.2	56.8
1974	49.3	49.3	11.0	55.5	55.1	57.1	56.5	62.2	60.7	55.2	35.9	47.8	49.8	61.1
1975	53.8	53.8	9.1	60.2	59.8	61.8	62.9	67.0	62.6	56.9	41.3	55.4	54.5	65.9
1976	56.9	56.9	5.8	62.1	61.6	63.1	61.5	68.0	67.7	58.4	49.4	56.4	58.2	68.1
1977	60.6	60.6	6.5	65.8	65.5	66.8	62.5	67.4	69.5	63.8	74.4	68.4	62.6	70.0
1978	65.2	65.2	7.6	72.2	72.0	73.8	68.1	77.6	74.2	70.9	78.7	73.6	68.3	74.1
1979	72.6	72.6	11.3	79.9	79.9	81.8	74.9	89.0	82.8	76.6	82.6	79.0	75.9	79.9
1980	82.4	82.4	13.5	86.7	86.8	88.4	83.9	92.0	90.9	82.1	91.4	88.4	83.4	86.4
1981	90.9	90.9	10.3	93.5	93.6	94.8	92.3	96.0	97.4	92.0	95.3	94.9	90.9	92.5
1982	96.5	96.5	6.2	97.3	97.4	98.1	96.5	99.6	98.8	97.0	97.9	97.3	95.8	96.7
1983	99.6	99.6	3.2	99.5	99.4	99.1	99.6	99.2	100.0	97.3	99.8	99.5	100.0	100.4
1984	103.9	103.9	4.3	103.2	103.2	102.8	103.9	101.3	101.3	105.7	102.3	103.1	104.2	103.0
1985	107.6	107.6	3.6	105.6	105.6	104.3	107.9	100.1	103.2	108.4	104.3	105.7	108.3	106.4
1986	109.6	109.6	1.9	109.1	109.0	107.3	110.9	104.5	103.3	109.4	110.4	109.4	112.5	111.1
1987	113.6	113.6	3.6	113.5	113.5	111.9	114.8	110.5	105.9	119.1	107.5	110.5	117.0	114.1
1988	118.3	118.3	4.1	118.2	118.2	116.6	122.1	114.3	108.4	128.1	107.5	113.1	121.8	118.6
1989	124.0	124.0	4.8	124.9	125.1	124.2	132.4	121.3	115.6	138.0	111.3	119.1	127.4	123.5
1990	130.7	130.7	5.4	132.1	132.4	132.3	140.0	130.0	126.5	149.0	113.5	123.4	133.4	129.3
1991	136.2	136.2	4.2	136.8	136.3	135.8	145.8	132.6	125.1	155.8	114.1	127.3	137.9	142.8
1992	140.3	140.3	3.0	138.7	137.9	136.8	151.5	130.9	128.5	155.4	114.3	128.8	140.7	147.3
1993	144.5	144.5	3.0	141.6	140.9	140.1	156.6	135.5	129.4	159.0	114.6	130.5	143.2	149.6
1994	148.2	148.2	2.6	144.9	144.3	144.1	163.0	137.2	131.7	165.0	123.2	135.6	145.7	151.5
1995	152.4	152.4	2.8	148.9	148.4	148.8	167.5	138.8	132.8	177.7	131.7	140.8	149.0	153.9
1996	156.9	156.9	3.0	153.7	153.3	154.3	174.0	144.8	142.1	183.9	128.6	142.9	152.7	158.5
1997	160.5	160.5	2.3	157.7	157.3	158.1	177.6	148.5	145.5	187.5	133.4	147.3	157.0	162.8
1998	163.0	163.0	1.6	161.1	160.7	161.1	181.1	147.3	150.8	198.2	133.0	150.8	161.1	165.7
1999	166.6	166.6	2.2	164.6	164.1	164.2	185.0	147.9	159.6	203.1	134.3	153.5	165.1	169.7
2000	172.2	172.2	3.4	168.4	167.8	167.9	188.3	154.5	160.7	204.6	137.8	155.6	169.0	174.7
2001	177.1	177.1	2.8	173.6	173.1	173.4	193.8	161.3	167.1	212.2	139.2	159.6	173.9	179.3
2002	179.9	179.9	1.6	176.8	176.2	175.6	198.0	162.1	168.1	220.9	139.2	160.8	178.3	183.6
2003	184.0	184.0	2.3	180.5	180.0	179.4	202.8	169.3	167.9	225.9	139.8	162.6	182.1	187.2
2004	188.9	188.9	2.7	186.6	186.2	186.2	206.0	181.7	180.2	232.7	140.4	164.9	187.5	192.1
2005	195.3	195.3	3.4	191.2	190.7	189.8	209.0	184.7	182.4	241.4	144.4	167.0	193.4	195.9
2006	201.6	201.6	3.2	195.7	195.2	193.1	212.8	186.6	181.4	252.9	147.4	169.6	199.4	200.7
2007	207.3	207.3	2.8	203.3	202.9	201.2	222.1	195.6	194.8	262.6	153.4	173.3	206.7	207.0
2008	215.3	215.3	3.8	214.2	214.1	214.1	244.9	204.7	210.4	278.9	160.0	184.2	215.8	214.5
2009	214.5	214.5	-0.4	218.2	218.0	215.1	252.6	203.8	197.0	272.9	163.0	191.2	223.3	220.8
2010	218.1	218.1	1.6	220.0	219.6	215.8	250.4	207.7	199.2	273.5	161.6	191.1	226.1	223.3
2011	224.9	224.9	3.2	227.9	227.8	226.2	260.3	223.2	212.7	284.7	166.8	197.4	231.4	226.7
2012	229.6	229.6	2.1	233.7	233.8	231.8	267.7	231.0	217.3	282.8	168.6	204.8	238.0	230.8
2011														
January	220.2	221.1	0.3	222.7	222.5	219.2	253.8	214.2	202.3	279.5	162.8	191.8	228.2	224.8
February	221.3	221.9	0.4	223.8	223.6	220.9	253.9	216.7	203.5	284.6	163.1	192.8	228.6	225.2
March	223.5	223.1	0.5	225.3	225.2	223.2	255.5	219.2	206.2	289.4	164.3	194.4	229.3	225.4
April	224.9	223.9	0.3	226.1	226.0	224.0	255.8	220.9	209.7	285.6	165.8	194.9	230.1	226.1
May	226.0	224.7	0.4	227.0	226.9	225.2	258.2	224.0	211.3	282.7	166.3	195.8	230.5	226.8
June	225.7	225.1	0.1	227.5	227.4	225.7	260.0	223.3	212.3	281.6	166.9	197.0	231.1	226.8
July	225.9	225.6	0.2	228.5	228.5	227.1	260.0	224.4	214.8	285.7	168.3	197.7	231.6	226.8
August	226.5	226.2	0.3	229.6	229.6	228.5	262.8	225.4	216.7	286.6	168.2	199.2	232.5	227.4
September	226.9	226.8	0.3	230.5	230.6	229.8	264.8	226.4	219.4	288.8	168.0	200.4	233.0	227.5
October	226.4	226.7	0.0	230.9	231.0	230.1	265.6	227.1	219.5	285.5	169.0	201.3	233.5	227.6
November	226.2	227.0	0.1	231.1	231.2	230.1	266.4	227.4	218.8	284.2	169.3	201.2	234.0	227.9
December	225.7	227.1	0.0	231.5	231.7	230.6	267.1	229.0	218.5	282.0	169.5	202.1	234.4	228.2
2012														
January	226.7	227.6	0.2	232.1	232.2	230.9	267.1	229.6	220.5	279.6	169.2	203.1	235.3	229.5
February	227.7	228.3	0.3	232.2	232.3	230.8	267.4	229.1	219.4	279.1	169.2	203.7	235.6	230.1
March	229.4	229.0	0.3	232.6	232.7	231.2	267.1	230.8	219.1	278.4	168.8	204.2	236.1	229.9
April	230.1	229.0	0.0	233.0	233.1	231.4	267.8	231.1	216.9	280.6	168.9	204.5	236.7	230.1
May	229.8	228.6	-0.1	233.1	233.2	231.3	267.7	230.2	216.1	281.5	168.3	205.1	237.3	230.5
June	229.5	228.9	0.1	233.5	233.6	231.6	266.7	230.7	215.5	284.4	168.5	205.0	237.8	231.0
July	229.1	228.8	0.0	233.7	233.8	231.6	267.6	231.4	214.4	283.9	167.9	205.0	238.3	231.0
August	230.4	230.0	0.5	234.1	234.2	231.8	267.6	232.3	214.5	284.7	167.6	204.9	239.1	230.9
September	231.4	231.2	0.5	234.2	234.4	231.7	267.3	230.8	215.3	283.8	168.6	205.3	239.6	231.2
October	231.3	231.6	0.2	234.7	234.8	232.4	268.0	232.1	217.1	285.2	168.4	205.2	239.7	231.1
November	230.2	231.1	-0.2	235.2	235.4	233.0	268.6	232.1	218.9	286.1	168.9	205.9	240.0	231.8
December	229.6	231.1	0.0	235.6	235.7	233.5	269.1	232.3	219.4	286.8	169.2	206.2	240.4	232.5

[1] Not seasonally adjusted.

Table 8-2. Consumer Price Indexes and Purchasing Power of the Dollar—*Continued*

(1982–1984 = 100, seasonally adjusted, except as noted.)

Year and month	Total	CPI-U, Housing — Shelter						Fuels and utilities				Household furnishings and operations	
		Total	Rent of shelter[2]	Rent of primary residence	Lodging away from home[3]	Owners' equivalent rent of primary residence[2]	Tenants' and household insurance[1,3]	Total	Fuel oil and other fuels	Energy services	Water and sewer and trash collection services[3]	Total	Household operations[1,3]
1970	36.4	35.5	...	46.5	...	...	...	29.1	17.0	25.4	...	46.8	...
1971	38.0	37.0	...	48.7	...	...	...	31.1	18.2	27.1	...	48.6	...
1972	39.4	38.7	...	50.4	...	...	...	32.5	18.3	28.5	...	49.7	...
1973	41.2	40.5	...	52.5	...	...	...	34.3	21.1	29.9	...	51.1	...
1974	45.8	44.4	...	55.2	...	...	...	40.7	33.2	34.5	...	56.8	...
1975	50.7	48.8	...	58.0	...	...	...	45.4	36.4	40.1	...	63.4	...
1976	53.8	51.5	...	61.1	...	...	...	49.4	38.8	44.7	...	67.3	...
1977	57.4	54.9	...	64.8	...	...	...	54.7	43.9	50.5	...	70.4	...
1978	62.4	60.5	...	69.3	...	...	...	58.5	46.2	55.0	...	74.7	...
1979	70.1	68.9	...	74.3	...	...	...	64.8	62.4	61.0	...	79.9	...
1980	81.1	81.0	...	80.9	...	...	...	75.4	86.1	71.4	...	86.3	...
1981	90.4	90.5	...	87.9	...	...	...	86.4	104.6	81.9	...	93.0	...
1982	96.9	96.9	...	94.6	...	...	...	94.9	103.4	93.2	...	98.0	...
1983	99.5	99.1	102.7	100.1	...	102.5	...	100.2	97.2	101.5	...	100.2	...
1984	103.6	104.0	107.7	105.3	...	107.3	...	104.8	99.4	105.4	...	101.9	...
1985	107.7	109.8	113.9	111.8	...	113.2	...	106.5	95.9	107.1	...	103.8	...
1986	110.9	115.8	120.2	118.3	...	119.4	...	104.1	77.6	105.7	...	105.2	...
1987	114.2	121.3	125.9	123.1	...	124.8	...	103.0	77.9	103.8	...	107.1	...
1988	118.5	127.1	132.0	127.8	...	131.1	...	104.4	78.1	104.6	...	109.4	...
1989	123.0	132.8	138.0	132.8	...	137.4	...	107.8	81.7	107.5	...	111.2	...
1990	128.5	140.0	145.5	138.4	...	144.8	...	111.6	99.3	109.3	...	113.3	...
1991	133.6	146.3	152.1	143.3	...	150.4	...	115.3	94.6	112.6	...	116.0	...
1992	137.5	151.2	157.3	146.9	...	155.5	...	117.8	90.7	114.8	...	118.0	...
1993	141.2	155.7	162.0	150.3	...	160.5	...	121.3	90.3	118.5	...	119.3	...
1994	144.8	160.5	167.0	154.0	...	165.8	...	122.8	88.8	119.2	...	121.0	...
1995	148.5	165.7	172.4	157.8	...	171.3	...	123.7	88.1	119.2	...	123.0	...
1996	152.8	171.0	178.0	162.0	...	176.8	...	127.5	99.2	122.1	...	124.7	...
1997	156.8	176.3	183.4	166.7	...	181.9	...	130.8	99.8	125.1	...	125.4	...
1998	160.4	182.1	189.6	172.1	109.0	187.8	99.8	128.5	90.0	121.2	101.6	126.6	101.5
1999	163.9	187.3	195.0	177.5	112.3	192.9	101.3	128.8	91.4	120.9	104.0	126.7	104.5
2000	169.6	193.4	201.3	183.9	117.5	198.7	103.7	137.9	129.7	128.0	106.5	128.2	110.5
2001	176.4	200.6	208.9	192.1	118.6	206.3	106.2	150.2	129.3	142.4	109.6	129.1	115.6
2002	180.3	208.1	216.7	199.7	118.3	214.7	108.7	143.6	115.5	134.4	113.0	128.3	119.0
2003	184.8	213.1	221.9	205.5	119.3	219.9	114.8	154.5	139.5	145.0	117.2	126.1	121.8
2004	189.5	218.8	227.9	211.0	125.9	224.9	116.2	161.9	160.5	150.6	124.0	125.5	125.0
2005	195.7	224.4	233.7	217.3	130.3	230.2	117.6	179.0	208.6	166.5	130.3	126.1	130.3
2006	203.2	232.1	241.9	225.1	136.0	238.2	116.5	194.7	234.9	182.1	136.8	127.0	136.6
2007	209.6	240.6	250.8	234.7	142.8	246.2	117.0	200.6	251.5	186.3	143.7	126.9	140.6
2008	216.3	246.7	257.2	243.3	143.7	252.4	118.8	220.0	334.4	202.2	152.1	127.8	147.5
2009	217.1	249.4	259.9	248.8	134.2	256.6	121.5	210.7	239.8	193.6	161.1	128.7	150.3
2010	216.3	248.4	258.8	249.4	133.7	256.6	125.7	214.2	275.1	192.9	170.9	125.5	150.3
2011	219.1	251.6	262.2	253.6	137.4	259.6	127.4	220.4	337.1	194.4	179.6	124.9	151.8
2012	222.7	257.1	267.8	260.4	140.5	264.8	131.3	219.0	335.9	189.7	189.3	125.7	155.2
2011													
January	217.1	249.6	260.2	251.1	135.2	257.6	126.2	215.9	314.1	191.3	175.7	124.4	151.2
February	217.5	249.9	260.4	251.5	134.8	258.0	126.5	217.9	326.9	192.8	176.8	124.5	151.4
March	217.9	250.2	260.6	251.9	135.8	258.2	125.9	219.3	341.9	193.4	177.6	124.4	150.5
April	218.3	250.4	260.8	252.2	135.9	258.4	126.6	220.7	348.7	194.6	178.1	124.6	151.3
May	218.6	250.8	261.2	252.6	136.6	258.7	126.8	221.6	347.0	195.6	178.7	124.8	151.7
June	218.9	251.2	261.7	252.9	138.4	259.1	127.2	221.1	340.8	195.2	179.3	124.8	151.7
July	219.3	251.9	262.3	253.5	140.6	259.7	127.3	221.1	336.9	195.2	179.9	124.9	151.9
August	219.7	252.3	262.8	254.4	139.0	260.2	127.6	221.3	336.0	195.4	180.0	125.2	152.1
September	220.1	252.7	263.2	255.0	138.3	260.5	127.9	222.4	334.7	196.4	181.3	125.3	152.0
October	220.3	253.1	263.7	255.7	136.9	261.0	128.4	221.6	335.1	195.2	181.9	125.4	152.4
November	220.6	253.6	264.3	256.2	138.3	261.4	128.8	220.9	342.8	193.8	182.4	125.5	152.6
December	220.8	254.0	265.0	256.8	138.5	261.9	129.5	220.5	340.5	193.1	183.3	125.6	152.7
2012													
January	221.1	254.5	265.2	257.2	139.0	262.4	129.9	220.0	344.6	192.2	184.0	125.7	153.6
February	221.4	254.9	265.7	257.8	140.4	262.7	129.2	219.5	350.5	190.9	185.1	126.0	154.2
March	221.7	255.5	266.2	258.3	140.6	263.3	130.0	219.4	356.6	190.1	186.1	125.8	154.4
April	222.1	256.0	266.7	258.9	140.7	263.8	130.9	219.5	352.2	190.0	187.4	125.8	155.0
May	222.1	256.5	267.1	259.4	141.7	264.2	131.1	218.0	340.8	188.7	187.9	125.5	154.9
June	222.4	256.8	267.5	259.8	142.5	264.4	131.2	218.1	316.9	189.6	189.1	125.8	155.6
July	222.4	257.2	267.8	260.6	140.2	264.9	131.6	216.2	312.4	187.3	189.8	126.0	155.5
August	222.9	257.7	268.4	261.1	139.8	265.4	131.7	217.6	321.8	188.1	191.1	125.7	155.6
September	223.4	258.3	269.1	261.8	140.3	266.1	131.5	218.6	330.4	188.8	191.6	125.6	155.5
October	223.9	258.8	269.7	262.7	140.5	266.5	131.8	219.3	334.1	189.1	192.4	125.5	155.4
November	224.4	259.2	270.1	263.1	140.4	267.0	132.5	220.5	335.1	190.3	193.2	125.9	155.9
December	224.7	259.6	270.7	263.6	139.9	267.3	133.9	221.1	335.6	190.9	193.9	125.6	156.1

[1]Not seasonally adjusted.
[2]December 1982 = 100.
[3]December 1997 = 100.
. . . = Not available.

Table 8-2. Consumer Price Indexes and Purchasing Power of the Dollar—*Continued*

(1982–1984 = 100, seasonally adjusted [preliminary], except as noted.)

Year and month	CPI-U, Apparel					CPI-U, Transportation								
							Private transportation						Motor vehicle parts and equipment	Motor vehicle maintenance and repair [1]
								New and used motor vehicles			Motor fuel			
	Total	Men's and boys' apparel	Women's and girls' apparel	Infants' and toddlers' apparel	Footwear	Total	Total	Total [3]	New vehicles	Used cars and trucks	Total	Gasoline (all types)		
1970	59.2	62.2	71.8	39.2	56.8	37.5	37.5	. . .	53.1	31.2	27.9	27.9	. . .	36.6
1971	61.1	63.9	74.4	40.0	58.6	39.5	39.4	. . .	55.3	33.0	28.1	28.1	. . .	39.3
1972	62.3	64.7	76.2	41.1	60.3	39.9	39.7	. . .	54.8	33.1	28.4	28.4	. . .	41.1
1973	64.6	67.1	78.8	42.5	62.8	41.2	41.0	. . .	54.8	35.2	31.2	31.2	. . .	43.2
1974	69.4	72.4	83.5	54.2	66.6	45.8	46.2	. . .	58.0	36.7	42.2	42.2	. . .	47.6
1975	72.5	75.5	85.5	64.5	69.6	50.1	50.6	. . .	63.0	43.8	45.1	45.1	. . .	53.7
1976	75.2	78.1	87.9	68.0	72.3	55.1	55.6	. . .	67.0	50.3	47.0	47.0	. . .	57.6
1977	78.6	81.7	90.6	74.6	75.7	59.0	59.7	. . .	70.5	54.7	49.7	49.7	. . .	61.9
1978	81.4	83.5	92.4	77.4	79.0	61.7	62.5	. . .	75.9	55.8	51.8	51.8	77.6	67.0
1979	84.9	85.4	94.0	79.0	85.3	70.5	71.7	. . .	81.9	60.2	70.1	70.2	85.1	73.7
1980	90.9	89.4	96.0	85.5	91.8	83.1	84.2	. . .	88.5	62.3	97.4	97.5	95.3	81.5
1981	95.3	94.2	97.5	92.9	96.7	93.2	93.8	. . .	93.9	76.9	108.5	108.5	101.0	89.2
1982	97.8	97.6	98.5	96.3	99.1	97.0	97.1	. . .	97.5	88.8	102.8	102.8	103.6	96.0
1983	100.2	100.3	100.2	101.1	99.8	99.3	99.3	. . .	99.9	98.7	99.4	99.4	100.7	100.3
1984	102.1	102.1	101.3	102.6	101.1	103.7	103.6	. . .	102.6	112.5	97.9	97.8	95.6	103.8
1985	105.0	105.0	104.9	107.2	102.3	106.4	106.2	. . .	106.1	113.7	98.7	98.6	95.9	106.8
1986	105.9	106.2	104.0	111.8	101.9	102.3	101.2	. . .	110.6	108.8	77.1	77.0	95.4	110.3
1987	110.6	109.1	110.4	112.1	105.1	105.4	104.2	. . .	114.4	113.1	80.2	80.1	96.1	114.8
1988	115.4	113.4	114.9	116.4	109.9	108.7	107.6	. . .	116.5	118.0	80.9	80.8	97.9	119.7
1989	118.6	117.0	116.4	119.1	114.4	114.1	112.9	. . .	119.2	120.4	88.5	88.5	100.2	124.9
1990	124.1	120.4	122.6	125.8	117.4	120.5	118.8	. . .	121.4	117.6	101.2	101.0	100.9	130.1
1991	128.7	124.2	127.6	128.9	120.9	123.8	121.9	. . .	126.0	118.1	99.4	99.2	102.2	136.0
1992	131.9	126.5	130.4	129.3	125.0	126.5	124.6	. . .	129.2	123.2	99.0	99.0	103.1	141.3
1993	133.7	127.5	132.6	127.1	125.9	130.4	127.5	91.8	132.7	133.9	98.0	97.7	101.6	145.9
1994	133.4	126.4	130.9	128.1	126.0	134.3	131.4	95.5	137.6	141.7	98.5	98.2	101.4	150.2
1995	132.0	126.2	126.9	127.2	125.4	139.1	136.3	99.4	141.0	156.5	100.0	99.8	102.1	154.0
1996	131.7	127.7	124.7	129.7	126.6	143.0	140.0	101.0	143.7	157.0	106.3	105.9	102.2	158.4
1997	132.9	130.1	126.1	129.0	127.6	144.3	141.0	100.5	144.3	151.1	106.2	105.8	101.9	162.7
1998	133.0	131.8	126.0	126.1	128.0	141.6	137.9	100.1	143.4	150.6	92.2	91.6	101.1	167.1
1999	131.3	131.1	123.3	129.0	125.7	144.4	140.5	100.1	142.9	152.0	100.7	100.1	100.5	171.9
2000	129.6	129.7	121.5	130.6	123.8	153.3	149.1	100.8	142.8	155.8	129.3	128.6	101.5	177.3
2001	127.3	125.7	119.3	129.2	123.0	154.3	150.0	101.3	142.1	158.7	124.7	124.0	104.8	183.5
2002	124.0	121.7	115.8	126.4	121.4	152.9	148.8	99.2	140.0	152.0	116.6	116.0	106.9	190.2
2003	120.9	118.0	113.1	122.1	119.6	157.6	153.6	96.5	137.9	142.9	135.8	135.1	107.8	195.6
2004	120.4	117.5	113.0	118.5	119.3	163.1	159.4	94.2	137.1	133.3	160.4	159.7	108.7	200.2
2005	119.5	116.1	110.8	116.7	122.6	173.9	170.2	95.6	137.9	139.4	195.7	194.7	111.9	206.9
2006	119.5	114.1	110.7	116.5	123.5	180.9	177.0	95.6	137.6	140.0	221.0	219.9	117.3	215.6
2007	119.0	112.4	110.3	113.9	122.4	184.7	180.8	94.3	136.3	135.7	239.1	238.0	121.6	223.0
2008	118.9	113.0	107.5	113.8	124.2	195.5	191.0	93.3	134.2	134.0	279.7	277.5	128.7	233.9
2009	120.1	113.6	108.1	114.5	126.9	179.3	174.8	93.5	135.6	127.0	202.0	201.6	134.1	243.3
2010	119.5	111.9	107.1	114.2	128.0	193.4	188.7	97.1	138.0	143.1	239.2	238.6	137.0	248.0
2011	122.1	114.7	109.2	113.6	128.5	212.4	207.6	99.8	141.9	149.0	302.6	301.7	143.9	253.1
2012	126.3	119.5	113.0	119.7	131.8	217.3	212.8	100.6	144.2	150.3	312.7	311.5	148.6	257.6
2011														
January	119.9	111.9	107.2	111.1	128.1	203.6	198.7	97.5	138.6	144.6	276.0	275.5	140.5	250.7
February	119.7	111.9	106.9	110.7	128.0	205.5	200.5	97.8	139.3	144.7	281.8	280.9	140.9	250.9
March	119.5	111.8	106.4	110.8	128.1	209.7	204.7	98.3	140.0	145.5	297.5	296.2	140.7	250.8
April	119.5	111.5	106.4	111.0	127.1	212.0	207.2	99.0	140.9	146.9	304.8	303.8	141.6	251.5
May	120.8	113.1	107.6	111.8	128.5	214.1	209.5	99.8	142.1	148.4	310.9	310.1	143.3	252.4
June	122.0	115.2	108.7	111.8	128.7	214.1	209.6	100.7	143.0	150.6	308.1	307.2	144.6	252.5
July	122.8	115.8	109.8	114.1	128.6	214.6	210.0	100.9	143.1	151.5	308.8	308.0	145.0	252.8
August	124.3	115.8	112.2	115.6	129.4	214.9	210.3	101.0	143.1	152.3	309.1	308.3	145.5	253.3
September	123.5	116.3	110.4	115.5	129.6	216.4	211.7	100.8	143.2	151.5	314.7	314.0	145.6	255.2
October	123.9	117.1	110.8	115.1	128.5	214.8	210.1	100.7	143.2	151.2	307.7	306.7	145.3	255.8
November	124.6	118.0	111.7	116.8	128.5	214.9	210.2	100.5	143.1	150.7	308.4	307.3	146.3	255.7
December	124.8	117.9	111.8	118.3	128.7	213.7	208.9	100.3	143.1	149.9	303.2	301.3	147.5	255.6
2012														
January	125.3	118.3	112.5	119.5	128.7	214.1	209.5	100.1	143.1	149.3	304.0	302.9	148.1	256.4
February	124.9	117.6	112.1	118.9	128.9	216.9	212.5	100.1	143.5	148.8	316.0	315.0	148.2	257.0
March	125.6	118.9	112.4	119.2	129.7	218.9	214.5	100.4	143.5	150.2	322.6	321.3	148.3	256.6
April	125.8	119.3	113.0	118.0	130.4	217.3	212.6	101.0	143.9	152.1	313.0	311.9	148.3	256.5
May	126.2	119.5	113.6	119.6	131.2	214.6	209.7	101.3	144.0	153.5	299.6	298.3	148.5	257.4
June	126.6	119.7	113.4	120.3	132.5	214.0	209.3	101.5	144.2	154.0	296.8	295.9	148.5	257.6
July	126.4	120.3	113.0	120.3	132.4	213.0	208.3	101.2	144.3	153.1	293.0	291.9	149.0	257.4
August	126.2	120.3	112.0	120.1	132.8	218.1	213.8	100.9	144.5	151.3	315.2	314.1	148.9	257.6
September	126.8	120.0	112.9	120.1	132.9	222.8	218.6	100.4	144.6	149.1	334.9	333.9	148.8	258.0
October	127.5	119.7	114.6	120.6	133.7	223.1	218.7	100.1	144.7	148.0	335.0	333.7	148.7	258.6
November	126.9	120.1	113.2	119.5	134.0	218.4	213.7	100.1	145.1	147.4	314.8	313.6	148.5	258.9
December	127.0	120.4	112.9	119.8	134.5	217.5	212.7	100.2	145.4	147.0	309.8	307.7	148.8	258.8

[1] Not seasonally adjusted.
[3] December 1997 = 100.
. . . = Not available.

Table 8-2. Consumer Price Indexes and Purchasing Power of the Dollar—*Continued*

(1982–1984 = 100, seasonally adjusted [preliminary], except as noted.)

| Year and month | CPI-U, Transportation—Continued | | CPI-U, Medical care | | | | | CPI-U, Recreation | | CPI-U, Education and communication | | | |
| | | | | | Medical care services | | | | | | Education | | |
	Public transportation	Transportation services	Medical care, total	Medical care commodities	Total	Professional services	Hospital and related services	Total [3]	Video and audio [3]	Total [3]	Total [3]	Educational books and supplies	Tuition, other school fees, and childcare
1970	35.2	40.6	34.1	46.4	32.5	37.0	...	...	...	...	...	38.8	...
1971	37.8	43.8	36.3	47.2	34.9	39.4	...	...	...	...	...	41.4	...
1972	39.3	44.8	37.5	47.3	36.2	40.8	...	...	...	...	...	44.2	...
1973	39.7	45.1	39.0	47.4	37.8	42.1	...	...	...	...	...	45.6	...
1974	40.6	46.8	42.6	49.1	41.7	45.8	...	...	...	...	...	47.2	...
1975	43.5	50.3	47.7	53.2	46.9	50.8	...	...	...	...	...	50.3	...
1976	47.8	57.5	52.3	56.4	51.6	55.4	...	...	...	...	...	53.7	...
1977	50.0	62.1	57.3	60.1	56.8	59.9	...	...	...	...	...	56.9	...
1978	51.5	65.2	62.1	64.5	61.6	64.6	55.1	...	...	...	...	61.6	59.8
1979	54.9	70.3	68.0	69.3	67.7	70.6	61.0	...	...	...	...	65.7	64.7
1980	69.0	79.8	75.6	75.6	75.7	78.7	69.2	...	...	...	...	71.4	71.2
1981	85.6	89.2	83.5	84.0	83.4	86.5	79.1	...	...	...	...	80.3	79.9
1982	94.9	96.5	92.5	92.4	92.6	93.1	90.3	...	...	...	...	91.0	90.5
1983	99.5	98.9	100.5	100.2	100.6	99.9	100.5	...	...	...	...	100.3	99.7
1984	105.7	104.6	106.9	107.4	106.8	107.0	109.2	...	...	...	...	108.7	109.8
1985	110.5	109.5	113.6	114.8	113.3	113.6	116.1	...	...	...	...	118.2	119.7
1986	117.0	115.4	122.0	122.2	122.0	120.9	123.1	...	...	...	...	128.1	129.6
1987	121.1	120.8	130.2	130.2	130.3	129.0	131.6	...	...	...	...	138.1	140.0
1988	123.3	127.1	139.0	139.0	139.0	137.7	143.9	...	...	...	...	148.1	151.0
1989	129.5	134.8	149.6	149.7	149.6	146.7	160.5	...	...	...	...	158.0	162.7
1990	142.6	142.7	162.7	162.2	162.8	156.4	178.0	...	...	...	...	171.3	175.7
1991	148.9	149.8	176.5	175.4	176.7	166.1	196.1	...	...	...	...	180.3	191.4
1992	151.4	154.3	189.6	186.5	190.3	176.3	214.0	...	...	...	...	190.3	208.5
1993	167.0	160.0	200.9	193.2	202.7	185.2	231.9	90.7	96.5	85.5	78.4	197.6	225.3
1994	172.0	165.7	210.4	198.6	213.0	193.4	245.6	92.7	95.4	88.8	83.3	205.5	239.8
1995	175.9	173.6	219.8	202.2	223.8	202.0	257.8	94.5	95.1	92.2	88.0	214.4	253.8
1996	181.9	178.3	227.6	207.8	232.1	209.5	269.5	97.4	96.6	95.3	92.7	226.9	267.1
1997	186.7	182.6	234.0	212.6	238.8	216.7	278.4	99.6	99.4	98.4	97.3	238.4	280.4
1998	190.3	185.4	241.4	218.6	246.6	223.7	287.5	101.1	101.1	100.3	102.1	250.8	294.2
1999	197.7	187.9	249.7	226.8	254.9	230.8	299.5	102.0	100.7	101.2	107.0	261.7	308.4
2000	209.6	192.9	259.9	233.6	265.9	239.6	317.3	103.3	101.0	102.5	112.5	279.9	324.0
2001	210.6	199.1	271.8	242.7	278.5	248.7	338.3	104.9	101.5	105.2	118.5	295.9	341.1
2002	207.4	207.7	284.6	251.1	292.5	256.0	367.8	106.2	102.8	107.9	126.0	317.6	362.1
2003	209.3	216.2	296.3	257.4	305.9	263.4	394.8	107.5	103.6	109.8	134.4	335.4	386.7
2004	209.1	220.9	309.5	263.2	321.5	274.0	417.9	108.6	104.2	111.6	143.7	351.0	414.3
2005	217.3	225.9	322.8	269.2	337.3	284.3	439.9	109.4	104.2	113.7	152.7	365.6	440.9
2006	226.6	230.6	335.7	279.0	351.1	291.7	468.1	110.9	104.6	116.8	162.1	388.9	468.1
2007	230.0	233.4	350.9	282.6	370.1	303.2	498.9	111.4	102.9	119.6	171.4	420.4	494.1
2008	250.5	242.6	364.2	288.0	386.3	313.4	534.0	113.3	102.6	123.6	181.3	450.2	522.1
2009	236.3	251.0	376.1	296.7	399.2	322.1	567.9	114.3	101.3	127.4	190.9	482.1	549.0
2010	251.4	260.0	389.8	306.3	414.3	331.5	607.7	113.3	99.1	129.9	199.3	505.6	573.2
2011	269.4	268.2	402.2	315.8	427.6	339.3	641.5	113.4	98.4	131.5	207.8	529.5	597.2
2012	271.4	274.2	417.8	325.6	445.2	345.7	672.1	114.7	99.4	133.8	216.3	562.6	621.0
2011													
January	265.0	264.9	394.0	319.3	417.1	331.9	625.7	112.9	97.9	130.5	203.7	519.8	585.3
February	268.6	266.0	395.5	320.2	418.8	333.5	628.8	113.2	98.3	130.7	204.4	519.4	587.5
March	271.3	267.1	396.4	321.3	419.5	334.3	630.9	113.2	98.4	130.9	205.1	522.4	589.4
April	270.3	267.3	397.7	323.0	420.7	334.8	634.1	113.2	98.4	131.0	205.7	524.4	591.4
May	268.8	267.6	398.7	323.5	421.8	335.0	637.8	113.5	98.3	131.1	206.5	526.3	593.5
June	266.6	267.6	399.4	324.0	422.6	335.2	639.5	113.5	98.1	131.3	207.2	528.4	595.5
July	268.3	267.9	400.4	324.6	423.9	335.8	642.7	113.4	98.5	131.4	208.1	529.7	598.1
August	270.1	268.5	401.5	324.8	425.3	336.2	646.6	113.5	98.1	131.7	209.2	529.1	601.6
September	271.6	269.5	402.2	325.4	426.0	336.5	648.1	113.4	98.5	131.8	209.6	535.0	602.5
October	271.6	269.9	404.1	326.5	428.2	337.6	652.0	113.3	98.8	132.1	210.5	537.9	604.9
November	271.1	269.9	405.8	327.6	430.1	338.1	655.0	113.4	98.8	132.4	211.3	540.7	607.3
December	270.5	270.0	407.3	328.8	431.7	339.0	656.8	113.8	98.8	132.6	212.0	541.6	609.3
2012													
January	269.2	270.3	408.3	329.7	432.7	338.7	659.1	114.4	99.3	132.9	212.6	545.2	611.0
February	268.9	270.1	408.9	330.9	433.0	338.3	659.9	114.4	99.4	133.2	213.2	546.7	612.7
March	270.1	270.8	410.2	331.8	434.5	339.1	661.4	114.5	99.5	133.4	213.9	549.7	614.6
April	272.6	271.7	411.4	331.8	436.2	339.7	664.5	114.4	99.4	133.6	214.6	552.8	616.4
May	274.7	272.6	413.0	332.3	438.2	340.9	667.7	114.5	99.5	134.0	215.4	556.8	618.5
June	271.1	272.4	415.1	333.2	440.8	341.9	673.2	114.9	99.4	134.2	216.0	559.3	620.3
July	269.0	272.3	416.8	335.4	442.2	342.5	676.5	114.8	99.4	134.1	217.1	563.1	623.3
August	266.5	272.4	417.8	336.4	443.1	343.5	675.2	114.9	99.7	133.8	217.2	569.3	623.2
September	269.7	273.7	418.7	336.0	444.6	344.3	678.4	114.9	99.7	133.9	217.7	573.6	624.5
October	273.3	275.3	419.1	336.2	445.0	344.5	679.6	114.9	99.3	134.2	218.6	575.0	627.0
November	274.9	275.8	419.6	335.3	446.2	344.9	682.6	115.0	99.3	134.4	219.4	579.2	629.1
December	276.9	277.0	420.3	334.3	447.6	345.5	686.9	114.7	99.1	134.5	220.1	579.9	631.2

[3]December 1997 = 100.
. . . = Not available.

Table 8-2. Consumer Price Indexes and Purchasing Power of the Dollar—*Continued*

(1982–1984 = 100, seasonally adjusted [preliminary], except as noted.)

Year and month	CPI-U, Education and communication—*Continued*					CPI-U, Other goods and services					CPI-W, All items, not seasonally adjusted	Purchasing power of the dollar, CPI-U, 1982–1984 = $1.00, not seasonally adjusted
	Communication					Total	Tobacco and smoking products [1]	Personal care				
	Total [3]	Information and information processing						Total	Personal care products [1]	Personal care services [1]		
		Total [3]	Telephone services [1,3]	Information technology, hardware, and services								
				Total [1,4]	Personal computers and peripheral equipment [1,5]							
1970	...	...	...	...	...	40.9	43.1	43.5	42.7	44.2	39.0	2.574
1971	...	...	...	...	...	42.9	45.0	44.9	44.0	45.7	40.7	2.466
1972	...	...	...	...	...	44.7	47.4	46.0	45.2	46.8	42.1	2.391
1973	...	...	...	...	...	46.4	48.8	48.1	46.4	49.7	44.7	2.251
1974	...	...	...	...	...	49.8	51.2	52.8	51.5	53.9	49.6	2.029
1975	...	...	...	...	...	53.9	54.8	57.9	58.0	57.7	54.1	1.859
1976	...	...	...	...	...	57.0	57.1	61.7	61.3	61.9	57.2	1.757
1977	...	...	...	...	...	60.4	59.9	65.7	64.7	66.4	60.9	1.649
1978	...	...	...	...	...	64.3	63.1	69.9	68.2	71.3	65.6	1.532
1979	...	...	...	...	...	68.9	66.9	75.2	72.9	77.2	73.1	1.380
1980	...	...	...	...	...	75.2	72.1	81.9	79.6	83.7	82.9	1.215
1981	...	...	...	...	...	82.6	77.7	89.1	87.8	90.2	91.4	1.098
1982	...	...	...	...	...	91.1	86.4	95.4	95.1	95.7	96.9	1.035
1983	...	...	...	...	...	101.1	103.4	100.3	100.7	100.0	99.8	1.003
1984	...	...	...	...	...	107.9	110.2	104.3	104.2	104.4	103.3	0.961
1985	...	...	...	...	...	114.5	116.8	108.3	107.6	108.9	106.9	0.928
1986	...	...	...	...	...	121.4	124.8	111.9	111.3	112.5	108.6	0.913
1987	...	...	...	...	...	128.5	133.7	115.1	113.9	116.2	112.5	0.880
1988	...	...	...	...	...	137.0	146.0	119.4	118.1	120.7	117.0	0.846
1989	...	...	...	96.3	...	147.7	164.2	125.0	123.2	126.8	122.6	0.807
1990	...	...	...	93.5	...	159.0	181.2	130.4	128.2	132.8	129.0	0.766
1991	...	...	...	88.6	...	171.6	202.5	134.9	132.8	137.0	134.3	0.734
1992	...	...	...	83.7	...	183.3	219.7	138.3	136.5	140.0	138.2	0.713
1993	96.7	97.7	...	78.8	...	192.9	228.3	141.5	139.0	144.0	142.1	0.692
1994	97.6	98.6	...	72.0	...	198.5	220.1	144.6	141.5	147.9	145.6	0.675
1995	98.8	98.7	...	63.8	...	206.9	225.9	147.1	143.1	151.5	149.8	0.656
1996	99.6	99.5	...	57.2	...	215.4	232.5	150.1	144.3	156.6	154.1	0.638
1997	100.3	100.4	...	50.1	...	224.8	243.3	152.7	144.2	162.4	157.6	0.623
1998	98.7	98.5	100.7	39.9	875.1	237.7	274.8	156.7	148.3	166.0	159.7	0.614
1999	96.0	95.5	100.2	30.5	598.7	258.3	356.2	161.1	151.8	171.4	163.2	0.600
2000	93.6	92.8	98.7	25.9	459.9	271.1	395.2	165.6	153.7	178.1	168.9	0.581
2001	93.3	92.3	99.4	21.3	330.1	282.6	426.1	170.5	155.1	184.3	173.5	0.565
2002	92.3	90.8	99.9	18.3	248.4	293.2	463.2	174.7	154.7	188.4	175.9	0.556
2003	89.7	87.8	98.5	16.1	196.9	298.7	470.5	178.0	153.5	193.2	179.8	0.544
2004	86.7	84.6	96.0	14.8	171.2	304.7	478.8	181.7	153.9	197.6	184.5	0.530
2005	84.7	82.6	95.0	13.6	143.2	313.4	504.2	185.6	154.4	203.9	191.0	0.512
2006	84.1	81.7	95.9	12.5	120.9	321.7	521.6	190.2	155.8	209.7	197.1	0.496
2007	83.4	80.7	98.4	10.6	108.4	333.3	555.5	195.6	158.3	216.6	202.8	0.482
2008	84.2	81.4	100.5	10.1	94.9	345.4	591.1	201.3	159.3	223.7	211.1	0.465
2009	85.0	81.9	102.3	9.7	82.3	368.6	735.1	204.6	162.6	227.6	209.6	0.466
2010	84.7	81.5	102.1	9.4	76.4	381.3	812.3	206.6	161.1	229.6	214.0	0.459
2011	83.3	80.0	100.6	9.0	68.9	387.2	839.7	208.6	160.5	230.8	221.6	0.445
2012	83.1	79.5	101.0	8.7	62.3	394.4	859.6	212.1	162.2	234.2	226.2	0.436
2011												
January	83.8	80.4	101.4	9.2	72.9	385.0	828.1	207.5	160.9	229.9	216.4	0.454
February	83.7	80.4	101.3	9.2	72.3	385.5	829.5	207.8	161.3	230.2	217.5	0.452
March	83.7	80.3	101.3	9.2	71.4	385.3	830.7	207.5	161.0	230.0	220.0	0.447
April	83.6	80.2	101.2	9.1	71.0	385.6	827.3	208.0	161.4	230.4	221.7	0.445
May	83.4	80.0	101.2	9.1	70.5	385.4	825.7	208.1	159.5	230.5	223.0	0.443
June	83.4	80.0	101.2	9.0	69.3	386.1	828.9	208.3	160.2	230.6	222.5	0.443
July	83.2	79.8	101.0	9.0	68.7	386.6	833.1	208.2	159.8	230.5	222.7	0.443
August	83.1	79.7	101.0	9.0	67.1	387.5	837.4	208.5	159.0	230.8	223.3	0.441
September	83.1	79.7	101.1	8.9	66.4	388.8	843.1	209.0	160.2	231.0	223.7	0.441
October	83.1	79.7	101.3	8.9	65.9	389.1	842.8	209.3	160.7	231.2	223.0	0.442
November	83.1	79.7	101.3	8.9	66.2	390.6	843.6	210.2	161.6	232.2	222.8	0.442
December	83.1	79.6	101.4	8.8	64.9	391.1	847.1	210.3	160.8	232.3	222.2	0.443
2012												
January	83.3	79.9	101.7	8.9	64.3	391.8	851.0	210.5	161.3	232.0	223.2	0.441
February	83.4	79.9	101.7	8.9	64.3	391.4	847.9	210.4	160.6	232.9	224.3	0.439
March	83.4	79.9	101.8	8.8	63.5	392.0	845.8	211.0	162.6	233.3	226.3	0.436
April	83.4	79.9	101.9	8.8	62.6	392.7	847.0	211.4	163.1	233.7	227.0	0.435
May	83.5	80.0	102.0	8.9	63.0	392.9	845.6	211.7	161.5	234.0	226.6	0.435
June	83.5	80.0	102.1	8.8	63.7	394.0	849.1	212.2	162.1	234.0	226.0	0.436
July	83.1	79.6	101.6	8.8	62.9	395.5	858.7	212.5	162.4	234.2	225.6	0.436
August	82.6	79.1	101.2	8.7	62.2	396.6	857.7	213.3	163.1	234.8	227.1	0.434
September	82.6	79.1	101.3	8.6	61.5	396.3	859.1	213.0	163.1	234.9	228.2	0.432
October	82.6	79.1	101.6	8.6	60.8	396.4	858.1	213.2	162.7	235.1	228.0	0.432
November	82.6	79.0	101.6	8.6	59.9	396.5	858.5	213.2	162.4	235.2	226.6	0.434
December	82.6	79.0	101.7	8.5	59.3	396.9	862.9	213.1	161.1	236.5	225.9	0.436

[1]Not seasonally adjusted.
[3]December 1997 = 100.
[4]December 1988 = 100.
[5]December 2007 = 100.
. . . = Not available.

Table 8-3. Alternative Measures of Total and Core Consumer Prices: Index Levels

(Various bases; monthly data seasonally adjusted, except as noted.)

Year and month	CPIs, all items						CPIs, all items less food and energy			Chain-type price indexes for personal consumption expenditures (PCE), 2009 = 100			
	CPI-U, 1982–1984 = 100	CPI-W, 1982–1984 = 100	CPI-U-X1, 1982–1984 = 100	CPI-E, Dec. 1982 = 100, not seasonally adjusted	CPI-U-RS, Dec. 1977 = 100, not seasonally adjusted	C-CPI-U, Dec. 1999 = 100, not seasonally adjusted	CPI-U, 1982–1984 = 100	CPI-U-RS, Dec. 1977 = 100, not seasonally adjusted	C-CPI-U, Dec. 1999 = 100, not seasonally adjusted	PCE, total	PCE, market-based	Excluding food and energy	
												PCE, total	PCE, market-based
1965	31.5	31.7	34.2	. . .	. . .	. . .	32.7	. . .	. . .	18.7	. . .	19.3	. . .
1966	32.4	32.6	35.2	. . .	. . .	. . .	33.5	. . .	. . .	19.2	. . .	19.8	. . .
1967	33.4	33.6	36.3	. . .	. . .	. . .	34.7	. . .	. . .	19.6	. . .	20.4	. . .
1968	34.8	35.0	37.7	. . .	. . .	. . .	36.3	. . .	. . .	20.4	. . .	21.2	. . .
1969	36.7	36.9	39.4	. . .	. . .	. . .	38.4	. . .	. . .	21.3	. . .	22.2	. . .
1970	38.8	39.0	41.3	. . .	. . .	. . .	40.8	. . .	. . .	22.3	. . .	23.3	. . .
1971	40.5	40.7	43.1	. . .	. . .	. . .	42.7	. . .	. . .	23.3	. . .	24.4	. . .
1972	41.8	42.1	44.4	. . .	. . .	. . .	44.0	. . .	. . .	24.1	. . .	25.2	. . .
1973	44.4	44.7	47.2	. . .	. . .	. . .	45.6	. . .	. . .	25.4	. . .	26.1	. . .
1974	49.3	49.6	51.9	. . .	. . .	. . .	49.4	. . .	. . .	28.0	. . .	28.2	. . .
1975	53.8	54.1	56.2	. . .	. . .	. . .	53.9	. . .	. . .	30.3	. . .	30.6	. . .
1976	56.9	57.2	59.4	. . .	. . .	. . .	57.4	. . .	. . .	32.0	. . .	32.4	. . .
1977	60.6	60.9	63.2	. . .	. . .	. . .	61.0	. . .	. . .	34.1	. . .	34.5	. . .
1978	65.2	65.6	67.5	. . .	104.4	. . .	65.5	103.6	. . .	36.5	. . .	36.8	. . .
1979	72.6	73.1	74.0	. . .	114.4	. . .	71.9	111.0	. . .	39.7	. . .	39.5	. . .
1980	82.4	82.9	82.3	. . .	127.1	. . .	80.8	120.9	. . .	44.0	. . .	43.1	. . .
1981	90.9	91.4	90.1	. . .	139.2	. . .	89.2	132.2	. . .	47.9	. . .	46.9	. . .
1982	96.5	96.9	95.6	. . .	147.6	. . .	95.8	142.4	. . .	50.6	. . .	49.9	. . .
1983	99.6	99.8	99.6	102.1	153.9	. . .	99.6	150.4	. . .	52.7	. . .	52.5	. . .
1984	103.9	103.3	103.9	106.5	160.2	. . .	104.6	157.9	. . .	54.7	. . .	54.6	. . .
1985	107.6	106.9	107.6	110.5	165.7	. . .	109.1	164.8	. . .	56.7	. . .	56.9	. . .
1986	109.6	108.6	109.6	113.3	168.7	. . .	113.5	171.4	. . .	57.9	. . .	58.8	. . .
1987	113.6	112.5	113.6	117.7	174.4	. . .	118.2	178.1	. . .	59.6	59.1	60.7	60.2
1988	118.3	117.0	118.3	122.7	180.8	. . .	123.4	185.2	. . .	62.0	61.4	63.3	62.8
1989	124.0	122.6	124.0	128.9	188.6	. . .	129.0	192.6	. . .	64.6	64.3	65.9	65.6
1990	130.7	129.0	130.7	136.6	198.0	. . .	135.5	201.4	. . .	67.4	67.4	68.5	68.6
1991	136.2	134.3	136.2	143.0	205.1	. . .	142.1	209.9	. . .	69.7	70.0	70.9	71.5
1992	140.3	138.2	140.3	147.6	210.3	. . .	147.3	216.4	. . .	71.5	72.0	73.0	73.9
1993	144.5	142.1	144.5	152.2	215.5	. . .	152.2	222.5	. . .	73.3	73.7	75.0	75.8
1994	148.2	145.6	148.2	156.6	220.1	. . .	156.5	227.7	. . .	74.8	75.2	76.7	77.4
1995	152.4	149.8	152.4	161.2	225.4	. . .	161.2	233.4	. . .	76.4	76.7	78.3	79.1
1996	156.9	154.1	156.9	166.1	231.4	. . .	165.6	239.1	. . .	78.0	78.2	79.8	80.3
1997	160.5	157.6	160.5	170.1	236.4	. . .	169.5	244.4	. . .	79.3	79.4	81.2	81.5
1998	163.0	159.7	163.0	173.2	239.7	. . .	173.4	249.7	. . .	79.9	79.8	82.2	82.4
1999	166.6	163.2	166.6	177.3	244.7	. . .	177.0	254.8	. . .	81.1	81.0	83.3	83.5
2000	172.2	168.9	172.2	183.5	252.9	102.0	181.3	260.8	101.4	83.1	82.9	84.7	84.7
2001	177.1	173.5	177.1	189.2	260.0	104.3	186.1	267.8	103.5	84.7	84.5	86.3	86.2
2002	179.9	175.9	179.9	192.7	264.2	105.6	190.5	273.9	105.4	85.9	85.4	87.7	87.5
2003	184.0	179.8	184.0	197.4	270.1	107.8	193.2	277.9	106.6	87.6	87.1	89.0	88.7
2004	188.9	184.5	188.9	203.3	277.4	110.5	196.6	282.9	108.4	89.7	89.1	90.8	90.3
2005	195.3	191.0	195.3	210.4	286.7	113.7	200.9	289.0	110.4	92.3	91.6	92.7	92.0
2006	201.6	197.1	201.6	217.3	296.1	117.0	205.9	296.2	112.9	94.7	94.1	94.8	94.0
2007	207.3	202.8	207.3	223.8	304.5	120.0	210.7	303.1	115.0	97.1	96.4	96.8	96.0
2008	215.3	211.1	215.3	232.4	316.2	124.4	215.6	310.1	117.3	100.1	99.6	98.8	98.1
2009	214.5	209.6	214.5	231.9	315.0	123.9	219.2	315.4	119.1	100.0	100.0	100.0	100.0
2010	218.1	214.0	218.1	235.0	320.2	125.6	221.3	318.4	120.0	101.7	101.5	101.3	101.0
2011	224.9	221.6	224.9	241.8	330.3	129.5	225.0	323.7	121.9	104.1	104.0	102.7	102.5
2012	229.6	226.2	229.6	246.7	337.2	¹131.8	229.8	330.5	¹124.3	106.0	105.9	104.6	104.3
2011													
January	221.1	217.3	221.1	237.2	323.4	126.8	222.7	319.6	120.4	102.7	102.5	101.8	101.5
February	221.9	218.2	221.9	238.3	325.0	127.4	223.1	320.8	120.8	103.0	102.9	102.0	101.7
March	223.1	219.6	223.1	240.3	328.2	128.6	223.4	321.8	121.1	103.4	103.3	102.1	101.8
April	223.9	220.5	223.9	241.5	330.3	129.5	223.8	322.4	121.5	103.7	103.6	102.3	102.0
May	224.7	221.5	224.7	242.5	331.8	130.0	224.4	323.0	121.6	104.0	104.0	102.5	102.3
June	225.1	221.7	225.1	242.5	331.5	129.8	224.9	323.5	121.8	104.1	104.1	102.7	102.5
July	225.6	222.3	225.6	242.8	331.8	130.0	225.4	323.9	121.9	104.3	104.3	102.9	102.6
August	226.2	222.9	226.2	243.3	332.7	130.4	225.9	324.9	122.3	104.5	104.5	103.1	102.8
September	226.8	223.6	226.8	243.6	333.2	130.6	226.1	325.5	122.6	104.7	104.7	103.2	102.9
October	226.7	223.5	226.7	243.3	332.5	130.4	226.5	326.2	122.9	104.8	104.7	103.3	103.0
November	227.0	223.8	227.0	243.1	332.2	130.2	226.9	326.3	122.9	104.9	104.8	103.5	103.2
December	227.1	223.8	227.1	242.8	331.4	129.8	227.2	326.2	122.8	105.0	105.0	103.6	103.4
2012													
January	227.6	224.3	227.6	243.8	332.9	¹130.4	227.7	326.9	¹123.1	105.2	105.2	103.9	103.6
February	228.3	225.0	228.3	244.8	334.3	¹130.8	227.9	327.8	¹123.4	105.5	105.5	104.0	103.8
March	229.0	225.8	229.0	246.3	336.9	¹131.6	228.4	329.0	¹123.9	105.7	105.7	104.2	103.9
April	229.0	225.6	229.0	247.0	337.9	¹132.0	228.9	329.8	¹124.2	105.7	105.7	104.3	104.0
May	228.6	225.2	228.6	246.8	337.5	¹131.9	229.4	330.3	¹124.3	105.7	105.6	104.5	104.2
June	228.9	225.4	228.9	246.7	337.0	¹131.8	229.9	330.7	¹124.4	105.8	105.7	104.7	104.4
July	228.8	225.3	228.8	246.5	336.4	¹131.6	230.1	330.7	¹124.4	105.9	105.7	104.8	104.5
August	230.0	226.7	230.0	247.6	338.3	¹132.2	230.2	331.1	¹124.5	106.2	106.1	104.8	104.5
September	231.2	228.1	231.2	248.5	339.8	¹132.7	230.6	332.0	¹124.8	106.5	106.5	104.9	104.6
October	231.6	228.4	231.6	248.4	339.7	¹132.7	231.0	332.7	¹125.1	106.7	106.6	105.1	104.7
November	231.1	227.6	231.1	247.5	338.1	¹132.2	231.3	332.7	¹125.1	106.6	106.4	105.2	104.8
December	231.1	227.6	231.1	247.1	337.2	¹131.9	231.5	332.3	¹124.9	106.6	106.4	105.2	104.8

¹Interim values.

. . . = Not available.

Table 8-4. Alternative Measures of Total and Core Consumer Prices: Inflation Rates

(Percent changes from year earlier, except as noted; monthly data seasonally adjusted, except as noted.)

Year and month	CPIs, all items						CPIs, all items less food and energy			Chain-type price indexes for personal consumption expenditures (PCE), 2009 = 100			
	CPI-U, 1982–1984 = 100	CPI-W, 1982–1984 = 100	CPI-U-X1, 1982–1984 = 100	CPI-E, Dec. 1982 = 100, not seasonally adjusted	CPI-U-RS, Dec. 1977 = 100, not seasonally adjusted	C-CPI-U, Dec. 1999 = 100, not seasonally adjusted	CPI-U, 1982–1984 = 100	CPI-U-RS, Dec. 1977 = 100, not seasonally adjusted	C-CPI-U, Dec. 1999 = 100, not seasonally adjusted	PCE, total	PCE, market-based	Excluding food and energy	
												PCE, total	PCE, market-based
1960	1.7	1.7	1.9	...	...	...	1.3	...	...	...	...	1.7	...
1961	1.0	1.0	0.9	...	...	...	1.3	...	...	...	...	1.3	...
1962	1.0	1.0	0.9	...	...	...	1.3	...	...	1.2	...	1.4	...
1963	1.3	1.3	1.5	...	...	...	1.3	...	...	1.0	...	1.3	...
1964	1.3	1.3	1.2	...	...	...	1.6	...	...	1.2	...	1.5	...
1965	1.6	1.6	1.5	...	...	...	1.2	...	...	1.2	...	1.3	...
1966	2.9	2.8	2.9	...	...	...	2.4	...	...	1.5	...	2.3	...
1967	3.1	3.1	3.1	...	...	...	3.6	...	...	1.4	...	3.1	...
1968	4.2	4.2	3.9	...	...	...	4.6	...	...	2.5	...	4.3	...
1969	5.5	5.4	4.5	...	...	...	5.8	...	...	2.5	...	4.7	...
1970	5.7	5.7	4.8	...	...	...	6.3	...	...	3.9	...	4.7	...
1971	4.4	4.4	4.4	...	...	...	4.7	...	...	4.5	...	4.7	...
1972	3.2	3.4	3.0	...	...	...	3.0	...	...	4.7	...	3.2	...
1973	6.2	6.2	6.3	...	...	...	3.6	...	...	4.3	...	3.8	...
1974	11.0	11.0	10.0	...	...	...	8.3	...	...	3.4	...	7.9	...
1975	9.1	9.1	8.3	...	...	...	9.1	...	...	5.4	...	8.4	...
1976	5.8	5.7	5.7	...	...	...	6.5	...	...	10.4	...	6.1	...
1977	6.5	6.5	6.4	...	...	...	6.3	...	...	8.4	...	6.4	...
1978	7.6	7.7	6.8	...	...	...	7.4	...	...	5.5	...	6.7	...
1979	11.3	11.4	9.6	...	9.6	...	9.8	7.1	...	6.5	...	7.3	...
1980	13.5	13.4	11.2	...	11.1	...	12.4	8.9	...	7.0	...	9.2	...
1981	10.3	10.3	9.5	...	9.5	...	10.4	9.3	...	8.9	...	8.7	...
1982	6.2	6.0	6.1	...	6.0	...	7.4	7.7	...	10.7	...	6.5	...
1983	3.2	3.0	4.2	...	4.3	...	4.0	5.6	...	8.9	...	5.2	...
1984	4.3	3.5	4.3	4.3	4.1	...	5.0	5.0	...	5.5	...	4.2	...
1985	3.6	3.5	3.6	3.8	3.4	...	4.3	4.4	...	4.3	...	4.1	...
1986	1.9	1.6	1.9	2.5	1.8	...	4.0	4.0	...	3.8	...	3.4	...
1987	3.6	3.6	3.6	3.9	3.4	...	4.1	3.9	...	3.5	...	3.2	...
1988	4.1	4.0	4.1	4.2	3.7	...	4.4	4.0	...	2.2	...	4.2	4.3
1989	4.8	4.8	4.8	5.0	4.3	...	4.5	4.0	...	3.0	4.6	4.1	4.4
1990	5.4	5.2	5.4	6.0	5.0	...	5.0	4.6	...	3.9	4.9	4.0	4.6
1991	4.2	4.1	4.2	4.7	3.6	...	4.9	4.2	...	4.3	3.8	3.5	4.2
1992	3.0	2.9	3.0	3.2	2.5	...	3.7	3.1	...	4.3	2.8	3.0	3.3
1993	3.0	2.8	3.0	3.2	2.5	...	3.3	2.8	...	3.3	2.4	2.7	2.6
1994	2.6	2.5	2.6	2.9	2.1	...	2.8	2.3	...	2.6	1.9	2.2	2.1
1995	2.8	2.9	2.8	2.9	2.4	...	3.0	2.5	...	2.5	2.0	2.1	2.1
1996	3.0	2.9	3.0	3.1	2.7	...	2.7	2.4	...	2.1	1.9	1.9	1.6
1997	2.3	2.3	2.3	2.4	2.2	...	2.4	2.2	...	2.1	1.5	1.7	1.5
1998	1.6	1.3	1.6	1.8	1.4	...	2.3	2.2	...	2.1	0.6	1.2	1.1
1999	2.2	2.2	2.2	2.3	2.1	...	2.1	2.0	...	1.7	1.4	1.3	1.2
2000	3.4	3.5	3.4	3.5	3.4	...	2.4	2.4	...	0.8	2.4	1.7	1.5
2001	2.8	2.7	2.8	3.1	2.8	2.3	2.6	2.7	2.1	1.5	1.9	1.8	1.8
2002	1.6	1.4	1.6	1.8	1.6	1.2	2.4	2.3	1.8	2.5	1.1	1.7	1.5
2003	2.3	2.2	2.3	2.5	2.2	2.1	1.4	1.5	1.1	1.9	1.9	1.5	1.4
2004	2.7	2.6	2.7	3.0	2.7	2.5	1.8	1.8	1.7	1.3	2.4	1.9	1.7
2005	3.4	3.5	3.4	3.5	3.4	2.9	2.2	2.2	1.8	2.0	2.8	2.2	2.0
2006	3.2	3.2	3.2	3.3	3.3	2.9	2.5	2.5	2.3	2.4	2.7	2.2	2.2
2007	2.8	2.9	2.8	3.0	2.8	2.5	2.3	2.3	1.8	2.9	2.5	2.2	2.0
2008	3.8	4.1	3.8	3.8	3.8	3.7	2.3	2.3	2.0	2.7	3.4	2.1	2.3
2009	-0.4	-0.7	-0.4	-0.2	-0.4	-0.5	1.7	1.7	1.5	2.5	0.4	1.2	1.9
2010	1.6	2.1	1.6	1.4	1.7	1.4	1.0	1.0	0.7	3.1	1.5	1.3	1.0
2011	3.2	3.6	3.2	2.9	3.2	3.1	1.7	1.7	1.6	-0.1	2.5	1.4	1.4
2012	2.1	2.1	2.1	2.1	2.1	[1]1.8	2.1	2.1	[1]2.0	1.7	1.8	1.8	1.8
Percent change, annual rate:													
1978–2012	3.8	3.7	3.7	...	3.5	...	3.8	3.5	...	3.2	...	3.1	...
1983–2012	2.9	2.9	2.9	3.1	2.7	...	2.9	2.8	...	2.4	...	2.4	...
2000–2012	2.4	2.5	2.4	2.5	2.4	[1]2.2	2.0	2.0	[1]1.7	2.0	2.1	1.8	1.7
2012													
January	3.0	3.2	3.0	2.8	2.9	[1]2.8	2.3	2.3	[1]2.2	2.5	2.6	2.0	2.1
February	2.9	3.1	2.9	2.7	2.9	[1]2.7	2.2	2.2	[1]2.2	2.4	2.5	2.0	2.0
March	2.6	2.8	2.6	2.5	2.7	[1]2.4	2.3	2.2	[1]2.3	2.3	2.3	2.0	2.0
April	2.3	2.3	2.3	2.3	2.3	[1]1.9	2.3	2.3	[1]2.2	2.0	2.0	2.0	2.0
May	1.7	1.7	1.7	1.8	1.7	[1]1.5	2.3	2.3	[1]2.2	1.6	1.6	1.9	1.9
June	1.7	1.6	1.7	1.7	1.7	[1]1.5	2.2	2.2	[1]2.2	1.6	1.6	1.9	1.9
July	1.4	1.3	1.4	1.5	1.4	[1]1.3	2.1	2.1	[1]2.0	1.5	1.4	1.9	1.8
August	1.7	1.7	1.7	1.8	1.7	[1]1.4	1.9	1.9	[1]1.8	1.6	1.5	1.7	1.6
September	2.0	2.0	2.0	2.0	2.0	[1]1.6	2.0	2.0	[1]1.8	1.7	1.7	1.7	1.7
October	2.2	2.2	2.2	2.1	2.2	[1]1.8	2.0	2.0	[1]1.8	1.8	1.8	1.8	1.7
November	1.8	1.7	1.8	1.8	1.8	[1]1.5	1.9	2.0	[1]1.8	1.6	1.5	1.7	1.5
December	1.8	1.7	1.8	1.8	1.8	[1]1.6	1.9	1.9	[1]1.7	1.5	1.4	1.6	1.4

[1]Interim values.
. . . = Not available.

Table 8-5. Producer Price Indexes by Stage of Processing

(1982 = 100, seasonally adjusted.)

Year and month	Finished goods Total	Percent change from previous period	Finished consumer goods Total	Finished consumer foods Total	Crude	Processed	Finished consumer goods, except foods Total	Durable goods	Nondurable goods less foods	Capital equipment Total	Manufacturing industries	Nonmanufacturing industries
1965	34.1	1.8	34.2	36.8	39.0	36.8	33.6	43.2	28.8	33.8	31.5	35.4
1966	35.2	3.2	35.4	39.2	41.5	39.2	34.1	43.4	29.3	34.6	32.5	36.0
1967	35.6	1.1	35.6	38.5	39.6	38.8	34.7	44.1	30.0	35.8	33.8	37.0
1968	36.6	2.8	36.5	40.0	42.5	40.0	35.5	45.1	30.6	37.0	35.0	38.2
1969	38.0	3.8	37.9	42.4	45.9	42.3	36.3	45.9	31.5	38.3	36.2	39.5
1970	39.3	3.4	39.1	43.8	46.0	43.9	37.4	47.2	32.5	40.1	38.1	41.3
1971	40.5	3.1	40.2	44.5	45.8	44.7	38.7	48.9	33.5	41.7	39.6	43.0
1972	41.8	3.2	41.5	46.9	48.0	47.2	39.4	50.0	34.1	42.8	40.5	44.2
1973	45.6	9.1	46.0	56.5	63.6	55.8	41.2	50.9	36.1	44.2	42.2	45.3
1974	52.6	15.4	53.1	64.4	71.6	63.9	48.2	55.5	44.0	50.5	48.8	51.2
1975	58.2	10.6	58.2	69.8	71.7	70.3	53.2	61.0	48.9	58.2	56.5	58.9
1976	60.8	4.5	60.4	69.6	76.7	69.0	56.5	63.7	52.4	62.1	60.3	62.9
1977	64.7	6.4	64.3	73.3	79.5	72.7	60.6	67.4	56.8	66.1	64.5	66.8
1978	69.8	7.9	69.4	79.9	85.8	79.4	64.9	73.6	60.0	71.3	70.1	71.8
1979	77.6	11.2	77.5	87.3	92.3	86.8	73.5	80.8	69.3	77.5	77.1	77.7
1980	88.0	13.4	88.6	92.4	93.9	92.3	87.1	91.0	85.1	85.8	86.0	85.7
1981	96.1	9.2	96.6	97.8	104.4	97.2	96.1	96.4	95.8	94.6	94.9	94.4
1982	100.0	4.1	100.0	100.0	100.0	100.0	100.0	100.0	100.0	100.0	100.0	100.0
1983	101.6	1.6	101.3	101.0	102.4	100.9	101.2	102.8	100.5	102.8	102.3	103.0
1984	103.7	2.1	103.3	105.4	111.4	104.9	102.2	104.5	101.1	105.2	104.9	105.4
1985	104.7	1.0	103.8	104.6	102.9	104.8	103.3	106.5	101.7	107.5	107.4	107.6
1986	103.2	-1.4	101.4	107.3	105.6	107.4	98.5	108.9	93.3	109.7	109.7	109.7
1987	105.4	2.1	103.6	109.5	107.1	109.6	100.7	111.5	94.9	111.7	111.8	111.6
1988	108.0	2.5	106.2	112.6	109.8	112.7	103.1	113.8	97.3	114.3	115.5	113.9
1989	113.6	5.2	112.1	118.7	119.6	118.6	108.9	117.6	103.8	118.8	120.3	118.2
1990	119.2	4.9	118.2	124.4	123.0	124.4	115.3	120.4	111.5	122.9	124.5	122.2
1991	121.7	2.1	120.5	124.1	119.3	124.4	118.7	123.9	115.0	126.7	127.8	126.3
1992	123.2	1.2	121.7	123.3	107.6	124.4	120.8	125.7	117.3	129.1	129.3	129.0
1993	124.7	1.2	123.0	125.7	114.4	126.5	121.7	128.0	117.6	131.4	131.2	131.4
1994	125.5	0.6	123.3	126.8	111.3	127.9	121.6	130.9	116.2	134.1	133.2	134.3
1995	127.9	1.9	125.6	129.0	118.8	129.8	124.0	132.7	118.8	136.7	135.8	137.0
1996	131.3	2.7	129.5	133.6	129.2	133.8	127.6	134.2	123.3	138.3	137.2	138.6
1997	131.8	0.4	130.2	134.5	126.6	135.1	128.2	133.7	124.3	138.2	137.7	138.4
1998	130.7	-0.8	128.9	134.3	127.2	134.8	126.4	132.9	122.2	137.6	137.9	137.4
1999	133.0	1.8	132.0	135.1	125.5	135.9	130.5	133.0	127.9	137.6	138.5	137.3
2000	138.0	3.8	138.2	137.2	123.5	138.3	138.4	133.9	138.7	138.8	139.5	138.6
2001	140.7	2.0	141.5	141.3	127.7	142.4	141.4	134.0	142.8	139.7	140.4	139.4
2002	138.9	-1.3	139.4	140.1	128.5	141.0	138.8	133.0	139.8	139.1	140.0	138.7
2003	143.3	3.2	145.3	145.9	130.0	147.2	144.7	133.1	148.4	139.5	139.9	139.3
2004	148.5	3.6	151.7	152.7	138.2	153.9	150.9	135.0	156.6	141.4	142.4	141.0
2005	155.7	4.8	160.4	155.7	140.2	156.9	161.9	136.6	172.0	144.6	146.0	144.1
2006	160.4	3.0	166.0	156.7	151.3	157.1	169.2	136.9	182.6	146.9	149.2	145.9
2007	166.6	3.9	173.5	167.0	170.2	166.7	175.6	138.3	191.7	149.5	152.5	148.3
2008	177.1	6.3	186.3	178.3	175.5	178.6	189.1	141.2	210.5	153.8	157.3	152.5
2009	172.5	-2.6	179.1	175.5	157.8	177.3	179.4	144.3	194.1	156.7	159.2	155.8
2010	179.8	4.2	189.1	182.4	172.6	183.3	190.4	144.9	210.1	157.3	159.6	156.4
2011	190.5	6.0	203.3	193.9	182.3	195.0	205.5	147.4	231.5	159.7	162.5	158.7
2012	194.2	1.9	207.3	199.0	167.9	202.0	209.1	151.0	235.0	162.8	165.1	161.8
2011												
January	185.6	0.7	196.9	187.5	188.7	186.8	199.1	145.2	222.5	158.2	160.9	157.1
February	187.6	1.1	199.6	194.4	233.8	189.4	200.3	145.7	224.1	158.6	161.3	157.5
March	188.9	0.7	201.2	193.7	202.9	192.1	202.7	146.2	227.4	159.0	161.8	157.9
April	190.2	0.7	202.9	193.7	189.2	193.7	205.0	146.7	230.6	159.4	162.3	158.3
May	191.0	0.4	204.0	191.8	172.1	193.5	207.1	146.9	233.6	159.6	162.4	158.4
June	190.9	-0.1	203.7	192.9	179.2	193.8	206.3	147.5	232.2	160.0	162.8	158.9
July	192.0	0.6	205.0	194.6	175.6	196.1	207.5	148.0	233.7	160.4	163.3	159.3
August	191.4	-0.3	204.3	196.2	176.3	197.9	206.0	148.0	231.4	160.3	163.3	159.1
September	193.1	0.9	206.5	197.1	181.4	198.2	208.7	148.5	235.2	160.7	163.5	159.5
October	192.5	-0.3	205.5	197.0	181.8	198.1	207.4	148.9	233.1	160.9	163.4	159.8
November	193.3	0.4	206.6	198.9	187.9	199.5	208.2	149.0	234.2	161.1	163.5	160.0
December	193.1	-0.1	206.2	197.7	175.8	199.6	208.0	149.2	233.8	161.4	163.7	160.4
2012												
January	193.3	0.1	206.3	197.8	164.4	200.7	208.2	149.7	233.7	161.9	164.2	160.9
February	193.9	0.3	206.9	197.6	160.9	200.8	209.1	150.0	235.0	162.3	164.8	161.2
March	194.0	0.1	206.9	198.2	170.5	200.5	208.9	150.3	234.5	162.5	165.0	161.5
April	193.6	-0.2	206.2	198.0	170.8	200.3	208.0	150.5	233.1	162.7	165.1	161.7
May	192.4	-0.6	204.4	197.7	168.5	200.2	205.7	150.6	229.6	162.8	165.3	161.8
June	192.5	0.1	204.6	198.5	173.2	200.6	205.6	151.1	229.3	163.0	165.2	162.1
July	193.2	0.4	205.3	198.9	171.0	201.3	206.4	151.9	230.1	163.5	165.5	162.6
August	195.2	1.0	208.3	200.3	181.4	201.9	210.0	151.8	235.5	163.4	165.6	162.5
September	197.2	1.0	211.1	200.5	179.6	202.3	213.7	151.9	240.9	163.4	165.7	162.4
October	196.9	-0.2	210.8	201.6	170.7	204.2	212.9	151.7	239.8	163.4	165.8	162.4
November	196.0	-0.5	209.5	203.8	178.2	206.0	210.3	152.0	235.8	163.5	165.8	162.5
December	195.8	-0.1	209.1	202.6	171.2	205.3	210.2	152.2	235.6	163.6	165.8	162.6

Table 8-5. Producer Price Indexes by Stage of Processing—*Continued*

(1982 = 100, seasonally adjusted.)

Year and month	Intermediate materials, supplies, and components												
	Total	Materials and components for manufacturing					Materials and components for construction	Processed fuels and lubricants			Containers, nonreturnable	Supplies	
		Total	Materials for food manufacturing	Materials for nondurable manufacturing	Materials for durable manufacturing	Components for manufacturing		Total	Manufacturing industries	Nonmanufacturing industries		Total	Manufacturing industries
1965	31.2	33.6	38.3	35.2	31.2	34.2	32.8	16.5	19.6	14.4	33.5	35.0	36.1
1966	32.0	34.3	40.0	35.4	31.8	35.4	33.6	16.8	19.9	14.7	34.5	36.5	37.1
1967	32.2	34.5	39.2	35.2	32.3	36.5	34.0	16.9	20.1	14.8	35.0	36.8	37.6
1968	33.0	35.3	39.8	35.6	33.4	37.3	35.7	16.5	19.8	14.2	35.9	37.1	38.7
1969	34.1	36.5	42.0	36.0	35.2	38.5	37.7	16.6	20.0	14.4	37.2	37.8	39.8
1970	35.4	38.0	44.3	36.5	37.0	40.6	38.3	17.7	21.5	15.2	39.0	39.7	41.4
1971	36.8	38.9	45.7	37.0	38.1	41.9	40.8	19.5	23.6	16.6	40.8	40.8	42.5
1972	38.2	40.4	47.0	38.5	39.9	42.9	43.0	20.1	24.5	16.9	42.7	42.5	43.3
1973	42.4	44.1	57.2	42.6	43.1	44.3	46.5	22.2	26.4	19.4	45.2	51.7	45.6
1974	52.5	56.0	82.0	54.6	55.4	51.1	55.0	33.6	35.5	32.7	53.3	56.8	53.3
1975	58.0	61.7	82.1	61.4	60.8	57.8	60.1	39.4	41.9	38.0	60.0	61.8	59.4
1976	60.9	64.0	70.6	64.8	64.8	60.8	64.1	42.3	44.8	41.1	63.1	65.8	62.6
1977	64.9	67.4	71.9	66.8	70.2	64.5	69.3	47.7	51.0	46.2	65.9	69.3	66.6
1978	69.5	72.0	81.0	69.2	76.2	69.2	76.5	49.9	53.7	48.1	71.0	72.9	71.2
1979	78.4	80.9	89.9	78.3	87.3	75.8	84.2	61.6	64.3	60.4	79.4	80.2	78.1
1980	90.3	91.7	103.7	91.2	97.1	84.6	91.3	85.0	85.5	84.7	89.1	89.9	87.2
1981	98.6	98.7	102.1	100.5	100.7	94.7	97.9	100.6	100.2	101.0	96.7	96.9	95.2
1982	100.0	100.0	100.0	100.0	100.0	100.0	100.0	100.0	100.0	100.0	100.0	100.0	100.0
1983	100.6	101.2	101.3	98.5	103.0	102.4	102.8	95.4	96.2	94.9	100.4	101.8	101.5
1984	103.1	104.1	106.3	102.1	104.9	105.0	105.6	95.7	97.1	94.6	105.9	104.1	105.0
1985	102.7	103.3	101.5	100.5	103.3	106.4	107.3	92.8	93.8	92.0	109.0	104.4	107.3
1986	99.1	102.2	98.4	98.1	101.2	107.5	108.1	72.7	75.1	71.2	110.3	105.6	108.3
1987	101.5	105.3	100.8	102.2	106.2	108.8	109.8	73.3	75.9	71.7	114.5	107.7	110.0
1988	107.1	113.2	106.0	112.9	118.7	112.3	116.1	71.2	73.3	69.9	120.1	113.7	114.8
1989	112.0	118.1	112.7	118.5	123.6	116.4	121.3	76.4	78.3	75.3	125.4	118.1	119.8
1990	114.5	118.7	117.9	118.0	120.7	119.0	122.9	85.9	87.3	85.0	127.7	119.4	122.1
1991	114.4	118.1	115.3	116.7	117.2	121.0	124.5	85.3	88.4	83.4	128.1	121.4	124.4
1992	114.7	117.9	113.9	115.4	117.2	122.0	126.5	84.5	87.5	82.6	127.7	122.7	125.9
1993	116.2	118.9	115.6	115.5	119.1	123.0	132.0	84.7	88.1	82.6	126.4	125.0	128.5
1994	118.5	122.1	118.5	119.2	125.2	124.3	136.6	83.1	86.1	81.1	129.7	127.0	130.7
1995	124.9	130.4	119.5	135.1	135.6	126.5	142.1	84.2	87.1	82.3	148.8	132.1	137.0
1996	125.7	128.6	125.3	130.5	131.3	126.9	143.6	90.0	92.4	88.4	141.1	135.9	138.7
1997	125.6	128.3	123.2	129.6	132.8	126.4	146.5	89.3	92.0	87.6	136.0	135.9	139.4
1998	123.0	126.1	123.2	126.7	128.0	125.9	146.8	81.1	85.8	78.1	140.8	134.8	140.6
1999	123.2	124.6	120.8	124.9	125.1	125.7	148.9	84.6	87.9	82.5	142.5	134.2	140.7
2000	129.2	128.1	119.2	132.6	129.0	126.2	150.7	102.0	100.9	102.3	151.6	136.9	143.5
2001	129.7	127.4	124.3	131.8	125.1	126.4	150.6	104.5	105.7	103.5	153.1	138.7	145.4
2002	127.8	126.1	123.2	129.2	124.7	126.1	151.3	96.3	98.7	94.8	152.1	138.9	144.7
2003	133.7	129.7	134.4	137.2	127.9	125.9	153.6	112.6	116.0	110.5	153.7	141.5	146.5
2004	142.6	137.9	145.0	147.8	146.6	127.4	166.4	124.3	125.1	123.8	159.3	146.7	149.2
2005	154.0	146.0	146.0	163.2	158.3	129.9	176.6	150.0	148.6	150.9	167.1	151.9	155.7
2006	164.0	155.9	146.2	175.0	180.5	134.5	188.4	162.8	158.1	165.7	175.0	157.0	161.1
2007	170.7	162.4	161.4	184.0	189.8	136.3	192.5	173.9	172.6	175.0	180.3	161.7	162.9
2008	188.3	177.2	180.4	214.3	203.3	140.3	205.4	206.2	199.4	209.6	191.8	173.8	170.5
2009	172.5	162.7	165.1	191.6	168.9	141.0	202.9	161.9	165.7	160.9	195.8	172.2	168.0
2010	183.4	174.0	174.4	215.4	186.6	142.2	205.7	185.2	184.8	185.8	201.2	175.0	172.2
2011	199.8	189.8	193.4	249.2	204.2	145.8	212.8	215.0	213.2	216.2	205.4	184.2	180.5
2012	200.7	189.0	198.1	245.4	199.1	147.7	218.4	213.2	212.0	214.2	206.9	188.9	182.9
2011													
January	191.6	181.9	181.8	232.2	196.8	143.7	208.7	199.3	193.6	202.4	203.3	179.7	176.0
February	194.7	185.4	187.8	238.8	202.2	144.2	209.7	204.0	197.3	207.4	203.8	181.0	176.7
March	197.3	187.7	191.6	244.3	203.9	144.6	210.8	209.6	201.6	213.5	204.4	182.3	178.2
April	200.0	191.0	193.5	252.1	207.4	145.3	211.9	212.7	204.6	216.8	204.9	183.9	179.8
May	201.7	192.4	192.4	257.6	206.6	145.7	212.4	217.1	209.1	221.1	206.4	184.4	181.1
June	202.3	192.3	193.2	256.6	206.1	146.1	213.5	218.7	213.1	221.7	206.8	185.1	182.4
July	203.2	193.3	195.8	258.1	207.5	146.4	214.5	219.9	217.5	221.7	207.1	185.6	182.5
August	201.8	192.7	198.4	255.3	207.0	146.5	214.6	214.4	212.8	215.9	206.0	185.9	182.0
September	202.8	192.8	198.1	256.5	206.0	146.5	214.6	218.0	215.3	220.0	206.1	186.5	182.3
October	200.5	190.8	196.8	251.8	202.6	146.7	214.8	212.5	208.4	215.0	205.6	185.8	182.3
November	200.8	189.8	198.1	248.1	202.1	146.8	214.7	216.3	210.8	219.4	205.5	185.6	181.9
December	200.0	188.1	197.2	242.7	200.8	146.9	214.8	216.6	213.4	218.7	205.5	185.1	181.5
2012													
January	199.9	189.0	197.1	244.9	201.9	147.0	215.7	213.3	206.4	216.7	205.5	185.7	181.6
February	200.9	190.6	196.7	249.7	203.2	147.2	217.0	213.0	203.7	217.3	206.7	186.2	182.1
March	202.9	192.6	196.4	256.6	203.2	147.4	217.3	216.8	209.6	220.3	206.8	187.2	182.9
April	201.8	192.6	195.9	257.1	202.3	147.6	218.1	210.5	204.4	213.6	207.0	187.8	183.8
May	200.2	191.2	194.8	253.1	200.5	147.8	218.6	205.1	199.0	208.2	207.0	188.3	183.8
June	198.8	187.7	195.6	242.1	198.1	147.8	218.9	206.0	205.0	207.4	206.8	188.4	183.6
July	198.1	186.6	197.3	238.7	196.5	147.8	218.4	204.9	205.5	205.6	206.3	189.0	183.1
August	200.0	186.9	198.7	240.4	195.1	147.8	218.8	211.5	209.7	213.2	206.1	190.4	182.2
September	202.3	188.1	199.8	242.7	197.4	147.9	219.5	218.8	215.0	221.2	206.0	191.1	182.6
October	202.2	188.2	202.5	243.0	196.7	147.9	219.6	217.9	212.6	220.8	206.4	191.1	183.1
November	200.5	187.5	204.6	240.5	195.8	148.1	220.1	210.8	207.5	212.9	209.5	190.9	183.4
December	200.6	187.6	202.6	240.2	197.0	148.1	220.5	211.2	207.9	213.4	210.1	190.9	183.6

Table 8-5. Producer Price Indexes by Stage of Processing—*Continued*

(1982 = 100, seasonally adjusted.)

Year and month	Intermediate materials, supplies, and components—*Continued*			Crude materials for further processing								
	Supplies—*Continued*			Total	Foodstuffs and feedstuffs	Crude nonfood materials						
	Nonmanufacturing industries					Total	Crude nonfood materials except fuel 2			Crude fuel 3		
	Total	Feeds	Other supplies				Total 2	Manu-facturing 2	Construc-tion	Total	Manu-facturing industries	Nonmanu-facturing industries
1965	34.5	45.9	33.0	31.1	39.2	. . .	27.7	27.2	36.1	10.6	9.0	11.9
1966	36.2	50.0	33.8	33.1	42.7	. . .	28.3	27.8	36.3	10.9	9.3	12.3
1967	36.3	48.3	34.5	31.3	40.3	21.1	26.5	25.8	37.0	11.3	9.7	12.8
1968	36.4	46.5	35.4	31.8	40.9	21.6	27.1	26.3	38.4	11.5	9.9	13.1
1969	36.9	46.4	36.0	33.9	44.1	22.5	28.4	27.6	39.8	12.0	10.2	13.8
1970	38.9	49.9	37.6	35.2	45.2	23.8	29.1	28.3	42.1	13.8	11.3	16.6
1971	39.9	50.4	38.9	36.0	46.1	24.7	29.4	28.4	44.1	15.7	12.6	19.3
1972	42.0	56.1	39.8	39.9	51.5	27.0	32.3	31.5	45.0	16.8	13.5	20.6
1973	54.7	97.3	42.7	54.5	72.6	34.3	42.9	42.7	46.2	18.6	14.8	22.9
1974	58.4	90.2	50.5	61.4	76.4	44.1	54.5	55.0	50.0	24.8	19.1	31.8
1975	62.9	84.0	58.9	61.6	77.4	43.7	50.0	49.7	55.9	30.6	24.4	38.0
1976	67.3	95.1	62.0	63.4	76.8	48.2	54.9	54.7	59.6	34.5	29.0	40.5
1977	70.7	99.3	65.2	65.5	77.5	51.7	56.3	56.0	63.1	42.0	37.2	47.4
1978	73.8	95.5	69.7	73.4	87.3	57.5	61.9	61.5	68.7	48.2	43.1	53.8
1979	81.2	106.9	76.3	85.9	100.0	69.6	75.5	75.6	76.6	57.3	53.1	62.0
1980	91.1	110.6	87.5	95.3	104.6	84.6	91.8	92.3	87.9	69.4	66.7	72.5
1981	97.8	111.3	95.4	103.0	103.9	101.8	109.8	110.9	96.8	84.8	83.6	86.2
1982	100.0	100.0	100.0	100.0	100.0	100.0	100.0	100.0	100.0	100.0	100.0	100.0
1983	102.0	109.1	101.0	101.3	101.8	100.7	98.8	98.6	100.1	105.1	105.8	104.4
1984	103.7	104.2	103.7	103.5	104.7	102.2	101.0	100.8	103.1	105.1	105.6	104.6
1985	103.0	86.6	105.3	95.8	94.8	96.9	94.3	93.1	105.7	102.7	102.7	102.5
1986	104.2	90.5	106.2	87.7	93.2	81.6	76.0	72.6	106.5	92.2	91.1	93.6
1987	106.6	94.6	108.3	93.7	96.2	87.9	88.5	84.7	114.8	84.1	82.1	86.3
1988	113.2	115.0	112.7	96.0	106.1	85.5	85.9	81.5	126.5	82.1	80.1	84.5
1989	117.2	114.4	117.5	103.1	111.2	93.4	95.8	91.0	136.9	85.3	83.9	87.0
1990	118.0	102.8	120.2	108.9	113.1	101.5	107.3	102.5	145.2	84.8	82.9	87.0
1991	119.9	101.3	122.5	101.2	105.5	94.6	97.5	92.2	147.5	82.9	82.3	84.1
1992	121.1	103.0	123.7	100.4	105.1	93.5	94.2	87.9	162.1	84.0	83.1	85.2
1993	123.2	105.4	125.8	102.4	108.4	94.7	94.1	85.6	193.6	87.1	85.9	88.6
1994	125.1	105.8	127.9	101.8	106.5	94.8	97.0	88.3	199.1	82.4	81.7	83.6
1995	129.5	103.4	133.2	102.7	105.8	96.8	105.8	97.3	201.7	72.1	72.5	72.9
1996	134.4	133.1	134.6	113.8	121.5	104.5	105.7	97.6	195.7	92.6	90.7	94.3
1997	134.1	129.1	134.8	111.1	112.2	106.4	103.5	95.0	201.4	101.3	98.4	103.3
1998	132.2	100.2	136.2	96.8	103.9	88.4	84.5	76.7	196.0	86.7	84.8	88.5
1999	131.4	89.2	136.5	98.2	98.7	94.3	91.1	83.0	195.7	91.2	90.0	92.9
2000	134.1	94.6	138.8	120.6	100.2	130.4	118.0	108.7	193.4	136.9	136.9	139.3
2001	135.8	96.8	140.5	121.0	106.1	126.8	101.5	93.2	181.7	151.4	150.2	154.2
2002	136.3	98.1	140.9	108.1	99.5	111.4	101.0	92.5	181.4	117.3	113.4	119.8
2003	139.0	106.6	143.1	135.3	113.5	148.2	116.9	107.5	180.8	185.7	176.4	189.9
2004	144.9	119.1	148.4	159.0	127.0	179.2	149.2	137.7	191.8	211.4	200.5	216.2
2005	149.7	107.4	154.9	182.2	122.7	223.4	176.7	163.4	199.3	279.7	263.9	286.3
2006	154.7	110.9	160.1	184.8	119.3	230.6	210.0	194.5	201.1	241.5	229.2	247.0
2007	160.1	138.4	163.2	207.1	146.7	246.3	238.7	221.6	201.7	236.8	224.9	242.2
2008	173.2	182.4	173.4	251.8	163.4	313.9	308.5	287.3	199.0	298.3	283.5	305.0
2009	171.4	170.7	173.0	175.2	134.5	197.5	211.1	197.1	200.5	166.3	185.0	169.0
2010	174.0	166.6	176.2	212.2	152.4	249.3	280.8	265.0	203.0	188.0	202.3	191.3
2011	183.3	203.2	183.3	249.4	188.4	284.0	342.0	324.6	206.6	181.5	206.0	184.3
2012	188.3	227.9	186.7	241.3	196.3	263.1	332.4	314.9	212.3	143.9	184.2	145.5
2011												
January	178.8	191.2	179.4	239.8	173.1	280.2	335.3	317.5	204.4	185.5	203.4	188.6
February	180.2	196.5	180.6	247.9	184.9	283.8	338.9	321.1	204.0	188.9	207.1	192.0
March	181.5	200.9	181.6	246.8	185.8	280.9	343.1	325.2	204.0	175.7	199.4	178.3
April	183.0	208.8	182.6	256.8	192.6	293.2	356.2	337.9	204.1	186.2	206.4	189.2
May	183.4	211.0	182.8	252.1	187.1	289.6	348.4	330.4	204.7	189.1	208.2	192.1
June	184.1	213.4	183.3	254.0	191.4	289.1	346.5	328.4	206.5	190.5	209.6	193.6
July	184.6	209.8	184.3	254.4	189.6	291.6	350.2	332.0	206.8	191.2	211.1	194.3
August	185.1	210.3	184.7	250.5	194.9	279.1	330.0	312.3	206.6	190.6	211.7	193.7
September	185.6	213.5	185.0	252.8	191.8	286.4	349.7	331.6	206.7	179.3	205.3	181.9
October	184.8	204.8	184.9	246.9	188.7	278.4	341.3	323.3	207.0	172.4	200.5	174.9
November	184.7	200.8	185.1	252.6	191.1	286.7	360.1	341.6	207.6	164.7	195.5	166.9
December	184.2	197.6	184.8	247.8	187.3	281.4	353.5	335.2	207.9	161.8	193.6	163.9
2012												
January	184.8	198.8	185.4	249.3	190.5	281.5	359.1	340.6	207.8	152.9	187.3	154.8
February	185.3	200.4	185.8	250.2	191.3	282.4	368.1	349.4	209.4	140.8	179.2	142.2
March	186.4	208.0	186.3	246.1	195.6	271.7	355.3	336.7	210.8	133.5	174.7	134.7
April	186.9	213.3	186.5	236.7	189.8	259.9	341.3	323.0	210.7	125.4	170.4	126.3
May	187.5	220.4	186.6	232.1	186.8	254.3	332.9	314.8	210.5	124.3	171.0	125.1
June	187.6	224.0	186.4	225.3	185.2	243.5	310.0	292.2	211.3	133.3	177.0	134.5
July	188.4	234.2	186.4	231.7	192.9	248.4	312.8	294.8	212.6	141.6	180.7	143.1
August	190.2	254.1	186.7	242.7	200.0	261.9	330.5	312.2	212.9	148.1	183.8	149.8
September	190.8	260.0	186.9	246.4	201.4	267.4	342.9	324.5	212.3	142.2	182.1	143.7
October	190.8	254.8	187.3	246.5	205.6	264.1	333.2	314.8	213.5	149.5	186.3	151.2
November	190.5	245.0	187.8	247.3	206.6	264.6	326.4	308.2	213.7	161.6	194.3	163.7
December	190.5	245.5	187.7	250.4	207.4	269.5	329.7	311.4	213.5	169.2	201.3	171.5

2Includes crude petroleum.
3Excludes crude petroleum.
. . . = Not available.

Table 8-6. Producer Price Indexes by Major Commodity Groups

(1982 = 100.)

Year and month	All commodities	Farm products	Processed foods and feeds	Industrial commodities													
				Total	Textile products and apparel	Hides, leather, and related products	Fuels and related products and power	Chemicals and allied products	Rubber and plastics products	Lumber and wood products	Pulp, paper, and allied products	Metals and metal products	Machinery and equipment	Furniture and household durables	Nonmetallic mineral products	Transportation equipment	Miscellaneous products
1950	27.3	44.0	33.2	25.0	50.2	32.9	12.6	30.4	35.6	31.4	25.7	22.0	22.6	40.9	23.5	. . .	28.6
1951	30.4	51.2	36.9	27.6	56.0	37.7	13.0	34.8	43.7	34.1	30.5	24.5	25.3	44.4	25.0	. . .	30.3
1952	29.6	48.4	36.4	26.9	50.5	30.5	13.0	33.0	39.6	33.2	29.7	24.5	25.3	43.5	25.0	. . .	30.2
1953	29.2	43.8	34.8	27.2	49.3	31.0	13.4	33.4	36.9	33.1	29.6	25.3	25.9	44.4	26.0	. . .	31.0
1954	29.3	43.2	35.4	27.2	48.2	29.5	13.2	33.8	37.5	32.5	29.6	25.5	26.3	44.9	26.6	. . .	31.3
1955	29.3	40.5	33.8	27.8	48.2	29.4	13.2	33.7	42.4	34.1	30.4	27.2	27.2	45.1	27.3	. . .	31.3
1956	30.3	40.0	33.8	29.1	48.2	31.2	13.6	33.9	43.0	34.6	32.4	29.6	29.3	46.3	28.5	. . .	31.7
1957	31.2	41.1	34.8	29.9	48.3	31.2	14.3	34.6	42.8	32.8	33.0	30.2	31.4	47.5	29.6	. . .	32.6
1958	31.6	42.9	36.5	30.0	47.4	31.6	13.7	34.9	42.8	32.5	33.4	30.0	32.1	47.9	29.9	. . .	33.3
1959	31.7	40.2	35.6	30.5	48.1	35.9	13.7	34.8	42.6	34.7	33.7	30.6	32.8	48.0	30.3	. . .	33.4
1960	31.7	40.1	35.6	30.5	48.6	34.6	13.9	34.8	42.7	33.5	34.0	30.6	33.0	47.8	30.4	. . .	33.6
1961	31.6	39.7	36.2	30.4	47.8	34.9	14.0	34.5	41.1	32.0	33.0	30.5	33.0	47.5	30.5	. . .	33.7
1962	31.7	40.4	36.5	30.4	48.2	35.3	14.0	33.9	39.9	32.2	33.4	30.2	33.0	47.2	30.5	. . .	33.9
1963	31.6	39.6	36.8	30.3	48.2	34.3	13.9	33.5	40.1	32.8	33.1	30.3	33.1	46.9	30.3	. . .	34.2
1964	31.6	39.0	36.7	30.5	48.5	34.4	13.5	33.6	39.6	33.5	33.0	31.1	33.3	47.1	30.4	. . .	34.4
1965	32.3	40.7	38.0	30.9	48.8	35.9	13.8	33.9	39.7	33.7	33.3	32.0	33.7	46.8	30.4	. . .	34.7
1966	33.3	43.7	40.2	31.5	48.9	39.4	14.1	34.0	40.5	35.2	34.2	32.8	34.7	47.4	30.7	. . .	35.3
1967	33.4	41.3	39.8	32.0	48.9	38.1	14.4	34.2	41.4	35.1	34.6	33.2	35.9	48.3	31.2	. . .	36.2
1968	34.2	42.3	40.6	32.8	50.7	39.3	14.3	34.1	42.8	39.8	35.0	34.0	37.0	49.7	32.4	. . .	37.0
1969	35.6	45.0	42.7	33.9	51.8	41.5	14.6	34.2	43.6	44.0	36.0	36.0	38.2	50.7	33.6	40.4	38.1
1970	36.9	45.8	44.6	35.2	52.4	42.0	15.3	35.0	44.9	39.9	37.5	38.7	40.0	51.9	35.3	41.9	39.8
1971	38.1	46.6	45.5	36.5	53.3	43.4	16.6	35.6	45.2	44.7	38.1	39.4	41.4	53.1	38.2	44.2	40.8
1972	39.8	51.6	48.0	37.8	55.5	50.0	17.1	35.6	45.3	50.7	39.3	40.9	42.3	53.8	39.4	45.5	41.5
1973	45.0	72.7	58.9	40.3	60.5	54.5	19.4	37.6	46.6	62.2	42.3	44.0	43.7	55.7	40.7	46.1	43.3
1974	53.5	77.4	68.0	49.2	68.0	55.2	30.1	50.2	56.4	64.5	52.5	57.0	50.0	61.8	47.8	50.3	48.1
1975	58.4	77.0	72.6	54.9	67.4	56.5	35.4	62.0	62.2	62.1	59.0	61.5	57.9	67.5	54.4	56.7	53.4
1976	61.1	78.8	70.8	58.4	72.4	63.9	38.3	64.0	66.0	72.2	62.1	65.0	61.3	70.3	58.2	60.5	55.6
1977	64.9	79.4	74.0	62.5	75.3	68.3	43.6	65.9	69.4	83.0	64.6	69.3	65.2	73.2	62.6	64.6	59.4
1978	69.9	87.7	80.6	67.0	78.1	76.1	46.5	68.0	72.4	96.9	67.7	75.3	70.3	77.5	69.6	69.5	66.7
1979	78.7	99.6	88.5	75.7	82.5	96.1	58.9	76.0	80.5	105.5	75.9	86.0	76.7	82.8	77.6	75.3	75.5
1980	89.8	102.9	95.9	88.0	89.7	94.7	82.8	89.0	90.1	101.5	86.3	95.0	86.0	90.7	88.4	82.9	93.6
1981	98.0	105.2	98.9	97.4	97.6	99.3	100.2	98.4	96.4	102.8	94.8	99.6	94.4	95.9	96.7	94.3	96.1
1982	100.0	100.0	100.0	100.0	100.0	100.0	100.0	100.0	100.0	100.0	100.0	100.0	100.0	100.0	100.0	100.0	100.0
1983	101.3	102.4	101.8	101.1	100.3	103.2	95.9	100.3	100.8	107.9	103.3	101.8	102.7	103.4	101.6	102.8	104.8
1984	103.7	105.5	105.4	103.3	102.7	109.0	94.8	102.9	102.3	108.0	110.3	104.8	105.1	105.7	105.4	105.2	107.0
1985	103.2	95.1	103.5	103.7	102.9	108.9	91.4	103.7	101.9	106.6	113.3	104.4	107.2	107.1	108.6	107.9	109.4
1986	100.2	92.9	105.4	100.0	103.2	113.0	69.8	102.6	101.9	107.2	116.1	103.2	108.8	108.2	110.0	110.5	111.6
1987	102.8	95.5	107.9	102.6	105.1	120.4	70.2	106.4	103.0	112.8	121.8	107.1	110.4	109.9	110.0	112.5	114.9
1988	106.9	104.9	112.7	106.3	109.2	131.4	66.7	116.3	109.3	118.9	130.4	118.7	113.2	113.1	111.2	114.3	120.2
1989	112.2	110.9	117.8	111.6	112.3	136.3	72.9	123.0	112.6	126.7	137.8	124.1	117.4	116.9	112.6	117.7	126.5
1990	116.3	112.2	121.9	115.8	115.0	141.7	82.3	123.6	113.6	129.7	141.2	122.9	120.7	119.2	114.7	121.5	134.2
1991	116.5	105.7	121.9	116.5	116.3	138.9	81.2	125.6	115.1	132.1	142.9	120.2	123.0	121.2	117.2	126.4	140.8
1992	117.2	103.6	122.1	117.4	117.8	140.4	80.4	125.9	115.1	146.6	145.2	119.2	123.4	122.2	117.3	130.4	145.3
1993	118.9	107.1	124.0	119.0	118.0	143.7	80.0	128.2	116.0	174.0	147.3	119.2	124.0	123.7	120.0	133.7	145.4
1994	120.4	106.3	125.5	120.7	118.3	148.5	77.8	132.1	117.6	180.0	152.5	124.8	125.1	126.1	124.2	137.2	141.9
1995	124.7	107.4	127.0	125.5	120.8	153.7	78.0	142.5	124.3	178.1	172.2	134.5	126.6	128.2	129.0	139.7	145.4
1996	127.7	122.4	133.3	127.3	122.4	150.5	85.8	142.1	123.8	176.1	168.7	131.0	126.5	130.4	131.0	141.7	147.7
1997	127.6	112.9	134.0	127.7	122.6	154.2	86.1	143.6	123.2	183.8	167.9	131.8	125.9	130.8	133.2	141.6	150.9
1998	124.4	104.6	131.6	124.8	122.9	148.0	75.3	143.9	122.6	179.1	171.7	127.8	124.9	131.3	135.4	141.2	156.0
1999	125.5	98.4	131.1	126.5	121.1	146.0	80.5	144.2	122.5	183.6	174.1	124.6	124.3	131.7	138.9	141.8	166.6
2000	132.7	99.5	133.1	134.8	121.4	151.5	103.5	151.0	125.5	178.2	183.7	128.1	124.0	132.6	142.5	143.8	170.8
2001	134.2	103.8	137.3	135.7	121.3	158.4	105.3	151.8	127.2	174.4	184.8	125.4	123.7	133.2	144.3	145.2	181.3
2002	131.1	99.0	136.2	132.4	119.9	157.6	93.2	151.9	126.8	173.3	185.9	125.9	122.9	133.5	146.2	144.6	182.4
2003	138.1	111.5	143.4	139.1	119.8	162.3	112.9	161.8	130.1	177.4	190.0	129.2	121.9	133.9	148.2	145.7	179.6
2004	146.7	123.3	151.2	147.6	121.0	164.5	126.9	174.4	133.8	195.6	195.7	149.6	122.1	135.1	153.2	148.6	183.2
2005	157.4	118.5	153.1	160.2	122.8	165.4	156.4	192.0	143.8	196.5	202.6	160.8	123.7	139.4	164.2	151.0	195.1
2006	164.7	117.0	153.8	168.8	124.5	168.4	166.7	205.8	153.8	194.4	209.8	181.6	126.2	142.6	179.9	152.6	205.6
2007	172.6	143.4	165.1	175.1	125.8	173.6	177.6	214.8	155.0	192.4	216.9	193.5	127.3	144.7	186.2	155.0	210.3
2008	189.6	161.3	180.5	192.3	128.9	173.1	214.6	245.5	165.9	191.3	226.8	213.0	129.7	148.9	197.1	158.6	216.6
2009	172.9	134.6	176.2	174.8	129.5	157.0	158.7	229.4	165.2	182.8	225.6	186.8	131.3	153.1	202.4	162.2	217.5
2010	184.7	151.0	182.3	187.0	131.7	181.4	185.8	246.6	170.7	192.7	236.9	207.6	131.1	153.2	201.8	163.4	221.5
2011	201.0	186.7	197.5	202.0	141.7	199.9	215.9	275.1	182.7	194.7	245.1	225.9	132.7	156.4	205.0	166.1	229.2
2012	202.2	192.5	205.2	202.1	142.2	202.3	212.1	276.6	186.9	201.6	244.2	219.9	134.2	160.6	211.0	169.8	235.6

. . . = Not available.

Table 8-7. Producer Price Indexes for the Net Output of Selected NAICS Industry Groups

(Various index bases, not seasonally adjusted.)

Year and month	Mining		Manufacturing (Dec. 1984 = 100)									
	Total (Dec. 1984 = 100)	Oil and gas extraction (Dec. 1985 = 100)	Total	Food manufacturing	Leather and products	Petroleum and coal products	Chemicals	Plastics and rubber products	Nonmetallic mineral products	Primary metals	Fabricated metal products	Furniture and related products
1990	81.8	82.7	114.5	116.2	122.6	91.4	121.0	111.3	110.0	116.5	115.1	119.1
1991	78.4	77.9	115.9	116.5	124.8	83.1	124.4	113.7	112.3	113.1	116.6	121.6
1992	76.9	76.5	117.4	116.9	127.0	80.3	125.8	114.2	112.8	111.7	117.2	122.9
1993	76.4	76.2	119.1	118.7	129.0	77.6	127.2	115.4	115.4	111.4	118.2	125.4
1994	73.3	71.1	120.7	120.1	130.6	74.8	130.0	117.1	119.6	117.0	120.3	129.7
1995	71.0	66.6	124.2	121.7	134.1	77.2	143.4	123.3	124.3	128.2	124.8	133.3
1996	84.4	84.8	127.1	127.1	134.7	87.4	145.8	123.1	125.8	123.7	126.2	136.2
1997	86.1	87.5	127.5	127.9	137.1	85.6	147.1	122.8	127.4	124.7	127.6	138.2
1998	70.8	68.3	126.2	126.3	137.1	66.3	148.7	122.1	129.3	120.9	128.7	139.7
1999	78.0	78.5	128.3	126.3	136.5	76.8	149.7	122.2	132.6	115.8	129.1	141.3
2000	113.5	126.8	133.5	128.5	137.9	112.8	156.7	124.6	134.7	119.8	130.3	143.3
2001	114.3	127.5	134.6	132.8	141.3	105.3	158.4	125.9	136.0	116.1	131.0	145.1
2002	96.6	107.0	133.7	132.0	141.1	98.8	157.3	125.5	137.1	116.2	131.7	146.3
2003	131.3	160.1	137.1	137.4	142.8	122.0	164.6	128.4	138.0	118.4	132.9	147.4
2004	153.4	192.7	142.9	144.3	143.6	149.9	172.8	131.7	142.7	142.8	141.3	151.5
2005	201.0	262.0	150.8	146.1	144.5	200.4	187.3	141.2	152.0	156.3	149.5	157.8
2006	208.7	252.5	156.9	146.8	146.6	235.5	196.8	149.7	163.4	179.3	155.7	162.5
2007	220.1	267.1	162.9	158.6	149.7	260.3	203.3	150.6	166.8	190.5	162.3	165.7
2008	274.7	347.5	175.8	173.8	153.5	329.2	228.2	161.3	170.9	211.9	174.4	171.7
2009	178.2	187.3	167.1	169.5	153.8	218.8	224.7	161.3	174.0	172.5	175.2	176.6
2010	214.4	240.5	175.4	175.5	156.2	285.8	233.7	166.1	172.5	196.1	176.5	177.1
2011	242.6	274.6	189.1	191.3	164.0	374.4	252.1	176.3	174.9	217.2	182.8	181.0
2012	226.0	240.9	193.1	198.6	167.7	379.2	260.3	180.6	180.2	207.6	185.4	185.0
2012												
January	238.0	264.4	191.1	194.9	165.3	371.1	258.4	178.5	178.2	211.6	184.5	183.5
February	234.9	257.1	192.1	194.9	165.4	377.5	259.7	179.3	179.2	215.0	184.8	184.0
March	236.7	259.7	194.3	195.7	166.9	401.2	261.7	180.2	179.6	214.6	185.2	184.0
April	229.9	247.7	194.7	196.0	167.9	403.5	262.0	181.2	179.6	213.2	185.6	184.5
May	218.5	227.4	193.6	196.6	167.8	387.6	262.0	181.6	179.9	211.1	185.9	184.7
June	208.4	208.4	191.7	197.1	167.5	366.7	259.6	181.7	180.0	207.1	185.9	185.0
July	213.8	219.4	191.2	198.2	167.8	357.3	259.6	181.3	180.6	204.8	185.5	185.4
August	224.6	240.3	193.5	200.6	168.0	380.8	260.2	180.4	180.9	201.6	185.4	185.4
September	227.4	242.8	195.4	202.1	168.7	401.1	259.9	180.5	180.8	204.8	185.5	185.7
October	226.0	240.3	195.1	202.4	169.1	391.5	260.8	180.8	180.9	203.6	185.6	186.2
November	226.3	241.2	192.6	202.6	169.2	360.0	259.9	181.0	181.2	201.6	185.6	186.2
December	227.7	242.6	191.8	201.7	169.5	352.1	259.3	180.9	181.6	202.9	185.8	185.7

Year and month	Transportation and warehousing					Health care and social assistance			Other services industries (Dec. 1996 = 100)			
	Air transportation (Dec. 1992 = 100)	Rail transportation (Dec. 1996 = 100)	Pipeline transportation (June 1986 = 100)		Postal service (June 1989 = 100)	Offices of physicians (Dec. 1996 = 100)	Home health care (Dec. 1996 = 100)	Hospitals (Dec. 1992 = 100)	Legal services	Architectural, engineering, and related services	Employment services	Accommodation
			Crude oil	Refined petr. products								
1990	. . .	. . .	94.2	100.8	100.0	. . .	. . .	. . .	. . .	. . .	. . .	. . .
1991	. . .	. . .	94.4	101.1	117.9	. . .	. . .	. . .	. . .	. . .	. . .	. . .
1992	. . .	. . .	94.8	101.2	119.8	. . .	. . .	. . .	. . .	. . .	. . .	. . .
1993	105.6	. . .	95.0	101.3	119.8	. . .	. . .	102.5	. . .	. . .	. . .	. . .
1994	108.5	. . .	102.5	103.4	119.8	. . .	. . .	106.2	. . .	. . .	. . .	. . .
1995	113.7	. . .	113.4	104.6	132.2	. . .	. . .	110.0	. . .	. . .	. . .	. . .
1996	121.1	. . .	104.7	104.3	132.3	. . .	. . .	112.6	. . .	. . .	. . .	. . .
1997	125.3	100.5	96.0	105.3	132.3	101.0	103.3	113.6	102.5	102.2	101.0	104.2
1998	124.5	101.7	96.8	104.8	132.3	103.2	106.2	114.4	106.1	105.1	103.2	108.1
1999	130.8	101.3	95.5	104.9	135.3	105.5	107.1	116.4	108.7	108.5	105.2	112.7
2000	147.7	102.6	101.0	105.3	135.2	107.3	111.1	119.4	112.5	111.8	107.3	116.2
2001	157.2	104.5	111.1	108.5	143.4	110.4	114.0	123.0	117.9	115.9	108.2	121.3
2002	157.8	106.6	112.3	111.0	150.2	110.3	116.6	127.5	121.7	121.1	108.9	121.3
2003	162.1	108.8	111.1	112.7	155.0	112.1	117.0	134.9	125.6	124.3	111.4	122.0
2004	162.3	113.4	115.2	116.0	155.0	114.3	119.8	141.5	131.8	126.8	113.9	125.2
2005	171.0	125.2	125.5	120.3	155.0	116.4	121.1	146.9	138.5	129.2	116.3	131.9
2006	180.4	135.9	135.3	123.8	164.7	117.5	121.8	153.3	145.2	134.4	119.2	136.7
2007	183.7	140.9	138.9	131.7	171.9	122.3	124.0	158.6	153.6	140.0	121.7	142.9
2008	203.8	157.3	152.0	139.2	178.9	123.6	126.1	163.4	161.6	141.0	123.2	146.0
2009	188.5	148.5	156.3	147.3	185.0	126.6	128.0	168.3	166.2	142.9	123.5	141.5
2010	202.9	156.2	203.3	153.1	187.7	129.7	129.5	173.3	171.9	143.5	124.9	140.6
2011	218.3	169.8	204.7	157.1	190.6	131.6	129.5	177.0	177.9	145.5	125.5	142.8
2012	227.6	177.4	216.7	165.6	195.7	133.2	130.5	181.4	182.8	147.5	126.3	146.3
2012												
January	224.3	173.4	210.1	161.8	191.6	133.1	130.3	179.9	182.0	146.6	125.5	142.4
February	228.2	174.5	210.1	161.6	196.0	133.1	130.3	179.9	182.1	146.6	126.1	143.9
March	232.3	174.7	210.1	161.4	196.0	133.2	130.3	180.0	182.3	146.7	126.0	149.0
April	233.3	176.1	208.0	161.4	196.0	133.2	130.4	180.5	182.7	147.1	126.6	147.6
May	230.4	179.8	208.0	161.4	196.0	133.1	130.3	180.6	182.8	147.4	126.1	146.0
June	233.7	179.5	208.0	161.4	196.0	133.1	130.2	180.8	182.9	147.2	126.2	147.2
July	230.0	178.2	222.9	169.5	196.0	133.3	130.3	181.7	182.9	147.9	126.6	148.0
August	230.5	176.6	224.2	169.6	196.0	133.2	130.4	181.9	183.0	147.6	126.4	148.7
September	219.2	177.0	224.2	169.6	196.0	133.4	130.7	181.9	183.0	148.1	126.2	148.4
October	224.2	179.2	224.8	169.6	196.0	133.5	131.0	182.9	183.0	148.3	126.5	148.2
November	222.7	180.3	224.8	169.6	196.0	133.1	131.0	182.9	183.2	148.4	126.8	144.2
December	221.8	180.2	224.8	169.7	196.0	133.0	131.0	183.9	183.2	148.7	126.7	142.1

. . . = Not available.

NOTES AND DEFINITIONS, CHAPTER 8

Tables 8-1 through 8-4: Consumer Price Indexes

SOURCES: U.S. DEPARTMENT OF LABOR, BUREAU OF LABOR STATISTICS (BLS) AND U.S. DEPARTMENT OF COMMERCE, BUREAU OF ECONOMIC ANALYSIS (BEA)

The Consumer Price Index (CPI), which is compiled by the Bureau of Labor Statistics (BLS), was originally conceived as a statistical measure of the average change in the cost to consumers of a market basket of goods and services purchased by urban wage earners and clerical workers. In 1978, its scope was broadened to also provide a measure of the change in the cost of the average market basket for all urban consumers. There was still a demand for a wage-earner index, so both versions have been calculated and published since then. The most commonly cited measure in this system is the Consumer Price Index for All Urban Consumers (CPI-U). The wage-earner alternative, used according to law for calculating cost of living adjustments in many government programs, including Social Security, and also used by choice of the contracting parties in wage agreements, is called the Consumer Price Index for Urban Wage Earners and Clerical Workers (CPI-W). Both are presented by the BLS back to 1913, and reproduced in *Business Statistics*; however, the movements (percent changes) in the two indexes before 1978 are identical and are based on the wage-earner market basket. (The pre-1978 levels of the two indexes differ because of differences between 1978 and the reference base period.)

These CPIs have typically been called "cost-of-living" indexes, even though the original fixed market basket concept does not correspond to economists' definition of a cost-of-living index, which is the cost of maintaining a constant standard of living or level of satisfaction. In recent years, the concept measured in practice in the CPI has developed into something intended to be closer to the theoretical definition of a cost-of-living index. In addition, a new variation of the CPI—the Chained Consumer Price Index for All Urban Consumers (C-CPI-U)—is intended to provide an even closer approximation.

The reference base for the total BLS Consumer Price Index and most of its components is currently 1982–1984 = 100. However, new products that have been introduced into the index since January 1982 are shown on later reference bases, as is the entire C-CPI-U.

Price indexes for personal consumption expenditures (PCE) are calculated and published by the Bureau of Economic Analysis (BEA) as a part of the national income and product accounts (NIPAs). (See Chapters 1 and 4 and their notes and definitions.) The reference base for these indexes is the average in the NIPA base year, 2009. These indexes differ in a number of other respects from the CPIs, and are often emphasized by the Federal Reserve in its analyses of the nation's economy. Because NIPA data for personal income, spending, and prices are also available monthly, four important NIPA aggregate price indexes can be shown in Tables 8-3 and 8-4 for convenient comparison with the CPIs. See the definitions for those tables for more information.

The CPI-U and the CPI-W

The *CPI-U*, which is displayed in Tables 8-1 through 8-4 and also provides all of the component category sub-indexes shown in Table 8-2, uses the consumption patterns for all urban consumers, who comprise about 88 percent of the population.

A slightly different index that is widely used for adjusting wages and government benefits is the *CPI-W*, of which the all-items total is shown in each of Tables 8-1 through 8-4. It represents the buying habits of only urban wage earners and clerical workers, who comprise about 29 percent of the population. The weights are derived from the same Consumer Expenditure Surveys (CES) used for the CPI-U weights, and are changed on the same schedule. However, they include only consumers from the specified categories instead of all urban consumers.

Beginning with January 2012, the weights in both indexes are based on consumer expenditures in the 2009–2010 period. From January 2010 to December 2011, 2007–2008 weights were used; from January 2008 to December 2009, 2005–2006 weights; from January 2006 to December 2007, 2003–2004 weights; from January 2004 to December 2005, 2001–2002 weights; from January 2002 to December 2003, 1999–2000 weights; and from January 1998 to December 2001, 1993–1995 weights. The weights will continue to be updated at two-year intervals, with new weights introduced in the January indexes of each even-numbered year. Previously, new weights were introduced only at the time of a major revision, which translated into a lag of a decade or more.

Specifically, the CPI weights for 1964 through 1977 were derived from reported expenditures of a sample of wage-earner and clerical-worker families and individuals in 1960–1961 and adjusted for price changes between the survey dates and 1963. Weights for the 1978–1986 period were derived from a survey undertaken during the 1972–1974 period and adjusted for price change between the survey dates and December 1977. For 1987 through 1997, the spending patterns reflected in the CPI were derived from a survey undertaken during the 1982–1984 period. The reported expenditures were adjusted for price change between the survey dates and December 1986.

The CPI was overhauled and updated in the latest major revision, which took effect in January 1998. In addition, new products and improved methods are regularly introduced into the index, usually in January.

The latest change in methods was the introduction of a geometric mean formula for calculating many of the basic components of the index. Beginning with the index for January 1999, this formula is used for categories comprising approximately 61 percent of total consumer spending. The new formula allows for the possibility that some consumers may react to changing relative prices within a category by substituting items whose relative prices have declined for products whose relative prices have risen, while maintaining their overall level of satisfaction. The geometric mean formula is not used for a few categories in which consumer substitution in the short term is not feasible, currently housing rent and utilities.

The CPI-U was introduced in 1978. Before that time, only CPI-W data were available. The movements of the CPI-U before 1978 are therefore based on the changes in the CPI-W. However, the index levels are different because the two indexes differed in the 1982–1984 base period.

Because the official CPI-U and CPI-W are so widely used in "escalation"—the calculation of cost-of-living adjustments for wages and other private contracts, and for government payments and tax parameters—these price indexes are not retrospectively revised to incorporate new information and methods. (An exception is occasionally made for outright error, which happened in September 2000 and affected the data for January through August of that year.) Instead, the new information and methods of calculation are introduced in the current index and affect future index changes only. In Tables 8-3 and 8-4, PCE indexes, which are subject to routine revision, and special CPI indexes that have been retrospectively revised are presented. These indexes can be used by researchers to provide more consistent historical information.

Notes on the CPI data

The CPI is based on prices of food, clothing, shelter, fuel, utilities, transportation, medical care, and other goods and services that people buy for day-to-day living. The quantity and quality of these priced items are kept essentially constant between revisions to ensure that only price changes will be measured. All taxes directly associated with the purchase and use of these items, such as sales and property taxes, are

included in the index; the effects of income and payroll tax changes are not included.

Data are collected on about 83,400 individually defined goods and services from about 25,600 retail and service establishments and about 4,000 housing units in 87 urban areas across the country. These data are used to develop the U.S. city average.

Periodic major revisions of the indexes update the content and weights of the market basket of goods and services; update the statistical sample of urban areas, outlets, and unique items used in calculating the CPI; and improve the statistical methods used. In addition, retail outlets and items are resampled on a rotating 5-year basis. Adjustments for changing quality are made at times of major product changes, such as the annual auto model changeover. Other methodological changes are introduced from time to time.

The CES provides the weights—that is, the relative importance—used to combine the individual price changes into subtotals and totals. This survey is composed of two separate surveys: an interview survey and a diary survey, both of which are conducted by the Census Bureau for BLS. Each expenditure reported in the two surveys is classified into a series of detailed categories, which are then combined into expenditure classes and ultimately into major expenditure groups. CPI data as of 1998 are grouped into eight such categories: (1) food and beverages, (2) housing, (3) apparel, (4) transportation, (5) medical care, (6) recreation, (7) education and communication, and (8) other goods and services.

Seasonally adjusted national CPI indexes are published for selected series for which there is a significant seasonal pattern of price change. The factors currently in use were derived by the X-12-ARIMA seasonal adjustment method. Some series with extreme or sharp movements are seasonally adjusted using X-12-ARIMA Intervention Analysis Seasonal Adjustment. Seasonally adjusted indexes and seasonal factors for the preceding five years are updated annually based on data through the previous December. Due to these revisions, BLS advises against the use of seasonally adjusted data for escalation. Detailed descriptions of seasonal adjustment procedures are available upon request from BLS.

BLS estimates the "standard error"—the error due to collecting data from a sample instead of the universe—of the one-month percent change in the not-seasonally-adjusted U.S. all-items index at 0.04 percentage point. This means that, for example, according to the BLS monthly release, "for a 1-month change of 0.2 percent in the All Items CPI-U, we are 95 percent confident that the actual percent change based on all retail prices would fall between 0.12 and 0.28 percent."

Monthly percent changes in the seasonally adjusted indexes, in contrast, may be revised by 0.1 percentage point when reviewed at the end of the year, and occasionally by even more.

CPI definitions

Definitions of the major CPI groupings were modified beginning with the data for January 1998. These modifications were carried back to 1993. The following definitions are the current definitions currently used for the CPI components.

The *food and beverage index* includes both food at home and food away from home (restaurant meals and other food bought and eaten away from home).

The *housing index* measures changes in rental costs and expenses connected with the acquisition and operation of a home. The CPI-U, beginning with data for January 1983, and the CPI-W, beginning with data for January 1985, reflect a change in the methodology used to compute the homeownership component. A rental equivalence measure replaced an asset-price approach, which included purchase prices and interest costs. The intent of the change was to separate shelter costs from the investment component of homeownership, so that the index would only reflect the cost of the shelter services provided by owner-occupied homes. In addition to measures of the cost of shelter, the housing category includes insurance, fuel, utilities, and household furnishings and operations.

The *apparel index* includes the purchase of apparel and footwear.

The *private transportation index* includes prices paid by urban consumers for such items as new and used automobiles and other vehicles, gasoline, motor oil, tires, repairs and maintenance, insurance, registration fees, driver's licenses, parking fees, and the like. Auto finance charges, like mortgage interest payments, are considered to be a cost of asset acquisition, not of current consumption. Therefore, they are no longer included in the CPI. City bus, streetcar, subway, taxicab, intercity bus, airplane, and railroad coach fares are some of the components of the *public transportation index*.

The *medical care index* includes prices for professional medical services, hospital and related services, prescription and nonprescription drugs, and other medical care commodities. The weight for the portion of health insurance premiums that is used to cover the costs of these medical goods and services is distributed among the items; the weight for the portion of health insurance costs attributable to administrative expenses and profits of insurance providers constitutes a separate health insurance item. Effective with the

January 1997 data, the method of calculating the hospital cost component was changed from the pricing of individual commodities and services to a more comprehensive cost-of-treatment approach.

Recreation includes components formerly listed in housing, apparel, entertainment, and "other goods and services."

Education and communication is a new group including components formerly categorized in housing and "other goods and services," such as telephone services and computers.

Other goods and services now includes tobacco, personal care, and miscellaneous.

Table 8-2: Purchasing Power of the Dollar

SOURCE: U.S. DEPARTMENT OF LABOR, BUREAU OF LABOR STATISTICS (BLS)

The purchasing power of the dollar measures changes in the quantity of goods and services a dollar will buy at a particular date compared with a selected base date. It must be defined in terms of the following: (1) the specific commodities and services that are to be purchased with the dollar; (2) the market level (producer, retail, etc.) at which they are purchased; and (3) the dates for which the comparison is to be made. Thus, the purchasing power of the dollar for a selected period, compared with another period, may be measured in terms of a single commodity or a large group of commodities such as all goods and services purchased by consumers at retail.

The purchasing power of the dollar is computed by dividing the price index number for the base period by the price index number for the comparison date and expressing the result in dollars and cents. The base period is the period in which the price index equals 100; the average purchasing power in that base period—1982–1984 in the case of the measure shown here—is therefore $1.00.

Purchasing power estimates in terms of both the CPI-U and the CPI-W are calculated by BLS, based on indexes not adjusted for seasonal variation, and published in the CPI press release. The CPI-U version is shown here.

Alternative price measures in Tables 8-3 and 8-4

Table 8-3 shows the all-items CPI-U and CPI-W, along with a number of other indexes that various analysts of price trends have preferred as measures of the price level. Table 8-4 shows the inflation rates (percent changes in price levels) implied by each of the indexes in Table 8-3.

As food and energy prices are volatile and frequently determined by forces separate from monetary aggregate demand pressures, many analysts prefer an index of prices excluding those components. Indexes *excluding food and energy* are known as *core* indexes, and inflation rates calculated from them are known as *core inflation rates.*

The *CPI-U-X1* is a special experimental version of the CPI that researchers have used to provide a more historically consistent series. As explained above, the official CPI-U treated homeownership on an asset-price basis until January 1983. It then changed to a rental equivalence method. The CPI-U-X1 incorporates a rental equivalence approach to homeowners' costs for the years 1967–1982 as well. It is rebased to the December 1982 value of the CPI-U (1982–1984 = 100); thus, it is identical to the CPI-U in December 1982 and all subsequent periods, as can be seen in Table 8-3. For this reason, it is not updated or published in the CPI news release or on the BLS Web site. We continue to present it here because it provides the only available data before 1978 on changes in an improved and more consistent CPI.

The *CPI-E* is an experimental re-weighting of components of the CPI-U to represent price change for the goods and services purchased by Americans age 62 years and over, who accounted for 16.5 percent of the total number of urban consumer units in the 2001–2002 CES.

BLS does not consider the CPI-E to be an ideal measure of price change for older Americans. Because the sample is small, the sampling error in the weights is greater than the error in the all-urban index. The products and outlets sampled are those characteristic of the general urban population rather than older residents. In addition, senior discounts are not included in the prices collected. Such discounts are included—appropriately—in the weights, which are based on the expenditures reported by the older consumers' households. Therefore, such discounts are only a problem if they do not move proportionately to general prices.

The *CPI-U-RS* is a "research series" CPI that retroactively incorporates estimates of the effects of most of the methodological changes implemented since 1978, including the rental equivalence method, new or improved quality adjustments, and improvement of formulas to eliminate bias and allow for some consumer substitution within categories. This index is calculated from 1977 onward. Its reference base is December 1977 = 100. Thus, although it generally shows less increase than the official index, its current levels are considerably higher because the earlier reference base period had lower prices. Unlike the official CPIs and the CPI-U-X1, its historical values will be revised each time a significant change is made in the calculation of the current index. This

index is not seasonally adjusted and is not included in the CPI news release. It is available on the BLS Web site, along with an explanation and background material. The CPI-U-RS is used by BLS in the calculation of historical trends in real compensation per hour in its Productivity and Costs system; see Table 9-3 and its notes and definitions. It is also now used by the Census Bureau to convert household incomes into constant dollars, as seen in Chapter 3. And it is used by the editor in some analytical calculations in this volume.

The *C-CPI-U* (Chained Consumer Price Index for All Urban Consumers) is a new, supplemental index that has been published in the monthly CPI news release since August 2002. It is available only from December 1999 to date and is calculated with the base December 1999 = 100; it is not seasonally adjusted. It is designed to be a still-closer approximation to a true cost-of-living index than the CPI-U and the CPI-W, in that it assumes that consumers substitute between as well as within categories as relative prices change, in order to maintain a fixed basket of "consumer satisfaction."

The C-CPI-U is technically a "superlative" index, using a method known as the "Tornqvist formula" to incorporate the composition of consumer spending in the current period as well as in the earlier base period. (All of the other Consumer Price Indexes use a "Laspeyres" formula; see the General Notes at the beginning of this volume.) As it requires consumer expenditure data for the current as well as the earlier period, its final version can only be calculated after the expenditure data become available—about two years later—and is approximated in more recent periods by making more extensive use of the geometric mean formula (see above). With the release of January 2012 data, the indexes for 2010 were revised to their final form, and the initial indexes for 2011 were revised to "interim" levels, shown in Tables 8-3 and 8-4.

Personal consumption expenditure (PCE) chain-type price indexes are calculated by the Bureau of Economic Analysis (BEA) in the framework of the national income and product accounts (NIPAs). (See the notes and definitions for Chapters 1 and 4.) The scope of NIPA PCE is broader than the scope of the CPI. PCE includes the rural as well as the urban population and also covers the consumption spending of nonprofit entities. The CPI includes only consumer out-of-pocket cash spending, whereas PCE includes some imputed services and includes expenditures financed by government and private insurance, particularly in the medical care area. For this reason, there is a large difference between the relatively small weight of medical care spending in the CPI and the markedly greater percentage of PCE that is accounted for by total medical care spending. Housing, on the other hand, has a somewhat smaller weight in PCE while all nonhousing components have a higher weight. The reason for this is that the CES—the survey on which the CPI weights are based—tends to report housing expenditures accurately and somewhat underestimate other spending. This suggests that the weight of housing relative to all other products may be overestimated in the CPI but measured more correctly in the PCE price index.

PCE chain-type indexes use the expenditure weights of both the earlier and the later period to determine the aggregate price change between the two periods. (See the notes and definitions for Chapter 1, as well as the General Notes on index number formulas.) Thus, they are subject to revision as improved data on the composition of consumption spending become available, and in this respect resemble the C-CPI-U.

For a large share of PCE, the price movements for basic individual spending categories are determined by CPI components. Hence, the differences between the rates of change in the aggregate CPI and PCE indexes are largely the result of the different weights, but also reflect some alternative methodologies and the previously mentioned differences in scope.

Market-based PCE indexes are based on household expenditures for which there are observable price measures. They exclude most implicit prices (for example, the services furnished without payment by financial intermediaries) and they exclude items not deflated by a detailed component of either the Consumer Price Index (CPI) or the Producer Price Index (PPI). This means that the price observations that make up these new aggregate measures are all based on observed market transactions, making them "market-based price indexes." The imputed rent for owner-occupied housing is included in the market-based price index, since it is based on observed rentals of comparable homes. Household insurance premiums are also included in the market-based index, since they are deflated by the CPI for tenants' and household insurance. Excluded are services furnished without payment by financial intermediaries, most insurance purchases, expenses of NPISHs (nonprofit institutions serving households), legal gambling (illegal gambling is excluded from all measures), margins on used light motor vehicles, and expenditures by U.S. residents working and traveling abroad. Also excluded are medical, hospitalization, and income loss insurance; expense of handling life insurance; motor vehicle insurance; and workers' compensation.

The *inflation rates* shown in Table 8-4 are percent changes in the price indexes introduced in Table 8-3. For annual indexes, the rate is the percent change from the previous year. For monthly indexes, the rate is the percent change from the same month a year earlier. To give an indication of the longer-run

implications of these different price indicators, comparisons of compound annual inflation rates, calculated by the editor, are also shown for the 1978–2011, 1983–2011, and 2000–2011 periods, using the growth rate formula presented in the article at the beginning of this volume.

Data availability and references

The CPI-U, CPI-W, and C-CPI-U are initially issued in a press release two to three weeks after the end of the month for which the data were collected. This release and detailed and complete current and historical data on the CPI and its variants and components, along with extensive documentation, are available on the BLS Web site at http://www.bls.gov/cpi. Seasonal factors and seasonally adjusted indexes are revised once a year with the issuance of the January index.

Information available on the BLS Web site includes "Common Misconceptions about the Consumer Price Index: Questions and Answers;" another fact sheet on frequently asked questions; a fact sheet on seasonal adjustment; Chapter 17 of the *BLS Handbook of Methods*, entitled "The Consumer Price Index"; a section entitled "Note on Chained Consumer Price Index for All Urban Consumers"; and a number of explanatory CPI fact sheets on specific subjects.

As previously indicated, the CPI-U-X1 is not currently published because its recent values are identical to the CPI-U. The CPI-E is presented in articles in the CPI section of the BLS Web site, the most recent of which is "Experimental Consumer Price Index for Americans 62 Years of Age and Older, 1998–2005"; recent values are available by request from BLS. The CPI-U-RS is updated each month in a report entitled "CPI Research Series Using Current Methods" on the site. In both cases, the reports describe the indexes and provide references.

The monthly PCE indexes are included in the personal income report issued by BEA, which is published near the end of the following month. These indexes are revised month-by-month to reflect new information and annually to reflect the annual and quinquennial benchmarking of the NIPAs. The complete historical record can be found on the BEA Web site at http://www.bea.gov in the Personal Income and Outlays section of the NIPA tables, in tables entitled "Price Indexes for Personal Consumption Expenditures by Major Type of Product."

Two special editions of the *Monthly Labor Review* were devoted to CPI issues. The December 1996 issue describes the subsequently implemented 1997 and 1998 revisions in a series of articles, and the December 1993 issue, entitled *The*

Anatomy of Price Change, includes the following articles: "The Consumer Price Index: Underlying Concepts and Caveats"; "Basic Components of the CPI: Estimation of Price Changes"; "The Commodity Substitution Effect in CPI Data, 1982–1991"; and "Quality Adjustment of Price Indexes."

The new formula for calculating basic components is described in "Incorporating a Geometric Mean Formula into the CPI," *Monthly Labor Review* (October 1998). For a detailed discussion of the treatment of homeownership, see "Changing the Homeownership Component of the Consumer Price Index to Rental Equivalence," *CPI Detailed Report* (January 1983).

For a comprehensive professional review of CPI concepts and methodology, see Charles Schultze and Christopher Mackie, ed., *At What Price? Conceptualizing and Measuring Cost-of-Living and Price Indexes* (Washington, DC: National Academy Press, 2001). Earlier references include: "Using Survey Data to Assess Bias in the Consumer Price Index," *Monthly Labor Review* (April 1998); Joel Popkin, "Improving the CPI: The Record and Suggested Next Steps," *Business Economics*, Vol. XXXII, No. 3 (July 1997), pages 42–47; *Measurement Issues in the Consumer Price Index* (Bureau of Labor Statistics, U.S. Department of Labor, June 1997); *Toward a More Accurate Measure of the Cost of Living* (Final Report to the Senate Finance Committee from the Advisory Commission to Study the Consumer Price Index, December 4, 1996)—also known as the "Boskin Commission" report; and *Government Price Statistics* (U.S. Congress Joint Economic Committee, 87th Congress, 1st Session, January 24, 1961)—also known as the "Stigler Committee" report.

For an explanation of the differences between the CPI-U and the PCE index, see Clinton P. McCully, Brian C. Moyer, and Kenneth J. Stewart, "Comparing the Consumer Price Index and the Personal Consumption Expenditures Price Index," *Survey of Current Business*, November 2007, pp. 26–33.

Tables 8-1 and 8-5 through 8-7: Producer Price Indexes

SOURCE: U.S. DEPARTMENT OF LABOR, BUREAU OF LABOR STATISTICS (BLS)

Producer Price Indexes (PPI) measure average changes in prices received by domestic producers. The prices of individual commodities are organized into three different, separate systems: stage of processing, commodity group, and industry. Most of the indexes currently are published on a base of 1982 = 100. However, there are a number of exceptions for products and industries introduced into the index system since 1982. In this book, alternative base periods are identified in the column headings for the individual series.

Tables 8-1A, 8-1B, and 8-5 present price indexes for commodities by stage of processing. Table 8-6 and 8-1C presents data by major commodity groups; these are the groupings that have the longest continuous history. In recent years, the major commodity groups—particularly the totals for all commodities and industrial commodities—have been de-emphasized, as they aggregate successive stages of processing and thus often exaggerate price trends. This effect was particularly acute in the energy price crisis of the early 1970s. To avoid this problem, the stage-of-processing groups were introduced in 1978, and the finished goods components, in total and minus food and energy, have been the headline Producer Price Indexes. However, the individual commodity groups (for example, textile products and apparel) provide a much longer historical perspective on individual industrial sectors than the current industry groupings; annual indexes for these groups are presented in Table 8-6 for that reason.

Table 8-7 presents PPIs for the net output of selected industry groups. As the coverage of the PPI is expanded, indexes for additional industries are frequently introduced, and new industries may only go back to December of the most recent year. This volume includes only those industry groupings with 16 years or more of historical data.

Definitions

The *stage-of-processing* PPI indexes (Tables 8-1 and 8-5) organize commodities by class of buyer and degree of fabrication. These have been the featured measures since 1978. The three major indexes are: (1) *finished goods*, or commodities that will not undergo further processing and are ready for sale to the ultimate user (such as automobiles, meats, apparel, and machine tools, and also unprocessed foods such as eggs and fresh vegetables, that are ready for the consumer); (2) *intermediate materials, supplies, and components*, or commodities that have been processed but require further processing before they become finished goods (such as steel mill products, cotton yarns, lumber, and flour), as well as physically complete goods that are purchased by business firms as inputs for their operations (such as diesel fuel and paper boxes); and (3) *crude materials* for further processing, or products entering the market for the first time that have not been manufactured or fabricated and are not sold directly to consumers (such as ores, scrap metals, crude petroleum, raw cotton, and livestock).

PPIs for the *net output* of industries and their products (Table 8-7) are grouped according to the North American Industry Classification System (NAICS). For each industry, they include both measures of price change for the products "primary" to that industry (products made primarily but not necessarily exclusively by that industry), and measures of changes in prices received by establishments classified in the industry for products or services chiefly made in some other industry. Thus, they are designed to be compatible with other economic time series organized by industry, such as data on shipments, employment, wages, and productivity.

Notes on the data

The probability sample used for calculating the PPI provides more than 100,000 price quotations per month, selected to represent the movement of prices of all commodities produced in the manufacturing; agriculture, forestry, and fishing; mining; and gas, electricity, and public utility sectors.

In addition, new PPIs are gradually being introduced for the products and services produced by industries in the construction, transportation, trade, finance, and services sectors. These are only used for industry indexes and are not incorporated in the commodity indexes or the published commodity by stage of processing indexes. In February 2011, BLS announced the development of an experimental aggregation system that will incorporate new services and construction data in an experimental aggregation system for the different portions of final and intermediate demand. For further information, see http://www.bls.gov/ppi/experimentalaggregation.htm.

To the greatest extent possible, prices used in calculating the PPI represent prices received by domestic producers in the first important commercial transaction for each commodity. These indexes attempt to measure only price changes (changes in receipts per unit of measurement not influenced by changes in quality, quantity sold, terms of sale, or level of distribution). Most quotations are the selling prices of selected manufacturers or other producers, although a few prices are those quoted on organized exchanges or markets. Transaction prices are sought instead of list or book prices.

Price data are generally collected monthly, primarily by mail questionnaire. Most prices are obtained directly from producing companies on a voluntary and confidential basis. Prices are generally reported for the Tuesday of the week containing the 13th day of the month.

The name "Producer Price Index" became effective with the release of March 1978 data and replaced the term "Wholesale Price Index." The change was made to more accurately reflect the coverage of the data. At the same time, there was a shift in analytical emphasis from the All Commodities Index and other traditional commodity grouping indexes (as shown in Table 8-6) to the Finished Goods Index and other stage-of-processing indexes.

The BLS revises the PPI weighting structure when data from economic censuses become available. Beginning with data for January 2012, the weights used to construct the PPI reflect 2007 shipments values as measured by the 2007 Economic Censuses. Data for January 2007 through December 2011 used 2002 values; 2002 through 2006, 1997 shipments values; 1996 through 2001, 1992 values; 1992 through 1995, 1987 values; 1987 through 1991, 1982 values; 1976 through 1986, 1972 values; and 1967 through 1975, 1963 values.

BLS has been working for a number of years on a comprehensive overhaul of the theory, methodology, and procedures used to construct the PPI. One aspect of this overhaul was the previously mentioned shift in emphasis to the stage-of-processing measures, which began in 1978. Other changes phased in since 1978 include the replacement of judgment sampling with probability sampling techniques; expansion to systematic coverage of the net output of virtually all industries in the mining and manufacturing sectors; introduction of measures for selected services industries, including retail trade; a shift from a commodity to an industry orientation; and the exclusion of imports from, and the inclusion of exports in, the survey universe.

The commodity components of the stage-of-processing indexes, in addition to being available in unadjusted form, are also adjusted for seasonal variation using the X-12-ARIMA method. Since January 1988, BLS has also used X-12-ARIMA Intervention Analysis Seasonal Adjustment for a small number of series to remove unusual values that might distort seasonal patterns before calculating the seasonal adjustment factors. Seasonal factors for the PPI are revised annually to take into account the most recent 12 months of data. Seasonally adjusted data for the previous 5 years are subject to these annual revisions. The industry net output indexes are not seasonally adjusted.

Data availability and references

The indexes are initially issued in a press release two to three weeks after the end of the month for which the data were collected. Data are subsequently published in greater detail in a monthly BLS publication, *PPI Detailed Report*. Each month, data for the fourth previous month (both unadjusted and seasonally adjusted) are revised to reflect late reports and corrections.

The press release, the *PPI Detailed Report*, detailed and complete current and historical data, and extensive documentation are available at http://www.bls.gov/ppi. The items available on this Web site include Chapter 14 of the *BLS Handbook of Methods*, "Producer Price Indexes"; a selection of *Monthly Labor Review* articles on the PPI; and fact sheets on a number of issues and index components.

CHAPTER 9: EMPLOYMENT COSTS, PRODUCTIVITY, AND PROFITS

Section 9a: Employment Cost Indexes

Figure 9-1. Changes in Wages and Salaries and in Benefit Costs, Private Nonfarm Industry, 1980–2012 (December values, not seasonally adjusted; percent change from year earlier)

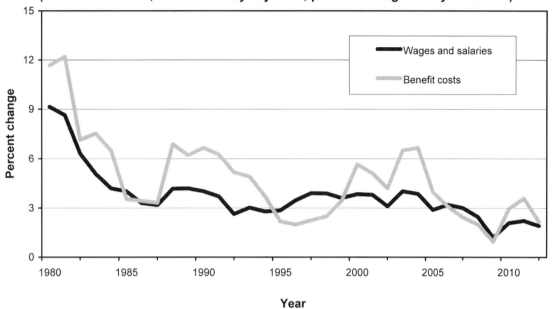

- The Employment Cost Index measures average increases in the dollar value of hourly compensation for nonfarm wage and salary workers, holding the composition of employment constant so as to reflect only the aggregate of changes affecting individual defined jobs. (The analogy is to the Consumer Price Index which holds the market basket constant in any individual time period so as to reflect only an aggregate of price changes affecting individual defined products.) This makes the ECI the most accurate indicator of changes in price for a typical unit of labor.

- Between the last two business cycle peaks, 2000 to 2007, average compensation for private industry workers rose at a 3.5 percent annual rate. Compensation includes wages, salaries, and benefits, but not stock options. The chain price index for personal consumption expenditures (PCE) rose at a 2.2 percent rate, implying an average real compensation increase of 1.3 percent per year. (Tables 9-1, 9-2, and 8-3)

- From 2007 to 2012, compensation rose at a 1.9 percent rate while PCE prices rose at a 1.8 percent pace, implying that real compensation per hour rose just 0.1 percent per year. (Tables 9-1, 9-2, and 8-3)

- It is often claimed that worker productivity pays off in real worker compensation, but as will be seen in a following table, nonfarm business productivity rose markedly more than real compensation in both periods—at a 2.7 percent rate from 2000 to 2007 and 1.9 percent from 2007 to 2012. (Table 9-3A)

- The ECI reports separately the rates of increase for wages and salaries and for benefits such as health insurance, as shown in Figure 9-1. (Tables 9-1 and 9-2)

Table 9-1. Employment Cost Indexes, NAICS Basis

(December 2005 [not seasonally adjusted] = 100; annual values are for December, not seasonally adjusted; quarterly values, seasonally adjusted, except as noted.)

Year and month	All civilian workers [1]	State and local government workers	All private industry workers	Excluding incentive paid occupations [2]	Management, professional, and related	Sales and office	Natural resources, construction, and maintenance	Production, transportation, and material moving	Service occupations	Total	Manufacturing	Service-providing	Union [2]	Non-union [2]
TOTAL COMPENSATION														
2001	87.1	86.2	87.3	...	87.4	86.9	86.6	87.4	89.4	86.0	85.5	87.8	84.8	87.8
2002	90.0	89.7	90.0	...	89.7	89.8	89.7	90.3	92.0	89.0	88.7	90.4	88.2	90.3
2003	93.5	92.8	93.6	...	93.8	93.1	93.3	93.6	95.0	92.6	92.4	94.0	92.3	93.9
2004	97.0	96.1	97.2	...	97.1	96.8	97.1	97.8	97.7	96.9	96.9	97.3	97.3	97.2
2005	100.0	100.0	100.0	100.0	100.0	100.0	100.0	100.0	100.0	100.0	100.0	100.0	100.0	100.0
2006	103.3	104.1	103.2	103.2	103.5	102.9	103.6	102.3	103.1	102.5	101.8	103.4	103.0	103.2
2007	106.7	108.4	106.3	106.4	106.8	106.1	106.7	104.5	107.0	105.0	103.8	106.7	105.1	106.5
2008	109.5	111.6	108.9	109.5	109.9	107.9	109.6	106.9	109.8	107.5	105.9	109.4	108.0	109.1
2009	111.0	114.2	110.2	110.8	110.7	109.2	111.2	108.9	111.8	108.6	107.0	110.8	111.1	110.1
2010	113.2	116.2	112.5	113.1	113.0	111.6	113.3	111.5	113.5	111.1	110.0	113.0	114.8	112.1
2011	115.5	117.7	115.0	115.5	115.4	114.2	115.8	114.2	115.4	113.8	113.1	115.3	117.9	114.5
2012	117.7	119.9	117.2	117.6	117.7	116.5	117.8	116.1	117.4	115.6	114.9	117.7	120.5	116.7
2001														
March	84.7	83.6	85.0	...	...	...	...	...	...	84.0	83.7	85.3	82.0	...
June	85.5	84.5	85.8	...	...	...	...	...	...	84.7	84.4	86.1	82.9	...
September	86.4	85.5	86.7	...	...	...	...	...	...	85.4	84.9	87.1	83.7	...
December	87.2	86.1	87.5	...	...	...	...	...	...	86.2	85.8	87.9	84.8	...
2002														
March	87.9	86.8	88.2	...	88.2	87.8	87.6	88.5	90.3	87.1	86.8	88.6	85.7	88.7
June	88.8	87.5	89.1	...	89.0	88.9	88.6	89.1	90.7	87.7	87.5	89.6	86.5	89.6
September	89.5	88.7	89.6	...	89.4	89.3	89.3	89.8	91.6	88.2	88.0	90.1	87.5	90.0
December	90.1	89.6	90.2	...	90.0	90.1	90.2	90.5	92.1	89.2	89.0	90.5	88.2	90.3
2003														
March	91.2	90.4	91.4	...	91.5	90.9	91.0	91.6	93.0	90.6	90.6	91.7	89.5	91.8
June	92.0	91.3	92.2	...	92.2	91.7	92.0	92.4	93.5	91.4	91.3	92.4	90.7	92.5
September	92.9	92.0	93.2	...	93.2	92.8	92.8	93.2	94.4	92.1	92.0	93.5	91.6	93.5
December	93.6	92.7	93.8	...	94.1	93.4	93.7	93.7	95.1	92.8	92.6	94.1	92.3	93.9
2004														
March	94.6	93.5	94.9	...	94.7	94.5	95.0	95.4	95.9	94.5	94.6	95.0	94.5	95.0
June	95.5	94.4	95.8	...	95.5	95.5	95.9	96.5	96.7	95.4	95.6	96.0	95.9	95.9
September	96.4	95.1	96.7	...	96.4	96.5	96.4	97.4	97.2	96.4	96.7	96.8	96.7	96.7
December	97.1	95.9	97.3	...	97.4	97.0	97.3	97.9	97.8	97.1	97.1	97.4	97.3	97.2
2005														
March	98.0	97.0	98.2	...	98.4	97.9	98.0	98.5	98.4	98.0	98.2	98.3	97.9	98.3
June	98.6	97.8	98.8	...	99.0	98.4	98.7	99.0	99.0	98.9	99.0	98.8	98.8	98.9
September	99.3	98.7	99.5	...	99.6	99.2	99.4	99.6	99.6	99.7	99.7	99.4	99.6	99.5
December	100.1	99.8	100.2	...	100.3	100.1	100.2	100.1	100.1	100.2	100.2	100.2	100.0	100.0
2006														
March	100.7	100.5	100.8	100.9	101.0	100.6	100.9	100.4	100.8	100.3	99.9	100.9	100.5	100.9
June	101.6	101.5	101.6	101.7	101.8	101.5	102.0	101.0	101.5	101.2	100.9	101.8	101.8	101.7
September	102.6	102.8	102.5	102.5	102.9	102.2	102.9	101.7	102.2	101.9	101.4	102.7	102.4	102.6
December	103.4	103.9	103.3	103.2	103.8	103.0	103.7	102.4	103.2	102.7	102.0	103.5	103.0	103.2
2007														
March	104.2	105.1	103.9	104.0	104.5	103.8	104.1	102.5	104.4	102.9	101.9	104.3	102.7	104.2
June	105.1	106.2	104.8	105.0	105.5	104.5	104.9	103.3	105.2	103.8	102.8	105.2	103.9	105.1
September	105.9	107.2	105.6	105.8	106.3	105.2	105.8	103.9	106.3	104.4	103.2	106.0	104.4	105.9
December	106.8	108.3	106.5	106.4	107.1	106.2	106.8	104.7	107.2	105.2	104.0	106.9	105.1	106.5
2008														
March	107.6	109.0	107.2	107.6	108.0	106.8	107.7	105.5	107.8	106.0	104.6	107.6	105.9	107.5
June	108.3	109.8	108.0	108.3	108.8	107.4	108.2	106.0	108.7	106.7	105.0	108.4	106.7	108.3
September	109.1	110.9	108.6	109.0	109.6	107.8	109.0	106.5	109.4	107.2	105.6	109.1	107.4	108.9
December	109.6	111.5	109.1	109.5	110.2	108.0	109.7	107.0	109.9	107.7	106.1	109.5	108.0	109.1
2009														
March	109.9	112.4	109.3	110.0	110.2	108.1	109.9	107.7	110.6	107.9	106.3	109.8	109.1	109.4
June	110.3	113.2	109.5	110.2	110.4	108.1	110.2	108.0	110.9	108.1	106.6	110.0	109.8	109.6
September	110.7	113.5	110.0	110.6	110.6	108.8	110.8	108.6	111.6	108.4	106.8	110.5	110.5	109.9
December	111.1	114.1	110.4	110.8	111.0	109.3	111.3	109.0	112.0	108.8	107.4	110.9	111.1	110.1
2010														
March	111.8	114.5	111.1	111.8	111.6	110.0	112.3	109.9	112.2	109.7	108.3	111.5	112.8	110.9
June	112.3	115.1	111.6	112.3	112.1	110.6	112.5	110.4	112.7	110.1	108.9	112.1	113.7	111.4
September	112.8	115.5	112.1	112.8	112.7	111.0	113.0	111.2	113.2	110.9	109.9	112.5	114.6	111.8
December	113.4	116.1	112.7	113.1	113.3	111.7	113.4	111.7	113.7	111.3	110.5	113.1	114.8	112.1
2011														
March	114.0	116.7	113.3	114.0	113.9	112.3	113.9	112.2	114.4	112.0	111.2	113.8	115.6	113.0
June	114.7	117.0	114.2	114.9	114.7	113.2	114.8	113.4	114.7	113.0	112.5	114.5	117.1	113.8
September	115.1	117.3	114.6	115.1	115.1	113.7	115.4	113.7	114.9	113.3	112.8	115.0	117.4	114.2
December	115.7	117.6	115.2	115.5	115.8	114.2	115.9	114.5	115.6	114.1	113.6	115.5	117.9	114.5
2012														
March	116.2	118.4	115.7	116.2	116.2	115.1	116.5	114.5	115.9	114.0	113.3	116.3	118.3	115.3
June	116.8	119.0	116.3	116.8	117.0	115.7	116.8	114.9	116.4	114.5	113.8	116.9	119.3	116.0
September	117.3	119.4	116.8	117.2	117.4	116.4	117.6	115.6	116.8	115.3	114.6	117.3	120.2	116.4
December	117.9	119.9	117.4	117.6	118.1	116.5	118.0	116.3	117.6	115.9	115.3	117.9	120.5	116.7

[1] Excludes farm workers, private household workers, and federal government employees.
[2] Not seasonally adjusted.
. . . = Not available.

Table 9-1. Employment Cost Indexes, NAICS Basis—*Continued*

(December 2005 [not seasonally adjusted] = 100; annual values are for December, not seasonally adjusted; quarterly values, seasonally adjusted, except as noted.)

Year and month	All civilian workers [1]	State and local government workers	Private industry workers											Union [2]	Non-union [2]
			All private industry workers	Excluding incentive paid occupations [2]	By occupational group					By industry				
					Management, professional, and related	Sales and office	Natural resources, construction, and maintenance	Production, transportation, and material moving	Service occupations	Goods-producing industries		Service-providing		
										Total	Manufacturing			
WAGES AND SALARIES														
2001	89.9	90.2	89.9	. . .	89.5	89.1	90.0	91.0	91.7	90.0	90.2	89.8	89.6	89.9
2002	92.4	93.0	92.2	. . .	91.7	91.7	92.6	93.3	93.9	92.6	92.8	92.1	92.6	92.2
2003	95.1	95.0	95.1	. . .	95.3	94.3	95.2	95.4	96.1	94.9	95.1	95.2	94.9	95.1
2004	97.5	97.0	97.6	. . .	97.8	97.2	97.5	97.8	97.9	97.2	97.4	97.7	97.6	97.6
2005	100.0	100.0	100.0	100.0	100.0	100.0	100.0	100.0	100.0	100.0	100.0	100.0	100.0	100.0
2006	103.2	103.5	103.2	103.2	103.6	103.0	103.4	102.4	102.9	102.9	102.3	103.3	102.3	103.3
2007	106.7	107.1	106.6	106.7	107.2	106.2	107.1	105.0	107.1	106.0	104.9	106.8	104.7	106.9
2008	109.6	110.4	109.4	110.1	110.5	108.0	110.5	107.8	110.1	109.0	107.7	109.6	108.1	109.6
2009	111.2	112.5	110.8	111.6	111.5	109.4	112.0	109.6	112.3	110.0	108.9	111.1	110.9	110.9
2010	113.0	113.8	112.8	113.4	113.7	111.5	113.3	111.3	113.5	111.6	110.7	113.1	112.9	112.7
2011	114.6	114.9	114.6	115.2	115.5	113.6	115.4	112.8	115.1	113.5	112.7	114.9	114.9	114.6
2012	116.5	116.2	116.6	117.0	117.7	115.8	116.7	115.1	116.8	115.4	114.8	117.0	117.4	116.5
2001														
March	87.6	87.6	87.6	. . .	. . .	. . .	. . .	. . .	. . .	87.9	88.2	87.4	86.5	87.7
June	88.4	88.4	88.4	. . .	. . .	. . .	. . .	. . .	. . .	88.7	89.0	88.3	87.4	88.6
September	89.2	89.4	89.2	. . .	. . .	. . .	. . .	. . .	. . .	89.3	89.5	89.1	88.3	89.3
December	90.0	90.0	90.0	. . .	. . .	. . .	. . .	. . .	. . .	90.1	90.3	90.0	89.6	89.9
2002														
March	90.7	90.5	90.7	. . .	90.4	90.1	90.7	91.9	. . .	90.8	91.2	90.7	90.2	90.8
June	91.5	91.2	91.6	. . .	91.2	91.1	91.6	92.4	. . .	91.3	91.7	91.6	91.1	91.7
September	92.0	92.1	92.0	. . .	91.5	91.3	92.2	92.8	. . .	91.8	92.2	92.0	91.9	92.0
December	92.4	92.8	92.3	. . .	91.9	92.0	92.8	93.3	. . .	92.7	93.0	92.2	92.6	92.2
2003														
March	93.3	93.5	93.3	. . .	93.3	92.5	93.4	94.1	. . .	93.3	93.8	93.2	93.0	93.3
June	93.9	94.1	93.8	. . .	93.9	93.2	94.0	94.6	. . .	94.0	94.4	93.8	93.8	94.0
September	94.6	94.4	94.7	. . .	94.8	94.1	94.6	95.1	. . .	94.5	94.8	94.7	94.4	94.9
December	95.1	94.9	95.2	. . .	95.4	94.5	95.3	95.4	. . .	95.0	95.3	95.2	94.9	95.1
2004														
March	95.7	95.5	95.7	. . .	95.9	95.2	95.9	96.0	. . .	95.6	95.7	95.8	95.6	95.8
June	96.3	96.0	96.4	. . .	96.4	96.0	96.5	96.7	. . .	96.2	96.4	96.5	96.4	96.5
September	97.0	96.3	97.2	. . .	97.2	97.0	97.0	97.6	. . .	97.2	97.4	97.2	97.1	97.3
December	97.5	96.9	97.7	. . .	98.0	97.3	97.6	97.9	. . .	97.4	97.6	97.8	97.6	97.6
2005														
March	98.2	97.7	98.3	. . .	98.6	98.0	98.0	98.4	. . .	97.9	98.2	98.4	97.9	98.3
June	98.7	98.3	98.8	. . .	99.1	98.4	98.6	98.9	. . .	98.6	98.8	98.9	98.7	98.9
September	99.3	98.8	99.4	. . .	99.5	99.2	99.3	99.5	. . .	99.4	99.6	99.4	99.5	99.5
December	100.1	99.8	100.1	. . .	100.2	100.1	100.1	100.1	. . .	100.2	100.2	100.1	100.0	100.0
2006														
March	100.7	100.4	100.8	100.8	101.0	100.6	100.8	100.6	100.6	100.7	100.6	100.8	100.3	100.8
June	101.5	101.2	101.6	101.7	101.9	101.5	101.8	101.1	101.3	101.7	101.6	101.6	101.2	101.8
September	102.5	102.4	102.5	102.5	102.9	102.2	102.7	101.7	101.9	102.2	101.8	102.6	101.7	102.7
December	103.3	103.4	103.3	103.2	103.8	103.0	103.4	102.5	103.0	103.0	102.5	103.4	102.3	103.3
2007														
March	104.3	104.2	104.3	104.3	104.9	104.0	104.3	103.2	104.6	103.9	103.2	104.4	102.8	104.5
June	105.1	105.0	105.1	105.2	105.7	104.7	105.1	103.8	105.4	104.6	103.8	105.2	103.7	105.3
September	105.9	106.0	105.9	106.1	106.6	105.2	106.1	104.4	106.4	105.4	104.4	106.1	104.4	106.2
December	106.8	107.0	106.7	106.7	107.4	106.2	107.1	105.0	107.2	106.1	105.1	106.9	104.7	106.9
2008														
March	107.6	107.8	107.6	107.9	108.4	106.9	108.2	106.0	107.9	107.1	105.9	107.7	105.5	107.9
June	108.4	108.6	108.4	108.7	109.2	107.6	108.9	106.8	108.9	107.9	106.6	108.6	106.7	108.7
September	109.2	109.8	109.1	109.5	110.1	107.9	109.7	107.4	109.6	108.5	107.3	109.2	107.4	109.4
December	109.7	110.3	109.5	110.1	110.7	108.0	110.5	107.9	110.2	109.1	107.9	109.7	108.1	109.6
2009														
March	110.0	111.0	109.8	110.6	110.9	108.2	110.7	108.3	110.9	109.2	108.0	110.0	108.8	110.0
June	110.4	111.7	110.1	110.8	111.1	108.2	111.0	108.8	111.3	109.4	108.3	110.3	109.6	110.2
September	110.8	111.9	110.5	111.3	111.3	108.9	111.5	109.3	112.0	109.7	108.6	110.7	110.2	110.6
December	111.2	112.4	110.9	111.6	111.7	109.4	112.0	109.7	112.4	110.2	109.1	111.2	110.9	110.9
2010														
March	111.7	112.8	111.4	112.2	112.3	109.9	112.6	109.9	112.5	110.5	109.3	111.7	111.5	111.4
June	112.2	113.2	111.9	112.6	112.9	110.5	112.8	110.3	112.8	110.8	109.9	112.2	112.1	111.9
September	112.5	113.3	112.3	113.1	113.4	110.8	113.0	111.0	113.2	111.4	110.5	112.6	112.7	112.4
December	113.0	113.7	112.8	113.4	113.9	111.5	113.3	111.3	113.6	111.7	110.9	113.2	112.9	112.7
2011														
March	113.4	114.1	113.2	114.0	114.3	111.9	113.8	111.6	114.1	112.1	111.4	113.5	113.6	113.2
June	113.9	114.4	113.8	114.4	114.8	112.5	114.4	112.0	114.3	112.7	112.0	114.1	114.0	113.8
September	114.3	114.5	114.2	114.8	115.2	113.1	115.1	112.4	114.5	113.1	112.4	114.6	114.6	114.3
December	114.7	114.8	114.7	115.2	115.7	113.6	115.4	112.9	115.2	113.6	113.0	115.0	114.9	114.6
2012														
March	115.3	115.3	115.3	115.7	116.1	114.6	115.8	113.8	115.3	114.0	113.5	115.7	115.6	115.2
June	115.8	115.6	115.8	116.2	116.9	115.1	115.9	114.1	115.9	114.5	114.0	116.3	116.2	115.9
September	116.2	115.8	116.3	116.6	117.2	115.7	116.5	114.5	116.1	115.1	114.5	116.6	116.9	116.3
December	116.6	116.1	116.7	117.0	117.9	115.7	116.7	115.1	116.9	115.5	115.1	117.1	117.4	116.5

[1]Excludes farm workers, private household workers, and federal government employees.
[2]Not seasonally adjusted.
. . . = Not available.

Table 9-1. Employment Cost Indexes, NAICS Basis—*Continued*

(December 2005 [not seasonally adjusted] = 100; annual values are for December, not seasonally adjusted; quarterly values, seasonally adjusted, except as noted.)

Year and month	All civilian workers [1]	State and local government workers	All private industry workers	Excluding incentive paid occupations [2]	By occupational group Management, professional, and related	Sales and office	Natural resources, construction, and maintenance	Production, transportation, and material moving	Service occupations	By industry Goods-producing industries Total	Manufacturing	Service-providing	Union [2]	Non-union [2]
TOTAL BENEFITS														
2001	80.6	78.1	81.3	...	82.0	81.1	79.8	80.7	82.5	78.5	77.2	82.4	77.3	82.2
2002	84.3	83.0	84.7	...	84.7	84.7	84.1	84.5	86.5	82.3	81.3	85.8	81.2	85.5
2003	89.7	88.2	90.2	...	90.1	90.0	89.8	90.2	91.7	88.2	87.3	91.0	88.1	90.6
2004	95.7	94.1	96.2	...	95.4	95.8	96.4	97.7	97.0	96.3	96.0	96.1	96.8	96.0
2005	100.0	100.0	100.0	...	100.0	100.0	100.0	100.0	100.0	100.0	100.0	100.0	100.0	100.0
2006	103.6	105.2	103.1	...	103.4	102.9	104.0	102.0	103.6	101.7	100.8	103.7	104.2	102.9
2007	106.8	111.0	105.6	...	106.0	106.0	105.9	103.7	106.7	103.2	101.7	106.6	105.8	105.6
2008	109.1	114.2	107.7	...	108.5	107.8	107.7	105.1	108.8	104.7	102.5	108.9	107.8	107.6
2009	110.7	117.7	108.7	...	108.8	108.7	109.5	107.4	110.5	105.8	103.6	109.9	111.4	108.2
2010	113.9	121.1	111.9	...	111.2	111.8	113.2	112.0	113.5	110.1	108.8	112.6	117.9	110.6
2011	117.5	123.6	115.9	...	115.2	115.5	116.8	117.0	116.4	114.4	113.9	116.4	122.8	114.4
2012	120.4	127.8	118.4	...	117.9	118.4	120.3	118.0	119.3	116.0	115.0	119.4	125.6	116.9
2001														
March	78.0	75.2	78.8	...	...	...	...	...	...	76.5	75.4	79.7	74.8	79.9
June	78.8	76.3	79.5	...	...	...	...	...	...	77.0	75.8	80.5	75.7	80.5
September	79.9	77.4	80.6	...	...	...	...	...	...	77.8	76.4	81.7	76.6	81.6
December	80.8	78.0	81.5	...	...	...	...	...	...	78.7	77.4	82.6	77.3	82.2
2002														
March	81.5	78.8	82.3	...	82.7	81.8	81.2	81.8	83.5	79.9	78.8	83.2	78.6	83.2
June	82.5	79.9	83.3	...	83.7	83.2	82.1	82.7	84.4	80.6	79.7	84.4	79.3	84.3
September	83.5	81.4	84.1	...	84.2	84.2	83.3	83.7	86.0	81.2	80.3	85.2	80.5	84.9
December	84.6	82.9	85.0	...	85.2	85.1	84.6	84.8	86.8	82.5	81.5	86.0	81.2	85.5
2003														
March	86.3	84.1	87.0	...	87.1	86.6	86.0	86.7	88.5	85.2	84.7	87.7	83.9	87.8
June	87.5	85.4	88.1	...	88.0	88.0	87.6	88.1	89.4	86.5	85.7	88.8	85.7	88.8
September	88.9	86.9	89.4	...	89.5	89.3	88.7	89.4	90.8	87.5	86.8	90.2	87.2	89.9
December	90.0	88.0	90.5	...	90.7	90.4	90.3	90.4	92.0	88.4	87.5	91.4	88.1	90.6
2004														
March	92.1	89.5	92.9	...	91.9	92.5	92.9	94.4	94.3	92.4	92.7	93.0	92.8	93.0
June	93.7	91.1	94.4	...	93.4	94.2	94.5	96.0	95.9	93.8	94.1	94.6	95.0	94.5
September	94.8	92.5	95.4	...	94.5	95.2	95.4	97.1	96.7	95.0	95.4	95.5	96.0	95.2
December	95.9	93.9	96.5	...	95.9	96.1	96.9	98.0	97.3	96.5	96.1	96.5	96.8	96.0
2005														
March	97.5	95.6	98.0	...	97.9	97.5	98.0	98.7	98.0	98.3	98.2	97.9	98.0	98.2
June	98.4	96.8	98.8	...	98.8	98.4	98.9	99.2	98.8	99.5	99.4	98.6	98.9	99.0
September	99.4	98.4	99.7	...	99.8	99.3	99.7	99.9	99.5	100.3	100.1	99.4	99.8	99.6
December	100.2	99.9	100.3	...	100.4	100.2	100.4	100.1	100.3	100.2	100.1	100.3	100.0	100.0
2006														
March	100.8	100.8	100.8	...	101.0	100.7	101.1	100.0	101.3	99.4	98.6	101.3	100.8	101.0
June	101.7	102.0	101.6	...	101.7	101.5	102.4	100.8	102.1	100.3	99.6	102.2	102.7	101.5
September	102.7	103.5	102.5	...	102.8	102.1	103.4	101.6	103.0	101.3	100.7	103.0	103.4	102.3
December	103.7	105.1	103.4	...	103.8	103.0	104.4	102.3	103.9	102.0	101.1	104.0	104.2	102.9
2007														
March	104.0	107.1	103.1	...	103.5	103.3	103.5	101.1	104.0	100.9	99.4	104.0	102.4	103.4
June	105.2	108.7	104.2	...	104.8	104.2	104.5	102.3	105.0	102.1	100.8	105.1	104.1	104.3
September	106.0	109.7	105.0	...	105.5	105.2	105.2	102.7	106.0	102.4	100.9	106.0	104.3	105.1
December	107.0	110.9	105.9	...	106.4	106.1	106.3	103.9	107.0	103.4	101.9	106.9	105.8	105.6
2008														
March	107.5	111.5	106.4	...	107.0	106.5	106.6	104.3	107.4	103.9	102.1	107.4	106.6	106.5
June	108.1	112.4	106.9	...	107.8	107.0	106.7	104.4	108.3	104.3	102.1	108.0	106.6	107.1
September	108.8	113.3	107.5	...	108.4	107.6	107.4	104.8	108.7	104.6	102.4	108.7	107.2	107.6
December	109.3	114.1	108.0	...	109.0	108.0	108.0	105.4	109.2	105.0	102.9	109.1	107.8	107.6
2009														
March	109.6	115.3	108.0	...	108.5	108.0	108.3	106.3	109.5	105.3	103.2	109.2	109.5	107.9
June	109.9	116.2	108.2	...	108.7	108.0	108.5	106.6	109.8	105.4	103.3	109.3	110.3	108.0
September	110.4	116.8	108.7	...	108.9	108.6	109.2	107.1	110.4	105.7	103.4	109.9	110.9	108.2
December	110.9	117.6	109.1	...	109.4	108.9	109.8	107.8	110.9	106.3	104.2	110.2	111.4	108.2
2010														
March	112.0	118.2	110.3	...	109.9	110.1	111.6	109.8	111.4	108.2	106.3	111.1	114.8	109.5
June	112.6	119.1	110.8	...	110.3	110.9	112.0	110.5	112.2	108.7	107.1	111.7	116.2	110.0
September	113.5	120.2	111.7	...	111.0	111.6	112.9	111.7	113.3	110.0	108.7	112.3	117.6	110.4
December	114.2	121.0	112.3	...	111.8	112.1	113.5	112.5	114.0	110.6	109.6	112.9	117.9	110.6
2011														
March	115.4	122.1	113.5	...	113.0	113.3	114.2	113.4	115.1	111.6	110.8	114.3	119.0	112.6
September	116.7	122.6	115.1	...	114.5	114.8	115.5	116.1	115.8	113.7	113.4	115.7	122.3	113.9
December	117.1	123.1	115.4	...	114.8	115.3	116.2	116.2	116.1	113.8	113.4	116.0	122.0	114.0
December	117.9	123.6	116.3	...	115.9	115.8	117.2	117.5	117.0	115.1	114.7	116.8	122.8	114.4
2012														
March	118.5	124.9	116.7	...	116.4	116.6	117.9	116.0	117.7	114.0	112.9	117.8	122.9	115.6
June	119.2	126.0	117.4	...	117.1	117.4	118.7	116.7	118.0	114.5	113.4	118.5	124.3	116.2
September	120.1	127.0	118.2	...	117.7	118.1	120.0	117.6	119.0	115.7	114.8	119.1	125.5	116.6
December	120.8	127.8	118.9	...	118.6	118.7	120.7	118.5	119.9	116.7	115.9	119.8	125.6	116.9

[1]Excludes farm workers, private household workers, and federal government employees.
[2]Not seasonally adjusted.
. . . = Not available.

Table 9-2. Employment Cost Indexes, SIC Basis

(Not seasonally adjusted, December 2005 = 100; annual values are for December.)

Year	All civilian workers [1,2]	State and local government workers [2]	Private industry workers		By occupational group				Private industry workers — By industry division								
			All private industry workers [2]	Private industry workers excluding sales occupations	Production and nonsupervisory occupations	White-collar occupations	Blue-collar occupations	Service occupations [2]	Goods-producing industries Total [2]	Construction [2]	Manufacturing [2]	Service-providing Total [2]	Transportation and utilities	Wholesale trade	Retail trade	Finance, insurance, and real estate [2]	Services
TOTAL COMPENSATION																	
1979	...	...	32.8	32.5	...	31.2	35.0	33.9	33.7	...	33.1	32.0	...	...	...	...	...
1980	...	...	35.9	35.9	...	34.2	38.5	37.1	37.0	...	36.4	35.1	...	...	...	...	...
1981	39.0	36.8	39.5	39.4	40.1	37.6	42.2	40.5	40.7	...	40.0	38.6	...	...	...	...	...
1982	41.5	39.4	42.0	42.0	42.8	40.1	44.7	43.9	43.2	...	42.4	41.1	...	...	...	...	...
1983	43.9	41.8	44.4	44.4	45.2	42.7	47.0	46.3	45.3	...	44.6	43.8	...	...	...	...	...
1984	46.2	44.6	46.6	46.7	47.3	44.8	49.0	49.4	47.4	...	46.9	46.0	...	...	...	...	...
1985	48.2	47.1	48.4	48.3	49.1	47.0	50.5	50.9	49.0	50.8	48.4	48.1	50.6	...	52.4	44.7	46.1
1986	49.9	49.6	49.9	49.9	50.5	48.6	51.9	52.4	50.5	52.3	50.0	49.6	51.8	48.5	53.5	46.1	48.1
1987	51.7	51.8	51.6	51.7	52.2	50.4	53.5	53.7	52.1	54.2	51.5	51.4	53.3	50.4	54.8	47.0	50.5
1988	54.2	54.7	54.1	54.1	54.8	52.9	55.9	56.5	54.4	56.5	53.8	54.0	54.9	52.5	58.0	50.0	53.5
1989	56.9	58.1	56.7	56.5	57.6	55.7	58.2	59.0	56.7	59.0	56.3	56.8	56.9	57.1	59.9	52.7	56.4
1990	59.7	61.5	59.3	59.3	60.1	58.4	60.7	61.8	59.4	60.9	59.1	59.4	59.1	58.2	62.5	54.9	59.9
1991	62.3	63.7	61.9	62.0	62.7	61.0	63.4	64.7	62.1	63.3	61.9	61.9	61.7	60.7	65.2	57.2	62.5
1992	64.4	66.0	64.1	64.2	64.9	63.1	65.6	66.7	64.5	65.6	64.3	63.9	63.9	62.5	66.9	57.9	65.2
1993	66.7	67.9	66.4	66.6	67.3	65.4	68.1	68.8	67.0	67.1	66.9	66.2	66.1	64.4	68.9	60.5	67.5
1994	68.7	69.9	68.5	68.6	69.2	67.5	70.0	70.8	69.0	69.6	69.0	68.1	68.7	66.4	70.8	61.8	69.4
1995	70.6	72.0	70.2	70.4	71.0	69.4	71.7	72.1	70.7	71.1	70.8	70.0	71.2	69.4	72.3	64.0	70.9
1996	72.6	73.9	72.4	72.4	73.1	71.7	73.6	74.2	72.7	72.9	72.9	72.3	73.4	71.5	75.1	65.5	73.1
1997	75.0	75.6	74.9	74.9	75.4	74.4	75.5	77.2	74.5	74.8	74.6	75.1	75.5	73.8	77.7	69.9	75.9
1998	77.6	77.8	77.5	77.2	78.1	77.3	77.6	79.4	76.5	77.4	76.6	78.0	78.4	78.0	80.0	74.1	78.2
1999	80.2	80.5	80.2	80.0	80.4	79.9	80.2	82.1	79.1	79.9	79.2	80.6	80.1	81.1	83.0	77.1	80.9
2000	83.6	82.9	83.6	83.6	84.0	83.6	83.6	85.3	82.6	84.6	82.3	84.2	83.5	84.4	86.4	81.0	84.5
2001	87.0	86.4	87.1	87.0	87.4	87.1	86.7	89.1	87.8	88.2	85.3	87.8	87.5	87.2	90.3	83.9	88.3
2002	90.0	89.9	90.0	89.9	90.2	89.9	89.8	92.0	88.9	91.0	88.5	90.5	91.0	91.1	91.9	87.6	90.7
2003	93.5	92.9	93.6	93.6	93.6	93.6	93.4	94.9	92.4	94.1	92.2	94.2	94.0	94.0	94.9	94.1	94.0
2004	96.9	96.1	97.1	97.2	97.2	96.9	97.5	97.7	96.8	96.4	96.7	97.3	97.6	96.5	97.1	96.7	97.5
2005	100.0	100.0	100.0	100.0	100.0	100.0	100.0	100.0	100.0	100.0	100.0	100.0	100.0	100.0	100.0	100.0	100.0
WAGES AND SALARIES																	
1979	...	...	36.1	36.1	36.8	34.1	39.4	37.9	38.2	41.4	37.5	34.9	39.1	33.7	39.7	32.8	31.7
1980	...	...	39.4	39.3	40.3	37.1	43.1	41.0	41.8	45.0	41.0	38.0	43.5	37.1	42.5	35.2	34.5
1981	42.3	40.1	42.8	42.9	43.9	40.4	46.8	44.4	45.4	49.0	44.5	41.4	47.1	40.0	45.6	38.8	38.1
1982	45.0	42.7	45.5	45.6	46.7	43.1	49.4	48.2	48.0	51.5	47.0	44.2	50.5	42.5	47.5	41.3	41.2
1983	47.3	45.0	47.8	47.9	48.9	45.7	51.3	50.4	49.9	53.0	49.0	46.7	53.0	45.1	49.5	44.3	43.9
1984	49.4	47.7	49.8	50.1	50.8	47.6	53.1	53.5	51.8	53.7	51.2	48.7	54.8	47.6	52.0	43.9	46.7
1985	51.5	50.3	51.8	51.9	52.9	50.0	55.0	54.8	53.6	55.3	53.0	51.0	56.9	49.7	54.5	47.9	48.4
1986	53.3	53.0	53.5	53.6	54.3	51.7	56.4	56.2	53.5	56.7	54.8	52.5	57.9	51.5	55.7	49.2	50.3
1987	55.2	55.2	55.2	55.5	56.0	53.6	58.1	57.6	57.1	58.6	56.6	54.3	59.1	53.6	57.2	49.8	53.0
1988	57.5	57.9	57.5	57.5	58.4	56.1	59.9	60.1	58.9	60.7	58.3	56.9	60.6	55.6	60.1	52.9	55.6
1989	60.1	61.0	59.9	59.8	61.0	58.7	62.0	62.3	61.2	62.8	60.6	59.5	62.2	60.7	62.0	55.7	58.3
1990	62.6	64.2	62.3	62.4	63.2	61.2	64.2	64.8	63.4	64.1	63.1	61.8	64.3	61.2	64.2	57.6	61.6
1991	64.9	66.4	64.6	64.7	65.4	63.5	66.4	67.4	65.8	66.0	65.6	64.1	66.6	63.6	66.6	59.6	63.8
1992	66.6	68.4	66.3	66.5	67.2	65.2	68.1	68.8	67.6	67.3	67.6	65.7	68.7	65.5	68.2	59.5	66.0
1993	68.7	70.2	68.3	68.5	69.2	67.4	70.0	70.3	69.6	68.6	69.7	67.8	70.9	67.1	70.2	62.1	68.0
1994	70.6	72.4	70.2	70.5	71.1	69.3	72.0	72.4	71.7	70.8	71.8	69.6	73.5	69.1	71.9	62.8	70.0
1995	72.7	74.7	72.2	72.5	73.0	71.3	74.1	74.0	73.7	72.5	73.9	71.7	76.0	72.4	73.6	65.1	71.7
1996	75.1	76.8	74.7	74.9	75.5	73.8	76.3	76.6	76.0	74.6	76.3	74.2	78.1	74.7	76.8	67.2	74.2
1997	77.9	78.9	77.6	77.7	78.3	77.0	78.8	79.9	78.3	77.1	78.6	77.4	80.7	77.0	79.7	71.8	77.5
1998	80.8	81.3	80.6	80.4	81.4	80.3	81.3	82.4	81.1	79.9	81.3	80.5	83.0	81.5	82.2	76.9	80.1
1999	83.6	84.2	83.5	83.4	83.8	83.1	84.0	85.1	83.8	82.5	84.1	83.4	84.8	84.5	85.2	79.8	83.0
2000	86.7	87.0	86.7	86.7	87.1	86.4	87.1	88.3	87.1	86.9	87.1	86.6	87.5	87.4	88.6	83.4	86.3
2001	90.0	90.2	90.0	90.0	90.4	89.6	90.5	91.8	90.2	90.4	90.2	89.9	91.7	89.3	91.9	85.8	90.0
2002	92.6	93.1	92.4	92.5	92.6	92.0	92.8	94.1	92.9	92.8	93.0	92.3	94.7	92.8	93.2	89.4	92.0
2003	95.2	95.0	95.2	95.4	95.1	95.2	95.2	96.2	95.1	95.1	95.2	95.3	96.2	95.3	95.5	95.9	94.8
2004	97.5	97.0	97.5	97.8	97.5	97.5	97.6	97.9	97.4	97.0	97.5	97.7	98.6	96.6	97.2	97.7	97.8
2005	100.0	100.0	100.0	100.0	100.0	100.0	100.0	100.0	100.0	100.0	100.0	100.0	100.0	100.0	100.0	100.0	100.0

[1] Excludes farm workers, private household workers, and federal government employees.
[2] Roughly continuous and comparable with new NAICS-based series. See notes and definitions for more information.
. . . = Not available.

Table 9-2. Employment Cost Indexes, SIC Basis—*Continued*

(Not seasonally adjusted, December 2005 = 100; annual values are for December.)

					Private industry workers													
		State and local govern- ment work- ers [2]		Private industry workers exclud- ing sales occupa- tions	By occupational group				By industry division									
Year	All civilian work- ers [1,2]		All private industry work- ers [2]						Goods-producing industries			Service-providing industries						
					Produc- tion and nonsup- ervisory occupa- tions	White- collar occupa- tions	Blue- collar occupa- tions	Service occupa- tions [2]	Total [2]	Con- struc- tion [2]	Manu- fac- turing [2]	Total [2]	Trans- portation and utilities	Whole- sale trade	Retail trade	Finance, insurance, and real estate [2]	Services

TOTAL BENEFITS

Year	All civilian	State/local	All private	Priv excl sales	Prod/nonsup	White-collar	Blue-collar	Service	Goods Total	Construction	Manufacturing	Service Total	Transp	Wholesale	Retail	Finance	Services
1979	. . .	. . .	25.7	. . .	. . .	24.7	27.4	. . .	26.0	. . .	25.8	25.4	. . .	. . .	. . .	. . .	. . .
1980	. . .	. . .	28.7	. . .	. . .	27.7	30.4	. . .	28.8	. . .	28.5	28.6	. . .	. . .	. . .	. . .	. . .
1981	31.8	. . .	32.2	. . .	. . .	31.1	34.0	. . .	32.4	. . .	32.1	31.9	. . .	. . .	. . .	. . .	. . .
1982	34.2	. . .	34.5	. . .	. . .	33.3	36.5	. . .	34.8	. . .	34.4	34.1	. . .	. . .	. . .	. . .	. . .
1983	36.8	. . .	37.1	. . .	. . .	35.8	39.1	. . .	37.2	. . .	36.9	36.8	. . .	. . .	. . .	. . .	. . .
1984	39.3	. . .	39.5	. . .	. . .	38.3	41.4	. . .	39.6	. . .	39.3	39.4	. . .	. . .	. . .	. . .	. . .
1985	40.8	. . .	40.9	. . .	. . .	40.0	42.5	41.2	40.8	. . .	40.4	40.9	. . .	. . .	. . .	. . .	. . .
1986	42.4	. . .	42.3	. . .	. . .	41.4	43.8	42.9	42.0	. . .	41.6	42.5	. . .	. . .	. . .	. . .	. . .
1987	44.0	. . .	43.7	. . .	. . .	42.9	45.3	43.9	43.2	. . .	42.7	44.2	. . .	. . .	. . .	. . .	. . .
1988	47.0	. . .	46.7	. . .	. . .	45.6	48.6	47.4	46.3	. . .	46.0	47.1	. . .	. . .	. . .	. . .	. . .
1989	50.1	52.2	49.6	. . .	. . .	48.6	51.2	50.5	48.8	. . .	48.7	50.2	. . .	. . .	. . .	. . .	. . .
1990	53.5	55.8	52.9	. . .	. . .	52.0	54.4	53.8	52.3	. . .	52.1	53.4	. . .	. . .	. . .	. . .	. . .
1991	56.5	58.0	56.2	. . .	. . .	55.2	57.8	57.7	55.5	. . .	55.2	56.7	. . .	. . .	. . .	. . .	. . .
1992	59.5	61.1	59.1	. . .	. . .	57.8	61.0	61.0	58.7	. . .	58.3	59.4	. . .	. . .	. . .	. . .	. . .
1993	62.2	62.9	62.0	. . .	. . .	60.5	64.4	64.4	62.0	. . .	61.8	62.0	. . .	. . .	. . .	. . .	. . .
1994	64.4	64.6	64.3	. . .	. . .	63.2	66.2	66.0	64.1	. . .	63.9	64.4	. . .	. . .	. . .	. . .	. . .
1995	65.8	66.3	65.7	. . .	. . .	64.8	67.2	66.6	65.2	. . .	65.0	66.0	. . .	. . .	. . .	. . .	. . .
1996	67.1	67.8	67.0	. . .	. . .	66.2	68.4	67.3	66.4	. . .	66.5	67.3	. . .	. . .	. . .	. . .	. . .
1997	68.5	68.6	68.5	. . .	. . .	68.0	69.4	69.6	67.3	. . .	67.4	69.2	. . .	. . .	. . .	. . .	. . .
1998	70.3	70.7	70.2	. . .	. . .	69.9	70.7	70.9	68.1	. . .	67.9	71.4	. . .	. . .	. . .	. . .	. . .
1999	72.6	72.7	72.6	. . .	. . .	72.3	73.0	73.4	70.5	. . .	70.3	73.8	. . .	. . .	. . .	. . .	. . .
2000	76.2	74.4	76.7	. . .	. . .	76.5	76.9	76.6	74.3	. . .	73.6	78.1	. . .	. . .	. . .	. . .	. . .
2001	80.2	78.5	80.6	. . .	. . .	81.1	79.5	81.3	77.3	. . .	76.3	82.5	. . .	. . .	. . .	. . .	. . .
2002	84.2	83.3	84.4	. . .	. . .	84.6	83.8	85.7	81.3	. . .	80.4	86.1	. . .	. . .	. . .	. . .	. . .
2003	89.5	88.4	89.8	. . .	. . .	89.7	89.8	91.3	87.4	. . .	86.7	91.2	. . .	. . .	. . .	. . .	. . .
2004	95.7	94.3	96.0	. . .	. . .	95.3	97.3	97.1	95.7	. . .	95.3	96.2	. . .	. . .	. . .	. . .	. . .
2005	100.0	100.0	100.0	. . .	. . .	100.0	100.0	100.0	100.0	. . .	100.0	100.0	. . .	. . .	. . .	. . .	. . .

[1] Excludes farm workers, private household workers, and federal government employees.
[2] Roughly continuous and comparable with new NAICS-based series. See notes and definitions for more information.
. . . = Not available.

Section 9b: Productivity and Related Data

Figure 9-2. Change in Labor Productivity, Nonfarm Business, 1948–2012

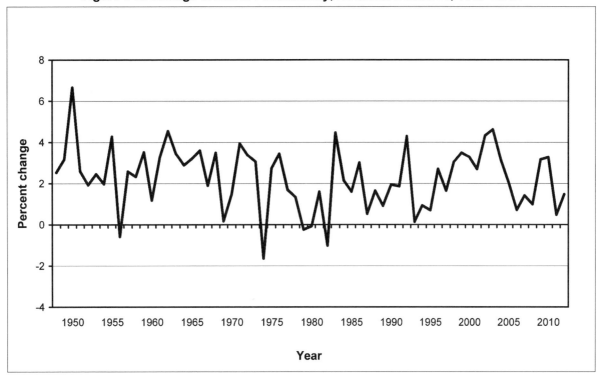

- As Figure 9-2 demonstrates, the rate of change in U.S. nonfarm labor productivity has often been quite variable from year to year. Up through the 1980s, productivity tended to decline (growth rates were less than zero) in recession years but rebound sharply in recovery. One explanation of this was that firms expected that declines in demand would be temporary, and therefore held on to their experienced workers in order to be prepared for the recovery. (Table 9-3A and B)

- In the 1990s and 2000s, productivity growth rates were still variable, but output per hour no longer declined even in a severe recession. This suggests that the steepness of this decline in demand was not regarded as temporary. (Table 9-3A)

- On average, measuring between cyclically high growth years, productivity grew at a 2.8 percent annual rate from 1948 to 1973. Productivity growth slowed between 1973 and 1989, averaging just 1.3 percent. From 1989 to 2012, however, productivity growth has speeded up to an average of 2.3 percent per year. These trends are the same as estimated last year, not changed by the comprehensive revision. (Table 9-3A and B)

- Real hourly compensation—measured differently in this data set, including stock options and affected by changes in the composition of employment—shows the same lag behind productivity as did the ECI: it rises at a 1.1 percent rate from 2000 to 2007, versus 2.7 percent for productivity; and it increases only 0.1 percent per year from 2007 to 2012, versus 1.9 percent for productivity. This lag reflects an unprecedented decline to unprecedented levels in the labor share of the total value of sector output. The labor share index was essentially trendless from 1950 to 2000—in fact, it was identical in those two years. But it fell 6 percent over the completed 2000–2007 cycle and another 5 percent since then. (Table 9-3A)

Table 9-3A. Productivity and Related Data: Recent Data

(2009 = 100, seasonally adjusted.)

Year and quarter	Business sector														
	Output per hour of all persons	Output	Hours of all persons	Employ-ment	Average weekly hours	Unit labor costs	Compen-sation per hour	Real hourly compen-sation	Labor share	Unit nonlabor payments	Implicit price deflator	Current dollar output	Compen-sation	Nonlabor payments	Output per job
1950	24.6	13.9	56.5	48.3	117.0	18.4	4.5	36.7	108.5	14.9	16.9	2.4	2.6	2.1	28.8
1951	25.4	14.8	58.3	49.6	117.6	19.5	5.0	37.3	107.1	16.4	18.2	2.7	2.9	2.4	29.9
1952	26.1	15.3	58.4	49.8	117.3	20.1	5.3	38.8	109.1	16.1	18.4	2.8	3.1	2.5	30.7
1953	27.1	16.0	59.2	50.5	117.2	20.6	5.6	41.0	111.0	15.8	18.6	3.0	3.3	2.5	31.8
1954	27.7	15.9	57.2	49.3	116.1	20.8	5.8	42.0	111.5	15.7	18.7	3.0	3.3	2.5	32.2
1955	28.9	17.1	59.3	50.7	117.0	20.5	5.9	43.2	108.3	16.7	18.9	3.2	3.5	2.9	33.8
1956	29.0	17.4	60.2	51.7	116.4	21.8	6.3	45.4	111.4	16.4	19.5	3.4	3.8	2.9	33.7
1957	29.9	17.8	59.4	51.6	115.0	22.5	6.7	46.8	111.5	17.0	20.2	3.6	4.0	3.0	34.4
1958	30.8	17.4	56.7	49.7	114.2	22.8	7.0	47.5	111.1	17.3	20.5	3.6	4.0	3.0	35.1
1959	31.9	18.8	59.1	51.2	115.4	22.9	7.3	49.1	110.4	17.7	20.7	3.9	4.3	3.3	36.8
1960	32.4	19.2	59.2	51.5	114.9	23.5	7.6	50.3	111.8	17.5	21.0	4.0	4.5	3.4	37.3
1961	33.6	19.6	58.3	50.9	114.4	23.5	7.9	51.7	111.3	17.8	21.1	4.1	4.6	3.5	38.5
1962	35.2	20.9	59.3	51.6	115.0	23.5	8.3	53.5	110.0	18.4	21.3	4.4	4.9	3.8	40.4
1963	36.5	21.8	59.7	51.9	115.1	23.4	8.5	54.6	109.0	18.8	21.5	4.7	5.1	4.1	42.0
1964	37.7	23.2	61.5	52.8	116.3	23.5	8.9	56.0	108.3	19.2	21.7	5.0	5.4	4.5	43.9
1965	39.1	24.8	63.5	54.4	116.9	23.5	9.2	57.1	106.7	20.0	22.0	5.5	5.8	5.0	45.7
1966	40.7	26.5	65.2	56.0	116.5	24.1	9.8	59.3	106.8	20.5	22.6	6.0	6.4	5.4	47.4
1967	41.7	27.1	65.0	56.7	114.6	24.9	10.4	60.8	107.4	20.8	23.2	6.3	6.7	5.6	47.7
1968	43.1	28.5	66.0	57.9	114.0	25.9	11.2	62.9	107.7	21.5	24.1	6.9	7.4	6.1	49.2
1969	43.3	29.3	67.7	59.7	113.4	27.6	12.0	63.8	109.6	21.8	25.2	7.4	8.1	6.4	49.1
1970	44.2	29.3	66.3	59.5	111.5	29.1	12.9	64.9	110.8	22.3	26.3	7.7	8.5	6.6	49.3
1971	46.0	30.4	66.2	59.6	111.0	29.7	13.6	65.9	108.3	24.2	27.4	8.3	9.0	7.4	51.0
1972	47.5	32.4	68.2	61.4	111.2	30.5	14.5	67.9	107.7	25.3	28.3	9.2	9.9	8.2	52.8
1973	48.9	34.6	70.8	64.0	110.7	32.0	15.6	68.9	107.3	26.8	29.8	10.3	11.1	9.3	54.1
1974	48.1	34.1	71.0	65.0	109.2	35.6	17.1	67.9	108.7	28.8	32.7	11.2	12.1	9.8	52.5
1975	49.8	33.8	67.9	63.0	107.7	38.1	18.9	68.9	105.9	33.0	35.9	12.1	12.9	11.1	53.6
1976	51.4	36.0	70.1	65.0	107.9	39.8	20.4	70.3	105.2	35.1	37.8	13.6	14.3	12.6	55.5
1977	52.3	38.1	72.8	67.8	107.4	42.2	22.1	71.3	105.4	37.1	40.1	15.3	16.1	14.1	56.2
1978	52.9	40.5	76.6	71.5	107.0	45.2	23.9	72.2	105.6	39.5	42.9	17.4	18.3	16.0	56.6
1979	53.0	41.9	79.1	74.3	106.5	49.6	26.3	72.3	106.7	42.1	46.5	19.5	20.8	17.7	56.4
1980	52.9	41.5	78.5	74.5	105.3	54.9	29.1	72.1	108.5	44.6	50.6	21.0	22.8	18.5	55.7
1981	54.1	42.7	79.0	75.2	105.0	58.8	31.8	72.0	106.5	50.3	55.3	23.6	25.1	21.5	56.8
1982	53.7	41.5	77.2	74.0	104.3	63.6	34.2	72.9	108.8	51.3	58.5	24.2	26.4	21.3	56.0
1983	55.7	43.7	78.6	74.7	105.2	64.1	35.7	73.1	106.0	55.4	60.5	26.5	28.1	24.2	58.6
1984	57.2	47.6	83.2	78.4	106.0	65.2	37.3	73.3	104.7	58.2	62.2	29.6	31.0	27.7	60.7
1985	58.5	49.8	85.1	80.4	105.9	67.0	39.2	74.5	104.7	59.8	64.0	31.9	33.3	29.8	61.9
1986	60.2	51.6	85.8	81.7	105.0	68.8	41.4	77.3	106.1	59.4	64.9	33.5	35.5	30.6	63.2
1987	60.5	53.4	88.3	83.9	105.2	71.0	43.0	77.6	107.4	59.4	66.1	35.3	38.0	31.7	63.7
1988	61.4	55.7	90.8	86.5	104.9	73.7	45.2	78.8	108.0	60.7	68.2	38.0	41.1	33.8	64.4
1989	62.1	57.9	93.1	88.4	105.4	75.0	46.6	77.9	106.1	64.7	70.7	40.9	43.4	37.5	65.5
1990	63.5	58.8	92.6	88.9	104.1	78.2	49.6	79.0	107.0	65.9	73.1	43.0	46.0	38.8	66.1
1991	64.6	58.5	90.4	87.6	103.3	80.5	52.1	79.9	107.1	67.7	75.1	43.9	47.1	39.6	66.8
1992	67.5	60.9	90.2	87.1	103.6	81.6	55.1	82.6	106.9	69.0	76.3	46.5	49.8	42.0	70.0
1993	67.6	62.7	92.7	88.9	104.2	82.8	56.0	81.8	106.0	71.6	78.1	49.0	51.9	44.9	70.5
1994	68.2	65.7	96.4	92.0	104.8	82.9	56.5	80.9	104.3	74.8	79.5	52.2	54.5	49.2	71.5
1995	68.4	67.8	99.1	94.6	104.8	84.2	57.6	80.5	104.1	76.3	80.9	54.8	57.1	51.7	71.7
1996	70.5	70.9	100.7	96.6	104.2	85.2	60.0	81.7	103.7	78.0	82.2	58.3	60.4	55.3	73.4
1997	71.8	74.7	104.0	99.3	104.8	86.6	62.2	82.9	103.9	78.8	83.3	62.3	64.7	58.9	75.3
1998	74.0	78.5	106.1	101.3	104.7	89.0	65.9	86.6	106.2	76.5	83.8	65.8	69.9	60.1	77.5
1999	76.7	83.1	108.2	103.0	105.1	89.6	68.8	88.5	106.3	76.9	84.3	70.0	74.4	63.9	80.7
2000	79.4	86.8	109.4	104.7	104.4	93.0	73.8	91.9	108.3	75.9	85.9	74.5	80.7	65.9	82.9
2001	81.5	87.3	107.1	104.0	103.0	94.7	77.2	93.5	108.3	77.3	87.4	76.3	82.7	67.5	84.0
2002	85.0	88.9	104.5	101.7	102.8	92.8	78.9	94.1	105.4	81.4	88.0	78.2	82.5	72.3	87.4
2003	89.1	92.5	103.9	101.5	102.3	91.9	81.9	95.5	103.9	83.6	88.4	81.8	85.1	77.3	91.2
2004	92.0	96.7	105.2	102.8	102.3	93.2	85.7	97.3	103.0	86.7	90.5	87.5	90.1	83.8	94.1
2005	93.9	100.4	106.9	104.7	102.1	94.6	88.8	97.6	101.4	91.5	93.3	93.6	94.9	91.8	95.9
2006	94.6	103.3	109.2	106.7	102.3	97.5	92.3	98.2	101.6	94.0	96.1	99.2	100.8	97.1	96.8
2007	95.8	105.3	109.9	107.6	102.1	100.6	96.4	99.7	102.2	95.5	98.5	103.7	105.9	100.5	97.8
2008	96.8	104.3	107.7	106.0	101.6	102.2	99.0	98.6	102.5	96.3	99.7	104.0	106.6	100.5	98.3
2009	100.0	100.0	100.0	100.0	100.0	100.0	100.0	100.0	100.0	100.0	100.0	100.0	100.0	100.0	100.0
2010	103.3	103.1	99.9	98.8	101.1	98.8	102.0	100.3	97.7	104.4	101.1	104.3	101.9	107.7	104.4
2011	103.6	105.6	101.9	100.3	101.6	100.8	104.4	99.6	97.6	106.8	103.3	109.1	106.4	112.8	105.3
2012	105.1	109.4	104.1	102.3	101.8	102.0	107.2	100.1	97.0	109.6	105.2	115.1	111.6	119.9	107.0
2010															
1st quarter	102.5	101.4	98.9	98.5	100.4	98.2	100.7	99.3	97.7	103.7	100.5	101.9	99.6	105.2	102.9
2nd quarter	102.9	102.7	99.8	98.8	101.0	99.0	101.9	100.6	98.1	103.5	100.9	103.6	101.6	106.3	104.0
3rd quarter	103.6	103.7	100.2	98.8	101.4	98.9	102.5	100.8	97.7	104.6	101.3	105.1	102.6	108.5	105.0
4th quarter	104.0	104.7	100.7	99.2	101.5	99.0	102.9	100.5	97.1	106.0	101.9	106.7	103.6	111.0	105.6
2011															
1st quarter	103.1	104.2	101.0	99.7	101.3	101.4	104.5	101.0	99.0	103.7	102.4	106.6	105.6	108.1	104.5
2nd quarter	103.5	105.2	101.6	100.1	101.5	100.8	104.4	99.7	97.8	106.2	103.0	108.4	106.0	111.8	105.1
3rd quarter	103.5	105.7	102.1	100.5	101.6	101.5	105.0	99.6	97.8	107.0	103.8	109.7	107.2	113.1	105.2
4th quarter	104.4	107.3	102.9	101.0	101.8	99.5	103.8	98.1	95.7	110.2	104.0	111.6	106.8	118.3	106.3
2012															
1st quarter	104.7	108.6	103.7	101.7	102.0	101.3	106.0	99.6	97.0	108.6	104.4	113.4	110.0	118.0	106.8
2nd quarter	105.0	109.1	103.8	102.1	101.7	101.4	106.5	99.9	96.7	109.7	104.9	114.4	110.6	119.6	106.8
3rd quarter	105.6	110.0	104.2	102.5	101.7	101.1	106.7	99.5	95.8	111.7	105.5	116.1	111.2	122.9	107.3
4th quarter	105.1	110.1	104.7	102.9	101.8	104.1	109.4	101.4	98.3	108.3	105.8	116.5	114.5	119.2	107.0

Table 9-3A. Productivity and Related Data: Recent Data—*Continued*

(2009 = 100, seasonally adjusted.)

Year and quarter	Output per hour of all persons	Output	Hours of all persons	Employ-ment	Average weekly hours	Unit labor costs	Compen-sation per hour	Real hourly compen-sation	Labor share	Unit nonlabor payments	Implicit price deflator	Current dollar output	Compen-sation	Nonlabor payments	Output per job
1950	27.9	13.6	48.9	41.2	118.6	17.5	4.9	39.5	108.3	14.3	16.1	2.2	2.4	1.9	33.1
1951	28.6	14.6	51.2	43.1	118.8	18.5	5.3	39.8	107.7	15.4	17.2	2.5	2.7	2.2	34.0
1952	29.1	15.1	51.8	43.6	118.7	19.2	5.6	41.2	109.2	15.3	17.6	2.6	2.9	2.3	34.6
1953	29.8	15.8	53.1	44.9	118.2	19.8	5.9	43.2	110.4	15.3	17.9	2.8	3.1	2.4	35.3
1954	30.4	15.6	51.3	43.7	117.3	20.0	6.1	44.3	110.7	15.3	18.1	2.8	3.1	2.4	35.7
1955	31.7	16.9	53.4	45.0	118.5	19.9	6.3	46.0	108.2	16.3	18.4	3.1	3.4	2.8	37.6
1956	31.5	17.2	54.7	46.3	118.0	21.2	6.7	48.1	111.5	16.0	19.0	3.3	3.7	2.8	37.2
1957	32.4	17.6	54.4	46.6	116.7	21.9	7.1	49.3	111.4	16.5	19.6	3.5	3.8	2.9	37.8
1958	33.1	17.3	52.1	44.9	115.9	22.2	7.4	49.8	111.6	16.7	19.9	3.4	3.8	2.9	38.4
1959	34.3	18.7	54.5	46.6	117.1	22.3	7.6	51.4	110.2	17.3	20.2	3.8	4.2	3.2	40.1
1960	34.7	19.0	54.8	47.1	116.5	23.0	8.0	52.7	112.3	17.0	20.5	3.9	4.4	3.2	40.4
1961	35.8	19.4	54.2	46.7	116.1	23.0	8.2	53.9	111.5	17.3	20.6	4.0	4.5	3.4	41.6
1962	37.4	20.8	55.4	47.6	116.5	22.9	8.6	55.5	109.9	17.9	20.8	4.3	4.7	3.7	43.6
1963	38.7	21.7	56.0	48.1	116.5	22.9	8.9	56.7	109.0	18.3	21.0	4.6	5.0	4.0	45.1
1964	39.9	23.2	58.1	49.3	117.9	22.9	9.1	57.7	107.9	18.9	21.2	4.9	5.3	4.4	47.0
1965	41.1	24.8	60.4	51.0	118.3	23.0	9.4	58.7	106.7	19.5	21.5	5.3	5.7	4.8	48.7
1966	42.6	26.6	62.4	53.0	117.8	23.5	10.0	60.4	106.6	20.0	22.0	5.9	6.2	5.3	50.2
1967	43.4	27.1	62.4	53.9	115.8	24.4	10.6	62.0	107.4	20.4	22.7	6.2	6.6	5.5	50.3
1968	44.9	28.5	63.5	55.2	115.1	25.3	11.4	64.0	107.4	21.1	23.6	6.7	7.2	6.0	51.7
1969	45.0	29.4	65.4	57.2	114.3	27.0	12.2	64.8	109.6	21.3	24.6	7.2	7.9	6.3	51.5
1970	45.7	29.4	64.3	57.2	112.5	28.5	13.0	65.6	110.7	21.9	25.7	7.6	8.4	6.4	51.4
1971	47.5	30.5	64.2	57.4	111.9	29.1	13.8	66.7	108.4	23.7	26.8	8.2	8.9	7.2	53.1
1972	49.1	32.5	66.3	59.1	112.1	29.9	14.7	68.8	108.2	24.5	27.7	9.0	9.7	8.0	55.0
1973	50.6	34.9	69.0	61.7	111.7	31.3	15.8	69.7	109.1	25.0	28.7	10.0	10.9	8.7	56.5
1974	49.7	34.4	69.1	62.7	110.1	34.8	17.3	68.7	110.0	27.2	31.6	10.9	12.0	9.3	54.8
1975	51.1	33.8	66.1	60.9	108.5	37.4	19.1	69.6	107.0	31.6	35.0	11.8	12.6	10.7	55.5
1976	52.9	36.2	68.5	63.0	108.7	39.0	20.6	70.9	105.6	34.0	36.9	13.4	14.1	12.3	57.4
1977	53.7	38.2	71.2	65.9	108.0	41.5	22.3	72.0	105.8	36.1	39.2	15.0	15.9	13.8	58.1
1978	54.5	40.8	74.9	69.5	107.7	44.5	24.2	73.1	106.3	38.2	41.8	17.1	18.1	15.6	58.6
1979	54.3	42.1	77.6	72.5	107.0	48.8	26.5	73.1	107.7	40.5	45.4	19.1	20.6	17.1	58.1
1980	54.3	41.8	76.9	72.7	105.8	54.1	29.4	72.8	108.9	43.5	49.7	20.7	22.6	18.2	57.4
1981	55.2	42.7	77.5	73.5	105.4	58.4	32.2	72.9	107.4	48.8	54.4	23.3	25.0	20.8	58.1
1982	54.6	41.4	75.8	72.4	104.7	63.3	34.6	73.7	109.4	50.2	57.8	23.9	26.2	20.8	57.2
1983	57.0	44.1	77.3	73.1	105.7	63.4	36.1	74.0	106.1	54.6	59.7	26.3	27.9	24.1	60.3
1984	58.2	47.7	82.0	77.0	106.4	64.7	37.7	74.1	105.3	56.8	61.4	29.3	30.9	27.1	62.0
1985	59.2	49.8	84.1	79.2	106.2	66.8	39.5	75.1	105.3	58.8	63.4	31.6	33.2	29.3	62.8
1986	61.0	51.7	84.8	80.6	105.2	68.6	41.8	78.0	106.5	58.5	64.4	33.3	35.4	30.2	64.1
1987	61.3	53.5	87.3	82.9	105.4	70.8	43.4	78.4	107.9	58.4	65.6	35.1	37.9	31.2	64.6
1988	62.3	56.0	89.8	85.5	105.1	73.2	45.6	79.5	108.3	59.8	67.6	37.8	41.0	33.4	65.5
1989	62.9	58.0	92.3	87.4	105.6	74.7	46.9	78.4	106.6	63.6	70.1	40.6	43.3	36.9	66.4
1990	64.1	58.9	91.9	88.1	104.4	77.8	49.9	79.3	107.4	64.9	72.4	42.7	45.8	38.2	66.9
1991	65.3	58.6	89.7	86.6	103.6	80.2	52.3	80.4	107.4	66.9	74.7	43.7	47.0	39.2	67.6
1992	68.1	60.9	89.5	86.2	103.9	81.5	55.5	83.1	107.4	68.0	75.9	46.2	49.7	41.5	70.7
1993	68.2	62.8	92.2	88.2	104.5	82.4	56.2	82.1	106.1	71.0	77.7	48.8	51.8	44.6	71.2
1994	68.8	65.7	95.5	91.1	104.9	82.6	56.9	81.4	104.5	74.1	79.1	52.0	54.3	48.7	72.2
1995	69.3	68.0	98.2	93.7	104.8	83.7	58.0	81.1	104.0	76.0	80.5	54.7	56.9	51.7	72.6
1996	71.2	71.1	99.9	95.9	104.2	84.8	60.4	82.2	104.0	77.0	81.6	58.0	60.3	54.7	74.1
1997	72.3	74.8	103.4	98.6	104.9	86.4	62.5	83.3	104.1	78.2	83.0	62.1	64.6	58.5	75.9
1998	74.5	78.7	105.7	100.8	104.8	88.7	66.1	86.9	106.3	76.2	83.5	65.7	69.8	60.0	78.1
1999	77.1	83.3	108.0	102.7	105.2	89.3	68.9	88.7	106.1	76.9	84.1	70.1	74.4	64.1	81.1
2000	79.7	86.9	109.1	104.5	104.5	92.9	74.0	92.1	108.3	75.9	85.8	74.6	80.7	66.0	83.2
2001	81.8	87.5	107.0	103.9	103.0	94.4	77.2	93.5	108.2	77.2	87.2	76.4	82.6	67.6	84.3
2002	85.4	89.1	104.4	101.5	102.8	92.5	79.0	94.2	105.2	81.5	87.9	78.3	82.4	72.6	87.8
2003	89.3	92.7	103.8	101.4	102.3	91.8	81.9	95.6	104.0	83.4	88.3	81.8	85.0	77.3	91.4
2004	92.1	96.8	105.2	102.8	102.3	93.0	85.7	97.3	103.2	86.0	90.1	87.3	90.1	83.3	94.2
2005	94.0	100.5	106.9	104.7	102.1	94.5	88.8	97.6	101.4	91.3	93.2	93.6	94.9	91.8	96.0
2006	94.6	103.4	109.3	106.7	102.4	97.5	92.3	98.2	101.6	93.9	96.0	99.3	100.9	97.2	96.9
2007	96.0	105.6	110.0	107.7	102.2	100.3	96.3	99.6	102.2	95.1	98.2	103.7	105.9	100.5	98.1
2008	96.9	104.5	107.8	106.1	101.6	102.0	98.9	98.5	102.6	95.8	99.4	103.9	106.6	100.1	98.5
2009	100.0	100.0	100.0	100.0	100.0	100.0	100.0	100.0	100.0	100.0	100.0	100.0	100.0	100.0	100.0
2010	103.3	103.2	99.9	98.8	101.1	98.8	102.1	100.4	97.9	104.0	101.0	104.2	102.0	107.3	104.4
2011	103.8	105.7	101.9	100.3	101.6	100.8	104.6	99.7	98.1	105.5	102.7	108.6	106.6	111.5	105.5
2012	105.3	109.7	104.1	102.3	101.8	102.0	107.4	100.3	97.5	108.3	104.6	114.7	111.8	118.7	107.2
2010															
1st quarter	102.6	101.5	98.9	98.5	100.4	98.2	100.7	99.4	97.9	103.4	100.4	101.9	99.7	104.9	103.0
2nd quarter	102.9	102.7	99.7	98.7	101.0	99.1	102.0	100.7	98.3	103.2	100.8	103.4	101.7	105.9	104.0
3rd quarter	103.5	103.7	100.2	98.8	101.4	99.0	102.5	100.9	97.9	104.1	101.2	104.9	102.7	108.0	105.0
4th quarter	104.1	104.8	100.7	99.1	101.6	99.0	103.1	100.6	97.4	105.3	101.6	106.5	103.8	110.3	105.7
2011															
1st quarter	103.2	104.2	101.0	99.6	101.3	101.5	104.7	101.2	99.6	102.5	101.9	106.2	105.7	106.8	104.6
2nd quarter	103.7	105.4	101.7	100.0	101.6	100.7	104.4	99.8	98.3	105.0	102.5	108.0	106.2	110.7	105.4
3rd quarter	103.7	105.9	102.1	100.4	101.7	101.5	105.2	99.8	98.4	105.5	103.2	109.2	107.4	111.8	105.4
4th quarter	104.4	107.4	102.8	101.0	101.8	99.6	104.0	98.3	96.2	108.9	103.4	111.1	106.9	117.0	106.4
2012															
1st quarter	104.8	108.7	103.7	101.6	102.0	101.3	106.3	99.8	97.6	107.4	103.8	112.9	110.2	116.7	107.0
2nd quarter	105.2	109.2	103.8	102.0	101.8	101.5	106.8	100.1	97.2	108.4	104.4	114.0	110.8	118.3	107.0
3rd quarter	105.8	110.3	104.2	102.5	101.7	101.1	106.9	99.7	96.3	110.4	105.0	115.8	111.4	121.8	107.6
4th quarter	105.4	110.5	104.8	103.0	101.8	103.9	109.5	101.5	98.8	107.0	105.2	116.2	114.8	118.1	107.3

Table 9-3A. Productivity and Related Data: Recent Data—*Continued*

(2009 = 100, seasonally adjusted.)

Year and quarter	Manufacturing					
	Output per hour of all persons	Output	Hours of all persons	Compensation per hour	Real compensation per hour	Unit labor costs
1950	. . .	. . .	. . .	. . .	. . .	. . .
1951	. . .	. . .	. . .	. . .	. . .	. . .
1952	. . .	. . .	. . .	. . .	. . .	. . .
1953	. . .	. . .	. . .	. . .	. . .	. . .
1954	. . .	. . .	. . .	. . .	. . .	. . .
1955	. . .	. . .	. . .	. . .	. . .	. . .
1956	. . .	. . .	. . .	. . .	. . .	. . .
1957	. . .	. . .	. . .	. . .	. . .	. . .
1958	. . .	. . .	. . .	. . .	. . .	. . .
1959	. . .	. . .	. . .	. . .	. . .	. . .
1960	. . .	. . .	. . .	. . .	. . .	. . .
1961	. . .	. . .	. . .	. . .	. . .	. . .
1962	. . .	. . .	. . .	. . .	. . .	. . .
1963	. . .	. . .	. . .	. . .	. . .	. . .
1964	. . .	. . .	. . .	. . .	. . .	. . .
1965	. . .	. . .	. . .	. . .	. . .	. . .
1966	. . .	. . .	. . .	. . .	. . .	. . .
1967	. . .	. . .	. . .	. . .	. . .	. . .
1968	. . .	. . .	. . .	. . .	. . .	. . .
1969	. . .	. . .	. . .	. . .	. . .	. . .
1970	. . .	. . .	. . .	. . .	. . .	. . .
1971	. . .	. . .	. . .	. . .	. . .	. . .
1972	. . .	. . .	. . .	. . .	. . .	. . .
1973	. . .	. . .	. . .	. . .	. . .	. . .
1974	. . .	. . .	. . .	. . .	. . .	. . .
1975	. . .	. . .	. . .	. . .	. . .	. . .
1976	. . .	. . .	. . .	. . .	. . .	. . .
1977	. . .	. . .	. . .	. . .	. . .	. . .
1978	. . .	. . .	. . .	. . .	. . .	. . .
1979	. . .	. . .	. . .	. . .	. . .	. . .
1980	. . .	. . .	. . .	. . .	. . .	. . .
1981	. . .	. . .	. . .	. . .	. . .	. . .
1982	. . .	. . .	. . .	. . .	. . .	. . .
1983	. . .	. . .	. . .	. . .	. . .	. . .
1984	. . .	. . .	. . .	. . .	. . .	. . .
1985	. . .	. . .	. . .	. . .	. . .	. . .
1986	. . .	. . .	. . .	. . .	. . .	. . .
1987	49.1	73.1	148.8	44.4	80.3	90.5
1988	50.1	76.8	153.3	46.2	80.4	92.1
1989	50.6	78.1	154.3	47.7	79.7	94.3
1990	51.7	77.8	150.4	50.1	79.7	96.8
1991	53.1	76.5	144.1	52.8	81.2	99.6
1992	55.1	79.0	143.3	55.6	83.3	100.9
1993	56.5	82.1	145.3	56.3	82.3	99.7
1994	58.5	87.0	148.7	57.2	81.9	97.8
1995	61.2	91.5	149.7	58.3	81.5	95.3
1996	63.4	94.7	149.4	60.0	81.7	94.8
1997	66.8	101.6	152.0	62.1	82.8	93.0
1998	70.5	106.9	151.7	65.2	85.7	92.5
1999	73.9	111.3	150.6	68.2	87.7	92.2
2000	77.1	114.7	148.7	73.3	91.3	95.0
2001	78.6	109.2	139.0	75.5	91.5	96.1
2002	84.2	108.8	129.2	78.0	93.0	92.6
2003	89.5	109.9	122.9	82.2	95.8	91.8
2004	91.5	111.9	122.2	85.2	96.7	93.1
2005	95.9	115.9	120.8	88.4	97.1	92.1
2006	96.8	117.8	121.7	90.6	96.3	93.6
2007	100.5	120.3	119.7	94.1	97.4	93.6
2008	99.9	114.8	114.9	96.7	96.3	96.7
2009	100.0	100.0	100.0	100.0	100.0	100.0
2010	106.3	106.3	99.9	102.4	100.7	96.3
2011	107.3	109.5	102.1	103.8	98.9	96.7
2012	109.2	114.1	104.4	105.7	98.7	96.8
2010						
1st quarter	104.6	103.4	98.8	100.6	99.3	96.2
2nd quarter	106.6	106.2	99.7	102.3	101.0	96.0
3rd quarter	106.8	107.5	100.6	102.7	101.1	96.2
4th quarter	107.2	107.9	100.6	103.9	101.5	96.9
2011						
1st quarter	107.4	108.7	101.2	104.2	100.7	97.1
2nd quarter	106.4	108.5	102.0	103.6	99.0	97.4
3rd quarter	107.7	109.8	101.9	104.2	98.8	96.7
4th quarter	107.8	111.2	103.1	102.9	97.3	95.5
2012						
1st quarter	108.9	113.4	104.1	105.5	99.1	96.9
2nd quarter	109.2	114.0	104.4	105.7	99.1	96.8
3rd quarter	109.1	114.0	104.5	105.3	98.2	96.5
4th quarter	109.7	114.8	104.6	106.3	98.6	96.9

. . . = Not available.

Table 9-3B. Productivity and Related Data: Historical

(2009 = 100, seasonally adjusted.)

Year and quarter	Business sector								Nonfarm business sector							
	Output per hour of all persons	Output	Hours of all persons	Compensation per hour	Real compensation per hour	Unit labor costs	Unit nonlabor payments	Implicit price deflator	Output per hour of all persons	Output	Hours of all persons	Compensation per hour	Real compensation per hour	Unit labor costs	Unit nonlabor payments	Implicit price deflator
1947	21.3	12.2	57.2	3.8	33.7	18.0	13.0	15.9	24.7	12.0	48.5	4.1	36.1	16.6	12.3	14.8
1948	22.3	12.8	57.6	4.2	33.8	18.7	14.4	16.9	25.3	12.5	49.3	4.5	36.3	17.6	13.3	15.8
1949	22.8	12.7	55.7	4.2	34.7	18.6	14.2	16.7	26.1	12.4	47.4	4.6	37.8	17.6	13.7	16.0
1947																
1st quarter	21.3	12.1	56.9	3.7	33.3	17.4	12.8	15.4	24.4	11.8	48.3	4.0	35.7	16.2	11.8	14.4
2nd quarter	21.4	12.2	56.8	3.8	33.8	17.8	12.7	15.6	25.0	12.1	48.3	4.0	36.0	16.2	12.3	14.6
3rd quarter	21.2	12.1	57.2	3.9	33.6	18.2	13.1	16.0	24.2	11.7	48.5	4.2	36.2	17.2	12.5	15.2
4th quarter	21.5	12.4	57.7	4.0	33.8	18.6	13.5	16.5	25.2	12.4	49.0	4.3	36.1	16.9	12.7	15.2
1948																
1st quarter	22.0	12.6	57.4	4.1	33.6	18.5	14.1	16.6	25.3	12.5	49.3	4.4	36.2	17.2	12.9	15.4
2nd quarter	22.4	12.9	57.4	4.1	33.4	18.3	14.6	16.7	25.3	12.4	49.2	4.4	36.1	17.5	13.2	15.7
3rd quarter	22.3	12.9	57.9	4.2	33.8	18.9	14.5	17.1	25.3	12.5	49.6	4.5	36.2	17.8	13.4	16.0
4th quarter	22.4	12.9	57.6	4.3	34.8	19.2	14.2	17.1	25.4	12.5	49.1	4.6	36.9	18.0	13.8	16.2
1949																
1st quarter	22.3	12.7	56.8	4.2	34.4	18.9	14.3	16.9	25.6	12.4	48.3	4.6	37.5	17.9	13.6	16.1
2nd quarter	22.4	12.6	56.2	4.2	34.2	18.6	14.1	16.7	25.9	12.3	47.5	4.6	37.6	17.7	13.5	16.0
3rd quarter	23.1	12.8	55.3	4.2	34.9	18.3	14.3	16.6	26.5	12.5	47.0	4.6	38.0	17.4	13.9	15.9
4th quarter	23.2	12.6	54.6	4.3	35.3	18.4	14.0	16.6	26.4	12.4	46.8	4.6	38.0	17.4	13.7	15.9
1950																
1st quarter	24.2	13.3	54.8	4.4	36.7	18.3	14.2	16.6	27.3	12.9	47.2	4.7	39.1	17.3	14.0	15.9
2nd quarter	24.5	13.7	56.0	4.5	36.8	18.3	14.4	16.6	27.6	13.4	48.3	4.8	39.6	17.4	14.0	16.0
3rd quarter	24.9	14.3	57.4	4.6	36.8	18.3	15.2	17.0	28.2	14.1	49.9	4.9	39.7	17.4	14.4	16.2
4th quarter	25.0	14.4	57.8	4.6	36.7	18.6	15.8	17.4	28.3	14.2	50.3	5.0	39.9	17.8	14.7	16.5
1951																
1st quarter	25.0	14.6	58.4	4.8	36.5	19.2	16.4	18.0	28.3	14.5	51.2	5.2	39.2	18.2	15.2	16.9
2nd quarter	25.1	14.7	58.7	4.9	37.2	19.7	16.2	18.2	28.2	14.6	51.6	5.3	39.7	18.7	15.1	17.2
3rd quarter	25.8	15.0	58.0	5.0	37.8	19.4	16.5	18.2	28.9	14.7	51.1	5.3	40.2	18.4	15.6	17.3
4th quarter	25.7	15.0	58.2	5.1	37.7	19.7	16.6	18.4	28.9	14.8	51.1	5.4	40.4	18.8	15.5	17.4
1952																
1st quarter	25.8	15.1	58.5	5.1	37.8	19.8	16.3	18.3	29.1	14.9	51.4	5.5	40.6	18.9	15.4	17.4
2nd quarter	26.1	15.1	57.9	5.2	38.5	20.0	16.0	18.3	29.0	14.9	51.2	5.5	40.8	19.0	15.2	17.4
3rd quarter	26.1	15.2	58.0	5.3	38.9	20.3	16.1	18.5	28.9	14.9	51.6	5.6	41.0	19.3	15.2	17.6
4th quarter	26.5	15.8	59.5	5.4	39.7	20.4	16.0	18.5	29.5	15.6	53.0	5.7	42.0	19.4	15.4	17.7
1953																
1st quarter	27.0	16.1	59.7	5.5	40.5	20.5	15.9	18.5	29.7	15.9	53.5	5.8	42.6	19.5	15.4	17.8
2nd quarter	27.2	16.2	59.7	5.6	40.8	20.5	15.8	18.5	29.8	16.0	53.6	5.9	43.0	19.7	15.4	17.9
3rd quarter	27.2	16.1	59.1	5.6	41.2	20.8	15.6	18.6	30.0	15.9	53.1	5.9	43.2	19.8	15.4	17.9
4th quarter	27.1	15.8	58.2	5.6	41.1	20.8	15.6	18.6	29.9	15.6	52.2	6.0	43.6	20.1	15.0	18.0
1954																
1st quarter	27.1	15.7	57.8	5.7	41.3	21.0	15.6	18.7	29.9	15.4	51.5	6.0	43.9	20.2	15.0	18.0
2nd quarter	27.5	15.7	57.0	5.8	41.9	21.0	15.4	18.7	30.1	15.4	51.1	6.0	44.0	20.1	15.2	18.1
3rd quarter	27.9	15.9	56.8	5.8	42.1	20.7	15.8	18.7	30.7	15.6	50.9	6.1	44.4	19.9	15.5	18.0
4th quarter	28.4	16.2	57.2	5.9	42.9	20.7	15.9	18.7	31.0	16.0	51.6	6.2	45.0	19.8	15.7	18.1
1955																
1st quarter	28.8	16.8	58.2	5.8	42.6	20.3	16.7	18.8	31.6	16.6	52.4	6.2	45.3	19.6	16.2	18.2
2nd quarter	29.0	17.1	58.9	5.9	43.2	20.4	16.6	18.8	31.7	16.8	53.1	6.2	45.7	19.7	16.2	18.3
3rd quarter	29.0	17.3	59.8	5.9	43.4	20.5	16.8	18.9	31.8	17.1	53.6	6.4	46.5	20.0	16.3	18.4
4th quarter	28.8	17.4	60.4	6.0	43.6	20.8	16.8	19.1	31.7	17.2	54.3	6.4	46.8	20.2	16.4	18.6
1956																
1st quarter	28.7	17.3	60.3	6.1	44.8	21.4	16.4	19.3	31.4	17.1	54.6	6.5	47.5	20.8	16.0	18.8
2nd quarter	28.9	17.4	60.4	6.3	45.4	21.7	16.2	19.4	31.5	17.2	54.7	6.6	48.1	21.1	15.9	18.9
3rd quarter	28.9	17.4	60.2	6.3	45.4	21.9	16.5	19.7	31.5	17.2	54.5	6.7	48.3	21.4	16.0	19.1
4th quarter	29.5	17.7	60.0	6.5	46.0	22.0	16.6	19.7	31.8	17.5	54.8	6.9	48.7	21.5	16.1	19.3
1957																
1st quarter	29.7	17.8	60.0	6.6	46.6	22.3	16.9	20.0	32.2	17.7	54.9	7.0	49.0	21.6	16.5	19.5
2nd quarter	29.7	17.7	59.7	6.7	46.6	22.5	16.9	20.1	32.1	17.6	54.8	7.0	49.1	21.9	16.4	19.6
3rd quarter	30.0	17.9	59.6	6.7	46.6	22.5	17.2	20.3	32.5	17.7	54.5	7.1	49.3	21.9	16.6	19.7
4th quarter	30.3	17.6	58.2	6.9	47.2	22.6	16.9	20.2	32.6	17.4	53.4	7.2	49.7	22.1	16.5	19.8
1958																
1st quarter	30.1	17.0	56.7	6.9	47.0	23.0	16.9	20.4	32.2	16.8	52.2	7.2	49.2	22.4	16.2	19.8
2nd quarter	30.5	17.1	56.2	6.9	46.8	22.7	17.3	20.4	32.8	16.9	51.4	7.3	49.3	22.2	16.6	19.8
3rd quarter	31.1	17.6	56.6	7.1	48.1	22.9	17.3	20.6	33.4	17.4	52.0	7.5	50.4	22.3	16.7	19.9
4th quarter	31.4	18.1	57.4	7.1	48.2	22.7	17.8	20.7	34.0	18.0	52.8	7.5	50.6	22.0	17.3	20.0
1959																
1st quarter	31.7	18.5	58.3	7.2	48.8	22.8	17.7	20.7	34.0	18.3	53.8	7.6	51.0	22.2	17.2	20.1
2nd quarter	31.8	19.0	59.7	7.2	48.7	22.7	17.9	20.7	34.4	18.9	54.8	7.6	51.3	22.1	17.5	20.2
3rd quarter	32.0	18.9	59.2	7.3	49.1	22.9	17.8	20.8	34.4	18.8	54.7	7.7	51.4	22.3	17.4	20.3
4th quarter	32.0	18.9	59.1	7.4	49.4	23.2	17.6	20.8	34.3	18.8	54.7	7.7	51.5	22.6	17.3	20.4
1960																
1st quarter	32.9	19.4	58.9	7.6	50.7	23.1	17.8	20.9	35.1	19.3	55.0	7.9	52.6	22.5	17.4	20.4
2nd quarter	32.3	19.2	59.5	7.6	50.2	23.5	17.4	21.0	34.6	19.1	55.1	8.0	52.6	23.0	16.9	20.4
3rd quarter	32.4	19.2	59.4	7.6	50.1	23.4	17.6	21.0	34.7	19.0	54.8	8.0	52.9	23.0	17.0	20.5
4th quarter	32.1	18.9	58.8	7.7	50.3	23.8	17.2	21.0	34.3	18.6	54.3	8.0	52.8	23.4	16.6	20.6

Table 9-3B. Productivity and Related Data: Historical—*Continued*

(2009 = 100, seasonally adjusted.)

Year and quarter	Business sector								Nonfarm business sector							
	Output per hour of all persons	Output	Hours of all persons	Compensation per hour	Real compensation per hour	Unit labor costs	Unit nonlabor payments	Implicit price deflator	Output per hour of all persons	Output	Hours of all persons	Compensation per hour	Real compensation per hour	Unit labor costs	Unit nonlabor payments	Implicit price deflator
1961																
1st quarter	32.5	19.0	58.4	7.7	50.6	23.8	17.3	21.1	34.7	18.8	54.0	8.1	53.2	23.3	16.8	20.6
2nd quarter	33.6	19.4	57.8	7.9	51.8	23.5	17.8	21.1	35.7	19.2	53.9	8.2	53.9	23.0	17.3	20.6
3rd quarter	34.0	19.8	58.2	8.0	51.9	23.4	18.0	21.1	36.2	19.6	54.2	8.3	54.1	22.9	17.5	20.6
4th quarter	34.3	20.2	58.7	8.0	52.5	23.4	18.1	21.2	36.6	20.1	54.9	8.3	54.4	22.8	17.6	20.7
1962																
1st quarter	34.7	20.6	59.4	8.1	52.8	23.4	18.4	21.3	37.2	20.5	55.1	8.5	55.1	22.8	17.9	20.8
2nd quarter	34.9	20.8	59.7	8.2	53.2	23.6	18.2	21.3	37.1	20.7	55.7	8.5	55.2	23.0	17.8	20.8
3rd quarter	35.4	21.0	59.4	8.3	53.5	23.4	18.5	21.4	37.6	20.9	55.6	8.6	55.5	22.9	18.0	20.9
4th quarter	35.7	21.1	58.9	8.4	54.0	23.5	18.4	21.3	37.9	21.0	55.3	8.7	55.8	22.9	18.0	20.8
1963																
1st quarter	35.9	21.3	59.4	8.4	54.1	23.5	18.5	21.4	38.0	21.1	55.6	8.8	56.2	23.0	18.0	20.9
2nd quarter	36.2	21.6	59.8	8.5	54.3	23.4	18.6	21.4	38.4	21.5	56.0	8.8	56.4	22.9	18.2	21.0
3rd quarter	37.0	22.1	59.7	8.6	54.7	23.3	18.9	21.4	39.2	22.0	56.1	8.9	56.6	22.7	18.5	20.9
4th quarter	37.0	22.2	60.1	8.7	55.1	23.4	19.0	21.6	39.2	22.2	56.5	9.0	57.1	22.9	18.5	21.1
1964																
1st quarter	37.5	22.8	60.8	8.7	55.3	23.3	19.3	21.6	39.6	22.8	57.6	9.0	56.8	22.7	18.9	21.1
2nd quarter	37.6	23.1	61.3	8.8	55.6	23.4	19.2	21.7	39.9	23.1	57.8	9.1	57.4	22.8	19.0	21.2
3rd quarter	38.0	23.4	61.7	8.9	56.2	23.5	19.3	21.7	40.2	23.4	58.2	9.2	58.0	22.9	19.0	21.3
4th quarter	37.8	23.5	62.1	9.0	56.4	23.8	19.1	21.8	39.8	23.4	58.8	9.3	58.2	23.3	18.7	21.4
1965																
1st quarter	38.5	24.2	62.8	9.1	56.8	23.6	19.6	21.9	40.4	24.1	59.7	9.3	58.2	23.1	19.2	21.4
2nd quarter	38.5	24.5	63.6	9.1	56.7	23.7	19.7	22.0	40.6	24.5	60.3	9.4	58.2	23.1	19.2	21.5
3rd quarter	39.4	25.0	63.5	9.2	57.2	23.4	20.1	22.1	41.4	25.0	60.4	9.5	58.7	22.9	19.7	21.6
4th quarter	40.0	25.7	64.2	9.4	57.6	23.4	20.5	22.2	42.1	25.7	61.0	9.6	59.2	22.8	20.0	21.6
1966																
1st quarter	40.7	26.4	64.8	9.6	58.4	23.5	20.6	22.3	42.7	26.4	61.9	9.8	59.7	22.9	20.0	21.7
2nd quarter	40.5	26.5	65.3	9.7	58.9	24.0	20.3	22.5	42.4	26.5	62.5	9.9	60.1	23.4	19.9	21.9
3rd quarter	40.6	26.6	65.4	9.9	59.4	24.4	20.3	22.7	42.5	26.7	62.8	10.1	60.4	23.7	19.8	22.1
4th quarter	41.0	26.7	65.3	10.1	59.9	24.6	20.6	22.9	42.8	26.8	62.6	10.2	60.8	23.9	20.2	22.3
1967																
1st quarter	41.3	27.0	65.2	10.1	60.2	24.6	20.7	23.0	43.2	27.0	62.5	10.4	61.4	24.0	20.3	22.5
2nd quarter	41.7	26.9	64.6	10.3	61.0	24.8	20.6	23.0	43.3	26.9	62.2	10.5	62.1	24.3	20.2	22.6
3rd quarter	41.7	27.1	65.0	10.4	61.0	25.0	20.8	23.3	43.5	27.1	62.4	10.7	62.3	24.5	20.4	22.8
4th quarter	41.9	27.3	65.3	10.6	61.1	25.2	21.0	23.5	43.7	27.4	62.6	10.8	62.4	24.7	20.5	23.0
1968																
1st quarter	42.8	27.9	65.3	10.9	62.3	25.4	21.4	23.7	44.6	28.0	62.8	11.1	63.5	24.9	21.0	23.2
2nd quarter	43.2	28.5	65.8	11.1	62.7	25.6	21.7	24.0	45.1	28.6	63.4	11.3	63.9	25.0	21.3	23.5
3rd quarter	43.3	28.6	66.2	11.3	63.0	26.1	21.5	24.2	45.1	28.7	63.8	11.5	64.1	25.4	21.1	23.6
4th quarter	43.2	28.8	66.6	11.5	63.5	26.6	21.5	24.5	45.0	28.9	64.2	11.7	64.6	26.0	21.1	24.0
1969																
1st quarter	43.3	29.3	67.5	11.6	63.1	26.7	22.1	24.8	45.3	29.4	64.8	11.8	64.6	26.1	21.6	24.3
2nd quarter	43.3	29.3	67.7	11.9	63.7	27.4	21.9	25.1	45.0	29.4	65.4	12.0	64.7	26.8	21.4	24.5
3rd quarter	43.4	29.5	67.9	12.1	64.1	27.9	21.8	25.3	45.0	29.6	65.7	12.3	64.9	27.2	21.3	24.8
4th quarter	43.3	29.3	67.6	12.4	64.5	28.5	21.6	25.6	44.8	29.3	65.5	12.5	65.2	27.9	21.0	25.0
1970																
1st quarter	43.5	29.2	67.2	12.6	64.7	29.0	21.6	25.9	44.9	29.3	65.3	12.7	65.3	28.3	21.0	25.3
2nd quarter	44.0	29.3	66.5	12.8	64.6	29.0	22.3	26.2	45.6	29.4	64.4	12.9	65.4	28.3	21.9	25.7
3rd quarter	44.8	29.6	66.1	13.0	65.1	29.0	22.7	26.4	46.3	29.7	64.1	13.1	65.8	28.4	22.2	25.8
4th quarter	44.5	29.1	65.5	13.1	64.9	29.5	22.8	26.7	45.9	29.2	63.6	13.3	65.5	28.9	22.3	26.2
1971																
1st quarter	45.8	30.1	65.8	13.4	65.6	29.2	23.8	27.0	47.2	30.2	63.9	13.5	66.3	28.7	23.3	26.4
2nd quarter	45.8	30.3	66.2	13.5	65.7	29.5	24.2	27.3	47.4	30.4	64.1	13.7	66.7	29.0	23.6	26.8
3rd quarter	46.4	30.6	66.0	13.8	66.2	29.7	24.5	27.5	47.8	30.6	64.1	13.9	66.9	29.1	24.0	27.0
4th quarter	46.0	30.7	66.7	13.9	66.2	30.2	24.3	27.7	47.4	30.7	64.8	14.0	66.9	29.6	23.7	27.1
1972																
1st quarter	46.4	31.4	67.6	14.2	67.3	30.6	24.4	28.0	48.1	31.5	65.6	14.4	68.2	29.9	24.0	27.4
2nd quarter	47.6	32.3	67.9	14.4	67.6	30.2	25.3	28.2	49.1	32.4	66.0	14.6	68.5	29.7	24.6	27.6
3rd quarter	47.7	32.6	68.4	14.5	67.8	30.5	25.6	28.4	49.3	32.8	66.4	14.8	68.9	29.9	24.7	27.7
4th quarter	48.2	33.3	69.0	14.8	68.5	30.8	25.9	28.7	49.8	33.4	67.1	15.0	69.5	30.2	24.6	27.9
1973																
1st quarter	49.1	34.3	70.0	15.3	69.4	31.1	26.2	29.0	50.9	34.6	68.1	15.4	70.2	30.3	24.9	28.1
2nd quarter	49.2	34.8	70.7	15.5	68.9	31.4	26.7	29.5	50.9	35.0	68.8	15.6	69.7	30.7	25.1	28.4
3rd quarter	48.6	34.5	71.1	15.8	68.8	32.5	26.8	30.1	50.4	34.9	69.3	15.9	69.5	31.6	24.8	28.7
4th quarter	48.7	34.9	71.5	16.1	68.4	32.9	27.6	30.7	50.1	34.9	69.6	16.2	69.2	32.4	25.2	29.4
1974																
1st quarter	48.1	34.4	71.5	16.3	67.6	34.0	27.7	31.4	50.0	34.7	69.3	16.6	68.7	33.2	25.7	30.1
2nd quarter	48.2	34.4	71.4	16.9	67.9	34.9	28.3	32.2	49.9	34.7	69.5	17.0	68.7	34.2	27.0	31.2
3rd quarter	47.8	33.9	71.0	17.4	68.2	36.4	28.8	33.2	49.3	34.2	69.3	17.6	68.8	35.6	27.3	32.2
4th quarter	48.2	33.7	69.9	17.8	67.8	37.0	30.4	34.2	49.8	33.9	68.1	18.0	68.6	36.2	28.8	33.1
1975																
1st quarter	48.9	33.1	67.7	18.4	68.6	37.7	31.4	35.1	50.2	33.1	66.0	18.6	69.2	37.0	30.2	34.2
2nd quarter	49.7	33.4	67.2	18.8	69.2	37.9	32.4	35.6	51.0	33.3	65.4	19.0	69.8	37.2	31.2	34.7
3rd quarter	50.2	34.0	67.8	19.1	68.7	38.0	33.7	36.2	51.6	34.0	66.0	19.3	69.6	37.5	32.2	35.3
4th quarter	50.3	34.6	68.8	19.4	68.8	38.6	34.2	36.8	51.6	34.6	67.1	19.6	69.5	38.0	32.6	35.8

Table 9-3B. Productivity and Related Data: Historical—*Continued*

(2009 = 100, seasonally adjusted.)

Year and quarter	Business sector								Nonfarm business sector							
	Output per hour of all persons	Output	Hours of all persons	Compen- sation per hour	Real compen- sation per hour	Unit labor costs	Unit nonlabor pay- ments	Implicit price deflator	Output per hour of all persons	Output	Hours of all persons	Compen- sation per hour	Real compen- sation per hour	Unit labor costs	Unit nonlabor pay- ments	Implicit price deflator
1976																
1st quarter	51.0	35.6	69.8	19.9	69.5	38.9	34.6	37.1	52.4	35.7	68.2	20.0	70.0	38.2	33.4	36.2
2nd quarter	51.4	36.0	70.0	20.2	70.1	39.4	34.9	37.5	52.9	36.1	68.2	20.4	70.7	38.5	33.9	36.6
3rd quarter	51.4	36.1	70.3	20.6	70.3	40.1	35.1	38.0	53.0	36.3	68.5	20.8	71.1	39.3	34.1	37.1
4th quarter	51.8	36.5	70.5	21.1	71.0	40.8	35.7	38.6	53.2	36.6	68.9	21.3	71.5	40.0	34.7	37.8
1977																
1st quarter	52.1	37.0	71.2	21.5	71.0	41.3	36.4	39.2	53.5	37.2	69.6	21.7	71.6	40.5	35.3	38.3
2nd quarter	52.2	37.9	72.8	21.8	71.0	41.9	36.8	39.8	53.7	38.1	70.9	22.1	71.8	41.1	35.9	39.0
3rd quarter	52.8	38.7	73.3	22.3	71.4	42.2	37.4	40.2	54.2	38.9	71.7	22.5	72.2	41.5	36.6	39.5
4th quarter	52.2	38.7	74.1	22.7	71.6	43.4	37.7	41.0	53.5	38.8	72.4	22.9	72.4	42.8	36.5	40.2
1978																
1st quarter	52.0	38.7	74.4	23.4	72.8	45.0	37.3	41.8	53.6	39.0	72.7	23.7	73.7	44.2	36.0	40.8
2nd quarter	53.1	40.6	76.6	23.7	72.0	44.6	39.5	42.5	54.6	40.9	74.9	23.9	72.9	43.8	38.0	41.4
3rd quarter	53.2	41.0	77.2	24.0	71.8	45.2	40.2	43.1	54.6	41.2	75.5	24.3	72.7	44.5	38.8	42.1
4th quarter	53.4	41.6	78.0	24.6	72.1	46.1	41.1	44.0	55.0	42.0	76.4	24.9	72.9	45.3	39.7	43.0
1979																
1st quarter	53.1	41.7	78.6	25.4	72.7	47.8	40.7	44.9	54.5	41.9	77.0	25.6	73.4	47.0	39.0	43.7
2nd quarter	53.0	41.7	78.8	25.9	72.4	49.0	42.0	46.1	54.3	42.0	77.3	26.2	73.1	48.2	40.4	45.0
3rd quarter	53.0	42.1	79.5	26.5	72.2	50.1	42.8	47.0	54.3	42.3	77.9	26.8	72.9	49.4	41.1	45.9
4th quarter	52.9	42.1	79.7	27.2	72.1	51.4	43.0	47.9	54.2	42.3	78.1	27.5	72.9	50.7	41.4	46.8
1980																
1st quarter	53.2	42.2	79.4	28.0	72.0	52.7	43.8	48.9	54.5	42.4	77.9	28.3	72.7	51.9	42.6	48.0
2nd quarter	52.6	41.0	78.0	28.7	72.1	54.6	43.6	50.0	53.9	41.2	76.5	29.0	72.8	53.8	43.1	49.4
3rd quarter	52.6	40.9	77.7	29.4	72.1	55.9	44.6	51.1	54.1	41.2	76.2	29.7	72.8	55.0	43.4	50.1
4th quarter	53.2	41.9	78.7	30.2	72.2	56.7	46.5	52.4	54.7	42.2	77.1	30.6	73.1	55.9	44.7	51.2
1981																
1st quarter	54.3	43.0	79.1	31.0	72.0	57.0	49.3	53.8	55.6	43.1	77.5	31.4	73.0	56.4	47.8	52.8
2nd quarter	53.8	42.5	79.0	31.5	72.1	58.5	49.6	54.8	54.9	42.6	77.6	31.9	72.9	58.1	48.0	53.9
3rd quarter	54.5	43.1	79.0	32.2	72.2	59.0	51.3	55.8	55.4	42.9	77.5	32.6	73.0	58.9	49.6	55.0
4th quarter	53.8	42.4	78.8	32.7	72.0	60.8	51.1	56.7	54.7	42.3	77.2	33.1	72.9	60.5	49.8	56.0
1982																
1st quarter	53.4	41.4	77.5	33.6	73.0	62.8	50.0	57.5	54.3	41.3	76.0	33.9	73.8	62.5	48.9	56.8
2nd quarter	53.6	41.6	77.7	33.9	73.0	63.2	51.0	58.1	54.4	41.5	76.3	34.2	73.7	62.9	50.0	57.5
3rd quarter	53.6	41.4	77.2	34.4	72.8	64.1	51.7	58.9	54.5	41.3	75.7	34.8	73.6	63.8	50.5	58.2
4th quarter	54.1	41.4	76.5	34.9	73.0	64.4	52.5	59.4	55.0	41.3	75.1	35.3	73.8	64.1	51.5	58.8
1983																
1st quarter	54.7	42.0	76.9	35.2	73.3	64.4	53.5	59.8	55.8	42.1	75.5	35.7	74.2	63.9	52.3	59.1
2nd quarter	55.7	43.2	77.7	35.6	73.2	63.9	54.9	60.2	57.1	43.6	76.3	36.0	74.1	63.1	54.0	59.3
3rd quarter	55.9	44.3	79.2	35.8	72.8	64.0	56.3	60.8	57.5	44.7	77.8	36.2	73.8	63.0	55.8	60.0
4th quarter	56.4	45.4	80.5	36.2	73.1	64.3	56.7	61.1	57.7	45.8	79.3	36.6	73.9	63.4	56.1	60.4
1984																
1st quarter	56.7	46.5	82.1	36.7	73.0	64.7	57.3	61.6	57.8	46.8	80.8	37.1	73.8	64.1	55.9	60.7
2nd quarter	57.2	47.5	83.1	37.0	73.0	64.8	58.3	62.0	58.2	47.7	81.9	37.4	73.8	64.3	56.9	61.2
3rd quarter	57.5	48.0	83.5	37.6	73.5	65.3	58.4	62.5	58.4	48.1	82.3	38.0	74.3	64.9	57.2	61.7
4th quarter	57.6	48.3	84.0	37.9	73.5	65.8	58.7	62.8	58.5	48.4	82.8	38.3	74.2	65.4	57.3	62.0
1985																
1st quarter	57.8	48.9	84.6	38.4	73.8	66.4	59.5	63.5	58.6	48.9	83.5	38.8	74.5	66.2	58.2	62.9
2nd quarter	58.0	49.4	85.1	38.8	73.9	66.8	59.8	63.9	58.8	49.4	84.0	39.1	74.6	66.6	58.7	63.3
3rd quarter	59.0	50.2	85.2	39.4	74.7	66.8	60.4	64.1	59.5	50.2	84.3	39.7	75.2	66.7	59.6	63.8
4th quarter	59.2	50.6	85.5	40.2	75.4	67.9	59.6	64.4	59.8	50.6	84.7	40.5	75.9	67.7	58.6	63.9
1986																
1st quarter	59.8	51.1	85.5	40.7	76.0	68.1	59.8	64.6	60.5	51.1	84.5	41.1	76.7	67.9	59.1	64.2
2nd quarter	60.1	51.3	85.3	41.1	77.2	68.4	59.7	64.8	61.0	51.4	84.3	41.5	77.9	68.1	58.9	64.3
3rd quarter	60.5	51.9	85.8	41.6	77.7	68.8	59.4	64.9	61.3	51.9	84.8	42.0	78.4	68.6	58.4	64.3
4th quarter	60.3	52.1	86.4	42.2	78.2	69.9	58.5	65.1	61.1	52.2	85.4	42.6	78.9	69.7	57.5	64.6
1987																
1st quarter	60.0	52.5	87.4	42.4	77.7	70.6	58.5	65.5	60.8	52.6	86.4	42.8	78.4	70.4	57.5	65.0
2nd quarter	60.4	53.1	88.0	42.7	77.4	70.6	59.3	65.9	61.2	53.2	86.9	43.1	78.2	70.4	58.4	65.4
3rd quarter	60.5	53.6	88.5	43.1	77.5	71.3	59.6	66.4	61.3	53.6	87.5	43.6	78.3	71.1	58.6	65.9
4th quarter	61.0	54.5	89.4	43.7	77.8	71.6	59.9	66.7	61.8	54.6	88.4	44.1	78.5	71.3	58.9	66.2
1988																
1st quarter	61.2	54.8	89.5	44.5	78.7	72.7	59.8	67.3	62.0	54.9	88.5	44.9	79.4	72.3	58.7	66.6
2nd quarter	61.3	55.6	90.7	45.0	78.8	73.4	60.0	68.2	62.2	55.8	89.8	45.4	79.5	73.0	59.1	67.2
3rd quarter	61.5	55.9	90.9	45.6	79.0	74.2	61.0	68.7	62.4	56.1	90.0	45.9	79.6	73.6	60.0	68.0
4th quarter	61.6	56.6	91.9	45.9	78.8	74.5	61.8	69.2	62.6	57.0	91.0	46.3	79.4	73.9	61.2	68.6
1989																
1st quarter	61.7	57.3	92.8	46.1	78.3	74.6	63.2	69.9	62.5	57.5	91.9	46.4	78.9	74.3	61.9	69.1
2nd quarter	62.1	57.7	93.0	46.3	77.5	74.6	65.0	70.6	62.7	57.9	92.3	46.6	78.0	74.3	63.9	69.9
3rd quarter	62.3	58.2	93.4	46.7	77.6	75.0	65.5	71.0	63.1	58.3	92.5	47.0	78.1	74.5	64.6	70.4
4th quarter	62.4	58.2	93.4	47.4	78.0	75.9	65.2	71.4	63.1	58.4	92.5	47.7	78.5	75.6	64.0	70.8
1990																
1st quarter	63.0	58.9	93.5	48.4	78.5	76.8	65.7	72.2	63.6	59.0	92.7	48.7	78.9	76.4	64.5	71.5
2nd quarter	63.6	59.1	92.9	49.5	79.5	77.8	66.0	72.8	64.2	59.2	92.2	49.7	79.8	77.3	64.9	72.1
3rd quarter	64.0	59.0	92.2	50.2	79.3	78.4	66.3	73.4	64.5	59.1	91.6	50.4	79.6	78.1	65.2	72.7
4th quarter	63.4	58.3	91.9	50.5	78.7	79.7	65.8	73.9	64.0	58.3	91.2	50.8	79.1	79.4	64.9	73.3

Table 9-3B. Productivity and Related Data: Historical—*Continued*

(2009 = 100, seasonally adjusted.)

Year and quarter	Business sector								Nonfarm business sector							
	Output per hour of all persons	Output	Hours of all persons	Compensation per hour	Real compensation per hour	Unit labor costs	Unit nonlabor payments	Implicit price deflator	Output per hour of all persons	Output	Hours of all persons	Compensation per hour	Real compensation per hour	Unit labor costs	Unit nonlabor payments	Implicit price deflator
1991																
1st quarter	63.6	57.8	90.9	50.9	78.8	80.1	66.8	74.5	64.2	57.9	90.2	51.2	79.2	79.8	66.0	71.5
2nd quarter	64.6	58.4	90.4	51.8	79.9	80.2	67.6	74.9	65.2	58.5	89.7	52.1	80.4	79.9	66.7	72.1
3rd quarter	65.0	58.7	90.3	52.4	80.3	80.6	68.2	75.4	65.7	58.8	89.6	52.7	80.8	80.3	67.5	72.7
4th quarter	65.4	59.0	90.1	53.1	80.8	81.1	68.1	75.7	66.0	59.1	89.5	53.4	81.2	80.9	67.3	73.3
1992																
1st quarter	66.8	59.9	89.6	54.4	82.3	81.5	67.9	75.8	67.3	59.9	89.0	54.7	82.8	81.3	66.9	75.3
2nd quarter	67.3	60.6	90.1	54.8	82.4	81.5	68.7	76.1	67.8	60.6	89.4	55.2	83.0	81.4	67.7	75.7
3rd quarter	67.9	61.3	90.3	55.5	82.8	81.7	69.2	76.5	68.4	61.2	89.6	55.8	83.4	81.6	68.2	76.0
4th quarter	68.2	62.0	90.9	55.9	82.8	81.9	70.2	77.0	68.8	62.0	90.2	56.2	83.3	81.7	69.3	76.6
1993																
1st quarter	67.7	62.0	91.5	55.4	81.8	81.9	71.2	77.4	68.3	62.1	90.9	55.7	82.1	81.6	70.7	77.0
2nd quarter	67.4	62.4	92.5	55.9	81.9	83.0	70.9	77.9	67.9	62.5	92.0	56.1	82.2	82.7	70.2	77.5
3rd quarter	67.4	62.7	93.0	56.0	81.6	83.1	71.8	78.4	68.1	62.9	92.5	56.2	81.9	82.6	71.3	77.9
4th quarter	68.0	63.7	93.8	56.5	81.8	83.1	72.6	78.7	68.5	63.8	93.3	56.7	82.1	82.8	71.8	78.2
1994																
1st quarter	68.3	64.5	94.5	56.2	81.1	82.3	74.3	79.0	68.8	64.5	93.6	56.5	81.6	82.0	73.5	78.5
2nd quarter	68.2	65.6	96.1	56.5	81.2	82.9	74.3	79.3	68.8	65.5	95.2	56.9	81.8	82.7	73.5	78.9
3rd quarter	67.8	66.0	97.2	56.5	80.5	83.3	74.6	79.7	68.4	65.9	96.4	56.9	81.1	83.1	74.1	79.4
4th quarter	68.4	66.9	97.8	56.8	80.6	83.0	75.9	80.0	69.1	67.0	96.9	57.2	81.2	82.8	75.4	79.7
1995																
1st quarter	68.1	67.1	98.5	57.0	80.4	83.7	75.7	80.4	68.9	67.3	97.6	57.4	81.0	83.2	75.5	80.0
2nd quarter	68.2	67.3	98.6	57.3	80.3	84.0	76.1	80.7	69.2	67.5	97.6	57.8	80.9	83.5	76.0	80.4
3rd quarter	68.3	68.0	99.6	57.7	80.4	84.5	76.4	81.1	69.2	68.3	98.7	58.1	81.0	84.0	76.0	80.6
4th quarter	68.9	68.7	99.6	58.3	80.9	84.6	76.9	81.4	69.8	68.9	98.8	58.7	81.4	84.1	76.2	80.8
1996																
1st quarter	69.6	69.2	99.5	59.2	81.4	85.0	77.1	81.7	70.4	69.4	98.6	59.6	82.0	84.7	76.1	81.1
2nd quarter	70.5	70.7	100.2	59.8	81.6	84.8	78.3	82.1	71.2	70.8	99.4	60.2	82.2	84.6	77.0	81.4
3rd quarter	70.8	71.5	100.9	60.4	82.0	85.3	78.0	82.2	71.5	71.6	100.2	60.7	82.4	84.9	77.2	81.7
4th quarter	70.9	72.4	102.1	60.7	81.7	85.6	78.5	82.6	71.5	72.6	101.5	61.0	82.1	85.3	77.6	82.1
1997																
1st quarter	70.7	73.0	103.2	61.2	81.9	86.5	78.3	83.1	71.3	73.1	102.5	61.5	82.4	86.3	77.3	82.5
2nd quarter	71.6	74.3	103.8	61.7	82.4	86.1	79.2	83.2	72.2	74.4	103.1	62.0	82.9	85.9	78.6	82.9
3rd quarter	72.3	75.4	104.4	62.4	82.9	86.3	79.5	83.4	72.7	75.5	103.8	62.6	83.3	86.1	79.0	83.1
4th quarter	72.6	76.1	104.7	63.6	84.1	87.5	78.2	83.6	73.0	76.2	104.3	63.7	84.4	87.3	77.8	83.3
1998																
1st quarter	73.0	76.9	105.3	64.7	85.5	88.5	76.9	83.7	73.5	77.1	104.8	64.9	85.7	88.2	76.5	83.3
2nd quarter	73.5	77.7	105.8	65.5	86.3	89.2	76.1	83.7	74.0	78.0	105.3	65.7	86.6	88.8	75.8	83.4
3rd quarter	74.5	78.9	105.9	66.5	87.2	89.3	76.4	83.9	75.0	79.2	105.5	66.8	87.6	89.0	76.0	83.6
4th quarter	75.0	80.5	107.4	66.8	87.3	89.0	76.8	83.9	75.5	80.8	107.0	67.0	87.5	88.7	76.4	83.6
1999																
1st quarter	76.0	81.4	107.2	68.0	88.5	89.5	76.5	84.1	76.4	81.7	107.0	68.1	88.6	89.2	76.1	83.7
2nd quarter	76.2	82.2	108.0	68.2	88.1	89.5	76.6	84.1	76.5	82.4	107.7	68.3	88.2	89.2	76.6	84.0
3rd quarter	76.8	83.4	108.6	68.8	88.1	89.5	77.2	84.4	77.2	83.7	108.5	68.8	88.3	89.2	77.3	84.2
4th quarter	78.0	85.1	109.1	70.1	89.2	89.8	77.4	84.6	78.5	85.4	108.8	70.3	89.4	89.6	77.5	84.6
2000																
1st quarter	77.8	85.3	109.6	72.6	91.6	93.4	73.7	85.1	78.2	85.4	109.2	72.9	91.9	93.2	73.7	85.1
2nd quarter	79.5	87.1	109.6	72.9	91.3	91.8	77.1	85.6	79.8	87.3	109.4	73.1	91.5	91.6	77.0	85.5
3rd quarter	79.5	87.2	109.6	74.4	92.3	93.6	75.7	86.1	79.8	87.3	109.3	74.6	92.5	93.5	75.7	86.1
4th quarter	80.4	87.6	109.0	74.9	92.3	93.2	77.2	86.5	80.6	87.7	108.9	75.0	92.4	93.1	77.1	86.4
2001																
1st quarter	80.1	87.2	108.8	76.8	93.6	95.9	74.6	87.0	80.3	87.3	108.7	76.9	93.7	95.7	74.5	86.8
2nd quarter	81.4	87.6	107.7	77.0	93.3	94.7	77.4	87.5	81.7	87.9	107.6	77.0	93.3	94.3	77.4	87.3
3rd quarter	81.8	87.1	106.5	77.2	93.2	94.3	78.2	87.5	82.1	87.4	106.4	77.1	93.1	93.9	78.1	87.3
4th quarter	82.9	87.4	105.4	77.8	94.0	93.8	78.9	87.6	83.1	87.5	105.2	77.8	94.1	93.6	79.0	87.5
2002																
1st quarter	84.5	88.3	104.5	78.1	94.1	92.5	80.8	87.6	85.0	88.7	104.3	78.2	94.2	92.0	80.9	87.4
2nd quarter	84.8	88.8	104.7	78.8	94.2	93.0	80.6	87.8	85.1	89.0	104.6	78.9	94.3	92.8	81.0	87.8
3rd quarter	85.5	89.2	104.4	79.2	94.2	92.7	81.8	88.1	85.7	89.4	104.2	79.3	94.3	92.5	82.0	88.1
4th quarter	85.3	89.2	104.5	79.4	93.8	93.1	82.2	88.5	85.6	89.3	104.3	79.5	93.9	92.9	82.2	88.4
2003																
1st quarter	86.6	90.1	104.0	79.9	93.5	92.3	83.1	88.4	86.9	90.1	103.8	80.0	93.6	92.1	83.1	88.4
2nd quarter	88.4	91.5	103.4	81.5	95.5	92.2	82.7	88.2	88.4	91.5	103.5	81.4	95.4	92.1	82.5	88.1
3rd quarter	90.3	93.7	103.7	82.6	96.0	91.4	84.3	88.4	90.5	93.8	103.6	82.6	96.1	91.3	84.0	88.2
4th quarter	91.0	94.9	104.3	83.6	96.9	91.9	84.3	88.7	91.4	95.2	104.2	83.7	97.0	91.6	83.7	88.3
2004																
1st quarter	91.2	95.5	104.7	83.6	96.1	91.7	86.4	89.5	91.3	95.5	104.6	83.6	96.1	91.6	85.6	89.1
2nd quarter	91.8	96.2	104.8	85.2	97.2	92.8	86.6	90.2	92.1	96.4	104.7	85.3	97.2	92.5	85.7	89.7
3rd quarter	92.1	97.1	105.5	86.7	98.2	94.1	86.0	90.7	92.3	97.3	105.4	86.7	98.2	93.9	85.5	90.4
4th quarter	92.7	98.0	105.7	87.3	97.8	94.1	87.7	91.4	92.6	98.1	105.9	87.1	97.6	94.0	87.2	91.2
2005																
1st quarter	93.7	99.3	106.0	87.9	98.0	93.8	89.9	92.1	93.7	99.4	106.1	87.8	97.9	93.7	89.6	92.0
2nd quarter	93.4	99.9	106.9	88.1	97.6	94.3	90.6	92.8	93.6	100.0	106.8	88.2	97.7	94.2	90.4	92.6
3rd quarter	94.2	100.8	107.0	89.3	97.4	94.8	92.3	93.7	94.3	100.9	107.0	89.3	97.5	94.7	92.1	93.6
4th quarter	94.3	101.4	107.6	89.9	97.2	95.4	93.2	94.5	94.3	101.5	107.7	89.9	97.2	95.3	93.1	94.4

Table 9-3B. Productivity and Related Data: Historical—*Continued*

(2009 = 100, seasonally adjusted.)

Year and quarter	Business sector								Nonfarm business sector							
	Output per hour of all persons	Output	Hours of all persons	Compensation per hour	Real compensation per hour	Unit labor costs	Unit nonlabor payments	Implicit price deflator	Output per hour of all persons	Output	Hours of all persons	Compensation per hour	Real compensation per hour	Unit labor costs	Unit nonlabor payments	Implicit price deflator
2006																
1st quarter	94.9	102.9	108.5	91.9	98.8	96.9	92.6	95.1	94.8	103.1	108.7	91.8	98.7	96.8	92.6	95.0
2nd quarter	94.8	103.2	108.9	91.8	97.9	96.9	94.4	95.8	94.7	103.2	109.0	91.8	97.9	97.0	94.4	95.9
3rd quarter	94.2	103.1	109.5	91.9	97.1	97.6	95.0	96.5	94.2	103.2	109.6	91.9	97.0	97.6	95.0	96.5
4th quarter	94.7	104.1	109.9	93.5	99.2	98.8	93.9	96.7	94.9	104.3	109.9	93.6	99.2	98.7	93.8	96.6
2007																
1st quarter	94.6	104.1	110.0	95.8	100.6	101.2	93.1	97.8	94.9	104.3	110.0	95.9	100.7	101.1	92.7	97.6
2nd quarter	95.4	105.0	110.1	96.1	99.7	100.7	95.2	98.4	95.5	105.3	110.4	95.9	99.5	100.4	95.0	98.2
3rd quarter	96.5	105.8	109.7	96.4	99.5	100.0	96.9	98.7	96.5	106.2	110.0	96.2	99.2	99.6	96.5	98.3
4th quarter	96.8	106.2	109.6	97.3	99.2	100.5	96.8	99.0	97.0	106.5	109.8	97.2	99.1	100.2	96.3	98.6
2008																
1st quarter	96.1	105.1	109.4	98.2	99.0	102.2	95.1	99.2	96.2	105.3	109.4	98.2	99.0	102.1	94.3	98.8
2nd quarter	97.1	105.6	108.8	98.3	97.9	101.3	97.2	99.6	97.2	105.9	108.9	98.2	97.8	101.1	96.5	99.2
3rd quarter	97.4	104.8	107.6	99.2	97.2	101.9	97.9	100.2	97.5	105.1	107.8	99.1	97.1	101.6	97.4	99.9
4th quarter	96.8	101.7	105.0	100.2	100.5	103.5	95.2	100.0	96.9	101.7	105.0	100.2	100.5	103.4	94.9	99.9
2009																
1st quarter	97.5	99.7	102.3	97.7	98.7	100.2	100.3	100.3	97.6	99.8	102.3	97.7	98.7	100.1	100.5	100.3
2nd quarter	99.4	99.5	100.1	100.1	100.6	100.7	98.8	99.9	99.5	99.5	100.0	100.1	100.6	100.6	98.8	99.9
3rd quarter	101.0	99.8	98.8	100.8	100.5	99.9	99.7	99.8	100.9	99.7	98.8	100.8	100.4	99.9	99.8	99.9
4th quarter	102.2	101.0	98.8	101.4	100.3	99.3	101.2	100.1	102.1	101.0	98.9	101.4	100.2	99.3	100.9	100.0
2010																
1st quarter	102.5	101.4	98.9	100.7	99.3	98.2	103.7	100.5	102.6	101.5	98.9	100.7	99.4	98.2	103.4	100.4
2nd quarter	102.9	102.7	99.8	101.9	100.6	99.0	103.5	100.9	102.9	102.7	99.7	102.0	100.7	99.1	103.2	100.8
3rd quarter	103.6	103.7	100.2	102.5	100.8	98.9	104.6	101.3	103.5	103.7	100.2	102.5	100.9	99.0	104.1	101.2
4th quarter	104.0	104.7	100.7	102.9	100.5	99.0	106.0	101.9	104.1	104.8	100.7	103.1	100.6	99.0	105.3	101.6
2011																
1st quarter	103.1	104.2	101.0	104.5	101.0	101.4	103.7	102.4	103.2	104.2	101.0	104.7	101.2	101.5	102.5	101.9
2nd quarter	103.5	105.2	101.6	104.4	99.7	100.8	106.2	103.0	103.7	105.4	101.7	104.4	99.8	100.7	105.0	102.5
3rd quarter	103.5	105.7	102.1	105.0	99.6	101.5	107.0	103.8	103.7	105.9	102.1	105.2	99.8	101.5	105.5	103.2
4th quarter	104.4	107.3	102.9	103.8	98.1	99.5	110.2	104.0	104.4	107.4	102.8	104.0	98.3	99.6	108.9	103.4
2012																
1st quarter	104.7	108.6	103.7	106.0	99.6	101.3	108.6	104.4	104.8	108.7	103.7	106.3	99.8	101.3	107.4	103.8
2nd quarter	105.0	109.1	103.8	106.5	99.9	101.4	109.7	104.9	105.2	109.2	103.8	106.8	100.1	101.5	108.4	104.4
3rd quarter	105.6	110.0	104.2	106.7	99.5	101.1	111.7	105.5	105.8	110.3	104.2	106.9	99.7	101.1	110.4	105.0
4th quarter	105.1	110.1	104.7	109.4	101.4	104.1	108.3	105.8	105.4	110.5	104.8	109.5	101.5	103.9	107.0	105.2

Section 9c: Returns and Profits by Industry

Figure 9-3. Rates of Return, Nonfinancial Industry Groups, 1997–2010

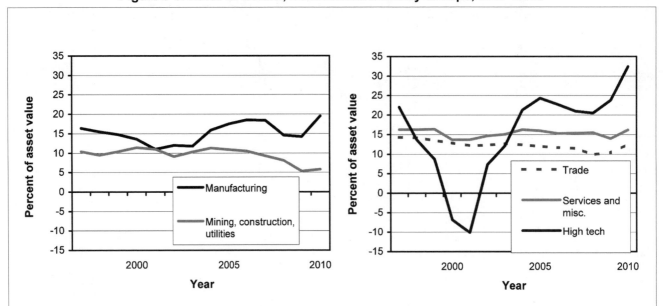

- Corporate profits have commanded an increasing, though cyclically variable, share of national income in recent years. At their low in 2008, economic profits were 10.3 percent of national income, compared with 8.2 percent at the previous cyclical low point in 2001. In 2012, profits were 14.4 percent of national income in a year of 8.1 percent unemployment, compared with a profit share of 13.7 percent in 2006, a year of much stronger economic activity when the unemployment rate was 4.6 percent. (Tables 1-13A and 10-1A)

- Rates of return on physical capital in domestic nonfinancial industry groups are shown in Figure 9-3. The rate of return is the net operating surplus—the sum of corporate profits, net interest, transfer payments, and proprietors' income—as a percentage of the value of the net stock of capital plus inventories. The net operating surplus is a more comprehensive measure of the return to capital than corporate profits. As the figure indicates, rates of return generally declined from 1997 through 2001, rose into the mid-2000s, and declined again as recession set in. By 2010, however—the latest year available—rates of return recovered in most industries and hit spectacular new highs in high-tech. (Table 9-4)

- Comparable rate of return data are not available for financial industries, presumably because of greater difficulty in identifying and measuring the capital base. Aggregate profits at domestic financial industries (leaving out the Federal Reserve System) rose an average 9.2 percent per year from 1999 to 2012, compared with 7.8 percent for domestic nonfinancial industries. (Table 9-5)

Table 9-4. Rates of Return and Related Data for Major Nonfinancial Industry Groups, NAICS Basis

Year	Nonfinancial corporations	Nonfinancial industries					
		Total	Mining, construction, and utilities	Manufacturing	Wholesale and retail trade	Other industries [1]	ICT-producing industries [2]
NET OPERATING SURPLUS BEFORE TAX (Billions of dollars)							
1997	736.3	1 278.1	164.0	320.1	202.9	591.1	71.3
1998	725.7	1 305.2	153.9	313.7	213.2	624.4	47.1
1999	745.1	1 367.5	173.1	311.8	215.2	667.4	32.1
2000	708.2	1 320.1	197.9	298.8	219.4	604.0	-28.2
2001	626.7	1 310.4	204.5	248.7	215.2	642.1	-45.3
2002	647.1	1 395.6	181.6	272.3	221.8	719.9	33.2
2003	699.2	1 492.3	215.9	269.5	237.8	769.1	55.5
2004	877.5	1 756.4	257.0	373.7	248.6	877.1	98.9
2005	1 025.1	1 900.9	279.1	432.9	260.9	928.0	118.3
2006	1 163.7	2 017.5	303.7	482.7	273.5	957.7	115.9
2007	1 137.4	2 109.5	293.7	507.4	285.9	1 022.5	112.2
2008	1 070.8	2 040.3	278.4	422.7	255.2	1 084.1	114.6
2009	964.2	1 849.8	186.0	411.4	263.4	989.0	134.1
2010	1 167.8	2 216.8	201.8	560.0	311.7	1 143.3	179.6
2011	1 260.2	. . .	. . .	. . .	. . .	. . .	. . .
PRODUCED ASSETS, AVERAGE OF YEAR-END VALUES (Billions of dollars)							
1997	7 056.0	8 580.9	1 584.2	1 951.6	1 422.5	3 622.8	323.7
1998	7 341.4	8 968.6	1 613.5	2 028.6	1 498.4	3 828.1	344.0
1999	7 729.9	9 438.4	1 658.6	2 111.9	1 591.1	4 076.8	371.2
2000	8 219.5	10 036.4	1 736.4	2 200.7	1 698.8	4 400.6	413.4
2001	8 648.3	10 574.7	1 859.1	2 253.4	1 760.8	4 701.5	448.0
2002	8 952.1	10 973.8	1 989.1	2 275.2	1 802.9	4 906.7	455.9
2003	9 238.2	11 360.3	2 096.4	2 290.4	1 877.3	5 096.3	453.6
2004	9 746.6	12 019.3	2 267.4	2 350.2	2 007.0	5 394.8	464.1
2005	10 550.8	13 030.7	2 565.9	2 474.8	2 179.7	5 810.3	486.0
2006	11 405.9	14 101.2	2 884.9	2 610.7	2 339.4	6 266.3	510.3
2007	12 155.1	15 048.0	3 161.3	2 762.1	2 477.4	6 647.2	534.1
2008	12 838.6	15 900.0	3 447.9	2 899.1	2 577.9	6 975.2	559.6
2009	12 906.1	16 004.0	3 501.7	2 900.0	2 537.5	7 064.9	564.2
2010	12 807.2	15 913.5	3 493.0	2 875.5	2 503.9	7 041.0	554.1
2011	13 507.5	. . .	. . .	. . .	. . .	. . .	. . .
RATES OF RETURN BEFORE TAX (Percent)							
1997	10.4	14.9	10.4	16.4	14.3	16.3	22.0
1998	9.9	14.6	9.5	15.5	14.2	16.3	13.7
1999	9.6	14.5	10.4	14.8	13.5	16.4	8.7
2000	8.6	13.2	11.4	13.6	12.9	13.7	-6.8
2001	7.2	12.4	11.0	11.0	12.2	13.7	-10.1
2002	7.2	12.7	9.1	12.0	12.3	14.7	7.3
2003	7.6	13.1	10.3	11.8	12.7	15.1	12.2
2004	9.0	14.6	11.3	15.9	12.4	16.3	21.3
2005	9.7	14.6	10.9	17.5	12.0	16.0	24.3
2006	10.2	14.3	10.5	18.5	11.7	15.3	22.7
2007	9.4	14.0	9.3	18.4	11.5	15.4	21.0
2008	8.3	12.8	8.1	14.6	9.9	15.5	20.5
2009	7.5	11.6	5.3	14.2	10.4	14.0	23.8
2010	9.1	13.9	5.8	19.5	12.5	16.2	32.4
2011	9.3	. . .	. . .	. . .	. . .	. . .	. . .
NET OPERATING SURPLUS BEFORE TAX AS A SHARE OF NET VALUE ADDED (Percent)							
1997	18.7	20.2	32.1	28.1	19.7	16.2	22.7
1998	17.4	22.7	29.1	26.6	19.1	21.3	14.1
1999	16.9	22.4	29.9	25.8	18.6	21.1	8.9
2000	15.1	20.4	30.9	23.9	17.9	18.1	-7.9
2001	13.6	20.0	30.5	21.3	17.4	18.4	-14.0
2002	13.9	20.7	27.6	23.1	17.6	19.8	9.1
2003	14.5	21.1	30.3	22.5	18.1	20.1	14.5
2004	16.9	23.1	32.8	28.6	18.0	21.3	22.6
2005	18.4	23.5	32.7	31.2	17.9	21.2	24.8
2006	19.6	23.7	32.5	34.1	17.8	20.7	23.3
2007	18.6	23.6	30.8	34.9	18.0	20.7	21.8
2008	17.5	22.6	28.9	30.7	16.4	21.2	21.9
2009	16.8	21.7	23.5	32.0	17.7	20.0	25.5
2010	19.3	24.5	25.5	38.7	19.9	21.8	30.4
2011	19.8	. . .	. . .	. . .	. . .	. . .	. . .

[1]Consists of agriculture, forestry, fishing and hunting; transportation and warehousing; information; rental and leasing services and lessors of intangible assets; professional, scientific, and technical services; administrative and waste management services; educational services; health care and social assistance; arts, entertainment, and recreation; accommodation and food services; and "other services, except government."
[2]Information-communication-technology (ICT) producing industries consists of computer and electronic products; publishing industries (includes software); information and data processing services; and computer systems design and related services. Computer and electronic products are included in manufacturing; the other ICT-producing industries are included in "other" industries.
. . . = Not available.

Table 9-5. Corporate Profits with Inventory Valuation Adjustment by Industry Group, NAICS Basis

(Billions of dollars, quarterly data are at seasonally adjusted annual rates.)   NIPA Table 6.16D

Year and quarter	Total	Financial Total	Federal Reserve banks	Other financial	Nonfinancial Total	Utilities	Manufacturing Total	Fabricated metal products	Machinery	Computer and electronic products	Electrical equipment, appliances, and components	Motor vehicles, bodies and trailers, and parts	Other durable goods
1999	762.2	640.2	26.7	127.9	485.6	34.4	184.5	16.4	12.7	6.6	10.2	13.8	37.4
2000	730.3	584.1	31.2	118.5	434.4	24.3	175.6	15.6	9.4	20.5	6.9	4.0	25.8
2001	698.7	528.3	28.9	166.1	333.3	22.5	75.1	9.2	2.2	-29.1	1.1	-6.8	14.0
2002	795.1	636.3	23.5	247.2	365.6	11.1	75.1	8.7	3.2	-24.3	-2.1	-3.0	20.6
2003	959.9	793.3	20.1	286.5	486.7	13.5	125.3	8.6	3.2	-6.3	1.5	7.9	17.8
2004	1 215.2	1 010.1	20.0	329.4	660.7	20.5	182.7	12.3	8.5	1.2	-0.2	-5.0	33.8
2005	1 621.2	1 382.1	26.6	383.1	972.4	30.8	277.7	18.2	18.0	15.7	-1.8	0.3	56.8
2006	1 815.7	1 559.6	33.8	381.3	1 144.4	55.1	349.7	18.4	23.2	29.0	10.7	-5.3	68.0
2007	1 708.9	1 355.5	36.0	265.5	1 054.0	49.5	321.9	21.0	25.0	24.7	-1.5	-15.7	65.2
2008	1 345.5	938.8	35.1	60.4	843.4	30.1	240.6	16.5	18.8	26.1	4.4	-39.6	38.1
2009	1 474.8	1 122.0	47.3	315.5	759.2	23.8	171.4	11.7	9.4	26.4	8.9	-54.3	32.3
2010	1 793.8	1 398.6	71.6	333.8	993.3	29.8	284.9	15.2	17.3	46.7	10.2	-10.3	47.2
2011	1 791.3	1 354.8	75.9	308.1	970.7	11.1	303.9	17.9	24.7	34.0	5.2	-4.6	58.4
2012	2 180.0	1 761.1	71.7	405.7	1 283.7	37.1	404.3	24.3	33.5	39.5	10.3	12.1	77.3
2010 1st quarter	1 751.6	1 354.1	71.6	315.5	967.0	44.6	228.4	12.7	12.5	43.8	9.2	-19.7	45.1
2nd quarter	1 762.2	1 367.8	74.0	288.6	1 005.2	14.5	283.9	12.5	15.2	42.3	11.9	-9.3	46.9
3rd quarter	1 861.5	1 476.8	71.4	344.3	1 061.2	35.3	324.3	17.3	20.0	48.8	11.4	-2.0	48.0
4th quarter	1 800.0	1 395.9	69.3	386.6	939.9	24.8	303.0	18.4	21.5	51.7	8.4	-10.3	49.0
2011 1st quarter	1 672.2	1 244.3	72.4	305.4	866.5	3.9	278.1	15.9	20.3	33.1	7.0	-9.2	47.6
2nd quarter	1 782.3	1 354.9	80.0	284.6	990.3	29.7	291.5	16.4	23.3	33.0	4.7	-6.4	52.7
3rd quarter	1 805.4	1 354.6	76.6	272.2	1 005.8	3.2	314.5	18.5	25.4	31.1	4.4	-5.5	64.7
4th quarter	1 905.4	1 465.2	74.7	370.4	1 020.1	7.9	331.7	20.8	29.6	38.9	4.8	2.6	68.6
2012 1st quarter	2 142.5	1 726.7	73.4	389.1	1 264.2	34.5	408.7	24.2	32.4	40.8	11.0	13.1	78.4
2nd quarter	2 169.8	1 740.5	72.6	375.1	1 292.8	39.4	410.5	24.9	34.8	41.7	8.3	13.3	76.9
3rd quarter	2 186.6	1 774.0	67.5	439.8	1 266.8	40.8	387.8	24.5	37.1	38.7	9.5	8.7	74.1
4th quarter	2 221.1	1 803.0	73.3	418.7	1 310.9	33.6	410.1	23.7	29.5	36.6	12.2	13.4	79.8

Domestic industries—Continued / Nonfinancial—Continued

Year and quarter	Nondurable goods Total	Food and beverage and tobacco products	Petroleum and coal products	Chemical products	Other nondurable goods	Wholesale trade	Retail trade	Transportation and warehousing	Information	Other nonfinancial	Rest of the world, net
1999	87.5	31.7	2.4	31.8	21.7	55.6	59.5	7.2	20.8	123.5	122.0
2000	93.3	25.8	25.9	25.1	16.6	59.5	51.3	9.5	-11.9	126.1	146.2
2001	84.5	28.5	27.5	22.0	6.6	51.1	71.3	-0.7	-26.4	140.2	170.4
2002	72.0	26.9	3.8	29.9	11.4	55.8	83.7	-6.0	-3.1	149.0	158.8
2003	92.6	25.9	26.0	32.2	8.5	59.3	90.5	4.8	16.3	177.1	166.6
2004	132.1	26.8	50.1	39.2	16.0	74.7	93.2	12.0	52.7	224.9	205.0
2005	170.5	29.5	79.9	41.2	19.9	96.2	121.7	27.7	91.3	327.2	239.1
2006	205.7	35.0	73.5	70.0	27.1	105.9	132.5	41.2	107.0	353.1	256.2
2007	203.0	31.7	78.7	69.3	23.3	103.2	119.0	23.9	108.4	328.2	353.4
2008	176.3	31.0	89.9	50.1	5.4	90.6	80.3	28.8	92.2	280.8	406.7
2009	137.0	46.4	13.7	58.6	18.2	89.3	108.7	22.4	81.2	262.3	352.8
2010	158.6	45.8	24.7	64.4	23.7	102.2	118.3	44.6	94.7	318.7	395.2
2011	168.3	40.7	48.4	56.8	22.4	96.3	116.1	32.1	87.4	323.7	436.6
2012	207.3	49.7	60.0	65.3	32.4	137.8	149.2	51.5	110.6	393.2	418.9
2010 1st quarter	124.8	43.0	18.5	42.8	20.5	99.2	120.9	39.1	93.7	341.1	397.5
2nd quarter	164.4	45.8	33.5	61.6	23.6	118.0	119.0	50.3	94.5	324.9	394.5
3rd quarter	180.7	51.6	20.1	82.2	26.8	114.5	118.0	51.9	101.0	316.2	384.7
4th quarter	164.2	43.0	26.7	70.8	23.7	77.2	115.4	37.1	89.8	292.7	404.1
2011 1st quarter	163.3	41.7	36.4	60.9	24.3	74.4	112.2	29.8	85.3	283.0	427.8
2nd quarter	167.7	42.1	56.5	49.0	20.1	94.7	109.1	33.3	92.4	339.5	427.3
3rd quarter	175.8	35.5	62.7	57.1	20.6	110.3	114.9	30.3	86.7	346.0	450.8
4th quarter	166.3	43.5	38.0	60.1	24.7	105.9	128.2	35.1	85.1	326.2	440.2
2012 1st quarter	208.7	50.3	58.9	68.7	30.9	128.8	149.9	53.4	110.3	378.6	415.9
2nd quarter	210.5	47.4	58.8	72.5	31.8	146.5	145.3	53.5	116.6	381.0	429.3
3rd quarter	195.2	52.9	53.0	56.1	33.2	131.6	142.5	52.2	112.9	399.0	412.5
4th quarter	214.8	48.0	69.1	64.0	33.6	144.4	159.0	47.1	102.5	414.2	418.1

NOTES AND DEFINITIONS, CHAPTER 9

General note on data on compensation per hour

This chapter includes two data series with similar names—the Employment Cost Index for total compensation and the index of compensation per hour—that often display different behavior. Both are compiled and published by the Bureau of Labor Statistics (BLS), but the definitions, sources, and methods of compilation are different. Users should be aware of these differences and of the consequent differences in the appropriate uses and interpretations for each of the two series.

The *Employment Cost Index (ECI)* (Tables 9-1 and 9-2) measures changes in hourly compensation for "all civilian workers", which is not quite as broad as it sounds, as it excludes federal government workers, farm workers, and private household workers. Indexes are also published for subgroups including state and local workers, "all private industry" (again excluding farm and private household workers), and a number of industry and occupational subgroups.

The ECI is calculated and published separately for *total compensation* and for the two components of hourly compensation, *wages and salaries* and the employer cost of employee *benefits*. It is constructed by analogy with the Consumer Price Index (CPI); that is, it holds the composition of employment constant in order to isolate hourly compensation trends that take place for individual occupations, which are then aggregated, using fixed relative importance weights. The ECI is based on a sample survey and may be revised from time to time, due to updated classification, weighting, and seasonal adjustments. However, it is not subject to major benchmark revision of the underlying wage, salary, and benefit rate observations. By design, it excludes any representation of employee stock options. As it is based on a sample survey, the ECI is measured "from the bottom up," aggregating from individual employers' reports to higher levels. The ECI is frequently and appropriately used as the best available measure of the general trend of wages and of the extent of inflationary pressure exerted on prices by labor costs.

The *compensation per hour* component of the report on "Productivity and Costs" (Table 9-3) is calculated and published for total compensation in total business, nonfarm business, nonfinancial corporations, and manufacturing. The nonfarm business category is similar in scope to the "all private industry" category in the ECI. The measures in Table 9-3, however, are compiled "from the top down," starting with aggregate estimates of compensation and hours, then dividing the former by the latter. Compensation per hour is affected by changes in the composition of employment. If the composition of employment shifts toward a larger proportion of higher-paid employees and/or industries, compensation per hour will rise even if there is no increase in hourly compensation for any individual worker.

In addition, *compensation per hour* includes the value of exercised stock options as expensed by companies. Also included are other transitory payments, many of which may be of little relevance to the typical worker or to ongoing production costs. These values are not reported immediately. Instead, they are incorporated when later, more comprehensive reports are received. This process can lead to dramatic revisions in compensation per hour and in the unit labor costs index, which is based on compensation. For example, the fourth-quarter 2004 increase in compensation per hour in nonfarm business was initially reported at an annual rate of 3.1 percent. Four months later, the reported rate for the same time period was 10.2 percent. The rate of increase from a year earlier was revised from 3.6 to 5.9 percent. According to then-Federal Reserve Chairman Alan Greenspan, in testimony before the Joint Economic Committee on June 9, 2005, this reflected "a large but apparently transitory surge in bonuses and the proceeds of stock option exercises," not a potentially inflationary acceleration in the rate of labor compensation increase. More recently, it was reported in August 2009 that "first-quarter unit labor costs were revised to negative 2.7% from positive 3%." (*Wall Street Journal,* August 12, 2009, p. A2.)

These characteristics suggest that *compensation per hour* should not be considered a reliable or appropriate indicator of wage or compensation trends for typical workers. It is useful in conjunction with the productivity series, because aggregate productivity is subject to the same composition shifts—higher-productivity industries also tend to have higher-paid employees. Hence, the measure of *unit labor costs* (derived by dividing compensation per hour by output per hour in this system) is not distorted when the composition of output shifts toward higher-productivity industries. The shift affects the numerator and denominator of the ratio similarly. However, both compensation and unit labor costs can still be distorted by transitory payments, such as those discussed above.

There are other, probably less important differences between the two measures. Compensation per hour refers to the entire quarter, while the ECI is observed in the terminal month of each quarter. Tips and other forms of compensation not provided by employers are included in hourly compensation but not in the ECI. The ECI excludes persons working for token wages, business owners and others who set their own wage, and family workers who do not earn a market wage; all of these workers are included in the productivity and cost accounts. Hourly compensation excludes employees of nonprofit institutions serving individuals—about 10 percent of private workers (mostly in education and medical care) who are within the scope of the ECI. Hourly compensation measures include an estimate for the unincorporated self-employed, who are assumed to earn the same hourly compensation as other employees in the sector. Implicitly, unpaid family workers also are included in the hourly compensation measures with the assumption that their hourly compensation is zero. Both of these groups are also excluded from the ECI.

Tables 9-1 and 9-2: Employment Cost Indexes

SOURCE: U.S. DEPARTMENT OF LABOR, BUREAU OF LABOR STATISTICS (BLS)

The Employment Cost Index (ECI) is a quarterly measure of the change in the cost of labor, independent of the influence of employment shifts among occupations and industries. It uses a fixed market basket of labor—similar in concept to the Consumer Price Index's fixed market basket of goods and services—to measure changes over time in employer costs of employing labor. Data are quarterly in all cases and are reported for the final month of each quarter. These measures are expressed as indexes, with the not-seasonally-adjusted value for December 2005 set at 100.

Care should be used in comparing the ECI with other data sets. The "all private industry" category in the ECI excludes farm and household workers (it is sometimes, and more precisely, called "private nonfarm industry"), and the "all civilian workers" category excludes federal government, farm, and household workers.

The data for 1979 through 2005, which are presented in Table 9-2 and are the official ECI measures for that time period, were based on the 1987 Standard Industrial Classification (SIC) and 1990 Occupational Classification System (OCS).

Currently the ECI is compiled based on the 2007 North American Industry Classification System (NAICS) and the 2000 Standard Occupational Classification Manual (SOC). These data, along with comparable data for 2001 through 2005, are shown in Table 9-1.

For certain broad categories shown in this volume—indicated by footnote 2 in Table 9-2—the old SIC categories are roughly comparable and continuous with the data for 2006 and subsequent years. (However, they differ slightly on overlap dates, and should be "linked" if a continuous time series is desired; see the article at the beginning of this volume.) Many of the new industry and occupational

categories are not continuous with the old series shown here, and some of the old categories are not being continued because BLS finds them obsolete and no longer meaningful.

Definitions

Total compensation comprises wages, salaries, and the employer's costs for employee benefits. Excluded from wages and salaries and employee benefits are the value of stock option exercises and items such as payment-in-kind, free room and board, and tips.

Wages and salaries consists of straight-time earnings per hour before payroll deductions, including production bonuses, incentive earnings, commissions, and cost-of-living adjustments. These wage rates exclude premium pay for overtime and for work on weekends and holidays, shift differentials, and nonproduction bonuses such as lump-sum payments provided in lieu of wage increases. According to BLS, wages and salaries are about 70 percent of total compensation.

Benefits includes the cost to employers for paid leave—vacations, holidays, sick leave, and other leave; for supplemental pay—premium pay for work in addition to the regular work schedule (such as overtime, weekends, and holidays), shift differentials, and nonproduction bonuses (such as referral bonuses and lump-sum payments provided in lieu of wage increases); for insurance benefits—life, health, short-term disability, and long-term disability; for retirement and savings benefits—defined benefit and defined contribution plans; and for legally required benefits—Social Security, Medicare, federal and state unemployment insurance, and workers' compensation. Severance pay and supplemental unemployment benefit (SUB) plans are included in the data through December 2005 but were dropped beginning with the March 2006 data. The combined cost of these two benefits accounted for less than one-tenth of one percent of compensation, and according to BLS, dropping these benefits has had virtually no impact on the index. According to BLS, benefit costs are about 30 percent of total compensation.

Civilian workers are private industry workers, as defined below, and workers in state and local government. Federal workers are not included.

Private industry workers are paid workers in private industry excluding farms and private households. To be included in the ECI, employees in occupations must receive cash payments from the establishment for services performed and the establishment must pay the employer's portion of Medicare taxes on that individual's wages. Major exclusions from the survey are the self-employed, individuals who set their own pay (for example, proprietors, owners, major stockholders, and partners in unincorporated firms), volunteers, unpaid workers, family members being paid token wages, individuals receiving long-term disability compensation, and U.S. citizens working overseas.

Private industry workers excluding incentive paid occupations is a new category introduced in the 2006 revision to eliminate the quarter-to-quarter variability related to the way workers (for example, salespersons working on commission) are paid. (The category *private industry workers excluding sales occupations* was intended to serve a similar purpose in the previous SIC-based classification system, but was much less accurate in separately identifying workers with highly variable compensation.)

Goods-producing industries include mining, construction, and manufacturing.

Service-providing industries include the following NAICS industries: wholesale trade; retail trade; transportation and warehousing; utilities; information; finance and insurance; real estate and rental and leasing; professional, scientific, and technical services; management of companies and enterprises; administrative and support and waste management and remediation services; education services; health care and social assistance; arts, entertainment, and recreation; accommodation and food services; and other services, except public administration.

Notes on the data

Employee benefit costs are calculated as cents per hour worked.

The December 2012 data were collected from probability samples of approximately 46,300 occupational observations in about 9,300 sample establishments in private industry, and approximately 9,200 occupations within about 1,400 establishments in state and local governments. The private industry sample is rotated over approximately five years. The state and local government sample is replaced less frequently; the latest sample was introduced in September 2007.

Currently, the sample establishments are classified in industry categories based on the NAICS. Within an establishment, specific job categories are selected and classified into approximately 800 occupational classifications according to the SOC. Similar procedures were followed under the previous classification systems. Data are collected each quarter for the pay periods including the 12th day of March, June, September, and December.

Aggregate indexes are calculated using fixed employment weights. Beginning with March 2006, ECI weights are based on fixed employment counts for 2002 from the BLS Occupational Employment Statistics survey. ECI measures were based on 1990 employment counts from March 1995 through December 2005 and 1980 census employment counts from June 1986 through December 1994. Prior to June 1986, they were based on 1970 census employment counts. Use of fixed weights ensures that changes in the indexes reflect only changes in hourly compensation, not employment shifts among industries or occupations with different levels of wages and compensation. This feature distinguishes the ECI from other compensation series such as average hourly earnings (see Chapter 10 and its notes and definitions) and the compensation per hour component of the productivity series (see Table 9-3 and its notes and definitions, and the general note above), each of which is affected by such employment shifts.

Data availability

Data for wages and salaries for the private nonfarm economy are available beginning with the data for 1975; data for compensation begin with the 1980 data. The series for state and local government and for the civilian nonfarm economy begin with the 1981 data. All series are available on the BLS Web site at http://www.bls.gov.

Wage and salary change and compensation cost change data also are available by major occupational and industry groups, as well as by region and collective bargaining status. Information on wage and salary change is available from 1975 to the present for most of these series. Compensation cost change data are available from 1980 to the present for most series. For 10 occupational and industry series, benefit cost change data are available from the early 1980s to the present. For state and local governments and the civilian economy (state and local governments plus private industry), wage and salary change and compensation cost change data are available for major occupational and industry series. BLS provides data for all these series from June 1981 to the present.

Updates are available about four weeks after the end of the reference quarter. Reference quarters end in March, June, September, and December. Seasonal adjustment factors and seasonally adjusted indexes are released in late April.

References

Explanatory notes, including references, are included in a Technical Note in each quarter's ECI news release, and can be found on the BLS Web site, in the PDF version of the release.

More detailed information on the ECI is available from Chapter 8, "National compensation measures," (http://www.bls.gov/opub/hom/pdf/homch8.pdf) from the BLS Handbook of Methods, and several articles published in the *Monthly Labor Review* and *Compensation and Working Conditions*. The articles and other descriptive pieces are available at http://www.bls.gov/ect/#publications, by calling (202) 691-6199, or sending e-mail to NCSinfo@bls.gov.

Table 9-3A and 9-3B: Productivity and Related Data

The indexes of productivity and costs for private business and private nonfarm business for the entire postwar period, 1947 through 2012, were revised by BLS in August 2013, incorporating the 2013 comprehensive revision of the National Income and Product Accounts, which are the source of the output and compensation components of this family of statistical measures. The indexes for manufacturing were also revised in their entirety. The revision also incorporated the latest data on employment and hours that supply the labor input measures. For details about the NIPA revisions, which included an expansion of the investment component of GDP to include spending on research, development, and entertainment, literary, and artistic originals, see the Notes and Definitions to Chapter 1.

The revised productivity and costs measures are also rebased to 2009 = 100. The previous base was 2005. Rebasing in itself has no effect on the rates of change recorded in these statistics.

Productivity and costs measures for nonfinancial corporations had not been revised to reflect the NIPA revision at the time *Business Statistics* went to press, and are therefore not shown in this year's edition.

Productivity measures relate real physical output to real input. They encompass a family of measures that includes single-factor input measures, such as output per unit of labor input or output per unit of capital input, as well as measures of multifactor productivity—that is, output per unit of combined labor and capital inputs. The indexes published in this book are indexes of labor productivity expressed in terms of output per hour of labor input. (A larger group of BLS productivity measures can be found in Bernan Press's *Handbook of U.S.*

Labor Statistics.) All data are presented as indexes with a base of 2009 = 100.

Definitions

Current dollar output is the current-dollar value of the goods and services produced in the specified sector. *Output* is the constant-dollar value of the same goods and services, derived as current-dollar output divided by the sector *implicit price deflator*. All these data are derived from components of the NIPAs; see Notes on the data below, and for general information on the NIPAs, see the Notes and Definitions to Chapter 1.

Output per hour of all persons (labor productivity) is the value of goods and services in constant dollars produced per hour of labor input. By definition, nonfinancial corporations include no self-employed persons. Productivity in this sector is expressed as *output per hour of all employees. Output per person* is output divided by the index for employment instead of by the index for hours of all persons.

Compensation is the total value of the wages and salaries of employees, plus employers' contributions for social insurance and private benefit plans, plus wages, salaries, and supplementary payments for the self-employed. *Compensation per hour* is compensation divided by *hours of all persons*. Included in compensation is the value of exercised stock options that companies report as a charge against earnings. Stock option values are reported with a delay; consequently, recent values are estimated based on extrapolation. They are revised to actual values when the data become available; sometimes the revisions are very large. The labor compensation of proprietors cannot be explicitly identified and must be estimated. This is done by assuming that proprietors have the same hourly compensation as employees in the same sector. The quarterly labor productivity and cost measures do not contain estimates of compensation for unpaid family workers.

Real compensation per hour is compensation per hour deflated by the Consumer Price Index Research Series (CPI-U-RS) for the period 1978 through 2012. (For current quarters, before the CPI-U-RS becomes available, changes in the CPI-U are used.) Changes in the Consumer Price Index for Urban Wage Earners and Clerical Workers (CPI-W) are used for data before 1978, as there was no CPI-U (or CPIU-RS) for that period. See the Notes and Definitions to Chapter 8 for explanation of the CPI-U, the CPI-W, and the CPI-U-RS.

Unit labor costs are the current-dollar labor costs expended in the production of a unit of output. They are derived by dividing compensation by output.

Unit nonlabor payments include profits, depreciation, interest, rental income of persons, and indirect taxes per unit of output. They are computed by subtracting current-dollar compensation of all persons from current-dollar value of output, providing the data for the index of total *nonlabor payments,* which is then divided by output.

Unit nonlabor costs are available for nonfinancial corporations only. They contain all the components of unit nonlabor payments except unit profits (and rental income of persons, which is zero by definition for nonfinancial corporations).

Unit profits, the other component of unit nonlabor payments, are also only available for nonfinancial corporations.

Hours of all persons (labor input) consists of the total hours at work (*employment* multiplied by *average weekly hours*) of payroll workers, self-employed persons, and unpaid family workers. For the nonfinancial corporations data, there are no self-employed persons; the data represent *employee hours.*

Labor share is the total dollar amount of labor compensation divided by the total current-dollar value of output.

Notes on the data

Output for the business sector is equal to constant-dollar gross domestic product minus: the rental value of owner-occupied dwellings, the output of nonprofit institutions, the output of paid employees of private households, and general government output. The measures are derived from national income and product account (NIPA) data supplied by the U.S. Department of Commerce's Bureau of Economic Analysis (BEA). For manufacturing, BLS produces annual estimates of sectoral output. Quarterly manufacturing output indexes derived from the Federal Reserve Board of Governors' monthly indexes of industrial production (see Chapter 2) are adjusted to these annual measures by the BLS, and are also used to project the quarterly values in the current period. The business sector accounted for 75 percent of the value of GDP in 2012; nonfarm business, for 74 percent.

Nonfinancial corporate output excludes unincorporated businesses and financial corporations from business sector output and accounted for approximately 49 percent of the value of GDP in 2012. Unit profits and unit nonlabor costs can be calculated separately for this sector and are shown in this table.

Compensation and hours data are developed from BLS and BEA data. The primary source for hours and employment is BLS's Current Employment Statistics (CES) program (see the notes and definitions for Chapter 10). Other data sources are

the Current Population Survey (CPS) and the National Compensation Survey (NCS). Weekly paid hours are adjusted to hours at work using the NCS. For paid employees, hours at work differ from hours paid, in that they exclude paid vacation and holidays, paid sick leave, and other paid personal or administrative leave.

Although the labor productivity measures relate output to labor input, they do not measure the contribution of labor or any other specific factor of production. Instead, they reflect the joint effect of many influences, including changes in technology; capital investment; level of output; utilization of capacity, energy, and materials; the organization of production; managerial skill; and the characteristics and efforts of the work force.

Revisions

Data for recent years are revised frequently to take account of revisions in the output and labor input measures that underlie the estimates. Customarily, all revisions to source data are reflected in the release following the source data revision. Data in this volume were released August 16, 2013, and reflect the midyear 2013 revisions to the NIPAs and all revisions in labor input and compensation available up to that release date, including the annual benchmark revision of the CES and updated seasonal factors.

Data availability

Series are available quarterly and annually. Quarterly measures are based entirely on seasonally adjusted data. For some detailed manufacturing series (not shown here), only annual averages are available. Productivity indexes are published early in the second and third months of each quarter, reflecting new data for preceding quarters. Complete historical data are available on the BLS Web site at http://www.bls.gov.

BLS also publishes productivity estimates for a number of individual industries. A release entitled "Productivity and Costs by Industry" is available on the BLS Web site at http://www.bls.gov.

References

Further information is available in the Technical Notes and footnotes on the most current monthly release, available on the Web site, and from the following sources: Chapter 10, "Productivity Measures: Business Sector and Major Subsectors," *BLS Handbook of Methods*—Bulletin 2490 (April 1997) and the following *Monthly Labor Review* articles: "Alternative Measures of Supervisory Employee Hours and Productivity Growth" (April 2004); "Possible Measurement Bias in Aggregate Productivity Growth" (February 1999); "Improvements to the Quarterly Productivity Measures" (October 1995); "Hours of Work: A New Base for BLS Productivity Statistics" (February 1990); and "New Sector Definitions for Productivity Series" (October 1976).

Table 9-4: Rates of Return and Related Data for Major Nonfinancial Industry Groups

SOURCE: U.S. DEPARTMENT OF COMMERCE, BUREAU OF ECONOMIC ANALYSIS

This table presents data on the net operating surplus and rate of return for five major nonfinancial industry groups from 1997 through 2010, based on the NAICS. The industry groups include both corporations and proprietors. Therefore, their data differ from the data for nonfinancial corporations alone, which are available through 2011 and shown for comparison purposes in the first column of this table. (Nonfinancial corporation rates of return and related data can also be found in Table 1-16.)

Definitions

Net operating surplus for the nonfinancial industries includes corporate profits, net interest, business current transfer payments, and proprietors' income (mainly the income of unincorporated self-employed workers).

Produced assets is the average of the end-year values for the current and previous year of the net stock of capital plus inventories, valued at current cost.

Rate of return is net operating surplus as a percent of the average value of produced assets at the beginning and end of the year.

Share of net value added is the net operating surplus as a percent of total value added in the industry. Value added is the portion of total national gross domestic product (GDP) produced in the industry and includes the net operating surplus, compensation of employees, taxes on production and imports less subsidies, and consumption of fixed capital.

Data availability, revisions, and references

These data were presented for the first time and described in "Returns for Domestic Nonfinancial Business," *Survey of Current Business,* May 2007, pp. 6-10. The data were most recently revised and updated in the June 2012 *Survey of Current Business*, and therefore do not reflect the 2013 revision of the NIPAs.

Table 9-5: Corporate Profits with Inventory Valuation Adjustment by Industry Group

SOURCE: U.S. DEPARTMENT OF COMMERCE, BUREAU OF ECONOMIC ANALYSIS

These profits measures are derived from the NIPAs and classified according to the NAICS. They are as revised in the 2013 comprehensive revision. See the notes and definitions to Chapter 1 for definitions, data availability, and references. Note that this industry breakdown of profits incorporates the inventory valuation adjustment (IVA), which eliminates any capital gain element in profits arising from changes in the prices at which inventories are valued, but does not incorporate the capital consumption adjustment (CCAdj), which adjusts historical costs of fixed capital to replacement costs and uses actual rather than tax-based service lives. This is because the CCAdj is calculated by BEA at an aggregate level, whereas the IVA is calculated at an industry level.

CHAPTER 10: EMPLOYMENT, HOURS, AND EARNINGS

Section 10a: Labor Force, Employment, and Unemployment

Figure 10-1. Labor Force Participation Rate and Employment—Population Ratio, 1948–2012

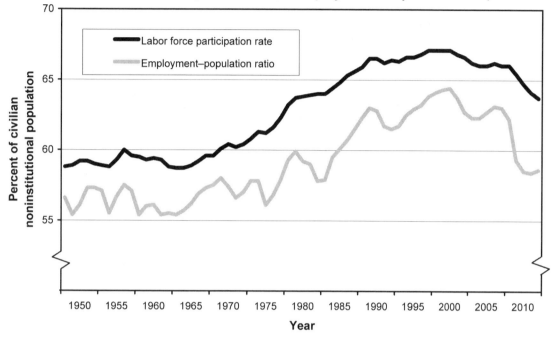

- From a high point in January 2008 to a low in December 2009, 8.1 million Americans lost jobs, based on total civilian employment smoothed for population adjustments. (Table 10-6) The employment/population ratio, charted in Figure 10-1 above, registered the steepest plunge of the postwar period. (Tables 10-1A and B) However, this 5.5 percent employment decline during 2008 and 2009 was nowhere near the length and scale of job loss in the Great Depression, when jobs dropped 22 percent from 1929 to 1932. (Table 10-21)

- By May 2013—the latest month available as this was written—there were 6.4 million more persons employed than at the December 2009 low, using the December 2009 figure in Table 10-6, which is based on population controls consistent with the current estimates. The employment/population ratio, which got as low as 58.2 percent in some months in 2010 and 2011, was 58.6 percent. (Tables 10-1A and B,10-6, and recent data)

- Beginning in 2001, the number of people who either had jobs or were unemployed and looking for a job began to decline relative to the size of the total working-age population. This drop in labor force participation, unprecedented in the period since 1948 during which these data have been collected, accelerated in 2009 through 2011—even as the recovery was beginning—and continued through early 2013. In May, labor force participation ticked up slightly, from 63.3 to 63.4 percent. (Tables 10-1A and B and recent data)

Table 10-1A. Summary Labor Force, Employment, and Unemployment: Recent Data

(Thousands of persons, percent, seasonally adjusted, except as noted.)

Year and month	Civilian noninstitutional population [1]	Civilian labor force		Employment, thousands of persons						Employment-population ratio, percent	Unemployment		
		Thousands of persons	Participation rate (percent)	Total	Men, 20 years and over	Women, 20 years and over	Both sexes, 16 to 19 years	Agricultural	Nonagricultural		Total	Unemployed 15 weeks and over	Rate (percent)
1965	126 513	74 455	58.9	71 088	43 422	22 630	5 036	4 361	66 726	56.2	3 366	755	4.5
1966	128 058	75 770	59.2	72 895	43 668	23 510	5 721	3 979	68 915	56.9	2 875	526	3.8
1967	129 874	77 347	59.6	74 372	44 294	24 397	5 682	3 844	70 527	57.3	2 975	448	3.8
1968	132 028	78 737	59.6	75 920	44 859	25 281	5 781	3 817	72 103	57.5	2 817	412	3.6
1969	134 335	80 734	60.1	77 902	45 388	26 397	6 117	3 606	74 296	58.0	2 832	375	3.5
1970	137 085	82 771	60.4	78 678	45 581	26 952	6 144	3 463	75 215	57.4	4 093	663	4.9
1971	140 216	84 382	60.2	79 367	45 912	27 246	6 208	3 394	75 972	56.6	5 016	1 187	5.9
1972	144 126	87 034	60.4	82 153	47 130	28 276	6 746	3 484	78 669	57.0	4 882	1 167	5.6
1973	147 096	89 429	60.8	85 064	48 310	29 484	7 271	3 470	81 594	57.8	4 365	826	4.9
1974	150 120	91 949	61.3	86 794	48 922	30 424	7 448	3 515	83 279	57.8	5 156	955	5.6
1975	153 153	93 775	61.2	85 846	48 018	30 726	7 104	3 408	82 438	56.1	7 929	2 505	8.5
1976	156 150	96 158	61.6	88 752	49 190	32 226	7 336	3 331	85 421	56.8	7 406	2 366	7.7
1977	159 033	99 009	62.3	92 017	50 555	33 775	7 688	3 283	88 734	57.9	6 991	1 942	7.1
1978	161 910	102 251	63.2	96 048	52 143	35 836	8 070	3 387	92 661	59.3	6 202	1 414	6.1
1979	164 863	104 962	63.7	98 824	53 308	37 434	8 083	3 347	95 477	59.9	6 137	1 241	5.8
1980	167 745	106 940	63.8	99 303	53 101	38 492	7 710	3 364	95 938	59.2	7 637	1 871	7.1
1981	170 130	108 670	63.9	100 397	53 582	39 590	7 225	3 368	97 030	59.0	8 273	2 285	7.6
1982	172 271	110 204	64.0	99 526	52 891	40 086	6 549	3 401	96 125	57.8	10 678	3 485	9.7
1983	174 215	111 550	64.0	100 834	53 487	41 004	6 342	3 383	97 450	57.9	10 717	4 210	9.6
1984	176 383	113 544	64.4	105 005	55 769	42 793	6 444	3 321	101 685	59.5	8 539	2 737	7.5
1985	178 206	115 461	64.8	107 150	56 562	44 154	6 434	3 179	103 971	60.1	8 312	2 305	7.2
1986	180 587	117 834	65.3	109 597	57 569	45 556	6 472	3 163	106 434	60.7	8 237	2 232	7.0
1987	182 753	119 865	65.6	112 440	58 726	47 074	6 640	3 208	109 232	61.5	7 425	1 983	6.2
1988	184 613	121 669	65.9	114 968	59 781	48 383	6 805	3 169	111 800	62.3	6 701	1 610	5.5
1989	186 393	123 869	66.5	117 342	60 837	49 745	6 759	3 199	114 142	63.0	6 528	1 375	5.3
1990	189 164	125 840	66.5	118 793	61 678	50 535	6 581	3 223	115 570	62.8	7 047	1 525	5.6
1991	190 925	126 346	66.2	117 718	61 178	50 634	5 906	3 269	114 449	61.7	8 628	2 357	6.8
1992	192 805	128 105	66.4	118 492	61 496	51 328	5 669	3 247	115 245	61.5	9 613	3 408	7.5
1993	194 838	129 200	66.3	120 259	62 355	52 099	5 805	3 115	117 144	61.7	8 940	3 094	6.9
1994	196 814	131 056	66.6	123 060	63 294	53 606	6 161	3 409	119 651	62.5	7 996	2 860	6.1
1995	198 584	132 304	66.6	124 900	64 085	54 396	6 419	3 440	121 460	62.9	7 404	2 363	5.6
1996	200 591	133 943	66.8	126 708	64 897	55 311	6 500	3 443	123 264	63.2	7 236	2 316	5.4
1997	203 133	136 297	67.1	129 558	66 284	56 613	6 661	3 399	126 159	63.8	6 739	2 062	4.9
1998	205 220	137 673	67.1	131 463	67 135	57 278	7 051	3 378	128 085	64.1	6 210	1 637	4.5
1999	207 753	139 368	67.1	133 488	67 761	58 555	7 172	3 281	130 207	64.3	5 880	1 480	4.2
2000	212 577	142 583	67.1	136 891	69 634	60 067	7 189	2 464	134 427	64.4	5 692	1 318	4.0
2001	215 092	143 734	66.8	136 933	69 776	60 417	6 740	2 299	134 635	63.7	6 801	1 752	4.7
2002	217 570	144 863	66.6	136 485	69 734	60 420	6 332	2 311	134 174	62.7	8 378	2 904	5.8
2003	221 168	146 510	66.2	137 736	70 415	61 402	5 919	2 275	135 461	62.3	8 774	3 378	6.0
2004	223 357	147 401	66.0	139 252	71 572	61 773	5 907	2 232	137 020	62.3	8 149	3 072	5.5
2005	226 082	149 320	66.0	141 730	73 050	62 702	5 978	2 197	139 532	62.7	7 591	2 619	5.1
2006	228 815	151 428	66.2	144 427	74 431	63 834	6 162	2 206	142 221	63.1	7 001	2 266	4.6
2007	231 867	153 124	66.0	146 047	75 337	64 799	5 911	2 095	143 952	63.0	7 078	2 303	4.6
2008	233 788	154 287	66.0	145 362	74 750	65 039	5 573	2 168	143 194	62.2	8 924	3 188	5.8
2009	235 801	154 142	65.4	139 877	71 341	63 699	4 837	2 103	137 775	59.3	14 265	7 272	9.3
2010	237 830	153 889	64.7	139 064	71 230	63 456	4 378	2 206	136 858	58.5	14 825	8 786	9.6
2011	239 618	153 617	64.1	139 869	72 182	63 460	4 327	2 254	137 615	58.4	13 747	8 077	8.9
2012	243 284	154 975	63.7	142 469	73 403	64 640	4 426	2 186	140 283	58.6	12 506	6 996	8.1
2011													
January	238 704	153 244	64.2	139 253	71 575	63 339	4 339	2 267	137 033	58.3	13 992	8 433	9.1
February	238 851	153 269	64.2	139 471	71 866	63 295	4 310	2 263	137 225	58.4	13 798	8 205	9.0
March	239 000	153 358	64.2	139 643	71 874	63 418	4 350	2 241	137 457	58.4	13 716	8 156	8.9
April	239 146	153 478	64.2	139 606	71 959	63 373	4 274	2 117	137 459	58.4	13 872	7 984	9.0
May	239 313	153 552	64.2	139 681	72 116	63 294	4 271	2 228	137 435	58.4	13 871	8 205	9.0
June	239 489	153 369	64.0	139 405	72 004	63 110	4 292	2 235	137 112	58.2	13 964	8 081	9.1
July	239 671	153 325	64.0	139 509	71 998	63 282	4 229	2 232	137 214	58.2	13 817	8 135	9.0
August	239 871	153 707	64.1	139 870	72 151	63 379	4 340	2 378	137 410	58.3	13 837	8 209	9.0
September	240 071	154 074	64.2	140 164	72 363	63 419	4 382	2 245	137 904	58.4	13 910	8 285	9.0
October	240 269	154 010	64.1	140 314	72 357	63 572	4 385	2 225	138 182	58.4	13 696	7 843	8.9
November	240 441	154 096	64.1	140 771	72 871	63 502	4 398	2 251	138 525	58.5	13 325	7 753	8.6
December	240 584	153 945	64.0	140 896	73 050	63 446	4 400	2 380	138 508	58.6	13 049	7 583	8.5
2012													
January	242 269	154 356	63.7	141 608	73 138	64 080	4 391	2 205	139 446	58.5	12 748	7 466	8.3
February	242 435	154 825	63.9	142 019	73 179	64 457	4 383	2 188	139 856	58.6	12 806	7 366	8.3
March	242 604	154 707	63.8	142 020	73 238	64 422	4 360	2 217	139 871	58.5	12 686	7 179	8.2
April	242 784	154 451	63.6	141 934	73 145	64 454	4 334	2 166	139 734	58.5	12 518	7 023	8.1
May	242 966	154 998	63.8	142 302	73 230	64 653	4 419	2 274	140 033	58.6	12 695	7 088	8.2
June	243 155	155 149	63.8	142 448	73 299	64 616	4 533	2 200	140 218	58.6	12 701	7 149	8.2
July	243 354	154 995	63.7	142 250	73 288	64 437	4 525	2 224	140 013	58.5	12 745	6 923	8.2
August	243 566	154 647	63.5	142 164	73 097	64 716	4 351	2 146	139 918	58.4	12 483	6 846	8.1
September	243 772	155 056	63.6	142 974	73 612	64 934	4 429	2 198	140 767	58.7	12 082	6 736	7.8
October	243 983	155 576	63.8	143 328	73 845	65 014	4 469	2 195	141 245	58.7	12 248	6 829	7.9
November	244 174	155 319	63.6	143 277	73 821	64 988	4 468	2 121	141 149	58.7	12 042	6 604	7.8
December	244 350	155 511	63.6	143 305	73 949	64 954	4 402	2 088	141 190	58.6	12 206	6 661	7.8

[1]Not seasonally adjusted.

Table 10-1B. Unemployment Rate Estimates, 1890–1929

(Percent.)

Year	Lebergott unemployment rate estimates
1890	4.0
1891	5.4
1892	3.0
1893	11.7
1894	18.4
1895	13.7
1896	14.4
1897	14.5
1898	12.4
1899	6.5
1900	5.0
1901	4.0
1902	3.7
1903	3.9
1904	5.4
1905	4.3
1906	1.7
1907	2.8
1908	8.0
1909	5.1
1910	5.9
1911	6.7
1912	4.6
1913	4.3
1914	7.9
1915	8.5
1916	5.1
1917	4.6
1918	1.4
1919	1.4
1920	5.2
1921	11.7
1922	6.7
1923	2.4
1924	5.0
1995	3.2
1926	1.8
1927	3.3
1928	4.2
1929	3.2

Table 10-1C. Summary Labor Force, Employment, and Unemployment: Historical

(Thousands of persons, percent, seasonally adjusted, except as noted.)

| Year and month | Civilian noninstitutional population [1] | Civilian labor force | | Employment, thousands of persons | | | | | | Employment-population ratio, percent | Unemployment [2] | | |
| | | Thousands of persons | Participation rate (percent) | Total | By age and sex | | | By industry | | | Thousands of persons | | Rate (percent) |
					Men, 20 years and over	Women, 20 years and over	Both sexes, 16 to 19 years	Agricultural	Nonagricultural		Total	Unemployed 15 weeks and over	
14 Years and Over													
1929	...	49 180	...	47 630	...	...	...	10 450	37 180	...	1 550	...	3.2
1930	...	49 820	...	45 480	...	...	...	10 340	35 140	...	4 340	...	8.7
1931	...	50 420	...	42 400	...	...	...	10 290	32 110	...	8 020	...	15.9 (15.3)
1932	...	51 000	...	38 940	...	...	...	10 170	28 770	...	12 060	...	23.6 (22.5)
1933	...	51 590	...	38 760	...	...	...	10 090	28 670	...	12 830	...	24.9 (20.6)
1934	...	52 230	...	40 890	...	...	...	9 900	30 990	...	11 340	...	21.7 (16.0)
1935	...	52 870	...	42 260	...	...	...	10 110	32 150	...	10 610	...	20.1 (14.2)
1936	...	53 440	...	44 410	...	...	...	10 000	34 410	...	9 030	...	16.9 (9.9)
1937	...	54 000	...	46 300	...	...	...	9 820	36 480	...	7 700	...	14.3 (9.1)
1938	...	54 610	...	44 220	...	...	...	9 690	34 530	...	10 390	...	19.0 (12.5)
1939	...	55 230	...	45 750	...	...	...	9 610	36 140	...	9 480	...	17.2 (11.3)
1940	99 840	55 640	55.7	47 520	...	...	...	9 540	37 980	47.6	8 120	...	14.6 (9.5)
1941	99 900	55 910	56.0	50 350	...	...	...	9 100	41 250	50.4	5 560	...	9.9 (6.0)
1942	98 640	56 410	57.2	53 750	...	...	...	9 250	44 500	54.5	2 660	...	4.7 (3.1)
1943	94 640	55 540	58.7	54 470	...	...	...	9 080	45 390	57.6	1 070	...	1.9 (1.8)
1944	93 220	54 630	58.6	53 960	...	...	...	8 950	45 010	57.9	670	...	1.2
1945	94 090	53 860	57.2	52 820	...	...	...	8 580	44 240	56.1	1 040	...	1.9
1946	103 070	57 520	55.8	55 250	...	...	...	8 320	46 930	53.6	2 270	...	3.9
1947	106 018	60 168	56.8	57 812	...	...	...	8 256	49 557	54.5	2 356	...	3.9
16 Years and Over													
1947	101 827	59 350	58.3	57 038	...	...	4 026	7 890	49 148	56.0	2 311	...	3.9
1948	103 068	60 621	58.8	58 343	39 382	14 936	4 026	7 629	50 714	56.6	2 276	309	3.8
1949	103 994	61 286	58.9	57 651	38 803	15 137	3 712	7 658	49 993	55.4	3 637	684	5.9
1950	104 995	62 208	59.2	58 918	39 394	15 824	3 703	7 160	51 758	56.1	3 288	782	5.3
1951	104 621	62 017	59.2	59 961	39 626	16 570	3 767	6 726	53 235	57.3	2 055	303	3.3
1952	105 231	62 138	59.0	60 250	39 578	16 958	3 719	6 500	53 749	57.3	1 883	232	3.0
1953	107 056	63 015	58.9	61 179	40 296	17 164	3 720	6 260	54 919	57.1	1 834	210	2.9
1954	108 321	63 643	58.8	60 109	39 634	17 000	3 475	6 205	53 904	55.5	3 532	812	5.5
1955	109 683	65 023	59.3	62 170	40 526	18 002	3 642	6 450	55 722	56.7	2 852	702	4.4
1956	110 954	66 552	60.0	63 799	41 216	18 767	3 818	6 283	57 514	57.5	2 750	533	4.1
1957	112 265	66 929	59.6	64 071	41 239	19 052	3 778	5 947	58 123	57.1	2 859	560	4.3
1958	113 727	67 639	59.5	63 036	40 411	19 043	3 582	5 586	57 450	55.4	4 602	1 452	6.8
1959	115 329	68 369	59.3	64 630	41 267	19 524	3 838	5 565	59 065	56.0	3 740	1 040	5.5
1960	117 245	69 628	59.4	65 778	41 543	20 105	4 129	5 458	60 318	56.1	3 852	957	5.5
1961	118 771	70 459	59.3	65 746	41 342	20 296	4 108	5 200	60 546	55.4	4 714	1 532	6.7
1962	120 153	70 614	58.8	66 702	41 815	20 693	4 195	4 944	61 759	55.5	3 911	1 119	5.5
1963	122 416	71 833	58.7	67 762	42 251	21 257	4 255	4 687	63 076	55.4	4 070	1 088	5.7
1964	124 485	73 091	58.7	69 305	42 886	21 903	4 516	4 523	64 782	55.7	3 786	973	5.2
1948													
January	102 603	60 095	58.6	58 061	39 386	14 556	4 119	8 077	49 984	56.6	2 034	311	3.4
February	102 698	60 524	58.9	58 196	39 480	14 621	4 095	7 696	50 500	56.7	2 328	283	3.8
March	102 771	60 070	58.5	57 671	39 098	14 481	4 092	7 333	50 338	56.1	2 399	292	4.0
April	102 831	60 677	59.0	58 291	39 157	15 001	4 133	7 557	50 734	56.7	2 386	324	3.9
May	102 923	59 972	58.3	57 854	39 139	14 712	4 003	7 141	50 713	56.2	2 118	329	3.5
June	102 992	60 957	59.2	58 743	39 392	15 213	4 138	7 591	51 152	57.0	2 214	322	3.6
July	103 216	61 181	59.3	58 968	39 607	15 348	4 013	7 602	51 366	57.1	2 213	295	3.6
August	103 240	60 806	58.9	58 456	39 510	14 994	3 952	7 562	50 894	56.6	2 350	332	3.9
September	103 291	60 815	58.9	58 513	39 324	15 207	3 982	7 865	50 648	56.6	2 302	298	3.8
October	103 361	60 646	58.7	58 387	39 522	14 956	3 909	7 626	50 761	56.5	2 259	324	3.7
November	103 424	60 702	58.7	58 417	39 459	15 054	3 904	7 624	50 793	56.5	2 285	282	3.8
December	103 468	61 169	59.1	58 740	39 539	15 137	4 064	7 984	50 756	56.8	2 429	305	4.0
1949													
January	103 529	60 771	58.7	58 175	39 233	14 991	3 951	7 790	50 385	56.2	2 596	315	4.3
February	103 559	61 057	59.0	58 208	39 117	15 117	3 974	8 022	50 186	56.2	2 849	374	4.7
March	103 665	61 073	58.9	58 043	39 015	15 069	3 959	8 008	50 035	56.0	3 030	414	5.0
April	103 739	61 007	58.8	57 747	38 993	14 978	3 776	7 911	49 836	55.7	3 260	483	5.3
May	103 845	61 259	59.0	57 552	38 701	15 066	3 785	8 067	49 485	55.4	3 707	602	6.1
June	103 930	60 948	58.6	57 172	38 632	15 003	3 537	7 802	49 370	55.0	3 776	705	6.2
July	104 042	61 301	58.9	57 190	38 405	15 244	3 541	8 021	49 169	55.0	4 111	848	6.7
August	104 121	61 590	59.2	57 397	38 610	15 181	3 606	7 604	49 793	55.1	4 193	917	6.8
September	104 219	61 633	59.1	57 584	38 744	15 129	3 711	7 297	50 287	55.3	4 049	973	6.6
October	104 338	62 185	59.6	57 269	38 394	15 260	3 615	6 814	50 455	54.9	4 916	1 000	7.9
November	104 421	62 005	59.4	58 009	38 860	15 422	3 727	7 497	50 512	55.6	3 996	1 056	6.4
December	104 524	61 908	59.2	57 845	38 908	15 300	3 637	7 379	50 466	55.3	4 063	961	6.6

[1] Not seasonally adjusted.
[2] In 1930 through 1943, the official BLS data count persons on work relief as unemployed. The unemployment rates for those years shown in parentheses count persons on work relief as employed, which is more consistent with the postwar practice. See notes and definitions.
... = Not available.

Table 10-1C. Summary Labor Force, Employment, and Unemployment: Historical—*Continued*

(Thousands of persons, percent, seasonally adjusted, except as noted.)

Year and month	Civilian noninstitutional population [1]	Civilian labor force		Employment, thousands of persons						Employment-population ratio, percent	Unemployment		
					By age and sex			By industry			Thousands of persons		
		Thousands of persons	Participation rate (percent)	Total	Men, 20 years and over	Women, 20 years and over	Both sexes, 16 to 19 years	Agricultural	Nonagricultural		Total	Unemployed 15 weeks and over	Rate (percent)
1950													
January	104 619	61 661	58.9	57 635	38 780	15 255	3 600	7 065	50 570	55.1	4 026	947	6.5
February	104 737	61 687	58.9	57 751	38 818	15 339	3 594	7 057	50 694	55.1	3 936	947	6.4
March	104 844	61 604	58.8	57 728	38 851	15 366	3 511	7 116	50 612	55.1	3 876	912	6.3
April	104 943	62 158	59.2	58 583	39 100	15 831	3 652	7 264	51 319	55.8	3 575	920	5.8
May	105 014	62 083	59.1	58 649	39 416	15 628	3 605	7 277	51 372	55.8	3 434	890	5.5
June	105 104	62 419	59.4	59 052	39 476	15 953	3 623	7 285	51 767	56.2	3 367	868	5.4
July	105 194	62 121	59.1	59 001	39 517	15 793	3 691	7 126	51 875	56.1	3 120	769	5.0
August	105 282	62 596	59.5	59 797	39 879	16 124	3 794	7 248	52 549	56.8	2 799	633	4.5
September	105 269	62 349	59.2	59 575	39 865	15 902	3 808	6 992	52 583	56.6	2 774	648	4.4
October	105 096	62 428	59.4	59 803	39 737	16 175	3 891	7 371	52 432	56.9	2 625	545	4.2
November	104 979	62 286	59.3	59 697	39 668	16 195	3 834	7 163	52 534	56.9	2 589	507	4.2
December	104 872	62 068	59.2	59 429	39 536	16 149	3 744	6 760	52 669	56.7	2 639	482	4.3
1951													
January	104 844	61 941	59.1	59 636	39 595	16 279	3 762	6 828	52 808	56.9	2 305	438	3.7
February	104 604	61 778	59.1	59 661	39 695	16 257	3 709	6 738	52 923	57.0	2 117	386	3.4
March	104 629	62 526	59.8	60 401	40 013	16 557	3 831	6 858	53 543	57.7	2 125	355	3.4
April	104 541	61 808	59.1	59 889	39 804	16 426	3 659	6 722	53 167	57.3	1 919	294	3.1
May	104 491	62 044	59.4	60 188	39 752	16 581	3 855	6 752	53 436	57.6	1 856	269	3.0
June	104 488	61 615	59.0	59 620	39 538	16 368	3 714	6 529	53 091	57.1	1 995	258	3.2
July	104 504	62 106	59.4	60 156	39 483	16 898	3 775	6 601	53 555	57.6	1 950	260	3.1
August	104 536	61 927	59.2	59 994	39 508	16 665	3 821	6 790	53 204	57.4	1 933	249	3.1
September	104 588	61 780	59.1	59 713	39 416	16 504	3 793	6 558	53 155	57.1	2 067	223	3.3
October	104 690	62 204	59.4	60 010	39 555	16 674	3 781	6 636	53 374	57.3	2 194	269	3.5
November	104 740	62 014	59.2	59 836	39 504	16 669	3 663	6 699	53 137	57.1	2 178	316	3.5
December	104 810	62 457	59.6	60 497	39 691	16 946	3 860	7 065	53 432	57.7	1 960	269	3.1
1952													
January	104 862	62 432	59.5	60 460	39 714	17 001	3 745	7 148	53 312	57.7	1 972	282	3.2
February	104 868	62 419	59.5	60 462	39 772	16 935	3 755	7 020	53 442	57.7	1 957	248	3.1
March	104 860	61 721	58.9	59 908	39 580	16 627	3 701	6 468	53 440	57.1	1 813	234	2.9
April	104 906	61 720	58.8	59 909	39 542	16 659	3 708	6 525	53 384	57.1	1 811	242	2.9
May	104 996	62 058	59.1	60 195	39 588	16 844	3 763	6 334	53 861	57.3	1 863	219	3.0
June	105 118	62 103	59.1	60 219	39 558	16 837	3 824	6 529	53 690	57.3	1 884	210	3.0
July	105 246	61 962	58.9	59 971	39 496	16 778	3 697	6 334	53 637	57.0	1 991	194	3.2
August	105 346	61 877	58.7	59 790	39 289	16 867	3 634	6 174	53 616	56.8	2 087	211	3.4
September	105 436	62 457	59.2	60 521	39 386	17 477	3 658	6 537	53 984	57.4	1 936	249	3.1
October	105 591	61 971	58.7	60 132	39 451	17 032	3 649	6 363	53 769	56.9	1 839	230	3.0
November	105 706	62 491	59.1	60 748	39 549	17 450	3 749	6 509	54 239	57.5	1 743	216	2.8
December	105 812	62 621	59.2	60 954	40 011	17 181	3 762	6 361	54 593	57.6	1 667	238	2.7
1953													
January	106 594	63 439	59.5	61 600	40 256	17 482	3 862	6 642	54 958	57.8	1 839	268	2.9
February	106 678	63 520	59.5	61 884	40 546	17 321	4 017	6 463	55 421	58.0	1 636	208	2.6
March	106 744	63 657	59.6	62 010	40 648	17 397	3 965	6 420	55 590	58.1	1 647	213	2.6
April	106 826	63 167	59.1	61 444	40 346	17 242	3 856	6 362	55 082	57.5	1 723	180	2.7
May	106 910	62 615	58.6	61 019	40 323	16 983	3 713	5 937	55 082	57.1	1 596	176	2.5
June	106 978	63 063	58.9	61 456	40 358	17 301	3 797	6 361	55 095	57.4	1 607	213	2.5
July	107 034	63 057	58.9	61 397	40 378	17 341	3 678	6 267	55 130	57.4	1 660	168	2.6
August	107 132	62 816	58.6	61 151	40 352	17 108	3 691	6 319	54 832	57.1	1 665	177	2.7
September	107 253	62 727	58.5	60 906	40 192	17 063	3 651	6 198	54 708	56.8	1 821	178	2.9
October	107 383	62 867	58.5	60 893	40 155	17 236	3 502	6 096	54 797	56.7	1 974	190	3.1
November	107 504	62 949	58.6	60 738	40 163	16 974	3 601	6 345	54 393	56.5	2 211	259	3.5
December	107 623	62 795	58.3	59 977	39 885	16 599	3 493	5 929	54 048	55.7	2 818	309	4.5
1954													
January	107 763	63 101	58.6	60 024	39 834	16 574	3 616	6 073	53 951	55.7	3 077	372	4.9
February	107 880	63 994	59.3	60 663	39 899	17 162	3 602	6 590	54 073	56.2	3 331	532	5.2
March	107 987	63 793	59.1	60 186	39 497	17 022	3 667	6 395	53 791	55.7	3 607	765	5.7
April	108 080	63 934	59.2	60 185	39 613	17 015	3 557	6 142	54 043	55.7	3 749	774	5.9
May	108 184	63 675	58.9	59 908	39 467	16 975	3 466	6 210	53 698	55.4	3 767	879	5.9
June	108 267	63 343	58.5	59 792	39 476	16 894	3 422	6 162	53 630	55.2	3 551	880	5.6
July	108 344	63 302	58.4	59 643	39 467	16 777	3 399	6 222	53 421	55.0	3 659	932	5.8
August	108 440	63 707	58.7	59 853	39 582	16 868	3 403	6 087	53 766	55.2	3 854	1 002	6.0
September	108 546	64 209	59.2	60 282	39 702	17 133	3 447	6 453	53 829	55.5	3 927	1 017	6.1
October	108 668	63 936	58.8	60 270	39 618	17 209	3 443	6 242	54 028	55.5	3 666	1 009	5.7
November	108 798	63 759	58.6	60 357	39 745	17 213	3 399	5 934	54 423	55.5	3 402	975	5.3
December	108 892	63 312	58.1	60 116	39 763	17 121	3 232	5 848	54 268	55.2	3 196	827	5.0

[1] Not seasonally adjusted.

Table 10-1C. Summary Labor Force, Employment, and Unemployment: Historical—*Continued*

(Thousands of persons, percent, seasonally adjusted, except as noted.)

Year and month	Civilian noninstitutional population [1]	Civilian labor force		Employment, thousands of persons						Employment-population ratio, percent	Unemployment		
					By age and sex			By industry			Thousands of persons		
		Thousands of persons	Participation rate (percent)	Total	Men, 20 years and over	Women, 20 years and over	Both sexes, 16 to 19 years	Agricultural	Nonagricultural		Total	Unemployed 15 weeks and over	Rate (percent)
1955													
January	109 059	63 910	58.6	60 753	39 937	17 375	3 441	6 113	54 640	55.7	3 157	882	4.9
February	109 078	63 696	58.4	60 727	39 964	17 413	3 350	5 854	54 873	55.7	2 969	826	4.7
March	109 254	63 882	58.5	60 964	40 111	17 415	3 438	6 242	54 722	55.8	2 918	816	4.6
April	109 377	64 564	59.0	61 515	40 120	17 867	3 528	6 363	55 152	56.2	3 049	811	4.7
May	109 544	64 381	58.8	61 634	40 410	17 665	3 559	6 327	55 307	56.3	2 747	734	4.3
June	109 680	64 482	58.8	61 781	40 444	17 837	3 500	6 243	55 538	56.3	2 701	668	4.2
July	109 792	65 145	59.3	62 513	40 751	18 123	3 639	6 438	56 075	56.9	2 632	640	4.0
August	109 882	65 581	59.7	62 797	40 747	18 377	3 673	6 575	56 222	57.1	2 784	535	4.2
September	109 977	65 628	59.7	62 950	40 920	18 285	3 745	6 819	56 131	57.2	2 678	558	4.1
October	110 085	65 821	59.8	62 991	40 858	18 327	3 806	6 728	56 263	57.2	2 830	572	4.3
November	110 177	66 037	59.9	63 257	40 936	18 422	3 899	6 655	56 602	57.4	2 780	564	4.2
December	110 296	66 445	60.2	63 684	41 063	18 630	3 991	6 653	57 031	57.7	2 761	581	4.2
1956													
January	110 390	66 419	60.2	63 753	41 203	18 691	3 859	6 590	57 163	57.8	2 666	561	4.0
February	110 478	66 124	59.9	63 518	41 175	18 582	3 761	6 457	57 061	57.5	2 606	545	3.9
March	110 582	66 175	59.8	63 411	41 199	18 496	3 716	6 221	57 190	57.3	2 764	521	4.2
April	110 650	66 264	59.9	63 614	41 289	18 629	3 696	6 460	57 154	57.5	2 650	476	4.0
May	110 810	66 722	60.2	63 861	41 166	18 844	3 851	6 375	57 486	57.6	2 861	506	4.3
June	110 903	66 702	60.1	63 820	41 196	18 748	3 876	6 335	57 485	57.5	2 882	516	4.3
July	111 019	66 752	60.1	63 800	41 216	18 718	3 866	6 320	57 480	57.5	2 952	523	4.4
August	111 099	66 673	60.0	63 972	41 265	18 864	3 843	6 280	57 692	57.6	2 701	543	4.1
September	111 222	66 714	60.0	64 079	41 221	19 019	3 839	6 375	57 704	57.6	2 635	577	3.9
October	111 335	66 546	59.8	63 975	41 261	18 928	3 786	6 137	57 838	57.5	2 571	530	3.9
November	111 432	66 657	59.8	63 796	41 208	18 846	3 742	5 997	57 799	57.3	2 861	575	4.3
December	111 526	66 700	59.8	63 910	41 192	18 859	3 859	5 806	58 104	57.3	2 790	567	4.2
1957													
January	111 626	66 428	59.5	63 632	41 168	18 740	3 724	5 790	57 842	57.0	2 796	509	4.2
February	111 711	66 879	59.9	64 257	41 341	19 115	3 801	6 125	58 132	57.5	2 622	530	3.9
March	111 824	66 913	59.8	64 404	41 500	19 066	3 838	5 963	58 441	57.6	2 509	514	3.7
April	111 933	66 647	59.5	64 047	41 345	18 937	3 765	5 836	58 211	57.2	2 600	516	3.9
May	112 031	66 695	59.5	63 985	41 334	18 897	3 754	5 999	57 986	57.1	2 710	538	4.1
June	112 172	67 052	59.8	64 196	41 411	18 973	3 812	6 002	58 194	57.2	2 856	526	4.3
July	112 317	67 336	60.0	64 540	41 472	19 262	3 806	6 401	58 139	57.5	2 796	535	4.2
August	112 421	66 706	59.3	63 959	41 243	19 020	3 696	5 898	58 061	56.9	2 747	542	4.1
September	112 554	67 064	59.6	64 121	41 213	19 116	3 792	5 728	58 393	57.0	2 943	559	4.4
October	112 710	67 066	59.5	64 046	41 069	19 160	3 817	5 875	58 171	56.8	3 020	650	4.5
November	112 874	67 123	59.5	63 669	40 853	19 082	3 734	5 686	57 983	56.4	3 454	674	5.1
December	113 013	67 398	59.6	63 922	40 884	19 285	3 753	6 037	57 885	56.6	3 476	731	5.2
1958													
January	113 138	67 095	59.3	63 220	40 617	19 035	3 568	5 831	57 389	55.9	3 875	879	5.8
February	113 234	67 201	59.3	62 898	40 336	18 951	3 611	5 654	57 244	55.5	4 303	1 005	6.4
March	113 337	67 223	59.3	62 731	40 180	18 968	3 583	5 561	57 170	55.3	4 492	1 128	6.7
April	113 415	67 647	59.6	62 631	40 129	18 969	3 533	5 602	57 029	55.2	5 016	1 387	7.4
May	113 534	67 895	59.8	62 874	40 253	18 978	3 643	5 647	57 227	55.4	5 021	1 493	7.4
June	113 647	67 674	59.5	62 730	40 208	19 008	3 514	5 510	57 220	55.2	4 944	1 677	7.3
July	113 727	67 824	59.6	62 745	40 270	19 039	3 436	5 525	57 220	55.2	5 079	1 796	7.5
August	113 835	68 037	59.8	63 012	40 343	19 103	3 566	5 673	57 339	55.4	5 025	1 888	7.4
September	113 977	68 002	59.7	63 181	40 564	19 033	3 584	5 453	57 728	55.4	4 821	1 795	7.1
October	114 138	68 045	59.6	63 475	40 699	19 091	3 685	5 563	57 912	55.6	4 570	1 708	6.7
November	114 283	67 658	59.2	63 470	40 684	19 157	3 629	5 571	57 899	55.5	4 188	1 570	6.2
December	114 429	67 740	59.2	63 549	40 666	19 170	3 713	5 521	58 028	55.5	4 191	1 490	6.2
1959													
January	114 582	67 936	59.3	63 868	40 769	19 292	3 807	5 481	58 387	55.7	4 068	1 396	6.0
February	114 712	67 649	59.0	63 684	40 699	19 167	3 818	5 429	58 255	55.5	3 965	1 277	5.9
March	114 849	68 068	59.3	64 267	41 079	19 379	3 809	5 677	58 590	56.0	3 801	1 210	5.6
April	114 986	68 339	59.4	64 768	41 419	19 498	3 851	5 893	58 875	56.3	3 571	1 039	5.2
May	115 144	68 178	59.2	64 699	41 355	19 565	3 779	5 792	58 907	56.2	3 479	965	5.1
June	115 287	68 278	59.2	64 849	41 387	19 658	3 804	5 712	59 137	56.3	3 429	963	5.0
July	115 429	68 539	59.4	65 011	41 596	19 595	3 820	5 564	59 447	56.3	3 528	889	5.1
August	115 555	68 432	59.2	64 844	41 485	19 568	3 791	5 442	59 402	56.1	3 588	889	5.2
September	115 668	68 545	59.3	64 770	41 351	19 531	3 888	5 447	59 323	56.0	3 775	895	5.5
October	115 798	68 821	59.4	64 911	41 362	19 702	3 847	5 355	59 556	56.1	3 910	883	5.7
November	115 916	68 533	59.1	64 530	41 062	19 594	3 874	5 480	59 050	55.7	4 003	982	5.8
December	116 040	68 994	59.5	65 341	41 651	19 717	3 973	5 458	59 883	56.3	3 653	920	5.3

[1] Not seasonally adjusted.

Table 10-1C. Summary Labor Force, Employment, and Unemployment: Historical—*Continued*

(Thousands of persons, percent, seasonally adjusted, except as noted.)

Year and month	Civilian noninstitutional population [1]	Civilian labor force		Employment, thousands of persons						Employment-population ratio, percent	Unemployment		
		Thousands of persons	Participation rate (percent)	Total	By age and sex			By industry			Thousands of persons		Rate (percent)
					Men, 20 years and over	Women, 20 years and over	Both sexes, 16 to 19 years	Agricultural	Nonagricultural		Total	Unemployed 15 weeks and over	
1960													
January	116 594	68 962	59.1	65 347	41 637	19 686	4 024	5 458	59 889	56.0	3 615	915	5.2
February	116 702	68 949	59.1	65 620	41 729	19 765	4 126	5 443	60 177	56.2	3 329	841	4.8
March	116 827	68 399	58.5	64 673	41 320	19 388	3 965	4 959	59 714	55.4	3 726	959	5.4
April	116 910	69 579	59.5	65 959	41 641	20 110	4 208	5 471	60 488	56.4	3 620	896	5.2
May	117 033	69 626	59.5	66 057	41 668	20 186	4 203	5 359	60 698	56.4	3 569	797	5.1
June	117 167	69 934	59.7	66 168	41 553	20 290	4 325	5 416	60 752	56.5	3 766	854	5.4
July	117 281	69 745	59.5	65 909	41 490	20 257	4 162	5 542	60 367	56.2	3 836	921	5.5
August	117 431	69 841	59.5	65 895	41 503	20 316	4 076	5 520	60 375	56.1	3 946	927	5.6
September	117 521	70 151	59.7	66 267	41 604	20 493	4 170	5 755	60 512	56.4	3 884	982	5.5
October	117 643	69 884	59.4	65 632	41 464	20 076	4 092	5 436	60 196	55.8	4 252	1 189	6.1
November	117 829	70 439	59.8	66 109	41 543	20 384	4 182	5 513	60 596	56.1	4 330	1 223	6.1
December	118 001	70 395	59.7	65 778	41 416	20 332	4 030	5 622	60 156	55.7	4 617	1 142	6.6
1961													
January	118 155	70 447	59.6	65 776	41 363	20 325	4 088	5 422	60 354	55.7	4 671	1 328	6.6
February	118 250	70 420	59.6	65 588	41 177	20 392	4 019	5 472	60 116	55.5	4 832	1 416	6.9
March	118 358	70 703	59.7	65 850	41 273	20 459	4 118	5 406	60 444	55.6	4 853	1 463	6.9
April	118 503	70 267	59.3	65 374	41 206	20 145	4 023	5 037	60 337	55.2	4 893	1 598	7.0
May	118 638	70 452	59.4	65 449	41 139	20 261	4 049	5 099	60 350	55.2	5 003	1 686	7.1
June	118 767	70 878	59.7	65 993	41 349	20 446	4 198	5 220	60 773	55.6	4 885	1 651	6.9
July	118 889	70 536	59.3	65 608	41 245	20 252	4 111	5 153	60 455	55.2	4 928	1 830	7.0
August	119 006	70 534	59.3	65 852	41 362	20 279	4 211	5 366	60 486	55.3	4 682	1 649	6.6
September	119 107	70 217	59.0	65 541	41 400	20 112	4 029	5 021	60 520	55.0	4 676	1 531	6.7
October	119 202	70 492	59.1	65 919	41 509	20 338	4 072	5 203	60 716	55.3	4 573	1 481	6.5
November	119 153	70 376	59.1	66 081	41 556	20 330	4 195	5 090	60 991	55.5	4 295	1 388	6.1
December	119 214	70 077	58.8	65 900	41 534	20 287	4 079	4 992	60 908	55.3	4 177	1 361	6.0
1962													
January	119 300	70 189	58.8	66 108	41 547	20 501	4 060	5 094	61 014	55.4	4 081	1 235	5.8
February	119 360	70 409	59.0	66 538	41 745	20 693	4 100	5 289	61 249	55.7	3 871	1 244	5.5
March	119 476	70 414	58.9	66 493	41 696	20 567	4 230	5 157	61 336	55.7	3 921	1 162	5.6
April	119 702	70 278	58.7	66 372	41 647	20 567	4 158	5 009	61 363	55.4	3 906	1 122	5.6
May	119 813	70 551	58.9	66 688	41 847	20 558	4 283	4 964	61 724	55.7	3 863	1 134	5.5
June	119 943	70 514	58.8	66 670	41 761	20 547	4 362	4 943	61 727	55.6	3 844	1 079	5.5
July	120 128	70 302	58.5	66 483	41 671	20 592	4 220	4 840	61 643	55.3	3 819	1 049	5.4
August	120 323	70 981	59.0	66 968	41 900	20 841	4 227	4 866	62 102	55.7	4 013	1 081	5.7
September	120 653	71 153	59.0	67 192	42 020	20 982	4 190	4 867	62 325	55.7	3 961	1 096	5.6
October	120 856	70 917	58.7	67 114	42 086	20 856	4 172	4 816	62 298	55.5	3 803	1 022	5.4
November	121 045	70 871	58.5	66 847	41 985	20 794	4 068	4 831	62 016	55.2	4 024	1 051	5.7
December	121 236	70 854	58.4	66 947	41 934	20 831	4 182	4 647	62 300	55.2	3 907	1 068	5.5
1963													
January	121 463	71 146	58.6	67 072	41 938	20 933	4 201	4 882	62 190	55.2	4 074	1 122	5.7
February	121 633	71 262	58.6	67 024	41 876	21 046	4 102	4 652	62 372	55.1	4 238	1 137	5.9
March	121 824	71 423	58.6	67 351	42 047	21 162	4 142	4 696	62 655	55.3	4 072	1 087	5.7
April	121 986	71 697	58.8	67 642	42 131	21 281	4 230	4 670	62 972	55.5	4 055	1 071	5.7
May	122 162	71 832	58.8	67 615	42 145	21 225	4 245	4 729	62 886	55.3	4 217	1 157	5.9
June	122 352	71 626	58.5	67 649	42 268	21 185	4 196	4 642	63 007	55.3	3 977	1 067	5.6
July	122 521	71 956	58.7	67 905	42 427	21 268	4 210	4 694	63 211	55.4	4 051	1 070	5.6
August	122 667	71 786	58.5	67 908	42 400	21 185	4 323	4 604	63 304	55.4	3 878	1 114	5.4
September	122 821	72 131	58.7	68 174	42 500	21 317	4 357	4 650	63 524	55.5	3 957	1 069	5.5
October	123 014	72 281	58.8	68 294	42 437	21 456	4 401	4 702	63 592	55.5	3 987	1 071	5.5
November	123 192	72 418	58.8	68 267	42 415	21 553	4 299	4 694	63 573	55.4	4 151	1 054	5.7
December	123 360	72 188	58.5	68 213	42 427	21 481	4 305	4 629	63 584	55.3	3 975	1 007	5.5
1964													
January	123 560	72 356	58.6	68 327	42 510	21 462	4 355	4 603	63 724	55.3	4 029	1 057	5.6
February	123 707	72 683	58.8	68 751	42 579	21 652	4 520	4 563	64 188	55.6	3 932	1 015	5.4
March	123 857	72 713	58.7	68 763	42 600	21 685	4 478	4 366	64 397	55.5	3 950	1 039	5.4
April	124 019	73 274	59.1	69 356	42 885	22 110	4 361	4 414	64 942	55.9	3 918	934	5.3
May	124 204	73 395	59.1	69 631	43 025	22 103	4 503	4 603	65 028	56.1	3 764	975	5.1
June	124 386	73 032	58.7	69 218	42 760	21 995	4 463	4 556	64 662	55.6	3 814	1 047	5.2
July	124 567	73 007	58.6	69 399	42 998	21 846	4 555	4 591	64 808	55.7	3 608	1 002	4.9
August	124 731	73 118	58.6	69 463	42 963	22 002	4 498	4 573	64 890	55.7	3 655	934	5.0
September	124 920	73 290	58.7	69 578	43 009	21 863	4 706	4 619	64 959	55.7	3 712	917	5.1
October	125 108	73 308	58.6	69 582	43 023	21 984	4 575	4 550	65 032	55.6	3 726	903	5.1
November	125 291	73 286	58.5	69 735	43 171	21 954	4 610	4 496	65 239	55.7	3 551	922	4.8
December	125 468	73 465	58.6	69 814	43 109	22 136	4 569	4 322	65 492	55.6	3 651	873	5.0

[1] Not seasonally adjusted.

Table 10-1C. Summary Labor Force, Employment, and Unemployment: Historical—*Continued*

(Thousands of persons, percent, seasonally adjusted, except as noted.)

Year and month	Civilian noninsti-tutional popu-lation [1]	Civilian labor force		Employment, thousands of persons						Employ-ment-population ratio, percent	Unemployment		
		Thousands of persons	Participa-tion rate (percent)	Total	By age and sex			By industry			Thousands of persons		Rate (percent)
					Men, 20 years and over	Women, 20 years and over	Both sexes, 16 to 19 years	Agri-cultural	Nonagri-cultural		Total	Unem-ployed 15 weeks and over	
1965													
January	125 647	73 569	58.6	69 997	43 237	22 282	4 478	4 271	65 726	55.7	3 572	793	4.9
February	125 810	73 857	58.7	70 127	43 279	22 276	4 572	4 322	65 805	55.7	3 730	919	5.1
March	125 985	73 949	58.7	70 439	43 370	22 373	4 696	4 318	66 121	55.9	3 510	796	4.7
April	126 155	74 228	58.8	70 633	43 397	22 416	4 820	4 424	66 209	56.0	3 595	796	4.8
May	126 320	74 466	59.0	71 034	43 579	22 494	4 961	4 724	66 310	56.2	3 432	736	4.6
June	126 499	74 412	58.8	71 025	43 487	22 759	4 779	4 444	66 581	56.1	3 387	786	4.6
July	126 573	74 761	59.1	71 460	43 489	22 841	5 130	4 390	67 070	56.5	3 301	683	4.4
August	126 756	74 616	58.9	71 362	43 447	22 783	5 132	4 355	67 007	56.3	3 254	733	4.4
September	126 906	74 502	58.7	71 286	43 371	22 684	5 231	4 271	67 015	56.2	3 216	732	4.3
October	127 043	74 838	58.9	71 695	43 461	22 819	5 415	4 418	67 277	56.4	3 143	672	4.2
November	127 171	74 797	58.8	71 724	43 447	22 829	5 448	4 093	67 631	56.4	3 073	645	4.1
December	127 294	75 093	59.0	72 062	43 513	22 983	5 566	4 159	67 903	56.6	3 031	659	4.0
1966													
January	127 394	75 186	59.0	72 198	43 495	23 098	5 605	4 077	68 121	56.7	2 988	623	4.0
February	127 514	74 954	58.8	72 134	43 528	23 089	5 517	4 078	68 056	56.6	2 820	594	3.8
March	127 626	75 075	58.8	72 188	43 576	23 109	5 503	4 069	68 119	56.6	2 887	583	3.8
April	127 744	75 338	59.0	72 510	43 679	23 227	5 604	4 108	68 402	56.8	2 828	575	3.8
May	127 879	75 447	59.0	72 497	43 710	23 282	5 505	3 930	68 567	56.7	2 950	534	3.9
June	127 983	75 647	59.1	72 775	43 662	23 359	5 754	3 967	68 808	56.9	2 872	475	3.8
July	128 102	75 736	59.1	72 860	43 574	23 422	5 864	3 920	68 940	56.9	2 876	427	3.8
August	128 240	76 046	59.3	73 146	43 636	23 605	5 905	3 921	69 225	57.0	2 900	464	3.8
September	128 359	76 056	59.3	73 258	43 718	23 881	5 659	3 952	69 306	57.1	2 798	488	3.7
October	128 494	76 199	59.3	73 401	43 776	23 881	5 744	3 912	69 489	57.1	2 798	494	3.7
November	128 627	76 610	59.6	73 840	43 804	24 130	5 906	3 945	69 895	57.4	2 770	464	3.6
December	128 730	76 641	59.5	73 729	43 820	24 025	5 884	3 906	69 823	57.3	2 912	488	3.8
1967													
January	128 909	76 639	59.5	73 671	44 029	23 872	5 770	3 890	69 781	57.1	2 968	489	3.9
February	129 032	76 521	59.3	73 606	43 997	23 919	5 690	3 723	69 883	57.0	2 915	459	3.8
March	129 190	76 328	59.1	73 439	43 922	23 832	5 685	3 757	69 682	56.8	2 889	436	3.8
April	129 344	76 777	59.4	73 882	44 061	24 161	5 660	3 748	70 134	57.1	2 895	428	3.8
May	129 515	76 773	59.3	73 844	44 100	24 172	5 572	3 658	70 186	57.0	2 929	417	3.8
June	129 722	77 270	59.6	74 278	44 230	24 303	5 745	3 689	70 589	57.3	2 992	422	3.9
July	129 918	77 464	59.6	74 520	44 364	24 416	5 740	3 833	70 687	57.4	2 944	412	3.8
August	130 187	77 712	59.7	74 767	44 410	24 600	5 757	3 963	70 804	57.4	2 945	441	3.8
September	130 392	77 812	59.7	74 854	44 535	24 683	5 636	3 851	71 003	57.4	2 958	448	3.8
October	130 582	78 194	59.9	75 051	44 610	24 802	5 639	4 008	71 043	57.5	3 143	472	4.0
November	130 754	78 191	59.8	75 125	44 625	24 914	5 586	3 933	71 192	57.5	3 066	490	3.9
December	130 936	78 491	59.9	75 473	44 719	25 104	5 650	4 076	71 397	57.6	3 018	485	3.8
1968													
January	131 112	77 578	59.2	74 700	44 606	24 581	5 513	3 908	70 792	57.0	2 878	503	3.7
February	131 277	78 230	59.6	75 229	44 659	24 881	5 689	3 959	71 270	57.3	3 001	468	3.8
March	131 412	78 256	59.6	75 379	44 663	25 019	5 697	3 904	71 475	57.4	2 877	447	3.7
April	131 553	78 270	59.5	75 561	44 753	25 072	5 736	3 875	71 686	57.4	2 709	393	3.5
May	131 712	78 847	59.9	76 107	44 841	25 513	5 753	3 814	72 293	57.8	2 740	395	3.5
June	131 872	79 120	60.0	76 182	44 914	25 466	5 802	3 806	72 376	57.8	2 938	405	3.7
July	132 053	78 970	59.8	76 087	44 935	25 347	5 805	3 820	72 267	57.6	2 883	426	3.7
August	132 251	78 811	59.6	76 043	44 897	25 201	5 945	3 736	72 307	57.5	2 768	393	3.5
September	132 446	78 858	59.5	76 172	44 893	25 445	5 834	3 758	72 414	57.5	2 686	375	3.4
October	132 617	78 913	59.5	76 224	44 884	25 475	5 865	3 741	72 483	57.5	2 689	386	3.4
November	132 903	79 209	59.6	76 494	44 996	25 674	5 824	3 758	72 736	57.6	2 715	357	3.4
December	133 120	79 463	59.7	76 778	45 262	25 712	5 804	3 746	73 032	57.7	2 685	351	3.4
1969													
January	133 324	79 523	59.6	76 805	45 154	25 777	5 874	3 704	73 101	57.6	2 718	339	3.4
February	133 465	80 019	60.0	77 327	45 339	26 092	5 896	3 770	73 557	57.9	2 692	358	3.4
March	133 639	80 079	59.9	77 367	45 305	26 115	5 947	3 668	73 699	57.9	2 712	353	3.4
April	133 821	80 281	60.0	77 523	45 262	26 233	6 028	3 629	73 894	57.9	2 758	386	3.4
May	134 027	80 125	59.8	77 412	45 278	26 283	5 851	3 706	73 706	57.8	2 713	387	3.4
June	134 213	80 696	60.1	77 880	45 313	26 429	6 138	3 663	74 217	58.0	2 816	368	3.5
July	134 414	80 827	60.1	77 959	45 305	26 516	6 138	3 548	74 411	58.0	2 868	377	3.5
August	134 597	81 106	60.3	78 250	45 513	26 556	6 181	3 613	74 637	58.1	2 856	373	3.5
September	134 774	81 290	60.3	78 250	45 447	26 572	6 231	3 551	74 699	58.1	3 040	391	3.7
October	135 012	81 494	60.4	78 445	45 488	26 658	6 299	3 517	74 928	58.1	3 049	374	3.7
November	135 239	81 397	60.2	78 541	45 505	26 652	6 384	3 477	75 064	58.1	2 856	392	3.5
December	135 489	81 624	60.2	78 740	45 577	26 832	6 331	3 409	75 331	58.1	2 884	413	3.5

[1]Not seasonally adjusted.

Table 10-1C. Summary Labor Force, Employment, and Unemployment: Historical—*Continued*

(Thousands of persons, percent, seasonally adjusted, except as noted.)

Year and month	Civilian noninsti-tutional popu-lation [1]	Civilian labor force		Employment, thousands of persons						Employ-ment-population ratio, percent	Unemployment		
		Thousands of persons	Participa-tion rate (percent)	Total	By age and sex			By industry			Thousands of persons		Rate (percent)
					Men, 20 years and over	Women, 20 years and over	Both sexes, 16 to 19 years	Agri-cultural	Nonagri-cultural		Total	Unem-ployed 15 weeks and over	
1970													
January	135 713	81 981	60.4	78 780	45 654	26 908	6 218	3 422	75 358	58.0	3 201	431	3.9
February	135 957	82 151	60.4	78 698	45 627	26 828	6 243	3 439	75 259	57.9	3 453	470	4.2
March	136 179	82 498	60.6	78 863	45 668	26 933	6 262	3 499	75 364	57.9	3 635	534	4.4
April	136 416	82 727	60.6	78 930	45 679	27 114	6 137	3 568	75 362	57.9	3 797	602	4.6
May	136 686	82 483	60.3	78 564	45 666	26 739	6 159	3 547	75 017	57.5	3 919	591	4.8
June	136 928	82 484	60.2	78 413	45 554	26 904	5 955	3 555	74 858	57.3	4 071	657	4.9
July	137 196	82 901	60.4	78 726	45 516	27 083	6 127	3 517	75 209	57.4	4 175	662	5.0
August	137 455	82 880	60.3	78 624	45 495	27 011	6 118	3 418	75 206	57.2	4 256	705	5.1
September	137 717	82 954	60.2	78 498	45 535	26 784	6 179	3 451	75 047	57.0	4 456	788	5.4
October	137 988	83 276	60.4	78 685	45 508	27 058	6 119	3 337	75 348	57.0	4 591	771	5.5
November	138 264	83 548	60.4	78 650	45 540	27 020	6 090	3 372	75 278	56.9	4 898	871	5.9
December	138 529	83 670	60.4	78 594	45 466	27 038	6 090	3 380	75 214	56.7	5 076	1 102	6.1
1971													
January	138 795	83 850	60.4	78 864	45 527	27 173	6 164	3 393	75 471	56.8	4 986	1 113	5.9
February	139 021	83 603	60.1	78 700	45 455	27 040	6 205	3 288	75 412	56.6	4 903	1 068	5.9
March	139 285	83 575	60.0	78 588	45 520	26 967	6 101	3 356	75 232	56.4	4 987	1 098	6.0
April	139 566	83 946	60.1	78 987	45 789	26 984	6 214	3 574	75 413	56.6	4 959	1 149	5.9
May	139 826	84 135	60.2	79 139	45 917	27 056	6 166	3 449	75 690	56.6	4 996	1 173	5.9
June	140 090	83 706	59.8	78 757	45 879	27 013	5 865	3 334	75 423	56.2	4 949	1 167	5.9
July	140 343	84 340	60.1	79 305	46 000	27 054	6 251	3 386	75 919	56.5	5 035	1 251	6.0
August	140 596	84 673	60.2	79 539	46 041	27 171	6 327	3 395	76 144	56.6	5 134	1 261	6.1
September	140 869	84 731	60.1	79 689	46 090	27 390	6 209	3 367	76 322	56.6	5 042	1 239	6.0
October	141 146	84 872	60.1	79 918	46 132	27 538	6 248	3 405	76 513	56.6	4 954	1 268	5.8
November	141 393	85 458	60.4	80 297	46 209	27 721	6 367	3 410	76 887	56.8	5 161	1 277	6.0
December	141 666	85 625	60.4	80 471	46 280	27 791	6 400	3 371	77 100	56.8	5 154	1 283	6.0
1972													
January	142 736	85 978	60.2	80 959	46 471	27 956	6 532	3 366	77 593	56.7	5 019	1 257	5.8
February	143 017	86 036	60.2	81 108	46 600	28 016	6 492	3 358	77 750	56.7	4 928	1 292	5.7
March	143 263	86 611	60.5	81 573	46 821	28 126	6 626	3 438	78 135	56.9	5 038	1 232	5.8
April	143 483	86 614	60.4	81 655	46 863	28 114	6 678	3 382	78 273	56.9	4 959	1 203	5.7
May	143 760	86 809	60.4	81 887	46 950	28 184	6 753	3 412	78 475	57.0	4 922	1 168	5.7
June	144 033	87 006	60.4	82 083	47 147	28 175	6 761	3 402	78 681	57.0	4 923	1 141	5.7
July	144 285	87 143	60.4	82 230	47 244	28 225	6 761	3 461	78 769	57.0	4 913	1 154	5.6
August	144 522	87 517	60.6	82 578	47 321	28 382	6 875	3 603	78 975	57.1	4 939	1 156	5.6
September	144 761	87 392	60.4	82 543	47 394	28 417	6 732	3 568	78 975	57.0	4 849	1 131	5.5
October	144 988	87 491	60.3	82 616	47 354	28 438	6 824	3 634	78 982	57.0	4 875	1 123	5.6
November	145 211	87 592	60.3	82 990	47 529	28 567	6 894	3 517	79 473	57.2	4 602	1 040	5.3
December	145 446	87 943	60.5	83 400	47 747	28 698	6 955	3 596	79 804	57.3	4 543	1 006	5.2
1973													
January	145 720	87 487	60.0	83 161	47 701	28 596	6 864	3 456	79 705	57.1	4 326	947	4.9
February	145 943	88 364	60.5	83 912	47 884	28 995	7 033	3 415	80 497	57.5	4 452	894	5.0
March	146 230	88 846	60.8	84 452	48 117	29 110	7 225	3 469	80 983	57.8	4 394	889	4.9
April	146 459	89 018	60.8	84 559	48 098	29 304	7 157	3 407	81 152	57.7	4 459	809	5.0
May	146 719	88 977	60.6	84 648	48 068	29 432	7 148	3 376	81 272	57.7	4 329	816	4.9
June	146 981	89 548	60.9	85 185	48 244	29 505	7 436	3 509	81 676	58.0	4 363	779	4.9
July	147 233	89 604	60.9	85 299	48 452	29 592	7 255	3 540	81 759	57.9	4 305	756	4.8
August	147 471	89 509	60.7	85 204	48 353	29 578	7 273	3 425	81 779	57.8	4 305	788	4.8
September	147 731	89 838	60.8	85 488	48 408	29 710	7 370	3 342	82 146	57.9	4 350	785	4.8
October	147 980	90 131	60.9	85 987	48 631	29 885	7 471	3 424	82 563	58.1	4 144	793	4.6
November	148 219	90 716	61.2	86 320	48 764	30 071	7 485	3 593	82 727	58.2	4 396	832	4.8
December	148 479	90 890	61.2	86 401	48 902	29 991	7 508	3 658	82 743	58.2	4 489	767	4.9
1974													
January	148 753	91 199	61.3	86 555	49 107	29 893	7 555	3 756	82 799	58.2	4 644	799	5.1
February	148 982	91 485	61.4	86 754	49 057	30 146	7 551	3 824	82 930	58.2	4 731	829	5.2
March	149 225	91 453	61.3	86 819	48 986	30 293	7 540	3 726	83 093	58.2	4 634	849	5.1
April	149 478	91 287	61.1	86 669	48 853	30 376	7 440	3 582	83 087	58.0	4 618	889	5.1
May	149 750	91 596	61.2	86 891	49 039	30 424	7 428	3 529	83 362	58.0	4 705	880	5.1
June	150 012	91 868	61.2	86 941	48 946	30 512	7 483	3 386	83 555	58.0	4 927	926	5.4
July	150 248	92 212	61.4	87 149	48 883	30 869	7 397	3 436	83 713	58.0	5 063	924	5.5
August	150 493	92 059	61.2	87 037	48 950	30 662	7 425	3 429	83 608	57.8	5 022	960	5.5
September	150 753	92 488	61.4	87 051	48 978	30 569	7 504	3 460	83 591	57.7	5 437	1 021	5.9
October	151 009	92 518	61.3	86 995	48 959	30 570	7 466	3 431	83 564	57.6	5 523	1 072	6.0
November	151 256	92 766	61.3	86 626	48 833	30 424	7 369	3 405	83 221	57.3	6 140	1 128	6.6
December	151 494	92 780	61.2	86 144	48 458	30 431	7 255	3 361	82 783	56.9	6 636	1 326	7.2

[1] Not seasonally adjusted.

Table 10-1C. Summary Labor Force, Employment, and Unemployment: Historical—*Continued*

(Thousands of persons, percent, seasonally adjusted, except as noted.)

Year and month	Civilian noninstitutional population [1]	Civilian labor force		Employment, thousands of persons						Employment-population ratio, percent	Unemployment		
		Thousands of persons	Participation rate (percent)	Total	By age and sex			By industry			Thousands of persons		Rate (percent)
					Men, 20 years and over	Women, 20 years and over	Both sexes, 16 to 19 years	Agricultural	Nonagricultural		Total	Unemployed 15 weeks and over	
1975													
January	151 755	93 128	61.4	85 627	48 086	30 343	7 198	3 401	82 226	56.4	7 501	1 555	8.1
February	151 990	92 776	61.0	85 256	47 927	30 215	7 114	3 361	81 895	56.1	7 520	1 841	8.1
March	152 217	93 165	61.2	85 187	47 776	30 334	7 077	3 358	81 829	56.0	7 978	2 074	8.6
April	152 443	93 399	61.3	85 189	47 759	30 410	7 020	3 315	81 874	55.9	8 210	2 442	8.8
May	152 704	93 884	61.5	85 451	47 835	30 483	7 133	3 560	81 891	56.0	8 433	2 643	9.0
June	152 976	93 575	61.2	85 355	47 754	30 618	6 983	3 368	81 987	55.8	8 220	2 843	8.8
July	153 309	94 021	61.3	85 894	48 050	30 794	7 050	3 457	82 437	56.0	8 127	2 943	8.6
August	153 580	94 162	61.3	86 234	48 239	30 966	7 029	3 429	82 805	56.1	7 928	2 862	8.4
September	153 848	94 202	61.2	86 279	48 126	30 979	7 174	3 508	82 771	56.1	7 923	2 906	8.4
October	154 082	94 267	61.2	86 370	48 165	31 121	7 084	3 397	82 973	56.1	7 897	2 689	8.4
November	154 338	94 250	61.1	86 456	48 203	31 135	7 118	3 331	83 125	56.0	7 794	2 789	8.3
December	154 589	94 409	61.1	86 665	48 266	31 268	7 131	3 259	83 406	56.1	7 744	2 868	8.2
1976													
January	154 853	94 934	61.3	87 400	48 592	31 595	7 213	3 387	84 013	56.4	7 534	2 713	7.9
February	155 066	94 998	61.3	87 672	48 721	31 680	7 271	3 304	84 368	56.5	7 326	2 519	7.7
March	155 306	95 215	61.3	87 985	48 836	31 842	7 307	3 296	84 689	56.7	7 230	2 441	7.6
April	155 529	95 746	61.6	88 416	49 097	31 951	7 368	3 438	84 978	56.8	7 330	2 210	7.7
May	155 765	95 847	61.5	88 794	49 193	32 147	7 454	3 367	85 427	57.0	7 053	2 115	7.4
June	156 026	95 885	61.5	88 563	49 010	32 267	7 286	3 310	85 253	56.8	7 322	2 332	7.6
July	156 276	96 583	61.8	89 093	49 236	32 334	7 523	3 358	85 735	57.0	7 490	2 316	7.8
August	156 525	96 741	61.8	89 223	49 417	32 437	7 369	3 380	85 843	57.0	7 518	2 378	7.8
September	156 779	96 553	61.6	89 173	49 485	32 390	7 298	3 278	85 895	56.9	7 380	2 296	7.6
October	156 993	96 704	61.6	89 274	49 524	32 412	7 338	3 316	85 958	56.9	7 430	2 292	7.7
November	157 235	97 254	61.9	89 634	49 561	32 753	7 320	3 263	86 371	57.0	7 620	2 354	7.8
December	157 438	97 348	61.8	89 803	49 599	32 914	7 290	3 251	86 552	57.0	7 545	2 375	7.8
1977													
January	157 688	97 208	61.6	89 928	49 738	32 872	7 318	3 185	86 743	57.0	7 280	2 200	7.5
February	157 913	97 785	61.9	90 342	49 838	32 997	7 507	3 222	87 120	57.2	7 443	2 174	7.6
March	158 131	98 115	62.0	90 808	50 031	33 246	7 531	3 212	87 596	57.4	7 307	2 057	7.4
April	158 371	98 330	62.1	91 271	50 185	33 470	7 616	3 313	87 958	57.6	7 059	1 936	7.2
May	158 657	98 665	62.2	91 754	50 280	33 851	7 623	3 432	88 322	57.8	6 911	1 928	7.0
June	158 928	99 093	62.4	91 959	50 544	33 678	7 737	3 340	88 619	57.9	7 134	1 918	7.2
July	159 185	98 913	62.1	92 084	50 597	33 749	7 738	3 247	88 837	57.8	6 829	1 907	6.9
August	159 430	99 366	62.3	92 441	50 745	33 809	7 887	3 260	89 181	58.0	6 925	1 836	7.0
September	159 674	99 453	62.3	92 702	50 825	34 218	7 659	3 201	89 501	58.1	6 751	1 853	6.8
October	159 915	99 815	62.4	93 052	51 046	34 187	7 819	3 272	89 780	58.2	6 763	1 789	6.8
November	160 129	100 576	62.8	93 761	51 316	34 536	7 909	3 375	90 386	58.6	6 815	1 804	6.8
December	160 376	100 491	62.7	94 105	51 492	34 668	7 945	3 320	90 785	58.7	6 386	1 717	6.4
1978													
January	160 617	100 873	62.8	94 384	51 542	34 948	7 894	3 434	90 950	58.8	6 489	1 643	6.4
February	160 831	100 837	62.7	94 519	51 578	35 118	7 823	3 320	91 199	58.8	6 318	1 584	6.3
March	161 038	101 092	62.8	94 755	51 635	35 310	7 810	3 351	91 404	58.8	6 337	1 531	6.3
April	161 263	101 574	63.0	95 394	51 912	35 546	7 936	3 349	92 045	59.2	6 180	1 502	6.1
May	161 518	101 896	63.1	95 769	52 050	35 597	8 122	3 325	92 444	59.3	6 127	1 420	6.0
June	161 794	102 371	63.3	96 343	52 240	35 828	8 275	3 483	92 860	59.5	6 028	1 352	5.9
July	162 034	102 399	63.2	96 090	52 190	35 764	8 136	3 441	92 649	59.3	6 309	1 373	6.2
August	162 259	102 511	63.2	96 431	52 228	35 856	8 347	3 401	93 030	59.4	6 080	1 242	5.9
September	162 502	102 795	63.3	96 670	52 284	36 274	8 112	3 400	93 270	59.5	6 125	1 308	6.0
October	162 783	103 080	63.3	97 133	52 448	36 525	8 160	3 409	93 724	59.7	5 947	1 319	5.8
November	163 017	103 562	63.5	97 485	52 802	36 559	8 124	3 284	94 201	59.8	6 077	1 242	5.9
December	163 272	103 809	63.6	97 581	52 807	36 686	8 088	3 396	94 185	59.8	6 228	1 269	6.0
1979													
January	163 516	104 057	63.6	97 948	53 072	36 697	8 179	3 305	94 643	59.9	6 109	1 250	5.9
February	163 726	104 502	63.8	98 329	53 233	36 904	8 192	3 373	94 956	60.1	6 173	1 297	5.9
March	164 027	104 589	63.8	98 480	53 120	37 159	8 201	3 368	95 112	60.0	6 109	1 365	5.8
April	164 162	104 172	63.5	98 103	53 085	36 944	8 074	3 291	94 812	59.8	6 069	1 272	5.8
May	164 459	104 171	63.3	98 331	53 178	37 134	8 019	3 272	95 059	59.8	5 840	1 239	5.6
June	164 720	104 638	63.5	98 679	53 309	37 221	8 149	3 331	95 348	59.9	5 959	1 171	5.7
July	164 970	105 002	63.6	99 006	53 384	37 514	8 108	3 335	95 671	60.0	5 996	1 123	5.7
August	165 198	105 096	63.6	98 776	53 336	37 548	7 892	3 374	95 402	59.8	6 320	1 203	6.0
September	165 431	105 530	63.8	99 340	53 510	37 798	8 032	3 371	95 969	60.0	6 190	1 172	5.9
October	165 813	105 700	63.7	99 404	53 478	37 931	7 995	3 325	96 079	59.9	6 296	1 219	6.0
November	166 051	105 812	63.7	99 574	53 435	38 065	8 074	3 436	96 138	60.0	6 238	1 239	5.9
December	166 300	106 258	63.9	99 933	53 555	38 259	8 119	3 400	96 533	60.1	6 325	1 277	6.0

[1] Not seasonally adjusted.

Table 10-1C. Summary Labor Force, Employment, and Unemployment: Historical—*Continued*

(Thousands of persons, percent, seasonally adjusted, except as noted.)

Year and month	Civilian noninsti- tutional popu- lation [1]	Civilian labor force		Employment, thousands of persons						Employ- ment- population ratio, percent	Unemployment		
		Thousands of persons	Participa- tion rate (percent)	Total	By age and sex			By industry			Thousands of persons		Rate (percent)
					Men, 20 years and over	Women, 20 years and over	Both sexes, 16 to 19 years	Agri- cultural	Nonagri- cultural		Total	Unem- ployed 15 weeks and over	
1980													
January	166 544	106 562	64.0	99 879	53 501	38 367	8 011	3 316	96 563	60.0	6 683	1 353	6.3
February	166 759	106 697	64.0	99 995	53 686	38 389	7 920	3 397	96 598	60.0	6 702	1 358	6.3
March	166 984	106 442	63.7	99 713	53 353	38 406	7 954	3 418	96 295	59.7	6 729	1 457	6.3
April	167 197	106 591	63.8	99 233	53 035	38 427	7 771	3 326	95 907	59.4	7 358	1 694	6.9
May	167 407	106 929	63.9	98 945	52 915	38 335	7 695	3 382	95 563	59.1	7 984	1 740	7.5
June	167 643	106 780	63.7	98 682	52 712	38 312	7 658	3 296	95 386	58.9	8 098	1 760	7.6
July	167 932	107 159	63.7	98 796	52 733	38 374	7 689	3 319	95 477	58.8	8 363	1 995	7.8
August	168 103	107 105	63.7	98 824	52 815	38 511	7 498	3 234	95 590	58.8	8 281	2 162	7.7
September	168 297	107 098	63.6	99 077	52 866	38 595	7 616	3 443	95 634	58.9	8 021	2 309	7.5
October	168 503	107 405	63.7	99 317	53 094	38 620	7 603	3 372	95 945	58.9	8 088	2 306	7.5
November	168 695	107 568	63.8	99 545	53 210	38 795	7 540	3 396	96 149	59.0	8 023	2 329	7.5
December	168 883	107 352	63.6	99 634	53 333	38 737	7 564	3 492	96 142	59.0	7 718	2 406	7.2
1981													
January	169 104	108 026	63.9	99 955	53 392	39 042	7 521	3 429	96 526	59.1	8 071	2 389	7.5
February	169 280	108 242	63.9	100 191	53 445	39 280	7 466	3 345	96 846	59.2	8 051	2 344	7.4
March	169 453	108 553	64.1	100 571	53 662	39 464	7 445	3 365	97 206	59.4	7 982	2 276	7.4
April	169 641	108 925	64.2	101 056	53 886	39 628	7 542	3 529	97 527	59.6	7 869	2 231	7.2
May	169 829	109 222	64.3	101 048	53 879	39 759	7 410	3 369	97 679	59.5	8 174	2 221	7.5
June	170 042	108 396	63.7	100 298	53 576	39 682	7 040	3 334	96 964	59.0	8 098	2 250	7.5
July	170 246	108 556	63.8	100 693	53 814	39 683	7 196	3 296	97 397	59.1	7 863	2 166	7.2
August	170 399	108 725	63.8	100 689	53 718	39 723	7 248	3 379	97 310	59.1	8 036	2 241	7.4
September	170 593	108 294	63.5	100 064	53 625	39 342	7 097	3 361	96 703	58.7	8 230	2 261	7.6
October	170 809	109 024	63.8	100 378	53 482	39 843	7 053	3 412	96 966	58.8	8 646	2 303	7.9
November	170 996	109 236	63.9	100 207	53 335	39 908	6 964	3 415	96 792	58.6	9 029	2 345	8.3
December	171 166	108 912	63.6	99 645	53 149	39 708	6 788	3 227	96 418	58.2	9 267	2 374	8.5
1982													
January	171 335	109 089	63.7	99 692	53 103	39 821	6 768	3 393	96 299	58.2	9 397	2 409	8.6
February	171 489	109 467	63.8	99 762	53 172	39 859	6 731	3 375	96 387	58.2	9 705	2 758	8.9
March	171 667	109 567	63.8	99 672	53 054	39 936	6 682	3 372	96 300	58.1	9 895	2 965	9.0
April	171 844	109 820	63.9	99 576	53 081	39 848	6 647	3 351	96 225	57.9	10 244	3 086	9.3
May	172 026	110 451	64.2	100 116	53 234	40 121	6 761	3 434	96 682	58.2	10 335	3 276	9.4
June	172 190	110 081	63.9	99 543	52 933	40 219	6 391	3 331	96 212	57.8	10 538	3 451	9.6
July	172 364	110 342	64.0	99 493	52 896	40 228	6 369	3 402	96 091	57.7	10 849	3 555	9.8
August	172 511	110 514	64.1	99 633	52 797	40 336	6 500	3 408	96 225	57.8	10 881	3 696	9.8
September	172 690	110 721	64.1	99 504	52 760	40 275	6 469	3 385	96 119	57.6	11 217	3 889	10.1
October	172 881	110 744	64.1	99 215	52 624	40 105	6 486	3 489	95 726	57.4	11 529	4 185	10.4
November	173 058	111 050	64.2	99 112	52 537	40 111	6 464	3 510	95 602	57.3	11 938	4 485	10.8
December	173 199	111 083	64.1	99 032	52 497	40 164	6 371	3 414	95 618	57.2	12 051	4 662	10.8
1983													
January	173 354	110 695	63.9	99 161	52 487	40 268	6 406	3 439	95 722	57.2	11 534	4 668	10.4
February	173 505	110 634	63.8	99 089	52 453	40 336	6 300	3 382	95 707	57.1	11 545	4 641	10.4
March	173 656	110 587	63.7	99 179	52 615	40 368	6 196	3 360	95 819	57.1	11 408	4 612	10.3
April	173 794	110 828	63.8	99 560	52 814	40 542	6 204	3 341	96 219	57.3	11 268	4 370	10.2
May	173 953	110 796	63.7	99 642	52 922	40 538	6 182	3 328	96 314	57.3	11 154	4 538	10.1
June	174 125	111 879	64.3	100 633	53 515	40 695	6 423	3 462	97 171	57.8	11 246	4 470	10.1
July	174 306	111 756	64.1	101 208	53 835	41 041	6 332	3 481	97 727	58.1	10 548	4 329	9.4
August	174 440	112 231	64.3	101 608	53 837	41 314	6 457	3 502	98 106	58.2	10 623	4 070	9.5
September	174 602	112 298	64.3	102 016	53 983	41 314	6 383	3 347	98 669	58.4	10 282	3 854	9.2
October	174 779	111 926	64.0	102 039	54 146	41 597	6 296	3 303	98 736	58.4	9 887	3 648	8.8
November	174 951	112 228	64.1	102 729	54 499	41 788	6 442	3 291	99 438	58.7	9 499	3 535	8.5
December	175 121	112 327	64.1	102 996	54 662	41 852	6 482	3 332	99 664	58.8	9 331	3 379	8.3
1984													
January	175 533	112 209	63.9	103 201	54 975	41 812	6 414	3 293	99 908	58.8	9 008	3 254	8.0
February	175 679	112 615	64.1	103 824	55 213	42 196	6 415	3 353	100 471	59.1	8 791	2 991	7.8
March	175 824	112 713	64.1	103 967	55 281	42 328	6 358	3 233	100 734	59.1	8 746	2 881	7.8
April	175 969	113 098	64.3	104 336	55 373	42 512	6 451	3 291	101 045	59.3	8 762	2 858	7.7
May	176 123	113 649	64.5	105 193	55 661	43 071	6 461	3 343	101 850	59.7	8 456	2 884	7.4
June	176 284	113 817	64.6	105 591	55 996	42 944	6 651	3 383	102 208	59.9	8 226	2 612	7.2
July	176 440	113 972	64.6	105 435	55 921	42 979	6 535	3 344	102 091	59.8	8 537	2 638	7.5
August	176 583	113 682	64.4	105 163	55 930	42 885	6 348	3 286	101 877	59.6	8 519	2 604	7.5
September	176 763	113 857	64.4	105 490	56 095	42 967	6 428	3 393	102 097	59.7	8 367	2 538	7.3
October	176 956	114 019	64.4	105 638	56 183	43 052	6 403	3 194	102 444	59.7	8 381	2 526	7.4
November	177 135	114 170	64.5	105 972	56 274	43 244	6 454	3 394	102 578	59.8	8 198	2 438	7.2
December	177 306	114 581	64.6	106 223	56 313	43 472	6 438	3 385	102 838	59.9	8 358	2 401	7.3

[1]Not seasonally adjusted.

Table 10-1C. Summary Labor Force, Employment, and Unemployment: Historical—*Continued*

(Thousands of persons, percent, seasonally adjusted, except as noted.)

Year and month	Civilian noninsti- tutional popu- lation [1]	Civilian labor force		Employment, thousands of persons						Employ- ment- population ratio, percent	Unemployment		
		Thousands of persons	Participa- tion rate (percent)	Total	By age and sex			By industry			Thousands of persons		Rate (percent)
					Men, 20 years and over	Women, 20 years and over	Both sexes, 16 to 19 years	Agri- cultural	Nonagri- cultural		Total	Unem- ployed 15 weeks and over	
1985													
January	177 384	114 725	64.7	106 302	56 184	43 589	6 529	3 317	102 985	59.9	8 423	2 284	7.3
February	177 516	114 876	64.7	106 555	56 216	43 787	6 552	3 317	103 238	60.0	8 321	2 389	7.2
March	177 667	115 328	64.9	106 989	56 356	44 035	6 598	3 250	103 739	60.2	8 339	2 394	7.2
April	177 799	115 331	64.9	106 936	56 374	44 000	6 562	3 306	103 630	60.1	8 395	2 393	7.3
May	177 944	115 234	64.8	106 932	56 531	43 905	6 496	3 280	103 652	60.1	8 302	2 292	7.2
June	178 096	114 965	64.6	106 505	56 288	43 958	6 259	3 161	103 344	59.8	8 460	2 310	7.4
July	178 263	115 320	64.7	106 807	56 435	43 975	6 397	3 143	103 664	59.9	8 513	2 329	7.4
August	178 405	115 291	64.6	107 095	56 655	44 103	6 337	3 121	103 974	60.0	8 196	2 258	7.1
September	178 572	115 905	64.9	107 657	56 845	44 395	6 417	3 064	104 593	60.3	8 248	2 242	7.1
October	178 770	116 145	65.0	107 847	56 969	44 565	6 313	3 051	104 796	60.3	8 298	2 295	7.1
November	178 940	116 135	64.9	108 007	56 972	44 617	6 418	3 062	104 945	60.4	8 128	2 207	7.0
December	179 112	116 354	65.0	108 216	56 995	44 889	6 332	3 141	105 075	60.4	8 138	2 208	7.0
1986													
January	179 670	116 682	64.9	108 887	57 637	44 944	6 306	3 287	105 600	60.6	7 795	2 089	6.7
February	179 821	116 882	65.0	108 480	57 269	44 804	6 407	3 083	105 397	60.3	8 402	2 308	7.2
March	179 985	117 220	65.1	108 837	57 353	44 960	6 524	3 200	105 637	60.5	8 383	2 261	7.2
April	180 148	117 316	65.1	108 952	57 358	45 081	6 513	3 153	105 799	60.5	8 364	2 162	7.1
May	180 311	117 528	65.2	109 089	57 287	45 289	6 513	3 150	105 939	60.5	8 439	2 232	7.2
June	180 503	118 084	65.4	109 576	57 471	45 621	6 484	3 193	106 383	60.7	8 508	2 320	7.2
July	180 682	118 129	65.4	109 810	57 514	45 837	6 459	3 141	106 669	60.8	8 319	2 269	7.0
August	180 828	118 150	65.3	110 015	57 597	45 926	6 492	3 082	106 933	60.8	8 135	2 276	6.9
September	180 997	118 395	65.4	110 085	57 630	45 972	6 483	3 171	106 914	60.8	8 310	2 318	7.0
October	181 186	118 516	65.4	110 273	57 660	46 046	6 567	3 128	107 145	60.9	8 243	2 188	7.0
November	181 363	118 634	65.4	110 475	57 941	46 070	6 464	3 220	107 255	60.9	8 159	2 202	6.9
December	181 547	118 611	65.3	110 728	58 185	46 132	6 411	3 148	107 580	61.0	7 883	2 161	6.6
1987													
January	181 827	118 845	65.4	110 953	58 264	46 219	6 470	3 143	107 810	61.0	7 892	2 168	6.6
February	181 998	119 122	65.5	111 257	58 279	46 444	6 534	3 208	108 049	61.1	7 865	2 117	6.6
March	182 179	119 270	65.5	111 408	58 362	46 549	6 497	3 214	108 194	61.2	7 862	2 070	6.6
April	182 344	119 336	65.4	111 794	58 503	46 746	6 545	3 246	108 548	61.3	7 542	2 091	6.3
May	182 533	120 008	65.7	112 434	58 713	47 052	6 669	3 345	109 089	61.6	7 574	2 104	6.3
June	182 703	119 644	65.5	112 246	58 581	47 102	6 563	3 216	109 030	61.4	7 398	2 087	6.2
July	182 885	119 902	65.6	112 634	58 740	47 229	6 665	3 235	109 399	61.6	7 268	1 921	6.1
August	183 002	120 318	65.7	113 057	58 810	47 322	6 925	3 112	109 945	61.8	7 261	1 878	6.0
September	183 161	120 011	65.5	112 909	58 964	47 285	6 660	3 189	109 720	61.6	7 102	1 866	5.9
October	183 311	120 509	65.7	113 282	59 073	47 533	6 676	3 219	110 063	61.8	7 227	1 794	6.0
November	183 470	120 540	65.7	113 505	59 210	47 622	6 673	3 145	110 360	61.9	7 035	1 797	5.8
December	183 620	120 729	65.7	113 793	59 217	47 781	6 795	3 213	110 580	62.0	6 936	1 767	5.7
1988													
January	183 822	120 969	65.8	114 016	59 346	47 862	6 808	3 247	110 769	62.0	6 953	1 714	5.7
February	183 969	121 156	65.9	114 227	59 535	47 919	6 773	3 201	111 026	62.1	6 929	1 738	5.7
March	184 111	120 913	65.7	114 037	59 393	48 090	6 554	3 169	110 868	61.9	6 876	1 744	5.7
April	184 232	121 251	65.8	114 650	59 832	48 147	6 671	3 224	111 426	62.2	6 601	1 563	5.4
May	184 374	121 071	65.7	114 292	59 644	47 946	6 702	3 121	111 171	62.0	6 779	1 647	5.6
June	184 562	121 473	65.8	114 927	59 751	48 146	7 030	3 111	111 816	62.3	6 546	1 531	5.4
July	184 729	121 665	65.9	115 060	59 888	48 186	6 986	3 060	112 000	62.3	6 605	1 601	5.4
August	184 830	122 125	66.1	115 282	59 877	48 467	6 938	3 119	112 163	62.4	6 843	1 639	5.6
September	184 962	121 960	65.9	115 356	59 980	48 511	6 865	3 165	112 191	62.4	6 604	1 569	5.4
October	185 114	122 206	66.0	115 638	60 023	48 859	6 756	3 231	112 407	62.5	6 568	1 562	5.4
November	185 244	122 637	66.2	116 100	60 042	49 254	6 804	3 241	112 859	62.7	6 537	1 468	5.3
December	185 402	122 622	66.1	116 104	60 059	49 257	6 788	3 194	112 910	62.6	6 518	1 490	5.3
1989													
January	185 644	123 390	66.5	116 708	60 477	49 529	6 702	3 287	113 421	62.9	6 682	1 480	5.4
February	185 777	123 135	66.3	116 776	60 588	49 497	6 691	3 234	113 542	62.9	6 359	1 304	5.2
March	185 897	123 227	66.3	117 022	60 795	49 503	6 724	3 198	113 824	62.9	6 205	1 353	5.0
April	186 024	123 565	66.4	117 097	60 764	49 565	6 768	3 162	113 935	62.9	6 468	1 397	5.2
May	186 181	123 474	66.3	117 099	60 795	49 583	6 721	3 125	113 974	62.9	6 375	1 348	5.2
June	186 329	123 995	66.5	117 418	61 054	49 542	6 822	3 068	114 350	63.0	6 577	1 300	5.3
July	186 483	123 967	66.5	117 472	60 947	49 693	6 832	3 227	114 245	63.0	6 495	1 435	5.2
August	186 598	124 166	66.5	117 655	60 915	49 804	6 936	3 284	114 371	63.1	6 511	1 302	5.2
September	186 726	123 944	66.4	117 354	60 668	50 015	6 671	3 219	114 135	62.8	6 590	1 360	5.3
October	186 871	124 211	66.5	117 581	60 958	49 871	6 752	3 215	114 366	62.9	6 630	1 392	5.3
November	187 017	124 637	66.6	117 912	60 958	50 221	6 733	3 132	114 780	63.0	6 725	1 418	5.4
December	187 165	124 497	66.5	117 830	61 068	50 116	6 646	3 188	114 642	63.0	6 667	1 375	5.4

[1]Not seasonally adjusted.

Table 10-1C. Summary Labor Force, Employment, and Unemployment: Historical—*Continued*

(Thousands of persons, percent, seasonally adjusted, except as noted.)

Year and month	Civilian noninsti- tutional popu- lation [1]	Civilian labor force — Thousands of persons	Civilian labor force — Participa- tion rate (percent)	Employment — Total	By age and sex — Men, 20 years and over	By age and sex — Women, 20 years and over	By age and sex — Both sexes, 16 to 19 years	By industry — Agri- cultural	By industry — Nonagri- cultural	Employ- ment- population ratio, percent	Unemployment — Thousands of persons — Total	Unemployment — Unem- ployed 15 weeks and over	Rate (percent)
1990													
January	188 413	125 833	66.8	119 081	61 742	50 436	6 903	3 210	115 871	63.2	6 752	1 412	5.4
February	188 516	125 710	66.7	119 059	61 805	50 438	6 816	3 188	115 871	63.2	6 651	1 350	5.3
March	188 630	125 801	66.7	119 203	61 832	50 463	6 908	3 260	115 943	63.2	6 598	1 331	5.2
April	188 778	125 649	66.6	118 852	61 579	50 457	6 816	3 231	115 621	63.0	6 797	1 376	5.4
May	188 913	125 893	66.6	119 151	61 778	50 646	6 727	3 266	115 885	63.1	6 742	1 415	5.4
June	189 058	125 573	66.4	118 983	61 762	50 550	6 671	3 245	115 738	62.9	6 590	1 436	5.2
July	189 188	125 732	66.5	118 810	61 683	50 514	6 613	3 192	115 618	62.8	6 922	1 534	5.5
August	189 342	125 990	66.5	118 802	61 715	50 635	6 452	3 197	115 605	62.7	7 188	1 607	5.7
September	189 528	125 892	66.4	118 524	61 608	50 587	6 329	3 206	115 318	62.5	7 368	1 695	5.9
October	189 710	125 995	66.4	118 536	61 606	50 616	6 314	3 270	115 266	62.5	7 459	1 689	5.9
November	189 872	126 070	66.4	118 306	61 545	50 541	6 220	3 189	115 117	62.3	7 764	1 831	6.2
December	190 017	126 142	66.4	118 241	61 506	50 530	6 205	3 245	114 996	62.2	7 901	1 804	6.3
1991													
January	190 163	125 955	66.2	117 940	61 383	50 472	6 085	3 208	114 732	62.0	8 015	1 866	6.4
February	190 271	126 020	66.2	117 755	61 117	50 523	6 115	3 270	114 485	61.9	8 265	1 955	6.6
March	190 381	126 238	66.3	117 652	61 144	50 422	6 086	3 177	114 475	61.8	8 586	2 137	6.8
April	190 517	126 548	66.4	118 109	61 280	50 760	6 069	3 241	114 868	62.0	8 439	2 206	6.7
May	190 650	126 176	66.2	117 440	61 052	50 457	5 931	3 275	114 165	61.6	8 736	2 252	6.9
June	190 800	126 331	66.2	117 639	61 147	50 585	5 907	3 300	114 339	61.7	8 692	2 533	6.9
July	190 946	126 154	66.1	117 568	61 179	50 636	5 753	3 319	114 249	61.6	8 586	2 388	6.8
August	191 116	126 150	66.0	117 484	61 122	50 601	5 761	3 313	114 171	61.5	8 666	2 460	6.9
September	191 302	126 650	66.2	117 928	61 279	50 864	5 785	3 319	114 609	61.6	8 722	2 497	6.9
October	191 497	126 642	66.1	117 800	61 174	50 811	5 815	3 289	114 511	61.5	8 842	2 638	7.0
November	191 657	126 701	66.1	117 770	61 201	50 759	5 810	3 296	114 474	61.4	8 931	2 718	7.0
December	191 798	126 664	66.0	117 466	61 074	50 728	5 664	3 146	114 320	61.2	9 198	2 892	7.3
1992													
January	191 953	127 261	66.3	117 978	61 116	51 095	5 767	3 155	114 823	61.5	9 283	3 060	7.3
February	192 067	127 207	66.2	117 753	61 062	51 033	5 658	3 239	114 514	61.3	9 454	3 182	7.4
March	192 204	127 604	66.4	118 144	61 363	51 204	5 577	3 236	114 908	61.5	9 460	3 196	7.4
April	192 354	127 841	66.5	118 426	61 468	51 323	5 635	3 245	115 181	61.6	9 415	3 130	7.4
May	192 503	128 119	66.6	118 375	61 513	51 245	5 617	3 213	115 162	61.5	9 744	3 444	7.6
June	192 663	128 459	66.7	118 419	61 537	51 383	5 499	3 297	115 122	61.5	10 040	3 758	7.8
July	192 826	128 563	66.7	118 713	61 641	51 458	5 614	3 285	115 428	61.6	9 850	3 614	7.7
August	193 018	128 613	66.6	118 826	61 681	51 386	5 759	3 279	115 547	61.6	9 787	3 579	7.6
September	193 229	128 501	66.5	118 720	61 663	51 359	5 698	3 274	115 446	61.4	9 781	3 504	7.6
October	193 442	128 026	66.2	118 628	61 550	51 373	5 705	3 254	115 374	61.3	9 398	3 505	7.3
November	193 621	128 441	66.3	118 876	61 644	51 535	5 697	3 207	115 669	61.4	9 565	3 397	7.4
December	193 784	128 554	66.3	118 997	61 721	51 524	5 752	3 259	115 738	61.4	9 557	3 651	7.4
1993													
January	193 962	128 400	66.2	119 075	61 895	51 505	5 675	3 222	115 853	61.4	9 325	3 346	7.3
February	194 108	128 458	66.2	119 275	61 963	51 573	5 739	3 125	116 150	61.4	9 183	3 190	7.1
March	194 248	128 598	66.2	120 007	61 808	51 808	5 727	3 119	116 423	61.5	9 056	3 115	7.0
April	194 398	128 584	66.1	119 474	62 032	51 732	5 710	3 074	116 400	61.5	9 110	3 014	7.1
May	194 549	129 264	66.4	120 115	62 309	51 996	5 810	3 100	117 015	61.7	9 149	3 101	7.1
June	194 719	129 411	66.5	120 290	62 409	52 183	5 698	3 108	117 182	61.8	9 121	3 141	7.0
July	194 882	129 397	66.4	120 467	62 497	52 088	5 882	3 126	117 341	61.8	8 930	3 046	6.9
August	195 063	129 619	66.4	120 856	62 634	52 294	5 928	3 026	117 830	62.0	8 763	3 026	6.8
September	195 259	129 268	66.2	120 554	62 437	52 241	5 876	3 174	117 380	61.7	8 714	3 042	6.7
October	195 444	129 573	66.3	120 823	62 614	52 379	5 830	3 084	117 739	61.8	8 750	3 029	6.8
November	195 625	129 711	66.3	121 169	62 732	52 531	5 906	3 157	118 012	61.9	8 542	2 986	6.6
December	195 794	129 941	66.4	121 464	62 760	52 813	5 891	3 116	118 348	62.0	8 477	2 968	6.5
1994													
January	195 953	130 596	66.6	121 966	62 798	53 052	6 116	3 302	118 664	62.2	8 630	3 060	6.6
February	196 090	130 669	66.6	122 086	62 708	53 266	6 112	3 339	118 747	62.3	8 583	3 118	6.6
March	196 213	130 400	66.5	121 930	62 780	53 099	6 051	3 354	118 576	62.1	8 470	3 055	6.5
April	196 363	130 621	66.5	122 290	62 906	53 274	6 110	3 428	118 862	62.3	8 331	2 921	6.4
May	196 510	130 779	66.6	122 864	63 116	53 624	6 124	3 409	119 455	62.5	7 915	2 836	6.1
June	196 693	130 561	66.4	122 634	63 041	53 393	6 200	3 299	119 335	62.3	7 927	2 735	6.1
July	196 859	130 652	66.4	122 706	63 034	53 531	6 141	3 333	119 373	62.3	7 946	2 822	6.1
August	197 043	131 275	66.6	123 342	63 294	53 744	6 304	3 451	119 891	62.6	7 933	2 750	6.0
September	197 248	131 421	66.6	123 687	63 631	53 991	6 065	3 430	120 257	62.7	7 734	2 746	5.9
October	197 430	131 744	66.7	124 112	63 818	54 071	6 223	3 490	120 622	62.9	7 632	2 955	5.8
November	197 607	131 891	66.7	124 516	64 080	54 168	6 268	3 574	120 942	63.0	7 375	2 666	5.6
December	197 765	131 951	66.7	124 721	64 359	54 054	6 308	3 577	121 144	63.1	7 230	2 488	5.5

[1]Not seasonally adjusted.

Table 10-1C. Summary Labor Force, Employment, and Unemployment: Historical—*Continued*

(Thousands of persons, percent, seasonally adjusted, except as noted.)

Year and month	Civilian noninsti-tutional popu-lation 1	Civilian labor force		Employment, thousands of persons						Employ-ment-population ratio, percent	Unemployment		
					By age and sex			By industry			Thousands of persons		Rate (percent)
		Thousands of persons	Participa-tion rate (percent)	Total	Men, 20 years and over	Women, 20 years and over	Both sexes, 16 to 19 years	Agri-cultural	Nonagri-cultural		Total	Unem-ployed 15 weeks and over	
1995													
January	197 753	132 038	66.8	124 663	64 185	54 087	6 391	3 519	121 144	63.0	7 375	2 396	5.6
February	197 886	132 115	66.8	124 928	64 378	54 226	6 324	3 620	121 308	63.1	7 187	2 345	5.4
March	198 007	132 108	66.7	124 955	64 321	54 141	6 493	3 634	121 321	63.1	7 153	2 287	5.4
April	198 148	132 590	66.9	124 945	64 165	54 366	6 414	3 566	121 379	63.1	7 645	2 473	5.8
May	198 286	131 851	66.5	124 421	63 829	54 272	6 320	3 349	121 072	62.7	7 430	2 577	5.6
June	198 452	131 949	66.5	124 522	63 992	54 020	6 510	3 461	121 061	62.7	7 427	2 266	5.6
July	198 615	132 343	66.6	124 816	63 962	54 476	6 378	3 379	121 437	62.8	7 527	2 311	5.7
August	198 801	132 336	66.6	124 852	63 875	54 434	6 543	3 374	121 478	62.8	7 484	2 391	5.7
September	199 005	132 611	66.6	125 133	64 179	54 507	6 447	3 285	121 848	62.9	7 478	2 306	5.6
October	199 192	132 716	66.6	125 388	64 272	54 692	6 424	3 438	121 950	62.9	7 328	2 272	5.5
November	199 355	132 614	66.5	125 188	63 931	54 850	6 407	3 338	121 850	62.8	7 426	2 339	5.6
December	199 508	132 511	66.4	125 088	64 041	54 674	6 373	3 352	121 736	62.7	7 423	2 331	5.6
1996													
January	199 634	132 616	66.4	125 125	64 180	54 580	6 365	3 483	121 642	62.7	7 491	2 371	5.6
February	199 772	132 952	66.6	125 639	64 398	54 844	6 397	3 547	122 092	62.9	7 313	2 307	5.5
March	199 921	133 180	66.6	125 862	64 506	54 994	6 362	3 489	122 373	63.0	7 318	2 454	5.5
April	200 101	133 409	66.7	125 994	64 481	55 067	6 446	3 406	122 588	63.0	7 415	2 455	5.6
May	200 278	133 667	66.7	126 244	64 683	55 034	6 527	3 473	122 771	63.0	7 423	2 403	5.6
June	200 459	133 697	66.7	126 602	64 940	55 177	6 485	3 424	123 178	63.2	7 095	2 355	5.3
July	200 641	134 284	66.9	126 947	65 068	55 362	6 517	3 433	123 514	63.3	7 337	2 297	5.5
August	200 847	134 054	66.7	127 172	65 216	55 525	6 431	3 395	123 777	63.3	6 882	2 267	5.1
September	201 060	134 515	66.9	127 536	65 169	55 669	6 698	3 448	124 088	63.4	6 979	2 220	5.2
October	201 273	134 921	67.0	127 890	65 460	55 750	6 680	3 463	124 427	63.5	7 031	2 268	5.2
November	201 463	135 007	67.0	127 771	65 320	55 896	6 555	3 356	124 415	63.4	7 236	2 159	5.4
December	201 636	135 113	67.0	127 860	65 435	55 849	6 576	3 445	124 415	63.4	7 253	2 124	5.4
1997													
January	202 285	135 456	67.0	128 298	65 679	56 024	6 595	3 449	124 849	63.4	7 158	2 162	5.3
February	202 388	135 400	66.9	128 298	65 758	55 955	6 585	3 353	124 945	63.4	7 102	2 140	5.2
March	202 513	135 891	67.1	128 891	65 974	56 270	6 647	3 419	125 472	63.6	7 000	2 110	5.2
April	202 674	136 016	67.1	129 143	66 092	56 347	6 704	3 462	125 681	63.7	6 873	2 176	5.1
May	202 832	136 119	67.1	129 464	66 328	56 446	6 690	3 437	126 027	63.8	6 655	2 121	4.9
June	203 000	136 211	67.1	129 412	66 308	56 573	6 531	3 409	126 003	63.7	6 799	2 085	5.0
July	203 166	136 477	67.2	129 822	66 422	56 785	6 615	3 422	126 400	63.9	6 655	2 119	4.9
August	203 364	136 618	67.2	130 010	66 508	56 852	6 650	3 359	126 651	63.9	6 608	2 004	4.8
September	203 570	136 675	67.1	130 019	66 483	56 931	6 605	3 392	126 627	63.9	6 656	2 074	4.9
October	203 767	136 633	67.1	130 179	66 511	56 982	6 686	3 312	126 867	63.9	6 454	1 950	4.7
November	203 941	136 961	67.2	130 653	66 765	57 039	6 849	3 386	127 267	64.1	6 308	1 817	4.6
December	204 098	137 155	67.2	130 679	66 643	57 219	6 817	3 405	127 274	64.0	6 476	1 901	4.7
1998													
January	204 238	137 095	67.1	130 726	66 750	56 941	7 035	3 299	127 389	64.0	6 368	1 833	4.6
February	204 400	137 112	67.1	130 807	66 856	56 992	6 959	3 284	127 522	64.0	6 306	1 809	4.6
March	204 546	137 236	67.1	130 814	66 721	57 080	7 014	3 146	127 650	64.0	6 422	1 772	4.7
April	204 731	137 150	67.0	131 209	67 151	57 074	6 985	3 334	127 852	64.1	5 941	1 476	4.3
May	204 899	137 372	67.0	131 325	67 164	57 155	7 007	3 360	127 959	64.1	6 047	1 490	4.4
June	205 085	137 455	67.0	131 244	67 054	57 156	7 033	3 380	127 874	64.0	6 212	1 613	4.5
July	205 270	137 588	67.0	131 329	67 119	57 192	7 018	3 455	127 913	64.0	6 259	1 577	4.5
August	205 479	137 570	67.0	131 390	66 985	57 332	7 074	3 509	127 970	63.9	6 179	1 626	4.5
September	205 699	138 286	67.2	131 986	67 254	57 520	7 212	3 500	128 399	64.2	6 300	1 688	4.6
October	205 919	138 279	67.2	131 999	67 433	57 529	7 036	3 593	128 389	64.1	6 280	1 582	4.5
November	206 104	138 381	67.1	132 280	67 591	57 638	7 052	3 375	128 897	64.2	6 100	1 590	4.4
December	206 270	138 634	67.2	132 602	67 548	57 840	7 214	3 246	129 320	64.3	6 032	1 559	4.4
1999													
January	206 719	139 003	67.2	133 027	67 679	58 256	7 092	3 233	129 802	64.4	5 976	1 490	4.3
February	206 873	138 967	67.2	132 856	67 498	58 129	7 229	3 246	129 647	64.2	6 111	1 551	4.4
March	207 036	138 730	67.0	132 947	67 660	58 132	7 155	3 238	129 656	64.2	5 783	1 472	4.2
April	207 236	138 959	67.1	132 955	67 542	58 260	7 153	3 336	129 615	64.2	6 004	1 480	4.3
May	207 427	139 107	67.1	133 311	67 539	58 440	7 331	3 335	129 937	64.3	5 796	1 505	4.2
June	207 632	139 329	67.1	133 378	67 700	58 641	7 037	3 386	129 982	64.2	5 951	1 624	4.3
July	207 828	139 439	67.1	133 414	67 731	58 490	7 193	3 346	130 146	64.2	6 025	1 513	4.3
August	208 038	139 430	67.0	133 591	67 768	58 707	7 117	3 234	130 366	64.2	5 838	1 455	4.2
September	208 265	139 622	67.0	133 707	67 882	58 735	7 090	3 173	130 434	64.2	5 915	1 449	4.2
October	208 483	139 771	67.0	133 993	67 840	58 921	7 232	3 229	130 758	64.3	5 778	1 438	4.1
November	208 666	140 025	67.1	134 309	68 094	59 018	7 198	3 343	130 989	64.4	5 716	1 378	4.1
December	208 832	140 177	67.1	134 523	68 217	59 056	7 251	3 260	131 257	64.4	5 653	1 375	4.0

1Not seasonally adjusted.

Table 10-1C. Summary Labor Force, Employment, and Unemployment: Historical—*Continued*

(Thousands of persons, percent, seasonally adjusted, except as noted.)

Year and month	Civilian noninsti-tutional popu-lation [1]	Civilian labor force		Employment, thousands of persons						Employ-ment-population ratio, percent	Unemployment		
		Thousands of persons	Participa-tion rate (percent)	Total	Men, 20 years and over	Women, 20 years and over	Both sexes, 16 to 19 years	Agri-cultural	Nonagri-cultural		Total	Unem-ployed 15 weeks and over	Rate (percent)
2000													
January	211 410	142 267	67.3	136 559	69 419	59 842	7 298	2 613	133 863	64.6	5 708	1 380	4.0
February	211 576	142 456	67.3	136 598	69 505	59 887	7 206	2 731	133 912	64.6	5 858	1 300	4.1
March	211 772	142 434	67.3	136 701	69 482	59 977	7 241	2 579	134 022	64.6	5 733	1 312	4.0
April	212 018	142 751	67.3	137 270	69 519	60 358	7 393	2 505	134 806	64.7	5 481	1 261	3.8
May	212 242	142 388	67.1	136 630	69 399	59 951	7 280	2 480	134 144	64.4	5 758	1 325	4.0
June	212 466	142 591	67.1	136 940	69 629	60 027	7 284	2 445	134 528	64.5	5 651	1 242	4.0
July	212 677	142 278	66.9	136 531	69 525	60 011	6 995	2 408	134 196	64.2	5 747	1 343	4.0
August	212 916	142 514	66.9	136 662	69 823	59 719	7 120	2 433	134 311	64.2	5 853	1 394	4.1
September	213 163	142 518	66.9	136 893	69 700	60 083	7 110	2 384	134 489	64.2	5 625	1 290	3.9
October	213 405	142 622	66.8	137 088	69 762	60 238	7 088	2 319	134 808	64.2	5 534	1 337	3.9
November	213 540	142 962	66.9	137 322	69 910	60 269	7 143	2 330	134 921	64.3	5 639	1 315	3.9
December	213 736	143 248	67.0	137 614	69 939	60 503	7 172	2 389	135 194	64.4	5 634	1 329	3.9
2001													
January	213 888	143 800	67.2	137 778	70 064	60 609	7 104	2 360	135 304	64.4	6 023	1 372	4.2
February	214 110	143 701	67.1	137 612	69 959	60 615	7 038	2 370	135 291	64.3	6 089	1 491	4.2
March	214 305	143 924	67.2	137 783	69 881	60 902	7 001	2 350	135 372	64.3	6 141	1 521	4.3
April	214 525	143 569	66.9	137 299	69 916	60 523	6 860	2 336	135 036	64.0	6 271	1 499	4.4
May	214 732	143 318	66.7	137 092	69 865	60 509	6 717	2 353	134 735	63.8	6 226	1 502	4.3
June	214 950	143 357	66.7	136 873	69 690	60 371	6 812	2 082	134 755	63.7	6 484	1 532	4.5
July	215 180	143 654	66.8	137 071	69 808	60 480	6 784	2 295	134 858	63.7	6 583	1 653	4.6
August	215 420	143 284	66.5	136 241	69 585	60 301	6 356	2 305	133 944	63.2	7 042	1 861	4.9
September	215 665	143 989	66.8	136 846	69 933	60 265	6 649	2 322	134 558	63.5	7 142	1 950	5.0
October	215 903	144 086	66.7	136 392	69 621	60 168	6 602	2 327	134 098	63.2	7 694	2 082	5.3
November	216 117	144 240	66.7	136 238	69 444	60 174	6 620	2 203	133 955	63.0	8 003	2 318	5.5
December	216 315	144 305	66.7	136 047	69 551	60 095	6 400	2 293	133 751	62.9	8 258	2 444	5.7
2002													
January	216 506	143 883	66.5	135 701	69 308	60 032	6 361	2 385	133 233	62.7	8 182	2 578	5.7
February	216 663	144 653	66.8	136 438	69 534	60 479	6 425	2 397	134 127	63.0	8 215	2 608	5.7
March	216 823	144 481	66.6	136 177	69 480	60 190	6 507	2 368	133 816	62.8	8 304	2 719	5.7
April	217 006	144 725	66.7	136 126	69 574	60 204	6 349	2 371	133 833	62.7	8 599	2 852	5.9
May	217 198	144 938	66.7	136 539	69 981	60 226	6 332	2 260	134 278	62.9	8 399	2 967	5.8
June	217 407	144 808	66.6	136 415	69 769	60 297	6 348	2 161	134 135	62.7	8 393	3 023	5.8
July	217 630	144 803	66.5	136 413	69 806	60 290	6 317	2 324	134 107	62.7	8 390	2 966	5.8
August	217 866	145 009	66.6	136 705	69 937	60 560	6 208	2 127	134 593	62.7	8 304	2 887	5.7
September	218 107	145 552	66.7	137 302	70 207	60 679	6 416	2 285	135 102	63.0	8 251	2 971	5.7
October	218 340	145 314	66.6	137 008	69 948	60 663	6 397	2 471	134 580	62.7	8 307	3 042	5.7
November	218 548	145 041	66.4	136 521	69 615	60 697	6 209	2 261	134 171	62.5	8 520	3 062	5.9
December	218 741	145 066	66.3	136 426	69 620	60 667	6 139	2 352	134 071	62.4	8 640	3 271	6.0
2003													
January	219 897	145 937	66.4	137 417	69 919	61 406	6 091	2 337	135 045	62.5	8 520	3 166	5.8
February	220 114	146 100	66.4	137 482	70 262	61 159	6 060	2 234	135 306	62.5	8 618	3 161	5.9
March	220 317	146 022	66.3	137 434	70 243	61 317	5 874	2 263	135 232	62.4	8 588	3 161	5.9
April	220 540	146 474	66.4	137 633	70 311	61 374	5 948	2 150	135 561	62.4	8 842	3 348	6.0
May	220 768	146 500	66.4	137 544	70 215	61 393	5 936	2 183	135 370	62.3	8 957	3 318	6.1
June	221 014	147 056	66.5	137 790	70 159	61 747	5 884	2 185	135 419	62.3	9 266	3 552	6.3
July	221 252	146 485	66.2	137 474	70 190	61 437	5 847	2 187	135 242	62.1	9 011	3 633	6.2
August	221 507	146 445	66.1	137 549	70 237	61 442	5 870	2 313	135 200	62.1	8 896	3 557	6.1
September	221 779	146 530	66.1	137 609	70 631	61 119	5 860	2 349	135 355	62.0	8 921	3 486	6.1
October	222 039	146 716	66.1	137 984	70 685	61 451	5 848	2 479	135 571	62.1	8 732	3 451	6.0
November	222 279	147 000	66.1	138 424	70 935	61 494	5 995	2 373	136 003	62.3	8 576	3 420	5.8
December	222 509	146 729	65.9	138 411	71 170	61 396	5 845	2 243	136 145	62.2	8 317	3 366	5.7
2004													
January	222 161	146 842	66.1	138 472	71 318	61 183	5 971	2 196	136 228	62.3	8 370	3 364	5.7
February	222 357	146 709	66.0	138 542	71 122	61 514	5 906	2 210	136 362	62.3	8 167	3 248	5.6
March	222 550	146 944	66.0	138 453	71 155	61 534	5 764	2 180	136 302	62.2	8 491	3 314	5.8
April	222 757	146 850	65.9	138 680	71 121	61 647	5 912	2 241	136 474	62.3	8 170	2 971	5.6
May	222 967	147 065	66.0	138 852	71 180	61 762	5 911	2 300	136 556	62.3	8 212	3 103	5.6
June	223 196	147 460	66.1	139 174	71 562	61 793	5 819	2 237	136 748	62.4	8 286	3 130	5.6
July	223 422	147 692	66.1	139 556	71 780	61 884	5 891	2 222	137 354	62.5	8 136	2 918	5.5
August	223 677	147 564	66.0	139 573	71 808	61 836	5 930	2 333	137 230	62.4	7 990	2 846	5.4
September	223 941	147 415	65.8	139 487	71 744	61 859	5 884	2 251	137 323	62.3	7 927	2 910	5.4
October	224 192	147 793	65.9	139 732	71 860	61 942	5 931	2 216	137 598	62.3	8 061	3 041	5.5
November	224 422	148 162	66.0	140 231	72 110	62 088	6 033	2 206	137 978	62.5	7 932	2 960	5.4
December	224 640	148 059	65.9	140 125	72 058	62 136	5 931	2 171	137 947	62.4	7 934	2 927	5.4

[1]Not seasonally adjusted.

Table 10-1C. Summary Labor Force, Employment, and Unemployment: Historical—*Continued*

(Thousands of persons, percent, seasonally adjusted, except as noted.)

Year and month	Civilian noninstitutional population [1]	Civilian labor force		Employment, thousands of persons						Employment-population ratio, percent	Unemployment		
					By age and sex			By industry			Thousands of persons		
		Thousands of persons	Participation rate (percent)	Total	Men, 20 years and over	Women, 20 years and over	Both sexes, 16 to 19 years	Agricultural	Nonagricultural		Total	Unemployed 15 weeks and over	Rate (percent)
2005													
January	224 837	148 029	65.8	140 245	72 063	62 260	5 922	2 112	138 111	62.4	7 784	2 851	5.3
February	225 041	148 364	65.9	140 385	72 299	62 253	5 832	2 129	138 267	62.4	7 980	2 896	5.4
March	225 236	148 391	65.9	140 654	72 478	62 222	5 954	2 180	138 462	62.4	7 737	2 817	5.2
April	225 441	148 926	66.1	141 254	72 860	62 483	5 912	2 248	138 992	62.7	7 672	2 678	5.2
May	225 670	149 261	66.1	141 609	73 133	62 557	5 920	2 225	139 379	62.8	7 651	2 683	5.1
June	225 911	149 238	66.1	141 714	73 223	62 516	5 975	2 302	139 276	62.7	7 524	2 405	5.0
July	226 153	149 432	66.1	142 026	73 337	62 691	5 999	2 308	139 789	62.8	7 406	2 449	5.0
August	226 421	149 779	66.2	142 434	73 513	62 844	6 077	2 183	140 277	62.9	7 345	2 569	4.9
September	226 693	149 954	66.1	142 401	73 333	63 035	6 033	2 181	140 276	62.8	7 553	2 537	5.0
October	226 959	150 001	66.1	142 548	73 445	63 127	5 976	2 191	140 435	62.8	7 453	2 492	5.0
November	227 204	150 065	66.0	142 499	73 341	63 127	6 031	2 174	140 299	62.7	7 566	2 486	5.0
December	227 425	150 030	66.0	142 752	73 467	63 209	6 076	2 094	140 635	62.8	7 279	2 429	4.9
2006													
January	227 553	150 214	66.0	143 150	73 892	63 151	6 106	2 164	140 933	62.9	7 064	2 270	4.7
February	227 763	150 641	66.1	143 457	73 972	63 304	6 182	2 178	141 254	63.0	7 184	2 546	4.8
March	227 975	150 813	66.2	143 741	74 228	63 353	6 160	2 153	141 604	63.1	7 072	2 373	4.7
April	228 199	150 881	66.1	143 761	74 204	63 413	6 144	2 249	141 388	63.0	7 120	2 353	4.7
May	228 428	151 069	66.1	144 089	74 229	63 656	6 204	2 194	141 859	63.1	6 980	2 303	4.6
June	228 671	151 354	66.2	144 353	74 261	63 866	6 226	2 256	142 019	63.1	7 001	2 127	4.6
July	228 912	151 377	66.1	144 202	74 011	64 030	6 162	2 278	142 066	63.0	7 175	2 289	4.7
August	229 167	151 716	66.2	144 625	74 384	64 139	6 102	2 240	142 440	63.1	7 091	2 293	4.7
September	229 420	151 662	66.1	144 815	74 866	63 922	6 026	2 182	142 661	63.1	6 847	2 231	4.5
October	229 675	152 041	66.2	145 314	74 833	64 298	6 183	2 183	143 222	63.3	6 727	2 062	4.4
November	229 905	152 406	66.3	145 534	74 962	64 328	6 244	2 164	143 350	63.3	6 872	2 159	4.5
December	230 108	152 732	66.4	145 970	75 232	64 518	6 220	2 233	143 716	63.4	6 762	2 083	4.4
2007													
January	230 650	153 144	66.4	146 028	75 238	64 621	6 169	2 214	143 785	63.3	7 116	2 156	4.6
February	230 834	152 983	66.3	146 057	75 239	64 750	6 068	2 295	143 741	63.3	6 927	2 211	4.5
March	231 034	153 051	66.2	146 320	75 386	64 928	6 006	2 178	144 153	63.3	6 731	2 255	4.4
April	231 253	152 435	65.9	145 586	75 342	64 366	5 877	2 069	143 385	63.0	6 850	2 281	4.5
May	231 480	152 670	66.0	145 903	75 386	64 724	5 793	2 081	143 773	63.0	6 766	2 231	4.4
June	231 713	153 041	66.0	146 063	75 327	64 788	5 948	1 946	144 112	63.0	6 979	2 281	4.6
July	231 958	153 054	66.0	145 905	75 247	64 766	5 892	2 016	144 041	62.9	7 149	2 364	4.7
August	232 211	152 749	65.8	145 682	75 195	64 838	5 649	1 863	143 865	62.7	7 067	2 333	4.6
September	232 461	153 414	66.0	146 244	75 273	65 086	5 885	2 095	144 148	62.9	7 170	2 355	4.7
October	232 715	153 183	65.8	145 946	75 146	64 842	5 958	2 121	143 926	62.7	7 237	2 300	4.7
November	232 939	153 835	66.0	146 595	75 683	64 985	5 927	2 148	144 413	62.9	7 240	2 366	4.7
December	233 156	153 918	66.0	146 273	75 510	64 910	5 853	2 219	144 018	62.7	7 645	2 501	5.0
2008													
January	232 616	154 063	66.2	146 378	75 551	65 058	5 770	2 205	144 168	62.9	7 685	2 540	5.0
February	232 809	153 653	66.0	146 156	75 450	65 021	5 684	2 190	143 943	62.8	7 497	2 446	4.9
March	232 995	153 908	66.1	146 086	75 294	65 074	5 719	2 172	143 871	62.7	7 822	2 491	5.1
April	233 198	153 769	65.9	146 132	75 182	65 107	5 843	2 115	143 874	62.7	7 637	2 687	5.0
May	233 405	154 303	66.1	145 908	74 953	65 137	5 817	2 113	143 737	62.5	8 395	2 780	5.4
June	233 627	154 313	66.1	145 737	74 975	65 169	5 594	2 127	143 629	62.4	8 575	2 913	5.6
July	233 864	154 469	66.1	145 532	74 950	65 103	5 478	2 134	143 519	62.2	8 937	3 114	5.8
August	234 107	154 641	66.1	145 203	74 658	65 008	5 537	2 148	143 086	62.0	9 438	3 420	6.1
September	234 360	154 570	66.0	145 076	74 456	65 078	5 542	2 231	142 796	61.9	9 494	3 626	6.1
October	234 612	154 876	66.0	144 802	74 263	65 103	5 436	2 199	142 689	61.7	10 074	3 990	6.5
November	234 828	154 639	65.9	144 100	73 943	64 885	5 272	2 207	141 962	61.4	10 538	3 923	6.8
December	235 035	154 655	65.8	143 369	73 311	64 813	5 246	2 209	141 139	61.0	11 286	4 547	7.3
2009													
January	234 739	154 232	65.7	142 153	72 729	64 207	5 218	2 147	140 022	60.6	12 079	4 767	7.8
February	234 913	154 526	65.8	141 644	72 268	64 194	5 182	2 131	139 500	60.3	12 881	5 452	8.3
March	235 086	154 142	65.6	140 721	71 643	64 027	5 050	2 026	138 666	59.9	13 421	5 882	8.7
April	235 271	154 479	65.7	140 652	71 605	64 022	5 025	2 137	138 447	59.8	13 826	6 381	9.0
May	235 452	154 742	65.7	140 250	71 412	63 807	5 031	2 144	138 044	59.6	14 492	7 023	9.4
June	235 655	154 710	65.7	140 005	71 329	63 734	4 942	2 158	137 835	59.4	14 705	7 820	9.5
July	235 870	154 505	65.5	139 898	71 267	63 762	4 870	2 126	137 822	59.3	14 607	7 834	9.5
August	236 087	154 300	65.4	139 481	71 097	63 636	4 748	2 098	137 360	59.1	14 819	7 824	9.6
September	236 322	153 815	65.1	138 810	70 828	63 330	4 652	2 036	136 728	58.7	15 005	8 402	9.8
October	236 550	153 804	65.0	138 421	70 693	63 281	4 447	2 044	136 453	58.5	15 382	8 667	10.0
November	236 743	153 887	65.0	138 665	70 777	63 422	4 465	2 102	136 645	58.6	15 223	8 776	9.9
December	236 924	153 120	64.6	138 025	70 477	63 098	4 450	2 091	135 925	58.3	15 095	8 851	9.9
2010													
January	236 832	153 455	64.8	138 439	70 517	63 489	4 433	2 130	136 382	58.5	15 016	8 909	9.8
February	236 998	153 702	64.9	138 624	70 624	63 514	4 487	2 308	136 353	58.5	15 078	8 925	9.8
March	237 159	153 960	64.9	138 767	70 902	63 372	4 494	2 200	136 580	58.5	15 192	9 078	9.9
April	237 329	154 577	65.1	139 296	71 365	63 414	4 518	2 269	136 982	58.7	15 281	9 117	9.9
May	237 499	154 110	64.9	139 255	71 380	63 440	4 435	2 196	137 024	58.6	14 856	8 902	9.6
June	237 690	153 623	64.6	139 148	71 358	63 540	4 250	2 129	136 961	58.5	14 475	8 874	9.4
July	237 890	153 709	64.6	139 167	71 450	63 406	4 311	2 175	136 935	58.5	14 542	8 693	9.5
August	238 099	154 078	64.7	139 405	71 571	63 437	4 396	2 183	137 158	58.5	14 673	8 399	9.5
September	238 322	153 966	64.6	139 388	71 562	63 554	4 272	2 168	137 208	58.5	14 577	8 444	9.5
October	238 530	153 681	64.4	139 097	71 395	63 402	4 301	2 347	136 829	58.3	14 584	8 646	9.5
November	238 715	154 140	64.6	139 046	71 145	63 502	4 398	2 194	136 882	58.2	15 094	8 730	9.8
December	238 889	153 649	64.3	139 295	71 472	63 516	4 307	2 195	137 110	58.3	14 354	8 572	9.3

[1] Not seasonally adjusted.

Table 10-2. Labor Force and Employment by Major Age and Sex Groups

(Thousands of persons, percent, seasonally adjusted.)

Year and month	Civilian labor force (thousands)			Participation rate (percent)			Employment (thousands)			Employment-population ratio, percent		
	Men, 20 years and over	Women, 20 years and over	Both sexes, 16 to 19 years	Men, 20 years and over	Women, 20 years and over	Both sexes, 16 to 19 years	Men, 20 years and over	Women, 20 years and over	Both sexes, 16 to 19 years	Men, 20 years and over	Women, 20 years and over	Both sexes, 16 to 19 years
1965	44 857	23 686	5 910	83.9	39.4	45.7	43 422	22 630	5 036	81.2	37.6	38.9
1966	44 788	24 431	6 558	83.6	40.1	48.2	43 668	23 510	5 721	81.5	38.6	42.1
1967	45 354	25 475	6 521	83.4	41.1	48.4	44 294	24 397	5 682	81.5	39.3	42.2
1968	45 852	26 266	6 619	83.1	41.6	48.3	44 859	25 281	5 781	81.3	40.0	42.2
1969	46 351	27 413	6 970	82.8	42.7	49.4	45 388	26 397	6 117	81.1	41.1	43.4
1970	47 220	28 301	7 249	82.6	43.3	49.9	45 581	26 952	6 144	79.7	41.2	42.3
1971	48 009	28 904	7 470	82.1	43.3	49.7	45 912	27 246	6 208	78.5	40.9	41.3
1972	49 079	29 901	8 054	81.6	43.7	51.9	47 130	28 276	6 746	78.4	41.3	43.5
1973	49 932	30 991	8 507	81.3	44.4	53.7	48 310	29 484	7 271	78.6	42.2	45.9
1974	50 879	32 201	8 871	81.0	45.3	54.8	48 922	30 424	7 448	77.9	42.8	46.0
1975	51 494	33 410	8 870	80.3	46.0	54.0	48 018	30 726	7 104	74.8	42.3	43.3
1976	52 288	34 814	9 056	79.8	47.0	54.5	49 190	32 226	7 336	75.1	43.5	44.2
1977	53 348	36 310	9 351	79.7	48.1	56.0	50 555	33 775	7 688	75.6	44.8	46.1
1978	54 471	38 128	9 652	79.8	49.6	57.8	52 143	35 836	8 070	76.4	46.6	48.3
1979	55 615	39 708	9 638	79.8	50.6	57.9	53 308	37 434	8 083	76.5	47.7	48.5
1980	56 455	41 106	9 378	79.4	51.3	56.7	53 101	38 492	7 710	74.6	48.1	46.6
1981	57 197	42 485	8 988	79.0	52.1	55.4	53 582	39 590	7 225	74.0	48.6	44.6
1982	57 980	43 699	8 526	78.7	52.7	54.1	52 891	40 086	6 549	71.8	48.4	41.5
1983	58 744	44 636	8 171	78.5	53.1	53.5	53 487	41 004	6 342	71.4	48.8	41.5
1984	59 701	45 900	7 943	78.3	53.7	53.9	55 769	42 793	6 444	73.2	50.1	43.7
1985	60 277	47 283	7 901	78.1	54.7	54.5	56 562	44 154	6 434	73.3	51.0	44.4
1986	61 320	48 589	7 926	78.1	55.5	54.7	57 569	45 556	6 472	73.3	52.0	44.6
1987	62 095	49 783	7 988	78.0	56.2	54.7	58 726	47 074	6 640	73.8	53.1	45.5
1988	62 768	50 870	8 031	77.9	56.8	55.3	59 781	48 383	6 805	74.2	54.0	46.8
1989	63 704	52 212	7 954	78.1	57.7	55.9	60 837	49 745	6 759	74.5	54.9	47.5
1990	64 916	53 131	7 792	78.2	58.0	53.7	61 678	50 535	6 581	74.3	55.2	45.3
1991	65 374	53 708	7 265	77.7	57.9	51.6	61 178	50 634	5 906	72.7	54.6	42.0
1992	66 213	54 796	7 096	77.7	58.5	51.3	61 496	51 328	5 669	72.1	54.8	41.0
1993	66 642	55 388	7 170	77.3	58.5	51.5	62 355	52 099	5 805	72.3	55.0	41.7
1994	66 921	56 655	7 481	76.8	59.3	52.7	63 294	53 606	6 161	72.6	56.2	43.4
1995	67 324	57 215	7 765	76.7	59.4	53.5	64 085	54 396	6 419	73.0	56.5	44.2
1996	68 044	58 094	7 806	76.8	59.9	52.3	64 897	55 311	6 500	73.2	57.0	43.5
1997	69 166	59 198	7 932	77.0	60.5	51.6	66 284	56 613	6 661	73.7	57.8	43.4
1998	69 715	59 702	8 256	76.8	60.4	52.8	67 135	57 278	7 051	73.9	58.0	45.1
1999	70 194	60 840	8 333	76.7	60.7	52.0	67 761	58 555	7 172	74.0	58.5	44.7
2000	72 010	62 301	8 271	76.7	60.6	52.0	69 634	60 067	7 189	74.2	58.4	45.2
2001	72 816	63 016	7 902	76.5	60.6	49.6	69 776	60 417	6 740	73.3	58.1	42.3
2002	73 630	63 648	7 585	76.3	60.5	47.4	69 734	60 420	6 332	72.3	57.5	39.6
2003	74 623	64 716	7 170	75.9	60.6	44.5	70 415	61 402	5 919	71.7	57.5	36.8
2004	75 364	64 923	7 114	75.8	60.3	43.9	71 572	61 773	5 907	71.9	57.4	36.4
2005	76 443	65 714	7 164	75.8	60.4	43.7	73 050	62 702	5 978	72.4	57.6	36.5
2006	77 562	66 585	7 281	75.9	60.5	43.7	74 431	63 834	6 162	72.9	58.0	36.9
2007	78 596	67 516	7 012	75.9	60.6	41.3	75 337	64 799	5 911	72.8	58.2	34.8
2008	79 047	68 382	6 858	75.7	60.9	40.2	74 750	65 039	5 573	71.6	57.9	32.6
2009	78 897	68 856	6 390	74.8	60.8	37.5	71 341	63 699	4 837	67.6	56.2	28.4
2010	78 994	68 990	5 906	74.1	60.3	34.9	71 230	63 456	4 378	66.8	55.5	25.9
2011	79 080	68 810	5 727	73.4	59.8	34.1	72 182	63 360	4 327	67.0	55.0	25.8
2012	79 387	69 765	5 823	73.0	59.3	34.3	73 403	64 640	4 426	67.5	55.0	26.1
2011												
January	78 648	68 772	5 824	73.4	60.0	34.5	71 575	63 339	4 339	66.8	55.3	25.7
February	78 855	68 745	5 669	73.5	59.9	33.7	71 866	63 295	4 310	67.0	55.2	25.6
March	78 810	68 790	5 758	73.4	59.9	34.2	71 874	63 418	4 350	66.9	55.2	25.9
April	78 980	68 825	5 673	73.5	59.9	33.7	71 959	63 373	4 274	67.0	55.2	25.4
May	79 136	68 796	5 620	73.6	59.8	33.5	72 116	63 294	4 271	67.0	55.1	25.4
June	79 083	68 586	5 700	73.5	59.6	34.0	72 004	63 110	4 292	66.9	54.9	25.6
July	78 976	68 716	5 633	73.3	59.7	33.6	71 998	63 282	4 229	66.8	55.0	25.2
August	79 075	68 830	5 802	73.3	59.7	34.6	72 151	63 379	4 340	66.9	55.0	25.9
September	79 227	69 048	5 799	73.4	59.9	34.6	72 363	63 419	4 382	67.0	55.0	26.2
October	79 218	69 014	5 777	73.3	59.8	34.5	72 357	63 572	4 385	66.9	55.1	26.2
November	79 437	68 880	5 778	73.4	59.6	34.6	72 871	63 502	4 398	67.3	55.0	26.3
December	79 420	68 815	5 709	73.3	59.5	34.2	73 050	63 446	4 400	67.5	54.9	26.4
2012												
January	79 203	69 420	5 733	73.3	59.3	33.5	73 138	64 080	4 391	67.7	54.7	25.7
February	79 301	69 775	5 748	73.3	59.5	33.7	73 179	64 457	4 383	67.6	55.0	25.7
March	79 313	69 580	5 814	73.2	59.3	34.1	73 238	64 422	4 360	67.6	54.9	25.6
April	79 103	69 580	5 768	73.0	59.3	33.9	73 145	64 454	4 334	67.5	54.9	25.4
May	79 373	69 777	5 847	73.2	59.4	34.4	73 230	64 653	4 419	67.5	55.0	26.0
June	79 432	69 777	5 940	73.1	59.4	34.9	73 299	64 616	4 533	67.5	55.0	26.7
July	79 376	69 673	5 945	73.0	59.2	35.0	73 288	64 437	4 525	67.4	54.8	26.7
August	79 085	69 800	5 763	72.7	59.3	34.0	73 097	64 716	4 351	67.2	55.0	25.7
September	79 436	69 813	5 807	72.9	59.2	34.3	73 612	64 934	4 429	67.6	55.1	26.2
October	79 679	70 041	5 856	73.0	59.4	34.6	73 845	65 014	4 469	67.7	55.1	26.4
November	79 568	69 907	5 845	72.9	59.2	34.6	73 821	64 988	4 468	67.6	55.0	26.5
December	79 695	70 059	5 756	72.9	59.3	34.1	73 949	64 954	4 402	67.7	55.0	26.1

Table 10-3. Employment by Type of Job

(Thousands of persons, seasonally adjusted, except as noted.)

Year and month	By class of worker								Multiple jobholders		Employed and at work part-time	
	Agricultural	Nonagricultural industries										
		Total	Wage and salary				Self-employed (unincor-porated)	Unpaid family workers [1]	Total (thousands)	Percent of total employed	Economic reasons	Non-economic reasons
			Total	Government	Private industries							
					Private house-holds [1]	Other private industries						
1965	4 361	66 726	60 031	9 608	...	...	6 097	600	...	...	2 209	8 466
1966	3 979	68 915	62 362	10 323	...	...	5 991	564	...	...	1 960	8 112
1967	3 844	70 527	64 848	11 146	...	...	5 174	505	...	...	2 163	8 701
1968	3 817	72 103	66 519	11 590	...	...	5 102	485	...	...	1 970	9 075
1969	3 606	74 296	68 528	12 025	...	...	5 252	517	...	...	2 056	9 652
1970	3 463	75 215	69 491	12 431	...	...	5 221	502	...	...	2 446	9 999
1971	3 394	75 972	70 120	12 799	...	...	5 327	522	...	...	2 688	10 152
1972	3 484	78 669	72 785	13 393	...	...	5 365	519	...	...	2 648	10 612
1973	3 470	81 594	75 580	13 655	...	...	5 474	540	...	...	2 554	10 972
1974	3 515	83 279	77 094	14 124	...	...	5 697	489	...	...	2 988	11 153
1975	3 408	82 438	76 249	14 675	...	...	5 705	483	...	...	3 804	11 228
1976	3 331	85 421	79 175	15 132	...	...	5 783	464	...	...	3 607	11 607
1977	3 283	88 734	82 121	15 361	...	...	6 114	498	...	...	3 608	12 120
1978	3 387	92 661	85 753	15 525	...	...	6 429	479	...	...	3 516	12 650
1979	3 347	95 477	88 222	15 635	...	...	6 791	463	...	...	3 577	12 893
1980	3 364	95 938	88 525	15 912	...	...	7 000	413	...	...	4 321	13 067
1981	3 368	97 030	89 543	15 689	...	...	7 097	390	...	...	4 768	13 025
1982	3 401	96 125	88 462	15 516	...	...	7 262	401	...	...	6 170	12 953
1983	3 383	97 450	89 500	15 537	...	...	7 575	376	...	...	6 266	12 911
1984	3 321	101 685	93 565	15 770	...	...	7 785	335	...	...	5 744	13 169
1985	3 179	103 971	95 871	16 031	...	...	7 811	289	...	...	5 590	13 489
1986	3 163	106 434	98 299	16 342	...	...	7 881	255	...	...	5 588	13 935
1987	3 208	109 232	100 771	16 800	...	...	8 201	260	...	...	5 401	14 395
1988	3 169	111 800	103 021	17 114	...	...	8 519	260	...	...	5 206	14 963
1989	3 199	114 142	105 259	17 469	...	...	8 605	279	...	...	4 894	15 393
1990	3 223	115 570	106 598	17 769	...	...	8 719	253	...	...	5 204	15 341
1991	3 269	114 449	105 373	17 934	...	...	8 851	226	...	...	6 161	15 172
1992	3 247	115 245	106 437	18 136	...	...	8 575	233	...	...	6 520	14 918
1993	3 115	117 144	107 966	18 579	...	...	8 959	218	...	...	6 481	15 240
1994	3 409	119 651	110 517	18 293	...	...	9 003	131	7 260	5.9	4 625	17 638
1995	3 440	121 460	112 448	18 362	...	...	8 902	110	7 693	6.2	4 473	17 734
1996	3 443	123 264	114 171	18 217	...	...	8 971	122	7 832	6.2	4 315	17 770
1997	3 399	126 159	116 983	18 131	...	...	9 056	120	7 955	6.1	4 068	18 149
1998	3 378	128 085	119 019	18 383	...	...	8 962	103	7 926	6.0	3 665	18 530
1999	3 281	130 207	121 323	18 903	...	...	8 790	95	7 802	5.8	3 357	18 758
2000	2 464	134 427	125 114	19 248	718	105 148	9 205	108	7 604	5.6	3 227	18 814
2001	2 299	134 635	125 407	19 335	694	105 378	9 121	107	7 357	5.4	3 715	18 790
2002	2 311	134 174	125 156	19 636	757	104 764	8 923	95	7 291	5.3	4 213	18 843
2003	2 275	135 461	126 015	19 634	764	105 616	9 344	101	7 315	5.3	4 701	19 014
2004	2 232	137 020	127 463	19 983	779	106 701	9 467	90	7 473	5.4	4 567	19 380
2005	2 197	139 532	129 931	20 357	812	108 761	9 509	93	7 546	5.3	4 350	19 491
2006	2 206	142 221	132 449	20 337	803	111 309	9 685	87	7 576	5.2	4 162	19 591
2007	2 095	143 952	134 283	21 003	813	112 467	9 557	112	7 655	5.2	4 401	19 756
2008	2 168	143 194	133 882	21 258	805	111 819	9 219	93	7 620	5.2	5 875	19 343
2009	2 103	137 775	128 713	21 178	783	106 752	8 995	66	7 271	5.2	8 913	18 710
2010	2 206	136 858	127 914	21 003	667	106 244	8 860	84	6 878	4.9	8 874	18 251
2011	2 254	137 615	128 934	20 536	722	107 676	8 603	78	6 880	4.9	8 560	18 334
2012	2 186	140 283	131 452	20 360	738	110 355	8 749	81	6 943	4.9	8 122	18 806
2011												
January	2 267	137 033	128 149	20 637	610	106 841	8 813	91	6 803	4.9	8 432	17 796
February	2 263	137 225	128 475	20 806	688	106 892	8 697	87	6 750	4.8	8 398	18 219
March	2 241	137 457	128 542	20 773	695	107 076	8 773	105	6 746	4.8	8 525	18 436
April	2 117	137 459	128 692	20 684	671	107 312	8 677	94	6 812	4.9	8 649	18 300
May	2 228	137 435	128 698	20 416	799	107 535	8 662	79	6 865	4.9	8 562	18 374
June	2 235	137 112	128 531	20 439	766	107 469	8 524	76	6 943	5.0	8 536	18 497
July	2 232	137 214	128 707	20 425	822	107 505	8 513	82	6 834	4.9	8 416	18 274
August	2 378	137 410	128 857	20 311	769	107 791	8 583	66	6 950	5.0	8 816	18 211
September	2 245	137 904	129 453	20 511	756	108 171	8 320	55	7 001	5.0	9 101	18 395
October	2 225	138 182	129 572	20 489	771	108 276	8 553	50	6 925	4.9	8 726	18 409
November	2 251	138 525	129 799	20 414	674	108 701	8 574	57	6 967	4.9	8 436	18 544
December	2 380	138 508	129 811	20 523	640	108 599	8 550	91	6 982	5.0	8 168	18 489
2012												
January	2 205	139 446	130 589	20 506	569	109 449	8 756	112	7 011	5.0	8 220	18 700
February	2 188	139 856	131 312	20 557	621	110 064	8 483	106	6 979	4.9	8 127	18 868
March	2 217	139 871	131 221	20 226	656	110 353	8 547	79	6 976	4.9	7 664	18 530
April	2 166	139 734	131 104	19 957	724	110 427	8 557	72	6 873	4.8	7 896	18 868
May	2 274	140 033	131 321	20 079	834	110 486	8 640	78	6 941	4.9	8 116	19 356
June	2 200	140 218	131 342	19 995	832	110 638	8 818	82	6 790	4.8	8 210	18 825
July	2 224	140 013	131 154	20 100	818	110 255	8 845	74	6 871	4.8	8 245	18 846
August	2 146	139 918	131 215	20 411	796	109 987	8 754	67	6 931	4.9	8 043	18 954
September	2 198	140 767	131 743	20 647	811	110 289	8 863	76	6 882	4.8	8 607	18 728
October	2 195	141 245	132 326	20 555	707	111 058	8 819	76	6 927	4.8	8 286	18 896
November	2 121	141 149	132 038	20 598	754	110 659	8 959	69	7 109	5.0	8 138	18 594
December	2 088	141 190	132 113	20 686	732	110 632	8 935	85	7 017	4.9	7 918	18 763

[1] Not seasonally adjusted.
. . . = Not available.

Figure 10-2. Unemployment Rate, 1948–2012

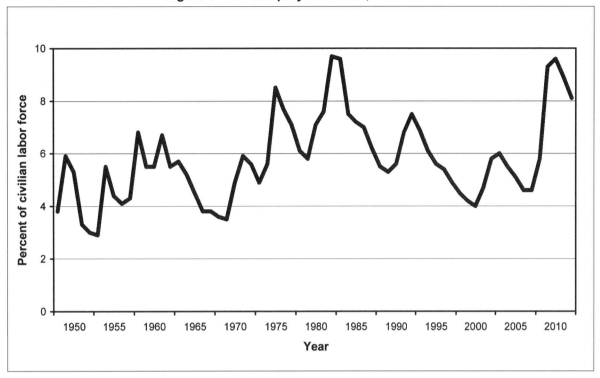

- The unemployment rate peaked at 10.0 percent in October 2009 (lagging, as it usually does, the business cycle trough, which was in June 2009). This was below the postwar record high of 10.8 percent, set in November and December 1982. Yet the employment losses of 2008–2009 were proportionately greater than the 2 percent drop in 1981–1982. The discrepancy is in labor force behavior. Recently, workers responded to job losses by dropping out of the labor force; in 1982, in contrast, labor force participation rates actually increased slightly. (Tables 10-1A and B)

- Unemployment hovered near 10 percent through early 2010, but has declined significantly since then to 7.6 percent in May 2013, as employment growth outpaced labor force growth. (Tables 10-1A and B and recent data)

- Unemployment rates in December 2012 for adult men were 3.1 percentage points higher than before the recession in 2007. For adult women, the rise was 3.3 percentage points, implying a somewhat greater impact. Over that period men's job losses, relative to population, were significantly higher than women's, but men were more likely to give up looking for work, and therefore not be counted as unemployed. (Tables 10-2 and 10-4)

- In December 2012, the median unemployed worker had been out of work 18.0 weeks—nearly double the median length of unemployment in the recession years 1983 and 2003. Median duration is more representative of the typical job-seeker than "average duration," which is distorted by the presence of a few extremely long-term unemployed and recently by a technical statistical problem. Nevertheless, the rise in long-term unemployment has been very large—and even understates the problem, since it does not include discouraged workers. (Table 10-5)

- Adding discouraged workers, workers marginally attached to the labor force, and persons on involuntary part time to get a comprehensive measure of the jobs gap, BLS calculates an underutilization rate that rose from 8.3 percent in 2007 to 16.7 percent in 2010, but has declined to 13.8 percent in May 2013. (Table 10-5 and recent data)

Table 10-4. Unemployment by Demographic Group

(Unemployment in thousands of persons and as a percent of the civilian labor force in group, seasonally adjusted, except as noted.)

| Year and month | Unemployment (thousands of persons) | | | | Unemployment rate (percent) | | | | | | | | |
| | Total | Men, 20 years and over | Women, 20 years and over | Both sexes, 16 to 19 years | All civilian workers | By age and sex | | | By race | | | | Hispanic or Latino ethnicity |
						Men, 20 years and over	Women, 20 years and over	Both sexes, 16 to 19 years	White	Black and other	Black or African American	Asian [1]	
1965	3 366	1 435	1 056	874	4.5	3.2	4.5	14.8	4.1	8.1	...	...	...
1966	2 875	1 120	921	837	3.8	2.5	3.8	12.8	3.4	7.3	...	...	...
1967	2 975	1 060	1 078	839	3.8	2.3	4.2	12.9	3.4	7.4	...	...	...
1968	2 817	993	985	838	3.6	2.2	3.8	12.7	3.2	6.7	...	...	...
1969	2 832	963	1 015	853	3.5	2.1	3.7	12.2	3.1	6.4	...	...	...
1970	4 093	1 638	1 349	1 106	4.9	3.5	4.8	15.3	4.5	8.2	...	...	...
1971	5 016	2 097	1 658	1 262	5.9	4.4	5.7	16.9	5.4	9.9	...	...	...
1972	4 882	1 948	1 625	1 308	5.6	4.0	5.4	16.2	5.1	10.0	10.4	...	...
1973	4 365	1 624	1 507	1 235	4.9	3.3	4.9	14.5	4.3	9.0	9.4	...	7.5
1974	5 156	1 957	1 777	1 422	5.6	3.8	5.5	16.0	5.0	9.9	10.5	...	8.1
1975	7 929	3 476	2 684	1 767	8.5	6.8	8.0	19.9	7.8	13.8	14.8	...	12.2
1976	7 406	3 098	2 588	1 719	7.7	5.9	7.4	19.0	7.0	13.1	14.0	...	11.5
1977	6 991	2 794	2 535	1 663	7.1	5.2	7.0	17.8	6.2	13.1	14.0	...	10.1
1978	6 202	2 328	2 292	1 583	6.1	4.3	6.0	16.4	5.2	11.9	12.8	...	9.1
1979	6 137	2 308	2 276	1 555	5.8	4.2	5.7	16.1	5.1	11.3	12.3	...	8.3
1980	7 637	3 353	2 615	1 669	7.1	5.9	6.4	17.8	6.3	13.1	14.3	...	10.1
1981	8 273	3 615	2 895	1 763	7.6	6.3	6.8	19.6	6.7	14.2	15.6	...	10.4
1982	10 678	5 089	3 613	1 977	9.7	8.8	8.3	23.2	8.6	17.3	18.9	...	13.8
1983	10 717	5 257	3 632	1 829	9.6	8.9	8.1	22.4	8.4	17.8	19.5	...	13.7
1984	8 539	3 932	3 107	1 499	7.5	6.6	6.8	18.9	6.5	14.4	15.9	...	10.7
1985	8 312	3 715	3 129	1 468	7.2	6.2	6.6	18.6	6.2	13.7	15.1	...	10.5
1986	8 237	3 751	3 032	1 454	7.0	6.1	6.2	18.3	6.0	13.1	14.5	...	10.6
1987	7 425	3 369	2 709	1 347	6.2	5.4	5.4	16.9	5.3	11.6	13.0	...	8.8
1988	6 701	2 987	2 487	1 226	5.5	4.8	4.9	15.3	4.7	10.4	11.7	...	8.2
1989	6 528	2 867	2 467	1 194	5.3	4.5	4.7	15.0	4.5	10.0	11.4	...	8.0
1990	7 047	3 239	2 596	1 212	5.6	5.0	4.9	15.5	4.8	10.1	11.4	...	8.2
1991	8 628	4 195	3 074	1 359	6.8	6.4	5.7	18.7	6.1	11.1	12.5	...	10.0
1992	9 613	4 717	3 469	1 427	7.5	7.1	6.3	20.1	6.6	12.7	14.2	...	11.6
1993	8 940	4 287	3 288	1 365	6.9	6.4	5.9	19.0	6.1	11.7	13.0	...	10.8
1994	7 996	3 627	3 049	1 320	6.1	5.4	5.4	17.6	5.3	10.5	11.5	...	9.9
1995	7 404	3 239	2 819	1 346	5.6	4.8	4.9	17.3	4.9	9.6	10.4	...	9.3
1996	7 236	3 146	2 783	1 306	5.4	4.6	4.8	16.7	4.7	9.3	10.5	...	8.9
1997	6 739	2 882	2 585	1 271	4.9	4.2	4.4	16.0	4.2	8.8	10.0	...	7.7
1998	6 210	2 580	2 424	1 205	4.5	3.7	4.1	14.6	3.9	7.8	8.9	...	7.2
1999	5 880	2 433	2 285	1 162	4.2	3.5	3.8	13.9	3.7	7.0	8.0	...	6.4
2000	5 692	2 376	2 235	1 081	4.0	3.3	3.6	13.1	3.5	6.7	7.6	3.6	5.7
2001	6 801	3 040	2 599	1 162	4.7	4.2	4.1	14.7	4.2	7.7	8.6	4.5	6.6
2002	8 378	3 896	3 228	1 253	5.8	5.3	5.1	16.5	5.1	9.2	10.2	5.9	7.5
2003	8 774	4 209	3 314	1 251	6.0	5.6	5.1	17.5	5.2	...	10.8	6.0	7.7
2004	8 149	3 791	3 150	1 208	5.5	5.0	4.9	17.0	4.8	...	10.4	4.4	7.0
2005	7 591	3 392	3 013	1 186	5.1	4.4	4.6	16.6	4.4	...	10.0	4.0	6.0
2006	7 001	3 131	2 751	1 119	4.6	4.0	4.1	15.4	4.0	...	8.9	3.0	5.2
2007	7 078	3 259	2 718	1 101	4.6	4.1	4.0	15.7	4.1	...	8.3	3.2	5.6
2008	8 924	4 297	3 342	1 285	5.8	5.4	4.9	18.7	5.2	...	10.1	4.0	7.6
2009	14 265	7 555	5 157	1 552	9.3	9.6	7.5	24.3	8.5	...	14.8	7.3	12.1
2010	14 825	7 763	5 534	1 528	9.6	9.8	8.0	25.9	8.7	...	16.0	7.5	12.5
2011	13 747	6 898	5 450	1 400	8.9	8.7	7.9	24.4	7.9	...	15.8	7.0	11.5
2012	12 506	5 984	5 125	1 397	8.1	7.5	7.3	24.0	7.2	...	13.8	5.9	10.3
2011													
January	13 992	7 073	5 433	1 486	9.1	9.0	7.9	25.5	8.1	...	15.8	6.9	12.1
February	13 798	6 989	5 450	1 359	9.0	8.9	7.9	24.0	8.1	...	15.5	6.8	11.6
March	13 716	6 936	5 372	1 408	8.9	8.8	7.8	24.4	8.0	...	15.7	7.1	11.4
April	13 872	7 022	5 452	1 399	9.0	8.9	7.9	24.7	8.1	...	16.3	6.4	11.9
May	13 871	7 021	5 502	1 349	9.0	8.9	8.0	24.0	8.0	...	16.3	7.0	11.8
June	13 964	7 079	5 476	1 408	9.1	9.0	8.0	24.7	8.1	...	16.2	6.8	11.6
July	13 817	6 978	5 434	1 404	9.0	8.8	7.9	24.9	8.0	...	15.8	7.7	11.3
August	13 837	6 923	5 452	1 462	9.0	8.8	7.9	25.2	7.9	...	16.5	7.1	11.2
September	13 910	6 864	5 628	1 417	9.0	8.7	8.2	24.4	7.9	...	15.8	7.8	11.3
October	13 696	6 861	5 442	1 392	8.9	8.7	7.9	24.1	8.0	...	14.9	7.3	11.4
November	13 325	6 567	5 378	1 380	8.6	8.3	7.8	23.9	7.7	...	15.5	6.5	11.3
December	13 049	6 370	5 369	1 310	8.5	8.0	7.8	22.9	7.5	...	15.6	6.8	11.0
2012													
January	12 748	6 065	5 341	1 342	8.3	7.7	7.7	23.4	7.4	...	13.6	6.7	10.5
February	12 806	6 123	5 318	1 365	8.3	7.7	7.6	23.7	7.4	...	14.1	6.3	10.6
March	12 686	6 075	5 158	1 453	8.2	7.7	7.4	25.0	7.3	...	14.0	6.2	10.3
April	12 518	5 958	5 126	1 434	8.1	7.5	7.4	24.9	7.4	...	13.1	5.2	10.3
May	12 695	6 143	5 124	1 428	8.2	7.7	7.3	24.4	7.4	...	13.6	5.2	11.0
June	12 701	6 133	5 161	1 406	8.2	7.7	7.4	23.7	7.3	...	14.4	6.3	11.0
July	12 745	6 089	5 236	1 420	8.2	7.7	7.5	23.9	7.4	...	14.1	6.2	10.3
August	12 483	5 988	5 083	1 412	8.1	7.6	7.3	24.5	7.2	...	14.0	5.9	10.2
September	12 082	5 825	4 879	1 378	7.8	7.3	7.0	23.7	7.0	...	13.4	4.8	9.9
October	12 248	5 834	5 027	1 387	7.9	7.3	7.2	23.7	6.9	...	14.5	4.9	10.0
November	12 042	5 747	4 918	1 376	7.8	7.2	7.0	23.6	6.8	...	13.2	6.4	9.9
December	12 206	5 746	5 105	1 355	7.8	7.2	7.3	23.5	6.9	...	14.0	6.6	9.6

[1] Not seasonally adjusted.
. . . = Not available.

Table 10-5. Unemployment Rates and Related Data

(Seasonally adjusted, except as noted.)

Year and month	Unemployment rates by marital status (percent of labor force in group)			Unemployment rates by reason for unemployment (percent of total civilian labor force in group.)					Duration of unemployment		Alternative measures of labor under-utilization (percent)		
	Married men, spouse present	Married women, spouse present	Women who maintain families[1]	Total	Job losers and persons who completed temporary jobs	Job leavers	Reentrants	New entrants	Average (mean) weeks unemployed	Median weeks unemployed	Including discouraged workers (U-4)	Including all marginally attached workers (U-5)	Including marginally attached and under-employed (U-6)
1965	2.4	4.5	...	4.5	...	...	...	...	11.8	...	...	...	...
1966	1.9	3.7	...	3.8	...	...	...	...	10.4	...	...	...	...
1967	1.8	4.5	4.9	3.8	1.6	0.6	1.2	0.5	8.7	2.3	...	...	...
1968	1.6	3.9	4.4	3.6	1.4	0.5	1.2	0.5	8.4	4.5	...	...	...
1969	1.5	3.9	4.4	3.5	1.3	0.5	1.2	0.5	7.8	4.4	...	...	...
1970	2.6	4.9	5.4	4.9	2.2	0.7	1.5	0.6	8.6	4.9	...	...	...
1971	3.2	5.7	7.3	5.9	2.8	0.7	1.7	0.7	11.3	6.3	...	...	...
1972	2.8	5.4	7.2	5.6	2.4	0.7	1.7	0.8	12.0	6.2	...	...	...
1973	2.3	4.7	7.1	4.9	1.9	0.8	1.5	0.7	10.0	5.2	...	...	...
1974	2.7	5.3	7.0	5.6	2.4	0.8	1.6	0.7	9.8	5.2	...	...	...
1975	5.1	7.9	10.0	8.5	4.7	0.9	2.0	0.9	14.2	8.4	...	...	...
1976	4.2	7.1	10.1	7.7	3.8	0.9	2.0	0.9	15.8	8.2	...	...	...
1977	3.6	6.5	9.4	7.1	3.2	0.9	2.0	1.0	14.3	7.0	...	...	...
1978	2.8	5.5	8.5	6.1	2.5	0.9	1.8	0.9	11.9	5.9	...	...	...
1979	2.8	5.1	8.3	5.8	2.5	0.8	1.7	0.8	10.8	5.4	...	...	...
1980	4.2	5.8	9.2	7.1	3.7	0.8	1.8	0.8	11.9	6.5	...	...	...
1981	4.3	6.0	10.4	7.6	3.9	0.8	1.9	0.9	13.7	6.9	...	...	...
1982	6.5	7.4	11.7	9.7	5.7	0.8	2.2	1.1	15.6	8.7	...	...	...
1983	6.5	7.0	12.2	9.6	5.6	0.7	2.2	1.1	20.0	10.1	...	...	...
1984	4.6	5.7	10.3	7.5	3.9	0.7	1.9	1.0	18.2	7.9	...	...	...
1985	4.3	5.6	10.4	7.2	3.6	0.8	2.0	0.9	15.6	6.8	...	...	...
1986	4.4	5.2	9.8	7.0	3.4	0.9	1.8	0.9	15.0	6.9	...	...	...
1987	3.9	4.3	9.2	6.2	3.0	0.8	1.6	0.8	14.5	6.5	...	...	...
1988	3.3	3.9	8.1	5.5	2.5	0.8	1.5	0.7	13.5	5.9	...	...	...
1989	3.0	3.7	8.1	5.3	2.4	0.8	1.5	0.5	11.9	4.8	...	...	...
1990	3.4	3.8	8.3	5.6	2.7	0.8	1.5	0.5	12.0	5.3	...	...	...
1991	4.4	4.5	9.3	6.8	3.7	0.8	1.7	0.6	13.7	6.8	...	...	...
1992	5.1	5.0	10.0	7.5	4.2	0.8	1.8	0.7	17.7	8.7	...	...	...
1993	4.4	4.6	9.7	6.9	3.8	0.8	1.7	0.7	18.0	8.3	...	...	...
1994	3.7	4.1	8.9	6.1	2.9	0.6	2.1	0.5	18.8	9.2	6.5	7.4	10.9
1995	3.3	3.9	8.0	5.6	2.6	0.6	1.9	0.4	16.6	8.3	5.9	6.7	10.1
1996	3.0	3.6	8.2	5.4	2.5	0.6	1.9	0.4	16.7	8.3	5.7	6.5	9.7
1997	2.7	3.1	8.1	4.9	2.2	0.6	1.7	0.4	15.8	8.0	5.2	5.9	8.9
1998	2.4	2.9	7.2	4.5	2.1	0.5	1.5	0.4	14.5	6.7	4.7	5.4	8.0
1999	2.2	2.7	6.4	4.2	1.9	0.6	1.4	0.3	13.4	6.4	4.4	5.0	7.4
2000	2.0	2.7	5.9	4.0	1.8	0.5	1.4	0.3	12.6	5.9	4.2	4.8	7.0
2001	2.7	3.1	6.6	4.7	2.4	0.6	1.4	0.3	13.1	6.8	4.9	5.6	8.1
2002	3.6	3.7	8.0	5.8	3.2	0.6	1.6	0.4	16.6	9.1	6.0	6.7	9.6
2003	3.8	3.7	8.5	6.0	3.3	0.6	1.7	0.4	19.2	10.1	6.3	7.0	10.1
2004	3.1	3.5	8.0	5.5	2.8	0.6	1.6	0.5	19.6	9.8	5.8	6.5	9.6
2005	2.8	3.3	7.8	5.1	2.5	0.6	1.6	0.4	18.4	8.9	5.4	6.1	8.9
2006	2.4	2.9	7.1	4.6	2.2	0.5	1.5	0.4	16.8	8.3	4.9	5.5	8.2
2007	2.5	2.8	6.5	4.6	2.3	0.5	1.4	0.4	16.8	8.5	4.9	5.5	8.3
2008	3.4	3.6	8.0	5.8	3.1	0.6	1.6	0.5	17.9	9.4	6.1	6.8	10.5
2009	6.6	5.5	11.5	9.3	5.9	0.6	2.1	0.7	24.4	15.1	9.7	10.5	16.2
2010	6.8	5.9	12.3	9.6	6.0	0.6	2.3	0.8	33.0	21.4	10.3	11.1	16.7
2011	5.8	5.6	12.4	8.9	5.3	0.6	2.2	0.8	39.3	21.4	9.5	10.4	15.9
2012	4.9	5.3	11.4	8.1	4.4	0.6	2.2	0.8	39.4	19.3	8.6	9.5	14.7
2011													
January	5.9	5.6	12.7	9.1	5.5	0.6	2.2	0.9	37.3	21.5	9.7	10.8	16.2
February	5.9	5.4	13.0	9.0	5.5	0.6	2.2	0.8	37.4	21.3	9.6	10.6	16.0
March	6.0	5.8	12.3	8.9	5.4	0.6	2.2	0.9	39.2	21.8	9.5	10.4	15.8
April	6.0	5.7	11.7	9.0	5.4	0.6	2.2	0.8	38.6	21.0	9.6	10.5	16.0
May	5.9	5.8	12.7	9.0	5.4	0.6	2.2	0.8	39.5	21.8	9.5	10.3	15.8
June	6.2	5.6	12.8	9.1	5.3	0.6	2.3	0.8	39.6	21.8	9.7	10.7	16.1
July	6.0	5.6	12.1	9.0	5.3	0.6	2.2	0.8	40.4	21.5	9.7	10.6	16.0
August	5.7	5.8	11.9	9.0	5.2	0.6	2.3	0.8	40.3	22.2	9.6	10.5	16.1
September	5.8	5.9	12.4	9.0	5.2	0.6	2.3	0.9	40.4	21.9	9.6	10.5	16.3
October	5.8	5.7	12.3	8.9	5.1	0.7	2.2	0.8	38.9	20.4	9.5	10.4	16.0
November	5.3	5.4	12.4	8.6	4.9	0.7	2.2	0.8	40.7	21.1	9.3	10.2	15.5
December	5.2	5.4	12.9	8.5	4.9	0.6	2.2	0.8	40.7	20.8	9.0	10.0	15.2
2012													
January	5.1	5.5	12.0	8.3	4.7	0.6	2.1	0.8	40.2	20.8	8.9	9.9	15.1
February	5.0	5.4	11.7	8.3	4.6	0.7	2.2	0.9	39.9	20.1	8.9	9.8	15.0
March	5.1	5.3	10.8	8.2	4.5	0.7	2.1	0.9	39.5	19.7	8.7	9.6	14.5
April	5.1	5.3	10.2	8.1	4.5	0.6	2.2	0.9	39.1	19.3	8.7	9.5	14.5
May	5.3	4.9	10.9	8.2	4.5	0.6	2.2	0.9	39.6	20.1	8.7	9.6	14.8
June	4.9	5.4	11.8	8.2	4.6	0.6	2.1	0.8	39.7	19.4	8.7	9.6	14.8
July	4.9	5.7	11.7	8.2	4.6	0.6	2.2	0.8	38.8	16.8	8.7	9.7	14.9
August	4.9	5.1	12.3	8.1	4.5	0.6	2.1	0.8	39.3	18.2	8.6	9.6	14.7
September	4.7	5.0	11.3	7.8	4.2	0.6	2.1	0.8	39.6	18.7	8.3	9.3	14.7
October	4.6	5.1	11.5	7.9	4.2	0.6	2.1	0.8	39.9	19.6	8.4	9.3	14.5
November	4.7	5.1	10.7	7.8	4.1	0.6	2.1	0.9	39.7	18.9	8.3	9.2	14.4
December	4.7	5.2	11.3	7.8	4.1	0.6	2.3	0.8	38.1	18.0	8.5	9.4	14.4

[1]Not seasonally adjusted.
. . . = Not available.

Table 10-6. Labor Force and Employment Estimates Smoothed for Population Adjustments

(Thousands of persons, seasonally adjusted.)

Year	January	February	March	April	May	June	July	August	September	October	November	December
CIVILIAN LABOR FORCE												
1990	125 845	125 734	125 837	125 697	125 953	125 645	125 816	126 087	126 001	126 116	126 203	126 287
1991	126 112	126 189	126 420	126 742	126 382	126 549	126 384	126 392	126 905	126 909	126 981	126 956
1992	127 566	127 524	127 934	128 184	128 475	128 829	128 945	129 008	128 908	128 444	128 872	128 998
1993	128 856	128 926	129 079	129 077	129 772	129 932	129 931	130 166	129 826	130 145	130 296	130 539
1994	131 210	131 296	131 038	131 272	131 444	131 237	131 341	131 980	132 139	132 477	132 637	132 710
1995	132 811	132 901	132 906	133 404	132 673	132 784	133 193	133 199	133 489	133 607	133 517	133 426
1996	133 545	133 896	134 138	134 381	134 654	134 697	135 302	135 083	135 560	135 982	136 082	136 202
1997	136 560	136 517	137 025	137 164	137 281	137 387	137 668	137 824	137 894	137 865	138 209	138 418
1998	138 370	138 401	138 539	138 465	138 703	138 800	138 947	138 942	139 679	139 685	139 801	140 070
1999	140 456	140 433	140 207	140 452	140 615	140 852	140 977	140 981	141 189	141 353	141 623	141 790
2000	142 260	142 443	142 414	142 724	142 355	142 551	142 232	142 461	142 458	142 556	142 889	143 168
2001	143 713	143 607	143 823	143 462	143 204	143 237	143 527	143 150	143 848	143 938	144 085	144 143
2002	143 715	144 477	144 299	144 536	144 742	144 605	144 593	144 792	145 327	145 083	144 803	144 822
2003	145 054	145 193	145 091	145 517	145 519	146 047	145 456	145 392	145 453	145 614	145 871	145 579
2004	146 111	145 963	146 182	146 074	146 273	146 651	146 867	146 724	146 561	146 922	147 274	147 156
2005	147 161	147 480	147 493	148 010	148 329	148 292	148 470	148 800	148 960	148 992	149 041	148 992
2006	149 292	149 704	149 862	149 917	150 091	150 361	150 371	150 695	150 629	150 993	151 342	151 653
2007	151 885	151 711	151 764	151 138	151 356	151 709	151 708	151 390	152 035	151 791	152 422	152 490
2008	153 260	152 844	153 090	152 943	153 466	153 466	153 614	153 777	153 698	153 994	153 750	153 758
2009	153 781	154 070	153 683	154 014	154 273	154 236	154 028	153 819	153 332	153 317	153 395	152 627
2010	153 212	153 460	153 720	154 337	153 873	153 388	153 476	153 846	153 736	153 453	153 913	153 424
2011	153 531	153 561	153 656	153 782	153 862	153 684	153 645	154 033	154 407	154 348	154 440	154 294
2012	154 450	154 923	154 809	154 556	155 108	155 263	155 112	154 768	155 181	155 705	155 452	155 648
CIVILIAN EMPLOYMENT, TOTAL												
1990	119 093	119 082	119 238	118 898	119 209	119 052	118 891	118 894	118 628	118 651	118 432	118 379
1991	118 089	117 915	117 823	118 293	117 634	117 845	117 785	117 712	118 169	118 052	118 033	117 740
1992	118 265	118 050	118 454	118 748	118 709	118 764	119 071	119 195	119 101	119 020	119 280	119 413
1993	119 503	119 715	119 995	119 938	120 594	120 781	120 970	121 373	121 081	121 363	121 722	122 031
1994	122 547	122 679	122 534	122 908	123 497	123 277	123 362	124 013	124 372	124 811	125 230	125 448
1995	125 402	125 681	125 720	125 722	125 207	125 321	125 629	125 677	125 972	126 241	126 052	125 963
1996	126 013	126 542	126 779	126 924	127 189	127 562	127 922	128 161	128 540	128 909	128 801	128 904
1997	129 358	129 370	129 981	130 247	130 584	130 544	130 970	131 172	131 194	131 368	131 859	131 898
1998	131 958	132 053	132 072	132 484	132 614	132 545	132 643	132 718	133 333	133 359	133 655	133 994
1999	134 436	134 276	134 381	134 402	134 775	134 855	134 905	135 097	135 227	135 529	135 862	136 092
2000	136 552	136 585	136 681	137 243	136 597	136 900	136 485	136 609	136 833	137 022	137 249	137 534
2001	137 691	137 519	137 683	137 193	136 979	136 754	136 945	136 109	136 707	136 246	136 086	135 889
2002	135 536	136 266	135 998	135 941	136 347	136 216	136 207	136 492	137 082	136 781	136 289	136 187
2003	136 580	136 622	136 552	136 727	136 616	136 838	136 501	136 553	136 590	136 940	137 354	137 318
2004	137 771	137 827	137 724	137 935	138 092	138 398	138 763	138 766	138 666	138 895	139 377	139 257
2005	139 407	139 533	139 786	140 369	140 708	140 798	141 094	141 486	141 439	141 571	141 508	141 746
2006	142 251	142 544	142 814	142 821	143 135	143 385	143 222	143 630	143 806	144 289	144 495	144 915
2007	144 807	144 821	145 068	144 326	144 626	144 770	144 599	144 364	144 907	144 597	145 226	144 892
2008	145 583	145 354	145 276	145 314	145 083	144 905	144 693	144 358	144 223	143 943	143 237	142 502
2009	141 692	141 180	140 256	140 183	139 778	139 530	139 419	138 999	138 326	137 935	138 174	137 532
2010	138 190	138 376	138 520	139 049	139 010	138 904	138 925	139 164	139 148	138 859	138 809	139 059
2011	139 495	139 718	139 896	139 864	139 944	139 672	139 781	140 148	140 447	140 603	141 066	141 196
2012	141 695	142 110	142 115	142 032	142 404	142 553	142 359	142 276	143 090	143 448	143 401	143 432

Table 10-7. Insured Unemployment

(Averages of weekly data; thousands of persons, except as noted.)

Year and month	State programs, seasonally adjusted			Federal programs, not seasonally adjusted					
				Initial claims		Persons claiming benefits			
	Initial claims	Insured unemployment	Insured unemployment rate (percent) [1]	Federal employees	Newly discharged veterans	Federal employees	Newly discharged veterans	Railroad retirement	Extended benefits
1970	297	1 848	...	...	...	...	...	...	...
1971	296	2 152	4.1	...	...	...	...	...	...
1972	263	1 844	3.5	...	...	...	...	...	...
1973	244	1 629	2.7	...	...	...	...	...	...
1974	352	2 278	3.5	...	...	...	...	...	...
1975	474	3 965	6.0	...	...	...	...	...	...
1976	383	2 978	4.5	...	...	...	...	...	...
1977	374	2 644	3.9	...	...	...	...	...	...
1978	341	2 337	3.3	...	...	...	...	...	...
1979	383	2 428	3.0	...	...	...	...	...	...
1980	488	3 365	3.9	...	...	...	...	...	...
1981	451	3 032	3.5	...	...	...	...	...	...
1982	586	4 094	4.7	...	...	...	...	...	...
1983	441	3 337	3.9	...	...	...	...	...	...
1984	374	2 452	2.8	...	...	...	...	...	...
1985	392	2 584	2.9	...	...	...	...	...	...
1986	378	2 632	2.8	2.13	2.52	20.24	17.11	...	...
1987	325	2 273	2.4	2.19	2.57	21.29	17.71	...	9.51
1988	309	2 075	2.1	2.32	2.74	22.91	18.13	13.28	1.17
1989	330	2 174	2.1	2.14	2.31	22.17	15.09	10.37	0.61
1990	385	2 539	2.4	2.45	2.54	23.89	18.43	10.56	2.36
1991	447	3 338	3.2	2.55	2.93	30.50	22.12	10.73	32.16
1992	409	3 208	3.1	2.75	4.95	32.10	60.25	8.77	4.61
1993	344	2 768	2.6	2.55	3.94	32.06	54.90	7.40	7.59
1994	340	2 667	2.5	2.54	3.02	32.21	37.65	6.21	31.09
1995	359	2 590	2.4	4.57	2.51	31.68	29.78	5.48	14.27
1996	352	2 552	2.3	7.33	2.13	29.84	24.30	5.40	5.53
1997	322	2 300	2.0	2.01	1.75	23.58	19.66	4.00	5.35
1998	317	2 213	1.9	1.64	1.41	19.60	15.68	3.19	6.43
1999	298	2 186	1.8	1.48	1.18	16.85	14.25	3.24	3.05
2000	299	2 112	1.7	1.73	1.05	18.60	12.54	3.92	0.58
2001	406	3 016	2.4	1.47	1.15	18.57	13.98	...	0.57
2002	404	3 570	2.8	1.46	1.22	17.54	16.07	...	10.79
2003	402	3 532	2.8	1.56	1.46	18.22	19.68	...	22.30
2004	342	2 930	2.3	1.50	1.89	18.14	26.90	...	4.22
2005	331	2 660	2.1	1.46	2.03	16.92	27.58	...	1.69
2006	312	2 456	1.9	1.34	1.96	15.51	26.37	...	1.38
2007	321	2 548	1.9	1.29	1.67	14.90	22.80	...	0.00
2008	418	3 337	2.5	1.25	1.64	14.53	22.16	...	3.43
2009	574	5 808	4.4	1.62	2.03	19.91	30.41	...	380.75
2010	459	4 544	3.6	2.73	2.56	28.31	39.21	...	571.30
2011	409	3 744	3.0	2.22	2.57	31.18	39.14	...	633.42
2012	374	3 319	2.6	1.46	2.56	20.42	39.72	...	179.91
2010									
January	484	4 878	3.8	1.86	2.27	26.47	36.85	...	237.98
February	485	4 869	3.7	1.28	2.24	23.67	36.29	...	174.32
March	468	4 851	3.7	1.26	2.53	22.05	36.18	...	153.82
April	468	4 840	3.7	1.30	2.43	19.78	36.98	...	238.14
May	459	4 812	3.7	1.61	2.46	17.28	36.35	...	385.72
June	461	4 804	3.7	2.31	2.61	18.45	36.76	...	467.55
July	458	4 781	3.7	3.43	2.80	22.18	41.71	...	612.63
August	474	4 765	3.7	4.37	3.10	25.28	41.12	...	913.35
September	449	4 744	3.7	4.13	3.09	29.60	41.56	...	945.21
October	449	4 746	3.7	5.43	2.68	40.90	42.55	...	963.76
November	428	4 736	3.7	2.96	2.30	46.87	42.11	...	898.12
December	425	4 731	3.7	2.49	2.24	48.86	41.96	...	886.25
2011									
January	432	3 964	3.2	3.28	2.63	49.25	41.50	...	887.49
February	405	3 883	3.1	1.80	2.30	44.18	40.10	...	782.46
March	406	3 788	3.0	1.58	2.23	38.55	38.66	...	739.79
April	421	3 768	3.0	1.67	2.33	30.86	37.23	...	686.68
May	422	3 752	3.0	1.78	2.42	23.60	36.15	...	617.12
June	419	3 727	3.0	2.25	2.68	23.27	36.84	...	605.31
July	411	3 722	3.0	2.58	2.68	25.15	37.64	...	545.14
August	408	3 714	3.0	1.90	2.68	25.48	38.16	...	544.98
September	410	3 711	3.0	2.13	2.72	24.35	38.39	...	526.36
October	402	3 674	2.9	2.86	2.86	27.68	40.42	...	536.24
November	389	3 627	2.9	2.27	2.46	29.18	41.60	...	553.12
December	382	3 594	2.8	2.14	2.73	30.71	42.41	...	553.75
2012									
January	382	3 503	2.8	1.81	2.81	30.47	42.84	...	498.94
February	367	3 431	2.7	1.27	2.50	28.02	41.96	...	471.98
March	367	3 367	2.7	1.20	2.44	23.88	41.33	...	436.39
April	379	3 315	2.6	1.20	2.40	19.63	40.14	...	355.66
May	373	3 303	2.6	1.30	2.39	16.38	38.61	...	250.37
June	380	3 314	2.6	1.49	2.57	16.29	38.19	...	60.58
July	369	3 304	2.6	1.38	2.56	17.63	39.38	...	15.23
August	371	3 312	2.6	1.22	2.60	17.39	38.69	...	3.89
September	373	3 277	0.0	1.41	2.82	16.88	38.14	...	19.36
October	369	2 798	2.5	1.77	2.74	18.13	39.08	...	36.02
November	401	3 284	2.6	1.84	2.50	19.40	39.33	...	38.14
December	366	3 208	2.5	1.68	2.39	21.67	39.45	...	18.59

[1] Insured unemployed as a percent of employment covered by state programs.
... = Not available.

Section 10b: Payroll Employment, Hours, and Earnings

Figure 10-3. Total Nonfarm Payroll Employment, 1946–2012

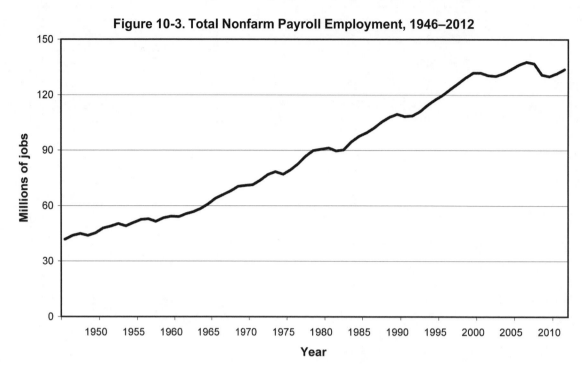

- Nonfarm payroll employment peaked in January 2008 and plunged 6.4 percent, a postwar record, between then and its lowest point in February 2010. The total number of jobs lost by this measure was 8.74 million. (Table 10-8A and B)

- Preliminary data for May 2013 indicate a nonfarm payroll job gain of 6.3 million since the February 2010 low, comparable to the recent gains in the household survey featured in the previous section. Differences in concepts and measurement practice between these two employment surveys are discussed in the Notes and Definitions to this chapter. (Table 10-8A and recent data)

- Based on annual average data, payroll employment grew by 5.8 million jobs between the 2000 and 2007 business cycle high points, an average growth rate of 0.6 percent per year during the latest completed cycle. The previous business cycle lasted 10 years between high points, from 1990 to 2000. During that period, 22.4 million jobs were added to U.S. nonfarm payrolls, for an annual average growth rate of 1.9 percent per year. (Table 10-8B)

- The diffusion index shows the percentage of industries in which employment is higher than six months earlier. Diffusion indexes measure the extent to which expansion and contraction have spread throughout the economy; indexes below 50 percent indicate recession. This index reached a low of 12.2 percent in April 2009—lower than the lowest points reached in any of the previous four recessions (1980, 1981–1982, 1990–1991, and 2001), and thus indicating the most widespread and pervasive decline in 30 years or more. Gains have been widespread during the recovery, with 77 percent of industries showing increases in early 2012, and a still-high 67 percent in May 2013. (Tables 10-8A and B and recent data)

Table 10-8A. Nonfarm Payroll Employment by NAICS Supersector: Recent Data

(Thousands; seasonally adjusted, except as noted.)

Year and month	Total	Private							Service-providing				
		Total	Goods-producing						Total	Private			
			Total	Mining and logging	Construc-tion	Manufacturing				Total	Trade, transportation, and utilities		
						Total	Durable	Nondurable			Total	Wholesale trade	Retail trade
2005	133 747	111 943	22 190	628	7 336	14 227	8 956	5 271	111 557	89 753	25 959	5 764	15 280
2006	136 125	114 151	22 530	684	7 691	14 155	8 981	5 174	113 594	91 621	26 276	5 905	15 353
2007	137 645	115 427	22 233	724	7 630	13 879	8 808	5 071	115 412	93 194	26 630	6 015	15 520
2008	136 852	114 342	21 335	767	7 162	13 406	8 463	4 943	115 517	93 008	26 293	5 943	15 283
2009	130 876	108 321	18 558	694	6 016	11 847	7 284	4 564	112 318	89 764	24 906	5 587	14 522
2010	129 917	107 427	17 751	705	5 518	11 528	7 064	4 464	112 166	89 676	24 636	5 452	14 440
2011	131 497	109 411	18 047	788	5 533	11 726	7 273	4 453	113 450	91 363	25 065	5 543	14 668
2012	133 739	111 822	18 410	851	5 641	11 919	7 462	4 456	115 329	93 411	25 516	5 673	14 875
2008													
January	138 056	115 668	21 947	746	7 476	13 725	8 693	5 032	116 109	93 721	26 714	6 036	15 570
February	137 971	115 554	21 898	748	7 453	13 697	8 674	5 023	116 073	93 656	26 663	6 026	15 528
March	137 892	115 449	21 820	755	7 406	13 659	8 646	5 013	116 072	93 629	26 633	6 015	15 506
April	137 677	115 227	21 680	755	7 327	13 598	8 596	5 002	115 997	93 547	26 539	5 993	15 429
May	137 491	115 008	21 599	761	7 274	13 564	8 579	4 985	115 892	93 409	26 460	5 980	15 379
June	137 322	114 805	21 483	766	7 213	13 504	8 542	4 962	115 839	93 322	26 395	5 966	15 335
July	137 106	114 538	21 360	770	7 160	13 430	8 488	4 942	115 746	93 178	26 332	5 946	15 299
August	136 836	114 269	21 250	778	7 114	13 358	8 430	4 928	115 586	93 019	26 241	5 926	15 245
September	136 377	113 840	21 101	782	7 044	13 275	8 372	4 903	115 276	92 739	26 123	5 914	15 172
October	135 905	113 356	20 897	781	6 967	13 149	8 277	4 872	115 008	92 459	26 004	5 876	15 103
November	135 130	112 570	20 625	776	6 813	13 036	8 195	4 841	114 505	91 945	25 802	5 838	14 981
December	134 425	111 869	20 323	771	6 701	12 851	8 066	4 785	114 102	91 546	25 625	5 797	14 870
2009													
January	133 631	111 048	19 874	764	6 554	12 556	7 826	4 730	113 757	91 174	25 471	5 760	14 784
February	132 936	110 356	19 588	749	6 453	12 386	7 706	4 680	113 348	90 768	25 338	5 717	14 717
March	132 106	109 544	19 232	728	6 291	12 213	7 580	4 633	112 874	90 312	25 164	5 673	14 621
April	131 402	108 723	18 890	711	6 149	12 030	7 428	4 602	112 512	89 833	25 007	5 628	14 557
May	131 050	108 435	18 661	692	6 103	11 866	7 292	4 574	112 389	89 774	24 959	5 602	14 554
June	130 578	107 993	18 414	685	6 008	11 721	7 178	4 543	112 164	89 579	24 894	5 576	14 530
July	130 227	107 711	18 264	677	5 928	11 659	7 137	4 522	111 963	89 447	24 798	5 552	14 485
August	130 017	107 489	18 142	668	5 851	11 623	7 109	4 514	111 875	89 347	24 766	5 535	14 478
September	129 784	107 327	18 037	666	5 785	11 586	7 081	4 505	111 747	89 290	24 702	5 521	14 436
October	129 614	107 094	17 923	660	5 724	11 539	7 047	4 492	111 691	89 171	24 616	5 502	14 380
November	129 593	107 060	17 863	663	5 693	11 507	7 019	4 488	111 730	89 197	24 588	5 490	14 371
December	129 373	106 893	17 786	665	5 650	11 471	6 998	4 473	111 587	89 107	24 539	5 475	14 334
2010													
January	129 360	106 876	17 710	669	5 581	11 460	6 990	4 470	111 650	89 166	24 536	5 450	14 385
February	129 320	106 850	17 657	675	5 522	11 460	6 990	4 470	111 663	89 193	24 541	5 446	14 397
March	129 474	106 961	17 691	683	5 542	11 466	7 005	4 461	111 783	89 270	24 571	5 445	14 421
April	129 703	107 131	17 738	687	5 554	11 497	7 030	4 467	111 965	89 393	24 574	5 443	14 419
May	130 224	107 233	17 754	696	5 527	11 531	7 057	4 474	112 470	89 479	24 595	5 439	14 434
June	130 094	107 327	17 751	700	5 512	11 539	7 067	4 472	112 343	89 576	24 607	5 443	14 427
July	130 008	107 430	17 762	707	5 497	11 558	7 088	4 470	112 246	89 668	24 639	5 446	14 443
August	129 971	107 559	17 782	715	5 519	11 548	7 084	4 464	112 189	89 777	24 646	5 447	14 451
September	129 928	107 672	17 774	721	5 499	11 554	7 095	4 459	112 154	89 898	24 688	5 453	14 471
October	130 156	107 860	17 787	731	5 501	11 555	7 102	4 453	112 369	90 073	24 740	5 462	14 503
November	130 300	108 014	17 809	735	5 497	11 577	7 119	4 458	112 491	90 205	24 742	5 470	14 486
December	130 395	108 128	17 792	734	5 468	11 590	7 130	4 460	112 603	90 336	24 774	5 476	14 492
2011													
January	130 464	108 208	17 797	738	5 435	11 624	7 171	4 453	112 667	90 411	24 821	5 483	14 547
February	130 660	108 451	17 880	740	5 478	11 662	7 199	4 463	112 780	90 571	24 868	5 497	14 557
March	130 865	108 674	17 923	756	5 485	11 682	7 218	4 464	112 942	90 751	24 896	5 513	14 564
April	131 169	108 977	17 972	768	5 497	11 707	7 238	4 469	113 197	91 005	24 990	5 523	14 634
May	131 284	109 160	18 015	776	5 524	11 715	7 257	4 458	113 269	91 145	25 013	5 531	14 639
June	131 493	109 337	18 042	788	5 530	11 724	7 274	4 450	113 451	91 295	25 076	5 540	14 676
July	131 571	109 543	18 093	799	5 547	11 747	7 290	4 457	113 478	91 450	25 116	5 546	14 710
August	131 703	109 672	18 109	803	5 546	11 760	7 298	4 462	113 594	91 563	25 152	5 556	14 711
September	131 928	109 928	18 156	811	5 583	11 762	7 307	4 455	113 772	91 772	25 166	5 560	14 733
October	132 094	110 102	18 165	819	5 576	11 770	7 324	4 446	113 929	91 937	25 196	5 575	14 741
November	132 268	110 299	18 169	823	5 577	11 769	7 334	4 435	114 099	92 130	25 246	5 586	14 769
December	132 498	110 548	18 242	833	5 612	11 797	7 362	4 435	114 256	92 306	25 285	5 605	14 775
2012													
January	132 809	110 871	18 314	844	5 629	11 841	7 400	4 441	114 495	92 557	25 372	5 623	14 829
February	133 080	111 136	18 365	851	5 644	11 870	7 426	4 444	114 715	92 771	25 377	5 635	14 805
March	133 285	111 344	18 402	852	5 640	11 910	7 452	4 458	114 883	92 942	25 381	5 641	14 799
April	133 397	111 464	18 408	852	5 636	11 920	7 460	4 460	114 989	93 056	25 409	5 654	14 830
May	133 522	111 616	18 396	855	5 615	11 926	7 467	4 459	115 126	93 220	25 463	5 667	14 839
June	133 609	111 694	18 410	853	5 622	11 935	7 476	4 459	115 199	93 284	25 467	5 676	14 836
July	133 762	111 871	18 436	852	5 627	11 957	7 496	4 461	115 326	93 435	25 485	5 686	14 839
August	133 927	112 002	18 422	849	5 630	11 943	7 482	4 461	115 505	93 580	25 520	5 692	14 850
September	134 065	112 120	18 405	847	5 633	11 925	7 465	4 460	115 660	93 715	25 550	5 691	14 876
October	134 225	112 337	18 421	841	5 649	11 931	7 466	4 465	115 804	93 916	25 623	5 699	14 928
November	134 472	112 593	18 464	853	5 673	11 938	7 483	4 455	116 008	94 129	25 720	5 709	14 998
December	134 691	112 817	18 522	860	5 711	11 951	7 494	4 457	116 169	94 295	25 769	5 715	15 004

Table 10-8A. Nonfarm Payroll Employment by NAICS Supersector: Recent Data—*Continued*

(Thousands; seasonally adjusted, except as noted.)

Year and month	Service-providing—*Continued*													Diffusion index, 6-month span, private nonfarm [2]
	Private—*Continued*						Government							
								Federal		State		Local		
	Information	Financial activities	Profes-sional and business services	Education and health services	Leisure and hospitality	Other services	Total	Total	Depart-ment of Defense [1]	Total	Education	Total	Education	
2005	3 061	8 197	16 954	17 372	12 816	5 395	21 804	2 732	488	5 032	2 260	14 041	7 856	62.8
2006	3 038	8 367	17 566	17 826	13 110	5 438	21 974	2 732	493	5 075	2 293	14 167	7 913	60.0
2007	3 032	8 348	17 942	18 322	13 427	5 494	22 218	2 734	491	5 122	2 318	14 362	7 987	56.8
2008	2 984	8 206	17 735	18 838	13 436	5 515	22 509	2 762	496	5 177	2 354	14 571	8 084	27.1
2009	2 804	7 838	16 579	19 193	13 077	5 367	22 555	2 832	519	5 169	2 360	14 554	8 079	17.7
2010	2 707	7 695	16 728	19 531	13 049	5 331	22 490	2 977	545	5 137	2 373	14 376	8 013	60.5
2011	2 674	7 697	17 332	19 883	13 353	5 360	22 086	2 859	559	5 078	2 374	14 150	7 873	69.9
2012	2 678	7 786	17 930	20 319	13 746	5 437	21 917	2 814	550	5 052	2 385	14 051	7 779	59.4
2008														
January	3 026	8 275	18 037	18 605	13 542	5 522	22 388	2 738	489	5 148	2 331	14 502	8 054	53.8
February	3 018	8 267	17 989	18 643	13 543	5 533	22 417	2 747	489	5 145	2 327	14 525	8 065	50.6
March	3 021	8 267	17 947	18 691	13 531	5 539	22 443	2 752	490	5 153	2 335	14 538	8 068	52.1
April	3 012	8 258	17 942	18 745	13 511	5 540	22 450	2 755	492	5 157	2 337	14 538	8 062	49.1
May	3 007	8 247	17 877	18 784	13 498	5 536	22 483	2 757	493	5 162	2 340	14 564	8 078	42.7
June	3 001	8 235	17 847	18 837	13 482	5 525	22 517	2 759	494	5 179	2 355	14 579	8 086	37.2
July	2 987	8 221	17 772	18 882	13 463	5 521	22 568	2 767	497	5 191	2 365	14 610	8 119	32.3
August	2 974	8 206	17 715	18 939	13 431	5 513	22 567	2 766	499	5 214	2 383	14 587	8 092	30.1
September	2 961	8 170	17 654	18 940	13 379	5 512	22 537	2 768	499	5 184	2 367	14 585	8 085	27.1
October	2 949	8 140	17 540	18 958	13 352	5 516	22 549	2 772	501	5 182	2 360	14 595	8 090	27.8
November	2 931	8 098	17 346	18 992	13 300	5 476	22 560	2 778	502	5 194	2 369	14 588	8 083	24.8
December	2 909	8 063	17 220	19 027	13 256	5 446	22 556	2 775	503	5 191	2 368	14 590	8 084	22.2
2009														
January	2 886	8 019	17 077	19 072	13 221	5 428	22 583	2 789	505	5 207	2 384	14 587	8 086	19.2
February	2 877	7 969	16 900	19 089	13 185	5 410	22 580	2 796	507	5 192	2 371	14 592	8 098	14.1
March	2 865	7 925	16 763	19 088	13 124	5 383	22 562	2 798	507	5 181	2 364	14 583	8 094	13.0
April	2 834	7 872	16 611	19 089	13 048	5 372	22 679	2 921	510	5 182	2 367	14 576	8 094	12.2
May	2 806	7 845	16 547	19 145	13 105	5 367	22 615	2 860	514	5 189	2 373	14 566	8 084	12.6
June	2 795	7 820	16 442	19 175	13 080	5 373	22 585	2 815	518	5 174	2 365	14 596	8 114	13.0
July	2 781	7 807	16 419	19 194	13 079	5 369	22 516	2 828	521	5 121	2 316	14 567	8 065	15.0
August	2 768	7 783	16 391	19 237	13 043	5 359	22 528	2 825	524	5 170	2 360	14 533	8 050	15.0
September	2 767	7 768	16 407	19 245	13 050	5 351	22 457	2 825	525	5 142	2 336	14 490	8 024	17.7
October	2 764	7 754	16 417	19 285	13 001	5 334	22 520	2 845	527	5 154	2 355	14 521	8 075	20.1
November	2 751	7 755	16 467	19 318	12 996	5 322	22 533	2 841	531	5 154	2 362	14 538	8 099	21.4
December	2 741	7 743	16 477	19 353	12 934	5 320	22 480	2 827	533	5 151	2 360	14 502	8 073	24.2
2010														
January	2 739	7 732	16 521	19 373	12 943	5 322	22 484	2 862	535	5 142	2 357	14 480	8 065	27.1
February	2 734	7 724	16 549	19 395	12 935	5 315	22 470	2 871	537	5 149	2 368	14 450	8 053	28.2
March	2 720	7 705	16 545	19 453	12 949	5 327	22 513	2 923	538	5 142	2 360	14 448	8 052	34.2
April	2 716	7 710	16 617	19 465	12 976	5 335	22 572	2 985	540	5 138	2 365	14 449	8 057	43.4
May	2 709	7 701	16 650	19 491	13 004	5 329	22 991	3 415	542	5 137	2 371	14 439	8 056	49.6
June	2 697	7 691	16 713	19 517	13 036	5 315	22 767	3 194	544	5 135	2 371	14 438	8 071	54.9
July	2 701	7 683	16 725	19 536	13 057	5 327	22 578	3 056	547	5 136	2 376	14 386	8 034	58.8
August	2 702	7 679	16 772	19 572	13 082	5 324	22 412	2 944	549	5 129	2 371	14 339	7 986	60.2
September	2 698	7 686	16 796	19 569	13 130	5 331	22 256	2 869	550	5 121	2 367	14 266	7 929	60.5
October	2 694	7 685	16 845	19 628	13 123	5 358	22 296	2 864	551	5 141	2 387	14 291	7 963	59.2
November	2 690	7 679	16 944	19 668	13 137	5 345	22 286	2 865	553	5 141	2 391	14 280	7 959	61.7
December	2 684	7 680	17 014	19 685	13 163	5 336	22 267	2 872	556	5 136	2 392	14 259	7 951	64.7
2011														
January	2 683	7 677	17 044	19 705	13 152	5 329	22 256	2 874	558	5 136	2 397	14 246	7 943	65.2
February	2 673	7 674	17 102	19 723	13 196	5 335	22 209	2 877	559	5 110	2 380	14 222	7 924	64.5
March	2 673	7 678	17 191	19 741	13 242	5 330	22 191	2 878	560	5 101	2 380	14 212	7 919	68.2
April	2 676	7 680	17 239	19 798	13 281	5 341	22 192	2 872	560	5 094	2 378	14 226	7 940	67.7
May	2 676	7 701	17 298	19 816	13 293	5 348	22 124	2 872	560	5 084	2 371	14 168	7 892	68.6
June	2 684	7 692	17 289	19 857	13 345	5 352	22 156	2 859	559	5 078	2 372	14 219	7 949	70.5
July	2 678	7 697	17 319	19 900	13 382	5 358	22 028	2 859	558	5 054	2 375	14 115	7 847	72.9
August	2 633	7 704	17 384	19 936	13 399	5 375	22 031	2 851	557	5 077	2 385	14 103	7 832	69.0
September	2 675	7 702	17 451	19 988	13 410	5 380	22 000	2 846	558	5 076	2 375	14 078	7 811	69.9
October	2 677	7 710	17 485	20 028	13 459	5 382	21 992	2 846	560	5 058	2 373	14 088	7 824	68.8
November	2 677	7 721	17 528	20 052	13 515	5 391	21 969	2 841	559	5 052	2 368	14 076	7 814	67.3
December	2 682	7 728	17 588	20 080	13 541	5 402	21 950	2 841	558	5 042	2 358	14 067	7 804	68.2
2012														
January	2 670	7 730	17 677	20 106	13 585	5 417	21 938	2 834	557	5 042	2 364	14 062	7 796	72.7
February	2 681	7 740	17 753	20 175	13 632	5 413	21 944	2 832	556	5 051	2 376	14 061	7 796	77.3
March	2 679	7 763	17 796	20 221	13 684	5 418	21 941	2 830	553	5 059	2 384	14 052	7 785	77.3
April	2 679	7 768	17 841	20 243	13 698	5 418	21 933	2 828	555	5 064	2 390	14 041	7 776	75.9
May	2 681	7 782	17 878	20 290	13 702	5 424	21 906	2 821	554	5 049	2 378	14 036	7 766	74.1
June	2 675	7 788	17 913	20 296	13 716	5 429	21 915	2 818	552	5 050	2 380	14 047	7 765	71.8
July	2 684	7 788	17 965	20 331	13 743	5 439	21 891	2 805	551	5 042	2 378	14 044	7 766	66.5
August	2 682	7 795	17 994	20 363	13 788	5 438	21 925	2 810	549	5 049	2 388	14 066	7 793	64.5
September	2 670	7 806	18 009	20 412	13 818	5 450	21 945	2 810	548	5 072	2 411	14 063	7 796	59.4
October	2 671	7 817	18 062	20 446	13 840	5 457	21 888	2 807	546	5 052	2 395	14 029	7 756	63.3
November	2 685	7 822	18 117	20 460	13 861	5 464	21 879	2 798	545	5 047	2 391	14 034	7 763	64.7
December	2 676	7 831	18 152	20 496	13 901	5 470	21 874	2 799	544	5 040	2 381	14 035	7 763	69.2

[1] Not seasonally adjusted.
[2] See notes and definitions for explanation. September value used to represent year.

Table 10-8B. Nonfarm Payroll Employment by NAICS Supersector: Historical Annual

(Thousands.)

Year and month	Total	Private								Service-providing				
		Total	Goods-producing							Total	Private			
			Total	Mining and logging	Construc-tion	Manufacturing					Total	Trade, transportation, and utilities		
						Total	Durable	Nondurable				Total	Wholesale trade	Retail trade
1939	30 645	26 606	11 511	856	1 205	9 450	4 654	4 796		19 134	15 094	6 739	1 508	3 158
1940	32 407	28 156	12 378	927	1 352	10 099	5 261	4 839		20 029	15 778	7 043	1 571	3 324
1941	36 600	31 874	14 940	967	1 852	12 121	6 778	5 343		21 660	16 934	7 550	1 679	3 552
1942	40 213	34 621	17 275	1 010	2 234	14 030	8 502	5 528		22 938	17 347	7 607	1 635	3 522
1943	42 574	36 353	18 738	958	1 627	16 153	10 583	5 570		23 837	17 615	7 628	1 566	3 479
1944	42 006	35 819	17 981	926	1 152	15 903	10 372	5 531		24 026	17 839	7 805	1 585	3 516
1945	40 510	34 428	16 308	864	1 190	14 255	8 732	5 523		24 203	18 121	8 048	1 672	3 624
1946	41 759	36 054	16 122	885	1 724	13 513	7 535	5 978		25 637	19 932	8 945	1 962	4 118
1947	43 945	38 379	17 314	976	2 051	14 287	8 079	6 208		26 631	21 064	9 452	2 116	4 393
1948	44 954	39 213	17 579	1 014	2 241	14 324	8 028	6 296		27 376	21 634	9 716	2 230	4 524
1949	43 843	37 893	16 464	948	2 236	13 281	7 240	6 041		27 379	21 430	9 579	2 227	4 520
1950	45 287	39 167	17 343	924	2 405	14 013	7 809	6 204		27 945	21 824	9 694	2 255	4 580
1951	47 930	41 427	18 703	956	2 678	15 070	8 738	6 332		29 227	22 725	10 089	2 335	4 758
1952	48 909	42 182	18 928	928	2 709	15 291	8 979	6 312		29 981	23 254	10 302	2 408	4 880
1953	50 310	43 552	19 733	902	2 700	16 131	9 690	6 441		30 577	23 820	10 504	2 444	5 012
1954	49 093	42 235	18 515	825	2 688	15 002	8 773	6 229		30 578	23 720	10 357	2 454	4 998
1955	50 744	43 722	19 234	828	2 881	15 524	9 161	6 363		31 510	24 489	10 612	2 505	5 158
1956	52 473	45 087	19 799	859	3 082	15 858	9 435	6 424		32 674	25 288	10 921	2 583	5 315
1957	52 959	45 235	19 669	864	3 007	15 798	9 452	6 346		33 290	25 566	10 942	2 593	5 328
1958	51 426	43 480	18 319	801	2 862	14 656	8 480	6 176		33 107	25 161	10 656	2 551	5 266
1959	53 374	45 182	19 163	789	3 050	15 325	8 988	6 337		34 211	26 018	10 960	2 638	5 453
1960	54 296	45 832	19 182	771	2 973	15 438	9 071	6 367		35 114	26 650	11 147	2 690	5 589
1961	54 105	45 399	18 647	728	2 908	15 011	8 711	6 300		35 458	26 752	11 040	2 681	5 560
1962	55 659	46 655	19 203	709	2 997	15 498	9 099	6 399		36 455	27 451	11 215	2 737	5 672
1963	56 764	47 423	19 385	694	3 060	15 631	9 226	6 405		37 379	28 038	11 367	2 780	5 781
1964	58 391	48 680	19 733	697	3 148	15 888	9 414	6 474		38 658	28 947	11 677	2 856	5 977
1965	60 874	50 683	20 595	694	3 284	16 617	9 973	6 644		40 279	30 089	12 139	2 967	6 262
1966	64 020	53 110	21 740	690	3 371	17 680	10 803	6 878		42 280	31 370	12 611	3 080	6 530
1967	65 931	54 406	21 882	679	3 305	17 897	10 952	6 945		44 049	32 524	12 950	3 158	6 711
1968	68 023	56 050	22 292	671	3 410	18 211	11 137	7 074		45 731	33 759	13 334	3 236	6 977
1969	70 512	58 181	22 893	683	3 637	18 573	11 396	7 177		47 619	35 288	13 853	3 344	7 295
1970	71 006	58 318	22 179	677	3 654	17 848	10 762	7 086		48 827	36 139	14 144	3 418	7 463
1971	71 335	58 323	21 602	658	3 770	17 174	10 229	6 944		49 734	36 721	14 318	3 424	7 657
1972	73 798	60 333	22 299	672	3 957	17 669	10 630	7 039		51 499	38 034	14 788	3 547	8 038
1973	76 912	63 050	23 450	693	4 167	18 589	11 414	7 176		53 462	39 600	15 349	3 688	8 371
1974	78 389	64 086	23 364	755	4 095	18 514	11 432	7 082		55 025	40 721	15 693	3 823	8 536
1975	77 069	62 250	21 318	802	3 608	16 909	10 266	6 643		55 751	40 932	15 606	3 810	8 600
1976	79 502	64 501	22 025	832	3 662	17 531	10 640	6 891		57 477	42 476	16 128	3 920	8 966
1977	82 593	67 334	22 972	865	3 940	18 167	11 132	7 035		59 620	44 362	16 765	4 055	9 359
1978	86 826	71 014	24 156	902	4 322	18 932	11 770	7 162		62 670	46 858	17 658	4 280	9 879
1979	89 932	73 864	24 997	1 008	4 562	19 426	12 220	7 206		64 935	48 868	18 303	4 485	10 180
1980	90 528	74 154	24 263	1 077	4 454	18 733	11 679	7 054		66 265	49 891	18 413	4 557	10 244
1981	91 289	75 109	24 118	1 180	4 304	18 634	11 611	7 023		67 172	50 991	18 604	4 634	10 364
1982	89 677	73 695	22 550	1 163	4 024	17 363	10 610	6 753		67 127	51 145	18 457	4 575	10 371
1983	90 280	74 269	22 110	997	4 065	17 048	10 326	6 722		68 171	52 160	18 668	4 559	10 634
1984	94 530	78 371	23 435	1 014	4 501	17 920	11 050	6 870		71 095	54 936	19 653	4 788	11 222
1985	97 511	80 978	23 585	974	4 793	17 819	11 034	6 784		73 926	57 393	20 379	4 915	11 733
1986	99 474	82 636	23 318	829	4 937	17 552	10 795	6 757		76 156	59 318	20 795	4 935	12 078
1987	102 088	84 932	23 470	771	5 090	17 609	10 767	6 842		78 618	61 462	21 302	5 003	12 418
1988	105 345	87 806	23 909	770	5 233	17 906	10 969	6 938		81 436	63 897	21 974	5 153	12 808
1989	108 014	90 087	24 045	750	5 309	17 985	11 004	6 981		83 969	66 042	22 510	5 284	13 107
1990	109 487	91 072	23 723	765	5 263	17 695	10 737	6 958		85 764	67 349	22 666	5 268	13 182
1991	108 377	89 832	22 588	739	4 780	17 068	10 220	6 848		85 790	67 244	22 281	5 185	12 896
1992	108 745	89 958	22 095	689	4 608	16 799	9 946	6 853		86 650	67 863	22 125	5 110	12 827
1993	110 876	91 887	22 219	666	4 779	16 774	9 901	6 872		88 657	69 668	22 378	5 093	13 020
1994	114 333	95 058	22 774	659	5 095	17 020	10 132	6 889		91 559	72 284	23 128	5 247	13 490
1995	117 336	97 904	23 156	641	5 274	17 241	10 373	6 868		94 181	74 748	23 834	5 433	13 896
1996	119 757	100 218	23 409	637	5 536	17 237	10 486	6 751		96 348	76 809	24 239	5 522	14 142
1997	122 853	103 190	23 886	654	5 813	17 419	10 705	6 714		98 967	79 304	24 700	5 664	14 388
1998	126 033	106 124	24 354	645	6 149	17 560	10 911	6 649		101 679	81 770	25 186	5 795	14 609
1999	129 098	108 791	24 465	598	6 545	17 322	10 831	6 491		104 633	84 326	25 771	5 893	14 970
2000	131 881	111 091	24 649	599	6 787	17 263	10 877	6 386		107 232	86 442	26 225	5 933	15 279
2001	131 919	110 800	23 873	606	6 826	16 441	10 336	6 105		108 045	86 927	25 983	5 773	15 238
2002	130 450	108 937	22 557	583	6 716	15 259	9 485	5 774		107 893	86 380	25 497	5 652	15 025
2003	130 100	108 517	21 816	572	6 735	14 510	8 964	5 546		108 284	86 701	25 287	5 608	14 917
2004	131 509	109 888	21 882	591	6 976	14 315	8 925	5 390		109 627	88 006	25 533	5 663	15 058
2005	133 747	111 943	22 190	628	7 336	14 227	8 956	5 271		111 557	89 753	25 959	5 764	15 280
2006	136 125	114 151	22 530	684	7 691	14 155	8 981	5 174		113 594	91 621	26 276	5 905	15 353
2007	137 645	115 427	22 233	724	7 630	13 879	8 808	5 071		115 412	93 194	26 630	6 015	15 520
2008	136 852	114 342	21 335	767	7 162	13 406	8 463	4 943		115 517	93 008	26 293	5 943	15 283
2009	130 876	108 321	18 558	694	6 016	11 847	7 284	4 564		112 318	89 764	24 906	5 587	14 522

Table 10-8B. Nonfarm Payroll Employment by NAICS Supersector: Historical Annual—*Continued*

(Thousands.)

Year and month	Service-providing—*Continued*													Diffusion index, 6-month span, private nonfarm [2]
	Private—*Continued*						Government							
								Federal		State		Local		
	Information	Financial activities	Professional and business services	Education and health services	Leisure and hospitality	Other services	Total	Total	Department of Defense [1]	Total	Education	Total	Education	
1939	1 141	1 386	1 976	1 405	1 896	553	4 040	950	133	...	...	...	...	...
1940	1 196	1 424	2 073	1 470	1 995	578	4 251	1 045	182	...	...	...	...	...
1941	1 342	1 466	2 265	1 566	2 130	616	4 726	1 406	375	...	...	...	...	...
1942	1 470	1 455	2 410	1 632	2 133	641	5 592	2 322	920	...	...	...	...	...
1943	1 605	1 431	2 518	1 660	2 122	652	6 222	3 047	1 361	...	...	...	...	...
1944	1 635	1 414	2 523	1 667	2 142	654	6 187	3 071	1 352	...	...	...	...	...
1945	1 581	1 435	2 495	1 698	2 200	664	6 082	2 945	1 234	...	...	...	...	...
1946	1 594	1 619	2 666	1 885	2 485	737	5 705	2 365	746	...	...	...	...	...
1947	1 658	1 674	2 828	2 015	2 650	788	5 567	1 985	499	...	...	...	...	...
1948	1 669	1 742	2 893	2 077	2 726	812	5 742	1 954	511	...	...	...	...	...
1949	1 583	1 768	2 853	2 097	2 729	820	5 950	2 001	531	...	...	...	...	...
1950	1 625	1 825	2 928	2 144	2 769	839	6 120	2 023	533	...	...	...	...	...
1951	1 718	1 890	3 061	2 221	2 877	870	6 502	2 415	797	...	...	...	...	...
1952	1 736	1 964	3 128	2 281	2 950	894	6 727	2 539	868	...	...	...	...	...
1953	1 785	2 036	3 215	2 335	3 030	916	6 758	2 418	818	...	...	...	...	...
1954	1 693	2 118	3 197	2 385	3 034	936	6 858	2 295	744	...	...	...	...	...
1955	1 735	2 212	3 320	2 491	3 140	978	7 021	2 295	744	1 168	308	3 558	1 751	...
1956	1 778	2 299	3 437	2 593	3 242	1 018	7 386	2 318	749	1 249	334	3 819	1 884	...
1957	1 780	2 348	3 504	2 676	3 267	1 050	7 724	2 326	729	1 328	363	4 071	2 026	...
1958	1 674	2 386	3 449	2 695	3 243	1 058	7 946	2 298	695	1 415	389	4 232	2 115	...
1959	1 718	2 454	3 591	2 822	3 365	1 107	8 192	2 342	699	1 484	420	4 366	2 198	...
1960	1 728	2 532	3 694	2 937	3 460	1 152	8 464	2 381	681	1 536	448	4 547	2 314	...
1961	1 693	2 590	3 744	3 030	3 468	1 188	8 706	2 391	683	1 607	474	4 708	2 411	...
1962	1 723	2 656	3 885	3 172	3 557	1 243	9 004	2 455	697	1 669	511	4 881	2 522	...
1963	1 735	2 731	3 990	3 288	3 639	1 288	9 341	2 473	687	1 747	557	5 121	2 674	...
1964	1 766	2 811	4 137	3 438	3 772	1 346	9 711	2 463	676	1 856	609	5 392	2 839	...
1965	1 824	2 878	4 306	3 587	3 951	1 404	10 191	2 495	679	1 996	679	5 700	3 031	...
1966	1 908	2 961	4 517	3 770	4 127	1 475	10 910	2 690	741	2 141	775	6 080	3 297	...
1967	1 955	3 087	4 720	3 986	4 269	1 558	11 525	2 852	802	2 302	873	6 371	3 490	...
1968	1 991	3 234	4 918	4 191	4 453	1 638	11 972	2 871	801	2 442	958	6 660	3 649	...
1969	2 048	3 404	5 156	4 428	4 670	1 731	12 330	2 893	815	2 533	1 042	6 904	3 785	...
1970	2 041	3 532	5 267	4 577	4 789	1 789	12 687	2 865	756	2 664	1 104	7 158	3 912	...
1971	2 009	3 651	5 328	4 675	4 914	1 827	13 012	2 828	731	2 747	1 149	7 437	4 091	...
1972	2 056	3 784	5 523	4 863	5 121	1 900	13 465	2 815	720	2 859	1 188	7 790	4 262	...
1973	2 135	3 920	5 774	5 092	5 341	1 990	13 862	2 794	696	2 923	1 205	8 146	4 433	...
1974	2 160	4 023	5 974	5 322	5 471	2 078	14 303	2 858	698	3 039	1 267	8 407	4 584	...
1975	2 061	4 047	6 034	5 497	5 544	2 144	14 820	2 882	704	3 179	1 323	8 758	4 722	...
1976	2 111	4 155	6 287	5 756	5 794	2 244	15 001	2 863	693	3 273	1 371	8 865	4 786	...
1977	2 185	4 348	6 587	6 052	6 065	2 359	15 258	2 859	676	3 377	1 385	9 023	4 859	77.5
1978	2 287	4 599	6 972	6 427	6 411	2 505	15 812	2 893	661	3 474	1 367	9 446	4 958	75.6
1979	2 375	4 843	7 312	6 767	6 631	2 637	16 068	2 894	649	3 541	1 378	9 633	4 989	57.7
1980	2 361	5 025	7 544	7 072	6 721	2 755	16 375	3 000	645	3 610	1 398	9 765	5 090	61.2
1981	2 382	5 163	7 782	7 357	6 840	2 865	16 180	2 922	655	3 640	1 420	9 619	5 095	39.0
1982	2 317	5 209	7 848	7 515	6 874	2 924	15 982	2 884	690	3 640	1 433	9 458	5 049	34.8
1983	2 253	5 334	8 039	7 766	7 078	3 021	16 011	2 915	699	3 662	1 450	9 434	5 020	78.2
1984	2 398	5 553	8 464	8 193	7 489	3 186	16 159	2 943	716	3 734	1 488	9 482	5 076	64.9
1985	2 437	5 815	8 871	8 657	7 869	3 366	16 533	3 014	738	3 832	1 540	9 687	5 221	59.5
1986	2 445	6 128	9 211	9 061	8 156	3 523	16 838	3 044	736	3 893	1 561	9 901	5 358	62.4
1987	2 507	6 385	9 608	9 515	8 446	3 699	17 156	3 089	736	3 967	1 586	10 100	5 469	73.5
1988	2 585	6 500	10 090	10 063	8 778	3 907	17 540	3 124	719	4 076	1 621	10 339	5 590	66.3
1989	2 622	6 562	10 555	10 616	9 062	4 116	17 927	3 136	735	4 182	1 668	10 609	5 740	54.6
1990	2 688	6 614	10 848	10 984	9 288	4 261	18 415	3 196	722	4 305	1 730	10 914	5 902	36.7
1991	2 677	6 561	10 714	11 506	9 256	4 249	18 545	3 110	702	4 355	1 768	11 081	5 994	44.0
1992	2 641	6 559	10 970	11 891	9 437	4 240	18 787	3 111	702	4 408	1 799	11 267	6 076	62.4
1993	2 668	6 742	11 495	12 303	9 732	4 350	18 989	3 063	670	4 488	1 834	11 438	6 206	72.2
1994	2 738	6 910	12 174	12 807	10 100	4 428	19 275	3 018	657	4 576	1 882	11 682	6 329	80.6
1995	2 843	6 866	12 844	13 289	10 501	4 572	19 432	2 949	627	4 635	1 919	11 849	6 453	68.6
1996	2 940	7 018	13 462	13 683	10 777	4 690	19 539	2 877	597	4 606	1 911	12 056	6 592	78.0
1997	3 084	7 255	14 335	14 087	11 018	4 825	19 664	2 806	588	4 582	1 904	12 276	6 759	80.1
1998	3 218	7 565	15 147	14 446	11 232	4 976	19 909	2 772	550	4 612	1 922	12 525	6 921	69.5
1999	3 419	7 753	15 957	14 798	11 543	5 087	20 307	2 769	525	4 709	1 983	12 829	7 120	69.5
2000	3 630	7 783	16 666	15 109	11 862	5 168	20 790	2 865	510	4 786	2 031	13 139	7 294	57.7
2001	3 629	7 900	16 476	15 645	12 036	5 258	21 118	2 764	504	4 905	2 113	13 449	7 479	32.3
2002	3 395	7 956	15 976	16 199	11 986	5 372	21 513	2 766	499	5 029	2 243	13 718	7 654	37.0
2003	3 188	8 078	15 987	16 588	12 173	5 401	21 583	2 761	486	5 002	2 255	13 820	7 709	40.0
2004	3 118	8 105	16 394	16 953	12 493	5 409	21 621	2 730	473	4 982	2 238	13 909	7 765	59.6
2005	3 061	8 197	16 954	17 372	12 816	5 395	21 804	2 732	488	5 032	2 260	14 041	7 856	62.8
2006	3 038	8 367	17 566	17 826	13 110	5 438	21 974	2 732	493	5 075	2 293	14 167	7 913	60.0
2007	3 032	8 348	17 942	18 322	13 427	5 494	22 218	2 734	491	5 122	2 318	14 362	7 987	56.8
2008	2 984	8 206	17 735	18 838	13 436	5 515	22 509	2 762	496	5 177	2 354	14 571	8 084	27.1
2009	2 804	7 838	16 579	19 193	13 077	5 367	22 555	2 832	519	5 169	2 360	14 554	8 079	17.7

[1] Not seasonally adjusted.
[2] See notes and definitions for explanation. September value used to represent year.
. . . = Not available.

Table 10-9. Employment, Hours, and Earnings, Total Nonfarm and Manufacturing, Historical Annual and Monthly

(Wage and salary workers on nonfarm payrolls, seasonally adjusted.)

Year and month	All wage and salary workers (thousands)					Production and nonsupervisory workers on private payrolls							
	Total	Private			Service-providing	Number (thousands)		Average hours per week		Average hourly earnings, dollars		Average weekly earnings, dollars	
		Total	Goods-producing			Total private	Manufacturing	Total private	Manufacturing	Total private	Manufacturing	Total private	Manufacturing
			Total	Manufacturing									
1939	30 645	26 606	11 511	9 450	19 134	. . .	8 163	. . .	37.7	. . .	0.49	. . .	18.47
1940	32 407	28 156	12 378	10 099	20 029	. . .	8 737	. . .	38.2	. . .	0.53	. . .	20.25
1941	36 600	31 874	14 940	12 121	21 660	. . .	10 641	. . .	40.7	. . .	0.61	. . .	24.83
1942	40 213	34 621	17 275	14 030	22 938	. . .	12 447	. . .	43.2	. . .	0.74	. . .	31.97
1943	42 574	36 353	18 738	16 153	23 837	. . .	14 407	. . .	45.1	. . .	0.86	. . .	38.79
1944	42 006	35 819	17 981	15 903	24 026	. . .	14 031	. . .	45.4	. . .	0.91	. . .	41.31
1945	40 510	34 428	16 308	14 255	24 203	. . .	12 445	. . .	43.6	. . .	0.90	. . .	39.24
1946	41 759	36 054	16 122	13 513	25 637	. . .	11 781	. . .	40.4	. . .	0.95	. . .	38.38
1947	43 945	38 379	17 314	14 287	26 631	. . .	12 453	. . .	40.5	. . .	1.10	. . .	44.55
1948	44 954	39 213	17 579	14 324	27 376	. . .	12 383	. . .	40.1	. . .	1.20	. . .	48.12
1949	43 843	37 893	16 464	13 281	27 379	. . .	11 355	. . .	39.2	. . .	1.25	. . .	49.00
1950	45 287	39 167	17 343	14 013	27 945	. . .	12 032	. . .	40.6	. . .	1.32	. . .	53.59
1951	47 930	41 427	18 703	15 070	29 227	. . .	12 808	. . .	40.7	. . .	1.45	. . .	59.02
1952	48 909	42 182	18 928	15 291	29 981	. . .	12 797	. . .	40.8	. . .	1.53	. . .	62.42
1953	50 310	43 552	19 733	16 131	30 577	. . .	13 437	. . .	40.6	. . .	1.63	. . .	66.18
1954	49 093	42 235	18 515	15 002	30 578	. . .	12 300	. . .	39.7	. . .	1.66	. . .	65.90
1955	50 744	43 722	19 234	15 524	31 510	. . .	12 735	. . .	40.8	. . .	1.74	. . .	70.99
1956	52 473	45 087	19 799	15 858	32 674	. . .	12 869	. . .	40.5	. . .	1.84	. . .	74.52
1957	52 959	45 235	19 669	15 798	33 290	. . .	12 640	. . .	39.9	. . .	1.93	. . .	77.01
1958	51 426	43 480	18 319	14 656	33 107	. . .	11 532	. . .	39.2	. . .	1.99	. . .	78.01
1959	53 374	45 182	19 163	15 325	34 211	. . .	12 089	. . .	40.3	. . .	2.08	. . .	83.82
1960	54 296	45 832	19 182	15 438	35 114	. . .	12 074	. . .	39.8	. . .	2.15	. . .	85.57
1961	54 105	45 399	18 647	15 011	35 458	. . .	11 612	. . .	39.9	. . .	2.20	. . .	87.78
1962	55 659	46 655	19 203	15 498	36 455	. . .	11 986	. . .	40.5	. . .	2.27	. . .	91.94
1963	56 764	47 423	19 385	15 631	37 379	. . .	12 051	. . .	40.6	. . .	2.34	. . .	95.00
1964	58 391	48 680	19 733	15 888	38 658	40 575	12 298	38.5	40.8	2.53	2.41	97.41	98.33
1946													
January	39 839	34 054	15 031	12 719	24 808	. . .	10 990	. . .	40.9	. . .	0.86	. . .	35.17
February	39 250	33 472	14 308	11 922	24 942	. . .	10 292	. . .	40.4	. . .	0.85	. . .	34.34
March	40 192	34 434	15 017	12 545	25 175	. . .	10 989	. . .	40.6	. . .	0.89	. . .	36.13
April	40 908	35 147	15 439	13 200	25 469	. . .	11 616	. . .	40.4	. . .	0.92	. . .	37.17
May	41 348	35 616	15 875	13 389	25 473	. . .	11 758	. . .	39.8	. . .	0.93	. . .	37.01
June	41 732	36 052	16 206	13 598	25 526	. . .	11 905	. . .	40.0	. . .	0.94	. . .	37.60
July	42 153	36 471	16 461	13 771	25 692	. . .	12 065	. . .	40.2	. . .	0.96	. . .	38.59
August	42 642	36 961	16 728	13 981	25 914	. . .	12 241	. . .	40.6	. . .	0.98	. . .	39.79
September	42 908	37 239	16 912	14 135	25 996	. . .	12 311	. . .	40.4	. . .	0.99	. . .	40.00
October	43 094	37 430	17 002	14 182	26 092	. . .	12 302	. . .	40.4	. . .	1.00	. . .	40.40
November	43 396	37 757	17 157	14 310	26 239	. . .	12 421	. . .	40.3	. . .	1.02	. . .	41.11
December	43 379	37 751	17 164	14 301	26 215	. . .	12 419	. . .	40.5	. . .	1.02	. . .	41.31
1947													
January	43 545	37 926	17 213	14 328	26 332	. . .	12 445	. . .	40.5	. . .	1.03	. . .	41.72
February	43 563	37 957	17 200	14 278	26 363	. . .	12 487	. . .	40.4	. . .	1.04	. . .	42.02
March	43 605	38 017	17 196	14 259	26 409	. . .	12 518	. . .	40.3	. . .	1.06	. . .	42.72
April	43 491	37 933	17 178	14 240	26 313	. . .	12 531	. . .	40.5	. . .	1.06	. . .	42.93
May	43 637	38 086	17 176	14 189	26 461	. . .	12 449	. . .	40.4	. . .	1.08	. . .	43.63
June	43 808	38 284	17 253	14 200	26 555	. . .	12 389	. . .	40.4	. . .	1.10	. . .	44.44
July	43 742	38 218	17 106	14 076	26 636	. . .	12 265	. . .	40.4	. . .	1.10	. . .	44.44
August	43 958	38 439	17 280	14 200	26 678	. . .	12 370	. . .	40.0	. . .	1.11	. . .	44.40
September	44 201	38 662	17 398	14 315	26 803	. . .	12 430	. . .	40.5	. . .	1.11	. . .	44.96
October	44 415	38 849	17 499	14 393	26 916	. . .	12 464	. . .	40.5	. . .	1.13	. . .	45.77
November	44 486	38 901	17 517	14 414	26 969	. . .	12 494	. . .	40.5	. . .	1.14	. . .	46.17
December	44 578	38 973	17 563	14 428	27 015	. . .	12 526	. . .	40.8	. . .	1.16	. . .	47.33
1948													
January	44 686	39 062	17 625	14 438	27 061	. . .	12 520	. . .	40.5	. . .	1.16	. . .	46.98
February	44 537	38 922	17 447	14 339	27 090	. . .	12 437	. . .	40.2	. . .	1.16	. . .	46.63
March	44 680	39 057	17 544	14 364	27 136	. . .	12 489	. . .	40.4	. . .	1.16	. . .	46.86
April	44 369	38 726	17 302	14 183	27 067	. . .	12 304	. . .	40.1	. . .	1.17	. . .	46.92
May	44 795	39 114	17 508	14 235	27 287	. . .	12 344	. . .	40.2	. . .	1.18	. . .	47.44
June	45 032	39 296	17 633	14 318	27 399	. . .	12 402	. . .	40.3	. . .	1.19	. . .	47.96
July	45 160	39 386	17 649	14 359	27 511	. . .	12 417	. . .	40.2	. . .	1.21	. . .	48.64
August	45 175	39 384	17 655	14 353	27 520	. . .	12 397	. . .	40.2	. . .	1.23	. . .	49.45
September	45 294	39 489	17 741	14 441	27 553	. . .	12 450	. . .	40.1	. . .	1.24	. . .	49.72
October	45 250	39 421	17 683	14 390	27 567	. . .	12 364	. . .	39.8	. . .	1.25	. . .	49.75
November	45 194	39 325	17 599	14 292	27 595	. . .	12 302	. . .	39.8	. . .	1.26	. . .	50.15
December	45 028	39 140	17 417	14 086	27 611	. . .	12 127	. . .	39.6	. . .	1.26	. . .	49.90
1949													
January	44 675	38 781	17 170	13 867	27 505	. . .	11 905	. . .	39.4	. . .	1.26	. . .	49.64
February	44 500	38 607	17 019	13 734	27 481	. . .	11 792	. . .	39.4	. . .	1.26	. . .	49.64
March	44 238	38 323	16 848	13 581	27 390	. . .	11 654	. . .	39.1	. . .	1.26	. . .	49.27
April	44 230	38 282	16 685	13 439	27 545	. . .	11 517	. . .	38.8	. . .	1.25	. . .	48.50
May	43 982	38 020	16 492	13 269	27 490	. . .	11 352	. . .	38.9	. . .	1.25	. . .	48.63
June	43 739	37 783	16 351	13 178	27 388	. . .	11 266	. . .	39.0	. . .	1.26	. . .	49.14
July	43 530	37 568	16 222	13 067	27 308	. . .	11 168	. . .	39.2	. . .	1.26	. . .	49.39
August	43 621	37 636	16 327	13 158	27 294	. . .	11 251	. . .	39.2	. . .	1.25	. . .	49.00
September	43 784	37 794	16 403	13 225	27 381	. . .	11 284	. . .	39.4	. . .	1.25	. . .	49.25
October	42 950	36 980	15 739	12 891	27 211	. . .	10 940	. . .	39.6	. . .	1.24	. . .	49.10
November	43 244	37 294	16 040	12 882	27 204	. . .	10 964	. . .	39.1	. . .	1.24	. . .	48.48
December	43 516	37 564	16 217	13 062	27 299	. . .	11 173	. . .	39.4	. . .	1.25	. . .	49.25

. . . = Not available.

Table 10-9. Employment, Hours, and Earnings, Total Nonfarm and Manufacturing, Historical Annual and Monthly—*Continued*

(Wage and salary workers on nonfarm payrolls, seasonally adjusted.)

Year and month	All wage and salary workers (thousands)					Production and nonsupervisory workers on private payrolls							
	Total	Private			Service-providing	Number (thousands)		Average hours per week		Average hourly earnings, dollars		Average weekly earnings, dollars	
		Total	Goods-producing			Total private	Manufacturing	Total private	Manufacturing	Total private	Manufacturing	Total private	Manufacturing
			Total	Manufacturing									
1950													
January	43 530	37 596	16 255	13 161	27 275	...	11 258	...	39.6	...	1.27	...	50.29
February	43 298	37 372	16 035	13 169	27 263	...	11 262	...	39.7	...	1.26	...	50.02
March	43 952	37 874	16 482	13 290	27 470	...	11 362	...	39.7	...	1.28	...	50.82
April	44 376	38 282	16 718	13 471	27 658	...	11 528	...	40.3	...	1.29	...	51.99
May	44 717	38 674	17 080	13 780	27 637	...	11 855	...	40.3	...	1.30	...	52.39
June	45 084	39 062	17 288	13 923	27 796	...	11 979	...	40.6	...	1.30	...	52.78
July	45 453	39 363	17 464	14 072	27 989	...	12 107	...	40.9	...	1.31	...	53.58
August	46 187	40 000	17 917	14 461	28 270	...	12 476	...	41.3	...	1.33	...	54.93
September	46 442	40 214	18 040	14 561	28 402	...	12 519	...	40.8	...	1.33	...	54.26
October	46 712	40 463	18 249	14 737	28 463	...	12 659	...	41.1	...	1.36	...	55.90
November	46 778	40 516	18 288	14 762	28 490	...	12 682	...	41.0	...	1.37	...	56.17
December	46 855	40 541	18 283	14 782	28 572	...	12 710	...	40.9	...	1.39	...	56.85
1951													
January	47 289	40 937	18 518	14 950	28 771	...	12 816	...	41.0	...	1.40	...	57.40
February	47 577	41 195	18 666	15 076	28 911	...	12 929	...	40.9	...	1.41	...	57.67
March	47 871	41 461	18 754	15 125	29 117	...	12 936	...	41.0	...	1.42	...	58.22
April	47 856	41 405	18 810	15 166	29 046	...	12 960	...	41.0	...	1.43	...	58.63
May	47 952	41 535	18 829	15 164	29 123	...	12 941	...	41.0	...	1.44	...	59.04
June	48 067	41 568	18 826	15 176	29 241	...	12 934	...	40.9	...	1.45	...	59.31
July	48 061	41 523	18 747	15 110	29 314	...	12 848	...	40.6	...	1.45	...	58.87
August	48 008	41 489	18 709	15 061	29 299	...	12 772	...	40.4	...	1.46	...	58.98
September	47 955	41 403	18 622	14 996	29 333	...	12 659	...	40.4	...	1.46	...	58.98
October	48 009	41 432	18 630	14 973	29 379	...	12 615	...	40.3	...	1.47	...	59.24
November	48 149	41 523	18 617	14 999	29 532	...	12 628	...	40.4	...	1.48	...	59.79
December	48 308	41 620	18 698	15 045	29 610	...	12 667	...	40.7	...	1.49	...	60.64
1952													
January	48 299	41 710	18 719	15 067	29 580	...	12 675	...	40.8	...	1.49	...	60.79
February	48 522	41 872	18 813	15 105	29 709	...	12 689	...	40.8	...	1.49	...	60.79
March	48 504	41 842	18 775	15 127	29 729	...	12 695	...	40.6	...	1.51	...	61.31
April	48 616	41 954	18 806	15 162	29 810	...	12 713	...	40.3	...	1.51	...	60.85
May	48 645	41 951	18 784	15 143	29 861	...	12 676	...	40.5	...	1.51	...	61.16
June	48 286	41 574	18 419	14 828	29 867	...	12 353	...	40.6	...	1.51	...	61.31
July	48 144	41 407	18 268	14 707	29 876	...	12 233	...	40.2	...	1.50	...	60.30
August	48 922	42 204	18 928	15 279	29 994	...	12 764	...	40.7	...	1.53	...	62.27
September	49 319	42 585	19 206	15 553	30 113	...	13 007	...	41.1	...	1.55	...	63.71
October	49 598	42 782	19 312	15 690	30 286	...	13 122	...	41.2	...	1.56	...	64.27
November	49 816	43 015	19 473	15 843	30 343	...	13 262	...	41.2	...	1.58	...	65.10
December	50 164	43 229	19 610	15 973	30 554	...	13 375	...	41.2	...	1.58	...	65.10
1953													
January	50 145	43 351	19 721	16 067	30 424	...	13 447	...	41.1	...	1.59	...	65.35
February	50 339	43 542	19 841	16 158	30 498	...	13 529	...	41.0	...	1.61	...	66.01
March	50 474	43 690	19 909	16 270	30 565	...	13 620	...	41.2	...	1.61	...	66.33
April	50 432	43 662	19 908	16 293	30 524	...	13 629	...	40.9	...	1.62	...	66.26
May	50 491	43 774	19 930	16 341	30 561	...	13 645	...	41.0	...	1.62	...	66.42
June	50 522	43 788	19 909	16 343	30 613	...	13 636	...	40.9	...	1.63	...	66.67
July	50 536	43 813	19 910	16 353	30 626	...	13 653	...	40.7	...	1.64	...	66.75
August	50 487	43 733	19 834	16 278	30 653	...	13 564	...	40.7	...	1.64	...	66.75
September	50 365	43 616	19 726	16 151	30 639	...	13 419	...	40.1	...	1.65	...	66.17
October	50 242	43 478	19 578	15 981	30 664	...	13 244	...	40.1	...	1.65	...	66.17
November	49 906	43 157	19 315	15 728	30 591	...	12 990	...	40.0	...	1.65	...	66.00
December	49 702	42 959	19 173	15 581	30 529	...	12 847	...	39.7	...	1.65	...	65.51
1954													
January	49 467	42 707	18 963	15 440	30 504	...	12 706	...	39.5	...	1.65	...	65.18
February	49 381	42 598	18 880	15 307	30 501	...	12 593	...	39.7	...	1.65	...	65.51
March	49 158	42 362	18 748	15 197	30 410	...	12 493	...	39.6	...	1.65	...	65.34
April	49 177	42 371	18 602	15 065	30 575	...	12 361	...	39.7	...	1.65	...	65.51
May	48 965	42 136	18 476	14 974	30 489	...	12 282	...	39.7	...	1.67	...	66.30
June	48 896	42 050	18 400	14 910	30 496	...	12 220	...	39.7	...	1.67	...	66.30
July	48 834	41 966	18 280	14 799	30 554	...	12 121	...	39.7	...	1.66	...	65.90
August	48 825	41 933	18 251	14 772	30 574	...	12 089	...	39.8	...	1.66	...	66.07
September	48 881	41 987	18 261	14 805	30 620	...	12 104	...	39.9	...	1.66	...	66.23
October	48 944	42 044	18 321	14 841	30 623	...	12 142	...	39.7	...	1.67	...	66.30
November	49 179	42 215	18 438	14 913	30 741	...	12 206	...	40.1	...	1.68	...	67.37
December	49 331	42 374	18 508	14 967	30 823	...	12 254	...	40.1	...	1.68	...	67.37
1955													
January	49 497	42 544	18 609	15 034	30 888	...	12 309	...	40.4	...	1.69	...	68.28
February	49 644	42 721	18 726	15 138	30 918	...	12 408	...	40.6	...	1.70	...	69.02
March	49 963	43 025	18 910	15 258	31 053	...	12 524	...	40.7	...	1.71	...	69.60
April	50 246	43 287	19 067	15 375	31 179	...	12 626	...	40.8	...	1.71	...	69.77
May	50 512	43 521	19 223	15 493	31 289	...	12 731	...	41.1	...	1.73	...	71.10
June	50 790	43 770	19 331	15 585	31 459	...	12 810	...	40.8	...	1.73	...	70.58
July	50 985	43 936	19 376	15 614	31 609	...	12 818	...	40.7	...	1.75	...	71.23
August	51 112	44 089	19 432	15 679	31 680	...	12 866	...	40.7	...	1.76	...	71.63
September	51 262	44 195	19 427	15 668	31 835	...	12 830	...	40.7	...	1.77	...	72.04
October	51 431	44 313	19 482	15 740	31 949	...	12 896	...	41.0	...	1.77	...	72.57
November	51 592	44 509	19 554	15 813	32 038	...	12 967	...	41.1	...	1.78	...	73.16
December	51 805	44 673	19 608	15 859	32 197	...	13 009	...	40.9	...	1.78	...	72.80

. . . = Not available.

Table 10-9. Employment, Hours, and Earnings, Total Nonfarm and Manufacturing, Historical Annual and Monthly—*Continued*

(Wage and salary workers on nonfarm payrolls, seasonally adjusted.)

Year and month	All wage and salary workers (thousands)					Production and nonsupervisory workers on private payrolls							
	Total	Private			Service-providing	Number (thousands)		Average hours per week		Average hourly earnings, dollars		Average weekly earnings, dollars	
		Total	Goods-producing			Total private	Manufac-turing	Total private	Manufac-turing	Total private	Manufac-turing	Total private	Manufac-turing
			Total	Manufac-turing									
1956													
January	51 975	44 808	19 665	15 882	32 310	. . .	13 011	. . .	40.8	. . .	1.78	. . .	72.62
February	52 167	44 955	19 731	15 889	32 436	. . .	12 986	. . .	40.7	. . .	1.79	. . .	72.85
March	52 295	45 043	19 691	15 829	32 604	. . .	12 905	. . .	40.6	. . .	1.80	. . .	73.08
April	52 375	45 099	19 811	15 909	32 564	. . .	12 970	. . .	40.5	. . .	1.82	. . .	73.71
May	52 506	45 139	19 825	15 893	32 681	. . .	12 925	. . .	40.4	. . .	1.83	. . .	73.93
June	52 583	45 216	19 905	15 835	32 678	. . .	12 836	. . .	40.3	. . .	1.83	. . .	73.75
July	51 954	44 549	19 390	15 468	32 564	. . .	12 435	. . .	40.3	. . .	1.82	. . .	73.35
August	52 632	45 181	19 922	15 893	32 710	. . .	12 860	. . .	40.3	. . .	1.85	. . .	74.56
September	52 600	45 119	19 860	15 863	32 740	. . .	12 822	. . .	40.5	. . .	1.87	. . .	75.74
October	52 781	45 262	19 918	15 937	32 863	. . .	12 908	. . .	40.6	. . .	1.88	. . .	76.33
November	52 822	45 269	19 886	15 916	32 936	. . .	12 864	. . .	40.4	. . .	1.88	. . .	75.95
December	52 930	45 346	19 926	15 957	33 004	. . .	12 882	. . .	40.6	. . .	1.91	. . .	77.55
1957													
January	52 888	45 268	19 833	15 970	33 055	. . .	12 881	. . .	40.4	. . .	1.90	. . .	76.76
February	53 098	45 452	19 933	15 998	33 165	. . .	12 885	. . .	40.5	. . .	1.91	. . .	77.36
March	53 156	45 484	19 936	15 994	33 220	. . .	12 855	. . .	40.4	. . .	1.92	. . .	77.57
April	53 238	45 537	19 887	15 970	33 351	. . .	12 811	. . .	40.0	. . .	1.91	. . .	76.40
May	53 149	45 436	19 834	15 931	33 315	. . .	12 762	. . .	40.0	. . .	1.92	. . .	76.80
June	53 066	45 364	19 777	15 873	33 289	. . .	12 697	. . .	40.0	. . .	1.92	. . .	76.80
July	53 122	45 368	19 735	15 854	33 387	. . .	12 669	. . .	40.0	. . .	1.93	. . .	77.20
August	53 128	45 371	19 728	15 867	33 400	. . .	12 673	. . .	40.0	. . .	1.94	. . .	77.60
September	52 932	45 183	19 545	15 710	33 387	. . .	12 528	. . .	39.7	. . .	1.95	. . .	77.42
October	52 765	44 997	19 421	15 599	33 344	. . .	12 437	. . .	39.4	. . .	1.96	. . .	77.22
November	52 557	44 788	19 260	15 466	33 297	. . .	12 301	. . .	39.2	. . .	1.96	. . .	76.83
December	52 385	44 539	19 111	15 332	33 274	. . .	12 170	. . .	39.1	. . .	1.95	. . .	76.25
1958													
January	52 077	44 256	18 902	15 130	33 175	. . .	11 969	. . .	38.9	. . .	1.95	. . .	75.86
February	51 576	43 744	18 529	14 908	33 047	. . .	11 757	. . .	38.7	. . .	1.95	. . .	75.47
March	51 300	43 452	18 335	14 670	32 965	. . .	11 532	. . .	38.8	. . .	1.96	. . .	76.05
April	51 026	43 158	18 120	14 506	32 906	. . .	11 373	. . .	38.9	. . .	1.96	. . .	76.24
May	50 913	43 019	18 008	14 414	32 905	. . .	11 294	. . .	38.9	. . .	1.97	. . .	76.63
June	50 912	42 986	17 984	14 408	32 928	. . .	11 300	. . .	39.1	. . .	1.98	. . .	77.42
July	51 037	43 065	18 038	14 450	32 999	. . .	11 349	. . .	39.3	. . .	1.98	. . .	77.81
August	51 233	43 221	18 147	14 524	33 086	. . .	11 412	. . .	39.5	. . .	2.01	. . .	79.40
September	51 506	43 490	18 331	14 658	33 175	. . .	11 556	. . .	39.5	. . .	2.00	. . .	79.00
October	51 485	43 454	18 218	14 503	33 267	. . .	11 394	. . .	39.6	. . .	2.00	. . .	79.20
November	51 943	43 915	18 610	14 827	33 333	. . .	11 702	. . .	39.9	. . .	2.03	. . .	81.00
December	52 088	43 988	18 592	14 877	33 496	. . .	11 743	. . .	39.9	. . .	2.04	. . .	81.40
1959													
January	52 481	44 376	18 796	14 998	33 685	. . .	11 849	. . .	40.2	. . .	2.04	. . .	82.01
February	52 687	44 571	18 890	15 115	33 797	. . .	11 950	. . .	40.3	. . .	2.05	. . .	82.62
March	53 016	44 884	19 069	15 259	33 947	. . .	12 078	. . .	40.4	. . .	2.07	. . .	83.63
April	53 320	45 178	19 269	15 385	34 051	. . .	12 185	. . .	40.5	. . .	2.08	. . .	84.24
May	53 549	45 396	19 378	15 487	34 171	. . .	12 277	. . .	40.7	. . .	2.08	. . .	84.66
June	53 678	45 535	19 462	15 554	34 216	. . .	12 330	. . .	40.6	. . .	2.09	. . .	84.85
July	53 803	45 630	19 529	15 623	34 274	. . .	12 366	. . .	40.3	. . .	2.09	. . .	84.23
August	53 337	45 156	19 049	15 202	34 288	. . .	11 936	. . .	40.4	. . .	2.07	. . .	83.63
September	53 428	45 189	19 052	15 254	34 376	. . .	11 984	. . .	40.4	. . .	2.08	. . .	84.03
October	53 359	45 094	18 925	15 158	34 434	. . .	11 864	. . .	40.1	. . .	2.07	. . .	83.01
November	53 635	45 351	19 108	15 300	34 527	. . .	11 991	. . .	39.9	. . .	2.07	. . .	82.59
December	54 175	45 807	19 425	15 573	34 750	. . .	12 254	. . .	40.3	. . .	2.11	. . .	85.03
1960													
January	54 274	45 967	19 491	15 687	34 783	. . .	12 362	. . .	40.6	. . .	2.13	. . .	86.48
February	54 513	46 187	19 605	15 765	34 908	. . .	12 434	. . .	40.3	. . .	2.14	. . .	86.24
March	54 458	45 933	19 373	15 707	35 085	. . .	12 362	. . .	40.0	. . .	2.14	. . .	85.60
April	54 812	46 278	19 446	15 654	35 366	. . .	12 299	. . .	40.0	. . .	2.14	. . .	85.60
May	54 472	46 040	19 374	15 575	35 098	. . .	12 218	. . .	40.1	. . .	2.14	. . .	85.81
June	54 347	45 915	19 240	15 466	35 107	. . .	12 102	. . .	39.9	. . .	2.14	. . .	85.39
July	54 303	45 861	19 170	15 413	35 133	. . .	12 047	. . .	39.9	. . .	2.14	. . .	85.39
August	54 272	45 800	19 105	15 360	35 167	. . .	11 986	. . .	39.7	. . .	2.15	. . .	85.36
September	54 228	45 734	19 057	15 330	35 171	. . .	11 956	. . .	39.4	. . .	2.16	. . .	85.10
October	54 144	45 642	18 952	15 231	35 192	. . .	11 846	. . .	39.7	. . .	2.16	. . .	85.75
November	53 962	45 446	18 799	15 112	35 163	. . .	11 726	. . .	39.3	. . .	2.15	. . .	84.50
December	53 743	45 146	18 548	14 947	35 195	. . .	11 556	. . .	38.4	. . .	2.16	. . .	82.94
1961													
January	53 683	45 119	18 508	14 863	35 175	. . .	11 473	. . .	39.3	. . .	2.16	. . .	84.89
February	53 556	44 969	18 418	14 801	35 138	. . .	11 414	. . .	39.4	. . .	2.16	. . .	85.10
March	53 662	45 051	18 438	14 802	35 224	. . .	11 410	. . .	39.5	. . .	2.16	. . .	85.32
April	53 626	44 997	18 432	14 825	35 194	. . .	11 444	. . .	39.5	. . .	2.18	. . .	86.11
May	53 783	45 119	18 523	14 932	35 260	. . .	11 544	. . .	39.7	. . .	2.19	. . .	86.94
June	53 977	45 289	18 618	14 981	35 359	. . .	11 593	. . .	40.0	. . .	2.20	. . .	88.00
July	54 124	45 400	18 640	15 029	35 484	. . .	11 639	. . .	40.0	. . .	2.21	. . .	88.40
August	54 299	45 535	18 725	15 093	35 574	. . .	11 701	. . .	40.1	. . .	2.22	. . .	89.02
September	54 387	45 591	18 730	15 080	35 657	. . .	11 679	. . .	39.5	. . .	2.20	. . .	86.90
October	54 521	45 716	18 805	15 143	35 716	. . .	11 731	. . .	40.3	. . .	2.23	. . .	89.87
November	54 743	45 931	18 927	15 259	35 816	. . .	11 842	. . .	40.7	. . .	2.23	. . .	90.76
December	54 871	46 035	18 981	15 309	35 890	. . .	11 872	. . .	40.4	. . .	2.24	. . .	90.50

. . . = Not available.

Table 10-9. Employment, Hours, and Earnings, Total Nonfarm and Manufacturing, Historical Annual and Monthly—*Continued*

(Wage and salary workers on nonfarm payrolls, seasonally adjusted.)

Year and month	All wage and salary workers (thousands)					Production and nonsupervisory workers on private payrolls							
	Total	Private			Service-providing	Number (thousands)		Average hours per week		Average hourly earnings, dollars		Average weekly earnings, dollars	
		Total	Goods-producing			Total private	Manufac-turing	Total private	Manufac-turing	Total private	Manufac-turing	Total private	Manufac-turing
			Total	Manufac-turing									
1962													
January	54 891	46 040	18 936	15 322	35 955	. . .	11 865	. . .	40.0	. . .	2.25	. . .	90.00
February	55 187	46 309	19 109	15 411	36 078	. . .	11 950	. . .	40.4	. . .	2.26	. . .	91.30
March	55 276	46 375	19 109	15 451	36 167	. . .	11 970	. . .	40.6	. . .	2.26	. . .	91.76
April	55 601	46 679	19 258	15 524	36 343	. . .	12 034	. . .	40.6	. . .	2.26	. . .	91.76
May	55 626	46 668	19 253	15 513	36 373	. . .	12 011	. . .	40.6	. . .	2.27	. . .	92.16
June	55 644	46 644	19 186	15 518	36 458	. . .	12 006	. . .	40.5	. . .	2.26	. . .	91.53
July	55 746	46 720	19 248	15 522	36 498	. . .	12 004	. . .	40.5	. . .	2.27	. . .	91.94
August	55 838	46 775	19 251	15 517	36 587	. . .	11 990	. . .	40.5	. . .	2.28	. . .	92.34
September	55 977	46 888	19 305	15 568	36 672	. . .	12 033	. . .	40.5	. . .	2.28	. . .	92.34
October	56 041	46 927	19 301	15 569	36 740	. . .	12 034	. . .	40.3	. . .	2.29	. . .	92.29
November	56 055	46 910	19 260	15 530	36 795	. . .	11 977	. . .	40.5	. . .	2.29	. . .	92.75
December	56 027	46 901	19 219	15 520	36 808	. . .	11 961	. . .	40.3	. . .	2.29	. . .	92.29
1963													
January	56 116	46 912	19 257	15 545	36 859	. . .	11 974	. . .	40.5	. . .	2.30	. . .	93.15
February	56 231	47 000	19 228	15 542	37 003	. . .	11 965	. . .	40.5	. . .	2.31	. . .	93.56
March	56 322	47 077	19 233	15 564	37 089	. . .	11 990	. . .	40.5	. . .	2.32	. . .	93.96
April	56 580	47 316	19 343	15 602	37 237	. . .	12 029	. . .	40.5	. . .	2.32	. . .	93.96
May	56 616	47 328	19 399	15 641	37 217	. . .	12 066	. . .	40.5	. . .	2.33	. . .	94.37
June	56 658	47 356	19 371	15 624	37 287	. . .	12 050	. . .	40.7	. . .	2.34	. . .	95.24
July	56 795	47 461	19 423	15 646	37 372	. . .	12 080	. . .	40.6	. . .	2.35	. . .	95.41
August	56 910	47 542	19 437	15 644	37 473	. . .	12 060	. . .	40.6	. . .	2.34	. . .	95.00
September	57 078	47 661	19 483	15 674	37 595	. . .	12 088	. . .	40.6	. . .	2.36	. . .	95.82
October	57 284	47 805	19 517	15 714	37 767	. . .	12 131	. . .	40.7	. . .	2.36	. . .	96.05
November	57 255	47 771	19 456	15 675	37 799	. . .	12 072	. . .	40.7	. . .	2.37	. . .	96.46
December	57 360	47 863	19 493	15 712	37 867	. . .	12 108	. . .	40.6	. . .	2.38	. . .	96.63
1964													
January	57 487	47 925	19 406	15 715	38 081	39 914	12 132	38.2	40.1	2.50	2.38	95.50	95.44
February	57 752	48 171	19 530	15 742	38 182	40 123	12 165	38.5	40.7	2.50	2.38	96.25	96.87
March	57 898	48 287	19 587	15 770	38 311	40 171	12 190	38.5	40.6	2.50	2.38	96.25	96.63
April	57 923	48 279	19 593	15 785	38 330	40 208	12 211	38.6	40.7	2.52	2.40	97.27	97.68
May	58 089	48 419	19 630	15 812	38 459	40 332	12 231	38.6	40.8	2.52	2.40	97.27	97.92
June	58 221	48 552	19 682	15 839	38 539	40 448	12 255	38.6	40.8	2.53	2.41	97.66	98.33
July	58 412	48 735	19 740	15 887	38 672	40 624	12 309	38.5	40.8	2.53	2.41	97.41	98.33
August	58 620	48 888	19 810	15 948	38 810	40 770	12 354	38.5	40.9	2.55	2.42	98.18	98.98
September	58 903	49 117	19 943	16 073	38 960	41 026	12 479	38.5	40.9	2.55	2.44	98.18	99.80
October	58 794	48 949	19 723	15 821	39 071	40 827	12 224	38.5	40.7	2.55	2.40	98.18	97.68
November	59 217	49 338	20 026	16 096	39 191	41 157	12 477	38.6	41.0	2.56	2.42	98.82	99.22
December	59 420	49 523	20 111	16 176	39 309	41 308	12 551	38.7	41.2	2.58	2.44	99.85	100.53
1965													
January	59 583	49 646	20 173	16 245	39 410	41 453	12 603	38.7	41.3	2.58	2.45	99.85	101.19
February	59 800	49 826	20 216	16 291	39 584	41 583	12 644	38.7	41.3	2.59	2.46	100.23	101.60
March	60 003	49 993	20 292	16 353	39 711	41 675	12 701	38.7	41.3	2.60	2.47	100.62	102.01
April	60 258	50 207	20 317	16 418	39 941	41 886	12 752	38.7	41.2	2.60	2.47	100.62	101.76
May	60 492	50 398	20 444	16 477	40 048	42 044	12 792	38.8	41.3	2.62	2.49	101.66	102.84
June	60 690	50 562	20 522	16 554	40 168	42 183	12 854	38.6	41.2	2.62	2.49	101.13	102.59
July	60 963	50 762	20 611	16 669	40 352	42 364	12 962	38.6	41.2	2.63	2.49	101.52	102.59
August	61 228	50 957	20 726	16 732	40 502	42 537	12 994	38.5	41.1	2.64	2.50	101.64	102.75
September	61 490	51 152	20 808	16 802	40 682	42 726	13 046	38.6	41.1	2.65	2.51	102.29	103.16
October	61 718	51 340	20 895	16 864	40 823	42 870	13 100	38.5	41.2	2.66	2.52	102.41	103.82
November	61 997	51 561	21 021	16 962	40 976	43 045	13 175	38.6	41.3	2.67	2.52	103.06	104.08
December	62 321	51 822	21 151	17 051	41 170	43 270	13 243	38.6	41.3	2.68	2.53	103.45	104.49
1966													
January	62 528	51 987	21 214	17 143	41 314	43 401	13 301	38.6	41.5	2.68	2.54	103.45	105.41
February	62 796	52 185	21 315	17 288	41 481	43 552	13 426	38.7	41.7	2.69	2.56	104.10	106.75
March	63 191	52 499	21 515	17 400	41 676	43 801	13 508	38.7	41.6	2.70	2.56	104.49	106.50
April	63 436	52 677	21 568	17 517	41 868	43 959	13 598	38.7	41.8	2.71	2.58	104.88	107.84
May	63 711	52 890	21 675	17 625	42 036	44 138	13 678	38.5	41.5	2.72	2.58	104.72	107.07
June	64 110	53 208	21 846	17 733	42 264	44 390	13 753	38.5	41.4	2.72	2.58	104.72	106.81
July	64 301	53 327	21 872	17 760	42 429	44 484	13 758	38.4	41.2	2.74	2.60	105.22	107.12
August	64 507	53 501	21 972	17 882	42 535	44 596	13 843	38.4	41.4	2.75	2.61	105.60	108.05
September	64 645	53 582	21 948	17 886	42 697	44 659	13 841	38.3	41.2	2.76	2.63	105.71	108.36
October	64 854	53 727	21 991	17 956	42 863	44 789	13 906	38.4	41.3	2.77	2.64	106.37	109.03
November	65 019	53 816	21 988	17 981	43 031	44 834	13 918	38.3	41.2	2.78	2.65	106.47	109.18
December	65 199	53 943	22 008	17 998	43 191	44 916	13 906	38.2	40.9	2.78	2.64	106.20	107.98
1967													
January	65 407	54 092	22 057	18 033	43 350	45 050	13 925	38.3	41.1	2.79	2.65	106.86	108.92
February	65 427	54 074	21 987	17 978	43 440	44 967	13 853	37.9	40.4	2.81	2.67	106.50	107.87
March	65 530	54 133	21 919	17 940	43 611	44 991	13 797	37.9	40.5	2.81	2.67	106.50	108.14
April	65 467	54 032	21 842	17 878	43 625	44 871	13 712	37.8	40.4	2.82	2.68	106.60	108.27
May	65 618	54 144	21 779	17 832	43 839	44 961	13 664	37.8	40.4	2.83	2.69	106.97	108.68
June	65 750	54 216	21 761	17 812	43 989	45 004	13 632	37.8	40.4	2.84	2.69	107.35	108.68
July	65 887	54 343	21 772	17 784	44 115	45 105	13 602	37.8	40.5	2.86	2.71	108.11	109.76
August	66 142	54 552	21 887	17 905	44 255	45 267	13 681	37.8	40.6	2.87	2.73	108.49	110.84
September	66 163	54 540	21 775	17 794	44 388	45 236	13 559	37.8	40.6	2.88	2.73	108.86	110.84
October	66 225	54 583	21 779	17 800	44 446	45 278	13 587	37.8	40.6	2.89	2.74	109.24	111.24
November	66 703	55 008	21 996	17 985	44 707	45 701	13 777	37.9	40.6	2.91	2.75	110.29	111.65
December	66 900	55 165	22 037	18 025	44 863	45 800	13 782	37.7	40.7	2.92	2.77	110.08	112.74

. . . = Not available.

Table 10-9. Employment, Hours, and Earnings, Total Nonfarm and Manufacturing, Historical Annual and Monthly—Continued

(Wage and salary workers on nonfarm payrolls, seasonally adjusted.)

Year and month	All wage and salary workers (thousands)					Production and nonsupervisory workers on private payrolls							
		Private				Number (thousands)		Average hours per week		Average hourly earnings, dollars		Average weekly earnings, dollars	
	Total	Total	Goods-producing		Service-providing	Total private	Manufacturing	Total private	Manufacturing	Total private	Manufacturing	Total private	Manufacturing
			Total	Manufacturing									
1968													
January	66 805	55 011	21 917	18 040	44 888	45 655	13 798	37.6	40.4	2.94	2.81	110.54	113.52
February	67 214	55 395	22 117	18 054	45 097	45 980	13 793	37.8	40.8	2.95	2.82	111.51	115.06
March	67 296	55 454	22 119	18 067	45 177	46 041	13 803	37.7	40.8	2.97	2.84	111.97	115.87
April	67 555	55 677	22 207	18 131	45 348	46 239	13 858	37.6	40.3	2.98	2.85	112.05	114.86
May	67 652	55 747	22 255	18 190	45 397	46 267	13 900	37.7	40.9	3.00	2.87	113.10	117.38
June	67 904	55 917	22 264	18 228	45 640	46 402	13 921	37.8	40.9	3.01	2.88	113.78	117.79
July	68 126	56 108	22 329	18 265	45 797	46 562	13 953	37.7	40.8	3.03	2.89	114.23	117.91
August	68 328	56 286	22 350	18 254	45 978	46 669	13 903	37.7	40.7	3.03	2.89	114.23	117.62
September	68 487	56 420	22 390	18 252	46 097	46 792	13 914	37.7	40.9	3.06	2.92	115.36	119.43
October	68 720	56 619	22 419	18 293	46 301	46 989	13 974	37.7	41.0	3.07	2.94	115.74	120.54
November	68 985	56 878	22 512	18 346	46 473	47 244	14 028	37.5	40.9	3.09	2.96	115.88	121.06
December	69 245	57 100	22 617	18 410	46 628	47 384	14 044	37.5	40.7	3.11	2.97	116.63	120.88
1969													
January	69 438	57 229	22 644	18 432	46 794	47 528	14 086	37.7	40.8	3.12	2.99	117.62	121.99
February	69 698	57 474	22 755	18 502	46 943	47 697	14 134	37.5	40.4	3.14	3.00	117.75	121.20
March	69 906	57 677	22 813	18 558	47 093	47 852	14 169	37.6	40.8	3.15	3.01	118.44	122.81
April	70 072	57 827	22 815	18 554	47 257	47 959	14 144	37.7	41.0	3.17	3.03	119.51	124.23
May	70 328	58 044	22 899	18 588	47 429	48 122	14 161	37.6	40.7	3.19	3.04	119.94	123.73
June	70 636	58 277	22 981	18 640	47 655	48 330	14 206	37.5	40.7	3.20	3.05	120.00	124.14
July	70 730	58 390	22 990	18 642	47 740	48 434	14 194	37.5	40.6	3.22	3.08	120.75	125.05
August	71 005	58 632	23 111	18 767	47 894	48 616	14 287	37.5	40.6	3.24	3.10	121.50	125.86
September	70 918	58 539	22 988	18 620	47 930	48 524	14 159	37.5	40.6	3.26	3.12	122.25	126.67
October	71 119	58 689	22 976	18 613	48 143	48 669	14 174	37.4	40.5	3.28	3.13	122.67	126.77
November	71 088	58 640	22 840	18 467	48 248	48 589	14 035	37.5	40.5	3.29	3.14	123.38	127.17
December	71 240	58 763	22 884	18 485	48 356	48 638	14 013	37.5	40.6	3.30	3.15	123.75	127.89
1970													
January	71 176	58 680	22 726	18 424	48 450	48 564	13 964	37.3	40.4	3.31	3.16	123.46	127.66
February	71 302	58 784	22 747	18 361	48 555	48 600	13 897	37.3	40.2	3.33	3.17	124.21	127.43
March	71 453	58 850	22 738	18 360	48 715	48 690	13 917	37.2	40.1	3.35	3.19	124.62	127.92
April	71 348	58 643	22 552	18 207	48 796	48 479	13 785	37.0	39.8	3.36	3.19	124.32	126.96
May	71 122	58 454	22 336	18 029	48 786	48 287	13 616	37.0	39.8	3.38	3.22	125.06	128.16
June	71 028	58 361	22 241	17 930	48 787	48 226	13 554	36.9	39.8	3.39	3.24	125.09	128.95
July	71 055	58 358	22 195	17 877	48 860	48 242	13 527	37.0	40.0	3.41	3.25	126.17	130.00
August	70 932	58 221	22 105	17 779	48 827	48 089	13 449	37.0	39.8	3.43	3.26	126.91	129.75
September	70 949	58 208	21 988	17 692	48 961	48 101	13 401	36.8	39.6	3.45	3.29	126.96	130.28
October	70 519	57 726	21 477	17 173	49 042	47 619	12 905	36.8	39.5	3.46	3.26	127.33	128.77
November	70 409	57 579	21 345	17 024	49 064	47 466	12 781	36.7	39.5	3.47	3.26	127.35	128.77
December	70 790	57 945	21 673	17 309	49 117	47 778	13 062	36.8	39.5	3.50	3.32	128.80	131.14
1971													
January	70 866	57 988	21 594	17 280	49 272	47 859	13 069	36.8	39.9	3.52	3.36	129.54	134.06
February	70 805	57 928	21 514	17 216	49 291	47 779	13 033	36.7	39.7	3.54	3.39	129.92	134.58
March	70 859	57 951	21 491	17 154	49 368	47 819	12 984	36.7	39.8	3.56	3.39	130.65	134.92
April	71 037	58 092	21 552	17 149	49 485	47 966	12 993	36.8	39.9	3.57	3.41	131.38	136.06
May	71 247	58 277	21 645	17 225	49 602	48 153	13 081	36.7	40.0	3.60	3.43	132.12	137.20
June	71 253	58 245	21 568	17 139	49 685	48 109	13 012	36.8	39.9	3.62	3.45	133.22	137.66
July	71 316	58 305	21 564	17 126	49 752	48 167	13 001	36.7	40.0	3.63	3.46	133.22	138.40
August	71 368	58 327	21 570	17 115	49 798	48 164	12 993	36.7	39.8	3.66	3.48	134.32	138.50
September	71 620	58 552	21 650	17 154	49 970	48 362	13 038	36.7	39.7	3.67	3.48	134.69	138.16
October	71 642	58 527	21 604	17 126	50 038	48 305	13 027	36.8	39.9	3.68	3.50	135.42	139.65
November	71 844	58 696	21 684	17 166	50 160	48 442	13 064	36.9	40.0	3.69	3.49	136.16	139.60
December	72 108	58 918	21 741	17 202	50 367	48 613	13 078	36.9	40.2	3.73	3.55	137.64	142.71
1972													
January	72 445	59 179	21 865	17 283	50 580	49 035	13 173	36.9	40.2	3.80	3.57	140.22	143.51
February	72 652	59 354	21 915	17 361	50 737	49 143	13 235	36.9	40.4	3.82	3.61	140.96	145.84
March	72 945	59 616	22 036	17 447	50 909	49 437	13 316	36.9	40.4	3.84	3.63	141.70	146.65
April	73 163	59 805	22 099	17 508	51 064	49 561	13 373	36.9	40.5	3.86	3.65	142.43	147.83
May	73 467	60 051	22 222	17 602	51 245	49 745	13 451	36.8	40.5	3.87	3.67	142.42	148.64
June	73 760	60 355	22 282	17 641	51 478	49 997	13 475	36.9	40.6	3.88	3.68	143.17	149.41
July	73 709	60 227	22 162	17 556	51 547	49 842	13 387	36.8	40.5	3.90	3.69	143.52	149.45
August	74 137	60 607	22 400	17 741	51 737	50 156	13 562	36.8	40.6	3.92	3.73	144.26	151.44
September	74 268	60 693	22 456	17 774	51 812	50 224	13 572	36.9	40.6	3.94	3.75	145.39	152.25
October	74 672	61 066	22 613	17 893	52 059	50 552	13 681	37.0	40.7	3.97	3.78	146.89	153.85
November	74 965	61 322	22 688	18 005	52 277	50 790	13 783	36.9	40.7	3.98	3.79	146.86	154.25
December	75 270	61 586	22 772	18 158	52 498	51 054	13 902	36.8	40.6	4.01	3.83	147.57	155.50
1973													
January	75 620	61 930	22 955	18 276	52 665	51 349	14 006	36.8	40.4	4.03	3.86	148.30	155.94
February	76 017	62 306	23 160	18 410	52 857	51 686	14 127	36.9	40.9	4.04	3.87	149.08	158.28
March	76 286	62 541	23 262	18 493	53 024	51 901	14 181	37.0	40.9	4.06	3.88	150.22	158.69
April	76 456	62 679	23 316	18 530	53 140	51 982	14 192	36.9	40.8	4.08	3.91	150.55	159.53
May	76 646	62 829	23 382	18 564	53 264	52 082	14 217	36.9	40.7	4.10	3.93	151.29	159.95
June	76 886	63 014	23 485	18 606	53 401	52 234	14 253	36.9	40.7	4.12	3.95	152.03	160.77
July	76 911	63 046	23 522	18 598	53 389	52 238	14 232	36.9	40.7	4.15	3.98	153.14	161.99
August	77 166	63 262	23 559	18 629	53 607	52 393	14 251	36.9	40.6	4.16	4.00	153.50	162.40
September	77 281	63 389	23 548	18 609	53 733	52 410	14 213	36.8	40.7	4.19	4.03	154.19	164.02
October	77 605	63 628	23 641	18 702	53 964	52 655	14 289	36.7	40.6	4.21	4.05	154.51	164.43
November	77 909	63 874	23 719	18 773	54 190	52 847	14 342	36.9	40.6	4.23	4.07	156.09	165.24
December	78 035	63 965	23 779	18 820	54 256	52 954	14 386	36.7	40.6	4.25	4.09	155.98	166.05

Table 10-9. Employment, Hours, and Earnings, Total Nonfarm and Manufacturing, Historical Annual and Monthly—*Continued*

(Wage and salary workers on nonfarm payrolls, seasonally adjusted.)

Year and month	All wage and salary workers (thousands)					Production and nonsupervisory workers on private payrolls							
	Total	Private			Service-providing	Number (thousands)		Average hours per week		Average hourly earnings, dollars		Average weekly earnings, dollars	
		Total	Goods-producing			Total private	Manufac-turing	Total private	Manufac-turing	Total private	Manufac-turing	Total private	Manufac-turing
			Total	Manufac-turing									
1974													
January	78 104	64 014	23 709	18 788	54 395	52 896	14 340	36.6	40.5	4.26	4.10	155.92	166.05
February	78 253	64 118	23 718	18 727	54 535	52 971	14 269	36.6	40.4	4.29	4.13	157.01	166.85
March	78 295	64 143	23 687	18 700	54 608	52 951	14 223	36.6	40.4	4.31	4.15	157.75	167.66
April	78 384	64 193	23 670	18 702	54 714	53 003	14 225	36.4	39.5	4.34	4.16	157.98	164.32
May	78 547	64 326	23 635	18 688	54 912	53 095	14 199	36.5	40.3	4.39	4.25	160.24	171.28
June	78 602	64 363	23 591	18 690	55 011	53 107	14 197	36.5	40.2	4.43	4.30	161.70	172.86
July	78 634	64 346	23 462	18 656	55 172	53 044	14 152	36.5	40.1	4.45	4.33	162.43	173.63
August	78 619	64 291	23 396	18 570	55 223	53 025	14 089	36.5	40.2	4.49	4.38	163.89	176.08
September	78 614	64 192	23 274	18 492	55 340	52 915	14 025	36.4	40.0	4.53	4.42	164.89	176.80
October	78 627	64 143	23 118	18 364	55 509	52 836	13 884	36.3	40.0	4.56	4.48	165.53	179.20
November	78 259	63 727	22 773	18 077	55 486	52 413	13 607	36.1	39.5	4.57	4.49	164.98	177.36
December	77 657	63 098	22 303	17 693	55 354	51 856	13 259	36.1	39.3	4.61	4.52	166.42	177.64
1975													
January	77 297	62 673	21 974	17 344	55 323	51 439	12 933	36.1	39.2	4.61	4.54	166.42	177.97
February	76 919	62 172	21 512	17 004	55 407	50 934	12 622	35.9	38.9	4.63	4.58	166.22	178.16
March	76 649	61 895	21 274	16 853	55 375	50 666	12 483	35.7	38.8	4.66	4.63	166.36	179.64
April	76 463	61 668	21 109	16 759	55 354	50 439	12 407	35.8	39.0	4.66	4.63	166.83	180.57
May	76 623	61 796	21 097	16 746	55 526	50 558	12 406	35.9	39.0	4.68	4.65	168.01	181.35
June	76 519	61 735	21 018	16 690	55 501	50 537	12 371	35.9	39.2	4.72	4.68	169.45	183.46
July	76 768	61 907	20 981	16 678	55 787	50 726	12 374	35.9	39.4	4.73	4.71	169.81	185.57
August	77 154	62 284	21 176	16 824	55 978	51 070	12 538	36.1	39.7	4.77	4.75	172.20	188.58
September	77 232	62 408	21 284	16 904	55 948	51 183	12 617	36.1	39.8	4.79	4.78	172.92	190.24
October	77 535	62 635	21 384	16 984	56 151	51 376	12 687	36.1	39.9	4.81	4.80	173.64	191.52
November	77 679	62 776	21 442	17 025	56 237	51 458	12 700	36.1	39.9	4.85	4.83	175.09	192.72
December	78 017	63 071	21 602	17 140	56 415	51 759	12 811	36.2	40.2	4.87	4.86	176.29	195.37
1976													
January	78 506	63 537	21 799	17 287	56 707	52 182	12 945	36.3	40.3	4.90	4.90	177.87	197.47
February	78 817	63 836	21 893	17 384	56 924	52 430	13 030	36.3	40.4	4.94	4.94	179.32	199.58
March	79 049	64 062	21 980	17 470	57 069	52 615	13 092	36.0	40.2	4.96	4.98	178.56	200.20
April	79 293	64 308	22 050	17 541	57 243	52 810	13 160	36.0	39.6	4.98	4.98	179.28	197.21
May	79 311	64 340	21 988	17 513	57 323	52 802	13 130	36.1	40.3	5.02	5.04	181.22	203.11
June	79 376	64 413	21 982	17 521	57 394	52 830	13 121	36.1	40.2	5.04	5.07	181.94	203.81
July	79 546	64 553	21 988	17 524	57 558	52 973	13 124	36.1	40.3	5.07	5.11	183.03	205.93
August	79 704	64 697	22 038	17 596	57 666	53 072	13 195	36.0	40.2	5.12	5.16	184.32	207.43
September	79 892	64 921	22 142	17 665	57 750	53 268	13 253	36.0	40.2	5.15	5.20	185.40	209.04
October	79 905	64 877	22 037	17 548	57 868	53 165	13 109	35.9	40.0	5.17	5.19	185.60	207.60
November	80 237	65 164	22 207	17 682	58 030	53 362	13 199	35.9	40.1	5.21	5.25	187.04	210.53
December	80 448	65 373	22 261	17 719	58 187	53 543	13 230	35.9	39.9	5.23	5.29	187.76	211.07
1977													
January	80 692	65 636	22 320	17 803	58 372	53 756	13 305	35.6	39.4	5.26	5.35	187.26	210.79
February	80 987	65 931	22 478	17 843	58 509	54 016	13 331	36.0	40.2	5.30	5.36	190.80	215.47
March	81 391	66 341	22 672	17 941	58 719	54 390	13 424	35.9	40.3	5.33	5.40	191.35	217.62
April	81 730	66 655	22 807	18 024	58 923	54 670	13 490	36.0	40.4	5.37	5.45	193.32	220.18
May	82 089	66 957	22 919	18 107	59 170	54 940	13 567	36.0	40.5	5.40	5.49	194.40	222.35
June	82 488	67 281	23 046	18 192	59 442	55 195	13 622	36.0	40.5	5.43	5.54	195.48	224.37
July	82 836	67 537	23 106	18 259	59 730	55 395	13 670	35.9	40.4	5.46	5.58	196.01	225.43
August	83 074	67 746	23 124	18 276	59 950	55 543	13 679	35.9	40.4	5.48	5.61	196.73	226.64
September	83 532	68 129	23 244	18 334	60 288	55 859	13 714	35.9	40.4	5.51	5.65	197.81	228.26
October	83 794	68 331	23 279	18 356	60 515	56 004	13 722	36.0	40.6	5.56	5.69	200.16	231.01
November	84 173	68 658	23 371	18 419	60 802	56 281	13 771	35.9	40.5	5.59	5.72	200.68	231.66
December	84 408	68 870	23 371	18 531	61 037	56 466	13 861	35.8	40.4	5.61	5.75	200.84	232.30
1978													
January	84 595	68 984	23 374	18 593	61 221	56 547	13 917	35.3	39.5	5.66	5.83	199.80	230.29
February	84 948	69 277	23 453	18 639	61 495	56 768	13 950	35.6	39.9	5.69	5.86	202.56	233.81
March	85 461	69 730	23 649	18 699	61 812	57 176	13 992	35.8	40.5	5.73	5.88	205.13	238.14
April	86 163	70 366	24 008	18 772	62 155	57 709	14 037	35.8	40.4	5.79	5.93	207.28	239.57
May	86 509	70 675	24 082	18 848	62 427	57 941	14 096	35.8	40.4	5.82	5.96	208.36	240.78
June	86 951	71 099	24 238	18 919	62 713	58 263	14 129	35.9	40.6	5.87	6.01	210.73	244.01
July	87 205	71 304	24 300	18 951	62 905	58 422	14 152	35.9	40.6	5.90	6.06	211.81	246.04
August	87 481	71 590	24 374	19 006	63 107	58 626	14 187	35.8	40.5	5.93	6.09	212.29	246.65
September	87 618	71 799	24 444	19 068	63 174	58 819	14 241	35.8	40.5	5.97	6.15	213.73	249.08
October	87 954	72 096	24 548	19 142	63 406	59 017	14 291	35.8	40.5	6.03	6.20	215.87	251.10
November	88 391	72 497	24 678	19 257	63 713	59 377	14 388	35.7	40.6	6.06	6.26	216.34	254.16
December	88 674	72 763	24 758	19 334	63 916	59 599	14 459	35.7	40.5	6.10	6.31	217.77	255.56
1979													
January	88 811	72 874	24 740	19 388	64 071	59 659	14 497	35.6	40.4	6.14	6.36	218.58	256.94
February	89 054	73 107	24 784	19 409	64 270	59 840	14 501	35.7	40.5	6.18	6.40	220.63	259.20
March	89 480	73 524	24 998	19 453	64 482	60 216	14 526	35.8	40.6	6.22	6.45	222.68	261.87
April	89 418	73 441	24 958	19 450	64 460	60 067	14 515	35.3	39.3	6.22	6.43	219.57	252.70
May	89 790	73 800	25 071	19 509	64 719	60 368	14 551	35.6	40.2	6.28	6.52	223.57	262.10
June	90 108	74 063	25 161	19 553	64 947	60 583	14 566	35.6	40.2	6.32	6.56	224.99	263.71
July	90 214	74 064	25 163	19 531	65 051	60 558	14 536	35.6	40.2	6.36	6.59	226.42	264.92
August	90 296	74 067	25 059	19 406	65 237	60 516	14 397	35.6	40.1	6.40	6.63	227.84	265.86
September	90 323	74 195	25 088	19 442	65 235	60 629	14 440	35.6	40.1	6.45	6.67	229.62	267.47
October	90 480	74 344	25 038	19 390	65 442	60 746	14 384	35.6	40.2	6.47	6.71	230.33	269.74
November	90 574	74 401	24 947	19 299	65 627	60 778	14 295	35.6	40.1	6.51	6.74	231.76	270.27
December	90 669	74 489	24 970	19 301	65 699	60 860	14 300	35.5	40.1	6.57	6.80	233.24	272.68

Table 10-9. Employment, Hours, and Earnings, Total Nonfarm and Manufacturing, Historical Annual and Monthly—*Continued*

(Wage and salary workers on nonfarm payrolls, seasonally adjusted.)

Year and month	All wage and salary workers (thousands)					Production and nonsupervisory workers on private payrolls							
	Total	Private			Service-providing	Number (thousands)		Average hours per week		Average hourly earnings, dollars		Average weekly earnings, dollars	
		Total	Goods-producing			Total private	Manufac-turing	Total private	Manufac-turing	Total private	Manufac-turing	Total private	Manufac-turing
			Total	Manufac-turing									
1980													
January	90 800	74 599	24 949	19 282	65 851	60 896	14 241	35.4	40.0	6.57	6.82	232.58	272.80
February	90 879	74 653	24 874	19 219	66 005	60 964	14 170	35.4	40.1	6.63	6.88	234.70	275.89
March	90 991	74 695	24 818	19 217	66 173	60 987	14 165	35.3	39.9	6.70	6.95	236.51	277.31
April	90 846	74 263	24 507	18 973	66 339	60 540	13 914	35.2	39.8	6.72	6.97	236.54	277.41
May	90 415	73 961	24 234	18 726	66 181	60 194	13 632	35.1	39.3	6.76	7.02	237.28	275.89
June	90 095	73 654	23 968	18 490	66 127	59 892	13 405	35.0	39.2	6.82	7.10	238.70	278.32
July	89 832	73 414	23 698	18 276	66 134	59 693	13 227	34.9	39.1	6.86	7.16	239.41	279.96
August	90 092	73 682	23 860	18 414	66 232	59 908	13 349	35.1	39.5	6.91	7.24	242.54	285.98
September	90 205	73 875	23 931	18 445	66 274	60 075	13 396	35.1	39.6	6.95	7.30	243.95	289.08
October	90 485	74 099	24 012	18 506	66 473	60 239	13 437	35.2	39.8	7.02	7.38	247.10	293.72
November	90 741	74 350	24 123	18 601	66 618	60 449	13 528	35.3	39.9	7.09	7.47	250.28	298.05
December	90 936	74 563	24 182	18 640	66 754	60 606	13 550	35.3	40.1	7.13	7.52	251.69	301.55
1981													
January	91 031	74 671	24 152	18 639	66 879	60 710	13 545	35.4	40.1	7.19	7.58	254.53	303.96
February	91 098	74 752	24 118	18 613	66 980	60 736	13 518	35.2	39.8	7.23	7.62	254.50	303.28
March	91 202	74 910	24 203	18 647	66 999	60 875	13 550	35.3	40.0	7.29	7.68	257.34	307.20
April	91 276	75 016	24 151	18 711	67 125	60 973	13 594	35.3	40.1	7.33	7.76	258.75	311.18
May	91 286	75 088	24 148	18 766	67 138	60 973	13 633	35.3	40.2	7.37	7.81	260.16	313.96
June	91 482	75 323	24 290	18 789	67 192	61 134	13 632	35.2	40.0	7.42	7.85	261.18	314.00
July	91 594	75 419	24 302	18 785	67 292	61 222	13 629	35.2	39.9	7.46	7.89	262.59	314.81
August	91 558	75 448	24 258	18 748	67 300	61 216	13 573	35.2	40.0	7.53	7.97	265.06	318.80
September	91 471	75 440	24 210	18 712	67 261	61 235	13 565	35.0	39.6	7.57	8.03	264.95	317.99
October	91 371	75 302	24 051	18 566	67 320	61 066	13 399	35.1	39.6	7.59	8.06	266.41	319.18
November	91 162	75 084	23 875	18 409	67 287	60 817	13 235	35.1	39.4	7.64	8.08	268.16	318.35
December	90 884	74 811	23 656	18 223	67 228	60 511	13 033	34.9	39.2	7.64	8.09	266.64	317.13
1982													
January	90 557	74 516	23 362	18 047	67 195	60 206	12 874	34.1	37.3	7.72	8.26	263.25	308.10
February	90 551	74 540	23 361	17 981	67 190	60 277	12 831	35.1	39.6	7.73	8.21	271.32	325.12
March	90 422	74 398	23 214	17 857	67 208	60 140	12 727	34.9	39.1	7.76	8.24	270.82	322.18
April	90 141	74 311	22 996	17 683	67 145	59 867	12 566	34.8	39.1	7.77	8.28	270.40	323.75
May	90 096	74 093	22 884	17 588	67 212	59 840	12 506	34.8	39.1	7.83	8.33	272.48	325.70
June	89 853	73 837	22 643	17 430	67 210	59 589	12 365	34.8	39.2	7.85	8.37	273.18	328.10
July	89 510	73 620	22 434	17 278	67 076	59 411	12 261	34.8	39.2	7.89	8.40	274.57	329.28
August	89 352	73 422	22 268	17 160	67 084	59 203	12 153	34.7	39.0	7.94	8.43	275.52	328.77
September	89 171	73 248	22 146	17 074	67 025	59 069	12 104	34.8	39.0	7.94	8.45	276.31	329.55
October	88 894	72 938	21 879	16 853	67 015	58 750	11 880	34.6	38.9	7.96	8.44	275.42	328.32
November	88 770	72 793	21 736	16 722	67 034	58 613	11 766	34.6	39.0	7.98	8.46	276.11	329.94
December	88 756	72 775	21 688	16 690	67 068	58 585	11 746	34.7	39.0	8.02	8.49	278.29	331.11
1983													
January	88 981	72 958	21 757	16 705	67 224	58 813	11 783	34.8	39.3	8.06	8.52	280.49	334.84
February	88 903	72 899	21 676	16 706	67 227	58 792	11 794	34.5	39.3	8.10	8.59	279.45	337.59
March	89 076	73 071	21 649	16 711	67 427	58 958	11 817	34.7	39.6	8.10	8.59	281.07	340.16
April	89 352	73 362	21 729	16 794	67 623	59 201	11 894	34.8	39.7	8.13	8.61	282.92	341.82
May	89 629	73 624	21 829	16 885	67 800	59 444	11 987	34.9	40.0	8.17	8.64	285.13	345.60
June	90 007	73 987	21 949	16 960	68 058	59 806	12 054	34.9	40.1	8.19	8.66	285.83	347.27
July	90 425	74 414	22 103	17 059	68 322	60 189	12 155	34.9	40.3	8.23	8.71	287.23	351.01
August	90 117	74 101	22 207	17 118	67 910	59 820	12 200	34.9	40.3	8.20	8.71	286.18	351.01
September	91 231	75 189	22 381	17 255	68 850	60 849	12 318	35.0	40.6	8.26	8.76	289.10	355.66
October	91 502	75 516	22 546	17 367	68 956	61 095	12 408	35.2	40.6	8.31	8.80	292.51	357.28
November	91 854	75 857	22 698	17 479	69 156	61 378	12 503	35.1	40.6	8.32	8.84	292.03	358.90
December	92 210	76 202	22 803	17 551	69 407	61 664	12 553	35.1	40.5	8.33	8.87	292.38	359.24
1984													
January	92 657	76 647	22 942	17 630	69 715	61 906	12 617	35.1	40.6	8.38	8.91	294.14	361.75
February	93 136	77 111	23 146	17 728	69 990	62 329	12 703	35.3	41.1	8.37	8.92	295.46	366.61
March	93 411	77 381	23 209	17 806	70 202	62 516	12 768	35.1	40.7	8.41	8.96	295.19	364.67
April	93 774	77 699	23 305	17 872	70 469	62 801	12 814	35.2	40.8	8.45	8.98	297.44	366.38
May	94 082	77 979	23 389	17 916	70 693	63 012	12 840	35.1	40.7	8.44	8.99	296.24	365.89
June	94 461	78 334	23 497	17 967	70 964	63 296	12 871	35.1	40.6	8.48	9.03	297.65	366.62
July	94 773	78 601	23 571	18 013	71 202	63 517	12 901	35.1	40.6	8.52	9.05	299.05	367.43
August	95 014	78 790	23 608	18 034	71 406	63 654	12 906	35.0	40.5	8.52	9.09	298.20	368.15
September	95 325	79 070	23 617	18 019	71 708	63 874	12 880	35.1	40.5	8.56	9.12	300.46	369.36
October	95 611	79 337	23 626	18 024	71 985	64 083	12 868	34.9	40.5	8.55	9.15	298.40	370.58
November	95 960	79 649	23 639	18 016	72 321	64 325	12 846	35.0	40.4	8.57	9.19	299.95	371.28
December	96 087	79 805	23 673	18 023	72 414	64 441	12 848	35.1	40.5	8.61	9.22	302.21	373.41
1985													
January	96 353	80 017	23 672	18 009	72 681	64 657	12 833	34.9	40.3	8.61	9.27	300.49	373.58
February	96 477	80 128	23 621	17 966	72 856	64 758	12 784	34.8	40.1	8.64	9.29	300.67	372.53
March	96 823	80 428	23 661	17 939	73 162	65 007	12 758	34.9	40.4	8.67	9.32	302.58	376.53
April	97 018	80 588	23 644	17 886	73 374	65 113	12 701	34.9	40.5	8.69	9.35	303.28	378.68
May	97 292	80 818	23 632	17 855	73 660	65 307	12 673	34.9	40.4	8.70	9.37	303.63	378.55
June	97 437	80 939	23 592	17 819	73 845	65 382	12 635	34.9	40.5	8.74	9.39	305.03	380.30
July	97 626	81 006	23 549	17 776	74 077	65 432	12 596	34.8	40.4	8.74	9.42	304.15	380.57
August	97 819	81 200	23 546	17 756	74 273	65 615	12 593	34.8	40.6	8.77	9.43	305.20	382.86
September	98 023	81 385	23 528	17 718	74 495	65 750	12 556	34.8	40.6	8.80	9.44	306.24	383.26
October	98 210	81 556	23 529	17 708	74 681	65 917	12 556	34.8	40.7	8.79	9.46	305.89	385.02
November	98 419	81 745	23 520	17 697	74 899	66 069	12 545	34.8	40.7	8.82	9.49	306.94	386.24
December	98 587	81 893	23 518	17 693	75 069	66 197	12 550	34.9	40.9	8.87	9.55	309.56	390.60

Table 10-9. Employment, Hours, and Earnings, Total Nonfarm and Manufacturing, Historical Annual and Monthly—*Continued*

(Wage and salary workers on nonfarm payrolls, seasonally adjusted.)

Year and month	All wage and salary workers (thousands)					Production and nonsupervisory workers on private payrolls							
		Private			Service-providing	Number (thousands)		Average hours per week		Average hourly earnings, dollars		Average weekly earnings, dollars	
	Total	Total	Goods-producing			Total private	Manufac-turing	Total private	Manufac-turing	Total private	Manufac-turing	Total private	Manufac-turing
			Total	Manufac-turing									
1986													
January	98 710	81 995	23 530	17 686	75 180	66 293	12 546	35.0	40.7	8.85	9.53	309.75	387.87
February	98 817	82 058	23 485	17 663	75 332	66 365	12 530	34.8	40.7	8.88	9.56	309.02	389.09
March	98 910	82 155	23 428	17 624	75 482	66 403	12 498	34.8	40.7	8.89	9.58	309.37	389.91
April	99 098	82 333	23 427	17 616	75 671	66 531	12 495	34.7	40.5	8.89	9.56	308.48	387.18
May	99 223	82 433	23 349	17 593	75 874	66 606	12 474	34.8	40.7	8.90	9.59	309.72	390.31
June	99 130	82 351	23 263	17 530	75 867	66 533	12 424	34.7	40.7	8.91	9.58	309.18	389.91
July	99 448	82 669	23 235	17 497	76 213	66 810	12 389	34.6	40.6	8.92	9.60	308.63	389.76
August	99 561	82 761	23 225	17 489	76 336	66 909	12 399	34.7	40.7	8.94	9.61	310.22	391.13
September	99 907	82 997	23 216	17 498	76 691	67 108	12 411	34.6	40.7	8.94	9.60	309.32	390.72
October	100 094	83 125	23 208	17 477	76 886	67 206	12 396	34.6	40.6	8.96	9.62	310.02	390.57
November	100 280	83 275	23 204	17 472	77 076	67 344	12 407	34.7	40.7	9.00	9.64	312.30	392.35
December	100 484	83 463	23 237	17 478	77 247	67 493	12 425	34.6	40.8	9.01	9.66	311.75	394.13
1987													
January	100 655	83 610	23 232	17 465	77 423	67 614	12 405	34.7	40.8	9.02	9.67	312.99	394.54
February	100 887	83 851	23 296	17 499	77 591	67 845	12 438	34.9	41.2	9.05	9.69	315.85	399.23
March	101 136	84 072	23 307	17 507	77 829	67 991	12 446	34.7	41.0	9.07	9.71	314.73	398.11
April	101 474	84 365	23 342	17 525	78 132	68 237	12 465	34.7	40.8	9.08	9.71	315.08	396.17
May	101 701	84 589	23 390	17 542	78 311	68 426	12 481	34.8	41.0	9.11	9.73	317.03	398.93
June	101 872	84 748	23 390	17 537	78 482	68 552	12 482	34.7	40.9	9.11	9.74	316.12	398.37
July	102 218	85 058	23 455	17 593	78 763	68 798	12 521	34.7	41.0	9.12	9.74	316.46	399.34
August	102 388	85 216	23 506	17 630	78 882	68 926	12 560	34.9	40.9	9.18	9.80	320.38	400.82
September	102 617	85 482	23 566	17 691	79 051	69 139	12 614	34.7	40.8	9.19	9.85	318.89	401.88
October	103 109	85 840	23 655	17 729	79 454	69 416	12 637	34.8	41.1	9.22	9.84	320.86	404.42
November	103 340	86 041	23 711	17 775	79 629	69 594	12 678	34.8	41.0	9.27	9.87	322.60	404.67
December	103 634	86 287	23 772	17 809	79 862	69 826	12 707	34.6	41.0	9.28	9.89	321.09	405.49
1988													
January	103 728	86 363	23 668	17 790	80 060	69 833	12 684	34.6	41.1	9.29	9.91	321.43	407.30
February	104 180	86 791	23 769	17 823	80 411	70 228	12 706	34.7	41.1	9.29	9.92	322.36	407.71
March	104 456	87 009	23 824	17 844	80 632	70 371	12 712	34.5	40.9	9.31	9.94	321.20	406.55
April	104 701	87 249	23 880	17 874	80 821	70 578	12 733	34.6	41.0	9.36	9.99	323.86	409.59
May	104 928	87 447	23 896	17 892	81 032	70 693	12 747	34.6	41.0	9.41	10.02	325.59	410.82
June	105 291	87 776	23 951	17 916	81 340	71 000	12 767	34.6	41.1	9.42	10.04	325.93	412.64
July	105 514	88 020	23 966	17 926	81 548	71 210	12 774	34.7	41.1	9.45	10.05	327.92	413.06
August	105 635	88 091	23 926	17 891	81 709	71 273	12 752	34.5	40.9	9.46	10.07	326.37	411.86
September	105 975	88 341	23 942	17 914	82 033	71 456	12 764	34.5	41.0	9.51	10.12	328.10	414.92
October	106 243	88 573	23 987	17 966	82 256	71 649	12 812	34.7	41.1	9.56	10.16	331.73	417.58
November	106 582	88 836	24 030	18 003	82 552	71 872	12 851	34.5	41.1	9.58	10.19	330.51	418.81
December	106 871	89 135	24 054	18 025	82 817	72 144	12 864	34.6	40.9	9.60	10.20	332.16	417.18
1989													
January	107 133	89 359	24 097	18 057	83 036	72 361	12 882	34.7	41.1	9.65	10.23	334.86	420.45
February	107 391	89 579	24 080	18 055	83 311	72 545	12 880	34.5	41.2	9.68	10.26	333.96	422.71
March	107 583	89 761	24 069	18 060	83 514	72 663	12 878	34.5	41.1	9.70	10.29	334.65	422.92
April	107 756	89 916	24 100	18 055	83 656	72 788	12 867	34.6	41.1	9.75	10.28	337.35	422.51
May	107 874	89 998	24 089	18 040	83 785	72 826	12 852	34.4	41.0	9.73	10.30	334.71	422.30
June	107 991	90 079	24 052	18 013	83 939	72 906	12 822	34.4	40.9	9.77	10.33	336.09	422.50
July	108 030	90 125	24 027	17 980	84 003	72 943	12 790	34.5	40.9	9.82	10.36	338.79	423.72
August	108 077	90 088	24 048	17 964	84 029	72 931	12 790	34.5	40.9	9.83	10.39	339.14	424.95
September	108 326	90 299	24 000	17 922	84 326	73 080	12 745	34.4	40.8	9.87	10.41	339.53	424.73
October	108 437	90 404	23 997	17 895	84 440	73 176	12 723	34.6	40.8	9.93	10.43	343.58	425.54
November	108 714	90 657	24 009	17 886	84 705	73 392	12 713	34.4	40.7	9.93	10.44	341.59	424.91
December	108 809	90 734	23 949	17 881	84 860	73 468	12 705	34.3	40.5	9.98	10.49	342.31	424.85
1990													
January	109 145	90 994	23 981	17 796	85 164	73 705	12 738	34.5	40.5	10.02	10.52	345.69	426.06
February	109 394	91 217	24 071	17 893	85 323	73 900	12 848	34.4	40.6	10.07	10.64	346.41	431.98
March	109 609	91 315	24 023	17 868	85 586	73 960	12 821	34.4	40.7	10.11	10.70	347.78	435.49
April	109 650	91 273	23 967	17 846	85 683	73 925	12 804	34.3	40.5	10.13	10.68	347.46	432.54
May	109 800	91 201	23 887	17 796	85 913	73 837	12 755	34.3	40.6	10.16	10.74	348.49	436.04
June	109 822	91 266	23 850	17 777	85 972	73 830	12 739	34.4	40.7	10.21	10.78	351.22	438.75
July	109 776	91 216	23 745	17 703	86 031	73 771	12 673	34.2	40.6	10.22	10.80	349.52	438.48
August	109 570	91 113	23 648	17 649	85 922	73 709	12 624	34.2	40.5	10.24	10.81	350.21	437.81
September	109 484	91 047	23 571	17 609	85 913	73 600	12 596	34.2	40.5	10.28	10.86	351.58	439.83
October	109 325	90 882	23 473	17 577	85 852	73 466	12 577	34.1	40.4	10.30	10.92	351.23	441.17
November	109 178	90 728	23 283	17 428	85 895	73 314	12 439	34.2	40.2	10.32	10.89	352.94	437.78
December	109 120	90 652	23 203	17 395	85 917	73 247	12 415	34.2	40.3	10.35	10.93	353.97	440.48
1991													
January	108 997	90 523	23 060	17 329	85 937	73 107	12 351	34.1	40.2	10.38	10.98	353.96	441.40
February	108 692	90 210	22 900	17 211	85 792	72 816	12 242	34.1	40.1	10.39	10.97	354.30	439.90
March	108 534	90 046	22 779	17 140	85 755	72 663	12 191	34.0	40.0	10.41	11.00	353.94	440.00
April	108 322	89 837	22 688	17 094	85 634	72 492	12 157	34.0	40.1	10.46	11.05	355.64	443.11
May	108 196	89 698	22 617	17 069	85 579	72 395	12 148	34.0	40.1	10.49	11.09	356.66	444.71
June	108 286	89 725	22 571	17 044	85 715	72 415	12 135	34.1	40.5	10.52	11.13	358.73	450.77
July	108 236	89 638	22 507	17 015	85 729	72 381	12 130	34.1	40.5	10.54	11.17	359.41	452.39
August	108 255	89 688	22 493	17 001	85 762	72 441	12 153	34.1	40.6	10.56	11.18	360.10	453.91
September	108 289	89 746	22 466	17 010	85 823	72 455	12 140	34.1	40.6	10.58	11.22	360.78	455.53
October	108 305	89 712	22 418	16 999	85 887	72 429	12 138	34.2	40.6	10.59	11.25	362.18	456.75
November	108 248	89 621	22 316	16 961	85 932	72 357	12 102	34.1	40.7	10.61	11.26	361.80	458.28
December	108 272	89 631	22 274	16 916	85 998	72 400	12 075	34.1	40.7	10.64	11.27	362.82	458.69

Table 10-9. Employment, Hours, and Earnings, Total Nonfarm and Manufacturing, Historical Annual and Monthly—*Continued*

(Wage and salary workers on nonfarm payrolls, seasonally adjusted.)

Year and month	All wage and salary workers (thousands)					Production and nonsupervisory workers on private payrolls							
		Private				Number (thousands)		Average hours per week		Average hourly earnings, dollars		Average weekly earnings, dollars	
	Total	Total	Goods-producing		Service-providing	Total private	Manufac-turing	Total private	Manufac-turing	Total private	Manufac-turing	Total private	Manufac-turing
			Total	Manufac-turing									
1992													
January	108 324	89 636	22 214	16 840	86 110	72 439	12 013	34.1	40.6	10.65	11.24	363.17	456.34
February	108 257	89 568	22 141	16 828	86 116	72 415	12 015	34.1	40.7	10.67	11.30	363.85	459.91
March	108 313	89 598	22 127	16 805	86 186	72 433	12 006	34.1	40.7	10.70	11.32	364.87	460.72
April	108 472	89 733	22 132	16 831	86 340	72 585	12 029	34.3	40.9	10.72	11.36	367.70	464.62
May	108 598	89 845	22 135	16 835	86 463	72 699	12 046	34.3	40.9	10.74	11.39	368.38	465.85
June	108 659	89 897	22 097	16 826	86 562	72 736	12 042	34.2	40.8	10.77	11.41	368.33	465.53
July	108 731	89 914	22 075	16 820	86 656	72 754	12 049	34.2	40.8	10.79	11.43	369.02	466.34
August	108 872	89 989	22 045	16 783	86 827	72 832	12 020	34.2	40.8	10.82	11.46	370.04	467.57
September	108 909	90 080	22 020	16 761	86 889	72 936	12 002	34.3	40.7	10.82	11.45	371.13	466.02
October	109 088	90 260	22 028	16 750	87 060	73 091	11 999	34.2	40.8	10.86	11.47	371.41	467.98
November	109 227	90 386	22 042	16 758	87 185	73 242	12 012	34.2	40.9	10.87	11.49	371.75	469.94
December	109 440	90 562	22 075	16 768	87 365	73 428	12 031	34.2	40.9	10.90	11.51	372.78	470.76
1993													
January	109 750	90 849	22 133	16 791	87 617	73 702	12 060	34.3	41.1	11.21	11.55	375.24	474.71
February	109 991	91 089	22 188	16 805	87 803	73 959	12 072	34.3	41.1	11.25	11.57	375.59	475.53
March	109 942	91 035	22 142	16 795	87 800	73 877	12 074	34.1	40.8	11.25	11.59	374.76	472.87
April	110 251	91 313	22 131	16 772	88 120	74 102	12 056	34.4	41.5	11.27	11.64	378.40	483.06
May	110 519	91 568	22 189	16 766	88 330	74 358	12 056	34.3	41.1	11.30	11.66	377.99	479.23
June	110 693	91 724	22 165	16 742	88 528	74 460	12 039	34.3	40.9	11.32	11.67	378.67	477.30
July	110 992	91 932	22 184	16 740	88 808	74 650	12 043	34.4	41.1	11.34	11.69	380.46	480.46
August	111 154	92 126	22 203	16 741	88 951	74 825	12 050	34.3	41.1	11.36	11.72	380.04	481.69
September	111 396	92 355	22 252	16 769	89 144	75 017	12 080	34.4	41.3	11.39	11.76	381.84	485.69
October	111 676	92 634	22 306	16 778	89 370	75 262	12 092	34.4	41.3	11.43	11.79	382.87	486.93
November	111 938	92 870	22 347	16 800	89 591	75 480	12 119	34.4	41.3	11.45	11.83	383.56	488.58
December	112 250	93 141	22 413	16 815	89 837	75 704	12 140	34.4	41.4	11.48	11.88	384.59	491.83
1994													
January	112 519	93 372	22 465	16 855	90 054	75 913	12 181	34.4	41.4	11.49	11.89	385.62	492.25
February	112 722	93 572	22 451	16 862	90 271	76 116	12 198	34.2	40.9	11.53	11.97	384.75	489.57
March	113 188	93 998	22 550	16 897	90 638	76 480	12 234	34.5	41.7	11.55	11.95	388.13	498.32
April	113 538	94 315	22 641	16 933	90 897	76 777	12 276	34.5	41.7	11.57	11.96	388.82	498.73
May	113 869	94 605	22 704	16 962	91 165	77 054	12 304	34.5	41.8	11.60	11.98	389.85	500.76
June	114 179	94 905	22 764	17 010	91 415	77 303	12 351	34.5	41.8	11.63	12.01	390.54	502.02
July	114 541	95 240	22 806	17 025	91 735	77 600	12 367	34.6	41.8	11.67	12.02	392.36	502.44
August	114 839	95 533	22 876	17 081	91 963	77 839	12 428	34.5	41.7	11.70	12.05	391.92	502.49
September	115 193	95 856	22 947	17 114	92 246	78 106	12 459	34.5	41.6	11.73	12.09	392.96	502.94
October	115 400	96 056	22 975	17 145	92 425	78 288	12 489	34.5	41.8	11.76	12.11	394.34	506.20
November	115 818	96 451	23 050	17 186	92 768	78 634	12 529	34.5	41.8	11.78	12.15	395.03	507.87
December	116 094	96 706	23 095	17 217	92 999	78 876	12 558	34.5	41.8	11.81	12.17	396.06	508.71
1995													
January	116 414	97 017	23 146	17 261	93 268	79 119	12 593	34.5	41.8	11.87	12.19	396.41	509.54
February	116 621	97 214	23 103	17 265	93 518	79 273	12 602	34.4	41.7	11.87	12.24	396.63	510.41
March	116 844	97 417	23 151	17 263	93 693	79 454	12 600	34.3	41.5	11.89	12.25	396.17	508.38
April	117 005	97 571	23 174	17 278	93 831	79 586	12 608	34.3	41.1	11.96	12.25	396.85	503.48
May	116 991	97 573	23 120	17 259	93 871	79 609	12 590	34.2	41.2	11.98	12.28	396.72	505.94
June	117 223	97 778	23 137	17 247	94 086	79 777	12 574	34.3	41.2	12.04	12.31	398.91	507.17
July	117 302	97 865	23 118	17 217	94 184	79 846	12 538	34.3	41.1	12.06	12.38	400.28	508.82
August	117 577	98 148	23 164	17 240	94 413	80 094	12 566	34.3	41.2	12.10	12.39	401.31	510.47
September	117 821	98 391	23 207	17 246	94 614	80 293	12 567	34.3	41.2	12.14	12.41	402.34	511.29
October	117 971	98 507	23 207	17 217	94 764	80 413	12 535	34.3	41.2	12.16	12.43	403.37	512.12
November	118 119	98 656	23 200	17 209	94 919	80 488	12 515	34.3	41.3	12.21	12.45	404.05	514.19
December	118 251	98 785	23 208	17 230	95 043	80 638	12 551	34.2	40.9	12.25	12.49	403.90	510.84
1996													
January	118 229	98 779	23 196	17 208	95 033	80 563	12 517	33.8	39.7	12.30	12.60	401.21	500.22
February	118 664	99 179	23 281	17 230	95 383	80 952	12 533	34.3	41.3	12.32	12.55	407.14	518.32
March	118 928	99 396	23 276	17 193	95 652	81 129	12 488	34.3	41.1	12.37	12.50	407.83	513.75
April	119 090	99 575	23 316	17 204	95 774	81 295	12 505	34.2	41.1	12.39	12.69	409.03	521.56
May	119 413	99 884	23 357	17 221	96 056	81 556	12 518	34.3	41.4	12.43	12.71	410.91	526.19
June	119 694	100 166	23 399	17 226	96 295	81 768	12 522	34.4	41.5	12.47	12.76	414.18	529.54
July	119 928	100 381	23 417	17 222	96 511	81 966	12 517	34.3	41.4	12.50	12.79	413.66	529.51
August	120 127	100 623	23 479	17 255	96 648	82 166	12 546	34.4	41.5	12.57	12.83	416.24	532.45
September	120 347	100 780	23 497	17 252	96 850	82 285	12 544	34.4	41.6	12.61	12.85	417.62	534.56
October	120 594	101 040	23 546	17 268	97 048	82 531	12 559	34.4	41.4	12.67	12.83	418.30	531.16
November	120 893	101 328	23 585	17 278	97 308	82 714	12 560	34.4	41.5	12.72	12.88	420.02	534.52
December	121 061	101 490	23 598	17 284	97 463	82 881	12 571	34.4	41.7	12.76	12.95	421.40	540.02
1997													
January	121 293	101 700	23 619	17 298	97 674	83 023	12 579	34.3	41.4	12.80	12.99	421.89	537.79
February	121 595	101 997	23 686	17 316	97 909	83 305	12 592	34.4	41.6	12.85	13.00	423.81	540.80
March	121 910	102 302	23 739	17 340	98 171	83 535	12 613	34.5	41.8	12.89	13.04	426.77	545.07
April	122 201	102 598	23 766	17 350	98 435	83 783	12 618	34.6	41.8	12.93	13.03	428.69	544.65
May	122 461	102 860	23 809	17 362	98 652	84 007	12 633	34.6	41.7	12.97	13.07	430.08	545.02
June	122 718	103 058	23 834	17 387	98 884	84 143	12 647	34.3	41.5	13.00	13.09	427.72	543.24
July	123 007	103 321	23 862	17 389	99 145	84 388	12 645	34.5	41.6	13.01	13.09	431.25	544.54
August	122 996	103 379	23 952	17 452	99 044	84 339	12 699	34.6	41.7	13.09	13.17	434.92	549.19
September	123 504	103 825	23 996	17 465	99 508	84 731	12 711	34.6	41.7	13.12	13.17	436.31	549.19
October	123 844	104 106	24 053	17 513	99 791	84 941	12 746	34.6	41.8	13.15	13.29	438.38	555.52
November	124 148	104 387	24 112	17 556	100 036	85 133	12 777	34.6	41.8	13.18	13.32	440.11	556.78
December	124 452	104 686	24 184	17 588	100 268	85 366	12 800	34.6	41.9	13.22	13.35	441.50	559.37

Table 10-9. Employment, Hours, and Earnings, Total Nonfarm and Manufacturing, Historical Annual and Monthly—*Continued*

(Wage and salary workers on nonfarm payrolls, seasonally adjusted.)

Year and month	All wage and salary workers (thousands)					Production and nonsupervisory workers on private payrolls							
	Total	Private			Service-providing	Number (thousands)		Average hours per week		Average hourly earnings, dollars		Average weekly earnings, dollars	
		Total	Goods-producing			Total private	Manufac-turing	Total private	Manufac-turing	Total private	Manufac-turing	Total private	Manufac-turing
			Total	Manufac-turing									
1998													
January	124 725	104 955	24 262	17 619	100 463	85 523	12 818	34.6	41.9	13.28	13.35	442.88	559.37
February	124 919	105 133	24 283	17 627	100 636	85 691	12 828	34.6	41.7	13.30	13.39	444.61	558.36
March	125 065	105 273	24 264	17 637	100 801	85 718	12 822	34.5	41.6	13.34	13.43	444.71	558.69
April	125 344	105 528	24 340	17 637	101 004	85 936	12 814	34.4	41.3	13.39	13.40	444.79	553.42
May	125 744	105 869	24 361	17 624	101 383	86 214	12 790	34.6	41.5	13.43	13.45	448.76	558.18
June	125 954	106 075	24 387	17 608	101 567	86 358	12 769	34.4	41.4	13.48	13.43	447.20	556.00
July	126 074	106 144	24 238	17 422	101 836	86 368	12 558	34.5	41.4	13.52	13.34	448.85	552.28
August	126 425	106 466	24 420	17 563	102 005	86 655	12 702	34.5	41.4	13.55	13.46	451.61	557.24
September	126 644	106 659	24 420	17 558	102 224	86 817	12 715	34.4	41.3	13.62	13.52	451.33	558.38
October	126 838	106 837	24 405	17 511	102 433	86 965	12 673	34.5	41.4	13.64	13.53	453.68	560.14
November	127 119	107 075	24 394	17 465	102 725	87 128	12 634	34.4	41.4	13.66	13.54	453.39	560.56
December	127 466	107 387	24 454	17 449	103 012	87 394	12 625	34.5	41.5	13.71	13.56	456.09	562.74
1999													
January	127 589	107 505	24 401	17 427	103 188	87 449	12 605	34.4	41.3	13.76	13.59	456.83	561.27
February	127 998	107 854	24 434	17 395	103 564	87 764	12 575	34.4	41.4	13.80	13.63	457.52	564.28
March	128 106	107 938	24 378	17 368	103 728	87 826	12 562	34.3	41.3	13.85	13.69	457.56	565.40
April	128 479	108 242	24 424	17 343	104 055	88 059	12 540	34.4	41.3	13.91	13.73	460.62	567.05
May	128 692	108 463	24 445	17 333	104 247	88 249	12 534	34.3	41.4	13.94	13.80	460.65	571.32
June	128 955	108 683	24 434	17 295	104 521	88 419	12 503	34.4	41.3	13.99	13.86	463.71	572.42
July	129 248	108 909	24 474	17 308	104 774	88 619	12 525	34.4	41.4	14.03	13.92	465.09	576.29
August	129 439	109 064	24 468	17 288	104 971	88 731	12 502	34.4	41.5	14.07	13.93	466.12	578.10
September	129 642	109 238	24 485	17 281	105 157	88 865	12 495	34.3	41.5	14.13	13.99	467.17	580.59
October	130 045	109 588	24 506	17 273	105 539	89 177	12 484	34.4	41.4	14.18	13.99	469.22	579.19
November	130 336	109 840	24 561	17 282	105 775	89 395	12 488	34.4	41.4	14.24	14.01	469.90	580.01
December	130 636	110 096	24 582	17 280	106 054	89 612	12 490	34.4	41.4	14.29	14.06	471.62	582.08
2000													
January	130 869	110 298	24 627	17 283	106 242	89 773	12 491	34.4	41.5	14.30	14.13	473.34	586.40
February	130 999	110 400	24 608	17 284	106 391	89 847	12 481	34.4	41.5	14.37	14.15	474.72	587.23
March	131 470	110 737	24 705	17 302	106 765	90 118	12 490	34.4	41.4	14.43	14.18	476.44	587.05
April	131 757	110 955	24 688	17 298	107 069	90 345	12 477	34.4	41.6	14.46	14.23	478.50	591.97
May	131 982	110 835	24 647	17 279	107 335	90 250	12 464	34.3	41.3	14.50	14.23	478.14	587.70
June	131 936	111 049	24 674	17 298	107 262	90 418	12 468	34.3	41.3	14.55	14.30	479.86	590.59
July	132 102	111 235	24 717	17 322	107 385	90 554	12 474	34.3	41.5	14.56	14.32	481.23	594.28
August	132 104	111 267	24 684	17 288	107 420	90 579	12 431	34.2	41.0	14.60	14.36	481.19	588.76
September	132 231	111 496	24 642	17 230	107 589	90 735	12 382	34.3	41.1	14.65	14.40	484.66	591.84
October	132 219	111 476	24 639	17 218	107 580	90 712	12 357	34.3	41.1	14.67	14.49	486.37	595.54
November	132 442	111 682	24 624	17 203	107 818	90 840	12 336	34.2	41.1	14.73	14.52	487.01	596.77
December	132 580	111 776	24 576	17 182	108 004	90 885	12 307	34.0	40.4	14.76	14.50	485.86	585.80
2001													
January	132 548	111 713	24 531	17 102	108 017	90 834	12 229	34.2	40.6	14.77	14.48	489.06	587.89
February	132 617	111 711	24 473	17 027	108 144	90 784	12 155	34.1	40.5	14.79	14.55	490.02	589.28
March	132 588	111 643	24 408	16 937	108 180	90 738	12 085	34.1	40.5	14.83	14.58	492.06	590.49
April	132 307	111 315	24 254	16 802	108 053	90 502	11 982	34.0	40.5	14.84	14.64	491.64	592.92
May	132 266	111 237	24 119	16 661	108 147	90 426	11 859	34.0	40.4	14.89	14.69	493.00	593.48
June	132 140	111 003	23 967	16 517	108 173	90 229	11 739	34.0	40.3	14.95	14.74	494.70	594.02
July	132 018	110 833	23 836	16 381	108 182	90 113	11 632	34.0	40.6	14.99	14.82	495.04	601.69
August	131 862	110 644	23 668	16 233	108 194	89 966	11 495	33.9	40.3	15.03	14.85	494.94	598.46
September	131 618	110 376	23 537	16 117	108 081	89 697	11 400	33.8	40.2	15.08	14.89	495.17	598.58
October	131 291	110 016	23 379	15 973	107 912	89 405	11 286	33.7	40.1	15.13	14.90	494.38	597.49
November	130 995	109 669	23 210	15 826	107 785	89 081	11 175	33.8	40.1	15.16	14.96	497.87	599.90
December	130 823	109 468	23 095	15 712	107 728	88 991	11 081	33.9	40.2	15.22	15.01	500.36	603.40
2002													
January	130 680	109 303	22 959	15 585	107 721	88 933	10 993	33.8	40.1	15.23	15.05	499.23	603.51
February	130 545	109 155	22 875	15 514	107 670	88 893	10 951	33.8	40.3	15.30	15.11	499.90	608.93
March	130 523	109 092	22 786	15 443	107 737	88 851	10 901	33.9	40.6	15.30	15.15	502.74	615.09
April	130 440	108 997	22 689	15 392	107 751	88 692	10 859	33.9	40.6	15.29	15.17	503.08	615.90
May	130 434	108 920	22 604	15 337	107 830	88 558	10 824	33.9	40.6	15.34	15.24	504.77	618.74
June	130 486	108 937	22 579	15 299	107 907	88 474	10 797	33.9	40.7	15.37	15.27	506.81	621.49
July	130 394	108 850	22 521	15 256	107 873	88 328	10 764	33.8	40.4	15.41	15.29	506.66	617.72
August	130 380	108 791	22 450	15 172	107 930	88 255	10 697	33.9	40.5	15.43	15.34	509.52	621.27
September	130 322	108 776	22 398	15 120	107 924	88 234	10 668	33.9	40.5	15.43	15.38	511.21	622.89
October	130 446	108 887	22 326	15 061	108 120	88 307	10 631	33.8	40.3	15.44	15.46	511.39	623.04
November	130 453	108 872	22 283	14 993	108 170	88 265	10 583	33.8	40.4	15.48	15.48	512.41	625.39
December	130 291	108 703	22 189	14 912	108 102	88 074	10 523	33.8	40.5	15.48	15.53	514.44	628.97
2003													
January	130 380	108 754	22 149	14 869	108 231	88 119	10 484	33.8	40.3	15.23	15.59	514.77	628.28
February	130 222	108 598	22 024	14 782	108 198	87 967	10 416	33.7	40.3	15.30	15.63	515.61	629.89
March	130 007	108 397	21 946	14 722	108 061	87 677	10 357	33.8	40.4	15.30	15.64	517.14	631.86
April	129 956	108 361	21 864	14 609	108 092	87 625	10 256	33.6	40.1	15.29	15.62	513.74	626.36
May	129 946	108 379	21 831	14 556	108 115	87 591	10 218	33.7	40.2	15.34	15.69	516.96	630.74
June	129 943	108 337	21 788	14 493	108 155	87 562	10 165	33.7	40.3	15.37	15.72	517.97	633.52
July	129 963	108 330	21 707	14 401	108 256	87 544	10 093	33.6	40.1	15.41	15.76	517.78	631.98
August	129 919	108 363	21 707	14 377	108 212	87 605	10 084	33.7	40.2	15.43	15.79	519.99	634.76
September	130 024	108 520	21 700	14 347	108 324	87 725	10 059	33.6	40.5	15.43	15.84	518.45	641.52
October	130 221	108 663	21 691	14 334	108 530	87 807	10 054	33.7	40.6	15.44	15.82	520.33	642.29
November	130 234	108 699	21 687	14 315	108 547	87 853	10 039	33.8	40.9	15.48	15.89	523.22	649.90
December	130 353	108 807	21 703	14 300	108 650	87 919	10 031	33.6	40.7	15.48	15.91	520.13	647.54

Table 10-9. Employment, Hours, and Earnings, Total Nonfarm and Manufacturing, Historical Annual and Monthly—*Continued*

(Wage and salary workers on nonfarm payrolls, seasonally adjusted.)

Year and month	All wage and salary workers (thousands)					Production and nonsupervisory workers on private payrolls							
	Total	Private			Service-providing	Number (thousands)		Average hours per week		Average hourly earnings, dollars		Average weekly earnings, dollars	
		Total	Goods-producing			Total private	Manufac-turing	Total private	Manufac-turing	Total private	Manufac-turing	Total private	Manufac-turing
			Total	Manufac-turing									
2004													
January	130 512	108 974	21 716	14 291	108 796	88 028	10 027	33.7	40.9	15.51	15.94	522.69	651.95
February	130 555	109 005	21 692	14 278	108 863	88 041	10 012	33.8	41.0	15.55	15.98	525.59	655.18
March	130 888	109 300	21 758	14 287	109 130	88 298	10 025	33.7	40.9	15.57	16.01	524.71	654.81
April	131 135	109 521	21 803	14 316	109 332	88 541	10 060	33.7	40.7	15.60	16.06	525.72	653.64
May	131 441	109 827	21 881	14 342	109 560	88 848	10 091	33.8	41.1	15.65	16.07	528.97	660.60
June	131 519	109 918	21 885	14 332	109 634	88 988	10 087	33.6	40.7	15.68	16.11	526.85	655.68
July	131 556	109 950	21 899	14 329	109 657	89 091	10 095	33.7	40.8	15.71	16.14	529.43	658.51
August	131 681	110 055	21 943	14 344	109 738	89 228	10 115	33.8	40.8	15.75	16.20	532.35	660.96
September	131 836	110 201	21 956	14 330	109 880	89 410	10 104	33.8	40.8	15.79	16.30	533.70	665.04
October	132 179	110 523	22 004	14 332	110 175	89 721	10 103	33.8	40.6	15.83	16.27	535.05	660.56
November	132 244	110 552	21 998	14 308	110 246	89 751	10 078	33.7	40.5	15.85	16.30	534.15	660.15
December	132 372	110 679	22 006	14 288	110 366	89 904	10 063	33.8	40.6	15.88	16.34	536.74	663.40
2005													
January	132 502	110 767	21 959	14 258	110 543	90 011	10 045	33.7	40.6	15.92	16.38	536.50	665.03
February	132 742	110 998	22 037	14 274	110 705	90 232	10 052	33.8	40.6	15.94	16.43	538.77	667.06
March	132 877	111 137	22 066	14 269	110 811	90 410	10 056	33.7	40.4	15.98	16.44	538.53	664.18
April	133 239	111 485	22 136	14 250	111 103	90 748	10 048	33.8	40.4	16.02	16.46	541.48	664.98
May	133 407	111 626	22 171	14 255	111 236	90 867	10 061	33.7	40.4	16.05	16.53	540.89	667.81
June	133 653	111 890	22 186	14 228	111 467	91 127	10 047	33.7	40.4	16.09	16.54	542.23	668.22
July	134 025	112 168	22 204	14 225	111 821	91 357	10 039	33.7	40.5	16.17	16.58	544.93	671.49
August	134 217	112 354	22 227	14 202	111 990	91 543	10 043	33.7	40.5	16.18	16.63	545.27	673.52
September	134 282	112 437	22 226	14 175	112 056	91 613	10 046	33.8	40.7	16.21	16.59	547.90	675.21
October	134 363	112 534	22 292	14 192	112 071	91 730	10 073	33.8	41.1	16.30	16.69	550.94	685.96
November	134 698	112 839	22 357	14 187	112 341	92 076	10 093	33.8	40.9	16.32	16.67	551.62	681.80
December	134 856	112 977	22 377	14 194	112 479	92 240	10 112	33.7	40.8	16.37	16.67	551.67	680.14
2006													
January	135 130	113 283	22 468	14 211	112 662	92 584	10 153	33.9	40.6	16.44	16.69	557.32	684.29
February	135 446	113 568	22 536	14 210	112 910	92 852	10 164	33.8	40.6	16.49	16.69	557.36	684.29
March	135 726	113 823	22 572	14 214	113 154	93 147	10 174	33.8	40.4	16.55	16.71	559.39	686.78
April	135 907	113 988	22 631	14 226	113 276	93 322	10 190	33.9	40.4	16.65	16.75	564.44	691.78
May	135 928	114 002	22 596	14 202	113 332	93 386	10 179	33.8	40.4	16.66	16.77	563.11	689.25
June	136 008	114 086	22 597	14 212	113 411	93 456	10 190	33.9	40.4	16.74	16.79	567.49	691.75
July	136 218	114 245	22 590	14 188	113 628	93 592	10 177	33.9	40.5	16.80	16.80	569.52	695.52
August	136 397	114 386	22 571	14 158	113 826	93 737	10 158	33.9	40.5	16.84	16.83	570.88	693.40
September	136 556	114 474	22 537	14 125	114 019	93 793	10 120	33.8	40.7	16.88	16.83	570.54	691.71
October	136 553	114 485	22 455	14 074	114 098	93 793	10 071	33.9	41.1	16.95	16.90	574.61	696.28
November	136 758	114 675	22 408	14 041	114 350	94 018	10 047	33.8	40.9	16.99	16.91	574.26	693.31
December	136 927	114 839	22 404	14 014	114 523	94 192	10 041	33.9	40.8	17.06	16.97	578.33	695.77
2007													
January	137 161	115 066	22 439	14 008	114 722	94 421	10 036	33.8	41.0	17.10	17.02	577.98	697.82
February	137 251	115 120	22 334	13 997	114 917	94 454	10 035	33.7	41.0	17.17	17.06	578.63	699.46
March	137 437	115 288	22 391	13 970	115 046	94 661	10 011	33.9	41.3	17.24	17.10	584.44	706.23
April	137 513	115 338	22 350	13 945	115 163	94 744	10 006	33.9	41.3	17.30	17.21	586.47	710.77
May	137 654	115 461	22 322	13 928	115 332	94 895	10 007	33.8	41.2	17.35	17.23	586.43	709.88
June	137 734	115 527	22 322	13 910	115 412	95 013	9 996	33.9	41.4	17.43	17.28	590.88	715.39
July	137 699	115 528	22 277	13 889	115 422	95 088	9 990	33.8	41.3	17.48	17.29	590.82	714.08
August	137 675	115 449	22 166	13 829	115 509	95 033	9 944	33.8	41.3	17.52	17.35	592.18	716.56
September	137 752	115 473	22 093	13 790	115 659	95 116	9 933	33.8	41.3	17.58	17.37	594.20	717.38
October	137 838	115 541	22 055	13 763	115 783	95 218	9 911	33.8	41.2	17.59	17.35	594.54	714.82
November	137 949	115 615	22 015	13 757	115 934	95 312	9 920	33.8	41.3	17.66	17.43	596.91	719.86
December	138 042	115 666	21 976	13 746	116 066	95 398	9 924	33.8	41.1	17.71	17.44	598.60	716.78
2008													
January	138 056	115 668	21 947	13 725	116 109	95 405	9 914	33.7	41.1	17.76	17.50	598.51	719.25
February	137 971	115 554	21 898	13 697	116 073	95 308	9 888	33.8	41.2	17.82	17.57	602.32	723.88
March	137 892	115 449	21 820	13 659	116 072	95 261	9 866	33.8	41.3	17.89	17.63	604.68	728.12
April	137 677	115 227	21 680	13 598	115 997	95 080	9 810	33.8	41.1	17.94	17.62	606.37	724.18
May	137 491	115 008	21 599	13 564	115 892	94 920	9 779	33.7	41.1	18.00	17.69	606.60	727.06
June	137 322	114 805	21 483	13 504	115 839	94 722	9 721	33.7	41.1	18.06	17.75	608.62	729.53
July	137 106	114 538	21 360	13 430	115 746	94 512	9 655	33.6	41.0	18.13	17.80	609.17	729.80
August	136 836	114 269	21 250	13 358	115 586	94 286	9 586	33.7	40.9	18.20	17.80	613.34	728.02
September	136 377	113 840	21 101	13 275	115 276	93 926	9 504	33.6	40.5	18.23	17.83	612.53	722.12
October	135 905	113 356	20 897	13 149	115 008	93 525	9 384	33.6	40.5	18.28	17.91	614.21	725.36
November	135 130	112 570	20 625	13 036	114 505	92 813	9 290	33.4	40.1	18.34	17.95	612.56	719.80
December	134 425	111 869	20 323	12 851	114 102	92 220	9 137	33.3	39.8	18.40	18.00	612.72	716.40
2009													
January	133 631	111 048	19 874	12 556	113 757	91 488	8 891	33.3	39.7	18.43	18.01	613.72	715.00
February	132 936	110 356	19 588	12 386	113 348	90 907	8 744	33.2	39.6	18.47	18.08	613.20	715.97
March	132 106	109 544	19 232	12 213	112 874	90 236	8 593	33.1	39.3	18.52	18.13	613.01	712.51
April	131 402	108 723	18 890	12 030	112 512	89 513	8 455	33.1	39.5	18.54	18.16	613.67	717.32
May	131 050	108 435	18 661	11 866	112 389	89 306	8 310	33.1	39.3	18.55	18.13	614.01	712.51
June	130 578	107 993	18 414	11 721	112 164	88 925	8 198	33.0	39.6	18.58	18.18	613.14	719.93
July	130 227	107 711	18 264	11 659	111 963	88 715	8 165	33.1	39.9	18.63	18.30	616.65	730.17
August	130 017	107 489	18 142	11 623	111 875	88 543	8 145	33.1	40.0	18.68	18.34	618.31	733.60
September	129 784	107 327	18 037	11 586	111 747	88 400	8 129	33.1	40.0	18.73	18.42	619.96	736.80
October	129 614	107 094	17 923	11 539	111 691	88 203	8 098	33.0	40.2	18.77	18.38	619.41	738.88
November	129 593	107 060	17 863	11 507	111 730	88 206	8 077	33.2	40.5	18.82	18.41	624.82	745.61
December	129 373	106 893	17 786	11 471	111 587	88 107	8 049	33.2	40.6	18.86	18.42	626.15	747.85

Table 10-9. Employment, Hours, and Earnings, Total Nonfarm and Manufacturing, Historical Annual and Monthly—*Continued*

(Wage and salary workers on nonfarm payrolls, seasonally adjusted.)

Year and month	All wage and salary workers (thousands)					Production and nonsupervisory workers on private payrolls							
	Total	Private			Service-providing	Number (thousands)		Average hours per week		Average hourly earnings, dollars		Average weekly earnings, dollars	
		Total	Goods-producing			Total private	Manufacturing	Total private	Manufacturing	Total private	Manufacturing	Total private	Manufacturing
			Total	Manufacturing									
2010													
January	129 360	106 876	17 710	11 460	111 650	88 095	8 042	33.3	40.9	18.92	18.44	630.04	754.20
February	129 320	106 850	17 657	11 460	111 663	88 042	8 038	33.2	40.4	18.94	18.46	628.81	745.78
March	129 474	106 961	17 691	11 466	111 783	88 182	8 034	33.3	41.0	18.95	18.47	631.04	757.27
April	129 703	107 131	17 738	11 497	111 965	88 307	8 054	33.4	41.2	18.98	18.50	633.93	762.20
May	130 224	107 233	17 754	11 531	112 470	88 377	8 080	33.5	41.4	19.03	18.59	637.51	769.63
June	130 094	107 327	17 751	11 539	112 343	88 468	8 095	33.4	41.0	19.06	18.58	636.60	761.78
July	130 008	107 430	17 762	11 558	112 246	88 551	8 106	33.5	41.1	19.08	18.63	639.18	765.69
August	129 971	107 559	17 782	11 548	112 189	88 641	8 091	33.5	41.2	19.13	18.66	640.86	768.79
September	129 928	107 672	17 774	11 554	112 154	88 740	8 089	33.5	41.3	19.15	18.72	641.53	773.14
October	130 156	107 860	17 787	11 555	112 369	88 926	8 090	33.6	41.2	19.23	18.71	646.13	770.85
November	130 300	108 014	17 809	11 577	112 491	89 028	8 098	33.5	41.3	19.24	18.75	644.54	774.38
December	130 395	108 128	17 792	11 590	112 603	89 144	8 112	33.5	41.3	19.24	18.79	644.54	776.03
2011													
January	130 464	108 208	17 797	11 624	112 667	89 160	8 137	33.4	41.0	19.33	18.90	645.62	774.90
February	130 660	108 451	17 880	11 662	112 780	89 348	8 168	33.5	41.3	19.34	18.90	647.89	780.57
March	130 865	108 674	17 923	11 682	112 942	89 582	8 190	33.6	41.5	19.34	18.90	649.82	784.35
April	131 169	108 977	17 972	11 707	113 197	89 828	8 215	33.7	41.4	19.39	18.90	653.44	782.46
May	131 284	109 160	18 015	11 715	113 269	89 969	8 217	33.6	41.5	19.44	18.93	653.18	785.60
June	131 337	109 337	18 042	11 724	113 451	90 145	8 223	33.6	41.4	19.45	18.91	653.52	782.87
July	131 571	109 543	18 093	11 747	113 478	90 333	8 243	33.7	41.4	19.51	18.93	657.49	783.70
August	131 703	109 672	18 109	11 760	113 594	90 435	8 253	33.6	41.3	19.50	18.90	655.20	780.57
September	131 928	109 928	18 156	11 762	113 772	90 694	8 257	33.7	41.4	19.52	18.92	657.82	783.29
October	132 094	110 102	18 165	11 770	113 929	90 852	8 269	33.7	41.5	19.56	18.96	659.17	786.84
November	132 268	110 299	18 169	11 769	114 099	91 030	8 264	33.7	41.5	19.59	18.96	660.18	786.84
December	132 498	110 548	18 242	11 797	114 256	91 259	8 293	33.7	41.6	19.58	18.99	659.85	789.98
2012													
January	132 809	110 871	18 314	11 841	114 495	91 555	8 328	33.8	41.8	19.61	19.03	662.82	795.45
February	133 080	111 136	18 365	11 870	114 715	91 838	8 368	33.8	41.8	19.64	19.02	663.83	795.04
March	133 285	111 344	18 402	11 910	114 883	91 989	8 398	33.7	41.6	19.68	19.02	663.22	791.23
April	133 397	111 464	18 408	11 920	114 989	92 102	8 404	33.7	41.7	19.72	19.08	664.56	795.64
May	133 522	111 616	18 396	11 926	115 126	92 207	8 409	33.7	41.6	19.70	19.03	663.89	791.65
June	133 609	111 694	18 410	11 935	115 199	92 273	8 408	33.7	41.6	19.75	19.08	665.58	793.73
July	133 762	111 871	18 436	11 957	115 326	92 421	8 435	33.7	41.7	19.77	19.11	666.25	796.89
August	133 927	112 002	18 422	11 943	115 505	92 561	8 413	33.6	41.6	19.76	19.07	663.94	793.31
September	134 065	112 120	18 405	11 925	115 660	92 680	8 392	33.7	41.5	19.80	19.07	667.26	791.41
October	134 225	112 337	18 421	11 931	115 804	92 886	8 399	33.6	41.5	19.82	19.08	665.95	791.82
November	134 472	112 593	18 464	11 938	116 008	93 041	8 403	33.7	41.6	19.88	19.17	669.96	797.47
December	134 691	112 817	18 522	11 951	116 169	93 237	8 408	33.7	41.8	19.93	19.17	671.64	801.31

Figure 10-4. Average Weekly Hours of All Employees, Monthly

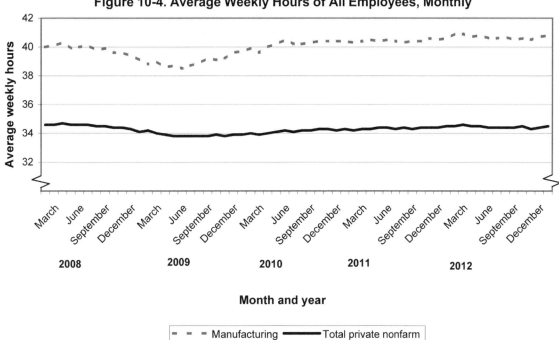

Month and year

- - - Manufacturing   Total private nonfarm

- The payroll survey now includes hours and earnings data for all nonfarm jobs, as well as the hours and earnings for production and nonsupervisory worker jobs that have been collected for many years. The newer, more comprehensive series are available beginning with March 2006. The new monthly data on the workweek for all nonfarm jobs and for manufacturing are shown in Figure 10-4. (Table 10-10)

- Firms experiencing increases in demand are likely to meet that demand, at first, by having their existing employees work longer hours. If the demand increase is sustained, they become more likely to hire more people. This is the basis for the long-time reputation of the workweek as a leading indicator for employment. As Figure 10-4 demonstrates, the workweek at manufacturing—the most cyclical sector—has been trending upward, though irregularly, since a low point of 38.5 hours in May 2009. In May 2013, according to preliminary data, it reached 40.8 hours. The workweek for all private nonfarm industry began to edge up in November 2009, from a low point of 33.8 hours, and was 34.5 hours long in May 2013. (Table 10-10 and recent data)

- It is important to note that the "average" all-employee workweek of about 34 1/2 hours reported in the payroll survey is not necessarily an accurate representation of how many hours per week a typical American worker works. This is because it is based on a count of jobs, as reported by employers. Suppose a full-time worker takes a second, "moonlighting" part-time job, newly created in another industry. This reduces the average workweek reported by the payroll survey, even though the individual is working longer hours than before. If a new labor force entrant takes a half-time job, it reduces the average workweek even if no other workers are working less. For measures of the workweek as reported by persons in the Current Population Survey, see Table 10-19, Figure 10-5, and the discussions of each.

Table 10-10. Average Weekly Hours of All Employees on Private Nonfarm Payrolls by NAICS Supersector

(Hours per week, seasonally adjusted.)

Year and month	Total private	Mining and logging	Construc-tion	Manufacturing		Trade, transportation, and utilities			Informa-tion	Financial activities	Profes-sional and business services	Education and health services	Leisure and hospitality	Other services
				Average weekly hours	Overtime hours	Total	Wholesale trade	Retail trade						
2007	34.6	44.0	38.0	40.0	3.3	34.5	38.1	31.7	36.1	36.6	35.4	33.5	26.1	32.9
2008	34.5	43.7	37.8	39.8	3.0	34.4	38.4	31.4	36.5	36.5	35.2	33.7	25.9	32.9
2009	33.9	42.1	37.1	39.0	2.3	34.1	37.9	31.3	36.5	36.6	35.0	33.0	25.6	31.6
2010	34.1	43.4	37.8	40.2	3.0	34.2	38.1	31.3	36.5	36.9	35.4	32.8	25.7	31.6
2011	34.4	44.5	38.3	40.5	3.2	34.6	38.6	31.6	36.6	37.3	35.7	32.8	25.9	31.7
2012	34.5	43.9	38.8	40.7	3.3	34.6	38.7	31.6	36.6	37.4	36.0	32.9	26.1	31.6
2008														
January	34.6	43.7	38.3	40.0	3.3	34.6	38.3	31.7	36.5	36.5	35.2	33.6	26.0	32.6
February	34.6	43.8	38.3	40.1	3.3	34.6	38.4	31.7	36.5	36.6	35.2	33.7	25.9	32.9
March	34.7	44.8	38.2	40.3	3.2	34.6	38.5	31.7	36.5	36.6	35.4	34.0	25.9	33.1
April	34.6	42.9	38.1	39.9	3.2	34.5	38.4	31.5	36.6	36.6	35.2	33.8	26.0	33.0
May	34.6	43.5	38.0	40.0	3.1	34.5	38.4	31.5	36.5	36.7	35.3	33.8	26.0	32.9
June	34.6	44.0	38.0	40.1	3.1	34.5	38.5	31.5	36.6	36.6	35.2	33.8	25.9	32.8
July	34.5	43.3	37.8	39.8	3.0	34.5	38.6	31.4	36.6	36.5	35.3	33.8	25.8	32.9
August	34.5	43.7	37.9	39.9	3.0	34.5	38.7	31.4	36.6	36.7	35.3	33.7	25.9	33.0
September	34.4	42.8	37.5	39.6	2.9	34.4	38.5	31.4	36.7	36.5	35.2	33.7	25.8	32.9
October	34.4	44.3	38.3	39.6	2.7	34.4	38.4	31.3	36.7	36.6	35.3	33.6	25.9	32.8
November	34.3	44.0	37.2	39.4	2.5	34.3	38.3	31.3	36.6	36.6	35.2	33.6	25.7	32.9
December	34.1	43.3	37.4	39.1	2.4	34.0	38.3	30.7	36.7	36.6	35.1	33.5	25.6	32.9
2009														
January	34.2	43.0	37.2	38.8	2.3	34.3	38.4	31.3	36.5	36.7	35.1	33.6	25.6	32.6
February	34.0	42.9	37.3	39.0	2.3	34.2	38.2	31.2	36.5	36.6	35.0	33.2	25.5	32.1
March	33.9	42.5	37.2	38.6	2.1	34.2	38.0	31.2	36.4	36.6	35.0	33.1	25.5	31.5
April	33.8	41.9	37.1	38.7	2.2	34.1	37.9	31.2	36.3	36.6	35.0	33.0	25.5	31.3
May	33.8	41.5	37.2	38.5	2.1	34.2	37.9	31.3	36.5	36.6	35.1	32.9	25.5	31.5
June	33.8	41.9	37.2	38.7	2.2	34.0	37.8	31.2	36.4	36.4	35.0	32.8	25.5	31.4
July	33.8	42.0	37.4	38.9	2.3	34.0	37.7	31.2	36.5	36.6	35.0	32.9	25.5	31.4
August	33.8	42.2	37.3	39.2	2.3	34.0	37.7	31.1	36.3	36.5	35.0	32.9	25.5	31.5
September	33.9	42.2	37.0	39.1	2.4	34.2	37.6	31.5	36.4	36.6	35.0	32.9	25.6	31.4
October	33.8	42.0	37.2	39.2	2.5	34.1	37.7	31.3	36.4	36.7	34.9	32.7	25.5	31.4
November	33.9	42.5	37.4	39.6	2.7	34.1	37.8	31.3	36.6	36.6	35.2	32.7	25.6	31.5
December	33.9	42.4	37.2	39.7	2.8	34.0	37.7	31.1	36.5	36.7	35.2	32.8	25.6	31.6
2010														
January	34.0	43.0	37.4	39.9	2.8	34.0	37.8	31.2	36.6	36.8	35.4	33.0	25.6	31.6
February	33.9	43.0	36.4	39.6	2.7	34.0	37.8	31.3	36.4	36.8	35.1	32.8	25.7	31.6
March	34.0	43.3	37.3	40.0	2.9	34.0	37.9	31.2	36.5	36.9	35.4	32.8	25.7	31.6
April	34.1	43.6	38.0	40.2	2.9	34.2	38.1	31.3	36.5	36.9	35.3	32.8	25.8	31.7
May	34.2	43.9	37.7	40.5	3.1	34.2	38.1	31.3	36.6	37.0	35.4	32.8	25.8	31.7
June	34.1	43.3	37.7	40.2	3.0	34.2	38.1	31.3	36.6	37.2	35.2	32.8	25.7	31.6
July	34.2	43.8	37.6	40.2	3.0	34.4	38.2	31.5	36.6	37.0	35.5	32.8	25.8	31.7
August	34.2	43.9	37.9	40.3	3.1	34.4	38.2	31.5	36.7	37.0	35.4	32.8	25.8	31.8
September	34.3	43.4	38.2	40.4	3.2	34.4	38.4	31.4	36.6	37.1	35.6	32.8	25.8	31.9
October	34.3	43.7	38.1	40.4	3.2	34.5	38.4	31.5	36.8	37.1	35.7	32.8	25.9	31.8
November	34.2	42.9	38.1	40.4	3.1	34.4	38.3	31.4	36.6	37.1	35.5	32.8	25.9	31.7
December	34.3	44.0	37.9	40.4	3.2	34.6	38.4	31.6	36.5	37.1	35.7	32.7	25.8	31.7
2011														
January	34.2	44.5	37.6	40.3	3.1	34.4	38.5	31.4	36.5	37.1	35.6	32.7	25.8	31.7
February	34.3	44.1	37.7	40.4	3.2	34.5	38.5	31.4	36.6	37.1	35.7	32.7	25.9	31.7
March	34.3	44.4	37.9	40.5	3.3	34.6	38.6	31.5	36.6	37.0	35.7	32.8	25.8	31.8
April	34.4	44.5	38.1	40.4	3.2	34.7	38.6	31.7	36.6	37.2	35.7	32.9	26.0	31.8
May	34.4	44.8	38.5	40.5	3.1	34.5	38.6	31.5	36.7	37.2	35.7	33.0	25.8	31.8
June	34.3	44.6	38.3	40.4	3.1	34.6	38.7	31.5	36.6	37.3	35.7	32.8	25.8	31.8
July	34.4	44.2	38.4	40.3	3.1	34.6	38.7	31.6	36.7	37.4	35.8	33.0	25.9	31.8
August	34.3	44.1	38.2	40.4	3.2	34.5	38.6	31.5	36.5	37.2	35.7	32.7	25.9	31.6
September	34.4	44.6	38.3	40.4	3.2	34.7	38.8	31.7	36.7	37.5	35.8	32.8	25.9	31.7
October	34.4	45.4	38.2	40.6	3.3	34.6	38.8	31.7	36.7	37.4	35.8	32.8	26.1	31.7
November	34.4	43.9	38.2	40.5	3.2	34.6	38.8	31.7	36.8	37.4	35.8	32.8	26.1	31.7
December	34.5	44.6	38.5	40.6	3.3	34.7	38.8	31.8	36.7	37.3	35.9	32.8	26.1	31.7
2012														
January	34.5	45.4	38.6	40.9	3.3	34.7	38.8	31.8	36.7	37.3	35.8	32.8	26.2	31.7
February	34.6	44.6	38.8	40.9	3.3	34.7	38.8	31.9	36.8	37.3	35.9	32.9	26.1	31.7
March	34.5	44.0	38.6	40.7	3.3	34.7	38.7	31.9	36.6	37.2	35.9	32.9	26.1	31.8
April	34.5	43.9	38.8	40.8	3.3	34.6	38.7	31.7	36.6	37.2	36.0	32.9	26.1	31.7
May	34.4	43.6	38.5	40.6	3.3	34.6	38.7	31.6	36.6	37.1	35.9	32.9	26.0	31.6
June	34.4	44.0	38.5	40.6	3.2	34.6	38.7	31.6	36.6	37.1	35.9	32.9	26.1	31.6
July	34.4	44.1	38.5	40.7	3.2	34.5	38.6	31.5	36.5	37.1	36.0	32.9	26.0	31.7
August	34.4	43.5	38.6	40.5	3.2	34.5	38.6	31.5	36.5	37.2	36.0	32.8	26.0	31.5
September	34.5	43.5	38.9	40.6	3.2	34.5	38.6	31.5	36.5	37.3	36.1	32.9	26.0	31.5
October	34.3	43.4	38.7	40.5	3.2	34.4	38.5	31.4	36.2	37.1	35.8	32.8	26.0	31.5
November	34.4	43.2	39.0	40.7	3.3	34.6	38.5	31.6	36.4	37.2	35.9	32.8	26.0	31.5
December	34.5	43.5	39.3	40.8	3.3	34.5	38.6	31.4	36.5	37.2	36.0	32.8	26.1	31.5

Table 10-11. Indexes of Aggregate Weekly Hours of All Employees on Private Nonfarm Payrolls by NAICS Supersector

(2007 =100, seasonally adjusted.)

Year and month	Total private	Mining and logging	Construction	Manu-facturing	Trade, transportation, and utilities			Information	Financial activities	Profes-sional and business services	Education and health services	Leisure and hospitality	Other services
					Total	Wholesale trade	Retail trade						
2007	100.0	100.0	100.0	100.0	100.0	100.0	100.0	100.0	100.0	100.0	100.0	100.0	100.0
2008	98.7	105.2	93.3	96.0	98.5	99.6	97.6	99.6	98.2	98.2	103.3	99.1	100.4
2009	92.0	91.9	77.0	83.1	92.5	92.4	92.2	93.5	94.0	91.4	103.1	95.4	94.1
2010	91.8	96.1	71.9	83.4	91.7	90.6	91.9	90.3	93.0	93.1	104.2	95.9	93.4
2011	94.2	110.2	73.1	85.4	94.2	93.4	94.1	89.4	93.9	97.4	106.2	98.7	94.2
2012	96.7	117.5	75.3	87.3	96.0	95.8	95.6	89.6	95.3	101.6	108.8	102.4	95.3
2008													
January	100.3	102.4	98.7	98.8	100.5	100.9	100.3	100.9	98.9	99.9	101.8	100.5	99.7
February	100.2	102.9	98.4	98.8	100.3	101.0	100.0	100.6	99.1	99.6	102.3	100.1	100.9
March	100.3	106.3	97.5	99.0	100.2	101.0	99.8	100.7	99.1	99.9	103.5	100.0	101.6
April	99.9	101.8	96.2	97.6	99.6	100.4	98.7	100.7	99.0	99.3	103.1	100.2	101.3
May	99.7	104.0	95.3	97.6	99.3	100.2	98.4	100.2	99.1	99.3	103.4	100.1	100.9
June	99.5	105.9	94.5	97.4	99.0	100.2	98.1	100.3	98.7	98.8	103.7	99.6	100.4
July	99.0	104.8	93.3	96.2	98.8	100.1	97.6	99.8	98.3	98.7	103.9	99.1	100.6
August	98.8	106.8	92.9	95.9	98.5	100.1	97.2	99.4	98.6	98.4	103.9	99.3	100.8
September	98.1	105.2	91.1	94.6	97.7	99.3	96.8	99.2	97.7	97.7	103.9	98.5	100.5
October	97.7	108.7	92.0	93.7	97.3	98.5	96.0	98.8	97.6	97.4	103.7	98.7	100.2
November	96.7	107.3	87.4	92.4	96.3	97.6	95.2	98.0	97.1	96.0	103.9	97.5	99.8
December	95.6	104.9	86.4	90.4	94.8	96.9	92.7	97.5	96.6	95.1	103.8	96.8	99.3
2009													
January	95.1	103.2	84.0	87.6	95.0	96.5	94.0	96.2	96.4	94.3	104.3	96.6	98.0
February	94.0	101.0	83.0	86.9	94.2	95.3	93.3	95.9	95.5	93.0	103.2	95.9	96.2
March	93.0	97.2	80.7	84.8	93.6	94.1	92.7	95.2	95.0	92.3	102.9	95.5	93.9
April	92.1	93.6	78.6	83.8	92.7	93.1	92.3	94.0	94.4	91.4	102.6	94.9	93.2
May	91.8	90.2	78.3	82.2	92.8	92.6	92.5	93.5	94.0	91.3	102.5	95.4	93.7
June	91.4	90.2	77.0	81.6	92.1	92.0	92.1	92.9	93.2	90.5	102.4	95.2	93.5
July	91.2	89.3	76.4	81.6	91.7	91.3	91.8	92.7	93.6	90.4	102.8	95.2	93.4
August	91.0	88.6	75.2	82.0	91.6	91.0	91.5	91.8	93.0	90.2	103.0	94.9	93.5
September	91.1	88.3	73.8	81.5	91.9	90.6	92.4	92.0	93.1	90.3	103.1	95.3	93.1
October	90.7	87.1	73.4	81.4	91.3	90.5	91.4	91.9	93.2	90.1	102.7	94.6	92.8
November	90.9	88.5	73.4	82.0	91.2	90.5	91.4	92.0	93.0	91.2	102.8	94.9	92.9
December	90.8	88.6	72.5	81.9	90.7	90.1	90.6	91.4	93.1	91.2	103.3	94.5	93.1
2010													
January	91.0	90.4	72.0	82.3	90.7	89.9	91.2	91.6	93.2	92.0	104.1	94.5	93.2
February	90.7	91.2	69.3	81.6	90.7	89.8	91.5	90.9	93.1	91.4	103.6	94.9	93.1
March	91.1	92.9	71.3	82.5	90.9	90.0	91.4	90.7	93.1	92.1	103.9	95.0	93.3
April	91.5	94.1	72.8	83.1	91.4	90.5	91.7	90.5	93.2	92.3	103.9	95.5	93.7
May	91.9	96.0	71.8	84.0	91.5	90.4	91.8	90.5	93.3	92.7	104.1	95.7	93.6
June	91.7	95.2	71.6	83.5	91.5	90.5	91.7	90.1	93.7	92.5	104.2	95.6	93.1
July	92.0	97.3	71.2	83.6	92.2	90.8	92.4	90.3	93.1	93.4	104.3	96.1	93.6
August	92.1	98.6	72.1	83.7	92.2	90.8	92.5	90.6	93.1	93.4	104.5	96.3	93.8
September	92.5	98.3	72.4	84.0	92.4	91.4	92.3	90.2	93.4	94.0	104.5	96.7	94.2
October	92.7	100.4	72.2	84.0	92.8	91.5	92.8	90.5	93.4	94.6	104.8	97.0	94.4
November	92.5	99.1	72.2	84.1	92.6	91.4	92.4	89.9	93.3	94.6	105.0	97.1	93.9
December	92.9	101.5	71.4	84.2	93.2	91.7	93.0	89.5	93.3	95.5	104.8	96.9	93.7
2011													
January	92.7	103.2	70.4	84.3	92.9	92.1	92.8	89.4	93.3	95.4	104.9	96.8	93.6
February	93.2	102.5	71.2	84.8	93.3	92.3	92.9	89.3	93.2	96.0	105.0	97.5	93.7
March	93.4	105.5	71.7	85.1	93.7	92.8	93.2	89.3	93.0	96.5	105.4	97.5	93.9
April	93.9	107.4	72.2	85.1	94.3	93.0	94.2	89.4	93.6	96.8	106.0	98.5	94.1
May	94.1	109.2	73.3	85.4	93.9	93.2	93.7	89.7	93.8	97.1	106.5	97.9	94.2
June	93.9	110.4	73.0	85.2	94.4	93.6	93.9	89.7	94.0	97.1	106.0	98.2	94.3
July	94.4	111.0	73.4	85.2	94.5	93.6	94.4	89.8	94.3	97.5	106.9	98.9	94.4
August	94.2	111.3	73.0	85.5	94.3	93.6	94.1	87.8	93.9	97.6	106.1	99.0	94.1
September	94.7	113.7	73.7	85.5	95.0	94.1	94.9	89.7	94.6	98.3	106.7	99.1	94.5
October	94.9	116.8	73.4	86.0	94.8	94.4	94.9	89.7	94.4	98.5	106.9	100.2	94.5
November	95.0	113.5	73.4	85.8	95.0	94.6	95.1	90.0	94.6	98.7	107.1	100.6	94.7
December	95.5	116.7	74.5	86.2	95.4	94.9	95.4	89.9	94.4	99.3	107.2	100.8	94.9
2012													
January	95.8	120.4	74.9	87.1	95.8	95.2	95.8	89.5	94.4	99.5	107.4	101.6	95.1
February	96.3	119.3	75.5	87.3	95.8	95.4	95.9	90.1	94.6	100.2	108.1	101.5	95.1
March	96.2	117.8	75.0	87.2	95.8	95.2	95.9	89.5	94.6	100.5	108.3	101.9	95.5
April	96.3	117.5	75.4	87.5	95.6	95.5	95.5	89.5	94.6	101.0	108.4	102.0	95.2
May	96.2	117.1	74.5	87.1	95.8	95.7	95.2	89.6	94.6	100.9	108.7	101.6	95.0
June	96.2	117.9	74.6	87.2	95.8	95.8	95.2	89.4	94.6	101.1	108.7	102.1	95.1
July	96.4	118.1	74.7	87.6	95.6	95.8	94.9	89.5	94.6	101.7	108.9	102.0	95.5
August	96.5	116.1	74.9	87.0	95.8	95.9	95.0	89.4	95.0	101.9	108.7	102.3	94.9
September	96.9	115.8	75.5	87.1	95.9	95.8	95.2	89.0	95.4	102.3	109.3	102.5	95.1
October	96.5	114.7	75.4	86.9	95.9	95.7	95.2	88.3	95.0	101.7	109.2	102.7	95.2
November	97.0	115.8	76.3	87.4	96.8	95.9	96.3	89.3	95.3	102.3	109.3	102.8	95.4
December	97.5	117.6	77.4	87.7	96.7	96.3	95.7	89.2	95.4	102.8	109.4	103.5	95.5

Table 10-12. Average Hourly Earnings of All Employees on Private Nonfarm Payrolls by NAICS Supersector

(Dollars, seasonally adjusted.)

Year and month	Total private	Mining and logging	Construction	Manufacturing	Trade, transportation, and utilities			Information	Financial activities	Professional and business services	Education and health services	Leisure and hospitality	Other services
					Total	Wholesale trade	Retail trade						
2007	20.97	24.91	23.02	21.50	18.58	23.96	15.13	28.09	25.64	24.68	21.35	12.39	17.62
2008	21.62	26.20	23.96	22.16	18.93	24.37	15.21	28.66	26.18	25.82	22.12	12.77	18.17
2009	22.22	27.29	24.83	23.04	19.32	25.41	15.39	29.40	26.53	27.03	22.41	12.97	19.54
2010	22.60	27.39	25.19	23.31	19.65	26.13	15.56	30.53	27.21	27.24	22.96	13.08	20.16
2011	23.06	28.10	25.41	23.69	20.04	26.38	15.86	31.59	27.90	27.76	23.62	13.23	20.50
2012	23.53	28.75	25.75	23.93	20.50	26.89	16.29	31.81	29.27	28.11	24.23	13.37	20.85
2008													
January	21.27	25.43	23.43	21.71	18.71	24.09	15.11	28.42	26.02	25.15	21.79	12.62	17.87
February	21.34	24.85	23.52	21.82	18.78	24.15	15.16	28.34	26.07	25.21	21.92	12.67	17.92
March	21.44	26.46	23.58	21.98	18.79	24.21	15.14	28.59	26.12	25.34	22.02	12.74	17.97
April	21.44	24.97	23.64	21.88	18.83	24.21	15.20	28.65	26.12	25.48	21.98	12.74	18.02
May	21.53	25.48	23.80	22.00	18.92	24.28	15.24	28.48	26.16	25.63	22.02	12.75	18.06
June	21.61	25.87	23.90	22.18	18.97	24.40	15.22	28.67	26.19	25.73	22.07	12.78	18.15
July	21.65	26.28	23.98	22.10	18.98	24.43	15.21	28.83	26.26	25.83	22.11	12.79	18.23
August	21.76	26.69	24.20	22.22	19.08	24.63	15.29	28.87	26.29	26.03	22.21	12.82	18.26
September	21.78	26.63	24.21	22.26	19.03	24.43	15.27	28.85	26.42	26.10	22.27	12.83	18.29
October	21.83	26.58	24.24	22.45	19.01	24.43	15.24	28.76	26.31	26.30	22.30	12.82	18.35
November	21.94	27.57	24.41	22.60	19.07	24.61	15.26	28.78	26.27	26.54	22.43	12.82	18.42
December	22.01	27.31	24.58	22.63	19.15	24.71	15.28	28.89	26.31	26.66	22.45	12.84	18.47
2009													
January	22.02	27.45	24.55	22.79	19.15	24.85	15.31	28.84	26.29	26.71	22.43	12.87	18.64
February	22.08	27.51	24.57	22.91	19.20	24.92	15.32	28.82	26.28	26.84	22.42	12.88	18.83
March	22.11	27.69	24.75	23.01	19.23	25.01	15.34	28.83	26.27	26.95	22.20	12.88	19.50
April	22.14	27.58	24.79	23.03	19.23	25.17	15.31	28.92	26.27	27.05	22.27	12.90	19.51
May	22.14	27.54	24.78	23.01	19.27	25.29	15.37	29.19	26.38	27.00	22.27	12.86	19.57
June	22.17	27.43	24.86	23.03	19.24	25.31	15.34	29.36	26.47	27.04	22.36	12.91	19.54
July	22.22	27.29	24.85	23.10	19.28	25.35	15.38	29.67	26.52	27.07	22.39	12.97	19.61
August	22.27	27.37	24.90	23.13	19.44	25.73	15.50	29.63	26.60	27.04	22.41	13.00	19.66
September	22.29	27.15	24.86	23.14	19.41	25.69	15.50	29.62	26.70	27.18	22.40	13.04	19.82
October	22.35	27.30	24.99	23.13	19.42	25.74	15.42	29.82	26.79	27.11	22.57	13.10	19.89
November	22.39	27.06	25.04	23.19	19.47	25.82	15.45	29.93	26.91	27.07	22.59	13.16	19.97
December	22.41	26.97	25.01	23.14	19.51	25.91	15.46	29.88	26.93	27.12	22.57	13.15	20.03
2010													
January	22.46	27.09	25.11	23.17	19.60	26.17	15.50	29.90	27.00	27.15	22.59	13.13	20.06
February	22.47	27.14	25.22	23.22	19.58	26.17	15.49	30.16	27.00	27.22	22.62	13.11	20.11
March	22.50	27.12	25.16	23.18	19.62	26.15	15.55	30.18	27.06	27.18	22.71	13.09	20.13
April	22.54	27.23	25.10	23.20	19.65	26.13	15.62	30.18	27.19	27.18	22.86	13.07	20.11
May	22.57	27.44	25.16	23.31	19.62	26.13	15.51	30.30	27.24	27.24	22.91	13.08	20.12
June	22.56	27.41	25.13	23.23	19.61	26.09	15.53	30.41	27.17	27.26	22.93	13.06	20.14
July	22.62	27.57	25.19	23.36	19.63	26.12	15.55	30.48	27.38	27.27	23.01	13.08	20.09
August	22.66	27.57	25.18	23.44	19.61	26.03	15.52	30.68	27.33	27.37	23.09	13.10	20.08
September	22.70	27.78	25.19	23.44	19.72	26.19	15.59	30.97	27.35	27.38	23.10	13.10	20.15
October	22.76	27.64	25.30	23.46	19.77	26.23	15.65	31.15	27.40	27.42	23.19	13.10	20.25
November	22.76	27.75	25.32	23.41	19.75	26.20	15.63	31.26	27.41	27.39	23.23	13.10	20.38
December	22.80	27.56	25.36	23.49	19.79	26.23	15.66	31.08	27.57	27.33	23.34	13.10	20.32
2011													
January	22.89	27.96	25.48	23.64	19.86	26.30	15.72	31.47	27.54	27.51	23.35	13.17	20.42
February	22.89	28.04	25.41	23.50	19.89	26.28	15.75	31.54	27.61	27.54	23.34	13.18	20.40
March	22.91	28.11	25.32	23.55	19.89	26.19	15.74	31.82	27.65	27.54	23.41	13.18	20.34
April	22.96	28.29	25.37	23.60	19.96	26.30	15.80	31.76	27.71	27.62	23.46	13.21	20.38
May	23.03	28.25	25.35	23.68	19.99	26.30	15.84	31.58	27.73	27.66	23.61	13.25	20.44
June	23.04	27.74	25.36	23.68	20.03	26.38	15.82	31.50	27.81	27.75	23.58	13.23	20.46
July	23.13	27.68	25.37	23.74	20.10	26.44	15.95	31.48	27.89	27.94	23.74	13.21	20.53
August	23.10	28.00	25.47	23.71	20.08	26.42	15.86	31.59	27.95	27.84	23.68	13.21	20.53
September	23.14	28.07	25.48	23.76	20.04	26.37	15.81	31.39	28.09	27.85	23.76	13.27	20.55
October	23.22	28.23	25.47	23.88	20.17	26.52	15.95	31.70	28.25	27.93	23.82	13.30	20.59
November	23.22	28.30	25.46	23.75	20.20	26.53	16.01	31.63	28.35	27.95	23.82	13.32	20.61
December	23.26	28.39	25.50	23.84	20.22	26.52	16.03	31.72	28.36	27.92	23.88	13.33	20.63
2012													
January	23.28	28.07	25.51	23.87	20.21	26.50	16.03	31.63	28.60	27.87	24.05	13.32	20.63
February	23.33	28.52	25.56	23.85	20.23	26.53	16.08	31.64	28.74	27.91	24.12	13.32	20.65
March	23.40	28.70	25.64	23.88	20.30	26.67	16.11	31.66	28.88	28.03	24.17	13.35	20.70
April	23.42	28.68	25.67	23.91	20.36	26.69	16.17	31.75	28.90	27.97	24.15	13.35	20.75
May	23.43	28.62	25.71	23.80	20.40	26.73	16.20	31.73	29.10	28.03	24.10	13.33	20.76
June	23.50	28.70	25.74	23.92	20.50	26.82	16.33	31.78	29.12	28.05	24.21	13.38	20.78
July	23.54	28.73	25.78	23.94	20.53	26.84	16.33	31.82	29.22	28.09	24.22	13.40	20.83
August	23.53	28.65	25.77	23.91	20.54	26.88	16.35	31.49	29.33	28.04	24.26	13.39	20.90
September	23.60	28.88	25.84	23.97	20.57	26.93	16.39	31.77	29.44	28.14	24.31	13.40	20.98
October	23.58	28.64	25.84	23.92	20.58	27.00	16.41	31.70	29.51	28.10	24.29	13.39	20.98
November	23.67	28.93	25.93	24.03	20.63	27.20	16.37	31.85	29.66	28.22	24.40	13.39	21.01
December	23.75	29.14	25.97	24.07	20.73	27.36	16.48	32.18	29.80	28.29	24.47	13.38	21.10

Table 10-13. Average Weekly Earnings of All Employees on Private Nonfarm Payrolls by NAICS Supersector

(Dollars, seasonally adjusted.)

| Year and month | Total private | Mining and logging | Construc-tion | Manu-facturing | Trade, transportation, and utilities | | | Information | Financial activities | Profes-sional and business services | Education and health services | Leisure and hospitality | Other services |
					Total	Wholesale trade	Retail trade						
2007	725.25	1 094.81	875.06	861.19	641.51	913.03	479.81	1 014.35	937.69	874.68	715.66	323.54	578.84
2008	745.00	1 144.63	905.68	882.19	651.96	936.17	478.00	1 047.50	956.24	909.23	745.03	330.32	597.13
2009	753.54	1 150.12	922.54	898.44	659.78	963.44	481.18	1 073.27	971.73	947.10	739.27	331.64	618.18
2010	770.82	1 189.32	952.78	937.34	672.58	994.71	487.66	1 114.65	1 004.14	963.57	752.26	336.83	637.65
2011	792.71	1 250.91	973.85	958.84	692.51	1 019.05	500.75	1 156.56	1 039.66	991.87	774.76	342.67	649.87
2012	811.99	1 263.46	997.82	974.29	708.84	1 041.35	515.22	1 165.28	1 093.60	1 012.88	797.13	348.96	659.48
2008													
January	735.94	1 111.29	897.37	868.40	647.37	922.65	478.99	1 037.33	949.73	885.28	732.14	328.12	582.56
February	738.36	1 088.43	900.82	874.98	649.79	927.36	480.57	1 034.41	954.16	887.39	738.70	328.15	589.57
March	743.97	1 185.41	900.76	885.79	650.13	932.09	479.94	1 043.54	955.99	897.04	748.68	329.97	594.81
April	741.82	1 071.21	900.68	873.01	649.64	929.66	478.80	1 048.59	955.99	896.90	742.92	331.24	594.66
May	744.94	1 108.38	904.40	880.00	652.74	932.35	480.06	1 039.52	960.07	904.74	744.28	331.50	594.17
June	747.71	1 138.28	908.20	889.42	654.47	939.40	479.43	1 049.32	958.55	905.70	745.97	331.00	595.32
July	746.93	1 137.92	906.44	879.58	654.81	943.00	477.59	1 055.18	958.49	911.80	747.32	329.98	599.77
August	750.72	1 166.35	917.18	886.58	658.26	953.18	480.11	1 056.64	964.84	918.86	748.48	332.04	602.58
September	749.23	1 139.76	907.88	881.50	654.63	940.56	479.48	1 058.80	964.33	918.72	750.50	331.01	601.74
October	750.95	1 177.49	928.39	889.02	653.94	938.11	477.01	1 055.49	962.95	928.39	749.28	332.04	601.88
November	752.54	1 213.08	908.05	890.44	654.10	942.56	477.64	1 053.35	961.48	934.21	753.65	329.47	606.02
December	750.54	1 182.52	919.29	884.83	651.10	946.39	469.10	1 060.26	962.95	935.77	752.08	328.70	607.66
2009													
January	753.08	1 180.35	913.26	884.25	656.85	954.24	479.20	1 052.66	964.84	937.52	753.65	329.47	607.66
February	750.72	1 180.18	916.46	893.49	656.64	951.94	477.98	1 051.93	961.85	939.40	744.34	328.44	604.44
March	749.53	1 176.83	920.70	888.19	657.67	950.38	478.61	1 049.41	961.48	943.25	734.82	328.44	614.25
April	748.33	1 155.60	919.71	891.26	655.74	953.94	477.67	1 049.80	961.48	946.75	734.91	328.95	610.66
May	748.33	1 142.91	921.82	885.89	659.03	958.49	481.08	1 065.44	965.51	947.70	732.68	327.93	616.46
June	749.35	1 149.32	924.79	891.26	654.16	956.72	478.61	1 068.70	963.51	946.40	733.41	329.21	613.56
July	751.04	1 146.18	929.39	898.59	655.52	955.70	479.86	1 082.96	970.63	947.45	736.63	330.74	615.75
August	752.73	1 155.01	928.77	906.70	660.96	970.02	482.05	1 075.57	970.90	946.40	737.29	331.50	619.29
September	755.63	1 145.73	919.82	904.77	663.82	965.94	488.25	1 078.17	977.22	951.30	736.96	333.82	622.35
October	755.43	1 146.60	929.63	906.70	662.22	970.40	482.65	1 085.45	983.19	946.14	738.04	334.05	624.55
November	759.02	1 150.05	936.50	918.32	663.93	976.00	483.59	1 095.44	984.91	952.86	738.69	336.90	629.06
December	759.70	1 143.53	930.37	918.66	663.34	976.81	480.81	1 090.62	988.33	954.62	740.30	336.64	632.95
2010													
January	763.64	1 164.87	939.11	924.48	666.40	989.23	483.60	1 094.34	993.60	961.11	745.47	336.13	633.90
February	761.73	1 167.02	918.01	919.51	665.72	989.23	484.84	1 097.82	993.60	955.42	741.94	336.93	635.48
March	765.00	1 174.30	938.47	927.20	667.08	991.09	485.16	1 101.57	998.51	962.17	744.89	336.41	636.11
April	768.61	1 187.23	953.80	932.64	672.03	995.55	488.91	1 101.57	1 003.31	959.45	749.81	337.21	637.49
May	771.89	1 204.62	948.53	944.06	671.00	995.55	485.46	1 108.98	1 007.88	964.30	751.45	337.46	637.80
June	769.30	1 186.85	947.40	933.85	670.66	994.03	486.09	1 113.01	1 010.72	959.55	752.10	335.64	636.42
July	773.60	1 207.57	947.14	939.07	675.27	997.78	489.83	1 115.57	1 013.06	968.09	754.73	337.46	636.85
August	774.97	1 210.32	954.32	944.63	674.58	994.35	488.88	1 125.96	1 011.21	968.90	757.35	337.98	638.54
September	778.61	1 205.65	962.26	946.98	678.37	1 005.70	489.53	1 133.50	1 014.69	974.73	757.68	337.98	642.79
October	780.67	1 207.87	963.93	947.78	682.07	1 007.23	492.98	1 146.32	1 016.54	978.89	760.63	339.29	643.95
November	778.39	1 190.48	964.69	945.76	679.40	1 003.46	490.78	1 144.12	1 016.91	972.35	761.94	339.29	646.05
December	782.04	1 212.64	961.14	949.00	684.73	1 007.23	494.86	1 134.42	1 022.85	975.68	763.22	337.98	644.14
2011													
January	782.84	1 244.22	958.05	952.69	683.18	1 012.55	493.61	1 148.66	1 021.73	979.36	763.55	339.79	647.31
February	785.13	1 236.56	957.96	949.40	686.21	1 011.78	494.55	1 154.36	1 024.33	983.18	763.22	341.36	646.68
March	785.81	1 248.08	959.63	953.78	688.19	1 010.93	495.81	1 164.61	1 023.05	983.18	767.85	340.04	646.81
April	789.82	1 258.91	966.60	953.44	692.61	1 015.18	500.86	1 162.42	1 030.81	986.03	771.83	343.46	648.08
May	792.23	1 265.60	975.98	959.04	689.66	1 015.18	498.96	1 158.99	1 031.56	987.46	779.13	341.85	649.99
June	790.27	1 237.20	971.29	956.67	693.04	1 020.91	498.33	1 152.90	1 037.31	990.68	773.42	341.33	650.63
July	795.67	1 223.46	974.21	956.72	695.46	1 023.23	504.02	1 155.32	1 043.09	1 000.25	783.42	342.14	652.85
August	792.33	1 234.80	972.95	957.88	692.76	1 019.61	499.59	1 153.04	1 039.74	993.89	774.34	342.14	648.75
September	796.02	1 251.92	975.88	959.90	695.39	1 023.16	501.18	1 152.01	1 053.38	997.03	779.33	343.69	651.44
October	798.77	1 281.64	972.95	969.53	697.88	1 028.98	505.62	1 163.39	1 056.55	999.89	781.30	347.13	652.70
November	798.77	1 242.37	972.57	961.88	698.92	1 029.36	507.52	1 163.98	1 060.29	1 000.61	781.30	347.65	653.34
December	802.47	1 266.19	981.75	967.90	701.63	1 028.98	509.75	1 164.12	1 057.83	1 002.33	783.26	347.91	653.97
2012													
January	803.16	1 274.38	984.69	976.28	701.29	1 028.20	509.75	1 160.82	1 066.78	997.75	788.84	348.98	653.97
February	807.22	1 271.99	991.73	975.47	701.98	1 029.36	512.95	1 164.35	1 072.00	1 001.97	793.55	347.65	654.61
March	807.30	1 262.80	989.70	971.92	704.41	1 032.13	513.91	1 158.76	1 074.34	1 006.28	795.19	348.44	658.26
April	807.99	1 259.05	996.00	975.53	704.46	1 032.90	512.59	1 162.05	1 075.08	1 006.92	794.54	348.44	657.78
May	805.99	1 247.83	989.84	966.28	705.84	1 034.45	511.92	1 161.32	1 079.61	1 006.28	792.89	348.58	656.02
June	808.40	1 262.80	990.99	971.15	709.30	1 037.93	516.03	1 163.15	1 080.35	1 007.00	796.51	349.22	656.65
July	809.78	1 266.99	992.53	974.36	708.29	1 036.02	514.40	1 161.43	1 084.06	1 011.24	796.84	348.40	660.31
August	809.43	1 246.28	994.72	968.36	708.63	1 037.57	515.03	1 149.39	1 091.08	1 009.44	795.73	348.14	658.35
September	814.20	1 256.28	1 005.18	973.18	709.67	1 039.50	516.29	1 159.61	1 098.11	1 015.85	799.80	348.40	660.87
October	808.79	1 242.98	1 000.01	968.76	707.95	1 039.50	515.27	1 147.54	1 094.82	1 005.98	796.71	348.14	660.87
November	814.25	1 249.78	1 011.27	978.02	713.80	1 047.20	517.29	1 159.34	1 103.35	1 013.10	800.32	348.14	661.82
December	819.38	1 267.59	1 020.62	982.06	715.19	1 056.10	517.47	1 174.57	1 108.56	1 018.44	802.62	349.22	664.65

Table 10-14. Production and Nonsupervisory Workers on Private Nonfarm Payrolls by NAICS Supersector

(Thousands, seasonally adjusted.)

Year and month	Total private	Mining and logging	Construction	Manufacturing	Trade, transportation, and utilities			Information	Financial activities	Professional and business services	Education and health services	Leisure and hospitality	Other services
					Total	Wholesale trade	Retail trade						
1965	42 302	523	2 906	12 905	10 702	...	...	1 268	2 434	3 515	3 443	3 443	1 161
1966	44 292	517	2 977	13 703	11 095	...	...	1 334	2 492	3 715	3 623	3 607	1 230
1967	45 185	501	2 903	13 714	11 369	...	...	1 365	2 585	3 890	3 818	3 734	1 306
1968	46 519	491	2 986	13 908	11 688	...	...	1 394	2 700	4 067	4 008	3 898	1 379
1969	48 246	501	3 177	14 147	12 152	...	...	1 438	2 841	4 252	4 196	4 089	1 452
1970	48 180	496	3 158	13 490	12 388	...	...	1 422	2 922	4 321	4 305	4 185	1 494
1971	48 151	474	3 238	13 034	12 502	...	...	1 392	2 978	4 354	4 372	4 286	1 521
1972	49 971	494	3 425	13 497	12 954	2 920	7 257	1 437	3 066	4 518	4 531	4 467	1 583
1973	52 235	502	3 576	14 227	13 437	3 041	7 551	1 504	3 164	4 748	4 747	4 664	1 666
1974	52 846	550	3 469	14 040	13 700	3 148	7 673	1 516	3 217	4 907	4 941	4 766	1 740
1975	51 010	581	2 990	12 576	13 578	3 121	7 714	1 416	3 227	4 939	5 088	4 821	1 795
1976	52 916	606	2 999	13 127	14 038	3 212	8 048	1 459	3 300	5 153	5 309	5 046	1 880
1977	55 207	636	3 209	13 591	14 579	3 323	8 396	1 514	3 452	5 404	5 561	5 284	1 978
1978	58 188	658	3 544	14 150	15 329	3 509	8 861	1 586	3 645	5 717	5 874	5 588	2 099
1979	60 403	737	3 760	14 458	15 843	3 667	9 113	1 650	3 825	5 993	6 157	5 772	2 209
1980	60 372	785	3 623	13 667	15 907	3 708	9 158	1 626	3 957	6 197	6 442	5 850	2 318
1981	60 960	861	3 469	13 492	16 004	3 753	9 238	1 633	4 052	6 396	6 694	5 944	2 414
1982	59 465	834	3 208	12 315	15 821	3 662	9 254	1 564	4 055	6 421	6 812	5 976	2 458
1983	60 005	698	3 240	12 121	15 999	3 639	9 494	1 502	4 128	6 581	7 032	6 161	2 542
1984	63 316	714	3 614	12 821	16 797	3 821	9 964	1 631	4 289	6 918	7 368	6 491	2 672
1985	65 436	686	3 868	12 648	17 427	3 935	10 399	1 660	4 476	7 258	7 770	6 817	2 827
1986	66 802	577	3 984	12 449	17 769	3 941	10 704	1 663	4 698	7 532	8 107	7 066	2 957
1987	68 700	541	4 088	12 537	18 196	3 989	10 986	1 717	4 861	7 859	8 488	7 310	3 104
1988	71 029	545	4 199	12 765	18 771	4 132	11 306	1 775	4 894	8 256	8 956	7 587	3 280
1989	72 927	526	4 257	12 805	19 230	4 235	11 565	1 807	4 931	8 648	9 432	7 833	3 459
1990	73 684	538	4 115	12 669	19 032	4 198	11 308	1 866	4 973	8 889	9 748	8 299	3 555
1991	72 522	515	3 674	12 164	18 640	4 122	11 008	1 871	4 914	8 748	10 212	8 247	3 539
1992	72 802	478	3 546	12 020	18 506	4 071	10 931	1 871	4 924	8 971	10 555	8 406	3 526
1993	74 618	462	3 704	12 070	18 752	4 072	11 104	1 896	5 084	9 451	10 908	8 667	3 623
1994	77 419	461	3 973	12 361	19 392	4 196	11 502	1 928	5 220	10 078	11 338	8 979	3 689
1995	79 879	458	4 113	12 567	19 984	4 361	11 841	2 007	5 199	10 645	11 765	9 330	3 812
1996	81 816	461	4 325	12 532	20 325	4 423	12 057	2 096	5 322	11 161	12 123	9 565	3 907
1997	84 225	479	4 546	12 673	20 698	4 523	12 274	2 181	5 482	11 896	12 478	9 780	4 013
1998	86 404	473	4 807	12 729	21 059	4 605	12 440	2 217	5 692	12 566	12 791	9 947	4 124
1999	88 520	438	5 105	12 524	21 576	4 673	12 772	2 351	5 818	13 184	13 089	10 216	4 219
2000	90 418	446	5 295	12 428	21 965	4 686	13 040	2 502	5 819	13 790	13 362	10 516	4 296
2001	90 061	457	5 332	11 677	21 709	4 555	12 952	2 531	5 888	13 588	13 846	10 662	4 373
2002	88 484	436	5 196	10 768	21 337	4 474	12 774	2 398	5 964	13 049	14 311	10 576	4 449
2003	87 744	420	5 123	10 189	21 078	4 396	12 655	2 347	6 052	12 911	14 532	10 666	4 426
2004	89 000	440	5 309	10 072	21 319	4 444	12 788	2 371	6 052	13 287	14 771	10 955	4 425
2005	91 171	473	5 611	10 060	21 830	4 584	13 030	2 386	6 127	13 854	15 129	11 263	4 438
2006	93 483	519	5 903	10 137	22 166	4 724	13 110	2 399	6 312	14 446	15 539	11 568	4 494
2007	94 941	547	5 883	9 975	22 546	4 851	13 317	2 403	6 365	14 784	15 999	11 861	4 578
2008	94 322	574	5 521	9 629	22 337	4 822	13 134	2 388	6 320	14 585	16 488	11 873	4 606
2009	89 231	510	4 567	8 322	21 116	4 506	12 472	2 240	6 066	13 520	16 841	11 560	4 488
2010	88 548	525	4 172	8 077	20 874	4 378	12 425	2 170	5 942	13 699	17 125	11 507	4 458
2011	90 221	594	4 184	8 228	21 234	4 443	12 647	2 148	5 900	14 251	17 421	11 772	4 491
2012	92 393	643	4 243	8 394	21 654	4 567	12 825	2 165	5 988	14 805	17 819	12 134	4 547
2011													
January	89 160	553	4 127	8 137	20 987	4 388	12 512	2 155	5 894	13 991	17 270	11 581	4 465
February	89 348	554	4 146	8 168	21 028	4 399	12 525	2 152	5 889	14 045	17 278	11 620	4 468
March	89 582	567	4 153	8 190	21 069	4 413	12 545	2 152	5 890	14 133	17 295	11 666	4 467
April	89 828	578	4 158	8 215	21 164	4 422	12 614	2 151	5 892	14 150	17 342	11 706	4 472
May	89 969	585	4 175	8 217	21 175	4 433	12 607	2 152	5 898	14 209	17 352	11 728	4 478
June	90 145	594	4 180	8 223	21 239	4 442	12 650	2 155	5 888	14 220	17 389	11 776	4 481
July	90 333	603	4 196	8 243	21 275	4 443	12 680	2 150	5 894	14 257	17 437	11 793	4 485
August	90 435	607	4 184	8 253	21 309	4 452	12 694	2 103	5 898	14 306	17 462	11 816	4 497
September	90 694	614	4 219	8 257	21 344	4 457	12 720	2 148	5 901	14 354	17 509	11 843	4 505
October	90 852	621	4 213	8 269	21 368	4 469	12 726	2 148	5 912	14 395	17 542	11 872	4 512
November	91 030	623	4 211	8 264	21 422	4 483	12 756	2 152	5 919	14 424	17 577	11 918	4 520
December	91 259	629	4 243	8 293	21 457	4 501	12 761	2 159	5 926	14 477	17 606	11 942	4 527
2012													
January	91 555	640	4 272	8 328	21 506	4 521	12 780	2 148	5 935	14 556	17 637	11 989	4 544
February	91 838	648	4 266	8 368	21 532	4 533	12 782	2 161	5 947	14 642	17 701	12 038	4 535
March	91 989	644	4 272	8 398	21 534	4 539	12 768	2 161	5 959	14 663	17 737	12 083	4 538
April	92 102	647	4 260	8 404	21 568	4 549	12 795	2 163	5 966	14 705	17 759	12 095	4 535
May	92 207	651	4 221	8 409	21 612	4 560	12 802	2 165	5 979	14 739	17 799	12 097	4 535
June	92 273	647	4 217	8 408	21 611	4 566	12 796	2 163	5 990	14 789	17 803	12 104	4 541
July	92 421	643	4 217	8 435	21 620	4 578	12 784	2 172	5 995	14 845	17 833	12 114	4 547
August	92 561	642	4 215	8 413	21 663	4 585	12 804	2 171	6 005	14 882	17 861	12 162	4 547
September	92 680	641	4 217	8 392	21 693	4 585	12 824	2 164	6 015	14 907	17 894	12 203	4 554
October	92 886	637	4 233	8 399	21 758	4 592	12 869	2 163	6 023	14 968	17 917	12 226	4 562
November	93 041	638	4 265	8 403	21 825	4 604	12 913	2 172	6 021	14 972	17 941	12 234	4 570
December	93 237	639	4 300	8 408	21 877	4 609	12 919	2 170	6 026	15 009	17 965	12 273	4 570

. . . = Not available.

Table 10-15. Average Weekly Hours of Production and Nonsupervisory Workers on Private Nonfarm Payrolls by NAICS Supersector

(Hours per week, seasonally adjusted.)

Year and month	Total private	Mining and logging	Construc-tion	Manufacturing — Average weekly hours	Manufacturing — Overtime hours	Trade, transportation, and utilities — Total	Trade, transportation, and utilities — Wholesale trade	Trade, transportation, and utilities — Retail trade	Informa-tion	Financial activities	Profes-sional and business services	Education and health services	Leisure and hospitality	Other services
1965	38.6	43.7	37.9	41.2	3.6	39.6	. . .	. . .	38.3	37.1	37.3	35.5	32.5	36.1
1966	38.5	44.1	38.1	41.4	3.9	39.1	. . .	. . .	38.3	37.2	37.0	35.2	31.9	35.8
1967	37.9	43.9	38.1	40.6	3.3	38.5	. . .	. . .	37.6	36.9	36.6	34.9	31.3	35.4
1968	37.7	44.0	37.8	40.7	3.6	38.2	. . .	. . .	37.6	36.8	36.3	34.5	30.8	35.0
1969	37.5	44.3	38.4	40.6	3.6	37.9	. . .	. . .	37.6	36.9	36.3	34.1	30.4	35.0
1970	37.0	43.9	37.8	39.8	2.9	37.6	. . .	. . .	37.2	36.6	35.9	34.1	30.0	34.7
1971	36.7	43.7	37.6	39.9	2.9	37.4	. . .	. . .	37.0	36.4	35.5	33.8	29.9	34.2
1972	36.9	44.1	37.0	40.6	3.4	37.4	39.8	35.1	37.3	36.4	35.5	33.3	29.7	34.2
1973	36.9	43.8	37.2	40.7	3.8	37.2	39.6	34.8	37.3	36.4	35.5	33.3	29.4	34.1
1974	36.4	43.7	37.1	40.0	3.2	36.8	39.2	34.3	37.0	36.3	35.3	33.3	29.1	33.9
1975	36.0	43.7	36.9	39.5	2.6	36.4	39.1	34.0	36.6	36.2	35.1	33.1	28.8	33.8
1976	36.1	44.2	37.3	40.1	3.1	36.3	39.1	33.8	36.7	36.2	34.9	33.0	28.5	33.6
1977	35.9	44.7	37.0	40.3	3.4	36.0	39.2	33.3	36.8	36.2	34.7	32.7	28.1	33.4
1978	35.8	44.9	37.3	40.4	3.6	35.6	39.2	32.7	36.8	36.1	34.6	32.5	27.7	33.2
1979	35.6	44.7	37.5	40.2	3.3	35.4	39.2	32.4	36.6	35.9	34.4	32.3	27.4	33.0
1980	35.2	44.9	37.5	39.6	2.8	35.0	38.8	31.9	36.4	36.0	34.3	32.2	27.0	33.0
1981	35.2	45.1	37.4	39.8	2.8	35.0	38.9	31.9	36.3	36.0	34.3	32.1	26.9	33.0
1982	34.7	44.1	37.2	38.9	2.3	34.6	38.7	31.7	35.8	36.0	34.2	32.1	26.8	33.0
1983	34.9	43.9	37.6	40.1	2.9	34.6	38.8	31.6	36.2	35.9	34.4	32.1	26.8	33.0
1984	35.1	44.6	38.2	40.6	3.4	34.7	38.9	31.6	36.6	36.2	34.3	32.1	26.7	32.9
1985	34.9	44.6	38.2	40.5	3.3	34.4	38.8	31.2	36.5	36.1	34.2	32.0	26.4	32.8
1986	34.7	43.6	37.9	40.7	3.4	34.1	38.7	31.0	36.4	36.1	34.3	31.9	26.2	32.9
1987	34.7	43.5	38.2	40.9	3.7	34.1	38.5	31.0	36.5	36.0	34.3	32.0	26.3	32.8
1988	34.6	43.3	38.2	41.0	3.8	33.8	38.5	30.9	36.1	35.6	34.2	32.0	26.3	32.9
1989	34.5	44.1	38.3	40.9	3.8	33.8	38.4	30.7	36.1	35.6	34.2	32.0	26.1	32.9
1990	34.3	45.0	38.3	40.5	3.9	33.7	38.4	30.6	35.8	35.5	34.2	32.0	26.0	32.8
1991	34.1	45.3	38.1	40.4	3.8	33.6	38.4	30.4	35.6	35.5	34.0	31.9	25.6	32.7
1992	34.2	44.6	38.0	40.7	4.0	33.8	38.5	30.7	35.8	35.6	34.0	31.9	25.7	32.6
1993	34.3	44.9	38.4	41.1	4.4	34.1	38.5	30.7	36.0	35.5	34.0	32.0	25.9	32.6
1994	34.5	45.3	38.8	41.7	5.0	34.3	38.8	30.9	36.0	35.5	34.1	32.0	26.0	32.7
1995	34.3	45.3	38.8	41.3	4.7	34.1	38.6	30.8	36.0	35.5	34.0	32.0	25.9	32.6
1996	34.3	46.0	38.9	41.3	4.8	34.1	38.6	30.7	36.3	35.6	34.1	32.0	25.9	32.5
1997	34.5	46.2	38.9	41.7	5.1	34.3	38.8	30.9	36.3	35.8	34.3	31.9	26.1	32.7
1998	34.5	44.9	38.8	41.4	4.9	34.2	38.6	30.9	36.6	36.0	34.3	32.2	26.2	32.6
1999	34.3	44.2	39.0	41.4	4.9	33.9	38.6	30.8	36.7	35.8	34.4	32.2	26.1	32.5
2000	34.3	44.4	39.2	41.3	4.7	33.8	38.8	30.7	36.8	35.9	34.5	32.1	26.1	32.5
2001	34.0	44.6	38.7	40.3	4.0	33.5	38.4	30.7	36.9	35.8	34.2	32.2	25.8	32.3
2002	33.9	43.2	38.4	40.5	4.2	33.6	38.0	30.9	36.5	35.6	34.2	32.3	25.8	32.1
2003	33.7	43.6	38.4	40.4	4.2	33.6	37.9	30.9	36.2	35.5	34.1	32.4	25.6	31.4
2004	33.7	44.5	38.3	40.8	4.6	33.5	37.8	30.7	36.3	35.6	34.2	32.3	25.7	31.0
2005	33.8	45.6	38.6	40.7	4.6	33.4	37.7	30.6	36.5	36.0	34.2	32.4	25.7	30.9
2006	33.9	45.6	39.0	41.1	4.4	33.4	38.0	30.5	36.6	35.8	34.6	32.6	25.7	30.9
2007	33.9	45.9	39.0	41.2	4.2	33.3	38.2	30.2	36.5	35.9	34.8	32.5	25.5	30.9
2008	33.6	45.1	38.5	40.8	3.7	33.2	38.2	30.0	36.7	35.9	34.8	32.6	25.2	30.8
2009	33.1	43.2	37.6	39.8	2.9	32.9	37.6	29.9	36.6	36.1	34.7	32.5	24.8	30.5
2010	33.4	44.6	38.4	41.1	3.8	33.3	37.9	30.2	36.3	36.2	35.1	32.2	24.8	30.7
2011	33.6	46.7	39.0	41.4	4.1	33.7	38.5	30.5	36.2	36.4	35.2	32.1	24.8	30.8
2012	33.7	46.6	39.3	41.7	4.2	33.8	38.7	30.5	36.0	36.8	35.3	32.3	25.0	30.7
2011														
January	33.4	45.6	37.7	41.0	4.1	33.5	38.3	30.3	36.3	36.4	35.2	32.1	24.6	30.7
February	33.5	45.7	38.6	41.3	4.2	33.6	38.3	30.3	36.4	36.4	35.2	32.2	24.7	30.8
March	33.6	45.8	38.6	41.5	4.2	33.7	38.5	30.4	36.3	36.2	35.2	32.2	24.8	30.8
April	33.7	46.5	38.8	41.4	4.1	33.8	38.5	30.6	36.5	36.3	35.3	32.3	24.8	30.8
May	33.6	46.7	39.2	41.5	4.1	33.6	38.5	30.4	36.4	36.4	35.2	32.3	24.7	30.8
June	33.6	47.2	39.0	41.4	4.0	33.7	38.5	30.5	36.3	36.5	35.2	32.3	24.7	30.9
July	33.7	46.4	39.1	41.4	4.1	33.8	38.5	30.7	36.4	36.5	35.2	32.4	24.8	30.7
August	33.6	46.4	39.1	41.3	4.1	33.6	38.4	30.4	35.9	36.4	35.1	32.3	24.8	30.7
September	33.7	46.7	39.0	41.4	4.1	33.7	38.6	30.5	36.1	36.6	35.2	32.4	24.8	30.8
October	33.7	47.6	38.8	41.5	4.1	33.8	38.7	30.7	36.3	36.6	35.3	32.3	24.9	30.9
November	33.7	47.0	38.9	41.5	4.1	33.8	38.6	30.6	36.2	36.5	35.2	32.4	24.8	30.8
December	33.7	47.4	39.2	41.6	4.1	33.8	38.7	30.7	36.0	36.6	35.2	32.3	24.9	30.8
2012														
January	33.8	47.9	39.2	41.8	4.2	33.9	38.6	30.8	36.2	36.6	35.3	32.3	25.0	30.8
February	33.8	47.3	39.3	41.8	4.2	33.9	38.8	30.7	36.1	36.6	35.3	32.4	24.9	30.7
March	33.7	47.2	39.3	41.6	4.2	33.8	38.6	30.7	36.0	36.6	35.2	32.4	25.0	30.8
April	33.7	47.3	39.3	41.7	4.2	33.8	38.6	30.6	35.9	36.6	35.3	32.3	24.9	30.7
May	33.7	46.3	39.0	41.6	4.2	33.7	38.6	30.5	35.8	36.6	35.2	32.3	24.9	30.6
June	33.7	46.6	39.1	41.6	4.2	33.8	38.7	30.5	36.0	36.6	35.2	32.4	25.0	30.6
July	33.7	46.8	39.1	41.7	4.2	33.7	38.6	30.4	35.8	36.6	35.3	32.2	24.9	30.7
August	33.6	45.9	39.1	41.6	4.1	33.7	38.5	30.5	35.7	36.7	35.2	32.3	24.9	30.5
September	33.7	46.0	39.4	41.5	4.2	33.6	38.6	30.3	35.7	36.7	35.3	32.3	24.9	30.6
October	33.6	45.6	39.3	41.5	4.1	33.6	38.6	30.2	35.6	36.7	35.0	32.3	24.9	30.5
November	33.7	45.4	39.5	41.6	4.1	33.8	38.6	30.5	35.8	36.9	35.2	32.3	24.9	30.5
December	33.7	45.8	39.7	41.8	4.3	33.8	38.7	30.4	35.8	36.9	35.3	32.3	25.0	30.6

. . . = Not available.

Table 10-16. Indexes of Aggregate Weekly Hours of Production and Nonsupervisory Workers on Private Nonfarm Payrolls by NAICS Supersector

(2002 = 100, seasonally adjusted.)

Year and month	Total private	Mining and logging	Construc-tion	Manu-facturing	Trade, transportation, and utilities			Information	Financial activities	Profes-sional and business services	Education and health services	Leisure and hospitality	Other services
					Total	Wholesale trade	Retail trade						
1965	54.5	121.6	55.2	122.1	59.0	...	...	55.5	42.6	29.4	26.2	41.0	29.4
1966	56.9	121.1	56.8	130.2	60.5	...	...	58.3	43.6	30.8	27.3	42.2	30.9
1967	57.1	117.0	55.4	127.8	61.1	...	...	58.6	44.9	31.9	28.4	42.9	32.4
1968	58.5	114.9	56.5	130.1	62.2	...	...	59.9	46.8	33.1	29.5	44.0	33.9
1969	60.4	118.1	61.0	131.9	64.3	...	...	61.8	49.4	34.6	30.9	45.6	35.6
1970	59.4	115.7	59.8	123.3	64.9	...	...	60.4	50.3	34.7	31.3	46.1	36.3
1971	59.1	109.9	61.0	119.3	65.1	...	...	58.7	51.1	34.7	31.4	46.9	36.5
1972	61.5	115.6	63.4	125.7	67.5	68.4	64.4	61.1	52.5	36.0	32.6	48.5	37.9
1973	64.3	117.0	66.7	132.9	69.6	71.0	66.4	64.1	54.2	37.8	34.1	50.3	39.9
1974	64.3	127.7	64.5	129.0	70.2	72.7	66.7	64.0	54.9	38.8	35.3	50.8	41.4
1975	61.2	134.9	55.2	113.9	68.9	71.8	66.4	59.1	55.0	38.9	36.2	50.9	42.6
1976	63.7	142.4	56.0	120.8	70.9	73.9	68.8	61.2	56.2	40.3	37.5	52.8	44.3
1977	66.2	151.1	59.4	125.8	73.1	76.7	70.7	63.5	58.8	42.1	39.0	54.4	46.3
1978	69.4	156.9	66.2	131.3	76.1	81.0	73.4	66.6	62.0	44.3	40.9	56.6	48.8
1979	71.7	175.2	70.6	133.3	78.3	84.6	74.7	69.0	64.7	46.3	42.7	57.9	51.2
1980	70.9	187.2	68.0	124.4	77.6	84.8	74.0	67.5	67.0	47.7	44.6	57.8	53.6
1981	71.5	206.2	64.9	123.1	78.0	86.0	74.5	67.7	68.6	49.2	46.3	58.7	55.8
1982	68.9	195.5	59.7	109.9	76.4	83.4	74.2	64.0	68.6	49.2	47.1	58.7	56.8
1983	69.9	162.8	61.0	111.6	77.2	83.3	76.0	62.1	69.8	50.7	48.8	60.4	58.9
1984	74.2	169.3	69.1	119.6	81.2	87.5	79.8	68.0	73.0	53.2	50.9	63.6	61.7
1985	76.1	162.7	73.9	117.5	83.5	89.9	82.2	69.1	76.1	55.6	53.5	66.0	65.0
1986	77.4	133.5	75.5	116.3	84.5	89.8	83.9	69.1	79.9	57.8	55.9	67.9	68.1
1987	79.6	125.2	78.1	117.8	86.5	90.5	86.3	71.5	82.3	60.3	58.5	70.5	71.5
1988	82.0	125.6	80.4	120.3	88.6	93.6	88.5	73.1	82.0	63.3	61.8	73.0	75.6
1989	84.0	123.2	81.7	120.3	90.5	95.9	90.0	74.4	82.6	66.3	65.2	74.9	79.7
1990	84.3	128.6	78.8	117.7	89.5	94.9	87.5	76.2	83.1	68.1	67.2	78.9	81.8
1991	82.5	123.8	70.1	112.8	87.4	93.3	84.8	76.1	82.0	66.7	70.2	77.3	81.1
1992	83.0	113.3	67.5	112.4	87.3	92.4	85.1	76.5	82.4	68.4	72.9	79.2	80.6
1993	85.4	110.3	71.3	113.9	89.1	92.4	86.3	78.0	84.9	71.9	75.4	82.1	82.8
1994	89.2	111.0	77.3	118.3	92.7	95.8	89.8	79.2	87.2	77.0	78.3	85.5	84.5
1995	91.5	110.3	79.9	119.0	95.1	99.2	92.3	82.5	86.9	81.2	81.2	88.5	87.0
1996	93.7	112.7	84.3	118.8	96.6	100.7	93.7	86.9	89.1	85.2	83.4	90.7	89.1
1997	97.1	117.6	88.6	121.4	98.9	103.4	95.9	90.4	92.3	91.5	86.7	93.4	91.9
1998	99.4	112.8	93.4	121.0	100.3	104.8	97.2	92.6	96.5	96.7	88.9	95.5	94.3
1999	101.5	102.9	99.7	119.0	101.9	106.2	99.5	98.5	98.1	101.7	90.6	97.8	96.2
2000	103.6	105.1	104.0	117.8	103.5	107.0	101.3	105.0	98.4	106.6	92.8	100.5	97.8
2001	102.1	108.3	103.2	108.1	101.5	102.9	100.5	106.7	99.3	104.0	96.6	100.6	99.0
2002	100.0	100.0	100.0	100.0	100.0	100.0	100.0	100.0	100.0	100.0	100.0	100.0	100.0
2003	98.7	97.4	98.4	94.5	98.6	98.0	98.9	97.0	101.3	98.7	101.4	100.0	97.4
2004	100.2	104.0	101.7	94.3	99.6	98.8	99.4	98.2	101.4	101.8	103.3	103.0	96.1
2005	102.7	114.7	108.3	93.9	101.6	101.8	100.8	99.4	103.7	106.3	106.4	106.2	96.2
2006	105.7	125.8	115.4	95.6	103.3	105.7	101.1	100.2	106.3	112.1	109.0	108.8	97.4
2007	107.3	133.5	114.7	94.4	104.8	109.2	101.8	100.1	107.6	115.3	112.5	110.8	99.3
2008	105.9	137.6	106.5	90.2	103.3	108.6	99.8	100.0	106.8	113.9	115.7	109.7	99.5
2009	98.7	117.2	85.9	76.1	96.8	99.9	94.3	93.5	103.2	105.2	117.2	105.1	96.0
2010	98.7	124.5	80.2	76.2	96.8	97.7	95.0	90.0	101.3	107.6	118.7	104.6	96.0
2011	101.3	147.4	81.7	78.3	99.7	100.7	97.7	88.9	101.2	112.4	121.3	106.9	96.8
2012	104.1	159.3	83.5	80.3	102.0	104.1	99.2	88.8	103.8	117.2	124.4	111.1	97.8
2011													
January	99.4	134.0	77.9	76.6	98.0	99.0	96.0	89.3	101.0	110.4	119.6	104.4	96.1
February	99.9	134.5	80.1	77.4	98.5	99.2	96.1	89.4	100.9	110.8	120.0	105.1	96.5
March	100.5	138.0	80.3	78.0	99.0	100.1	96.5	89.2	100.4	111.5	120.1	106.0	96.5
April	101.0	142.8	80.8	78.1	99.7	100.3	97.7	89.6	100.7	111.9	120.8	106.3	96.6
May	100.9	145.2	81.9	78.3	99.2	100.5	97.0	89.4	101.1	112.1	120.9	106.1	96.7
June	101.1	149.0	81.6	78.1	99.8	100.7	97.7	89.3	101.2	112.2	121.2	106.5	97.1
July	101.6	148.7	82.1	78.3	100.2	100.7	98.5	89.3	101.3	112.5	121.9	107.1	96.6
August	101.4	149.7	81.9	78.2	99.8	100.7	97.7	86.2	101.1	112.5	121.7	107.3	96.8
September	102.0	152.4	82.4	78.5	100.3	101.3	98.2	88.5	101.7	113.2	122.4	107.6	97.3
October	102.2	157.1	81.8	78.8	100.7	101.9	98.9	89.0	101.9	113.9	122.2	108.3	97.8
November	102.4	155.6	82.0	78.7	100.9	101.9	98.8	88.9	101.7	113.8	122.9	108.3	97.6
December	102.6	158.4	83.3	79.2	101.1	102.6	99.2	88.7	102.1	114.2	122.7	108.9	97.8
2012													
January	103.3	162.9	83.8	79.9	101.6	102.8	99.6	88.7	102.3	115.2	122.9	109.8	98.2
February	103.6	162.9	83.9	80.3	101.8	103.6	99.3	89.0	102.5	115.8	123.7	109.8	97.6
March	103.5	161.5	84.1	80.2	101.5	103.2	99.2	88.8	102.7	115.7	124.0	110.6	98.0
April	103.6	162.6	83.8	80.4	101.6	103.4	99.1	88.6	102.8	116.3	123.7	110.3	97.6
May	103.7	160.2	82.4	80.3	101.5	103.7	98.8	88.5	103.0	116.3	124.0	110.3	97.3
June	103.8	160.2	82.6	80.3	101.8	104.1	98.8	88.9	103.2	116.7	124.4	110.8	97.5
July	104.0	159.9	82.6	80.7	101.6	104.1	98.4	88.7	103.3	117.4	123.9	110.5	97.9
August	103.8	156.6	82.5	80.3	101.8	104.0	98.9	88.5	103.7	117.4	124.5	110.9	97.3
September	104.2	156.7	83.2	79.9	101.6	104.2	98.4	88.2	103.9	117.9	124.7	111.3	97.7
October	104.2	154.4	83.3	80.0	101.9	104.4	98.4	87.9	104.1	117.4	124.8	111.5	97.6
November	104.7	153.9	84.4	80.2	102.8	104.7	99.7	88.7	104.6	118.1	125.0	111.6	97.8
December	104.9	155.5	85.5	80.7	103.1	105.0	99.4	88.7	104.7	118.7	125.2	112.4	98.1

. . . = Not available.

Table 10-17. Average Hourly Earnings of Production and Nonsupervisory Workers on Private Nonfarm Payrolls by NAICS Supersector

(Dollars, seasonally adjusted.)

Year and month	Total private	Mining and logging	Construction	Manu-facturing	Trade, transportation, and utilities			Information	Financial activities	Profes-sional and business services	Education and health services	Leisure and hospitality	Other services
					Total	Wholesale trade	Retail trade						
1965	2.63	2.87	3.23	2.49	2.94	...	...	4.47	2.38	3.28	2.12	1.17	1.25
1966	2.73	3.00	3.41	2.60	3.04	...	...	4.56	2.47	3.39	2.23	1.26	1.37
1967	2.85	3.14	3.63	2.71	3.15	...	...	4.68	2.58	3.51	2.36	1.37	1.49
1968	3.02	3.30	3.92	2.89	3.32	...	...	4.85	2.75	3.65	2.49	1.53	1.62
1969	3.22	3.54	4.30	3.07	3.48	...	...	5.05	2.92	3.84	2.68	1.69	1.81
1970	3.40	3.77	4.74	3.24	3.65	...	...	5.25	3.07	4.04	2.88	1.82	2.01
1971	3.63	3.99	5.17	3.45	3.86	...	...	5.53	3.23	4.26	3.11	1.95	2.24
1972	3.90	4.28	5.55	3.70	4.23	4.58	3.52	5.87	3.37	4.50	3.33	2.08	2.46
1973	4.14	4.59	5.89	3.97	4.46	4.80	3.69	6.17	3.55	4.72	3.54	2.20	2.67
1974	4.43	5.09	6.29	4.31	4.74	5.11	3.92	6.52	3.80	5.01	3.82	2.40	2.95
1975	4.73	5.68	6.78	4.71	5.01	5.45	4.14	6.92	4.08	5.29	4.09	2.58	3.21
1976	5.06	6.19	7.17	5.10	5.31	5.75	4.36	7.37	4.30	5.60	4.39	2.78	3.51
1977	5.44	6.70	7.56	5.55	5.67	6.12	4.65	7.84	4.58	5.95	4.72	3.03	3.84
1978	5.88	7.44	8.11	6.05	6.11	6.61	5.00	8.34	4.93	6.32	5.07	3.33	4.19
1979	6.34	8.20	8.71	6.57	6.56	7.12	5.34	8.86	5.31	6.71	5.44	3.63	4.56
1980	6.85	8.97	9.37	7.15	7.04	7.68	5.71	9.47	5.82	7.22	5.93	3.98	5.05
1981	7.44	9.89	10.24	7.87	7.55	8.28	6.09	10.21	6.34	7.80	6.49	4.36	5.61
1982	7.87	10.64	11.04	8.36	7.91	8.81	6.34	10.76	6.82	8.30	7.00	4.63	6.11
1983	8.20	11.14	11.36	8.70	8.23	9.27	6.60	11.18	7.32	8.70	7.39	4.89	6.51
1984	8.49	11.54	11.56	9.05	8.45	9.61	6.73	11.50	7.65	8.98	7.67	4.99	6.79
1985	8.74	11.87	11.75	9.40	8.60	9.88	6.83	11.81	7.97	9.28	7.98	5.10	7.10
1986	8.93	12.14	11.92	9.60	8.74	10.07	6.93	12.08	8.37	9.55	8.25	5.20	7.38
1987	9.14	12.17	12.15	9.77	8.92	10.32	7.02	12.36	8.73	9.85	8.57	5.30	7.69
1988	9.44	12.45	12.52	10.05	9.15	10.71	7.23	12.63	9.07	10.22	8.96	5.50	8.08
1989	9.80	12.90	12.98	10.35	9.46	11.12	7.46	12.99	9.54	10.69	9.46	5.76	8.58
1990	10.20	13.40	13.42	10.78	9.83	11.58	7.71	13.40	9.98	11.14	10.00	6.02	9.08
1991	10.52	13.82	13.65	11.13	10.08	11.95	7.89	13.90	10.43	11.50	10.49	6.22	9.39
1992	10.77	14.09	13.81	11.40	10.30	12.21	8.12	14.29	10.86	11.78	10.87	6.36	9.66
1993	11.05	14.12	14.04	11.70	10.55	12.57	8.36	14.86	11.38	11.96	11.21	6.48	9.90
1994	11.34	14.41	14.38	12.04	10.80	12.93	8.61	15.32	11.84	12.15	11.50	6.62	10.18
1995	11.66	14.78	14.73	12.34	11.10	13.34	8.85	15.68	12.31	12.53	11.80	6.79	10.51
1996	12.05	15.09	15.11	12.75	11.46	13.80	9.21	16.30	12.75	13.00	12.17	6.99	10.85
1997	12.51	15.57	15.67	13.14	11.90	14.41	9.59	17.14	13.28	13.57	12.56	7.32	11.29
1998	13.02	16.20	16.23	13.45	12.40	15.07	10.05	17.67	14.00	14.27	13.00	7.67	11.79
1999	13.49	16.33	16.80	13.85	12.82	15.62	10.45	18.40	14.55	14.85	13.44	7.96	12.26
2000	14.02	16.55	17.48	14.32	13.31	16.28	10.87	19.07	15.04	15.52	13.95	8.32	12.73
2001	14.55	17.00	18.00	14.76	13.70	16.77	11.29	19.80	15.65	16.33	14.64	8.57	13.27
2002	14.97	17.19	18.52	15.29	14.02	16.98	11.67	20.20	16.25	16.80	15.21	8.81	13.72
2003	15.38	17.56	18.95	15.74	14.34	17.36	11.90	21.01	17.21	17.21	15.64	9.00	13.84
2004	15.70	18.07	19.23	16.14	14.58	17.65	12.08	21.40	17.58	17.48	16.15	9.15	13.98
2005	16.13	18.72	19.46	16.56	14.92	18.16	12.36	22.06	17.98	18.08	16.71	9.38	14.34
2006	16.76	19.90	20.02	16.81	15.39	18.91	12.57	23.23	18.83	19.13	17.38	9.75	14.77
2007	17.44	20.97	20.95	17.26	15.78	19.59	12.75	23.96	19.67	20.15	18.11	10.41	15.42
2008	18.08	22.50	21.87	17.75	16.16	20.13	12.87	24.78	20.32	21.18	18.87	10.84	16.09
2009	18.63	23.29	22.66	18.24	16.48	20.84	13.01	25.45	20.90	22.35	19.49	11.12	16.59
2010	19.07	23.82	23.22	18.61	16.82	21.54	13.25	25.87	21.55	22.78	20.12	11.31	17.06
2011	19.46	24.50	23.65	18.93	17.15	21.97	13.51	26.62	21.93	23.12	20.77	11.45	17.32
2012	19.77	25.79	23.98	19.08	17.42	22.24	13.81	27.01	22.83	23.28	21.09	11.62	17.59
2011													
January	19.33	24.24	23.53	18.90	17.05	21.90	13.39	26.36	21.76	23.04	20.49	11.35	17.26
February	19.34	24.17	23.53	18.90	17.08	21.93	13.40	26.45	21.67	23.03	20.52	11.37	17.21
March	19.34	24.29	23.47	18.90	17.07	21.85	13.43	26.51	21.76	22.98	20.56	11.39	17.24
April	19.39	23.89	23.58	18.90	17.10	21.93	13.46	26.70	21.85	23.08	20.57	11.41	17.28
May	19.44	24.40	23.57	18.93	17.11	21.98	13.42	26.66	21.80	23.10	20.71	11.50	17.29
June	19.45	24.39	23.59	18.91	17.11	21.97	13.45	26.46	21.80	23.18	20.75	11.47	17.33
July	19.51	24.55	23.63	18.93	17.18	22.12	13.52	26.54	21.91	23.25	20.85	11.49	17.35
August	19.50	24.63	23.77	18.90	17.18	22.02	13.50	26.59	21.93	23.13	20.92	11.48	17.32
September	19.52	24.67	23.77	18.92	17.19	22.00	13.50	26.68	22.02	23.10	20.91	11.49	17.37
October	19.56	24.87	23.72	18.96	17.24	22.06	13.60	26.78	22.09	23.15	20.95	11.50	17.39
November	19.59	24.95	23.71	18.96	17.27	22.01	13.69	26.78	22.23	23.22	20.96	11.53	17.41
December	19.58	24.91	23.76	18.99	17.25	21.98	13.68	26.81	22.32	23.09	20.96	11.54	17.43
2012													
January	19.61	24.85	23.73	19.03	17.28	22.09	13.68	26.78	22.39	23.12	21.00	11.56	17.43
February	19.64	25.49	23.80	19.02	17.31	22.03	13.74	26.74	22.47	23.11	21.01	11.57	17.47
March	19.68	25.58	23.91	19.02	17.37	22.14	13.79	26.83	22.50	23.23	21.02	11.60	17.50
April	19.72	25.92	23.90	19.08	17.40	22.17	13.78	26.93	22.60	23.22	21.05	11.62	17.50
May	19.70	25.68	23.93	19.03	17.41	22.14	13.82	26.80	22.68	23.19	21.03	11.61	17.54
June	19.75	25.81	23.95	19.08	17.47	22.22	13.88	26.85	22.75	23.19	21.10	11.63	17.57
July	19.77	25.99	24.02	19.11	17.46	22.22	13.83	27.04	22.82	23.21	21.08	11.64	17.60
August	19.76	25.75	23.98	19.07	17.41	22.18	13.80	27.00	22.86	23.23	21.09	11.65	17.63
September	19.80	25.74	24.01	19.07	17.45	22.23	13.83	27.16	22.96	23.29	21.14	11.64	17.66
October	19.82	25.93	24.06	19.08	17.47	22.23	13.87	27.06	23.06	23.28	21.16	11.66	17.69
November	19.88	26.13	24.08	19.17	17.49	22.40	13.84	27.24	23.21	23.40	21.19	11.65	17.71
December	19.93	26.21	24.15	19.17	17.49	22.40	13.85	27.48	23.37	23.48	21.25	11.67	17.77

. . . = Not available.

Table 10-18. Average Weekly Earnings of Production and Nonsupervisory Workers on Private Nonfarm Payrolls by NAICS Supersector

(Dollars, seasonally adjusted.)

| Year and month | Total private | Mining and logging | Construc-tion | Manu-facturing | Trade, transportation, and utilities | | | Information | Financial activities | Profes-sional and business services | Education and health services | Leisure and hospitality | Other services |
					Total	Wholesale trade	Retail trade						
1965	101.51	125.48	122.35	102.69	116.36	...	...	171.24	88.50	122.30	74.84	38.06	45.30
1966	105.23	132.50	130.11	107.47	118.78	...	...	174.52	91.83	125.53	78.04	40.34	48.94
1967	108.07	137.76	138.55	109.85	121.57	...	...	176.09	95.35	128.34	81.34	43.06	52.69
1968	113.82	145.26	148.22	117.73	126.69	...	...	182.65	101.18	132.47	85.02	47.07	56.81
1969	120.70	157.11	164.88	124.74	132.13	...	...	190.18	107.91	139.37	91.46	51.29	63.44
1970	125.79	165.82	179.11	128.84	137.15	...	...	195.24	112.32	144.76	97.23	54.57	69.67
1971	133.22	174.18	194.70	137.59	144.11	...	...	204.50	117.60	151.51	103.57	58.39	76.58
1972	143.87	188.76	205.04	150.23	158.09	181.98	123.57	218.72	122.86	159.88	111.12	61.78	84.14
1973	152.59	201.43	219.32	161.59	165.61	190.33	128.16	230.48	129.32	167.40	117.85	64.92	91.06
1974	161.61	222.24	233.24	172.37	174.18	200.53	134.39	241.07	137.71	176.47	126.50	69.90	99.98
1975	170.29	248.38	249.70	185.69	182.61	212.85	140.99	253.21	147.75	185.81	134.83	74.49	108.67
1976	182.65	273.69	267.00	204.41	192.62	224.66	147.21	270.80	155.54	195.61	143.47	79.47	117.85
1977	195.58	299.46	279.61	224.01	203.87	239.57	154.51	288.29	165.47	206.78	153.38	85.20	128.12
1978	210.29	334.27	302.27	244.49	217.53	258.75	163.74	306.71	177.96	218.42	163.48	92.16	138.74
1979	225.69	366.58	326.55	263.99	232.36	278.74	173.18	324.51	190.72	231.16	174.80	99.47	150.47
1980	241.07	402.51	351.49	283.35	246.60	298.24	182.25	344.38	209.21	247.64	190.16	107.52	166.32
1981	261.53	446.10	382.75	312.74	263.93	322.08	193.97	370.36	228.21	267.46	208.06	117.49	184.77
1982	273.10	469.10	410.39	325.07	274.09	340.84	200.74	385.82	245.16	284.11	224.53	124.14	201.49
1983	286.43	488.89	427.00	348.89	284.76	359.98	208.81	404.89	262.83	298.74	237.50	130.82	214.87
1984	298.26	514.77	441.28	367.77	292.99	373.78	212.82	420.45	276.50	308.24	245.48	133.49	223.33
1985	304.62	529.62	448.35	380.60	295.81	383.22	213.38	430.86	287.66	317.41	254.50	134.71	232.81
1986	309.78	529.20	451.22	390.46	298.07	389.73	214.52	439.84	302.32	327.30	263.73	136.34	242.33
1987	317.39	529.72	463.78	400.00	304.10	397.39	218.05	450.77	314.01	337.57	273.81	139.45	252.58
1988	326.48	539.63	478.74	412.62	309.58	411.71	223.67	455.59	322.87	349.89	286.89	144.51	265.83
1989	338.34	568.55	497.43	423.58	319.40	427.40	229.14	468.77	339.46	365.93	303.02	150.29	282.09
1990	349.72	602.43	513.43	436.13	331.55	444.48	235.56	479.50	354.63	380.61	319.27	156.32	297.88
1991	358.51	625.46	520.41	449.83	339.10	459.17	240.13	495.14	369.75	391.06	334.55	159.20	306.75
1992	368.25	628.94	525.13	464.43	348.60	470.41	249.66	511.95	386.34	400.64	348.29	163.70	315.08
1993	378.94	634.77	539.81	480.80	359.51	484.46	256.89	535.19	403.68	406.20	359.08	167.54	322.69
1994	391.28	653.13	558.53	501.95	370.38	501.14	265.74	551.21	420.18	414.16	368.14	172.27	332.44
1995	400.22	670.40	571.57	509.26	378.79	515.14	272.63	564.92	437.26	426.54	377.73	175.74	342.36
1996	413.47	695.04	588.48	526.55	390.67	533.36	282.74	592.45	453.16	442.81	388.30	181.02	352.68
1997	432.05	720.07	609.48	548.26	407.63	559.39	295.94	622.37	475.03	465.51	404.65	190.66	368.63
1998	448.76	727.19	629.75	557.12	423.33	582.21	310.33	646.52	504.06	490.13	418.82	200.82	384.25
1999	463.35	721.77	655.11	573.29	434.31	602.77	321.71	675.47	520.98	510.99	431.35	208.05	398.77
2000	481.36	734.88	685.78	591.01	449.96	631.24	333.41	700.92	540.39	535.07	449.29	217.20	413.30
2001	494.05	757.96	695.86	595.19	459.53	643.45	346.16	731.18	560.46	557.84	473.39	220.73	428.64
2002	507.03	741.97	711.82	618.62	471.27	644.38	360.84	737.94	578.94	574.60	492.74	227.31	439.87
2003	518.41	765.94	727.00	636.03	481.14	657.29	367.18	760.84	611.65	587.02	505.69	230.49	434.41
2004	529.23	804.01	735.55	658.52	488.51	666.79	371.13	776.72	625.50	597.54	523.78	234.86	433.04
2005	544.44	853.87	750.37	673.30	498.46	685.00	377.58	805.11	646.48	618.71	544.59	241.36	443.40
2006	567.89	907.95	781.59	690.88	514.37	718.50	383.12	850.64	673.48	662.27	564.94	250.34	456.50
2007	590.24	962.63	816.23	711.53	525.91	748.94	385.00	874.45	706.33	700.82	590.09	265.54	477.06
2008	608.11	1 014.69	842.61	724.46	536.11	769.62	386.21	908.78	729.61	737.90	613.73	273.39	495.57
2009	617.50	1 006.67	851.76	726.12	541.88	784.49	388.57	931.08	755.08	775.81	628.45	275.95	506.26
2010	637.18	1 063.11	891.83	765.18	559.63	816.50	400.07	939.85	780.19	798.54	646.65	280.87	523.70
2011	654.73	1 144.64	921.84	784.29	577.71	845.44	412.09	964.85	798.71	813.37	670.24	283.82	532.63
2012	666.99	1 201.92	942.75	794.81	588.70	860.74	421.85	971.22	840.57	822.19	682.74	290.43	539.31
2011													
January	645.62	1 105.34	887.08	774.90	571.18	838.77	405.72	956.87	792.06	811.01	657.73	279.21	529.88
February	647.89	1 104.57	908.26	780.57	573.89	839.92	406.02	962.78	788.79	810.66	660.74	280.84	530.07
March	649.82	1 112.48	905.94	784.35	575.26	841.23	408.27	962.31	787.71	808.90	662.03	282.47	530.99
April	653.44	1 110.89	914.90	782.46	577.98	844.31	411.88	974.55	793.16	814.72	664.41	282.97	532.22
May	653.18	1 139.48	923.94	785.60	574.90	846.23	407.97	970.42	793.52	813.12	668.93	284.05	532.53
June	653.52	1 151.21	920.01	782.87	576.61	845.85	410.23	960.50	795.70	815.94	670.23	283.31	535.50
July	657.49	1 139.12	923.93	783.70	580.68	851.62	415.06	966.06	799.72	818.40	675.54	284.95	532.65
August	655.20	1 142.83	929.41	780.57	577.25	845.57	410.40	954.58	798.25	811.86	675.72	284.70	531.72
September	657.82	1 152.09	927.03	783.29	579.30	849.20	411.75	963.15	805.93	813.12	677.48	284.95	535.00
October	659.17	1 183.81	920.34	786.84	582.71	853.72	417.52	972.11	808.49	817.20	676.69	286.35	537.35
November	660.18	1 172.65	922.32	786.84	583.73	849.59	418.91	969.44	811.40	817.34	679.10	285.94	536.23
December	659.85	1 180.73	931.39	789.98	583.05	850.63	419.98	965.16	816.91	812.77	677.01	287.35	536.84
2012													
January	662.82	1 190.32	930.22	795.45	585.79	852.67	421.34	969.44	819.47	816.14	678.30	289.00	536.84
February	663.83	1 205.68	935.34	795.04	586.81	854.76	421.82	965.31	822.40	815.78	680.72	288.09	536.33
March	663.22	1 207.38	939.66	791.23	587.11	854.60	423.35	965.88	823.50	817.70	681.05	290.00	539.00
April	664.56	1 226.02	939.27	795.64	588.12	855.76	421.67	966.79	827.16	819.67	679.92	289.34	537.25
May	663.89	1 188.98	933.27	791.65	586.72	854.60	421.51	959.44	830.09	816.29	679.27	289.09	536.72
June	665.58	1 202.75	936.45	793.73	590.49	859.91	423.34	966.60	832.65	816.29	683.64	290.75	537.64
July	666.25	1 216.33	939.18	796.89	588.40	857.69	420.43	968.03	835.21	819.31	678.78	289.84	540.32
August	663.94	1 181.93	937.62	793.31	586.72	853.93	420.90	963.90	838.96	817.70	681.21	290.09	537.72
September	667.26	1 184.04	945.99	791.41	586.32	858.08	419.05	969.61	842.63	822.14	682.82	289.84	540.40
October	665.95	1 182.41	945.56	791.82	586.99	858.08	418.87	963.34	846.30	814.80	683.47	290.33	539.55
November	669.96	1 186.30	951.16	797.47	591.16	864.64	422.12	975.19	856.45	823.68	684.44	290.09	540.16
December	671.64	1 200.42	958.76	801.31	591.16	866.88	421.04	983.78	862.35	828.84	686.38	291.75	543.76

. . . = Not available.

Section 10c: Other Significant Labor Market Data

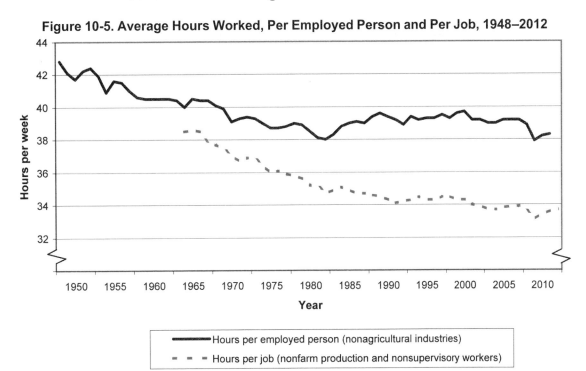

Figure 10-5. Average Hours Worked, Per Employed Person and Per Job, 1948–2012

- This section of *Business Statistics* includes indicators of hours and earnings from the Current Population Statistics (household) survey that are, for some purposes, more appropriate than similarly-named indicators produced by the payroll survey and shown in the previous section. It also includes annual employment data from the Bureau of Economic Analysis, produced as part of the National Income and Product Accounts (NIPAS), that provide a consistent historical record of U.S. employment from 1929 through 2000.

- Figure 10-5 above shows annual averages of hours worked per week reported by all persons in the household survey employed in nonagricultural industries. (Table 10-19 reports average workweeks for several worker groups; this one was chosen for the graph because it has the longest history.) Along with the recession dips expected in any measure of the average workweek, it displays a clear downward trend through the early 1970s, but no trend since then. The recession low in 2009 was actually higher than the recession low in 1982. The 2000 peak is equal to the 1969 level. (Table 10-19)

- For comparison, average weekly hours for nonfarm production and nonsupervisory workers are also graphed in Figure 10-5. These are the workweeks reported by employers in the Current Employment Statistics (payroll) survey and they pertain to jobs, not to workers. (Table 10-15) This CES measure of "hours per job" represents roughly the same workers as those in the "hours per employed person" measure shown in the graph, and was selected for the graph because it has the longest available history. But it is increasingly pulled downward by the increasing prevalence of part-time work. It is not a good indicator of either the level or the trend of the amount of work being done each week by the typical American worker. (Table 10-19)

- A look at some of the other categories in Table 10-19 confirms the absence of any downtrend in the workers' workweek in recent years. Note, for example, that men reported working an average of 41.7 hours in both 2007 and 1976, and women actually reported working longer—36.1 hours in 2007—against 34.1 hours in 1976. (Table 10-19)

Table 10-19. Hours at Work, Current Population Survey

(Hours per week.)

Year and month	Hours per person, all industries				Hours per person, nonagricultural industries			Memorandum: average weekly hours per job, total private nonfarm, from CES survey	
					All workers		Wage and salary workers		
	Total	Men	Women	Persons who usually work full-time	Total	Usually work full-time		All employees	Production and nonsupervisory workers
1948	42.8	...	...	...	41.6	...	...	...	...
1949	42.1	...	...	...	40.9	...	...	...	...
1950	41.7	...	...	...	40.7	...	...	...	...
1951	42.2	...	...	...	41.3	...	...	...	...
1952	42.4	...	...	...	41.6	...	...	...	...
1953	41.9	...	...	...	41.1	...	...	...	...
1954	40.9	...	...	...	40.0	...	...	...	...
1955	41.6	...	...	...	40.9	...	...	...	...
1956	41.5	43.8	36.5	...	40.9	...	...	...	...
1957	41.0	43.4	36.1	...	40.5	...	...	...	...
1958	40.6	42.9	35.8	...	40.1	...	...	...	...
1959	40.5	42.8	35.6	...	40.0	...	...	...	...
1960	40.5	43.0	35.4	...	40.0	...	...	...	...
1961	40.5	43.0	35.3	...	40.1	...	...	...	...
1962	40.5	43.2	35.2	...	40.1	...	...	...	...
1963	40.4	43.2	35.1	...	40.1	...	...	...	...
1964	40.0	42.8	34.7	...	39.7	...	...	...	38.5
1965	40.5	43.3	35.1	...	40.2	...	...	...	38.6
1966	40.4	43.2	35.2	...	40.1	...	...	...	38.5
1967	40.4	43.3	35.2	...	40.0	...	...	...	37.9
1968	40.1	43.0	34.9	...	39.7	...	...	...	37.7
1969	39.9	42.9	34.9	...	39.5	...	...	...	37.5
1970	39.1	42.0	34.2	...	38.7	...	...	...	37.0
1971	39.3	42.2	34.3	...	38.9	...	...	...	36.7
1972	39.4	42.3	34.5	...	39.0	...	...	...	36.9
1973	39.3	42.4	34.4	...	39.0	...	...	...	36.9
1974	39.0	42.0	34.3	...	38.7	...	...	...	36.4
1975	38.7	41.6	34.1	...	38.4	...	...	...	36.0
1976	38.7	41.7	34.1	...	38.4	...	38.1	...	36.1
1977	38.8	41.9	34.2	...	38.5	...	38.3	...	35.9
1978	39.0	42.1	34.5	...	38.7	...	38.4	...	35.8
1979	38.9	42.0	34.5	...	38.6	...	38.4	...	35.6
1980	38.5	41.5	34.5	...	38.3	...	38.1	...	35.2
1981	38.1	41.1	34.1	...	37.9	...	37.7	...	35.2
1982	38.0	40.9	34.1	...	37.7	...	37.6	...	34.7
1983	38.3	41.2	34.5	...	38.1	...	37.9	...	34.9
1984	38.8	41.8	34.9	...	38.6	...	38.4	...	35.1
1985	39.0	42.0	35.2	...	38.9	...	38.7	...	34.9
1986	39.1	42.1	35.4	...	38.9	...	38.8	...	34.7
1987	39.0	42.0	35.3	...	38.8	...	38.7	...	34.7
1988	39.4	42.4	35.7	...	39.3	...	39.1	...	34.6
1989	39.6	42.6	35.8	...	39.4	...	39.3	...	34.5
1990	39.4	42.3	35.8	...	39.3	...	39.2	...	34.3
1991	39.2	42.0	35.8	...	39.1	...	39.0	...	34.1
1992	38.9	41.7	35.6	...	38.8	...	38.7	...	34.2
1993	39.4	42.2	36.0	...	39.3	...	39.2	...	34.3
1994	39.2	42.2	35.5	43.4	39.1	43.3	39.1	...	34.5
1995	39.3	42.3	35.6	43.4	39.2	43.2	39.2	...	34.3
1996	39.3	42.3	35.7	43.3	39.2	43.2	39.2	...	34.3
1997	39.5	42.4	36.0	43.4	39.4	43.3	39.4	...	34.5
1998	39.3	42.2	35.8	43.2	39.2	43.1	39.2	...	34.5
1999	39.6	42.4	36.2	43.4	39.5	43.3	39.5	...	34.3
2000	39.7	42.5	36.4	43.4	39.6	43.3	39.6	...	34.3
2001	39.2	41.9	36.1	42.9	39.2	42.8	39.2	...	34.0
2002	39.2	41.8	36.0	42.9	39.1	42.8	39.1	...	33.9
2003	39.0	41.7	35.9	42.9	39.0	42.7	39.0	...	33.7
2004	39.0	41.7	35.9	42.9	39.0	42.8	39.0	...	33.7
2005	39.2	41.8	36.1	42.9	39.1	42.8	39.1	...	33.8
2006	39.2	41.8	36.2	42.9	39.2	42.8	39.2	...	33.9
2007	39.2	41.7	36.1	42.8	39.1	42.7	39.2	34.6	33.9
2008	38.9	41.3	36.1	42.6	38.8	42.5	39.0	34.5	33.6
2009	37.9	40.2	35.3	41.9	37.8	41.8	38.0	33.9	33.1
2010	38.2	40.5	35.5	42.2	38.1	42.2	38.3	34.1	33.4
2011	38.3	40.6	35.6	42.4	38.2	42.3	38.4	34.4	33.6
2012	38.5	...	...	...	...	...	...	34.5	33.7

. . . = Not available.

Figure 10-6. Real Median Weekly Earnings, 1979–2012
(full-time workers, age 25 years and over)

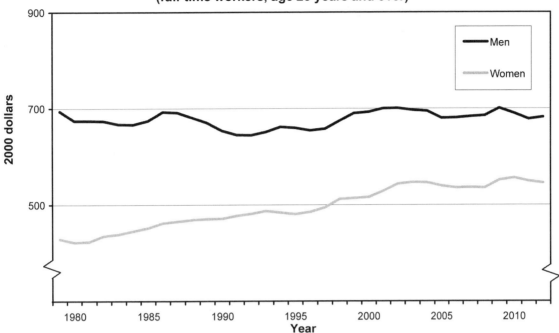

- "Median usual weekly earnings of full-time wage and salary workers," as shown in Table 10-20, are derived quarterly from the Current Population Survey, not from the payroll survey that provides the weekly earnings shown in Tables 10-9, 10-13, and 10-18. That is, they are collected from individual households in the CPS sample, providing better approximations of the paychecks of typical breadwinners than the payroll data on average weekly earnings (AWE). (See the Notes and Definitions to this chapter.)

- Focusing on workers 25 and over, women's earnings were moving closer to men's over most of the period covered in this survey, rising from 61.8 percent in 1979 to 78.5 percent in 2007, the latest high-employment year. Since then the ratio gained even further—to 80 percent in 2012—as men experienced real income losses. (Table 10-20)

- As Figure 10-6 shows, typical workers age 25 and over of both sexes lost ground in real terms in many recent years. The median man's real earnings in 2012 were slightly below those in 2000, and the median woman's only up at a 0.5 percent annual rate since then. (Table 10-20) In contrast, business productivity growth over that 12-year period was 2.3 percent per year. (Table 9-3A)

- Taking a longer look at the entire period shown here, men's real earnings have been essentially stagnant for the entire 33 years, while women's have increased 0.7 percent per year. For both sexes these earnings fall short of what might have been expected from the 2.0 percent rate of increase in productivity over those 33 years. (Tables 10-20 and 9-3A)

Table 10-20. Median Usual Weekly Earnings of Full-Time Wage and Salary Workers

(Current dollars, except as noted; not seasonally adjusted.)

Year and quarter	Total, 16 years and over	Sex and age								Race and ethnicity			
		Men, 16 years and over				Women, 16 years and over				White	Black or African American	Asian	Hispanic or Latino ethnicity
		Total	16 to 24 years	25 years and over		Total	16 to 24 years	25 years and over					
				Current dollars	2000 dollars [1]			Current dollars	2000 dollars [1]				
1979	241	292	196	314	694	182	154	194	429	247	198	. . .	. . .
1980	262	313	208	339	675	201	167	212	422	268	212	. . .	. . .
1981	284	340	218	371	674	219	180	233	423	290	234	. . .	. . .
1982	302	364	224	393	673	239	191	254	435	309	245	. . .	. . .
1983	313	379	223	406	667	252	197	267	439	319	261	. . .	. . .
1984	326	392	231	422	666	265	203	282	445	336	269	. . .	. . .
1985	344	407	240	442	675	277	210	296	452	355	277	. . .	. . .
1986	359	419	245	462	693	291	218	308	462	370	291	. . .	277
1987	374	434	257	477	692	303	226	321	465	383	301	. . .	284
1988	385	449	261	487	681	315	235	335	469	394	314	. . .	290
1989	399	468	271	500	670	328	246	351	471	409	319	. . .	298
1990	412	481	282	512	654	346	254	369	471	424	329	. . .	304
1991	426	493	285	523	645	366	266	387	477	442	348	. . .	312
1992	440	501	284	536	645	380	267	400	481	458	357	. . .	322
1993	459	510	288	555	651	393	273	415	487	475	369	. . .	331
1994	467	522	294	576	662	399	276	421	484	484	371	. . .	324
1995	479	538	303	588	660	406	275	428	480	494	383	. . .	329
1996	490	557	307	599	655	418	284	444	485	506	387	. . .	339
1997	503	579	317	615	658	431	292	462	494	519	400	. . .	351
1998	523	598	334	639	674	456	305	485	512	545	426	. . .	370
1999	549	618	356	668	690	473	324	497	514	573	445	. . .	385
2000	576	641	375	693	693	493	344	516	516	590	474	615	399
2001	596	670	391	720	700	512	353	543	528	610	491	639	417
2002	608	679	391	732	701	529	367	568	544	623	498	658	424
2003	620	695	398	744	697	552	371	584	547	636	514	693	440
2004	638	713	400	762	695	573	375	599	546	657	525	708	456
2005	651	722	409	771	680	585	381	612	540	672	520	753	471
2006	671	743	418	797	681	600	395	627	536	690	554	784	486
2007	695	766	443	823	684	614	409	646	537	716	569	830	503
2008	722	798	461	857	685	638	420	670	536	742	589	861	529
2009	739	819	458	873	701	657	424	687	552	757	601	880	541
2010	747	824	443	874	690	669	422	704	556	765	611	855	535
2011	756	832	455	886	678	684	421	718	550	775	615	866	549
2012	768	854	468	910	683	691	416	727	545	792	621	920	568
2005													
1st quarter	653	729	401	775	696	586	380	610	547	677	513	738	470
2nd quarter	643	713	407	762	675	580	374	608	538	663	518	743	473
3rd quarter	649	716	407	768	672	585	379	615	538	667	520	761	462
4th quarter	659	731	418	778	677	588	389	614	534	682	533	767	479
2006													
1st quarter	668	744	417	793	686	600	388	624	540	688	560	766	487
2nd quarter	659	731	421	783	667	593	395	619	527	678	534	765	485
3rd quarter	675	749	409	808	684	599	393	629	532	692	555	798	485
4th quarter	682	749	429	800	683	609	403	638	545	702	569	809	489
2007													
1st quarter	693	759	451	811	686	615	414	646	546	714	561	798	502
2nd quarter	690	763	436	819	679	607	404	635	527	713	562	827	503
3rd quarter	695	767	430	831	687	616	398	654	541	713	578	842	502
4th quarter	700	774	459	831	682	618	421	649	533	722	574	856	507
2008													
1st quarter	719	790	466	848	688	637	419	666	541	742	582	842	520
2nd quarter	719	800	469	862	685	634	415	668	531	738	591	855	537
3rd quarter	720	796	446	857	673	631	406	666	523	739	589	854	529
4th quarter	728	807	462	859	694	650	449	679	549	748	593	889	535
2009													
1st quarter	738	823	461	879	714	649	448	679	552	758	577	869	545
2nd quarter	734	815	450	872	701	652	413	679	546	754	592	909	547
3rd quarter	738	812	448	870	695	657	415	691	552	753	607	877	527
4th quarter	748	825	476	871	694	670	436	700	558	763	629	877	547
2010													
1st quarter	754	844	473	887	704	665	422	698	554	772	610	859	554
2nd quarter	740	810	442	861	680	672	417	704	556	756	607	873	529
3rd quarter	740	813	424	869	686	662	419	702	554	759	611	854	522
4th quarter	752	830	449	878	691	679	436	709	558	772	614	828	539
2011													
1st quarter	755	829	470	880	684	683	426	716	556	774	604	831	549
2nd quarter	753	825	446	884	675	689	417	720	550	770	623	872	565
3rd quarter	753	827	440	888	675	673	422	713	542	772	616	869	545
4th quarter	764	843	466	893	680	688	420	724	551	786	621	880	537
2012													
1st quarter	769	848	469	904	683	697	421	731	552	793	635	918	567
2nd quarter	771	865	460	918	688	689	409	727	545	792	637	930	576
3rd quarter	758	828	459	891	666	685	414	725	542	780	606	915	556
4th quarter	775	875	480	926	692	692	422	725	542	802	615	910	571

[1]Converted to 2000 dollars by the editor using CPI-U-RS. See notes and definitions.
. . . = Not available.

Table 10-21. Employment by SIC Industry, Historical Annual

(Full-time and part-time employees, thousands.)

NIPA Table 6.4A, B, and C

Year	Total employ-ment	Total domestic	Total private industries	Agriculture, forestry, and fisheries	Mining	Construc-tion	Manufacturing — Total manu-facturing	Durable goods	Nondur-able goods	Transpor-tation and public utilities	Wholesale trade	Retail trade	Finance, insurance, and real estate	Services
1942 SIC														
1929	37 699	37 699	34 088	3 556	993	1 484	10 428	5 238	5 190	3 989	1 757	4 684	1 520	5 677
1930	35 590	35 590	31 811	3 337	932	1 366	9 309	4 457	4 852	3 742	1 693	4 469	1 491	5 472
1931	32 724	32 723	28 590	3 252	813	1 198	7 895	3 497	4 398	3 282	1 530	4 148	1 423	5 049
1932	29 445	29 444	25 071	3 028	672	907	6 678	2 724	3 954	2 826	1 380	3 688	1 358	4 534
1933	30 940	30 939	25 038	2 995	693	703	7 204	2 893	4 311	2 684	1 377	3 699	1 309	4 374
1934	34 238	34 237	27 417	2 986	822	806	8 364	3 587	4 777	2 774	1 492	4 075	1 332	4 766
1935	35 577	35 576	28 426	3 013	840	866	8 904	3 941	4 963	2 808	1 507	4 200	1 352	4 936
1936	38 599	38 598	30 548	3 106	897	1 104	9 645	4 460	5 185	2 973	1 612	4 543	1 401	5 267
1937	39 701	39 700	32 508	3 083	955	1 082	10 591	5 130	5 461	3 140	1 770	4 904	1 445	5 538
1938	38 322	38 321	30 124	2 949	859	1 055	9 131	4 085	5 046	2 837	1 767	4 780	1 436	5 310
1939	39 633	39 632	31 612	2 859	832	1 219	9 967	4 609	5 358	2 943	1 833	4 992	1 470	5 497
1940	41 437	41 435	33 518	2 809	927	1 285	10 882	5 367	5 515	3 064	1 899	5 321	1 518	5 813
1941	45 785	45 782	37 210	2 779	975	1 774	13 137	6 999	6 138	3 311	2 014	5 754	1 559	5 907
1942	50 219	50 214	39 728	2 692	985	2 131	15 284	8 846	6 438	3 458	1 916	5 623	1 531	6 108
1943	55 995	56 016	40 723	2 563	917	1 566	17 402	10 924	6 478	3 652	1 808	5 570	1 475	5 770
1944	57 221	57 276	39 749	2 372	879	1 110	17 050	10 722	6 328	3 822	1 828	5 529	1 447	5 712
1945	55 548	55 614	38 183	2 259	829	1 135	15 186	8 933	6 253	3 926	1 927	5 717	1 477	5 727
1946	49 643	49 690	40 379	2 343	871	1 739	14 493	7 742	6 751	4 113	2 286	6 769	1 692	6 073
1947	49 936	49 941	42 458	2 427	933	2 062	15 205	8 330	6 875	4 173	2 480	7 061	1 744	6 373
1948	51 332	51 325	43 431	2 498	981	2 278	15 276	8 309	6 967	4 212	2 573	7 223	1 811	6 579
1972 SIC														
1948	51 332	51 325	43 431	2 505	993	2 324	15 521	8 343	7 178	4 212	2 731	6 585	1 776	6 784
1949	50 358	50 373	41 857	2 418	923	2 212	14 429	7 508	6 921	4 026	2 653	6 552	1 805	6 839
1950	52 424	52 428	43 626	2 499	926	2 448	15 241	8 121	7 120	4 064	2 670	6 727	1 883	7 168
1951	56 415	56 470	46 112	2 418	939	2 727	16 453	9 144	7 309	4 267	2 817	7 123	1 970	7 398
1952	57 702	57 770	46 668	2 338	916	2 763	16 752	9 466	7 286	4 279	2 870	7 270	2 044	7 436
1953	58 918	58 996	47 873	2 277	876	2 743	17 587	10 144	7 443	4 326	2 901	7 403	2 125	7 635
1954	57 387	57 514	46 400	2 301	798	2 729	16 395	9 194	7 201	4 120	2 875	7 336	2 199	7 647
1955	59 080	59 218	48 036	2 233	804	2 879	16 965	9 617	7 348	4 182	2 930	7 547	2 302	8 194
1956	60 845	60 987	49 573	2 141	843	3 025	17 327	9 894	7 433	4 290	3 054	7 812	2 406	8 675
1957	61 308	61 441	49 732	2 114	840	2 945	17 245	9 894	7 351	4 276	3 078	7 881	2 459	8 894
1958	59 839	59 967	48 211	2 153	749	2 865	15 919	8 839	7 080	4 011	3 066	7 785	2 513	9 150
1959	61 587	61 721	49 781	2 133	717	3 001	16 656	9 385	7 271	4 015	3 129	8 046	2 578	9 506
1960	62 680	62 823	50 548	2 097	699	2 969	16 779	9 453	7 326	4 024	3 205	8 305	2 660	9 810
1961	62 881	63 006	50 374	2 121	666	2 946	16 333	9 075	7 258	3 920	3 218	8 276	2 719	10 175
1962	64 573	64 664	51 672	2 075	649	3 024	16 901	9 514	7 387	3 920	3 268	8 508	2 781	10 546
1963	65 619	65 691	52 444	2 043	632	3 112	17 028	9 631	7 397	3 919	3 314	8 737	2 857	10 802
1964	67 275	67 338	53 655	1 879	628	3 234	17 330	9 856	7 474	3 972	3 394	9 068	2 939	11 211
1965	69 692	69 713	55 598	1 775	634	3 382	18 120	10 445	7 675	4 050	3 518	9 466	3 047	11 606
1966	73 516	73 531	58 209	1 662	631	3 485	19 319	11 359	7 960	4 192	3 667	9 937	3 136	12 180
1967	75 442	75 457	59 288	1 568	614	3 441	19 544	11 507	8 037	4 289	3 759	10 234	3 245	12 594
1968	77 602	77 618	60 948	1 545	610	3 570	19 898	11 700	8 198	4 352	3 851	10 638	3 412	13 072
1969	79 850	79 872	62 877	1 530	624	3 738	20 306	11 982	8 324	4 472	3 981	11 115	3 564	13 547
1970	79 750	79 770	62 702	1 545	628	3 676	19 442	11 270	8 172	4 525	4 061	11 362	3 696	13 767
1971	79 554	79 573	62 529	1 535	615	3 735	18 611	10 636	7 975	4 488	4 087	11 615	3 777	14 066
1972	81 583	81 604	64 568	1 551	625	3 927	19 080	11 010	8 070	4 538	4 206	11 982	3 917	14 742
1973	85 202	85 226	67 939	1 637	639	4 217	20 139	11 884	8 255	4 689	4 422	12 589	4 138	15 469
1974	86 573	86 594	68 947	1 738	699	4 151	20 121	11 964	8 157	4 746	4 540	12 847	4 270	15 835
1975	85 044	85 069	67 069	1 711	753	3 675	18 379	10 724	7 655	4 581	4 465	12 977	4 319	16 209
1976	87 402	87 427	69 430	1 815	782	3 728	19 082	11 123	7 959	4 600	4 609	13 570	4 443	16 801
1977	90 421	90 444	72 275	1 760	827	4 006	19 801	11 665	8 136	4 734	4 781	14 195	4 641	17 530
1978	94 777	94 805	76 313	1 763	876	4 443	20 668	12 372	8 296	4 955	5 056	15 031	4 947	18 573
1979	98 017	98 039	79 137	1 816	948	4 710	21 182	12 848	8 334	5 167	5 295	15 461	5 198	19 359
1980	98 370	98 394	79 121	1 865	1 032	4 493	20 433	12 270	8 163	5 178	5 346	15 487	5 362	19 924
1981	99 225	99 287	80 139	1 844	1 151	4 338	20 328	12 194	8 134	5 219	5 466	15 659	5 488	20 646
1982	97 305	97 369	78 220	1 718	1 138	4 013	18 923	11 122	7 800	5 131	5 350	15 471	5 528	20 949
1983	98 041	98 111	78 939	1 835	964	4 070	18 527	10 784	7 742	5 027	5 323	15 916	5 667	21 610
1984	102 458	102 531	83 103	1 747	980	4 527	19 473	11 560	7 913	5 192	5 614	16 908	5 894	22 768
1985	104 987	105 059	85 264	1 632	935	4 809	19 348	11 552	7 795	5 269	5 757	17 654	6 132	23 728
1986	106 873	106 940	86 770	1 611	784	4 960	19 035	11 269	7 766	5 283	5 799	18 188	6 435	24 675
1987	109 754	109 820	89 270	1 671	727	5 069	19 091	11 222	7 869	5 412	5 916	18 788	6 707	25 887
1987 SIC														
1987	109 754	109 820	89 270	1 671	727	5 069	19 091	11 193	7 898	5 412	5 937	18 767	6 719	25 875
1988	112 864	112 939	92 033	1 765	729	5 212	19 450	11 437	8 012	5 553	6 085	19 345	6 806	27 089
1989	115 501	115 584	94 300	1 723	704	5 269	19 482	11 435	8 046	5 659	6 319	19 843	6 846	28 456
1990	116 964	117 046	95 233	1 740	721	5 226	19 173	11 153	8 020	5 811	6 251	19 912	6 876	29 522
1991	115 525	115 607	93 763	1 735	700	4 794	18 507	10 618	7 889	5 785	6 097	19 604	6 835	29 705
1992	115 968	116 046	94 151	1 694	644	4 635	18 148	10 310	7 837	5 748	6 090	19 710	6 761	30 721
1993	117 604	118 030	96 106	1 724	617	4 790	18 141	10 268	7 874	5 861	6 018	20 110	6 851	31 993
1994	120 379	120 858	98 853	1 761	608	5 121	18 388	10 485	7 902	6 049	6 197	20 811	6 993	32 924
1995	123 236	123 713	101 636	1 819	590	5 304	18 548	10 698	7 849	6 177	6 437	21 498	6 899	34 365
1996	125 461	125 901	103 832	1 841	583	5 579	18 529	10 815	7 714	6 298	6 522	21 869	7 011	35 601
1997	128 316	128 788	106 698	1 919	599	5 859	18 706	11 030	7 676	6 470	6 711	22 240	7 212	36 983
1998	131 563	132 031	109 709	1 961	591	6 178	18 849	11 231	7 618	6 680	6 876	22 595	7 491	38 488
1999	134 350	134 864	112 253	2 055	537	6 570	18 605	11 141	7 465	6 895	6 951	23 140	7 649	39 850
2000	137 228	137 691	114 597	2 068	537	6 870	18 500	11 142	7 358	7 089	7 058	23 643	7 674	41 157

Table 10-21. Employment by SIC Industry, Historical Annual—*Continued*

(Full-time and part-time employees, thousands.)

NIPA Table 6.4A, B, and C

Year	Total government	Domestic industries												Rest of the world
		Federal government						State and local government						
		Total federal	General government				Government enterprises	Total state and local	General government				Government enterprises	
			General gov't total	Civilian 1	Military	Work relief			General gov't total	Education	Other 1	Work relief		
1942 SIC														
1929	3 611	981	644	267	377	. . .	337	2 630	2 509	1 067	1 442	. . .	121	0
1930	3 779	1 034	695	310	385	. . .	339	2 745	2 618	1 095	1 503	20	127	0
1931	4 133	1 019	683	296	387	. . .	336	3 114	2 984	1 105	1 580	299	130	1
1932	4 373	1 006	673	290	383	. . .	333	3 367	3 249	1 093	1 564	592	118	1
1933	5 901	1 470	1 135	294	370	471	335	4 431	4 317	1 069	1 524	1 724	114	1
1934	6 820	2 227	1 868	357	371	1 140	359	4 593	4 473	1 069	1 570	1 834	120	1
1935	7 150	2 209	1 835	449	396	990	374	4 941	4 815	1 097	1 621	2 097	126	1
1936	8 050	4 993	4 612	521	438	3 653	381	3 057	2 922	1 118	1 713	91	135	1
1937	7 192	4 085	3 698	517	474	2 707	387	3 107	2 967	1 149	1 762	56	140	1
1938	8 197	4 987	4 583	507	504	3 572	404	3 210	3 070	1 180	1 871	19	140	1
1939	8 020	4 754	4 342	560	566	3 216	412	3 266	3 123	1 207	1 877	39	143	1
1940	7 917	4 652	4 227	642	793	2 792	425	3 265	3 104	1 194	1 872	38	161	2
1941	8 572	5 281	4 829	944	1 693	2 192	452	3 291	3 119	1 256	1 846	17	172	3
1942	10 486	7 252	6 765	1 702	4 154	909	487	3 234	3 063	1 264	1 794	5	171	5
1943	15 293	12 155	11 611	2 497	9 029	85	544	3 138	2 965	1 256	1 709	. . .	173	-21
1944	17 527	14 405	13 885	2 520	11 365	. . .	520	3 122	2 956	1 256	1 700	. . .	166	-55
1945	17 431	14 258	13 722	2 420	11 302	. . .	536	3 173	3 007	1 273	1 734	. . .	166	-66
1946	9 311	5 902	5 294	1 822	3 472	. . .	608	3 409	3 236	1 347	1 889	. . .	173	-47
1947	7 483	3 808	3 268	1 436	1 832	. . .	540	3 675	3 481	1 445	2 036	. . .	194	-5
1948	7 894	4 007	3 437	1 428	2 009	. . .	570	3 887	3 657	1 504	2 153	. . .	230	7
1972 SIC														
1948	7 894	4 007	3 437	1 428	2 009	. . .	570	3 887	3 657	1 504	2 153	. . .	230	7
1949	8 516	4 462	3 857	1 448	2 409	. . .	605	4 054	3 815	1 581	2 234	. . .	239	-15
1950	8 802	4 603	4 016	1 468	2 548	. . .	587	4 199	3 947	1 636	2 311	. . .	252	-4
1951	10 358	6 131	5 519	1 817	3 702	. . .	612	4 227	3 967	1 684	2 283	. . .	260	-55
1952	11 102	6 737	6 081	1 910	4 171	. . .	656	4 365	4 067	1 762	2 305	. . .	298	-68
1953	11 123	6 611	5 976	1 823	4 153	. . .	635	4 512	4 209	1 851	2 358	. . .	303	-78
1954	11 114	6 394	5 759	1 702	4 057	. . .	635	4 720	4 415	1 946	2 469	. . .	305	-127
1955	11 182	6 234	5 601	1 711	3 890	. . .	633	4 948	4 637	2 076	2 561	. . .	311	-138
1956	11 414	6 202	5 563	1 738	3 825	. . .	639	5 212	4 900	2 199	2 701	. . .	312	-142
1957	11 709	6 277	5 618	1 734	3 884	. . .	659	5 432	5 117	2 310	2 807	. . .	315	-133
1958	11 756	6 044	5 373	1 691	3 682	. . .	671	5 712	5 375	2 430	2 945	. . .	337	-128
1959	11 940	6 030	5 349	1 721	3 628	. . .	681	5 910	5 516	2 559	2 957	. . .	394	-134
1960	12 275	6 090	5 390	1 770	3 620	. . .	700	6 185	5 777	2 732	3 045	. . .	408	-143
1961	12 632	6 200	5 481	1 772	3 709	. . .	719	6 432	6 022	2 863	3 159	. . .	410	-125
1962	12 992	6 349	5 618	1 833	3 785	. . .	731	6 643	6 228	3 012	3 216	. . .	415	-91
1963	13 247	6 302	5 568	1 852	3 716	. . .	734	6 945	6 521	3 214	3 307	. . .	424	-72
1964	13 683	6 382	5 641	1 838	3 803	. . .	741	7 301	6 861	3 431	3 430	. . .	440	-63
1965	14 115	6 387	5 625	1 856	3 769	. . .	762	7 728	7 276	3 705	3 571	. . .	452	-21
1966	15 322	7 057	6 222	1 978	4 244	. . .	835	8 265	7 800	4 049	3 751	. . .	465	-15
1967	16 169	7 497	6 623	2 100	4 523	. . .	874	8 672	8 199	4 321	3 878	. . .	473	-15
1968	16 670	7 551	6 669	2 112	4 557	. . .	882	9 119	8 625	4 582	4 043	. . .	494	-16
1969	16 995	7 492	6 599	2 083	4 516	. . .	893	9 503	8 991	4 828	4 163	. . .	512	-22
1970	17 068	7 129	6 217	2 042	4 175	. . .	912	9 939	9 404	5 060	4 344	. . .	535	-20
1971	17 044	6 717	5 807	2 002	3 805	. . .	910	10 327	9 778	5 298	4 480	. . .	549	-19
1972	17 036	6 308	5 427	2 017	3 410	. . .	881	10 728	10 164	5 467	4 697	. . .	564	-21
1973	17 287	6 174	5 293	2 001	3 292	. . .	881	11 113	10 524	5 641	4 883	. . .	589	-24
1974	17 647	6 146	5 251	2 049	3 202	. . .	895	11 501	10 879	5 858	5 021	. . .	622	-21
1975	18 000	6 060	5 183	2 075	3 108	. . .	877	11 940	11 280	6 052	5 228	. . .	660	-25
1976	17 997	5 934	5 080	2 085	2 995	. . .	854	12 063	11 400	6 124	5 276	. . .	663	-25
1977	18 169	5 871	5 027	2 090	2 937	. . .	844	12 298	11 638	6 251	5 387	. . .	660	-23
1978	18 492	5 881	5 031	2 117	2 914	. . .	850	12 611	11 922	6 292	5 630	. . .	689	-28
1979	18 902	5 881	5 016	2 126	2 890	. . .	865	13 021	12 289	6 361	5 928	. . .	732	-22
1980	19 273	6 010	5 140	2 221	2 919	. . .	870	13 263	12 506	6 481	6 025	. . .	757	-24
1981	19 148	6 006	5 133	2 131	3 002	. . .	873	13 142	12 389	6 466	5 923	. . .	753	-62
1982	19 149	6 084	5 207	2 113	3 094	. . .	877	13 065	12 307	6 421	5 886	. . .	758	-64
1983	19 172	6 095	5 246	2 117	3 129	. . .	849	13 077	12 315	6 478	5 837	. . .	762	-70
1984	19 428	6 196	5 316	2 143	3 173	. . .	880	13 232	12 459	6 581	5 878	. . .	773	-73
1985	19 795	6 311	5 401	2 180	3 221	. . .	910	13 484	12 692	6 759	5 933	. . .	792	-72
1986	20 170	6 384	5 427	2 164	3 263	. . .	957	13 786	12 981	6 940	6 041	. . .	805	-67
1987	20 550	6 475	5 493	2 190	3 303	. . .	982	14 075	13 258	6 992	6 266	. . .	817	-66
1987 SIC														
1987	20 550	6 475	5 493	2 190	3 303	. . .	982	14 075	13 258	6 992	6 266	. . .	817	-66
1988	20 906	6 470	5 465	2 192	3 273	. . .	1 005	14 436	13 608	7 257	6 351	. . .	828	-75
1989	21 284	6 483	5 471	2 207	3 264	. . .	1 012	14 801	13 955	7 458	6 497	. . .	846	-83
1990	21 813	6 532	5 520	2 315	3 205	. . .	1 012	15 281	14 403	7 670	6 733	. . .	878	-82
1991	21 844	6 349	5 356	2 211	3 145	. . .	993	15 495	14 605	7 787	6 818	. . .	890	-82
1992	21 895	6 177	5 211	2 231	2 980	. . .	966	15 718	14 863	7 887	6 976	. . .	855	-78
1993	21 924	5 929	4 976	2 176	2 800	. . .	953	15 995	15 126	8 070	7 056	. . .	869	-426
1994	22 005	5 719	4 749	2 101	2 648	. . .	970	16 286	15 380	8 227	7 153	. . .	906	-479
1995	22 077	5 556	4 571	2 027	2 544	. . .	985	16 521	15 593	8 392	7 201	. . .	928	-477
1996	22 069	5 386	4 398	1 952	2 446	. . .	988	16 683	15 754	8 526	7 228	. . .	929	-440
1997	22 090	5 266	4 276	1 900	2 376	. . .	990	16 824	15 890	8 740	7 150	. . .	934	-472
1998	22 322	5 191	4 200	1 878	2 322	. . .	991	17 131	16 191	8 932	7 259	. . .	940	-468
1999	22 611	5 136	4 146	1 855	2 291	. . .	990	17 475	16 530	9 152	7 378	. . .	945	-514
2000	23 094	5 235	4 260	1 976	2 284	. . .	975	17 859	16 904	9 389	7 515	. . .	955	-463

1Excluding work relief 1930–1943.
. . . = Not available.

NOTES AND DEFINITIONS, CHAPTER 10

General note on monthly employment data

This chapter presents data from two different data sets that measure employment monthly. Both are compiled and published by the Bureau of Labor Statistics (BLS), but each set has different characteristics. Users should be aware of these dissimilarities and the consequent differences in the appropriate uses and interpretations of data from the two systems.

One set of monthly employment estimates comes from the Current Population Survey (CPS), a large sample survey of approximately 60,000 U.S. households. The numbers in the sample are expanded to match the latest estimates of the total U.S. population. These are the most comprehensive estimates in their scope—that is, in the universe that they are designed to measure. These estimates represent all civilian workers, including the following groups that are excluded by definition from the other set of estimates: all farm workers; household workers (domestic servants); nonagricultural, nonincorporated self-employed workers; and nonagricultural unpaid family workers.

However, official CPS data are characterized by periodic discontinuities, which occur when new benchmarks for Census measures of the total population are introduced. These updates take place in a single month—usually January—and the official data for previous months are typically not modified to provide a smooth transition. Therefore, shorter-term comparisons (for a year or two or for a business cycle phase) will be misleading if such a discontinuity is included in the period. A recent example will illustrate. Beginning with January 2010, the estimates for civilian noninstitutional population, civilian labor force, and employment were all adjusted downward by about 250,000 persons. The reported seasonally adjusted change in employment from December 2009 to January 2010 was an increase of 541,000. If there had been no population control adjustment, the increase in employment would have been 784,000. Such discontinuities occur throughout the history of the series.

For users who would like to examine monthly CPS data in which these discontinuities have been smoothed, BLS now provides unofficial smoothed estimates of total labor force and total employment from January 1990 through December 2012 on its Web site, http://www.bls.gov. These two series are shown in Table 10-6.

The CPS is a count of persons employed, rather than a count of jobs. A person is counted as employed in this data set only once, no matter how many jobs he or she may hold. The CPS count is limited to persons 16 years of age and over.

The second set of employment estimates—the payroll survey—comes from a very large sample survey of about 145,000 business and government employers at approximately 557,000 worksites, the Current Employment Statistics (CES) survey. It is benchmarked annually to a survey of all employers. Benchmark data are introduced with a smooth adjustment back to the previous benchmark, thus preserving the continuity of the series and making it more appropriate for measurement of employment change over a year or two, a business cycle, or other short- to medium-length periods. This sample is much larger than the CPS sample, including about one-third of all nonfarm payroll employees, and consequently the threshold of statistical significance for changes is lower. The minimum size of the over-the-month change required to be statistically significant is about 90,000 jobs in the payroll survey, versus about 400,000 persons in the household survey.

Over recent years, benchmark revisions to payroll survey employment have ranged in magnitude from an upward revision of 0.6 percent, in 2006, to the March 2009 benchmark, which reduced the seasonally adjusted level of payroll employment in that month by 902,000 persons, or 0.7 percent. The most recent revision increased the level of employment in March 2012 by 424,000, or 0.3 percent. In absolute terms (that is, disregarding the sign), revisions have ranged from 0.1 to 0.7 percentage points over the latest 12 years and averaged 0.3 percentage points. Within that range, relatively large upward revisions have been seen for strong economies, and relatively large downward revisions for weak ones.

The scope of the CES survey is smaller than that of the CPS survey, as it is limited to wage and salary workers on nonfarm payrolls. There is also a significant definitional difference, because the CES survey is a count of jobs. Thus, a person with more than one nonfarm wage or salary job is counted as employed in each job. In addition, workers are not classified by age; as a result, there may be some workers younger than 16 years old in the job count.

Persons with a job but not at work (absent due to bad weather, work stoppages, personal reasons, and the like) are included in the household survey. However, they are excluded from the payroll survey if on leave without pay for the entire payroll period.

In addition to the differences in definitions and scope between the two series, there are also differences in sample design, collection methodology, and the sampling variability inherent in the surveys.

The payroll survey provides the most reliable and detailed information on the breakdown of employment by industry (for example, the data shown in Table 15-1). In addition, it provides data on weekly hours per job and hourly and weekly earnings per job.

The CPS employment estimates provide information not collected in the CES on the breakdown of employment by demographic characteristics, such as age, race, and Hispanic ethnicity; by education levels; and by occupation. A few of these breakdowns are shown in *Business Statistics*. Many more breakdowns, in richer detail, can be found in the *Handbook of U.S. Labor Statistics*, also published by Bernan Press.

The differences between these two employment measures are discussed in an article on the BLS Web site, "Employment from the BLS household and payroll surveys: summary of recent trends," which is updated monthly along with the release of the monthly data, and can be found under "Publications" on the CPS homepage at http://www.bls.gov. This article also includes references to further relevant studies.

Additional annual employment data

In addition to the CPS and CES monthly and annual data series, a third set of historical, annual-only estimates of employment is presented at the end of this chapter. These estimates of "full-time and part-time employees" by industry are compiled by the U.S. Department of Commerce, Bureau of Economic Analysis, as part of the National Income and Product Accounts (NIPAs). These estimates provide the most comprehensive and consistent employment estimates for the years before 1948.

Further detail on the historical and other characteristics of all of these employment series is presented below in the notes associated with specific data tables.

Tables 10-1 through 10-5: Labor Force, Employment, and Unemployment

SOURCE: U.S. DEPARTMENT OF LABOR, BUREAU OF LABOR STATISTICS (BLS)

Labor force, employment, and unemployment data are derived from the Current Population Survey (CPS), a sample survey of households conducted each month by the Census Bureau for the Bureau of Labor Statistics (BLS). The data pertain to the U.S. civilian noninstitutional population age 16 years and over.

Due to changes in questionnaire design and survey methodology, data for 1994 and subsequent years are not fully comparable with data for 1993 and earlier years. Additionally, discontinuities in the reported number of persons in the population, and consequently in the estimated numbers of employed and unemployed persons and the number of persons in the labor force, are introduced whenever periodic updates are made to U.S. population estimates.

For example, population controls based on Census 2000 were introduced beginning with the data for January 2000. These data are therefore not comparable with data for December 1999 and earlier. Data for 1990 through 1999 incorporate 1990 census–based population controls and are not comparable with the preceding years. An additional large population adjustment was introduced in January 2004, making the data from that time forward not comparable with data for December 2003 and earlier; further adjustments have been made in each subsequent January and other discontinuities have been introduced in various earlier years, usually with January data. See "Notes on the Data," below, for information on adjustments in other years, including the incorporation of the 2010 Census count beginning in January 2012.

For the most part, these population adjustments distort comparisons involving the numbers of persons in the population, labor force, and employment. They generally have negligible effects on the percentages that comprise the most important features of the CPS: the unemployment rates, the labor force participation rates, and the employment-population ratios.

BLS now makes available unofficial smoothed data for the total number of persons in the civilian labor force and the number of persons employed for 1990 through 2012, which introduce the population adjustments gradually within the period shown. These data are shown in Table 10-6.

Beginning with the data for January 2000, data classified by industry and occupation use the North American Industry Classification System (NAICS) and the 2000 Standard Occupational Classification System. This creates breaks in the time series between December 1999 and January 2000 for occupational and industry data at all levels of aggregation. Since the recent history is so short, most CPS industry and occupation data have been dropped from *Business Statistics* in favor of other important and economically meaningful data for which a longer consistent history can be supplied. However, detailed employment data by occupation and industry can be found in Bernan Press's *Handbook of U.S. Labor Statistics*.

Pre-1948 data

The Census Bureau began the survey of households that provides labor force data in 1942, and the Census of Population supplied data for 1940. For the years before that, annual data for labor force, employment, and unemployment are retrospective estimates. The 1929–1947 estimates were made by BLS. The 1890–1929 estimates shown in Table 10-1B were made by Stanley Lebergott. Both of those used trend interpolation of labor force participation between Census years, and the Census and Lebergott estimates are identical in 1929.

From 1929 to 1947, the data collected pertained to persons 14 years of age and over. From 1947 to the present the survey pertains to persons 16 years of age and over. Table 10-1C shows summary data for both age definitions in the overlap year, 1947. In that year, the unemployment rates are the same (3.9 percent) for both age definitions. However, the labor force participation rate and the employment/population ratio are higher when the 14- and 15-year-olds are excluded. Naturally, the raw numbers for population, labor force, and employment are smaller when the 14- and 15-year-olds are excluded.

The 1940 Census and the BLS data for 1931 through 1942 did not treat government work relief employment as employment; persons engaged in such work were counted as unemployed. In the labor force survey used today, anyone who worked for pay or profit is counted as employed (see the definitions below). Therefore, today's survey would count work relief as employment and not unemployment, and the BLS figures for the period before 1942 are not consistent with today's unemployment rates. Michael Darby calculated an alternative unemployment rate in which such workers are counted as employed, and this rate is shown in parentheses in Table 10-1C. Work relief employment is included in the BEA total employment figures in Table 10-21.

Race and ethnic origin

Data for two broad racial categories were made available beginning in 1954: *White* and *Black and other.* The latter included Asians and all other "nonwhite" races, and was discontinued after 2002. Data for *Blacks* only are available beginning with 1972; this category is now called *Black or African American.* Data for *Asians* are shown beginning with 2000. Persons in the remaining race categories—American Indian or Alaska Native, Native Hawaiian or Other Pacific Islanders, and persons who selected more than one race category when that became possible, beginning in 2003 (see below)—are included in the estimates of total employment

and unemployment, but are not shown separately because their numbers are too small to yield quality estimates.

Hispanic or Latino ethnicity, previously labeled *Hispanic origin*, is not a racial category and is established in a survey question separate from the question about race. Persons of Hispanic or Latino ethnicity may be of any race.

In January 2003, changes that affected classification by race and Hispanic ethnicity were introduced. These changes caused discontinuities in race and ethnic group data between December 2002 and January 2003.

• Individuals in the sample are now asked whether they are of Hispanic ethnicity before being asked about their race. Prior to 2003, individuals were asked their ethnic origin after they were asked about their race. Furthermore, respondents are now asked directly if they are Spanish, Hispanic, or Latino. Previously, they were identified based on their or their ancestors' country of origin.

• Individuals in the sample are now allowed to choose more than one race category. Before 2003, they were required to select a single primary race. This change had no impact on the size of the overall civilian noninstitutional population and labor force. It did reduce the population and labor force levels of Whites and Blacks beginning in January 2003, as individuals who reported more than one race are now excluded from those groups.

BLS has estimated, based on a special survey, that these changes reduced the population and labor force levels for Whites by about 950,000 and 730,000 persons, respectively, and for Blacks by about 320,000 and 240,000 persons, respectively, while having little or no impact on either of their unemployment rates. The changes did not affect the size of the Hispanic population or labor force, but they did cause an increase of about half a percentage point in the Hispanic unemployment rate.

Definitions

The employment status of the civilian population is surveyed each month with respect to a specific week in mid-month—not for the entire month. This is known as the "reference week." For a precise definition and explanation of the reference week, see Notes on the Data, which follows these definitions.

The *civilian noninstitutional population* comprises all civilians 16 years of age and over who are not inmates of penal or mental institutions, sanitariums, or homes for the aged, infirm, or needy.

Civilian employment includes those civilians who (1) worked for pay or profit at any time during the Sunday-through-Saturday week that includes the 12th day of the month (the reference week), or who worked for 15 hours or more as an unpaid worker in a family-operated enterprise; or (2) were temporarily absent from regular jobs because of vacation, illness, industrial dispute, bad weather, or similar reasons. Each employed person is counted only once; those who hold more than one job are counted as being in the job at which they worked the greatest number of hours during the reference week.

Unemployed persons are all civilians who were not employed (according to the above definition) during the reference week, but who were available for work—except for temporary illness—and who had made specific efforts to find employment sometime during the previous four weeks. Persons who did not look for work because they were on layoff are also counted as unemployed.

The *civilian labor force* comprises all civilians classified as employed or unemployed.

Civilians 16 years of age and over in the noninstitutional population who are not classified as employed or unemployed are defined as *not in the labor force*. This group includes those engaged in own-home housework; in school; unable to work because of long-term illness, retirement, or age; seasonal workers for whom the reference week fell in an "off" season (if not qualifying as unemployed by looking for a job); persons who became discouraged and gave up the search for work; and the voluntarily idle. Also included are those doing only incidental work (less than 15 hours) in a family-operated business during the reference week.

The civilian *labor force participation rate* represents the percentage of the civilian noninstitutional population (age 16 years and over) that is in the civilian labor force.

The *employment-population ratio* represents the percentage of the civilian noninstitutional population (age 16 years and over) that is employed. This is traditionally called a "ratio," although it is also traditionally expressed as a percent and therefore would be more appropriately called a "rate," as is the case with the labor force participation rate.

Employment is shown by *class of worker,* including a breakdown of total employment into *agricultural* and *nonagricultural* industries. Employment in *nonagricultural industries* includes *wage and salary workers*, the *self-employed*, and *unpaid family workers.*

Wage and salary workers receive wages, salaries, commissions, tips, and/or pay-in-kind. This category includes owners of self-owned incorporated businesses.

Self-employed workers are those who work for profit or for fees in their own business, profession, trade, or farm. This category includes only the unincorporated; a person whose business is incorporated is considered to be a wage and salary worker since he or she is a paid employee of a corporation, even if he or she is the corporation's president and sole employee. These categories are now labeled "Self-employed workers, unincorporated" to clarify this definition.

Wage and salary employment comprises *government* and *private industry* wage and salary workers. Domestic workers and other employees of *private households*, who are not included in the payroll employment series, are shown separately from *all other private industries*. The series for *government* and *other private industries* wage and salary workers are the closest in scope to similar categories in the payroll employment series.

Multiple jobholders are employed persons who, during the reference week, either had two or more jobs as a wage and salary worker, were self-employed and also held a wage and salary job, or worked as an unpaid family worker and also held a wage and salary job. This category does not include self-employed persons with multiple businesses or persons with multiple jobs as unpaid family workers. For purposes of industry and occupational classification, multiple jobholders are counted as being in the job at which they worked the greatest number of hours during the reference week.

Employed and at work part time does not include employed persons who were absent from their jobs during the entire reference week for reasons such as vacation, illness, or industrial dispute.

At work part time for economic reasons ("involuntary" part time) refers to individuals who worked 1 to 34 hours during the reference week because of slack work, unfavorable business conditions, an inability to find full-time work, or seasonal declines in demand. To be included in this category, workers must also indicate that they want and are available for full-time work.

At work part time for noneconomic reasons ("voluntary" part time) refers to persons who usually work part time and were at work for 1 to 34 hours during the reference week for reasons such as illness, other medical limitations, family obligations, education, retirement, Social Security limits on earnings, or working in an industry where the workweek is less than 35 hours. It also includes respondents who gave an economic reason but were not available for, or did not want, full-time work. At work part time for noneconomic reasons excludes persons who usually work full time, but who worked only 1 to 34 hours during the reference week for reasons such as holidays, illnesses, and bad weather.

The *long-term unemployed* are persons currently unemployed (searching or on layoff) who have been unemployed for 15 consecutive weeks or longer. If a person ceases to look for work for two weeks or more, or becomes temporarily employed, the continuity of long-term unemployment is broken. If he or she starts searching for work or is laid off again, the monthly CPS will record the length of his or her unemployment from the time the search recommenced or since the latest layoff.

The civilian *unemployment rate* is the number of unemployed as a percentage of the civilian labor force. The unemployment rates for groups within the civilian population (such as males age 20 years and over) are the number of unemployed in a group as a percent of that group's labor force.

Unemployment rates by reason provides a breakdown of the total unemployment rate. Each unemployed person is classified into one of four groups.

Job losers and persons who completed temporary jobs includes persons on temporary layoff, permanent job losers, and persons who completed temporary jobs and began looking for work after those jobs ended. These three categories are shown separately without seasonal adjustment in the BLS's "Employment Situation" news release and on its Web site. They are combined, under the title shown here, for the purpose of seasonal adjustment. This is the category of unemployment that responds most strongly to the business cycle.

Job leavers terminated their employment voluntarily and immediately began looking for work.

Reentrants are persons who previously worked, but were out of the labor force prior to beginning their current job search.

New entrants are persons searching for a first job who have never worked.

Each of these categories is expressed as a proportion of the entire civilian labor force, so that the sum of the four rates equals the unemployment rate for all civilian workers, except for possible discrepancies due to rounding or separate seasonal adjustment.

Median and average weeks unemployed are summary measures of the length of time that persons classified as unemployed have been looking for work. For persons on layoff, the duration represents the number of full weeks of the

layoff. The *average (mean)* number of weeks is computed by aggregating all the weeks of unemployment experienced by all unemployed persons during their current spell of unemployment and dividing by the number of unemployed. The average can be distorted by what is called "top coding" because the length of unemployment is reported in ranges, including a top range of "over ___ weeks", rather than exact numbers. See the paragraph below for further explanation. The *median* number of weeks unemployed is the number of weeks of unemployment experienced by the person at the midpoint of the distribution of all unemployed persons, as ranked by duration of unemployment, and is not distorted by top coding. Like medians in other economic time series, it is likely to be a better measure of typical experience.

Beginning with the data for January 2011 and phasing in through April 2011, respondents could report unemployment durations of up to 5 years; before that time, the "top code" was up to 2 years. This change causes a sharp increase in January 2011 and continued rises through April for *average weeks unemployed.* It did not affect total unemployment, total long-term unemployment, or the *median weeks unemployed.* Comparisons of the average weeks statistics on the old and new basis are available on the BLS Web site.

Alternative measures of labor underutilization are calculated by BLS and published in the monthly Employment Situation release. They measure alternative concepts of unused working capacity, and are numbered "U-1" through "U-6" in order of increasing breadth of the definition of underutilization.

"U-1" is persons unemployed 15 weeks or longer, as a percent of the civilian labor force. It is not shown in *Business Statistics.*

"U-2" is job losers and persons who completed temporary jobs, as a percent of the civilian labor force; it is shown in *Business Statistics* in the fifth column of Table 10-5.

"U-3" is the official rate, described above and shown in the final columns of Tables 10-1, the fifth column of Table 10-4, and the fourth column of Table 10-5.

"U-4" through "U-6" are shown in the last three columns of Table 10-5. They are based on additional labor force status questions, now included in the CPS survey, that were introduced beginning in 1994. U-4 and U-5 are increasingly broader rates of unemployment, while U-6 can be described as an "unemployment and underemployment rate."

"U-4" adds discouraged workers to unemployment and the labor force. Discouraged workers are persons not in the officially defined labor force who have given a job-market-related reason for not looking currently for a job—for example, they have not looked for a job because they believed that no jobs were available.

"U-5" adds both discouraged workers and all other "marginally attached" workers to unemployment and the labor force. "Marginally attached" workers are all persons who currently are neither working nor looking for work but indicate that they want and are available for a job and have looked for work some time in the recent past.

"U-6" adds persons employed part time for economic reasons, as shown in Table 10-3, to the number of persons counted as unemployed in "U-5", with the same labor force definition as in "U-5." Recently this statistic, measuring combined unemployment and underemployment, has often been cited in press reports on the employment situation.

For more information, see "BLS introduced new range of alternative unemployment measures" in the October 1995 issue of the *Monthly Labor Review.*

Notes on the data

The CPS data are collected by trained interviewers from about 60,000 sample households selected to represent the U.S. civilian noninstitutional population. The sample size was about 60,000 households from mid-1989 to mid-1995, but was reduced for budgetary reasons in two stages to about 50,000 households, beginning in January 1996. This sample size was maintained from 1996 through 2000. The sample size was increased back to 60,000 households, beginning with the data for July 2001, as part of a plan to meet the requirements of the State Children's Health Insurance Program legislation. The CPS provides data for other data series in addition to the BLS employment status data, such as household income and poverty (see Chapter 3) and health insurance.

The employment status data are based on the activity or status reported for the calendar week, Sunday through Saturday, that includes the 12th day of the month (the reference week). Households are interviewed in the week following the reference week. Sample households are phased in and out of the sample on a rotating basis. Consequently, three-fourths of the sample is the same for any two consecutive months. One-half of the sample is the same as the sample in the same month a year earlier.

Data relating to 1994 and subsequent years are not strictly comparable with data for 1993 and earlier years because of the major 1994 redesign of the survey questionnaire and collection methodology. The redesign included new and revised questions for the classification of individuals as employed or unemployed, the collection of new data on multiple jobholding, a change in the definition of discouraged

workers, and the implementation of a more completely automated data collection.

The 1994 redesign of the CPS was the most extensive since 1967. However, there are many other significant periods of year-to-year noncomparability in the labor force data. These typically result from the introduction of new decennial census data into the CPS estimation procedures, expansions of the sample, or other improvements made to increase the reliability of the estimates. Each change introduces a new discontinuity, usually between December of the previous year and January of the newly altered year. The discontinuities are usually minor or negligible with respect to figures expressed as nationwide percentages (such as the unemployment rate or the labor force participation rate), but can be significant with respect to levels (such as labor force and employment in thousands of persons). A list of the dates of the major discontinuities follows, with BLS estimates of their quantitative impact on the national totals. (There are likely to be larger impacts on population subgroups.) The discontinuities occur in January unless otherwise indicated. Note that some of the changes caused adjustments that were carried back to an earlier year.

• 1953: 1950 census data introduced. Labor force and employment were raised by about 350,000.

• 1960: Alaska and Hawaii included. The labor force was increased by about 300,000, mainly in nonagricultural employment.

• 1962: 1960 census data introduced. Labor force and employment were reduced by about 200,000.

• 1972: 1970 census data introduced. Labor force and employment were raised by about 300,000.

• March 1973: Further 1970 census data were introduced, reducing White labor force and employment by about 150,000 and raising Black and other labor force and employment by approximately 210,000.

• July 1975: Adjustment for Vietnamese refugee inflow, raising total and Black and other population by 76,000.

• 1978: Sample expansion and revised estimation procedures increased labor force and employment by about 250,000.

• 1982: Change in estimation procedures introduced. To avoid major breaks, many series were reestimated back to 1970. This did not smooth the breaks occurring between 1972 and 1979.

• 1986, with revisions carried back to 1980: Adjustment for better estimates of immigration, raising labor force by nearly

400,000 and employment by 350,000, mainly among Hispanics.

• 1994: 1990 census data introduced and carried back to 1990, when employment was increased by about 880,000 and the unemployment rate was raised by about 0.1 percentage point.

• 1997: New estimates of immigration and emigration, raising labor force and employment by about 300,000, again mainly among Hispanics.

• 1998: New population estimates and estimation procedures, reducing labor force and employment by around 250,000.

• 1999: New information on immigration, raising labor force and employment by around 60,000, but lowering Hispanic employment by about 200,000.

• 2000: Census 2000 data introduced, using the 2002 NAICS and the 2000 Standard Occupational Classification System. The labor force was increased by about 1.6 million in January 2000, growing to around 2.5 million by December 2002.

• 2003: Further population estimates introduced (based on an annual population update and therefore not carried back to 2000), raising the labor force by 614,000.

• 2004: Population controls updated to reflect revised migration estimates, reducing labor force and employment by around 400,000, mostly among Hispanics.

• 2005: Updated migration and vital statistics data decreased labor force and employment by around 45,000.

• 2006: Updated migration and vital statistics data decreased labor force and employment by about 125,000.

• 2007: Updated migration and vital statistics data increased labor force and employment by about 150,000.

• 2008: Updated migration and vital statistics data decreased labor force by 637,000 and employment by 598,000.

• 2009: Updated migration adjustments, new vital statistics data, and methodological changes decreased labor force by 449,000 and employment by 407,000.

• 2010: Updated information on migration, vital statistics, and other data and methodological changes decreased labor force by 249,000 and employment by 243,000.

• 2011: Updated estimates reduced the labor force by 504,000, employment by 472,000, and unemployment by 32,000; raised the number of persons not in the labor force by 157,000; and had no effect on the unemployment rate.

• 2012: Reflecting the 2010 Census, the civilian noninstitutional population was increased by 1,510,000; the civilian labor force by 258,000; employment by 216,000; and unemployment by 42,000. BLS states, "Although the total unemployment rate was unaffected, the labor force participation rate and the employment-population ratio were each reduced by 0.3 percentage point. This was because the population increase was primarily among persons 55 and older and, to a lesser degree, persons 16 to 24 years of age. Both these age groups have lower levels of labor force participation than the general population."

• 2013: Updated population estimates increased the population by 138,000, the labor force by 136,000, and employment by 127,000. The rates and ratios were not affected.

For further information on these changes, see "Publications and Other Documentation" at http://www.bls.gov/cps.

The monthly labor force, employment, and unemployment data are seasonally adjusted by the X-12-ARIMA method. All seasonally adjusted civilian labor force and unemployment rate statistics, as well as major employment and unemployment estimates, are computed by aggregating independently adjusted series. For example, the seasonally adjusted level of total unemployment is the sum of the seasonally adjusted levels of unemployment for the four age/sex groups (men and women age 16 to 19 years, and men and women age 20 years and over). Seasonally adjusted employment is the sum of the seasonally adjusted levels of employment for the same four groups. The seasonally adjusted civilian labor force is the sum of all eight components. Finally, the seasonally adjusted civilian worker unemployment rate is calculated by taking total seasonally adjusted unemployment as a percent of the total seasonally adjusted civilian labor force.

To minimize subsequent revisions, BLS uses a concurrent technique that estimates factors for the latest month using the most recent data. Then, seasonal adjustment factors are fully revised at the end of each year to reflect recent experience. The revisions also affect the preceding four years. An article describing the seasonal adjustment methodology for the household survey data is available at http://www.bls.gov/cps/cpsrs2010.pdf.

Breakdowns other than the basic age/sex classification described above—such as the employment data by class of worker in Table 10-3—will not necessarily add to totals because of independent seasonal adjustment.

Data availability

Data for each month are usually released on the first Friday of the following month in the "Employment Situation" press release, which also includes data from the establishment survey (Tables 10-8 through 10-18 and Chapter 15). (The release date actually is determined by the timing of the survey week.) The press release and data are available on the BLS Web site at http://www.bls.gov. The *Monthly Labor Review*, also available online at the BLS Web site, features frequent articles analyzing developments in the labor force, employment, and unemployment.

Monthly and annual data on the current basis are available beginning with 1948. Historical unadjusted data are published in *Labor Force Statistics Derived from the Current Population Survey* (BLS Bulletin 2307). Historical seasonally adjusted data are available from BLS upon request. Complete historical data are available on the BLS Web site at http://www.bls.gov/cps.

Seasonal adjustment factors are revised each year for the five previous years, with the release of December data in early January. New population controls are introduced with the release of January data in early February.

BLS annual data for 1940 through 1947 are published on their Web site at http://www.bls.gov. The data for 1929 through 1939 were published in *Employment and Earnings*, May 1972, and in U.S. Commerce Department, Bureau of Economic Analysis, *Long-Term Economic Growth, 1860–1970*, June 1973, p. 163. The Lebergott estimates are also found in the latter volume.

The Darby alternative unemployment rate is found in Michael Darby, "Three-and-a-Half Million U.S. Employees Have Been Mislaid," *Journal of Political Economy,* February 1976, v. 84, no. 1. It is also displayed and discussed in Robert A. Margo, "Employment and Unemployment in the 1930s," *Journal of Economic Perspectives,* v. 7, no. 2, Spring 1993.

References

Comprehensive descriptive material can be found at http://www.bls.gov/cps under the "Publications and Other Documentation" section. Historical background on the CPS, as well as a description of the 1994 redesign, can be found in three articles from the September 1993 edition of *Monthly Labor Review*: "Why Is It Necessary to Change?"; "Redesigning the Questionnaire"; and "Evaluating Changes in the Estimates." The redesign is also described in the February 1994 issue of *Employment and Earnings*. See also Chapter 1, "Labor Force Data Derived from the Current Population

Survey," *BLS Handbook of Methods*, Bulletin 2490 (April 1997).

Table 10-6: Labor Force and Employment Estimates Smoothed for Population Adjustments

SOURCE: U.S. DEPARTMENT OF LABOR, BUREAU OF LABOR STATISTICS

This table presents seasonally adjusted monthly estimates of total civilian labor force and total civilian employment in which discontinuities caused by the introduction of new population controls in the official series—as described above—have been smoothed (see box above). The method of smoothing is described in Marisa L. Di Natale, "Creating Comparability in CPS Employment Series," on the BLS Web site at http://www.bls.gov/cps/cpscomp.pdf. BLS notes that these series do not match the official estimates in BLS publications, which are also the data shown in all other tables in this volume.

Table 10-7: Insured Unemployment

SOURCE: U.S. DEPARTMENT OF LABOR, EMPLOYMENT AND TRAINING ADMINISTRATION

Definitions

State programs of unemployment insurance cover operations of regular programs under state unemployment insurance laws. In 1976, the law was amended to extend coverage to include virtually all state and local government employees, as well as many agricultural and domestic workers. (This took effect on January 1, 1978.) Benefits under state programs are financed by taxes levied by the states on employers.

Federal programs are those directly financed by the federal government. They include unemployment benefits for *federal employees* (Unemployment Compensation for Federal Employees, or UCFE), *newly discharged veterans* (Unemployment Compensation for Ex-Service Members, or UCX), *railroad retirement,* and *extended benefits,* which are sometimes enacted by Congress in times of widespread or protracted unemployment.

UCX pays benefits, based on service, to veterans who were on active duty and honorably separated. In the case of both UCFE and UCX, state laws determine the benefit amounts, number of weeks benefits can be paid, and other eligibility conditions.

An *initial claim* is the first claim in a benefit year filed by a worker after losing his or her job, or the first claim filed at the beginning of a subsequent period of unemployment in the same benefit year. The initial claim establishes the starting date for any insured unemployment that may result if the claimant is unemployed for one week or longer. Transitional claims (filed by claimants as they start a new benefit year in a continuing spell of unemployment) are excluded; therefore, these data more closely represent instances of new unemployment and are widely followed as a leading indicator of job market conditions.

Insured unemployment and *persons claiming benefits* both describe the average number of persons receiving benefits in the indicated month or year.

The *insured unemployment rate* for state programs is the level of insured unemployment as a percentage of employment covered by state programs.

Monthly averages in this book are averages, calculated by the editor, of the weekly data published by the Employment and Training Administration. Annual data are averages of the monthly data.

Data availability

Data are published in weekly press releases from the Employment and Training Administration. These releases are available on their Web site at http://www.doleta.gov under "Labor Market Data," as are historical data, under the category "UI/Program Statistics."

Tables 10-8, 10-9, 10-14, 15-1, and 15-2: Nonfarm Payroll Employment

SOURCE: U.S. DEPARTMENT OF LABOR, BUREAU OF LABOR STATISTICS (BLS)

These nonfarm employment data, as well as the hours and earnings data in Tables 10-9 through 10-13, 10-15 through 10-18, and 15-3 through 15-6, are compiled from payroll records. Information is reported monthly on a voluntary basis to BLS and its cooperating state agencies by a large sample of establishments, representing all industries except farming. These data, formally known as the Current Employment Statistics (CES) survey, are often referred to as the "establishment data" or the "payroll data." They are also known as the BLS-790 survey.

The survey, originally based on a stratified quota sample, has been replaced on a phased-in basis by a stratified probability sample. The new sampling procedure went into effect for wholesale trade in June 2000; for mining, construction, and manufacturing in June 2001; and for retail trade, transportation and public utilities, and finance, insurance, and real estate in June 2002. The phase-in was completed in June

2003, upon its extension to the service industries. The phase-in schedule was slightly different for the state and area series.

The sample has always been very large. Currently, it includes approximately 145,000 businesses and government agencies covering about 557,000 individual worksites, which account for about one-third of total benchmark employment of payroll workers. The sample is drawn from a sampling frame of over 8 million unemployment insurance tax accounts.

Data are classified according to the North American Industry Classification System. BLS has reconstructed historical time series to conform with NAICS, to ensure that all published series have a NAICS-based history extending back to at least January 1990. NAICS-based history extends back to January 1939 for total nonfarm and other high-level aggregates. For more detailed series, the starting date for NAICS data varies depending on the extent of the definitional changes between the old Standard Industrial Classification (SIC) and NAICS.

Definitions

An *establishment* is an economic unit, such as a factory, store, or professional office, that produces goods or services at a single location and is engaged in one type of economic activity.

Employment comprises all persons who received pay (including holiday and sick pay) for any part of the payroll period that includes the 12th day of the month. The definition of the payroll period for each reporting respondent is that used by the employer; it could be weekly, biweekly, monthly, or other. Included are all full-time and part-time workers in nonfarm establishments, including salaried officers of corporations. Persons holding more than one job are counted in each establishment that reports them. Not covered are proprietors, the self-employed, unpaid volunteer and family workers, farm workers, domestic workers in households, and military personnel. Employees of the Central Intelligence Agency, the Defense Intelligence Agency, the National Geospatial-Intelligence Agency, and the National Security Agency are not included.

Persons on an establishment payroll who are on paid sick leave (when pay is received directly from the employer), on paid holiday or vacation, or who work during a portion of the pay period despite being unemployed or on strike during the rest of the period, are counted as employed. Not counted as employed are persons who are laid off, on leave without pay, on strike for the entire period, or hired but not paid during the period.

Intermittent workers are counted if they performed any service during the month. BLS considers regular full-time teachers (private and government) to be employed during the summer vacation period, regardless of whether they are specifically paid during those months.

The *government* division includes federal, state, and local activities such as legislative, executive, and judicial functions, as well as the U.S. Postal Service and all government-owned and government-operated business enterprises, establishments, and institutions (arsenals, navy yards, hospitals, state-owned utilities, etc.), and government force account construction. However, as indicated earlier, members of the armed forces and employees of certain national-security-related agencies are not included.

The monthly *diffusion index of employment change*, currently based on 271 private nonfarm NAICS industries, represents the percentage of those industries in which the seasonally adjusted level of employment in that month was higher than six months earlier, plus one-half of the percentage of industries with unchanged employment. Therefore, the diffusion index reported for September represents the change from March to September. *Business Statistics* uses the September value to represent the year as a whole, since it spans the year's midpoint. Diffusion indexes measure the dispersion of economic gains and losses, with values below 50 percent associated with recessions. The current NAICS-based series begins with January 1991. For October 1976 through December 1990, an earlier series is available based on 347 SIC industries (there are more industries using the older classification system because in SIC manufacturing industries were represented in greater detail). September values from this series are used here to represent the years 1977 through 1990.

Production and nonsupervisory workers include all *production and related workers* in mining and manufacturing; *construction workers* in construction; and *nonsupervisory workers* in transportation, communication, electric, gas, and sanitary services; wholesale and retail trade; finance, insurance, and real estate; and services. These groups account for about four-fifths of the total employment on private nonagricultural payrolls. Previously, this category was called "production or nonsupervisory workers." The definitions have not changed.

Production and related workers include working supervisors and all nonsupervisory workers (including group leaders and trainees) engaged in fabricating, processing, assembling, inspecting, receiving, storing, handling, packing, warehousing, shipping, trucking, hauling, maintenance, repair, janitorial, guard services, product development, auxiliary production for plant's own use (such as a power plant), record

keeping, and other services closely associated with these production operations.

Construction workers include the following employees in the construction division of the NAICS: working supervisors, qualified craft workers, mechanics, apprentices, laborers, and the like, who are engaged in new work, alterations, demolition, repair, maintenance, and other tasks, whether working at the site of construction or working in shops or yards at jobs (such as precutting and preassembling) ordinarily performed by members of the construction trades.

Nonsupervisory employees include employees (not above the working supervisory level) such as office and clerical workers, repairers, salespersons, operators, drivers, physicians, lawyers, accountants, nurses, social workers, research aides, teachers, drafters, photographers, beauticians, musicians, restaurant workers, custodial workers, attendants, line installers and repairers, laborers, janitors, guards, and other employees at similar occupational levels whose services are closely associated with those of the employees listed.

Notes on the data

Benchmark adjustments. The establishment survey data are adjusted annually to comprehensive counts of employment, called "benchmarks." Benchmark information on employment by industry is compiled by state agencies from reports of establishments covered under state unemployment insurance laws; these form an annual compilation of administrative data known as the ES-202. These tabulations cover about 97 percent of all employees on nonfarm payrolls. Benchmark data for the residual are obtained from alternate sources, primarily from Railroad Retirement Board records and the Census Bureau's *County Business Patterns*. The latest benchmark adjustment, which is incorporated into the data in this volume, increased the employment level in the benchmark month March 2012 by 424,000 jobs, which was 0.3 percent.

The estimates for the benchmark month are compared with new benchmark levels for each industry. If revisions are necessary, the monthly series of estimates between benchmark periods are adjusted by graduated amounts between the new benchmark and the preceding one ("wedged back"), and the new benchmark level for each industry is then carried forward month by month based on the sample.

More specifically, the month-to-month changes for each estimation cell are based on changes in a matched sample for that cell, plus an estimate of net business births and deaths. The matched sample for each pair of months consists of establishments that have reported data for both months (which automatically excludes establishments that have gone out of business by the second month). Since new businesses are not immediately incorporated into the sample, a model-based estimate of net business births and deaths in that estimating cell is added. The birth/death adjustment factors are re-estimated quarterly based on the Quarterly Census of Employment and Wages.

Not-seasonally-adjusted data for all months since the last benchmark date are subject to revision.

Beginning in 1959, the data include Alaska and Hawaii. This inclusion resulted in an increase of 212,000 (0.4 percent) in total nonfarm employment for the March 1959 benchmark month.

Seasonal adjustment. The seasonal movements that recur periodically—such as warm and cold weather, holidays, and vacations—are generally the largest single component of month-to-month changes in employment. After adjusting the data to remove such seasonal variation, basic trends become more evident. BLS uses X-12-ARIMA software to produce seasonal factors and perform concurrent seasonal adjustment, using the most recent 10 years of data. New factors are developed each month adding the most current data.

For most series, a special procedure called REGARIMA (regression with autocorrelated errors) is used before calculating the seasonal factors; this adjusts for the length of the interval (which can be either four or five weeks) between the survey weeks. REGARIMA has also been used to isolate extreme weather effects that distort the measurement of seasonal patterns in the construction industry, and to identify variations in local government employment due to the presence or absence of election poll workers.

Seasonal adjustment factors are directly applied to the component levels. Seasonally adjusted totals for employment series are then obtained by aggregating the seasonally adjusted components directly, while hours and earnings series represent weighted averages of the seasonally adjusted component series. Seasonally adjusted data are not published for a small number of series characterized by small seasonal components relative to their trend and/or irregular components. However, these series are used in aggregating to broader seasonally adjusted levels.

Revisions of the seasonally adjusted data, usually for the most recent five-year period, are made once a year coincident with the benchmark revisions. This means that these revisions typically extend back farther than the benchmark revisions.

Data availability

Employment data by industry division are available beginning with 1919. Data for each month usually are released on the first Friday of the following month in a press release that also contains data from the household survey (Tables 10-1 through 10-5). (The release date actually is determined by the timing of the survey week.) The *Monthly Labor Review* frequently contains articles analyzing developments in the labor force, employment, and unemployment. The *Monthly Labor Review*, press releases, and complete historical data are available on the BLS Web site at http://www.bls.gov.

Benchmark revisions and revised seasonally adjusted data for recent years are made each year with the release of January data in early February. Before 2004, the benchmark revisions were not made until June; the acceleration is due to earlier availability of the benchmark UI (ES-202) data.

References

References can be found at http://www.bls.gov/ces under the headings "Special Notices," "Benchmark Information," and "Technical Notes." Extensive changes incorporated in June 2003 are described in "Recent Changes in the National Current Employment Statistics Survey," *Monthly Labor Review*, June 2003. The latest benchmark revision is discussed in an article available on the Website. See also Chapter 2, "Employment, Hours, and Earnings from the Establishment Survey," *BLS Handbook of Methods*, Bulletin 2490 (April 1997).

Tables 10-9 through 10-11, 10-15, 10-16, 15-3, and 15-6: Average Hours Per Week; Aggregate Employee Hours

SOURCE: U.S. DEPARTMENT OF LABOR, BUREAU OF LABOR STATISTICS (BLS)

See the notes and definitions to Tables 10-8 and related tables, above, for an overall description of the "establishment" or "payroll" survey that is the source of hours data.

Hours and earnings have been reported for production and nonsupervisory workers, as defined above, since the inception of the CES. Beginning with data for March 2006, such data have also been collected for all payroll employees. With sufficient history for calculation of seasonal adjustment factors, BLS began publishing all-employee hours and earnings in February 2010, and these new data are presented in *Business Statistics* Tables 10-10 through 10-13.

Definitions

Average weekly hours represents the average hours paid per worker during the pay period that includes the 12th of the month. Included are hours paid for holidays and vacations, as well as those paid for sick leave when pay is received directly from the firm.

Average weekly hours are different from standard or scheduled hours. Factors such as unpaid absenteeism, labor turnover, part-time work, and work stoppages can cause average weekly hours to be lower than scheduled hours of work for an establishment.

An important characteristic of these data is that average weekly hours pertain to jobs, not to persons; thus, a person with half-time jobs in two different establishments is represented in this series as two jobs that have 20-hour workweeks, not as one person with a 40-hour workweek.

Overtime hours represent the portion of average weekly hours worked in excess of regular hours, for which overtime premiums were paid. Weekend and holiday hours are included only if overtime premiums were paid. Hours for which only shift differential, hazard, incentive, or other similar types of premiums were paid are excluded.

Aggregate hours provide measures of changes over time in labor input to the industry, in index-number form. The indexes are obtained by multiplying seasonally adjusted employment by seasonally adjusted average weekly hours, dividing the resulting series by their monthly averages for a base period, and multiplying the results by 100, so that the annual average for the base period equals 100. For total private, goods-producing, service-providing, and major industry divisions, the indexes are obtained by summing the seasonally adjusted aggregate weekly employee hours for the component industries, dividing by the monthly average for the base period, and multiplying by 100. For the series covering production and nonsupervisory workers, the base period is 2002; for the all-employee series, the base period is 2007.

Notes on the data

Benchmark adjustments. Independent benchmarks are not available for the hours and earnings series. However, at the time of the annual adjustment of the employment series to new benchmarks, the levels of hours and earnings may be affected by the revised employment weights (which are used in computing the industry averages for hours and earnings), as well as by the changes in seasonal adjustment factors introduced with the benchmark revision.

Method of computing industry series. "Average weekly hours" for individual industries are computed by dividing worker hours (reported by establishments classified in each industry) by the number of workers reported for the same establishments. Estimates for divisions and major industry groups are averages (weighted by employment) of the figures for component industries.

Seasonal adjustment. Hours and earnings series are seasonally adjusted by applying factors directly to the corresponding unadjusted series. Data for some industries are not seasonally adjusted because the seasonal component is small relative to the trend-cycle and/or irregular components. Consequently, they cannot be separated with sufficient precision.

Special adjustments are made to average weekly hours to account for the presence or absence of religious holidays in the April survey reference period and the occasional occurrence of Labor Day in the September reference period. In addition, REGARIMA modeling is used prior to seasonal adjustment to correct for reporting and processing errors associated with the number of weekdays in a month (rather than to correct for the 4- and 5-week effect, which is less significant for hours than it is for employment). This is of particular importance for average weekly hours in the service-providing industries other than retail trade. For this reason, BLS advises that calculations of over-the-year changes (for example, the change for the current month from a year earlier) should use seasonally adjusted data, since the actual not-seasonally-adjusted monthly data may be distorted.

Data availability

See data availability for Tables 10-8 and related, above.

References

See references for Tables 10-8 and related, above.

Tables 10-9, 10-12, 10-13, 10-17, 10-18, 15-4, and 15-5: Hourly and Weekly Earnings

SOURCE: U.S. DEPARTMENT OF LABOR, BUREAU OF LABOR STATISTICS (BLS)

See the notes and definitions to Tables 10-8 and related for an overall description of the "establishment" or "payroll" survey that is the source of these earnings data.

Hours and earnings have been reported for production and nonsupervisory workers, as defined above, since the inception of the CES. Beginning with data for March 2006, such data have also been collected for all payroll employees. With sufficient history for calculation of seasonal adjustment factors, BLS began publishing all-employee hours and earnings in February 2010, and these data are presented in new *Business Statistics* Tables 10-10 through 10-13.

Definitions

Earnings are the payments that workers receive during the survey period (before deductions for taxes and other items), including premium pay for overtime or late-shift work but excluding irregular bonuses and other special payments. After being previously excluded, tips were asked to be reported beginning in September 2005. This made little difference in most industries, and BLS asserts that many respondents had already been including tips. In two industries, full-service restaurants and cafeterias, there was a substantial difference, and the historical earnings data for those industries have been reconstructed to reflect the new higher level of earnings.

Notes on the data

The hours and earnings series are based on reports of gross payroll and corresponding paid hours for full- and part-time workers who received pay for any part of the pay period that included the 12th of the month.

Total payrolls are before deductions, such as for the employee share of old-age and unemployment insurance, group insurance, withholding taxes, bonds, and union dues. The payroll figures also include pay for overtime, holidays, vacations, and sick leave (paid directly by the employer for the period reported). Excluded from the payroll figures are fringe benefits (health and other types of insurance and contributions to retirement, paid by the employer, and the employer share of payroll taxes), bonuses (unless earned and paid regularly each pay period), other pay not earned in the pay period reported (retroactive pay), and the value of free rent, fuel, meals, or other payment-in-kind.

Average hourly earnings data reflect not only changes in basic hourly and incentive wage rates, but also such variable factors as premium pay for overtime and late-shift work and changes in output of workers paid on an incentive basis. Shifts in the volume of employment between relatively high-paid and low-paid work also affect the general average of hourly earnings.

Averages of hourly earnings should not be confused with wage rates, which represent the rates stipulated for a given unit of work or time, while earnings refer to the actual return to the worker for a stated period of time. The earnings series do not represent total labor cost to the employer because of the inclusion of tips and the exclusion of irregular bonuses, retroactive items, the cost of employer-provided benefits, and payroll taxes paid by employers.

Average weekly earnings are not the amounts available to workers for spending, since they do not reflect deductions such as income taxes and Social Security taxes. It is also important to understand that average weekly earnings represent earnings per job, not per worker (since a worker may have more than one job) and not per family (since a family may have more than one worker). A person with two half-time jobs will be reflected as two earners with low weekly earnings rather than as one person with the total earnings from his or her two jobs.

Method of computing industry series. Average hourly earnings are obtained by dividing the reported total worker payroll by total worker hours. Estimates for both hours and hourly earnings for nonfarm divisions and major industry groups are employment-weighted averages of the figures for component industries.

Average weekly earnings are computed by multiplying average hourly earnings by average weekly hours. In addition to the factors mentioned above, which exert varying influences upon average hourly earnings, average weekly earnings are affected by changes in the length of the workweek, part-time work, work stoppages, labor turnover, and absenteeism. Persistent long-term uptrends in the proportion of part-time workers in retail trade and many of the service industries have reduced average workweeks (as measured here), and have similarly affected the average weekly earnings series.

Benchmark adjustments. Independent benchmarks are not available for the hours and earnings series. At the time of the annual adjustment of the employment series to new benchmarks, the levels of hours and earnings may be affected by the revised employment weights (which are used in computing the industry averages for hours and earnings), as well as by the changes in seasonal adjustment factors that were also introduced with the benchmark revision.

Seasonal adjustment. Hours and earnings series are seasonally adjusted by applying factors directly to the corresponding unadjusted series; seasonally adjusted average weekly earnings are the product of seasonally adjusted hourly earnings and weekly hours.

REGARIMA modeling is used to correct for reporting and processing errors associated with variations in the number of weekdays in a month (rather than for the 4- and 5-week effect, which is less significant for earnings than for employment). This is of particular importance for average hourly earnings in wholesale trade, financial activities, professional and business services, and other services. For this reason, BLS advises that calculations of over-the-year changes, for example the change for the current month from a year earlier, should use seasonally adjusted data, since the actual not seasonally adjusted monthly data may be distorted.

Data availability

See data availability for Tables 10-8 and related, above.

References

See references for Tables 10-8 and related, above.

Table 10-19: Hours at Work, Current Population Survey

This table presents annual average measures of hours worked per week reported by workers in the Current Population Survey, in response to questions asking for the hours worked in the survey week by each worker in the household on all his or her jobs combined. These measures are not published in regular BLS reports but are available on request. *Business Statistics* obtained these numbers from BLS staff and presents them here in annual average form.

A study published in the *Monthly Labor Review*, June 2011, indicates that CPS survey respondents may tend to overestimate the length of their workweeks, with greater overestimates the longer the actual workweek. This means that the level of the CPS data series may be overestimated, though not necessarily the time pattern of the series. In the judgment of the editor, the CPS data nevertheless give a more accurate picture of trends in the workweeks of typical American workers.

Table 10-20: Median Usual Weekly Earnings of Full-Time Wage and Salary Workers

SOURCE: U.S. DEPARTMENT OF LABOR, BUREAU OF LABOR STATISTICS

These data are from the Current Population Survey, which was described in the notes to Tables 10-1 through 10-6. Because they are earnings per worker, not per job, and are limited to full-time workers, the data are not distorted by the increasing proportion of part-time workers, as the CES earnings data are.

Definitions

Full-time wage and salary workers are those workers reported as "employed" in the CPS who receive wages, salaries, commissions, tips, pay in kind, or piece rates, and usually work 35 hours or more per week at their sole or principal job. Both private-sector and public-sector employees are included.

All self-employed persons are excluded (even those whose businesses are incorporated). The number of full-time wage and salary workers was 103.7 million, seasonally adjusted, in the fourth quarter of 2012; these workers made up 72 percent of total civilian employment.

Usual weekly earnings are earnings before taxes and other deductions and include any overtime pay, commissions, or tips usually received. In the case of multiple jobholders they refer to the main job. The wording of the question was changed in January 1994 to better deal with persons who found it easier to report earnings on other than a weekly basis. Such reports are then converted to the weekly equivalent. According to BLS, "the term 'usual' is as perceived by the respondent. If the respondent asks for a definition of usual, interviewers are instructed to define the term as more than half the weeks worked during the past 4 or 5 months."

The *median* is the amount that divides a given earnings distribution into two equal groups, one having earnings above the median and the other having earnings below the median.

2000 dollars. For men 25 and older and women 25 and older, median usual weekly earnings are shown on both a current-dollar and a constant-dollar basis. The editor has converted the current-dollar figures to 2000 dollars using the CPI-U-RS, which is shown and described in Chapter 8. The CPI-U-RS was chosen because it is the deflator used by the Census Bureau to convert household income and earnings to constant dollars and by the Bureau of Labor Statistics to convert compensation per hour to constant dollars. It corrects historical values of the CPI to be consistent with current CPI methodology.

Race and ethnicity. See the notes to Tables 10-1 through 10-6 for the definitions of these categories.

Data availability

These data become available about 3 weeks after the end of each quarter in the "Usual Weekly Earnings of Wage and Salary Workers" press release, available on the BLS Web site at http://www.bls.gov/cps. Recent data are available at that location. Also available are greater detail by demographic and age groups, by occupation, by union status, and by education; distributional data, by deciles and quartiles; and earnings for part-time workers. Also available are earnings in 1982 dollars using the CPI-U. (In the opinion of the editor, these give a less accurate depiction of longer-term trends, which is why *Business Statistics* provides the CPI-U-RS data explained above.) Historical data are available upon request from BLS by telephone at (202) 691-6378.

Table 10-21: Full-Time and Part-Time Employees by SIC Industry, Historical Annual

These estimates, which are made only annually for the full year, are found in Tables 6-4 of the National Income and Product Accounts (NIPAs). They are like the payroll series in counting the number of jobs rather than the number of persons employed. However, they are broader than the payroll series in that they include private household employment (domestic service) in the "service" industry category. They exclude most of the agricultural employment reported in the CPS, but include members of the armed forces and all other government employment including work-relief agencies such as the Works Progress Administration and the Civilian Conservation Corps; these categories are shown separately in Table 10-21. This treatment is consistent with the rest of the NIPAs, in which GDP includes, as output, the work done by relief workers, and the buildings they constructed are included in investment and capital stock. The industry estimates are based on various versions of the Standard Industrial Classification system that were in effect at the time of compilation.

CHAPTER 11: ENERGY

Figure 11-1. Energy Consumption and Prices, 1950–2012

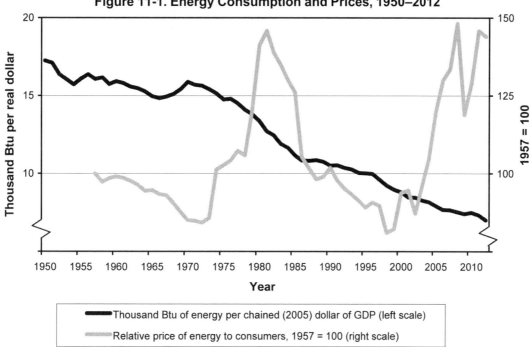

The downward trend in energy use per dollar of real GDP, which can also be described as an increase in the energy efficiency of national production, may seem surprising in light of long-term trend increases in motor vehicle use, air conditioning, air travel, and other consumer uses of energy. Evidently, these increases are more than offset by factors such as the rising share of services and high-tech goods in GDP; the declining relative importance of energy-intensive materials production processes such as primary metals production; and the movement of population and economic activity to warmer states, which cuts more energy in heating costs than it increases on air-conditioning. Also, upswings in relative energy prices—measured as the ratio of the CPI for energy to the total CPI—appear to have been associated with somewhat faster declines in the energy/GDP trend. (Figure 11-1, from Tables 8-1 and 11-2)

- Net imports supplied 13.8 percent of total energy supply (production plus net imports) in 2012, down dramatically from a high of 30.3 percent in 2005, and marked the highest degree of energy independence since 1972. Compared with 2005, domestic production was up 14 percent in 2012, reflecting increases in production of crude oil, natural gas plant liquids, renewable energy, and especially natural gas, which together outweighed a decrease in coal production. In addition, over the same period, energy imports dropped 23 percent. (Table 11-1)

- Nuclear power, almost nonexistent in 1965, supplied 10.2 percent of total U.S. energy production in 2012. Renewable energy sources, which provided 6.7 percent in 1965, accounted for 11.2 percent in 2012. The remaining 78.6 percent in 2012 was accounted for by domestic fossil fuel production, compared with 93.2 percent in 1965. (Table 11-1)

Table 11-1. Energy Supply and Consumption

(Quadrillion Btu.)

Year and month	Imports	Exports	Production, by source								Consumption, by end-use sector			
			Total	Fossil fuels					Nuclear electric power	Renewable energy, total	Total	Residential and commercial	Industrial	Transport-ation
				Total	Coal	Natural gas	Crude oil	Natural gas plant liquids						
1965	5.892	1.829	50.676	47.234	13.055	15.775	16.521	1.883	0.043	3.399	54.017	16.509	25.075	12.434
1966	6.146	1.829	53.534	50.036	13.468	17.011	17.561	1.996	0.064	3.434	57.017	17.517	26.397	13.102
1967	6.159	2.115	56.379	52.596	13.825	17.943	18.651	2.177	0.088	3.695	58.908	18.541	26.616	13.752
1968	6.905	1.998	58.225	54.306	13.609	19.068	19.308	2.321	0.142	3.777	62.419	19.665	27.888	14.866
1969	7.676	2.126	60.541	56.285	13.863	20.446	19.556	2.420	0.154	4.102	65.621	21.000	29.114	15.506
1970	8.342	2.632	63.501	59.186	14.607	21.666	20.401	2.512	0.239	4.076	67.844	22.105	29.641	16.098
1971	9.535	2.151	62.723	58.043	13.186	22.280	20.033	2.544	0.413	4.267	69.289	22.959	29.601	16.729
1972	11.387	2.118	63.920	58.939	14.092	22.208	20.041	2.598	0.584	4.397	72.704	24.036	30.953	17.716
1973	14.613	2.033	63.563	58.241	13.992	22.187	19.493	2.569	0.910	4.411	75.676	24.440	32.623	18.613
1974	14.304	2.203	62.345	56.331	14.074	21.210	18.575	2.471	1.272	4.742	73.955	24.048	31.787	18.120
1975	14.032	2.323	61.320	54.733	14.989	19.640	17.729	2.374	1.900	4.687	71.964	24.306	29.413	18.245
1976	16.760	2.172	61.561	54.723	15.654	19.480	17.262	2.327	2.111	4.727	75.967	25.474	31.393	19.101
1977	19.948	2.052	62.012	55.101	15.755	19.565	17.454	2.327	2.702	4.209	77.954	25.869	32.263	19.822
1978	19.106	1.920	63.104	55.074	14.910	19.485	18.434	2.245	3.024	5.005	79.949	26.644	32.688	20.617
1979	19.460	2.855	65.904	58.006	17.540	20.076	18.104	2.286	2.776	5.123	80.857	26.461	33.925	20.472
1980	15.796	3.695	67.175	59.008	18.598	19.908	18.249	2.254	2.739	5.428	78.068	26.332	32.039	19.697
1981	13.719	4.307	66.951	58.529	18.377	19.699	18.146	2.307	3.008	5.414	76.103	25.877	30.712	19.514
1982	11.861	4.608	66.569	57.458	18.639	18.319	18.309	2.191	3.131	5.980	73.095	26.391	27.614	19.089
1983	11.752	3.693	64.114	54.416	17.247	16.593	18.392	2.184	3.203	6.496	72.968	26.363	27.428	19.177
1984	12.471	3.786	68.840	58.849	19.719	18.008	18.848	2.274	3.553	6.438	76.629	27.403	29.570	19.656
1985	11.781	4.196	67.698	57.539	19.325	16.980	18.992	2.241	4.076	6.084	76.396	27.493	28.816	20.088
1986	14.151	4.021	67.066	56.575	19.509	16.541	18.376	2.149	4.380	6.111	76.644	27.581	28.274	20.789
1987	15.398	3.812	67.542	57.167	20.141	17.136	17.675	2.215	4.754	5.622	79.057	28.209	29.379	21.469
1988	17.296	4.366	68.919	57.875	20.738	17.599	17.279	2.260	5.587	5.457	82.706	29.711	30.677	22.318
1989	18.766	4.661	69.320	57.483	21.360	17.847	16.117	2.158	5.602	6.235	84.777	30.979	31.320	22.478
1990	18.817	4.752	70.705	58.560	22.488	18.326	15.571	2.175	6.104	6.041	84.494	30.265	31.810	22.420
1991	18.335	5.141	70.362	57.872	21.636	18.229	15.701	2.306	6.422	6.069	84.437	30.920	31.399	22.118
1992	19.372	4.937	69.956	57.655	21.694	18.375	15.223	2.363	6.479	5.821	85.783	30.797	32.571	22.415
1993	21.273	4.258	68.315	55.822	20.336	18.584	14.494	2.408	6.410	6.083	87.434	32.037	32.629	22.768
1994	22.390	4.061	70.726	58.044	22.202	19.348	14.103	2.391	6.694	5.988	89.097	32.210	33.521	23.366
1995	22.260	4.511	71.174	57.540	22.130	19.082	13.887	2.442	7.075	6.558	91.026	33.209	33.971	23.846
1996	23.702	4.633	72.486	58.387	22.790	19.344	13.723	2.530	7.087	7.012	94.018	34.676	34.904	24.437
1997	25.215	4.514	72.472	58.857	23.310	19.394	13.658	2.495	6.597	7.018	94.596	34.646	35.200	24.750
1998	26.581	4.299	72.876	59.314	24.045	19.613	13.235	2.420	7.068	6.494	95.021	34.922	34.843	25.256
1999	27.252	3.715	71.742	57.614	23.295	19.341	12.451	2.528	7.610	6.517	96.646	35.933	34.764	25.949
2000	28.973	4.006	71.332	57.366	22.735	19.662	12.358	2.611	7.862	6.104	98.812	37.600	34.664	26.548
2001	30.157	3.771	71.735	58.541	23.547	20.166	12.282	2.547	8.029	5.164	96.174	37.179	32.720	26.275
2002	29.408	3.669	70.713	56.834	22.732	19.382	12.160	2.559	8.145	5.734	97.640	38.136	32.662	26.842
2003	31.061	4.054	69.927	56.022	22.094	19.633	11.948	2.346	7.959	5.947	97.944	38.470	32.555	26.919
2004	33.544	4.434	70.220	55.930	22.852	19.074	11.538	2.466	8.222	6.069	100.160	38.751	33.519	27.895
2005	34.709	4.560	69.443	55.053	23.185	18.556	10.978	2.334	8.161	6.229	100.280	39.483	32.446	28.353
2006	34.679	4.872	70.754	55.940	23.790	19.022	10.772	2.356	8.215	6.599	99.630	38.399	32.401	28.830
2007	34.703	5.482	71.419	56.435	23.493	19.786	10.748	2.409	8.455	6.528	101.310	39.796	32.403	29.117
2008	32.992	7.060	73.235	57.588	23.851	20.703	10.615	2.419	8.427	7.219	99.292	40.097	31.364	27.831
2009	29.706	6.965	72.680	56.669	21.624	21.139	11.332	2.574	8.356	7.655	94.598	39.000	28.491	27.108
2010	29.877	8.234	74.786	58.224	22.038	21.806	11.598	2.781	8.434	8.128	97.966	39.904	30.502	27.561
2011	28.855	10.458	78.001	60.562	22.221	23.406	11.965	2.970	8.269	9.170	97.462	39.401	30.843	27.218
2012	26.608	11.452	79.154	62.237	20.600	24.592	13.809	3.235	8.050	8.867	95.105	37.704	30.696	26.705
2011														
January	2.656	0.841	6.494	4.985	1.854	1.901	0.989	0.241	0.761	0.747	9.334	4.431	2.677	2.225
February	2.126	0.759	5.892	4.504	1.736	1.684	0.879	0.207	0.678	0.710	8.143	3.698	2.397	2.048
March	2.545	0.880	6.667	5.163	1.958	1.950	1.006	0.250	0.687	0.816	8.395	3.407	2.675	2.313
April	2.411	0.878	6.294	4.911	1.795	1.909	0.965	0.241	0.571	0.813	7.548	2.815	2.486	2.247
May	2.497	0.847	6.429	5.000	1.760	1.977	1.009	0.254	0.597	0.832	7.621	2.764	2.535	2.323
June	2.418	0.818	6.425	4.917	1.804	1.903	0.970	0.241	0.683	0.825	7.932	3.072	2.530	2.330
July	2.505	0.854	6.490	4.941	1.736	1.979	0.975	0.251	0.757	0.792	8.411	3.481	2.583	2.347
August	2.406	0.879	6.697	5.208	1.937	2.003	1.015	0.254	0.746	0.742	8.434	3.398	2.660	2.377
September	2.292	0.892	6.430	5.054	1.907	1.935	0.973	0.239	0.700	0.677	7.594	2.852	2.498	2.245
October	2.352	0.891	6.672	5.301	1.919	2.063	1.056	0.263	0.663	0.708	7.619	2.749	2.587	2.282
November	2.274	0.894	6.649	5.237	1.909	2.022	1.045	0.261	0.675	0.738	7.818	3.005	2.612	2.201
December	2.372	1.026	6.861	5.339	1.908	2.079	1.084	0.268	0.752	0.770	8.614	3.731	2.603	2.280
2012														
January	2.328	0.863	6.930	5.389	1.925	2.089	1.104	0.271	0.757	0.783	8.720	3.942	2.639	2.139
February	2.102	0.837	6.343	4.976	1.738	1.931	1.051	0.255	0.668	0.699	8.033	3.427	2.513	2.093
March	2.258	0.963	6.642	5.203	1.736	2.062	1.134	0.271	0.646	0.792	7.730	2.963	2.527	2.241
April	2.176	0.999	6.290	4.938	1.572	2.007	1.096	0.263	0.585	0.768	7.295	2.619	2.462	2.215
May	2.353	1.010	6.614	5.150	1.659	2.079	1.140	0.271	0.650	0.814	7.684	2.772	2.598	2.314
June	2.324	0.998	6.473	5.013	1.660	2.005	1.090	0.258	0.682	0.778	7.783	2.984	2.515	2.284
July	2.305	0.981	6.723	5.250	1.751	2.084	1.150	0.265	0.723	0.749	8.348	3.439	2.593	2.316
August	2.324	0.941	6.757	5.317	1.841	2.070	1.136	0.270	0.728	0.711	8.272	3.287	2.621	2.365
September	2.172	0.914	6.423	5.104	1.658	2.029	1.146	0.272	0.675	0.643	7.407	2.800	2.445	2.161
October	2.146	0.954	6.668	5.368	1.726	2.108	1.251	0.284	0.625	0.674	7.607	2.756	2.596	2.255
November	2.070	0.940	6.538	5.259	1.707	2.043	1.232	0.278	0.593	0.685	7.811	3.085	2.561	2.166
December	2.051	1.052	6.755	5.268	1.626	2.086	1.280	0.276	0.718	0.769	8.413	3.636	2.622	2.156

Table 11-2. Energy Consumption per Dollar of Real Gross Domestic Product

Year	Primary energy consumption (quadrillion Btu)			Gross domestic product (billions of chained [2005] dollars)	Energy consumption per real dollar of GDP (thousand Btu per chained [2005] dollar)		
	Total	Petroleum and natural gas	Other energy		Total	Petroleum and natural gas	Other energy
1950	34.616	19.284	15.332	2 006.0	17.26	9.61	7.64
1951	36.974	21.477	15.497	2 161.1	17.11	9.94	7.17
1952	36.748	22.505	14.243	2 243.9	16.38	10.03	6.35
1953	37.664	23.462	14.202	2 347.2	16.05	10.00	6.05
1954	36.639	24.169	12.470	2 332.4	15.71	10.36	5.35
1955	40.208	26.253	13.955	2 500.3	16.08	10.50	5.58
1956	41.754	27.551	14.203	2 549.7	16.38	10.81	5.57
1957	41.787	28.122	13.665	2 601.1	16.07	10.81	5.25
1958	41.645	29.190	12.455	2 577.6	16.16	11.32	4.83
1959	43.466	31.040	12.426	2 762.5	15.73	11.24	4.50
1960	45.087	32.305	12.782	2 830.9	15.93	11.41	4.52
1961	45.739	33.143	12.596	2 896.9	15.79	11.44	4.35
1962	47.828	34.780	13.048	3 072.4	15.57	11.32	4.25
1963	49.646	36.104	13.542	3 206.7	15.48	11.26	4.22
1964	51.817	37.589	14.228	3 392.3	15.27	11.08	4.19
1965	54.017	39.014	15.003	3 610.1	14.96	10.81	4.16
1966	57.017	41.396	15.621	3 845.3	14.83	10.77	4.06
1967	58.908	43.228	15.680	3 942.5	14.94	10.96	3.98
1968	62.419	46.189	16.230	4 133.4	15.10	11.17	3.93
1969	65.621	49.016	16.605	4 261.8	15.40	11.50	3.90
1970	67.844	51.315	16.529	4 269.9	15.89	12.02	3.87
1971	69.289	53.030	16.259	4 413.3	15.70	12.02	3.68
1972	72.704	55.645	17.059	4 647.7	15.64	11.97	3.67
1973	75.684	57.350	18.334	4 912.8	15.41	11.67	3.73
1974	73.962	55.186	18.776	4 885.7	15.14	11.30	3.84
1975	71.965	52.680	19.284	4 875.4	14.76	10.81	3.96
1976	75.975	55.523	20.452	5 136.9	14.79	10.81	3.98
1977	77.961	57.054	20.907	5 373.1	14.51	10.62	3.89
1978	79.950	57.963	21.987	5 672.8	14.09	10.22	3.88
1979	80.859	57.788	23.070	5 850.1	13.82	9.88	3.94
1980	78.067	54.440	23.627	5 834.0	13.38	9.33	4.05
1981	76.106	51.680	24.426	5 982.1	12.72	8.64	4.08
1982	73.099	48.588	24.511	5 865.9	12.46	8.28	4.18
1983	72.971	47.273	25.698	6 130.9	11.90	7.71	4.19
1984	76.632	49.447	27.185	6 571.5	11.66	7.52	4.14
1985	76.392	48.628	27.764	6 843.4	11.16	7.11	4.06
1986	76.647	48.790	27.857	7 080.5	10.83	6.89	3.93
1987	79.054	50.504	28.551	7 307.0	10.82	6.91	3.91
1988	82.709	52.671	30.038	7 607.4	10.87	6.92	3.95
1989	84.786	53.811	30.975	7 879.2	10.76	6.83	3.93
1990	84.485	53.155	31.330	8 027.1	10.52	6.62	3.90
1991	84.438	52.879	31.559	8 008.3	10.54	6.60	3.94
1992	85.783	54.239	31.544	8 280.0	10.36	6.55	3.81
1993	87.424	54.973	32.450	8 516.2	10.27	6.46	3.81
1994	89.091	56.289	32.803	8 863.1	10.05	6.35	3.70
1995	91.029	57.110	33.920	9 086.0	10.02	6.29	3.73
1996	94.022	58.760	35.262	9 425.8	9.97	6.23	3.74
1997	94.602	59.382	35.221	9 845.9	9.61	6.03	3.58
1998	95.018	59.646	35.372	10 274.7	9.25	5.81	3.44
1999	96.652	60.747	35.905	10 770.7	8.97	5.64	3.33
2000	98.814	62.086	36.729	11 216.4	8.81	5.54	3.27
2001	96.168	60.958	35.210	11 337.5	8.48	5.38	3.11
2002	97.645	61.734	35.911	11 543.1	8.46	5.35	3.11
2003	97.943	61.642	36.301	11 836.4	8.27	5.21	3.07
2004	100.160	63.215	36.945	12 246.9	8.18	5.16	3.02
2005	100.282	62.953	37.328	12 623.0	7.94	4.99	2.96
2006	99.629	62.194	37.435	12 958.5	7.69	4.80	2.89
2007	101.315	63.437	37.878	13 206.4	7.67	4.80	2.87
2008	99.292	61.123	38.169	13 161.9	7.54	4.64	2.90
2009	94.598	58.819	35.779	12 757.9	7.41	4.61	2.80
2010	97.974	60.584	37.389	13 063.0	7.50	4.64	2.86
2011	97.469	60.325	37.144	13 299.1	7.33	4.54	2.79
2012	95.100	60.688	34.412	13 593.2	7.00	4.46	2.53

NOTES AND DEFINITIONS, CHAPTER 11

Tables 11-1 and 11-2: Energy Supply and Consumption

SOURCES: U.S. DEPARTMENT OF ENERGY, ENERGY INFORMATION ADMINISTRATION; U.S. DEPARTMENT OF COMMERCE, BUREAU OF ECONOMIC ANALYSIS

Definitions

The *British thermal unit (Btu)* is a measure used to combine data for different energy sources into a consistent aggregate. It is the amount of energy required to raise the temperature of 1 pound of water 1 degree Fahrenheit when the water is near a temperature of 39.2 degrees Fahrenheit. To illustrate one of the factors used to convert volumes to Btu, conventional motor gasoline has a heat content of 5.253 million Btu per barrel. For further information, see the Energy Information Administration's *Monthly Energy Review*, Appendix A.

Production: Crude oil includes lease condensates.

Renewable energy, total includes conventional hydroelectric power, geothermal, solar thermal and photovoltaic, wind, and biomass. Hydroelectric power includes conventional electrical utility and industrial generation. Biomass includes wood, waste, and alcohol fuels (ethanol blended into motor gasoline).

The sum of domestic energy *production* and net imports of energy (*imports* minus *exports*) does not exactly equal domestic energy *consumption*. The difference is attributed to inventory changes; losses and gains in conversion, transportation, and distribution; the addition of blending compounds; shipments of anthracite to U.S. armed forces in Europe; and adjustments to account for discrepancies between reporting systems.

Consumption by end-use sector is based on total, not net, consumption—that is, each sector's consumption includes its electricity purchases as well as its own energy production. Electric utilities are not treated as a separate end-use sector. However, they are counted as primary producers in the production accounts, which measure only primary production. As a result, total national supply and consumption are in rough balance, though components may not add to exact totals, not only because of the miscellaneous adjustments described above, but also because of different sector-specific conversion factors.

References and notes on the data

All of these data are published each month in Tables 1.1, 1.2, 1.7, and 2.1 in the *Monthly Energy Review*. Annual data before 1973 are published in the *Annual Energy Review*. These two publications are no longer published in printed form but are available, along with all current and historical data, on the EIA Web site at http://www.eia.doe.gov.

The real gross domestic product (GDP) data used to calculate energy consumption per dollar of real GDP are from the Bureau of Economic Analysis; see Table 1-2 and the applicable notes and definitions in this volume of *Business Statistics*. The GDP numbers shown in this table do not reflect the comprehensive revision of July 2013, due to deadline pressures. However, the editor believes that the revision is not likely to change the general direction of these trends.

CHAPTER 12: MONEY, INTEREST, ASSETS, LIABILITIES, AND ASSET PRICES

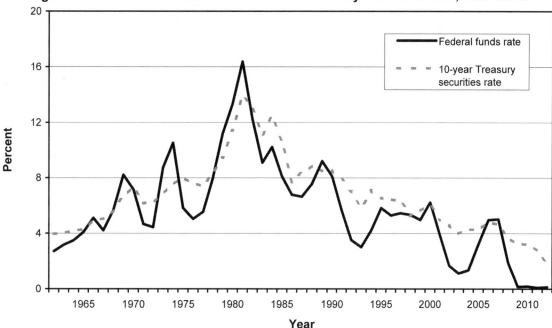

Figure 12-1: Federal Funds Rate and 10-Year Treasury Securities Rate, 1962–2012

- As the recession deepened, the Federal Reserve brought short-term interest rates lower than at any time since the Great Depression, World War II, and its aftermath. The federal funds rate—shown in Figure 12-1—has been held under 0.2 percent since then, and the "real" fed funds and other short-term interest rates (subtracting out current underlying inflation rates) have been negative since early 2008. (Tables 12-9A and B)

- Longer-term rates have also declined dramatically. The nominal rate on Treasury 10-year securities, the ultimate in safe longer-term investments, is also shown in Figure 12-1. It was 1.7 percent at the end of 2012. Despite the huge volume of federal borrowing (see Tables 6-1, 6-14 and 12-5), this interest rate was lower than at any time in the postwar period. (Tables 12-9A and B)

- The rate spread between Aaa-rated and Baa-rated corporate bonds, representing a market evaluation of risk, was more than 3 percentage points (300 "basis points") in December 2008. This exceeded the previous record postwar spreads seen in 1982. At the end of 2012, the spread had contracted back to 0.98 percentage point. (Table 12-9A and B)

- Looking at the easing in quantitative terms, the Federal Reserve added $1.3 trillion to its balance sheet during 2008 and another $668 billion by the end of 2012. The size of the monetary base has grown at a 26.5 percent annual rate over the 5 years since December 2007. (Table 12-3) But with financial institutions reluctant to lend and thereby create deposits, the money supply grew more tamely; M1 grew at a 12 percent annual rate over those years, while M2, the aggregate most closely associated with the dollar value of GDP and hence with economic activity and inflationary pressure, only increased at a 7 percent rate. (Table 12-1)

Table 12-1A. Money Stock Measures and Components of M1: Recent Data

(Billions of dollars, monthly data are averages of daily figures, annual data are for December.)

Year and month	Not seasonally adjusted		Seasonally adjusted					Other checkable deposits		
	M1	M2	M1	M2	Currency	Traveler's checks	Demand deposits	At commercial banks	At thrift institutions	Total
1960	144.5	315.3	140.7	312.4	28.7	0.3	111.6	0.0	0.0	0.0
1961	149.2	338.5	145.2	335.5	29.3	0.4	115.5	0.0	0.0	0.0
1962	151.9	365.8	147.8	362.7	30.3	0.4	117.1	0.0	0.0	0.0
1963	157.5	396.4	153.3	393.2	32.2	0.4	120.6	0.0	0.1	0.1
1964	164.9	428.3	160.3	424.7	33.9	0.5	125.8	0.0	0.1	0.1
1965	172.6	463.1	167.8	459.2	36.0	0.5	131.3	0.0	0.1	0.1
1966	176.9	483.7	172.0	480.2	38.0	0.6	133.4	0.0	0.1	0.1
1967	188.4	528.0	183.3	524.8	40.0	0.6	142.5	0.0	0.1	0.1
1968	202.8	569.7	197.4	566.8	43.0	0.7	153.6	0.0	0.1	0.1
1969	209.3	590.1	203.9	587.9	45.7	0.8	157.3	0.0	0.1	0.1
1970	220.1	627.8	214.4	626.5	48.6	0.9	164.7	0.0	0.1	0.1
1971	234.5	711.2	228.3	710.3	52.0	1.0	175.1	0.0	0.2	0.2
1972	256.1	803.1	249.2	802.3	56.2	1.2	191.6	0.0	0.2	0.2
1973	270.2	856.5	262.9	855.5	60.8	1.4	200.3	0.0	0.3	0.3
1974	281.8	903.5	274.2	902.1	67.0	1.7	205.1	0.2	0.4	0.4
1975	295.3	1 017.8	287.1	1 016.2	72.8	2.1	211.3	0.4	0.5	0.9
1976	314.5	1 153.5	306.2	1 152.0	79.5	2.6	221.5	1.3	1.4	2.7
1977	340.0	1 273.0	330.9	1 270.3	87.4	2.9	236.4	1.8	2.3	4.2
1978	367.9	1 370.8	357.3	1 366.0	96.0	3.3	249.5	5.3	3.1	8.5
1979	393.2	1 479.0	381.8	1 473.7	104.8	3.5	256.6	12.7	4.2	16.8
1980	419.5	1 604.8	408.5	1 599.8	115.3	3.9	261.2	20.8	7.3	28.1
1981	447.0	1 760.3	436.7	1 755.5	122.5	4.1	231.4	63.0	15.6	78.7
1982	485.8	1 914.3	474.8	1 906.4	132.5	4.1	234.1	80.5	23.6	104.1
1983	533.3	2 134.3	521.4	2 123.8	146.2	4.7	238.5	97.3	34.8	132.1
1984	564.6	2 318.8	551.6	2 306.8	156.1	5.0	243.4	104.7	42.4	147.1
1985	633.3	2 504.6	619.8	2 492.6	167.7	5.6	266.9	124.7	54.9	179.5
1986	739.8	2 741.9	724.7	2 729.2	180.4	6.1	302.9	161.0	74.2	235.2
1987	765.4	2 840.8	750.2	2 828.8	196.7	6.6	287.7	178.2	81.0	259.2
1988	803.1	3 003.0	786.7	2 990.6	212.0	7.0	287.1	192.5	88.1	280.6
1989	810.6	3 167.5	792.9	3 154.4	222.3	6.9	278.6	197.4	87.7	285.1
1990	842.7	3 286.0	824.7	3 272.7	246.5	7.7	276.8	208.7	85.0	293.7
1991	915.6	3 385.8	897.0	3 371.6	267.1	7.7	289.6	241.6	90.9	332.5
1992	1 045.6	3 439.7	1 024.9	3 423.1	292.1	8.2	340.0	280.8	103.8	384.6
1993	1 153.3	3 493.0	1 129.8	3 472.4	321.7	8.0	385.4	302.6	112.0	414.6
1994	1 174.5	3 506.3	1 150.8	3 484.9	354.7	8.6	383.6	297.4	106.6	404.0
1995	1 152.7	3 650.4	1 127.5	3 626.5	372.8	9.0	389.0	249.0	107.6	356.6
1996	1 105.8	3 826.0	1 081.3	3 804.8	394.5	8.8	402.2	172.1	103.7	275.8
1997	1 097.5	4 039.4	1 072.8	4 018.1	425.2	8.4	393.9	148.3	96.9	245.2
1998	1 121.2	4 380.8	1 096.1	4 358.9	460.4	8.5	377.1	143.8	106.2	250.0
1999	1 148.2	4 643.4	1 122.9	4 617.1	517.9	8.6	353.3	139.7	103.5	243.2
2000	1 111.7	4 931.1	1 087.9	4 900.4	531.3	8.3	310.0	133.2	105.1	238.2
2001	1 208.5	5 436.4	1 182.9	5 403.2	581.3	8.0	336.0	142.1	115.4	257.5
2002	1 245.5	5 772.5	1 220.4	5 742.0	626.3	7.8	307.0	154.3	125.1	279.3
2003	1 332.2	6 067.0	1 306.6	6 039.6	662.5	7.7	326.3	175.2	134.8	310.0
2004	1 401.2	6 417.5	1 375.9	6 390.9	697.6	7.6	343.0	187.0	140.8	327.8
2005	1 396.9	6 678.4	1 374.9	6 656.8	724.3	7.2	324.7	180.7	138.1	318.8
2006	1 387.3	7 068.9	1 366.5	7 042.0	749.8	6.7	305.0	176.7	128.2	304.9
2007	1 394.5	7 476.6	1 374.3	7 450.5	760.3	6.3	302.4	172.8	132.6	305.4
2008	1 632.0	8 205.4	1 604.9	8 183.8	816.3	5.5	471.9	178.5	132.6	311.1
2009	1 724.0	8 512.2	1 695.8	8 487.4	864.1	5.1	443.4	234.0	149.2	383.2
2010	1 871.0	8 823.2	1 836.7	8 782.4	919.1	4.7	512.8	238.9	161.2	400.1
2011	2 207.4	9 691.2	2 160.9	9 638.3	1 001.9	4.3	742.5	237.1	175.2	412.3
2012	2 503.6	10 482.5	2 445.6	10 408.9	1 090.8	3.8	907.4	248.1	195.6	443.6
2011										
January	1 855.2	8 815.7	1 854.8	8 801.3	923.7	4.7	525.1	236.1	165.3	401.3
February	1 858.3	8 853.3	1 876.4	8 857.3	929.9	4.6	539.4	236.3	166.2	402.5
March	1 908.9	8 966.7	1 890.4	8 899.9	937.7	4.6	544.9	236.5	166.7	403.1
April	1 917.5	9 021.7	1 902.5	8 948.2	946.9	4.6	552.6	229.6	168.9	398.4
May	1 933.7	8 991.8	1 940.6	9 000.7	956.6	4.6	577.8	234.4	167.3	401.7
June	1 953.6	9 080.2	1 952.4	9 081.2	963.6	4.5	583.5	235.6	165.2	400.8
July	1 993.9	9 232.6	1 998.8	9 267.4	970.1	4.5	621.1	235.7	167.4	403.1
August	2 101.2	9 427.0	2 112.5	9 490.8	976.9	4.4	718.6	239.8	172.7	412.5
September	2 098.5	9 465.2	2 123.6	9 520.5	982.5	4.4	724.8	238.3	173.6	411.9
October	2 127.5	9 514.4	2 142.2	9 550.2	986.6	4.4	740.8	235.7	174.7	410.4
November	2 163.7	9 596.2	2 159.9	9 602.4	994.7	4.3	747.3	238.8	174.9	413.6
December	2 207.4	9 691.2	2 160.9	9 638.3	1 001.9	4.3	742.5	237.1	175.2	412.3
2012										
January	2 208.4	9 723.5	2 201.9	9 712.3	1 010.6	4.2	769.5	238.2	179.4	417.6
February	2 193.6	9 748.7	2 216.8	9 747.8	1 019.1	4.2	772.1	239.6	181.8	421.4
March	2 245.1	9 864.8	2 223.5	9 784.3	1 027.3	4.1	769.1	239.8	183.1	422.9
April	2 267.6	9 910.3	2 252.6	9 828.7	1 033.7	4.1	789.7	240.1	185.0	425.1
May	2 247.4	9 843.7	2 262.6	9 870.3	1 039.5	4.0	793.2	240.6	185.2	425.8
June	2 265.3	9 921.3	2 267.4	9 921.0	1 045.8	4.0	797.2	235.6	184.7	420.4
July	2 305.5	9 958.6	2 312.6	10 012.8	1 052.7	4.0	824.9	242.9	188.1	431.0
August	2 326.7	10 021.2	2 340.0	10 085.3	1 059.9	3.9	843.8	243.2	189.2	432.4
September	2 350.4	10 117.3	2 374.3	10 160.9	1 068.6	3.9	868.2	242.0	191.5	433.6
October	2 408.2	10 196.5	2 420.9	10 245.8	1 077.6	3.9	901.4	246.2	191.8	438.0
November	2 408.6	10 294.4	2 406.5	10 298.2	1 083.0	3.9	887.6	240.4	191.6	432.0
December	2 503.6	10 482.5	2 445.6	10 408.9	1 090.8	3.8	907.4	248.1	195.6	443.6

Table 12-1B. Money Stock: Historical, 1892–1946

(Not seasonally adjusted, millions of dollars.)

Classification	1892	1893	1894	1895	1896	1897	1898	1899	1900	1901	1902
June 30											
Currency outside banks	1 015	1 081	972	971	974	1 013	1 150	1 181	1 331	1 395	1 431
Demand deposits adjusted	2 880	2 766	2 807	2 960	2 839	2 871	3 432	4 162	4 420	5 204	5 719
M1	3 895	3 847	3 779	3 931	3 813	3 884	4 582	5 343	5 751	6 599	7 150
Time deposits	1 929	2 007	1 994	2 088	2 220	2 305	2 397	2 617	3 015	3 315	3 565
M2	5 824	5 854	5 773	6 019	6 033	6 189	6 979	7 960	8 766	9 914	10 715
December 31											
Currency outside banks	. . .	. . .	. . .	. . .	. . .	. . .	. . .	. . .	. . .	. . .	. . .
Demand deposits adjusted	. . .	. . .	. . .	. . .	. . .	. . .	. . .	. . .	. . .	. . .	. . .
M1	. . .	. . .	. . .	. . .	. . .	. . .	. . .	. . .	. . .	. . .	. . .
Time deposits	. . .	. . .	. . .	. . .	. . .	. . .	. . .	. . .	. . .	. . .	. . .
M2	. . .	. . .	. . .	. . .	. . .	. . .	. . .	. . .	. . .	. . .	. . .

Classification	1903	1904	1905	1906	1907	1908	1909	1910	1911	1912	1913
June 30											
Currency outside banks	1 543	1 562	1 629	1 759	1 700	1 711	1 691	1 725	1 709	1 762	1 858
Demand deposits adjusted	5 962	6 256	7 069	7 504	7 872	7 384	7 768	8 254	8 668	9 156	9 140
M1	7 505	7 818	8 698	9 263	9 572	9 095	9 459	9 979	10 377	10 918	10 998
Time deposits	3 800	4 045	4 464	4 769	5 350	5 493	6 265	6 944	7 337	7 889	8 356
M2	11 305	11 863	13 162	14 032	14 922	14 588	15 724	16 923	17 714	18 807	19 354
December 31											
Currency outside banks	. . .	. . .	. . .	. . .	. . .	. . .	. . .	. . .	. . .	. . .	. . .
Demand deposits adjusted	. . .	. . .	. . .	. . .	. . .	. . .	. . .	. . .	. . .	. . .	. . .
M1	. . .	. . .	. . .	. . .	. . .	. . .	. . .	. . .	. . .	. . .	. . .
Time deposits	. . .	. . .	. . .	. . .	. . .	. . .	. . .	. . .	. . .	. . .	. . .
M2	. . .	. . .	. . .	. . .	. . .	. . .	. . .	. . .	. . .	. . .	. . .

Classification	1914	1915	1916	1917	1918	1919	1920	1921	1922	1923	1924
June 30											
Currency outside banks	1 533	1 575	1 876	2 276	3 298	3 593	4 105	3 677	3 346	3 739	3 650
Demand deposits adjusted	10 082	9 828	11 973	13 501	14 843	17 624	19 616	17 113	18 045	18 958	19 412
M1	11 615	11 403	13 849	15 777	18 141	21 217	23 721	20 790	21 391	22 697	23 062
Time deposits	8 350	9 231	10 313	11 543	11 717	13 423	15 834	16 583	17 437	19 722	21 259
M2	19 965	20 634	24 162	27 320	29 858	34 640	39 555	37 373	48 828	42 419	44 321
December 31											
Currency outside banks	. . .	. . .	. . .	. . .	. . .	. . .	. . .	. . .	. . .	3 726	3 696
Demand deposits adjusted	. . .	. . .	. . .	. . .	. . .	. . .	. . .	. . .	. . .	19 144	20 898
M1	. . .	. . .	. . .	. . .	. . .	. . .	. . .	. . .	. . .	22 870	24 594
Time deposits	. . .	. . .	. . .	. . .	. . .	. . .	. . .	. . .	. . .	20 379	22 232
M2	. . .	. . .	. . .	. . .	. . .	. . .	. . .	. . .	. . .	43 249	46 826

. . . = Not available.

Table 12-1B. Money Stock: Historical, 1892–1946—*Continued*

(Not seasonally adjusted, millions of dollars.)

Classification	1925	1926	1927	1928	1929	1930	1931	1932	1933	1934	1935
June 30											
Currency outside banks	3 573	3 601	3 556	3 622	3 639	3 369	3 651	4 616	4 761	4 659	4 783
Demand deposits adjusted	21 376	22 000	21 983	22 259	22 540	21 706	19 832	15 625	14 411	16 694	20 433
M1	24 949	25 601	25 539	25 881	26 179	25 075	23 483	20 241	19 172	21 353	25 216
Time deposits	23 194	24 741	26 465	28 526	28 611	28 992	28 961	24 756	21 656	22 875	23 854
M2	48 143	50 342	52 004	54 407	54 790	54 067	52 444	44 997	40 828	44 228	49 070
December 31											
Currency outside banks	3 771	3 827	3 700	3 593	3 557	3 605	4 470	4 669	4 782	4 655	4 917
Demand deposits adjusted	22 288	21 271	22 730	23 081	22 809	20 967	17 412	15 728	15 035	18 459	22 115
M1	26 059	25 548	26 430	26 674	26 366	24 572	21 882	20 397	19 817	23 114	27 032
Time deposits	23 922	25 328	27 372	28 681	28 189	28 676	25 979	24 457	21 715	23 156	24 241
M2	49 981	50 876	53 802	55 355	54 555	53 248	47 861	44 854	41 532	46 270	51 273

Classification	1936	1937	1938	1939	1940	1941	1942	1943	1944	1945	1946
June 30											
Currency outside banks	5 222	5 489	5 417	6 005	6 699	8 204	10 936	15 814	20 881	25 097	26 516
Demand deposits adjusted	23 780	25 198	24 313	27 355	31 962	37 317	41 870	56 039	60 065	69 053	79 476
M1	29 002	30 687	29 730	33 360	38 661	45 521	52 806	71 853	80 946	94 150	105 992
Time deposits	24 908	25 905	26 236	26 791	27 463	27 879	27 320	30 260	35 720	44 253	51 829
M2	53 910	56 592	55 966	60 151	66 124	73 400	80 126	102 113	116 666	138 403	157 821
December 31											
Currency outside banks	5 516	5 638	5 775	6 401	7 325	9 615	13 946	18 837	23 505	26 490	26 730
Demand deposits adjusted	25 483	23 959	25 986	29 793	34 945	38 992	48 922	60 803	66 930	75 851	83 814
M1	30 999	29 597	31 761	36 194	42 270	48 607	62 868	79 640	90 435	102 341	110 044
Time deposits	25 361	26 218	26 305	27 059	27 738	27 729	28 431	32 748	39 790	48 452	53 960
M2	56 360	55 815	58 066	63 253	70 008	76 336	91 299	112 388	130 225	150 793	164 004

Table 12-1C. Money Stock: Historical, January 1947–January 1959

(Averages of daily figures; seasonally adjusted, billions of dollars.)

Year and month	Money stock (M1)			Time deposits adjusted	M2 (M1 plus time deposits)
	Total	Currency component	Demand deposit component		
1947					
January	109.5	26.7	82.8	33.3	142.8
February	109.7	26.7	83.0	33.5	143.2
March	110.3	26.7	83.7	33.6	143.9
April	111.1	26.6	84.5	33.7	144.8
May	111.7	26.6	85.1	33.8	145.5
June	112.1	26.6	85.5	33.9	146.0
July	112.2	26.5	85.7	34.0	146.2
August	112.6	26.5	86.1	34.4	147.0
September	113.0	26.7	86.3	34.7	147.7
October	112.9	26.5	86.4	35.0	147.9
November	113.3	26.5	86.8	35.2	148.5
December	113.1	26.4	86.7	35.4	148.5
1948					
January	113.4	26.4	87.0	35.5	148.9
February	113.2	26.3	86.8	35.7	148.9
March	112.6	26.2	86.4	35.7	148.3
April	112.3	26.1	86.3	35.7	148.0
May	112.1	26.0	86.0	35.7	147.8
June	112.0	26.0	86.0	35.8	147.8
July	112.2	26.0	86.2	35.8	148.0
August	112.3	26.0	86.2	35.9	148.2
September	112.2	26.0	86.2	35.9	148.1
October	112.1	26.0	86.1	35.9	148.0
November	111.8	26.0	85.9	36.0	147.8
December	111.5	25.8	85.8	36.0	147.5
1949					
January	111.2	25.7	85.5	36.1	147.3
February	111.2	25.7	85.5	36.1	147.3
March	111.2	25.7	85.6	36.1	147.3
April	113.3	25.7	85.6	36.2	149.5
May	111.5	25.7	85.8	36.3	147.8
June	111.3	25.6	85.7	36.4	147.7
July	111.2	25.5	85.7	36.4	147.6
August	111.0	25.5	85.6	36.4	147.4
September	110.9	25.3	85.6	36.4	147.3
October	110.9	25.3	85.6	36.4	147.3
November	111.0	25.2	85.8	36.4	147.4
December	111.2	25.1	86.0	36.4	147.6
1950					
January	111.5	25.1	86.4	36.4	147.9
February	112.1	25.1	86.9	36.6	148.7
March	112.5	25.2	87.3	36.6	149.1
April	113.2	25.3	88.0	36.7	149.9
May	113.7	25.2	88.5	36.9	150.6
June	114.1	25.1	89.0	36.9	151.0
July	114.6	25.0	89.6	36.8	151.4
August	115.0	24.9	90.1	36.7	151.7
September	115.2	24.9	90.3	36.6	151.8
October	115.7	24.9	90.8	36.5	152.2
November	115.9	24.9	90.9	36.6	152.5
December	116.2	25.0	91.2	36.7	152.9
1951					
January	116.7	25.0	91.7	36.7	153.4
February	117.1	25.1	92.0	36.6	153.7
March	117.6	25.2	92.4	36.6	154.2
April	117.8	25.2	92.6	36.7	154.5
May	118.2	25.3	92.8	36.8	155.0
June	118.6	25.4	93.2	36.9	155.5
July	119.1	25.6	93.4	37.2	156.3
August	119.6	25.7	93.8	37.4	157.0
September	120.4	25.8	94.5	37.7	158.1
October	121.0	26.0	95.1	37.8	158.8
November	122.0	26.0	96.0	38.0	160.0
December	122.7	26.1	96.5	38.2	160.9
1952					
January	123.1	26.2	96.9	38.4	161.5
February	123.6	26.3	97.3	38.7	162.3
March	123.8	26.4	97.5	38.9	162.7
April	124.1	26.4	97.6	39.1	163.2
May	124.5	26.5	98.0	39.3	163.8
June	125.0	26.7	98.4	39.5	164.5
July	125.3	26.7	98.6	39.7	165.0
August	125.7	26.8	98.9	40.0	165.7
September	126.4	26.9	99.4	40.3	166.7
October	126.7	27.0	99.7	40.5	167.2
November	127.1	27.2	99.9	40.9	168.0
December	127.4	27.3	100.1	41.1	168.5

Table 12-1C. Money Stock: Historical, January 1947–January 1959—*Continued*

(Averages of daily figures; seasonally adjusted, billions of dollars.)

Year and month	Money stock (M1)			Time deposits adjusted	M2 (M1 plus time deposits)
	Total	Currency component	Demand deposit component		
1953					
January	127.3	27.4	99.9	41.4	168.7
February	127.4	27.5	99.9	41.6	169.0
March	128.0	27.6	100.4	41.9	169.9
April	128.3	27.7	100.7	42.1	170.4
May	128.5	27.7	100.7	42.4	170.9
June	128.5	27.7	100.7	42.6	171.1
July	128.6	27.8	100.8	42.9	171.5
August	128.7	27.8	100.9	43.2	171.9
September	128.6	27.8	100.8	43.5	172.1
October	128.7	27.8	100.9	43.9	172.6
November	128.7	27.8	100.9	44.2	172.9
December	128.8	27.7	101.1	44.5	173.3
1954					
January	129.0	27.7	101.3	44.8	173.8
February	129.1	27.7	101.5	45.2	174.3
March	129.2	27.6	101.6	45.6	174.8
April	128.6	27.6	101.0	46.1	174.7
May	129.7	27.6	102.1	46.5	176.2
June	129.9	27.5	102.3	46.8	176.7
July	130.3	27.5	102.8	47.3	177.6
August	130.7	27.5	103.2	47.8	178.5
September	130.9	27.4	103.5	47.9	178.8
October	131.5	27.4	104.1	48.1	179.6
November	132.1	27.4	104.7	48.2	180.3
December	132.3	27.4	104.9	48.3	180.6
1955					
January	133.0	27.4	105.6	48.5	181.5
February	133.9	27.5	106.4	48.7	182.6
March	133.6	27.5	106.0	48.8	182.4
April	133.9	27.5	106.3	49.0	182.9
May	134.6	27.6	107.0	49.0	183.6
June	134.4	27.6	106.8	49.2	183.6
July	134.8	27.7	107.2	49.3	184.1
August	134.8	27.7	107.0	49.3	184.1
September	135.0	27.7	107.3	49.6	184.6
October	135.2	27.8	107.4	49.7	184.9
November	134.9	27.8	107.1	49.9	184.8
December	135.2	27.8	107.4	50.0	185.2
1956					
January	135.5	27.9	107.7	49.9	185.4
February	135.5	27.9	107.7	49.9	185.4
March	135.7	27.9	107.8	50.1	185.8
April	136.0	27.9	108.1	50.3	186.3
May	135.8	27.9	107.9	50.4	186.2
June	136.0	27.9	108.1	50.7	186.7
July	136.0	28.0	108.0	50.9	186.9
August	135.7	28.0	107.8	51.2	186.9
September	136.2	28.0	108.2	51.5	187.7
October	136.3	28.0	108.2	51.6	187.9
November	136.6	28.1	108.4	51.8	188.4
December	136.9	28.2	108.7	51.9	188.8
1957					
January	136.9	28.2	108.6	52.6	189.5
February	136.8	28.2	108.6	53.1	189.9
March	136.9	28.2	108.7	53.7	190.6
April	136.9	28.2	108.7	54.0	190.9
May	137.0	28.2	108.8	54.5	191.5
June	136.9	28.3	108.6	54.8	191.7
July	137.0	28.3	108.7	55.3	192.3
August	137.1	28.3	108.8	55.7	192.8
September	136.8	28.3	108.4	56.1	192.9
October	136.5	28.3	108.2	56.6	193.1
November	136.3	28.3	108.0	57.0	193.3
December	135.9	28.3	107.6	57.4	193.3
1958					
January	135.5	28.3	107.2	57.6	193.1
February	136.2	28.2	107.9	59.2	195.4
March	136.5	28.2	108.3	60.5	197.0
April	137.0	28.2	108.7	61.5	198.5
May	137.5	28.3	109.2	62.3	199.8
June	138.4	28.3	110.1	63.2	201.6
July	138.4	28.4	110.0	64.0	202.4
August	139.1	28.4	110.7	64.6	203.7
September	139.5	28.5	111.1	64.8	204.3
October	140.1	28.5	111.6	64.9	205.0
November	140.9	28.5	112.4	65.2	206.1
December	141.1	28.6	112.6	65.4	206.5
1959					
January	142.2	28.7	113.5	66.3	208.5

Table 12-1D. Money Stock, Reserves, and Monetary Base: Historical, from January 1959

(Averages of daily figures; seasonally adjusted, except as noted.)

| Year and month | Money stock measures, billions of dollars | | Reserves and monetary base, adjusted for change in reserve requirements, millions of dollars | | | | | |
	M1	M2	Total reserves	Nonborrowed reserves	Nonborrowed reserves plus extended credit [1]	Required reserves	Excess reserves, not seasonally adjusted	Monetary base
1959								
January	138.9	286.6	11 112	10 560	10 560	10 614	498	40 425
February	139.4	287.7	11 129	10 624	10 624	10 675	454	40 605
March	139.7	289.2	11 081	10 482	10 482	10 621	460	40 615
April	139.7	290.1	11 116	10 424	10 424	10 684	431	40 694
May	140.7	292.2	11 058	10 317	10 317	10 637	421	40 731
June	141.2	294.1	10 972	10 043	10 043	10 566	407	40 750
July	141.7	295.2	11 109	10 148	10 148	10 693	416	40 896
August	141.9	296.4	11 168	10 177	10 177	10 720	448	40 992
September	141.0	296.7	11 128	10 202	10 202	10 686	443	41 034
October	140.5	296.5	11 057	10 150	10 150	10 616	441	40 903
November	140.4	297.1	11 052	10 194	10 194	10 609	444	40 822
December	140.0	297.8	11 109	10 168	10 168	10 603	506	40 880
1960								
January	140.0	298.2	11 081	10 194	10 194	10 567	514	40 794
February	139.9	298.5	10 884	10 074	10 074	10 430	454	40 666
March	139.8	299.4	10 796	10 155	10 155	10 373	423	40 616
April	139.6	300.1	10 767	10 161	10 161	10 341	426	40 621
May	139.6	300.9	10 840	10 344	10 344	10 396	445	40 639
June	139.6	302.3	10 885	10 451	10 451	10 406	479	40 689
July	140.2	304.1	10 994	10 615	10 615	10 493	501	40 794
August	141.3	306.9	11 078	10 782	10 782	10 536	542	40 895
September	141.2	308.4	11 147	10 932	10 932	10 520	627	41 040
October	140.9	309.5	11 216	11 049	11 049	10 554	662	41 097
November	140.9	310.9	11 299	11 166	11 166	10 556	743	41 130
December	140.7	312.4	11 247	11 172	11 172	10 503	743	40 977
1961								
January	141.1	314.1	11 324	11 259	11 259	10 553	772	40 960
February	141.6	316.5	11 229	11 096	11 096	10 580	649	40 945
March	141.9	318.3	11 108	11 038	11 038	10 563	546	40 851
April	142.1	319.9	11 123	11 066	11 066	10 507	616	40 823
May	142.7	322.2	11 035	10 940	10 940	10 480	556	40 791
June	142.9	324.3	11 087	11 024	11 024	10 497	590	40 902
July	142.9	325.6	11 124	11 070	11 070	10 508	616	40 980
August	143.5	327.6	11 234	11 169	11 169	10 655	579	41 227
September	143.8	329.5	11 289	11 251	11 251	10 709	580	41 417
October	144.1	331.1	11 413	11 342	11 342	10 881	532	41 651
November	144.8	333.4	11 482	11 384	11 384	10 891	591	41 782
December	145.2	335.5	11 499	11 366	11 366	10 915	584	41 853
1962								
January	145.2	337.5	11 490	11 403	11 403	10 867	623	41 864
February	145.7	340.1	11 301	11 233	11 233	10 799	502	41 810
March	146.0	343.1	11 259	11 170	11 170	10 788	472	41 923
April	146.4	345.5	11 330	11 258	11 258	10 838	492	42 096
May	146.8	347.5	11 384	11 323	11 323	10 867	517	42 194
June	146.6	349.3	11 328	11 226	11 226	10 855	473	42 259
July	146.5	350.8	11 394	11 302	11 302	10 860	534	42 398
August	146.6	352.8	11 355	11 231	11 231	10 826	530	42 491
September	146.3	354.9	11 383	11 303	11 303	10 893	490	42 537
October	146.7	357.2	11 450	11 387	11 387	10 972	477	42 700
November	147.3	359.8	11 492	11 372	11 372	10 936	557	42 861
December	147.8	362.7	11 604	11 344	11 344	11 033	572	42 957
1963								
January	148.3	365.2	11 567	11 421	11 421	11 062	505	43 008
February	148.9	367.9	11 456	11 290	11 290	10 995	461	43 155
March	149.2	370.7	11 404	11 255	11 255	10 970	434	43 289
April	149.7	373.3	11 449	11 319	11 319	10 992	457	43 444
May	150.4	376.1	11 426	11 216	11 216	10 996	430	43 586
June	150.4	378.4	11 398	11 139	11 139	10 981	417	43 780
July	151.3	381.1	11 530	11 232	11 232	11 075	454	44 058
August	151.8	383.6	11 484	11 155	11 155	11 039	445	44 149
September	152.0	386.0	11 503	11 184	11 184	11 075	428	44 339
October	152.6	388.3	11 457	11 137	11 137	11 060	397	44 444
November	153.6	391.5	11 547	11 198	11 198	11 106	441	44 744
December	153.3	393.2	11 730	11 397	11 397	11 239	490	45 003
1964								
January	153.7	395.2	11 643	11 369	11 369	11 204	440	45 042
February	154.3	397.6	11 547	11 261	11 261	11 150	397	45 112
March	154.5	399.8	11 563	11 285	11 285	11 177	386	45 371
April	154.8	401.7	11 537	11 326	11 326	11 185	352	45 470
May	155.3	404.2	11 523	11 263	11 263	11 169	354	45 651
June	155.6	407.1	11 595	11 326	11 326	11 220	375	45 959
July	156.8	410.1	11 651	11 387	11 387	11 275	376	46 143
August	157.8	413.4	11 795	11 480	11 480	11 374	421	46 410
September	158.7	416.9	11 863	11 518	11 518	11 432	431	46 714
October	159.2	419.1	11 888	11 567	11 567	11 490	398	46 823
November	160.0	422.0	11 998	11 598	11 598	11 591	408	47 106
December	160.3	424.7	12 011	11 747	11 747	11 605	406	47 161

[1]Extended credit program discontinued January 9, 2003. See notes and definitions for more information.

Table 12-1D. Money Stock, Reserves, and Monetary Base: Historical, from January 1959—*Continued*

(Averages of daily figures; seasonally adjusted, except as noted.)

Year and month	Money stock measures, billions of dollars		Reserves and monetary base, adjusted for change in reserve requirements, millions of dollars					
	M1	M2	Total reserves	Nonborrowed reserves	Nonborrowed reserves plus extended credit [1]	Required reserves	Excess reserves, not seasonally adjusted	Monetary base
1965								
January	160.7	427.5	11 952	11 653	11 653	11 537	415	47 281
February	160.9	430.4	11 883	11 479	11 479	11 472	412	47 500
March	161.5	433.2	11 884	11 472	11 472	11 518	366	47 584
April	162.0	435.4	12 043	11 571	11 571	11 701	341	47 721
May	161.7	437.1	11 912	11 417	11 417	11 578	334	47 799
June	162.2	440.1	12 005	11 467	11 467	11 643	362	48 061
July	163.0	442.9	12 073	11 544	11 544	11 720	353	48 281
August	163.7	445.8	12 079	11 531	11 531	11 682	396	48 453
September	164.9	449.5	12 071	11 517	11 517	11 662	410	48 712
October	166.0	452.6	12 118	11 630	11 630	11 759	358	49 029
November	166.7	455.7	12 087	11 655	11 655	11 735	352	49 234
December	167.8	459.2	12 316	11 872	11 872	11 892	423	49 620
1966								
January	169.1	462.0	12 295	11 875	11 875	11 916	379	49 850
February	169.6	464.6	12 193	11 711	11 711	11 846	347	50 054
March	170.5	467.2	12 164	11 604	11 604	11 822	342	50 171
April	171.8	469.3	12 258	11 621	11 621	11 903	355	50 439
May	171.3	470.1	12 263	11 575	11 575	11 922	341	50 591
June	171.6	471.2	12 256	11 549	11 549	11 901	356	50 754
July	170.3	470.9	12 371	11 629	11 629	11 993	378	51 019
August	170.8	472.6	12 165	11 430	11 430	11 798	367	50 989
September	172.0	475.4	12 229	11 460	11 460	11 858	371	51 154
October	171.2	475.7	12 199	11 465	11 465	11 867	333	51 200
November	171.4	477.3	12 205	11 598	11 598	11 820	385	51 422
December	172.0	480.2	12 223	11 690	11 690	11 884	339	51 565
1967								
January	171.9	481.6	12 334	11 924	11 924	11 931	403	51 876
February	173.0	485.1	12 280	11 916	11 916	11 911	369	52 173
March	174.8	489.7	12 438	12 237	12 237	12 024	414	52 494
April	174.2	492.1	12 488	12 342	12 342	12 138	350	52 517
May	175.7	497.2	12 418	12 329	12 329	12 053	365	52 682
June	177.0	502.0	12 457	12 351	12 351	12 104	352	52 867
July	178.1	506.3	12 722	12 607	12 607	12 304	418	53 165
August	179.7	510.8	12 678	12 598	12 598	12 313	365	53 347
September	180.7	514.7	12 846	12 758	12 758	12 504	342	53 670
October	181.6	518.2	13 088	12 959	12 959	12 752	335	54 044
November	182.4	521.2	13 131	12 999	12 999	12 773	358	54 241
December	183.3	524.8	13 180	12 952	12 952	12 805	375	54 579
1968								
January	184.3	527.4	13 239	12 993	12 993	12 852	387	54 892
February	184.7	530.4	13 188	12 815	12 815	12 801	386	55 171
March	185.5	533.2	13 186	12 527	12 527	12 849	337	55 436
April	186.6	535.7	13 117	12 432	12 432	12 782	335	55 692
May	188.0	538.9	13 130	12 389	12 389	12 771	360	55 872
June	189.4	542.6	13 251	12 557	12 557	12 923	328	56 323
July	190.5	545.6	13 455	12 928	12 928	13 105	351	56 626
August	191.8	549.4	13 440	12 875	12 875	13 110	329	56 976
September	192.7	553.6	13 435	12 931	12 931	13 074	361	57 160
October	194.0	557.6	13 529	13 086	13 086	13 283	245	57 477
November	196.0	562.4	13 649	13 104	13 104	13 340	308	57 887
December	197.4	566.8	13 767	13 021	13 021	13 341	426	58 357
1969								
January	198.7	569.3	13 629	12 893	12 893	13 383	246	58 597
February	199.3	571.9	13 714	12 879	12 879	13 460	254	58 917
March	200.0	574.4	13 653	12 751	12 751	13 434	219	58 999
April	200.7	575.7	13 471	12 468	12 468	13 304	167	59 062
May	200.8	576.5	13 844	12 470	12 470	13 589	255	59 552
June	201.3	578.5	13 795	12 410	12 410	13 491	304	59 794
July	201.7	579.5	13 491	12 239	12 239	13 266	225	59 713
August	201.7	580.1	13 784	12 565	12 565	13 547	237	60 137
September	202.1	582.1	13 822	12 743	12 743	13 549	274	60 357
October	202.9	583.4	13 904	12 754	12 754	13 741	163	60 633
November	203.6	585.4	14 172	12 969	12 969	13 943	229	61 229
December	203.9	587.9	14 168	13 049	13 049	13 882	286	61 569
1970								
January	206.2	589.6	14 087	13 128	13 128	13 914	174	61 792
February	205.0	586.3	14 099	13 019	13 019	13 891	208	61 931
March	205.7	587.3	14 071	13 173	13 173	13 908	163	62 205
April	206.7	588.4	14 209	13 364	13 364	14 057	152	62 653
May	207.2	591.5	14 007	13 040	13 040	13 850	157	62 977
June	207.6	595.2	14 078	13 197	13 197	13 888	190	63 189
July	208.0	599.1	14 159	12 799	12 799	13 993	166	63 444
August	209.9	604.9	14 282	13 445	13 445	14 108	174	63 725
September	211.8	611.2	14 447	13 847	13 847	14 203	244	64 087
October	212.9	616.4	14 480	14 017	14 017	14 274	205	64 303
November	213.7	621.1	14 470	14 055	14 055	14 236	234	64 574
December	214.4	626.5	14 558	14 225	14 225	14 309	249	65 013

[1]Extended credit program discontinued January 9, 2003. See notes and definitions for more information.

Table 12-1D. Money Stock, Reserves, and Monetary Base: Historical, from January 1959—*Continued*

(Averages of daily figures; seasonally adjusted, except as noted.)

Year and month	Money stock measures, billions of dollars		Reserves and monetary base, adjusted for change in reserve requirements, millions of dollars					
	M1	M2	Total reserves	Nonborrowed reserves	Nonborrowed reserves plus extended credit [1]	Required reserves	Excess reserves, not seasonally adjusted	Monetary base
1971								
January	215.5	632.9	14 604	14 240	14 240	14 371	234	65 545
February	217.4	641.0	14 819	14 488	14 488	14 565	254	66 037
March	218.8	649.9	14 798	14 479	14 479	14 603	195	66 378
April	220.0	658.4	14 759	14 606	14 606	14 591	168	66 731
May	222.0	666.7	14 982	14 698	14 698	14 763	219	67 315
June	223.5	673.0	15 057	14 564	14 564	14 855	201	67 678
July	224.9	679.6	15 125	14 302	14 302	14 941	184	68 155
August	225.6	685.5	15 190	14 380	14 380	14 994	196	68 413
September	226.5	692.5	15 423	14 928	14 928	15 234	189	68 751
October	227.2	698.4	15 211	14 854	14 854	15 049	163	68 603
November	227.8	704.6	15 247	14 864	14 864	15 010	237	68 894
December	228.3	710.3	15 230	15 104	15 104	15 049	182	69 108
1972								
January	230.1	717.7	15 369	15 347	15 347	15 163	206	69 853
February	232.3	725.7	15 363	15 331	15 331	15 211	152	70 368
March	234.3	733.5	15 480	15 382	15 382	15 291	190	70 820
April	235.6	738.4	15 651	15 534	15 534	15 495	156	71 031
May	235.9	743.3	15 739	15 628	15 628	15 600	139	71 525
June	236.6	749.7	15 909	15 809	15 809	15 706	203	71 817
July	238.8	759.5	15 835	15 597	15 597	15 642	193	72 173
August	240.9	768.7	16 010	15 623	15 623	15 822	188	72 623
September	243.2	778.3	16 000	15 459	15 459	15 788	212	72 984
October	245.0	786.9	16 193	15 637	15 637	15 981	211	73 644
November	246.4	793.9	16 441	15 833	15 833	16 088	354	74 370
December	249.2	802.3	16 645	15 595	15 595	16 361	284	75 167
1973								
January	251.5	810.3	16 708	15 548	15 548	16 450	258	75 925
February	252.2	814.1	16 714	15 120	15 120	16 516	197	76 160
March	251.7	815.3	16 923	15 099	15 099	16 714	209	76 663
April	252.7	819.7	16 731	15 020	15 020	16 508	223	76 962
May	254.9	826.8	16 672	14 829	14 830	16 533	138	77 393
June	256.7	833.3	16 746	14 895	14 903	16 528	217	77 842
July	257.5	836.5	16 988	15 035	15 067	16 705	283	78 531
August	257.7	838.8	16 796	14 631	14 657	16 624	172	78 781
September	257.9	839.3	16 735	14 883	14 909	16 505	231	79 316
October	259.0	842.6	16 924	15 448	15 464	16 672	252	80 173
November	261.0	848.9	16 978	15 585	15 585	16 753	225	80 479
December	262.9	855.5	17 021	15 723	15 723	16 717	304	81 073
1974								
January	263.8	859.7	17 222	16 171	16 174	17 060	162	81 850
February	265.3	864.2	17 125	15 933	15 933	16 941	184	82 341
March	266.7	870.1	17 131	15 817	15 817	16 997	134	82 835
April	267.2	872.9	17 298	15 561	15 561	17 116	182	83 621
May	267.6	874.6	17 423	14 833	15 491	17 263	160	84 432
June	268.5	877.8	17 367	14 361	15 587	17 169	198	84 895
July	269.3	881.4	17 486	14 185	15 615	17 323	162	85 439
August	270.1	884.1	17 391	14 055	15 592	17 203	188	85 974
September	271.0	887.9	17 385	14 102	15 731	17 204	181	86 377
October	272.3	893.3	17 349	15 536	16 021	17 228	120	86 513
November	273.7	898.6	17 453	16 201	16 361	17 248	205	87 043
December	274.2	902.1	17 550	16 823	16 970	17 292	258	87 535
1975								
January	273.9	906.3	17 273	16 874	17 010	17 126	147	87 756
February	275.0	914.1	17 271	17 123	17 176	17 077	194	88 192
March	276.4	925.0	17 439	17 333	17 370	17 239	200	88 916
April	276.2	935.1	17 498	17 387	17 398	17 340	158	89 116
May	279.2	947.9	17 353	17 288	17 291	17 198	155	89 610
June	282.4	963.0	17 715	17 488	17 504	17 513	201	90 817
July	283.7	975.1	17 632	17 331	17 351	17 445	188	91 373
August	284.1	983.1	17 660	17 449	17 461	17 465	195	91 700
September	285.7	991.5	17 834	17 438	17 452	17 643	191	92 119
October	285.4	997.8	17 587	17 397	17 408	17 380	207	92 448
November	286.8	1 006.9	17 849	17 789	17 794	17 566	283	93 373
December	287.1	1 016.2	17 822	17 692	17 704	17 556	266	93 887
1976								
January	288.4	1 026.6	17 616	17 537	17 549	17 376	240	94 281
February	290.8	1 040.3	17 806	17 725	17 734	17 587	219	95 039
March	292.7	1 050.0	17 875	17 821	17 824	17 651	223	95 786
April	294.7	1 060.8	17 719	17 675	17 675	17 564	155	96 479
May	295.9	1 072.1	17 940	17 826	17 826	17 731	210	97 251
June	296.2	1 077.6	17 946	17 820	17 820	17 732	214	97 732
July	297.2	1 086.3	17 846	17 714	17 714	17 612	234	98 234
August	299.0	1 098.7	18 053	17 953	17 953	17 846	207	98 888
September	299.6	1 110.8	18 009	17 948	17 948	17 808	201	99 446
October	302.0	1 125.0	18 077	17 983	17 983	17 858	219	100 066
November	303.6	1 138.2	18 340	18 268	18 268	18 083	257	100 892
December	306.2	1 152.0	18 388	18 335	18 335	18 115	274	101 515

[1] Extended credit program discontinued January 9, 2003. See notes and definitions for more information.

Table 12-1D. Money Stock, Reserves, and Monetary Base: Historical, from January 1959—*Continued*

(Averages of daily figures; seasonally adjusted, except as noted.)

Year and month	Money stock measures, billions of dollars		Reserves and monetary base, adjusted for change in reserve requirements, millions of dollars					
	M1	M2	Total reserves	Nonborrowed reserves	Nonborrowed reserves plus extended credit [1]	Required reserves	Excess reserves, not seasonally adjusted	Monetary base
1977								
January	308.3	1 165.2	18 421	18 353	18 353	18 156	266	102 237
February	311.5	1 177.6	18 299	18 227	18 227	18 100	198	102 654
March	313.9	1 188.5	18 405	18 301	18 301	18 190	215	103 337
April	316.0	1 199.6	18 479	18 406	18 406	18 287	192	104 076
May	317.2	1 209.0	18 585	18 379	18 379	18 377	208	104 630
June	318.8	1 217.8	18 471	18 208	18 208	18 324	147	105 186
July	320.2	1 226.7	18 748	18 425	18 425	18 473	275	106 394
August	322.3	1 237.0	18 919	17 858	17 858	18 719	200	107 185
September	324.5	1 246.2	18 873	18 247	18 247	18 664	209	107 923
October	326.4	1 254.0	18 963	17 658	17 658	18 753	210	108 750
November	328.6	1 262.4	19 012	18 150	18 150	18 761	251	109 560
December	330.9	1 270.3	18 990	18 420	18 420	18 800	190	110 324
1978								
January	334.4	1 279.7	19 290	18 806	18 806	19 023	267	111 449
February	335.3	1 285.5	19 561	19 155	19 155	19 319	241	112 450
March	337.0	1 292.2	19 286	18 958	18 958	19 087	199	112 778
April	339.9	1 300.4	19 408	18 851	18 851	19 260	148	113 377
May	344.9	1 310.5	19 655	18 443	18 443	19 436	219	114 418
June	346.9	1 318.5	19 868	18 774	18 774	19 691	178	115 376
July	347.6	1 324.1	20 118	18 801	18 801	19 921	197	116 273
August	349.6	1 333.5	19 912	18 772	18 772	19 744	168	116 904
September	352.2	1 345.0	19 994	18 934	18 934	19 801	193	118 112
October	353.3	1 352.3	20 109	18 832	18 832	19 947	162	119 044
November	355.4	1 359.1	19 872	19 169	19 169	19 650	222	119 733
December	357.3	1 366.0	19 753	18 885	18 885	19 521	232	120 445
1979								
January	358.6	1 371.6	19 821	18 818	18 818	19 606	214	121 272
February	359.9	1 377.8	19 396	18 423	18 423	19 187	209	121 504
March	362.5	1 387.8	19 429	18 439	18 439	19 271	158	122 065
April	368.0	1 402.1	19 504	18 587	18 587	19 328	176	122 819
May	369.6	1 410.2	19 553	17 788	17 788	19 412	141	123 487
June	373.4	1 423.0	19 808	18 390	18 390	19 587	221	124 635
July	377.2	1 434.8	19 992	18 822	18 822	19 782	211	125 810
August	378.8	1 446.6	20 008	18 923	18 923	19 786	222	127 079
September	379.3	1 454.1	20 007	18 667	18 667	19 816	191	128 309
October	380.8	1 460.4	20 375	18 353	18 353	20 103	272	129 458
November	380.8	1 465.9	20 398	18 492	18 492	20 153	245	130 369
December	381.8	1 473.7	20 720	19 248	19 248	20 279	442	131 143
1980								
January	385.8	1 482.7	20 693	19 452	19 452	20 442	251	131 998
February	390.1	1 494.6	20 682	19 027	19 027	20 471	211	132 785
March	388.4	1 499.8	20 703	17 879	17 978	20 517	186	133 607
April	383.8	1 502.2	20 629	18 174	18 726	20 432	197	134 740
May	384.8	1 512.3	20 440	19 421	20 164	20 262	178	134 998
June	389.1	1 529.2	20 575	20 196	20 503	20 372	203	135 679
July	394.0	1 545.5	20 796	20 401	20 654	20 511	284	136 637
August	399.2	1 561.5	21 011	20 352	20 594	20 709	302	137 977
September	404.8	1 574.0	21 232	19 921	20 011	20 977	256	139 220
October	409.0	1 584.8	21 147	19 837	19 837	20 941	206	140 150
November	410.7	1 595.8	22 150	20 091	20 091	21 629	521	141 566
December	408.5	1 599.8	22 015	20 325	20 328	21 501	514	142 004
1981								
January	411.3	1 606.9	21 673	20 278	20 348	21 298	374	141 462
February	414.8	1 618.7	21 840	20 536	20 557	21 489	350	142 270
March	419.0	1 636.6	22 072	21 072	21 086	21 791	280	143 029
April	427.4	1 659.2	22 187	20 849	20 857	22 018	169	143 917
May	424.7	1 664.2	22 442	20 219	20 224	22 184	257	144 587
June	425.2	1 670.3	22 326	20 289	20 295	21 988	338	145 001
July	426.9	1 681.9	22 329	20 650	20 653	21 989	340	145 839
August	426.9	1 694.3	22 356	20 936	21 017	22 064	292	146 467
September	427.0	1 706.0	22 487	21 031	21 332	22 073	414	146 941
October	428.4	1 721.8	22 296	21 115	21 553	22 018	278	147 062
November	431.3	1 736.1	22 338	21 675	21 840	21 993	344	147 749
December	436.7	1 755.5	22 443	21 807	21 956	22 124	319	149 021
1982								
January	442.7	1 770.4	22 669	21 152	21 349	22 251	418	149 991
February	441.9	1 774.5	22 551	20 762	20 994	22 248	304	150 459
March	442.7	1 786.5	22 452	20 898	21 206	22 091	361	150 660
April	447.1	1 803.9	22 337	20 769	21 014	22 064	273	151 606
May	446.7	1 815.4	22 402	21 285	21 461	22 043	359	152 868
June	447.5	1 826.0	22 368	21 164	21 268	22 060	308	153 861
July	448.0	1 831.8	22 182	21 490	21 541	21 868	314	154 385
August	451.4	1 845.6	22 348	21 833	21 926	22 036	312	155 470
September	456.9	1 858.8	22 686	21 752	21 871	22 302	384	156 629
October	464.5	1 870.1	22 889	22 412	22 553	22 485	404	157 716
November	471.5	1 884.1	23 354	22 733	22 921	22 952	402	158 667
December	474.8	1 906.4	23 600	22 966	23 152	23 100	500	160 127

[1] Extended credit program discontinued January 9, 2003. See notes and definitions for more information.

Table 12-1D. Money Stock, Reserves, and Monetary Base: Historical, from January 1959—*Continued*

(Averages of daily figures; seasonally adjusted, except as noted.)

Year and month	Money stock measures, billions of dollars		Reserves and monetary base, adjusted for change in reserve requirements, millions of dollars					
	M1	M2	Total reserves	Nonborrowed reserves	Nonborrowed reserves plus extended credit [1]	Required reserves	Excess reserves, not seasonally adjusted	Monetary base
1983								
January	477.2	1 959.8	23 226	22 697	22 854	22 678	548	161 136
February	484.3	1 997.2	23 901	23 319	23 597	23 466	435	163 170
March	490.6	2 015.5	24 414	23 621	23 939	23 981	433	165 052
April	493.2	2 028.9	24 900	23 890	24 295	24 424	476	166 549
May	500.0	2 043.4	24 860	23 907	24 420	24 411	449	167 842
June	504.0	2 053.8	25 277	23 641	24 599	24 797	480	169 393
July	507.8	2 065.1	25 356	23 903	24 480	24 848	507	170 129
August	510.5	2 074.3	25 376	23 830	24 320	24 929	446	171 208
September	512.8	2 083.5	25 435	23 994	24 509	24 937	498	172 411
October	517.2	2 099.5	25 454	24 610	24 866	24 949	505	173 584
November	519.0	2 112.6	25 396	24 491	24 497	24 867	529	174 605
December	521.4	2 123.8	25 367	24 593	24 595	24 806	561	175 467
1984								
January	525.1	2 138.5	25 451	24 736	24 740	24 838	613	176 896
February	527.5	2 158.6	25 829	25 262	25 266	24 923	906	177 838
March	531.4	2 175.5	25 763	24 812	24 838	25 095	668	178 872
April	535.0	2 192.1	25 691	24 457	24 501	25 218	473	179 898
May	536.7	2 204.5	25 882	22 894	22 931	25 313	570	180 723
June	540.2	2 215.4	26 094	22 794	24 666	25 334	760	181 995
July	540.9	2 223.9	25 981	20 057	25 064	25 351	630	182 991
August	541.0	2 230.7	26 040	18 023	25 066	25 359	681	183 754
September	543.1	2 244.8	26 090	18 848	25 306	25 440	650	184 661
October	543.7	2 259.2	26 259	20 242	25 299	25 641	618	185 220
November	547.5	2 281.7	26 518	21 901	25 738	25 820	699	186 105
December	551.6	2 306.8	26 913	23 727	26 331	26 078	835	187 253
1985								
January	557.0	2 332.7	27 077	25 683	26 732	26 334	743	188 081
February	563.6	2 354.4	27 596	26 307	27 110	26 746	850	189 636
March	566.6	2 366.6	27 591	25 998	27 056	26 916	675	190 321
April	570.4	2 375.7	27 871	26 548	27 416	27 134	736	191 353
May	575.1	2 389.9	28 156	26 822	27 355	27 402	753	192 690
June	582.3	2 413.0	28 849	27 644	28 309	27 926	923	194 762
July	589.1	2 429.9	29 142	28 035	28 541	28 301	840	195 947
August	596.2	2 444.4	29 653	28 580	29 149	28 818	835	198 013
September	603.3	2 456.8	30 031	28 742	29 397	29 333	698	199 307
October	607.8	2 468.5	30 490	29 303	29 932	29 746	745	200 740
November	612.2	2 478.2	30 916	29 176	29 706	29 998	919	202 120
December	619.8	2 492.6	31 569	30 251	30 749	30 505	1 064	203 556
1986								
January	621.4	2 502.7	31 564	30 794	31 290	30 481	1 083	204 222
February	625.2	2 513.4	31 659	30 775	31 267	30 645	1 014	205 315
March	633.5	2 533.7	32 091	31 330	31 848	31 207	883	206 930
April	641.0	2 558.4	32 518	31 625	32 259	31 745	773	208 125
May	652.0	2 585.5	33 266	32 390	32 974	32 387	879	210 155
June	660.6	2 605.8	33 947	33 144	33 674	33 028	920	211 795
July	670.3	2 627.5	34 657	33 917	34 294	33 784	873	213 407
August	678.7	2 647.4	35 192	34 319	34 784	34 451	741	215 273
September	687.4	2 668.9	35 622	34 613	35 183	34 932	690	216 764
October	694.9	2 688.7	36 262	35 421	35 917	35 545	718	218 635
November	705.4	2 702.5	37 271	36 519	36 937	36 369	902	220 714
December	724.7	2 729.2	38 841	38 014	38 317	37 667	1 174	223 417
1987								
January	730.2	2 745.0	39 244	38 664	38 889	38 173	1 071	225 347
February	730.7	2 748.6	39 007	38 450	38 733	37 813	1 193	226 568
March	733.8	2 754.9	38 828	38 301	38 564	37 907	921	227 084
April	743.9	2 769.1	39 534	38 541	38 811	38 677	857	228 964
May	745.8	2 774.4	39 812	38 777	39 064	38 744	1 068	230 521
June	743.2	2 776.1	39 462	38 686	38 958	38 228	1 234	231 303
July	743.0	2 780.6	39 081	38 408	38 602	38 221	859	231 973
August	744.9	2 789.8	39 209	38 562	38 693	38 157	1 052	233 529
September	747.6	2 801.2	39 118	38 178	38 586	38 333	785	234 709
October	756.2	2 816.8	39 827	38 884	39 333	38 737	1 090	237 110
November	753.2	2 821.4	39 335	38 710	39 103	38 394	940	238 807
December	750.2	2 828.8	38 913	38 136	38 618	37 893	1 020	239 830
1988								
January	756.2	2 849.8	39 465	38 383	38 754	38 213	1 252	241 825
February	757.7	2 872.7	39 407	39 010	39 215	38 268	1 138	242 804
March	761.8	2 893.0	39 267	37 515	38 993	38 321	945	243 751
April	768.1	2 913.1	39 622	36 629	39 252	38 737	885	245 760
May	771.7	2 928.5	39 958	37 381	39 487	38 911	1 047	247 435
June	778.3	2 940.7	40 278	37 195	39 748	39 382	896	249 161
July	781.4	2 949.5	40 515	37 075	39 613	39 623	891	251 001
August	783.3	2 954.5	40 470	37 230	39 882	39 500	970	252 064
September	783.7	2 959.4	40 343	37 504	39 562	39 326	1 017	253 359
October	783.3	2 967.8	40 423	38 124	39 904	39 370	1 053	254 579
November	784.9	2 982.7	40 548	37 687	40 009	39 374	1 174	255 676
December	786.7	2 990.6	40 454	38 738	39 982	39 392	1 062	256 897

[1]Extended credit program discontinued January 9, 2003. See notes and definitions for more information.

Table 12-1D. Money Stock, Reserves, and Monetary Base: Historical, from January 1959—*Continued*

(Averages of daily figures; seasonally adjusted, except as noted.)

Year and month	Money stock measures, billions of dollars		Reserves and monetary base, adjusted for change in reserve requirements, millions of dollars					
	M1	M2	Total reserves	Nonborrowed reserves	Nonborrowed reserves plus extended credit [1]	Required reserves	Excess reserves, not seasonally adjusted	Monetary base
1989								
January	785.7	2 994.0	40 422	38 773	39 811	39 278	1 144	257 915
February	783.8	2 994.4	40 339	38 852	39 901	39 184	1 155	258 309
March	783.0	3 002.1	39 845	38 032	39 366	38 926	919	259 160
April	779.2	3 008.3	39 533	37 244	38 950	38 719	814	259 559
May	775.0	3 013.9	39 301	37 581	38 778	38 258	1 043	260 264
June	773.5	3 030.2	39 085	37 595	38 512	38 177	909	261 108
July	777.8	3 054.7	39 438	38 744	38 850	38 455	983	262 226
August	779.4	3 076.7	39 398	38 723	38 764	38 505	892	262 843
September	781.0	3 094.8	39 674	38 981	39 002	38 728	945	263 760
October	786.6	3 116.4	40 163	39 608	39 629	39 123	1 040	264 899
November	787.9	3 135.3	40 170	39 821	39 841	39 221	949	265 615
December	792.9	3 154.4	40 487	40 222	40 241	39 545	942	267 761
1990								
January	795.4	3 168.5	40 731	40 292	40 317	39 688	1 043	269 469
February	798.1	3 180.9	40 744	39 296	39 830	39 743	1 001	271 088
March	801.5	3 191.7	40 650	38 527	40 477	39 769	882	272 965
April	806.1	3 203.2	40 845	39 237	40 621	39 974	872	275 134
May	804.2	3 202.1	40 751	39 419	40 291	39 796	954	276 707
June	808.8	3 215.0	40 667	39 786	40 131	39 879	788	278 903
July	810.1	3 225.6	40 576	39 818	40 098	39 707	869	280 974
August	815.7	3 243.2	40 873	39 947	40 074	39 997	876	284 115
September	820.2	3 255.8	41 090	40 466	40 472	40 177	914	287 366
October	819.9	3 260.4	40 809	40 398	40 416	39 968	841	289 265
November	822.1	3 263.6	40 971	40 741	40 765	40 043	928	291 165
December	824.7	3 272.7	41 767	41 441	41 463	40 101	1 665	293 339
1991								
January	827.2	3 288.4	42 294	41 760	41 786	40 153	2 141	297 776
February	832.6	3 304.8	42 072	41 820	41 853	40 267	1 805	300 808
March	838.7	3 322.2	41 805	41 564	41 616	40 623	1 182	302 731
April	843.1	3 332.5	41 862	41 631	41 716	40 833	1 029	302 943
May	848.8	3 343.1	42 411	42 108	42 196	41 376	1 035	304 180
June	856.7	3 352.0	42 712	42 372	42 379	41 716	996	305 481
July	861.6	3 355.9	42 985	42 378	42 423	42 080	905	307 302
August	866.7	3 354.7	43 393	42 629	42 928	42 308	1 085	309 333
September	869.7	3 354.6	43 558	42 913	43 214	42 625	934	310 726
October	878.0	3 359.6	44 007	43 746	43 758	42 950	1 057	312 696
November	887.6	3 365.0	44 615	44 507	44 508	43 722	893	314 970
December	897.0	3 371.6	45 516	45 324	45 325	44 526	990	317 523
1992								
January	910.4	3 380.3	46 374	46 141	46 141	45 381	993	319 621
February	925.2	3 399.0	47 602	47 525	47 526	46 557	1 046	322 449
March	936.7	3 402.9	48 274	48 183	48 185	47 249	1 026	324 383
April	943.8	3 398.7	49 042	48 952	48 953	47 908	1 134	326 734
May	950.6	3 397.5	49 337	49 182	49 182	48 333	1 004	328 827
June	954.3	3 392.3	49 271	49 041	49 041	48 346	924	330 201
July	963.3	3 392.6	49 756	49 471	49 471	48 780	976	333 357
August	973.7	3 397.5	50 479	50 229	50 228	49 540	940	336 941
September	988.0	3 409.0	51 395	51 107	51 107	50 380	1 015	340 646
October	1 003.7	3 422.4	52 767	52 625	52 624	51 704	1 063	344 496
November	1 015.7	3 424.9	53 750	53 646	53 646	52 707	1 043	347 671
December	1 024.9	3 423.1	54 422	54 298	54 298	53 267	1 155	350 885
1993								
January	1 030.4	3 417.3	54 971	54 805	54 806	53 708	1 263	353 715
February	1 033.5	3 412.8	54 687	54 641	54 641	53 593	1 093	355 350
March	1 038.6	3 410.2	54 971	54 879	54 879	53 737	1 233	357 923
April	1 047.7	3 409.6	55 359	55 285	55 285	54 255	1 103	360 960
May	1 065.9	3 434.7	56 655	56 534	56 533	55 656	999	364 922
June	1 075.1	3 440.6	57 086	56 905	56 905	56 191	896	367 885
July	1 084.5	3 439.9	57 730	57 486	57 485	56 662	1 068	371 511
August	1 094.2	3 443.5	58 184	57 832	57 831	57 231	953	374 554
September	1 104.1	3 449.9	58 871	58 444	58 443	57 784	1 087	378 113
October	1 112.9	3 454.3	59 595	59 309	59 309	58 517	1 078	381 504
November	1 124.2	3 468.0	60 304	60 215	60 214	59 184	1 120	384 074
December	1 129.8	3 472.4	60 567	60 485	60 484	59 497	1 070	386 720
1994								
January	1 131.6	3 472.4	60 896	60 822	60 822	59 436	1 460	390 246
February	1 136.3	3 473.3	60 516	60 446	60 445	59 367	1 149	393 242
March	1 140.3	3 478.5	60 299	60 244	60 244	59 315	984	396 074
April	1 141.1	3 481.1	60 504	60 380	60 379	59 361	1 142	398 978
May	1 143.3	3 490.4	59 972	59 772	59 772	59 103	870	401 442
June	1 145.1	3 479.1	60 048	59 715	59 715	58 931	1 117	404 339
July	1 150.6	3 487.4	60 321	59 863	59 863	59 205	1 117	407 876
August	1 150.6	3 484.6	59 960	59 491	59 490	58 949	1 010	409 520
September	1 151.8	3 484.7	59 800	59 313	59 313	58 751	1 049	411 695
October	1 150.1	3 483.0	59 374	58 994	58 993	58 576	798	413 936
November	1 151.0	3 486.0	59 412	59 163	59 163	58 415	997	416 785
December	1 150.8	3 484.9	59 466	59 257	59 257	58 295	1 171	418 474

[1]Extended credit program discontinued January 9, 2003. See notes and definitions for more information.

Table 12-1D. Money Stock, Reserves, and Monetary Base: Historical, from January 1959—*Continued*

(Averages of daily figures; seasonally adjusted, except as noted.)

Year and month	Money stock measures, billions of dollars		Reserves and monetary base, adjusted for change in reserve requirements, millions of dollars					
	M1	M2	Total reserves	Nonborrowed reserves	Nonborrowed reserves plus extended credit [1]	Required reserves	Excess reserves, not seasonally adjusted	Monetary base
1995								
January	1 151.5	3 490.4	59 404	59 268	59 272	58 071	1 333	421 138
February	1 147.5	3 487.6	58 653	58 593	58 593	57 683	970	421 670
March	1 146.8	3 488.8	58 210	58 141	58 140	57 386	824	424 823
April	1 149.2	3 496.6	57 974	57 863	57 862	57 216	758	427 833
May	1 145.3	3 521.3	57 641	57 492	57 491	56 768	874	430 461
June	1 144.0	3 546.1	57 377	57 104	57 104	56 393	984	429 995
July	1 145.4	3 564.5	57 818	57 446	57 446	56 711	1 107	430 757
August	1 145.5	3 586.1	57 538	57 257	57 256	56 532	1 007	431 218
September	1 142.0	3 599.2	57 310	57 033	57 032	56 338	972	431 955
October	1 137.3	3 610.4	56 720	56 474	56 474	55 640	1 080	432 637
November	1 134.1	3 617.0	56 306	56 102	56 101	55 360	946	432 977
December	1 127.5	3 626.5	56 484	56 226	56 226	55 193	1 291	434 645
1996								
January	1 123.5	3 644.7	55 884	55 846	55 846	54 417	1 468	434 865
February	1 118.5	3 658.8	54 622	54 588	54 587	53 761	861	432 548
March	1 122.6	3 683.8	55 295	55 274	55 273	54 153	1 142	435 994
April	1 124.8	3 694.2	55 179	55 088	55 088	54 052	1 127	436 886
May	1 116.6	3 705.3	54 041	53 914	53 913	53 130	911	437 512
June	1 115.1	3 718.8	54 145	53 759	53 758	53 031	1 115	440 014
July	1 112.4	3 733.7	53 377	53 010	53 009	52 356	1 022	442 588
August	1 101.5	3 740.5	52 162	51 828	51 828	51 201	961	444 609
September	1 096.2	3 748.9	51 313	50 945	50 945	50 262	1 051	446 085
October	1 086.3	3 765.3	50 038	49 751	49 750	49 030	1 008	446 897
November	1 083.4	3 783.4	49 780	49 566	49 565	48 724	1 056	448 825
December	1 081.3	3 804.8	50 185	50 030	50 030	48 766	1 419	451 935
1997								
January	1 081.3	3 819.7	49 684	49 639	49 639	48 456	1 228	453 574
February	1 078.9	3 831.3	48 716	48 673	48 673	47 681	1 035	454 512
March	1 072.1	3 845.1	47 851	47 694	47 694	46 681	1 169	456 242
April	1 064.0	3 862.2	47 354	47 093	47 093	46 339	1 015	457 930
May	1 064.1	3 874.2	46 657	46 414	46 414	45 374	1 283	459 500
June	1 065.6	3 888.6	46 938	46 571	46 570	45 593	1 344	462 200
July	1 066.3	3 910.7	46 756	46 347	46 346	45 518	1 238	464 742
August	1 074.2	3 939.2	46 913	46 316	46 315	45 653	1 260	467 078
September	1 067.6	3 959.2	46 248	45 810	45 809	44 950	1 297	469 213
October	1 065.6	3 976.1	45 960	45 690	45 690	44 544	1 416	471 912
November	1 070.1	3 997.4	46 411	46 258	46 258	44 742	1 669	475 921
December	1 072.8	4 018.1	46 876	46 551	46 551	45 189	1 687	479 798
1998								
January	1 074.2	4 041.0	46 659	46 449	46 448	44 894	1 765	482 094
February	1 078.0	4 072.6	45 743	45 685	45 684	44 208	1 535	483 160
March	1 077.1	4 099.1	45 854	45 813	45 812	44 503	1 351	484 814
April	1 076.7	4 124.0	46 131	46 059	46 058	44 739	1 391	486 891
May	1 078.3	4 145.1	45 532	45 379	45 379	44 241	1 291	488 929
June	1 076.9	4 170.1	45 417	45 166	45 166	43 798	1 619	491 830
July	1 075.0	4 187.0	44 893	44 636	44 635	43 519	1 375	494 720
August	1 075.2	4 209.5	44 956	44 686	44 685	43 423	1 533	497 990
September	1 080.2	4 251.0	44 850	44 599	44 599	43 152	1 698	502 775
October	1 086.1	4 289.5	44 888	44 714	44 714	43 312	1 576	506 859
November	1 094.3	4 325.8	44 816	44 732	44 732	43 205	1 611	510 295
December	1 096.1	4 358.9	45 174	45 058	45 055	43 662	1 513	513 821
1999								
January	1 097.4	4 380.1	45 030	44 824	44 801	43 540	1 490	516 887
February	1 097.1	4 406.2	44 926	44 810	44 801	43 731	1 194	520 761
March	1 097.2	4 415.4	44 471	44 406	44 474	43 202	1 269	524 941
April	1 102.0	4 442.2	43 661	43 495	43 553	42 506	1 155	528 385
May	1 102.8	4 462.7	44 006	43 879	43 828	42 785	1 221	533 398
June	1 099.7	4 488.3	43 064	42 919	42 843	41 766	1 298	537 095
July	1 098.5	4 514.3	41 992	41 683	41 596	41 028	964	540 372
August	1 099.2	4 531.6	42 302	41 958	41 931	41 141	1 162	545 002
September	1 097.0	4 547.5	41 958	41 620	41 695	40 744	1 214	550 063
October	1 102.2	4 566.3	41 572	41 291	41 329	40 424	1 148	557 281
November	1 111.4	4 591.5	41 771	41 535	41 520	40 442	1 329	570 825
December	1 122.9	4 617.1	42 149	41 829	41 853	40 855	1 295	593 383
2000								
January	1 121.6	4 642.6	42 533	42 159	42 133	40 519	2 014	590 941
February	1 109.1	4 660.9	41 445	41 338	41 326	40 332	1 113	572 957
March	1 107.6	4 689.9	40 727	40 548	40 608	39 519	1 208	571 685
April	1 114.6	4 741.1	40 484	40 180	40 234	39 317	1 167	572 184
May	1 105.6	4 734.8	40 684	40 322	40 267	39 713	971	573 800
June	1 102.9	4 751.6	40 171	39 692	39 608	39 056	1 115	575 897
July	1 102.8	4 765.6	40 091	39 521	39 437	38 947	1 143	577 066
August	1 100.9	4 799.2	39 813	39 234	39 207	38 759	1 054	577 879
September	1 099.5	4 830.6	39 555	39 078	39 149	38 409	1 146	578 269
October	1 098.7	4 848.3	39 369	38 951	38 982	38 221	1 148	580 216
November	1 092.7	4 860.1	39 384	39 100	39 078	38 180	1 203	582 051
December	1 087.9	4 900.4	38 685	38 475	38 493	37 359	1 326	584 928

[1]Extended credit program discontinued January 9, 2003. See notes and definitions for more information.

Table 12-1D. Money Stock, Reserves, and Monetary Base: Historical, from January 1959—*Continued*

(Averages of daily figures; seasonally adjusted, except as noted.)

Year and month	Money stock measures, billions of dollars		Reserves and monetary base, adjusted for change in reserve requirements, millions of dollars					
	M1	M2	Total reserves	Nonborrowed reserves	Nonborrowed reserves plus extended credit [1]	Required reserves	Excess reserves, not seasonally adjusted	Monetary base
2001								
January	1 097.1	4 954.8	37 885	37 812	37 785	36 621	1 264	587 941
February	1 101.2	4 991.2	38 585	38 534	38 522	37 240	1 345	589 711
March	1 109.1	5 049.2	38 406	38 348	38 405	37 155	1 251	592 279
April	1 116.1	5 108.5	38 375	38 325	38 379	37 118	1 258	595 512
May	1 119.2	5 111.9	38 628	38 415	38 350	37 609	1 019	598 773
June	1 126.1	5 148.4	38 834	38 604	38 519	37 585	1 249	602 131
July	1 139.0	5 179.9	39 475	39 192	39 106	38 073	1 402	608 001
August	1 149.9	5 211.9	39 961	39 778	39 750	38 757	1 203	615 553
September	1 204.8	5 319.7	57 917	54 532	54 609	38 902	19 015	639 414
October	1 166.2	5 311.2	45 461	45 334	45 358	44 135	1 327	630 163
November	1 171.3	5 354.1	40 952	40 868	40 838	39 513	1 439	629 865
December	1 182.9	5 403.2	41 384	41 317	41 336	39 740	1 643	635 575
2002								
January	1 191.3	5 429.6	41 680	41 630	41 600	40 274	1 406	641 219
February	1 190.5	5 456.0	41 813	41 783	41 772	40 440	1 373	646 134
March	1 192.4	5 462.9	41 053	40 974	41 049	39 650	1 403	650 001
April	1 187.7	5 470.1	40 538	40 468	40 543	39 333	1 205	653 796
May	1 189.3	5 491.9	39 508	39 396	39 332	38 249	1 259	657 855
June	1 192.4	5 514.0	39 120	38 978	38 906	37 882	1 238	662 906
July	1 199.8	5 562.1	39 277	39 085	39 019	37 900	1 377	668 568
August	1 186.7	5 599.7	39 862	39 529	39 528	38 255	1 607	670 140
September	1 195.7	5 622.2	38 875	38 646	38 761	37 391	1 484	671 340
October	1 204.7	5 674.0	39 115	38 972	39 025	37 582	1 533	673 743
November	1 209.3	5 717.9	39 774	39 502	39 503	38 136	1 638	676 947
December	1 220.4	5 742.0	40 275	40 195	40 240	38 267	2 008	681 486
2003								
January	1 227.1	5 773.3	40 722	40 695	10 364	39 015	1 708	685 308
February	1 238.0	5 810.0	41 206	41 180	. . .	39 242	1 964	690 397
March	1 238.6	5 826.0	41 169	41 148	. . .	39 540	1 629	694 616
April	1 250.3	5 869.6	40 568	40 538	. . .	39 028	1 539	697 996
May	1 268.7	5 926.7	40 909	40 853	. . .	39 292	1 617	701 234
June	1 280.0	5 962.0	42 256	42 094	. . .	40 216	2 040	703 576
July	1 288.3	6 017.0	43 083	42 952	. . .	41 148	1 934	705 482
August	1 294.5	6 061.3	45 775	45 447	. . .	42 011	3 764	709 776
September	1 297.6	6 044.7	44 141	43 960	. . .	42 633	1 508	710 959
October	1 297.3	6 033.0	43 402	43 295	. . .	41 935	1 467	714 777
November	1 297.8	6 032.7	42 856	42 788	. . .	41 373	1 483	717 526
December	1 306.6	6 039.6	42 542	42 496	. . .	41 495	1 047	720 115
2004								
January	1 306.0	6 045.5	42 981	42 875	. . .	42 093	888	721 832
February	1 320.7	6 081.6	42 993	42 951	. . .	41 801	1 192	723 653
March	1 329.3	6 122.7	44 868	44 816	. . .	43 061	1 807	726 360
April	1 333.2	6 164.3	45 613	45 527	. . .	43 808	1 805	730 176
May	1 332.6	6 231.1	45 422	45 311	. . .	43 739	1 684	733 636
June	1 342.2	6 242.8	45 869	45 689	. . .	43 938	1 931	738 478
July	1 340.6	6 255.2	46 126	45 882	. . .	44 405	1 721	746 235
August	1 353.2	6 276.7	45 536	45 284	. . .	43 954	1 581	747 823
September	1 362.1	6 314.6	46 477	46 142	. . .	44 823	1 654	752 415
October	1 360.7	6 337.7	46 289	46 110	. . .	44 534	1 756	755 102
November	1 374.9	6 374.5	46 003	45 820	. . .	44 218	1 785	759 021
December	1 375.9	6 390.9	46 425	46 362	. . .	44 517	1 908	759 085
2005								
January	1 366.4	6 390.2	47 449	47 387	. . .	45 710	1 739	760 377
February	1 371.6	6 406.0	45 901	45 859	. . .	44 411	1 489	762 840
March	1 371.9	6 418.3	46 816	46 767	. . .	45 036	1 781	765 108
April	1 358.2	6 426.5	46 132	46 001	. . .	44 468	1 664	766 132
May	1 366.0	6 442.0	45 447	45 307	. . .	43 921	1 526	766 893
June	1 379.2	6 478.0	46 103	45 854	. . .	44 364	1 739	770 674
July	1 366.9	6 502.5	46 411	45 986	. . .	44 620	1 791	773 727
August	1 377.2	6 536.3	45 357	44 994	. . .	43 737	1 620	775 852
September	1 377.5	6 574.1	46 400	46 068	. . .	44 405	1 995	779 546
October	1 375.6	6 604.7	45 486	45 202	. . .	43 603	1 883	781 396
November	1 376.1	6 628.7	45 100	44 974	. . .	43 320	1 781	784 170
December	1 374.9	6 656.8	44 963	44 795	. . .	43 063	1 900	787 369
2006								
January	1 379.9	6 694.5	44 377	44 267	. . .	42 801	1 576	791 509
February	1 379.3	6 722.3	44 136	44 083	. . .	42 586	1 550	795 748
March	1 383.7	6 733.9	43 878	43 709	. . .	42 371	1 507	798 044
April	1 381.0	6 767.2	44 553	44 305	. . .	42 728	1 825	800 877
May	1 387.5	6 778.4	44 937	44 762	. . .	43 139	1 798	804 831
June	1 373.8	6 816.0	45 535	45 282	. . .	43 754	1 782	805 085
July	1 370.0	6 850.4	44 564	44 214	. . .	43 011	1 553	804 375
August	1 371.8	6 880.7	43 167	42 798	. . .	41 647	1 520	804 702
September	1 362.7	6 907.5	43 321	42 918	. . .	41 560	1 760	805 798
October	1 370.3	6 963.2	42 795	42 566	. . .	41 102	1 693	806 192
November	1 370.5	7 001.5	42 921	42 762	. . .	41 232	1 689	808 801
December	1 366.5	7 042.0	43 124	42 933	. . .	41 261	1 863	812 367

[1] Extended credit program discontinued January 9, 2003. See notes and definitions for more information.
. . . = Not available.

Table 12-1D. Money Stock, Reserves, and Monetary Base: Historical, from January 1959—*Continued*

(Averages of daily figures; seasonally adjusted, except as noted.)

Year and month	Money stock measures, billions of dollars		Reserves and monetary base, adjusted for change in reserve requirements, millions of dollars					
	M1	M2	Total reserves	Nonborrowed reserves	Nonborrowed reserves plus extended credit [1]	Required reserves	Excess reserves, not seasonally adjusted	Monetary base
2007								
January	1 372.8	7 080.4	41 998	41 787	. . .	40 453	1 545	813 189
February	1 364.2	7 100.4	42 178	42 149	. . .	40 725	1 453	812 127
March	1 366.9	7 130.6	41 943	41 889	. . .	40 325	1 618	812 856
April	1 378.2	7 199.2	42 328	42 248	. . .	40 740	1 587	815 881
May	1 381.6	7 221.5	43 439	43 336	. . .	41 984	1 455	818 352
June	1 365.4	7 245.4	44 195	44 007	. . .	42 441	1 753	820 002
July	1 368.9	7 277.4	42 570	42 308	. . .	40 936	1 634	821 646
August	1 375.2	7 341.5	45 602	44 627	. . .	40 775	4 827	825 257
September	1 373.4	7 365.1	43 333	41 767	. . .	41 601	1 733	823 400
October	1 379.9	7 391.2	43 013	42 758	. . .	41 553	1 459	825 969
November	1 371.0	7 420.4	43 195	42 830	. . .	41 502	1 694	826 657
December	1 374.3	7 450.5	43 133	27 702	. . .	41 348	1 785	824 809
2008								
January	1 379.5	7 483.0	42 515	-3 145	. . .	40 867	1 648	821 327
February	1 381.5	7 569.2	43 519	-16 638	. . .	41 904	1 615	821 214
March	1 388.3	7 625.3	44 939	-49 585	. . .	42 294	2 645	824 326
April	1 392.6	7 676.5	44 713	-90 696	. . .	42 976	1 737	823 212
May	1 393.9	7 686.2	45 990	-109 790	. . .	44 152	1 838	827 259
June	1 401.2	7 695.5	46 034	-125 244	. . .	43 809	2 225	833 192
July	1 418.5	7 750.1	45 796	-119 867	. . .	43 884	1 913	840 143
August	1 405.0	7 739.4	46 534	-121 545	. . .	44 658	1 875	843 597
September	1 461.8	7 833.7	103 326	-186 779	. . .	43 844	59 482	905 134
October	1 474.2	7 941.5	315 394	-332 926	. . .	48 237	267 157	1 130 219
November	1 512.5	7 990.2	609 306	-89 480	. . .	50 497	558 808	1 435 070
December	1 604.9	8 183.8	820 187	166 621	. . .	52 868	767 318	1 654 974
2009								
January	1 584.4	8 246.5	857 389	293 893	. . .	60 554	796 835	1 704 691
February	1 568.7	8 284.6	700 286	117 789	. . .	58 215	642 071	1 555 526
March	1 579.2	8 342.7	779 411	167 300	. . .	56 308	723 103	1 639 985
April	1 612.7	8 345.3	880 883	322 689	. . .	58 286	822 598	1 745 920
May	1 616.8	8 389.2	901 237	375 789	. . .	59 093	842 144	1 768 242
June	1 656.6	8 408.5	809 812	371 089	. . .	60 411	749 401	1 679 798
July	1 658.6	8 408.0	796 091	429 130	. . .	63 846	732 245	1 667 915
August	1 657.6	8 389.1	829 048	497 598	. . .	63 422	765 626	1 704 097
September	1 663.3	8 410.5	922 173	615 346	. . .	62 286	859 887	1 800 396
October	1 678.7	8 441.6	1 056 387	791 329	. . .	61 885	994 502	1 936 059
November	1 680.3	8 473.1	1 140 806	923 499	. . .	63 795	1 077 011	2 018 999
December	1 695.8	8 487.4	1 138 682	968 755	. . .	63 483	1 075 199	2 019 228
2010								
January	1 675.4	8 419.5	1 109 328	967 186	. . .	63 528	1 045 801	1 990 330
February	1 701.9	8 483.2	1 224 708	1 113 481	. . .	62 856	1 161 852	2 109 893
March	1 712.3	8 475.7	1 185 945	1 094 300	. . .	65 575	1 120 370	2 073 917
April	1 700.4	8 503.2	1 116 640	1 036 415	. . .	66 424	1 050 215	2 008 256
May	1 710.6	8 546.9	1 109 957	1 034 332	. . .	65 178	1 044 779	2 005 699
June	1 728.4	8 571.1	1 099 851	1 029 954	. . .	64 925	1 034 927	1 998 659
July	1 721.4	8 582.3	1 088 095	1 022 248	. . .	66 449	1 021 646	1 991 729
August	1 747.1	8 623.9	1 085 834	1 025 750	. . .	66 275	1 019 559	1 994 664
September	1 764.1	8 665.3	1 047 759	995 239	. . .	66 928	980 831	1 962 397
October	1 780.5	8 710.9	1 039 893	991 320	. . .	66 302	973 591	1 962 569
November	1 826.0	8 752.7	1 038 725	992 036	. . .	67 160	971 565	1 968 840
December	1 836.7	8 782.4	1 077 359	1 031 871	. . .	70 723	1 006 636	2 011 078
2011								
January	1 854.8	8 801.3	1 106 871	1 074 624	. . .	70 404	1 036 466	2 045 246
February	1 876.4	8 857.3	1 262 561	1 240 628	. . .	72 559	1 190 001	2 206 968
March	1 890.4	8 899.9	1 436 155	1 416 273	. . .	74 008	1 362 146	2 388 588
April	1 902.5	8 948.2	1 526 629	1 508 786	. . .	74 682	1 451 947	2 488 232
May	1 940.6	9 000.7	1 587 841	1 572 695	. . .	75 353	1 512 488	2 559 330
June	1 952.4	9 081.2	1 666 615	1 653 372	. . .	77 890	1 588 726	2 644 873
July	1 998.8	9 267.4	1 696 633	1 684 238	. . .	78 516	1 618 117	2 681 180
August	2 112.5	9 490.8	1 666 698	1 654 864	. . .	83 354	1 583 344	2 657 705
September	2 123.6	9 520.5	1 642 237	1 630 662	. . .	91 260	1 550 977	2 638 154
October	2 142.2	9 550.2	1 638 130	1 626 919	. . .	92 993	1 545 136	2 638 313
November	2 159.9	9 602.4	1 591 703	1 581 362	. . .	93 934	1 497 769	2 599 462
December	2 160.9	9 638.3	1 597 100	1 587 574	. . .	94 894	1 502 206	2 612 081
2012								
January	2 201.9	9 712.3	1 614 301	1 605 687	. . .	94 850	1 519 451	2 638 114
February	2 216.8	9 747.8	1 657 931	1 649 998	. . .	97 811	1 560 121	2 690 184
March	2 223.5	9 784.3	1 607 819	1 600 490	. . .	98 226	1 509 593	2 648 070
April	2 252.6	9 828.7	1 584 770	1 577 905	. . .	98 593	1 486 176	2 631 478
May	2 262.6	9 870.3	1 556 689	1 550 503	. . .	99 230	1 457 460	2 609 131
June	2 267.4	9 921.0	1 557 175	1 551 961	. . .	99 699	1 457 475	2 615 664
July	2 312.6	10 012.8	1 584 049	1 579 791	. . .	101 000	1 483 049	2 649 396
August	2 340.0	10 085.3	1 582 288	1 579 017	. . .	104 538	1 477 750	2 654 458
September	2 374.3	10 160.9	1 515 888	1 513 923	. . .	106 447	1 409 441	2 597 251
October	2 420.9	10 245.8	1 525 145	1 523 679	. . .	106 870	1 418 275	2 615 620
November	2 406.5	10 298.2	1 546 809	1 545 758	. . .	111 505	1 435 304	2 643 297
December	2 445.6	10 408.9	1 569 017	1 568 221	. . .	110 266	1 458 751	2 672 578

[1]Extended credit program discontinued January 9, 2003. See notes and definitions for more information.
. . . = Not available.

Table 12-2. Components of Non-M1 M2

(Billions of dollars, seasonally adjusted; monthly data are averages of daily figures, annual data are for December.)

Year and month	Savings deposits			Small-denomination time deposits			Retail money funds	Total non-M1 M2	Memorandum: Institutional money funds
	At commercial banks	At thrift institutions	Total	At commercial banks	At thrift institutions	Total			
1960	58.3	100.8	159.1	9.7	2.8	12.5	0.0	171.7	0.0
1961	64.2	111.3	175.5	11.1	3.7	14.8	0.0	190.3	0.0
1962	71.3	123.4	194.8	15.5	4.6	20.1	0.0	214.9	0.0
1963	76.8	137.6	214.4	19.9	5.7	25.5	0.0	240.0	0.0
1964	82.9	152.4	235.2	22.4	6.8	29.2	0.0	264.4	0.0
1965	92.4	164.5	256.9	26.7	7.8	34.5	0.0	291.3	0.0
1966	89.9	163.3	253.1	38.7	16.3	55.0	0.0	308.1	0.0
1967	94.1	169.6	263.7	50.7	27.1	77.8	0.0	341.5	0.0
1968	96.1	172.8	268.9	63.5	37.1	100.5	0.0	369.4	0.0
1969	93.8	169.8	263.7	71.6	48.8	120.4	0.0	384.0	0.0
1970	98.6	162.3	261.0	79.3	71.9	151.2	0.0	412.1	0.0
1971	112.8	179.4	292.2	94.7	95.1	189.7	0.0	481.9	0.0
1972	124.8	196.6	321.4	108.2	123.5	231.6	0.0	553.0	0.0
1973	128.0	198.7	326.8	116.8	149.0	265.8	0.1	592.6	0.0
1974	136.8	201.8	338.6	123.1	164.8	287.9	1.4	627.9	0.2
1975	161.2	227.6	388.9	142.3	195.5	337.9	2.4	729.1	0.5
1976	201.8	251.4	453.2	155.5	235.2	390.7	1.8	845.8	0.6
1977	218.8	273.4	492.2	167.5	278.0	445.5	1.8	939.4	1.0
1978	216.5	265.4	481.9	185.1	335.8	521.0	5.8	1 008.7	3.5
1979	195.0	228.8	423.8	235.5	398.7	634.3	33.9	1 092.0	10.4
1980	185.7	214.5	400.3	286.2	442.3	728.5	62.5	1 191.3	16.0
1981	159.0	184.9	343.9	347.7	475.4	823.1	151.7	1 318.8	38.2
1982	190.1	210.0	400.1	379.9	471.0	850.9	180.5	1 431.5	48.8
1983	363.2	321.7	684.9	350.9	433.1	784.1	133.4	1 602.4	40.9
1984	389.3	315.4	704.7	387.9	500.9	888.8	161.7	1 755.2	65.6
1985	456.6	358.6	815.3	386.4	499.3	885.7	171.8	1 872.8	68.6
1986	533.5	407.4	940.9	369.4	489.0	858.4	205.3	2 004.5	89.7
1987	534.8	402.6	937.4	391.7	529.3	921.0	220.2	2 078.6	96.6
1988	542.4	383.9	926.4	451.2	585.9	1 037.1	240.4	2 203.9	97.9
1989	541.1	352.6	893.7	533.8	617.6	1 151.3	316.5	2 361.5	116.3
1990	581.3	341.6	922.9	610.7	562.6	1 173.3	351.8	2 448.0	145.4
1991	664.8	379.6	1 044.5	602.2	463.1	1 065.3	364.9	2 474.7	196.1
1992	754.2	433.1	1 187.2	508.1	359.7	867.7	343.2	2 398.2	222.4
1993	785.3	434.0	1 219.3	467.9	313.6	781.5	341.9	2 342.7	228.7
1994	752.8	398.5	1 151.3	503.6	313.9	817.5	365.4	2 334.1	226.2
1995	774.8	361.0	1 135.9	575.8	356.5	932.4	430.8	2 499.0	281.5
1996	906.1	368.8	1 274.8	594.2	353.7	947.9	500.7	2 723.4	344.0
1997	1 022.9	378.8	1 401.8	625.5	342.2	967.6	576.0	2 945.4	418.9
1998	1 188.6	416.5	1 605.1	626.4	324.9	951.3	706.4	3 262.8	573.8
1999	1 288.7	451.1	1 739.8	636.9	318.3	955.2	799.2	3 494.2	679.2
2000	1 423.7	453.8	1 877.4	700.8	345.3	1 046.0	889.0	3 812.5	831.8
2001	1 738.8	570.8	2 309.6	636.0	338.5	974.6	936.1	4 220.2	1 250.9
2002	2 058.7	713.4	2 772.1	591.3	303.5	894.7	854.8	4 521.6	1 312.5
2003	2 337.3	824.7	3 162.0	541.9	276.2	818.1	752.8	4 733.0	1 161.4
2004	2 632.6	876.2	3 508.8	551.9	276.5	828.4	677.8	5 014.9	1 105.9
2005	2 776.9	829.6	3 606.5	646.7	347.0	993.7	681.7	5 281.9	1 176.7
2006	2 910.4	783.3	3 693.7	780.6	425.3	1 205.9	776.0	5 675.5	1 391.4
2007	3 042.5	827.5	3 870.1	858.7	417.1	1 275.8	930.3	6 076.1	1 961.2
2008	3 330.0	771.0	4 101.0	1 078.0	378.7	1 456.7	1 021.2	6 578.9	2 459.3
2009	3 991.6	838.8	4 830.4	862.5	319.4	1 181.9	779.3	6 791.6	2 254.4
2010	4 419.8	925.5	5 345.3	656.3	270.5	926.8	673.6	6 945.7	1 894.1
2011	5 048.6	1 001.7	6 050.3	536.8	228.4	765.2	661.8	7 477.4	1 763.1
2012	5 731.8	960.5	6 692.3	454.5	176.4	630.9	640.1	7 963.3	1 742.9
2011									
January	4 436.7	930.5	5 367.3	643.5	265.2	908.7	670.5	6 946.5	1 846.8
February	4 476.0	943.8	5 419.8	634.2	262.1	896.3	664.8	6 980.9	1 825.3
March	4 507.7	956.7	5 464.4	623.6	259.8	883.4	661.6	7 009.5	1 846.6
April	4 559.4	957.3	5 516.7	614.7	256.9	871.6	657.4	7 045.7	1 875.7
May	4 576.5	968.9	5 545.4	604.4	254.1	858.5	656.2	7 060.1	1 895.5
June	4 657.6	969.5	5 627.1	593.0	250.5	843.5	658.3	7 128.8	1 872.9
July	4 802.9	977.9	5 780.8	581.9	246.8	828.7	659.2	7 268.7	1 838.4
August	4 909.0	983.7	5 892.7	569.9	242.5	812.4	673.3	7 378.4	1 746.5
September	4 945.4	985.6	5 931.0	559.0	238.7	797.7	668.2	7 397.0	1 768.2
October	4 961.6	989.1	5 950.7	549.9	234.8	784.7	672.6	7 408.0	1 765.2
November	5 006.0	997.4	6 003.4	541.5	231.0	772.5	666.6	7 442.5	1 758.1
December	5 048.6	1 001.7	6 050.3	536.8	228.4	765.2	661.8	7 477.4	1 763.1
2012									
January	5 097.5	1 000.1	6 097.7	533.7	221.9	755.7	657.1	7 510.4	1 759.7
February	5 159.1	980.6	6 139.7	532.7	212.5	745.2	646.1	7 531.1	1 746.5
March	5 198.2	990.1	6 188.2	525.0	207.6	732.6	640.0	7 560.8	1 750.8
April	5 222.1	995.0	6 217.1	515.8	205.2	721.1	637.9	7 576.1	1 738.9
May	5 256.9	1 007.0	6 263.9	506.9	202.6	709.5	634.4	7 607.7	1 735.0
June	5 312.8	1 011.3	6 324.1	498.9	200.1	698.9	630.6	7 653.7	1 727.1
July	5 360.7	1 024.0	6 384.6	491.7	196.3	688.0	627.5	7 700.2	1 730.0
August	5 413.0	1 029.5	6 442.4	484.8	193.0	677.8	625.0	7 745.3	1 741.5
September	5 464.0	1 030.8	6 494.8	478.0	189.3	667.3	624.5	7 786.6	1 750.7
October	5 507.8	1 035.9	6 543.7	469.8	186.0	655.8	625.4	7 824.9	1 742.3
November	5 665.6	953.5	6 619.1	463.5	179.2	642.7	629.9	7 891.7	1 735.2
December	5 731.8	960.5	6 692.3	454.5	176.4	630.9	640.1	7 963.3	1 742.9

Table 12-3. Aggregate Reserves, Monetary Base, and FR Balance Sheet

(Millions of dollars; reserves and monetary base adjusted for seasonality and changes in reserve requirements, except as noted; annual data are for December.)

Year and month	Reserves					Monetary base	Federal Reserve balance sheet: total assets
	Total	Nonborrowed	Nonborrowed plus extended credit [1]	Required	Excess reserves, not seasonally adjusted		
1960	11 247	11 172	11 172	10 503	743	40 977	. . .
1961	11 499	11 366	11 366	10 915	584	41 853	. . .
1962	11 604	11 344	11 344	11 033	572	42 957	. . .
1963	11 730	11 397	11 397	11 239	490	45 003	. . .
1964	12 011	11 747	11 747	11 605	406	47 161	. . .
1965	12 316	11 872	11 872	11 892	423	49 620	. . .
1966	12 223	11 690	11 690	11 884	339	51 565	. . .
1967	13 180	12 952	12 952	12 805	375	54 579	. . .
1968	13 767	13 021	13 021	13 341	426	58 357	. . .
1969	14 168	13 049	13 049	13 882	286	61 569	. . .
1970	14 558	14 225	14 225	14 309	249	65 013	. . .
1971	15 230	15 104	15 104	15 049	182	69 108	. . .
1972	16 645	15 595	15 595	16 361	284	75 167	. . .
1973	17 021	15 723	15 723	16 717	304	81 073	. . .
1974	17 550	16 823	16 970	17 292	258	87 535	. . .
1975	17 822	17 692	17 704	17 556	266	93 887	. . .
1976	18 388	18 335	18 335	18 115	274	101 515	. . .
1977	18 990	18 420	18 420	18 800	190	110 324	. . .
1978	19 753	18 885	18 885	19 521	232	120 445	. . .
1979	20 720	19 248	19 248	20 279	442	131 143	. . .
1980	22 015	20 325	20 328	21 501	514	142 004	. . .
1981	22 443	21 807	21 956	22 124	319	149 021	. . .
1982	23 600	22 966	23 152	23 100	500	160 127	. . .
1983	25 367	24 593	24 595	24 806	561	175 467	. . .
1984	26 913	23 727	26 331	26 078	835	187 253	. . .
1985	31 569	30 251	30 749	30 505	1 064	203 556	. . .
1986	38 841	38 014	38 317	37 667	1 174	223 417	. . .
1987	38 913	38 136	38 618	37 893	1 020	239 830	. . .
1988	40 454	38 738	39 982	39 392	1 062	256 897	. . .
1989	40 487	40 222	40 241	39 545	942	267 761	. . .
1990	41 767	41 441	41 463	40 101	1 665	293 339	. . .
1991	45 516	45 324	45 325	44 526	990	317 523	. . .
1992	54 422	54 298	54 298	53 267	1 155	350 885	. . .
1993	60 567	60 485	60 484	59 497	1 070	386 720	. . .
1994	59 466	59 257	59 257	58 295	1 171	418 474	. . .
1995	56 484	56 226	56 226	55 193	1 291	434 645	. . .
1996	50 185	50 030	50 030	48 766	1 419	451 935	. . .
1997	46 876	46 551	46 551	45 189	1 687	479 798	. . .
1998	45 174	45 058	45 053	43 662	1 513	513 821	. . .
1999	42 149	41 829	41 787	40 855	1 295	593 383	. . .
2000	38 685	38 475	38 465	37 359	1 326	584 928	. . .
2001	41 384	41 317	41 338	39 740	1 643	635 575	. . .
2002	40 275	40 195	40 207	38 267	2 008	681 486	. . .
2003	42 542	42 496	. . .	41 495	1 047	720 115	. . .
2004	46 425	46 362	. . .	44 517	1 908	759 085	. . .
2005	44 963	44 795	. . .	43 063	1 900	787 369	. . .
2006	43 124	42 933	. . .	41 261	1 863	812 367	. . .
2007	43 133	27 702	. . .	41 348	1 785	824 809	890 662
2008	820 187	166 621	. . .	52 868	767 318	1 654 974	2 239 457
2009	1 138 682	968 755	. . .	63 483	1 075 199	2 019 228	2 234 067
2010	1 077 359	1 031 871	. . .	70 723	1 006 636	2 011 078	2 420 570
2011	1 597 100	1 587 574	. . .	94 894	1 502 206	2 612 081	2 926 095
2012	1 569 017	1 568 221	. . .	110 266	1 458 751	2 672 578	2 907 300
2011							
January	1 106 871	1 074 624	. . .	70 404	1 036 466	2 045 246	2 443 527
February	1 262 561	1 240 628	. . .	72 559	1 190 001	2 206 968	2 533 221
March	1 436 155	1 416 273	. . .	74 008	1 362 146	2 388 588	2 622 523
April	1 526 629	1 508 786	. . .	74 682	1 451 947	2 488 232	2 690 985
May	1 587 841	1 572 695	. . .	75 353	1 512 488	2 559 330	2 774 996
June	1 666 615	1 653 372	. . .	77 890	1 588 726	2 644 873	2 865 251
July	1 696 633	1 684 238	. . .	78 516	1 618 117	2 681 180	2 863 576
August	1 666 698	1 654 864	. . .	83 354	1 583 344	2 657 705	2 853 888
September	1 642 237	1 630 662	. . .	91 260	1 550 977	2 638 154	2 850 921
October	1 638 130	1 626 919	. . .	92 993	1 545 136	2 638 313	2 845 685
November	1 591 703	1 581 362	. . .	93 934	1 497 769	2 599 462	2 814 235
December	1 597 100	1 587 574	. . .	94 894	1 502 206	2 612 081	2 926 095
2012							
January	1 614 301	1 605 687	. . .	94 850	1 519 451	2 638 114	2 919 545
February	1 657 931	1 649 998	. . .	97 811	1 560 121	2 690 184	2 925 722
March	1 607 819	1 600 490	. . .	98 226	1 509 593	2 648 070	2 878 137
April	1 584 770	1 577 905	. . .	98 593	1 486 176	2 631 478	2 866 561
May	1 556 689	1 550 503	. . .	99 230	1 457 460	2 609 131	2 842 654
June	1 557 175	1 551 961	. . .	99 699	1 457 475	2 615 664	2 863 547
July	1 584 049	1 579 791	. . .	101 000	1 483 049	2 649 396	2 846 757
August	1 582 288	1 579 017	. . .	104 538	1 477 750	2 654 458	2 812 806
September	1 515 888	1 513 923	. . .	106 447	1 409 441	2 597 251	2 804 457
October	1 525 145	1 523 679	. . .	106 870	1 418 275	2 615 620	2 823 137
November	1 546 809	1 545 758	. . .	111 505	1 435 304	2 643 297	2 851 362
December	1 569 017	1 568 221	. . .	110 266	1 458 751	2 672 578	2 907 300

[1]Extended credit program discontinued January 9, 2003. See notes and definitions for more information.
. . . = Not available.

Table 12-4A. Commercial Banks: Bank Credit and Selected Liabilities: Recent Data

(All commercial banks in the United States, billions of dollars, seasonally adjusted, annual data are for December.)

Year and month	Bank credit									
	Total	Securities in bank credit			Loans and leases in bank credit					
		Total	U.S. Treasury and agency securities	Other securities	Total	Commercial and industrial	Real estate			
							Total	Revolving home equity	Other residential	Commercial
1960	197.1	78.3	63.1	15.2	118.9	42.1	28.1	...	...	...
1961	213.3	86.8	69.4	17.4	126.4	43.8	29.5	...	...	...
1962	232.0	90.8	69.9	20.9	141.1	47.4	33.3	...	...	...
1963	252.0	91.4	66.8	24.6	160.6	52.2	38.1	...	...	...
1964	272.5	93.7	66.2	27.4	178.9	58.3	42.5	...	...	...
1965	300.5	95.1	63.9	31.2	205.4	69.2	47.8	...	...	...
1966	319.5	96.8	61.5	35.4	222.6	79.0	52.5	...	...	...
1967	352.2	111.1	71.5	39.6	241.1	86.1	56.8	...	...	...
1968	391.8	121.6	74.8	46.8	270.2	96.2	63.3	...	...	...
1969	401.6	112.1	65.1	46.9	289.5	106.6	68.4	...	...	...
1970	435.8	129.3	74.5	54.8	306.5	111.4	71.3	...	...	...
1971	488.9	147.3	81.5	65.8	341.5	117.8	80.0	...	...	...
1972	561.8	159.7	86.9	72.8	402.0	133.1	96.9	...	...	...
1973	643.1	166.9	90.1	76.8	476.2	161.2	117.0	...	...	...
1974	707.5	172.1	88.2	83.9	535.4	191.3	129.8	...	...	...
1975	737.8	204.9	118.1	86.8	532.9	183.4	134.1	...	...	...
1976	798.6	226.7	137.5	89.1	571.9	185.2	148.5	...	...	...
1977	885.6	234.3	137.5	96.8	651.3	204.7	175.1	...	...	...
1978	1 003.7	240.2	138.4	101.9	763.5	237.2	210.5	...	...	...
1979	1 118.1	257.8	146.1	111.7	860.3	279.7	241.7	...	...	...
1980	1 216.9	293.4	171.5	121.9	923.5	312.0	262.3	...	...	...
1981	1 297.7	306.8	179.8	127.0	990.9	350.3	283.6	...	...	...
1982	1 397.6	333.8	202.4	131.4	1 063.8	392.0	299.7	...	...	...
1983	1 549.6	398.1	260.4	137.8	1 151.5	413.9	330.4	...	...	...
1984	1 715.9	401.1	260.0	141.1	1 314.8	473.4	376.2	...	...	...
1985	1 883.5	440.5	264.2	176.3	1 443.1	499.1	422.1	...	...	...
1986	2 077.6	498.9	310.3	188.6	1 578.7	539.2	490.6	...	...	...
1987	2 226.4	526.1	336.3	189.8	1 700.3	565.1	585.8	30.6	...	...
1988	2 399.8	549.7	360.5	189.2	1 850.1	604.7	663.2	41.2	...	...
1989	2 562.9	571.1	401.6	169.5	1 991.8	637.1	760.6	51.5	...	...
1990	2 700.0	619.2	460.2	159.1	2 080.8	640.1	842.5	63.5	...	...
1991	2 807.5	727.5	564.3	163.2	2 080.0	617.9	868.6	71.9	...	...
1992	2 907.2	824.1	664.7	159.5	2 083.0	596.8	887.7	75.0	...	...
1993	3 059.8	894.5	730.0	164.4	2 165.4	583.8	928.6	74.2	...	...
1994	3 233.6	891.6	721.9	169.7	2 342.0	644.0	987.6	76.0	...	...
1995	3 461.2	892.9	703.3	189.6	2 568.2	715.2	1 061.7	79.8	...	...
1996	3 634.8	893.3	698.6	194.8	2 741.5	778.7	1 122.2	86.3	...	...
1997	3 956.4	985.6	750.2	235.4	2 970.8	845.6	1 220.1	98.8	...	...
1998	4 368.4	1 096.8	795.3	301.6	3 271.5	939.0	1 311.0	97.2	...	...
1999	4 627.6	1 144.5	811.1	333.4	3 483.2	1 001.7	1 460.3	101.2	...	...
2000	5 022.5	1 174.2	787.7	386.5	3 848.4	1 087.1	1 638.4	129.3	...	...
2001	5 206.9	1 307.5	838.8	468.7	3 899.3	1 023.9	1 757.6	153.8	...	...
2002	5 639.6	1 490.4	1 004.2	486.2	4 149.2	962.4	2 008.4	212.4	...	...
2003	5 999.1	1 621.9	1 088.8	533.2	4 377.1	889.6	2 206.1	278.7	...	...
2004	6 582.4	1 741.4	1 145.8	595.6	4 841.0	913.4	2 551.9	395.4	1 075.0	1 081.5
2005	7 301.2	1 852.5	1 135.3	717.2	5 448.6	1 043.6	2 922.6	443.2	1 207.6	1 271.8
2006	8 088.4	1 985.2	1 187.2	797.9	6 103.3	1 191.4	3 365.4	467.8	1 438.1	1 459.5
2007	8 892.2	2 102.7	1 108.6	994.1	6 789.4	1 430.7	3 592.1	484.5	1 524.5	1 583.1
2008	9 342.4	2 095.5	1 236.7	858.7	7 246.9	1 572.7	3 815.3	587.9	1 501.5	1 725.9
2009	8 982.6	2 324.1	1 444.4	879.7	6 658.5	1 278.8	3 773.4	602.9	1 532.7	1 637.9
2010	9 179.5	2 426.7	1 637.8	788.8	6 752.8	1 208.2	3 609.6	581.5	1 531.5	1 496.6
2011	9 401.0	2 494.9	1 697.5	797.4	6 906.1	1 331.5	3 490.2	548.2	1 527.8	1 414.2
2012	9 948.7	2 736.6	1 877.6	859.0	7 212.1	1 505.0	3 542.9	514.3	1 607.5	1 421.1
2011										
January	9 159.6	2 426.4	1 642.8	783.6	6 733.2	1 212.2	3 597.9	577.5	1 534.1	1 486.3
February	9 119.9	2 416.7	1 635.6	781.1	6 703.2	1 216.4	3 565.6	574.4	1 512.4	1 478.8
March	9 119.5	2 430.2	1 646.6	783.6	6 689.2	1 226.1	3 535.4	572.3	1 494.8	1 468.2
April	9 153.7	2 443.7	1 671.2	772.5	6 710.0	1 236.4	3 516.6	568.6	1 488.3	1 459.7
May	9 154.6	2 439.6	1 669.4	770.2	6 714.9	1 249.6	3 504.6	565.7	1 483.3	1 455.6
June	9 159.6	2 433.4	1 659.8	773.6	6 726.2	1 256.7	3 500.2	562.9	1 487.9	1 449.4
July	9 202.1	2 432.0	1 651.3	780.6	6 770.1	1 269.4	3 495.9	559.7	1 495.5	1 440.8
August	9 245.1	2 446.8	1 658.0	788.7	6 798.3	1 290.0	3 489.0	556.9	1 498.6	1 433.5
September	9 264.3	2 456.1	1 666.9	789.3	6 808.1	1 295.7	3 486.5	555.0	1 502.8	1 428.7
October	9 323.1	2 462.4	1 676.5	785.9	6 860.7	1 309.8	3 494.3	552.6	1 519.2	1 422.5
November	9 386.4	2 477.7	1 686.7	791.0	6 908.7	1 318.9	3 497.7	550.2	1 527.2	1 420.2
December	9 401.0	2 494.9	1 697.5	797.4	6 906.1	1 331.5	3 490.2	548.2	1 527.8	1 414.2
2012										
January	9 471.2	2 529.5	1 725.6	803.9	6 941.7	1 349.4	3 507.1	549.1	1 544.1	1 413.9
February	9 563.4	2 566.5	1 756.7	809.8	6 996.8	1 372.3	3 536.5	550.3	1 561.7	1 424.6
March	9 590.3	2 579.5	1 778.3	801.2	7 010.7	1 382.8	3 541.7	546.8	1 571.6	1 423.3
April	9 634.6	2 595.0	1 798.0	797.0	7 039.6	1 402.8	3 539.2	543.7	1 572.8	1 422.7
May	9 677.3	2 604.5	1 808.0	796.5	7 072.9	1 410.9	3 538.0	540.4	1 578.9	1 418.8
June	9 706.4	2 608.5	1 807.4	801.1	7 097.9	1 432.7	3 529.7	537.0	1 575.0	1 417.7
July	9 755.0	2 639.0	1 828.3	810.8	7 116.0	1 450.7	3 527.4	532.8	1 576.3	1 418.3
August	9 780.0	2 644.8	1 832.7	812.1	7 135.2	1 461.7	3 527.1	529.4	1 579.9	1 417.8
September	9 805.1	2 656.8	1 835.4	821.4	7 148.3	1 464.8	3 531.8	525.3	1 588.6	1 417.9
October	9 821.7	2 666.1	1 835.3	830.9	7 155.6	1 479.4	3 522.6	520.5	1 584.1	1 418.0
November	9 871.3	2 690.6	1 851.0	839.6	7 180.8	1 483.8	3 546.1	517.8	1 609.5	1 418.8
December	9 948.7	2 736.6	1 877.6	859.0	7 212.1	1 505.0	3 542.9	514.3	1 607.5	1 421.1

. . . = Not available.

Table 12-4A. Commercial Banks: Bank Credit and Selected Liabilities: Recent Data—*Continued*

(All commercial banks in the United States, billions of dollars, seasonally adjusted, annual data are for December.)

Year and month	Bank credit					Selected liabilities			
	Loans and leases in bank credit				Deposits	Borrowings			
		Consumer loans							
	Total	Credit cards and other revolving plans	Other consumer loans	Other loans and leases		Total	From banks in the United States	From others
1960	26.3	. . .	. . .	22.4	. . .	. . .	. . .	. . .
1961	27.6	. . .	. . .	25.5	. . .	. . .	. . .	. . .
1962	30.2	. . .	. . .	30.2	. . .	. . .	. . .	. . .
1963	34.2	. . .	. . .	36.2	. . .	. . .	. . .	. . .
1964	39.5	. . .	. . .	38.5	. . .	. . .	. . .	. . .
1965	45.0	. . .	. . .	43.4	. . .	. . .	. . .	. . .
1966	47.8	. . .	. . .	43.4	. . .	. . .	. . .	. . .
1967	51.2	. . .	. . .	46.9	. . .	. . .	. . .	. . .
1968	57.7	. . .	. . .	53.0	. . .	. . .	. . .	. . .
1969	62.5	. . .	. . .	52.0	. . .	. . .	. . .	. . .
1970	65.2	. . .	. . .	58.6	. . .	. . .	. . .	. . .
1971	73.2	. . .	. . .	70.6	. . .	. . .	. . .	. . .
1972	85.3	. . .	. . .	86.8	. . .	. . .	. . .	. . .
1973	98.4	. . .	. . .	99.7	663.7	14.9	. . .	. . .
1974	102.1	. . .	. . .	112.2	731.4	19.5	. . .	. . .
1975	104.3	. . .	. . .	111.1	768.0	20.5	. . .	. . .
1976	115.8	. . .	. . .	122.3	825.9	22.4	. . .	. . .
1977	138.0	. . .	. . .	133.5	910.9	29.0	. . .	. . .
1978	164.4	. . .	. . .	151.3	1 004.0	53.3	. . .	. . .
1979	183.8	. . .	. . .	155.1	1 072.7	176.0	. . .	. . .
1980	178.7	. . .	. . .	170.5	1 185.1	211.5	. . .	. . .
1981	182.1	. . .	. . .	174.8	1 248.2	254.8	. . .	. . .
1982	187.9	. . .	. . .	184.2	1 365.5	280.6	. . .	. . .
1983	212.9	. . .	. . .	194.3	1 479.1	280.8	. . .	. . .
1984	253.8	. . .	. . .	211.3	1 612.4	315.2	. . .	. . .
1985	291.1	. . .	. . .	230.8	1 762.5	347.4	. . .	. . .
1986	314.8	. . .	. . .	234.1	1 925.7	391.5	. . .	. . .
1987	327.1	. . .	. . .	222.4	1 986.6	408.9	. . .	. . .
1988	355.2	. . .	. . .	226.9	2 116.9	457.6	. . .	. . .
1989	373.4	. . .	. . .	220.7	2 243.0	514.9	. . .	. . .
1990	375.2	. . .	. . .	222.9	2 336.8	525.2	. . .	. . .
1991	363.3	. . .	. . .	230.2	2 467.7	464.8	. . .	. . .
1992	354.5	. . .	. . .	244.1	2 499.1	464.5	. . .	. . .
1993	385.9	. . .	. . .	267.1	2 534.6	498.1	. . .	. . .
1994	443.3	. . .	. . .	267.1	2 533.4	583.6	. . .	. . .
1995	484.0	. . .	. . .	307.3	2 651.8	646.0	. . .	. . .
1996	506.9	. . .	. . .	333.7	2 832.7	679.7	295.9	383.9
1997	500.0	. . .	. . .	405.1	3 079.0	806.4	299.9	506.5
1998	497.7	. . .	. . .	524.0	3 293.7	945.2	315.0	630.2
1999	506.7	. . .	. . .	514.4	3 475.8	1 079.0	342.8	736.1
2000	556.3	228.9	327.4	566.6	3 724.7	1 170.1	377.0	793.1
2001	574.4	242.2	332.2	543.3	4 078.2	1 168.3	405.6	762.7
2002	610.5	254.7	355.7	567.9	4 351.1	1 318.6	422.4	896.2
2003	664.8	281.3	383.6	616.6	4 627.5	1 365.3	392.1	973.2
2004	690.8	297.3	393.5	684.9	5 150.4	1 478.6	398.8	1 079.9
2005	702.4	303.7	398.7	780.0	5 591.0	1 638.2	370.9	1 267.3
2006	736.4	313.3	423.1	810.1	6 092.6	1 868.6	407.5	1 461.0
2007	798.0	341.8	456.2	968.7	6 665.1	2 131.3	475.9	1 655.4
2008	875.0	384.7	490.3	983.9	7 206.6	2 456.1	382.0	2 074.1
2009	835.3	336.3	499.1	770.9	7 679.8	1 900.7	259.6	1 641.1
2010	1 113.2	604.5	508.7	821.8	7 860.1	1 885.2	227.5	1 657.7
2011	1 089.7	597.6	492.1	994.7	8 413.0	1 611.4	131.7	1 479.7
2012	1 114.5	601.8	512.8	1 049.8	9 225.8	1 548.8	150.2	1 398.6
2011								
January	1 080.4	600.1	480.4	842.6	7 889.8	1 809.3	203.3	1 606.0
February	1 076.5	597.1	479.3	844.8	7 937.2	1 791.2	193.1	1 598.2
March	1 075.3	595.9	479.4	852.5	7 986.7	1 775.2	184.1	1 591.1
April	1 079.3	594.3	485.0	877.6	8 067.9	1 713.3	156.6	1 556.7
May	1 079.3	593.9	485.4	881.4	8 152.8	1 679.9	154.9	1 525.0
June	1 083.4	596.8	486.7	885.9	8 188.7	1 685.4	173.3	1 512.1
July	1 088.1	597.7	490.4	916.7	8 282.6	1 664.3	145.7	1 518.7
August	1 085.8	596.9	488.9	933.6	8 342.3	1 654.7	153.9	1 500.8
September	1 085.2	596.9	488.4	940.7	8 364.1	1 624.5	147.3	1 477.2
October	1 086.7	596.7	490.1	969.8	8 367.4	1 604.7	138.9	1 465.8
November	1 087.7	596.6	491.0	1 004.5	8 378.9	1 621.8	139.7	1 482.1
December	1 089.7	597.6	492.1	994.7	8 413.0	1 611.4	131.7	1 479.7
2012								
January	1 088.9	594.9	493.9	996.3	8 483.8	1 598.1	128.2	1 469.9
February	1 090.2	593.1	497.0	997.8	8 566.6	1 599.9	127.2	1 472.7
March	1 093.8	593.9	499.9	992.5	8 612.1	1 576.9	129.0	1 447.9
April	1 096.9	595.5	501.5	1 000.7	8 643.2	1 552.6	131.2	1 421.3
May	1 106.8	604.2	502.6	1 017.1	8 656.7	1 585.2	132.6	1 452.6
June	1 107.1	603.8	503.3	1 028.3	8 732.0	1 586.6	133.3	1 453.3
July	1 106.9	602.1	504.8	1 030.9	8 813.6	1 584.5	136.7	1 447.9
August	1 108.0	602.8	505.2	1 038.4	8 862.7	1 569.4	135.6	1 433.8
September	1 109.3	602.0	507.3	1 042.4	8 915.0	1 576.6	135.6	1 441.0
October	1 110.8	601.4	509.4	1 042.8	8 977.4	1 568.2	141.0	1 427.2
November	1 112.9	602.0	510.9	1 038.0	9 084.6	1 561.0	142.5	1 418.5
December	1 114.5	601.8	512.8	1 049.8	9 225.8	1 548.8	150.2	1 398.6

. . . = Not available.

Table 12-4B. Bank Credit and Other Credit Instruments: Historical

(Millions of dollars, year end, not seasonally adjusted.)

Year	Loans and investments, all commercial banks[1]	Commercial and finance paper	Commercial paper only	Bankers' acceptances
1914	16 854	. . .	. . .	. . .
1915	17 473	. . .	. . .	. . .
1916	20 411	. . .	. . .	. . .
1917	23 863	. . .	. . .	. . .
1918	27 380	. . .	881	. . .
1919	31 760	. . .	1 186	. . .
1920	36 294	. . .	948	. . .
1921	34 219	. . .	663	. . .
1922	33 893	. . .	722	. . .
1923	37 296	. . .	763	. . .
1924	39 836	. . .	798	821
1925	43 011	. . .	621	774
1926	43 927	. . .	526	755
1927	46 780	. . .	555	1 081
1928	49 339	. . .	383	1 284
1929	49 467	. . .	334	1 732
1930	46 700	. . .	358	1 556
1931	39 653	. . .	120	974
1932	35 083	. . .	81	710
1933	30 789	. . .	109	764
1934	33 735	. . .	166	543
1935	35 982	. . .	171	397
1936	39 472	. . .	215	373
1937	38 333	. . .	279	343
1938	38 699	. . .	187	270
1939	40 667	. . .	210	233
1940	43 922	. . .	218	209
1941	50 722	. . .	375	194
1942	67 393	. . .	230	118
1943	85 095	. . .	202	117
1944	105 530	. . .	166	129
1945	124 019	. . .	159	154
1946	113 993	. . .	228	227
1947	116 284	. . .	287	261
1948	114 298	674	269	259
1949	120 197	838	257	272
1950	126 675	921	333	394
1951	132 610	1 333	434	490
1952	141 624	1 749	539	492
1953	145 687	1 973	. . .	574
1954	155 916	1 933	. . .	873
1955	160 881	2 035	. . .	642
1956	165 123	2 183	. . .	967
1957	170 068	2 672	. . .	1 307
1958	185 165	2 751	. . .	1 194
1959	190 270	3 202	. . .	1 151
1960	199 509	4 497	. . .	2 027
1961	215 441	4 686	. . .	2 683
1962	235 839	6 000	. . .	2 650
1963	254 162	6 790	. . .	2 890
1964	277 376	8 442	. . .	3 385
1965	306 060	9 300	. . .	3 392
1966	322 661	13 645	. . .	3 604
1967	359 903	17 085	. . .	4 317
1968	401 262	21 173	. . .	4 428

[1]December 31, 1922 to date; before that, June 30
. . . = Not available.

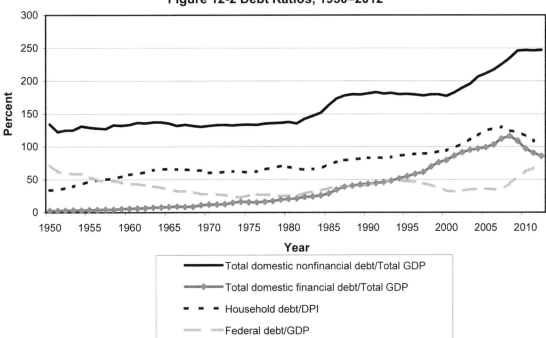

Figure 12-2 Debt Ratios, 1950–2012

- Unsustainable debt growth was the source of the credit crisis and economic decline in 2007–2009. Traditionally, analysts have focused on the debt of nonfinancial sectors. Among the major nonfinancial divisions of the economy, the most striking expansion in debt relative to income occurred in the household sector. Household debt in 1984 was no higher, relative to income, than it had been in 1964—but then it began a rapid and uninterrupted expansion. In 2001, debt rose above 100 percent of the annual rate of income, and it reached 130 percent at the end of 2007. Debt and the ratio declined after that, and by the end of 2012, the ratio to DPI was down to 102.4 percent—still higher than anything seen before 2002. (Table 12-5)

- During the expansion period, financial sector debt—much of it reflecting the securitization of nonfinancial sector debt, especially mortgages, in other words debt built upon other debt—grew somewhat more rapidly than nonfinancial sector debt. Between 1985 and 2007, financial sector debt rose from 29 percent to 112 percent of GDP, while total nonfinancial sector debt only grew from 164 to 225 percent.

- Up through 2003, the debt of federal government-related financial entities—government-sponsored enterprises (GSEs) such as "Fannie Mae" and "Freddie Mac" and mortgage pools backed by federal agencies and GSEs—and the debt of private financial sectors both rose rapidly. From 2003 to 2007, growth slowed in the government portion but accelerated in the private segment. After 2008, total private financial debt dropped dramatically and total financial debt fell to 86 percent of GDP at the end of 2012. (Tables 1-1 and 12-5)

- Debt of the federal government itself—that is, Treasury securities issued to fund budget deficits—contributed little, on balance, to the rising trend of aggregate debt—until the recession struck in 2008, revenues fell, and spending rose because of both recession-sensitive programs like unemployment insurance and new moves to stabilize credit markets and the economy. (Tables 12-5, 6-1 and 6-15)

Table 12-5. Credit Market Debt Outstanding, by Borrower and Lender

(Billions of dollars, except as noted; end of period; not seasonally adjusted.)

Year and quarter	Total	Credit market debt outstanding												
		Owed by:												
		Domestic financial sectors			Domestic nonfinancial sectors									
		Total	Federal govern- ment- related	Private	Total		Federal government			Households		Nonfinancial business		
									Budget agency securities and mortgages				Corporate	
					Billions of dollars	Percent of GDP	Total	Treasury securities		Billions of dollars	Percent of DPI	Total	Total	Percent of sector value added
1955	582.0	15.1	3.2	11.9	550.5	129.2	230.0	228.4	1.6	138.4	47.4	136.0	101.1	45.7
1956	611.5	17.8	4.0	13.8	576.5	128.1	224.1	222.8	1.4	153.2	49.1	148.7	110.8	46.7
1957	642.7	20.7	5.1	15.5	603.5	127.1	221.9	220.1	1.7	165.8	50.3	160.8	120.4	48.6
1958	681.6	20.8	5.2	15.6	640.2	132.8	231.1	229.0	1.6	176.5	51.8	171.9	127.7	52.7
1959	738.7	27.4	7.5	20.0	689.9	132.0	238.0	236.2	0.9	198.5	55.0	186.7	136.4	50.2
1960	780.2	32.3	8.1	24.2	724.7	133.4	236.0	234.0	0.7	216.5	57.5	200.1	145.0	51.3
1961	828.5	34.7	8.9	25.8	768.4	136.4	243.2	240.7	1.0	233.9	59.4	213.6	151.9	52.3
1962	888.2	39.3	10.5	28.8	821.4	135.7	250.0	246.8	1.5	255.8	61.3	231.8	162.5	51.3
1963	954.2	46.4	12.0	34.3	877.0	137.3	253.8	250.7	1.4	282.9	64.5	251.0	173.1	51.2
1964	1 028.5	52.7	12.7	40.0	940.9	137.2	259.9	255.9	2.2	312.7	65.6	272.7	186.4	51.1
1965	1 106.9	61.4	15.1	46.4	1 008.0	135.5	261.5	257.0	2.7	340.6	66.4	302.7	207.2	51.7
1966	1 187.3	72.3	20.3	52.0	1 075.5	132.0	265.1	259.3	4.0	363.1	65.5	337.2	232.0	52.7
1967	1 268.0	73.2	20.4	52.8	1 151.5	133.6	278.1	268.2	8.2	386.8	65.3	369.2	253.6	54.7
1968	1 372.9	83.5	24.4	59.1	1 243.3	131.9	290.6	277.6	11.3	415.2	64.5	411.4	284.8	55.8
1969	1 490.6	111.0	33.8	77.2	1 330.4	130.4	287.4	276.8	9.0	445.0	63.9	459.7	317.8	57.3
1970	1 599.6	127.3	43.6	83.7	1 420.2	132.0	299.5	289.9	8.1	460.3	60.4	510.1	361.6	63.1
1971	1 749.5	137.8	49.5	88.2	1 555.2	133.2	324.4	315.9	7.0	503.2	60.6	560.9	389.7	63.1
1972	1 933.5	161.3	57.9	103.3	1 711.2	133.4	339.4	330.1	7.9	558.2	62.0	632.9	430.3	62.7
1973	2 170.8	207.9	77.9	130.0	1 895.5	132.7	346.3	336.7	8.4	628.2	62.4	726.2	496.0	64.5
1974	2 408.0	257.6	98.6	159.0	2 069.1	133.6	358.2	348.8	8.2	684.5	62.3	818.2	550.9	66.4
1975	2 616.3	261.3	108.9	152.4	2 259.8	133.8	443.9	434.9	7.9	741.5	60.8	855.0	567.4	63.2
1976	2 904.1	285.5	123.1	162.3	2 503.0	133.3	513.1	503.7	8.3	828.5	62.5	923.5	606.4	59.8
1977	3 291.7	339.1	145.5	193.6	2 824.0	135.4	569.4	560.9	7.6	956.1	65.6	1 042.3	682.5	59.5
1978	3 776.3	412.7	182.6	230.1	3 207.9	136.1	621.9	614.9	6.2	1 111.2	68.2	1 179.3	761.1	58.4
1979	4 273.7	508.9	231.8	277.1	3 596.3	136.6	657.7	652.1	4.9	1 278.5	70.7	1 337.9	845.9	58.3
1980	4 722.4	584.7	276.6	308.1	3 944.3	137.8	735.0	730.0	4.4	1 396.0	69.2	1 468.9	913.8	58.0
1981	5 255.0	689.2	324.0	365.2	4 351.9	135.5	820.5	815.9	4.1	1 505.9	66.9	1 653.4	1 033.6	57.8
1982	5 766.8	785.5	388.9	396.6	4 773.1	142.7	981.8	978.1	3.4	1 575.8	65.0	1 801.8	1 124.1	60.6
1983	6 462.9	890.1	456.6	433.5	5 348.6	147.0	1 167.0	1 163.4	3.3	1 731.1	66.1	1 989.5	1 240.5	62.5
1984	7 422.5	1 054.9	531.2	523.7	6 134.8	151.8	1 364.2	1 360.8	3.2	1 943.1	66.9	2 313.8	1 451.2	65.2
1985	8 612.0	1 259.0	631.7	627.2	7 110.6	163.6	1 589.9	1 586.6	3.2	2 277.7	73.5	2 565.1	1 632.1	68.9
1986	9 801.5	1 596.6	810.3	786.3	7 953.0	173.3	1 805.9	1 802.2	3.6	2 534.2	77.1	2 860.8	1 860.6	75.5
1987	10 814.8	1 899.7	977.6	922.1	8 656.1	177.7	1 949.8	1 944.6	5.1	2 752.5	79.4	3 111.2	2 053.0	77.7
1988	11 856.3	2 149.5	1 098.4	1 051.2	9 437.0	179.7	2 104.9	2 082.3	22.6	3 039.8	80.6	3 399.3	2 257.3	78.5
1989	12 830.0	2 402.8	1 247.8	1 155.0	10 139.3	179.2	2 251.2	2 227.0	24.2	3 309.2	81.7	3 638.6	2 448.4	81.1
1990	13 757.1	2 613.8	1 418.4	1 195.4	10 825.1	181.0	2 498.1	2 465.8	32.4	3 571.6	82.8	3 767.9	2 577.4	81.5
1991	14 412.3	2 766.8	1 564.2	1 202.6	11 295.2	182.9	2 776.4	2 757.8	18.6	3 758.5	83.8	3 681.7	2 519.7	78.0
1992	15 204.0	3 018.9	1 720.4	1 298.5	11 812.7	180.6	3 080.3	3 061.6	18.8	3 961.7	82.5	3 675.6	2 540.0	75.2
1993	16 280.2	3 317.2	1 885.7	1 431.5	12 494.8	181.6	3 336.5	3 309.9	26.6	4 203.5	84.1	3 801.8	2 686.9	76.0
1994	17 373.9	3 789.7	2 173.4	1 616.3	13 141.1	179.8	3 492.3	3 465.6	26.7	4 527.0	86.3	4 014.3	2 885.0	75.6
1995	18 604.3	4 226.3	2 377.7	1 848.5	13 810.4	180.2	3 636.7	3 608.5	28.2	4 846.1	87.6	4 280.9	3 106.2	76.9
1996	19 923.3	4 749.5	2 609.2	2 140.3	14 516.5	179.2	3 781.7	3 755.1	26.6	5 183.8	88.9	4 524.8	3 279.7	76.3
1997	21 331.5	5 299.7	2 822.8	2 476.9	15 308.2	177.8	3 804.8	3 778.3	26.5	5 489.4	89.3	4 937.0	3 590.0	77.9
1998	23 416.0	6 326.2	3 294.4	3 031.8	16 306.7	179.4	3 752.2	3 723.7	28.5	5 902.9	90.0	5 507.9	3 981.8	81.7
1999	25 477.9	7 376.5	3 887.7	3 488.8	17 353.2	179.5	3 681.0	3 652.7	28.3	6 377.6	92.7	6 113.6	4 393.7	85.0
2000	27 211.0	8 168.4	4 319.7	3 848.7	18 228.1	177.1	3 385.1	3 357.8	27.3	6 963.5	94.1	6 681.6	4 769.3	86.5
2001	29 395.9	9 156.8	4 962.3	4 194.5	19 373.7	182.3	3 379.5	3 352.7	26.8	7 627.8	98.4	7 063.0	4 987.3	91.2
2002	31 913.2	10 038.2	5 509.0	4 529.2	20 802.2	189.5	3 637.0	3 609.8	27.3	8 439.1	104.2	7 278.2	5 050.6	91.2
2003	34 716.6	10 944.5	5 944.5	5 000.0	22 518.8	195.6	4 033.1	4 008.2	24.9	9 462.0	111.5	7 455.3	5 153.9	90.0
2004	38 683.5	11 898.3	6 060.3	5 838.1	25 346.4	206.5	4 395.0	4 370.7	24.3	10 536.1	117.0	7 967.1	5 411.0	88.6
2005	42 160.8	12 957.3	6 140.7	6 816.5	27 689.6	211.4	4 701.9	4 678.0	23.8	11 716.4	124.6	8 681.5	5 783.7	88.5
2006	46 202.3	14 260.5	6 468.9	7 791.6	30 059.2	216.9	4 885.3	4 861.7	23.5	12 833.3	127.9	9 649.9	6 336.9	90.7
2007	50 953.0	16 204.5	7 374.6	8 829.9	32 622.3	225.3	5 122.3	5 099.2	23.1	13 689.3	130.3	10 973.1	7 198.5	99.9
2008	53 353.2	17 101.0	8 143.4	8 957.7	34 543.4	234.7	6 361.5	6 338.2	23.3	13 669.0	124.3	11 657.4	7 564.0	104.2
2009	53 252.5	15 688.5	8 083.3	7 605.2	35 473.7	246.0	7 805.4	7 781.9	23.5	13 397.0	122.5	11 302.8	7 329.5	106.8
2010	53 620.8	14 486.0	7 574.0	6 912.0	36 909.5	246.7	9 385.6	9 361.5	24.2	13 059.9	116.2	11 426.0	7 485.9	103.4
2011	54 589.6	14 045.4	7 552.1	6 493.2	38 267.5	246.4	10 453.6	10 428.3	25.3	12 863.7	109.1	11 965.0	8 012.6	104.9
2012	56 447.3	13 911.3	7 529.7	6 381.5	40 121.4	247.0	11 593.7	11 568.9	24.9	12 819.3	104.7	12 728.3	8 704.7	108.5
2010														
1st quarter	52 780.9	14 831.2	7 633.4	7 197.8	35 832.6	244.2	8 283.2	8 259.6	23.6	13 243.0	119.9	11 312.9	7 353.1	103.9
2nd quarter	52 740.4	14 581.9	7 637.6	6 944.3	36 059.7	242.3	8 627.7	8 603.8	23.9	13 165.3	117.5	11 281.4	7 329.3	101.9
3rd quarter	53 149.9	14 426.8	7 594.1	6 832.7	36 498.5	242.5	9 017.8	8 993.8	24.0	13 108.5	116.1	11 383.6	7 435.3	101.2
4th quarter	53 620.8	14 486.0	7 574.0	6 912.0	36 909.5	242.3	9 385.6	9 361.5	24.2	13 059.9	114.3	11 426.0	7 485.9	101.8
2011														
1st quarter	53 887.4	14 424.4	7 624.3	6 800.1	37 153.3	243.7	9 645.9	9 621.4	24.5	12 948.2	111.1	11 541.1	7 610.1	102.0
2nd quarter	53 898.7	14 265.5	7 553.3	6 712.2	37 275.3	241.1	9 738.6	9 714.1	24.5	12 865.3	109.5	11 687.4	7 757.5	101.6
3rd quarter	54 218.2	14 153.5	7 560.0	6 593.4	37 757.0	241.8	10 127.6	10 102.6	25.0	12 842.7	108.3	11 812.8	7 879.3	102.1
4th quarter	54 589.6	14 045.4	7 552.1	6 493.2	38 267.5	241.9	10 453.6	10 428.3	25.3	12 863.7	108.2	11 965.0	8 012.6	103.7
2012														
1st quarter	55 022.6	13 989.3	7 508.5	6 480.7	38 715.1	241.3	10 851.9	10 827.5	24.4	12 791.0	105.8	12 085.9	8 125.4	102.3
2nd quarter	55 232.1	13 833.8	7 517.2	6 316.6	39 100.4	242.0	11 050.1	11 025.6	24.5	12 823.0	105.3	12 234.0	8 257.6	103.2
3rd quarter	55 755.3	13 951.5	7 519.5	6 432.0	39 437.8	241.1	11 279.9	11 255.5	24.4	12 726.0	104.3	12 446.7	8 459.6	105.8
4th quarter	56 447.3	13 911.3	7 529.7	6 381.5	40 121.4	244.3	11 593.7	11 568.9	24.9	12 819.3	102.4	12 728.3	8 704.7	106.8

Table 12-5. Credit Market Debt Outstanding, by Borrower and Lender—*Continued*

(Billions of dollars, except as noted; end of period; not seasonally adjusted.)

Year and quarter	Credit market debt outstanding owed by: —Continued — Nonfinancial business —Continued — Noncorporate	State and local governments	Foreign credit market debt held in United States	Credit market assets held by: — Total	Selected government-related sectors — Total	Federal government	Government-sponsored enterprises	Federally related mortgage pools	State and local governments	State and local retirement funds	Federal government retirement funds	Selected domestic financial sectors — Total, selected sectors	Monetary authority
1955	34.8	46.1	16.4	582.0	51.3	21.0	5.0	0.1	14.7	10.5	0.0	367.9	24.4
1956	37.9	50.4	17.3	611.5	55.4	21.6	6.0	0.1	15.9	11.7	0.0	389.4	24.7
1957	40.4	55.0	18.5	642.7	58.9	22.2	7.3	0.2	15.9	13.3	0.0	409.8	23.8
1958	44.2	60.7	20.5	681.6	62.6	23.6	7.7	0.2	16.1	15.0	0.0	443.4	26.3
1959	50.2	66.7	21.4	738.7	70.1	25.7	9.9	0.2	17.5	16.8	0.0	470.8	26.7
1960	55.0	72.2	23.2	780.2	76.0	26.7	11.1	0.2	19.1	18.9	0.0	502.2	27.0
1961	61.7	77.8	25.4	828.5	82.0	28.4	12.1	0.3	20.1	21.1	0.0	540.7	28.8
1962	69.3	83.8	27.5	888.2	89.4	30.3	13.7	0.4	21.7	23.2	0.0	586.9	30.5
1963	78.0	89.2	30.8	954.2	96.6	31.9	15.3	0.5	23.3	25.6	0.0	638.6	33.7
1964	86.3	95.6	35.0	1 028.5	104.7	34.7	16.0	0.6	25.0	28.3	0.0	695.6	36.6
1965	95.6	103.2	37.4	1 106.9	115.5	37.6	18.3	0.9	27.5	31.3	0.0	758.4	40.6
1966	105.3	110.0	39.4	1 187.3	129.8	42.7	23.3	1.3	27.5	34.9	0.0	804.0	43.7
1967	115.6	117.4	43.3	1 268.0	138.5	47.3	23.3	2.0	27.6	38.3	0.0	868.9	49.1
1968	126.6	126.1	46.0	1 372.9	154.4	52.2	26.5	2.5	31.4	41.6	0.0	941.8	53.0
1969	141.9	138.3	49.2	1 490.6	175.6	55.4	35.1	3.2	36.4	45.5	0.0	993.0	57.2
1970	148.6	150.3	52.0	1 599.6	191.5	58.2	43.9	4.8	35.1	49.6	0.0	1 064.6	62.2
1971	171.2	166.7	56.5	1 749.5	201.1	60.3	45.0	9.5	33.4	52.9	0.0	1 175.4	69.6
1972	202.6	180.7	61.1	1 933.5	223.0	62.1	49.0	14.4	40.1	57.4	0.0	1 317.7	71.2
1973	230.1	194.8	67.4	2 170.8	260.2	64.8	64.4	18.0	49.8	63.1	0.0	1 478.2	80.5
1974	267.3	208.2	81.2	2 408.0	304.6	72.1	85.3	21.5	56.4	69.4	0.0	1 606.2	85.3
1975	287.6	219.4	95.3	2 616.3	345.9	85.5	89.8	28.5	63.8	78.3	0.0	1 736.6	93.5
1976	317.1	237.8	115.7	2 904.1	398.6	93.7	94.5	40.7	82.0	87.7	0.0	1 925.7	100.3
1977	359.8	256.2	128.6	3 291.7	471.6	103.6	101.4	56.8	110.6	99.2	0.0	2 177.2	108.9
1978	418.2	295.6	155.7	3 776.3	582.6	120.6	128.1	70.4	147.5	116.0	0.0	2 454.5	117.4
1979	492.0	322.2	168.5	4 273.7	696.0	141.4	158.1	94.8	175.2	126.6	0.0	2 752.3	124.5
1980	555.1	344.4	193.4	4 722.4	804.5	165.5	184.5	114.0	193.4	147.2	0.0	2 999.2	128.0
1981	619.8	372.1	214.0	5 255.0	931.1	189.9	217.7	129.0	225.6	169.0	0.0	3 292.5	136.9
1982	677.6	413.8	208.1	5 766.8	1 058.9	205.8	233.7	178.5	250.1	190.7	0.0	3 561.8	144.5
1983	749.0	461.1	224.1	6 462.9	1 177.7	215.3	236.4	244.8	282.4	198.8	0.0	3 968.1	159.2
1984	862.6	513.6	232.8	7 422.5	1 339.7	232.6	265.9	289.0	319.0	233.2	0.0	4 522.1	167.6
1985	933.0	677.9	242.5	8 612.0	1 618.0	251.2	291.0	367.9	455.6	252.4	0.0	5 081.7	186.0
1986	1 000.2	752.1	251.9	9 801.5	1 920.0	258.0	307.6	531.6	525.8	297.1	0.0	5 766.6	205.5
1987	1 058.2	842.6	259.0	10 814.8	2 156.6	242.8	330.9	669.4	583.6	328.8	1.1	6 279.7	226.5
1988	1 142.0	893.0	269.8	11 856.3	2 298.7	217.4	364.2	745.3	618.6	350.5	2.7	6 797.8	241.2
1989	1 190.2	940.4	287.9	12 830.0	2 489.2	209.4	359.9	869.5	664.1	381.5	4.9	7 212.1	233.3
1990	1 190.5	987.4	318.2	13 757.1	2 749.6	243.1	373.9	1 019.9	703.4	402.0	7.4	7 551.1	241.4
1991	1 162.0	1 078.6	350.4	14 412.3	2 961.6	251.0	388.9	1 156.5	750.6	404.6	10.0	7 777.6	272.5
1992	1 135.5	1 095.1	372.4	15 204.0	3 176.3	239.0	458.1	1 272.0	752.3	441.8	13.1	8 136.3	300.4
1993	1 114.9	1 153.0	468.2	16 280.2	3 400.7	227.5	546.7	1 356.8	784.9	468.6	16.2	8 749.1	336.7
1994	1 129.3	1 107.5	443.1	17 373.9	3 590.9	222.1	667.9	1 472.4	729.9	478.7	19.9	9 214.5	368.2
1995	1 174.6	1 046.7	567.6	18 604.3	3 702.7	197.6	762.8	1 570.7	638.6	509.8	23.3	9 871.1	380.8
1996	1 245.1	1 026.2	657.2	19 923.3	3 916.0	201.6	833.8	1 711.7	604.8	538.4	25.6	10 412.0	393.1
1997	1 347.1	1 076.9	723.6	21 331.5	4 204.3	213.1	934.2	1 826.3	605.0	598.3	27.5	11 202.9	431.4
1998	1 526.1	1 143.8	783.2	23 416.0	4 895.5	218.8	1 251.5	2 019.0	714.6	661.5	30.2	12 381.2	452.5
1999	1 719.9	1 181.0	748.2	25 477.9	5 645.2	256.3	1 538.8	2 293.5	816.5	707.0	33.1	13 531.0	478.1
2000	1 912.3	1 197.9	814.5	27 211.0	6 216.5	263.1	1 794.4	2 493.2	887.3	743.2	35.1	14 422.9	511.8
2001	2 075.7	1 303.4	865.4	29 395.9	6 913.3	267.0	2 099.1	2 831.8	981.2	689.4	44.8	15 545.9	551.7
2002	2 227.6	1 447.9	1 072.8	31 913.2	7 520.8	275.0	2 323.1	3 158.6	1 067.4	638.7	58.0	16 828.4	629.4
2003	2 301.4	1 568.4	1 253.3	34 716.6	8 012.0	272.4	2 564.1	3 343.3	1 109.9	657.5	64.8	18 208.4	666.7
2004	2 556.1	2 448.2	1 438.8	38 683.5	8 258.6	274.7	2 613.0	3 384.0	1 237.4	679.4	70.0	19 827.2	717.8
2005	2 897.7	2 589.8	1 513.9	42 160.8	8 517.4	273.8	2 543.9	3 548.5	1 356.2	717.0	78.0	21 744.1	744.2
2006	3 313.0	2 690.8	1 882.6	46 202.3	9 040.0	275.2	2 590.5	3 841.1	1 437.4	809.1	86.7	23 834.5	778.9
2007	3 774.6	2 837.5	2 126.3	50 953.0	10 058.8	281.1	2 829.5	4 464.4	1 534.8	849.5	99.4	25 758.3	740.6
2008	4 093.4	2 855.4	1 708.8	53 353.2	10 642.1	366.4	3 037.5	4 961.4	1 330.6	823.0	123.3	26 355.5	986.0
2009	3 973.3	2 968.4	2 090.3	53 252.5	10 876.6	661.8	2 714.4	5 376.7	1 255.7	737.2	130.7	26 033.0	1 987.7
2010	3 940.0	3 038.0	2 225.3	53 620.8	10 438.7	746.9	6 360.5	1 139.5	1 291.1	759.3	141.5	25 654.5	2 259.2
2011	3 952.4	2 985.3	2 276.7	54 589.6	10 332.8	746.2	6 158.2	1 304.8	1 200.6	761.5	161.6	26 467.9	2 635.6
2012	4 023.6	2 980.0	2 414.7	56 447.3	10 287.6	828.5	5 935.1	1 437.0	1 148.5	763.0	175.5	27 306.8	2 670.1
2010													
1st quarter	3 959.8	2 993.5	2 117.1	52 780.9	10 410.9	677.7	6 607.0	980.2	1 271.8	742.1	132.1	25 827.7	2 151.8
2nd quarter	3 952.1	2 985.4	2 098.8	52 740.4	10 380.5	680.3	6 521.3	1 046.5	1 259.9	736.4	136.1	25 603.1	2 187.3
3rd quarter	3 948.4	2 988.6	2 224.5	53 149.9	10 372.6	726.3	6 414.6	1 096.0	1 265.9	729.0	140.8	25 590.6	2 150.3
4th quarter	3 940.0	3 038.0	2 225.3	53 620.8	10 438.7	746.9	6 360.5	1 139.5	1 291.1	759.3	141.5	25 654.5	2 259.2
2011													
1st quarter	3 931.0	3 018.1	2 309.7	53 887.4	10 513.8	778.2	6 353.4	1 187.0	1 277.0	772.9	145.3	25 805.7	2 479.2
2nd quarter	3 929.9	2 984.1	2 357.8	53 898.7	10 440.1	757.0	6 270.1	1 236.0	1 253.1	774.3	149.5	26 039.0	2 700.4
3rd quarter	3 933.5	2 973.9	2 307.7	54 218.2	10 365.9	761.6	6 194.7	1 277.3	1 215.6	758.9	157.8	26 161.2	2 686.1
4th quarter	3 952.4	2 985.3	2 276.7	54 589.6	10 332.8	746.2	6 158.2	1 304.8	1 200.6	761.5	161.6	26 467.9	2 635.6
2012													
1st quarter	3 960.5	2 986.3	2 318.3	55 022.6	10 325.6	755.8	6 121.9	1 329.9	1 184.6	770.4	163.0	26 588.1	2 613.4
2nd quarter	3 976.3	2 993.3	2 297.9	55 232.1	10 300.3	775.0	6 033.0	1 377.3	1 183.4	764.3	167.2	26 690.1	2 610.9
3rd quarter	3 987.1	2 985.3	2 366.0	55 755.3	10 287.0	811.5	5 971.7	1 408.0	1 170.3	756.1	169.5	26 838.2	2 565.1
4th quarter	4 023.6	2 980.0	2 414.7	56 447.3	10 287.6	828.5	5 935.1	1 437.0	1 148.5	763.0	175.5	27 306.8	2 670.1

Table 12-5. Credit Market Debt Outstanding, by Borrower and Lender—*Continued*

(Billions of dollars, except as noted; end of period; not seasonally adjusted.)

Year and quarter	Credit market assets held by:—*Continued*											
	Selected domestic financial sectors—*Continued*									House-holds	Foreign holdings in United States	All other financial and non-financial sectors
	U.S. chartered depository institutions	Credit unions	Life insurance companies	Property-casualty insurance companies	Private pension funds	Money market mutual funds	Mutual funds	Asset-backed security issuers	Finance companies			
1955	220.5	2.0	80.5	11.5	11.2	0.0	0.8	0.0	17.0	117.6	6.7	38.6
1956	233.0	2.4	85.6	11.9	12.7	0.0	1.1	0.0	18.0	124.9	7.3	34.5
1957	245.2	2.9	90.5	12.6	14.5	0.0	1.2	0.0	19.3	131.9	7.5	34.6
1958	268.4	3.1	95.5	13.4	16.2	0.0	1.5	0.0	19.0	132.7	7.5	35.4
1959	283.2	3.8	100.5	14.6	17.9	0.0	1.8	0.0	22.4	142.8	11.7	43.3
1960	302.0	4.5	105.6	15.5	19.7	0.0	2.0	0.0	25.9	150.9	12.6	38.5
1961	329.0	4.9	110.9	16.5	21.2	0.0	2.4	0.0	27.0	154.9	13.1	37.9
1962	361.2	5.6	116.9	18.0	22.9	0.0	2.6	0.0	29.2	158.2	14.8	38.9
1963	395.2	6.3	123.3	18.7	24.8	0.0	2.8	0.0	33.7	159.8	15.9	43.3
1964	433.8	7.2	130.3	19.5	27.2	0.0	3.2	0.0	37.9	166.2	16.9	45.1
1965	475.6	8.2	137.8	20.6	29.1	0.0	3.9	0.0	42.7	170.0	17.4	45.5
1966	501.1	9.4	145.9	22.0	31.9	0.0	5.1	0.0	44.9	190.0	17.3	46.1
1967	550.3	10.2	153.3	23.5	32.8	0.0	4.3	0.0	45.5	195.2	20.0	45.4
1968	602.4	11.7	160.7	25.4	33.8	0.0	4.1	0.0	50.6	203.5	22.6	50.6
1969	628.4	13.8	167.6	27.0	34.6	0.0	5.1	0.0	59.2	241.4	23.2	57.5
1970	677.9	15.2	174.6	30.9	36.6	0.0	5.7	0.0	61.5	242.4	35.0	66.1
1971	763.1	17.2	182.8	34.6	35.0	0.0	5.5	0.0	67.6	233.2	62.8	77.0
1972	871.6	20.1	192.5	38.3	40.5	0.0	6.0	0.0	77.5	230.0	73.2	89.7
1973	984.7	23.7	204.8	41.8	46.8	0.0	6.6	0.0	89.4	254.7	74.7	103.0
1974	1 071.8	26.4	217.7	46.4	55.6	0.8	7.4	0.0	94.8	299.5	79.8	117.8
1975	1 147.2	31.7	234.6	53.7	71.2	1.5	8.0	0.0	95.0	320.7	88.3	124.8
1976	1 267.7	38.4	258.3	66.2	77.8	2.1	8.4	0.0	106.6	331.3	99.4	149.1
1977	1 422.1	45.6	285.8	83.7	88.2	1.9	12.3	0.0	128.6	358.4	135.4	149.1
1978	1 595.4	52.0	318.9	100.2	98.7	5.1	12.5	0.0	154.2	406.7	161.3	171.2
1979	1 764.8	53.8	352.0	113.7	120.8	24.9	14.5	0.0	183.4	486.1	149.7	189.6
1980	1 903.2	53.0	385.1	123.5	151.4	42.0	17.1	0.0	195.8	521.0	169.7	228.0
1981	2 023.9	55.0	419.8	132.0	178.6	107.5	20.2	0.0	218.6	546.6	197.0	287.9
1982	2 140.0	57.3	463.2	139.6	225.4	137.6	25.4	0.0	228.9	612.2	240.0	294.0
1983	2 399.0	69.4	513.8	147.6	267.5	119.7	34.9	3.0	254.0	703.8	263.3	349.9
1984	2 691.1	85.0	570.1	162.0	305.9	164.1	53.9	19.8	302.5	808.7	340.4	411.7
1985	2 933.7	98.4	646.6	191.8	329.0	178.2	129.9	34.8	353.2	967.4	419.9	525.1
1986	3 190.3	113.9	734.5	234.6	333.6	213.1	259.9	71.4	409.9	1 001.0	536.4	577.5
1987	3 409.2	131.3	823.1	274.6	347.2	215.0	291.1	113.2	448.3	1 176.4	586.5	615.6
1988	3 634.5	148.8	927.2	306.0	369.2	225.5	304.5	147.6	493.3	1 381.8	689.1	689.0
1989	3 678.8	156.0	1 028.3	335.6	420.8	293.7	327.2	201.1	537.3	1 479.6	815.8	833.3
1990	3 633.6	166.6	1 134.5	364.2	464.3	371.3	360.1	250.3	564.8	1 741.2	881.7	833.4
1991	3 506.8	179.4	1 218.9	394.1	489.7	403.9	440.2	299.5	572.5	1 824.9	909.6	938.7
1992	3 500.4	197.1	1 304.4	410.6	515.7	408.6	566.4	357.9	575.0	1 886.5	983.1	1 021.7
1993	3 627.4	218.7	1 415.5	443.3	551.9	429.0	725.9	437.8	563.1	1 995.5	1 095.0	1 039.9
1994	3 781.1	246.8	1 487.5	465.6	591.5	459.0	718.8	501.0	595.1	2 377.7	1 162.8	1 028.1
1995	3 954.9	263.0	1 587.5	493.1	608.4	545.5	771.3	612.0	654.6	2 379.8	1 464.8	1 185.9
1996	4 093.0	288.5	1 657.0	514.2	602.3	634.3	820.2	712.2	697.1	2 545.6	1 795.6	1 254.1
1997	4 359.8	305.3	1 751.1	538.2	646.8	721.9	901.1	826.5	720.8	2 503.0	2 035.6	1 385.7
1998	4 697.2	324.2	1 828.0	548.9	639.7	970.8	1 028.4	1 078.8	812.8	2 556.3	2 202.0	1 381.0
1999	5 098.5	351.7	1 886.0	536.5	746.9	1 156.4	1 076.8	1 253.3	946.6	2 671.6	2 196.1	1 434.0
2000	5 486.8	379.7	1 943.9	534.3	621.9	1 325.8	1 103.1	1 413.6	1 101.9	2 565.5	2 451.1	1 555.1
2001	5 720.7	421.2	2 071.5	536.6	587.0	1 594.3	1 229.5	1 662.6	1 170.7	2 476.5	2 850.2	1 610.1
2002	6 143.7	465.4	2 300.3	584.7	581.7	1 564.8	1 368.1	1 897.8	1 292.5	2 631.2	3 303.0	1 629.9
2003	6 642.5	516.6	2 478.8	660.5	653.5	1 491.0	1 505.1	2 125.1	1 468.7	2 851.0	3 836.1	1 809.1
2004	7 311.0	556.4	2 643.9	746.5	654.6	1 346.3	1 619.8	2 555.1	1 675.9	3 896.2	4 634.7	2 066.9
2005	8 011.3	592.5	2 753.9	819.3	699.9	1 348.6	1 743.8	3 289.9	1 740.6	4 226.5	5 191.3	2 481.5
2006	8 628.6	622.6	2 786.4	864.1	796.1	1 570.2	1 928.7	4 049.6	1 809.2	4 392.3	6 199.7	2 735.8
2007	9 201.0	657.9	2 871.2	869.3	1 043.4	1 962.0	2 196.7	4 399.8	1 816.3	4 865.4	7 272.2	2 998.4
2008	9 442.9	701.1	2 882.8	853.4	833.0	2 689.9	2 229.2	4 002.8	1 734.4	5 204.1	7 523.7	3 627.7
2009	9 131.1	734.6	3 022.6	886.7	843.3	2 070.0	2 616.3	3 224.0	1 516.7	5 648.4	7 723.4	2 971.0
2010	9 341.5	758.6	3 174.2	890.6	968.0	1 673.4	2 969.9	2 179.0	1 440.1	5 928.1	8 498.9	3 100.5
2011	9 468.4	796.2	3 297.9	926.8	1 020.5	1 663.6	3 329.3	1 935.3	1 394.3	5 401.6	9 122.0	3 265.4
2012	9 815.1	842.3	3 367.3	924.3	983.0	1 580.9	4 036.9	1 725.7	1 361.2	5 468.8	9 640.1	3 744.0
2010												
1st quarter	9 373.2	740.9	3 042.6	886.8	874.5	1 863.3	2 736.2	2 547.4	1 611.1	5 665.4	7 866.4	3 010.5
2nd quarter	9 265.2	753.4	3 083.7	887.2	906.2	1 742.0	2 781.6	2 418.7	1 577.6	5 685.3	8 049.3	3 022.1
3rd quarter	9 308.9	744.5	3 134.3	892.2	937.3	1 639.6	2 915.8	2 309.4	1 558.6	5 469.7	8 528.9	3 188.1
4th quarter	9 341.5	758.6	3 174.2	890.6	968.0	1 673.4	2 969.9	2 179.0	1 440.1	5 928.1	8 498.9	3 100.5
2011												
1st quarter	9 211.3	770.8	3 211.1	895.2	988.1	1 640.3	3 091.1	2 098.9	1 419.5	5 888.5	8 595.7	3 083.7
2nd quarter	9 185.9	780.3	3 237.3	890.3	1 023.5	1 576.4	3 201.0	2 050.8	1 393.2	5 520.7	8 775.1	3 123.8
3rd quarter	9 299.0	788.3	3 284.3	890.6	1 046.9	1 559.8	3 234.5	1 984.5	1 387.0	5 390.7	9 091.6	3 208.7
4th quarter	9 468.4	796.2	3 297.9	926.8	1 020.5	1 663.6	3 329.3	1 935.3	1 394.3	5 401.6	9 122.0	3 265.4
2012												
1st quarter	9 462.8	814.6	3 333.6	923.4	998.2	1 600.7	3 581.7	1 877.5	1 382.3	5 438.4	9 190.6	3 479.9
2nd quarter	9 564.3	829.1	3 307.7	920.6	1 002.3	1 528.4	3 741.5	1 819.6	1 365.7	5 414.7	9 291.8	3 535.2
3rd quarter	9 622.3	837.8	3 349.5	920.9	991.9	1 520.2	3 907.7	1 759.1	1 363.8	5 419.1	9 543.7	3 667.3
4th quarter	9 815.1	842.3	3 367.3	924.3	983.0	1 580.9	4 036.9	1 725.7	1 361.2	5 468.8	9 640.1	3 744.0

Figure 12-3. Rations of Household Debt Service and Financial Obligations to Disposable Personal Income (1980–2012)

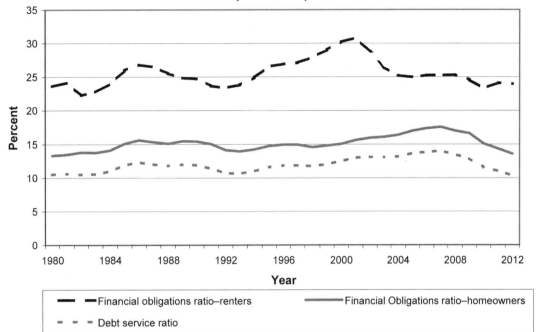

- The Federal Reserve calculates aggregate household debt service (payments of principal and interest) and total financial obligations as a percentage of aggregate disposable personal income (DPI) for the period 1980 to the present. These measures provide supplements to the ratio of the total level of household debt to DPI (shown in Figure 12-2 and Table 12-5), and are important because lengthening maturities and lower interest rates can mitigate much of the burden of a high level of debt. Unlike the debt/income ratio, the debt service ratio leveled off between 2002 and 2004, reflecting the decline in interest rates. However, the debt service ratio rose to a new record high of 14.0 percent in 2006 and 2007. Since then it has dropped back to 10.3 percent at the end of 2012, the lowest ever recorded in this series that goes back to 1980. (Table 12-6)

- Financial obligations ratios are higher than the debt service ratio. They are calculated separately for homeowners and renters and include all debt service plus rental payments on primary residences, property taxes, homeowners' insurance, and automobile lease payments. The financial obligations ratio for homeowners stood at a record high 17.6 percent of income in the third quarter of 2007, but has dropped back to 13.5 percent since then, the lowest since 1981. (Table 12-6)

- Reflecting the lower average incomes of the renters' group, the financial obligations ratio for renters is about double the ratio for homeowners. But the renters' ratio peaked in 2001. It then declined rapidly in the early 2000s. At the end of 2012 the ratio was about the same as in the early 1980s. (Table 12-6)

- Additional evidence on debt trends is seen in the ratio of aggregate household debt to aggregate household financial and nonfinancial assets, which rose from around 10 percent in 1960 to 20 percent in 2008, and was 15.9 percent at the end of 2012. (Table 12-6) Narrowing the comparison to mortgage debt alone, home mortgage debt as a percent of the value of real estate has increased from a range of 30 to 35 percent that prevailed from 1960 through 1987 to 63 percent in the years 2008 through 2011, before falling back to 56 percent in 2012. In other words, homeowners as a group now have only 44 percent equity in their homes, compared with the nearly 70 percent that they had as recently as 1982. (Table 12-7)

Table 12-6. Household Assets, Liabilities, Net Worth, Financial Obligations, and Delinquency Rates

(Billions of dollars, except as noted; end of period; not seasonally adjusted, except as noted.)

Year and quarter	Total 2	Checkable deposits and currency	Time and savings deposits	Money market fund shares	U.S. savings bonds	Other Treasury securities	Agency- and GSE-backed securities	Municipal securities	Corporate and foreign bonds	Mortgages	Corporate equities	Mutual fund shares	Security credit	Life insurance reserves
1955	1 018.6	70.0	105.8	0.0	50.2	18.6	0.6	19.2	5.0	22.7	248.2	7.8	0.9	69.3
1956	1 087.4	71.9	115.2	0.0	50.1	20.1	1.0	21.9	6.1	24.3	271.0	9.0	0.9	72.7
1957	1 100.1	71.0	127.2	0.0	48.2	23.3	1.5	23.9	7.2	26.2	244.5	8.7	0.9	75.5
1958	1 228.8	73.7	141.3	0.0	47.7	20.9	0.8	24.6	7.9	28.8	322.3	13.2	1.2	78.5
1959	1 304.2	75.6	152.5	0.0	45.9	25.7	2.3	28.4	8.2	30.7	357.3	15.8	1.0	82.0
1960	1 352.7	77.6	164.5	0.0	45.6	26.6	1.0	31.0	10.6	33.5	359.8	17.0	1.1	85.2
1961	1 497.8	77.0	182.8	0.0	46.4	25.5	0.6	32.5	10.8	36.8	443.2	22.9	1.2	88.6
1962	1 540.6	77.2	208.8	0.0	47.0	26.8	0.2	32.1	10.2	39.0	431.2	20.9	1.2	92.4
1963	1 639.3	82.1	234.9	0.0	48.1	24.7	0.0	32.1	10.1	40.5	469.9	24.8	1.2	96.6
1964	1 794.0	84.9	261.0	0.0	49.1	24.5	0.2	34.9	10.3	42.0	544.1	28.4	1.7	101.1
1965	1 960.4	91.6	288.5	0.0	49.7	25.1	1.1	36.5	9.0	42.6	616.1	34.4	2.5	105.9
1966	1 982.4	93.5	307.1	0.0	50.2	28.8	5.9	41.2	11.1	44.6	548.3	33.9	2.7	110.6
1967	2 232.6	103.8	342.3	0.0	51.2	27.8	6.3	38.2	15.1	46.5	682.1	43.0	4.9	115.5
1968	2 496.0	112.7	372.5	0.0	51.9	29.9	6.1	36.5	18.0	49.0	815.3	49.5	7.0	120.3
1969	2 440.1	110.9	381.3	0.0	51.8	41.4	11.3	47.2	22.0	49.1	667.4	45.6	5.2	125.4
1970	2 532.9	118.6	423.5	0.0	52.1	31.0	15.9	47.1	29.7	50.0	650.2	44.5	4.4	130.7
1971	2 821.5	132.1	491.0	0.0	54.4	19.8	14.6	46.0	37.4	47.3	743.7	53.0	4.9	137.1
1972	3 231.1	144.4	564.2	0.0	57.7	19.7	8.9	47.7	38.5	48.2	921.4	56.4	5.0	143.9
1973	3 238.3	152.5	624.9	0.0	60.4	28.1	8.3	55.1	41.5	47.2	693.9	43.7	4.9	151.3
1974	3 213.8	157.4	681.0	2.4	63.3	32.9	13.7	62.2	54.4	50.5	445.0	31.8	3.9	158.4
1975	3 678.8	158.7	762.2	3.7	67.4	44.4	7.6	66.8	64.3	50.4	584.6	38.7	4.5	168.6
1976	4 161.2	169.2	860.8	3.4	72.0	30.7	11.7	72.9	74.3	52.8	731.6	41.4	5.7	177.8
1977	4 439.3	184.2	963.0	3.2	76.8	27.8	8.4	78.8	79.8	55.3	631.3	40.4	5.7	187.8
1978	4 967.8	200.7	1 058.3	8.9	80.7	29.6	9.9	104.2	73.6	62.4	640.0	41.1	8.5	199.4
1979	5 692.6	220.5	1 126.1	39.5	79.9	76.0	12.5	123.6	66.6	71.6	768.1	44.8	10.4	210.3
1980	6 574.1	238.1	1 248.0	64.4	72.5	101.3	18.6	130.1	59.0	87.2	1 010.4	52.1	16.2	220.6
1981	6 970.9	284.4	1 319.5	154.6	68.2	100.6	14.2	160.3	60.0	101.4	905.2	52.6	14.7	230.1
1982	7 582.9	303.9	1 447.8	186.7	68.3	116.8	13.4	201.1	53.0	110.9	966.3	65.1	17.8	238.0
1983	8 342.5	313.6	1 644.7	149.9	71.5	159.2	14.5	246.6	57.0	111.2	1 088.6	98.0	20.6	246.7
1984	8 848.3	327.0	1 864.2	193.0	74.5	203.2	27.7	290.4	44.7	102.5	1 008.7	117.5	21.6	252.8
1985	9 994.9	344.8	2 001.9	196.3	79.8	202.5	23.4	395.1	94.7	115.5	1 229.5	213.8	35.1	264.3
1986	11 129.9	461.9	2 102.5	235.1	93.3	177.6	23.3	410.9	127.8	111.9	1 494.0	378.7	44.0	282.6
1987	11 775.2	460.8	2 217.4	256.0	101.1	207.1	32.1	516.6	144.6	119.5	1 462.6	424.5	39.1	309.5
1988	12 908.9	460.5	2 392.7	273.0	109.6	283.9	51.8	586.0	135.1	121.8	1 757.1	439.1	40.9	335.7
1989	14 236.9	462.2	2 466.9	351.1	117.7	277.2	74.8	613.3	178.1	130.7	2 147.5	513.0	53.2	365.3
1990	14 695.0	450.8	2 512.1	389.4	126.2	377.8	117.3	647.7	237.6	140.9	1 961.4	511.5	62.4	391.7
1991	16 249.1	505.0	2 440.8	407.7	138.1	397.4	115.5	701.8	270.9	142.7	2 759.2	645.0	87.0	418.6
1992	17 084.3	616.4	2 333.0	365.5	157.3	470.1	114.4	672.2	283.2	136.8	3 094.2	799.4	76.2	447.7
1993	18 467.2	667.5	2 218.3	363.5	171.9	501.3	58.3	640.8	428.8	129.4	3 437.0	1 098.0	102.3	484.8
1994	19 202.3	636.3	2 181.4	373.1	179.9	691.1	187.6	594.1	534.8	120.5	3 294.2	1 096.6	109.0	520.3
1995	21 783.4	586.5	2 317.2	472.4	185.0	643.0	216.4	533.4	616.9	113.3	4 434.2	1 253.0	127.6	566.2
1996	23 548.8	544.8	2 457.9	500.9	187.0	701.9	332.8	493.0	649.3	105.8	4 712.2	1 561.9	162.9	610.6
1997	27 031.2	503.8	2 594.9	571.3	186.5	611.4	389.7	497.6	641.9	98.7	6 144.1	1 949.3	215.5	665.0
1998	30 353.4	528.6	2 696.9	667.4	186.6	546.4	441.7	498.4	708.6	94.3	7 506.8	2 352.2	276.7	718.3
1999	34 828.1	508.9	2 792.3	769.5	186.4	623.7	541.8	526.9	605.6	101.6	9 763.0	2 894.6	323.9	783.9
2000	33 770.9	405.3	3 046.8	937.3	184.8	394.0	589.3	531.5	663.4	103.4	8 140.2	2 708.0	412.4	819.1
2001	32 715.2	480.1	3 333.1	1 101.0	190.3	242.1	388.3	587.9	868.4	108.7	6 825.9	2 618.0	454.3	880.0
2002	30 898.8	464.1	3 643.3	1 068.4	194.9	68.3	256.1	671.5	1 238.8	116.6	5 163.5	2 222.9	412.7	920.9
2003	35 999.9	458.0	3 971.5	954.5	203.8	203.4	385.4	687.2	1 169.8	120.9	6 788.0	2 914.1	475.4	1 013.2
2004	41 007.5	399.8	4 444.5	898.4	204.4	263.2	417.9	1 522.7	1 267.1	131.3	7 516.9	3 411.2	578.3	1 060.4
2005	44 906.3	285.8	4 928.8	942.7	205.1	234.9	585.9	1 600.8	1 353.3	139.4	8 179.0	3 636.2	575.3	1 082.6
2006	49 875.3	239.6	5 439.8	1 106.8	202.4	146.6	635.6	1 636.1	1 523.0	122.1	10 331.3	4 195.2	655.7	1 055.2
2007	52 898.0	154.9	5 912.7	1 346.7	196.4	-13.4	874.3	1 674.1	1 899.3	109.8	10 448.0	4 869.1	866.4	1 076.8
2008	43 436.0	364.9	6 102.6	1 581.8	194.0	75.4	1 097.8	1 722.0	1 968.1	111.1	5 954.4	3 313.9	742.7	1 049.8
2009	46 303.7	393.5	6 265.1	1 313.2	191.2	714.7	435.7	1 829.1	2 314.9	101.4	7 518.3	4 130.7	668.6	1 109.2
2010	50 385.8	437.9	6 384.0	1 129.7	187.9	1 077.3	389.9	1 873.3	2 251.6	90.2	8 843.9	4 617.8	694.3	1 137.2
2011	51 310.1	754.5	6 734.3	1 109.9	185.2	630.6	372.8	1 807.7	2 273.3	79.5	8 866.3	4 453.0	752.4	1 203.6
2012	55 595.2	884.6	7 096.9	1 110.2	182.4	1 015.4	96.9	1 656.5	2 402.0	66.1	10 178.4	5 372.4	776.0	1 186.1
2010														
1st quarter	47 085.0	343.7	6 365.4	1 198.6	190.2	889.5	392.1	1 866.9	2 168.7	99.8	7 711.4	4 285.3	680.0	1 115.4
2nd quarter	45 611.7	339.6	6 346.4	1 140.0	189.6	1 059.5	358.8	1 865.6	2 058.7	96.5	6 962.4	4 017.9	686.0	1 098.5
3rd quarter	47 668.1	347.5	6 405.9	1 125.9	188.7	1 039.2	337.7	1 844.5	1 908.2	93.4	7 967.6	4 352.7	696.8	1 122.8
4th quarter	50 385.8	437.9	6 384.0	1 129.7	187.9	1 077.3	389.9	1 873.3	2 251.6	90.2	8 843.9	4 617.8	694.3	1 137.2
2011														
1st quarter	52 115.4	449.3	6 478.5	1 098.6	186.8	953.5	482.4	1 890.6	2 228.4	87.8	9 566.5	5 025.0	703.3	1 160.3
2nd quarter	52 049.1	500.4	6 612.8	1 086.8	186.0	683.7	419.8	1 850.2	2 238.2	84.6	9 514.0	5 140.6	757.7	1 174.1
3rd quarter	49 251.9	629.4	6 636.9	1 103.3	185.1	605.7	378.7	1 832.1	2 250.7	82.8	7 902.4	4 436.5	804.9	1 174.5
4th quarter	51 310.1	754.5	6 734.3	1 109.9	185.2	630.6	372.8	1 807.7	2 273.3	79.5	8 866.3	4 453.0	752.4	1 203.6
2012														
1st quarter	53 720.7	741.0	6 844.5	1 052.2	184.7	822.4	273.2	1 781.3	2 244.4	75.9	9 892.2	5 039.4	762.3	1 199.4
2nd quarter	53 097.9	733.0	6 904.1	1 024.2	184.3	867.9	237.6	1 774.4	2 226.0	72.4	9 534.3	4 893.1	777.7	1 172.6
3rd quarter	54 581.3	727.7	6 930.6	1 045.4	183.6	898.1	176.0	1 709.1	2 331.1	69.4	9 960.5	5 196.5	780.2	1 180.6
4th quarter	55 595.2	884.6	7 096.9	1 110.2	182.4	1 015.4	96.9	1 656.5	2 402.0	66.1	10 178.4	5 372.4	776.0	1 186.1

1Includes nonprofit organizations.
2Includes components not shown separately.

Table 12-6. Household Assets, Liabilities, Net Worth, Financial Obligations, and Delinquency Rates—*Continued*

(Billions of dollars, except as noted; end of period; not seasonally adjusted, except as noted.)

Year and quarter	Financial assets of the household sector [1] —*Continued*		Nonfinancial assets of the household sector		Debt as a percent of total assets [1]	Total liabilities [1]	Net worth [1]	Ratios to disposable personal income (percent, seasonally adjusted)				Consumer credit card accounts held at banks (percent, seasonally adjusted)	
	Pension fund reserves	Equity in non-corporate business	Total [1]	House-hold real estate [3]				House-hold debt service	Household financial obligations			Delinquency rate	Charge-off rate
									Total	Home-owners	Renters		
1955	52.0	334.8	565.3	367.4	8.7	144.3	1 439.6	...	...	...	...	...	...
1956	58.2	351.0	607.8	394.3	9.0	159.5	1 535.7	...	...	...	...	...	...
1957	64.6	362.9	643.4	417.2	9.5	172.0	1 571.5	...	...	...	...	...	...
1958	74.9	377.8	669.9	438.4	9.3	184.0	1 714.7	...	...	...	...	...	...
1959	85.0	378.4	705.4	463.6	9.9	206.6	1 803.0	...	...	...	...	...	...
1960	93.9	388.4	737.1	486.9	10.4	224.7	1 865.0	...	...	...	...	...	...
1961	107.2	405.0	769.1	511.1	10.3	243.5	2 023.3	...	...	...	...	...	...
1962	113.7	421.3	802.9	533.2	10.9	265.6	2 077.8	...	...	...	...	...	...
1963	128.0	425.8	838.3	553.2	11.4	294.7	2 182.9	...	...	...	...	...	...
1964	144.8	444.7	883.1	579.8	11.7	324.4	2 352.7	...	...	...	...	...	...
1965	162.0	470.8	929.7	605.6	11.8	353.4	2 536.7	...	...	...	...	...	...
1966	172.5	504.0	1 004.5	649.0	12.2	376.6	2 610.4	...	...	...	...	...	...
1967	195.6	528.5	1 072.7	685.7	11.7	404.2	2 901.1	...	...	...	...	...	...
1968	218.7	572.8	1 198.8	768.2	11.2	436.2	3 258.7	...	...	...	...	...	...
1969	230.9	606.3	1 306.2	832.4	11.9	463.7	3 282.6	...	...	...	...	...	...
1970	253.7	636.3	1 387.9	874.5	11.7	478.7	3 442.0	...	...	...	...	...	...
1971	293.5	701.9	1 514.8	957.2	11.6	525.5	3 810.8	...	...	...	...	...	...
1972	349.3	782.5	1 710.9	1 098.6	11.3	585.5	4 356.6	...	...	...	...	...	...
1973	358.5	917.0	1 939.3	1 251.4	12.1	652.4	4 525.1	...	...	...	...	...	...
1974	367.5	1 026.8	2 059.7	1 261.1	13.0	709.1	4 564.4	...	...	...	...	...	...
1975	467.0	1 126.1	2 281.5	1 413.7	12.4	768.1	5 192.2	...	...	...	...	...	...
1976	534.5	1 255.5	2 537.6	1 590.0	12.4	860.1	5 838.6	...	...	...	...	...	...
1977	589.9	1 418.2	2 941.3	1 886.8	13.0	991.0	6 389.5	...	...	...	...	...	...
1978	691.4	1 648.5	3 401.6	2 210.9	13.3	1 150.6	7 218.9	...	...	...	...	...	...
1979	801.1	1 913.5	3 954.1	2 603.3	13.3	1 320.3	8 326.4	...	...	...	...	...	...
1980	969.7	2 154.3	4 441.6	2 943.2	12.7	1 447.4	9 568.2	10.5	15.4	13.3	23.6	...	...
1981	1 063.5	2 312.2	4 906.0	3 293.0	12.7	1 558.5	10 318.4	10.6	15.6	13.5	24.2	...	...
1982	1 289.1	2 357.4	5 136.2	3 447.4	12.4	1 632.7	11 086.4	10.5	15.6	13.8	22.3	...	...
1983	1 535.8	2 421.3	5 397.5	3 605.9	12.6	1 799.4	11 940.5	10.6	15.6	13.7	22.8	...	...
1984	1 707.5	2 425.1	6 052.5	4 126.3	13.0	2 011.3	12 889.5	11.0	16.1	14.1	24.0	...	...
1985	2 088.6	2 498.8	6 768.0	4 698.7	13.6	2 367.9	14 395.0	11.9	17.3	15.1	26.0	...	2.98
1986	2 326.8	2 627.0	7 402.9	5 147.3	13.7	2 632.1	15 900.7	12.3	17.8	15.6	26.8	...	3.42
1987	2 504.8	2 718.5	8 021.1	5 597.2	13.9	2 840.7	16 955.7	12.0	17.5	15.3	26.5	...	3.26
1988	2 738.3	2 862.4	8 741.2	6 117.8	14.0	3 140.2	18 510.0	11.8	17.2	15.1	25.6	...	3.22
1989	3 169.0	2 983.5	9 439.4	6 641.1	14.0	3 425.5	20 250.9	12.0	17.3	15.5	24.9	...	3.27
1990	3 310.3	3 096.8	9 722.9	6 801.1	14.6	3 693.6	20 724.3	11.9	17.3	15.4	24.7	...	3.84
1991	3 830.6	3 051.2	9 928.3	6 968.1	14.4	3 905.5	22 271.9	11.4	16.9	15.0	23.7	5.30	4.65
1992	4 139.4	3 027.4	10 251.1	7 258.3	14.5	4 113.0	23 222.5	10.7	16.0	14.1	23.4	4.69	4.54
1993	4 617.5	3 170.9	10 607.1	7 499.5	14.5	4 383.9	24 690.4	10.6	16.0	13.9	23.8	3.90	3.35
1994	4 898.3	3 385.8	11 048.1	7 771.4	15.0	4 712.1	25 538.3	11.0	16.4	14.2	24.9	3.27	3.07
1995	5 725.1	3 569.7	11 472.2	8 055.2	14.6	5 043.3	28 212.3	11.6	17.0	14.8	26.6	3.93	3.93
1996	6 386.7	3 690.9	11 964.2	8 432.0	14.6	5 405.7	30 107.2	11.8	17.2	15.0	26.9	4.59	4.64
1997	7 360.7	4 134.8	12 693.3	8 865.0	13.8	5 757.2	33 967.4	11.8	17.2	14.9	27.1	4.78	5.38
1998	8 265.4	4 386.2	13 760.4	9 694.3	13.4	6 199.6	37 914.2	11.7	16.9	14.6	27.9	4.70	5.14
1999	9 264.1	4 643.2	14 945.7	10 645.1	12.8	6 755.9	43 018.0	12.0	17.2	14.8	29.0	4.50	4.44
2000	9 171.3	5 137.9	16 863.5	12 193.4	13.8	7 352.9	43 281.5	12.5	17.5	15.0	30.2	4.56	4.47
2001	8 764.3	5 335.5	18 411.9	13 566.5	14.9	7 976.2	43 151.0	13.0	18.1	15.6	30.8	4.69	6.19
2002	8 189.8	5 687.1	19 976.7	14 851.7	16.6	8 759.2	42 116.3	13.1	18.0	15.9	28.7	4.85	5.39
2003	9 719.4	6 301.6	21 848.8	16 453.6	16.4	9 822.2	48 026.6	13.1	17.8	16.1	26.4	4.43	5.87
2004	10 642.9	7 547.8	24 882.0	18 949.6	16.0	10 995.8	54 893.7	13.2	17.8	16.4	25.2	4.03	4.57
2005	11 512.2	8 868.5	28 451.7	22 023.2	16.0	12 157.5	61 200.5	13.6	18.3	17.0	25.0	3.54	6.01
2006	12 557.2	9 191.0	29 542.2	22 693.2	16.2	13 348.1	66 069.3	13.9	18.7	17.4	25.3	3.95	3.69
2007	13 236.1	9 329.1	28 216.9	20 823.8	16.9	14 253.2	66 861.7	14.0	18.8	17.5	25.2	4.60	4.34
2008	10 567.7	7 730.8	24 825.6	17 582.8	20.0	14 097.6	54 163.9	13.5	18.4	17.0	25.3	5.64	6.52
2009	11 959.2	6 459.8	23 769.0	17 155.7	19.1	13 874.8	56 197.9	12.9	18.1	16.6	24.6	6.34	10.44
2010	13 209.9	7 120.5	23 472.8	16 623.9	17.7	13 636.9	60 221.6	11.6	16.6	15.1	23.3	4.15	7.95
2011	13 434.1	7 673.2	23 432.6	16 233.2	17.2	13 415.0	61 327.7	11.0	16.1	14.3	24.1	3.26	4.77
2012	14 444.1	8 141.4	25 188.9	17 690.9	15.9	13 437.7	67 346.5	10.3	15.4	13.5	24.0	2.72	4.07
2010													
1st quarter	12 376.8	6 507.2	23 782.5	17 201.0	18.7	13 722.1	57 145.4	12.4	17.5	16.1	24.1	5.79	10.52
2nd quarter	11 695.3	6 792.3	23 831.0	17 099.1	19.0	13 671.2	55 771.5	12.1	17.1	15.7	23.7	5.09	10.59
3rd quarter	12 398.0	6 919.0	23 488.4	16 729.0	18.4	13 633.5	57 523.0	11.9	16.9	15.4	23.4	4.57	8.64
4th quarter	13 209.9	7 120.5	23 472.8	16 623.9	17.7	13 636.9	60 221.6	11.6	16.6	15.1	23.3	4.15	7.95
2011													
1st quarter	13 564.8	7 293.2	23 330.3	16 361.4	17.2	13 568.2	61 877.5	11.2	16.2	14.6	23.2	3.83	6.99
2nd quarter	13 509.7	7 343.1	23 290.2	16 275.7	17.1	13 486.4	61 852.9	11.1	16.1	14.5	23.5	3.64	5.22
3rd quarter	12 809.9	7 455.8	23 359.7	16 305.1	17.7	13 405.1	59 206.5	11.0	16.1	14.4	23.8	3.45	5.72
4th quarter	13 434.1	7 673.2	23 432.6	16 233.2	17.2	13 415.0	61 327.7	11.0	16.1	14.3	24.1	3.26	4.77
2012													
1st quarter	14 117.1	7 713.7	23 839.0	16 592.9	16.5	13 374.7	64 185.0	10.8	15.9	14.1	24.0	3.07	4.41
2nd quarter	13 943.1	7 784.0	24 218.3	16 913.7	16.6	13 386.0	63 930.3	10.7	15.8	14.0	24.0	2.90	3.88
3rd quarter	14 402.2	8 016.5	24 682.1	17 258.2	16.1	13 314.1	65 949.3	10.6	15.7	13.9	24.1	2.81	3.90
4th quarter	14 444.1	8 141.4	25 188.9	17 690.9	15.9	13 437.7	67 346.5	10.3	15.4	13.5	24.0	2.72	4.07

[1] Includes nonprofit organizations.
[3] Excludes nonprofit organizations.
. . . = Not available.

Table 12-7. Mortgage Debt Outstanding

(Billions of dollars, except as noted; end of period; not seasonally adjusted.)

Year and quarter	Total	By type of property					By type of holder						
		Home		Multi-family residences	Commercial	Farm	U.S.-chartered depository institutions	Life insurance companies	Federal and related agencies	Mortgage pools or trusts			Other
		Billions of dollars	Percent of value of real estate							Total [1]	Federally related agencies	ABS issuers	
1950	73	45	19	9	12	6	35	16	3	0	0	0	19
1951	83	52	19	11	13	7	40	19	3	0	0	0	20
1952	92	58	20	11	14	7	45	21	4	0	0	0	21
1953	101	66	21	12	16	8	51	23	5	0	0	0	22
1954	114	75	22	13	17	8	59	26	5	0	0	0	24
1955	130	88	24	13	19	9	69	29	5	0	0	0	26
1956	144	99	25	14	22	10	77	33	6	0	0	0	28
1957	157	107	26	15	24	10	83	35	7	0	0	0	30
1958	172	117	27	17	27	11	93	37	8	0	0	0	34
1959	191	130	28	19	30	12	105	39	10	0	0	0	37
1960	208	141	29	21	33	13	115	42	11	0	0	0	41
1961	229	154	30	24	37	14	127	44	12	0	0	0	46
1962	252	168	32	27	42	15	143	47	12	0	0	0	49
1963	279	185	33	30	47	17	164	51	11	1	1	0	53
1964	307	202	35	35	51	19	183	55	12	1	1	0	56
1965	334	219	36	38	56	21	202	60	13	1	1	0	59
1966	358	233	36	41	61	23	214	65	16	1	1	0	62
1967	382	246	36	45	66	25	228	68	19	2	2	0	65
1968	411	263	34	48	73	27	247	70	23	3	3	0	69
1969	440	279	33	53	79	29	264	72	28	3	3	0	73
1970	469	292	33	60	87	30	278	74	34	5	5	0	79
1971	518	318	33	70	97	32	313	75	37	10	10	0	83
1972	590	357	33	83	114	35	366	77	40	14	14	0	92
1973	666	400	32	93	134	40	418	81	47	18	18	0	102
1974	728	435	35	100	148	45	451	86	61	21	21	0	108
1975	786	474	34	101	161	50	485	89	73	29	29	0	110
1976	870	535	34	106	174	55	547	92	76	41	41	0	115
1977	999	628	33	114	193	64	637	97	84	57	57	0	125
1978	1 151	738	33	125	215	73	730	106	100	70	70	0	144
1979	1 317	856	33	135	239	87	808	118	121	95	95	0	175
1980	1 458	958	33	143	260	97	853	131	143	114	114	0	217
1981	1 579	1 030	31	142	300	107	890	138	160	129	129	0	262
1982	1 661	1 070	31	146	334	111	871	142	177	179	179	0	293
1983	1 850	1 186	33	161	389	114	950	151	188	245	245	0	316
1984	2 092	1 321	32	186	472	112	1 084	157	202	300	289	11	349
1985	2 368	1 526	32	206	542	94	1 189	172	213	392	368	25	401
1986	2 655	1 729	34	239	602	84	1 279	194	202	549	532	18	431
1987	2 956	1 928	34	258	694	76	1 403	212	189	701	669	31	451
1988	3 273	2 162	35	275	766	71	1 540	233	192	786	745	40	522
1989	3 526	2 369	36	287	801	69	1 609	254	198	922	870	53	542
1990	3 781	2 606	38	287	820	68	1 601	268	239	1 086	1 020	66	587
1991	3 932	2 774	40	284	806	67	1 527	260	266	1 270	1 156	113	610
1992	4 043	2 942	41	271	763	68	1 471	242	286	1 440	1 272	168	604
1993	4 175	3 101	41	268	738	68	1 494	224	326	1 561	1 357	204	570
1994	4 339	3 278	42	268	723	70	1 560	216	316	1 697	1 472	225	551
1995	4 525	3 445	43	274	734	72	1 642	213	308	1 812	1 571	242	550
1996	4 806	3 682	44	286	764	74	1 731	208	294	1 989	1 712	278	583
1997	5 118	3 916	44	298	826	79	1 840	207	285	2 166	1 826	339	620
1998	5 603	4 272	44	331	916	83	1 948	214	292	2 487	2 019	468	663
1999	6 210	4 698	44	372	1 053	87	2 133	231	320	2 832	2 294	539	694
2000	6 769	5 122	42	402	1 160	85	2 350	236	340	3 098	2 493	604	745
2001	7 476	5 674	42	444	1 269	89	2 511	243	372	3 557	2 832	725	793
2002	8 377	6 429	43	483	1 370	95	2 799	250	432	3 995	3 159	836	901
2003	9 389	7 252	44	557	1 496	83	3 084	261	694	4 352	3 343	1 009	997
2004	10 663	8 291	44	607	1 668	96	3 605	273	703	4 836	3 384	1 452	1 245
2005	12 103	9 415	43	667	1 916	105	4 055	285	665	5 702	3 548	2 153	1 395
2006	13 512	10 487	46	706	2 210	108	4 416	304	687	6 626	3 841	2 784	1 479
2007	14 589	11 207	54	793	2 476	113	4 659	326	725	7 432	4 464	2 968	1 446
2008	14 656	11 097	63	841	2 584	135	4 615	342	801	7 577	4 961	2 615	1 321
2009	14 359	10 893	63	848	2 487	131	4 372	326	816	7 622	5 377	2 245	1 223
2010	13 739	10 426	63	838	2 333	141	4 195	317	5 128	3 055	1 139	1 916	1 044
2011	13 413	10 171	63	843	2 253	146	4 050	332	5 035	3 002	1 305	1 697	995
2012	13 154	9 925	56	859	2 218	153	3 997	344	4 936	2 928	1 437	1 490	949
2010													
1st quarter	14 177	10 748	62	841	2 454	134	4 311	321	5 211	3 123	980	2 143	1 210
2nd quarter	14 059	10 678	62	838	2 408	136	4 253	318	5 193	3 114	1 046	2 067	1 182
3rd quarter	13 937	10 595	63	839	2 365	139	4 221	318	5 142	3 089	1 096	1 993	1 167
4th quarter	13 739	10 426	63	838	2 333	141	4 195	317	5 128	3 055	1 139	1 916	1 044
2011													
1st quarter	13 645	10 352	63	837	2 314	142	4 082	318	5 162	3 049	1 187	1 862	1 033
2nd quarter	13 556	10 285	63	837	2 290	144	4 046	323	5 128	3 037	1 236	1 801	1 023
3rd quarter	13 475	10 227	63	838	2 265	145	4 038	329	5 074	3 027	1 277	1 749	1 007
4th quarter	13 413	10 171	63	843	2 253	146	4 050	332	5 035	3 002	1 305	1 697	995
2012													
1st quarter	13 304	10 085	61	833	2 239	148	3 985	337	5 035	2 968	1 330	1 638	980
2nd quarter	13 237	10 026	59	839	2 223	150	3 986	341	4 982	2 963	1 377	1 586	965
3rd quarter	13 142	9 937	58	847	2 207	151	3 945	344	4 957	2 939	1 408	1 531	959
4th quarter	13 154	9 925	56	859	2 218	153	3 997	344	4 936	2 928	1 437	1 490	949

[1]Outstanding principal balances of mortgage-backed securities issued or guaranteed by the holder indicated.

Table 12-8. Consumer Credit

(Outstanding at end of period, billions of dollars.)

Year and month	Seasonally adjusted			Not seasonally adjusted						
	Total	By major credit type		Total	By major holder					
		Revolving	Non-revolving		Depository institutions	Finance companies [1]	Credit unions	Federal government [1]	Nonfinancial businesses	Securitized pools [2]
1960	60.0	...	60.0	61.2	28.9	15.4	3.4	0.0	13.5	0.0
1961	62.2	...	62.2	63.4	30.7	15.5	3.6	0.0	13.6	0.0
1962	68.1	...	68.1	69.3	33.6	17.3	4.1	0.0	14.3	0.0
1963	76.6	...	76.6	77.9	38.3	19.6	4.5	0.0	15.5	0.0
1964	86.0	...	86.0	87.4	43.4	21.6	5.4	0.0	16.8	0.0
1965	96.0	...	96.0	97.5	49.1	23.9	6.5	0.0	18.1	0.0
1966	101.8	...	101.8	103.4	52.2	24.8	7.5	0.0	19.0	0.0
1967	106.8	...	106.8	108.6	55.8	24.6	8.3	0.0	19.9	0.0
1968	117.4	2.0	115.4	119.3	62.7	26.1	9.7	0.0	20.8	0.0
1969	127.2	3.6	123.6	129.2	67.8	27.8	11.7	0.0	21.9	0.0
1970	131.6	5.0	126.6	133.7	70.1	27.6	13.0	0.0	23.0	0.0
1971	146.9	8.2	138.7	149.2	79.0	29.2	14.8	0.0	26.2	0.0
1972	166.2	9.4	156.8	168.8	92.1	31.9	17.0	0.0	27.8	0.0
1973	190.1	11.3	178.7	193.0	108.1	35.4	19.6	0.0	29.8	0.0
1974	198.9	13.2	185.7	201.9	112.1	36.1	21.9	0.0	31.8	0.0
1975	204.0	14.5	189.5	207.0	116.2	32.6	25.7	0.0	32.6	0.0
1976	225.7	16.5	209.2	229.0	128.9	33.7	31.2	0.0	35.2	0.0
1977	260.6	37.4	223.1	264.9	152.1	37.3	37.6	0.5	37.4	0.0
1978	306.1	45.7	260.4	311.3	179.6	44.4	45.2	0.9	41.2	0.0
1979	348.6	53.6	295.0	354.6	205.7	55.4	47.4	1.5	44.6	0.0
1980	351.9	55.0	297.0	358.0	202.9	62.2	44.1	2.6	46.2	0.0
1981	371.3	60.9	310.4	377.9	208.2	70.1	46.7	4.8	48.1	0.0
1982	389.8	66.3	323.5	396.7	217.5	75.3	48.8	6.4	48.7	0.0
1983	437.1	79.0	358.0	444.9	245.2	83.3	56.1	4.6	55.7	0.0
1984	517.3	100.4	416.9	526.6	303.1	89.9	67.9	5.6	60.2	0.0
1985	599.7	124.5	475.2	610.6	354.8	111.7	74.0	6.8	63.3	0.0
1986	654.8	141.1	513.7	666.4	383.1	134.0	77.1	8.2	64.0	0.0
1987	686.3	160.9	525.5	698.6	399.4	140.0	81.0	10.0	68.1	0.0
1988	731.9	184.6	547.3	745.2	427.6	144.7	88.3	13.2	71.4	0.0
1989	794.6	211.2	583.4	809.3	445.8	138.9	91.7	16.0	69.6	47.3
1990	808.2	238.6	569.6	824.4	431.6	133.4	91.6	19.2	71.9	76.7
1991	798.0	263.8	534.3	815.6	412.3	121.6	90.3	21.1	67.3	103.0
1992	806.1	278.4	527.7	824.8	400.3	118.1	91.7	24.2	70.3	120.3
1993	865.7	309.9	555.7	886.2	433.6	116.1	101.6	27.2	77.2	130.5
1994	997.3	365.6	631.7	1 021.2	497.2	134.4	119.6	37.2	86.6	146.1
1995	1 140.7	443.9	696.8	1 168.2	542.4	152.1	131.9	43.5	85.1	213.1
1996	1 253.4	507.5	745.9	1 273.9	572.2	154.9	144.1	51.4	77.7	273.5
1997	1 324.8	540.0	784.8	1 344.2	562.2	167.5	152.4	57.2	84.4	320.5
1998	1 421.0	581.4	839.6	1 441.3	564.4	183.3	155.4	64.9	79.3	393.9
1999	1 531.1	610.7	920.4	1 553.6	569.5	201.6	167.9	81.8	76.1	456.7
2000	1 717.0	682.6	1 034.3	1 741.3	615.8	234.4	184.4	96.7	81.5	528.4
2001	1 867.9	714.8	1 153.0	1 891.8	639.5	280.0	189.6	111.9	73.1	597.8
2002	1 972.1	750.9	1 221.2	1 997.0	671.3	307.5	195.7	117.3	74.8	630.4
2003	2 077.4	768.3	1 309.1	2 102.9	747.3	393.0	205.9	102.9	59.1	594.8
2004	2 192.2	799.6	1 392.7	2 220.1	795.6	492.3	215.4	86.1	59.2	571.5
2005	2 290.9	829.5	1 461.4	2 320.6	816.1	516.5	228.6	89.8	59.6	609.9
2006	2 361.8	924.9	1 436.9	2 361.8	836.7	531.9	236.1	86.9	50.0	617.2
2007	2 506.3	1 002.9	1 503.4	2 506.3	894.9	572.1	236.6	93.0	51.5	652.5
2008	2 525.9	1 005.2	1 520.7	2 525.9	965.0	554.3	236.2	104.3	48.9	610.2
2009	2 420.2	917.2	1 503.0	2 420.2	906.3	471.9	237.1	178.6	45.0	572.5
2010	2 522.2	840.7	1 681.5	2 522.2	1 185.5	705.0	226.5	308.8	46.2	50.3
2011	2 615.7	842.5	1 773.2	2 615.7	1 192.6	688.0	223.0	417.4	48.5	46.2
2012	2 768.1	845.8	1 922.3	2 768.1	1 218.7	680.7	243.6	526.8	48.5	49.9
2011										
January	2 519.5	837.7	1 681.8	2 517.5	1 165.0	700.4	224.2	333.1	46.2	48.6
February	2 531.8	836.0	1 695.7	2 499.1	1 147.2	694.3	221.9	341.3	45.6	48.7
March	2 539.0	837.9	1 701.1	2 494.1	1 143.6	692.0	218.1	347.5	45.5	47.3
April	2 543.5	834.0	1 709.5	2 500.3	1 150.8	684.9	220.3	351.8	45.7	46.8
May	2 551.9	837.3	1 714.6	2 508.8	1 154.4	684.3	221.4	357.3	45.9	45.6
June	2 562.5	839.0	1 723.5	2 518.6	1 159.8	684.5	220.9	362.4	46.1	44.9
July	2 578.3	837.8	1 740.5	2 536.0	1 159.6	684.5	222.5	378.1	46.4	45.0
August	2 570.8	837.9	1 732.9	2 551.0	1 166.1	684.9	224.6	384.2	47.1	44.2
September	2 580.8	839.0	1 741.9	2 563.2	1 163.1	685.1	223.9	398.5	47.2	45.4
October	2 586.8	839.4	1 747.4	2 563.7	1 160.5	683.5	224.6	402.2	47.3	45.6
November	2 602.7	842.4	1 760.3	2 584.8	1 171.3	685.8	225.1	408.7	47.7	46.2
December	2 615.7	842.5	1 773.2	2 615.7	1 192.6	688.0	223.0	417.4	48.5	46.2
2012										
January	2 628.3	841.2	1 787.2	2 626.3	1 175.4	684.4	225.5	445.3	48.3	47.3
February	2 640.2	842.0	1 798.2	2 607.0	1 161.8	681.8	223.8	445.6	47.5	46.3
March	2 650.9	842.2	1 808.7	2 605.8	1 155.7	680.7	223.0	452.6	47.2	46.7
April	2 663.3	840.2	1 823.1	2 619.7	1 156.0	682.6	227.7	458.7	47.2	47.6
May	2 683.2	847.1	1 836.0	2 639.5	1 175.0	676.2	229.4	464.9	47.2	46.8
June	2 691.0	844.3	1 846.7	2 646.4	1 174.5	675.9	231.2	470.7	47.3	47.0
July	2 695.2	842.3	1 853.0	2 651.4	1 176.9	674.4	234.7	471.8	47.3	46.3
August	2 713.8	846.8	1 867.0	2 693.0	1 188.5	677.8	237.1	495.7	47.8	46.1
September	2 723.7	845.1	1 878.5	2 705.4	1 186.1	677.4	236.7	509.5	47.8	47.9
October	2 739.9	848.0	1 891.9	2 716.3	1 187.3	677.7	238.8	516.4	47.7	48.4
November	2 753.8	848.0	1 905.8	2 735.8	1 195.6	679.2	242.6	521.3	47.9	49.1
December	2 768.1	845.8	1 922.3	2 768.1	1 218.7	680.7	243.6	526.8	48.5	49.9

[1]Student Loan Marketing Association (Sallie Mae) included in federal government sector until end of 2004, and in finance companies since then.
[2]Outstanding balances of pools upon which securities have been issued; these balances are no longer carried on the balance sheets of the loan originators.
. . . = Not available.

Table 12-9A. Summary Interest Rates, Bond Yields, and Stock Prices: Recent Data

(Percent per annum, except as noted.)

Year and month	Federal funds interest rate	Federal Reserve discount rate[1]	U.S. Treasury bills, secondary market, 3-month	Inflation: percent change from year earlier in PCE chain-type price index excluding food and energy	Real 3-month Treasury bill rate	Commercial paper, 3-month [2]	Bank prime rate	Treasury 10-year nominal yields	Bond yields Domestic corporate (Moody's) Aaa	Baa	State and local bonds (Bond Buyer)	Standard and Poor's composite (500 stocks) Index, 1941-1943 = 10	Dividend-price ratio	Earnings-price ratio
1970	7.17	5.87	6.39	4.69	1.70	. . .	7.91	7.35	8.04	9.11	6.33	83.22	3.83	6.45
1971	4.67	5.95	4.33	4.71	-0.38	5.25	5.73	6.16	7.39	8.56	5.47	98.29	3.14	5.41
1972	4.44	4.88	4.06	3.23	0.83	4.66	5.25	6.21	7.21	8.16	5.26	109.20	2.84	5.50
1973	8.74	4.50	7.04	3.82	3.22	8.21	8.03	6.85	7.44	8.24	5.19	107.43	3.06	7.12
1974	10.51	6.45	7.85	7.93	-0.08	10.05	10.81	7.56	8.57	9.50	6.17	82.85	4.47	11.59
1975	5.82	7.83	5.79	8.37	-2.58	6.26	7.86	7.99	8.83	10.61	7.05	86.16	4.31	9.15
1976	5.05	6.25	4.98	6.08	-1.10	5.24	6.84	7.61	8.43	9.75	6.64	102.01	3.77	8.90
1977	5.54	5.50	5.26	6.42	-1.16	5.54	6.83	7.42	8.02	8.97	5.68	98.20	4.62	10.79
1978	7.94	5.46	7.18	6.69	0.49	7.93	9.06	8.41	8.73	9.49	6.02	96.02	5.28	12.03
1979	11.20	7.46	10.05	7.27	2.78	10.95	12.67	9.43	9.63	10.69	6.52	103.01	5.47	13.46
1980	13.35	10.29	11.39	9.15	2.24	12.61	15.26	11.43	11.94	13.67	8.59	118.78	5.26	12.66
1981	16.39	11.77	14.04	8.73	5.31	15.34	18.87	13.92	14.17	16.04	11.33	128.05	5.20	11.96
1982	12.24	13.42	10.60	6.45	4.15	11.90	14.85	13.01	13.79	16.11	11.66	119.71	5.81	11.60
1983	9.09	11.01	8.62	5.18	3.44	8.88	10.79	11.10	12.04	13.55	9.51	160.41	4.40	8.03
1984	10.23	8.50	9.54	4.15	5.39	10.12	12.04	12.46	12.71	14.19	10.10	160.46	4.64	10.02
1985	8.10	8.80	7.47	4.12	3.35	7.95	9.93	10.62	11.37	12.72	9.10	186.84	4.25	8.12
1986	6.80	7.69	5.97	3.43	2.54	6.49	8.33	7.67	9.02	10.39	7.32	236.34	3.49	6.09
1987	6.66	6.32	5.78	3.17	2.61	6.82	8.21	8.39	9.38	10.58	7.64	286.83	3.08	5.48
1988	7.57	5.66	6.67	4.23	2.44	7.66	9.32	8.85	9.71	10.83	7.68	265.79	3.64	8.01
1989	9.21	6.20	8.11	4.08	4.03	8.99	10.87	8.49	9.26	10.18	7.23	322.84	3.45	7.42
1990	8.10	6.93	7.50	3.98	3.52	8.06	10.01	8.55	9.32	10.36	7.27	334.59	3.61	6.47
1991	5.69	6.98	5.38	3.50	1.88	5.87	8.46	7.86	8.77	9.80	6.92	376.18	3.24	4.79
1992	3.52	5.45	3.43	3.01	0.42	3.75	6.25	7.01	8.14	8.98	6.44	415.74	2.99	4.22
1993	3.02	3.25	3.00	2.72	0.28	3.22	6.00	5.87	7.22	7.93	5.60	451.41	2.78	4.46
1994	4.21	3.00	4.25	2.23	2.02	4.66	7.15	7.09	7.97	8.63	6.18	460.42	2.82	5.83
1995	5.83	3.60	5.49	2.14	3.35	5.93	8.83	6.57	7.59	8.20	5.95	541.72	2.56	6.09
1996	5.30	5.21	5.01	1.88	3.13	5.41	8.27	6.44	7.37	8.05	5.76	670.50	2.19	5.24
1997	5.46	5.02	5.06	1.75	3.31	5.49	8.44	6.35	7.27	7.87	5.52	873.43	1.77	4.57
1998	5.35	5.00	4.78	1.24	3.54	5.34	8.35	5.26	6.53	7.22	5.09	1 085.50	1.49	3.46
1999	4.97	4.92	4.64	1.33	3.31	5.18	8.00	5.65	7.05	7.88	5.43	1 327.33	1.25	3.17
2000	6.24	4.62	5.82	1.75	4.07	6.31	9.23	6.03	7.62	8.37	5.71	1 427.22	1.15	3.63
2001	3.88	5.73	3.40	1.81	1.59	3.65	6.91	5.02	7.08	7.95	5.15	1 194.18	1.32	2.95
2002	1.67	3.40	1.61	1.71	-0.10	1.69	4.67	4.61	6.49	7.80	5.04	993.94	1.61	2.92
2003	1.13	. . .	1.01	1.48	-0.47	1.11	4.12	4.01	5.66	6.76	4.75	965.23	1.77	3.84
2004	1.35	2.34	1.37	1.91	-0.54	1.41	4.34	4.27	5.63	6.39	4.68	1 130.65	1.72	4.89
2005	3.22	4.19	3.15	2.16	0.99	3.42	6.19	4.29	5.23	6.06	4.40	1 207.23	1.83	5.36
2006	4.97	5.96	4.73	2.24	2.49	5.10	7.96	4.80	5.59	6.48	4.40	1 310.46	1.87	5.78
2007	5.02	5.86	4.36	2.16	2.20	4.92	8.05	4.63	5.56	6.48	4.40	1 477.19	1.86	5.29
2008	1.92	2.39	1.37	2.06	-0.69	2.13	5.09	3.66	5.63	7.44	4.86	1 220.04	2.37	3.54
2009	0.16	0.50	0.15	1.19	-1.04	0.26	3.25	3.26	5.31	7.29	4.62	948.05	2.40	1.86
2010	0.18	0.72	0.14	1.29	-1.15	0.24	3.25	3.22	4.94	6.04	4.29	1 139.97	1.98	6.04
2011	0.10	0.75	0.05	1.44	-1.39	0.17	3.25	2.78	4.64	5.66	4.51	1 267.64	2.05	6.77
2012	0.14	0.75	0.09	1.84	-1.75	0.19	3.25	1.80	3.67	4.94	3.73	1 379.35	2.24	6.20
2011														
January	0.17	0.75	0.15	1.00	-0.85	0.26	3.25	3.39	5.04	6.09	5.28	1 282.62	1.84	. . .
February	0.16	0.75	0.13	1.07	-0.94	0.25	3.25	3.58	5.22	6.15	5.15	1 321.12	1.80	. . .
March	0.14	0.75	0.10	1.05	-0.95	0.23	3.25	3.41	5.13	6.03	4.92	1 304.49	1.90	6.13
April	0.10	0.75	0.06	1.23	-1.17	0.22	3.25	3.46	5.16	6.02	4.99	1 331.51	1.92	. . .
May	0.09	0.75	0.04	1.35	-1.31	0.18	3.25	3.17	4.96	5.78	4.59	1 338.31	1.95	. . .
June	0.09	0.75	0.04	1.40	-1.36	0.17	3.25	3.00	4.99	5.75	4.51	1 287.29	2.04	6.35
July	0.07	0.75	0.04	1.50	-1.46	0.17	3.25	3.00	4.93	5.76	4.52	1 325.18	1.99	. . .
August	0.10	0.75	0.02	1.62	-1.60	0.21	3.25	2.30	4.37	5.36	4.02	1 185.31	2.20	. . .
September ...	0.08	0.75	0.01	1.65	-1.64	0.22	3.25	1.98	4.09	5.27	4.01	1 173.88	2.25	7.69
October	0.07	0.75	0.02	1.71	-1.69	0.24	3.25	2.15	3.98	5.37	4.13	1 207.22	2.28	. . .
November	0.08	0.75	0.01	1.77	-1.76	0.21	3.25	2.01	3.87	5.14	4.05	1 226.41	2.22	. . .
December	0.07	0.75	0.01	1.89	-1.88	0.18	3.25	1.98	3.93	5.25	3.95	1 243.32	2.24	6.91
2012														
January	0.08	0.75	0.03	2.01	-1.98	0.26	3.25	1.97	3.85	5.23	3.68	1 300.58	2.17	. . .
February	0.10	0.75	0.09	1.99	-1.90	0.21	3.25	1.97	3.85	5.14	3.66	1 352.49	2.11	. . .
March	0.13	0.75	0.08	2.04	-1.96	0.20	3.25	2.17	3.99	5.23	3.91	1 389.24	2.09	6.29
April	0.14	0.75	0.08	1.96	-1.88	0.20	3.25	2.05	3.96	5.19	3.95	1 386.43	2.20	. . .
May	0.16	0.75	0.09	1.86	-1.77	0.20	3.25	1.80	3.80	5.07	3.77	1 341.27	2.31	. . .
June	0.16	0.75	0.09	1.92	-1.83	0.21	3.25	1.62	3.64	5.02	3.94	1 323.48	2.38	6.45
July	0.16	0.75	0.10	1.86	-1.76	0.24	3.25	1.53	3.40	4.87	3.78	1 359.78	2.33	. . .
August	0.13	0.75	0.10	1.70	-1.60	0.19	3.25	1.68	3.48	4.91	3.74	1 403.44	2.26	. . .
September ...	0.14	0.75	0.11	1.71	-1.60	0.17	3.25	1.72	3.49	4.84	3.73	1 443.42	2.21	6.00
October	0.16	0.75	0.10	1.76	-1.66	0.19	3.25	1.75	3.47	4.58	3.65	1 437.82	2.24	. . .
November	0.16	0.75	0.09	1.67	-1.58	0.21	3.25	1.65	3.50	4.51	3.46	1 394.51	2.33	. . .
December	0.16	0.75	0.07	1.60	-1.53	0.17	3.25	1.72	3.65	4.63	3.48	1 422.29	2.28	6.07

[1] Federal Reserve Bank of New York. Through 2002, represents the rate for adjustment credit. Beginning in 2003, represents the rate for primary credit. See notes and definitions for more information.
[2] Prior to September 1997, this series represents both nonfinancial and financial commercial paper rates. Beginning September 1997, rates for financial companies only are shown. See notes and definitions for more information.
. . . = Not available.

Table 12-9B. Summary Interest Rates, Bond Yields, and Stock Prices: Historical

(Percent per annum, except as noted.)

Year and month	Federal funds interest rate	Federal Reserve discount rate[1]	U.S. Treasury bills, secondary market, 3-month	Inflation[2]	Real 3-month Treasury bill rate	Commercial paper, 3-month[3]	Bank prime rate	Treasury 10-year nominal yields	Bond yields Domestic corporate (Moody's) Aaa	Baa	State and local bonds (Bond Buyer)	Standard and Poor's composite (500 stocks) Index, 1941-1943 = 10	Dividend-price ratio	Earnings-price ratio
1919	...	...	...	...	...	5.37	...	4.73	5.49	7.25	4.46	8.78	...	...
1920	...	...	5.42	...	...	7.50	...	5.32	6.12	8.20	4.98	7.98	...	...
1921	...	...	4.83	...	...	6.62	...	5.09	5.97	8.35	5.09	6.86	...	...
1922	...	...	3.47	...	...	4.52	...	4.30	5.10	7.08	4.23	8.41	...	...
1923	...	...	3.93	...	...	5.07	...	4.36	5.12	7.24	4.25	8.57	...	...
1924	...	...	2.77	...	...	3.98	...	4.06	5.00	6.83	4.20	9.05	...	...
1925	...	...	3.03	...	...	4.02	...	3.86	4.88	6.27	4.09	11.15	...	...
1926	...	...	3.23	...	...	4.34	...	3.68	4.73	5.87	4.08	12.59	4.94	9.19
1927	...	...	3.10	...	...	4.11	...	3.34	4.57	5.48	3.98	15.34	4.76	6.29
1928	...	...	3.97	...	...	4.85	...	3.33	4.55	5.48	4.05	19.95	3.98	5.67
1929	...	5.17	4.42	...	...	5.85	5.5–6	3.60	4.73	5.90	4.27	26.02	3.47	7.51
1930	...	3.04	2.23	...	...	3.59	3.5–6	3.29	4.55	5.90	4.07	21.03	4.51	6.33
1931	...	2.11	1.40	...	...	2.64	2.75–5	3.34	4.58	7.62	4.01	13.66	6.15	7.51
1932	...	2.82	0.88	...	...	2.73	3.25–4	3.68	5.01	9.30	4.65	6.93	7.43	5.95
1933	...	2.56	0.52	...	...	1.73	1.5–4	3.31	4.49	7.76	4.71	8.96	4.21	4.36
1934	...	1.54	0.28	...	...	1.02	1.50	3.12	4.00	6.32	4.03	9.84	3.72	5.16
1935	...	1.50	0.17	...	...	0.76	1.50	2.79	3.60	5.75	3.41	10.60	3.82	7.23
1936	...	1.50	0.17	...	...	0.75	1.50	2.65	3.24	4.77	3.07	15.47	3.44	6.57
1937	...	1.33	0.28	...	...	0.94	1.50	2.68	3.26	5.03	3.10	15.41	4.86	8.25
1938	...	1.00	0.07	...	...	0.81	1.50	2.56	3.19	5.80	2.91	11.49	5.18	5.55
1939	...	1.00	0.05	...	...	0.59	1.50	2.36	3.01	4.96	2.76	12.06	4.05	7.34
1940	...	1.00	0.04	...	...	0.56	1.50	2.21	2.84	4.75	2.50	11.02	5.59	9.80
1941	...	1.00	0.13	...	...	0.53	1.50	2.12	2.77	4.33	2.10	9.82	6.82	12.14
1942	...	1.00	0.34	...	...	0.66	1.50	2.46	2.83	4.28	2.36	8.67	7.24	11.42
1943	...	1.00	0.38	...	...	0.69	1.50	2.47	2.73	3.91	2.06	11.50	4.93	7.82
1944	...	1.00	0.38	...	...	0.73	1.50	2.48	2.72	3.61	1.86	12.47	4.86	7.34
1945	...	1.00	0.38	...	...	0.75	1.50	2.37	2.62	3.29	1.67	15.16	4.17	6.39
1946	...	1.00	0.38	...	...	0.81	1.50	2.19	2.53	3.05	1.64	17.08	3.85	6.31
1947	...	1.00	0.61	...	...	1.03	1.63	2.25	2.61	3.24	2.01	15.17	4.93	10.69
1948	...	1.34	1.05	...	...	1.44	1.88	2.44	2.82	3.47	2.40	15.53	5.54	14.60
1949	...	1.50	1.10	...	...	1.49	2.00	2.31	2.66	3.42	2.21	15.23	6.59	15.48
1950	...	1.59	1.22	...	...	1.45	2.07	2.32	2.62	3.24	1.98	18.40	6.57	13.99
1951	...	1.75	1.55	...	...	2.16	2.56	2.57	2.86	3.41	2.00	22.34	6.13	11.82
1952	...	1.75	1.77	...	...	2.33	3.00	2.68	2.96	3.52	2.19	24.50	5.80	9.47
1953	...	1.99	1.94	...	...	2.52	3.17	2.94	3.20	3.73	2.74	24.73	5.80	10.26
1954	...	1.60	0.94	...	...	1.58	3.05	2.55	2.90	3.51	2.39	29.69	4.95	8.57
1955	1.79	1.89	1.72	...	...	2.18	3.16	2.84	3.05	3.53	2.48	40.49	4.08	7.95
1956	2.73	2.77	2.62	...	...	3.31	3.77	3.08	3.36	3.88	2.76	46.62	4.09	7.55
1957	3.11	3.12	3.22	...	...	3.81	4.20	3.47	3.89	4.71	3.28	44.38	4.35	7.89
1958	1.57	2.15	1.77	...	...	2.46	3.83	3.43	3.79	4.73	3.16	46.24	3.97	6.23
1959	3.31	3.36	3.39	...	...	3.97	4.48	4.07	4.38	5.05	3.56	57.38	3.23	5.78
1960	3.21	3.53	2.87	1.79	1.08	3.85	4.82	4.01	4.41	5.19	3.52	55.85	3.47	5.90
1961	1.95	3.00	2.35	1.26	1.10	2.97	4.50	3.90	4.35	5.08	3.45	66.27	2.98	4.62
1962	2.71	3.00	2.77	1.36	1.40	3.26	4.50	3.95	4.33	5.02	3.15	62.38	3.37	5.82
1963	3.18	3.23	3.16	1.30	1.86	3.55	4.50	4.00	4.26	4.86	3.17	69.87	3.17	5.50
1964	3.50	3.55	3.55	1.53	2.02	3.97	4.50	4.19	4.41	4.83	3.21	81.37	3.01	5.32
1965	4.07	3.55	3.95	1.27	2.69	...	4.54	4.28	4.49	4.87	3.26	88.17	3.00	5.59
1966	5.11	4.04	4.86	2.26	2.60	...	5.63	4.93	5.13	5.67	3.81	85.26	3.40	6.63
1967	4.22	4.50	4.29	3.07	1.23	...	5.63	5.07	5.51	6.23	3.94	91.93	3.20	5.73
1968	5.66	4.19	5.34	4.29	1.05	...	6.31	5.64	6.18	6.94	4.45	98.70	3.07	5.67
1969	8.21	5.17	6.67	4.69	1.98	...	7.96	6.67	7.03	7.81	5.72	97.84	3.24	6.08
1945														
January	...	1.00	0.38	...	...	...	1.50	...	2.69	3.46	...	13.49	...	...
February	...	1.00	0.38	...	...	...	1.50	...	2.65	3.41	...	13.94	...	...
March	...	1.00	0.38	...	...	...	1.50	...	2.62	3.38	...	13.93	...	...
April	...	1.00	0.38	...	...	...	1.50	...	2.61	3.36	...	14.28	...	...
May	...	1.00	0.38	...	...	...	1.50	...	2.62	3.32	...	14.82	...	...
June	...	1.00	0.38	...	...	...	1.50	...	2.61	3.29	...	15.09	...	...
July	...	1.00	0.38	...	...	...	1.50	...	2.60	3.26	...	14.78	...	...
August	...	1.00	0.38	...	...	...	1.50	...	2.61	3.26	...	14.83	...	...
September	...	1.00	0.38	...	...	...	1.50	...	2.62	3.24	...	15.84	...	...
October	...	1.00	0.38	...	...	...	1.50	...	2.62	3.20	...	16.50	...	...
November	...	1.00	0.38	...	...	...	1.50	...	2.62	3.15	...	17.04	...	...
December	...	1.00	0.38	...	...	...	1.50	...	2.61	3.10	...	17.33	...	...
1946														
January	...	1.00	0.38	...	...	...	1.50	...	2.54	3.01	...	18.02	...	...
February	...	1.00	0.38	...	...	...	1.50	...	2.48	2.95	...	18.07	...	...
March	...	1.00	0.38	...	...	...	1.50	...	2.47	2.94	...	17.53	...	...
April	...	1.00	0.38	...	...	...	1.50	...	2.46	2.96	...	18.66	...	...
May	...	1.00	0.38	...	...	...	1.50	...	2.51	3.02	...	18.70	...	...
June	...	1.00	0.38	...	...	...	1.50	...	2.49	3.03	...	18.58	...	...
July	...	1.00	0.38	...	...	...	1.50	...	2.48	3.03	...	18.05	...	...
August	...	1.00	0.38	...	...	...	1.50	...	2.51	3.03	...	17.70	...	...
September	...	1.00	0.38	...	...	...	1.50	...	2.58	3.10	...	15.09	...	...
October	...	1.00	0.38	...	...	...	1.50	...	2.60	3.15	...	14.75	...	...
November	...	1.00	0.38	...	...	...	1.50	...	2.59	3.17	...	14.69	...	...
December	...	1.00	0.38	...	...	...	1.50	...	2.61	3.17	...	15.13	...	...

[1]Federal Reserve Bank of New York. Through 2002, represents the rate for adjustment credit. Beginning in 2003, represents the rate for primary credit. See notes and definitions for more information.
[2]Beginning 1960, PCE except food and energy; before then, CPI-U.
[3]Prior to September 1997, this series represents both nonfinancial and financial commercial paper rates. Beginning September 1997, rates for financial companies only are shown. See notes and definitions for more information.
... = Not available.

Table 12-9B. Summary Interest Rates, Bond Yields, and Stock Prices: Historical—*Continued*

(Percent per annum, except as noted.)

Year and month	Federal funds interest rate	Federal Reserve discount rate[1]	U.S. Treasury bills, secondary market, 3-month	Inflation[2]	Real 3-month Treasury bill rate	Commercial paper, 3-month[3]	Bank prime rate	Treasury 10-year nominal yields	Bond yields Domestic corporate (Moody's) Aaa	Bond yields Domestic corporate (Moody's) Baa	State and local bonds (Bond Buyer)	Standard and Poor's composite (500 stocks) Index, 1941-1943 = 10	Dividend-price ratio	Earnings-price ratio
1947														
January	...	1.00	0.38	...	...	...	1.50	...	2.57	3.13	...	15.21	...	...
February	...	1.00	0.38	...	...	...	1.50	...	2.55	3.12	...	15.80	...	...
March	...	1.00	0.38	...	...	...	1.50	...	2.55	3.15	...	15.16	...	...
April	...	1.00	0.38	...	...	...	1.50	...	2.53	3.16	...	14.60	...	...
May	...	1.00	0.38	...	...	...	1.50	...	2.53	3.17	...	14.34	...	...
June	...	1.00	0.38	...	...	...	1.50	...	2.55	3.21	...	14.84	...	...
July	...	1.00	0.66	...	...	...	1.50	...	2.55	3.18	...	15.77	...	...
August	...	1.00	0.75	...	...	...	1.50	...	2.56	3.17	...	15.46	...	...
September	...	1.00	0.80	...	...	...	1.50	...	2.61	3.23	...	15.06	...	...
October	...	1.00	0.85	...	...	...	1.50	...	2.70	3.35	...	15.45	...	...
November	...	1.00	0.92	...	...	...	1.50	...	2.77	3.44	...	15.27	...	...
December	...	1.00	0.95	...	...	...	1.75	...	2.86	3.52	...	15.03	...	...
1948														
January	...	1.25	0.97	...	...	...	1.75	...	2.86	3.52	...	14.83	...	...
February	...	1.25	1.00	...	...	...	1.75	...	2.85	3.53	...	14.10	...	...
March	...	1.25	1.00	...	...	...	1.75	...	2.83	3.53	...	14.30	...	...
April	...	1.25	1.00	...	...	...	1.75	...	2.78	3.47	...	15.40	...	...
May	...	1.25	1.00	...	...	...	1.75	...	2.76	3.38	...	16.15	...	...
June	...	1.25	1.00	...	...	...	1.75	...	2.76	3.34	...	16.82	...	...
July	...	1.25	1.00	...	...	...	1.75	...	2.81	3.37	...	16.42	...	...
August	...	1.50	1.06	...	...	...	2.00	...	2.84	3.44	...	15.94	...	...
September	...	1.50	1.09	...	...	...	2.00	...	2.84	3.45	...	15.76	...	...
October	...	1.50	1.12	...	...	...	2.00	...	2.84	3.50	...	16.19	...	...
November	...	1.50	1.14	...	...	...	2.00	...	2.84	3.53	...	15.29	...	...
December	...	1.50	1.16	...	...	...	2.00	...	2.79	3.53	...	15.19	...	...
1949														
January	...	1.50	1.17	...	...	...	2.00	...	2.71	3.46	...	15.36	...	...
February	...	1.50	1.17	...	...	...	2.00	...	2.71	3.45	...	14.77	...	...
March	...	1.50	1.17	...	...	...	2.00	...	2.70	3.47	...	14.91	...	...
April	...	1.50	1.17	...	...	...	2.00	...	2.70	3.45	...	14.89	...	...
May	...	1.50	1.17	...	...	...	2.00	...	2.71	3.45	...	14.78	...	...
June	...	1.50	1.17	...	...	...	2.00	...	2.71	3.47	...	13.97	...	...
July	...	1.50	1.02	...	...	...	2.00	...	2.67	3.46	...	14.76	...	...
August	...	1.50	1.04	...	...	...	2.00	...	2.62	3.40	...	15.29	...	...
September	...	1.50	1.07	...	...	...	2.00	...	2.60	3.37	...	15.49	...	...
October	...	1.50	1.05	...	...	...	2.00	...	2.61	3.36	...	15.89	...	...
November	...	1.50	1.08	...	...	...	2.00	...	2.60	3.35	...	16.11	...	...
December	...	1.50	1.10	...	...	...	2.00	...	2.58	3.31	...	16.54	...	...
1950														
January	...	1.50	1.07	...	...	...	2.00	...	2.57	3.24	...	16.88	...	...
February	...	1.50	1.12	...	...	...	2.00	...	2.58	3.24	...	17.21	...	...
March	...	1.50	1.12	...	...	...	2.00	...	2.58	3.24	...	17.35	...	...
April	...	1.50	1.15	...	...	...	2.00	...	2.60	3.23	...	17.84	...	...
May	...	1.50	1.16	...	...	...	2.00	...	2.61	3.25	...	18.44	...	...
June	...	1.50	1.15	...	...	...	2.00	...	2.62	3.28	...	18.74	...	...
July	...	1.50	1.16	...	...	...	2.00	...	2.65	3.32	...	17.38	...	...
August	...	1.59	1.20	...	...	...	2.00	...	2.61	3.23	...	18.43	...	...
September	...	1.75	1.30	...	...	...	2.08	...	2.64	3.21	...	19.08	...	...
October	...	1.75	1.31	...	...	...	2.25	...	2.67	3.22	...	19.87	...	...
November	...	1.75	1.36	...	...	...	2.25	...	2.67	3.22	...	19.83	...	...
December	...	1.75	1.34	...	...	...	2.25	...	2.67	3.20	...	19.75	...	...
1951														
January	...	1.75	1.34	...	...	...	2.44	...	2.66	3.17	...	21.21	...	...
February	...	1.75	1.36	...	...	...	2.50	...	2.66	3.16	...	22.00	...	...
March	...	1.75	1.40	...	...	...	2.50	...	2.78	3.23	...	21.63	...	...
April	...	1.75	1.47	...	...	...	2.50	...	2.87	3.35	...	21.92	...	...
May	...	1.75	1.55	...	...	...	2.50	...	2.89	3.40	...	21.93	...	...
June	...	1.75	1.45	...	...	...	2.50	...	2.94	3.49	...	21.55	...	...
July	...	1.75	1.56	...	...	...	2.50	...	2.94	3.53	...	21.93	...	...
August	...	1.75	1.62	...	...	...	2.50	...	2.88	3.50	...	22.89	...	...
September	...	1.75	1.63	...	...	...	2.50	...	2.84	3.46	...	23.48	...	...
October	...	1.75	1.54	...	...	...	2.62	...	2.89	3.50	...	23.36	...	...
November	...	1.75	1.56	...	...	...	2.75	...	2.96	3.56	...	22.71	...	...
December	...	1.75	1.73	...	...	...	2.85	...	3.01	3.61	...	23.41	...	...
1952														
January	...	1.75	1.57	...	...	...	3.00	...	2.98	3.59	...	24.19	...	...
February	...	1.75	1.54	...	...	...	3.00	...	2.93	3.53	...	23.75	...	...
March	...	1.75	1.59	...	...	...	3.00	...	2.96	3.51	...	23.81	...	...
April	...	1.75	1.57	...	...	...	3.00	...	2.93	3.50	...	23.74	...	...
May	...	1.75	1.67	...	...	...	3.00	...	2.93	3.49	...	23.73	...	...
June	...	1.75	1.70	...	...	...	3.00	...	2.94	3.50	...	24.38	...	...
July	...	1.75	1.81	...	...	...	3.00	...	2.95	3.50	...	25.08	...	...
August	...	1.75	1.83	...	...	...	3.00	...	2.94	3.51	...	25.18	...	...
September	...	1.75	1.71	...	...	...	3.00	...	2.95	3.52	...	24.78	...	...
October	...	1.75	1.74	...	...	...	3.00	...	3.01	3.54	...	24.26	...	...
November	...	1.75	1.85	...	...	...	3.00	...	2.98	3.53	...	25.03	...	...
December	...	1.75	2.09	...	...	...	3.00	...	2.97	3.51	...	26.04	...	...

[1] Federal Reserve Bank of New York. Through 2002, represents the rate for adjustment credit. Beginning in 2003, represents the rate for primary credit. See notes and definitions for more information.
[2] Beginning 1960, PCE except food and energy; before then, CPI-U.
[3] Prior to September 1997, this series represents both nonfinancial and financial commercial paper rates. Beginning September 1997, rates for financial companies only are shown. See notes and definitions for more information.
... = Not available.

Table 12-9B. Summary Interest Rates, Bond Yields, and Stock Prices: Historical—*Continued*

(Percent per annum, except as noted.)

Year and month	Federal funds interest rate	Federal Reserve discount rate[1]	U.S. Treasury bills, secondary market, 3-month	Inflation[2]	Real 3-month Treasury bill rate	Commercial paper, 3-month[3]	Bank prime rate	Treasury 10-year nominal yields	Bond yields Domestic corporate (Moody's) Aaa	Baa	State and local bonds (Bond Buyer)	Standard and Poor's composite (500 stocks) Index, 1941-1943 = 10	Dividend-price ratio	Earnings-price ratio
1953														
January	. . .	1.88	1.96	. . .	. . .	. . .	3.00	. . .	3.02	3.51	2.44	26.18	. . .	. . .
February	. . .	2.00	1.97	. . .	. . .	. . .	3.00	. . .	3.07	3.53	2.59	25.86	. . .	. . .
March	. . .	2.00	2.01	. . .	. . .	. . .	3.00	. . .	3.12	3.57	2.65	25.99	. . .	. . .
April	. . .	2.00	2.19	. . .	. . .	2.83	3.03	. . .	3.23	3.65	2.67	24.71	. . .	. . .
May	. . .	2.00	2.16	. . .	. . .	3.05	3.25	. . .	3.34	3.78	2.82	24.84	. . .	. . .
June	. . .	2.00	2.11	. . .	. . .	3.11	3.25	. . .	3.40	3.86	3.03	23.95	. . .	. . .
July	. . .	2.00	2.04	. . .	. . .	2.93	3.25	. . .	3.28	3.86	2.95	24.29	. . .	. . .
August	. . .	2.00	2.04	. . .	. . .	2.95	3.25	. . .	3.24	3.85	2.90	24.39	. . .	. . .
September	. . .	2.00	1.79	. . .	. . .	2.87	3.25	. . .	3.29	3.88	2.87	23.27	. . .	. . .
October	. . .	2.00	1.38	. . .	. . .	2.66	3.25	. . .	3.16	3.82	2.71	23.97	. . .	. . .
November	. . .	2.00	1.44	. . .	. . .	2.68	3.25	. . .	3.11	3.75	2.60	24.50	. . .	. . .
December	. . .	2.00	1.60	. . .	. . .	2.59	3.25	. . .	3.13	3.74	2.59	24.83	. . .	. . .
1954														
January	. . .	2.00	1.18	. . .	. . .	. . .	3.25	2.48	3.06	3.71	2.50	25.46	. . .	. . .
February	. . .	1.79	0.97	. . .	. . .	. . .	3.25	2.47	2.95	3.61	2.42	26.02	. . .	. . .
March	. . .	1.75	1.03	. . .	. . .	. . .	3.13	2.37	2.86	3.51	2.39	26.57	. . .	. . .
April	. . .	1.63	0.97	. . .	. . .	. . .	3.00	2.29	2.85	3.47	2.47	27.63	. . .	. . .
May	. . .	1.50	0.76	. . .	. . .	. . .	3.00	2.37	2.88	3.47	2.49	28.73	. . .	. . .
June	. . .	1.50	0.64	. . .	. . .	. . .	3.00	2.38	2.90	3.49	2.47	28.96	. . .	. . .
July	0.80	1.50	0.72	. . .	. . .	. . .	3.00	2.30	2.89	3.50	2.32	30.13	. . .	. . .
August	1.22	1.50	0.92	. . .	. . .	. . .	3.00	2.36	2.87	3.49	2.26	30.73	. . .	. . .
September	1.06	1.50	1.01	. . .	. . .	. . .	3.00	2.38	2.89	3.47	2.31	31.45	. . .	. . .
October	0.85	1.50	0.98	. . .	. . .	. . .	3.00	2.43	2.87	3.46	2.34	32.18	. . .	. . .
November	0.83	1.50	0.93	. . .	. . .	. . .	3.00	2.48	2.89	3.45	2.32	33.44	. . .	. . .
December	1.28	1.50	1.15	. . .	. . .	. . .	3.00	2.51	2.90	3.45	2.36	34.97	. . .	. . .
1955														
January	1.39	1.50	1.22	. . .	. . .	. . .	3.00	2.61	2.93	3.45	2.40	35.60	. . .	. . .
February	1.29	1.50	1.17	. . .	. . .	. . .	3.00	2.65	2.93	3.47	2.43	36.79	. . .	. . .
March	1.35	1.50	1.28	. . .	. . .	. . .	3.00	2.68	3.02	3.48	2.44	36.50	. . .	. . .
April	1.43	1.63	1.59	. . .	. . .	. . .	3.00	2.75	3.01	3.49	2.41	37.76	. . .	. . .
May	1.43	1.75	1.45	. . .	. . .	. . .	3.00	2.76	3.04	3.50	2.38	37.60	. . .	. . .
June	1.64	1.75	1.41	. . .	. . .	. . .	3.00	2.78	3.05	3.51	2.41	39.78	. . .	. . .
July	1.68	1.75	1.60	. . .	. . .	. . .	3.00	2.90	3.06	3.52	2.54	42.69	. . .	. . .
August	1.96	1.97	1.90	. . .	. . .	. . .	3.23	2.97	3.11	3.56	2.60	42.43	. . .	. . .
September	2.18	2.18	2.07	. . .	. . .	. . .	3.25	2.97	3.13	3.59	2.58	44.34	. . .	. . .
October	2.24	2.25	2.23	. . .	. . .	. . .	3.40	2.88	3.10	3.59	2.51	42.11	. . .	. . .
November	2.35	2.36	2.24	. . .	. . .	. . .	3.50	2.89	3.10	3.58	2.45	44.95	. . .	. . .
December	2.48	2.50	2.54	. . .	. . .	. . .	3.50	2.96	3.15	3.62	2.57	45.37	. . .	. . .
1956														
January	2.45	2.50	2.41	. . .	. . .	. . .	3.50	2.90	3.11	3.60	2.50	44.15	. . .	. . .
February	2.50	2.50	2.32	. . .	. . .	. . .	3.50	2.84	3.08	3.58	2.44	44.43	. . .	. . .
March	2.50	2.50	2.25	. . .	. . .	. . .	3.50	2.96	3.10	3.60	2.57	47.49	. . .	. . .
April	2.62	2.65	2.60	. . .	. . .	. . .	3.65	3.18	3.24	3.68	2.70	48.05	. . .	. . .
May	2.75	2.75	2.61	. . .	. . .	. . .	3.75	3.07	3.28	3.73	2.68	46.54	. . .	. . .
June	2.71	2.75	2.49	. . .	. . .	. . .	3.75	3.00	3.26	3.76	2.54	46.27	. . .	. . .
July	2.75	2.75	2.31	. . .	. . .	. . .	3.75	3.11	3.28	3.80	2.65	48.78	. . .	. . .
August	2.73	2.81	2.60	. . .	. . .	. . .	3.84	3.33	3.43	3.93	2.80	48.49	. . .	. . .
September	2.95	3.00	2.84	. . .	. . .	. . .	4.00	3.38	3.56	4.07	2.93	46.84	. . .	. . .
October	2.96	3.00	2.90	. . .	. . .	. . .	4.00	3.34	3.59	4.17	2.95	46.24	. . .	. . .
November	2.88	3.00	2.99	. . .	. . .	. . .	4.00	3.49	3.69	4.24	3.16	45.76	. . .	. . .
December	2.94	3.00	3.21	. . .	. . .	. . .	4.00	3.59	3.75	4.37	3.22	46.44	. . .	. . .
1957														
January	2.84	3.00	3.11	. . .	. . .	. . .	4.00	3.46	3.77	4.49	3.18	45.43	. . .	. . .
February	3.00	3.00	3.10	. . .	. . .	. . .	4.00	3.34	3.67	4.47	3.00	43.47	. . .	. . .
March	2.96	3.00	3.08	. . .	. . .	. . .	4.00	3.41	3.66	4.43	3.09	44.03	. . .	. . .
April	3.00	3.00	3.07	. . .	. . .	. . .	4.00	3.48	3.67	4.44	3.13	45.05	. . .	. . .
May	3.00	3.00	3.06	. . .	. . .	. . .	4.00	3.60	3.74	4.52	3.27	46.78	. . .	. . .
June	3.00	3.00	3.29	. . .	. . .	. . .	4.00	3.80	3.91	4.63	3.41	47.55	. . .	. . .
July	2.99	3.00	3.16	. . .	. . .	. . .	4.00	3.93	3.99	4.73	3.39	48.51	. . .	. . .
August	3.24	3.15	3.37	. . .	. . .	. . .	4.42	3.93	4.10	4.82	3.54	45.84	. . .	. . .
September	3.47	3.50	3.53	. . .	. . .	. . .	4.50	3.92	4.12	4.93	3.53	43.98	. . .	. . .
October	3.50	3.50	3.58	. . .	. . .	. . .	4.50	3.97	4.10	4.99	3.42	41.24	. . .	. . .
November	3.28	3.23	3.31	. . .	. . .	. . .	4.50	3.72	4.08	5.09	3.37	40.35	. . .	. . .
December	2.98	3.00	3.04	. . .	. . .	. . .	4.50	3.21	3.81	5.03	3.04	40.33	. . .	. . .
1958														
January	2.72	2.94	2.44	. . .	. . .	. . .	4.34	3.09	3.60	4.83	2.91	41.12	. . .	. . .
February	1.67	2.75	1.53	. . .	. . .	. . .	4.00	3.05	3.59	4.66	3.02	41.26	. . .	. . .
March	1.20	2.35	1.30	. . .	. . .	. . .	4.00	2.98	3.63	4.68	3.06	42.11	. . .	. . .
April	1.26	2.03	1.13	. . .	. . .	. . .	3.83	2.88	3.60	4.67	2.96	42.34	. . .	. . .
May	0.63	1.75	0.91	. . .	. . .	. . .	3.50	2.92	3.57	4.62	2.92	43.70	. . .	. . .
June	0.93	1.75	0.83	. . .	. . .	. . .	3.50	2.97	3.57	4.55	2.97	44.75	. . .	. . .
July	0.68	1.75	0.91	. . .	. . .	. . .	3.50	3.20	3.67	4.53	3.09	45.98	. . .	. . .
August	1.53	1.75	1.69	. . .	. . .	. . .	3.50	3.54	3.85	4.67	3.35	47.70	. . .	. . .
September	1.76	1.91	2.44	. . .	. . .	. . .	3.83	3.76	4.09	4.87	3.54	48.96	. . .	. . .
October	1.80	2.00	2.63	. . .	. . .	. . .	4.00	3.80	4.11	4.92	3.45	50.95	. . .	. . .
November	2.27	2.40	2.67	. . .	. . .	. . .	4.00	3.74	4.09	4.87	3.32	52.50	. . .	. . .
December	2.42	2.50	2.77	. . .	. . .	. . .	4.00	3.86	4.08	4.85	3.33	53.49	. . .	. . .

[1]Federal Reserve Bank of New York. Through 2002, represents the rate for adjustment credit. Beginning in 2003, represents the rate for primary credit. See notes and definitions for more information.
[2]Beginning 1960, PCE except food and energy; before then, CPI-U.
[3]Prior to September 1997, this series represents both nonfinancial and financial commercial paper rates. Beginning September 1997, rates for financial companies only are shown. See notes and definitions for more information.
. . . = Not available.

Table 12-9B. Summary Interest Rates, Bond Yields, and Stock Prices: Historical—*Continued*

(Percent per annum, except as noted.)

Year and month	Federal funds interest rate	Federal Reserve discount rate[1]	U.S. Treasury bills, secondary market, 3-month	Inflation[2]	Real 3-month Treasury bill rate	Commercial paper, 3-month[3]	Bank prime rate	Treasury 10-year nominal yields	Bond yields: Domestic corporate (Moody's) Aaa	Bond yields: Domestic corporate (Moody's) Baa	State and local bonds (Bond Buyer)	S&P Index, 1941-1943 = 10	S&P Dividend-price ratio	S&P Earnings-price ratio
1959														
January	2.48	2.50	2.82	...	...	...	4.00	4.02	4.12	4.87	3.42	55.62	...	...
February	2.43	2.50	2.70	...	...	...	4.00	3.96	4.14	4.89	3.36	54.77	...	...
March	2.80	2.92	2.80	...	...	...	4.00	3.99	4.13	4.85	3.30	56.15	...	...
April	2.96	3.00	2.95	...	...	...	4.00	4.12	4.23	4.86	3.39	57.10	...	...
May	2.90	3.05	2.84	...	...	...	4.23	4.31	4.37	4.96	3.57	57.96	...	...
June	3.39	3.50	3.21	...	...	...	4.50	4.34	4.46	5.04	3.71	57.46	...	...
July	3.47	3.50	3.20	...	...	...	4.50	4.40	4.47	5.08	3.71	59.74	...	...
August	3.50	3.50	3.38	...	...	...	4.50	4.43	4.43	5.09	3.58	59.40	...	...
September	3.76	3.83	4.04	...	...	...	5.00	4.68	4.52	5.18	3.78	57.05	...	...
October	3.98	4.00	4.05	...	...	...	5.00	4.53	4.57	5.28	3.62	57.00	...	...
November	4.00	4.00	4.15	...	...	...	5.00	4.53	4.56	5.26	3.55	57.23	...	...
December	3.99	4.00	4.49	...	...	...	5.00	4.69	4.58	5.28	3.70	59.06	...	...
1960														
January	3.99	4.00	4.35	2.02	2.33	...	5.00	4.72	4.61	5.34	3.72	58.03	...	...
February	3.97	4.00	3.96	2.14	1.82	...	5.00	4.49	4.56	5.34	3.60	55.78	...	...
March	3.84	4.00	3.31	2.05	1.26	...	5.00	4.25	4.49	5.25	3.57	55.02	...	...
April	3.92	4.00	3.23	1.99	1.24	...	5.00	4.28	4.45	5.20	3.56	55.73	...	...
May	3.85	4.00	3.29	2.04	1.25	...	5.00	4.35	4.46	5.28	3.60	55.22	...	...
June	3.32	3.65	2.46	1.81	0.65	...	5.00	4.15	4.45	5.26	3.55	57.26	...	...
July	3.23	3.50	2.30	1.76	0.54	...	5.00	3.90	4.41	5.22	3.50	55.84	...	...
August	2.98	3.18	2.30	1.75	0.55	...	4.85	3.80	4.28	5.08	3.33	56.51	...	...
September	2.60	3.00	2.48	1.57	0.91	...	4.50	3.80	4.25	5.01	3.42	54.81	...	...
October	2.47	3.00	2.30	1.45	0.85	...	4.50	3.89	4.30	5.11	3.53	53.73	...	...
November	2.44	3.00	2.37	1.54	0.83	...	4.50	3.93	4.31	5.08	3.40	55.47	...	...
December	1.98	3.00	2.25	1.36	0.89	...	4.50	3.84	4.35	5.10	3.40	56.80	...	...
1961														
January	1.45	3.00	2.24	1.34	0.90	...	4.50	3.84	4.32	5.10	3.39	59.72	...	...
February	2.54	3.00	2.42	1.26	1.16	...	4.50	3.78	4.27	5.07	3.31	62.17	...	...
March	2.02	3.00	2.39	1.28	1.11	...	4.50	3.74	4.22	5.02	3.45	64.12	...	...
April	1.49	3.00	2.29	1.24	1.05	...	4.50	3.78	4.25	5.01	3.48	65.83	...	...
May	1.98	3.00	2.29	1.21	1.08	...	4.50	3.71	4.27	5.01	3.43	66.50	...	...
June	1.73	3.00	2.33	1.29	1.04	...	4.50	3.88	4.33	5.03	3.52	65.62	...	...
July	1.17	3.00	2.24	1.27	0.97	...	4.50	3.92	4.41	5.09	3.51	65.44	...	...
August	2.00	3.00	2.39	1.23	1.16	...	4.50	4.04	4.45	5.11	3.52	67.79	...	...
September	1.88	3.00	2.28	1.35	0.93	...	4.50	3.98	4.45	5.12	3.53	67.26	...	...
October	2.26	3.00	2.30	1.32	0.98	...	4.50	3.92	4.42	5.13	3.42	68.00	...	...
November	2.61	3.00	2.48	1.07	1.41	...	4.50	3.94	4.39	5.11	3.41	71.08	...	...
December	2.33	3.00	2.60	1.19	1.41	...	4.50	4.06	4.42	5.10	3.47	71.74	...	...
1962														
January	2.15	3.00	2.72	1.30	1.42	...	4.50	4.08	4.42	5.08	3.34	69.07	...	...
February	2.37	3.00	2.73	1.37	1.36	...	4.50	4.04	4.42	5.07	3.21	70.22	...	...
March	2.85	3.00	2.72	1.56	1.16	...	4.50	3.93	4.39	5.04	3.14	70.29	...	...
April	2.78	3.00	2.73	1.44	1.29	...	4.50	3.84	4.33	5.02	3.06	68.05	...	...
May	2.36	3.00	2.69	1.45	1.24	...	4.50	3.87	4.28	5.00	3.11	62.99	...	...
June	2.68	3.00	2.73	1.49	1.24	...	4.50	3.91	4.28	5.02	3.25	55.63	...	...
July	2.71	3.00	2.92	1.40	1.52	...	4.50	4.01	4.34	5.05	3.27	56.97	...	...
August	2.93	3.00	2.82	1.30	1.52	...	4.50	3.98	4.35	5.06	3.23	58.52	...	...
September	2.90	3.00	2.78	1.29	1.49	...	4.50	3.98	4.32	5.03	3.11	58.00	...	...
October	2.90	3.00	2.74	1.25	1.49	...	4.50	3.93	4.28	4.99	3.02	56.17	...	...
November	2.94	3.00	2.83	1.29	1.54	...	4.50	3.92	4.25	4.96	3.04	60.04	...	...
December	2.93	3.00	2.87	1.23	1.64	...	4.50	3.86	4.24	4.92	3.07	62.64	...	...
1963														
January	2.92	3.00	2.91	1.31	1.60	...	4.50	3.83	4.21	4.91	3.10	65.06	...	...
February	3.00	3.00	2.92	1.25	1.67	...	4.50	3.92	4.19	4.89	3.15	65.92	...	...
March	2.98	3.00	2.89	1.07	1.82	...	4.50	3.93	4.19	4.88	3.05	65.67	...	...
April	2.90	3.00	2.90	1.16	1.74	...	4.50	3.97	4.21	4.87	3.10	68.76	...	...
May	3.00	3.00	2.93	1.20	1.73	...	4.50	3.93	4.22	4.85	3.11	70.14	...	...
June	2.99	3.00	2.99	1.18	1.81	...	4.50	3.99	4.23	4.84	3.21	70.11	...	...
July	3.02	3.24	3.18	1.19	1.99	...	4.50	4.02	4.26	4.84	3.22	69.07	...	...
August	3.49	3.50	3.32	1.27	2.05	...	4.50	4.00	4.29	4.83	3.13	70.98	...	...
September	3.48	3.50	3.38	1.26	2.12	...	4.50	4.08	4.31	4.84	3.20	72.85	...	...
October	3.50	3.50	3.45	1.50	1.95	...	4.50	4.11	4.32	4.83	3.20	73.03	...	...
November	3.48	3.50	3.52	1.52	2.00	...	4.50	4.12	4.33	4.84	3.30	72.62	...	...
December	3.38	3.50	3.52	1.64	1.88	...	4.50	4.13	4.35	4.85	3.27	74.17	...	...
1964														
January	3.48	3.50	3.52	1.59	1.93	...	4.50	4.17	4.39	4.83	3.22	76.45	...	...
February	3.48	3.50	3.53	1.68	1.85	...	4.50	4.15	4.36	4.83	3.14	77.39	...	...
March	3.43	3.50	3.54	1.72	1.82	...	4.50	4.22	4.38	4.83	3.28	78.80	...	...
April	3.47	3.50	3.47	1.71	1.76	...	4.50	4.23	4.40	4.85	3.28	79.94	...	...
May	3.50	3.50	3.48	1.62	1.86	...	4.50	4.20	4.41	4.85	3.20	80.72	...	...
June	3.50	3.50	3.48	1.53	1.95	...	4.50	4.17	4.41	4.85	3.20	80.24	...	...
July	3.42	3.50	3.46	1.54	1.92	...	4.50	4.19	4.40	4.83	3.18	83.22	...	...
August	3.50	3.50	3.50	1.59	1.91	...	4.50	4.19	4.41	4.82	3.19	82.00	...	...
September	3.45	3.50	3.53	1.46	2.07	...	4.50	4.20	4.42	4.82	3.23	83.41	...	...
October	3.36	3.50	3.57	1.28	2.29	...	4.50	4.19	4.42	4.81	3.25	84.85	...	...
November	3.52	3.62	3.64	1.33	2.31	...	4.50	4.15	4.43	4.81	3.18	85.44	...	...
December	3.85	4.00	3.84	1.33	2.51	...	4.50	4.18	4.44	4.81	3.13	83.96	...	...

[1]Federal Reserve Bank of New York. Through 2002, represents the rate for adjustment credit. Beginning in 2003, represents the rate for primary credit. See notes and definitions for more information.
[2]Beginning 1960, PCE except food and energy; before then, CPI-U.
[3]Prior to September 1997, this series represents both nonfinancial and financial commercial paper rates. Beginning September 1997, rates for financial companies only are shown. See notes and definitions for more information.
. . . = Not available.

Table 12-9B. Summary Interest Rates, Bond Yields, and Stock Prices: Historical—*Continued*

(Percent per annum, except as noted.)

Year and month	Federal funds interest rate	Federal Reserve discount rate[1]	U.S. Treasury bills, secondary market, 3-month	Inflation[2]	Real 3-month Treasury bill rate	Commercial paper, 3-month[3]	Bank prime rate	Treasury 10-year nominal yields	Domestic corporate (Moody's) Aaa	Domestic corporate (Moody's) Baa	State and local bonds (Bond Buyer)	Index, 1941-1943 = 10	Dividend-price ratio	Earnings-price ratio
1965														
January	3.90	4.00	3.81	1.31	2.50	. . .	4.50	4.19	4.43	4.80	3.06	86.12	. . .	. . .
February	3.98	4.00	3.93	1.23	2.70	. . .	4.50	4.21	4.41	4.78	3.09	86.75	. . .	. . .
March	4.04	4.00	3.93	1.19	2.74	. . .	4.50	4.21	4.42	4.78	3.17	86.83	. . .	. . .
April	4.09	4.00	3.93	1.21	2.72	. . .	4.50	4.20	4.43	4.80	3.15	87.97	. . .	. . .
May	4.10	4.00	3.89	1.30	2.59	. . .	4.50	4.21	4.44	4.81	3.17	89.28	. . .	. . .
June	4.04	4.00	3.80	1.20	2.60	. . .	4.50	4.21	4.46	4.85	3.24	85.04	. . .	. . .
July	4.09	4.00	3.84	1.19	2.65	. . .	4.50	4.20	4.48	4.88	3.27	84.91	. . .	. . .
August	4.12	4.00	3.84	1.25	2.59	. . .	4.50	4.25	4.49	4.88	3.24	86.49	. . .	. . .
September	4.01	4.00	3.92	1.32	2.60	. . .	4.50	4.29	4.52	4.91	3.35	89.38	. . .	. . .
October	4.08	4.00	4.03	1.24	2.79	. . .	4.50	4.35	4.56	4.93	3.40	91.39	. . .	. . .
November	4.10	4.00	4.09	1.28	2.81	. . .	4.50	4.45	4.60	4.95	3.45	92.15	. . .	. . .
December	4.32	4.42	4.38	1.45	2.93	. . .	4.92	4.62	4.68	5.02	3.54	91.73	. . .	. . .
1966														
January	4.42	4.50	4.59	1.35	3.24	. . .	5.00	4.61	4.74	5.06	3.52	93.32	. . .	. . .
February	4.60	4.50	4.65	1.48	3.17	. . .	5.00	4.83	4.78	5.12	3.64	92.69	. . .	. . .
March	4.65	4.50	4.59	1.56	3.03	. . .	5.35	4.87	4.92	5.32	3.72	88.88	. . .	. . .
April	4.67	4.50	4.62	1.80	2.82	. . .	5.50	4.75	4.96	5.41	3.56	91.60	. . .	. . .
May	4.90	4.50	4.64	1.89	2.75	. . .	5.50	4.78	4.98	5.48	3.65	86.78	. . .	. . .
June	5.17	4.50	4.50	2.25	2.25	. . .	5.52	4.81	5.07	5.58	3.77	86.06	. . .	. . .
July	5.30	4.50	4.80	2.45	2.35	. . .	5.75	5.02	5.16	5.68	3.95	85.84	. . .	. . .
August	5.53	4.50	4.96	2.44	2.52	. . .	5.88	5.22	5.31	5.83	4.12	80.65	. . .	. . .
September	5.40	4.50	5.37	2.64	2.73	. . .	6.00	5.18	5.49	6.09	4.12	77.81	. . .	. . .
October	5.53	4.50	5.35	3.02	2.33	. . .	6.00	5.01	5.41	6.10	3.93	77.13	. . .	. . .
November	5.76	4.50	5.32	3.09	2.23	. . .	6.00	5.16	5.35	6.13	3.86	80.99	. . .	. . .
December	5.40	4.50	4.96	3.09	1.87	. . .	6.00	4.84	5.39	6.18	3.86	81.33	. . .	. . .
1967														
January	4.94	4.50	4.72	3.15	1.57	. . .	5.96	4.58	5.20	5.97	3.54	84.45	. . .	. . .
February	5.00	4.50	4.56	3.08	1.48	. . .	5.75	4.63	5.03	5.82	3.52	87.36	. . .	. . .
March	4.53	4.50	4.26	3.09	1.17	. . .	5.71	4.54	5.13	5.85	3.55	89.42	. . .	. . .
April	4.05	4.10	3.84	3.02	0.82	. . .	5.50	4.59	5.11	5.83	3.60	90.96	. . .	. . .
May	3.94	4.00	3.60	2.97	0.63	. . .	5.50	4.85	5.24	5.96	3.89	92.59	. . .	. . .
June	3.98	4.00	3.54	2.89	0.65	. . .	5.50	5.02	5.44	6.15	3.96	91.43	. . .	. . .
July	3.79	4.00	4.21	2.93	1.28	. . .	5.50	5.16	5.58	6.26	4.02	93.01	. . .	. . .
August	3.90	4.00	4.27	3.06	1.21	. . .	5.50	5.28	5.62	6.33	3.99	94.49	. . .	. . .
September	3.99	4.00	4.42	3.10	1.32	. . .	5.50	5.30	5.65	6.40	4.12	95.81	. . .	. . .
October	3.88	4.00	4.56	3.14	1.42	. . .	5.50	5.48	5.82	6.52	4.29	95.66	. . .	. . .
November	4.13	4.18	4.73	3.20	1.53	. . .	5.68	5.75	6.07	6.72	4.34	92.66	. . .	. . .
December	4.51	4.50	4.97	3.14	1.83	. . .	6.00	5.70	6.19	6.93	4.43	95.30	. . .	. . .
1968														
January	4.60	4.50	5.00	3.49	1.51	. . .	6.00	5.53	6.17	6.84	4.29	95.04	. . .	. . .
February	4.71	4.50	4.98	3.75	1.23	. . .	6.00	5.56	6.10	6.80	4.31	90.75	. . .	. . .
March	5.05	4.66	5.17	4.01	1.16	. . .	6.00	5.74	6.11	6.85	4.54	89.09	. . .	. . .
April	5.76	5.20	5.38	4.10	1.28	. . .	6.20	5.64	6.21	6.97	4.34	95.67	. . .	. . .
May	6.11	5.50	5.66	4.26	1.40	. . .	6.50	5.87	6.27	7.03	4.54	97.87	. . .	. . .
June	6.07	5.50	5.52	4.40	1.12	. . .	6.50	5.72	6.28	7.07	4.49	100.53	. . .	. . .
July	6.02	5.50	5.31	4.40	0.91	. . .	6.50	5.50	6.24	6.98	4.33	100.30	. . .	. . .
August	6.03	5.48	5.09	4.49	0.60	. . .	6.50	5.42	6.02	6.82	4.21	98.11	. . .	. . .
September	5.78	5.25	5.19	4.55	0.64	. . .	6.45	5.46	5.97	6.79	4.38	101.34	. . .	. . .
October	5.91	5.25	5.35	4.59	0.76	. . .	6.25	5.58	6.09	6.84	4.49	103.76	. . .	. . .
November	5.82	5.25	5.45	4.65	0.80	. . .	6.25	5.70	6.19	7.01	4.60	105.40	. . .	. . .
December	6.02	5.36	5.96	4.71	1.25	. . .	6.60	6.03	6.45	7.23	4.82	106.48	. . .	. . .
1969														
January	6.30	5.50	6.14	4.67	1.47	. . .	6.95	6.04	6.59	7.32	4.85	102.04	. . .	. . .
February	6.61	5.50	6.12	4.58	1.54	. . .	7.00	6.19	6.66	7.30	4.98	101.46	. . .	. . .
March	6.79	5.50	6.02	4.66	1.36	. . .	7.24	6.30	6.85	7.51	5.26	99.30	. . .	. . .
April	7.41	5.95	6.11	4.68	1.43	. . .	7.50	6.17	6.89	7.54	5.19	101.26	. . .	. . .
May	8.67	6.00	6.04	4.71	1.33	. . .	7.50	6.32	6.79	7.52	5.33	104.62	. . .	. . .
June	8.90	6.00	6.44	4.66	1.78	. . .	8.23	6.57	6.98	7.70	5.75	99.14	. . .	. . .
July	8.61	6.00	7.00	4.80	2.20	. . .	8.50	6.72	7.08	7.84	5.75	94.71	. . .	. . .
August	9.19	6.00	6.98	4.69	2.29	. . .	8.50	6.69	6.97	7.86	6.00	94.18	. . .	. . .
September	9.15	6.00	7.09	4.69	2.40	. . .	8.50	7.16	7.14	8.05	6.26	94.51	. . .	. . .
October	9.00	6.00	7.00	4.71	2.29	. . .	8.50	7.10	7.33	8.22	6.09	95.52	. . .	. . .
November	8.85	6.00	7.24	4.72	2.52	. . .	8.50	7.14	7.35	8.25	6.30	96.21	. . .	. . .
December	8.97	6.00	7.82	4.78	3.04	. . .	8.50	7.65	7.72	8.65	6.82	91.11	. . .	. . .
1970														
January	8.98	6.00	7.87	4.72	3.15	. . .	8.50	7.79	7.91	8.86	6.63	90.31	. . .	. . .
February	8.98	6.00	7.13	4.76	2.37	. . .	8.50	7.24	7.93	8.78	6.22	87.16	. . .	. . .
March	7.76	6.00	6.63	4.66	1.97	. . .	8.39	7.07	7.84	8.63	6.05	88.65	. . .	. . .
April	8.10	6.00	6.51	4.67	1.84	. . .	8.00	7.39	7.83	8.70	6.65	85.95	. . .	. . .
May	7.94	6.00	6.84	4.61	2.23	. . .	8.00	7.91	8.11	8.98	7.00	76.06	. . .	. . .
June	7.60	6.00	6.68	4.63	2.05	. . .	8.00	7.84	8.48	9.25	6.93	75.59	. . .	. . .
July	7.21	6.00	6.45	4.54	1.91	. . .	8.00	7.46	8.44	9.40	6.42	75.72	. . .	. . .
August	6.61	6.00	6.41	4.61	1.80	. . .	8.00	7.53	8.13	9.44	6.17	77.92	. . .	. . .
September	6.29	6.00	6.12	4.62	1.50	. . .	7.83	7.39	8.09	9.39	6.31	82.58	. . .	. . .
October	6.20	6.00	5.91	4.69	1.22	. . .	7.50	7.33	8.03	9.33	6.37	84.37	. . .	. . .
November	5.60	5.85	5.28	4.82	0.46	. . .	7.28	6.84	8.05	9.38	5.71	84.28	. . .	. . .
December	4.90	5.52	4.87	4.96	-0.09	. . .	6.92	6.39	7.64	9.12	5.47	90.05	. . .	. . .

[1]Federal Reserve Bank of New York. Through 2002, represents the rate for adjustment credit. Beginning in 2003, represents the rate for primary credit. See notes and definitions for more information.
[2]Beginning 1960, PCE except food and energy; before then, CPI-U.
[3]Prior to September 1997, this series represents both nonfinancial and financial commercial paper rates. Beginning September 1997, rates for financial companies only are shown. See notes and definitions for more information.
. . . = Not available.

Table 12-9B. Summary Interest Rates, Bond Yields, and Stock Prices: Historical—*Continued*

(Percent per annum, except as noted.)

Year and month	Federal funds interest rate	Federal Reserve discount rate[1]	U.S. Treasury bills, secondary market, 3-month	Inflation[2]	Real 3-month Treasury bill rate	Commercial paper, 3-month [3]	Bank prime rate	Treasury 10-year nominal yields	Bond yields Domestic corporate (Moody's)		State and local bonds (Bond Buyer)	Standard and Poor's composite (500 stocks)		
									Aaa	Baa		Index, 1941-1943 = 10	Dividend-price ratio	Earnings-price ratio
1971														
January	4.14	5.23	4.44	5.03	-0.59	...	6.29	6.24	7.36	8.74	5.35	93.49	...	...
February	3.72	4.91	3.70	5.03	-1.33	...	5.88	6.11	7.08	8.39	5.23	97.11	...	...
March	3.71	4.75	3.38	4.97	-1.59	...	5.44	5.70	7.21	8.46	5.17	99.60	...	...
April	4.15	4.75	3.86	4.95	-1.09	4.57	5.28	5.83	7.25	8.45	5.37	103.04	...	...
May	4.63	4.75	4.14	5.04	-0.90	5.06	5.46	6.39	7.53	8.62	5.90	101.64	...	...
June	4.91	4.75	4.75	5.07	-0.32	5.38	5.50	6.52	7.64	8.75	5.95	99.72	...	...
July	5.31	4.88	5.40	5.07	0.33	5.75	5.91	6.73	7.64	8.76	6.06	99.00	...	...
August	5.56	5.00	4.94	4.86	0.08	5.74	6.00	6.58	7.59	8.76	5.82	97.24	...	...
September	5.55	5.00	4.69	4.60	0.09	5.69	6.00	6.14	7.44	8.59	5.37	99.40	...	...
October	5.20	5.00	4.46	4.25	0.21	5.42	5.90	5.93	7.39	8.48	5.06	97.29	...	...
November	4.91	4.90	4.22	3.95	0.27	4.84	5.53	5.81	7.26	8.38	5.20	92.78	...	...
December	4.14	4.63	4.01	3.75	0.26	4.66	5.49	5.93	7.25	8.38	5.21	99.17	...	...
1972														
January	3.50	4.50	3.38	3.79	-0.41	4.03	5.18	5.95	7.19	8.23	5.12	103.30	...	...
February	3.29	4.50	3.20	3.68	-0.48	3.81	4.75	6.08	7.27	8.23	5.28	105.24	...	...
March	3.83	4.50	3.73	3.55	0.18	4.10	4.75	6.07	7.24	8.24	5.31	107.69	...	...
April	4.17	4.50	3.71	3.40	0.31	4.55	4.97	6.19	7.30	8.24	5.43	108.81	...	...
May	4.27	4.50	3.69	3.19	0.50	4.45	5.00	6.13	7.30	8.23	5.30	107.65	...	...
June	4.46	4.50	3.91	2.99	0.92	4.60	5.04	6.11	7.23	8.20	5.33	108.01	...	...
July	4.55	4.50	3.98	2.90	1.08	4.83	5.25	6.11	7.21	8.23	5.41	107.21	...	...
August	4.80	4.50	4.02	2.97	1.05	4.75	5.27	6.21	7.19	8.19	5.30	111.01	...	...
September	4.87	4.50	4.66	3.14	1.52	5.07	5.50	6.55	7.22	8.09	5.36	109.39	...	...
October	5.04	4.50	4.74	3.04	1.70	5.21	5.73	6.48	7.21	8.06	5.18	109.56	...	...
November	5.06	4.50	4.78	3.08	1.70	5.18	5.75	6.28	7.12	7.99	5.02	115.05	...	...
December	5.33	4.50	5.07	3.06	2.01	5.40	5.79	6.36	7.08	7.93	5.05	117.50	...	...
1973														
January	5.94	4.77	5.41	2.69	2.72	5.77	6.00	6.46	7.15	7.90	5.05	118.42	...	...
February	6.58	5.05	5.60	2.74	2.86	6.17	6.02	6.64	7.22	7.97	5.13	114.16	...	...
March	7.09	5.50	6.09	2.95	3.14	6.76	6.30	6.71	7.29	8.03	5.29	112.42	...	...
April	7.12	5.50	6.26	3.31	2.95	7.13	6.61	6.67	7.26	8.09	5.15	110.27	...	...
May	7.84	5.90	6.36	3.47	2.89	7.26	7.01	6.85	7.29	8.06	5.15	107.22	...	...
June	8.49	6.33	7.19	3.71	3.48	8.00	7.49	6.90	7.37	8.13	5.17	104.75	...	...
July	10.40	6.98	8.01	3.85	4.16	9.26	8.30	7.13	7.45	8.24	5.40	105.83	...	...
August	10.50	7.29	8.67	4.11	4.56	10.26	9.23	7.40	7.68	8.53	5.48	103.80	...	...
September	10.78	7.50	8.29	4.29	4.00	10.31	9.86	7.09	7.63	8.63	5.10	105.61	...	...
October	10.01	7.50	7.22	4.64	2.58	9.14	9.94	6.79	7.60	8.41	5.05	109.84	...	...
November	10.03	7.50	7.83	4.87	2.96	9.11	9.75	6.73	7.67	8.42	5.18	102.03	...	...
December	9.95	7.50	7.45	5.13	2.32	9.28	9.75	6.74	7.68	8.48	5.12	94.78	...	...
1974														
January	9.65	7.50	7.77	5.57	2.20	8.86	9.73	6.99	7.83	8.48	5.22	96.11	...	...
February	8.97	7.50	7.12	5.92	1.20	8.00	9.21	6.96	7.85	8.53	5.20	93.45	...	...
March	9.35	7.50	7.96	6.30	1.66	8.64	8.85	7.21	8.01	8.62	5.40	97.44	...	...
April	10.51	7.60	8.33	6.49	1.84	9.92	10.02	7.51	8.25	8.87	5.73	92.46	...	...
May	11.31	8.00	8.23	7.09	1.14	10.82	11.25	7.58	8.37	9.05	6.02	89.67	...	...
June	11.93	8.00	7.90	7.73	0.17	11.18	11.54	7.54	8.47	9.27	6.13	89.79	...	...
July	12.92	8.00	7.55	8.22	-0.67	11.93	11.97	7.81	8.72	9.48	6.68	82.82	...	...
August	12.01	8.00	8.96	8.76	0.20	11.79	12.00	8.04	9.00	9.77	6.71	76.03	...	...
September	11.34	8.00	8.06	9.19	-1.13	11.36	12.00	8.04	9.24	10.18	6.76	68.12	...	...
October	10.06	8.00	7.46	9.61	-2.15	9.55	11.68	7.90	9.27	10.48	6.57	69.44	...	...
November	9.45	8.00	7.47	9.88	-2.41	8.95	10.83	7.68	8.89	10.60	6.61	71.74	...	...
December	8.53	7.81	7.15	10.05	-2.90	9.18	10.50	7.43	8.89	10.63	7.05	67.07	...	...
1975														
January	7.13	7.40	6.26	10.16	-3.90	7.39	10.05	7.50	8.83	10.81	6.82	72.56	...	...
February	6.24	6.82	5.50	10.23	-4.73	6.36	8.96	7.39	8.62	10.65	6.39	80.10	...	...
March	5.54	6.40	5.49	9.96	-4.47	6.06	7.93	7.73	8.67	10.48	6.73	83.78	...	...
April	5.49	6.25	5.61	9.68	-4.07	6.11	7.50	8.23	8.95	10.58	6.95	84.72	...	...
May	5.22	6.12	5.23	9.09	-3.86	5.70	7.40	8.06	8.90	10.69	6.97	90.10	...	...
June	5.55	6.00	5.34	8.51	-3.17	5.67	7.07	7.86	8.77	10.62	6.94	92.40	...	...
July	6.10	6.00	6.13	8.22	-2.09	6.32	7.15	8.06	8.84	10.55	7.07	92.49	...	...
August	6.14	6.00	6.44	7.56	-1.12	6.59	7.66	8.40	8.95	10.59	7.17	85.71	...	...
September	6.24	6.00	6.42	7.18	-0.76	6.79	7.88	8.43	8.95	10.61	7.44	84.67	...	...
October	5.82	6.00	5.96	6.88	-0.92	6.35	7.96	8.14	8.86	10.62	7.39	88.57	...	...
November	5.22	6.00	5.48	6.80	-1.32	5.78	7.53	8.05	8.78	10.56	7.43	90.07	...	...
December	5.20	6.00	5.44	6.69	-1.25	5.88	7.26	8.00	8.79	10.56	7.31	88.70	...	...
1976														
January	4.87	5.79	4.87	6.62	-1.75	5.16	7.00	7.74	8.60	10.41	7.07	96.86	...	...
February	4.77	5.50	4.88	6.29	-1.41	5.13	6.75	7.79	8.55	10.24	6.94	100.64	...	...
March	4.84	5.50	5.00	6.08	-1.08	5.25	6.75	7.73	8.52	10.12	6.91	101.08	...	...
April	4.82	5.50	4.86	5.98	-1.12	5.09	6.75	7.56	8.40	9.94	6.60	101.93	...	...
May	5.29	5.50	5.20	6.03	-0.83	5.44	6.75	7.90	8.58	9.86	6.87	101.16	...	...
June	5.48	5.50	5.41	5.94	-0.53	5.83	7.20	7.86	8.62	9.89	6.87	101.77	...	...
July	5.31	5.50	5.23	5.86	-0.63	5.54	7.25	7.83	8.56	9.82	6.79	104.20	...	...
August	5.29	5.50	5.14	6.11	-0.97	5.36	7.01	7.77	8.45	9.64	6.61	103.29	...	...
September	5.25	5.50	5.08	6.15	-1.07	5.33	7.00	7.59	8.38	9.40	6.51	105.45	...	...
October	5.02	5.50	4.92	6.14	-1.22	5.10	6.77	7.41	8.32	9.29	6.30	101.89	...	...
November	4.95	5.43	4.75	5.92	-1.17	4.98	6.50	7.29	8.25	9.23	6.29	101.19	...	...
December	4.65	5.25	4.35	5.85	-1.50	4.66	6.35	6.87	7.98	9.12	5.94	104.66	...	...

[1] Federal Reserve Bank of New York. Through 2002, represents the rate for adjustment credit. Beginning in 2003, represents the rate for primary credit. See notes and definitions for more information.
[2] Beginning 1960, PCE except food and energy; before then, CPI-U.
[3] Prior to September 1997, this series represents both nonfinancial and financial commercial paper rates. Beginning September 1997, rates for financial companies only are shown. See notes and definitions for more information.
. . . = Not available.

Table 12-9B. Summary Interest Rates, Bond Yields, and Stock Prices: Historical—*Continued*

(Percent per annum, except as noted.)

Year and month	Federal funds interest rate	Federal Reserve discount rate[1]	U.S. Treasury bills, secondary market, 3-month	Inflation[2]	Real 3-month Treasury bill rate	Commercial paper, 3-month[3]	Bank prime rate	Treasury 10-year nominal yields	Bond yields Domestic corporate (Moody's) Aaa	Bond yields Domestic corporate (Moody's) Baa	State and local bonds (Bond Buyer)	Standard and Poor's composite (500 stocks) Index, 1941-1943 = 10	Dividend-price ratio	Earnings-price ratio
1977														
January	4.61	5.25	4.62	5.94	-1.32	4.72	6.25	7.21	7.96	9.08	5.87	103.81	. . .	. . .
February	4.68	5.25	4.67	6.16	-1.49	4.76	6.25	7.39	8.04	9.12	5.88	100.96	. . .	. . .
March	4.69	5.25	4.60	6.26	-1.66	4.75	6.25	7.46	8.10	9.12	5.89	100.57	. . .	. . .
April	4.73	5.25	4.54	6.37	-1.83	4.75	6.25	7.37	8.04	9.07	5.72	99.05	. . .	. . .
May	5.35	5.25	4.96	6.42	-1.46	5.26	6.41	7.46	8.05	9.01	5.75	98.76	. . .	. . .
June	5.39	5.25	5.02	6.62	-1.60	5.42	6.75	7.28	7.95	8.91	5.62	99.29	. . .	. . .
July	5.42	5.25	5.19	6.70	-1.51	5.39	6.75	7.33	7.94	8.87	5.63	100.18	. . .	. . .
August	5.90	5.27	5.49	6.61	-1.12	5.76	6.83	7.40	7.98	8.82	5.62	97.75	. . .	. . .
September ...	6.14	5.75	5.81	6.44	-0.63	6.10	7.13	7.34	7.92	8.80	5.51	96.23	. . .	. . .
October	6.47	5.80	6.16	6.44	-0.28	6.51	7.52	7.52	8.04	8.89	5.64	93.74	. . .	. . .
November	6.51	6.00	6.10	6.51	-0.41	6.54	7.75	7.58	8.08	8.95	5.49	94.28	. . .	. . .
December	6.56	6.00	6.07	6.51	-0.44	6.61	7.75	7.69	8.19	8.99	5.57	93.82	. . .	. . .
1978														
January	6.70	6.37	6.44	6.52	-0.08	6.75	7.93	7.96	8.41	9.17	5.71	90.25	. . .	. . .
February	6.78	6.50	6.45	6.29	0.16	6.76	8.00	8.03	8.47	9.20	5.62	88.98	. . .	. . .
March	6.79	6.50	6.29	6.42	-0.13	6.75	8.00	8.04	8.47	9.22	5.61	88.82	. . .	. . .
April	6.89	6.50	6.29	6.58	-0.29	6.82	8.00	8.15	8.56	9.32	5.79	92.71	. . .	. . .
May	7.36	6.84	6.41	6.66	-0.25	7.06	8.27	8.35	8.69	9.49	6.03	97.41	. . .	. . .
June	7.60	7.00	6.73	6.63	0.10	7.59	8.63	8.46	8.76	9.60	6.22	97.66	. . .	. . .
July	7.81	7.23	7.01	6.59	0.42	7.85	9.00	8.64	8.88	9.60	6.28	97.19	. . .	. . .
August	8.04	7.43	7.08	6.64	0.44	7.83	9.01	8.41	8.69	9.48	6.12	103.92	. . .	. . .
September ...	8.45	7.83	7.85	6.80	1.05	8.39	9.41	8.42	8.69	9.42	6.09	103.86	. . .	. . .
October	8.96	8.26	7.99	7.06	0.93	8.98	9.94	8.64	8.89	9.59	6.13	100.58	. . .	. . .
November	9.76	9.50	8.64	7.08	1.56	10.14	10.94	8.81	9.03	9.83	6.19	94.71	. . .	. . .
December	10.03	9.50	9.08	6.93	2.15	10.37	11.55	9.01	9.16	9.94	6.50	96.11	. . .	. . .
1979														
January	10.07	9.50	9.35	6.81	2.54	10.25	11.75	9.10	9.25	10.13	6.46	99.71	. . .	. . .
February	10.06	9.50	9.32	6.74	2.58	9.95	11.75	9.10	9.26	10.08	6.31	98.23	. . .	. . .
March	10.09	9.50	9.48	6.77	2.71	9.90	11.75	9.12	9.37	10.26	6.33	100.11	. . .	. . .
April	10.01	9.50	9.46	7.06	2.40	9.85	11.75	9.18	9.38	10.33	6.28	102.07	. . .	. . .
May	10.24	9.50	9.61	7.35	2.26	9.95	11.75	9.25	9.50	10.47	6.25	99.73	. . .	. . .
June	10.29	9.50	9.06	7.35	1.71	9.76	11.65	8.91	9.29	10.38	6.12	101.73	. . .	. . .
July	10.47	9.69	9.24	7.25	1.99	9.87	11.54	8.95	9.20	10.29	6.13	102.71	. . .	. . .
August	10.94	10.24	9.52	7.38	2.14	10.42	11.91	9.03	9.23	10.35	6.20	107.36	. . .	. . .
September ...	11.43	10.70	10.26	7.49	2.77	11.63	12.90	9.33	9.44	10.54	6.52	108.60	. . .	. . .
October	13.77	11.77	11.70	7.48	4.22	13.23	14.39	10.30	10.13	11.40	7.08	104.47	. . .	. . .
November	13.18	12.00	11.79	7.59	4.20	13.57	15.55	10.65	10.76	11.99	7.30	103.66	. . .	. . .
December	13.78	12.00	12.04	7.94	4.10	13.24	15.30	10.39	10.74	12.06	7.22	107.78	. . .	. . .
1980														
January	13.82	12.00	12.00	8.21	3.79	13.04	15.25	10.80	11.09	12.42	7.35	110.87	. . .	. . .
February	14.13	12.52	12.86	8.93	3.93	13.78	15.63	12.41	12.38	13.57	8.16	115.34	. . .	. . .
March	17.19	13.00	15.20	9.31	5.89	16.81	18.31	12.75	12.96	14.45	9.16	104.69	. . .	. . .
April	17.61	13.00	13.20	8.87	4.33	15.78	19.77	11.47	12.04	14.19	8.63	102.97	. . .	. . .
May	10.98	12.94	8.58	8.80	-0.22	9.49	16.57	10.18	10.99	13.17	7.59	107.69	. . .	. . .
June	9.47	11.40	7.07	8.91	-1.84	8.27	12.63	9.78	10.58	12.71	7.63	114.55	. . .	. . .
July	9.03	10.87	8.06	9.13	-1.07	8.41	11.48	10.25	11.07	12.65	8.13	119.83	. . .	. . .
August	9.61	10.00	9.13	9.20	-0.07	9.57	11.12	11.10	11.64	13.15	8.67	123.50	. . .	. . .
September ...	10.87	10.17	10.27	9.48	0.79	10.97	12.23	11.51	12.02	13.70	8.94	126.51	. . .	. . .
October	12.81	11.00	11.62	9.58	2.04	12.52	13.79	11.75	12.31	14.23	9.11	130.22	. . .	. . .
November	15.85	11.47	13.73	9.74	3.99	15.18	16.06	12.68	12.97	14.64	9.56	135.65	. . .	. . .
December	18.90	12.87	15.49	9.62	5.87	18.07	20.35	12.84	13.21	15.14	10.20	133.48	. . .	. . .
1981														
January	19.08	13.00	15.02	9.74	5.28	16.58	20.16	12.57	12.81	15.03	9.66	132.97	. . .	. . .
February	15.93	13.00	14.79	9.46	5.33	15.49	19.43	13.19	13.35	15.37	10.09	128.40	. . .	. . .
March	14.70	13.00	13.36	9.06	4.30	13.94	18.05	13.12	13.33	15.34	10.16	133.19	. . .	. . .
April	15.72	13.00	13.69	9.18	4.51	14.56	17.15	13.68	13.88	15.56	10.62	134.43	. . .	. . .
May	18.52	13.87	16.30	9.05	7.25	17.56	19.61	14.10	14.32	15.95	10.77	131.73	. . .	. . .
June	19.10	14.00	14.73	8.87	5.86	16.32	20.03	13.47	13.75	15.80	10.67	132.28	. . .	. . .
July	19.04	14.00	14.95	8.77	6.18	17.00	20.39	14.28	14.38	16.17	11.14	129.13	. . .	. . .
August	17.82	14.00	15.51	8.71	6.80	17.23	20.50	14.94	14.89	16.34	12.26	129.63	. . .	. . .
September ...	15.87	14.00	14.70	8.40	6.30	16.09	20.08	15.32	15.49	16.92	12.92	118.27	. . .	. . .
October	15.08	14.00	13.54	8.15	5.39	14.85	18.45	15.15	15.40	17.11	12.83	119.80	. . .	. . .
November	13.31	13.03	10.86	7.93	2.93	12.16	16.84	13.39	14.22	16.39	11.89	122.92	. . .	. . .
December	12.37	12.10	10.85	7.67	3.18	12.12	15.75	13.72	14.23	16.55	12.91	123.79	. . .	. . .
1982														
January	13.22	12.00	12.28	7.39	4.89	13.09	15.75	14.59	15.18	17.10	13.28	117.28	. . .	. . .
February	14.78	12.00	13.48	7.02	6.46	14.53	16.56	14.43	15.27	17.18	12.97	114.50	. . .	. . .
March	14.68	12.00	12.68	6.89	5.79	13.80	16.50	13.86	14.58	16.82	12.82	110.84	. . .	. . .
April	14.94	12.00	12.70	6.64	6.06	14.06	16.50	13.87	14.46	16.78	12.58	116.31	. . .	. . .
May	14.45	12.00	12.09	6.49	5.60	13.42	16.50	13.62	14.26	16.64	11.95	116.35	. . .	. . .
June	14.15	12.00	12.47	6.49	5.98	13.96	16.50	14.30	14.81	16.92	12.44	109.70	. . .	. . .
July	12.59	11.81	11.35	6.54	4.81	12.94	16.26	13.95	14.61	16.80	12.28	109.38	. . .	. . .
August	10.12	10.68	8.68	6.32	2.36	10.15	14.39	13.06	13.71	16.32	11.23	109.65	. . .	. . .
September ...	10.31	10.00	7.92	6.03	1.89	10.36	13.50	12.34	12.94	15.63	10.66	122.43	. . .	. . .
October	9.71	9.68	7.71	6.07	1.64	9.20	12.52	10.91	12.12	14.73	9.68	132.66	. . .	. . .
November	9.20	9.35	8.07	5.86	2.21	8.69	11.85	10.55	11.68	14.30	10.06	138.10	. . .	. . .
December	8.95	8.73	7.94	5.82	2.12	8.51	11.50	10.54	11.83	14.14	9.96	139.37	. . .	. . .

[1]Federal Reserve Bank of New York. Through 2002, represents the rate for adjustment credit. Beginning in 2003, represents the rate for primary credit. See notes and definitions for more information.
[2]Beginning 1960, PCE except food and energy; before then, CPI-U.
[3]Prior to September 1997, this series represents both nonfinancial and financial commercial paper rates. Beginning September 1997, rates for financial companies only are shown. See notes and definitions for more information.
. . . = Not available.

Table 12-9B. Summary Interest Rates, Bond Yields, and Stock Prices: Historical—*Continued*
(Percent per annum, except as noted.)

Year and month	Federal funds interest rate	Federal Reserve discount rate[1]	U.S. Treasury bills, secondary market, 3-month	Inflation[2]	Real 3-month Treasury bill rate	Commer-cial paper, 3-month[3]	Bank prime rate	Treasury 10-year nominal yields	Bond yields Domestic corporate (Moody's) Aaa	Baa	State and local bonds (Bond Buyer)	Standard and Poor's composite (500 stocks) Index, 1941-1943 = 10	Dividend-price ratio	Earnings-price ratio
1983														
January	8.68	8.50	7.86	5.93	1.93	8.17	11.16	10.46	11.79	13.94	9.50	144.27	...	...
February	8.51	8.50	8.11	5.93	2.18	8.34	10.98	10.72	12.01	13.95	9.58	146.80	...	...
March	8.77	8.50	8.35	5.62	2.73	8.52	10.50	10.51	11.73	13.61	9.20	151.88	...	...
April	8.80	8.50	8.21	5.53	2.68	8.53	10.50	10.40	11.51	13.29	9.04	157.71	...	...
May	8.63	8.50	8.19	5.11	3.08	8.33	10.50	10.38	11.46	13.09	9.11	164.10	...	...
June	8.98	8.50	8.79	5.08	3.71	9.00	10.50	10.85	11.74	13.37	9.52	166.39	...	...
July	9.37	8.50	9.08	5.11	3.97	9.25	10.50	11.38	12.15	13.39	9.53	166.96	...	...
August	9.56	8.50	9.34	5.17	4.17	9.54	10.89	11.85	12.51	13.64	9.72	162.42	...	...
September	9.45	8.50	9.00	5.20	3.80	9.24	11.00	11.65	12.37	13.55	9.58	167.16	...	...
October	9.48	8.50	8.64	4.73	3.91	8.99	11.00	11.54	12.25	13.46	9.66	167.65	...	...
November	9.34	8.50	8.76	4.57	4.19	9.10	11.00	11.69	12.41	13.61	9.74	165.23	...	...
December	9.47	8.50	9.00	4.31	4.69	9.53	11.00	11.83	12.57	13.75	9.89	164.36	...	...
1984														
January	9.56	8.50	8.90	3.91	4.99	9.20	11.00	11.67	12.20	13.65	9.63	166.39	...	...
February	9.59	8.50	9.09	4.17	4.92	9.32	11.00	11.84	12.08	13.59	9.64	157.25	...	...
March	9.91	8.50	9.52	4.43	5.09	9.83	11.21	12.32	12.57	13.99	9.94	157.44	...	...
April	10.29	8.87	9.69	4.60	5.09	10.18	11.93	12.63	12.81	14.31	9.96	157.60	...	...
May	10.32	9.00	9.83	4.69	5.14	10.65	12.39	13.41	13.28	14.74	10.49	156.55	...	...
June	11.06	9.00	9.87	4.45	5.42	10.98	12.60	13.56	13.55	15.05	10.67	153.12	...	...
July	11.23	9.00	10.12	4.20	5.92	11.19	13.00	13.36	13.44	15.15	10.42	151.08	...	...
August	11.64	9.00	10.47	4.00	6.47	11.18	13.00	12.72	12.87	14.63	9.99	164.42	...	...
September	11.30	9.00	10.37	3.74	6.63	11.04	12.97	12.52	12.66	14.35	10.10	166.11	...	...
October	9.99	9.00	9.74	3.79	5.95	10.12	12.58	12.16	12.63	13.94	10.25	164.82	...	...
November	9.43	8.83	8.61	3.78	4.83	9.03	11.77	11.57	12.29	13.48	10.17	166.27	...	...
December	8.38	8.37	8.06	4.11	3.95	8.44	11.06	11.50	12.13	13.40	9.95	164.48	...	...
1985														
January	8.35	8.00	7.76	4.35	3.41	8.03	10.61	11.38	12.08	13.26	9.51	171.61	...	...
February	8.50	8.00	8.27	4.26	4.01	8.54	10.50	11.51	12.13	13.23	9.65	180.88	...	...
March	8.58	8.00	8.52	4.24	4.28	8.90	10.50	11.86	12.56	13.69	9.77	179.42	...	...
April	8.27	8.00	7.95	3.89	4.06	8.37	10.50	11.43	12.23	13.51	9.42	180.62	...	...
May	7.97	7.81	7.48	4.02	3.46	7.83	10.31	10.85	11.72	13.15	9.01	184.90	...	...
June	7.53	7.50	6.95	4.12	2.83	7.35	9.78	10.16	10.94	12.40	8.69	188.89	...	...
July	7.88	7.50	7.08	3.98	3.10	7.56	9.50	10.31	10.97	12.43	8.81	192.54	...	...
August	7.90	7.50	7.14	4.15	2.99	7.72	9.50	10.33	11.05	12.50	9.08	188.31	...	...
September	7.92	7.50	7.10	4.20	2.90	7.83	9.50	10.37	11.07	12.48	9.27	184.06	...	...
October	7.99	7.50	7.16	4.12	3.04	7.80	9.50	10.24	11.02	12.36	9.08	186.18	...	...
November	8.05	7.50	7.24	4.14	3.10	7.77	9.50	9.78	10.55	11.99	8.54	197.45	...	...
December	8.27	7.50	7.10	4.02	3.08	7.75	9.50	9.26	10.16	11.58	8.42	207.26	...	...
1986														
January	8.14	7.50	7.07	4.00	3.07	7.71	9.50	9.19	10.05	11.44	8.08	208.19	...	...
February	7.86	7.50	7.06	3.72	3.34	7.63	9.50	8.70	9.67	11.11	7.44	219.37	...	...
March	7.48	7.10	6.56	3.65	2.91	7.20	9.10	7.78	9.00	10.50	7.08	232.33	...	...
April	6.99	6.83	6.06	3.69	2.37	6.60	8.83	7.30	8.79	10.19	7.19	237.98	...	...
May	6.85	6.50	6.15	3.49	2.66	6.62	8.50	7.71	9.09	10.29	7.54	238.46	...	...
June	6.92	6.50	6.21	3.44	2.77	6.71	8.50	7.80	9.13	10.34	7.87	245.30	...	...
July	6.56	6.16	5.83	3.31	2.52	6.33	8.16	7.30	8.88	10.16	7.51	240.18	...	...
August	6.17	5.82	5.53	3.01	2.52	5.92	7.90	7.17	8.72	10.18	7.21	245.00	...	...
September	5.89	5.50	5.21	3.13	2.08	5.68	7.50	7.45	8.89	10.20	7.11	238.27	...	...
October	5.85	5.50	5.18	3.32	1.86	5.68	7.50	7.43	8.86	10.24	7.08	237.36	...	...
November	6.04	5.50	5.35	3.29	2.06	5.76	7.50	7.25	8.68	10.07	6.84	245.09	...	...
December	6.91	5.50	5.53	3.14	2.39	6.10	7.50	7.11	8.49	9.97	6.87	248.61	...	...
1987														
January	6.43	5.50	5.43	2.81	2.62	5.84	7.50	7.08	8.36	9.72	6.66	264.51	...	...
February	6.10	5.50	5.59	2.76	2.83	6.05	7.50	7.25	8.38	9.65	6.61	280.93	...	...
March	6.13	5.50	5.59	2.76	2.83	6.16	7.50	7.25	8.36	9.61	6.65	292.47	...	...
April	6.37	5.50	5.64	3.01	2.63	6.45	7.75	8.02	8.85	10.04	7.55	289.32	...	...
May	6.85	5.50	5.66	3.12	2.54	6.93	8.14	8.61	9.33	10.51	8.00	289.12	...	...
June	6.73	5.50	5.67	3.10	2.57	6.92	8.25	8.40	9.32	10.52	7.79	301.38	...	...
July	6.58	5.50	5.69	3.18	2.51	6.65	8.25	8.45	9.42	10.61	7.72	310.09	...	...
August	6.73	5.50	6.04	3.32	2.72	6.71	8.25	8.76	9.67	10.80	7.82	329.36	...	...
September	7.22	5.95	6.40	3.40	3.00	7.37	8.70	9.42	10.18	11.31	8.26	318.66	...	...
October	7.29	6.00	6.13	3.51	2.62	7.89	9.07	9.52	10.52	11.62	8.70	280.16	...	...
November	6.69	6.00	5.69	3.51	2.18	7.17	8.78	8.86	10.01	11.23	7.95	245.01	...	...
December	6.77	6.00	5.77	3.59	2.18	7.61	8.75	8.99	10.11	11.29	7.96	240.96	...	...
1988														
January	6.83	6.00	5.81	3.84	1.97	6.87	8.75	8.67	9.88	11.07	7.69	250.48	...	...
February	6.58	6.00	5.66	3.83	1.83	6.58	8.51	8.21	9.40	10.62	7.49	258.13	...	...
March	6.58	6.00	5.70	3.96	1.74	6.62	8.50	8.37	9.39	10.57	7.74	265.74	...	...
April	6.87	6.00	5.91	4.04	1.87	6.86	8.50	8.72	9.67	10.90	7.81	262.61	...	...
May	7.09	6.00	6.26	4.11	2.15	7.19	8.84	9.09	9.90	11.04	7.91	256.12	...	...
June	7.51	6.00	6.46	4.27	2.19	7.49	9.00	8.92	9.86	11.00	7.78	270.68	...	...
July	7.75	6.00	6.73	4.43	2.30	7.82	9.29	9.06	9.96	11.11	7.76	269.05	...	...
August	8.01	6.37	7.06	4.34	2.72	8.26	9.84	9.26	10.11	11.21	7.79	263.73	...	...
September	8.19	6.50	7.24	4.48	2.76	8.17	10.00	8.98	9.82	10.90	7.66	267.97	...	...
October	8.30	6.50	7.35	4.42	2.93	8.24	10.00	8.80	9.51	10.41	7.46	277.40	...	...
November	8.35	6.50	7.76	4.48	3.28	8.66	10.05	8.96	9.45	10.48	7.46	271.02	...	...
December	8.76	6.50	8.07	4.59	3.48	9.11	10.50	9.11	9.57	10.65	7.61	276.51	...	...

[1]Federal Reserve Bank of New York. Through 2002, represents the rate for adjustment credit. Beginning in 2003, represents the rate for primary credit. See notes and definitions for more information.
[2]Beginning 1960, PCE except food and energy; before then, CPI-U.
[3]Prior to September 1997, this series represents both nonfinancial and financial commercial paper rates. Beginning September 1997, rates for financial companies only are shown. See notes and definitions for more information.
. . . = Not available.

Table 12-9B. Summary Interest Rates, Bond Yields, and Stock Prices: Historical—*Continued*

(Percent per annum, except as noted.)

Year and month	Federal funds interest rate	Federal Reserve discount rate[1]	U.S. Treasury bills, secondary market, 3-month	Inflation[2]	Real 3-month Treasury bill rate	Commercial paper, 3-month[3]	Bank prime rate	Treasury 10-year nominal yields	Bond yields Domestic corporate (Moody's) Aaa	Baa	State and local bonds (Bond Buyer)	Standard and Poor's composite (500 stocks) Index, 1941-1943 = 10	Dividend-price ratio	Earnings-price ratio
1989														
January	9.12	6.50	8.27	4.62	3.65	9.04	10.50	9.09	9.62	10.65	7.35	285.41	. . .	. . .
February	9.36	6.59	8.53	4.67	3.86	9.37	10.93	9.17	9.64	10.61	7.44	294.01	. . .	. . .
March	9.85	7.00	8.82	4.52	4.30	9.95	11.50	9.36	9.80	10.67	7.59	292.71	. . .	. . .
April	9.84	7.00	8.65	4.36	4.29	9.81	11.50	9.18	9.79	10.61	7.49	302.25	. . .	. . .
May	9.81	7.00	8.43	4.31	4.12	9.47	11.50	8.86	9.57	10.46	7.25	313.93	. . .	. . .
June	9.53	7.00	8.15	4.14	4.01	9.11	11.07	8.28	9.10	10.03	7.02	323.73	. . .	. . .
July	9.24	7.00	7.88	3.97	3.91	8.68	10.98	8.02	8.93	9.87	6.96	331.93	. . .	. . .
August	8.99	7.00	7.90	3.86	4.04	8.57	10.50	8.11	8.96	9.88	7.06	346.61	. . .	. . .
September	9.02	7.00	7.75	3.65	4.10	8.70	10.50	8.19	9.01	9.91	7.26	347.33	. . .	. . .
October	8.84	7.00	7.64	3.64	4.00	8.53	10.50	8.01	8.92	9.81	7.22	347.40	. . .	. . .
November	8.55	7.00	7.69	3.63	4.06	8.35	10.50	7.87	8.89	9.81	7.14	340.22	. . .	. . .
December	8.45	7.00	7.63	3.60	4.03	8.29	10.50	7.84	8.86	9.82	6.98	348.57	. . .	. . .
1990														
January	8.23	7.00	7.64	3.47	4.17	8.10	10.11	8.21	8.99	9.94	7.10	339.97	. . .	. . .
February	8.24	7.00	7.74	3.71	4.03	8.14	10.00	8.47	9.22	10.14	7.22	330.45	. . .	. . .
March	8.28	7.00	7.90	3.90	4.00	8.28	10.00	8.59	9.37	10.21	7.29	338.47	. . .	. . .
April	8.26	7.00	7.77	3.87	3.90	8.30	10.00	8.79	9.46	10.30	7.39	338.18	. . .	. . .
May	8.18	7.00	7.74	3.87	3.87	8.25	10.00	8.76	9.47	10.41	7.35	350.25	. . .	. . .
June	8.29	7.00	7.73	4.00	3.73	8.14	10.00	8.48	9.26	10.22	7.24	360.39	. . .	. . .
July	8.15	7.00	7.62	3.99	3.63	7.99	10.00	8.47	9.24	10.20	7.19	360.03	. . .	. . .
August	8.13	7.00	7.45	4.29	3.16	7.88	10.00	8.75	9.41	10.41	7.32	330.75	. . .	. . .
September ...	8.20	7.00	7.36	4.31	3.05	7.96	10.00	8.89	9.56	10.64	7.43	315.41	. . .	. . .
October	8.11	7.00	7.17	4.27	2.90	7.98	10.00	8.72	9.53	10.74	7.49	307.12	. . .	. . .
November	7.81	7.00	7.06	4.12	2.94	7.91	10.00	8.39	9.30	10.62	7.18	315.29	. . .	. . .
December	7.31	6.79	6.74	3.96	2.78	7.80	10.00	8.08	9.05	10.43	7.09	328.75	. . .	. . .
1991														
January	6.91	6.50	6.22	4.08	2.14	7.10	9.52	8.09	9.04	10.45	7.08	325.49	. . .	. . .
February	6.25	6.00	5.94	3.85	2.09	6.49	9.05	7.85	8.83	10.07	6.91	362.26	. . .	. . .
March	6.12	6.00	5.91	3.57	2.34	6.41	9.00	8.11	8.93	10.09	7.10	372.28	. . .	. . .
April	5.91	5.98	5.65	3.46	2.19	6.07	9.00	8.04	8.86	9.94	7.02	379.68	. . .	. . .
May	5.78	5.50	5.46	3.57	1.89	5.92	8.50	8.07	8.86	9.86	6.95	377.99	. . .	. . .
June	5.90	5.50	5.57	3.39	2.18	6.11	8.50	8.28	9.01	9.96	7.13	378.29	. . .	. . .
July	5.82	5.50	5.58	3.46	2.12	6.05	8.50	8.27	9.00	9.89	7.05	380.23	. . .	. . .
August	5.66	5.50	5.33	3.31	2.02	5.72	8.50	7.90	8.75	9.65	6.90	389.40	. . .	. . .
September ...	5.45	5.20	5.22	3.35	1.87	5.57	8.20	7.65	8.61	9.51	6.80	387.20	. . .	. . .
October	5.21	5.00	4.99	3.23	1.76	5.35	8.00	7.53	8.55	9.49	6.68	386.88	. . .	. . .
November	4.81	4.58	4.56	3.30	1.26	4.98	7.58	7.42	8.48	9.45	6.73	385.92	. . .	. . .
December	4.43	4.11	4.07	3.42	0.65	4.61	7.21	7.09	8.31	9.26	6.69	388.51	. . .	. . .
1992														
January	4.03	3.50	3.80	3.19	0.61	4.07	6.50	7.03	8.20	9.13	6.54	416.08	. . .	. . .
February	4.06	3.50	3.84	3.20	0.64	4.11	6.50	7.34	8.29	9.23	6.74	412.56	. . .	. . .
March	3.98	3.50	4.04	3.25	0.79	4.30	6.50	7.54	8.35	9.25	6.76	407.36	. . .	. . .
April	3.73	3.50	3.75	3.39	0.36	4.04	6.50	7.48	8.33	9.21	6.67	407.41	. . .	. . .
May	3.82	3.50	3.63	3.13	0.50	3.88	6.50	7.39	8.28	9.13	6.57	414.81	. . .	. . .
June	3.76	3.50	3.66	2.98	0.68	3.92	6.50	7.26	8.22	9.05	6.49	408.27	. . .	. . .
July	3.25	3.02	3.21	3.06	0.15	3.44	6.02	6.84	8.07	8.84	6.13	415.05	. . .	. . .
August	3.30	3.00	3.13	2.87	0.26	3.38	6.00	6.59	7.95	8.65	6.16	417.93	. . .	. . .
September ...	3.22	3.00	2.91	2.63	0.28	3.24	6.00	6.42	7.92	8.62	6.25	418.48	. . .	. . .
October	3.10	3.00	2.86	2.81	0.05	3.33	6.00	6.59	7.99	8.84	6.41	412.50	. . .	. . .
November	3.09	3.00	3.13	2.85	0.28	3.66	6.00	6.87	8.10	8.96	6.36	422.84	. . .	. . .
December	2.92	3.00	3.22	2.79	0.43	3.67	6.00	6.77	7.98	8.81	6.22	435.64	. . .	. . .
1993														
January	3.02	3.00	3.00	2.82	0.18	3.25	6.00	6.60	7.91	8.67	6.16	435.23	. . .	. . .
February	3.03	3.00	2.93	2.74	0.19	3.18	6.00	6.26	7.71	8.39	5.87	441.70	. . .	. . .
March	3.07	3.00	2.95	2.70	0.25	3.17	6.00	5.98	7.58	8.15	5.64	450.16	. . .	. . .
April	2.96	3.00	2.87	2.67	0.20	3.14	6.00	5.97	7.46	8.14	5.76	443.08	. . .	. . .
May	3.00	3.00	2.96	2.87	0.09	3.14	6.00	6.04	7.43	8.21	5.73	445.25	. . .	. . .
June	3.04	3.00	3.07	2.89	0.18	3.25	6.00	5.96	7.33	8.07	5.63	448.06	. . .	. . .
July	3.06	3.00	3.04	2.72	0.32	3.20	6.00	5.81	7.17	7.93	5.57	447.29	. . .	. . .
August	3.03	3.00	3.02	2.82	0.20	3.18	6.00	5.68	6.85	7.60	5.45	454.13	. . .	. . .
September ...	3.09	3.00	2.95	2.81	0.14	3.16	6.00	5.36	6.66	7.34	5.29	459.24	. . .	. . .
October	2.99	3.00	3.02	2.57	0.45	3.26	6.00	5.33	6.67	7.31	5.25	463.90	. . .	. . .
November	3.02	3.00	3.10	2.61	0.49	3.40	6.00	5.72	6.93	7.66	5.47	462.89	. . .	. . .
December	2.96	3.00	3.06	2.46	0.60	3.36	6.00	5.77	6.93	7.69	5.35	465.95	. . .	. . .
1994														
January	3.05	3.00	2.98	2.24	0.74	3.19	6.00	5.75	6.92	7.65	5.31	472.99	. . .	. . .
February	3.25	3.00	3.25	2.27	0.98	3.49	6.00	5.97	7.08	7.76	5.40	471.58	. . .	. . .
March	3.34	3.00	3.50	2.40	1.10	3.85	6.06	6.48	7.48	8.13	5.91	463.81	. . .	. . .
April	3.56	3.00	3.68	2.25	1.43	4.05	6.45	6.97	7.88	8.52	6.23	447.23	. . .	. . .
May	4.01	3.24	4.14	2.13	2.01	4.57	6.99	7.18	7.99	8.62	6.19	450.90	. . .	. . .
June	4.25	3.50	4.14	2.25	1.89	4.57	7.25	7.10	7.97	8.65	6.11	454.83	. . .	. . .
July	4.26	3.50	4.33	2.26	2.07	4.75	7.25	7.30	8.11	8.80	6.23	451.40	. . .	. . .
August	4.47	3.76	4.48	2.17	2.31	4.84	7.51	7.24	8.07	8.74	6.21	464.24	. . .	. . .
September ...	4.73	4.00	4.62	2.17	2.45	5.02	7.75	7.46	8.34	8.98	6.28	466.96	. . .	. . .
October	4.76	4.00	4.95	2.25	2.70	5.51	7.75	7.74	8.57	9.20	6.52	463.81	. . .	. . .
November	5.29	4.40	5.29	2.18	3.11	5.81	8.15	7.96	8.68	9.32	6.97	461.01	. . .	. . .
December	5.45	4.75	5.60	2.17	3.43	6.26	8.50	7.81	8.46	9.10	6.80	455.19	. . .	. . .

[1]Federal Reserve Bank of New York. Through 2002, represents the rate for adjustment credit. Beginning in 2003, represents the rate for primary credit. See notes and definitions for more information.
[2]Beginning 1960, PCE except food and energy; before then, CPI-U.
[3]Prior to September 1997, this series represents both nonfinancial and financial commercial paper rates. Beginning September 1997, rates for financial companies only are shown. See notes and definitions for more information.
. . . = Not available.

Table 12-9B. Summary Interest Rates, Bond Yields, and Stock Prices: Historical—*Continued*
(Percent per annum, except as noted.)

Year and month	Federal funds interest rate	Federal Reserve discount rate[1]	U.S. Treasury bills, secondary market, 3-month	Inflation[2]	Real 3-month Treasury bill rate	Commercial paper, 3-month[3]	Bank prime rate	Treasury 10-year nominal yields	Bond yields Domestic corporate (Moody's) Aaa	Baa	State and local bonds (Bond Buyer)	Standard and Poor's composite (500 stocks) Index, 1941-1943 = 10	Dividend-price ratio	Earnings-price ratio
1995														
January	5.53	4.75	5.71	2.34	3.37	6.22	8.50	7.78	8.46	9.08	6.53	465.25	. . .	. . .
February	5.92	5.25	5.77	2.28	3.49	6.15	9.00	7.47	8.26	8.85	6.22	481.92	. . .	. . .
March	5.98	5.25	5.73	2.17	3.56	6.15	9.00	7.20	8.12	8.70	6.10	493.15	. . .	. . .
April	6.05	5.25	5.65	2.25	3.40	6.12	9.00	7.06	8.03	8.60	6.02	507.91	. . .	. . .
May	6.01	5.25	5.67	2.19	3.48	6.06	9.00	6.63	7.65	8.20	5.95	523.81	. . .	. . .
June	6.00	5.25	5.47	2.05	3.42	5.94	9.00	6.17	7.30	7.90	5.84	539.35	. . .	. . .
July	5.85	5.25	5.42	1.99	3.43	5.79	8.80	6.28	7.41	8.04	5.92	557.37	. . .	. . .
August	5.74	5.25	5.40	2.13	3.27	5.82	8.75	6.49	7.57	8.19	6.06	559.11	. . .	. . .
September ...	5.80	5.25	5.28	2.11	3.17	5.74	8.75	6.20	7.32	7.93	5.91	578.77	. . .	. . .
October	5.76	5.25	5.28	2.11	3.17	5.82	8.75	6.04	7.12	7.75	5.80	582.92	. . .	. . .
November	5.80	5.25	5.36	1.99	3.37	5.74	8.75	5.93	7.02	7.68	5.64	595.53	. . .	. . .
December	5.60	5.25	5.14	2.10	3.04	5.64	8.65	5.71	6.82	7.49	5.45	614.57	. . .	. . .
1996														
January	5.56	5.24	5.00	1.98	3.02	5.40	8.50	5.65	6.81	7.47	5.43	614.42	. . .	. . .
February	5.22	5.00	4.83	1.95	2.88	5.15	8.25	5.81	6.99	7.63	5.43	649.54	. . .	. . .
March	5.31	5.00	4.96	1.94	3.02	5.31	8.25	6.27	7.35	8.03	5.79	647.07	. . .	. . .
April	5.22	5.00	4.95	1.84	3.11	5.39	8.25	6.51	7.50	8.19	5.94	647.17	. . .	. . .
May	5.24	5.00	5.02	1.85	3.17	5.39	8.25	6.74	7.62	8.30	5.98	661.23	. . .	. . .
June	5.27	5.00	5.09	1.85	3.24	5.49	8.25	6.91	7.71	8.40	6.02	668.50	. . .	. . .
July	5.40	5.00	5.15	1.88	3.27	5.53	8.25	6.87	7.65	8.35	5.92	644.07	. . .	. . .
August	5.22	5.00	5.05	1.73	3.32	5.42	8.25	6.64	7.46	8.18	5.76	662.68	. . .	. . .
September ...	5.30	5.00	5.09	1.90	3.19	5.52	8.25	6.83	7.66	8.35	5.87	674.88	. . .	. . .
October	5.24	5.00	4.99	1.89	3.10	5.43	8.25	6.53	7.39	8.07	5.72	701.45	. . .	. . .
November	5.31	5.00	5.03	1.96	3.07	5.41	8.25	6.20	7.10	7.79	5.59	735.67	. . .	. . .
December	5.29	5.00	4.91	1.85	3.06	5.51	8.25	6.30	7.20	7.89	5.64	743.25	. . .	. . .
1997														
January	5.25	5.00	5.03	1.84	3.19	5.30	8.25	6.58	7.42	8.09	5.72	766.22	. . .	. . .
February	5.19	5.00	5.01	1.92	3.09	5.27	8.25	6.42	7.31	7.94	5.63	798.39	. . .	. . .
March	5.39	5.00	5.14	1.92	3.22	5.39	8.30	6.69	7.55	8.18	5.76	792.16	. . .	. . .
April	5.51	5.00	5.16	1.98	3.18	5.57	8.50	6.89	7.73	8.34	5.88	763.93	. . .	. . .
May	5.50	5.00	5.05	1.89	3.16	5.57	8.50	6.71	7.58	8.20	5.70	833.09	. . .	. . .
June	5.56	5.00	4.93	1.96	2.97	5.54	8.50	6.49	7.41	8.02	5.53	876.29	. . .	. . .
July	5.52	5.00	5.05	1.83	3.22	5.49	8.50	6.22	7.14	7.75	5.35	925.29	. . .	. . .
August	5.54	5.00	5.14	1.70	3.44	5.48	8.50	6.30	7.22	7.82	5.41	927.74	. . .	. . .
September ...	5.54	5.00	4.95	1.59	3.36	5.48	8.50	6.21	7.15	7.70	5.39	937.02	. . .	. . .
October	5.50	5.00	4.97	1.51	3.46	5.51	8.50	6.03	7.00	7.57	5.38	951.16	. . .	. . .
November	5.52	5.00	5.14	1.41	3.73	5.60	8.50	5.88	6.87	7.42	5.33	938.92	. . .	. . .
December	5.50	5.00	5.16	1.44	3.72	5.67	8.50	5.81	6.76	7.32	5.19	962.37	. . .	. . .
1998														
January	5.56	5.00	5.04	1.47	3.57	5.42	8.50	5.54	6.61	7.19	5.06	963.36	. . .	. . .
February	5.51	5.00	5.09	1.34	3.75	5.42	8.50	5.57	6.67	7.25	5.10	1 023.74	. . .	. . .
March	5.49	5.00	5.03	1.20	3.83	5.46	8.50	5.65	6.72	7.32	5.21	1 076.83	. . .	. . .
April	5.45	5.00	4.95	1.20	3.75	5.46	8.50	5.64	6.69	7.33	5.23	1 112.20	. . .	. . .
May	5.49	5.00	5.00	1.22	3.78	5.48	8.50	5.65	6.69	7.30	5.20	1 108.42	. . .	. . .
June	5.56	5.00	4.98	0.95	4.03	5.48	8.50	5.50	6.53	7.13	5.12	1 108.39	. . .	. . .
July	5.54	5.00	4.96	1.16	3.80	5.48	8.50	5.46	6.55	7.15	5.14	1 156.58	. . .	. . .
August	5.55	5.00	4.90	1.40	3.50	5.48	8.50	5.34	6.52	7.14	5.10	1 074.63	. . .	. . .
September ...	5.51	5.00	4.61	1.18	3.43	5.31	8.49	4.81	6.40	7.09	4.99	1 020.64	. . .	. . .
October	5.07	4.86	3.96	1.22	2.74	5.04	8.12	4.53	6.37	7.18	4.93	1 032.47	. . .	. . .
November	4.83	4.63	4.41	1.19	3.22	5.06	7.89	4.83	6.41	7.34	5.03	1 144.43	. . .	. . .
December	4.68	4.50	4.39	1.31	3.08	5.00	7.75	4.65	6.22	7.23	4.98	1 190.05	. . .	. . .
1999														
January	4.63	4.50	4.34	1.36	2.98	4.77	7.75	4.72	6.24	7.29	5.01	1 248.77	. . .	. . .
February	4.76	4.50	4.44	1.29	3.15	4.79	7.75	5.00	6.40	7.39	5.03	1 246.58	. . .	. . .
March	4.81	4.50	4.44	1.21	3.23	4.81	7.75	5.23	6.62	7.53	5.10	1 281.66	. . .	. . .
April	4.74	4.50	4.29	1.26	3.03	4.79	7.75	5.18	6.64	7.48	5.08	1 334.76	. . .	. . .
May	4.74	4.50	4.50	1.23	3.27	4.81	7.75	5.54	6.93	7.72	5.18	1 332.07	. . .	. . .
June	4.76	4.50	4.57	1.39	3.18	4.98	7.75	5.90	7.23	8.02	5.37	1 322.55	. . .	. . .
July	4.99	4.50	4.55	1.29	3.26	5.11	8.00	5.79	7.19	7.95	5.36	1 380.99	. . .	. . .
August	5.07	4.56	4.72	1.15	3.57	5.25	8.06	5.94	7.40	8.15	5.58	1 327.49	. . .	. . .
September ...	5.22	4.75	4.68	1.43	3.25	5.32	8.25	5.92	7.39	8.20	5.69	1 318.17	. . .	. . .
October	5.20	4.75	4.86	1.40	3.46	5.88	8.25	6.11	7.55	8.38	5.92	1 300.01	. . .	. . .
November	5.42	4.86	5.07	1.48	3.59	5.81	8.37	6.03	7.36	8.15	5.86	1 391.00	. . .	. . .
December	5.30	5.00	5.20	1.44	3.76	5.87	8.50	6.28	7.55	8.19	5.95	1 428.68	. . .	. . .
2000														
January	5.45	5.00	5.32	1.51	3.81	5.74	8.50	6.66	7.78	8.33	6.08	1 425.59	. . .	. . .
February	5.73	5.24	5.55	1.66	3.89	5.87	8.73	6.52	7.68	8.29	6.00	1 388.87	. . .	. . .
March	5.85	5.34	5.69	1.84	3.85	6.00	8.83	6.26	7.68	8.37	5.83	1 442.21	. . .	. . .
April	6.02	5.50	5.66	1.66	4.00	6.11	9.00	5.99	7.64	8.40	5.75	1 461.36	. . .	. . .
May	6.27	5.71	5.79	1.69	4.10	6.54	9.24	6.44	7.99	8.90	6.00	1 418.48	. . .	. . .
June	6.53	6.00	5.69	1.71	3.98	6.57	9.50	6.10	7.67	8.48	5.80	1 461.96	. . .	. . .
July	6.54	6.00	5.96	1.75	4.21	6.52	9.50	6.05	7.65	8.35	5.63	1 473.00	. . .	. . .
August	6.50	6.00	6.09	1.83	4.26	6.49	9.50	5.83	7.55	8.26	5.51	1 485.46	. . .	. . .
September ...	6.52	6.00	6.00	1.82	4.18	6.47	9.50	5.80	7.62	8.35	5.56	1 468.05	. . .	. . .
October	6.51	6.00	6.11	1.80	4.31	6.51	9.50	5.74	7.55	8.34	5.59	1 390.14	. . .	. . .
November	6.51	6.00	6.17	1.88	4.29	6.50	9.50	5.72	7.45	8.28	5.54	1 375.04	. . .	. . .
December	6.40	6.00	5.77	1.80	3.97	6.34	9.50	5.24	7.21	8.02	5.22	1 330.93	. . .	. . .

[1]Federal Reserve Bank of New York. Through 2002, represents the rate for adjustment credit. Beginning in 2003, represents the rate for primary credit. See notes and definitions for more information.
[2]Beginning 1960, PCE except food and energy; before then, CPI-U.
[3]Prior to September 1997, this series represents both nonfinancial and financial commercial paper rates. Beginning September 1997, rates for financial companies only are shown. See notes and definitions for more information.
. . . = Not available.

Table 12-9B. Summary Interest Rates, Bond Yields, and Stock Prices: Historical—*Continued*

(Percent per annum, except as noted.)

Year and month	Federal funds interest rate	Federal Reserve discount rate[1]	U.S. Treasury bills, secondary market, 3-month	Inflation[2]	Real 3-month Treasury bill rate	Commercial paper, 3-month[3]	Bank prime rate	Treasury 10-year nominal yields	Bond yields Domestic corporate (Moody's) Aaa	Baa	State and local bonds (Bond Buyer)	S&P composite Index, 1941-1943 = 10	Dividend-price ratio	Earnings-price ratio
2001														
January	5.98	5.52	5.15	1.87	3.28	5.49	9.05	5.16	7.15	7.93	5.10	1 335.63	...	...
February	5.49	5.00	4.88	1.88	3.00	5.14	8.50	5.10	7.10	7.87	5.18	1 305.75	...	...
March	5.31	4.81	4.42	1.77	2.65	4.78	8.32	4.89	6.98	7.84	5.13	1 185.85	...	...
April	4.80	4.28	3.87	1.89	1.98	4.44	7.80	5.14	7.20	8.07	5.27	1 189.84	...	...
May	4.21	3.73	3.62	1.82	1.80	3.93	7.24	5.39	7.29	8.07	5.29	1 270.37	...	...
June	3.97	3.47	3.49	2.00	1.49	3.67	6.98	5.28	7.18	7.97	5.20	1 238.71	...	...
July	3.77	3.25	3.51	2.04	1.47	3.59	6.75	5.24	7.13	7.97	5.20	1 204.45	...	...
August	3.65	3.16	3.36	1.98	1.38	3.42	6.67	4.97	7.02	7.85	5.03	1 178.50	...	...
September	3.07	2.77	2.64	1.17	1.47	2.81	6.28	4.73	7.17	8.03	5.09	1 044.64	...	...
October	2.49	2.02	2.16	1.76	0.40	2.28	5.53	4.57	7.03	7.91	5.05	1 076.59	...	...
November	2.09	1.58	1.87	1.79	0.08	1.97	5.10	4.65	6.97	7.81	5.04	1 129.68	...	...
December	1.82	1.33	1.69	1.74	-0.05	1.78	4.84	5.09	6.77	8.05	5.25	1 144.93	...	...
2002														
January	1.73	1.25	1.65	1.44	0.21	1.70	4.75	5.04	6.55	7.87	5.16	1 140.21	...	...
February	1.74	1.25	1.73	1.48	0.25	1.79	4.75	4.91	6.51	7.89	5.11	1 100.67	...	...
March	1.73	1.25	1.79	1.51	0.28	1.86	4.75	5.28	6.81	8.11	5.29	1 153.79	...	...
April	1.75	1.25	1.72	1.64	0.08	1.81	4.75	5.21	6.76	8.03	5.22	1 112.03	...	...
May	1.75	1.25	1.73	1.74	-0.01	1.78	4.75	5.16	6.75	8.09	5.19	1 079.27	...	...
June	1.75	1.25	1.70	1.66	0.04	1.76	4.75	4.93	6.63	7.95	5.09	1 014.05	...	...
July	1.73	1.25	1.68	1.59	0.09	1.75	4.75	4.65	6.53	7.90	5.02	903.59	...	...
August	1.74	1.25	1.62	1.72	-0.10	1.70	4.75	4.26	6.37	7.58	4.95	912.55	...	...
September	1.75	1.25	1.63	2.44	-0.81	1.72	4.75	3.87	6.15	7.40	4.74	867.81	...	...
October	1.75	1.25	1.58	1.80	-0.22	1.70	4.75	3.94	6.32	7.73	4.88	854.63	...	...
November	1.34	0.83	1.23	1.70	-0.47	1.36	4.35	4.05	6.31	7.62	4.95	909.93	...	...
December	1.24	0.75	1.19	1.75	-0.56	1.31	4.25	4.03	6.21	7.45	4.85	899.18	...	...
2003														
January	1.24	...	1.17	1.74	-0.57	1.26	4.25	4.05	6.17	7.35	4.90	895.84	...	...
February	1.26	2.25	1.17	1.68	-0.51	1.26	4.25	3.90	5.95	7.06	4.81	837.62	...	...
March	1.25	2.25	1.13	1.70	-0.57	1.19	4.25	3.81	5.89	6.95	4.76	846.62	...	...
April	1.26	2.25	1.13	1.51	-0.38	1.20	4.25	3.96	5.74	6.85	4.74	890.03	...	...
May	1.26	2.25	1.07	1.52	-0.45	1.19	4.25	3.57	5.22	6.38	4.41	935.96	...	...
June	1.22	2.20	0.92	1.42	-0.50	1.01	4.22	3.33	4.97	6.19	4.33	988.00	...	...
July	1.01	2.00	0.90	1.45	-0.55	1.01	4.00	3.98	5.49	6.62	4.74	992.54	...	...
August	1.03	2.00	0.95	1.35	-0.40	1.04	4.00	4.45	5.88	7.01	5.10	989.53	...	...
September	1.01	2.00	0.94	1.30	-0.36	1.04	4.00	4.27	5.72	6.79	4.92	1 019.44	...	...
October	1.01	2.00	0.92	1.34	-0.42	1.05	4.00	4.29	5.70	6.73	4.89	1 038.73	...	...
November	1.00	2.00	0.93	1.36	-0.43	1.06	4.00	4.30	5.65	6.66	4.73	1 049.90	...	...
December	0.98	2.00	0.90	1.41	-0.51	1.05	4.00	4.27	5.62	6.60	4.65	1 080.64	...	...
2004														
January	1.00	2.00	0.88	1.61	-0.73	1.01	4.00	4.15	5.54	6.44	4.61	1 132.52	...	...
February	1.01	2.00	0.93	1.68	-0.75	1.01	4.00	4.08	5.50	6.27	4.55	1 143.36	...	...
March	1.00	2.00	0.94	1.72	-0.78	1.00	4.00	3.83	5.33	6.11	4.41	1 123.98	...	...
April	1.00	2.00	0.94	1.86	-0.92	1.05	4.00	4.35	5.73	6.46	4.82	1 133.08	...	...
May	1.00	2.00	1.02	1.87	-0.85	1.07	4.00	4.72	6.04	6.75	5.07	1 102.78	...	...
June	1.03	2.01	1.27	2.02	-0.75	1.34	4.01	4.73	6.01	6.78	5.05	1 132.76	...	...
July	1.26	2.25	1.33	1.95	-0.62	1.50	4.25	4.50	5.82	6.62	4.87	1 105.85	...	...
August	1.43	2.43	1.48	1.94	-0.46	1.62	4.43	4.28	5.65	6.46	4.70	1 088.94	...	...
September	1.61	2.58	1.65	2.02	-0.37	1.75	4.58	4.13	5.46	6.27	4.56	1 117.66	...	...
October	1.76	2.75	1.76	2.06	-0.30	1.95	4.75	4.10	5.47	6.21	4.49	1 118.07	...	...
November	1.93	2.93	2.07	2.10	-0.03	2.18	4.93	4.19	5.52	6.20	4.52	1 168.94	...	...
December	2.16	3.15	2.19	2.12	0.07	2.34	5.15	4.23	5.47	6.15	4.48	1 199.21	...	...
2005														
January	2.28	3.25	2.33	2.18	0.15	2.53	5.25	4.22	5.36	6.02	4.41	1 181.41	...	...
February	2.50	3.49	2.54	2.17	0.37	...	5.49	4.17	5.20	5.82	4.35	1 199.63	...	...
March	2.63	3.58	2.74	2.23	0.51	2.82	5.58	4.50	5.40	6.06	4.57	1 194.90	...	...
April	2.79	3.75	2.78	2.10	0.68	2.97	5.75	4.34	5.33	6.05	4.46	1 164.42	...	...
May	3.00	3.98	2.84	2.19	0.65	3.09	5.98	4.14	5.15	6.01	4.31	1 178.28	...	...
June	3.04	4.01	2.97	2.05	0.92	3.27	6.01	4.00	4.96	5.86	4.23	1 202.26	...	...
July	3.26	4.25	3.22	2.04	1.18	3.47	6.25	4.18	5.06	5.95	4.31	1 222.24	...	...
August	3.50	4.44	3.44	2.06	1.38	3.64	6.44	4.26	5.09	5.96	4.32	1 224.27	...	...
September	3.62	4.59	3.42	2.11	1.31	3.72	6.59	4.20	5.13	6.03	4.29	1 225.91	...	...
October	3.78	4.75	3.71	2.21	1.50	4.01	6.75	4.46	5.35	6.30	4.49	1 191.96	...	...
November	4.00	5.00	3.88	2.29	1.59	4.23	7.00	4.54	5.42	6.39	4.57	1 237.37	...	...
December	4.16	5.15	3.89	2.28	1.61	...	7.15	4.47	5.37	6.32	4.46	1 262.07	...	...
2006														
January	4.29	5.26	4.24	2.15	2.09	...	7.26	4.42	5.29	6.24	4.37	1 278.72	...	...
February	4.49	5.50	4.43	2.12	2.31	4.55	7.50	4.57	5.35	6.27	4.41	1 276.65	...	...
March	4.59	5.53	4.51	2.11	2.40	4.76	7.53	4.72	5.53	6.41	4.44	1 293.74	...	...
April	4.79	5.75	4.60	2.24	2.36	4.87	7.75	4.99	5.84	6.68	4.58	1 302.18	...	...
May	4.94	5.93	4.72	2.20	2.52	5.01	7.93	5.11	5.95	6.75	4.59	1 290.00	...	...
June	4.99	6.02	4.79	2.37	2.42	5.29	8.02	5.11	5.89	6.78	4.60	1 253.12	...	...
July	5.24	6.25	4.95	2.34	2.61	...	8.25	5.09	5.85	6.76	4.61	1 260.24	...	...
August	5.25	6.25	4.96	2.45	2.51	5.21	8.25	4.88	5.68	6.59	4.39	1 287.15	...	...
September	5.25	6.25	4.81	2.39	2.42	5.21	8.25	4.72	5.51	6.43	4.27	1 317.81	...	...
October	5.25	6.25	4.92	2.27	2.65	5.19	8.25	4.73	5.51	6.42	4.30	1 363.38	...	...
November	5.25	6.25	4.94	2.07	2.87	5.17	8.25	4.60	5.33	6.20	4.14	1 388.63	...	...
December	5.24	6.25	4.85	2.13	2.72	5.19	8.25	4.56	5.32	6.22	4.11	1 416.42	...	...

[1]Federal Reserve Bank of New York. Through 2002, represents the rate for adjustment credit. Beginning in 2003, represents the rate for primary credit. See notes and definitions for more information.
[2]Beginning 1960, PCE except food and energy; before then, CPI-U.
[3]Prior to September 1997, this series represents both nonfinancial and financial commercial paper rates. Beginning September 1997, rates for financial companies only are shown. See notes and definitions for more information.
. . . = Not available.

Table 12-9B. Summary Interest Rates, Bond Yields, and Stock Prices: Historical—*Continued*

(Percent per annum, except as noted.)

Year and month	Federal funds interest rate	Federal Reserve discount rate[1]	U.S. Treasury bills, secondary market, 3-month	Inflation[2]	Real 3-month Treasury bill rate	Commercial paper, 3-month[3]	Bank prime rate	Treasury 10-year nominal yields	Bond yields Domestic corporate (Moody's) Aaa	Bond yields Domestic corporate (Moody's) Baa	State and local bonds (Bond Buyer)	Standard and Poor's composite (500 stocks) Index, 1941-1943 = 10	Standard and Poor's composite (500 stocks) Dividend-price ratio	Standard and Poor's composite (500 stocks) Earnings-price ratio
2007														
January	5.25	6.25	4.98	2.35	2.63	5.17	8.25	4.76	5.40	6.34	4.23	1 424.16	1.81	...
February	5.26	6.25	5.03	2.45	2.58	5.18	8.25	4.72	5.39	6.28	4.22	1 444.79	1.82	...
March	5.26	6.25	4.94	2.29	2.65	5.20	8.25	4.56	5.30	6.27	4.15	1 406.95	1.89	5.85
April	5.25	6.25	4.87	2.13	2.74	5.20	8.25	4.69	5.47	6.39	4.26	1 463.65	1.84	...
May	5.25	6.25	4.73	2.03	2.70	5.19	8.25	4.75	5.47	6.39	4.31	1 511.14	1.81	...
June	5.25	6.25	4.61	1.95	2.66	5.23	8.25	5.10	5.79	6.70	4.60	1 514.49	1.81	5.65
July	5.26	6.25	4.82	1.98	2.84	5.22	8.25	5.00	5.73	6.65	4.56	1 520.70	1.80	...
August	5.02	6.01	4.20	1.94	2.26	5.25	8.25	4.67	5.79	6.65	4.64	1 454.62	1.92	...
September ...	4.94	5.53	3.89	2.04	1.85	4.92	8.03	4.52	5.74	6.59	4.51	1 497.12	1.88	5.15
October	4.76	5.24	3.90	2.14	1.76	4.63	7.74	4.53	5.66	6.48	4.39	1 539.66	1.84	...
November	4.49	5.00	3.27	2.27	1.00	4.42	7.50	4.15	5.44	6.40	4.46	1 463.39	1.95	...
December	4.24	4.83	3.00	2.32	0.68	4.23	7.33	4.10	5.49	6.65	4.42	1 479.23	1.93	4.51
2008														
January	3.94	4.48	2.75	2.14	0.61	3.25	6.98	3.74	5.33	6.54	4.27	1 378.76	2.06	...
February	2.98	3.50	2.12	2.02	0.10	2.72	6.00	3.74	5.53	6.82	4.64	1 354.87	2.10	...
March	2.61	3.04	1.26	2.16	-0.90	2.35	5.66	3.51	5.51	6.89	4.93	1 316.94	2.17	4.57
April	2.28	2.49	1.29	2.19	-0.90	1.99	5.24	3.68	5.55	6.97	4.70	1 370.47	2.09	...
May	1.98	2.25	1.73	2.28	-0.55	2.00	5.00	3.88	5.57	6.93	4.58	1 403.22	2.07	...
June	2.00	2.25	1.86	2.32	-0.46	2.21	5.00	4.10	5.68	7.07	4.69	1 341.25	2.15	4.01
July	2.01	2.25	1.63	2.31	-0.68	2.18	5.00	4.01	5.67	7.16	4.68	1 257.33	2.27	...
August	2.00	2.25	1.72	2.26	-0.54	2.08	5.00	3.89	5.64	7.15	4.69	1 281.47	2.23	...
September ...	1.81	2.25	1.13	2.11	-0.98	2.13	5.00	3.69	5.65	7.31	4.86	1 217.01	2.36	3.94
October	0.97	1.81	0.67	1.85	-1.18	2.07	4.56	3.81	6.28	8.88	5.50	968.80	2.83	...
November	0.39	1.25	0.19	1.69	-1.50	1.45	4.00	3.53	6.12	9.21	5.23	883.04	3.11	...
December	0.16	0.86	0.03	1.41	-1.38	0.97	3.61	2.42	5.05	8.43	5.56	877.56	3.00	1.65
2009														
January	0.15	0.50	0.13	1.23	-1.10	0.31	3.25	2.52	5.05	8.14	5.07	865.58	3.01	...
February	0.22	0.50	0.30	1.21	-0.91	0.48	3.25	2.87	5.27	8.08	4.90	805.23	3.07	...
March	0.18	0.50	0.21	1.11	-0.90	0.37	3.25	2.82	5.50	8.42	4.99	757.13	2.92	0.86
April	0.15	0.50	0.16	1.25	-1.09	0.28	3.25	2.93	5.39	8.39	4.78	848.15	2.60	...
May	0.18	0.50	0.18	1.16	-0.98	0.23	3.25	3.29	5.54	8.06	4.56	902.41	2.41	...
June	0.21	0.50	0.18	1.10	-0.92	0.26	3.25	3.72	5.61	7.50	4.81	926.12	2.35	0.82
July	0.16	0.50	0.18	0.97	-0.79	0.28	3.25	3.56	5.41	7.09	4.72	935.82	2.31	...
August	0.16	0.50	0.17	0.97	-0.80	0.24	3.25	3.59	5.26	6.58	4.60	1 009.72	2.12	...
September ...	0.15	0.50	0.12	1.03	-0.91	0.19	3.25	3.40	5.13	6.31	4.24	1 044.55	2.06	1.19
October	0.12	0.50	0.07	1.33	-1.26	0.19	3.25	3.39	5.15	6.29	4.20	1 067.66	2.02	...
November	0.12	0.50	0.05	1.42	-1.37	0.15	3.25	3.40	5.19	6.32	4.37	1 088.07	1.99	...
December	0.12	0.50	0.05	1.49	-1.44	0.16	3.25	3.59	5.26	6.37	4.21	1 110.38	1.95	4.57
2010														
January	0.11	0.50	0.06	1.56	-1.50	0.13	3.25	3.73	5.26	6.25	4.33	1 123.58	1.92	...
February	0.13	0.59	0.11	1.54	-1.43	0.15	3.25	3.69	5.35	6.34	4.36	1 089.16	2.00	...
March	0.16	0.75	0.15	1.56	-1.41	0.20	3.25	3.73	5.27	6.27	4.36	1 152.05	1.90	5.21
April	0.20	0.75	0.16	1.33	-1.17	0.23	3.25	3.85	5.29	6.25	4.41	1 197.32	1.84	...
May	0.20	0.75	0.16	1.35	-1.19	0.28	3.25	3.42	4.96	6.05	4.29	1 125.06	1.98	...
June	0.18	0.75	0.12	1.32	-1.20	0.32	3.25	3.20	4.88	6.23	4.36	1 083.36	2.09	6.51
July	0.18	0.75	0.16	1.36	-1.20	0.27	3.25	3.01	4.72	6.01	4.32	1 079.80	2.10	...
August	0.19	0.75	0.16	1.33	-1.17	0.25	3.25	2.70	4.49	5.66	4.03	1 087.28	2.10	...
September ...	0.19	0.75	0.15	1.20	-1.05	0.24	3.25	2.65	4.53	5.66	3.87	1 122.08	2.06	6.30
October	0.19	0.75	0.13	0.98	-0.85	0.23	3.25	2.54	4.68	5.72	3.87	1 171.58	1.97	...
November	0.19	0.75	0.14	0.99	-0.85	0.23	3.25	2.76	4.87	5.92	4.40	1 198.89	1.94	...
December	0.18	0.75	0.14	0.95	-0.81	0.23	3.25	3.29	5.02	6.10	4.92	1 241.53	1.90	6.15
2011														
January	0.17	0.75	0.15	1.00	-0.85	0.24	3.25	3.39	5.04	6.09	5.28	1 282.62	1.84	...
February	0.16	0.75	0.13	1.07	-0.94	0.23	3.25	3.58	5.22	6.15	5.15	1 321.12	1.80	...
March	0.14	0.75	0.10	1.05	-0.95	0.23	3.25	3.41	5.13	6.03	4.92	1 304.49	1.90	6.13
April	0.10	0.75	0.06	1.23	-1.17	0.20	3.25	3.46	5.16	6.02	4.99	1 331.51	1.92	...
May	0.09	0.75	0.04	1.35	-1.31	0.16	3.25	3.17	4.96	5.78	4.59	1 338.31	1.95	...
June	0.09	0.75	0.04	1.40	-1.36	0.15	3.25	3.00	4.99	5.75	4.51	1 287.29	2.04	6.35
July	0.07	0.75	0.04	1.50	-1.46	0.14	3.25	3.00	4.93	5.76	4.52	1 325.18	1.99	...
August	0.10	0.75	0.02	1.62	-1.60	0.16	3.25	2.30	4.37	5.36	4.02	1 185.31	2.20	...
September ...	0.08	0.75	0.01	1.65	-1.64	0.14	3.25	1.98	4.09	5.27	4.01	1 173.88	2.25	7.69
October	0.07	0.75	0.02	1.71	-1.69	0.15	3.25	2.15	3.98	5.37	4.13	1 207.22	2.28	...
November	0.08	0.75	0.01	1.77	-1.76	0.14	3.25	2.01	3.87	5.14	4.05	1 226.41	2.22	...
December	0.07	0.75	0.01	1.89	-1.88	0.14	3.25	1.98	3.93	5.25	3.95	1 243.32	2.24	6.91

[1]Federal Reserve Bank of New York. Through 2002, represents the rate for adjustment credit. Beginning in 2003, represents the rate for primary credit. See notes and definitions for more information.
[2]Beginning 1960, PCE except food and energy; before then, CPI-U.
[3]Prior to September 1997, this series represents both nonfinancial and financial commercial paper rates. Beginning September 1997, rates for financial companies only are shown. See notes and definitions for more information.
. . . = Not available.

Table 12-10. Selected Interest Rates

(Percent per annum; interest rates are nominal [not adjusted for inflation], except as noted.)

Year and month	Eurodollar deposits, 1-month	U.S. Treasury bills, secondary market, 6-month	CDs (secondary market) 3-month	Interest rate swaps		U.S. Treasury securities, constant maturities							
						Nominal yields					Inflation-indexed yields		
				1-year	30-year	1-year	5-year	10-year	20-year	30-year	5-year	20-year	Long-term average
1960	. . .	3.20	. . .	. . .	. . .	. . .	. . .	. . .	. . .	. . .	. . .	. . .	. . .
1961	. . .	2.59	. . .	. . .	. . .	. . .	. . .	. . .	. . .	. . .	. . .	. . .	. . .
1962	. . .	2.90	. . .	. . .	. . .	3.10	3.70	3.95	. . .	. . .	. . .	. . .	. . .
1963	. . .	3.26	. . .	. . .	. . .	3.36	3.83	4.00	. . .	. . .	. . .	. . .	. . .
1964	. . .	3.68	3.92	. . .	. . .	3.85	4.07	4.19	. . .	. . .	. . .	. . .	. . .
1965	. . .	4.05	4.36	. . .	. . .	4.15	4.25	4.28	. . .	. . .	. . .	. . .	. . .
1966	. . .	5.06	5.45	. . .	. . .	5.20	5.11	4.93	. . .	. . .	. . .	. . .	. . .
1967	. . .	4.61	4.99	. . .	. . .	4.88	5.10	5.07	. . .	. . .	. . .	. . .	. . .
1968	. . .	5.47	5.82	. . .	. . .	5.69	5.70	5.64	. . .	. . .	. . .	. . .	. . .
1969	. . .	6.86	7.23	. . .	. . .	7.12	6.93	6.67	. . .	. . .	. . .	. . .	. . .
1970	. . .	6.51	7.55	. . .	. . .	6.90	7.38	7.35	. . .	. . .	. . .	. . .	. . .
1971	6.40	4.52	5.00	. . .	. . .	4.89	5.99	6.16	. . .	. . .	. . .	. . .	. . .
1972	5.00	4.47	4.66	. . .	. . .	4.95	5.98	6.21	. . .	. . .	. . .	. . .	. . .
1973	9.19	7.20	9.30	. . .	. . .	7.32	6.87	6.85	. . .	. . .	. . .	. . .	. . .
1974	10.79	7.95	10.29	. . .	. . .	8.20	7.82	7.56	. . .	. . .	. . .	. . .	. . .
1975	6.35	6.10	6.44	. . .	. . .	6.78	7.78	7.99	. . .	. . .	. . .	. . .	. . .
1976	5.26	5.26	5.27	. . .	. . .	5.88	7.18	7.61	. . .	. . .	. . .	. . .	. . .
1977	5.75	5.52	5.63	. . .	. . .	6.08	6.99	7.42	. . .	7.75	. . .	. . .	. . .
1978	8.33	7.58	8.21	. . .	. . .	8.34	8.32	8.41	. . .	8.49	. . .	. . .	. . .
1979	11.66	10.04	11.20	. . .	. . .	10.65	9.51	9.43	. . .	9.28	. . .	. . .	. . .
1980	13.77	11.32	13.02	. . .	. . .	12.00	11.45	11.43	. . .	11.27	. . .	. . .	. . .
1981	16.72	13.81	15.93	. . .	. . .	14.80	14.25	13.92	. . .	13.45	. . .	. . .	. . .
1982	12.74	11.06	12.27	. . .	. . .	12.27	13.01	13.01	. . .	12.76	. . .	. . .	. . .
1983	9.38	8.74	9.07	. . .	. . .	9.58	10.79	11.10	. . .	11.18	. . .	. . .	. . .
1984	10.45	9.78	10.39	. . .	. . .	10.91	12.26	12.46	. . .	12.41	. . .	. . .	. . .
1985	8.12	7.65	8.04	. . .	. . .	8.42	10.12	10.62	. . .	10.79	. . .	. . .	. . .
1986	6.78	6.02	6.51	. . .	. . .	6.45	7.30	7.67	. . .	7.78	. . .	. . .	. . .
1987	6.88	6.03	6.87	. . .	. . .	6.77	7.94	8.39	. . .	8.59	. . .	. . .	. . .
1988	7.69	6.91	7.73	. . .	. . .	7.65	8.48	8.85	. . .	8.96	. . .	. . .	. . .
1989	9.16	8.03	9.09	. . .	. . .	8.53	8.50	8.49	. . .	8.45	. . .	. . .	. . .
1990	8.15	7.46	8.15	. . .	. . .	7.89	8.37	8.55	. . .	8.61	. . .	. . .	. . .
1991	5.81	5.44	5.83	. . .	. . .	5.86	7.37	7.86	. . .	8.14	. . .	. . .	. . .
1992	3.62	3.54	3.68	. . .	. . .	3.89	6.19	7.01	. . .	7.67	. . .	. . .	. . .
1993	3.07	3.12	3.17	. . .	. . .	3.43	5.14	5.87	6.29	6.59	. . .	. . .	. . .
1994	4.34	4.64	4.63	. . .	. . .	5.32	6.69	7.09	7.49	7.37	. . .	. . .	. . .
1995	5.86	5.56	5.92	. . .	. . .	5.94	6.38	6.57	6.95	6.88	. . .	. . .	. . .
1996	5.32	5.08	5.39	. . .	. . .	5.52	6.18	6.44	6.83	6.71	. . .	. . .	. . .
1997	5.52	5.18	5.62	. . .	. . .	5.63	6.22	6.35	6.69	6.61	. . .	. . .	. . .
1998	5.45	4.83	5.47	. . .	. . .	5.05	5.15	5.26	5.72	5.58	. . .	. . .	. . .
1999	5.15	4.75	5.33	. . .	. . .	5.08	5.55	5.65	6.20	5.87	. . .	. . .	. . .
2000	6.33	5.90	6.46	6.73	6.93	6.11	6.16	6.03	6.23	5.94	. . .	. . .	. . .
2001	3.81	3.34	3.71	3.87	6.20	3.49	4.56	5.02	5.63	5.49	. . .	. . .	. . .
2002	1.71	1.68	1.73	2.21	5.80	2.00	3.82	4.61	5.43	5.43	. . .	. . .	. . .
2003	1.14	1.05	1.15	1.36	5.24	1.24	2.97	4.01	4.96	. . .	1.27	. . .	2.54
2004	1.43	1.58	1.57	2.13	5.38	1.89	3.43	4.27	5.04	. . .	1.04	2.14	2.21
2005	3.33	3.39	3.51	4.04	5.03	3.62	4.05	4.29	4.64	. . .	1.50	1.97	1.94
2006	5.09	4.81	5.16	5.33	5.44	4.94	4.75	4.80	5.00	4.91	2.28	2.31	2.27
2007	5.28	4.44	5.27	5.09	5.45	4.53	4.43	4.63	4.91	4.84	2.15	2.36	2.34
2008	3.03	1.62	2.97	2.75	4.57	1.83	2.80	3.66	4.36	4.28	1.30	2.18	2.20
2009	0.61	0.28	0.55	0.90	3.87	0.47	2.20	3.26	4.11	4.08	1.06	2.21	2.24
2010	0.34	0.20	0.31	0.55	4.00	0.32	1.93	3.22	4.03	4.25	0.26	1.73	1.72
2011	0.30	0.10	0.30	0.48	3.65	0.18	1.52	2.78	3.62	3.91	-0.41	1.19	1.19
2012	0.31	0.13	0.28	0.45	2.66	0.17	0.76	1.80	2.54	2.92	-1.19	0.22	0.17
2011													
January	0.32	0.18	0.29	0.46	4.26	0.27	1.99	3.39	4.28	4.52	0.06	1.70	1.73
February	0.32	0.17	0.28	0.47	4.42	0.29	2.26	3.58	4.42	4.65	0.25	1.85	1.90
March	0.30	0.16	0.28	0.44	4.29	0.26	2.11	3.41	4.27	4.51	-0.09	1.58	1.65
April	0.26	0.12	0.23	0.41	4.27	0.25	2.17	3.46	4.28	4.50	-0.14	1.48	1.56
May	0.26	0.09	0.21	0.37	4.05	0.19	1.84	3.17	4.01	4.29	-0.34	1.47	1.49
June	0.24	0.10	0.22	0.39	3.96	0.18	1.58	3.00	3.91	4.23	-0.38	1.53	1.48
July	0.22	0.08	0.24	0.43	3.96	0.19	1.54	3.00	3.95	4.27	-0.49	1.36	1.31
August	0.25	0.06	0.29	0.44	3.31	0.11	1.02	2.30	3.24	3.65	-0.75	0.81	0.76
September ...	0.33	0.04	0.33	0.49	2.93	0.10	0.90	1.98	2.83	3.18	-0.72	0.69	0.71
October	0.35	0.05	0.37	0.57	2.90	0.11	1.06	2.15	2.87	3.13	-0.63	0.72	0.74
November	0.35	0.05	0.41	0.66	2.77	0.11	0.91	2.01	2.72	3.02	-0.85	0.55	0.52
December	0.35	0.05	0.49	0.67	2.70	0.12	0.89	1.98	2.67	2.98	-0.78	0.56	0.51
2012													
January	0.35	0.07	0.40	0.58	2.73	0.12	0.84	1.97	2.70	3.03	-0.92	0.51	0.45
February	0.34	0.12	0.30	0.50	2.80	0.16	0.83	1.97	2.75	3.11	-1.11	0.45	0.36
March	0.34	0.14	0.29	0.50	2.96	0.19	1.02	2.17	2.94	3.28	-1.03	0.56	0.51
April	0.33	0.14	0.29	0.52	2.89	0.18	0.89	2.05	2.82	3.18	-1.06	0.50	0.42
May	0.30	0.15	0.29	0.55	2.65	0.19	0.76	1.80	2.53	2.93	-1.12	0.44	0.26
June	0.30	0.15	0.32	0.52	2.44	0.19	0.71	1.62	2.31	2.70	-1.05	0.10	0.11
July	0.31	0.15	0.30	0.45	2.35	0.19	0.62	1.53	2.22	2.59	-1.15	-0.01	0.02
August	0.31	0.14	0.26	0.42	2.55	0.18	0.71	1.68	2.40	2.77	-1.19	0.06	0.09
September ...	0.30	0.14	0.24	0.36	2.64	0.18	0.67	1.72	2.49	2.88	-1.47	0.02	0.01
October	0.28	0.15	0.23	0.33	2.67	0.18	0.71	1.75	2.51	2.90	-1.47	-0.01	-0.05
November	0.27	0.14	0.23	0.33	2.55	0.18	0.67	1.65	2.39	2.80	-1.38	-0.06	-0.10
December	0.27	0.12	0.24	0.33	2.67	0.16	0.70	1.72	2.47	2.88	-1.40	0.00	-0.12

. . . = Not available.

**Figure 12-4. S&P Stock Price Index and "Hybrid" FHFA House Price Index, 1975–2012
(ratio scale, price indexes, 1975 = 100)**

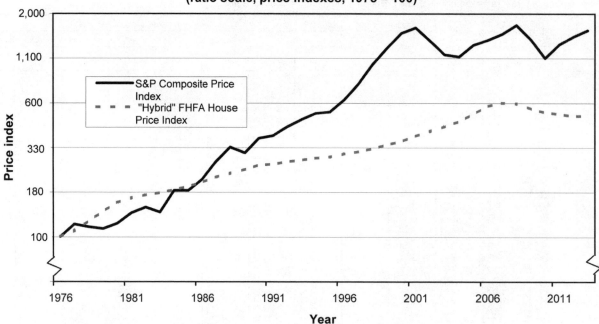

- The rise in prices of existing homes sold, as measured by the Federal Housing Finance Agency (FHFA) Purchase-Only House Price Index, ended in 2006, after annual rates of appreciation of 10 percent in 2004 and 2005. From the end of 2006 through the end of 2011, these prices declined 19 percent, then rose 5.5 percent in 2012. (A different, privately compiled index, the Standard & Poor's Case-Shiller Home Price Index, is the measure most frequently quoted in the press. See the Notes and Definitions for a discussion of the characteristics of these different indexes.) (Table 12-11)

- In Figure 12-4 we show an index line that displays the national average changes in the prices of purchased houses for the years 1992 through 2012. Such a purchase-only measure is not available for earlier years, so for the purpose of longer-term comparisons this index has been extended back to 1975 using changes in a similar FHFA index for houses purchased or refinanced. The two FHFA indexes, both of which are shown in their original form in Table 12-11, have been linked to each other to make the "hybrid" index shown here, rebased to 1975 = 100.

- The long-terms gains in national average housing prices as estimated here have been no match for those in the prices of common stocks. This is demonstrated in Figure 12-4 above, where our "hybrid" FHFA house price index is compared with the S&P 500 stock index, both rebased to 1975=100 so that their growth since then can be directly compared. Over the 37 years, house prices rose at an average 4.5 percent annual rate, while the index of stock prices, though more volatile than home prices, rose at a 7.8 percent rate. (This price increase comparison does not take account of tax considerations, stock dividends, or the value of shelter provided by the owner-occupied home. Past history is no guarantee of future results.) (Table 12-11)

Table 12-11. Selected Stock and Housing Market Data

| Year and month | Stock price indexes | | | | FHFA House Price Indexes | | | |
| | Dow Jones industrials (30 stocks) | Standard and Poor's composite (500 stocks) (1941–1943 = 10) | Nasdaq composite (Feb. 5, 1971 = 100) | Interest rate on fixed-rate first mortgages | House Price Index (purchases and refinance) | | Purchase-Only Index | |
					Level at end of period (1980:I = 100)	Appreciation from same quarter one year earlier (percent)	Level at end of period (1991:I = 100)	Appreciation from same quarter one year earlier (percent)
1960	618.04	55.85	. . .	. . .	. . .	. . .	. . .	. . .
1961	691.55	66.27	. . .	. . .	. . .	. . .	. . .	. . .
1962	639.76	62.38	. . .	. . .	. . .	. . .	. . .	. . .
1963	714.81	69.87	. . .	. . .	. . .	. . .	. . .	. . .
1964	834.05	81.37	. . .	. . .	. . .	. . .	. . .	. . .
1965	910.88	88.17	. . .	. . .	. . .	. . .	. . .	. . .
1966	873.60	85.26	. . .	. . .	. . .	. . .	. . .	. . .
1967	879.12	91.93	. . .	. . .	. . .	. . .	. . .	. . .
1968	906.00	98.70	. . .	. . .	. . .	. . .	. . .	. . .
1969	876.72	97.84	. . .	. . .	. . .	. . .	. . .	. . .
1970	753.19	83.22	. . .	. . .	. . .	. . .	. . .	. . .
1971	884.76	98.29	107.44	. . .	. . .	. . .	. . .	. . .
1972	950.71	109.20	128.52	7.38	. . .	. . .	. . .	. . .
1973	923.88	107.43	109.90	8.04	. . .	. . .	. . .	. . .
1974	759.37	82.85	76.29	9.19	. . .	. . .	. . .	. . .
1975	802.49	86.16	77.20	9.04	62.31	. . .	. . .	. . .
1976	974.92	102.01	89.90	8.86	67.54	8.39	. . .	. . .
1977	894.63	98.20	98.71	8.84	77.16	14.24	. . .	. . .
1978	820.23	96.02	117.53	9.63	87.43	13.31	. . .	. . .
1979	844.40	103.01	136.57	11.19	98.35	12.49	. . .	. . .
1980	891.41	118.78	168.61	13.77	104.74	6.50	. . .	. . .
1981	932.92	128.05	203.18	16.63	109.15	4.21	. . .	. . .
1982	884.36	119.71	188.97	16.08	112.20	2.79	. . .	. . .
1983	1 190.34	160.41	285.43	13.23	116.99	4.27	. . .	. . .
1984	1 178.48	160.46	248.88	13.87	122.44	4.66	. . .	. . .
1985	1 328.23	186.84	290.19	12.42	129.41	5.69	. . .	. . .
1986	1 792.76	236.34	366.96	10.18	138.76	7.23	. . .	. . .
1987	2 275.99	286.83	402.57	10.20	146.22	5.38	. . .	. . .
1988	2 060.82	265.79	374.43	10.34	154.49	5.66	. . .	. . .
1989	2 508.91	322.84	437.81	10.32	163.10	5.57	. . .	. . .
1990	2 678.94	334.59	409.17	10.13	165.06	1.20	. . .	. . .
1991	2 929.33	376.18	491.69	9.25	170.21	3.12	101.46	. . .
1992	3 284.29	415.74	599.26	8.40	174.32	2.41	104.25	2.75
1993	3 522.06	451.41	715.16	7.33	178.93	2.64	107.09	2.72
1994	3 793.77	460.42	751.65	8.35	181.76	1.58	110.19	2.89
1995	4 493.76	541.72	925.19	7.95	190.04	4.56	113.12	2.66
1996	5 742.89	670.50	1 164.96	7.80	194.88	2.55	116.28	2.79
1997	7 441.15	873.43	1 469.49	7.60	203.49	4.42	120.14	3.32
1998	8 625.52	1 085.50	1 794.91	6.94	213.80	5.07	126.97	5.69
1999	10 464.88	1 327.33	2 728.15	7.43	224.33	4.93	134.87	6.22
2000	10 734.90	1 427.22	3 783.67	8.06	240.22	7.08	144.30	6.99
2001	10 189.13	1 194.18	2 035.00	6.97	257.29	7.11	154.03	6.74
2002	9 226.43	993.94	1 539.73	6.54	274.55	6.71	165.87	7.69
2003	8 993.59	965.23	1 647.17	5.82	293.60	6.94	178.91	7.86
2004	10 317.39	1 130.65	1 986.53	5.84	323.78	10.28	197.09	10.16
2005	10 547.67	1 207.23	2 099.32	5.86	360.02	11.19	217.17	10.19
2006	11 408.67	1 310.46	2 263.41	6.41	376.52	4.58	223.84	3.07
2007	13 169.98	1 477.19	2 578.47	6.34	372.79	-0.99	218.43	-2.42
2008	11 252.62	1 220.04	2 161.65	6.04	347.61	-6.75	197.16	-9.74
2009	8 876.15	948.05	1 845.38	5.04	329.94	-5.08	192.86	-2.18
2010	10 662.80	1 139.97	2 349.89	4.69	324.16	-1.75	184.88	-4.14
2011	11 966.36	1 267.64	2 677.44	4.46	314.37	-3.02	180.56	-2.34
2012	12 967.08	1 379.35	2 965.56	3.66	316.63	0.72	190.48	5.49
2011								
January	11 802.37	1 282.62	2 717.21	4.76	. . .	. . .	. . .	. . .
February	12 190.00	1 321.12	2 783.54	4.95	. . .	. . .	. . .	. . .
March	12 081.48	1 304.49	2 722.29	4.84	315.24	-3.31	178.87	-5.44
April	12 434.88	1 331.51	2 797.07	4.84	. . .	. . .	. . .	. . .
May	12 579.99	1 338.31	2 815.08	4.64	. . .	. . .	. . .	. . .
June	12 097.31	1 287.29	2 687.76	4.51	310.10	-4.07	181.55	-5.52
July	12 512.33	1 325.18	2 810.58	4.55	. . .	. . .	. . .	. . .
August	11 326.62	1 185.31	2 504.62	4.27	. . .	. . .	. . .	. . .
September	11 175.45	1 173.88	2 524.14	4.11	312.85	-4.17	182.69	-3.37
October	11 515.93	1 207.22	2 594.78	4.07	. . .	. . .	. . .	. . .
November	11 804.33	1 226.41	2 606.29	3.99	. . .	. . .	. . .	. . .
December	12 075.68	1 243.32	2 601.67	3.96	314.37	-3.02	180.56	-2.34
2012								
January	12 550.89	1 300.58	2 743.80	3.92	. . .	. . .	. . .	. . .
February	12 889.05	1 352.49	2 928.98	3.89	. . .	. . .	. . .	. . .
March	13 079.47	1 389.24	3 035.92	3.95	311.15	-1.30	179.96	0.61
April	13 030.75	1 386.43	3 035.10	3.91	. . .	. . .	. . .	. . .
May	12 721.08	1 341.27	2 900.41	3.80	. . .	. . .	. . .	. . .
June	12 544.90	1 323.48	2 850.35	3.68	310.17	0.02	187.89	3.49
July	12 814.10	1 359.78	2 920.11	3.55	. . .	. . .	. . .	. . .
August	13 134.90	1 403.44	3 032.67	3.60	. . .	. . .	. . .	. . .
September	13 418.50	1 443.42	3 136.80	3.50	314.13	0.41	190.10	4.06
October	13 380.65	1 437.82	3 060.26	3.38	. . .	. . .	. . .	. . .
November	12 896.44	1 394.51	2 941.02	3.35	. . .	. . .	. . .	. . .
December	13 144.18	1 422.29	3 003.79	3.35	316.63	0.72	190.48	5.49

. . . = Not available.

NOTES AND DEFINITIONS, CHAPTER 12

Most of the data in this chapter are found on the Federal Reserve Board Web site, http://www.federalreserve.gov. Current releases and most historical data are found at that site by selecting Economic Research & Data/Statistical Releases and Historical Data and then selecting the appropriate report. This is the location for all data not otherwise specified.

Historical data not found online are taken from two printed volumes of statistical data that were published by the Board of Governors of the Federal Reserve System: *Banking and Monetary Statistics,* 1943, and *Banking and Monetary Statistics, 1941-1970,* 1976. These will be referred to as *B&MS* 1943 and *B&MS* 1976.

Tables 12-1 and 12-2: Money Stock Measures and Components

SOURCE: BOARD OF GOVERNORS OF THE FEDERAL RESERVE SYSTEM

Estimates of two monetary aggregates (M1 and M2) and the components of these measures are published weekly. The monthly data are averages of daily figures.

The Federal Reserve Board ceased publication of the M3 aggregate on March 23, 2006. Weekly publication was also discontinued for the following components of M3: large-denomination time deposits, repurchase agreements (RPs), and Eurodollars. The Board continues to publish institutional money market mutual funds as a memorandum item in this release. Measures of large-denomination time deposits continue to be published in the Financial Accounts (Z.1 release) and in the H.8 release weekly for commercial banks.

The Board stated that "M3 does not appear to convey any additional information about economic activity that is not already embodied in M2 and has not played a role in the monetary policy process for many years. Consequently, the Board judged that the costs of collecting the underlying data and publishing M3 outweigh the benefits." ("Discontinuance of M3," H.6, Money Stock Measures [November 10, 2005, revised March 9, 2006]. [Accessed November 6, 2006.]

Definitions

M1 consists of (1) currency, (2) traveler's checks of nonbank issuers, (3) demand deposits, and (4) other checkable deposits.

M2 consists of M1 plus savings deposits (including money market deposit accounts), small-denomination time deposits, and balances in retail money market mutual funds.

Currency consists of currency outside the U.S. Treasury, the Federal Reserve Banks, and the vaults of depository institutions.

Traveler's checks is the outstanding amount of U.S. dollar-denominated traveler's checks of nonbank issuers. Traveler's checks issued by depository institutions are included in demand deposits.

Demand deposits consists of demand deposits at domestically chartered commercial banks, U.S. branches and agencies of foreign banks, and Edge Act corporations (excluding those amounts held by depository institutions, the U.S. government, and foreign banks and official institutions) less cash items in the process of collection and Federal Reserve float. A "demand deposit" is a deposit that the depositor has a right to withdraw at any time without prior notice to the depository institution—most commonly, a checking account. "Federal Reserve float" is Federal Reserve credit that appears on the books of the depository institution of both the check writer and the check receiver while a check is being processed. This amount and cash items in the process of collection are subtracted to avoid double counting of deposits, so that they will not be counted both at the bank in which the check is deposited and at the bank on which the check is drawn.

Other checkable deposits at commercial banks consists of negotiable order of withdrawal (NOW) and automatic transfer service (ATS) balances at domestically chartered commercial banks, U.S. branches and agencies of foreign banks, and Edge Act corporations.

Other checkable deposits at thrift institutions consists of NOW and ATS balances at thrift institutions, credit union share draft balances, and demand deposits at thrift institutions.

Savings deposits includes money market deposit accounts and other savings deposits at *commercial banks* and *thrift institutions*.

Small time deposits are deposits issued at *commercial banks* and *thrift institutions* in amounts less than $100,000. All Individual Retirement Account (IRA) and Keogh account balances at commercial banks and thrift institutions are subtracted from small time deposits.

Retail money funds exclude IRA and Keogh account balances at money market mutual funds.

Institutional money funds are included in the money stock report for informational purposes. They are not part of M1 or M2.

Notes on the data

Seasonal adjustment. Seasonally adjusted M1 is calculated by summing currency, traveler's checks, demand deposits, and other checkable deposits (each seasonally adjusted separately). Seasonally adjusted M2 is computed by adjusting each of its non-M1 components and then adding this result to seasonally adjusted M1.

Revisions. Money stock measures are revised frequently and have a benchmark and seasonal factor review in the middle of the year; this review typically extends back a number of years. The monetary aggregates were redefined in major revisions introduced in 1980.

Historical: January 1947-January 1959. These data are not currently maintained online and are found in *B&MS* 1976. They are not continuous with the current data series; for that reason the values for January 1959 are shown so that users can link to the current data. The *demand deposit component* includes demand deposits held in commercial banks by individuals, partnerships, and corporations both domestic and foreign, and demand deposits held by nonbank financial institutions and foreign banks. Note that this includes demand deposit liabilities to foreign governments, central banks, and international institutions—said to be "relatively small" in the source document. *Time deposits adjusted* is time and savings deposits at commercial banks, other than large negotiable certificates of deposit (CDs), and excluding all deposits due to the U.S. government and domestic commercial banks. The editor has added this to the *Money stock (M1)* to approximate *M2*, which is not shown as such in the source document.

Historical: 1892-1946. These data are from *B&MS* 1943 and *B&MS* 1976. They pertain only to the last day of June and, after 1922, the last day of December, the "call dates" on which banks reported to the federal government. For more data and analysis concerning monetary developments in this period, including monthly money supply estimates, see Milton Friedman and Anna Jacobson Schwartz, *A Monetary History of the United States, 1867-1960,* Princeton, Princeton University Press, 1963. In Table 12-1B, *Demand deposits adjusted* refers to the elimination of interbank and U.S. government deposits and cash items in process of collection, not to seasonal adjustment, which is not applicable to call report data because they are only reported once or twice a year. The editor has retitled as *M1* the "Total" money stock shown in the source document, and has added time deposits to it in order to approximate *M2*, which is not shown in the source document.

Data availability

Estimates are released weekly in Federal Reserve Statistical Release H.6, "Money Stock Measures." Current and historical data are available on the Federal Reserve Web site.

References

Board of Governors of the Federal Reserve System, *The Federal Reserve System: Purposes and Functions,* available online at http://www.federalreserve.gov in the category "About the Fed/Features," includes a chapter discussing monetary policy and the monetary aggregates and a glossary of terms as an appendix.

An explanation of the 1980 redefinition of the monetary aggregates is found in the *Federal Reserve Bulletin* for February 1980.

Tables 12-3 and 12-1D: Aggregate Reserves, Monetary Base, and FR Balance Sheet

SOURCE: BOARD OF GOVERNORS OF THE FEDERAL RESERVE SYSTEM

In July 2013 the Federal Reserve Board issued a substantially revised format for reporting reserves of depository institutions and the monetary base. The revisions were made in response to the substantial growth in reserves undertaken beginning in 2008 to mitigate the effects of the financial crisis, and to recent changes in the administration of bank reserves. The concepts and procedures incorporated in the data in this volume and described below will not apply to the data that the Fed will be showing in the H.3 release going forward. Seasonally adjusted data (apparently no longer relevant in a situation of vastly expanded reserves) will no longer be published. New aggregates and interest rates will be published to "give the public insight into how depository institutions collectively manage their reserves within the current framework for the implementation of monetary policy." However, the new format will enable calculations of concepts similar to "excess reserves," and a new simplified monetary base is nearly identical with the historical time series of that name. For further information, see "Aggregate Reserves of Depository Institutions and the Monetary Base - H.3" at www.federalreserve.gov under Economic Research & Data/Statistical Releases and Historical Data.

The data on reserves and the monetary base presented here are in millions of dollars, seasonally adjusted (with one exception), and adjusted for changes in reserve requirements ("break-adjusted") in order to provide a consistent gauge of the effect of Federal Reserve open-market operations. Break adjustment is required because an observed increase in reserves will not represent an easing in monetary conditions if it is simply equal to the increase in reserves required by the Federal Reserve. Therefore, the mandated increases and decreases are deducted to provide the break-adjusted series. Monthly data are averages of daily figures. Annual data are for December.

The series "Federal Reserve balance sheet: total assets" was introduced in the 14th edition of *Business Statistics*. It demonstrates the extent to which the Federal Reserve has, beginning in 2007, undertaken "quantitative easing"—direct purchases of financial assets—in addition to conventional easing, which has consisted of reducing short-term interest rates to near zero and supporting that rate level with purchases and sales of short-term securities on the open market. The balance sheet data are accessed on a different part of the Federal Reserve Web site—"Monetary Policy" instead of "Economic Research and Data"—which features an extensive explanation and discussion of the meaning and importance of this indicator. The balance sheet is reported in millions of dollars for each Wednesday, and is shown here with the last Wednesday of the month representing the month and the last Wednesday of December representing the year. These values are not adjusted for seasonal variation.

Definitions

Total reserves consists of reserve balances with the Federal Reserve Banks plus vault cash used to satisfy reserve requirements. Seasonally adjusted, break-adjusted total reserves equal seasonally adjusted, break-adjusted required reserves plus unadjusted excess reserves.

Seasonally adjusted, break-adjusted *nonborrowed reserves* equal seasonally adjusted, break-adjusted total reserves less unadjusted total borrowings of depository institutions from the Federal Reserve.

Extended credit consisted of borrowing at the discount window under the terms and conditions established for the extended credit program to help depository institutions deal with sustained liquidity pressures. Since there was not the same need to repay such borrowing promptly as there was with traditional short-term adjustment credit, the money market impact of extended credit was similar to that of nonborrowed reserves. The extended credit program was significant in the 1980s but used infrequently in subsequent years. It ended with the 2002 revision of the discount window program, effective January 9, 2003. See the explanation of the discount rate in the notes and definitions for Table 12-9A.

To adjust *required reserves* for discontinuities due to regulatory changes in reserve requirements, a multiplicative procedure is used to estimate what required reserves would have been in past periods, had current reserve requirements been in effect. Break-adjusted required reserves include required reserves against transactions deposits and personal time and savings deposits (but not reservable nondeposit liabilities).

Excess reserves, not seasonally adjusted equals unadjusted total reserves less unadjusted required reserves.

The seasonally adjusted, break-adjusted *monetary base* consists of (1) seasonally adjusted, break-adjusted total reserves; plus (2) the seasonally adjusted currency component of the money stock; plus (3) the seasonally adjusted, break-adjusted difference between current vault cash and the amount applied to satisfy current reserve requirements for all quarterly reporters on the "Report of Transaction Accounts, Other Deposits and Vault Cash" and for all weekly reporters whose vault cash exceeds their required reserves.

Federal Reserve balance sheet: total assets is total assets from the Consolidated Statement of Condition of All Federal Reserve Banks, which is reported each Wednesday. The last Wednesday of the month is used to represent the month, and the last Wednesday in December is used to represent the year. Currently, the principal components of total assets are Treasury, federal agency, and mortgage-backed securities. Other types of assets representing Federal Reserve credit extension, some of which have varied during the course of the crisis, have been repurchase agreements; term auction credit; portfolio holdings of various limited liability companies (LLCs) set up to manage assets taken over from other institutions; liquidity swaps with foreign central banks; and other loans, including traditional loans to member commercial banks made at the discount rate (see the definitions for Table 12-9). Total assets are equal to the sum of Federal Reserve liabilities and capital. The principal components of liabilities are Federal Reserve notes and the deposits of member banks representing their reserves.

Revisions

The data on reserves and the monetary base are revised annually around midyear to reflect the result of annual reviews of seasonal factors and break factors. The Federal Reserve balance sheet is not subject to revision.

Data availability

Reserve and monetary base data are released weekly in Federal Reserve Release H.3, "Aggregate Reserves of

Depository Institutions and the Monetary Base." Current and historical data are available on the Federal Reserve Web site.

The Federal Reserve balance sheet appears each week in the H.4.1 release, Factors Affecting Reserve Balances, released each Thursday at 4:30 p.m., and available on the Federal Reserve Web site under Economic Research and Data/Statistical Releases and Historical Data. However, to obtain the full historical data for total assets, the user must go to Monetary policy/Credit and liquidity programs and the balance sheet/Recent balance sheet trends/Total assets/View as table/All/Copy data. Other explanatory material, including a monthly report on changes in these programs, is available at the Monetary policy location.

Table 12-4A: Commercial Banks: Bank Credit and Selected Liabilities

SOURCE: BOARD OF GOVERNORS OF THE FEDERAL RESERVE SYSTEM

Definitions and notes on the data

This table presents selected balance sheet items (not a complete balance sheet with total assets and liabilities) for all commercial banks in the United States. This category covers the following types of institutions in the 50 states and the District of Columbia: domestically chartered commercial banks that report weekly (large domestic), other domestically chartered commercial banks (small domestic), branches and agencies of foreign banks, and Edge Act and Agreement corporations (foreign related institutions). International Banking Facilities are excluded.

Data are collected weekly for Wednesday values, and monthly data are pro rata averages of Wednesday values. Annual data represent December figures.

Data are complete for large domestic banks. Data for other institutions are estimated on the basis of weekly samples and end-of-quarter condition reports. Data are adjusted for breaks caused by the reclassifications of assets and liabilities.

Data before 1988 are based on previous versions of this survey—the G.7 release, "Loans and Securities at Commercial Banks," and the G.10 release, "Major Nondeposit Funds of Commercial Banks."

Most of the categories of credit and liabilities are self-explanatory.

U.S. Treasury and agency securities includes liabilities of the U.S. Treasury, liabilities of U.S. government agencies, and liabilities of U.S. government-sponsored enterprises.

Loans and leases in bank credit excludes various forms of credit extended to other commercial banks in the United States.

Security loans, previously shown as a separate category under "Loans and leases in bank credit", are now included in "*Other loans and leases.*"

Allowances for loan and lease losses, interbank loans, cash assets, trading assets including derivatives, and other assets are not components of bank credit and are omitted from Table 12-4. Interbank loans include loans made to commercial banks, reverse RPs with commercial banks, and federal funds sold to commercial banks.

Selected liabilities show *deposits* and *borrowings*. Other components of total liabilities, "trading liabilities" and "other liabilities," are omitted.

Revisions

Data are revised annually around midyear to reflect new benchmark information and revised seasonal factors.

Data availability

Federal Reserve Statistical Release H.8, "Assets and Liabilities of Commercial Banks in the United States," is issued each Friday around 4:30 p.m. (EST). Current and historical data are available on the Federal Reserve Web site.

Table 12-4B: Bank Credit and Other Credit Instruments: Historical

December data are taken from *B&MS* 1976 and *B&MS* 1943.

Loans and investments, all commercial banks is the sum of these items from commercial bank balance sheets, including total loans, holdings of U.S. Government securities, and holdings of other securities, which according to the 1976 source book "consist mainly of State and municipal issues."

Commercial paper reflects outstanding values of these short-term securities.

Bankers' acceptances reflects amounts of these short-term borrowing instruments reported by banks and dealers in the United States as well as by agencies of foreign banks located in the United States. From 1924 through 1934, acceptances includes acceptances held by Federal Reserve Banks, both for their own account ($391 million in December 1929) and for account of foreign correspondent banks ($548 million in December 1929). These Federal Reserve holdings declined rapidly after 1931 and amounted to zero by December 1934.

By then, most of the outstanding acceptances were held by banks.

Table 12-5: Credit Market Debt Outstanding, by Borrower and Lender

SOURCE: BOARD OF GOVERNORS OF THE FEDERAL RESERVE SYSTEM

"The Financial Accounts of the United States," an expanded version of what was known before 2013 as the "Flow of Funds Accounts," are compiled quarterly by the Federal Reserve Board. They supplement the national income and product accounts (NIPAs) by providing a comprehensive and detailed accounting of financial transactions and a balance sheet for each financial and nonfinancial sector of the economy. Table 12-5 is taken from these accounts. It shows the *credit market debt outstanding owed* by the major sectors in the economy, and it shows the major lending sectors in the credit markets under *credit market assets held*. One purpose of these statistics is to show the comparative growth of the various lending sectors.

Aggregates of these data can include multiple layers of financial intermediation, such as banks making advances to finance companies that subsequently lend to households. Adding bank data to finance company data involves duplication of such debt. In macroeconomic analysis, the most widely used flow of funds measure is the total debt of domestic nonfinancial sectors. By eliminating the financial sectors, this measure has little duplication due to financial intermediation. The Federal Reserve uses this along with the monetary aggregates as an indicator of monetary conditions.

Definitions and notes on the data

Quarterly data on debt outstanding are shown on an end-of-period basis, not adjusted for seasonal variation or for "breaks" or discontinuities in the series. Due to these discontinuities, caution should be used in interpreting changes in debt levels. Break-adjusted values of changes, representing best estimates of actual fund flows, can be found in the quarterly flow of funds report, along with a suggested method for calculating percentage changes.

The data on credit market debt exclude corporate equities and mutual fund shares. However, these values of these instruments held by households and nonprofits appear as assets in the household sector accounts in Table 12-6.

Data for the current and several preceding years are revised each year to reflect revisions in source data, including the NIPAs; the revisions are issued about a month after the release of the annual NIPA revisions.

Sectors owing debt

Domestic financial sectors

Federal government-related sectors include government-sponsored enterprises (GSEs) such as Fannie Mae (originally the Federal National Mortgage Association), Freddie Mac (originally the Federal Home Loan Mortgage Corporation), and Ginnie Mae (originally the Government National Mortgage Association); agency and GSE-backed mortgage pools; and the monetary authority (Federal Reserve). However, the Federal Reserve usually owes no credit market debt.

The *private* sector includes a broad category introduced recently into the Flow of Funds accounts, "U.S.-chartered depository institutions", which replaces and comprises two earlier categories, commercial banks and bank holding companies and savings institutions; it also includes credit unions, life insurance companies, asset-backed securities (ABS) issuers, brokers and dealers, finance and mortgage companies, REITs (real estate investment trusts), and funding corporations.

Domestic nonfinancial sectors

Federal government consists of all federal government agencies and funds included in the unified budget. However, the District of Columbia government is included in the state and local sector.

Treasury securities as shown here excludes securities issued by the Treasury but held by agencies within the U.S. government (e.g., in the Social Security trust funds). In this respect, it corresponds to the "Federal debt" shown in Table 6-15, except that the latter table uses a fiscal-year basis rather than a calendar-year basis. Federal government debt as shown here is smaller than the official total public debt and the "debt subject to limit." Both of those include the securities held by U.S. government agencies. The value shown here is considered to be a more accurate measure of the effect of government borrowing in relation to the economy and credit markets than those obtained from the larger aggregates.

Budget agency securities and mortgages are those issued by government-owned corporations and agencies, such as the Export-Import Bank, that issue securities individually. There are no mortgages currently included in the debt of agencies.

Households also includes personal trusts, nonprofit organizations, and domestic hedge funds.

Nonfinancial noncorporate business now includes noncorporate farm business, formerly shown separately.

State and local governments represent operating funds only. State and local government retirement funds are included in the financial sector.

Foreign credit market debt held in the United States shows the foreign credit market debt owed to U.S. residents. This debt is included along with the debt of domestic financial and nonfinancial sectors in total credit market debt outstanding.

Percentage measures

Table 12-5 includes three measures of relative debt burdens, calculated by the editor.

Domestic nonfinancial debt as a percent of GDP is the total debt owed by domestic nonfinancial sectors as a percent of the current-dollar value of total Gross Domestic Product. (Table 1-1)

Household debt as a percent of DPI is the value of debt owed by households as a percent of the current-dollar value of disposable personal income. (Table 4-1)

Corporate nonfinancial business debt as a percent of sector value added is the total debt owed by domestic corporate nonfinancial business as a percent of the current-dollar gross value added of domestic corporate nonfinancial business. (Table 1-15)

For the annual ratios, debt outstanding at the end of the year is taken as a percent of the product or income data for the full preceding year. For the quarterly ratios, the debt outstanding at the end of the quarter is taken as a percent of the annual rate of the product or income flow for that quarter. This means that the end-year ratios will almost inevitably be higher than the corresponding end-quarter ratios and should therefore not be compared with them.

Credit market assets held by sector

Selected government-related sectors

This grouping includes two nonfinancial and four financial sectors. The nonfinancial sectors are the *federal government*, as reflected in the U.S. Budget accounts, and the operations of *state and local governments*, including the District of Columbia. *State and local employee retirement funds* and *federal government retirement funds* are shown separately and considered to be financial sectors. The other two government-related financial sectors are *government-sponsored enterprises (GSEs)* and *federally related mortgage pools.*

Government-sponsored enterprises (GSEs) are financial institutions that provide credit to housing, agriculture, and

other specific areas of the economy, such as Federal Home Loan Banks, Fannie Mae, and Freddie Mac (see above for explanation of the latter two terms).

Federally related mortgage pools are entities established for bookkeeping purposes that record the issuance of pooled securities representing an interest in mortgages backed by federal agencies and GSEs. Rather than being composed of a group of institutions, the sector is made up of a set of contractual arrangements in regard to pooled mortgages.

Selected domestic financial sectors

The former categories "commercial banks" and "savings institutions" are now combined in the category *U.S.-chartered depository institutions.* The *monetary authority* (the Federal Reserve) has been put in this group because it is sometimes included in banking sector totals. Other important financial sectors are *credit unions, life insurance companies, property-casualty insurance companies,* and *private pension funds.* Additional private financial sectors are *money market mutual funds,* which issue shares and invest in short-term liquid assets; *mutual funds,* whose investments are not restricted to the short-term area; *asset-backed security (ABS) issuers,* which issue debt obligations that are backed by pooled assets, a financial procedure similar to that of federally related mortgage pools; and *finance companies,* which provide credit to businesses and individuals.

Private domestic nonfinancial sectors

Households were the dominant private domestic nonfinancial lenders in earlier years, but lending by domestic households has now been surpassed by *foreign holdings* of assets representing claims on U.S. entities.

A number of lending sectors of smaller importance are included in the category *"All other financial and nonfinancial."* One of those is nonfinancial business, a sector that is important on the borrowing side but not on the lending side. The financial sectors included in this total are closed-end funds, exchange-traded funds, real estate investment trusts (REITs), brokers and dealers, and funding corporations.

Data availability

Debt estimates are released quarterly, about nine weeks following the end of the quarter. The data can be found in Federal Reserve Statistical Release Z.1, "Financial Accounts of the United States," available on the Federal Reserve Web site. The data in Table 12-5 are found in Tables L.1 and L.2 of that release. Current and historical data are also available on the same Federal Reserve Web site.

References

A *Guide to the Flow of Funds (Financial) Accounts* can be ordered; ordering information is available on the Federal Reserve Web site along with the Z.1 release. Individual table descriptions can be accessed at the same location. The *Federal Reserve Bulletin* for July 2001 includes an article entitled "The U.S. Flow of Funds Accounts and Their Uses." To access *Bulletin* articles on the Federal Reserve Web site, select Economic Research & Data/Federal Reserve Bulletin and select the year.

Table 12-6: Household Assets, Liabilities, Net Worth, Financial Obligations, and Delinquency Rates

SOURCE: BOARD OF GOVERNORS OF THE FEDERAL RESERVE SYSTEM

The quarterly data on household sector assets, liabilities, and net worth are also obtained from the Federal Reserve Board's Financial Accounts, which are described above. These data appear in Table B.100 of the Z.1 statistical release, also cited above.

The household credit ratios and rates are also compiled by the Federal Reserve. The household debt service ratio relates required debt service (interest and principal) payments to disposable personal income (DPI). The financial obligations ratios include not only required debt payments, but also rental payments, automobile lease payments, homeowners' insurance, and property taxes. They are also expressed as a percentage of DPI. Unlike the debt service ratio, the financial obligations ratios are not distorted by the trend toward debt-financed homeownership in preference to rental or the trend toward auto leasing in preference to loan financing.

The delinquency and charge-off rates relate delinquent (past due 30 days or more) and charged-off consumer credit card credit at commercial banks to total bank holdings of that type of credit.

Definitions and notes on the data

Quarterly data on holdings of *financial assets* are shown on an end-of-period basis, not adjusted for seasonal variations. Data for the current and preceding years are revised annually to reflect revisions in source data.

It is important to note that for most categories in this reporting system, the values for the household sector are

calculated as residuals. That is, starting with a known total (such as total Treasury securities outstanding), the amounts in that category reported or estimated to be held by other sectors are subtracted and the remainder is assigned to the household sector. This means that any error in estimating one of the other sectors causes an equal and opposite error in the household sector.

It should also be noted that the Financial Accounts "household" balance sheet includes nonprofit organizations, personal trusts, farm households, and domestic hedge funds, the last of which may account for the astonishing drop in "household" holdings of checkable deposits and currency in 2007 and the equally astonishing rise in 2011. Household sector assets exclude holdings by unincorporated businesses.

The table shows total household ownership of *checkable deposits and currency, time and savings deposits, money market fund shares, U.S. savings bonds, other Treasury securities, agency- and GSE-backed securities, municipal securities, corporate and foreign bonds, mortgages, corporate equities* (at market value), *mutual fund shares* (with equities at market value and other assets at book value), *security credit, life insurance reserves, pension fund reserves,* and *equity in noncorporate business.* Note that the reserves of life insurance companies and pension funds, though held by institutions, are counted here as assets of the household sector. *Pension fund reserves* includes insurance and pension fund reserves of federal, state, and local government employee funds—but not the Social Security system—as well as private industry funds. Bank personal trusts were formerly included as a type of household financial asset. However, in a recent revision of the flow of funds accounts, the various assets in these trusts were instead included in the appropriate categories, such as bonds, equities, and so forth. Included in total *financial assets,* but not shown separately, are foreign deposits, open market paper, and claims on insurance companies, such as unearned premium reserves of other insurance companies and health insurance reserves of life insurance companies.

Nonfinancial assets complete the asset side of the household balance sheet. Nonfinancial assets comprise equipment and software owned by nonprofit organizations, real estate, and consumer durable goods. *Household real estate* includes farm homes, mobile homes, second homes not rented, vacant homes for sale, vacant land, and owner-occupied housing. It is valued at market value, while equipment, software, and consumer durables are valued at replacement (current) cost.

Debt as a percent of total assets is calculated by the editor as household credit market debt outstanding, from Table 12-5, as a percent of the total of nonfinancial and financial assets in this table. It covers both households and nonprofit organizations, as defined above.

Total liabilities consists of household credit market debt, as shown in Table 12-5, plus security credit, trade payables of nonprofit organizations, and deferred and unpaid life insurance premiums.

Net worth is the sum of the value of financial and nonfinancial assets minus total liabilities.

The *household debt-service* and *financial obligations ratios* are estimated on a quarterly basis by the Federal Reserve based on aggregate and consumer survey data. They are seasonally adjusted, unlike almost all of the other data in Table 12-6. Fourth-quarter values are shown to represent the calendar year. The denominator for the aggregate ratio is disposable personal income (DPI) from the NIPAs. (See Chapter 4.) The allocation of the NIPA data between *renters* and *homeowners* is estimated by the Federal Reserve based on data from its triennial Survey of Consumer Finances and the Census Bureau's Current Population Survey (CPS). (For more information on the CPS, see the notes and definitions to Chapters 3 and 10.)

Debt service payments are the minimum required monthly payments of principal and interest on mortgage debt (including home equity loans), revolving credit (credit card debt), and auto, student, mobile home, recreational vehicle, marine, and personal loans.

The *financial obligations ratios* include, in addition to debt service, rental payments on primary residences, property taxes, homeowners' insurance, and automobile lease payments.

Delinquency and *charge-off rates of credit card accounts held at banks* are compiled from the quarterly FFIEC (Federal Financial Institutions Examination Council) Consolidated Reports of Condition and Income (FFIEC 031 through 034) and pertain to all insured U.S.-chartered commercial banks. The *delinquency rate* concerns loans past due 30 days or more and still accruing interest as well as those in nonaccrual status, measured as a percentage of end-of-period loans. The *charge-off rate* is the value of net charge-offs (loans removed from the books and charged against loss reserves, minus recoveries) as a percentage of average loans outstanding over the quarter, annualized.

Data availability

Household balance sheet estimates are released quarterly, about nine weeks following the end of a quarter, in the Federal Reserve Statistical Release Z.1, "Financial Accounts

of the United States." Further information on data availability is given in the notes to Table 12-5, a table which is also derived from these accounts.

The revised debt service ratio and the new financial obligations ratios are described in "Recent Changes to a Measure of U.S. Household Debt Service," *Federal Reserve Bulletin,* October 2003. The data are estimated by the Federal Reserve about three months after the end of each quarter. Current and historical data and articles from the *Bulletin* are available on the Federal Reserve Web site by selecting Economic Research and Data and either Statistical Releases and Historical Data or Federal Reserve Bulletin, then selecting the year.

Delinquency and charge-off rates of credit card accounts held at banks are also available on the Federal Reserve Web site, listed under "Charge-off and Delinquency Rates on Loans at Commercial Banks." Rates are posted approximately 60 days after the end of the quarter.

Table 12-7: Mortgage Debt Outstanding

SOURCE: BOARD OF GOVERNORS OF THE FEDERAL RESERVE SYSTEM

These data are also published in the Federal Reserve's Statistical Release Z.1, "Financial Accounts of the United States," Table L.217. They are based on reports from various government and private organizations.

Definitions and notes on the data

By type of property

Home mortgages includes home equity loans; these are also shown separately elsewhere in this Federal Reserve statistical report.

Multifamily residences refers to mortgages on structures of five or more units.

By type of holder

Federal and related agencies shows mortgages held directly by the federal government and GSEs (see notes and definitions for Table 12-5 above).

Mortgage pools or trusts show mortgages that were refinanced by their holders through the issuance of mortgage-backed securities. They are shown in two columns: refinancings by *federally related agencies*—mainly the GSEs Fannie Mae, Freddie Mac, and Ginnie Mae (see above)—and refinancings by private conduits (these are referred to as *ABS issuers* in these accounts, which stands for issuers of asset-backed securities).

Other holders encompasses a variety of groups, including finance companies, individuals, state and local governments, credit unions, and others.

Home mortgage debt as a percentage of the value of real estate is calculated by the editor, using total home mortgage debt as a percentage of the value of household real estate, which is shown in Table 12-6.

Data availability

Mortgage debt data are compiled quarterly about nine weeks following the end of the quarter in Federal Reserve Statistical Release Z.1, "Financial Accounts of the United States." The release and current and historical data are available on the Federal Reserve Web site.

Table 12-8: Consumer Credit

SOURCE: BOARD OF GOVERNORS OF THE FEDERAL RESERVE SYSTEM

The consumer credit series cover most short- and intermediate-term credit extended to individuals through regular business channels, excluding loans secured by real estate (such as first and second mortgages and home equity credit). In October 2003, the scope of this survey was expanded to incorporate student loans extended by the federal government and by SLM Holding Corporation (SLM), the parent company of Sallie Mae (Student Loan Marketing Association). The historical data have been revised back to 1977 to reflect this inclusion.

The failure to include home equity credit is an important limitation of this data set. The household debt series presented in Table 12-5 are more comprehensive, comprising both mortgage and consumer debt.

Consumer credit is categorized by major types of credit and by major holders.

Definitions and notes on the data

The major types of consumer credit are *revolving* and *nonrevolving*. *Revolving credit* includes credit arising from purchases on credit card plans of retail stores and banks, cash advances and check credit plans of banks, and some overdraft credit arrangements. *Nonrevolving credit* includes automobile loans, mobile home loans, and all other loans not included in revolving credit, such as loans for education, boats, trailers, or vacations. These loans may be secured or unsecured.

Debt secured by real estate (including first liens, junior liens, and home equity loans) is excluded. Credit extended to governmental agencies and nonprofit or charitable organizations, as well as credit extended to business or to individuals exclusively for business purposes, is excluded.

Categories of *holders* include *U.S.-chartered depository institutions* (comprising commercial banks and savings institutions), *finance companies, credit unions, federal government, nonfinancial businesses*, and *pools of securitized assets*. The Student Loan Marketing Association (Sallie Mae) is included in "Federal government" until the end of 2004, at which time it became fully privatized. Beginning with the end of 2004, Sallie Mae is included in "Finance companies." Retailers and gasoline companies are included in the nonfinancial businesses category. *Pools of securitized assets* comprises the outstanding balances of pools upon which securities have been issued; these balances are no longer carried on the balance sheets of the loan originators.

The consumer credit series are benchmarked to comprehensive data that periodically become available. Current monthly estimates are brought forward from the latest benchmarks in accordance with weighted changes indicated by sample data. Classifications are made on a "holder" basis. Thus, installment paper sold by retail outlets is included in the figures for the banks and finance companies that purchased the paper.

The amount of outstanding credit represents the sum of the balances in the installment receivable accounts of financial institutions and retail outlets at the end of each month.

The estimates of the amount of credit outstanding include any finance and insurance charges included as part of the installment contract. Unearned income on loans is included in some cases when lenders cannot separate the components.

The seasonally-adjusted data are adjusted for differences in the number of trading days and for seasonal influences.

Data availability

Current data are available monthly in the Federal Reserve Statistical Release G.19, "Consumer Credit," available along with all current and historical data on the Federal Reserve Web site. In the autumn of each year there is a revision of several years of past data reflecting benchmarking and seasonal factor review.

Tables 12-9, 12-10 and 12-11: Interest Rates, Bond Yields, Stock Prices, and Housing Market Data

SOURCES: BOARD OF GOVERNORS OF THE FEDERAL RESERVE SYSTEM; BUREAU OF ECONOMIC ANALYSIS; MOODY'S INVESTORS SERVICE; THE BOND BUYER; DOW JONES, INC.; STANDARD AND POOR'S CORPORATION; NEW YORK STOCK EXCHANGE; FEDERAL HOUSING FINANCE AGENCY (FHFA), PREVIOUSLY OFHEO (OFFICE OF FEDERAL HOUSING ENTERPRISE OVERSIGHT)

Definitions and notes on the data

Interest rates and bond yields are percents per year and are averages of business day figures, except as noted. With a few exceptions, they are nominal rates or yields not adjusted for inflation.

The daily effective *federal funds rate*—the rate that currently serves as the principal marker for Federal Reserve monetary policy —is a weighted average of rates on trades through New York brokers. Monthly figures include each calendar day in the month. Annualized figures use a 360-day year.

The *Federal Reserve discount rate* is the rate for discount window borrowing at the Federal Reserve Bank of New York. Monthly figures include each calendar day in the month. Annualized figures use a 360-day year. Before 1945, annual averages calculated by editor.

Beginning in January 2003, the rules governing the discount window programs were revised. "Adjustment credit," which had been extended at a below-market rate (as can be seen in the average discount rates from 1978 through 2002 shown in Table 12-9, which are below the federal funds rate), was replaced by a new type of credit called "primary credit." Primary credit is available for very short terms as a backup source of liquidity to depository institutions in generally sound financial condition, as judged by the lending Federal Reserve Bank. Primary credit is extended at a rate above the federal funds rate, eliminating the incentive for institutions to exploit the spread of money market rates over the discount rate.

Through December 2002, Table 12-9 displays the adjustment credit rate. Beginning in February 2003, the new primary credit rate is shown. The rule change, and the change in discount rates shown, did not entail a change in the stance of monetary policy at that time. The overall stance of monetary policy is consistently measured by the level of the federal funds rate.

The *U.S. Treasury bills, 3-month rate* and the *U.S. Treasury bills, 6-month rate* are the yields on these securities based on their prices as traded in the secondary market. The rates are quoted on a discount basis. Annualized figures use a 360-day year. Early data are taken from *B&MS* 1943 and 1976. From 1934 to 1944, the 3-month rate is based on dealers' quotations. From 1931 through 1933, it is the average rate on new issues. For 1920 through 1930, it is the rate on 3- to 6-month Treasury notes and certificates.

The *inflation* column shown here, calculated by the editor, is the rate of change in the PCE chain-type price index, excluding food and energy. For monthly entries, it is the change from the same month a year earlier. This price index is calculated by the Bureau of Economic Analysis (BEA) and shown in Table 8-3. This inflation rate is shown along with other rates in Table 8-4; see the notes and definitions for that table.

The *real 3-month Treasury bill rate* is calculated by the editor by subtracting the inflation estimate from the nominal interest rate. Note that subtraction means changing the sign and adding; hence negative inflation (that is, price decline or deflation), as experienced in the 1930s, contributes to large positive real interest rates.

Commercial paper, 3-month rates are interpolated from data on certain commercial paper trades settled by the Depository Trust Company. This company is a clearinghouse and custodian for nearly all domestic commercial paper activity. The trades, which are on a discount basis, represent sales of commercial paper by dealers or direct issuers. Annualized figures use a 360-day year. From 1971 through September 1997, the series represented both nonfinancial and financial commercial paper. Since September 1997, rates have been reported separately for nonfinancial and financial companies; only rates for financial companies are shown here. This introduces a slight discontinuity in this series between August and September 1997. Before 1971, the prevailing rate in New York City for 4- to 6-month commercial paper; hence, this series is also discontinuous between December 1970 and January 1971, and is obtained from *B&MS* 1943 and 1976.

The *bank prime rate* is one of several base rates used by banks to price short-term business loans. It is the rate posted by a majority of the top 25 (by amount of assets in domestic offices) insured U.S.-chartered commercial banks. Monthly figures include each calendar day in the month. Annualized figures use a 360-day year. Before 1949, the data are not on the Federal Reserve Web site but have been reproduced from *B&MS* 1976. In that volume, the prime rate is described as "the rate that banks charge their most creditworthy business customers on short-term loans", as posted by the largest banks. The same source goes on to write, "A nationally publicized and uniform prime rate did not emerge until the depression of the 1930s. The rate in that period—1 ½ percent—represented a floor below which banks were said to regard lending as unprofitable. The date shown [for the beginning of a changed rate] is that on which the new rate was put into effect by the first bank to make the change. The table shows a range of rates for 1929-1933 because no information is available to indicate when the rate changed in that period." For further information, the source document cites "The Prime Rate," *Monthly Review,* Federal Reserve Bank of New York, April and May 1962, pp. 54-59 and 70-73, respectively.

U.S. Treasury securities, constant maturities. The rates shown for 1-year, 5-year, 10-year, 20-year, and 30-year securities are yields on actively traded issues adjusted to constant maturities. Yields on Treasury securities at "constant maturity" are interpolated by the Treasury Department from the daily yield curve. This curve, which relates the yield on a security to its time to maturity, is based on the closing market bid yields on actively traded Treasury securities in the over-the-counter market. These market yields are calculated from composites of quotations reported by U.S. Government securities dealers to the Federal Reserve Bank of New York. The constant maturity yield values are read from the yield curve at fixed maturities. For example, this method provides a yield for a 10-year maturity, even if no outstanding security has exactly 10 years remaining to maturity. The 30-year series was discontinued as of February 2002, because the Treasury Department was no longer issuing such bonds at that time. However, issuance of 30-year bonds was resumed in 2005 as an additional means of financing rising deficits, and the 30-year interest rate series resumes in 2006. The current 20-year series begins with 1993 and is not comparable with an earlier 20-year series. For further information, see the historical data series on the Federal Reserve Web site.

Before 1962, the *Treasury 10-year* is not available on the constant-maturity basis. The entries in that column are from *B&MS* 1943 and 1976 where they are labeled "United States government bonds (long-term)." Before 1941, they represent yields on bonds that were partly tax exempt. In 1941, the yield for the partly tax-exempt series was 1.95 percent—comparable with the entries for previous years—while the entry comparable with subsequent years was 2.12 percent.

Domestic corporate bond yields, Aaa and Baa. The rates shown are for general obligation bonds based on Thursday figures, and are provided by Moody's Investors Service and republished by the Federal Reserve. The Aaa rates through December 6, 2001 are averages of Aaa utility and Aaa industrial bond rates. As of December 7, 2001, these rates are averages of Aaa industrial bonds only.

The *state and local bond yields* are the Bond Buyer index as republished by the Federal Reserve. The index is based on 20 state and local government general obligation bonds of mixed quality maturing in 20 years or less. Quotes are as of the Thursday of each week. These rates have typically in the past been lower than those on U.S. Treasury or private long-term bonds because the interest on them is exempt from U.S. income taxes, but some recent data display different patterns because of changing assessments of credit risks relative to Treasury securities. Before 1953, the source is Standard and Poor's yields on high-grade municipal bonds as republished in *B&MS* 1943 and 1976.

Stock price indexes and yields. The *Dow Jones industrial average* is an average price of 30 stocks compiled by Dow Jones, Inc. The *Standard and Poor's composite* is an index of the prices of 500 stocks that are weighted by the volume of shares outstanding, accounting for about 90 percent of New York Stock Exchange value, with a base of 1941–1943 = 10, compiled by Standard and Poor's Corporation. (Before February 1957, these data are based on a conversion of an earlier 90-stock index, and are obtained from *B&MS* 1943 and 1976.) The *dividend-price ratio* is compiled by Standard and Poor's, covering the 500 stocks in the S&P index. It represents aggregate cash dividends (based on the latest known annual rate) divided by aggregate market value based on Wednesday closing prices. The *earnings/price ratio* measures earnings (after taxes) for four quarters, ending with the indicated quarter, as a ratio to stock prices for the last day of that quarter. Monthly data are averages of weekly figures; annual data are averages of monthly or quarterly figures. The *Nasdaq composite index* is an average price of over 5,000 stocks traded on the Nasdaq exchange.

The *Eurodollar deposits* rate shown is the bid rate at about 9:30 a.m. (EST) for 1-month Eurodollar deposits. Annualized figures use a 360-day year.

CDs (secondary market), 3-month rates are averages of dealer offering rates on nationally traded certificates of deposit. Annualized figures use a 360-day year.

Interest rate swaps. An interest rate swap is a type of financial market derivative in which two parties, known as "counterparties," exchange two streams of cash flows. The rates shown here are the results of transactions in which streams of fixed-rate interest flows are exchanged for streams of floating-rate interest flows. The rates shown are the fixed interest rates which are exchanged for floating-rate flows paying the three-month LIBOR (London Interbank Offered Rate, a rate at which highly-rated banks can borrow short-term). They are International Swaps and Derivatives Association (ISDA ®) mid-market par swap rates, collected at 11 a.m. EST by Garban Intercapital plc and published on Reuters Page ISDAFIX ®1. ISDAFIX is a registered service mark of ISDA. Reprinted by the Federal Reserve from Reuters Limited.

Inflation-indexed yields. In recent years, the Treasury Department has issued Treasury Inflation-Protected Securities (TIPS), which are marketable long-term bonds whose redemption value is increased by the change in the CPI-U from the date of purchase. (See notes and definitions to Chapter 8.) The purchaser of these bonds, unlike with ordinary securities, is guaranteed that the real value of his or her principal will remain intact. He or she need not make his or her own estimate of future inflation in order to make a rational bid. Therefore, the observed purchase price represents a real rate of interest that purchasers and sellers are mutually willing to accept. Inflation-indexed yields are shown here for 5 and 20 years (adjusted to constant maturities by the Treasury) and for the long-term average, which is the unweighted average of the bid yields for all TIPS with remaining terms to maturity over 10 years.

The *fixed-rate first mortgage* rates are primary market contract interest rates on commitments for fixed-rate conventional 30-year first mortgages. The rates are obtained by the Federal Reserve from the Federal Home Loan Mortgage Corporation (FHLMC, or Freddie Mac).

FHFA (formerly OFHEO) House Price Indexes. The value of single-family owner-occupied houses has been an increasingly important element in household wealth and credit expansion and the subsequent collapse. The Federal Housing Finance Agency (FHFA), a government agency charged with regulation of the government-sponsored mortgage finance institutions Fannie Mae and Freddie Mac and the 12 Federal Home Loan Banks, uses data from those institutions to compile quarterly House Price Indexes of the value of existing single-family homes. Not included are condominiums, cooperatives, multi-unit properties, and planned unit developments. These indexes were developed by the predecessor agency, the Office of Federal Housing Enterprise Oversight (OFHEO), and has been published since the fourth quarter of 1995.

The data come from all properties for which a conventional, "conforming" mortgage has been purchased or securitized by Fannie Mae or Freddie Mac since January 1975. (Conventional mortgages are those not insured or guaranteed by the FHA, VA, or other federal government entities. A conforming mortgage is one no larger than the maximum that the insuring institution will insure. The limit has increased over time and has been $417,000 since the beginning of 2006. Loan limits for mortgages originated in the latter half of 2007 through Dec. 31, 2008, were raised to as much as $729,750 in high-cost areas in the continental United States. Legislation

generally extended those limits for 2009-originated mortgages, and the limits for 2010 originations were further extended for certain places.) Every new mortgage transaction that can be matched against a previous transaction for that property yields a rate of price change over the period between the two transactions, which enters into the calculation of the index. This data set is very large, with about 32 million repeat transactions over the 32-year span. The index is computed using a modified version of the Case-Shiller geometric weighted repeat-sales procedure.

Due to the size of this data set, indexes so defined can be calculated, and are published, not only for the United States as a whole but also for regions, states, metropolitan statistical areas (MSAs) and metropolitan divisions (subdivisions of MSAs). Obviously, the national average price trend shown here is not representative of price behavior in some "hot" local markets.

In addition, FHFA now publishes Purchase-Only Indexes for the house purchase subgroup of new mortgage transactions, excluding refinancing transactions. Nation-wide, this index is based on 4.7 million transactions over the latest 16 years. While this is still a very large statistical base, it is subject to somewhat greater revision and is less reliable for smaller geographical areas.

The FHFA price indexes are subject to revision for preceding quarters and years, because each new transaction, when reported, affects the rate of price change for all periods since the last time that the property involved in the new transaction changed hands or was refinanced. Indeed, last year's indexes indicated that prices peaked in 2007, but this year's revised data show a 2006 peak.

Seasonally adjusted data are also available for the purchase-only indexes. Seasonal price patterns appear to have some significance, especially for regional indexes. The seasonally adjusted indexes are not shown here because the year-over-change, calculated from not-seasonally-adjusted data, is the main focus of attention in these data.

The FHFA indexes do not come from a random sample of house prices, and users need to consider possible sources of bias. Expensive houses are under-represented in general because the transactions are limited to conforming mortgages. This is important if the price trends for expensive houses are different.

It has also been suspected that prices of houses that are refinanced may behave differently from the prices of houses sold. However, data for the period since 1991 in which both series are available does not support this. Between the end of 1991 and the peak at the end of 2006, the total House Price

Index rose 121 percent, identical with the Purchase-Only Index. Since then the total index has declined 16 percent and the prices of purchased homes, 15 percent.

New privately-developed house price indexes are now receiving regular media attention, and even provide the basis for a futures contract trading on the Chicago Mercantile Exchange. Standard & Poor's now issues S&P/Case-Shiller® Home Price Indexes each month. They cover resales only for houses at all price ranges, based on information obtained from county assessor and recorder offices. They are value-weighted, meaning that price trends for more expensive homes have greater influence on changes in the index. The FHFA index weights price trends equally for all properties. S&P/Case-Shiller data are only collected for 20 major metropolitan statistical areas. Series description and data can be found at http://www.homeprice.standardandpoors.com.

Data availability and references

Interest rates and bond yields are published weekly in the Federal Reserve's H.15 release, "Selected Interest Rates"; the release and current and historical data are available on the Federal Reserve Web site and in *B&MS* 1943 and 1976. The starting dates for individual interest rate series vary; some date back to 1911, and many begin in the 1950s and 1960s.

Stock market data are published monthly in *Economic Indicators,* and annually in *Economic Report of the President,* available online at http://www.gpo.gov/fdsys. Some historical interest rate data that are not available on the Federal Reserve Web site were also taken from the *Economic Report of the President.*

The FHFA house price indexes for the United States as a whole, regions, states, and metropolitan and sub-metropolitan groups are published every 3 months, approximately 2 months after the end of the previous quarter. The release and supporting data and explanatory material are available at http://www.fhfa.gov.

The OFHEO (now FHFA) and other price indexes for houses are discussed and compared in Jordan Rappaport, "Comparing Aggregate Housing Price Measures," *Business Economics,* October 2007, pp. 55–65.

CHAPTER 13: INTERNATIONAL COMPARISONS

Figure 13-1. Real GDP Per Capita, United States and Three Other Countries, 1960–2011 (ratio scale)

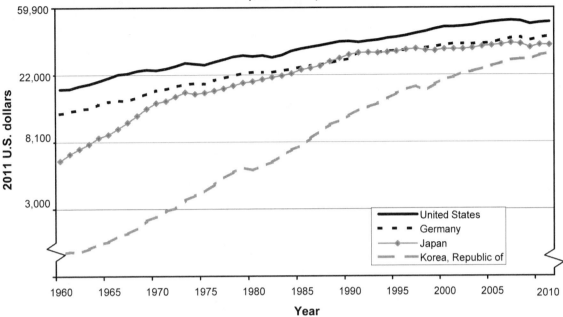

- In the United States, gross domestic product (GDP) per capita grew at an annual rate of 2.2 percent between 1960 and 2007. Canada and Australia had similar growth rates. European rates ranged from 2.4 percent in Germany and the Netherlands to 2.7 percent in Italy and Spain. Japan grew at a 3.8 percent rate and the Republic of Korea achieved 6.2 percent average growth. The growth paths of the United States, Germany, Japan, and Korea are compared in Figure 13-1. (Table 13-2)

- Korea was least affected by the recession, its growth rate slowing to 2.8 percent after 2008. Australia and Germany saw output declines but had recovered and surpassed previous highs by 2011. The other nations shown in Table 13-2 were still below their previous peaks in 2011, by percentages ranging from 1.1 percent in Canada to 5 percent or more in Spain, the United Kingdom, and Italy. (Table 13-2)

- In 2012, consumer price change in the 14 countries shown in Table 13-4B, made comparable by the calculation of "Harmonized Indexes," ranged from a decline of 0.8 percent in Switzerland to an increase of 3.3 percent in Italy. (Table 13-4A)

- The countries shown employ different percentages of their working-age populations. In 2012, Canada and Australia were highest, with over 62 percent of their populations at work. The Netherlands was close at 61.4 percent, and the United States and United Kingdom next at 58.6 percent and 58.3 percent respectively. These were followed by Germany and Japan at 56 percent. The lowest was Italy at 43.7 percent, next to France at 50.3 percent. (Table 13-6)

Table 13-1. International Comparisons: Growth Rates in Real Gross Domestic Product

(Percent change at annual rate.)

Area and country	1994–2003 annual average	2004	2005	2006	2007	2008	2009	2010	2011	2012 [1]	2013 [1]
World	3.4	4.9	4.6	5.3	5.4	2.8	-0.6	5.1	3.9	3.2	3.5
Advanced economies	2.8	3.1	2.6	3.0	2.8	0.1	-3.5	3.0	1.6	1.3	1.4
Of which:											
United States	3.3	3.5	3.1	2.7	1.9	-0.3	-3.1	2.4	1.8	2.3	2.0
Euro area [2]	2.2	2.2	1.7	3.2	3.0	0.4	-4.4	2.0	1.4	-0.4	-0.2
Germany	1.5	0.7	0.8	3.9	3.4	0.8	-5.1	4.0	3.1	0.9	0.6
France	2.2	2.5	1.8	2.5	2.3	-0.1	-3.1	1.7	1.7	0.2	0.3
Italy	1.7	1.7	0.9	2.2	1.7	-1.2	-5.5	1.8	0.4	-2.1	-1.0
Spain	3.6	3.3	3.6	4.1	3.5	0.9	-3.7	-0.3	0.4	-1.4	-1.5
Japan	0.9	2.4	1.3	1.7	2.2	-1.0	-5.5	4.5	-0.6	2.0	1.2
United Kingdom	3.5	2.9	2.8	2.6	3.6	-1.0	-4.0	1.8	0.9	-0.2	1.0
Canada	3.5	3.1	3.0	2.8	2.2	0.7	-2.8	3.2	2.6	2.0	1.8
Memorandum:											
Newly industrialized Asian economies [3]	5.1	5.9	4.8	5.8	5.9	1.8	-0.7	8.5	4.0	1.8	3.2
Emerging and developing economies	4.4	7.5	7.3	8.2	8.7	6.1	2.7	7.4	6.3	5.1	5.5
Regional groups:											
Central and eastern Europe	3.4	7.3	5.9	6.4	5.4	3.2	-3.6	4.6	5.3	1.8	2.4
Commonwealth of Independent States [4]	0.6	8.2	6.7	8.8	9.0	5.4	-6.4	4.8	4.9	3.6	3.8
Russia	0.7	7.2	6.4	8.2	8.5	5.2	-7.8	4.3	4.3	3.6	3.7
Developing Asia	7.0	8.5	9.5	10.3	11.4	7.9	7.0	9.5	8.0	6.6	7.1
China	9.4	10.1	11.3	12.7	14.2	9.6	9.2	10.4	9.3	7.8	8.2
India	6.0	7.6	9.0	9.5	10.0	6.9	5.9	10.1	7.9	4.5	5.9
Latin America and the Caribbean	2.5	6.0	4.7	5.7	5.8	4.2	-1.5	6.2	4.5	3.0	3.6
Brazil	2.5	5.7	3.2	4.0	6.1	5.2	-0.3	7.5	2.7	1.0	3.5
Mexico	2.6	4.0	3.2	5.1	3.2	1.2	-6.0	5.6	3.9	3.8	3.5
Middle East and North Africa	4.0	6.2	5.3	6.3	5.7	4.5	2.6	5.0	3.5	5.2	3.4
Sub-Saharan Africa	4.0	7.1	6.2	6.4	7.1	5.6	2.8	5.3	5.3	4.8	5.8

[1]All figures are forecasts as published by the International Monetary Fund as of early 2013.
[2]Euro area consists of: Austria, Belgium, Cyprus, Estonia, Finland, France, Germany, Greece, Ireland, Italy, Luxembourg, Malta, Netherlands, Portugal, Slovak Republic, Slovenia, and Spain.
[3]Consists of Hong Kong SAR (Special Adminsitrative Region of China), Korea (Republic of), Singapore, and Taiwan Province of China.
[4]Includes Georgia and Mongolia, which are not members of the Commonwealth of Independent States, but are included for reasons of geography and similarities in economic structure.

Table 13-2. International Comparisons: Real GDP Per Capita

(2011 U.S. dollars.)

Year	United States	Australia	Canada	France	Germany [1]	Italy	Japan	Korea, Republic of	Netherlands	Spain	United Kingdom
1960	17 747	15 320	14 733	11 272	12 352	9 841	6 109	1 537	14 244	. . .	11 879
1961	17 862	14 849	14 894	11 688	12 753	10 577	6 772	1 579	14 463	. . .	12 107
1962	18 655	15 397	15 642	12 268	13 193	11 158	7 285	1 567	14 875	. . .	12 172
1963	19 192	16 018	16 168	12 805	13 433	11 698	7 846	1 663	15 157	. . .	12 662
1964	20 023	16 737	16 894	13 485	14 184	11 927	8 633	1 777	16 242	10 726	13 316
1965	21 044	17 200	17 647	14 000	14 779	12 213	9 022	1 832	16 869	11 275	13 571
1966	22 158	17 398	18 472	14 603	15 055	12 844	9 862	2 004	17 116	11 964	13 803
1967	22 472	18 268	18 672	15 195	14 974	13 667	10 840	2 073	17 820	12 334	14 110
1968	23 326	18 942	19 284	15 752	15 734	14 469	11 995	2 255	18 821	13 016	14 687
1969	23 816	19 847	19 966	16 736	16 748	15 265	13 274	2 510	19 871	14 010	14 972
1970	23 585	20 732	20 286	17 612	17 422	15 991	14 471	2 671	20 834	14 429	15 308
1971	24 071	20 571	20 507	18 376	17 777	16 206	14 909	2 892	21 466	14 901	15 582
1972	25 080	20 675	21 375	19 041	18 430	16 709	15 941	3 024	21 998	15 923	16 135
1973	26 281	21 305	22 585	20 138	19 216	17 779	16 983	3 410	23 009	16 974	17 298
1974	25 898	21 313	23 094	20 946	19 363	18 634	16 549	3 666	23 616	17 768	17 100
1975	25 590	21 509	23 175	20 615	19 265	18 136	16 848	3 870	23 414	17 703	17 016
1976	26 707	22 090	24 061	21 433	20 316	19 332	17 330	4 321	24 257	18 076	17 456
1977	27 656	22 226	24 603	22 099	21 041	19 743	17 918	4 757	24 719	18 333	17 886
1978	28 891	22 469	25 323	22 861	21 700	20 310	18 692	5 168	25 235	18 358	18 477
1979	29 467	23 085	26 027	23 547	22 589	21 458	19 551	5 517	25 569	18 231	18 981
1980	29 041	23 495	26 250	23 810	22 830	22 148	19 943	5 329	25 703	18 370	18 571
1981	29 488	24 096	26 836	23 909	22 907	22 308	20 625	5 635	25 325	18 241	18 328
1982	28 638	23 700	25 761	24 341	22 833	22 384	21 172	6 008	24 897	18 370	18 762
1983	29 662	23 295	26 200	24 511	23 273	22 638	21 672	6 642	25 313	18 607	19 472
1984	31 519	24 436	27 463	24 758	24 027	23 363	22 492	7 207	25 989	18 862	20 013
1985	32 531	25 448	28 514	25 033	24 648	24 009	23 768	7 670	26 540	19 229	20 733
1986	33 353	25 676	28 916	25 470	25 194	24 695	24 312	8 523	27 131	19 794	21 576
1987	34 114	26 529	29 751	25 941	25 543	25 480	25 188	9 475	27 472	20 841	22 640
1988	35 196	27 228	30 828	26 999	26 329	26 536	26 873	10 476	28 233	21 854	23 854
1989	36 111	27 965	31 073	27 966	27 085	27 415	28 208	11 074	29 310	22 865	24 405
1990	36 378	27 967	30 668	28 546	27 971	27 954	29 679	11 985	30 330	23 694	24 779
1991	35 812	27 373	29 655	28 700	30 761	28 355	30 549	13 019	30 820	24 241	24 253
1992	36 537	27 750	29 563	28 983	31 112	28 563	30 683	13 627	31 110	24 386	24 399
1993	37 094	28 593	29 923	28 668	30 579	28 399	30 638	14 344	31 279	24 060	25 097
1994	38 139	29 630	31 019	29 206	31 241	29 045	30 819	15 446	32 015	24 567	26 178
1995	38 640	30 264	31 562	29 699	31 672	29 885	31 340	16 656	32 844	25 185	26 935
1996	39 623	31 067	31 740	29 913	31 831	30 232	32 083	17 684	33 818	25 735	27 707
1997	40 897	32 025	32 754	30 461	32 322	30 706	32 518	18 529	35 082	26 660	28 703
1998	42 183	33 261	33 814	31 376	32 933	31 075	31 789	17 345	36 236	27 754	29 630
1999	43 716	34 255	35 396	32 246	33 526	31 432	31 669	19 070	37 679	28 922	30 459
2000	45 026	34 910	36 903	33 207	34 508	32 661	32 322	20 575	38 886	30 128	31 640
2001	45 046	35 303	37 157	33 574	34 966	33 257	32 346	21 235	39 336	30 883	32 428
2002	45 418	36 256	37 836	33 643	34 909	33 305	32 382	22 627	39 112	31 264	33 102
2003	46 137	36 963	38 199	33 709	34 762	32 979	32 876	23 146	39 059	31 700	34 230
2004	47 307	38 017	39 020	34 316	35 174	33 255	33 621	24 124	39 803	32 207	35 055
2005	48 312	38 677	39 818	34 683	35 431	33 351	34 056	25 027	40 515	32 818	35 792
2006	49 130	39 169	40 526	35 295	36 785	33 900	34 634	26 196	41 816	33 636	36 511
2007	49 571	40 357	40 973	35 882	38 036	34 261	35 392	27 406	43 360	34 182	37 588
2008	48 951	40 644	40 773	35 656	38 515	33 612	35 040	27 834	43 971	33 941	36 975
2009	47 041	40 447	39 161	34 351	36 649	31 543	33 144	27 791	42 143	32 432	35 279
2010	47 772	40 910	39 951	34 734	38 057	32 050	34 519	29 411	42 610	32 309	35 689
2011	48 282	41 340	40 489	35 133	39 186	32 100	34 294	30 254	42 824	32 501	35 688

[1]Before 1991, data are based on growth in West Germany alone.
. . . = Not available.

Table 13-3. International Comparisons: Real GDP Per Employed Person

(2011 U.S. dollars.)

Year	United States	Australia	Canada	France	Germany [1]	Italy	Japan	Korea, Republic of	Netherlands	Spain	United Kingdom
1960	46 951	37 876	42 310	25 811	26 243	23 608	12 101	. . .	34 524	. . .	26 064
1961	48 026	37 578	42 986	27 057	27 081	25 384	13 348	. . .	35 015	. . .	26 476
1962	50 049	38 753	44 726	28 931	28 246	27 038	14 311	. . .	35 803	. . .	26 716
1963	51 519	39 954	46 032	30 486	28 971	29 036	15 437	5 996	36 487	. . .	27 894
1964	53 332	41 168	47 335	32 094	30 874	29 952	16 942	6 460	38 942	. . .	29 141
1965	55 397	41 799	48 569	33 541	32 344	31 705	17 619	6 483	40 660	. . .	29 597
1966	57 295	41 245	49 767	35 023	33 349	34 160	19 035	7 086	41 476	. . .	30 197
1967	57 383	43 014	49 664	36 640	34 366	36 162	20 745	7 244	43 809	. . .	31 412
1968	58 922	44 271	51 048	38 378	36 209	38 548	22 835	7 676	46 314	. . .	32 994
1969	59 294	46 210	51 982	40 489	38 314	41 195	25 372	8 528	48 654	. . .	33 771
1970	59 075	47 317	52 924	42 426	39 741	43 182	27 684	8 955	50 862	. . .	34 726
1971	60 822	48 001	53 779	44 478	40 800	43 953	28 696	9 563	52 517	36 966	35 561
1972	62 223	48 322	55 048	46 208	42 321	45 693	30 950	9 761	54 684	39 491	36 826
1973	63 727	49 132	56 030	48 583	43 815	48 266	32 697	10 628	57 271	41 506	38 957
1974	62 213	49 386	55 720	50 399	44 627	50 141	32 433	11 137	58 845	43 678	38 422
1975	62 785	50 564	55 708	50 236	45 379	49 056	33 518	11 678	58 887	44 802	38 372
1976	64 064	51 952	57 455	52 014	47 824	52 025	34 568	12 480	61 035	46 795	39 591
1977	64 693	52 009	58 433	53 407	49 313	53 194	35 657	13 519	62 511	48 436	40 510
1978	65 508	53 108	58 948	55 182	50 300	54 735	37 175	14 244	63 362	50 392	41 619
1979	65 717	54 218	58 643	56 735	51 395	57 359	38 814	15 223	63 295	51 579	42 368
1980	65 217	54 320	58 207	57 426	51 259	58 481	39 636	14 847	62 966	53 512	41 700
1981	66 133	55 430	58 541	58 087	51 469	59 023	40 980	15 560	62 753	54 753	42 281
1982	65 380	55 484	58 727	59 379	51 665	59 146	42 020	16 433	62 916	55 916	44 095
1983	67 453	56 282	59 893	60 175	52 959	59 645	42 660	18 275	64 792	57 104	46 125
1984	69 475	57 999	61 822	61 433	53 988	61 573	44 413	20 182	66 234	59 453	46 485
1985	70 921	59 379	62 800	62 583	54 480	62 702	46 972	20 906	66 694	61 463	47 681
1986	71 766	58 393	62 454	63 665	54 677	64 055	48 056	22 655	66 974	62 026	49 422
1987	72 217	59 953	63 398	64 643	54 680	65 949	49 832	24 114	66 837	62 474	50 956
1988	73 586	60 281	64 596	67 023	55 911	67 985	52 781	26 103	67 909	63 434	52 079
1989	74 712	60 370	64 830	68 650	57 020	69 812	54 808	26 769	69 057	64 171	52 074
1990	75 227	60 209	64 510	69 831	58 183	70 128	56 912	28 409	69 816	64 160	52 781
1991	75 754	61 099	64 284	70 461	63 557	69 895	57 632	30 226	70 172	65 013	53 248
1992	77 920	63 018	65 497	72 000	65 670	70 950	57 456	31 363	70 379	66 543	55 012
1993	79 081	65 245	66 712	72 358	65 853	72 534	57 337	32 958	70 966	67 780	57 244
1994	80 521	66 290	68 511	73 670	67 531	75 441	57 767	34 740	72 564	69 724	59 392
1995	81 408	65 954	69 203	74 480	68 418	77 779	58 701	36 793	73 178	70 309	60 535
1996	83 305	67 745	69 704	74 857	69 014	78 261	60 188	38 607	74 017	70 989	61 840
1997	85 154	69 881	71 145	75 978	70 317	79 278	60 726	40 138	74 865	71 645	63 099
1998	87 605	71 749	72 286	77 223	70 815	79 471	60 219	40 267	75 824	72 036	64 661
1999	90 477	73 540	74 412	77 975	71 073	79 532	60 937	43 812	77 388	72 816	65 793
2000	91 921	73 969	76 417	78 808	72 017	81 107	62 703	45 717	78 668	73 916	67 791
2001	92 858	75 003	76 837	79 072	72 917	80 999	63 406	46 617	78 211	74 227	69 178
2002	94 791	76 433	77 233	79 396	73 348	80 005	64 357	48 605	77 319	74 407	70 328
2003	96 243	77 125	76 858	80 010	73 709	78 664	65 422	50 035	78 023	74 324	72 332
2004	98 505	78 774	77 975	81 925	74 343	79 759	66 589	51 376	79 922	74 063	73 657
2005	99 803	78 498	79 318	82 873	74 963	80 122	66 983	52 711	81 506	73 663	74 937
2006	100 602	78 651	80 136	84 010	77 308	80 327	67 827	54 734	82 742	73 729	76 210
2007	101 409	79 803	79 976	84 746	78 504	80 764	69 007	56 836	83 928	74 052	78 430
2008	101 522	79 547	79 198	84 266	78 394	79 629	68 605	57 787	84 159	74 844	77 112
2009	102 185	80 038	78 242	82 695	74 344	76 438	65 844	58 147	81 039	77 209	75 275
2010	105 235	79 884	79 676	84 122	76 724	78 606	69 087	60 984	84 583	79 220	76 431
2011	106 541	80 330	80 357	85 152	77 978	78 813	68 537	62 119	85 437	81 417	76 638

[1]Before 1991, data are based on growth in West Germany alone.

. . . = Not available.

Table 13-4A. International Comparisons: Consumer Price Indexes

(1982–1984 = 100.)

Year	United States Index	Percent change	Australia Index	Percent change	Canada Index	Percent change	France Index	Percent change	Germany [1] Index	Percent change	Italy Index	Percent change	Japan Index	Percent change	Netherlands Index	Percent change	Spain Index	Percent change	United Kingdom Index	Percent change
1950	24.1	. . .	12.6	. . .	21.6	. . .	11.2	. . .	34.0	. . .	. . .	. . .	. . .	. . .	21.0	. . .	5.5	. . .	9.8	. . .
1951	26.0	7.9	15.0	19.4	23.8	10.4	13.1	16.9	36.6	7.6	. . .	. . .	. . .	. . .	23.1	9.6	6.0	9.4	10.7	9.1
1952	26.5	1.9	17.6	17.2	24.5	2.9	14.7	11.8	37.3	2.1	. . .	. . .	. . .	. . .	23.1	0.0	5.9	-2.0	11.7	9.2
1953	26.7	0.8	18.4	4.5	24.2	-1.4	14.5	-1.2	36.7	-1.7	10.3	. . .	. . .	. . .	23.1	0.0	6.0	1.6	12.1	3.1
1954	26.9	0.7	18.7	1.6	24.4	0.7	14.4	-0.4	36.8	0.4	10.6	2.8	. . .	. . .	24.0	4.0	6.1	1.2	12.3	2.0
1955	26.8	-0.4	19.0	1.5	24.4	0.0	14.6	1.2	37.3	1.4	10.9	2.3	. . .	. . .	24.5	1.9	6.3	4.0	12.8	4.4
1956	27.2	1.5	20.1	5.7	24.7	1.4	14.9	2.0	38.4	2.8	11.2	3.4	. . .	. . .	24.9	1.9	6.7	5.9	13.5	5.1
1957	28.1	3.3	20.7	2.9	25.6	3.5	15.3	2.7	39.1	2.0	11.4	1.3	. . .	. . .	26.5	6.5	7.4	10.8	14.0	3.5
1958	28.9	2.8	20.8	0.7	26.3	2.7	17.6	15.0	40.0	2.3	11.7	2.8	. . .	. . .	27.0	1.7	8.4	13.4	14.4	3.2
1959	29.1	0.7	21.2	2.1	26.4	0.7	18.7	6.2	40.3	0.6	11.7	-0.4	. . .	. . .	27.2	0.8	9.0	7.3	14.5	0.4
1960	29.6	1.7	22.0	3.7	26.8	1.3	19.4	3.7	40.9	1.6	11.9	2.3	. . .	. . .	27.9	2.5	9.1	1.2	14.6	1.0
1961	29.9	1.0	22.5	2.3	27.1	1.3	20.0	3.3	42.0	2.5	12.2	2.1	. . .	. . .	28.4	1.7	9.2	0.8	15.1	3.5
1962	30.2	1.0	22.5	-0.3	27.5	1.3	21.0	4.7	43.1	2.8	12.7	4.7	. . .	. . .	28.9	1.9	9.7	5.7	15.8	4.3
1963	30.6	1.3	22.6	0.6	27.8	1.3	22.0	4.8	44.4	3.0	13.7	7.5	. . .	. . .	30.0	3.8	10.6	8.7	16.1	1.9
1964	31.0	1.3	23.2	2.9	28.3	1.9	22.7	3.4	45.5	2.4	14.5	5.9	. . .	. . .	31.7	5.5	11.3	7.0	16.6	3.3
1965	31.5	1.6	24.0	3.4	29.0	2.4	23.3	2.5	46.9	3.2	15.2	4.6	. . .	. . .	33.3	5.2	12.8	13.2	17.4	4.7
1966	32.4	2.9	24.8	3.3	30.2	4.2	23.9	2.7	48.5	3.3	15.5	2.3	. . .	. . .	35.3	5.8	13.6	6.2	18.1	3.9
1967	33.4	3.1	25.7	3.5	31.3	3.4	24.6	2.6	49.4	1.9	16.1	3.7	. . .	. . .	36.4	3.1	14.5	6.4	18.6	2.6
1968	34.8	4.2	26.3	2.5	32.5	3.9	25.7	4.6	50.2	1.6	16.3	1.4	. . .	. . .	37.7	3.7	15.2	5.0	19.4	4.7
1969	36.7	5.5	27.2	3.3	34.0	4.8	27.3	6.5	51.1	1.8	16.7	2.7	. . .	. . .	40.5	7.4	15.5	2.2	20.5	5.4
1970	38.8	5.7	28.1	3.4	35.1	3.0	28.8	5.2	52.9	3.6	17.5	4.9	38.4	. . .	42.3	4.4	16.4	5.7	21.8	6.4
1971	40.5	4.4	29.9	6.1	36.1	3.0	30.3	5.5	55.7	5.2	18.4	4.8	41.0	6.7	45.5	7.5	17.7	8.2	23.8	9.4
1972	41.8	3.2	31.7	6.0	37.8	4.8	32.2	6.2	58.7	5.4	19.4	5.7	42.9	4.6	49.1	7.8	19.2	8.3	25.5	7.1
1973	44.4	6.2	34.5	9.1	40.8	7.8	34.6	7.3	62.8	7.1	21.6	10.8	48.0	11.8	53.0	8.0	21.4	11.4	27.8	9.1
1974	49.3	11.0	39.9	15.4	45.3	11.0	39.3	13.7	67.2	6.9	25.7	19.1	59.0	23.1	58.1	9.6	24.8	15.7	32.3	16.0
1975	53.8	9.1	45.9	15.2	50.1	10.7	43.9	11.8	71.2	6.0	30.0	17.0	66.0	11.8	64.0	10.2	29.0	17.0	40.1	24.2
1976	56.9	5.8	52.0	13.3	53.7	7.2	48.2	9.6	74.2	4.2	35.1	16.8	72.2	9.5	69.6	8.8	34.1	17.6	46.8	16.5
1977	60.6	6.5	58.4	12.3	58.1	8.0	52.7	9.4	77.0	3.7	41.0	17.0	78.0	8.0	74.3	6.7	42.4	24.5	54.2	15.8
1978	65.2	7.6	63.1	8.0	63.2	8.9	57.5	9.1	79.1	2.7	46.0	12.1	81.4	4.4	77.3	4.1	50.8	19.8	58.7	8.3
1979	72.6	11.3	68.9	9.1	69.1	9.3	63.6	10.8	82.3	4.1	52.8	14.8	84.4	3.6	80.6	4.2	58.8	15.7	66.6	13.4
1980	82.4	13.5	75.8	10.1	76.0	10.0	72.3	13.6	86.8	5.4	64.0	21.2	91.0	7.8	85.8	6.5	67.9	15.6	78.5	18.0
1981	90.9	10.3	83.0	9.5	85.5	12.5	82.0	13.4	92.2	6.3	75.4	17.8	95.3	4.8	91.6	6.7	77.8	14.5	87.9	11.9
1982	96.5	6.2	92.5	11.4	94.9	10.9	91.6	11.8	97.1	5.2	87.8	16.5	98.0	2.8	97.1	6.0	89.0	14.4	95.4	8.6
1983	99.6	3.2	101.8	10.0	100.4	5.8	100.5	9.6	100.2	3.2	100.7	14.7	99.8	1.8	99.8	2.8	99.9	12.2	99.8	4.6
1984	103.9	4.3	105.8	4.0	104.7	4.3	107.9	7.4	102.7	2.5	111.5	10.8	102.2	2.4	103.1	3.3	111.1	11.3	104.8	5.0
1985	107.6	3.6	112.9	6.7	108.9	4.0	114.2	5.8	104.8	2.0	121.8	9.2	104.2	2.0	105.4	2.2	120.9	8.8	111.1	6.1
1986	109.6	1.9	123.1	9.1	113.4	4.1	117.2	2.7	104.7	-0.1	129.0	5.9	104.9	0.7	105.6	0.2	131.6	8.8	114.9	3.4
1987	113.6	3.6	133.6	8.5	118.4	4.4	120.9	3.1	104.9	0.2	135.1	4.7	104.9	0.0	105.1	-0.5	138.5	5.2	119.7	4.2
1988	118.3	4.1	143.3	7.2	123.0	3.9	124.2	2.7	106.2	1.2	141.9	5.0	105.7	0.8	105.8	0.7	145.2	4.8	125.6	4.9
1989	124.0	4.8	154.1	7.5	129.3	5.1	128.6	3.6	109.2	2.8	150.8	6.3	108.1	2.2	107.0	1.1	155.0	6.8	135.4	7.8
1990	130.7	5.4	165.4	7.3	135.5	4.8	133.0	3.4	112.1	2.6	160.5	6.5	111.4	3.1	109.6	2.5	165.4	6.7	148.2	9.5
1991	136.2	4.2	170.6	3.2	143.1	5.6	137.3	3.2	116.3	3.7	170.6	6.3	115.0	3.3	113.8	3.9	175.2	5.9	156.9	5.9
1992	140.3	3.0	172.3	1.0	145.2	1.4	140.5	2.4	122.3	5.1	179.6	5.3	117.0	1.7	118.1	3.7	185.6	5.9	162.7	3.7
1993	144.5	3.0	175.4	1.8	147.9	1.9	143.5	2.1	127.6	4.4	187.8	4.6	118.5	1.3	120.5	2.1	194.1	4.6	165.3	1.6
1994	148.2	2.6	178.8	2.0	148.1	0.1	145.8	1.6	131.2	2.8	195.5	4.1	119.2	0.6	123.8	2.8	203.3	4.7	169.3	2.4
1995	152.4	2.8	187.1	4.6	151.4	2.2	148.4	1.8	133.4	1.8	205.8	5.3	119.1	-0.1	126.0	1.8	212.8	4.7	175.2	3.5
1996	156.9	3.0	192.0	2.6	153.6	1.5	151.3	2.0	135.3	1.4	214.0	4.0	119.2	0.1	128.7	2.1	220.3	3.6	179.4	2.4
1997	160.5	2.3	192.4	0.2	156.2	1.7	153.2	1.2	137.9	1.9	218.3	2.0	121.5	1.9	131.5	2.2	224.7	2.0	185.1	3.1
1998	163.0	1.6	194.1	0.9	157.8	1.0	154.3	0.7	139.3	1.0	222.6	2.0	122.2	0.6	134.1	2.0	228.8	1.8	191.4	3.4
1999	166.6	2.2	197.0	1.5	160.5	1.8	155.0	0.5	140.0	0.6	226.3	1.7	121.8	-0.3	137.0	2.2	234.1	2.3	194.3	1.5
2000	172.2	3.4	205.7	4.5	164.9	2.7	157.7	1.7	142.0	1.4	232.1	2.5	121.0	-0.7	140.2	2.3	242.1	3.4	200.1	3.0
2001	177.1	2.8	214.8	4.4	169.0	2.5	160.3	1.7	144.8	1.9	238.5	2.7	120.1	-0.8	146.1	4.2	250.8	3.6	203.6	1.8
2002	179.9	1.6	221.2	3.0	172.8	2.2	163.4	1.9	146.9	1.5	244.5	2.5	119.0	-0.9	150.9	3.3	259.6	3.5	207.0	1.7
2003	184.0	2.3	227.2	2.7	177.6	2.8	166.8	2.1	148.5	1.0	251.0	2.7	118.7	-0.3	154.0	2.1	267.5	3.0	213.0	2.9
2004	188.9	2.7	232.6	2.3	180.9	1.8	170.3	2.1	150.9	1.7	256.6	2.2	118.7	0.0	156.0	1.2	275.6	3.0	219.4	3.0
2005	195.3	3.4	238.8	2.7	184.9	2.2	173.4	1.8	153.2	1.5	261.5	1.9	118.3	-0.3	158.6	1.7	284.9	3.4	225.6	2.8
2006	201.6	3.2	247.3	3.6	188.5	2.0	176.2	1.6	155.7	1.6	267.1	2.1	118.7	0.3	160.4	1.2	294.9	3.5	232.8	3.2
2007	207.3	2.8	253.1	2.3	192.7	2.2	178.9	1.5	159.2	2.3	272.0	1.8	118.7	0.0	163.0	1.6	303.1	2.8	242.7	4.3
2008	215.3	3.8	264.1	4.4	197.2	2.3	183.9	2.8	163.3	2.6	281.1	3.3	120.3	1.4	167.1	2.5	315.5	4.1	252.4	4.0
2009	214.5	-0.4	268.8	1.8	197.7	0.3	184.1	0.1	163.9	0.4	283.3	0.8	118.7	-1.4	169.0	1.2	314.6	-0.3	251.1	-0.5
2010	218.1	1.6	276.6	2.9	201.3	1.8	186.9	1.5	165.8	1.1	287.7	1.5	117.8	-0.7	171.2	1.3	320.2	1.8	262.7	4.6
2011	224.9	3.2	285.8	3.3	207.2	2.9	190.8	2.1	169.6	2.3	295.7	2.8	117.5	-0.3	175.2	2.3	330.5	3.2	276.3	5.2
2012	229.6	2.1	290.8	1.8	210.3	1.5	194.6	2.0	173.0	2.0	304.6	3.0	117.5	0.0	179.5	2.5	338.6	2.4	285.2	3.2

[1] Data prior to 1991 are for West Germany only.
. . . = Not available.

Table 13-4B. International Comparisons: Harmonized Indexes of Consumer Prices

(2005 = 100.)

Year	United States Index	United States Percent change	Japan Index	Japan Percent change	European Union Index	European Union Percent change	Euro Area Index	Euro Area Percent change	Austria Index	Austria Percent change	Belgium Index	Belgium Percent change	Denmark Index	Denmark Percent change	France Index	France Percent change
1996	. . .	. . .	101.8	. . .	84.9	. . .	84.6	. . .	87.2	. . .	85.3	. . .	84.3	. . .	86.6	. . .
1997	. . .	. . .	103.4	1.6	86.4	1.7	85.9	1.6	88.2	1.2	86.5	1.5	85.9	1.9	87.8	1.3
1998	84.1	. . .	104.1	0.7	87.5	1.3	86.9	1.1	89.0	0.8	87.3	0.9	87.0	1.3	88.3	0.7
1999	85.8	2.0	103.7	-0.4	88.5	1.2	87.9	1.1	89.4	0.5	88.3	1.1	88.8	2.1	88.8	0.6
2000	88.7	3.4	102.8	-0.9	90.2	1.9	89.7	2.1	91.2	2.0	90.7	2.7	91.2	2.7	90.5	1.8
2001	90.8	2.3	101.9	-0.9	92.2	2.2	91.8	2.4	93.3	2.3	92.9	2.4	93.3	2.3	92.1	1.8
2002	91.6	0.9	100.7	-1.2	94.1	2.1	93.9	2.2	94.8	1.7	94.3	1.6	95.6	2.5	93.9	1.9
2003	93.7	2.3	100.4	-0.3	96.0	2.0	95.8	2.1	96.1	1.3	95.8	1.5	97.5	2.0	95.9	2.2
2004	96.3	2.8	100.4	0.0	97.9	2.0	97.9	2.1	97.9	2.0	97.5	1.9	98.3	0.8	98.1	2.3
2005	100.0	3.9	100.0	-0.4	100.0	2.2	100.0	2.2	100.0	2.1	100.0	2.5	100.0	1.7	100.0	1.9
2006	103.2	3.2	100.3	0.3	102.2	2.2	102.2	2.2	101.7	1.7	102.3	2.3	101.8	1.8	101.9	1.9
2007	105.9	2.6	100.4	0.1	104.6	2.3	104.4	2.1	103.9	2.2	104.2	1.8	103.5	1.7	103.6	1.6
2008	110.6	4.4	102.0	1.6	108.4	3.7	107.8	3.3	107.3	3.2	108.9	4.5	107.3	3.7	106.8	3.2
2009	109.7	-0.9	100.5	-1.5	109.5	1.0	108.1	0.3	107.7	0.4	108.9	0.0	108.4	1.0	106.9	0.1
2010	112.4	2.5	99.7	-0.8	111.8	2.1	109.8	1.6	109.5	1.7	111.4	2.3	110.8	2.2	108.8	1.7
2011	116.8	3.9	99.4	-0.3	115.2	3.1	112.8	2.7	113.4	3.6	115.3	3.5	113.8	2.7	111.3	2.3
2012	119.4	2.2	99.4	0.0	118.3	2.6	115.7	2.5	116.3	2.6	118.3	2.6	116.5	2.4	113.8	2.2

Year	Germany Index	Germany Percent change	Italy Index	Italy Percent change	Netherlands Index	Netherlands Percent change	Norway Index	Norway Percent change	Spain Index	Spain Percent change	Sweden Index	Sweden Percent change	Switzerland Index	Switzerland Percent change	United Kingdom Index	United Kingdom Percent change
1996	88.6	. . .	81.8	. . .	80.4	. . .	84.3	. . .	77.9	. . .	87.5	. . .	. . .	. . .	88.1	. . .
1997	90.0	1.6	83.3	1.8	81.9	1.9	86.5	2.6	79.4	1.9	89.1	1.8	. . .	. . .	89.7	1.8
1998	90.5	0.6	85.0	2.0	83.4	1.8	88.2	2.0	80.8	1.8	90.0	1.0	. . .	. . .	91.1	1.6
1999	91.1	0.7	86.4	1.6	85.1	2.0	90.0	2.0	82.6	2.2	90.5	0.6	. . .	. . .	92.3	1.3
2000	92.4	1.4	88.6	2.5	87.1	2.3	92.8	3.1	85.5	3.5	91.7	1.3	. . .	. . .	93.1	0.9
2001	94.1	1.8	90.7	2.4	91.5	5.1	95.3	2.7	87.9	2.8	94.1	2.7	. . .	. . .	94.2	1.2
2002	95.4	1.4	93.1	2.6	95.1	3.9	96.1	0.8	91.0	3.6	95.9	1.9	. . .	. . .	95.4	1.3
2003	96.4	1.0	95.7	2.8	97.2	2.2	97.9	1.9	93.9	3.1	98.2	2.3	. . .	. . .	96.7	1.4
2004	98.1	1.8	97.8	2.2	98.5	1.4	98.5	0.6	96.7	3.1	99.2	1.0	. . .	. . .	98.0	1.3
2005	100.0	1.9	100.0	2.2	100.0	1.5	100.0	1.5	100.0	3.4	100.0	0.8	100.0	. . .	100.0	2.0
2006	101.8	1.8	102.2	2.2	101.7	1.7	102.5	2.5	103.6	3.6	101.5	1.5	101.0	1.0	102.3	2.3
2007	104.1	2.3	104.3	2.1	103.3	1.6	103.2	0.7	106.5	2.8	103.2	1.7	101.8	0.8	104.7	2.3
2008	107.0	2.8	108.0	3.5	105.5	2.2	106.7	3.4	110.9	4.1	106.7	3.3	104.2	2.4	108.5	3.6
2009	107.2	0.2	108.8	0.7	106.6	1.0	109.2	2.3	110.6	-0.2	108.7	1.9	103.4	-0.8	110.8	2.1
2010	108.4	1.1	110.6	1.7	107.6	0.9	111.8	2.4	112.9	2.0	110.8	1.9	104.1	0.7	114.5	3.3
2011	111.1	2.5	113.8	2.9	110.2	2.5	113.1	1.2	116.4	3.1	112.3	1.4	104.2	0.1	119.6	4.5
2012	113.5	2.2	117.5	3.3	113.3	2.8	113.6	0.4	119.2	2.4	113.4	0.9	103.4	-0.8	123.0	2.8

. . . = Not available.

Table 13-5. International Comparisons: Civilian Working Age Population

(Approximating U.S. concepts, thousands of persons.)

Year	United States	Australia	Canada	France	Germany [1]	Italy	Japan	Netherlands	United Kingdom
1960	117 245	. . .	11 494	31 369	43 436	37 130	64 990	. . .	38 952
1961	118 771	. . .	11 708	31 596	43 647	37 358	65 820	. . .	39 287
1962	120 153	. . .	11 940	32 319	43 972	37 815	67 330	. . .	39 804
1963	122 416	. . .	12 179	33 166	44 232	38 083	69 170	. . .	40 036
1964	124 485	7 668	12 453	33 717	44 525	38 515	71 000	. . .	40 281
1965	126 513	7 830	12 755	34 219	44 909	38 724	72 650	. . .	40 481
1966	128 058	8 023	13 083	34 606	45 174	39 276	74 090	. . .	40 631
1967	129 874	8 208	13 444	34 995	45 111	39 456	75 340	. . .	40 779
1968	132 028	8 403	13 805	35 362	45 163	39 833	76 550	. . .	40 874
1969	134 335	8 612	14 162	35 742	45 570	39 781	77 580	. . .	41 006
1970	137 085	8 819	14 528	36 980	46 094	40 279	78 616	. . .	41 101
1971	140 216	9 036	14 872	37 410	46 688	40 385	79 556	. . .	40 410
1972	144 126	9 238	15 186	37 803	47 101	40 780	80 467	. . .	40 578
1973	147 096	9 425	15 526	38 192	47 594	41 186	82 147	9 750	40 754
1974	150 120	9 614	15 924	38 560	47 904	41 745	83 173	9 885	40 925
1975	153 153	9 763	16 323	38 872	48 018	42 131	84 192	9 803	41 115
1976	156 150	9 957	16 582	39 182	48 128	42 312	85 164	9 960	41 344
1977	159 033	10 136	16 964	39 527	48 419	42 529	86 070	10 103	41 620
1978	161 910	10 406	17 302	39 858	48 789	43 000	87 021	10 256	41 916
1979	164 863	10 575	17 663	40 233	49 254	43 436	88 000	10 415	42 240
1980	167 745	10 778	18 032	40 601	49 848	43 860	89 078	10 588	42 582
1981	170 130	10 994	18 398	40 961	50 344	44 184	89 927	10 744	42 881
1982	172 271	11 204	18 716	41 295	50 714	44 847	90 918	10 871	43 095
1983	174 215	11 401	18 981	41 630	50 928	45 457	92 075	10 996	43 340
1984	176 383	11 602	19 220	41 966	51 084	45 853	93 226	11 131	43 608
1985	178 206	11 826	19 460	42 303	51 252	46 174	94 405	11 271	43 876
1986	180 587	12 074	19 715	42 660	51 448	46 628	95 626	11 403	44 099
1987	182 753	12 323	19 985	43 035	51 645	46 986	96 955	11 561	44 308
1988	184 613	12 593	20 257	43 404	51 894	47 778	98 243	11 667	44 468
1989	186 393	12 823	20 540	43 762	52 283	47 660	99 493	11 766	44 613
1990	189 164	13 051	20 852	44 152	53 438	48 016	100 656	11 865	44 717
1991	190 925	13 227	21 176	44 396	66 487	48 044	101 750	11 979	44 804
1992	192 805	13 391	21 459	44 651	67 083	48 203	102 592	12 077	44 859
1993	194 838	13 561	21 731	44 919	67 709	47 375	103 466	12 162	44 899
1994	196 814	13 729	21 994	45 164	68 022	47 520	104 200	12 246	44 973
1995	198 584	13 936	22 274	45 419	68 240	47 646	104 857	12 319	45 091
1996	200 591	14 117	22 567	45 676	68 498	47 748	105 467	12 387	45 249
1997	203 133	14 321	22 858	45 954	68 797	47 820	106 367	12 455	45 423
1998	205 220	14 525	23 124	46 217	68 914	47 904	107 044	12 538	45 609
1999	207 753	14 698	23 385	46 521	69 187	47 960	107 594	12 614	45 818
2000	212 577	14 902	23 687	46 871	69 365	48 029	108 120	12 703	46 085
2001	215 092	15 140	24 028	47 278	69 600	48 107	108 620	12 803	46 413
2002	217 570	15 390	24 383	47 681	69 900	48 232	109 030	12 892	46 707
2003	221 168	15 611	24 703	48 067	70 160	48 562	109 381	12 962	47 007
2004	223 357	15 802	25 028	48 469	70 432	49 080	109 661	13 019	47 364
2005	226 082	16 099	25 345	48 885	70 752	49 606	109 838	13 075	47 792
2006	228 815	16 371	25 711	49 250	70 892	49 913	110 059	13 128	48 197
2007	231 867	16 701	26 094	49 559	70 968	50 301	110 419	13 190	48 611
2008	233 788	17 020	26 486	49 826	71 021	50 711	110 630	13 271	48 998
2009	235 801	17 400	26 883	50 057	70 943	51 064	110 761	13 368	49 355
2010	237 830	17 773	27 250	50 294	70 858	51 311	110 881	13 460	49 726
2011	239 618	18 052	27 578	50 557	70 978	51 579	110 882	13 540	50 095
2012	243 284	18 332	27 922	50 782	71 274	51 729	110 752	13 629	50 473

[1]Data prior to 1991 are for West Germany only.
. . . = Not available.

Table 13-6. International Comparisons: Civilian Employment-Population Ratios

(Approximating U.S. concepts. Civilian employment as a percent of civilian working-age population.)

Year	United States	Australia	Canada	France	Germany [1]	Italy	Japan	Netherlands	United Kingdom
1960	56.1	...	52.6	58.6	59.2	54.0	66.7	...	60.6
1961	55.4	...	52.4	58.2	59.6	54.0	66.8	...	60.8
1962	55.5	...	52.8	57.1	59.3	53.2	66.0	...	60.4
1963	55.4	...	53.0	56.6	59.2	51.9	64.9	...	60.2
1964	55.7	58.6	53.7	56.9	58.8	51.1	64.1	...	60.7
1965	56.2	59.1	54.4	56.4	58.5	49.6	63.6	...	61.0
1966	56.9	59.6	55.4	56.4	58.0	48.1	63.7	...	60.9
1967	57.3	60.0	55.4	56.2	56.3	48.5	64.0	...	60.0
1968	57.5	60.1	55.0	55.5	56.2	47.9	64.1	...	59.6
1969	58.0	60.2	55.3	55.9	56.6	47.6	63.9	...	59.5
1970	57.4	61.1	54.5	54.8	56.6	47.4	63.8	...	59.2
1971	56.6	61.0	54.5	54.6	56.2	47.1	63.4	...	60.2
1972	57.0	60.6	54.9	54.3	55.8	45.9	62.9	...	60.1
1973	57.8	61.2	56.4	54.6	55.9	45.8	63.2	51.8	60.8
1974	57.8	61.3	57.3	54.5	54.8	46.2	62.2	51.6	60.7
1975	56.1	60.1	56.9	53.7	53.2	46.0	61.2	51.7	60.2
1976	56.8	59.7	58.2	53.7	52.8	46.1	61.1	51.2	59.6
1977	57.9	59.2	57.9	53.7	52.5	46.2	61.3	51.6	59.2
1978	59.3	58.0	58.5	53.5	52.6	45.9	61.3	51.3	59.1
1979	59.9	57.8	59.8	53.2	52.9	45.9	61.4	51.4	59.3
1980	59.2	58.3	60.3	52.8	53.1	46.0	61.3	52.1	58.5
1981	59.0	58.4	60.8	52.1	52.5	45.9	61.2	51.7	56.6
1982	57.8	57.3	58.0	53.7	51.6	45.1	61.2	50.8	55.2
1983	57.9	55.3	57.6	53.2	50.6	44.7	61.4	49.3	54.5
1984	59.5	56.0	58.3	52.3	50.6	44.5	61.0	49.3	55.3
1985	60.1	56.6	59.4	51.9	50.8	44.4	60.6	50.1	55.7
1986	60.7	57.8	60.3	51.9	51.3	44.2	60.4	50.3	55.8
1987	61.5	57.8	61.2	51.5	51.5	43.8	60.1	49.8	56.6
1988	62.3	58.8	62.2	51.2	51.6	43.7	60.4	50.7	58.3
1989	63.0	60.2	62.7	51.5	52.0	43.6	60.8	51.4	59.6
1990	62.8	60.2	62.2	51.3	52.3	43.9	61.3	52.7	59.8
1991	61.7	58.0	60.2	50.8	55.5	44.5	61.8	53.6	58.1
1992	61.5	57.0	58.9	50.4	54.2	44.0	62.0	54.3	56.6
1993	61.7	56.6	58.5	49.7	53.2	44.5	61.7	53.9	56.1
1994	62.5	57.7	59.0	49.3	52.6	43.6	61.3	54.0	56.4
1995	62.9	59.1	59.3	49.6	52.4	43.1	60.9	55.3	57.0
1996	63.2	59.1	59.1	49.6	52.0	43.2	60.9	56.2	57.3
1997	63.8	58.9	59.7	49.2	51.6	43.2	61.0	57.7	58.1
1998	64.1	59.3	60.4	49.3	52.3	43.5	60.2	59.0	58.5
1999	64.3	59.6	61.3	49.7	52.1	43.9	59.4	60.2	59.0
2000	64.4	60.3	62.0	50.6	52.2	44.5	59.0	61.4	59.4
2001	63.7	60.0	61.8	50.9	52.2	45.1	58.4	62.5	59.5
2002	62.7	60.2	62.4	51.0	51.5	45.6	57.5	62.8	59.6
2003	62.3	60.8	63.1	50.7	50.8	45.3	57.1	62.2	59.8
2004	62.3	61.1	63.3	50.4	50.6	45.1	57.1	61.8	59.9
2005	62.7	62.1	63.3	50.3	51.1	44.9	57.3	61.5	60.0
2006	63.1	62.7	63.5	50.3	52.1	45.5	57.5	62.4	60.0
2007	63.0	63.3	64.0	50.9	53.2	45.6	57.7	63.6	60.0
2008	62.2	63.9	64.1	51.3	54.0	45.6	57.4	64.2	59.9
2009	59.3	63.0	62.2	50.6	54.0	44.6	56.5	63.8	58.5
2010	58.5	63.0	62.3	50.5	54.4	44.0	56.3	61.7	58.2
2011	58.4	63.1	62.5	50.4	55.7	44.0	56.2	61.3	58.0
2012	58.6	62.7	62.5	50.3	55.9	43.7	56.1	61.4	58.3

[1] Data prior to 1991 are for West Germany only.
. . . = Not available.

Table 13-7. International Comparisons: Civilian Unemployment Rates

(Approximating U.S. concepts. Civilian unemployment as a percent of civilian labor force.)

Year	United States	Australia	Canada	France	Germany [1]	Italy	Japan	Netherlands	United Kingdom
1960	5.5	1.6	6.5	1.5	1.1	3.7	1.7	. . .	2.2
1961	6.7	3.0	6.7	1.2	0.6	3.2	1.5	. . .	2.0
1962	5.5	2.9	5.5	1.4	0.6	2.8	1.3	. . .	2.7
1963	5.7	2.3	5.2	1.6	0.5	2.4	1.3	. . .	3.3
1964	5.2	1.4	4.4	1.2	0.4	2.7	1.2	. . .	2.5
1965	4.5	1.3	3.6	1.6	0.3	3.5	1.2	. . .	2.1
1966	3.8	1.6	3.3	1.6	0.3	3.7	1.4	. . .	2.3
1967	3.8	1.9	3.8	2.1	1.3	3.4	1.3	. . .	3.3
1968	3.6	1.8	4.5	2.7	1.1	3.5	1.2	. . .	3.2
1969	3.5	1.8	4.4	2.3	0.6	3.5	1.1	. . .	3.1
1970	4.9	1.7	5.7	2.5	0.5	3.2	1.2	. . .	. . .
1971	5.9	1.9	6.2	2.8	0.6	3.3	1.3	. . .	4.2
1972	5.6	2.6	6.2	2.9	0.7	3.8	1.4	. . .	4.4
1973	4.9	2.3	5.6	2.8	0.7	3.7	1.3	3.1	3.7
1974	5.6	2.7	5.3	2.9	1.6	3.1	1.4	3.6	3.7
1975	8.5	4.9	6.9	3.6	3.4	3.4	1.9	5.1	4.5
1976	7.7	4.8	6.9	4.0	3.4	3.9	2.0	5.4	5.4
1977	7.1	5.6	7.8	4.5	3.4	4.1	2.0	4.9	5.6
1978	6.1	6.3	8.1	4.6	3.3	4.1	2.3	5.1	5.5
1979	5.8	6.3	7.3	5.2	2.9	4.4	2.1	5.1	5.4
1980	7.1	6.1	7.3	5.6	2.8	4.4	2.0	6.0	6.8
1981	7.6	5.8	7.3	6.6	4.0	4.9	2.2	8.9	9.7
1982	9.7	7.2	10.7	6.9	5.6	5.4	2.4	10.2	10.8
1983	9.6	10.0	11.6	7.3	6.9	5.9	2.7	11.4	11.5
1984	7.5	9.0	10.9	8.5	7.1	5.9	2.8	11.5	11.8
1985	7.2	8.3	10.1	9.0	7.2	6.0	2.5	9.6	11.4
1986	7.0	8.1	9.2	9.0	6.6	7.5	2.7	10.0	11.4
1987	6.2	8.1	8.4	9.2	6.3	7.9	2.6	9.8	10.5
1988	5.5	7.2	7.4	8.9	6.3	7.9	2.4	9.3	8.6
1989	5.3	6.2	7.1	8.3	5.7	7.8	2.2	8.4	7.3
1990	5.6	6.9	7.7	8.0	5.0	7.0	2.0	7.6	7.1
1991	6.8	9.6	9.8	8.2	5.6	6.9	2.0	7.1	8.9
1992	7.5	10.8	10.6	9.1	6.7	7.3	2.1	6.8	10.0
1993	6.9	10.9	10.8	10.2	8.0	9.8	2.4	6.3	10.4
1994	6.1	9.7	9.6	10.8	8.5	10.7	2.6	6.9	9.5
1995	5.6	8.5	8.6	10.2	8.2	11.3	2.9	7.1	8.7
1996	5.4	8.5	8.8	10.7	9.0	11.3	3.1	6.6	8.1
1997	4.9	8.5	8.4	10.8	9.9	11.3	3.1	5.6	7.0
1998	4.5	7.7	7.7	10.4	9.3	11.4	3.8	4.4	6.3
1999	4.2	6.9	7.0	10.1	8.5	11.0	4.2	3.5	6.0
2000	4.0	6.3	6.1	8.6	7.8	10.1	4.4	3.1	5.5
2001	4.7	6.8	6.5	7.8	7.9	9.1	4.5	2.5	5.1
2002	5.8	6.4	7.0	8.0	8.6	8.6	4.9	3.0	5.2
2003	6.0	5.9	6.9	8.6	9.3	8.5	4.6	4.1	5.0
2004	5.5	5.4	6.4	9.0	10.3	8.1	4.2	5.0	4.8
2005	5.1	5.0	6.0	9.0	11.2	7.8	3.8	5.2	4.9
2006	4.6	4.8	5.5	8.9	10.3	6.9	3.6	4.3	5.5
2007	4.6	4.4	5.2	8.1	8.7	6.2	3.6	3.5	5.4
2008	5.8	4.2	5.3	7.5	7.6	6.8	3.7	3.0	5.7
2009	9.3	5.6	7.3	9.2	7.8	7.9	4.8	3.7	7.6
2010	9.6	5.2	7.1	9.4	7.1	8.5	4.7	4.5	7.9
2011	8.9	5.1	6.5	9.3	5.9	8.5	4.2	4.5	8.1
2012	8.1	5.2	6.3	10.0	5.5	10.8	3.9	5.3	8.0

[1] Data prior to 1991 are for West Germany only.
. . . = Not available.

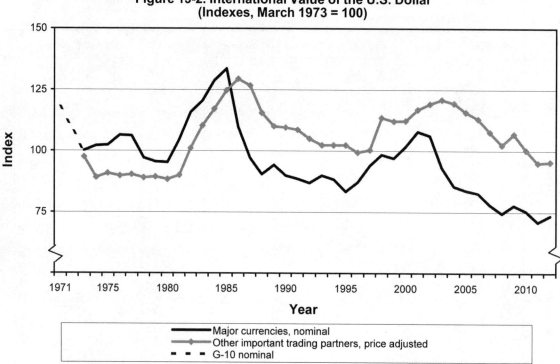

Figure 13-2. International Value of the U.S. Dollar
(Indexes, March 1973 = 100)

- Figure 13-2 above displays two indexes of the dollar's value. One is relative to a weighted average of seven "major" currencies—the euro, the British pound, the Canadian dollar, the Japanese yen, the Swiss franc, the Australian dollar, and the Swedish krona. These are all major industrial countries whose currencies are freely traded on world markets. Measured against these major currencies in terms of annual averages, the dollar has depreciated 32 percent from 2001 to 2012, comparable to the 32 percent drop from 1985 to 1988. This dollar depreciation trend seems unsurprising in light of the large current-account deficits detailed in Chapter 7. (Table 13-8 and Chapter 7)

- However, the major-currency index does not well represent U.S. competitiveness relative to the emerging-market currencies ("Other important trading partners" or OITP) that account for much of the U.S. trade deficit. Many emerging-market countries, especially China, are able to control the international values of their currencies (through, for example, direct capital controls) and keep their currencies from appreciating relative to the dollar to maintain their competitiveness in the U.S. market. Since the mid-decade, the Chinese have allowed some yuan appreciation, as can be seen in the lower yuan value of the dollar in Table 13-8, and inflation in China has also affected its real exchange rate. An index of the real (price-adjusted) value of the dollar relative to OITP, including China, is also shown in Figure 13-2. Overall, there was an 18 percent decline in the price-adjusted OITP index from 2001 to 2012. This represents an appreciable increase in overall U.S. price competitiveness with those countries, but not as great as that indicated by the major currencies index. (Table 13-8)

Table 13-8. Foreign Exchange Rates

(Not seasonally adjusted.)

Year and month	Foreign currency per U.S. dollar							Trade-weighted exchange indexes of value of U.S. dollar					
								Nominal				Price-adjusted	
	Canada, dollar	China (P.R.), yuan (renminbi)	EMU members, euro	Germany, mark	Japan, yen	Switzerland, franc	United Kingdom, pound	G-10 countries (March 1973 = 100)	Broad (January 1997 = 100)	Major currencies (March 1973 = 100)	Other important trading partners (January 1997 = 100)	Broad (March 1973 = 100)	Other important trading partners (March 1973 = 100)
1971	1.0099	. . .	. . .	3.4673	348.05	4.1158	0.4091	117.81	. . .	. . .	. . .	. . .	. . .
1972	0.9908	. . .	. . .	3.1889	303.11	3.8181	0.3995	109.07	. . .	. . .	. . .	. . .	. . .
1973	1.0002	. . .	. . .	2.6719	271.40	3.1698	0.4077	99.14	31.70	100.17	2.03	98.97	97.47
1974	0.9781	. . .	. . .	2.5873	291.94	2.9791	0.4273	101.41	32.58	102.03	2.14	95.63	89.11
1975	1.0173	. . .	. . .	2.4614	296.77	2.5834	0.4501	98.50	33.68	102.39	2.39	94.45	90.88
1976	0.9861	. . .	. . .	2.5184	296.48	2.5003	0.5541	105.63	35.83	106.44	2.71	94.51	89.84
1977	1.0635	. . .	. . .	2.3225	268.38	2.4038	0.5731	103.35	36.88	106.10	3.02	92.88	90.38
1978	1.1408	. . .	. . .	2.0089	210.46	1.7899	0.5213	92.39	35.09	97.13	3.18	87.30	89.04
1979	1.1716	. . .	. . .	1.8331	219.21	1.6635	0.4712	88.07	35.36	95.59	3.41	88.61	89.43
1980	1.1694	. . .	. . .	1.8183	226.58	1.6776	0.4302	87.39	36.35	95.35	3.75	89.75	88.43
1981	1.1989	1.7090	. . .	2.2606	220.45	1.9647	0.4940	103.26	40.34	104.76	4.27	96.58	90.03
1982	1.2339	1.8973	. . .	2.4281	249.05	2.0318	0.5721	116.50	46.83	115.75	5.52	106.10	101.03
1983	1.2326	1.9809	. . .	2.5545	237.45	2.1004	0.6597	125.32	52.81	120.46	7.44	110.57	110.30
1984	1.2952	2.3346	. . .	2.8403	237.50	2.3517	0.7481	138.34	60.11	128.69	9.78	117.91	117.12
1985	1.3659	2.9446	. . .	2.9443	238.47	2.4576	0.7708	143.24	67.16	133.55	13.14	122.73	124.63
1986	1.3898	3.4610	. . .	2.1711	168.50	1.7988	0.6813	112.27	62.35	109.77	16.49	107.40	129.33
1987	1.3262	3.7314	. . .	1.7976	144.62	1.4916	0.6098	96.95	60.42	97.16	19.92	98.66	126.62
1988	1.2309	3.7314	. . .	1.7561	128.14	1.4633	0.5614	92.75	60.92	90.43	24.07	92.07	115.57
1989	1.1841	3.7690	. . .	1.8792	137.99	1.6354	0.6104	98.52	66.90	94.29	29.61	93.80	110.04
1990	1.1670	4.7955	. . .	1.6159	144.82	1.3898	0.5605	89.05	71.41	89.91	40.10	91.22	109.56
1991	1.1460	5.3348	. . .	1.6585	134.51	1.4338	0.5658	89.73	74.35	88.59	46.69	89.68	108.58
1992	1.2088	5.5266	. . .	1.5624	126.75	1.4069	0.5662	86.64	76.91	87.00	53.13	87.79	104.96
1993	1.2902	5.7767	. . .	1.6537	111.23	1.4780	0.6660	93.17	83.78	89.90	63.37	89.13	102.33
1994	1.3659	8.6401	. . .	1.6219	102.20	1.3668	0.6528	91.32	90.87	88.43	80.54	88.96	102.34
1995	1.3727	8.3709	. . .	1.4331	94.11	1.1822	0.6335	84.30	92.65	83.41	92.51	86.51	102.40
1996	1.3637	8.3387	. . .	1.5049	108.80	1.2364	0.6407	87.34	97.46	87.25	98.24	88.52	99.40
1997	1.3849	8.3193	. . .	1.7339	121.09	1.4508	0.6106	96.35	104.43	93.93	104.64	93.23	100.45
1998	1.4836	8.3006	. . .	1.7593	130.82	1.4497	0.6034	98.82	115.89	98.45	125.89	101.20	113.61
1999	1.4858	8.2783	0.9375	1.8359	113.71	1.5027	0.6184	. . .	116.16	97.06	129.20	100.34	112.18
2000	1.4855	8.2784	1.0830	. . .	107.82	1.6899	0.6598	. . .	119.55	101.76	129.81	104.16	112.24
2001	1.5490	8.2770	1.1167	. . .	121.52	1.6880	0.6946	. . .	126.06	107.87	135.92	110.16	116.80
2002	1.5706	8.2771	1.0579	. . .	125.27	1.5571	0.6656	. . .	126.82	106.18	140.41	110.32	119.25
2003	1.4012	8.2772	0.8836	. . .	115.92	1.3452	0.6117	. . .	119.26	93.15	143.57	103.66	120.87
2004	1.3016	8.2768	0.8039	. . .	108.16	1.2428	0.5456	. . .	113.76	85.51	143.38	99.03	119.46
2005	1.2115	8.1940	0.8034	. . .	110.14	1.2462	0.5493	. . .	110.84	83.87	138.86	97.37	115.80
2006	1.1344	7.9720	0.7962	. . .	116.35	1.2535	0.5425	. . .	108.71	82.62	135.40	96.25	113.09
2007	1.0742	7.6059	0.7294	. . .	117.77	1.1999	0.4995	. . .	103.58	77.98	130.23	91.66	107.51
2008	1.0668	6.9482	0.6801	. . .	103.38	1.0829	0.5392	. . .	99.88	74.47	126.79	87.81	102.31
2009	1.1414	6.8307	0.7177	. . .	93.60	1.0861	0.6389	. . .	105.66	77.66	135.89	91.40	106.78
2010	1.0301	6.7690	0.7532	. . .	87.75	1.0426	0.6466	. . .	101.82	75.30	130.37	87.11	100.21
2011	0.9890	6.4633	0.7184	. . .	79.71	0.8876	0.6236	. . .	97.15	70.85	125.76	82.61	95.01
2012	0.9994	6.3085	0.7774	. . .	79.81	0.9374	0.6307	. . .	99.82	73.48	128.28	84.35	95.48
2011													
January	0.9939	6.5964	0.7479	. . .	82.63	0.9565	0.6336	. . .	98.60	72.87	126.30	83.73	95.74
February	0.9876	6.5761	0.7323	. . .	82.54	0.9500	0.6202	. . .	97.85	71.93	125.89	83.18	95.40
March	0.9766	6.5645	0.7133	. . .	81.65	0.9185	0.6189	. . .	96.92	70.74	125.39	82.52	95.15
April	0.9580	6.5267	0.6916	. . .	83.18	0.8972	0.6105	. . .	95.32	69.48	123.45	81.18	93.66
May	0.9680	6.4957	0.6976	. . .	81.13	0.8740	0.6123	. . .	95.28	69.57	123.22	81.24	93.50
June	0.9766	6.4746	0.6943	. . .	80.43	0.8401	0.6166	. . .	95.25	69.48	123.28	81.12	93.21
July	0.9553	6.4575	0.7005	. . .	79.24	0.8214	0.6189	. . .	94.59	69.04	122.38	80.52	92.40
August	0.9817	6.4036	0.6977	. . .	76.97	0.7800	0.6114	. . .	95.13	69.01	123.68	81.03	93.39
September	1.0025	6.3885	0.7274	. . .	76.80	0.8767	0.6341	. . .	97.98	71.14	127.28	83.41	96.09
October	1.0198	6.3710	0.7282	. . .	76.64	0.8958	0.6342	. . .	98.89	71.57	128.78	83.94	96.87
November	1.0248	6.3564	0.7376	. . .	77.56	0.9079	0.6327	. . .	99.52	72.21	129.35	84.41	97.16
December	1.0235	6.3482	0.7602	. . .	77.80	0.9334	0.6416	. . .	100.45	73.22	130.09	85.09	97.50
2012													
January	1.0130	6.3172	0.7746	. . .	76.96	0.9376	0.6442	. . .	99.83	73.35	128.49	84.43	96.02
February	0.9967	6.2997	0.7554	. . .	78.47	0.9118	0.6328	. . .	98.10	72.26	126.01	83.23	94.61
March	0.9938	6.3125	0.7571	. . .	82.47	0.9131	0.6320	. . .	98.70	72.91	126.48	83.69	94.76
April	0.9928	6.3043	0.7599	. . .	81.25	0.9133	0.6250	. . .	99.01	72.79	127.37	83.78	95.21
May	1.0097	6.3242	0.7809	. . .	79.67	0.9383	0.6280	. . .	100.74	73.92	129.78	85.03	96.59
June	1.0280	6.3633	0.7974	. . .	79.32	0.9576	0.6428	. . .	102.18	75.03	131.56	86.26	97.80
July	1.0142	6.3717	0.8145	. . .	78.93	0.9783	0.6413	. . .	101.70	75.22	130.21	85.72	96.60
August	0.9924	6.3593	0.8061	. . .	78.69	0.9681	0.6361	. . .	100.82	74.24	129.52	85.10	96.15
September	0.9783	6.3200	0.7761	. . .	78.14	0.9386	0.6201	. . .	99.24	72.58	128.19	83.96	95.34
October	0.9872	6.2627	0.7708	. . .	79.01	0.9323	0.6219	. . .	98.96	72.74	127.32	83.71	94.65
November	0.9970	6.2338	0.7790	. . .	81.03	0.9388	0.6263	. . .	99.59	73.60	127.58	83.96	94.44
December	0.9898	6.2328	0.7623	. . .	83.79	0.9213	0.6194	. . .	99.01	73.10	126.93	83.29	93.63

. . . = Not available.

NOTES AND DEFINITIONS, CHAPTER 13

Table 13-1: International Comparisons: Growth Rates in Real Gross Domestic Product

SOURCE: ECONOMIC REPORT OF THE PRESIDENT, ANNUAL REPORT OF THE COUNCIL OF ECONOMIC ADVISERS, FEBRUARY 2013

Table 13-1 is reprinted from the February 2013 *Annual Report of the U.S. Council of Economic Advisers*, where it appears as Table B-112. It is based on data from the Department of Commerce's Bureau of Economic Analysis (BEA) and the International Monetary Fund. The report is found at http://www.whitehouse.gov/administration/eop/cea/economic-report-of-the-President. Note that all of the 2013 data are based on forecasts, and the U.S. data are now superseded by later BEA estimates shown elsewhere in the volume and expected subsequently as well.

As a result of the spending cuts (commonly referred to as sequestration) required by the Balanced Budget and Emergency Deficit Control Act, as amended, the Bureau of Labor Statistics was required to cut its current budget by more than $30 million. In order to achieve these savings and protect its core programs (such as U.S. price indexes and measures of the U.S. labor market), BLS has eliminated several programs, including the International Labor Comparisons program, which adjusts foreign data to a common framework of concepts, definitions, and classifications to facilitate comparisons between the United States and other countries. Therefore, some of the series adjusted for comparability presented in Tables 13-2 through 13-7 will not be updated going forward, although the historical data shown here will still be valid.

Tables 13-2 and 13-3: International Comparisons: Real Gross Domestic Product Per Capita, Real Gross Domestic Product Per Employed Person

SOURCE: U.S. DEPARTMENT OF LABOR, BUREAU OF LABOR STATISTICS (BLS)

Definitions and notes on the data

Real gross domestic product (GDP) per capita can be taken as a rough measure of potential economic welfare; that is, the potential standard of living available to each of a country's residents. Because income distributions are typically skewed, GDP per capita (which is an average or "mean") should not be taken as a representation of the value of the standard of living actually enjoyed by a typical ("median") individual. See the

subsection entitled "Whose standard of living?" in the article at the beginning of this volume.

Real gross domestic product per employed person is a rough measure of productivity (ignoring any differences in hours worked by employees).

The GDP, population, and employment measures for each country come from the country's own national accounts and population sources. Not all countries use annual chain-weighted methods such as those incorporated in U.S. GDP. (See notes and definitions to Chapter 1.) Some of the employment and population figures have been recalculated for greater comparability by BLS. GDP figures are converted from national currency values to U.S. 2011-dollar equivalents using 2011 purchasing power parities (PPPs) published by the OECD (Organisation for Economic Co-operation and Development) in the OECD-Eurostat PPP Program.

PPPs are currency conversion rates that allow output in different currency units to be expressed in a common unit of value (in this case, U.S. dollars). They are preferable to international market exchange rates for this purpose. According to BLS, "At best, market exchange rates represent only the relative prices of goods and services that are traded internationally, not the relative value of total domestic output, which also consists of goods, and particularly services, that are not traded internationally, or which are isolated from the effects of foreign trade. Market exchange rates also are affected by… currency traders' views of the stability of governments in various countries, relative interest rates among countries, and other incentives for holding financial assets in one currency rather than another."

Measuring PPPs is difficult and subject to error, and BLS emphasizes that statistics using PPPs should be used with caution: "The per capita GDPs of most OECD countries fall within a relatively narrow range, and changes in rankings can occur as a result of relatively minor adjustments to PPP estimates."

In addition to the 11 countries shown here, BLS also calculates and publishes similar data for Austria, Belgium, Czech Republic, Denmark, Finland, Ireland, Norway, Sweden, and Singapore. In the latest report, referenced below, there are also data, graphs, and discussion on hours worked, GDP per hour worked and gross national income per capita.

References

These data and related information are contained in Department of Labor, Bureau of Labor Statistics, Division of International Labor Comparisons, "International comparisons of gross domestic product per capita and per hour,

1960–2011" (November 7, 2012), available online at http://www.bls.gov/ilc.

Tables 13-4A and 13-4B: International Comparisons: Consumer Price Indexes

SOURCE: U.S. DEPARTMENT OF LABOR, BUREAU OF LABOR STATISTICS

Notes on the data

These data are prepared by the BLS Division of International Labor Comparisons. The update presented here was issued August 1, 2013.

In Table 13-4A, the indexes are not adjusted for comparability across countries (except insofar as they are rebased to the common base 1982–1984 =100, which preserves the year-to-year changes in the original index). National differences exist with respect to population coverage, frequency of market basket weight changes, and treatment of homeowner costs. For some countries, BLS publishes indexes for all households and for workers' households; in such cases, *Business Statistics* shows the all-households index.

BLS links published indexes together to form historical series and rebases the foreign indexes to the U.S. base 1982–1984 = 100. Percent changes may differ from changes published elsewhere due to rounding differences.

Table 13-4B shows Harmonized Indexes of Consumer Prices (HICP), internationally comparable measures covering all households and excluding owner-occupied housing costs, conforming to the conceptual basis of the European Union's Harmonized Index of Consumer Prices. This is the index that EU member states must produce for comparisons across countries, and that is used by the European Central Bank for the conduct of monetary policy. The U.S. entry is an "experimental" BLS series, expanded to cover the entire non-institutional population and narrowed to remove owner-occupied housing costs. As can be seen, these changes do alter year-to-year comparisons. These data are produced outside of regular BLS production systems, so the BLS points out that they may have "less than full production quality." These indexes have all been rebased to 2005 = 100.

The European Union index covers the following 27 countries: Austria, Belgium, Bulgaria, Cyprus, the Czech Republic, Denmark, Estonia, Finland, France, Germany, Greece, Hungary, Ireland, Italy, Latvia, Lithuania, Luxembourg, Malta, the Netherlands, Poland, Portugal, Romania, Slovakia, Slovenia, Spain, Sweden, and the United Kingdom. Its geographic coverage has expanded as the EU membership

expands; data for new member countries are linked in to the earlier series.

The Euro area index covers the following 16 countries: Austria, Belgium, Cyprus, Finland, France, Germany, Greece, Ireland, Italy, Luxembourg, Malta, the Netherlands, Portugal, Slovakia, Slovenia, and Spain. As with the EU index, the newer countries have been linked in as membership has expanded.

References

For a description of the official U.S. index, see the notes and definitions for Table 8-1.

The indexes for the other countries and the harmonized indexes are presented and described in "International Indexes of Consumer Prices, 18 countries and areas, 1996–2009" (August 3, 2010), available at http://www.bls.gov/ilc. They were updated in August, 2013.

For more information on the HICP, see "International comparisons of Harmonized Indexes of Consumer Prices," at http://www.bls.gov/opub/mlr/2007/02/ressum.pdf. For more information on the United States HICP, see "Comparing U.S. and European inflation: the CPI and the HICP," at http://www.bls.gov/opub/mlr/2006/05/art3full.pdf.

Tables 13-5 through 13-7: International Comparisons: Working-Age Population, Employment-Population Ratios, and Unemployment Rates

SOURCE: U.S. DEPARTMENT OF LABOR, BUREAU OF LABOR STATISTICS

Notes on the data

Current and historical data on working-age population, labor force, employment, and unemployment for 10 industrial countries are collected and adjusted by BLS to approximate U.S. concepts and definitions. (For the U.S. concepts and definitions, see the notes and definitions for Tables 10-1 through 10-6.) Nine of those countries are shown in Tables 13-5 through 13-7; the tenth is Sweden. The German data are for the former West Germany through 1990, and for unified Germany from 1991 to the present. Adding the former East Germany raised the 1991 unemployment rate from 4.3 percent (for West Germany alone) to 5.6 percent for unified Germany.

It should be noted that there is also a set of employment-population ratios, quite different from the ones shown here, published by BLS in the report for "International comparisons of gross domestic product per capita and per hour" that is referenced above in the notes for Tables 13-2 and 13-3. The ratios in that report are for employment divided by the total resident population (including children). The ratios shown and described here are for employment divided by the working-age population.

Historically, there were large differences between published and BLS-adjusted unemployment rates; however, in recent years, the two unemployment rate series have nearly converged for most countries. Major differences between the country's own official unemployment rates and those adjusted by BLS remain for Canada, Germany, the Netherlands, and Sweden.

There are many qualifications to the adjustments for comparability. Many of the adjusted measures still use a lower age limit than the U.S. limit of 16 years, if the age at which compulsory schooling ends in that country is lower than 16. Currently, however, no country's age limit is lower than 15 years. In Japan and Germany, the institutional population is included. In some countries where the customary significance of layoffs is different, workers on layoff are counted as employed, although in the United States they are considered unemployed. In addition, each country except Japan has some break in historical continuity because of methodological change. The source document includes documentation of each country's series breaks and deviations from exact comparability.

Data availability and references

In addition to the series shown here, BLS calculates and publishes comparative labor force participation rates, employment-population ratios, and unemployment rates by sex; employment by sex and by economic sector; and unemployment rates by age. Data for 1960 through 1969 are from the BLS report "International comparisons of annual labor force statistics: 10 countries, 1960–2007" (October 21, 2008). The data for 1970 through 2012 are from BLS, Division of International Labor Comparisons, "International comparisons of annual labor force statistics, 1970–2012" (June 7, 2013). This report, related data, and monthly updates to unemployment rates are available on the International Labor Comparisons Web site at http://www.bls.gov/ilc.

Table 13-8: Foreign Exchange Rates

SOURCE: BOARD OF GOVERNORS OF THE FEDERAL RESERVE SYSTEM

Definitions and notes on the data

This table shows measures of the U.S. dollar relative to the currencies of some important individual countries and also relative to average values for major groups of countries. In Business Statistics, all of these measures are defined as the foreign currency price of the U.S. dollar. When the measure is relatively high, the dollar is relatively strong—but less competitive (in the sense of price competition)—and the other currency or group of currencies named in the measure is relatively weak and more competitive.

For consistency, this definition is used in Business Statistics even in the case of currencies that are commonly quoted in the financial press and elsewhere as dollars per foreign currency unit instead of foreign currency units per dollar. Notably, this is the case for the euro and for the British pound. Where Business Statistics shows the average 2010 value of the dollar as 0.7540 euros, the more usual statement—and the one found on the Federal Reserve release used as a source for this information—is that in 2010, the euro was worth on average $1.3261. (The value shown in the table is 1 divided by 1.3261, with slight rounding differences.) Where Business Statistics shows the 2010 value of the dollar as 0.6472 British pounds, the more usual statement is that the pound was worth $1.5452. The Canadian dollar is also sometimes quoted relative to the U.S. dollar, rather than as shown here and in documents from the Federal Reserve.

The definition of the dollar's value used in Business Statistics is the most useful for economic analysis from the U.S. point of view and for foreign tourists in the United States. For American tourists overseas, it is easier to use the inverse of this measure, the value of the other currency; for example, the traveler in Paris can more easily translate prices into dollars by multiplying by the dollar value of the euro than by dividing by the euro value of the dollar.

The foreign exchange rates shown are averages of the daily noon buying rates for cable transfers in New York City certified for customs purposes by the Federal Reserve Bank of New York.

The introduction of the euro in January 1999 as the common currency for 11 European countries—Austria, Belgium, Finland, France, Germany, Ireland, Italy, Luxembourg, Netherlands, Portugal, and Spain—marked a major change in the international currency system, and the use of the euro subsequently spread to five more countries. Greece entered the European Monetary Union (EMU) in January 2001 and Slovenia entered in January 2007. Cyprus and Malta joined in January 2008 and the Slovak Republic in January 2009. The euro is also the national currency in Monaco, the Vatican City and San Marino, and is the de facto currency in Andorra, Kosovo, and Montenegro. The values of the currencies of these countries no longer fluctuate relative to each other, but the value of the euro still fluctuates relative to the dollar and to currencies for countries outside the EMU. The currency and coins of the individual countries continued to circulate from 1999 through the end of 2001, but in January 2002, new euro currency and coins were introduced, replacing the currency and coins of the individual countries. Once a country has entered the monetary union, its values relative to the dollar will continue to fluctuate—but only due to fluctuations in the value of the euro relative to the dollar.

There is no fully satisfactory historical equivalent to the euro. For comparisons over time, the Federal Reserve Board uses a "restated German mark," derived simply by dividing each historical value of the mark by the euro conversion factor, 1.95583. The G-10 dollar index described below includes five of the currencies that later merged into the euro, but also includes the currencies of Canada, Japan, the United Kingdom, Switzerland, and Sweden.

Trade-weighted indexes of the value of the dollar against groups of foreign currencies also appear in this table. In each case, weighted averages of the individual currency values of the dollar are set at 100 in a base period. The weights are based on goods trade only and exclude trade in services. Base periods differ for different indexes.

The first four columns show the more familiar type of foreign exchange indexes, which use *nominal* values of each currency. The last two columns are *price-adjusted* (indexes of "real" exchange rates), aggregating values of the dollar in terms of each currency that have been adjusted for inflation, using each country's consumer price index.

Where any currency has had an episode of hyperinflation with consequent huge depreciation in terms of the dollar, the nominal index will not reflect the actual competitiveness of the dollar in terms of that currency over the longer term. As there have been hyperinflations in some of the countries making up the broad index and its "other important trading partners" component (see below), price-adjusted indexes are also shown for those two groupings in the final two columns.

The *G-10 Index (March 1973 = 100)*. This measure is an index of the exchange value of the U.S. dollar in terms of the weighted average currencies of the G-10 ("Other industrialized") countries, which are Belgium, Canada, France, Germany, Italy, Japan, the Netherlands, Sweden, Switzerland, and the United Kingdom. Unlike the three indexes that follow, the weights in this index—which represented "multilateral" (world market) trade shares—were fixed. The Federal Reserve stopped calculating this index as of December 1998.

The three newer indexes, introduced in December 1998, use weights that focus more directly on U.S. competitiveness and that change as trade flows shift. Each country's weight is based on an average of the country's share of U.S. imports, the country's share of U.S. exports, and the country's share of exports that go to other countries that are large importers of U.S. goods. The weights are updated each year; the latest weights were introduced on October 10, 2012. The index formula uses geometric averaging.

The *broad index (January 1997 = 100)*. The new overall index includes currencies of all economies that have a share of U.S. non-oil goods imports or goods exports of at least 0.5 percent. These economies encompass the euro area and 25 other countries. The list of currencies is updated each year, though no changes have been made in the list of included countries. These countries are then classified in either the major currency index or the other important trading partners as outlined below.

The *major currency index (March 1973 = 100)*. This index serves purposes similar to those of the discontinued G-10 index, and its level and movements are similar. It is a measure of the competitiveness of U.S. products in the major industrial countries and a gauge of financial pressure on the dollar. The index includes countries whose currencies are traded in deep and relatively liquid financial markets and circulate widely outside the country of issue. These are also countries for which information on short and long-term interest rates is readily available. This index includes the euro, Canada, Japan, the United Kingdom, Switzerland, Australia, and Sweden. This list has not changed since the introduction of the new indexes in 1998.

The *other important trading partners (OITP) index (January 1997 = 100)*. This index captures the competitiveness of U.S. products in key emerging markets in Latin America, Asia, the Middle East, and Eastern Europe, whose currencies do not circulate widely outside the country of issue. Hyperinflations and large depreciations for some of these countries have led to a persistent upward trend in the nominal version of this index. Hence, the nominal OITP index is mainly useful for analysis of short-term developments, and the price-adjusted index is shown to give a more appropriate measure of longer-term competitiveness. This index includes Mexico, China, Taiwan, South Korea, Singapore, Hong Kong, Malaysia, Brazil, Thailand, Philippines, Indonesia, India, Israel, Saudi Arabia, Russia, Argentina, Venezuela, Chile, and Colombia.

Data availability and references

Current press releases, historical data, and information on weights and methods for exchange rates and exchange rate indexes are available on the Federal Reserve Web site at http://www.federalreserve.gov/; go to "Economic Research and Data", then "Statistical Releases and Historical Data," and select the G.5 release. The dollar value indexes are described in the article "Indexes of the Foreign Exchange Value of the Dollar," *Federal Reserve Bulletin* (Winter 2005), also available on the Federal Reserve Web site.

Additional information on exchange rates can be found on the Federal Reserve Bank of St. Louis Web site at http://www.stls.frb.org/fred/data/exchange.html.

PART B

INDUSTRY PROFILES

CHAPTER 14: PRODUCT AND INCOME BY INDUSTRY

Figure 14-1: Major Industry Groups, Long-Term, Recession, and Early Recovery (percent change in real GDP, annual rate)

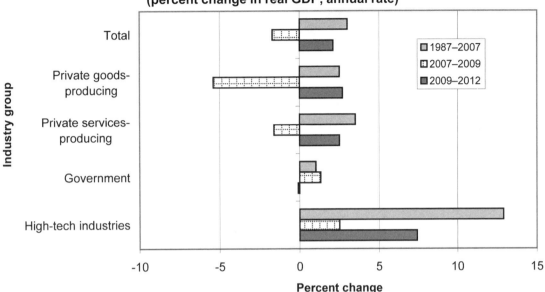

- Between 1987 and 2007 (the peak of the most recent business cycle), total real gross domestic product (GDP) rose at an average annual rate of 3.0 percent. The goods-producing sector grew at a 2.6 percent rate, while private service-producing industries grew at a 3.5 percent rate. The high-tech sector (information-communications-technology-producing industries), which accounted for just 3.4 percent of total GDP in 1987—the first year in which they can be identified separately—grew at a 12.9 percent annual rate over the subsequent 20 years, but still only accounted for 4.2 percent of total GDP. (Tables 14-1 and 14-2; Figure 14-1)

- The latest recession began in December 2007 and ended in June 2009. From 2007 to 2009, using annual figures, total real GDP fell at a 1.7 percent per year rate, with goods output down at a sharp 5.4 percent rate and private services, a 1.6 percent rate. The high-tech subgroup still grew during the recession, though more slowly. In the first three years of recovery, goods recovered at a 2.7 percent rate according to preliminary 2012 data, and private services 2.5 percent; high-tech speeded up to 7.4 percent. (Table 14-2, Figure 14-1)

- Table 14-3 can be used to assess the share of each industry group in total gross domestic factor income and the shares paid to employees and accruing to land and capital in each industry. Factor income is a better measure for such purposes than the BEA definition of value added because value added includes, but factor income excludes, taxes on production and imports. In the U.S. accounts these taxes are assigned to industries that do not bear their ultimate burden (see the Notes to this chapter).

- In private goods-producing industries in 2011, employee compensation received 53.4 percent of gross factor income, while in private services-producing industries excluding real estate and rental and leasing, compensation received 66.0 percent of total value. ("Real estate and rental and leasing" is recorded as an extremely capital-intensive industry; one reason is because industry values include the value of owner-occupied housing, which has no paid labor counterpart.) (Table 14-3)

Table 14-1. Gross Domestic Product (Value Added) by NAICS Industry Group

(Billions of dollars.)

Year	Total gross domestic product	Private industries					Manufacturing							
		Total	Agriculture, forestry, fishing, and hunting	Mining	Utilities	Construction	Durable goods	Nondurable goods	Wholesale trade	Retail trade	Transportation and warehousing	Information	Finance and insurance	Real estate and rental and leasing
1947	244.1	213.7	19.9	5.8	3.5	8.9	32.0	30.5	15.5	23.1	14.1	6.8	5.9	19.7
1948	269.1	239.2	23.2	7.7	3.9	11.1	36.2	33.8	17.1	24.5	15.5	7.5	6.7	21.6
1949	267.2	235.9	18.6	6.6	4.4	11.2	35.7	32.7	16.7	24.9	15.1	8.1	7.6	23.1
1950	293.7	262.2	19.9	7.7	4.9	12.8	43.8	35.5	18.7	26.0	16.8	8.7	8.2	25.5
1951	339.3	300.4	23.0	8.5	5.6	15.3	53.7	41.0	21.3	28.5	19.0	9.6	9.3	28.3
1952	358.3	313.8	22.1	8.3	6.1	16.4	56.9	41.5	21.5	29.9	19.8	10.3	10.4	30.9
1953	379.3	332.8	20.0	8.8	6.8	17.1	64.0	43.5	22.1	30.8	20.6	11.3	11.5	33.9
1954	380.4	332.1	19.6	8.9	7.5	17.2	58.9	42.8	22.3	31.4	19.2	11.5	12.3	36.8
1955	414.7	363.8	18.8	10.1	8.1	18.4	68.0	47.1	25.1	33.4	21.0	12.4	13.4	39.7
1956	437.4	383.1	18.6	10.9	8.6	20.3	70.3	49.1	27.0	34.6	22.0	13.2	14.5	42.2
1957	461.1	403.0	18.4	11.0	9.3	21.3	74.7	49.7	28.5	36.6	22.9	14.1	15.6	45.2
1958	467.2	405.4	20.6	10.1	10.0	21.0	67.1	50.3	29.2	37.3	21.8	14.8	16.8	48.3
1959	506.6	441.4	19.0	9.9	11.0	22.7	77.8	54.3	33.4	40.6	22.9	16.2	18.1	51.7
1960	526.4	457.1	19.9	10.1	12.0	23.1	78.4	55.1	34.9	41.5	23.2	17.1	19.5	55.2
1961	544.8	471.2	20.1	10.2	12.7	24.1	77.6	56.4	35.9	42.6	23.5	18.0	20.6	58.7
1962	585.7	506.9	20.3	10.4	13.4	25.9	87.6	59.7	38.3	45.7	25.0	19.3	21.1	63.4
1963	617.8	533.2	20.5	10.6	14.0	27.7	93.3	62.4	39.9	47.7	25.9	20.8	22.0	67.4
1964	663.6	572.9	19.6	11.0	15.0	30.3	101.0	66.3	43.0	52.4	27.5	22.6	24.1	71.6
1965	719.1	622.2	22.4	11.2	15.6	33.3	113.4	71.5	46.5	56.2	29.7	24.4	26.4	76.3
1966	787.7	680.3	23.4	11.8	16.7	36.6	126.5	78.4	51.0	60.5	32.4	26.7	29.0	81.4
1967	832.4	714.2	22.9	12.0	17.6	38.2	129.1	80.4	53.9	64.9	33.1	28.7	32.3	86.4
1968	909.8	778.2	23.6	12.9	19.0	41.8	140.4	87.8	59.2	71.6	35.9	31.1	36.3	93.1
1969	984.4	840.7	26.3	13.5	20.4	46.7	147.4	91.7	63.8	77.6	38.1	34.3	40.9	101.2
1970	1 038.3	880.0	27.3	15.1	21.7	49.5	140.4	95.1	67.7	83.0	40.2	37.4	44.1	108.7
1971	1 126.8	954.5	29.4	15.2	24.7	54.5	148.3	100.6	73.4	90.7	44.3	40.6	48.7	121.0
1972	1 237.9	1 050.6	34.3	16.0	27.0	60.2	165.7	108.3	81.7	98.3	48.8	45.4	53.1	132.1
1973	1 382.3	1 180.1	52.2	19.2	29.0	68.2	187.0	115.8	91.8	108.2	53.8	50.2	57.0	146.9
1974	1 499.5	1 276.8	50.0	29.6	30.3	73.0	194.2	124.2	104.2	113.6	59.1	54.3	64.6	159.4
1975	1 637.7	1 390.9	51.4	34.2	38.5	73.7	200.4	136.9	113.9	127.5	60.0	60.3	73.6	175.3
1976	1 824.6	1 555.5	50.1	37.9	42.9	84.2	232.2	154.8	122.0	144.1	69.4	67.8	80.5	192.7
1977	2 030.1	1 738.7	51.2	43.9	47.5	92.8	267.6	171.6	134.1	158.7	77.0	75.8	95.0	210.1
1978	2 293.8	1 976.4	59.5	50.3	52.1	109.7	306.0	184.4	152.2	177.4	87.5	87.5	112.7	237.1
1979	2 562.2	2 216.8	70.2	59.1	53.8	124.8	334.6	210.3	174.4	193.0	97.5	96.9	125.0	268.5
1980	2 788.1	2 404.8	62.1	90.8	61.0	131.5	339.2	219.2	186.3	198.3	102.6	108.3	137.7	309.2
1981	3 126.8	2 701.6	75.6	121.5	72.0	133.1	376.2	243.4	206.2	218.0	110.1	123.5	155.0	347.8
1982	3 253.2	2 791.4	71.6	118.5	83.2	131.0	359.2	247.3	206.6	226.9	106.3	135.3	168.0	376.8
1983	3 534.6	3 041.7	57.2	102.8	94.4	139.6	385.5	272.0	222.4	255.3	118.0	152.5	193.9	417.7
1984	3 930.9	3 393.0	77.0	107.2	105.7	160.7	451.0	280.7	249.8	286.8	131.4	160.0	213.4	464.1
1985	4 217.5	3 634.6	76.6	106.2	113.0	177.0	458.6	292.8	269.2	309.1	137.1	176.4	233.1	506.3
1986	4 460.1	3 840.4	73.7	70.3	117.5	197.2	468.4	308.9	279.3	331.4	147.0	185.6	262.2	541.9
1987	4 736.4	4 077.9	78.8	73.1	125.8	210.1	492.5	330.6	285.6	345.7	152.6	197.4	282.4	567.8
1988	5 100.4	4 395.3	78.1	74.1	125.1	226.5	537.9	362.2	314.3	366.8	161.4	205.4	301.5	614.2
1989	5 482.1	4 729.7	91.6	78.6	138.2	238.6	562.4	387.7	335.7	390.7	166.3	222.4	322.0	658.9
1990	5 800.5	4 994.3	95.7	88.4	145.5	243.6	558.9	410.1	347.7	400.4	172.8	235.6	346.5	702.6
1991	5 992.1	5 133.2	88.3	79.5	153.8	228.8	554.2	422.5	362.6	407.9	182.3	244.3	382.0	727.8
1992	6 342.3	5 442.0	99.3	73.6	159.7	233.2	574.5	442.2	380.1	430.0	192.0	260.5	414.3	777.8
1993	6 667.4	5 735.9	90.6	74.4	164.3	250.4	603.0	456.0	402.5	462.9	206.4	279.6	441.3	818.0
1994	7 085.2	6 119.9	105.6	75.9	171.2	277.2	650.2	477.1	444.5	500.5	223.7	299.4	456.3	865.3
1995	7 414.7	6 420.0	91.3	76.7	175.3	294.2	675.4	505.5	460.2	525.0	231.7	311.5	489.6	916.2
1996	7 838.5	6 812.6	114.2	90.0	173.4	320.9	705.0	503.5	492.5	556.8	241.3	338.6	527.1	963.2
1997	8 332.4	7 271.0	108.4	94.8	169.9	346.7	748.9	528.3	524.9	589.9	261.8	349.4	582.4	1 028.2
1998	8 793.5	7 694.4	100.3	81.0	165.1	383.7	781.2	545.6	557.3	626.9	275.6	386.1	634.7	1 062.1
1999	9 353.5	8 199.6	92.8	82.0	172.7	428.4	802.4	565.6	579.1	653.4	287.1	438.5	681.7	1 152.3
2000	9 951.5	8 736.1	95.6	108.9	173.9	467.3	839.1	576.5	617.7	686.2	301.4	417.8	762.0	1 235.7
2001	10 286.2	9 010.8	98.6	119.3	177.6	490.5	758.8	585.2	613.3	703.9	302.6	451.1	838.7	1 316.1
2002	10 642.3	9 289.3	94.4	109.5	181.0	494.3	767.8	587.8	614.9	731.2	302.4	499.7	863.5	1 358.7
2003	11 142.2	9 706.9	115.5	134.9	192.0	516.1	766.4	607.9	638.1	769.5	319.8	506.6	902.4	1 414.1
2004	11 853.3	10 345.6	142.7	159.3	208.0	554.2	822.0	660.6	684.2	795.1	347.0	558.8	919.0	1 481.4
2005	12 623.0	11 037.1	127.1	192.3	205.9	612.5	878.3	691.0	725.5	837.6	369.5	586.5	1 019.4	1 579.4
2006	13 377.2	11 709.4	122.5	229.8	236.0	651.0	921.3	727.1	769.7	875.8	394.0	590.6	1 092.7	1 672.6
2007	14 028.7	12 268.8	144.5	254.5	248.6	653.8	939.9	758.1	816.7	887.9	404.9	635.5	1 080.0	1 777.0
2008	14 291.5	12 437.1	159.4	319.2	257.7	614.2	904.1	724.4	824.1	848.6	415.0	636.8	1 041.5	1 875.2
2009	13 973.7	12 056.7	142.4	221.7	264.7	542.9	787.0	753.2	766.3	846.8	396.6	604.8	1 093.6	1 848.3
2010	14 498.9	12 532.3	157.6	251.9	284.5	523.3	866.7	763.8	799.0	876.0	422.6	612.2	1 157.3	1 864.5
2011	15 075.7	13 081.8	173.5	289.9	297.9	529.5	910.1	821.3	845.1	905.7	447.9	646.6	1 159.3	1 898.8
2012	15 684.8	13 657.6	168.6	285.2	304.3	558.7	1 000.2	866.5	897.9	949.1	469.3	690.6	1 242.3	1 926.3

Table 14-1. Gross Domestic Product (Value Added) by NAICS Industry Group—*Continued*

(Billions of dollars.)

Year	Professional, scientific, and technical services	Management of companies and enterprises	Administrative and waste management services	Educational services	Health care and social assistance	Arts, entertainment, and recreation	Accommodation and food services	Other services except government	Government			Private goods-producing industries	Private services-producing industries	Information-communications-technology-producing industries[1]
									Total government	Federal	State and local			
1947	3.2	3.6	1.3	0.8	3.8	1.6	6.4	7.4	30.4	20.3	10.1	97.0	116.7	. . .
1948	3.6	4.0	1.4	1.0	4.2	1.6	6.8	7.8	30.0	18.4	11.5	112.0	127.2	. . .
1949	3.8	4.0	1.5	1.0	4.4	1.7	7.0	8.0	31.3	18.7	12.6	104.7	131.2	. . .
1950	4.1	4.4	1.7	1.1	4.8	1.7	7.2	8.6	31.6	18.2	13.4	119.7	142.4	. . .
1951	4.8	5.1	2.0	1.2	5.4	1.8	7.8	9.3	38.9	23.9	15.0	141.4	159.0	. . .
1952	5.3	5.4	2.2	1.2	5.9	2.0	8.2	9.6	44.5	28.0	16.5	145.3	168.5	. . .
1953	5.8	5.7	2.4	1.3	6.5	2.1	8.5	10.2	46.5	28.8	17.8	153.4	179.4	. . .
1954	6.2	5.7	2.6	1.4	6.7	2.2	8.7	10.4	48.2	28.9	19.3	147.3	184.8	. . .
1955	6.9	6.3	2.8	1.5	7.9	2.3	9.2	11.4	50.9	30.0	20.9	162.4	201.4	. . .
1956	7.6	6.6	3.1	1.7	8.4	2.5	9.5	12.4	54.3	31.1	23.2	169.1	214.0	. . .
1957	8.5	7.0	3.4	1.8	9.2	2.6	10.1	13.2	58.1	32.6	25.5	175.0	228.0	. . .
1958	8.9	6.8	3.7	2.0	10.1	2.7	10.3	13.7	61.8	34.0	27.8	169.1	236.3	. . .
1959	10.0	7.6	4.0	2.2	11.3	3.1	11.2	14.5	65.2	35.1	30.1	183.7	257.8	. . .
1960	10.5	7.8	4.3	2.4	11.8	3.3	11.4	15.6	69.3	36.4	32.9	186.6	270.5	. . .
1961	11.4	8.0	4.7	2.6	12.6	3.5	11.8	16.3	73.5	37.8	35.7	188.4	282.8	. . .
1962	12.5	8.7	5.1	3.0	13.7	3.7	12.6	17.3	78.8	40.1	38.6	204.0	302.9	. . .
1963	13.4	9.1	5.5	3.2	14.7	4.0	13.3	18.0	84.5	42.6	42.0	214.5	318.8	. . .
1964	14.8	9.8	6.0	3.6	16.3	4.3	14.5	19.2	90.7	45.1	45.6	228.2	344.7	. . .
1965	16.3	10.6	6.6	4.0	17.6	4.5	15.7	20.1	96.9	47.1	49.7	251.7	370.5	. . .
1966	18.6	11.7	7.4	4.6	19.8	4.8	17.0	21.9	107.4	52.1	55.3	276.8	403.4	. . .
1967	20.3	12.2	7.9	5.0	22.6	5.0	18.4	23.2	118.3	56.7	61.5	282.6	431.6	. . .
1968	21.9	13.4	8.6	5.6	25.5	5.4	20.3	24.8	131.6	62.5	69.1	306.5	471.8	. . .
1969	24.5	14.3	9.7	6.6	29.1	5.6	22.1	26.7	143.8	66.7	77.1	325.7	515.0	. . .
1970	26.9	14.7	10.4	7.5	32.9	6.1	23.7	27.8	158.3	71.1	87.2	327.4	552.7	. . .
1971	29.2	15.7	11.3	8.4	36.4	6.5	25.8	29.7	172.3	75.4	96.9	348.0	606.5	. . .
1972	32.7	17.2	12.7	9.6	40.9	6.9	28.1	31.7	187.3	80.5	106.8	384.4	666.2	. . .
1973	37.7	19.0	14.5	10.4	46.0	8.0	31.0	34.3	202.2	83.0	119.2	442.4	737.7	. . .
1974	41.6	20.6	16.3	11.1	52.4	8.8	32.6	37.0	222.6	90.4	132.2	471.0	805.8	. . .
1975	45.9	22.7	17.7	12.0	61.1	9.7	36.6	39.6	246.8	98.2	148.7	496.5	894.4	. . .
1976	51.4	25.7	20.4	12.5	70.2	11.0	41.6	44.1	269.0	107.4	161.7	559.2	996.3	. . .
1977	61.0	28.9	24.1	13.0	79.4	13.1	46.4	47.6	291.4	116.1	175.4	627.1	1 111.6	. . .
1978	70.4	32.9	28.3	14.2	90.2	14.6	54.0	55.3	317.3	125.5	191.8	709.9	1 266.5	. . .
1979	82.7	36.1	33.3	15.7	102.5	16.4	61.5	60.6	345.4	135.3	210.1	799.0	1 417.8	. . .
1980	95.8	39.8	37.5	17.6	116.5	17.7	65.2	68.5	383.3	150.4	233.0	842.8	1 562.0	. . .
1981	109.3	45.3	42.7	19.3	133.6	20.0	72.9	76.0	425.2	170.7	254.5	949.9	1 751.7	. . .
1982	120.4	47.2	45.5	20.9	148.3	21.2	78.9	78.3	461.8	185.6	276.2	927.7	1 863.7	. . .
1983	137.4	53.4	51.6	23.8	165.8	23.3	88.1	86.8	492.9	197.4	295.6	957.1	2 084.6	. . .
1984	158.5	61.3	61.2	26.3	180.8	24.8	96.0	96.3	537.9	219.8	318.1	1 076.7	2 316.3	. . .
1985	179.6	67.9	68.8	28.4	197.0	27.6	104.4	105.3	582.9	235.8	347.1	1 111.2	2 523.4	. . .
1986	201.5	74.1	76.9	30.2	215.1	29.9	114.1	115.3	619.7	244.6	375.1	1 118.6	2 721.8	. . .
1987	221.1	76.9	86.4	33.3	244.4	32.6	119.7	121.1	658.4	256.6	401.8	1 185.0	2 892.9	161.3
1988	254.5	73.2	96.6	35.6	265.9	35.2	133.6	133.0	705.1	272.1	433.1	1 278.8	3 116.5	176.1
1989	284.6	77.5	108.3	38.7	298.7	41.0	143.0	144.8	752.4	285.9	466.5	1 358.9	3 370.8	188.4
1990	315.1	80.3	121.2	41.2	335.4	47.6	152.0	153.9	806.2	298.9	507.3	1 396.5	3 597.7	197.3
1991	320.6	81.4	122.0	45.4	368.0	49.3	156.6	155.9	858.9	320.8	538.0	1 373.2	3 760.0	203.8
1992	347.4	84.7	134.5	48.9	404.0	56.2	162.7	166.3	900.3	333.0	567.4	1 422.8	4 019.2	215.9
1993	365.5	92.4	143.1	51.7	424.7	58.0	172.9	178.3	931.4	334.7	596.7	1 474.3	4 261.6	227.4
1994	386.5	96.4	156.7	55.5	444.7	60.6	181.7	190.7	965.3	337.2	628.1	1 586.1	4 533.8	253.4
1995	411.9	103.2	172.3	58.9	465.1	65.9	189.5	200.7	994.6	337.0	657.6	1 643.1	4 776.9	275.9
1996	454.3	111.3	191.0	62.5	482.9	70.8	202.0	211.2	1 025.9	341.6	684.3	1 733.6	5 079.0	304.0
1997	504.0	124.1	214.0	66.9	504.5	79.7	220.5	223.8	1 061.3	347.1	714.2	1 827.2	5 443.8	343.2
1998	555.0	138.0	234.0	73.0	528.3	81.2	239.8	245.6	1 099.1	351.9	747.2	1 891.7	5 802.7	372.0
1999	607.0	148.1	255.1	79.5	559.0	91.0	264.4	259.3	1 153.9	361.5	792.4	1 971.3	6 228.3	405.6
2000	662.4	171.1	283.3	85.9	592.1	98.6	283.0	277.6	1 215.4	378.4	837.0	2 087.4	6 648.7	409.9
2001	701.1	174.6	295.0	88.7	640.5	94.8	296.4	264.2	1 275.4	385.1	890.3	2 052.3	6 958.5	380.8
2002	718.9	178.3	301.0	98.9	690.9	102.1	309.0	285.0	1 353.0	416.6	936.4	2 053.7	7 235.6	422.6
2003	744.6	192.4	322.9	106.1	741.0	106.1	321.7	288.8	1 435.3	447.3	988.0	2 140.8	7 566.1	437.9
2004	808.7	203.3	335.6	116.0	790.1	114.7	344.0	300.8	1 507.7	478.4	1 029.3	2 338.9	8 006.6	494.4
2005	870.3	218.4	371.4	120.2	833.3	118.9	366.5	313.0	1 585.9	501.8	1 084.1	2 501.2	8 535.8	535.0
2006	947.5	234.5	385.1	129.1	886.2	127.7	384.7	331.6	1 667.8	526.5	1 141.3	2 651.6	9 057.8	560.0
2007	1 024.7	257.7	415.2	137.9	939.0	137.2	411.7	343.8	1 759.9	552.3	1 207.6	2 750.9	9 517.9	587.4
2008	1 100.2	263.2	419.8	147.6	1 006.3	132.4	404.9	342.7	1 854.4	580.9	1 273.5	2 721.2	9 715.9	599.1
2009	1 045.8	248.2	399.1	163.1	1 062.4	130.6	394.8	344.4	1 917.0	613.0	1 304.0	2 447.1	9 609.6	588.9
2010	1 084.0	262.7	423.0	166.4	1 102.7	139.4	418.6	356.0	1 966.6	647.2	1 319.5	2 563.4	9 968.9	635.3
2011	1 151.5	283.6	448.8	174.2	1 136.9	148.0	443.1	369.9	1 993.8	658.1	1 335.8	2 724.4	10 357.0	647.7
2012	1 192.3	295.6	464.5	179.9	1 164.8	153.3	471.6	376.7	2 026.2	668.3	1 357.9	2 879.2	10 778.0	687.1

[1]Consists of computer and electronic products manufacturing; publishing, including software; information and data processing services; and computer systems design and related services.
. . . = Not available.

Table 14-2. Chain-Type Quantity Indexes for Value Added by NAICS Industry Group

(2005 = 100.)

Year	Total gross domestic product	Private industries											
		Total	Agriculture, forestry, fishing, and hunting	Mining	Utilities	Construc-tion	Manufacturing		Wholesale trade	Retail trade	Transpor-tation and ware-housing	Information	Finance and insurance	Real estate and rental and leasing
							Durable goods	Nondurable goods						
1947	14.1	13.2	20.2	65.2	10.2	34.8	10.6	19.0	6.4	12.7	19.5	4.9	10.1	10.5
1948	14.7	13.9	23.2	66.7	11.5	40.4	11.2	20.3	6.6	12.9	18.9	5.2	10.2	10.8
1949	14.6	13.7	22.2	58.4	12.9	40.5	10.5	20.1	6.7	13.6	17.0	5.4	10.5	11.4
1950	15.9	15.0	23.4	65.5	14.0	45.1	12.5	22.0	7.4	14.8	18.5	5.5	10.9	12.1
1951	17.1	16.0	22.2	71.7	16.3	50.3	14.3	23.6	7.6	14.9	20.7	5.9	11.8	12.8
1952	17.8	16.5	23.3	69.9	17.4	52.4	15.1	23.7	7.9	15.3	20.0	6.1	12.3	13.7
1953	18.6	17.3	24.4	72.2	18.9	54.4	16.5	24.6	8.1	15.9	20.2	6.5	12.8	14.5
1954	18.5	17.1	25.1	69.6	20.7	56.3	14.8	24.2	8.2	16.0	18.9	6.5	13.2	15.3
1955	19.8	18.5	25.8	78.3	21.7	60.0	16.7	26.0	9.0	17.3	20.8	6.9	14.4	16.3
1956	20.2	18.9	25.8	81.1	23.0	63.3	16.3	26.5	9.4	17.4	21.3	7.1	15.3	17.0
1957	20.6	19.3	24.8	80.5	24.7	63.5	16.5	26.8	9.6	17.7	21.3	7.4	16.1	17.9
1958	20.4	18.9	25.5	74.0	25.8	65.9	14.3	26.8	9.7	17.7	19.7	7.6	15.8	18.7
1959	21.9	20.4	25.5	76.7	28.2	71.4	16.2	29.2	11.0	18.8	20.8	8.1	16.0	20.0
1960	22.4	20.9	26.8	78.5	30.2	72.2	16.2	29.3	11.5	19.0	21.1	8.4	16.8	21.1
1961	22.9	21.3	27.0	79.0	31.8	73.3	16.0	29.9	11.8	19.0	21.1	8.7	17.7	22.1
1962	24.3	22.7	26.5	81.4	33.5	76.8	17.8	31.8	12.6	20.3	22.2	9.3	18.2	23.6
1963	25.4	23.9	27.5	84.9	35.1	78.9	19.4	34.3	13.1	20.9	23.4	9.9	18.6	24.6
1964	26.9	25.3	27.0	88.0	37.7	82.9	21.0	36.0	13.9	22.3	24.3	10.6	19.6	25.8
1965	28.6	27.1	28.7	91.7	39.3	86.5	23.6	38.3	15.0	23.6	26.4	11.4	20.1	27.3
1966	30.4	28.8	27.9	97.2	42.1	87.3	25.9	41.1	16.0	24.9	28.8	12.4	20.8	28.6
1967	31.2	29.3	29.8	98.6	44.2	85.4	25.7	40.7	16.7	25.2	28.6	13.1	22.0	29.4
1968	32.7	30.6	29.0	101.4	48.2	84.9	27.0	43.3	17.8	26.4	30.0	13.9	23.1	30.9
1969	33.7	31.7	29.9	104.6	51.1	82.0	27.6	44.7	18.5	26.6	31.1	15.0	25.3	32.7
1970	33.8	31.6	30.7	108.4	52.7	75.2	25.2	44.4	19.0	27.0	30.8	16.0	26.0	33.4
1971	34.9	32.7	32.2	106.1	56.8	73.0	25.6	46.5	20.1	28.2	31.4	16.7	26.4	35.6
1972	36.8	34.7	32.6	105.4	58.0	74.1	28.1	50.1	21.6	30.0	34.0	17.9	27.8	37.5
1973	38.9	37.0	32.4	108.8	65.0	76.8	31.5	53.8	22.4	31.8	36.2	19.2	29.6	39.4
1974	38.7	36.6	31.7	104.0	66.1	74.0	30.4	50.4	22.1	30.4	36.5	19.8	31.8	41.0
1975	38.6	36.5	36.8	105.7	70.4	67.0	27.4	49.2	22.6	30.6	34.0	20.5	34.0	42.7
1976	40.7	38.6	35.7	105.5	69.7	71.9	30.3	54.8	23.4	33.0	36.9	21.6	34.1	44.4
1977	42.6	40.5	37.1	113.5	69.3	72.8	32.7	58.9	24.6	34.3	38.5	23.2	34.5	44.9
1978	44.9	42.9	35.9	117.4	68.9	77.0	34.8	60.8	27.1	36.3	40.5	25.9	37.7	47.3
1979	46.3	44.5	38.9	104.7	63.3	79.6	35.4	64.7	29.2	36.3	42.8	28.0	39.2	50.5
1980	46.2	44.2	38.4	115.6	59.1	75.1	33.5	61.4	29.0	34.3	41.8	30.4	41.6	52.7
1981	47.4	45.4	48.4	114.9	59.0	68.5	34.4	66.3	30.7	35.3	40.8	32.0	42.6	53.2
1982	46.5	44.3	51.0	109.8	57.7	60.5	31.0	64.2	30.9	35.2	38.8	32.0	43.8	53.3
1983	48.6	46.3	36.4	104.3	60.8	62.8	33.1	70.5	32.2	38.5	43.8	34.2	43.6	55.3
1984	52.1	49.8	47.1	114.5	66.3	70.7	38.4	70.8	34.8	42.2	45.9	33.9	45.3	57.3
1985	54.2	52.0	55.8	121.1	70.5	75.8	39.5	73.2	36.7	44.5	46.6	34.8	45.7	59.3
1986	56.1	53.5	54.9	116.8	74.0	77.5	39.8	72.3	40.3	47.8	46.7	35.0	47.2	59.6
1987	57.9	55.5	56.8	122.4	82.7	79.1	42.6	78.0	39.2	46.1	49.0	37.4	51.0	60.5
1988	60.3	58.1	50.7	136.9	82.0	83.0	46.9	80.1	41.3	50.7	50.4	38.6	52.4	62.9
1989	62.4	60.2	56.7	132.3	90.4	85.3	47.6	80.5	43.3	53.0	52.4	41.3	53.2	64.8
1990	63.6	61.3	60.1	130.8	95.6	84.8	46.7	80.1	42.7	53.8	55.1	42.6	54.8	66.1
1991	63.4	61.2	60.8	133.1	96.8	78.6	45.2	80.7	44.4	53.7	57.7	43.1	56.5	66.6
1992	65.6	63.5	68.0	129.0	97.7	80.4	46.2	84.7	48.5	56.5	61.3	45.4	56.4	69.8
1993	67.5	65.3	59.0	131.2	96.4	82.6	48.1	87.9	50.0	59.2	64.0	47.8	58.5	71.6
1994	70.2	68.4	70.4	142.4	99.4	87.3	51.8	92.4	53.1	63.5	69.2	50.3	58.8	74.0
1995	72.0	70.1	59.6	143.5	102.6	88.2	55.8	91.8	52.9	66.7	71.2	52.0	59.8	76.4
1996	74.7	73.1	66.3	133.7	101.7	93.0	59.3	91.2	57.8	72.9	75.1	55.3	61.1	78.2
1997	78.0	76.8	71.6	138.1	97.1	95.2	64.2	93.7	64.1	79.2	79.0	56.4	64.4	81.3
1998	81.4	80.5	69.8	148.8	95.0	98.3	70.6	92.1	74.2	84.2	78.1	62.1	68.6	82.1
1999	85.3	84.8	73.0	137.8	104.7	103.6	76.0	94.1	78.1	86.6	80.8	70.5	74.1	86.7
2000	88.9	88.7	81.6	121.0	108.3	107.0	84.4	94.0	83.5	89.9	86.2	67.8	82.5	90.0
2001	89.8	89.8	78.9	136.8	93.9	104.5	79.3	91.6	87.7	92.7	83.1	72.9	92.0	92.6
2002	91.4	91.3	82.1	138.4	97.4	100.9	82.2	92.4	88.5	95.8	81.9	81.0	91.8	92.4
2003	93.8	93.5	90.6	120.5	100.9	101.2	85.1	95.1	93.9	98.0	86.1	82.5	92.9	93.9
2004	97.0	96.9	96.5	119.2	104.8	101.1	93.0	101.5	98.9	98.0	93.9	92.7	92.0	96.2
2005	100.0	100.0	100.0	100.0	100.0	100.0	100.0	100.0	100.0	100.0	100.0	100.0	100.0	100.0
2006	102.7	103.0	100.8	108.4	100.5	97.0	106.7	101.1	103.0	102.2	104.0	101.5	106.4	102.5
2007	104.6	105.0	93.1	111.4	104.0	91.6	110.7	104.4	108.6	102.5	105.2	109.3	102.6	106.7
2008	104.3	103.9	101.3	107.2	108.8	85.5	108.9	93.0	107.4	96.6	106.2	111.2	95.9	109.7
2009	101.1	99.9	114.5	134.3	99.0	74.5	91.1	92.7	93.1	94.7	95.4	105.0	104.0	106.7
2010	103.5	102.6	111.2	122.0	109.0	73.6	103.2	93.0	96.2	101.4	101.7	108.3	101.8	108.8
2011	105.4	104.7	96.1	122.0	111.8	73.4	110.2	91.1	99.1	101.5	106.6	114.7	101.1	109.8
2012	107.7	107.7	92.5	126.5	112.8	75.7	120.3	93.8	103.8	105.4	108.0	121.3	104.7	111.1

Table 14-2. Chain-Type Quantity Indexes for Value Added by NAICS Industry Group—*Continued*

(2005 = 100.)

Year	Private industries—*Continued*								Government			Private goods-producing industries	Private services-producing industries	Information-communi-cations-technology-producing industries[1]
	Profes-sional, scientific, and technical services	Manage-ment of companies and enterprises	Adminis-trative and waste manage-ment services	Educational services	Health care and social assistance	Arts, entertain-ment, and recreation	Accom-modation and food services	Other services except govern-ment	Total govern-ment	Federal	State and local			
1947	7.7	17.7	4.9	18.1	9.2	14.2	17.3	40.5	33.4	64.4	19.5	18.5	11.1	. . .
1948	7.8	18.4	5.0	20.9	9.6	13.9	17.3	41.4	32.2	60.4	19.8	20.0	11.3	. . .
1949	7.9	18.2	5.1	21.5	9.9	13.7	17.9	41.2	32.1	58.2	20.8	19.2	11.5	. . .
1950	8.2	19.6	5.5	21.7	10.5	13.8	19.0	41.9	32.5	58.3	21.4	21.6	12.3	. . .
1951	8.6	21.0	5.8	21.7	10.9	14.6	19.2	42.3	38.3	75.8	21.8	23.4	13.0	. . .
1952	8.8	21.9	6.1	21.6	11.5	14.5	19.7	42.4	41.4	84.5	22.3	24.2	13.3	. . .
1953	9.1	23.1	6.4	22.1	12.1	14.8	20.4	42.9	42.1	84.9	23.2	25.6	13.9	. . .
1954	9.3	22.5	6.4	22.3	12.9	14.8	20.5	42.6	42.0	82.8	24.0	24.5	14.0	. . .
1955	9.7	24.3	6.8	23.2	13.2	15.3	21.9	45.3	42.2	81.2	25.0	26.8	15.1	. . .
1956	10.0	24.6	7.2	23.5	13.7	16.0	22.1	46.8	42.9	80.4	26.3	26.9	15.6	. . .
1957	10.9	25.2	7.7	25.3	14.5	16.2	22.9	48.3	43.8	80.3	27.7	27.0	16.2	. . .
1958	11.2	24.5	8.1	26.5	15.6	16.5	22.7	49.8	44.2	78.5	29.1	25.5	16.3	. . .
1959	12.0	26.6	8.7	27.1	16.6	17.7	23.9	51.1	45.0	78.0	30.4	27.9	17.5	. . .
1960	12.2	27.1	9.0	28.3	17.3	18.6	24.3	53.1	46.6	79.8	32.0	28.2	18.1	. . .
1961	13.0	27.6	9.5	29.7	18.0	19.1	24.3	54.3	48.2	81.5	33.5	28.3	18.6	. . .
1962	13.6	29.3	10.0	31.5	19.5	19.6	25.9	55.4	50.0	84.7	34.7	30.3	19.7	. . .
1963	14.3	31.1	10.5	32.8	20.7	20.4	26.9	56.6	51.6	85.6	36.5	32.4	20.6	. . .
1964	15.0	32.8	11.1	33.8	23.1	21.4	28.5	58.5	53.4	86.9	38.6	34.3	21.7	. . .
1965	15.9	35.6	11.9	36.2	24.0	21.8	30.4	60.4	55.4	88.1	40.9	37.2	23.0	. . .
1966	17.4	38.5	12.9	38.5	25.4	22.2	31.9	63.6	58.8	94.3	43.1	39.6	24.4	. . .
1967	18.4	38.8	13.3	40.6	26.4	22.4	32.7	65.0	61.7	100.1	44.8	39.6	25.2	. . .
1968	19.1	41.1	14.0	42.2	28.2	23.0	33.9	65.9	64.3	102.6	47.4	41.1	26.5	. . .
1969	20.1	42.5	15.0	43.8	30.3	22.7	34.3	67.2	65.9	103.0	49.4	41.8	27.7	. . .
1970	20.8	42.1	15.3	45.8	32.2	23.4	35.1	66.6	66.0	98.6	51.4	39.8	28.4	. . .
1971	21.2	43.7	15.5	48.4	34.3	23.8	36.3	67.3	66.2	94.7	53.4	40.5	29.7	. . .
1972	22.5	46.9	16.9	49.1	36.3	24.6	38.5	69.8	66.5	91.5	55.3	43.2	31.4	. . .
1973	24.3	51.1	18.1	50.0	38.9	27.2	40.7	72.2	66.7	87.8	57.2	46.5	33.3	. . .
1974	25.0	47.4	19.0	51.8	40.5	27.6	39.3	68.6	68.5	88.6	59.4	44.6	33.6	. . .
1975	24.6	46.6	18.2	53.0	43.3	28.2	39.5	68.0	69.3	87.2	61.3	42.5	34.3	. . .
1976	25.6	50.8	19.2	53.5	45.6	30.2	42.5	71.0	70.4	88.9	62.1	45.9	35.9	. . .
1977	28.0	54.3	20.8	54.0	49.0	34.1	44.7	71.3	71.0	88.8	63.1	48.9	37.3	. . .
1978	30.2	57.0	22.7	56.2	51.3	36.0	47.9	74.7	72.7	90.8	64.6	51.1	39.8	. . .
1979	32.7	57.7	24.9	56.5	53.8	38.0	48.9	75.3	73.6	90.8	66.0	52.5	41.6	. . .
1980	34.1	56.6	25.9	57.7	55.8	38.8	46.4	76.0	74.9	92.5	67.0	50.6	42.0	. . .
1981	35.2	56.9	26.6	56.8	57.2	41.4	47.7	73.7	75.2	93.5	67.0	52.4	43.0	. . .
1982	35.1	57.8	26.0	56.9	57.0	41.8	49.1	70.9	75.3	93.0	67.4	48.9	42.9	. . .
1983	37.1	62.8	28.1	61.1	58.9	43.7	53.3	74.1	76.0	95.3	67.3	50.2	45.2	. . .
1984	40.6	70.3	32.0	64.3	60.4	44.2	56.0	78.1	76.8	96.8	67.8	55.9	47.8	. . .
1985	43.9	74.9	34.8	66.3	61.8	47.9	58.3	80.6	78.8	99.1	69.7	58.7	49.8	. . .
1986	47.4	80.5	37.7	66.7	63.1	49.7	62.6	82.4	80.7	100.5	71.8	58.7	51.9	. . .
1987	49.5	82.9	41.4	70.1	67.2	52.2	61.2	83.9	82.2	102.8	73.0	62.2	53.3	10.6
1988	54.0	76.2	43.8	70.4	67.8	54.4	64.9	88.0	84.3	104.1	75.5	65.7	55.7	11.9
1989	57.7	78.4	47.4	72.4	70.5	60.4	66.0	92.0	86.4	105.6	77.9	66.9	58.2	12.9
1990	60.5	78.8	50.1	72.7	73.4	66.5	66.7	94.0	88.5	107.5	80.0	66.4	59.7	13.6
1991	58.6	75.2	48.4	75.8	74.9	65.7	64.5	91.2	89.0	107.6	80.7	65.0	60.1	13.9
1992	60.6	73.8	50.8	78.4	77.2	73.0	65.2	93.3	89.5	107.0	81.7	67.2	62.5	15.1
1993	61.7	76.3	52.8	80.6	77.2	73.5	67.8	96.6	89.5	104.7	82.7	68.8	64.3	16.4
1994	63.4	76.7	56.7	83.3	77.3	74.6	70.2	101.1	89.8	102.6	84.0	73.8	66.8	19.1
1995	64.7	78.8	61.1	86.2	78.3	78.8	72.0	103.0	89.7	98.3	85.9	75.4	68.6	23.1
1996	68.8	84.0	66.1	87.7	79.2	81.4	75.2	103.9	90.1	96.3	87.4	78.1	71.7	27.6
1997	73.1	91.4	71.1	90.4	80.4	88.8	77.5	102.7	91.1	95.6	89.1	82.2	75.3	33.4
1998	78.2	93.0	74.6	92.3	81.4	88.2	80.7	108.4	92.3	95.4	90.9	85.8	79.0	41.6
1999	82.1	93.1	78.8	94.6	83.4	93.5	85.7	109.3	93.4	94.8	92.8	89.9	83.3	50.7
2000	85.6	98.4	83.8	96.5	85.4	96.6	89.3	111.0	95.1	96.1	94.7	94.4	87.0	56.9
2001	88.3	102.6	83.5	95.0	88.0	89.8	89.7	99.3	95.9	94.7	96.5	91.4	89.3	58.1
2002	89.4	103.1	83.1	99.6	91.5	94.2	90.4	102.4	97.8	96.7	98.3	92.4	91.0	67.1
2003	90.7	103.5	89.5	100.1	94.8	94.4	93.4	100.4	98.7	98.5	98.9	94.0	93.3	74.0
2004	96.0	101.3	90.8	102.7	97.7	99.5	97.2	100.7	99.4	99.9	99.3	99.2	96.3	89.0
2005	100.0	100.0	100.0	100.0	100.0	100.0	100.0	100.0	100.0	100.0	100.0	100.0	100.0	100.0
2006	104.7	100.9	101.1	101.0	103.6	104.5	101.9	101.7	100.4	99.7	100.8	102.5	103.1	108.3
2007	108.2	99.5	105.5	102.0	105.4	108.6	104.7	101.7	101.2	99.9	101.8	103.2	105.5	119.4
2008	113.9	101.5	107.3	104.3	110.7	102.3	99.6	97.4	103.0	102.6	103.2	98.0	105.7	126.7
2009	107.0	101.7	97.7	107.7	112.7	98.9	92.5	93.2	103.9	106.3	102.8	92.4	102.1	125.5
2010	109.8	96.8	103.0	105.8	114.7	105.0	98.6	93.9	104.6	109.4	102.4	95.1	104.9	139.8
2011	115.7	96.3	110.1	107.0	116.7	110.8	103.8	95.1	103.8	109.1	101.4	95.6	107.4	145.9
2012	117.1	99.8	112.7	107.2	117.2	114.5	107.5	95.2	103.5	108.5	101.2	100.1	109.9	155.4

[1]Consists of computer and electronic products manufacturing; publishing, including software; information and data processing services; and computer systems design and related services.
. . . = Not available.

Table 14-3. Gross Domestic Factor Income by NAICS Industry Group

(Billions of current dollars.)

NAICS industry	2000	2001	2002	2003	2004	2005	2006	2007	2008	2009	2010	2011
Gross domestic factor income, total	9 288.7	9 617.2	9 920.9	10 384.5	11 036.3	11 753.7	12 441.8	13 056.1	13 305.8	13 010.2	13 500.9	14 039.4
Compensation of employees	5 793.5	5 984.5	6 116.4	6 388.3	6 699.6	7 071.5	7 483.6	7 863.0	8 079.1	7 807.2	7 977.2	8 303.2
Gross operating surplus	3 495.2	3 632.7	3 804.5	3 996.2	4 336.7	4 682.2	4 958.2	5 193.1	5 226.7	5 203.0	5 523.7	5 736.2
Private industries	8 061.9	8 329.2	8 553.2	8 933.5	9 511.9	10 150.8	10 756.5	11 277.5	11 431.1	11 070.8	11 513.4	12 023.5
Compensation of employees	4 773.3	4 905.2	4 966.0	5 162.4	5 408.4	5 715.6	6 063.4	6 364.0	6 499.5	6 175.8	6 303.7	6 610.1
Gross operating surplus	3 288.6	3 424.0	3 587.2	3 771.1	4 103.5	4 435.2	4 693.1	4 913.5	4 931.6	4 895.0	5 209.7	5 413.4
Agriculture, forestry, fishing, and hunting	110.0	113.1	99.6	123.7	147.6	141.8	129.1	146.8	161.5	144.9	160.0	173.8
Compensation of employees	30.2	31.6	31.9	31.9	35.4	35.6	39.7	42.4	43.0	43.5	42.4	43.6
Gross operating surplus	79.8	81.5	67.7	91.8	112.2	106.2	89.4	104.4	118.5	101.4	117.6	130.2
Mining	95.2	103.9	94.3	117.6	139.5	167.2	201.2	222.0	277.2	191.2	217.2	251.3
Compensation of employees	35.6	38.1	35.9	37.9	42.6	47.6	57.5	62.6	73.5	65.0	69.2	80.6
Gross operating surplus	59.6	65.8	58.4	79.7	96.9	119.6	143.7	159.4	203.7	126.2	148.0	170.7
Utilities	139.5	148.0	142.5	150.8	164.4	159.7	185.6	194.9	201.9	207.9	226.4	238.5
Compensation of employees	47.5	51.6	54.3	53.6	56.4	56.5	60.4	61.5	66.9	68.4	68.6	71.3
Gross operating surplus	92.0	96.4	88.2	97.2	108.0	103.2	125.2	133.4	135.0	139.5	157.8	167.2
Construction	462.3	485.3	488.6	510.1	547.6	605.3	643.4	646.0	606.8	535.1	515.7	521.7
Compensation of employees	307.3	325.5	327.8	339.9	357.4	390.7	425.8	441.8	440.3	373.8	352.7	363.5
Gross operating surplus	155.0	159.8	160.8	170.2	190.2	214.6	217.6	204.2	166.5	161.3	163.0	158.2
Durable goods manufacturing	821.4	740.4	748.7	746.8	801.8	857.3	899.5	917.2	880.8	763.6	844.8	887.5
Compensation of employees	605.8	577.0	556.1	574.2	575.5	591.9	611.8	622.1	615.2	544.4	550.0	589.9
Gross operating surplus	215.6	163.4	192.6	172.6	226.3	265.4	287.7	295.1	265.6	219.2	294.8	297.6
Nondurable goods manufacturing	548.1	556.3	557.0	577.1	628.6	657.0	691.2	721.7	687.3	705.8	714.8	771.6
Compensation of employees	297.3	297.1	301.4	305.1	306.4	308.6	313.6	316.5	325.9	304.1	309.5	315.0
Gross operating surplus	250.8	259.2	255.6	272.0	322.2	348.4	377.6	405.2	361.4	401.7	405.3	456.6
Wholesale trade	479.8	476.4	474.9	491.0	527.2	559.1	594.6	640.7	649.9	606.7	630.2	663.3
Compensation of employees	327.8	330.1	330.1	338.8	358.8	381.7	407.1	431.1	438.5	408.1	415.6	438.0
Gross operating surplus	152.0	146.3	144.8	152.2	168.4	177.4	187.5	209.6	211.4	198.6	214.6	225.3
Retail trade	550.9	568.0	591.0	621.4	636.2	665.4	692.5	704.7	669.1	676.7	695.7	718.4
Compensation of employees	404.2	415.9	428.1	445.1	459.3	477.6	493.0	506.5	501.0	476.9	482.5	499.4
Gross operating surplus	146.7	152.1	162.9	176.3	176.9	187.8	199.5	198.2	168.1	199.8	213.2	219.0
Transportation and warehousing	283.9	290.4	285.3	304.4	328.5	349.2	372.5	381.9	390.3	373.2	400.1	420.5
Compensation of employees	202.3	206.6	204.0	209.7	222.7	233.8	243.4	255.1	257.9	244.7	251.2	264.2
Gross operating surplus	81.6	83.8	81.3	94.7	105.8	115.4	129.1	126.8	132.4	128.5	148.9	156.3
Information	381.7	413.3	461.2	467.7	518.9	544.6	548.4	591.9	597.5	565.5	573.9	607.7
Compensation of employees	242.2	240.8	224.3	228.5	235.5	237.5	245.8	258.4	259.9	250.9	248.8	260.7
Gross operating surplus	139.5	172.5	236.9	239.2	283.4	307.1	302.6	333.5	337.6	314.6	325.1	347.0
Finance and insurance	734.3	809.9	832.9	868.9	882.1	980.2	1 051.5	1 035.8	996.0	1 044.7	1 107.8	1 107.2
Compensation of employees	407.1	442.3	447.3	467.3	497.4	541.8	584.4	610.3	610.4	561.4	582.6	613.1
Gross operating surplus	327.2	367.6	385.6	401.6	384.7	438.4	467.1	425.5	385.6	483.3	525.2	494.1
Real estate and rental and leasing	1 104.1	1 176.1	1 206.9	1 254.0	1 311.2	1 401.9	1 478.6	1 574.3	1 662.8	1 632.2	1 644.0	1 678.6
Compensation of employees	78.9	81.1	86.2	87.6	95.3	101.7	108.4	112.5	110.7	104.4	106.1	109.7
Gross operating surplus	1 025.2	1 095.0	1 120.7	1 166.4	1 215.9	1 300.2	1 370.2	1 461.8	1 552.1	1 527.8	1 537.9	1 568.9
Professional, scientific, and technical services	645.9	683.2	699.1	721.3	781.6	836.6	914.4	993.3	1 074.0	1 023.2	1 060.7	1 127.3
Compensation of employees	462.3	476.4	469.4	479.8	508.3	555.8	607.5	654.0	694.2	672.3	690.4	732.5
Gross operating surplus	183.6	206.8	229.7	241.5	273.3	280.8	306.9	339.3	379.8	350.9	370.3	394.8
Management of companies and enterprises	165.6	168.9	172.3	185.8	195.9	210.7	226.1	248.5	252.0	238.4	252.9	273.5
Compensation of employees	146.2	149.5	152.1	164.0	173.0	185.8	200.6	219.4	222.5	207.6	222.2	238.4
Gross operating surplus	19.4	19.4	20.2	21.8	22.9	24.9	25.5	29.1	29.5	30.8	30.7	35.1
Administrative and waste management services	277.2	288.8	294.6	316.2	328.4	363.9	377.0	406.2	410.6	389.8	413.3	438.8
Compensation of employees	218.9	224.0	227.5	239.7	248.3	274.7	292.4	310.2	314.6	290.3	303.7	324.2
Gross operating surplus	58.3	64.8	67.1	76.5	80.1	89.2	84.6	96.0	96.0	99.5	109.6	114.6
Educational services	82.3	84.7	94.5	101.3	110.8	114.6	123.0	131.3	140.5	154.9	158.2	165.7
Compensation of employees	74.3	79.7	88.8	94.6	102.5	106.1	113.4	121.2	128.9	139.5	141.7	149.4
Gross operating surplus	8.0	5.0	5.7	6.7	8.3	8.5	9.6	10.1	11.6	15.4	16.5	16.3
Health care and social assistance	577.9	625.6	674.7	723.4	771.0	812.4	863.7	914.3	981.0	1 035.6	1 075.7	1 112.6
Compensation of employees	485.2	521.3	564.2	608.5	649.1	687.4	733.2	773.8	825.0	864.4	898.3	922.9
Gross operating surplus	92.7	104.3	110.5	114.9	121.9	125.0	130.5	140.5	156.0	171.4	177.4	189.7
Arts, entertainment, and recreation	89.9	85.7	92.5	95.8	103.6	107.1	115.0	122.6	117.9	116.4	124.6	133.0
Compensation of employees	55.1	57.8	61.4	64.1	67.5	69.2	75.9	80.6	80.9	79.1	80.2	83.2
Gross operating surplus	34.8	27.9	31.1	31.7	36.1	37.9	39.1	42.0	37.0	37.3	44.4	49.8
Accommodation and food services	246.5	259.4	270.9	281.1	300.8	319.5	334.3	357.0	348.4	338.8	359.9	381.5
Compensation of employees	175.0	183.0	188.2	197.8	211.8	222.0	231.4	253.7	251.0	241.4	250.9	265.0
Gross operating surplus	71.5	76.4	82.7	83.3	89.0	97.5	102.9	103.3	97.4	97.4	109.0	116.5
Other services, except government	265.5	251.5	271.8	275.0	286.0	297.2	314.6	326.7	325.6	326.1	337.6	351.0
Compensation of employees	170.1	175.7	187.0	194.2	205.0	209.5	217.8	230.4	239.0	235.5	237.1	245.6
Gross operating surplus	95.4	75.8	84.8	80.8	81.0	87.7	96.8	96.3	86.6	90.6	100.5	105.4
Government	1 226.9	1 288.0	1 367.7	1 451.0	1 524.2	1 603.0	1 685.4	1 778.5	1 874.7	1 030.4	1 907.5	2 016.0
Compensation of employees	1 020.3	1 079.3	1 150.4	1 225.9	1 291.1	1 355.9	1 420.3	1 499.0	1 579.5	1 631.4	1 673.5	1 693.1
Gross operating surplus	206.6	208.7	217.3	225.1	233.1	247.1	265.1	279.5	295.2	308.0	314.0	322.9
Addenda:												
Private goods-producing industries	2 036.9	1 999.1	1 988.3	2 075.3	2 265.2	2 428.6	2 564.6	2 653.5	2 613.5	2 340.4	2 452.5	2 606.0
Compensation of employees	1 276.1	1 269.3	1 253.2	1 289.0	1 317.3	1 374.4	1 448.5	1 485.3	1 497.9	1 330.7	1 323.9	1 392.6
Gross operating surplus	760.8	729.8	735.1	786.3	947.9	1 054.2	1 116.1	1 168.2	1 115.6	1 009.7	1 128.6	1 213.4
Private services-producing industries	6 025.0	6 330.1	6 564.9	6 858.2	7 246.8	7 722.2	8 191.8	8 624.0	8 817.6	8 730.4	9 060.9	9 417.6
Compensation of employees	3 497.2	3 635.9	3 712.8	3 873.4	4 091.1	4 341.2	4 614.8	4 878.7	5 001.6	4 845.1	4 979.8	5 217.6
Gross operating surplus	2 527.8	2 694.2	2 852.1	2 984.8	3 155.7	3 381.0	3 577.0	3 745.3	3 816.0	3 885.3	4 081.1	4 200.0
Information-communications-technology-producing industries [1]	400.7	371.2	412.8	427.9	484.0	524.0	548.4	574.7	586.2	575.0	621.4	633.5
Compensation of employees	378.0	359.9	321.7	315.9	329.0	348.1	370.1	389.0	394.5	379.8	394.7	424.6
Gross operating surplus	22.7	11.3	91.1	112.0	155.0	175.9	178.3	185.7	191.7	195.2	226.7	208.9

[1]Consists of computer and electronic products manufacturing; publishing, including software; information and data processing services; and computer systems design and related services.

NOTES AND DEFINITIONS, CHAPTER 14

Tables 14-1 through 14-3: Gross Domestic Product (Value Added) and Gross Factor Income by Industry

SOURCE: U.S. DEPARTMENT OF COMMERCE, BUREAU OF ECONOMIC ANALYSIS (BEA)

In the introduction to the notes and definitions for Chapter 1, it was observed that gross domestic product (GDP), while primarily measured as the sum of final demands for goods and services, is also the sum of the values created by each industry in the economy. In this chapter, selected data are presented from the industry accounts in the national income and product accounts (NIPAs). The industry accounts measure the contribution of each major industry to GDP.

Currently these are only calculated on an annual basis. However, BEA is working on quarterly GDP by industry statistics, which they plan to make available within 30 days of BEA's third release of quarterly GDP, that is, within 120 days after the end of the reference quarter. These plans, with "prototype" estimates for 2007 through 2011, are described in "Prototype Quarterly Statistics on U.S. GDP by Industry, 2007–2011", June 2012, a "BEA Briefing," available on the BEA website, http://www.bea.gov.

In recent years, estimates of GDP by industry have been prepared using a methodology integrated with annual input-output accounts in order to produce estimates of gross industry output, industry input, and the difference between the two—industry value added—with greater consistency and timeliness than was previously possible. The current integrated industry accounts also include a wealth of related information too extensive for inclusion here, such as quantity and price indexes for gross output and intermediate inputs, cost per unit of real value added allocated to the three components of value added, and components of domestic supply (domestic output, imports, exports, and inventory change).

The estimates of GDP by NAICS industry have been extended back to 1947, using approximations of current methods in earlier years when the source data were less comprehensive. Table 14-1 presents current-dollar GDP for NAICS industry groups. Table 14-2 presents indexes of real value added for each industry group.

In Table 14-3, the editor presents a measure derived from the components of current-dollar value added as published by BEA. This measure, "gross domestic factor income," enables users to obtain a clearer picture of the quantitative impact of each industry on the economy and of the shares of capital and labor in each industry.

The 2004 revision incorporated a change in terminology. An industry's contribution to total GDP, formerly referred to as "gross product originating" (GPO) or "gross product by industry," is now called "value added." This is consistent with the use of the term "value added" in most economic writing. However, it should not be confused with a concept known as "Census value added," which is used in U.S. censuses and surveys of manufactures. Census value added is calculated at the individual establishment level and, for that reason, necessarily does not exclude purchased business services. This means that census value added is not a true measure of economic value added.

Definitions and notes on the data

An industry's *gross domestic product (value added)*, formerly *GPO*, is equal to the market value of its gross output (which consists of the value, including taxes, of sales or receipts and other operating income plus the value of inventory change) minus the value of its intermediate inputs (energy, raw materials, semifinished goods, and services that are purchased from domestic industries or from foreign sources).

In concept, this is also equal to the sum of *compensation of employees, taxes on production and imports less subsidies,* and *gross operating surplus.* (See Chapter 1 and its notes and definitions for more information.)

Compensation of employees consists of wage and salary accruals and supplements to wages and salaries. This approximates the labor share of production, subject to the note below about proprietors' income.

Taxes on production and imports less subsidies. Although this is shown in BEA source data as a single net line item, it represents two separate components.

Taxes on production and imports are included in the market value of the goods and services sold to final consumers and therefore in the consumer valuation of those goods. Since they are not part of the payments to the labor and capital inputs in the producing industries, they must be added to the sum of the returns to those inputs in order to account for the total value to consumers. Taxes that fall into this classification include property taxes, sales and excise taxes, and Customs duties.

BEA allocates these taxes to the industry level at which they are assessed by law. Most sales taxes are considered by BEA to be part of the value added by retail trade. Some sales taxes, most fuel taxes, and all customs duties are allocated by BEA to wholesale trade. Residential real property taxes, including those on owner-occupied dwellings, are allocated by BEA to the real estate industry.

Subsidies to business by government are included in the labor and/or capital payments made by that industry. Since they are payments to the industry in addition to the market values paid by consumers, they are *subtracted* from the values of the labor and capital inputs to make them consistent with the market values as defined in value added. The role of subsidies is obvious in the source data for the agricultural sector, where the net "taxes on production and imports less subsidies" has a negative sign: farm subsidies more than offset this industry's taxes on production and imports, which mainly consist of property taxes, since sales, excise, and import taxes are not levied on farms.

For private sector businesses, *gross operating surplus* consists of business income (corporate profits before tax, proprietors' income, and rental income of persons), net interest and miscellaneous payments, business current transfer payments (net), and capital consumption allowances. For government, households, and institutions, it consists of consumption of fixed capital and (for government) government enterprises' current surplus. This approximates the share of the value of production ascribable to capital and land as measured in the NIPAs accounts; however, as BEA notes, "an unknown portion [of proprietors' income] reflects the labor contribution of proprietors." (*Survey of Current Business*, June 2004, p. 27, footnote 7.) Another aspect to be noted is that gross operating surplus includes the return to owner-occupied housing in the real estate sector. Because there is in the NIPAs no employee compensation attributed to owner-occupied housing, the capital share in that industry as measured by gross operating surplus is very large.

Quantity indexes for value added. Measures of the constant-dollar change in each industry's gross output minus its intermediate input use are calculated by BEA, using a Fisher index-number formula which incorporates weights from two adjacent years. The changes for successive years are chained together in indexes, with the value for the year 2005 set at 100. The indexes are multiplied by 2005 current-dollar value added to provide estimates of value added in "chained 2005 dollars," but because the actual weights used change from year to year, components in chained 2005 dollars typically do not add up to total GDP in 2005 dollars—and do not contain any information not already summarized in the indexes. For that reason, only the indexes are published here.

Gross domestic factor income (not a category published as such in the NIPAs) is calculated by the editor as the sum of "compensation of employees" and "gross operating surplus," which the same as value added minus "taxes on production

and imports less subsidies." The effect of this procedure is to take out the specified taxes, and to leave in the subsidies embedded in the employee compensation and gross operating surplus components. The editor believes that this provides a valuable alternative basis for assessing the importance of different industries in the economy and the shares of labor and capital in each industry's output. The components shown in this table are found on the BEA website in a table entitled "Components of Value Added by Industry."

The editor's reasoning is based on the facts that more than half of these taxes are sales, excise, and import taxes, and the assignment of these taxes to industries is economically arbitrary. BEA assigns them to the industry with the legal liability to pay, not to the entity bearing the major incidence of the tax. Yet economists have demonstrated that most of the burdens of sales and excise taxes and import duties are not borne by the factors in the legally liable industry; instead, they are passed on to consumers. In addition, because the wholesale and retail trade industries are classified as "services-producing," BEA's allocation of those taxes has a very peculiar result: taxes on goods are represented as paid by "service" industries. The process adopted instead by the editor in Table 14-3, which excludes these taxes and focuses on "gross domestic factor income," has the effect (for example) of keeping the wholesale trade industry from appearing to be both larger and more heavily taxed than it really is.

Private goods-producing industries consists of agriculture, forestry, fishing, and hunting; mining; construction; and manufacturing.

Private services-producing industries consists of utilities; wholesale trade; retail trade; transportation and warehousing; information; finance, insurance, real estate, rental, and leasing; professional and business services; educational services, health care, and social assistance; arts, entertainment, recreation, accommodation, and food services; and other services, except government.

Information-communications-technology-producing industries is a category that cuts across the goods and services framework, consisting of computer and electronic products manufacturing; publishing industries (which includes software) from the information sector; information and data processing services; and computer systems design and related services.

Data availability and references

The GDP by industry data shown here have been recalculated back to 1947 consistent with the 2009 comprehensive revision of the NIPAs. They are most recently presented and described in "Annual Industry Statistics: Revised Statistics for 2009-2011," *Survey of Current Business*, December 2012. The data for 2012 in Tables 14-1 and 14-2 are advance estimates, with considerably less detail and using approximations of the detailed methods, released on April 25, 2013. All data and *Survey of Current Business* articles are available on the BEA Web site at http://www.bea.gov. Click on "Annual Industry Accounts." For the tables, click on "Interactive Tables" under "Gross Domestic Product (GDP) by Industry."

CHAPTER 15: EMPLOYMENT, HOURS, AND EARNINGS BY NAICS INDUSTRY

Figure 15-1. Net Nonfarm Payroll Jobs by Major NAICS Industry Groups

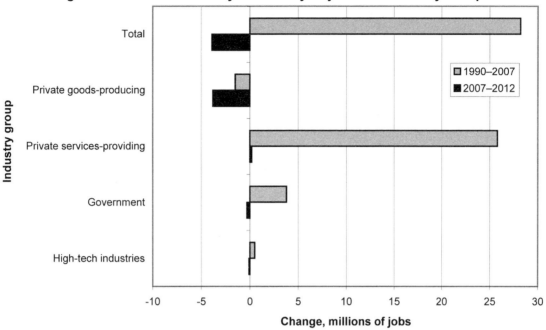

- From 1990 to the year of the business cycle peak in 2007, U.S. nonfarm employers added a net total of 28.2 million jobs, based on the annual averages displayed in this chapter. Employment began to decline in February 2008 and didn't begin to increase until March 2010, nine months after the recession's end, which the National Bureau of Economic Research Business Cycle Dating Committee places at June 2009. In 2012, total payroll employment was still 3.9 million jobs less than the 2007 average, almost entirely because of continued losses in the goods-producing industries. Government employment was also down, while private services show a small gain. ("Business Cycle Perspectives" at the beginning of this volume, Table 10-9, and Table 15-1)

- Based on the annual averages, a number of industries have had employment turnarounds since 2009, including mining, many durable goods manufacturing industries, and temporary help agencies. Some other industries experienced continued growth even during recession, such as Internet publishing, management and technical consulting services, computer systems design, and private education, health care, and social assistance. (Table 15-1)

- The average workweek for production and nonsupervisory workers is up since 2009 in nearly all industries and industry groups. (Table 15-3)

- Average hourly earnings for production and nonsupervisory workers in 2012 ranged from $11.62 in the leisure and hospitality sector to over $31 in petroleum and coal products manufacturing and utilities. (Table 15-4)

Table 15-1. Nonfarm Employment by NAICS Sector and Industry

(Wage and salary workers on nonfarm payrolls, thousands.)

Industry	1990	1991	1992	1993	1994	1995	1996	1997	1998	1999
TOTAL NONFARM	109 487	108 377	108 745	110 876	114 333	117 336	119 757	122 853	126 033	129 098
Total Private	91 072	89 832	89 958	91 887	95 058	97 904	100 218	103 190	106 124	108 791
Goods-Producing	23 723	22 588	22 095	22 219	22 774	23 156	23 409	23 886	24 354	24 465
Mining and logging	765	739	689	666	659	641	637	654	645	598
Logging	84.6	78.7	78.7	81.0	82.0	82.5	80.7	82.1	80.0	80.8
Mining	680.1	660.5	609.8	584.9	576.5	558.1	556.4	571.3	564.7	517.4
Oil and gas extraction	190.2	191.0	182.2	170.9	162.4	151.7	146.9	144.1	140.8	131.2
Mining, except oil and gas [1]	302.2	285.1	271.8	250.9	255.2	252.4	249.4	249.5	243.1	234.5
Coal mining	136.0	125.6	117.5	100.2	103.5	96.7	90.5	89.4	85.3	78.6
Support activities for mining	187.6	184.5	155.7	163.1	158.8	154.0	160.1	177.7	180.8	151.7
Construction	5 263	4 780	4 608	4 779	5 095	5 274	5 536	5 813	6 149	6 545
Construction of buildings	1 413.0	1 252.9	1 187.3	1 227.4	1 300.8	1 325.4	1 380.2	1 435.4	1 508.8	1 586.3
Heavy and civil engineering	813.0	759.1	734.2	738.4	761.7	774.7	800.1	824.9	865.3	908.7
Specialty trade contractors	3 037.3	2 768.4	2 686.0	2 813.6	3 032.5	3 174.1	3 355.1	3 552.6	3 775.1	4 049.6
Manufacturing	17 695	17 068	16 799	16 774	17 020	17 241	17 237	17 419	17 560	17 322
Durable goods	10 737	10 220	9 946	9 901	10 132	10 373	10 486	10 705	10 911	10 831
Wood products	543.0	500.7	504.1	526.4	562.9	576.1	585.2	597.8	611.6	622.7
Nonmetallic mineral products	528.4	494.7	487.3	491.1	505.3	513.1	517.3	525.7	535.3	540.8
Primary metals	688.6	656.1	630.3	618.4	630.4	641.7	639.3	638.8	641.5	625.0
Fabricated metal products	1 610.0	1 541.3	1 497.2	1 509.5	1 565.3	1 623.4	1 647.5	1 695.8	1 739.5	1 728.4
Machinery	1 409.8	1 347.9	1 311.2	1 330.9	1 381.4	1 442.3	1 468.9	1 495.9	1 514.1	1 468.3
Computer and electronic products [1]	1 902.5	1 809.3	1 707.3	1 655.9	1 651.1	1 688.4	1 746.6	1 803.3	1 830.9	1 780.5
Computer and peripheral equipment	367.4	348.6	328.5	305.7	297.7	295.6	304.6	316.7	322.1	310.1
Communications equipment	223.0	212.5	202.0	202.6	210.0	224.3	228.9	235.0	237.4	228.7
Semiconductors and electronic components	574.0	546.6	519.4	519.4	535.4	571.0	606.6	639.8	649.8	630.5
Electronic instruments	634.8	598.0	556.2	525.3	501.4	490.5	497.8	502.8	509.2	498.3
Electrical equipment and appliances	633.1	597.7	579.4	575.8	588.5	592.8	591.0	586.3	591.6	588.0
Transportation equipment [1]	2 134.5	2 029.3	1 978.1	1 915.0	1 937.4	1 978.5	1 975.1	2 027.6	2 078.4	2 088.6
Motor vehicles and parts	1 054.2	1 017.6	1 047.0	1 077.8	1 168.5	1 241.5	1 240.3	1 253.9	1 271.5	1 312.5
Furniture and related products	601.7	561.5	563.2	575.7	600.4	607.0	604.2	615.5	641.6	665.2
Miscellaneous manufacturing	685.7	681.8	687.7	702.5	709.0	709.7	710.7	718.2	726.8	724.0
Nondurable goods [1]	6 958	6 848	6 853	6 872	6 889	6 868	6 751	6 714	6 649	6 491
Food manufacturing	1 507.3	1 515.2	1 518.3	1 534.6	1 539.2	1 560.0	1 562.0	1 557.9	1 554.9	1 549.8
Textile mills	491.8	479.9	479.0	478.7	477.6	468.5	443.2	436.2	424.5	397.1
Textile product mills	235.6	225.1	228.0	232.6	242.9	242.1	237.1	236.4	234.7	232.4
Apparel	902.8	876.9	879.3	857.3	831.9	791.1	722.3	680.8	621.4	540.5
Paper and paper products	647.2	638.5	639.6	639.7	639.4	639.5	631.4	630.6	624.9	615.6
Printing and related support activities	808.5	792.3	780.3	785.2	802.3	817.3	815.8	821.1	827.9	814.6
Petroleum and coal products	152.8	154.8	152.3	146.2	144.0	140.4	137.3	136.0	134.5	127.8
Chemicals	1 035.7	1 024.1	1 028.9	1 024.9	1 004.7	987.9	984.5	986.8	992.6	982.5
Plastics and rubber products	824.8	802.1	817.9	847.8	888.1	913.7	918.7	932.7	941.4	947.0
Service-Providing	85 764	85 790	86 650	88 657	91 559	94 181	96 348	98 967	101 679	104 633
Private Service-Providing	67 349	67 244	67 863	69 668	72 284	74 748	76 809	79 304	81 770	84 326
Trade, transportation, and utilities	22 666	22 281	22 125	22 378	23 128	23 834	24 239	24 700	25 186	25 771
Wholesale trade	5 268.4	5 185.3	5 109.7	5 093.2	5 247.3	5 433.1	5 522.0	5 663.9	5 795.2	5 892.5
Durable goods	2 833.7	2 766.6	2 698.8	2 687.0	2 786.0	2 908.8	2 977.8	3 071.9	3 162.4	3 219.6
Nondurable goods	1 900.2	1 891.3	1 891.5	1 888.3	1 927.0	1 969.3	1 977.5	2 007.9	2 032.7	2 061.1
Electronic markets, agents, and brokers	534.5	527.4	519.4	517.9	534.4	555.0	566.7	584.1	600.1	611.8

[1] Includes other industries, not shown separately.

Table 15-1. Nonfarm Employment by NAICS Sector and Industry—*Continued*

(Wage and salary workers on nonfarm payrolls, thousands.)

Industry	2000	2001	2002	2003	2004	2005	2006	2007	2008	2009	2010	2011	2012
TOTAL NONFARM	131 881	131 919	130 450	130 100	131 509	133 747	136 125	137 645	136 852	130 876	129 917	131 497	133 739
Total Private	111 091	110 800	108 937	108 517	109 888	111 943	114 151	115 427	114 342	108 321	107 427	109 411	111 822
Goods-Producing	24 649	23 873	22 557	21 816	21 882	22 190	22 530	22 233	21 335	18 558	17 751	18 047	18 410
Mining and logging	599	606	583	572	591	628	684	724	767	694	705	788	851
Logging	79.0	73.5	70.4	69.4	67.6	65.2	64.4	60.1	56.6	50.4	49.7	48.7	50.4
Mining	520.2	532.5	512.2	502.7	523.0	562.2	619.7	663.8	709.8	643.3	654.8	739.2	800.4
Oil and gas extraction	124.9	123.7	121.9	120.2	123.4	125.7	134.5	146.2	160.5	159.8	158.7	172.0	186.8
Mining, except oil and gas [1]	224.8	218.7	210.6	202.7	205.1	212.8	220.3	223.4	226.0	208.3	204.5	218.4	222.6
Coal mining	72.2	74.3	74.4	70.0	70.6	73.9	78.0	77.2	81.2	81.5	80.8	87.3	86.6
Support activities for mining	170.6	190.1	179.8	179.8	194.6	223.7	264.9	294.3	323.4	275.2	291.6	348.8	391.1
Construction	6 787	6 826	6 716	6 735	6 976	7 336	7 691	7 630	7 162	6 016	5 518	5 533	5 641
Construction of buildings	1 632.5	1 588.9	1 574.8	1 575.8	1 630.0	1 711.9	1 804.9	1 774.2	1 641.7	1 357.2	1 229.7	1 222.1	1 235.8
Heavy and civil engineering	937.0	953.0	930.6	903.1	907.4	951.2	985.1	1 005.4	964.5	851.3	825.1	836.8	870.7
Specialty trade contractors	4 217.0	4 283.9	4 210.4	4 255.7	4 438.6	4 673.1	4 901.1	4 850.2	4 555.8	3 807.9	3 463.4	3 474.4	3 534.2
Manufacturing	17 263	16 441	15 259	14 509	14 315	14 227	14 155	13 879	13 406	11 847	11 528	11 726	11 919
Durable goods	10 877	10 336	9 485	8 964	8 925	8 956	8 981	8 808	8 463	7 284	7 064	7 273	7 462
Wood products	615.4	576.3	557.0	539.5	551.6	561.0	560.6	517.1	457.7	360.2	342.1	337.1	337.9
Nonmetallic mineral products	554.2	544.5	516.0	494.2	505.5	505.3	509.6	500.5	465.0	394.3	370.9	366.6	363.8
Primary metals	621.8	570.9	509.4	477.4	466.8	466.0	464.0	455.8	442.0	362.1	362.3	388.3	401.8
Fabricated metal products	1 752.6	1 676.4	1 548.5	1 478.9	1 497.1	1 522.0	1 553.1	1 562.8	1 527.5	1 311.6	1 281.7	1 347.3	1 411.3
Machinery	1 457.0	1 370.6	1 231.8	1 151.6	1 145.2	1 165.5	1 183.2	1 187.1	1 187.6	1 028.6	996.1	1 055.8	1 098.2
Computer and electronic products [1]	1 820.0	1 748.8	1 507.2	1 355.2	1 322.8	1 316.4	1 307.5	1 272.5	1 244.2	1 136.9	1 094.6	1 103.5	1 093.7
Computer and peripheral equipment	301.9	286.2	250.0	224.0	210.0	205.1	196.2	186.2	183.2	166.4	157.6	157.4	158.6
Communications equipment	238.6	225.4	179.0	149.2	143.0	141.4	136.2	128.1	127.3	120.5	117.4	115.3	109.5
Semiconductors and electronic components	676.3	645.4	524.5	461.1	454.1	452.0	457.9	447.5	431.8	378.1	369.4	383.4	384.4
Electronic instruments	487.7	483.6	456.8	435.4	436.9	441.0	444.5	443.2	441.0	421.6	406.4	404.2	400.4
Electrical equipment and appliances	590.9	556.9	496.5	459.6	445.1	433.5	432.7	429.4	424.3	373.6	359.5	366.1	370.1
Transportation equipment [1]	2 057.1	1 939.1	1 830.0	1 775.1	1 766.7	1 772.3	1 768.9	1 711.9	1 608.0	1 347.9	1 333.1	1 381.5	1 456.0
Motor vehicles and parts	1 313.6	1 212.9	1 151.2	1 125.3	1 112.8	1 096.7	1 070.0	994.2	875.5	664.1	678.5	717.7	772.9
Furniture and related products	680.1	642.9	604.7	573.7	574.1	566.3	558.3	529.4	478.0	384.3	357.2	353.1	350.1
Miscellaneous manufacturing	728.0	709.5	683.3	658.3	650.6	647.2	643.7	641.7	628.9	584.4	566.8	573.7	579.5
Nondurable goods [1]	6 386	6 105	5 774	5 546	5 390	5 271	5 174	5 071	4 943	4 564	4 464	4 453	4 456
Food manufacturing	1 553.1	1 551.2	1 525.7	1 517.5	1 493.7	1 477.6	1 479.4	1 484.1	1 480.9	1 456.4	1 450.6	1 458.8	1 468.7
Textile mills	378.2	332.9	290.9	261.3	236.9	217.6	195.0	169.7	151.2	124.4	119.0	120.1	118.0
Textile product mills	229.6	217.0	204.2	187.7	183.2	176.4	166.7	157.7	147.2	125.7	119.0	117.6	116.6
Apparel	483.5	415.2	350.0	303.9	278.0	250.5	232.4	214.6	199.0	167.5	156.6	151.7	148.1
Paper and paper products	604.7	577.6	546.6	516.2	495.5	484.2	470.5	458.2	444.9	407.0	394.7	387.4	379.0
Printing and related support activities	806.8	768.3	706.6	680.4	662.6	646.3	634.4	622.0	594.1	521.9	487.6	471.8	462.1
Petroleum and coal products	123.2	121.1	118.1	114.3	111.7	112.1	113.2	114.5	117.4	115.3	113.9	111.8	113.2
Chemicals	980.4	959.0	927.5	906.1	887.0	872.1	865.9	860.9	847.1	804.1	786.5	783.6	783.6
Plastics and rubber products	950.9	896.2	846.8	814.3	804.7	802.3	785.5	757.2	729.4	624.9	624.8	635.2	645.2
Service-Providing	107 232	108 045	107 893	108 284	109 627	111 557	113 594	115 412	115 517	112 318	112 166	113 450	115 329
Private Service-Providing	86 442	86 927	86 380	86 701	88 006	89 753	91 621	93 194	93 008	89 764	89 676	91 363	93 411
Trade, transportation, and utilities	26 225	25 983	25 497	25 287	25 533	25 959	26 276	26 630	26 293	24 906	24 636	25 065	25 516
Wholesale trade	5 933.2	5 772.7	5 652.3	5 607.5	5 662.9	5 764.4	5 904.5	6 015.2	5 942.7	5 586.6	5 452.1	5 543.1	5 672.7
Durable goods	3 250.7	3 130.4	3 007.9	2 940.6	2 950.5	2 999.2	3 074.8	3 121.5	3 052.0	2 809.9	2 713.5	2 765.2	2 830.3
Nondurable goods	2 064.8	2 031.3	2 015.0	2 004.6	2 010.0	2 022.4	2 041.3	2 062.2	2 047.7	1 966.1	1 928.1	1 939.0	1 971.9
Electronic markets, agents, and brokers	617.7	611.1	629.4	662.2	702.4	742.8	788.5	831.5	842.9	810.7	810.5	839.0	870.6

[1] Includes other industries, not shown separately.

Table 15-1. Nonfarm Employment by NAICS Sector and Industry—*Continued*

(Wage and salary workers on nonfarm payrolls, thousands.)

Industry	1990	1991	1992	1993	1994	1995	1996	1997	1998	1999
Retail trade	13 182	12 896	12 828	13 021	13 491	13 897	14 143	14 389	14 609	14 970
Motor vehicle and parts dealers [1]	1 494.4	1 435.1	1 428.1	1 475.3	1 564.7	1 627.1	1 685.6	1 723.4	1 740.9	1 796.6
Automobile dealers	983.3	938.3	934.8	970.4	1 031.8	1 071.6	1 113.0	1 134.5	1 142.0	1 179.7
Furniture and home furnishings stores	431.5	412.8	410.3	418.6	441.6	461.2	474.2	484.7	499.1	524.4
Electronics and appliance stores	450.7	449.4	446.3	459.4	495.7	534.7	555.5	575.2	590.6	623.8
Building material and garden supply stores	890.9	863.0	872.1	891.9	946.2	981.8	1 007.2	1 043.1	1 062.3	1 101.0
Food and beverage stores	2 778.8	2 767.9	2 743.9	2 774.8	2 825.0	2 879.8	2 927.8	2 956.9	2 965.7	2 984.5
Health and personal care stores	792.0	788.5	780.2	778.6	797.0	811.9	826.4	853.3	876.0	898.2
Gasoline stations	910.2	889.3	876.4	881.2	902.3	922.3	946.4	956.2	961.3	943.5
Clothing and clothing accessories stores	1 313.0	1 275.8	1 249.1	1 259.9	1 261.7	1 246.3	1 220.6	1 235.9	1 268.6	1 306.6
Sporting goods, hobby, book, and music stores	463.6	459.5	466.2	472.8	498.9	519.8	528.8	545.1	555.1	582.7
General merchandise stores [1]	2 499.8	2 416.7	2 414.2	2 450.2	2 541.0	2 635.4	2 657.3	2 657.6	2 686.5	2 751.8
Department stores	1 493.9	1 440.8	1 445.2	1 486.8	1 560.4	1 629.8	1 645.0	1 653.5	1 679.2	1 709.2
Miscellaneous store retailers	738.2	734.7	736.8	752.9	795.7	841.1	874.3	913.2	950.3	985.5
Nonstore retailers	419.2	403.7	404.5	404.9	421.2	435.4	438.5	444.5	453.0	471.6
Transportation and warehousing	3 475.6	3 462.8	3 461.8	3 553.8	3 701.0	3 837.8	3 935.3	4 026.5	4 168.0	4 300.3
Air transportation	529.2	525.4	519.6	516.6	511.2	510.9	525.7	542.0	562.7	586.3
Rail transportation	271.8	255.6	248.1	242.2	234.6	232.5	225.2	221.0	225.0	228.8
Water transportation	56.8	57.4	56.7	52.8	52.3	50.8	51.0	50.7	50.5	51.7
Truck transportation	1 122.4	1 104.6	1 107.4	1 154.8	1 206.2	1 249.1	1 282.4	1 308.2	1 354.4	1 391.5
Transit and ground passenger transportation	274.2	283.9	287.9	299.9	316.6	327.9	339.1	349.6	362.7	371.0
Pipeline transportation	59.8	60.7	60.1	58.7	57.0	53.6	51.4	49.7	48.1	46.9
Scenic and sightseeing transportation	15.7	16.5	17.7	19.3	21.3	22.0	23.2	24.5	25.4	26.1
Support activities for transportation	364.1	376.6	369.9	381.8	404.7	430.4	445.8	473.4	496.8	518.1
Couriers and messengers	375.0	378.9	388.8	414.3	466.2	516.8	539.9	546.0	568.2	585.9
Warehousing and storage	406.6	403.2	405.6	413.4	431.0	443.8	451.8	461.5	474.2	494.1
Utilities	740.0	736.1	726.0	710.7	689.3	666.2	639.6	620.9	613.4	608.5
Information	2 688	2 677	2 641	2 668	2 738	2 843	2 940	3 084	3 218	3 419
Publishing industries, except Internet	870.6	863.4	854.2	873.1	891.0	910.7	927.2	955.5	982.3	1 004.8
Motion picture and sound recording industries	254.6	258.9	254.3	259.6	278.4	311.1	334.7	353.0	369.5	384.4
Broadcasting, except Internet	283.8	281.2	279.7	284.0	290.1	298.1	309.1	313.0	321.2	329.4
Telecommunications	1 008.5	999.9	972.9	969.5	989.5	1 009.3	1 038.1	1 108.0	1 167.4	1 270.8
Data processing, hosting, and related services	211.4	212.8	219.6	223.4	226.9	242.6	252.0	268.4	282.8	307.1
Other information services [1]	59.3	61.2	60.5	58.1	62.5	71.8	79.0	85.5	95.3	121.9
Internet publishing and broadcasting	29.4	28.3	28.2	28.7	29.7	33.7	39.6	45.4	53.9	78.1
Financial activities	6 614	6 561	6 559	6 742	6 910	6 866	7 018	7 255	7 565	7 753
Finance and insurance	4 976.4	4 937.9	4 931.0	5 065.2	5 175.3	5 107.5	5 200.6	5 378.9	5 631.7	5 770.2
Monetary authorities–central bank	24.0	24.2	23.7	23.4	23.4	23.0	22.8	22.1	21.7	22.6
Credit intermediation and related activities [1]	2 424.8	2 352.4	2 317.3	2 360.7	2 375.7	2 314.4	2 368.2	2 433.6	2 531.9	2 591.0
Depository credit intermediation [1]	1 908.5	1 830.7	1 769.0	1 760.5	1 736.7	1 700.2	1 691.4	1 696.6	1 708.9	1 709.7
Commercial banking	1 361.8	1 333.7	1 302.8	1 308.7	1 297.4	1 281.7	1 275.1	1 277.9	1 286.0	1 281.2
Securities, commodity contracts, investments	457.9	455.0	475.7	507.9	553.4	562.2	589.6	636.1	692.2	737.3
Insurance carriers and related activities	2 016.1	2 051.0	2 058.0	2 114.8	2 161.7	2 146.7	2 157.2	2 220.4	2 312.5	2 341.4
Funds, trusts, and other financial vehicles	53.5	55.3	56.2	58.5	61.2	61.2	62.8	66.8	73.4	78.0
Real estate and rental and leasing	1 637.1	1 623.0	1 627.7	1 676.3	1 734.2	1 758.1	1 817.1	1 875.9	1 933.7	1 982.5
Real estate	1 109.0	1 109.8	1 116.7	1 148.6	1 185.9	1 181.7	1 208.6	1 243.8	1 277.7	1 302.6
Rental and leasing services	514.2	499.4	496.4	511.0	529.9	557.4	587.7	600.5	630.8	653.1
Lessors of nonfinancial intangible assets	13.9	13.9	14.6	16.7	18.4	19.0	20.8	22.6	25.3	26.8

[1] Includes other industries, not shown separately.

Table 15-1. Nonfarm Employment by NAICS Sector and Industry—*Continued*

(Wage and salary workers on nonfarm payrolls, thousands.)

Industry	2000	2001	2002	2003	2004	2005	2006	2007	2008	2009	2010	2011	2012
Retail trade	15 280	15 239	15 025	14 917	15 058	15 280	15 353	15 520	15 283	14 522	14 440	14 668	14 875
Motor vehicle and parts dealers [1]	1 846.9	1 854.6	1 879.4	1 882.9	1 902.3	1 918.6	1 909.7	1 908.3	1 831.2	1 637.5	1 629.2	1 691.2	1 732.3
Automobile dealers	1 216.5	1 225.1	1 252.8	1 254.4	1 257.3	1 261.4	1 246.7	1 242.2	1 176.7	1 018.2	1 011.5	1 056.9	1 091.3
Furniture and home furnishings stores	543.5	541.2	538.7	547.3	563.4	576.1	586.9	574.6	531.1	449.2	437.9	438.9	441.7
Electronics and appliance stores	647.3	632.6	594.8	573.9	571.5	585.0	580.5	582.5	569.6	515.7	522.3	527.4	511.6
Building material and garden supply stores	1 142.1	1 151.8	1 176.5	1 185.0	1 227.1	1 276.1	1 324.1	1 309.3	1 248.0	1 155.6	1 131.8	1 145.7	1 169.9
Food and beverage stores	2 993.0	2 950.5	2 881.6	2 838.4	2 821.6	2 817.8	2 821.1	2 843.6	2 862.0	2 830.0	2 808.2	2 822.8	2 859.1
Health and personal care stores	927.6	951.5	938.8	938.1	941.1	953.7	961.1	993.1	1 002.8	986.0	980.5	980.9	1 002.7
Gasoline stations	935.7	925.3	895.9	882.0	875.6	871.1	864.1	861.5	842.4	825.5	819.3	831.0	841.1
Clothing and clothing accessories stores	1 321.6	1 321.1	1 312.5	1 304.5	1 364.3	1 414.6	1 450.9	1 500.0	1 468.0	1 363.9	1 352.5	1 360.9	1 407.9
Sporting goods, hobby, book, and music stores	602.7	601.1	591.8	584.7	585.9	597.9	606.0	623.3	621.9	589.2	579.1	577.9	579.3
General merchandise stores [1]	2 819.8	2 842.2	2 812.0	2 822.4	2 863.1	2 934.3	2 935.0	3 020.6	3 025.6	2 966.2	2 997.7	3 085.2	3 088.4
Department stores	1 755.0	1 768.3	1 684.0	1 620.6	1 605.3	1 595.1	1 557.2	1 591.5	1 540.5	1 472.9	1 501.6	1 538.6	1 501.0
Miscellaneous store retailers	1 007.1	993.3	959.5	930.7	913.5	899.9	881.0	865.4	842.5	782.4	761.5	772.4	797.5
Nonstore retailers	492.4	473.5	443.7	427.3	428.8	434.6	432.8	437.9	438.0	421.1	420.6	433.5	443.4
Transportation and warehousing	4 410.3	4 372.0	4 223.6	4 185.4	4 248.6	4 360.9	4 469.6	4 540.9	4 508.3	4 236.4	4 190.7	4 301.6	4 414.5
Air transportation	614.4	615.3	563.5	528.3	514.5	500.8	487.0	491.8	490.7	462.8	458.3	456.9	458.3
Rail transportation	231.7	226.7	217.8	217.7	225.7	227.8	225.5	233.7	231.0	218.2	216.4	228.1	230.2
Water transportation	56.0	54.0	52.6	54.5	56.4	60.6	62.7	65.5	67.1	63.4	62.3	61.3	63.1
Truck transportation	1 405.8	1 386.8	1 339.3	1 325.6	1 351.7	1 397.6	1 435.8	1 439.2	1 389.0	1 268.2	1 250.4	1 300.5	1 351.0
Transit and ground passenger transportation	372.1	374.8	380.8	382.2	384.9	389.2	399.3	412.1	423.3	421.7	429.7	439.9	447.6
Pipeline transportation	46.0	45.4	41.7	40.2	38.4	37.8	38.7	39.9	41.7	42.6	42.3	42.9	43.9
Scenic and sightseeing transportation	27.5	29.1	25.6	26.6	27.2	28.8	27.5	28.6	28.0	27.6	27.3	27.5	27.3
Support activities for transportation	537.4	539.2	524.7	520.3	535.1	552.2	570.6	584.2	592.0	548.5	542.5	562.2	578.3
Couriers and messengers	605.0	587.0	560.9	561.7	556.6	571.4	582.4	580.7	573.4	546.3	528.1	529.2	532.8
Warehousing and storage	514.4	513.8	516.7	528.3	558.1	594.7	638.1	665.2	672.1	637.1	633.4	653.1	682.0
Utilities	601.3	599.4	596.2	577.0	563.8	554.0	548.5	553.4	558.9	560.0	552.8	552.6	554.1
Information	3 630	3 629	3 395	3 188	3 118	3 061	3 038	3 032	2 984	2 804	2 707	2 674	2 678
Publishing industries, except Internet	1 035.0	1 020.7	964.1	924.8	909.1	904.1	902.4	901.2	880.4	796.4	759.0	748.6	737.7
Motion picture and sound recording industries	382.6	376.8	387.9	376.2	385.0	377.5	375.7	380.6	371.3	357.6	370.2	362.1	372.3
Broadcasting, except Internet	343.5	344.6	334.1	324.3	325.0	327.7	328.3	325.2	318.7	300.5	290.3	283.2	285.3
Telecommunications	1 396.6	1 423.9	1 280.9	1 166.8	1 115.1	1 071.3	1 047.6	1 030.6	1 019.4	965.7	902.9	873.6	858.1
Data processing, hosting, and related services	315.7	316.8	303.9	280.0	267.1	262.5	263.2	267.8	260.3	248.5	243.0	245.8	250.4
Other information services [1]	157.1	146.5	123.6	115.9	116.9	117.7	120.8	126.3	133.5	135.0	141.7	160.0	173.7
Internet publishing and broadcasting	110.8	100.4	76.3	67.2	66.1	67.2	69.1	72.9	80.6	83.3	92.0	109.6	121.4
Financial activities	7 783	7 900	7 956	8 078	8 105	8 197	8 367	8 348	8 206	7 838	7 695	7 697	7 786
Finance and insurance	5 772.8	5 862.0	5 922.2	6 020.5	6 019.4	6 062.9	6 194.0	6 179.1	6 076.3	5 843.9	5 761.0	5 769.0	5 834.3
Monetary authorities–central bank	22.8	23.0	23.4	22.6	21.8	20.8	21.2	21.6	22.4	21.0	20.0	18.3	17.2
Credit intermediation and related activities [1]	2 547.8	2 597.7	2 686.0	2 792.4	2 817.0	2 869.0	2 924.9	2 866.3	2 732.7	2 590.2	2 550.0	2 554.1	2 578.8
Depository credit intermediation [1]	1 681.2	1 701.2	1 733.0	1 748.5	1 751.5	1 769.2	1 802.0	1 823.5	1 815.2	1 753.8	1 728.8	1 735.1	1 738.1
Commercial banking	1 250.5	1 258.4	1 278.1	1 280.1	1 280.8	1 296.0	1 322.9	1 351.4	1 357.5	1 316.9	1 305.9	1 314.5	1 318.2
Securities, commodity contracts, investments	804.5	830.5	789.4	757.7	766.1	786.1	818.3	848.6	864.2	811.3	800.5	810.7	814.4
Insurance carriers and related activities	2 316.7	2 326.4	2 341.7	2 367.4	2 332.8	2 303.3	2 341.7	2 353.9	2 366.7	2 333.0	2 303.8	2 299.9	2 337.1
Funds, trusts, and other financial vehicles	81.1	84.4	81.7	80.4	81.7	83.7	87.9	88.7	90.5	88.4	86.8	85.9	86.8
Real estate and rental and leasing	2 010.6	2 038.4	2 033.3	2 057.5	2 085.5	2 133.5	2 172.5	2 169.1	2 129.6	1 994.0	1 933.8	1 927.4	1 952.0
Real estate	1 316.0	1 343.4	1 356.6	1 387.1	1 418.7	1 460.8	1 499.0	1 500.4	1 485.0	1 420.2	1 395.7	1 400.8	1 416.5
Rental and leasing services	666.8	666.3	649.1	643.1	641.1	645.8	645.5	640.3	616.9	547.3	513.5	502.2	511.4
Lessors of nonfinancial intangible assets	27.8	28.7	27.6	27.3	25.7	26.9	28.1	28.4	27.7	26.5	24.6	24.4	24.2

[1] Includes other industries, not shown separately.

Table 15-1. Nonfarm Employment by NAICS Sector and Industry—*Continued*

(Wage and salary workers on nonfarm payrolls, thousands.)

Industry	1990	1991	1992	1993	1994	1995	1996	1997	1998	1999
Professional and business services	10 848	10 714	10 970	11 495	12 174	12 844	13 462	14 335	15 147	15 957
Professional and technical services [1]	4 538.2	4 509.2	4 575.6	4 689.1	4 823.3	5 078.4	5 312.7	5 628.8	5 992.3	6 345.4
Legal services	943.6	946.0	949.8	963.9	965.6	959.2	968.4	987.5	1 021.1	1 051.4
Accounting and bookkeeping services	664.1	655.4	657.8	654.2	670.1	706.3	729.8	761.2	802.0	837.6
Architectural and engineering services	941.5	906.2	901.8	922.7	952.0	997.1	1 024.5	1 063.4	1 114.8	1 168.1
Computer systems design and related services	409.7	419.9	444.9	484.8	531.4	611.2	701.4	826.7	974.9	1 132.9
Management and technical consulting services	305.1	314.3	340.2	366.2	396.5	451.8	492.7	541.7	590.4	619.0
Management of companies and enterprises	1 667.4	1 638.1	1 623.4	1 640.1	1 665.9	1 685.8	1 702.7	1 729.7	1 756.1	1 773.8
Administrative and waste services	4 642.8	4 566.6	4 770.5	5 165.6	5 684.4	6 079.7	6 446.5	6 976.6	7 398.0	7 837.5
Administrative and support services [1]	4 413.3	4 334.3	4 533.8	4 917.0	5 423.7	5 806.4	6 164.5	6 686.0	7 098.7	7 527.0
Employment services [1]	1 512.1	1 466.0	1 610.4	1 884.3	2 246.8	2 448.1	2 625.3	2 953.9	3 245.8	3 581.6
Temporary help services	1 155.8	1 123.3	1 212.5	1 388.8	1 632.2	1 743.8	1 849.0	2 059.7	2 245.2	2 469.6
Business support services	504.6	503.3	524.5	549.0	574.4	629.8	678.3	733.9	772.2	780.5
Services to buildings and dwellings	1 174.6	1 150.9	1 159.7	1 197.9	1 267.2	1 302.4	1 361.5	1 424.1	1 460.0	1 534.7
Waste management and remediation services	229.4	232.4	236.7	248.6	260.7	273.3	282.0	290.5	299.3	310.5
Education and health services	10 984	11 506	11 891	12 303	12 807	13 289	13 683	14 087	14 446	14 798
Educational services	1 688.0	1 737.0	1 713.0	1 755.0	1 895.0	2 010.0	2 078.0	2 155.0	2 233.0	2 320.0
Health care and social assistance	9 295.8	9 769.8	10 178.0	10 548.1	10 911.7	11 278.4	11 604.9	11 932.2	12 213.5	12 477.1
Health care	8 210.7	8 617.7	8 954.8	9 253.6	9 529.7	9 808.9	10 092.6	10 358.0	10 540.9	10 690.9
Ambulatory health care services [1]	2 841.6	3 028.4	3 199.9	3 385.5	3 578.8	3 767.5	3 939.9	4 093.0	4 161.2	4 226.6
Offices of physicians	1 278.0	1 345.2	1 401.1	1 442.0	1 480.9	1 540.4	1 603.8	1 660.5	1 723.6	1 786.6
Outpatient care centers	260.5	271.4	286.5	303.1	314.5	328.8	340.2	352.1	363.3	375.4
Home health care services	287.5	340.7	393.4	463.8	553.2	621.8	667.2	702.8	659.5	629.6
Hospitals	3 512.6	3 617.3	3 711.4	3 740.0	3 724.0	3 733.7	3 772.8	3 821.6	3 892.4	3 935.5
Nursing and residential care facilities [1]	1 856.4	1 972.0	2 043.5	2 128.1	2 227.0	2 307.7	2 379.9	2 443.4	2 487.3	2 528.8
Nursing care facilities	1 169.8	1 240.2	1 273.4	1 319.3	1 377.1	1 413.0	1 448.4	1 474.6	1 489.3	1 501.0
Social assistance [1]	1 085.1	1 152.2	1 223.3	1 294.4	1 381.9	1 469.5	1 512.3	1 574.2	1 672.6	1 786.2
Child day care services	387.8	413.2	446.5	468.9	510.0	557.1	559.2	570.4	615.1	673.7
Leisure and hospitality	9 288	9 256	9 437	9 732	10 100	10 501	10 777	11 018	11 232	11 543
Arts, entertainment, and recreation	1 132.0	1 177.0	1 236.3	1 301.9	1 375.6	1 459.4	1 522.1	1 599.9	1 645.2	1 709.1
Performing arts and spectator sports	272.7	282.7	289.5	286.8	296.1	307.7	328.6	349.6	350.0	361.1
Museums, historical sites, zoos, and parks	68.0	71.0	75.0	78.3	81.8	83.9	88.9	93.8	97.4	103.1
Amusements, gambling, and recreation	791.3	823.4	871.8	936.8	997.7	1 067.8	1 104.5	1 156.5	1 197.9	1 244.9
Accommodation and food services	8 155.6	8 078.9	8 200.5	8 430.4	8 724.1	9 041.6	9 254.3	9 417.9	9 586.2	9 833.7
Accommodation	1 616.0	1 574.3	1 561.5	1 580.5	1 615.3	1 652.5	1 698.9	1 729.5	1 773.5	1 831.7
Food services and drinking places	6 539.6	6 504.6	6 639.0	6 849.9	7 108.7	7 389.1	7 555.4	7 688.5	7 812.7	8 002.0
Other services	4 261	4 249	4 240	4 350	4 428	4 572	4 690	4 825	4 976	5 087
Repair and maintenance	1 009.0	960.0	964.0	998.0	1 023.5	1 078.9	1 135.5	1 169.3	1 189.2	1 222.0
Personal and laundry services	1 119.9	1 109.2	1 098.9	1 116.0	1 120.3	1 143.9	1 165.7	1 180.4	1 205.6	1 220.3
Membership associations and organizations	2 132.2	2 179.5	2 177.1	2 236.4	2 284.5	2 348.9	2 389.1	2 474.9	2 581.3	2 644.4
Government	18 415	18 545	18 787	18 989	19 275	19 432	19 539	19 664	19 909	20 307
Federal	3 196	3 110	3 111	3 063	3 018	2 949	2 877	2 806	2 772	2 769
Federal, except U.S. Postal Service	2 370.5	2 296.2	2 310.7	2 269.4	2 197.2	2 098.8	2 009.8	1 940.2	1 891.3	1 879.5
U.S. Postal Service	825.1	813.2	800.0	793.2	820.6	849.9	867.2	866.0	880.5	889.7
State government	4 305	4 355	4 408	4 488	4 576	4 635	4 606	4 582	4 612	4 709
State government education	1 729.9	1 767.6	1 798.6	1 834.1	1 881.9	1 919.0	1 910.7	1 904.0	1 922.2	1 983.2
State government, excluding education	2 574.6	2 587.3	2 609.7	2 653.8	2 693.6	2 715.5	2 695.1	2 677.9	2 690.2	2 725.6
Local government	10 914	11 081	11 267	11 438	11 682	11 849	12 056	12 276	12 525	12 829
Local government education	5 902.1	5 994.1	6 075.9	6 206.3	6 329.4	6 453.1	6 592.3	6 758.5	6 920.9	7 120.4
Local government, excluding education	5 012.4	5 086.9	5 191.6	5 231.9	5 352.2	5 396.0	5 464.1	5 516.9	5 603.9	5 708.6

[1]Includes other industries, not shown separately.

Table 15-1. Nonfarm Employment by NAICS Sector and Industry—*Continued*

(Wage and salary workers on nonfarm payrolls, thousands.)

Industry	2000	2001	2002	2003	2004	2005	2006	2007	2008	2009	2010	2011	2012
Professional and business services	16 666	16 476	15 976	15 987	16 394	16 954	17 566	17 942	17 735	16 579	16 728	17 332	17 930
Professional and technical services [1]	6 701.7	6 871.1	6 648.8	6 602.7	6 747.1	7 024.6	7 356.7	7 659.5	7 799.4	7 508.5	7 441.3	7 666.2	7 892.6
Legal services	1 065.7	1 091.3	1 115.3	1 142.1	1 163.1	1 168.0	1 173.2	1 175.4	1 161.5	1 124.9	1 114.2	1 115.7	1 122.1
Accounting and bookkeeping services	866.4	872.2	837.3	815.3	805.9	849.3	889.0	935.9	951.0	914.2	886.5	898.9	912.7
Architectural and engineering services	1 237.9	1 274.7	1 246.1	1 226.9	1 258.2	1 310.9	1 385.7	1 432.2	1 439.4	1 324.7	1 275.4	1 293.5	1 323.3
Computer systems design and related services	1 254.3	1 297.8	1 152.8	1 116.6	1 148.6	1 195.2	1 284.6	1 372.1	1 439.6	1 422.6	1 449.0	1 535.9	1 620.3
Management and technical consulting services	672.7	715.1	707.7	718.0	763.0	824.2	886.4	952.7	1 002.0	994.9	999.4	1 065.2	1 121.1
Management of companies and enterprises	1 796.0	1 779.0	1 705.4	1 687.2	1 724.4	1 758.9	1 810.9	1 866.4	1 904.5	1 866.9	1 872.3	1 933.6	2 008.3
Administrative and waste services	8 168.3	7 826.0	7 621.9	7 696.8	7 922.9	8 170.2	8 398.3	8 416.3	8 031.5	7 203.3	7 414.0	7 731.9	8 029.4
Administrative and support services [1]	7 855.4	7 508.7	7 303.6	7 374.7	7 594.4	7 832.5	8 050.2	8 061.3	7 674.7	6 851.6	7 056.7	7 366.7	7 656.7
Employment services [1]	3 849.3	3 468.2	3 273.2	3 326.4	3 455.5	3 606.9	3 680.9	3 545.9	3 133.0	2 480.8	2 722.5	2 942.1	3 147.9
Temporary help services	2 635.6	2 337.7	2 193.7	2 224.2	2 387.2	2 549.4	2 637.4	2 597.4	2 348.4	1 823.3	2 093.6	2 313.0	2 507.7
Business support services	786.7	779.7	756.6	749.7	757.8	766.4	792.9	817.4	832.3	820.0	808.6	814.5	827.9
Services to buildings and dwellings	1 570.5	1 606.2	1 606.1	1 636.1	1 693.7	1 737.5	1 801.4	1 849.5	1 839.8	1 753.3	1 745.0	1 788.6	1 829.5
Waste management and remediation services	312.9	317.3	318.3	322.1	328.6	337.6	348.1	355.0	356.8	351.7	357.3	365.3	372.7
Education and health services	15 109	15 645	16 199	16 588	16 953	17 372	17 826	18 322	18 838	19 193	19 531	19 883	20 319
Educational services	2 390.0	2 511.0	2 643.0	2 695.0	2 763.0	2 836.0	2 901.0	2 941.0	3 040.0	3 090.0	3 155.0	3 249.6	3 347.0
Health care and social assistance	12 718.0	13 134.0	13 555.7	13 892.6	14 190.2	14 536.3	14 925.3	15 380.2	15 798.3	16 102.7	16 375.4	16 633.5	16 971.5
Health care	10 857.8	11 188.1	11 536.0	11 817.1	12 055.3	12 313.9	12 601.8	12 946.8	13 289.9	13 543.0	13 776.9	14 025.9	14 302.4
Ambulatory health care services [1]	4 320.3	4 461.5	4 633.2	4 786.4	4 952.3	5 113.5	5 285.8	5 473.5	5 646.6	5 793.4	5 974.7	6 136.2	6 317.8
Offices of physicians	1 839.9	1 911.2	1 967.8	2 002.5	2 047.8	2 093.5	2 147.8	2 201.6	2 252.6	2 279.1	2 312.7	2 344.1	2 391.1
Outpatient care centers	386.4	399.7	413.0	426.8	450.5	473.2	492.6	512.0	533.3	557.5	599.9	620.8	651.6
Home health care services	633.3	638.6	679.8	732.6	776.6	821.0	865.6	913.8	961.4	1 027.1	1 084.6	1 140.3	1 198.6
Hospitals	3 954.3	4 050.9	4 159.6	4 244.6	4 284.7	4 345.4	4 423.4	4 515.0	4 627.3	4 667.4	4 678.5	4 721.7	4 791.0
Nursing and residential care facilities [1]	2 583.2	2 675.8	2 743.3	2 786.2	2 818.4	2 855.0	2 892.5	2 958.3	3 016.1	3 082.2	3 123.7	3 168.1	3 193.6
Nursing care facilities	1 513.6	1 546.8	1 573.2	1 579.8	1 576.9	1 577.4	1 581.4	1 602.6	1 618.7	1 644.9	1 657.1	1 669.6	1 664.8
Social assistance [1]	1 860.2	1 945.9	2 019.7	2 075.4	2 134.8	2 222.3	2 323.5	2 433.4	2 508.4	2 559.8	2 598.5	2 607.6	2 669.2
Child day care services	695.8	714.6	744.1	755.3	764.7	789.7	818.3	850.4	859.4	852.8	848.0	849.4	855.5
Leisure and hospitality	11 862	12 036	11 986	12 173	12 493	12 816	13 110	13 427	13 436	13 077	13 049	13 353	13 746
Arts, entertainment, and recreation	1 787.9	1 824.4	1 782.6	1 812.9	1 849.6	1 892.3	1 928.5	1 969.2	1 970.1	1 915.5	1 913.3	1 919.1	1 965.4
Performing arts and spectator sports	381.8	382.3	363.7	371.7	367.5	376.3	398.5	405.0	405.7	396.8	406.2	394.2	404.4
Museums, historical sites, zoos, and parks	110.4	115.0	114.0	114.7	118.3	120.7	123.8	130.3	131.6	129.4	127.7	132.7	135.6
Amusements, gambling, and recreation	1 295.7	1 327.1	1 305.0	1 326.5	1 363.8	1 395.3	1 406.3	1 433.9	1 432.8	1 389.2	1 379.4	1 392.2	1 425.5
Accommodation and food services	10 073.5	10 211.3	10 203.2	10 359.8	10 643.2	10 923.0	11 181.1	11 457.4	11 466.3	11 161.9	11 135.4	11 433.6	11 780.2
Accommodation	1 884.4	1 852.2	1 778.6	1 775.4	1 789.5	1 818.6	1 832.1	1 866.9	1 868.7	1 763.0	1 759.6	1 800.5	1 817.0
Food services and drinking places	8 189.1	8 359.1	8 424.6	8 584.4	8 853.7	9 104.4	9 349.0	9 590.4	9 597.5	9 398.9	9 375.8	9 633.1	9 963.2
Other services	5 168	5 258	5 372	5 401	5 409	5 395	5 438	5 494	5 515	5 367	5 331	5 360	5 437
Repair and maintenance	1 241.5	1 256.5	1 246.9	1 233.6	1 228.8	1 236.0	1 248.5	1 253.4	1 227.0	1 150.4	1 138.8	1 168.7	1 190.5
Personal and laundry services	1 242.9	1 255.0	1 257.2	1 263.5	1 272.9	1 276.6	1 288.4	1 309.7	1 322.6	1 280.6	1 265.3	1 288.6	1 312.7
Membership associations and organizations	2 683.3	2 746.4	2 867.8	2 903.6	2 907.5	2 882.2	2 901.2	2 931.1	2 965.7	2 936.0	2 926.4	2 903.0	2 933.4
Government	20 790	21 118	21 513	21 583	21 621	21 804	21 974	22 218	22 509	22 555	22 490	22 086	21 917
Federal	2 865	2 764	2 766	2 761	2 730	2 732	2 732	2 734	2 762	2 832	2 977	2 859	2 814
Federal, except U.S. Postal Service	1 984.8	1 891.0	1 923.8	1 952.4	1 947.5	1 957.3	1 962.6	1 964.7	2 014.4	2 128.5	2 318.1	2 227.6	2 203.4
U.S. Postal Service	879.7	873.0	842.4	808.6	782.1	774.2	769.7	769.1	747.4	703.4	658.5	630.9	611.2
State government	4 786	4 905	5 029	5 002	4 982	5 032	5 075	5 122	5 177	5 169	5 137	5 078	5 052
State government education	2 030.6	2 112.9	2 242.8	2 254.7	2 238.1	2 259.9	2 292.5	2 317.5	2 354.4	2 360.2	2 373.1	2 374.0	2 385.4
State government, excluding education	2 755.9	2 791.8	2 786.3	2 747.6	2 743.9	2 771.6	2 782.0	2 804.3	2 822.5	2 808.8	2 764.1	2 703.7	2 666.7
Local government	13 139	13 449	13 718	13 820	13 909	14 041	14 167	14 362	14 571	14 554	14 376	14 150	14 051
Local government education	7 293.9	7 479.3	7 654.4	7 709.4	7 765.2	7 856.1	7 913.0	7 986.8	8 083.9	8 078.8	8 013.4	7 872.5	7 779.3
Local government, excluding education	5 844.6	5 970.0	6 063.2	6 110.2	6 144.1	6 184.6	6 253.8	6 375.5	6 486.5	6 474.9	6 362.9	6 277.7	6 271.8

[1]Includes other industries, not shown separately.

Table 15-2. Production and Nonsupervisory Workers on Private Nonfarm Payrolls by NAICS Industry

(Wage and salary workers on nonfarm payrolls, thousands.)

Industry	1990	1991	1992	1993	1994	1995	1996	1997	1998	1999
Total Private	73 684	72 522	72 802	74 618	77 419	79 879	81 816	84 225	86 404	88 520
Goods-Producing	17 322	16 352	16 044	16 236	16 795	17 137	17 318	17 698	18 008	18 067
Mining and logging	538	515	478	462	461	458	461	479	473	438
Construction	4 115	3 674	3 546	3 704	3 973	4 113	4 325	4 546	4 807	5 105
Manufacturing	12 669	12 164	12 020	12 070	12 361	12 567	12 532	12 673	12 729	12 524
Durable goods	7 397	7 001	6 853	6 880	7 134	7 352	7 426	7 599	7 721	7 651
Wood products	451.5	414.3	418.6	438.5	470.4	479.3	486.6	498.3	509.6	516.2
Nonmetallic mineral products	413.2	384.1	378.4	380.7	392.3	399.7	404.8	412.5	420.6	426.0
Primary metals	525.1	496.9	478.7	473.0	487.4	500.3	500.3	501.6	505.3	491.9
Fabricated metal products	1 190.1	1 131.6	1 101.0	1 116.9	1 172.0	1 223.0	1 241.6	1 285.3	1 319.6	1 304.9
Machinery	938.9	884.9	857.7	875.5	922.5	969.9	984.5	1 006.9	1 016.1	978.4
Computer and electronic products	980.2	925.6	876.3	856.0	864.0	890.3	915.3	951.1	964.7	932.9
Electrical equipment and appliances	465.2	435.6	425.0	422.0	434.7	438.4	433.9	427.7	431.8	433.2
Transportation equipment [1]	1 473.4	1 406.4	1 388.6	1 367.0	1 415.6	1 472.2	1 481.0	1 521.9	1 530.2	1 526.5
Motor vehicles and parts	869.5	840.1	868.0	896.0	978.4	1 048.9	1 052.4	1 062.4	1 050.2	1 075.8
Furniture and related products	475.2	440.1	442.9	454.0	475.7	480.0	477.9	489.8	512.2	532.4
Miscellaneous manufacturing	484.2	481.2	486.0	495.0	499.0	499.1	500.1	503.4	511.0	508.9
Nondurable goods [1]	5 272	5 163	5 167	5 191	5 227	5 214	5 106	5 075	5 008	4 872
Food manufacturing	1 165.0	1 174.2	1 182.0	1 195.3	1 200.4	1 221.0	1 227.7	1 227.7	1 227.6	1 228.7
Textile mills	417.9	407.2	406.0	404.0	403.3	393.2	371.7	367.1	357.2	333.7
Textile product mills	194.9	185.0	187.4	191.0	199.0	197.9	192.5	192.6	189.7	186.8
Apparel	805.2	781.0	785.3	764.2	740.1	697.9	631.1	593.7	534.0	458.3
Paper and paper products	493.2	488.4	489.9	490.9	492.8	493.8	487.5	488.7	484.1	474.0
Printing and related support activities	597.6	581.7	573.6	579.7	591.4	599.1	594.0	597.0	598.4	585.1
Petroleum and coal products	97.5	97.4	96.8	93.0	90.9	88.8	87.2	87.8	87.1	84.6
Chemicals	620.3	599.7	586.2	590.1	595.6	598.4	595.1	593.3	600.6	595.2
Plastics and rubber products	646.7	623.9	638.9	663.8	698.5	718.7	720.3	731.7	739.3	746.0
Private Service-Providing	56 362	56 170	56 759	58 382	60 624	62 742	64 499	66 527	68 396	70 453
Trade, transportation, and utilities	19 032	18 640	18 506	18 752	19 392	19 984	20 325	20 698	21 059	21 576
Wholesale trade	4 198.3	4 122.0	4 071.0	4 072.2	4 196.4	4 360.8	4 423.2	4 523.2	4 605.0	4 673.1
Retail trade	11 308.4	11 007.9	10 931.4	11 104.0	11 502.1	11 841.0	12 056.7	12 273.6	12 439.8	12 771.5
Transportation and warehousing	2 940.8	2 928.4	2 934.3	3 019.4	3 152.8	3 260.2	3 339.3	3 406.8	3 521.6	3 641.9
Utilities	584.9	581.5	569.5	556.5	540.9	521.8	505.5	493.8	492.2	489.2
Information	1 866	1 871	1 871	1 896	1 928	2 007	2 096	2 181	2 217	2 351
Financial activities	4 973	4 914	4 924	5 084	5 220	5 199	5 322	5 482	5 692	5 818
Professional and business services	8 889	8 748	8 971	9 451	10 078	10 645	11 161	11 896	12 566	13 184
Education and health services	9 748	10 212	10 555	10 908	11 338	11 765	12 123	12 478	12 791	13 089
Leisure and hospitality	8 299	8 247	8 406	8 667	8 979	9 330	9 565	9 780	9 947	10 216
Other services	3 555	3 539	3 526	3 623	3 689	3 812	3 907	4 013	4 124	4 219

[1]Includes other industries, not shown separately.

Table 15-2. Production and Nonsupervisory Workers on Private Nonfarm Payrolls by NAICS Industry—*Continued*

(Wage and salary workers on nonfarm payrolls, thousands.)

Industry	2000	2001	2002	2003	2004	2005	2006	2007	2008	2009	2010	2011	2012
Total Private	90 418	90 061	88 484	87 744	89 000	91 171	93 483	94 941	94 322	89 231	88 548	90 221	92 393
Goods-Producing	18 169	17 466	16 400	15 732	15 821	16 145	16 559	16 405	15 724	13 399	12 774	13 005	13 280
Mining and logging	446	457	436	420	440	473	519	547	574	510	525	594	643
Construction	5 295	5 332	5 196	5 123	5 309	5 611	5 903	5 883	5 521	4 567	4 172	4 184	4 243
Manufacturing	12 428	11 677	10 768	10 189	10 072	10 060	10 137	9 975	9 629	8 322	8 077	8 228	8 394
Durable goods	7 659	7 164	6 530	6 152	6 140	6 220	6 355	6 250	5 975	4 990	4 829	4 986	5 146
Wood products	507.4	470.0	450.3	434.4	445.4	454.4	451.2	407.0	357.5	277.8	269.0	268.7	270.8
Nonmetallic mineral products	439.5	427.1	398.8	374.7	387.8	387.0	391.2	383.6	363.4	302.7	283.5	277.6	272.3
Primary metals	490.0	446.9	396.2	370.3	363.7	362.7	362.6	357.5	347.7	272.5	275.3	301.2	316.5
Fabricated metal products	1 325.8	1 253.5	1 147.0	1 092.5	1 108.6	1 129.3	1 161.8	1 170.9	1 142.9	960.5	935.3	993.6	1 051.4
Machinery	961.4	890.7	786.9	732.3	729.7	748.9	769.8	774.0	771.7	641.0	615.9	662.3	699.6
Computer and electronic products	949.3	875.8	744.1	672.7	655.8	700.1	755.6	743.8	730.0	654.3	629.3	630.0	630.6
Electrical equipment and appliances	433.1	402.2	351.9	319.5	307.2	300.1	302.9	305.2	305.3	266.1	251.1	247.8	247.1
Transportation equipment [1]	1 497.8	1 398.7	1 310.2	1 269.3	1 265.2	1 276.8	1 303.7	1 274.5	1 177.2	948.1	937.0	972.0	1 020.8
Motor vehicles and parts	1 073.0	986.8	931.0	906.3	902.9	893.7	872.7	804.2	695.5	510.0	524.9	556.2	594.5
Furniture and related products	544.4	509.2	475.1	444.5	444.3	435.7	432.8	409.0	364.2	284.3	263.0	260.0	257.9
Miscellaneous manufacturing	509.8	489.8	469.2	442.1	432.2	424.4	423.4	424.6	415.6	382.2	370.2	372.8	379.3
Nondurable goods [1]	4 769	4 513	4 238	4 037	3 932	3 841	3 782	3 725	3 653	3 332	3 248	3 241	3 248
Food manufacturing	1 227.9	1 221.3	1 202.3	1 192.5	1 177.8	1 170.0	1 172.2	1 183.5	1 183.9	1 161.1	1 152.2	1 158.0	1 168.7
Textile mills	315.2	275.8	242.2	216.9	193.9	174.2	157.8	137.3	122.0	98.6	95.9	98.2	95.8
Textile product mills	183.4	173.7	162.0	148.3	147.1	143.0	134.9	123.2	115.3	97.7	91.7	89.2	85.0
Apparel	403.8	341.4	286.0	241.5	218.6	192.7	182.0	173.4	163.3	132.3	120.4	111.6	108.6
Paper and paper products	467.5	446.3	421.4	392.7	373.7	365.2	357.4	350.5	343.7	313.0	302.2	295.3	287.0
Printing and related support activities	575.7	544.4	492.6	471.2	459.5	447.3	446.6	442.6	424.5	369.3	341.7	327.1	316.0
Petroleum and coal products	83.1	80.9	78.0	74.4	76.7	75.4	72.2	72.6	77.1	69.7	69.5	69.8	73.1
Chemicals	587.7	562.2	531.9	524.9	520.2	510.0	507.7	504.4	512.5	478.7	473.8	479.8	491.0
Plastics and rubber products	752.6	704.4	661.9	633.4	625.6	620.4	607.6	592.3	571.5	476.5	472.0	481.7	486.9
Private Service-Providing	72 249	72 595	72 084	72 012	73 179	75 027	76 924	78 537	78 598	75 832	75 774	77 217	79 112
Trade, transportation, and utilities	21 965	21 709	21 337	21 078	21 319	21 830	22 166	22 546	22 337	21 116	20 874	21 234	21 654
Wholesale trade	4 686.4	4 555.1	4 473.5	4 395.9	4 443.5	4 583.6	4 724.3	4 850.9	4 822.1	4 505.6	4 377.5	4 442.6	4 567.4
Retail trade	13 039.9	12 952.3	12 774.0	12 654.9	12 788.0	13 029.6	13 110.3	13 317.1	13 134.0	12 471.8	12 425.3	12 647.3	12 824.7
Transportation and warehousing	3 753.2	3 718.2	3 611.3	3 563.1	3 637.1	3 774.0	3 889.1	3 934.6	3 930.7	3 688.1	3 627.1	3 703.4	3 819.6
Utilities	485.1	482.8	478.4	463.7	449.9	443.0	442.6	443.5	450.4	451.0	443.5	440.8	442.2
Information	2 502	2 531	2 398	2 347	2 371	2 386	2 399	2 403	2 388	2 240	2 170	2 148	2 165
Financial activities	5 819	5 888	5 964	6 052	6 052	6 127	6 312	6 365	6 320	6 066	5 942	5 900	5 988
Professional and business services	13 790	13 588	13 049	12 911	13 287	13 854	14 446	14 784	14 585	13 520	13 699	14 251	14 805
Education and health services	13 362	13 846	14 311	14 532	14 771	15 129	15 539	15 999	16 488	16 841	17 125	17 421	17 819
Leisure and hospitality	10 516	10 662	10 576	10 666	10 955	11 263	11 568	11 861	11 873	11 560	11 507	11 772	12 134
Other services	4 296	4 373	4 449	4 426	4 425	4 438	4 494	4 578	4 606	4 488	4 458	4 491	4 547

[1]Includes other industries, not shown separately.

Table 15-3. Average Weekly Hours of Production and Nonsupervisory Workers on Private Nonfarm Payrolls by NAICS Industry

(Hours.)

Industry	1990	1991	1992	1993	1994	1995	1996	1997	1998	1999	2000
Total Private	34.3	34.1	34.2	34.3	34.5	34.3	34.3	34.5	34.5	34.3	34.3
Goods-Producing	40.1	40.1	40.2	40.6	41.1	40.8	40.8	41.1	40.8	40.8	40.7
Mining and logging	45.0	45.3	44.6	44.9	45.3	45.3	46.0	46.2	44.9	44.2	44.4
Construction	38.3	38.1	38.0	38.4	38.8	38.8	38.9	38.9	38.8	39.0	39.2
Manufacturing	40.5	40.4	40.7	41.1	41.7	41.3	41.3	41.7	41.4	41.4	41.3
Overtime hours	3.9	3.8	4.0	4.4	5.0	4.7	4.8	5.1	4.9	4.9	4.7
Durable goods	41.1	40.9	41.3	41.9	42.6	42.1	42.1	42.6	42.1	41.9	41.8
Overtime hours	3.9	3.7	3.9	4.5	5.3	5.0	5.0	5.4	5.0	5.0	4.8
Wood products	40.4	40.2	40.9	41.2	41.7	41.0	41.2	41.4	41.4	41.3	41.0
Nonmetallic mineral products	40.9	40.5	41.0	41.5	42.2	41.8	42.0	41.9	42.2	42.1	41.6
Primary metals	42.1	41.5	42.4	43.1	44.1	43.4	43.6	44.3	43.5	43.8	44.2
Fabricated metal products	41.0	40.8	41.2	41.6	42.3	41.9	41.9	42.3	41.9	41.7	41.9
Machinery	42.1	41.9	42.4	43.2	43.9	43.5	43.3	44.0	43.1	42.3	42.3
Computer and electronic products	41.3	40.9	41.4	41.7	42.2	42.2	41.9	42.5	41.9	41.5	41.4
Electrical equipment and appliances	41.2	41.4	41.8	42.4	43.0	41.9	42.1	42.1	41.8	41.8	41.6
Transportation equipment [1]	42.0	41.9	41.9	43.0	44.3	43.7	43.8	44.2	43.3	43.6	43.3
Motor vehicles and parts	41.4	41.5	41.6	43.3	44.8	43.8	43.8	43.9	42.6	43.8	43.4
Furniture and related products	38.0	37.8	38.6	39.0	39.3	38.5	38.2	39.1	39.4	39.3	39.2
Miscellaneous manufacturing	39.0	39.2	39.3	39.2	39.4	39.2	39.1	39.7	39.2	39.3	39.0
Nondurable goods [1]	39.6	39.7	40.0	40.1	40.5	40.1	40.1	40.5	40.5	40.5	40.3
Overtime hours	3.9	4.0	4.2	4.3	4.6	4.3	4.4	4.7	4.6	4.6	4.5
Food manufacturing	39.3	39.2	39.2	39.3	39.8	39.6	39.5	39.8	40.1	40.2	40.1
Textile mills	40.2	40.7	41.3	41.6	41.9	40.9	40.8	41.6	41.0	41.0	41.4
Textile product mills	38.5	38.6	38.7	39.2	39.4	38.6	38.8	39.2	39.2	39.1	38.7
Apparel	34.7	35.4	35.6	35.6	35.7	35.3	35.2	35.6	35.5	35.4	35.7
Paper and paper products	43.6	43.6	43.8	43.8	44.2	43.4	43.5	43.9	43.6	43.6	42.8
Printing and related support activities	38.7	38.6	39.0	39.2	39.6	39.1	39.1	39.5	39.3	39.1	39.2
Petroleum and coal products	44.4	43.9	43.6	44.0	44.3	43.7	43.7	43.1	43.6	42.6	42.7
Chemicals	42.8	43.1	43.3	43.2	43.4	43.4	43.3	43.4	43.2	42.8	42.2
Plastics and rubber products	40.6	40.5	41.2	41.4	41.8	41.1	41.0	41.4	41.3	41.3	40.8
Private Service-Providing	32.5	32.4	32.5	32.5	32.7	32.6	32.6	32.8	32.8	32.7	32.7
Trade, transportation, and utilities	33.7	33.6	33.8	34.1	34.3	34.1	34.1	34.3	34.2	33.9	33.8
Wholesale trade	38.4	38.4	38.5	38.5	38.8	38.6	38.6	38.8	38.6	38.6	38.8
Retail trade	30.6	30.4	30.7	30.7	30.9	30.8	30.7	30.9	30.9	30.8	30.7
Transportation and warehousing	37.7	37.3	37.4	38.9	39.5	38.9	39.1	39.4	38.7	37.6	37.4
Utilities	41.6	41.5	41.7	42.1	42.3	42.3	42.0	42.0	42.0	42.0	42.0
Information	35.8	35.6	35.8	36.0	36.0	36.0	36.3	36.3	36.6	36.7	36.8
Financial activities	35.5	35.5	35.6	35.5	35.5	35.5	35.6	35.8	36.0	35.8	35.9
Professional and business services	34.2	34.0	34.0	34.0	34.1	34.0	34.1	34.3	34.3	34.4	34.5
Education and health services	31.9	31.9	32.0	32.0	32.0	32.0	31.9	32.2	32.2	32.1	32.2
Leisure and hospitality	26.0	25.6	25.7	25.9	26.0	25.9	25.9	26.1	26.2	26.1	26.1
Other services	32.8	32.7	32.6	32.6	32.7	32.6	32.5	32.7	32.6	32.5	32.5

[1] Includes other industries, not shown separately.

Table 15-3. Average Weekly Hours of Production and Nonsupervisory Workers on Private Nonfarm Payrolls by NAICS Industry—*Continued*

(Hours.)

Industry	2001	2002	2003	2004	2005	2006	2007	2008	2009	2010	2011	2012
Total Private	34.0	33.9	33.7	33.7	33.8	33.9	33.9	33.6	33.1	33.4	33.6	33.7
Goods-Producing	39.9	39.9	39.8	40.0	40.1	40.5	40.6	40.2	39.2	40.4	40.9	41.2
Mining and logging	44.6	43.2	43.6	44.5	45.6	45.6	45.9	45.1	43.2	44.6	46.7	46.6
Construction	38.7	38.4	38.4	38.3	38.6	39.0	39.0	38.5	37.6	38.4	39.0	39.3
Manufacturing	40.3	40.5	40.4	40.8	40.7	41.1	41.2	40.8	39.8	41.1	41.4	41.7
Overtime hours	4.0	4.2	4.2	4.6	4.6	4.4	4.2	3.7	2.9	3.8	4.1	4.2
Durable goods	40.6	40.8	40.8	41.3	41.1	41.4	41.5	41.1	39.8	41.4	41.9	42.0
Overtime hours	3.9	4.2	4.3	4.7	4.6	4.4	4.2	3.7	2.7	3.8	4.2	4.3
Wood products	40.2	39.9	40.4	40.7	40.0	39.8	39.4	38.6	37.4	39.1	39.7	41.1
Nonmetallic mineral products	41.6	42.0	42.2	42.4	42.2	43.0	42.3	42.1	40.8	41.7	42.3	42.2
Primary metals	42.4	42.4	42.3	43.1	43.1	43.6	42.9	42.2	40.7	43.7	44.6	43.8
Fabricated metal products	40.7	40.6	40.7	41.1	41.0	41.4	41.6	41.3	39.4	41.4	42.0	42.1
Machinery	40.9	40.5	40.8	41.9	42.1	42.4	42.6	42.3	40.1	42.1	43.1	42.8
Computer and electronic products	39.8	39.7	40.4	40.4	40.0	40.5	40.6	41.0	40.4	40.9	40.5	40.4
Electrical equipment and appliances	39.8	40.1	40.6	40.7	40.6	41.0	41.2	40.9	39.3	41.1	40.8	41.6
Transportation equipment [1]	41.9	42.5	41.9	42.5	42.4	42.7	42.8	41.9	41.2	42.9	43.2	43.8
Motor vehicles and parts	41.6	42.6	42.0	42.6	42.3	42.2	42.3	41.4	40.1	43.4	43.4	44.2
Furniture and related products	38.3	39.1	38.9	39.5	39.2	38.8	39.2	38.1	37.7	38.5	39.9	40.0
Miscellaneous manufacturing	38.8	38.7	38.4	38.5	38.7	38.7	38.9	38.9	38.5	38.7	38.9	39.3
Nondurable goods [1]	39.9	40.0	39.8	40.0	39.9	40.6	40.8	40.4	39.8	40.8	40.8	41.1
Overtime hours	4.1	4.2	4.1	4.4	4.4	4.4	4.2	3.7	3.3	3.8	4.0	4.1
Food manufacturing	39.6	39.6	39.3	39.3	39.0	40.1	40.7	40.5	40.0	40.7	40.2	40.6
Textile mills	40.0	40.6	39.1	40.1	40.3	40.6	40.3	38.7	37.7	41.2	41.7	42.6
Textile product mills	38.4	39.0	39.4	38.7	38.9	39.8	39.7	38.6	37.9	39.0	39.1	39.7
Apparel	36.0	36.7	35.6	36.1	35.8	36.5	37.2	36.4	36.0	36.6	38.2	37.1
Paper and paper products	42.1	41.8	41.5	42.1	42.5	42.9	43.1	42.9	41.8	42.9	42.9	42.9
Printing and related support activities	38.7	38.4	38.2	38.4	38.4	39.2	39.1	38.3	38.0	38.2	38.0	38.5
Petroleum and coal products	43.8	43.0	44.5	44.9	45.5	45.0	44.1	44.6	43.4	43.0	43.8	47.1
Chemicals	41.9	42.3	42.4	42.8	42.3	42.5	41.9	41.5	41.4	42.2	42.5	42.4
Plastics and rubber products	40.0	40.6	40.4	40.4	40.0	40.6	41.3	41.0	40.2	41.9	42.0	41.8
Private Service-Providing	32.5	32.5	32.4	32.3	32.4	32.5	32.4	32.3	32.1	32.2	32.4	32.5
Trade, transportation, and utilities	33.5	33.6	33.6	33.5	33.4	33.4	33.3	33.2	32.9	33.3	33.7	33.8
Wholesale trade	38.4	38.0	37.9	37.8	37.7	38.0	38.2	38.2	37.6	37.9	38.5	38.7
Retail trade	30.7	30.9	30.9	30.7	30.6	30.5	30.2	30.0	29.9	30.2	30.5	30.5
Transportation and warehousing	36.7	36.8	36.8	37.2	37.0	36.9	37.0	36.4	36.0	37.1	37.8	38.0
Utilities	41.4	40.9	41.1	40.9	41.1	41.4	42.4	42.7	42.0	42.0	42.1	41.1
Information	36.9	36.5	36.2	36.3	36.5	36.6	36.5	36.7	36.6	36.3	36.2	36.0
Financial activities	35.8	35.6	35.5	35.6	36.0	35.8	35.9	35.9	36.1	36.2	36.4	36.8
Professional and business services	34.2	34.2	34.1	34.2	34.2	34.6	34.8	34.8	34.7	35.1	35.2	35.3
Education and health services	32.3	32.4	32.3	32.4	32.6	32.5	32.6	32.5	32.2	32.1	32.3	32.4
Leisure and hospitality	25.8	25.8	25.6	25.7	25.7	25.7	25.5	25.2	24.8	24.8	24.8	25.0
Other services	32.3	32.1	31.4	31.0	30.9	30.9	30.9	30.8	30.5	30.7	30.8	30.7

[1] Includes other industries, not shown separately.

Table 15-4. Average Hourly Earnings of Production and Nonsupervisory Workers on Private Nonfarm Payrolls by NAICS Industry

(Dollars.)

Industry	1990	1991	1992	1993	1994	1995	1996	1997	1998	1999	2000
Total Private	10.20	10.52	10.77	11.05	11.34	11.66	12.05	12.51	13.02	13.49	14.02
Goods-Producing	11.46	11.76	11.99	12.28	12.63	12.96	13.38	13.82	14.23	14.71	15.27
Mining and logging	13.40	13.82	14.09	14.12	14.41	14.78	15.09	15.57	16.20	16.33	16.55
Construction	13.42	13.65	13.81	14.04	14.38	14.73	15.11	15.67	16.23	16.80	17.48
Manufacturing	10.78	11.13	11.40	11.70	12.04	12.34	12.75	13.14	13.45	13.85	14.32
Excluding overtime [1]	10.28	10.63	10.86	11.10	11.36	11.68	12.05	12.37	12.70	13.08	13.55
Durable goods	11.40	11.81	12.09	12.41	12.78	13.05	13.45	13.83	14.07	14.46	14.92
Wood products	8.82	9.02	9.24	9.40	9.66	9.92	10.24	10.52	10.85	11.18	11.63
Nonmetallic mineral products	11.11	11.34	11.57	11.83	12.11	12.39	12.80	13.17	13.59	13.97	14.53
Primary metals	12.97	13.37	13.72	14.08	14.47	14.75	15.12	15.39	15.66	16.00	16.64
Fabricated metal products	10.64	10.97	11.17	11.40	11.64	11.91	12.26	12.64	12.97	13.34	13.77
Machinery	11.73	12.12	12.40	12.72	12.94	13.13	13.49	13.94	14.23	14.77	15.21
Computer and electronic products	10.89	11.35	11.64	11.95	12.19	12.29	12.75	13.24	13.85	14.37	14.73
Electrical equipment and appliances	10.00	10.30	10.50	10.65	10.94	11.25	11.80	12.24	12.51	12.90	13.23
Transportation equipment [2]	14.44	15.12	15.59	16.21	16.93	17.21	17.66	17.99	17.91	18.24	18.89
Motor vehicles and parts	15.00	15.67	15.92	16.56	17.38	17.72	18.14	18.43	18.21	18.49	19.11
Furniture and related products	8.53	8.75	9.01	9.25	9.52	9.76	10.09	10.50	10.89	11.28	11.73
Miscellaneous manufacturing	8.87	9.15	9.43	9.64	9.90	10.23	10.59	10.89	11.18	11.55	11.93
Nondurable goods [2]	9.87	10.18	10.45	10.70	10.96	11.30	11.68	12.04	12.45	12.85	13.31
Food manufacturing	9.04	9.32	9.59	9.82	10.00	10.27	10.50	10.77	11.09	11.40	11.77
Textile mills	8.17	8.49	8.82	9.12	9.35	9.63	9.88	10.22	10.58	10.90	11.23
Textile product mills	7.37	7.60	7.85	8.10	8.29	8.60	8.95	9.30	9.61	10.04	10.31
Apparel	6.22	6.43	6.60	6.75	6.96	7.22	7.45	7.76	8.05	8.35	8.61
Paper and paper products	12.06	12.45	12.78	13.13	13.49	13.94	14.38	14.76	15.20	15.58	15.91
Printing and related support activities	11.11	11.32	11.53	11.67	11.89	12.08	12.41	12.78	13.20	13.67	14.09
Petroleum and coal products	17.00	17.90	18.83	19.43	19.96	20.24	20.18	21.10	21.75	22.22	22.80
Chemicals	12.85	13.30	13.70	13.97	14.33	14.86	15.37	15.78	16.23	16.40	17.09
Plastics and rubber products	9.76	10.07	10.35	10.56	10.66	10.86	11.17	11.48	11.79	12.25	12.70
Private Service-Providing	9.72	10.06	10.35	10.62	10.89	11.21	11.60	12.08	12.62	13.10	13.63
Trade, transportation, and utilities	9.83	10.08	10.30	10.55	10.80	11.10	11.46	11.90	12.40	12.82	13.31
Wholesale trade	11.58	11.95	12.21	12.57	12.93	13.34	13.80	14.41	15.07	15.62	16.28
Retail trade	7.71	7.89	8.12	8.36	8.61	8.85	9.21	9.59	10.05	10.45	10.87
Transportation and warehousing	12.50	12.61	12.77	12.71	12.84	13.18	13.45	13.78	14.12	14.56	15.05
Utilities	16.14	16.70	17.17	17.95	18.66	19.19	19.78	20.59	21.48	22.03	22.75
Information	13.40	13.90	14.29	14.86	15.32	15.68	16.30	17.14	17.67	18.40	19.07
Financial activities	9.98	10.43	10.86	11.38	11.84	12.31	12.75	13.28	14.00	14.55	15.04
Professional and business services	11.14	11.50	11.78	11.96	12.15	12.53	13.00	13.57	14.27	14.85	15.52
Education and health services	10.00	10.49	10.87	11.21	11.50	11.80	12.17	12.56	13.00	13.44	13.95
Leisure and hospitality	6.02	6.22	6.36	6.48	6.62	6.79	6.99	7.32	7.67	7.96	8.32
Other services	9.08	9.39	9.66	9.90	10.18	10.51	10.85	11.29	11.79	12.26	12.73

[1] Derived by assuming that overtime hours are paid at the rate of time and one-half.
[2] Includes other industries, not shown separately.

Table 15-4. Average Hourly Earnings of Production and Nonsupervisory Workers on Private Nonfarm Payrolls by NAICS Industry—*Continued*

(Dollars.)

Industry	2001	2002	2003	2004	2005	2006	2007	2008	2009	2010	2011	2012
Total Private	14.55	14.97	15.38	15.70	16.13	16.76	17.44	18.08	18.63	19.07	19.46	19.77
Goods-Producing	15.78	16.33	16.80	17.19	17.60	18.02	18.67	19.33	19.90	20.28	20.67	20.95
Mining and logging	17.00	17.19	17.56	18.07	18.72	19.90	20.97	22.50	23.29	23.82	24.50	25.79
Construction	18.00	18.52	18.95	19.23	19.46	20.02	20.95	21.87	22.66	23.22	23.65	23.98
Manufacturing	14.76	15.29	15.74	16.14	16.56	16.81	17.26	17.75	18.24	18.61	18.93	19.08
Excluding overtime [1]	14.06	14.54	14.96	15.29	15.68	15.96	16.43	16.97	17.59	17.78	18.03	18.16
Durable goods	15.38	16.02	16.45	16.82	17.33	17.68	18.20	18.71	19.36	19.80	20.11	20.19
Wood products	11.99	12.33	12.71	13.03	13.16	13.39	13.68	14.19	14.92	14.85	14.81	14.98
Nonmetallic mineral products	14.86	15.39	15.76	16.25	16.61	16.59	16.93	16.90	17.28	17.48	18.16	18.15
Primary metals	17.06	17.68	18.13	18.57	18.94	19.36	19.66	20.19	20.10	20.13	19.94	20.72
Fabricated metal products	14.19	14.68	15.01	15.31	15.80	16.17	16.53	16.99	17.48	17.94	18.13	18.26
Machinery	15.48	15.92	16.29	16.67	17.02	17.20	17.72	17.97	18.39	18.96	19.54	20.17
Computer and electronic products	15.42	16.20	16.68	17.27	18.39	18.94	19.94	21.04	21.87	22.78	23.32	23.34
Electrical equipment and appliances	13.78	13.98	14.36	14.90	15.24	15.53	15.93	15.78	16.27	16.87	17.96	18.03
Transportation equipment [2]	19.47	20.63	21.22	21.48	22.09	22.41	23.04	23.86	24.98	25.23	25.34	24.59
Motor vehicles and parts	19.66	21.09	21.68	21.71	22.26	22.14	22.00	22.21	21.86	22.02	21.93	21.29
Furniture and related products	12.14	12.62	12.99	13.16	13.45	13.80	14.32	14.54	15.04	15.06	15.24	15.46
Miscellaneous manufacturing	12.45	12.91	13.30	13.84	14.07	14.36	14.66	15.20	16.13	16.56	16.82	17.06
Nondurable goods [2]	13.75	14.15	14.63	15.05	15.26	15.33	15.67	16.15	16.56	16.80	17.06	17.30
Food manufacturing	12.18	12.55	12.80	12.98	13.04	13.13	13.55	14.00	14.39	14.41	14.63	15.02
Textile mills	11.40	11.73	11.99	12.13	12.38	12.55	13.00	13.58	13.71	13.56	13.79	13.51
Textile product mills	10.49	10.85	11.15	11.31	11.61	11.86	11.78	11.73	11.73	11.44	12.21	12.77
Apparel	8.83	9.11	9.58	9.77	10.26	10.65	11.05	11.40	11.37	11.43	11.96	12.89
Paper and paper products	16.38	16.85	17.33	17.91	17.99	18.01	18.44	18.89	19.29	20.04	20.28	20.43
Printing and related support activities	14.48	14.93	15.37	15.71	15.74	15.80	16.15	16.75	16.75	16.91	17.28	17.28
Petroleum and coal products	22.90	23.04	23.63	24.39	24.47	24.11	25.21	27.41	29.61	31.31	31.75	32.13
Chemicals	17.57	17.97	18.50	19.17	19.67	19.60	19.55	19.50	20.30	21.07	21.45	21.45
Plastics and rubber products	13.21	13.55	14.18	14.59	14.80	14.97	15.39	15.85	16.01	15.71	15.95	16.05
Private Service-Providing	14.19	14.59	15.00	15.30	15.74	16.42	17.11	17.77	18.36	18.81	19.21	19.52
Trade, transportation, and utilities	13.70	14.02	14.34	14.58	14.92	15.39	15.78	16.16	16.48	16.82	17.15	17.42
Wholesale trade	16.77	16.98	17.36	17.65	18.16	18.91	19.59	20.13	20.84	21.54	21.97	22.24
Retail trade	11.29	11.67	11.90	12.08	12.36	12.57	12.75	12.87	13.01	13.25	13.51	13.81
Transportation and warehousing	15.33	15.76	16.25	16.52	16.70	17.27	17.72	18.41	18.81	19.16	19.49	19.54
Utilities	23.58	23.96	24.77	25.61	26.68	27.40	27.88	28.83	29.48	30.04	30.82	31.61
Information	19.80	20.20	21.01	21.40	22.06	23.23	23.96	24.78	25.45	25.87	26.62	27.01
Financial activities	15.65	16.25	17.21	17.58	17.98	18.83	19.67	20.32	20.90	21.55	21.93	22.83
Professional and business services	16.33	16.80	17.21	17.48	18.08	19.13	20.15	21.18	22.35	22.78	23.12	23.28
Education and health services	14.64	15.21	15.64	16.15	16.71	17.38	18.11	18.87	19.49	20.12	20.77	21.09
Leisure and hospitality	8.57	8.81	9.00	9.15	9.38	9.75	10.41	10.84	11.12	11.31	11.45	11.62
Other services	13.27	13.72	13.84	13.98	14.34	14.77	15.42	16.09	16.59	17.06	17.32	17.59

[1]Derived by assuming that overtime hours are paid at the rate of time and one-half.
[2]Includes other industries, not shown separately.

Table 15-5. Average Weekly Earnings of Production and Nonsupervisory Workers on Private Nonfarm Payrolls by NAICS Industry

(Dollars.)

Industry	1990	1991	1992	1993	1994	1995	1996	1997	1998	1999
Total Private	349.72	358.51	368.25	378.94	391.28	400.22	413.47	432.05	448.76	463.35
Goods-Producing	459.52	471.32	482.58	498.79	519.58	528.51	546.44	568.43	580.99	599.99
Mining and logging	602.43	625.46	628.94	634.77	653.13	670.40	695.04	720.07	727.19	721.77
Construction	513.43	520.41	525.13	539.81	558.53	571.57	588.48	609.48	629.75	655.11
Manufacturing	436.13	449.83	464.43	480.80	501.95	509.26	526.55	548.26	557.12	573.29
Durable goods	468.43	483.24	499.56	519.89	544.63	549.49	566.53	589.06	591.80	606.55
Wood products	356.32	362.46	377.73	387.28	402.83	406.53	422.30	435.66	449.77	461.46
Nonmetallic mineral products	453.91	459.17	474.45	490.67	510.95	517.75	538.10	551.65	573.04	587.42
Primary metals	545.36	555.34	581.45	606.49	637.73	639.70	658.81	681.52	681.68	700.93
Fabricated metal products	436.00	448.01	459.67	474.21	492.07	498.48	513.47	534.38	543.20	555.86
Machinery	493.25	507.79	525.32	549.76	567.93	571.19	584.62	613.19	613.77	625.07
Computer and electronic products	450.06	464.31	482.05	498.95	514.98	518.19	534.39	562.68	579.85	596.37
Electrical equipment and appliances	412.42	426.81	439.04	451.44	470.24	471.72	496.69	515.77	522.54	538.98
Transportation equipment [1]	606.68	633.96	652.75	697.14	750.29	751.45	773.73	795.74	774.77	795.57
Motor vehicles and parts	621.68	650.36	662.82	717.68	779.29	776.41	794.09	808.28	775.56	809.31
Furniture and related products	324.37	330.64	348.07	360.81	373.90	375.18	385.82	410.48	428.67	443.68
Miscellaneous manufacturing	345.82	358.54	370.67	378.21	389.64	400.88	413.94	431.72	437.95	454.14
Nondurable goods [1]	390.65	404.25	417.95	429.15	443.85	452.77	467.91	487.04	504.02	520.02
Food manufacturing	355.80	364.90	375.69	386.07	398.53	406.75	414.74	428.58	444.72	458.73
Textile mills	328.11	345.48	364.45	379.74	391.64	394.17	403.08	425.53	434.15	447.38
Textile product mills	283.76	293.60	303.68	317.69	326.47	332.12	347.05	364.12	376.37	392.46
Apparel	215.89	227.82	235.13	239.88	248.51	254.91	261.99	276.01	286.17	295.62
Paper and paper products	525.58	542.08	559.98	575.60	595.85	604.66	625.38	647.64	662.27	679.05
Printing and related support activities	429.93	437.00	450.02	457.91	470.74	472.37	484.99	504.46	518.32	534.15
Petroleum and coal products	754.13	786.05	821.72	855.36	883.81	883.68	881.24	908.50	949.28	947.60
Chemicals	550.25	573.27	593.24	603.75	622.53	644.46	666.28	685.43	700.53	701.06
Plastics and rubber products	396.26	408.25	426.65	436.85	445.99	446.01	458.29	475.04	487.04	505.45
Private Service-Providing	316.03	325.87	336.11	345.68	355.79	364.93	377.51	395.73	414.14	428.41
Trade, transportation, and utilities	331.55	339.10	348.60	359.51	370.38	378.79	390.67	407.63	423.33	434.31
Wholesale trade	444.48	459.17	470.41	484.46	501.14	515.14	533.36	559.39	582.21	602.77
Retail trade	235.56	240.13	249.66	256.89	265.74	272.63	282.74	295.94	310.33	321.71
Transportation and warehousing	471.82	471.02	477.81	494.54	507.13	513.40	525.72	542.51	546.89	548.00
Utilities	670.80	693.61	716.65	756.50	790.13	811.72	831.24	865.02	902.44	924.40
Information	479.50	495.14	511.95	535.19	551.21	564.92	592.45	622.37	646.52	675.47
Financial activities	354.63	369.75	386.34	403.68	420.18	437.26	453.16	475.03	504.06	520.98
Professional and business services	380.61	391.06	400.64	406.20	414.16	426.54	442.81	465.51	490.13	510.99
Education and health services	319.27	334.55	348.29	359.08	368.14	377.73	388.30	404.65	418.82	431.35
Leisure and hospitality	156.32	159.20	163.70	167.54	172.27	175.74	181.02	190.66	200.82	208.05
Other services	297.88	306.75	315.08	322.69	332.44	342.36	352.68	368.63	384.25	398.77

[1] Includes other industries, not shown separately.

Table 15-5. Average Weekly Earnings of Production and Nonsupervisory Workers on Private Nonfarm Payrolls by NAICS Industry—*Continued*

(Dollars.)

Industry	2000	2001	2002	2003	2004	2005	2006	2007	2008	2009	2010	2011	2012
Total Private	481.36	494.05	507.03	518.41	529.23	544.44	567.89	590.24	608.11	617.50	637.18	654.73	666.99
Goods-Producing	621.86	629.91	651.61	669.13	688.32	705.31	730.16	757.50	776.63	779.68	818.96	844.89	862.09
Mining and logging	734.88	757.96	741.97	765.94	804.01	853.87	907.95	962.63	1 014.69	1 006.67	1 063.11	1 144.64	1 201.92
Construction	685.78	695.86	711.82	727.00	735.55	750.37	781.59	816.23	842.61	851.76	891.83	921.84	942.75
Manufacturing	591.01	595.19	618.62	636.03	658.52	673.30	690.88	711.53	724.46	726.12	765.18	784.29	794.81
Durable goods	624.35	624.54	652.84	671.35	694.06	712.81	732.00	754.58	767.99	771.39	819.02	841.89	848.70
Wood products	476.97	481.33	492.07	514.06	530.15	526.65	533.12	539.41	547.53	557.65	580.74	587.77	615.58
Nonmetallic mineral products	604.76	618.91	647.00	664.96	688.33	700.63	712.67	716.78	711.11	705.54	728.22	768.35	765.98
Primary metals	734.79	723.82	749.32	767.45	799.77	815.90	843.63	843.26	851.29	817.67	880.50	889.27	908.06
Fabricated metal products	576.71	576.71	596.42	610.40	628.80	647.21	668.94	687.16	701.57	689.06	742.76	762.17	767.99
Machinery	643.81	632.81	645.38	664.51	699.31	716.13	728.84	754.34	759.94	737.97	797.62	842.96	863.99
Computer and electronic products	609.97	613.18	642.77	674.69	697.97	735.59	766.75	809.10	861.58	883.02	932.26	943.88	943.99
Electrical equipment and appliances	550.48	548.03	560.33	583.27	607.00	618.88	637.04	656.46	645.60	639.34	693.49	732.16	749.84
Transportation equipment [1]	817.48	816.58	877.46	889.42	912.63	937.75	957.69	986.79	1 000.71	1 028.37	1 081.53	1 094.46	1 076.09
Motor vehicles and parts	828.73	818.68	898.54	910.02	924.72	940.64	934.41	930.51	920.57	876.45	956.36	952.12	941.50
Furniture and related products	459.95	464.87	493.95	505.26	519.61	527.49	535.90	561.08	553.90	566.75	579.66	608.00	617.70
Miscellaneous manufacturing	464.80	483.07	499.01	510.54	533.27	545.01	555.87	570.12	591.95	620.74	640.85	654.90	669.49
Nondurable goods [1]	536.85	548.30	566.72	582.61	602.56	609.04	622.00	639.99	652.22	658.54	685.07	696.03	710.30
Food manufacturing	472.09	481.81	497.25	502.92	509.55	508.55	526.02	551.21	566.88	575.40	586.52	588.19	609.72
Textile mills	464.51	456.64	476.52	469.33	486.68	498.47	509.39	524.40	525.00	516.86	559.13	574.61	575.77
Textile product mills	398.93	402.53	423.05	438.67	437.89	451.36	472.10	467.80	453.06	433.09	459.46	477.49	507.10
Apparel	307.51	317.63	334.24	340.73	352.04	366.93	389.05	411.57	415.10	408.86	418.28	456.97	478.30
Paper and paper products	681.38	689.76	705.20	719.55	754.17	764.15	772.57	795.58	809.57	806.19	858.65	870.53	877.50
Printing and related support activities	552.15	560.89	573.05	587.58	603.97	604.73	618.92	632.02	642.50	635.68	646.11	655.81	665.47
Petroleum and coal products	973.53	1 003.34	990.88	1 052.32	1 095.00	1 114.51	1 085.50	1 112.73	1 222.07	1 284.44	1 345.72	1 390.80	1 512.11
Chemicals	721.41	735.57	759.56	784.26	819.93	831.79	833.84	819.51	809.29	841.18	888.25	910.88	910.03
Plastics and rubber products	517.56	528.62	550.14	572.53	589.99	591.59	608.37	635.63	649.02	643.91	658.55	669.54	671.28
Private Service-Providing	446.01	461.32	474.31	485.26	494.71	509.69	532.92	555.00	574.63	588.54	606.19	622.28	634.60
Trade, transportation, and utilities	449.96	459.53	471.27	481.14	488.51	498.46	514.37	525.91	536.11	541.88	559.63	577.71	588.70
Wholesale trade	631.24	643.45	644.38	657.29	666.79	685.00	718.50	748.94	769.62	784.49	816.50	845.44	860.74
Retail trade	333.41	346.16	360.84	367.18	371.13	377.58	383.12	385.00	386.21	388.57	400.07	412.09	421.85
Transportation and warehousing	562.56	562.57	579.91	598.41	614.89	618.55	636.80	654.95	670.22	677.56	710.85	737.00	742.23
Utilities	955.09	977.25	979.26	1 017.44	1 048.01	1 095.91	1 135.57	1 182.65	1 230.65	1 239.34	1 262.89	1 296.92	1 298.19
Information	700.92	731.18	737.94	760.84	776.72	805.11	850.64	874.45	908.78	931.08	939.85	964.85	971.22
Financial activities	540.39	560.46	578.94	611.65	625.50	646.48	673.48	706.33	729.61	755.08	780.19	798.71	840.57
Professional and business services	535.07	557.84	574.60	587.02	597.54	618.71	662.27	700.82	737.90	775.81	798.54	813.37	822.19
Education and health services	449.29	473.39	492.74	505.69	523.78	544.59	564.94	590.09	613.73	628.45	646.65	670.24	682.74
Leisure and hospitality	217.20	220.73	227.31	230.49	234.86	241.36	250.34	265.54	273.39	275.95	280.87	283.82	290.43
Other services	413.30	428.64	439.87	434.41	433.04	443.40	456.50	477.06	495.57	506.26	523.70	532.63	539.31

[1] Includes other industries, not shown separately.

Table 15-6. Indexes of Aggregate Weekly Hours of Production and Nonsupervisory Workers on Private Nonfarm Payrolls by NAICS Industry

(2002 = 100.)

Industry	1990	1991	1992	1993	1994	1995	1996	1997	1998	1999
Total Private	84.3	82.5	83.0	85.4	89.2	91.5	93.7	97.1	99.4	101.5
Goods-Producing	106.1	100.1	98.7	100.8	105.6	106.8	108.1	111.2	112.3	112.6
Mining and logging	128.6	123.8	113.3	110.3	111.0	110.3	112.7	117.6	112.8	102.9
Construction	78.8	70.1	67.5	71.3	77.3	79.9	84.3	88.6	93.4	99.7
Manufacturing	117.7	112.8	112.4	113.9	118.3	119.0	118.8	121.4	121.0	119.0
Durable goods	114.2	107.6	106.4	108.3	114.2	116.4	117.5	121.6	122.0	120.6
Wood products	101.5	92.6	95.2	100.5	109.1	109.3	111.6	114.8	117.5	118.5
Nonmetallic mineral products	100.7	92.8	92.6	94.2	98.8	99.7	101.5	103.1	105.8	106.9
Primary metals	131.5	122.9	120.8	121.5	128.0	129.3	129.9	132.3	131.1	128.4
Fabricated metal products	104.6	99.1	97.3	99.7	106.3	109.9	111.6	116.6	118.6	116.7
Machinery	123.8	116.2	113.9	118.6	126.9	132.2	133.7	138.9	137.4	129.8
Computer and electronic products	137.2	128.2	122.9	121.1	123.6	127.1	130.0	136.8	136.7	131.1
Electrical equipment and appliances	136.0	127.9	125.9	126.8	132.4	130.3	129.4	127.7	127.8	128.3
Transportation equipment [1]	111.1	105.8	104.4	105.5	112.6	115.4	116.5	120.8	118.8	119.5
Motor vehicles and parts	90.9	87.9	91.1	97.9	110.6	115.9	116.1	117.5	112.8	118.7
Furniture and related products	97.1	89.4	92.0	95.3	100.5	99.2	98.3	102.9	108.4	112.6
Miscellaneous manufacturing	104.1	103.9	105.3	107.0	108.3	107.8	107.7	110.1	110.4	110.3
Nondurable goods [1]	123.0	120.8	121.7	122.7	124.7	123.1	120.5	120.9	119.4	116.1
Food manufacturing	96.2	96.5	97.2	98.6	100.4	101.6	101.8	102.6	103.3	103.7
Textile mills	170.4	168.4	170.3	170.8	171.6	163.5	154.1	155.2	148.9	139.1
Textile product mills	118.8	113.1	114.8	118.7	124.0	121.0	118.1	119.4	117.7	115.6
Apparel	266.5	263.6	266.6	259.0	252.1	234.8	211.6	201.3	180.9	154.6
Paper and paper products	121.9	120.6	121.7	122.0	123.5	121.5	120.2	121.6	119.6	117.2
Printing and related support activities	122.3	118.7	118.4	120.3	123.8	123.9	122.8	124.6	124.3	120.9
Petroleum and coal products	128.9	127.5	126.0	122.0	120.0	115.5	113.5	112.7	113.4	107.6
Chemicals	118.2	115.0	112.9	113.5	115.1	115.4	114.8	114.7	115.4	113.2
Plastics and rubber products	97.7	94.1	98.0	102.3	108.7	109.8	110.0	112.7	113.7	114.6
Private Service-Providing	78.2	77.6	78.7	81.1	84.5	87.2	89.6	93.1	95.8	98.3
Trade, transportation, and utilities	89.5	87.4	87.3	89.1	92.7	95.1	96.6	98.9	100.3	101.9
Wholesale trade	94.9	93.3	92.4	92.4	95.8	99.2	100.7	103.4	104.8	106.2
Retail trade	87.5	84.8	85.1	86.3	89.8	92.3	93.7	95.9	97.2	99.5
Transportation and warehousing	83.5	82.3	82.6	88.4	93.7	95.6	98.3	101.0	102.6	103.2
Utilities	124.3	123.5	121.6	119.9	117.1	112.9	108.6	106.1	105.7	105.0
Information	76.2	76.1	76.5	78.0	79.2	82.5	86.9	90.4	92.6	98.5
Financial activities	83.1	82.0	82.4	84.9	87.2	86.9	89.1	92.3	96.5	98.1
Professional and business services	68.1	66.7	68.4	71.9	77.0	81.2	85.2	91.5	96.7	101.7
Education and health services	67.2	70.2	72.9	75.4	78.3	81.2	83.4	86.7	88.9	90.6
Leisure and hospitality	78.9	77.3	79.2	82.1	85.5	88.5	90.7	93.4	95.5	97.8
Other services	81.8	81.1	80.6	82.8	84.5	87.0	89.1	91.9	94.3	96.2

[1] Includes other industries, not shown separately.

Table 15-6. Indexes of Aggregate Weekly Hours of Production and Nonsupervisory Workers on Private Nonfarm Payrolls by NAICS Industry—*Continued*

(2002 = 100.)

Industry	2000	2001	2002	2003	2004	2005	2006	2007	2008	2009	2010	2011	2012
Total Private	103.6	102.1	100.0	98.7	100.2	102.7	105.7	107.3	105.9	98.7	98.7	101.3	104.1
Goods-Producing	113.1	106.5	100.0	95.7	96.8	98.9	102.5	101.7	96.5	80.2	78.8	81.2	83.5
Mining and logging	105.1	108.3	100.0	97.4	104.0	114.7	125.8	133.5	137.6	117.2	124.5	147.4	159.3
Construction	104.0	103.2	100.0	98.4	101.7	108.3	115.4	114.7	106.5	85.9	80.2	81.7	83.5
Manufacturing	117.8	108.1	100.0	94.5	94.3	93.9	95.6	94.4	90.2	76.1	76.2	78.3	80.3
Durable goods	120.4	109.3	100.0	94.3	95.2	96.1	98.9	97.4	92.2	74.7	75.0	78.4	81.3
Wood products	115.8	105.0	100.0	97.8	100.8	101.2	99.9	89.3	76.7	57.8	58.5	59.3	61.9
Nonmetallic mineral products	109.1	106.1	100.0	94.3	98.0	97.4	100.3	96.9	91.2	73.8	70.5	70.1	68.6
Primary metals	128.9	113.0	100.0	93.4	93.3	93.1	94.1	91.4	87.4	66.0	71.7	80.0	82.7
Fabricated metal products	119.1	109.3	100.0	95.3	97.7	99.2	103.1	104.5	101.3	81.2	83.1	89.6	94.9
Machinery	127.5	114.1	100.0	93.6	95.9	98.8	102.2	103.3	102.3	80.6	81.2	89.6	93.9
Computer and electronic products	133.1	117.9	100.0	92.1	89.8	94.8	103.6	102.2	101.2	89.4	87.2	86.4	86.4
Electrical equipment and appliances	127.7	113.4	100.0	92.0	88.7	86.4	88.0	89.1	88.5	74.1	73.2	71.6	72.9
Transportation equipment [1]	116.3	105.3	100.0	95.5	96.5	97.3	100.0	98.0	88.6	70.1	72.1	75.3	80.2
Motor vehicles and parts	117.3	103.6	100.0	95.9	97.0	95.2	92.9	85.8	72.7	51.6	57.5	60.9	66.3
Furniture and related products	114.7	104.8	100.0	93.0	94.3	91.9	90.4	86.1	74.6	57.6	54.4	55.8	55.4
Miscellaneous manufacturing	109.5	104.7	100.0	93.6	91.8	90.6	90.4	91.0	89.2	81.1	79.0	80.0	82.1
Nondurable goods [1]	113.3	106.0	100.0	94.7	92.7	90.3	90.4	89.6	86.9	78.1	78.0	77.9	78.6
Food manufacturing	103.4	101.4	100.0	98.4	97.1	95.8	98.6	101.1	100.6	97.5	98.5	97.7	99.6
Textile mills	132.4	112.2	100.0	86.3	79.0	71.3	65.1	56.3	47.9	37.8	40.2	41.6	41.5
Textile product mills	112.3	105.5	100.0	92.4	90.2	88.0	85.0	77.5	70.5	58.5	56.5	55.2	53.4
Apparel	137.5	117.1	100.0	81.9	75.1	65.7	63.4	61.5	56.7	45.4	42.0	40.7	38.4
Paper and paper products	113.5	106.6	100.0	92.5	89.2	88.0	86.9	85.8	83.5	74.2	73.5	71.9	69.9
Printing and related support activities	119.4	111.5	100.0	95.3	93.4	90.9	92.5	91.6	86.1	74.1	69.0	65.6	64.4
Petroleum and coal products	105.8	105.6	100.0	98.7	102.6	102.4	96.9	95.6	102.4	90.2	89.1	91.2	102.6
Chemicals	110.4	104.7	100.0	99.0	99.0	95.9	96.1	94.1	94.6	88.3	88.9	90.6	92.7
Plastics and rubber products	114.2	104.9	100.0	95.2	94.2	92.3	91.9	91.1	87.1	71.3	73.6	75.3	75.8
Private Service-Providing	100.9	100.8	100.0	99.5	101.0	103.7	106.5	108.7	108.5	103.8	104.2	106.8	109.8
Trade, transportation, and utilities	103.5	101.5	100.0	98.6	99.6	101.6	103.3	104.8	103.3	96.8	96.8	99.7	102.0
Wholesale trade	107.0	102.9	100.0	98.0	98.8	101.8	105.7	109.2	108.6	99.9	97.7	100.7	104.1
Retail trade	101.3	100.5	100.0	98.9	99.4	100.8	101.1	101.8	99.8	94.3	95.0	97.7	99.2
Transportation and warehousing	105.6	102.7	100.0	98.8	101.9	105.2	107.9	109.4	107.7	100.0	101.3	105.4	109.2
Utilities	104.1	102.3	100.0	97.4	94.2	93.1	93.8	96.2	98.3	97.0	95.4	94.9	92.9
Information	105.0	106.7	100.0	97.0	98.2	99.4	100.2	100.1	100.0	93.5	90.0	88.9	88.8
Financial activities	98.4	99.3	100.0	101.3	101.4	103.7	106.3	107.6	106.8	103.2	101.3	101.2	103.8
Professional and business services	106.6	104.0	100.0	98.7	101.8	106.3	112.1	115.3	113.9	105.2	107.6	112.4	117.2
Education and health services	92.8	96.6	100.0	101.4	103.3	106.4	109.0	112.5	115.7	117.2	118.7	121.3	124.4
Leisure and hospitality	100.5	100.6	100.0	100.0	103.0	106.2	108.8	110.8	109.7	105.1	104.6	106.9	111.1
Other services	97.8	99.0	100.0	97.4	96.1	96.2	97.4	99.3	99.5	96.0	96.0	96.8	97.8

[1]Includes other industries, not shown separately.

NOTES AND DEFINITIONS, CHAPTER 15

Tables 15-1 through 15-6: Employment, Hours, and Earnings by NAICS Industry

SOURCE: U.S. DEPARTMENT OF LABOR, BUREAU OF LABOR STATISTICS

See the notes and definitions for Tables 10-8 through 10-18 regarding definitions of *employment*, *production and* *nonsupervisory workers*, *average weekly hours*, *overtime hours*, *average hourly earnings*, *average weekly earnings*, and the *indexes of aggregate weekly hours*. Availability and reference information is also provided in those notes and definitions.

CHAPTER 16: KEY SECTOR STATISTICS

Figure 16-1. Housing Starts, 1960–2012

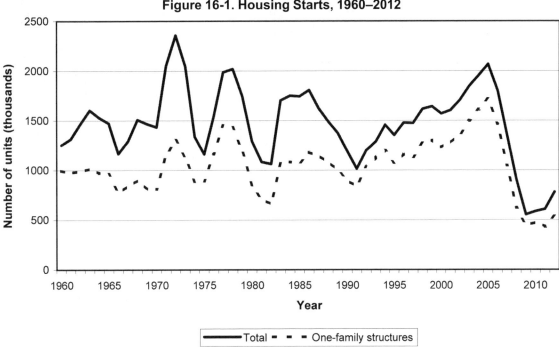

- The housing sector was the source of the boom and bust cycle of 2001–2009. In 2005, as shown in Figure 16-1, 2.1 million housing units were started, the highest since 1972. Of those, 1.7 million were one-family homes, an all-time record. By 2009, both total and single-family starts had plunged to the lowest levels of their 50-year history. With very modest recovery since then, starts remain at recessionary levels. (Table 16-3)

- New orders for nondefense capital goods excluding aircraft and parts at U.S. manufacturing firms is a widely followed advance indicator for production of investment goods. The value of such orders fell 24 percent from 2007 to 2009, similar to their decline between 2000 and 2002. Their recovery since 2009 has been faster than it was in the 3 years following 2002, and the value of new orders in 2012 was not far short of the peak in 2007. (Table 16-6)

- Sales of cars and light trucks were 10.4 million in 2009, down 6.5 million from their recent high in 2005; they recovered by 4 million from 2009 to 2012. (Table 16-8)

- Service industries were affected later and less. They experienced revenue declines in late 2008 and early 2009 but then resumed growth. In the fourth quarter of 2012, information industry revenues were up 17 percent from the first quarter of 2007; professional, scientific, and technical services were up 23 percent; and administrative and support and waste management, which includes temporary help firms, were up 17 percent. Hospital revenues were up 34 percent. (Table 16-15)

- As a percentage of the total supply of petroleum and products (domestic crude oil and natural gas liquids production plus net imports), net imports increased from 10 percent in 1955 to 65 percent in 2005, but were reduced to 45 percent by 2012. (Table 16-1)

- Sales by electronic shopping and mail order grew from 1.9 percent of total retail sales in 1992 to 7.4 percent in 2012. (Table 16-9) E-commerce alone grew from 0.6 percent of total retail sales at the end of 1999 to 5.4 percent at the end of 2012. (Table 16-10)

Table 16-1. Petroleum and Petroleum Products—Prices, Imports, Domestic Production, and Stocks

(Not seasonally adjusted.)

Year and month	Crude oil futures price (dollars per barrel)		Imports				Supply (thousands of barrels per day)					Stocks (end of period, millions of barrels)		
			Total energy-related petroleum products (thousands of barrels)	Crude petroleum			Petroleum and products			Domestic production		Crude oil and petroleum products	Crude petroleum	
	Current dollars	2009 dollars		Thousands of barrels		Unit price (dollars per barrel)	Exports	Imports	Net imports	Crude oil	Natural gas plant liquids		Non-SPR	Strategic petroleum reserve
				Total	Average per day									
1955	. . .	. . .	. . .	. . .	. . .	. . .	368	1 248	880	6 807	771	715	266	. . .
1956	. . .	. . .	. . .	. . .	. . .	. . .	430	1 436	1 006	7 151	800	780	266	. . .
1957	. . .	. . .	. . .	. . .	. . .	. . .	568	1 574	1 006	7 170	808	841	282	. . .
1958	. . .	. . .	. . .	. . .	. . .	. . .	276	1 700	1 424	6 710	808	789	263	. . .
1959	. . .	. . .	. . .	. . .	. . .	. . .	211	1 780	1 569	7 054	879	809	257	. . .
1960	. . .	. . .	. . .	. . .	. . .	. . .	202	1 815	1 613	7 035	929	785	240	. . .
1961	. . .	. . .	. . .	. . .	. . .	. . .	174	1 917	1 743	7 183	991	825	245	. . .
1962	. . .	. . .	. . .	. . .	. . .	. . .	168	2 082	1 914	7 332	1 021	834	252	. . .
1963	. . .	. . .	. . .	. . .	. . .	. . .	208	2 123	1 915	7 542	1 098	836	237	. . .
1964	. . .	. . .	. . .	. . .	. . .	. . .	202	2 259	2 057	7 614	1 154	839	230	. . .
1965	. . .	. . .	. . .	. . .	. . .	. . .	187	2 468	2 281	7 804	1 210	836	220	. . .
1966	. . .	. . .	. . .	. . .	. . .	. . .	198	2 573	2 375	8 295	1 284	874	238	. . .
1967	. . .	. . .	. . .	. . .	. . .	. . .	307	2 537	2 230	8 810	1 409	944	249	. . .
1968	. . .	. . .	. . .	. . .	. . .	. . .	231	2 840	2 609	9 096	1 504	1 000	272	. . .
1969	. . .	. . .	. . .	. . .	. . .	. . .	233	3 166	2 933	9 238	1 590	980	265	. . .
1970	. . .	. . .	. . .	. . .	. . .	. . .	259	3 419	3 160	9 637	1 660	1 018	276	. . .
1971	. . .	. . .	. . .	. . .	. . .	. . .	224	3 926	3 702	9 463	1 693	1 044	260	. . .
1972	. . .	. . .	. . .	. . .	. . .	. . .	222	4 741	4 519	9 441	1 744	959	246	. . .
1973	. . .	. . .	. . .	1 392 970	3 816	3.30	231	6 256	6 025	9 208	1 738	1 008	242	. . .
1974	. . .	. . .	. . .	1 367 081	3 745	11.17	221	6 112	5 892	8 774	1 688	1 074	265	. . .
1975	. . .	. . .	. . .	1 584 730	4 342	11.59	209	6 056	5 846	8 375	1 633	1 133	271	. . .
1976	. . .	. . .	. . .	2 050 424	5 618	12.43	223	7 313	7 090	8 132	1 604	1 112	285	. . .
1977	. . .	. . .	. . .	2 519 806	6 904	13.33	243	8 807	8 565	8 245	1 618	1 312	340	7
1978	. . .	. . .	. . .	2 392 350	6 554	13.43	362	8 363	8 002	8 707	1 567	1 278	309	67
1979	. . .	. . .	. . .	2 467 315	6 760	18.68	471	8 456	7 985	8 552	1 584	1 341	339	91
1980	. . .	. . .	. . .	1 977 247	5 417	31.36	544	6 909	6 365	8 597	1 573	1 392	358	108
1981	. . .	. . .	. . .	1 763 072	4 830	35.13	595	5 996	5 401	8 572	1 609	1 484	363	230
1982	. . .	. . .	. . .	1 420 753	3 892	33.39	815	5 113	4 298	8 649	1 550	1 430	350	294
1983	30.66	58.15	. . .	1 293 819	3 545	29.51	739	5 051	4 312	8 688	1 559	1 454	344	379
1984	29.44	53.80	. . .	1 319 683	3 616	27.68	722	5 437	4 715	8 879	1 630	1 556	345	451
1985	27.89	49.22	. . .	1 260 856	3 454	26.20	781	5 067	4 286	8 971	1 609	1 519	321	493
1986	15.05	26.00	. . .	1 634 567	4 478	13.90	785	6 224	5 439	8 680	1 551	1 593	331	512
1987	19.15	32.10	. . .	1 744 977	4 781	16.80	764	6 678	5 914	8 349	1 595	1 607	349	541
1988	15.96	25.75	. . .	1 887 860	5 172	13.69	815	7 402	6 587	8 140	1 625	1 597	330	560
1989	19.58	30.29	. . .	2 146 552	5 881	16.49	859	8 061	7 202	7 613	1 546	1 581	341	580
1990	24.50	36.33	. . .	2 216 604	6 073	19.75	857	8 018	7 161	7 355	1 559	1 621	323	586
1991	21.50	30.87	2 828 953	2 146 064	5 880	17.46	1 001	7 627	6 626	7 417	1 659	1 617	325	569
1992	20.58	28.79	2 947 582	2 294 570	6 269	16.80	950	7 888	6 938	7 171	1 697	1 592	318	575
1993	18.48	25.22	3 257 008	2 543 374	6 968	15.13	1 003	8 620	7 618	6 847	1 736	1 647	335	587
1994	17.19	22.98	3 416 045	2 704 196	7 409	14.23	942	8 996	8 054	6 662	1 727	1 653	337	592
1995	18.40	24.10	3 361 882	2 767 312	7 582	15.81	949	8 835	7 886	6 560	1 762	1 563	303	592
1996	22.03	28.25	3 622 385	2 893 647	7 906	18.98	981	9 478	8 498	6 465	1 830	1 507	284	566
1997	20.61	25.98	3 802 574	3 069 430	8 409	17.67	1 003	10 162	9 158	6 452	1 817	1 560	305	563
1998	14.40	18.01	4 088 027	3 242 711	8 884	11.49	945	10 708	9 764	6 252	1 759	1 647	324	571
1999	19.30	23.80	4 081 181	3 228 092	8 844	15.76	940	10 852	9 912	5 881	1 850	1 493	284	567
2000	30.26	36.40	4 314 825	3 399 239	9 288	26.44	1 040	11 459	10 419	5 822	1 911	1 468	286	541
2001	25.95	30.63	4 475 026	3 471 067	9 510	21.40	971	11 871	10 900	5 801	1 868	1 586	312	550
2002	26.15	30.45	4 337 075	3 418 022	9 364	22.61	984	11 530	10 546	5 744	1 880	1 548	278	599
2003	30.99	35.39	4 654 638	3 676 005	10 071	26.98	1 027	12 264	11 238	5 644	1 719	1 568	269	638
2004	41.47	46.23	4 917 591	3 820 979	10 440	34.48	1 048	13 145	12 097	5 435	1 809	1 645	286	676
2005	56.70	61.46	5 004 339	3 754 671	10 287	46.81	1 165	13 714	12 549	5 186	1 717	1 698	324	685
2006	66.25	69.94	4 880 734	3 734 226	10 231	58.01	1 317	13 707	12 390	5 089	1 739	1 720	312	689
2007	72.41	74.57	4 807 811	3 690 568	10 111	64.28	1 433	13 468	12 036	5 077	1 783	1 665	286	697
2008	99.75	99.69	4 613 444	3 590 628	9 810	95.22	1 802	12 915	11 114	5 000	1 784	1 737	326	702
2009	62.09	62.09	4 266 007	3 314 787	9 082	56.93	2 024	11 691	9 667	5 353	1 910	1 776	325	727
2010	79.61	78.31	4 279 611	3 377 077	9 252	74.67	2 353	11 793	9 441	5 479	2 074	1 794	333	727
2011	95.11	91.38	4 164 180	3 321 918	9 101	99.82	2 986	11 504	8 518	5 652	2 216	1 751	331	696
2012	94.15	88.81	3 842 137	3 092 232	8 449	101.16	3 184	10 596	7 412	6 496	2 399	1 807	365	695
2012														
January	100.32	95.34	343 782	269 702	8 700	103.78	2 839	10 944	8 104	6 132	2 376	1 772	340	696
February	102.26	96.95	282 490	225 032	7 760	103.63	2 980	10 464	7 484	6 246	2 388	1 765	347	696
March	106.21	100.46	331 131	271 817	8 768	108.03	3 064	10 610	7 547	6 297	2 375	1 778	368	696
April	103.35	97.75	325 576	270 361	9 012	109.69	3 263	10 634	7 370	6 290	2 382	1 777	377	696
May	94.72	89.63	330 015	270 684	8 732	108.06	3 194	11 132	7 939	6 346	2 376	1 794	386	696
June	82.41	77.86	331 551	263 436	8 781	100.13	3 209	11 393	8 184	6 259	2 335	1 808	386	696
July	87.93	83.05	337 797	277 462	8 950	93.71	3 211	10 748	7 537	6 387	2 323	1 809	370	696
August	94.16	88.66	340 506	272 836	8 801	94.48	3 017	10 898	7 881	6 317	2 367	1 801	363	696
September	94.56	88.78	306 424	245 712	8 190	98.90	3 150	10 533	7 383	6 577	2 458	1 818	369	695
October	89.57	83.94	322 737	259 383	8 367	99.76	3 255	10 088	6 833	6 942	2 485	1 810	375	695
November	86.73	81.38	306 117	242 956	8 099	97.45	3 404	10 103	6 698	7 052	2 516	1 809	379	695
December	88.25	82.80	284 011	222 852	7 189	95.16	3 623	9 610	5 987	7 095	2 414	1 807	365	695

. . . = Not available.

Table 16-2. New Construction Put in Place

(Billions of dollars, monthly data are at seasonally adjusted annual rates.)

Year and month	Total	Private											
		Total [1]	Residential	Office	Commercial		Health care	Educational	Amusement and recreation	Transportation	Communication	Power	Manufacturing
					Total [1]	Multi-retail							
1975	152.6	109.3	51.6	. . .	. . .	. . .	. . .	. . .	. . .	. . .	. . .	. . .	. . .
1976	172.1	128.2	68.3	. . .	. . .	. . .	. . .	. . .	. . .	. . .	. . .	. . .	. . .
1977	200.5	157.4	92.0	. . .	. . .	. . .	. . .	. . .	. . .	. . .	. . .	. . .	. . .
1978	239.9	189.7	109.8	. . .	. . .	. . .	. . .	. . .	. . .	. . .	. . .	. . .	. . .
1979	272.9	216.2	116.4	. . .	. . .	. . .	. . .	. . .	. . .	. . .	. . .	. . .	. . .
1980	273.9	210.3	100.4	. . .	. . .	. . .	. . .	. . .	. . .	. . .	. . .	. . .	. . .
1981	289.1	224.4	99.2	. . .	. . .	. . .	. . .	. . .	. . .	. . .	. . .	. . .	. . .
1982	279.3	216.3	84.7	. . .	. . .	. . .	. . .	. . .	. . .	. . .	. . .	. . .	. . .
1983	311.9	248.4	125.8	. . .	. . .	. . .	. . .	. . .	. . .	. . .	. . .	. . .	. . .
1984	370.2	300.0	155.0	. . .	. . .	. . .	. . .	. . .	. . .	. . .	. . .	. . .	. . .
1985	403.4	325.6	160.5	. . .	. . .	. . .	. . .	. . .	. . .	. . .	. . .	. . .	. . .
1986	433.5	348.9	190.7	. . .	. . .	. . .	. . .	. . .	. . .	. . .	. . .	. . .	. . .
1987	446.6	356.0	199.7	. . .	. . .	. . .	. . .	. . .	. . .	. . .	. . .	. . .	. . .
1988	462.0	367.3	204.5	. . .	. . .	. . .	. . .	. . .	. . .	. . .	. . .	. . .	. . .
1989	477.5	379.3	204.3	. . .	. . .	. . .	. . .	. . .	. . .	. . .	. . .	. . .	. . .
1990	476.8	369.3	191.1	. . .	. . .	. . .	. . .	. . .	. . .	. . .	. . .	. . .	. . .
1991	432.6	322.5	166.3	. . .	. . .	. . .	. . .	. . .	. . .	. . .	. . .	. . .	. . .
1992	463.7	347.8	199.4	. . .	. . .	. . .	. . .	. . .	. . .	. . .	. . .	. . .	. . .
1993	485.5	358.2	208.2	20.0	34.4	11.5	14.9	4.8	4.6	4.7	9.8	23.6	23.4
1994	531.9	401.5	241.0	20.4	39.6	12.2	15.4	5.0	5.1	4.7	10.1	21.0	28.8
1995	548.7	408.7	228.1	23.0	44.1	12.0	15.3	5.7	5.9	4.8	11.1	22.0	35.4
1996	599.7	453.0	257.5	26.5	49.4	13.3	15.4	7.0	7.0	5.8	11.8	17.4	38.1
1997	631.9	478.4	264.7	32.8	53.1	12.2	17.4	8.8	8.5	6.2	12.5	16.4	37.6
1998	688.5	533.7	296.3	40.4	55.7	13.3	17.7	9.8	8.6	7.3	12.5	21.7	40.5
1999	744.6	575.5	326.3	45.1	59.4	15.2	18.4	9.8	9.6	6.5	18.4	22.0	35.1
2000	802.8	621.4	346.1	52.4	64.1	14.9	19.5	11.7	8.8	6.9	18.8	29.3	37.6
2001	840.2	634.4	396.7	35.3	59.0	15.6	22.4	13.1	7.5	6.8	18.4	32.6	22.7
2002	847.9	634.4	396.7	35.3	59.0	15.6	22.4	13.1	7.5	6.8	18.4	32.6	22.7
2003	891.5	675.4	446.0	30.6	57.5	15.4	24.2	13.4	7.8	6.6	14.5	33.6	21.4
2004	991.4	771.2	532.9	32.9	63.2	18.8	26.3	12.7	8.4	6.8	15.5	27.6	23.2
2005	1 104.1	870.0	611.9	37.3	66.6	22.8	28.5	12.8	7.5	7.1	18.8	29.2	28.4
2006	1 167.2	911.8	613.7	45.7	73.4	29.2	32.0	13.8	9.3	8.7	22.2	33.7	32.3
2007	1 152.4	863.3	493.2	53.8	85.9	34.8	35.6	16.7	10.2	9.0	27.5	54.1	40.2
2008	1 067.6	758.8	350.3	55.5	82.7	32.0	38.4	18.6	10.5	9.9	26.3	69.2	52.8
2009	903.2	588.3	245.9	37.3	50.5	18.4	35.3	16.9	8.4	9.1	19.7	76.1	56.3
2010	804.6	500.6	238.8	24.4	36.5	12.5	29.6	13.4	6.5	9.9	17.7	66.1	39.8
2011	778.2	495.0	237.0	22.5	40.0	13.4	28.6	14.2	7.0	9.8	17.4	63.9	40.6
2012	854.5	578.8	275.5	26.2	43.9	15.5	29.7	17.1	6.6	10.8	16.9	88.1	48.2
2010													
January	816.1	520.3	255.0	27.4	40.0	13.8	30.2	14.2	5.9	9.2	17.4	56.9	43.3
February	795.8	505.5	240.9	28.2	38.6	13.5	29.2	14.3	6.1	9.5	18.3	56.4	43.8
March	806.0	508.2	242.8	25.5	38.1	13.3	29.1	14.5	7.1	9.5	16.5	57.0	48.6
April	824.0	517.6	251.8	24.8	37.5	13.1	29.5	13.9	7.3	9.4	17.7	61.7	45.0
May	816.3	507.0	244.2	24.2	36.2	12.3	29.7	13.7	6.7	9.6	18.0	63.8	42.4
June	816.3	504.2	241.4	23.9	37.0	12.6	29.1	13.6	6.6	10.1	17.2	65.7	42.0
July	788.5	484.2	233.8	22.4	34.5	12.3	29.0	12.9	6.2	10.2	17.7	60.8	39.0
August	791.7	483.3	229.4	23.3	36.1	12.2	29.6	13.2	6.4	10.1	18.4	61.6	37.9
September	798.9	483.9	231.2	24.3	35.4	12.5	30.2	12.9	6.9	9.7	17.4	62.3	36.7
October	800.3	493.7	236.6	23.7	35.2	11.3	29.5	12.4	6.1	10.5	17.6	70.6	35.3
November	798.3	499.5	235.7	22.4	35.1	11.6	29.8	12.9	6.4	10.2	18.1	79.3	33.3
December	779.9	488.4	229.3	23.2	34.6	11.2	29.8	13.0	6.2	10.1	17.5	77.4	31.4
2011													
January	752.6	464.6	237.7	22.0	35.4	11.9	27.1	12.5	6.0	9.4	17.2	53.5	29.5
February	746.1	461.5	231.2	21.5	36.1	12.2	28.1	12.6	5.9	9.3	17.5	54.1	31.9
March	753.4	467.1	226.8	21.6	36.9	12.6	28.3	13.3	5.8	9.2	17.4	58.6	35.1
April	755.4	475.3	236.0	21.6	38.6	13.1	27.6	13.2	7.0	9.0	17.8	57.5	33.3
May	775.8	495.3	243.1	22.9	39.9	13.2	27.4	13.5	7.4	9.2	17.4	62.7	38.3
June	786.8	502.1	236.9	23.4	40.9	13.4	28.8	14.8	7.3	9.6	17.8	64.9	43.8
July	763.5	485.8	222.4	23.0	41.7	13.4	29.1	14.8	7.3	9.6	17.9	64.9	41.5
August	786.3	501.5	232.2	23.2	42.5	14.0	29.0	14.3	7.3	10.0	17.3	67.5	44.2
September	790.3	507.2	236.5	22.6	40.9	13.8	29.5	15.0	7.7	10.3	17.7	66.5	46.5
October	795.7	512.8	243.7	23.0	41.1	14.0	28.6	14.8	7.4	10.3	17.0	67.8	45.4
November	804.0	520.4	248.2	22.6	41.9	14.0	29.5	15.6	7.4	10.6	16.3	69.1	44.9
December	820.6	534.6	249.4	23.0	41.9	15.0	29.9	15.6	7.3	11.2	17.6	73.8	50.0
2012													
January	824.7	547.5	249.6	23.7	43.6	15.2	30.0	16.4	6.5	10.0	17.2	90.9	44.8
February	820.7	544.6	252.6	23.3	42.8	15.3	30.6	16.8	6.4	8.6	16.6	85.8	46.6
March	817.8	544.8	249.5	24.6	43.2	16.0	29.6	17.5	6.4	9.3	16.7	85.8	46.8
April	825.1	552.3	254.1	24.3	43.4	16.3	30.4	17.3	6.6	10.7	16.7	85.5	47.9
May	838.8	562.1	262.6	25.3	44.2	16.6	30.3	17.4	6.6	11.0	16.7	82.8	49.4
June	845.1	566.4	271.3	25.4	43.4	15.4	30.2	17.6	6.2	11.1	17.3	80.0	48.1
July	846.6	572.4	274.7	25.7	43.3	15.2	30.2	17.4	6.6	11.7	17.1	82.7	46.6
August	855.9	578.0	282.4	27.1	44.4	16.2	31.1	17.0	7.0	11.0	16.4	78.4	47.0
September	862.2	587.5	290.5	26.8	44.6	15.6	28.6	17.4	6.9	11.5	17.7	79.6	48.2
October	876.2	601.9	299.8	28.5	45.4	15.0	29.2	17.5	7.1	12.2	16.5	80.5	48.6
November	892.4	618.0	299.5	29.0	44.3	14.7	28.6	16.4	7.0	10.7	17.0	99.9	49.6
December	893.6	624.7	297.1	28.7	43.8	13.9	28.8	17.3	6.3	10.5	16.8	106.6	52.2

[1] Includes categories not shown separately.
. . . = Not available.

Table 16-2. New Construction Put in Place—*Continued*

(Billions of dollars, monthly data are at seasonally adjusted annual rates.)

Year and month	Total	Public — State and local — Total ¹	Residential	Office	Health care	Educational	Public safety	Amusement and recreation	Transportation	Power	Highway and street	Sewage and waste disposal	Water supply	Federal
1975	43.3	37.2	...	...	...	...	...	...	...	...	...	...	...	6.1
1976	44.0	37.2	...	...	...	...	...	...	...	...	...	...	...	6.8
1977	43.1	36.0	...	...	...	...	...	...	...	...	...	...	...	7.1
1978	50.1	42.0	...	...	...	...	...	...	...	...	...	...	...	8.1
1979	56.6	48.1	...	...	...	...	...	...	...	...	...	...	...	8.6
1980	63.6	54.0	...	...	...	...	...	...	...	...	...	...	...	9.6
1981	64.7	54.3	...	...	...	...	...	...	...	...	...	...	...	10.4
1982	63.1	53.1	...	...	...	...	...	...	...	...	...	...	...	10.0
1983	63.5	52.9	...	...	...	...	...	...	...	...	...	...	...	10.6
1984	70.2	59.0	...	...	...	...	...	...	...	...	...	...	...	11.2
1985	77.8	65.8	...	...	...	...	...	...	...	...	...	...	...	12.0
1986	84.6	72.2	...	...	...	...	...	...	...	...	...	...	...	12.4
1987	90.6	76.6	...	...	...	...	...	...	...	...	...	...	...	14.1
1988	94.7	82.5	...	...	...	...	...	...	...	...	...	...	...	12.3
1989	98.2	86.0	...	...	...	...	...	...	...	...	...	...	...	12.2
1990	107.5	95.4	...	...	...	...	...	...	...	...	...	...	...	12.1
1991	110.1	97.3	...	...	...	...	...	...	...	...	...	...	...	12.8
1992	115.8	101.5	...	...	...	...	...	...	...	...	...	...	...	14.4
1993	127.4	112.9	3.4	2.8	2.3	24.2	4.6	4.3	9.8	7.4	34.5	11.2	6.4	14.4
1994	130.4	116.0	4.2	3.0	2.4	25.3	4.5	4.7	9.2	5.1	37.3	12.0	6.4	14.4
1995	140.0	124.3	4.5	3.3	2.6	27.5	5.0	5.1	9.6	5.7	38.6	13.0	7.3	15.8
1996	146.7	131.4	3.7	3.6	2.8	31.0	5.5	5.0	10.4	4.8	40.6	13.6	7.7	15.3
1997	153.4	139.4	3.3	3.8	2.9	34.3	5.6	5.7	10.3	4.4	44.4	13.1	8.1	14.1
1998	154.8	140.5	3.2	3.7	2.3	35.1	6.1	6.2	10.5	2.8	45.4	13.2	8.9	14.3
1999	169.1	155.1	3.2	3.6	2.5	39.8	6.2	7.2	11.4	2.9	51.0	14.5	9.6	14.0
2000	181.3	167.2	3.0	4.5	2.8	46.8	5.9	7.6	13.0	5.5	51.6	14.0	9.5	14.2
2001	213.4	196.9	3.8	6.3	3.5	59.5	6.0	9.2	17.3	3.8	56.7	15.3	11.7	16.6
2002	213.4	196.9	3.8	6.3	3.5	59.5	6.0	9.2	17.3	3.8	56.7	15.3	11.7	16.6
2003	216.1	198.2	3.7	6.1	4.0	59.3	5.8	8.4	16.5	6.8	56.3	15.6	11.7	17.9
2004	220.2	201.8	4.1	6.0	5.0	59.7	5.5	7.8	16.4	7.0	57.4	17.1	12.0	18.3
2005	234.2	216.9	4.0	5.2	5.1	65.8	6.0	7.3	16.3	8.3	63.2	18.3	13.5	17.3
2006	255.4	237.8	4.3	5.6	5.6	69.8	6.6	9.4	17.7	7.8	71.0	21.5	14.3	17.6
2007	289.1	268.5	5.1	7.2	7.0	78.4	8.4	10.7	21.1	11.4	75.5	23.3	15.0	20.6
2008	308.7	285.0	4.9	8.5	7.0	84.5	9.7	10.9	23.2	11.0	80.4	24.1	16.0	23.7
2009	314.9	286.5	5.8	9.2	6.8	83.7	9.4	10.6	25.5	11.8	81.3	23.5	14.8	28.4
2010	304.0	272.8	7.6	8.3	6.2	71.9	7.6	9.7	26.5	10.8	81.3	24.6	14.4	31.1
2011	283.3	252.9	6.2	7.4	6.9	67.4	7.3	8.5	23.2	8.6	78.0	21.0	13.4	30.4
2012	275.7	250.2	5.0	6.1	7.0	65.4	7.6	9.0	24.5	9.0	78.6	20.7	12.7	25.5
2010														
January	295.9	268.1	6.0	8.6	6.2	76.0	8.3	10.2	24.5	9.3	76.6	26.2	12.3	27.7
February	290.3	261.0	5.8	8.2	6.1	74.2	8.3	9.4	25.6	8.4	76.8	22.1	12.8	29.3
March	297.8	268.2	6.6	8.4	6.4	72.4	7.9	9.1	27.7	10.1	78.5	23.8	13.7	29.6
April	306.4	273.6	7.2	8.6	6.0	72.0	7.8	9.6	28.2	10.7	80.4	25.2	14.4	32.8
May	309.3	277.1	7.6	8.1	5.9	72.8	7.8	9.3	28.1	9.0	85.1	24.5	15.2	32.2
June	312.1	278.5	8.2	8.1	5.7	74.2	7.5	9.5	27.2	11.4	82.7	24.6	15.5	33.5
July	304.0	273.0	7.9	8.2	6.3	74.7	7.3	9.8	26.6	11.2	77.2	25.3	15.0	30.8
August	308.4	278.6	8.2	8.6	6.5	73.1	7.2	10.3	25.6	11.2	82.4	26.2	15.2	29.8
September	315.0	281.8	8.1	8.8	6.5	72.5	7.4	10.2	29.3	11.5	83.3	25.1	14.9	33.3
October	306.6	274.0	8.8	8.1	6.4	67.6	7.3	9.9	25.3	12.3	84.3	24.8	14.7	32.5
November	298.9	267.0	8.5	8.1	6.1	66.6	7.4	9.3	24.7	11.5	82.3	23.5	14.5	31.9
December	291.5	263.1	7.4	8.1	6.4	65.7	7.1	9.2	25.9	12.0	80.0	22.9	14.2	28.4
2011														
January	288.1	256.7	6.9	8.0	6.6	66.0	6.9	15.7	35.8	64.7	80.2	23.0	15.0	31.4
February	284.5	253.1	6.5	8.0	6.7	64.9	7.0	16.1	35.1	65.3	78.7	22.4	14.7	31.4
March	286.3	254.9	6.4	7.8	7.0	66.5	7.0	16.0	35.7	69.4	78.1	23.5	13.9	31.4
April	280.2	249.8	6.7	7.9	7.3	66.5	7.1	16.2	35.0	67.7	75.1	21.9	14.1	30.4
May	280.5	248.8	6.4	7.5	7.0	66.9	7.3	16.8	34.6	71.9	76.8	22.3	13.2	31.7
June	284.6	253.8	6.4	7.8	7.2	66.8	7.7	16.4	35.2	76.2	77.3	23.2	13.5	30.8
July	277.7	247.4	5.6	6.9	7.4	66.7	7.0	16.4	33.6	74.0	77.1	22.1	14.7	30.2
August	284.8	253.0	6.3	6.9	7.0	69.3	7.4	15.9	35.8	76.3	78.0	22.0	14.7	31.8
September	283.1	253.8	6.4	7.6	7.2	69.3	7.2	16.0	34.7	75.3	80.3	22.0	14.2	29.3
October	282.9	253.7	6.0	7.0	6.5	69.1	7.2	16.1	34.2	77.2	80.8	22.3	14.6	29.2
November	283.6	255.5	5.7	7.2	6.7	66.8	7.5	16.6	34.1	79.7	82.8	22.9	14.3	28.1
December	286.1	256.1	5.8	6.7	6.9	67.7	7.7	16.7	35.6	84.4	82.4	23.8	13.3	29.9
2012														
January	277.2	251.1	5.8	6.9	6.7	67.5	8.1	9.3	23.0	8.6	75.2	22.0	13.7	26.1
February	276.1	249.4	5.2	6.4	6.8	66.7	8.0	9.0	22.7	8.3	76.7	22.1	13.1	26.7
March	273.0	245.9	4.9	6.3	6.8	65.9	7.9	9.0	21.7	7.6	76.8	21.2	12.9	27.1
April	272.8	247.3	4.8	6.5	6.8	65.1	7.7	8.7	22.5	7.8	78.8	21.0	13.0	25.5
May	276.6	249.8	4.6	6.3	6.9	64.3	8.0	9.3	24.4	8.4	79.5	20.6	13.0	26.9
June	278.7	252.8	4.7	6.1	7.0	67.1	7.7	9.2	24.4	8.0	81.5	20.0	12.4	25.8
July	274.2	249.4	4.8	5.9	6.8	66.4	7.6	9.0	24.0	8.4	80.1	19.6	12.0	24.8
August	278.0	252.6	4.9	6.1	7.5	66.0	7.4	8.7	25.2	10.0	79.1	20.5	12.0	25.3
September	274.7	251.0	5.0	6.1	6.9	64.9	7.4	9.4	25.5	10.0	77.7	20.7	12.6	23.7
October	274.3	248.3	5.1	5.8	6.9	63.4	7.3	9.1	26.7	9.8	76.7	20.3	12.5	26.0
November	274.4	249.7	5.3	5.8	7.0	63.6	7.0	8.5	26.0	10.8	77.3	21.0	12.5	24.7
December	269.0	244.2	4.8	5.5	7.3	62.7	7.1	8.4	26.0	8.8	76.6	19.7	12.9	24.8

¹ Includes categories not shown separately.
. . . = Not available.

Table 16-3. Housing Starts and Building Permits; New House Sales and Prices

Year and month	Housing starts and building permits										New house sales and prices			
	New private housing units (thousands)									Shipments of manufactured homes (thousands, seasonally adjusted annual rate)	Seasonally adjusted		Median sales price (dollars)	Price index (2005 = 100)
	Started (not seasonally adjusted)			Seasonally adjusted annual rate							Sold (thousands, annual rate)	For sale, end-of-period (thousands)		
				Started			Authorized by building permits							
	Total	One-family structures	Five units or more	Total	One-family structures	Five units or more	Total	One-family structures	Five units or more					
1975	1 160	892	204	1 160	892	204	939	675	200	213	549	316	39 300	22.1
1976	1 538	1 162	289	1 538	1 162	289	1 296	894	309	246	646	358	44 200	24.0
1977	1 987	1 451	414	1 987	1 451	414	1 690	1 126	443	266	819	408	48 800	27.0
1978	2 020	1 433	462	2 020	1 433	462	1 801	1 183	487	276	817	419	55 700	30.9
1979	1 745	1 194	429	1 745	1 194	429	1 552	982	445	277	709	402	62 900	35.3
1980	1 292	852	331	1 292	852	331	1 191	710	366	222	545	342	64 600	38.9
1981	1 084	705	288	1 084	705	288	986	564	319	241	436	278	68 900	42.0
1982	1 062	663	320	1 062	663	320	1 000	546	366	240	412	255	69 300	43.0
1983	1 703	1 068	522	1 703	1 068	522	1 605	901	570	296	623	304	75 300	43.9
1984	1 750	1 084	544	1 750	1 084	544	1 682	922	617	295	639	358	79 900	45.7
1985	1 742	1 072	576	1 742	1 072	576	1 733	957	657	284	688	350	84 300	46.2
1986	1 805	1 179	542	1 805	1 179	542	1 769	1 078	583	244	750	361	92 000	48.0
1987	1 621	1 146	409	1 621	1 146	409	1 535	1 024	421	233	671	370	104 500	50.6
1988	1 488	1 081	348	1 488	1 081	348	1 456	994	386	218	676	371	112 500	52.5
1989	1 376	1 003	318	1 376	1 003	318	1 338	932	340	198	650	366	120 000	54.6
1990	1 193	895	260	1 193	895	260	1 111	794	263	188	534	321	122 900	55.7
1991	1 014	840	138	1 014	840	138	949	754	152	171	509	284	120 000	56.4
1992	1 200	1 030	139	1 200	1 030	139	1 095	911	138	211	610	267	121 500	57.2
1993	1 288	1 126	133	1 288	1 126	133	1 199	987	160	254	666	295	126 500	59.4
1994	1 457	1 198	224	1 457	1 198	224	1 372	1 068	241	304	670	340	130 000	62.9
1995	1 354	1 076	244	1 354	1 076	244	1 333	997	272	340	667	374	133 900	64.3
1996	1 477	1 161	271	1 477	1 161	271	1 426	1 069	290	363	757	326	140 000	66.0
1997	1 474	1 134	296	1 474	1 134	296	1 441	1 062	310	354	804	287	146 000	67.5
1998	1 617	1 271	303	1 617	1 271	303	1 612	1 188	355	373	886	300	152 500	69.2
1999	1 641	1 302	307	1 641	1 302	307	1 664	1 247	351	348	880	315	161 000	72.8
2000	1 569	1 231	299	1 569	1 231	299	1 592	1 198	329	250	877	301	169 000	75.6
2001	1 603	1 273	293	1 603	1 273	293	1 637	1 236	335	193	908	310	175 200	77.9
2002	1 705	1 359	308	1 705	1 359	308	1 748	1 333	341	169	973	344	187 600	81.4
2003	1 848	1 499	315	1 848	1 499	315	1 889	1 461	346	131	1 086	377	195 000	86.0
2004	1 956	1 611	303	1 956	1 611	303	2 070	1 613	366	131	1 203	431	221 000	92.8
2005	2 068	1 716	311	2 068	1 716	311	2 155	1 682	389	147	1 283	515	240 900	100.0
2006	1 801	1 465	293	1 801	1 465	293	1 839	1 378	384	117	1 051	537	246 500	104.7
2007	1 355	1 046	277	1 355	1 046	277	1 398	980	359	96	776	496	247 900	104.9
2008	906	622	266	906	622	266	905	576	295	82	485	352	232 100	99.5
2009	554	445	97	554	445	97	583	441	121	50	375	232	216 700	95.1
2010	587	471	104	587	471	104	605	447	135	50	323	188	221 800	95.0
2011	609	431	167	609	431	167	624	418	184	52	306	150	227 200	94.3
2012	781	535	234	781	535	234	830	519	285	55	368	148	245 200	97.6
2010														
January	39	32	7	614	510	97	636	504	111	51	345	233	218 200	. . .
February	41	35	4	604	526	62	650	510	120	53	336	231	221 900	. . .
March	55	47	7	636	542	86	687	536	128	54	381	227	224 800	94.8
April	62	52	9	687	566	108	637	476	143	55	422	217	208 300	. . .
May	56	45	11	583	457	114	575	435	120	57	280	216	230 500	. . .
June	54	46	8	536	445	86	587	425	139	55	305	212	219 500	95.2
July	52	41	9	546	426	101	579	411	147	52	283	209	212 100	. . .
August	56	39	16	599	417	168	580	402	156	50	282	206	226 600	. . .
September	53	39	13	594	449	139	563	404	131	47	317	201	228 000	94.2
October	45	36	8	543	438	93	558	408	129	43	291	199	204 200	. . .
November	41	33	6	545	452	79	560	418	122	43	287	195	219 600	. . .
December	34	27	7	539	429	101	632	447	160	40	326	190	241 200	96.3
2011														
January	40	27	13	630	430	188	576	420	134	44	307	187	240 100	. . .
February	35	27	8	517	391	109	542	379	147	44	270	183	220 100	. . .
March	50	36	13	600	429	160	583	399	168	46	300	179	220 500	93.7
April	49	38	10	554	415	125	581	403	155	47	310	173	224 700	. . .
May	54	41	13	561	414	140	618	411	185	49	305	168	222 000	. . .
June	61	45	15	608	435	166	636	413	201	49	301	166	240 200	94.5
July	58	41	16	623	432	181	621	416	182	48	296	166	229 900	. . .
August	55	39	15	585	422	156	647	428	192	50	299	162	219 600	. . .
September	59	37	21	650	418	226	610	425	164	56	304	160	217 000	93.0
October	53	36	16	610	439	157	671	439	209	63	316	158	224 800	. . .
November	53	33	20	711	465	237	706	449	235	65	328	155	214 300	. . .
December	43	31	10	694	522	149	697	458	216	58	341	151	218 600	94.0
2012														
January	47	33	13	723	513	194	714	461	231	59	338	149	221 700	. . .
February	50	32	17	713	462	243	739	486	227	58	366	146	239 900	. . .
March	58	40	17	707	483	214	785	477	285	56	349	145	239 800	94.0
April	67	47	20	754	505	240	749	484	242	55	352	145	236 400	. . .
May	68	50	16	711	515	181	806	499	284	54	369	144	239 200	. . .
June	75	54	20	757	530	219	785	501	260	54	360	145	232 600	95.2
July	69	49	19	741	512	217	839	520	290	54	369	142	237 400	. . .
August	69	49	19	749	537	205	827	520	279	54	374	143	253 200	. . .
September	76	51	24	854	591	254	921	559	333	53	384	145	254 600	98.9
October	77	50	25	864	595	252	908	570	312	53	365	146	247 200	. . .
November	62	40	21	842	576	256	933	574	330	54	398	149	245 000	. . .
December	63	38	24	983	620	345	943	584	329	56	396	150	258 300	100.0

1Includes structures with 2 to 4 units, not shown separately.
. . . = Not available.

Table 16-4. Manufacturers' Shipments

(Millions of dollars, seasonally adjusted.)

Year and month	Total	Total durable goods¹	Total nondurable goods¹	Construction materials and supplies	Information technology industries	Capital goods — Total	Nondefense — Total	Nondefense — Excluding aircraft and parts	Defense	Consumer goods — Total	Durable	Nondurable
1992	2 904 024	1 518 862	1 385 162	281 232	236 015	566 268	471 485	435 696	94 783	1 098 480	253 111	845 369
1993	3 020 497	1 604 544	1 415 953	303 391	241 680	580 859	493 875	463 753	86 984	1 127 629	274 813	852 816
1994	3 238 112	1 764 061	1 474 051	332 734	264 092	616 435	538 203	512 327	78 232	1 192 098	314 931	877 167
1995	3 479 677	1 902 815	1 576 862	353 198	291 885	666 167	590 578	565 729	75 589	1 256 611	324 036	932 575
1996	3 597 188	1 978 597	1 618 591	371 401	311 028	704 635	630 932	605 295	73 703	1 292 955	328 402	964 553
1997	3 834 699	2 147 384	1 687 315	399 880	349 846	779 232	702 971	665 074	76 261	1 358 516	360 193	998 323
1998	3 899 813	2 231 588	1 668 225	418 756	362 564	821 736	747 046	695 717	74 690	1 351 812	373 404	978 408
1999	4 031 887	2 326 736	1 705 151	434 138	374 384	839 754	768 799	713 042	70 955	1 424 828	412 646	1 012 182
2000	4 208 584	2 373 688	1 834 896	444 812	399 751	875 396	808 345	757 617	67 051	1 500 532	391 463	1 109 069
2001	3 970 499	2 174 406	1 796 093	424 517	353 237	801 999	728 495	678 288	73 504	1 480 495	367 522	1 112 973
2002	3 914 723	2 123 621	1 791 102	424 008	284 799	728 585	652 342	609 595	76 243	1 494 575	395 953	1 098 622
2003	4 015 388	2 142 589	1 872 799	429 183	274 829	719 602	634 273	600 616	85 329	1 584 329	418 821	1 165 508
2004	4 308 970	2 264 667	2 044 303	463 148	287 837	752 905	661 740	629 146	91 165	1 700 835	419 182	1 281 653
2005	4 742 077	2 424 844	2 317 233	509 865	295 447	821 906	730 368	686 939	91 538	1 895 119	422 555	1 472 564
2006	5 015 552	2 562 194	2 453 358	546 866	319 890	884 199	794 638	744 282	89 561	1 980 031	421 860	1 558 171
2007	5 319 457	2 687 028	2 632 429	560 208	322 846	936 404	836 426	768 662	99 978	2 106 081	421 822	1 684 259
2008	5 468 095	2 619 931	2 848 164	543 769	315 383	953 501	838 116	772 231	115 385	2 252 714	359 362	1 893 352
2009	4 419 501	2 062 631	2 356 870	426 353	264 405	815 857	692 374	636 669	123 483	1 846 487	271 838	1 574 649
2010	4 905 445	2 290 796	2 614 649	443 253	259 772	851 851	720 928	666 730	130 923	2 055 025	329 120	1 725 905
2011	5 498 601	2 502 606	2 995 995	475 536	262 914	918 431	798 003	733 603	120 428	2 376 973	355 404	2 021 569
2012	5 733 291	2 671 564	3 061 727	498 975	262 955	983 028	865 252	777 887	117 776	2 472 827	394 202	2 078 625
2009												
January	366 106	176 264	189 842	37 238	21 969	70 303	61 750	55 314	8 553	148 756	22 777	125 979
February	368 542	175 768	192 774	37 684	22 939	70 307	60 224	55 774	10 083	149 585	22 468	127 117
March	357 984	172 069	185 915	35 931	22 623	69 088	59 501	54 764	9 587	144 937	22 327	122 610
April	353 510	167 131	186 379	35 011	21 391	66 684	56 623	51 915	10 061	145 811	22 160	123 651
May	353 385	163 922	189 463	34 701	21 407	66 314	56 277	51 839	10 037	147 497	21 154	126 343
June	362 350	163 203	199 147	34 641	21 920	67 120	56 675	52 562	10 445	154 658	19 674	134 984
July	363 563	168 403	195 160	35 363	22 463	66 820	56 621	52 495	10 199	152 240	22 081	130 159
August	369 376	169 652	199 724	35 177	22 163	65 668	55 101	51 430	10 567	157 072	22 811	134 261
September	375 257	174 527	200 730	35 425	21 801	68 465	57 602	52 231	10 863	157 854	23 272	134 582
October	378 656	174 930	203 726	35 269	22 390	67 705	56 721	52 476	10 984	160 839	23 698	137 141
November	384 922	177 528	207 394	35 400	22 467	68 530	57 380	52 937	11 150	163 711	24 791	138 920
December	389 942	181 235	208 707	35 038	21 234	69 369	58 746	53 482	10 623	165 488	25 209	140 279
2010												
January	393 487	184 201	209 286	35 406	21 826	69 059	57 116	52 900	11 943	166 363	26 384	139 979
February	392 368	180 225	212 143	35 700	21 630	69 311	57 824	53 804	11 487	165 219	24 521	140 698
March	400 225	182 256	217 969	36 255	21 792	70 289	58 971	54 679	11 318	170 148	25 293	144 855
April	404 564	188 065	216 499	37 340	21 597	69 962	58 645	54 333	11 317	168 327	25 809	142 518
May	402 668	188 796	213 872	37 712	21 393	69 453	58 721	54 965	10 732	167 001	26 405	140 596
June	401 947	187 744	214 203	37 148	21 181	70 575	59 953	55 616	10 622	167 466	26 791	140 675
July	410 189	195 339	214 850	36 884	21 694	72 153	61 308	55 214	10 845	170 101	29 270	140 831
August	412 315	195 292	217 023	36 992	21 621	71 329	61 017	56 083	10 312	171 052	28 944	142 108
September	416 524	197 276	219 248	37 033	21 701	72 340	61 316	57 082	11 024	172 755	29 471	143 284
October	417 900	196 267	221 633	37 338	21 882	71 941	61 444	56 717	10 497	175 141	29 241	145 900
November	423 677	196 057	227 620	37 708	22 211	71 786	61 400	57 148	10 386	179 569	28 364	151 205
December	432 464	199 681	232 783	37 570	21 868	74 142	63 487	58 535	10 655	184 447	29 191	155 256
2011												
January	440 049	200 964	239 085	38 160	21 940	72 887	62 625	58 233	10 262	189 519	29 384	160 135
February	441 053	200 907	240 146	38 111	21 577	72 941	62 294	57 515	10 647	190 922	29 571	161 351
March	457 331	209 077	248 254	39 307	21 675	75 847	64 824	59 916	11 023	199 004	31 513	167 491
April	455 758	203 954	251 804	38 702	21 941	74 908	64 361	59 527	10 547	199 375	28 705	170 670
May	455 632	204 931	250 701	39 049	21 933	75 289	64 958	60 263	10 331	196 722	28 353	168 369
June	458 333	206 139	252 194	39 686	21 744	75 907	65 899	61 003	10 008	198 147	28 735	169 412
July	464 174	211 270	252 904	39 965	21 640	76 305	66 766	60 996	9 539	202 326	31 896	170 430
August	466 076	213 180	252 896	40 306	22 358	79 805	69 777	63 787	10 028	199 519	29 168	170 351
September	463 638	210 950	252 688	40 186	22 218	78 596	68 828	63 241	9 768	199 616	28 576	171 040
October	465 411	214 598	250 813	40 567	21 823	78 849	69 754	62 903	9 095	200 147	30 858	169 289
November	467 060	213 368	253 692	40 681	21 829	77 331	68 207	62 351	9 124	202 825	30 130	172 695
December	469 881	216 915	252 966	41 253	22 406	79 963	69 977	64 394	9 986	201 442	30 060	171 382
2012												
January	473 046	219 487	253 559	41 589	22 335	80 897	71 046	63 266	9 851	202 608	30 886	171 722
February	473 877	217 950	255 927	41 168	22 413	79 844	70 740	63 973	9 104	205 054	30 986	174 068
March	477 673	219 515	258 158	42 007	22 276	81 718	72 005	65 779	9 713	206 717	31 669	175 048
April	475 592	221 515	254 077	41 867	22 430	80 766	71 700	64 649	9 066	205 308	33 444	171 864
May	477 594	224 384	253 210	41 808	23 059	82 381	72 470	65 302	9 911	204 848	33 353	171 495
June	466 816	222 107	244 709	41 266	21 745	82 015	71 887	65 312	10 128	198 038	33 088	164 950
July	475 210	224 060	251 150	41 153	21 484	81 718	72 054	64 438	9 664	204 780	34 464	170 316
August	476 102	220 751	255 351	41 324	21 025	80 360	70 836	63 990	9 524	206 917	33 019	173 898
September	481 499	222 172	259 327	41 150	21 296	82 081	72 107	63 888	9 974	210 668	33 371	177 297
October	481 887	222 560	259 327	41 660	21 531	82 191	72 352	64 257	9 839	209 535	32 487	177 048
November	482 241	225 316	256 925	41 693	21 522	83 318	73 238	65 473	10 080	207 613	33 591	174 022
December	482 478	226 396	256 082	41 760	21 630	83 541	73 113	65 469	10 428	207 684	33 901	173 783

¹Includes categories not shown separately.

Table 16-5. Manufacturers' Inventories

(Current cost basis, end of period; seasonally adjusted, millions of dollars.)

Year and month	Total	Total durable goods	Durables total by stage of fabrication			Total nondurable goods	Nondurables total by stage of fabrication		
			Materials and supplies	Work in process	Finished goods		Materials and supplies	Work in process	Finished goods
1992	378 412	237 788	69 639	104 130	64 019	140 624	53 033	23 382	64 209
1993	379 705	238 716	72 631	102 014	64 071	140 989	54 123	23 384	63 482
1994	399 867	253 078	78 551	106 578	67 949	146 789	57 044	24 427	65 318
1995	424 819	267 425	85 508	106 718	75 199	157 394	60 800	25 774	70 820
1996	430 451	272 485	86 256	110 656	75 573	157 966	59 141	26 497	72 328
1997	443 551	280 986	92 279	109 945	78 762	162 565	60 181	28 535	73 849
1998	448 738	290 403	93 494	115 150	81 759	158 335	58 181	27 066	73 088
1999	463 454	296 413	97 833	114 032	84 548	167 041	60 976	28 781	77 284
2000	481 091	306 322	106 000	111 023	89 299	174 769	61 530	30 017	83 222
2001	427 663	267 617	91 245	93 856	82 516	160 046	55 716	27 070	77 260
2002	422 815	260 338	88 455	92 345	79 538	162 477	56 575	27 857	78 045
2003	408 175	246 781	82 257	88 615	75 909	161 394	56 898	27 034	77 462
2004	440 736	264 952	92 053	91 091	81 808	175 784	61 784	29 877	84 123
2005	473 484	283 619	98 440	98 677	86 502	189 865	66 816	32 757	90 292
2006	522 126	317 416	111 534	106 560	99 322	204 710	70 334	36 912	97 464
2007	560 985	334 648	116 464	117 651	100 533	226 337	74 960	44 710	106 667
2008	541 115	330 233	117 613	111 864	100 756	210 882	71 980	40 993	97 909
2009	502 020	295 259	100 472	107 512	87 275	206 761	70 952	41 667	94 142
2010	551 348	323 100	106 763	124 204	92 133	228 248	75 458	45 328	107 462
2011	607 500	358 139	119 466	138 452	100 221	249 361	80 362	50 531	118 468
2012	622 299	374 147	123 675	145 953	104 519	248 152	80 336	48 514	119 302
2009									
January	536 462	328 342	117 856	111 654	98 832	208 120	70 325	41 701	96 094
February	528 677	324 338	116 943	110 361	97 034	204 339	68 808	40 820	94 711
March	522 237	317 751	113 762	108 934	95 055	204 486	68 213	41 543	94 730
April	516 106	314 075	111 736	108 248	94 091	202 031	66 889	41 436	93 706
May	512 308	309 649	109 406	108 007	92 236	202 659	67 614	41 383	93 662
June	506 980	303 350	105 279	107 539	90 532	203 630	67 998	41 311	94 321
July	503 556	300 596	103 325	107 823	89 448	202 960	68 299	40 937	93 724
August	500 396	296 421	101 958	106 025	88 438	203 975	68 208	41 428	94 339
September	496 888	294 417	101 617	105 656	87 144	202 471	67 675	41 379	93 417
October	499 908	294 861	100 990	106 988	86 883	205 047	68 162	41 690	95 195
November	502 217	295 606	100 546	107 989	87 071	206 611	69 635	41 699	95 277
December	502 020	295 259	100 472	107 512	87 275	206 761	70 952	41 667	94 142
2010									
January	503 502	296 341	100 061	108 681	87 599	207 161	70 318	40 991	95 852
February	508 527	298 301	100 759	109 857	87 685	210 226	71 627	41 640	96 959
March	511 570	299 738	101 192	110 504	88 042	211 832	72 019	42 321	97 492
April	514 391	302 155	101 433	112 198	88 524	212 236	71 013	42 435	98 788
May	514 570	304 523	102 170	113 082	89 271	210 047	69 393	41 417	99 237
June	519 062	308 343	103 859	114 470	90 014	210 719	69 676	41 323	99 720
July	522 284	309 847	103 688	115 273	90 886	212 437	70 273	41 384	100 780
August	525 205	311 460	103 718	116 435	91 307	213 745	69 739	42 180	101 826
September	531 118	314 656	103 954	118 770	91 932	216 462	70 975	42 088	103 399
October	537 162	317 158	104 924	120 055	92 179	220 004	71 758	43 087	105 159
November	543 257	320 395	105 900	121 769	92 726	222 862	73 034	43 459	106 369
December	551 348	323 100	106 763	124 204	92 133	228 248	75 458	45 328	107 462
2011									
January	558 692	327 120	108 192	125 712	93 216	231 572	76 105	45 839	109 628
February	565 583	330 995	109 050	126 793	95 152	234 588	77 899	46 313	110 376
March	573 556	337 071	110 323	130 422	96 326	236 485	78 135	46 493	111 857
April	583 372	341 122	112 248	131 852	97 022	242 250	78 814	48 537	114 899
May	590 135	345 672	113 768	134 049	97 855	244 463	79 454	48 638	116 371
June	593 440	347 712	114 600	134 767	98 345	245 728	78 904	49 476	117 348
July	597 076	350 783	115 439	136 001	99 343	246 293	78 687	49 212	118 394
August	599 689	353 399	116 519	136 580	100 300	246 290	79 701	48 356	118 233
September	598 553	353 565	116 772	136 097	100 696	244 988	78 486	48 542	117 960
October	604 705	355 421	117 431	137 279	100 711	249 284	80 848	49 814	118 622
November	607 397	357 445	118 207	138 504	100 734	249 952	80 527	50 061	119 364
December	607 500	358 139	119 466	138 452	100 221	249 361	80 362	50 531	118 468
2012									
January	611 035	360 635	120 810	139 365	100 460	250 400	80 464	51 641	118 295
February	613 530	362 003	120 990	140 186	100 827	251 527	80 434	51 770	119 323
March	614 569	364 194	122 403	140 547	101 244	250 375	80 690	50 982	118 703
April	614 094	365 289	122 397	140 981	101 911	248 805	81 760	49 157	117 888
May	614 029	366 705	122 507	141 207	102 991	247 324	81 036	49 626	116 662
June	613 690	367 308	122 420	141 977	102 911	246 382	80 814	49 292	116 276
July	616 309	369 858	122 968	143 256	103 634	246 451	81 489	48 278	116 684
August	619 464	371 694	123 245	144 228	104 221	247 770	81 576	48 667	117 527
September	623 432	372 471	123 817	144 327	104 327	250 961	81 846	50 526	118 589
October	622 417	373 736	124 027	144 623	105 086	248 681	81 089	49 359	118 233
November	621 940	374 423	123 931	145 486	105 006	247 517	80 198	49 013	118 306
December	622 299	374 147	123 675	145 953	104 519	248 152	80 336	48 514	119 302

Table 16-5. Manufacturers' Inventories—*Continued*

(Current cost basis, end of period; seasonally adjusted, millions of dollars.)

Year and month	Construction materials and supplies	Information technology industries	By topical categories						
			Capital goods				Consumer goods		
			Total	Nondefense		Defense	Total	Durable	Nondurable
				Total	Excluding aircraft and parts				
1992	36 728	40 177	120 467	97 323	78 886	23 144	103 142	20 826	82 316
1993	38 307	39 192	118 480	97 163	79 606	21 317	104 732	21 835	82 897
1994	40 884	41 559	123 397	103 381	85 743	20 016	109 440	23 946	85 494
1995	43 416	46 952	129 743	111 622	94 692	18 121	116 361	25 301	91 060
1996	44 122	43 572	132 802	115 277	93 458	17 525	116 340	24 739	91 601
1997	45 722	48 142	137 635	122 654	98 866	14 981	119 708	24 906	94 802
1998	46 502	45 329	145 084	127 106	97 330	17 978	117 410	24 910	92 500
1999	48 545	46 216	146 369	126 331	99 640	20 038	124 287	26 114	98 173
2000	50 500	52 773	149 162	131 749	110 177	17 413	130 843	27 292	103 551
2001	46 330	42 992	128 772	114 971	93 327	13 801	121 470	25 419	96 051
2002	46 566	39 016	122 477	108 028	88 525	14 449	124 711	25 692	99 019
2003	45 309	35 214	115 026	99 191	81 746	15 835	124 984	25 017	99 967
2004	51 181	33 128	117 782	99 010	83 765	18 772	133 905	26 267	107 638
2005	55 048	39 153	127 256	110 678	92 901	16 578	144 473	28 091	116 382
2006	60 871	39 890	139 588	122 540	101 823	17 048	153 116	27 754	125 362
2007	62 599	38 721	150 346	131 485	104 704	18 861	170 827	27 672	143 155
2008	61 790	37 454	150 849	134 291	107 240	16 558	153 919	24 461	129 458
2009	51 402	35 643	145 563	125 488	96 699	20 075	157 226	21 638	135 588
2010	54 399	36 419	160 588	139 661	102 815	20 927	173 181	23 053	150 128
2011	59 325	38 871	176 971	156 157	114 497	20 814	187 605	24 800	162 805
2012	60 647	39 286	188 673	167 124	120 290	21 549	188 002	25 654	162 348
2009									
January	61 131	36 953	151 189	133 804	106 860	17 385	153 093	24 377	128 716
February	59 181	36 926	151 230	133 782	106 145	17 448	150 488	23 890	126 598
March	57 460	36 516	149 605	131 878	104 338	17 727	151 458	23 620	127 838
April	55 900	36 887	149 966	131 825	103 712	18 141	150 818	23 385	127 433
May	54 500	36 644	149 019	130 595	102 286	18 424	152 346	22 963	129 383
June	53 294	35 561	147 555	129 179	100 248	18 376	152 992	22 146	130 846
July	52 610	35 354	146 719	128 007	98 470	18 712	152 921	21 852	131 069
August	51 950	35 190	144 899	126 067	97 552	18 832	154 233	21 736	132 497
September	51 722	35 258	143 626	124 664	96 962	18 962	152 400	21 439	130 961
October	51 600	35 272	145 119	125 532	96 584	19 587	154 741	21 200	133 541
November	51 504	35 344	146 406	126 400	96 507	20 006	156 012	21 276	134 736
December	51 402	35 643	145 563	125 488	96 699	20 075	157 226	21 638	135 588
2010									
January	51 615	35 817	146 837	126 171	96 690	20 666	157 126	21 911	135 215
February	51 149	36 069	147 756	126 932	96 906	20 824	160 272	22 265	138 007
March	51 894	35 444	147 318	126 507	96 330	20 811	160 661	22 351	138 310
April	52 183	35 412	148 333	127 886	96 590	20 447	160 442	22 472	137 970
May	52 393	35 572	149 237	128 985	97 419	20 252	157 395	22 768	134 627
June	53 232	36 218	151 186	130 740	98 520	20 446	157 900	22 905	134 995
July	53 475	36 015	152 021	131 544	99 217	20 477	159 581	23 029	136 552
August	53 661	36 101	152 901	132 510	99 747	20 391	160 753	23 179	137 574
September	53 985	36 183	155 455	135 198	100 547	20 257	163 117	23 051	140 066
October	53 900	36 407	157 231	136 784	101 567	20 447	166 129	22 965	143 164
November	54 146	36 403	159 139	138 169	102 247	20 970	168 510	23 231	145 279
December	54 399	36 419	160 588	139 661	102 815	20 927	173 181	23 053	150 128
2011									
January	54 985	36 635	162 591	141 640	103 972	20 951	174 541	23 414	151 127
February	55 472	37 141	163 998	143 086	105 450	20 912	177 061	23 786	153 275
March	56 129	37 983	167 965	146 110	107 221	21 855	178 646	23 813	154 833
April	56 936	38 465	169 781	148 246	108 581	21 535	183 154	23 886	159 268
May	57 767	38 918	172 021	150 192	110 187	21 829	184 102	23 995	160 107
June	57 761	39 196	172 938	151 579	111 029	21 359	184 246	24 031	160 215
July	57 971	39 422	174 207	152 840	111 969	21 367	184 355	24 408	159 947
August	58 415	39 627	175 397	153 951	112 951	21 446	183 735	24 507	159 228
September	58 516	39 560	174 786	153 957	113 315	20 829	182 233	24 786	157 447
October	58 725	39 623	176 211	155 188	114 407	21 023	186 045	24 765	161 280
November	59 221	39 528	177 244	156 094	115 082	21 150	187 427	24 668	162 759
December	59 325	38 871	176 971	156 157	114 497	20 814	187 605	24 800	162 805
2012									
January	59 174	39 296	178 852	158 099	116 533	20 753	188 437	24 863	163 574
February	59 210	39 484	179 880	159 045	117 298	20 835	189 598	24 721	164 877
March	59 123	39 659	181 163	160 635	118 023	20 528	188 621	25 010	163 611
April	59 333	39 645	182 467	161 639	118 754	20 828	187 070	24 953	162 117
May	59 466	39 371	183 651	162 665	119 206	20 986	185 924	25 070	160 854
June	59 737	38 994	184 049	163 083	119 030	20 966	185 666	25 118	160 548
July	59 890	39 080	186 175	164 768	120 371	21 407	185 987	25 162	160 825
August	59 843	39 073	187 813	166 123	120 678	21 690	187 726	25 302	162 424
September	59 963	39 184	188 157	166 951	120 826	21 206	190 876	25 278	165 598
October	60 106	39 346	188 724	167 680	121 052	21 044	189 012	25 470	163 542
November	60 182	39 439	189 731	168 084	121 048	21 647	187 557	25 411	162 146
December	60 647	39 286	188 673	167 124	120 290	21 549	188 002	25 654	162 348

Table 16-6. Manufacturers' New Orders

(Net, millions of dollars, seasonally adjusted.)

Year and month	Total [1]	Total durable goods [1]	By topical categories								
			Construction materials and supplies	Information technology industries	Capital goods				Consumer goods		
					Total	Nondefense		Defense	Total	Durable	Nondurable
						Total	Excluding aircraft and parts				
1993	2 960 015	1 544 062	304 264	239 387	561 097	488 166	466 433	72 931	1 128 447	275 631	852 816
1994	3 199 686	1 725 635	335 962	265 010	616 252	542 094	523 461	74 158	1 192 584	315 417	877 167
1995	3 426 503	1 849 641	355 161	297 605	680 857	612 132	576 769	68 725	1 256 721	324 146	932 575
1996	3 567 384	1 948 793	373 536	310 074	737 268	648 797	607 174	88 471	1 293 537	328 984	964 553
1997	3 779 835	2 092 520	403 860	352 700	792 859	728 362	676 119	64 497	1 360 010	361 687	998 323
1998	3 808 143	2 139 918	419 330	365 723	809 727	745 600	698 279	64 127	1 352 708	374 300	978 408
1999	3 957 242	2 252 091	435 034	389 160	840 603	772 703	728 089	67 900	1 425 617	413 435	1 012 182
2000	4 161 472	2 326 576	446 792	409 500	910 933	831 335	767 754	79 598	1 501 810	392 741	1 109 069
2001	3 868 660	2 072 567	420 790	336 836	775 248	691 492	656 814	83 756	1 477 128	364 155	1 112 973
2002	3 822 991	2 031 889	423 548	273 763	698 748	622 276	588 972	76 472	1 494 103	395 481	1 098 622
2003	3 975 747	2 102 948	431 541	282 261	737 032	636 807	608 120	100 225	1 585 009	419 501	1 165 508
2004	4 288 963	2 244 660	468 721	293 790	787 749	688 832	643 954	98 917	1 701 561	419 908	1 281 653
2005	4 764 162	2 446 929	516 763	300 327	896 786	814 352	703 677	82 434	1 894 076	421 512	1 472 564
2006	5 089 750	2 636 392	549 455	332 582	992 650	889 475	775 033	103 175	1 979 178	421 007	1 558 171
2007	5 397 459	2 765 030	564 718	324 207	1 061 843	957 866	786 659	103 977	2 105 790	421 531	1 684 259
2008	5 447 245	2 599 081	543 201	314 940	1 005 209	877 753	779 411	127 456	2 251 447	358 095	1 893 352
2009	4 191 026	1 834 156	412 779	257 556	684 941	581 015	601 561	103 926	1 846 059	271 410	1 574 649
2010	4 875 719	2 261 070	447 724	263 946	881 906	742 398	678 558	139 508	2 054 785	328 880	1 725 905
2011	5 504 599	2 508 604	480 737	269 452	985 531	856 239	757 023	129 292	2 377 351	355 782	2 021 569
2012	5 681 458	2 619 731	499 297	269 715	1 018 299	891 037	775 671	127 262	2 472 899	394 274	2 078 625
2009											
January	341 587	151 745	34 371	20 888	55 614	49 470	48 926	6 144	148 641	22 662	125 979
February	337 877	145 103	35 431	22 329	52 976	44 531	49 563	8 445	149 385	22 268	127 117
March	330 371	144 456	33 408	22 421	53 206	45 636	49 149	7 570	144 867	22 257	122 610
April	330 787	144 408	33 283	20 605	53 025	43 100	46 353	9 925	145 698	22 047	123 651
May	339 379	149 916	33 345	21 306	60 438	49 111	48 226	11 327	147 370	21 027	126 343
June	345 267	146 120	32 918	21 390	56 014	48 977	50 223	7 037	154 568	19 584	134 984
July	352 283	157 123	34 245	21 648	61 935	53 085	50 330	8 850	152 314	22 155	130 159
August	357 254	157 530	34 516	21 176	57 876	49 045	49 575	8 831	157 125	22 864	134 261
September	358 697	157 967	35 053	21 387	59 285	49 957	51 924	9 328	157 856	23 274	134 582
October	366 119	162 393	35 975	21 940	61 009	52 405	51 877	8 604	160 816	23 675	137 141
November	368 668	161 274	35 509	21 814	59 188	50 704	52 246	8 484	163 736	24 816	138 920
December	367 214	158 507	34 901	20 947	56 034	47 082	53 176	8 952	165 613	25 334	140 279
2010											
January	388 683	179 397	35 406	21 177	69 433	56 749	51 172	12 684	166 623	26 644	139 979
February	387 411	175 268	35 952	20 794	70 401	58 834	52 305	11 567	165 109	24 411	140 698
March	397 231	179 262	36 917	22 318	69 357	57 032	55 516	12 325	170 088	25 233	144 855
April	403 560	187 061	37 891	21 982	75 125	62 952	54 024	12 173	168 498	25 980	142 518
May	399 887	186 015	37 551	21 457	72 686	60 659	56 148	12 027	166 932	26 336	140 596
June	401 314	187 111	37 635	22 056	75 258	64 450	59 385	10 808	167 340	26 665	140 675
July	406 214	191 364	37 351	21 881	73 319	62 069	55 852	11 250	169 909	29 078	140 831
August	407 979	190 956	37 669	22 892	72 874	61 656	58 194	11 218	170 836	28 728	142 108
September	421 308	202 060	37 682	23 259	81 910	69 772	59 283	12 138	172 687	29 403	143 284
October	415 952	194 319	36 990	20 980	77 466	67 192	57 289	10 274	175 126	29 226	145 900
November	424 624	197 004	38 281	22 946	74 909	63 003	59 442	11 906	179 607	28 402	151 205
December	426 231	193 448	38 337	22 827	70 282	58 972	60 747	11 310	184 538	29 282	155 256
2011											
January	441 479	202 394	39 472	22 334	78 882	64 334	59 604	14 548	189 442	29 307	160 135
February	433 827	193 681	38 895	22 759	72 680	62 636	58 325	10 044	191 041	29 690	161 351
March	460 671	212 417	39 799	21 618	84 055	71 795	62 056	12 260	199 096	31 605	167 491
April	453 697	201 893	39 222	21 437	78 974	66 742	61 417	12 232	199 389	28 719	170 670
May	457 336	206 635	39 456	22 306	81 761	70 234	63 205	11 527	196 666	28 297	168 369
June	455 994	203 800	40 102	22 803	80 371	68 983	63 509	11 388	198 156	28 744	169 412
July	465 134	212 230	40 290	21 883	81 975	71 574	64 038	10 401	202 335	31 905	170 430
August	467 478	214 582	40 204	23 182	86 927	76 161	64 129	10 766	199 377	29 026	170 351
September	464 308	211 620	40 467	23 326	84 261	72 953	65 636	11 308	199 587	28 547	171 040
October	461 054	210 241	40 726	23 142	80 048	71 092	66 571	8 956	200 271	30 982	169 289
November	471 788	218 096	41 330	22 359	86 020	76 868	63 174	9 152	203 028	30 333	172 695
December	478 319	225 353	41 315	22 589	90 393	83 744	66 764	6 649	201 553	30 171	171 382
2012											
January	471 692	218 133	41 758	22 918	88 711	80 141	65 086	8 570	202 521	30 799	171 722
February	475 158	219 231	41 410	23 584	88 005	78 669	66 481	9 336	205 044	30 976	174 068
March	475 369	217 211	41 963	23 356	83 784	73 553	66 868	10 231	206 597	31 549	175 048
April	471 381	217 304	41 802	23 863	82 010	73 604	65 677	8 406	205 356	33 492	171 864
May	467 933	214 723	42 077	23 960	80 590	72 041	66 178	8 549	204 915	33 420	171 495
June	465 112	220 403	41 494	22 154	88 138	73 349	64 906	14 789	198 003	33 053	164 950
July	478 363	227 213	41 630	21 803	93 525	80 735	62 293	12 790	204 777	34 461	170 316
August	453 195	197 844	40 351	21 552	67 229	60 314	62 342	6 915	206 918	33 020	173 898
September	476 580	217 253	41 147	21 020	83 872	73 845	61 708	10 027	210 735	33 438	177 297
October	478 059	218 732	41 884	21 725	85 272	76 384	63 933	8 888	209 632	32 584	177 048
November	474 814	217 889	41 317	22 016	80 777	72 388	64 870	8 389	207 680	33 658	174 022
December	485 183	229 101	41 924	21 487	93 834	74 146	63 644	19 688	207 652	33 869	173 783

[1] Includes categories not shown separately.

Table 16-7. Manufacturers' Unfilled Orders, Durable Goods Industries

(End of period, millions of dollars, seasonally adjusted.)

Year and month	Total [1]	Transportation equipment		Construction materials and supplies	Information technology industries	By topical categories				Consumer durable goods
		Nondefense aircraft and parts	Defense aircraft and parts			Capital goods				
							Nondefense			
						Total	Total	Excluding aircraft and parts	Defense	
1992	451 086	127 514	49 542	20 895	80 301	319 108	179 611	92 528	139 497	3 871
1993	425 792	110 933	46 595	21 764	77 989	299 302	173 903	95 303	125 399	4 705
1994	435 074	101 162	44 678	25 083	79 076	299 314	178 015	106 780	121 299	5 241
1995	447 669	109 515	42 375	27 156	84 934	314 031	199 669	118 050	114 362	5 346
1996	489 246	130 593	45 198	29 436	84 235	346 647	217 657	120 309	128 990	5 884
1997	513 168	143 399	40 824	33 608	87 330	360 319	243 063	131 667	117 256	7 376
1998	496 197	137 403	37 692	34 263	90 579	348 099	241 203	134 005	106 896	8 308
1999	505 395	126 403	35 593	35 261	105 502	349 111	245 165	149 197	103 946	9 129
2000	549 235	138 339	42 398	37 387	115 390	384 500	267 953	159 428	116 547	10 460
2001	509 983	124 964	51 988	33 564	98 813	357 401	230 435	137 401	126 966	7 074
2002	479 723	114 906	57 994	33 109	87 954	327 883	200 567	116 953	127 316	6 632
2003	506 462	110 211	64 367	35 540	95 502	345 340	203 117	124 540	142 223	7 303
2004	558 692	123 551	57 574	41 271	101 350	379 870	229 989	139 495	149 881	8 147
2005	654 513	189 112	55 351	48 276	106 342	453 487	312 724	156 395	140 763	7 196
2006	798 177	266 596	59 933	50 771	119 026	561 096	406 555	187 468	154 541	6 400
2007	947 437	378 366	63 275	55 260	120 031	685 201	526 467	205 586	158 734	6 079
2008	996 261	418 723	72 566	54 606	119 633	737 607	566 264	212 903	171 343	4 623
2009	825 269	344 185	61 684	40 683	112 717	607 834	456 146	177 252	151 688	4 164
2010	869 481	351 941	62 134	45 259	116 890	638 514	478 284	189 533	160 230	3 868
2011	956 812	392 653	64 876	50 564	123 544	706 233	537 130	213 832	169 103	4 245
2012	992 007	426 235	71 551	50 876	130 236	741 150	562 751	212 022	178 399	4 305
2009										
January	976 324	416 537	70 908	51 739	118 552	722 918	553 984	206 515	168 934	4 508
February	949 901	406 105	70 121	49 486	117 942	705 587	538 291	200 304	167 296	4 308
March	926 837	397 741	69 965	46 963	117 740	689 705	524 426	194 689	165 279	4 238
April	909 084	389 716	70 028	45 235	116 954	676 046	510 903	189 127	165 143	4 125
May	900 062	386 178	68 981	43 879	116 853	670 170	503 737	185 514	166 433	3 998
June	886 764	380 797	69 504	42 156	116 323	659 064	496 039	183 175	163 025	3 908
July	880 593	378 905	69 287	41 038	115 508	654 179	492 503	181 010	161 676	3 982
August	873 320	374 985	68 518	40 377	114 521	646 387	486 447	179 155	159 940	4 035
September	861 532	366 889	65 783	40 005	114 107	637 207	478 802	178 848	158 405	4 037
October	854 060	362 912	64 760	40 711	113 657	630 511	474 486	178 249	156 025	4 014
November	842 627	357 451	62 923	40 820	113 004	621 169	467 810	177 558	153 359	4 039
December	825 269	344 185	61 684	40 683	112 717	607 834	456 146	177 252	151 688	4 164
2010										
January	827 899	344 675	63 633	40 683	112 068	608 208	455 779	175 524	152 429	4 424
February	828 389	346 378	63 353	40 935	111 232	609 298	456 789	174 025	152 509	4 314
March	829 292	343 098	63 098	41 597	111 758	608 366	454 850	174 862	153 516	4 254
April	835 048	347 555	62 684	42 148	112 143	613 529	459 157	174 553	154 372	4 425
May	838 264	348 059	62 475	41 987	112 207	616 762	461 095	175 736	155 667	4 356
June	841 307	348 335	62 390	42 474	113 082	621 445	465 592	179 505	155 853	4 230
July	843 943	348 714	62 180	42 941	113 269	622 611	466 353	180 143	156 258	4 038
August	846 229	346 985	61 868	43 618	114 540	624 156	466 992	182 254	157 164	3 822
September	857 525	353 365	62 834	44 267	116 098	633 726	475 448	184 455	158 278	3 754
October	861 850	358 511	62 371	43 919	115 196	639 251	481 196	185 027	158 055	3 739
November	869 324	358 137	62 737	44 492	115 931	642 374	482 799	187 321	159 575	3 777
December	869 481	351 941	62 134	45 259	116 890	638 514	478 284	189 533	160 230	3 868
2011										
January	877 595	352 954	63 125	46 571	117 284	644 509	479 993	190 904	164 516	3 791
February	877 496	352 784	63 178	47 355	118 466	644 248	480 335	191 714	163 913	3 910
March	887 440	357 703	63 688	47 847	118 409	652 456	487 306	193 854	165 150	4 002
April	892 231	358 974	64 289	48 367	117 905	656 522	489 687	195 744	166 835	4 016
May	900 988	361 738	65 559	48 774	118 278	662 994	494 963	198 686	168 031	3 960
June	905 112	362 823	65 314	49 190	119 337	667 458	498 047	201 192	169 411	3 969
July	912 628	365 507	65 214	49 515	119 580	673 128	502 855	204 234	170 273	3 978
August	921 103	371 993	66 702	49 413	120 404	680 250	509 239	204 576	171 011	3 836
September	928 324	373 684	65 734	49 694	121 512	685 915	513 364	206 971	172 551	3 807
October	930 653	371 925	65 484	49 853	122 831	687 114	514 702	210 639	172 412	3 931
November	942 526	380 200	65 665	50 502	123 361	695 803	523 363	211 462	172 440	4 134
December	956 812	392 653	64 876	50 564	123 544	706 233	537 130	213 832	169 103	4 245
2012										
January	962 269	399 209	64 276	50 733	124 127	714 047	546 225	215 652	167 822	4 158
February	970 746	405 065	65 173	50 975	125 298	722 208	554 154	218 160	168 054	4 148
March	973 844	406 304	66 711	50 931	126 378	724 274	555 702	219 249	168 572	4 028
April	976 684	407 461	66 996	50 866	127 811	725 518	557 606	220 277	167 912	4 076
May	974 397	406 973	66 392	51 135	128 712	723 727	557 177	221 153	166 550	4 143
June	979 831	409 317	66 866	51 363	129 121	729 850	558 639	220 747	171 211	4 108
July	991 465	420 566	67 341	51 840	129 440	741 657	567 320	218 602	174 337	4 105
August	975 675	411 815	67 016	50 867	129 967	728 526	556 798	216 954	171 728	4 106
September	978 058	416 502	68 110	50 864	129 691	730 317	558 536	214 774	171 781	4 173
October	982 069	420 896	68 998	51 088	129 885	733 398	562 568	214 450	170 830	4 270
November	981 752	423 017	69 134	50 712	130 379	730 857	561 718	213 847	169 139	4 337
December	992 007	426 235	71 551	50 876	130 236	741 150	562 751	212 022	178 399	4 305

[1] Includes categories not shown separately.

Table 16-8. Motor Vehicle Sales and Inventories

(Units.)

Year and month	Retail sales of new passenger cars						Retail inventories of new domestic passenger cars (thousands of units, end of period)		
	Thousands of units, not seasonally adjusted			Millions of units, seasonally adjusted annual rate			Not seasonally adjusted	Seasonally adjusted	Inventory to sales ratio
	Total	Domestic	Foreign	Total	Domestic	Foreign			
1970	8 402.6	7 119.4	1 283.2	8.403	7.119	1.283	. . .	. . .	. . .
1971	10 227.9	8 661.8	1 566.0	10.228	8.662	1.566	. . .	. . .	. . .
1972	10 873.4	9 252.6	1 620.7	10.873	9.253	1.621	1 311.0	1 379.0	1.700
1973	11 350.2	9 588.6	1 761.5	11.350	9.589	1.762	1 600.0	1 654.0	2.500
1974	8 773.7	7 361.8	1 411.9	8.774	7.362	1.412	1 672.0	1 730.0	3.400
1975	8 537.9	6 950.9	1 586.9	8.538	6.951	1.587	1 419.0	1 468.0	2.200
1976	9 994.0	8 492.0	1 502.0	9.994	8.492	1.502	1 465.0	1 494.0	1.900
1977	11 046.0	8 971.2	2 074.8	11.046	8.971	2.075	1 731.0	1 743.0	2.300
1978	11 164.0	9 163.9	2 000.1	11.164	9.164	2.000	1 729.0	1 731.0	2.300
1979	10 558.8	8 230.1	2 328.7	10.559	8.230	2.329	1 691.0	1 667.0	2.400
1980	8 981.8	6 581.4	2 400.4	8.982	6.581	2.401	1 448.0	1 440.0	2.600
1981	8 534.3	6 208.8	2 325.5	8.534	6.209	2.326	1 471.0	1 495.0	3.600
1982	7 979.4	5 758.2	2 221.2	7.980	5.758	2.221	1 126.0	1 127.0	2.200
1983	9 178.6	6 793.0	2 385.6	9.179	6.793	2.386	1 352.0	1 350.0	2.000
1984	10 390.2	7 951.7	2 438.5	10.390	7.952	2.439	1 415.0	1 411.0	2.100
1985	10 978.4	8 204.7	2 773.7	10.978	8.205	2.774	1 630.0	1 619.0	2.500
1986	10 418.3	8 215.0	3 190.7	11.406	8.215	3.191	1 499.0	1 515.0	2.000
1987	10 170.9	7 080.9	3 090.0	10.171	7.081	3.090	1 680.0	1 716.0	2.800
1988	10 545.6	7 539.4	3 006.2	10.546	7.539	3.006	1 601.0	1 601.0	2.300
1989	9 776.8	7 078.1	2 698.7	9.777	7.078	2.699	1 669.0	1 687.0	3.100
1990	9 300.2	6 896.9	2 403.3	9.300	6.897	2.403	1 408.0	1 418.0	2.600
1991	8 175.0	6 136.9	2 038.1	8.175	6.137	2.038	1 283.0	1 296.0	2.600
1992	8 214.4	6 276.6	1 937.8	8.214	6.277	1.938	1 276.0	1 288.0	2.300
1993	8 517.7	6 734.0	1 783.7	8.518	6.734	1.784	1 364.9	1 377.3	2.359
1994	8 990.4	7 255.2	1 735.2	8.990	7.255	1.735	1 436.6	1 449.3	2.325
1995	8 636.2	7 128.8	1 507.4	8.637	7.129	1.508	1 618.5	1 631.2	2.550
1996	8 526.8	7 253.7	1 273.1	8.527	7.254	1.273	1 363.4	1 375.9	2.378
1997	8 272.5	6 906.2	1 366.3	8.273	6.907	1.366	1 329.9	1 342.4	2.249
1998	8 142.1	6 763.9	1 378.2	8.143	6.764	1.378	1 324.4	1 383.0	2.214
1999	8 696.5	6 981.7	1 714.8	8.697	6.982	1.715	1 367.6	1 421.9	2.366
2000	8 852.1	6 832.8	2 019.3	8.852	6.833	2.019	1 377.0	1 408.7	2.815
2001	8 422.1	6 322.7	2 099.4	8.422	6.323	2.099	955.7	993.4	2.284
2002	8 108.7	5 877.6	2 231.1	8.102	5.871	2.231	1 132.0	1 245.3	2.538
2003	7 610.5	5 527.5	2 083.0	7.615	5.527	2.087	1 115.8	1 234.1	2.702
2004	7 545.1	5 396.2	2 148.9	7.545	5.396	2.149	1 034.2	1 152.0	2.385
2005	7 719.8	5 533.0	2 186.8	7.720	5.533	2.187	930.6	1 032.3	2.304
2006	7 820.7	5 476.1	2 344.6	7.821	5.476	2.345	1 031.7	1 109.5	2.468
2007	7 618.4	5 253.4	2 365.0	7.618	5.253	2.365	906.8	978.2	2.226
2008	6 813.5	4 535.3	2 278.2	6.813	4.535	2.278	1 144.1	1 217.4	4.146
2009	5 456.1	3 613.0	1 843.1	5.456	3.613	1.843	686.4	751.3	2.165
2010	5 728.6	3 884.3	1 844.3	5.729	3.884	1.845	759.1	817.1	2.362
2011	6 193.8	4 246.9	1 946.9	6.193	4.247	1.946	813.0	826.8	2.200
2012	7 359.3	5 234.0	2 125.3	7.373	5.243	2.130	1 069.5	1 077.1	2.292
2010									
January	361.7	245.5	116.2	5.530	3.737	1.793	719.4	759.9	2.440
February	399.2	278.8	120.4	5.181	3.521	1.660	768.1	808.9	2.757
March	541.1	382.8	158.3	5.641	3.965	1.676	755.2	804.8	2.435
April	501.3	351.2	150.1	5.432	3.791	1.641	729.4	819.4	2.594
May	562.7	397.3	165.4	5.709	3.979	1.730	682.4	849.5	2.562
June	500.0	341.8	158.2	5.713	3.892	1.821	698.5	855.7	2.638
July	524.0	345.8	178.2	5.823	3.943	1.880	620.9	864.5	2.631
August	498.9	327.1	171.8	5.883	3.906	1.977	640.4	876.5	2.693
September	471.3	313.7	157.6	5.925	3.928	1.997	690.6	882.4	2.696
October	445.1	288.4	156.7	5.917	3.880	2.037	767.2	870.3	2.692
November	403.5	264.1	139.4	5.880	3.919	1.961	822.6	869.6	2.663
December	519.8	347.8	172.0	6.112	4.151	1.961	759.1	817.1	2.362
2011									
January	387.5	265.8	121.7	5.926	4.043	1.883	775.7	811.2	2.408
February	490.5	346.1	144.4	6.328	4.344	1.984	756.5	788.6	2.179
March	652.9	449.7	203.2	6.499	4.440	2.059	708.5	771.0	2.084
April	608.1	417.6	190.5	6.465	4.413	2.052	629.4	742.2	2.018
May	543.5	371.1	172.4	5.835	3.914	1.921	580.2	748.3	2.294
June	524.4	359.4	165.0	5.798	3.954	1.844	591.2	766.1	2.325
July	504.0	336.1	167.9	5.853	3.998	1.855	529.2	770.4	2.312
August	505.6	348.5	157.1	5.869	4.096	1.773	558.3	778.7	2.281
September	483.1	335.6	147.5	6.144	4.252	1.892	595.6	769.1	2.170
October	477.3	328.2	149.1	6.485	4.498	1.987	694.9	774.8	2.067
November	459.8	309.5	150.3	6.567	4.497	2.070	786.6	786.1	2.097
December	557.1	379.3	177.8	6.541	4.511	2.030	813.0	826.8	2.200
2012									
January	465.1	328.0	137.1	7.105	4.990	2.115	886.6	876.5	2.108
February	608.7	434.9	173.8	7.624	5.313	2.311	902.9	871.8	1.969
March	758.2	538.3	219.9	7.314	5.156	2.158	876.2	889.6	2.070
April	628.1	445.3	182.8	7.143	5.021	2.122	857.9	923.3	2.207
May	681.8	495.6	186.2	6.891	4.934	1.957	840.3	973.2	2.367
June	654.4	472.4	182.0	7.192	5.176	2.016	858.8	986.9	2.288
July	578.8	404.6	174.2	7.079	5.051	2.028	822.7	1 075.5	2.555
August	645.3	464.4	180.9	7.326	5.352	1.974	845.4	1 068.5	2.396
September	595.5	422.3	173.2	7.608	5.375	2.233	888.0	1 062.5	2.372
October	539.9	378.8	161.1	7.385	5.233	2.152	1 025.5	1 067.5	2.448
November	560.3	391.3	169.0	8.000	5.700	2.300	1 112.3	1 073.0	2.268
December	643.2	458.1	185.1	7.800	5.600	2.200	1 069.5	1 077.1	2.292

. . . = Not available.

Table 16-8. Motor Vehicle Sales and Inventories—*Continued*

(Units.)

Year and month	Retail sales of new trucks and buses								Unit sales of cars and light trucks (millions of units, seasonally adjusted annual rate)		
	Thousands of units, not seasonally adjusted				Millions of units, seasonally adjusted annual rate						
	Total	0–14,000 pounds		14,001 pounds and over	Total	0–14,000 pounds		14,001 pounds and over	Total	Domestic	Foreign
		Domestic	Foreign			Domestic	Foreign				
1970	...	1 408.5	...	337.3	...	1.408	...	0.335	...	8.527	...
1971	...	1 693.0	...	338.9	...	1.700	...	0.339	...	10.362	...
1972	...	2 122.5	...	437.4	...	2.116	...	0.437	...	11.369	...
1973	...	2 509.4	...	495.7	...	2.513	...	0.495	...	12.102	...
1974	...	2 180.1	...	423.9	...	2.176	...	0.424	...	9.538	...
1975	...	2 052.6	...	298.3	...	2.055	...	0.298	...	9.006	...
1976	3 300.5	2 738.3	237.5	324.7	3.296	2.733	0.239	0.324	12.966	11.225	1.741
1977	3 813.0	3 112.8	323.1	377.1	3.818	3.116	0.324	0.378	14.486	12.088	2.399
1978	4 256.8	3 481.1	335.9	439.8	4.249	3.469	0.340	0.440	14.973	12.633	2.340
1979	3 589.7	2 730.2	469.4	390.1	3.599	2.740	0.469	0.390	13.768	10.970	2.798
1980	2 487.4	1 731.1	484.6	271.7	2.482	1.731	0.480	0.271	11.192	8.312	2.881
1981	2 255.6	1 581.7	447.6	226.3	2.255	1.585	0.444	0.226	10.564	7.794	2.770
1982	2 562.8	1 967.5	410.4	184.9	2.569	1.971	0.413	0.185	10.363	7.729	2.634
1983	3 117.3	2 465.2	463.3	188.8	3.130	2.480	0.461	0.189	12.120	9.273	2.846
1984	4 093.1	3 207.2	607.7	278.2	4.085	3.199	0.609	0.278	14.197	11.150	3.047
1985	4 741.7	3 618.4	828.3	295.0	4.759	3.634	0.831	0.295	15.443	11.838	3.604
1986	4 912.1	3 671.4	967.2	273.5	4.918	3.676	0.969	0.273	16.051	11.891	4.160
1987	4 991.5	3 792.0	912.2	287.3	4.977	3.783	0.907	0.288	14.861	10.864	3.997
1988	5 231.9	4 199.7	697.9	334.3	5.225	4.194	0.697	0.334	15.436	11.733	3.703
1989	5 055.9	4 113.6	630.3	312.0	5.065	4.123	0.629	0.313	14.529	11.201	3.328
1990	4 837.0	3 956.8	602.7	277.5	4.841	3.960	0.602	0.278	13.863	10.857	3.006
1991	4 355.4	3 605.6	528.8	221.0	4.360	3.612	0.528	0.221	12.314	9.748	2.566
1992	4 892.2	4 247.0	395.9	249.3	4.894	4.247	0.398	0.248	12.860	10.524	2.336
1993	5 667.8	5 000.5	364.5	302.8	5.658	4.991	0.365	0.302	13.874	11.725	2.148
1994	6 407.3	5 658.2	396.3	352.8	6.408	5.659	0.395	0.354	15.044	12.914	2.130
1995	6 469.8	5 690.9	390.5	388.4	6.486	5.703	0.393	0.390	14.732	12.832	1.900
1996	6 921.8	6 131.8	430.9	359.1	6.914	6.127	0.429	0.357	15.083	13.381	1.702
1997	7 217.8	6 270.4	571.2	376.2	7.229	6.283	0.570	0.376	15.126	13.190	1.936
1998	7 815.8	6 745.3	646.2	424.3	7.788	6.720	0.644	0.425	15.506	13.484	2.022
1999	8 704.2	7 420.0	762.9	521.3	8.713	7.429	0.763	0.521	16.888	14.411	2.478
2000	8 953.5	7 650.8	840.8	461.9	8.951	7.649	0.841	0.461	17.342	14.481	2.861
2001	9 046.3	7 718.4	977.8	350.1	9.043	7.715	0.978	0.350	17.115	14.038	3.078
2002	9 035.6	7 646.9	1 066.3	322.4	9.035	7.647	1.066	0.322	16.816	13.518	3.298
2003	9 357.0	7 801.4	1 227.2	328.4	9.356	7.802	1.227	0.328	16.643	13.329	3.315
2004	9 753.3	8 075.5	1 246.2	431.6	9.751	8.076	1.246	0.429	16.867	13.472	3.395
2005	9 724.9	8 012.9	1 215.5	496.5	9.725	8.012	1.215	0.497	16.948	13.545	3.402
2006	9 227.8	7 336.8	1 346.6	544.4	9.229	7.337	1.347	0.545	16.504	12.813	3.691
2007	8 841.8	7 082.6	1 388.1	371.1	8.843	7.083	1.388	0.373	16.089	12.336	3.753
2008	6 680.0	5 285.0	1 096.5	298.5	6.680	5.285	1.097	0.298	13.195	9.820	3.375
2009	5 145.1	4 061.1	884.2	199.8	5.145	4.061	0.884	0.199	10.402	7.674	2.728
2010	6 043.6	4 927.3	898.7	217.6	6.043	4.927	0.899	0.217	11.555	8.812	2.743
2011	6 846.8	5 558.2	982.5	306.1	6.866	5.558	0.982	0.326	12.733	9.805	2.928
2012	7 426.4	6 019.8	1 060.8	345.8	7.404	5.999	1.060	0.346	14.432	11.242	3.190
2010											
January	350.8	279.6	55.3	15.9	5.384	4.374	0.786	0.224	10.690	8.111	2.579
February	394.0	321.5	57.6	14.9	5.141	4.174	0.763	0.204	10.118	7.695	2.423
March	542.8	434.4	88.1	20.3	6.049	4.874	0.959	0.216	11.474	8.839	2.635
April	496.1	408.8	70.4	16.9	5.871	4.829	0.838	0.204	11.099	8.620	2.479
May	554.8	464.9	73.1	16.8	6.216	5.161	0.846	0.209	11.716	9.140	2.576
June	500.5	415.0	66.3	19.2	5.888	4.838	0.839	0.211	11.390	8.730	2.660
July	541.7	441.3	81.7	18.7	6.087	4.953	0.899	0.235	11.675	8.896	2.779
August	512.6	413.7	81.7	17.2	6.154	5.000	0.938	0.216	11.821	8.906	2.915
September	502.6	410.1	74.5	18.0	6.070	4.910	0.939	0.221	11.774	8.838	2.936
October	520.1	424.0	77.6	18.5	6.496	5.316	0.963	0.217	12.196	9.196	3.000
November	484.5	389.0	77.1	18.4	6.541	5.304	1.010	0.227	12.194	9.223	2.971
December	643.1	525.0	95.3	22.8	6.621	5.395	1.003	0.223	12.510	9.546	2.964
2011											
January	447.3	357.8	71.5	18.0	6.838	5.572	1.014	0.252	12.512	9.615	2.897
February	518.8	418.9	80.5	19.4	6.763	5.434	1.063	0.266	12.825	9.778	3.047
March	614.9	489.4	100.0	25.5	6.527	5.216	1.038	0.273	12.753	9.656	3.097
April	569.1	464.3	81.8	23.0	6.730	5.482	0.962	0.286	12.909	9.895	3.014
May	539.9	443.3	71.5	25.1	6.342	5.161	0.875	0.306	11.871	9.075	2.796
June	552.1	452.9	71.7	27.5	6.186	5.008	0.874	0.304	11.680	8.962	2.718
July	576.2	472.2	80.3	23.7	6.817	5.588	0.921	0.308	12.362	9.586	2.776
August	591.0	478.5	84.9	27.6	6.878	5.600	0.950	0.328	12.419	9.696	2.723
September	594.5	482.1	85.1	27.3	7.284	5.893	1.056	0.335	13.093	10.145	2.948
October	569.6	462.8	77.8	29.0	7.149	5.804	1.005	0.340	13.294	10.302	2.992
November	558.2	453.1	78.4	26.7	7.273	5.944	0.999	0.330	13.510	10.441	3.069
December	715.2	582.9	99.0	33.3	7.363	5.994	1.031	0.338	13.566	10.505	3.061
2012											
January	469.6	370.8	74.3	24.5	7.159	5.771	1.053	0.335	13.929	10.761	3.168
February	564.0	455.1	82.0	26.9	7.154	5.752	1.053	0.349	14.429	11.065	3.364
March	673.7	537.1	104.8	31.8	7.123	5.725	1.049	0.349	14.088	10.881	3.207
April	581.5	470.5	82.6	28.4	7.301	5.875	1.063	0.363	14.081	10.896	3.185
May	680.1	553.0	95.3	31.8	7.375	5.915	1.091	0.369	13.897	10.849	3.048
June	657.2	536.0	90.9	30.3	7.485	6.063	1.079	0.343	14.334	11.239	3.095
July	599.6	484.4	86.3	28.9	7.328	5.913	1.049	0.366	14.041	10.964	3.077
August	665.2	544.4	90.5	30.3	7.497	6.169	0.967	0.361	14.462	11.521	2.941
September	614.8	502.1	86.2	26.5	7.620	6.178	1.093	0.349	14.879	11.553	3.326
October	576.2	472.3	75.1	28.8	7.159	5.880	0.967	0.312	14.232	11.113	3.119
November	604.8	489.1	90.0	25.7	7.815	6.371	1.124	0.320	15.482	12.047	3.435
December	739.7	605.0	102.8	31.9	7.837	6.372	1.126	0.339	15.325	12.012	3.313

. . . = Not available.

Table 16-9. Retail and Food Services Sales

(All retail establishments and food services; millions of dollars; not seasonally adjusted.)

Year and month	Retail and food services, total [1]	Retail (NAICS industry categories)											Food services and drinking places
		GAFO (department store type goods), total [2]	Motor vehicles and parts	Furniture and home furnishings	Electronics and appliances	Building materials and garden	Food and beverages	Health and personal care	Gasoline	Clothing and accessories	General merchandise	Nonstore retailers	
1992	2 014 096	533 388	418 393	52 336	42 631	130 989	370 513	89 699	156 324	120 103	247 876	78 501	202 865
1993	2 153 090	570 782	472 916	55 456	48 614	140 964	374 516	92 589	162 376	124 749	265 996	85 811	215 467
1994	2 330 231	616 347	541 141	60 416	57 266	157 228	384 340	96 359	171 222	129 083	285 190	96 280	225 000
1995	2 450 625	650 040	579 715	63 470	64 770	164 561	390 386	101 632	181 113	131 333	300 498	103 516	233 012
1996	2 603 791	682 613	627 507	67 707	68 363	176 683	401 073	109 554	194 425	136 581	315 305	117 761	242 245
1997	2 726 129	713 387	653 817	72 715	70 061	191 063	409 373	118 670	199 700	140 293	331 363	126 190	257 364
1998	2 852 955	757 936	688 415	77 412	74 527	202 423	416 525	129 582	191 727	149 151	351 081	133 904	271 194
1999	3 086 988	815 665	764 204	84 294	78 977	218 290	433 699	142 697	212 524	159 751	380 179	151 797	283 900
2000	3 287 536	862 739	796 210	91 170	82 206	228 994	444 764	155 233	249 816	167 674	404 228	180 453	304 261
2001	3 378 905	882 700	815 579	91 484	80 240	239 379	462 429	166 532	251 383	167 287	427 468	180 563	316 638
2002	3 459 077	912 707	818 811	94 438	83 740	248 539	464 856	179 983	250 619	172 304	446 520	189 279	330 525
2003	3 612 704	946 361	841 588	96 736	86 689	263 463	474 385	192 426	275 187	178 694	468 771	206 359	349 726
2004	3 847 125	1 004 411	866 372	103 757	94 416	295 274	490 380	199 290	324 006	190 253	497 382	228 977	373 557
2005	4 086 625	1 060 478	888 307	109 120	101 340	320 802	508 484	210 085	378 923	200 969	528 385	255 579	396 463
2006	4 296 871	1 112 667	899 997	112 795	107 989	334 130	525 232	223 336	421 976	213 189	554 256	284 343	422 786
2007	4 443 807	1 147 500	910 139	111 144	110 673	320 854	547 837	237 164	451 822	221 205	578 582	308 767	444 551
2008	4 402 508	1 143 031	787 079	99 560	108 663	304 556	569 735	246 787	502 983	215 776	596 358	319 283	456 102
2009	4 082 092	1 097 323	674 002	86 258	98 030	266 975	569 314	253 245	389 774	204 813	591 682	311 891	451 684
2010	4 307 947	1 125 548	746 120	87 290	99 128	267 950	581 929	261 128	445 962	213 720	607 989	342 041	466 493
2011	4 631 122	1 169 526	819 929	90 073	101 455	279 068	612 012	272 073	529 093	229 312	630 256	378 712	494 770
2012	4 881 385	1 221 410	882 951	97 393	100 987	294 255	631 970	278 080	550 585	242 495	655 970	408 151	531 107
2010													
January	316 127	80 725	49 975	6 466	7 587	15 714	47 147	20 799	34 007	13 234	44 144	27 591	35 517
February	312 513	82 236	51 988	6 617	7 836	15 853	44 335	20 195	31 763	14 841	45 054	25 913	35 361
March	362 497	90 696	67 683	7 447	7 736	22 236	48 209	22 557	37 067	17 418	48 980	28 841	39 380
April	358 296	87 735	64 609	6 898	7 115	27 490	47 146	21 548	38 112	17 073	48 072	26 517	39 392
May	367 552	92 195	65 484	7 102	7 578	26 990	49 760	21 410	38 954	17 764	50 833	25 518	40 775
June	360 583	89 064	64 921	7 079	7 934	26 193	47 929	21 535	38 020	16 170	48 638	26 796	39 396
July	363 815	90 329	67 289	7 426	7 905	23 731	49 849	21 401	38 850	16 871	48 977	25 216	40 992
August	364 503	94 132	66 343	7 514	8 086	22 301	48 511	21 652	38 336	17 932	49 679	27 212	40 265
September	347 868	86 556	61 956	7 274	7 618	21 866	47 620	21 344	36 944	16 256	46 005	27 294	38 313
October	357 197	90 122	61 712	6 957	7 305	22 581	48 737	21 832	38 241	17 449	49 390	27 679	40 076
November	367 894	103 676	59 187	7 814	9 470	22 110	48 989	21 893	36 836	20 058	55 976	31 982	37 372
December	429 102	138 082	64 973	8 696	12 958	20 885	53 697	24 962	38 832	28 654	72 241	41 482	39 654
2011													
January	337 608	81 299	58 406	6 377	7 530	16 469	48 590	22 217	37 758	13 730	44 624	31 040	36 837
February	339 459	84 637	63 255	6 619	7 757	16 462	45 748	21 272	36 418	15 954	46 099	28 889	37 257
March	389 616	93 397	76 046	7 682	8 179	22 641	49 948	23 600	44 036	18 276	49 994	32 049	41 877
April	383 323	92 789	70 352	7 042	7 305	25 223	50 835	22 227	45 470	18 681	50 810	28 652	41 610
May	394 799	94 603	70 085	7 243	7 620	28 725	51 741	22 753	47 858	18 816	51 795	29 333	42 858
June	391 511	93 473	70 954	7 204	7 869	28 028	51 336	22 377	47 150	17 827	51 287	29 262	41 920
July	387 259	93 548	69 900	7 426	8 005	24 274	52 830	21 879	47 774	17 982	51 084	27 181	43 194
August	397 392	98 619	71 940	7 904	8 428	24 548	51 865	23 015	47 907	19 293	51 741	30 512	42 338
September	377 707	91 921	67 434	7 686	7 711	23 300	50 185	22 240	45 033	18 042	48 716	29 674	41 392
October	382 545	93 814	66 283	7 223	7 829	24 036	51 127	22 609	44 729	18 325	51 434	30 928	42 484
November	394 377	107 561	64 184	8 248	10 145	23 259	51 552	22 460	42 614	21 056	57 865	36 557	39 875
December	455 526	143 865	71 090	9 419	13 077	22 103	56 255	25 424	42 346	31 330	74 807	44 635	43 128
2012													
January	358 313	85 134	62 182	7 207	7 671	18 733	49 995	22 967	41 024	14 449	46 463	32 721	39 987
February	376 066	93 177	70 375	7 554	8 089	19 292	49 008	22 871	41 826	18 074	50 587	31 917	41 374
March	418 324	100 946	81 129	8 238	8 317	25 251	52 765	24 151	47 899	20 318	54 191	33 279	46 202
April	397 263	93 878	73 313	7 320	7 043	27 300	51 066	22 936	47 192	18 769	51 671	30 615	44 373
May	423 323	100 264	79 512	8 204	7 772	30 812	54 213	23 725	48 722	20 181	54 247	32 456	46 117
June	405 484	97 949	75 587	7 892	7 789	26 988	52 977	22 382	46 033	18 926	53 440	30 555	45 510
July	400 379	95 945	74 800	8 081	7 962	24 983	53 168	22 525	46 222	18 480	51 863	30 435	45 152
August	422 544	104 401	80 204	8 656	8 228	25 242	53 792	23 356	49 726	20 963	54 889	33 094	45 607
September	390 169	94 340	70 863	7 960	7 572	23 323	51 501	21 723	46 782	18 643	50 410	31 109	43 697
October	404 534	96 422	71 857	7 785	7 409	25 774	52 666	23 225	48 658	19 119	52 507	34 371	44 206
November	416 397	112 361	69 299	8 783	10 077	24 503	53 352	22 676	44 150	22 368	60 292	40 053	43 074
December	468 589	146 593	73 830	9 713	13 058	22 054	57 467	25 543	42 351	32 205	75 410	47 546	45 808

[1]Includes store categories not shown separately.
[2]Includes furniture, home furnishings, electronics, appliances, clothing, sporting goods, hobby, book, music, general merchandise, office supplies, stationery, and gifts.

Table 16-9. Retail and Food Services Sales—*Continued*

(All retail establishments and food services; millions of dollars; seasonally adjusted.)

Year and month	Total	Retail and food services										
		Retail (NAICS industry categories)										
		Total	GAFO (department store type goods) [2]	Motor vehicles and parts	Furniture and home furnishings	Electronics and appliances	Building materials and garden	Food and beverages			Health and personal care	Gasoline
								Total [1]	Groceries	Beer, wine, and liquor		
1992	2 014 096	1 811 231	533 388	418 393	52 336	42 631	130 989	370 513	337 370	21 687	89 699	156 324
1993	2 153 090	1 937 623	570 782	472 916	55 456	48 614	140 964	374 516	341 318	21 538	92 589	162 376
1994	2 330 231	2 105 231	616 347	541 141	60 416	57 266	157 228	384 340	350 523	22 101	96 359	171 222
1995	2 450 625	2 217 613	650 040	579 715	63 470	64 770	164 561	390 386	356 409	22 007	101 632	181 113
1996	2 603 791	2 361 546	682 613	627 507	67 707	68 363	176 683	401 073	365 547	23 157	109 554	194 425
1997	2 726 129	2 468 765	713 387	653 817	72 715	70 061	191 063	409 373	372 570	24 081	118 670	199 700
1998	2 852 955	2 581 761	757 936	688 415	77 412	74 527	202 423	416 525	378 188	25 382	129 582	191 727
1999	3 086 988	2 803 088	815 665	764 204	84 294	78 977	218 290	433 699	394 250	26 476	142 697	212 524
2000	3 287 536	2 983 275	862 739	796 210	91 170	82 206	228 994	444 764	402 515	28 507	155 233	249 816
2001	3 378 905	3 062 267	882 700	815 579	91 484	80 240	239 379	462 429	418 127	29 621	166 532	251 383
2002	3 459 077	3 128 552	912 707	818 811	94 438	83 740	248 539	464 856	419 813	29 894	179 983	250 619
2003	3 612 704	3 262 978	946 361	841 588	96 736	86 689	263 463	474 385	427 987	30 469	192 426	275 187
2004	3 847 125	3 473 568	1 004 411	866 372	103 757	94 416	295 274	490 380	441 136	32 189	199 290	324 006
2005	4 086 625	3 690 162	1 060 478	888 307	109 120	101 340	320 802	508 484	457 667	33 567	210 085	378 923
2006	4 296 871	3 874 085	1 112 667	899 997	112 795	107 989	334 130	525 232	471 699	36 016	223 336	421 976
2007	4 443 807	3 999 256	1 147 500	910 139	111 144	110 673	320 854	547 837	491 360	38 128	237 164	451 822
2008	4 402 508	3 946 406	1 143 031	787 079	99 560	108 663	304 556	569 735	511 388	39 522	246 787	502 983
2009	4 082 092	3 630 408	1 097 323	674 002	86 258	98 030	266 975	569 314	510 330	40 283	253 245	389 774
2010	4 307 947	3 841 454	1 125 548	746 120	87 290	99 128	267 950	581 929	521 233	41 460	261 128	445 962
2011	4 631 122	4 136 352	1 169 526	819 929	90 073	101 455	279 068	612 012	549 109	42 603	272 073	529 093
2012	4 881 385	4 350 278	1 221 410	882 951	97 393	100 987	294 255	631 970	565 602	44 134	278 080	550 585
2010												
January	347 854	310 389	92 619	57 412	7 137	8 209	21 079	47 999	43 089	3 391	21 116	37 085
February	348 269	309 958	93 476	55 881	7 295	8 443	20 940	48 777	43 747	3 456	21 280	36 720
March	356 067	317 572	93 852	60 880	7 381	8 136	22 390	48 425	43 368	3 457	21 422	36 919
April	358 200	319 505	93 713	61 474	7 330	8 239	24 083	48 206	43 126	3 471	21 570	36 930
May	356 231	317 582	93 242	62 031	7 269	8 305	22 313	48 289	43 289	3 420	21 410	36 440
June	355 935	317 159	93 400	61 717	7 253	8 420	22 140	48 069	43 043	3 440	21 753	35 666
July	356 446	317 517	93 163	63 083	7 266	8 268	22 075	47 765	42 797	3 384	21 793	35 642
August	359 108	319 825	93 740	62 994	7 324	8 178	21 955	48 557	43 456	3 490	21 937	36 098
September	361 534	322 239	93 672	63 552	7 289	8 350	22 167	48 680	43 571	3 480	22 050	37 204
October	366 758	327 313	94 261	65 587	7 270	8 279	22 794	48 836	43 689	3 512	22 164	38 511
November	369 001	329 370	95 801	65 440	7 276	8 164	22 542	49 289	44 134	3 500	22 294	38 898
December	371 152	331 498	94 691	65 582	7 211	8 250	22 829	49 396	44 325	3 447	22 347	40 662
2011												
January	373 430	334 074	94 342	66 986	7 093	8 219	22 117	49 853	44 757	3 478	22 487	41 311
February	376 425	336 147	95 645	67 677	7 282	8 315	21 751	50 210	45 017	3 537	22 392	41 860
March	380 141	340 141	96 619	68 024	7 539	8 476	22 543	50 268	45 151	3 501	22 584	43 343
April	382 726	342 210	97 297	67 574	7 507	8 446	22 651	50 976	45 828	3 486	22 294	44 232
May	382 866	341 932	96 752	66 295	7 376	8 370	23 064	50 799	45 636	3 498	22 595	45 064
June	385 784	344 524	97 585	67 512	7 404	8 392	23 589	51 132	45 884	3 549	22 672	44 356
July	386 747	345 531	97 440	68 050	7 441	8 464	23 619	51 242	45 987	3 561	22 673	44 607
August	387 099	345 591	97 690	66 656	7 535	8 481	23 685	51 484	46 216	3 574	22 878	44 857
September	389 985	348 048	98 727	68 899	7 633	8 424	23 581	51 251	45 946	3 605	22 928	44 809
October	394 706	352 349	98 971	70 480	7 684	8 902	24 134	51 595	46 222	3 595	23 023	44 954
November	395 729	353 399	99 168	70 949	7 708	8 664	23 813	51 725	46 370	3 615	22 942	45 142
December	394 282	351 833	98 528	71 576	7 797	8 346	24 364	51 385	46 098	3 542	22 925	44 249
2012												
January	397 083	354 040	99 915	70 976	7 955	8 386	24 518	51 941	46 507	3 631	22 990	45 032
February	402 385	358 925	101 378	72 220	7 994	8 353	24 495	51 811	46 429	3 616	23 149	46 319
March	405 211	361 459	101 842	72 557	8 014	8 527	25 561	52 148	46 678	3 642	23 178	46 594
April	403 892	359 696	100 783	72 230	8 053	8 295	24 525	52 547	47 079	3 657	23 309	46 403
May	403 815	359 810	101 380	73 021	8 131	8 413	24 011	52 359	46 850	3 684	23 192	45 620
June	400 197	356 353	101 180	72 650	8 094	8 322	23 514	52 414	46 930	3 660	22 839	43 509
July	402 831	358 780	101 848	72 665	8 171	8 452	23 862	52 656	47 153	3 645	23 222	43 483
August	407 723	363 616	101 892	74 211	8 158	8 302	24 349	52 533	47 065	3 608	23 171	46 128
September	412 031	367 488	102 104	75 461	8 172	8 397	24 890	53 075	47 541	3 660	23 085	47 112
October	411 939	367 332	102 238	73 909	8 118	8 360	24 627	53 312	47 748	3 695	23 064	48 464
November	413 435	368 379	102 236	75 795	8 170	8 503	24 981	53 129	47 512	3 727	23 115	46 182
December	414 652	368 935	102 563	76 798	8 302	8 458	25 062	53 337	47 563	3 830	23 412	44 959

[1] Includes store categories not shown separately.
[2] Includes furniture, home furnishings, electronics, appliances, clothing, sporting goods, hobby, book, music, general merchandise, office supplies, stationery, and gifts.

Table 16-10. Quarterly Retail Sales: Total and E-Commerce

Year and quarter	Retail sales (millions of dollars)		E-commerce as a percent of total sales	Percent change from prior quarter		Percent change from same quarter a year ago	
	Total	E-commerce		Total sales	E-commerce sales	Total sales	E-commerce sales
NOT SEASONALLY ADJUSTED							
2010							
1st quarter	888 667	37 166	4.2	-8.9	-18.6	6.6	14.4
2nd quarter	978 726	37 718	3.9	10.1	1.5	7.4	14.6
3rd quarter	970 155	39 230	4.0	-0.9	4.0	5.7	14.9
4rd quarter	1 051 917	53 225	5.1	8.4	35.7	7.8	16.5
2011							
1st quarter	965 068	43 713	4.5	-8.3	-17.9	8.6	17.6
2nd quarter	1 061 124	44 224	4.2	10.0	1.2	8.4	17.2
3rd quarter	1 049 523	44 550	4.2	-1.1	0.7	8.2	13.6
4rd quarter	1 112 422	61 765	5.6	6.9	37.6	7.2	15.8
2012							
1st quarter	1 029 472	50 295	4.9	-7.5	-18.6	7.9	15.4
2nd quarter	1 093 057	51 203	4.7	6.2	1.8	4.4	15.1
3rd quarter	1 080 510	52 492	4.9	-1.1	2.5	3.9	17.0
4rd quarter	1 156 898	71 554	6.2	7.1	36.3	4.0	15.8
SEASONALLY ADJUSTED							
1999							
4th quarter	724 737	4 571	0.6	2.2	. . .	9.0	. . .
2000							
1st quarter	742 333	5 824	0.8	2.4	27.4	9.3	. . .
2nd quarter	741 582	6 504	0.9	-0.1	11.7	7.0	. . .
3rd quarter	747 819	7 388	1.0	0.8	13.6	5.4	. . .
4th quarter	753 245	7 858	1.0	0.7	6.4	3.9	71.9
2001							
1st quarter	756 957	8 253	1.1	0.5	5.0	2.0	41.7
2nd quarter	764 827	8 418	1.1	1.0	2.0	3.1	29.4
3rd quarter	759 081	8 355	1.1	-0.8	-0.7	1.5	13.1
4th quarter	787 100	9 422	1.2	3.7	12.8	4.5	19.9
2002							
1st quarter	772 932	10 097	1.3	-1.8	7.2	2.1	22.3
2nd quarter	779 542	10 870	1.4	0.9	7.7	1.9	29.1
3rd quarter	789 978	11 631	1.5	1.3	7.0	4.1	39.2
4th quarter	792 817	12 409	1.6	0.4	6.7	0.7	31.7
2003							
1st quarter	799 504	13 003	1.6	0.8	4.8	3.4	28.8
2nd quarter	806 000	14 011	1.7	0.8	7.8	3.4	28.9
3rd quarter	829 025	15 062	1.8	2.9	7.5	4.9	29.5
4th quarter	832 261	15 855	1.9	0.4	5.3	5.0	27.8
2004							
1st quarter	847 868	17 097	2.0	1.9	7.8	6.0	31.5
2nd quarter	857 215	17 872	2.1	1.1	4.5	6.4	27.6
3rd quarter	870 400	18 926	2.2	1.5	5.9	5.0	25.7
4th quarter	892 367	20 025	2.2	2.5	5.8	7.2	26.3
2005							
1st quarter	900 378	21 227	2.4	0.9	6.0	6.2	24.2
2nd quarter	918 660	22 523	2.5	2.0	6.1	7.2	26.0
3rd quarter	935 577	24 043	2.6	1.8	6.7	7.5	27.0
4rd quarter	939 298	24 712	2.6	0.4	2.8	5.3	23.4
2006							
1st quarter	966 148	26 770	2.8	2.9	8.3	7.3	26.1
2nd quarter	968 895	27 717	2.9	0.3	3.5	5.5	23.1
3rd quarter	975 174	29 184	3.0	0.6	5.3	4.2	21.4
4th quarter	975 660	30 670	3.1	0.0	5.1	3.9	24.1
2007							
1st quarter	989 144	32 350	3.3	1.4	5.5	2.4	20.8
2nd quarter	997 157	34 032	3.4	0.8	5.2	2.9	22.8
3rd quarter	1 005 154	34 975	3.5	0.8	2.8	3.1	19.8
4th quarter	1 016 641	36 207	3.6	1.1	3.5	4.2	18.1
2008							
1st quarter	1 010 490	36 244	3.6	-0.6	0.1	2.2	12.0
2nd quarter	1 016 290	36 691	3.6	0.6	1.2	1.9	7.8
3rd quarter	1 002 911	36 180	3.6	-1.3	-1.4	-0.2	3.4
4th quarter	915 673	33 393	3.6	-8.7	-7.7	-9.9	-7.8
2009							
1st quarter	895 260	34 151	3.8	-2.2	2.3	-11.4	-5.8
2nd quarter	896 957	35 133	3.9	0.2	2.9	-11.7	-4.2
3rd quarter	918 917	36 909	4.0	2.4	5.1	-8.4	2.0
4rd quarter	928 333	38 269	4.1	1.0	3.7	1.4	14.6
2010							
1st quarter	948 172	39 159	4.1	2.1	2.3	5.9	14.7
2nd quarter	963 389	40 472	4.2	1.6	3.4	7.4	15.2
3rd quarter	972 440	42 381	4.4	0.9	4.7	5.8	14.8
4th quarter	1 003 118	44 485	4.4	3.1	4.9	8.1	16.2
2011							
1st quarter	1 029 862	46 131	4.5	2.7	3.7	8.6	17.8
2nd quarter	1 041 406	47 352	4.5	1.1	2.6	8.1	17.2
3rd quarter	1 053 190	48 567	4.6	1.1	2.6	8.3	14.5
4th quarter	1 064 205	51 497	4.8	1.9	6.0	7.4	14.9
2012							
1st quarter	1 080 064	53 091	4.9	1.5	3.1	6.2	15.3
2nd quarter	1 076 950	54 936	5.1	-0.3	3.5	4.3	15.5
3rd quarter	1 091 897	57 034	5.2	1.4	3.8	4.6	17.4
4rd quarter	1 106 823	59 545	5.4	1.4	4.4	4.0	15.6

. . . = Not available.

Table 16-11. Retail Inventories

(All retail stores; end of period, millions of dollars.)

Year and month	Not seasonally adjusted			Seasonally adjusted							General merchandise	
	Total	Excluding motor vehicles and parts	Motor vehicles and parts	Total	Excluding motor vehicles and parts	Motor vehicles and parts	Furniture, home furnishings, electronics, and appliances	Building materials and garden	Food and beverages	Clothing and accessories	Total	Department stores [1]
1992	256 166	184 700	71 466	260 276	191 118	69 158	16 183	21 099	27 408	27 390	49 306	37 878
1993	274 071	196 418	77 653	278 444	203 310	75 134	18 113	22 621	27 498	28 080	53 283	40 458
1994	299 812	211 223	88 589	304 519	218 757	85 762	20 397	24 857	28 112	29 518	56 581	41 908
1995	317 304	220 921	96 383	322 216	228 842	93 374	21 817	26 337	28 718	29 298	59 530	43 455
1996	328 160	227 888	100 272	333 255	236 015	97 240	22 253	27 447	29 658	29 778	60 591	44 124
1997	338 789	234 269	104 520	343 824	242 517	101 307	22 109	28 897	29 891	31 079	60 715	44 309
1998	351 252	245 397	105 855	356 515	253 885	102 630	22 662	30 921	30 837	32 308	61 542	43 438
1999	378 809	259 875	118 934	384 074	268 563	115 511	24 093	33 005	32 635	33 735	64 297	43 835
2000	400 391	268 979	131 412	405 928	277 826	128 102	25 620	34 269	32 108	36 753	64 929	42 667
2001	387 858	266 369	121 489	393 637	274 795	118 842	24 496	34 235	33 165	35 627	64 790	40 464
2002	409 314	271 757	137 557	415 018	280 121	134 897	25 853	36 086	32 907	37 361	65 978	38 750
2003	425 790	277 513	148 277	431 201	285 670	145 531	27 195	37 398	32 504	38 462	66 655	36 823
2004	454 938	297 651	157 287	460 364	305 970	154 394	30 164	41 593	33 433	41 372	70 969	37 230
2005	466 267	310 609	155 658	472 075	319 217	152 858	30 713	45 150	33 773	43 113	74 349	38 140
2006	481 302	324 779	156 523	487 380	333 759	153 621	31 177	47 176	34 681	47 504	75 938	37 354
2007	495 794	335 693	160 101	501 959	344 654	157 305	31 915	49 381	36 448	47 745	76 339	36 752
2008	474 040	325 487	148 553	480 050	333 877	146 173	28 405	47 289	37 234	46 518	73 563	33 533
2009	427 235	311 610	115 625	433 271	319 164	114 107	26 300	44 022	37 211	41 534	70 656	31 367
2010	453 825	324 375	129 450	460 062	332 131	127 931	27 955	44 770	38 571	42 818	74 568	31 584
2011	471 369	336 043	135 326	477 993	344 136	133 857	27 121	45 876	40 278	45 504	77 868	31 800
2012	509 252	346 684	162 568	516 297	355 294	161 003	27 540	47 804	41 312	47 872	79 751	30 783
2009												
January	461 691	320 536	141 155	471 681	332 003	139 678	28 031	46 700	37 603	46 033	73 175	33 154
February	459 040	320 944	138 096	465 947	330 948	134 999	27 627	46 511	37 634	46 231	72 635	32 999
March	460 939	324 416	136 523	460 883	328 786	132 097	27 324	46 382	37 717	45 255	72 953	33 244
April	456 584	323 055	133 529	455 454	326 722	128 732	27 195	45 732	37 720	44 579	72 337	32 960
May	442 788	318 427	124 361	447 181	324 396	122 785	26 872	45 185	37 799	44 070	72 014	32 747
June	436 030	316 504	119 526	442 444	323 466	118 978	26 695	44 533	37 618	43 641	72 141	32 958
July	426 520	316 218	110 302	437 204	322 449	114 755	26 492	44 187	37 696	43 186	71 758	32 574
August	417 160	317 459	99 701	425 896	320 918	104 978	26 456	43 909	37 563	42 716	71 228	32 525
September	431 369	326 742	104 627	429 000	318 936	110 064	26 528	43 745	37 626	42 073	70 903	32 528
October	454 559	343 483	111 076	431 576	319 664	111 912	27 038	43 564	37 773	41 816	71 143	32 248
November	461 009	345 585	115 424	432 101	318 778	113 323	26 381	42 961	37 879	41 752	71 104	32 012
December	427 235	311 610	115 625	433 271	319 164	114 107	26 300	44 022	37 211	41 534	70 656	31 367
2010												
January	423 799	308 274	115 525	433 302	318 855	114 447	26 359	43 652	37 707	41 317	70 323	31 815
February	427 638	308 864	118 774	434 742	318 591	116 151	26 307	43 619	37 783	41 272	69 918	31 600
March	437 390	316 835	120 555	438 126	321 214	116 912	26 645	43 785	38 013	41 364	71 322	31 330
April	440 069	319 533	120 536	439 833	323 192	116 641	26 761	44 047	37 856	41 644	71 951	31 489
May	435 348	317 846	117 502	439 869	323 567	116 302	27 206	44 492	37 790	41 802	71 854	31 322
June	438 431	317 590	120 841	444 847	324 336	120 511	27 291	44 100	37 867	41 895	72 416	31 355
July	437 142	318 899	118 243	448 421	325 357	123 064	27 328	43 905	37 842	42 012	73 143	31 640
August	442 731	323 016	119 715	452 088	326 323	125 765	27 474	43 811	37 866	42 035	73 434	31 555
September	459 132	335 946	123 186	457 345	328 065	129 280	27 650	43 946	38 073	42 142	73 869	31 299
October	479 646	352 130	127 516	456 337	328 168	128 169	27 580	44 000	38 165	42 274	73 769	31 417
November	487 013	356 599	130 414	457 330	329 433	127 897	27 793	44 345	38 332	42 070	74 291	31 851
December	453 825	324 375	129 450	460 062	332 131	127 931	27 955	44 770	38 571	42 818	74 568	31 584
2011												
January	450 734	322 139	128 595	460 343	332 941	127 402	27 812	44 920	38 837	43 015	74 357	31 615
February	450 690	322 843	127 847	457 993	332 876	125 117	27 481	45 054	38 861	43 332	74 244	31 597
March	463 804	332 539	131 265	464 648	337 142	127 506	27 824	45 422	38 970	43 811	76 147	31 991
April	465 372	333 827	131 545	465 263	337 649	127 614	27 703	45 495	39 434	44 058	75 789	31 808
May	462 088	332 665	129 423	466 553	338 343	128 210	27 448	45 450	39 488	44 375	75 934	31 954
June	460 507	332 325	128 182	467 120	339 160	127 960	27 519	45 448	39 565	44 386	76 260	31 723
July	454 525	331 799	122 726	466 223	338 639	127 584	27 398	45 399	39 801	44 442	75 999	31 667
August	461 857	337 851	124 006	471 065	341 079	129 986	27 425	45 494	40 042	44 990	76 767	31 847
September	475 075	349 778	125 297	472 780	341 705	131 075	27 062	45 851	40 131	45 333	77 012	31 971
October	497 214	366 239	130 975	473 271	341 862	131 409	27 121	45 928	40 098	45 692	76 974	31 826
November	506 654	370 919	135 735	476 468	343 360	133 108	27 077	45 947	40 250	45 732	77 140	31 684
December	471 369	336 043	135 326	477 993	344 136	133 857	27 121	45 876	40 278	45 504	77 868	31 800
2012												
January	471 766	333 414	138 352	481 106	344 285	136 821	27 228	46 115	40 334	45 780	77 834	31 424
February	478 376	336 254	142 122	485 232	346 080	139 152	27 354	46 507	40 641	45 801	78 174	31 272
March	487 642	341 837	145 805	488 169	346 322	141 847	27 361	46 472	40 942	46 097	77 686	30 735
April	492 256	342 891	149 365	492 002	346 916	145 086	27 407	46 829	40 756	46 024	77 823	30 988
May	493 228	343 846	149 382	497 192	349 236	147 956	27 628	46 999	40 868	46 277	78 652	31 043
June	493 169	342 465	150 704	499 817	349 378	150 439	27 667	46 945	40 942	47 108	78 159	30 936
July	492 529	344 202	148 327	505 696	351 350	154 346	27 467	47 236	41 095	47 528	78 586	30 844
August	498 307	348 970	149 337	508 506	352 058	156 448	27 357	47 505	41 086	47 411	78 821	30 714
September	511 301	359 973	151 328	510 163	352 120	158 043	27 180	47 737	41 235	47 383	78 184	30 107
October	537 221	378 508	158 713	513 002	353 731	159 271	27 408	47 819	41 094	47 236	79 256	30 626
November	544 455	381 416	163 039	513 758	353 819	159 939	27 515	47 738	41 216	47 372	78 546	30 319
December	509 252	346 684	162 568	516 297	355 294	161 003	27 540	47 804	41 312	47 872	79 751	30 783

[1] Excluding leased departments.

Table 16-12. Merchant Wholesalers—Sales and Inventories

(Millions of dollars.)

Classification basis, year, and month	Not seasonally adjusted						Seasonally adjusted					
	Sales			Inventories (current cost, end of period)			Sales			Inventories (current cost, end of period)		
	Total	Durable goods establishments	Nondurable goods establishments	Total	Durable goods establishments	Nondurable goods establishments	Total	Durable goods establishments	Nondurable goods establishments	Total	Durable goods establishments	Nondurable goods establishments
1992	1 767 130	861 182	905 948	197 793	121 809	75 984	1 767 130	861 182	905 948	196 914	123 435	73 479
1993	1 848 215	939 945	908 270	205 815	127 094	78 721	1 848 215	939 945	908 270	204 842	128 851	75 991
1994	1 974 899	1 037 638	937 261	222 826	139 941	82 885	1 974 899	1 037 638	937 261	221 978	141 975	80 003
1995	2 158 980	1 141 701	1 017 279	239 275	151 709	87 566	2 158 980	1 141 701	1 017 279	238 392	154 089	84 303
1996	2 284 343	1 190 342	1 094 001	241 396	154 207	87 189	2 284 343	1 190 342	1 094 001	241 058	156 683	84 375
1997	2 377 845	1 256 384	1 121 461	258 900	165 371	93 529	2 377 845	1 256 384	1 121 461	258 454	168 089	90 365
1998	2 427 120	1 306 545	1 120 575	272 575	175 994	96 581	2 427 120	1 306 545	1 120 575	272 297	178 918	93 379
1999	2 599 159	1 406 371	1 192 788	290 407	187 763	102 644	2 599 159	1 406 371	1 192 788	290 207	190 924	99 283
2000	2 814 554	1 486 673	1 327 881	309 764	198 579	111 185	2 814 554	1 486 673	1 327 881	309 246	201 852	107 394
2001	2 785 152	1 422 195	1 362 957	298 651	182 595	116 056	2 785 152	1 422 195	1 362 957	297 588	185 592	111 996
2002	2 835 528	1 421 503	1 414 025	302 807	182 242	120 565	2 835 528	1 421 503	1 414 025	301 436	185 168	116 268
2003	2 971 816	1 461 729	1 510 087	309 856	186 248	123 608	2 971 816	1 461 729	1 510 087	308 055	189 163	118 892
2004	3 316 403	1 680 871	1 635 532	340 823	212 937	127 886	3 316 403	1 680 871	1 635 532	339 431	215 994	123 437
2005	3 613 381	1 814 405	1 798 976	368 842	232 362	136 480	3 613 381	1 814 405	1 798 976	367 505	235 515	131 990
2006	3 904 209	1 982 844	1 921 365	399 872	255 356	144 516	3 904 209	1 982 844	1 921 365	398 586	258 709	139 877
2007	4 174 286	2 074 466	2 099 820	426 664	261 895	164 769	4 174 286	2 074 466	2 099 820	424 806	265 317	159 489
2008	4 431 775	2 076 292	2 355 483	442 903	276 183	166 720	4 431 775	2 076 292	2 355 483	442 249	279 821	162 428
2009	3 699 214	1 669 710	2 029 504	391 532	225 794	165 738	3 699 214	1 669 710	2 029 504	389 908	229 047	160 861
2010	4 132 327	1 875 793	2 256 534	432 070	245 126	186 944	4 132 327	1 875 793	2 256 534	429 260	248 656	180 604
2011	4 677 337	2 093 773	2 583 564	473 737	270 277	203 460	4 677 337	2 093 773	2 583 564	471 549	273 932	197 617
2012	4 917 053	2 209 254	2 707 799	499 350	291 033	208 317	4 917 053	2 209 254	2 707 799	498 617	296 390	202 227
2009												
January	285 273	127 460	157 813	439 622	274 541	165 081	303 793	138 908	164 885	437 149	276 170	160 979
February	275 290	125 387	149 903	431 101	268 267	162 834	307 019	142 104	164 915	428 205	268 074	160 131
March	307 718	142 345	165 373	420 549	258 941	161 608	295 975	135 547	160 428	419 310	260 086	159 224
April	302 964	135 168	167 796	412 284	253 287	158 997	297 636	133 612	164 024	413 387	254 063	159 324
May	297 782	129 668	168 114	403 261	247 658	155 603	300 286	133 753	166 533	407 902	248 490	159 412
June	320 293	145 101	175 192	398 392	243 903	154 489	303 299	135 353	167 946	400 549	243 690	156 859
July	312 954	140 291	172 663	393 589	240 947	152 642	306 855	137 693	169 162	394 516	239 148	155 368
August	308 908	139 060	169 848	385 665	235 306	150 359	309 842	139 226	170 616	389 443	234 872	154 571
September	319 451	146 586	172 865	384 720	234 068	150 652	311 756	140 577	171 179	384 913	232 481	152 432
October	326 959	149 679	177 280	388 990	234 617	154 373	314 528	142 102	172 426	386 270	232 216	154 054
November	312 021	138 971	173 050	394 236	232 363	161 873	323 648	144 375	179 273	391 806	231 271	160 535
December	329 601	149 994	179 607	391 532	225 794	165 738	324 983	146 015	178 968	389 908	229 047	160 861
2010												
January	299 417	130 256	169 161	393 383	227 679	165 704	327 364	146 690	180 674	390 649	229 174	161 475
February	297 448	131 058	166 390	394 687	230 408	164 279	331 658	148 602	183 056	391 435	230 238	161 197
March	359 964	162 949	197 015	395 175	231 526	163 649	336 103	150 520	185 583	393 490	232 864	160 626
April	348 835	157 124	191 711	393 721	232 513	161 208	341 364	154 373	186 991	394 596	233 543	161 053
May	337 917	150 849	187 068	392 039	233 863	158 176	340 153	155 679	184 474	395 833	234 779	161 054
June	357 010	166 453	190 557	394 079	235 291	158 788	338 780	156 095	182 685	396 106	235 086	161 020
July	340 666	155 952	184 714	400 334	239 055	161 279	342 513	157 213	185 300	401 395	237 148	164 247
August	354 056	163 489	190 567	401 437	239 947	161 490	344 468	158 028	186 440	406 020	239 350	166 670
September	352 836	165 060	187 776	410 725	243 088	167 637	346 293	158 842	187 451	412 226	241 354	170 872
October	357 257	163 104	194 153	424 846	247 043	177 803	354 528	160 381	194 147	421 311	244 266	177 045
November	358 994	161 624	197 370	426 159	247 069	179 090	361 015	162 670	198 345	423 206	245 833	177 373
December	367 927	167 875	200 052	432 070	245 126	186 944	363 906	163 732	200 174	429 260	248 656	180 604
2011												
January	345 734	149 369	196 365	438 921	249 071	189 850	376 856	168 122	208 734	434 085	250 761	183 324
February	336 398	146 728	189 670	443 425	252 437	190 988	374 427	166 312	208 115	437 988	252 397	185 591
March	413 865	185 368	228 497	446 738	252 144	194 594	385 965	171 199	214 766	443 400	253 561	189 839
April	387 872	167 507	220 365	446 154	254 378	191 776	388 422	170 447	217 975	446 698	255 169	191 529
May	396 558	169 324	227 234	450 017	259 192	190 825	387 450	169 355	218 095	454 999	259 858	195 141
June	407 610	182 970	224 640	452 861	263 133	189 728	390 895	173 118	217 777	457 671	262 722	194 949
July	376 195	168 341	207 854	457 918	267 569	190 349	391 887	176 497	215 390	460 836	265 039	195 797
August	417 221	192 248	224 973	455 522	268 534	186 988	397 050	180 839	216 211	462 975	268 234	194 741
September	402 955	187 199	215 756	457 333	270 679	186 654	396 544	179 790	216 754	459 782	269 321	190 461
October	400 006	181 802	218 204	469 385	274 489	194 896	399 229	179 780	219 449	466 544	271 658	194 886
November	394 417	178 051	216 366	468 732	272 654	196 078	397 164	179 187	217 977	466 509	271 822	194 687
December	398 506	184 866	213 640	473 737	270 277	203 460	403 969	184 713	219 256	471 884	274 357	197 527
2012												
January	381 845	169 639	212 206	477 405	274 566	202 839	403 268	183 802	219 466	473 570	276 745	196 825
February	382 933	171 209	211 724	483 658	278 153	205 505	407 542	185 096	222 446	478 904	278 532	200 372
March	429 747	194 493	235 254	484 307	279 351	204 956	409 458	183 768	225 690	480 584	280 841	199 743
April	412 547	179 358	233 189	483 820	283 904	199 916	412 940	183 495	229 445	482 838	284 479	198 359
May	431 708	190 239	241 469	479 839	285 534	194 305	408 492	184 281	224 211	482 756	285 882	196 874
June	409 934	188 347	221 587	477 315	287 173	190 142	402 730	182 539	220 191	481 897	286 525	195 372
July	396 689	178 232	218 457	482 513	291 325	191 188	401 942	181 142	220 800	484 939	288 155	196 784
August	424 186	193 737	230 449	480 023	288 872	191 151	405 897	182 695	223 202	488 787	288 720	200 067
September	396 767	180 245	216 522	490 461	292 462	197 999	413 437	184 180	229 257	494 350	291 499	202 851
October	432 374	196 003	236 371	500 115	297 046	203 069	409 784	183 354	226 430	496 077	293 825	202 252
November	415 963	187 123	228 840	501 830	295 836	205 994	418 755	188 023	230 732	498 252	294 872	203 380
December	402 360	180 629	221 731	499 350	291 033	208 317	418 923	186 644	232 279	498 617	296 390	202 227

. . . = Not available.

Table 16-13. Manufacturing and Trade Sales and Inventories

| Year and month | Sales, billions of dollars | | | | | Inventories, billions of dollars, end of period, seasonally adjusted | | | | Ratios, inventories to sales, seasonally adjusted [1] | | | |
	Not seasonally adjusted, total	Total	Manufacturing	Retail trade	Merchant wholesalers	Total	Manufacturing	Retail trade	Merchant wholesalers	Total	Manufacturing	Retail trade	Merchant wholesalers
1992	6 482.4	6 462.1	2 896.1	1 805.1	1 760.9	835.6	378.4	260.3	196.9	1.53	1.57	1.67	1.31
1993	6 806.3	6 804.0	3 019.7	1 936.4	1 847.8	863.0	379.7	278.4	204.8	1.50	1.50	1.68	1.30
1994	7 318.2	7 321.8	3 241.6	2 103.3	1 976.9	926.4	399.9	304.5	222.0	1.46	1.44	1.66	1.29
1995	7 856.3	7 865.2	3 481.3	2 220.3	2 163.7	985.4	424.8	322.2	238.4	1.48	1.44	1.72	1.29
1996	8 243.1	8 217.6	3 585.9	2 355.6	2 276.0	1 004.8	430.5	333.3	241.1	1.45	1.44	1.67	1.27
1997	8 681.3	8 683.6	3 835.8	2 470.8	2 377.1	1 045.8	443.6	343.8	258.5	1.42	1.37	1.64	1.26
1998	8 908.7	8 906.6	3 897.6	2 582.6	2 426.3	1 077.6	448.7	356.5	272.3	1.43	1.39	1.62	1.32
1999	9 434.1	9 430.7	4 032.3	2 801.4	2 597.0	1 137.7	463.5	384.1	290.2	1.40	1.35	1.59	1.30
2000	10 006.4	9 998.3	4 201.7	2 979.4	2 817.3	1 196.2	481.1	405.9	309.2	1.41	1.35	1.59	1.29
2001	9 817.9	9 819.3	3 971.2	3 062.3	2 785.8	1 118.8	427.7	393.6	297.5	1.42	1.38	1.58	1.32
2002	9 878.8	9 881.0	3 916.7	3 129.7	2 834.5	1 139.2	422.8	415.1	301.3	1.36	1.29	1.55	1.26
2003	10 254.6	10 253.4	4 016.2	3 262.0	2 975.3	1 147.7	408.2	431.2	308.2	1.34	1.25	1.56	1.22
2004	11 107.7	11 065.1	4 293.3	3 461.4	3 310.4	1 241.3	440.7	460.5	340.1	1.30	1.19	1.56	1.18
2005	12 061.6	12 064.5	4 742.3	3 687.6	3 634.6	1 314.2	473.5	472.1	368.6	1.27	1.17	1.51	1.17
2006	12 816.1	12 828.2	5 016.1	3 880.2	3 932.0	1 409.9	522.1	487.4	400.3	1.28	1.20	1.50	1.18
2007	13 520.5	13 521.4	5 320.8	4 001.0	4 199.6	1 489.7	561.0	502.0	426.7	1.29	1.22	1.49	1.18
2008	13 874.2	13 828.4	5 447.4	3 939.0	4 442.0	1 465.7	541.1	480.1	444.5	1.32	1.26	1.52	1.21
2009	11 775.9	11 780.7	4 423.6	3 631.0	3 726.1	1 327.2	502.0	433.3	391.9	1.39	1.39	1.47	1.31
2010	12 928.4	12 925.3	4 908.3	3 839.9	4 177.0	1 444.4	551.3	460.1	433.0	1.28	1.28	1.40	1.17
2011	14 336.9	14 349.8	5 504.4	4 135.8	4 709.6	1 558.3	607.5	478.0	472.8	1.27	1.29	1.36	1.17
2012	15 001.2	14 980.2	5 724.0	4 344.5	4 911.7	1 637.4	622.3	516.3	498.8	1.29	1.29	1.38	1.19
2008													
January	1 099.7	1 176.5	466.8	337.9	371.8	1 505.5	568.6	504.5	432.5	1.28	1.22	1.49	1.16
February	1 099.1	1 168.0	462.8	334.8	370.4	1 511.7	570.3	504.6	436.7	1.29	1.23	1.51	1.18
March	1 187.5	1 169.3	460.2	335.3	373.8	1 510.9	573.7	499.9	437.3	1.29	1.25	1.49	1.17
April	1 196.5	1 193.2	474.8	337.0	381.4	1 518.7	573.3	501.2	444.2	1.27	1.21	1.49	1.16
May	1 244.4	1 202.1	476.3	338.1	387.7	1 521.1	574.2	500.0	446.9	1.27	1.21	1.48	1.15
June	1 257.9	1 220.2	483.3	339.6	397.2	1 533.1	581.5	499.0	452.6	1.26	1.20	1.47	1.14
July	1 225.6	1 218.8	487.1	337.8	394.0	1 543.4	582.1	503.1	458.2	1.27	1.19	1.49	1.16
August	1 212.9	1 194.0	471.5	335.7	386.8	1 543.6	583.5	497.9	462.1	1.29	1.24	1.48	1.19
September	1 170.8	1 158.9	453.7	328.8	376.4	1 534.9	577.1	497.9	459.8	1.32	1.27	1.51	1.22
October	1 143.1	1 105.8	431.2	315.6	358.9	1 519.1	569.0	497.0	453.1	1.37	1.32	1.57	1.26
November	991.0	1 030.9	399.6	303.5	327.8	1 496.9	559.1	487.8	450.1	1.45	1.40	1.61	1.37
December	1 045.9	990.8	380.0	294.9	315.8	1 465.7	541.1	480.1	444.5	1.48	1.42	1.63	1.41
2009													
January	898.2	970.8	366.1	299.5	305.2	1 447.6	536.5	471.7	439.4	1.49	1.47	1.58	1.44
February	883.1	976.5	368.5	299.0	309.0	1 425.1	528.7	465.9	430.5	1.46	1.43	1.56	1.39
March	976.5	949.7	358.0	294.0	297.7	1 404.6	522.2	460.9	421.5	1.48	1.46	1.57	1.42
April	952.5	947.4	353.5	294.7	299.2	1 386.9	516.1	455.5	415.4	1.46	1.46	1.55	1.39
May	966.7	954.1	353.4	298.3	302.4	1 369.5	512.3	447.2	410.0	1.44	1.45	1.50	1.36
June	1 015.2	971.4	362.4	302.9	306.1	1 352.6	507.0	442.4	403.2	1.39	1.40	1.46	1.32
July	983.2	977.4	363.6	304.2	309.7	1 337.6	503.6	437.2	396.8	1.37	1.39	1.44	1.28
August	1 003.9	993.4	369.4	311.5	312.6	1 318.0	500.4	425.9	391.7	1.33	1.35	1.37	1.25
September	1 000.4	992.2	375.3	302.7	314.3	1 312.4	496.9	429.0	386.5	1.32	1.32	1.42	1.23
October	1 020.6	1 001.3	378.7	305.4	317.2	1 319.5	499.9	431.6	388.0	1.32	1.32	1.41	1.22
November	992.1	1 019.0	384.9	308.8	325.3	1 328.2	502.2	432.1	393.8	1.30	1.30	1.40	1.21
December	1 083.5	1 027.4	389.9	310.1	327.4	1 327.2	502.0	433.3	391.9	1.29	1.29	1.40	1.20
2010													
January	941.7	1 033.2	393.5	310.4	329.3	1 328.7	503.5	433.3	391.9	1.29	1.28	1.40	1.19
February	939.0	1 036.6	392.4	310.0	334.3	1 336.3	508.5	434.7	393.0	1.29	1.30	1.40	1.18
March	1 110.2	1 056.8	400.2	317.6	339.0	1 344.6	511.6	438.1	394.9	1.27	1.28	1.38	1.16
April	1 079.7	1 068.3	404.6	319.5	344.2	1 349.6	514.4	439.8	395.4	1.26	1.27	1.38	1.15
May	1 076.0	1 063.8	402.7	317.6	343.5	1 351.5	514.6	439.9	397.1	1.27	1.28	1.39	1.16
June	1 109.7	1 063.2	401.9	317.2	344.1	1 362.7	519.1	444.8	398.8	1.28	1.29	1.40	1.16
July	1 065.6	1 075.4	410.2	317.5	347.7	1 374.3	522.3	448.4	403.5	1.28	1.27	1.41	1.16
August	1 107.0	1 082.4	412.3	319.8	350.3	1 385.9	525.2	452.1	408.6	1.28	1.27	1.41	1.17
September	1 098.5	1 090.2	416.5	322.2	351.5	1 403.1	531.1	457.3	414.6	1.29	1.28	1.42	1.18
October	1 104.6	1 105.6	417.9	327.3	360.4	1 418.0	537.2	456.3	424.5	1.28	1.29	1.39	1.18
November	1 107.0	1 118.1	423.7	329.4	365.1	1 427.1	543.3	457.3	426.5	1.28	1.28	1.39	1.17
December	1 189.3	1 131.5	432.5	331.5	367.6	1 444.4	551.3	460.1	433.0	1.28	1.27	1.39	1.18
2011													
January	1 053.6	1 154.9	440.0	334.1	380.8	1 456.1	558.7	460.3	437.0	1.26	1.27	1.38	1.15
February	1 049.4	1 154.9	441.1	336.1	377.7	1 464.8	565.6	458.0	441.2	1.27	1.28	1.36	1.17
March	1 251.0	1 185.8	457.3	340.1	388.3	1 484.9	573.6	464.6	446.7	1.25	1.25	1.37	1.15
April	1 189.4	1 189.2	455.8	342.2	391.3	1 497.1	583.4	465.3	448.5	1.26	1.28	1.36	1.15
May	1 217.1	1 186.4	455.6	341.9	388.8	1 513.9	590.1	466.6	457.2	1.28	1.30	1.36	1.18
June	1 245.0	1 195.8	458.3	344.5	392.9	1 521.3	593.4	467.1	460.7	1.27	1.29	1.36	1.17
July	1 169.3	1 204.6	464.2	345.5	394.9	1 526.2	597.1	466.2	462.9	1.27	1.29	1.35	1.17
August	1 257.7	1 210.4	466.1	345.6	398.7	1 536.0	599.7	471.1	465.2	1.27	1.29	1.36	1.17
September	1 218.0	1 208.1	463.6	348.0	396.4	1 531.6	598.6	472.8	460.2	1.27	1.29	1.36	1.16
October	1 212.7	1 217.9	465.4	352.3	400.1	1 545.1	604.7	473.3	467.1	1.27	1.30	1.34	1.17
November	1 203.6	1 217.5	467.1	353.4	397.0	1 550.7	607.4	476.5	466.9	1.27	1.30	1.35	1.18
December	1 270.1	1 224.6	469.9	351.8	402.9	1 558.3	607.5	478.0	472.8	1.27	1.29	1.36	1.17
2012													
January	1 136.3	1 230.0	473.0	354.0	402.9	1 566.2	611.0	481.1	474.0	1.27	1.29	1.36	1.18
February	1 172.3	1 239.7	473.9	358.9	406.9	1 578.4	613.5	485.2	479.7	1.27	1.29	1.35	1.18
March	1 305.0	1 248.1	477.7	361.5	409.0	1 584.9	614.6	488.2	482.2	1.27	1.29	1.35	1.18
April	1 242.4	1 249.3	475.6	360.1	413.6	1 590.9	614.1	491.9	485.0	1.27	1.29	1.37	1.17
May	1 302.9	1 245.2	477.6	359.5	408.0	1 595.9	614.0	497.0	484.9	1.28	1.29	1.38	1.19
June	1 259.8	1 226.1	466.8	356.1	403.2	1 599.1	613.7	499.8	485.6	1.30	1.31	1.40	1.20
July	1 211.5	1 236.8	475.2	358.6	403.0	1 609.8	616.3	505.7	487.8	1.30	1.30	1.41	1.21
August	1 297.8	1 245.5	476.1	363.6	405.8	1 618.0	619.5	508.5	490.0	1.30	1.30	1.40	1.21
September	1 229.6	1 262.5	481.5	367.5	413.5	1 628.3	623.4	510.2	494.7	1.29	1.29	1.39	1.20
October	1 292.0	1 258.2	481.9	367.3	409.0	1 633.5	622.4	513.0	498.1	1.30	1.29	1.40	1.22
November	1 259.0	1 268.4	482.2	368.4	417.8	1 635.5	621.9	513.8	499.8	1.29	1.29	1.39	1.20
December	1 292.5	1 270.3	482.5	368.9	418.9	1 637.4	622.3	516.3	498.8	1.29	1.29	1.40	1.19

[1] Annual data are averages of monthly ratios.

Table 16-14. Real Manufacturing and Trade Sales and Inventories

(Billions of chained [2005] dollars, ratios; seasonally adjusted; annual sales figures are averages of seasonally adjusted monthly data.)

NIPA Tables 1BU, 2BU, 3BU

Year and month	Sales, monthly average				Inventories, end of period				Ratios, end-of-period inventories to monthly average sales			
	Total	Manufac-turing	Retail trade	Merchant wholesalers	Total	Manufac-turing	Retail trade	Merchant wholesalers	Total	Manufac-turing	Retail trade	Merchant wholesalers
1997	807.5	365.1	228.0	209.8	1 110.9	490.0	349.5	276.0	1.38	1.34	1.53	1.32
1998	846.7	377.1	241.6	224.7	1 165.0	507.6	364.7	297.3	1.38	1.35	1.51	1.32
1999	893.8	389.1	259.4	242.8	1 225.8	523.8	390.5	315.3	1.37	1.35	1.51	1.30
2000	920.3	393.8	269.3	255.7	1 271.2	531.9	411.1	331.4	1.38	1.35	1.53	1.30
2001	907.2	371.9	275.6	256.4	1 226.2	505.7	400.5	322.6	1.35	1.36	1.45	1.26
2002	919.9	369.8	283.9	263.5	1 246.7	500.5	424.2	323.2	1.36	1.35	1.49	1.23
2003	937.2	370.6	295.6	268.8	1 256.5	492.0	441.5	323.3	1.34	1.33	1.49	1.20
2004	972.0	378.4	307.9	284.7	1 304.9	498.0	465.2	341.7	1.34	1.32	1.51	1.20
2005	1 014.3	395.2	320.7	298.4	1 344.9	519.0	469.8	356.0	1.33	1.31	1.47	1.19
2006	1 043.7	400.0	332.6	311.6	1 387.5	536.0	480.6	370.8	1.33	1.34	1.45	1.19
2007	1 056.7	400.4	337.9	319.3	1 413.2	551.4	484.8	376.6	1.34	1.38	1.44	1.18
2008	1 012.2	377.0	323.8	311.3	1 376.2	537.3	458.3	379.3	1.36	1.43	1.42	1.22
2009	921.2	327.6	307.7	284.0	1 262.8	511.7	411.5	337.9	1.37	1.56	1.34	1.19
2010	961.2	345.1	318.6	296.6	1 312.3	528.8	426.6	355.1	1.37	1.53	1.34	1.20
2011	995.2	357.0	331.6	306.9	1 342.2	547.7	422.3	368.9	1.35	1.53	1.27	1.20
2012	1 024.7	364.6	344.1	317.5	1 393.5	559.3	445.3	386.0	1.36	1.53	1.29	1.22
2008												
January	1 060.0	406.2	335.3	319.4	1 418.2	557.4	483.5	376.7	1.34	1.37	1.44	1.18
February	1 044.9	398.4	331.3	315.7	1 415.1	557.3	480.6	376.4	1.35	1.40	1.45	1.19
March	1 035.5	388.8	331.3	315.6	1 409.2	558.0	476.5	373.6	1.36	1.44	1.44	1.18
April	1 046.2	395.7	332.3	318.8	1 406.6	554.8	474.0	376.6	1.34	1.40	1.43	1.18
May	1 036.6	387.0	331.6	318.7	1 401.2	551.2	472.8	376.2	1.35	1.42	1.43	1.18
June	1 036.1	386.2	329.1	320.9	1 403.3	552.9	471.8	377.4	1.35	1.43	1.43	1.18
July	1 018.4	380.9	323.7	313.7	1 406.4	549.8	476.2	379.8	1.38	1.44	1.47	1.21
August	1 007.7	372.0	323.4	312.2	1 400.7	548.5	470.0	380.9	1.39	1.48	1.45	1.22
September	983.5	361.6	317.7	303.8	1 393.9	544.5	467.8	380.5	1.42	1.51	1.47	1.25
October	974.3	358.8	309.6	304.6	1 390.5	544.0	466.6	378.8	1.43	1.52	1.51	1.24
November	954.1	345.8	311.1	295.7	1 388.1	544.6	462.4	379.8	1.46	1.58	1.49	1.28
December	949.1	343.1	309.0	296.1	1 376.2	537.3	458.3	379.3	1.45	1.57	1.48	1.28
2009												
January	929.1	330.1	312.8	284.9	1 368.9	537.3	451.2	378.8	1.47	1.63	1.44	1.33
February	932.8	333.5	308.9	289.3	1 356.6	533.6	448.1	373.5	1.45	1.60	1.45	1.29
March	915.2	326.3	304.8	282.1	1 343.7	530.2	444.5	367.6	1.47	1.63	1.46	1.30
April	908.9	320.0	305.1	281.8	1 333.4	526.3	442.4	363.4	1.47	1.65	1.45	1.29
May	907.6	316.7	307.3	281.4	1 319.5	524.3	435.4	358.4	1.45	1.66	1.42	1.27
June	905.5	319.0	305.5	278.8	1 303.6	520.6	430.5	351.1	1.44	1.63	1.41	1.26
July	920.8	325.0	307.0	287.0	1 290.2	518.1	424.9	345.7	1.40	1.59	1.38	1.21
August	919.9	322.7	313.4	282.3	1 272.9	516.0	414.1	341.2	1.38	1.60	1.32	1.21
September	920.9	330.4	303.8	284.3	1 265.5	511.9	415.4	336.7	1.37	1.55	1.37	1.18
October	924.2	333.9	305.9	282.3	1 266.8	513.0	415.2	337.2	1.37	1.54	1.36	1.19
November	932.6	334.4	308.5	287.8	1 268.6	513.5	412.4	341.0	1.36	1.54	1.34	1.19
December	936.3	339.0	309.6	285.8	1 262.8	511.7	411.5	337.9	1.35	1.51	1.33	1.18
2010												
January	931.9	338.0	309.2	282.9	1 262.2	511.4	412.0	337.3	1.35	1.51	1.33	1.19
February	938.0	338.0	309.1	288.4	1 266.6	514.3	413.1	337.5	1.35	1.52	1.34	1.17
March	947.4	340.8	315.7	289.5	1 269.7	514.5	414.5	339.1	1.34	1.51	1.31	1.17
April	954.9	341.5	318.3	294.2	1 272.3	514.1	416.9	339.8	1.33	1.51	1.31	1.16
May	953.8	338.4	317.3	297.1	1 270.9	510.9	417.7	341.0	1.33	1.51	1.32	1.15
June	958.2	339.4	316.8	301.3	1 276.7	513.4	420.8	341.2	1.33	1.51	1.33	1.13
July	972.0	350.3	317.0	304.2	1 284.7	515.2	422.9	345.3	1.32	1.47	1.33	1.14
August	969.6	347.1	319.2	302.5	1 291.6	516.8	425.2	348.1	1.33	1.49	1.33	1.15
September	972.8	351.3	321.5	299.5	1 300.6	520.1	427.7	351.4	1.34	1.48	1.33	1.17
October	973.5	348.8	324.4	300.0	1 307.5	523.1	426.4	356.2	1.34	1.50	1.31	1.19
November	980.1	350.7	327.3	301.9	1 306.4	525.6	425.3	353.8	1.33	1.50	1.30	1.17
December	982.6	357.2	327.3	298.1	1 312.3	528.8	426.6	355.1	1.34	1.48	1.30	1.19
2011												
January	992.3	358.5	329.1	304.6	1 314.5	530.8	426.3	355.5	1.33	1.48	1.30	1.17
February	979.2	353.8	329.3	296.1	1 313.6	532.0	424.1	355.4	1.34	1.50	1.29	1.20
March	990.1	357.3	329.2	303.7	1 319.5	534.1	426.8	356.6	1.33	1.50	1.30	1.17
April	983.3	350.8	329.4	302.9	1 323.8	538.1	426.5	356.9	1.35	1.53	1.30	1.18
May	982.7	348.6	328.5	305.4	1 328.9	539.0	425.5	361.8	1.35	1.55	1.30	1.19
June	989.2	351.8	329.1	308.1	1 327.3	538.2	424.4	362.1	1.34	1.53	1.29	1.18
July	996.8	359.0	329.8	307.8	1 329.6	539.3	423.4	364.1	1.33	1.50	1.28	1.18
August	1 000.9	358.7	329.4	312.7	1 332.2	540.2	424.4	364.9	1.33	1.51	1.29	1.17
September	997.0	357.1	332.4	308.1	1 326.4	538.8	423.2	361.8	1.33	1.51	1.27	1.17
October	1 008.7	361.6	336.3	311.7	1 335.4	544.7	421.5	366.0	1.32	1.51	1.25	1.17
November	1 006.7	360.9	338.2	308.9	1 339.0	547.6	422.7	365.6	1.33	1.52	1.25	1.18
December	1 015.8	365.9	338.8	312.8	1 342.2	547.7	422.3	368.9	1.32	1.50	1.25	1.18
2012												
January	1 016.4	365.6	339.9	312.4	1 349.1	550.5	425.1	370.3	1.33	1.51	1.25	1.19
February	1 019.7	365.2	341.6	314.4	1 354.2	550.7	427.0	373.3	1.33	1.51	1.25	1.19
March	1 015.2	360.3	341.7	314.6	1 355.4	550.7	427.6	373.9	1.34	1.53	1.25	1.19
April	1 017.5	359.2	340.6	318.9	1 358.9	550.0	429.2	376.4	1.34	1.53	1.26	1.18
May	1 024.6	362.5	342.6	320.9	1 363.4	549.8	432.6	378.0	1.33	1.52	1.26	1.18
June	1 019.9	360.6	340.7	319.8	1 366.1	550.2	434.9	378.1	1.34	1.53	1.28	1.18
July	1 028.4	369.0	343.5	317.3	1 376.8	553.8	439.2	380.9	1.34	1.50	1.28	1.20
August	1 023.1	364.4	344.7	315.8	1 382.0	556.8	440.5	381.8	1.35	1.53	1.28	1.21
September	1 024.6	363.2	346.9	316.1	1 385.8	559.3	439.7	383.6	1.35	1.54	1.27	1.21
October	1 022.1	364.3	345.8	313.5	1 387.7	558.9	441.3	384.4	1.36	1.53	1.28	1.23
November	1 041.3	369.8	349.6	323.8	1 390.9	559.0	442.4	386.4	1.34	1.51	1.27	1.19
December	1 043.6	371.2	351.9	322.6	1 393.5	559.3	445.3	386.0	1.34	1.51	1.27	1.20

Table 16-15. Selected Services—Quarterly Estimated Revenue for Employer Firms

(Millions of dollars.)

2007 NAICS code	Kind of business	2007 1st quarter	2nd quarter	3rd quarter	4th quarter	2008 1st quarter	2nd quarter	3rd quarter	4th quarter
SEASONALLY ADJUSTED									
51	**Information**	263 776	266 272	270 025	272 054	276 013	278 199	280 692	273 583
5112	Software publishers	34 516	33 470	33 207	34 131	35 907	36 254	36 103	34 416
512	Motion picture and sound recording industries	23 946	23 621	24 120	23 408	23 913	24 586	24 099	22 800
54	**Professional, Scientific, and Technical Services**	305 042	310 473	314 187	320 775	325 287	331 907	332 753	326 507
5411	Legal services	61 592	58 628	58 881	60 503	60 382	62 578	61 749	60 113
5412	Accounting, tax preparation, bookkeeping, and payroll services	26 864	28 389	29 148	30 181	30 112	30 098	29 906	29 959
56	**Administrative and Support and Waste Management and Remediation Services**	154 383	158 462	158 782	159 102	163 786	163 680	161 923	158 751
5613	Employment services	51 341	52 711	52 362	53 174	54 120	54 124	52 921	50 970
5615	Travel arrangement and reservation services	9 342	9 282	9 231	9 238	9 732	9 727	9 500	8 986
562	Waste management and remediation services	18 874	18 725	18 746	18 941	20 046	20 167	19 261	19 504
622	**Hospitals**	172 065	174 331	177 024	179 809	182 928	183 849	184 748	186 529
NOT SEASONALLY ADJUSTED									
51	**Information**	257 973	265 739	267 325	281 304	270 217	277 643	277 604	282 885
511	Publishing industries (except Internet)	67 376	69 318	70 108	75 421	69 292	70 935	71 487	72 899
51111	Newspaper publishers	11 252	12 089	11 757	12 465	11 022	11 167	10 844	10 886
51112	Periodical publishers	10 642	11 613	11 731	12 017	10 969	11 103	11 623	11 290
5111 pt	Book, directory and mailing list, and other publishers	11 725	12 380	15 073	14 078	12 292	12 592	14 830	13 278
5112	Software publishers	33 757	33 236	31 547	36 861	35 009	36 073	34 190	37 445
512	Motion picture and sound recording industries	23 204	23 408	22 649	25 725	23 243	24 291	22 725	25 012
515	Broadcasting (except Internet)	23 530	25 117	24 662	26 610	25 322	26 448	26 077	26 737
5151	Radio and television broadcasting	13 376	13 970	13 146	14 501	13 962	14 196	13 655	13 202
5152	Cable and other subscription programming	10 154	11 147	11 516	12 109	11 360	12 252	12 422	13 535
517	Telecommunications [1]	. . .	. . .	. . .	. . .	. . .	. . .	. . .	. . .
5171	Wired telecommunications carriers	. . .	. . .	. . .	. . .	. . .	. . .	. . .	. . .
5172	Wireless telecommunications carriers (except satellite)	41 131	41 927	43 327	44 199	44 211	44 969	46 009	46 287
54	**Professional, Scientific, and Technical Services** [1]	301 992	312 957	307 903	328 153	321 384	334 230	327 429	333 690
5411	Legal services	56 849	58 335	57 115	67 098	55 853	62 140	60 514	66 004
5412	Accounting, tax preparation, bookkeeping, and payroll services	32 183	29 922	24 601	27 404	35 773	31 844	25 450	26 993
5413	Architectural, engineering, and related services	61 203	62 235	64 468	66 295	63 827	67 145	68 377	68 566
5415	Computer systems design and related services	57 194	61 083	62 114	63 998	65 529	66 869	66 582	66 739
5416	Management, scientific, and technical consulting services	33 387	35 684	35 030	35 704	35 385	37 199	37 118	37 294
5417	Scientific research and development services	22 433	23 492	23 602	24 991	24 148	26 067	26 515	25 173
5418	Advertising and related services	20 353	22 032	21 915	23 134	21 757	22 121	22 637	22 685
56	**Administrative and Support and Waste Management and Remediation Services** [1]	149 638	159 966	160 513	160 653	158 910	165 057	163 838	160 168
561	Administrative and support services	131 840	141 054	141 223	141 466	139 967	144 588	143 980	140 586
5613	Employment services	50 057	52 395	52 257	54 982	52 767	53 691	52 921	52 652
5615	Travel arrangement and reservation services	9 127	9 904	9 268	8 813	9 469	10 359	9 614	8 564
562	Waste management and remediation services	17 798	18 912	19 290	19 187	18 943	20 469	19 858	19 582
622	Hospitals	173 958	175 377	175 254	178 371	185 123	184 952	183 085	185 037
623	Nursing and residential care facilities	41 060	41 890	42 674	43 437	44 041	44 756	44 191	44 518

. . . = Not available.
[1] Includes components not shown separately.

Table 16-15. Selected Services—Quarterly Estimated Revenue for Employer Firms—*Continued*

(Millions of dollars.)

2007 NAICS code	Kind of business	2009				2010			
		1st quarter	2nd quarter	3rd quarter	4th quarter	1st quarter	2nd quarter	3rd quarter	4th quarter
SEASONALLY ADJUSTED									
51	**Information**	267 567	267 416	268 461	271 132	273 221	275 247	279 408	281 844
5112	Software publishers	33 567	34 126	34 495	36 371	35 506	36 105	36 607	37 010
512	Motion picture and sound recording industries	22 706	22 558	22 484	22 600	23 748	23 542	24 014	23 797
54	**Professional, Scientific, and Technical Services**	315 669	311 717	311 960	313 105	320 219	321 460	327 080	330 049
5411	Legal services	59 063	59 339	59 950	59 149	60 184	59 169	60 749	60 429
5412	Accounting, tax preparation, bookkeeping, and payroll services	29 302	29 780	29 673	29 498	30 181	29 031	28 571	28 075
56	**Administrative and Support and Waste Management and Remediation Services**	151 446	148 155	149 399	152 911	156 064	160 090	161 626	164 753
5613	Employment services	47 480	46 123	47 642	49 117	50 417	52 805	53 688	55 861
5615	Travel arrangement and reservation services	8 585	8 214	8 409	8 660	8 916	9 358	9 360	9 327
562	Waste management and remediation services	18 025	17 640	18 132	19 066	19 604	20 888	20 831	20 607
622	**Hospitals**	190 939	196 340	199 010	200 958	198 095	204 141	208 069	212 460
NOT SEASONALLY ADJUSTED									
51	**Information**	261 948	266 881	265 508	280 622	267 483	274 697	276 055	291 990
511	Publishing industries (except Internet)	62 629	65 105	64 988	71 472	62 372	65 427	66 121	71 798
51111	Newspaper publishers	8 779	9 230	8 980	9 369	8 252	8 708	8 594	9 141
51112	Periodical publishers	9 692	9 604	9 466	10 337	9 309	9 348	9 660	10 078
5111 pt	Book, directory and mailing list, and other publishers	11 699	12 213	14 013	11 831	10 761	11 302	13 420	11 720
5112	Software publishers	32 459	34 058	32 529	39 935	34 050	36 069	34 447	40 859
512	Motion picture and sound recording industries	22 093	22 265	21 225	24 815	23 107	23 165	22 717	26 129
515	Broadcasting (except Internet)	23 684	24 577	24 247	26 426	25 855	26 961	25 710	28 994
5151	Radio and television broadcasting	11 248	11 813	11 303	13 139	12 885	12 595	12 219	14 653
5152	Cable and other subscription programming	12 436	12 764	12 944	13 287	12 970	14 366	13 491	14 341
517	Telecommunications [1]	. . .	. . .	. . .	. . .	. . .	. . .	. . .	. . .
5171	Wired telecommunications carriers	. . .	. . .	. . .	. . .	. . .	. . .	. . .	. . .
5172	Wireless telecommunications carriers (except satellite)	45 495	45 998	46 862	47 330	47 706	48 100	49 695	50 025
54	**Professional, Scientific, and Technical Services** [1]	311 565	313 587	307 905	318 741	316 697	323 067	323 155	335 660
5411	Legal services	54 810	58 864	59 231	64 295	56 152	58 696	60 081	65 384
5412	Accounting, tax preparation, bookkeeping, and payroll services	34 781	31 567	25 489	26 194	36 036	30 657	24 771	24 678
5413	Architectural, engineering, and related services	61 068	59 213	58 169	56 510	53 500	55 711	57 697	59 291
5415	Computer systems design and related services	63 134	64 711	64 461	68 160	68 789	69 123	71 147	74 731
5416	Management, scientific, and technical consulting services	33 217	33 449	34 416	34 643	34 769	37 266	36 849	37 455
5417	Scientific research and development services	24 812	25 784	26 928	28 232	27 977	28 820	30 563	30 013
5418	Advertising and related services	20 331	19 976	20 017	22 194	20 656	21 951	21 945	24 292
56	**Administrative and Support and Waste Management and Remediation Services** [1]	146 996	149 411	151 268	154 192	151 510	161 317	163 951	165 903
561	Administrative and support services	129 926	131 418	132 519	135 202	132 906	139 990	142 328	145 523
5613	Employment services	46 340	45 662	47 690	50 738	49 257	52 224	53 849	57 537
5615	Travel arrangement and reservation services	8 319	8 740	8 560	8 244	8 604	9 957	9 566	8 870
562	Waste management and remediation services	17 070	17 993	18 749	18 990	18 604	21 327	21 623	20 380
622	Hospitals	193 230	197 322	197 219	199 350	200 472	205 162	206 196	210 760
623	Nursing and residential care facilities	44 613	46 139	46 331	46 833	46 936	47 908	47 705	49 486

. . . = Not available.

[1]Includes components not shown separately.

Table 16-15. Selected Services—Quarterly Estimated Revenue for Employer Firms—*Continued*

(Millions of dollars.)

2007 NAICS code	Kind of business	2011				2012			
		1st quarter	2nd quarter	3rd quarter	4th quarter	1st quarter	2nd quarter	3rd quarter	4th quarter
SEASONALLY ADJUSTED									
51	**Information**	284 136	290 132	292 370	293 684	296 657	298 058	300 019	309 655
5112	Software publishers	37 858	38 584	39 398	39 165	39 014	38 997	38 907	39 912
512	Motion picture and sound recording industries	22 061	24 104	25 197	24 308	23 904	24 077	24 311	24 917
54	**Professional, Scientific, and Technical Services**	330 535	337 243	344 132	351 328	362 416	366 905	368 698	374 475
5411	Legal services	59 940	61 415	62 192	62 885	66 488	66 641	66 969	70 161
5412	Accounting, tax preparation, bookkeeping, and payroll services	28 988	29 679	30 853	31 477	32 069	32 732	33 270	33 883
56	**Administrative and Support and Waste Management and Remediation Services**	168 254	171 003	173 337	173 808	178 679	178 044	181 083	181 246
5613	Employment services	58 129	58 606	59 479	59 894	62 243	62 281	63 677	63 603
5615	Travel arrangement and reservation services	9 276	9 724	9 928	10 322	10 479	10 279	10 534	9 888
562	Waste management and remediation services	21 296	20 939	21 495	20 844	21 003	20 734	20 282	20 079
622	**Hospitals**	211 958	216 292	212 868	220 808	223 179	224 341	227 013	230 007
NOT SEASONALLY ADJUSTED									
51	**Information**	277 885	289 552	288 862	304 550	290 131	297 462	296 119	321 112
511	Publishing industries (except Internet)	64 365	68 051	68 199	73 287	64 387	66 632	64 759	73 788
51111	Newspaper publishers	8 001	8 453	8 092	8 618	7 675	8 056	7 762	8 548
51112	Periodical publishers	9 448	9 739	9 967	10 349	9 535	9 684	9 380	10 288
5111 pt	Book, directory and mailing list, and other publishers	10 724	11 352	13 145	10 925	9 880	10 012	11 122	10 650
5112	Software publishers	36 192	38 507	36 995	43 395	37 297	38 880	36 495	44 302
512	Motion picture and sound recording industries	21 443	23 694	23 862	26 763	23 163	23 620	23 071	27 458
515	Broadcasting (except Internet)	27 178	28 640	27 158	29 809	29 021	30 243	30 055	32 466
5151	Radio and television broadcasting	12 921	12 965	12 220	14 361	13 635	13 853	14 465	15 761
5152	Cable and other subscription programming	14 257	15 675	14 938	15 448	15 386	16 390	15 590	16 705
517	Telecommunications [1]	...	...	...	...	...	...	139 266	144 138
5171	Wired telecommunications carriers	...	...	...	...	...	...	75 923	77 772
5172	Wireless telecommunications carriers (except satellite)	50 893	51 754	52 443	53 842	53 938	54 527	55 442	58 178
54	**Professional, Scientific, and Technical Services** [1]	327 560	339 604	339 314	356 598	359 879	369 840	362 430	380 092
5411	Legal services	56 284	60 924	61 197	68 104	62 698	66 175	65 429	76 265
5412	Accounting, tax preparation, bookkeeping, and payroll services	34 728	31 311	26 873	27 542	38 483	34 500	28 978	29 648
5413	Architectural, engineering, and related services	55 945	58 607	59 802	59 709	58 825	63 672	63 174	60 881
5415	Computer systems design and related services	72 574	74 128	75 392	81 097	81 162	82 074	81 002	85 979
5416	Management, scientific, and technical consulting services	36 964	39 266	39 439	41 018	40 226	44 034	42 129	45 469
5417	Scientific research and development services	30 263	32 211	32 611	32 552	34 240	33 997	36 043	33 876
5418	Advertising and related services	21 355	22 538	23 356	25 583	22 767	23 180	23 297	25 540
56	**Administrative and Support and Waste Management and Remediation Services** [1]	163 321	172 221	176 092	174 708	173 545	179 300	184 145	182 042
561	Administrative and support services	143 090	150 800	153 716	154 218	153 550	158 068	162 971	162 405
5613	Employment services	56 850	57 903	59 776	61 571	60 936	61 534	64 059	65 257
5615	Travel arrangement and reservation services	8 914	10 346	10 186	9 816	10 039	10 937	10 850	9 384
562	Waste management and remediation services	20 231	21 421	22 376	20 490	19 995	21 232	21 174	19 637
622	Hospitals	214 502	217 157	211 165	219 262	225 634	225 238	225 197	228 397
623	Nursing and residential care facilities	49 263	50 301	50 362	50 181	50 654	50 920	51 029	51 857

. . . = Not available.
[1] Includes components not shown separately.

NOTES AND DEFINITIONS, CHAPTER 16

Table 16-1: Petroleum and Petroleum Products—Prices, Imports, Domestic Production, and Stocks

SOURCES: FUTURES PRICES—U.S. DEPARTMENT OF ENERGY, ENERGY INFORMATION ADMINISTRATION (EIA), AND U.S. DEPARTMENT OF COMMERCE, BUREAU OF ECONOMIC ANALYSIS; IMPORTS—U.S. DEPARTMENT OF COMMERCE, CENSUS BUREAU (SEE NOTES AND DEFINITIONS FOR TABLES 7-9 THROUGH 7-14); SUPPLY (NET IMPORTS AND DOMESTIC PRODUCTION) AND STOCKS—EIA.

Definitions and notes on the data

The *crude oil futures price* in *current dollars per barrel* is the price for next-month delivery in Cushing, Oklahoma (a pipeline hub), of light, sweet crude oil, as determined by trading on the New York Mercantile Exchange (NYMEX). Official daily closing prices are reported each day at 2:30 p.m., and are tabulated weekly in Table 13 of *EIA's Weekly Petroleum Status Report*. The monthly averages shown in this volume are the average prices for the nearest future from each trading day of the month. For example, for most days in January, the futures contract priced will be for February; for the last few days in January, the February contract will have expired and the March contract will be quoted. The annual averages are averages of the monthly averages.

The *crude oil futures price* in *2009 dollars* is calculated by the editors, by dividing each month's current-dollar price by that month's chain price index for total personal consumption expenditures (PCE), with the price index average for the year 2009 set at 1.0000. The PCE chain price index is compiled by the Bureau of Economic Analysis (BEA). It is described in the notes and definitions for Chapter 1 and is also presented in Chapter 8, Table 8-2, and discussed in its notes and definitions.

The import data in Columns 3 through 6 of this table are those published as Exhibit 16, "Imports of Energy-related Petroleum Products, including Crude Petroleum," in the monthly Census-BEA foreign trade press release, FT900. *Total energy-related petroleum products* includes the following Standard International Trade Classification (SITC) commodity groupings: crude oil, petroleum preparations, and liquefied propane and butane gas.

The data in Columns 7 through 11, on exports, imports, and net imports (imports minus exports) of petroleum and products and domestic production of crude oil and natural gas plant liquids (all expressed as thousands of barrels per day), and in Columns 12 through 14, depicting stocks of crude oil in millions of barrels, are derived from the Department of Energy's weekly petroleum supply reporting system. They are published in EIA's *Monthly Energy Review*, which is

classified under Reports and Products/Multifuel Energy Overview on the Web site, and can be found there in Tables 3.1 and 3.4. Stock totals are as of the end of the period. Geographic coverage includes the 50 states and the District of Columbia.

Data availability

Data on futures prices, petroleum supply and stocks are available from the EIA Web site at http://www.eia.doe.gov, under the categories "Publications and Reports/Monthly Energy Review" and "Petroleum/Weekly Petroleum Status Report." The *Monthly Energy Review* is no longer published in printed form.

The import data are available in the FT900 report from the Census Bureau at www.census.gov. See the notes and definitions for Tables 7-9 through 7-14 for further information.

Table 16-2: Construction Put in Place

SOURCE: U.S. DEPARTMENT OF COMMERCE, CENSUS BUREAU

The Census Bureau's estimates of the value of new construction put in place are intended to provide monthly estimates of the total dollar value of construction work done in the United States.

Definitions and notes on the data

The estimates cover all construction work done each month on new private residential and nonresidential buildings and structures, public construction, and improvements to existing buildings and structures. Included are the cost of labor, materials, and equipment rental; cost of architectural and engineering work; overhead costs assigned to the project; interest and taxes paid during construction; and contractor's profits.

The total value put in place for a given period is the sum of the value of work done on all projects underway during this period, regardless of when work on each individual project was started or when payment was made to the contractors. For some categories, estimates are derived by distributing the total construction cost of the project by means of historic construction progress patterns. Published estimates represent payments made during a period for some categories.

The statistics on the value of construction put in place result from direct measurement and indirect estimation. A series results from direct measurement when it is based on reports of the actual value of construction progress or construction expenditures obtained in a complete census or a sample survey. All other series are developed by indirect estimation using related construction statistics. On an annual basis, estimates for series directly measured monthly, quarterly, or annually accounted for about 71 percent of total construction in 1998 (private multifamily residential, private residential improvements, private nonresidential buildings, farm nonresidential construction, public utility construction, all other private construction, and virtually all of public construction). On a monthly basis, directly measured data are available for about 55 percent of the value in place estimates.

Beginning in 1993, the Construction Expenditures Branch of the Census Bureau's Manufacturing and Construction Division began collecting these data using a new classification system, which bases project types on their end usage instead of on building/nonbuilding types. Data collection on this system for federal construction began in January 2002.

With the changes in project classifications, data presented in these tables for 1993 to date are not directly comparable with data for previous years, except at aggregate levels. For that reason, *Business Statistics* shows earlier historical data only at these aggregate levels. Although some categories, such as lodging, office, education, and religion, have the same names as categories in previously published data, there have been changes within the classifications that make these values noncomparable. For example, private medical office buildings were classified as "office" buildings previously, but are categorized as "health care" under the new classification.

The seasonally adjusted data are obtained by removing normal seasonal movement from the unadjusted data to bring out underlying trends and business cycles, which is accomplished by using the Census X-12-ARIMA method. Seasonal adjustment accounts for month-to-month variations resulting from normal or average changes in any phenomena affecting the data, such as weather conditions, the differing lengths of months, and the varying number of holidays, weekdays, and weekends within each month. It does not adjust for abnormal conditions within each month or for year-to-year variations in weather. The seasonally adjusted annual rate is the seasonally adjusted monthly rate multiplied by 12.

Residential consists of new houses, town houses, apartments, and condominiums for sale or rent; these dwellings are built by the owner or for the owner on contract. It includes improvements inside and outside residential structures, such as remodeling, additions, major replacements, and additions of swimming pools and garages. Manufactured housing, houseboats, and maintenance and repair work are not included.

Office includes general office buildings, administration buildings, professional buildings, and financial institution buildings. Office buildings at manufacturing sites are classified as *manufacturing,* but office buildings owned by manufacturing companies but not at such a site are included in the *office* category. In the state and local government category, *office* includes capitols, city halls, courthouses, and similar buildings.

Commercial includes buildings and structures used by the retail, wholesale, farm, and selected service industries. One of the subgroups of this category is *multi-retail,* which consists of department and variety stores, shopping centers and malls, and warehouse-type retail stores.

Health care includes hospitals, medical buildings, nursing homes, adult day-care centers, and similar institutions.

Educational includes schools at all levels, higher education facilities, trade schools, libraries, museums, and similar institutions.

Amusement and recreation includes theme and amusement parks, sports structures not located at educational institutions, fitness centers and health clubs, neighborhood centers, camps, movie theaters, and similar establishments.

Transportation includes airport facilities; rail facilities, track, and bridges; bus, rail, maritime, and air terminals; and docks, marinas, and similar structures.

Communication includes telephone, television, and radio distribution and maintenance structures.

Power includes electricity production and distribution and gas and crude oil transmission, storage, and distribution.

Manufacturing includes all buildings and structures at manufacturing sites but not the installation of production machinery or special-purpose equipment.

Included in *total private construction*, but not shown separately in these pages, are lodging facilities (hotels and motels), religious structures, and private public safety, sewage and waste disposal, water supply, highway and street, and conservation and development spending.

Included in *total state and local construction,* but not shown separately in these pages, are state and local construction of commercial buildings, conservation and development (dams, levees, jetties, and dredging), lodging, religious facilities, and communication structures.

Public safety includes correctional facilities, police and sheriffs' stations, fire stations, and similar establishments.

Highway and street includes pavement, lighting, retaining walls, bridges, tunnels, toll facilities, and maintenance and rest facilities.

Sewage and waste disposal includes sewage systems, solid waste disposal, and recycling.

Water supply includes water supply, transmission, and storage facilities.

Among the data sources for construction expenditures are the Census Bureau's Survey of Construction, Building Permits Survey, Consumer Expenditure Survey (conducted for the Bureau of Labor Statistics), Annual Capital Expenditures Survey, and Construction Progress Reporting Survey; also included are data from the F.W. Dodge Division of the McGraw-Hill Information Systems Company, the U.S. Department of Agriculture, and utility regulatory agencies.

Data availability

Each month's "Construction Spending" press release is released on the last workday of the following month. The release, more detailed data, and a discussion of methodologies can be found on the Census Bureau's Web site at http://www.census.gov/constructionspending.

Table 16-3: Housing Starts and Building Permits; New House Sales and Prices

SOURCES: U.S. DEPARTMENT OF COMMERCE, CENSUS BUREAU

These data are mainly found in two major Census Bureau reports, "New Residential Construction" and "New Residential Sales." They cover new housing units intended for occupancy and maintained by the occupants, excluding hotels, motels, and group residential structures. Manufactured home units are reported in a separate survey.

Definitions

A *housing unit* is a house, an apartment, or a group of rooms or single room intended for occupancy as separate living quarters. Occupants must live separately from other individuals in the building and have direct access to the housing unit from the outside of the building or through a common hall. Each apartment unit in an apartment building is counted as one housing unit. As of January 2000, a previous requirement for residents to have the capability to eat separately has been eliminated. (Based on the old definition, some senior housing projects were excluded from the multifamily housing statistics because individual units did not have their own eating facilities.) Housing starts exclude group

quarters such as dormitories or rooming houses, transient accommodations such as motels, and manufactured homes. Publicly owned housing units are excluded, but units in structures built by private developers with subsidies or for sale to local public housing authorities are both classified as private housing.

The *start* of construction of a privately owned housing unit is when excavation begins for the footings or foundation of a building primarily intended as a housekeeping residential structure and designed for nontransient occupancy. All housing units in a multifamily building are defined as being started when excavation for the building begins.

One-family structures includes fully detached, semi-detached, row houses, and townhouses. In the case of attached units, each must be separated from the adjacent unit by a ground-to-roof wall to be classified as a one-unit structure and must not share facilities such as heating or water supply. Units built one on top of another and those built side-by-side without a ground-to-roof wall and/or with common facilities are classified by the number of units in the structure.

Apartment buildings are defined as buildings containing *five units or more*. The type of ownership is not the criterion—a condominium apartment building is not classified as one-family structures but as a multifamily structure.

A *manufactured* home is a moveable dwelling, 8 feet or more wide and 40 feet or more long, designed to be towed on its own chassis with transportation gear integral to the unit when it leaves the factory, and without need of a permanent foundation. Multiwides and expandable manufactured homes are included. Excluded are travel trailers, motor homes, and modular housing. The shipments figures are based on reports submitted by manufacturers on the number of homes actually shipped during the survey month. Shipments to dealers may not necessarily be placed for residential use in the same month as they are shipped. The number of manufactured "homes" used for nonresidential purposes (for example, those used for offices) is not known.

Units authorized by building permits represents the approximately 97 percent of housing in permit-requiring areas.

The *start* occurs when excavation begins for the footing or foundation. Starts are estimated for all areas, regardless of whether permits are required.

New house *sales* are reported only for new single-family residential structures. The sales transaction must intend to include both house and land. Excluded are houses built for rent, houses built by the owner, and houses built by a contractor on the owner's land. A sale is reported when a deposit is taken or a sales agreement is signed; this can occur prior to a permit being issued.

> Once the sale is reported, the sold housing unit drops out of the survey. Consequently the Census Bureau does not find out if the sales contract is cancelled or if the house is ever resold. As a result, if conditions are worsening and cancellations are high, sales are temporarily overestimated. When conditions improve and the cancelled sales materialize as actual sales, the Census sales estimates are then underestimated because the case did not re-enter the survey. In the long run, cancellations do not cause the survey to overestimate or underestimate sales; but in the short run, cancellations and ultimate resales are not reflected in this survey, and fluctuations can appear less severe than in reality.

A house is *for sale* when a permit to build has been issued (or work begun in non-permit areas) and a sales contract has not been signed nor a deposit accepted.

The *sales price* used in this survey is the price agreed upon between the purchaser and the seller at the time the first sales contract is signed or deposit made. It includes the price of the improved lot. The *median sales price* is the sales price of the house that falls on the middle point of a distribution by price of the total number of houses sold. Half of the houses sold have a price lower than the median; half have a price higher than the median. Changes in the *sales price* data reflect changes in the distribution of houses by region, size, and the like, as well as changes in the prices of houses with identical characteristics.

The *price index* measures the change in price of a new single-family house of constant physical characteristics, using the characteristics of houses built in 2005. Characteristics held constant include floor area, whether inside or outside a metropolitan area, number of bedrooms, number of bathrooms, number of fireplaces, type of parking facility, type of foundation, presence of a deck, construction method, exterior wall material, type of heating, and presence of air-conditioning. The indexes are calculated separately for attached and detached houses and combined with base period weights. The price measured includes the value of the lot.

See the notes and definitions to Table 12-11 for a discussion of the characteristics of other price indexes for single-family houses.

Notes on the data

Monthly permit authorizations are based on data collected by a mail survey from a sample of about 9,000 permit-issuing places, selected from and representing a universe of 20,000 such places in the United States. The remaining places are surveyed annually. Data for 1994 through 2003 represented 19,000 places; data for 1984 through 1993 represented 17,000 places; data for 1978 through 1983 represented 16,000 places; data for 1972 through 1977 represented 14,000 places; data for 1967 through 1971 represented 13,000 places; data for 1963 through 1966 represented 12,000 places; and data for 1959 through 1962 represented 10,000 places.

Housing starts and sales data are obtained from the Survey of Construction, for which Census Bureau field representatives sample both permit-issuing and non-permit-issuing places.

Effective with the January 2005 data release, the Survey of Construction implemented a new sample of building permit offices, replacing a previous sample selected in 1985. As a result, writes the Census Bureau, "Data users should uses caution when analyzing year over year changes in housing prices and characteristics between 2004 and 2005." In the newer sample, land may be more abundant, lot sizes larger, and sales prices lower.

For 2004, the permit data were compiled for both the new 20,000 place universe and the old 19,000 place universe. Ratios of the new estimates to the old were calculated by state for total housing units, structures by number of units, and valuation. For the United States as a whole, the new estimate was 100.9 percent of the old estimate. The complete table of ratios can be found on the Census Bureau Web site at http://www.census.gov/const/www/permitsindex.

Effective with the data for April 2001, the Census Bureau made changes to the methodology used for new house sales, including discontinuing an adjustment for construction in areas in which building permits are required without a permit being issued. It was believed that such unauthorized construction has virtually ceased. The upward adjustment was not phased out but dropped completely in revised estimates as of January 1999. The total effect of these changes was to lower the number of sales by about 2.9 percent relative to those published for earlier years.

The data used in the price index are collected in the Survey of Construction, through monthly interviews with the builders or owners. The size of the sample is currently about 20,000 observations per year.

Data availability and references

Housing starts and building permit data have been collected monthly by the Bureau of the Census since 1959.

The monthly report for "New Residential Construction" (permits, starts, and completions) is issued in the middle of the following month. The monthly report and associated descriptions and historical data can be found at http://www.census.gov/construction/nrc.

The monthly report for "New Residential Sales" (sales, houses for sale, and prices) is issued toward the end of the following month. The monthly report and associated descriptions and historical data can be found at http://www.census.gov/construction/nrs.

The manufactured housing data (not seasonally adjusted) and background information can be found at http://www.manufacturedhousing.org/statistics. Data with and without seasonal adjustment can be found at http://www.census.gov/construction/mhs.

Data and background on the price index for new one-family houses can be found at http://www.census/gov, in the alphabetical index under the category "Construction price indexes."

Tables 16-4 through 16-7: Manufacturers' Shipments, Inventories, and Orders

SOURCE: U.S. DEPARTMENT OF COMMERCE, CENSUS BUREAU

These data are from the Census Bureau's monthly M3 survey, a sample-based survey that provides measures of changes in the value of domestic manufacturing activity and indications of future production commitments. The sample is not a probability sample. It includes approximately 4,300 reporting units, including companies with $500 million or more in annual shipments and a selection of smaller companies. Currently, reported monthly data represent approximately 60 percent of shipments at the total manufacturing level.

One important technology industry, semiconductors, is represented in the shipments and inventories data in this report but not in new or unfilled orders. This affects the new and unfilled orders totals for computers and electronic products, durable goods industries, and total manufacturing. Based on shipments data, semiconductors accounted for about 15 percent of computers and electronic products, 3 percent of durable goods industries, and 1.5 percent of total manufacturing. Since semiconductors are intermediate materials and components rather than finished final products, the absence of these data does not distort new and unfilled

orders data for important final demand categories, such as capital goods and information technology.

Definitions and notes on the data

Shipments. The value of shipments data represent net selling values, f.o.b. (free on board) plant, after discounts and allowances and excluding freight charges and excise taxes. For multi-establishment companies, the M3 reports are typically company- or division-level reports that encompass groups of plants or products. The data reported are usually net sales and receipts from customers and do not include the value of interplant transfers. The reported sales are used to calculate month-to-month changes that bring forward the estimates for the entire industry (that is, estimates of the statistical "universe") that have been developed from the Annual Survey of Manufactures (ASM). The value of products made elsewhere under contract from materials owned by the plant is also included in shipments, along with receipts for contract work performed for others, resales, miscellaneous activities such as the sale of scrap and refuse, and installation and repair work performed by employees of the plant.

Inventories. Inventories in the M3 survey are collected on a current cost or pre-LIFO (last in, first out) basis. As different inventory valuation methods are reflected in the reported data, the estimates differ slightly from replacement cost estimates. Companies using the LIFO method for valuing inventories report their pre-LIFO value; the adjustment to their base-period prices is excluded. In the ASM, inventories are collected according to this same definition.

Inventory data are requested from respondents by three stages of fabrication: finished goods, work in process, and raw materials and supplies. Response to the stage of fabrication inquiries is lower than for total inventories; not all companies keep their monthly data at this level of detail. It should be noted that a product considered to be a finished good in one industry, such as steel mill shapes, may be reported as a raw material in another industry, such as stamping plants. For some purposes, this difference in definitions is an advantage. When a factory accumulates inventory that it considers to be raw materials, it can be expected that that accumulation is intentional. But when a factory—whether a materials-making or a final-product producer—has a buildup of finished goods inventories, it may indicate involuntary accumulation as a result of sales falling short of expectations. Hence, the two types of accumulation can have different economic interpretations, even if they represent identical types of goods.

Like total inventories, stage of fabrication inventories are benchmarked to the ASM data. Stage of fabrication data are benchmarked at the major group level, as opposed to the level of total inventories, which is benchmarked at the individual industry level.

New orders, as reported in the monthly survey, are net of order cancellations and include orders received and filled during the month as well as orders received for future delivery. They also include the value of contract changes that increase or decrease the value of the unfilled orders to which they relate. Orders are defined to include those supported by binding legal documents such as signed contracts, letters of award, or letters of intent, although this definition may not be strictly applicable in some industries.

Unfilled orders includes new orders (as defined above) that have not been reflected as shipments. Generally, unfilled orders at the end of the reporting period are equal to unfilled orders at the beginning of the period plus net new orders received less net shipments.

Series are adjusted for seasonal variation and variation in the number of trading days in the month using the X-12-ARIMA version of the Census Bureau's seasonal adjustment program.

Benchmarking and revisions

The data shown in the volume have been benchmarked to the 2007 Economic Census and to ASMs through 2011. In each benchmark revision, new and unfilled orders are adjusted to be consistent with the benchmarked shipments and inventory data, seasonal adjustment factors are revised and updated, and other corrections are made.

Data availability and references

Data have been collected monthly since 1958.

The "Advance Report on Durable Goods Manufacturers' Shipments, Inventories and Orders" is available as a press release about 18 working days after the end of each month. It includes seasonally adjusted and not seasonally adjusted estimates of shipments, new orders, unfilled orders, and inventories for durable goods industries.

The monthly "Manufacturers' Shipments, Inventories, and Orders" report is released on the 23rd working day after the end of the month. Content includes revisions to the advance durable goods data, estimates for nondurable goods industries, tabulations by market category, and ratios of shipments to inventories and to unfilled orders. Revisions may affect selected data for the two previous months.

Press releases, historical data, descriptions of the survey, and documentation are available on the Census Bureau Web site at

http://www.census.gov, under the category "Manufacturing" in the alphabetic listing there.

Table 16-8: Motor Vehicle Sales and Inventories

SOURCE: U.S. DEPARTMENT OF COMMERCE, BUREAU OF ECONOMIC ANALYSIS

Retail sales and *inventories of cars, trucks, and buses*. These estimates are prepared by the Bureau of Economic Analysis (BEA), based on data from the American Automobile Manufacturers Association, Ward's Automotive Reports, and other sources. Seasonal adjustments are recalculated annually. Data are available on the BEA Web site at http://www.bea.gov as a part of the national income and product accounts data set; they are found under the "Supplemental Estimates" heading. They are also available on the STAT-USA subscription Web site at http://www.stat-usa.gov.

Tables 16-9 and 16-11: Retail and Food Services Sales; Retail Inventories

SOURCE: U.S. DEPARTMENT OF COMMERCE, CENSUS BUREAU

Every month, the Census Bureau prepares estimates of retail sales and inventories by kind of business, based on a mail-out/mail-back survey of about 12,500 retail businesses with paid employees.

Retail sales and inventories are now compiled using the new NAICS classification system, which replaced the old SIC system. Historical data have been restated on the NAICS basis back to January 1992. In NAICS, Eating and drinking places and Mobile food services have been reclassified out of retail trade and into sector 72, Accommodation and food services, which also includes Hotels. The retail sales survey still collects and publishes sales data for Food services and drinking places. It no longer includes them in the Retail total, but they are included in a new Retail and food services total.

Subtotals of durable and nondurable goods are no longer published. They were always imprecise for retail sales, since general merchandise stores (including department stores) were included in nondurable goods, yet obviously sold substantial quantities of durable goods.

Definitions

Sales is the value of merchandise sold for cash or credit at retail or wholesale. Services that are incidental to the sale of merchandise, and excise taxes that are paid by the manufacturer or wholesaler and passed along to the retailer, are also included. Sales are net, after deductions for refunds and merchandise returns. They exclude sales taxes collected directly from customers and paid directly to a local, state, or federal tax agency. The sales estimates include only sales by establishments primarily engaged in retail trade, and are not intended to measure the total sales for a given commodity or merchandise line.

Inventories is the value of stocks of goods held for sale through retail stores, valued at cost, as of the last day of the report period. Stocks may be held either at the store or at warehouses that maintain supplies primarily intended for distribution to retail stores within the organization.

Leased departments consists of the operations of one company conducted within the establishment of another company, such as jewelry counters or optical centers within department stores. The values for sales and inventories at department stores in Tables 16-9 and 16-10 exclude sales of leased departments.

GAFO (department store type goods) is a special aggregate grouping of sales at general merchandise stores and at other stores that sell merchandise normally sold in department stores—clothing and accessories, furniture and home furnishings, electronics, appliances, sporting goods, hobby, book, music, office supplies, stationery, and gifts.

Notes on the data

The data published here have been benchmarked to the 2007, 2002, 1997, and 1992 Economic Censuses and the Annual Retail Trade Surveys for 2011 and previous years. Each year, the monthly series are benchmarked to the latest annual survey and new factors are incorporated to adjust for seasonal, trading-day, and holiday variations, using the Census Bureau's X-12-ARIMA program.

The survey sample is stratified by kind of business and estimated sales. All firms with sales above applicable size cutoffs are included. Firms are selected randomly from the remaining strata. The sample used for the end-of-month inventory estimates is a sub-sample of the monthly sales sample, about one-third of the size of the whole sample.

New samples, designed to produce NAICS estimates, were introduced with the 1999 Annual Retail Trade Survey and the March 2001 Monthly Retail Trade Survey. On November 30, 2006, another new sample was introduced, affecting the data for September 2006 and the following months. The sample is updated quarterly to take account of business births and deaths.

Data availability and references

An "Advance Monthly Retail Sales" report is released about nine working days after the close of the reference month, based on responses from a sub-sample of the complete retail sample.

The revised and more complete monthly "Retail Trade, Sales, and Inventories" reports are released six weeks after the close of the reference month. They contain preliminary figures for the current month and final figures for the prior 12 months. Statistics include retail sales, inventories, and ratios of inventories to sales. Data are both seasonally adjusted and unadjusted.

The "Annual Benchmark Report for Retail Trade" is released each spring. It includes updated seasonal adjustment factors; revised and benchmarked monthly estimates of sales and inventories; monthly data for the most recent 10 or more years; detailed annual estimates and ratios for the United States by kind of business; and comparable prior-year statistics and year-to-year changes. The latest such report available when *Business Statistics* was compiled was U.S. Census Bureau, *Annual Revision of Monthly Retail and Food Services: Sales and inventories—January 1992 through March 2012,* available on the Census Bureau Web site at http://www.census.gov/retail/mrts, along with the latest data releases and complete historical data.

Table 16-10: Quarterly Retail Sales: Total and E-Commerce

SOURCE: U.S. DEPARTMENT OF COMMERCE, CENSUS BUREAU

Beginning with the fourth quarter of 1999, the Census Bureau has conducted a quarterly survey of retail e-commerce sales from the Monthly Retail Trade Survey sample. (The monthly survey does not report electronic shopping separately; it is combined with mail order.) E-commerce sales are the sales of goods and services in which an order is placed by the buyer or the price and terms of sale are negotiated over the Internet or an extranet, Electronic Data Interchange (EDI) network, electronic mail, or other online system. Payment may or may not be made online. The quarterly release is issued around the 20th of February, May, August, and November, and is available along with full historical data on the Census Bureau Web site at http://www.census.gov. It can be located under the heading "Retail" in the alphabetical Web site index, under "E" for "Economic data and information."

These estimates reflect the NAICS definition of retail sales, which excludes food service. Online travel services, financial brokers and dealers, and ticket sales agencies are not classified as retail and are not included in these estimates; they are, however, included in the annual survey of selected services.

Table 16-12: Merchant Wholesalers—Sales and Inventories

SOURCE: U.S. DEPARTMENT OF COMMERCE, CENSUS BUREAU

These data are based on a monthly mail-out/mail-back sample survey conducted by the Census Bureau. The sample consists of about 4,500 establishments, with a response rate of about 75 percent; missing reports are imputed based on reports of similar reporters.

These data are now based on the new NAICS classification system, which replaced the old SIC system. Historical data have been restated on the NAICS basis back to January 1992.

Classification changes in NAICS

NAICS shifts a significant number of businesses from the Wholesale to the Retail sector. An important new criterion for classification concerns whether or not the establishment is intended to solicit walk-in traffic. If it is, and if it uses mass-media advertising, it is now classified as Retail, even if it also serves business and institutional clients.

Definitions

Merchant wholesalers includes merchant wholesalers that take title of the goods they sell, as well as jobbers, industrial distributors, exporters, and importers. The survey does not cover marketing sales offices and branches of manufacturing, refining, and mining firms, nor does it include NAICS 4251: Wholesale Electronic Markets and Agents and Brokers.

Notes on the data

Inventories are valued using methods other than LIFO (last in, first out) in order to better reflect the current costs of goods held as inventory.

A survey has been conducted monthly since 1946. New samples are drawn every 5 years, most recently in 2006. The samples are updated every quarter to add new businesses and to drop companies that are no longer active.

Data availability and references

"Monthly Wholesale Trade, Sales and Inventories" reports are released six weeks after the close of the reference month. They contain preliminary current-month figures and final

figures for the previous month. Statistics include sales, inventories, and stock/sale ratios, along with standard errors. Data are both seasonally adjusted and unadjusted.

The "Annual Benchmark Report for Wholesale Trade" is released each spring. It contains estimated annual sales, monthly and year-end inventories, inventory/sales ratios, purchases, gross margins, and gross margin/sales ratios by kind of business. Annual estimates are benchmarked to annual surveys and the most recent census of wholesale trade. Monthly sales and inventories estimates are revised consistent with the annual data, seasonal adjustment factors are updated, and revised data for both seasonally adjusted and unadjusted values are published.

Data and documentation are available on the Census Bureau Web site at http://www.census.gov, under "Economic Indicators" and in the alphabetic index under "E" for economic data.

Tables 16-13 and 16-14: Manufacturing and Trade Sales and Inventories

SOURCES: U.S. DEPARTMENT OF COMMERCE, CENSUS BUREAU (CURRENT-DOLLAR SERIES) AND U.S. DEPARTMENT OF COMMERCE, BUREAU OF ECONOMIC ANALYSIS (BEA; CONSTANT-DOLLAR SERIES)

The current-dollar data on which these tables are based bring together summary data from the separate series on manufacturers' shipments, inventories, and orders; merchant wholesalers' sales and inventories; and retail sales and inventories, all of which are included in this chapter. Generally, current-dollar inventories are collected on a current cost (or pre-LIFO [last in, first out]) basis. See the notes and definitions for Tables 16-4, 16-5, 16-9, 16-11, and 16-12 for further information about these data.

Based on these current-dollar values and relevant price data, BEA makes estimates of real sales, inventories, and inventory-sales ratios. Note, however, that annual figures for sales are shown as annual totals in Table 16-13 but as averages of the monthly data in Table 16-14, reflecting the practices of the respective source agencies. Also note that constant-dollar detail may not add to constant-dollar totals because of the chain-weighting formula; see the discussion of chain-weighted measures in the notes and definitions for Chapter 1. The constant-dollar estimates shown in this volume of *Business Statistics* were made before BEA completed its 2013 comprehensive revision, and consequently are stated in 2005 rather than 2009 dollars.

Inventory values are as of the end of the month or year. In Table 16-13, annual values for monthly current-dollar inventory-sales ratios are averages of seasonally adjusted monthly ratios. However, for the real ratios in Table 16-14, annual figures for inventory-sales ratios are calculated by BEA as year-end (December) inventories divided by the monthly average of sales for the entire year. In all cases, the ratios in these two tables (like those in Table 1-8) represent the number of months' sales on hand as inventory at the end of the reporting period.

Data availability

Sales, inventories, and inventory-sales ratios for manufacturers, merchant wholesalers, and retailers are published monthly by the Census Bureau in a press release entitled "Manufacturing and Trade Inventories and Sales." Recent and historical data are available on the Census Bureau Web site at http://www.census.gov/mtis/www/mtis.html. They can also be found by going to the general Census Web site, http://www.census.gov, going to the alphabetical index, finding "Economic Data and Information" under "E" and then finding "Manufacturing and trade" under "Manufacturing" or "Sales."

Sales and inventories in constant dollars are available on the BEA Web site at http://www.bea.gov. To locate these data on that site, click on "National Economic Accounts." Scroll down to "Supplemental Estimates," click "Underlying Detail Tables," and then click on "List of Underlying Detail Tables." For the most recent data, if there is more than one table with the same title, select the last table listed.

References

For information about the 1996 historical revisions to sales and inventories in constant dollars, see "Real Inventories, Sales, and Inventory-Sales Ratios for Manufacturing and Trade, 1977–95," Survey of Current Business (May 1996).

Table 16-15: Selected Services, Quarterly: Estimated Revenue for Employer Firms

SOURCE: U.S. DEPARTMENT OF COMMERCE, CENSUS BUREAU

Census data on quarterly revenue for selected service industries are based on information collected from a probability sample that has been expanded over recent years to approximately 19,000 employer firms (firms with employees), chosen from the sample for the larger Service Annual Survey and expanded to represent totals—for employer firms only—for the selected industries. The sample is updated quarterly to account for business births, deaths, and other changes. Industries are defined according to the 2007 NAICS.

The scope of the survey and the size of the sample have increased several times since the inception of this survey in 2004. More industries are now available than are shown here in Table 16-15, which focuses on industries with a longer statistical history.

Definitions and notes on the data

These data are collected in current dollars only. See the Producer Price Indexes in Chapter 8 for indicators of price trends in various sectors.

Both taxable and tax-exempt firms are covered unless otherwise specified.

Generally, government enterprises are not within the scope (that is, the industries it is designed to cover) of the survey. *Utilities* excludes government-owned utilities and *Transportation and warehousing* excludes the U.S. Postal Service.

Private industries that are not within the scope of the survey are NAICS 482, rail transportation; 525, funds, trusts, and other financial vehicles; 51112, offices of notaries; 6111, 6112, and 6113, elementary, secondary, and post-secondary schools; 8131, religious organizations; 81393 (labor unions and similar), 81394 (political organizations, and 814 (private households).

Totals shown for sectors and subsectors may include data for kinds of business that are in the scope of the survey but are not shown separately in the detail beneath.

Data for selected industry groups are adjusted for seasonal variation using the Census Bureau's X-13 ARIMA-SEATS program.

Data availability and references

The quarterly release "U.S. Government Estimates of Quarterly Revenue for Selected Services" is available on the Census Web site at http://www.census.gov/, as "Quarterly Services Survey" listed under Q in the alphabetic index; historical, technical, and background information, including sampling errors, is also available there.

The revised and updated data through the fourth quarter of 2012 shown in this volume, benchmarked to Service Annual Surveys through 2011, were released in early 2013.

INDEX